CONTENTS

INTRODUCTION

The *RHS Plant Finder* exists to put enthusiastic gardeners in touch with suppliers of plants, many of them unusual. The book is divided into two related sections – PLANTS and NURSERIES. PLANTS includes an A–Z Plant Directory of some 65,000 plant names, against which are listed a series of nursery codes. These codes point the reader to the full nursery details contained in the NURSERIES section towards the back of the book.

The *RHS Plant Finder* is comprehensively up-dated every year and provides the plant lover with the richest source of suppliers known to us, whether you are looking for plants locally, shopping from your armchair or touring the country in search of the rare and unusual.

NEW IN THIS EDITION

Following readers suggestions, this year we have asked nurseries to indicate if their premises are suitable for wheelchair users. The assesment of ease-of-access is entirely the individual nursery's responsibility.

AVAILABLE FROM THE COMPILER

APPLICATION FOR ENTRY

Nurseries appearing in the *RHS Plant Finder* for the first time this year are printed in bold type in the Nursery Index by Name starting on p.907.

If any other nursery wishes to be considered for inclusion in the next edition of the *RHS Plant Finder* (2004-05), please write for details to the Compiler at the address below.

PLANTS LAST LISTED IN EARLIER EDITIONS

Plants cease to be listed for a variety of reasons. For more information turn to How to Use the Plant Directory on p.19.

A listing of the 23,400 or so plants last listed in earlier editions, and for which we currently have no known supplier, is available from the Compiler. Please send a £1 stamp.

LISTS OF NURSERIES FOR PLANTS WITH MORE THAN 30 SUPPLIERS

To prevent the *RHS Plant Finder* from becoming still larger, if more than 30 nurseries offer the same plant we cease to print the nursery codes and instead list the plant as having 'more than 30 suppliers'. This is detailed more fully in How to Use the Plant Directory on p.19.

If any readers have difficulty in finding such a plant, we will be pleased to send a full list of all the nurseries that we have on file as stockists. All such enquiries must include the full name of the plant being sought, as shown in the *RHS Plant Finder*, together with an A5 size SAE. For more than one plant, please send an A4 1st class SAE.

The above may all be obtained from:
The Compiler,
RHS Plant Finder,
RHS Garden Wisley,
Woking,
Surrey
GU23 6QB

THE RHS PLANT FINDER ONLINE

The *RHS Plant Finder* is available on the Internet. Visit the Royal Horticultural Society's website **www.rhs.org.uk** and search the *RHS Plant Finder* database online.

> IT IS NOT WITHIN THE REMIT OF THIS BOOK TO CHECK that nurseries are applying the right names to the right plants or to ensure nurseries selling plants with Plant Breeders' Rights are licensed to do so.

ACKNOWLEDGMENTS

For this year's edition, Judith Merrick, together with June Skinner, and assisted by Gerda Pope, Patty Boardman and Emma Cox, co-ordinated the compilation of nursery information and plant data, while Richard Sanford oversaw the editing of plant names on the database. Rupert Wilson and Lynda Collett managed the Horticultural Database from which the book is produced.

The team at Wisley also acknowledges the help of Simon Maughan of the RHS' Publications Department in London, Adrian Whiteley for his essay on The Naming of Plants, Dr Kerry Walter of BG-BASE Inc. and Max Phillips of Strange Software.

Senior Botanist Janet Cubey and RHS botanists Mike Grant, James Armitage and Jo Osborne have carried out the editing of all plant names new to the book.

Once again this year we are indebted to our colleagues on the RHS Advisory Panel on Nomenclature and Taxonomy, along with the RHS's International Registrars and the RHS' Keeper of the Herbarium, Diana Miller, all of whom have provided much valuable guidance and information. Scores of nurseries have sent helpful information about asterisked plants which has proved immensely useful in verifying some of the most obscure names, as well as suggesting corrections to existing entries. Some of these suggested corrections remain to be checked and entered in our next edition, though those that contravene the Codes of Nomenclature have had to be rejected for reasons covered in the section on nomenclature. We are grateful, too, to our regular correspondents.

Actaea	J. Compton ('94)
Camellia	T.J. Savige, International Registrar, NSW, Australia ('96)
Cistus	R. Page ('97, '99 & '02)
Clematis	V. Mathews, International Registrar, RHS ('00-'02)
Conifers	P. Trehane, International Registrar, RHS Wisley ('94 & '99)
Cotoneaster	Jeanette Fryer, NCCPG Collection Holder ('99)
Dahlia	R. Hedge, RHS Wisley ('96-'00 & '02)
Delphinium	Dr A.C. Leslie, International Registrar, RHS Wisley ('97-'00 & '02)
Dianthus	Dr A.C. Leslie, International Registrar, RHS Wisley ('91-'00 & '02)
Geranium	D.X. Victor, International Registrar ('03)
Hebe	Mrs J. Hewitt ('94-'99)
Hypericum	Dr N.K.B. Robson ('94-'97)
Ilex	Ms S. Andrews ('92-'98)
Iris	Mrs J. Hewitt ('95-'99 & '02)
Jovibarba & *Sempervivum*	P.J. Mitchell, International Registrar, Sempervivum Society ('98)
Lavandula	Ms S. Andrews ('92-'99)
Lilium	Dr A.C. Leslie, International Registrar, RHS Wisley ('91-'00 & '02)
Liriope	Dr P.R. Fantz ('99)
Meconopsis	Dr E. Stevens ('02 & '03)
Narcissus	Mrs S. Kington, International Registrar, RHS ('91-'00 & '02)
Ophiopogon	Dr P.R. Fantz ('99)
Rhododendron	Dr A.C. Leslie, International Registrar, RHS Wisley ('91-'00 & '02)
Sorbus	Dr H. McAllister ('01)

To all these, as well as the many readers and nurseries who have also made comments and suggestions, we are, once again, sincerely grateful.

Tony Lord, February 2003

TO AVOID DISAPPOINTMENT, WE SUGGEST THAT YOU ALWAYS check with the nursery before visiting or ordering and always use the current edition of the book.

THE NAMING
OF PLANTS

To make the best use of the *RHS Plant Finder*, it is helpful to understand some of the complexities of botanical names.

COMMON NAMES VS BOTANICAL NAMES

Common Names
The most common question asked by gardeners is 'Why can't we just use common names?'. While, on the face of it, this is an attractive proposition, there are several factors that make this impractical for garden plants. The main hurdle is that plants are introduced from all over the world and therefore do not have common names in the language of the recipient country. Although common names could be introduced along with the plant, in whatever language, experience teaches us that acceptance of such names is likely to be resisted, and the possible need to transliterate the names from non-Roman scripts, such as Japanese or Hebrew, is a further complication. Additionally, there will often be more than one name available and there is no system to decide which one to use. Many plants attract a plethora of common names of very local usage, even within a small country and, of course, widespread plants have common names in many languages. Also, there will be plants that do not have a common name in any language if they have never been found to be useful to man.

It would naturally be possible to invent common names in suitable languages for recipient countries. In fact this is already done extensively in the United States, but with no system to regulate or standardise names, confusion can easily arise through 'common' names having no regard for the relationships between plants. For example, fragrant Himalayan champaca, banana shrub and Jack Fogg michelia are common names listed in a recent catalogue for *Michelia champaca*, *Michelia figo* and *Michelia × foggii* 'Jack Fogg' respectively. These are three closely related plants whose botanical names identify them precisely *and* reveal their relatedness. With no other point of reference, the common names chosen are forced to draw upon unrelated elements of the botanical names and can end up as more complex constructions without conveying as

much information. The 'common' names do not show that these are similar plants yet do not avoid 'difficult' botanical elements. An added problem in an alphabetical list like the *RHS Plant Finder* is that common names of related plants would appear in different parts of the book.

On a slightly different but related tack, familiar and well-loved common names tend to get used for more than one plant. A classic example in the English-speaking world is bluebell, referring to *Hyacinthoides non-scripta* in England, *Campanula rotundifolia* in Scotland, *Sollya heterophylla* in Australia and species of *Mertensia* in North America. The scope for confusion is enormous.

Botanical Names
Most people do not think twice about using rhododendron, chrysanthemum or fuchsia as the common names for three large, popular groups of plants, but these are also their botanical names. The fact that they have passed into common usage demonstrates the great strength of botanical names – they are intended to be universal. The aim of the botanical naming system is to provide each different plant with a single name which can be recognised by anyone, whatever their own language.

Botanical names are often referred to as Latin names, but this is slightly misleading. While it is true that the rules governing the formation and spelling of names are based on Latin, any word, in any language, can form the basis of a plant name. Thus many plant names commemorate people and places or are derived from common names used in the country of origin. These are indiscriminately mixed with Latin and Greek words, all of them 'latinized' by following the rules of Latin grammar.

WHAT BOTANICAL NAMES REPRESENT

To understand how botanical names are applied, it is necessary briefly to describe how plants are classified, since the units into which they are separated determine the structure of names.

Species

The basic unit of plant classification is the **species** (not 'specie' – species is both singular and plural in biology) which can be defined as a group of interbreeding individuals producing more-or-less similar offspring and differing from other similar groups by a number of key characters.

Genera

Species which share a number of significant features are grouped together to form a **genus** (plural **genera**). The characteristics of a genus are often quite easy to recognise, making this perhaps the most generally useful level at which plants can be identified for practical purposes. It is common for a plant to be referred to as, for instance, *Malva* sp., the **sp.** being an abbreviation of species and indicating an unidentified species of a particular genus. Genera can vary in size from a single species to over a thousand, depending on their distinctive characteristics. Compare *Rhodochiton* with *Rhododendron* in this book, for example.

Families

Genera are grouped into larger entities called **families**, some of which are easily recognised, others less so. Although families may appear at first to be of only academic interest, knowledge of the family to which an unknown plant belongs is the springboard to identifying it, and for the gardener, it can give an indication of the conditions required for successful cultivation.

The majority of families have always had names ending with the same group of letters, *-aceae*, and based on a genus within the family. This neatly distinguishes family names from genera and other plant groups. However, there are eight families with very well-known names which do not conform to this pattern. While it is perfectly acceptable to continue to use these names, the modern trend is to use alternative names with *-aceae* endings and this is what has been adopted in the *RHS Plant Finder*. The families are *Compositae* (*Asteraceae*), *Cruciferae* (*Brassicaceae*), *Gramineae* (*Poaceae*), *Guttiferae* (*Clusiaceae*), *Labiatae* (*Lamiaceae*), *Leguminosae* (split into three families based on well-known sub-families: *Caesalpiniaceae*, *Mimosaceae* and *Papilionaceae*), *Palmae* (*Arecaceae*) and *Umbelliferae* (*Apiaceae*). Also, the traditionally large family *Liliaceae* is split into a number of smaller, more natural families that may be unfamiliar to readers.

HOW NAMES WORK

At higher levels: genus, species and family

The name of a species is made up of two elements and is known as a **binomen** or **binominal name**, commonly referred to as a **binomial**. First comes the name of the genus, for example, *Malva*. Added to this is the **specific epithet**, for example, *moschata*. Put together, they form the name of a species, *Malva moschata*, which is in the family *Malvaceae*. To make them stand out in text, plant names are printed in italics (or underlined in handwriting) and the genus and family start with capital letters. Each species in a genus is given a different specific epithet, for example, *Malva verticillata* and *M. sylvestris* (abbreviation of a genus name to a single letter, once established in a piece of text, is perfectly acceptable). While genus names are uniquely associated with related plants, specific epithets can each be used once in as many genera as botanists decide appropriate. Repetition of an epithet within a genus would naturally cause confusion and is not allowed.

At lower levels: subspecies, variety and form

Things start to get complicated when variation within species needs recognition by use of further names. When plants have a wide distribution in the wild, natural selection and evolution work at different rates in different areas, especially if populations become geographically isolated. Such populations are often distinguished as **subspecies** (abbreviated to **subsp.** or occasionally **ssp.** but this can easily be confused with **spp.**, the abbreviation for species plural, so is not recommended), easily attributable to the species but differing in significant characters. Once a particular population is recognised as a subspecies and given a name, plants typical of the species automatically become a subspecies bearing the name of the species. Thus *Malva sylvestris* subsp. *mauritanica* differs from the typical subsp. *sylvestris* in having a more robust habit and larger, deeper purple flowers with darker veins.

Populations and individuals that exhibit less striking differences are named as varieties and forms (technically **varietas** and **forma**, abbreviated to **var.** and **f.** respectively). Their designation as a varietas or forma relates partly to the degree of difference exhibited and partly to the botanical tradition of the country in which a botanist was trained. So *Malva alcea* var. *fastigiata* differs from typical plants in having an upright habit (although other characters may vary too) and *M. moschata* f. *alba* simply has white rather than mauve flowers. Botanically, these are not very significant differences, but in the garden they can be crucial to achieving the desired effect.

Although subspecies, varietas and forma tend to be used somewhat erratically and interchangeably, they are technically ranked in order of difference and one plant can have a name at each rank – for example, the diminutive daffodil *Narcissus romieuxii* subsp. *albidus* var. *zaianicus* f. *lutescens*.

As can be seen, there are five ranked elements to this name which, when fully presented, gives a very precise idea to the daffodil enthusiast as to the characters of the plant in question. Mercifully, this situation is rare! Such complex names are rarely used and indeed are not really essential from a naming point of view – the trinomen *N. romieuxii* f. *lutescens* provides a perfectly precise name for the plant. Where cultivars are derived from such a plant, it is not generally necessary to cite every rank but simply sufficient to add the cultivar name to the species binomial (or even just the genus). In this book, all ranks are given where known to emphasise the relationships of the plants listed.

Sometimes, a second epithet is quoted without indication of rank, an invalid construction known as an **unranked trinomen** or **trinomial**. In these cases, either the rank is not known or it is unclear whether or not the name should be treated as a cultivar. This is an unsatisfactory situation but requires considerable research to resolve.

Hybrids
Some plant species, when grown together, either in the wild or in gardens, are found to interbreed. The resulting offspring are known as **hybrids** and the majority occur between species within a single genus. For example, hybrids between *Erica ciliaris* and *E. tetralix* have been given the hybrid name *Erica* × *watsonii*, the multiplication sign denoting hybrid origin. Some hybrids have not been given a hybrid name but are referred to by quoting the parent species linked by a multiplication sign, for instance *Drosera pulchella* × *D. nitidula*. This is termed a **hybrid formula**. Hybrids between different genera are given a new hybrid genus name and the different combinations of species are treated as species in their own right. Thus the hybrid *Mahonia aquifolium* × *Berberis sargentiana* has been named × *Mahoberberis aquisargentii* and *M. aquifolium* × *B. julianae* is × *Mahoberberis meithkeana*.

There are also a few special-case hybrids called graft hybrids, where the tissues of two plants are physically rather than genetically mixed. These are indicated by an addition rather than a multiplication sign, so *Laburnum* + *Cytisus* becomes + *Laburnocytisus*.

Cultivars
In cultivation, variation within species and that generated by hybridisation is particularly valued. Plants exhibiting desirable characteristics of flower colour, habit, size, variegation, fruit colour, flavour etc. are often given names. These are termed **cultivar** names (from <u>culti</u>vated <u>var</u>iety) and can be added to a binomial or simply a generic name. To make them stand out from the purely botanical part of a name, they are enclosed in single quotation marks and are not written in italics, resulting in names like *Malva sylvestris* 'Primley Blue' and + *Laburnocytisus* 'Adamii'. Additionally, new cultivar names coined since 1959 should follow international rules and be in a modern language — i.e., they should not be Latin or latinized, as many were in the past – to make them stand out even more clearly. As with specific epithets, cultivar names should not be repeated within a genus, although it is easy to find historical examples where this has occurred.

Cultivars are often popularly referred to as varieties, which is fine if they have names like 'Mavoureen Nesmith' or 'Techny Spider', but could be confused with a botanical varietas if they are older, latinized names. Consistent use of the term cultivar is therefore helpful in promoting clarity when using plant names.

Group, Grex and Series
When dealing with some genera where there are a lot of cultivars or where a well-known cultivar becomes variable through poor selection of propagation material or gives rise to a lot of new ones through breeding work, it has been found useful to use a collective name, the **cultivar-group name**, to identify them. Such a name always includes the word Group and, when used in conjunction with a cultivar name, is enclosed in round brackets (never single quotation marks). For example, *Actaea simplex* (Atropurpurea Group) 'Brunette' is a distinct cultivar within a group of purple-leaved cultivars. It is also possible to recognise as a cultivar-group a species, subspecies or varietas no longer felt by botanists to be worthy of recognition as a separate entity when the whole range of variation in related plants is considered. Such a species becomes part of another species, and botanically its name becomes a synonym. However, its characteristics are often horticulturally significant and the transfer of its name to a cultivar-group is useful to gardeners. For example, while *Rhododendron scintillans* is no longer recognised as a separate species and is botanically 'sunk' into *R. polycladum*, it is recognised horticulturally as *R. polycladum* Scintillans Group.

In some plant groups, notably within orchids, where complex hybrid parentages are carefully recorded, the group system is further refined. Each hybrid is given a **grex** name (Latin for flock) which covers all offspring from that particular cross, however different they may be from one another. Individual cultivars may then be named and propagated by division or micropropagation. Although a grex is similar to a botanical hybrid in principal, backcrossing a member of a grex with one of its parents results in a new grex, with a new name, whereas backcrossing a hybrid makes no difference to the hybrid name. In contrast to groups, with grex names no brackets are used and grex is abbreviated to **g.** – for example, *Pleione* Shantung g. is a popular grex of hardy ground-living orchids while *P.* Shantung g. 'Muriel Harberd' is a particularly good cultivar, selected from the grex.

With seed-raised plants, particularly F1 hybrid flowers, **series** have become increasingly popular. A series is like a group in that it contains a number of similar cultivars, but it differs in being created specifically as a marketing device, with cultivars added to create a range of flower colours on plants of similar habit. The identities of individual cultivars are often undisclosed, and the individual colour elements may be represented by slightly different cultivars over the years. Series names are treated similarly to group names. Unfortunately, the term series also has a precise botanical usage, but one that is unlikely to affect gardeners.

Synonyms

Although the ideal is for each species or cultivar to have only one name, anyone dealing with plants soon comes across a situation where one plant has received two or more names, or two plants have received the same name. In each case, only one name and application, for reasons of precision and stability, can be regarded as correct. Additional names are known as **synonyms**, constant thorns in the sides of gardeners! Two major factors leading to name changes and the creation of synonyms are rarely understood and require some explanation. Firstly, in the past and during the 19th century in particular, when a huge amount of botanical exploration was taking place, it was possible for botanists to be beavering away describing and naming plants in different parts of the world, blissfully unaware that they were duplicating someone else's work. This is perhaps difficult to understand in these days of instant global communication, but it led to many cases of a single species with two or more names or two or more species with the same name. The simplest way to resolve the problem of duplicated and superfluous names is to invoke a rule of **priority** – the earliest name correctly published wins and new names are therefore needed for some plants with later, incorrect names. This is a basically sound idea but has led to changes of some very familiar, yet incorrect names due to the discovery of earlier, correct ones in very obscure texts. This can have a destabilising effect, contrary to the intention of the rule of priority, so there is now a much more pragmatic view being taken, with some of the more destabilising proposed name changes vetted by an international panel and often rejected if the

technically wrong name is widely known. For example, the popular heather, *Erica carnea* was saved from a change to *E. herbacea*. An even more dramatic example was the retention of the genus name *Freesia* instead of the technically correct *Anomatheca*.

Cultivars acquire extra names in similar ways to wild plants and also through deliberate re-naming when the original name is felt not to promote good sales. The same principle of priority applies for cultivars as for wild plants so there are always cases where correction is needed. However, it is not always appropriate to provide a new, unique name for a cultivar which has been given the same name as an existing plant. Where there are large groups of cultivars, such as in *Fuchsia* and *Pelargonium*, repetition of cultivar names has proved difficult to avoid. In these cases, names can be qualified with the name of the raiser, the date of introduction or the plant type to help pinpoint their identity.

The second factor leading to name changes is misidentification. In gardens, many plants are distributed with the wrong name, usually through simple error, and it is important that these mistakes are corrected so that the plant you buy agrees with the description that goes with the name.

In the case of wild plants, correct identification and naming relies on knowing what species exist and how they are related. We have by no means discovered every plant species on the planet, and every discovery sheds new light on plant relationships. Add to this the increasingly reliable evidence of evolutionary trends provided by DNA and molecular studies and the fact that, for better or worse, the naming system aims to reflect the classification and therefore relationships, and it can be seen that some changes are inevitable. The most obvious results of new knowledge are changes to the membership of genera, some being split, with new ones created, others amalgamated – 'lumped' or 'sunk' in botanical slang. However, the closer we get to cataloguing the whole plant kingdom, the fewer new changes should occur.

Authorities

In the light of the problems raised by the existence of synonyms, and in order that plant names can be used with precision within the scientific world, there is a system whereby the name of the person who coined the name of a plant species (its **author** or **authority**) is added to the plant name, often in abbreviated form. For instance, *Malva moschata* L. was named by the prolific botanist Linnaeus, whose own name is abbreviated by international convention to **L**. Most of the time, this information is irrelevant to the gardener, except in cases where the same name has been given to two different plants. Although only one usage is correct, both may be encountered in books and catalogues, so indicating the author is the only way to be certain about which plant is being referred to. The same can happen with cultivars and, although authors are not routinely attached to cultivar names, this is sometimes the only way to be certain which plant, with the desired characteristics, you are dealing with.

Trade Designations and Trade Marks

Until fairly recently, cultivars, grexes and groups were the end of the story with regard to garden plant names. However, the expanding use of Plant Breeders' Rights (PBR) has resulted in an increasing number of additional names known as **trade designations**, and the marketing of plants using trade marks has also added confusion.

To obtain PBR protection, a new plant must be registered and pass tests for distinctness, uniformity and stability under an approved name. The approved name is its cultivar name, which should be unique to that plant within the genus and must, by law, be used on labels at point-of-sale. However, it has become common practice for the names registered for PBR to be code or nonsense names which do nothing to promote healthy sales. An additional selling name is therefore given (or perhaps several, covering different countries in which the plant is sold) and this is the **trade designation**. It looks like a cultivar name and is often presented as such, but should not be enclosed in single quotation marks and should be printed in a contrasting typeface to the cultivar name. Rose growers started the trend for code names, but with the rapid expansion of PBR they can now be found attached to almost any plant. *Choisya ternata* Sundance is a good example of a common garden centre plant with both a trade designation and a coded cultivar name, *C. ternata* 'Lich'. In the Plant Directory section of this book, trade designations are linked to cultivar names by an equals sign (Sundance = 'Lich') for clarity.

There is a second category of trade designation, involving cultivar names originating in foreign languages. In many countries there is resistance to using foreign cultivar names which can easily be translated or given an alternative name. For the sake of stability, the correct form of a cultivar name is taken, with certain provisos, as that in which it was originally published, in a nursery catalogue or elsewhere. Translations are therefore classified as trade designations. In the *RHS Plant Finder*, translations are cross-referenced to their correct cultivar names, in the same way as synonyms.

Trade marks used in conjunction with, or apparently *as* cultivar names cause particular problems when assessing which words constitute a cultivar name and which are a marketing device. It seems that trade mark law is regularly misinterpreted when it comes to plants, since a trade mark is a device to identify goods from a particular source and cannot be used to identify a particular plant. However, the way names are presented on labels and in catalogues often leaves this as the only possible interpretation. Care is therefore needed when quoting trade marks alongside plant names. They are best treated as trade designations, i.e. printed in a different typeface but with the appropriate ™ or ® suffix.

USING COMMON NAMES

Having begun with a section on common names and why they are not the best way to communicate information about plants, let's end with one celebrating them. They are, after all, often charmingly descriptive and contribute richly to our vocabulary. In a context where their meaning is clear, there is nothing wrong with using common names. To refer to gardener's garters rather than *Phalaris arundinacea* var. *picta* and King Edward potatoes instead of *Solanum tuberosum* 'King Edward' is usually the only sensible option. The same is true when we talk about wallflowers, daffodils, pansies and other common garden plants, either among our friends or for an audience sharing the same language and gardening experience. Only when communicating with a large audience, as books and magazines must do, is it necessary to think more carefully about using precise botanical names. Or, perhaps, when ordering the latest introduction from a far-flung corner of the world, its common name (or names) might be even more difficult to get to grips with than, for instance, *Xysmalobium stockenstroemense* or *Romanzoffia unalaschcensis* – or would it?

Adrian Whiteley
March 2001

A QUESTION OF NOMENCLATURE

Though Adrian Whiteley's succinct and elegant explanation of the naming of plants sets out the general principles of plant nomenclature we use, it helps to explain how we have interpreted and applied some of the other rules of nomenclature required by the two Codes (the *International Code of Botanical Nomenclature 2000* (the Saint Louis Code or ICBN) and the *International Code of Nomenclature of Cultivated Plants 1995* (ICNCP)). Our aim has been to make plant names in *The RHS Plant Finder* as consistent, reliable and stable as possible, and acceptable to gardeners and botanists alike, not only in the British Isles but around the world.

Cases in which the most correct name or the interpretation of the codes is debatable are referred to the RHS's Advisory Panel on Nomenclature and Taxonomy. The Panel looks at all recent and current proposals to change or correct names and strives for a balance between the stability of well-known names and botanical and taxonomic correctness according to the codes of nomenclature. Unlike the independent Horticultural Taxonomy Group (Hortax), its aim is to consider individual problems of plant nomenclature rather than general principles. Chaired by Dr Alan Leslie, the panel includes

---

'The question of nomenclature is always a vexed one. The only thing certain is, that it is impossible to please everyone.'

W.J. BEAN - PREFACE TO FIRST EDITION OF *Trees & Shrubs Hardy in the British Isles.*

Susyn Andrews (Kew), Chris Brickell, Dr James Compton (University of Reading), Janet Cubey (RHS), Mike Grant (RHS), Dr Christopher Grey-Wilson, Dr Stephen Jury (University of Reading), Sabina Knees (Edinburgh), Tony Lord, Piers Trehane (Index Hortensis) and Adrian Whiteley.

Many name changes proposed by nurseries and Plant Finder users over the past year have been adopted but others have yet to be considered and approved by the Panel. We hope that all those who have generously told us about wrong names will be patient if the corrections they suggest are not immediately made: all such opinions are much valued but the volume of information is great and must be thoroughly checked before we make changes.

Families and genera used in *The RHS Plant Finder* are almost always those given in Brummitt's *Vascular Plant Families and Genera*. For spellings and genders of generic names, Greuter's *Names in Current Use for Extant Plant Genera* is being followed; there are rare cases in which this disagrees with some prominent recent publications such as its use of the spelling *Diplarrhena* as opposed to *Diplarrena* in the current *Flora of Australia*. However, the general effect will be to keep names in exactly the same form as they are already known to gardeners.

In some cases the Panel feels that the conflicting views about the naming of some groups of plants will not be easily resolved. Our policy is to wait until an absolutely clear consensus is reached, not to rush to rename plants only to have to change names a second time when opinions have shifted yet again.

This edition contains few major changes to plant names. However, *Bougainvillea* names have been brought into line with the recent International Checklist and *Galanthus* has been corrected according to the very welcome new work by Bishop, Davis and Grimshaw. The current trial at Wisley has occasioned a check on *Geranium* names and has highlighted a problem with the numerous dark-leaved variants of *G. pratense*; there seem to be two seed strains involved, Victor Reiter Junior and Midnight Reiter, but the taxonomic status of these and which one each of the purple-leaved cultivars derives from remain to be resolved during the trial. For the first time this year, we are following most North American authorities and Stace's *New Flora of the British Isles* in accepting *Chamerion* (the rosebay willowherbs) as a separate genus from *Epilobium* and are also treating *Calibrachoa* (for instance the Million Bells Series) as distinct from *Petunia*.

Once again, the Internet has proved a great boon in the checking of plant names and carries searchable sources of information in ever increasing number on both wild species and cultivated plants. The most extensive and reliable websites giving information on plant names are included in our Bibliography, though many of the addresses have changed in the last year.

All of us involved in the publication of *The RHS Plant Finder* remain committed to the use of plant names that are as correct as possible. As before, gardeners and nurserymen may still choose to differ and use what names they want, many preferring a more conservative and a few a more radical approach to naming. Except for those names in which we have made corrections of a couple of letters to bring them in line with the codes of nomenclature, we are responsible for none of the name changes in this or any other edition of *The RHS Plant Finder*.

RULES OF NOMENCLATURE

Throughout *The RHS Plant Finder* we try to follow the codes of nomenclature rigorously. Plant names that are clearly not permissible under these and for which there seems to be no valid alternative are marked I (for invalid), even if they have been accepted by the appropriate International Cultivar Registrar. The commonest sorts of invalid names seem to be those that are wholly or partly in Latin (not permissible since 1959, e.g. 'Pixie Alba', 'Superba', 'Variegata') and those which use a Latin generic name as a cultivar name (e.g. *Rosa* 'Corylus', *Viola* 'Gazania').

Apart from being discourteous to the plants' originators and their countries, the translating of foreign plant names into English is a bad and insular practice that is likely to cause confusion; it is also contrary to Article 28 of the 1995 ICNCP. The Code requires that such translations be considered trade designations and not cultivar names and so should be presented in a different font (here sans serif) and not in quotes. It may be years yet before we make sense of the host of German names and apparent English translations for a genus such as *Coreopsis*, many of which must be synonyms. Throughout *The RHS Plant Finder*, we have tried to give preference to the original name in every case, although English translations are also given as trade designations where they are in general use.

The substitution of slick selling names by nurseries which do not like, or have not bothered to find out, the correct names of the plants they sell is sharp practice not expected of any reputable nursery; it is also a probable breach of the Trades Description Act.

The publication of the ICNCP has done a great deal to clarify nomenclature without generally introducing rules that cause destabilising name changes. However, it significantly alters the sort of plant names that are allowed since 1 January 1996: nurseries that name plants are strongly urged to check that the names they want to use are acceptable under the new Code.

One Article of the 1995 Code that affects names published since 1995, is Art. 17.13, dealing in part with the use of botanical or common generic names within a cultivar or group name. This bans names in which the last word of the cultivar name is the common or botanical name of a genus or species. Two sorts of such names are commonly found: those based on colours (ending

Lilac, Lavender, Rose, Rosa, Apricot, Peach, Mauve (French for *Malva*)) and those based on personal names (Rosemary, Hazel). These will be marked I in The RHS Plant Finder if known to have been published after 1995 or marked with an asterisk if their date of publication is unknown. This rule does not preclude cultivar epithets ending with common names which apply to only part of a genus such as Cerise, Cherry, Lemon, Lime, Orange, Pink, or Violet, each of which refers to more than one species and/or their hybrids.

An Article of the new Code which the Panel has agreed it cannot implement is Art. 17.11, banning cultivar names consisting of solely adjectival words in a modern language, unless one of these words may be considered a substantive or unless the epithet is the recognized name of a colour. As this rule is retroactive, applying to all cultivar names whenever they were published, if applied strictly it could require rejection of several hundred cultivar names in *The RHS Plant Finder*, many of them very well known and widely used. Furthermore, it is difficult to apply: many adjectives also have substantive meanings, albeit sometimes obscure ones, that might or might not justify acceptance of the names; it is not easy to decide which names of colours are accepted and which are not. Our Panel's judgement is that, as currently worded, this Article is unintentionally restrictive and potentially destabilizing, so for the time being we will not use this Article as a basis for making changes, nor for declaring already established names unacceptable. The next edition of the Code, which should be published this year following the 2002 International Symposium on the Taxonomy of Cultivated Plants in Toronto, is expected to be much less restrictive in its treatment of both this article and Art. 17.13, though for this edition our Panel has decided that we should not change our interpretation and implementation of the current Code.

ORTHOGRAPHY

One of the most striking changes in the new Saint Louis edition of the *International Code of Botanical Nomenclature* is its clarification of what orthographic (spelling) corrections should be made to commemorative plant names. In the previous (Tokyo 1994) edition of the ICBN, this proved the most difficult part of the code to implement because of its ambiguous phrasing and aroused a great deal of debate at our Panel meetings. The present code rules that such epithets as *alcoquiana, glaziovii, bigelovii* and *bureavii*, commemorating Alcock, Glaziou, Bigelow and Bureau, are intentional and acceptable latinizations that do not affect merely the terminations of the names.

However, we are now told that in *fortuni*, *billardierii* and *backhousii*, only the termination is affected so these must be corrected to *fortunei*, *billardierei* and *backhousei* respectively. Though this makes the permitted spelling clear in a number of cases, many other cases seem still to be debatable, particularly those in which someone whose name was originally in a alphabet such as Cyrillic is commemorated: there are numerous examples of commemorands themselves having used transliterations of their own name when publishing in alphabets other than their own that differ from those approved by the code. Though we have made some orthographic corrections to accord with the new edition of the code where the code's intention is clear, in other cases the code is less clear and our Panel will have to deliberate carefully, only making changes if the intention of the code is certain.

VERIFICATION OF NAMES

Although we try to verify every name that appears in these pages, the amount of time that can be allotted to checking each of over 70,000 entries must be limited. There is always a proportion that does not appear in any of the reference sources used and those unverified names for which there may be scope for error are marked with an asterisk. Such errors may occur with species we cannot find listed (possibly synonyms for more recent and better known names) or may include misspellings (particularly of names transliterated from Japanese or Chinese, or commemorating a person). We are especially circumspect about names not known to the International Cultivar Registrar for a particular genus. We are always grateful to receive information about the naming and origin of any asterisked plant and once we feel reassured about the plant's pedigree, the asterisk will be removed. Of course, many such names will prove to be absolutely correct and buyers can be reassured if they know that the selling nursery takes great care with the naming of its plants. However, although we are able to check that names are valid, correctly styled and spelt, we have no means of checking that nurseries are applying them to the right plant; caveat emptor!

For *Hosta*, *Juniperus* and *Saxifraga*, gardeners and nurseries are often unfamiliar with the species to which a particular cultivar belongs and so these are listed by cultivar first, giving the species in parentheses.

ADJECTIVAL NAMES

Latin adjectival names, whether for species, subspecies, cultivar etc., must agree in gender with the genus, not with the specific name if the latter is a noun (as for *Styrax obassia*, *Lonicera caprifolium* etc.). Thus azaleas have to agree with *Rhododendron*, their true genus (neuter), rather than Azalea (feminine). For French cultivar names, adjectives should agree with whatever is being described; for roses, this is almost always la rose (feminine) but on rare occasions le rosier (when describing vegetative characteristics such as climbing forms), *l'oeillet* or *le pompon* (all masculine).

It is often the case that gardeners consider two plants to be distinct but botanists, who know of a whole range of intermediates linking the two, consider them to be the same species. The most notable example is for the rhododendrons, many species of which were 'sunk' in Cullen and Chamberlain's revision. In such cases we have always tried to provide names that retain important horticultural entities, even if not botanically distinct, often by calling the sunk species by a Cultivar-group name, such as *Rhododendron rubiginosum* Desquamatum Group. Cultivar-group names are also used for swarms of hybrids with the same parentage. These were formerly treated as grex names, a term now only used for orchids; thus grex names for lilies, bromeliads and begonias are now styled as Groups. A single clone from the Group may be given the same cultivar name, e.g. 'Polar Bear'. In many cases nursery catalogues do not specify whether the named clone is being offered or other selections from the hybrid swarm and entries are therefore given as e.g. *Rhododendron* Polar Bear Group & cl.

One requirement of the 1995 ICNCP is that cultivar-group names used after 1 January 1996 must have been validly published with a description or reference to a previously published description. Such publication is beyond the scope and purpose of *The RHS Plant Finder*. As principal editor, I may not style the more variable taxa that appear in this and subsequent editions as cultivar-groups unless they have been published elsewhere as Groups. Nevertheless, I still feel it is helpful to gardeners and other plant users to use cultivar names only for those plants that fulfil the Code's requirement that a cultivar be distinct, uniform and stable in its narrow sense. This applies particularly to mixtures and races of seed-raised plants that embrace significant variation, are often not distinct from similar named selections and may be changed in character from year to year. Any new entries that are of this nature are here styled neither as cultivars nor as cultivar-groups but simply as epithets or descriptions, without quotation marks and thus beyond the scope of the new Code. This applies especially to plants described as 'strains' or 'hybrids', though the latter term is sometimes merely a provenance rather than a sign of common parentage. Thus plants here appearing as cultivars with their names in quotes have, as far as I can tell, uniform and predictable characteristics. There are a few cases in which it is difficult to tell whether a 'sunk' species remains horticulturally distinct enough to merit a group name, as for many of the rhododendrons; we would be grateful if users would let us know of any plants that we have 'sunk' in synonymy but which still need to be distinguished by a separate name. In many cases, the plants gardeners grow will be the most extreme variants of a species; although one 'end' of the species will seem to be quite a different plant from the other 'end' to the gardener, the botanist will see them as the outer limits of a continuous range of variation and will give them the same species name. We often hear gardeners complain 'How can these two plants have the same name? They are different!' In such cases, although the botanist may have to 'lump' them under the same name, we will always try to provide an acceptable name to distinguish an important horticultural entity, even if it is not botanically distinct.

TAXONOMIC RANK

The ICBN requires the rank of each infraspecific botanical epithet to be given. In many cases, it is not at all clear whether a colour form shown as, say, alba is a true botanical forma or a cultivar of garden origin. Our inclination here is not to treat such plants as cultivars if they are recorded as being naturally occurring, nor if they embrace considerable variation: forma *alba* would be preferred if a valid publication is recorded, otherwise a previously-published Group name or a simple description such as "white-flowered". In the absence of conclusive evidence we will leave such names styled as they are at present and so some ranks remain to be added in future editions. In many cases, *alba* is assumed without any proof to be the correct name for a white-flowered variant though research often shows that the validly published name is something quite different such as *albiflora*, *leucantha* or *nivea*.

AUTHOR CITATIONS

Adrian Whiteley has explained the need to cite the author of a particular name if it has been used twice or more by different authors for different plants. This applies equally to botanical epithets and to cultivars, for instance of some fuchsias. Generally the more recent name will be invalid and may be cross-referenced to the plant's first validly published name. Author's names appear directly after the species name and if abbreviated follow

Brummitt and Powell's *Authors of Plant Names*; abbreviations are also listed in e.g. Mabberley's *The Plant-Book*. Such names appear in a smaller typeface, and neither in quotes nor in sans serif font, so should not be confused with cultivar names or trade designations.

HYPHENATION

The ICBN ruling on hyphenation (Article 60.9) forbids the use of hyphens after a 'compounding form' (i.e. *albo*, *pseudo*, *aureo*, *neo*). Hyphens are still permitted to divide separate words such as *novae-angliae* or *uva-crispa* and following the Tokyo Congress (1993), after a vowel terminating a compounding form when followed by the same vowel (e.g. *Gaultheria semi-infera*, *Gentiana sino-ornata*).

TERMINATIONS OF COMMEMORATIVE NAMES

According to Article 60.11 (referring to Recommendation 60C.1) of ICNCP, the genitive form of commemorative names ending in -a is always -*ae*, even if a man is being commemorated (as for *Picea koyamae*). This same article requires that the well known *Crocosmia* be spelt *masoniorum* and not *masonorum* and that *Rosa wichurana* be spelt thus and not *wichuraiana*. However, corrections do not have to be made to epithets derived from personal names already in Greek or Latin or possessing a well-established latinized form. The new edition of the code gives *edithae* (for Editha or Edith) and *murielae* (for Muriela or Muriel) as examples of this category.

The RHS Plant Finder is useful not only as a directory of plant sources but as a 'menu' of plants grown by British gardeners. Such a list is of great value not only to private gardeners; landscapers can use it to check the range of plants they can incorporate in designs; gardeners in countries of the European Union can check which plants they can import by Mail Order; botanists can discover the species grown in Britain, some of them from recorded natural sources; nurserymen can use it to select for propagation first-rate plants that are still not readily available; horticultural authors, who often only want to write about plants the public are able to buy, will find it invaluable. For all such users, *The RHS Plant Finder* can be recommended as a source of standard, up-to-date and reliable nomenclature.

Tony Lord, February 2003

SYMBOLS AND ABBREVIATIONS

SYMBOLS APPEARING TO THE LEFT OF THE NAME

* Name not validated. Not listed in the appropriate International Registration Authority checklist nor in works cited in the Bibliography. For fuller discussion see p.12
I Invalid name. See *International Code of Botanical Nomenclature 2000* and *International Code of Nomenclature for Cultivated Plants 1995*. For fuller discussion see p.12
N Refer to Nomenclature Notes on p.25
§ Plant listed elsewhere in the Plant Directory under a synonym
x Hybrid genus
+ Graft hybrid genus

SYMBOLS APPEARING TO THE RIGHT OF THE NAME

✿ National Council for the Conservation of Plants and Gardens (NCCPG) National Plant Collection® exists for all or part of this genus. Provisional Collections appear in brackets. Full details of the NCCPG Plant Collections are found in the *National Plant Collections® Directory 2003–2004* available from: www.nccpg.com or NCCPG, RHS Garden, Wisley, Woking, Surrey GU23 6QP
♀H4 The Royal Horticultural Society's Award of Garden Merit, see p.20.
(d) double-flowered

(F) Fruit
(f) female
(m) male
(v) variegated plant, see p.20
PBR Plant Breeders Rights see p.20
new New plant entry in this edition

For abbreviations relating to individual genera see **Classification of Genera** p.31
For **Collectors' References** see p.22
For symbols used in the **Nurseries** section see the reverse of the card insert

SYMBOLS AND ABBREVIATIONS USED AS PART OF THE NAME

x hybrid species
aff. affinis (allied to)
agg. aggregate, a single name used to cover a group of very similar plants, regarded by some as separate species
ambig. ambiguous, a name used by two authors for different plants and where it is unclear which is being offered
cl. clone
cv(s) cultivar(s)
f. forma (botanical form)
g. grex
sp. species
subsp. subspecies
subvar. subvarietas (botanical subvariety)
var. varietas (botanical variety)

IT IS NOT WITHIN THE REMIT OF THIS BOOK TO CHECK

that nurseries are applying the right names to the right plants or to ensure nurseries selling plants with Plant Breeders' Rights are licensed to do so.

Please, never use an old edition

PLANTS

WHATEVER PLANT YOU ARE LOOKING FOR,
MAYBE AN OLD FAVOURITE OR A MORE UNUSUAL
CULTIVAR, SEARCH HERE FOR A LIST OF THE
SUPPLIERS THAT ARE CLOSEST TO YOU.

How to Use the Plant Directory

Nursery Codes

Look up the plant you require in the alphabetical Plant Directory. Against each plant you will find one or more four-letter codes, for example SLan, each code represents one nursery offering that plant. The first letter of each code indicates the main area of the country in which the nursery is situated, based on their county. For this geographical key, refer to the **Nursery Codes and Symbols** on p.778.

Turn to the **Nursery Details by Code** starting on p.782 where, in alphabetical order of codes, you will find details of each nursery which offers the plant in question. If you wish to visit any nursery, you may find its location on one of the maps (following p.917). Please note, however, that not all nurseries, especially mail order only nurseries, choose to be shown on the maps. For a fuller explanation of how to use the nursery listings please turn to p.779. **Always check that the nursery you select has the plant in stock before you set out.**

Plants with more than 30 Suppliers

In some cases, against the plant name you will see the term 'more than 30 suppliers' instead of a nursery code. If we were to include every plant listed by all nurseries, the *RHS Plant Finder* would become unmanageably bulky. We therefore ask nurseries to restrict their entries to those plants that are not already well represented. As a result, if more than 30 nurseries offer any plant the Directory gives no nursery codes and the plant is listed instead as having 'more than 30 suppliers'. You should have little difficulty in locating these in local nurseries or garden centres. However, if you are unable to find such plants, we will be pleased to send a full list of all the nurseries that we have on file as stockists. To obtain a list, please see the Introduction on p.4.

Finding Fruit, Vegetables and Herbs

You will need to search for these by their botanical names. Common names are cross-referenced to their botanical names in the Plant Directory.

If you have Difficulty Finding your Plant

If you cannot immediately find the plant you seek, look through the various species of the genus. You may be using an incomplete name. The problem is most likely to arise in very large genera such as *Phlox* where there are a number of possible species, each with a large number of cultivars. A search through the whole genus may well bring success. Please note that, for space reasons, the following are not listed in the Plant Directory: annuals, orchids, except hardy terrestrial orchids; cacti, except hardy cacti.

Cross-references

It may be that the plant name you seek is a synonym. Our intention is to list nursery codes only against the correct botanical name. Where you find a synonym you will be cross-referred to the correct name. Occasionally you may find that the correct botanical name to which you have been referred is not listed. This is because it was last listed in an earlier edition as explained below.

Plants Last Listed in Earlier Editions

It may be that the plant you are seeking has no known suppliers and is thus not listed.

The loss of a plant name from the Directory may arise for a number of reasons – the supplier may have gone out of business, or may not have responded to our latest questionnaire and has therefore been removed from the book. Such plants may well be still available but we have no current knowledge of their whereabouts. Alternatively, some plants may have been misnamed by nurseries in previous editions, but are now appearing under their correct name.

To obtain a listing of plants last listed in earlier editions please see the Introduction on p.4.

> *Please, never use an old edition*

USING THE PLANT DIRECTORY

The main purpose of the Plant Directory is to help the reader correctly identify the plant they seek and find its stockist. Each nursery has a unique identification code which appears to the right of the plant name. Turn to Nursery Details by Code (p.782) for the address, opening times and other details of the nursery. The first letter of each nursery code denotes its geographical region.

Turn to the map on p.778 to find your region code and then identify the nurseries in your area.

Another purpose of the Directory is to provide more information about the plant through the symbols and other information. For example, if it has an alternative names, is new to this edition or has received the RHS Award of Garden Merit.

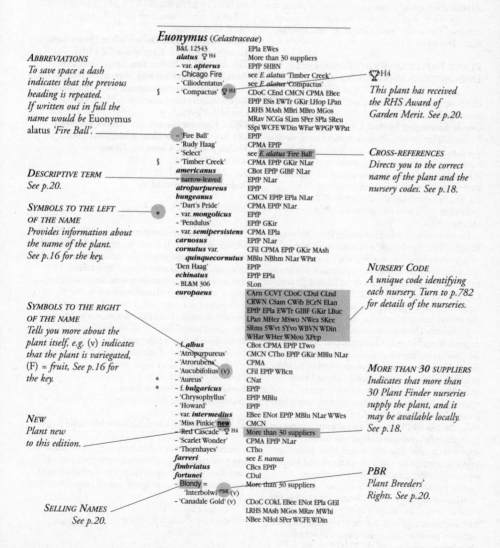

ABBREVIATIONS
To save space a dash indicates that the previous heading is repeated. If written out in full the name would be Euonymus *alatus 'Fire Ball'.*

DESCRIPTIVE TERM
See p.20.

SYMBOLS TO THE LEFT OF THE NAME
Provides information about the name of the plant. See p.16 for the key.

SYMBOLS TO THE RIGHT OF THE NAME
Tells you more about the plant itself, e.g. (v) indicates that the plant is variegated, (F) = fruit, See p.16 for the key.

NEW
Plant new to this edition.

SELLING NAMES
See p.20.

This plant has received the RHS Award of Garden Merit. See p.20.

CROSS-REFERENCES
Directs you to the correct name of the plant and the nursery codes. See p.18.

NURSERY CODE
A unique code identifying each nursery. Turn to p.782 for details of the nurseries.

MORE THAN 30 SUPPLIERS
Indicates that more than 30 Plant Finder nurseries supply the plant, and it may be available locally. See p.18.

PBR
Plant Breeders' Rights. See p.20.

Additional Plant Name Information in the Directory

Descriptive Terms

Terms which appear after the main part of the name are shown in a smaller font to distinguish name parts that are common names, collectors' codes and other descriptive terms. This descriptive element gives extra information about the plant, for example where it is from, or what colour it is. For example, *Penstemon* 'Sour Graphes' M. Fish, *Lobelia tupa* dark orange.

Plant Breeders' Rights and Trade Designations (Selling Names)

Plants covered by an active Plant Breeders' Rights grant are indicated in the *RHS Plant Finder*. Grants are awarded by both UK and EU Plant Variety Rights offices. Because grants can come into force and lapse at any time, this book can only represent the situation at one point in time, but it is hoped that the information presented will act as a useful guide to growers and gardeners. UK grants represent the position as of the end of December 2002 and EU grants as of the end of October 2002.

Plants granted protection under Plant Breeders' Rights (PBR) legislation, and those with high-volume international sales, are often given a code or nonsense name for registration purposes. Under the rules of the International Code of Nomenclature for Cultivated Plants 1995 (ICNCP), such a name, established by a legal process, has to be regarded as the correct cultivar name for the plant.

Unfortunately, the names are often unpronounceable and meaningless, so the plants are given other names designed to attract sales when they are released. These are often referred to as selling names but are officially termed trade designations. Also, when a cultivar name is translated from its original language, the translation is regarded as a trade designation.

In the case of PBRs, it is a legal requirement for both the cultivar name and the trade designation to appear on a label at point-of-sale. Most plants are sold under only one trade designation, but some, especially roses, are sold under a number of names, particularly when cultivars are introduced to other countries. Usually, the correct cultivar name is the only way to ensure that the same plant is not bought unwittingly under two or more different trade designations. The *RHS Plant Finder* follows the recommendations of the ICNCP when dealing with trade designations. These are always to quote the cultivar name and trade designation together and to style the trade designation in a different typeface, without single quotation marks. The *RHS Plant Finder* takes no responsibility for ensuring that nurseries selling plants with Plant Breeders' Rights are licensed to do so.

For further information on PBR contact:
Mr R Greenaway
Plant Variety Rights Office, White House Lane, Huntingdon Road, Cambridge CB3 0LF
Tel: (01223) 342350   Fax: (01223) 342386.
Website: www.defra.gov.uk/planth/pvs/pbrguide.htm

For details of plants covered by Community Rights contact the Community Plant Variety Office (CPVO):
Office Communautaire des Variétés Végétales,
PO Box 2141, 3 Boulevard Maréchal Foch,
F-49021 Angers, Cedex 02, France
Tel: 00 33 (02) 41 25 64 00
Fax: 00 33 (02) 41 25 64 10
Website: www.cpvo.eu.int

Variegated Plants

Following a suggestion from the Variegated Plant Group of the Hardy Plant Society, we have added a (v) to those plants which are 'variegated' although this may not be apparent from their name. The dividing line between variegation and less distinct colour marking is necessarily arbitrary and plants with light veins, pale, silver or dark zones or leaves flushed in paler colours are not shown as being variegated unless there is an absolutely sharp distinction between paler and darker zones. For further details of the Variegated Plant Group, please write to
Mrs Bee Newbold
Netherbury, 36 Worgret Road
Wareham, Dorset BH20 4PN

♥ The Award Of Garden Merit

The Award of Garden Merit (AGM) is intended to be of practical value to the ordinary gardener, and is therefore awarded only after a period of assessment by the Society's Standing and Joint Committees. An AGM plant:
- must be available
- must be of outstanding excellence for garden decoration or use
- must be of good constitution

- must not require highly specialist growing conditions or care
- must not be particularly susceptible to any pest or disease
- must not be subject to an unreasonable degree of reversion

The RHS publication *AGM Plants 2003* gives a full list of AGM plants with hardiness ratings. Copies can be ordered from **RHS Enterprises** on (01483) 211320. Information about AGM plants is also available on the RHS website at www.rhs.org.uk.

HARDINESS

Hardiness ratings are shown for AGM plants. The categories used are as follows:

H1 = plants requiring heated glass in the British Isles (roughly equivalent to Zones 10 and 11 according to the United States Department of Agriculture [USDA] system).

H2 = plants requiring unheated glass in the British Isles (USDA Zone 9 but sometimes resenting winter wet).

H3 = plants hardy outside in some regions of the British Isles or in particular situations, or which, while usually grown outside in summer, need frost-free protection in winter (e.g. dahlias)(USDA Zones 8 and 9).

H4 = plants hardy throughout the British Isles. (USDA Zone 7. Though most of the British Isles corresponds to USDA Zone 8, to be considered hardy here, plants must tolerate significantly colder than average, i.e. USDA Zone 7, winters.)

NOTES TO SUPPLEMENTARY KEYS

COLLECTORS' REFERENCES

Abbreviations (usually with numbers) following a plant name, refer to the collector(s) of the plant. These abbreviations are expanded, with a collector's name or expedition title, in the section Collectors' References starting on p.22.

A collector's reference may indicate a new, as yet unnamed range of variation within a species; their inclusion in the *RHS Plant Finder* supports the book's role in sourcing unusual plants.

Since the adoption of the *Convention on Biological Diversity* in 1993, collectors are normally required to have prior consent for the acquisition and commercialisation of collected material.

NOMENCLATURE NOTES

These refer to plants in the Directory that are marked with a 'N' to the left of the name. The notes add further information to names which are complex or may be confusing. They start on p.25.

CLASSIFICATION OF GENERA

Genera including a large number of species or with many cultivars are often subdivided into groups, each based on a particular characteristic or combination of characteristics. Colour of flower or fruit and shape of flower are common examples, and, with fruit, whether a cultivar is grown for culinary or dessert purposes. How such groups are named differs from genus to genus.

To help users of the *RHS Plant Finder* find exactly the plants they want, the majority of classifications used within cultivated genera are listed with codes and each species or cultivar is marked with the appropriate code in brackets after its name in the Plant Directory. The codes relating to edible fruits are listed with the more specialised classifications. These apply across several genera. To find the explanation of each code, simply look it up under the genus concerned in the Classification of Genera on p.31.

REVERSE SYNONYMS

It is likely that users of this book will come across names in certain genera which they did not expect to find. This may be because species have been transferred from another genus (or genera). In the list of Reverse Synonyms on p.36, the name on the left hand side is that of an accepted genus to which species have been transferred from the genus on the right. Sometimes all species will have been transferred, but in many cases only a few will be affected. Consulting Reverse Synonyms enables users to find the genera from which species have been transferred. If the right-hand genus is then found in the Plant Directory, the movements of species becomes clear through the cross-references in the nursery-code column.

SUPPLEMENTARY KEYS TO THE DIRECTORY

COLLECTORS' REFERENCES

Abbreviations following a plant name, refer to the collector(s) of the plant. These abbreviations are expanded below, with a collector's name or expedition title. For a fuller explanation, see p.21.

A&JW	A. & J. Watson
A&L	Ala, A.; Lancaster, Roy
AB&S	Archibald, James; Blanchard, John W; Salmon, M.
AC	Clark, Alan J.
AC&H	Apold, J.; Cox, Peter; Hutchison, Peter
AC&W	Albury; Cheese, M.; Watson, J.M.
ACE	AGS Expedition to China (1994)
ACL	Leslie, Alan C.
AGS/ES	AGS Expedition to Sikkim (1983)
AGSJ	AGS Expedition to Japan (1988)
Airth	Airth, Murray
Akagi	Akagi Botanical Garden
AL&JS	Sharman, Joseph L.; Leslie, Alan C.
ARG	Argent, G.C.G.
B L.	Beer, Len
B&L	Brickell, Christopher D.; Leslie, Alan C.
B&M & BM	Brickell, Christopher D.; Mathew, Brian
B&S	Bird P. & Salmon M.
B&SWJ	Wynn-Jones, Bleddyn; Wynn-Jones, Susan
BB	Bartholomew, B.
BC	Chudziak, W.
BC&W	Beckett; Cheese, M.; Watson, J.M.
BL&M	University of Bangor Expedition to NE Nepal
BM	Mathew, Brian F.
BM&W	Binns, David L.; Mason, M.; Wright, A.
BR	Rushbrooke, Ben
BS	Smith, Basil
BSBE	Bowles Scholarship Botanical Expedition (1963)
BSSS	Crûg Expedition, Jordan 1991
Bu	Bubert, S.
Burtt	Burtt, Brian L.
C	Cole, Desmond T.
C&C	Cox, P.A. & Cox, K.N.E.

C&Cu	Cox, K.N.E. & Cubey, J.
C&H	Cox, Peter; Hutchison, Peter
C&K	Chamberlain & Knott
C&R	Christian & Roderick
C&S	Clark, Alan; Sinclair, Ian W.J.
C&V	K.N.E. Cox & S. Vergera
C&W	Cheese, M.; Watson, J.M.
CC	Chadwell, Christopher
CC&H	Chamberlain, David F.; Cox, Peter; Hutchison, P.
CC&McK	Chadwell, Christopher; McKelvie, A.
CC&MR	Chadwell, Christopher; Ramsay
CCH&H	Chamberlain, D.F.; Cox, P.; Hutchison, P.; Hootman, S.
CCH&H	Chamberlain, Cox, Hootman & Hutchison
CD&R	Compton, J.; D'Arcy, J.; Rix, E.M.
CDB	Brickell, Christopher D.
CDC	Coode, Mark J.E.; Dockrill, Alexander
CDC&C	Compton, D'Arcy, Christopher & Coke
CDPR	Compton, D'Arcy, Pope & Rix
CE&H	Christian, P.J.; Elliott; Hoog
CEE	Chengdu Edinburgh Expedition China 1991
CGW	Grey-Wilson, Christopher
CH&M	Cox, P.; Hutchison, P.; Maxwell-MacDonald, D.
CHP&W	Kashmir Botanical Expedition
CL	Lovell, Chris
CLD	Chungtien, Lijiang & Dali Exped. China 1990
CM&W	Cheese M., Mitchel J. & Watson, J.
CN&W	Clark; Neilson; Wilson
CNDS	Nelson, C. & Sayers D.
Cooper	Cooper, R.E.
Cox	Cox, Peter A.
CPC	Cobblewood Plant Collection
CPN	Compton, James
CSE	Cyclamen Society Expedition (1990)
CT	Teune, Carla
DBG	Denver Botanic Garden, Colorado
DC	Cheshire, David
DF	Fox, D.
DJH	Hinkley, Dan

DJHC	Hinkley China
DM	Millais, David
Doleshy	Doleshy, F.L.
DS&T	Drake, Sharman J.; Thompson
DWD	Rose, D.
ECN	Nelson, E. Charles
EDHCH	Hammond, Eric D.
EGM	Millais, T.
EKB	Balls, Edward K.
EM	East Malling Research Station
EMAK	Edinburgh Makalu Expedition (1991)
EMR	Rix, E.Martyn
EN	Needham, Edward F.
ENF	Fuller, E. Nigel
ETE	Edinburgh Taiwan Expedition (1993)
ETOT	Kirkham, T.S.; Flanagan, Mark
F	Forrest, G.
F&W	Watson, J.; Flores, A.
Farrer	Farrer, Reginald
FK	Kinmonth, Fergus W.
FMB	Bailey, F.M.
G	Gardner, Martin F.
G&K	Gardner, Martin F.; Knees, Sabina G.
G&P	Gardner, Martin F.; Page, Christopher N.
GG	Gusman, G.
GS	Sherriff, George
Guitt	Guittoneau, G.G.
Guiz	Guizhou Expedition (1985)
G-W&P	Grey-Wilson, Christopher; Phillips
H	Huggins, Paul
H&B	Hilliard, Olive M.; Burtt, Brian L.
H&D	Howick, C.; Darby
H&M	Howick, Charles; McNamara, William A.
H&W	Hedge, Ian C.; Wendelbo, Per W.
Harry Smith	Smith, K.A.Harry
Hartside	Hartside Nursery
HCM	Heronswood Expedition to Chile, 1998
HH&K	Hannay, S&S & Kingsbury, N
HLMS	Springate, L.S.
HM&S	Halliwell, B., Mason, M. & Smallcombe
HOA	Hoog, Anton
Hummel	Hummel, D.
HW&E	Wendelbo, Per; Hedge, I.; Ekberg, L.
HWEL	Hirst, J.Michael; Webster, D.
HWJ	Crûg Heronswood Joint Expedition
HWJCM	Crûg Heronswood Expedition
HWJK	Crûg Heronswood Expedition, East Nepal 2002
HZ	Zetterlund, Henrik
IDS	International Dendrological Society
J&JA	Archibald, James; Archibald, Jennifer
J. Jurasek	Jurasek, J.
JCA	Archibald, James
JE	Jack Elliott
JJ	Jackson, J.
JJ&JH	Halda, J.; Halda, J.
JJH	Halda, Joseph J.
JLS	Sharman, J.L.
JMT	Mann Taylor, J.
JN	Nielson, Jens
JR	Russell, J.
JRM	Marr, John
JW	Watson, J.M.
K	Kirkpatrick, George
K&LG	Gillanders, Kenneth; Gillanders, L.
K&Mc	Kirkpatrick, George; McBeath, Ronald J.D.
K&P	Josef Kopec, Milan Prasil
K&T	Kurashige, Y.; Tsukie, S.
KC	Cox, Kenneth
KEKE	Kew/Edinburgh Kanchenjunga Expedition (1989)
KGB	Kunming/Gothenburg Botanical Expedition (1993)
KR	Rushforth, K.D.
KRW	Wooster, K.R. (distributed after his death by Kath Dryden)
KW	Kingdon-Ward, F.
L	Lancaster, Roy C.
L&S	Ludlow, Francis; Sherriff, George
LA	Long Ashton Research Station clonal selection scheme
LEG	Lesotho Edinburgh/Gothenburg Expedition (1997)
Lismore	Lismore Nursery, Breeder's Number
LM&S	Leslie, Mattern & Sharman
LP	Palmer, W.J.L.
LS&E	Ludlow, Frank; Sherriff, George; Elliott, E. E.
LS&H	Ludlow, Frank; Sherriff, George; Hicks, J. H.
LS&T	Ludlow, Frank; Sherriff, George; Taylor, George
M&PS	Mike & Polly Stone
M&T	Mathew; Tomlinson
Mac&W	McPhail & Watson
McB	McBeath, R.J.D.
McLaren	McLaren, H.D.
MDM	Myers, Michael D.
MESE	Alpine Garden Society Expedition, Greece 1999
MF	Foster, Maurice
MH	Heasman, Matthew T.
MK	Kammerlander, Michael
MP	Pavelka, Mojmir
MPF	Frankis, M.P.
MS	Salmon, M.
MS&CL	Salmon, M.; Lovell, C.
MSF	Fillan, M.S.
NJM	Macer, N.J.
NNS	Ratko, Ron
NS	Turland, Nick
NVFDE	Northern Vietnam First Darwin Expedition

Og	Ogisu, Mikinori
P&C	Paterson, David S.; Clarke, Sidney
P&W	Polastri; Watson, J. M.
PB	Bird, Peter
PC&H	Pattison, G.; Catt, P.; Hickson, M.
PD	Davis, Peter H.
PF	Furse, Paul
PJC	Christian, Paul J.
PJC&AH	P.J. Christian & A. Hogg
Polunin	Polunin, Oleg
Pras	Prasil, M.
PS&W	Polunin, Oleg; Sykes, William; Williams, John
PW	Wharton, Peter
R	Rock, J.F.C.
RB	Brown, R.
RCB/Arg	Brown, Robert, Argentina, 2002
RCB/Eq	Brown, Robert, Ecuador, 1988
RCB/TQ	Brown, Robert, Turkey 2001
RH	Hancock, R.
RMRP	Rocky Mountain Rare Plants, Denver, Colorado
RS	Suckow, Reinhart
RV	Richard Valder
S&B	Blanchard, J.W.; Salmon, M.
S&F	Salmon, M. & Fillan, M.
S&L	Sinclair, Ian W.J.; Long, David G.
S&SH	Sheilah and Spencer Hannay
Sandham	Sandham, John
SB&L	Salmon, Bird and Lovell
SBEC	Sino-British Expedition to Cangshan
SBEL	Sino-British Lijiang Expedition
SBQE	Sino-British Expedition to Quinghai
Sch	Schilling, Anthony D.

SD	Sashal Dayal
SDR	Rankin, Stella; Rankin, David
SEH	Hootman, Steve
SEP	Swedish Expedition to Pakistan
SF	Forde, P.
SG	Salmon, M. & Guy, P.
SH	Hannay, Spencer
Sich	Simmons, Erskine, Howick & Mcnamara
SLIZE	Swedish-Lithuanian-Iranian Zagros Expedition to Iran (May 1988)
SOJA	Kew / Quarryhill Expedition to Southern Japan
SS&W	Stainton, J.D.Adam; Sykes, William; Williams, John
SSNY	Sino-Scottish Expedition to NW Yunnan (1992)
T	Taylor, Nigel P.
T&K	Taylor, Nigel P.; Knees, Sabina
TS&BC	Smythe, T and Cherry, B
TSS	Spring Smyth, T.L.M.
TW	Tony Weston
USDAPI	US Department of Agriculture Plant Index Number
USDAPQ	US Dept. of Agriculture Plant Quarantine Number
USNA	United States National Arboretum
VHH	Vernon H. Heywood
W	Wilson, Ernest H.
WM	McLewin, William
Woods	Woods, Patrick J.B.
Wr	Wraight, David & Anke
Yu	Yu, Tse-tsun

NOMENCLATURE NOTES

These notes refer to plants in the main Plant Directory that are marked with a 'N'. 'Bean Supplement' refers to W.J. Bean *Trees & Shrubs Hardy in the British Isles* (Supplement to the 8th edition) edited by D L Clarke 1988.

Acer palmatum 'Sango-kaku'/ 'Senkaki'
Two or more clones are offered under these names. *A. palmatum* 'Eddisbury' is similar with brighter coral stems.

Achillea ptarmica The Pearl Group/ *A. ptarmica* (The Pearl Group) 'Boule de Neige' / *A. ptarmica* (The Pearl Group) 'The Pearl'
In the recent trial of achilleas at Wisley, only one of the several stocks submitted as 'The Pearl' matched the original appearance of this plant according to Graham Stuart Thomas, this being from Wisley's own stock. At rather less than 60cm (2ft), this needed little support, being the shortest of the plants bearing this name, with slightly grey, not glossy dark green, leaves and a non-invasive habit. This has been designated as the type for this cultivar and only this clone should bear the cultivar name 'The Pearl'. The Pearl Group covers all other double-flowered clones of this species, including seed-raised plants which are markedly inferior, sometimes scarcely double, often invasive and usually needing careful staking. It has been claimed that 'The Pearl' was a re-naming of Lemoine's 'Boule de Neige' but not all authorities agree: all plants submitted to the Wisley trial as 'Boule de Neige' were different from each other, not the same clone as Wisley's 'The Pearl' and referrable to The Pearl Group.

Anemone magellanica
According to *The European Garden Flora*, this is a variant of the very variable *A. multifida*.

Anemone nemorosa 'Alba Plena'
This name is used for several double white forms including *A. nemorosa* 'Flore Pleno' and *A. nemorosa* 'Vestal'.

Artemisia granatensis hort.
Possibly a variant of *A. absinthium*.

Artemisia ludoviciana var. latiloba / *A. ludoviciana* 'Valerie Finnis'
Leaves of the former are glabrous at maturity, those of the latter are not.

Artemisia stelleriana 'Boughton Silver'
This was thought to be the first validly published name for this plant, 'Silver Brocade' having been published earlier but invalidly in an undated publication. However, an earlier valid publication for the cultivar name 'Mori' has subsequently been found for the same plant. A proposal to conserve 'Boughton Silver' has been tabled because of its more widespread use.

Aster amellus Violet Queen
It is probable that more than one cultivar is sold under this name.

Aster dumosus
Many of the asters listed under *A. novi-belgii* contain varying amounts of *A. dumosus* blood in their parentage. It is not possible to allocate these to one species or the other and they are therefore listed under *A. novi-belgii*.

Aster × frikartii 'Mönch'
The true plant is very rare in British gardens. Most plants are another form of *A. × frikartii*, usually 'Wunder von Stäfa'.

Aster novi-belgii
See note under *A. dumosus*. *A. laevis* is also involved in the parentage of most cultivars.

Azara paraguayensis
This is an unpublished name for what seems to be a hybrid between *A. serrata* and *A. lanceolata*.

Berberis buxifolia 'Nana'/ 'Pygmaea'
See explanation in Bean Supplement.

Berberis stenophylla 'Lemon Queen'
This sport from 'Pink Pearl' was first named in 1982. The same mutation occurred again and was named 'Cream Showers'. The older name has priority.

Betula utilis var. jacquemontii
Plants are often the clones *B. utilis* var. *jacquemontii* 'Inverleith' or *B. utilis* var. *jacquemontii* 'Doorenbos'

Blechnum chilense/B. tabulare
The true *B. tabulare* has an AGM and is grown in the British Isles but is probably not presently offered by nurseries. This name is often misapplied to *B. chilense*.

Brachyscome
Originally published as *Brachyscome* by Cassini who later revised his spelling to *Brachycome*. The original spelling has been internationally adopted.

Calamagrostis × acutiflora 'Karl Foerster'
C. × acutiflora 'Stricta' differs in being 15cm taller, 10-15 days earlier flowering with a less fluffy inflorescence.

Caltha polypetala
This name is often applied to a large-flowered variant of C. *palustris*. The true species has more (7-10) petals.

Camassia leichtlinii 'Alba'
The true cultivar has blueish-white, not cream flowers.

Camassia leichtlinii 'Plena'
This has starry, transparent green-white flowers; creamy-white 'Semiplena' is sometimes offered under this name.

Camellia japonica 'Campbellii'
This name is used for five cultivars including 'Margherita Coleoni' but applies correctly to Guichard's 1894 cultivar, single to semi-double full rose pink.

Campanula lactiflora 'Alba'
This refers to the pure white flowered clone, not to blueish- or greyish-white flowered plants, nor to seed-raised plants.

Carex morrowii 'Variegata'
C. *oshimensis* 'Evergold' is sometimes sold under this name.

Carya illinoinensis
The correct spelling of this name is discussed in *Baileya*, **10**(1) (1962).

Cassinia retorta
Now included within C. *leptophylla*. A valid infra-specific epithet has yet to be published.

Ceanothus 'Italian Skies'
Many plants under this name are not true to name.

Chamaecyparis lawsoniana 'Columnaris Glauca'
Plants under this name might be C. *lawsoniana* 'Columnaris' or a new invalidly named cultivar.

Chamaecyparis pisifera 'Squarrosa Argentea'
There are two plants of this name, one (valid) with variegated foliage, the other (invalid) with silvery foliage.

Chrysanthemum 'Anastasia Variegated'
Despite its name, this seems to be derived from 'Mei-kyo', not 'Anastasia'.

Clematis chrysocoma
The true C. *chrysocoma* is a non-climbing erect plant with dense yellow down on the young growth, still uncommon in cultivation.

Clematis montana
This name should be used for the typical white-flowered variety only. Pink-flowered variants are referable to C. *montana* var. *rubens*.

Clematis 'Victoria'
There is also a Latvian cultivar of this name with petals with a central white bar.

Colchicum 'Autumn Queen'
Entries here might refer to the slightly different C. 'Prinses Astrid'.

Cornus 'Norman Hadden'
See note in Bean Supplement, p.184.

Cotoneaster dammeri
Plants sold under this name are usually C. *dammeri* 'Major'.

Cotoneaster frigidus 'Cornubia'
According to Hylmø this cultivar, like all other variants of this species, is fully deciduous. Several evergreen cotoneasters are also grown under this name, most are clones of C. × *watereri* or C. *salicifolius*.

Crataegus coccinea
C. *intricata*, C. *pedicellata* and C. *biltmoreana* are occasionally supplied under this name.

Crocus cartwrightianus 'Albus'
The plant offered is the true cultivar and not C. *hadriaticus*.

Dianthus fringed pink
D. 'Old Fringed Pink' and D. 'Old Fringed White' are also sometimes sold under this name.

Dianthus 'Musgrave's Pink' (p)
This is the registered name of this white-flowered cultivar.

Elymus magellanicus
Although this is a valid name, Roger Grounds has suggested that many plants might belong to a different, perhaps unnamed species.

Epilobium glabellum hort.
Plants under this name are not E. *glabellum* but are close to E. *wilsonii* Petrie or perhaps a hybrid of it.

Erodium glandulosum
Plants under this name are often hybrids.

Erodium guttatum
Doubtfully in commerce; plants under this name are usually E. *heteradenum*, E. *cheilanthifolium* or hybrids.

Erysimum cheiri 'Baden-Powell'
Plant of uncertain origin differing from E. *cheiri* 'Harpur Crewe' only in its shorter stature.

Fagus sylvatica Cuprea Group/Atropurpurea Group
It is desirable to provide a name, Cuprea Group, for less richly coloured forms, used in historic landscapes before the purple clones appeared.

Fagus sylvatica 'Pendula'
This name refers to the Knap Hill clone, the most common weeping form in English gardens. Other clones occur, particularly in Cornwall and Ireland.

Fuchsia loxensis
For a comparison of the true species with the hybrids 'Speciosa' and 'Loxensis' commonly grown under this name, see Boullemier's Check List (2nd ed.) p.268.

Gentiana cachemirica
Most plants sold are not true to type.

Geum 'Borisii'
This name refers to cultivars of *G. coccineum* Sibthorp & Smith, especially *G.* 'Werner Arends' and not to *G.* × *borisii* Kelleper.

Halimium alyssoides and *H. halimifolium*
Plants under these names are sometimes *H.* × *pauanum* or *H.* × *santae*.

Hebe 'C.P. Raffill'
See note in Bean Supplement, p.265.

Hebe 'Carl Teschner'
See note in Bean Supplement, p.264.

Hebe glaucophylla
A green reversion of the hybrid *H.* 'Glaucophylla Variegata' is often sold under this name.

Hedera helix 'Caenwoodiana' / 'Pedata'
Some authorities consider these to be distinct cultivars while others think them different morphological forms of the same unstable clone.

Hedera helix 'Oro di Bogliasco'
Priority between this name and 'Jubiläum Goldherz' and 'Goldheart' has yet to be finally resolved.

Helleborus × *hybridus* / *H. orientalis* hort.
The name *H.* × *hybridus* for acaulescent hellebore hybrids does not seem to follow the *International Code of Botanical Nomenclature* Article H.3.2 requiring one of the parent species to be designated and does not seem to have been typified, contrary to Article 7 of the Code. However, the illustration accompanying the original description in Vilmorin's *Blumengärtnerei* 3(1): 27 (1894) shows that one parent of the cross must have been *H. guttatus*, now treated as part of *H. orientalis*. Taking this illustration as the type for this hybrid species makes it possible to retain *H.* × *hybridus* formally as a hybrid binomial (rather than *H. hybridus* as in a previous edition), as the Code's requirement to distinguish one parent is now met.

Heuchera micrantha var. *diversifolia* 'Palace Purple'
This cultivar name refers only to plants with deep purple-red foliage. Seed-raised plants of inferior colouring should not be offered under this name.

Hosta montana
This name refers only to plants long grown in Europe, which differ from *H. elata*.

Hydrangea macrophylla Teller Series
This is used both as a descriptive common name for Lacecap hydrangeas (German *teller* = plate, referring to the more or less flat inflorescence) and for the series of hybrids raised by Wädenswill in Switzerland bearing German names of birds. It is not generally possible to link a hydrangea described by the series name plus a colour description (e.g. Teller Blau, Teller Rosa, Teller Rot) to a single cultivar.

Hypericum fragile
The true *H. fragile* is probably not available from British nurseries.

Hypericum 'Gemo'
Either a selection of *H. prolificum* or *H. prolificum* × *H. densiflorum*.

Ilex × *altaclerensis*
The argument for this spelling is given by Susyn Andrews, *The Plantsman*, 5(2) and is not superceded by the more recent comments in the Supplement to Bean's Trees and Shrubs.

Iris
Apart from those noted below, cultivar names marked 'N' are not registered. The majority of those marked 'I' have been previously used for a different cultivar.

Iris histrioides 'Major'
Two clones are offered under this name, the true one pale blue with darker spotting on the falls, the incorrect one violet-blue with almost horizontal falls.

Juniperus × *media*
This name is illegitimate if applied to hybrids of *J. chinensis* × *J. sabina*, having been previously used for a different hybrid (P.A. Schmidt, *IDS Yearbook 1993*, 47-48). Because of its importance to gardeners, a proposal to conserve its present use was tabled but subsequently rejected.

Lavandula angustifolia 'Lavender Lady' / *L.* 'Cambridge Lady'
Might be synonyms of *L. angustifolia* 'Lady'.

Lavandula × *intermedia* 'Arabian Night'
Plants under this name might be *L.* × *intermedia* 'Impress Purple'.

Lavandula spica
This name is classed as a name to be rejected (*nomen rejiciendum*) by the *International Code of Botanical Nomenclature*.

Lavandula 'Twickel Purple'
Two cultivars are sold under this name, one a form of *L.* × *intermedia*, the other of *L. angustifolia*.

Lavatera olbia and *L. thuringiaca*
Although *L. olbia* is usually shrubby and *L. thuringiaca* usually herbaceous, both

species are very variable. Cultivars formally ascribed to one species or the other have been shown to be hybrids and are referable to the recently-named hybrid species *L.* × *clementii*.

Lonicera periclymenum 'Serotina'
See note in Bean Supplement, p.315.

Lonicera sempervirens f. sulphurea
Plants in the British Isles usually a yellow-flowered form of *L. periclymenum*.

Malus domestica 'Dummellor's Seedling'
The phonetic spelling 'Dumelow's Seedling' contravenes the ICBN ruling on orthography, i.e. that, except for intentional latinizations, commemorative names should be based on the original spelling of the person's name (Article 60.11). The spelling adopted here is that used on the gravestone of the raiser in Leicestershire.

Meconopsis Fertile Blue Group
This Cultivar-group comprises seed-raised and intrinsically perennial tall blue poppies of as yet indeterminate origin (i.e. fertile forms other than the species *M. betonicifolia*, *M. grandis* and *M. simplicifolia*). The only cultivar so far established is *M.* 'Lingholm' (syns 'Blue Ice' and 'Correnie'). The bulk of seed-raised plants in cultivation and offered for sale are very likely to be *M.* 'Lingholm', although sometimes poorly selected. Many of these plants are currently being distributed erroneously as *M.* × *sheldonii* and as *M. grandis*.

Meconopsis George Sherriff Group
This Cultivar-group comprises a number of sterile (almost invariably) clones of large blue poppies previously (and erroneously) known collectively as *M. grandis* GS600.

Meconopsis grandis ambig.
See note under *M.* Fertile Blue Group. The true species has been recently reintroduced into cultivation in the British Isles but is still rarely offered.

Meconopsis Infertile Blue Group
This cultivar-group comprises long-established sterile (almost invariably) clones of large blue poppies other than George Sherriff Group and often given the epithet × *sheldonii*.

Meconopsis × sheldonii ambig.
See notes for *M.* Fertile Blue Group and *M.* Infertile Blue Group.

Melissa officinalis 'Variegata'
The true cultivar of this name had leaves striped with white.

Nemesia caerulea 'Joan Wilder'
The lavender blue clone 'Joan Wilder', described and illustrated in *The Hardy Plant*, 14(1), 11-14, does not come true from seed; it may only be propagated from cuttings.

Osmanthus heterophyllus 'Gulftide'
Probably correctly *O.* × *fortunei* 'Gulftide'.

Papaver orientale agg.
Plants listed as *P. orientale* agg. (i.e. aggregate) or as one of its cultivars may be *P. orientale* L,, *P. pseudo-orientale* or *P. bracteatum* or hybrids between them.

Pelargonium 'Lass o' Gowrie'
The American plant of this name has pointed, not rounded leaf lobes.

Pelargonium quercifolium
Plants under this name are mainly hybrids. The true species has pointed, not rounded leaf lobes.

Penstemon 'Taoensis'
This name for a small-flowered cultivar or hybrid of *P. isophyllus* originally appeared as 'Taoense' but must be corrected to agree in gender with *Penstemon* (masculine). Presumably an invalid name (published in Latin form since 1958), it is not synonymous with *P. crandallii* subsp. *glabrescens* var. *taosensis*.

Pernettya
Botanists now consider that *Pernettya* (fruit a berry) is not separable from *Gaultheria* (fruit a capsule) because in some species the fruit is intermediate between a berry and a capsule. For a fuller explanation see D. Middleton, *The Plantsman*, 12(3).

Picea pungens 'Glauca Pendula'
This name is used for several different glaucous cultivars.

Pinus ayacahuite
P. ayacahuite var. *veitchii* (syn. *P. veitchii)* is occasionally sold under this name.

Pinus nigra 'Cebennensis Nana'
A doubtful name, possibly a synonym for *P. nigra* 'Nana'.

Prunus laurocerasus 'Castlewellan'
We are grateful to Dr Charles Nelson for informing us that the name 'Marbled White' is
not valid because although it has priority of publication it does not have the approval of the originator who asked for it to be called 'Castlewellan'.

Prunus serrulata var. pubescens
See note in Bean Supplement, p.398.

Prunus × subhirtella 'Rosea'
Might be *P. pendula* var. *ascendens* 'Rosea', *P. pendula* 'Pendula Rosea', or *P.* × *subhirtella* 'Autumnalis Rosea'.

Rheum × cultorum
The name *R. × cultorum* was published without adequate description and must be abandoned in favour of the validly published *R. × hybridum*.

Rhododendron (azaleas)
All names marked 'N', except for the following, refer to more than one cultivar.

Rhododendron 'Hinomayo'
This name is based on a faulty transliteration (should be 'Hinamoyo') but the spelling 'Hinomayo' is retained in the interests of stability.

Rhus typhina
Linnaeus published both *R. typhina* and *R. hirta* as names for the same species. Though *R. hirta* has priority, it has been proposed that the name *R. typhina* should be conserved.

Rosa gentiliana
Plants under this name are usually the cultivar 'Polyantha Grandiflora' but might otherwise be *R. multiflora* 'Wilsonii', *R. multiflora* var. *cathayensis*, *R. henryi* or another hybrid.

Rosa 'Gros Choux de Hollande' hort. (Bb)
It is doubtful if this name is correctly applied.

Rosa 'Jacques Cartier' hort.
For a discussion on the correct identity of this rose see *Heritage Rose Foundation News*, Oct. 1989 & Jan. 1990.

Rosa 'Professeur Emile Perrot'
For a discussion on the correct identity of this rose see *Heritage Roses*, Nov. 1991.

Rosa Sweetheart
This is not the same as the Sweetheart Rose, a common name for *R.* 'Cécile Brünner'.

Rosa wichurana
This is the correct spelling according to the ICBN 1994 Article 60.11 (which enforces Recommendation 60C.1c) and not *wichuraiana* for this rose commemorating Max Wichura.

Rubus fruticosus L. agg.
Though some cultivated blackberries do belong to *Rubus fruticosus* L. *sensu stricto*, others are more correctly ascribed to other species of *Rubus* section *Glandulosus* (including *R. armeniacus*, *R. laciniatus* or *R. ulmifolius*) or are hybrids of species within this section. Because it is almost impossible to ascribe every cultivar to a single species or hybrid, they are listed under *R. fruticosus* L. agg. (i.e. aggregate) for convenience.

Salvia microphylla var. neurepia
The type of this variety is referable to the typical variety, *S. microphylla* var. *microphylla*.

Salvia officinalis 'Aurea'
S. officinalis var. *aurea* is a rare variant of the common sage with leaves entirely of gold. It is represented in cultivation by the cultivar 'Kew Gold'. The plant usually offered as *S. officinalis* 'Aurea' is the gold variegated sage *S. officinalis* 'Icterina'.

Sambucus nigra 'Aurea'
Plants under this name are usually not *S. nigra*.

Sedum nevii
The true species is not in cultivation. Plants under this name are usually either *S. glaucophyllum* or occasionally *S. beyrichianum*.

Skimmia japonica 'Foremanii'
The true cultivar, which belongs to *S. japonica* Rogersii Group, is believed to be lost to cultivation. Plants offered under this name are usually *S. japonica* 'Veitchii'.

Sorbus
Except for the following, *Sorbus* species marked N refer to names proposed by Dr Hugh McAllister for apomictic microspecies but not yet published.

Sorbus multijuga Sch 1132
Though this is an accepted name, this collection was obtained from outside the usual range of this species.

Spiraea japonica 'Shirobana'
Shirobana-shimotsuke is the common name for *S. japonica* var. *albiflora*. Shirobana means white-flowered and does not apply to the two-coloured form.

Staphylea holocarpa var. rosea
This botanical variety has woolly leaves. The cultivar 'Rosea', with which it is often confused, does not.

Stewartia ovata var. grandiflora.
Most, possibly all, plants available from British nurseries under this name are not true to name but are derived from the improved Nymans form.

Thymus serpyllum cultivars
Most cultivars are probably correctly cultivars of *T. polytrichus* or hybrids though they will remain listed under *T. serpyllum* pending further research.

Thymus 'Silver Posie'
The cultivar name 'Silver Posie' is applied to several different plants, not all of them *T. vulgaris*.

Tricyrtis Hototogisu
This is the common name applied generally to all Japanese *Tricyrtis* and specifically to *T. hirta*.

Tricyrtis macropoda
This name has been used for at least five different species.

Uncinia rubra
This name is also misapplied to *U. egmontiana* and *U. uncinata*.

Verbena
Entries marked (G) are considered by some botanists to belong to a separate genus, *Glandularia*. The principal differences are that verbenas have quadrangular, upright stems and terminal (rarely axillary) flowers in spikes or panicles of spikes; glandularias have cylindrical, creeping or semi-erect stems and flowers in terminal and axillary heads, sometimes elongating with age.

Verbena 'Kemerton'
Origin unknown, not from Kemerton.

Viburnum opulus 'Fructu Luteo'
See note below.

Viburnum opulus 'Xanthocarpum'
Some entries under this name might be the less compact *V. opulus* 'Fructu Luteo'.

Viburnum plicatum
Entries may include the 'snowball' form, *V. plicatum* f. *plicatum* (syn. *V. plicatum* 'Sterile'), as well as the 'lacecap' form, *V. plicatum* f. *tomentosum*.

Viola labradorica
See Note in *The Garden*, 110(2): 96.

CLASSIFICATION OF GENERA

Genera including a large number of species or with many cultivars are often subdivided into groups. Please turn to p.13 for a fuller explanation.

ACTINIDIA

(s-p)	Self-pollinating

BEGONIA

(C)	Cane
(R)	Rex
(S)	Semperflorens Cultorum
(T)	× *tuberhybrida* (Tuberous)

CHRYSANTHEMUM

(By the National Chrysanthemum Society)

(1)	Indoor Large (Exhibition)
(2)	Indoor Medium (Exhibition)
(3a)	Indoor Incurved: Large-flowered
(3b)	Indoor Incurved: Medium-flowered
(3c)	Indoor Incurved: Small-flowered
(4a)	Indoor Reflexed: Large-flowered
(4b)	Indoor Reflexed: Medium-flowered
(4c)	Indoor Reflexed: Small-flowered
(5a)	Indoor Intermediate: Large-flowered
(5b)	Indoor Intermediate: Medium-flowered
(5c)	Indoor Intermediate: Small-flowered (6a) Indoor Anemone: Large-flowered
(6b)	Indoor Anemone: Medium-flowered
(6c)	Indoor Anemone: Small-flowered
(7a)	Indoor Single: Large-flowered
(7b)	Indoor Single: Medium-flowered
(7c)	Indoor Single: Small-flowered
(8a)	Indoor True Pompon
(8b)	Indoor Semi-pompon
(9a)	Indoor Spray: Anemone
(9b)	Indoor Spray: Pompon
(9c)	Indoor Spray: Reflexed
(9d)	Indoor Spray: Single
(9e)	Indoor Spray: Intermediate
(9f)	Indoor Spray: Spider, Quill, Spoon or Any Other Type
(10a)	Indoor, Spider
(10b)	Indoor, Quill
(10c)	Indoor, Spoon
(11)	Any Other Indoor Type
(12a)	Indoor, Charm
(12b)	Indoor, Cascade
(13a)	October-flowering Incurved: Large-flowered
(13b)	October-flowering Incurved: Medium-flowered

(13c)	October-flowering Incurved: Small-flowered
(14a)	October-flowering Reflexed: Large-flowered
(14b)	October-flowering Reflexed: Medium-flowered
(14c)	October-flowering Reflexed: Small-flowered
(15a)	October-flowering Intermediate: Large-flowered
(15b)	October-flowering Intermediate: Medium-flowered
(15c)	October-flowered Intermediate: Small-flowered
(16)	October-flowering Large
(17a)	October-flowering Single: Large-flowered
(17b)	October-flowering Single: Medium-flowered
(17c)	October-flowering Single: Small-flowered
(18a)	October-flowering Pompon: True Pompon
(18b)	October-flowering Pompon: Semi-pompon
(19a)	October-flowering Spray: Anemone
(19b)	October-flowering Spray: Pompon
(19c)	October-flowering Spray: Reflexed
(19d)	October-flowering Spray: Single
(19e)	October-flowering Spray: Intermediate
(19f)	October-flowering Spray: Spider, Quill, Spoon or Any Other Type
(20)	Any Other October-flowering Type
(22a)	Charm: Anemone
(22b)	Charm: Pompon
(22c)	Charm: Reflexed
(22d)	Charm: Single
(22e)	Charm: Intermediate
(22f)	Charm: Spider, Quill, Spoon or Any Other Type
(23a)	Early-flowering Outdoor Incurved: Large-flowered
(23b)	Early-flowering Outdoor Incurved: Medium-flowered
(23c)	Early-flowering Outdoor Incurved: Small-flowered
(24a)	Early-flowering Outdoor Reflexed: Large-flowered
(24b)	Early-flowering Outdoor Reflexed: Medium-flowered
(24c)	Early-flowering Outdoor Reflexed: Small-flowered
(25a)	Early-flowering Outdoor Intermediate: Large-flowered

(25b)	Early-flowering Outdoor Intermediate: Medium-flowered
(25c)	Early-flowering Outdoor Intermediate: Small-flowered
(26a)	Early-flowering Outdoor Anemone: Large-flowered
(26b)	Early-flowering Outdoor Anemone: Medium-flowered
(27a)	Early-flowering Outdoor Single: Large-flowered
(27b)	Early-flowering Outdoor Single: Medium-flowered
(28a)	Early-flowering Outdoor Pompon: True Pompon
(28b)	Early-flowering Outdoor Pompon: Semi-pompon
(29a)	Early-flowering Outdoor Spray: Anemone
(29b)	Early-flowering Outdoor Spray: Pompon
(29c)	Early-flowering Outdoor Spray: Reflexed
(29d)	Early-flowering Outdoor Spray: Single
(29e)	Early-flowering Outdoor Spray: Intermediate
(29f)	Early-flowering Outdoor Spray: Spider, Quill, Spoon or Any Other Type
(29K)	Early-flowering Outdoor Spray: Korean
(29Rub)	Early-flowering Outdoor Spray: Rubellum
(30)	Any Other Early-flowering Outdoor Type

CLEMATIS

(A)	Alpina Group (Section Atragene)
(D)	Diversifolia Group
(Fl)	Florida Group (double-flowered)
(Fo)	Forsteri Group
(H)	Heracleifolia Group
(I)	Integrifolia Group
(J)	Jackmanii Group
(L)	Lanuginosa Group
(P)	Patens Group
(T)	Texensis Group
(Ta)	Tangutica Group
(Vt)	Viticella Group

DAHLIA

(By the National Dahlia Society with corresponding numerical classification according to the Royal Horticultural Society's International Register)

(Sin)	1 Single
(Anem)	2 Anemone-flowered

(Col)	3 Collerette
(WL)	4 Waterlily (unassigned)
(LWL)	4B Waterlily, Large
(MWL)	4C Waterlily, Medium
(SWL)	4D Waterlily, Small
(MinWL)	4E Waterlily, Miniature
(D)	5 Decorative (unassigned)
(GD)	5A Decorative, Giant
(LD)	5B Decorative, Large
(MD)	5C Decorative, Medium
(SD)	5D Decorative, Small
(MinD)	5E Decorative, Miniature
(SBa)	6A Small Ball
(MinBa)	6B Miniature Ball
(Pom)	7 Pompon
(C)	8 Cactus (unassigned)
(GC)	8A Cactus, Giant
(LC)	8B Cactus, Large
(MC)	8C Cactus, Medium
(SC)	8D Cactus, Small
(MinC)	8E Cactus, Miniature
(S-c)	9 Semi-cactus (unassigned)
(GS-c)	9A Semi-cactus, Giant
(LS-c)	9B Semi-cactus, Large
(MS-c)	9C Semi-cactus, Medium
(SS-c)	9D Semi-cactus, Small
(MinS-c)	9E Semi-cactus, Miniature
(Misc)	10 Miscellaneous
(O)	Orchid-flowering (in combination)
(B)	Botanical (in combination)
(DwB)	Dwarf Bedding (in combination)
(Fim)	Fimbriated (in combination)
(Lil)	Lilliput (in combination)

DIANTHUS

(By the Royal Horticultural Society)

(p)	Pink
(p,a)	Annual Pink
(pf)	Perpetual-flowering Carnation
(b)	Border Carnation
(M)	Malmaison Carnation

FRUIT

(B)	Black (*Vitis*), Blackcurrant (*Ribes*)
(Ball)	Ballerina (*Malus*)
(C)	Culinary (*Malus, Prunus, Pyrus, Ribes*)
(Cider)	Cider (*Malus*)
(D)	Dessert (*Malus, Prunus, Pyrus, Ribes*)
(F)	Fruit
(G)	Glasshouse (*Vitis*)
(O)	Outdoor (*Vitis*)
(P)	Pinkcurrant (*Ribes*)
(Perry)	Perry (*Pyrus*)
(R)	Red (*Vitis*), Redcurrant (*Ribes*)

(S)	Seedless (*Citrus, Vitis*)
(W)	White (*Vitis*), Whitecurrant (*Ribes*)

GLADIOLUS

(B)	Butterfly
(E)	Exotic
(G)	Giant
(L)	Large
(M)	Medium
(Min)	Miniature
(N)	Nanus
(P)	Primulinus
(S)	Small
(Tub)	Tubergenii

HYDRANGEA MACROPHYLLA

(H)	Hortensia
(L)	Lacecap

IRIS

(By the American Iris Society)

(AB)	Arilbred
(BB)	Border Bearded
(Cal-Sib)	Series *Californicae* × Series *Sibiricae*
(CH)	Californian Hybrid
(DB)	Dwarf Bearded (not assigned)
(Dut)	Dutch
(IB)	Intermediate Bearded
(La)	Louisiana Hybrid
(MDB)	Miniature Dwarf Bearded
(MTB)	Miniature Tall Bearded
(SDB)	Standard Dwarf Bearded
(Sino-Sib)	Series *Sibiricae*, chromosome number 2n=40
(Spuria)	Spuria
(TB)	Tall Bearded

LILIUM

(Classification according to *The International Lily Register* (ed. 3, 1982) with amendments from Supp. 10 (1992), Royal Horticultural Society)

(I)	Early-flowering Asiatic Hybrids derived from *L. amabile, L. bulbiferum, L. cernuum, L. concolor, L. davidii, L.* × *hollandicum, L. lancifolium, L. leichtlinii, L.* × *maculatum* and *L. pumilum*
(Ia)	Upright flowers, borne singly or in an umbel
(Ib)	Outward-facing flowers
(Ic)	Pendant flowers
(II)	Hybrids of Martagon type, one parent having been a form of *L. hansonii* or *L. martagon*

(III)	Hybrids from *L. candidum, L. chalcedonicum* and other related European species (excluding *L. martagon*)
(IV)	Hybrids of American species
(V)	Hybrids derived from *L. formosanum* and *L. longiflorum*
(VI)	Hybrid Trumpet Lilies and Aurelian hybrids from Asiatic species, including *L. henryi* but excluding those from *L. auratum, L. japonicum, L. rubellum* and *L. speciosum.*
(VIa)	Plants with trumpet-shaped flowers
(VIb)	Plants with bowl-shaped flowers
(VIc)	Plants with flat flowers (or only the tips recurved)
(VId)	Plants with recurved flowers
(VII)	Hybrids of Far Eastern species as *L auratum, L. japonicum, L. rubellum* and *L. speciosum* (Oriental Hybrids)
(VIIa)	Plants with trumpet-shaped flowers
(VIIb)	Plants with bowl-shaped flowers
(VIIc)	Plants with flat flowers
(VIId)	Plants with recurved flowers
(VIII)	All hybrids not in another division
(IX)	All species and their varieties and forms

MALUS *SEE* FRUIT

NARCISSUS

(By the Royal Horticultural Society, revised 1998)

(1)	Trumpet
(2)	Large-cupped
(3)	Small-cupped
(4)	Double
(5)	Triandrus
(6)	Cyclamineus
(7)	Jonquilla and Apodanthus
(8)	Tazetta
(9)	Poeticus
(10)	Bulbocodium
(11a)	Split-corona: Collar
(11b)	Split-corona: Papillon
(12)	Miscellaneous
(13)	Species

NYMPHAEA

(H)	Hardy
(D)	Day-blooming
(N)	Night-blooming
(T)	Tropical

PAEONIA

(S)	Shrubby

PELARGONIUM

(A)	Angel
(C)	Coloured Foliage (in combination)
(Ca)	Cactus (in combination)
(d)	Double (in combination)
(Dec)	Decorative
(Dw)	Dwarf
(DwI)	Dwarf Ivy-leaved
(Fr)	Frutetorum
(I)	Ivy-leaved
(Min)	Miniature
(MinI)	Miniature Ivy-leaved
(R)	Regal
(Sc)	Scented-leaved
(St)	Stellar (in combination)
(T)	Tulip (in combination)
(U)	Unique
(Z)	Zonal

PRIMULA

(Classification as per W.W. Smith & Forrest (1928) and W.W. Smith & Fletcher (1941-49))

(1)	Amethystina
(2)	Auricula
(3)	Bullatae
(4)	Candelabra
(5)	Capitatae
(6)	Carolinella
(7)	Cortusoides
(8)	Cuneifolia
(9)	Denticulata
(10)	Dryadifolia
(11)	Farinosae
(12)	Floribundae
(13)	Grandis
(14)	Malacoides
(15)	Malvacea
(16)	Minutissimae
(17)	Muscarioides
(18)	Nivales
(19)	Obconica
(20)	Parryi
(21)	Petiolares
(22)	Pinnatae
(23)	Pycnoloba
(24)	Reinii
(25)	Rotundifolia
(26)	Sikkimensis
(27)	Sinenses
(28)	Soldanelloideae
(29)	Souliei
(30)	Vernales
(A)	Alpine Auricula
(B)	Border Auricula
(Poly)	Polyanthus
(Prim)	Primrose
(S)	Show Auricula
(St)	Striped Auricula

PRUNUS SEE FRUIT

PYRUS SEE FRUIT

RHODODENDRON

(A)	Azalea (deciduous, species or unclassified hybrid)
(Ad)	Azaleodendron
(EA)	Evergreen azalea
(G)	Ghent azalea (deciduous)
(K)	Knap Hill or Exbury azalea (deciduous)
(M)	Mollis azalea (deciduous)
(O)	Occidentalis azalea (deciduous)
(R)	Rustica azalea (deciduous)
(V)	Vireya rhododendron
(Vs)	Viscosa azalea (deciduous)

RIBES SEE FRUIT

ROSA

(A)	Alba
(Bb)	Bourbon
(Bs)	Boursault
(Ce)	Centifolia
(Ch)	China
(Cl)	Climbing (in combination)
(D)	Damask
(DPo)	Damask Portland
(F)	Floribunda or Cluster-flowered
(G)	Gallica
(Ga)	Garnette
(GC)	Ground Cover
(HM)	Hybrid Musk
(HP)	Hybrid Perpetual
(HT)	Hybrid Tea or Large-flowered
(Min)	Miniature
(Mo)	Moss (in combination)
(N)	Noisette
(Patio)	Patio, Miniature Floribunda or Dwarf Cluster-flowered
(Poly)	Polyantha
(PiH)	Pimpinellifolia hybrid (Hybrid Scots Briar)
(Ra)	Rambler
(RH)	Rubiginosa hybrid (Hybrid Sweet Briar)
(Ru)	Rugosa
(S)	Shrub
(T)	Tea

SAXIFRAGA

(Classification from Gornall, R.J. (1987). *Botanical Journal of the Linnean Society*, 95(4): 273-292)

(1)	Ciliatae
(2)	Cymbalaria
(3)	Merkianae
(4)	Micranthes
(5)	Irregulares
(6)	Heterisia
(7)	Porphyrion
(8)	Ligulatae
(9)	Xanthizoon
(10)	Trachyphyllum
(11)	Gymnopera
(12)	Cotylea
(13)	Odontophyllae
(14)	Mesogyne
(15)	Saxifraga

TULIPA

(Classification from *Classified List and International Register of Tulip Names* by Koninklijke Algemeene Vereening voor Bloembollenculture 1996)

(1)	Single Early Group
(2)	Double Early Group
(3)	Triumph Group
(4)	Darwinhybrid Group
(5)	Single Late Group (including Darwin Group and Cottage Group)
(6)	Lily-flowered Group
(7)	Fringed Group
(8)	Viridiflora Group
(9)	Rembrandt Group
(10)	Parrot Group
(11)	Double Late Group
(12)	Kaufmanniana Group
(13)	Fosteriana Group
(14)	Greigii Group
(15)	Miscellaneous

VERBENA

(G)	Species and hybrids considered by some botanists to belong to the separate genus *Glandularia*.

VIOLA

(C)	Cornuta Hybrid
(dVt)	Double Violet
(ExVa)	Exhibition Viola
(FP)	Fancy Pansy
(PVt)	Parma Violet
(SP)	Show Pansy
(T)	Tricolor
(Va)	Viola
(Vt)	Violet
(Vtta)	Violetta

VITIS *SEE* FRUIT

REVERSE SYNONYMS

The following list of reverse synonyms is intended to help users find from which genus an unfamiliar plant name has been cross-referred. For a fuller explanation see p.13.

Acacia – Racosperma
Acanthocalyx – Morina
Acca – Feijoa
× Achicodonia – Eucodonia
Achillea – Anthemis
Acinos – Calamintha
Acinos – Micromeria
Actaea – Cimicifuga
Aethionema – Eunomia
Agapetes – Pentapterygium
Agarista – Leucothoe
Agastache – Cedronella
Aichryson – Aeonium
Ajania – Chrysanthemum
Ajania – Eupatorium
Albizia – Acacia
Alcea – Althaea
Allardia – Waldheimia
Allocasuarina – Casuarina
Aloysia – Lippia
Althaea – Malva
Alyogyne – Hibiscus
Alyssum – Ptilotrichum
× Amarygia – Amaryllis
Amaryllis – Brunsvigia
Amomyrtus – Myrtus
Amsonia – Rhazya
Anaphalis – Gnaphalium
Anchusa – Lycopsis
Androsace – Douglasia
Anemone – Eriocapitella
Anisodontea – Malvastrum
Anomatheca – Lapeirousia
Anredera – Boussingaultia
Antirrhinum – Asarina
Aphanes – Alchemilla
Apium – Apium × Petroselinum
Arctanthemum – Chrysanthemum
Arctostaphylos – Arbutus
Arctotis – × Venidioarctotis
Arctotis – Venidium
Arenga – Didymosperma
Argyranthemum – Anthemis
Argyranthemum – Chrysanthemum
Armoracia – Cochlearia
Arundinaria – Pseudosasa
Asarina – Antirrhinum

Asarum – Hexastylis
Asclepias – Gomphocarpus
Asparagus – Smilax
Asperula – Galium
Asphodeline – Asphodelus
Asplenium – Camptosorus
Asplenium – Ceterach
Asplenium – Phyllitis
Asplenium – Scolopendrium
Aster – Crinitaria
Aster – Doellingeria
Aster – Microglossa
Asteriscus – Pallenis
Astilboides – Rodgersia
Atropanthe – Scopolia
Aurinia – Alyssum
Austrocedrus – Libocedrus
Azorella – Bolax
Azorina – Campanula

Bambusa – Arundinaria
Bashania – Arundinaria
Bellevalia – Muscari
Bellis – Erigeron
Besseya – Veronica
Blechnum – Lomaria
Bolax – Azorella
Bolboschoenus – Scirpus
Borago – Anchusa
Borinda – Fargesia
Bothriochloa – Andropogon
Boykinia – Telesonix
Brachyglottis – Senecio
Brimeura – Hyacinthus
Brugmansia – Datura
Brunnera – Anchusa
Buglossoides – Lithospermum
Bulbine – Bulbinopsis
Buphthalmum – Inula

Cacalia – Adenostyles
Caiophora – Loasa
Caladium – Xanthosoma
Calamagrostis – Agrostis
Calamagrostis – Stipa
Calamintha – Clinopodium
Calibrachoa – Petunia
Calliergon – Acrocladium
Callisia – Phyodina
Callisia – Tradescantia
Calocedrus – Libocedrus
Calocephalus – Leucophyta
Calomeria – Humea
Caloscordum – Nothoscordum

Calytrix – Lhotzkya
Camellia – Thea
Campanula × Symphandra – Campanula
Cardamine – Dentaria
Carpobrotus – Lampranthus
Cassiope – Harrimanella
Catapodium – Desmazeria
Cayratia – Parthenocissus
Cedronella – Agastache
Centaurium – Erythraea
Centella – Hydrocotyle
Centranthus – Kentranthus
Centranthus – Valeriana
Cephalaria – Scabiosa
Ceratostigma – Plumbago
Cercestis – Rhektophyllum
Cestrum – Iochroma
Chaenomeles – Cydonia
Chaenorhinum – Linaria
Chamaecyparis – Cupressus
Chamaecytisus – Cytisus
Chamaedaphne – Cassandra
Chamaemelum – Anthemis
Chamerion – Chamaenerion
Chamerion – Epilobium
Chasmanthium – Uniola
Cheilanthes – Notholaena
Chiastophyllum – Cotyledon
Chimonobambusa – Arundinaria
Chimonobambusa – Gelidocalamus
Chimonobambusa – Quiongzhuea
Chionohebe – Pygmea
× Chionoscilla – Scilla
Chlorophytum – Diuranthera
Chondrosum – Bouteloua
Chrysanthemum – Dendranthema
Cicerbita – Lactuca
Cionura – Marsdenia
Cissus – Ampelopsis
Cissus – Parthenocissus
× Citrofortunella – Citrus
Citronella – Villaresia
Clarkia – Eucharidium
Clarkia – Godetia
Clavinodum – Arundinaria
Claytonia – Calandrinia
Claytonia – Montia
Clematis – Atragene
Cleyera – Eurya
Clinopodium – Acinos
Clinopodium – Calamintha
Clytostoma – Bignonia
Clytostoma – Pandorea

Cnicus – Carduus
Codonopsis – Campanumoea
Colobanthus – Arenaria
Consolida – Delphinium
× Coralia – Carmichaelia ×
  Corallospartium
Cordyline – Dracaena
Cornus – Chamaepericlymenum
Cornus – Dendrobenthamia
Coronilla – Securigera
Cortaderia – Gynerium
Corydalis – Fumaria
Corydalis – Pseudofumaria
Cosmos – Bidens
Cotinus – Rhus
Cotula – Leptinella
Crassula – Rochea
Crassula – Sedum
Crassula – Tillaea
Cremanthodium – Ligularia
Crinodendron – Tricuspidaria
Crocosmia – Antholyza
Crocosmia – Curtonus
Crocosmia – Montbretia
Cruciata – Galium
Ctenanthe – Calathea
Ctenanthe – Stromanthe
× Cupressocyparis –
  Chamaecyparis
Cyathodes – Leucopogon
Cyathodes – Styphelia
Cyclosorus – Pneumatopteris
Cymbalaria – Linaria
Cynara – Scolymus
Cynoglottis – Anchusa
Cyperus – Mariscus
Cypripedium – Criogenes
Cyrtanthus – Anoiganthus
Cyrtanthus – Vallota
Cyrtomium – Phanerophlebia
Cyrtomium – Polystichum
Cytisus – Argyrocytisus
Cytisus – Genista
Cytisus – Lembotropis
Cytisus – Spartocytisus

Daboecia – Menziesia
Dacrycarpus – Podocarpus
Dactylorhiza – Orchis
Danae – Ruscus
Darmera – Peltiphyllum
Dasypyrum – Haynaldia
Datura – Brugmansia
Davallia – Humata
Delairea – Senecio
Delosperma – Lampranthus
Delosperma – Mesembryanthemum
Dendrocalamus – Bambusa

Derwentia – Hebe
Desmodium – Lespedeza
Deuterocohnia – Abromeitiella
Dichelostemma – Brodiaea
Dicliptera – Barleria
Dicliptera – Justicia
Diervilla – Weigela
Dietes – Moraea
Diplazium – Athyrium
Disporopsis – Polygonatum
Distictis – Phaedranthus
Distylium – Sycopsis
Dolichothrix – Helichrysum
Dracaena – Pleomele
Dracunculus – Arum
Dregea – Wattakaka
Drepanostachyum – Arundinaria
Drepanostachyum –
  Thamnocalamus
Drepanostachyum –
  Chimonobambusa
Drimys – Tasmannia
Duchesnea – Fragaria
Dugaldia – Helenium
Dunalia – Acnistus
Dypsis – Chrysalidocarpus
Dypsis – Neodypsis

Echeveria – Cotyledon
Echinacea – Rudbeckia
Edraianthus – Wahlenbergia
Egeria – Elodea
Elatostema – Pellionia
Eleutherococcus – Acanthopanax
Elliottia – Botryostege
Elliottia – Cladothamnus
Elymus – Agropyron
Elymus – Leymus
Ensete – Musa
Epipremnum – Philodendron
Epipremnum – Scindapsus
Episcia – Alsobia
Eranthis – Aconitum
Erigeron – Aster
Erigeron – Haplopappus
Erysimum – Cheiranthus
Eucodonia – Achimenes
Eupatorium – Ageratina
Eupatorium – Ajania
Eupatorium – Ayapana
Eupatorium – Bartlettina
Euphorbia – Poinsettia
Euryops – Senecio
Eustoma – Lisianthus

Fallopia – Bilderdykia
Fallopia – Polygonum
Fallopia – Reynoutria

Farfugium – Ligularia
Fargesia – Arundinaria
Fargesia – Sinarundinaria
Fargesia – Thamnocalamus
Fatsia – Aralia
Felicia – Agathaea
Felicia – Aster
Fibigia – Farsetia
Filipendula – Spiraea
Foeniculum – Ferula
Fortunella – Citrus
Furcraea – Agave

Galium – Asperula
Galtonia – Hyacinthus
Gaultheria – Chiogenes
Gaultheria – × Gaulnettya
Gaultheria – Pernettya
Gelasine – Sisyrinchium
Genista – Chamaespartium
Genista – Cytisus
Genista – Echinospartum
Genista – Teline
Gentianopsis – Gentiana
Gerbera – Leibnitzia
Gladiolus – Acidanthera
Gladiolus – Anomalesia
Gladiolus – Homoglossum
Gladiolus – Petamenes
Glechoma – Nepeta
Gloxinia – Seemannia
Gomphocarpus – Asclepias
Goniolimon – Limonium
Graptopetalum – Sedum
Graptopetalum – Tacitus
Greenovia – Sempervivum
Gymnospermium – Leontice

Habranthus – Zephyranthes
Hacquetia – Dondia
× Halimiocistus – Cistus
× Halimiocistus – Halimium
Halimione – Atriplex
Halimium – Cistus
Halimium – × Halimiocistus
Halimium – Helianthemum
Halocarpus – Dacrydium
Haplopappus – Aster
Hechtia – Dyckia
Hedychium – Brachychilum
Hedyscepe – Kentia
Helianthella – Helianthus
Helianthemum – Cistus
Helianthus – Heliopsis
Helichrysum – Gnaphalium
Helictotrichon – Avena
Helictotrichon – Avenula
Heliopsis – Helianthus

Hepatica – Anemone
Herbertia – Alophia
Hermodactylus – Iris
Heterocentron – Schizocentron
Heterotheca – Chrysopsis
Hibbertia – Candollea
Hieracium – Andryala
Himalayacalamus –
   Arundinaria
Himalayacalamus –
   Drepanostachyum
Hippocrepis – Coronilla
Hippolytia – Achillea
Hippolytia – Tanacetum
Hoheria – Plagianthus
Homalocladium –
   Muehlenbeckia
Howea – Kentia
Hyacinthoides – Endymion
Hyacinthoides – Scilla
Hymenocallis – Elisena
Hymenocallis – Ismene
Hyophorbe – Mascarena
Hypochaeris – Hieracium
Hypoxis – Rhodohypoxis

Incarvillea – Amphicome
Indocalamus – Sasa
Iochroma – Acnistus
Iochroma – Cestrum
Iochroma – Dunalia
Ipheion – Tristagma
Ipheion – Triteleia
Ipomoea – Mina
Ipomoea – Pharbitis
Ipomopsis – Gilia
Ischyrolepis – Restio
Ismelia – Chrysanthemum
Isolepis – Scirpus

Jamesbrittenia – Sutera
Jeffersonia – Plagiorhegma
Jovibarba – Sempervivum
Juncus – Scirpus
Jurinea – Jurinella
Justicia – Beloperone
Justicia – Jacobinia
Justicia – Libonia

Kalanchoe – Bryophyllum
Kalanchoe – Kitchingia
Kalimeris – Aster
Kalimeris – Asteromoea
Kalimeris – Boltonia
Kalopanax – Eleutherococcus
Keckiella – Penstemon
Knautia – Scabiosa
Kniphofia – Tritoma

Kohleria – Isoloma
Kunzea – Leptospermum

Lablab – Dolichos
Lagarosiphon – Elodea
Lagarostrobos – Dacrydium
Lallemantia – Dracocephalum
Lamium – Galeobdolon
Lamium – Lamiastrum
Lampranthus –
   Mesembryanthemum
Lampranthus – Oscularia
Laurentia – Hippobroma
Lavatera – Malva
Ledebouria – Scilla
× Ledodendron – Rhododendron
Lepechinia – Sphacele
Lepidothamnus – Dacrydium
Leptinella – Cotula
Leptodactylon – Gilia
Leucanthemella –
   Chrysanthemum
Leucanthemella – Leucanthemum
Leucanthemopsis –
   Chrysanthemum
Leucanthemopsis – Tanacetum
Leucanthemum –
   Chrysanthemum
Leucochrysum – Helipterum
Leucophyta – Calocephalus
Leucopogon – Cyathodes
× Leucoraoulia – Raoulia
Leuzea – Centaurea
Leymus – Elymus
Ligularia – Senecio
Ligustrum – Parasyringa
Lilium – Nomocharis
Limonium – Statice
Linanthus – Linanthastrum
Lindelofia – Adelocaryum
Lindera – Parabenzoin
Liriope – Ophiopogon
Lithocarpus – Quercus
Lithodora – Lithospermum
Littorella – Plantago
Lophospermum – Asarina
Lophospermum – Maurandya
Lophostemon – Tristania
Lotus – Dorycnium
Lotus – Tetragonolobus
Ludwigia – Jussiaea
Luma – Myrtus
× Lycene – Lychnis
Lychnis – Agrostemma
Lychnis – Silene
Lychnis – Viscaria
Lycianthes – Solanum
Lytocaryum – Cocos

Lytocaryum – Microcoelum

Macfadyena – Bignonia
Macfadyena – Doxantha
Machaeranthera – Xylorhiza
Mackaya – Asystasia
Macleaya – Bocconia
Mahonia – Berberis
Mandevilla – Dipladenia
Mandragora – Atropa
Marrubium – Ballota
Matricaria – Chamomilla
Matricaria – Tripleurosperum
Maurandella – Asarina
Maurandella – Maurandya
Maurandya – Asarina
Melicytus – Hymenanthera
Melinis – Rhynchelytrum
Mentha – Preslia
Merremia – Ipomoea
Millettia – Wisteria
Mimulus – Diplacus
Minuartia – Arenaria
Modiolastrum – Malvastrum
Moltkia – Lithodora
Moltkia – Lithospermum
Morina – Acanthocalyx
Mukdenia – Aceriphyllum
Muscari – Hyacinthus
Muscari – Leopoldia
Muscari – Leopoldia
Muscari – Muscarimia
Muscari – Pseudomuscari
Myricaria – Tamarix
Myrteola – Myrtus

Naiocrene – Claytonia
Naiocrene – Montia
Nassella – Stipa
Nectaroscordum – Allium
Nematanthus – Hypocyrta
Nemesia – Diascia
Neopaxia – Claytonia
Neopaxia – Montia
Neoregelia – Guzmania
Neoregelia – Nidularium
Nepeta – Dracocephalum
Nepeta – Origanum
Nephrophyllidium – Fauria
Nertera – Coprosma
× Niduregelia – Guzmania
Nipponanthemum –
   Chrysanthemum
Nipponanthemum –
   Leucanthemum
Nymphoides – Villarsia

Oemleria – Osmaronia

Oenothera – Chamissonia
Olearia – Pachystegia
Olsynium – Phaiophleps
Olsynium – Sisyrinchium
Onixotis – Dipidax
Ophiopogon – Convallaria
Orchis – Dactylorhiza
Oreopteris – Thelypteris
Orostachys – Sedum
Osmanthus – × Osmarea
Osmanthus – Phillyrea
Osteospermum – Dimorphotheca
Othonna – Hertia
Othonna – Othonnopsis
Ozothamnus – Helichrysum

Pachyphragma – Cardamine
Packera – Senecio
Paederota – Veronica
Papaver – Meconopsis
Parahebe – Derwentia
Parahebe – Hebe
Parahebe – Veronica
Paraserianthes – Albizia
Paris – Daiswa
Parthenocissus – Ampelopsis
Parthenocissus – Vitis
Passiflora – Tetrapathaea
Paxistima – Pachystema
Pecteilis – Habenaria
Pelargonium – Geranium
Peltoboykinia – Boykinia
Penstemon – Chelone
Pentaglottis – Anchusa
Pentalinon – Urechites
Pericallis – Senecio
Persea – Machilus
Persicaria – Aconogonon
Persicaria – Bistorta
Persicaria – Polygonum
Persicaria – Tovara
Petrocoptis – Lychnis
Petrophytum – Spiraea
Petrorhagia – Tunica
Petroselinum – Carum
Phegopteris – Thelypteris
Phoenicaulis – Parrya
Photinia – Heteromeles
Photinia – Stranvaesia
Photinia – × Stravinia
Phuopsis – Crucianella
Phyla – Lippia
Phymosia – Sphaeralcea
Physoplexis – Phyteuma
Physostegia – Dracocephalum
Pieris – Arcterica
Pilosella – Hieracium
Piper – Macropiper

Pisonia – Heimerliodendron
Plagiomnium – Mnium
Plecostachys – Helichrysum
Plectranthus – Solenostemon
Pleioblastus – Arundinaria
Pleioblastus – Sasa
Podranea – Tecoma
Polianthes – Bravoa
Polygonum – Persicaria
Polypodium – Phlebodium
Polystichum – Phanerophlebia
Poncirus – Aegle
Potentilla – Comarum
Pratia – Lobelia
Prenanthes – Nabalus
Prumnopitys – Podocarpus
Prunus – Amygdalus
Pseudocydonia – Chaenomeles
Pseudopanax – Metapanax
Pseudopanax – Neopanax
Pseudopanax – Nothopanax
Pseudosasa – Arundinaria
Pseudotsuga – Tsuga
Pseudowintera – Drimys
Pterocephalus – Scabiosa
Ptilostemon – Cirsium
Pulicaria – Inula
Pulsatilla – Anemone
Pushkinia – Scilla
Pyrethropsis – Argyranthemum
Pyrethropsis – Chrysanthemum
Pyrethropsis – Leucanthemopsis
Pyrethropsis – Leucanthemum
Pyrrocoma – Haplopappus

Reineckea – Liriope
Retama – Genista
Rhapis – Chamaerops
Rhodanthe – Helipterum
Rhodanthemum –
    Chrysanthemopsis
Rhodanthemum –
    Chrysanthemum
Rhodanthemum –
    Leucanthemopsis
Rhodanthemum – Leucanthemum
Rhodanthemum – Pyrethropsis
Rhodiola – Clementsia
Rhodiola – Rosularia
Rhodiola – Sedum
Rhododendron – Azalea
Rhododendron – Azaleodendron
Rhododendron – Rhodora
Rhodophiala – Hippeastrum
× Rhodoxis – Hypoxis ×
    Rhodohypoxis
× Rhodoxis – Rhodohypoxis
Rosularia – Cotyledon

Rosularia – Sempervivella
Rothmannia – Gardenia
Ruellia – Dipteracanthus
Ruschia –
    Mesembryanthemum
Rytidosperma – Merxmuellera

Saccharum – Erianthus
Sagina – Minuartia
Salvia – Salvia
Sanguisorba – Dendriopoterium
Sanguisorba – Poterium
Sasa – Arundinaria
Sasa – Pleioblastus
Sasaella – Arundinaria
Sasaella – Pleioblastus
Sasaella – Sasa
Sasamorpha – Sasa
Satureja – Micromeria
Sauromatum – Arum
Saussurea – Jurinea
Scadoxus – Haemanthus
Schefflera – Brassaia
Schefflera – Dizygotheca
Schefflera – Heptapleurum
Schizachyrium – Andropogon
Schizostachyum – Arundinaria
Schizostachyum – Thamnocalamus
Schoenoplectus – Scirpus
Scirpoides – Scirpus
Scirpus – Eriophorum
Sedum – Hylotelephium
Sedum – Rhodiola
Sedum – Sedastrum
Sedum – Villadia
Semiaquilegia – Aquilegia
Semiaquilegia – Paraquilegia
Semiarundinaria – Arundinaria
Semiarundinaria – Oligostachyum
Senecio – Cineraria
Senecio – Kleinia
Senecio – Ligularia
Senna – Cassia
Seriphidium – Artemisia
Shortia – Schizocodon
Sibbaldiopsis – Potentilla
Sieversia – Geum
Silene – Lychnis
Silene – Melandrium
Silene – Saponaria
Sinacalia – Ligularia
Sinacalia – Senecio
Sinarundinaria –
    Semiarundinaria
Sinobambusa – Pleioblastus
Sinningia – Gesneria
Sinningia – Rechsteineria
Sisymbrium – Hesperis

Sisyrinchium – Phaiophleps
× Smithicodonia –
    × Achimenantha
Solanum – Lycianthes
Soleirolia – Helxine
Solenopsis, – Isotoma
Solenostemon, – Coleus
× Solidaster – Aster
× Solidaster – Solidago
Sorbaria – Spiraea
Sparaxis – Synnotia
Sphaeralcea – Iliamna
Sphaeromeria – Tanacetum
Spirodela – Lemna
Spraguea – Calyptridium
Stachys – Betonica
Steirodiscus – Gamolepis
Stemmacantha – Centaurea
Stemmacantha – Leuzea
Stenomesson – Urceolina
Stenotus – Haplopappus
Steptocarpus – Streptocarpella
Stewartia – Stuartia
Stipa – Achnatherum
Stipa – Anemanthele
Stipa – Lasiagrostis
Stipa – Oryzopsis
Strobilanthes – Pteracanthus
Succisa – Scabiosa
Sutera – Bacopa
Syagrus – Arecastrum
Syagrus – Cocos

Tanacetum – Achillea
Tanacetum – Balsamita
Tanacetum – Chrysanthemum
Tanacetum – Matricaria
Tanacetum – Pyrethrum
Tanacetum – Spathipappus

Tanacetum – Sphaeromeria
Tecoma – Tecomaria
Tecomaria – Tecoma
Telekia – Buphthalmum
Tephroseris – Senecio
Tetradium – Euodia
Tetraneuris – Actinella
Tetraneuris – Hymenoxys
Tetrapanax – Fatsia
Thamnocalamus – Arundinaria
Thamnocalamus –
    Sinarundinaria
Thlaspi – Hutchinsia
Thlaspi – Noccaea
Thuja – Platycladus
Thuja – Thujopsis
Thymus – Origanum
Tiarella – × Heucherella
Tonestus – Haplopappus
Toona – Cedrela
Trachelium – Diosphaera
Trachycarpus – Chamaerops
Tradescantia – Rhoeo
Tradescantia – Setcreasea
Tradescantia – Tradescantia
Tradescantia – Zebrina
Trichopetalum – Anthericum
Trichophorum – Scirpus
Tripetaleia – Elliottia
Tripleurospermum – Matricaria
Tripogandra – Tradescantia
Tristagma – Beauverdia
Tristaniopsis – Tristania
Triteleia – Brodiaea
Tritonia – Crocosmia
Tropaeolum – Nasturtium hort.
Tuberaria – Helianthemum
Tulipa – Amana
Tweedia – Oxypetalum

Ugni – Myrtus
Ullucus – Anredera
Ursinia – Euryops
Uvularia – Oakesiella

Vaccinium – Oxycoccus
Verbascum – Celsia
Verbascum –
    × Celsioverbascum
Verbena – Glandularia
Verbena – Lippia
Veronicastrum – Veronica
Vigna – Phaseolus
Villadia – Sedum
Viola – Erpetion
Vitaliana – Androsace
Vitaliana – Douglasia

Weigela – Diervilla
Weigela – Macrodiervilla

Xanthophthalmum –
    Chrysanthemum
Xanthorhiza – Zanthorhiza
Xerichrysum – Bracteantha
Xerichrysum – Helichrysum

Yushania – Arundinaria
Yushania – Sinarundinaria
Yushania – Thamnocalamus

Zantedeschia – Calla
Zauschneria – Epilobium
Zephyranthes – × Cooperanthes
Zephyranthes – Cooperia
Zephyranthes – Habranthus

THE PLANT DIRECTORY

A

Abelia ✿ (*Caprifoliaceae*)

biflora	NLar WWes
chinensis misapplied	see *A.* x *grandiflora*
§ *chinensis* R. Br.	CBcs CPle EBee ECre EPfP MAsh NBlu SDnm SMer SPer SPla WFar WHCG WPat WSHC WTel
dielsii	CTrw ECrN GQui
'Edward Goucher'	CBcs CDoC CPle EBee ECrN EGra ELan ENot EPfP LPan LRHS MGos MRav MSwo NBea NHol SEND SLim SPer SPlb SWvt WBVN WDin WFar WOld WPat WSHC
engleriana	CAbP CPle EBee EPfP MAsh WBcn WFar
floribunda ♀H3	CBcs CFil CMac CPLG CPle CSBt CSam CTrw CWib ELan EPfP IDee LRHS MAsh SDnm SIgm SMur SPer SPoG SSpi SSta WAbe WBcn WBod WFar WOld WPat
§ x *grandiflora* ♀H4	More than 30 suppliers
- 'Aurea'	see *A.* x *grandiflora* 'Gold Spot'
- 'Compacta'	LRHS WFar
- Confetti = 'Conti'PBR (v)	More than 30 suppliers
- dwarf	CDoC
§ - 'Francis Mason' (v)	More than 30 suppliers
§ - 'Gold Spot'	CBcs CDoC CWSG EBee EPfP LHop MAsh MWat SOWG SSto WBrE WOld WWeb
- 'Gold Strike'	see *A.* x *grandiflora* 'Gold Spot'
- 'Goldsport'	see *A.* x *grandiflora* 'Gold Spot'
- 'Hopleys'PBR (v)	LHop LRHS
- 'Panache' (v)	CPle MGos
- 'Sherwoodii'	WPat
- 'Sunrise'PBR (v)	CDoC CSBt EBee EHoe ELan EPfP LRHS SBod SBra SLim SMur SPer SPla WWeb
- 'Variegata'	see *A.* x *grandiflora* 'Francis Mason'
mosanensis **new**	NLar
rupestris hort.	see *A.* x *grandiflora*
rupestris Lindl.	see *A. chinensis*
schumannii ♀H4	More than 30 suppliers
- 'Saxon Gold' **new**	SSto
spathulata	WBcn WFar
triflora	CAbP CBot CFil CPLG CPle EBee EPfP LAst LRHS SLon SSta WFar WPat
zanderi	see *A. dielsii*

Abeliophyllum (*Oleaceae*)

distichum	More than 30 suppliers
- Roseum Group	CBcs CFil CPMA EBee EBre ELan EPfP GBuc LAst LHop LRHS MAsh MRav NSti SHBN SLon SPer SSpi WPGP

Abies ✿ (*Pinaceae*)

alba	CDul GKir GTSp MBar NWea WMou

- 'Compacta'	CKen
- 'King's Dwarf'	CKen
- 'Microphylla'	CKen
- 'Munsterland'	CKen
- 'Tortuosa'	CKen
amabilis	GKir GTSp LCon LRav
- 'Spreading Star'	NLar
arizonica	see *A. lasiocarpa* var. *arizonica*
x *arnoldiana*	MBar NLar
balsamea	CAgr GTSp LCon NWea WEve
- Hudsonia Group ♀H4	CDoC CDul CKen CMac EHul EPot GKir IMGH LCon LLin LRHS MAsh MBar MGos MOne NDlv NMen SLim WDin
- 'Le Feber' **new**	CKen
- 'Nana'	CKen EBre EHul EOrn GKir LBee LCon LRHS MAsh WDin WStI
- var. *phanerolepis* 'Bear Swamp' **new**	CKen
- 'Piccolo'	CDoC CKen EHul EMil IMGH NLar SLim WGor
- 'Prostrata'	ECho EHul LLin LRHS WEve
- 'Renswoude' **new**	CKen
- 'Verkade's Prostrate'	CKen
borisii-regis	GTSp LCon
* - 'Pendula'	CKen
brachyphylla dwarf	see *A. homolepis* 'Prostrata'
cephalonica	GTSp LCon
- 'Greg's Broom'	CKen
§ - 'Meyer's Dwarf'	EBre EHul IMGH LCon LLin LRHS MAsh MBar SCoo SLim WEve
- 'Nana'	see *A. cephalonica* 'Meyer's Dwarf'
concolor ♀H4	CBcs CDul CTho EHul GKir GTSp GWCH LCon LPan LRHS MBar NWea SEND WDin
- 'Archer's Dwarf'	CKen LCon MGos NLar
I - 'Argentea'	LCon
- 'Blue Spreader'	CKen MGos
§ - 'Compacta' ♀H4	CDoC CKen EBre EOrn GKir IMGH LCon LLin LRHS MAsh MBar MGos NLar SCoo SLim SPoG WEve WFar
- 'Fagerhult'	CKen
- 'Gable's Weeping'	CKen
- 'Glauca'	see *A. concolor* Violacea Group
- 'Glauca Compacta'	see *A. concolor* 'Compacta'
§ - 'Hillier's Dwarf'	CKen
- 'Husky Pup'	CKen
- Lowiana Group	LCon
- - 'Creamy'	CKen
- 'Masonic Broom'	CKen
- 'Mike Stearn'	CKen
- 'Ostrov Nad Ohri' **new**	CKen
- 'Piggelmee'	CKen LLin
* - 'Swift's Silver'	LBee WEve
§ - Violacea Group	CDoC CKen LCon LLin MAsh MBar WEve
- 'Wattez Prostrate' **new**	WFar
- 'Wattezii'	CKen LLin
- 'Wintergold'	CKen NLar
delavayi	CMCN GKir GTSp

– SF 360	ISea
– SF 656	ISea
– var. *delavayi*	see *A. fabri*
Fabri Group	
– 'Major Neishe'	CKen
I – 'Nana'	CKen
– 'Nana Headfort'	see *A. fargesii* 'Headfort'
§ *fabri*	CLnd LCon
fargesii var. *faxoniana*	GKir
§ – 'Headfort'	LCon MBar NLar
firma	GTSp
forrestii **new**	CKen
– var. *ferreana* SF 95168	ISea
– – SF 95226	ISea
– var. *georgei*	MBlu
fraseri	CTri GIBF GKir MBar NWea SEND WMou
– 'Raul's Dwarf'	CKen
grandis	CBcs ENot GIBF GKir LCon LRav MBar NWea SHBN WDin WEve WMou
– 'Compacta'	CKen
– 'van Dedem's Dwarf' **new**	CKen
holophylla	CMCN
homolepis	CDul CMCN GKir GTSp NWea
§ – 'Prostrata'	CKen
koreana	More than 30 suppliers
– 'Aurea'	see *A. koreana* 'Flava'
– 'Blaue Zwo'	CKen MAsh
– 'Blauer Eskimo'	CKen
– 'Blauer Pfiff'	CKen EBre GKir LPan MGos NLar SLim
– 'Blinsham Gold'	CKen
– blue	EHoe
– 'Blue Emperor'	CKen NLar
– 'Blue Magic'	CKen NLar
– 'Blue 'n' Silver'	LLin NLar
– 'Cis'	CKen NLar SLim
– 'Compact Dwarf'	LLin MBar MGos NLar
– 'Crystal Globe'	CKen NLar
§ – 'Flava'	CKen ECho IMGH LLin MAsh MBar MBri NHol SCoo SLim WEve
– 'Frosty' **new**	NLar
– 'Gait'	CKen NLar
– 'Golden Dream'	CKen
– 'Green Carpet'	CKen
– 'Inverleith'	CKen
– 'Kohout'	CKen
– 'Lippetal'	CKen
– 'Luminetta'	CKen LRHS NLar
– 'Nadelkissen'	CKen
– 'Nisbet'	EBre ECho IMGH LLin MAsh SLim WEve WGor
– 'Oberon'	CKen EHul LCon MAsh NLar
– 'Piccolo'	CKen NLar
– 'Pinocchio'	CKen NLar
– 'Prostrata'	see *A. koreana* 'Prostrate Beauty'
§ – 'Prostrate Beauty'	ECho EOrn IMGH WEve WGor
– 'Silberkugel'	CKen
– 'Silberlocke' ♀H4	CDoC CKen EBre ENot GKir LBee LCon LLin LPan LRHS MAsh MBar MBlu MBri MGos NBea NBlu NHol SLim SPer WEve
– 'Silbermavers'	CKen
– 'Silberperl'	CKen
– 'Silberschmeltzer'	LLin
– 'Silver Show'	CKen
– 'Starker's Dwarf'	CKen
– 'Taiga' **new**	NLar
– 'Threave'	CKen
– 'Tundra'	NLar
– 'Winter Goldtip' **new**	LLin

lasiocarpa	CDul NWea
– var. *arizonica*	LCon SCoo
I – – 'Argentea'	NWea
– – 'Compacta', ♀H4	CDoC CFee CKen CMac ECho EBre EHul GKir IMGH LBee LCon LLin LRHS MAsh MBar MBri MGos SCoo SLim SPoG WBrE WFar WEve WGor
– – 'Kenwith Blue'	CKen NLar
– 'Day Creek'	CKen
– 'Duflon'	CKen
– 'Green Globe'	CKen MBar
* – 'King's Blue'	CKen
– 'Logan Pass' **new**	CKen
– 'Mulligan's Dwarf'	CKen
– 'Roger Watson' **new**	WEve
– 'Toenisvorst' **new**	CKen
magnifica	LCon LPan LRav
I – 'Nana'	CKen NLar
– witches' broom **new**	CKen
nobilis	see *A. procera*
nordmanniana ♀H4	CDoC CDul CTri EHul EPfP GIBF GKir LBuc LCon LPan LRHS MBar MGos NWea SEND WDin WEve
– 'Barabits' Compact'	MBar NLar
– 'Barabits' Spreader'	CKen
– subsp. *equi-trojani*	GKir LCon
– – 'Archer'	CKen
– 'Golden Spreader' ♀H4	CDoC CKen EBre EOrn GKir IMGH LBee LCon LLin LRHS MAsh MBar MBri MGos NLar SLim SPoG WEve
– 'Jakobsen'	CKen
– 'Pendula'	GKir LPan
numidica	LPan
– 'Glauca'	CKen
I – 'Pendula'	LCon
I – 'Prostrata'	LPan
pindrow	CDul GTSp LCon
pinsapo	LPan LRHS MBar SEND
– 'Aurea'	CKen GKir LLin NLar WEve
I – 'Aurea Nana'	CKen
– 'Fastigiata' **new**	MPkF
– 'Glauca' ♀H4	CDoC CDul CKen CTho EHul ELan GKir LCon LPan MBar MBlu NLar SCoo WDin WEve WMou
– 'Hamondii'	CKen
I – 'Horstmann'	CKen LCon LLin WEve
– 'Kelleriis'	LCon
– 'Pendula'	MPkF
– 'Quicksilver'	CKen
§ *procera* ♀H4	CBcs CDoC CDul EHul GIBF GKir LCon MBar NWea WBVN WDin WEve WMou
– 'Blaue Hexe'	CKen EBre GKir SLim
– Glauca Group	CDoC CMac CTho EBre GKir LCon LLin LPan LRHS MAsh MBar MBlu MBri MGos WEve WFar WGer
– 'Glauca Prostrata'	GKir LBee LPan LRHS MBar MGos SCoo WEve
– 'Sherwoodii'	CKen
religiosa	LCon
Rosemoor hybrid	CKen
sibirica	LCon NWea
squamata	GKir LCon
veitchii	CBcs CDul GKir LCon MBar NWea
– 'Hedergott'	CKen
– 'Heine'	CKen NLar
I – 'Pendula'	CKen
– 'Rumburg'	CKen

Abromeitiella (Bromeliaceae)

brevifolia ♀H1	CFil EPem

Abrotanella (Asteraceae)

sp.   ECho

Abutilon ✿ (Malvaceae)

'Amiti'	MOak
'Amsterdam'	ERea
'Apricot Belle'	MOak
'Ashford Red'	LRHS MJnS SOWG SRms WKif
'Boule de Neige'	CBot CHal ERea LRHS MOak SOWG SYvo
'Canary Bird' ♀H2	CBcs CBot CHEx CHal ERea MJnS MLan MOak SHBN SYvo WKif WOld
'Canary Bird' misapplied	see A. 'Golden Fleece'
'Cannington Carol' (v) ♀H2	ERea MOak SDnm SDys
'Cannington Peter' (v) ♀H2	CHal MOak SDnm
'Cannington Sally' (v)	MLan SDnm SSte SWvt
'Cannington Sonia' (v)	ERea
'Cloth of Gold'	LRHS SOWG
'Cynthia Pike' (v)	LRHS
I 'Eric Rose' **new**	MTis
§ 'Feuerglocke'	MOak
Firebell	see A. 'Feuerglocke'
'Frances Elizabeth'	LRHS MOak
globosum	see A. x *hybridum*
§ 'Golden Fleece'	ERea MOak
'Heather Bennington'	LRHS
'Helen'	SMrm
'Henry Makepeace'	LRHS
'Hinton Seedling'	CRHN MOak
§ x *hybridum*	CHEx
- 'Savitzii'	see A. 'Savitzii'
indicum	WPic
'J. Morris'	LRHS MAsh
'Kentish Belle' ♀H2-3	CBcs CHEx CMHG CMac CPle CRHN EBee ECot ELan EPfP MOak SBra SHBN SPer
I 'Kentish Belle Variegatum' **new**	ELan
'Lemon Queen'	CHal
'Linda Vista Peach' ♀H2	MOak
'Louis Marignac'	MOak
'Marion' ♀H2	CHrt LRHS MOak SDys SOWG
'Master Michael'	CMac ERea
megapotamicum ♀H3	CBcs CBot CHEx CMHG CPLG CPle CRHN CSBt CTrC EBee ELan ENot EPfP EPla ERea GQui LRHS MAsh MGos MHer MLan MOak MRav SOWG SPer SRms WBod WFar WSHC XPep
- 'Variegatum' (v)	CBcs CBrm CPLG CSBt ELan EPfP GQui LRHS MAsh MGos MOak SBod SHBN SOWG SPer SSta SWvt WFar
x *milleri* ♀H2	CMac CPLG CRHN ERea MLan SHBN SVen WSHC
- 'Variegatum' (v)	CHEx CHal CMHG CMac LRHS MOak SEND
- 'Ventnor Gold'	SVen
'Moonchimes'	MOak
'Nabob' ♀H2	CHal ERea LRHS MBri MLan MOak MTis SAga SLdr SOWG SYvo
'Orange Glow' (v) ♀H2	MOak
'Orange Vein'	CHal
'Patrick Synge'	CMHG CPle EBee ERea LPhx MOak SOWG SVen
'Peaches and Cream'	LRHS
§ *pictum*	ERea
- 'Thompsonii' (v)	CHEx CHal ERea MJnS MLLN MOak SGar SSte WDyG
'Pink Lady'	CBcs ERea GQui

'Red Bells'	GQui MOak SVen
'Rotterdam'	MOak
§ 'Savitzii' (v) ♀H2	CHal MOak SOWG SRms SSte SVen
sellowianum var. *marmoratum*	ERea
'Snowfall'	MOak
'Souvenir de Bonn' (v) ♀H2	CHal EHol ERea EShb LRHS MLan MOak MTis SAga SSte
striatum hort.	see A. *pictum*
x *suntense*	CBcs CMHG CPLG CSBt EPfP ERea LHyd LRHS MJnS MWgw NPer SOWG SSta WBod WTel
- 'Jermyns' ♀H3	EPfP LRHS MFOX
- 'Violetta'	CEnd MSte SPer
theophrasti	MSal
variegated salmon (v) **new**	LAst
'Victory' **new**	SSpi
vitifolium	CBcs CBot ECot EPfP ERea IDee ISea MGos MHer NBid NCGa SAga SChu SPer SYvo WKif
- var. *album*	CBcs CMHG CPLG CRHN CTCP EPfP IDee ISea LAst LHyd MLan SChu SEND SGar SSpi SSta WCru WSpi
- 'Buckland'	CHll
- 'Ice Blue'	CBot
- 'Simcox White'	WEas WSPU
- 'Tennant's White' ♀H3	CAbP CBot ELan EPfP ERea LRHS NBur SDnm SOWG WCru
- 'Veronica Tennant' ♀H3	ERea MSte SDnm WGwG WKif

Acacia ✿ (Mimosaceae)

acinacea	SPlb
adunca	SPlb
alpina	WCel
armata	see A. *paradoxa*
baileyana ♀H2	CBcs CSBt CTrC CTrG ECot ELan EMil EPfP ERea EShb ESlt GQui LRHS MGol MPRe SPer SPlb WMul WPat
- var. *aurea*	SPlb
- 'Purpurea' ♀H2	CAbb CBcs CBos CDoC CEnd CFil CKno CTbh CTrC CWSG CWib EAmu EBee EMil EPfP ERea EShb GQui IDee MGos MLan MPRe MTis SPer SPlb SWvt WFar WMul WPGP
boormanii	CTrC WCel
cultriformis	ERea SEND
cyanophylla	see A. *saligna*
dealbata ♀H2	More than 30 suppliers
* - subsp. *subalpina*	CCVT LRHS WCel WMul WPGP
Exeter hybrid	CSBt
filicifolia	WCel
floribunda	CTrC
- 'Lisette'	EPfP LRHS
frigescens	WCel
galpinii	EShb
jonesii	CTrC
julibrissin	see Albizia julibrissin
juniperina	see A. *ulicifolia*
karroo	CArn WMul XPep
kybeanensis	CTrC WCel
longifolia	CAbb CBcs CHEx EBee IDee SEND SPer SRms
macradenia	SPlb
maidenii	MGol
mearnsii	WCel WMul
melanoxylon	CDul CTrC IDee ISea LRHS WCel WHer
motteana	ECot ERea
mucronata	CTrC
obliquinervia	WCel
§ *paradoxa* ♀H2	CTrC LRHS NBlu WPat
pataczekii	ENot EPfP ERea LRHS SKee SSpi

podalyriifolia	CDoC CFil IDee WPGP
pravissima ♀H2-3	More than 30 suppliers
retinodes ♀H2	CAbb CBcs CDoC CPle CTrC EBee EPfP ERea GQui IDee LRav MLan SEND WCFE WMul
riceana	CTrC CTrG GQui IDee LEdu LRav WPat
rivalis	ERea
rubida	IDee LRav MPRe WCel WMul
§ **saligna**	CBcs CTrC EBee EShb LRHS
senegal	ELau
sentis	see *A. victoriae*
sophorae	CTrC GGar
spectabilis	SPlb
suaveolens	SPlb
§ **ulicifolia**	CPLG CSBt CTrG
verticillata	CHll CTrG GGar
– riverine	CTrC
§ **victoriae**	ERea

Acaena (Rosaceae)

adscendens hort.	see *A. magellanica* subsp. *magellanica*, *A. saccaticupula* 'Blue Haze'
adscendens misapplied	see *A. affinis*
adscendens Vahl	see *A. magellanica* subsp. *laevigata*
– 'Glauca'	CMdw EMan NBir NFor SBla
§ **affinis**	COIW ECha SDix
anserinifolia hort.	see *A. novae-zelandiae*
§ **anserinifolia** (Forst. & Forst. f.) Druce	ECha GGar NHol WPer WWin
buchananii	CTri EBee EDAr EGoo GGar GTou IHMH MBar MLLN MWgw NBro NFor SRms WCom WFar WPer WShp
caerulea	see *A. caesiiglauca*
§ **caesiiglauca**	CTri GAbr GGar GTou NBid NFor NMRc SBla SCro SGar SVal WCom WEas WPer
caespitosa	EBee
fissistipula	EHoe GGar WHer
glaucophylla	see *A. magellanica* subsp. *magellanica*
'Greencourt Hybrid'	CLyd
inermis	CLyd EBee EPot GTou MLLN NFla SPlb WCom WPer
– 'Purpurea'	EBre EChP ECha EShb NLar WHoo
macrocephala	EBee
§ **magellanica**	GTou WWin WWpP
subsp. *laevigata*	
§ – subsp. *magellanica*	GTou LEdu WShp
microphylla ♀H4	EBee ECha IHMH LBee LRHS MBar MSPs NJOw NMen SHfr SIng SPlb SRms SVal WAbe WPer WShp
– Copper Carpet	see *A. microphylla* 'Kupferteppich'
– 'Glauca'	see *A. caesiiglauca*
§ – 'Kupferteppich'	CBrm EBee EBre EHoe EMan GGar GKir IHMH MBri MBro MRav MWgw NVic SIng WBea WCom WPat WPer WShp WWpP
– 'Pewter Carpet'	EGoo
– 'Pulchella'	EBre EMan LRHS
myriophylla	EBee ECho EDAr EGoo EMFP
§ **novae-zelandiae**	CTri EBee EDAr GGar GTou SDix SIng WCom WMoo WPer
ovalifolia	CNic EBee EDAr GTou NLAp
'Pewter'	see *A. saccaticupula* 'Blue Haze'
pinnatifida	GTou NBro
platycantha F&W 9293 **new**	WCot
profundeincisa	see *A. anserinifolia* Druce
'Purple Carpet'	see *A. microphylla* 'Kupferteppich'
saccaticupula	MWgw NLar

§ – 'Blue Haze'	CLyd COIW EBee ECha EDAr GFlt GGar GKir GTou LRHS MBar MBro MLLN NChi NVic SIng SPer SPlb SRms SWvt WBVN WCom WFar WHoo WMoo WPer
sanguisorbae	see *A. anserinifolia* Druce
viridior	see *A. anserinifolia* Druce

Acalypha (Euphorbiaceae)

hispaniolae ♀H1	ERea ESlt MOak
hispida ♀H1	LRHS MBri
pendula	see *A. reptans*
§ **reptans**	CHal SPet

Acanthocalyx see *Morina*

Acantholimon (Plumbaginaceae)

acerosum **new**	WLin
androsaceum	see *A. ulicinum*
caesareum **new**	WLin
glumaceum	MDHE MWat
hohenackeri	WLin
§ **ulicinum**	ECho EPot WLin

Acanthopanax see *Eleutherococcus*

ricinifolius	see *Kalopanax septemlobus*

Acanthostachys (Bromeliaceae)

pitcairnioides	EMan

Acanthus ✿ (Acanthaceae)

balcanicus	see *A. hungaricus*
caroli-alexandri	EBlw WHil
dioscoridis	CBot EBlw SMHy WSel
– var. *perringii*	CDes EBee LPio MSph MSte NChi SBla SIgm SSpi SSte WCot WFar WHil WPGP WSHC
– smooth-leaved	SIgm
hirsutus	CBot EBlw EMar EMon LPio MMil SCro SIgm SVal WCot
– JCA 109.700	MSph SBla
– f. *roseus*	SBla SIgm WFar
– subsp. *syriacus*	EHrv MAnH
– – JCA 106.500	LPhx
§ **hungaricus**	More than 30 suppliers
– AL&JS 90097YU	EBlw EMon WPrP
– 'Architect'	LRHS
longifolius	see *A. hungaricus*
mollis	More than 30 suppliers
– 'Feilding Gold'	see *A. mollis* 'Hollard's Gold'
– free-flowering	GCal
– 'Hollard's Gold'	CBAn CBct CFir CHad CKno EBee EBlw ECtt EFou EMan EPPr LPio MAnH MAvo MBri MLLN NCGa NPro SDix SHop SIgm SUsu SWat WCom WCot WFar WHil WSel
– 'Jardin en Face' **new**	CBot
– 'Jefalba'	see *A. mollis* 'Rue Ledan'
– Latifolius Group	EBee EBlw EFou EMan EPfP LRHS MRav MSte SChu SPer SRms WHil WHoo WWpP
– – 'Rue Ledan'	EBee EBlw EMon LPhx MAnH SUsu WHil
– 'Pride of Morvan' (v)	EMan
– 'Summerdance'	LHop
sennii	LPhx SIgm WCot
spinosus ♀H4	More than 30 suppliers
– 'Lady Moore' (v)	EBlw EMon IBlr NLar WCot WSPU
– 'Royal Haughty'	EFou
– Spinosissimus Group	CBct CMHG EBlw ECha EHrv ELan EMan EMon EOrc GCal LPhx LPio MMil MRav SAga SBla SMad SWat WCot WFar WHil WMnd WSel WTin

'Summer Beauty' EBre MBri NPro WCot
syriacus CPom EBlw EMan GCal NLar NPro
SAga SVal WCot WViv

Acca (Myrtaceae)

sellowiana (F) More than 30 suppliers
- 'Apollo' (F) CTrC ERea
- 'Coolidge' (F) ERea
- 'Mammoth' (F) CBcs ERea
- 'Triumph' (F) CBcs ERea
- 'Variegata' (F/v) ELan LAst

Acer ✿ (Aceraceae)

B&SWJ 6024 WHCr
B&SWJ 6245 WHCr
B&SWJ 6341 WHCr
acuminatum CMCN GKir WNor WWes
albopurpurascens WWes
argutum CMCN IMGH WCwm WNor
barbinerve CMCN EPfP WNor WWes
x *bornmuelleri* **new** WWes
buergerianum CBcs CDul CMCN CMen CPMA
ECrN GKir IMGH LRHS SBLw
SEND STre WCwm WDin WNor
- 'Goshiki-
  kosode' (v) **new** WWes
- 'Goshiki-kaede' (v) CPMA WWes
- 'Integrifolium' see *A. buergerianum*
'Subintegrum'
- 'Koshi-miyasama' **new** WWes
- 'Kyuden' **new** WWes
- 'Mino-yatsubusa' WWes
- 'Naruto' CMCN
- subsp. *ningpoense* **new** WWes
- 'Shirley Debacq' **new** WWes
§ - 'Subintegrum' CMCN WWes
* - 'Variegatum' (v) CMCN
caesium WWes
calcaratum CMCN
campbellii B&SWJ 7685 WCru
* - var. *fansipanense* WCru WHCr
B&SWJ 8270
- - B&SWJ 8276 WHCr
- - HWJ 569 WCru
§ - subsp. *flabellatum* WCru
B&SWJ 8057
- - var. *yunnanense* CDoC CFil WCwm
- subsp. *sinense* see *A. sinense*
- subsp. *wilsonii* see *A. wilsonii*
campestre ♀H4 More than 30 suppliers
- 'Carnival' (v) CBcs CDul CMCN CMCN CPMA
CWib EBee GKir LRHS MAsh MBlu
MBri MGos NHol SMad SPer SWvt
WCot WPGP WWes
- 'Elsrijk' CCVT CLnd SBLw
- 'Evenley Red' MBlu
- 'Pendulum' CEnd CTho GKir
- 'Postelense' CEnd CMCN CPMA GKir MBlu
MGos SLim SSpi WWes
- 'Pulverulentum' (v) CDoC CEnd CPMA GKir
MAsh SLim SMad SSta WBcn
- 'Queen Elizabeth' CCVT SEND
- 'Red Shine' MGos
- 'Royal Ruby' CTho GKir GTSp MAsh MGos
SKee SSta
* - 'Ruby Glow' CDoC CEnd CLnd GKir LRHS
- 'Silver Celebration' (v) CPMA
- 'William Caldwell' CEnd CTho GKir LRHS
capillipes ♀H4 CBcs CDul CMCN CTho CWib
ECrN EGFP ENot LRHS MBar
MDun NBea NPSI SBLw WDin
WNor WOrn
- 'Candy Stripe' GKir SLim SSpi SSta
- 'Gimborn' **new** WWes

- 'Golden Increase' **new** WWes
- var. *morifolium* see *A. morifolium*
cappadocicum CDul CMCN CSam GTSp LRHS
MDun MLan NBee NWea WDin
WNor WWes
- 'Aureum' ♀H4 More than 30 suppliers
- 'De Oirsprong' **new** WWes
- subsp. *divergens* **new** MPkF
- var. *mono* see *A. pictum*
- 'Rubrum' ♀H4 CDul CLnd CMCN ECrN ENot
EPfP GKir LBuc LPan LRHS MBlu
MGos MRav SBLw SKee SLim SPer
WDin WHer
- subsp. *sinicum* CFil CMCN EPfP
carpinifolium CBrd CMCN CTho ECrN NLar SSpi
WCwm WNor
- B&SWJ 5086 WHCr
- 'Esveld Select' **new** WWes
catalpifolium see *A. longipes* subsp.
catalpifolium
§ *caudatifolium* CFil CMCN CPle EBee WPGP
- B&SWJ 3531 WCru
- B&SWJ 6734 WCru WHCr
- B&SWJ 6761 WHCr
§ aff. *caudatifolium* WHCr
B&SWJ 1744
§ *caudatum* SSpi
- subsp. *ukurunduense* CMCN GIBF IArd WNor
cinnamomifolium see *A. coriaceifolium*
circinatum CBcs CDoC CDul CMCN CPMA
CSam EPfP LRHS MLan NBea NFor
NHol NLar SHBN SSpi SSta WDin
WFar WNor
- 'Little Gem' CPMA
- 'Monroe' WWes
- 'Sunglow' **new** WWes
circinatum GKir
x *palmatum* **new**
cissifolium CBcs CDoC CFil CMCN CTho EPfP
EPla GKir IArd IMGH LRHS WNor
WPGP
x *conspicuum* CPMA GKir
'Candy Stripe'
- 'Elephant's Ear' CPMA EPfP
I - 'Phoenix' CEnd CMCN CPMA CTho EPfP
GKir LRHS MBlu MBri NLar SSpi
- 'Silver Cardinal' see *A.* 'Silver Cardinal'
§ - 'Silver Vein' CDoC CDul CEnd CMCN CPMA
EBee EPfP GKir LRHS NLar SSpi
SSta
§ *cordatum* WWes
§ *coriaceifolium* WNor
crataegifolium CMCN IMGH WNor
- 'Veitchii' (v) CDoC CLnd CMCN CPMA EPfP
GKir SSpi WBcn WPGP WWes
creticum L., . see *A. sempervirens*
non f. Schmidt
dasycarpum see *A. saccharinum*
davidii More than 30 suppliers
- B&SWJ 8162 WHCr
- B&SWJ 8183 WCru WHCr
- 'Cantonspark' **new** MPkF WWes
- 'Ernest Wilson' CBcs CMCN LRHS MBlu NLar
- 'George Forrest' ♀H4 CBcs CDoC CDul CMCN CTho
EBee ECrN ELan EPfP GKir LPan
LRHS MAsh MBlu MBri MDun
NBea NWea SBod SEND SHBN
SKee SLim SPer WDin
- 'Hagelunie' **new** MPkF
- 'Karmen' CPMA GKir LRHS MBri WWes
- 'Madeline Spitta' CMCN GKir
- 'Rosalie' CDul EPfP GKir LRHS MBlu MBri
- 'Sekka' **new** WWes
- 'Serpentine' ♀H4 CBcs CDoC CMCN CPMA CTho

	EPfP GKir LRHS MBlu MBri NLar SSpi SSta WFar WOrn
- 'Silver Vein'	see *A.* x *conspicuum* 'Silver Vein'
- variegated **new**	WWes
diabolicum	CMCN WWes
- f. *purpurascens*	GIBF
distylum	WWes
divergens	CMCN
elegantulum	CDoC CMCN WCwm WNor
erianthum	CPne CTho SSpi SSta WNor WWes
fabri	CBcs CMCN WNor
flabellatum	see *A. campbellii* subsp. *flabellatum*
§ *forrestii*	CDul CMCN CTho EPfP IArd NBea NHol WNor
- 'Alice'	CBcs CDul CEnd CMCN CPMA GKir SSpi SSta WBcn
§ - 'Sirene'	CPMA
§ - 'Sparkling'	CPMA GKir LRHS MBri SSpi
x *freemanii*	CMCN
- 'Armstrong'	SBLw WFar WWes
- Autumn Blaze	CCVT CDoC CDul CLnd CMCN
= 'Jeffersred'	EPfP LRHS MBlu SBLw SKee SMad WDin WFar WOrn
- 'Autumn Fantasy'	GKir MBlu
- Celebration	LRHS WFar
= 'Celzam' **new**	
§ - 'Elegant'	CBcs SBLw
- Indian Summer	CEnd CLnd CPMA GKir LRHS
= 'Morgan'	WWes
fulvescens	see *A. longipes*
ginnala	see *A. tataricum* subsp. *ginnala*
glabrum	WNor
globosum	see *A. platanoides* 'Globosum'
grandidentatum	see *A. saccharum* subsp. *grandidentatum*
griseum ♀H4	More than 30 suppliers
grosseri	CBcs CDul CMCN CTri GKir IArd
- var. *hersii* ♀H4	More than 30 suppliers
- 'Leiden'	MBlu
heldreichii	CMCN EPfP
henryi	CBcs CDul CLnd CMCN CTho ECrN ENot EPfP WBVN WCwm WNor
hookeri	CMCN
hyrcanum	CMCN WWes
- 'Alma Mater' **new**	WWes
japonicum	CDul CMCN LRHS MBar NHol SKee SSta WNor
- B&SWJ 5950	WCru
§ - 'Aconitifolium' ♀H4	More than 30 suppliers
- 'Attaryi'	CMCN NLar
- 'Aureum'	see *A. shirasawanum* 'Aureum'
- 'Ezo-no-momiji'	see *A. shirasawanum* 'Ezo-no-momiji'
- 'Fairy Lights' **new**	WWes
- 'Filicifolium'	see *A. japonicum* 'Aconitifolium'
- 'Green Cascade'	CEnd CMCN CPMA ECho NLar WPGP WPat WWes
- 'Kujaku-nishiki' (v) **new**	WWes
- 'Laciniatum'	see *A. japonicum* 'Aconitifolium'
- f. *microphyllum*	see *A. shirasawanum* 'Microphyllum'
- 'Mikasa-yama'	GKir LRHS
- 'Ogurayama'	see *A. shirasawanum* 'Ogurayama'
- 'Ô-isami'	CMCN EPfP GKir LRHS WWes
- 'Ô-taki'	ECho
- 'Vitifolium' ♀H4	CDoC CEnd CMCN CPMA CSBt ELan EPfP GKir LPan LRHS MBlu NPSI NPal SPer SSpi SSta WPGP WPat
kawakamii	see *A. caudatifolium*
laevigatum	CMCN
laxiflorum	CBcs SSta
lobelii Tenore	CLnd CTho NRog WWes
lobelii Bunge	see *A. turkestanicum*
§ *longipes*	CMCN
§ - subsp. *catalpifolium*	CMCN
- 'Gold Coin' **new**	WWes
macrophyllum	CFil CMCN CTho EPfP IDee ISea LHyd LRHS SMad
mandschuricum	CBcs EPfP IArd MBlu WCwm WDin WNor
§ *maximowiczianum*	CBcs CMCN CSam CTho ELan GIBF SSpi SSta WFar WNor
maximowiczii	CMCN ECrN LRHS WNor
§ *metcalfii*	WNor
micranthum	CDoC CFil CMCN CPLG EPfP GKir IMGH MBlu MDun SSpi WNor WPGP
miyabei	WWes
mono	see *A. pictum*
monspessulanum	CBcs CDul CFil CMCN CTho IArd SEND XPep
§ *morifolium*	CCVT MPkF WWes
morrisonense	see *A. caudatifolium*
negundo	CCVT CDul CLnd CMCN CTho CWib ECrN ENot NWea SBLw SCrf WNor WOrn
- IDS 2000	WHCr
- 'Argenteovariegatum'	see *A. negundo* 'Variegatum'
- 'Auratum'	CMCN MBar SBLw WDin WPat
- 'Aureomarginatum' (v)	LBuc SPer
- 'Aureovariegatum' (v)	CBcs MBar
- subsp. *californicum*	WNor WWes
- - var. *texanum* **new**	WWes
§ - 'Elegans' (v)	CDul CEnd CLnd CMCN COtt EBee EBre ECrN ENot EPfP LPan LRHS NHol SHBN SKee SPer WWes
- 'Elegantissimum'	see *A. negundo* 'Elegans'
- 'Flamingo' (v)	More than 30 suppliers
- 'Kelly's Gold'	CBcs CTho EBre EGra ENot LRHS MAsh MDun MGos NPro SCoo SKee SLim SPoG WFar WOrn
	WWes
- 'Sensation' **new**	WWes
§ - 'Variegatum' (v)	CBcs CLnd EBee ECrN ENot LAst LPan LRHS NWea SBLw SPer WDin WFar
- var. *violaceum*	CBcs CEnd CMCN WBcn WWes
nikoense	see *A. maximowiczianum*
nipponicum	WWes
oblongum	CMCN
§ *obtusifolium*	WBcn WWes
olivaceum **new**	WWes
oliverianum	CFil EPfP WNor WPGP WWes
- subsp. *formosanum*	WWes
- - B&SWJ 6773	WCru
- - B&SWJ 6797	WCru
opalus	CMCN SSpi WCwm WWes
orientale	see *A. sempervirens*
'Pacific Sunset'	GKir LRHS
palmatum	More than 30 suppliers
§ - 'Aka Shigitatsusawa'	CBcs CBdw CMCN CMac CMen CPMA GKir LRHS MAsh MGos NLar SSpi WFar WPat
- 'Akane'	CBdw CMen
- 'Akegarasu'	LRHS MAsh NLar
- 'Alloys' **new**	WWes
- 'Alpine Surprise' **new**	WWes
- 'Ao Kanzashi' (v) **new**	CBdw MPkF NLar
- 'Aoba-jo'	CMen CPMA NLar
- 'Aoshime-no-uchi'	see *A. palmatum* 'Shinobugaoka'
- 'Aoyagi'	CEnd CMCN CMen CPMA EPfP GKir LAst LMil LRHS MAsh NHol WFoF WPat WWes
§ - 'Arakawa'	CEnd CMCN CMen ECho GKir WWes

- 'Aratama'   CBdw CPMA WPat WWes
- 'Ariake-nomura'   WWes
- 'Asahi-zuru' (v)   CBcs CBdw CMCN CMen CPMA EBee ECho GKir LPan LRHS MGos NHol NLar NPSI WFar WFoF WPat WWes
- 'Ashurst Wood' **new**   LMil
- 'Atrolineare'   WPat
- 'Atropurpureum'   CBrm CMen CSBt CTho CTri CWib EBee ECrN ISea MDun MSwo SPer SWvt WBod WHil WWes
- f. **atropurpureum**   More than 30 suppliers
- 'Atropurpureum = 'Celzam' **new**   MPkF
- 'Attraction'   CMCN CMac WWes
- 'Aureum'   CBdw CMCN CMen CWib ECho EPfP GKir LRHS NLar SCoo SSpi WFar WWes
- Autumn Glory Group   CEnd CPMA SSpi WWes
- 'Autumn Red'   LPan LRHS
- * - 'Autumn Showers'   CEnd CPMA
- 'Azuma-murasaki'   CPMA NLar WWes
- 'Barrie Bergman' **new**   CBdw WWes
- * - 'Beni K Sport'   CPMA
- 'Beni-chidori'   CBdw CMen ECho WWes
- 'Beni-gasa'   CPMA
- 'Beni-hime'   CBdw CPMA NLar
- 'Beni-kagami'   CEnd CMCN CPMA EPfP GKir LRHS MBlu MGos NLar WWes
- 'Beni-kawa'   CBdw GKir LMil SSpi WWes
- 'Beni-komachi'   CBcs CEnd CMCN CMac CMen CPMA ECho GKir LRHS MAsh WPat WWes
- 'Beni-maiko'   CBdw CEnd CMCN CMen CPMA EBee GKir LRHS WPGP WPat WWes
- 'Beni-otake'   CBcs CBdw CMCN CMen CPMA ECho LRHS MAsh MGos NLar NPSI SBod WPat WWes
- 'Beni-schichihenge' (v)   CBdw CEnd CMCN CMen CPMA EPfP GKir LRHS MAsh NHol SCoo SMur SSta WPGP WPat
- I - 'Beni-shidare Tricolor' (v) **new**   CBdw
- 'Beni-shigitatsu-sawa'   see *A. palmatum* 'Aka Shigitatsusawa'
- 'Beni-tsukasa' (v)   CBdw CEnd CMen CPMA ECho GKir LMil LPan LRHS MAsh SSpi SSta WPGP WPat WWes
- 'Beni-tsukasa-shidare' **new**   CBdw
- 'Beni-ubi-gohon' **new**   MPkF WWes
- 'Beni-yatsubusa' **new**   WWes
- 'Beni-zuru' **new**   CBdw
- 'Berry Dwarf'   WPat
- 'Bloodgood' ♀H4   More than 30 suppliers
- * - 'Bonfire' **new**   LRHS
- 'Bonnie Bergman' **new**   WWes
- 'Boskoop Glory' **new**   WWes
- 'Brandt's Dwarf' **new**   CBdw
- 'Burgundy Lace' ♀H4   CBcs CDoC CEnd CMCN CPMA CSBt CWib ECrN EMil GKir LRHS MAsh MBlu MBri MGos NHol NPSI SPer WFar WPat
- 'Butterfly' (v)   CBcs CDoC CEnd CFil CMCN CPMA CWSG CWib EBre EPfP GKir LPan LRHS MBar MGos NBea NHol SLdr SLim SReu SSta WDin WFar WStl WWes
- 'Carminium'   see *A. palmatum* 'Corallinum'
- 'Chikuma-no' **new**   MPkF
- 'Chirimen-nishiki' (v)   CMCN
- 'Chishio'   see *A. palmatum* 'Shishio'

- 'Chishio Improved'   see *A. palmatum* 'Shishio Improved'
- 'Chishio-hime' **new**   CBdw
- 'Chitoseyama' ♀H4   CEnd CMCN CMen CPMA EPfP GKir LRHS MBar MBri MGos NLar SCoo SLim SMur SSpi WFar WPat WWes
- 'Collingwood Ingram' **new**   WWes
- 'Coonara Pygmy'   CBdw CMCN CMen CPMA ECho LRHS MAsh WFar WPat WWes
- 'Coral Pink'   CBdw CPMA WWes
- § - 'Corallinum'   CBdw CEnd CMCN CMen CPMA NLar SSpi WPat
- var. **coreanum**   CMCN CSam WNor
- B&SWJ 4474   WCru
- B&SWJ 8606   WCru
- 'Korean Gem'   ECho MAsh
- 'Crippsii'   CDoC CMen ECho EMil LRHS MBri SCoo SPer WFar WPat WWes
- 'Demi-sec' **new**   CBdw WWes
- 'Deshôjô'   CBcs CBdw CMCN CMen LPan MBar MBlu MGos NHol SHBN
- 'Diana'   NLar WWes
- 'Diane Verkade' **new**   CBdw
- var. **dissectum** ♀H4   CDoC CDul CEnd CTri CWSG CWib EBee ENot EPfP EWTr GKir LBuc LHyd LRHS MBar MBri MGos NBee NHol NWea SHBN SLim SReu WCFE WDin WFar WNor WPat WStl
- - 'Ao-shidare'   CBdw WWes
- - 'Ariadne' (v)   CBdw CPMA GKir NLar WPat WWes
- - 'Baby Lace'   CPMA
- - 'Baldsmith'   CBdw CPMA
- - 'Beni-fushigi'   CBdw NLar WWes
- - 'Beni-shidare Variegated' (v)   CMCN CPMA
- - 'Berrima Bridge'   CPMA
- - 'Brocade'   CMCN WPat WWes
- - 'Chantilly Lace' **new**   CPMA
- - 'Crimson Queen' ♀H4   More than 30 suppliers
- - Dissectum Atropurpureum Group   CBcs CDul CPMA CTri EBre ELan ENot EPfP GKir LHyd LPan LRHS MAsh MGos NBea NHol NWea SHBN SLim SPer SPlb SReu SSpi SSta WBod WDin WFar WOrn WPat
- - 'Dissectum Flavescens'   CBdw CEnd CMac CPMA MBlu
- § - 'Dissectum Nigrum'   CPMA CWSG LPan LRHS MGos NBea NBee NHol SSpi WWes
- - 'Dissectum Palmatifidum'   CDoC LRHS MPkF NPSI SPer WFar WPat WWes
- - 'Dissectum Rubrifolium'   WWes
- § - 'Dissectum Variegatum' (v)   CBcs CPMA EPfP LRHS SSta
- - Dissectum Viride Group   CBcs CMCN CMen CPMA CSBt CWSG ECrN ELan EMui EPfP LPan LRHS MAsh MBro MDun MGos MSwo NBPC NBea NBlu NPSI NPri SKee SLim SPer SPla SSta WBod WFar WOrn
- - 'Ellen'   WPat WWes
- - 'Emerald Lace' **new**   WWes
- - 'Felice' **new**   CBdw MPkF WPat
- - 'Filigree' (v)   CBdw CMCN CMen CPMA EPfP GKir LRHS MAsh MGos NLar SSpi WPat WWes
- - 'Garnet'   More than 30 suppliers
- - 'Goshiki-shidare' (v)   CEnd CPMA WWes
- - 'Green Globe'   CBdw LPan LRHS NLar WWes
- - 'Green Lace'   LPan NLar
- - 'Green Mist'   CPMA WWes
- - 'Inaba-shidare' ♀H4   CBcs CDoC CEnd CMCN CMen COtt CPMA CSBt CWib EBee EBre

	EMil ENot EPfP GKir IMGH LPan LRHS MAsh MBar MBri MGos NHol SBod SPer SSta WGer WPGP WPat
– – 'Kiri-nishiki'	CMen CPMA ECho NLar
* – – 'Lionheart'	CBdw CPMA ECho EMil LRHS MGos NPSI SBod SCoo SPer WFar WPat
– – 'Nomura-nishiki' (v)	WWes
– – 'Octopus'	CBdw CPMA
– – 'Orangeola'	CBdw CPMA NLar WPat WWes
– – 'Ornatum'	CDoC CMCN CMen COtt CWib EBee ECho IMGH LPan MBar MDun MGos NBea NBlu SCoo WDin WFar WGer WHar
– – 'Pendulum Julian'	CMCN NLar
– – 'Pink Filigree'	CBdw LPan WWes
– – 'Red Autumn Lace'	WWes
– – 'Red Dragon'	CBcs CBdw CDoC CMen CPMA ECho ECrN LRHS MGos NPSI WPat
– – 'Red Filgree Lace'	CBdw CEnd CMCN CMen CPMA ECho EPfP GKir LRHS MBlu SSta WPat
– – 'Red Select'	MGos WWes
– – 'Seiryû'	More than 30 suppliers
§ – – 'Shôjô-shidare'	CEnd ECho LRHS NLar WWes
– – 'Sunset'	CBdw CMCN CPMA MDun WPat
– – 'Tamukeyama'	CMCN CMen CPMA EMil LRHS MAsh MBri MDun NLar SBod SKee SSpi WBVN WFar WPat
– – 'Toyama-nishiki' (v)	CMCN CMen NLar
– – 'Waterfall'	CMCN CPMA
– – 'Watnong'	CBdw CPMA
– – 'Zaaling'	CPMA ECho
– 'Dragon's Fire'	CBdw EMui MDun
– 'Eddisbury'	CEnd CPMA MDun NLar SSta WBod WPat WWes
– 'Edna Bergman'	CPMA
– 'Effegi'	see A. palmatum 'Fireglow'
– 'Eimini'	CBdw WWes
– 'Elegans'	ECho EPfP NLar WDin
– 'Englishtown' new	CBdw WWes
– 'Enkan'	CBdw CPMA WPat WWes
– 'Ever Red'	see A. palmatum var. dissectum 'Dissectum Nigrum'
– 'Fall's Fire'	CBdw CPMA
– 'Filigree Rouge' new	CBdw WWes
– 'Fior d'Arancio'	CPMA WWes
§ – 'Fireglow'	CDoC CEnd CMCN CMen CPMA CSBt CWib ECho EMil LPan LRHS MAsh MGos NBlu NLar SBod SCoo WFar WPGP WPat WWes
– 'Fjellheim'	CBdw CPMA
– 'Flushing' new	WWes
– 'Frederici Guglielmi'	see A. palmatum var. dissectum 'Dissectum Variegatum'
– 'Garyu' new	WWes
– 'Gasshoh' new	CBdw WWes
– 'Gekko-nishiki' new	CBdw WWes
– 'Germaine's Gyration' new	CBdw
– 'Glowing Embers' new	WWes
– 'Golden Pond'	CBdw WWes
– 'Goshiki-kotohime' (v)	CMCN CPMA
– 'Green Trompenburg'	CMCN CMen NLar
– 'Groundcover' new	CBdw WWes
§ – 'Hagoromo'	CMen ECho NPSI WFar
– 'Hanami-nishiki'	CMen MPkF
– 'Hatsushigure' new	CBdw
– 'Heartbeat' new	CBdw WWes
– 'Helena'	NLar WWes
– var. heptalobum	CDul CMCN WWes
§ – 'Heptalobum Elegans'	CMCN LRHS MBlu SHBN SSpi
– 'Heptalobum Elegans Purpureum'	see A. palmatum 'Hessei'
– 'Herbstfeuer' new	CPMA
§ – 'Hessei'	CEnd CMCN ECho GKir LRHS MAsh MBlu NLar WWes
– 'Higasayama' (v)	CBcs CEnd CMCN CMen CPMA GKir LRHS MAsh NHol WPGP WPat WWes
– 'Hi-no-tsukasa' new	CBdw
– 'Hiryu' new	WWes
– 'Hôgyoku'	CMCN CPMA
– 'Hondoshi' new	CBdw WWes
– 'Hoshi-kuzu' new	CBdw
– 'Hupp's Dwarf'	WWes
– 'Ibo-nishiki' new	CMen MPkF
– 'Ichigyôji'	CDul CEnd CMCN CPMA LRHS MAsh WPGP WWes
– 'Improved Shishio'	see A. palmatum 'Shishio Improved'
– 'Inazuma'	CBcs CMCN ECho LRHS NLar WWes
– 'Irish Lace' new	CBdw
– 'Issai-nishiki' new	MPkF
* – 'Issai-nishiki-kawazu' new	MPkF
– 'Itami-nishiki' new	CBdw WWes
– 'Jane' new	MPkF WWes
– 'Japanese Sunrise'	CBdw WWes
– 'Jirô-shidare'	EPfP LRHS MAsh
– 'Junihitoe'	see A. shirasawanum 'Jûnihitoe'
– 'Kaba'	WWes
– 'Kagero' (v)	MPkF WFar
§ – 'Kagiri-nishiki' (v)	CBcs CBdw CDul CMCN CMen CPMA CWSG ECho LRHS MGos NHol SCoo WFar WNor
– 'Kamagata'	CBdw CEnd CMCN CMen CPMA EPfP GKir LMil LRHS MAsh MBri MGos NLar NPSI SSta WBod WPGP WPat WWes
– 'Kandy Kitchen'	CBdw WWes
– 'Karaori' new	WWes
– 'Karaori-nishiki' (v)	CMen ECho MBlu NLar
– 'Karasugawa' (v)	CBdw CMen CPMA NLar
– 'Kasagiyama'	CBdw CEnd CMCN CMen COtt CPMA LRHS NLar WPGP
– 'Kasen-nishiki'	CBdw CMen ECho
– 'Kashima'	CBdw CEnd CMCN CMen CPMA ECho LRHS MBNS NLar WFar WWes
– 'Kashima-yatsubusa' new	CBdw
– 'Katja'	WWes
– 'Katsura' ♀H4	CBcs CBdw CDoC CEnd CMCN CMen CPMA EPfP GKir LMil LPan LRHS MAsh MBlu MBri MGos NBlu NHol SPer SPla SSpi SSta WFar WNor WStI
– 'Kenko-nishiki' new	CMCN CMen CPMA NLar WWes
– 'Ki-hachijô'	CMCN CMen CPMA NLar WWes
– 'Kingsville Variegated' (v)	WWes
– 'Kinran'	CMCN CMen ECho GKir LRHS MAsh WPat WWes
– 'Kinshi'	CEnd CMCN CPMA GKir LRHS MAsh NLar SSta WPat
– 'Kiyohime'	CBdw CDoC CMCN CMen ECho GKir MBlu WFar WPat
– 'Ko-chidori'	WWes
– 'Kogane-nishiki' new	WWes
– 'Koko' new	WWes
– 'Komache-hime'	CBdw CPMA
– 'Komaru'	NLar
– 'Komon-nishiki' (v)	CBdw CPMA WWes
– 'Koriba'	CBdw NLar
§ – 'Koshimino'	CPMA LPan
– 'Kotohime'	CBcs CBdw CMCN CMen CPMA NLar WWes
– 'Koto-ito-komachi'	CBdw CEnd CMen CPMA ECho NLar WPat

- 'Koto-maru' **new**	CBdw MPkF
- 'Koto-no-ito'	CBdw CMCN NLar
- 'Koya-san' **new**	CBdw MPkF
- 'Kurabu-yama'	CMCN
- 'Kurui-jishi'	CBdw NLar WPat
- 'Kyra' **new**	WWes
- 'Lemon Lime Lace' **new**	CBdw WWes
- 'Linearilobum'	CDoC EPfP GKir LHyd LRHS MBlu NBea NHol NLar SSpi WFar WNor WPat
- 'Linearilobum Atropurpureum'	LRHS WNor
- 'Lin-ling' **new**	LMil
- 'Little Princess'	see *A. palmatum* 'Mapi-no-machihime'
- 'Lozita' **new**	WWes
- 'Lutescens'	ECho
- 'Lydia' **new**	MPkF
- 'Maiko'	CMen ECho
- 'Mai-mori' (v)	WWes
§ - 'Mapi-no-machihime'	CBdw CEnd CMCN CMen CPMA ELan GKir LRHS MAsh NHol SMur WPGP WPat
- 'Marakumo' **new**	MPkF
- 'Margaret' **new**	WWes
- 'Margaret Bee' **new**	WWes
- 'Marjan'	NLar WWes
- 'Masamurasaki'	WPat
- 'Masukagami' (v)	CEnd CPMA NLar
- 'Matsuga-e' (v)	MAsh
- 'Matsukaze'	CMCN CMen COtt CPMA GKir WWes
- 'Mei-ho-nishiki' **new**	CBdw
- 'Melanie'	SSpi
- 'Meoto' **new**	WWes
- 'Mikawa-yatsubusa'	CMCN CMen CPMA ECho LRHS NBhm NLar WPat WWes
- 'Mini Mondo'	WPat WWes
- 'Mirte'	WWes
- 'Misty Moon' **new**	WWes
- 'Mizuho-beni'	CBdw CPMA
- 'Mizu-kuguri'	CMCN NLar WPat
- 'Momenshide'	CBdw WWes
- 'Momoiro-koya-san'	NLar WPat
- 'Mon Papa'	CPMA WWes
- 'Mono-zigawa' **new**	WWes
- 'Monzukushi'	CMCN CPMA
- 'Moonfire'	CMCN CPMA EPfP GKir LRHS MAsh NLar SSpi WWes
- 'Mufuri' **new**	WWes
- 'Murasaki-kiyohime'	CBdw CEnd CMCN CMen CPMA ECho NLar WPat
- 'Murasaki-shikibu' **new**	CBdw
- 'Mure-hibari'	CMCN CPMA
- var. **nakai new**	WWes
- 'Nanase-gawa' **new**	MPkF
- 'Nathan'	WWes
- 'Nicholsonii'	CMCN EPfP LRHS MBri NLar WFar WPat WWes
- 'Nigrum' ♀H4	CMCN WPat
- 'Nishiki-gasane' (v) **new**	CBdw MPkF
§ - 'Nishiki-gawa'	CEnd CMCN CMen CPMA GKir WPGP WWes
- 'Nishiki-momiji'	CMen
- 'Nomurishidare' misapplied	see *A. palmatum* 'Shôjô-shidare'
- 'Nomurishidare' Wada	SSpi
- 'Nuresagi'	CBdw CEnd CPMA
- 'Ôgi-nagashi' (v)	WWes
- 'Ôgon-sarasa'	CPMA
- 'Ojishi' **new**	CMen
- 'Ô-kagami'	CEnd CMen CPMA ECho GKir LRHS MGos SSta WPat
- 'Okina'	CBdw WWes
- 'Okukuji-nishiki'	CBdw CPMA MAsh
- 'Okushimo'	CBdw CEnd CMCN CMen CPMA LRHS NHol NLar WPGP WPat
- 'Olga' **new**	WWes
- 'Omato'	WFar
- 'Omurayama'	CDoC CEnd CMCN CMen CPMA ECho EPfP LRHS MAsh MGos NBhm NBlu NLar SCoo SSta WPat WWes
§ - 'Ô-nishiki'	CBdw CMCN CMen CWib
- 'Orange Dream'	CBcs CBdw CEnd CMCN CMen CPMA GKir LPan LRHS MAsh MBlu NLar SCoo WPat WWes
- 'Oregon Sunset'	CBdw CMen
- 'Orido-nishiki' (v)	CBcs CEnd CMCN CMen CPMA ELan EPfP LMil LRHS MAsh MBar MBlu MBri MGos NBea NBee NBlu SCoo SSpi SSta
- 'Ori-zuru' **new**	LMil
- 'Ôsakazuki' ♀H4	More than 30 suppliers
- 'Ôshio-beni'	CPMA ECho MAsh NLar WWes
- 'Ôshû-shidare'	CBdw CPMA WFar WPat
- 'Otome-zakura'	CBdw CMCN CMen WPat
I - 'Paul's Variegated' **new**	CBdw
- 'Peaches and Cream' (v)	CBdw CPMA WWes
- 'Peve Multicolor' **new**	MPkF
- 'Phoenix' **new**	MPkF
- 'Pine Bark Maple'	see *A. palmatum* 'Nishiki-gawa'
- 'Pixie'	CBdw CMCN CPMA NLar
- var. **pubescens** B&SWJ 6886	WCru
- 'Pung-kil' **new**	CBdw
- 'Purpureum' **new**	WWes
- 'Red Baron' **new**	WWes
- 'Red Flash'	LPan LRHS WWes
- 'Red Jonas' **new**	WWes
- 'Red Pygmy' ♀H4	CBcs CDoC CEnd CMCN CMen COtt CPMA CWib EMil GKir LRHS MAsh MBar MBlu MBri MGos NBea NBee SBod SCoo SMur SPer SSpi SSta WBod WFar WPat
- 'Red Shadow' **new**	LMil
- 'Red Wood' **new**	CDoC MPkF WPat WWes
- 'Renjaku-maru' **new**	CBdw
- 'Reticulatum'	see *A. palmatum* 'Shigitatsu-sawa'
- 'Ribesifolium'	see *A. palmatum* 'Shishigashira'
- 'Roseomarginatum'	see *A. palmatum* 'Kagiri-nishiki'
- 'Roseum Ornatum' **new**	CBdw
- 'Rough Bark Maple'	see *A. palmatum* 'Arakawa'
- 'Royle' **new**	CBdw WWes
- 'Ryumon-nishiki' **new**	CBdw
- 'Ryuzu'	CPMA
- 'Sagara-nishiki' (v)	CBdw CEnd CMen CPMA ECho WWes
- 'Samidare'	CPMA EPfP NLar WWes
- 'Sandra'	WWes
N - 'Sango-kaku' ♀H4	More than 30 suppliers
- 'Saoshika'	CDul CMCN CPMA
- 'Sa-otome' **new**	MPkF
- 'Satsuki-beni'	WWes
- 'Sawa-chidori' **new**	CBdw
- 'Sazanami'	CEnd CPMA NLar WNor
- 'Scolopendriifolium'	WPat WWes
- 'Seigen'	CBdw CEnd CMCN CMen CPMA ECho WPat
I - 'Seigen Aureum' **new**	CBdw CPMA
- 'Seiun Kaku'	CBdw CPMA WWes
- 'Sekimori'	CMCN CPMA
- 'Sekka-yatsubusa'	CMCN CMen
- 'Senkaki'	see *A. palmatum* 'Sango-kaku'
- 'Septemlobum Elegans'	see *A. palmatum* 'Heptalobum Elegans'
- 'Septemlobum Purpureum'	see *A. palmatum* 'Hessei'
- 'Sessilifolium' dwarf	see *A. palmatum* 'Hagoromo'

- 'Sessilifolium' tall	see *A. palmatum* 'Koshimino'
- 'Shaina'	CBcs CEnd CMen CPMA LPan LRHS NBhm NBlu NLar WFar WPat WWes
- 'Sharp's Pygmy'	CBdw WWes
- 'Sherwood Flame'	CMCN CPMA CWib LRHS MAsh MBlu MBri MGos NLar WFar WPat WWes
- 'Shichigosan' **new**	CMen
- 'Shidava Gold'	CBdw CPMA GKir WPat
- 'Shigarami'	MPkF
§ - 'Shigitatsu-sawa' (v)	CBcs CBdw CEnd CMCN CMen CPMA EMil GKir LPan LRHS MGos NLar SCoo
- 'Shigure-bato'	CMCN CPMA WWes
- 'Shigurezome'	CMCN WWes
- 'Shikageori-nishiki'	LRHS
- 'Shime-no-uchi'	CMCN LMil
- 'Shindeshôjô'	CBcs CBdw CDoC CEnd CMCN CMen COtt CPMA ECrN GKir LRHS MAsh MBri MGos MLan NPSI SBod SCoo SHBN SPer SReu SSta WFoF WNor WPat
§ - 'Shinobugaoka'	CMCN CMen CPMA
- 'Shinonome'	WWes
- 'Shin-seyu' **new**	WWes
§ - 'Shishigashira'	CBcs CDoC CMCN CMen COtt CPMA ECho EPfP LPan LRHS MBar MBlu MBri MDun MGos NLar WFar WPat
§ - 'Shishio'	CBcs CMCN CMen ECho GKir LAst LHyd LRHS MAsh SSpi WPat
§ - 'Shishio Improved'	CBdw CEnd CMCN CPMA CTho CWSG LMil MBlu MGos NBhm NLar SSta SWvt
- 'Shôjô'	CMCN CPMA WWes
- 'Shôjô-no-mai'	CBdw
- 'Shôjô-nomura'	CAbP CEnd CMen COtt CPMA LRHS MAsh NLar WPGP
- 'Skeeters'	CBdw CDoC MBri WPat
- 'Skeeter's Broom' **new**	LRHS
* - 'Sode-nishiki' **new**	CBdw MPkF
- 'Spreading Star' **new**	WWes
- 'Saint Jean' **new**	CBdw
- 'Stanley's Unknown' **new**	WWes
- 'Stella Rossa'	CEnd CMCN CPMA LPan LRHS MBlu NLar WPat WWes
- 'Suminagashi'	CDoC CMCN LRHS MBri MDun SBod SMur WPat
- 'Susan'	WWes
- 'Taiyo-nishiki' **new**	CBdw
- 'Takao' **new**	WWes
- 'Takinogawa'	LRHS MAsh
- 'Tamahime'	CMCN CMen CPMA ECho WWes
- 'Tana'	CBdw CMCN CPMA EPfP WFar WPat WWes
- 'Taro-yama'	CBdw WPat
- 'Tatsuta'	ECho WWes
- 'Tennyo-no-hoshi'	NLar
- 'The Bishop' **new**	WWes
- 'Tiny Tim'	CBdw CPMA WPat
- 'Trompenburg' ♀H4	More than 30 suppliers
- 'Tsuchigumo'	CMCN CMen CPMA ECho
- 'Tsukushigata'	CMCN
- 'Tsuma-beni'	CMCN CMen CPMA EPfP LRHS MAsh WPat
- 'Tsuma-gaki'	CBdw CMCN CMen CPMA ECho NLar WPat WWes
- 'Tsuri-nishiki' (v)	CBdw CPMA ECho WWes
- 'Ueno-homare' **new**	CBdw MPkF
- 'Ueno-yama' **new**	CBdw
- 'Ukigumo' (v)	CBcs CBdw CEnd CMCN CMen CPMA CSBt CWSG ELan EMil LRHS MGos NBlu NHol NPSI SBod SCoo SMur SPer SSta WPat
- 'Ukon'	CBdw CMCN CMen CPMA EMil MBri
- 'Umegae'	CPMA
- 'Usu-midori' **new**	CBdw
- 'Utsu-semi'	CPMA WWes
- 'Vanderhoss Red' **new**	WWes
- 'Vens Broom'	WPat
- 'Versicolor' (v)	CEnd CMCN CPMA LRHS WWes
- 'Vic Broom'	CBdw WPat
- 'Vic Pink'	CBdw WPat
- 'Villa Taranto'	CBdw CDoC CEnd CMCN CMen CPMA CSBt EPfP GKir LRHS MAsh MBlu NLar SCoo SSpi WPGP WPat WWes
- 'Volubile'	CMCN CMen ECho EPfP LRHS MAsh SMur SSta
- 'Wabito'	CMCN CPMA
- 'Waka-midori' **new**	ECho
- 'Waka-momiji' (v) **new**	CBdw
- 'Wakehurst Pink' (v)	CBdw CMCN CMen NLar WWes
- 'Wendy'	NLar WWes
- 'Wilson's Pink Dwarf'	CBdw CEnd CMen CPMA ECho EPfP MBri NLar
- 'Winter Flame'	CBdw CPMA MAsh WBod WPat
- 'Wolff's Broom' **new**	CBdw
- 'Wou-nishiki'	see *A. palmatum* 'Ô-nishiki'
- 'Yana-gawa' **new**	CMen ECho
- 'Yasemin'	CBdw CMen MBri MPkF WWes
- 'Yatsubusa'	WWes
- 'Yezo-nishiki'	CMCN LRHS MAsh MBri WFar
- 'Yuba e'	CMen MBri WFar
- 'Yûgure'	NLar WFar WWes
papilio	see *A. caudatum*
paxii	CMCN WWes
pectinatum	WWes
- subsp. *forrestii*	see *A. forrestii*
- 'Sirene'	see *A. forrestii* 'Sirene'
- 'Sparkling'	see *A. forrestii* 'Sparkling'
pensylvanicum ♀H4	More than 30 suppliers
- 'Erythrocladum'	CEnd CMCN CPMA EPfP GKir IMGH LRHS MAsh MBri MGos NBea NHol NLar SLim SMad SSpi SSta
pentaphyllum	CMCN LRHS SKee SSpi
§ *pictum*	CMCN CTho EPfP GIBF LRHS WNor WWes
- subsp. *okamotoanum*	CMCN WWes
- - B&SWJ 8516	WCru
- 'Shufu-nishiki'	CMCN
platanoides ♀H4	CCVT CDoC CDul CLnd CMCN CTri CWib EBee ECrN ENot EPfP GKir LBuc LPan MGos MSwo NBee NWea SBLw SKee SPer WDin WHar WMou WNor WWes
- 'Charles Joly' **new**	WWes
- 'Cleveland'	CBcs ENot
- 'Columnare'	CDoC CLnd CMCN CWib EBee ECrN ENot EPfP GKir LPan LRHS WOrn
- 'Crimson King' ♀H4	More than 30 suppliers
- 'Crimson Sentry'	CDoC CDul CEnd CLnd CMCN COtt CTri CWSG CWib EBee EBre ECrN EGra ENot GKir IArd LBuc LRHS MAsh MBri MGos MLan MRav NBee SKee SLim WDin WFar WHar WOrn
- 'Cucullatum'	CMCN CTho
- 'Deborah'	CBcs CLnd CTho LPan SHBN WWes
- 'Dissectum'	CTho GKir
- 'Drummondii' (v)	More than 30 suppliers
- 'Emerald Queen'	CDoC CLnd CWib EBee ECrN ENot SBLw SHBN WDin

- 'Faassen's Black'		GKir LPan SBLw
§	- 'Globosum'	CLnd CMCN ECrN ENot LBuc LPan SBLw SWvt
- 'Goldsworth Purple'		CLnd
- 'Laciniatum'		CEnd CMCN ECrN ENot GKir SHBN
- 'Lorbergii'		see *A. platanoides* 'Palmatifidum'
- 'Meyering' **new**		WWes
- 'Olmsted'		ENot WWes
§	- 'Palmatifidum'	CLnd GKir
- Princeton Gold		CDoC ECrN ELan ENot GKir LPan
= 'Prigo'PBR		LRHS SCoo SKee SPoG
- 'Reitenbachii'		CDul WWes
- 'Royal Red'		CDul CWib EBee ECrN ENot GKir LPan MGos MRav SKee WOrn WWes
- 'Ruby'		GKir
- 'Schwedleri' ♀H4		CDul CMCN ECrN MGos NBee NWea SPer WDin
- 'Tharandt'		CMCN
- 'Walderseei'		CLnd
pseudoplatanus		CBcs CCVT CDul CLnd CMCN CSBt CTri ECrN ENot GKir LBuc LPan MBar MGos NBee NWea SBLw SKee SPer WDin WHar WMou
§	- 'Atropurpureum'	CDoC CDul CLnd CTho ECrN ENot NBee NWea SBLw WDin WGer WOrn
- 'Brilliantissimum' ♀H4		More than 30 suppliers
- 'Corstorphinense'		CMCN
- 'Erectum'		ENot WFar
- 'Esk Sunset' (v) **new**		LRHS
- 'Leopoldii' ambig. (v)		CBcs CDoC CDul CLnd CMCN COtt CTho EBee ECrN ELan ENot EPfP LAst LPan NBee SBLw SEND SHBN SKee SLim SPer SWvt WDin WFar WOrn WWes
- 'Negenia'		ENot
- 'Nizetii' (v)		CMCN LRHS SBLw WWes
- 'Prinz Handjéry'		CBcs CDul CEnd CLnd CMCN CTri CWib EBee LPan LRHS MAsh MBar MGos NWea SBLw SKee SPer SSpi
- 'Purpureum' **new**		SEND
- 'Simon-Louis Frères' (v)		CCVT CDul CEnd CLnd CMCN CWSG CWib ECrN EMui EPfP LPan LRHS MAsh MBar MBri MDun MGos MWat NBea SKee SLim SPer SWvt WFar WFoF WHar WOrn WStI
- 'Spaethii' misapplied		see *A. pseudoplatanus* 'Atropurpureum'
- 'Spring Gold'		MGos
- 'Worley'		CBcs CDoC CDul CLnd CMCN COtt CSBt CTho CTri EBee ECrN ENot EPfP GKir LPan LRHS MRav NBee NWea SBLw SEND SHBN SKee SLim SPer SWvt WDin WHar WOrn WStI
pseudosieboldianum		CFil CMCN GIBF GKir MBlu SSpi WNor WPGP
- var. microsieboldianum B&SWJ 8766 **new**		WCru
pubipalmatum		WNor
pycnanthum		CMCN WWes
robustum		CMCN WNor WWes
rubescens		CLnd
- B&SWJ 6710		WHCr
- B&SWJ 6735		WCru WHCr
rubrum		More than 30 suppliers
- 'Autumn Flame' **new**		WWes
- 'Bowhall'		CMCN SBir
- 'Candy Ice' (v)		CPMA

- 'Columnare'		CDul CMCN
- 'October Glory' ♀H4		CBcs CDoC CDul CEnd CLnd CMCN CPMA CTho CTri EPfP GKir LPan LRHS MAsh MBlu MBri MDun NWea SBir SCoo SKee SMad SSpi SSta WFar WPGP WPat
- Red Sunset		CDoC CDul CEnd CMCN CPMA
= 'Franksred'		CTho EPfP GKir LPan LRHS MBlu SBir SCoo SKee SMad SSpi SSta
- 'Schlesingeri'		CDul CEnd CLnd CMCN CMac CPMA NLar
- 'Tilford'		GKir SSta WWes
§	**rufinerve** ♀H4	CBcs CCVT CDoC CDul CFil CLnd CMCN CTho CTri ECrN EPfP EPla EWTr LPan LRHS MAsh MBri NBea NWea SBLw SKee SPer WBVN WDin WGer WNor WOrn WPGP WStI WWes
- B&SWJ 5108		WHCr
- 'Albolimbatum'		see *A. rufinerve* 'Hatsuyuki'
- 'Albomarginatum'		see *A. rufinerve* 'Hatsuyuki'
- 'Erythrocladum'		CPMA
§	- 'Hatsuyuki' (v)	CDoC CEnd CMCN CPMA GKir LRHS WBcn WPGP
- 'Winter Gold'		CPMA GKir LRHS SCoo SKee SSpi
§	**saccharinum**	CBcs CCVT CDul CLnd CMCN CTri EBee ECrN ELan ENot EPfP EWTr LRHS MGos MLan MWat NBee NWea SBLw SHBN SKee SPer WDin WFar WNor WStI
- 'Fastigiatum'		see *A. saccharinum* f. *pyramidale*
- f. *laciniatum*		CMCN EBee ENot LRHS MBlu MGos SPer WDin
- 'Laciniatum Wieri'		CDul CLnd CMCN CTho LPan MGos SBLw WDin
- f. *lutescens*		CDul CMCN CTho ENot MBlu SBLw
§	- f. *pyramidale*	CDoC CLnd CMCN EBee ECrN ENot LPan SBLw SPer WDin
saccharum		CAgr CBcs CDoC CDul CLnd CMCN CTho ECrN EPfP GKir IDee LPan MBlu MLan NWea SBLw SPer WNor
- subsp. *barbatum*		see *A. saccharum* subsp. *floridanum*
- 'Brocade' **new**		MPkF WWes
§	- subsp. *floridanum*	CMCN
§	- subsp. *grandidentatum*	CMCN
- subsp. *leucoderme*		CMCN
- 'Louisa Lad' **new**		WWes
- subsp. *nigrum*		CMCN
- - 'Temple's Upright'		CMCN
- subsp. *skutchii*		CMCN
'Scanlon'		CBcs CDoC CEnd CMCN CTho GKir LRHS SBLw
schneiderianum new		WWes
seiboldianum		WWes
'Osiris' **new**		
§	**sempervirens**	CFil CMCN WPGP
serrulatum B&SWJ 6760		WCru
- B&SWJ 6773		WHCr
§	**shirasawanum**	CMCN WNor
§	- 'Aureum' ♀H4	More than 30 suppliers
- 'Autumn Moon'		CPMA WWes
§	- 'Ezo-no-momiji'	CMCN CMen CPMA WWes
- 'Gloria' **new**		WWes
§	- 'Jūnihitoe'	WNor
§	- 'Microphyllum'	CMCN WNor
§	- 'Ogurayama'	CPMA
- 'Palmatifolium'		CMCN CPMA GKir MGos WStI
- var. *tenuifolium*		GKir WNor WWes
sieboldianum		CMCN CMen CTho CTri ECho ECrN EPfP GKir GTSp MDun SSpi WNor

- 'Isis' **new**   WWes
- 'Sode-no-uchi'   CMCN CMen WPat
sikkimense   see *A. metcalfii*
    subsp. *metcalfii*
§ 'Silver Cardinal' (v)   CEnd CMCN CPMA EPfP GKir
                                        MBlu MBri MGos NBhm NLar
                                        SMad SSpi
'Silver Vein'   see *A.* x *conspicuum* 'Silver Vein'
§ *sinense*   CMCN GIBF IArd WCwm WNor
spicatum   CMCN WNor
§ *stachyophyllum*   GQui WWes
§ *sterculiaceum*   CFil CMCN EBee WPGP
syriacum   see *A. obtusifolium*
taronense   CMCN
tataricum   CMCN WWes
- IDS 97   WHCr
- subsp. *aidzuense* **new**   WWes
- 'Emerald Elf' **new**   WWes
§ - subsp. *ginnala*   CBcs CDul CLnd CMCN CTho
                                        CTri ECrN ENot EPfP LRHS MGos
                                        NBea NWea SBLw SHBN SKee
                                        SLim SPer WCwm WDin WMoo
                                        WNor
- - 'Fire'   LRHS
- - 'Flame'   CPMA CWSG ECrN ELan EPfP
                                        GKir MGos NWea SHBN SKee
- subsp. *semenovii*   WWes
tegmentosum   CMCN CPMA EPfP MBlu WNor
- B&SWJ 8421   WCru
- subsp.   see *A. rufinerve*
    glaucorufinerve
tenuifolium   CMCN
tetramerum   see *A. stachyophyllum*
tonkinense **new**   WWes
trautvetteri   CMCN EPfP WNor
triflorum ♀H4   CMCN CPMA CTho EPfP GKir
                                        IArd IMGH LRHS NLar SSpi WDin
                                        WFar WWes
truncatum   CMCN WNor
- 'Akaji-nishiki' (v)   LRHS
- 'Akikaze-nishiki' (v)   CPMA GKir
tschonoskii   GQui WNor WWes
- subsp. *koreanum*   CTho LRHS NLar WNor
§ *turkestanicum*   CDul CFil CMCN EBee
velutinum   CMCN WWes
villosum   see *A. sterculiaceum*
'White Tigress'   CTho LRHS WWes
§ *wilsonii*   CDul CMCN GIBF WNor
x *zoeschense*   CMCN
- 'Annae'   CPMA SBLw WWes

Aceras (Orchidaceae)
anthropophorum   EFEx

Aceriphyllum see *Mukdenia*

x *Achicodonia* (Gesneriaceae)
'Dark Velvet'   WDib

Achillea ✿ (Asteraceae)
ageratifolia ♀H4   ECha ECtt LBee MTho NJOw SRms
                                        WFar
- subsp. *serbica*   XPep
§ *ageratum*   CArn CHby CSev ELau GBar GPoy
                                        MHer MSal NArg NPri SIde SRms
                                        WHHs WHer WJek WLHH WPer
                                        WWpP WWye
- 'W.B. Childs'   CPlt CSli CSpe EBee ECha ECtt
                                        EGle ELan EOrc GBuc MAvo
                                        MNrw NDov SHar WCot WEas
'Alabaster'   CDes CKno CSli EFou GBuc LPhx
Anthea = 'Anblo'PBR   CKno CSam EBee EBre EGle EMan
                                        EWsh GKir GSki LRHS MCLN
                                        MLLN NCGa SCro WAul WFar XPep

'Apfelblüte'   More than 30 suppliers
Appleblossom   see *A.* 'Apfelblüte'
'Apricot Beauty'   CElw CFir CFwr EChP EMan EMar
                                        EOMN NPro SSvw SVil WShp
argentea misapplied   see *A. clavennae, A. umbellata*
argentea Lamarck   see *Tanacetum argenteum*
aurea   see *A. chrysocoma*
'Bahama'   EBee EPPr GFlt NBro WWpP
'Belle Epoque' ♀H4   CDes CSli
'Bloodstone'   CSli ECtt EMan EPPr EWes EWsh
                                        GBar GMac MRav NPPs WOut
brachyphylla   EPot
'Brilliant'   WWeb
cartilaginea   CDes CSli EFou EPPr WFar WMoo
                                        WOut
- 'Silver Spray'   EBee EMan SDnm WOut WWpP
chamaemelifolia   WHil
'Christine's Pink' ♀H4   CDes CKno CSli EBee EMan EPPr
§ *chrysocoma*   ETow GAbr MWat WMoo WTel
                                        XPep
- 'Grandiflora'   CHad CHar ECha ELan NGdn
§ *clavennae*   CBrm ECtt EMlt EPot LPio MLLN
                                        MWat NRya SAga SBla SRms
                                        WCom WCot WFar
clypeolata Sibth. & Sm.   CSli EPPr LPio NLar SMad SPlb
                                        SRms WPer
coarctata   NBir WPer XPep
'Coral Beauty'   EBee
'Coronation Gold' ♀H4   CDoC CPrp CWCL EBee ECtt EFou
                                        ELan ENot EPfP ERou GKir GMac
                                        GSki LPVe LRHS MBri MCLN MRav
                                        MWat MWgw WCAu WEas WFar
                                        WMnd WShp XPep
'Credo' ♀H4   More than 30 suppliers
crithmifolia **new**   XPep
'Croftway'   SCro
decolorans   see *A. ageratum*
erba-rotta   ECho NBro
    subsp. *moschata*
- subsp. *rupestris*   MDHE
§ 'Fanal'   More than 30 suppliers
'Faust'   CDes CElw CHar CKno CMil CPlt
                                        CSli EBee EFou LPhx SMrm STes
                                        SUsu WPGP
'Feuerland'   More than 30 suppliers
filipendulina   NLRH NSti WHrl WWpP
- 'Cloth of Gold' ♀H4   More than 30 suppliers
- 'Gold Plate' ♀H4   CDoC CHad EBre EChP ECha ECtt
                                        EFou ELan EPfP ERou GKir GSki
                                        MMil MRav MWgw NDov NOrc
                                        SCro SHel SPer SRms WCot WFar
                                        WMnd
- 'Parker's Variety' ♀H4   EBee LRHS MLan WFar
Flowers of Sulphur   see *A.* 'Schwefelblüte'
'Forncett Beauty'   CSli EFou MDKP NBrk SChu
'Forncett Bride'   CSli EFou NDov
'Forncett Candy'   CSli EFou MAvo NDov
I 'Forncett Citrus'   CSli EBee EFou WPGP
'Forncett Fletton'   CFir CSli CWCL EBee EFou EGle
                                        EMan EMar EPPr GBri MAvo MBnl
                                        MCLN MNrw NBrk NGdn NHol
                                        NPPs NPro SAga SCro SMrm STes
                                        WCAu WHil WTMC WViv
'Forncett Ivory'   CSli EFou EPPr LPhx
fraasii   MDKP
glaberrima hybrid   EMan EPPr WCot
'Gloria Jean'   EBee SHar
'Gold and Grey'   CSli
grandifolia misapplied   see *Tanacetum macrophyllum*
§ *grandifolia* Friv.   CFwr CSam EBee EChP EGle
                                        EMon EPPr GBuc GCal LEdu LPhx
                                        MWgw NBro NSti SMad SMrm
                                        SSvw WBea WFar WHer WHil
                                        WMnd WMoo WOld WWye

'Great Expectations'	see *A.* 'Hoffnung'
'Grey and Gold'	EFou
'Hannelore Pahl'	EBee
'Hartington White'	GBuc
'Heidi' ♀H4	CSli GBri
'Helios' ♀H4	GBin
'Hella Glashoff' ♀H4	CDes CSli EBee ECho EGle LPhx MBri NBrk NCGa NDov SCro WCot WHoo WPrP WWeb
§ 'Hoffnung'	CPrp CSli CWCL EBee ECtt EGle EMan ERou GSki MBri MRav NBrk NPPs NPro SCro SPer SSpe WCAu WMnd WPer WWin
'Huteri'	CLyd CPBP EBre ECtt EDAr EGoo EPot ESis LBee MBro MHer MRav NFor NJOw SBla SChu WCom WEas WFar WPer WWin
'Inca Gold'	CKno CSli EBee ECha ECtt EGle EHrv EMan EMar EPPr GBuc MBnl MCLN MHar MRav NBro NDov NGdn NPro SAga SBla SChu WTMC WWpP
'Jacqueline'	CFwr EBee
'Judith'	WWeb
x **kellereri**	MBro MDHE NLar XPep
Kirschkönigin	see *A. millefolium* 'Cerise Queen'
x **kolbiana**	EMan MWat NHol NJOw NMen SRms WHoo WLin WPat
§ 'Lachsschönheit' ♀H4	More than 30 suppliers
x **lewisii**	NMen
- 'King Edward' ♀H4	CMHG CSam EBre ECha EDAr EMlt ESis LRHS NBir NJOw NPro SBla SChu SIng WCom WFar WCot
ligustica	WCot
'Lucky Break' ♀H4	ECha SDix SMHy SUsu
macrophylla	EBee EMar
'Marie Ann'	CHea EPPr ERou LPio MBnl MBri MCLN NLar NPro WCAu WHil
'Marmalade'	CMdw CSli EBee WPGP
'Martina' ♀H4	More than 30 suppliers
'McVities'	More than 30 suppliers
millefolium	CArn COld EFWa ELau GBar GPoy GWCH MBow MHer NLan NMir NSco SPlb WHHs WHbs WHer WJek WLHH WSel WWye XPep
- 'Bright Cerise' **new**	WFar
- 'Carla Hussey'	WFar
- 'Cassis'	CBrm ECoo EOMN GFlt SDnm SWal WGMN WOut
§ - 'Cerise Queen'	More than 30 suppliers
- 'Cherry Queen'	LPVe MAvo MBow WSan
- 'Christel'	CDes CSli EBee SUsu
- 'Christine'	EMan
- 'Colorado'	COIW CPen CSam CWCL GAbr LPVe MFir NChi SSvw WHrl WWeb
- dark red	CSli
- 'Debutante'	WHil
- 'Fire King'	CHal
- 'Goldstar' **new**	WFar
- 'Kelwayi' ♀H4	CSli
- 'Lansdorferglut' ♀H4	CKno CSli EPPr LRHS MBri MDKP MRav NDov NPro SUsu WWpP
- 'Lavender Beauty'	see *A. millefolium* 'Lilac Beauty'
- 'Lemon Curd'	LDai
§ - 'Lilac Beauty'	More than 30 suppliers
* - 'Lilac Queen'	CSli SWat
- 'Lollypop'	LDai
- 'Martha' **new**	EBee
- 'Paprika'	More than 30 suppliers
- 'Red Beauty'	CFwr CSli CWCL EBee EMan EMar EWTr LRHS MTis NBro NDov SRms SWat XPep
- 'Red Velvet'	CSpe EBlw EChP ECha EPPr MBnl MBri MLLN NCGa WCot WHoo
- 'Rosie'	GBar
- 'Rougham Beauty'	CSli ERou
- 'Rougham Cream'	CSli
- 'Rougham White'	CSli
- 'Salmon Pink' **new**	WFar
- 'Salmon Queen'	WCra
- 'Sammetriese'	CSli EBre EGle GBuc LPhx LRHS MCLN MHar MSte SMad WCAu WCot WFar WHoo WPrP WRHF WTin WWpP
- 'Serenade'	EBee
- 'Summertime'	SBod
- 'Tickled Pink'	SSvw WPer
- 'White Beauty' **new**	SPoG
- 'White Queen'	EBee EGle EMar EWTr LBuc MSPs WPer
'Mondpagode' ♀H4	CHar CPrp CSli EBee EChP EGle EMan EMar EPPr LPhx MAvo MBNS MCLN NDov SAsh SLon SUsu SVil WWpP
'Moonlight'	MBro
'Moonshine' ♀H3	More than 30 suppliers
'Moonwalker'	CAbP EBee LRHS MLLN SIde WBVN WFar WPer WWeb WWpP
nana	LPVe
nobilis new	XPep
- subsp. **neilreichii**	CSli CSpe EBee EChP EDAr EGoo EHrv EMon GBri LPio MLLN NDov NSti SAga SPer WCAu WCot WHal WHil WPrP WTin
'Nostalgia' **new**	EBee
odorata	XPep
'Old Brocade'	CHea CSli EFou EPPr LPhx
'Peter Davis'	see *Hippolytia berderi*
pindicola	EWes WCom
subsp. **integrifolia**	
'Pink Candy' **new**	CSpe
pink island form	CKno
'Pink Lady' **new**	EMan
'Prospero'	CMea MSte WCot WCra
ptarmica	CArn ELau EMFW GBar MGol MHer MSal NMir SIde SPer WLHH WWye
* - 'Ballerina'	EPPr MGol MWrn NDov NLar WRHF
- Innocence	see *A. ptarmica* 'Unschuld'
- 'Major'	WCAu
- 'Nana Compacta'	CSli CSpe EBee EChP ECha EFou EGle EMan EMlt EPPr GSki IGor LHop LRHS MLLN NBir NCGa SMrm SOkh SPlb SUsu WCAu WCFE WCot WOld
- 'Perry's White'	CBre EBee EGle GCal NGHP NHol WCot
- 'Stephanie Cohen'	see *A. sibirica* 'Stephanie Cohen'
N - The Pearl Group seed-raised (d)	CBcs EBre ECha EFou EGra ELan EPar GKir LHop MFOX MFir NBlu NJOw NVic SPlb SWat WBea WFar WMoo WPer WShp WTin WWpP
N - - 'Boule de Neige' (clonal) (d)	CHal GSki MBri NPer NSti SPer SPet SPla WFar WMnd
N - - 'The Pearl' (clonal) (d) ♀H4	CDes CSBt EBee EPfP ERou IHMM MRav MSte MWat MWgw NBPC NBid NBir NBro NCGa NGHP SCro SRms WBVN WBrk WCAu WCot WEas WFar WHer WHil WOld WWeb
§ - 'Unschuld'	NBir
I 'Rose Madder'	More than 30 suppliers
'Rougham Bright Star'	CSli
'Rougham Salmon'	CSli ERou
'Sally'	EBee EPPr
'Sandstone'	see *A.* 'Wesersandstein'
§ 'Schwefelblüte'	NBir SBla SMrm

'Schwellenburg' CDes CHar CSli
sibirica LPio
- var. *camschatica* CBrm CSli ECtt EMan EPfP EWTr
'Love Parade' GBar GMac GSki LPVe LRHS
MDKP MGol MRav MSPs MTis
MWrn NJOw SGar SSvw WBea
WBro WBry WGMN WMoo WSSM
WSan WViv WWpP
§ - 'Stephanie Cohen' CHVG CStr EBee EFou EGle EMan
MAvo MBnl MCLN MDKP MLLN
MSph NBhm SCro SOkh WCAu
WCot WFar WTMC WWpP
'Stephanie' **new** EPPr MAvo
'Summer Glory' SCro
Summer Pastels Group CBri CBrm CHrt CM&M COlW
EGra EMil EShb GKir LRHS MLan
NArg NBPC NBir NBlu NMir NOrc
SECG SGar SMac SPet SRms SWat
WFar WMnd WPer WRha WWeb
'Summerwine' ♀H4 More than 30 suppliers
I 'Taygetea' CSam CSli EBee EChP ELan EMan
EPPr EPfP EWTr MSte MTis NCGa
NSti SChu SDix SPer WCAu WCom
WCot WFar WKif WPer WSHC
'Terracotta' More than 30 suppliers
'The Beacon' see *A.* 'Fanal'
tomentosa ♀H4 CTri ECha ECtt EPfP WShp
§ - 'Aurea' CHal ELau IHMH LPVe NBlu NBro
NJOw SRms WPer
- 'Maynard's Gold' see *A. tomentosa* 'Aurea'
§ *umbellata* CLyd EBee EMlt ETow GBri WCot
XPep
'Walther Funcke' More than 30 suppliers
§ 'Wesersandstein' More than 30 suppliers
'Wilczekii' NChi SRms

x *Achimenantha* (Gesneriaceae)
'Inferno' ♀H1 WDib

Achimenes (Gesneriaceae)
'Ambroise Verschaffelt' LAma WDib
  ♀H1
'Cattleya' LAma
'Crummock Water' WDib
erecta WDib
'Flamingo' SDeJ
'Harry Williams' LAma
'Hilda Michelssen' ♀H1 WDib
'Himalayan Yellow Cloud' LAma
'Little Beauty' **new** WDib
'Maxima' LAma
'Orange Delight' WDib
'Peach Blossom' LAma
'Snow Princess' SDeJ
'Stan's Delight' (d) ♀H1 WDib
'Tarantella' WDib
'Vivid' LAma

Achlys (Berberidaceae)
californica IBlr
japonica WCru
triphylla EBee GBuc GGar IBlr WCru

Achnatherum see *Stipa*

Achyranthes (Amaranthaceae)
bidentata CArn MSal

Acidanthera see *Gladiolus*

Acinos (Lamiaceae)
§ *alpinus* CAgr CArn CBrm EBre EMan ESis
LPVe LTwo MSPs MWgw NLar SBla
WJek WWeb

§ *arvensis* MHer MSal WBWf
§ *corsicus* CStu MBro NLAp NWCA WHoo
WPat WWin

Aciphylla (Apiaceae)
aurea CTrC GCal GCrs ITim LRav MCCP
NWCA SMad SPlb WPat
congesta EMan NMen
crenulata WCot
crosby-smithii EMan
dieffenbachii **new** ITim
dobsonii EMan
glaucescens GCrs
hectorii EMan NMen WCot
horrida GCal WCot
kirkii EMan WCot
monroi GCal LTwo NMen NWCA WCot
montana NMen WCot
- var. *gracilis* NMen
pinnatifida GCrs GGar NMen
similis EMan NMen
simplex NMen
squarrosa EMan GCal
subflabellata GCal

Acmella (Asteraceae)
§ *oleracea* CArn EOHP MSal
- 'Peek-a-boo' **new** NPri

Acmena (Myrtaceae)
smithii EShb

Acnistus (Solanaceae)
australis see *Iochroma australe*

Acoelorrhaphe (Arecaceae)
wrightii CBrP LPal WMul

Aconitum ❀ (Ranunculaceae)
ACE 1449 GBuc
B&SWJ 2954 from Nepal WCru
CNDS 036 from Burma WCru
alboviolaceum GCal
- var. *albiflorum* WCru
  B&SWJ 4105
anglicum see *A. napellus* subsp. *napellus*
Anglicum Group
anthora LPio MLLN WAul
arcuatum B&SWJ 774 WCru
austroyunnanense WCru
  BWJ 7902 **new**
autumnale misapplied see *A. carmichaelii* Wilsonii
Group
autumnale ambig. NBir
bartlettii B&SWJ 337 EBee EMan WCru
'Blue Opal' EBee EWes
'Blue Sceptre' EMan MBNS MBri NPro SUsu WAul
WCAu WSel
'Bressingham Spire' ♀H4 More than 30 suppliers
x *cammarum* More than 30 suppliers
- 'Bicolor' ♀H4
- 'Grandiflorum Album' EBee ERou LPhx MSte SAga
§ *carmichaelii* CArn CBot CBri CMea EBee EFou
EMan GAbr GKir GSki IBlr LRHS
MBri MBro MRav MWgw NBro
NChi NFor NOrc SCro SMrm SRms
WBod WCom WHoo WPnP WSel
WTin
- 'Arendsii' ♀H4 More than 30 suppliers
- 'Pink Sensation' EMan MBNS MCLN MTis NBPC
NSti WHil
- 'Royal Flush' **new** WCot
- var. *truppelianum* WCru
  HWJ 732 **new**

§ – Wilsonii Group CHar EBee GGar LPhx LRHS MRav MSte MWat NChi SBla SChu WFar WPGP WPer WSel WWin WWye

§ – – 'Barker's Variety' CKno CPou CRow EBee EChP EGle EMan EPfP EWTr GBuc GMac LPhx MAnH NHol NSti SMrm WAul WCot WViv

– – 'Kelmscott' ♀H4 EBee ECGN EGle EMon GMac MRav MSte MWgw SAga SDix WFar WRHF

– – 'Spätlese' CAbP EBee EChP EGle EMan EMar GCal MAnH MEHN NBPC NDov NMyG WCot WHHs WWhi

– – 'The Grim Reaper' EMon

cilicicum see *Eranthis hyemalis* Cilicica Group

compactum see *A. napellus* subsp. *vulgare*

'Eleonara' CFir EBee EChP ECtt EGle EMan EMar EPPr EPfP GBuc GKir LRHS MAvo NGHP NGby NLar NSti SSvw WAul WFar

elliotii GBin

elwesii EBee GGar

episcopale EBee WCru WFar

aff. *episcopale* WSHC

aff. *episcopale* CLD 1426 GBuc WFar

'Faun' EBee

ferox EBee MLLN

fischeri misapplied see *A. carmichaelii*

fukutomei WCot WCru

var. *formosanum*
B&SWJ 3057

§ *hemsleyanum* CBot CBri CPLG CRHN CRow EBee EPot ETow GAbr GEil IBlr LPhx LRHS MDun MNrw MTis MWrn NBid NCGa SMad WAul WBVN WBrE WCru WEas WFar WFoF WHoo WOld WWhi

– dark blue CMea

– var. *latisectum* IBlr

heterophyllum LPhx

hyemale see *Eranthis hyemalis*

'Ivorine' More than 30 suppliers

aff. *jaluense* WCru
B&SWJ 8741 **new**

japonicum EBee

– subsp. *subcuneatum* WCru
B&SWJ 6228

lamarckii see *A. lycoctonum* subsp. *neapolitanum*

longecassidatum WCru
B&SWJ 4105

lycoctonum GCrs SRms WBVN WCAu

– 'Dark Eyes' CMdw EBee ECGN NBrk WCot

§ – subsp. *lycoctonum* CM&M MSal SRms

– subsp. *moldavicum* EBee

§ – subsp. *neapolitanum* EBee EChP ELan EMFP EMan EMar EPfP GCal GSki LRHS MBow MLLN MRav MTis NFla NGHP NHol NLar NSti SBla SSpi SWat WBor WFar WSan

– subsp. EBee
platanifolium **new**

§ – subsp. *vulparia* CArn ECGN EFou GCal GPoy MSal MTed NMRc WCot WEas WPer WSel WWhi WWye

napellus More than 30 suppliers

– 'Albiflorus' see *A. napellus* subsp. *vulgare* 'Albidum'

– 'Bergfürst' EBee EBre EGle LPhx LPio MBri MTed

– 'Blue Valley' EBee EChP EFou EGle EMan EPfP NMyG NPro WLow

– 'Carneum' see *A. napellus* subsp. *vulgare* 'Carneum'

§ – subsp. *napellus* CRow CSev EBee EChP EGbc IBlr
Anglicum Group MGol MSal MSte NHol SMac SSpi WBWf WCot WPen

– 'Rubellum' CRez EChP EGle ELan EMan EPPr LAst MBow NBir NBro NFla NGHP NOrc NPri SSvw WAul WPnP WSpi SSvw

– 'Schneewittchen' **new** SSvw

– 'Sphere's Variety' NOrc

– subsp. *tauricum* EBee

§ – subsp. *vulgare* CPrp EBee EChP EFou EHrv EMar 'Albidum' EPfP GFlt GSki LAst LRHS MRav MTis MWrn NBid NChi NDov NGHP NHol NLar NPri NSti SCro SLon WAul WCAu WCot WCra WFar WWye

§ – – 'Carneum' EBee EGle EMan GKir MLLN MRav NSti WCAu WEas WGMN WHer WHoo WKif WLin WSel WWin WWye

napiforme LPio WPnP

– B&SWJ 943 WCru

neapolitanum see *A. lycoctonum* subsp. *neapolitanum*

'Newry Blue' CBos CHad EMon ERou GBuc GKir ITim MRav MWhi NBir NHol SRms WCAu WCra WFar WPer

orientale hort. see *A. lycoctonum* subsp. *vulparia*

orientale ambig. **new** NPro

paniculatum EBee MBri

– 'Roseum' LRHS MBNS MTis WAul WFar

'Pink Sensation' PBR IPot

proliferum WCru
B&SWJ 4107 **new**

pseudolaeve EBee LPhx

pyrenaicum see *A. lycoctonum* subsp. *neapolitanum*

ranunculifolius see *A. lycoctonum* subsp. *neapolitanum*

sczukinii EMon WCru

seoulense B&SWJ 694 WCru

– B&SWJ 864 WCru

septentrionale see *A. lycoctonum* subsp. *lycoctonum*

'Spark's Variety' ♀H4 More than 30 suppliers

spicatum EBee

'Stainless Steel' More than 30 suppliers

'Tissington Pearl' MTis

x *tubergenii* see *Eranthis hyemalis* Tubergenii Group

uchiyamai B&SWJ 1005 WCru

– B&SWJ 1216 WCru

vilmorinianum MFir

volubile hort. see *A. hemsleyanum*, *A. ciliare*

vulparia see *A. lycoctonum* subsp. *vulparia*

yamazakii WCru

Aconogonon see *Persicaria*

Acorus ✿ (*Acoraceae*)

calamus CAgr CArn CDWL CRow CWat EHon ELau EMFW EPza GPoy LNCo LPBA MCCP MGol MSal MSta NArg NBlu NPer SWat WHer WMAq WWpP

– 'Argenteostriatus' (v) CBcs CBen CRow CWat EBee EChP ECha ECtt EHon EMFW EPfP EPza LNCo LPBA MSta NOrc SHel SLon SWal SWat WMAq WMoo WWpP

gramineus CPne CRow LPBA MLan NPer SWat WHer WTin WWpP

– 'Golden Edge' (v) ENot

– 'Hakuro-nishiki' (v)	More than 30 suppliers	
I – 'Licorice'	CBgR CWil EBee EPPr IFro LBuc	
	LRHS MBNS MSal SHel WBea	
	WCHb WCot WLeb WPnP WWpP	
– 'Masamune' (v)	EGle EMan EPla GCal WBrk WCot	
	WTin	
– 'Minimus Aureus'	CBgR CBre CWCL	
– 'Oborozuki' (v)	CPne CRow CWil EPla WCot WPrP	
– 'Oborozuki' misapplied	see *A. gramineus* 'Ogon'	
§ – 'Ogon' (v)	More than 30 suppliers	
– var. *pusillus*	CRow CStu EPla NBro SWal	
– 'Variegatus' (v)	More than 30 suppliers	
– 'Yodo-no-yuki' (v)	CRow EPla	
* *intermedius*	NPer	
tatarinowii	EBee	

Acradenia (*Rutaceae*)

frankliniae	CBcs CFil CMHG CPLG CPle CTrC
	CTrG GEil GGar IArd IDee LRHS
	SEND SSpi WBod WFar WPGP
	WSHC

Acridocarpus (*Malpighiaceae*)

natalitius	CTCP

Actaea (*Ranunculaceae*)

alba	see *A. pachypoda*, *A. rubra*
	f. *neglecta*
arizonica	GCal LPhx SAga
asiatica	CDes GBin
– B&SWJ 616	WCru
biternata	CLAP MSte
– B&SWJ 5591	WCru
cimicifuga	GBin GCal GPoy
– B&SWJ 2966	WCru
cordifolia	EBee EMan LPhx MSal WCru WPnP
– 'Blickfang' **new**	GBin
dahurica	EBee GCal GKir MSal NLar SWat
	WCru
elata	EBee WCru
erythrocarpa	see *A. rubra*
europaea	LPhx WCru
frigida B&SWJ 2657	WCru
heracleifolia	GKir GSki
– B&SWJ 8843	WCru
japonica	CLAP CMea CRow EBee EBre
	EChP GCal GKir LPhx LRHS NSti
	WCot
– B&SWJ 5828	WCru
– B&SWJ 8758a	WCru
from Cheju Do	
– var. *acerina*	GBin
'Compacta' **new**	
matsumurae	CFil CRow ECha EPar GCal LPhx
'Elstead' ♀H4	MRav NDov SOkh SSpi SUsu
	WPGP
– 'Frau Herms'	GKir LPhx
– 'White Pearl'	CRow EBee EBre EChP ECha EHrv
	ELan EPfP GGar GKir LHop LPhx
	LRHS MBri NGdn NSti SMad SPer
	SPet SPla SSpi WCAu WCra WFar
	WLow WMnd WMoo WPGP WPnP
§ *pachypoda* ♀H4	CLyd CPom ECGN ECGP ECha
	EGle ELan EMan EPar GBBs GBuc
	GEdr GPoy GTou IBlr MFir MSal
	MSte MTed MTis NBPC NBid NLar
	NSti SSpi WCot WCru WMoo
– f. *rubrocarpa*	EBee ELan
podocarpa	GCal MSal SRms
racemosa ♀H4	CArn CBos CMea CRow CSam
	EBre EChP ELan EPfP ERou GBBs
	GCal GKir GPoy LRHS MSal NGdn
	SECG SPer WCot WFar WMnd
* – 'Purple Torch'	CBos

§ *rubra* ♀H4	CBro CHid CMHG EChP ECha	
	EPar GBuc GCal GGar GKir	
	GPoy IBlr LRHS MLLN MSte	
	NChi NHol NSti SMad SSpi	
	WCru WEas WFar WMoo WPGP	
	WWin	
– *alba*	see *A. pachypoda*, *A. rubra* f.	
	neglecta	
§ – f. *neglecta*	EBee EChP EMan GBuc GKir NLar	
	SMad SSpi	
simplex	CFil CSam EBee GKir LRHS MWgw	
	NPri SLon SPer SWat WCot	
– B&SWJ 6355	WCru	
– Atropurpurea Group	More than 30 suppliers	
– – 'Bernard Mitchell'	CFir MTed	
– – 'Brunette' ♀H4	More than 30 suppliers	
– – 'Hillside Black Beauty'	CBAn CBct CElw CLAP EBee EBlw	
	EChP ECtt EGle ELan EMan GFlt	
	GMac IBal IPot LHop LRHS MAvo	
	MCLN MNrw NBPC NBir NGdn	
	SOkh WAul WCAu WCot WGMN	
	WHil WLin	
– – 'James Compton'	More than 30 suppliers	
– 'Mountain Wave'	CLAP EBee WPnP	
– 'Pink Spike' **new**	EBee	
§ – 'Prichard's Giant'	CLAP CPlt EBee ECha GBuc GKir	
	LPhx LRHS MBri MRav MSte NHol	
	WCot WFar WShp	
– *ramosa*	see *A. simplex* 'Prichard's Giant'	
– 'Scimitar'	LPhx	
– 'Silver Axe'	GCal	
§ *spicata*	GBuc GKir GPoy MFOX MSal	
	MSte NLar NSti NWoo WCot	
	WCru	
– var. *acuminata*	WCru	
B&SWJ 6257 **new**		
– var. *rubra*	see *A. rubra*	
taiwanensis	CDes	
– B&SWJ 3413	EBee WCru	
– B&SWJ 343	CLAP	
vaginata **new**	GKev	
yesoensis	GCal	
yunnanensis ACE 1880	GBuc	

Actinella (*Asteraceae*)

scaposa	see *Tetraneuris scaposa*

Actinidia (*Actinidiaceae*)

arguta	CAgr CFil MRav SSte WPGP
– (m)	SHBN
– B&SWJ 569	WCru
– 'Bayern'	EBee MRav
– 'Issai' (s-p/F)	CBcs EBee ERea LBuc MGos MRav
– LL#2 (f)	CAgr
– LL#3 (m)	CAgr
– 'Weiki'	MGos
callosa var.	WCru
ephippioidea	
B&SWJ 1790	
– var. *formosana*	WCru
B&SWJ 3806	
chinensis misapplied	see *A. deliciosa*
§ *deliciosa*	CDul ERom MGos SLon WBVN
	WCru WSHC WStI
– (f/F)	MRav SHBN
– 'Atlas' (m)	MBri SLim
– 'Bruno' (f/F)	SLim
– 'Hayward' (f/F)	CBcs CDoC CHEx COtt EBee ELan
	EMil EMui EPfP ERea LRHS MBri
	MGos MWat NPal SDea SHBN SPer
	SWvt WCru WStI
– 'Jenny' (s-p/F)	CSBt EBee LBuc LRHS MCoo MGos
	MLan SDea SKee
– 'Solo'	CDoC SSte

- 'Tomuri' (m)	CBcs CDoC CHEx COtt EBee ELan EMil EMui EPfP ERea LRHS MGos MWat NPal SHBN SPer WCru WStI
hypoleuca B&SWJ 5942	WCru
kolomikta ♀H4	More than 30 suppliers
- (m) **new**	CAgr
- B&SWJ 4243	WCru
- 'Tomoko' (F) **new**	WCru
- 'Yazuaki' (m) **new**	WCru
latifolia B&SWJ 3563	WCru
petelotii HWJ 628 **new**	WCru
pilosula	CBcs CFil CPLG CSPN EMil GCal LHop SCoo SLon SSte WCru WPGP WPat WSHC
polygama (F)	CBcs SSte WCru
- B&SWJ 5444	WCru
purpurea (f/F)	CAgr
rubricaulis B&SWJ 3111	WCru
rufa B&SWJ 3525	WCru
tetramera B&SWJ 3564	WCru

Adansonia (*Bombacaceae*)

gregorii **new**	SPlb

Adelocaryum see *Lindelofia*

Adenium (*Apocynaceae*)

obesum ♀H1	CRoM ESlt MOak

Adenocarpus (*Papilionaceae*)

decorticans	CArn CTrC WSHC

Adenophora (*Campanulaceae*)

BWJ 7696 from China **new**	WCru
'Afterglow'	see *Campanula rapunculoides* 'Afterglow'
'Amethyst'	CBos MAnH
* *asiatica*	WFar
aurita	CBcs CFir CMea EBee EChP EMan EPPr MLLN NWoo WCot
bulleyana	CBri CHar COIW EBre EGle ELan EMan EWTr EWsh GBuc LRHS MLwd NBid NChi SDnm SMac SPet SPlb SRot WBea WCAu WCot WFar WGwG WHHs WPer
* *campanulata*	WPer
coelestis	EBee EMan SRot
- ACE 2455	EPot GBuc
- B&SWJ 7998	WCru
confusa	EBee EMan LHop LRHS MAnH MDKP SDnm WFar WGMN WHer WSHC
cymerae	EBee
divaricata	EMan WFoF
forrestii	WFar
- var. *handeliana*	EBee
grandiflora	WCru
B&SWJ 8555 **new**	
himalayana	GBri MNrw SAga WCot WPer
khasiana	CBri CFir CHby GMac LDai LTwo MAnH MDKP MNrw NLar WPrP WWin
koreana	EBee SDnm
kurilensis	SIng
latifolia hort.	see *A. pereskiifolia*
latifolia Fischer	GBri NBir WFar
liliifolia	CBri CHar ECtt ELan EMan GAbr GCal GEil LHop LRHS MLwd NPer NSti SRot WFar WPer WTin
§ *nikoensis*	CTCP EBee MNrw NBid NWCA
§ - var. *stenophylla*	WCot
nipponica	see *A. nikoensis* var. *stenophylla*
§ *pereskiifolia*	EBee SEND SHar SPlb WCot WFar WPer

polyantha	CHar EBee EChP EHrv EMan EWsh GBuc LRHS MAnH MNrw SBod SRms WFar WPic WPnP
polymorpha	see *A. nikoensis*
potaninii	CFir CHea EBee EChP EGra EMan GBuc LBBr MNrw NSti SBla SDnm SGar WBVN WCHb WFar WHal WPnP
remotiflora B&SWJ 8562	WCru
stricta	LRHS MLan
- subsp. *sessilifolia*	EBee EPyc GBuc SPla
sublata	WFar
takedae	MAnH
- var. *howozana*	EBee LHop SCro WPrP
taquetii	GMac
- B&SWJ 1303	WCru
tashiroi	CNic CPrp EBee ECtt EPfP GAbr GBri GBuc GFlt LHop MNrw NPro SHel SMac WCHb WGwG WHHs WPat
triphylla	EMan GCal NBir WFar
- var. *hakusanensis*	EBee
- var. *japonica*	EBee
- - B&SWJ 8835	WCru
uehatae	MAvo
- B&SWJ 126	WCru

Adiantum ✿ (*Adiantaceae*)

aethiopicum	NWoo WHer WRic
§ *aleuticum* ♀H4	CBcs CFil CLAP EBee EDAr EFer ELan EMon GBin NBro NHol NMar WAbe WFib WHal WPGP WRic WTMC
- 'Imbricatum'	CBcs EBee EChP ECha LRHS NHol NLar SBla SPla SRms WFar WFib
- 'Japonicum'	CBos CDes CLAP CMil CWil EBee EFtx ELan GCal MAsh MBri NBir NHol SRms SSpi WCot WCru WFar WFib WHal WPGP WRic
- 'Laciniatum'	SRms
* - f. *minimum*	SRms
- 'Miss Sharples'	CLAP EBee ELan GCal LRHS MAsh MBnl NHol NLar NMar SRms WCru WFar WPrP WRic
- 'Subpumilum' ♀H4	CBos CLAP GBin MRav WAbe WCot
capillus-veneris	MWat WCot WFib
- 'Mairisii'	see *A.* x *mairisii*
cuneatum	see *A. raddianum*
diaphanum	NMar
formosanum	WRic
hispidulum	NMar SRms
§ x *mairisii* ♀H3	EFtx NMar
* *monocolor*	MBri
pedatum ♀H4	CBcs CFil CHEx CLAP EBee ECha EFer ELan ENot EPfP EPza LEur LPBA LRHS MBri MSPs NHol SChu SPer SRot SSpi SWat WFar WPGP WTMC
- var. *aleuticum*	see *A. aleuticum*
- Asiatic form	see *A. aleuticum* 'Japonicum'
- 'Japonicum'	see *A. aleuticum* 'Japonicum'
- 'Roseum'	see *A. aleuticum* 'Japonicum'
- var. *subpumilum*	see *A. aleuticum* 'Subpumilum'
peruvianum	MBri
pubescens	MBri NMar
§ *raddianum* ♀H2	CHal EFtx NMar
- 'Crested Majus'	NMar
- 'Crested Micropinnulum'	NMar
- 'Deflexum'	NMar
- 'Double Leaflet'	NMar
- 'Elegans'	NMar
- 'Feltham Beauty'	NMar
- 'Fluffy Ruffles' **new**	EFtx

- 'Fragrans'	see *A. raddianum* 'Fragrantissimum'
§ - 'Fragrantissimum'	MBri
- 'Fritz Lüthi' ♀H2	CHal MBri NMar
- 'Gracilis'	see *A. raddianum* 'Gracillimum'
§ - 'Gracillimum'	NMar
- 'Grandiceps'	NMar
- 'Gympie Gold'	NMar
- 'Kensington Gem' ♀H1	NMar
- 'Legrandii'	NMar
- 'Micropinnulum'	EFtx NMar
- 'Pacific Maid'	NMar
- 'Pacottii'	NMar
- 'Tuffy Tips'	NMar
- 'Variegated Pacottii' (v)	NMar
- 'Variegated Tessellate' (v)	NMar
- 'Victoria's Elegans'	NMar
- 'Weigandii'	NMar
tenerum 'Green Glory'	NMar
venustum ♀H4	CBos CFil CHEx CLAP CWil EFer
	EFtx EGle EHyt EMon GCal LEur
	NMar NVic SDix SHFr SMad SRms
	SSpi SWat WAbe WCom WCot
	WEas WFib WPGP WRic
whitei	NMar

Adina (Rubiaceae)
rubella	IArd

Adlumia (Papaveraceae)
fungosa	CHid CSpe GFlt LRHS

Adonis (Ranunculaceae)
amurensis	CMea EBee ECho EPar EPot GCrs
	LAma LTwo SCnR WCot WLin
- 'Fukujukai'	ECha WFar
- 'Pleniflora' (d)	EBee EPar MBri MTed NLar SBod
	SPer WCot WFar
brevistyla	EBee EHyt ETow GBuc GCrs NSla
	WCru
chrysocyathus	EBee
coerulea	EBee
sibirica **new**	LAma
sutchuenensis	EBee LAma
tianschanica	EBee LAma
vernalis	EPar EPot GPoy MMHG

Adoxa (Adoxaceae)
moschatellina	CRWN NMen WHer WPnP WShi
	WWye

Adromischus (Crassulaceae)
cooperi	WEas

Aechmea (Bromeliaceae)
distichantha	CFir
var. *schlumbergeri*	
fasciata ♀H1	LRHS MBri

Aegle (Rutaceae)
sepiaria	see *Poncirus trifoliata*

Aegopodium (Apiaceae)
podagraria 'Bengt'	EMon
- 'Dangerous' (v)	CHid CNat WCHb
- gold-margined (v)	EMon
- 'Lacock Blush'	CNat
- 'Variegatum' (v)	More than 30 suppliers

Aeonium (Crassulaceae)
arboreum ♀H1	CAbb CHEx EPem EShb MWya
	WHal WIvy WRos
- 'Atropurpureum' ♀H1	CHEx EAmu EBee EPem ERea
	EShb IBlr MBri MLan MOak NPer
	SEND WCot

- green-leaved **new**	SEND
* - 'Magnificum'	EBee EPfP EWll SAPC SArc
- 'Variegatum' (v)	EWll LPio NPer SSte
balsamiferum	CHEx CTbh CTrC EBee EPfP EWll
	SAPC SArc SChr WCom WCot
	WHal
'Blush' **new**	EBee
canariense	CAbb CBrP CHEx EBee WHal
	WLow
- var. *palmense* **new**	EBee
castello-paivae	EBee EShb SChr
cuneatum	CTbh MLan SChr SEND SPet
decorum **new**	SEND
* - 'Variegatum' (v)	WCot
'Dinner Plate'	CHEx
x *domesticum*	see *Aichryson* x *domesticum*
glandulosum	SChr
goochiae	EBee
haworthii ♀H1	CAbb CBrP CHEx CHal CTbh
	CTrC MLan SEND
- 'Variegatum' (v)	EBee SChr
holochrysum	IBlr
Webb & Berth.	
lindleyi	SChr
- var. *viscatum* **new**	EBee
nobile	CBrP
simsii	CHal CTbh EBee SChr
- variegated **new**	EPem
tabuliforme ♀H1	CSpe EPem SSte
- 'Cristatum'	EPem
undulatum ♀H1	CHEx
urbicum	CHEx
'Zwartkop' ♀H1	More than 30 suppliers

Aeschynanthus (Gesneriaceae)
'Big Apple'	CHal WDib
Black Pagoda Group	WDib
'Fire Wheel'	WDib
hildebrandii	WDib
'Hot Flash'	WDib
lobbianus	see *A. radicans*
longicalyx	WDib
§ *longicaulis* ♀H1	LRHS WDib
marmoratus	see *A. longicaulis*
'Mira'	MBri
'Mona'	MBri
parvifolius	see *A. radicans*
§ *radicans* ♀H1	EBak MBri WDib
- *lobbianus*	see *A. radicans*
speciosus ♀H1	CHal WDib

Aesculus ✿ (Hippocastanaceae)
arguta	see *A. glabra* var. *arguta*
x *arnoldiana*	CMCN SBir
- 'Autumn Splendor'	CDul
assamica	CFil
§ x *bushii*	CDul CMCN CTho MGos
californica	CBcs CDul CFil CMCN CTrw ECrN
	EPfP ERod IArd IDee ISea NPal
	SMad SSpi WPGP
- 'Blue Haze' **new**	SSpi
x *carnea*	ELan MBar SBLw
- 'Aureomarginata' (v)	ERod SMad WPat
- 'Briotii' ♀H4	More than 30 suppliers
- 'Plantierensis'	CDul ECrN ENot SBLw
* - 'Variegata' (v)	CBcs CDul CMCN LRHS MGos
	WDin
chinensis	CMCN NLar
'Dallimorei'	SMad
(graft-chimaera)	
§ *flava* ♀H4	CFil CMCN CTho ECrN ENot EPfP
	GTSp NWea SBLw SPer SSpi WPGP
- f. *vestita*	CDoC CDul MBlu
flava x *pavia*	see *A.* x *hybrida*

georgiana	see *A. sylvatica*
glabra	CDul CFil CMCN CTho LRHS
§ - var. *arguta*	CFil CMCN GKir WDin
- 'October Red'	MBlu WPGP
glaucescens	see *A.* x *neglecta*
hippocastanum ♀H4	More than 30 suppliers
§ - 'Baumannii' (d) ♀H4	CDoC CDul CLnd COtt EBee ECrN
	ENot EPfP ERod GKir LPan LRHS
	MGos MSwo NWea SBLw SHBN
	SPer WDin WStI
- 'Digitata'	CDul CMCN GKir SBLw SMad
- 'Flore Pleno'	see *A. hippocastanum* 'Baumannii'
- 'Hampton Court Gold'	CBcs CDul CEnd CMCN GKir
	NBhm
- 'Honiton Gold'	CTho
- 'Laciniata'	CBcs CDul CMCN ERod GKir
	LRHS MBlu SMad
- 'Monstrosa'	SMad
- 'Pyramidalis'	CDul CLnd LPan SBLw SMad
- 'Wisselink'	CDul CLnd CMCN MBlu SMad
§ x *hybrida*	SSpi
indica	CDul CHEx CLnd CMCN CTho
	EBee ECrN ELan ENot EPfP GGGa
	GKir IArd LPan LRHS NWea SLdr
	SMHT SPer SSpi WDin WPGP
- 'Sydney Pearce' ♀H4	CDul CEnd CFil CMCN EBee ERod
	MBlu MGos NLar SBir SMad SPer
	SSpi
x *marylandica*	CDul
memmingeri	SBir
x *mississippiensis*	see *A.* x *bushii*
x *mutabilis* 'Harbisonii'	WWes
- 'Induta'	CLnd CMCN EBee EPfP GTSp IArd
	LRHS MBlu MBri SDix SKee SSpi
	WWes
§ - 'Penduliflora'	CBcs CDul CEnd EPfP LRHS MBlu
	NPal
§ x *neglecta*	CBcs CLnd CMCN
- 'Erythroblastos' ♀H4	CBcs CDoC CDul CEnd CLnd
	CMCN CTho EBee EMil EPfP ERod
	GKir IDee LRHS MBlu SBir SHBN
	SKee SMad SSpi WDin WPat
parviflora ♀H4	More than 30 suppliers
§ *pavia* ♀H4	CBcs CDul CMCN CTho EPfP GKir
	IDee ISea LRHS SSpi WDin WWes
- 'Atrosanguinea'	CDul CEnd CLnd CMCN EPfP
	ERod LRHS MBlu NPal SMad SSpi
- var. *discolor*	SBLw WDin
- - 'Koehnei'	CDul CMCN LRHS MBlu SKee
	SPoG WOrn
- var. *flavescens*	NPal
- 'Penduliflora'	see *A.* x *mutabilis* 'Penduliflora'
- 'Purple Spring'	MBlu
- 'Rosea Nana'	CBcs CMCN WPat
splendens	see *A. pavia*
§ *sylvatica*	CLnd CMCN CTho
turbinata	CDul CLnd CMCN IDee LRHS
	MBlu WBVN
- var. *pubescens*	MBlu WPGP
wilsonii	CFil WPGP
x *woerlitzensis*	CLnd ISea WCwm

Aethionema (Brassicaceae)

armenum	MOne WLin
coridifolium	WPer
* *glaucum*	WLin
§ *grandiflorum* ♀H4	CElw NBro SBla SRms WPer
- Pulchellum Group ♀H4	CLyd EPot GKev GKir MBro NMen
	SGar WWin
iberideum	ETow MDKP MOne MWat SRms
I *kotschyi* hort. **new**	ECho NMen NWCA WAbe
oppositifolium	CLyd GTou MBro MWat WAbe
	WHoo
pulchellum	see *A. grandiflorum*

§ *saxatile*	CBrm
schistosum	WLin
'Warley Rose' ♀H4	CLyd CSpe CWCL EDAr ELan EPot
	GKir LHop MBro MWat NLAp
	NMen NWCA SIng SRms WPat
	WWin
'Warley Ruber'	CLyd CStu EDAr NBir NHol SBla
	SIng WAbe

Afrocarpus (Podocarpaceae)

falcatus	ECou GGar

Agalinis (Scrophulariaceae)

linariodes **new**	EMan

Agapanthus ✿ (Alliaceae)

'Aberdeen'	CPne XDoo
I 'Adonis'	IBlr
§ *africanus* ♀H1	CAbb CElw CM&M EBee EHrv
	EPfP GSki IBlr LRHS MBNS NBlu
	NScw SAPC SArc SBod SPer SWat
	WBrE WFar WPer WShp XPep
* - 'Albus' ♀H1	CBcs CDoC CFwr CHad CHid
	EBee EMan ENot EPfP GSki IBlr
	IHMH LPhx LRHS MBNS NBlu
	SBod SEND SYvo WHil WPer XDoo
	XPep
* - 'Big Blue'	CKno CPrp EBee GGar
* 'Albus'	CAvo CBri CPLG CSBt GFlt IBal
	MGos MHer SAga WLow
'Amsterdam'	CFwr XDoo
'Angela'	CPne
'Aphrodite'	IBlr
'Aquamarine' **new**	EBee
'Arctic Star'	GSki
Ardernei hybrid	CDes CFil CPne EBee ECha EWes
	GCal IBlr LPhx LPio MSte MTed
	SAga SRos SSpi SUsu WCot WPGP
	XDoo
'Baby Blue'	CLyd IBlr LRHS XDoo
'Ballyrogan'	IBlr LPio
'Basutoland' **new**	LRHS
'Beeches Dwarf'	EBee
'Ben Hope'	EBee GBuc IBlr SDnm WCot WHil
	XDoo
'Bethlehem Star'	CPne GSki SRos
'Bicton Bluebell'	IBlr
'Blue Baby'	EBee LRHS WFar
'Blue Brush'	CAbb CPne EMil SVil
'Blue Cascade'	IBlr
'Blue Companion'	IBlr
'Blue Diamond'	EHrv SRos
'Blue Dot'	CPne EBee EFou EMan
'Blue Fortune'	WGer
'Blue Giant'	CBro CHid CPen EBee EBre ELan
	EUJe EWTr IBal IBlr LRHS MNFA
	MSte NGby SAga SWat WDav WFar
	WPGP WSpi WWpP
'Blue Globe'	CHid CM&M EBee EChP EMan
	ERou IBal MBct NGdn STes WCAu
	WHil WMnd WTMC
'Blue Gown'	CPne
'Blue Haze'	SRos
'Blue Imp'	CBro GBuc GSki IBlr LRHS MMHG
	NHol SLon XDoo
'Blue Méoni'	XDoo
'Blue Moon'	CBro CHad CPen EBee EGle IBal
	IBlr LRHS MTed NPri SEND WCot
	XDoo
'Blue Nile'	CPne
'Blue Skies'	CBcs EBee IBlr NCGa WTMC XDoo
'Blue Triumphator'	CHid CSBt EBee EPfP EWTr EWll
	IBlr LPhx LPio LRHS NGby SBod
	SMrm WCot XDoo

'Blue Velvet' — CPne

'Bressingham Blue' — CBro CPne CTri EBre GCal IBlr LRHS MRav MSte NVic SChu SSpe SWat WGer XDoo

'Bressingham Bounty' — EBre

'Bressingham White' — CHad CPne EBee EBre ECtt EFou EHrv EMan LPio LRHS MRav MTed NCGa SLon SOkh SSpe SWat XDoo

'Bristol' — XDoo

'Buckingham Palace' — CBro CDes CFil CKno EBee IBlr WPGP XDoo

'Caeruleus' **new** — XDoo

'Cally Blue' **new** — GCal

'Cambridge' — CPne XDoo

§ *campanulatus* — CElw CPLG CPrp CWCL EBee EBlw ELan EPfP GFlt GGar GSki IBlr ISea LRHS MRav NCGa SWat SYvo WCot WFar WWpP XPep

- var. *albidus* — More than 30 suppliers

- 'Albovittatus' — CBot CLAP CSam ECho LPhx

- bright blue — CWCL GCal

- 'Buckland' — IBlr

- 'Cobalt Blue' — EBla ECha

- 'Isis' — CBro CFil CFir CTri CWCL EBla EBre ECha GBuc IBal IBlr LRHS SRos WCAu

- 'Meibont' (v) — WCot

- 'Oxbridge' — IBlr

- 'Oxford Blue' — CFil CPen EBee GBri GBuc IBlr LRHS SRos WPGP

- subsp. *patens* ♀H3 — EBee EBla EMan EPfP GBri GBuc LPio SSpi SWat WPGP

- - deep blue — CFir IBlr LRHS

- 'Premier' — CFil EBee IBlr WPGP

- 'Profusion' — CBro CWCL EBre ECha IBal IBlr LRHS SRos SSpi WFar

- 'Slieve Donard Variety' — IBlr WFar

- 'Spokes' — IBlr

- variegated (v) — EBla ECha NPer

- 'Wedgwood Blue' — CPen IBal IBlr XDoo

- 'Wendy' — CPen IBlr

- 'White Hope' — IBlr SRos

- 'White Triumphator' — WCot

'Castle of Mey' — CFil CPlt EBee EGle GAbr GBuc IBlr LPhx MTho SBla SRos WPGP XDoo

'Catharina' — CPne XDoo

caulescens ♀H1 — CFil EBee IBlr WBrE WPGP

- subsp. *angustifolius* — CBrm IBlr WCot XPep

- subsp. *caulescens* — SWat

'Cedric Morris' — ERea IBlr SRos XDoo

'Chandra' — IBlr

'Charlotte' — XDoo

'Cherry Holley' — LPio SRos

'Clarence House' — CBro

coddii — EMan IBlr LPio LRHS SChu WCot WHil

'Columba' **new** — XDoo

comptonii — CAvo CFil CPou IBlr WPGP XDoo

- subsp. *comptonii* — CBrm SWat

- subsp. *longitubus* — CPne LPio SWat WCot WHil

'Crystal Drop' **new** — CPne

Danube — see A. 'Donau'

'Dark Star' **new** — WFar

'Dawn Star' — XDoo

'Debbie' — CFwr CPne XDoo

'Delft' — IBlr

'Dell Garden' **new** — LRHS

'Density' — IBlr

'Devon Dawn' — CPne

'Dnjepr' **new** — GSki

'Doktor Brouwer' — CPen CPne EBee GSki MDKP NGby XDoo

§ 'Donau' — CBro CDoC CHid EBee EFou EMan WFar XDoo

dyeri — CBro IBlr

'Ed Carman' (v) **new** — WCot

'Elisabeth' — CPne

'Ethel's Joy' **new** — CPen

'Eve' — EBee IBlr

'Evening Star' — ECha GSki LRHS

'Findlay's Blue' — CFil CLCN EBee GBuc WPGP

from Gary Dunlop **new** — XDoo

'Gayle's Lilac' — CBcs CBro CDoC CElw CFai CFwr CPne CPrp CSam EBee EBre EChP EGle ELan EMan EMil GSki IBal LPio LRHS MAvo MRav NCGa NSti SDnm SPoG WCot WGer WPnn WWhi

'Glacier Stream' — EBee GSki IPot WSpi

'Glenavon' — CAbb CFir CPne CPrp EBee ENor IBal NLar WSpi

'Golden Rule' (v) — CDes CFir CPne CRow EBee EHoe GBuc IBlr SAga SSpi WPGP

§ Headbourne hybrids — More than 30 suppliers

'Helen' — IBlr

'Holbeach' — CFwr CPne XDoo

'Holbrook' — CSam

'Hydon Mist' — XDoo

'Ice Blue Star' — CPne SRos

'Ice Lolly' — CBro EBee

inapertus — CBro CFil LRHS SBla SSpi SWat WCot WPGP XPep

- dwarf **new** — IBlr

- subsp. *hollandii* — CAvo CPne GCal GGar IBlr MSte SWat

- - 'Lydenburg' — IBlr

- subsp. *inapertus* — EChP ERea IBlr SWat WCot

I - - 'Albus' — IBlr

- - 'Cyan' — IBlr

- - 'Indigo Cascade' **new** — SWat

- subsp. *intermedius* — CFil EBee EChP GCal IBlr SSpi SWat

- - 'Wolkberg' — IBlr

- subsp. *parviflorus* — IBlr

- subsp. *pendulus* — CBrm CFir CKno EBee IBlr WPGP

'Innocence' — IBlr

'Intermedius' van Tubergen — EBee GSki XDoo

'Ivory' **new** — MLLN

'Jack's Blue' — More than 30 suppliers

'Jersey Giant' — EBee LEdu

'Jodie' — CPne

'Johanna' — CPne

'Kew White' — EWTr

'Kingston Blue' — EBla EHrv IBlr SMHy SUsu WFar WPrP WSHC XDoo

'Kobold' — EBee EGle SBod WFar

'Lady Edith' — IBlr

'Lady Moore' — EBee EGle IBlr XDoo

'Latent Blue' — IBlr

'Leicester' **new** — XDoo

'Lilac Time' — CPne IBlr

'Lilliput' — More than 30 suppliers

'Little Diamond' **new** — EBee

'Loch Hope' ♀H3 — CAbb CAvo CBro CCtw CDoC CFil CHid CPne CPrp EBee EBlw EGle EMan GAbr IBal LAst MAvo MFOX NBPC SRos SSpi SVil WCot WPnn WWhi XDoo

'Luly' — CPne XDoo

'Mabel Grey' — IBlr

'Magnifico' — IBlr

'Malvern Hills' — WSpi

'Marcus' — CPne

'Mariètte' — CFwr CPen CPne XDoo

'Marjorie' — CLCN CWCL

'Martine' — CFwr CPne XDoo

'Midnight' — CHad SAga

'Midnight Blue' ambig. — CDoC CPne ELan EPfP GBuc GSki LPhx LPio LRHS MSte SMHy WFar

'Midnight Blue' P.Wood	GCal IBlr
'Midnight Star'	CBro CPen ECha ERea GSki IBal
	LRHS MSte SRos WFar WPrP XDoo
mixed whites	WCFE
* 'Mooreanus' misapplied	CFil EPfP GCal IBlr WPGP XDoo
'Morning Star'	CPne GSki SRos
'Naomi'	LAst
'Navy Blue'	CAbb CBot CCtw CDoC CFai
	CMdw CPne CPrp EBee EChP
	EMan EOrc EWll GBin GMac GSki
	IBal IPot MAvo MBri MCLN MNrw
	MSph NChi SPer WCot WKif WPnn
	WWhi XDoo
'New Blue'	CPen ENot IBal
'Norman Hadden'	IBlr
'Nottingham'	CFwr XDoo
nutans	EBre IBlr LRHS WCot
- 'Albus'	GCal
'Nyx'	IBlr
'Oslo'	CFwr CPne XDoo
Palmer's hybrids	see *A.* Headbourne hybrids
'Patent Blue'	IBlr
'Penelope Palmer'	IBlr
'Penny Slade'	SRos
'Peter Pan'	CBcs CBro CElw CFwr CHid CMea
	COlW CPen CPne CPrp CRow
	CSWP CTrC CWib EBee EChP
	EOrc GBuc GGar GSki IBal LPhx
	LPio LRHS MRav WCAu WFar
	WOBN WSpi XPep
'Phantom'	CPne IBlr
'Pinchbeck'	CPne XDoo
'Pinocchio'	CFwr EBee GSki IPot MLan NHol
'Plas Merdyn Blue'	IBlr
'Plas Merdyn White'	CFir IBlr
'Podge Mill'	CWCL EGle IBlr XDoo
'Polar Ice'	CFir CPne EBee EFou GSki IBlr
	NHol WFar WHil XDoo
'Porcelain' **new**	IBlr
praecox	CFil CLAP EBee GAbr IBlr WViv
- 'Atlas'	IBlr
- 'Bangor Blue'	IBlr
- 'Blue Formality'	IBlr
I - 'Blue Mercury'	IBlr
- 'Dwarf White'	see *Agapanthus* white dwarf
	hybrids
- 'Flore Pleno' (d)	CDes CFai CKno CPne CPrp EBee
	ECha EHrv ELan EMan IBlr MBNS
	SSpi WCot WFar WPGP WPrP
- subsp. *floribundus*	SWat
- subsp. *maximus* 'Albus'	CPou IBlr SSpi
- 'Miniature Blue'	SWat
- subsp. *minimus*	CElw CPne GSki IBlr SWat XDoo
- - 'Adelaide'	SWat
- - blue	ERea SWat
I - - 'Supreme'	IBlr
- - white	ERea SWat
- 'Mount Stewart'	IBlr
§ - subsp. *orientalis*	CSut EBee EHrv ERea EUJe GGar
	GSki IBlr NPal SWat WPic XPep
- - var. *albiflorus*	CBro CPne CPou CSut EBee GSki
	NPal
- - 'Weaver' **new**	WHil
- subsp. *praecox*	IBlr IGor
- - azure	SWat
- - 'Silver Sceptre'	IBlr
- - 'Variegatus' (v) ♀H1	CDes WSPU
- Slieve Donard form	IBlr
- 'Storms River'	SWat XPep
- 'Titan'	IBlr
- 'Vittatus' (v)	ERea LAst WCot WFar
'Pride of Bicton' **new**	CPne
'Purple Cloud'	More than 30 suppliers
'Purple Star'	SVil

'Rhône'	IBlr WSpi
rich blue	XDoo
'Rosewarne'	CAbb CBcs CPne CPrp EBee
	EBre GQui IBlr NLar SVil WGer
'Rotterdam'	XDoo
'Royal Blue'	CBro CWCL GBuc LPio MSte NHol
	SVil WSpi
'Sandringham'	CDes CFil CRow EBee IBlr WPGP
	XDoo
'Sapphire'	IBlr XDoo
'Sea Coral'	CAbb CBcs CDoC CFai CFir CPne
	EBee IBal XDoo
'Sea Foam'	CBcs CPne EBee IBal MBNS NLar
	WCAu WSpi
'Sea Mist'	CBcs CPne IBal WSpi XDoo
'Sea Spray'	CKno CPne GGar IBal XDoo
'Septemberhemel' **new**	XDoo
'Silver Baby'	CAbb ERea
'Silver Mist'	CPne IBlr
Silver Moon	EHan ELan EMan ENot EPfP LBuc
= 'Notfred' (v)	
silver variegated (v)	SMrm
'Sky Rocket'	IBlr
'Snowball'	CBcs CDoC CFai CLAP COlW
	CPne CPrp EBee ERea GAbr IBal
	MSte NBPC SCro SVil WSpi XDoo
'Snowcloud'	CAbb CBro CPne EBee IBal WSpi
I 'Snowdrops'	More than 30 suppliers
'Snowy Eyes'	EBee
'Snowy Owl'	CLAP EBee
'Starburst'	IBlr
'Stéphanie Charm'	XDoo
'Storm Cloud' (d)	CBro CFir
'Streamline'	More than 30 suppliers
'Summer Clouds'	ENot EPfP LRHS
'Summer Skies'	ENot EPfP LRHS
'Sunfield'	CPne EBee GSki IBal LRHS WBro
	WCAu WDav WHil WWeb XDoo
'Super Star'	XDoo
'Sylvine'	XDoo
'Tall Boy'	IBlr
'Timaru'	More than 30 suppliers
'Tinkerbell' (v)	More than 30 suppliers
'Torbay'	CElw CPne EBee ECtt EMar EOMN
	EWll IBlr SLon XDoo
Tresco hybrid	CHEx
I 'Tresco Select'	EBee
'Twilight'	IBlr
umbellatus L'Hérit.	see *A. africanus*
umbellatus Redouté	see *A. praecox* subsp. *orientalis*
'Underway'	EFou GCal IBlr
I 'Virgineus'	XDoo
white	GFlt GGar
'White Christmas'	EBee ERea
'White Dwarf'	see *A.* white dwarf hybrids
§ white dwarf hybrids	CBro CPen CPne EBee ECha EFou
	EMan EMar EPfP IBal LRHS SMrm
	WFar XDoo
'White Ice'	CAbb CBcs CPne EBee GQui WSpi
	XDoo
'White Starlet'	IBal XDoo
'White Superior'	CM&M CPne CSpe EBee EChP
	EMan ERou LAst NGdn WCAu
	WMnd WTMC WWye
'White Umbrella'	EBee WPrP
'Whitney' **new**	IBlr
'Windlebrooke'	EBee ECha
'Windsor Castle'	IBlr XDoo
'Windsor Grey'	CDes IBlr SSpi WPGP XDoo
'Winsome'	IBlr
'Wolga'	EBee
'Yves Klein'	IBlr
'Zella Thomas'	EBee LHyd XDoo

Agapetes (Ericaceae)
serpens ♀H1	CKob SLon
- 'Nepal Cream'	SLon
- 'Scarlet Elf'	CDoC
smithiana	GGGa
var. *major* **new**	

Agarista (Ericaceae)
§ *populifolia*	WFar

Agastache (Lamiaceae)
B&SWJ 4187 from Korea	WCru
anethiodora	see *A. foeniculum*
anisata	see *A. foeniculum*
'Apache Sunset'	MAnH SDnm
'Apricot Sprite'	CFwr CSpe EWll LDai MHar MWrn
	NGHP NPps SBri SDnm SUsu
	WCHb WGwG WHHs WWeb
	WWpP
'Apricot Sunrise'	EMan
'Apricot Surprise' **new**	WHer
aurantiaca	CTCP LHop NDov
'Black Adder'	EBee LHop
'Blue Fortune'	CBcs EBee EBre ECha ECtt EMan
	EMil EMon ENot EPfP GBri IBal
	LRHS MBow MCLN MLLN NCGa
	NDov SMrm SOkh WFar WShp
	WWeb WWhi
'Bridal Veil' **new**	WHer
§ *cana*	EBee ECtt EMan LDai LPhx MAnH
	MDKP MLLN MSph MWrn SPoG
	WCHb WCot WFar WRos WShp
- 'Cinnabar Rose'	NBir WFar
- 'Heather Queen'	EOHP WGMN
- 'Purple Pygmy' **new**	MSph
canariensis misapplied	see *Cedronella canariensis*
cusickii	WLin
'Firebird'	More than 30 suppliers
§ *foeniculum*	CArn CBod CPrp ECha EFou ELan
	ELau EOHP GPoy LPhx LRHS
	MHer MRav NFor SBla SRms WCAu
	WFar WHHs WPer WWye XPep
- 'Alabaster'	CBcs EBee EBre EGoo ELau IHMH
	LPhx LRHS SAga WCHb
- 'Alba'	EFou MLLN NGHP SHDw WFar
- 'Fragrant Delight'	SRms
- 'Golden Jubilee' **new**	ECoo MAnH MAvo MCCP MWrn
- 'Honey' **new**	WGwG WHHs
'Globetrotter'	EBee LHop NDov
'Glowing Embers'	EBee ECtt ELan EMan ENot EPfP
	LRHS
'Honey Bee Blue'	EWll LRHS
'Honey Bee White'	WBry
§ *mexicana*	CSev EBee LDai MHar MSal SCro
	SDnm SMHy SMrm WCom WGwG
	WHHs WJek WSan
- 'Carille Carmine'	EMan
- 'Champagne'	EGoo EMan WCHb
- 'Mauve Beauty'	EBee NNor WPer
- 'Red Fortune'PBR	ENot MBri WShp
- 'Rose Beauty'	SMrm
- 'Rosea'	see *A. cana*
- 'Toronjil Morado'	EBee LHop
nepetoides	CArn EBee EMan EPPr LPhx
	MDKP MSal MWrn NBPC NLar
	SDnm SWal WCHb WWpP WWye
'New Blue'	EPfP
'Painted Lady'	CSpe EBee ECtt EMan LPhx SMrm
	WCot WWpP
pallidiflora	EBee
var. *pallidiflora*	
- var. *neomexicana* **new**	GEil
- - 'Lavender Haze'	WGwG WHHs

palmeri	LHop
'Pink Panther'	EBee ECtt EMan MDKP WShp
	WWpP
pringlei	EChP GEil MDKP MWrn NLar
	SWat WCHb WWpP
'Purple Candle'	EFou EWes EWll MTis NCGa SPla
'Purple Haze' **new**	EBee
rugosa	CArn CBod CFir CSev CTCP ELau
	EMan EOHP GBar GPoy LPhx
	LRHS MAnH MLLN MSal MWrn
	NLRH SCro SDnm SECG SSth SWat
	WHHs WJek WLin WMoo WPer
	WSel WWye XPep
- B&SWJ 4187	WCru
- subsp. *albiflora*	SDnm WCAu WHil
- pink-flowered	CPom CSam
rupestris	EBee EChP EMan EMar EShb LHop
	LPhx MSPs MWrn WCot WHil
	WKif WLin WSan WShp
scrophulariifolia	EBee EWll WCHb WRos WWpP
'Serpentine'	EBee EMon
'Tangerine Dreams'	CSpe EBee ECtt EMan LPhx SAga
	WCot
'Tutti-frutti'	EBee ECtt EHrv EMan LDai SDnm
	SPoG WGwG WHHs WHil WShp
urticifolia	CArn CSpe LRHS MSal WOut
- 'Alba'	CSpe CTCP EBee WPer
- 'Liquorice Blue'	EChP ECtt EOMN EWTr LRHS
	MLan MWgw NBid NDov NGdn
	NLar SDnm SPoG SWat WFar
	WHHs WPer
- 'Liquorice White'	EBee LRHS NBur NDov NLar SWat
	WHHs WWhi

Agathaea see *Felicia*

Agathis (Araucariaceae)
australis	CDoC LCon

Agathosma (Rutaceae)
crenulata	ELau

Agave ✿ (Agavaceae)
albicans	EOas
americana ♀H1	More than 30 suppliers
- 'Marginata' (v)	CBrP CHal CHll EOas IBlr MPRe
	NPri SDnm WMul
- 'Mediopicta' (v) ♀H1	CHEx CTbh SAPC SArc STop WEas
	WMul
§ - 'Mediopicta	CBrP EAmu EOas MPRe SChr
Alba' (v) ♀H1	WMul
- 'Mediopicta' misapplied	see *A. americana* 'Mediopicta Alba'
- 'Striata' (v)	NBlu
- 'Variegata' (v) ♀H1	More than 30 suppliers
angustifolia	MPRe
var. *marginata* hort.	
attenuata	CBrP EOas LRHS SAPC SArc WMul
bracteosa	EOas EPem MPRe
§ *celsii*	CBrP CHEx CTbh CTrC EBee EOas
	SAPC SArc SChr
chrysantha	CAbb CTrC EOas WCot
cupreata **new**	EBee
deserti	CBrP EOas MPRe
ferdinandi-regis	see *A. scabra* x *A. victoriae-*
	reginae
ferox	CBrP CTrC CWil EBee EOas MPRe
	WHPE WMul
filifera ♀H1	CBcs CHEx EOas EPem MPRe
	SChr WMul
fourcroydes **new**	MPRe
geminiflora **new**	WCot
ghiesbreghtii	CBrP EOas MPRe
guadalajarana	MPRe
'Trelease' **new**	

guiengiola **new**	EOas
havardiana	CTrC
horrida	SChr
- 'Perotensis' **new**	MPRe
kerchovei	EOas WCot
lechuguilla	CTrC EOas SChr
lophantha	CWil MPRe
- var. coerulescens	EOas
§ - var. univittata	EOas
lurida Aiton	MPRe
mckelveyana	EOas
mitis	see *A. celsii*
§ mitriformis **new**	WMul
montana	EBee
neomexicana	CTrC MPRe SIgm
nizandensis	CHEx
obscura **new**	EOas
palmeri	CTrC EOas EPem IDee SChr
parryi	CAbb CDoC CTrC EBee EOas IDee
	LEdu MSPs SChr SIgm SSte WCot
	WMul WPGP
- var. couesii	see *A. parryi* var. *parryi*
- var. huachucensis	CBrP
§ - var. parryi	CBrP CFir CFwr EOas MPRe
parviflora ♀H1	CTrC EBee SChr
aff. pelona	EBee
polyacantha var.	MPRe
xalapensis **new**H1	
potatorum ♀	SChr
- var. verschaffeltii	MPRe
salmiana	WMul
- var. ferox	EOas SAPC SArc SChr
scabra	EBee EOas EPem
scabra	EPem SChr
x victoriae-reginae	
schidigera	CBrP CFir EMan GCal
schottii	WCot
shawii	EOas
sisalana	EOas WMul
striata	CTrC IDee XPep
stricta ♀H1	EBee EOas MPRe WMul
I - 'Minor' **new**	CBrP
titanota	EOas
toumeyana	SChr
triangularis **new**	EOas
univittata	see *A. lophantha* var. *univittata*
utahensis ♀H1	EOas SEND SIgm
- var. discreta	SChr
- var. eborispina	EOas
victoriae-reginae ♀H1	CBrP CTrC EBee EOas SEND
xylonacantha	EOas

Ageratina see *Eupatorium*

Ageratum (Asteraceae)

corymbosum	CSpe

Aglaonema (Araceae)

§ crispum	MBri
- 'Marie'	MBri
'Malay Beauty'	MBri
roebelinii	see *A. crispum*
'Silver Queen' ♀H1	MBri

Agonis (Myrtaceae)

flexuosa	CPLG CTrC
juniperina	LRav

Agrimonia (Rosaceae)

eupatoria	CArn COld CRWN EBee ELau
	GPoy MGas MHer NMir SECG SIde
	SWat WBri WCHb WHHs WHbs
	WHer WWye
- 'Topas'	ELau

grandiflora	EBee
gryposepala	EBee
odorata misapplied	see *A. procera*
odorata (L.) Mill.	see *A. repens*
pilosa	CArn EBee ELau MSal
§ procera	WBWf
§ repens	CTCP GBar MSal WCHb

Agropyron (Poaceae)

glaucum	see *Elymus hispidus*
magellanicum	see *Elymus magellanicus*
pubiflorum	see *Elymus magellanicus*
scabrum	see *Elymus scabrus*

Agrostemma (Caryophyllaceae)

coronaria	see *Lychnis coronaria*
githago	GWCH MBow MWgw WHer WJek

Agrostis (Poaceae)

calamagrostis	see *Stipa calamagrostis*
§ canina	CBre EChP EGra EHoe EHul EMan
'Silver Needles' (v)	EWes GCal GKir LRHS MMoz NBir
	NHol WFar WRos
'Lago Lago' **new**	EBee
nebulosa	EFWa EPza LIck

Aichryson (Crassulaceae)

§ x domesticum	CHal EBee
- 'Variegatum' (v) ♀H1	CHal EBak EBee

Ailanthus (Simaroubaceae)

§ altissima	CBcs CDul CHEx CLnd CTho EBee
	ECrN EMil ENot EPat EPfP EWTr
	GKir LPan MBlu MGos NBee SAPC
	SArc SBLw SDnm SMad SPer SPlb
	SWvt WBVN WDin WNor WOrn
	WStI
- var. sutchuenensis	CFil
- var. tanakae	WCru
B&SWJ 6777	
glandulosa	see *A. altissima*

Ainsliaea (Asteraceae)

acerifolia B&SWJ 4795	WCru
fragrans	EBee

Aiphanes (Arecaceae)

aculeata	LPal

Ajania (Asteraceae)

§ pacifica	CHal EBee ECtt ELan EMFP EMan
	LDai LRHS MBow MOak NBlu
	SPoG XPep
- 'Silver Edge' **new**	MTis
pallasiana	GIBF
tibetica JJH 9308103	NWCA

Ajuga (Lamiaceae)

ciliata var. villosior	CFir EBee GCal
genevensis **new**	EWTr MSPs
- 'Tottenham'	EBee WOut
'Little Court Pink'	LRHS
metallica hort.	see *A. pyramidalis*
'Monmotaro San'	EMan
'Pink Spires'	EBee NCot
§ pyramidalis	CFee CLyd EBee ECho NBrk SCro
	WHer WMoo
- 'Metallica Crispa'	CRez EBee EMan EMar EWes GKir
	MBro NLar NRya WFar WWeb
	WWpP
reptans	CAgr CNic CRWN ECtt ELau
	EMFW EWTr GPoy LGro LPBA
	MHer MSal NBrk NMir NSco SGar
	WFar WHHs WRHF WWpP

- f. *albiflora* 'Alba'	CArn CMea CRow EBee ECtt EMan EPfP GCal GGar IHMH MNrw NBro NPro NSti SRms WCAu WCHb WFar WHil WLHH WMoo WWye
- - 'Schneekerze'	EBee
- - 'Silver Shadow'	GBBs MAvo
- 'Arctic Fox' (v)	More than 30 suppliers
- 'Argentea'	see *A. reptans* 'Variegata'
§ - 'Atropurpurea'	More than 30 suppliers
- 'Braunherz'	More than 30 suppliers
- 'Brean Down' **new**	CNat
- 'Burgundy Glow' (v)	More than 30 suppliers
§ - 'Catlin's Giant' ♀H4	More than 30 suppliers
- 'Chocolate Chip'	see *A. reptans* 'Valfredda'
- 'Delight' (v)	ECot SBod WEas
- 'Ebony'	EBee WShp
- 'Ermine' (v)	EBee EChP EMan EMil LAst MBNS MNrw MTPN NLar WCot WShp
- 'Evening Glow'	CFwr
- 'Flisteridge' **new**	CNat
- 'Green Splash' (v)	EBee
- 'Grey Lady'	EMan GBuc ITer WLin
- 'Harlequin' (v)	SWvt
- 'John Pierpoint'	SHar WCot
- 'Jumbo'	see *A. reptans* 'Jungle Beauty'
§ - 'Jungle Beauty'	CHid CSev ECtt EMan EPar EPfP IHMH MRav WHen
- 'Little Pink Court' **new**	EBee
- 'Macrophylla'	see *A. reptans* 'Catlin's Giant'
§ - 'Multicolor' (v)	CArn CHEx COkL COIW EBre EDAr ELan EPar GGar IHMH LAst LGro LPBA MBar MLLN MRav NArg NFor SBod SPer SPlb SRms SWvt WFar WHil WMoo WTel
- 'Palisander'	EBee GSki LRHS NLar NSti
I - 'Pat's Selection' (v)	EMan
- 'Pink Elf'	CBre CLyd CMCo CMHG CRow EMan ENot EOrc MRav NBro SHel SIng SUsu SWat WBea WFar WHoo WLin WMoo WWpP
- 'Pink Splendour'	CBre NChi WBry
- 'Pink Surprise'	CHid CNic CRow ECha ECtt EHoe EMar GBar GBuc LRHS MHer NRya SCro SSvw WCHb WEas WFar WMoo WTMC
- 'Purple Brocade'	CStr EHoe WBro
- 'Purple Torch'	CBgR COIW EBee WEas WOut WTMC WWpP
- 'Purpurea'	see *A. reptans* 'Atropurpurea'
- 'Rainbow'	see *A. reptans* 'Multicolor'
- 'Rosea'	EBee NPro WHil WMoo
- 'Rowden Amethyst' **new**	CRow
- 'Rowden Appleblossom' **new**	CRow
- 'Rowden Blue Mist' **new**	CRow
- 'Rowden Royal Purple'	CRow
- 'Tricolor'	see *A. reptans* 'Multicolor'
§ - 'Valfredda'	CBAn CBgR COkL EBee EBre EDAr EMan EMar ESis EWll GBin NCot NLar NPro SHar SLon WCot WOut
- 'Vanilla Chip' (v) **new**	EMan
§ - 'Variegata' (v)	COkL EBre ECtt EDAr EHoe EMFW EMar EPar LGro LHop MHer MLLN NBid NPPs SBod SPer SPet SRms SWat WCot WEas WFar WMoo WWpP
'Variegated Glacier' (v)	WShp

Akebia (*Lardizabalaceae*)

longeracemosa	WCot
- B&SWJ 3606	WCru
x *pentaphylla*	ELan EMil EPfP ERea GQui LRHS MAsh SBra WBcn WSHC

- B&SWJ 2829	WCru
quinata	More than 30 suppliers
- B&SWJ 4425	WCru
- 'Alba'	CBcs CSPN
- cream-flowered	EPfP ERea LRHS MAsh SBra SSta SWvt WCru
- variegated (v)	CBcs WCru
- 'White Chocolate' **new**	WCru
trifoliata	CBcs EBee EPfP GKir LBuc LRHS MDun SLim WBcn
- B&SWJ 2829	WCru
- B&SWJ 5063	WCru

Alangium (*Alangiaceae*)

chinense	CFil EPla LAst WBVN WBcn WPGP
platanifolium	CBot CFil CMCN EPla IArd IDee MBlu NLar SMad WBod WPGP
- var. *genuinum* **new**	NLar

Albizia (*Mimosaceae*)

distachya	see *Paraserianthes lophantha*
§ *julibrissin*	CArn CFil CTrC IDee LAst LRHS MGol MPRe MWat SHFr SPlb WDin WMul WPat
- 'Ombrella'	NPSI
- f. *rosea* ♀H2-3	More than 30 suppliers
lophantha	see *Paraserianthes lophantha*
saman	MGol

Albuca (*Hyacinthaceae*)

from Lesotho	GCal
altissima	CStu SScr WCot
batteniana **new**	CFir
canadensis	CStu WCot
clanwilliamigloria **new**	CDes WPrP
humilis	CNic CStu ECho ESis ETow NMen WAbe WCot
juncifolia	EMan WCot
maxima **new**	WCot
nelsonii	CAvo LRHS WCot
rupestris **new**	WCot
setosa	WCot
shawii	CDes CPrp CStu EBee EMan ERos IFro ITer NSla SAga SBla SOkd WAbe WCot WHil WOBN WPGP WPrP
spiralis	CDes
trichophylla **new**	WCot
unifolia **new**	WCot

Alcea (*Malvaceae*)

'Arabian Nights'	WBry
'Blackcurrant Whirl'	WBry
'Double Moonlight' (d)	WBry WRHF
ficifolia	EChP EMan EWTr MAnH MCCP MWgw NBPC NPPs NPri SDnm WHil WMoo
pallida	EMan NPri
'Park Rondel' **new**	ECha
'Peaches and Cream' **new**	WRHF
'Peaches 'n' Dreams' **new**	CWib MBri SSvw WHil
§ *rosea*	GWCH LAst MBow MWgw SECG WFar XPep
- 'Black Beauty'	NBur
- Chater's Double Group (d)	EBre ECtt EPfP GKir LPVe MBri MLan NBlu NFor NNor SCoo SRms SRob WMnd WRHF
- - chamois (d)	WViv
- - chestnut brown (d)	WViv
- - pink (d)	ECtt NPri SPer WViv
- - red (d)	CWCL ECtt NPri WViv
- - salmon pink (d)	EMar NPri WViv
- - violet (d)	NPri SPer
- - white (d)	NPri SPer WViv

- - yellow (d)	ECtt EMar LAst NPri SPer WViv
- 'Crème de Cassis'	MAnH MSph
- double apricot (d)	NBur
- double pink (d)	MHer WShp
- double red (d)	MHer WShp
- double rose (d)	SPer
- double scarlet (d)	SPer
- double white (d)	EBee MHer WShp
- double yellow (d)	EBee MHer WShp
- 'Jet Black' **new**	WMnd
- 'Lemon Light'	EBee EOMN LHop NBur
- 'Nigra'	More than 30 suppliers
- single	COlW LPVe MWgw
- single pink	LHop LRHS
- single white	WCAu
- Summer Carnival Group	CWib SRms WGor
- 'Victoria Ann' (v)	CPla
- yellow	IHMH MMHG
§ *rugosa*	CHad CSam EMan EMar EOrc MSte
	MWgw NPri SDix WPGP
- *alba*	CBri

Alcea × *Althaea* (Malvaceae)

'Parkallee'	EMon WCot

Alchemilla ✿ (Rosaceae)

§ *abyssinica*	CHid WBro WHen WHrl
alpina misapplied	see *A. conjuncta*, *A. plicatula*
alpina L.	CFee CLyd CMea EPar EPfP GKir
	GTou LRHS MCLN MRav MTho
	NBrk NChi NFor NGHP NMir SHel
	SIng SPet SRms SWat WCom WFar
	WMoo WPer WWhi WWin
aroanica	EBee EBla
arvensis	see *Aphanes arvensis*
§ *conjuncta*	More than 30 suppliers
elisabethae	ECGP EMon NBrk WCHb
ellenbeckii	CFee CMCo EBee EDAr EMon ESis
	EWsh GAbr GBar GGar GKir MBar
	MHer MTho SWat WCHb WCom
	WFar WHen WPGP WPat WPer
epipsila	EBee LPhx MSte NLar WPer
erythropoda ♀H4	More than 30 suppliers
faeroensis	CMCo NChi WPer
- var. *pumila*	CLyd EBee EBla EHyt NMen
filicaulis 'Minima'	CNat
§ *fulgens*	EWTr LEdu WHen
glaucescens	CNat EBla EMon GFlt
hoppeana hort.	see *A. plicatula*
hoppeana Della Torre	GCal
iniquiformis	EBee WPGP
lapeyrousei	EBla EMon EPPr SIng
mollis ♀H4	More than 30 suppliers
I - 'Auslese'	EPza LPVe LRHS WHil WWpP
* - 'Robusta'	EBee ECha EPla LRHS MTho NBrk
	NBur SEND SPlb SWat WFar WMnd
	WMoo WPnP WWpP
* - 'Senior'	EMil IHMM WMnd
- 'Thriller'	IBal NArg NBlu NBur WSpi WWeb
- 'Variegata' (v)	EBee IBlr
monticola	WPer
'Mr Poland's Variety'	see *A. venosa*
pedata	see *A. abyssinica*
pentaphylla	EBla
§ *plicatula*	WPer
psilomischa	EBee EMon LRHS
pumila	EFou
robusta	SWvt
saxatilis	EBee WPer
speciosa	SHel
splendens misapplied	see *A. fulgens*
straminea	EFou EMFP
§ *venosa*	EBee SCro
aff. *venosa*	EPla

vetteri	EBee EBla
vulgaris hort.	see *A. xanthochlora*
§ *xanthochlora*	CArn EBee GBar GPoy MSal NLar
	NSco WFar WHer WPer

Aldrovanda (Droseraceae)

vesiculosa **new**	EFEx

Aletris (Melanthiaceae)

farinosa	EBee
spicata	EBee

Alisma (Alismataceae)

lanceolatum	EPAt
plantago-aquatica	CRow EHon EMFW LNCo LPBA
	MSta NArg NPer SLon SWat WFar
	WMAq WPnP WWpP
- var. *parviflorum*	EMFW LPBA MSta NArg SPlb SWat

Alkanna (Boraginaceae)

orientalis	WCot
tinctoria	MSal SAga SECG
- HH&K 345	CMdw

Allamanda (Apocynaceae)

§ *blanchetii*	SOWG
cathartica	ERea LRHS MBri
- 'Birthe'	MBri
- 'Halley's Comet'	SOWG
- 'Hendersonii' ♀H1	LRHS SOWG
'Jamaican Sunset'	SOWG
neriifolia	see *A. schottii*
§ *schottii* ♀H1	LRHS SOWG
violacea	see *A. blanchetii*

Allardia (Asteraceae)

tomentosa	EHyt

Alliaria (Brassicaceae)

petiolata	CArn GPoy NLan WHbs WHer

Allium ✿ (Alliaceae)

aciphyllum	EBee LAma
§ *acuminatum*	CPom EHyt GIBF GKir GSki NBir
	NMen
I - 'Album' **new**	ECho
acutiflorum	CPom
aflatunense misapplied	see *A. hollandicum*, *A. stipitatum*
aflatunense B. Fedtsch.	CBrm EBee EMon GBBs WBrE
akaka	EHyt GCrs
albidum	see *A. denudatum*
albopilosum	see *A. cristophii*
altaicum	EBee GIBF
altissimum 'Goliath'	EBee EMan
amabile	see *A. mairei* var. *amabile*
ampeloprasum	CFil EBee ECha GIBF WHer WShi
- var. *babingtonii*	CArn CNat GPoy ILis LEdu MLLN
	WHer WShi
amphibolum	EBee EHrv
§ *angulosum*	CMea EBee GIBF MMil MSph SDix
	SMrm WCot WHil
angustitepalum	see *A. jesdianum* subsp.
	angustitepalum
atropurpureum	CPom EBee EChP ECha EHrv ELan
	EMan EMon EPar GIBF LAma LEdu
	LPhx LRHS MLLN NRog SGar WHrl
atroviolaceum	EBee GIBF
azureum	see *A. caeruleum*
balansae	SOkd
barszczewskii	EBee
'Beau Regard' ♀H4	EBee LAma
beesianum hort.	see *A. cyaneum*
beesianum W.W. Smith	CLAP CLyd CPom EHyt GIBF GKir
	NBir NRya

- from Zheduo Pass, Sichuan SBla
blandum GIBF
brevicaule LRHS
bucharicum JJH 94805 WCot
bulgaricum see *Nectaroscordum siculum* subsp. *bulgaricum*
§ *caeruleum* 🏆H4 More than 30 suppliers
- *azureum* see *A. caeruleum*
caesium 🏆H4 EBee EHyt WWst
callimischon CBro
- subsp. *callimischon* EBee
- subsp. *haemostictum* EHyt NMen SBla SIng
canadense CArn EBee SHar
caricoides EBee
§ *carinatum* EBee
§ - subsp. *pulchellum* 🏆H4 More than 30 suppliers
- - f. *album* 🏆H4 CAvo CBro CHar CPom CSWP CStr EBee EChP ECha EGle EHyt EMon EPar EPot ERos LLWP LPhx LRHS MBow MBro MNrw NChi NDov NMen NRog NSti WCom WCot WWin
§ *carolinianum* EBee GCrs GIBF MGol
cepa NGHP
- Aggregatum Group ELau ILis
- 'Kew White' WCot
- 'Perutile' CArn GBar GPoy ILis LEdu MHer
- Proliferum Group CArn CBod CHby CPrp CSev ELau GBar GPoy ILis LEdu MBow MHer NWoo WBrk WCHb WHer WJek WLHH WSel
cernuum More than 30 suppliers
§ - 'Hidcote' 🏆H4 CLAP EMon MBct MSte WBVN WCot WKif
- 'Major' see *A. cernuum* 'Hidcote'
- var. *obtusum* **new** WCot
- pink-flowered CLyd CPLG GBBs GSki SIng
cirrhosum see *A. carinatum* subsp. *pulchellum*
cowanii see *A. neapolitanum* Cowanii Group
crenulatum EHyt
§ *cristophii* 🏆H4 More than 30 suppliers
cupanii EBee
§ *cyaneum* 🏆H4 CGra CLyd CPBP CPne CPom EMlt ERos GBBs GCrs GKir LBee LPhx LRHS NChi NJOw NMen NRya SBla SRot WBea WCom WCot WWin
cyathophorum GBBs GCrs
§ - var. *farreri* CArn CAvo CBre CBro CLyd CNic EBee EBre EMlt EPot ERos GCrs GEdr GIBF GKir GSki LLWP MBro MRav MSte NChi NMen NRya SIng WCot WPrP WWin
darwasicum EBee
decipiens EBee
delicatulum EBee
§ *denudatum* EBee
dichlamydeum CPom EBee ERos
elatum see *A. macleanii*
ericetorum ERos
eusperma EBee LAma
falcifolium EBee EChP EPot GCrs LAma NMen WCot
farreri see *A. cyathophorum* var. *farreri*
fasciculatum EBee LAma
fetisowii EBee
fimbriatum EBee
'Firmament' CAvo CElw CMea EBee EChP EMan EMon LAma LRHS MSte
fistulosum CArn CBod CHby EBee ELau GBar GPoy GSki ILis LEdu MHer NFor NGHP NHol NPri SIde WCHb WCot WPer WWye
- red CBod
- 'Red Welsh' ILis WJek WLHH
flavum 🏆H4 CArn CAvo CBro CPom ECha EGle EPar GIBF GKir GSki LAma LHop MRav NRog NSti SCro SHBN SPer SRob WBVN WGor WGwG
§ - 'Blue Leaf' EPot ERos GKir LEdu NBir
- subsp. *flavum* EBee LEdu LPhx MBow MNrw
- - var. *minus* EHyt MTho NWCA
- 'Glaucum' see *A. flavum* 'Blue Leaf'
- var. *nanum* CNic GEdr GKir
- subsp. *tauricum* EBee ECho LPhx
forrestii CLyd CPom GCrs MDKP
galanthum EBee
geyeri EHyt WCot
giganteum 🏆H4 More than 30 suppliers
'Gladiator' 🏆H4 CBro CFir CHar CPen CPou EBee EChP ECtt EMan EMon LAma LRHS MLLN NRog SPer SPet WDav
glaucum see *A. senescens* subsp. *montanum* var. *glaucum*
'Globemaster' 🏆H4 CAvo CBro CFir CMea EBee ECtt EHrv ELan EMan LAma LPhx LRHS MBri MMHG MSte NFor SPer WBry WCot WFar
globosum EBee
'Globus' CMea EBee EMan LAma LRHS
goodingii CNic CPom EHyt
grisellum EBee
gultschense GIBF
guttatum subsp. *dalmaticum* EBee
- subsp. *sardoum* EBee ECho
haematochiton WCot
'Hair' see *A. vineale* 'Hair'
heldreichii EBee
* *hirtifolium* var. *album* EBee LAma
'His Excellency' CFir EBee ECho EMan LAma LRHS SVil
§ *hollandicum* 🏆H4 More than 30 suppliers
- 'Purple Sensation' 🏆H4 More than 30 suppliers
hookeri ACE 2430 WCot
- var. *muliense* GEdr
humile CLyd WCot
hyalinum EBee EHyt
- pink EMan WCot
§ *insubricum* 🏆H4 ECho ERos GCrs GEdr LPhx NBir NMen NSti SIng WDav
jajlae see *A. rotundum* subsp. *jajlae*
jesdianum CBro CPom EMon
§ - 'Akbulak' EBee LAma LPhx LRHS WCot
- subsp. *angustitepalum* EBee
- 'Michael Hoog' see *A. rosenbachianum* 'Michael Hoog'
- 'Purple King' EMan EPyc LAma WCot
- white-flowered EBee
kansuense see *A. sikkimense*
karataviense 🏆H3 More than 30 suppliers
- 'Ivory Queen' CBro CElw CMea CStu EBee EChP ECtt EMar EMon EPfP EPyc GBBs GFlt LAma LRHS MBow MCCP MDKP MSph MSte MTed MWgw SPer SPlb WAul WDav WFar WWhi LRHS
- 'Kara Tau' LRHS
komarovianum see *A. thunbergii*
ledebourianum EBee ECho WCra
lenkoranicum EBee
libani WPer WPrP
lineare CPom GIBF IHMH
longicuspis GIBF
loratum EPar
'Lucy Ball' CMea CPou EBee ECtt EMan EMon

		EPot LAma LRHS MLLN MSte NBir
		NRog SPet WBry
§	*macleanii*	CArn CPom EBee ELau EMan
		EMon EPar LAma LRHS NRog
		WDav
	macranthum	CLyd CPom EBee GBBs GEdr GFlt
		MSte WLin
	macrochaetum	LAma
	mairei	CElw CLyd EBee EHyt ERos GBBs
		LHop LLWP LRHS MBar NMen
		NRya WGwG WTin
§	– var. *amabile*	CLyd ERos GEdr GIBF LTwo NChi
		NJOw NRya SIng WCot
	'Mars'	CFir EBee LRHS MLLN
	maximowiczii	EBee ECho EWes
	meteoricum	LRHS
	moly	CArn CBri CBro EPar EPfP GBBs
		GFlt GSki LAma MBow MBri MRav
		NGHP NJOw NRog NRya NSti
		SGar SRms WCHb WCom WCot
		WTin WWin
	– 'Jeannine' ♀H4	CBro CMea EBee EPot LAma LPhx
		MLLN
	'Mont Blanc'	CMea EBee ELan LAma
	'Mount Everest'	CAvo CBro CFir CHar CPen EBee
		EChP EMan EMon EPot LAma
		LRHS MSte SPer WCra WDav WShi
	multibulbosum	see *A. nigrum*
	murrayanum misapplied	see *A. unifolium*
	murrayanum Reg.	see *A. acuminatum*
	narcissiflorum misapplied	see *A. insubricum*
§	*narcissiflorum* Villars	CLyd CPom GCrs GEdr GIBF NChi
		WCot WDav
	neapolitanum	CArn EBee EPar EPot LAma LRHS
		MBri NRog NSti SPer SRms
§	– Cowanii Group	CBro EBee EHrv ERos GIBF LRHS
		MNrw WCot WCra WLin
	– 'Grandiflorum'	CSam EBee LPhx LRHS MLLN
		MNrw WBrE
	nevskianum	EBee LAma
§	*nigrum*	CArn CBro CHar CHea EBee EHrv
		EMan EMar EMon EPar EPot GIBF
		LAma LPhx LRHS MBow MLLN
		MNrw MRav NBir NJOw NRog
		WAul WCot
	nutans	CBgR CBod EBee EHol IHMH LEdu
		NGHP SHDw WHal WJek WPrP
§	*obliquum*	EBee ECha ECho EGle GSki LRHS
		WCot WTin
	odorum L.	see *A. ramosum* L.
	oleraceum	WHer
	olympicum	SScr
§	*oreophilum*	CArn CAvo CBri CBro CMdw ECha
		ECtt EHrv EHyt EPar EPfP GBBs
		GSki LAma LRHS MBow MLLN
		NJOw NRog NRya NWCA SPer
		SRms WCom WCot WTin
	– 'Zwanenburg' ♀H4	CBro CMea EBee ECho EMar EPot
		GEdr LPhx NMen NRog WCot
	oreoprasum	EBee GIBF LAma
	orientale	GIBF
	ostrowskianum	see *A. oreophilum*
	pallasii	EBee LAma
	pallens	CBre CHea MTho NBir
§	*paniculatum*	CAvo CPom EChP EHyt GKir MMil
	paradoxum	EBee LRHS NBir
	– var. *normale*	CBgR CBro CMea EBee EHyt EMan
		EMon NMen WCot WDav
	pedemontanum	see *A. narcissiflorum* Villars
	platycaule new	WCot
	platyspathum	EBee
	plurifoliatum	EBee LAma
	polyphyllum	see *A. carolinianum*

	polyrhizum	EBee
	protensum	WWst
	przewalskianum	EBee
	pskemense	GIBF
	pulchellum	see *A. carinatum* subsp.
		pulchellum
	pyrenaicum misapplied	see *A. angulosum*
	pyrenaicum	ELan EMan
	Costa & Vayreda	
	ramosum Jacquin	see *A. obliquum*
§	*ramosum* L.	LAma NGHP WJek WPer
	'Rien Poortvliet'	CArn EBee EMan LAma LRHS
		NRog
§	*rosenbachianum*	CArn CBro CHar EBee EBlw EMan
		EPar EPot GIBF LAma MLLN NRog
		WDav
	– 'Akbulak'	see *A. jesdianum* 'Akbulak'
	– 'Album'	EBee ECha ECho EPar EPot LAma
		MLLN NRog WCot WDav
§	– 'Michael Hoog'	EBee LAma LRHS WCot
	– 'Purple King'	EBee LRHS
	– 'Shing'	LRHS
	roseum	CAgr CArn CMea CPBP EBee ECtt
		ERos GFlt LAma LRav MDKP NRog
	– var. *bulbiferum*	WCot
	– 'Grandiflorum'	see *A. roseum* var. *bulbiferum*
§	*rotundum* subsp. *jajlae*	EBee LLWP
	rubens	CPom
	sarawschanicum	EBee LRHS
	'Chinoro'	
	sativum	CArn EOHP MHer SIde WJek WSel
		WWye
	– 'Arno' **new**	CPrp
	– 'Corail' **new**	CPrp
	– golden	GPoy
	– var. *ophioscorodon*	EBee GPoy ILis LAma
	– 'Printanor'	CBod
	– 'Thermidrome'	CBod
	saxatile	EBee LPhx
	schmitzii	EMon
	schoenoprasum	More than 30 suppliers
	– 'Black Isle Blush'	GPoy MHer
	– 'Corsican White'	EMon SUsu
	– fine-leaved	ELau IHMH WHHs
	– 'Forescate'	CBod CM&M CPrp ECha EFou
		ELau EWes GBar GCal GSki LRHS
		MLLN MRav SPet SSpe SSvw WBea
		WCHb WCot
	– 'Forncett Forescate' **new**	CBgR
	– medium-leaved	ELau NPri
	– 'Pink Perfection'	GPoy MHer
	– 'Polyphant'	CBre EBee WCHb WRha WWpP
	– var. *sibiricum*	GBar GPoy MBri SDix WSel WShi
	– 'Silver Chimes'	CMil EBee ELau MBri SHDw
		WWpP
	– 'Wallington White'	GBar
	– white-flowered	CArn CSWP ECha ELau IHMH
		LEdu LPhx MBro MHer MSte NBir
		NCGa NHol SIde SSvw WBea
		WCHb WCot WEas WHer WRha
		WWpP WWye
	schubertii	More than 30 suppliers
	scorodoprasum	CAgr GIBF WCHb
	– subsp. *jajlae*	see *A. rotundum* subsp. *jajlae*
	senescens	CArn EBee CTri EBee ECGP EPar
		ERos GIBF IHMH MRav NChi
		NJOw SIng SRms SSpe SSvw WBea
		WTin
	– var. *calcareum*	IHMH
§	– subsp. *montanum*	CBro CPom CSpe ECha ECho EFou
		EGoo EMFP EPot LEdu NMen SDix
		SIng WAbe WMoo
§	– – var. *glaucum*	CArn CLyd CMea CPBP CPrp CStr
		EBee EBre ECha EMan EMar EPar

	EPla GEdr LEdu SAga SIng WCot
	WHer WPer WTin WWye
- subsp. *senescens*	EMon MLLN SUsu WPrP
sibthorpianum	see *A. paniculatum*
siculum	see *Nectaroscordum siculum*
sieheanum	EBee
§ *sikkimense*	CHea CPlt CPom EBee EBre EMan
	ERos GIBF GKir LRHS MDKP
	NMen NSla NWCA SBla SSvw
	WBea WCot WPer
sinkiangense	EBee
songpanicum	EBee LAma
sphaerocephalon	More than 30 suppliers
splendens	CPom
stellatum	LRHS WGwG WPrP
stellerianum	WPer
- var. *kurilense*	CLyd CNic
§ *stipitatum*	CPom EBee EChP EMon GIBF
	LAma LRHS MLLN NRog WCot
- 'Album'	CArn CBro EBee EMon EPot LAma
	LRHS NRog
- 'Glory of Pamir'	EMan LRHS
- 'Violet Beauty' **new**	EBee LPhx WCot
stracheyi	WCot
strictum Ledeb.	see *A. szovitsii*
strictum Schrad.	see *A. lineare*
suaveolens	GIBF
subhirsutum	CLyd EBee
subvillosum	EBee WCot
'Summer Beauty'	see *A. senescens* subsp.
	montanum
§ *szovitsii*	EBee
tanguticum	LRHS
§ *thunbergii* ♀H4	EBee GCrs GIBF NBir
- 'Nanum'	EPot WCot
- 'Ozawa'	EBee EHyt NMen SBla SIng WCot
tibeticum	see *A. sikkimense*
* *tournefortii*	EBee ECho
tricoccum	GIBF
triquetrum	CAgr CAvo CStu EBee ELan EPfP
	EPot GGar GIBF IBlr ILis LAma
	LPhx MBow NBir NRog NSti SYvo
	WCHb WCot WCru WHer WMoo
	WPnP WShi WWin
tuberosum	More than 30 suppliers
- purple/mauve	CHby ELau GWCH WMoo
- variegated (v)	ELau
tubiflorum	EBee LPhx
turcomanicum	EBee
turkestanicum	GIBF
§ *unifolium* ♀H4	CArn CAvo CBro CPom EHyt EPot
	GBBs LAma LLWP LPhx LRHS
	MBow MBri MLLN MNrw MRav
	MSPs NBir NPPs NRog NSti SGar
	SPer STes WAbe WBea WBrE WCot
	WFar WPer
ursinum	CArn CAvo GKir GPoy LAma
	MBow NArg NGHP NMir NRog
	NTHB WAul WCHb WFar WHen
	WJek WShi WWye
'Valerie Finnis'	EBee SAga SBla
victorialis	GCal GIBF
- 'Kemerovo'	EBee
vineale	CArn EBee ECtt WHer
- 'Hair'	CFwr EChP EMan EPfP ITer LAma
	NJOw WHil
violaceum	see *A. carinatum*
'Violet Beauty'	see *A. stipitatum* 'Violet Beauty'
virgunculae	EBee EHyt SBla SCnR SRot
wallichii	CLyd CPou EBee EHyt EMon GBuc
	LAma MBNS MGol NBir WCot
	WLin WTin
- ACE 2458	WCot
- CC&McK 1025	WCot

- plum	GEdr
'White Giant' **new**	LPhx
'World Cup'	LRHS
zaprjagajevii	EBee LEdu
zebdanense	ERos LAma LRHS MNrw

Allocasuarina (*Casuarinaceae*)

campestris	SPlb
monilifera	ECou GGar
nana	CTrC IDee
§ *verticillata*	CTrC

Allophylus (*Sapindaceae*)

natalensis **new**	EShb

almond see *Prunus dulcis*

Alnus ✿ (*Betulaceae*)

B&SWJ 5414	WPGP
cordata ♀H4	More than 30 suppliers
cremastogyne **new**	NLar
crispa	see *A. viridis* subsp. *crispa*
firma	CDul CMCN IArd IDee
formosana	GIBF
fruticosa	see *A. viridis* subsp. *fruticosa*
glutinosa	CBcs CCVT CDoC CDul CLnd
	CRWN CSBt CSam CTri EBee ECrN
	ENot EPfP GKir LBuc LPan MGos
	NBee NBlu NRog NWea SBLw
	SHBN SHFr WDin WMou WOrn
	WStI
- 'Aurea'	CDul CEnd CLnd CTho ECrN GKir
	LRHS MBlu MDun SBLw SPer SSpi
- var. *barbata*	GIBF
- 'Imperialis' ♀H4	CDoC CDul CEnd CLnd CTho
	EBee ELan ENot EPfP EWTr GKir
	LPan LRHS MAsh MBri MDun
	NBee SBLw SPer SSpi WDin WMoo
	WOrn
- 'Laciniata'	CDoC CDul CTho ECrN MBlu
	NBlu SBLw WFar WMoo
hirsuta	CMCN
- var. *sibirica*	GIBF
x *hybrida*	GIBF
incana	CDoC CDul CLnd CMCN CWib
	EBee ECrN ENot GKir LBuc MBar
	MGos NRog NWea SBLw SHBN
	SKee SPer WDin WMou
- 'Aurea'	CBcs CDul CEnd CLnd COtt CTho
	EBee ECrN ELan ENot EPfP EPla
	GKir IArd LPan LRHS MBar MBlu
	MBri MGos NRog SBLw SHBN
	SPer SSpi WDin WOrn
- 'Laciniata'	CDul CLnd CTho ENot IDee SBLw
	WDin WFar
- 'Pendula'	CLnd CTho SBLw
japonica	CLnd
- var. *arguta*	GIBF
lanata	CMCN WHCr
nepalensis	WCwm
nitida	CFil CMCN IArd IDee NLar
oregana	see *A. rubra*
orientalis	GIBF
rhombifolia	CMCN
§ *rubra*	CCVT CDoC CDul CLnd CMCN
	CTho EBee ECrN ELan ENot NLar
	NWea SBLw SKee WDin WMou
- 'Pinnatifida'	see *A. rubra* f. *pinnatisecta*
§ - f. *pinnatisecta*	CLnd CMCN CTho
§ *rugosa*	CMCN
serrulata	see *A. rugosa*
sinuata	see *A. viridis* subsp. *sinuata*
x *spaethii*	CDoC CTho GKir LRHS SBLw
	SEND

subcordata	CLnd
viridis	CAgr CMCN ECrN NWea SBLw
- subsp. *crispa*	GIBF
- - var. *mollis*	CMCN
- subsp. *fruticosa*	GIBF
§ - subsp. *sinuata*	CAgr CMCN NWea

Alocasia ✿ (*Araceae*)

x *amazonica* ♀H1	ERea LRHS MBri MNew XBlo
- 'Polly'	MNew
'Aquino'	MNew
'Black Velvet'	MNew
'Calidora' **new**	MJnS
'Crinkles'	MNew
cucullata	MNew WMul
culionensis	MNew
cuprea	MNew
'Elaine'	MNew
gageana	MNew WMul
'Green Shield'	MNew
'Green Velvet'	MNew
guttata var. *imperialis*	MNew
'Hilo Beauty'	MNew
lancifolia	MNew
longiloba	MNew
macrorrhiza	EAmu EUJe LEur MJnS MNew WMul
- 'Lutea'	MJnS MNew
- 'Variegata' (v) ♀H1	MJnS MNew
maximiliana	MNew
micholitziana	MNew
'Mindanao'	MNew
nigra	see *A. plumbea* 'Nigra'
odora	CKob EAmu EUJe LEur MJnS MNew MOak WMul
plumbea	MNew
§ - 'Nigra'	MNew
portei	MNew
'Portodora' **new**	EAmu MJnS WMul
'Portora'	MNew
sanderiana 'Nobilis'	MNew
x *sedenii*	MNew
'Tigrina Superba'	MNew
watsoniana	MNew
wentii	EAmu MNew
'White Knight'	MNew
zebrina	MNew
- 'Reticulata'	MNew

Aloe (*Aloaceae*)

aculeata	WCot
arborescens	CAbb CHEx CTrC EOas MBro SChr SSte WMul
- yellow-flowered	CTrC EOas
aristata ♀H1	CAbb CHEx CHal EOas MBri SAPC SArc SChr SEND SPet SSte SWvt WHer
barbadensis	see *A. vera*
barberae	IDee WMul
boylei	CFir
branddraaiensis	WCot
brevifolia ♀H1	CRoM CTbh EOas SArc
broomii	EOas EPem SChr
camperi 'Maculata'	CTrC MBri SChr
candelabrum	SMrm
ciliaris	EMan EOas ERea SChr WCot
cooperi	CAbb
dichotoma	CAbb GBin
distans **new**	SEND
dumetorum	EPem
ecklonis	CTrC EOas SChr SPlb WCot
erinacea	EOas
excelsa	SChr
ferox	CBrP CTrC MSal SChr SEND WMul

fosteri	CTrC EOas
globuligemma	WCot
greatheadii **new**	CTrC
- var. *davyana*	CCtw CTrC EOas
humilis	CTrC EPem
juvenna	EPem
littoralis	EPem
marlothii	EOas WCot WMul
mitriformis	EOas MPRe NPri SChr SEND
mutabilis	CHEx CTrC EOas SChr
plicatilis	CAbb CTrC EOas
polyphylla **new**	EOas
pratensis	CFir CTrC EOas SChr SPlb
- glaucous-leaved	EOas
prinslooi	EPem
reitzii	CTrC EOas IDee
saponaria	CHEx CRoM CTrC EOas
spectabilis	EOas
x *spinosissima* **new**	SChr
striata	XPep
striatula	CAbb CBrP CFil CHEx CTbh CTrC EOas EPla IBlr SAPC SArc SChr WGer WMul WPGP XPep
- var. *caesia*	IBlr
tenuior **new**	EOas
thraskii **new**	WMul
variegata (v) ♀H1	EOas SWvt WEas
§ *vera* ♀H1	CArn CDoC CHby COld CSpe ELau EOHP EOas EPem ERea ESlt GPoy IFro ILis MPRe MSal NPer NPri NScw SIde SSte SWal WCot WHHs WHer
'Walmsley's Blue'	MBri

Alonsoa (*Scrophulariaceae*)

'Bright Spark'	CSpe EMan
meridionalis	LRav NJOw WWeb
- 'Shell Pink' **new**	WWeb
'Pink Beauty'	CSpe CWCL NBur
'Snowflake'	LRav
unilabiata	CSpe
warscewiczii	CHll ELan NBlu SHFr
- pale-flowered	see *A. warscewiczii* 'Peachy-keen'
§ - 'Peachy-keen'	CSpe EMan SPet

Alopecurus (*Poaceae*)

alpinus	EBre EHoe EMan EOMN EPPr LRHS NBur
- subsp. *glaucus*	CBrm CFwr CPen CSLe EBee EBre EHoe EPPr MBri SPer
borealis subsp. *glaucus* **new**	GCal
geniculatus **new**	CRWN
lanatus	NBea
pratensis	NOrc
- 'Aureovariegatus' (v)	EBee EHoe ENot EPPr EPla EPza EUJe EWsh GCal GKir GSki IHMH MBar MBnl MBri MMoz MPRe MSte MWgw NBid NFor NHol SLim SPer WFar WMoo WPnP
- 'Aureus'	EBee EBlw EChP ECha EFou EGle EGra GBin LRHS MRav MWhi NBro NGdn NSti SPlb WFar WLin WPer WRHF WWin
- 'No Overtaking' (v)	EMan EMon EPPr WWpP

Alophia (*Iridaceae*)

drummondii	ERos
lahue	see *Herbertia lahue*

Aloysia (*Verbenaceae*)

chamaedrifolia	CPle XPep
citriodora	see *A. triphylla*
§ *triphylla* ♀H2	More than 30 suppliers

Alpinia (*Zingiberaceae*)

chinensis	EBee LEur
galanga	MGol WMul
§ **hainanensis**	LEur
japonica	EBee F&W MSal
katsumadai	see *A. hainanensis*
malaccensis	WCru
B&SWJ 7196 **new**	
officinarum	CArn
purpurata	MJnS
- pink **new**	MJnS
speciosa	see *A. zerumbet*
§ **vittata** (v)	MOak
§ **zerumbet**	EAmu LEur MOak WMul
- 'Variegata' (v)	EAmu MOak WMul XBlo

Alsobia see *Episcia*

Alstroemeria ✿ (*Alstroemeriaceae*)

'Aimi'	CBcs COtt EBee LRHS MBri SBai SPer SWvt WFar WViv
'Angelina'	SBai SVil SWvt
'Apollo' ♀H4	COtt GKir LRHS MBNS MBri MTed SBai SPer SWvt WViv
aurantiaca	see *A. aurea*
§ **aurea**	CTri EMar EPfP EWoo GGar MDun MRav MWrn NLar SMrm SRms SSpi WCot WGMN
- 'Apricot'	GCal
- 'Cally Fire'	GCal WCot
- 'Dover Orange'	CPrp EBee EChP EMan EPfP EPza LRHS MWgw SCoo
- 'Lutea'	CDoC CTri EChP ENot EWTr EWll LRHS MWrn SPlb
- 'Orange King'	CDoC EBee ELan EPfP EWll LRHS MBow MTed NLar SDeJ WCom WCot WShp WTin
'Blushing Bride'	CBcs CDoC LBuc MBNS MBri SBai SVil SWvt WViv
brasiliensis	GCal MDKP SSpi WCot WSHC
Butterfly hybrids	SWal
'Charm'	LRHS WFar
'Coronet' ♀H4	COtt LRHS MBNS SPer WViv
I 'Crusader Lily'	EMui
'Dayspring Delight' (v)	WCot
Diana, Princess of Wales = 'Stablaco'	EMui
diluta	WCot
- subsp. **chrysantha** F&W 8700	WCot
Doctor Salter's hybrids	ECGP EFou SRms SWal
'Eternal Love'	COtt
'Evening Song'	CDoC LBuc LRHS MBNS MBri SBai SWvt WViv
aff. **exserens**	WCot
'Firefly'	LRHS SPer
'Flaming Star'	EBee LBuc LIck SBai WViv
'Fortune'	LRHS
'Frances' (v)	LHop
'Friendship' ♀H4	CBcs CDoC SBai SWal SWvt WCot WViv
'Fury'	EBee
garaventae	MDKP WCot
gayana	MDKP WCot
'Golden Delight'	COtt MBri SBai SPla SVil WViv
haemantha	MDKP
Hawera Seedlings	CDes EBee SMrm
hookeri	ECho GCal MTho SCnR SIgm
- subsp. **cummingiana**	WCot
- subsp. **hookeri**	CFil
huemulina	MDKP
'Inca Blaze'	WViv
'Inca Dream'	WViv WWeb

'Inca Ice'	WViv WWeb
'Inca Moonlight'	WViv WWeb
'Inca Tropic'	WViv WWeb
kingii	see *A. versicolor*
leporina	WCot
- F&W 9550	MDKP
ligtu hybrids	More than 30 suppliers
- var. **ligtu**	LPhx
'Lilac Wonder'	NBhm
'Little Eleanor'PBR	COtt GKir LRHS WCot WFar WViv
'Little Miss Charlotte'	COtt LRHS WFar WViv
'Little Miss Christina'	MBNS SBai SVil SWvt WViv
'Little Miss Gloria'	CDoC LBuc MBNS SBai SVil SWvt
'Little Miss Isabel'	WViv
'Little Miss Lucy'	COtt
'Little Miss Matilda'	COtt WViv
'Little Miss Olivia'	WViv
'Little Miss Rosanna'	COtt LRHS WViv
'Little Miss Roselind'	LBuc MBNS SBai SVil SWvt WViv
'Little Miss Sophie'	CDoC LBuc MBNS SBai SVil SWvt WViv
'Little Miss Tara'	CDoC MBNS MMil SBai SWvt WViv
'Little Miss Veronica'	MBNS SVil WViv
'Lucinda'	LBuc MBri SBai SVil SWvt WViv
magnifica	MDKP WCot
- subsp. **magnifica new**	WCot
- subsp. **maxima**	WCot
'Marina'	LRHS MBNS SPer
'Marissa'	LRHS
'Mars'	LRHS SWal
Meyer hybrids	MTho
'Moulin Rouge' **new**	MBNS SBai SVil WViv
'Orange Gem' ♀H4	COtt LRHS MBNS WFar
'Orange Glory' ♀H4	CBcs CDoC COtt EBee IArd LRHS MBNS MBri SBai SMrm SPla SWvt WCot WFar WViv
'Oriana'	SBai SVil SWvt
pallida	CBro CFil CPBP SIgm
- JCA 2.028.500	WCot
patagonica	EHyt WCot
- P&W 6226	ETow
- 'Maxi'	WCot
- - F&W 9337	CPBP
§ **paupercula**	CSev
pelegrina	ECho MTho SIgm WCot
- 'Alba'	ELan SIgm WCot
- var. **humilis**	WCot
- 'Rosea'	ELan
'Perfect Love'	COtt EBee
philipii	WCot
'Phoenix'	EBee LBuc SBai SPla SVil SWvt WViv
'Pink Perfection'	LRHS NLar
'Polka'	EBee MBNS SBai SVil WViv
presliana	EBee
- RB 94103	WCot
- subsp. **australis**	CPou SIgm
- - JCA 12590	SSpi
Princess Aiko = 'Zapriko' **new**	EBee LIck MMil SPla
Princess Angela = 'Staprilan'PBR	COtt EBee LIck MBNS SCoo
Princess Astrid = 'Stabopink'PBR	EMui
Princess Beatrix = 'Stadoran'	EMui
Princess Caroline = 'Stakaros'	EMui
Princess Charlotte = 'Staprizsa'PBR	EMui
Princess Daniela = 'Stapridani'PBR	CBcs SCoo
Princess Ella = 'Staprirange'PBR	NLar

Princess Freckles	EMui
Princess Frederika	EMui
= 'Stabronza'	
Princess Grace	EMui
= 'Starodo'PBR	
Princess Ileana	EMui
= 'Stalvir'	
Princess Ivana	EBee EMui NLar
= 'Staprivane'	
Princess Juliana	EMui SPla
= 'Staterpa'	
Princess Julieta	EBee LIck
= 'Zaprijul' **new**	
Princess Leyla	CBcs EBee MBNS WCot
= 'Stapriley'PBR	
Princess Marie-Louise	EMui
= 'Zelanon'	
Princess Marilene	COtt EBee MBNS
= 'Staprilene'PBR	
Princess Monica	COtt EMui MBNS MMil SPla
= 'Staprimon'PBR	
Princess Morana	COtt EMui
= 'Staprirana'PBR	
Princess Oxana	SCoo
= 'Staprioxa'PBR	
Princess Paola	CBcs COtt EBee MBNS SCoo SPla
= 'Stapripal'	
Princess Sarah	EMui MBNS MMil
= 'Stalicamp'	
Princess Sissi	COtt EBee EMui
= 'Staprisis'PBR	
Princess Sophia	EMui
= 'Stajello'PBR	
Princess Stephanie	CBcs EBee EMui LBuc NLar SPla
= 'Stapirag'	
Princess Susana	EBee EMui NLar SCoo
= 'Staprisusa'PBR	
Princess Victoria	see *A.* 'Victoria'
Princess Zavina	CFir COtt EMui MBNS MMil NLar
= 'Staprivina'PBR	
pseudospathulata	WCot
RB 94010	
§ *psittacina*	CBro CFil CFwr CHar CSev CStu EBee EHrv ELan EPar ERos EWoo GCal LHop MBri MHer MSte NChi SIgm SMrm SSpi SWal WCot WFar WPGP WSHC WTin
- 'Mona Lisa'	EShb EWll WCot WViv
- 'Royal Star' (v)	CFwr EBee ELan EMan EMar EMon ENot EPPr EPfP LBuc LRHS SIgm SSpi WCom WCot WFar WHil WPrP WWeb
- variegated	see *A. psittacina* 'Royal Star'
pulchella Sims	see *A. psittacina*
pulchra	CFil MDKP SIgm
- JCA 2.029.410	WCot
'Purple Rain'	CBcs CDoC LBuc MBri SBai SVil SWvt WViv
pygmaea	EHyt MTho
Queen Elizabeth PBR	EMui
The Queen Mother	
= 'Stamoli'	
'Red Beauty' (v)	EBee GKir LRHS MBNS MBri NBir SBai SPer SPlb SVil SWvt WCot WSpi WViv
'Red Elf'	CDoC CPlt EFou GKir LRHS MBNS MBri SBai SVil SWvt WFar WViv
'Regina'	see *A.* 'Victoria'
revoluta	CFil
- F&W 8722	WCot
schizanthoides	MDKP
'Selina'	EBee LIck LRHS MBNS SPer SVil WFar WViv
'Short Purple'	CDes WCot WPGP

'Solent Candy'	WFar
'Solent Crest'	WFar
'Solent Dawn'	WFar
'Solent Pride'	WFar
'Solent Wings'	WFar
'Sovereign'	MDKP
'Spitfire' (v)	CDoC EBee LIck SBai SWvt
'Spring Delight' (v)	EMan WCot
'Sunstar'	LRHS
'Sweet Laura'PBR	MMHG NOrc WHil
'Tapestry' **new**	SWal
'Tessa'	LRHS MBNS WViv
umbellata	WCot
'Verona'	LRHS
§ *versicolor*	GCrs MDKP WCot
- BC&W 4624	GBin
- F&W 8721	SIgm
§ 'Victoria'PBR	EMui
violacea	see *A. paupercula*
werdermannii F&W 869	WCot
- F&W 9589	SIgm
- var. *flavicans*	MDKP
F&W 956289	
- var. *werdermannii*	MDKP
F&W 9585	
'White Apollo'	EBee SPla WCot
'Yellow Friendship' ♀H4	CDoC COtt GKir LRHS MBNS NLar SBai SPer SPlb SWvt WFar WViv
'Yellow Queen'	WFar
zoellneri F&W 9608 **new**	WCot

Althaea (*Malvaceae*)

armeniaca	EBee EMan EMon LPio WCot
cannabina	CBri CFir CFis EChP ELan EMon GBri GCal GQui MAnH MBro MFir MGol NBPC SOkh WBor WHal WHoo WOld WSHC WWhi XPep
- MESE 510	EBee
officinalis	CAgr CArn CPrp CSev ELan EMon EWTr GBar GMac GPoy ILis ITer MHer MMil MSal SECG SIde WHHs WPer WWye XPep
- *alba*	EChP NLar WCom WHer
§ - 'Romney Marsh'	CFwr EBee EWll GCal MRav NCot SMad WSHC
rosea	see *Alcea rosea*
rugosostellulata	see *Alcea rugosa*

Altingia (*Hamamelidaceae*)

gracilipes **new**	CMCN

Alyogyne (*Malvaceae*)

hakeifolia	CSpe ECou ERea
- 'Elle Maree'	ERea SOWG
§ *huegelii*	EMan MOak WDyG
- 'Santa Cruz'	CBcs CHll CMdw CPLG CSpe EOrc ERea MSte SOWG SSpi WCot WOld WPGP
'Melissa Anne' **new**	SOWG

Alyssoides (*Brassicaceae*)

utriculata	WPer

Alyssum (*Brassicaceae*)

argenteum hort.	see *A. murale*
caespitosum	WLin
corymbosum	see *Aurinia corymbosa*
idaeum	LRHS
markgrafii	WCom
montanum	CArn ECha MWat NBir NBlu SECG SPlb SRms WCom WMoo WShp
§ - 'Berggold'	CBcs CHrt EBre EPfP LPVe LRHS LRav NFla
- Mountain Gold	see *A. montanum* 'Berggold'

§ *murale* | IHMH NLar
oschtenicum | WLin
oxycarpum | NMen SBla WAbe
pulvinare | NLAp
repens subsp. *repens* | GIBF
saxatile | see *Aurinia saxatilis*
- 'Plena' (d) | CFir GEdr
scardicum **new** | LTwo
serpyllifolium | CLyd MOne NWCA
spinosum | CMea MBro WAbe WFar WLin
| XPep
§ - 'Roseum' ♀H4 | CTri EBre ECha EDAr EHyt ELan
| EPot LBee LRHS LSpr MWat
| NMen SBla WAbe WCot WPat WPer
| WWin
- 'Strawberries | WAbe
and Cream'
wulfenianum | NLar NMen NRya

Amana see *Tulipa*

x *Amarcrinum* (*Amaryllidaceae*)
memoria-corsii | CFir EBee EMan LPio LRHS WCot
'Howardii'

x *Amarine* (*Amaryllidaceae*)
tubergenii | CAvo LPio
- 'Zwanenburg' | EBee EMan WCot

x *Amarygia* (*Amaryllidaceae*)
§ *parkeri* 'Alba' | CAvo EBee ECho EMan LPio MSte
| SSpi WCot

Amaryllis (*Amaryllidaceae*)
§ *belladonna* ♀H2-3 | CBcs CBro CFil CStu EMan EMon
| EPar EPfP LAma LRHS MBri NRog
| SChr SDeJ SDnm SPer SSpi WCot
| WGer
- 'Bloemfontein' | CAvo
- 'Johannesburg' | CAvo EMon LRHS WCot
- 'Kimberley' | EMon
- 'Major' | CAvo
- 'Parkeri Alba' | see x *Amarygia parkeri* 'Alba'
- 'Purpurea' | EBee
- white-flowered | SDnm SSpi WCot
- 'Windhoek' | CAvo

Amelanchier ✿ (*Rosaceae*)
alnifolia | CTho EPla LRHS WBcn
- 'Obelisk' 'PBR | EBee SKee
- pink-fruited | NLar
§ - var. *pumila* | CPle CTho GSki LHop MSte NHol
| NLar SSta WDin WNor
- 'Smokey' | CDul ECrN
* *alpina* | EHyt
arborea | CBcs CPle CTho EGFP LRHS WNor
asiatica **new** | CBcs
bartramiana | CTho LRHS SSta
- 'Eskimo' | NLar
canadensis (L.) Medik. | More than 30 suppliers
x *grandiflora* | CEnd GKir LRHS NHol NLar
'Autumn Brilliance'
- 'Ballerina' ♀H4 | More than 30 suppliers
- 'Cole's Select' | SReu
- 'Princess Diana' | NLar SMad
- 'Robin Hill' | CBcs GKir LBuc LPan LRHS MAsh
| MBlu MGos NLar SBLw SHBN
| SKee SLim SMad WFar
- 'Rubescens' | CDul CEnd GKir LRHS
humilis **new** | CBcs
'La Paloma' | MBri NLar
laevis | CBcs CDul CTri EPfP LRHS MGos
| SKee SPer WGor
- 'Cumulus' **new** | NLar

- 'Prince Charles' **new** | NLar
- 'R.J. Hilton' | MBri MGos MLan
- 'Snow Cloud' | CDoC
- 'Snowflakes' | CEnd CWSG GKir LRHS MAsh
| MDun MGos NPro SKee SLim
| WBVN
lamarckii ♀H4 | More than 30 suppliers
ovalis **new** | CBcs XPep
pumila | see *A. alnifolia* var. *pumila*
rotundifolia 'Edelweiss' | CEnd CPMA GKir MBlu MGos
- 'Helvetia' | CEnd GKir LRHS MAsh WEas
spicata | CPle ECrN GIBF

x *Amelasorbus* (*Rosaceae*)
jackii | MBlu

Amicia (*Papilionaceae*)
zygomeris | CAbb CBot CHEx CHll CMdw
| CPle CPom CSpe EMan EWes
| GBuc GCal SMad SMrm WSHC
| WWye

Ammi (*Apiaceae*)
majus | CArn EMan MSal WEas
visnaga | CArn GPoy LPio MSal

Ammobium (*Asteraceae*)
calyceroides | EMan WCot

Ammocharis (*Amaryllidaceae*)
coranica | WCot

Ammophila (*Poaceae*)
arenaria | CRWN GQui
breviligulata **new** | GBin

Amomum (*Zingiberaceae*)
dealbatum | CKob EUJe LEur MOak
subulatum | CKob EUJe LEur MOak WMul

Amomyrtus (*Myrtaceae*)
§ *luma* | CDoC CTbh CTrG CTri CTrw ELan
| EPfP IDee SArc WBod WFar WJek
| WPic

Amorpha (*Papilionaceae*)
canescens | CBcs CPle EMan IDee NSti SEND
| WBVN WSHC
fruticosa | CBcs CFil CPle EWTr LEdu MBlu
| MGol MNrw SLon SPlb
ouachitensis **new** | NLar

Amorphophallus (*Araceae*)
albus LEur
bulbifer | CKob EAmu EUJe LAma LEur
| LRHS MOak WMul
dunnii | EBee LEur
kerrii | CKob EBee EUJe LEur
konjac | CHEx CKob CStu EUJe ITer LEur
| SSpi
paeoniifolius **new** | CKob
rivieri | EBee GCal LEur WMul
stipitatus | EBee EUJe SSpi
titanum **new** | LAma
yunnanensis | CKob LEur

Ampelocalamus (*Poaceae*)
scandens | CFil EPla WPGP

Ampelodesmos (*Poaceae*)
mauritanica | CBig CBrm CHar CHrt COIW CPen
| EBee ECha EFou EHoe EMan LEdu
| LRav MCCP MWrn NOGN SEND
| SMad SPlb SSvw XPep

Ampelopsis (Vitaceae)

aconitifolia	SBra
brevipedunculata	see *A. glandulosa* var. *brevipedunculata*
chaffanjonii	SMur
§ **glandulosa** var.	CBcs CRHN ELan SCoo SGar SLim
brevipedunculata	SPer WDin WFar
- - f. **citrulloides** B&SWJ 1173	WCru
§ - - 'Elegans' (v)	CBcs CBrm CHEx CMac CRHN CWib EBee EBre ELan EPfP GEil LHop MBar MGos MRav MSwo NBlu SAdn SAga SBra SHBN SPer SPla SWvt WCot WDin WPat WSHC WStI
- - 'Tricolor'	see *A. glandulosa* var. *brevipedunculata* 'Elegans'
- var. **hancei** B&SWJ 3855	WCru
henryana	see *Parthenocissus henryana*
megalophylla	CBcs CBot CFil CHEx EBee ELan EPfP EShb ISea LRHS MBlu NCGa SMHy SPer WBcn WCru WFar WNor WOVN WPGP
sempervirens hort.ex Veitch.	see *Cissus striata*
tricuspidata 'Veitchii'	see *Parthenocissus tricuspidata* 'Veitchii'

Amphicome see *Incarvillea*

Amsonia (Apocynaceae)

ciliata	CFee CFir EBee ECGN ELan LPhx WCot WFar WPer
hubrichtii	CBcs CMdw CPom EBee EGle EMan MGol MSPs NBPC NLar SIgm SMac SMad WHil
illustris	CPom EBee EFou EMan GEil LRHS MSte SMHy WPer WTin
jonesii	EBee SIgm
§ **orientalis**	More than 30 suppliers
tabernaemontana	CFir EBee ECha EGle ELan EMan EWTr GBuc GEil LRHS MNrw MWrn NDov SAga SIgm SMac SMrm SOkh SRms WCot WFar WMoo WOld WPer WPnP WSHC
- var. **salicifolia**	EBee EChP EGle EOrc GKir GSki LPhx LRHS MSte WCAu WTin

Amygdalus see *Prunus*

Anacamptis (Orchidaceae)

laxiflora	see *Orchis laxiflora*
pyramidalis	CHdy EFEx WHer

Anacyclus (Asteraceae)

pyrethrum	GPoy WShp
- var. **depressus**	CTri EBre ECtt EDAr ELan EMlt EPfP GKir GTou IHMM LRHS MSte NBlu NFor NLAp NScw NVic NWCA SBla SIng SPet SPlb WCFE WFar WHoo WPer WWin
- - 'Garden Gnome'	CTri NJOw NPri SRms

Anadenanthera (Mimosaceae)

colubrina	MGol

Anagallis (Primulaceae)

arvensis	MHer MSal WHbs
foemina	MSal
linifolia	see *A. monellii* subsp. *linifolia*
§ **monellii** ♀H4	CNic SAga SBla WWin
- subsp. **linifolia**	EHyt
- - 'Blue Light' **new**	CSpe

- 'Sunrise'	CPBP EHyt LAst SBla SUsu
'Skylover'	EMan LAst MLan SMrm SPet
tenella	SIng
- 'Studland'	CWCL EDAr EMlt NJOw NMen NSla NWCA SBla SIng WAbe WHoo

Anagyris (Leguminosae)

foetida **new**	XPep

Ananas (Bromeliaceae)

comosus (F)	CKob LRHS
- var. **variegatus** (v)	CKob MBri SMur

Anaphalis (Asteraceae)

CC 3725	WCot
alpicola	EPot NMen
margaritacea	COlW CSBt ECha ECtt EWTr GBin GGar IHMM ITer MBri MLLN NBid NOak SMer SRms WFar WMoo
§ - var. **cinnamomea**	EMon WEas
§ - 'Neuschnee'	CTri EBee GKir LBBr MWgw NArg NBPC NGdn NMir NPri SPla WBea WPer
- New Snow	see *A. margaritacea* 'Neuschnee'
§ - var. **yedoensis** ♀H4	CBre CTri EBee ECot EFou EGle MWat SDix WBrE WTin
§ **nepalensis** var. **monocephala**	ELan EMon MWat NSti WCAu
nubigena	see *A. nepalensis* var. *monocephala*
sinica 'Moon's Silver'	WCot
transnokoensis **new**	EWes
§ **trinervis**	NJOw
triplinervis ♀H4	More than 30 suppliers
- CC 1620	WCot
- dwarf	WShp
§ - 'Sommerschnee' ♀H4	CSLe EBee EBre EChP ECha ECot ECtt EFou EGle EPfP ERou LRHS MBri MTis NFor SAga SChu SPer WBea WMnd WPer
- Summer Snow	see *A. triplinervis* 'Sommerschnee'

Anarrhinum (Scrophulariaceae)

bellidifolium	SPet

Anchusa (Boraginaceae)

angustissima	see *A. leptophylla* subsp. *incana*
§ **azurea**	GKir IHMM MGol MWrn WPer WWeb XPep
- 'Blue Angel'	EBee IBal LRHS NJOw WWeb
- 'Dropmore'	CTri EBee ELan EMar EPfP EWTr GFlt LAst LRHS MAnH MEHN MGol MWgw NOrc NPer SRms SSth WBry WPer WShp
- 'Feltham Pride'	CMdw CSBt EBre EWTr GKir MAnH MSte NBPC NPri SRms SWvt WFar WHil WHoo WPGP WPer WWeb WWhi
- 'Little John'	COtt EBee ECot ERou SAga SRms WTel
- 'Loddon Royalist' ♀H4	More than 30 suppliers
- 'Opal'	EBee ECGP EChP ECot EMan EPfP ERou LRHS MNFA MWat NCGa SChu SMrm SPla WCAu
- 'Royal Blue'	LRHS
caespitosa hort.	see *A. leptophylla* subsp. *incana*
capensis	CTCP LAst WHil
cespitosa Lam.	ECho EHyt ELan EWes SBla SIng
italica	see *A. azurea*
laxiflora	see *Borago pygmaea*
leptophylla subsp. **incana**	EBee LRHS MSph
- - F&W 9550	MDKP
myosotidiflora	see *Brunnera macrophylla*

officinalis — CArn LRHS MGol MSal WHil
sempervirens — see *Pentaglottis sempervirens*
undulata — SIgm

Ancrumia (Alliaceae)

cuspidata F&W 8233 — WCot

Ancylostemon (Gesneriaceae)

convexus — WCru
  B&SWJ 6624 **new**

Andrachne (Euphorbiaceae)

colchica — EMan WCot

Andromeda (Ericaceae)

glaucophylla — MBar WDin
polifolia — CMHG EMil EPot GCrs GKir NJOw
  WDin WFar
- 'Alba' — EBee ELan GEdr GKir LRHS MAsh
  MBar MBro MRav NHol NRya SBod
  SPer SPlb SWvt WFar WPat WWin
- 'Blue Ice' — CWib ELan EPfP EPot GKir LRHS
  MAsh NMen SPer SSpi WAbe WFar
  WPat
- 'Compacta' ♀H4 — CDoC CWib EBee EHoe EMil GCrs
  GKir LRHS MBar MBri NHol NLRH
  NMen SRms SWvt WGwG WPat
  WSHC WWin
- 'Grandiflora' — ELan GKir ITim LRHS MAsh MBri
  SBod SPer
- 'Hayachine' — EPot
- 'Kirigamine' — GKir LRHS MAsh MBri NHol WPat
- 'Macrophylla' ♀H4 — GEdr ITim MBro NDlv NHol WAbe
  WPat
- 'Nana' — CSBt ELan EPfP GEil GKir LRHS
  MAsh NMen STre WStI
- 'Nikko' — CWib ITim NHol WPat
- 'Shibutsu' — NMen

Andropogon (Poaceae)

gerardii — CBig CBrm CKno CPen CRWN
  CWCL EBee EBre ECGN EHoe
  EHul EMan EPPr EPla EPza LPhx
  LRav MAnH MWhi SMad WDyG
  WWpP
hallii hybrid — EPPr
ischaemum — see *Bothriochloa ischaemum*
saccharoides — EBee
scoparius — see *Schizachyrium scoparium*
virginicus — CBig CBrm LPhx

Androsace (Primulaceae)

albana — ITim
alpina — SPlb
axillaris ACE 1060 — EHyt
baltistanica — CGra EHyt GCrs
barbulata — EPot
bulleyana — CStu WLin WPat
carnea — CPBP EBre SIng WWin
- *alba* — LRHS NWCA WLin
- subsp. *brigantiaca* — GCrs GTou ITim MBro NJOw NSla
  WAbe WHoo
- var. *halleri* — see *A. carnea* subsp. *rosea*
- subsp. *laggeri* ♀H4 — ECho GCrs GTou LTwo NSla
  NWCA SIng WAbe
§ - subsp. *rosea* ♀H4 — CPBP
carnea x *pyrenaica* — ITim NMen SOkd WAbe
chaixii — ITim
chamaejasme — ECho
ciliata — GCrs GTou ITim NSla
cylindrica — CGra CPBP EPot GCrs GTou ITim
  LRHS NMen WAbe WFar WPat
- 'Val d'Ossue' — EPot
cylindrica x *hirtella* — CGra EPot GTou ITim LRHS WAbe

- x - ENF **new** — WAbe
dasyphylla **new** — WLin
delavayi — WAbe
geraniifolia — CPLG EBee ECha LHop WAbe
  WCru
globifera — CGra CPBP EHyt EPot GKev ITim
  NMen WAbe
hausmannii — GTou ITim
hedraeantha — CLyd ITim MWat NMen SIng WAbe
x *heeri* pink — CGra
- white — SBla
himalaica — CNic CPBP EHyt EPot
hirtella — ETow GTou ITim NMen
idahoensis — CGra WAbe
jacquemontii — see *A. villosa* var. *jacquemontii*
* *kochii tauricola* — ITim
lactea — CNic GCrs GTou ITim WAbe
§ *laevigata* — CGra CNic EHyt GCrs NMen WAbe
- var. *ciliolata* — GTou SIng WLin
- from Columbia River — EHyt
  Gorge, USA **new**
- 'Gothenburg' — EHyt WPat
lanuginosa ♀H4 — CLyd CMea CPlt EHyt EPot GCrs
  GEdr MBro MWat NMen NWCA
  SBla SIng SRms WAbe WWin
- compact — EPot SScr
- 'Wisley Variety' — SIgm
lehmannii — WLin
limprichtii — see *A. sarmentosa* var. *watkinsii*
x *marpensis* — EPot WAbe
mathildae — EHyt GTou ITim NMen NWCA
  WAbe
microphylla — see *A. mucronifolia* Watt
'Millstream' **new** — EHyt
§ *mollis* — CPBP SIgm SIng WCom
§ *montana* — NWCA
mucronifolia hort. — see *A. sempervivoides*
§ *mucronifolia* G. Watt — EHyt EPot GTou NJOw
- Schacht's form **new** — EHyt
mucronifolia — EHyt EPot NJOw WOBN
  x *sempervivoides*
muscoidea — EPot WAbe
- C&R 188 — GTou
- 'Breviscapa' — EPot
- f. *longiscapa* — CGra ITim NWCA
- Schacht's form — EHyt GCrs SBla SIgm
§ *nivalis* — EHyt
- var. *dentata* **new** — EHyt
pavlovskyi **new** — WLin
x *pedemontana* — ITim
primuloides — see *A. studiosorum*
pubescens — CGra ITim LRHS LTwo NMen
  WAbe
pyrenaica — CGra EHyt GTou ITim LRHS NMen
  NWCA SIng WAbe
rigida KGB 168 — EPot
robusta — GCrs
* - subsp. *purpurea* — SIgm WAbe
rotundifolia — GTou WCru
sarmentosa misapplied — see *A. studiosorum*
sarmentosa Wall. — EDAr EHyt ELan GTou MBro MWat
  NMen NSla SRms WCom WHoo
  WTel
- CC 2627 — WOBN
- CC 407 — LRHS
- 'Chumbyi' — see *A. studiosorum* 'Chumbyi'
- from Namche, Nepal — EHyt WAbe
- 'Salmon's Variety' — see *A. studiosorum* 'Salmon's
  Variety'
- 'Sherriffii' — CFee EPot GEdr MOne NLAp SIgm
  SRms WLin WWin
§ - var. *watkinsii* — EPot NMen
- var. *yunnanensis* — see *A. studiosorum*
  misapplied

- var. *yunnanensis* Knuth	see *A. mollis*
selago	WAbe
§ *sempervivoides* ♀H4	CLyd CMea ECha EDAr EHyt ELan
	EPot GKev LHop LRHS MBro NDlv
	NHol NLAp NMen NWCA SBla
	SIgm SIng SRms WCom WHoo
	WLin WPat WRHF WWin
- dark	ITim
- 'Greystone'	EPot
- scented	CWCL
- 'Susan Joan' (v)	CPBP EHyt WAbe
septentrionalis 'Stardust'	CBrm ECho NJOw
sericea	EHyt
spinulifera	GKev NLAp WPat
strigillosa	GCrs WAbe
§ *studiosorum* ♀H4	CWCL NLAp
- 'Brilliant'	CNic
- 'Chumbyi'	EHol ETow GEdr LTwo MBro
	MOne NHol NWCA SBla SIng
	SRms WOBN WPat
- 'Doksa'	EHyt EPot GCrs NMen SOkd WAbe
§ - 'Salmon's Variety'	CMea CTri ECho NRya SIgm WAbe
sublanata	WAbe
tapete	WAbe
– ACE 1725	EPot
vandellii	CGra EPot GTou ITim NSla WAbe
villosa	WLin
- var. *arachnoidea*	EHyt
- - 'Superba'	NMen
- var. *congesta*	CGra EHyt
§ - var. *jacquemontii*	ETow GCrs NMen SBla SIgm WLin
- - lilac	CPBP EPot WAbe
- - pink	EPot NLAp WAbe
- subsp. *taurica*	CLyd EHyt
vitaliana	see *Vitaliana primuliflora*
watkinsii	see *A. sarmentosa* var. *watkinsii*
yargongensis ACE 1722	EPot
zambalensis **new**	WAbe

Andryala (*Asteraceae*)

agardhii	NJOw WPat
lanata	see *Hieracium lanatum*

Anemanthele see *Stipa*

lessoniana	see *Stipa arundinacea*

Anemarrhena (*Anthericaceae*)

asphodeloides	MSal WCot

Anemone ✿ (*Ranunculaceae*)

B&SWJ 1452	WCru
aconitifolia ambig.	CSpe
aconitifolia Michx.	see *A. narcissiflora*
afghanica **new**	EBre
altaica	GAbr MSal SRms
amurensis	EBee
apennina ♀H4	CAvo CBos CLAP EBee ECha EPar
	IBlr SCro WTin
- var. *albiflora*	CDes CFwr CLAP EBee ECha EPot
	ERos IBlr LPhx LRHS MSte WCot
	WPGP WPnP
- 'Ballyrogan Park' **new**	IBlr
- double	ECha IBlr SBla
- 'Petrovac'	CDes CLAP IBlr
- - C&H 538	EBee LRHS WCot
baicalensis	EWll NSti WLin
baldensis	CTCP ECho EPyc GAbr GKir LBee
	LRHS NBur NMen NOak NWCA
	SRms WCom
barbulata	CLAP EBee EChP EMan GBuc
	LPhx MWrn NLar
blanda ♀H4	CBri EOrc GBBs GKir LAma MBri
	NBlu NChi NRog SChu WBea
	WCom WFar WPer WShi

- blue	CAvo CBri CBro CMea CPLG CTri
	ELan EPar EPot GAbr GKir LAma
	LRHS MBri SMrm SRms WBVN
	WFar
- 'Blue Shades'	CFwr ECho EMar EPfP GEdr IGor
	LPhx LRHS SPer WBrE WHil WPGP
- 'Charmer'	EPar EPot MBNS MNrw NMen
- 'Ingramii' CE&H 626	EPar LAma NRog WCot
- 'Pink Shades' **new**	SPer
- 'Pink Star'	CBro EPot LAma LRHS MBNS NBir
	NRog WHil
- 'Radar' ♀H4	CBro CDes CLAP CMea ECho EPar
	EPot LAma MNrw NBir NMen
	NRog SVal
- var. *rosea* ♀H4	CAvo CFwr CNic ECho ELan EPfP
	LAma MLLN WFar WPer
- 'Violet Star'	CFwr EPot LPhx LRHS MMil WCot
- 'White Splendour' ♀H4	More than 30 suppliers
canadensis	CHar CNic CSpe CTCP EBee EBre
	GBBs GBuc GKir MBrN MNrw
	MSte MWrn NBur NWoo WBVN
	WCot WLin WRos
caroliniana	CLyd EBre EMFP ESis GBuc GCrs
	GKir LRHS NOak WCru
caucasica	SBla SCnR
chapaensis	WCru
HWJ 631 **new**	
coronaria	CTri EPfP LAma LHop NRog SPer
De Caen Group	WFar
- - 'Die Braut'	GFlt LPhx NMyG NRog SPer WFar
	WRHF
- - 'His Excellency'	see *A. coronaria* (De Caen Group)
	'Hollandia'
§ - - 'Hollandia'	SPer
- - 'Mister Fokker'	GFlt LAma LPhx NRog SPer WFar
- - The Bride	see *A. coronaria* (De Caen Group)
	'Die Braut'
- - 'The Governor'	NRog SPer WFar
- 'Jerusalem'	WFar
- Saint Bridgid Group (d)	CTri EPfP LAma MBri NRog SDeJ
	SPet WFar
- - 'Lord Lieutenant' (d)	LPhx NBir NBur NRog SPer WFar
- - 'Mount Everest' (d)	GFlt NBir SPer
- - 'The Admiral' (d)	LPhx NBir NRog SPer WFar WHil
- Saint Piran Group	SDeJ
- 'Sylphide'	LPhx NBir NRog SPer WFar
(Mona Lisa Series)	
crinita	EBee GBuc WBVN WLin
cylindrica	CFir CMHG CTCP EBee EBlw
	EChP MDKP MNrw NLar
davidii	EBee
- B&SWJ 7508	WCru
decapetala	GCal WBVN WLin
demissa	CTCP EBee EMan GBuc NRya
dichotoma	EBee
drummondii	CCge CLyd CTCP EBee EBre EChP
	EMan GSki LRHS MBrN NBur NChi
	WBVN WWeb
elongata B&SWJ 2975	WCru
eranthoides	CLAP EBee
fasciculata	see *A. narcissiflora*
flaccida	CBro CDes CLAP CMea EBee EHrv
	GBuc GMac LPhx LRHS MSte
	WCot WCru WFar WWhi
x *fulgens*	ECha SAga SIgm SVal
- 'Annulata Grandiflora'	ECGP
- 'Multipetala'	GEdr NRog
- Saint Bavo Group	ECGP
globosa	see *A. multifida*
'Guernica'	ECho GBuc MOne SRot
'Hatakeyama Double' (d)	CDes GCal
'Hatakeyama Single'	CDes GCal
hepatica	see *Hepatica nobilis*
§ *hortensis*	LPhx SBla WHil

- subsp. *heldreichii*	CDes SAga SCnR
§ *hupehensis*	CBos EBee EWll GBBs GKir LRHS NOrc SVal WFar
- BWJ 8190	WCru
- f. *alba*	CDes CMil EBee WPGP
§ - 'Bowles' Pink' ♀H4	CMil CStr EBee EGle EPPr MBri MBro MWat NPPs WBrk WCru WHoo WPGP WTin WWhi
- 'Crispa'	see *A.* x *hybrida* 'Lady Gilmour'
- 'Eugenie'	CMil CStr CWCL EBee EChP EMan GBuc GSki LRHS MBNS NBir WWeb
- 'Hadspen Abundance' ♀H4	More than 30 suppliers
§ - var. *japonica*	CBos CPou GCal NFor WEas
- - B&SWJ 4886	WCru
- - 'Bodnant Burgundy'	CDes CPen CPrp EBee EChP ECtt EGle EMan IPot LRHS MBri MCCP WCAu WHil WPnP
§ - - 'Bressingham Glow'	More than 30 suppliers
§ - - 'Pamina' ♀H4	More than 30 suppliers
- - Prince Henry	see *A. hupehensis* var. *japonica* 'Prinz Heinrich'
§ - - 'Prinz Heinrich' ♀H4	More than 30 suppliers
§ - - 'Rotkäppchen'	CPar EBee EMan EMar EWTr MRav NBur NPro NSti SLon WAul WBrk WRHF WWeb
- 'Praecox'	CBot CKno CMea EBee EBlw EHrv EPfP GBri GBuc GSki LRHS MAvo MBNS MBri MWgw NBir NGdn NPri NSti SCro SWvt WAbb WCru WHal WMnd WPnP WWeb WWin
- 'September Charm'	see *A.* x *hybrida* 'September Charm'
- 'Splendens'	CMHG COlW EBee EMan ENot GBBs GBuc LAst LHop LRHS SPer SWal SWvt WAbb WBro WFar WHal WShp
- 'Superba'	EBee WKif
§ x *hybrida*	EPar MWrn NChi NOak SChu SGar WCru WFar WMoo WRHF WWpP
- 'Alba' hort. (UK)	see *A.* x *hybrida* 'Honorine Jobert'
- 'Andrea Atkinson'	CPrp EChP EMan EPfP GBBs GBuc GSki LAst LGro LPVe LRHS MBri MCLN MNFA NBid NGdn NPSI NSti SChu SMrm SPla WBrk WCot WCra WFar WHil WHoo WMnd WMoo
- 'Bowles' Pink'	see *A. hupehensis* 'Bowles' Pink'
- 'Bressingham Glow'	see *A. hupehensis* var. *japonica* 'Bressingham Glow'
- 'Coupe d'Argent'	EBee
§ - 'Elegans' ♀H4	CWCL EBee EFou EMan ERou GFlt MBnl MDKP MLLN MRav NBir SWat WBcn WCAu WCru WHil WHoo
§ - 'Géante des Blanches'	CBos CHar CMil CStr EBee EBre GKir GMac LRHS MAnH MSph NPPs SHop SMrm WFar WHoo
§ - 'Honorine Jobert' ♀H4	More than 30 suppliers
§ - 'Königin Charlotte' ♀H4	More than 30 suppliers
- 'Kriemhilde'	GCal GMac
§ - 'Lady Gilmour' Wolley-Dod	CElw CFai CSpe EBee EBre EChP ECtt EGle EHol EHrv EPfP GCal GKir GMac LRHS MAnH MCCP MRav NBir NChi NGdn SAga SOkh WBro WCAu WCot WCru WFar WHil WPnP
- 'Lady Gilmour' misapplied	see *A.* x *hybrida* 'Margarete'
- 'Loreley'	CM&M CMea CPrp EBee EChP EMan GBuc IPot LPVe MBNS MBnl MSte MWat NPSI NSti SMrm WHil WWpP
- 'Luise Uhink'	CPou LRHS MDKP NBir SSpi WEas
- 'Margarete' Kayser & Seibert **new**	LRHS
- 'Max Vogel'	see *A.* x *hybrida* 'Elegans'
- 'Monterosa'	see *A.* x *hybrida* 'Margarete'
- 'Montrose'	CMil CPLG CPar CPou EBre EChP EFou EHrv EWTr EWes GCal GKir LRHS NBir SChu SCro SMrm SRms STes SWat WCot WCru WFar WHoo WPnP
- 'Pamina'	see *A. hupehensis* var. *japonica* 'Pamina'
- Prince Henry	see *A. hupehensis* var. *japonica* 'Prinz Heinrich'
- 'Prinz Heinrich'	see *A. hupehensis* var. *japonica* 'Prinz Heinrich'
- 'Profusion'	CTri LBuc LRHS MLan MBlu SHBN
- Queen Charlotte	see *A.* x *hybrida* 'Königin Charlotte'
- 'Richard Ahrens'	CDoC EChP ECtt EGle ERou GBuc GKir LHop LRHS MAvo MNFA NDov NOrc SAga SMrm SPla SWat WBro WCru WFar WLin WMnd WPnP WWeb
- 'Robustissima'	CSpe EBee EChP ECtt EGra ENot EPfP ERou IHMH LRHS MBri MRav MSte MWgw NBir NBlu NPri NSti SHBN SPer SPla SWat SWvt WAbb WAul WFar WMnd WMoo WShp
- 'Rosenschale'	CBos CFwr EBee EBre EGle GCal LRHS MBri NCGa WCru WFar
- 'Rotkäppchen'	see *A. hupehensis* var. *japonica* 'Rotkäppchen'
§ - 'September Charm' ♀H4	More than 30 suppliers
- 'Serenade'	CPar EBee EBlw EBre ECtt EFou EGle EMan ENot EPfP ERou GBBs LPVe LRHS MBri NBPC NBir NPSI SHBN SSvw SVil WAul WCAu WCot WFar WHil WMoo
- 'Terry's Pink'	WCot
- Tourbillon	see *A.* x *hybrida* 'Whirlwind'
§ - 'Whirlwind'	More than 30 suppliers
- 'White Queen'	see *A.* x *hybrida* 'Géante des Blanches'
- Wirbelwind	see *A.* x *hybrida* 'Whirlwind'
japonica	see *A.* x *hybrida*, *A. hupehensis*
keiskeana **new**	WCru
x *lesseri*	CBro CFir CLyd CSpe EChP ECha ECtt EDAr EHrv ELan ESis GBBs MBro MHer MRav NChi NMen NSti SBla SGar SOkh SRms WAul WBVN WCom WCru WFar WHoo WPat WWin
leveillei	More than 30 suppliers
§ x *lipsiensis*	More than 30 suppliers
- 'Pallida' ♀H4	CBos CHad CPlt EBee ECho ERos GBuc GCrs GEdr GKev MAvo MNFA NPar WCot
lyallii	EBee EPPr GBuc
N *magellanica* hort. ex Wehrh.	see *A. multifida*
mexicana B&SWJ 8414	WCru
multifida misapplied red	see *A.* x *lesseri*
§ *multifida*	More than 30 suppliers
- JCA 2050.5	SBla
- 'Major'	CFir CHar CLyd CMea LAst LPhx LRHS MBNS NPro SAga SBla SMac WBVN WCFE WCom WMoo WPnP
- pink	GBuc WSan
* - 'Rubra'	CPLG EHrv EWll GBuc GGar LAst LPhx LRHS MBNS MNrw NBir NDlv NWCA SMad SPet WWeb
§ *narcissiflora*	EBee ECGP GBuc GKir NChi SVal WCom

*	– *citrina*	SBla
	nemorosa ♀H4	More than 30 suppliers
N	– 'Alba Plena' (d)	CBro CHea CSWP CSam EBee EBlw ECha EPPr ERos ETow GBuc GGar GMac LRHS MTho NMen SIng SUsu WAbb WCot WCru WEas WFar WHil WLin WPnP
	– 'Allenii' ♀H4	CBro CHea CLAP CSpe ECha EHyt EPar ERos GEdr GKir ITim LPhx MAvo MLwd MNFA MRav NMen NPar NRya SIgm SIng SMac SSpi WCom WCot WCru WHil WPGP WPnP
	– 'Atrocaerulea'	CLAP EBee EPar GBuc IBlr NHol NLar WCru
	– 'Bill Baker's Pink'	CDes CLAP
	– 'Blue Beauty'	CLAP EBee EGle EPot ERos ETow GBuc IBlr MAvo MNFA MNrw NMen SSpi WCru
	– 'Blue Bonnet'	CElw CStu EBee ECho GBuc ITim MAvo MNrw WCot
	– 'Blue Eyes' (d)	CDes CLAP EGle ETow GBuc GCrs IBlr MAvo MSte SBla SIgm WCot WCru WPGP
	– 'Blue Queen'	CStu GBuc
	– 'Bowles' Purple'	CBos CStu EBee EPPr EPar EPot ETow GBuc GMac IBlr MNFA MNrw NDov NGar NMyG NRya SIgm SIng WBor WCot WCru WFar WIvy WPGP WTin
	– 'Bracteata'	CAvo EBee EHrv ERos GEdr NDov
	– 'Bracteata Pleniflora' (d)	CLAP CStu EBee ECha EGle GBuc IBlr LHop MAvo MBro MNFA MNrw NBir NGar WBor WCot WCru WFar
	– 'Buckland'	CDes CLAP ECha EHrv IBlr WCru
	– 'Cedric's Pink'	CLAP EPPr ERos IBlr MNrw WCru
	– 'Celestial'	GBuc
	– 'Danica'	EBee
	– 'Dee Day'	CLAP EBee EHrv EPPr GBuc MAvo MNrw NGar WCru
	– 'Flore Pleno' (d)	EBee EBre EHyt EOrc EPar GBBs GKir MBro NBir NGar NMen WPGP
	– 'Green Fingers'	CDes CLAP EBee ECho EHrv EPPr EPot GBuc GEdr ITim LPhx MNrw NGby NPar SCnR WCot WCru WIvy
	– 'Hannah Gubbay'	CLAP EBee EGle EPar GBuc IBlr MNrw MSte SSpi
	– 'Hilda'	CLAP EBee EGle EPar EPot ERos ETow GBuc MNFA MNrw NDlv NDov NGar NMen NRya NSla SSpi WCru
	– 'Jack Brownless'	IBlr
	– 'Kentish Pink'	GBBs GBuc GCrs
	– 'Knightshayes Vestal' (d)	CLAP GMac MAvo MRav WCot WCru WIvy
	– 'Lady Doneraile'	CDes CLAP EBee ECha ETow GBuc NBir NPar WCru WFar
	– 'Leeds' Variety'	EBee EGle GCrs ITim LPhx MNrw MTho NBrk NHol NSla SBla WCot
	– 'Lismore Blue'	EBee EPot
§	– 'Lismore Pink'	EHrv GEdr
	– 'Lychette'	EBee ECha EGle EHrv EPar GBuc IBlr ITim LPhx NDov NSla NWCA WCru
	– 'Martin' **new**	CStu
	– 'Merlin'	WCot
	– 'Monstrosa'	EBee EPar EPot GBuc WCot
	– 'New Pink'	CLAP IBlr
	– 'Parlez Vous'	CMil EGle EHrv EPPr MNrw NGar WCru
	– 'Pentre Pink'	IBlr MNrw MTho WBVN WCru WIvy
	– 'Picos Pink'	EHrv
	– pink	CLAP CPlt LPhx WCru
	– 'Pink Carpet' **new**	GBuc GEdr
	– x *ranunculoides*	see *A.* x *lipsiensis*
	– 'Robinsoniana' ♀H4	More than 30 suppliers
	– 'Rosea'	CAvo CLAP GEdr GMac MNFA WCru
	– 'Royal Blue'	CAvo CLAP CMil CNic CStu EBee ECha EHrv EPPr EPar EPot ETow GBuc GEdr GMac LAma MNFA NDov NGar NHol NMen SBla WCot WCru WFar WPnP WTin SSpi
	– 'Tinney's Blush'	SSpi
	– 'Tinney's Double' (d)	NPar
	– 'Tomas'	CDes EBee GMac
	– 'Vestal' (d) ♀H4	More than 30 suppliers
	– 'Virescens' ♀H4	CAvo CLAP CStu EChP ECha EGle EHrv EPPr EPot ERos GCrs GEdr MNFA NGar NPar NSla SIng WIvy WLin WPGP
	– 'Viridiflora'	CLAP EBee GBuc LHop LPhx MNrw MRav MTed MTho NBir NSti SSpi WCot WCru WFar WSHC
	– 'Westwell Pink'	CDes EBee MSte SIgm WCot WPGP
	– 'Wilks' Giant'	EBee WCot WCru
	– 'Wilks' White'	CLAP EBee EGle EPar GEdr LBuc WCru
	– 'Wyatt's Pink'	CLAP GBuc LPhx MAvo WCru WPnP WTin
	– 'Yerda Ramusem'	ECho
	obtusiloba	CLAP GBuc GCrs GTou IMGH LEur MTho SBla SRms WLin
	– CLD 1549	GEdr
	– J&JA 4.044.010	NWCA
	– *alba*	GMac LEur SBla
	– var. *polysepala* **new**	GEdr
I	– 'Sulphurea' **new**	GEdr
	– yellow	GBuc LEur SBla
	palmata	CLAP EPot MDKP SSpi WBVN WCru
	parviflora	CHea GBuc
	pavonina	CSpe ECha ERos MAsh MTho SBla SIgm SRot SVal
	– 'Chapeau de Napoléon'	SBla
	– 'Grecian Sunset'	MAsh
	polyanthes	EBee EBre GTou LRHS
	aff. *polyanthes* ex ACE	SIgm
	prattii	EBee
	protracta	EBee
	pseudoaltaica	NGar WCru
	– pale blue-flowered **new**	CLAP
	pulsatilla	see *Pulsatilla vulgaris*
	raddeana	EBee
	ranunculoides ♀H4	More than 30 suppliers
	– 'Frank Waley'	WCot
*	– *laciniata*	CLAP GBuc MSte NGar
	– 'Pleniflora' (d)	CBgR CFwr CHea CLAP ECha EHrv EHyt EPar EPot MRav NGar NLar NMen SBla WCot WFar WIvy
	– subsp. *wockeana*	CBgR CDes CFwr EBee LPhx
	richardsonii	CPla
	riparia	see *A. virginiana* var. *alba*
	rivularis	More than 30 suppliers
	– B&SWJ 7611	WCru
	– CLD 573	CDes WLin
	rossii	EBee
	rupicola	GMac NBir NWCA SRot SSpi
	x *seemannii*	see *A.* x *lipsiensis*
	sibirica	EBee
	smithiana	EBee
	stellata	see *A. hortensis*

subpinnata **new**	EBee
sulphurea	see *Pulsatilla alpina* subsp. *apiifolia*
sylvestris	More than 30 suppliers
§ - 'Elise Fellmann' (d)	CDes CLAP EBee EMan GBuc LPhx MTed SHar WCot
- 'Flore Pleno'	see *A. sylvestris* 'Elise Fellmann'
- 'Macrantha'	CLAP CPen CPrp EBee EChP EMan EPfP GMac LAst NBid SMrm SSpi WBor WPGP
'Taiwan's Tiny Treasure' **new**	WCru
tetrasepala	CDes CLAP EBee WPGP
§ *tomentosa*	EBee ECha EMan EMar GGar GSki LRHS SCro SDix SRms SWat WFar WGwG WRha
§ - 'Albadura'	EBee EPza GSki
- 'Robustissima'	see *A.* x *hybrida* 'Robustissima'
trifolia	CBos CTCP EBee ECha EHyt EMan EPPr EPot ERos GMac NDov NGar NMen SCnR SCro SRms SSpi SUsu WCot WPGP
- pink	CDes CLAP MSte WFar
- 'Semiplena' (d)	CDes EBee WCot
trullifolia	EPfP ETow GCrs GMac ITim MTis SBla
- *alba*	GBBs GGar GTou
- blue	CDes GBBs GBuc GTou NBir
- *coelestina*	EBee
vernalis	see *Pulsatilla vernalis*
virginiana	CBri CCge CFir EWll LDai MDKP MFOX MSte MTed MWrn NBid NBur NChi WBVN WFar WOut
§ - var. *alba*	EBee NBPC NLar NSti SHar WBVN
vitifolia misapplied.	see *A. tomentosa*
vitifolia DC. B&SWJ 2320	WCru
- HWJ 682	WCru

Anemonella (Ranunculaceae)

thalictroides	CFir CLAP EChP EFEx EHrv EHyt EMan EPar EPot GEdr GFlt GGar GSki ITim LAma LEur NGar NMen NRya SBla SMHy WAbe WCru WFar WPrP
- 'Alba Plena' (d)	GBuc
- 'Amelia'	GEdr NPar SOkd WAbe
- 'Betty Blake' (d)	MS&S
- 'Cameo'	EFEx
- 'Double Green' (d)	EFEx
- 'Full Double White'	CWCL EFEx
- 'Green Hurricane'	EFEx
- f. *rosea*	CElw CLAP CPom CWCL EPar EPot GBuc LEur
- - double pink (d)	SBla
- - 'Oscar Schoaff' (d)	CLAP WAbe
- semi-double pink (d)	CLAP
- semi-double white (d)	CLAP EPar ETow GBuc SBla SRot WCot
- 'Snowball' **new**	CGra
- 'Snowflakes' (d)	NPar

Anemonopsis (Ranunculaceae)

macrophylla	CBro CLAP CPlt EMan EPPr ETow GBuc GCal LEur LPhx LRHS MNrw MSte MTed MTho NLar SBla SOkd SSpi WCru WSHC

Anemopsis (Saururaceae)

californica	EMan NLar WCru

Anethum (Apiaceae)

graveolens	CArn CHrt GPoy LRHS MBow MHer NBlu SECG SIde SWal WPer WSel WShp

- 'Bouquet'	NPri
- 'Dukat'	CSev ELau NGHP
- 'Fern Leaved'	CBod EOHP WHHs WJek

Angelica (Apiaceae)

PC&H 129	WBry
acutiloba	SIgm WCot
archangelica	More than 30 suppliers
- 'Corinne Tremaine' (v)	EMan GBri NGHP NSti WBry WCHb WCot WHil WWpP
arguta	EBee WCot
atropurpurea	CPom EChP ECtt EMan EMar EWll EWsh ITer LEdu MHer MNrw NBur NGHP NLar NSti SWat WCAu WCHb WFar WJek WMnd
dahurica	CArn EBee
- B&SWJ 8603	WCru
decursiva	EBee LPio
- B&SWJ 5746	WCru
florentii	EBee GIBF
gigas	More than 30 suppliers
- B&SWJ 4170	WCru
- 'Gold Leaf'	EBee
grayi	EBee WCot
* *hispanica*	CArn CBod CBri CHid CSpe EBee EChP ELan EMFP EMar EPyc EWll GBar GKir LEdu LPhx MCCP MHer MLLN NBir NGHP SIde SMad WBry WCHb WCru WHHs WLin WSHC
japonica B&SWJ 8816a **new**	WCru
keiskei B&SWJ 7086 **new**	WCru
- B&SWJ 8816b	WCru
linearilobа	WLin
montana	see *A. sylvestris*
pachycarpa	CBct EBee EChP ELan EMan EOHP LPio MAvo NCGa NChi SCro SIgm SMad SWat WCot WFar WJek WPer WWye
paniculata	see *Trochiscanthes nodiflora*
polymorpha **new**	WCom
pubescens	CTCP MSte
- B&SWJ 5593	WCru
- var. *matsumurae* B&SWJ 6387	WCru
razulii	EBee
sachalinensis	EBee GIBF
saxatilis	EBee GIBF
sinensis	EBee GPoy WCHb
'Summer Delight'	CSpe EMFP EMan ITim MDKP MSPs SPoG WWpP
§ *sylvestris*	CAgr CArn CRWN GBar NSco WCHb WHer WWpP
- 'Purpurea'	see *A. sylvestris* 'Vicar's Mead'
§ - 'Vicar's Mead'	CMil CSpe EBee EWes GKir IBlr LPhx NCGa NChi SBla SDnm SUsu WGMN WHil WPGP WSHC
taiwaniana	EBee ELan LPhx SWat WCot WOut
ursina	EBee GIBF NBPC

angelica see *Angelica archangelica*

Angelonia (Scrophulariaceae)

'Angelface Blue Bi-Colour' (Angelface Series) **new**	LAst
angustifolia	NPri
Angel Mist White = 'Balangwhit' **new**	
- Angel Mist Lavender Pink = 'Balanglapi' **new**	NPri
- Angel Mist Purple Stripe **new**	NBlu NPri
'Stella Gem'	LRHS SMrm

Anigozanthos (*Haemodoraceae*)

flavidus	CBcs CTrC EBee ECre EOHP EPAt MBri SPlb WCot WDyG
- 'Ember' **new**	SVil
- 'Illusion' **new**	SVil
- 'Opal' **new**	SPoG SVil
- 'Pearl' **new**	SPoG SVil
- 'Splendour' **new**	SPoG SVil
- yellow	WBrE
manglesii ♀H1	CHEx GGar SPlb WBrE

anise see *Pimpinella anisum*

Anisodontea (*Malvaceae*)

§ *capensis*	CBcs CPLG EBee EChP ELan EMan ERea GGar GKir LAst MBNS NBir SChu SLim SMrm SOWG SRms SVen SWvt WDyG XPep
- 'Tara's Pink'	EPfP LPhx MAsh MBNS SAga SMrm
elegans	CSpe SAga
'Elegant Lady' **new**	GFai
huegelii	see *Alyogyne huegelii*
x *hypomadara* misapplied	see *A. capensis*
§ x *hypomadara* (Sprague) D.M. Bates	CMHG ECtt SRms
malvastroides	XPep
scabrosa	CChe XPep

Anisodus (*Solanaceae*)

§ *luridus*	MGol MSal WWye

Anisotome (*Apiaceae*)

sp.	NSti

Annona (*Annonaceae*)

cherimola (F)	CTrG SSte XBlo
muricata (F)	XBlo
squamosa (F)	SSte

Anoiganthus see *Cyrtanthus*

Anomalesia see *Gladiolus*

Anomatheca (*Iridaceae*)

cruenta	see *A. laxa*
grandiflora	CDes CHll CPLG ERos
§ *laxa* ♀H2-3	CArn CMHG CPLG CRHN CSpe CStu CTri ECha ELan EPfP EPot ERos GFlt MNrw MTho NMen NPPs SBri SDix SRms SSpi WAbe WBrk WCom WCru WFar WPat WPer WWeb WWin
- var. *alba* ♀H2-3	CNic CPLG CPom CRHN CSpe CStu EHrv ELan ERos MTho NMen SSpi WAbe WBrk WCom WOBN WWeb
- *alba-maculata*	LRHS
- blue	ERos SIng WAbe
- 'Joan Evans'	CElw CNic CRHN ECtt ELan ERos LTwo NMen SRms WAbe WBrk WHrl WOBN
- red spot	CPLG EDif LHop WLFP
viridis	CPLG CPou CStu EBee ERos LRHS WBrk WCot

Anopterus (*Escalloniaceae*)

glandulosus	IBlr WCru

Anredera (*Basellaceae*)

§ *cordifolia*	CRHN ECho LEdu LRHS

Antennaria (*Asteraceae*)

aprica	see *A. parvifolia*
dioica	CTri GPoy MBro MHer NFla NJOw SPlb SRms WFar WWye
- 'Alba'	EDAr EHoe
- 'Alex Duguid'	CPlt GCrs LBee LRHS SAga SBla WCom
- 'Aprica'	see *A. parvifolia*
§ - var. *hyperborea*	LGro
- 'Minima'	ECho NBro NJOw NMen SIng WAbe
- 'Nyewoods Variety'	EPot NLAp
- red	SIng
- var. *rosea*	see *A. rosea*
* - 'Rubra'	CTri EBre ECha EDAr MHer NMen NPri SBla WAbe WDyG WHen WShp
- *tomentosa*	see *A. dioica* var. *hyperborea*
'Joy'	SBla
macrophylla hort.	see *A. microphylla*
§ *microphylla*	CBrm EDAr EHoe LGro MBar NFla NHol SRms WBea WEas WPat WPer
neglecta **new**	ECho
§ *parvifolia*	CLyd CNic CTri EBre MBar NLar SRms WAbe WBea WMoo WPer
- var. *rosea*	see *A. microphylla*
plantaginifolia	EBee
'Red Wonder'	CMea
§ *rosea* ♀H4	ECho GBBs GKir NLAp NMen NVic SPlb SRms WBVN

Anthemis ✿ (*Asteraceae*)

from Turkey	LLWP
arvensis	SECG
§ 'Beauty of Grallagh'	ECtt EFou GBuc GCal GMac MDKP NDov NGdn SDix WCot WWpP
'Cally Cream'	GCal
'Cally White'	GCal
carpatica	NBro WLin
- 'Karpatenschnee'	EBre EMlt MSPs MWrn SCro
cretica	SMrm
- subsp. *columnae* MESE 377	WAbe
§ - subsp. *cretica*	CLyd
- - NS 754	NWCA
* *cuphiana* **new**	WFar
frutescens	see *Argyranthemum frutescens*
§ 'Grallagh Gold'	EBee ECha ECtt EMon EOrc EWes LDai LHop LPhx LRHS MBri MWat NPer SAga SCro WBea WCAu WFar WSpi WTel
'Grallagh Gold' misapplied (orange-yellow)	see *A.* 'Beauty of Grallagh'
§ *marschalliana*	CPBP EBee ECha EDAr EPot IHMH LBee MSte SMrm WPer WWeb
montana	see *A. cretica* subsp. *cretica*
nobilis	see *Chamaemelum nobile*
punctata	CSLe
- subsp. *cupaniana* ♀H3-4	More than 30 suppliers
- - 'Nana'	EMon GKir NPer SHar
rudolphiana	see *A. marschalliana*
sancti-johannis	CWib EBee EGle EGoo ERou GFlt IGor LDai MBri NArg NPer SBri SPer SRms WBry WFar WMnd WPer WWpP
'Sauce Béarnaise'	EMon WMnd
Susanna Mitchell = 'Blomit'	CHar CHea EBee EBre EChP ECtt EMan EPfP EWll GKir GMac LRHS MMil MNrw MSph MSte SBla SCro SMrm WCAu WCom WSHC WSpi WTin WWeb WWhi XPep

	'Tetworth'	CStr EBee EChP ECha EHrv ELan EMan EMon GBuc GMac MSte SChu SMad WCot WFar WPer WWpP
	tinctoria	CArn CHby EBee ECha ELau EMon EPza GKir GMac GPoy LRHS MBow MHer NFor NPer SPet SWvt WBea WJek WWeb WWye
	- 'Alba'	COIW EMan GKir LPhx SChu SHar WHen WPer WWpP
*	- 'Compacta'	EFou EWes LPhx SAsh SMrm
	- dwarf	CBgR EBee GMac SBla SBri SUsu WCot WFar WWpP
	- 'E.C. Buxton'	More than 30 suppliers
	- 'Eva'	EBee EMon LRHS MBNS NDov NLar WEas WWhi WWpP
	- from Judaea	EMon
	- 'Golden Rays'	EBee MDKP NPro
	- 'Grallagh Gold'	see *A.* 'Grallagh Gold'
	- 'Kelwayi'	CFwr CHrt CSBt CTri EBee ECtt EMar EPfP ERou GKir LRHS MBNS NBPC NBro NPer SMer SPer SPla SRms WBea WFar WHen WMnd WPer WShp WWpP
	- 'Lemon Maid'	EFou EPPr GCal SChu SMrm
	- 'Pride of Grallagh'	see *A.* 'Beauty of Grallagh'
	- 'Sauce Hollandaise'	More than 30 suppliers
	- 'Wargrave Variety'	More than 30 suppliers
	triumfettii	NPer
	tuberculata	EBre EMan LRHS NChi SBla SIng

Anthericum (*Anthericaceae*)

	algeriense	see *A. liliago* var. *major*
*	*fistulosum*	EBee GSki
	liliago	CBro CFil EBee EBre ELan ERos EWTr GCal GKir LHop MLLN MSte NCGa SPer SSvw WPer
§	- var. *major* ♀H4	CAvo CDes ECha EHrv GBuc IBlr LPhx SSpi WPGP
	ramosum	CAvo CBos CDes EBee ECGN EChP ECha ELan EMan EPot ERos EWes GSki LPhx LRHS MBrN MLLN NBid NBir NCGa NWCA SHel SIng SMrm SUsu WPer
	- *plumosum*	see *Trichopetalum plumosum*
	undulatum	ERos

Antholyza (*Iridaceae*)

	coccinea	see *Crocosmia paniculata*
	crocosmioides	see *Crocosmia latifolia*
	paniculata	see *Crocosmia paniculata*

Anthoxanthum (*Poaceae*)

	odoratum	CArn CBig CPen CRWN ELau GBar GIBF GPoy NNor WWye

Anthriscus (*Apiaceae*)

	cerefolium	CArn CBod CSev EOHP GPoy ILis MBow MDun MHer NPri SECG WHHs WHbs WJek WLHH WPer WSel
	sylvestris	CArn NSco WShi
	- 'Broadleas Blush'	CNat
	- 'Hullavington' (v)	CNat
	- 'Kabir' **new**	CNat
	- 'Moonlit Night'	EHoe
	- 'Ravenswing'	More than 30 suppliers

Anthurium (*Araceae*)

	amazonicum	MBri
	andraeanum ♀H1	MBri
	'Crimson' **new**	XBlo
	'Magenta' **new**	XBlo
	'Porcelaine White' **new**	XBlo

	scherzerianum ♀H1	MBri

Anthyllis (*Papilionaceae*)

	barba-jovis	CSpe EMan XPep
	hermanniae	XPep
	- 'Compacta'	see *A. hermanniae* 'Minor'
§	- 'Minor'	EPot NLar WAbe
	montana	SBla
	- subsp. *atropurpurea*	LRHS
	- 'Rubra' ♀H4	CWCL EChP ECho EDAr EGle EMan EPot LTwo NJOw NMen WWin
	vulneraria	CFee GTou NJOw NMir NSco SSpi WBVN WBWf WHer
	- var. *coccinea*	CHar CMil CSpe EMan EMlt GGar MBro MCCP MLLN MNrw MSte MTho NJOw NSla NWCA SGar SScr WAbe WBVN WCom WFar WHil

Antigonon (*Polygonaceae*)

	leptopus	MJnS SOWG

Antirrhinum (*Scrophulariaceae*)

	asarina	see *Asarina procumbens*
	barrelieri	EMon
	braun-blanquetii	CHal EBee EMFP EMan ERou GBBs MLLN MOne MSPs STes WCAu WCot
	'Candy Snap' (v) **new**	LAst
	'Candy Stripe' **new**	EMan
	glutinosum	see *A. hispanicum* subsp. *hispanicum*
	graniticum	EBee LRav
§	*hispanicum*	EBee NBir SBla
	- 'Avalanche'	CHal ECtt EMan LAst MLan SPet
	- subsp. *hispanicum*	CSpe WSPU XPep
§	- - 'Roseum'	CMea CPom CSpe EDAr EMan SPet
	latifolium **new**	XPep
	'Luminaire Pink' (Luminaire Series) **new**	NPri
	majus	XPep
	- 'Black Prince'	CHad CSpe EMan LHop SAga WEas WMoo
	- subsp. *majus*	EWll
	- 'Taff's White' (v)	LRHS
	molle	CBri CPom CSpe EBee ECtt EHyt EOrc MSte NBir NPer NWCA SAga SIng SRot SUsu WAbe
	- pink	CBri CSWP EOrc MSte SAga
I	'Pendula Lampion Appleblossom' **new**	LAst
I	'Pendula Lampion Purple' **new**	LAst
I	'Pendula Lampion Salmon/Orange' **new**	LAst
	'Powys Pride' (v)	EWll
	pulverulentum	LHop LPhx NPPs SAga
	sempervirens	EBee EMan WAbe WWeb
	siculum	EBee WMoo

añu see *Tropaeolum tuberosum*

Aphanes (*Rosaceae*)

§	*arvensis*	MSal WWye

Aphelandra (*Acanthaceae*)

	squarrosa	CHal LRHS MBri

Aphyllanthes (*Aphyllanthaceae*)

	monspeliensis	CFee EBee ECho SBla

Apios (*Papilionaceae*)

§	*americana*	CMdw CPom EBee EChP EMan

EMon EOrc GBin LEdu MCCP NBir
NSti SSpi WCot WCru WSHC

tuberosa — see *A. americana*

Apium (Apiaceae)

graveolens — CArn CBgR CBod ELau EOHP
GPoy MBow MHer MSal SIde WBri
WJek

- (Secalinum Group) — MHer NGHP
'Par-cel'

Apium x *Petroselinum* (Apiaceae)

hybrid — see *A. graveolens* Secalinum Group

Apocynum (Apocynaceae)

cannabinum — CArn GPoy MGol MSal WWye

Aponogeton (Aponogetonaceae)

distachyos — CDWL CRow CWat EHon ELan
EMFW EPfP LNCo LPBA MSta
NArg NBlu NPer SCoo SLon SWat
WFar WMAq WMyn WPnP WTin
WWpP

apple see *Malus domestica*

apricot see *Prunus armeniaca*

Aptenia (Aizoaceae)

cordifolia ♀H1-2 — CSev EOHP LRav NPer SChr SDnm
SEND SPet SSte SVen WRos XPep

- 'Variegata' (v) — MRav

Aquilegia ✿ (Ranunculaceae)

akitensis hort. — see *A. flabellata*, *A. flabellata* var. *pumila*
'Alaska' (State Series) — CThr
* *alba variegata* (v) — WEas
alpina — CBot CMea ECtt EDAr ELau EMlt
EPfP EWTr GKir GTou MHer MLan
MWgw NBlu NFor NJOw NPPs
SPer SPet SRms WCAu WFar WHen
WMoo WPer WStI
- 'Alba' — CM&M MWgw NOak WLow
- 'Hensol Harebell' — see *A.* 'Hensol Harebell'
'Alpine Blue' — WLow
amaliae — see *A. ottonis* subsp. *amaliae*
'Anja' (v) **new** — WCot
'Apple Blossom' — GFlt GKev SPoG
aragonensis — see *A. pyrenaica*
§ *atrata* — CPou EBee EWTr GSki MDKP
NOak SMHy WAbe WBVN WPer
atrovinosa — EBee WLin
aurea misapplied — see *A. vulgaris* golden-leaved
aurea Janka — EBee
'Ballerina' — EBee NPPs WHer
barnebyi — CMea
bernardii — NJOw NOak WHil
bertolonii ♀H4 — EHyt EPot GCrs GTou LBee LHop
LRHS MBro NMen NOak SBla
SRms WAbe WHoo WPat
Biedermeier Group — EMil GKir IHMH LPVe LRHS MBNS
MDKP NHol NNor NOrc SWal
WPer WWpP
'Blue Berry' — EBee MBro WPat
'Blue Jay' (Songbird Series) — CFai NPri SSvw SWvt
'Blue Star' (Star Series) — EBee ECtt LRHS SBri WPer
'Bluebird' (Songbird Series) — AGM CThr SWvt
brevicalcarata — EBee
buergeriana — EBee MDKP NChi STes WPer WPrP
- 'Calimero' — EBee MDKP NGby NLar WHil
WPrP
- var. *oxysepala* — see *A. oxysepala*

'Bunting' — EWll SLon SSvw SWvt
(Songbird Series) ♀H2
'Burnished Rose' — CBel CPla NPro WGMN WHil
canadensis ♀H4 — CMHG CPom CSpe EBee EDAr
EFWa ELan GSki MHer MSte NBid
NBir NBro NOak SGar SMac SRms
SSpi WPer WPrP
- 'Corbett' — GBuc WHil
- 'Little Lanterns' — CMdw EBee EPyc MDKP MSte
WHil
- 'Nana' — CStu EPot GBuc MDKP NLAp
WPat
'Cardinal' (Songbird Series) — CFai EWll NPri SLon SPer SSvw
SWvt
'Chaffinch' — CThr
(Songbird Series) **new**
§ *chaplinei* — EBee NBir SIgm WEas
chrysantha — CBot CHea CHrt EBee ECGN
EWTr GBin MLLN NOak SRms
WBrE WCot WEas WLin WPer
- var. *chaplinei* — see *A. chaplinei*
- 'Flore Pleno' (d) — MDKP
- 'Yellow Queen' — CBot CHea CSpe EBee EPfP LAst
MAvo MDKP SOkh SPla SSvw WHil
WSan
clematiflora — see *A. vulgaris* var. *stellata*
coerulea ♀H4 — EFWa EWTr GKev SIgm SRms
WLin
- 'Mrs Nicholls' — EPar MBri
- var. *ochroleuca* — WLin
'Colorado' (State Series) — CFai CThr EMar
'Crimson Star' — CHea CPen EBee EBre ENor ENot
EPfP GKir MDKP NCGa NFla SOkh
SPer WMoo WWeb
'Debutante' — MDKP
desertorum — CPom EBee MDKP SMac
discolor — GEdr GSki GTou LBee LHop LRHS
LTwo NMen SIng WPat
'Double Chocolate' — LRHS
Double Rubies (d) — EGoo EMan WCom WCot
'Dove' — CFai CThr EWll GBuc MHer NPri
(Songbird Series) ♀H2 — SPer SWat SWvt WCra WGMN
I 'Dragonfly' — CBcs EPfP MBri NJOw NMir NOak
SPer WFar
ecalcarata — see *Semiaquilegia ecalcarata*
elegantula — EBee GCrs
eximia — EBee WLin
'Firewheel' — see *A. vulgaris* var. *stellata*
'Firewheel'
§ *flabellata* ♀H4 — CTri EBlw MBro WPat WPer
§ - f. *alba* — CTri ELan NWCA SBla WEas
- 'Blue Angel' — CBcs EDAr WPer
* - 'White Angel' — WPer
- Cameo Series — EBre EWll MAvo SIng WCra WFar
WGor WHil WRos
- - 'Cameo Blue' — LPVe
- - 'Cameo Pink and White' — MHer
- - 'Cameo Pink' — MDKP
- - 'Cameo Rose' — NBir
- Jewel Series — CSpe EBre ECho NBlu SPet WHil
WPer
- - 'Blue Jewel' — SPla
- - 'Pink Jewel' — SPla
- - 'White Jewel' — GKev SPla
- 'Ministar' — ECho EDAr EMlt EPfP GKir GSki
LRHS MBNS MBro MHer NOak
NVic SPet SRot WFar WHil WPer
WShp WWin
- 'Nana Alba' — see *A. flabellata* var. *pumila* f. *alba*
I - *nana yezoense* **new** — GFlt
§ - var. *pumila* ♀H4 — ECha EHyt GFlt GTou LHop LPVe
MAvo NOak SBla SIng WCom WFar
WHil WLin WPat WPer

§ - - f. *alba* ♀H4	CBot ECha GEdr LBee LHop LRHS MBNS MFOX MSte SIng SRms WHil WWin
- - f. *kurilensis*	MSte
- - 'Silver Edge' (v)	CElw CPla ITer MNrw WCom
* - - 'Snowflakes'	EHyt
flavescens	EBee WPer
- var. *miniana*	LTwo
'Florida' (State Series) ♀H2 **new**	CThr
formosa	EBee MDKP NChi NPri NWCA WPer
- var. *truncata*	GBuc MLLN
§ *fragrans*	CBot EBee ECGN EMan GBin GEdr MBro MTho NOak NWCA SBla STes WCra WHoo WLin WRha
- white-flowered	ELan
glandulosa	CMHG EBee NLar WEas
glauca	see *A. fragrans*
'Golden Guiness' **new**	ECoo
'Goldfinch' (Songbird Series)	CBot CFai CThr EWll NBir NPri SPer SWvt
grata	EBee MBNS MDKP
Harbutt's hybrids	ERou
§ 'Hensol Harebell' ♀H4	CPou CSWP EBee GBuc MBow MBro MFir SHar SPer SRms WHoo
hirsutissima	see *A. viscosa* subsp. *hirsutissima*
'Ice Blue'	WCot
'Irish Elegance'	EGoo WRha
japonica	see *A. flabellata* var. *pumila*
'Jenny' **new**	MDKP
jonesii	CGra ITim LBee NLAp WAbe WPat
jonesii x *saximontana*	GFlt ITim
'Kansas' (State Series)	CThr
karelinii	MWrn SRob
kitaibelii	EBee
'Koralle'	MDKP WFar WHil
'Kristall'	EBee ERou LAst MDKP NOak SSvw STes WHil
Langdon's Rainbow hybrids	MDKP
laramiensis	CGra CPBP MDKP
'Lavender and White' (Songbird Series)	see *A.* 'Nuthatch'
longissima ♀H4	CHar CMea CMil GBri GBuc MHer MLLN SBla SBri SHar SSte STes WEas WHoo
'Louisiana' (State Series) ♀H2	CThr
'Magpie'	see *A. vulgaris* 'William Guiness'
'Maxi'	MDKP WHil
McKana Group	CWCL EBre ELan EMlt ENot EPfP LAst LHop LPVe LRHS MBow MWgw NBlu NFor NGdn NOak NVic SPer SPlb SRms WCAu WMnd
'Mellow Yellow'	CPla ECGP ECoo ECtt EMan GBuc MAnH MBNS MCLN MDKP SIgm WBea WMoo WPer WPnP
micrantha	EBee
'Milk and Honey'	CBre EBee EMan SPer SPoG WCot WHil
'Montana' (State Series) **new**	CThr
moorcroftiana	EBee
Mrs Scott-Elliot hybrids	COlW CSBt EBee EHol IGor LHop LIck MLan NHol SPer WFar
Music Series ♀H4	NOak SMrm SRms
nigricans	see *A. atrata*
§ 'Nuthatch' (Songbird Series)	CFai CThr EMar WCra
olympica	EBee EWes LPhx MDHE WPer
ottonis	LHop
- subsp. *amaliae*	EBee MWrn WAbe
§ *oxysepala*	CPLG EBee WPrP
'Perfumed Garden'	CPla

'Purple Emperor'	LRHS
§ *pyrenaica*	WLin
'Raspberry Ice' **new**	ITim
'Red Hobbit'	CBrm CSpe EMlt EOMN GAbr ITim LRHS MDKP NBPC NHol NWCA WHil WWeb
'Red Star' (Star Series)	EBee ECtt ERou MDKP NOak SHar SPer WHil WPer
'Redwing' (Songbird Series)	CThr SWvt
'Robin' (Songbird Series)	CBot CFai CThr EMar NPri SWat SWvt
rockii	EBee EWTr MBNS MDKP WLin
- B&SWJ 7965	WCru
'Roman Bronze'	CPla EMan MAvo NCGa NOak NPro SSte WCom WCot WWhi WWpP
'Rose Queen'	MDKP MWrn Whil WHoo
'Roundway Chocolate' **new**	CBot
saximontana	CGra CStu EHyt GTou ITim NLar NWCA WPer
§ 'Schneekönigin'	NFla NOak WHen WPer
scopulorum	CGra EBee MDHE SBla WCom
shockleyi	EBee ETow GBuc MLan SBri
sibirica	CPLG EBee WPer
'Silver Queen'	EBee ELan MDKP MLan SOkh
'Simone's White'	EBee
skinneri	CHea CHrt CTCP EBee EBlw EChP EFWa EWsh GBin GSki LHop MBNS MBct MHer SAga STes WCot WCra WCru WMnd WMoo WRha WRos
- from Mexico	CHar NCGa
- 'Ruby Francis'	MWrn
'Skylark' (Songbird Series) **new**	CThr WCra
Snow Queen	see *A.* 'Schneekönigin'
Songbird Series	CSpe LRHS MLLN NPri SWat WSan WHil
'Spring Magic Blue and White' (Spring Magic Series) **new**	
stellata	see *A. vulgaris* var. *stellata*
'Stoulton Blue'	CHea EBee WCom WSPU
'Sunburst Ruby'	CPla EMan MAvo MDKP NOak NPPs NPro SMad WHoo WMoo WRos WWpP
'Sweet Lemon Drops'	CPla EBee GBuc MAvo MWrn SPer STes WHoo
'Sweet Rainbows' (d)	CPla
thalictrifolia	EBee LPhx
triternata	EBee GCal NNor NWCA SIgm
'Virginia' (State Series) **new**	CThr
viridiflora	CBot CHar CTri EShb GBuc GFlt LPhx MHer MTho NDov SBla SMad WCom WCru WEas WFar WHil WMnd WPer WPnP WPrP WTMC
- bronze **new**	SMHy
- hybrid	SMHy
- yellow **new**	SMHy
§ *viscosa*	EBee
subsp. *hirsutissima*	
vulgaris	CArn CHrt CMHG CRWN EPfP GPoy LLWP MBow MGol NBro NPPs NSco SGar SPlb WBWf WBri WCAu WGwG WMoo WPer WSSM WShi WTin WWye
- 'Adelaide Addison'	CPlt ECha GBri GBuc SBla WEas WFar
- var. *alba*	CMea EMan LLWP SEND SGar WCAu WMnd
- 'Altrosa'	CBri
- 'Aureovariegata'	see *A. vulgaris* Vervaeneana Group

- *clematiflora*	see *A. vulgaris* var. *stellata*
- var. *flore-pleno* (d)	EChP LLWP WHen WLin WPer
- - black (d)	WCot
- - blue (d)	WCot
- - 'Blue Bonnet' (d)	EMan ERou
- - 'Burgundy' (d)	CMil
- - Dorothy Series	GBuc LHop LRHS
- - - 'Dorothy Rose' (d)	EBee SAga
- - 'Double Pleat' (d)	WHer
- - 'Double Pleat' blue/white (d)	MWrn WHil WPer
- - 'Double Pleat' pink/white (d)	NGdn WHil WPer
- - 'Frilly Dilly Blue' (d)	WBry
* - - 'Frilly Dilly Rose' (d)	STes
* - - 'Frilly Dilly Sky Blue' (d)	STes
- - 'Jane Hollow' (d)	CPou
- - pale blue (d)	LLWP
- - pink (d)	GGar
- - 'Pink Bonnet' (d)	WMnd
- - 'Powder Blue' (d)	CHea
- - purple (d)	LLWP
- - red (d)	GGar
- - 'Tower White' (d) **new**	MWrn
- - white (d)	LLWP LPhx NOak
* - - 'White Bonnet' (d)	EBee EBre SRos
§ - golden-leaved	ECha ECho
- 'Grandmother's Garden'	EWll
- 'Granny's Gold'	EBre
- 'Heidi'	CBot EBee EWll WPer
- 'Magpie'	see *A. vulgaris* 'William Guiness'
- 'Miss Coventry'	SMHy
- Munstead White	see *A. vulgaris* 'Nivea'
§ - 'Nivea' ♀H4	CBot CPou CSam EBee ECha LAst MBro SBla WHoo
- 'Pink Spurless'	see *A. vulgaris* var. *stellata* pink
- 'Pom Pom Crimson' (Pom Pom Series)	NBro NBur NPPs WCot
§ - var. *stellata*	EBee ECGN ELan EMan EPot EWTr EWsh GBuc MBNS NBPC NBro SLon SMac WLin WMoo WPer WWeb WWin
- - Barlow Series (d)	WFar
- - - 'Black Barlow' (d)	CBcs EBee EBlw ECGP EChP ECtt EGoo EMar EPar EWll GKir LHop MBri MWrn NOrc SPer SSte WAul WSan WWeb
- - - 'Blue Barlow' (d)	CBgR ECtt EWTr EWll GCal GKir MBri SCro SPer WMnd WPer WSan
- - - 'Christa Barlow' (d)	EChP LRHS SCro WWeb
- - - 'Nora Barlow' (d) ♀H4	More than 30 suppliers
- - - 'Rose Barlow' (d)	CBgR EWTr GCal SCro
§ - - 'Firewheel'	CBri EBee EGoo EMan MDKP MWrn SBri STes WMoo
- - 'Greenapples'	CMil EBee EMan ITer MCCP MDKP MFOX MWrn NPro WBar WBry WCot WWhi
* - - 'Iceberg'	EMan WSpi
§ - - pink	LLWP
- - purple	LLWP
- - red	LLWP WHen WWeb
- - 'Royal Purple' (d)	EMan MBNS MLwd NBro SMac SPoG WBVN
- - 'Ruby Port' (d)	CBri EBee EBlw EMan GCal GKir LAst LPhx MBri NChi NPri SBri SPla SSvw STes SUsu WFar WHen WMnd WPrP
- - 'Ruby Port' crimped (d)	NDov WPnP
- - 'Sunlight White' (d)	SWat WMnd WPer
§ - - white	LHop NBro WFar WHal
* - - 'Woodside Blue'	ECtt MFOX
- 'Strawberry'	CPen EBee EGoo EMan GBri NBro

Ice Cream' (d)	NBur
- 'The Bride'	EBee
- variegated foliage	see *A. vulgaris* Vervaeneana Group
§ - Vervaeneana Group (v)	More than 30 suppliers
- - 'Graeme Iddon' (v)	EBee GBuc SAga
- - 'Woodside'	see *A. vulgaris* Vervaeneana Group
- - 'Woodside Blue' (v)	COIW EGoo
- - 'Woodside White' (v)	MFOX NBir
- 'Warwick'	WCot
- 'Westfaeld'	MTed NOak
- 'White Spurless'	see *A. vulgaris* var. *stellata* white
§ - 'William Guiness'	More than 30 suppliers
- - white	WWeb
'White Rock' **new**	GFlt
'White Star' (Star Series)	CHea EBee EPfP ERou NPSI WHil WPer
Winky Series 'Winky Blue and White'	LAst WHil WWeb
- 'Winky Purple and White'	WWeb
- 'Winky Red and White'	LAst WHil WWeb
yabeana	EBee GFlt MWrn SBri WHil
'Yellow Star' (Star Series)	EGra

Aquilegia x *Semiaquilegia* (Ranunculaceae)

blue	NPPs WCru
Cally hybrids	GCal

Arabis (Brassicaceae)

albida	see *A. alpina* subsp. *caucasica*
alpina	SPlb
§ - subsp. *caucasica*	WFar WShp
- - 'Corfe Castle'	ECtt
- - 'Douler Angevine' (v)	LIck NPri NPro
§ - - 'Flore Pleno' (d) ♀H4	CTri CWCL ECha ECtt ELan EOrc LGro MFir MTho NWoo SBod SIng SRms SScr WCom WEas WFar WShp WWin
- - 'Pink Pearl'	NBlu WFar
- - 'Rosea'	MRav NBir NJOw NPri SRms WFar WMoo WShp
§ - - 'Schneehaube' ♀H4	CTri ECtt EPfP EShb GKir MBar NBlu NJOw NMir NOrc SRms WMoo WPer
- - Snowcap	see *A. alpina* subsp. *caucasica* 'Schneehaube'
- - 'Snowdrop'	MRav NPri WFar
- - 'Variegata' (v)	EBre ECtt EHoe ELan EPot LBee MBri MHer MTho NFor SRms WCom WEas WFar WShp WWin
androsacea	GTou SRms
x *arendsii* 'Compinkie'	EBre ECtt MBow NPri SPlb SRms
- 'Rosabella' (v)	EBre GKir LRHS MBNS
blepharophylla	EPfP MWat SIng SPet
- 'Alba'	WShp
§ - 'Frühlingszauber' ♀H4	CBcs EBre GKir IHMH LPVe MOne NBir NBlu NPri SRms WBVN WFar
- Spring Charm	see *A. blepharophylla* 'Frühlingszauber'
bryoides	EPot GTou LRHS NMen WLin
caerulea	CBrm
carduchorum	NMen
caucasica	see *A. alpina* subsp. *caucasica*
§ *collina* subsp. *rosea*	IHMH
dispar **new**	WLin
double white	CFee
'Doulier Anguine' **new**	EPot
ferdinandi-coburgi	EPot SScr WEas
- 'Aureovariegata' (v)	CTri ECtt EDAr EHoe GKir IHMH LGro SPet SWvt
- 'Old Gold'	EBre ECtt EDAr EMlt EPfP EPot GKir LBee MBar MHer MRav NHol NJOw NVic SBla SRms SWvt WCom WFar WHoo WPat WWin

- 'Variegata'	see *A. procurrens* 'Variegata'
glabra	WPer
x **kellereri**	NMen
lucida 'Variegata' (v) **new**	NPro
§ **procurrens**	CTri EBre ECha ECtt ELan EMlt
'Variegata' (v) ♀H4	EPot EWes GKir GTou LBee MBar
	MHer MWat NFor NJOw NWCA
	SBla SHFr SPlb SRms WCom WFar
	WTel
rosea	see *A. collina* subsp. *rosea*
§ **scabra**	CNat
§ **soyeri** subsp. **coriacea**	NDlv
stricta	see *A. scabra*
x **sturii**	ETow

Arachniodes (Dryopteridaceae)

simplicior	WCot WRic

Aralia ✿ (Araliaceae)

armata B&SWJ 3137	WCru
bipinnata B&SWJ 6719	WCru
cachemirica	CDes CHad EBee EWes GCal GIBF
	MTed NBid NLar SDix SMad SSpi
	WPGP
californica	EBee GCal GPoy LEdu MSal MSte
	NLar SIgm SSpi WCru
chapaensis	WCru
HWJ 723 **new**	
chinensis misapplied	see *A. elata*
chinensis L.	MBNS MSal SPer
- BWJ 8102	WCru
continentalis	EBee EPPr GCal WCru
- B&SWJ 4152	WCru
- B&SWJ 8524	WCru
cordata	CHEx EWes GCal GFlt LEdu MSal
	NLar
- B&SWJ 5511	WCru
decaisneana	WCru
B&SWJ 3588	
§ **elata** ♀H4	More than 30 suppliers
- B&SWJ 5480	WCru
- 'Albomarginata'	see *A. elata* 'Variegata'
- 'Aureovariegata' (v)	CBcs CDoC ELan ENot EPfP
	NMoo NPal WCot WDin WOrn
	WPat
- 'Golden Umbrella' (v)	NLar
- 'Silver Umbrella'	EPfP MGos NLar
§ - 'Variegata' (v) ♀H4	CBcs CBot CDoC CDul ELan ENot
	EPfP LRHS MBlu MGos NMoo
	NPSI NPal SHBN WCot WDin
	WGer WPat
foliolosa B&SWJ 8360	WCru
racemosa	CBrm EBee GCal GPoy LEdu MLLN
	MNrw MSal MSte MWgw NLar
	SRms WFar WHal WPnP
sieboldii	see *Fatsia japonica*
spinosa	CHEx IArd MBlu NLar WHer

Araucaria (Araucariaceae)

angustifolia	LCon
§ **araucana**	More than 30 suppliers
bidwillii **new**	LCon
§ **columnaris** **new**	LCon
cunninghamii	LCon
excelsa hort.	see *A. heterophylla*
§ **heterophylla** ♀H1	CDoC GTSp LCon LRHS MBri
	WNor
imbricata	see *A. araucana*

Araujia (Asclepiadaceae)

sericifera	CBcs CHEx CMHG CMac CRHN
	CTrG EMil ERea GQui ITer SBra
	SDnm SGar SSpi WBor WSHC
	XPep

Arbutus ✿ (Ericaceae)

andrachne	CDul EPfP XPep
x **andrachnoides** ♀H4	CAbP CBcs CDul CFil CMHG
	CPMA ELan EPfP GKir MAsh SAPC
	SArc SDnm SHBN SPer SReu SSpi
	SSta WHCG WPGP WPat XPep
glandulosa	see *Arctostaphylos glandulosa*
'Marina'	CAbP CDoC CDul CEnd CFil
	CPMA EBee ELan EPfP ISea LRHS
	MAsh MBlu MBro SEND SMad SPer
	SReu SSpi SSta WFar WPGP WPat
menziesii ♀H3	CDoC CEnd CFil CMCN CTho
	ECrN EPfP IDee MLan SLon SMad
	SSpi WFar
unedo ♀H4	More than 30 suppliers
- 'Atlantic'	EBee EMil IArd MBri SLim SSpi
	SWvt WGer WPat WWeb
- 'Compacta'	CBcs CDoC EBee EBre GKir LPio
	LRHS MAsh MGos SHBN WBcn
	WDin XPep
- 'Elfin King'	ELan MAsh SDnm SSpi SSta SWvt
- 'Quercifolia'	EPfP NLar SDnm SReu SSpi SSta
	WPat
- f. **rubra** ♀H4	More than 30 suppliers

Archontophoenix (Arecaceae)

alexandrae	CRoM LPal WMul
cunninghamiana ♀H1	CBrP CRoM CTrC LPal WMul

Arctanthemum (Asteraceae)

§ **arcticum**	CKno ECha EFou EMFP MAvo
	NChi
- 'Roseum'	EBee EFou
- 'Schwefelglanz'	EFou

Arcterica see *Pieris*

Arctium (Asteraceae)

lappa	CAgr CArn GBar GPoy MHer MSal
	SIde WHer
minus	MSal NSco

Arctostaphylos (Ericaceae)

§ **glandulosa**	SAPC SArc
x **media** 'Wood's Red'	GEil GKir MBar MGos WFar
myrtifolia	MBar
nevadensis	see *Arenaria tetraquetra* subsp.
	amabilis
stanfordiana C&H 105	GGGa
uva-ursi	CArn CTri GPoy GTSp MBar NBlu
	NLar NMen SHBN SPer SSta WBod
	WDin
- 'Massachusetts'	EWTr GKir GQui MAsh SMur SReu
	SSta
- 'Snowcap'	WWes
- 'Vancouver Jade'	CDoC CEnd EBee GKir LRHS
	MAsh MBar MGos NHol SPer SPoG
	SReu SSta SWvt WWeb

Arctotheca (Asteraceae)

calendula **new**	XPep

Arctotis (Asteraceae)

fastuosa	MOak
var. **alba** 'Zulu Prince'	
x **hybrida** 'Apricot'	CHEx CTbh LAst SAga SMrm
	WWol
- 'Bacchus'	SMrm
- 'China Rose'	CTbh SAga SMrm
- cream	SAga
- 'Flame' ♀H1+3	CBrm CPlt CSpe CWCL LAst
	MBNS MLan MOak MSte SAga
	SMrm WEas WWol

* - 'Mahogany' ♀H1+3	CHrt CTbh EShb MBNS SAga SUsu WWol
- 'Red Devil'	CHEx CSpe CTbh CWCL LAst MBNS SAga SMrm
- white	CHEx
- 'Wine'	CBrm CWCL LAst MBNS MLan MSte SAga SMrm
'Prostrate Raspberry'	CSpe SAga

Ardisia (*Myrsinaceae*)

crenata	LRHS MBri SMur
japonica B&SWJ 3809	WCru
- var. *angusta* **new**	WCot
- 'Miyo-nishiki' (v)	WCot
maclurei B&SWJ 3772	LRHS

Areca (*Arecaceae*)

catechu	MBri
concinna	LPal
vestiaria	LPal

Arecastrum see *Syagrus*

Arenaria (*Caryophyllaceae*)

alfacarensis	see *A. lithops*
balearica	LBee LRHS NRya SIng SPlb SRms
bertolonii	LRHS
edgeworthiana **new**	WLin
festucoides	CPBP GTou
ledebouriana	EHyt MWat NLar
§ *lithops*	CLyd
montana ♀H4	More than 30 suppliers
norvegica **new**	GFlt
pinifolia	see *Minuartia circassica*
pulvinata	see *A. lithops*
purpurascens	CPBP CStu ECho EDAr EHyt MBrN NWCA SBla SRms SRot
- 'Elliott's Variety'	NHol WPat
tetraquetra	GCrs WAbe
§ - subsp. *amabilis*	CPBP EHyt LRHS MBar NJOw NMen NSla NWCA SReu
tmolea	NMen
verna	see *Minuartia verna*

Arenga (*Arecaceae*)

§ *caudata*	WMul
engleri	CRoM LPal WMul
pinnata	CRoM

Argemone (*Papaveraceae*)

grandiflora	ELan
mexicana	ELan

Argyranthemum ✿ (*Asteraceae*)

'Anastasia'	LIck MAJR WPnn
'Apricot Surprise'	see *A.* 'Peach Cheeks'
'Blanche'	IHMH
(Courtyard Series)	
'Blanche Petite'	WGor
(Courtyard Series) **new**	
§ 'Blizzard' (d)	ECtt LIck MAJR WPnn
'Bofinger'	LIck MAJR
Boston yellow daisy	see *A. callichrysum*
broussonetii	LIck MAJR
'Butterfly' ♀H1+3	LIck MAJR MBNS SVil WPnn WWol
§ *callichrysum*	LIck MAJR
- 'Penny'	LIck MAJR
- 'Prado'	LIck
'Camilla Ponticelli'	LIck MAJR
canariense hort.	see *A. frutescens* subsp. *canariae*
'Champagne'	LIck MAJR
'Cheek's Peach'	see *A.* 'Peach Cheeks'
* *compactum*	LIck MAJR
'Comtesse de Chambord'	LIck MAJR SPet

'Cornish Gold' ♀H1+3	CBcs LIck MAJR MBNS MSte
coronopifolium	LIck MAJR XPep
Daisy Crazy Series	SVil
- Blushing Rose	
= 'Supaellic' **new**	
- Bright Carmine	SVil
= 'Supalight' **new**	
- Strawberry Pink	SVil
= 'Suparosa' **new**	
- Vanilla Ripple	SVil
= 'Supabright' **new**	
'Donington Hero' ♀H1+3	ECtt LIck MAJR MHom WPnn
double cream (d)	LIck
double white (d)	LIck MAJR
double yellow (d)	WPnn
'Edelweiss' (d)	LIck MAJR MHom WHen
'Flamingo'	see *Rhodanthemum gayanum*
§ *foeniculaceum* hort.	CSLe CTri EHol ELan LIck WHen WKif
§ *foeniculaceum*	CHal GMac
(Willd.) Webb & Sch.Bip.	
- pink	see *A.* 'Petite Pink'
§ - 'Royal Haze' ♀H1+3	LIck MAJR NPer
'Frosty'	LIck MBNS
§ *frutescens*	CHEx ECtt LIck LRHS MAJR WEas
* - 'Album Plenum' (d)	SEND
§ - subsp. *canariae* ♀H1+3	CHal ECtt LIck MAJR
- 'Lemon Delight'	CHal LAst LIck
- 'Primrose Petite'ᴾᴮᴿ **new**	WGor
- subsp.	MAJR
succulentum **new**	
- - 'Margaret Lynch'	LIck MAJR
- 'Sugar and Ice'ᴾᴮᴿ	LIck
- 'Sugar Button'ᴾᴮᴿ	CBcs LIck WWeb
(d) ♀H1+3	
- 'Summer Pink'ᴾᴮᴿ	LAst LIck
'Fuji Sundance'	LIck MAJR
'George'	LIck MAJR
'Gill's Pink'	CElw ECtt GMac LIck MAJR MHom WPnn
'Golden Treasure'	LIck MAJR
gracile	CHal ECtt EHol LIck MAJR MHom MLan MSte WPnn
'Chelsea Girl' ♀H1+3	
'Guernsey Pink' **new**	MAJR
'Harvest Snow'	LAst LIck MBNS
'Hopleys Double	LIck
Cream' (d)	
§ 'Jamaica Primrose' ♀H1+3	CBot CElw CSpe ECtt GMac LIck MHar SDix WBod WHen WPnn
'Jamaica Snowstorm'	see *A.* 'Snow Storm'
'Julie Anna' (d)	CBcs LAst MBNS
'Lemon Chiffon'	LIck MAJR
'Lemon Meringue' (d)	ECtt LIck MAJR
'Lemon Soufflé'	LIck MAJR
lemsii	LIck MAJR
§ 'Levada Cream' ♀H1+3	LIck MAJR MHom
'Libby Brett' **new**	MAJR
'Lilliput'	LIck MAJR
§ *maderense* ♀H1+3	CHal CSam LIck LRHS MAJR MSte SUsu
- pale	CHal
'Mary Cheek' (d) ♀H1+3	LIck MAJR SPet WPnn
'Mary Wootton' (d)	CElw ECtt LIck MAJR MHom MSte
mawii	see *Rhodanthemum gayanum*
'Mike's Pink'	LIck MAJR
'Mini-snowflake'	see *A.* 'Blizzard'
§ 'Mrs F. Sander' (d)	LIck MAJR MHom
'Nevada Cream'	see *Argyranthemum* 'Levada Cream'
ochroleucum	see *A. maderense*
'Patches Pink'	LIck MAJR
§ 'Peach Cheeks' (d)	CHal ECtt LIck MAJR MSte SPet WWol

§ 'Petite Pink' ♀H1+3	CHal ECtt LAst LIck MAJR MHom MSte SEND WHen
'Pink Australian' (d)	LIck MAJR MHom
'Pink Break'	CHal LIck MAJR
I 'Pink Dahlia'	LIck MAJR
'Pink Delight'	see A. 'Petite Pink'
'Pink Pixie'	LIck MAJR
pinnatifidium subsp. *succulentum* **new**	MAJR
'Powder Puff' (d)	ECtt LIck MAJR MRav WPnn
prostrate double pink	LIck MAJR
§ 'Qinta White' (d) ♀H1+3	GMac LIck MAJR WPnn
'Rising Sun'	GMac LIck MAJR
'Romance' **new**	WWol
'Rosa Dwarf'	LIck
'Royal Haze'	see A. *foeniculaceum* 'Royal Haze'
'Royal Yellow'	LIck
'Saimi'	LIck
'Saute'	LIck MAJR
'Serenade' **new**	WWol
'Silver Leaf'	LIck MAJR
'Silver Queen'	see A. *foeniculaceum* hort.
single pink	LIck MAJR
§ 'Snow Storm' ♀H1+3	LAst LIck MAJR MHom WPnn
'Snowball' **new**	MAJR
'Snowflake' (d)	MSte WHen
'Snowflake' misapplied	see A. 'Mrs F. Sander'
'Starlight'	LIck MAJR
'Sugar Baby'PBR	LIck SMrm WWeb
'Sugar Lace'	CBcs LIck
'Summer Angel'PBR (d)	LIck
'Summer Eyes'	CBcs LIck
'Summer Melody'PBR (d)	CSpe LIck WPnn WWeb
'Summer Stars Pink' (d)	LIck
'Sweety'	LIck WPnn
'Tenerife'	LIck MSte
'Tony Holmes'	LIck MAJR
'Vancouver' (d) ♀H1+3	CElw CWCL ECtt EShb LAst LIck MHom SChu SPet WEas WHen WPnn WWol
* 'Vera' **new**	LIck MAJR
'Wellwood Park'	LIck MAJR
'Weymouth Pink'	LIck MAJR
'Weymouth Surprise'	LIck MAJR
'White Spider'	ELan LIck MAJR MHom
'White Star'	WWol
'Whiteknights' ♀H1+3	LIck MAJR
'Yellow Australian' (d)	LIck MAJR

Argyreia (*Convolvulaceae*)

nervosa	MGol

Argyrocytisus see *Cytisus*

Arisaema (*Araceae*)

ACE 2130	NGar
C&H 7026	NMen
CC 382	WCot
amurense	CFil CFir CHEx CLAP CStu EBee GCal GIBF GKir ITer LAma LEur MLLN WCot WFar WPGP
- B&SWJ 947	WCru
- dark-flowered	WWst
- green-flowered	WWst
- subsp. *robustum*	WWst
- - B&SWJ 1186	WCru
- subsp. *serratum* B&SWJ 711	WCru
angustatum	LAma
var. *amurense*	
- var. *peninsulae*	EBee LEur
- - B&SWJ 841	LAma WCru
* - - f. *variegatum* (v) B&SWJ 4321	WCru

- var. *serratum*	LAma
aridum	EBee
asperatum	EBee LAma
auriculatum	EBee LAma
austroyunnanense **new**	EBee
bathycoleum	EBee LAma
biauriculatum	EBee
brachyspathum **new**	EBee
brevipes	EBee LAma
calcareum **new**	EBee
candidissimum ♀H4	More than 30 suppliers
- green	EBee LAma
- white	CPne EBee LAma LEur NBPC WCot
ciliatum	CBro CDes CFil CPom CStu EBee GEdr ITer LAma LEur MLLN MNrw NLar SBla SRot SSpi WCot WIvy
- CT 369	SCnR
- GG 93167	WCot
- var. *liubaense*	CLAP EBee EUJe MGol WCru WWst
- - CT 369	WCot
clavatum	EBee LAma
concinnum	CFir CStu EBee EMar EPot EUJe LAma LEur MGol MOak NLar WCru WPnP WSan WViv
- GG 94152	WCot
consanguineum	CBro CDes CFil CHEx CLAP CMea CPom CRow EBee GBuc GKir ITer LAma LEur MGol NWoo SGar SSpi WCot WPGP
- B&SWJ 071	WCru
- CC 3635	WCot
- CLD 1519	GKir
- GG 92112	WCot
- GG 97083	WCot
- PJ 277	WCot
* - bicolour	GCrs
- 'J. Balis'	WCot
- marbled leaf **new**	WCot
- 'Qinling' **new**	WCot
costatum	CFil CHEx CLAP EBee EPot EUJe GBuc ITer LAma LEur LRHS MOak WCru WMul WPGP WSan
- CC 2924	WCot
danzhuense **new**	EBee
decipiens	EBee
dilatatum	EBee LAma LEur
- *yunnanense* **new**	CLAP
dracontium	CLAP EBee ITer LAma NLar WCru
du-bois-reymondiae	EBee EUJe LAma
ehimense **new**	EBee LAma
elephas	EBee LAma WCru
engleri	EBee EUJe ITer LEur
- GG 98173	WCot
erubescens	EBee EPot ERos EUJe LAma LEur NLar
exappendiculatum	CDes CFil EPar SSpi WCru WPGP
fargesii	CLAP EBee EPot EUJe ITer LAma LEur WCru WWst
flavum	CBro CDes CFil CLAP CMea CStu EBee EHyt EPot EUJe GCal GEdr GIBF GKir ITer ITim LAma LRHS NMen NSla SSpi WBVN WCot WCru WPGP
- CC 1782	WCot WCra
- subsp. *abbreviatum*	WCot
- - GG 84193	WWst
* - *minus* **new**	NWCA
- tall	CLAP ITer
- subsp. *tibeticum*	EBee LEur
formosanum	EBee ITer LAma
- B&SWJ 280	WCru
- B&SWJ 390	CPou

- GG 95166 — WCot
- var. **bicolorifolium** — WCru
  B&SWJ 3528
- f. **stenophyllum** — WCru
  B&SWJ 1477
franchetianum — EBee ITer LAma LEur MGol WCot
fraternum — WCot
- CC 465 — WCot
galeatum — CFir EBee EPot EUJe LAma LEur MGol MOak WCot WCru WViv
§ **griffithii** — EBee EPar EPot EUJe GGar LAma LRHS NMyG SSpi WCru WMul WOBN WPnP WSan WViv
- var. **pradhanii** — EBee
hachijoense new — EBee LAma
handelii — EBee LEur
hatizyoense — WWst
heterophyllum — EBee EUJe ITer LAma LEur
- B&SWJ 2028 — WCru
- 'Baguo' **new** — WCot
ilanense B&SWJ 3030 — WCru
inkiangense — EBee LAma LEur
- **maculatum** — EBee
intermedium — EBee EMar EPot ITer LAma MNrw NMyG SSpi
- CC 3102 — WCot
- GG 96283 — WCot
- var. **biflagellatum** — ITer
- - HWJCM 161 — WCru
- - PB 022 — WCot
iyoanum — EBee LAma WCru
- subsp. **nakaianum new** — EBee
jacquemontii — CAvo CBro CFil CLAP EBee ECho EHyt EPot ETow GBuc GCrs GEdr GGar GKir ITer LAma LRHS NLar NMen WCot
- B&SWJ 2719 — WCru
- GG 94120 — WCot
aff. **jacquemontii** MECCN 29 **new** — NMen
- MECCN 76 — NMen
japonicum — see *A. serratum*
jingdongense new — EBee
jinshajiangense — LAma
kelung-insulare — WCru
  B&SWJ 256
kishidae new — EBee LAma
kiushianum — CFil EBee EFEx LAma SOkd WCru
lichiangense — EBee LAma
lingyunense — EBee LAma WCru
lobatum — EBee EUJe LAma LEur WWst
maximowiczii — EBee LAma WCru
meleagris new — EBee LAma
multisectum — EBee
negishii — EBee LAma WCru WWst
§ **nepenthoides** — CBro CFir EBee EMar EPar EPot EUJe GEdr LAma MGol WCot WMul WSan WViv
- B&SWJ 2614b — WCru
ochraceum — see *A. nepenthoides*
omeiense — EBee LAma
onoticum — EBee LAma
ovale — CLAP
penicillatum — EBee
polyphyllum — EBee
- B&SWJ 3904 — WCru
prazeri new — EBee
propinquum — CLAP EBee EHyt EPot GKir LAma NMen SSpi WCru WViv
purpureogaleatum — EBee LAma
rhizomatum — EBee EUJe LAma LEur WCru
rhombiforme — EBee LAma WCot
ringens misapplied — see *A. robustum*

ringens — CDes EFEx EPot GIBF ITer LAma WPGP
  (Thunberg) Schott
- f. **praecox** — EBee
- - B&SWJ 1515 — WCru
- f. **sieboldii** B&SWJ 551 — WCru
§ **robustum** — CFil CStu EBee LRHS WCot WPGP
saxatile — EBee EUJe LAma
sazensoo — EBee LAma WCru
§ **serratum** — CDes CFil EBee GIBF ITer LAma MNrw SBla WPGP
- AGSJ 249 — WWst
- B&SWJ 5894 — WCru
shihmienense — EBee LAma
§ **sikokianum** — CBro CDes CFil EBee EFEx EPot GIBF LAma LRHS SOkd WCot WCru WPGP WViv
- var. **henryanum** — EBee
- var. **serratum** — EBee
- variegated (v) — WCru
silvestrii new — EBee
souliei new — EBee
speciosum — CHEx EBee EMar EPar EPot EUJe GBuc GGar GSki LAma LEur MOak SSpi WCot WFar WMul WPnP WSan WViv
- B&SWJ 2403 — WCru
- CC 3100 — WCot
- **magnificum new** — WSan
- var. **mirabile** — WCru
  B&SWJ 2712
* - var. **sikkimense** — LAma
taiwanense — CFil SSpi WCot
- B&SWJ 269 — WCru
- B&SWJ 356 — CPou
- var. **brevipedunculatum** B&SWJ 1859 — WCru
- f. **cinereum** B&SWJ 19121 — WCru
- silver leaf — WCot
tashiroi — EBee LAma WCru
ternatipartitum — EBee LAma WDav
- B&SWJ 5790 — WCru
thunbergii — EFEx WCot WViv
- subsp. **autumnale** B&SWJ 1425 — WCru
- subsp. **thunbergii** — WCru
- - variegated (v) — WCru
- subsp. **urashima** — CLAP EBee EFEx GIBF LAma WCru WWst
§ **tortuosum** — CBro CFil CLAP EBee EHyt EMar EPar EPot ERos GEdr GIBF GKir ITer LAma LEur MNrw MOak NLar NMyG SBla WCot WPnP
- CC 1452 — CPou
- CC 1760 — WCot
- CC 3211 — WCot
- CC 3340 — WCot
- GG 892230 — WCot
- GG 94082 — WCot
- GG 97148 — WCot
- var. **helleborifolium** CC 3641 **new** — WCot
- high altitude — EUJe GBuc NMen
- - B&SWJ 2386 — WCru
- low altitude — WSan
- - B&SWJ 2298 — WCru
tosaense — EBee LAma
- B&SWJ 5761 — WCru
- GG 91224 — WCru
triphyllum — CFil CHEx CLAP CPom EBee EMFP EPar EUJe GGar GSki ITer LAma LEdu LRHS MSal SMad SSpi WCru WFar WPGP WPnP WSan

- var. *atrorubens*	CLAP WPGP
unzenense B&SWJ 6226	WCru
§ *utile*	EBee LAma
- CC 3101	WCot
- HWJCM 161	WCru
verrucosum	see *A. griffithii*
- var. *utile*	see *A. utile*
wardii **new**	EBee
wattii **new**	EBee
wumengense **new**	EBee
yamatense	WCru
- subsp. *sugimotoi*	EBee GIBF LAma
- - B&SWJ 5092	WCru
yunnanense	EBee ITer LAma LEur MGol WCot

Arisarum (*Araceae*)

proboscideum	More than 30 suppliers
- MS 958	EMar
vulgare	SIgm
* - f. *maculatum*	LEur
- subsp. *simorrhinum*	EBla LEur WCot
- - SF 296	LEur
- subsp. *vulgare*	LEur WCot

Aristea (*Iridaceae*)

S&SH 88	SAga
* *capensis* **new**	EBee
capitata	CPne
confusa	SWat
ecklonii	CDoC CFil CHEx CPLG CPou EChP EDif EMan GGar GSki IGor SChr SCro SSpi SWat WCot WDyG WWin
- 'Blue Stars' **new**	CBct
ensifolia	CMdw WPrP WSHC
grandis	CFir WCot
§ *major*	CCtw CFir CPne CTrC EMan GGar GSki WHil
- pink	CDes EBee WPGP
montana **new**	CTrC
spiralis	SWat
thyrsiflora	see *A. major*

Aristida (*Poaceae*)

purpurea	CBrm

Aristolochia ✿ (*Aristolochiaceae*)

CC 962	CPLG
baetica	CArn SSpi WCru
californica	LEdu
clematitis	CArn EBee EChP GPoy LEdu MSal WCot WCru WWye
contorta	CBcs SSpi
debilis	EBee
delavayi	CHEx
durior	see *A. macrophylla*
elegans	see *A. littoralis*
fangchi **new**	EBee
gigantea	SMur
griffithii B&SWJ 2118	WCru
heterophylla B&SWJ 3109	WCru
kaempferi B&SWJ 293	WCru
§ *littoralis* ♀H1	SHFr SMur SOWG
§ *macrophylla*	CBcs CBot CHEx EBee ENot GKir IDee NBlu NPal SHBN SLim SPer WCru WDin WSpi
mandschurica	GIBF SSpi
manshuriensis B&SWJ 962	WCru
onoei B&SWJ 4960	WCru
paucinervis	WCru
- AB&S 4393	WCot
pearcei	CPla

sempervirens	SSpi WSHC
sipho	see *A. macrophylla*
tomentosa	ITer WCru
zollingeriana B&SWJ 7030	WCru

Aristotelia (*Elaeocarpaceae*)

§ *chilensis*	WPic
- 'Variegata' (v)	CBcs CSam CWib EBee LAst SEND SLim SPlb WCom WEas
fruticosa	CPne
- (f)	ECou
- (m)	ECou
macqui	see *A. chilensis*
serrata	ECou
- (f)	ECou
- (m)	ECou

Armeria (*Plumbaginaceae*)

§ *alliacea*	CSpe ECha EPPr MWgw NJOw
- f. *leucantha*	SRms WMoo
§ *alpina*	MWat
Bees' hybrids	SRms WAul WMoo
'Bees' Ruby'	WPer
caespitosa	see *A. juniperifolia*
euscadiensis	CSpe EMFP
formosa hybrids	CTri ELan MWgw NBlu NMir
§ *girardii*	EPot NJOw
Joystick Series	NArg NPPs
- 'Joystick Lilac Shades'	IGor NLar
- 'Joystick Red'	CWCL SBri WHil
- 'Joystick White' **new**	WHil
§ *juniperifolia* ♀H4	CLyd CMea CTri EBre ECtt EDAr ELan EPfP ESis LBee LRHS MTho NMen NVic NWCA SIng SRms WWin
- 'Alba'	CMea EDAr ELan EPfP NMen NPri NRya SRms WAbe
- 'Beechwood'	LRHS NHol SBla
- 'Bevan's Variety' ♀H4	EBre ECha ECtt ELan EPfP EPot GCrs GGar GKir LRHS MNrw MWat NHol NJOw NLAp NMen NPri NRya SBla SRms SRot WAbe WLin WPat
- dark	EWes SBla WAbe
- rose	EPot ITim
- spiny dwarf	EPot ITim
juniperifolia x *maritima*	SIng
§ *maritima*	CArn EBre EPfP GKir LRHS MBar MBow NArg NBlu NFor SPet SWal WBea WFar WMoo XPep
- 'Alba'	More than 30 suppliers
- subsp. *alpina*	see *A. alpina*
- 'Bloodstone'	CTri ECot ELan MWat
- 'Corsica'	CMea CTri ECha EPot MBNS MHer NBir NRya SMer XPep
- Düsseldorf Pride	see *A. maritima* 'Düsseldorfer Stolz'
§ - 'Düsseldorfer Stolz'	CElw CPBP EBre ECha ECtt EDAr ELan EPfP GGar GKir ITim LRHS MBri NJOw NMen NPri WBea WPat WWye
- 'Glory of Holland'	EPot
- 'Laucheana'	CBod WHoo WMoo
I - 'Rubrifolia'	CBgR CMea CPlt CSpe EHoe EMan EPPr MSph NJOw NLar WAbe WCot WShp
- 'Ruby Glow'	CTri LBuc
- 'Splendens'	CBcs COIW EMil EMlt ENot EPfP GGar GWCH LAst MBow MHer MLan MWgw NBlu NMir NRya NVic WFar WMoo WPer WShp WWin

- 'Vindictive' ♀H4	CMea CTri EDAr EPfP LGro
'Nifty Thrifty' (v)	CBod CMea EBee EBre EDAr EHoe
	EWes LRHS NLAp NPri NSla SCoo
	SIde SRot WCom WMoo WPat
'Ornament'	ECtt LRav NJOw WFar WHen
plantaginea	see *A. alliacea*
pseudarmeria	EBee ELan MLan
- 'Drumstick Red'	GBBs WPer
- 'Drumstick White'	GBBs WPer
pungens **new**	EBee
setacea	see *A. girardii*
tweedyi	CLyd GTou NLAp WCom
vulgaris	see *A. maritima*
welwitschii	SRms
'Westacre Beauty'	EWes

Armoracia (Brassicaceae)

§ *rusticana*	CArn CBod COld CPrp CSev ELau
	GAbr GPoy IHMH ILis MBri MHer
	MSal NBlu NGHP NPri SIde WHHs
	WHer WJek WLHH WSel WWye
- 'Variegata' (v)	CPrp EBee ELau EMan EMar EMon
	GBar ITer LHop LRHS MAvo NSti
	SMad SPla WBar WCHb WCot
	WPnP WSel

Arnica (Asteraceae)

angustifolia	EBee SRms
subsp. *alpina*	
- subsp. *iljinii*	EBee NBir
chamissonis Schmidt	see *A. sachalinensis*
chamissonis Less.	CHby EBee ELau GBar MNrw MSal
	NLar WJek WPer WWye
lessingii	EBee
longifolia	EBee
montana	CArn GBar GPoy GTou MHer
	MLan NSti SRms SWat WPer WWye
- yellow	MLan
nevadensis	EBee
§ *sachalinensis*	EBee

Arnoglossum (Asteraceae)

§ *plantagineum*	EBee

Aronia (Rosaceae)

arbutifolia	CBcs CDul EPfP EPla GBin MBlu
	MWhi NBlu SHBN SLdr SLon
	WBod WDin
- 'Erecta'	CDul EBee ECrN ELan EPfP LAst
	LEdu LHop LPio MBNS MBlu MBri
	NLar SLPl SMac SPoG SRms SSpi
	WBor WFar
melanocarpa	CAgr CBcs CMCN CMHG EGra
	ELan EPfP EWTr GKir LEdu LPan
	LRHS MAsh MBar MBlu MRav SSpi
	WDin WFar WHCG
- 'Autumn Magic'	CDoC CFai CPMA EBee EPfP LAst
	LRHS MAsh MBlu NLar NPSI SPer
	WBor
- var. *elata*	EPla
* - 'Red Viking'	NPSI
x *prunifolia*	CDoC CMHG CPLG EWTr GKir
	LEdu WHCG
- 'Brilliant'	CDoC COtt CTri EBee LRHS SPer
	WBcn WBod WWes
- 'Nero' (F)	ESim
- 'Viking' (F)	CAgr EBee ECrN ENot EPfP GEil
	GKir LBuc MRav WDin WWes

Arrhenatherum (Poaceae)

elatius subsp. *bulbosum*	CFwr SPer WFar
- - 'Variegatum' (v)	CElw CFwr EChP EGra EHoe ELan
	EPot EPza GBin LAst LEdu LRHS
	MBrN MBri MMoz MWgw MWhi

	NBid NGdn NHol NOrc NSti SHFr
	WFar WMoo WPer WPnP WSSM

Artemisia ✿ (Asteraceae)

§ *abrotanum* ♀H4	More than 30 suppliers
* - 'Variegata' (v)	WWeb
absinthium	CArn CPrp CSLe CSev ELau GPoy
	MBar MBow MHer MLLN MWgw
	NFor NSti SIde SPer SWat WGwG
	WHHs WHbs WPer WWye XPep
* - 'Argentea' **new**	XPep
- 'Corinne Tremaine' (v)	WHer
- 'Lambrook Mist' ♀H3-4	CSLe CSev EBee EChP ELan EMan
	EPfP EPza GBri GMac LRHS MMil
	MRav NCiC NDov NSti NWoo
	SWat WCAu WMnd
- 'Lambrook Silver' ♀H4	More than 30 suppliers
* - 'Variegata' (v)	CBcs
afra	CArn EBee EMan GBar IFro XPep
§ *alba*	CSev EMan EMon EOHP GBar
	GPoy ILis MHer NBur NSti SIde
	SMad WPer WRha XPep
§ - 'Canescens' ♀H4	More than 30 suppliers
annua	CArn MGol MSal SIde WJek WWye
arborescens ♀H3	CArn CMHG CTri ECha SDix SDry
	SPer WDin WHer XPep
- 'Brass Band'	see *A.* 'Powis Castle'
- 'Faith Raven'	CArn EBee ERou GBuc NLar
	WCAu WFar WHer
- 'Little Mice'	EBee EFou
- 'Porquerolles'	CSLe XPep
arctica	GIBF
- subsp. *arctica*	EBee
var. *saxatilis*	
§ *armeniaca*	WWin XPep
assoana	see *A. caucasica*
brachyloba	CFis CSLe MLLN WCHb
californica	IFro XPep
campestris	WRha WSel
subsp. *borealis*	
- var. *borealis* NNS 96-19	WCot
- subsp. *campestris*	XPep
- subsp. *glutinosa* **new**	XPep
- subsp. *maritima*	XPep
camphorata	see *A. alba*
cana	see *Seriphidium canum*
canescens hort.	see *A. alba* 'Canescens'
canescens Willd.	see *A. armeniaca*
capillaris	EBee MSal XPep
§ *caucasica* ♀H3-4	CSLe EBee EBre EDAr EMlt EWes
	GKir LGro LPhx MBrN MHer
	NLRH SBla SRms SRot WCHb WEas
	WJek WPer XPep
- *caucasica*	WFar
chamaemelifolia	CArn IGor MHer WPer WWye
	XPep
cretacea	see *Seriphidium nutans*
discolor Dougl. ex Besser	see *A. michauxiana*
douglasiana	see *A. ludoviciana* 'Valerie Finnis'
'Valerie Finnis'	
dracunculus	CAgr CArn CHad CHby CSev ECha
	ELan ELau GAbr GBar GPoy
	GWCH MBar MBow MHer MRav
	NFor NGHP NPri NVic SIde SPlb
	WBrk WEas WFar WHHs WPer
	WSel WWye XPep
- *dracunculoides*	CArn GBar NPri
filifolia	EBee XPep
frigida ♀H3-4	EBee GBar ILis WHCG XPep
genipi	MSal
glacialis	ECha XPep
gmelinii	EBee GBar GIBF
gnaphalodes	see *A. ludoviciana*
N *granatensis* hort.	MSte

herba-alba	XPep
'Huntington'	CHad
kawakamii B&SWJ 088	WCru
kitadakensis 'Guizhou'	see *A. lactiflora* Guizhou Group
lactiflora ♀H4	CPrp ECha ECtt EFou ELan ELau
	EMon EPar ERou EWTr GBar MRav
	NFor NGdn NOrc NSti SDix SHel
	SMrm SPer SRms WFar WMoo
	WTin WWpP
– dark	see *A. lactiflora* Guizhou Group
– 'Elfenbein'	LHop
§ – Guizhou Group	More than 30 suppliers
– 'Jim Russell'	CElw EBee EWes LPhx NDov
– **purpurea**	see *A. lactiflora* Guizhou Group
– 'Variegata'	see *A. vulgaris* 'Variegata'
– 'Weisses Wunder' **new**	EBee
lagocephala	EMan WCot
lagopus	EBee GIBF
lanata Willd. non Lam.	see *A. caucasica*
leucophylla	EBee
longifolia new	XPep
§ **ludoviciana**	CSLe EBee EBlw ELan ELau ERou
	GBar MBrN MEHN MHer MRav
	MWat NBid NOak NOrc SGar
	SRms WWin WWpP
N – var. **latifolia**	see *A. ludoviciana* subsp.
	ludoviciana var. *latiloba*
– subsp. **ludoviciana**	ECha EGle EMan MRav WHer
var. **incompta**	
§ – – var. **latiloba**	EHoe GBuc GMac LHop LRHS MBro
	MRav NBro NOak NSti SWvt WCot
	WCra WEas WHoo WPer WWpP
– subsp. **mexicana**	WFar
var. **albula**	
– 'Silver Queen' ♀H4	More than 30 suppliers
N – 'Valerie Finnis' ♀H4	More than 30 suppliers
manshurica	EBee EMan WCot
maritima	see *Seriphidium maritimum*
§ **michauxiana**	EBee NBur NSti WHer WKif
molinieri	XPep
niitakayamensis	GBar XPep
nutans	see *Seriphidium nutans*
'Okra'	MMil
palmeri hort.	see *A. ludoviciana*
aff. **parviflora** CLD 1531	EMon
pedemontana	see *A. caucasica*
pontica	CArn ECGN ECha EHoe ELan GBar
	GGar GMac GPoy MBNS MBro
	MHer MRav MWgw NBro NJOw
	NSti SDix SPer SSvw WCom WFar
	WHil WHoo WPer WWeb WWin
	WWye XPep
'Powis Castle' ♀H3	More than 30 suppliers
princeps	CArn
procera Willd.	see *A. abrotanum*
purshiana	see *A. ludoviciana*
pycnocephala	SMad
'David's Choice'	
'Rosenschleier'	CBre EBee EFou EMon EPPr LPhx
	NCGa WPGP
schmidtiana ♀H4	CFis ECha ECot EFou EMan GKir
	MOne MWat NOrc SRms
– 'Nana' ♀H4	More than 30 suppliers
splendens misapplied	see *A. alba* 'Canescens'
splendens Willd.	ELan LPhx NSti WEas
stelleriana	GGar MHer MTho MWgw NBro
	NFor NSti SPet SRms WAul WCAu
	WEas XPep
N – 'Boughton Silver'	More than 30 suppliers
N – 'Mori'	see *A. stelleriana* 'Boughton Silver'
– 'Nana'	EMan NLRH SBla SWvt
– 'Prostata'	see *A. stelleriana* 'Boughton Silver'
– 'Silver Brocade'	see *A. stelleriana* 'Boughton Silver'
tilesii	EBee GIBF

tridentata	see *Seriphidium tridentatum*
vallesiaca	see *Seriphidium vallesiacum*
verlotiorum	GBar
vulgaris	CAgr CArn CPrp ELau GBar GPoy
	GWCH IHMH MGol MHer WHbs
	WHer WJek WLHH WWye
– 'Cragg-Barber Eye' (v)	EBee EChP GSki NBid NPro SAga
	WBar WBry WCHb WCom WHer
	WRha
– 'Crispa'	ELau EMon
– 'Obelisk'	EFou
– Oriental Limelight	More than 30 suppliers
= 'Janlim' (v)	
– 'Peddar's Gold' (v)	EChP EWes
§ – 'Variegata' (v)	EBee GBar GLil NBir NMRc NPro
	NSti SMad WBea WCHb WCom
	WFar WHer WJek WPer WRha
– 'Woolaston' (v)	EMan WCot

Arthrocnemum (Chenopodiaceae)

glaucum new	XPep

Arthropodium (Anthericaceae)

candidum	CBot CRow CStu ECha ECou EPAt
	GAbr GEdr ITim MBrN MWgw
	NWCA SHBN SRot WFar WHal
	WPer WRos
– **maculatum**	GEdr SPlb
– **purpureum**	CBcs CBrm CPLG CPom CTCP
	EBee EChP EMan EPza GBri GCal
	GGar LRHS MLan NJOw NLAp
	WCot WFar WHrl WPGP
* **carlesii**	CRHN
cirratum	CHEx CTrC ECou ERea GGar IDee
	MFOX MLan WSHC
– 'Matapouri Bay'	CBcs CHEx EBee EMan EMil WCot
	WPGP
milleflorum	GGar WCot

Arthrostylidium (Poaceae)

naibuense	CFil

artichoke, globe see *Cynara cardunculus* Scolymus Group

artichoke, Jerusalem see *Helianthus tuberosus*

Arum (Araceae)

alpinum	CFil WPGP
§ **besserianum**	WWst
'Chameleon'	CDes CLAP EFou EMan EMon LEur
	MAvo MBct MMil MNrw MTho
	NBir SIgm SMad SPer SSpi WCot
	WFar WHal WHil WTin WViv
§ **concinnatum**	CFil CStu EBee EMon EPot GIBF
	ITer LAma LEur SChr SSpi WPGP
	WPrP
cornutum	see *Sauromatum venosum*
creticum	CArn CBro CFir EChP ECha EHyt
	EMan EPar ETow GBuc IBlr ITer
	MAvo MMil MNrw MRav MTho
	SCnR SDix SRot SSpi WCot WPGP
– MS 696	MNrw
– FCC form	EPot MTed SBla WCot
– white	MNrw
– yellow	NBir NPar WFar WIvy
creticum x **italicum**	LEur MAvo MDKP
cyrenaicum	CDes CStu EBee EHyt MNrw WCot
– NS 21	LEur
§ **dioscoridis**	CDes CStu EBee EWes MMil MTho
	NLar WCot WPGP
– JCA 195.197	WCot
– MS&CL 524	ITer
– W 5658	LEur

- var. *cyprium*	EBee LEur
§ - var. *dioscoridis*	LEur WCot
- - JCA 195200	WPrP
- var. *liepoldtii*	see *A. dioscoridis* var. *dioscoridis*
- var. *philistaeum*	WWst
- var. *smithii*	see *A. dioscoridis* var. *dioscoridis*
dracunculus	see *Dracunculus vulgaris*
elongatum RS 274/87	WCot
hygrophilum	EMon
idaeum	SSpi
italicum	CFwr CLAP CTri EBee EHyt EWTr
	GEil GFlt LAma MBri MTho NJOw
	NLar NRog SBod SEND SWat WAbe
	WCot WFar WPnP WSHC WShi WStI
- subsp. *albispathum*	CDes CFil CHid CStu EBee EMon
	LAma LEur MTed WCot WPGP
- black-spotted	EHyt LEur WFar
- 'Green Marble'	SBla WFar
- subsp. *italicum*	EPla IHMH WTin
- - 'Bill Baker'	EMon LEur
- - 'Cyclops' EAF 7701	CHid CLAP MNrw WCot
§ - - 'Marmoratum' ♀H4	More than 30 suppliers
- - 'Sparkler'	WCot
- - 'Spotted Jack'	MNrw WCot WCru
- - 'Tiny'	CFir EMon GCal LEur
§ - - 'White Winter'	ECGP EMon GBuc MAvo WSPU
- 'Nancy Lindsay'	EMar EMon WPrP
- subsp. *neglectum*	SChr
- - 'Miss Janay Hall' (v)	MAvo WCot
- 'Pictum'	see *A. italicum* subsp. *italicum*
	'Marmoratum'
- 'Whitegate' **new**	CMea
jacquemontii	WWst
korolkowii	NRog
maculatum	CArn CRWN EPar EPot EUJe GPoy
	LAma MBow MHer MRav MSal
	WHer WShi WWye
- 'Painted Lady' (v)	WCot
- 'Pleddel'	MRav WCot
* - 'Variegatum' (v)	GPoy
nickelii	see *A. concinnatum*
§ *nigrum*	CDes LEur WCot
- CE&H 524	LEur
orientale	EHyt EPot ETow LEur
- subsp. *amoenum*	MNrw
- subsp. *besserianum*	see *A. besserianum*
- subsp. *orientale* **new**	CPom
palaestinum	EMon
petteri hort.	see *A. nigrum*
pictum	CLAP EBee LAma LEur LRHS NRog
	SBla WCot WIvy WTin
- 'Taff's Form'	see *A. italicum* subsp. *italicum*
	'White Winter'
purpureospathum	CDes EHyt LEur WCot WPGP
§ *rupicola* var. *rupicola*	WWst
- var. *virescens*	EBee WCot
sintenisii	EBee WCot WWst
'Streaked Spectre'	EMon

Aruncus ✿ (*Rosaceae*)

AGSJ 214	NHol
aethusifolius ♀H4	More than 30 suppliers
- 'Little Gem' B&SWJ 4475	WCru
asiaticus	EBee
§ *dioicus*	CTri ECGP EChP EGle EMFW EMil
	EPfP EWTr GGar GKir GSki LHop
	LPBA LRHS NBlu NChi NGdn NPri
	SPet SPlb SSpe WBea WCAu WFar
	WHoo WLow WPnP WWpP
- (m) ♀H4	CDoC CRow EBre ECha ELan ENot
	EPla GSki LLck MBNS MRav
	MWgw NBro NFor NHol NSti SGar
	SMad SPer SRms SSpi SWat WFar
	WMoo WPer

- var. *acuminatus*	EBee
- Child of Two Worlds	see *A. dioicus* 'Zweiweltenkind'
- 'Glasnevin'	CRow CSev ECha ECtt EMan MRav
	NHol WFar
- var. *kamtschaticus*	EChP EWes NHol NLar WWpP
- - AGSJ 238	NHol
- - B&SWJ 8624	WCru
- 'Kneiffii'	More than 30 suppliers
§ - 'Zweiweltenkind'	CBrm CFwr EBee EHrv EWTr GCal
	GSki NGby NLar SMad
'Horatio'	EBee EMon LPhx WCot
'Johannifest'	EBee EMon
'Noble Spirit' **new**	NLar
plumosus	see *A. dioicus*
sinensis	EWll WFar
sylvestris	see *A. dioicus*
'Woldemar Meier'	EMon

Arundinaria ✿ (*Poaceae*)

amabilis	see *Pseudosasa amabilis*
anceps	see *Yushania anceps*
angustifolia	see *Pleioblastus chino*
	'Murakamianus'
auricoma	see *Pleioblastus viridistriatus*
chino	see *Pleioblastus chino*
disticha	see *Pleioblastus pygmaeus* var.
	distichus
falconeri	see *Himalayacalamus falconeri*
fargesii	see *Bashania fargesii*
fastuosa	see *Semiarundinaria fastuosa*
fortunei	see *Pleioblastus variegatus*
funghomii	see *Schizostachyum funghomii*
§ *gigantea*	SDry WJun
- subsp. *tecta*	CBcs MGos
hindsii	see *Pleioblastus hindsii* hort.
hookeriana misapplied	see *Himalayacalamus falconeri*
	'Damarapa'
hookeriana Munro	see *Himalayacalamus*
	hookerianus
humilis	see *Pleioblastus humilis*
japonica	see *Pseudosasa japonica*
jaunsarensis	see *Yushania anceps*
maling	see *Yushania maling*
marmorea	see *Chimonobambusa*
	marmorea
murielae	see *Fargesia murielae*
nitida	see *Fargesia nitida*
oedogonata	see *Clavinodum oedogonatum*
palmata	see *Sasa palmata*
pumila	see *Pleioblastus argenteostriatus*
	f. *pumilus*
pygmaea	see *Pleioblastus pygmaeus*
quadrangularis	see *Chimonobambusa*
	quadrangularis
simonii	see *Pleioblastus simonii*
spathiflora	see *Thamnocalamus spathiflorus*
tessellata	see *Thamnocalamus tessellatus*
vagans	see *Sasaella ramosa*
variegata	see *Pleioblastus variegatus*
veitchii	see *Sasa veitchii*
viridistriata	see *Pleioblastus auricomus*
'Wang Tsai'	see *Bambusa multiplex*
	'Floribunda'

Arundo (*Poaceae*)

donax	More than 30 suppliers
- 'Golden Chain'	EPPr
- 'Macrophylla'	CBig CFil CRow EPPr EPla LEdu
	LPJP WPGP
- 'Variegata'	see *A. donax* var. *versicolor*
§ - var. *versicolor* (v)	More than 30 suppliers
- yellow variegated (v)	CKno SEND
formosana	CKno CRez EMan EPPr
pliniana	CMCo CRow EPPr LEdu

Asarina (Scrophulariaceae)

antirrhiniflora	see *Maurandella antirrhiniflora*
barclayana	see *Maurandya barclayana*
erubescens	see *Lophospermum erubescens*
hispanica	see *Antirrhinum hispanicum*
lophantha	see *Lophospermum scandens*
lophospermum	see *Lophospermum scandens*
§ procumbens	CBri CBrm CTCP EBee EBre EMan EPfP GAbr GBBs GKir GTou MTho NRya SHFr SIng SRms SSpi WFar WGwG WHer WPer WWin
– compact	GKev
'Victoria Falls'	see *Maurandya* 'Victoria Falls'

Asarum ✿ (Aristolochiaceae)

albomaculatum B&SWJ 1726	WCru
arifolium	CDes CHid CLAP EBee EHrv EPar GBBs LEur NLar
* campaniforme	CLAP EBee LAma LEur WCru
canadense	CArn EBee EChP EMar EPot EUJe GBBs GGar GPoy GSki LRHS MSal NLar NMyG WCru
caudatum	CAvo CDes CHid CLAP CRow CStu EBee ECha EHyt EMan EPPr GBuc LEdu LEur MTed NBro NLar NSti NWCA SRms WCot WCru WFar WPGP WPnP
– white	CDes CLAP SSpi
caudigerum	EBee LAma LEur
– B&SWJ 1517	WCru
caulescens	CLAP EBee LAma LEur WCru
– B&SWJ 5886	WCru
chinense	EBee LEur
debile	EBee LAma SSpi
delavayi	EBee LAma LEur WCot WCru
epigynum B&SWJ 3443	WCru
– 'Silver Web'	CLAP
– – B&SWJ 3442	WCru
europaeum	More than 30 suppliers
fauriei	WCru
forbesii	EBee LEur
geophilum	EBee
hartwegii	CDes CLAP EBee EHyt EMan EMar EPar EPot ERos GBuc WCot WCru WPGP
– NNS 00-78	WCot
heterotropoides	EBee
– f. mandshuricum	LEur
hexalobum	WCot
hirsutisepalum	CLAP
hypogynum B&SWJ 3628	WCru
ichangense **new**	EBee
infrapurpureum	WCot
– B&SWJ 1994	WCru
insigne **new**	EBee
kumageanum	WCot
lemmonii	EMan LEdu WCru
leptophyllum B&SWJ 1983	WCru
longirhizomatosum	EBee WCru
macranthum	WCot
– B&SWJ 1691	WCru
maculatum	WCot
– B&SWJ 1114	WCru
magnificum	CLAP EBee EPot LAma LEur WCru
maximum	CLAP EBee EMar EPot LAma LEur WCru WMul
minamitanianum	WCru
* minor 'Honeysong' **new**	EBee
* naniflorum	EBee
'Eco Decor' **new**	
pulchellum	EBee EHrv EMan EPar WCot WCru

shuttleworthii	CLAP NLar WCru
sieboldii	CLAP WCru
speciosum	EBee
'Buxom Beauty' **new**	
splendens	CBos CDes CFee CStu EBee EHoe EHrv EMan EPot GMac LAma LEdu LEur LHop MCCP NGdn NMyG NSti NVic SBla SMad SMrm SSpi WCot WCru WHer WMul WPGP WShp
taipingshanianum B&SWJ 1688	WCru
takaoi	SSpi
– 'Galaxy' **new**	EBee
virginicum	EBee
wulingense	EBee LEur WCru

Asclepias (Asclepiadaceae)

'Cinderella'	CSev EBee LBuc SGar SIgm WWin SSte
curassavica	CHrt CSev LRHS MSPs SHFr SSpi SSte
– 'Red Butterfly' **new**	EBee
§ fascicularis	SIgm
fasciculata	see *A. fascicularis*
fruticosa	see *Gomphocarpus fruticosus*
incarnata	CAgr CSev EBee ELan ERou GKir MTis SMHy SPer SSte WAul WOld WPer
– 'Alba'	EChP ELan EMon
– 'Ice Ballet'	EBee EMan ERou LBuc LHop LRHS SAga SIgm SSte SWat WMnd WMoo WWin
– 'Iceberg'	EBee
– 'Soulmate'	CFai EBee EChP EPfP EWll LRHS LRav MLLN MMHG NJOw WMoo WWeb
– 'White Superior'	EBee
physocarpa	see *Gomphocarpus physocarpus*
purpurascens	CArn CTCP EChP SSte
speciosa	CAgr EBee NLar SScr
sullivantii	EBee EMan SSte
syriaca	CAgr CArn EBee LRHS MSte SSte WWin
tuberosa	CArn CBcs COlW CPom CTCP EBee ELau EMan GKir GPoy LHop LRHS MHer MMHG MNrw MSal NBir NDov SMad SPet SSpi SSte WCot WMnd WShp WWin
– Gay Butterflies Group	EBee MLan NLar SMrm
– 'Hello Yellow'	LRHS SSte WWeb
verticillata	SIgm SSte

Asimina (Annonaceae)

triloba (F)	IArd MBlu NLar WNor
– 'Davis' (F) **new**	CAgr

Askidiosperma (Restionaceae)

chartaceum	CTrC
esterhuyseniae	CTrC WNor
paniculatum	CTrC

Asparagus (Asparagaceae)

asparagoides ♀H1	ERea EShb SEND
§ – 'Myrtifolius'	CHal SYvo
cochinchinensis B&SWJ 3425	ELau WCru
crassicladus	EShb
densiflorus 'Mazeppa'	EShb
– 'Myersii' ♀H1	CHal ERea SRms
– Sprengeri Group ♀H1	CHal LRHS MBri
– – 'Variegatus' **new**	EShb
falcatus	MBri SEND
officinalis	ERea SEND WFar
– 'Atlas'	EMui

- 'Backlim' ♀H4 — EMui
- 'Butler' — SDea
- 'Cito' (m) — SDea
- 'Dariana' — SDea
- 'Franklim' — CTri EMui WFar
- 'Gijnlim' ♀H4 — EMui SDea
- 'Purple Jacq Ma' — EMui
- 'Purple Jumbo' — EBee

plumosus — see *A. setaceus*
pseudoscaber — EMan EShb SMad
  'Spitzenschleier'
retrofractus — CFil WPGP
scandens — EShb
schoberioides — WCru
  B&SWJ 871
§ *setaceus* ♀H1 — CHal LRHS MBri
- 'Pyramidalis' ♀H1 — MBri
suaveolens — EShb
verticillatus — SRms

Asperula (*Rubiaceae*)

§ *arcadiensis* ♀H3 — CLyd EHyt EPot NWCA SBla
- JCA 201-100 — CStu
aristata subsp. *scabra* — EBee ECha ELan EMan EMon
- subsp. *thessala* — see *A. sintenisii*
cyanchica — MSal
daphneola — CNic ECho EHyt EWes SBla
gussonei — CLyd CMea CStu EPot GAbr GCrs
  LRHS MBro MWat NLAp NMen
  NWCA SBla SScr WAbe WPat
hirta — CNic
lilaciflora — see *A. lilaciflora* subsp. *lilaciflora*
  var. *caespitosa*
§ - subsp. *lilaciflora* — CLyd CPBP EDAr NMen WWin
nitida — ECho
- subsp. *puberula* — see *A. sintenisii*
odorata — see *Galium odoratum*
orientalis — WPGP
§ *sintenisii* ♀H2-3 — CLyd LBee LRHS MBro NMen
  NWCA SBla SScr WAbe WHoo
suberosa misapplied — see *A. arcadiensis*
suberosa Sibth. & Sm. — ECho WAbe
taurina — NLar NSti WCHb
  subsp. *caucasica*
tinctoria — CArn EOHP GBar GPoy MHer MSal
  SRms WCHb

Asphodeline (*Asphodelaceae*)

liburnica — CBro EBee ECGN EChP ECha ELan
  EMan EMar ERos ERou GSki MBro
  MRav MWgw SAga SEND SGar
  SSpi WCAu WCot WFar WGwG
  WPer
§ *lutea* — More than 30 suppliers
§ - 'Gelbkerze' — GBBs LRHS WBVN
- Yellow Candle — see *A. lutea* 'Gelbkerze'
taurica — ECho EMan SMrm SVal WPer
- JJ 96-100 — WCot

Asphodelus (*Asphodelaceae*)

acaulis — EHyt SIgm SSpi WAbe WCot
§ *aestivus* — CDes EBee ECha GAbr GSki NBur
  SMad SSvw SWat WBVN WPer
albus — CArn CBot CBri CPLG EBee ECha
  GBuc GIBF GSki NBid SPlb SRms
  WCot WPer
cerasiferus — see *A. ramosus*
fistulosus — ECGN MMHG NBir WPer WPrP
  WWin XPep
lusitanicus — see *A. ramosus*
luteus — see *Asphodeline lutea*
microcarpus — see *A. aestivus*
§ *ramosus* — CBrm CPar EBee ECGN ECGP
  EChP EGoo EMan GSki MNrw

MTho SGar SIgm SMrm WBVN
WCot WPer XPep

Aspidistra (*Convallariaceae*)

attenuata — CKob
- B&SWJ 377 — WCru
caespitosa — IBlr LEur WCot
  'Jade Ribbons'
'China Star' — WCot
'China Sun' — WCot
daibuensis — CKob
- B&SWJ 312b — WCru
elatior ♀H1 — CBct CHEx CHal EBak IBlr LRHS
  MBri NPal SAPC SArc SEND SMad
  SYvo WCot
- 'Akebono' (v) — WCot
- 'Asahi' (v) — WCot
- 'Hoshi-zora' (v) — WCot
- 'Milky Way' (v) — CBct CHid CKob EBee EMan IBlr
  IFro LEur MSPs MTho SEND SMur
  WCot WHil
- 'Okame' (v) — WCot
- 'Variegata' (v) ♀H1 — CBct CHEx CHal EShb IBlr IFro
  MTho NBir SMad SYvo WCot
linearifolia 'Leopard' — WCot
longiloba — EBee LEur
lurida — EBee IBlr LEur
- 'Irish Mist' (v) — IBlr
minutiflora — EBee LEur
saxicola — WCru
  'Uan Fat Lady' **new**

Asplenium ✿ (*Aspleniaceae*)

adiantum-nigrum — LRHS SRms WAbe
bulbiferum ♀H1-2 — CHEx CPLG CTrC EFtx ESlt NMar
  SMur
bulbiferum — EAmu
  × *oblongifolium* **new**
§ *ceterach* — EBee SRms WAbe WHer
dareoides — SOkd SRot SSpi WAbe
ebenoides **new** — WAbe
flaccidum — CTrC
'Maori Princess' **new** — CTrC
nidus ♀H1 — LRHS MBri
oblongifolium — CTrC
platyneuron — EBee WAbe
ruta-muraria — EFer SRms
§ *scolopendrium* ♀H4 — More than 30 suppliers
- 'Angustatum' — CLAP CMil CWCL EBee GBin GEdr
  LRHS MAsh MAvo MBct MCCP
  MGos MMoz MTed MWgw NHol
  NLar NVic SMac WBor WCru WPnP
- 'Capitatum' — MDun
* - 'Circinatum' — CRow WPGP
- 'Conglomeratum' — SRms
- 'Cornutoabruptum' — NMar
- Crispum Group — CLAP CRow CSBt CWCL EBee
  EBre ECha EFer ELan EPza NHol
  SRms WAbe WFib WPGP
- - 'Golden Queen' — CLAP
- 'Crispum Bolton's — NBro WFib WPGP
  Nobile' ♀H4
- Crispum Cristatum — CLAP EChP SCro
  Group
- Crispum Fimbriatum — GQui
  Group
- Cristatum Group — CElw CFwr CHEx CLAP CPrp
  CRow EBee EHrv ELan EMar EPfP
  EWTr LRHS MBri MGos MRav
  MWgw NDlv NHol NMar SNut
  SPer SPla SRms SWat WFib WRic
- 'Cristatum' — EBlw MAsh SSto
- Fimbriatum Group — CLAP WRic
- 'Furcatum' — CFwr CLAP CPrp EBee GEdr

– 'Kaye's Lacerated' ♀H4	CLAP CRow EFer ELan NHol NMar SChu
– Laceratum Group	CLAP SRms
– Marginatum Group	NMar SWat WPGP
– – 'Irregulare'	NHol SChu SRms WFib
– 'Muricatum'	CLAP ELan GBin NMar SChu WFib WTin
– 'Ramocristatum'	CLAP CRow NMar
– Ramomarginatum Group	CLAP ELan SRms WAbe WFar WRic
– 'Sagittatocristatum'	WPGP
– 'Sagittato-projectum Sclater' **new**	WFib
– Undulatum Group	CLAP CPLG EBee ECGP EFtx EMFW MAsh NBir NMar NSti SPla SRms SSpi SWat WPnP WRic
– Undulatum Cristatum Group	CLAP MBri NDlv
septentrionale	SRms
trichomanes ♀H4	More than 30 suppliers
– 'Bipinnatum'	WRic
– Cristatum Group	SRms
– Grandiceps Group	EFer
– Incisum Group	CLAP EBee NHol NMar NOrc
– subsp. *pachyrachis*	NMar
viride	SRms

Astartea (Myrtaceae)
fascicularis	CPLG CTrC SOWG

Astelia (Asteliaceae)
alpina **new**	IBlr
banksii	CBos CDoC CPen CTrC IBal LEdu LPio WAbe WDyG
§ *chathamica* ♀H3	More than 30 suppliers
– 'Silver Spear'	see *A. chathamica*
cunninghamii	see *A. solandri*
fragrans	ECou GGar IBlr LEdu WCot WDyG
graminea	IBlr
grandis	CHEx CTrC IBlr LEdu WCot
'Lodestone' **new**	CStu
'Luzulliea Johnsen' **new**	LPBA
nervosa	CAbb CFil EBee EGra IBlr LEdu SAPC SArc WCot WMul WPGP
– 'Bronze Giant'	IBlr
– 'Westland'	CBcs CBod CDoC CPen CTrC EMan GCal IBlr SSpi WLeb WMul
nivicola	EBee IBlr
– 'Red Gem'	GCal IBlr LEdu
petriei	IBlr
§ *solandri*	CHEx IBlr LEdu
trinervia	IBlr

Aster ✿ (Asteraceae)
ACE 425	WOBN
acris see *A. sedifolius*	
§ *albescens*	CPle
alpigenus	CPBP
var. *alpigenus*	
– var. *haydenii*	NBid
alpinus ♀H4	CHrt CTri CWCL EPfP GKir IHMH MNrw MWgw NJOw SBla SECG SPet SRms WBrk WFar WPer WShp WStl WWin
– var. *albus*	EMil EPfP IHMH WCAu WPer WShp WWeb
– Dark Beauty	see *A. alpinus* 'Dunkle Schöne'
§ – 'Dunkle Schöne'	CBrm CHrt GAbr GKir LDai SRms WCra WPer WWeb
– 'Goliath'	ECho GAbr SPlb WFar WWeb
– 'Happy End'	CHrt CM&M EBee EMil IHMH LDai NLar NOak SRms WWeb
– 'Pinkie'	CBrm GAbr ITim MSPs MWrn NLar WWeb

– 'Trimix'	EMlt ESis LPVe NArg NBir SRms WFar
– violet	WPer
– 'White Beauty'	SRms
* – 'Wolfii'	SRms
amelloides	see *Felicia amelloides*
amellus	ITim NFor SPer WMoo
– 'Blue King'	EWsh MLLN SWvt WCAu
– 'Breslau'	EBee
– 'Brilliant'	EBee EChP ECtt EFou EGle EMan MLLN MMil MNFA MRav MWat WOld WWin
– 'Butzemann'	GMac
– 'Doktor Otto Petschek'	EBee WFar WViv
– 'Fourncett Flourish'	EFou
– 'Framfieldii' ♀H4	WFar WOld
– 'Jacqueline Genebrier' ♀H4	CHar CMil EGle EPPr SChu SCro WCot WIvy WSHC
– 'Joseph Lakin'	EBee WFar
– 'King George' ♀H4	CBel CDoC CMHG EBee EBre ECtt EFou EGle EHrv ELan EPfP ERou GKir LRHS MBri MMil MRav MSte MWat SChu SPer SPla SRms SWat WBVN WCAu WCot WFar WMnd WOld
– 'Kobold'	LRHS WFar
– 'Lac de Genève'	EBee LRHS MRav NLar SUsu WCot WFar WOld
– 'Lady Hindlip'	WEas WFar
– 'Moerheim Gem'	WEas
– 'Nocturne'	EGle ERou WCot WOld
– 'Peach Blossom'	EBee WCAu
– 'Pink Pearl'	WFar
– Pink Zenith	see *A. amellus* 'Rosa Erfüllung'
§ – 'Rosa Erfüllung'	CDoC CHrt EBee EBre ECtt EFou ELan EMar EPfP ERou GBuc GKir LHop MLLN MNFA MRav NFor SChu SPla SWvt WCAu WCot WMnd WOld WPer WTin
– 'Rotfeuer'	EFou
– 'Rudolph Goethe'	CBri CHar EBee EBlw EMil LRHS MLLN MMil MRav MWhi NVic SHBN STes WFar WMoo WOld WShp WWye
– 'September Glow'	EFou EGle
– 'Sonia'	ECha EGle NLar WCAu WCra WFar
– 'Sonora'	EBee ECGP EGle ERou LHop MAnH MSte NChi NDov SAga WHoo WKif WOld
– 'Sternkugel'	WOld
– 'Ultramarine'	WFar
– 'Vanity'	GBuc WOld
§ – 'Veilchenkönigin' ♀H4	More than 30 suppliers
N – Violet Queen	see *A. amellus* 'Veilchenkönigin'
– 'Weltfriede'	WOld
'Anja's Choice'	EBee EMon EPPr WOld
asper	see *A. bakerianus*
asperulus	EPPr LPhx MBri SBla SMHy
'Bahamas' **new**	MBri
§ *bakerianus*	EBee SUsu WFar WPer
'Barbados' **new**	MBri
capensis 'Variegatus'	see *Felicia amelloides* variegated
§ *carolinianus*	WOld
'Cassandra' **new**	MBri
'Cassy' **new**	MBri
'Chelsea' **new**	MBri
chilensis	EBee
ciliolatus 'Bigwig'	EBee
'Cirina Dark' PBR **new**	MBri
'Climax' misapplied	see *A. laevis* 'Calliope', *A. laevis* 'Arcturus'
'Climax' Vicary Gibbs	WOld
'Climax' ambig.	EBee GBuc GCal LPhx MRav NSti SAga SMrm

	coelestis	see *Felicia amelloides*
	coloradoensis	CPBP NSla
	concolor	EBee
	'Connecticut Snow Flurry'	see *A. ericoides* f. *prostratus* 'Snow Flurry'
	'Coombe Fishacre' ♀H4	CHrt ColW EBee EChP EMan EPPr ERou GBuc GCal MMil MOne MRav MSte SAga SHel SOkh SPla SSvw SUsu WCom WCot WFar WMnd WOld WTin
	cordifolius	WFar
	- 'Aldebaran'	LPhx
	- 'Chieftain' ♀H4	LPhx MNrw MTed SAga WIvy WOld
	- 'Elegans'	CStr EBee EFou MBri MSte NSti WBro WIvy WMnd WMoo WOld
	- 'Ideal'	EBee EFou WOld WPer
	- 'Little Carlow'	see *A.* 'Little Carlow' (*cordifolius* hybrid)
	- 'Little Dorrit'	see *A.* 'Little Dorrit' (*cordifolius* hybrid)
	- 'Photograph'	see *A.* 'Photograph'
	- 'Silver Queen'	EBee WOld
	- 'Silver Spray'	CPrp EFou EMan ERou GMac MLLN MNFA MWat WOld WPer
	- 'Sweet Lavender' ♀H4	EBee ERou WOld
	corymbosus	see *A. divaricatus*
	'Cotswold Gem'	WCot
§	'Dark Pink Star'	WOld
	'Deep Pink Star'	see *A.* 'Dark Pink Star'
	delavayi	EBee SUsu
	diffusus	see *A. lateriflorus*
	diplostephioides	EChP NLar SCro WAul
§	*divaricatus*	More than 30 suppliers
§	- 'Eastern Star'	NDov WBVN WCot WOld
	- Raiche form	see *A. divaricatus* 'Eastern Star'
	drummondii	EBee
N	*dumosus*	SHel WFar WPer
	eatonii	EBee
	ericoides	CHrt CSam EShb MFOX NPPs NWCA WFar WMoo WWin XPep
	- 'Blue Star' ♀H4	CPrp CWCL EBee EFou GBuc LPVe LRHS MBnl MLLN MSte NLar NSti SChu SHel SPoG WBor WCAu WCot WMnd WOld
	- 'Brimstone' ♀H4	EPPr MRav WOld
	- 'Cinderella'	ColW GBuc GMac MNFA NSti WOld
	- 'Cirylle'	EFou SMHy SMrm
	- 'Constance'	WOld
	- 'Enchantress'	ERou
	- 'Erlkönig'	CPrp EBee EChP EFou EMan EPPr GAbr LAst LRHS MBnl MMil MNFA MSte MWgw NCGa SChu SPla SSpe SWat WMnd WOld WPer WWin
	- 'Esther'	CHea EBee ECha EFou EGle ELan EOrc ERou MSte NLar SDix WOld
	- 'Golden Spray' ♀H4	EBee EFou MBow NLar NSti SHel WFar WMnd WOld WOut
	- 'Herbstmyrte'	EBee GBuc MLLN NGby
	- 'Hon. Edith Gibbs'	WOld
	- 'Maidenhood'	WOld
	- 'Monte Cassino'	see *A. pilosus* var. *pringlei* 'Monte Cassino'
	- 'Pink Cloud' ♀H4	More than 30 suppliers
	- f. *prostratus*	EBee EMon EOrc EPot LRHS SGar WFar
§	- - 'Snow Flurry' ♀H4	CBre CMea CSam EBee ECha ECtt EFou EGle EMan LPVe MBnl MLLN MNrw SPla SUsu WBor WCAu WCom WCot WEas WMnd WOld
	- 'Rosy Veil'	CHea GMac MHom MNFA NBir NGdn WOld WTin
	- 'Ruth McConnell'	NSti
	- 'Schneegitter'	MLLN MSte WFar
	- 'Sulphurea'	MWat
	- 'White Heather'	CPrp EBee GMac MNFA NLar WCot WIvy WMnd WOld WRHF WTin
	- 'Yvette Richardson'	MHom MSte SMHy WOld
	'Fanny's Fall'	see *A. oblongifolius* 'Fanny's'
	farreri	SSpi
*	- 'Blue Moon'	WCom
§	*flaccidus*	EBee GKir LRHS WCot
	foliaceus	EBee
	- from Montana	EPPr
	x *frikartii*	EBee EBre EFou EGle ELan EPar EPfP ERou LAst MBro MRav SAga SChu SHBN SRms SWvt WEas WMnd WOld WPer WWin
	- 'Eiger'	WOld
	- 'Flora's Delight'	EBre EMan GKir MRav WOld
	- 'Jungfrau'	CFis EBee MRav MSte NLar WOld WWhi
N	- 'Mönch' ♀H4	More than 30 suppliers
	- Wonder of Stafa	see *A.* x *frikartii* 'Wunder von Stäfa'
§	- 'Wunder von Stäfa' ♀H4	CEnd EBee ECtt ELan EMan EMar EPfP GBuc GKir LHop LRHS MAvo MBNS MRav NBlu NLar SChu SLon WCAu WCot WMnd WOld WPGP WPnP WTel
	'Herfstweelde'	CMil CWCL EBee EFou EMon GBuc LRHS MSte NCGa WFar WOld
	x *herveyi*	EMan EMon LPhx LRHS MSph SAga WOld
	himalaicus	EBee GTou MWrn SRms
*	'Hittlemaar'	WCot
§	'Hon. Vicary Gibbs' (*ericoides* hybrid)	EBee GMac MHom MNFA MSte WOld WOut
	hybridus luteus	see x *Solidaster luteus*
	ibericus	EBee
§	'Kylie' ♀H4	EBee EMon EPPr GBuc MHom MSte NCGa WBor WCot WFar WOld WTin
	laevis	MSte NLar WTin
§	- 'Arcturus'	CFir EBee MFir MHar MLLN MMil NMRc NSti SSvw WCot WFar
	- 'Blauhügel'	GCal
§	- 'Calliope'	More than 30 suppliers
	- var. *geyeri*	MNrw
	lanceolatus Kuntze	see *Pyrrocoma lanceolata*
	lanceolatus Willd.	WCot
	- 'Edwin Beckett'	CBre EMan GMac MNFA WOld
§	*lateriflorus*	EBee WOld WPer
	- 'Bleke Bet'	WOld
	- 'Buck's Fizz'	CHrt EBee ELan NLar SHar WOld
	- 'Datschii'	WFar
	- 'Delight'	MLLN
	- 'Horizontalis' ♀H4	More than 30 suppliers
	- 'Jan'	WOld
	- 'Lady in Black'	More than 30 suppliers
	- 'Lovely'	EBee EMan LRHS MBow MBro MLLN WOld
	- 'Prince'	More than 30 suppliers
	laterifolius	see *A. ericoides* f. *prostratus* 'Snow Flurry'
	'Snow Flurry'	'Snow Flurry'
	linariifolius	EBee
§	*linosyris*	EBee MSte NLar NSti SPer WHer WOld
	- 'Goldilocks'	see *A. linosyris*
§	'Little Carlow' (*cordifolius* hybrid) ♀H4	More than 30 suppliers
§	'Little Dorrit' (*cordifolius* hybrid)	EBee MAvo MLLN NBro NOak WHil WOld
	maackii	EBee

macrophyllus	CPou EBee ELan EMon GFlt LRHS	
	NLar WOld	
- 'Albus'	EMon EPPr GFlt WFar WIvy WOld	
- 'Twilight'	CMea EBee EChP ECha ECtt EFou	
	EGle EMan EOrc EPla GCal LLWP	
	MBnl MLLN MNFA MSte NDov	
	NSti SDix SSpe WCAu WCot WIvy	
	WMnd WOld WTin	
'Midget'	NNor	
mongolicus	see *Kalimeris mongolica*	
natalensis	see *Felicia rosulata*	
novae-angliae	ELau SECG WMoo WOld	
- 'Andenken an Alma Pötschke'	More than 30 suppliers	
- 'Andenken an Paul Gerbe'	EMon NGby	
- 'Annabelle de Chazal'	WOld	
- Autumn Snow	see *A. novae-angliae* 'Herbstschnee'	
- 'Barr's Blue'	EFou EMon EWsh LRHS MAvo	
	MBNS MSte MTed MWat NFla NSti	
	SRms SSvw WCAu WFar WMoo	
	WOld	
- 'Barr's Pink'	CBre CBri EChP ECtt EFou EMon	
	MRav MWat NFla SEND SHel WBrk	
	WCAu WFar WHrl WOld WPer	
* - 'Barr's Purple'	WOld	
- 'Barr's Violet'	EGle EPPr MAvo MSPs NFor SHel	
	SRms WCot WHoo WHrl WOld	
	WPer WTin WWpP	
- 'Bishop Colenso'	EFou	
- 'Christopher Harbutt'	EGle ERou NPro WOld	
- 'Crimson Beauty'	CBri CStr EMon EPPr MAvo MNFA	
	MWat WBrk WOld	
- 'Dwarf Alma Pötschke' **new**	WCot	
- 'Evensong'	WOld	
- 'Harrington's Pink' ♀H4	More than 30 suppliers	
- 'Helen Picton'	WOld	
§ - 'Herbstschnee'	CPrp CSBt EBre EChP ECtt EFou	
	EHrv EMon ERou GMac MRav	
	MSte MWat NFor NSti SChu SHel	
	SPer SPet SSpe WBrk WCAu WFar	
	WMnd WMoo WOld WPer WTin	
	WWye	
- 'James Ritchie' **new**	WHoo	
- 'John Davies'	WOld	
- 'Lou Williams'	WOld	
I - 'Lucida' **new**	WRHF	
- 'Lye End Beauty'	CPou EGle EMon EOrc LRHS	
	MAvo MFir MRav MSte MWat NFor	
	SChu WCom WCot WHoo WMoo	
	WOld WTin	
- 'Marina Wolkonsky'	WCot	
- 'Millennium Star'	WOld	
- 'Mrs S.T. Wright'	EFou EGle EMon ERou GMac	
	MAnH MBrN MHom MNFA MSte	
	WFar WFoF WOld	
- 'Mrs S.W. Stern'	WOld	
- 'Pink Parfait'	EFou GMac NGdn WCot WOld	
	WWpP	
- 'Pink Victor'	CTri EBre EPPr NLar SEND SHel	
	WWpP	
- 'Primrose Upward'	WCot	
- 'Purple Cloud'	EMon ERou GMac LHop MHer	
	MNFA MWat MWgw NGdn WCom	
	WFoF WOld	
I - 'Purple Dome'	More than 30 suppliers	
- 'Quinton Menzies'	WCom WOld	
- 'Red Cloud'	CBri EFou SMrm WOld	
- 'Rosa Sieger' ♀H4	CBre CPlt EBee EBre EFou EGle	
	EMon GMac MHom NGdn SChu	
	SHel SUsu WBor WBrk WOld WViv	
- 'Rose Williams'	WOld	

- 'Rubinschatz'	EOrc WOld	
- 'Rudelsburg'	EMon	
- 'Sayer's Croft'	EFou EGle EMon MHom MWat	
	WBrk WCot WHoo WOld WTin	
- September Ruby	see *A. novae-angliae* 'Septemberrubin'	
§ - 'Septemberrubin'	CBri CMea EBee ECtt EGle EMon	
	ERou EWsh LHop MAnH MRav	
	MSte NSti SChu SUsu WFar WMoo	
	WOld WPnP WWin	
- 'Treasure'	CBre EFou EMon WFar WMoo	
	WOld	
- 'Violetta'	CMea CStr EBee EFou EGle EMon	
	LPhx MHom MSte MTed SHel	
	WOld WTin WWye	
- 'Wow'	EFou SMrm	
N *novi-belgii*	GWCH NSco WHer WMoo	
- 'Ada Ballard'	ENot ERou LRHS NGdn SPer SPet	
	WOld WWye	
- 'Albanian'	WOld	
- 'Alderman Vokes'	WOld	
- 'Alex Norman'	ERou WOld	
- 'Algar's Pride'	CHrt EBee ERou NBro WOld	
- 'Alice Haslam'	ECtt EFou EPPr GBri GKir IHMH	
	LRHS MCCP MWgw NOrc NPri	
	STes WOld WPer	
- 'Anita Ballard'	WOld	
- 'Anita Webb'	ERou GBri NBir NOak WOld	
- 'Anneke'	EBee EPfP SHel WWeb	
- 'Apollo'	NLar NPri	
- 'Apple Blossom'	SHel WOld	
- 'Arctic'	EBee ERou	
- 'Audrey'	CM&M CRez ECtt EFou EPPr ERou	
	GKir LRHS MLLN MWgw NBro	
	NCGa NOrc SChu SPla STes WBar	
	WOld WTel	
- 'Autumn Beauty'	WOld	
- 'Autumn Days'	EBee WOld	
- 'Autumn Glory'	CSam ERou WOld	
- 'Autumn Rose'	CHea WOld	
- 'Baby Climax'	WOld	
- 'Beauty of Colwall'	WOld	
- 'Beechwood Challenger'	ERou MOne WOld	
- 'Beechwood Charm'	WOld	
- 'Beechwood Rival'	EBee MAvo	
- 'Beechwood Supreme'	ERou WOld	
- 'Bewunderung'	NBro WOld	
- 'Blandie'	CHea CTri EFou ERou MSte MWat	
	MWgw NBro SHel WCAu WOld	
- 'Blauglut'	EFou NBro WOld	
- 'Blue Baby'	WPer WWye	
- 'Blue Bouquet'	ERou SRms WBro WOld	
- 'Blue Boy'	WBrk WOld	
- 'Blue Danube'	CMdw WOld	
- 'Blue Eyes'	CElw EBee ERou LPhx SAga WOld	
	WWye	
- 'Blue Gown'	ERou GCal WOld	
- 'Blue Lagoon'	EBee LPVe LRHS MBow MBri	
	WOld WWeb	
- 'Blue Patrol'	ERou WOld	
- 'Blue Radiance'	WOld	
- 'Blue Whirl'	ERou NBro WOld	
- 'Bonanza'	WOld WTel	
- 'Boningale Blue'	EBee WOld	
- 'Boningale White'	CBel ERou WOld	
- 'Bridesmaid'	WOld	
- 'Brightest and Best'	WOld	
- 'Caborn Pink'	LLWP	
- 'Cameo'	WOld	
- 'Cantab'	WOld	
- 'Cantonese Queen' (v)	EMon	
- 'Carlingcott'	EBee ERou MOne WOld	
- 'Carnival'	CM&M ECtt EFou ERou MMHG	
	NOrc SPer SSpe WOld	

- 'Cecily'	EBee NBro WOld
- 'Charles Wilson'	WOld
- 'Chatterbox'	COlW CPrp EDAr LRHS MRav MWat NLar SChu SRms WOld
- 'Chelwood'	WOld
- 'Chequers'	CBrm CM&M EBee ECot ERou MSte WOld
- 'Christina'	see *A. novi-belgii* 'Kristina'
- 'Christine Soanes'	EFou WOld
- 'Cliff Lewis'	ERou NBro WOld
- 'Climax Albus'	see *A.* 'White Climax'
- 'Cloudy Blue'	EBee WOld
- 'Colonel F.R. Durham'	EBee ERou
- 'Coombe Delight'	ERou
- 'Coombe Gladys'	EBee ERou WOld
- 'Coombe Joy'	ERou WOld
- 'Coombe Margaret'	EBee WOld WOut
- 'Coombe Pink'	ERou
- 'Coombe Queen'	WOld
- 'Coombe Radiance'	ERou MSte WOld
- 'Coombe Ronald'	ERou MWat WOld
- 'Coombe Rosemary'	ECtt ERou LRHS NLar WBor WOld WRHF WTel
- 'Coombe Violet'	MWat WOld
- 'Countess of Dudley'	WOld WPer
- 'Court Herald'	WOld
- 'Crimson Brocade'	EBee ENot EPfP ERou MRav MWat NLar WOld
- 'Dandy'	EBee ECot ELan EMar LRHS NBir NGdn SChu WOld
- 'Daniela'	CBel EFou WBrk WOld
- 'Daphne Anne'	WOld
- 'Dauerblau'	WOld
- 'Davey's True Blue'	CTri EFou ERou MSte WOld
- 'David Murray'	WOld
- 'Dazzler'	WOld
- 'Destiny'	WOld
- 'Diana'	CNic ERou MOne NBro WOld WViv
- 'Diana Watts'	ERou WOld
- 'Dietgard'	WOld
- 'Dolly'	NBir WOld
- 'Dusky Maid'	MBri WBor WOld
- 'Elizabeth'	WOld
- 'Elizabeth Bright'	WOld
- 'Elizabeth Hutton'	WOld
- 'Elsie Dale'	EBee WOld
- 'Elta'	WOld
- 'Erica'	CElw MWat WOld
- 'Ernest Ballard'	ERou WOld
- 'Eva'	WOld
- 'Eventide'	CBcs CElw EBee ENot ERou NOak SPer WMoo WOld WRHF
- 'F.M. Simpson'	ERou
- 'Fair Lady'	ERou MWat WOld
- 'Faith'	WOld
- 'Farnecombe Lilac'	EBee
- 'Farrington'	WOld
- 'Fellowship'	CBcs CDes CFir CStr EBee EFou ENot ERou IHMH LPhx MAvo MSte MWat SAga SPer SRms WBrk WCot WOld WShp WTel
- 'Fontaine'	WOld
- 'Fran'	MFir
- 'Freda Ballard'	EBee ECtt EPPr ERou EWll LRHS MWat NGdn WBor WCAu WOld
- 'Freya'	WOld
- 'Fuldatal'	EFou WOld WOut
- 'Gayborder Blue'	WOld
- 'Gayborder Royal'	CFir EBee ERou MOne WOld
- 'Glory of Colwall'	WOld
- 'Goliath'	WOld
- 'Grey Lady'	WOld
- 'Guardsman'	EBee ERou GKir WOld
- 'Gulliver'	WOld
- 'Gurney Slade'	CStr EBee ERou GKir WOld
- 'Guy Ballard'	ERou
- 'Harrison's Blue'	ERou LPhx SAga WBrk WOld WPer
- 'Heinz Richard'	CM&M COlW EBee ECha EFou MSte NBir NGdn SBla SChu SPet WOld WWpP
- 'Helen'	WOld
- 'Helen Ballard'	CHea CPlt CRez CStr ERou WBrk WOld
- 'Herbstpurzel'	EBee MOne
- 'Hilda Ballard'	ERou WOld
- 'Ilse Brensell'	EBee MOne MSte WOld
- 'Irene'	WOld
- 'Isabel Allen'	WOld
- 'Janet Watts'	ERou NBro WOld
- 'Jean'	EBee MWat WOld
- 'Jean Gyte'	WOld
- 'Jenny'	More than 30 suppliers
- 'Jollity'	WOld
- 'Julia'	WOld
- 'Karminkuppel'	WOld
- 'King of the Belgians'	WOld
- 'King's College'	GKir WOld
§ - 'Kristina'	COlW EBee ECha EFou ERou GKir LRHS MOne MRav SPet WCot WOld WRHF WTel WWpP
- 'Lady Evelyn Drummond'	WOld
- 'Lady Frances'	EBee WOld
- 'Lady in Blue'	COlW CSBt EBee EChP ECtt ELan ENot EPfP GKir LRHS MBNS MWat MWgw NVic SPer SPet SRms SSpe STes SWat SWvt WFar WMoo WOld WPer WTel WTin WWin
- 'Lady Paget'	WOld
- 'Lassie'	CHea EBee ERou LLWP MWat SBri WCot WOld
- 'Lavender Dream'	WOld
- 'Lawrence Chiswell'	SHel WOld
- 'Lederstrumpf' **new**	EFou
- 'Lilac Time'	WOld
- 'Lisa Dawn'	WOld
- 'Little Boy Blue'	CBcs ERou SHBN WOld
- 'Little Man in Blue'	WOld
- 'Little Pink Beauty'	CBrm COlW CPrp EBee ECtt EFou ELan ERou GKir LHop LRHS MBNS MRav NBid NMir NVic SHel SPer SSpe STes WMoo WOld WTel WViv WWin
- 'Little Pink Lady'	ERou SAga WOld
- 'Little Pink Pyramid'	SRms
- 'Little Red Boy'	CBcs ERou WOld
- 'Little Treasure'	WOld
- 'Lucy'	WOld
- 'Madge Cato'	WOld
- 'Malvern Castle'	EBee ERou
- 'Mammoth'	WOld
- 'Margaret Rose'	NCiC NOrc WOld
- 'Margery Bennett'	ERou GBri WOld
- 'Marie Ballard'	CBcs CHea CSBt CSam EChP ENot EPfP ERou GKir MFir MWat NBro NGdn NOrc SHBN SPer SRms STes SWat WBrk WCAu WEas WOld WPer WShp WTMC WTel WWpP
- 'Marie's Pretty Please'	WOld
- 'Marjorie'	WOld
- 'Marjory Ballard'	WOld
- 'Mark Ballard'	MOne
- 'Martonie'	WOld WPer
- 'Mary Ann Neil'	WOld
- 'Mary Deane'	MSte WOld WPer
- 'Mauve Magic'	WOld
- 'Melbourne Belle'	WOld

- 'Melbourne Magnet'   CHea ERou MOne WOld
- 'Michael Watts'   ERou WOld
- 'Mistress Quickly'   CRez EBee ERou GBri MAvo MBri
                        WOld
- 'Mittelmeer'   EFou
- 'Mount Everest'   ERou WOld WPer
- 'Mrs Leo Hunter'   WOld
- 'Nesthäkchen'   EBee ECho
- 'Nobilis'   WOld
- 'Norman's Jubilee'   ERou NBir WOld
- 'Nursteed Charm'   WOld
- 'Oktoberschneekuppel'   ERou LRHS MBri NBro
- 'Orlando'   ERou WCot WOld
- 'Pamela'   ERou WOld
- 'Patricia Ballard'   CElw CPrp CSBt EBee ERou GKir
                        MWat NBro SPer SSpe WBVN
                        WCAu WFar WOld WPer WTel
- 'Peace'   WOld
- 'Percy Thrower'   ERou WOld
- 'Peter Chiswell'   MBri WOld
- 'Peter Harrison'   GMac NBir NBro WOld WPer
- 'Peter Pan'   EBee WOld
- 'Picture'   WOld
- 'Pink Gown'   WOld
- 'Pink Lace'   ERou MBNS MLLN WOld WPer
- 'Pink Pyramid'   WOld
- 'Plenty'   ERou MBri WOld
- 'Porzellan'   CElw CM&M ColW ECtt EMar
                 MAvo NCGa WCot
- 'Pride of Colwall'   EBee ERou MOne MWat WBrk
- 'Priory Blush'   CHea CRez ERou WOld WWeb
- 'Professor Anton   CSBt EBee EFou EPfP ERou GKir
   Kippenberg'   IHMH LRHS MBow MHer MRav
                  NBro SHel SPer WMoo WOld WTel
- 'Prosperity'   ERou GKir NMRc WOld
* - 'Prunella'   ERou WOld
- 'Purple Dome'   ECha MCCP WOld
- 'Queen Mary'   ERou WOld
- 'Queen of Colwall'   WOld
- 'Ralph Picton'   WOld
- 'Raspberry Ripple'   ECot ERou NCiC WOld
- 'Red Robin'   MWat
- 'Red Sunset'   CBcs ERou SRms WOld
- 'Rembrandt'   EBee ECtt EWll GKir LBuc
- 'Remembrance'   GKir WBrk WOld
- 'Reverend Vincent Dale'   WOld
- 'Richness'   ERou SAga WOld
- 'Robin Adair'   WOld
- 'Roland Smith'   WOld
- 'Rose Bonnet'   CSBt EFou ENot MWat SHBN SPlb
- 'Rose Bouquet'   WOld
- 'Rosebud'   WOld
- 'Rosemarie Sallmann'   MOne
- 'Rosenwichtel'   EBee EFou EMar LPVe MCLN NLar
                    WBrk WOld
- 'Royal Ruby'   ECtt WOld
- 'Royal Velvet'   ENot ERou WOld
- 'Rozika'   WOld
- 'Rufus'   ERou WOld
- 'Sailor Boy'   EBee EFou ERou WOld
- 'Saint Egwyn'   WOld
- 'Sam Banham'   EBee ERou MAvo NBro WOld
- 'Sandford White Swan'   EBee ERou GBuc GKir MHom
                           WBrk WEas WPer
- 'Sarah Ballard'   ERou IHMH MWat SCro WOld
                     WShp
§ - 'Schneekissen'   CPrp CStu EBee EFou ECtt EGoo EOMN
                      EPfP EPla MHer MWgw NPri SEND
                      SPer STes SWvt WOld
- 'Schneezicklein' **new**   GBin
- 'Schöne von Dietlikon'   CKno EBee EFou WOld
- 'Schoolgirl'   EBee ERou GKir WOld
- 'Sheena'   ERou MBri WOld
- 'Silberblaukissen' **new**   GBin

§ - 'Silberteppich'   GMac
- Silver Carpet   see *A. novi-belgii* 'Silberteppich'
- Snow Cushion   see *A. novi-belgii* 'Schneekissen'
- 'Snowdrift'   WOld
- 'Snowsprite'   CBcs CSBt EBee ELan EPfP MBow
                  MWat NBro NLar NOrc NPro SWat
                  WBrk WOld WTin
- 'Sonata'   ERou NOak SPer WCra WOld
- 'Sophia'   ERou NOak WOld
- 'Starlight'   EBee ENot ERou LPVe MAvo
                 MBNS WFar WMoo WOld
- 'Steinebrück'   WOld
- 'Sterling Silver'   EBee ERou WOld
- 'Storm Clouds'   EFou
- 'Strahlenmeer'   EFou
- 'Sunset'   EBee WOld
- 'Susan'   WOld
- 'Sweet Briar'   CElw WOld
- 'Tapestry'   WOld
- 'Terry's Pride'   WOld
- 'The Archbishop'   WOld
- 'The Bishop'   ERou WOld
- 'The Cardinal'   ERou WOld
- 'The Choristers'   WOld
- 'The Dean'   ERou WOld
§ - 'The Rector'   WOld
- 'The Sexton'   ERou WOld
- 'Thundercloud'   EBee WOld
- 'Timsbury'   WOld
- 'Tony'   WOld
- 'Tovarich'   GMac WOld
- 'Trudi Ann'   NBir WOld
- 'Twinkle'   NBro WOld WOut
- 'Victor'   EBee MOne WOld
- 'Vignem'   NSti
- 'Violet Lady'   ERou WOld
- 'Waterperry'   MWat
- 'Weisses Wunder'   EFou WOld WOut
- 'White Ladies'   EBee EFou ERou LLWP MWat
                    NOrc SPer WShp
- 'White Swan'   CPou EPPr LPhx WOld
- 'White Wings'   MBri WOld
- 'Winston S. Churchill'   CM&M ColW CTri ELan ENot EPfP
                            ERou LRHS MWat NOrc SHBN
                            SPer SPlb SSpe WBro WOld WPnP
                            WShp WTel
                            SUsu WOld

oblongifolius   EBee EMan MBnl MMil MNFA
- 'Fanny's'   SPoG WCot WFar WGMN WOld
'Ochtendgloren'   EFou EGle EMon EPPr GBuc GKir
   (*pringlei* hybrid) ♀H4   GMac MAvo MBri MMil MNrw
                              MSte NCGa SAga SMrm WCot
                              WFar WOld WWye
Octoberlight   see *A.* 'Oktoberlicht'
§ 'Oktoberlicht'   EMon SAga WOld
oolentangiensis   EBee EMan EPPr
'Orchidee' **new**   EBee
pappei   see *Felicia amoena*
'Pearl Star' **new**   GMac WOld
petiolatus   see *Felicia petiolata*
§ 'Photograph' ♀H4   CStr GCal MAvo MSte MTed MWat
                      SMrm WFar WMnd WOld
§ *pilosus*   EChP ECha EMon EWes MLLN
   var. *demotus* ♀H4   MRav MSte NHol SHel WFar WOld
                         WTin
§ - var. *pringlei*   More than 30 suppliers
   'Monte Cassino' ♀H4
- - 'October Glory' **new**   WFar
I - - 'Phoebe'   WOld
- - 'Pink Cushion'   WCot
'Pink Cassino'   WCAu
'Pink Star'   CMea CStr EBee EFou EMan GKir
               GMac LPhx MRav MWgw NSti
               WBrk WFar WHoo WOld WTin

'Plowden's Pink' | WOld
'Poollicht' | EFou
§ *ptarmicoides* | CM&M EMon MBrN MLLN WCot WOld WPer
purdomii | see *A. flaccidus*
pyrenaeus 'Lutetia' | CHea EBee EChP ECha EFou EMan EOrc EPPr GAbr GBuc GCal LRHS MAnH MBnl MNFA MSte MWgw NDov NLar SBla WCAu WCot WFar WOld
radula | EBee EChP EMan EMon GCal NLar NSti SUsu WOld
'Ringdove' (*ericoides* hybrid) ♀H4 | EBee EFou EPfP ERou GMac LRHS MBnl MNFA MNrw MTis MWat MWgw NSti NVic SLon WCAu WCot WOld
'Rosa Star' | SHel WOld
rotundifolius | see *Felicia amelloides* variegated
'Variegatus' |
rugulosus 'Asrugo' | EBee
x *salignus* | WOld
- Scottish form | WOld
'Samoa' **new** | MBri
§ *scaber* | EBee WCot WPGP
scandens | see *A. carolinianus*
schreberi | CHea MHom MLLN WCot WOld
§ *sedifolius* | ELan EMan EPPr MSte MWat NBid SBla SChu SDix SOkh SPla WBea WEas WFar WMnd WOld WPer
- 'Nanus' | CElw CSam EBee EOrc ERou LRHS MLLN MSte NBir NLar NSti SPer WCot WFar WMnd WOld WSpi WTin
- 'Snow Flurries' | see *A. ericoides* f. *prostrata* 'Snow Flurry'
sericeus | EBee
§ *sibiricus* | NLar WOld
'Snow Flurry' | see *A. ericoides* f. *prostrata* 'Snow Flurry'
'Snow Star' | WOld
souliei | EBre
- B&SWJ 7655 | WCru
spathulifolius | NBir
spectabilis | GAbr WOld
stracheyi | EHyt GEil
subcaeruleus | see *A. tongolensis*
subspicatus | WPer
'Sunhelene' | WViv
Sunplum | WViv
= 'Danasplum' PBR |
'Sunqueen' | WViv
'Sunsky' | WViv
tataricus | EBee ECha WOld WWye
- 'Jindai' | WCot WFar
thomsonii 'Nanus' | CMdw CSam EBee EBre EFou EOrc LPhx MSte NBid SPer WCot WFar WOld WSHC
thunbergii | WCru
var. *thunbergii*
f. *rosea*
B&SWJ 8811 **new**
tibeticus | see *A. flaccidus*
'Tonga' **new** | MBri
§ *tongolensis* | EPfP GKir MSPs SRms WCFE WFar WWeb WWin
- 'Berggarten' | CHar EBre GKir MBri MMil SUsu WAbe WFar WWeb
- 'Dunkleviolette' | GBuc NBro SRms
- 'Lavender Star' | EFou GBuc
- 'Leuchtenburg' | ERou
- 'Napsbury' | CDes EBee ECha ERou GKir LRHS WPGP
- 'Wartburgstern' | EBee EChP EPfP LRHS MDKP MMil NDov NGdn NPri SCro WBea WFar WMnd WPer

tradescantii misapplied | see *A. pilosus* var. *demotus*
tradescantii L. | EFou EGra ELan EMan EPAt MBNS MBnl MFir MWgw NOak NSti SHel WCot WOld WTin
§ *trinervius* | CPou EBee
subsp. *ageratoides*
- - 'Asran' | EBee SSvw WFar
- var. *harae* | WOld
- var. *ovatus* **new** | GEil
tripolium | MBow WHer
§ 'Triumph' | WCot
turbinellus hort. ♀H4 | CBrm ECGN EChP EFou EMan EMon GBuc LRHS MBNS MBct MBro MNFA MSte NDov SChu SDix SMHy WCot WFar WHer WHoo WMoo WOld WTin WWeb
turbinellus Lindl. | EPPr
- hybrid | CMea NPPs
umbellatus | CBre EMon EPPr NCGa NSti SRms WCAu WCot WOld WTin
'Vasterival' **new** | WCot
vimineus Lam. | see *A. lateriflorus*
- 'Ptarmicoides' | see *A. ptarmicoides*
§ 'White Climax' | MSte MTed WBrk WCot WOld
yunnanensis | EBee WSHC
'Yvonne' | CBre EBee

Asteranthera (*Gesneriaceae*)
ovata | CFil CPen GGGa GGar LAst NCGa SSpi WAbe WBod WBor WCru WGMN WGwG WPrP WSHC

Asteriscus (*Asteraceae*)
maritimus | see *Pallenis maritima*

Asteromoea (*Asteraceae*)
mongolica | see *Kalimeris mongolica*
pinnatifida | see *Kalimeris pinnatifida*

Asteropyrum (*Ranunculaceae*)
cavaleriei | EBee LEur WCru

Astilbe ✿ (*Saxifragaceae*)
'America' | CMHG ECtt MBnl
'Aphrodite' | CMCo CPlt CWCL EBee EBlw EChP ENot LAst MDKP NCGa NHol NPro SChu SMac SSpi WBrE WGor
(*simplicifolia* hybrid)
x *arendsii* | CWat MBro NJOw SMac SPet WMoo WPer
- 'Amethyst' | CMHG EBee EMFW GSki LRHS MRav NPSI SBod SMac SPer WAul WCAu WFar WHoo WMoo
- 'Anita Pfeifer' | CMHG GKir LPBA LRHS WFar WPnP
- 'Augustleuchen' **new** | EBee
- Bella Group | SLon WWeb
- 'Bergkristall' | CMHG EBee EMil
§ - 'Brautschleier' ♀H4 | CM&M CMHG CMac CPrp CTri CWCL EChP ECtt EFou ENot EPfP MOne NPSI NPri WPnP
- 'Bressingham Beauty' | CDoC CMHG CPrp CSam CWCL EBre ECtt EHon ELan EMFW ENot EPar EPfP EPla GBBs GKir LPBA LRHS MCLN MRav NGdn NHol NPro NSti SPer SSpe SWvt WFar WMoo WWpP
- Bridal Veil | see *A.* x *arendsii* 'Brautschleier'
- 'Bronzlaub' **new** | EBee
- 'Bumalda' | CFir CFwr CMCo COtt CSam ENot GSki LRHS NDlv NOrc NPro SPlb SSpi WAul WFar WMoo WWeb
- 'Cattleya' | CMHG CWCL EBee EFou MBnl NCGa NLar WFar WMoo

§ = section symbol

- 'Cattleya Dunkel' — CMHG WFar
- 'Ceres' — CMHG NHol
- 'Darwin's Favourite' — CWCL
§ - 'Diamant' — CMHG EBee EBre LAst LRHS NGdn NHol WFar
- Diamond — see A. x arendsii 'Diamant'
- 'Drayton Glory' — see A. x rosea 'Peach Blossom'
- Elizabeth Bloom = 'Eliblo'PBR — EBee EBre GSki LRHS MCLN SLon SVil WFar
- 'Ellie' — see A. x arendsii 'Ellie van Veen'
§ - 'Ellie van Veen' — CFai CM&M CMHG CWCL EChP GBin MAvo MBri NHol NPSI NPro SVil
- 'Erica' — CMHG CSBt CTri EBee EWll GKir LRHS MBri MRav NPro WCAu WFar WMoo
- 'Fanal' ♀H4 — More than 30 suppliers
§ - 'Federsee' — CBcs CMHG CWCL EBee EBre ECha EFou ELan EMil ENot LRHS NBro NGdn NPro WFar
§ - 'Feuer' — CM&M CMCo CMHG CPrp CWCL EBee EBlw ELan EPfP MAvo MBnl NCGa NHol NOrc NPro NVic SPer
- Fire — see A. x arendsii 'Feuer'
- 'Flamingo'PBR — MBNS MBnl MBri NCGa NPro SBod
- 'Gertrud Brix' — CBcs EBee EPar NBir NGdn NPro SBod
- 'Gladstone' — see A. 'W.E. Gladstone' (japonica hybrid)
- 'Gloria' — CMHG CTri GFlt LPBA LRHS MRav WFar
§ - 'Gloria Purpurea' — CMHG EBlw GKir LRHS MDun NHol WMoo WWpP
- Glow — see A. x arendsii 'Glut'
§ - 'Glut' — CMHG CWCL ECtt GKir LRHS NHol NMyG SRms WFar
- 'Granat' — CDoC CM&M CMHG CMac EBee EMFW MCLN NBPC NBir NPro WBor WMoo WWin
* - 'Grande' — NPro
- 'Grete Püngel' — EBee ECha MLLN WFar
- 'Harmony' — CMHG
- Hyacinth — see A. x arendsii 'Hyazinth'
§ - 'Hyazinth' — CDoC CFai CMHG CPLG CPrp EBee EGra EMFW GSki LRHS MLan NFor NGdn NHol NPro WFar
- 'Irrlicht' — CBcs CMHG CSBt EBee EHon ELan EMFW EPfP EPla EWTr GGar GKir LHop LPBA LRHS NFor NHol SMac SPer SWat WAul WPnP WWpP
- 'Kvele' — CMHG GKir SOkh WFar WMoo
§ - 'Lachskönigin' — CMHG EBee
- 'Lilli Goos' — CMHG EBee
- 'Mars' — CMHG EBee
- 'Moerheim's Glory' — CM&M LAst
- 'Mont Blanc' — CMHG
- 'Obergärtner Jürgens' — CM&M EBee EChP GBin
- 'Paul Gaärder' — CMHG
- Pink Pearl — see A. x arendsii 'Rosa Perle'
- 'Queen of Holland' — see A. 'Queen of Holland' (japonica hybrid)
- Red Light — see A. x arendsii 'Rotlicht'
§ - 'Rosa Perle' — CMHG CSam NHol
- 'Rot Straussenfeder' new — EBee
I - 'Rote Cattleya' new — EBee
§ - 'Rotlicht' — CMHG CPlt EBee ECot GKir LRHS NLar NMyG NPro NSti WFar WGor
- 'Salmon Queen' — see A. x arendsii 'Lachskönigin'
- 'Showstar Group' — LRHS SWvt
- 'Snowdrift' — CBrm CMHG CSBt CWat EBre EPla GKir GSki LRHS MBNS NFor NOak NOrc NPro SWat WFar
- 'Solferino' — CMHG
- 'Spartan' — see A. x arendsii 'Rotlicht'

- 'Spinell' — CWCL EBee NOrc WPnP
- 'Venus' — CBrm CHar CSBt CSam EBee ECha ECtt EFou EGra EMFW EPla EWTr GGar GKir LPBA MCLN MSte NHol NOrc NVic SPer SSpe SWat WCAu WFar WMoo
- 'Walküre' — CMHG
- 'Washington' — see A. 'Washington' (japonica hybrid)
§ - 'Weisse Gloria' — CMHG EBee ECha EPPr EPar EWTr LPBA MBnl MBow MLan MRav NBPC NHol NOrc NSti SBod WMoo WTin
- White Gloria — see A. x arendsii 'Weisse Gloria'
- 'White Queen' — NHol NWoo
- 'William Reeves' — CMHG MFir NHol
- 'Zuster Theresa' — CMHG EBee EBre GKir LRHS MAvo MBNS MBnl NBro WFar

astilboides — CMHG NHol SWvt
'Atrorosea' (simplicifolia hybrid) — NCot SRms
'Avalanche' — EBee NHol
'Betsy Cuperus' (thunbergii hybrid) — CMHG CMil LBuc MRav MSte NPro SLon WCAu
biternata — EBee EMon
'Bonn' (japonica hybrid) — CBcs EPar LPBA NBlu SCoo SRms WWol
'Bremen' (japonica hybrid) — CM&M CMHG EBre LPBA
§ 'Bronce Elegans' (simplicifolia hybrid) ♀H4 — CBcs CMHG EChP ECha EFou EPar EPfP GBBs GBuc GKir GSki LAst LRHS MBNS MDHE MDun MRav NHol NOrc NPro SChu SMac SPer WBea WCAu WFar WHoo WMoo
* **bumalda** 'Bronze Pygmy' — COlW EWTr NArg NHol STes
'Carnea' (simplicifolia hybrid) — CMHG
'Catherine Deneuve' — see A. x arendsii 'Federsee'
'Cherry Ripe' — see A. x arendsii 'Feuer'
chinensis — CMCo CMHG CWat GKir GSki IBlr LRHS WLin WSHC WWeb
- B&SWJ 8178 — WCru
- 'Christian' **new** — EBee
- var. **davidii** — CMHG GSki
- - B&SWJ 8583 — WCru
- - B&SWJ 8645 — WCru
- 'Finale' — EMFW GLil NArg NHol NPro SPer WFar WLin WShp
- 'Frankentroll' — CMHG
- from Russia — GCal
- 'Intermezzo' — EBee
§ - var. **pumila** ♀H4 — More than 30 suppliers
- - 'Serenade' — EBee GSki LRHS MBri NGdn WFar
- 'Purple Glory' — CMHG
- 'Purpurkerze' — EBee EChP LDai MBNS MBri MNrw NBPC NBid NBro
- 'Spätsommer' — CMHG
- var. **taquetii** — EChP NSti SRms WWeb
- - Purple Lance — see A. chinensis var. taquetii 'Purpurlanze'
§ - - 'Purpurlanze' — CMHG CWCL EBee EBre ECha ECtt EFou EGra EMFW EMan EPPr GKir LLWP LPhx MBri MRav NBir NChi NDov NGdn NPro WCAu WCot WFar WMoo WWin WWpP
- - 'Rowden Sunstar' — CRow
§ - - 'Superba' ♀H4 — CM&M CMHG CRow CTri CWCL ECha ENot EPfP GGar IHMM MCCP MLLN MSte NArg NBro NHol SChu SDix SPer SRms WEas WFar WMoo WOld WPGP WShp
- 'Veronica Klose' — CMHG GKir NLar NPro SMrm WCAu
- 'Vision in Pink'PBR — MCLN

- 'Vision in Red'	MBNS MBnl MBri MCLN NFor NPro
- 'Visions'	CFai CMHG EBee EBre EChP EMan ENot LRHS MBNS MBri MSte NBro NGdn NPSI NPro STes WCot WFar WLin
Cologne	see *A.* 'Köln' (japonica hybrid)
'Crimson Feather'	see *A.* x *arendsii* 'Gloria Purpurea'
x *crispa*	IBlr WFar
- 'Gnom'	EMFW
- 'Lilliput'	CLAP GEdr GKir LRHS NLar NPro
§ - 'Perkeo' ♀H4	COtt EBee EBre ECha ELan EPfP GBBs GGar GKir GSki IMGH LHop LRHS MDun MRav MSte NBir NLar NMen NOak NPro NSla SRms SSpi WAul WBVN WBro WFar WMoo WWeb
- 'Peter Pan'	see *A.* x *crispa* 'Perkeo'
- 'Snow Queen'	LRHS NBir NMen NPro WFar
'Darwin's Dream'	MBnl NPri NPro
'Deutschland' (*japonica* hybrid)	More than 30 suppliers
'Dunkellachs' (*simplicifolia* hybrid)	CFwr CM&M NHol NPro WFar WSSM
'Düsseldorf' (*japonica* hybrid)	CMHG CSam CWCL EBee EPar GKir
'Dutch Treat' (*japonica* hybrid)	CMea
'Eden's Odysseus'	EChP EFou MOne
'Elegans' (*simplicifolia* hybrid)	CMHG WFar
'Elizabeth' (*japonica* hybrid)	CMHG
'Etna' (*japonica* hybrid)	CBcs CMHG CRez CSam CWCL EBee EGra EWTr GBri GSki NPro SRms WPnP
'Europa' (*japonica* hybrid)	CM&M CMHG CMac CSBt EBee EBre ECtt EMFW LHop LPBA MRav NOak SPla SSpe WFar WMoo
'Fata Morgana' (x *arendsii* hybrid)	CMHG
§ *glaberrima*	EPar NHol NMen
- var. *saxatilis* ♀H4	CLyd CRow EBee EHyt EPfP ETow IFro IMGH NOak NSla NWoo SAga WAbe WHal
- *saxosa*	see *A.* 'Saxosa'
* - - *minor*	NJOw
grandis	CMHG WHer
'Hennie Graafland' (*simplicifolia* hybrid)	CBcs CMHG COtt CWCL EChP EFou EMan EMil GKir MBNS MDHE NCGa NLar NPro WLin WShp
'Holden Clough' (*japonica* hybrid)	NHol
'Inshriach Pink' (*simplicifolia* hybrid)	CMHG EBee EBre EFou EHoe ELan EMFW GCrs GKir GLil LRHS MBri MDHE NBir NCGa NHol NMen NOak SAga WBro WCot WFar WHal WLin
japonica var. *terrestris*	see *A. glaberrima*
'Jo Ophorst' (*davidii* hybrid)	CMHG EBee EMan EPPr GSki LPBA MRav NGdn NLar NPro
'Koblenz' (*japonica* hybrid)	CMHG CWCL EBee MDKP
§ 'Köln' (*japonica* hybrid)	CMHG EBee EMil LPBA SMrm WFar
'König Albert'	EBee
davidii hybrid **new**	
koreana	EBee WCot
- B&SWJ 8611	WCru
- B&SWJ 8680	WCru
'Koster'	LPBA
'Kriemhilde'	CMHG
'Lady Digby'	LPBA
'Lollipop'	MBNS MBnl MBri MCLN NPro WShp
longicarpa B&SWJ 6711	WCru

'Maggie Daley'	EBee MBri NBro NPro WMoo
'Mainz' (*japonica* hybrid)	CMHG EBee ELan EMil LPBA MBow
microphylla	CMHG EBee NHol
- pink	CMHG EBee NHol
'Moerheimii' (*thunbergii* hybrid)	CMHG
'Montgomery' (japonica hybrid)	CMHG EBee EBre EChP GKir LRHS MBri MRav NFor NGdn NHol WBVN
Ostrich Plume	see *A.* 'Straussenfeder' (*thunbergii* hybrid)
'Peaches and Cream'	EBee GKir LRHS MMHG MRav NBro NLar WAul WPnP
'Peter Barrow' (*glaberrima* hybrid)	SRms
'Pink Lightening' (*simplicifolia* hybrid)	CWCL MBNS MBnl WShp
'Poschka'	CFir NPro
I 'Poschka Alba'	CFir NPro
'Professor van der Wielen' (*thunbergii* hybrid)	CMHG CMil CWCL EBee EGle EMon ETow GCal GGar GKir LAst MSte SDix SPer SRms SSpi WCAu WFar WHoo
pumila	see *A. chinensis* var. *pumila*
* 'Queen'	LPBA
§ 'Queen of Holland' (*japonica* hybrid)	EBee WWol
'Radius'	MBri SVil
* 'Red Admiral'	NFor
'Red Sentinel' (*japonica* hybrid)	CBcs CFai CM&M CWCL EChP EMFW EMil EPar LAst MOne MTis NBro NCGa NHol NOrc NPro SMrm SVil WFar WLow WSan WWeb
'Rheinland' (*japonica* hybrid) ♀H4	CM&M CMHG CWCL EPfP IHMH LPBA MBro NArg NFla NPri STes WCAu WEas WFar WHoo WPnP WShp
rivularis	CMHG WCot
- var. *myriantha* BWJ 8076a **new**	WCru
§ x *rosea* 'Peach Blossom'	CBcs CM&M CMHG EBee EChP EPar EWTr GBuc LPBA MBro NArg NBir NHol NPro NSti WFar WHoo WLow WMoo WMyn WWeb WWpP
- 'Queen Alexandra'	WFar
'Rosea' (*simplicifolia* hybrid)	NHol WFar
Rosemary Bloom = 'Rosblo'	NHol
'Salmonea' (*simplicifolia* hybrid)	CMHG
§ 'Saxosa'	GGar SPla
simplicifolia ♀H4	CRow GKir NMen SSpi WFar
- 'Alba'	CMHG EBee NHol NPro
- Bronze Elegance	see *A.* 'Bronce Elegans' (*simplicifolia* hybrid)
- 'Darwin's Snow Sprite'	CHVG CLAP CMac CRez ECho GKir MBnl MBri MSte NHol NLar NPri NPro WFar WLin WMyn
- 'Jacqueline'	ECho EFou NHol NLar WFar
* - 'Nana Alba'	NPro
- 'Praecox Alba'	CMCo EBee EChP ENot NHol SMac SVil WHoo
- 'Sheila Haxton'	EBre
'Sprite' (*simplicifolia* hybrid) ♀H4	More than 30 suppliers
§ 'Straussenfeder' (*thunbergii* hybrid) ♀H4	CM&M CMHG CTri CWCL EBee EChP EFou EMan EPfP EPla ETow GCal GFlt LAst LHop LRHS NBid NBro NHol NOrc SMac SPer SSpi WAul WCAu WMoo WPnP WShp

'Sugar Plum'	LAst SVil
(*simplicifolia* hybrid)	
'Superba'	see *A. chinensis* var. *taquetii*
	'Superba'
thunbergii var.	EBee
hachijoensis new	
- var. **terrestris**	WCru
B&SWJ 6125	
'Vesuvius'	CBcs GKir MDKP NBlu NBro NSti
(*japonica* hybrid)	WSan
§ 'W.E. Gladstone'	CWat EBee GSki LBBr MSte NBlu
(*japonica* hybrid)	NCiC NGby NHol NPro WAbe
	WGor WWpP
'Walter Bitner'	EPPr MBNS NLRH SVil
§ 'Washington'	IHMH LAst MDKP NGdn WWeb
(*japonica* hybrid)	
'White Wings'	NPro WShp
(*simplicifolia* hybrid)	
'Willie Buchanan'	CMHG CPrp EBee EBlw ECtt EHoe
(*simplicifolia* hybrid)	EPza GKir GSki LRHS MBar MDHE
	MTis NFor NHol NMen NOak
	SChu SIng SPer SPla SRms SSpi
	WAbe WBea WFar WMoo WWeb
	WWin

Astilboides (*Saxifragaceae*)

§ **tabularis**	More than 30 suppliers

Astragalus (*Papilionaceae*)

arnotianus JCA 9128	CPBP
canadensis	EMan GKir
candelarius new	CPBP
danicus	WBWf
glycyphyllos	CAgr CArn MSal WBWf WWye
lusitanicus	LRav
membranaceus	CArn ELau MSal
norvegicus	SLon
purshii	WLin
sinicus	WHer
utahensis	CPBP

Astrantia ✿ (*Apiaceae*)

bavarica	CCge EBee EBlw EMan EMar GCal
	MDKP MTed SMrm WCot WOut
	WWpP
§ 'Buckland'	More than 30 suppliers
carniolica	EBlw EMon SBri WTel WWpP
- **major**	see *A. major*
- 'Rubra' **new**	MWrn
- 'Variegata'	see *A. major* 'Sunningdale
	Variegata'
'Hadspen Blood'	More than 30 suppliers
helleborifolia hort.	see *A. maxima*
§ **major**	More than 30 suppliers
* - **alba**	CMHG EBee EBlw ECGN ECha
	EGle EHrv EMon GFlt GSki MBnl
	MRav MWrn NBir NGdn NPer
	WMnd
- 'Ann Cann' **new**	CBct
- 'Berendien Stam'	CCge EBlw EMon MAvo WWpP
- subsp. **biebersteinii**	CCge EBla EBlw EMon NBir
- 'Buckland'	see *A.* 'Buckland'
- 'Celtic Star'	CBcs CBct CElw CFai CFir CKno
	EBla EChP ELan EMan LHop MAvo
	MBNS MBnl MSph NCot NGdn
	NMyG NOak NSti SPla WCot
- 'Claret'	More than 30 suppliers
- Cliff's form	MTed
- 'Compton Lane'	WCom
- 'Cyril James' **new**	CBct
- 'Dulcie Scott'	WOut
- 'Elmblut'	EBlw EMon
- 'Enduring Love' **new**	SCro
- 'Gill Richardson'	EFou

- Gwen's form	MTed
- 'Hillview Red'	CCge CElw EBee SHel
- subsp. **involucrata**	EBlw EHrv GSki LRHS MBro MTis
	NHol SWat WFar
- - 'Barrister'	CBct CDes CSam EBee GBuc SSpi
	WFar WOut WPGP
- - 'Canneman'	CBct EBee EBla EBlw EMon EWes
	LPhx MAvo MBct NSti SCro SMrm
	SOkh WCot WWpP
- - 'Margery Fish'	see *A. major* subsp. *involucrata*
	'Shaggy'
- - 'Moira Reid'	EBee EBla EBlw GBri MFOX SHar
- - 'Orlando'	EBee EBlw
§ - - 'Shaggy' ♀H4	More than 30 suppliers
- 'Jade Lady' **new**	WFar
- 'Lars'	More than 30 suppliers
- 'Lars' seedlings	GCal
- 'Maureen'	NOak
- 'Primadonna'	CBct CCge CHea CKno CSam
	EBee EBlw EHrv EMan ERou EWsh
	GSki MBNS MTis MWrn NArg
	NHol NLar SCro SIgm SPlb WFar
	WMnd WMoo WPer WViv
- 'Prockter'	WCra
- 'Roma'PBR	CBct CCge CHad COtt EBee EFou
	EHrv EMan EMon LPhx MBri MTed
	MWrn NBhm NCGa NCot NDov
	NOak SMHy SSpi SUsu WCAu
	WFar WViv
- var. **rosea**	More than 30 suppliers
- 'Rosensinfonie'	EBee EBlw GSki MBct MWrn NBro
	NOak NPro WFar WMnd WMoo
	WViv WWpP
§ - 'Rubra'	More than 30 suppliers
- 'Ruby Cloud'	CBri CCge CHea CHid CM&M
	EBee ECGN EHrv EMan GAbr ITim
	MNrw MSPs MWgw MWrn NBro
	NSti SVil WCAu WFoF WHil WWol
- 'Ruby Wedding'	More than 30 suppliers
- 'Starburst'	EBee WFar
- 'Sue Barnes' (v)	EMon
§ - 'Sunningdale	More than 30 suppliers
Variegated' (v) ♀H4	
- 'Titoki Point'	EBlw WCot
- 'Variegata'	see *A. major* 'Sunningdale
	Variegated'
§ **maxima** ♀H4	More than 30 suppliers
- 'Mark Fenwick'	NBir
* - **rosea**	CKno ECtt MTis NBir NGdn SPet
	WSan WWol
minor	CPrp GAbr WCru
'Rainbow'	NLar
rubra	see *A. major* 'Rubra'
'Snow Star'	EHrv GBin IPot MAvo MBnl MBri
	MCLN MWrn NCot NSti
'Warren Hills'	MWrn

Asyneuma (*Campanulaceae*)

canescens	ELan EMan MBNS MLLN WWin
limonifolium	CPom
prenanthoides	ELan MLwd MWrn
pulvinatum	EHyt WAbe

Asystasia (*Acanthaceae*)

bella	see *Mackaya bella*
§ **gangetica**	CSev
violacea	see *A. gangetica*

Athamanta (*Apiaceae*)

cretensis	EBee LPhx
macedonica	EBee
subsp. **arachnoidea**	
turbith	SIgm
- subsp. **haynaldii**	EBee

vestina LPhx
  – JCA 224300 SIgm SSpi

Athanasia (Asteraceae)
§ *parviflora* GGar SPlb

Atherosperma (Monimiaceae)
moschatum CBcs CPne WSHC

Athrotaxis (Cupressaceae)
cupressoides CDul CKen MBar WCwm
laxifolia CDoC CKen LCon MBar WCwm
selaginoides CDoC CDul CTrG WCwm

Athyrium ❀ (Woodsiaceae)
'Branford Beauty' WRic
'Branford Rambler' WRic
drepanopterum WRic
filix-femina ♀H4 More than 30 suppliers
  – var. **angustum** WRic
    'Lady in Red'
  – 'Clarissimum' WIvy WRic
* – *congestum cristatum* CLAP WFib
  – 'Corymbiferum' GQui NMar SRms
  – 'Crispum SRms
    Grandiceps Kaye'
  – Cristatum Group CLAP EBee EBlw EFer EFtx ELan
    EMon EPza MMoz NHol SBla SWat
    WAbe WFib WRic
§ – Cruciatum Group CBos CFwr CLAP CRow EBee
    EGol ELan EMar EMon EPfP MAsh
    MBct MMoz MWgw NHol NOGN
    SLon SPer SRms WCot WCru WFib
    WMoo WRic
  – 'Fieldii' CLAP CRow EFer NHol SChu
    SRms WFib
  – 'Frizelliae' ♀H4 More than 30 suppliers
  – 'Frizelliae Capitatum' CLAP CRow NMar WFib WPGP
  – 'Frizelliae Cristatum' EFtx SRms
  – 'Grandiceps' CLAP EBee NMar SRms
  – 'Minutissimum' CFil CLAP CPlt EBee ECha EGol
    EHon ELan EMon LPBA MMoz
    NMar SBla WPGP
* – 'Nudicaule' **new** SRms
  – 'Percristatum' EMon
  – Plumosum Group CFil CLAP GBri GQui NMar WFib
  – 'Plumosum Axminster' CFil CLAP
  – 'Plumosum Cristatum' CLAP NMar
  – 'Plumosum GQui
    Percristatum'
  – Ramocristatum Group NMar
  – Red Stem see *A. filix-femina* 'Rotstiel'
§ – 'Rotstiel' CFwr CLAP EBee MMoz NLar WFar
    WMoo WPnP
  – 'Setigerum Cristatum' NMar
* – *superbum* 'Druery' CLAP
  – 'Vernoniae' ♀H4 CLAP ELan EMon LEur LPBA
    MWgw SGar WRic
  – 'Vernoniae Cristatum' CLAP GBin NHol NMar WFib
  – 'Victoriae' **new** LPBA
  – Victoriae Group see *A. filix-femina* Cruciatum Group
'Ghost' WRic
goeringianum 'Pictum' see *A. niponicum* var. *pictum*
niponicum SLdr
  – f. **metallicum** see *A. niponicum* var. *pictum*
§ – var. **pictum** ♀H3 More than 30 suppliers
* – – 'Cristatoflabellatum' CBos CLAP ELan EMon
  – – 'Red Beauty' **new** EBee
  – – 'Silver Falls' CFwr CLAP EBee LRHS MBnl NCot
    SSpi WCot
  – – 'Ursula's Red' CLAP EBee WCot
  – – 'Wildwood Twist' CLAP MAvo
otophorum ♀H4 EMon LEur NHol NMar NVic SChu
    SRms WPGP WRic

  – var. **okanum** CElw CFwr CLAP CMHG CMil
    CPrp EBee EFer EFtx ELan EWTr
    GBin GCal GEdr LEur MAsh MBct
    MBri MSte NBlu NHol SBla SMad
    SNut SRot SSto WCot WCru WMoo
    WPnP
vidalii CLAP EBee MBri WFib WRic

Atractylodes (Asteraceae)
japonica EFEx
macrocephala CArn EFEx

Atragene see *Clematis*

Atriplex (Chenopodiaceae)
canescens WDin XPep
cinerea GGar
halimus CArn CBcs CBot CSLe ECha EHoe
    ENot EPPr LRHS MBlu MBri MRav
    NLar SLon SPer SWat WCot WDin
    WHer WKif WPGP WTel WTin
    XPep
hortensis gold-leaved WLHH
  – var. **rubra** CArn CHad CSpe EGra ELan EOHP
    MHer NChi NDov NGHP SIde
    WCHb WCot WEas WJek WWye
nummularia **new** XPep
portulacoides see *Halimione portulacoides*

Atropa (Solanaceae)
bella-donna CArn GBar GPoy MGol MSal
    WWye
  – var. **lutea** MSal
mandragora see *Mandragora officinarum*

Atropanthe (Solanaceae)
§ *sinensis* MSal

Aubrieta ❀ (Brassicaceae)
'Alba' see *A.* 'Fiona'
albomarginata see *A.* 'Argenteovariegata'
'Alix Brett' CMea CPBP EBre EDAr ELan LRHS
    NPer
'April Joy' ECho ECot ELan
§ 'Argenteovariegata' ELan SBla SIgm WAbe WHoo WShp
  (v) ♀H4
'Astolat' (v) EBre ECtt NSla SBla SRms WEas
    WPat
§ 'Aureovariegata' (v) ♀H4 CMea EBre ECtt EDAr ELan GKir
    IHMH LRHS MHer NJOw NPer
    NWCA SBla WAbe WFar
'Belisha Beacon' ECho ECtt MBri
Bengal hybrids STre WGor
Blaue Schönheit see *A.* 'Blue Beauty'
'Blaumeise' IHMH
§ 'Blue Beauty' CFai NBlu
'Blue Emperor' MBow
'Blue Midnight' EDAr
* 'Blue Mist' ECho EDAr
'Blue Sky' EDAr
§ 'Bob Saunders' (d) CMea EBre ECtt LTwo
'Bonfire' ECho ECtt
'Bressingham CMea EBre ECho ECtt ELan LRHS
  Pink' (d) ♀H4
'Bressingham Red' EBre LRHS SIng WRHF
campbellii ECho
canescens WLin
  subsp. **cilicica**
Cascade Series WFar WShp
  – 'Blue Cascade' ECho ECtt EPfP GKir LPVe SPlb
    WGor
  – 'Lilac Cascade' ECho
  – 'Purple Cascade' CWib ECtt EPfP LRHS NBlu NPro
    SCoo SPlb SRms WFar WGor

	'Red Cascade' ♀H4	CTri CWib ECtt EPfP GKir SCoo SPlb
	'Dantra' **new**	ECho
	deltoidea	CMea ECtt EPot NJOw WGor
	'Nana Variegata' (v)	
	– Variegata Group (v)	ECtt EPot GKir LHop LRHS NSla SIng WFar WPat
	'Doctor Mules' ♀H4	EBre ECho EDAr LRHS SIng SRms WPat
	'Doctor Mules Variegata' (v)	CWCL EBre EDAr EMlt LAst LGro MHer NPri SIng SWvt WLin
	'Dream'	SIng
	'Elsa Lancaster'	EHyt EPot
	'Fiona'	EDAr SIng
§	'Frühlingszauber'	SRms WGor
	'Gloriosa'	CFai SIng
	'Godstone'	ECho
	'Golden Carpet'	SIng
	'Golden King'	see *A.* 'Aureovariegata'
*	'Graeca'	EBre NPri
	'Greencourt Purple' ♀H4	ECho EDAr ELan MHer MWat SIng WWin
	'Gurgedyke'	ECho ELan SRms
	'Hamburger Stadtpark'	CBAn ECho EDAr WShp
	'Harknoll Red'	EPot
	'Hartswood'	SIng
	'Hemswell Purity' PBR	see *A.* 'Snow Maiden'
	'Hendersonii'	SRms WShp
	'J.S. Baker'	SRms
	'Jeeves' **new**	EBre
	'Joan Allen'	EDAr
	'Joy' (d)	ECho ECtt LTwo
	'Kitte' **new**	ECho
	'Leichtlinii'	EBre ECho NJOw NLar
	'Lemon and Lime'	EBre EDAr LRHS
	'Little Gem'	ECho
	'Lodge Crave'	SIng
	macedonica	EPot
	'Maurice Prichard'	EBre ECtt LRHS
	'Mrs Lloyd Edwards'	ECho
	'Mrs Rodewald' ♀H4	ECho EDAr SRms
	'Novalis Blue'	SRms
	'Oakington Lavender'	ECho EDAr ELan
	parviflora	CStu
	'Pike's Pink' **new**	EPot
	'Pike's Variegated' (v)	ECho
	pinardii	EHyt WLin
	'Purple Charm'	SRms
	'Purple Emperor'	SIng
	'Red Carpet'	EBre ELan EPot LGro LRHS MHer SIng SRms WShp WWin
	'Red Dyke'	SIng
	'Riverslea'	SIng
	'Rosanna Miles'	SIng
	'Rose Queen'	CMea CPBP LRHS SMrm
	Royal Series 'Royal Blue'	EBre ECho LRHS NJOw WMoo
	– 'Royal Red'	CWCL EBre NJOw NPri SRms WFar WGor WMoo
	– 'Royal Violet'	EBre ECho LRHS NJOw WPer
	'Schofield's Double'	see *A.* 'Bob Saunders'
	'Silberrand'	ECha ECtt EDAr NSla
§	'Snow Maiden' PBR	ECho ECtt LAst LRHS
	'Somerfield Silver'	SIng
	'Somerford Lime' (v)	ECtt WPat
	Spring Charm	see *A.* 'Frühlingszauber'
	'Swan Red' (v)	EPot LAst
	thessala	CPBP
	'Toby Saunders'	ECho
	'Triumphante'	EBre ECho ECtt LRHS LTwo
	'Wanda'	ECho ELan SIng
	'Whitewell Gem'	EBre NJOw SRms

Aucuba ✿ (*Aucubaceae*)

	japonica (f)	CDul EBee EWTr SMer

	– (m)	CHEx SReu
	– 'Crassifolia' (m)	MRav SAPC SArc
	– 'Crotonifolia' (f/v) ♀H4	More than 30 suppliers
	– 'Crotonifolia' (m/v) **new**	MAsh SRms
	– 'Dentata'	CHEx WWes
	– 'Fructu Albo' (f/v)	SPer
	– 'Gold Dust' (f/v)	LRHS
	– 'Golden King' (m/v) ♀H4	CBcs CDoC CHEx CMac CSBt CTrw EBee ELan ENot EPfP GKir LRHS MGos MSwo MWat SLim SPla SPoG WBcn WFar WWeb
	– 'Golden Spangles' (f/v)	CBcs CDoC EBee ECot EPla SWvt
	– 'Goldstrike' (v)	EBee EHoe
	– 'Lance Leaf' (m)	SLon WCru
	– f. **longifolia** ♀H4	CMac SAPC SArc SDix WCru WStI
	– – 'Salicifolia' (f)	CHEx EBee ENot EPla LRHS MRav NLar SLon SMad WBcn WCru WDin WGer WPGP
	– 'Maculata' hort.	see *A. japonica* 'Variegata'
	– 'Marmorata'	EPla LRHS
	– 'Nana Rotundifolia' (f)	EPla WStI
	– 'Pepperpot' (m/v)	CHEx
	– 'Picturata' (m/v)	CBcs CDul CHEx CMac CSBt ELan ENot EPfP EPla LRHS MAsh MRav NHol SAga SHBN SLim SPer WCFE WFar
	– 'Rozannie' (f/m) ♀H4	CBcs CDoC CDul CSBt EBee ECrN ELan ENot EPfP EPla EWTr GKir LRHS MAsh MBlu MGos MLan MRav MWat SLim SPer SPla SReu SWvt WDin WFar WStI
	– 'Speckles'	GSki
	– 'Sulphurea Marginata' (f/v)	CBcs CDoC CMac EMil EPla NPro SPer WBcn WBod
§	– 'Variegata' (f/v)	More than 30 suppliers
	– Windsor form (f)	EPla LRHS MBri WWes
	– 'Wykehurst' (v)	MTed

Aurinia (*Brassicaceae*)

§	**corymbosa**	LTwo
§	**saxatilis** ♀H4	EBre EMlt GKir MBar MWat NBlu SIng SPet SPlb STre WBVN WFar WTel
	– 'Citrina' ♀H4	CHal ECha ECtt MWat SRms WCom
	– 'Compacta'	CTri EBre ECtt MBro WShp
	– 'Dudley Nevill'	ECho EHol LRHS MWat SBla WTin
	– 'Dudley Nevill Variegated' (v)	EBre ECha EWes MHer NBir SBla
	– 'Flore Pleno' (d)	EHol
	– Gold Ball	see *A. saxatilis* 'Goldkugel'
	– 'Gold Dust'	ECtt LGro SRms
	– 'Golden Queen'	ECtt MHer
§	– 'Goldkugel'	GKir IHMH LRHS SRms
	– 'Silver Queen'	WEas
	– 'Variegata' (v)	NPri SIng
	sinuata 'Pebbles'	LRav

Austrocedrus (*Cupressaceae*)

§	**chilensis**	CKen CPne CTho LRHS

Austromyrtus (*Myrtaceae*)

§	**dulcis**	ECou

Avena (*Poaceae*)

	candida	see *Helictotrichon sempervirens*
	sativa	SWal
	sterilis	SWal

Avenula see *Helictotrichon*

Ayapana see *Eupatorium*

Azalea see *Rhododendron*

Azara ✿ (Flacourtiaceae)

alpina	CFil CPLG ISea
- G&P 5015	WPGP
dentata	CBcs CFil CHll CMac EBee ERea IDee LAst WPGP WSHC
- 'Variegata'	see *A. integrifolia* 'Variegata' (v)
* **integerrima**	GQui
integrifolia	CFil CRez WPGP
- 'Variegata' (v)	CFil CWib ERea SDnm SSpi
lanceolata	CBcs CFil CMCN CPLG CTri ISea LAst LEdu NSti SLon SPer WGer WPGP WPic
- G 3502	WPGP
microphylla ♀H3	CBcs CDul CFil CLnd CMCN CMHG CPLG CPle CSBt CTri EPfP EPla GKir ISea LAst NSti SArc SBra SDnm SDry SSpi WBod WFar WPGP WSHC WTel
- 'Variegata' (v)	CBcs CDoC CFil CMac CPLG CPle CSBt CWib EBee EHoe EPfP GQui LAst MLan NHol NSti SDnm SSpi SSta STre WCru WFar WGer WPGP WSHC
N **paraguayensis**	GGar ISea SDnm
petiolaris	CFai CFil CPle EPfP WGer WPic
- G&P 5026	WPGP
serrata ♀H3	CBcs CDul CEnd CFil CMCN CPLG CPle CSBt CTbh CWib EPfP EPla GGar GKir IDee ISea NCGa SDix SPer SRms SSta WBod WBor WCru WDin WFar WGer WHar WPGP WTel
- 'Patagonica'	ISea
uruguayensis	CPLG EBee

Azorella (Apiaceae)

compacta	SPlb
filamentosa	ECou
glebaria hort.	see *A. trifurcata*
glebaria A.Gray	see *Bolax gummifer*
gummifera	see *Bolax gummifer*
§ **trifurcata**	CPar CTri ECtt GAbr GEdr GKir GTou IHMH NLAp NWCA SBla SIgm WAbe WPer WShp
- 'Nana'	CNic GGar MBro MWat NJOw NMen WPat

Azorina (Campanulaceae)

§ **vidalii**	CBot CSpe EBee ERea EShb IDee LPio SAPC SAga SArc SVen
- 'Rosea'	CKob

B

Babiana (Iridaceae)

ambigua	CStu EGrW
angustifolia	CPLG EGrW
disticha	see *B. plicata*
dregei	EGrW WCot
ecklonii new	WCot
framesii	CStu
hybrids new	EGrW
nana	CStu EGrW WCot
odorata	WCot
§ **plicata**	SYvo WCot
pulchra	EPot
pygmaea	WCot
rubrocyanea	WCot
sambucina	CStu WCot
sinuata	EGrW WCot
striata	EMui

stricta ♀H1-2	EGrW WCot
- 'Purple Star'	CPLG ECho
thunbergii	EGrW
truncata	CStu EGrW WCot
tubulosa	EGrW WCot
vanzyliae	CStu EGrW WCot
villosa	EGrW WCot
'Zwanenburg's Glory'	EMan

Baccharis (Asteraceae)

genistelloides	SMad WCot
halimifolia	CBcs CPle CTrC GQui LRav
- 'Twin Peaks'	SDry XPep
patagonica	CTrC GEil GGar LEdu LPhx LSpr SAPC SAga SArc SScr WKif
'Sea Foam'	EChP EMan SBod SMad

Bacopa (Scrophulariaceae)

caroliniana	EMan EOHP
monnieri new	EOHP
'Snowflake'	see *Sutera cordata* 'Snowflake'

Baeckea (Myrtaceae)

densifolia	ECou
virgata	CTrC ECou SPlb

Baillonia (Verbenaceae)

juncea	WSHC

Balbisia (Geraniaceae)

peduncularis	WFoF

Baldellia (Alismataceae)

ranunculoides	CRow EMFW EMan WMAq WWpP
- f. **repens**	EMan LHop

Ballota ✿ (Lamiaceae)

acetabulosa ♀H3-4	EBee ECha EFou EGoo EMan EWes MWgw MWrn SDix WCom WCot WKif WWeb XPep
'All Hallows Green'	CFee EBee EFou EGoo EMan EPfP EPza GBuc LAst LHop LRHS NSti SBla SChu
hirsuta	XPep
nigra	CArn EBee GPoy GWCH MHer MSal SECG SMoo WWye XPep
§ - 'Archer's Variegated' (v)	EBee EChP ECtt EMan ERou EWes WCot
- 'Intakes White'	MInt
- 'Variegata'	see *B. nigra* 'Archer's Variegated'
- 'Zanzibar' (v)	EMon
pseudodictamnus ♀H3-4	More than 30 suppliers
- 'Candia'	MSph SBla
- from Crete	ECha

Balsamita see Tanacetum

Balsamorhiza (Asteraceae)

sagittata	ECho

Bambusa ✿ (Poaceae)

glaucescens	see *B. multiplex*
gracilis	see *Drepanostachyum falcatum*
gracillima	COtt EPla
§ **multiplex**	EFul GKir MAsh
- 'Alphonso-Karrii'	CFil GKir LPal MMoz NMoo SDry WPGP
- 'Elegans'	see *B. muliplex* 'Floribunda'
- 'Fernleaf'	see *B. muliplex* 'Floribunda'
§ - 'Floribunda'	CHEx COtt EFul NMoo SDry
- 'Golden Goddess'	NMoo
- 'Wang Tsai'	see *B. muliplex* 'Floribunda'
textilis	WJun
ventricosa	NMoo SDry

banana see *Musa*

Banisteriopsis (*Malpighiaceae*)
caapi	MGol

Banksia (*Proteaceae*)
burdettii	SOWG
canei	CTrC SPlb
coccinea	SOWG
ericifolia	CTrC SOWG
grandis	CCtw CTrC IDee SOWG
integrifolia	CBcs CCtw CTrC GQui
marginata	CTrC ECou SPlb
- mauve-flowered	SOWG
media	CTrC SPlb
oblongifolia	CTrC SPlb
occidentalis	CCtw SOWG
paludosa	CTrC SPlb
robur	CTrC
serrata	CCtw SOWG SPlb
serratifolia	CPla
speciosa	CCtw CTrC SPlb
spinulosa var. **collina**	CCtw CTrC
- pink	SOWG
violacea	SPlb

Baptisia (*Papilionaceae*)
§ **alba**	CPom EMan MSPs SIgm
§ - var. **macrophylla**	CMdw CPle LRHS MLLN NBir NLar
australis ♀H4	More than 30 suppliers
- 'Caspian Blue'	NBPC SPla
- 'Exaltata'	ELan GBuc LHop LRHS
- var. **minor**	EBee LPVe LPhx
§ **bracteata** var. **leucophaea**	SIgm
'Carolina Moonlight' **new**	EBee
lactea	see *B. alba* var. *macrophylla*
leucantha	see *B. alba* var. *macrophylla*
leucophaea	see *B. bracteata* var. *leucophaea*
pendula	see *B. alba*
'Purple Smoke'	EBee
tinctoria	CArn

Barbarea (*Brassicaceae*)
praecox	see *B. verna*
§ **verna**	CArn GPoy MHer NGHP WHer
vulgaris 'Variegata' (v)	CArn CBrm CHal EBee ELan EMan IHMH LDai MDun MWrn NBid NBro NOak NSti SWal WCAu WCHb WCot WMoo

Barleria (*Acanthaceae*)
repens	SOWG
suberecta	see *Dicliptera suberecta*

Barnadesia (*Asteraceae*)
caryophylla RCB/Eq T-5 **new**	WCot

Barosma see *Agathosma*

Bartlettina see *Eupatorium*

Bashania (*Poaceae*)
faberi Og 94053	EPla
§ **fargesii**	CDoC CDul EPla ERod GKir MRav MWht SEND WJun
I **qingchengshanensis**	CFil EPla WJun

basil see *Ocimum*

Bassia (*Chenopodiaceae*)
scoparia	MSal
- f. **trichophylla**	LPVe

Bauera (*Cunoniaceae*)
rubioides var. **alba**	ECou
- 'Candy Stripe'	SOWG
- pink	ECou SOWG
- 'Ruby Glow'	SOWG
sessiliflora	SOWG

Bauhinia (*Caesalpiniaceae*)
alba	see *B. variegata*
corymbosa	LRHS SOWG
galpinii	SOWG SPlb
monandra	SOWG WMul
natalensis	SPlb
tomentosa	EShb
§ **variegata** (v)	MGol
yunnanensis	SOWG

Baumea see *Machaerina*

bay see *Laurus nobilis*

Beaucarnea see *Nolina*

Beaufortia (*Myrtaceae*)
micrantha	SOWG
orbifolia	SOWG
sparsa	CTrC SOWG
squarrosa	SPlb

Beaumontia (*Apocynaceae*)
grandiflora	LRHS SOWG

Beauverdia see *Leucocoryne*

Beccariophoenix (*Arecaceae*)
madagascariensis	LPal

Beckmannia (*Poaceae*)
eruciformis	WRos

Bedfordia (*Asteraceae*)
salicina	ECou

Beesia (*Ranunculaceae*)
calthifolia	EBee WCru
- DJHC 98447	CDes

Begonia ✿ (*Begoniaceae*)
from China	NShi
from Vietnam **new**	ER&R
- BWJ 7840 **new**	WCru
- DJHC 98479	SSpi
'Abel Carrière'	CHal ER&R NShi WDib
acerifolia	see *B. vitifolia*
acetosa	ER&R
acida	ER&R NShi
aconitifolia	ER&R NShi
acutifolia	ER&R NShi
'Aladdin'	ER&R
'Alamo III' **new**	ER&R
albopicta (C)	CHal EBak ER&R LRHS
- 'Rosea'	CHal WDib
alice-clarkiae	ER&R NShi
'Allan Langdon' (T)	CBla
'Alleryi' (C)	ER&R NShi
alnifolia	ER&R
'Alto Scharff' ♀H1	ER&R NShi
'Alzasco' (C)	ER&R NShi
'Amigo Pink' (C)	ER&R

'Amigo Variegated' (v) — ER&R
ampla — ER&R
'Amy' (T) — CBla
angularis — see *B. stipulacea*
'Anita Roseanna' (C) — ER&R NShi
'Ann Anderson' (C) — ER&R NShi
'Anna Christine' (C) — ER&R
'Anniversary' (T) — CBla
§ *annulata* — ER&R NShi
'Apollo' (T) — CBla
'Apricot Delight' (T) — CBla
'Aquarius' — ER&R NShi
'Arabian Sunset' (C) — ER&R NShi
'Argentea' (R) — EBak MBri
× *argenteoguttata* (C) — CHal ER&R NShi
'Aries' — ER&R
'Art Monday' (C) — NShi
'Arthur Mallet' — ER&R
'Aruba' — ER&R
augustinei **new** — EBee
'Autumn Glow' (T) — ER&R NShi
'Avalanche' (T) — ER&R NShi
'Axel Lange' (R) **new** — NShi
'Aya' (C) — NShi WDib
'Baby Perfection' — NShi WDib
'Bahamas' — ER&R NShi
'Bantam Delight' — ER&R NShi
'Barbara Ann' (C) — ER&R
'Barbara Hamilton' (C) — ER&R
'Barbara Parker' — ER&R
'Barclay Griffiths' — ER&R NShi
'Beatrice Haddrell' — CHal ER&R NShi WDib
* *benichoma* — WDib
'Benitochiba' (R) — ER&R NShi
'Bernat Klein' (T) — CBla
'Bess' — ER&R NShi
'Bessie Buxton' — ER&R NShi
'Bethlehem Star' — ER&R NShi WDib
§ 'Bettina Rothschild' (R) — CHal ER&R NShi WDib
'Beverly Jean' — ER&R NShi
'Big Mac' — ER&R NShi
'Billie Langdon' (T) — CBla
'Bill's Beauty' — ER&R NShi
'Bishop's Irish Eyes' (C) — NShi
'Black Jack' (C) — ER&R NShi
'Black Knight' (R) — CHal NShi
'Black Raspberry' — ER&R NShi
'Blanc de Neige' — ER&R
'Blue Vein' — ER&R
'Blue Wave' **new** — NShi
'Bokit' — ER&R NShi WDib
boliviensis **new** — WCru
'Bonaire' — CHal
'Boomer' (C) — ER&R NShi
'Botato' — NShi
'Bouton de Rose' (T) — NRog SDeJ
bowerae — CHal ER&R LRHS
§ – var. *nigramarga* — ER&R NShi
'Boy Friend' — ER&R NShi
bracteosa — ER&R
brevirimosa — ER&R
'Brown Lace' **new** — NShi
'Brown Twist' — NShi WDib
'Bunchii' — ER&R NShi
'Burgundy Velvet' — ER&R NShi WDib
'Burle Marx' ♀H1 — CHal ER&R EShb NShi SDix WDib
'Bush Baby' — CHal NShi
'Butter Cup' **new** — NShi
'Buttermilk' (T) — CBla
'Calico Kew' — ER&R
'Calla Queen' (S) — ER&R
'Camelliiflora' (T) — NRog
'Can-can' (R) — see *B.* 'Herzog von Sagan'
'Can-can' (T) — CBla NShi

'Candy Floss' **new** — WCru
'Captain Nemo' **new** — ER&R
cardiocarpa **new** — ER&R
'Carol Mac' — ER&R
'Carol Wilkins
   of Ballarat' (T) — CBla
'Carolina Moon' (R) — ER&R NShi
carolineifolia — NShi WDib
carrieae — ER&R NShi
× *carrierei* — see *B.* Semperflorens Cultorum
   Group
'Cathedral' — ER&R NShi WDib
'Chantilly Lace' — CHal ER&R NShi
chapaensis HWJ 642 — WCru
'Charles Chevalier' — ER&R NShi
'Charles Jaros' — ER&R NShi
'Charm' (S) — CHal ER&R NShi WDib
'Cherry Jubilee' (C) — NShi
'Cherry Sundae' **new** — ER&R
'Chesson' — ER&R
'China Curl' **new** — ER&R
'China Doll' — NShi
'China Swirl' **new** — NShi
'Chocolate Box' — ER&R
'Chocolate Chip' — ER&R
'Christmas Candy' — ER&R EShb WDib
'Christy White' — NShi
'Chumash' — ER&R NShi
circumlobata **new** — EBee
'Cistine' **new** — ER&R
'Clara' (R) — MBri NShi
'Cleopatra' ♀H1 — CHal ER&R MRav NShi WDib
'Clifton' — ER&R NShi
coccinea (C) — ER&R NShi WDib
'Coconut Ice' **new** — LAst SPoG
compta — see *B. stipulacea*
'Comte de Lesseps' (C) — NShi WDib
conchifolia — ER&R NShi
   var. *rubrimacula*
'Concord' — ER&R
'Connee Boswell' — ER&R NShi WDib
convolvulacea — ER&R NShi
cooperi — ER&R NShi
'Coppelia' (T) — CBla
'Cora Anne' — ER&R
'Cora Miller' (R) — ER&R NShi
× *corallina* — EBak
§ – 'Lucerna' (C) — CHal EBak ER&R LRav NShi
– 'Lucerna Amazon' (C) — CHal ER&R IBlr NShi
'Corbeille de Feu' — CHal ER&R NShi
'Cosie' (C) — NShi
'Cowardly Lion' (R) — ER&R NShi
'Cracklin' Rosie' (C) — ER&R NShi
crassicaulis — ER&R NShi
'Crestabruchii' — ER&R
'Crimson Cascade' — CBla
'Crystal Brook' — ER&R NShi
* 'Crystal Cascade' — CBla
cubensis — ER&R NShi
cucullata — CHal ER&R NShi
'Curly Fireflush' (R) — ER&R
'Curly Locks' (S) — CHal
'Dales' Delight' (C) — ER&R NShi
'Dancin' Fred' — ER&R
'Dancing Girl' — ER&R NShi
'Dannebo' — MBri
'D'Artagnan' — ER&R NShi
'David Blais' (R) — NShi WDib
'Dawnal Meyer' (C) — ER&R NShi WDib
'De Elegans' — ER&R WDib
'Decker's Select' — ER&R NShi
decora — ER&R NShi
deliciosa — ER&R
'Delray Silver' — NShi

'Dewdrop' (R) — ER&R NShi WDib
diadema — ER&R
'Di-anna' (C) — ER&R
dichotoma — ER&R NShi
dichroa (C) — ER&R
'Dielytra' **new** — ER&R
'Di-erna' — ER&R NShi
dietrichiana Irmsch. — ER&R
'Digswelliana' — ER&R
dipetala — ER&R
discolor — see *B. grandis* subsp. *evansiana*
domingensis — ER&R
'Don Miller' — ER&R NShi WDib
'Doublet Pink' — ER&R
'Doublet Red' — ER&R
'Doublet White' — ER&R
'Douglas Nisbet' (C) — ER&R
Dragon Wing Red — NShi
   = 'Bepared'[PBR] ♀H1+3
dregei (T) ♀H1 — ER&R NShi
- 'Bonsai' **new** — STre
- 'Glasgow' **new** — ER&R
- var. *macbethii* — NShi
'Druryi' — ER&R NShi
'Dwarf Houghtonii' — ER&R NShi
'Earl of Pearl' **new** — ER&R
* 'Ebony' (C) — CHal ER&R NShi
echinosepala — ER&R NShi
echinosepala — NShi
   x *sanguinea*
I 'Edinburgh Brevirimosa' — ER&R NShi
edmundoi — ER&R
egregia — ER&R
'Elaine' — ER&R NShi
'Elaine Ayres' (C) — ER&R NShi
§ 'Elaine Wilkerson' — ER&R NShi
'Elaine's Baby' — see *B.* 'Elaine Wilkerson'
'Elda' — ER&R NShi
'Elda Haring' (R) — ER&R NShi
'Elizabeth Hayden' — ER&R
'Elsie M. Frey' — ER&R
'Emerald Giant' (R) — ER&R NShi WDib
'Emerald Isle' — NShi
'Emma Watson' — CHal ER&R NShi
'Enchantment' — ER&R
'Enech' — ER&R NShi
'English Knight' — ER&R NShi
'English Lace' — ER&R NShi
epipsila — ER&R
x *erythrophylla* — NShi
- 'Bunchii' — ER&R NShi
§ - 'Helix' — CHal ER&R NShi
'Essie Hunt' — ER&R
'Esther Albertine' (C) ♀H1 — CHal ER&R NShi
'Eureka' (T) — CBla
'Evening Star' — ER&R
'Exotica' — ER&R
'Fairy' — ER&R NShi
'Fairylight' (T) — CBla
feastii 'Helix' — see *B.* x *erythrophylla* 'Helix'
fernando-costae — ER&R NShi
'Festiva' (T) — CBla
§ 'Feuerkönigin' (S) — ER&R
'Filigree' — ER&R NShi
fimbriata — WWol
fimbristipula (T) **new** — EBee
'Fire Flush' — see *B.* 'Bettina Rothschild'
'Firedance' (T) — CBla
'Fireworks' (R) — ER&R NShi WDib
'Five and Dime' — ER&R NShi
'Flamboyant' (T) — ER&R MBri NShi
Flaming Queen — see *B.* 'Feuerkönigin'
'Flamingo' — ER&R NShi
'Flamingo Queen' — ER&R

'Flo'Belle Moseley' (C) — CHal ER&R NShi WDib
'Florence Carrell' — ER&R NShi
'Florence Rita' (C) — ER&R NShi
'Flying High' **new** — ER&R
foliosa — CHal ER&R NShi WDib
- var. *amplifolia* — CHal ER&R NShi
§ - var. *miniata* 'Rosea' — CDoC CHal LRHS
formosana B&SWJ 7041 — WCru
'Frances Lyons' **new** — ER&R
'Freckles' (R) — ER&R
'Fred Bedson' — ER&R NShi
'Fred Martin' (R) **new** — NShi
friburgensis — ER&R
'Friendship' — ER&R
from Sikkim, India — EMan
   B&SWJ 2692 **new**
'Frosty' (T) — NShi WDib
'Frosty Fairyland' — ER&R
'Frosty Knight' — ER&R NShi
'Fuchsifoliosa' — ER&R
fuchsioides ♀H1 — CDoC EBak ER&R Llck MOak NShi
   SDix SYvo WDib
- pink-flowered **new** — LAst
- red-flowered — MOak WFar
- 'Rosea' — see *B. foliosa* var. *miniata* 'Rosea'
- 'Full Moon' (T) — CBla
'Fuscomaculata' — ER&R
'Gaystar' — NShi
gehrtii — ER&R NShi
geranioides — ER&R
glabra — ER&R
glandulosa — ER&R
glaucophylla — see *B. radicans*
'Glen Daniels' — NShi
'Gloire de Sceaux' — ER&R NShi
goegoensis — ER&R NShi
'Gold Cascade' — CBla
'Gold Doubloon' (T) — CBla
'Goldilocks' (T) — CBla
'Good 'n' Plenty' — ER&R NShi
gracilis — NShi
   var. *martiana* **new**
'Granada' — ER&R NShi
§ *grandis* subsp. — CDoC CHEx CHal CSam CWCL
   evansiana ♀H3-4 — EBee ELan EMan EMon ER&R GCal
   LEdu MLLN MOak MSte MTho
   NCiC NShi SDix SMad SMrm SSpi
   WBrk WCot WCru WFar WHen
   WCru
- - B&SWJ 5702
- - var. *alba* hort. — CDoC CHal CMdw EBee EMon
   ER&R GCal MOak MSte MTho
   SMad SSpi WCot WPGP
- - 'Claret Jug' — EMan EMon WCot WPGP
- 'Maria' — EBee WCot
- 'Sapporo' — EPPr GCal MSte
- 'Simsii' — WFar
* 'Great Beverly' — ER&R NShi
'Green Gold' (R) — NShi WDib
'Green Lace' — ER&R NShi
'Grey Feather' — ER&R NShi
griffithii — see *B. annulata*
'Gustav Lind' (S) — CHal ER&R NShi
'Guy Savard' (C) — NShi WDib
'Gypsy Maiden' (T) — CBla
haageana — see *B. scharffii*
handelii — ER&R NShi
* 'Happy Heart' — ER&R NShi
'Harbison Canyon' **new** — NShi
* 'Harry's Beard' — ER&R NShi
'Hastor' — ER&R NShi
hatacoa — ER&R NShi
- silver — CHal ER&R NShi
- spotted — ER&R NShi
'Hazel's Front Porch' (C) — ER&R NShi

'Helen Lewis'	ER&R NShi	
'Helen Teupel' (R)	ER&R NShi WDib	
'Helene Jaros' **new**	ER&R	
hemsleyana **new**	EBee	
henryii **new**	EBee	
'Her Majesty' (R)	ER&R	
heracleifolia	ER&R	
var. *longipila*		
- var. *nigricans*	NShi	
- 'Wisley'	NShi	
§ 'Herzog von Sagan' (R)	ER&R NShi	
x *hiemalis* 'Elatior'	LRHS	
hispida var. *cucullifera*	ER&R NShi	
'Holmes Chapel'	ER&R NShi	
homonyma (T)	ER&R	
'Honeysuckle' (C)	ER&R NShi	
'Hot Tamale' **new**	ER&R	
'Hottentot'	NShi	
hydrocotylifolia	ER&R NShi	
hypolipara	ER&R NShi	
Illumination Series	WWol	
'Illumination Apricot'		
- 'Illumination Rose'	SCoo WWol	
- 'Illumination	SCoo	
Salmon Pink' ♀H2-3		
- 'Illumination White'	WWol	
imperialis	ER&R NShi	
imperialis x 'Bokit'	NShi WDib	
incarnata (C)	ER&R NShi	
- 'Metallica'	see *B. metallica*	
'Ingramii'	ER&R NShi	
'Interlaken' (C)	ER&R NShi	
'Irene Nuss' (C) ♀H1	ER&R NShi	
'Ironstone' (R)	NShi	
'Ivanhoe' (T)	CBla	
'Ivy Ever'	ER&R NShi	
'Jade'	NShi	
'Jean Blair' (T)	CBla	
'Jelly Roll Morton'	ER&R	
'Joe Hayden'	CHal ER&R NShi	
'John Tonkin' (C)	ER&R NShi	
johnstonii	ER&R	
'Joy Porter' (C)	NShi	
'Jubilee Mine'	ER&R	
juliana **new**	ER&R	
'Jumbo Jeans'	ER&R NShi	
'Jumbo Jet' (C)	ER&R NShi	
'Kagaribi' (C)	ER&R NShi	
kellermanii (C)	ER&R NShi	
'Ken Lau Ren' (C)	NShi	
keniensis **new**	GCal	
'Kentwood' (C)	ER&R	
kenworthyae	ER&R	
kingiana	WDib	
'Kit Jeans'	ER&R NShi	
'Kit Jeans Mounger'	ER&R NShi	
'Knutsford' **new**	NShi	
'Kookaburra' (T)	CBla	
'Krakatoa'	CBla	
'Kyoto'	NShi	
'La Paloma' (C)	WDib	
'Lacewing' **new**	ER&R	
'Lady Carol'	CHal	
'Lady Clare'	ER&R NShi SDix	
* 'Lady France'	ER&R MBri	
'Lady Rowena' (T)	CBla	
'Lady Snow'	CHal	
'Lana' (C)	ER&R NShi	
'Lancelot' (T)	CBla	
langeana	NShi	
'Laurie's Love' (C)	ER&R	
'Lawrence H. Fewkes'	ER&R	
leathermaniae (C)	ER&R	
'Legia'	ER&R	

'Lenore Olivier' (C)	ER&R NShi	
'Leopard'	ER&R MBri NShi	
'Lexington'	ER&R	
'Libor' (C)	ER&R	
'Lillian' (R)	NShi	
'Lime Swirl'	ER&R NShi	
limmingheana	see *B. radicans*	
'Linda Dawn' (C)	ER&R NShi	
'Linda Harley'	ER&R	
'Linda Myatt'	ER&R NShi	
lindeniana	ER&R NShi	
listada ♀H1	CHal ER&R MBri NShi WDib	
'Lithuania'	ER&R	
'Little Brother	CHal ER&R NShi SDix WDib	
Montgomery' ♀H1		
'Little Darling'	ER&R NShi	
'Little Iodine'	NShi	
'Lois Burks' (C)	CHal ER&R NShi WDib	
'Loma Alta'	ER&R	
'Looking Glass' (C)	ER&R NShi WDib	
'Lospe-tu'	ER&R NShi	
'Lou Anne'	CBla	
'Lubbergei' (C)	ER&R NShi	
'Lucerna'	see *B.* x *corallina* 'Lucerna'	
'Lulu Bower' (C)	ER&R	
luxurians	ER&R NShi	
- 'Ziesenhenne'	ER&R	
lyman-smithii	ER&R	
'Mabel Corwin'	ER&R NShi	
'Mac MacIntyre'	NShi	
macdougallii	CHal NShi WDib	
var. *purpurea*		
macduffieana	NShi	
macrocarpa	ER&R	
'Mac's Gold'	ER&R NShi	
maculata ♀H1	ER&R NShi	
- 'Wightii' (C)	CHal CSpe ER&R NShi WDib	
'Mad Hatter'	ER&R NShi	
'Madame Butterfly' (C)	ER&R NShi	
'Magic Carpet'	ER&R NShi	
'Magic Lace'	ER&R NShi	
'Majesty' (T)	CBla	
'Manacris' **new**	ER&R	
'Mandarin	NShi	
Orange' (C) **new**		
manicata	ER&R NShi WDib	
'Maphil'	MBri NShi	
'Mardi Gras' (T)	CBla	
'Margaritae'	ER&R NShi	
'Marmaduke' ♀H1	CHal NShi WDib	
'Marmorata' (T)	LRHS NRog	
'Martha Floro' (C)	ER&R	
'Martin Johnson' (R)	ER&R NShi WDib	
'Martin's Mystery'	ER&R NShi	
masoniana ♀H1	CHal ER&R ERea MOak NShi WDib	
I 'Matador' (T)	CBla	
'Maurice Amey'	ER&R NShi	
'Maverick'	ER&R NShi	
maxima	ER&R NShi	
mazae	ER&R NShi	
'Medora' (C)	ER&R NShi	
'Melissa' (T)	CBla NShi	
'Merry Christmas' (R) ♀H1	ER&R WDib	
metachroa	ER&R	
§ *metallica* ♀H1	CHal ER&R NShi	
'Michaele' **new**	ER&R	
'Midnight Sun'	ER&R NShi	
'Midnight Twister'	ER&R NShi	
'Mikado' (R)	ER&R NShi	
minor	ER&R	
'Mirage' ♀H1	ER&R NShi	
'Miss Priss' (C)	NShi	
mollicaulis	ER&R	
'Moon Maid'	ER&R	

* 'Moulin Rouge'	CBla
'Mr Steve' (T)	CBla
'Mrs Hashimoto' (C)	ER&R NShi
'Mrs Hatcher' **new**	ER&R
'Mrs Schinkle' (C)	NShi
multinervia	ER&R
'Munchkin' ♀H1	CHal ER&R NShi WDib
* 'Mystic'	ER&R NShi
'Mystique'	ER&R NShi
'Nancy Cummings'	ER&R
natalensis (T)	ER&R NShi
'Nell Gwynne' (T)	CBla
'Nelly Bly'	ER&R
nelumbifolia	ER&R NShi
nigramarga	see *B. bowerae* var. *nigramarga*
nigritarum	ER&R
* *nitida alba* **new**	ER&R
'Nokomis' (C)	ER&R NShi
'Norah Bedson'	ER&R NShi
'Northern Lights' (S)	ER&R NShi
obliqua **new**	ER&R
obscura	ER&R
'Obsession'	ER&R
odorata	ER&R
- var. *rosea*	NShi
'Odorata Alba'	ER&R NShi
olbia	ER&R
'Old Gold' (T)	ER&R
'Oliver Twist'	ER&R
'Ophelia' (T)	CBla
'Orange Cascade' (T)	CBla
'Orange Dainty'	ER&R
'Orange Pinafore (C)'	ER&R
'Orange Rubra' (C) ♀H1	CHal ER&R NShi
'Orococo'	NShi
'Orpha C. Fox' (C)	ER&R NShi
'Orrell' (C)	ER&R NShi
'Othello'	ER&R NShi
'Otto Forster'	ER&R NShi
oxyphylla	ER&R
'Pachea' (R)	NShi
paleata	ER&R NShi
palmata	CDes EBee EMan GCal WPGP
- var. *palmata*	NShi SSpi
- - B&SWJ 7175	WCru
'Palomar Prince'	ER&R NShi
'Panasoffkee'	ER&R NShi
'Pantaloon'	NShi
'Panther'	ER&R
'Papillon' (T)	ER&R NShi
paranaensis	ER&R NShi
* 'Parilis'	ER&R NShi
partita	ER&R NShi
'Passing Storm'	ER&R NShi
'Patricia Ogdon'	ER&R NShi
'Paul Harley'	ER&R NShi
'Paul Henry'	NShi
'Paul-bee'	ER&R NShi
paulensis	ER&R NShi
'Peace' (R)	NShi
'Peach Parfait' (C)	ER&R NShi
pearcei	ER&R NShi
'Pearl Ripple'	ER&R NShi
'Pearls' (C)	ER&R NShi
pedatifida **new**	EBee
'Peggy Stevens' (C)	ER&R
peltata	ER&R NShi
* 'Penelope Jane'	ER&R
'Persephone' (T)	CBla
'Persian Brocade'	ER&R NShi
'Petite Marie' (C) **new**	ER&R
'Phil Corwin' (R)	NShi
'Piccolo'	ER&R NShi
'Pickobeth' (C)	ER&R NShi

'Picotee' (T)	CSut
'Pinafore' (C) ♀H1	ER&R NShi
'Pink Basket'	NShi
'Pink Champagne' (R)	CBla NShi WDib
'Pink Frosted'	NShi
'Pink Jade' (C)	NShi
'Pink Lady' (R) **new**	WCru
'Pink Nacre'	CHal ER&R NShi
'Pink Parade' (C)	ER&R NShi
'Pink Parfan'	NShi
'Pink Shasta' (C)	NShi
'Pink Slate' (C)	NShi
'Pink Spot Lucerne' (C)	ER&R NShi SYvo
'Pink Taffeta'	ER&R NShi
plagioneura	ER&R
platanifolia	ER&R
var. *acuminatissima*	
'Plum Rose'	ER&R NShi
plumieri **new**	ER&R
polyantha	ER&R NShi
polygonoides	ER&R
popenoei	ER&R
'Posy Wahl' (C)	NShi
'Potpourri'	ER&R
'Président Carnot' (C)	ER&R NShi SYvo
'Pretty Rose'	ER&R
'Preussen'	ER&R NShi
'Primrose' (T)	CBla
'Princess of Hanover' (R)	ER&R NShi WDib
'Princessa	ER&R
Rio de Plata' **new**	
prismatocarpa	ER&R NShi
procumbens	see *B. radicans*
pustulata 'Argentea'	ER&R NShi
putii B&SWJ 7245 **new**	WCru
'Queen Mother' (R)	ER&R NShi
'Queen Olympus'	ER&R NShi WDib
'Quinebaug'	ER&R NShi
§ *radicans* ♀H1	CHal ER&R LRHS MBri NShi
'Raquel Wood'	ER&R NShi
'Raspberry Swirl' (R) ♀H1	CHal ER&R NShi WDib
ravenii	GCal NShi SSpi WCot
- B&SWJ 1954	WCru
'Raymond George Nelson' ♀H1	CHal ER&R NShi
'Razzmatazz' (R)	NShi WDib
'Red Berry' (R)	ER&R NShi
'Red Planet'	ER&R NShi WDib
'Red Reign'	ER&R NShi
'Red Robin' (R)	NShi WDib
'Red Spider'	ER&R NShi
'Red Undies' **new**	WCru
'Red Wing' (R)	NShi
'Regal Minuet' (R)	NShi WDib
'Regalia'	ER&R
'Reine des Neiges' (R)	NShi
rex	LRHS MBri MRav NShi
- 'Orient'	ER&R
'Richard Robinson'	ER&R
'Richmondensis'	ER&R NShi
'Ricinifolia'	ER&R NShi
'Ricky Minter' ♀H1	ER&R NShi
'Rip van Winkle'	ER&R NShi
'Robert Blais' (R)	NShi
'Robin' (R)	ER&R NShi
'Robin's Red' (C)	ER&R NShi
'Roi de Roses' (R)	ER&R NShi
roxburghii	ER&R NShi
'Roy Hartley' (T)	CBla
'Royal Lustre'	ER&R NShi
'Royalty' (T)	CBla
'Rubacon'	ER&R NShi
rubro-setulosa	ER&R
'Sabre Dance' (R)	ER&R NShi

'Sachsen'	ER&R NShi
'Saint Albans Grey' **new**	NShi
salicifolia (C)	ER&R
sanguinea	ER&R NShi
'Scarlet Pimpernel' (T)	CBla
'Scarlett O'Hara' (T)	CBla ER&R
'Sceptre' (T)	CBla
scharffiana	ER&R
§ *scharffii*	CHal EBak ER&R SDix
'Scherzo'	CHal ER&R NShi WDib
'Scottish Star'	NShi
'Sea Captain' **new**	NShi
'Sea Coral' (T)	CBla
'Sea Serpent'	NShi
'Secpuoc' **new**	ER&R
semperflorens hort.	see *B.* Semperflorens Cultorum Group
§ Semperflorens Cultorum Group	MBri NShi
– double (d)	CHal
'Serlis'	ER&R NShi
serratipetala	CHal EBak ER&R MBri NShi WDib
'Shamus' **new**	ER&R
* *sheperdii*	CHal WDib
'Shiloh' (R)	ER&R NShi
* 'Shinihart' **new**	ER&R
'Shoppy'	NShi
'Sierra Mist' (C)	ER&R NShi
'Silbreen'	NShi
'Silver Cloud' (R)	ER&R NShi WDib
* 'Silver Dawn'	ER&R NShi
'Silver Dollar' **new**	NShi
'Silver Dots' **new**	NShi
'Silver Giant' (R) **new**	ER&R
'Silver Jewell'	NShi WDib
'Silver Lace'	NShi
'Silver Mist' (C)	ER&R NShi
'Silver Points'	ER&R NShi
'Silver Queen' (R) ♀H1	NShi
'Silver Sweet' (R)	ER&R NShi
'Silver Wings'	ER&R NShi
'Sinbad' (C)	ER&R NShi
sinensis	EBee EMan EMon NShi WCot
– B&SWJ 8011A	WCru
– BWJ 8011	WCru
* 'Sir Charles'	ER&R
'Sir John Falstaff'	ER&R NShi
Skeezar Group	ER&R
– 'Brown Lake'	ER&R NShi
* 'Snowcap' (C) ♀H1	ER&R EShb NShi WDib
socotrana	ER&R
solananthera ♀H1	CHal ER&R NShi WDib
soli-mutata	NShi
sonderiana	ERea GCal
'Sophie Cecile' (C) ♀H1	CHal ER&R NShi
'Sophie's Jenny'	NShi
'Speckled Roundabout' **new**	NShi
'Speculata' (R)	ER&R NShi
'Spellbound'	ER&R NShi WDib
'Spindrift'	ER&R NShi
'Spotches'	ER&R NShi
'Stained Glass' (R)	NShi WDib
'Stichael Maeae' **new**	ER&R
§ *stipulacea*	CHal ER&R NShi
subvillosa (S)	ER&R
'Sugar Candy' (T)	CBla
'Sugar Plum' **new**	ER&R
'Sun God'	NShi
'Superba Azella' (C)	NShi
sutherlandii ♀H1	CAvo CHEx CHal EBak EOHP ER&R ERea ERos LRHS MOak NBir NPer NShi SDix SYvo WCot WCru WDib WEas WFar WHer

– 'Papaya'	CSpe
'Swan Song'	ER&R
'Sweet Dreams' (T)	CBla
'Sweet Magic'	CHal ER&R NShi
'Swirly Top' (C)	ER&R NShi
'Sylvan Triumph' (C)	ER&R NShi
'Tahiti' (T)	CBla
taiwaniana **new**	NShi
'Tapestry' (R)	NShi
'Tar Baby' (T) **new**	ER&R
* *taya*	WDib
'Tea Rose'	ER&R NShi
'Tequesta'	NShi
teuscheri (C)	ER&R NShi
'Texastar'	ER&R NShi WDib
'The Wiz'	ER&R NShi
thelmae	ER&R NShi
'Think Pink'	NShi
'Thrush' (R)	NShi
'Thumotec'	ER&R
'Thunderclap'	CHal ER&R NShi
'Thurstonii' ♀H1	CHal ER&R NShi
'Tiger Paws' ♀H1	CHal ER&R MBri NShi
'Tingley Mallet' (C)	ER&R NShi
'Tiny Bright' (R)	ER&R NShi
'Tiny Gem'	ER&R NShi
'Tom Ment' (C)	ER&R NShi
'Tom Ment II' (C)	ER&R
'Tomoshiba' **new**	ER&R
'Tondelayo' (R)	ER&R NShi
'Tornado' (R)	NShi
'Tribute'	ER&R NShi
'Trinidad' **new**	ER&R
tripartita (T)	ER&R NShi WDib
'Twilight'	ER&R NShi
'Two Face'	ER&R NShi WDib
ulmifolia (C)	ER&R NShi
undulata (C)	CHal ER&R NShi
'Universe'	ER&R NShi
'Venetian Red' (R)	NShi
venosa	CHal ER&R NShi
'Venus'	CHal ER&R NShi
'Vera Wyatt'	NShi
x *verschaffeltii*	ER&R NShi
versicolor	ER&R
'Vesuvius' (R)	NShi WDib
'Viaudii'	ER&R NShi
'Viau-Scharff'	ER&R
§ *vitifolia*	ER&R NShi
'Wally's World'	NShi
'Weltoniensis'	ER&R NShi
'Weltoniensis Alba' (T)	ER&R
'White Cascade'	ER&R
'Wild Swan' **new**	WCru
'Witch Craft' (T)	ER&R NShi
'Withlacoochee'	ER&R NShi WDib
wollnyi	ER&R
'Wood Nymph' (R)	ER&R NShi
'Yellow Sweety' (T)	CBla
'Zuensis'	ER&R
'Zulu' (T)	CBla

Belamcanda (Iridaceae)

chinensis	CArn CBro EBee EChP ECha EGra EMan GEdr GPoy LRHS MAvo MLLN MSal SDnm SPlb SSto SYvo WBVN WBrE WCFE WCru WLun WPer WWye
– 'Hello Yellow'	GBuc MSte

Bellevalia (Hyacinthaceae)

dubia	WCot
fominii **new**	WWst
forniculata	EHyt GTou

gracilis	WCot
hackelii	ERos
hyacinthoides	CStu
kurdistanica	ERos
longipes	WCot
longistyla	WCot
§ *paradoxa*	CHar CPLG CPom EBee EChP EHrv EHyt EMan EPar ERos ITim LTwo MAvo MLwd MSPs NJOw NRog WCot
pycnantha hort.	see *B. paradoxa*
romana	CNic EBee ERos LPhx MTho NRog WCot
sarmatica **new**	ERos
tabriziana	ERos
webbiana **new**	ERos

Bellis (Asteraceae)

perennis	NSco SECG
- 'Alba Plena' (d)	ECho ELan
- 'Alice'	SUsu
- 'Blue Moon' **new**	WCHb
- 'Dresden China'	CCge ELan GAbr MTho NBlu SIng WCot WOut
- Hen and Chickens	see *B. perennis* 'Prolifera'
- 'Hullavington'	CNat
- 'Jocelyn Castle' (d)	WWye
- 'Lower Minety' (v)	CNat
- 'Miss Mason'	GAbr WBro WOut
§ - 'Prolifera'	WHer
- 'Red Buttons' **new**	NBlu
- 'Robella' **new**	SECG
- 'Robert'	GAbr
- 'Rusher Rose'	EPfP
- 'Single Blue'	see *B. rotundifolia* 'Caerulescens'
- 'Tasso Strawberries and Cream'	SECG WRHF
§ *rotundifolia*	CElw CNic ELan GAbr NBir NBro
'Caerulescens'	SIng WCot WOut
sylvestris	CArn

Bellium (Asteraceae)

bellidioides	GEdr
* *crassifolium canescens*	WPer
minutum	MTho

Beloperone see *Justicia*

Bensoniella (Saxifragaceae)

oregona	EBee EMon

Berberidopsis (Flacourtiaceae)

beckleri	CFil
corallina	More than 30 suppliers

Berberis ✿ (Berberidaceae)

ACE 2237	EPot
aetnensis	GIBF
aggregata	EPla GKir NBir SPer SRms WDin
amurensis 'Flamboyant'	WBcn
- var. *latifolia* B&SWJ 4353	WCru
x *antoniana*	ESis LRHS MBri WBcn
aquifolium	see *Mahonia aquifolium*
- 'Fascicularis'	see *Mahonia x wagneri* 'Pinnacle'
N *aristata* ambig.	CAgr CArn CMCN
- Parker	see *B. glaucocarpa*
asiatica	CPLG GPoy
bealei	see *Mahonia japonica* Bealei Group
bergmanniae	SLPl
'Blenheim'	WFar
'Boughton Red'	MBri
brevipedunculata Bean	see *B. prattii*

x *bristolensis*	EPla SLon SPla SRms
buxifolia	CPle MRav WCFE
- 'Nana'	see *B. buxifolia* 'Pygmaea'
N - 'Pygmaea'	CABP CSBt CTri EBee EMil ENot GGar GKir LRHS MAsh MBNS MBar MRav NHol SLim SMer SPer STre WCom WDin WFar WStI
calliantha	CPle WBcn WFar
candidula	EBee ECrN ENot EPfP GKir LAst MBar MGos MRav MSwo NHol SLon SPer WDin WGwG WStI
- 'Jytte'	see *B.* 'Jytte'
x *carminea* 'Barbarossa'	SPer WDin
- 'Buccaneer'	ENot SPer
- 'Pirate King'	CSBt EBee ENot LRHS MRav SPer SWvt WPat
chrysosphaera	WFar
§ *concinna*	IMGH
- CC 3302	CPLG
congestiflora	CPle
cooperi	GIBF
coxii	GGar WCwm
darwinii ♀H4	More than 30 suppliers
dictyophylla ♀H4	CFil CPMA EPfP EPla MGos NLar SLon SSpi WCwm WDin WPGP WPat WSHC
dulcis 'Nana'	see *B. buxifolia* 'Pygmaea'
empetrifolia	CPle
erythroclada	see *B. concinna*
'Fireball'	CMac
franchetiana var. *macrobotrys*	GIBF
francisci-ferdinandii	SMad
x *frikartii*	CDoC CMac CSBt CSam EBee EBre ELan ENot EPfP GKir LAst MBNS MRav NLar WDin WFar
'Amstelveen' ♀H4	
- 'Telstar'	EBee ENot LAst LBuc MRav NPro WStI
gagnepainii hort.	see *B. gagnepainii* var. *lanceifolia*
gagnepainii C.K. Schneid.	CMac GKir LRav MRav NHol SLPl WBVN WGwG WTel
- 'Fernspray'	CDul EPfP EPla LRHS MRav SBod SRms WBod
§ - var. *lanceifolia*	CBcs CTri ENot EPla GKir MBar MDun MGos MWhi NWea SPer WDin WFar
- 'Purpurea'	see *B. x interposita* 'Wallich's Purple'
'Georgei' ♀H4	CMHG CWib EPfP GKir LRHS SMur SPoG SSpi WBcn
gilgiana	CPLG
§ *glaucocarpa*	EPfP EPla NHol
'Goldilocks'	CABP CDul CFil CPMA EPfP GKir LAst LRHS MBlu MBri SPoG SSpi WBcn WGer
gyalaica	GIBF
holocraspedon **new**	CPle
hookeri var. *latifolia*	see *B. manipurana*
x *hybridogagnepainii* 'Chenaultii'	ELan SPer
hypokerina	CMac
insignis	WFar
- subsp. *insignis* var. *insignis* B&SWJ 2432	WCru
§ x *interposita*	EBee ENot EPfP MBar MDun MRav MSwo NHol SPer WDin WStI
'Wallich's Purple'	
jamesiana	WCFE
julianae ♀H4	CBcs CSBt EBee ECrN ELan ENot EPfP EWTr GKir LAst LRav MBar MGos MRav MSwo NBee NHol NWea SHBN SHFr SLPl SPer SWvt WBVN WDin WFar WHCG WHar WSHC WTel

- 'Mary Poppins'	LRHS MBri WSPU
§ 'Jytte'	EBee MRav MWhi WDin
kawakamii	CPle SLPl
knightii	see *B. manipurana*
koreana	CDul CFil CMCN EPfP EPla GIBF
	NLar WCom WPGP
lecomtei	GIBF
lempergiana	CMCN
lepidifolia	GBin
linearifolia	CMac
- 'Orange King'	CBcs CDoC CMac EBee ECrN ELan
	ENot EPfP GKir LRHS MAsh MGos
	NBee NHol SHBN SIgm SPer WDin
	WFar WHar WPat WStI
'Little Favourite'	see *B. thunbergii* 'Atropurpurea
	Nana'
x *lologensis*	MGos NHol WDin
- 'Apricot Queen' ♀H4	CBcs CMac EPfP GKir LRHS MAsh
	MGos NBea NBee NLar SHBN SPer
	SPoG WDin WStI
- 'Mystery Fire'	CDoC COtt GKir LRHS MAsh MBar
	MBlu MBri MDun MGos NBlu
	NHol NLar SCoo SWvt WDin WFar
	WHar
- 'Stapehill'	ELan EPfP GKir LRHS MAsh MBri
	SSpi WBcn
lycium	CAgr MMil WHCr
- CC 1729	CPLG
macrosepala	WCru
var. *macrosepala*	
B&SWJ 2124	
§ *manipurana*	ENot
x *media* Park Jewel	see *B.* x *media* 'Parkjuweel'
§ - 'Parkjuweel'	CBcs EBee ENot EPfP GKir IArd
	MRav NLar WDin WFar
- 'Red Jewel' ♀H4	CDoC CMac CSBt EBee EBre EPfP
	LRHS MAsh MGos MWat NBee
	NHol NPro NScw SPer WBod
	WDin WFar WMoo
montana	WPat
morrisonensis	CFil WCom WPGP
morrisonicola	GIBF
aff. *nepalensis*	GIBF
nummularia	GIBF
x *ottawensis*	MWhi WStI
- 'Auricoma'	EBee LRHS MAsh MRav
- f. *purpurea*	CWib EBee MGos SBod WDin WHar
§ - - 'Superba' ♀H4	More than 30 suppliers
§ - 'Silver Miles' (v)	EHoe EPfP LRHS MRav NHol SPoG
	WBVN WFar WPat
§ *panlanensis*	EBee ENot MBar MRav SLon WWes
poiretii	CPLG NBhm
polyantha hort.	see *B. prattii*
§ *prattii*	CMHG CPle MBri MWat NLRH
pruinosa	CFil
'Red Tears'	CPMA CSam LRHS MBlu MBri
	MGos MLan NLar SPer WHCG
'Rubrostilla'	GEil
x *rubrostilla*	CMac
'Cherry Ripe'	
- 'Wisley'	EPfP LRHS
sanguinea hort.	see *B. panlanensis*
sargentiana	CPle NFor SLPl
sherriffii	CPle WCwm
sieboldii	WPat
x *stenophylla* ♀H4	More than 30 suppliers
- 'Claret Cascade'	EBee EPfP GKir LRHS MAsh MBri
	MGos NHol SPer WBod WDin
	WFar WGwG
- 'Corallina'	WBcn
- 'Corallina	CFee CLyd ELan EPfP EPot GCrs
Compacta' ♀H4	GKir LHop LRHS MAsh MBro
	NHol NLAp NRya SChu SPer SPoG
	SRms WAbe WPat

- 'Cornish Cream'	see *B.* x *stenophylla* 'Lemon
	Queen'
- 'Crawley Gem'	CMHG LRHS MBar NHol WDin
	WFar WStI
- Cream Showers	see *B.* x *stenophylla* 'Lemon
	Queen'
- 'Etna'	ELan LRHS MAsh
- 'Irwinii'	CMHG CMac CTri GKir LAst MBar
	MGos MSwo NHol SLon SPer
	WDin WFar WTel
N - 'Lemon Queen'	SMer SPer WTel
- 'Nana'	SRms WAbe
- 'Pink Pearl' (v)	CMHG LRHS MGos
temolaica ♀H4	CFil CPMA ENot EPfP GKir LRHS
	NLar SDnm SPer SSpi SSta WDin
	WPat
thunbergii ♀H4	CDoC CDul CSBt ENot GBin GKir
	LBuc MAsh MRav NWea SMer SPer
	SPlb WBod WDin WFar WStI
- f. *atropurpurea*	CBcs CDul CTri EBee EBre ENot
	EPfP EWTr GKir ISea LAst LBuc
	MAsh MBar MGos MSwo MWat
	NBee NBlu NFor NWea SGar SPer
	WBVN WBod WDin WFar WMoo
	WStI
§ - - 'Atropurpurea	More than 30 suppliers
Nana' ♀H4	
- - 'Bagatelle' ♀H4	More than 30 suppliers
- - 'Carmen'	LRHS MGos
- - 'Dart's Purple'	LRHS MAsh MBri WFar
- - 'Dart's Red Lady'	CPLG CSBt CWib EBee EBre ECrN
	ECtt ELan ENot EPfP ESis GKir
	LRHS MAsh MBri MRav NPro SLim
	SPer SWvt WDin WFar WPat
- - 'Golden Ring' ♀H4	More than 30 suppliers
- - 'Harlequin' (v)	More than 30 suppliers
- - 'Helmond Pillar'	More than 30 suppliers
- - 'Red Chief' ♀H4	CBcs CBrm CMHG EBee EBre
	ECrN ECtt ELan ENot EPfP GKir
	LRHS MAsh MGos MRav MWat
	SLim SLon SPer SPla SWvt WDin
	WFar WHCG WHar WPat WStI
	WTel WWeb
- - 'Red King'	EBee MRav WDin
- - 'Red Pillar'	CChe CDoC CPle EBee EBre EHoe
	ELan GKir LRHS MAsh MBar MGos
	MWat NHol SHBN SPla WDin WFar
	WPat WStI
- - 'Red Rocket'	EMil MBri
- - 'Rose Glow' (v) ♀H4	More than 30 suppliers
- 'Atropurpurea Superba'	see *B.* x *ottawensis* f. *purpurea*
	'Superba'
- 'Aurea'	More than 30 suppliers
- Bonanza Gold	CAbP CBcs CDoC COtt EBee ELan
= 'Bogozam'PBR	ENot EPfP GKir LRHS MAsh MRav
	NLar SMur WDin WFar
	WHar
- 'Carpetbagger'	WHar
- 'Crimson Pygmy'	see *B. thunbergii* f. *atropurpurea*
	'Atropurpurea Nana'
- 'Erecta'	CMac EBee ENot EPfP LRHS MBar
	MGos MRav SPer WBod WCFE
	WDin
- 'Golden Torch'	MBri SWvt WWeb
- 'Green Carpet'	CDul ENot LHop LRHS MBar MRav
- 'Green Mantle'	see *B. thunbergii* 'Kelleriis'
- 'Green Marble'	see *B. thunbergii* 'Kelleriis'
§ - 'Kelleriis' (v)	CDoC EPfP MBar NPro SLon SPoG
	WDin WFar WRHF WStI
- 'Kobold'	EBee ECrN ENot EPfP GKir LHop
	LRHS MAsh MBar MGos MRav
	NHol SLim SPer SPla WFar WStI
- 'Pink Attraction' (v)	CBcs
- 'Pink Queen' (v)	CBcs EBee ENot EPfP LAst MAsh
	MGos MRav WDin WHar WPat

- 'Pow-wow' — CBcs MGos MMil NLar WBcn
- 'Silver Beauty' (v) — CMHG EBee ELan LRHS MGos WDin
- 'Silver Carpet' — NLar
- 'Silver Mile' — see *B.* x *ottawensis* 'Silver Miles'
- 'Somerset' — CMac WBcn
* - 'Tricolor' (v) — CMac EHoe NHol WFar WPat
tischleri var. *abbreviata* — GIBF
tsangpoensis — SLPl
valdiviana — CDul CFil EPfP IArd SMad SSpi WPGP
veitchii — SLPl
verruculosa ♀H4 — CBcs CTri EBee ENot EPfP GKir LAst MBar MGos MRav MSwo NHol NWea SGar SPer SRms WCFE WDin WFar
virescens B&SWJ 2646D — WCru
vulgaris — CArn CNat GPoy SECG
- 'Wiltshire Wonder' (v) — CNat
wardii — CPle
wilsoniae — CBcs CDul CFil CPle CTri EBee EBre ENot EPfP EPla EWTr GEil GKir MBar MWhi NHol NWea SHBN SPer WCFE WDin WFar
- ACE 1847 — EPot
- ACE 2462 — EHyt
- L 650 — WPGP
- blue — LRHS NPro WBcn WFar WGer
- 'Graciella' — LRHS NPro
- var. *guhtzunica* — EPla EWes

Berchemia (*Rhamnaceae*)
racemosa — WSHC

bergamot see *Citrus bergamia*

Bergenia ❀ (*Saxifragaceae*)
'Abendglocken' — ECGP ECha ECtt EGle EPfP GKir LGro LRHS MBri MNFA MWat MWgw NGdn NHol NSti SChu SPla SWat WEas WFar
§ 'Abendglut' — More than 30 suppliers
'Admiral' — CBct ECha
* *agavifolia* — CBct
'Apple Court White' — CBct
'Autumn Magic' — SPoG
'Baby Doll' — CBct CKno COlW COtt EBre ECha EGle EPla EWTr GKir GSki LHop LRHS MAvo MRav MSte NBir NMRc NOrc NPer NPro NSti SMrm SPla WCAu WFar WMnd WShp WSpi WTin
'Bach' — SSpi
§ 'Ballawley' clonal ♀H4 — CFir ECha ENot IBlr MRav SSpi SWat WCAu WCot WFar
'Ballawley' seed-raised — see *Bergenia* Ballawley hybrids
'Ballawley Guardsman' — CBct EHrv ERou MTed
Ballawley hybrids — EPar GFlt LGro NSti SDix SPer SWat WCot
'Bartók' — SSpi
beesiana — see *B. purpurascens*
'Beethoven' — CBct CDes CLAP CPlt EBee ECha EGle EPla IGor MRav MTed NBir NPar SSpi SWat WCot WPGP WSHC
Bell Tower — see *B.* 'Glockenturm'
'Bizet' — CBct MTed SSpi
'Borodin' — CBct
'Brahms' — CBct GBuc SSpi
'Bressingham Bountiful' — CBct WCot
'Bressingham Ruby'PBR — CBct EBee EBre ECGP ECha ECtt GKir LRHS MRav MTed NBir NCGa NHol SChu SHBN SPer SWat WCAu WCot WPGP WSpi

'Bressingham Salmon' — CBct CHar EBee EGle ELan ENot EPfP ERou GSki LRHS MBri MRav NLar SHBN WCot WMnd WWeb
'Bressingham White' ♀H4 — More than 30 suppliers
'Britten' — CMac LPio SSpi
ciliata — CDes CFee CHEx CKno CLAP EBee EChP EPfP GCal LEdu MRav MSte NBir NHol NLar SBla SDix SSpi SUsu WCot WEas WKif WPGP WPer WSHC
- f. *ciliata* — CBct
- f. *ligulata* — see *B. pacumbis*
- 'Wilton' — WCot
ciliata x *crassifolia* — see *B.* x *schmidtii*
'Claire Maxine' — GCal
cordifolia — More than 30 suppliers
- 'Flore Pleno' — CBct
- 'Purpurea' ♀H4 — CBcs CDoC CSBt EBee ECha ELan EMFW ENot EPfP GKir GSki IHMH LBuc LGro LRHS MRav NBir SHBN SPer SPla SRms SWat WCAu WFar WPnP WShp
- 'Rosa Schwester' **new** — GBin
- 'Rosa Zeiten' **new** — GBin
- 'Tubby Andrews' (v) — CBct EBla EGle MLLN NLar NPro WGMN WHil
- 'Winterglut' — IBal ITim LPVe MSPs SWvt WHil WWeb
crassifolia — EPla EWTr SRms
- DF 90028 — EMon
- 'Autumn Red' — CBct EBee ECha
- 'Orbicularis' — see *B.* x *schmidtii*
- var. *pacifica* — CFil EBee GIBF
* *cyanea* — WCot
'David' — ECha EMon EWes MTed
delavayi — see *B. purpurascens* var. *delavayi*
'Delbees' — see *B.* 'Ballawley' clonal
'Eden's Dark Margin' — EBee
'Eden's Magic Carpet' — CFir
'Eden's Magic Giant' — EBee EChP
emeiensis — CDes EBee SBla
- hybrid — CBct MWat
'Eric Smith' — CBct CLAP EBee ECha EPar GCal MBri MTed WCot
'Eroica' — CBct CSpe EBee EChP ECha ELan EMon GBin MBri MRav NSti SWat WCAu WLow WMnd
'Evening Glow' — see *B.* 'Abendglut'
§ 'Glockenturm' — CBct GCal
'Hellen Dillon' **new** — CBct
'Herbstblute' — EBee EMon
'Jo Watanabe' — ECha
'Lambrook' — see *B.* 'Margery Fish'
§ 'Margery Fish' — CBct ECha
milesii — see *B. stracheyi*
§ 'Morgenröte' ♀H4 — CBcs CBct EBee EBre ECha EMil EPfP GKir IHMH LRHS MBNS MGos MRav NHol NSti SHBN SPer SRms SSvw SWat SWvt WCFE WCot
'Morning Light' — NPro
Morning Red — see *B.* 'Morgenröte'
'Mozart' — CLAP
'Mrs Crawford' — CBct ECha
'Oeschberg' — CBct WCAu
'Opal' — CBct
'Overture' — CBct WCAu WCot WFar
§ *pacumbis* — CHEx CLAP CPLG EBee GEdr LEdu MWgw NBid NBir NSti SSpi WCot
- B&SWJ 2693 — WCru
- CC 3616 — ITer WCot
'Perfect' — CBct EBee WMnd WWeb
'Pink Dragonfly' **new** — GBin

'Pinneberg' — EBee
'Profusion' — WCAu
'Pugsley's Pink' — CBct ECha LPio SHBN
§ **purpurascens** ♀H4 — CMac ECha EWTr GBuc GCrs GKir GSki NFla SDix SMad SPer SSpi WCot WWin
- ACE 2175 — WCot
- CC 3285 — WCot
§ - var. **delavayi** ♀H4 — MBri SRms WPnP
- - CLD 1366 — WPer
aff. **purpurascens** ACE 2175 — WCot
'Purpurglocken' — GCal
'Red Beauty' — GFlt MGos WShp
'Reitheim' **new** — CBct
'Rosette' — LPio
'Rosi Klose' — CFee EBee EChP ECha EMon EWes GAbr GBin GCal MBri MNFA MRav NMyG SBla WCot WShp
'Rotblum' — CBct EBee ECtt EPfP EPla GBin GSki GWCH LAst MDun NBir NGdn NOrc NPri NVic WBor WFar WPer WRHF WWeb
§ × **schmidtii** ♀H4 — CMac EBee ENot EWll NBir SDix WCot
'Schneekissen' — CBct EBee EGle LAst MRav SWat WCAu
§ 'Schneekönigin' — CBct ECha LPio MRav WGer
§ 'Silberlicht' ♀H4 — More than 30 suppliers
Silverlight — see *B.* 'Silberlicht'
Snow Queen — see *B.* 'Schneekönigin'
'Snowblush' — SSpi
§ **stracheyi** — CBct EBee ECha EGle EGoo NBid SDix WEas
- Alba Group — CBct CDes ECha EPfP GCal MSte WSHC
'Sunningdale' — CBcs CBct EBee ECha ELan EMFW EPar EPfP EWTr GKir GSki LRHS MLLN MRav NBir SChu SPer SSpi SWat SWvt WCAu WMnd
Winter Fairy Tales — see *B.* 'Wintermärchen'
§ 'Wintermärchen' — CBct CM&M EBee ECha ELan ENot EPfP GKir GSki LRHS MGos MRav MSte MWgw NCGa NOrc NPro SWat WCAu WCot WMnd
'Winterzauber' — EBee MTed

Bergeranthus (Aizoaceae)
glenensis — EDAr
multiceps — SChr

Berkheya (Asteraceae)
macrocephala — EMon WCot
multijuga — EOMN
purpurea — CPom EMan GBri GGar MDKP SIgm WCot WRos

Berlandiera (Asteraceae)
lyrata — CFwr EBee EMan GCal NJOw WCot

Berneuxia (Diapensiaceae)
thibetica — IBlr

Berula (Apiaceae)
erecta — EHon EMFW NPer WWpP

Berzelia (Bruniaceae)
galpinii — SPlb
lanuginosa — CTrC IDee

Beschorneria (Agavaceae)
septentrionalis — CFil CFir CTrC EBee EMan EOas MSPs WCot WPGP

tubiflora — CFil CHEx EBee EOas LEdu WPGP
yuccoides ♀H3 — CAbb CBcs CFil CHEx CPne CTrC EAmu EBee EOas EPAt EPla IBlr IDee ISea LEdu MSte SAPC SArc SChr SDnm SIgm SLim WKif WMul XPep
- 'Quicksilver' — CBcs CBod CDoC CFil CKno CTbh CTrC EBee EMan MDun MSte SDnm SSpi WCot WGer WPat

Bessera (Alliaceae)
elegans — CFir EBee EMan EPot LPhx LRHS MSte WCot

Beta (Chenopodiaceae)
trigyna — WCot
vulgaris — WHer
- 'Bull's Blood' — CSpe EMan MSte WCot WJek
- subsp. **cicla** var.
flavescens 'Rhubarb Chard' ♀H3 — WJek

Betonica see Stachys

Betula ✿ (Betulaceae)
alba L. — see *B. pendula, B. pubescens*
albosinensis misapplied — see *B. utilis*
albosinensis ♀H4 — CBcs CCVT CDul CMCN EBee EPfP GIBF GKir ISea MGos NWea SBLw SPer WCwm WDin WFar WNor WOrn
- 'Bowling Green' — CPMA CTho
- 'China Ruby' — GKir LRHS MBri SSpi
- 'Chinese Garden' — CPMA CTho
- clone F — see *B. albosinensis* 'Ness'
- 'K.Ashburner' — CPMA CTho
- 'Kansu' — GKir
§ - 'Ness' — CPMA CTho
- var. **septentrionalis** ♀H4 — CDoC CDul CEnd CLnd CTho EBee ECrN ENot EPfP GBin GKir IMGH LRHS MAsh MBlu MBri MDun NWea SCoo SKee SLim SPer SSpi SSta WCwm WMoo
- - 'Purdom' — CLnd CPMA GKir
§ **alleghaniensis** — CDul CLnd CMCN ECrN GKir GTSp IArd IDee NWea SPoG WDin
alnoides — GIBF WNor
apoiensis — GIBF SSta WNor
- 'Mount Apoi' — SSpi
austrosinensis — WNor
borealis — see *B. pumila*
§ × **caerulea** — CDul CLnd CPMA CTho LRHS
caerulea-grandis — see *B.* × *caerulea*
chichibuensis — EPla GIBF SBir WHer
chinensis — CMCN GIBF WNor
'Conyngham' — CTho MBlu
costata misapplied — see *B. ermanii* 'Grayswood Hill'
costata Trautv. — CDul CLnd CTho EBee EPfP GTSp LRHS MAsh SBLw SKee WDin WOrn
* - 'Fincham Cream' — EPfP ERea GKir SSpi
dahurica — CDul CMCN IArd LRHS WNor
- B&SWJ 4247 — WHCr
- 'Maurice Foster' — CPMA CTho
- 'Stone Farm' **new** — CPMA CTho
divaricata — GIBF
ermanii — CBcs CDoC CDul CLnd CMCN CMHG CSBt CSam CTho EBee ECrN ELan ENot EPfP EWTr GKir GQui LPan LRHS MAsh MBlu MGos MRav NBea NWea SBir WDin WMoo WNor WOrn
- 'Blush' — see *B. ermanii* 'Grayswood Hill'

- - 'Silver Shadow' ♀H4 | CLnd CMCN CPMA CTho EPfP GKir LRHS MAsh MBlu MBri NWea SHBN SKee SLim SMad SPer SPoG SSpi SSta
- - 'Snowqueen' | CDul CEnd CLnd CMCN COtt CPMA CSBt CWSG EMui EPfP GKir IMGH LBuc LRHS MAsh MBri MDun MGos MLan NWea SCoo SKee SLim WHCr WOrn
- 'Knightshayes' | CTho
- 'Moonbeam' | CLnd CMCN CPMA GKir SSpi
- var. *occidentalis* 'Kyelang' | CPMA CTho
- 'Polar Bear' | GKir
- var. *prattii* | CEnd CTho GKir MDun
- 'Ramdana River' | CTho MBlu
- 'Schilling' | CEnd GKir LRHS
- 'Silver Queen' | SSpi
- 'Thyangboche Monastery' | MDun
- 'Trinity College' | CLnd CMCN CPMA GKir LRHS SSpi
- 'Wakehurst Place Chocolate' | CPMA GKir LRHS MBri SMad SSpi
verrucosa | see *B. pendula*

Biarum (Araceae)
davisii | EHyt GCrs LAma SSpi
dispar | WCot
ochridense | WCot
spruneri S&L 229 | SSpi
tenuifolium | CStu ECho SSpi WCot
- AB&S 4356 | GCrs

Bidens (Asteraceae)
atrosanguinea | see *Cosmos atrosanguineus*
§ *aurea* | CHad CMil CStr ECtt EMon EPPr EWes GCal LAst LIck LRHS MAnH MDKP MNrw MOak SAga SBla SGar SMrm SPet STes WBor WFar WOld WWye
- B&SWJ 9049 from Guatemala | WCru
- cream | MAnH MNrw MSte
- 'Hannay's Lemon Drop' | CHea CMdw CMea CPen CSev CSpe CStr EBee GBri MAnH MBnl MDKP MHar MNrw MSph MSte STes SUsu
ferulifolia ♀H1+3 | ECtt NPer SChu SMrm SPet
- Golden Flame = 'Samsawae' | LAst
- 'Peters Goldteppich' PBR | LAst SMrm
heterophylla Ortega | see *B. aurea*
heterophylla hort. | CKno ECtt EDif EMlt NCGa SCoo SOkh WMoo
humilis | see *B. triplinervia* var. *macrantha*
integrifolia | EChP SMad
ostruthioides | MOak
§ *triplinervia* var. *macrantha* | LHop

Bignonia (Bignoniaceae)
capreolata | SBra WCru WSHC XPep
§ - 'Atrosanguinea' | LRHS
- 'Tangerine Beauty' | SSpi
lindleyana | see *Clytostoma calystegioides*
unguis-cati | see *Macfadyena unguis-cati*

Bilderdykia see *Fallopia*

Billardiera (Pittosporaceae)
cymosa | SOWG
longiflora ♀H3 | More than 30 suppliers

- 'Cherry Berry' | CBcs EBee ECou ELan ERea IArd LPio LRHS MAsh MCCP SBra SLim SMur SPer SPoG SSpi SWvt WSHC
- *fructu-albo* | CBcs CPle EBee ELan EWes LRHS MAsh SLim SPer
- red-berried | CPle
scandens | ECou

Billbergia (Bromeliaceae)
x *gireaudiana* ♀H1 | SSte
morelii **new** | CFir
nutans | CHEx CHal EBak EGra EOHP EShb ESlt IBlr IDee MBri SAPC SArc SChr SRms SSte WGwG WHer WMul XPep
* - 'Variegata' (v) | ESlt WCot
nutans x *pyramidalis* **new** | CFir
I *pyramidalis* 'Variegata' (v) | SSte
'Santa Barbara' (v) | SSte
x *windii* ♀H1 | CHEx CHal EBak ESlt SRms

Bismarckia (Arecaceae)
nobilis | EAmu LPal

Bistorta see *Persicaria*

Bixa (Bixaceae)
orellana | ELau MGol

blackberry see *Rubus fruticosus* agg.

blackcurrant see *Ribes nigrum*

Blastus (Melastomataceae)
dunnianus | EBee

Blechnum (Blechnaceae)
alpinum | see *B. penna-marina* subsp. *alpinum*
capense | CTrC
N *chilense* ♀H3 | CDes CHEx CLAP CRow CWil ECha EPfP GGar IBlr LEur NMar NVic SAPC SArc SChu SDix SSpi WAbe WCru WPGP WRic
discolor | CLAP CTrC IDee LPal LPan
- 'Silver Lady' **new** | CTrC
durum **new** | CTrC
fluviatile | CTrC IDee
gibbum | EFtx LRHS MBri
magellanicum misapplied | see *B. chilense*
minus | EFtx NMar WRic
minus x *wattsii* | WRic
moorei | NMar
novae-zelandiae | CTrC GGar WRic
nudum | EAmu EFtx EPfP NMoo WRic
penna-marina ♀H4 | CBro CFil CLAP CPLG CWil EBee EFer EMon EPar GAbr GGar LEdu LEur MBri NMar NRya NVic NWCA SChu SDix SIng SRms SSpi WEas WMoo WPGP WRic WWye
§ - subsp. *alpinum* | CFil CLAP GEdr NMar WAbe WPGP
- 'Cristatum' | CFil CLAP GAbr GGar SRms WAbe WPGP
procerum **new** | CTrC GGar
punctulatum | WRic
spicant ♀H4 | More than 30 suppliers
- 'Cristatum' | WRic
tabulare misapplied | see *B. chilense*
N *tabulare* (Thunb.) Kuhn ♀H1 | WRic
vulcanicum | CLAP
wattsii | CDes WRic

Blepharocalyx (Myrtaceae)

cruckshanksii	CPLG LRHS WGer
- 'Heaven Scent'	CSam LAst MCCP NLar

Blephilia (Lamiaceae)

'Cherokee' **new**	EBee
ciliata	EBee IFro MSal
hirsuta	EBee

Bletilla ✿ (Orchidaceae)

Brigantes g.	CHdy LEur
* - 'Moonlight'	LEur
Coritani g.	LAma LEur WCot
formosana	LAma LEur
* - *alba*	CHdy
hyacinthina	see *B. striata*
ochracea	LAma LEur WCot
Penway Dragon g.	CHdy EPot
* Penway Imperial g.	CHdy EPot
Penway Paris g.	CHdy EMan EPot
Penway Princess g.	EPot LEur
Penway Rainbow g.	EPot LEur
* Penway Rose g.	LEur
Penway Starshine g.	CHdy LEur
Penway Sunset g.	LEur WCot
§ *striata*	CBct CDes CPom ERea ERos GSki IBlr IHMH ITer LAma LEdu LPhx MSal NHol NRog SBla SChr WCot WFar WPGP WViv
- *alba*	see *B. striata* var. *japonica* f. *gebina*
- 'Albostriata'	CBct CDes EBee ELan EMan IBlr LAma LEur NRog WCot WOBN
- var. *japonica*	EPot LEur
§ - - f. *gebina*	CDes CHdy EBee GSki IBlr IHMH LAma LEdu LEur LRHS NRog SBla SChr SSpi WCot WFar WViv
- - - variegated (v)	CHdy LEur WCot
szetschuanica	LAma LEur
'Yokohama'	CHdy EPot LAma LEur

Bloomeria (Alliaceae)

crocea	WHil
- var. *aurea*	LRHS WCot
- var. *montana* NNS 98-84	WCot

blueberry see *Vaccinium corymbosum*

Bocconia (Papaveraceae)

cordata	see *Macleaya cordata*
microcarpa	see *Macleaya microcarpa*

Boehmeria (Urticaceae)

nivea MSal	

Boenninghausenia (Rutaceae)

albiflora	CWCL EMan WCot
- B&SWJ 1479	WCru
japonica B&SWJ 4876	WCru

Boesenbergia (Zingiberaceae)

longiflora	CKob

Bolax (Apiaceae)

glebaria	see *Azorella trifurcata*
§ *gummifer*	EPot SBla WAbe

Bolboschoenus (Cyperaceae)

caldwellii	EPPr
§ *maritimus*	CRWN LPBA WFar

Boltonia (Asteraceae)

asteroides	CFee CSam ECtt EHrv EMon GFlt

	GMac GSki LRHS NGdn NSti SPer SWat WBVN WCAu WDyG WRHF
- var. *latisquama*	EBee EPPr MBrN MRav MSte MWat SSvw WBor WCot WFar WHal
- - 'Nana'	CBre EBee EBee ECGN EGoo EMan LRHS MLLN MRav MWgw NBid NChi WBVN WMoo WPer
- 'Pink Beauty'	CBre EMon
- var. *recognita*	EBee EMon LRHS
- 'Snowbank'	ELan EMan EWTr EWsh
decurrens	EBee
incisa	see *Kalimeris incisa*

Bomarea (Alstroemeriaceae)

acutifolia	WCru
B&SWJ 9094 **new**	
caldasii ♀H1	CFil CHEx CPne CRHN ERea SIgm SOWG SSpi WBor WPGP WSHC WTre
edulis	ERea
hirtella	CFil CHEx CRHN EBee SSpi WCot WHil WSPU
- B&SWJ 9017	WCru
isopetala	CFil SSpi
kalbreyeri	WCot
multiflora	CFil EShb
- JCA 13761	SSpi
ovata	ERea
patacocensis	CPle
- JCA 13987	WCot
salsilla	CFil GCal SIgm WCot WSHC

Bongardia (Berberidaceae)

chrysogonum	CAvo EHyt EPot LRHS WCot

Bonia (Poaceae)

solida	CBig CHEx EPla ERod LPal MMoz MWht NPal SDry SEND WJun WMul

borage see *Borago officinalis*

Borago (Boraginaceae)

alba	EOHP WBry WCHb
laxiflora	see *B. pygmaea*
officinalis	CArn CBod CSev EChP EDAr ELau GKir GPoy LRHS MBow MBri MHer NPri NVic SECG WCot WHHs WHer WPer WSel WWye
- 'Alba'	CBre CSev EChP ELau ILis MBow MHer NBid NGHP SDnm SIde WCHb WHHs WHer WJek WLHH WPer WRha WSel
- 'Bill Archer' (v)	CNat
§ *pygmaea*	CArn CCge CHid CPLG CSev EChP ELan EMon EOHP GBar GEil LHop MAnH MFir MHar MHer MTho NGHP NLar NMRc NSti STes SWat WCHb WHHs WMoo WOld WWin WWpP

Borinda (Poaceae)

SSNY 2	WPGP
albocerea	CFil EPla ERod WJun
edulis **new**	WJun

Boronia (Rutaceae)

citriodora	SOWG
denticulata	ECou
heterophylla	CBcs CPLG CSWP ECou IArd IDee SOWG
- white-flowered	ECou
megastigma	CBcs ECou
- 'Brown Meg'	CBcs

	mollis	SOWG
	pinnata	ECou SOWG
	serrulata	ECou

Bothriochloa (Poaceae)

	barbinodies	CKno
§	*bladhii*	EPPr
	caucasica	see *B. bladhii*
§	*ischaemum*	CBig CBrm EHoe EMan EPPr EWes LRav MCCP MWod WWpP

Botryostege see *Elliottia*

Bougainvillea (Nyctaginaceae)

	'Ailsa Lambe'	see *B.* (Spectoperuviana Group) 'Mary Palmer'
	'Alabama Sunset'	CWDa
	'Alexandra'	MBri
	'Apple Blossom'	see *B.* 'Elizabeth Doxey'
	'Audrey Grey'	see *B.* 'Elizabeth Doxey'
	'Aussie Gold'	see *B.* 'Carson's Gold'
	'Begum Sikander'	CWDa ERea
	'Betty Lavers'	ERea
§	'Blondie'	CWDa
	'Bridal Bouquet'	see *B.* 'Cherry Blossom'
	'Brilliance'	CWDa ERea LRHS
	'Brilliant' misapplied	see *B.* x *buttiana* 'Raspberry Ice'
	x *buttiana* 'Afterglow'	CWDa
	– 'Ametyst'	MBri
	– 'Asia'	ERea
	– 'Audrey Grey'	see *B.* 'Elizabeth Doxey'
	– 'Barbara Karst'	CWDa ERea SOWG
	– 'Chitra'	ERea
	– 'Coconut Ice'	CWDa SOWG
	– 'Daphne Mason'	ERea
§	– 'Enid Lancaster'	ERea LRHS
	– 'Golden Glow'	see *B.* x *buttiana* 'Enid Lancaster'
	– 'Golden McClean'	CWDa
§	– 'Jamaica Red'	ERea
	– 'Killie Campbell' ♀H1	ERea MBri
§	– 'Lady Mary Baring'	ERea LRHS SOWG
§	– 'Louise Wathen'	CWDa
§	– 'Mahara' (d)	CWDa ERea SOWG
	– 'Mahara Double Red'	see *B.* x *buttiana* 'Mahara'
	– 'Mahara Off-white'	see *B.* 'Cherry Blossom'
	– 'Mahara Pink'	see *B.* 'Los Banos Beauty'
§	– 'Mardi Gras' (v)	CWDa ERea
§	– 'Mrs Butt' ♀H1	CWDa ERea
	– 'Mrs McClean'	ERea
§	– 'Poultonii'	ERea
§	– 'Poulton's Special' ♀H1	ERea
	– 'Rainbow Gold'	ERea
§	– 'Raspberry Ice' (v)	ERea LRHS SOWG
	– 'Ratana Red' (v)	ERea
§	– 'Rosenka'	CWDa ERea
§	– 'Roseville's Delight' (d)	ERea LRHS SOWG
§	– 'Scarlet Glory'	ERea
§	– Texas Dawn = 'Monas'	ERea
	– 'Tiggy' **new**	ERea
	'California Gold'	see *B.* x *buttiana* 'Enid Lancaster'
	Camarillo Fiesta = 'Monle'	CWDa ERea SOWG
	(*spectabilis* hybrid)	
	'Captain Caisy'	CWDa ERea
§	'Carson's Gold' (d)	CWDa ERea
	'Cherry Blossoms'	CWDa ERea
§	'Chiang Mai Beauty'	ERea
	'Closeburn'	ERea SOWG
	'Crimson Lake' misapplied	see *B.* x *buttiana* 'Mrs Butt'
	'Dauphine'	see *B.* 'Los Banos Beauty'
	'David Lemmer'	CWDa ERea
	'Delicate'	see *B.* 'Blondie'
	'Dixie'	ERea
	'Donya'	CWDa ERea

	'Double Yellow'	see *B.* 'Carson's Gold'
	'Durban'	see *B. glabra* 'Jane Snook'
§	'Elizabeth Angus'	CWDa ERea
§	'Elizabeth Doxey'	ERea SOWG
	'Elizabeth'	ERea
	(*spectabilis* hybrid)	
*	'Elsbet'	CWDa
	'Enchantment'	see *B.* (Spectoperuviana Group) 'Mary Palmer's Enchantment'
	'Fair Lady'	see *B.* 'Blondie'
	'Flamingo Pink'	see *B.* 'Chiang Mai Beauty'
	'Floribunda'	CWDa ERea
	'Gillian Greensmith'	ERea
	glabra ♀H1	ERea LRHS MBri XPep
§	– 'Doctor David Barry'	CWDa ERea
	– 'Elizabeth Angus'	see *B.* 'Elizabeth Angus'
§	– 'Harrissii' (v)	CWDa ERea LRHS
§	– 'Jane Snook'	CWDa ERea
	– 'Jennifer Fernie'	see *B.* 'Jennifer Fernie'
§	– 'Magnifica'	SOWG
§	– 'Magnifica Traillii' **new**	ERea
	– 'Peggy Redman' (v) **new**	ERea
§	– 'Pride of Singapore'	ERea
§	– 'Sanderiana'	ERea LPan
§	– 'Sanderiana Variegata' (v)	SVen
	'Gloucester Royal'	CWDa SOWG
	'Glowing Flame' (v)	CWDa ERea
	'Golden Doubloon'	see *B.* x *buttiana* 'Roseville's Delight'
	'Golden Glow'	see *B.* x *buttiana* 'Enid Lancaster'
	'Golden MacLean'	see *B.* x *buttiana* 'Golden McLean'
	'Golden Tango'	CWDa ERea
	'Harrissii'	see *B. glabra* 'Harrissii'
	'Hawaiian Scarlet'	see *B.* 'San Diego Red'
	'Hugh Evans'	see *B.* 'Blondie'
	'Indian Flame'	see *B.* 'Partha'
	'Isabel Greensmith'	CWDa ERea
	'Jamaica Orange'	CWDa ERea
	'Jamaica Red'	see *B.* x *buttiana* 'Jamaica Red'
	'James Walker'	ERea
	'Jane Snook'	see *B. glabra* 'Jane Snook'
§	'Jennifer Fernie'	ERea
	'Juanita Hatten'	CWDa ERea
	'Kauai Royal'	see *B.* 'Elizabeth Angus'
	'Klong Fire'	see *B.* x *buttiana* 'Mahara'
	'La Jolla'	ERea
	'Lady Mary Baring'	see *B.* x *buttiana* 'Lady Mary Baring'
	'Lavender Girl'	CWDa ERea
	'Lemmer's Special'	see *B.* 'Partha'
	'Limberlost Beauty'	see *B.* 'Cherry Blossom'
	'Little Caroline'	CWDa SOWG
	'Lord Willingdon' misapplied	see *B.* 'Pixie'
§	'Los Banos Beauty' (d)	CWDa ERea
	'Magnifica'	see *B. glabra* 'Magnifica'
	'Mahara Double Red'	see *B.* x *buttiana* 'Mahara'
	'Mahara Off-white'	see *B.* 'Cherry Blossom'
	'Mahara Orange'	see *B.* x *buttiana* 'Roseville's Delight'
	'Mahara Pink'	see *B.* 'Los Banos Beauty'
	'Mahara White'	see *B.* 'Cherry Blossom'
	'Manila Magic Red'	see *B.* x *buttiana* 'Mahara'
	'Mardi Gras'	see *B.* x *buttiana* 'Mardi Gras'
	'Mariel Fitzpatrick'	ERea
	'Mary Palmer's Enchantment'	see *B.* (Spectoperuviana Group) 'Mary Palmer's Enchantment'
*	'Michael Lemmer'	CWDa
	'Mini-Thai'	see *B.* 'Pixie'
§	'Miss Manila'	CWDa ERea SOWG
	'Mrs Butt'	see *B.* x *buttiana* 'Mrs Butt'
	'Mrs Helen McLean'	see *B.* x *buttiana* 'Mrs McLean'
	'Mrs McLean'	see *B.* x *buttiana* 'Mrs McLean'
	Natalii Group	CWDa ERea

'Nina Mitton' CWDa ERea
* 'Orange Flame' **new** SOWG
'Orange Glow' see *B.* Camarillo Fiesta = 'Monle'
'Orange King' see *B.* x *buttiana* 'Louise Wathen'
'Orange Stripe' (v) ERea
'Pagoda Pink' see *B.* 'Los Banos Beauty'
§ 'Partha' CWDa
'Penelope' see *B.* (Spectoperuviana Group)
 'Mary Palmer's Enchantment'
pink ESlt
'Pink Champagne' see *B.* 'Los Banos Beauty'
'Pink Clusters' CWDa ERea
§ 'Pixie' ERea
'Poultonii' see *B.* x *buttiana* 'Poultonii'
'Poultonii Special' see *B.* x *buttiana* 'Poulton's
 Special'
'Pride of Singapore' see *B. glabra* 'Pride of Singapore'
'Princess Mahara' see *B.* x *buttiana* 'Mahara'
'Purple Robe' CWDa ERea
'Rainbow Gold' see *B.* x *buttiana* 'Rainbow Gold'
'Raspberry Ice' (v) see *B.* x *buttiana* 'Raspberry Ice'
'Ratana Orange' (v) ERea
'Red Diamond' ERea
'Red Fantasy' (v) ERea
'Red Glory' CWDa ERea
'Reggae Gold' (v) CWDa ERea
'Robyn's Glory' see *B.* x *buttiana* Texas Dawn
 = 'Monas'
'Rosenka' see *B.* x *buttiana* 'Rosenka'
'Royal Purple' CWDa ERea
'Rubyana' CWDa ERea SOWG
§ 'San Diego Red' ERea ESlt SOWG
'Sanderiana' see *B. glabra* 'Sanderiana'
'Scarlet Glory' see *B.* x *buttiana* 'Scarlet Glory'
Scarlett O'Hara see *B.* 'San Diego Red'
'Singapore Pink' see *B. glabra* 'Doctor David Barry'
'Singapore White' CWDa ERea
'Smartipants' see *B.* 'Pixie'
'Snow Cap' see *B.* (Spectoperuviana Group)
 'Mary Palmer'
spectabilis 'Speciosa ERea
 Floribunda'
- 'Wallflower' CWDa
§ Spectoperuviana ERea
 Group (v)
§ - 'Mary Palmer' CWDa LRHS
§ - 'Mary Palmer's CWDa ERea
 Enchantment'
- 'Mischief' CWDa
§ - 'Mrs H.C. Buck' CWDa ERea
'Summer Snow' CWDa
Surprise see *B.* (Spectoperuviana Group)
 'Mary Palmer'
'Tango' see *B.* 'Miss Manila'
* 'Tango Supreme' CWDa
'Thai Gold' see *B.* x *buttiana* 'Roseville's
 Delight'
* 'Tom Thumb' CWDa
'Tropical Bouquet' CWDa
'Tropical Rainbow' see *B.* x *buttiana* 'Raspberry Ice'
* 'Turkish Delight' CWDa ESlt
'Variegata' see *B. glabra* 'Harrissii', *B. glabra*
 'Sanderiana Variegata'
'Vera Blakeman' CWDa ERea ESlt SOWG
'Wac Campbell' (d) CWDa SOWG
'Weeping Beauty' ERea
* 'White Cascade' CWDa ERea

Boussingaultia (Basellaceae)
basselloides Hook. see *Anredera cordifolia*

Bouteloua (Poaceae)
curtipendula CBig CBrm CRWN EBee EChP
 EMan EPPr LEdu LRav NHol

§ *gracilis* CBig CBrm CHrt CRWN EBre
 EChP EMon ENor ENot EPPr EPza
 EWsh MBNS MCCP MLLN MWgw
 MWod NBea NHol NJOw NSti
 SUsu WMoo WPGP WPer XPep

Bouvardia (Rubiaceae)
longiflora ERea LRHS SOWG

Bowenia (Boweniaceae)
serrulata CBrP

Bowiea (Hyacinthaceae)
volubilis CHal EBee WCot

Bowkeria (Scrophulariaceae)
citrina CPle

Boykinia (Saxifragaceae)
aconitifolia CAbP EBee GAbr GBuc GGar
 GTou MLLN MRav NLar NRya SSpi
 WCru WMoo WSHC
elata see *B. occidentalis*
heucheriformis see *B.jamesii*
§ *jamesii* CGra EBee EDAr NJOw NLAp
major WCru
§ *occidentalis* EBee GFlt GGar WCru WMoo WPat
rotundifolia EBee GBuc NBir SLon WCru
 WMoo WPnP
- JLS 86269LACA EMon
tellimoides see *Peltoboykinia tellimoides*

boysenberry see *Rubus* Boysenberry

Brachychilum see *Hedychium*

Brachychiton (Sterculiaceae)
acerifolius CHEx
bidwillii EShb
discolor **new** EShb
rupestris **new** ESlt

Brachyelytrum (Poaceae)
japonicum **new** GFlt

Brachyglottis ✿ (Asteraceae)
§ *bidwillii* CBcs CPLG SDry
- 'Basil Fox' WAbe
brunonis **new** CPle
§ *buchananii* GEil SDry WSHC
- 'Silver Shadow' GGar GKir
§ *compacta* ECou EPfP LRHS MAsh NPro SDry
 SPer WBcn WEas
compacta x *monroi* ECou LRHS
'County Park' ECou
'Drysdale' EBee ELan EPfP GGar GKir LRHS
 MAsh MBri MRav NPri SDry SLon
 SPoG
§ (Dunedin Group) CPLG EGoo SDry SGar
 'Moira Reid' (v)
- 'Sunshine' ♥H4 More than 30 suppliers
'Frosty' ECou
greyi misapplied see *B.* (Dunedin Group) 'Sunshine'
§ *greyi* (Hook. f.) B. Nord. CTrG EBee EPfP ISea MBar MWhi
§ *hectoris* CHEx
§ *huntii* CPLG GGar
laxifolia misapplied see *B.* (Dunedin Group) 'Sunshine'
'Leith's Gold' **new** CTrC
§ 'Leonard Cockayne' SLim
§ *monroi* ♥H4 CChe CSBt CWib EBee EBre ECou
 EGoo EHoe EHol ELan EOHP EPfP
 GGar GKir LAst MAsh MBar MLLN
 MRav NHol SLon SMer SPer WBrE
 WCom WDin WEas XPep

– 'Clarence'	ECou
repanda	CBcs CHEx CPle CTrC CTrG
– 'Purpurea'	CHEx
– var. **rangiora**	LEdu
repanda x **greyi**	CDoC CHEx CPle GGar SAPC SArc
§ **rotundifolia**	CDoC CPle CTrC EPfP GGar NLar
	WCru WEas
sciadophila <u>**new**</u>	ITim
'Silver Waves'	ECou
§ **spedenii**	GGar GTou
I 'Sunshine Improved'	WSPU
'Sunshine Variegated'	see *B.* (Dunedin Group) 'Moira Reid'

Brachypodium (*Poaceae*)

pinnatum	EHoe
retusum <u>**new**</u>	XPep
sylvaticum	CBig CBod CPen EHul

Brachyscome (*Asteraceae*)

'Blue Mist'	SPet
curvicarpa	ECou
formosa	ECou
melanocarpa	WCom
'Metallic Blue' <u>**new**</u>	SVil
'Mini Mauve Delight' <u>**new**</u>	SVil
'Mini Yellow'	NPri
multifida	MBri NPri
nivalis var. **alpina**	see *B. tadgellii*
'Pink Mist'	LAst SPet
rigidula	ECou GKev MDHE
'Strawberry Mousse'	LAst SPet
§ **tadgellii**	MTPN
'Tinkerbell'	SPoG

Brachysema (*Papilionaceae*)

celsianum	SOWG

Brachystachyum (*Poaceae*)

densiflorum	EPla NLar SDry

Bracteantha see *Xerochrysum*

Brahea (*Arecaceae*)

aculeata	EAmu
armata	CAbb CBrP CDoC CRoM CTrC
	EAmu EPfP LPal LPan MPRe NPal
	SAPC SArc SChr SPer WHPE WMul
brandegeei	EAmu
edulis	CBrP CRoM EAmu LPal MPRe
	WMul

Brassaia see *Schefflera*

Brassica (*Brassicaceae*)

japonica	see *B. juncea* var. *crispifolia*
§ **juncea** var. **crispifolia**	CArn WJek
oleracea	WHer
* **rapa** var. **japonica**	WJek
* – var. **purpurea**	WJek

Breynia (*Euphorbiaceae*)

nivosa 'Rosea Picta' (v)	ESlt

Briggsia (*Gesneriaceae*)

aurantiaca	SOkd

Brillantaisia (*Acanthaceae*)

subulugurica	GFai

Brimeura (*Hyacinthaceae*)

§ **amethystina**	CAvo CPom ERos GCrs LPhx LRHS
– 'Alba'	CAvo CBri ERos LPhx LRHS
§ **fastigiata**	ERos

Briza (*Poaceae*)

maxima	CHrt COlW EChP EFWa EGoo
	EHoe EPla EPza LHop LIck MFOX
	NGdn NSti SSth SWal WHal WHer
	WRos WWye
media	More than 30 suppliers
– 'Limouzi'	CElw CFir CKno EBee EBre EFou
	EGle EHoe EMan EMon EPPr GCal
	LRHS MAvo MSph NSti SDys SHel
	SOkh SSth WDyG WPGP WPrP
	WWpP
minor	EGoo EPza SWal WRos
subaristata	EBee WHal WWpP
triloba	CPen EChP EHoe EMan EPPr EWes
	EWsh GBin NOGN SBod SCro
	SWal WHal WMoo WRos WWpP
– RB 94154	EBee

Brodiaea (*Alliaceae*)

§ **californica**	CNic EBee ECho ERos NMen WCot
capitata	see *Dichelostemma capitatum*
coronaria	CPBP
– NNS 97-37	WCot
'Corrina'	see *Triteleia* 'Corrina'
elegans	ERos WCot
ida-maia	see *Dichelostemma ida-maia*
jolonensis	ERos
laxa	see *Triteleia laxa*
§ **minor**	WCot
pallida <u>**new**</u>	WCot
peduncularis	see *Triteleia peduncularis*
purdyi	see *B. minor*
stellaris	EHyt WCot
terrestris	WCot
subsp. **kernensis**	
NNS 98-88	
– subsp. **terrestris** <u>**new**</u>	NMen

Bromus (*Poaceae*)

carinatus	WCru
B&SWJ 9100 <u>**new**</u>	
inermis	CBrm CFwr CWCL EBee EGra
'Skinner's Gold' (v)	EHoe EHul EMan EOMN EWes
	EWsh NSti SPer WCot
morrisonensis	EMan
ramosus	EHoe

Broussonetia (*Moraceae*)

kazinoki	CBcs IArd NLar WDin
papyrifera	CAbP CBcs CFil CMCN ELan IDee
	LPan SPer SSpi WDin WPGP WSPU
– 'Laciniata'	NLar

Bruckenthalia see *Erica*

Brugmansia ✿ (*Solanaceae*)

'Apricot Goldilocks' <u>**new**</u>	WVKB
§ **arborea**	CArn CHEx MGol SRms WVKB
§ – 'Knightii' (d) ♀H1	CHEx CHal EBak ELan EPfP ERea
	ESlt LRHS MJnS MOak SOWG
	WMul WVKB
aurea	CHEx LRHS WVKB
'Butterfly' <u>**new**</u>	WVKB
x **candida**	EBak ERea SSte WMul WVKB
– 'Blush'	ERea
– 'Culebra'	MGol WVKB
* – 'Ecuador Pink'	EPfP ERea WVKB
§ – 'Grand Marnier' ♀H1	CBot CHEx CHll ECot ELan EPfP
	ERea ESlt LRHS MJnS SOWG SVen
	WVKB
– 'Knightii'	see *B. arborea* 'Knightii'
– 'Plena'	see *B. arborea* 'Knightii'
– 'Primrose'	ERea

§ - 'Variegata' (v) — CKob ERea MJnS MOak SSte WVKB
§ **chlorantha** — MJnS
I 'Citronella'**new** — WVKB
  x **cubensis** — WVKB
  'Charles Grimaldi'**new**
  'Equador Pink'**new** — MJnS
I 'Flore Pleno Tiara' (d) **new** — WVKB
  'Glockenfontaine'**new** — WVKB
  'Golden Lady'**new** — WVKB
  'Goldrichter'**new** — WVKB
  'Herrenhausen Garten'**new** — WVKB
  hybrids — WMul
§ x **insignis** — CHll
  - 90-9 **new** — WVKB
§ - pink — CHEx EPfP MJnS
  'Jean Pasco'**new** — WVKB
  'Logees'**new** — WVKB
  'Lorely Chameleon'**new** — WVKB
  'Marrakech'**new** — WVKB
  'Maya'**new** — WVKB
  meteloides — see *Datura inoxia*
  'Ochre'**new** — WVKB
* pink — LIck WFar WWol
  'Pink Delight'**new** — WVKB
  'Rosabella'**new** — WVKB
  rosei — see *B. sanguinea* subsp. *sanguinea* var. *flava*
  'Rosenrot'**new** — WVKB
  'Rothkirch'**new** — WVKB
§ **sanguinea** — CHEx CHll EBak EShb MGol MOak MSal SOWG SSte SVen WMul
  - 'Feuerwerk'**new** — WVKB
  - red-flowered — CHEx
  - 'Rosea' — see *B.* x *insignis* pink
  - 'Sangre'**new** — WVKB
§ - subsp. **sanguinea** var. *flava* — WMul WVKB
  - subsp. *vulcanicola* — WVKB
  'Roter Vulkan'**new**
  - 'White Flame'**new** — WVKB
§ **suaveolens** ♀H1 — CHEx CHll ELan ERea MGol WMul WVKB
  - pink-flowered **new** — WVKB
  - **rosea** — see *B.* x *insignis* pink
  - 'Variegata' (v) — CKob ERea WMul
  suaveolens x **versicolor** — see *B.* x *insignis*
  'Variegata Sunset' — see *B.* x *candida* 'Variegata'
  versicolor misapplied — see *B. arborea*
§ **versicolor** Lagerh. — ERea SOWG WVKB
  - 'Lacks'**new** — WVKB
  - 'Pride of Hanover' **new** — WVKB
  'White Marble'**new** — WVKB
  yellow — LIck WFar WWol
* 'Yellow Trumpet' — EPfP

Brunfelsia (Solanaceae)
  americana — SOWG
  calycina — see *B. pauciflora*
  jamaicensis — SOWG
§ **pauciflora** ♀H1 — ELan ESlt LRHS MBri
  - 'Floribunda' — SOWG
  - 'Macrantha' — SOWG

Brunnera (Boraginaceae)
§ **macrophylla** ♀H4 — More than 30 suppliers
  - 'Alba' — see *B. macrophylla* 'Betty Bowring'
§ - 'Betty Bowring' — CDes CLAP CPlt CPom ECha EGle EPPr GBuc LPhx MAvo MHar NBhm NLar NSti SBla WCot WFar WHal WPGP WPnP WTin
  - 'Blaukuppel' **new** — EMon

§ - 'Dawson's White' (v) — More than 30 suppliers
  - 'Gordano Gold' (v) — EHoe EMon WCom WHal
  - 'Hadspen Cream' (v) ♀H4 — More than 30 suppliers
  - 'Jack Frost'^PBR — More than 30 suppliers
  - 'Langford Hewitt' (v) — CLAP WCom WPrP
  - 'Langtrees' — More than 30 suppliers
* - 'Marley's White' — CBAn EBee
  - 'Variegata' — see *B. macrophylla* 'Dawson's White'
  sibirica — CDes EMon

Brunonia (Goodeniaceae)
  australis — SPlb

Brunsvigia (Amaryllidaceae)
  radulosa — WCot
  rosea 'Minor' — see *Amaryllis belladonna*

Bryonia (Cucurbitaceae)
  dioica — GPoy MSal

Bryophyllum see *Kalanchoe*

Buchloe (Poaceae)
  dactyloides — CBig CPen CRWN

Buddleja ✿ (Buddlejaceae)
  B&SWJ 3853 — WCru
  from Philippines
  agathosma — CBot CFil CPle SLon WEas WLav WPGP WSHC XPep
  albiflora — CPle SLon WLav
  alternifolia ♀H4 — More than 30 suppliers
  - 'Argentea' — CBot CDoC CPMA CPle EBee ELan ENot EPfP LPio MBNS MBro MRav NLar NSti SHBN SPer SPla SSpi WCot WHCG WLav WPat WSHC XPep
  asiatica ♀H2 — CBot CPle ERea EShb ESlt SLon WLav
  - B&SWJ 7214 — WCru
  auriculata — CBcs CBot CFil CMCN CWib EHol EPfP ERea GQui LAst NSti SDix SLon SOWG SPer WCFE WCru WGwG WHCG WLav WPGP WPat XPep
  australis — CPle SLon
* 'Butterfly Ball' — SLon WBVN WBcn
  caryopteridifolia — CFai EHol GEil SLon
  colvilei — CDoC CFil CPle CSBt CTrw EPfP GKir LAst SDnm WBor WCot
  - B&SWJ 2121 — WCru
  - 'Kewensis' — CBot CFil CPLG CRHN CSam NSti SBra SLon SVen WBod WCru WCwm WLav WPGP WSHC
  cordata — SLon
  coriacea — CPle SLon
§ **crispa** — CBot CPle ECha ELan EPfP GEil LRHS NSti SAga SBra SDnm SDry SHBN SOWG SPer SSpi WCot WEas WFar WHCG WKif WPGP WSHC XPep
  - L 1544 — CFil
  crotonoides amplexicaulis — SLon
  curviflora f. **venenifera** — SSte
  - - B&SWJ 6036 — WCru
  davidii — CArn GWCH MBro NWea SGar SHFr STre WDin
  - B&SWJ 8083 — WCru
  - from Beijing, China — CDul SLon
  - Adonis Blue = 'Adokeep' — ENot WWeb
  - 'African Queen' — SLon SPer

- var. *alba*	CDul CNic CWib SHBN
- 'Autumn Beauty'	CPle
- 'Black Knight' ♀H4	More than 30 suppliers
- 'Blue Horizon'	CSam EGra SEND SLon WCot WLav WMoo WRHF
- 'Border Beauty'	CMac GKir
§ - 'Charming'	CDul WMoo WSHC
- 'Dartmoor' ♀H4	More than 30 suppliers
- 'Dart's Ornamental White'	ENot MRav
- 'Dart's Papillon Blue'	SLPl
- 'Dubonnet'	SLon WLav
- 'Ecolonia' **new**	MAsh
- 'Empire Blue' ♀H4	CBcs CDoC CSBt EBee EBre ECrN ECtt ENot EPfP GKir LRHS MAsh MBri MRav MWat NBee NPer NWea SPer SPlb WDin WFar WStl WTel WWeb
- 'Fascinating'	CTri MAsh WLav
- 'Flaming Violet'	SLon WLav
- 'Glasnevin Blue'	SDix SPer WLav
- 'Gonglepod'	SLon
- 'Harlequin' (v)	More than 30 suppliers
- 'Ile de France'	CBcs CWib GKir MGos NWea SBod SRms WLav
- Masquerade = 'Notbud'PBR (v)	EBee ENot MBri MGos SLon WGor WStl WWes
§ - 'Nanho Blue' ♀H4	More than 30 suppliers
- 'Nanho Petite Indigo'	see B. davidii 'Nanho Blue'
- Nanho Petite Plum	see B. davidii 'Nanho Purple'
- 'Nanho Petite Purple'	see B. davidii 'Nanho Purple'
§ - 'Nanho Purple' ♀H4	CDoC CMHG CTri CWib EBee ELan ENot EPfP GKir LRHS MAsh MBar MRav NBlu SLim SLon SPer SPla SPlb WHar WSHC
- var. *nanhoensis*	CPle MWhi SEND SIde SIgm SPer WHCG WLav
- - *alba*	ELan EPfP GKir MBar SPer SRms WFar WWeb
- - blue	SLon SPer
- Operette = 'Courtabud'	MBri NBlu
- 'Orchid Beauty'	MBNS WBod WLav
- 'Orpheus' **new**	WLav
- 'Peace'	CChe CDoC CPLG CSBt EBee ENot EPfP MBri NPer SPer WLav
- Peacock = 'Peakeep'	ENot
- 'Pink Beauty'	GKir SHBN WHCG
- 'Pink Charming'	see B. davidii 'Charming'
- 'Pink Pearl'	SLon WLav
- 'Pink Spreader' **new**	MAsh
- 'Pixie Blue'	MAsh NBlu NLar WWeb
- 'Pixie Red'	EBee EOMN GEil MAsh NLar NPri SLon WBcn WWeb
- 'Pixie White'	EOMN MAsh MBNS NBlu NLar WLav
- Purple Emperor = 'Pyrkeep'	ENot
- 'Purple Friend'	WLav
- 'Royal Purple'	GKir SLim
- 'Royal Red' ♀H4	More than 30 suppliers
- 'Salicifolia'	GEil
- 'Santana' (v)	CDul CFai LHop LRHS WCot
- 'Summer Beauty'	CWib EBee EGra EMil ENot GKir LRHS MGos WBcn WLav
- 'Variegata' (v)	LRHS SMrm WLav
- 'White Ball'	CFwr LRHS MAsh MBNS NLar SLon
- 'White Bouquet'	CSBt EBee EPfP GKir LAst LRHS MHer MSwo MWat NWea SEND SMer SPer SReu SWal WLav WLow WTel
- 'White Butterfly'	LRHS SLon
- 'White Cloud'	ECrN EPar GQui SGar SRms WGwG
- 'White Harlequin' (v)	CRow EBee SLon WBcn WCFE WCot WEas
- 'White Profusion' ♀H4	CBcs CSam EBee EBre ECtt ELan EPfP LRHS MBar MGos MRav NBPC NBee NBlu NFor NWea SHBN SLim SPla SWvt WBod WCFE WDin WEas WFar WHCG WHar WMoo WStl WWin
- 'White Wings'	SLon WLav
§ *delavayi*	CPle ERea WCru
fallowiana misapplied	see B. 'West Hill'
fallowiana Balf. f.	CBcs CPle GEil IFro LRHS NFor WLav
- ACE 2481	LRHS
- BWJ 7803	WCru
- CLD 1109	CFil WPGP
- var. *alba* ♀H3	CBot CDoC ECrN ELan ENot EPfP GEil LRHS MRav SLon SPer SPoG WBcn WEas WFar WPGP WSHC WWeb XPep
farreri	CBot CPle MSte SOWG WBod
forrestii	CBot CHEx CPle SSte WCru
globosa ♀H4	More than 30 suppliers
- RCB/Arg C-11	WCot
- 'Cally Orange'	GCal
- 'Lemon Ball'	WLav
glomerata	EShb XPep
heliophila	see B. delavayi
indica	CPle SLon
japonica	CPle IFro
- B&SWJ 8912	WCru
* 'Lady Curzon'	WRHF
x *lewisiana* 'Margaret Pike'	CBot SLon SOWG
limitanea	SLon
lindleyana	More than 30 suppliers
'Lochinch' ♀H3-4	More than 30 suppliers
loricata	CBot CFai CFil CPle ERea GQui MSte SGar SIgm SLon SOWG SPlb SSpi SVen WCFE WCot WEas WGwG WLav WPGP XPep
macrostachya	CFil CPle
- HWJ 602	WCru
§ *madagascariensis* ♀H1	CPle CRHN EShb SOWG SSte WCot XPep
marrubiifolia **new**	XPep
megalocephala B&SWJ 9106 **new**	WCru
myriantha	CFai GQui XPep
* - f. *fragrans*	WCot
nappii	SLon WPGP
nicodemia	see B. madagascariensis
nivea	CBot CMCN CPLG IFro SOWG SSte WLav XPep
- B&SWJ 2679	WCru
- BWJ 8146	WCru
- pink	SLon
- var. *yunnanensis*	CPle MSte WCFE
aff. *nivea* L 860	WPGP
officinalis ♀H2	CBot CPLG CPle CRHN EHol ERea XPep
paniculata	SLon
parvifolia MPF 148	WLav WPGP
§ x *pikei* 'Hever'	CHal CPle CStr GQui SPer
'Pink Delight' ♀H4	More than 30 suppliers
'Pink Perfection' **new**	WFar
saligna	CPle CTrC SLon XPep
'Salmon Spheres'	CPle SSte
salviifolia	CBot CFil CRHN CSWP CSam CTbh CTrG EBee ELan GEil GGar GQui IFro LAst MHer NSti SDnm SDry SIgm SPer SWal WCom WGwG WHer WLav XPep
- white	CRHN

stenostachya	CPle GEil
sterniana	see *B. crispa*
tibetica	see *B. crispa*
tubiflora	CBot ERea SLon SOWG WLav
venenifera B&SWJ 895	WCru
§ 'West Hill'	SLon WLav
x *weyeriana*	CDul CRHN CSam ECtt EOrc EPar
	EPfP GEil MNrw MSwo MTis MWat
	NBir SGar SPlb SSte SWvt WBVN
	WBea WBrE WDin WFar WHCG
	WLav WMoo WTel
- 'Flight's Fancy' (v)	WWeb
- 'Golden Glow' (v)	CChe CSBt CTri ECrN EPfP MAsh
	NFor SHel SLon WBrE WLav WStI
	WWin
- 'Lady de Ramsey'	SEND WPer
- 'Moonlight'	CPLG CPle CRow IFro SLon WLav
	WSel
- 'Sungold' ♀H4	CBrm CHrt CPle CWib EBee ELan
	EPfP GKir MAnH MBlu MCCP
	MGos MLLN MRav NBlu NHol
	SBod SLon SPer WBVN WBod
	WCot WHar WLav XPep

Buglossoides (Boraginaceae)

§ *purpurocaerulea*	CCge CMHG CPom EBee ECha ELan
	EMan EMar EWTr LHop LRHS MBro
	MSal MSte MWhi NBid SAga WCom
	WFar WMoo WSHC WWin WWye

Bukiniczia (Plumbaginaceae)

cabulica **new**	WLin

Bulbine (Asphodelaceae)

annua misapplied	see *B. semibarbata*
caulescens	see *B. frutescens*
§ *frutescens*	CHll CPLG EMan EOas GFlt NBur
	WWin XPep
- 'Hallmark' **new**	XPep
§ *semibarbata*	CPom NBro

Bulbinella (Asphodelaceae)

angustifolia	ECho EMan GCrs WCot
cauda-felis	WCot
eburnifolia	WCot
elata	WCot
floribunda	IBlr
gibbsii var. *balanifera*	ECho
hookeri	EMan GAbr GCrs GFlt GGar ITim
	NDlv NLap SYvo
latifolia	EBee
nutans **new**	CMil ECho
- var. *nutans*	EBee
setosa **new**	CPne
talbotii	WCot

Bulbinopsis see *Bulbine*

Bulbocodium (Colchicaceae)

vernum	EHyt EPot ERos GCrs LAma LPhx
	MBri NRog WCot
- white-flowered	ECho

bullace see *Prunus insititia*

Bunias (Brassicaceae)

orientalis **new**	MSal

Bunium (Apiaceae)

bulbocastanum	CAgr LEdu

Buphthalmum (Asteraceae)

§ *salicifolium*	CHrt CSam CSev EBee ELan EPfP
	GKir MBri NBid NBlu NBro NGdn

	NNor NOrc SPer SRms SWat WCAu
	WCot WFar WHil WPer WShp WWpP
- 'Alpengold'	ECha GKir GSki NLar SIgm
- 'Dora'	EMan WCot
- 'Sunwheel'	EFou EWll LRHS NPri SRms
speciosum	see *Telekia speciosa*

Bupleurum (Apiaceae)

angulosum	CFil CPom EBee MAvo SBla SIgm
	SMrm SSpi WCot WFar WPGP
- copper	see *B. longifolium*
benoistii	SIgm
falcatum	CArn EChP ECha EMan EPPr MBro
	MLLN MRav MSal NCGa NDov
	SBri SChu WAul WBWf WCot WFar
fruticosum	CBot CFil CPle EPfP MRav SChu
	SDix SDnm SIgm SMHy SSpi WCot
	WCru WDin WEas WPGP WPat
	WSHC WStI XPep
* *griffithii*	MSal
§ *longifolium*	CElw CFee CMea CSpe EBee EChP
	EGle GBin GBuc GGar MFOX
	MNrw NCGa NChi NLar SMrm
	WCot WTin WWhi
- short bronze	WCru
- subsp. *aureum*	NGby NLar
longiradiatum	WCru
B&SWJ 729	
multinerve	NChi
ranunculoides	CTCP EBee NChi SIgm
rotundifolium	MSal NDov WPGP
salicifolium	CFil SIgm
spinosum	NLar SIgm SMad
stellatum	GGar LRHS
tenue B&SWJ 2973	WCru
- var. *humile* B&SWJ 6470	WCru

Bursaria (Pittosporaceae)

spinosa	ECou GQui

Butia (Arecaceae)

bonnetii **new**	WMul
capitata	CAbb CBrP CHEx CPHo CRoM
	CTrC EAmu LEdu LPJP LPal LPan
	NPal SAPC SArc SChr WHPE WMul
eriospatha	CRoM
yatay	CRoM LPal WMul

Butomus (Butomaceae)

umbellatus ♀H4	CBen CDWL CFwr CRWN CRow
	CWat ECha ECtt EHon EMFW
	ENot EPAt EPfP LNCo LPBA MCCP
	MSta NArg NPer SLon SWat WFar
	WMAq WMoo WPnP WTin WWpP
- 'Rosenrot'	CRow
- 'Schneeweisschen'	CRow

butternut see *Juglans cinerea*

Buxus ✿ (Buxaceae)

aurea 'Marginata'	see *B. sempervirens* 'Marginata'
balearica ♀H4	CFil EPla SDry SLan SLon WPGP
	WPic WSHC WSPU XPep
bodinieri	EPla SLan
- 'David's Gold'	WPen WSHC
glomerata	SLan
'Green Gem'	EPla LEar NGHP NHol SLan WSel
'Green Mountain'	SLan
'Green Velvet'	EPfP NHol SLan STop
harlandii hort.	EPla LEar SIng SLan SRiv
* - f. *pendulus* **new**	SLan
- 'Richard'	SLan STre
henryi	SLan
japonica 'Nana'	see *B. microphylla*

	leonii	SLan
	macowanii	SLan
§	*microphylla*	CSWP LPan MHer NHol NWea SIng SLan STre WBVN
	- 'Asiatic Winter'	see *B. sinica* var. *insularis* 'Winter Gem'
§	- 'Compacta'	CFil NLAp SLan SRiv WCot WPat
	- 'Curly Locks'	EPla MHer NHol SLan
	- 'Faulkner'	EBee ELan EMil ENot EPfP EPla LBuc LEar LHop LPan LRHS MBNS MBlu MBri MRav NGHP NHol SLan SRiv STop WBcn
	- 'Grace Hendrick Phillips'	SLan
	- 'Green Jade'	SLan
	- 'Green Pillow'	NHol SLan SRiv
	- 'Helen Whiting'	SLan
	- var. *insularis*	see *B. sinica* var. *insularis*
	- var. *japonica*	SLan
	- - 'Gold Dust'	SLan
	- - 'Morris Dwarf'	SLan
	- - 'Morris Midget'	IArd NHol SLan
	- - 'National'	MHer SLan WPGP
	- - f. *yakushima*	SLan
	- 'Jim's Spreader' **new**	SLan
	- 'John Baldwin'	SLan SRiv STop WBcn
	- var. *koreana*	see *B. sinica* var. *insularis*
	- var. *riparia*	see *B. riparia*
	- var. *sinica*	see *B. sinica*
	- 'Winter Gem'	see *B. sinica* var. *insularis* 'Winter Gem'
	'Newport Blue'	see *B. sempervirens* 'Newport Blue'
	papillosa	SLan
§	*riparia*	EPla SLan
	rugulosa var. *intermedia*	SLan
	sempervirens ♀[H4]	More than 30 suppliers
	- 'Agram' **new**	SLan
§	- 'Angustifolia'	MHer NHol SLan SMad WCom
	- 'Arborescens'	LPan
	- 'Argentea'	see *B. sempervirens* 'Argenteovariegata'
§	- 'Argenteovariegata' (v)	EPfP GKir MRav NGHP NHol SLan WBcn WFar WSHC
	- 'Aurea'	see *B. sempervirens* 'Aureovariegata'
	- 'Aurea Maculata'	see *B. sempervirens* 'Aureovariegata'
	- 'Aurea Marginata'	see *B. sempervirens* 'Marginata'
	- 'Aurea Pendula' (v)	EPla SLan SLon WBcn WWye
§	- 'Aureovariegata' (v)	CBcs CSBt EBee ECrN EPfP GBar ISea MBar MBow MGos MHer MRav MWat NSti SChu SIng SLan SMer SPer SRiv WCom WDin WFar WMoo WTel WWye
	- 'Belleville' **new**	SLan
	- 'Bentley Blue'	MBNS NHol
	- 'Blauer Heinz'	ELan EMil LEar LRHS MBri MHer MTed SLan SRiv STop WSel
§	- 'Blue Cone'	CHar LEar
	- 'Blue Spire'	see *B. sempervirens* 'Blue Cone'
	- 'Bowles' Blue' **new**	SLan
	- clipped ball	CWib EPfP LEar LPan NBlu NGHP
	- clipped pyramid	CWib EPfP LEar LPan NBlu NGHP
	- clipped spiral **new**	NBlu
	- 'Dee Runk' **new**	SLan
§	- 'Elegantissima' (v) ♀[H4]	More than 30 suppliers
	- 'Gold Tip'	see *B. sempervirens* 'Notata'
	- 'Golden Frimley' (v)	LHop
§	- 'Graham Blandy'	LEar MHer NHol SLan SRiv STop WBcn
	- 'Green Balloon' **new**	LBuc
	- 'Greenpeace'	see *B. sempervirens* 'Graham Blandy'
	- 'Handsworthiensis'	EBee ECrN EMil LEar SEND SLan SPer STop

	- - blue **new**	SLan
	- 'Handsworthii'	CTri NWea SRms
	- subsp. *hyrcana*	SLan
	- 'Ickworth Giant'	SLan STop
	- 'Inverewe'	SLan WCom
	- 'Ipek' **new**	SLan
	- 'Japonica Aurea'	see *B. sempervirens* 'Latifolia Maculata'
	- 'Kensington Gardens'	SLan
	- 'Kingsville'	see *B. microphylla* 'Compacta'
	- 'Kingsville Dwarf'	see *B. microphylla* 'Compacta'
	- 'Lace'	NHol NSti SLan
§	- 'Langley Beauty'	SLan WBcn
	- 'Langley Pendula'	see *B. sempervirens* 'Langley Beauty'
	- 'Latifolia Macrophylla'	SLan SLon WLow WSel
§	- 'Latifolia Maculata' (v) ♀[H4]	CAbP CChe CDoC CWib EBee EPfP EPla LEar LRHS NGHP NHol NPer SLan SPoG SRiv STop STre WJek
*	- 'Latifolia Pendula'	NHol SLan
	- 'Lawson's Golden'	MAsh
	- 'Longifolia'	see *B. sempervirens* 'Angustifolia'
§	- 'Marginata' (v)	CBrm ECtt EPla GBar GKir LHop MAsh MHer MRav MSwo NHol NSti SHBN SHFr SLan SLon WBrE WHar WSel WStI
	- 'Memorial'	MHer NHol SLan SRiv STop
	- 'Molesworth' **new**	SLan
	- 'Myosotidifolia'	CFil CMHG EPla NPro SLan SRiv WPGP
	- 'Myrtifolia'	CBot EPla MHer NHol SLan SLon WCom
§	- 'Newport Blue'	MTed SLan
§	- 'Notata' (v)	CBcs CSBt CSWP EBee EGra GKir SHel SPlb
	- 'Parasol'	MHer SLan
	- 'Pendula'	CMHG GKir SLan SLon WCom
	- 'Prostrata'	NHol NWea SLan WBcn
	- 'Pyramidalis'	NBee SLan
	- 'Rosmarinifolia'	MRav SLan WCom
	- 'Rotundifolia'	CLnd EBee MHer SIde SLan STop WDin
	- 'Salicifolia Elata'	SLan
	- 'Silver Beauty' (v)	EMil MGos
	- 'Silver Variegated'	see *B. sempervirens* 'Elegantissima'
	- 'Suffruticosa' ♀[H4]	More than 30 suppliers
I	- 'Suffruticosa Blue'	NHol SVil
	- 'Suffruticosa Variegata' (v)	EBee ECrN EOHP SRms SWvt
	- 'Vardar Valley'	NPro SLan SRiv STop
*	- 'Variegata' (v)	ELan LRHS SLon
	- 'Waterfall'	SLan WBcn
§	*sinica*	SLan
§	- var. *insularis*	EPla SLan
	- - 'Filigree'	EPla NHol SLan WSel
	- - 'Justin Brouwers'	MHer SLan SRiv STop
	- - 'Pincushion'	SLan
	- - 'Tide Hill'	SLan SRiv STop WBcn WSel
§	- - 'Winter Gem'	EBee ENot LEar MHer MRav NHol NLar SLPl SLan
	wallichiana	CFil EPla SLan WPGP

C

Cacalia (Asteraceae)

atriplicifolia	LRHS
delphiniifolia B&SWJ 5789	WCru
firma B&SWJ 4650	WCru
kiusiana B&SWJ 5911	WCru
muhlenbergii **new**	MSal

plantaginea	see *Arnoglossum plantagineum*
suaveolens	EBee

Caesalpinia (*Caesalpiniaceae*)

gilliesii	CBot EBee MTPN SOWG SPlb WHPE XPep
– RCB/Arg N-1	WCot
pulcherrima	MGol SOWG SPlb

Caiophora (*Loasaceae*)

RCB/Arg M-1 **new**	WCot
prietea	CTCP

Caladium (*Araceae*)

'Aaron' (v)	MOak
§ *bicolor* (v)	MBri
– 'Mrs Arno Nehrling' (v)	MOak
– 'Postman Joyner'	MOak
– 'Rosebud' (v)	MOak
'Blaze'	MOak
'Brandywine'	see *C.* 'Irene Dank'
'Candidum' (v)	MOak
'Candidum Junior' (v)	MOak
'Carolyn Whorton' (v)	MOak
'Fannie Munson' (v)	MOak
'Festivia' (v)	MOak
'Fire Chief'	MOak
'Flash Rouge'	MOak
'Florida Cardinal' (v)	MOak
'Florida Elise'	MOak
'Freida Hemple'	MOak
'Galaxy'	MOak
'Gingerland' (v)	MOak
x *hortulanum*	see *C. bicolor*
§ 'Irene Dank'	MOak
'John Peed' (v)	MOak
'June Bride' (v)	MOak
'Kathleen'	MOak
'Lord Derby' (v)	MOak
'Miss Muffet'	MOak
'Mrs F.M. Joyner' (v)	MOak
'Mrs W.B. Haldeman' (v)	MOak
'Pink Beauty'	MOak
'Pink Cloud' (v)	MOak
'Pink Gem' (v)	MOak
'Poecile Anglais'	MOak
'Red Frill' (v)	MOak
'Rosalie' (v)	MOak
* 'Scarlet Pimpernell'	MOak
'Symphonic Rose'	MOak
'Thomas Tomlinson' (v)	MOak
'White Christmas' (v)	MOak
'White Queen' (v)	MOak
'White Wing' (v)	MOak

Calamagrostis (*Poaceae*)

x *acutiflora*	ECGN
N – 'Karl Foerster'	More than 30 suppliers
– 'Overdam' (v)	More than 30 suppliers
– 'Stricta'	EPPr EWsh GKir LPhx
argentea	see *Stipa calamagrostis*
§ *arundinacea*	More than 30 suppliers
§ *brachytricha*	More than 30 suppliers
emodensis	CBod CBrm CFwr CKno CMil CPen CWCL EBee EBre EPPr EPla LPan MMoz SYvo WPGP
§ *epigejos*	CBig CHrt CNat EMan EPPr EWsh GBin LPhx MWod NHol NOGN WRos WWpP
– CLD 1325	EPla
splendens misapplied	see *Stipa calamagrostis*
varia	EHoe EPPr

Calamintha (*Lamiaceae*)

alpina	see *Acinos alpinus*
§ *ascendens*	CTCP EBee MLLN SGar WBWf WMoo WOut
clinopodium	see *Clinopodium vulgare*
cretica	CLyd WOut WPer WWye
§ *grandiflora*	More than 30 suppliers
– 'Elfin Purple'	CBgR EBee MWrn
– 'Variegata' (v)	CRow EBee ELan EMan ERou GGar MAnH MMil NPri NSti SCro WCHb WCom WFar WHHs WWeb WWpP
§ *menthifolia*	CPom NLar WJek WOut
– HH&K 163	GBri
§ *nepeta*	More than 30 suppliers
– subsp. *glandulosa*	CTCP EBee WMoo
– – ACL 1050/90	LRHS WHoo
– – 'White Cloud'	CHea CSpe ECGN EFou EHrv ELan ERqu EWTr GBar GBuc LLWP MBro MRav MSte NBir NDov WCAu WMoo WWeb WWye XPep
– 'Gottfried Kuehn'	MRav WCAu
§ – subsp. *nepeta*	CSev EFou ELan EMon EPfP ERou EWTr GBar IHMH LHop MBri MHer MRav MWgw NSti SHel SPer SUsu WCHb WCom WEas WFar WTin WWpP
– – 'Blue Cloud'	CHea CSam ECGN EChP ECha EFou EHrv ILis LPhx NBir NDov NGar SAga SBla SOkh SWat WCAu WCHb WMoo XPep
nepetoides	see *C. nepeta* subsp. *nepeta*
officinalis misapplied	see *C. ascendens*
sylvatica	see *C. menthifolia*
I – 'Menthe'	EBee SSvw
vulgaris	see *Clinopodium vulgare*

calamondin see x *Citrofortunella microcarpa*

Calamovilfa (*Poaceae*)

longifolia	EBee

Calandrinia (*Portulacaceae*)

caespitosa	CTCP
colchaguensis **new**	WLin
depressa **new**	CTCP
discolor	LRHS
grandiflora	CTCP MLLN WWin
* *ranunculina*	CPBP
sericea	CGra CPBP
sibirica	see *Claytonia sibirica*
umbellata	EBre EMlt NJOw WPer WWin
* – *amarantha*	EDAr
– 'Ruby Tuesday'	NPri

Calanthe (*Orchidaceae*)

amamiana	EFEx
arisanenesis	EFEx
aristulifera	EFEx LAma
bicolor	see *C. discolor* var. *flava*
caudatilabella	EFEx
discolor	EFEx LAma WCot
§ – var. *flava*	CLAP LAma
hamata	EFEx
japonica	EFEx
mannii	EFEx
nipponica	EFEx LAma
reflexa	EBee EFEx LAma
§ *sieboldii*	EBee EFEx LAma WCot
striata	see *C. sieboldii*
tokunoshimensis	EFEx
tricarinata	EFEx LAma

Calathea (Marantaceae)

	crocata ♀H1	LRHS MBri
	'Greystar'	MBri
	louisae 'Maui Queen'	MBri
§	*majestica* ♀H1	LRHS
	makoyana ♀H1	MBri
	metallica	MBri
	oppenheimiana	see *Ctenanthe oppenheimiana*
	ornata	see *C. majestica*
	picturata 'Argentea' ♀H1	MBri
	roseopicta ♀H1	LRHS MBri
*	*stromata* **new**	XBlo
	veitchiana	MBri
	warscewiczii	MBri
	'Wavestar'	MBri
	zebrina ♀H1	MBri

Calceolaria (Scrophulariaceae)

	acutifolia	see *C. polyrhiza*
	alba	CPla EMan GFlt SScr WCom WCot WHil
	arachnoidea	NWoo WCot
	x *banksii*	EBee WCom
	bicolor	WCot
§	*biflora*	CLyd EDAr EHol EHyt GTou LEdu MBow MHer NWCA SIng
	- 'Goldcap'	EMlt WWeb
	- 'Goldcrest Amber'	WPer
	'Camden Hero'	MOak WCom
	chelidonioides	GGar MTho
	crenatiflora	NWoo
	falklandica	CNic CTCP NLAp SRms WHer WPer WWin
	fothergillii	MOne NArg
	'Goldcrest'	EBre EPfP SRms WWeb
	'Hall's Spotted' **new**	NWCA
§	*integrifolia* ♀H3	CBcs CHal CPLG EBee ELan SChu SEND SGar SIng SPer SRms WAbe WOld
	- var. *angustifolia*	MOak SDry WCom
	- bronze	SPer WAbe
	'John Innes'	ECho LRHS SChr WRha WWeb
	'Kentish Hero'	CElw CHal MOak MSte NPer SChu WCom
	mexicana	CPLG SHFr
	plantaginea	see *C. biflora*
§	*polyrhiza*	ECho NRya
	purpurea	WCom
	rugosa	see *C. integrifolia*
	Sunset Series	EPfP IHMH
	tenella	ECtt EDAr NLAp NMen NWCA WAbe
	uniflora **new**	GKev
	- var. *darwinii*	ECho EHyt GEdr GTou NMen SIng
	'Walter Shrimpton'	ECho EPot EWes WCom

Caldcluvia (Cunoniaceae)

paniculata	ISea

Calea (Asteraceae)

zacatechichi	MGol

Calendula (Asteraceae)

meuselii	CFee
officinalis	CArn EDAr ELau GPoy GWCH MHer MSal SIde WHHs WHbs WHer WJek WLHH WSel WWye
- 'Fiesta Gitana' ♀H4	CBod CPrp WJek
- 'Prolifera'	WHer

Calibrachoa (Solanaceae)

Carillon Series	WWol
'Carillon Burgundy'	

Million Bells Blue = 'Sunbelbu'PBR **new**	NBlu
Million Bells Cherry = 'Sunbelchipi'PBR	LAst
Million Bells Lemon = 'Sunbelkic'PBR	LAst NBlu WWol
Million Bells Red = 'Sunbelrc' **new**	LAst NPri WWol
Million Bells Terracotta = 'Sunbelkist'	LAst WWol
Million Bells Trailing Blue = 'Sunbelkubu'PBR	WWol
Million Bells Trailing Fuchsia = 'Sunbelrkup' **new**	WWol
Million Bells Trailing Lavender Vein = 'Sunbelbura' **new**	LAst WWol
Million Bells Trailing Pink = 'Sunbelkupi'PBR **new**	LAst
Million Bells Trailing White = 'Sunbelkuho'PBR **new**	LAst

Calicotome (Papilionaceae)

spinosa **new**	XPep

Calla (Araceae)

aethiopica	see *Zantedeschia aethiopica*
palustris	CRow CWat EHon EMFW EPAt EPfP LNCo LPBA MCCP MSta NPer SLon SPlb SWat WFar WMAq WPnP WTin WWpP

Calliandra (Mimosaceae)

*	*emarginata minima*	LRHS SOWG
	haematocephala	SOWG
	tweedii **new**	SOWG

Callianthemum (Ranunculaceae)

anemonoides	GCrs SBla
coriandrifolium	EPot SBla

Callicarpa (Verbenaceae)

	americana	NLar
	- var. *lactea*	CMCN
	bodinieri	NBir WFar
	- var. *giraldii*	CBrm GBin GIBF MRav SMac WBod WDin WWeb
	- - 'Profusion' ♀H4	More than 30 suppliers
	cathayana	NLar
	dichotoma	CPLG CPle CTrG EPfP GIBF LRHS WBcn WBod WFar WWin
	- f. *albifructa*	GIBF
	- 'Issai'	NLar WBcn
	- 'Shirobana'	WBcn
	aff. *formosana* B&SWJ 7127	WCru
	japonica	CPle WWes
	- B&SWJ 8587	WCru
	- f. *albibacca* **new**	NLar
	- 'Heavy Berry' **new**	WBcn
	- 'Leucocarpa'	CBcs CMac CPLG EBee ELan EPfP GEil LRHS NLar NVic WBcn WFar
	- var. *luxurians* **new**	NLar
	- - B&SWJ 8521	WCru
	kwangtungensis	CMCN NLar
	mollis	EBee NLar WPGP
*	*trichotoma*	GEil

Callirhoe (*Malvaceae*)

involucrata	CPLG EBee EMan NBur NWCA SMad SUsu
triangulata	EMan

Callisia (*Commelinaceae*)

elegans ♀H1	CHal
§ *navicularis*	CHal
repens	CHal MBri

Callistemon ✿ (*Myrtaceae*)

acuminatus <u>new</u>	XPep
'Burgundy'	SOWG
* 'Burning Bush'	SOWG
chisholmii	SOWG
citrinus	CHll CSBt EBee ECot ECou ERom GGar GSki ITim LAst SMer SOWG SPer SPlb SSte WBrE WDin WHar WWin
- 'Albus'	see *C. citrinus* 'White Anzac'
- 'Angela'	SOWG
- 'Canberra'	SOWG
- 'Firebrand'	CDoC LRHS MAsh SMur SOWG
- 'Horse Paddock'	SOWG
- 'Splendens' ♀H3	CBcs CBrm CDoC CDul CHEx CMac CTrC EBee EGra ELan EPfP GQui IArd MAsh MBri MGos NPal SBra SDry SHBN SHFr SOWG SPer SReu SSta WBod WFar WStI
§ - 'White Anzac'	LRHS SOWG SSte
comboynensis	SOWG
'Coochy Coochy Station'	SOWG
'Dawson River Weeper'	SOWG
flavescens	SOWG
flavovirens	SOWG
formosus	SOWG
glaucus	see *C. speciosus*
'Hannah's Child'	SOWG
'Happy Valley'	SOWG
'Harkness'	SOWG
'Injune'	SOWG
'Kings Park Special'	EHol LRHS SOWG
laevis hort.	see *C. rugulosus*
linearis ♀H3	CBcs CMac CSBt CTrC CTri EBee EBre ECou ECrN ELan EPfP EPla LRHS LRav MDun MHer SLim SLon SOWG SPlb SRms SSpi SWvt WMul WNor
macropunctatus	SOWG SPlb
'Mauve Mist'	CTrC LRHS MAsh SOWG
pachyphyllus	ECou SOWG
- var. *viridis*	SOWG SSte
pallidus	CMHG CMac CPLG CWib EBee ECou ELan EPfP GGar IDee ITim LRHS SMur SOWG SPer SPlb SSta SSte
paludosus	see *C. sieberi* DC.
pearsonii	SOWG
- prostrate	SOWG
'Perth Pink'	CBcs CDoC ELan SOWG SPoG SSte
phoeniceus	ECou SOWG
- 'Pink Ice'	SOWG
pinifolius	SOWG SPlb SSte
- green-flowered	SOWG
- red-flowered	SOWG
- 'Sockeye'	SOWG
'Pink Champagne'	SOWG
§ *pityoides*	CPLG CTrC ECou SOWG WBod XPep
- from Brown's Swamp, Australia	ECou
polandii	SOWG
- dwarf	SOWG

'Purple Splendour'	SOWG
'Red Clusters'	CBcs CDoC CTrC EBee ELan ERea IArd LAst MDun NLar NPer SMur SOWG SWvt WPat
'Reeve's Pink'	SOWG
rigidus	More than 30 suppliers
§ *rugulosus*	CBcs EBee EGra IArd LRHS SOWG XPep
salignus ♀H3	CBcs CDoC CSBt CTrC CTri EBee ECrN EPfP GEil GSki ISea LEur MHer SEND SHFr SLim SOWG SYvo WBVN WDin WSHC XPep
- 'Ruber'	CTrC
sieberi misapplied	see *C. pityoides*
§ *sieberi* DC.	CBcs CDoC CMHG CTrC ECou ELan EPfP GGar GSki LHop NBir SOWG SPlb SSpi WFar
§ *speciosus*	CDul CTrC EBee SMur SOWG SPer
subulatus	CDoC CTrC EBee ECou MCCP NHol NLar SAPC SArc SOWG SPlb WMoo
- 'Crimson Tail'	MDun
teretifolius	SOWG
viminalis	CBcs CTrC SGar SOWG SPlb
- 'Captain Cook'	ECou ERea EShb LAst LRHS NLar SLim SOWG
- 'Hannah Ray'	SOWG
- 'Little John'	CBcs CWSG IArd LRHS SLim SOWG SPoG XPep
- 'Malawi Giant'	SOWG
'Violaceus'	LRav XPep
viridiflorus	CTrC ECou GQui LEur MCCP SGar SOWG SWal WCru
- 'County Park Dwarf'	ECou
- 'Sunshine'	ECou
- 'White Anzac'	see *C. citrinus* 'White Anzac'

Callitriche (*Callitrichaceae*)

autumnalis	see *C. hermaphroditica*
§ *hermaphroditica*	EMFW NBlu WMAq
§ *palustris*	EHon
stagnalis <u>new</u>	NArg
verna	see *C. palustris*

Callitris (*Cupressaceae*)

oblonga	GTSp

Calluna ✿ (*Ericaceae*)

vulgaris	GWCH LRHS
- 'Aberdeen'	EHea
- 'Adrie'	EHea
- 'Alba Argentea'	EHea
- 'Alba Aurea'	EHea MBar
- 'Alba Carlton'	EHea
- 'Alba Dumosa'	EHea
- 'Alba Elata'	CNCN EHea MBar
- 'Alba Elegans'	EHea
- 'Alba Elongata'	see *C. vulgaris* 'Mair's Variety'
- 'Alba Erecta'	EHea
- 'Alba Jae'	EHea MBar
- 'Alba Minor'	EHea
- 'Alba Multiflora'	EHea
- 'Alba Pilosa'	EHea
§ - 'Alba Plena' (d)	CSBt EHea LRHS MBar WStI
- 'Alba Praecox'	EHea
- 'Alba Pumila'	EHea MBar
§ - 'Alba Rigida'	EHea LRHS MBar
- 'Alec Martin' (d)	EHea
- 'Alex Warwick'	EHea
- 'Alexandra'[PBR] ♀H4	EHea LRHS NHol SCoo
- 'Alice Knight'	EHea
- 'Alicia'[PBR] ♀H4	EDAr EHea LRHS
- 'Alieke'	EHea
- 'Alison Yates'	EHea MBar

- 'Allegretto'	EHea
- 'Allegro' ♀H4	EDAr EHea EPfP LRHS MBar NHol WStI
- 'Alportii'	CBrm EHea MBar WStI
- 'Alportii Praecox'	CNCN EHea LRHS MBar
- 'Alys Sutcliffe'	EHea
- 'Amanda Wain'	EHea
- 'Amethyst'PBR	EHea NHol
- 'Amilto'	CNCN EHea NHol
- 'Andrew Proudley'	EHea MBar
- 'Anette'PBR ♀H4	EHea LRHS NHol SCoo
- 'Angela Wain'	EHea
- 'Anna'	EHea
- 'Annabel' (d)	EHea
- 'Anne Dobbin'	EHea
- 'Annegret'	see *C. vulgaris* 'Marlies'
- 'Anneke'	EHea
- 'Annemarie' (d) ♀H4	CBcs CNCN EBre EHea EPfP LRHS NHol SCoo
- 'Anne's Zwerg'	EHea
- 'Anthony Davis' ♀H4	CNCN EHea MBar NHol
- 'Anthony Wain'	EHea
- 'Anton'	EHea
- 'Antrujo Gold'	EHea
- 'Aphrodite'PBR **new**	EHea
- 'Apollo'	EHea
- 'Applecross' (d)	CNCN EHea
- 'Arabella'PBR	EHea LRHS NHol
- 'Argentea'	EHea MBar
- 'Ariadne'	EHea
- 'Arina'	CNCN EHea LRHS MBri
- 'Arran Gold'	CNCN EHea MBar
- 'Ashgarth Amber'	EHea
- 'Ashgarth Amethyst'	EHea
- 'Ashgarth Shell Pink'	EHea
- 'Asterix'	EHea
- 'Atalanta'	EHea
- 'Atholl Gold'	EHea
- 'August Beauty'	CNCN EHea
- 'Aurea'	EHea LRHS
- 'Autumn Glow'	EHea
- 'Baby Ben'	EHea
- 'Baby Wicklow'	EHea
- 'Barbara Fleur'	EHea
- 'Barja'	EHea
- 'Barnett Anley'	CNCN EHea
- 'Battle of Arnhem'	CNCN EHea MBar
- 'Bayport'	EHea
- 'Beechwood Crimson'	CNCN EHea
- 'Ben Nevis'	EHea
- 'Bennachie Bronze' **new**	EHea
- 'Bennachie Prostrate' **new**	EHea
- 'Beoley Crimson'	CNCN EHea LRHS MBar
- 'Beoley Crimson Variegated' (v)	EHea
- 'Beoley Gold' ♀H4	CBrm CNCN CSBt CTri EHea EPfP GKir LRHS MBar MBri MGos NHol WStI
- 'Beoley Silver'	CNCN EHea MBar NBlu
- 'Bernadette'	EHea
- 'Betty Baum'	EHea
- 'Bispingen'	EHea
- 'Blazeaway'	CBrm CNCN CTri EHea EPfP GKir LRHS MBar MBri NHol WStI
- 'Blueness'	EHea
- 'Bognie'	CNCN EHea
- 'Bonfire Brilliance'	CNCN CSBt EHea MBar NHol
- 'Bonita'PBR **new**	EHea
- 'Bonne's Darkness'	EHea
- 'Bonsaï'	EHea
- 'Boreray'	CNCN EHea
- 'Boskoop'	CBrm CNCN EBre EHea LRHS MBar MBri NHol

- 'Bradford'	EHea
- 'Braemar'	CNCN EHea
- 'Braeriach'	EHea
- 'Branchy Anne'	EHea
- 'Bray Head'	CNCN EHea MBar
- 'Brita Elisabeth' (d)	EHea
- 'Bronze Beauty'	EHea
- 'Bud Lyle'	EHea
- 'Bunsall'	CNCN EHea
- 'Buxton Snowdrift'	EHea
- 'C.W. Nix'	CSBt EHea MBar
- 'Caerketton White'	EHea
- 'Caleb Threlkeld'	EHea NHol
- 'Calf of Man'	EHea
- 'Californian Midge'	EHea LRHS MBar NHol
- 'Carl Röders' (d)	EHea
- 'Carmen'	EHea
- 'Carngold'	EHea
- 'Carole Chapman'	EHea MBar
- 'Carolyn'	EHea
- 'Cassa'	EHea
- 'Catherine' **new**	EHea
- 'Catherine Anne'	EHea LRHS
- 'Celtic Gold'	EHea
- 'Charles Chapman'	EHea
- 'Chernobyl' (d)	EHea NHol
- 'Chindit'	EHea
- 'Christina'	EHea
- 'Cilcennin Common'	EHea
- 'Clare Carpet'	EHea
- 'Coby'	EHea
- 'Coccinea'	EHea MBar
- 'Colette'	EHea
- 'Con Brio'	CBcs CNCN EHea LRHS
- 'Copper Glow'	EHea
- 'Coral Island'	EHea MBar
- 'Corbett's Red'	EHea
- 'Corrie's White'	EHea
- 'Cottswood Gold'	EHea
- 'County Wicklow' (d) ♀H4	CBcs CNCN CTri EHea EPfP GKir LRHS MBar MBri MGos NBlu NHol
- 'Craig Rossie'	EHea
- 'Crail Orange'	EHea
- 'Cramond' (d)	CNCN EHea LRHS MBar
- 'Cream Steving'	EHea
- 'Crimson Glory'	EHea LRHS MBar NBlu NDlv WStI
- 'Crimson Sunset'	CNCN EHea WStI
- 'Crinkly Tuft'	EHea
- 'Crowborough Beacon'	EHea
- 'Cuprea'	CNCN EHea EPfP LRHS MBar MBri NHol WStI
- 'Dainty Bess'	EHea LRHS MBar MSwo NHol WStI
- 'Dark Beauty'PBR (d) ♀H4	CNCN EBre EDAr EHea EPfP ESis GKir LRHS MBar NDlv NHol WStI
- 'Dark Star' (d) ♀H4	CBcs CNCN EBre EHea EPfP LRHS MBar MGos NHol SCoo
- 'Darkness' ♀H4	CBcs CNCN CSBt CTri EHea EPfP GKir LRHS MBar MBri NHol SCoo WStI
- 'Darleyensis'	EHea
- 'Dart's Amethyst'	EHea
- 'Dart's Beauty'	EHea
- 'Dart's Brilliant'	EHea
- 'Dart's Flamboyant'	EHea
- 'Dart's Gold'	EHea MBar
- 'Dart's Hedgehog'	EHea
- 'Dart's Parakeet'	EHea
- 'Dart's Parrot'	EHea
- 'Dart's Silver Rocket'	EHea
- 'Dart's Squirrel'	EHea
- 'Dart's Surprise'	EHea
- 'David Eason'	CNCN EHea
- 'David Hagenaars'	EHea
- 'David Hutton'	EHea MBar

- 'David Platt' (d) — EHea
- 'Denkewitz' **new** — EHea
- 'Denny Pratt' — EHea
- 'Desiree' — EHea
- 'Devon' (d) — EHea
- 'Diana' — EHea
- 'Dickson's Blazes' — EHea
- 'Dirry' — CNCN EHea
- 'Doctor Murray's White' — see *C. vulgaris* 'Mullardoch'
- 'Doris Rushworth' — EHea
- 'Drum-ra' — EHea MBar SRms
- 'Dunnet Lime' — EHea SPlb
- 'Dunnydeer' — EHea
- 'Dunwood' — EHea MBar
- 'Durford Wood' — EHea
- 'Dwingeloo Delight' — EHea
- 'E.F. Brown' — EHea
- 'E. Hoare' — EHea MBar
- 'Easter-bonfire' — CNCN EHea NBlu NHol
- 'Eckart Miessner' — EHea
- 'Edith Godbolt' — EHea
- 'Elaine' — EHea
- 'Elegant Pearl' — EHea MBar
- 'Elegantissima' — CBcs EHea
- 'Elegantissima Walter Ingwersen' — see *C. vulgaris* 'Walter Ingwersen'
- 'Elkstone White' — CNCN EHea MBar
- 'Ellen' — EHea
- 'Ellie Barbour' — EHea
- 'Elly' — EHea
- 'Else Frye' (d) — EHea
- 'Elsie Purnell' (d) ♀H4 — CNCN CSBt EDAr EHea EPfP LRHS MBar MGos NHol SPlb WStI
- 'Emerald Jock' — EHea
- 'Emma Louise Tuke' — EHea
- 'Eric Easton' — EHea
- 'Eskdale Gold' — EHea
- 'Eurosa'PBR **new** — EHea
- 'Fairy' — EHea
- 'Falling Star' — EHea
- 'Feuerwerk' — EHea
§ - 'Finale' — EHea MBar
- 'Findling' — EHea
- 'Fire King' — EHea MBar
- 'Fire Star' — EHea
- 'Firebreak' — EHea MBar
- 'Firefly' ♀H4 — CBrm CNCN CSBt EBre EDAr EHea EPfP LRHS MBar MBri NBlu WStI
- 'Flamingo' — CBcs CNCN CSBt EDAr EHea LRHS MBar MBri MSwo NHol
- 'Flatling' — EHea NHol
- 'Flore Pleno' (d) — EHea MBar
- 'Floriferous' — EHea
- 'Florrie Spicer' — EHea
- 'Fokko' (d) — EHea
- 'Fort Bragg' — EHea
- 'Fortyniner Gold' — EHea
- 'Foxhollow Wanderer' — CNCN EHea MBar
- 'Foxii' — EHea
- 'Foxii Floribunda' — EHea LRHS MBar
- 'Foxii Lett's Form' — see *C. vulgaris* 'Velvet Dome', *C. vulgaris* 'Mousehole'
- 'Foxii Nana' — CNCN EHea ESis LRHS MBar NBlu NDlv NHol
- 'Foya' — EHea
- 'Fraser's Old Gold' — EHea
- 'Fred J. Chapple' — CNCN EHea LRHS MBar MBri NBlu WStI
- 'Fréjus' — EHea
- 'French Grey' — CNCN EHea
- 'Fritz Kircher'PBR — EHea NHol
- 'Gaia' — EHea
- 'Gerda' — EHea LRHS

- 'Ginkel's Glorie' — EHea
- 'Glasa' — EHea
- 'Glen Mashie' — EHea
- 'Glencoe' (d) — EHea LRHS MBar MBri
- 'Glendoick Silver' — EHea
- 'Glenfiddich' — CSBt EHea MBar
- 'Glenlivet' — EHea MBar
- 'Glenmorangie' — EHea MBar
- 'Gloucester Boy' — EHea
- 'Gnome Pink' — EHea
- 'Gold Charm' — EHea
- 'Gold Finch' — EHea
- 'Gold Flame' — EHea LRHS MBar
- Gold Hamilton — see *C. vulgaris* 'Chernobyl'
- 'Gold Haze' ♀H4 — CBcs CBrm CNCN CTri EHea EPfP GKir LRHS MBar MBri NHol SCoo WStI
- 'Gold Knight' — EDAr EHea EPfP LRHS MBar
- 'Gold Kup' — EHea MBar
- 'Gold Mist' — EHea LRHS NBlu NDlv
- 'Gold Spronk' — EHea
- 'Goldcarmen' — EHea
- 'Golden Blazeaway' — EHea
- 'Golden Carpet' — CNCN CSBt EHea ESis LRHS MBar MBri MGos NDlv NHol WStI
- 'Golden Dew' — EHea
- 'Golden Dream' (d) — EHea
- 'Golden Feather' — CNCN CSBt EHea LRHS MBar
- 'Golden Fleece' — CNCN EHea
- 'Golden Max' — EHea
- 'Golden Rivulet' — EHea LRHS MBar MSwo
- 'Golden Turret' — CNCN EHea LRHS
- 'Golden Wonder' (d) — EHea
- 'Goldsworth Crimson' — CSBt EHea
- 'Goldsworth Crimson Variegated' (v) — CNCN EHea MBar
- 'Goscote Wine' — EHea
- 'Grasmeriensis' — EHea MBar
- 'Great Comp' — MBar
- 'Green Cardinal' — EHea
- 'Grey Carpet' — CNCN EHea LRHS MBar
- 'Grijsje' — EHea
- 'Grizabella' — EHea
- 'Grizzly' — EHea
- 'Grönsinka' — EHea
- 'Grouse' — EHea
- 'Guinea Gold' — CNCN EHea LRHS MBar MBri
- 'Gunilla Uggla' **new** — EHea
§ - 'H.E. Beale' (d) — CNCN CSBt CTri EHea EPfP GKir LRHS MBar MBri MGos NHol
- 'Hamlet Green' — CNCN EHea MBar
- 'Hammondii' — CNCN EHea WStI
- 'Hammondii Aureifolia' — CNCN EHea LRHS MBar MBri SPlb
- 'Hammondii Rubrifolia' — EHea LRHS MBar MBri NBlu
- 'Harlekin' — EHea
- 'Harry Gibbon' (d) — EHea
- 'Harten's Findling' — EHea
- 'Hatje's Herbstfeuer' (d) — EHea
- 'Hayesensis' — EHea
- 'Heidberg' — EHea
- 'Heidepracht' — EHea
- 'Heidesinfonie' — EHea
- 'Heideteppich' — EHea
- 'Heidezwerg' — EHea
- 'Heike' (d) — EHea
- 'Herbert Mitchell' — EHea
- 'Hester' — EHea
- 'Hetty' — EHea
- 'Hibernica' — EHea MBar
- 'Hiemalis' — EHea MBar
- 'Hiemalis Southcote' — see *C. vulgaris* 'Durford Wood'
- 'Highland Cream' — CNCN
- Highland Cream — see *C. vulgaris* 'Punch's Dessert'
- 'Highland Rose' — CNCN EHea LRHS SPlb

– 'Highland Spring'	EHea	
– 'Hilda Turberfield'	EHea	
– 'Hillbrook Limelight'	EHea	
– 'Hillbrook Orange'	EHea MBar	
– 'Hillbrook Sparkler'	EHea	
– 'Hinton White'	EHea	
– 'Hirsuta Albiflora'	EHea	
– 'Hirsuta Typica'	CNCN EHea	
– 'Hollandia'	EHea	
– 'Holstein'	EHea	
– 'Hookstone'	EHea MBar	
– 'Hoyerhagen'	EHea	
§ – 'Hugh Nicholson'	CNCN EHea	
– 'Humpty Dumpty'	EHea NHol	
– 'Hypnoides'	EHea	
– 'Ide's Double' (d)	EHea	
– 'Inchcolm'	EHea	
– 'Inchkeith'	EHea	
– 'Ineke'	CNCN EHea MBar	
– 'Inge'	EHea	
– 'Ingrid Bouter' (d)	EHea	
– 'Inshriach Bronze'	CNCN EHea MBar	
– 'Iris van Leyen'	CNCN EHea LRHS	
– 'Islay Mist'	EHea	
– 'Isle of Hirta'	CNCN EHea MBar NHol	
– 'Isobel Frye'	EHea MBar	
– 'Isobel Hughes' (d)	EHea MBar	
– 'J.H. Hamilton' (d) ♀H4	CNCN CTri EHea GKir LRHS MBar MBri MGos NHol SRms WStI	
– 'Jan'	EHea	
– 'Jan Dekker'	CNCN EHea LRHS NBlu NHol	
– 'Janice Chapman'	EHea MBar	
– 'Japanese White'	EHea	
– 'Jenny'	EHea	
– 'Jill'	EHea	
– 'Jimmy Dyce' (d)	EHea	
– 'Joan Sparkes' (d)	CNCN EHea LRHS MBar WStI	
– 'Jochen'	EHea	
– 'Johan Slegers'	EHea	
– John Denver	see *C. vulgaris* 'Marleen Select'	
– 'John F. Letts'	CSBt EHea LRHS MBar SRms WStI	
– 'Johnson's Variety'	CBcs CNCN EHea MBar	
– 'Jos' Lemon'	EHea	
– 'Jos' Whitie'	EHea	
– 'Josefine'	EHea	
– 'Joseph's Coat'	EHea	
– 'Joy Vanstone' ♀H4	CNCN CSBt EHea EPfP GKir LRHS MBar MBri MGos NHol	
– 'Julia'	EHea	
– 'Julie Ann Platt'	EHea	
– 'Juno'	EHea	
– 'Kaiser'	EHea	
– 'Karin Blum'	EHea	
– 'Kermit'	EHea	
– 'Kerstin' ♀H4	CBcs CBrm EHea LRHS MBar MSwo NBlu NHol SPlb	
– 'Kinlochruel' (d) ♀H4	CNCN CSBt CTri EHea EPfP GKir LRHS MBar MBri MGos NBlu NHol SPlb SRms	
– 'Kir Royal'	EHea	
– 'Kirby White'	CNCN EHea LRHS MBar MBri NBlu NDlv NHol SPlb	
– 'Kirsty Anderson'	EHea LRHS	
– 'Kit Hill'	EHea MBar	
– 'Kontrast'	EHea	
– 'Kuphaldtii'	EHea MBar	
– 'Kuppendorf'	EHea	
– 'Kynance'	CNCN EHea MBar	
– 'Lady Maithe'	EHea	
– 'Lambstails'	EHea MBar	
– 'L'Ancresse'	EHea	
– 'Larissa'PBR	EHea	
– 'Late Crimson Gold'	EHea	
– 'Lemon Gem'	EHea	
– 'Lemon Queen'	EHea	
– 'Leslie Slinger'	EHea LRHS MBar	
– 'Lewis Lilac'	EHea	
– 'Liebestraum'	EHea	
– 'Lilac Elegance'	EHea	
– 'Lime Glade'	CNCN EHea	
– 'Lime Gold'	EHea	
– 'Little John'	EHea	
– 'Llanbedrog Pride' (d)	EHea MBar	
– 'Loch Turret'	EHea MBar MBri	
– 'Loch-na-Seil'	EHea MBar	
– 'London Pride'	EHea	
– 'Long White'	CNCN EHea MBar	
– 'Loni'	EHea	
– 'Lüneberg Heath'	EHea	
– 'Lyle's Late White'	CNCN EHea	
– 'Lyle's Surprise'	EHea MBar	
– 'Lyndon Proudley'	EHea	
– 'Macdonald of Glencoe'	EHea	
§ – 'Mair's Variety' ♀H4	EHea LRHS MBar	
– 'Mallard'	EHea	
– 'Manitoba'	EHea	
– 'Marianne'	EHea	
– 'Marie'	EHea	
– 'Marion Blum'	EHea MBar	
– 'Marleen'	CNCN EHea MBar NHol	
– 'Marleen Select'	EHea	
§ – 'Marlies'	EHea NHol	
– 'Martha Hermann'	EHea	
– 'Martine Langenberg'	EHea	
– 'Masquerade'	EHea MBar	
– 'Matita'	EHea	
– 'Mauvelyn'	EHea	
– 'Mazurka'	EHea	
– 'Melanie'	EHea LRHS MBar MSwo NHol	
– 'Mick Jamieson' (d)	EHea	
– 'Mies'	EHea	
– 'Minima'	EHea MBar	
– 'Minima Smith's Variety'	EHea MBar	
– 'Minty'	EHea	
– 'Mirelle'	CNCN EHea	
– 'Miss Muffet'	EHea NHol	
– 'Molecule'	EHea MBar	
– 'Monika' (d)	EHea	
– 'Monja' **new**	EHea	
– 'Moon Glow'	EHea	
– 'Mountain Snow'	EHea	
§ – 'Mousehole'	CNCN EHea LRHS MBar NHol	
– 'Mousehole Compact'	see *C. vulgaris* 'Mousehole'	
– 'Mrs Alf'	EHea	
– 'Mrs E. Wilson' (d)	EHea	
– 'Mrs Neil Collins'	EHea	
– 'Mrs Pat'	CNCN EHea LRHS MBar NHol	
– 'Mrs Pinxteren'	EHea	
– 'Mrs Ronald Gray'	CNCN EHea MBar	
– 'Mullach Mor'	EHea	
§ – 'Mullardoch'	EHea MBar	
– 'Mullion' ♀H4	EHea MBar	
– 'Multicolor'	CNCN EHea GKir LRHS MBar NDlv NHol SRms	
– 'Murielle Dobson'	EHea	
§ – 'My Dream' (d) ♀H4	CNCN CSBt EHea EPfP LRHS MBar NHol SCoo	
– 'Nana'	EHea	
– 'Nana Compacta'	CNCN EHea LRHS MBar SRms	
– 'Natasja'	EHea	
– 'Naturpark'	EHea MBar	
– 'Nico'	EHea	
– Nordlicht	see *C. vulgaris* 'Skone'	
– 'October White'	CNCN EHea	
– 'Odette'	EHea	
– 'Oiseval'	EHea	
– 'Old Rose'	EHea	

- 'Olive Turner'   EHea
- 'Olympic Gold'   EHea
- 'Orange and Gold'   EHea LRHS
- 'Orange Carpet'   EHea
- 'Orange Max'   EHea
- 'Orange Queen'   CNCN CSBt CWCL EHea LRHS
                          MBar
- 'Öxabäck'   EHea MBar
- 'Oxshott Common'   CNCN EHea GQui MBar
- 'Pallida'   EHea
- 'Parsons' Gold'   EHea
- 'Parsons' Grey Selected' EHea
- 'Pastell' (d)   EHea
- 'Pat's Gold'   EHea
- 'Peace'   EHea
- 'Pearl Drop'   EHea MBar
- 'Peggy'   EHea
- 'Penhale'   EHea
- 'Penny Bun'   EHea
- 'Pennyacre Gold'   EHea
- 'Pennyacre Lemon'   EHea
- 'Pepper and Salt'   see *C. vulgaris* 'Hugh Nicholson'
- 'Perestrojka'   EHea NHol
- 'Peter Sparkes' (d) ♀H4 CNCN CSBt CWCL EHea EPfP
                          LRHS MBar MBri MGos NHol SRms
- 'Petra'   EHea
- 'Pewter Plate'   EHea MBar
- 'Pink Beale'   see *C. vulgaris* 'H.E. Beale'
- 'Pink Dream' (d)   EHea
- 'Pink Gown'   EHea
- 'Pink Spreader'   EHea
- 'Pink Tips'   EHea
- 'Plantarium'   EHea
- 'Platt's Surprise' (d) EHea
- 'Polly'   EHea
- 'Poolster'   EHea
- 'Porth Wen White'   EHea
- 'Prizewinner'   EHea
- 'Prostrata Flagelliformis' EHea
- 'Prostrate Orange'   CNCN EHea ESis MBar
- 'Punch's Dessert'   EHea
- 'Purple Passion' **new** EPfP
- 'Pygmaea'   EHea MBar
- 'Pyramidalis'   EHea LRHS
- 'Pyrenaica'   EHea MBar
- 'Quail' **new**   EHea
- 'R.A. McEwan'   EHea
- 'Radnor' (d) ♀H4   CBcs CNCN CSBt EHea LRHS
                          MBar NBlu
- 'Radnor Gold' (d)   EHea MBar
- 'Raket'   EHea
- 'Ralph Purnell'   CNCN EHea MBar
- 'Ralph Purnell Select' EHea
- 'Ralph's Pearl'   EHea
- 'Ralph's Red'   EHea
- 'Randall's Crimson'   EHea
- 'Rannoch'   EHea
- 'Rebecca's Red' **new** EHea
- 'Red Carpet'   CNCN EHea LRHS MBar
- 'Red Favorit' (d)   CBcs EHea LRHS
- 'Red Fred'   EDAr EHea NHol SCoo
- 'Red Haze'   CBrm CNCN EHea EPfP LRHS
                          MBar NHol WStI
- 'Red Max'   EHea
- 'Red Pimpernel'   CNCN EHea EPfP MBar NHol
- 'Red Rug'   EHea
- 'Red Star' (d)   CNCN EHea LRHS MBar NHol
- 'Red Wings'   EHea
- 'Redbud'   EHea
- 'Redgauntlet'   EHea
- 'Reini'   EHea NHol
- 'Rica'   EHea
- 'Richard Cooper'   EHea MBar
- 'Rieanne'   EHea

- 'Rigida Prostrata'   see *C. vulgaris* 'Alba Rigida'
- 'Rivington'   EHea
- 'Robber Knight'   EHea
- 'Robert Chapman' ♀H4   CBrm CNCN CSBt CTri EBre EHea
                          GKir LRHS MBar MBri NHol
- 'Rock Spray'   EHea
- 'Röding' **new**   EHea
- 'Rokoko' **new**   EHea
- 'Roland Haagen' ♀H4   EHea ESis MBar
- 'Roma'   EHea LRHS MBar
- 'Romina'   CNCN EHea MSwo NHol
- 'Ronas Hill'   CNCN EHea
- 'Roodkapje'   EHea
- 'Rosalind' ambig.   CNCN CSBt EPfP LRHS MBar NHol
- 'Rosalind,   EHea
  Crastock Heath'
- 'Rosalind, Underwood's' EHea LRHS
- 'Ross Hutton'   EHea
- 'Roswitha'   EHea
§ - 'Roter Oktober'   EHea
- 'Rotfuchs'   EHea
- 'Ruby Slinger'   CNCN EHea LRHS MBar
- 'Rusty Triumph'   EHea
- 'Ruth Sparkes' (d)   CNCN EHea LRHS MBar NHol
- 'Sabrina' (d)   EHea
- 'Saima'   EHea
- 'Saint Nick'   EHea MBar
- 'Salland'   EHea
- 'Sally Anne Proudley'   CNCN EHea MBar
- 'Salmon Leap'   CBrm EHea MBar NHol
- 'Sam Hewitt'   EHea
- 'Sampford Sunset'   CSam EHea
- 'Sandhammaren'   EHea
- 'Sandwood Bay'   EHea
- 'Sandy' PBR   EHea
- 'Sarah Platt' (d)   EHea
- 'Saskia'   EHea
- 'Scaynes Hill'   EHea
- 'Scholje's Jimmy' **new** EHea
- 'Scholje's Rubin' (d)   EHea
- 'Scholje's Super   EHea
  Star' (d) **new**
- 'Schurig's Sensation' (d) CNCN EHea LRHS MBar MBri
- 'Schurig's Wonder' (d) EHea
- 'Scotch Mist'   EHea
- 'Sedloňov'   EHea
- 'Sellingsloh'   EHea
- 'September Pink'   EHea
- 'Serlei'   EDAr EHea LRHS MBar
- 'Serlei Aurea' ♀H4   CNCN CSBt EDAr EHea LRHS
                          MBar NHol
- 'Serlei Grandiflora'   EHea MBar
- 'Serlei Purpurea'   EHea
- 'Serlei Rubra'   EHea
- 'Sesam'   EHea
- 'Sesse'   EHea
- 'Shirley'   EHea MBar
I - 'Silberspargel'   EHea
- 'Silver Cloud'   CNCN EHea MBar
- 'Silver Fox'   EHea
- 'Silver King'   CNCN EHea LRHS MBar
- 'Silver Knight'   CNCN CSBt EDAr EHea EPfP GKir
                          LRHS MBar MBri MGos NHol SPlb
                          WStI
- 'Silver Pearl' **new** EHea
- 'Silver Queen' ♀H4   CNCN EHea GKir LRHS MBar MBri
                          NHol SRms
- 'Silver Rose' ♀H4   CNCN EHea LRHS MBar
- 'Silver Sandra'   EHea
- 'Silver Spire'   CNCN EHea MBar
- 'Silver Stream'   EHea LRHS MBar
- 'Silver White' **new** EHea
- 'Silvie' **new**   EHea
- 'Simone'   EHea

- 'Sir Anthony Hopkins'	EHea
- 'Sir John Charrington' ♀H4	CBcs CNCN CSBt EBre EHea EPfP ESis GKir LRHS MBar MBri MGos NHol WStI
- 'Sirsson'	EHea MBar MBri
- 'Sister Anne' ♀H4	CNCN CSBt EBre EHea EPfP LRHS MBri NBlu NDlv NHol SRms
- 'Skipper'	EHea MBar
- 'Skone' (v)	EHea
- 'Snowball'	see *C. vulgaris* 'My Dream'
- 'Snowflake'	EHea
- 'Soay'	EHea MBar
- 'Sonja' (d)	EHea
- 'Sonning' (d)	EHea
- 'Sonny Boy'	EHea
- 'Sophia' (d)	EHea
- 'Sparkling Stars'	EHea
- 'Spicata'	EHea
- 'Spicata Aurea'	CNCN EHea MBar
- 'Spicata Nana'	EHea
- 'Spider'	EHea
- 'Spitfire'	CNCN EHea ESis LRHS MBar NHol WStI
- 'Spook'	EHea
- 'Spring Cream' ♀H4	CBcs CNCN EBre EDAr EHea GKir LRHS MBar MBri NBlu NHol WStI
- 'Spring Glow'	CNCN EHea LRHS MBar MBri
- 'Spring Torch'	CBcs CNCN CWCL EBre EHea GKir LRHS MBar MBri NHol SCoo WStI
- 'Springbank'	EHea MBar
- 'Stag's Horn'	EHea
I - 'Startler'	EHea
- 'Stefanie'	EHea
- 'Stranger'	EHea
- 'Strawberry Delight' (d)	EDAr EHea EPfP NHol
- 'Summer Elegance'	EHea
- 'Summer Orange'	CNCN CSBt EHea LRHS MBar NHol
- 'Summer White' (d)	EHea
- 'Sunningdale'	see *C. vulgaris* 'Finale'
- 'Sunrise'	CNCN CSBt EHea LRHS MBar MGos NBlu NHol WStI
- 'Sunset' ♀H4	CBrm CNCN CSBt EHea LRHS MBar NHol SRms WStI
- 'Sunset Glow'	EHea
- 'Talisker'	EHea
- 'Tenella'	EHea
- 'Tenuis'	EHea MBar
- 'Terrick's Orange'	EHea
- 'The Pygmy'	EHea
- 'Tib' (d) ♀H4	CSBt EHea LRHS MBar MBri NBlu NDlv SRms WStI
- 'Tijdens Copper'	EHea
- 'Tino'	EHea
- 'Tom Thumb'	EHea MBar
- 'Tom's Fancy'	EHea
- 'Torogay'	EHea
- 'Torulosa'	EHea
- 'Tremans'	EHea
- 'Tricolorifolia'	CNCN EHea GKir LRHS NBlu NHol
- 'Underwoodii'	EHea LRHS MBar
- 'Unity'	EHea
- 'Valorian'	EHea
- 'Van Beek'	EHea
§ - 'Velvet Dome'	EHea LRHS MBar
- 'Velvet Fascination' ♀H4	CBcs CNCN EDAr EHea EPfP GKir LRHS MBar MGos NHol
- 'Violet Bamford'	EHea
- 'Visser's Fancy'	EHea
§ - 'Walter Ingwersen'	EHea
- 'Waquoit Brightness'	EHea

- 'Westerlee Gold'	EHea
- 'Westerlee Green'	EHea
- 'Westphalia'	EHea
- 'White Bouquet'	see *C. vulgaris* 'Alba Plena'
- 'White Carpet'	EHea MBar
- 'White Coral' (d)	EHea MGos
- 'White Gown'	EHea
- 'White Lawn' ♀H4	CNCN EHea LRHS MBar MSwo NBlu NDlv NHol SRms
- 'White Mite'	EHea LRHS MBar
- 'White Pearl' (d)	EHea
- 'White Princess'	see *C. vulgaris* 'White Queen'
§ - 'White Queen'	EHea MBar
- 'White Star' (d)	EHea LRHS
- 'Whiteness'	CNCN EHea
- 'Wickwar Flame' ♀H4	CBcs CBrm CNCN CSBt EHea EPAt EPfP LRHS MBar MBri MGos NBlu NHol SPlb WStI
- 'Wilma'	EHea
- 'Wingates Gem'	EHea
- 'Wingates Gold'	EHea
- 'Winter Chocolate'	CNCN CSBt EHea EPfP LRHS MBar MBri MSwo NDlv NHol WStI
- 'Winter Fire'	EHea
- 'Winter Red'	EHea
- 'Wollmer's Weisse' (d)	EHea
- 'Wood Close'	EHea
- 'Yellow Basket'	EHea
- 'Yellow Dome'	CNCN
- 'Yellow Globe'	EHea
- 'Yellow One'	EHea
- 'Yvette's Silver'	EHea
- 'Yvonne Clare'	EHea

Calocedrus (Cupressaceae)

§ *decurrens* ♀H4	CAgr CBcs CDoC CDul CMac CTho CTri EHul ENot EOrn EPfP GKir LCon LPan LRHS MBar MBlu MBri MGos NWea SLim WEve
- 'Aureovariegata' (v)	CDoC CKen EBre EHul LCon LPan LRHS MAsh MBar MBlu MBri NLar SLim WEve
- 'Berrima Gold'	CKen EBre ENot EPfP GKir LRHS MAsh MGos SLim WEve
§ - 'Depressa'	CKen
- 'Intricata'	CKen
- 'Nana'	see *C. decurrens* 'Depressa'
- 'Pillar'	CKen GTSp
macrolepis	EMon ISea

Calocephalus (Asteraceae)

brownii	see *Leucophyta brownii*

Calochortus (Liliaceae)

albus var. *rubellus*	ECho LAma
argillosus J&JA 1151500	CPBP
barbatus	EPot NWCA
luteus	EPot LAma WCot WLin
- 'Golden Orb' PBR	CBro CStu EChP ECho LRHS
luteus × *superbus* **new**	WCot
obispoensis	EPot
plummerae JA 94-104	EHyt
splendens	LAma
- 'Violet Queen'	CBro
striatus JA 93-21	EHyt
superbus	CBro EChP ECho EHyt EPot LRHS WGMN
tolmiei	EHyt
- JCA 1.178.020	WCot
umpquaensis	EHyt
uniflorus	EHyt EPot WCot
venustus	CBro EChP EHyt EPot GFlt LAma LRHS WCot WGMN WLin
vestae	EHyt WCot

Calomeria (Asteraceae)
§   **amaranthoides**   WJek

Calonyction see *Ipomoea*

Calopogon (Orchidaceae)
    tuberosus   SSpi

Calopsis (Restionaceae)
    paniculata   CBig CPne CTrC IArd WMul

Caloscordum (Alliaceae)
§   **neriniflorum**   EBur WAbe

Calothamnus (Myrtaceae)
    blepharospermus   SOWG
    gilesii   SOWG
    homolophyllus   SOWG
    quadrifidus   SOWG
    - yellow-flowered   SOWG
    rupestris   SOWG
    sanguineus   SOWG
    validus   CPLG SOWG SPlb

Caltha ✿ (Ranunculaceae)
    'Auenwald'   CLAP CRow SSpi
    'Honeydew'   CLAP CRow GBuc
    introloba   SWat
    laeta   see *C. palustris* var. *palustris*
    leptosepala   CLAP CRow EBee NWCA
    natans   CRow EBee
    palustris ♀H4   More than 30 suppliers
    - var. **alba**   More than 30 suppliers
    - **barthei**   CFir EBee SSpi
    - 'Flore Pleno' (d) ♀H4   More than 30 suppliers
    - var. **himalensis**   EBee ITim WCot WWpP
    - 'Marilyn'   CLAP GBuc
    - 'Multiplex' (d)   COtt EBee GBuc
§   - var. **palustris**   CBen CBre CRow ECha EHon
                               ELan EMFW EMon EPar EWTr
                               GGar LPBA MSta NArg SLon SMad
                               SSpi SWat WCra WFar WMAq
                               WWpP
    - - 'Plena' (d)   COIW CRow CSam CWat ENot
                               EPfP LNCo LRHS SMac WFar
                               WMAq
    - var. **polypetala**   CDWL LNCo NPer
    - var. **radicans**   CRow GCrs SSpi
    - - 'Flore Pleno' (d)   CRow
    - 'Semiplena' (d)   EMon
    - 'Stagnalis'   CRow WWpP
    - Trotter's form   GBuc
    - 'Tyermannii'   CRow
    - 'Yellow Giant'   CDWL SLon
N   **polypetala** hort.   see *C. palustris* var. *palustris*
N   **polypetala** Hochst.   CLAP CWat EBee EWll GBuc
                               LNCo
    sagittata   CLAP CRow
    - JCA 2.198.200   SSpi
    scaposa   EBee
    'Susan'   CRow

Calycanthus (Calycanthaceae)
    fertilis   see *C. floridus* var. *glaucus*
    - 'Purpureus'   see *C. floridus* var. *glaucus*
                               'Purpureus'
    floridus   CAgr CArn CBcs CDul CFil CFwr
                               CMCN CPMA CPle CTho CWib
                               EBee ECrN ELan EPfP EWTr IDee
                               LAst LEdu LRHS MBNS MBlu
                               MDun SDnm SMur SPer WBod
                               WDin WWin
*   - **ferox** **new**   NLar

§   - var. **glaucus**   CFil CPle EPfP LBuc MGos NBlu
                               NLar WSHC
§   - - 'Purpureus'   CPMA MBlu NLar WBcn
    - var. **laevigatus**   see *C. floridus* var. *glaucus*
    occidentalis   CAgr CArn CBcs CFil CMCN CPle
                               CWib ECrN EMil EPfP IDee MBlu
                               SIgm SMur SSpi WBVN WCot

Calydorea (Iridaceae)
    speciosa   see *C. xiphioides*
§   **xiphioides**   EWes

Calylophus (Onagraceae)
    serrulatus   SMad

Calystegia (Convolvulaceae)
    collina subsp. **venusta**   EMan WCot
§   **hederacea**   CFwr EBee EChP ECha ELan EMon
    'Flore Pleno' (d)   EOrc EPar MCCP MTho NLar NSti
                               SMad SSvw WCot WFar WHer
                               WShp
    japonica 'Flore Pleno' see *C. hederacea* 'Flore Pleno'
    macrostegia   EMan WCot
        subsp. **cyclostegia**
    silvatica 'Incarnata' EBee EMon EOrc EWes
    soldanella **new**   XPep
    - NNS 99-85   EBee WCot

Calytrix (Myrtaceae)
§   **alpestris**   SOWG
    fraseri **new**   SOWG
    longiflora   SOWG
        yellow-flowered
    sullivanii   SOWG
    tetragona   SPlb
    - compact, pink   SOWG

Camassia ✿ (Hyacinthaceae)
    biflora   EBee
    - F&W 8669   WCot
    cusickii   More than 30 suppliers
    - 'Zwanenburg'   EBee LRHS WCot WDav
    esculenta   see *C. quamash*
    fraseri   see *C. scilloides*
    howellii **new**   EBee
    leichtlinii misapplied see *C. leichtlinii* subsp. *suksdorfii*
    leichtlinii   ISea SSto
        (Bak.) S.Wats. **new**
N   - 'Alba' hort.   see *C. leichtlinii* subsp. *leichtlinii*
*   - 'Alba Plena'   NBir
    - 'Blauwe Donau'   see *C. leichtlinii* subsp. *suksdorfii*
                               'Blauwe Donau'
    - Blue Danube   see *C. leichtlinii* subsp. *suksdorfii*
                               'Blauwe Donau'
§   - subsp. **leichtlinii** ♀H4   More than 30 suppliers
N   - 'Plena' (d)   ECha MSte WCom
    - 'Semiplena' (d)   CAvo CBro CFai CFwr CMea CMil
                               EBee EChP EMan EMon EPar EPot
                               GEdr MSte NMen SAga WAul WCot
                               WDav WPnP WPrP
    - subsp. **suksdorfii**   CAvo CBri EPPr EPar EWTr GBBs
                               GBuc LRHS MSph NBPC SCro
                               WAul WHil
§   - - 'Blauwe Donau'   LAma LRHS WDav
    - - Caerulea Group   More than 30 suppliers
    - - 'Electra'   ECha LPio SMHy
§   **quamash**   More than 30 suppliers
    - 'Blue Melody' (v)   CBro CFwr CHid CMea EBee EBlw
                               EMan EMar EMon EPPr EPot GBuc
                               GMac LRHS MAvo MBNS NMen
                               WCot WPnP
    - 'Orion'   CBro CMea EBee EMon GBuc
                               GMac MAvo WCot WPrP
§   **scilloides**   EBee MBri WCot

Camellia ✿ (Theaceae)

'Auburn White'	see *C. japonica* 'Mrs Bertha A. Harms'
'Barbara Clark' (*saluenensis* x *reticulata*)	CTrG MAsh MBri MGos SCog WCwm WWeb
'Barbara Hillier' x *japonica* 'Juno'	CDoC
'Bertha Harms Blush'	see *C. japonica* 'Mrs Bertha A. Harms'
'Black Lace' (*reticulata* x *williamsii*) ♀H4	CBrm CDoC CTrh CTri MAsh MBri SCam SCog SPer SPoG WBVN WBcn WGwG WMoo WWeb
'Bonnie Marie' (hybrid)	CBcs SCam SCog
brevistyla **new**	CBcs
'Charles Cobb'	see *C. japonica* 'Mrs Charles Cobb'
* 'Chatsworth Belle' **new**	CTrh
'China Lady' (*reticulata* x *granthamiana*)	MBri
'Cinnamon Cindy' (hybrid)	SCog
'Contessa Lavinia Maggi'	see *C. japonica* 'Lavinia Maggi'
* 'Cornish Clay'	ISea
'Cornish Snow' (*cuspidata* x *saluenensis*) ♀H4	CDoC CSBt CSam CTrh EPfP LHyd MGos SCam SCog SHBN SReu SSpi SSta WFar WPGP
'Cornish Spring' (*japonica* x *cuspidata*) ♀H4	CBcs CDoC CSBt CTrh EPfP LHyd SCog WBcn WCot
'Corsica'	SHBN
cuspidata	LHyd
'Czar'	see *C. japonica* 'The Czar'
'Dainty Dale' (hybrid)	SCam
'Delia Williams'	see *C.* x *williamsii* 'Citation'
'Diana's Charm' **new**	CDoC
'Doctor Clifford Parks' (*reticulata* x *japonica*) ♀H2	LHyd SCog
'Donckelaeri'	see *C. japonica* 'Masayoshi'
'El Dorado' (*pitardii* x *japonica*)	CTrG
'Extravaganza' (*japonica* hybrid)	CBcs CTrh IArd MBri SBod SCog WBcn
'Felice Harris' (*sasanqua* x *reticulata*)	MBri SCog
'Fire 'n' Ice'	CDoC SCog
'Forty-niner' (*reticulata* x *japonica*)	CBcs CDoC SCog
'Fragrant Pink' (*rusticana* x *lutchuensis*)	CTrh WBcn
'Francie L' (*saluenensis* x *reticulata*) ♀H3-4	CDoC CTrh EPfP LHyd SCam SCog SSta
'Frau Minna Seidel'	see *C. japonica* 'Otome'
'Freedom Bell' (hybrid) ♀H4	CCtw CDoC CTrG CTrh GGGa ISea LHyd MAsh MBri SCam SCog WBcn
'Gay Baby' (hybrid)	MGos
'Golden Aniversary' **new**	SPer
grijsii	CTrh LHyd
handelii **new**	CBcs
§ *hiemalis* 'Bonanza' **new**	CTrh SCam
- 'Chansonette'	SCam
§ - 'Dazzler'	CDoC CPLG CSBt LHyd SCam SCog
- 'Kanjirô'	CTrh LHyd SCam
- 'Showa Supreme' **new**	SCam
§ - 'Sparkling Burgundy' ♀H3	CBcs CBrm CDoC LHyd SCam SCog
'Hooker' (hybrid)	CDoC
'Howard Asper' (*reticulata* x *japonica*)	SCam
'Ice Follies'	SCog
'Imbricata Rubra'	see *C. japonica* 'Imbricata'

'Innovation' (x *williamsii* x *reticulata*)	CBcs ISea MBri WWeb
'Inspiration' (*reticulata* [4] x *saluenensis*) ♀H	CBcs CDoC CMHG CMac CSBt CTrG CTrh CWSG EPfP GGGa GKir ISea LHyd MAsh MBri MGos SBod SCam SCog SHBN SSpi WBod
japonica 'Aaron's Ruby'	CBcs COtt
- 'Ace of Hearts' **new**	MBri
- 'Ada Pieper'	CTrh
- 'Adelina Patti' ♀H4	CBcs CCtw CTrh LHyd SCog WCwm
- 'Adolphe Audusson' ♀H4	More than 30 suppliers
- 'Adolphe Audusson Special'	CBcs
§ - 'Akashigata' ♀H4	CDoC CHEx CTrG CTrw ENot EPfP SCam SCog SSta WBod WCot WCwm WWeb
§ - 'Akebono'	CTrw MBri
- 'Alba Plena' ♀H4	CTrh CWSG ENot LHyd SBod SCam SCog WFar
- 'Alba Simplex'	CBcs CMac ELan EPfP SBod SCam SCog SHBN SMer SPer SSpi SSta WStI
- 'Alexander Hunter' ♀H4	LHyd SBod SCam SCog WWeb
- 'Alexis Smith' **new**	CBcs
§ - 'Althaeiflora'	CBcs CDoC SCam
- 'Ama-no-gawa'	LHyd
- 'Anemoniflora'	CBcs CDoC CTrG ELan SCam WBod WFar
- 'Angel'	CBcs SCam SCog
- 'Angela Cocchi'	MBri WBod
- 'Ann Sothern'	CTrh
- 'Annette Gehry'	CBcs
- 'Annie Wylam' ♀H4	CTrh LHyd SCog
I - 'Apollo' Paul	CBcs CDoC CSam CTrG CTrh EPfP MAsh MGos MSwo SCam SCog SHBN WBcn WBod
§ - 'Apple Blossom' ♀H4	CBcs CMac ELan MAsh WBod
- 'Arajishii'	see *C. rusticana* 'Arajishi'
* - 'Augustine Supreme'	CMac
- 'Augusto Leal de Gouveia Pinto'	WBod
- 'Australis' ♀H4	CTrh
- 'Ave Maria' ♀H4	CBrm CDoC CTrh
- 'Ballet Dancer' ♀H4	MGos SCam SCog WBcn WGwG
- 'Baron Gomer'	see *C. japonica* 'Comte de Gomer'
- 'Baronne Leguay'	SCam
- 'Beau Harp'	SCam
- 'Bella Romana'	SCam
- 'Benidaikagura'	SCam
- 'Benten' (v)	CTrG CTrw
- 'Berenice Boddy' ♀H4	CBcs CDoC CTrh MBri SCam
- 'Berenice Perfection'	LHyd LRHS MBri WFar
- 'Betty Foy Sanders'	CTrh
- 'Betty Sheffield'	CDoC COtt CTrG MDun MGos SCog SHBN WFar
- 'Betty Sheffield Pink'	CTrG SCam
- 'Betty Sheffield Supreme'	CBcs
- 'Billie McCaskill'	SCam
- 'Black Tie'	LHyd SCog
- 'Blackburnia'	see *C. japonica* 'Althaeiflora'
- 'Blaze of Glory'	CTrh SCog WBcn
§ - 'Blood of China'	CBcs CDoC CSBt CWSG LRHS MAsh MBri SBod SCam SCog SPer WBod WCwm
- 'Bob Hope' ♀H4	CBcs CDul CTrh LRHS MGos
- 'Bob's Tinsie' ♀H4	CDoC CSBt CTbh CTrw EPfP GBin ISea LRHS MBri SCam
§ - 'Bokuhan' ♀H4	CCtw CDoC EPfP SCog
- 'Bright Buoy'	CDoC
- 'Brushfield's Yellow' ♀H4	CBcs CDoC CMHG COtt CSBt EPfP GKir IArd IMGH LHyd MBri MDun MGos SCam SCog SPer SSta WFar

- 'Bush Hill Beauty' — see *C. japonica* 'Lady de Saumarez'
§ - 'C.M. Hovey' ♀H4 — CMHG CMac CTrh EPfP MAsh SCam SHBN WBcn WBod WGwG WWeb
- 'C.M. Wilson' — CMac SCog WBod
N - 'Campbellii' — CDoC
- 'Campsii Alba' — LRHS SMer WStI
- 'Can Can' — CBcs CTrG SCam SCog
- 'Canon Boscawen' — CTrG
- 'Cara Mia' — SCam
- 'Carter's Sunburst' ♀H4 — CBcs CTrh EPfP SCam SCog
- 'Chandleri Elegans' — see *C. japonica* 'Elegans'
- 'Charlotte de Rothschild' — CTrh CTri
- 'Cheryll Lynn' — CTrh
- 'Christmas Beauty' — SCam WBod
- 'Cinderella' — SCam SCog
- 'Clarise Carleton' — CTrh GGGa LHyd
- 'Clarissa' — SCam
§ - 'Coccinea' — LRHS
- 'Colonel Firey' — see *C. japonica* 'C.M. Hovey'
- 'Commander Mulroy' ♀H4 — CTrh MBri WBcn
- 'Compton's Brow' — see *C. japonica* 'Gauntlettii'
- 'Comte de Gomer' — ELan EPfP LRHS SCam WBcn
- 'Conspicua' — CBcs
§ - 'Coquettii' ♀H4 — CBcs CDoC SCam WWeb
- 'Coral Beauty' **new** — WFar
- 'Coral Pink Lotus' — SCam
- 'Coral Queen' — SCam
- 'Countess of Orkney' **new** — WBcn
- 'Dahlohnega' — CTrh
- 'Daikagura' — CBcs
- 'Dainty' — CBcs WBcn
- 'Daitairin' — see *C. japonica* 'Dewatairin'
- 'Dear Jenny' — CBcs CTrG MBri SCog
- 'Debbie' — CDoC EHol WGwG
- 'Debutante' — CBcs CDoC CMac CTrh LHyd LRHS MAsh MBri SCam WBcn WBod
- 'Desire' ♀H4 — CBcs CDoC CMHG CTrh MBri MDun SCam SPoG WWeb
- 'Devonia' — CBcs EPfP LHyd LRHS SCog
§ - 'Dewatairin' (Higo) — CMac SCam SCog
- 'Dixie Knight' — LRHS MGos SCam SCog SSta
- 'Dobreei' — CMac
- 'Doctor Burnside' — CBcs CMHG CTrh SCog
- 'Doctor Olga Petersen' **new** — SCog
- 'Doctor Tinsley' ♀H4 — CDoC CTrh LRHS MDun SCam WBcn WWeb
- 'Dona Herzilia de Freitas Magalhaes' — SCam WBcn
- 'Dona Jane Andresson' — SCam
- 'Donckelaeri' — see *C. japonica* 'Masayoshi'
- 'Donnan's Dream' — CTrh
- 'Double Rose' (d) — SCog
- 'Drama Girl' ♀H2 — CBcs CDoC CTrw SBod SCam SCog WBod
- 'Dream Time' — CBcs
- 'Duc de Bretagne' — ISea SCog
- 'Duchesse Decazes' — CBcs MBri
- 'Edelweiss' — MGos SCam SCog
- 'Effendee' — see *C. sasanqua* 'Rosea Plena'
- 'Eleanor Hagood' — CBcs WBcn
§ - 'Elegans' ♀H4 — CBcs CDoC CMac CTrG ENot EPfP ISea LRHS MAsh SBod SCam SCog SHBN SPer SReu SSta WBcn
- 'Elegans Champagne' — CTrh WBcn
- 'Elegans Splendor' — MBri WBcn
- 'Elegant Beauty' — see *C. x williamsii* 'Elegant Beauty'
- 'Elisabeth' — WFar
- 'Elizabeth Dowd' — CBcs SCog
- 'Elizabeth Hawkins' — CTrh LHyd MAsh MBri

- 'Ella Drayton' — SCog
- 'Emmett Barnes' — LHyd MBri SCam
- 'Emmett Pfingstl' — SCam WBcn
- 'Emperor of Russia' — LHyd LRHS WBod
- 'Erin Farmer' — CBcs
- 'Eugène Lizé' — SCam
- 'Evelyn' — SCam
- 'Fanny' **new** — SCam
- 'Fashionata' — SCam
- 'Feast Perfection' — CDoC
§ - 'Fimbriata' — SCam
- 'Fimbriata Alba' — see *C. japonica* 'Fimbriata'
- 'Finlandia Variegated' — SCam SCog
- 'Fire Dance' — CTrh
- 'Flame' — CBcs WBod
- 'Flashlight' — EPfP
§ - 'Fleur Dipater' — MBri SCam
- 'Flora' — WBod
- 'Flowerwood' — SCam SCog WFar
- 'Forest Green' — ELan LRHS MAsh
- 'Fortune Teller' — CDoC
- 'Fred Sander' — CBcs CWSG SCam SCog SMer
- 'Frosty Morn' — CBcs
- 'Furo-an' — MAsh SCam
§ - 'Gauntlettii' — CBcs SCam
- 'Geisha Girl' — SCam SCog
- 'Général Lamoricière' — WWeb
§ - 'Gigantea' — SCam
- 'Giuditta Rosani' — CDoC
- 'Giuseppina Pieri' **new** — LHyd
- 'Gladys Wannamaker' — SCog
- 'Glen 40' — see *C. japonica* 'Coquettii'
- 'Gloire de Nantes' ♀H4 — CBcs SCam SCog WBcn WBod
- 'Gold Tone' — SCam
* - 'Golden Wedding' (v) — LRHS MAsh
- 'Grace Bunton' — CBcs SCam SCog
- 'Granada' — SCog
- 'Grand Prix' ♀H4 — CDoC CTrh CTrw LHyd LRHS SCam SCog
- 'Grand Slam' ♀H2 — CBcs CBrm CDoC CMac CTrh EPfP LRHS MAsh MBri SCam SCog WBcn
- 'Guest of Honor' — CBcs
- 'Guilio Nuccio' ♀H4 — CBcs CDoC CTrG EPfP IArd LRHS MBri MGos SCam SCog SMer SPer WBod
- 'Gus Menard' — SCam
- 'Gwenneth Morey' — CBcs EPfP SCam
- 'H.A. Downing' — SCam
§ - 'Hagoromo' ♀H4 — CDoC CTrh ELan ENot EPfP LRHS SCam SCog SHBN SPer WBcn WBod WFar
§ - 'Hakurakuten' ♀H4 — CTrh IArd ISea MBri SBod SCam SCog
- 'Hanafûki' — SCam SCog
- 'Hanatachibana' — SCam WBcn
- 'Hatsuzakura' — see *C. japonica* 'Dewatairin'
- 'Hawaii' — CBcs CDoC CSBt CTrh LRHS SCam SCog
- Herme — see *C. japonica* 'Hikarugenji'
- 'High Hat' — CBcs LHyd
§ - 'Hikarugenji' — SCog
- 'Hinomaru' — CMac LRHS
- 'Holly Bright' — CTrh
- 'Huricotome' **new** — SCam
§ - 'Imbricata' — ENot ISea MAsh MGos SCog
§ - 'Incarnata' **new** — SCam
- 'Italiana Vera' — MAsh
- 'J.J. Whitfield' — CMac
- 'Jack Jones Scented' — CMHG
- 'Janet Waterhouse' — CBcs WFar
§ - 'Japonica Variegata' (v) — CMHG WBcn
- 'Jean Clere' — CTrG MGos SCog WBcn
- 'John Tooley' **new** — LBuc

	- 'Joseph Pfingstl' ♀H4	MAsh MBri SCam WWeb
	- 'Joshua E.Youtz'	LHyd LRHS SCam SCog
	- 'Jovey Carlyon' (hybrid)	CDoC WWeb
	- 'Joy Sander'	see *C. japonica* 'Apple Blossom'
§	- 'Julia Drayton'	LRHS
	- 'Julia France'	SCog
	- 'Juno'	CBcs SCam
I	- 'Jupiter' Paul ♀H4	CBcs CDoC CDul CMac CTrh CTri CTrw EPfP ISea LHyd MAsh MGos SCog SHBN WBVN WBod
	- 'Justine Heurtin'	SCam
§	- 'K. Sawada'	SCam SCog
	- 'Katie'	SCog
	- 'Kellingtoniana'	see *C. japonica* 'Gigantea'
	- 'Kenny'	CBcs
	- 'Kentucky' **new**	SCam
	- 'Kewpie Doll'	CTrh
	- 'Kick-off'	CBcs CTrh MBri WBcn
	- 'Kimberley'	CBcs CDoC EPfP MBri SCog WBcn WBod
	- 'King's Ransom'	CMac MAsh MBri
§	- 'Kingyo-tsubaki'	SSta WBod
	- 'Kitty Berry'	CTrh
	- 'Kokinran'	SCam
§	- 'Konronkoku' ♀H4	CCtw CDoC CTrh SCam SCog WBcn WBod
	- 'Kouron-jura'	see *C. japonica* 'Konronkoku'
	- 'Kramer's Beauty'	SCog
	- 'Kramer's Supreme'	CDoC CTrG CWSG MDun MGos SBod SCam SCog WFar
	- 'La Graciola'	see *C. japonica* 'Odoratissima'
	- 'La Pace Rubra'	SCam
	- 'Lady Campbell'	CTri SCam
	- 'Lady Clare'	see *C. japonica* 'Akashigata'
§	- 'Lady de Saumarez'	CDoC
	- 'Lady Erma' **new**	CBcs
	- 'Lady Loch'	CTrh MBri MGos
	- 'Lady McCulloch'	SCam
	- 'Lady Vansittart'	CBcs CBrm CDoC CSam CTrG EBee ELan ENot EPfP ISea LHyd LRHS MAsh SCog SPer WBcn WBod WWeb
§	- 'Lady Vansittart Pink'	MGos SCam SHBN
	- 'Lady Vansittart Red'	see *C. japonica* 'Lady Vansittart Pink'
	- 'Lady Vansittart Shell'	see *C. japonica* 'Yours Truly'
	- 'Latifolia'	SCam
	- 'Laurie Bray'	MBri WFar
§	- 'Lavinia Maggi' ♀H4	CTrG CTrh ELan EPfP LHyd LPan LRHS MAsh MBri MGos SBod SCam SCog SHBN SMer SPer SReu SRms SSta WBVN WWeb
	- 'Lavinia Maggi Rosea'	SCam
§	- 'Le Lys'	SCam
	- 'Lemon Drop'	CTrh
	- 'Lily Pons' ♀H4	CDoC CTrh LHyd MBri WBcn
	- 'Lipstick'	CTrh LHyd
	- 'Little Bit'	CBcs CDoC CTrh SCam SPer
	- 'Lotus'	see *C. japonica* 'Gauntlettii'
	- 'Lovelight' ♀H4	CTrh ISea
	- 'Lulu Belle'	SCog
	- 'Ma Belle'	CMHG
	- 'Mabel Blackwell'	SCam
	- 'Madame de Strekaloff'	CMac SCam
	- 'Madame Lebois'	CBcs SCam
	- 'Madame Martin Cachet'	CMHG SCog
	- 'Madge Miller'	LRHS
	- 'Magnoliiflora'	see *C. japonica* 'Hagoromo'
	- 'Magnoliiflora Alba'	see *C. japonica* 'Miyakodori'
	- 'Maiden's Blush'	CDoC CMac
	- 'Man Size'	CDoC
	- 'Margaret Davis'	CDoC CSBt CTrG EBee EPfP IMGH LHyd MAsh MBri MGos SCam WWeb

	- 'Margaret Davis Picotee' ♀H4	CBcs CMHG CTrh CTrw SCog SPer SSta WBcn
	- 'Margaret Rose'	SCam
	- 'Margaret Short'	MBri WWeb
	- 'Margherita Coleoni'	CBcs LHyd SHBN
	- 'Marguérite Gouillon'	ISea LHyd SCam
	- 'Marian Mitchell'	SCam
	- 'Mariana'	SCam
	- 'Mariann'	CTrh
	- 'Marie Bracey'	CBcs SCam
	- 'Marinka'	CBcs
	- 'Marjorie Magnificent'	CDoC LHyd LRHS WWeb
	- 'Maroon and Gold'	WBcn
	- 'Mars' ♀H4	CDoC MGos SCam SCog WWeb
	- 'Mary Costa'	CBcs CTrh WFar
	- 'Mary J.Wheeler'	CTrw
§	- 'Masayoshi' ♀H4	CMac CSBt CTrG LHyd MBri SCog WBod
§	- 'Mathotiana'	LRHS MBri
	- 'Mathotiana Alba' ♀H4	CBcs CDoC CMac CSBt EPfP LRHS NBlu SCam SCog SPer
	- 'Mathotiana Purple King'	see *C. japonica* 'Julia Drayton'
§	- 'Mathotiana Rosea' ♀H4	CBcs CMac SCam SHBN SPer WBod
	- 'Mathotiana Supreme'	SCam SCog
	- 'Matterhorn'	CTrh LRHS MBri WBcn
	- 'Mattie Cole'	LHyd SCam
	- 'Mattie O'Reilly'	MBri
	- 'Mercury' ♀H4	CBcs CDoC CMac COtt CTrG CWSG GGGa MBri SCog SHBN WBod
	- 'Mercury Variegated'	CMHG
	- 'Midnight'	CBcs CDoC CMHG WFar WWeb
	- 'Midnight Magic'	CTrh
	- 'Midnight Serenade'	CCtw CTrh
	- 'Midsummer's Day'	CBcs
§	- 'Mikenjaku'	CTrG ENot LRHS MAsh SCam SCog
	- 'Minnie Maddern Fiske'	SCam
	- 'Miriam Stevenson'	SCam
	- 'Miss Charleston'	CBcs LHyd MBri SCog
	- 'Miss Lyla'	SCam
	- 'Miss Universe'	CTrh
	- 'Mississippi Beauty'	CTrh
§	- 'Miyakodori'	EPfP LRHS
	- 'Monsieur Faucillon'	CBcs
	- 'Monte Carlo'	CDoC SCam SCog
	- 'Moonlight Bay'	SCog
	- 'Moshe Dayan'	MAsh SMer WWeb
§	- 'Mrs Bertha A. Harms'	SCam
§	- 'Mrs Charles Cobb'	LPan
	- 'Mrs D.W. Davis'	CBcs CTrw EPfP SCam SCog
	- 'Mrs Sander'	see *C. japonica* 'Gauntlettii'
	- 'Mrs William Thompson'	NBlu
I	- 'Mutabilis'	WBcn
	- 'Nagasaki'	see *C. japonica* 'Mikenjaku'
	- 'Nigra'	see *C. japonica* 'Konronkoku'
	- 'Nobilissima'	CBcs CDoC CMac CTrG CTrh CTri ENot EPfP ISea LRHS MAsh SCam SCog SHBN SPer WBcn WFar WWeb
	- 'Nuccio's Cameo'	CDoC CTrh MAsh WWeb
	- 'Nuccio's Gem' ♀H4	CDoC ELan LHyd LRHS SCam SCog SSta
	- 'Nuccio's Jewel' ♀H4	CDoC COtt CTrh CWSG IMGH LHyd LRHS MAsh SCog SPer SPoG WBcn WMoo WWeb
	- 'Nuccio's Pearl'	CBcs CDoC SCam SCog SMer WBcn WBod WMoo WWeb
§	- 'Odoratissima'	CTrG
	- 'Onetia Holland'	CBcs CBrm CDoC CTrw SCam SCog
§	- 'O-niji'	CDoC

- 'Optima' SCog
- 'Optima Rosea' CBcs CTrG ENot WBcn
§ - 'Otome' NBlu WBod
- 'Patricia Ann' CTrh
- 'Paulette Goddard' SCam
- 'Paul's Apollo' see *C. japonica* 'Apollo' Paul
- 'Peachblossom' see *C. japonica* 'Fleur Dipater'
- 'Pearl Harbor' SCam
- 'Pink Champagne' SBod
- 'Pink Clouds' CBcs SCog
- 'Pink Pearl' **new** MBri
- 'Pink Perfection' see *C. japonica* 'Otome'
- 'Preston Rose' CBcs CDoC CPLG WBcn
- 'Primavera' CTrh LHyd SCam SCog
- 'Princess Baciocchi' CBcs SCam
- 'Princess du Mahe' CMac
- 'Professor Sargent' WCwm
- 'Purple Emperor' see *C. japonica* 'Julia Drayton'
- 'R.L. Wheeler' ♀H4 CBcs CDoC CSBt CTrw LHyd
  MAsh MBri SCam SCog WBod
  WWeb
- 'Rafia' SCam
- 'Rainbow' see *C. japonica* 'O-niji'
- 'Red Dandy' SCam SCog
- 'Red Elephant' SCam
- 'Reg Ragland' SCam SCog
- 'Robert Strauss' SCam
- 'Roger Hall' CDoC ISea SCog WCwm
- 'Rôgetsu' SCam
- 'Roman Soldier' CBcs
- 'Rosularis' SCam SCog
- 'Rubescens Major' ♀H4 CBcs ISea LHyd MBri SCam WWeb
- 'Ruddigore' CTrh LRHS MBri
- 'Saint André' CMac MBri
- 'Sally Harrell' SCam
- 'San Dimas' ♀H4 CTrh SCam SCog SSta WBcn
- 'Saturnia' CDoC COtt MBri WWeb
- 'Sawada's Dream' ISea SCog
- 'Scented Red' CCtw SCog
- 'Scentsation' ♀H4 CMHG COtt SCog
- 'Sea Foam' LHyd SCam
- 'Sea Gull' CTrh SCam
- 'Seiji' CMac
- 'Shin-akebono' see *C. japonica* 'Akebono'
§ - 'Shiragiku' MDun SPer WBod
- 'Shiro Chan' SCam WBcn
- 'Shirobotan' CTrG GQui SCam SCog
- 'Shiro-daikagura' see *C. rusticana* 'Shiro-daikagura'
- 'Silver Anniversary' CBcs CBrm CDoC CMHG CSBt
  CTrG CTrh ELan GQui LHyd LRHS
  MAsh MBri MGos SCam SCog SPer
  SReu SSta WBVN WBod WWeb
- 'Silver Moon' see *C. japonica* 'K. Sawada'
- 'Silver Ruffles' SCam
- 'Silver Triumph' MBri
- 'Simeon' SCam
- 'Sleigh Ride' WBcn
- 'Southern Charm' WWeb
- 'Souvenir de CBcs SCam SCog WBod
  Bahuaud-Litou' ♀H4
- 'Spencer's Pink' CBcs CTrw SCam
- 'Splendens Carlyon' WWeb
- 'Spring Fever' SCam
- 'Spring Formal' CTrh
- 'Spring Frill' SCog
- 'Strawberry Blonde' SCog
- 'Sugar Babe' **new** SCog
- 'Susan Stone' **new** MBri
- 'Sweetheart' SCog
- 'Sylva' ♀H4 GGGa SCam SSpi
- 'Sylvia' CMac LRHS WBod
- 'Tammia' COtt EPfP SCam
- 'Tarô'an' CDoC
- 'Teresa Ragland' SCam

§ - 'The Czar' CBcs CTrw ISea SCog
- 'The Mikado' CDoC SCog
- 'Theo's Mini' SCam
- 'Tick Tock Blush' SCam
- 'Tickled Pink' CDoC SCam
- 'Tiffany' CBcs CDoC LHyd LRHS MBri
  SCam SHBN
- 'Tiki' **new** MBri
- 'Tinker Bell' CDoC MBri SCog
- 'Tom Thumb' ♀H4 CMHG CTrh ISea SCog SRms
- 'Tomorrow' CBcs CDoC CTrw LRHS SCam
  SCog
- 'Tomorrow Park Hill' SCog
§ - 'Tomorrow Variegated' SCam
- 'Tomorrow's Dawn' CBcs SCam
- 'Touchdown' SCam
- 'Tregye' CBcs
- 'Trewithen White' CSam
§ - 'Tricolor' ♀H4 CBcs CDoC CMHG CMac CSBt
  CTrh ENot EPfP LHyd SCam SCog
  SHBN WBod WBrE WFar WGwG
  WWeb
- 'Tricolor Red' see *C. japonica* 'Lady de Saumarez'
- 'Twilight' LRHS
- 'Victor de Bisschop' see *C. japonica* 'Le Lys'
- 'Victor Emmanuel' see *C. japonica* 'Blood of China'
- 'Ville de Nantes' CDoC SSta WBcn WBod
- 'Ville de Nantes Red' WBcn
- 'Virginia Carlyon' CBcs CCtw CDoC
- 'Virginia Robinson' MBri SCam
- 'Vittorio Emanuele II' CTrh
- 'Warrior' COtt SCam SCog
- 'White Nun' SCog
- 'White Swan' CMac COtt CSBt MAsh
- 'White Tulip' MBri
- 'Wilamina' ♀H4 CTrh SPoG
- 'Wildfire' SCam
- 'William Bartlett' CTrh MBri
- 'William Honey' CTrh
- 'Winter Cheer' **new** SCog
- 'Wisley White' see *C. japonica* 'Hakurakuten'
§ - 'Yours Truly' CBcs CMac CTrh LHyd LRHS MBri
  MDun SCam WBcn
- 'Yukimi-guruma' WBod
§ - 'Yukishiro' CTrw
'John Tooby' COtt WWeb
'Jury's Yellow' see *C.* x *williamsii* 'Jury's Yellow'
'Lasca Beauty' SCam
  (*reticulata* x *japonica*)
'Lavender Queen' see *C. sasanqua* 'Lavender Queen'
'Leonard Messel' CBcs CDoC CMHG CTrG CTrh
  (*reticulata* ENot EPfP GGGa LHyd NBlu SCam
  x *williamsii*) ♀H4 SCog SHBN SMer SPer SReu
  WCwm WStI
lutchuensis CTrh SCam
'Madame Victor see *C. japonica* 'Le Lys'
  de Bisschop'
§ *maliflora* (d) CBcs
'Maud Messel' SCam
  (x *williamsii*
  x *reticulata*)
'Milo Rowell' **new** SCam
'Nicky Crisp' LHyd
  (*japonica* x *pitardii*)
'Nijinski' CDoC ISea
  (*reticulata* hybrid)
oleifera CSam CTrh NLar SCam SCog WFar
'Paradise Little Liane'PBR CBcs
'Pink Spangles' see *C. japonica* 'Mathotiana Rosea'
pitardii **new** SCog
'Polar Ice' (*oleifera* hybrid) CDoC SCog
'Polyanna' (hybrid) CDoC SCog
'Portuense' see *C. japonica* 'Japonica
  Variegata'

'Quintessence'	SCog
(*japonica*	
x *lutchuensis*)	
reticulata	CTrG
'Arch of Triumph'	
- 'Mary Williams'	CBcs
- 'Miss Tulare'	LHyd
- 'Nuccio's Ruby'	LHyd
- 'William Hertrich'	CBcs
'Royalty' (*japonica*	CBcs CTrG
x *reticulata*) ♀H3	
§ **rusticana** 'Arajishi'	CBcs CDoC CMac COtt SCam
	SCog SCoo WBod
§ - 'Shiro-daikagura'	WBod
saluenensis 'Exbury	CCtw
Trumpet'	
- 'Trewithen Red'	CTrw WBod
'Salutation' (*reticulata*	CBcs ISea SCam SCog WBod
x *saluenensis*)	
sasanqua	CSBt CSam ISea LPan
- 'Baronesa de Soutelinho'	SCam SCog
- 'Ben'	SCog
- 'Bettie Patricia'	SCog
- 'Bonanza'	see *C. hiemalis* 'Bonanza'
- Borde Hill form **new**	SCam
- 'Cleopatra'	LPan
- 'Crimson King' ♀H3	GQui SCam SHBN WBcn
- 'Dazzler'	see *C. hiemalis* 'Dazzler'
- 'Flamingo'	see *C. sasanqua* 'Fukuzutsumi'
- 'Flore Pleno'	see *C. maliflora*
- 'Fragrans'	SCog
- 'Fuji-no-mine'	CTrh
§ - 'Fukuzutsumi'	CSBt CTrG ISea SCam SCog
	WCwm
- 'Gay Sue'	CTrh LHyd SCam
- 'Hugh Evans' ♀H3	CBcs CDoC COtt CTrh CTri LHyd
	SCam SCog SSta WBod
- 'Jean May' ♀H3	CDoC LHyd SCam SCog SSta WBcn
	WBod
- 'Kenkyô'	SCam SCog SSta
§ - 'Lavender Queen'	SCam
* - 'Little Liane'	SCog
- 'Little Pearl'	LHyd
- 'Lucinda'	SCog
- 'Maiden's Blush'	CSBt ISea SCog WFar WSpi
- 'Mignonne'	CTrh
- 'Mine-no-yuki'	SCog
- 'Narumigata'	CBcs CDoC CMac CTbh CTrw
	ENot EPfP LHyd MAsh SCam SCog
	SSta WBod WSHC
- 'Navajo'	CTrh
- 'New Dawn' **new**	SCam
- 'Nyewoods'	CMac
- 'Papaver'	SCam SCog
- 'Paradise Blush'	CBcs SCog
- 'Paradise Glow'	CBcs SCog
- 'Paradise Hilda'	CBcs SCog
- 'Paradise Pearl'	CBcs SCog
- 'Paradise Petite'PBR	SCog
- 'Paradise Venessa'PBR	CBcs SCog
- 'Peach Blossom'	CBcs LHyd
- 'Plantation Pink'	SCam SCog SPer
- 'Rainbow'	CTrG ISea SCam SCog WBcn WBod
	WFar
- 'Rosea'	SCam SSta
§ - 'Rosea Plena'	CBcs CMac CTrw SCog
- 'Sasanqua Rubra'	CMac
- 'Sasanqua Variegata' (v)	SCam SSta
- 'Setsugekka' **new**	SCam
I - 'Shishigashira'	CTrh SCam
- 'Snowflake'	SCam SSta
- 'Sparkling Burgundy'	see *C. hiemalis* 'Sparkling
	Burgundy'
- 'Winter's Snowman'	CDoC CPLG SCam SCog

'Satan's Robe'	CDoC SCam SCog WFar
(*reticulata* hybrid)	
'Scented Sun'	CTrh
'Scentuous' (*japonica*	SCog WBcn
x *lutchuensis*)	
'Sea Shell'	WWeb
'Show Girl' (*sasanqua*	LHyd SBod SCog WBcn WBod
x *reticulata*)	
§ 'Shôwa-wabisuke'	CTrh WBcn
(Wabisuke)	
§ **sinensis**	CTrG EShb GPoy SCam
'Snow Flurry'	CDoC SCam SCog
(*oleifera* hybrid)	
'Splendens'	see *C. japonica* 'Coccinea'
'Spring Festival'	CBcs CDoC CMHG LHyd WMoo
(*cuspidata* hybrid) ♀H4	
'Spring Mist' (*japonica*	CMHG CTrh LHyd SCam
x *lutchuensis*)	
'Swan Lake' (hybrid)	CTrG ISea
'Tarôkaja' (Wabisuke)	SCam
thea	see *C. sinensis*
'Tinsie'	see *C. japonica* 'Bokuhan'
'Tiny Princess'	CBcs
(*japonica* x *fraterna*)	
'Tom Knudsen'	CTrh MBri
(*reticulata*	
x *japonica*) ♀H3	
'Tomorrow Supreme'	see *C. japonica* 'Tomorrow
	Variegated'
transnokoensis	CTrh SCam
'Tricolor Sieboldii'	see *C. japonica* 'Tricolor'
'Tristrem Carlyon'	CBcs CCtw CDoC CTrG SPoG
(*reticulata* hybrid) ♀H4	
tsaii	CPLG
'Usu-ôtome'	see *C. japonica* 'Otome'
'Valley Knudsen'	SCog
(*saluenensis*	
x *reticulata*)	
x **vernalis** 'Hiryû'	SCog
- 'Yuletide'	SCam
x **williamsii**	CBcs CDoC CMHG CSBt CSam
'Anticipation' ♀H4	CTrG CTrh CTrw CWSG ENot
	EPfP GGGa GKir ISea LHyd LRHS
	MAsh MBri MDun MGos MSwo
	SCam SCog SHBN SPer SSpi WBcn
	WBod WFar WWeb
- 'Anticipation Variegated'	GGGa
- 'Ballet Queen'	CBcs CDoC CSBt GKir MGos
	SCam WBod WFar
- 'Ballet Queen Variegated'	SCog SSta
- 'Bartley Number Five'	CMac
- 'Beatrice Michael'	CBcs CMac
- 'Blue Danube'	MBri
- 'Bow Bells'	CDoC CDul CMac CTrh GKir LHyd
	LRHS MAsh SCam
- 'Bowen Bryant' ♀H4	CTrw GGGa SCog
- 'Bridal Gown'	LHyd
- 'Brigadoon' ♀H4	CDoC CMHG CTrG CTrh CTrw
	EPfP GGGa GKir LHyd LRHS MAsh
	MBri MDun MGos SCam SCog
- 'Burncoose'	CBcs
- 'Burncoose	CBcs
Apple Blossom'	
- 'C.F. Coates'	CDoC SSta
- 'Caerhays'	CBcs
- 'Carnation'	MAsh WWeb
- 'Carolyn Williams'	CBcs
- 'Celebration'	CBcs
- 'Charlean'	CDoC SCam
- 'Charles Colbert'	MBri WBcn
- 'Charles Michael'	CBcs
- 'Charles Puddle' **new**	WBod
- 'China Clay' ♀H4	CDoC CTrG EPfP LHyd LRHS SBod
	SCog WBcn WBod

§ – 'Citation'	CBcs CMac CTrw
– 'Clarrie Fawcett'	CDoC
– 'Contribution'	CTrh
– 'Crinkles'	SCam
– 'Daintiness' ♀H4	CDoC LHyd LRHS
– 'Dark Nite'	CMHG
– 'Debbie' ♀H4	More than 30 suppliers
– 'Debbie's Carnation'	CMHG
– 'Donation' ♀H4	More than 30 suppliers
– 'Dream Boat'	CBcs LHyd
– 'E.G.Waterhouse'	CBcs CDoC CMHG CTrG CTrh
	CTri CTrw EPfP GKir LHyd MAsh
	SBod SCam SCog SSta WBcn WBod
	WCot WCwm WWeb
– 'E.T.R. Carlyon' ♀H4	CBcs CCtw CTrh EBee EPfP LHyd
	LRHS NLar SCog SPoG WBVN
	WWeb
§ – 'Elegant Beauty' ♀H4	CDoC CTrG CTrh CTrw CWSG
	MBri SBod SCam SCog WBVN
	WCwm
– 'Elizabeth Anderson'	CTrh
– 'Ellamine'	CBcs
– 'Elsie Jury' ♀H3	CBcs CDoC CMac CTrG CTri CTrw
	CWSG GKir GQui LHyd LRHS
	MAsh MGos NBlu SBod SCam
	SCog WBVN WBcn WBod WGwG
– 'Francis Hanger'	CBcs CDoC CTrh LHyd MAsh
	SCam SCog SSpi
– 'Galaxie' ♀H4	CBcs ISea SCog
– 'Garden Glory'	CTrh GGGa
– 'George Blandford' ♀H4	CBcs CMHG CMac SCam
– 'Glenn's Orbit' ♀H4	CBcs CDoC CTrw SCam WBcn
– 'Golden Spangles' (v)	CBcs CDoC CDul CMac CTrG
	ELan EPfP GKir LHyd LRHS MGos
	SCam SReu SSta WBcn
– 'Gwavas'	CBcs CPLG LHyd SCog
– 'Hilo'	CTrw
– 'Hiraethlyn'	CBcs LHyd SCam WBod
– 'J.C. Williams' ♀H4	CBcs CMac CSam CTri CTrw
	CWSG ENot EPfP ISea LHyd SCog
	SPer SSpi WBod
– 'Jean Claris'	CDoC
– 'Jenefer Carlyon'	CCtw CDoC
– 'Jill Totty'	CTrh
– 'Joan Trehane' ♀H4	CTrw
– 'Joe Nuccio'	CTrh
– 'Julia Hamiter' ♀H4	CBcs CTrw
§ – 'Jury's Yellow' ♀H4	CBcs CDoC CTbh CTrG CTrh CTri
	CTrw ELan EPfP GGGa GKir GQui
	ISea LHyd LRHS MAsh MGos SCam
	SCog SHBN SPer SSta WBcn WFar
	WWeb
– 'Laura Boscawen'	CTrG CTrh LHyd
– 'Les Jury' ♀H4	CDoC CTrh SCog
– 'Margaret Waterhouse'	CDoC COtt SCam SCog
– 'Mary Christian' ♀H4	CBcs COtt EPfP LHyd SCam
– 'Mary Jobson'	CBcs CDoC SCam
– 'Mary Phoebe Taylor' ♀H4	CBcs CDoC CPLG CTrG CTrw CWSG GKir MBri SCog SHBN WBod
– 'Mirage'	CTrh
– 'Moira Reid'	CDoC
– 'Monica Dance'	CBcs
– 'Muskoka' ♀H4	CBcs CTrh ISea WCwm
– 'New Venture'	CBcs
– 'November Pink'	CBcs EHol
– 'Phillippa Forward'	CMac WBod
– 'Rendezvous'	CDoC SCam SCog SPer
– 'Rose Court'	WBod
– 'Rose Parade'	LHyd MAsh
– 'Rose Quartz'	MAsh
– 'Rosemary Williams'	CBcs CTrw SCam
– 'Rosie Anderson'	LRHS MAsh
– 'Ruby Bells'	CMHG
– 'Ruby Wedding'	CBrm CDoC CTrh GQui LHyd
	SCog WBcn WBod WWeb
– 'Saint Ewe' ♀H4	CBcs CDoC CTrG CTrh CTri CTrw
	EPfP GGar ISea LHyd MBri MGos
	NBlu SCam SCog SHBN SMer SPer
	WBod
– 'Sayonara'	SCog
– 'Senorita' ♀H4	CDoC CTrh LHyd MBri SCam SCog
– 'Simon Bolitho' **new**	LHyd
– 'Sun Song' **new**	SCog
– 'Taylor's Perfection'	CTrw
– 'The Duchess of Cornwall'	CCtw CDoC
– 'Tiptoe'	CTrh LHyd MBri
– 'Twinkle Star'	CDoC
– 'Water Lily' ♀H4	CBcs CDoC CTrh CTrw EPfP MBri
	MGos SCam WBcn WBod
– 'Wilber Foss' ♀H4	CDoC CTrh CTrw LHyd SCam
	SCog
– 'William Carlyon'	CWSG
– 'Wynne Rayner' **new**	SCam
– 'Yesterday'	SMur
'Winter's Charm' (*oleifera* x *sasanqua*)	SCog
'Winter's Dream' (*hiemalis* x *oleifera*)	SCog
'Winter's Interlude' (*oleifera* x *sinensis*)	CDoC CPLG SCog
'Winter's Joy'	SCog
'Winter's Toughie' (?*oleifera* x *sasanqua*)	SCam SCog
'Winton' (*cuspidata* x *saluenensis*)	CBcs CDoC SCam
'Wirlinga Belle'	SCog
'Yoimachi' (*fraterna* x *sasanqua*)	CTrh
'Yukihaki'	see *C. japonica* 'Yukishiro'

Campanula ✿ (*Campanulaceae*)

abietina	see *C. patula* subsp. *abietina*
alaskana	see *C. rotundifolia* var. *alaskana*
§ *alliariifolia*	More than 30 suppliers
– 'Ivory Bells'	see *C. alliariifolia*
allionii	see *C. alpestris*
§ *alpestris*	ECho GTou NMen SIgm
alpina	MDKP NBur
ardonensis	NSla
argaea	CTCP EChP MAnH
argyrotricha	ITim NBur
arvatica	CLyd EPot ETow LRHS MBro
	MDKP NHol NMen WAbe WPat
– 'Alba'	CLyd WAbe WPat
arvatica x *cochleariifolia*	WBea
aucheri	see *C. saxifraga* subsp. *aucheri*
§ 'Balchiniana' (v)	WEas
'Barbara Valentine' **new**	EMon
barbata	EBee EMlt GTou ITim LHop MAnH
	NBur NWCA WMoo WPer WWeb
– var. *alba*	GAbr NBur
beauverdiana	WCom
bellidifolia	NBir
§ *betulifolia* ♀H4	CGra CSam EHyt ITim MAnH
	MBro NBur
– JCA 252.005	SBla
betulifolia x *troegerae*	ITim
'Birch Hybrid' ♀H4	CMHG EBre ECtt EDAr ELan EPfP
	GKir LBee LRHS SCro WCom WFar
	WTel
bononiensis	EBee GBBs NBrk SRms
'Bumblebee'	CGra CNic SBla
'Burghaltii' ♀H4	CBri CElw CHar CMil CPom EBee
	EBlw EBre ECGP ECha EHrv ELan
	EMon GMac LRHS MAnH MBro

MSte SAga SBla SSpi WCot WFar
WPer WWhi WWin
calaminthifolia EBur
§ **carnica** ECho MSte
carpatha SBla
carpatica ♀H4 CWCL EBee ECho EPfP GKir ITim
MBar MBri MDKP MWgw NBro
NGdn SPlb SRms SWat WShp
WWin
- f. **alba** LPVe MWgw NFor NGdn SPlb
SWat WSSM
- - 'Bressingham White' EBre GKir SBla
§ - - 'Weisse Clips' COkL ECtt EDAr ELan ENot EPfP
GGar GKir GTou LAst LHop MDun
MWgw NGdn NJOw SPer SPla
SRms SWvt WFar WPat WPer WShp
WWeb
§ - 'Blaue Clips' ECtt EDAr ELan EMlt ENot EPar
EPfP ESis GGar GKir GTou LAst
MBNS MDun MWgw NBlu NGdn
NJOw SPer SPla SRms SWvt WFar
WGwG WPat WPer WRHF WShp
WWeb
- blue MRav
* - 'Blue and White LPVe
  Uniform'
- Blue Clips see *C. carpatica* 'Blaue Clips'
- 'Blue Moonlight' EBre EBur GKir LRHS SMer
- 'Caerulea' CBcs
- 'Chewton Joy' CLyd CTri EBre GKir LRHS
- dwarf EPot SScr
- 'Karpatenkrone' EBee
- 'Kathy' GBuc
- 'Kobaltglocke' EBee
- 'Maureen Haddon' EBre GKir LRHS
- 'Queen of Somerville' NJOw
- 'Suzie' SBla
- 'Take Me' **new** GKir
- var. **turbinata** EHyt MTho NSla SRms
- - f. *alba* 'Hannah' LRHS
- - 'Georg Arends' CLyd CNic
- - 'Isabel' EBee LRHS
- - 'Jewel' LRHS
- - 'Karl Foerster' EBee EBre GBuc GKir LRHS MTho
SBla SMer WHoo
- - 'Wheatley Violet' LRHS SBla
- White Clips see *C. carpatica* f. *alba* 'Weisse
Clips'
§ **cashmeriana** EBur MAnH NBur
- SEP 386 EHyt
- 'Blue Cloud' **new** CWib MBri WCFE
cephallenica see *C. garganica* subsp.
cephallenica
§ **chamissonis** EMlt NBur NSla SBla WCom WPat
§ - 'Major' CPBP EDAr EPot EWes LBee MBro
NBur SAga
- 'Oyobeni' NBur NLAp
§ - 'Superba' ♀H4 EBur ELan MTho NBur NMen NSla
choruhensis CGra ITim NBur
§ **cochlearifolia** ♀H4 CSpe CTri EDAr ELan EMlt EPfP
ESis GKir GTou MBro MDun MFir
MTho MWat NJOw SPet SSvw
WFar WHoo WPer WShp WTel
WWhi WWin
- var. *alba* CNic CSpe EDAr EMlt LRHS MBro
MHer MWat NChi NMen NRya
SBla SRms WAbe WHoo WPer
- - 'Bavaria White' ITim LPVe
- - double white (d) WPat
- - 'White Baby' EPfP GAbr GGar NBlu NFla NPri
(Baby Series)
- 'Bavaria Blue' ECho ITim LPVe NWCA
- 'Blue Baby' (Baby Series) ECho ECtt EPfP GGar MHer NPro
- 'Blue Tit' GBuc

- 'Blue Wonder' COtt EPot
- 'Cambridge Blue' EBre LRHS NBur WAbe
- 'Elizabeth Oliver' (d) More than 30 suppliers
- 'Flore Pleno' (d) ECtt NLAp
- 'Miss Willmott' CLyd EBur MTho NBir
- 'Oakington Blue' LRHS SBla WCom
- var. *pallida* 'Miranda' LRHS WIvy
- - 'Silver Chimes' ITim
- 'R.B. Loder' (d) EMlt
- 'Tubby' CLyd ECho LRHS MHer MTho
NJOw SRms
- 'Warleyensis' see *C.* x *haylodgensis* 'Warley
White'
collina CTri EBee GSki MAvo NBur NJOw
SIgm WCFE WPer
'Covadonga' CMea CPBP ECGP EMlt LHop
LRHS LTwo
'Crystal' ECtt MAvo
dasyantha see *C. chamissonis*
'E.K. Toogood' CElw CPBP EBee ECtt MDHE
MWat NBro NHol NVic SBla SCro
SMac SRms WRHF WWpP
'Elizabeth' see *C. takesimana* 'Elizabeth'
erinus CTCP
eriocarpa see *C. latifolia* 'Eriocarpa'
§ 'Faichem Lilac' CHar EBee ECtt NChi NLar NPro
STes WBar
fenestrellata ITim MTho NBro SRms WAbe
finitima see *C. betulifolia*
foliosa MSPs NBur WPer
formanekiana ♀H2-3 EBee EBur EChP ECoo EMan EPyc
GBBs MFOX NBur SMad STes
WCom WOut
fragilis EBur ECho EHyt
- subsp. *cavolinii* EHyt
- 'Hirsuta' ECho
'G.F. Wilson' ♀H4 EBur ECho EMlt LTwo WRHF
garganica ♀H4 EBre EGra EPfP EPza GAbr GBBs
GSki MDKP MRav NBlu NFla NFor
SPet SWvt WFar WLow WMoo
WPer WShp
- 'Aurea' see *C. garganica* 'Dickson's Gold'
- 'Blue Diamond' EDAr ELan LHop SBla WAbe
§ - subsp. *cephallenica* CElw NBro NJOw
§ - 'Dickson's Gold' More than 30 suppliers
- 'Major' ECho IHMH LAst NJOw
- 'W.H. Paine' ♀H4 CLyd EBre ECho ECtt EDAr LRHS
MDKP NMen NSla WHoo WRHF
§ 'Glandore' NMen NPro
glomerata CBot CBri CElw CRWN EDAr EGra
EPza GKir GTou LPVe MBNS
MBow MBrN MFir NBid NBlu
NBro NLan NMir SOkh SPet SRms
STes WBea WBrk WFar WGwG
WWin WWye
- var. *acaulis* CPrp EBee EMan EMlt EPfP ERou
GKir LRHS MBNS NArg NJOw
NWCA SPet SPla WFar WPer WShp
WWeb WWin
- var. *alba* More than 30 suppliers
§ - - 'Alba Nana' EBee LAst
§ - - 'Schneekrone' CBri ECha EFou EPfP ERou EWTr
NBrk NOak WBea WFar WShp
- 'Caroline' More than 30 suppliers
* - 'Compacta Alba' EPza
- Crown of Snow see *C. glomerata* var. *alba*
'Schneekrone'
- var. *dahurica* CTri EWTr LPVe MOne NLar SPet
WBea WPer
- 'Joan Elliott' CCge EBee EChP ECha EMan
GBuc IPot LRHS MNFA MRav
MWat NBrk NGdn SPet WAul
- 'Nana Alba' see *C. glomerata* var. *alba* 'Alba
Nana'

- 'Superba' ♀H4	More than 30 suppliers
- 'White Barn'	ECha NBrk NOak
grossekii	CBri EBee EChP EHrv EWll LTwo
	MFOX MWrn WBVN
'Hallii'	EBre LRHS MBro NWCA WPat
Hannay's form	CHar
x *haylodgensis*	see *C.* x *haylodgensis* 'Plena'
sensu stricto hort.	
§ x *haylodgensis*	CGra EDAr MBro SBla WAbe WCot
'Marion Fisher' (d)	WHoo
§ - 'Plena' (d)	EDAr ELan EPot LAst LBee LHop
	LRHS MBro NBro NMen NWCA
	SBla SRms WAbe WBVN WCom
	WCot WEas WHoo WKif WPat
§ - 'Warley White' (d)	CNic EBur ELan
- 'Yvonne'	COIW EBre EDAr NCGa WFar
'Hemswell Starlight'	CLyd NMen NPro
hercegovina 'Nana'	CPBP SBla WAbe
herminii	EHyt
'Hilltop Snow'	CGra CPBP WAbe
'Hillview Hose in Hose'	WHil
hypopolia	EPfP
§ *incurva*	CBri CPou CSpe EBur EMan EWTr
	GAbr GBBs ITim MAnH MLwd
	MNrw NBrk NOak WBea WPer
- *alba*	NBPC WPer
- 'Blue Ice'	WWin
x *innesi*	see *C.* 'John Innes'
isophylla ♀H2	ECho MBri SPet
- 'Alba' ♀H2	ECho SYvo
- 'Flore Pleno' (d)	EBur
- 'Mayi' ♀H2	CSpe
- 'Mayi' misapplied	see *C.* 'Balchiniana'
- 'Variegata'	see *C.* 'Balchiniana'
jaubertiana	CGra EHyt
'Joe Elliott' ♀H2-3	CStu ECho EWes LRHS
§ 'John Innes'	CLyd
kemulariae	ESis NBur NJOw SRms WCom
	WPer
'Kent Belle' ♀H4	More than 30 suppliers
'Kent Blue'	CBri
lactiflora	More than 30 suppliers
- *alba*	see *C. lactiflora* white
N - 'Alba' ♀H4	EChP EGle EMil ERou GKir GMac
	MAvo MTed STes
- 'Blue Avalanche'	EBee SMrm SOkh
- 'Blue Cross'	COtt EBre ECoo EFou GMac LRHS
	MAnH WHrl WTel
- 'Blue Lady' **new**	EBee EChP EFou
- dwarf pink **new**	MWrn WOut
- 'Loddon Anna' ♀H4	More than 30 suppliers
- 'Pouffe'	EBee EBre EChP ECha ECtt EGle
	ELan EMan EPfP GKir GMac LPVe
	LRHS MDKP MRav MWrn NBro
	NCGa NGdn SPer SPet SPla SWat
	SWvt WFar WShp WWin
- 'Prichard's Variety' ♀H4	More than 30 suppliers
- 'Senior'	EBee EFou LPio
- 'Superba' ♀H4	EBee GKir MCLN MTed
- 'Violet'	EBee SWat WPer
§ - white	CBot EBee ECha EFou LAst MAnH
	NBir NBro NBur NCot NFla SChu
	SPer WPer
- 'White Pouffe'	EBre EChP EGle ELan EOrc EPfP
	EWTr GKir GMac GSki LRHS MRav
	MWrn NCGa NChi NLar SMer SPer
	SPla STes SWat WFar
lanata	CTCP
lasiocarpa	EBur LRHS NBur WFar
§ *latifolia*	CArn EChP ECha GAbr GBBs GGar
	LRHS MCLN MWgw NBid NFor
	NMir NOrc NSti NVic SBla SMer
	SPer WBWf WCAu WCra WFar
	WMoo

- var. *alba*	ELan GAbr GBBs MAnH MBri
	MLwd MSte NGdn SBla SPer SSpi
- - 'White Ladies'	NBur
* - 'Amethyst'	EBee SDnm WMnd
- 'Brantwood'	CBri CFwr EChP EFWa EGle EMar
	ERou GAbr GMac MAnH MFir
	MRav MWat NBPC NBrk NChi
	NOak NPro SCro SDnm SMer SPer
	SRms SSpe STes WMnd WWin
- 'Buckland'	CHea SBla
§ - 'Eriocarpa'	EBee NBur
- 'Gloaming'	NBur
- var. *macrantha*	CSBt CWCL EBlw EFou ELan EPfP
	ERou GLil LHop LPVe LRHS MBri
	MHer MLwd MNrw MSte MWrn
	NBPC NCGa NJOw NSti SSvw
	SWvt WBea WCom WMoo WPer
	WShp WWeb WWye
- - *alba*	CM&M CMil ECha ECtt EHrv EMan
	ERou LHop LPhx LRHS MAnH
	MRav MSte NCGa WCAu WCot
	WMoo WPer
- 'Roger Wood'	MWgw WCot
§ *latiloba*	CBre CElw CMHG GKir LGro MFir
	NChi NWoo SAga WBrk WFar
	WHoo WWin
- 'Alba' ♀H4	CBre CElw CHar CPlt EFou EGle
	ELan EPPr EPfP GCal MAnH MDKP
	NChi NGdn SGar SHel WBrk WEas
	WRHF
- 'Hidcote Amethyst' ♀H4	More than 30 suppliers
- 'Highcliffe Variety' ♀H4	CHea CHee EBlw EChP EGle ELan
	EMan EMar EPfP GBuc GFlt MAnH
	MRav NCGa NDov NSti SPla SSpe
	SSpi WCot WEas WKif WMnd
* - 'Highdown'	MLLN WFar
- 'Percy Piper' ♀H4	CSam CStr ELan EWsh GBBs GBuc
	GKir LRHS MSph NBrk NBro NFor
	NLar WFar WOut
- 'Splash'	CElw CFee EBee ECtt MAvo MTed
	MWrn WCot
linifolia	see *C. carnica*
lusitanica **new**	SAga
- 'Mini Blue' **new**	MWrn
'Lynchmere'	ETow
makaschvilii	CPla ECtt EMan GBBs GFlt GIBF
	GMac IGor ITim LRHS MAnH
	MAvo MLwd MSph MTis MWrn
	NBPC NBur NLar SAga SBod SMac
	STes WCHb WCom WHil WHrl
	WPer
'Marion Fisher'	see *C.* x *haylodgensis* 'Marion
	Fisher'
medium	LAst NBlu
§ - var. *calycanthema*	ERou
- 'Cup and Saucer'	see *C. medium* var. *calycanthema*
'Mist Maiden'	CLyd EPot ETow LRHS WCom
	WFar
muralis	see *C. portenschlagiana*
'Mystery'	EBee EMan NLar
'Mystery Blue'	EBee EMan EPfP ERou NCot NLar
nitida	see *C. persicifolia* var. *planiflora*
- var. *planiflora*	see *C. persicifolia* var. *planiflora*
'Norman Grove'	CLyd LBee
ochroleuca	CMea EBee EBre EChP EFou EWTr
	GBBs GCal LRHS MAnH MWrn
	NBPC NBur NCGa SPoG STes SWat
	WCFE WHal WHrl WMoo WWeb
- 'White Beauty' **new**	CWib
- 'White Bells'	MWhi SPet WHHs WMnd
odontosepala	CElw EMon
'Oliver's Choice' **new**	WHrl
olympica hort.	see *C. rotundifolia* 'Olympica'
ossetica	see *Symphyandra ossetica*

	pallida CC 3684	GKev
	- subsp. ***tibetica***	see *C. cashmeriana*
	parviflora Lam.	see *C. sibirica*
	patula	NLar WBWf
§	- subsp. ***abietina***	MAnH MAvo NLar STes
	'Paul Furse'	ECtt LRHS MDKP MFir MLLN NLar NSti SHar STes WCot WSSM WTin WWin
	pelviformis	MNrw
	persicifolia	More than 30 suppliers
	- var. ***alba***	More than 30 suppliers
§	- 'Alba Coronata' (d)	CFir EBre EMon GAbr GBri LRHS NBir NBrk WEas WFar
	- 'Alba Plena'	see *C. persicifolia* 'Alba Coronata'
	- 'Beau Belle' **new**	EBee EChP MBNS MCLN NCot STes WHil
§	- 'Bennett's Blue' (d)	CSev EBee EChP ECtt EGle EOrc GBri GBuc GSki LAst LHop LPio LRHS MAvo MBnl MCCP MCLN MRav MTis MWgw MWrn NCiC NSti SPla SRms SWat WCAu WCra WViv
	- 'Best China'	MAvo
	- blue	EMan EOrc LAst MBow MRav NMen SMac SPlb WEas WFar
	- 'Blue Bell'	WSSM
	- 'Blue Bloomers' (d)	CElw CHar CHea CMil EBee EBre EChP EGle EMon EWes GBri GMac LLWP MAvo MRav MSph WCot WHal WPnP WRHF
	- blue cup-in-cup (d)	MDKP WFar WLin WWin
	- 'Boule de Neige' (d)	CHea CM&M EBee ECtt EGle NBrk NOak WCom WEas
	- 'Caerulea Coronata'	see *C. persicifolia* 'Coronata'
*	- 'Caerulea Plena' (d)	EWsh MBNS
	- 'Carillon'	GBri NBrk
§	- 'Chettle Charm' PBR ♀H4	More than 30 suppliers
§	- 'Coronata' (d)	MRav SPer WBrE
§	- 'Cristine'	MDKP
	- cup and saucer blue (d)	WHil
§	- cup and saucer white (d)	CElw ELan NBrk WFar WHil WPer WWye
	- double blue (d)	EGle NBro WEas
	- double white (d)	ELan NChi WMoo
	- 'Fleur de Neige' (d) ♀H4	CSam EBre ECtt LRHS MBro MLLN MSph NOak SPer WAul WCot WHoo
	- 'Flore Pleno' (d)	NBir
	- 'Frances' (d)	CLAP EGle EMon GBri WPnP
	- 'Frank Lawley' (d)	EBre LRHS SPer
	- 'George Chiswell' PBR	see *C. persicifolia* 'Chettle Charm'
	- 'Grandiflora Alba'	GBuc MAnH SMrm
	- 'Grandiflora Caerulea'	NLar
§	- 'Hampstead White' (d)	More than 30 suppliers
	- 'Hetty'	see *C. persicifolia* 'Hampstead White'
	- 'Kelly's Gold'	CFai CPou EBee MAvo MBNS MBnl NBPC NBhm NGdn NLar NPri NPro NSti SOkh WCAu WCot WCra WShp
	- 'La Belle'	EChP MAvo MBnl MCLN NCot SOkh WCAu WHil
	- 'Moerheimii' (d)	EOrc EPar ERou MBnl MDKP NBir NDov STes WCAu WHil WIvy WLin WWin
	- New Giant hybrids **new**	SMac
	- var. ***nitida***	see *C. persicifolia* var. *planiflora*
	- 'Peach Bells'	MBNS NOak
	- 'Perry's Boy Blue'	NPer
	- 'Pike's Supremo'	see *C.* 'Pike's Supremo'
§	- var. ***planiflora***	CPBP EBee ETow GTou SBla WAbe
§	- - f. ***alba***	GFlt WAbe WWin
	- 'Pride of Exmouth' (d)	CCge CHar CHea CSam EBee EChP ECtt EHrv ELan EMan EMar EMon

		GBuc LAst LRHS MAvo MBnl MBri MCCP NOak SPet WBrk WCot WCra WKif
	- 'Rearsby Belle' (d)	MDKP
	- subsp. ***sessiliflora***	see *C. latiloba*
	- 'Snowdrift'	ELan SRms
	- 'Telham Beauty' misapplied	CHea COtt CSBt CWCL EBee ECtt EFou ELan ENot EPfP EPza ERou GAbr GKir LRHS MRav MSte MWrn SMer SMrm SPer SPla SRms SWvt WMnd WMoo WPer WShp WWeb WWpP
	- 'Tinpenny Blue'	WTin
	- 'White Bell'	MWrn
	- 'White Cup and Saucer'	see *C. persicifolia* cup and saucer white
	- 'White Queen' (d)	NBur WEas WMnd
	- 'Wortham Belle'	see *C. persicifolia* 'Bennett's Blue'
	petrophila	EHyt
§	***'Pike's Supremo'*** (d)	NBir
	pilosa	see *C. chamissonis*
	piperi 'Townsend Ridge'	CGra
	planiflora	see *C. persicifolia* var. *planiflora*
§	***portenschlagiana*** ♀H4	More than 30 suppliers
	- 'Lieselotte'	CElw GBuc MDHE WPat
	- 'Major'	WFar
	- 'Resholdt's Variety'	CMea CSam EBre EDAr EFou EMlt EPfP LBee LHop LRHS NHol WPer
	poscharskyana	More than 30 suppliers
	- 'Blauranke'	EBee EOMN EWes MDHE WCom
	- 'Blue Gown'	EGle MAnH
	- 'Blue Waterfall'	EBre LRHS MAnH WWpP
	- 'E.H. Frost'	CBre CRez EBee ECtt EDAr EGle EPPr EPfP ESis EWTr LAst LHop MAnH MAvo MWat NBro NHol NJOw NRya SAga SRms SWvt WBea WBrk WFar WMoo WPer WShp WTel WWpP
	- 'Glandore'	see *C.* 'Glandore'
	- 'Lilacina'	CElw EPPr SCro SHel
	- 'Lisduggan Variety'	CElw EBur ECtt EDAr EGle EPPr EWes GKir MAvo NBro NCGa SBla SWat WBea WFar WMoo WPer WWin
	- 'Schneeranke'	SCro
	- 'Stella' ♀H4	CWCL EBee ECha ECtt EGle ENot ESis LRHS MAvo MRav NBro NJOw NVic SChu SDix SIng SPer SWvt WCom WFar WMoo WWpP
	- variegated (v)	EHoe IBlr WCot
	- white	ELan LAst MDKP WFar
	prenanthoides	see *Asyneuma prenanthoides*
	primulifolia	CHar CRez CTCP EBee ECoo ECtt ELan EMan GBBs IFro LRHS MAnH MMil MNrw MSte MWrn SAga SBod SMac SRms WCHb WCom WMoo WPer WSan WTin WWin
	- 'Blue Oasis'	CFwr CMHG EBee NBPC NJOw WMnd WWeb
	x pseudoraineri	EBur EDAr EHyt EWes NMen WCom
	'Puff of Smoke'	WCot
	pulla	CLyd CSpe EBur ECtt EDAr EHyt ELan ESis LAst MBro MTho NRya SBla SIng WCru WFar WLin WPat WPer
	- ***alba***	EBur ECtt EDAr EHyt LBee LRHS MBro SBla WCru WLin WPat
	x pulloides	CLyd EBre EDAr
	punctata	More than 30 suppliers
	- f. ***albiflora***	CM&M GKir LHop LRHS MAnH MLLN MNrw NChi WBro WFar WHil WWin
	- - 'Nana Alba'	CBri EBee LRHS MWrn NBur WFar

- 'Alina's Double' (d) — MAvo MNrw WBro WCot
- var. *hondoensis* — CHar EBee EPPr GEil IGor MBrN MNrw NSti SAga WBea WCot WHil WMoo WWpP
- - - 'Bossy Boots' — EFou
- - hose-in-hose (d) — CDes NLar SSte WFar
- - 'Hot Lips' — CElw CFai CFir CFwr CWCL EBee EChP EMan EPfP LAst MAvo MBNS MBnl MCCP NBPC NCot NPro NSti SOkh WCAu WCot WGMN WHil WSan WShp
- var. *microdonta* — EBre LRHS
- - - B&SWJ 5553 — WCru
- 'Millennium' — MAvo WCot WFar
- 'Milly' — CBri CDes EBee EMon MDKP WPGP
- 'Mottled' **new** — MWrn
* - 'Nana' — EChP
- 'Pantaloons' (d) — SHar
- 'Pink Chimes' — NBhm NPro
- 'Pink Eclipse' — WFar
- 'Reifrock' — EFou SMrm
- 'Rosea' — LPio SRms WFar WHil WSan
- f. *rubriflora* — More than 30 suppliers
- - 'Beetroot' — CBri CFwr CKno EBee EChP EMon GBri LHop MAnH MCCP MFOX MSph NBur NChi SSpi WPGP
- - - 'Bowl of Cherries' — SHar
- - - 'Cherry Bells' — CElw CFir EBee ECtt EFou EMan EPfP IPot LAst MAnH MAvo MNrw MTis NCot SHar WCAu WCot WSan
- - - 'Wine 'n' Rubies' — CElw CStr ECtt EFWa EHrv EMan MAvo MDKP MLwd MNrw MWrn SHar SUsu WCot

punctata — see *C. takesimana*
　var. *takesimana*
- 'Wedding Bells' — CElw CFai CFwr EBee EChP EFou EMan EPPr IPot LDai MAnH MBnl MBri MTis NCot NLar NPro NSti SMrm STes SUsu WBro WCAu WCot
- white hose-in-hose (d) — GMac MAnH MAvo MNrw SAga WCot WFar
pusilla — see *C. cochleariifolia*
pyramidalis — CBot CSpe EBee EPfP GIBF GWCH LIck MAnH MBNS MHer MLwd MRav NOrc SDnm SPlb SRob WOut WPer
- *alba* — CSpe CWib EBee ECtt EOMN EPfP EWTr GWCH LPio MAnH SDnm SPlb WBrE WPer
raddeana — CElw CLyd EBre ITim NJOw NLar WBrk WFar WLin
raineri ♀H4 — LRHS MBro NMen NWCA SBla WAbe
§ *rapunculoides* — EBee EGoo GAbr SWat WBea WHer WPer
§ - 'Afterglow' — MAvo WCot WFar
- 'Alba' — CStr EMon MAvo WBar
rapunculus — ILis MLLN MWgw
recurva — see *C. incurva*
reiseri — MLwd NBur
rhomboidalis Gorter — see *C. rapunculoides*
rigidipila — NBur
'Rosanna's Rainbow' (v) — WBar
rotundifolia — CArn CRWN EPfP GWCH MBow MBro MHer NBid NLan NMir NRya NSti SECG SIde SPlb SWal WBea WBrk WJek WPer
§ - var. *alaskana* — NWCA
§ - var. *alba* — MAnH
- 'Jotunheimen' — CPBP EHyt
§ - 'Olympica' — CWCL EBee EBur EMan EPfP GEdr

IGor MBNS NBur NJOw NPri WCot WFar WHoo
- 'White Gem' **new** — NChi SCro
rupestris — EBur LTwo
'Samantha' — LAst NCGa SHar WCot
'Sarastro' — More than 30 suppliers
sarmatica — CBri CTCP EBee ECoo EMan EMon GBuc MAnH MBrN MSte MWhi NBPC NBid NOak NPPs SRms STes WCAu WCHb WMoo WPer WPic
sartorii — EBur EMan ITim MWrn NMen WPer WWin
saxifraga — EBur ITim NBur NMen SIgm
§ - subsp. *aucheri* — EBur EHyt GEdr ITim WAbe
scabrella — CGra
scheuchzeri — EPot
shetleri — CGra EHyt
§ *sibirica* — EMan NBur SSvw WGwG WPer
- white — NLar
siegizmundii — GMac NBur
'Smokey Blue' — WCot
'Sojourner' — CGra
speciosa — EBee EChP MWhi MWrn
'Stansfieldii' — CPBP EBur EPot NMen WPat
'Summer Pearl' — LAst MBNS WLin
'Swannbles' — see *C. punctata* x *Symphyandra ossetica*, 'Swannbles'
§ *takesimana* — More than 30 suppliers
- B&SWJ 8499 — WCru
- *alba* — EBee GKir ITim LPio MAnH MDKP SMad WBry WMoo WOut
- 'Beautiful Truth' — CFai LAst MAvo NBPC NBhm NSti SHar WBro WCru WLFP
§ - 'Elizabeth' — More than 30 suppliers
- 'Elizabeth II' (d) **new** — WCot
- purple **new** — SOkh
thessala — WAbe
thyrsoides — CBri EBee EMan EWll GTou NBPC NBur SDnm WHal WPer
- subsp. *carniolica* — SGar
'Timsbury Perfection' — CGra
tommasiniana ♀H4 — EHyt LRHS NBur
trachelium — CBri CMHG EBee EChP ECoo EPfP GAbr ITim MAnH MBNS MBow MNrw MRav MWrn NBPC NJOw NLan SCou SGar WCAu WFar WHer WPer
- var. *alba* — EBee EChP EWTr GAbr LRHS MAnH MFir MMHG MNrw MWhi MWrn NPar SCou STes WBrE WCom WCot WFar WMoo WPer WWhi
- 'Alba Flore Pleno' (d) — CDes CFir CHar CHea CStr EMlt EMon LPhx LPio MAnH SBla SMac STes WBro WCot WFar WSan
- 'Bernice' (d) — More than 30 suppliers
- 'Faichem Lilac' — see *C.* 'Faichem Lilac'
- lilac-blue — NOrc WHHs
- 'Snowball' **new** — LAst SPoG SVil
tridentata — WPer
troegerae — LRHS SBla
'Tymonsii' — CPBP EBur ECho EHyt LRHS NBir NJOw
'Van-Houttei' — CElw CHar CMil CStr EBee GMac NBrk NLar SAga WBrk WCot WFar WPer
versicolor — EBee
- G&K 3347 — EMon
vidalii — see *Azorina vidalii*
waldsteiniana — CPBP LRHS LTwo NBur NWCA WFar
'Warley White' — see *C.* x *haylodgensis* 'Warley White'
'Warleyensis' — see *C.* x *haylodgensis* 'Warley White'

witasekiana	EBee
x *wockei* 'Puck'	EBee EBur ECtt EHyt EMlt EPot LRHS MBro NLar NWCA WAbe WPat
'Zierlotte' **new**	NJOw
zoysii	EHyt LRHS SBla

Campanula x *Symphyandra* (Campanulaceae)

§ *C. punctata* x *S. ossetica*,	CPou EGle EMan GMac MAnH
'Swannables'	MWrn NCGa NChi WCot

Campanumoea see *Codonopsis*

Camphorosma (Chenopodiaceae)
monspeliaca	XPep

Campsis (Bignoniaceae)

atrosanguinea	see *Bignonia capreolata* 'Atrosanguinea'
grandiflora	CArn CBcs CSPN EBee ELan ENot EPfP GSki IMGH LRHS SPer WCFE XPep
radicans	CArn CBcs CDul CMac CRHN CSBt CStu CWib EBee ECrN ELan EPfP GQui LAst LPan LRHS MHer MSwo MWat NBlu SHBN SLon SPer SPlb WBVN WBrE WDin XPep
- 'Flamenco'	CDoC EBee ELan GQui GSki LAst LRHS MAsh SBra SCoo SLim SWvt WBro WCot
§ - f. *flava* ♀H4	CDoC EBee EBre ELan ENot EPfP IMGH LHop LRHS MAsh MBri MCCP MGos MWat MWgw NBlu NHol NPal NSti SBra SLim SPer SPet SSta SWvt XPep
- 'Indian Summer'	CBcs EBee MBlu MGos NLar SLim WCot WWeb
- 'Yellow Trumpet'	see *C. radicans* f. *flava*
x *tagliabuana*	NLar
'Dancing Flame' **new**	
- 'Madame Galen' ♀H4	More than 30 suppliers

Camptosorus see *Asplenium*

Campylandra see *Tupistra*

Campylotropis (Papilionaceae)
macrocarpa	NLar WCot

Canarina (Campanulaceae)
canariensis ♀H1	CFil CStu EShb WPGP

Candollea see *Hibbertia*

Canna ✿ (Cannaceae)

'Adam's Orange'	CHEx
'Alberich'	CSam
altensteinii	XBlo
'Ambassador'	CHEx EBee LAma MOak
'America'	CHid EBee LAma WCot
'Angel Pink'	MJnS
'Annaeei' ♀H3	EAmu MOak
'Anthony and Cleopatra' (v)	WCot
'Apricot Dream'	MBri MOak
'Apricot Ice'	MOak
'Aranyálom'	LAma
'Assaut'	LPio MOak SAPC SArc
'Atlantis' **new**	XBlo
'Australia'	MJnS MOak WCot XBlo
'Black Knight'	CSpe EAmu EBee EChP ELan IPot LAma LPVe LPio MJnS MOak SPet SWal WCot WHil WMul XBlo
'Bonfire'	CHEx

brasiliensis	CHll WCot
'Brillant'	ELan LAma LPVe
'Canary'	XBlo
'Centurion'	LAma
'Cerise Davenport'	CFir MOak
'Champigny'	MOak
'Champion'	CHEx MOak
'China Doll' **new**	MOak
'Chinese Coral' Schmid	CHEx LAma
§ 'City of Portland'	CSut EBee ELan LAma MBri MOak SChr
§ 'Cleopatra'	EAmu LAma LPVe MBri MJnS MOak SPet WGwG
coccinea	MOak
§ 'Colibri'	EBee LAma
'Conestoga' **new**	MOak
'Confetti'	see *C.* 'Colibri'
'Creamy White'	CHEx XBlo
'Crimson Beauty'	LAma
Crozy hybrids	LRav
'Delaware' **new**	MOak
'Délibáb'	CSam EBee EChP IPot LAma LPVe MJnS MOak SPet SWal
'Di Bartolo'	LPio MJnS XBlo
I 'Durban' Cooke (v)	CHEx CHll CKob CSpe CTrC EBee EBlw ELan EOrc EWes LAst LHop LPJP MFan MJnS MOak SCoo SDix WCot WHal WMul XBlo
edulis	EUJe MOak
- 'Newlyn Green'	CHEx
§ x *ehemanii* ♀H3	CHEx CKob CSev EBee LPio MJnS MOak SAPC SArc SChr SDix SVen WCot WMul WPGP
'Ember'	XBlo
'En Avant'	CHEx LAma SPlb
'Endeavour'	CDWL CHEx EUJe LPJP MOak MSta WMAq WMul WPGP
'Erebus' ♀H3	CDWL LPio MOak MSta SDix SVen WMAq
'Ermine' **new**	WCot
'Étoile du Feu'	XBlo
'Eureka' **new**	MOak
'Evening Star'	LAma
'Extase'	XBlo
'Fatamorgana'	LAma WWeb
'Felix Ragout'	LAma
Firebird	see *C.* 'Oiseau de Feu'
flaccida	CDWL WMul
'Flame'	XBlo
§ 'Florence Vaughan'	MJnS MOak
'Gaiety' **new**	MOak
'General Eisenhower' ♀H3	MOak
x *generalis* hybrids	SHGC
glauca	EUJe MOak SDix WWpP
* 'Gold Ader'	LAma
'Gold Dream'	LAma LPVe
'Golden Inferno'	XBlo
'Golden Lucifer'	CSpe ELan LAma LPVe WWeb
'Grand Duc'	MOak
'Grande'	CFir MJnS MOak
'Heinrich Seidel'	CHEx
'Horn'	MOak
hybrids	ELan
§ *indica*	CBcs CBri CSev CTCP EFul EUJe IFro LPio MGol MOak SAPC SArc SPlb SYvo
- 'Purpurea'	EBlw ECha EOrc LEdu LPio MOak SDix SPlb SVen WCot WDyG WMul WPGP
'Inferno'	MJnS XBlo
'Ingeborg' ♀H3	CBri LAma LPVe
'Intrigue'	MOak
iridiflora misapplied	see *C.* x *ehemanii*
iridiflora Ruiz & Pav.	CDWL EBee

	'Kansas City' (v)	MJnS WCot
I	'King Humbert' (blood-red)	CBcs CHEx LAma MGol SYvo WCot XBlo
	King Humbert (orange-red)	see *C.* 'Roi Humbert'
	'King Midas'	see *C.* 'Richard Wallace'
	'La Bohème' (Grand Opera Series)	LAma
	'La Traviata' **new**	MOak
	'Lenape' **new**	MOak
	'Lesotho Lill'	CHll CMdw
	'Liberté'	see *C.* 'Wyoming'
	'Lippo's Kiwi' **new**	MOak
	'Louis Cayeux' ♀H3	SDix
	'Louis Cottin'	CSam EChP LAma LPVe LPio SChr WWol
	'Lucifer'	CBcs CBri CHVG CSpe EAmu EBee EPfP LAma LPVe LRHS MJnS MLan NPer SPet SYvo WBrE WWol
	lutea	CHEx XBlo
	'Madame Angèle Martin'	MOak XBlo
	'Malawiensis Variegata'	see *C.* 'Striata'
	'Marvel'	LAma
	'Monet' **new**	ECho
	'Mrs Oklahoma'	LAma LPVe MOak
	'Musifolia' ♀H3	CHEx CKob EAmu LPJP LPio MOak SChr SDix WCot WDyG WMul XBlo
	'Mystique' ♀H3	MOak SDix
§	'Oiseau de Feu'	LAma
	'Orange Blush'	MOak
	'Orange Futurity'	MOak
	'Orange Perfection'	CFir CHEx CSam LAma MOak
	'Orange Punch' **new**	MBri MOak
	'Orchid'	see *C.* 'City of Portland'
	'Panache'	CHEx CTrC MOak WCot WDyG WMul
	'Perkeo'	CTrC EBee LAma LPVe MOak SPet WWol
§	'Pfitzer's Salmon Pink'	CHEx
	'Picasso' ♀H3	CBcs CBri CHEx CSam EAmu EBee LAma MJnS MLan SPet SWal SYvo XBlo
	'Pink Futurity' (Futurity Series)	MOak
	'Pink Sunburst' (v)	CKob CSpe MJnS MOak
	'Plantagenet'	MOak
	'President'	CSut EBee ECho LAma LPVe LPio MOak SPet WBrE
	'Pretoria'	see *C.* 'Striata'
	'Princess Di'	MBri MOak
	'Pringle Bay' (v)	XBlo
	'Ra' ♀H3	CDWL MOak MSta WMAq
	'Red Futurity' (Futurity Series)	MOak
	'Red Wine'	MOak
§	'Richard Wallace'	CSam CSut EBee LAma LPio MOak SAPC SArc SPlb SVen SYvo WCot XBlo
	'Robert Kemp'	LAma
§	'Roi Humbert'	CBri CSam EBee MAvo MOak WMul
	'Roi Soleil' ♀H3	CHEx LAma MOak WPGP
	'Roitelet'	CHEx
I	'Rosa' **new**	MBri
	'Rose Futurity' (Futurity Series)	MOak
	'Rosemond Coles'	CBcs CHEx CSam EPfP LAma MJnS MLan MOak SWal SYvo
	'Saladin'	CSam
	'Salmon Pink'	see *C.* 'Pfitzer's Salmon Pink'
	'Sémaphore'	MJnS
	'Shenandoah' ♀H3	CTrC
	'Singapore Girl'	MOak
	'Snow-White' **new**	XBlo
	'Spartacus' **new**	SChr
	speciosa	EUJe XBlo
	'Strasbourg'	CSam LAma NPer WMul WPGP
§	'Striata' (v) ♀H3	CHEx CKob CRez CSev CSpe EBee EBlw EOrc EUJe LAst LPJP LPio MAvo MJnS MOak MSta NPSI SPet SYvo WCot WDyG WHal WMul WSPU XBlo
	'Striata' misapplied	see *C.* 'Stuttgart' (v)
	'Striped Beauty' (v)	CDWL CTrC EAmu MOak SHGC SVen
§	'Stuttgart' (v)	CSpe EAmu EBee EPfP MJnS MOak WCot WMul
	'Südfunk'	EAmu
	'Sunny Delight'	MOak
	'Talisman'	MJnS XBlo
	'Taney'	CDWL EUJe MSta WMAq
	'Tango'	SChr
	'Tashkent Red'	CHad
	'Tirol'	IPot LPVe MJnS MOak
	'Tricarinata'	CHEx
	'Tropical Rose'	EAmu LRHS SRms
	Tropicanna = 'Phasion'PBR (v) ♀H3	COtt EBee EPfP LRHS MOak NPer
*	'Variegata' (v)	LAma LRHS WCot WMul
	'Verdi' ♀H3	CSpe LAma MJnS
	warscewiczii	MOak SYvo WCot
	'Wine 'n' Roses'	MBri MOak
§	'Wyoming' ♀H3	CBcs CHEx CSam EBee LAma LPVe LPio MCCP MJnS MOak NVic SWal SYvo WCot WMul WPGP XBlo
	'Yellow Humbert'	CSev LAma LPVe MJnS MOak
	'Yellow Humbert' misapplied	see *C.* 'Richard Wallace', *C.* 'Cleopatra', *C.* 'Florence Vaughan'

Cannomois (*Restionaceae*)

virgata **new** — CBig

Cantua (*Polemoniaceae*)

buxifolia — CAbb CBcs CFee CPLG CPle CPne ECre GQui LRHS SIgm SOWG

Cape gooseberry see *Physalis peruviana*

Capparis (*Capparaceae*)

spinosa **new** — WJek XPep
- var. *inermis* **new** — XPep

Capsicum (*Solanaceae*)

annuum — MBri

Caragana (*Papilionaceae*)

arborescens — ECrN EPAt EPfP GKir MBar NBee NWea SBLw SEND SPer SPlb WBVN WDin WStI XPep
- 'Lorbergii' — CEnd CLnd EPfP EWTr GBin GKir LRHS MBlu SKee SPer WBcn WFoF
- 'Pendula' — CDul CWib EBee ECrN ELan ENot EPfP GKir LRHS MAsh MBar MBlu NBee NPri SBLw SCoo SLim SPer WDin WStI
- 'Walker' — CBcs COtt CWib EBee ELan EMil ENot EPfP GKir LPan LRHS MAsh MBar MBlu MBri MGos SBLw SLim SPer WOrn WStI
aurantiaca — MBar
frutex 'Globosa' — NBlu SPer
jubata — NLar
microphylla — WNor

caraway see *Carum carvi*

Cardamine ✿ (*Brassicaceae*)

alba	WEas
asarifolia hort.	see *Pachyphragma macrophyllum*
bulbifera	CLAP EBee EPPr IBlr LEdu NGar NRya WBri WCru WSHC
californica	EBee EMan EPar MAsh NGar NRya WCru
diphylla	CLAP EBee EPar MLLN NLar SSpi WCot WCru WFar
– 'Eco Cut Leaf'	CDes WCru
enneaphylla	EBee IBlr NGby SSpi SVal WCru
glanduligera	CDes CElw EBee EGle EPPr LEdu WCru WPGP
– MDM 94010	NGar
– MDM 94011	NGar
§ **heptaphylla**	CLAP ELan EPar IBlr MBri MRav NGar NHol SSpi SWat WBri WCru WHoo
– Guincho form	CDes CFir IBlr
– white	CPlt
§ **kitaibelii**	CLAP ECha EPar IBlr LEdu NGar NPol SIng SSpi WCru
laciniata	EBee NLar SSpi SVal SWat WCru
latifolia Vahl	see *C. raphanifolia*
lineariloba	IBlr
macrophylla	CLAP EBee NGar SDys SSpi SWat WCot WCru WFar WIvy
maxima new	WCru
§ **microphylla**	CLAP EHyt GCrs WAbe WCru
pachystigma NNS 98-149	WCot
pentaphylla ♀H4	CPom EBre EGle ELan EMar EPPr EPar EPla ERos EWTr GBBs GBuc GCrs GGar GKir LRHS MBri MRav NBir NDov NGar SBla SSpi SVal WCot WCru WLin WPnP WTin EWTr
* – 'Alba'	EWTr
– bright pink	CLAP NPol WCot
pratensis	CArn CRWN CRow EMFW EWTr GFlt MBow MGas MHer MLan NLan NMir NOrc NPri SIde SWat WFar WHHs WHbs WHer WMoo WShi WWpP WWye
– 'Edith' (d)	CDes CLAP EBee EPPr GBuc MNrw NChi WPrP WWpP
– 'Flore Pleno' (d)	More than 30 suppliers
– 'Improperly Dressed'	CNat
– 'William' (d)	EBee EPPr GBuc MNrw WMoo WPnP WPrP
quinquefolia	CDes CElw CLAP CMea CPlt CPom EBee EGle EHrv EMan EMar EPPr EPar GBuc NDov SBla SCro SDys SSpi SUsu WCot WCru WFar WPGP WRHF WRha WWye
§ **raphanifolia**	CBre CDes CRow EBee ECha EMan EOrc GAbr GBuc GCal GGar IBlr LEdu MFir MRav NBid NBro SSpi SWat WBor WCru WMoo WPGP WPnP WTin
trifolia	More than 30 suppliers
* – **digitata**	MTho
urbaniana	EBee
waldsteinii	CDes CElw CPlt CPom ECho EGle EHrv EPPr MBro NDov SCnR SRot SSpi WCru WHoo WIvy WTin WWhi
yezoensis	CDes IBlr NGar
– B&SWJ 4659	WCru

cardamon see *Elettaria cardamomum*

Cardiandra (*Hydrangeaceae*)

alternifolia	CLAP
– B&SWJ 5845	WCru

– B&SWJ 6354	WCru
formosana	CLAP
– B&SWJ 2005	WCru

Cardiocrinum (*Liliaceae*)

cathayanum	EBee LEur
cordatum B&SWJ 4841	WCru
– var. **glehnii**	CLAP GEdr SSpi
– – B&SWJ 4758	WCru
– red-veined	CLAP GEdr SSpi
giganteum	CBcs CBct CBot CBro CFil CHEx EBee EPar EPot EUJe GBuc GEdr GFlt GGar GKir IBlr ITer LAma MBri MDun SMad SSpi WBod WCru WHer WMul WPGP
– B&SWJ 2419	WCru
– var. **yunnanense**	CFil CLAP CPom EPfP GBuc GEdr GGGa IBlr LEur NBid SSpi WCru WPGP
– – CD&R 2491	WCru

cardoon see *Cynara cardunculus*

Carduus (*Asteraceae*)

benedictus	see *Cnicus benedictus*

Carex (*Cyperaceae*)

from Uganda	GBin GCal MMoz
no 4 (Nanking)	EPPr
acuta	CBig
acutiformis	CRWN GKir
alba	CBrm EPPr WDyG
albida	CHrt EBee EHul EMan EPla GKir LRHS SWal WWpP
albula	MMoz WHoo
annectans	EPPr
var. **xanthocarpa**	
appressa	CBig
arenaria	EPPr NNor
atrata	CCol CHrt EBee EHoe EPPr EPla ESis GKir LRHS MAnH MWrn WDyG WHrl
aurea	EBee EPPr GKir NHol
baccans	CBig EPPr EPla EShb GCal LRav MWod NOak WDyG
bebbii	EPPr
berggrenii	CLyd EChP ECou EHoe EHul ELan EMon ENot GKir GOrn GSki LPBA LRHS MBnl MNrw MWhi MWod NBro NHol NSti NWCA SMrm SPlb SWal SWat WMoo WPer WTin WWin WWye
– narrow-leaved	ITim
bicknellii	EPPr
binervis	CRWN
boottiana	EWes
brunnea	EHoe EPPr EWes
– 'Jenneke' **new**	CPen
– 'Variegata' (v)	CAbb CBrm EBee EHoe EPPr MMoz NGdn WCot
buchananii ♀H4	More than 30 suppliers
– 'Viridis'	EBee EHoe ELan EMan EPza LRHS MMoz WHer
bushii	EPPr
'Caldwell Blue' **new**	SSpi
caryophyllea	CElw EBee EChP EGoo EHoe EPPr EPla ESis MMoz NBir NBro NHol
'The Beatles'	
chathamica	CKno CRez EBee EMan EPPr MMoz NSti SMac
'China Blue'	CRez MMoz
comans	CBri COlW CTrC CWCL EBee EFul EHoe EMar EMon EPPr EPar GCal GKir GOrn GSki LRHS MAnH NBro NHol NOak NPol SHel

- bronze	More than 30 suppliers
- 'Dancing Flame'	CPrp CWCL EBee GBin MCCP
- 'Frosted Curls'	More than 30 suppliers
- 'Kupferflamme'	EFou
- 'Small Red'	see *C. comans* 'Taranaki'
§ - 'Taranaki'	CWCL EBee EBre EMan EPza GKir
	MAvo MBNS MLwd MMoz NGdn
	NHol SWal
comosa	EPPr
conica 'Hime-kan-suge'	see *C. conica* 'Snowline'
- 'Kiku-satura'	NHol
§ - 'Snowline' (v)	More than 30 suppliers
coriacea	CBig SWvt
- from Dunedin,	EPPr
New Zealand	
crinita	EPPr MNrw
cristatella	EBee EPPr
crus-corvi	EPPr
curta **new**	CRWN
dallii	EBee ECou EWes MAnH MMoz
	MWrn
davisii	EPPr
demissa	CRWN EBee EHoe EPPr WWye
depauperata	CRWN EHoe EMon WWye
digitata	CRWN WWye
dioica **new**	CRWN
dipsacea	More than 30 suppliers
dissita	CBig CTrC LEdu
divulsa	CRWN
subsp. *divulsa* **new**	
- subsp. *leersii*	EPPr
dolichostachya	CMil CPen CRez EBee EMan EMon
'Kaga-nishiki' (v)	EOMN EPPr LEdu LRHS MMoz
	SAga WCot WLin WPnP WPrP
duthiei KEKE 494	WPGP
echinata	CRWN GIBF
elata	EPPr
§ - 'Aurea' (v) ♀H4	More than 30 suppliers
- 'Bowles' Golden'	see *C. elata* 'Aurea'
- 'Knightshayes' ♀H4	CKno EMan GBin MMoz WCot
'Evergold'	see *C. oshimensis* 'Evergold'
fascicularis	CBig EPPr GGar
ferruginea	GBin
§ *flacca*	CBig CHrt CRWN EHoe EMan
	EPPr EWsh GBin GKir NPro SWal
	WPer WPnP
- 'Bias' (v)	CNat EMan EMon EPPr EPla GKir
	LRHS MMoz WDyG WRHF
§ - subsp. *flacca*	EBee EOMN EPza EWes MMoz
	MTed NHol WPGP WWye
flagellifera	More than 30 suppliers
- 'Auburn Cascade'	CMil EBee GCal NHol SMac
- 'Coca-Cola'	CPen GCal MAvo MBnl NOak
- 'Rapunzel'	EBee EPPr MMoz WPGP
flava	EBee EHoe EPPr WWpP
fortunei	see *C. morrowii*
fraseri	see *Cymophyllus fraserianus*
fraserianus	see *Cymophyllus fraserianus*
* *germinata* **new**	CBig
glauca Scopoli	see *C. flacca* subsp. *flacca*
glauca Bosc. ex Boott	CBig EBee EPla SHel WPGP
'Gold Fountains' **new**	LAst
granularis	EPPr
grayi	CBig CKno EBee EBlw EHoe EMar
	EMon EPGN EPPr EPla GCal GFlt
	GKir LBuc LEdu LRHS MBlu MTho
	NOak WCot WDyG WPer WSan
	WWye
- 'Morning Star' **new**	EPza
§ *hachijoensis*	EMon EPPr LAst LRHS WFar
- 'Evergold'	see *C. oshimensis* 'Evergold'

halleriana **new**	XPep
'Happy Wanderer'	SLPl
hirta	CRWN EPPr
hispida	CBig EPPr WMoo WRos
hordeistichos	EBee EPPr
hostiana **new**	CRWN
hystricina	EPPr
§ 'Ice Dance' (v)	CMea EBee EBre EFou EPPr GGar
	MAvo MMoz NCGa NOak SWvt
	WCot WPGP WPrP WWpP
intumescens	EBee
kaloides	EBee EBre EHoe EMan EMon LRHS
	MAvo
'Kan-suge'	see *C. morrowii* Boott
longebrachiata **new**	CBig
longebracteata	GGar
lupulina	EPPr NBPC
lurida	CBig CBod CPen EBee EPPr EPza
	GBin MAvo MBNS NLar WWpP
macloviana	EPPr
macrocephala	EPPr
'Majken' **new**	EBee
maorica	CBig LEdu
maritima **new**	CRWN
Milk Chocolate	CHar CMil CPen EOMN GCal NPro
= 'Milchoc'PBR (v)	WLeb
* *mimosa*	EPPr
molesta	EPPr
montana	EPPr GKir LRHS
morrowii hort.	see *C. oshimensis, C. hachijoensis*
§ *morrowii* Boott	MWhi
- 'Evergold'	see *C. oshimensis* 'Evergold'
- 'Fisher's Form' (v)	More than 30 suppliers
- 'Gilt' (v)	EMon EPPr LRHS MAvo
- 'Ice Dance'	see *C.* 'Ice Dance'
- 'Nana Variegata' (v)	CTri NBir NWoo WPGP
- var. *temnolepis*	EPPr WCot
'Silk Tassel'	
N - 'Variegata' (v)	More than 30 suppliers
muhlenbergii	EPPr
multifida	EPPr
muricata	EPPr
subsp. *muricata*	
muskingumensis	More than 30 suppliers
- 'Ice Fountains' (v)	EPPr WHil
- 'Little Midge'	EBee EFou EMan EPPr GKir LRHS
	MTed
- 'Oehme' (v)	CHar CWCL EBee EFou EMan
	EMon EPPr EPla EPyc GBin GCal
	LRHS MTed NBid WCot WDyG
	WTin
- 'Silberstreif' (v)	CBrm EMon MTed NLar
- 'Wachtposten'	GCal MFir
'Mystery'	GGar
nigra	CRWN EHon EPPr GSki WWpP
§ - 'On-line' (v)	EMon EOMN EPPr EWsh MMoz
	SMac WBrk WCot
- 'Variegata'	see *C. nigra* 'On-line'
normalis	EPPr
obnupta	CBrm EBee EPPr SMac
obtrubae **new**	CRWN
ornithopoda	EGle
- 'Aurea'	see *C. ornithopoda* 'Variegata'
§ - 'Variegata' (v)	CSam ECtt EHoe EHul EPPr EPar
	EPla EWsh MBrN MMoz MWhi
	NBro NGdn NHol SAga WCot WFar
	WMoo WTin WWye
§ *oshimensis*	EDAr WCot
§ - 'Evergold' (v) ♀H4	More than 30 suppliers
- 'Evergold Compact' **new**	SMac
- 'Variegata' (v)	EPot IHMH NBir
ovalis	CRWN SWal WRos
pallescens	EPPr GBin WWye
- 'Wood's Edge' (v)	CNat EPPr

panicea	CBri CKno CRWN CWCL EBee EBre EHoe EPPr EPla MMoz SMac WFar WWpP
paniculata	CBig CRWN
pauciflora	GKir
pendula	More than 30 suppliers
- 'Moonraker' (v)	CBot CFil CNat CWCL EHoe EMan EPPr EPla LEdu MAnH MAvo MBNS WCot WLeb WSpi
petriei	CFwr CWCL ECha ECoo EWes EWsh GBuc GGar GOrn LAst LLWP MAvo MBNS MMoz NBPC NVic SCro SGar SWal SYvo WCot WFar WHoo WPer WTin
phyllocephala	EHoe EPza WCot WDyG WRos
- 'Sparkler' (v)	More than 30 suppliers
pilulifera	EMan GKir LRHS NHol SOkd
'Tinney's Princess' (v)	WCot
plantaginea	CFil CFwr EBee EHoe EMar EMon EPPr EPla GBin LEdu NBea WCot WDyG WFar WHil WMoo WPGP
platyphylla	WWye
prairea	EPPr
projecta	EPPr
§ *pseudocyperus*	CElw CRWN EHoe EHon EPPr EPla EPza EWsh GBin GIBF GKir LPBA MAnH MBow MMoz MNrw MSta NArg NBlu NGdn NPer SCou SRms WFar WLeb WMoo WPer WPnP WWpP WWye
pulicaris	CRWN
remota	CBig CRWN EPPr GBin GKir LBuc LRHS WPer WWye
riparia	CRWN EMFW EPPr LPBA MBow MWhi NHol NPer SLon SWal WFar WRos WShi
- 'Bowles' Golden'	see *C. elata* 'Aurea'
- 'Variegata' (v)	CDWL CRow EBee ECha ECoo EGra EHoe EHon EMFW EMon EPPr EPla EWsh GCal LPBA LRHS MAvo MBrN MMoz NArg NBro NHol SAga SCro WAbb WCot WFar WHal WMoo WWpP
rostrata	CRWN NArg
* *saxatilis* 'Variegata' (v)	EBee EHoe EMan
scoparia	EPPr
secta	CBig CTrC EBee ECou EHoe EPPr GOrn MNrw WDyG WMoo WPer WRos
- from Dunedin, New Zealand	EPPr
- var. *tenuiculmis*	see *C. tenuiculmis*
shortiana	EPPr
siderosticha	CBcs CFil EPla SLPl WHrl WPGP WPer
- 'Elaine West' (v)	WCot
- 'Kisokaido' (v)	EMan EMon WCot
- 'Old Barn'	EBee EPPr
- 'Shima-nishiki' (v)	CBcs CHrt CMil CPen CPrp EBee EGle EHoe EMan EMar EPPr EPfP EPla EPyc EPza GBin GEil GFlt LAst MCCP MMoz NCGa NPro SMac SPoG WBor WCot WLin
- 'Variegata' (v)	More than 30 suppliers
- 'Silver Sceptre' (v)	More than 30 suppliers
solandri	CPen CSam CTrC EBee EChP EWsh LEdu MAvo MWrn NLar SHel SWal WMoo WWpP
'Spiky Lollipops' **new**	MCCP
spissa	MNrw
sprengelii	EPPr
sterilis	EPPr
stipata	EPPr
stricta Gooden.	see *C. elata*

- 'Bowles' Golden'	see *C. elata* 'Aurea'
stricta Lamarck	CBrm EPPr EPla WDyG
'Supergold' **new**	EBee
sylvatica	CRWN EBee ECGN WWye
'Taranaki'	EPPr
tasmanica **new**	CBig
tenuiculmis	CBod CWCL EBee ECGN EChP EHoe EMan EMon EPPr EPza EWsh GBin GWCH LAst LPVe LRHS MAvo MWhi NHol WTin WWpP
tereticaulis	GGar WCwm
testacea	More than 30 suppliers
- 'Old Gold'	CFwr CPrp EBee EPPr EWes MAnH MBnl MCCP NOak SMac SMer SPlb SVil WBrE WFar WPnP
texensis	EPPr
trifida	CHEx CHrt CTrC EBee EPPr EPla EPza EWsh GCal GGar ITim LRHS MMoz MNrw NSti SMad WCot WDyG WFar WMnd WWpP WWye
- 'Chatham Blue'	CMHG EChP LBuc NBPC NBir
tuckermanii	EPPr
typhina	EPPr
umbrosa	CBig
- subsp. *sabynensis* 'Thinny Thin' (v)	EBee EMon EPPr
uncifolia	ECou
utriculata	EPPr
virgata	CBig CTrC
viridula subsp. *viridula*	CRWN NArg
vulpina	CBig EPPr
vulpinoidea	EPPr

Carica (Caricaceae)

goudotiana	CKob
x *heilbornii*	CKob
papaya (F)	CKob MGol WHer
pubescens	CKob
quercifolia	CKob

Carissa (Apocynaceae)

grandiflora	see *C. macrocarpa*
§ *macrocarpa* (F)	CTCP ERea EShb ESlt MWya

Carlina (Asteraceae)

acanthifolia	CArn NSla SIgm
- subsp. *cyanara* JJA 274.101	NWCA
acaulis	EGoo ELan EPfP GAbr NPri NWCA SDnm SPlb WFar WHHs WJek WPer
- subsp. *acaulis*	GPoy
- bronze	EGoo EMan EWll LDai LPhx
- var. *caulescens*	see *C. acaulis* subsp. *simplex*
§ - subsp. *simplex*	EBee ECGP EChP ECha EMan GBuc GKir ITer LRHS SCro WCAu WCot WFar WJek WPer WWeb
- - bronze	NChi NSla SMad
vulgaris	WPer
- 'Silver Star'	EGoo EMan

Carmichaelia (Papilionaceae)

'Abundance'	ECou
'Angie'	ECou
angustata 'Buller'	ECou
appressa	ECou GEil GGar
- 'Ellesmere'	ECou
§ *arborea*	ECou
- 'Grand'	ECou
astonii	ECou
- 'Ben More'	ECou
- 'Chalk Ridge'	ECou
australis	ECou WBod
- 'Bright Eyes'	ECou

- 'Cunningham'	ECou
- Flagelliformis Group	ECou
- 'Mahurangi'	ECou
- Ovata Group	ECou
- 'Solander'	ECou
'Charm'	ECou
'Clifford Bay'	ECou
corrugata	ECou
'Culverden'	ECou
curta	ECou
enysii	EHyt
exsul	ECou
fieldii 'Westhaven'	ECou
flagelliformis 'Roro'	ECou
glabrata	CHEx CPLG CPle
'Hay and Honey'	ECou
juncea Nigrans Group	ECou
kirkii	ECou
'Lilac Haze'	ECou
monroi	ECou
- 'Rangitata'	ECou
- 'Tekapo'	ECou
nana	ECou
- 'Desert Road'	ECou
- 'Pringle'	ECou
- 'Waitaki'	ECou
nigrans 'Wanaka'	ECou
odorata	CPLG ECou
- Angustata Group	ECou
- 'Green Dwarf'	ECou
- 'Lakeside'	ECou
- 'Riverside'	ECou
ovata 'Calf Creek'	ECou
'Parson's Tiny'	ECou
petriei	ECou GEil SMad
- 'Aviemore'	ECou
- 'Lindis'	ECou
- 'Pukaki'	ECou
- Virgata Group	ECou
'Porter's Pass'	ECou
'Spangle'	ECou
'Tangle'	ECou
uniflora	ECou
- 'Bealey'	ECou
'Weka'	ECou
williamsii **new**	ECou
'Yellow Eyes'	ECou

x *Carmispartium* (Papilionaceae)

astens	see x *C. hutchinsii*
§ *hutchinsii*	ECou
- 'Butterfly'	ECou
- 'County Park'	ECou
- 'Delight'	ECou
- 'Pink Beauty'	ECou
- 'Wingletye'	ECou

Carpenteria (Hydrangeaceae)

californica ♀H3	More than 30 suppliers
- 'Bodnant'	LPio LRHS MBri MGos SPoG SSpi WGer WPGP
- 'Elizabeth'	CAbP CPMA EPfP GKir LRHS MAsh MBri SMur SPer SSpi SSta WPat
- 'Ladhams' Variety'	CBcs CPMA ENot EPfP MRav NLar SBra SSpi SSta WKif WPGP WSPU

Carpinus ✿ (Corylaceae)

betulus ♀H4	More than 30 suppliers
* - 'A. Beeckman' **new**	SBLw
- 'Columnaris'	CLnd CTho GKir LRHS SBLw
* - 'Columnaris Nana'	CMCN
§ - 'Fastigiata' ♀H4	More than 30 suppliers
- 'Frans Fontaine'	CDul CMCN CTho EBee ENot

	GKir IArd IMGH MAsh MBlu MBri MGos NBlu SBLw SCoo SKee SLim SPer SSta
- 'Horizontalis'	CMCN
- 'Pendula'	CDul CEnd CLnd CTho EBee GKir IDee SBLw WDin
- 'Purpurea'	CDul CEnd ENot SBLw
- 'Pyramidalis'	see *C. betulus* 'Fastigiata'
- 'Quercifolia'	CDul SBLw
caroliniana	CLnd CMCN WNor
cordata	CMCN SBir WCwm WDin
coreana	CLnd CMCN CTho WDin WNor
fangiana	CEnd CTho GKir
fargesii	see *C. viminea*
henryana	CMen SBir WDin WHCr WNor
japonica ♀H4	CEnd CMCN CMen CTho EPfP GKir IDee LRHS MBlu SKee SMad WDin
laxiflora	CMen ISea SMad WNor WPGP
- var. *longispica* B&SWJ 8772 **new**	WCru
- var. *macrostachya*	see *C. viminea*
orientalis	CMCN WNor
polyneura	CMCN SBir WNor
pubescens **new**	GKir
* *schisiensis*	CDul GKir
x *schuschaensis*	GKir
shensiensis **new**	CMCN
tschonoskii	CMCN
turczaninowii ♀H4	CBcs CDul CMCN CMHG CMen CTho GKir NPal NWea SBir STre WDin WNor
§ *viminea*	CDul CEnd CMCN CTho EPfP GKir SBir SSpi WNor

Carpobrotus (Aizoaceae)

acinaciformis **new**	SChr
§ *edulis*	CAgr CHEx CTrC SAPC SArc SChr SEND WHer
muirii	CTrC EShb
quadrifidus	CTrC
rossii	GGar
sauerae	CTrC

Carthamus (Asteraceae)

tinctorius	MSal

Carum (Apiaceae)

carvi	CArn CBod GPoy GWCH MHer NPri NVic SECG SIde WHHs WHer WJek WLHH WPer WSel WWye
copticum	MSal
petroselinum	see *Petroselinum crispum*

Carya ✿ (Juglandaceae)

aquatica	CTho
cordiformis	CMCN CTho EPfP MBlu
glabra	CMCN
N *illinoinensis* (F)	CMCN
laciniosa (F)	CTho EGFP EPfP LRHS SSpi
- 'Henry' (F)	CAgr
- 'Keystone' seedlings (F)	CAgr
myristiciformis	EGFP
ovata (F)	CAgr CLnd CMCN CTho EPfP MBlu SSpi WDin WWes
pallida	CMCN

Caryophyllus see *Syzygium*

Caryopteris ✿ (Verbenaceae)

x *clandonensis*	CTrw EBee ECtt ENot MWat NBir WBod WCFE WDin WFar WHCG WHar WSHC WStI WTel WWin WWye

- 'Arthur Simmonds' ♀H4 — CSam CTri EBee ECha EPfP LHop SPer WGor
- 'Blue Danube' — LAst
- 'Dark Night' — CHar LRHS MBri WBcn WHil
- 'Ferndown' — CDoC CWib EBee EPfP EWTr LRHS MGos NLar SPer SPla SReu SRms SSpi WWeb
- 'First Choice' ♀H3-4 — CAbP ECrN ELan EPfP LRHS MAsh MWat SChu SMad SMrm SMur SPer SPoG WBcn
- Grand Bleu = 'Inoveris'PBR — ELan ENot MBNS
- 'Heavenly Baby' **new** — MAsh
- 'Heavenly Blue' — More than 30 suppliers
- 'Kew Blue' — More than 30 suppliers
- 'Longwood Blue' — EPfP GCal LRHS WBcn
- 'Moody Blue' (v) **new** — EPfP SPoG
- 'Pershore' — MTis WSPU
- 'Summer Gold' **new** — MAsh SPoG
- 'Worcester Gold' ♀H3-4 — More than 30 suppliers
- *divaricata* — EBee EMon
- 'Electrum' — EMan EMon
- 'Jade Shades' — EBee EMan EMon WPGP
§ *incana* — CPle EBee ECrN EPfP MWhi SLon SPer SPoG WSHC XPep
- 'Blue Cascade' — ENot MRav
- weeping — CPle ELan GBuc GCal MBro MSte NLar SAdn WLeb WPat WSPU
- *mastacanthus* — see *C. incana*
- *mongolica* **new** — XPep

Caryota (Arecaceae)

- 'Hymalaya' — CRoM LPal WMul
- *mitis* ♀H1 — EAmu LPal WMul
- *obtusa* — LPal
- *ochlandra* — EAmu LPal
- *urens* — LPal

Cassandra see *Chamaedaphne*

Cassia (Caesalpiniaceae)

- *corymbosa* Lam. — see *Senna corymbosa*
- *marilandica* — see *Senna marilandica*
- *obtusifolia* — see *Senna obtusifolia*

Cassinia (Asteraceae)

- *aculeata* — GGar
- *leptophylla* — GGar SPer
- subsp. *fulvida* — CBcs ECou EHoe GGar GKir GTou MBar SPer WBcn
- subsp. *vauvilliersii* — CDoC GEil GGar SPer
- - var. *albida* — CBcs EGoo EPfP LRHS SPer WBcn WCwm
- - 'Silberschmelze' — SOWG
N *retorta* — CDoC ECou
- 'Ward Silver' — CBot CHar CRez ECou EHoe EMan EWes GEil GSki IArd

Cassinia x *Helichrysum* (Asteraceae)

* hybrid — WKif WSHC

Cassiope ✿ (Ericaceae)

* 'Askival' — EPot ITim
- 'Askival Arctic Fox' — GCrs
- 'Askival Freebird' — see *C.* Freebird Group
- 'Askival Snowbird' — EPot GCrs ITim
- 'Askival Snow-wreath' — see *C.* Snow-wreath Group
- 'Askival Stormbird' — GCrs ITim
- 'Badenoch' — ECho GCrs GEdr GKir ITim NDlv NLAp NLRH WAbe
- 'Bearsden' — CMHG MBar NDlv
- 'Edinburgh' ♀H4 — CMHG EPfP GCrs GEdr GKev GKir ITim MBar NDlv NHol NMen WPat
- *fastigiata* — ITim WAbe

§ Freebird Group — GCrs ITim
- 'George Taylor' — GGGa GKir
* *inermis* — NMen
- *lycopodioides* ♀H4 — GTou ITim MBar NHol
- 'Beatrice Lilley' — EPot GEdr GKir GTou ITim LTwo MBar NDlv NHol SRms WPat
- var. *crista-pilosa* — GKir
- 'Jim Lever' — GCrs ITim WAbe
- *minima* — GEdr
- 'Rokujô' — GKir ITim NHol NMen
- 'Medusa' — GTou NHol WPat
- *mertensiana* — ECho GTou MBar NDlv NJOw NMen SRms
- var. *californica* — EPot GKir
- var. *gracilis* — CMHG GEdr GKir NHol
- 'Muirhead' ♀H4 — CMHG EPot GEdr GKir GTou MBar MDun NDlv NHol NLAp NMen SRms WAbe WPat
- 'Randle Cooke' ♀H4 — CMHG GCrs GEdr GKir GTou MBar MBro MDun NDlv NHol NLAp SRms WAbe WPat
§ *selaginoides* LS&E 13284 — GCrs ITim WAbe
§ Snow-wreath Group — GCrs ITim
§ *stelleriana* — GCrs
- *tetragona* — GKir GTou MBar NLar SRms
- var. *saximontana* — ITim NHol
- *wardii* — GGGa GKir
- *wardii* x *fastigiata* — GCrs GGGa ITim
  Askival strain

Castanea ✿ (Fagaceae)

- 'Bouche de Betizac' (F) **new** — CAgr
- *henryi* **new** — CBcs
- 'Layeroka' (F) — CAgr
- 'Maraval' **new** — LRHS
- 'Maridonne' (F) — CAgr
- 'Marigoule' (F) — CAgr SKee
- 'Marlhac' (F) — CAgr
- 'Marsol' (F) **new** — CAgr
- *mollissima* — CAgr CMCN ISea
- x *neglecta* — CTho LRHS
- 'Précoce Migoule' (F) — CAgr
- *pumila* — CAgr CMCN
- 'Rousse de Nay' (F) — CAgr
- *sativa* ♀H4 — More than 30 suppliers
§ - 'Albomarginata' (v) ♀H4 — CDoC CDul CEnd CTho EBee EPfP IMGH LRHS MBlu MBri MDun MGos NBea SBLw SKee SPer WDin WWes
- 'Anny's Red' — MBlu
- 'Anny's Summer Red' — CDul LRHS MBri
- 'Argenteovariegata' — see *C. sativa* 'Albomarginata'
- 'Aspleniifolia' — CBcs CDul MBlu
- 'Aureomarginata' — see *C. sativa* 'Variegata'
- 'Belle Epine' (F) **new** — CAgr
- 'Bournette' (F) — CAgr
* - 'Doré de Lyon' — CAgr
- 'Laguépie' (F) — CAgr
- 'Marron de Goujounac' (F) **new** — CAgr
- 'Marron de Lyon' (F) — CAgr CDul CEnd CTho EMui EPfP MBlu MCoo SKee
- 'Numbo' (F) **new** — CAgr
- 'Pyramidalis' — WDin
§ - 'Variegata' (v) — CBcs CLnd CMCN COtt ECrN ELan EMil EPfP LPan LRHS MAsh SCoo SKee
- 'Vincent van Gogh' — SMad
- *seguinii* — LEdu LRHS
- 'Simpson' — CAgr
- 'Vignols' (F) — CAgr

Castanopsis (Fagaceae)

- *cuspidata* — CBcs

Castilleja (Scrophulariaceae)

miniata **new**	WAbe

Casuarina (Casuarinaceae)

cunninghamiana	CTrC ECou
glauca	CTrC
stricta	see *Allocasuarina verticillata*
* *zephrea* **new**	CTrC

Catalpa ✿ (Bignoniaceae)

bignonioides ♀H4	More than 30 suppliers
- 'Aurea' ♀H4	More than 30 suppliers
- 'Nana'	ECrN EUJe LRHS SBLw SKee
- 'Purpurea'	see *C.* x *erubescens* 'Purpurea'
- 'Variegata' (v)	CTho EPfP LRHS MBro MRav NHol SLim SPer SSta WPat
bungei	CLnd CTho LPan NPal WNor
- 'Purpurea'	ELan
x *erubescens*	SBLw
§ - 'Purpurea' ♀H4	More than 30 suppliers
fargesii	CFil CLnd
- f. *duclouxii*	CFil CTho NLar WPGP
ovata	CMCN CPle CTho
speciosa	CBcs CLnd CMCN CPle CTho EPfP LRHS SBLw
- 'Pulverulenta' (v)	CDoC CDul CEnd CMCN EMil LRHS MGos NLar WStI

Catananche (Asteraceae)

caerulea	More than 30 suppliers
- 'Alba'	CMea EBee EBla EChP ECha EMlt EPar EPfP ERou GKir LIck LRHS NBid NBir NPri SMac SPer WHHs WMoo WPer WWhi
- 'Amor White'	LRav
- 'Bicolor'	CM&M EMan LRHS MHer MNrw STes WFar WHer WHoo WMoo
- 'Major' ♀H4	EBee EBre EChP LRHS SRms WEas
caespitosa	SBla

Catha (Celastraceae)

edulis	CArn MGol WJek

Catharanthus (Apocynaceae)

roseus ♀H1	GPoy MBri MSal
- Ocellatus Group	MBri

Cathaya (Pinaceae)

argyrophylla **new**	CFil

Caulokaempferia (Zingiberaceae)

linearis **new**	CKob LEur

Caulophyllum (Berberidaceae)

thalictroides	CArn CLAP EBee GBBs GBuc GEdr LEur LRHS MSal WCot WCru WPnP
- subsp. *robustum*	EBee LEur WCru

Cautleya ✿ (Zingiberaceae)

cathcartii	WCru
B&SWJ 2281 **new**	
§ *gracilis*	CBct CKob CLAP EBee EUJe IBlr LEdu LEur MOak WMul
- B&SWJ 7186	WCru
- CC 1751	WCot
lutea	see *C. gracilis*
spicata	CBct CHEx CKob EBee EUJe IBlr ITim LPio MTed WCot
- B&SWJ 2103	WCru
- CC 3676	ITer
* - var. *lutea*	EUJe MOak
- 'Robusta'	CAvo CHEx CLAP CMdw CPne EBee EBre EMan GCal IBlr LEdu

Ceanothus ✿ (Rhamnaceae)

	LRav SBla SCro SMad WBor WCru WMul WPGP
'A.T. Johnson'	CDul EBee ECrN ENot MWya SHBN SLim SPer SRms
americanus	CArn CPle
arboreus	SAPC SArc
- 'Owlswood Blue'	LRHS
- 'Trewithen Blue' ♀H3	More than 30 suppliers
'Autumnal Blue' ♀H3	More than 30 suppliers
'Basil Fox'	LRHS
'Blue Buttons'	LRHS
* 'Blue Carpet'	CWSG
'Blue Cushion'	CBcs CDoC CPMA CWSG EBee ECtt GGar LAst LHop LPVe LRHS MGos MRav SMer SWvt WBVN WFar
'Blue Dreams' **new**	WFar
'Blue Jeans'	EBee IArd LHop LRHS WAbe WLeb
* 'Blue Moon'	LRHS
'Blue Mound' ♀H3	More than 30 suppliers
'Blue Sapphire'PBR	CBcs CWSG EMil LAst NLar NPro SPer SWvt
'Burkwoodii' ♀H3	CBcs CDoC CDul CMac CSBt CTri CWSG EBee EBre ENot EPfP GKir LRHS MAsh MBri MDun MGos MRav NBea NHol SHBN SPer SWvt WFar WRHF
'Burtonensis'	CBcs CTri CWSG EBee EBre ENot GEil GKir LRHS MGos MWat MWgw NBea NSti SLon SPer SPlb WBod WHCG WStI XPep
'Cascade' ♀H3	
'Comtesse de Paris'	see *C.* x *delileanus* 'Comtesse de Paris'
'Concha' ♀H3	More than 30 suppliers
§ *cuneatus* var. *rigidus*	EHol LRHS SDry SRms WAbe WSHC
- - 'Snowball'	EBee ELan EPfP LRHS MGos WBcn
cyaneus	CPle
'Cynthia Postan'	CAbP CMHG CPle CSBt CWSG EBee EBre ECrN EPfP IArd LRHS MBlu MRav MWat NCGa NHol NLar SCoo SDix
'Dark Star' ♀H3	CBcs CBrm CChe CDoC CMHG CPMA CSPN CTbh CWSG EBee EBre EPfP EWll LRHS MBro MWgw NBPC NPro SMad SOWG SPla SReu SSta WPat
'Delight'	CBcs ELan EPfP EPla LRHS MGos MRav NBea NLar SWvt WAbe WDin WFar
x *delileanus*	CBcs
§ - 'Comtesse de Paris'	EBee
- 'Gloire de Versailles' ♀H4	More than 30 suppliers
- 'Henri Desfossé'	CPle EBee EHol ELan IMGH LRHS MRav NCGa SOWG SPer WDin WKif
- 'Indigo'	WKif
- 'Topaze' ♀H4	CBcs CRez CWSG EBee ELan EMil EPfP GEil LRHS MRav SLon SOWG WDin WHar WKif
dentatus hort.	see *C.* x *lobbianus*
dentatus Torr & A.Gray	ENot MAsh MGos SPer
- var. *floribundus*	CSBt EBee ELan LRHS SDix
* - 'Superbus'	EBee
'Diamond Heights'	see *C. griseus* var. *horizontalis* 'Diamond Heights'
divergens	EBee
'Edinburgh' ♀H3	EBee EBre EPfP LRHS MGos NBlu
'Eleanor Taylor'	EBee
'Fallen Skies'	LRHS
foliosus	CPle
- var. *austromontanus*	CTrw

'Frosty Blue'	LRHS
'Gentian Plume'	LRHS
gloriosus	CFai EBee EWes LRHS SDry
- 'Anchor Bay'	COtt EBee ELan EPfP IArd LRHS SLon SOWG WCot WWeb
- 'Emily Brown'	CBcs CSPN EBee GEil NLar
§ *griseus* var. *horizontalis*	EBee LRHS MGos NPri SPer WFar
'Diamond Heights' (v)	
- - 'Hurricane Point'	WBcn WFar
- - 'Silver Surprise'PBR (v)	CBcs CFai CSPN EBee ELan ENot EPfP MGos NLar NPri SHBN SLim SPer SPoG WWeb
- - 'Yankee Point'	CBcs CChe CDoC CMac CSBt EBee ECrN EMil ENot EPfP GGar GKir LPVe LRHS MBri MGos MRav MSwo NBPC SHBN SLim SMer SPer SPlb SWvt WDin WFar XPep
impressus	CBcs CMHG CSBt CTri EBee ECrN ENot EPfP LRHS MAsh MRav SMer SPer SPla WCFE WCom WEas WFar WStI WWeb XPep
N 'Italian Skies' ♀H3	CBcs CChe CDoC CMac CSBt CWSG EBee ECrN EMil EPfP LAst LPVe LRHS MDun MGos MLan MRav MSwo NBlu NPri SLim SLon SMer SPer SPlb WBod WDin WFar WWeb XPep
'Joyce Coulter'	CBcs EBee ISea
'Julia Phelps'	CMHG EBee WEas WSPU
'Ken Taylor'	LRHS
§ x *lobbianus*	CBcs CTri ECtt EHol LAst MRav NJOw WDin
- 'Russellianus'	CAbP EBee MGos MWya SHBN WSPU
x *pallidus*	CFai WBcn
- 'Golden Elan'	WBcn
- 'Marie Simon'	CBcs CBot CBrm CChe CWib EBee EBre ECrN EHol ELan EMil EPfP GEil LHop LRHS NBlu NJOw SRms SSta WBod WCFE WDin WFar WGMN WKif WSHC WWeb
- 'Marie Simon Variegated' (v) **new**	CPMA
- 'Perle Rose'	CBcs CMac CPle EBee EPfP LRHS SHBN SOWG SPla WKif WSHC
papillosus	EBee
- var. *roweanus*	CPle
'Pershore Zanzibar'PBR (v)	CSPN CWSG EBee EBre EHoe ENot EPfP LAst LRHS MCCP MGos MSwo MTis MWat MWgw MWya NPri SHBN SPer SWvt WSPU WWeb
'Pin Cushion'	CDoC CWSG CWib EBee EPfP LRHS MRav WBcn WRHF WSPU
'Point Millerton'	see *C. thyrsiflorus* 'Millerton Point'
prostratus	MAsh SDry SHBN SMad WAbe
'Puget Blue' ♀H4	More than 30 suppliers
purpureus	WWeb
'Ray Hartman'	SMad WBcn XPep
repens	see *C. thyrsiflorus* var. *repens*
rigidus	see *C. cuneatus* var. *rigidus*
'Sierra Blue'	EBee
'Snow Flurries'	CBcs CWib EBee ECrN ECtt EMil EPfP LAst MGos MSwo MWat WAbe WFar WSPU
'Snow Showers'	NBPC NBlu WBod
'Southmead' ♀H3	CDoC CTri EBee ECrN ECtt EGra EMil EPfP GBuc LRHS MAsh MGos MSwo NBPC NBlu NHol NPri WBrE WDin WHCG
thyrsiflorus	CBcs CMac CTri CWSG CWib EBee EPfP LRHS MAsh NHol SGar SHBN SPer SRms SWvt WDin WFar WHar WTel
- 'Borne Again' (v)	WBcn WWpP
§ - 'Millerton Point'	CChe CWSG EBee EMil EPfP LAst LRHS MBlu NBlu NLar SLim WBod WWeb WWpP XPep
§ - var. *repens* ♀H3	More than 30 suppliers
- 'Skylark' ♀H3	More than 30 suppliers
'Tilden Park'	LRHS
x *veitchianus*	CMac CSBt EBee ELan ENot LAst LRHS MAsh MBar NHol SPer WWeb
velutinus	MSal
'Victoria'	EBee LBuc XPep
'White Cascade'	CSBt EBee EHol LRHS

Cedrela (Meliaceae)

sinensis	see *Toona sinensis*

Cedronella (Lamiaceae)

§ *canariensis*	CArn CBod CHby CSev CTCP EShb GBar GGar GPoy IFro ILis MBow MHer MSal NGHP SIde SOWG SWat WCHb WHHs WHer WPer WSel WWye XPep
mexicana	see *Agastache mexicana*
triphylla	see *C. canariensis*

Cedrus (Pinaceae)

atlantica	CDul CLnd CSBt ECrN EHul GKir MBar NWea SEND WBVN WEve WMou
- 'Aurea'	CMac LLin LPan MBar MGos NLar SCoo SSta WDin WHar
- 'Fastigiata'	CDoC CMac EHul LCon MBar MBri MGos NLar SCoo SLim WEve
- Glauca Group ♀H4	More than 30 suppliers
- - 'Silberspitz'	CKen
- 'Glauca Fastigiata'	CKen CMen ECho WEve
- 'Glauca Pendula'	CDoC CDul CKen CMen EBre ECrN EHul EOrn EPfP GKir IMGH LCon LPan LRHS MBar MBlu MBri MGos NBee NBlu NPSI NWea SHBN SKee SLim SMad SSta WDin
- 'Pendula'	CDul CMac ECho GBin MAsh SHBN WOrn
brevifolia	ECho LCon LLin LPan MBar MBri MGos NLar WEve
- 'Epstein'	MBar
- 'Hillier Compact'	CKen GTSp
- 'Kenwith'	CKen
deodara ♀H4	More than 30 suppliers
- 'Albospica' (v)	LCon LLin MAsh SWvt
- 'Argentea'	MBar MGos NLar
- 'Aurea' ♀H4	CDoC CDul CSBt CTho EBre ECrN EHul EOrn EPfP GFlt GKir IMGH LCon LLin LPan LRHS MAsh MBar MBri MGos NBlu SLim WDin WEve WFar WOrn
- 'Blue Dwarf'	CKen LCon LLin WEve
* - 'Blue Mountain Broom'	CKen
- 'Blue Snake' **new**	NLar
- 'Blue Triumph'	LPan WEve
- 'Cream Puff'	CSli ECho LLin MAsh MBar MGos
* - 'Dawn Mist' **new**	LLin
- 'Feelin' Blue'	CDoC CKen COtt CSli EBre EHul ENot EPla GKir IMGH LBee LCon LLin LPan LRHS MAsh MBar MBri MGos MLan NBlu NHol SCoo SHBN SLim SWvt WEve WStI
- 'Gold Cone'	MGos
- 'Gold Mound'	CKen CSBt LCon MAsh WEve
- 'Golden Horizon'	CDoC CKen CSBt EBre EHul EOrn GKir IMGH LBee LCon LLin LPan LRHS MAsh MBar MBri MGos NBee NBlu SHBN SLim SWvt WDin WEve

– 'Karl Fuchs'	CDoC EBre GKir LPan LRHS MAsh MBri NBlu NLar SCoo SMad WGor
– 'Kashmir'	CSli
– 'Kelly Gold'	GKir MBri
– 'Klondyke'	MAsh
– 'Mountain Beauty'	CKen
– 'Nana'	CKen
– 'Nivea'	CKen
– 'Pendula'	CDoC EHul LPan MBar MGos MWat NPSI WDin WEve WGor WStI
– 'Polar Winter'	SMad
– 'Pygmy'	CKen
– 'Raywood's Prostrate'	CKen
– 'Robusta'	WEve
– 'Roman Candle'	CSli ECho EOrn SHBN WEve
– 'Scott'	CKen
– 'Silver Mist'	CKen
– 'Silver Spring'	MAsh MGos NLar
* 'Home Park'	CKen
libani ♀H4	More than 30 suppliers
– 'Comte de Dijon'	EHul LLin LRHS SLim SPoG
– Nana Group	CKen ECho MAsh
– 'Sargentii'	CDoC CKen EHul EOrn IMGH LCon LLin LRHS MBar MBri MGos NPSI SHBN SLim WEve
– 'Taurus'	MBar NLar

Celastrus (*Celastraceae*)

angulatus	GIBF WPGP
orbiculatus	CBcs CDoC CFwr CMac EBee ELan GBin GEil LRHS MAsh MRav NSti SHGC SLon SReu SSta WBor WFar WSHC
– 'Diana' (f)	NBea NLar SSta
– 'Hercules' (m)	NBea NLar
– Hermaphrodite Group ♀H4	CBrm CSam GSki MCCP SBra SDix SPer SSpi
– var. *papillosus* B&SWJ 591	WCru
– var. *punctatus* B&SWJ 1931	WCru
rosthornianus	GIBF
scandens	CMac EBee ENot IMGH NLar SMur SPlb WDin

Celmisia ✿ (*Asteraceae*)

adamsii	IBlr
allanii	IBlr
alpina	IBlr SOkd
– large-leaved	IBlr
angustifolia	EPot GCrs IBlr
– silver-leaved	IBlr
argentea	GCrs GGar GTou IBlr ITim NDlv NLAp WAbe
armstrongii	ECho IBlr
asteliifolia	IBlr
Ballyrogan hybrids	IBlr
bellidioides	EPot EWes GCrs GEdr IBlr MDKP NLAp NMen WAbe
bonplandii	IBlr
brevifolia	IBlr
coriacea misapplied	see *C. semicordata*
coriacea Raoul	see *C. mackaui*
coriacea (G. Forst.) Hook. f.	GCal IBlr MDun NFor
costiniana	IBlr
dallii	IBlr
'David Shackleton'	IBlr
densiflora	GCrs IBlr ITim SOkd
– silver-leaved	IBlr
discolor	IBlr
durietzii	IBlr

'Edrom'	ITim
glandulosa	IBlr
gracilenta	GCrs IBlr ITim NLAp NMen NSla SOkd SRot
– CC 563	NWCA
graminifolia	IBlr
haastii	IBlr
§ 'Harry Bryce'	IBlr
hectorii	GCrs IBlr ITim SOkd
hectorii x *ramulosa* **new**	WAbe
holosericea	IBlr
hookeri	EPot GCal IBlr
inaccessa	IBlr
incana	GCrs IBlr ITim SOkd
Inshriach hybrids	GAbr IBlr
insignis	IBlr
Jury hybrids	IBlr
latifolia	IBlr
– large-leaved	IBlr
longifolia	GGar SSpi
– large-leaved	IBlr
– small-leaved	IBlr
§ *mackaui*	GGar IBlr
markii	IBlr
monroi	GCrs IBlr
morganii	IBlr
prorepens	IBlr ITim
pugioniformis	IBlr SOkd
ramulosa	EPot GEdr GGar ITim NLAp
§ – var. *tuberculata*	GCrs GTou IBlr NSla
saxifraga	IBlr ITim WAbe
§ *semicordata*	GBuc IBlr ITim NLAp NSla WPat
– subsp. *aurigans*	IBlr
– 'David Shackleton'	see *C.* 'David Shackleton'
– subsp. *stricta*	IBlr
sericophylla	IBlr
– large-leaved	IBlr
sessiliflora	EPot GTou IBlr ITim
– 'Mount Potts'	IBlr
spectabilis	IBlr MDun NLAp WCot WPat
– subsp. *magnifica*	IBlr
– subsp. *spectabilis* var. *angustifolia*	IBlr
spedenii	IBlr
Timpany hybrids	ITim
tomentella	IBlr
traversii	IBlr ITim WWeb
verbascifolia	GCrs IBlr
viscosa	IBlr
§ *walkeri*	EPot GCrs GGar GTou IBlr
webbiana	see *C. walkeri*

Celosia (*Amaranthaceae*)

argentea var. *cristata*	MBri
– – Plumosa Group	MBri

Celsia see *Verbascum*

x *Celsioverbascum* see *Verbascum*

Celtis (*Ulmaceae*)

australis	CBcs CDul CTho EGFP GKir LPan LRHS SBLw
bungeana	CMCN IDee
julianae	WCwm WNor
occidentalis	CAgr CTho ELan LRHS WBVN
– var. *pumila*	WNor
sinensis	EGFP NLar WNor
trinervia	GIBF

Cenolophium (*Apiaceae*)

denudatum	CDes EBee ECha SIgm WPGP

Centaurea ✿ (*Asteraceae*)

D&T 89061T	EBee
HH&K 271	NBid
from Turkey	WPGP
alba	EBee NCot
alpestris	CMHG EChP ECho NLar
argentea	CBot
atropurpurea	NLar SGar
bella	More than 30 suppliers
– 'Katherine' (v) **new**	MAvo
benoistii	CDes CHad CKno CPlt EBee EMan
	LPhx MRav SIgm WPGP
'Black Ball' **new**	CSpe WGwG WHHs
'Blue Dreams'	EMon LPVe MLLN SCro SUsu
cana	see *C. triumfettii* subsp. *cana*
candidissima hort.	see *C. cineraria*
'Caramia'	EBre EOMN SSvw SUsu
cheiranthifolia	CDes CElw EChP ECha EMon NBir
	WFar
§ – var. *purpurascens*	EMon
§ *cineraria*	EMan MOak SRms WCot WEas
cyanus	CArn GWCH MBow MHer NArg
	WBWf WFar WJek
dealbata	More than 30 suppliers
– 'Steenbergii'	CAbP CMHG EBre EChP EGle
	ELan ERou EWTr GCal GKir LRHS
	NBid NOak NPer NSti SMer SPer
	SSpe WAbb WCom WCot WFar
	WHoo WMnd
fischeri Willd.	CDes EMon MAvo
glastifolia	EBee EMon GCal MLLN WCot
	WPGP
gymnocarpa	see *C. cineraria*
'Hoar Frost'	CMil EMon
hypoleuca 'John Coutts'	More than 30 suppliers
jacea	EMan GAbr MBow NBid SYvo
	WCAu WCot WPer WSSM
kotschyana	CDes EBee NBid WPGP
macrocephala	More than 30 suppliers
marschalliana	NBid
mollis **new**	NBid
montana	More than 30 suppliers
– 'Alba'	More than 30 suppliers
§ – 'Carnea'	CElw CPom EBee EChP ECha EGle
	EMon LLWP LPhx MAnH MAvo
	NChi NCot SCro STes WCAu WFar
	WWin
– 'Coerulea'	CBot IHMH WBVN WShp
– 'Gold Bullion'	CDes CFai EBee EBre ECGP ECtt
	EGle EMon EPPr EWes GBuc LDai
	MAvo MBri MCCP NBid NBir NCot
	NSti SMad SSvw SUsu SVil WBcn
	WCAu WCot WWeb
– 'Grandiflora'	EBee GGar MBri
– 'Horwood Gold'	LHop WBro
– 'Joyce'	EMon MAvo
– 'Lady Flora Hastings'	CBot CBre CDes CElw CFee CKno
	CSam CSpe EBee GMac LPhx
	MAvo MTed SCro WPGP
– 'Ochroleuca'	EGle EGoo EMon GBuc MLLN
	WBcn
– pale pink **new**	NChi
– 'Parham'	CElw CMHG CPrp CSev EBee
	EBlw EMan ERou EWTr GCal
	LHop LLWP LRHS MCLN MRav
	NSti SChu SHel SPer SPla SPlb
	SWat WMnd
– 'Purple Prose'	EMon WBcn
– 'Purpurea'	CDes EBee MRav
– 'Rosea'	see *C. montana* 'Carnea'
* – *violacea*	IBlr
– 'Violetta'	CPom MAvo NBir WFar
nervosa	see *C. uniflora* subsp. *nervosa*
nigra	CArn COld CRWN EBee EMan
	ITim LAst MBow MOne NLan
	NMir NNor NSco SRob WMoo
– var. *alba*	CArn CBre NBid WWye
– 'Breakaway' (v)	EBee
– subsp. *rivularis*	ECha NBid
orientalis	CMdw CPou CRez CSam EBee
	EChP LPhx MHar MMHG NLar
	SBla SCro SIgm SSvw WPer
pannonica	CPom NBid WSHC
subsp. *pannonica*	
– – HH&K 259	CStr
pestalozzae **new**	EHyt
phrygia	EBee EMan GAbr MNrw NBid
	NLar WPer WRos
– subsp. *pseudophrygia*	CSam NBid
pulcherrima	EChP EMan EMon EWTr GCal
	MAvo MLLN NOak WPer XPep
'Pulchra Major'	see *Stemmacantha centauriodes*
rigidifolia	EGle
rothrockii	WSan
rupestris	CMHG CPou EBee EChP LPhx
	NLar SAga SBla SGar WBar WWeb
	WWin
ruthenica	CHea CPom EChP EMan LPhx
	MSte NLar SIgm SPer WCot
* – 'Alba'	MSte
salonitana	EMon
scabiosa	CArn CRWN ECoo GWCH MBow
	MHer MWhi NBid NJOw NLan
	NSco WPer
– f. *albiflora*	CNat ECGP EMan EMon EPza LAst
	LRHS MWgw
simplicicaulis	CKno CNic CPlt CSam EBee EGle
	EMan GAbr GBri MBct MBro
	MTho NMen SBla SIgm SRms SRot
	WCom WCot WEas WHoo WPGP
	WPer WWhi WWpP
stenolepis	CStr
subsp. *razgradensis*	
HH&K 297	
thracica	LPhx SAga SCro WCot
§ *triumfettii*	CBrm NJOw SBla WWin
subsp. *cana* 'Rosea'	
– subsp. *stricta*	CBgR CDes CKno CSLe CSam
	EBee EMon GAbr GBuc MSte SBla
	SCro WPGP
§ *uniflora* subsp. *nervosa*	GGar MGas NBid NBro WBea WPer

Centaurium (*Gentianaceae*)

chloodes	see *C. confertum*
§ *confertum*	WBVN
erythraea	CArn EDAr EMlt GPoy MHer MSal
	NJOw NLar NWCA SECG WHHs
	WWye
scilloides	EBre LRHS MTho NMen WAbe
	WCom

Centella (*Apiaceae*)

§ *asiatica*	CArn EBee EOHP GPoy ILis MGol
	MSal WJek

Centradenia (*Melastomataceae*)

floribunda	SYvo
inaequilateralis	CHal ECtt EMan LPVe MBri SHFr
'Cascade'	SPet

Centranthus (*Valerianaceae*)

§ *ruber*	More than 30 suppliers
* – 'Alba Pura'	NBPC
§ – 'Albus'	More than 30 suppliers
– 'Atrococcineus'	ECha EMan WPer WShp
– var. *coccineus*	CBcs EBee EBre EChP EGoo ELan
	ENot EPfP GAbr GKir IHMH LIck

	LPhx LRHS MRav MWgw NBlu
	NDov NPri SEND SMrm SPer SPla
	WCAu WCot WFar WHil WWeb
– mauve	LPhx MAnH NDov WEas XPep
– 'Roseus'	EBee WMoo WOVN
– 'Rosy Red' **new**	GFlt
– 'Snowcloud'	COIW CSev EWTr GFlt NPri SWvt
	WHil
– 'Swanage' **new**	CNat
'White Cloud'	WJek

Cephalanthera (*Orchidaceae*)

falcata	EFEx
longibracteata	EFEx

Cephalanthus (*Rubiaceae*)

occidentalis	CBcs CDul CPle EDAr EMil GEil
	IFro IMGH LRav MBNS MBlu
	MGos NBlu SPer SSpi WBVN WFar

Cephalaria (*Dipsacaceae*)

HWJ 695 **new**	LPhx
from Nepal 2800m	CSam
§ *alpina*	EBee EBre ECha EDAr EHrv EMan
	EMlt EPAt GKir IBal IHMH LAst
	LRHS MHer MNrw NHol NLar
	SOkh SRms SWat WBVN WFar
	WPer
– 'Nana'	CMil NMen NWCA
ambrosioides	MLLN
dipsacoides	CFee CKno CTCP EBee EChP
	ECha GFlt LDai LPhx MHer MWrn
	NLar SMHy WMoo
§ *flava*	EBee GKir
galpiniana	EBee
subsp. *simplicior*	
§ *gigantea*	More than 30 suppliers
graeca	see *C. flava*
leucantha	CHea EBee ECGN EMan GBuc
	MLLN MSph MWrn NLar SHel STes
litvinovii	CElw
natalensis	EBee
oblongifolia **new**	CTCP SPoG
radiata	ITer
tatarica	see *C. gigantea*
tchihatchewii	EBee MLLN

Cephalotaxus (*Cephalotaxaceae*)

fortunei	CDoC CDul SLon
– 'Prostrate Spreader'	EHul
harringtonii	ECho LEdu MRav SMur
– 'Fastigiata'	CBcs CDoC CKen EBre EHul ENot
	EOrn GKir IArd LCon LLin LRHS
	MAsh MBar MBlu MBri SLim WDin
	WFar WGer
– 'Gimborn's Pillow'	MBar
– 'Korean Gold'	CKen NLar
– 'Prostrata'	MBar

Cephalotus (*Cephalotaceae*)

follicularis	SHmp

Cerastium (*Caryophyllaceae*)

alpinum	SRms
– var. *lanatum*	EBre ECho ETow EWes MDKP
	NJOw WPer
arvense	NDlv
candidissimum	EWes XPep
tomentosum	CHal CTri EFer EPfP EWTr GKir
	GWCH IHMH LGro MHer NBlu
	NDlv NFor NJOw NPri SPer SPet
	SPlb WFar WPer XPep
– var. *columnae*	ECha ECho EHoe EPfP EWes WCot
	WShp

– 'Silberteppich'	EGoo LPVe

Ceratoides (*Chenopodiaceae*)

lanata	see *Krascheninnikovia lanata*

Ceratonia (*Caesalpiniaceae*)

siliqua	CAgr CFil MSal WHHs XPep

Ceratophyllum (*Ceratophyllaceae*)

demersum	CBen CRow EHon EMFW LNCo
	NArg SLon SWat WMAq

Ceratostigma ✿ (*Plumbaginaceae*)

abyssinicum	ELan
'Autumn Blue'	EPfP
griffithii	More than 30 suppliers
– SF 149/150	ISea
minus	CPLG
§ *plumbaginoides* ♀H3-4	More than 30 suppliers
willmottianum ♀H3-4	More than 30 suppliers
– Desert Skies	CBcs CBrm CFwr EBee EBre ELan
= 'Palmgold'PBR	EPfP GBuc LHop LRHS MAsh SCoo
	SHGC SMad SPer SSta SWvt WWeb
– Forest Blue = 'Lice'PBR	CAbP CDoC CFwr CSBt CWSG
	EBee EBre ECrN EGra ELan ENor
	ENot EPfP LHop LRHS MAsh MRav
	MWgw NPri NPro SCoo SHBN
	SMer SMrm SPer SPla SReu WPat
	WWeb

Cercidiphyllum ✿ (*Cercidiphyllaceae*)

japonicum ♀H4	More than 30 suppliers
– 'Heronswood Globe'	CMCN CPMA MBlu NLar
– f. *pendulum* ♀H4	CBcs CDul CEnd CLnd CMCN
	CPMA EPfP GKir LBuc LRHS MAsh
	MBlu NBea NLar SHBN SKee SLim
	SPer SSpi WDin WOrn WPGP
	WWes
– – 'Amazing Grace'	CTho LRHS
– Red Fox	see *C. japonicum* 'Rotfuchs'
§ – 'Rotfuchs'	CBcs CEnd CMCN CPMA CTho
	EBee EPfP GKir LRHS MAsh MBlu
	MDun MGos NLar NPal SKee SLim
	SSpi WBcn WPGP
– 'Ruby'	CPMA
I – 'Strawberry'	EPfP MBlu NLar
magnificum	CDul CEnd CFil CMCN EPfP MBlu
	NLar SSpi
– Og 95.111	CDoC
– Og 95.114	WCru
– Og 95.144	CFil EPla WPGP
– f. *pendulum*	see *C. japonicum* f. *pendulum*

Cercis (*Caesalpiniaceae*)

canadensis	CAgr CBcs CBrm CDul CHEx
	CLnd CMCN EMil EPfP EWTr GIBF
	MCCP MGos NHol SLim SPer
	WHCG WNor WPat
– f. *alba* **new**	LRHS
– – 'Royal White'	EPfP MBlu NLar
– 'Forest Pansy' ♀H4	More than 30 suppliers
* – 'Gigantea'	IArd
§ – var. *occidentalis*	LRav SOWG
– 'Rubye Atkinson'	NLar
chinensis	LRHS MCCP NLar SPer SSta WDin
	WMoo
– 'Avondale'	CBcs CDoC CEnd CPMA CWib
	EBee EMil EWes IArd LRHS MBlu
	MGos NLar SKee SLim SWvt
chingii	WPGP
griffithii	IArd NLar
occidentalis	see *C. canadensis* var. *occidentalis*
racemosa	NLar
reniformis 'Oklahoma'	CBcs CPMA EBee IArd MBlu NLar

- 'Texas White'	CBcs CPMA NLar WSpi
siliquastrum ♀H4	More than 30 suppliers
- f. *albida*	CBot CTho ECrN EPfP LPan LRHS
- 'Bodnant'	EPfP MBlu NLar
- 'Rubra'	WPat
yunnanensis	NLar

Cercocarpus (Rosaceae)

montanus	NLar
var. *glaber* new	

Cerinthe (Boraginaceae)

glabra	EMan NJOw SPlb
'Golden Bouquet'	NPSI
major	WEas WSan
- 'Kiwi Blue'	CHll CSpe MDKP
- 'Purpurascens'	More than 30 suppliers
- 'Yellow Gem'	CPla
minor new	CTCP
- subsp. *auriculata*	LIck
retorta	CTCP

Ceropegia (Asclepiadaceae)

barklyi	CHal
linearis	CHal EShb IBlr MBri SRms
subsp. *woodii* ♀H1	
sandersonii ♀H1	SSte

Ceroxylon (Arecaceae)

alpinum	CPHo LPJP LPal
ventricosum	LPal

Cestrum (Solanaceae)

aurantiacum	ERea
auriculatum	SOWG
x *cultum*	CHll CPle
- 'Cretan Purple'	CHll CPle EPfP ERea SMur SSpi
§ *elegans*	CHEx CHal CHll CPLG CSev MOak
	SOWG WCot WDin
fasciculatum	CBcs SIgm SMad SOWG
'Newellii' ♀H2	CAbb CBcs CHEx CMHG CPLG
	CSev CWib EBak ELan EPfP ERea
	MBlu NPSI SDnm SGar SIgm
	SOWG SSpi WBor WSHC
nocturnum	CBcs CDoC CHal CHll CPle EBak
	ERea ESlt LRHS SHBN SOWG XPep
parqui ♀H3	CAbb CHEx CHll CMHG CPLG
	CPle EBee ECha ELan EPfP ERea
	EShb MOak SDix SDnm SGar SLon
	SMad SMrm SMur SOWG SSte
	SVen SYvo WCot WKif WOld WPic
	WSHC XPep
- hybrid	SSpi
- 'Orange Essence' new	WCot
psittacinum	CPLG
purpureum misapplied	see *Iochroma cyaneum* 'Trebah'
purpureum	see *C. elegans*
(Lindley) Standley	
roseum	CPLG CSev
- 'Ilnacullin'	CPLG CTCP CTrC ERea IDee
* *splendens*	SOWG
violaceum misapplied	see *Iochroma cyaneum* 'Trebah'

Ceterach (Aspleniaceae)

officinarum	see *Asplenium ceterach*

Chaenomeles (Rosaceae)

cathayensis	CTho EPfP EPla LEdu SMad WBcn
	WHer
§ *japonica*	CCVT ENot MBar NFor WDin WFar
	XPep
- 'Orange Beauty'	WFar
- 'Sargentii'	CBcs CMac NLar
'John Pilger'	NHol NPro SLon

lagenaria	see *C. speciosa*
'Madame Butterfly'	COtt EBre GKir
maulei	see *C. japonica*
sinensis	see *Pseudocydonia sinensis*
§ *speciosa*	CSam ISea MBar NFor NWea WNor
- 'Apple Blossom'	see *C. speciosa* 'Moerloosei'
- 'Aurora'	LRHS MBri
- 'Brilliant'	EPfP
- 'Contorta'	WCot
- 'Falconnet Charlet' (d)	MRav
- 'Geisha Girl' ♀H4	More than 30 suppliers
- 'Grayshott Salmon'	EBee MCCP NCiC NHol NPro
	WFar WLeb
§ - 'Moerloosei' ♀H4	CBrm CDoC CEnd CPMA CSBt
	CSam CTri EBee ELan ENot EPfP
	GKir IMGH LAst LRHS MBri MRav
	MSwo MWat NSti SHBN SLim SPer
	SPla SSta WDin WGwG WMoo
- 'Nivalis'	More than 30 suppliers
- 'Port Eliot'	WBcn WWeb
- 'Rosea Plena' (d)	WBcn
- 'Rubra Grandiflora'	WBrE
- 'Simonii' (d)	CBcs EBee EHol ENot EPfP LRHS
	MGos MRav NWea SPer WFar
- 'Snow'	CChe CSBt EBee MRav MSwo
	MWat NHol NPro WCot WStI
- 'Umbilicata'	ENot SPer SRms WWes XPep
- 'Winter Snow'	ENot
- 'Yukigoten'	LRHS WBcn
x *superba*	NFor
- 'Boule de Feu'	CTri CWib ECtt GKir
- 'Cameo' (d)	CBot CChe ECrN EPfP LAst LRHS
	MAsh MBri NPri SLPl WWeb
- 'Coral Sea'	NFor
- 'Crimson and Gold' ♀H4	More than 30 suppliers
- 'Elly Mossel'	CBcs CMac CSBt GKir MAsh NBlu
	SMer WFar
- 'Ernst Finken'	EBee
- 'Etna'	GKir
- 'Fire Dance'	CMac EBee ECrN ECtt ENot IMGH
	MRav MSwo NBee NHol SPer
	SPoG WRHF
- 'Hollandia'	MGos
- 'Issai White'	LRHS WBcn
- 'Jet Trail'	CBcs CSBt EBee ECrN ELan ENot
	EPfP LAst LRHS MAsh MGos MRav
	MSwo NBlu NPro WFar
- 'Knap Hill Scarlet' ♀H4	CBrm CDoC EBee EBre ECot ENot
	EPfP GKir LRHS MAsh MRav NHol
	SEND SLim SPer SPoG SRms
	WBVN WBod WDin WFar WRHF
	WStI
- 'Lemon and Lime'	EBee ELan ENot EPfP MAsh MGos
	MRav NSti WBcn
- 'Nicoline' ♀H4	CBcs CDoC EBee ENot EPfP GKir
	LRHS MBri MRav MWat NPri SBra
	SPoG WDin WFar WStI
- 'Ohio Red'	WBod
- 'Pink Lady' ♀H4	More than 30 suppliers
- 'Red Joy' new	WBcn
- 'Red Trail'	EBee ENot MRav
- 'Rowallane' ♀H4	EBee ECrN ELan ENot EPfP IMGH
	MRav NLRH SHBN
- 'Salmon Horizon'	EWTr MGos WBcn
- 'Texas Scarlet'	WBcn
- 'Tortuosa'	SPoG WBcn
- 'Vermilion'	MBNS
- 'Vesuvius'	EWTr

Chaenorhinum (Scrophulariaceae)

§ *origanifolium*	CElw CNic EBee ESis LIck NBlu
	NWCA SPlb WGMN WWin XPep
- 'Blue Dream'	CBAn CSpe EBre ECtt EMan GBBs
	MBri MNrw MWgw MWrn NBlu

NBur NPri SPet SWvt WBVN WCot
WFar WPer WShp WWeb

Chaerophyllum (Apiaceae)

hirsutum   CRow ELan
- 'Roseum'   More than 30 suppliers

Chamaecyparis ✿ (Cupressaceae)

formosensis   CKen
funebris   see *Cupressus funebris*
lawsoniana   CDul EHul MBar NWea WBVN
    WDin WEve WMou
- 'Albospica' (v)   ECho EHul GKir MBar SBod WFar
- 'Albospica Nana'   see *C. lawsoniana* 'Nana
    Albospica'
- 'Albovariegata' (v)   ECho EHul EOrn LBee LRHS MBar
- 'Allumii Aurea'   see *C. lawsoniana* 'Alumigold'
- 'Allumii Magnificent'   CBcs MAsh
§ - 'Alumigold'   CDoC CSBt CSli CWib EBre GKir
    MAsh MBar MGos SBod SMer
    WDin WStI
- 'Alumii'   CMac CTri ECrN EHul ENot GKir
    MAsh MBar MGos NWea SPer WStI
- 'Argentea'   see *C. lawsoniana*
    'Argenteovariegata'
§ - 'Argenteovariegata' (v)   CDoC CMac ECho GKir SLim
§ - 'Aurea'   CDul
I - 'Aurea Compacta'   ECho
- 'Aurea Densa' ♀H4   CFee CKen CMac CNic CSBt CTri
    EHul EOrn GKir MAsh MBar MGos
    SBod SPoG STre WGor
- 'Aureovariegata' (v)   MBar WBcn
§ - 'Barabits' Globe'   MBar
- 'Barry's Gold'   EOrn
- 'Barry's Silver' **new**   EBre
- 'Beacon Silver'   WBcn
§ - 'Bleu Nantais'   CKen CMac CSBt EHul EOrn GKir
    LBee LCon LLin LRHS MAsh MBar
    MBro MGos MWat SBod SHBN
    SLim WCFE WEve
- 'Blom'   CKen EHul MBri
- 'Blue Gem'   NHol
§ - 'Blue Gown'   EHul LBee MBar MGos SRms
§ - 'Blue Jacket'   MBar NWea
- 'Blue Nantais'   see *C. lawsoniana* 'Bleu Nantais'
- 'Blue Surprise'   CKen ECrN EHul EOrn MBar MBro
    MOne SAga WFar
- 'Brégéon'   CKen
- 'Broomhill Gold'   CBrm CDoC CMac CSBt EBre EHul
    ENot GKir LCon LLin LRHS MAsh
    MBar MBri MGos MWat NHol
    SBod SLim SPer SPla WCFE WDin
    WEve WLow WStI
- 'Buckland Gold' **new**   CDoC
* - 'Burkwood's Blue'   MBar
- 'Caudata'   CKen MBar WBcn
- 'Chantry Gold'   CKen ECho EHul GKir
§ - 'Chilworth Silver' ♀H4   CSBt CTri EBre EHul EOrn EPot
    GKir LBee LRHS MAsh MBar MBri
    SBod SHBN SLim SPer SRms
    WBVN WDin WFar WStI
- 'Chingii'   EHul MAsh
- 'Columnaris'   CBcs CDoC CMac EBre ENot EPfP
    GKir LBee LRHS MBar MBri MGos
    NBlu NWea SHBN SLim WCFE
    WFar
- 'Columnaris Aurea'   see *C. lawsoniana* 'Golden Spire'
N - 'Columnaris Glauca'   CSBt CWib EBre EHul EOrn GKir
    LCon LPan MAsh MGos MWat
    NBee SBod SPer WDin WFar WStI
    WTel
- 'Crawford's Compact'   CMac
- 'Cream Crackers'   ECho EHul
- 'Cream Glow'   CKen EBre LRHS SLim WFar WGor

- 'Croftway'   EHul
- 'Dart's Blue
   Ribbon' **new**   MBri
- 'Dik's Weeping'   CDoC MBri SMad WEve
- 'Dorset Gold'   CMac
- 'Duncanii'   EHul
- 'Dutch Gold'   EHul GKir MAsh
- 'Dwarf Blue'   see *C. lawsoniana* 'Pick's Dwarf
    Blue'
- 'Eclipse'   CKen
- 'Elegantissima' ambig.   CKen CMac
- 'Ellwoodii' ♀H4   CMac CSBt CTri CWib EBre ECrN
    EHul ENot EPfP GKir LCon LRHS
    MAsh MBar MGos MWat NBlu
    NWea SBod SLim SMer SPer WCFE
    WDin WFar WMoo WTel
I - 'Ellwoodii Glauca' **new**   EBre EGra SPlb WLow
- 'Ellwood's Empire'   EHul LRHS MBri NHol WEve
- 'Ellwood's Gold' ♀H4   More than 30 suppliers
- 'Ellwood's Gold Pillar'   CSBt EBre ECho EHul ENot EOrn
    GKir LBee LLin MAsh MGos NHol
    SCoo SLim SPla WPat
§ - 'Ellwood's Nymph'   CKen CNic EOrn LLin MAsh MBar
    MOne SHBN SLim SPoG WGor
- Ellwood's Pillar
   = 'Flolar'   CChe CDoC CKen CSBt
    EBre EGra EHul EOrn EPfP GKir
    LBee LCon LRHS MAsh MBar MBri
    MGos MWat NHol SBod SLim SPla
    WBrE WCFE WDin WFar WStI
- 'Ellwood's Pygmy'   CMac ECho GKir MBar NHol
- 'Ellwood's Silver'   MAsh WFar
- 'Ellwood's
   Silver Threads'   CMac EGra GKir
* - 'Ellwood's Treasure'   ECho ENot MAsh
- 'Ellwood's Variegata'   see *C. lawsoniana* 'Ellwood's
    White'
§ - 'Ellwood's White' (v)   CKen CMac CSBt EHul EOrn EPfP
    LRHS MBar SHBN WFar WMoo
I - 'Emerald'   CKen MBar MBri NHol
- 'Emerald Spire'   CMac MAsh NHol
- 'Empire'   WFar
- 'Erecta
   Argenteovariegata' (v)   WEve
- 'Erecta Aurea'   ECho EHul LBee LRHS NBee
- 'Erecta Filiformis'   MBar MBri
§ - 'Erecta Viridis'   CMac CTrG EBre GKir MBar NBee
    NWea WCFE WDin WFar WStI
- 'Ericoides'   EHul GKir
- 'Erika'   MBar
- 'Filiformis Compacta'   EHul
- 'Fleckellwood'   CWib ECho EHul GKir MAsh MBar
    SAga SMer WEve WStI
- 'Fletcheri' ♀H4   CBcs CMac CWib EHul ENot GKir
    LBee LRHS MAsh MBar MGos
    NWea SBod SHBN SMer SPer WDin
    WFar WOrn WStI
- 'Fletcheri Aurea'   see *C. lawsoniana* 'Yellow
    Transparent'
- 'Fletcher's White'   ECho EHul LRHS MBar WBcn
- 'Forsteckensis'   CKen CSli EBre EHul EOrn GKir
    LLin LRHS MBar NBee NWea SLim
    SRms WEve WFar WGor
- 'Fraseri'   MBar NWea WDin
- 'Gimbornii' ♀H4   CDoC CMac EBre EHul EOrn GKir
    LBee LCon MAsh MBar MBri SBod
    SLim SRms WCFE WFar
- 'Glauca'   CDul
- 'Glauca Spek'   see *C. lawsoniana* 'Spek'
- 'Globosa'   MGos
- 'Globus'   see *C. lawsoniana* 'Barabits'
    Globe'
- 'Gnome'   CDoC CMac EBre EHul EOrn GEdr
    LLin MBar MGos MOne NHol SBod
    SCoo SLim

	- 'Gold Flake'	MBar MGos
	- 'Gold Splash'	MBar
	- 'Golden King'	MBar
§	- 'Golden Pot'	CBrm CDoC CKen CMac CSBt CWib EGra EHul EOrn GKir LBee LRHS MBar MGos MWat SMer WDin
§	- 'Golden Queen'	EHul
	- 'Golden Showers'	EHul
§	- 'Golden Spire'	GKir LRHS MAsh MBar MGos
	- 'Golden Triumph'	EHul
	- 'Golden Wonder'	CMac EHul LBee LRHS MAsh MBar MGos NBee NWea SRms WDin WEve WFar WStI
	- 'Grant's Gold'	EHul
	- 'Grayswood Feather'	CDoC CSBt EBre ECho EGra EHul GKir LBee LRHS MAsh MBar MGos SLim SMer WEve
	- 'Grayswood Gold'	EHul EOrn LBee LRHS MAsh MBar MGos WEve
	- 'Grayswood Pillar' ♀H4	CDul CMac ECho EHul EOrn GKir LCon LRHS MBar MGos
*	- 'Grayswood Spire'	CMac
	- 'Green Globe'	CDoC CKen CSBt CSli EBre EHul EOrn GKir LBee LCon LLin LRHS MAsh MBar MBri SAga SBod WDin WEve
§	- 'Green Hedger' ♀H4	CMac CSBt CTri EHul ENot GKir LBuc MBar SBod SRms WFar
§	- 'Green Pillar'	CBrm CSBt CWib ECrN LBee LRHS MBar MGos SHBN SPoG
	- 'Green Spire'	see *C. lawsoniana* 'Green Pillar'
	- 'Greycone'	CKen LRHS
	- 'Hillieri'	MBar NBee
	- 'Hogger's Blue Gown'	see *C. lawsoniana* 'Blue Gown'
	- 'Howarth's Gold'	GKir LRHS MBri
	- 'Ilona' **new**	WBcn
	- 'Imbricata Pendula'	CKen IDee LCon
	- 'Intertexta' ♀H4	EHul WBcn WCwm WEve
	- 'Ivonne'	EHul MGos NBee NBlu WEve WOrn
	- 'Jackman's Green Hedger'	see *C. lawsoniana* 'Green Hedger'
	- 'Jackman's Variety'	see *C. lawsoniana* 'Green Pillar'
	- 'Kelleriis Gold'	EHul MBar
	- 'Kilmacurragh' ♀H4	CMac ENot GKir MAsh MBar MGos NWea WOrn
	- 'Kilworth Column'	LLin MGos MOne SPoG
	- 'Kingswood'	LRHS WEve
	- 'Knowefieldensis'	CMac EHul LLin WBcn
	- 'Lane' hort.	see *C. lawsoniana* 'Lanei Aurea'
	- 'Lanei'	CSBt CWib ECrN MAsh WDin
§	- 'Lanei Aurea' ♀H4	CMac ECho EHul ENot EPfP GKir MBar MGos NWea WBVN WFar WOrn
	- 'Lemon Pillar'	WBcn WDin WEve WOrn
	- 'Lemon Queen'	CSBt ECho EGra EHul LBee LRHS WEve WGor
	- 'Limelight'	EHul MGos
	- 'Little Spire' ♀H4	CDoC CMHG EBre EOrn GKir LBee LCon LLin LRHS MBar MBri MGos SLim SPoG WEve WGor
	- 'Lombartsii'	EHul WBcn WFar
	- 'Lutea' ♀H4	CMac EHul MGos SBod
§	- 'Lutea Nana' ♀H4	CKen CMac ECho EHul MAsh MBar MBro MGos MOne NLar
§	- 'Lutea Smithii'	MBar
	- 'Luteocompacta'	LBee LRHS MGos SHBN
	- 'Lycopodioides'	EHul MBar WBcn
*	- 'MacPenny's Gold'	CMac
	- 'Miki'	WEve
	- 'Milford Blue Jacket'	see *C. lawsoniana* 'Blue Jacket'
§	- 'Minima'	MBar SRms WCFE
	- 'Minima Argentea'	see *C. lawsoniana* 'Nana Argentea'
	- 'Minima Aurea' ♀H4	More than 30 suppliers
	- 'Minima Densa'	see *C. lawsoniana* 'Minima'
	- 'Minima Glauca' ♀H4	CMac CSBt EBre EHul ENot EPfP GKir LRHS MAsh MBar MGos NHol NWea SBod SHBN SLim SPer SPla WDin WEve WFar
	- 'Moonlight'	MBar MGos
*	- 'Moonsprite' **new**	EBre LLin LRHS
	- 'Nana'	MBar
§	- 'Nana Albospica' (v)	CBrm EGra EHul EOrn EPfP GKir LBee LCon LRHS MBar MGos SCoo SLim WFar WGor WStI
§	- 'Nana Argentea'	CKen CMac ECho EHul EOrn EPfP WGor
	- 'Nana Lutea'	see *C. lawsoniana* 'Lutea Nana'
	- 'Nicole' **new**	SPoG
	- 'Nidiformis'	EBre EHul LBee LRHS MBar NWea SRms
	- 'Nyewoods'	see *C. lawsoniana* 'Chilworth Silver'
	- 'Nymph'	see *C. lawsoniana* 'Ellwood's Nymph'
§	- 'Pelt's Blue' ♀H4	CDoC CKen CSBt EBre EGra EHul LBee LCon LRHS MBar MBri MGos NBee SCoo SHBN SLim WDin WFar WOrn
	- 'Pembury Blue' ♀H4	CDoC CDul CMHG CMac CSBt CWib EBre ECrN EHul ENot EOrn EPfP GKir LBee LCon LRHS MAsh MBar MBro MGos MWat NBee NWea SBod SHBN SLim SPer WDin WFar
	- 'Pendula'	LLin MBar
	- 'Pick's Dwarf Blue'	EHul MBar MBri NHol WGor
	- Pot of Gold	see *C. lawsoniana* 'Golden Pot'
	- 'Pottenii'	CMac CSBt EBre ECrN EHul GKir LBee LCon LRHS MAsh MBar MGos NWea SBod SHBN SMer SPer WDin WEve WFar WOrn WStI
	- 'Pygmaea Argentea' (v) ♀H4	CKen CMac CWib EBre EGra EHul EOrn EPfP GEdr GKir LBee LCon LLin LRHS MAsh MBar MBri MGos NBee NHol SBod SLim SRms WCFE WDin WEve WFar
	- 'Pygmy'	CNic EBre ECho EHul MBar NHol NLar SLim
	- 'Rijnhof'	EHul LBee LLin WBcn
	- 'Rogersii'	EOrn MBar SRms WFar
	- 'Romana'	ENot MBri
	- 'Royal Gold'	ECho EHul EOrn
	- 'Silver Queen' (v)	CKen MBar NWea WBcn
	- 'Silver Threads' (v)	CMac CSli EBre EGra EHul ENot EOrn GKir LBee LRHS MAsh MBar MGos MWat SBod WBVN WStI
	- 'Silver Tip' (v)	EBre EHul SCoo SLim
	- 'Slocock'	SHBN
	- 'Smithii'	see *C. lawsoniana* 'Lutea Smithii'
	- 'Snow Flurry' (v)	EHul WFar
	- 'Snow White' PBR (v)	CDoC CSBt EBre EHul ENot GKir LBee LCon LRHS MAsh MBar MBri MGos SLim SPla WFar WGor WLow
	- 'Somerset'	CMac MBar
§	- 'Spek'	CBcs MBar
	- 'Springtime' PBR	CDoC EBre ECho EHul EOrn LBee LCon LRHS MAsh MBri SCoo SLim WGor
	- 'Stardust' ♀H4	CDoC CMac CSBt CTri CWib EBre EHul ENot GKir LCon LPan LRHS MAsh MBar MBri MGos NBee SBod SHBN SLim SMer SPer WDin WOrn
	- 'Stewartii'	CDul CMac CTri ENot GKir MBar MGos NBee NBlu NWea SBod SHBN SMer SPer WStI

	- 'Stilton Cheese'	MBar
*	- 'Summer Cream'	EHul
	- 'Summer Snow' (v)	CBcs CDoC CDul CMac EBre EHoe EHul ENot EPfP GKir LBee LLin LRHS MAsh MBar MBro MGos SBod SLim SPla SRms WEve WFar WStI
	- 'Sunkist'	CKen WFar
	- 'Tamariscifolia'	CDoC ECho EHul MBar MOne SBod SPoG WCFE WDin WFar WStI
	- 'Tharandtensis Caesia'	EOrn MBar WFar
	- 'Tilford'	EHul
	- 'Treasure' (v)	CKen CSli EBre EHoe EHul EOrn EPfP LBee LCon LRHS MAsh MBar NHol SLim WEve WFar
	- 'Triomf van Boskoop'	MBar
	- Van Pelt's Blue'	see *C. lawsoniana* 'Pelt's Blue'
	- 'Versicolor' (v)	MBar
	- 'Waterfall'	SMad
	- 'Westermannii' (v)	CMac EBre EHul LCon LLin SBod SCoo SLim WBcn
	- 'White Edge' **new**	WFar
	- 'White Spot' (v)	CDoC EBre EHul GKir LBee LRHS MBar MBri MGos NBlu SLim WBVN WStI
	- 'Winston Churchill'	CDul CSBt MBar MGos NWea SBod
	- 'Wisselii' ♀H4	CDoC CKen CMac CTrG EGra EHul ENot GKir LBee LLin LRHS MAsh MBar NWea SBod SRms WDin WFar
	- 'Wisselii Nana'	CKen EHul
	- 'Wissel's Saguaro'	CDoC CKen LCon LRHS NLar
	- 'Witzeliana'	CDoC CSBt ECho EOrn LRHS MBar MGos SCoo WOrn
	- 'Wyevale Silver'	MBar
	- 'Yellow Cascade'	ECho
	- 'Yellow Queen'	see *C. lawsoniana* 'Golden Queen'
	- 'Yellow Success'	see *C. lawsoniana* 'Golden Queen'
§	- 'Yellow Transparent'	CDoC CMac CSli LBee MBar SBod SHBN SPoG WEve
	- 'Yvonne'	EBre ECho GKir LLin LRHS MAsh MBar SCoo SLim WEve
	leylandii	see X *Cupressocyparis leylandii*
	nootkatensis	CDul MBar
	- 'Aurea'	ECrN GKir WDin WEve
	- 'Aureovariegata' (v)	EBre EHul SLim WBcn
	- 'Compacta'	CDul CTri MBar
	- 'Glauca'	CTho LCon MBar
	- 'Gracilis'	EHul
	- 'Green Arrow'	CKen SLim
	- 'Jubilee'	EBre SCoo SLim
	- 'Lutea'	CMHG CMac CTri MBar NWea SLim
	- 'Nidifera'	MBar WCwm
	- 'Pendula' ♀H4	CDoC CTho EBre ELan ENot EOrn GKir LCon LLin LPan LRHS MAsh MBar MBri MGos NBee NBlu NWea SLim SPer WCFE WCwm WDin WEve WMou WOrn
	- 'Strict Weeper'	CKen
	- 'Variegata' (v)	LRHS MBar SLim WBcn
	obtusa 'Albospica' (v)	ECho EHul
	- 'Albovariegata' (v)	CKen
	- 'Arneson's Compact'	CKen
	- 'Aurea'	CDoC
	- 'Aureovariegata'	see *C. obtusa* 'Opaal'
	- 'Aurora'	CKen EOrn LCon MAsh
*	- 'Autumn Gold'	MBar
	- 'Bambi'	CKen EOrn MGos
	- 'Barkenny'	CKen
	- 'Bartley'	CKen EPot
	- 'Bassett'	CKen
	- 'Bess'	CKen
	- 'Brigitt'	CKen

	- 'Buttonball'	CKen
	- 'Caespitosa'	CKen EPot
	- 'Chabo-yadori'	CDoC EHul EOrn LLin LRHS MBar MGos NHol SLim WFar WStI
	- 'Chilworth'	CKen LCon MBar MGos NLar
	- 'Chima-anihiba'	CKen
	- 'Chirimen'	CKen NLar SBla
	- 'Clarke's Seedling'	MGos NLar
	- 'Confucius'	EHul NHol
	- 'Contorta'	EOrn EPot MBar NLar
	- 'Cooper's Gem'	EPot
§	- 'Coralliformis'	CMac ECho EOrn LLin MBar NHol SMur WBcn
§	- 'Crippsii' ♀H4	CBcs CDoC CKen CMHG CMac EBre ECho EHul EOrn GBin LCon LLin LRHS MBar MGos NHol SBod SLim SPoG
	- 'Crippsii Aurea'	see *C. obtusa* 'Crippsii'
	- 'Dainty Doll'	CKen EOrn
	- 'Densa'	see *C. obtusa* 'Nana Densa'
	- 'Draht'	CDoC MBar NLar WBcn WEve
	- 'Elf'	CKen
	- 'Ellie B'	CKen EOrn
	- 'Ericoides'	CKen ECho EOrn
	- 'Erika'	ECho EOrn WBcn
	- 'Fernspray Gold'	CDoC CKen CMac CTri EBre EHul EOrn GKir LCon LLin MAsh MBar NHol SBod SLim SPer WFar
	- 'Flabelliformis'	CKen
	- 'Gnome'	CKen
	- 'Gold Fern'	CKen
	- 'Golden Fairy'	CKen EOrn
	- 'Golden Filament' (v)	CKen
	- 'Golden Nymph'	CKen EOrn MGos
	- 'Golden Sprite'	CKen MGos
	- 'Goldilocks'	ECho EHul WBcn
	- 'Gracilis Aurea'	CKen
	- 'Graciosa'	see *C. obtusa* 'Loenik'
	- 'Green Diamond'	CKen
	- 'Hage'	CKen EOrn LCon
	- 'Hypnoides Nana'	CKen EOrn
	- 'Intermedia'	CKen EOrn EPot MGos
	- 'Ivan's Column'	CKen
	- 'Junior'	CKen
	- 'Juniperoides'	CKen EOrn
	- 'Juniperoides Compacta'	CKen EPot
	- 'Kamarachiba'	CKen EBre LCon LLin LRHS NLar SLim WBcn
	- 'Kanaamihiba'	MBar NLar
	- 'Konijn'	EHul EOrn
	- 'Kosteri'	CDoC CKen CMac EBre EHul EOrn LBee LLin MAsh MBar MGos NDlv NHol SHBN SLim WEve WStI
	- 'Leprechaun'	NLar
	- 'Little Markey'	CKen EOrn
§	- 'Loenik'	ECho EOrn MBar NHol WBcn
	- 'Lycopodioides'	ECho EOrn
	- 'Lycopodioides Aurea'	SLim
	- 'Marian'	CKen
§	- 'Mariesii' (v)	CKen EHul EOrn SHBN
	- 'Minima'	CKen EOrn MGos SCoo SMer
	- 'Nana' ♀H4	CKen CMac ECho LBee LCon LRHS MBar MGos NHol
	- 'Nana Albospica'	ECho
	- 'Nana Aurea' ♀H4	CDoC CMac EBre EHul EOrn EPfP GKir MAsh MBar MGos NBee NHol NPro SHBN SMer WBrE WFar WStI
	- 'Nana Compacta'	EOrn NHol
§	- 'Nana Densa'	CKen CMac NLar WEve
	- 'Nana Gracilis' ♀H4	More than 30 suppliers
I	- 'Nana Gracilis Aurea'	EHul SMur WEve
I	- 'Nana Lutea'	CDoC CKen CSBt EBre EHul EOrn EPfP GKir LBee LCon LLin LRHS

	MAsh MBar MBri MGos NDlv NHol SBod SLim SPla WGer
- 'Nana Pyramidalis'	ECho
- 'Nana Rigida'	see *C. obtusa* 'Rigid Dwarf'
- 'Nana Variegata'	see *C. obtusa* 'Mariesii'
§ - 'Opaal' (v)	MBar WBcn
- 'Pygmaea'	CNic CSBt EBre EHul ENot EOrn LCon LLin MBar MGos SBod SLim SPoG WEve
- 'Pygmaea Aurescens'	MBar
- 'Repens'	ECho EOrn WBcn
§ - 'Rigid Dwarf'	CKen EHul EOrn IMGH LBee LCon LRHS MBar SCoo WEve
* - 'Saint Andrew'	CKen
- 'Snowflake' (v)	CDoC CKen EOrn MAsh MGos MOne WBcn WFar WGor
- 'Snowkist' (v)	CKen
- 'Spiralis'	CKen ECrN MBar
- 'Stoneham'	CKen LCon MBar
- 'Tempelhof'	CKen CSBt EBre EHul EOrn GKir LCon LLin LRHS MAsh MBar MGos NDlv SBod SCoo SLim WEve WStI
- 'Tetragona Aurea'	CBcs CBrm CMac ECho EGra EHul EOrn IMGH LLin LRHS MBar MGos SLim SPer SPoG WEve
- 'Tonia' (v)	CDoC CKen EHul EOrn MAsh MBri NHol SCoo SLim WEve WGor
- 'Topsie'	CKen
- 'Torulosa'	see *C. obtusa* 'Coralliformis'
- 'Tsatsumi Gold'	CKen NLar
- 'Verdon'	CKen
- 'Winter Gold' **new**	WEve
- 'Wissel'	CKen EOrn
- 'Wyckoff'	CKen
- 'Yellowtip' (v)	CKen EHul LCon MAsh MBar MGos NLar WBcn WEve
pisifera 'Aurea Nana' misapplied	see *C. pisifera* 'Strathmore'
- 'Avenue'	EHul LLin
- 'Baby Blue'	CKen EBre EPfP LLin SCoo SLim
- 'Blue Globe'	CKen EOrn
- 'Boulevard' ♥H4	More than 30 suppliers
- 'Compacta'	ECho EOrn NDlv
- 'Compacta Variegata' (v)	ECho EHul EOrn MAsh MBar NDlv
- 'Curly Tops'	EBre ECho GKir GTsp LCon LLin MGos MOne SLim WBcn WGor
- 'Devon Cream'	LBee LRHS MAsh MBar WFar
- 'Filifera'	CMac CSBt GKir MBar SCoo SLim WFar
- 'Filifera Aurea' ♥H4	CKen CMac CSBt CWib EBre EGra EHul EOrn GKir LBee LCon LLin LRHS MAsh MBar MBri NWea SBod SRms WCFE WDin WEve WFar
- 'Filifera Aureovariegata' (v)	CMac EBre EHul LLin MBar SLim
- 'Filifera Nana'	EBre EHul EOrn GKir MBar MBri NDlv STre WDin WFar
- 'Filifera Sungold'	see *C. pisifera* 'Sungold'
- 'Fuiri-tsukomo'	CKen
* - 'Gold Cascade'	MGos
- 'Gold Cushion'	CKen
- 'Gold Dust'	see *C. pisifera* 'Plumosa Aurea'
- 'Gold Spangle'	EHul EOrn MBar MGos MOne SBod WFar
- 'Golden Mop' ♥H4	CKen ECho EHul MAsh NDlv
- 'Green Pincushion' **new**	CKen
- 'Hime-himuro'	CKen
- 'Hime-sawara'	CKen EOrn
- 'Margaret'	CKen
- 'Nana'	CKen EBre EHul ENot EPfP LLin MAsh MBar MWat NDlv NHol SBod SMer WFar
I - 'Nana Albovariegata' (v)	CDoC CNic ECho EOrn LLin LRHS MAsh MBar MBri NPro
§ - 'Nana Aureovariegata' (v)	CDoC CMac CSBt EBre EGra EHul IMGH LBee LCon LLin LRHS MAsh MBar MBri NDlv NHol SLim SPoG WEve WFar
I - 'Nana Compacta'	CMac SRms
- 'Nana Variegata' (v)	EBre ECho LBee LRHS MBar SLim SPer WFar
I - 'Parslorii'	CKen
- 'Pici'	CKen
- 'Plumosa Albopicta' (v)	ECho MBar
§ - 'Plumosa Aurea'	CKen EHul GKir MAsh MBar NWea WDin WFar
- 'Plumosa Aurea Compacta'	CKen CMac NDlv
I - 'Plumosa Aurea Compacta Variegata' (v)	CMac
- 'Plumosa Aurea Nana'	ENot MAsh MBar MGos NDlv SMer
I - 'Plumosa Aurea Nana Compacta'	CMac
- 'Plumosa Aurescens'	CDoC CMac
§ - 'Plumosa Compressa'	CDoC CFee CKen EBre ECho EHul EOrn ESis LBee LCon MBar MGos NDlv SLim SPoG WGor
- 'Plumosa Densa'	see *C. pisifera* 'Plumosa Compressa'
- 'Plumosa Flavescens'	EHul LRHS MBar NDlv
I - 'Plumosa Juniperoides'	CKen EHul EOrn LLin MBar NDlv SLim WGor
- 'Plumosa Purple Dome'	see *C. pisifera* 'Purple Dome'
I - 'Plumosa Pygmaea'	ECho MGos NDlv WGor
§ - 'Plumosa Rogersii'	EHul EOrn LRHS MBar SBod WGor
§ - 'Purple Dome'	ECho EHul EOrn MBar
- 'Rogersii'	see *C. pisifera* 'Plumosa Rogersii'
- 'Silver and Gold' (v)	EHul MBar
- 'Silver Lode' (v)	CKen EOrn
- 'Snow' (v)	CKen CMac EOrn MBar SMer
- 'Snowflake'	CKen EHul
- 'Spaan's Cannon Ball'	CKen
§ - 'Squarrosa'	MBar WDin WFar
- 'Squarrosa Dumosa'	CKen EHul MBar
- 'Squarrosa Intermedia'	EHul MBar
I - 'Squarrosa Lombarts'	CMac CSBt EBre ECho EHul EOrn LBee MBar
- 'Squarrosa Lutea'	CKen MAsh MBar
- 'Squarrosa Sulphurea'	CSBt EBre ECrN EGra EHul EOrn EPfP LBee LCon LRHS MAsh MBar SLim SPla STre WBVN WDin WFar
- 'Squarrosa Veitchii'	see *C. pisifera* 'Squarrosa'
§ - 'Strathmore'	CKen EHul LLin MBar NHol WDin
§ - 'Sungold'	CDoC CKen CSBt CTri EBre EGra EHul ENot LCon LLin LRHS MAsh MBar MBri NBlu NDlv NWea SBod SLim SPla WEve
- 'Tama-himuro'	CKen WBcn
* - 'Tsukibeni'	WBcn
* - 'White Brocade'	CMac
- 'White Pygmy'	EOrn
thyoides 'Andelyensis'	CDoC CMac CSBt ECho EHul ENot EOrn GKir LLin MBar NDlv SCoo SPoG WEve
- 'Andelyensis Nana'	CKen
- 'Aurea'	EHul MBar WBcn
- 'Conica'	CKen MAsh
- 'Ericoides' ♥H4	CDoC CKen CMac CTri ECrN EHul ENot EOrn GKir LBee LLin MAsh MBar MWat SBod SPlb WDin WEve WFar
§ - 'Glauca'	EOrn
- 'Kewensis'	see *C. thyoides* 'Glauca'
- 'Little Jamie'	CKen
- 'Red Star'	see *C. thyoides* 'Rubicon'

§	- 'Rubicon'	CKen CMac CSBt EBre EHul EOrn EPfP ESis LBee LCon LLin LRHS MAsh MBar MGos NDlv SLim SPla WEve WGer
	- 'Schumaker's Blue Dwarf'	WBcn
	- 'Top Point'	CDoC CKen EBre EOrn LBee MAsh MBri MOne SCoo SLim WEve
	- 'Variegata' (v)	CDoC ECho EHul MBar
	- 'Winter Wonder'	EHul

Chamaecytisus (Papilionaceae)

§	*albus*	GKir GQui SPer WDin WStI
	austriacus	GEil
§	*hirsutus*	CFil WLin WPGP WWeb
	- var. *demissus*	see *C. polytrichus*
§	*polytrichus*	WLin
	prolifer	CPLG
§	*purpureus*	CWCL EBre EGra ELan EPfP GKir MAsh MBar MBri MGos MRav MSwo NBlu NWea SHBN SPer WBVN WDin WFar WPat
	- f. *albus*	CBcs EPfP MBar SHBN SPer WBcn
§	- 'Atropurpureus' ♀H4	ENot LAst NHol SPer WTel
	- 'Incarnatus'	see *C. purpureus* 'Atropurpureus'
	- 'Lilac Lady' **new**	MAsh
§	*supinus*	CPLG SRms

Chamaedaphne (Ericaceae)

§	*calyculata*	CBcs GEil LRHS LTwo SPer WSHC
	- 'Nana'	CBcs CMHG MBar MGos NBlu NLar SPer

Chamaedorea (Arecaceae)

	elegans ♀H1	LPal MBri
	erumpens	see *C. seifrizii*
	glaucifolia **new**	WMul
	linearis	LPal
	metallica misapplied	see *C. microspadix*
	metallica Cook ♀H1	LPal
§	*microspadix*	CRoM CTrC LPJP LPal WMul
	radicalis	CBrP CRoM EAmu LPJP LPal WMul
§	*seifrizii* ♀H1	LPal

Chamaemelum (Asteraceae)

§	*nobile*	CAgr CArn CHby CPrp CSev EDAr ELau GBar GKir GMac GPoy IHMM MBar MBow MBri MHer NDov NGdn NJOw SECG SPlb SRms WHHs WJek WPer WSel WWye
	- dwarf	GBar
	- dwarf, double-flowered (d)	GBar NLRH
	- 'Flore Pleno' (d)	More than 30 suppliers
	- 'Treneague'	More than 30 suppliers

Chamaenerion see *Chamerion*

Chamaepericlymenum see *Cornus*

Chamaerops (Arecaceae)

	excelsa misapplied	see *Trachycarpus fortunei*
	excelsa Thunb.	see *Rhapis excelsa*
	humilis ♀H3	More than 30 suppliers
§	- var. *argentea*	CBrP CPHo CTrC EAmu LPJP LPal NPal WHPE WMul
	- var. *cerifera*	see *C. humilis* var. *argentea*
	- 'Vulcano' **new**	EAmu MBri MGos WMul

Chamaespartium see *Genista*

Chamaesphacos (Lamiaceae)

	ilicifolius	CDes CPne WPGP

Chambeyronia (Arecaceae)

	macrocarpa	CBrP LPal

Chamelaucium (Myrtaceae)

	axillare	SOWG
	uncinatum	ESlt SOWG

Chamerion (Onagraceae)

§	*angustifolium*	GBar GWCH NSco SWat WHer
	- 'Album'	More than 30 suppliers
	- 'Isobel'	CSpe MLLN MRav WAbb WCom WCot
	- 'Stahl Rose'	CBot CHid CMea EBee EMar EWes LPhx SMrm SSpi WPGP WSHC
	dodonaei	EMan MLLN MTho NGar WEas WMoo WSHC WWin
	fleischeri	CNic EDAr WSHC

Chasmanthe (Iridaceae)

	aethiopica	CPou GGar SYvo
	bicolor	CPou WCot
	floribunda	CHEx ERea LRHS WCot WHil
	- var. *duckittii*	EBee ECho LRHS WCot WPGP

Chasmanthium (Poaceae)

§	*latifolium*	More than 30 suppliers

Cheilanthes (Adiantaceae)

	argentea	WRic
	distans	SRms
	hirta	WRic
	lanosa	EBee EDAr SRms WRic
	lindheimeri	WCot
§	*nivea*	WAbe
	siliquosa NNS 00-83 **new**	WCot
	sinuata	WRic
	tomentosa	SRms WRic

Cheiranthus see *Erysimum*

Cheiridopsis (Aizoaceae)

	derenbergiana	EMan WCot

Chelidonium (Papaveraceae)

	japonicum	see *Hylomecon japonica*
	majus	CArn CRWN CRow ELau GPoy MGas MGol MHer MSal WCHb WHer WShi WWye
	- 'Flore Pleno' (d)	CBre CRow ECoo GAbr MGol NBid NBro NSti WCHb WHer
	- var. *laciniatum*	EMon GBar NSti WCHb
	- 'Laciniatum Flore Pleno' (d)	CRow EMar IBlr MMHG

Chelone (Scrophulariaceae)

	barbata	see *Penstemon barbatus*
§	*glabra*	More than 30 suppliers
	- 'Black Ace' **new**	SSpi
	lyonii	EBee EChP LAst LEdu MBow NLar SHFr WCAu WLow WMoo WSan WShi
	- 'Hot Lips' **new**	WCot
	obliqua	More than 30 suppliers
	- var. *alba*	see *C. glabra*
	- 'Forncett Foremost' **new**	GQui
	- 'Forncett Poppet'	EFou
	- 'Ieniemienie'	EMon
	- 'Pink Sensation' **new**	EBee
*	- *rosea*	CHar EBee LRHS WHHs

Chelonopsis (Lamiaceae)

	moschata	CDes CPlt EBee ECha EMan MHar NGby WMoo WPGP

yagiharana	CFai EBee LPio MMHG WGMN WHil WPnP

Chenopodium (*Chenopodiaceae*)

ambrosioides	WJek
bonus-henricus	CAgr CArn CHby GBar GPoy GWCH ILis LRHS MHer NTHB SIde WCHb WHer WSel WWye
botrys	MSal
giganteum	WJek
- 'Magentaspreen'	ECoo

cherimoya see *Annona cherimola*

cherry, duke see *Prunus x gondouinii*

cherry, sour or Morello see *Prunus cerasus*

cherry, sweet see *Prunus avium*

chervil see *Anthriscus cerefolium*

chestnut, sweet see *Castanea*

Chiastophyllum (*Crassulaceae*)

§ *oppositifolium* ♀H4	More than 30 suppliers
- 'Frosted Jade'	see *C. oppositifolium* 'Jim's Pride'
§ - 'Jim's Pride' (v)	More than 30 suppliers
simplicifolium	see *C. oppositifolium*

Chiliotrichum (*Asteraceae*)

diffusum	GEil GGar GKir GSki ISea
- 'Siska'	CBcs EBee IArd SMad WCot WWes

Chimaphila (*Ericaceae*)

maculata	GBBs SSpi

Chimonanthus (*Calycanthaceae*)

fragrans	see *C. praecox*
§ *praecox*	More than 30 suppliers
* - 'Fragrance'	ERea
- 'Grandiflorus' ♀H4	CEnd ENot EPfP SPoG SSta WPat
- var. *luteus* ♀H4	CEnd CPMA ELan ENot EPfP LPio SPer
- 'Trenython'	CEnd

Chimonobambusa (*Poaceae*)

falcata	see *Drepanostachyum falcatum*
hejiangensis **new**	EPla
hookeriana hort.	see *Himalayacalamus falconeri* 'Damarapa'
macrophylla	EPla SDry
f. *intermedia*	
§ *marmorea*	CAbb CFil EPla ERod LPal MMoz NMoo SDry WDyG WJun WPGP
- 'Variegata' (v)	CFil EFul EPla ERod MTed SDry SLPl WJun WPGP
§ *quadrangularis*	CBcs CDoC CFil CHEx EFul EPfP EPla ERod LEdu MAsh MMoz MTed NMoo SDry WJun WPGP
- 'Nagaminea' (v)	EPla
- 'Suow' (v)	CFil EPla SDry WPGP
§ *tumidissinoda*	CAbb CFil EPla ERod MMoz SDry WDyG WJun WPGP

Chinese chives see *Allium tuberosum*

Chiogenes see *Gaultheria*

Chionanthus (*Oleaceae*)

retusus	CMCN EPfP IDee MPkF NLar SSpi WDin

virginicus	CBcs CDoC CDul CEnd CFil CMCN CPMA EBee ELan EPfP EWTr GKir IArd IDee IMGH LRHS MBlu MBri SMad SPer SSpi SSta WDin WHCG WOrn WPGP

Chionochloa (*Poaceae*)

conspicua	CElw CFil CKno EBee EChP EMan EWsh GCal GIBF GSki LEdu MAnH MAvo MNrw MWhi MWrn NBir NFor NOGN WHer WPGP WRHF WWye
- subsp. *conspicua*	GGar WCot
- subsp. *cunninghamii*	CPLG
- 'Rubra'	see *C. rubra*
flavescens	EBee EHoe EPza GSki
flavicans	CKno CTrC EChP EMan EWsh MAnH MAvo MLLN SMad
rigida	LEdu
§ *rubra*	More than 30 suppliers
- subsp. *cuprea*	EGle GGar

Chionodoxa ✿ (*Hyacinthaceae*)

§ *forbesii*	CBro CNic EPar EPfP EPot LRHS SPer SRms WHer WPer WPnP WShi
- 'Alba'	ECho EPar LAma NRog
- 'Blue Giant'	CRez EPot LRHS
- 'Rosea'	EPar LAma NRog
- Siehei Group	see *C. siehei*
gigantea	see *C. luciliae* Gigantea Group
luciliae misapplied	see *C. forbesii*
luciliae Boissier ♀H4	CAvo CBro EPar EPfP EPot LAma MBri NRog
- 'Alba'	CBro CFwr ECho LPhx LRHS WBry WLin
§ - Gigantea Group	ECho ELan EPar EPot LAma LPhx NJOw NRog
- - 'Alba'	EPar EPot GCrs MBNS
'Pink Giant'	CAvo CBro CFwr CRez EPar EPfP EPot GFlt LAma LRHS MAvo WCra
sardensis ♀H4	CBro ECho EPar EPot LAma LRHS MBNS NRog WLin WRHF WShi
§ *siehei* ♀H4	CBro
'Valentine Day'	EPot

Chionographis (*Melanthiaceae*)

japonica	EFEx WCru

Chionohebe (*Scrophulariaceae*)

armstrongii	EPot ITim
§ *densifolia*	CStu EPot GAbr GCrs ITim
pulvinaris	GCrs ITim NSla

x *Chionoscilla* (*Hyacinthaceae*)

§ *allenii*	ECho EPot

Chirita (*Gesneriaceae*)

'Aiko'	WDib
'Chastity'	WDib
'Diane Marie'	WDib
heterotricha	WDib
'Keiko'	WDib
linearifolia	WDib
linearifolia x *sinensis* **new**	WDib
longgangensis **new**	WDib
'New York'	WDib
sinensis ♀H1	CHal WDib
- 'Hisako'	WDib
'Stardust' **new**	WDib
tamiana	WDib

Chironia (*Gentianaceae*)

baccifera	SPlb

× *Chitalpa* (Bignoniaceae)

tashkentensis	CEnd CMCN EPfP IMGH MBlu NLar SMad WPGP XPep
- 'Summer Bells'	CDoC LRHS

chives see *Allium schoenoprasum*

Chlidanthus (Amaryllidaceae)

fragrans	CFwr CStu ECho LPhx NRog

Chloranthus (Chloranthaceae)

fortunei	EBee LEur SBla WCot WCru
henryi	EBee
japonicus	EBee SSpi WCru
multistachys	EBee
oldhamii B&SWJ 2019	EBee WCru WPrP
serratus	EBee WCru
sessifolius var.	EBee
austrosinensis **new**	

Chloris (Poaceae)

distichophylla	see *Eustachys distichophylla*
virgata	CWCL

Chlorophytum (Anthericaceae)

comosum	SEND
- 'Mandanum' (v)	CHal
- 'Variegatum' (v) ♀H1+3	CHal LRHS MBri SRms
- 'Vittatum' (v) ♀H1+3	CHEx SRms
intermedium	WCru
B&SWJ 6447	
krookianum	CFir WCot
macrophyllum	EShb
§ *majus*	WCot
nepalense	WCot
- B&SWJ 2393	WCru

Choisya (Rutaceae)

arizonica	SIgm
'Aztec Pearl' ♀H4	More than 30 suppliers
dumosa	LHop
- var. *arizonica*	SDry SLon
- var. *mollis*	SLon
Goldfingers = 'Limo'PBR	CAbP CBcs CBot CEnd CSBt EBee EBre EHan ELan ENor ENot EPfP LAst LRHS MAsh MBri MGos NLar NPri NPro SCoo SHGC SLim SLon SMer SPer SSta SWvt WRHF WWeb
ternata ♀H4	More than 30 suppliers
- 'Brica'	see *C.* ternata Sundance = 'Lich'
- Moonshine	LRHS
= 'Walcho'PBR	
- Moonsleeper	see *C.* ternata Sundance = 'Lich'
§ - Sundance	More than 30 suppliers
= 'Lich'PBR ♀H3	

Chondropetalum (Restionaceae)

mucronatum	CBig CTrC
tectorum	CAbb CBcs CBig CFir CFwr CKno CPen CSpe CTrC EBee EMan ENot LEdu MWod SPer WCot WHal WMul WNor WPrP

Chondrosum (Poaceae)

gracile	see *Bouteloua gracilis*

Chordospartium (Papilionaceae)

muritai	ECou
- 'Huia Gilpen'	ECou
- 'Ron Feron'	ECou
- 'Wayne Nichols'	ECou
stevensonii	CPle ECou EPfP NLar SMad WBVN
- 'Duncan'	ECou
- 'Kiwi'	ECou
- 'Miller'	ECou

Chorisia (Bombacaceae)

speciosa **new**	WMul

Chorizema (Papilionaceae)

cordatum ♀H1	ECou
diversifolium	ERea
ilicifolium	CAbb CSPN ERea SBra

Chronanthus see *Cytisus*

Chrysalidocarpus (Arecaceae)

lutescens	see *Dypsis lutescens*

Chrysanthemopsis see *Rhodanthemum*

Chrysanthemum ✿ (Asteraceae)

'Albert Broadhurst' (24b)	NHal
'Alec Bedser' (25a)	WWol
'Alehmer Rote' (29Rub) **new**	EMon
'Alex Young' (25b) **new**	WWol
'Alexandra' **new**	WWol
'Allouise' (25b) ♀H3	NHal WWol
alpinum	see *Leucanthemopsis alpina*
'Amber Gigantic' (1)	NHal WIvo
'Amber Matlock' (24b)	NHal
'Anastasia'PBR (28)	CHid ECtt EMon EPPr GMac LHop MNrw MRav NMRc NSti SChu SRms WCot WFar WIvy WPer WRHF WWin
N 'Anastasia Variegated' (28/v)	EMon
'Anastasia White' (28)	WCot WIvy
'Anne' (29K)	SAga
'Anne, Lady Brocket'	EBee EMon GBuc MNrw
'Annie Lea' (25b)	NHal
'Apollo' (29K)	EFou EMon EWll WCom
'Apricot' (29Rub)	CPrp EBee EBre EChP EFou EPPr GKir MNrw MRav SOkh
'Apricot Chessington' (25a)	NHal
'Apricot Courtier' (24a)	NHal
'Apricot Enbee Wedding' (29d)	see *C.* 'Bronze Enbee Wedding'
'Apricot Harry Gee' (1)	WIvo
arcticum L.	see *Arctanthemum arcticum*
argenteum	see *Tanacetum argenteum*
'Arona Gran' (25b)	NHal
'Astro' **new**	NHal
'Autumn Days' (25b)	NHal
'Balcombe Perfection' (5a)	NHal WWol
balsamita	see *Tanacetum balsamita*
Barbara = 'Yobarbara'PBR (22)	EPfP NHal
'Beacon' (5a) ♀H2	NHal
'Bella Pink' (29)	WAba
'Beppie' (29e)	WWol
'Beppie Bronze' (29)	WAba WWol
'Beppie Dark' (29)	WWol
'Beppie Lemon' **new**	WAba
'Beppie Purple' (29)	WAba WWol
'Beppie Red' **new**	WAba
'Beppie Yellow' (29)	WWol
'Bernadette Wade' (23a)	NHal
Beth = 'Yobeth' (22c) **new**	WWol
'Big Wheel'PBR (22) **new**	LAst
'Bill Wade' (25a)	NHal
* 'Billy Bell' (25a)	WWol
'Blenda' **new**	WAba
'Blenda Pink' **new**	WAba
'Blenda Purple' **new**	WAba

'Brautstrauss'	EFou
Bravo	EPfP NHal
= 'Yobra'PBR (22c) ♀H3	
* 'Breitner's Supreme'	MNrw WCAu
'Brennpunkt'	EFou WMnd
'Bright Eye' (28)	WMnd WPer WWol
'Brightness' (29K)	SChu SUsu
'Bronze Beauty' (25b)	WFar
'Bronze Cassandra' (5b) ♀H2	NHal
'Bronze Dee Gem' (29c)	NHal
§ 'Bronze Elegance' (28b)	CM&M CSam EBee EMon MLLN NBir NGdn NPPs NSti SPla SRms WEas WIvy WMnd
§ 'Bronze Enbee Wedding' (29d) ♀H3	NHal
'Bronze Margaret' (29c) ♀H3	NHal
'Bronze Matlock' (24b)	NHal
'Bronze Max Riley' (23b) ♀H3	NHal
'Bronze Mayford Perfection' (5a) ♀H2	NHal WWol
'Bronze Mei-kyo'	see *C.* 'Bronze Elegance'
'Bronze Pamela'	see *C.* 'Pamela'
'Bronze William Florentine' (15a)	NHal
'Bruera' (24b)	NHal
'Bruno' (24b) **new**	WAba
'Bruno Bronze' **new**	WAba
'Bryan Kirk' (4b)	WWol
'Buff Peter Rowe' (23b)	NHal
'Carlene Welby' (25b)	NHal
'Carmine Blush' (29Rub)	EBee EFou MNrw WCot
I 'Cassandra' (5b) ♀H2	NHal
'Cawthorne' (29d)	WWol
'Cerise Mayford Perfection' **new**	WWol
'Cezanne' **new**	WWol
'Cherry Chessington' (25a)	NHal
'Cherry Margaret' (29c)	NHal
'Chessington' (25a)	NHal
'Chesterfield' (13b) **new**	WWol
sinense	see *C. morifolium*
'Christopher Lawson' (24b)	NHal
'Cinderella' **new**	EFou
cinerariifolium	see *Tanacetum cinerariifolium*
'Citrus' (29K)	EFou
'Clapham Delight' (23a)	NHal
'Clara Curtis' (29Rub)	More than 30 suppliers
'Claudia' (24c)	WAba
'Claudia Red' (24c) **new**	WAba
clusii	see *Tanacetum corymbosum* subsp. *clusii*
coccineum	see *Tanacetum coccineum*
'Conjora' (22c)	LAst WWol
'Contralto' (22)	WCot
'Copper Margaret' (29c)	WAba
'Cornetto' (25b)	NHal
'Corngold' (5b)	NHal
corymbosum	see *Tanacetum corymbosum*
'Cossack' (2)	WWol
'Cottage Apricot'	CHea EBee EChP EWoo GMac LHop MBNS MNrw WEas
'Cottage Pink'	see *C.* 'Emperor of China'
'Cottage Yellow'	MSte WCot WHoo
'Courtier' (24a)	NHal
'Cream Duke of Kent' (1)	WIvo
'Cream Enbee Wedding' (29d)	WAba
'Cream Jessie Habgood' (1) **new**	WIvo

'Cream Margaret' (29c) ♀H3	NHal
'Cream Patricia) Millar' (14b)	NHal
'Cream Pennine Pink' (29c) **new**	WAba
'Creamist' (25b) ♀H3	WWol
'Crimson Gala'	WWol
Dana	NHal
= 'Yodana' (25b) ♀H3	
'Daniel Cooper' (29Rub)	MNrw
'Danielle Bronze' (29d) **new**	WAba
'Danielle White' (29d) **new**	WAba
'Dark Red Mayford Perfection' (4b) ♀H2	WWol
'Darlington Anniversary' (25b) **new**	WWol
'Darren Pugh' (3b)	NHal WWol
'David McNamara' (3b)	WWol
Debonair = 'Yodebo'PBR (22c) ♀H3	EPfP NBlu
'Dee Gem' (29c) ♀H3	NHal
'Delta Dark Cerise' **new**	WWol
'Delta Orange' (29)	WWol
* 'Delta Pink' (29)	WWol
'Delta Rose' (29c) **new**	WWol
* 'Delta White' (29)	WWol
'Delta Yellow' (29)	WWol
§ 'Doctor Tom Parr' (28)	ELan EMon IGor LHop SUsu
'Doreen Statham' (4b)	NHal
'Dorothy Stone' (25b)	NHal
'Dorridge Beauty' (24a)	WWol
'Dorridge Crystal' (24a)	NHal WWol
'Dorridge Vulcan' (23b)	WWol
'Duchess of Edinburgh' (30)	CPrp CSam EBee EBre EChP ECtt ELan EMon GKir LRHS MBri MRav MTis NCGa SSvw WCAu
'Duke of Kent' (1)	NHal WIvo
'Ed Hodgson' (25a)	NHal
'Edelweiss' (29K)	EFou EMon GMac WCot
'Egret' (23b)	NHal
'Elaine Johnson' (3b)	NHal
'Elegance' (9c)	WWol
'Elegance Yellow' (9e)	WWol
'Elizabeth Burton' (5a)	WWol
'Elizabeth Lawson' (5b)	NHal
'Elizabeth Shoesmith' (1)	NHal
'Ellen' (29c)	CHrt NHal WAba
* 'Emma Jane' (25a)	WWol
§ 'Emperor of China' (29Rub)	CElw CSam EBee EChP ECha EFou EMon EPPr GCal IGor LRHS MNrw MRav MSte NCGa SChu SSvw WBor WCAu WFar WMnd
'Enbee Wedding' (29d) ♀H3	NHal WAba
'Ermine' (23a)	NHal
'Ernst' **new**	NHal
'Esther' (29Rub) **new**	EMon
* 'Evesham Vale' (24b)	WWol
'Fieldfare' (22)	NHal
'Firecracker'PBR (22)	WWol
'Fitton's Reward' (1)	WIvo
'Florence Pope' (25b) **new**	WWol
foeniculaceum misapplied	see *Argyranthemum* *foeniculaceum* hort.
foeniculaceum (Willd.) Desf.	see *Argyranthemum* *foeniculaceum* (Willd.) Webb & Sch.Bip.
'Foxtrot'PBR **new**	LAst
'Frances Jeavons'	EBee
'Fred Shoesmith' (5a)	WWol
frutescens	see *Argyranthemum frutescens*
'Gala'PBR (22) **new**	LAst

'Gambit' (24a)	NHal
'Geof Brady' (5a)	NHal WWol
'George	NHal
Griffiths' (24b) ♀H3	
'Gerrie Hock' (29c) **new**	WAba
'Gigantic' (1)	WIvo
'Gladys' (24b)	EBee EChP ELan EWoo
'Gladys Emerson' (3b)	NHal
'Gold John	NHal
Wingfield' (14b)	
'Gold Margaret'	see *C.* 'Golden Margaret'
'Golden	NHal
Cassandra' (5b) ♀H2	
'Golden Courtier' (24a)	NHal
'Golden	NHal
Florentine' (15a) **new**	
'Golden Gigantic' (1)	NHal WIvo
§ 'Golden	NHal
Margaret' (29c) ♀H3	
'Golden Mayford	NHal WWol
Perfection' (5a) ♀H2	
'Golden Pamela' (29c)	NHal
'Golden Plover' (22)	NHal
'Golden Seal' (7b)	EMon GBuc
'Goldengreenheart'	EFou MNrw
(29Rub)	
'Gompie Bronze' **new**	WAba
'Gompie Red' **new**	WAba
I 'Gompie Rose' **new**	WAba
'Gompie Yellow' **new**	WAba
'Goodlife	NHal
Sombrero' (29a) ♀H3	
'Grace Wade' (25b)	NHal WWol
§ *grandiflorum*	SRms
'Green Boy' (10b)	WWol
* 'Green Envy' (10b)	WWol
'Green Nightingale' (10)	WWol
'Green Satin' (5b)	WWol
'Hanenburg'	NHal WWol
* 'Happy Days' (15b)	WWol
haradjanii	see *Tanacetum haradjanii*
'Harold Lawson' (5a)	NHal
'Harry Gee' (1)	WIvo WWol
'Harry Woolman' (3b)	NHal
'Hazy Days' (25b)	NHal
'Heather James' (3b)	NHal
'Heide' (29c) ♀H3	NHal WAba
'Helen Gravestock' (4a)	WWol
'Herbstrubin'	EFou IGor
'Hesketh Knight' (5b)	NHal
Holly	NHal
= 'Yoholly' (22b) ♀H3	
'Honey Enbee	NHal
Wedding' (29d)	
hosmariense	see *Rhodanthemum bosmariense*
'Innocence' (29Rub)	CSam EBee EChP ELan EMon IGor
	MNrw MRav NCGa NGdn NSti
	SAga SPla
* 'Iris Morris' (4b)	WWol
'Ivor Mace' (1)	WIvo
'Jan Horton' (3b)	WWol
'Janice'PBR (7a)	LAst
'Jante Wells' (28)	EMon WEas WTel
'Jessie Cooper'	see *C.* 'Mrs Jessie Cooper'
'Jessie Habgood' (1)	WIvo
'John Harrison' (25b)	NHal
'John Hughes' (3b)	NHal
'John Wingfield' (14b)	NHal
'Joyce Frieda' (23b)	WWol
'Julia' (28)	EFou
Julia = 'Yojulia'	CHea
'Julie Lagravère' (28)	EFou EMon GBuc WWhi
'Kay Woolman' (13b)	NHal WWol
'Ken Stubbins' (7b) **new**	WWol

'Kenneth Roy' (15a)	NHal
'Kimberley Marie' (15b)	NHal
x *koreanum*	see *C. grandiflorum*
'Kota Kinabalu' (1)	WIvo
'Lady in Pink' (29Rub)	GBuc
'Lakelanders' (3b)	NHal
'Lameet' (29)	WWol
'Lancashire Fold' (1)	WIvo
'Lancashire Lad' (1)	WIvo
'Laser' (24b)	WWol
'Laureate'	WWol
'Lautrec' ♀H3 **new**	WWol
'Le Bonheur Red'	WWol
'Leading Lady' (25b)	WWol
'Lemon Margaret' (29c)	NHal
♀H3	
'Leo' (28) **new**	EMon
leucanthemum	see *Leucanthemum vulgare*
'Lilac Chessington' (25a)	NHal
'Lilac Prince' (1) **new**	WIvo
'Lilian Hoek' (29c)	WAba
Linda = 'Lindayo'PBR	NBlu WWol
(22c)	
'Lindie' (28)	EFou
'Lizzie Dear' (25b)	NHal
'Long Island	WTel
Beauty' (6b) ♀H2	
'Lorna Wood' (13b)	NHal
'Louise Park' (24a)	NHal
'Lucy' (29a)	NHal
'Lundy' (2)	NHal
'Luv Purple'	WWol
'Lynn Johnson' (15a)	NHal
Lynn = 'Yolynn'PBR	NHal
(22c) ♀H3	
macrophyllum	see *T. macrophyllum*
'Majola' **new**	WAba
'Malcolm Perkins' (25a)	NHal
'Mancetta Comet' (29a)	NHal
'Mandarin' (5b)	EFou
maresii	see *Rhodanthemum bosmariense*
'Margaret' (29c) ♀H3	NHal
'Mark Woolman' (1)	NHal WIvo
'Mary Stoker' (29Rub)	More than 30 suppliers
'Matador' (14a)	WWol
'Matlock' (24b)	NHal
mawii	see *Rhodanthemum gayanum*
'Max Riley' (23b) ♀H3	NHal
maximum misapplied	see *Leucanthemum* x *superbum*
maximum Ramond	see *Leucanthemum maximum*
	(Ramond) DC
'Maxine Johnson' (25b)	NHal
'May Shoesmith' (5a) ♀H2	NHal
'Mayford	NHal
Perfection' (5a) ♀H2	
'Megan Woolman' (3b)	WWol
'Mei-kyo' (28b)	CM&M CMea EBee EFou EMon
	IGor LBBr MLLN MRav MWgw
	SPla SRms WFar
'Membury' (24b)	NHal
'Mermaid Yellow' **new**	LAst
'Michelle Preston' (13b)	NHal
'Migoli'	WWol
'Minstreel Bronze' (9)	WWol
'Minstreel Dark' (9)	WWol
'Minstreel Lilac' **new**	WWol
'Miral White' **new**	WWol
'Moonlight' (29d/K)	MRav
morifolium **new**	SSpi
§ 'Mrs Jessie Cooper'	ELan GMac MNrw MSte NBir SChu
(29Rub)	SSvw WCom WCot WHoo WHrl
	WTin
'Mrs Jessie Cooper No.1'	MSph
'Music' (23b)	NHal

'Myss Goldie' (29c)	NHal	
'Nancy Perry' (19Rub)	CSam ELan EMon MNrw MRav SChu	
§ ***nankingense***	WFar	
'Nantyderry' ♀H4 Sunshine' (28b)	CSam EBee EFou LBBr LRHS MNrw MWgw SMrm SPla WCot WEas WMnd WPer WRha	
'Nell Gwyn' (29Rub)	MNrw	
'Netherall Moonlight'	EBee	
'Netherhall Yellow' **new**	EMon	
Nicole = 'Yonicole'PBR (22c) ♀H3	NHal	
nipponicum	see *Nipponanthemum nipponicum*	
'Orange Allouise' (25b)	NHal WWol	
'Orange Enbee Wedding' (29d)	NHal	
'Oury' **new**	EFou EMon	
pacificum	see *Ajania pacifica*	
§ 'Pamela' (29c)	NHal WAba	
'Pandion'	WWol	
'Parkfield Tigger' (29c)	NHal	
parthenium	see *Tanacetum parthenium*	
'Pat Davison' (25b)	NHal	
'Paul Boissier' (30Rub)	CElw EFou LPhx MAnH NSti WMnd	
'Payton Dale' (29c) ♀H3	NHal	
'Payton Glow' (29c)	NBir	
'Payton Lady' (29c)	WAba	
'Payton Prince' (29c) ♀H3 **new**	WAba	
'Peach Allouise' (25b) ♀H3	NHal	
'Peach Courtier' (24a)	NHal	
'Peach Enbee Wedding' (29d) ♀H3	NHal	
'Peach John Wingfield' (14b)	NHal	
'Pearl Celebration' (24a)	NHal	
'Peggy Anne' (1)	WIvo	
'Pennine Bullion'	NHal WWol	
I 'Pennine Coconut' (29)	WWol	
'Pennine Dart' (29d)	NHal	
'Pennine Digger' (29c)	WWol	
'Pennine Drift'	NHal WWol	
'Pennine Eagle' (29c)	WWol	
'Pennine Gift' (29c)	NHal	
'Pennine Ginger' (29c) ♀H3	NHal	
'Pennine Goal' (29c) ♀H3	WWol	
'Pennine Grant'	WWol	
'Pennine Jane'	WWol	
'Pennine Marie' (29a) ♀H3	NHal	
'Pennine Oriel' (29a) ♀H3	NHal	
'Pennine Pageant' (29d)	NHal	
'Pennine Passion' (29c)	WWol	
'Pennine Perfecta' (29d)	WWol	
'Pennine Pilot' **new**	WWol	
'Pennine Pink' (29c)	WAba	
'Pennine Pink Purple' (29c) **new**	WAba	
'Pennine Point'	WWol	
'Pennine Polo' (29d) ♀H3	NHal WWol	
'Pennine Port'	WWol	
'Pennine Ranger' (29d)	NHal	
'Pennine Romeo' (19c)	NHal	
'Pennine Sally' (29c)	WAba	
'Pennine Ski' (29c)	WAba	
'Pennine Splash' (29d)	NHal	
'Pennine Sunlight' (19d)	WWol	

'Pennine Swan' (29c)	NHal	
'Pennine Toy'	NHal WWol	
'Pennine Volcano'	WWol	
'Perry's Peach'	MNrw NPer SUsu	
'Peter Rowe' (23b)	NHal	
'Peter Sare' (29d)	GMac	
'Peterkin'	CHea ECtt EMon GMac MNrw MWgw	
'Phil Houghton' (1)	WIvo WWol	
'Picasso' **new**	WWol	
'Pink Duke' (1)	NHal	
'Pink Duke of Kent' (1)	WIvo	
'Pink Ice' (5b)	WRha WSpi	
'Pink John Wingfield' (14b)	NHal	
'Pink Marvellous' (29f)	WWol	
'Pink Progression'	GMac MWgw NBir	
'Polar Gem' (3a)	NHal	
'Polaris' (9c)	EWll	
* 'Pompon Bronze' (28)	WWol	
* 'Pompon Pink' (28)	WWol	
* 'Pompon Purple' (28)	WWol	
* 'Pompon Yellow' (28)	WWol	
'Primrose Allouise' (24b) ♀H3	NHal	
'Primrose Chessington' (25a)	NHal	
'Primrose Courtier'	see *C.* 'Yellow Courtier'	
'Primrose Dorothy Stone' (25b)	NHal	
'Primrose Dorridge Crystal' (24a)	NHal	
'Primrose Enbee Wedding' (29d) ♀H3	NHal WAba	
'Primrose Ermine' (23a)	NHal	
'Primrose Jessie Habgood' (1)	WIvo	
'Primrose John Hughes' (3b)	NHal	
'Primrose Mayford Perfection' (5a) ♀H2	NHal WWol	
'Primrose West Bromwich' (14a)	NHal	
'Prince Bishop' (25a)	NHal	
'Promise' (25a)	NHal	
'Purleigh White' (28b)	EBee EFou GMac MNrw NSti SPla WBor WCot WRha	
'Purple Chempak Rose' (14b) **new**	NHal	
'Purple Glow' (5a)	NHal	
'Purple Margaret' (29c)	NHal	
'Rachel Fairweather' (3a)	NHal	
Radiant Lynn = 'Radiant Yolynn'PBR (22c)	NHal WWol	
'Ralph Lambert' (1)	WIvo	
'Ray Williams' (15b) **new**	WWol	
'Red Balcombe Perfection' (5a)	NHal WWol	
'Red Bella' (29c)	NBir	
'Red Pamela' (29c)	NHal	
'Red Payton Dale' (29c)	WAba	
'Red Pennine Gift' (29c)	NHal	
'Red Regal Mist' (25b)	WWol	
'Red Shirley Model' (3a)	NHal	
'Red Wendy' (29c) ♀H3	CHrt WAba	
'Regal Mist' (25b)	WWol	
'Regalia' (24b) ♀H3	WWol	
'Rehange' **new**	EMon	
'Rene Green' (25b) **new**	WWol	
'Renoir' **new**	WWol	
'Revert'PBR	WWol	
'Riley's Dynasty' (14a)	NHal	
'Rita May' (2)	NHal	
'Rita McMahon' (29d)	NHal	

Robin = 'Yorobi'^{PBR} (22c) NHal
'Romantika' CHea
'Romany' (2) CElw WEas
'Rose Enbee Wedding' NHal
  (29d)
'Rose Mayford NHal WWol
  Perfection' (5a) ♀^{H2}
'Rose Patricia Millar' NHal
  (14b) **new**
'Rose Payton Lady' WAba
  (29c) **new**
Rose Pink Debonair LAst
  = 'Rosepink
  Yodebo'^{PBR} (22c)
'Rosenmarguerite' **new** EFou
'Rosette' (29c) EFou
roseum see *Tanacetum coccineum*
'Royal Command' (29Rub) EBee EMon MNrw
  WWol
'Rubaiyat' WWol
rubellum see *C. zawadskii*
'Ruby Enbee Wedding' NHal WAba
  (29d) ♀^{H3}
'Ruby Mound' (29c/K) LPhx LRHS MNrw WEas
'Ruby Raynor' (29Rub) MNrw
'Rumpelstilzchen' CMdw CMea EBee MNrw WPer
'Russet Gown' EBee
'Salmon Allouise' (25b) NHal
'Salmon Chessington' NHal
  (25a)
'Salmon Enbee Wedding' NHal
  (29d) ♀^{H3}
'Salmon Harry Gee' WIvo
  (1) **new**
'Salmon Lilac Prince' (1) WIvo
'Salmon Payton Dale' WAba
  (29c) **new**
'Sam Vinter' (5a) NHal
'Sarah Louise' (25b) NHal
'Sarah's Yellow' CSam
Shelley = 'Yoshelley' WWol
  (22b)
'Shepherd' **new** WWol
'Shirley Primrose' (1) WIvo
'Silver Gigantic' (1) WIvo
'Skylark' (22a) **new** NPri
Soft Lynn NHal
  = 'Soft Yolynn' (22c)
'Sonnenschein' LHop WHen
'Sophie Elizabeth' (24a) NHal
'Southway Shiraz' (29d) NHal
'Southway Snoopy' (29d) NHal
'Southway Sonar' (29d) NHal
'Southway Spree' (29d) NHal
'Southway Sting' (29d) NHal
'Southway Stomp' (29d) NHal
'Southway Strontium' NHal WAba
  (29d)
'Spartan Fire' WWol
'Spartan Glory' (25b) WWol
'Spartan Leo' (29c) WWol
'Spartan Linnet' WWol
'Spartan Moon' (25b) WWol
'Spartan Seagull' WWol
'Spartan Sunrise' (29c) WWol
'Spartan Torch' WWol
'Stella' (29c) EFou
'Stockton' (3b) ♀^{H2} NHal
'Streamer' ambig. **new** WWol
Sundoro = 'Yosun'^{PBR} NHal
  (22d)
Sunny Linda = 'Sunny WWol
  Lindayo' (22c) ♀^{H3}
'Sunny Margaret' WAba
  (29c) **new**

Sunny Robin = 'Sunny WWol
  Yorobin' **new**
'Sutton White' (25a) WWol
'Syllabub' **new** LAst
'Taiga White' **new** WWol
'Talbot Bolero' (29c) NHal
'Talbot Ultra' (29f) NHal
'Tapestry Rose' (29K) CMea EBee EChP EMon IGor MMil
  MNrw NPPs
Target = 'Yotarget' (22) NHal
'Thoroughbred' (24a) NHal WWol
'Tightrope' ♀^{H3} **new** WWol
'Toledo' (25a) WWol
'Tom Parr' see *C.* 'Doctor Tom Parr'
'Tom Snowball' (3b) NHal
'Tracy Waller' (24b) NHal
'Trapeze' WWol
uliginosum see *Leucanthemella serotina*
'Universiade' (25a) NHal
'Vagabond Prince' CSam MBro MSte WHoo
'Venice' (24b) NHal
'Wedding Day' (29K) GBuc MMil MNrw WCAu WTin
'Wedding Sunshine' (29K) LRHS MMil
welwitschii see *Xanthophthalmum segetum*
'Wendy' (29c) ♀^{H3} WAba
'West Bromwich' (14a) NHal
'Westland Regal' **new** WWol
§ *weyrichii* EBre ECtt GAbr MHer MTho
  NJOw NWCA SBla SRms SScr
  WGwG
'Whitby' (5a) NHal
'White Allouise' (25b) NHal
  ♀^{H3}
'White Beppie' (29e) WWol
'White Bouquet' (28) WWol
'White Cassandra' (5b) NHal
'White Enbee Wedding' NHal
  (29d)
'White Gerrie Hoek' (29c) WAba
'White Gloss' (29K) LRHS
'White Lancashire WIvo
  Fold' (1)
'White Lilac Prince' (1) WIvo
'White Margaret' NHal WAba
  (29c) ♀^{H3}
'White Marvellous' (29f) WWol
'White Skylark' (22) NHal
'White Tower' MNrw
'William Florentine' (15a) NHal
'Windermere' (24a) NHal
'Wine Carlene Welby' NHal
  (25b)
'Winning's Red' (29Rub) EMon LHop MNrw SMad WWin
'Woolman's Century' (1) WWol
'Woolman's Prince' (3a) WWol
'Woolman's Star' (3a) NHal
'Woolman's Venture' (4b) NHal
'Yellow Allouise' (25b) NHal
§ 'Yellow Courtier' (24a) NHal
'Yellow Dorothy Stone' NHal
  (25b)
'Yellow Duke of Kent' (1) WIvo
'Yellow Egret' (23b) NHal
'Yellow Ellen' (29c) NHal WAba
'Yellow Fred WWol
  Shoesmith' (5a)
'Yellow Harold WWol
  Lawson' (5a) **new**
'Yellow Hazy Days' (25b) NHal
'Yellow Heide' (29c) ♀^{H3} NHal WAba
'Yellow John Hughes' NHal
  (3b) ♀^{H2}
'Yellow John NHal
  Wingfield' (14b)

'Yellow Lilian Hoek' (29c)   WAba
'Yellow Margaret'   NHal
   (29c) ♀H3
'Yellow May Shoesmith'   NHal
   (5a)
'Yellow Mayford   NHal WWol
   Perfection' (5a) ♀H2
'Yellow Megan   WWol
   Woolman' (3b)
'Yellow Pennine Oriel'   NHal
   (29a) ♀H3
'Yellow Phil Houghton'   WIvo WWol
   (1)
'Yellow Ralph Lambert'   WIvo
   (1)
'Yellow Whitby' (5b)   NHal
§ *yezoense* ♀H4   CSam CStu EBee ELan MNrw WEas
- 'Roseum'   CSam EBee MNrw NSti WBor
   WPGP
§ *zawadskii*   LBee NCGa WFar

Chrysocoma (Asteraceae)
ciliata JJH 9401633   NWCA
coma-aurea   NWCA

Chrysogonum (Asteraceae)
australe   EBee
virginianum   CHal CMea EBee ECha EMan EMar
   EWes LRHS MRav SPer SPet WFar
   WMoo

Chrysopogon (Poaceae)
gryllus   CBig CBrm CStu EBee WPGP

Chrysopsis (Asteraceae)
mariana   EMon WOld
villosa   see *Heterotheca villosa*

Chrysosplenium (Saxifragaceae)
alternifolium   EMFW IHMH MCCP
davidianum   CBre CPLG EBee ECha EMan EPar
   EPot GEdr GFlt LSpr NBir NSla
   SScr WBor WCot WCru WGer
   WMoo WPrP WTMC
- SBEC 231   NHol NWoo
lanuginosum   WCru
   var. *formosanum*
   B&SWJ 6979 **new**
macrophyllum   EBee WCru
macrostemon   WCru
   var. *shiobarense*
   B&SWJ 6173
oppositifolium   EBee WHer WShi

Chrysothemis (Gesneriaceae)
pulchella ♀H1   CHal

Chusquea ✿ (Poaceae)
coronalis   CFil WJun
culeou ♀H4   CAbb CBig CDoC CEnd CFil CHEx
   EFul EPfP EPla GFlt GKir LPal
   LRHS MAsh MAvo MMoz MWht
   NBea NMoo SArc SDix SDry SLon
   SMad SSta WCru WJun WMul
   WNor WPGP
- 'Breviglumis'   see *C. culeou* 'Tenuis'
§ - 'Tenuis'   CFil EPla ERod SDry WJun WMul
   WNor WPGP
cumingii   WJun
gigantea   CFil EPla WMul
macrostachya   CFil EPla WPGP
montana   CFil EPla WPGP
pittieri   WJun
quila   CFil MMoz SDry WPGP

ramosissima   CFil SDry
sulcata   WJun
uliginosa   WJun
valdiviensis   WJun

Cicerbita (Asteraceae)
B&SWJ 5162   WCru
B&SWJ 6588   WCru
BWJ 7891 from China   WCru
§ *alpina*   EPAt GFlt MSph NBid NLar SGar
   SPlb WRos
macrorhiza B&SWJ 2970   WCru
plumieri   CStr EMan SScr WCot WFar WRos
- 'Blott' (v)   LSpr

Cichorium (Asteraceae)
intybus   CHby CPrp EChP ECoo ELan ELau
   EWTr GAbr GMac ITer LHop
   MBow MRav NBlu NGHP NMir
   SECG SIde SPer SPlb WBVN WBro
   WCHb WHHs WHer WJek WMoo
   WSHC WWin
- f. *album*   CPrp EBee EChP ECha ECoo EGle
   EMan EMon EPfP GMac LHop
   LRHS MBow MRav NGdn NSti
   SWat WBro WCAu WCHb WHHs
- 'Roseum'   CBot CHad CPrp CSpe EBee ECGP
   EChP ECha ECoo ECot EGle ELan
   EMan EMon EPfP GBri GMac LHop
   LRHS MBow MRav NGdn SPer
   SWat WBro WCAu WCHb WHHs
   WHil WWin

Cimicifuga see *Actaea*
americana   see *Actaea podocarpa*
foetida   see *Actaea cimicifuga*
ramosa   see *Actaea simplex* 'Prichard's
   Giant'
rubifolia   see *Actaea cordifolia*

Cineraria (Asteraceae)
maritima   see *Senecio cineraria*
saxifraga **new**   EShb

Cinnamomum (Lauraceae)
camphora   CBcs CHEx CTrG ERea LPan
japonicum   CFil WPGP
micranthum **new**   CFil WPGP

Cionura (Asclepiadaceae)
oreophila   GCal WPGP WSHC

Circaea (Onagraceae)
lutetiana   EPAt MSal NSco WHer WShi
- 'Caveat Emptor' (v)   CBgR CHid EBee EMan EMon ITer
   NBid WCot WHer WWeb

Cirsium (Asteraceae)
* *atroroseum*   SWat
diacantha   see *Ptilostemon diacantha*
eriophorum   NLar WBWf
falconeri   NBur
helenioides   see *C. heterophyllum*
§ *heterophyllum*   CPom EBee EChP EMan EMon
   LDai NBur NLar SHar WCot WPGP
japonicum 'Early Pink   EWTr LDai MSPs
   Beauty'
- 'Early Rose Beauty'   MSPs NVic
* - 'Pink Beauty'   CMHG GKir WHil
- 'Rose Beauty'   LRHS MBri NBlu
oleraceum   LEdu NLar
palustre   WBWf
purpuratum   EMan WCot WPGP
- JCA 4.192.500   CDes

rivulare	More than 30 suppliers
'Atropurpureum'	
vulgare	GGar

Cissus (Vitaceae)

antarctica ♀H1	CTrC LRHS MBri
discolor	CHal
pedata B&SWJ 2371	WCru
rhombifolia ♀H1	MBri
- 'Ellen Danica'	CHal LRHS
♀H1 **new**	
§ *striata*	CBcs CDoC CDul CHEx CSam CTrC EBee EMil IFro IMGH LRHS SBra SLim WCot WCru WSHC WWeb

Cistus ✿ (Cistaceae)

x *aguilarii*	CChe CPLG CSBt CSam CTri EBee EPfP EWTr SIgm WSHC XPep
- 'Maculatus' ♀H3	More than 30 suppliers
albanicus	see *C. sintenisii*
albidus	CArn EGoo MLLN SDry SMrm SSpi WHer XPep
- f. *albus* **new**	XPep
algarvensis	see *Halimium ocymoides*
'Ann Baker'	SLPl WAbe XPep
'Anne Palmer'	see *C.* x *fernandesiae* 'Anne Palmer'
x *argenteus* 'Blushing Peggy Sammons'	CSBt LPhx MAsh WAbe WSPU WWeb XPep
- Golden Treasure = 'Nepond' (v)	CDoC EBee EPfP LAst MGos MRav MWat SLim SMur
- 'Paper Moon' **new**	XPep
§ - 'Peggy Sammons' ♀H3	More than 30 suppliers
- 'Silver Ghost'	CDoC SCoo WAbe XPep
- 'Silver Pink' misapplied	see *C.* x *argenteus* 'Peggy Sammons', *C.* 'Grayswood Pink', *C.* x *skanbergii*
- 'Silver Pink' ambig.	More than 30 suppliers
- 'Stripey' **new**	XPep
atriplicifolius	see *Halimium atriplicifolium*
'Blanche'	see *C. ladanifer* 'Blanche'
x *bornetianus* 'Jester'	CSBt EBee SHop WAbe XPep
'Candy Stripe' (v)	NPro WBcn
x *canescens* **new**	WAbe XPep
- f. *albus*	CWib SIgm WEas WHCG XPep
'Chelsea Pink'	see *C.* 'Grayswood Pink'
chinamadensis **new**	XPep
x *chnoodophyllus* **new**	XPep
x *clausonis* **new**	XPep
§ *clusii*	CHar MAsh SPla XPep
- subsp. *multiflorus* **new**	XPep
x *corbariensis*	see *C.* x *hybridus*
creticus	EBre LAst MWgw NBlu SGar SPoG WBVN
- subsp. *corsicus* **new**	XPep
- subsp. *creticus*	CFil CMHG CTrC EBee EGoo ELan ENot EPfP GEil LRHS MBri MSte SPer WAbe WBcn WGer WWin XPep
- - f. *albus*	XPep
§ - - - 'Tania Compton'	WAbe
* - - 'Ano Moulia' **new**	XPep
* - - 'Bali' **new**	XPep
- - 'Lasithi'	WAbe
- subsp. *eriocephalus* **new**	XPep
* - 'Michel Valantin' **new**	XPep
- subsp. *incanus*	EWTr LPhx MNrw WHCG
- var. *tauricus* **new**	XPep
x *crispatus* **new**	XPep
§ - 'Warley Rose'	NPPs NSti SHBN SHop SIgm WAbe WWeb XPep
crispus misapplied	see *C.* x *pulverulentus*

§ *crispus* L.	EGoo GEil SIgm WAbe WEas XPep
- 'Prostratus'	see *C. crispus* L.
- 'Sunset'	see *C.* x *pulverulentus* 'Sunset'
§ x *cyprius* ♀H4	CArn CBrm CDul CSBt EBee ECtt ELan ENot EPfP LHop MGos MRav MWat MWgw SDix SEND SHBN SLPl SRms WBod WBrE WDin WFar WPnn WWeb XPep
- f. *albiflorus*	MSte WBcn XPep
- var. *ellipticus* f. *bicolor* **new**	XPep
- - 'Elma' ♀H3	CMHG EBee ELan EPfP LPhx LRHS MAsh MWgw SDry SIgm SPla WAbe WBod WEas WGer WHCG XPep
§ x *dansereaui*	CHar CMHG CSBt CSam EOrc MAsh MRav MSte WFar WWpP XPep
- 'Albiflorus'	see *C.* x *dansereaui* 'Portmeirion'
- 'Decumbens' ♀H4	CBcs CMHG CTrC CTri EBee EBre ELan EPfP ESis MBNS MDun MRav MSwo MWgw NCGa NFor SArc SHBN SIgm SMer SPer SPla WAbe WBod WDin WGer WHCG WStI XPep
- 'Jenkyn Place'	EBee MBri SLPl SUsu WAbe WBor XPep
- 'Little Gem'	LPhx LRHS MAsh XPep
§ - 'Portmeirion'	WAbe WFar XPep
x *dubius* **new**	XPep
x *escartianus* **new**	XPep
x *fernandesiae* **new**	XPep
- 'Anne Palmer'	CFwr EPfP SIgm WAbe WBod WFar
§ x *florentinus* misapplied	see x *Halimiocistus* 'Ingwersenii'
x *florentinus* Lam.	CAbP CHar SChu XPep
* - 'Béziers' **new**	XPep
- 'Fontfroide'	WAbe WWeb
* - 'Tramontane' **new**	XPep
formosus	see *H. lasianthum* subsp. *formosum*
x *gardianus* **new**	XPep
'Gordon Cooper' **new**	WAbe XPep
§ 'Grayswood Pink' ♀H4	More than 30 suppliers
x *heterocalyx* 'Chelsea Bonnet'	CFai EBee EWTr LPhx MSte SIgm SLim WAbe WBrE WPen WWeb XPep
heterophyllus **new**	XPep
hirsutus Lam. 1786	see *C. inflatus*
- var. *psilosepalus*	see *C. inflatus*
x *hybridus*	More than 30 suppliers
* - 'Donadieu' **new**	XPep
- 'Gold Prize' (v) **new**	MBri WWeb
incanus	see *C. creticus* subsp. *incanus*
§ *inflatus*	NWoo SDry SEND WAbe WBod WHar WHer XPep
ingwerseniana	see x *Halimiocistus* 'Ingwersenii'
'Jessamy Beauty'	SHop SLPl SVen WAbe XPep
'Jessamy Bride'	SLPl XPep
'Jessamy Charm'	LPhx XPep
'John Hardy'	EBee
ladanifer misapplied	see *C.* x *cyprius*
ladanifer L. ♀H3	CDoC CFil CTri ECha ELan EPfP EWTr IMGH LEdu LRHS MRav MSwo SChu SGar SPer WBod WEas WFar WHar WLin WSHC WTel XPep
- var. *albiflorus*	CBcs SSpi WAbe XPep
* - - 'Bashful' **new**	XPep
§ - 'Blanche'	LRHS SHop SIgm WKif XPep
§ - 'Paladin'	SHop WAbe XPep
- Palhinhae Group	see *C. ladanifer* var. *sulcatus*
- 'Pat'	ELan EPfP LRHS MAsh
- var. *petiolatus* **new**	XPep
- - f. *immaculatus* **new**	XPep

§ – var. *sulcatus* — CHar LPhx LRHS MSte SDry WFar
– – f. *bicolor* **new** — XPep
– – f. *latifolius* **new** — XPep
– var. *tangerinus* **new** — XPep
lasianthus — see *Halimium lasianthum*
laurifolius ♀H4 — CDoC CFil CHar EBee ENot EPfP LPio MGos MNrw NBee NBir SLPl SLon SPer WHar XPep
– subsp. *atlanticus* **new** — XPep
§ x *laxus* 'Snow White' — CAbP CDoC EBee EPfP LHop LPhx LRHS MDun MSte MWgw NPer NPro NSti SChu SLPl SLim SLon SPer SSpi SUsu WKif WLeb XPep
x *ledon* — SLPl WWeb XPep
libanotis — CHar CPle XPep
x *longifolius* — see *C.* x *nigricans*
x *loretii* misapplied — see *C.* x *dansereaui*
x *loretii* Rouy & Fouc. — see *C.* x *stenophyllus*
x *lucasii* **new** — XPep
x *lusitanicus* Maund. — see *C.* x *dansereaui*
'Merrist Wood Cream' — see x *Halimiocistus wintonensis* 'Merrist Wood Cream'
x *mesoensis* **new** — XPep
monspeliensis — CAbP CPle ENot EPfP EWTr LPio LRHS SPer SSpi WFar XPep
– CMBS 62 — WPGP
– 'Densifolius' **new** — XPep
– 'Vicar's Mead' **new** — SPla XPep
munbyi **new** — XPep
§ x *nigricans* — EBre SLPl WCot XPep
x *oblongifolius* **new** — XPep
– 'Barr Common' — LRHS
x *obtusifolius* misapplied — see *C.* x *nigricans*
x *obtusifolius* Sweet — CAbP EPfP EWes MAsh SLPl WEas XPep
– 'Thrive' — MBri
ochreatus — see *C. symphytifolius* subsp. *leucophyllus*
ocymoides — see *Halimium ocymoides*
osbeckiifolius — SIgm XPep
'Paladin' — see *C. ladanifer* 'Paladin'
– 'Paladin' — see *C. ladanifer* var. *sulcatus*
palhinhae — see *C. ladanifer* var. *sulcatus*
parviflorus misapplied — see *C.* 'Grayswood Pink'
parviflorus Lam. — CBot LPhx NSti SChu WCFE WSHC XPep
x *pauranthus* **new** — XPep
* – 'Natacha' **new** — XPep
'Peggy Sammons' — see *C.* x *argenteus* 'Peggy Sammons'
x *penarcleusensis* **new** — XPep
x *picardianus* **new** — XPep
x *platysepalus* — LPhx SHop XPep
populifolius — CBot CBrd CMHG ECha LTwo SPer WAbe WHer
– var. *lasiocalyx* — see *C. populifolius* subsp. *major*
§ – subsp. *major* ♀H3 — CPle EPfP LPhx SMrm XPep
– subvar. *populifolius* **new** — XPep
pouzolzii **new** — XPep
psilosepalus — see *C. inflatus*
§ x *pulverulentus* — CDul CPLG CTri ECha EPfP MMHG MWgw SChu WAbe WDin WSHC
* – Delilei Group **new** — XPep
* – – 'Fiona' **new** — XPep
§ – 'Sunset' ♀H3 — More than 30 suppliers
– 'Warley Rose' — see *C.* x *crispatus* 'Warley Rose'
§ x *purpureus* ♀H3 — More than 30 suppliers
– 'Alan Fradd' — CBcs EBee ENot EPfP LHop LRHS MAsh MDun MGos MSwo MTis MWgw SCoo SEND SLim SMrm SPla WGer XPep
– var. *argenteus* — EBee WAbe WSPU XPep
f. *stictus*

– 'Betty Taudevin' — see *C.* x *purpureus*
– var. *holorhodos* **new** — XPep
x *ralletii* — XPep
– f. *subcreticus* **new** — XPep
x *rodiaei* 'Jessica' — WAbe WSPU XPep
rosmarinifolius — see *C. clusii*
'Ruby Cluster' — WLeb XPep
sahucii — see x *Halimiocistus sahucii*
salviifolius — CAbP CArn CPle EMil ISea LRHS NSla NWCA SSpi WAbe WCFE WFar WHCG WWeb XPep
– 'Avalanche' — EBee GEil MAsh MRav NPro WAbe
– 'Gold Star' **new** — XPep
* – 'Ivoire' **new** — XPep
salviifolius — see *C.* x *florentinus*
    x *monspeliensis*
– 'Prostratus' — ELan ESis LPhx LRHS NPro WHCG
* – 'Sirocco' **new** — XPep
* – 'Villeveyrac' **new** — XPep
x *sammonsii* 'Ida' **new** — XPep
'Silver Pink' Hillier — see *C.* x *argenteus* 'Silver Pink'
'Silver Pink' misapplied — see *C.* x *argenteus* 'Peggy Sammons', *C.* 'Grayswood Pink', *C.* x *skanbergii*
§ *sintenisii* — XPep
§ x *skanbergii* ♀H3 — CBcs CHar CSBt CSLe CTri CWib EBee ELan ENot EPfP IMGH LHop LRHS MGos MRav MWat MWgw NBir SDix SHBN SIgm SPer WCom WEas WFar XPep
* – 'Akamas' — XPep
    C. monspeliensis
    x *C. parviflorus* **new**
'Snow Fire' ♀H4 — CDoC CSBt EBee EPfP LPhx LRHS MBri NPro SHop SIgm SLPl SPoG SSpi SUsu WAbe WGer WLeb WSPU WWeb XPep
§ x *stenophyllus* — CWib SPer WAbe WKif XPep
– var. *albiflorus* — XPep
* – – 'Mistral' **new** — XPep
* – 'Elise' **new** — XPep
symphytifolius — CSLe WPGP XPep
§ – subsp. *leucophyllus* — CFil XPep
– – MSF 98.019 — WPGP
'Tania Compton' — see *C. creticus* subsp. *creticus* f. *albus* 'Tania Compton'
x *tephreus* **new** — XPep
'Thrive' — see *C.* x *obtusifolius* 'Thrive'
tomentosus — see *Helianthemum nummularium* subsp. *tomentosum*
x *verguinii* — EBee LHop LRHS SIgm XPep
– f. *albiflorus* — WAbe XPep
– var. *albiflorus* — see *C.* x *dansereaui* 'Portmeirion' misapplied
* – 'Salabert' **new** — XPep
villosus — see *C. creticus* subsp. *creticus*
wintonensis — see x *Halimiocistus wintonensis*

Citharexylum (Verbenaceae)
spicatum — CPLG CPle

x *Citrofortunella* (Rutaceae)
floridana 'Eustis' (F) — ERea SCit
– 'Lakeland' (F) — ERea
lemonquat (F) — SCit
§ *microcarpa* (F) ♀H1 — CDoC CWSG EMui EPfP ERea MBri SCit WBVN
§ – 'Tiger' (v/F) ♀H1 — EPfP ERea SCit
– 'Variegata' — see x *C. microcarpa* 'Tiger'
mitis — see x *C. microcarpa*
procimequat (F) — SCit
reticulata (F) — SCit
swinglei 'Tavares' (F) — ERea

citron see *Citrus medica*

x *Citroncirus* (*Rutaceae*)

citandarin **new**	MJnS
citremon	MJnS
'Swingle' (F)	SCit
webberi 'Benton'	SCit
– 'Carrizo'	SCit
– 'Morton' **new**	MJnS
– 'Rusk'	MJnS SCit
– 'US119' **new**	MJnS

Citrullus (*Cucurbitaceae*)

colocynthis **new**	CArn

Citrus ✿ (*Rutaceae*)

amblycarpa Djeruk lime (F)	ERea
aurantiifolia (F)	SCit
– Indian lime (F)	ERea
aurantium (F)	SCit
– 'Aber's Narrowleaf' (F)	SCit
– 'Bigaradier Apepu'	SCit
– 'Bittersweet' (F)	SCit
– 'Bouquet de Fleurs'	ERea SCit
– 'Bouquetier de Nice à Fleurs Doubles' (d)	SCit
– 'Gou-tou Cheng' (F)	SCit
– var. *myrtifolia* 'Chinotto' (F)	ERea SCit
– 'Sauvage' (F)	SCit
– 'Seville' (F)	ERea
– 'Smooth Flat Seville' (F)	SCit
– 'Willowleaf' (F)	SCit SPer
bergamia bergamot	ERea
– 'Fantastico'	SCit
calamondin	see x *Citrofortunella microcarpa*
deliciosa	see *C.* x *nobilis*
Ichang Lemon (F)	MJnS
ichangensis (F)	SCit
jambhiri 'Milam'	SCit
– red rough lemon (F)	SCit
– rough lemon (F)	SCit
– Schaub rough lemon (F)	SCit
japonica	see *Fortunella japonica*
kinokuni	SCit
kumquat	see *Fortunella margarita*
'La Valette'	EPfP ERea ESlt
latifolia (F/S)	CWSG EPfP ERea ESlt SPer
limettoides (F)	CArn SCit
limon (F)	LPan
– 'Eureka Variegated' (F/v)	SCit
– 'Fino' (F)	EPfP SCit
§ – 'Garey's Eureka' (F)	CDoC CWSG EPfP ERea
– 'Imperial' (F)	ERea
– 'Lemonade' (F)	ERea SCit
– 'Lisbon' (F)	ERea
– 'Quatre Saisons'	see *C. limon* 'Garey's Eureka'
– 'Toscana'	CWSG EPfP ERea
– 'Variegata' (F/v) ♀H1	ERea
– 'Verna' (F)	SCit
– 'Villa Franca' (F)	ERea
– 'Yen Ben' (F)	SCit
x *limonia* 'Rangpur' (F)	ERea
macrophylla	SCit
madurensis	see *Fortunella japonica*
maxima (F)	ERea SCit
medica (F)	SCit
– 'Cidro Digitado'	see *C. medica* var. *digitata*
§ – var. *digitata* (F)	ERea SCit
– 'Ethrog' (F)	ERea ESlt SCit
– var. *sarcodactylis*	see *C. medica* var. *digitata*
§ x *meyeri* **new**	CWSG MJnS

– 'Meyer' (F) ♀H1	CBcs CWSG EPfP ERea ESlt GTwe LRHS MJnS SCit SPer
microcarpa	see x *Citrofortunella microcarpa*
Philippine lime	
mitis	see x *Citrofortunella microcarpa*
natsudaidai	SCit
§ x *nobilis* (F)	CWSG LPan
– 'Blida' (F)	ERea SCit
– 'Ellendale' (F)	EPfP SCit
– 'Murcott' (F)	EPfP ERea SCit
– Ortanique Group (F)	EPfP SCit
– 'Silver Hill Owari' (F)	ERea
– Tangor Group (F)	ERea
x *paradisi* 'Foster' (F)	ERea
– 'Golden Special' (F)	ERea
– 'Navel' (F)	EPfP SCit
– 'Star Ruby' (F/S)	ERea ESlt SCit
– 'Wheeny' (F)	SCit
pennivesiculata (F)	SCit
'Ponderosa' (F)	ERea SCit
reshni Cleopatra mandarin (F)	SCit
reticulata (F)	CWSG SArc WMul
– 'Dancy' (F)	SCit
– 'Fina' (F/S)	SCit
– 'Hernandina' (F)	SCit
– Mandarin Group (F)	CDoC
– – 'Clementine' (F)	CDoC ERea
– – 'De Nules' (F/S)	ESlt SCit
– – 'Encore' (F)	ERea
– – 'Fortune' (F)	ESlt SCit
– 'Marisol' (F/S)	SCit
– 'Miyagawa' **new**	ERea
– 'Nour' (F)	SCit
– 'Nova'	see *C.* x *tangelo* 'Nova'
– Satsuma Group	see *C. unshiu*
– 'Suntina'	see *C.* x *tangelo* 'Nova'
sinensis (F)	ERea LPan SAPC SArc WMul
– 'Egg' (F)	ERea
– 'Embiguo' (F)	ERea
– 'Harwood Late' (F)	ERea
– 'Jaffa'	see *C. sinensis* 'Shamouti'
– 'Lane Late' (F)	EPfP SCit
– 'Malta Blood' (F)	ERea ESlt
– 'Moro Blood' (F)	ERea SCit
– 'Navelate' (F)	SCit
– 'Navelina' (F/S)	CDoC ERea ESlt SCit
– 'Newhall' (F)	SCit
– 'Parson Brown' (F)	ERea
– 'Prata' (F)	ERea
– 'Ruby' (F)	ERea
– 'Saint Michael' (F)	ERea
– 'Salustiana' (F/S)	SCit
– 'Sanguinelli' (F)	ERea SCit
§ – 'Shamouti' (F)	ERea
– 'Succari' (F)	SCit
– 'Tarocco' (F)	SCit
– 'Thomson' (F)	ERea
– 'Valencia' (F)	CWSG ECot ERea
– 'Valencia Late' (F)	ERea ESlt SCit
– 'Washington' (F/S)	ERea GTwe SCit
tachibana	SCit
x *tangelo* 'Minneola' (F)	SCit
– 'Nocatee' (F)	SCit
§ – 'Nova' (F/S)	SCit
– 'Orlando' (F)	SCit
– 'Samson' (F)	SCit
– 'Seminole' (F)	ERea
– 'Ugli' (F)	SCit
§ *unshiu* (F)	ERea
– 'Clausellina' (F/S)	ERea ESlt
– 'Hashimoto' (F/S)	SCit
– 'Okitsu' (F/S)	SCit
– 'Owari' (F/S)	SCit

volkameriana	ERea SCit

Cladothamnus see *Elliottia*

Cladrastis (*Papilionaceae*)

kentukea	CArn CBcs CDul CLnd CMCN
	CTho ELan EPfP LRHS MBlu NHol
	NLar SHBN SPer SSpi WBVN WBod
	WDin WNor
- 'Perkins Pink'	CMCN MBlu
- 'Rosea'	see *C. kentukea* 'Perkins Pink'
lutea	see *C. kentukea*
sinensis	CFil CMCN EPfP MBlu SSpi WPGP

Clarkia (*Onagraceae*)

* *repens*	CSpe

Clavinodum (*Poaceae*)

§ *oedogonatum*	EPla SDry WJun

Claytonia (*Portulacaceae*)

alsinoides	see *C. sibirica*
australasica	see *Neopaxia australasica*
caroliniana	EBee GFlt LAma NLar
§ *megarhiza* var. *nivalis*	NWCA
§ *nevadensis*	EMar
parvifolia	see *Naiocrene parvifolia*
§ *perfoliata*	CArn CPLG GPoy ILis WCHb WHer
§ *sibirica*	CAgr CArn CElw CNic CRow
	CTCP ECoo EMan NBid WBVN
	WHen WRHF WWye
- 'Alba'	CElw NBid
virginica	EBee EHrv LAma WFar WMoo

Clematis ✿ (*Ranunculaceae*)

B&SWJ 599	WCru
B&SWJ 8910 from Japan	WCru
BWJ 7630 from China	WCru
BWJ 8169 from China	WCru
CC 2713	CPLG
RCB TQ-H-7	WCot
RCB/Arg K2-3	WCot
'Abundance' (Vt) ♀H4	CDoC CElw CFRD CPev CRHN
	CSPN EBee EOrc EPfP ERob ESCh
	ETho LRHS MAsh MBri MCad
	NBea NTay SBra SDix SHBN SPer
	SPet WTel WTre
addisonii	CBcs CSPN ERob ESCh ETho
	MWhi NBrk WTre
aethusifolia	CSPN ERob
afoliata	CBcs CPev CSPN CStu ECou ERob
	ETho WTre
afoliata x *forsteri* (Fo)	ECou
'Aino' (Vt)	ERob
'Akaishi' (P)	ERob ESCh ETho MCad NBrk NTay
akebioides	CPLG EBee LRHS NBrk SBra SHBN
	SLim WCru WSpi
'Akemi' (L)	ERob MCad
Alabast = 'Poulala'PBR	CSPN EBee ERob ESCh ETho
(Fl) ♀H4	MBNS MCad MWgw NTay SBra
	SCoo SLim WTre
'Alba Luxurians' (Vt) ♀H4	More than 30 suppliers
'Albatross'	EHan ERob ESCh
'Albiflora'	CSPN ECtt ESCh NSti WTre
I 'Albina Plena' (A/d)	ESCh NBrk SLim WTre
'Aleksandrit' (P)	ERob
'Alice Fisk' (P)	CFRD CSPN EBee ERob ESCh
	ETho MCad MSwo NBea NBrk
	NTay SBra SHBN WGor WTre
'Alionushka' (D) ♀H4	More than 30 suppliers
'Allanah' (J)	CFRD CRHN EBee EPfP ERob ESCh
	ETho GKir LAst MGos MSwo NBea
	NTay SBra SCoo SLim WStI WTre
'Al-nor' **new**	ESCh

§ *alpina* (A) ♀H4	CMac CPev ECtt EPfP ESCh GKir
	GSki MBar MCad MDun MWhi
	NPer SHBN SLim SPlb WBVN
	WCot WFar
- 'Albiflora'	see *C. alpina* subsp. *sibirica*
- 'Burford White' (A)	CSPN EBee EOrc EPfP ERob ESCh
	NBrk NTay WTre
- 'Columbine' (A)	CFRD CPev CWSG EBee ENot
	ETho LBuc MAsh MBar MCad
	MSwo MWgw NBea NHol SCoo
	SDix SLim SPer WTre
- 'Columbine White'	see *C. alpina* 'White Columbine'
- 'Constance' (A) ♀H4	CElw CFRD CSPN EBee ENot EOrc
	EPfP ERob ESCh ETho LRHS NBrk
	NSti NTay SBra SPer SRms WPGP
	WTre
- 'Foxy' (A) ♀H4	EBre EPfP ERob ESCh NBrk NTay
	SLim SLon WTre
- 'Frances Rivis' (A) ♀H4	More than 30 suppliers
- 'Francesca' (A) **new**	ESCh
- 'Frankie' (A) ♀H4	CDoC CSPN EBee ELan ENot ERob
	ESCh ETho LRHS NTay SBra SLim
	SPer WTre
- 'Jacqueline du Pré'	CElw CFRD CHad CPev CSPN
(A) ♀H4	EBee EHan EOrc EPfP ERob ESCh
	ETho GEil MCad MGos NBea NTay
	SBra SPet WTre
- 'Jan Lindmark' (A)	see *C. macropetala* 'Jan Lindmark'
- 'Mary Whistler'	ESCh
- 'Odorata' (A)	CSPN ERob ESCh LBuc MGos
	NBea
§ - 'Pamela Jackman' (A)	CDoC CFRD CSPN CWSG EBee
	EBre EHan ELan ESCh GKir LAst
	LRHS MAsh MCad MGos NBea
	NCGa NHol NSti NTay SBra SDix
	SLim SPer SWvt WTre
- 'Pink Flamingo' (A) ♀H4	CElw CFRD CMHG CSPN EBee
	EBre ECtt ELan ENot EPfP ERob
	ESCh ETho LRHS MBri MWgw
	NBPC NPri NSti NTay SLim SMur
	SPet WTre
- 'Rosy Pagoda' (A)	EBee ELan EOrc EPfP ERob ESCh
	LRHS MCad NBea NBir WTel WTre
- 'Ruby' (A)	CFRD CMHG CPev CSPN CWSG
	EBee ELan EPfP ESCh ETho LRHS
	MAsh MCad MGos MWgw NBea
	NHol NSti SBra SChu SDix SHBN
	SLim SPer SPet WTMC WTel WTre
§ - subsp. *sibirica* (A)	CBcs CPev ERob NTay SPla WBVN
§ - - 'Altai' **new**	ESCh
§ - - 'Riga' (A)	ERob ESCh NTay WTre
§ - - 'White Moth' (A)	CElw CFRD CSPN CWSG EBee
	ELan EPfP ESCh ETho EWTr LRHS
	MGos NBrk NHol NTay SBra SLim
	SPer SPet SPla SRms WTel
- 'Tage Lundell'	see *C.* 'Tage Lundell'
- 'Violet Purple' (A)	ERob ESCh
§ - 'White Columbine'	EPfP ERob ESCh ETho LAst MSwo
(A) ♀H4	NBea NSti WTre
- 'Willy' (A)	More than 30 suppliers
'Alpinist' (L)	ERob
'Amelia Joan' (Ta)	ERob
* *ameshisuto* **new**	ETho
'Ametistina' (A)	ERob
'André Devillers'	see *C.* 'Directeur André Devillers'
I 'Andromeda' (Fl)	CSPN ERob ESCh ETho NBrk NTay
	SBra WFar
'Anita' (Ta)	EBee EMil ERob ESCh ETho MCad
	SBra SLim WTre
'Anna' (P)	ERob ESCh NTay
'Anna German' (L)	ERob ESCh
Anna Louise	CSPN EBee ERob ESCh ETho LRHS
= 'Evithree'PBR (P) ♀H4	MBri NTay SBra SCoo SLim WTre
'Annabel' (P)	CSPN ERob MAsh

'Annemieke' (Ta)　ERob ESCh MGos SBra WTre
'Annie Treasure'　ERob WTre
'Anniversary'　EBee EHan ENot ERob ESCh NBrk
anshunensis　see *C. clarkeana*
'Anti'　ESCh
'Aoife' (Fo)　ETho
'Aotearoa'　ERob ESCh
'Aphrodite'　ERob WTre
apiifolia　CPev ERob ESCh MWhi
- B&SWJ 4838　WCru
'Arabella' (D)　♀H4　More than 30 suppliers
Arctic Queen　CSPN EBee EHan ENot ESCh ETho
　= 'Evitwo'PBR (Fl) ♀H4　GKir LRHS MBNS MCad NPri SLim
　　SPer WTre WWes
armandii　More than 30 suppliers
- 'Apple Blossom'　♀H4　More than 30 suppliers
- var. ***biondiana***　ERob SBla
- 'Bowl of Beauty'　ERob ESCh MAsh MCad MGos
- 'Enham Star' **new**　MBri
- 'Little White Charm'　CSPN ERob MBlu MCad NLar
- 'Meyeniana'　see *C. armandii* 'Little White Charm'
§ - 'Snowdrift'　CBcs CPev CSBt CSPN CSam
　CWSG ELan EPfP ERob ESCh ETho
　EWTr LRHS MAsh MCad MGos
　MLan NSti NTay SHBN SLim SPer
　SReu SRms WTre
x ***aromatica***　CSPN EBee ELan EOrc EPfP ERob
　ESCh ETho GMac LAst LFol LRHS
　MBri MCad MWgw NBea NSti
　NTay SBra WTre
§ 'Asagasumi' (L)　ERob ESCh LBuc MCad NBrk
'Asao' (P)　CElw CFRD CRHN EBee EBre ELan
　ERob ESCh ETho LAst LRHS MAsh
　MCad NBPC NBea NTay SBra SLim
　SPer SPet WBVN WTre
'Ascotiensis' (J)　CElw CPev CRHN CSPN EBee EBre
　EPfP ESCh ETho LRHS MCad NBea
　NPri NTay SBra SDix SLim SPer
　WTre
§ 'Aureolin' (Ta)　CSPN CWSG EBee ENot EPfP
　ERob GKir LRHS MAsh MBar
　MGos NBrk NHol NPri SBra SLim
　WPGP WTre
australis　ERob ITim NLAp
'Bagatelle' (P)　ESCh
'Baltyk' (P)　CSPN ERob ESCh
'Barbara' **new**　ETho
'Barbara Dibley' (P)　CPev CTri CWSG EBee ERob ESCh
　LRHS MAsh MBNS MSwo NBea
　NTay SBra SDix SLim WBar WTre
'Barbara Jackman' (P)　CPev CRHN EBee ECtt ENot ERob
　ETho GKir LRHS MAsh MBar
　MCad MSwo NBea NBlu NTay SBra
　SLim SPer SPet WFar WFoF WStI
　WTre
'Barbara Wheeler'　ERob
barbellata (A)　EHyt ERob GCrs
- 'Pruinina'　see *C.* 'Pruinina'
'Basil Bartlett'　ECou ERob ESCh
'Beata' (L)　ESCh MCad
'Beauty of Richmond' (L)　CWSG ERob ESCh MCad
'Beauty of Worcester'　CFRD CPev CSPN CWSG EBee
　(Fl/L)　EBre ELan EPfP ESCh ETho GKir
　LAst LRHS MAsh MBar MCad
　MSwo MWgw NBea NTay SBra
　SDix SLim SPer SPet WFar WTre
　WWeb
'Bees' Jubilee' (P)　More than 30 suppliers
'Bella' (J)　ERob ESCh ETho
'Belle Nantaise' (L)　CElw CPev EBee ERob ESCh LRHS
　NBea NTay SBra SPet WTre
'Belle of Woking' (Fl/P)　CElw CPev CRHN CSPN CWSG
　EBee EBre ECtt EHan ELan ENot

EPfP ERob ESCh ETho LRHS MAsh
　MBar MCad NBPC NBea NTay SBra
　SDix SHBN SLim SPer SPet WTre
'Bessie Watkinson'　ERob ESCh
§ 'Beth Currie' (P)　CFRD CSPN EBee ERob ESCh
'Betina' (A)　CSPN ERob ESCh ETho LBuc
　MAsh MCad
'Betty Corning'　CHad CSPN EBee EBre ELan EMil
　(VtxT) ♀H4　EOrc EPfP ERob ESCh ETho LRHS
　MBri MCad NBea NBrk NTay SBra
　SLon WTMC WTel WTre WWhi
'Betty Risdon' (P)　ERob ESCh ETho MAsh NBrk
'Big Bird' (A/d)　ERob ESCh LBuc
§ 'Bill MacKenzie' (Ta)　♀H4　More than 30 suppliers
'Black Madonna' (P)　ERob
'Black Prince' (Vt)　CRHN ELan EPfP ERob ESCh ETho
　NBrk WTre
'Black Tea'　ERob
§ 'Blekitny Aniol' (J/Vt)　♀H4　CElw CFRD CRHN CSPN EBee
　EHan ERob ESCh ETho GEil GMac
　LRHS MAsh MCad NBea NBrk NPri
　NTay SBra SCoo SLim SPer SPet
　WTre
Blue Angel　see *C.* 'Blekitny Aniol'
'Blue Belle' (Vt)　CElw CFRD CPou CRHN EBee
　ELan ESCh LRHS MBri MCad NBea
　NBrk NSti NTay SBra SLim SPet
　WTre
'Blue Bird' (A/d)　CBcs CWSG EBee ECtt MAsh MBri
　MWgw NBea SBra SLim SPer SPet
　WTre
'Blue Boy' (D)　see *C.* x ***eriostemon*** 'Blue Boy' (D)
'Blue Boy' (L/P)　see *C.* 'Elsa Späth'
'Blue Dancer' (A)　CAbP CElw EBee EOrc EPfP ERob
　ESCh ETho GKir MWat MWgw
　NBea NBrk NTay SPet WTre WWes
'Blue Eclipse'　CSPN ERob WTre
'Blue Eyes'　CFRD CSPN EBee ERob ESCh
　NTay
'Blue Gem' (L)　ERob ESCh MCad NTay SBra SLim
'Blue Japan' (I)　NBrk
'Blue Light'PBR (L/d)　CSPN EHan ELan ENot ERob ESCh
　ETho LBuc MCad MGos NBrk NLar
　NTay SBra WFar WTre
Blue Moon = 'Evirin'PBR　EBee EBre ENot ESCh ETho LAst
　LRHS MBNS MWgw NBea NLar
　NPri NTay SBra SCoo WFar
Blue Rain　see *C.* 'Sinij Dozhdj'
'Blue Ravine' (P)　EBee EPfP ERob ESCh ETho MCad
　MGos NBPC NLar NTay SBra SCoo
　WTre
'Blue Stream' (A)　ESCh
x ***bonstedtii*** (H)　ESCh
§ - 'Campanile' (H)　CPev EBee ERob ESCh NBir NBrk
- 'Crépuscule' (H)　ERob ESCh GCal NBrk NTay SRms
　WCot WTre
'Boskoop Beauty' (PxL)　ERob ESCh NBrk
'Bracebridge Star' (L/P)　ECtt ERob ESCh
brachiata　ESCh SBra
brachyura　ERob
'Bravo' (Ta)　ERob WTre
brevicaudata　GIBF
'Brocade' (Vt)　CRHN ERob ESCh
'Broughton Bride' (A)　ERob ESCh
§ 'Brunette' (A)　CSPN ELan EPfP ERob ESCh ETho
　MCad MGos NBrk NTay SBra WTre
buchananiana　see *C. rehderiana*
　Finet & Gagnep.
buchananiana DC.　CPLG ERob ITim
'Budapest' (I)　ERob ESCh LBuc MWgw SBra
　WTre
'Burford Bell'　ERob WTre
* 'Burford Princess'　ERob
'Burford Variety' (Ta)　ERob ESCh MCad NTay WTre

'Burma Star' (P)	CElw CFRD CPev EHan EPfP ERob ESCh ETho GEil MCad NBea NBrk NTay SBra SPet WTre
'C.W. Dowman' (P)	ERob ETho
'Caddick's Cascade'	MCad
'Caerulea Luxurians'	CRHN ERob ESCh WTre
calycina	see *C. cirrhosa*
campaniflora	CBot CBgs CElw CFRD CMea CNic CPev CRHN CSPN EBee EHyt EOrc EPla ERob ESCh ETho MCad MWhi NBea NBrk NWCA SBra SDix SGar SLim SPer WPGP WSHC WTre
- 'Lisboa'	ERob ESCh NBrk SBra WSHC
'Campanile'	see *C.s* x *bonstedtii* 'Campanile'
I 'Campanulina Plena' (A/d)	ERob
'Candida' (L)	CFRD ESCh MCad
'Candle Glow'	CElw CSPN MAsh
'Candy Stripe'	EBee ERob ESCh GKir NTay SLim
'Capitaine Thuilleaux'	see *C.* 'Souvenir du Capitaine Thuilleaux'
'Cardinal Wyszynski'	see *C.* 'Kardynal Wyszynski'
'Carmen Rose' (A)	ERob
'Carmencita' (Vt)	CRHN CSPN EBee ERob ESCh ETho NBrk NTay SBra SLim WTre
'Carnaby' (L)	CDoC CRHN CSPN CWSG EBee EBre ENot EPfP ERob ESCh ETho LAst LRHS MAsh MBar MBri MCad MGos NBea NTay SBra SLim SPet WPGP WTre WWeb
'Carnival Queen'	CSPN CWSG ERob ESCh NBrk NTay
'Caroline' (J)	CHad CPev CSPN EBee ERob ESCh ETho LBuc MCad NBea NBrk NTay SBra WTre
'Caroline Lloyd' (Vt)	ERob
§ x *cartmanii* hort.	CSPN EHan ELan ERob LBuc LRHS SBla SLim
'Avalanche'PBR (Fo) ♀H3	
- 'Joe' (Fo)	More than 30 suppliers
- 'Snow Valley' (Fo)	SBla
- 'White Abundance' (Fo)	SBla
'Celebration'PBR	MCad
'Centre Attraction'	MCad
'Chalcedony' (FlxL)	CPev CSPN ERob ESCh ETho MAsh MCad MGos NBrk NTay SBra WTre
'Charissima' (P)	CBcs CElw CPev CSPN CSam EBee EHan EPfP ERob ESCh ETho MGos NTay SBra SCoo SPet WFar WTre
chiisanensis	CBcs CSPN ERob MWhi SBra WHrl WTre
- B&SWJ 4560	WCru
- B&SWJ 8706	WCru
- 'Lemon Bells' (A)	ELan LRHS SMur
- 'Love Child' (A)	CBcs CSPN ERob ESCh ETho LBuc MBlu NTay SBra SCoo SLim SPer WTre
chinensis misapplied	see *C. terniflora*
chinensis Retz	ERob
'Chinook' **new**	LRHS
'Christian Steven' (J)	CSPN ERob ESCh
chrysantha var. *paucidentata*	see *C. bilariae*
chrysocoma misapplied	see *C. montana* var. *sericea*
N *chrysocoma* Franchet	CPev EPfP ERob MBNS MBar MSwo NBPC NHol SBra WCru
- ACE 1093	CPou
- B&L 12237	NBea
- hybrid	ERob NTay
'Cicciolina' (Vt)	ERob
§ *cirrhosa*	CBot CPev CTri ELan ESCh LRHS MAsh MCad MGos MWhi NTay SArc WBVN WTre
- var. *balearica*	More than 30 suppliers
- 'Freckles' ♀H3	More than 30 suppliers
- 'Jingle Bells'	CElw EBee EBre EHan EPfP ERob ESCh ETho GEil LRHS MAsh MCad NTay SBra SCoo SLim SMur WFar WTre
- 'Lansdowne Gem'	CSPN LBuc MBlu
- 'Ourika Valley'	ERob
- subsp. *semitriloba*	ERob
- 'Wisley Cream' ♀H3	More than 30 suppliers
'Citra' (A)	ERob ESCh NBrk NTay
§ *clarkeana*	ETho
coactilis	ERob
'Colette Deville' (J)	EPfP ERob ESCh MCad NTay
columbiana	ERob
- var. *columbiana*	WCot
§ - var. *tenuiloba*	ITim SAga SOkd
- - 'Ylva'	EHyt WAbe
'Columella' (A)	ERob ESCh
'Comtesse de Bouchaud' (J) ♀H4	More than 30 suppliers
connata	EPfP ERob ESCh GQui NBrk SBra
- HWJCM 132	WCru
'Corona' (PxL)	CFRD CPev CSPN EBee ELan EPfP ERob LAst LRHS MAsh MBar MCad NBea NBlu NTay SBra SLim SPet WTre
'Corry' (Ta)	ERob ESCh NBrk
'Cotton Candy'	ERob
'Countess of Lovelace' (P)	CBcs CFRD CSPN CWSG EBee EHan EPfP ERob ESCh ETho LRHS MAsh MBar MBri MCad MGos MWgw NBea NTay SBra SDix SLim SPer SPet WTre
County Park Group (Fo)	ECou
- 'Fairy' (Fo/f)	ECou ESCh
- 'Fragrant Joy' (Fo/m)	ECou
§ - 'Pixie' (Fo/m)	CSPN CStu EBee EBre ECou ENot EPfP ESCh ETho LRHS MGos NLAp NLar NTay SBra SCoo SPet WGwG WStl WTre WWeb
'Cragside'	ETho
crassifolia B&SWJ 6700	WCru
'Crimson King' (L)	ERob ESCh MCad NTay SBod WGor
§ *crispa*	CFRD CPou CSPN EHyt ERob ESCh ETho MCad MWhi NBea
- 'Cylindrica'	ERob NBrk
- 'Rosea'	see *C. crispa* 'Cylindrica'
Crystal Fountain = 'Fairy Blue'	ESCh ETho LRHS NPri
cunninghamii	see *C. parviflora*
'Cyanea' (A)	EBee ERob ESCh
x *cylindrica*	CSPN ESCh NBrk WTre
'Daniel Deronda' (P) ♀H4	CPev CSPN CWSG EBee EBre ECtt ELan ENot ERob ESCh ETho EWTr GKir LAst LRHS MAsh MCad MWgw NBea NTay SBod SBra SDix SHBN SLim SPer SPet WTre
'Dark Secret'	CSPN ERob ESCh
'Dawn' (L/P)	CFRD CPev CSPN EBee ERob ESCh ETho LRHS MAsh MCad NBea NTay SBra SLim SPer SPet WGwG WTre
'Débutante'	ESCh ETho
'Denny's Double' (d)	CSPN CWSG ERob ESCh ETho MAsh NBrk NRib NTay WTre
'Diana'	ERob ESCh
dioscoreifolia	see *C. terniflora*
§ 'Directeur André Devillers' (P)	ERob ESCh MCad
'Docteur Le Bêle'	ERob NBrk NTay
'Doctor Ruppel' (P)	More than 30 suppliers
'Doggy' (Vt)	ERob
'Dominika' (J)	CSPN ERob ESCh ETho NTay SBra WTre

'Dorath' | ERob ESCh WTre
'Dorota' (L) | ERob
'Dorothy Tolver' (P) | ERob ESCh ETho WTre
'Dorothy Walton' (J) | CRHN CSPN EBee ERob ESCh MCad NBrk NTay SBra SCoo SLim WTre
douglasii | see *C. hirsutissima*
'Duchess of Albany' (T) | More than 30 suppliers
'Duchess of Edinburgh' (Fl) | More than 30 suppliers
'Duchess of Sutherland' (Vt/d) | CPev CRHN EBee ERob ESCh LRHS MCad NBea NTay SBra SDix SPet WTre
x *durandii* (D) ♀H4 | More than 30 suppliers
'Early Sensation' (Fo) | More than 30 suppliers
'Edith' (L) ♀H4 | EBee ECtt EPfP ERob ESCh ETho LRHS MAsh MWgw NBea NBrk NTay SBra SLim WGor WGwG WTre
'Edomurasaki' (L) | EBee ERob ESCh ETho NBrk NTay WTre
'Edouard Desfossé' (P) | EBee ERob ESCh NTay SBra
'Edward Prichard' (H) | CFRD CSPN EBee EPfP ERob ESCh ETho MAsh NBea NBrk SBra WTre
'Eetika' (Vt) | ERob ESCh
'Ekstra' (J) | ERob ESCh ETho NBrk
'Eleanor' | ECou ESCh
'Eleanor of Guildford' (P) | ENot ERob ESCh
'Elf' | CPev
'Elfin' (v) | ECou
§ x *eriostemon* (D) ♀ | More than 30 suppliers
'Elvan' (Vt) | CBgR CFRD CPev CRHN EBee ERob ESCh MCad NBrk NTay SPet WTre
'Emerald Stars' | ESCh
'Emilia Plater' (Vt) | CRHN CSPN ERob ESCh ETho MBri MCad NBea NBrk NTay SBra WBcn WTre
'Emogi' | ESCh
'Empress of India' (P) | ERob ESCh MWgw WTre
'Entel' (J) | ERob NBrk WTre
'Erik' (A) **new** | ESCh
§ x *eriostemon* (D) | CFRD CRHN EBee EOrc EPfP ESCh GEil GKir LRHS MBNS MCad MGos MSte NBPC NBrk NHol SBra SDix SGar SPer SPet WTre
§ - 'Blue Boy' (D) | CBgR CFRD CSPN EPfP ERob ESCh ETho MBri MCad MGos NBrk NTay SBra SPet WTre
 - 'Heather Herschell' (D) | CBgR CElw CFRD CPev CSPN ERob ESCh ETho SPet WTre
§ - 'Hendersonii' (D) | More than 30 suppliers
 - 'Lauren' (D) | ERob
§ - 'Olgae' (D) | CFRD CPev CSPN EBee EHan ESCh ETho MBow MCad MDKP NBea NBrk NTay SBra SCro SDix SLim WTre
'Ernest Markham' (J/Vt) ♀H4 | More than 30 suppliers
'Esperanto' (J) | ESCh
'Etoile de Malicorne' (P) | EBee ERob ESCh LRHS MCad NBea WGor WTre
'Etoile de Paris' (P) | EBee ERob ESCh NTay SBra WTre
'Etoile Nacrée' | ERob ESCh
'Etoile Rose' (T) | CFRD CPev CSPN CTri EBee EBre ELan ENot EOrc EPfP ERob ESCh ETho GKir LAst LRHS MAsh MCad NBea NTay SBra SDix SLim SMur SPer WFar WPGP WSHC WTre
'Etoile Violette' (Vt) ♀H4 | More than 30 suppliers
'Europa' | ERob
'Eva' | ERob ESCh NBrk
Evening Star = 'Evista'PBR | EPfP ERob ESCh MWgw NTay SBra SLim

'Eximia' (A/d) | ERob ESCh
'Fair Rosamond' (L/P) | CFRD CPev EBee EPfP ERob ESCh LRHS MAsh MCad NBea NTay SBra SCoo SDix SLim WTre
'Fairy Queen' (L) | ERob ESCh ETho SBra
fargesii | see *C. potaninii*
x *fargesioides* | see *C.* 'Paul Farges'
fasciculiflora | CBot CMHG CRHN CSPN ERob LRHS SSpi
 - L 657 | CFil SAga WCru WPGP
'Fascination' **new** | ESCh ETho LRHS MAsh SBra
fauriei (A) | ERob
finetiana hort. | see *C. paniculata* J.G. Gmel.
'Firefly' | ERob ESCh NTay
'Fireworks' (P) | COtt CSPN EBee ECtt ENot EPfP ESCh ETho LAst LRHS MAsh MBri MCad MGos NBea NBlu NPri NTay SBra SLim WFoF WGor WTre
'Flamingo' (L) | CWSG ERob
flammula | More than 30 suppliers
 - var. *flavescens* | ERob
 - 'Ithaca' (v) | ERob
 - 'Rubra Marginata' | see *C.* x *triternata* 'Rubromarginata'
§ 'Floralia' (A/d) | CFRD CSPN EBee EOrc ESCh LRHS NBea NBrk NTay SCoo SLim
florida | CSPN ERob ESCh ETho
 - 'Bicolor' | see *C. florida* var. *sieboldiana*
 - var. *flore-pleno* (d) | CPev CSPN EBee EBre ELan EOrc EPfP ESCh ETho GMac LAst LRHS MAsh MCad NBea NRib NTay SBod SBra SHBN SMad SPer SPla WCot WTre
 - Pistachio = 'Evirida'PBR (Fl) | COtt CSPN EHan EOrc EPfP ESCh ETho LBuc MBNS NLar NPri NTay SLim SPoG WWhi
 - var. *sieboldiana* (d) | More than 30 suppliers
foetida | CBcs CSPN NLAp
forrestii | see *C. napaulensis*
§ *forsteri* | CBcs CSPN EBee EOrc ERob ESCh ETho GSki IDee LFol MCad MWod NBrk NLAp SBra WPGP WSHC
forsteri x *indivisa* | WCru
'Foxtrot' (Vt) | CRHN ERob ESCh MAsh NBrk WTre
'Frau Mikiko' (P) | ERob ESCh
'Fryderyk Chopin' (P) | CSPN ERob ESCh ETho NTay
'Fuji-musume' (L) ♀H4 | CSPN EBee EHan ERob ESCh ETho MAsh MCad NBrk NTay SBra SLim WFar WTre
'Fujinami' (L) | ERob
fusca hort. | see *C. japonica*
fusca Turcz. | ERob MWhi
 - B&SWJ 4229 | WCru
 - var. *coreana* | WCru
 f. *umbrosa* B&SWJ 700 |
§ - subsp. *fusca* | ESCh ETho GIBF
 - var. *kamtschatica* | see *C. fusca* subsp. *fusca*
fusijamana | ERob
'G. Steffner' (A) | ERob ESCh NBrk
'Gabriëlle' (P) | CSPN ERob ESCh LBuc SLim WTre
'Gazelle' **new** | LRHS
'Gekkyuuden' | ERob
'Gemini' | ENot ERob ESCh WSpi
'General Sikorski' (L) | CBcs CElw CMac CRHN CSPN CSam CWSG EBee EBre ECtt ELan EPfP ESCh ETho LAst LRHS MAsh MBri MCad MGos NBea NTay SBra SDix SLim SPer SPet WTre
gentianoides | ERob SBla WAbe WCot
'Georg' (A/d) | ERob MGos WTre
'Georg Ots' (J) | ERob ESCh
'Gillian Blades' (P) ♀H4 | CFRD CRHN CSPN EBee EHan ELan ENot EPfP ERob ESCh ETho

	LAst LRHS MAsh MCad MWgw NBea NBrk NPri NTay SBra SLim SPet WTre
'Gipsy Queen' (J) ♀H4	More than 30 suppliers
'Gladys Picard' (P)	ERob ESCh MCad NTay SLim WFar WTre
glauca hort.	see *C. intricata*
'Glynderek' (L)	ERob ESCh MCad NTay SBra
'Golden Harvest' (Ta)	ERob ESCh NHol SBra WFar WTre
Golden Tiara	CSPN EBre EHan ENot ERob ESCh
= 'Kugotia'PBR (Ta) ♀H4	ETho LRHS MCad MGos MWgw NBea NBrk NPal NPri NTay SBra SPer WCot WTre
'Gornoye Ozero'	ERob ESCh
gouriana	ERob ESCh
- subsp. *lishanensis* B&SWJ 292	WCru
'Grace' (Ta)	CRHN CSPN ERob ESCh ETho NBrk WTre
gracilifolia	ERob ESCh WTre
- var. *dissectifolia*	ERob
'Grandiflora Sanguinea' (Vt)	ERob SLim
'Grandiflora Sanguinea' Johnson	see *C.* 'Södertälje'
grata hort.	see *C.* x *jouiniana*
grata Wall.	CElw CPLG CPev ERob NBrk WCot
- B&SWJ 6774	WCru
'Gravetye Beauty' (T)	More than 30 suppliers
'Green Velvet' (Fo)	ECou
grewiiflora B&SWJ 2956	WCru
'Guernsey Cream' (P)	CFRD CSPN CSam CWSG EBee EBre EHan EMil ESCh ETho GEil LAst LRHS MAsh MBri MCad NBea NTay SBra SDix SLim SPet WFar WTre WWes
'Guiding Star' (L)	ERob SBra
'H.F.Young' (L/P)	More than 30 suppliers
'Hagley Hybrid' (J)	More than 30 suppliers
'Hainton Ruby' (P)	ERob ESCh
'Haku-ōkan' (L)	CFRD CPev CSPN EBee EHan EPfP ERob ESCh ETho LRHS MAsh MCad NBea NTay SBra SLim WSpi WTre
'Hakuree'	ETho
'Hanaguruma' (P)	CSPN EBee ERob ESCh ETho MCad NBea NBrk NTay WFar WTre
'Hanajima' (I)	EHyt ERob ESCh ETho NBrk
'Hania' **new**	ETho
'Hanna' (Vt)	ERob ESCh ETho
Harlow Carr	LRHS
= 'Evipo-004' **new**	
'Harmony' (d)	ERob ESCh
'Haruyama'	ESCh MCad
Havering hybrids (Fo)	ECou
'Helen Cropper' (P)	ERob ESCh ETho MCad NBrk
'Helios' (Ta)	CFRD CSPN EBee EBre ENot EPfP ERob ESCh ETho GMac LRHS MCad MGos NBea NBrk NTay SBra WCot WTre
'Helsingborg' (A) ♀H4	CBcs CFRD CSPN EBee ECtt ELan ENot EPfP ERob ESCh ETho LAst LRHS MCad NBea NHol NPri NSti NTay SBra SLim SPet SPla WTel WTre WWes
hendersonii Stand.	see *C.* x *eriostemon*
hendersonii Koch	see *C.* x *eriostemon* 'Hendersonii'
'Hendersonii Rubra' (D)	CSPN
henryi	ENot
- B&SWJ 3402	WCru
'Henryi' (P) ♀H4	More than 30 suppliers
henryi var. *morii* B&SWJ 1668	WCru

heracleifolia (H)	CBcs CPou EChP ECtt EHol ESCh GKir GSki LPio MCad MFOX NLar WHil WMoo WTre
- Alan BloomPBR	see *C. tabulosa* Alan Bloom = 'Alblo'
- 'Blue Dwarf'	ETho
I - 'Cassandra' (H)	EBee EFou EHyt EPfP ESCh NBrk
- 'China Purple' (H)	CFai EBee ERob GBri MAvo NLar SSpi WAul WBor WCot WHil
- var. *davidiana*	see *C. tabulosa*
- 'New Love'PBR (H)	CBgR CSPN EFou EGle EHan ENot ERob ESCh ETho LAst LBuc LPio MBlu MGos NLar NSti SBra SPer WCAu WHil
- 'Roundway Blue Bird' (H)	CBot CFRD LHop
'Herbert Johnson' (P)	CPev ESCh NBrk SBra
hexapetala misapplied	see *C. recta* subsp. *recta* var. *lasiosepala*
hexapetala DC.	see *C. forsteri*
'Hikarugenji' (P)	CSPN ERob ESCh MCad NBrk NTay
§ *hilariae* (Ta)	ERob ESCh
§ *hirsutissima*	EHyt WLin
- var. *hirsutissima*	EBee
- var. *scottii*	ERob
'Honora' (P)	CSPN ERob ESCh MCad NTay SBra WTre
'Horn of Plenty' (L/P)	EBee EHan ERob ESCh LRHS MCad NBea NBrk NTay SBra SLim WTre
'Huldine' (Vt) ♀H4	More than 30 suppliers
'Huvi' (J)	ERob ESCh
§ 'Hybrida Sieboldii' (L)	CRHN EBee ERob ESCh ETho MCad NBea NBlu NBrk NTay SBra SLim WTre
Hyde Hall	LRHS
= 'Evipo-009' **new**	
'Hythe Chiffchaff' (Fo) **new**	EHyt
'Hythe Egret' (Fo)	EHyt LTwo SIng
'Hågelby White' (Vt)	ERob ESCh
ianthina	EHyt EPfP ERob ESCh SBra WPGP WSHC
- var. *kuripoensis*	ERob ETho
- - B&SWJ 700	WCru
'Ice Maiden'	ESCh
'Ice Queen' **new**	MAsh
'Ideal' (L)	ERob ESCh
'Ilka' (P)	ERob ESCh
'Imperial' (P/d)	ERob ESCh ETho NBrk
indivisa	see *C. paniculata* J.G. Gmel.
'Inglewood' (P)	ERob NTay
Inspiration = 'Zoin'PBR	CSPN EHan ELan ERob ESCh ETho LBuc MAsh MCad MGos NBrk NTay SBra SPer WTre
integrifolia	More than 30 suppliers
- 'Alba'	CElw CFRD CSPN ECtt EHan LAst LRHS NBea NTay SLim SPer
§ - var. *albiflora*	CBcs CHad EBee ESCh ETho GBuc MCad MDKP NBea NBir NBrk SBra SPet WCru WTre
- 'Amy'	ERob ESCh
- blue-flowered (I) **new**	CFRD
* - 'Finnis Form'	SChu
- 'Floris V'	CBAn EBee ERob ESCh NBrk
- 'Hendersonii' Koch	see *C.* x *eriostemon* 'Hendersonii'
I - 'Hendersonii'	ERob ESCh GKir LRHS MSte NTay SPet WTre
- subsp. *integrifolia* var. *latifolia*	ERob ESCh
- 'Olgae'	see *C.* x *eriostemon* 'Olgae'
- 'Ozawa's Blue' **new**	ETho
- 'Pangbourne Pink' ♀H4	CElw CFRD CHad CSPN EBee EBre EHan EOrc EPfP ERob ESCh ETho

	GBuc LRHS MAsh MCad NBPC NBea NBrk NTay SBra SLim WCru WTre
- 'Pastel Blue'	CPev ERob ESch ETho MCad NBea
- 'Pastel Pink'	CPev ERob ESch MCad WTre
- 'Rosea' ♀H4	CBcs CBot CM&M CPev CSPN EBee EBre EHan EPfP ERob ESch ETho EWTr LAst LHop LRHS MBri MCad MSwo MTho MWgw NBea NBrk NChi NTay SLim WSHC WTre
- 'Tapestry'	CPev ERob SBra
- white	see *C. integrifolia* var. *albiflora*
§ *intricata*	CBcs CFRD CSPN ECre EPfP ERob ERob ESch
- 'Harry Smith'	ERob ESch
- 'Vince Denny' **new**	ESch
'Iola Fair' (P)	CSPN ERob ESch ETho NTay
'Ishobel' (P)	ERob ESch NBrk
'Ivan Olsson' (PxL)	CFRD CSPN ERob ESch ETho
'Izumi' H. Hayakawa	ESch
'Jackmanii' (J) ♀H4	CBcs CMac CRHN CTri EBee ENot EPfP ERob ESch ETho GKir LRHS MAsh MCad NBea NBlu NWea SBod SBra SLim SPer SPet WFar WTel WTre
'Jackmanii Alba' (J)	CPev EBee EBre ELan EPfP ERob ESch ETho LAst LRHS MAsh MBar MCad NBea NBrk NTay SLim SPet WStI WTre
'Jackmanii Rubra' (J)	CPev ERob ESch MAsh MCad NBea SCoo SLim WTre
'Jackmanii Superba' ambig. (J)	More than 30 suppliers
'Jackmanii Superba' misapplied	see *C.* 'Gipsy Queen'
'Jadwiga Teresa' **new**	CFRD
'James Mason' (P)	CPev CSPN EBee EHan ESch MCad NBea NTay SBra SCoo SPet WTre
§ 'Jan Pawel II' (J)	CMac CWSG EBee ECtt ELan EPfP ESch ETho GKir LRHS MAsh MCad NBea NTay SBra SLim SPer SPet
Janis Ruplens no. 1	ERob
§ *japonica*	CPev CSPN ERob NBrk SBra WLin WTre
- B&SWJ 5017	WCru
- var. *obvallata*	see *C. obvallata*
aff. *japonica* B&SWJ 8900 **new**	WCru
'Jasper'	ERob ESch
'Jennifer Valentine'	MCad
'Jenny Caddick' (Vt)	CFRD CSPN ERob ESch ETho MCad NTay
'Jim Hollis' (Fl)	ERob ESch
'Joan Baker' (Vt)	ERob
'Joan Gray' (d)	ERob ESch
'Joan Picton' (P)	CWSG EBee ESch MAsh NBea NBrk NRib NTay SBra
'John Gould Veitch' (Fl)	ERob ESch
'John Gudmundsson' (L)	ERob ESch
'John Huxtable' (J) ♀H4	CDoC CPev CRHN EBee EPfP ERob ESch ETho LRHS MCad NBea NBrk NPri NTay SBra SLim WGor WTre
John Paul II	see *C.* 'Jan Pawel II'
'John Treasure'	WTre
'John Warren' (L)	CFRD CWSG EBee ERob ESch ETho EWTr LRHS MAsh MCad NTay SBra SCoo SLim WTre
'Jorma' (J)	ERob ESch
Josephine = 'Evijohill' PBR ♀H4	COtt CSPN EBre EHan ENot EOrc EPfP ESch ETho GKir LAst LRHS MBNS MCad MWgw NLar NPri NTay SBra SCoo SPer WWeb
§ x *jouiniana*	EBee ERob ESch MBlu MCad MWya NHol SPer WGwG WSHC WTre
- 'Chance'	ESch
- 'Côte d'Azur' (H)	EBee EOrc ERob ESch GCal GEil MAvo MCCP MCad MTed NBPC NBrk NLar WTre
- 'Praecox' ♀H4	More than 30 suppliers
'Jubileinyi 70'	ERob ESch
'Julka' **new**	ETho
'June Pyne'	ESch ETho LRHS NPri
'Juuli' (I)	ERob ESch ETho NBrk
'Kaaru' (Vt)	CSPN ERob ESch ETho WTre
'Kacper' (L)	CSPN ESch ETho MCad NBrk NTay
'Kaiu' (T x Vt)	ERob ESch
§ 'Kakio' (P)	CDoC CElw CFRD EBee ERob ESch ETho GKir LAst MAsh MCad MGos NBea NTay SBra SLim SPer SPet WFar WTre
'Kalina' (P)	ERob ESch NBrk
'Kamilla'	ERob ESch
§ 'Kardynal Wyszynski' (J)	CRHN EBee ERob ESch ETho MAsh MCad MGos NBea NBlu NBrk NTay SBra SCoo SLim WTre
'Kasmu' (Vt)	ERob ESch WTre
'Kasugayama' (L)	ERob
'Katharina'	ERob ESch
'Kathleen Dunford' (Fl)	CFRD EBee ERob ESch LAst LRHS MAsh MCad NBea NTay SCoo SLim SPet WTre
'Kathleen Wheeler' (P)	CPev EBee ERob ESch ETho MCad NBea NTay SCoo SDix SLim WTre
'Keith Richardson' (P)	CPev ERob ESch NBea NBrk NTay WTre
'Ken Donson' (L) ♀H4	CElw CFRD EBee EPfP ERob ESch NBrk NTay SPet
I 'Ken Hall's Form' (Fo) **new**	SBra
'Kermesina' (Vt) ♀H4	CElw CHad CPev CRHN CSam EBee EBre ELan EOrc EPfP ESch ETho GKir LRHS MAsh MBri MCad NBPC NBea NHol NSti NTay SBra SDix SLim SPer SPet WBVN WSHC WTre
'Ketu'	ERob
'Kiev' (Vt)	ERob ESch
'King Edward VII' (L)	EBee EPfP ERob ESch LRHS NBea NBrk NTay SBra WGor WStI WTre
'King George V' (L)	ERob ESch NBrk
'Kinokawa' (P)	ERob
'Kiri Te Kanawa'	CPev CSPN EHan EPfP ERob ESch ETho LAst MAsh MCad NBea NBrk NTay SBra SCoo SLim WTre
kirilovii	ERob
'Kirimäe' (P)	ERob ESch
'Kjell'	ERob ESch
'Klaara' (P)	ERob
'Kommerei' (Vt)	ERob ETho
'Königskind' (P)	CFRD CSPN ERob ESch ETho NBrk NTay WTre
'Königskind Rosa' (P)	ERob ESch
koreana	ERob NBea NHol WSHC
- *citra*	see *C.* 'Citra'
- f. *lutea*	CElw CFRD ESch MCad NBrk
'Kosmicheskaia Melodiia' (J)	CFRD CSPN ERob ESch NBrk NTay
'Kotkas' (J/L)	ERob
'Kuba' (P)	ERob ESch NBrk
'Küllus'	ERob ESch ETho NTay
kweichowensis **new**	ETho
ladakhiana (Ta)	CFRD CPev CSPN EBee EPfP ESch ETho GQui MCad MWhi NBea NBir SBra WCru

'Lady Betty Balfour' (J/Vt)	CElw CFRD CPev CSPN CWSG EBee ERob ESCh ETho GKir LRHS MAsh MBNS MBri MCad NTay SBra SDix SGar SLim SPet WFar WTre WWeb
'Lady Caroline Nevill' (L)	CPev CRHN EBee ERob ESCh MCad NBea NTay WTre
'Lady Katherine' (d)	ERob
'Lady Londesborough' (P)	CFRD CPev EPfP ERob ESCh LRHS NBea NBrk NTay SDix SLim WTre
'Lady Northcliffe' (L)	CPev CSPN CTri CWSG EHan EPfP ERob ESCh ETho LRHS MAsh MCad NBea NTay SBra SDix SLim WTre
'Ladybird Johnson' (T)	CFRD CPev EBee ERob ESCh ETho MCad NBrk NTay SBra SLim WTre
lasiandra	ERob
- B&SWJ 6775	WCru
- white	ERob
lasiantha	ESCh
'Last Dance' (Ta)	CRHN ERob ESCh
Lasting Love = 'Grazyna'	ESCh MAsh
'Lasurstern' (P) ♀H4	More than 30 suppliers
'Laura' (L)	ERob ESCh MCad NBrk
'Laura Denny' (P)	ESCh ETho MAsh NBrk
'Lavender Lace'	ERob ESCh MAsh
'Lawsoniana' (L)	CElw CFRD CRHN CWSG EBee EGra ESCh LAst MAsh MBar NBea NBlu NBrk NTay SLim SPet WTre
'Leione' **new**	ESCh
'Lemon Chiffon' (P)	CSPN EBee EBre ERob ESCh ETho NBrk NTay SBra SLim
Liberation = 'Evifive'PBR	EBee ERob ESCh ETho LAst LRHS NTay SBra SCoo SLim WTre
§ *ligusticifolia*	ERob ESCh GSki
'Liisu' (J)	ESCh
'Lilacina Floribunda' (L)	CBcs CFRD EBee ESCh LRHS MBNS MBar NBea NBrk NTay SBra SLim WTre
'Lilactime' (P)	ERob ESCh NBea SBra
'Lincoln Star' (P)	CPev CRHN EBee EHan EPfP ERob ESCh GKir LAst LRHS MAsh MBar MCad NBea NBrk NPri NTay SBra SDix SLim SPer SPet WTre
'Lincolnshire Lady' (A)	NTay
'Little Bas'	CSPN ERob ESCh NBrk
'Little Butterfly' (Vt)	ERob ESCh
'Little Nell' (Vt)	CElw CFRD CPev CRHN CSPN EBee EBre ELan EOrc ERob ESCh ETho GKir LRHS MAsh MCad NBea NBrk NHol NTay SBra SDix SLim SPer SPet WSHC WSpi WTre
'Lord Herschell'	CElw CPev EBee ERob ESCh ETho
'Lord Nevill' (P)	CPev CRHN CWSG EPfP ERob ESCh ETho LRHS MAsh MCad NBea NBlu NTay SBra SDix WTre
'Louise Rowe' (Fl)	CFRD EBee ELan ERob ESCh ETho LRHS MAsh MCad MGos NBea NTay SBra SLim SPet WTre
loureiroana HWJ 663	WCru
'Love Jewelry'	ETho
'Lucey' (J)	ESCh NBrk NTay
'Lucie' (P)	NBea WTre
'Lunar Lass' (Fo/f)	CRez CStu EBee ECho EHyt EPfP ESCh ETho GGar ITim LBee NLAp NSla SIng WAbe WPGP
'Lunar Lass' x *foetida* (Fo)	ECou
I 'Lunar Lass Variegata' (Fo/v)	ECho
'Luther Burbank' (J)	CFRD ERob ESCh ETho NTay
'Macrantha'	ERob
macropetala (A/d)	More than 30 suppliers
- 'Alborosea' (A/d)	EBee ERob ESCh GMac NTay
- 'Anders' (A/d)	ESCh
- 'Ballerina' (A/d)	MCad
- 'Ballet Skirt' (A/d)	ERob ESCh LBuc LRHS MCad MGos SLim WTre
- 'Blue Lagoon'	see *C. macropetala* 'Lagoon' Jackman 1959
§ - 'Chili' (A)	ERob NBrk
- 'Floralia'	see *C.* 'Floralia'
- 'Harry Smith'	see *C. macropetala* 'Chili'
§ - 'Jan Lindmark' (A/d)	EBee EBre EOrc ERob ESCh ETho LRHS MAsh MCad MGos NBea NBir NHol NSti NTay SBra SLim WCru WFar WTre
- 'Lagoon' Jackman 1956	see *C. macropetala* 'Maidwell Hall'
§ - 'Lagoon' (A/d) Jackman 1959 ♀H4	CSPN ERob ETho LRHS MAsh MSwo NBea NBrk NSti SBra SCoo SLim SMur WCru WTre
§ - 'Maidwell Hall') Jackman (A/d	CDoC CSPN CTri CWSG EBee ECtt EPfP ERob ESCh ETho LRHS MAsh MCad MGos NBea NBrk NHol SBra SHBN WCru WPGP WSHC WTel WTre
- 'Markham's Pink' (A/d) ♀H4	More than 30 suppliers
- 'Pauline' (A/d)	CWSG EBee ERob ESCh ETho LRHS MBri NBea NBrk NTay SBra SLim WTMC WTre
- 'Pearl Rose' (A/d)	CWSG EBee ERob ESCh
- 'Purple Spider' (A/d)	CBcs CElw CFRD CSPN EBee EBre EOrc ERob ESCh ETho GKir LBuc MAsh MBlu MWgw NBea NHol NTay SBra SLim SPer SPet WTre
- 'Snowbird' (A/d)	CPev CSPN ERob ESCh MAsh NHol SBra
- 'Wesselton' (A/d)	CSPN ERob ESCh ETho MCad NBrk NHol NTay WTre
- 'White Lady' (A/d)	EPfP ERob ESCh GKir NTay SBra WTre
- 'White Moth'	see *C. alpina* subsp. *sibirica* 'White Moth'
- 'White Swan'	see *C.* 'White Swan'
- 'White Wings' (A/d)	CBcs ERob ESCh ETho LAst MWgw
'Madame Baron Veillard' (J)	CFRD CPev EBee ECtt ESCh LAst LRHS MBar MCad NBrk NTay SBra SDix SLim WSpi WTre WWeb
'Madame Edouard) André' (J	CDoC CPev CRHN CSPN EBee EPfP ERob ESCh LRHS MAsh MCad NBea NTay SBra SDix SLim WTre
'Madame Grangé' (J) ♀H4	CPev CRHN CSPN EBee EPfP ESCh ETho LRHS NBea NBrk NTay SBra SDix SLim SPet WTre
'Madame Julia Correvon' (Vt) ♀H4	More than 30 suppliers
'Madame le Coultre'	see *C.* 'Marie Boisselot'
'Madame van Houtte' (L)	ERob ESCh MCad
'Magnus Johnson' (A)	ERob
'Majojo' (Fo)	CStu EBee ESCh
'Mammut' (P)	ERob ESCh
§ *mandschurica*	EBee ERob ETho GCal GEil GSki NLar SBra
- B&SWJ 1060	WCru
marata (Fo)	GCrs WCot
'Marcel Moser' (P)	CPev ERob ESCh MCad NBrk NTay SDix
'Margaret Hunt' (J)	CSPN EBee ELan ERob ESCh ETho LRHS MCad NBea NBrk NTay SBra SPla
'Margaret Wood' (P)	ERob ESCh MCad NTay
'Margot Koster' (Vt)	CDoC CElw CFRD CRHN CSam EBee EBre EPfP ESCh LRHS MBri MCad MSwo NBea NTay SBra SLim SPet WSHC WTre WWeb
§ 'Marie Boisselot' (L) ♀H4	More than 30 suppliers

'Marie Louise Jensen' (J)	ESCh NTay SBra WTre	
marmoraria (Fo) ♀H2-3	CPBP EBee EBre EHyt EPot ESCh GBin GCrs ITim LHop LRHS NLAp NSla SBla SIng WAbe WFar	
- hybrid (Fo)	ITim LBee NLAp	
marmoraria x *cartmanii* hort. 'Joe' (Fo)	MGos	
marmoraria x *petriei* (Fo/f)	ITim	
'Marmori'	ERob ESCh ETho	
'Mary Claire' (d)	ERob ESCh	
§ 'Maskarad' (Vt)	CSPN EBee ERob ESCh NBrk SBra WTre	
Masquerade (Vt)	see *C.* 'Maskarad' (Vt)	
'Masquerade' (P)	ETho LRHS MBri NTay SCoo SMur	
'Matka Siedliska' (Fl)	CFRD CSPN ERob ESCh NTay	
§ 'Matka Teresa'	ERob MCad	
'Matka Urszula Ledóchowska' (P)	ERob	
'Maureen' (L)	CPev CSPN CWSG ESCh ETho MAsh	
mauritiana	ERob	
maximowicziana	see *C. terniflora*	
'Medley' **new**	LRHS	
'Meeli' (J)	ESCh NBrk	
'Meloodia' (J)	WTre	
'Memm' (A/d)	ERob	
'Mia' (P/d)	ERob	
'Michelle' (I)	ERob	
microphylla	ECou	
'Miikla' (J)	ERob	
'Mikelite' (P)	ERob ESCh	
'Miniseelik' (J)	ERob ESCh ETho NBrk	
'Minister' (P)	CFRD ESCh ETho MCad NBrk	
'Minuet' (Vt) ♀H4	CHad CRHN CSPN EBee EPfP ERob ESCh ETho GKir LRHS MCad MSwo NBPC NBea NHol NTay SBra SDix SLim SPer SPla WSHC WSpi WTel WTre	
'Miriam Markham' (J)	CPev ERob ESCh MCad NBea NBrk SBra WTre	
'Miss Bateman' (P) ♀H4	More than 30 suppliers	
'Miss Crawshay' (P)	CPev EBee ERob ESCh MCad NTay SLim WTre	
N *montana*	CBcs CElw CPev CSBt EBee ECtt ENot ESCh EWTr GKir MBar MCad MGos MWat NBea NBlu NHol SBod SBra SDix SHBN SLim SPet SSta WFar WGwG WTre	
- B&SWJ 6930	WCru	
- BWJ 8189b from China	WCru	
- *alba*	see *C. montana*	
- 'Alexander'	CDoC CPou CWSG EBee ERob ESCh LRHS MBNS MCad MGos NTay WBrE WCru	
- 'Brookfield Clove'	ERob	
- 'East Malling'	ERob ESCh	
- 'Elten'	CSPN ERob ESCh	
- 'Fragrant Spring'	CSPN EBee ECtt ERob ESCh ETho MCad MGos NBlu NLar NTay SBra SLim WBcn WTre	
- 'Giant Star' **new**	CBcs NPer	
- 'Gothenburg'	EPfP ERob ESCh NBea SBra WTre	
- f. *grandiflora* ♀H4	More than 30 suppliers	
§ - 'Hidcote'	ERob ESCh SBra WTre	
- 'Jacqui' (d)	ERob ESCh ETho LRHS MGos SBra SCoo SLim WBcn	
- 'Jenny Keay' (d)	ERob ESCh LBuc SBra	
- 'Lilacina'	ESCh MAsh SBra WPen	
- 'Mrs Margaret Jones' (d)	EBee ERob ESCh NBrk SBra WTre	
- 'New Dawn'	CSPN ERob ESCh MCad NBlu SBra WTre	
- 'Odorata'	CDoC EBee EPfP ERob ETho GSki LFol MCad MGos NTay SCoo SLim WGor WGor	
* - 'Olga'	ERob ESCh	
- 'Peveril'	CPev CSPN EPAt ERob ESCh ETho MCad NBrk SBra	
- 'Pleniflora' (d)	CFRD ESCh MGos SBra	
- 'Rosebud' **new**	CBcs NPer	
- var. *rubens*	More than 30 suppliers	
- - 'Broughton Star' (d) ♀H4	More than 30 suppliers	
- - 'Continuity'	ERob MAsh NTay SBra SDix SLim SPla WSHC	
- - 'Elizabeth' ♀H4	More than 30 suppliers	
- - 'Freda' ♀H4	More than 30 suppliers	
- - 'Marjorie' (d)	More than 30 suppliers	
- - 'Mayleen' ♀H4	More than 30 suppliers	
- - 'Odorata'	ESCh SLim WTre	
- - 'Picton's Variety'	CDoC CPev CTri EBee EHan ERob ESCh ETho MBri MCad NHol SBra SHBN SRms WTre	
- - 'Pink Perfection'	CDoC CElw CWSG EBee EBre ECtt ELan EPfP ERob ESCh LAst LRHS MCad NBea NBlu NBrk NHol NTay SBra SLim SPer SPet WFar WGwG WStl WTre	
- 'Rubens Superba'	see *C. montana* var. *rubens* 'Superba'	
§ - var. *rubens* 'Superba'	CDul CMHG CWSG EBee ECtt ESCh GKir SHBN SLim WFar	
- - 'Tetrarose' ♀H4	More than 30 suppliers	
- - 'Vera'	CFRD CSPN EBee ECtt ERob ESCh ETho LRHS MCad NBea NBir NBrk NTay SBra SCoo SLim SPla WCru WStl WTre	
- - 'Warwickshire Rose'	CElw CFRD CRHN CSPN CWSG ECtt EHan ERob ESCh ETho GKir MAsh MCad NBea NBrk NCGa NHol NTay SBra WCot WFar WPGP WPen WSHC WTre WWeb WWhi	
§ - var. *sericea*	CElw CFRD CPev CTri CWSG EBee ECtt ELan ESCh GKir GQui LRHS MAsh MCad NBrk NTay SBra SLim SLon SRms WCru WFoF	
- 'Spooneri'	see *C. montana* var. *sericea*	
- 'Sunrise'PBR (d)	COtt CSPN EHan EOrc ESCh ETho MAsh MSwo NLar SBra WFar	
- 'Unity'	ESCh	
- var. *wilsonii*	More than 30 suppliers	
- - 'Hergest'	ESCh	
'Monte Cassino' (J)	CFRD CRHN CSPN ERob ESCh ETho MAsh MCad NBrk NTay SPet WTre	
'Moonbeam' (Fo)	CFRD EBre ECou EHyt ELan EOrc EPot ESCh GEdr GKir ITim MGos NBrk NLAp NSla NTay SBra SLon SMrm WCot	
§ 'Moonlight' (P)	CPev CSPN EBee ERob ESCh GEil LAst MAsh NBrk NTay SBra WTre	
'Moonman' (Fo)	ETho SIng	
Morning Cloud	see *C.* 'Yukikomachi'	
Mother Theresa	see *C.* 'Matka Teresa'	
'Mrs Bush' (L)	ERob ESCh LRHS NBea WTre WWes	
'Mrs Cholmondeley' (L) ♀H4	More than 30 suppliers	
'Mrs George Jackman' (P) ♀H4	CPev CSPN EBee ERob ESCh ETho MAsh MBri MCad MGos NBea NBlu NBrk NTay SBra SLim SPla WStl WTre	
'Mrs Hope' (L)	CPev ERob ESCh MCad NBea NBrk SBra WTre	
'Mrs James Mason'	CFRD CPev EBee ERob ESCh ETho MCad NBea NTay SBra SLim WTre	

'Mrs N. Thompson' (P) — More than 30 suppliers
'Mrs P.B. Truax' (P) — EBee EHan ERob ESCh LRHS MCad NBea NTay SBra SCoo SDix SLim WTre
'Mrs. P.T. James' — ERob
'Mrs Robert Brydon' (H) — CBgR EBee EPfP ERob GEil IPot MCad MWgw NBrk NHol NTay SCoo SGar SLim WCot WTre
'Mrs Spencer Castle' (Vt) — CPev CSPN ERob ESCh MCad NTay SBra WTre
'Mrs T. Lundell' (Vt) — CFRD CSPN ERob ESCh ETho MCad NBea NBrk NTay
'Multi Blue' — More than 30 suppliers
'My Angel'[PBR] (Ta) — CSPN EBee ELan ENot ESCh MBri MCad MGos NLar NTay SPer WSpi WTre
'Myôjô' (P) — CSPN EBee ERob ESCh LRHS MCad SBra SLim WTre
'Myôkô' (L) — SLim
'Nadezhda' (P) — CFRD ERob ESCh ETho NTay
§ *napaulensis* — CBcs CFRD CPev CSPN EBee EOrc ERob ESCh LEur LFol LRHS MCad NBea NTay SBra SLim WCru WGwG WSHC WTre
'Natacha' (P) — CElw ERob ESCh ETho NBea NBrk SBra SLim SPet WTre
'Negritjanka' (J) — CSPN ERob ESCh LBuc MBri NBrk NTay WTre
'Negus' (J) — ERob ESCh
'Nelly Moser' (L/P) ♀[H4] — More than 30 suppliers
Nettleton seedlings — EPot
New Zealand hybrids (Fo) — ECou
'Nikolai Rubtsov' — CSPN ERob ESCh NTay
'Niobe' (J) ♀[H4] — More than 30 suppliers
'Norfolk Queen' — ESCh
'North Star' — see *C.* 'Pôhjanael'
'Nuit de Chine' — ERob ESCh MCad NBrk
obscura — ERob
§ *obvallata* — ESCh
ochotensis (A) — CSPN ERob SDys
ochroleuca — NWCA
'Odoriba' — ESCh ETho
'Ola Howells' (A/d) — ERob ESCh
'Olimpiada-80' (L) — ERob ESCh NTay
'Omoshiro' **new** — ESCh
'Opaline' — see *C.* 'Asagasumi'
orientalis misapplied — see *C. tibetana* subsp. *vernayi*
orientalis L. (Ta) — CFRD CPLG EPfP ESCh GSki IMGH LRHS MCad NHol SBra SReu
– 'Bill MacKenzie' — see *C.* 'Bill MacKenzie'
– 'Orange Peel' — see *C. tibetana* subsp. *vernayi* 'Orange Peel'
– var. *orientalis* (Ta) — CStr ERob
* – 'Rubromarginata' (Ta) — CPev
– 'Sherriffii' — see *C. tibetana* subsp. *vernayi*
– var. *tenuifolia* (Ta) — ERob ESCh
– var. *tenuiloba* — see *C. columbiana* var. *tenuiloba*
'Otto Fröbel' (L) — CSPN ERob ESCh ETho MCad NBrk NTay
'Paala' — ERob
'Paddington' (P) — ERob ETho
'Pagoda' (PxVt) ♀[H4] — CDoC CElw CFRD CPev CRHN EBee EBre EHan EOrc EPfP ESCh ETho GMac LAst LRHS MAsh MBri MCad NBea NHol NPal NTay SBra SLim SPla SRms WSHC WTre
'Päkapikk' (Vt) — ERob
'Pamela' — CSPN ERob ESCh ETho LBuc NTay WTre
'Pamela Jackman' — see *C. alpina* 'Pamela Jackman'
'Pamiat Serdtsa' (I) — ERob ESCh ETho WTre
paniculata Thunb. — see *C. terniflora*
paniculata J.G. Gmel. — CPev CSPN EBee GGar LRHS SBra WPGP WSHC

– var. *lobata* — WTre
'Paola' (d) — ESCh MCad
'Paradise Queen' **new** — ESCh ETho
'Parasol' — CSPN ERob ESCh NBrk NTay
§ *parviflora* — ERob
parviflora x *forsteri* — ESCh
parviloba var. *bartlettii* — WCru
    B&SWJ 6788
'Pastel Princess' — CFRD ERob MCad NTay
'Pat Coleman' (P) — ESCh ETho
patens — NBea
– from China — ERob ESCh
– from Japan — ERob ESCh
– 'Korean Moon' **new** — WCru
– 'Nagoya' — ESCh
– 'Sanda' **new** — ESCh
Patricia Ann Fretwell — CPev CSPN ERob LRHS MCad
    = 'Pafar'[PBR] — NBea
§ 'Paul Farges' ♀[H4] — CBcs CFRD CSPN EBee EOrc ERob ETho GMac MBlu MBri MCad MWgw NBrk NHol NSti NTay SBra SLim WTel WTre WWeb
'Pendragon' — ERob ESCh
'Pennell's Purity' (L) — ERob ESCh ETho MCad NTay
'Percy Picton' (P) — ESCh MAsh
'Perle d'Azur' (J) — More than 30 suppliers
'Perrin's Pride' (Vt) — EBee ERob ESCh LRHS MCad NBrk NTay SBra SCoo WTre
'Peter Pan' (P) — ERob
peterae **new** — ERob
– var. *trichocarpa* — ERob
Petit Faucon — EBee EBre ECtt EHan ENot EPfP ERob ETho GMac LAst LRHS MAsh MBNS MBri MWgw NBea NPri NTay SBra SLim SPer WPGP WTre
    = 'Evisix'[PBR] ♀[H4] —
petriei (Fo) — ECou ETow LPio MBow NLAp
– 'Princess' (Fo/f) — ECou
– 'Steepdown' (F) — ECou
petriei x *foetida* (Fo) — ECou
'Peveril Peach' — CPev ESCh
'Peveril Pearl' (P) — CPev ERob ESCh ETho MCad NTay
'Peveril Pendant' — CPev
I 'Phoenix' (P) — ESCh
'Picardy' **new** — LRHS
pierotii — ERob
'Piilu' (P) — CFRD CSPN ELan ERob ESCh ETho LBuc LRHS MCad NBrk NPri NTay SBra SCoo SLim WTre
'Pink Champagne' — see *C.* 'Kakio'
'Pink Fantasy' (J) — CFRD CPev CRHN CSPN CTri CWSG EBee EBre ERob ESCh ETho LRHS MAsh MBar MCad NBea NBrk NTay SBra SLim WTre
'Pink Pearl' (P) — ESCh NBrk
'Pirko' (Vt) — ERob ESCh
§ *pitcheri* — CPev ERob ESCh NBrk
'Pixie' — see *C.* (County Park Group) 'Pixie'
'Pointy' (A) — ESCh
'Polish Spirit' (Vt) ♀[H4] — More than 30 suppliers
§ *potaninii* — CCge CRHN CSPN ECtt GIBF MCad MWhi WSHC WTMC
§ – var. *potaninii* — CPev EPfP ERob MCad NBea NTay SDix
– var. *souliei* — see *C. potaninii* var. *potaninii*
– 'Summer Snow' — see *C.* 'Paul Farges'
'Prairie' **new** — LRHS
'Prairie River' (A) — ERob
'Pretty in Blue' **new** — ESCh ETho SBra
'Pribaltika' (J) — ERob WTre
'Primrose Star' (d) — CDoC COtt CSPN EHan EOrc ERob ESCh ETho EWTr LAst LBuc LRHS MBlu MCad MGos MSwo NBrk NHol NLar NPri SBra SCoo SPer WFar WTre

'Prince Charles' (J) ♀H4 — CElw CHad CPou CRHN CSPN CTri EBee EBre ELan EPfP ESCh ETho LRHS MCad NBea NBir NTay SBra SDix SLim SPer SPet WSHC WTre

'Prince Philip' (P) — ERob ESCh NBrk NTay SBra WFar

§ 'Princess Diana' (T) ♀H4 — More than 30 suppliers

§ 'Princess of Wales' (L) — EPfP ERob LRHS MBNS MCad SBra WSHC WTre

'Prins Hendrik' (L/P) — ERob MCad WGor

'Propertius' (A) — CFRD ERob ESCh ETho NBrk

'Proteus' (Fl) — CPev CSPN EBee EBre EHan ELan EPfP ESCh ETho GKir LAst LRHS MAsh MBNS MCad NBea NTay SBra SDix SLim SPer SPet WTre

§ 'Pruinina' (A) — CSPN ERob WTre

§ 'Põhjanael' (J) — CSPN CWSG EBee ERob ESCh MCad NBea NBrk SCoo SLim WTre

'Pulmapäev' (L) — ERob ESCh

'Purple Haze' — CRHN

quadribracteolata — ECou

- 'Nancy's Lookout' — ECou

'Queen Alexandra' (P) — ERob ESCh MCad

'Radostj' (J) — ERob

'Ragamuffin' (d) — ENot ERob ESCh

'Rahvarinne' — ERob ESCh

'Ramona' — see *C.* 'Hybrida Sieboldii'

ranunculoides — WCru

CD&R 2345

recta — CFRD CFee CHad CPev CSPN EChP ECtt EPfP ERob ETho GKir GSki LPio LRHS MAsh MBro MCad MLLN MNrw MWgw MWhi NBea NLar SPer WHil WPer WTre WWye

- 'Lime Close' **new** — SMrm

- 'Peveril' — CFRD CPev EBee ERob ESCh ETho LAst NBre WTre

- 'Purpurea' — More than 30 suppliers

§ - subsp. *recta* — CSPN ERob GBBs WHil
  var. *lasiosepala*

* - 'Velvet Night' — CSpe ECtt ERob ESCh ETho LAst LHop MBri MTis NHol SMrm WCom WTre

'Red Ballon' (Ta) — ERob ESCh LBuc

'Red Cooler' — ERob ESCh NBrk

'Red Pearl' (P) — ERob ESCh ETho MGos NTay

§ *rehderiana* ♀H4 — More than 30 suppliers

- BWJ 7700 from China — WCru

- CC 3601 — CPLG

'Reiman' (L/J) — ERob

reticulata — ERob

'Rhapsody' F Watkinson (P) ♀H4 — CFRD CPev CSPN EBee ENor EPfP ERob ETho LRHS MAsh MBri MCad NBrk NTay SBra SCoo WBar WTre

'Richard Pennell' (P) ♀H4 — CPev EBee EHan ERob ESCh ETho LRHS MAsh MBri MCad MWgw NBea NBrk NPri NTay SBra SCoo SDix SLim WTre

'Ristimägi' (J) — ERob

'Rodomax' (A) — ERob ESCh

'Roko' (J) — ERob

'Roko-Kolla' (J) — CFRD CSPN ERob ESCh ETho NBea NBrk SBra WWes

'Romantika' (J) — CFRD CSPN EBee EBre EHan ELan ERob ESCh ETho MAsh NBea NTay SBra SLim SPer WTre

'Roogoja' (L) — ERob ESCh

'Rooguchi' (I) — CFRD ERob ESCh ETho LRHS NBrk

'Rose Supreme' — MCad

Rosemoor — LRHS
  = 'Evipo-002' **new**

'Rosy O'Grady' (A) ♀H4 — EBee ELan EOrc ESCh ETho MAsh MBar MCad MGos NBea NHol NSti SLim SPer WTre

'Rouge Cardinal' (J) — More than 30 suppliers

'Royal Velours' (Vt) ♀H4 — CDoC CElw CHad CPev CRHN CSPN CTri EBee EBre ELan EPfP ERob ESCh ETho GKir LRHS MCad NBea NHol NSti SBra SDix SHBN SLim SPer SPet WFar WTre WWhi

Royal Velvet — CSPN EBee ESCh ETho LAst MBri
  = 'Evifour'PBR — MCad NTay SBra SCoo SLim WTre

'Royalty' (LxP) ♀H4 — CElw CFRD CSPN EBee EBre ELan EPfP ERob ESCh LRHS MAsh MCad NBea NBir NPri NTay SBra SDix SLim SPer SPet WTre

'Rozalia' **new** — ESCh

'Ruby Glow' (L) — EBee EPfP ERob ESCh MCad NTay SCoo WTre

'Rüütel' (J) — CFRD ERob ESCh ETho MAsh MCad NBrk NTay SBra SCoo SLim WTre

'Saalomon' (J) — ERob

'Sakala' (P) — ERob ESCh

'Sally Cadge' (P) — CFRD ERob ESCh

'Samantha Denny' — CSPN ERob ESCh ETho MAsh NBrk NRib NTay SBra WTre

'Sander' (H) — CSPN ERob ESCh ETho WTre

'Sandra Denny' — ESCh MAsh

'Satsukibare' (P) — ERob ESCh NBrk WTre

I 'Saturn' (Vt) — ERob ESCh NBea SPla WTre

'Saturn' (P) — SCoo

'Scartho Gem' (P) — CFRD CPev EBee EPfP ERob ESCh MCad NBea NPri NTay SCoo WTre

'Schneeglanz' (P) — MCad

'Sealand Gem' (L) — CFRD CPev EBee ERob ESCh ETho LAst MCad NBea NBlu NTay SBra SCoo SLim WTre

'Semu' (J) — CSPN ERob ESCh ETho

'Serenata' (J) — ERob MCad NBea

serratifolia (Ta) — CElw CFRD CPev EHyt ERob ESCh ETho GFlt MCad MDKP MLLN MWhi NTay SDix WTre

- B&SWJ 8458 from Korea — WCru

'Sheila Thacker' (P) — ESCh ETho

'Sherriffii' (Ta) — ERob ESCh

'Shirakihane' — NBrk

'Shirayukihime' (L) — CSPN ESCh

§ 'Shiva' — ERob MAsh SPet

'Shorty' (Ta) — ERob ESCh

'Sho-un' (L) — EBee ERob ESCh NTay SBra

'Shropshire Blue' — ERob WTre

'Sialia' (A/d) — ERob ESCh NTay

sibirica — see *C. alpina* subsp. *sibirica*

'Signe' (Vt) — ERob ESCh ETho MCad

'Siirus' (L) — ERob

'Silmakivi' (L/J) — ERob ESCh

'Silver Moon' (L) — CSPN EBee EHan ERob ESCh ETho MAsh MCad NBea NTay SBra WTre

§ 'Simplicity' — CBgR CSPN ERob ESCh SPet

simsii Britt. & A. Br. — see *C. pitcheri*

simsii Sweet — see *C. crispa*

'Sinee Plamia' (J) — ERob ESCh

§ 'Sinij Dozhdj' (D) — CSPN ERob ESCh LBuc MBri NBrk NTay WTre

'Sir Garnet Wolseley' (P) — ERob ESCh MAsh NBrk NTay SDix WTre

'Sir Trevor Lawrence' (T) — CFRD CPev CSPN EBee ERob ESCh ETho LAst LRHS MAsh MCad NBea NHol NSti NTay SBra SDix SLim WPGP WTre

'Sizaia Ptitsa' (I) — ERob ESCh ETho

'Snow Queen' (P) — CElw CFRD CSPN EBee EBre EHan EPfP ESCh ETho LRHS MBri MCad MGos MSwo NBea NTay SBra SPet WTel WTre

'Snowdrift'   see *C.* 'Paul Farges', *C. armandii*
                                    'Snowdrift'
§ 'Södertälje' (Vt)   CFRD CRHN EBee ERob ESCh
                                    ETho MCad NBea NTay SBra
                                    WSHC
'Solveig' (P)   ERob
songarica   ESCh LRHS NBrk NHol NTay SBra
                                    WHil
- var. *songarica*   ERob
- 'Sundance'   CSPN ERob ESCh
'Souvenir   ERob ESCh NBrk NTay SBra
  de J.L. Delbard' (P)
§ 'Souvenir du Capitaine   CFRD CPev EBee ESCh GKir LAst
  Thuilleaux' (P)   MAsh MCad MGos NBea NBlu
                                    NTay SBra SLim WTre
'Special Occasion' (P)   CSPN ERob ESCh ETho LBuc
                                    MBNS NBea NLar NPri NTay SBra
                                    SCoo SLim WTre
spooneri   see *C. montana* var. *sericea*
- 'Rosea'   see *C.* x *vedrariensis* 'Rosea'
'Sputnik' (J)   CSPN EPfP ERob ESCh NBrk NTay
stans   CFRD CHea CPou EOrc EPfP
                                    ERob ESCh ETho GEil GSki IFro
                                    ITer LRHS MWhi NLar SIng
                                    WTre
- B&SWJ 4567   WCru
- B&SWJ 6345   WCru
- 'Rusalka'   ERob
'Star Fish' (L)   ERob ESCh
'Star of India' (P/J)   CFRD CPev CRHN EBee EPfP
                                    ERob ESCh ETho LRHS MAsh
                                    MCad NBea NTay SBra SDix SLim
                                    SPer WTre
'Stasik' (J)   ERob ESCh
'Strawberry Roan' (P)   ESCh
Sugar Candy   EBee EBre EMil ERob ESCh LAst
  = 'Evione'PBR (P)   MBri NPri NTay SBra SLim WTre
                                    WWes
Summer Snow   see *C.* 'Paul Farges'
'Sunset' (J) ♀H4   EBee EHan EOrc ERob ESCh LRHS
                                    MBri MCad NBea NTay SBra SMur
                                    WTre
'Susan Allsop' (L)   CPev ERob ESCh WTre
'Suzanne' **new**   LRHS
'Sylvia Denny' (Fl)   CWSG EBee EBre ELan EPfP ERob
                                    ESCh ETho GKir LAst LRHS MAsh
                                    MBar MCad NBea NBrk NRib NTay
                                    SBra SLim SPer WTre
'Sympathia' (L)   ERob ESCh MCad NTay SGar WTre
'Syrena' (J)   ESCh
szuyuanensis   WCru
  B&SWJ 6791
§ 'Tage Lundell' (A)   CElw CFRD CRHN CSPN EBre
                                    ERob ETho MCad MGos NBea
                                    NBrk NTay SPet WTre
'Tango' (T)   CElw CFRD CRHN ERob ESCh
                                    MCad NBrk SBra SPet WTre
tangutica   More than 30 suppliers
- 'Aureolin'   see *C.* 'Aureolin'
- 'Bill MacKenzie'   see *C.* 'Bill MacKenzie'
- 'Gravetye Variety'   ERob ESCh MWgw
- 'Lambton Park' ♀H4   CFRD EBee EPfP ERob ESCh ETho
                                    LRHS MCad NBea NBrk NTay WTre
                                    WWpP
- 'Radar Love'   WGwG
'Tartu' (L)   CSPN ERob ESCh
tashiroi   ERob ESCh
- B&SWJ 1423   WCru
- B&SWJ 7005 purple   WCru
- 'Yellow Peril' **new**   WCru
'Tateshina' (P)   MCad
'Teksa' (J)   ERob ESCh
'Tentel' (J)   ERob ETho
tenuiloba   see *C. columbiana* var. *tenuiloba*

§ *terniflora*   CFRD CPev EBee EHol EPfP ESCh
                                    ETho LFol LRHS MCad NBrk NSti
                                    SBra SLim SPer WCru
- B&SWJ 5751   WCru
- var. *mandshurica*   see *C. mandschurica*
- var. *robusta*   see *C. terniflora* var. *terniflora*
- var. *terniflora*   ERob ESCh LFol
'Teruko'   ERob
'Teshio' (Fl)   CSPN ERob ESCh ETho LBuc
                                    MCad NBrk SBra SLim WTre
texensis   ETho MCad WSHC
- 'Red Five'   CPev
- 'The Princess of Wales'   see *C.* 'Princess Diana'
'The Bride' (J)   CSPN EBee ERob ESCh ETho LBuc
                                    MCad NBea NBrk NTay SBra SLim
                                    WTre
'The Comet'   ERob
'The First Lady'   CSPN ERob ESCh ETho LBuc
                                    MAsh MCad NTay SLim WTre
'The President' (P) ♀H4   More than 30 suppliers
'The Princess of Wales' (L)   see *C.* 'Princess of Wales' (L)
'The Princess of Wales' (T)   see *C.* 'Princess Diana' (T)
'The Vagabond' (P)   CFRD CSPN CWSG EBee ELan
                                    ERob ETho MAsh MCad MSwo
                                    NBea NBrk NTay SBra WTre
'The Velvet'   ERob
'Theydon Belle'   ESCh
thunbergii hort.   see *C. terniflora*
'Thyrislund'   CSPN ESCh ETho
Tibetan mix   CSPN ERob ESCh
§ *tibetana*   CPev ETho MBar MCad MNrw
                                    NTay SCoo SLim SPer SSpi
- subsp. *vernayi*   CMHG EBee EHyt EPfP ERob GKir
                                    MCad MSte NSti SBra SCoo SPer
                                    WCru WWin
- - CC&McK 193   NWCA
- - var. *laciniifolia*   ERob ESCh NHol WTre
- - LS&E 13342   see *C. tibetana* subsp. *vernayi*
                                    'Orange Peel'
- - 'Orange Peel'   CBcs CDoC CPev EBee EBre EHan
    LS&E 13342   ENot EPfP ERob ESCh GKir GMac
                                    LAst LBuc LRHS MAsh MBNS
                                    MCad NBrk NHol SBra SGar SLim
                                    SPer WFar WTre
Timpany NZ hybrids (Fo)   ITim NLAp
'Tinkerbell'   see *C.* 'Shiva'
'Titania' (PxL)   EPfP ERob ESCh NBrk
'Toki'   ESCh ETho
tongluensis HWJCM 076   WCru
'Treasure Trove'   CFRD CSPN ESCh LBuc WTre
'Trianon' (P)   ERob NBrk
'Triibu'   ESCh
'Trikatrei'   ESCh NBrk
'Trine' (Vt)   ERob
§ x *triternata*   More than 30 suppliers
  'Rubromarginata' ♀H4
'Tsuzuki' (P)   CFRD CSPN ERob ESCh ETho
                                    NBea NTay
tubulosa   CFRD CPev CPle CSPN ESCh ETho
                                    NHol SRms
- Alan Bloom   EBre GBri GKir LRHS NLar
  = 'Alblo'PBR (H)
- 'Alba'   ERob
- 'Wyevale' (H) ♀H4   COIW CPev CSPN CStr EBee EChP
                                    ELan EPfP ERob ETho GKir LHop
                                    LRHS MBlu MRav MWgw NBea
                                    NTay SBra SDix SLim SMad SPer
                                    SPla WAul WCot WEas WHil WTre
'Tuczka' (J)   ERob .
'Twilight' (J)   CSPN EBee ESCh ETho MAsh
                                    MCad NBea NTay SBra SCoo SLim
                                    WTre
'Ulrique' (P)   EBee ERob
uncinata   CPev ERob SDix

- B&SWJ 1893	WCru
- var. *ovatifolia*	ERob
urophylla	ERob
urticifolia	WCru
B&SWJ 8640 **new**	
- B&SWJ 8651	WCru
'Valge Daam' (L)	ERob ESch ETho MCad NTay SCoo SLim
'Vanessa' (J)	CRHN ERob ESch ETho NBrk
'Vanilla Cream'	ECou
x *vedrariensis*	NBrk
- 'Dovedale'	CPev ESch
- 'Hidcote'	see *C. montana* 'Hidcote'
- 'Highdown'	ERob NBrk SBra
§ - 'Rosea'	CTrw ERob ESch NBrk
veitchiana	CPLG ERob
'Velutinea Purpurea' (J)	ERob
'Venosa Violacea'	CElw CFRD CRHN CSPN EBee
(Vt) ♀H4	EBre EHan ELan EOrc EPfP ERob ESch ETho LAst LRHS MAsh MCad NBea NHol NPri NSti SBra SDix SPer SPet SPla WFar WTre
vernayi	see *C. tibetana* subsp. *vernayi*
'Veronica's Choice' (L)	CPev CRHN CSPN EBee EHan ELan ENor EOrc ERob ESch LRHS MBri MCad MGos NBea NTay SBra WTre
versicolor	ERob ESch
'Vetke' (J)	ERob
N 'Victoria' (J) ♀H4	CFRD CPev CSPN EBee EBre ERob ESch ETho LAst LRHS MAsh MCad NBea NTay SBra SDix SLim SPet WSpi WTre
'Ville de Lyon' (Vt)	More than 30 suppliers
villosa	CTCP
Vino = 'Poulvo'PBR (J)	EBee ERob ESch LRHS MBri MCad NBea NTay SBra SCoo WTre
I 'Viola' (J)	CFRD CSPN ERob ESch ETho MAsh MCad NBea NBrk NTay WBcn WTre
'Violet Charm' (L)	CWSG EBee ENot ERob ESch NBrk NTay SBra SCoo
'Violet Elizabeth' (P)	ESch MCad NBrk SBra
'Violetta' (P)	ERob
viorna	EHyt ERob ESch NBea WSHC
virginiana misapplied	see *C. vitalba*
virginiana Hook.	see *C. ligusticifolia*
§ *vitalba*	CArn CPev CRWN ERob ESch ETho MBar MCad MHer NTay WHer
viticella ♀H4	CPev CWib ERob ESch ETho EWTr MBNS MCad NBea NBlu SBra SDix WSHC WStl WTel WTre
- 'Brocade'	CFRD CPev CRHN CSPN ETho
I - 'Danae'	ERob WTre
- 'Mary Rose' (d)	CPev ERob ESch ETho LAst LRHS MCad NBrk SBra WTre
- 'Purpurea Plena Elegans' (d) ♀H4	More than 30 suppliers
- 'Rosea' (Vt)	ERob
'Viticella Rubra' (Vt)	EWTr LBuc NBrk
Vivienne	see *C.* 'Beth Currie'
'Vivienne Lawson'	ERob ESch NTay
'Voluceau' (Vt)	CFRD CPou CRHN EBee EBre ELan ERob ESch LAst MCad NBea NTay SBra SLim SPer WStl WTre
'Vostok' (J)	ERob ESch NBrk
'Vyvyan Pennell' (Fl/P)	More than 30 suppliers
'W.E. Gladstone' (L)	CPev CRHN EBee ERob ESch ETho EWTr GKir LRHS MAsh MCad NBea NTay SBra SDix SPer WTre
'W.S. Callick' (P)	CFRD ERob ESch MCad NTay
'Wada's Primrose' (P)	More than 30 suppliers
'Walenburg' (Vt)	ERob ESch NBrk SBra

'Walter Pennell' (Fl/P)	CPev CWSG EBee ESch ETho MCad NBea NTay SBra SCoo SLim WGor WTre
'Warszawska Nike' (J) ♀H4	CElw CFRD CRHN EBee EBre EHan ELan EPfP ERob ESch ETho EWTr LAst MAsh MBri MCad MGos MWgw NBea NBlu NBrk NTay SBra SCoo SPer SPet WStl WTre
'Waterperry Star' (Ta)	ERob
'Western Virgin'	ERob ESch NTay
'Westerplatte' (P)	CSPN EBre EHan ERob ESch ETho LAst LBuc LRHS MAsh MCad NBea NBrk NTay SBra SCoo WFar WTre
§ 'White Swan' (A)	CSPN EBee EPfP ERob ESch LRHS MAsh MBri MCad MGos NBea NHol NPri NSti SDix SLim SPer SPla WFoF WPGP WTre
'White Tokyo' (A)	MGos
'Wilhelmina Tull' (L)	CSPN ERob ESch MCad NBrk
'Will Goodwin' (L) ♀H4	CBcs EBee ELan EPfP ERob ESch ETho GMac LAst LRHS MAsh MBri MCad MWgw NBea NBrk NPri SBra SLim WStl WTre
'William Kennett' (L)	CPev CWSG EBee EHan ELan EPfP ESch ETho LAst LRHS MBNS MBar MBri MCad MGos NBlu NTay SBod SBra SDix SLim SPet WTre
williamsii **new**	CFRD ESch
'Winter Beauty' **new**	ESch
Wisley = 'Evipo-001' **new**	LRHS
'Xerxes'	see *C.* 'Elsa Späth'
'Yatsuhashi'	ERob
'Yellow Queen'	see *C.* 'Moonlight'
'Yorkshire Pride'	ERob
§ 'Yukikomachi' (LxJ)	CSPN ERob ESch ETho MCad NBrk NTay WTre
'Yuki-no-yosooi'	ERob
'Yukiokoshi' (Fl)	ERob ESch ETho
yunnanensis	ERob
'Yvette Houry' (L)	ERob ESch NLar NTay WTre
'Zingaro' (Vt)	ERob
'Zolotoi Jubilei' (J)	ERob

Clematopsis see *Clematis*

Clementsia see *Rhodiola*

Clerodendrum (Verbenaceae)

bungei	More than 30 suppliers
- 'Herfstleu'	MGos
- 'Pink Diamond' (v) **new**	EPfP SPoG
§ *chinense*	ERea
var. *chinense* (d) ♀H1	
- 'Pleniflorum'	see *C. chinense* var. *chinense*
fragrans	see *C. chinense* var. *chinense*
var. *pleniflorum*	
* *mutabile* B&SWJ 6651	WCru
myricoides	CHll CKob CMdw CSpe ELan ERea
'Ugandense' ♀H1	EShb ESlt SOWG
philippinum	see *C. chinense* var. *chinense*
x *speciosum*	ERea SOWG
splendens ♀H1	SOWG
thomsoniae ♀H1	ELan LRHS MBri SOWG
trichotomum	More than 30 suppliers
- B&SWJ 4896A	WCru
- 'Carnival' (v)	CFil ELan EPAt EPfP EWes GKir IArd LRHS MAsh MBri NLar SLim SLon SMad SMur SPer SSta WBcn WCom
- var. *fargesii* ♀H4	More than 30 suppliers
- 'Hopleys' (v)	LHop
- white calyx B&SWJ 4896	WCru
wallichii **new**	SOWG

Clethra (*Clethraceae*)

B&SWJ 5416	WPGP
acuminata	EPfP NLar
alnifolia	CBcs CBrm CDul CEnd CMCN CMHG CPLG CSBt CTrC CTrG ECrN EPfP EWTr GKir IDee MBar SMur SPer SRms SSpi WBod WCFE WDin WFar WLow WPic WWin
- 'Anne Bidwell' **new**	NLar
- 'Creel's Calico' (v) **new**	NLar
- 'Fingle Dwarf'	SReu SSta
- 'Hummingbird'	CEnd EBee ELan EPfP GEil GKir LRHS MAsh MBlu MBri NLar SMur SSpi WFar
- 'Paniculata' ♀H4	CDoC CFwr CPLG SMac SPoG WFar
- 'Pink Spire'	CBcs CDoC CFwr EBee EPfP EWTr MRav NBlu SCoo SMac WBVN WBor WDin WFar WLow WOrn WStI
- 'Rosea'	CBot CDul CTri GKir GQui IMGH MBar MBlu MGos SHBN SPer WFar WSHC
- 'Ruby Spice'	CEnd CMHG CPLG EBee ELan EMil ENot EPfP GEil GKir IMGH LAst LRHS MAsh MBlu MBri NBee SMur SPer SSpi WBVN WBcn
- 'September Beauty'	NLar
arborea	CBcs CFil CHEx CMHG CPLG
barbinervis ♀H4	CBcs CFai CMCN CPLG EPfP GEil IDee IMGH MBlu NLar SPer SPoG WBVN WDin WFar WSHC
- B&SWJ 8915	WCru
delavayi	CDoC CPLG EPfP GGGa GQui NLar
- C&H 7067	GGGa
fargesii	EPfP IMGH MGos NLar
monostachya	GGGa
tomentosa	WWes
- 'Cottondale'	NLar SSpi

Cleyera (*Theaceae*)

fortunei	see *C. japonica* 'Fortunei'
- 'Variegata'	see *C. japonica* 'Fortunei'
§ *japonica* 'Fortunei' (v)	CFil CHal CMac CWib WFar
- var. *japonica*	CFil EMil WPGP
- var. *wallichii*	CFil EBee WPGP

Clianthus (*Papilionaceae*)

maximus	ECou
§ *puniceus* ♀H2	CAbb CBcs CCtw CHEx CHll CSBt CTCP CTrw CWib EBee ECou EMil EPfP ERea EShb GGar LAst LRHS MLan SHGC SOWG SPer SPlb SSpi WBrE WCFE WCru WKif WPGP WSHC
§ - 'Albus' ♀H2	CBcs CBot CHEx CHll CPLG CTrw CWib EBee EMil EPfP ERea EShb LAst LRHS MLan SDry SGar SOWG SPer SVen
- 'Flamingo'	see *C. puniceus* 'Roseus'
- 'Kaka King'	CBcs
- 'Red Admiral'	see *C. puniceus*
- 'Red Cardinal'	see *C. puniceus*
§ - 'Roseus'	CPLG EMil ERea LRHS MTPN SPer
- 'White Heron'	see *C. puniceus* 'Albus'

Clinopodium (*Lamiaceae*)

acinos	see *Acinos arvensis*
ascendens	see *Calamintha ascendens*
calamintha	see *Calamintha nepeta*
georgianum	SSpi
grandiflorum	see *Calamintha grandiflora*

§ *vulgare*	CArn CRWN ECoo EMan EPPr GBar MGas MHer MWrn NMir NSco SCro SIde WCAu WHer WOut

Clintonia (*Convallariaceae*)

andrewsiana	CBro CLAP GBuc GCrs GGGa GKir LEur SSpi WCru
borealis	SCnR WCru
udensis	WCru
umbellulata	CLAP WCru
uniflora	CLAP GKir

Clivia ❁ (*Amaryllidaceae*)

caulescens	ERea
x *cyrtanthiflora*	ERea
gardenii	ERea
miniata ♀H1	CBcs CHal LRHS MLan SChr SMur SRms SYvo WCot
- 'Aurea' ♀H1	CSpe
- var. *citrina* ♀H1	ECho
- - 'New Dawn'	ERea
- hybrids	ERea LAma MBri NPal SEND WBVN
- 'Striata' (v)	ERea
nobilis ♀H1	ERea

Clytostoma (*Bignoniaceae*)

§ *calystegioides*	CBcs CRHN ERea

Cneorum (*Cneoraceae*)

tricoccon	CKob SSpi XPep

Cnicus (*Asteraceae*)

§ *benedictus*	CArn GPoy MHer MSal SECG SIde WHer

Cobaea (*Cobaeaceae*)

pringlei	ERea WSHC
scandens ♀H3	CSpe ELan LRav SGar SMur WPen
- f. *alba* ♀H3	ELan EShb SMur WPen

cobnut see *Corylus avellana*

Coccothrinax (*Arecaceae*)

argentata **new**	WMul
argentea **new**	EAmu
crinita	LPal

Cocculus (*Menispermaceae*)

§ *orbiculatus*	EMon
- B&SWJ 535	WCru
trilobus	see *C. orbiculatus*

Cochlearia (*Brassicaceae*)

armoracia	see *Armoracia rusticana*
glastifolia	MSal
officinalis	MHer MSal WHer

Cocos (*Arecaceae*)

plumosa	see *Syagrus romanzoffiana*
weddelliana	see *Lytocaryum weddellianum*

Coddia (*Rubiaceae*)

rudis **new**	EShb

Codiaeum ❁ (*Euphorbiaceae*)

variegatum var. *pictum* 'Excellent' (v)	LRHS
- var. *pictum* 'Petra' (v)	LRHS MBri

Codonanthe (*Gesneriaceae*)

gracilis	EBak WDib
'Paula'	WDib

x *Codonatanthus* (*Gesneriaceae*)
'Golden Tambourine' **new**	WDib
'Sunset'	WDib
'Tambourine'	WDib

Codonopsis ✿ (*Campanulaceae*)
affinis HWJCM 70	LEur WCru
benthamii **new**	NChi
bhutanica	CHid EBee ITim WCot
bulleyana	EBee ITim NLar WCot WSan
cardiophylla	GCal ITim NLar NPPs WGMN WLin
clematidea	More than 30 suppliers
- 'Lilac Eyes'	MCCP NHol WRHF
convolvulacea misapplied	see *C. grey-wilsonii*
convolvulacea Kurz	GBuc GFlt MTho NSla WCru WHoo WPGP
- B&SWJ 7812	WCru
- B&SWJ 7847	WCru
- ex J&JA 4220705	LEur NWCA
- 'Alba'	see *C. grey-wilsonii* 'Himal Snow'
- Forrest's form	see *C. forrestii* Diels
dicentrifolia	EMan ITim
- HWJCM 267	WCru
forrestii misapplied	see *C. grey-wilsonii*
§ *forrestii* Diels	EHyt EMan ITim
§ *grey-wilsonii* ♀H4	CBro CLAP EChP GCrs GEdr ITim SBla
- B&SWJ 7532	WCru
§ - 'Himal Snow'	CLAP EHyt GCrs GEdr IMGH ITim SBla
handeliana	see *C. tubulosa*
§ *javanica* B&SWJ 380	WCru
- B&SWJ 8145	WCru
kawakamii	EPot
- B&SWJ 1592	WCru
§ *lanceolata*	EHyt EPot ITim LEur MCCP NChi
- B&SWJ 562	WCru
- B&SWJ 5099	WCru
lancifolia B&SWJ 3835	WCru
meleagris misapplied	see *C. meleagris* hybrid
§ *meleagris* hybrid	EBee
mollis	EBee EChP GSki NLar WFar
nepalensis Grey-Wilson	see *C. grey-wilsonii*
obtusa	NChi WCot
ovata	CFir CHid CLyd EBee GBuc MTho NBro NChi SBla SChr SIgm SRms
§ *pilosula*	EBee GPoy LEur MNrw MSal MTho WCot
rotundifolia	ITim LEur
- CC 1770	WCot
§ - var. *angustifolia*	LEur MDKP
silvestris	see *C. pilosula*
subsimplex	CLyd
tangshen misapplied	see *C. rotundifolia* var. *angustifolia*
tangshen Oliver	CArn MCCP MNrw MSal MTho NChi SHFr
thalictrifolia MECC 93	WCru
§ *tubulosa*	EMan LRHS
ussuriensis	see *C. lanceolata*
vinciflora	CNic CPne EHyt GEdr LEur SBla WCot WCru
viridiflora	CNic LEur

coffee see *Coffea*

Coix (*Poaceae*)
lacryma-jobi	CFwr CHrt MSal

Colchicum ✿ (*Colchicaceae*)
agrippinum ♀H4	CAvo CBro CFee ECha EHyt EPar

	EPot GCrs GKev LAma MRav NBir NRog NRya NSla SSpi WTin
'Antares'	ECha LAma LLWP NBir
atropurpureum	CBro EPot GEdr LAma
- Drake's form	EPot
'Attlee'	LAma
'Autumn Herald'	EPot LAma
N 'Autumn Queen'	CBro LAma
§ *autumnale*	CArn CAvo CBro CFee EPot GPoy ITim LAma LRHS NMen NRya WFar WShi
* - 'Albopilosum'	NBir
- 'Alboplenum'	CBro EPot LAma WTin
- 'Album'	CAvo CBro EHyt EPar EPot GEdr LAma LLWP LRHS NBir WHoo WPnP WShi WTin
- var. *major*	see *C. byzantinum*
- var. *minor*	see *C. autumnale*
- 'Nancy Lindsay' ♀H4	CBro ECho EPot GFlt SRot
§ - 'Pleniflorum' (d)	CBro EPar EPot LAma
- 'Roseum Plenum'	see *C. autumnale* 'Pleniflorum'
baytopiorum	EHyt EPot GEdr
§ *bivonae*	CBro ECha GFlt LAma
Blom's hybrid	WTin
§ *boissieri*	ERos SSpi
- MFF 2192	WCot
bornmuelleri hort.	see *C. speciosum* var. *bornmuelleri* hort.
bornmuelleri Freyn	CBro EPar EPot LAma
bowlesianum	see *C. bivonae*
§ *byzantinum* ♀H4	CBro ECho EPar EPot LAma LRHS MBri NBir NRog WTin
- *album*	see *C. byzantinum* 'Innocence'
- 'Innocence'	CBro EPot
cilicicum	CBro EPot LAma LRHS
- Bowles' form	GFlt
- 'Purpureum'	LAma
'Conquest'	see *C.* 'Glory of Heemstede'
corsicum	EHyt EPar ERos LAma NMen
'Daendels'	GFlt LAma
davisii **new**	GEdr
'Dick Trotter'	GFlt GKir LAma
'Disraeli'	CBro
doerfleri	see *C. hungaricum*
'E.A. Bowles'	GFlt LAma LRHS
§ *giganteum*	EPot GEdr GFlt LAma
'Glory of Heemstede'	GFlt LAma
hierosolymitanum	LAma
§ *hungaricum*	CBro EPot LAma SCnR
- f. *albiflorum*	EHyt
illyricum	see *C. giganteum*
kesselringii	WWst
kotschyi	LAma
laetum hort.	see *C. parnassicum*
'Lilac Wonder'	CBro EHyt EPot LAma LRHS MBri NRog WCot WHoo
lingulatum	WTin
§ *longiflorum*	LAma
lusitanicum	LAma
luteum	LAma NRog
macrophyllum	LAma
micranthum	EHyt LAma
neapolitanum	see *C. longiflorum*
'Oktoberfest'	EPot
§ *parnassicum*	CBro ECha GFlt
'Pink Goblet' ♀H4	CBro EHyt EPot GFlt LAma
polyphyllum	LAma
'Prinses Astrid'	GFlt LAma
procurrens	see *C. boissieri*
'Rosy Dawn' ♀H4	CBro ECha EPot GFlt LAma
sibthorpii	see *C. bivonae*
speciosum ♀H4	CAvo CBro EHyt EPot GEdr LAma LRHS NBir SSpi WCot

	- 'Album' ♀H4	CAvo CBro CFee ECha ECho EHyt
		EPar EPot ETow GAbr GEdr GFlt
		LAma LPhx LRHS MBri NBir
		WCot
	- 'Atrorubens'	ECha EPot GFlt LAma LRHS
I	- var. **bornmuelleri** hort.	GEdr
	- 'Huxley'	GFlt
	- var. *illyricum*	see *C. giganteum*
	- 'Maximum'	LAma
	tenorei ♀H4	EPot GFlt LAma NBir WCot
	'The Giant'	CBro EPot GAbr GFlt GKev LAma
		LRHS NRog
	troodi	ERos
	variegatum	CBro LAma
	'Violet Queen'	CBro EPot GAbr GFlt LAma LPhx
		LRHS
	'Waterlily' (d) ♀H4	CAvo CBro CLyd ELan EPar EPot
		GAbr GFlt LAma LPhx LRHS
		MBri NBir NRog WCot WHoo
		WPnP
	'William Dykes'	GFlt LAma
	'Zephyr'	LAma

Coleonema (Rutaceae)

	album	CTrC XPep
	pulchrum	CHEx CSpe NSti WCot XPep
	'Sunset Gold'	CPLG CSpe CTrC

Coleus see *Solenostemon*, *Plectranthus*

	caninus	see *Plectranthus ornatus*

Colletia (Rhamnaceae)

	RCB/Arg S-3 **new**	WCot
	armata	see *C. hystrix*
	cruciata	see *C. paradoxa*
§	***hystrix***	CBcs CHEx CTri GBin GGar SAPC
		SArc SLon SMad SOWG
	- 'Rosea'	CAbb CPle
§	***paradoxa***	CBcs CHEx CPle LPJP NLar SAPC
		SArc SIgm SMad
	spinosissima	CPle

Collinsonia (Lamiaceae)

	canadensis	CArn EBee ELan EMan MSal WWye

Collomia (Polemoniaceae)

	debilis	EHyt NPol NWCA
	- var. *larsenii*	see *C. larsenii*
	grandiflora	EMan NPol
§	***larsenii***	GTou
	mazama **new**	NPol

Colobanthus (Caryophyllaceae)

	canaliculatus	EPot

Colocasia (Araceae)

	affinis var. *jeningsii*	EAmu EUJe LEur MOak
	antiquorum	see *C. esculenta*
§	***esculenta*** ♀H1	CDWL CHEx EAmu EUJe LEur
		MJnS MOak SDix WMul
*	- var. ***aquatilis***	LEur
	- 'Black Magic'	EAmu MJnS MOak WMul
	- 'Bun-long' **new**	MJnS
	- burgundy stem **new**	WMul
	- 'Elepaio Keiki' **new**	MJnS
	- 'Fontanesii'	EAmu LEur MJnS SSpi WMul
	- 'Illustris'	MJnS
	- 'Nigrescens'	EAmu
	- 'Palau Keiki' **new**	MJnS
	- 'Ulaula Kumu-oha' **new**	MJnS
	formosana	WCru
	B&SWJ 6909 **new**	
	gigantea **new**	EAmu
	'Nancyana' **new**	MJnS

Colquhounia (Lamiaceae)

	coccinea	CArn CHEx CHal CTrC MRav SIgm
		WBod WCom WCru WHer WHil
		WPGP WSHC WWye
§	- var. ***vestita***	CBcs CFai CFil CFwr CPen CPle
		CWib EBee EPfP GGar IMGH MSte
		SBra SDnm SEND WBor WPGP
	- - B&SWJ 7222	WCru

Columnea (Gesneriaceae)

	'Aladdin's Lamp'	CHal WDib
	'Apollo'	WDib
	x ***banksii*** ♀H1	CHal EOHP WDib
	- variegated (v)	WCot
	'Bold Venture'	WDib
§	'Broget Stavanger' (v)	WDib
	'Chanticleer' ♀H1	CHal MBri WDib
I	'Firedragon'	WDib
	'Gavin Brown'	WDib
	gloriosa	EBak
	hirta ♀H1	MBri WDib
	- 'Variegata'	see *C.* 'Light Prince'
	'Inferno'	WDib
	'Katsura'	MBri WDib
I	'Kewensis Variegata'	MBri
	(v) ♀H1	
§	'Light Prince' (v)	WDib
	'Merkur'	WDib
	microphylla	MBri
	'Variegata' (v)	
I	'Midnight Lantern'	WDib
	'Rising Sun'	WDib
	'Robin'	WDib
	schiedeana	CHal MBri WDib
	'Stavanger' ♀H1	CHal EBak WDib
	'Stavanger Variegated'	see *C.* 'Broget Stavanger'
	Yellow Dragon Group	CHal

Colutea (Papilionaceae)

	arborescens	CAgr CArn CBcs CPLG EBee ELan
		GKir LHop LRHS MBlu MGos MSal
		NWea SHBN SLon SPer WBVN
		WDin WHer WWin XPep
§	***buhsei***	NLar SLPl SOWG
	istria	GEil
	x ***media***	LRav MBlu
	- 'Copper Beauty'	CBcs GEil MGos MRav WPat
	orientalis	CBcs CPLG CPle GEil LAst XPep
	persica hort.	see *C. buhsei*

Comarum see *Potentilla*

Combretum (Combretaceae)

	molle **new**	CTCP

Commelina (Commelinaceae)

	coelestis	see *C. tuberosa* Coelestis Group
	- 'Sleeping Beauty' **new**	WGMN
	communis	EMan
	dianthifolia	CNic EMan GCal GCrs GKir MTho
		NWCA SPet SYvo WCom WPer
	- 'Sapphirino'	EMon
	tuberosa	CAvo CBct CPLG ELan EMFP EPfP
		ERos MAvo MLan MSte NSti WWeb
	- 'Alba'	EBee ELan MLLN MSte WPer
	- 'Axminster Lilac'	WPer
§	- Coelestis Group	CFwr CWCL EBee EChP ECha
		EMan GEil IGor MLLN SPet SRms
		SYvo WCom WFar WPGP WPer
		WSHC WWin
	- - 'Hopleys	EMan
	Variegated' (v)	
	- 'Snowmelt'	CWCL

Comptonia (Myricaceae)
peregrina   CMac NLar WCru

Conandron (Gesneriaceae)
ramondoides   WCru
   B&SWJ 8929

Coniogramme (Adiantaceae)
intermedia   NMar

Conioselinum (Apiaceae)
morrisonense   WCru
   B&SWJ 173
schugnanicum   EBee

Conium (Apiaceae)
maculatum   CArn MGol MSal
- 'Golden Nemesis' (v)   EBee

Conopodium (Apiaceae)
majus   CRWN WShi

Conradina (Lamiaceae)
verticillata   WPat

Consolida (Ranunculaceae)
§ **ajacis**   MSal
ambigua   see *C. ajacis*
regalis   ECoo

Convallaria ✿ (Convallariaceae)
japonica   see *Ophiopogon jaburan*
keiskei   CLAP
majalis ♥H4   More than 30 suppliers
§ - 'Albostriata' (v)   CBct CFil CFwr CLAP CRow EBee
    EBre ECha EHrv ELan EMan EPar
    EPfP LEur LRHS MRav MTho NBir
    SMac SOkh WCHb WCot WCru
    WEas WHer WPGP
- 'Berlin Giant'   EBee NRya
- 'Dorien'   CBct CBre CFir EBee EChP LEur
- 'Flore Pleno' (d)   CBct EBee EBla EPar LEur MTho
    WCot
- 'Fortin's Giant'   CAvo CBct CBro CLAP CMea
    CRow EBee EMon EPar EPla EPot
    LEur MRav NGby SIng SMad WCot
    WPGP WSel
- 'Gerard Debureaux' (v)   see *C. majalis* 'Green Tapestry'
- 'Golden Slippers'   NPar
§ - 'Green Tapestry' (v)   CRow EMon
- 'Haldon Grange' (v)   CBct CLAP EBee EMon
- 'Hardwick Hall' (v)   CAvo CBct CLAP CRow EBee ECha
    EHoe EPar EPla EPot LEur MTed
    NPar WBro WCot WSan
- 'Hofheim' (v)   CRow EBee WTMC
- 'Prolificans'   CAvo CBct CBro CFir CLAP CRow
    EBee EMon EPar ERos LEur MRav
    NGar SIng
- var. **rosea**   More than 30 suppliers
- 'Variegata' (v)   CBro CHar EPar EPla ERou GCrs
    NMen SChu SMad WHil WSel
- 'Vic Pawlowski's   CLAP CPLG CRow SBla WCHb
   Gold' (v)
montana   LRHS
transcaucasica   EBee

Convolvulus (Convolvulaceae)
althaeoides   CBot CHad CPle EBre ECGP EChP
    ELan LPhx LRHS MNrw MTho
    NBir SBla SHFr SMad SPer WAbb
    WEas WHal WPGP WWin
§ - subsp. **tenuissimus**   CSWP CSpe EBee EMan EWes
    LHop MBri MHer WCFE WCot

- - 'Pink Fanfare' **new**   WSpi
§ **boissieri**   CFir CGra EMan EPot NWCA SBla
    WAbe
cantabricus   CHll EChP MDKP
chilensis   EMan GFlt
cneorum ♥H3   More than 30 suppliers
- 'Snow Angel' **new**   SVil
compactus   EPot
elegantissimus   see *C. althaeoides* subsp.
    tenuissimus
incanus   WCru
lineatus   ECho EHyt EMan LRHS MTho
    NMen NWCA SMrm SRot WCom
mauritanicus   see *C. sabatius*
nitidus   see *C. boissieri*
oleifolius **new**   XPep
§ **sabatius** ♥H3   More than 30 suppliers
- 'Compton Lane'   WCom
- dark   CSpe ELan EMan LIck MOak MSte
    SMrm SScr SUsu

---

x *Cooperanthes* see *Zephyranthes*

Cooperia see *Zephyranthes*

Copernicia (Arecaceae)
alba   EAmu LPal
prunifera   EAmu

Coprosma ✿ (Rubiaceae)
acerosa **new**   GGar
- 'Live Wire' (f)   ECou
areolata (m)   ECou
atropurpurea (f)   ECou NWCA
- (m)   ECou
'Autumn Orange' (f)   ECou
'Autumn Prince' (m)   ECou
baueri   see *C. repens*
'Beatson's Gold' (f/v)   CBcs CBot CChe CHal CMHG CPLG
    CTrG EBee ELan EMil EPfP ERea
    GEil GGar GQui ISea SAga STre
    WBod WDin WHen WSHC WStI
'Blue Pearls' (f)   ECou
'Brunette' (f)   ECou
§ **brunnea**   CTrC ECou
- 'Blue Beauty' (f)   ECou
- 'Violet Fleck' (f)   ECou
'Bruno' (m)   ECou
cheesemanii (f)   ECou
- (m)   ECou
- 'Hanmer Red' (f)   ECou
- 'Mack' (m)   ECou
- 'Red Mack' (f)   ECou
'Chocolate Soldier' (m)   ECou
'Coppershine'   CBcs CPLG CTrC ERea MOak
crassifolia x **repens** (m)   ECou
x **cunninghamii** (f)   ECou
x **cunninghamii**   ECou
   x **macrocarpa** (m)
'Cutie' (f)   ECou
depressa   ECou
- 'Orange Spread' (f)   ECou
'Evening Glow' (v)   CDoC COtt ECou LHop LRHS
    MAsh
'Green Girl' (f)   ECou
'Hinerua' (f)   ECou
'Indigo Lustre' (f)   ECou
'Jewel' (f)   ECou
'Karo Red' (v)   CDoC COtt LRHS MAsh
x **kirkii** 'Kirkii' (f)   ECou ERea STre XPep
- 'Kirkii Variegata' (f/v)   CBcs CBot CDoC CHal CStu CTrC
    EBee ECou ECrN ERea GEil GQui
    IFro MOak SOWG STre WBrE
    WSHC WStI

'Kiwi' (m) — ECou
'Kiwi-gold' (m/v) — ECou ERea
'Lemon Drops' (f) — ECou
linariifolia (m) — ECou
lucida (f) — ECou
- 'Mount White' (m) — ECou
- 'Wanaka' (f) — ECou
macrocarpa (f) — CTrC ECou
- (m) — ECou
'Middlemore' — CDoC
nitida (f) — ECou
parviflora (m) — CTrC ECou
- purple fruit (f) — ECou
- red fruit (f) — ECou
- white fruit (f) — ECou
'Pearl Drops' (f) — ECou
'Pearl's Sister' (f) — ECou
'Pearly Queen' (f) — ECou
petriei — ECou
- 'Don' (m) — ECou
- 'Lyn' (f) — ECou
'Pride' — CDoC CTrC
propinqua — SDry
- (f) — ECou
- (m) — ECou
- var. *latiuscula* (f) — ECou
- - (m) — ECou
'Prostrata' (m) — ECou
pseudocuneata (m) — ECou
'Rainbow Surprise' (v) — COtt LRHS MAsh SVen
§ *repens* — XPep
§ - (f) — CHEx ECou
- (m) — CBcs ECou SEND
- 'Apricot Flush' (f) — ECou
- 'County Park Purple' (f) — ECou ERea
- 'Exotica' (f/v) — ECou
- 'Marble King' (m/v) — ECou
- 'Marble Queen' (m/v) ♀H1-2 — CHll ECou EShb WCot WFar
- 'Orangeade' (f) — ECou
- 'Painter's Palette' (m) — CBcs ECou WDin
- 'Picturata' (m/v) ♀H1-2 — ECou ERea EShb
- 'Pink Splendour' (m/v) — CBcs CDoC ECou ERea LHop WDin
- 'Rangatiri' (f) — ECou
- 'Silver Queen' (m/v) — ECou SVen
- 'Variegata' (m/v) — CHEx ECou
rigida — ECou
- 'Ann' (f) — ECou
- 'Tan' (m) — ECou
robusta — CTrC ECou SDry
- 'Cullen's Point' (f) — ECou
- 'Sally Blunt' (f) — ECou
- 'Steepdown' (f) — ECou
- 'Tim Blunt' (m) — ECou
* - 'Variegata' (m/v) — ECou
- 'William' (m) — ECou
- 'Woodside' (f) — ECou
rotundifolia — ECou
'Roy's Red' (m) — CDoC ECou
rugosa (f) — ECou
I 'Snowberry' (f) — ECou
'Taiko' — CTrC
tenuifolia (m) — ECou
'Translucent Gold' (f) — ECou
'Violet Drops' (f) — ECou
virescens (f) — ECou
'Walter Brockie' — CHll CTrC SVen
'White Lady' (f) — ECou
'Winter Bronze' (f) — ECou

Coptis (Ranunculaceae)

japonica var. *dissecta*
　B&SWJ 6000 — WCru
- var. *major* — WCru

quinquefolia — WCru
　B&SWJ 1677

x *Coralia* (Papilionaceae)

'County Park' — ECou
'Essex' — ECou
'Havering' — ECou

Corallospartium (Papilionaceae)

crassicaule — ECou
- 'Jack Sprat' — ECou
- var. *racemosum* — ECou

Cordyline (Agavaceae)

australis ♀H3 — More than 30 suppliers
- 'Albertii' (v) ♀H3 — CBcs CWSG LAst LHop MBri MCCP NMoo NPri SAPC SArc SPoG WCot
* - 'Atropurpurea' — CDoC ECrN GKir SSto WDin WFar
- 'Black Tower' — CBcs CDoC ELan LRHS MGos
- 'Coffee Cream' — CTrC CWSG EAmu EBee ELan EPfP LRHS MBlu MLan WDin WFar WGer
- 'Karo Kiri' **new** — CTrC
- 'Krakatoa' — ENot
- 'Peko' PBR **new** — WCot
- 'Pink Stripe' (v) — CBcs CBrm CDoC COtt EBee EBre ELan EPfP ISea LRHS MAsh MCCP MLan NPri SAga SHGC SLim SNew SPla SSto SWvt WFar WPat
- 'Purple Heart' — CTrC WPat
- 'Purple Tower' — CBrm CDoC CHEx COtt CTrC CWSG EAmu EBee EBre EChP EMil ENot EPfP LRHS MCCP MPRe SLim SMad SNew WCot WPat
- Purpurea Group — CBcs CBot CChe CHEx CHar CMHG CTrC CWSG EBee EBre ENot EPfP ISea LAst LRHS MGos NBlu SEND SHBN SPer SPlb WFar WGer WStI
- 'Red Robin' — LRav
- 'Red Sensation' — CHEx CTrC EBre GKir ISea LRHS MAsh MPRe SHGC SWvt
- 'Red Star' — More than 30 suppliers
- 'Sundance' ♀H3 — More than 30 suppliers
- 'Torbay Dazzler' (v) ♀H3 — More than 30 suppliers
- 'Torbay Green' — ENot
* - 'Torbay Razzle Dazzle' — CTrC
- 'Torbay Red' ♀H3 — CAbb CBcs CBrm CDoC CMHG COtt CTrC CWSG EBee EBre ELan EPfP ISea LHop LPan LRHS MAsh MBlu MBri MJnS MWgw SPla SWvt WFar WPat WWeb
- 'Torbay Sunset' — CDoC COtt CTrC ELan LRHS WPat
- 'Variegata' (v) — CBot
'Autumn' — CTrC WFar
banksii — CTrC LEdu
- 'Purpurea' — LPVe
- 'Red Fountain' PBR — EBee ENot
'Dark Star' — CDoC LAst MCCP
fruticosa 'Atom' — MBri
- 'Baby Ti' (v) — MBri
- 'Calypso Queen' — MBri
- 'Kiwi' — MBri
- 'New Guinea Black' — CAbb CTrC EChP ELan LAst NCot WCot
- 'Orange Prince' — MBri
- 'Red Edge' ♀H1 — MBri
- 'Yellow King' — MBri
'Green Goddess' — CBcs CTrC MPRe
§ *indivisa* — CBrP EAmu EBak ITim LEdu LPan LRHS MBri NJOw SPlb SWal WGer WMul WPGP
- 'Perkeo' — EBee

kaspar	CAbb CHEx LEdu SAPC SArc
– bronze	LEdu
parryi 'Purpurea'	NPal
pumilio	CTrC LEdu
§ **stricta**	CHEx MBri
terminalis	see *C. fruticosa*

Coreopsis ✿ (Asteraceae)

auriculata Cutting Gold	see *C. auriculata* 'Schnittgold'
– 'Nana' **new**	EBre EFou WFar
§ – 'Schnittgold'	EBee EOMN MWgw WFar WPer
– 'Superba'	LRHS
'Baby Gold'	EBee EMlt EPfP MBNS MTis NBlu NFla NNor SWvt WFar WShp WWeb
Baby Sun	see *C.* 'Sonnenkind'
gigantea new	EWes
'Goldfink'	EBre GKir GSki LRHS MBrN MRav SRms
grandiflora	SRob SWat XPep
– 'Astolat'	CMdw CStr EMon MNrw SPer SUsu
– 'Badengold'	CBcs EBee EMil IHMH MLwd
– 'Bernwode' (v)	EBee EMan NBPC
I – 'Calypso' (v)	EBee EWes LRHS SCoo WWeb
– 'Domino'	EBee LHop NOak
– 'Early Sunrise'	CSBt CSam EBee ECtt EGra ERou LPVe LRHS MHer NBir NMir NPer SAga SGar SMer SPet SWal SWvt WFar WGwG WHen WMnd WPer WRHF
– Flying Saucers = 'Walcoreop'PBR	EBee EChP GBri GKir LRHS SCoo
– 'Kelvin Harbutt'	CStr EMan ERou
– 'Mayfield Giant'	CSBt EBee EFou EMan ERou LRHS MNrw MWat MWgw NBPC NPri SChu SMer SPer SRms SWat SWvt WMnd
lanceolata	EFou NSti
– 'Sterntaler'	CFir CPen EBee EFou EMil EPar ERou GAbr GKir IHMH LPVe LRHS MBri MSph NCGa NPri NVic SWvt WHil WMoo WPer WWeb
– 'Walter' **new**	EBee MBri
latifolia	EBee
'Limerock Ruby' **new**	EBre SPer
maximiliani	see *Helianthus maximiliani*
palmata	MDKP
pulchra	EBee
rosea	NLar WFar WPer
– 'American Dream'	More than 30 suppliers
– f. **leucantha**	CStr
– 'Sweet Dreams'	EBre GBri SPer WCot
§ 'Sonnenkind'	CPen EBee ECtt EMil EPar IHMH LRHS MHer MWgw NBro NJOw WPer
Sun Child	see *C.* 'Sonnenkind'
'Sunburst'	COtt EBee GSki LRHS NOak WMnd WPer WWpP
'Sunray'	More than 30 suppliers
'Tequila Sunrise' (v)	CFai EBee EChP EHoe EMan MBNS NSti WCot
tinctoria	MSal SECG WHer
– 'Tiger Flowered' **new**	GFlt
tripteris	CPou EBee EChP EMan EMon LPhx MDKP MSte SAga SSvw WMoo WPer
– 'Pierre Bennerup'	EMon
verticillata	EBee ECha EHrv ENot EPfP IHMH LRHS MBrN MBro MDun MHer MWat NPPs NPer SDix SRms SWat WFar WHal WShp WTin
– 'Golden Gain'	CTri EBee EBre ECtt EFou EMan EPla GBri GKir GSki LHop LRHS
	MLLN MMil NGdn NHol WBVN WMnd
– 'Golden Shower'	see *C. verticillata* 'Grandiflora'
§ – 'Grandiflora' ♥H4	CBcs CTri EBre EFou ELan EPfP EPza ERou GSki MCLN MRav NFor NGdn NHol NOak NVic SBla SChu SMad SPer SPla SSpe WCAu WMnd WOld WWin
– 'Moonbeam'	More than 30 suppliers
– 'Zagreb' ♥H4	More than 30 suppliers

coriander see *Coriandrum sativum*

Coriandrum (Apiaceae)

sativum	CArn CSev EOHP GPoy ILis LRHS MHer NBlu NVic SIde WHHs WHer WLHH WPer
– 'Leisure'	CBod CSev MBow NPri
– 'Moroccan'	WHHs
– 'Santo'	ELau NGHP WJek

Coriaria ✿ (Coriariaceae)

arborea	WCru
intermedia B&SWJ 019	WCru
japonica	WCot WCru
– B&SWJ 2833	WCru
kingiana	ECou WCru
§ **microphylla**	GEil WCru
– B&SWJ 8999	WCru
myrtifolia	CFil GCal GSki WCru WFar XPep
napalensis	GCal WCru
– BWJ 7755	WCru
pteridoides	WCru
ruscifolia	LEdu WCru
– HCM 98178	WCru
sarmentosa	GCal WCru
terminalis	CDes CTrG EBee EMan EPfP GBuc
var. **xanthocarpa**	GCal GEil SSpi WCot WCru WGwG WPGP
thymifolia	see *C. microphylla*

Coris (Primulaceae)

monspeliensis new	XPep

Cornus ✿ (Cornaceae)

alba	CCVT CDoC CDul CLnd ECrN ENot GKir IHMH ISea MAsh MHer MRav MSwo NWea SRms WDin WMou WStI
* – 'Albovariegata' (v)	ENot
– 'Argenteovariegata'	see *C. alba* 'Variegata'
– 'Aurea' ♥H4	More than 30 suppliers
– 'Elegantissima' (v) ♥H4	More than 30 suppliers
– 'Gouchaultii' (v)	CBcs EBee ECrN EPfP EWTr GKir LPan MBar MRav NBlu NPri SPer SRms WDin
– 'Hedgerow' **new**	SPoG
– 'Hessei'	GKir LRHS MRav
– 'Hessei' misapplied	see *C. sanguinea* 'Compressa'
– Ivory Halo = 'Bailhalo'PBR	EBee EBre ENot EPfP GKir LRHS MAsh MBNS MBri MGos MRav NMoo NPri NWea SPer WGer
– 'Kesselringii'	CAbP CBcs CDoC CDul CSBt EBee ECrN EHoe EMil ENot EPfP EPla EWTr GKir LBuc LRHS MBar MBri MGos MRav MSwo NCGa NWea SMad SPer WBod WDin WFar WMoo
– 'Red Gnome'	MAsh WPat
– 'Siberian Pearls'	CBcs EBee ELan GKir MBlu MGos NMoo SSta
§ – 'Sibirica' ♥H4	More than 30 suppliers
– 'Sibirica Variegata' (v)	CDoC CMac EBee EPfP EPla GEil GKir LPan LRHS MAsh MBlu MBri

	MGos MSwo NBee NPri SHBN SLim SPer SSpi SSta SWvt WFar
- 'Spaethii' (v) ♀H4	More than 30 suppliers
§ - 'Variegata' (v)	CBcs GEil LAst SPer WWin
- 'Westonbirt'	see *C. alba* 'Sibirica'
alternifolia	CDul CMCN CMHG COtt ELan EWTr GIBF GKir MDun SSpi WPat
§ - 'Argentea' (v) ♀H4	More than 30 suppliers
- 'Variegata'	see *C. alternifolia* 'Argentea'
amomum	CAbP CBcs NHol WBcn WWpP
angustata	CTho LRHS SPer SSpi
§ 'Ascona'	CPMA ELan EPfP LRHS MBlu MBri NLar SKee SSpi SSta SWvt WPat
Aurora = 'Rutban' (Stellar Series)	CPMA MPkF NLar
§ *canadensis* ♀H4	More than 30 suppliers
candidissima	see *C. racemosa*
capitata	CAgr CBcs CDoC CDul CMac CPne CTrG CTri EPfP GIBF LRHS MWya SEND SSpi WCwm WFar WMoo WPGP WPat
- JN 468	GGar
- subsp. *emeiensis*	SSpi
§ Celestial = 'Rutdan' (Stellar Series)	CPMA MPkF
Constellation = 'Rutcan' (Stellar Series)	CPMA
controversa	CBcs CDul CMCN CTho ECrN ELan EMil EPfP EWTr LPan MBar MBlu MDun NDlv NPSI SHBN SLPl SPer SReu SSpi SSta SWvt WDin WHar WOrn WPGP
- 'Frans Type' (v)	CBcs CBot CEnd ELan EMil ERom LPan MBlu MBri SHBN SPer SReu SSta SWvt WDin WHCG WPat
I - 'Marginata Nord'	CTho NLar SKee
- 'Pagoda'	MBlu NBhm NLar SSpi
- 'Variegata' (v) ♀H4	More than 30 suppliers
- 'Variegata' Frans type	see *C. controversa* 'Frans Type'
'Eddie's White Wonder' ♀H4	More than 30 suppliers
florida	CDul CLnd CMCN CTho EPfP GIBF ISea LRHS MBar NBlu SKee SPer WNor WPat
- 'Alba Plena' (d)	CPMA NLar
- 'Andrea Hart' **new**	CPMA
- Apple Blossom'	CMac CPMA ECho
- Cherokee Brave = 'Comco No. 1'	CBcs CPMA CWib LRHS NLar SSpi SSta
- 'Cherokee Chief' ♀H4	CAbP CBcs CEnd CPMA CTri CWib ECho EPfP GKir IArd IMGH LPan LRHS MGos MSwo NLar NPSI SHBN SKee WDin WOrn WPat
- 'Cherokee Daybreak' (v)	CBcs CWib
- 'Cherokee Princess'	CPMA EPfP GKir LPan LRHS MAsh SKee SMur SSpi
- 'Cherokee Sunset' (v)	NLar
- 'Clear Moon'	LPan
- 'Cloud Nine'	CBcs CDoC CPMA EMil LAst MGos NCGa NLar SLdr SSpi WOrn WPat
- 'Daybreak' (v)	CEnd CPMA LPan MGos WPat
- 'First Lady'	CBcs CPMA ECho LPan SSpi
- 'G.H. Ford' (v)	CPMA
- 'Golden Nugget'	CPMA
- 'Junior Miss'	CPMA EMil
- 'Junior Miss Variegated' (v)	CPMA
- 'Moonglow'	CPMA
- 'Pendula'	CPMA
- f. *pluribracteata* (d) **new**	NLar
- 'Purple Glory'	CPMA
- Rainbow = Marzelli' (v)	CAbP COtt CPMA CWib ECrN EPfP GKir LPan LRHS MAsh MBri
	MGos NPSI SHBN SKee SPla WDin WPat
- 'Red Giant'	CAbP CPMA ELan EPfP LRHS MAsh SMur SSpi SSta
- 'Royal Red'	CBcs CPMA
- f. *rubra*	CBcs CSBt CWib ELan EPfP LAst LPan LRHS MGos SSta WFar WGer WNor WPat
- 'Spring Song'	CMac CPMA ECho LRHS
- 'Stoke's Pink'	CEnd COtt CPMA ECho GKir
- 'Sunset' (v)	CEnd CPMA CWib MGos SHBN WPat
- 'Sweetwater'	CPMA EMil
- 'Tricolor'	see *C. florida* 'Welchii'
- 'Variegata' **new**	SSpi
- 'Weaver's White' **new**	MPkF
§ - 'Welchii' (v)	CEnd CPMA SSpi
- 'White Cloud'	CPMA
'Gloria Birkett' **new**	SSpi
'Greenlight'	NPro WWeb
hemsleyi	EPla
hessei misapplied	see *C. sanguinea* 'Compressa'
hongkongensis	CBcs
'Kelsey Dwarf'	see *C. sericea* 'Kelseyi'
kousa	CDoC CDul CMCN CTbh CTho CWSG ECrN ELan EPfP ERom GKir ISea LRHS MBar MLan MWat NFor NPSI SHBN SPer SPlb WDin WFar WHCG WHar WStI
- B&SWJ 5494	WCru
- 'Autumn Rose'	CPMA EPfP NLar
- 'Beni-fuji'	CPMA
- 'Blue Shadow' **new**	CPMA
- 'Bonfire' (v)	CPMA
- 'Bultinck's Beauty'	LRHS SSpi
- 'Bultinck's Giant' **new**	NLar
- var. *chinensis* ♀H4	More than 30 suppliers
- - 'Bodnant Form'	CEnd CPMA GKir
- - 'China Girl'	CAbP CEnd CPMA CWib ELan EPfP GKir LBuc LPan LRHS MAsh MBlu MBri MGos MSwo MWya SHBN SLim SSpi SSta WDin WOrn WPGP WPat
- - 'Greta's Gold' (v)	CPMA
- - 'Milky Way'	CMCN CPMA CWib GEil LBuc NLar SHBN WBod
- - 'Snowflake'	CPMA
- - Spinners form	CPMA WPat
- - 'Summer Stars' **new**	NLar
- - 'White Dusted'	EPfP
- - 'White Fountain'	NLar
- - 'Wieting's Select'	CPMA
- 'Claudine' **new**	CPMA
- 'Doubloon'	CPMA
- 'Ed Mezitt'	CPMA
- 'Elizabeth Lustgarten'	SSpi SSta
- 'Gold Cup' (v)	CPMA
- 'Gold Star' (v)	CAbP CBcs CEnd CMCN CMac COtt CTho CWib ELan EPfP LBuc LRHS MAsh MGos SHBN SKee SPla SSpi
- 'John Slocock'	MAsh SSpi
- 'Lustgarten Weeping'	LRHS NLar SSpi
- 'Madame Butterfly'	CEnd CPMA LRHS SSpi
- 'Minuma' **new**	NLar
- 'Moonbeam'	CPMA
- 'Mount Fuji' **new**	NLar
- 'National'	CPMA MGos WPat
- 'Nicole'	CDoC WDin
- 'Radiant Rose'	CPMA MBlu
- 'Rasen' **new**	NLar
- 'Rosea'	CPMA
- 'Satomi' ♀H4	CAbP CBcs CDoC CEnd CMCN CPMA EBee ELan EPfP GKir LBuc

	LPan LRHS MBlu MBri MDun
	MGos MRav NBea NBee SKee SLdr
	SLim SPer SReu SSpi SSta WDin
	WPGP WPat
- 'Schmetterling'	CPMA
- 'Snowboy' (v)	CBcs CEnd CPMA LRHS NLar SKee
- 'Southern Cross'	CPMA
- 'Summer Majesty'	CPMA
- 'Sunsplash' (v)	CPMA CTho
- 'Temple Jewel' (v)	LRHS SSpi
- 'Triple Crown'	CPMA
- 'Tsukubanomine'	CPMA NLar
- 'Weaver's Weeping'	CPMA
macrophylla	CMCN EPfP IArd SMad WCwm
mas	More than 30 suppliers
- 'Aurea' (v)	CAbP CDul CPMA EBee ELan EPfP
	GKir LPan MAsh MBri MBro MRav
	SLim SSpi WDin WPat
§ - 'Aureoelegantissima' (v)	CFil CPMA CWib EBee LRHS MAsh
	MBro NHol NLar SPer SSpi WFar
	WPGP WPat WSHC
- 'Elegantissima'	see *C. mas* 'Aureoelegantissima'
- 'Golden Glory' ♀H4	CBcs CPMA MBlu NLar
- 'Jolico' **new**	CPMA NLar
- 'Variegata' (v) ♀H4	CBcs CBot CDul CMCN CPMA
	CTho EBee EPfP GKir LRHS MAsh
	MBlu MBro MGos NPal SKee SPer
	SSpi WDin WFar WPat
N 'Norman Hadden' ♀H4	CAbP CDoC CDul CEnd CMCN
	CMac CPMA CSBt CTbh CTho
	EPfP GKir LAst LRHS MAsh MBro
	MRav MWya SHBN SHfr SPer SSpi
	SSta WAbe WDin WFar WPGP WPat
nuttallii	CBcs CTho CWib ELan EPfP EWTr
	LAst LPan LRHS MDun NWea
	SHBN SPer WDin WFar WNor
- 'Ascona'	see *C.* 'Ascona'
- 'Barrick' **new**	CPMA
- 'Colrigo Giant'	CPMA SSpi
- 'Gold Spot' (v)	CMac CPMA EPfP LPan LRHS
	MGos WPat
- 'Monarch'	CPMA CTho NLar
- 'North Star'	CPMA NLar
I - 'Osmunda' **new**	NCGa
- 'Portlemouth'	CEnd CPMA LRHS MAsh NLar SSpi
	WPat
obliqua	CFil WPGP
§ *occidentalis*	EPla
officinalis	CMCN CTho EPfP LPan LRHS MBri
	NLar WCwm WDin
'Ormonde'	CPMA ECho LRHS SSpi
paucinervis	GIBF
'Pink Blush'	CPMA
'Porlock' ♀H4	CDul CMCN CPMA ENot EPfP
	LRHS NLar SSpi WDin
pubescens	see *C. occidentalis*
pumila	CPMA NHol NLar WDin
§ *racemosa*	WFar
rugosa	WNor
x *rutgersiensis* Galaxy	see *C.* Celestial = 'Rutdan'
Ruth Ellen = 'Rutlan'	CPMA NLar
(Stellar Series)	
sanguinea	CBcs CCVT CDul CLnd CRWN
	CTri ECrN ENot EPfP LBuc MAsh
	MRav MSwo NFor NWea SKee SPer
	WDin WGwG WHar WMou XPep
- 'Anny's Winter	MBlu
Orange' **new**	
§ - 'Compressa'	GEil MBro NHol NLar WSPU WWes
- 'Magic Flame'	MBri
- 'Midwinter Fire'	More than 30 suppliers
§ - 'Winter Beauty'	CDoC CSBt EBee EBre EPfP MBlu
	MBro NBee SHBN SLon WFar WPat
	WSPU

§ *sericea*	CArn EPla MGos SMer
- 'Budd's Yellow' **new**	MGos
- 'Cardinal' **new**	MBri MGos
§ - 'Flaviramea' ♀H4	More than 30 suppliers
- 'Hedgerow Gold' **new**	SPoG WCot
- 'Kelseyi'	CBcs CFwr CMac EBee ENot EPla
	ESis GEil GKir MBNS MBar MRav
	NPri NPro SBod SLPl SMac SPer
	WWeb
- Kelsey's Gold = 'Rosco'	SLon WPat
- 'Sunshine'	CSpe
§ - 'White Gold' (v) ♀H4	CDoC CPMA EBee ECrN EHoe
	ENot LRHS MBri MGos MRav NPro
	SPer WBcn WDin WFar WMoo
Stellar Pink = 'Rutgan'	CPMA CWib MPkF NLar
(Stellar Series)	
stolonifera	see *C. sericea*
- 'Flaviramea'	see *C. sericea* 'Flaviramea'
- 'White Spot'	see *C. sericea* 'White Gold' (v)
suecica	GIBF
walteri	CMCN WCwm WFar

Corokia (Escalloniaceae)

buddlejoides	CDoC CMHG CWib ECou GGar
	SOWG SPer WBod WCru WFar
'Coppershine'	CBcs CMHG
cotoneaster	CAbP CMac CSBt CTrw ECou ELan
	EMan ENot EPfP EPot MAsh MGos
	SDry SIgm SLon SMad SMur SPer
	WBod WBrE WCot WFar WPat
	WSHC WWes
- 'Little Prince'	GGar
- 'Ohau Scarlet'	ECou
- 'Ohau Yellow'	ECou
- 'Swale Stream'	ECou
- 'Wanaka'	ECou
macrocarpa	CDoC ECou ISea SDix WSHC
x *virgata*	CAbP CBcs CDoC CMHG CTrC CTri
	EBee ECou ECrN ELan EPfP LRHS
	MBlu MCCP MWhi SAPC SAga SArc
	SPer WBVN WCom WCru WSHC
- 'Bronze King'	CBrm CDoC CTrC EBee ECrN SPer
- 'Cheesemanii'	ECou GGar
- 'County Park Lemon'	ECou SOWG
- 'County Park Orange'	ECou
- 'County Park Purple'	ECou
- 'County Park Red'	ECou
- 'Frosted Chocolate'	CBcs CDoC CTrC EBee ECou EPfP
	MGos WBcn WDin
- 'Havering'	ECou
- 'Mangatangi'	MGos
- 'Pink Delight'	CDoC ECou EPfP
- 'Red Wonder'	CBrm CMHG CPen CTrC EBee
	ECrN GGar LRHS SAga SDry SEND
	SMac SOWG WDin WStl
- 'Sunsplash' (v)	CBcs CDoC CTrC EBee ECou
	MGos SAga
- 'Virgata'	CChe CTrC ECou MGos
- 'Yellow Wonder'	CBcs CMHG CPen CTrC ECot
	ECou ECrN EMan GEil GGar MGos
	WDin

Coronilla (Papilionaceae)

cappadocica	see *C. orientalis*
comosa	see *Hippocrepis comosa*
emerus	see *Hippocrepis emerus*
glauca	see *C. valentina* subsp. *glauca*
minima	SBla WAbe XPep
§ *orientalis*	WWin
valentina	CDoC CMac CRHN CSPN EMil
	LHop SBra SDix XPep
- subsp. *glauca* ♀H3	CBot CDul CFee CHar CMac CPle
	CSBt CSam CTri CWib EBee ELan
	ENot EPfP ERea LAst LRHS MWhi

	SAga SGar SPer SRms SVen WAbe
	WBod WHCG WPic XPep
- - 'Citrina' ♀H3	More than 30 suppliers
* - - 'Pygmaea'	WCot
- - 'Variegata' (v)	More than 30 suppliers
§ *varia*	CAgr CArn CStr MWrn NLar SPet
	XPep

Correa (Rutaceae)

alba	CDoC CPLG CTrC ECou EPfP
	SMur WGwG XPep
- 'Pinkie' ♀H2	CPLG ECou LHop LRHS SDys
	SOWG
backhouseana ♀H2	CAbb CBcs CDoC CPLG CPle
	CTrG CTri ECre EPfP GCal GGar
	GQui LHop LRHS SAga SLon
	SOWG WBod WCot WPat WSHC
	WSPU
baeuerlenii	CMHG CPLG SOWG
decumbens	CAbb CPLG CPle CTrC ECou ESlt
	GSki SDys SMur SOWG
'Dusky Bells' ♀H2	CDoC CHll CSWP CTrC ECou EPfP
	LHop MOak SMur SOWG WCFE
'Dusky Maid'	CAbb
'Gwen' **new**	SOWG
'Harrisii'	see *C.* 'Mannii'
'Ivory Bells'	ECou SDys
lawrenceana	CDoC CTrC GQui SEND WAbe
§ 'Mannii' ♀H2	CBcs CPLG CPom CSev EBee
	ECou EPfP LRHS SOWG WCot
	WSHC
'Marian's Marvel' ♀H2	CAbb CMHG CPLG ECou GQui
	LRHS SDys SOWG SVen WAbe
	WGwG
'Peachy Cream'	CDoC SMur
'Poorinda Mary'	SOWG
pulchella ♀H2	CDoC CPLG CTri GQui LRHS
	SOWG
§ *reflexa* ♀H2	CDoC CPLG CPle ECou SOWG
	WAbe WBor
- 'Federation Bell'	SOWG
- var. *nummulariifolia*	WAbe
new	
- var. *reflexa*	CPLG
- *virens*	CPLG WEas
- 'Yanakie'	CPle SOWG
speciosa	see *C. reflexa*
* *spectabilis*	CPLG
viridiflora	GQui

Cortaderia ✿ (Poaceae)

RCB/Arg K2-2 **new**	WCot
argentea	see *C. selloana*
§ *fulvida*	CBig EBee EBre EWes IBlr MNrw
	SMad WDin WKif WSSM
richardii misapplied	see *C. fulvida*
§ *richardii* (Endl.)	CBcs CKno CMCo EBre EFou
Zotov ♀H3-4	EHoe EPPr EPla EPza EWes GGar
	IBlr NVic SAPC SArc SWal WBea
	WCot WCru
- BR 26	GGar
§ *selloana*	CBcs CHEx CTri EBee EHul ENot
	EPfP EUJe GKir MBar MRav NBee
	NBir NBlu NFor NHol SAPC SArc
	SPlb WMoo WMul WStI
§ - 'Albolineata' (v)	CBrm CKno EBee EBre EHoe EPza
	EWes EWsh LAst MBri MCCP
	MWht NOak SEND SLim SSto
	SWvt WLeb WMoo WPat
§ - 'Aureolineata' (v) ♀H3	CBrm CDoC CMac CMil CSam
	CWCL EHoe ELan ENot EPfP GKir
	LRHS MAsh MCCP MGos MMoz
	MRav SHBN SLim SPer SSto WFar
	WLeb WMoo WPGP WPat

- 'Elegans'	CBig
- 'Gold Band'	see *C. selloana* 'Aureolineata'
- 'Monstrosa'	SMad
- 'Patagonia'	EHoe EPPr
- 'Pink Feather'	EPfP EPza EWsh GKir SAdn SHBN
	SPer WFar WLow WStI WWeb
- 'Pumila' ♀H4	More than 30 suppliers
- 'Rendatleri'	CBcs CBig CDoC EBee ELan EPfP
	EWsh GKir LRHS MAsh SLim SPer
	WDin
- 'Rosea'	CBig EBee EUJe GSki IHMH LRHS
	MBar MGos NBlu NGdn NHol
	WFar WMoo
- 'Senior' **new**	IHMH
- 'Silver Comet'	GKir
- Silver Feather	ENot WWeb
= 'Notcort'	
- 'Silver Fountain'	ELan EPfP LRHS MAsh SPer
- 'Silver Stripe'	see *C. selloana* 'Albolineata'
- 'Sunningdale Silver' ♀H3	More than 30 suppliers
- 'White Feather'	EPza IHMH MWhi NGdn WFar
	WLow WWeb

Cortusa (Primulaceae)

brotheri	EHyt GEdr NWCA WLin
matthioli	CPom EPfP GBBs GEdr GGar GKir
	GTou LBee MBow NMen NWCA
	SRms WFar WLin WWhi
- 'Alba'	ECGN GBuc NLar NMen NSla
	NWCA SRms WLin
- subsp. *pekinensis*	CFir CLyd EMlt GBuc NJOw NLar
	NMen SRms
turkestanica	ECho ECoo GFlt

Corydalis (Papaveraceae)

from Sichuan, China	EMan MDKP NCot
alexeenkoana	see *C. vittae*
subsp. *vittae*	
x *allenii*	GCrs WWst
ambigua hort.	see *C. fumariifolia*
angustifolia	NDlv
- white	WWst
anthriscifolia **new**	CLAP
aquilegioides	EBee
'Blackberry Wine'	CBAn CHll CLAP CSpe EBee EDAr
	GBri MDKP NBPC
§ *blanda*	EHyt
subsp. *parnassica*	
'Blue Panda'	see *C. flexuosa* 'Blue Panda'
bracteata	GCrs
- white	WWst
bulbosa misapplied	see *C. cava*
bulbosa (L.) DC.	see *C. solida*
buschii	CDes CLAP CPom EBee EHyt ERos
	GCrs GEdr NDov NRya SBla SChu
	SCnR WAbe WPGP WPrP WWst
cashmeriana	EBee GCrs GEdr GTou NHol NLar
	SBla WAbe WIvy
- 'Kailash'	CLAP EMon GBuc MAvo
caucasica	ERos GBuc GCrs LAma NMen
- var. *alba* misapplied	see *C. malkensis*
§ *cava*	CLAP CPom EBee EChP ECho EPot
	GFlt GGar LAma NJOw
- *albiflora*	EPar EPot NMen SBla
chaerophylla	IBlr
- B&SWJ 2951	WCru
cheilanthifolia	More than 30 suppliers
curviflora **new**	EPot
- subsp. *rosthornii*	SMHy
DJHC 0615 **new**	
darwasica	WWst
davidii	EBee
decipiens Schott,	see *C. solida* subsp. *incisa*
Nyman & Kotschy	

I	**decipiens** hort. ♀H4	CFwr CPom EPot GAbr WPrP
I	– purple-flowered **new**	EBee ECho
§	**densiflora**	WWst
	'Early Bird'	EWes
	elata	More than 30 suppliers
	– 'Blue Summit'	CLAP SBla
	elata x **flexuosa** clone 1	CLAP CPom GCrs WCot
	flexuosa ♀H4	CFee CMil CPLG CPne CSpe
		CWCL ECGN EDAr EGle EMar
		EPot LAst MBro MNrw MTho SChu
		SGar SMac WAbe WCFE WFar
		WSHC WWin
	– CD&R 528	EHyt MBro MRav NRya SAga
	– 'Balang Mist'	CLAP EBee EGle LHop NDov SBla
		SMrm SOkh SUsu
	– 'Blue Dragon'	see *C. flexuosa* 'Purple Leaf'
§	– 'Blue Panda'	EBee EGle EPfP EWes GBuc IBlr
		ITim LRHS NDov NGar SBla SSpi
		WAbe
	– 'China Blue' CD&R 528c	More than 30 suppliers
	– 'Golden Panda' (v)	CBct EBee LAst MBNS SPoG
	– 'Nightshade'	CElw EBee ECtt EMan GBuc MAvo
		NBid NCot NDov NGar SWat WCot
		WCra WFar WIvy WPrP
I	– 'Norman's Seedling'	EBee EPPr NCot WCot WPGP
	– 'Père David' CD&R 528b	More than 30 suppliers
	– 'Purple Leaf' CD&R 528a	More than 30 suppliers
§	**fumariifolia**	EBee EPot GEdr LAma MTho NRog
	glauca	see *C. sempervirens*
	glaucescens	WWst
	'Early Beauty' **new**	
	– 'Moonlight Beauty' **new**	WWst
	– 'Pink Beauty' **new**	WWst
	gracilis	WWst
	haussknechtii	EHyt
	henrikii	EHyt
	heterocarpa	SScr
	integra	GCrs WCot WWst
	jingyuanensis	EBee
	'Kingfisher'	EBee WAbe
	kusnetzovii	EHyt
	ledebouriana	WWst
	leptocarpa **new**	EBee
	leucanthema	CLAP CPom
	– DJHC 752	CDes
	– 'Silver Sceptre'	SSpi
	lineariloba **new**	WWst
	linstowiana	CPom CTCP EBee EDAr EHyt EMan
		EMon EPPr IBlr LPhx NWCA WOBN
	– CD&R 605	CLAP
§	**lutea**	CBcs CRWN EBee EBre EChP
		EDAr EMar EPat EPfP GBuc IBlr
		LGro MBow MTis NPer NVic SEND
		SHFr SRms WCot WMoo
	macrocentra	WWst
	maculata B&SWJ 4417	WCru
	magadanica	GIBF
§	**malkensis** ♀H4	CPom EHyt ETow GBuc GCrs NBir
		SBla SCnR WWst
	nariniana white **new**	EHyt
	nemoralis **new**	EBee
	nobilis	CPom EBee MLLN SHBN WCot
	nudicaulis	WWst
	ochotensis	NCGa NLar
	– B&SWJ 3138	WCru
	– B&SWJ 917	WCru
§	**ochroleuca**	CDes CElw CHrt CRow CSpe
		CTCP EChP EMar EPot GCrs MTho
		MWgw NCot NJOw NPol WFar
		WMoo
	ophiocarpa	EHoe ELan EMan EMar GBBs GCal
		GIBF IBlr MBNS MLan MRav MWhi
		NBur SWal WBVN WBea WCot
		WFoF WMoo

	ornata	EHyt WWst
	– white	WWst
	pachycentra **new**	EPot
	paczoskii	EHyt ERos GBuc GKir LRHS NDlv
		NMen WAbe WOBN
*	**pallescens** **new**	MWrn
	pallida B&SWJ 395	WCru
	parnassica	see *C. blanda* subsp. *parnassica*
	paschei	EHyt
	popovii	GCrs MTho
	pseudocristata	EBee
	pseudofumaria alba	see *C. ochroleuca*
	pumila	EPot ETow WLin
	repens	EBee
	rosea	IBlr
	ruksansii	WWst
	scandens	see *Dicentra scandens*
	schanginii	WLin
	– subsp. **ainii** ♀H2	EHyt
	– subsp. **schanginii**	EHyt GCrs
	scouleri	EMFP NBir
	seisumsiana	WWst
§	**sempervirens**	EMan WCru WRos WSan
	– **alba**	ECho WFoF
	sewerzowii	WWst
	sheareri	EBee
	shimienensis **new**	EBee
	smithiana	CPom EDAr GKev WFar WTin
	– ACE 154	EHyt GBuc WOBN
§	**solida**	More than 30 suppliers
	– BM 8499	NHol
	– pink and red shades	CFwr
	– 'Ballade' **new**	WWst
	– 'Cantata' **new**	WWst
	– 'Cat's Paw' **new**	WWst
	– 'Christina' **new**	WWst
	– compact **new**	WWst
	– 'Evening Dream' **new**	WWst
	– 'First Kiss'	WWst
	– 'Harkov'	GCrs
	– 'Highland Sunset' **new**	GCrs
§	– subsp. **incisa** ♀H4	CMea EBee EHyt LRHS MNrw
		MTho WPrP WShi
	– – 'Lavender Lips' **new**	EBee
	– – 'Vermion Dawn'	WWst
	– 'Kissproof' **new**	WWst
	– 'Margaret' **new**	WWst
	– 'Maxima'	GCrs
	– 'Moonlight Shade' **new**	WWst
	– Nettleton seedlings	EPot
	– 'Pink Discovery' **new**	WWst
	– 'Pink Smile' **new**	WWst
	– 'Pink Splash' **new**	WWst
	– 'Punk Lips'	EHyt
	– 'Pussy' **new**	WWst
	– 'Rozula'	WWst
	– 'Snowlark' **new**	GCrs WWst
	– 'Soft Pink'	EPot
§	– subsp. **solida**	CLAP EHyt EPot NBir NMen NRya
		WAbe WCot WTin
	– – 'Alba' **new**	NSla
	– – 'Beth Evans'	CBro EBee EHyt EPot LTwo NMen
		SCnR SRot WCot WLin WWst
	– – 'Blue Dream'	WWst
	– – 'Blue Giant' **new**	WWst
	– – 'Blushing Girl'	WWst
	– – 'Charles Archbold'	NPar
	– – 'Dieter Schacht' ♀H4	EBee GCrs LAma NPar WAbe WCot
		WWst
	– – 'Evening Shade'	WWst
	– – from Penza, Russia	GBuc GCrs SBla
	– – 'George Baker' ♀H4	CBro CMea EBee EHyt EPar EPot
		ETow GBuc GCrs GEdr LAma LBee
		LRHS LTwo MTho NDov NGar

	NMen NSla SCnR SOkh SUsu WAbe WCom WCot WLin WWst
- - 'Highland Mist'	GCrs NGar
- - 'Lahovice'	EHyt GCrs WAbe
- - 'Munich Sunrise'	EHyt NRya
- - 'Prasil Sunset'	EHyt SOkh
- - 'Sixtus' **new**	WWst
- - 'White Knight'	GCrs
- - 'Spring Bird' **new**	WWst
- subsp. *subremota*	WWst
- 'White King'	WWst
- 'Yaroslavna' **new**	WWst
'Spinners'	CDes LPhx WHil
taliensis	CPom CTCP EBee GEdr
- ACE 2443	EPot NCot
tauricola	EPot GCrs
temulifolia	EBee
tomentella	GEdr SIng
'Tory MP'	CDes CHid CKno CLAP CSam EBee MNrw NChi WHoo WPGP WPrP
triternata ♀H4	EPot
turtschaninovii	EBee WWst
verticillaris	EHyt
§ *vittae*	EHyt
vivipara	EBee
wendelboi	EHyt GCrs
- subsp. *congesta*	WWst
- - 'Abant Wine'	WWst
wilsonii	EHyt GEdr IBlr MTho NWCA SBla SIng WEas
zetterlundii	GBuc NDlv

Corylopsis ✿ *(Hamamelidaceae)*

from Chollipo, South Korea	LRHS SSpi
§ *glabrescens*	CEnd CPMA GIBF IMGH LRHS NLar SMur WNor WWes
- var. *gotoana*	EPfP LRHS SMur SSpi SSta WBod
- - 'Chollipo'	MAsh SSta
himalayana	CBcs NLar
multiflora	SSpi SSta
pauciflora ♀H4	More than 30 suppliers
platypetala	see *C. sinensis* var. *calvescens*
- var. *laevis*	see *C. sinensis* var. *calvescens*
sinensis	GIBF SSta
§ - var. *calvescens*	CBcs CPMA CPne LRHS NLar
§ - - f. *veitchiana* ♀H4	CBcs CPMA EPfP IArd LRHS NLar SMur SPoG WDin
- - - purple selection	CPMA
§ - var. *sinensis* ♀H4	CBcs CBrm CDoC CMHG CPMA CWSG EPfP LAst MAsh SReu WAbe WBod WDin WFar
- - 'Spring Purple'	CAbP CMac CPMA EPfP IArd LRHS NLar SPla SPoG SSpi SSta WDin WPGP WPat
spicata	CBcs CPMA CSBt EBee GIBF LRHS MBlu NBlu SLim SPer WBod
- 'Red Eye'	NLar
veitchiana	see *C. sinensis* var. *calvescens* f. *veitchiana*
willmottiae	see *C. sinensis* var. *sinensis*

Corylus ✿ *(Corylaceae)*

avellana (F)	CBcs CCVT CDoC CDul CLnd CRWN CTri ECrN EMui ENot EPfP ERea GKir LBuc LRHS MAsh MBar MBow MBri NBee NRog NWea SKee SPer WDin WHar WMou WOrn WStI
- 'Aurea'	CDul CEnd CLnd COtt CSBt CTho EBee ECrN ELan ENot EPfP EWTr GKir LBuc LRHS MAsh MBlu MBri MGos NHol SKee SLim SPer SSta SWvt WDin WFar

- 'Bollwylle'	see *C. maxima* 'Halle'sche Riesennuss'
- 'Casina' (F) **new**	CAgr
- 'Contorta'	More than 30 suppliers
- 'Cosford Cob' (F)	CDoC CDul CSBt CTho CTri ECrN EMui ERea ESim GKir GTwe LBuc LRHS MBlu MBri MGos NRog SDea SKee SPer
- 'Fortin' (F)	ESim
§ - 'Fuscorubra' (F)	GKir MSwo SAga SWvt
§ - 'Heterophylla'	CEnd CTho EPfP GKir GTSp WMou WWes
- 'Laciniata'	see *C. avellana* 'Heterophylla'
- 'Merveille de Bollwyller'	see *C. maxima* 'Halle'sche Riesennuss'
- 'Nottingham Prolific'	see *C. avellana* 'Pearson's Prolific'
§ - 'Pearson's Prolific' (F)	ERea ESim GTwe LBuc SDea
- 'Pendula'	GKir SBLw
- 'Purpurea'	see *C. avellana* 'Fuscorubra'
- 'Red Majestic'PBR **new**	MPkF
- 'Webb's Prize Cob' (F)	CDoC ERea GTwe MBlu NRog SDea WMou
chinensis **new**	EGFP
colurna ♀H4	CDul CFil CLnd CMCN CTho EBee ECrN ENot EPfP GKir LPan LRHS MGos NBee NWea SBLw SKee SLPl SPer WDin WMou WOrn
- 'Granat' **new**	GKir
x *colurnoides*	ESim
- 'Laroka' (F)	ECrN ESim
maxima (F)	CDul CLnd ECrN EMui GTwe MSwo NWea SDea WDin
- 'Butler' (F)	CAgr CDul CTri ERea GTwe LRHS MBri SKee
- 'Ennis' (F)	CAgr ERea GTwe LRHS SDea SKee
- 'Fertile de Coutard'	see *C. maxima* 'White Filbert'
- 'Frizzled Filbert' (F)	ECrN EMil
- 'Frühe van Frauendorf'	see *C. maxima* 'Red Filbert'
- 'Garibaldi' (F)	MBlu
- 'Grote Lambertsnoot'	see *C. maxima* 'Kentish Cob'
- 'Gunslebert' (F)	CAgr CSBt ECrN ERea GKir GTwe LRHS MBri SDea SKee
- Halle Giant	see *C. maxima* 'Halle'sche Riesennuss'
§ - 'Halle'sche Riesennuss' (F)	ERea GTwe SKee
§ - 'Kentish Cob' (F)	CAgr CBcs CDoC CSBt CTho CWSG ECrN EMui EPfP ERea ESim GKir GTwe LBuc LRHS MBlu MBri MGos NBee NPri NRog SDea SFam SKee SPer SRms WHar WOrn
- 'Lambert's Filbert'	see *C. maxima* 'Kentish Cob'
- 'Longue d'Espagne'	see *C. maxima* 'Kentish Cob'
- 'Monsieur de Bouweller'	see *C. maxima* 'Halle'sche Riesennuss'
- 'Purple Filbert'	see *C. maxima* 'Purpurea'
§ - 'Purpurea' (F) ♀H4	More than 30 suppliers
§ - 'Red Filbert' (F)	CEnd CWSG ERea GKir GTwe IMGH LRHS MBlu MBri NRog SKee SLim
- 'Red Zellernut'	see *C. maxima* 'Red Filbert'
- 'Spanish White'	see *C. maxima* 'White Filbert'
§ - 'White Filbert' (F)	CDoC ERea GTwe MBri NRog SKee WHar
- 'White Spanish Filbert'	see *C. maxima* 'White Filbert'
- 'Witpit Lambertsnoot'	see *C. maxima* 'White Filbert'
sieboldiana var. *mandshurica*	CMCN
'Te Terra Red'	CMCN GKir MBlu SBLw SMad SSpi WMou

Corymbia see *Eucalyptus*

Corynephorus (Poaceae)

canescens	CBig CPen CStr EBee EHoe EMan EOMN EPza LPVe MCCP MLLN NBir NHol NJOw WWeb

Corynocarpus (Corynocarpaceae)

laevigatus	CHEx ECou MBri
I - 'Picturatus'	CHEx

Cosmos (Asteraceae)

§ **atrosanguineus**	More than 30 suppliers
bipinnatus 'Sonata Carmine' **new**	NBlu
- 'Sonata Pink' **new**	NBlu
- 'Sonata White' **new**	NBlu
peucedanifolius new	CSpe
sulphureus new	MSal

costmary see *Tanacetum balsamita*

Costus (Costaceae)

amazonicus	MOak
barbatus new	WMul
curvibracteatus	MOak
erythrophyllus	MOak
speciosus	CKob ELau MOak WMul
stenophyllus	MOak

Cotinus (Anacardiaceae)

americanus	see *C. obovatus*
§ **coggygria** ♀H4	More than 30 suppliers
- 'Foliis Purpureis'	see *C. coggygria* Rubrifolius Group
- Golden Spirit = 'Ancot'PBR	CAbP EBee EBre EHan ELan EMan ENot EPfP GKir MAsh MBri MGos MRav NPri NSti SCoo SKee SLim SPer
- 'Notcutt's Variety'	CMac ELan ENot EPfP GKir MAsh MGos MRav NSti WBod WWes
- 'Pink Champagne'	CPMA EPfP NLar
- Purpureus Group	EGra ENot
- 'Red Beauty'	LRHS
- 'Royal Purple' ♀H4	More than 30 suppliers
§ - Rubrifolius Group	CBcs CDul EBee EPfP GKir LRHS NFor SChu SDix SPer SWvt WDin
- 'Smokey Joe' **new**	EBre MAsh
- 'Velvet Cloak'	CAbP CPMA EBee EBre ELan ENot EPfP GKir LRHS MAsh MBri MGos MRav SLim SPla WHCG
'Flame' ♀H4	CDul CPMA EPfP LAst LRHS MAsh MBlu MBri MGos MRav SLim SPla SPoG SSpi WHCG WPat
'Grace'	More than 30 suppliers
§ **obovatus** ♀H4	CMCN CMHG CPle CTho ELan ENot EPfP IArd MRav NLar SHBN SPer SSpi SSta WWes

Cotoneaster ✿ (Rosaceae)

CC 4042	CPLG
CC&McK 465	NWCA
acuminatus	SRms WPGP
acutifolius	GIBF
adpressus ♀H4	EPfP GKir MGos MSwo MWgw NFor
§ - 'Little Gem'	ECho LRHS SRms
- var. **praecox**	see *C. nanshan*
- 'Tom Thumb'	see *C. adpressus* 'Little Gem'
affinis	SRms
albokermesinus	SRms
amoenus	SLPl SRms
- 'Fire Mountain'	LRHS NPro WFar
§ **apiculatus**	GKir MAsh MBar SRms
armenus	SRms
§ **ascendens**	SRms

assadii	SRms
assamensis	SRms
§ **astrophoros**	GEil MBlu
atropurpureus	SRms
§ - 'Variegatus' (v) ♀H4	More than 30 suppliers
atuntzensis	SRms
bis-ramianus	SRms
boisianus	SRms
bradyi	SRms
brickellii	SRms
§ **bullatus** ♀H4	CDul CLnd CTri ENot GKir MGos NFor SEND SLon SRms WCwm WOrn WSHC WTel
- 'Bjuv'	SRms
- 'Firebird'	see *C. ignescens*
- f. **floribundus**	see *C. bullatus*
- var. **macrophyllus**	see *C. rehderi*
- 'McLaren'	SRms
bumthangensis	SRms
buxifolius blue-leaved	see *C. lidjiangensis*
- f. **vellaeus**	see *C. astrophoros*
calocarpus	GIBF
camilli-schneideri	SRms
canescens	SRms
cardinalis	SRms
cavei	SRms
chungtiensis	SRms
cinerascens	SRms
cinnabarinus	SRms
cinovskisii	SRms
§ **cochleatus**	CPLG EBee EPot GIBF GKir LAst MBar MGos NBee NMen SRms WEas WLin
§ **congestus**	CSBt CWib EBee GKir LRHS MBar MBro MGos MRav MSwo NFor NHol SPer SPlb WBod WDin WHar WWin
- 'Nanus'	CLyd CMHG CTri ELan EOrn LRHS MBro MOne NBid NFor NHol NLAp WPat
conspicuus	CBcs CSam SRms
- 'Decorus' ♀H4	CCVT CDoC CMHG CSBt CWSG EBee EHol ENot EPfP GKir LRHS MBar MGos MRav MSwo MWhi NFor NHol NWea SLim SPer SPlb SWal WBVN WDin WStI WTel WWes
- 'Flameburst'	LRHS SHBN
- prostrate	SRms
- 'Red Alert'	SRms
cooperi	SRms
- 'Rumsey Gardens'	SRms
* - 'Coral'	SCoo
cornifolius	SRms
crispii	SRms
cuspidatus	SRms
N **dammeri** ♀H4	More than 30 suppliers
§ - 'Major'	LBuc MSwo NBlu SRms WCFE
§ - 'Mooncreeper'	LRHS MBNS MBri SCoo
- 'Oakwood'	see *C. radicans* 'Eichholz'
- var. **radicans** misapplied	see *C. dammeri* 'Major'
- var. **radicans** C.K.Schneid.	see *C. radicans*
- 'Streib's Findling'	see *C.* 'Streib's Findling'
dielsianus	GIBF NWea SPer SRms
distichus var. **tongolensis**	see *C. splendens*
divaricatus	ENot EPfP NWea SLon SRms WFar
duthieanus 'Boer'	see *C. apiculatus*
elatus	SRms
elegans	SRms
ellipticus	SRms
emeiensis	SRms

'Erlinda' — see *C.* x *suecicus* 'Erlinda'
falconeri — MGol SRms
fastigiatus — SRms
flinckii — SRms
floccosus — CSBt EBee GEil GKir LRHS MBri NWea SRms
floridus — SRms
forrestii — SRms
franchetii — CBcs CDul CSBt EBee EBre ECrN ELan EMil EPfP GIBF GKir LBuc LPan LRHS MGos MRav MSwo MWat MWgw NWea SLim SPer WCFE WDin WFar WGwG WHar WStI WTel WWeb
- var. *sternianus* — see *C. sternianus*
frigidus — CDul EBee NWea SRms
N - 'Cornubia' ♀H4 — More than 30 suppliers
- 'Fructu Luteo' — GKir MBri WWes
- 'Notcutt's Variety' — EBee ELan ENot MRav WWes
§ - 'Pershore Coral' — WSPU
- 'Saint Monica' — MBlu
froebelii — SRms
gamblei — WCwm
ganghobaensis — SRms
glabratus — SLPl SRms
glacialis — SRms
glaucophyllus — SEND SRms
§ *glomerulatus* — MBar SRms
gracia — SRms
gracilis — SRms
granatensis — SRms
harrovianus — NLar SLPl SRms
hedegaardii — SRms
yellow-fruited
henryanus — CDoC SRms
- 'Anne Cornwallis' — WBcn
'Herbstfeuer' — see *C. salicifolius* 'Herbstfeuer'
'Highlight' — see *C. pluriflorus*
hillieri — SRms
§ *hjelmqvistii* — LBuc SRms
- 'Robustus' — see *C. hjelmqvistii*
- 'Rotundifolius' — see *C. hjelmqvistii*
hodjingensis — SRms
horizontalis ♀H4 — More than 30 suppliers
- 'Peitz' — SRms
- 'Variegatus' — see *C. atropurpureus* 'Variegatus'
- var. *wilsonii* — see *C. ascendens*
hualiensis — SRms
humifusus — see *C. dammeri*
hummelii — CDul CPle SRms
hunanensis — SRms
§ 'Hybridus Pendulus' — More than 30 suppliers
§ *hylmoei* — SLPl SRms
hypocarpus — SRms
ignavus — SLPl SRms
ignescens — LRHS SPer
ignotus — SRms
incanus — SRms
induratus — GEil MBri SLPl SRms
insculptus — SRms
insolitus — SRms
integerrimus — SRms
- Mac&W 5916 from China — GIBF
§ *integrifolius* ♀H4 — CMHG EPfP EPla GKir LRHS MBar MWhi NBlu NMen SRms STre WMoo
kangdingensis — SRms
klotzii — SRms
kuanensis — SRms
lacteus ♀H4 — CDul CTri EBee ELan ENot EPfP EPla EWTr GKir LBuc LPan LRHS MGos MRav NBlu SEND SHBN SLon SPer SPla SRms WCFE WDin WFar XPep
- 'Variegatus' (v) — CEnd

lancasteri — SRms
langei — SRms
laxiflorus — SRms
lesliei — SRms
§ *lidjiangensis* — SRms WCot
§ *linearifolius* — CLyd EHol GEil GKir LRHS MWht SRms
lucidus — SRms
ludlowii — SRms
§ *mairei* — CSBt SRms
marginatus — SRms
marquandii — EPla SRms
§ *meiophyllus* — SRms
meuselii — SRms
microphyllus misapplied — see *C. purpurascens*
microphyllus Wall. ex Lindl. — CTri ENot GIBF MBar MGos NFor NScw NWea SDix SHBN SPer STre WDin WTel
- var. *cochleatus* — see *C. cochleatus*
- 'Donard Gem' — see *C. astrophoros*
- 'Ruby' — SRms
- 'Teulon Porter' — see *C. astrophoros*
- var. *thymifolius* misapplied — see *C. linearifolius*
- var. *thymifolius* (Lindl.) Koehne — see *C. integrifolius*
milkedandai — SRms
miniatus — SRms
mirabilis — SRms
moliensis Yu 14196 — GIBF
monopyrenus — SRms
'Mooncreeper' — see *C. dammeri* 'Mooncreeper'
morulus — SRms
moupinensis — SRms
mucronatus — SRms
multiflorus Bunge — SRms
'My Pet' — NLAp
§ *nanshan* — GEil NWea SRms WSPU
- 'Boer' — see *C. apiculatus*
newryensis — SRms
niger — GIBF
nitens — SRms
nitidifolius — see *C. glomerulatus*
nohelii — GIBF SRms
notabilis — SRms
nummarioides — SRms
nummularius — SRms
obscurus — SRms
obtusus — SRms
omissus — GIBF SRms
otto-schwarzii — SRms
pannosus — SLPl SRms WFar
- 'Speckles' — SRms
paradoxus — SRms
parkeri — SRms
pekinensis — SRms
permutatus — see *C. pluriflorus*
perpusillus — SRms WFar
'Pershore Coral' — see *C. frigidus* 'Pershore Coral'
§ *pluriflorus* — CDul GEil SRms
poluninii — SRms
polycarpus — SRms
praecox 'Boer' — see *C. apiculatus*
§ *procumbens* — EBee SRms WDin
- 'Queen of Carpets' — CDoC EBee GKir LRHS MAsh MBNS MGos MRav NHol SLim SRms SWvt WGwG
- 'Seattle' — SRms
- 'Streib's Findling' — see *C.* 'Streib's Findling'
prostratus — SRms
- 'Arnold Forster' — SRms
przewalskii — SRms
pseudo-obscurus — SRms
§ *purpurascens* — CSBt EBee MDun NHol WFar

	pyrenaicus	see *C. congestus*
	qungbixiensis	SRms
	racemiflorus	EHol
§	*radicans*	LRHS
§	- 'Eichholz'	EBee GKir IArd LRHS MGos WWeb
	rannensis	SRms
§	*rehderi*	SRms
	roseus	GIBF SRms
	'Rothschildianus'	see *C. salicifolius* 'Rothschildianus'
	rotundifolius	EBee SLon SRms
	'Royal Beauty'	see *C.* x *suecicus* 'Coral Beauty'
	rufus	SRms
	rugosus	SRms
	salicifolius	CLnd EMil GKir MSwo NBee SPer SRms WDin WFar
	- Autumn Fire	see *C. salicifolius* 'Herbstfeuer'
§	- 'Avonbank'	CDoC CEnd EBee MAsh WSPU
	- 'Bruno Orangeade'	SRms
	- 'Elstead'	MRav
	- 'Exburyensis'	CBcs CDoC EBee EPfP GKir LRHS MAsh MBri MGos SHBN SPer SPla WDin WFar WHCG WWin
	- 'Gnom'	EBee ELan EPfP GKir LRHS MAsh MBar MBlu MBri MGos MRav MWht NFor SRms WDin WFar
§	- 'Herbstfeuer'	EHol GKir MGos MRav MSwo SRms WDin WFar WRHF
	- 'Merriott Weeper'	CDoC
	- Park Carpet	see *C. salicifolius* 'Parkteppich'
§	- 'Parkteppich'	NWea SPer
	- 'Pendulus'	see *C.* 'Hybridus Pendulus'
	- 'Repens'	CDoC CWib EHol EPfP NScw NWea SPer SRms SSto WDin WFar
§	- 'Rothschildianus' ♀H4	CCVT CDoC CDul CSBt CTri CWib EBee EBre ECrN ECtt EMil ENot EPfP GKir LRHS MAsh MBar MRav MSwo NBlu SAga SLim SMac SPer SPla SWvt WMoo
	- var. *rugosus* hort.	see *C. hylmoei*
	- 'Scarlet Leader'	LRHS
	salwinensis	SLPl SRms
	sandakphuensis	SRms
	saxatilis	SRms
	scandinavicus	SRms
	schantungensis	SRms
	schubertii	SRms
	serotinus misapplied	see *C. meiophyllus*
	serotinus Hutchinson	CAbP SLPl SRms
	shannanensis	SRms
	shansiensis	LRHS SRms
	sherriffii	SRms
	sikangensis	GBin SLon SRms
	simonsii ♀H4	CDoC CLnd CTri EBee EBre ELan EPfP GKir LBuc LRHS MBar MGos NScw NWea SPoG SRms WDin WFar WHar
§	*splendens*	GEil GIBF WFar
	- 'Sabrina'	see *C. splendens*
	spongbergii	SRms
	staintonii	SRms
§	*sternianus* ♀H4	EPfP GKir LRHS MBar SLPl SRms
	- ACE 2200	EPot
	'Streib's Findling'	MAsh SRms
	subacutus	SRms
	subadpressus	SRms
§	x *suecicus* 'Coral Beauty'	More than 30 suppliers
§	- 'Erlinda' (v)	CEnd CWib EBee MBar SRms
	- 'Ifor'	SLPl SRms
	- 'Juliette' (v)	CWib MBar NBlu SLim WFar WOrn
	- 'Jürgl'	SRms
	- 'Skogholm'	CSBt CWSG CWib EBee GKir LRHS MBar MGos MWat NWea SPer SRms WDin WFar WHar WStl WWin
	taoensis	SRms

	tardiflorus	SRms
	tauricus	SRms
	teijiashanensis	SRms
	tengyuehensis	SRms
	thimphuensis	SRms
*	*thraciaensis*	SRms
	tomentosus	SRms
	trinervis	SRms
	- 'Bruno'	SRms
	tripyrenus	SRms
	tsarongensis	SRms
	turbinatus	SRms
	uzbezicus	SRms
	'Valkenburg'	SRms
	vandelaarii	SRms
	veitchii	NLar SRms
	verruculosus	SRms
	villosulus	EHol SRms
	vilmorinianus	SRms
	wardii misapplied	see *C. mairei*
	wardii W. W. Sm.	GIBF NBee
	x *watereri*	CCVT CDul CSBt CWib GEil LRHS MAsh MGos MSwo NWea WCFE WDin WTel
	- 'Avonbank'	see *C. salicifolius* 'Avonbank'
	- 'Coral Bunch' **new**	MBri
	- 'Corina'	SRms
	- 'Cornubia'	see *C. frigidus* 'Cornubia'
	- 'Goscote'	MGos
	- 'John Waterer' ♀H4	EPfP MGos WFar
	- 'Pendulus'	see *C.* 'Hybridus Pendulus'
	- 'Pink Champagne'	CAbP GEil GKir LRHS MBri SPer
	- 'Willeke'	SRms
	yakuticus	SRms
	yallungensis	SRms
	yinchangensis	SRms
	yui	SRms
	zabelii	GIBF SRms

Cotula (Asteraceae)

	C&H 452	NWCA
	atrata	see *Leptinella atrata*
	- var. *dendyi*	see *Leptinella dendyi*
	coronopifolia	CSev CWat LPBA MSta NBlu NPer SWat WWpP
§	*hispida*	More than 30 suppliers
	lineariloba	ECha EWes LBee LRHS
	minor	see *Leptinella minor*
	perpusilla	see *Leptinella pusilla*
	'Platt's Black'	see *Leptinella squalida* 'Platt's Black'
	potentilloides	see *Leptinella potentillina*
	pyrethrifolia	see *Leptinella pyrethrifolia*
	rotundata	see *Leptinella rotundata*
	sericea	see *Leptinella albida*
	serrulata	see *Leptinella serrulata*
	squalida	see *Leptinella squalida*

Cotyledon (Crassulaceae)

chrysantha	see *Rosularia chrysantha*
gibbiflora var. *metallica*	see *Echeveria gibbiflora* var. *metallica*
oppositifolia	see *Chiastophyllum oppositifolium*
orbiculata	CStu SDix SIgm
- B&SWJ 723	WCru
- var. *oblonga*	EBee EMan SChr WCot WEas
simplicifolia	see *Chiastophyllum oppositifolium*
undulata	WEas

Cowania (Rosaceae)

aff. *mexicana* B&SWJ 9040 **new**	WCru

Coxella (Apiaceae)

dieffenbachii	GCal

Crambe (Brassicaceae)

cordifolia ♀H4	More than 30 suppliers
koktebelica	GFlt
maritima ♀H4	More than 30 suppliers
- 'Lilywhite'	ILis LPio WCot WHer
orientalis	WCot
tatarica	CArn EMan NLar WPer

cranberry see *Vaccinium macrocarpon, V. oxycoccos*

Craspedia (Asteraceae)

alpina from Tasmania **new**	GGar

Crassula (Crassulaceae)

anomala	SChr
arborescens	SRms STre
argentea	see *C. ovata*
coccinea	CHEx CTrC WOld
falcata ♀H1	EShb IBlr MBri
justi-corderoyi	CHal
lactea	CHal STre
§ *milfordiae*	CTri GKir MBar MOne MWat NBir
	NJOw NLAp WPer
muscosa	SChr STre
obtusa	SRot
orbicularis **new**	EPem
§ *ovata* ♀H1	CHal EBak EPem MBri NPer SVen
	SWal
- 'Hummel's Sunset' (v) ♀H1	CHal EPem
* - *minima*	EPem
* - *nana*	STre
- 'Sunset' (v) **new**	SWal
- 'Variegata' (v)	CHal EBak WCot
pellucida	CHal
subsp. *marginalis*	
* - - 'Variegata' (v)	CHal
peploides	SChr
perforata	CHal
- 'Variegata' (v)	CHal
portulacea	see *C. ovata*
rupestris ♀H1	MBri
§ *sarcocaulis*	CHEx CHal CStu CTri ELan EMlt
	EOas ESis GGar GTou ITim MTho
	NMen NVic NWCA SIgm SIng SPlb
	SRms SRot SScr STre WAbe WEas
	WLow WPat WSHC WWin
- *alba*	CHal EMlt NJOw SHFr STre WPer
- 'Ken Aslet'	SPet STre
schmidtii	CHal MBri
sedifolia	see *C. milfordiae*
sediformis	see *C. milfordiae*
socialis	CHal WPat
tetragona	SEND
* *tomentosa* 'Variegata' (v)	EShb
'Très Bon'	STre

Crataegus ✿ (Rosaceae)

arnoldiana	CEnd CLnd CTho CTri ECrN EPfP
	GKir LRHS MBri MCoo MGos
	NWea SEND SKee SLPl WOrn
'Autumn Glory'	CEnd CLnd EBee ECrN GKir LRHS
	MGos
champlainensis	CLnd CTho
chlorosarca	GIBF
chungtienensis	CMCN GKir
- ACE 1624	SSpi
coccinea misapplied	see *C. biltmoreana, C. intricata,*
	C. pedicellata
coccinea ambig.	NWea

cordata	see *C. phaenopyrum*
crus-galli misapplied	see *C. persimilis* 'Prunifolia'
crus-galli L.	CCVT CDoC CDul CLnd CTho
	ECrN EPfP GKir LBuc LRHS MAsh
	SPer WDin
- var. *pyracanthifolia*	CLnd CTho
douglasii	GIBF
x *durobrivensis*	CLnd CTho GKir
ellwangeriana	CAgr CLnd CTho ECrN GKir
eriocarpa	CLnd
flabellata	CEnd GIBF GKir SSpi
gemmosa	CEnd CLnd CTho GKir NWea
greggiana	CLnd
x *grignonensis*	CBcs CCVT CDul CLnd ECrN EMil
	ENot MAsh SBLw SPer
jonesiae	EPfP
laciniata	see *C. orientalis*
§ *laevigata*	CDul NWea WMou
- 'Coccinea Plena'	see *C. laevigata* 'Paul's Scarlet'
- 'Crimson Cloud'	CDoC CEnd CLnd CWSG CWib
	EBee ECrN ELan EMui ENot EPfP
	GKir LRHS MAsh MBri MGos
	MSwo MWat NBlu NWea SCoo
	SKee SLim SLon SPer WOrn
- 'Flore Pleno'	see *C. laevigata* 'Plena'
- 'Mutabilis'	CLnd GKir SBLw SHBN
§ - 'Paul's Scarlet' (d) ♀H4	More than 30 suppliers
- 'Pink Corkscrew'	CTho GKir MBlu MGos WCot
	WPat WWes
§ - 'Plena' (d)	CBcs CDoC CDul CLnd CRez CSBt
	CTho CTri CWib EBee ECrN EWTr
	GKir LAst LPan LRHS MBri MSwo
	MWat NBee NWea SBLw SFam
	SHBN SKee SLim SPer WDin WOrn
- 'Punicea'	GKir
- 'Rosea'	SKee
- 'Rosea Flore Pleno' (d) ♀H4	CCVT CDoC CDul CLnd CSBt
	CTho CTri CWSG EBee EBre ECrN
	ELan ENot EPfP GKir LAst LBuc
	LRHS MBar MBri MDun MGos
	MSwo NWea SHBN SPer WDin
	WOrn WStI
x *lavalleei*	CCVT CDul CLnd CTri EBee ECrN
	ENot EPfP GKir LRHS MSwo NWea
	SKee SPer WDin
- 'Carrierei' ♀H4	CDoC CDul CTho ECrN EPfP GKir
	LPan LRHS MAsh MBri NWea
	SBLw SCoo SKee
maximowiczii	GIBF
x *media* 'Gireoudii' (v)	CDul CEnd CPMA CWib GKir
	GTSp MBlu MGos WPat
mexicana	see *C. pubescens* f. *stipulacea*
mollis	CTho ECrN EPfP NWea
monogyna	CBcs CCVT CDoC CDul CLnd
	CRWN ELan ENot EPfP GKir
	GWCH LBuc LRHS MBar MBri
	MGos NBee NBlu NWea SPer
	WDin WMou
§ - 'Biflora'	CDul CEnd CTho CTri EBee ECrN
	GKir LRHS MAsh MCoo MGos
	NWea SKee SLim WPGP WSPU
- 'Compacta'	MBlu SMad
- 'Ferox'	CTho
- 'Flexuosa'	MGos
- 'Praecox'	see *C. monogyna* 'Biflora'
- 'Stricta'	CCVT CDul CLnd CSBt CTho EBee
	ECrN ENot EPfP SBLw SPer
- 'Variegata' (v)	CDul ECrN WBcn WSPU
x *mordenensis*	CDoC CDul CLnd CTho SBLw
'Toba' (d)	
neofluvialis	GIBF
orientalis	CDul CEnd CLnd CMCN CTho
	CTri EBee ECrN EPfP GIBF GKir
	IArd LRHS MAsh MBri MCoo

	MGos NWea SHBN SKee SLPl SLim SPer SSpi WCFE WMou
oxyacantha	see *C. laevigata*
pedicellata	CLnd CTho EPfP GKir LRHS SKee
§ *persimilis* 'Prunifolia' ♀H4	More than 30 suppliers
- 'Prunifolia Splendens'	EWTr LPan SBLw
§ *phaenopyrum*	CDul CLnd CMCN CTho EPfP GIBF GKir SLPl SSpi
pinnatifida	SMad
- var. *major*	CEnd EPfP GKir NWea SKee SMad
- - 'Big Golden Star'	CAgr CTho ECrN ESim LRHS
'Praecox'	see *C. monogyna* 'Biflora'
prunifolia	see *C. persimilis* 'Prunifolia'
§ *pubescens* f. *stipulacea*	CDul SSpi
punctata	SLPl
sanguinea	GIBF
schraderiana	CLnd CTho
succulenta	GKir
var. *macracantha*	
tanacetifolia	CDul CLnd CTho ECrN GKir LRHS MBlu SPoG SSpi
uniflora	GIBF
viridis 'Winter King'	CDoC GKir LRHS MBlu SKee
wattiana	CTho

x *Crataemespilus* (*Rosaceae*)

grandiflora	CDul CTho GKir LRHS

Craterostigma (*Scrophulariaceae*)

wilmsii	SPlb

Crawfurdia (*Gentianaceae*)

speciosa B&SWJ 2138	WCru

Cremanthodium (*Asteraceae*)

sp.	EMan

Crenularia see *Aethionema*

Crepis (*Asteraceae*)

aurea	GAbr NJOw WCom
incana ♀H4	CFee CPla EGoo EMan GBri GKir GSki LPhx LRHS MAvo MTho NBid NChi NSla NWCA SIng SRms WAbe WPat WWin
rubra	LPio LRHS

Crinitaria see *Aster*

Crinodendron (*Elaeocarpaceae*)

§ *hookerianum* ♀H3	More than 30 suppliers
- 'Ada Hoffmann'	CPLG NLar
patagua	CBcs CPLG CPle CSam CStu CWib EBee GGar GQui IArd IDee LRHS MDun MLan SPer WAbe WBod WFar WSHC

Crinum (*Amaryllidaceae*)

amoenum	EUJe
asiaticum var. *sinicum*	CDes
§ *bulbispermum*	CFil CFir EBee ELan WCot
- 'Album'	EMan
§ *campanulatum*	EBee
capense	see *C. bulbispermum*
'Carolina Beauty'	WCot
'Ellen Bosanquet'	CDes CFir CKno EBee WCot WPGP
'Hanibal's Dwarf'	WCot
macowanii	WCot
moorei	CDes CFir EBee NRog SChr WPGP
- f. *album*	CAvo CFil EUJe WMul
§ x *powellii* ♀H3	More than 30 suppliers
- 'Album' ♀H3	CAvo CBct CDes CHEx CPne CTri

	EBee ECha ELan EMan EWes LAma LPhx LPio LRHS MOak MRav NRog SSpi WCot WCru WFar WPGP WPic WViv
- 'Harlemense'	SSpi
- 'Longifolium'	see *C. bulbispermum*
- 'Roseum'	see *C. x powellii*
variabile	WCot
yemense	WCot
zeylanicum **new**	EBee

Criogenes see *Cypripedium*

Crithmum (*Apiaceae*)

maritimum	CArn EBee GPoy MSal NLar NTHB SECG SIgm WBri WJek WWye XPep

Crocosmia ✿ (*Iridaceae*)

'Amberglow'	CElw CFwr CHar CMea EBee EWoo IBlr LAst MBNS MLan NPer WFar WSSM WWpP
'Anniversary'	SSpi
aurea misapplied	see *C. x crocosmiiflora* 'George Davison'
aurea ambig.	NBir SPlb
aurea Planchon	CPou CTCP NHol SSpi
- JCA 3.100.000	WCot
- var. *aurea*	GCal IBlr
aurea x *paniculata*	SWvt
Bressingham Beacon = 'Blos'	GGar GKir IBlr LRHS NHol WBea WRHF
'Bressingham Blaze'	CBre CMHG CPrp EBre GCal GKir IBlr LRHS NHol WCot WHil WWin
'Cadenza'	IBlr
'Carnival'	IBlr
'Cascade'	IBlr
'Chinatown'	IBlr WHil
'Comet' Knutty	GBuc IBlr NHol SIgm SSpi WHil WWhi
§ x *crocosmiiflora*	COIW EGra EPla IBlr LAst NOrc SIng SPlb SRms SWat WBrk WCHb WCot WFar WMoo WMyn WRHF WSSM WShi WWpP WWye
- 'A.J. Hogan'	IBal IBlr WHil
- 'Apricot Queen'	IBlr
- 'Baby Barnaby'	CAbx CBos CBre CKno EBee IBlr WPGP
- 'Babylon'	CBre CBro CFwr CPou EBee EChP ECtt EGra GBuc GKir IBlr MAvo MBNS MBri MTed NBir NGdn NHol SPet SSpi WCAu WFar WHil WLow WPer
- 'Burford Bronze'	IBlr WHil
- 'Buttercup'	CFwr EBee IBlr WBor
- 'Canary Bird'	CBro CCge CPrp CRow CSam EBee ECtt EGra GAbr GKir GMac IBlr LRHS NBPC NGdn NHol WHil WRHF
- 'Carmin Brillant' ♀H3-4	More than 30 suppliers
- 'Challa'	CFwr EBee
- 'Citronella' J.E. Fitt	CBro CCge CFwr CHar CPLG CPrp CSam CTri EBee EBre EChP EGra EHrv EPfP GKir LRHS NGdn NHol WBVN WCot WGMN WHoo WRha
- 'Columbus'	CFwr CM&M EBee EChP GMac LBBr LHop LRHS SSpe SVil WBor WCAu WLow WMnd
- 'Colwall'	CPou IBlr
- 'Constance'	CBre CBro CElw CFwr CSam EBee EChP EPot GKir IBlr LRHS MBNS MBri MNrw NCot NGdn NHol SRos WCHb WFar WHil
I - 'Corona'	IBlr WHil

– 'Corten'	IBlr
§ – 'Croesus'	CAbx EGra GBri IBlr MAvo MCLN MRav SCro WCot WHil
– 'Custard Cream'	GKir IBlr LRHS SRos WCot WFar WHil WOut
– 'D.H. Houghton'	IBlr
– 'Debutante'	CBos CMil IBlr MAvo MBnl SOkh WCot WSHC WWhi
– 'Dusky Maiden'	More than 30 suppliers
§ – 'E.A. Bowles'	CAbx CPou EBee GCal IBlr WCot
– 'Eastern Promise'	CBre CMea EBee GKir IBlr SMrm
– 'Elegans'	CBre CElw CStr ECtt IBlr
§ – 'Emily McKenzie'	More than 30 suppliers
– 'Etoile de Feu'	IBlr
– 'Fantasie'	CFwr EBee MBNS
– 'Firebrand'	CBos IBlr
– 'Flamethrower'	IBlr
§ – 'George Davison' Davison	More than 30 suppliers
§ – 'Gerbe d'Or'	More than 30 suppliers
– 'Gloria'	CPen IBlr
§ – 'Golden Glory'	CBri CHar CPrp CSBt CSam EBre EFou EHrv GFlt GKir IBlr MAvo MSwo NBid NBir NChi NHol NPPs SRos WBrE WCot WCra WFar WHil WLin WWeb
– 'Golden Sheaf'	GBri IBlr NGdn NHol SDys SUsu WBea
– 'Goldfinch'	IBlr WHil
– 'Hades'	IBlr
– 'His Majesty'	CBro CMil CPne CPou CRow CSam CSpe EBee GKir IBlr LRHS SAga SCro SDys WFar WHil WPer WWhi
§ – 'Jackanapes'	CBos CBro CFwr CMil CPrp CRow EBre EGra EHrv EPfP GCal GKir IBlr LRHS MBri NHol SDys SUsu WBro WHil WPnP WWeb WWhi WWpP WWye
– 'James Coey' J.E. Fitt	CHad CHar CM&M COlW CRow ECha ECha EHrv EPfP GCal GEil GGar GMac GSki LAma LAst LRHS MCLN MDun NDov NGdn NHol NPPs SIng SMrm SWvt WFar WOld WViv
* – 'Jesse van Dyke'	IBlr
§ – 'Jessie'	CElw CFwr EBee GCal IBlr WCot WHil WPer WWpP
– 'Kiatschou'	EBee EGra GMac IBlr LEur SDys
– 'Lady Hamilton'	More than 30 suppliers
– 'Lady McKenzie'	see *C.* x *crocosmiiflora* 'Emily McKenzie'
– 'Lady Oxford'	EBre EGra EMan GCal IBlr LRHS
– 'Lutea'	EBre ECtt EGra IBlr
– 'Marjorie'	LAma NHol WCot
– 'Mephistopheles'	IBlr
– 'Météore'	CFwr EBee GGar LAst MBNS NHol NOrc WWeb
– 'Morning Light'	CBos CPen ECtt IBlr MAvo MBnl SOkh WCot
§ – 'Mrs Geoffrey Howard'	CBos CPlt CSam EBee ECtt EGra GBri IBlr NCGa SUsu WCru WPGP WWhi
– 'Mrs Morrison'	see *C.* x *crocosmiiflora* 'Mrs Geoffrey Howard'
– 'Newry seedling'	see *C.* x *crocosmiiflora* 'Prometheus'
– 'Nimbus'	GBri IBlr WCot
§ – 'Norwich Canary'	More than 30 suppliers
I – 'Pepper'	IBlr
– 'Polo'	CFwr EBee
– 'Princess'	see *C.* x *crocosmiiflora* 'Red Knight'
– 'Princess Alexandra'	IBlr WCHb

– 'Prolificans'	IBlr
§ – 'Prometheus'	IBlr WHil
– 'Queen Alexandra' J.E. Fitt	EChP ECha IBlr LAma LHop NCGa SOkh SWat WHal WPer
– 'Queen Charlotte'	IBlr
– 'Queen Mary II'	CAvo CPar EMan IBlr WHil WWpP
– 'Queen of Spain'	CCge CPrp GKir IBlr LRHS MBri MDKP MLLN SCro SOkh SWat WHil WViv
– 'Rayon d'Or'	IBlr
– 'Red King'	CFwr CHar EBee EBla GGar IBlr LAst WWeb
§ – 'Red Knight'	CM&M IBlr MAvo MTed NHol WCot WSSM
– 'Rheingold'	see *C.* x *crocosmiiflora* 'Golden Glory'
– 'Rose Queen'	IBlr
– 'Saracen'	EBee EChP EMan GCal GMac IBal IBlr LAst MBNS MBnl SIgm SMad SMrm SOkh SPla SSpi WCot WFar
– 'Sir Matthew Wilson'	GBri IBlr WCot
– 'Solfatare' ♥H3	More than 30 suppliers
– 'Solfatare Coleton Fishacre'	see *C.* x *crocosmiiflora* 'Gerbe d'Or'
– 'Star of the East' ♥H3	More than 30 suppliers
§ – 'Sulphurea'	CPLG CPou CRow CSam EBee EGra EOrc GCal GGar GKir IBlr LAma NHol NPPs SDix SIng WAbe WBrk WCot WEas WHal WHil WPer
– 'Sultan'	CBro CCge CElw EBee IBlr LPio SOkh WCot WFar WPGP
– 'Venus'	CAbx CBre CFwr CPen CPou EBee EBre ECtt EGra GBuc IBlr LRHS NHol SRos STes WFar WLin WOut
– 'Vesuvius' W. Pfitzer	CElw GCal GKir IBlr WFar
'Culzean Peach'	GAbr GCal GFlt MRav NBir NPPs SMrm WCot WGMN
'Darkleaf Apricot'	see *C.* x *crocosmiiflora* 'Gerbe d'Or'
'Devil's Advocate' **new**	NHol
'Eclatant'	IBlr
'Eldorado'	see *C.* x *crocosmiiflora* 'E.A. Bowles'
'Emberglow'	More than 30 suppliers
'Fandango'	IBlr
'Festival Orange'	MAvo
* 'Feuerser'	NHol
'Fire King' misapplied	see *C.* x *crocosmiiflora* 'Jackanapes'
'Fire Sprite'	IBlr
'Firebird'	GBuc IBlr IGor LRHS MBri NHol SIgm SMer SRos WBea WCot
'Firefly' **new**	IBlr
'Fireglow'	ECtt EGra IBlr WFar WPer
fucata 'Jupiter'	see *C.* 'Jupiter'
* 'Fusilade'	IBlr
'George Davison' hort.	see *C.* x *crocosmiiflora* 'Golden Glory', 'Sulphurea'
Golden Fleece Lemoine	see *C.* x *crocosmiiflora* 'Gerbe d'Or'
'Goldsprite'	IBlr
'Highlight'	IBlr WHil
§ 'Honey Angels'	More than 30 suppliers
'Honey Bells' **new**	WBrk
'Irish Dawn'	EBre
'Irish Flame' **new**	EBre
'Irish Sunset' **new**	EBre
'Jennine'	NHol WHil
Jenny Bloom = 'Blacro'[PBR]	CHar CM&M EBee EBre ECtt GBuc GKir GSki LRHS NBir SMHy STes
'John Boots'	CFwr CPen CRez EBee EChP EHrv EPot GBuc LBBr MBNS NHol SMrm WBea WBor WCot WHil

§ 'Jupiter' — CBos CBot CBre CM&M CPou CWCL EBee EFou GBuc GMac IBlr LRHS NHol SMrm WCot WFar WGwG WLin WOld

'Kiaora' — IBlr

'Lady Wilson' hort. — see *Tritonia disticha* subsp. *rubrolucens*

'Lambrook Gold' — CAvo

'Lana de Savary' — CPen EMan GCal GEil IBlr WCot

'Late Cornish' — see *C.* × *crocosmiiflora* 'Queen Alexandra'

'Late Lucifer' — CHEx CTri CWCL GCal SDix

§ *latifolia* — IBlr

– 'Castle Ward Late' — CAbx CPou CRow ECha EFou EGra GBuc GCal GGar IBlr MNFA MSte WMoo WSHC

– 'Vulcan' T.Smith — GKir IBlr

'Loweswater' — MAvo WCot

'Lucifer' ♀H4 — More than 30 suppliers

'Mandarin' — IBlr

§ 'Marcotijn' — EBee EChP ECtt EGra EMan GCal GEil IBlr IGor MAvo NChi WGwG

'Mars' — CElw CFwr EBee EBla ECtt EGra EWes GBuc GCal GGar GMac IBlr LRHS MAnH NHol SPlb WCAu WCHb WFar WOld WPGP WPer

§ *masoniorum* ♀H3 — More than 30 suppliers

– 'Auricorn' — IBlr

– 'Dixter Flame' — IBlr SDix

– 'Fern Hill' — IBlr

– 'Flamenco' — GKir IBlr MTed

– 'Minotaur' — IBlr

– red — CHar IBlr

– Rowallane orange — IBlr MAvo NHol

– 'Rowallane Yellow' ♀H3-4 — CPen EBre GBri GKir IBlr LRHS MAvo MBri NHol SRos WCot WHil

mathewsiana — IBlr

'Merryman' — WWpP

'Mistral' — CAbx CFwr CSBt EBee EChP GBuc IBlr LRHS MAvo MNrw WBor WCot WFar WLin WMoo WWpP

'Moira Reed' **new** — NHol

'Mount Stewart' — see *C.* × *crocosmiiflora* 'Jessie'

'Mount Usher' — EGra GCal IBlr MAvo NHol WOut

'Mr Bedford' — see *C.* × *crocosmiiflora* 'Croesus'

Old Hat — see *C.* 'Walberton Red'

'Orange Devil' — CBre MBri WWpP

'Orange Lucifer' — EFou

'Orange Spirit' **new** — WFar

'Orangeade' — CAvo CHar EBee ECtt EGra GBri IBlr NHol

§ *paniculata* — CBcs CElw CHEx CPou EBla EChP ECtt GAbr GGar LRHS MNFA MNrw NBid NHol NOrc SAPC SChu SPet WBrk WCot WMoo WPen WSHi WTin

– brown/orange — IBlr

– 'Major' — CTri IBlr

– red — CPLG EBre GKir IBlr SWvt

* – 'Ruby Velvet' — IBlr

– triploid **new** — IBlr

aff. *paniculata* — ECtt IBlr

paniculata — IBlr
   × *masoniorum*
   'Shocking'

pearsei — IBlr

'Phillipa Browne' **new** — WCot

'Plaisir' — CFwr CRez EBee EPot IBlr MBNS WFar

§ *pottsii* — CAvo CFee CRow EChP ECtt GBin GMac IBlr LEur LHop NHol WFar

– CD&R 109 — CBre CPou

– 'Culzean Pink' — CPom EBre GBuc GKir IBlr LRHS WHil

– deep pink — IBlr IGor WSHC

– 'Grandiflora' — IBlr

– 'Lady Bangor' — ECtt

'Red Devils' **new** — NHol

rosea — see *Tritonia disticha* subsp. *rubrolucens*

'Rowden Bronze' — see *C.* × *crocosmiiflora* 'Gerbe d'Or'

'Rowden Chrome' — see *C.* × *crocosmiiflora* 'George Davison'

'Rubygold' — IBlr

'Sabena' **new** — WCot

'Saturn' — see *C.* 'Jupiter'

'Scarlatti' — IBlr WHil

'Severn Sunrise' ♀H3-4 — More than 30 suppliers

'Son of Lucifer' **new** — WFar

'Sonate' — ECtt NCot NGby NHol SPlb WPer

'Spitfire' — More than 30 suppliers

'Sunset' — GSki

'Sunzest' — WFar

'Tangerine Queen' — CAbx CPen CPlt ECtt EGra IBlr WCot WWpP

* 'Tiger' — CElw IBlr

'Vic's Yellow' — SGar SMrm SSpe

* 'Voyager' — CFwr EBee GKir IBlr LRHS MBow NPPs WHil

I 'Vulcan' A.Bloom — CMdw CPen CWSG EBre IBlr LRHS SAga WCot WFar WHil WWhi

§ 'Walberton Red' — CFwr IBlr MAvo MBri SAga SUsu

Walberton Yellow — CFwr SMHy SSpi WCot
   = 'Walcroy'PBR

'Zeal Giant' — IBlr

'Zeal Tan' — CElw CPen CSam EBee EChP ELan EMan GCal IBlr LAst MAvo MBNS MBnl MLLN SMad SPla WCAu WCot

Zeal unnamed — IBlr

Crocus ✿ (*Iridaceae*)

abantensis — EPot ERos

adanensis — ERos

alatavicus — WWst

albiflorus — see *C. vernus* subsp. *albiflorus*

§ *ancyrensis* — EHyt EPar EPot LAma NGar NRog

– 'Golden Bunch' — EPfP LPhx LRHS WShi

§ *angustifolius* ♀H4 — CBro EPot ERos GIBF LAma NRog

– 'Minor' — EPot LAma

antalyensis — EPot

asturicus — see *C. serotinus* subsp. *salzmannii*

asumaniae — ECho EPot ERos

aureus — see *C. flavus* subsp. *flavus*

banaticus ♀H4 — CAvo CBro EHyt EPot ERos GCrs GEdr LAma NGar WWst

– *albus* — ERos NGar

baytopiorum — EPot ERos

biflorus — LAma NRog

– subsp. *adamii* — ERos

– subsp. *alexandri* — EPot ERos LAma LRHS NRog

§ – subsp. *biflorus* — ERos LAma

§ – – 'Parkinsonii' — ERos

– subsp. *crewei* — ERos

– subsp. *isauricus* — ERos

– subsp. *melantherus* — ERos

– – JCA 341.353 — WCot

– 'Miss Vain' — CAvo EPot LAma LRHS

– var. *parkinsonii* — see *C. biflorus* subsp. *biflorus* 'Parkinsonii'

– subsp. *tauri* — WWst

– subsp. *weldenii* 'Albus' — EPot ERos LAma

– – 'Fairy' — CBro EPot ERos LAma LRHS

'Big Boy' — EHyt

boryi — CAvo EHyt

cambessedesii — ERos SBla

§ *cancellatus* — ERos LAma
   subsp. *cancellatus*

- var. *cilicicus* — see *C. cancellatus* subsp. *cancellatus*
- subsp. *mazziaricus* — CNic ERos
- subsp. *pamphylicus* — ERos
candidus var. *subflavus* — see *C. olivieri* subsp. *olivieri*
§ *cartwrightianus* ♀H4 — CAvo CBro EPot LAma
- 'Albus' Tubergen ♀H4 — EPot ERos
- 'Albus' misapplied — see *C. hadriaticus*
chrysanthus 'Advance' — CBro EPar EPfP EPot LAma NRog SPer
- 'Ard Schenk' — EPot LAma LRHS
- 'Aubade' — EPot
- 'Blue Bird' — CBro EPar EPot LAma LRHS
- 'Blue Pearl' — CAvo CBro EPar EPfP EPot LAma LPhx LRHS MBri NBir NRog SPer WShi
- 'Blue Peter' — LAma
- 'Brass Band' — LAma LRHS
- 'Cream Beauty' ♀H4 — CAvo CBro CMea EPar EPot LAma LPhx LRHS MBri NBir NRog SPer
- 'Dorothy' — EPot LAma LRHS NRog
- 'E.A. Bowles' ♀H4 — ECho LAma
- 'E.P. Bowles' — CBro EPot LAma LRHS MBri NRog
- 'Elegance' — LAma LRHS
- 'Eye-catcher' — EPot LAma LRHS
- var. *fuscotinctus* — EPot LAma MBri NRog
- 'Gipsy Girl' — CBro EPot LAma LRHS MBri NRog
- 'Goldilocks' — EPot LAma LRHS
- 'Herald' — EPot LAma LRHS
- 'Jeannine' **new** — EPot
- 'Ladykiller' ♀H4 — CAvo CBro EPar EPot LAma LRHS MBri NRog
- 'Moonlight' — LAma LRHS NRog
- 'Prins Claus' — EPot LAma
- 'Prinses Beatrix' — EPot LAma LRHS NRog
- 'Romance' — CAvo EPot LAma LRHS SPer
- 'Saturnus' — EPot LAma NRog
- 'Skyline' — CBro EPot LRHS
- 'Snow Bunting' ♀H4 — CAvo CBro EPar EPfP EPot LAma LPhx LRHS NBir NRog WShi
- 'Spring Pearl' — CBro LAma LRHS
- 'Sunspot' **new** — EPot
- 'Uschak Orange' **new** — EPot WWst
- 'Warley' — NRog
- 'White Beauty' — LAma
- 'White Triumphator' — CBro LAma NBir NRog
- 'Zenith' — LAma
- 'Zwanenburg Bronze' ♀H4 — EPar EPfP EPot LAma LRHS NRog
'Cloth of Gold' — see *C. angustifolius*
clusii — see *C. serotinus* subsp. *clusii*
corsicus ♀H4 — EPot ERos LAma
dalmaticus — EPot LAma
- 'Petrovac' — WWst
danfordiae — ERos ETow
'Dutch Yellow' — see *C.* x *luteus* 'Golden Yellow'
etruscus ♀H4 — ERos
- 'Rosalind' — EPot WLin
- 'Zwanenburg' — EPot LAma WCot
flavus — see *C. flavus* subsp. *flavus*
§ - subsp. *flavus* ♀H4 — EPot GIBF LAma LRHS WCot WShi
fleischeri — EPot ERos LAma NGar
gargaricus — ERos SCnR
- subsp. *gargaricus* — ERos
- subsp. *herbertii* — WWst
'Golden Mammoth' — see *C.* x *luteus* 'Golden Yellow'
goulimyi ♀H4 — CAvo CBro EPar EPot ERos LAma LRHS SIgm SSpi WCom WCot
§ - subsp. *goulimyi* ♀H4 — EHyt ERos
'Mani White' ♀H4
- subsp. *leucanthus* — EHyt
graveolens — EPot
'Haarlem Gem' — LAma
§ *hadriaticus* ♀H4 — CAvo ERos LAma

- var. *chrysobelonicus* — see *C. hadriaticus*
imperati ♀H4 — ERos
- subsp. *imperati* — CAvo EPot LAma LRHS
'De Jager'
- subsp. *suaveolens* — ERos
x *jessoppiae* — ERos WWst
karduchorum — CBro EPot LAma
korolkowii — EPar ERos GIBF LAma LPhx LRHS
- 'Golden Nugget' — GCrs
- 'Kiss of Spring' — EPot
- 'Unicoloratus' — WWst
kosaninii — EPot ERos
kotschyanus ♀H4 — ECho EPar NRya
- 'Albus' — ECho EHyt LRHS
§ - subsp. *kotschyanus* — CBro EPot LAma NRog
- var. *leucopharynx* — LRHS
laevigatus ♀H4 — LAma
- 'Fontenayi' — CBro EHyt EPot LAma LEdu WPnP
- from Crete — EHyt
'Large Yellow' — see *C.* x *luteus* 'Golden Yellow'
ligusticus — EPar
longiflorus ♀H4 — CAvo CBro EPot ERos GEdr WCot
§ x *luteus* 'Golden Yellow' ♀H4 — EPfP EPot LAma WShi
§ - 'Stellaris' — EPot ERos
malyi ♀H2-4 — EHyt ERos GCrs
'Mammoth Yellow' — see *C.* x *luteus* 'Golden Yellow'
mathewii JCA 347.910 — WCot
medius ♀H4 — CBro EPot ERos LAma
michelsonii — WWst
minimus — CBro CMea EHyt EPot ERos LAma LRHS NGar
niveus — CAvo CBro EHyt EPot ERos LAma SSpi WCot
nudiflorus — CAvo CBro ERos LAma NMen WCot WShi
ochroleucus ♀H4 — CBro EPot ERos LAma LRHS
olivieri — ERos LAma
- subsp. *balansae* — EPot
'Zwanenburg'
§ - subsp. *olivieri* — EHyt EPot ERos LAma LRHS
pallasii subsp. *pallasii* — ERos
pestalozzae — EHyt ERos
* - var. *caeruleus* — EHyt EPot ERos
pulchellus ♀H4 — ECho EPot ERos GCrs LAma LPhx MBow
- *albus* — EPot
'Purpureus' — see *C. vernus* 'Purpureus Grandiflorus'
reticulatus — WWst
subsp. *hittiticus*
- subsp. *reticulatus* — EPot
robertianus — EHyt
rujanensis — ERos
salzmannii — see *C. serotinus* subsp. *salzmannii*
sativus — CArn CAvo CBod CBro ELan EOHP EPar EPot GPoy LAma LPhx LRHS MBri MSal NBir NGHP NRog
- var. *cartwrightianus* — see *C. cartwrightianus*
- var. *cashmirianus* — LPhx
scepusiensis — see *C. vernus* subsp. *vernus* var. *scepusiensis*
§ *serotinus* subsp. *clusii* — CBro EHyt EPot LAma
§ - subsp. *salzmannii* — CBro EPar EPot ERos LAma LRHS
sibiricus — see *C. sieberi*
§ *sieberi* ♀H4 — EPot ERos
§ - 'Albus' ♀H4 — CAvo CBro ECho EHyt EPot LAma LRHS WLin
- subsp. *atticus* — LAma LRHS
- 'Bowles' White' — see *C. sieberi* 'Albus'
- 'Firefly' — CBro EPot LAma LRHS NRog
- 'Hubert Edelsten' ♀H4 — EHyt EPot ERos LAma
- subsp. *sublimis* — CAvo CBro ECho EHyt EPot ERos
'Tricolor' ♀H4 — GCrs LAma LRHS NMen WCot

- 'Violet Queen'	CBro EPot LAma LRHS MBri NRog
speciosus ♀H4	CAvo CBro EPar EPot LAma LRHS MBro NRog WCot WHoo WShi
- 'Aitchisonii'	CBro EPot LAma LRHS
- 'Albus' ♀H4	CBro EPar EPot LRHS
- 'Artabir'	CBro EPot LRHS
- 'Cassiope'	EPot LAma LRHS
- 'Conqueror'	CBro LAma LRHS
- 'Oxonian'	EPot LAma LPhx LRHS
x *stellaris*	see *C.* x *luteus* 'Stellaris'
susianus	see *C. angustifolius*
suterianus	see *C. olivieri* subsp. *olivieri*
tommasinianus ♀H4	CAvo CBro CMea ECho EPar EPot LAma MBri MRav SRms WShi
- f. *albus*	EHyt EPot LAma LRHS WCom
- 'Barr's Purple'	EPot LAma LRHS
- 'Eric Smith'	CAvo
- 'Lilac Beauty'	EPot LAma
- var. *pictus*	CAvo EPot ERos LAma WCom
- var. *roseus*	CMea EHyt EPot ERos LAma LPhx WCom WCot
- 'Ruby Giant'	CAvo CBro CNic EHyt EPar EPfP EPot LAma LRHS NRog SPer WShi
- subsp. *tommasinianus*	GIBF
- 'Whitewell Purple'	CAvo CBro ECho EPot LAma LPhx LRHS MBri NRog WCot WShi
tournefortii ♀H2-4	CAvo CBro EHyt ERos LAma WCot WWst
§ 'Vanguard'	CAvo CBro EPot LAma LPhx NRog
veluchensis	EPot WCot
§ *vernus* subsp. *albiflorus*	EPot ERos LAma
- 'Enchantress'	EPot LAma
- 'Flower Record'	EPfP EPot NBir
- 'Glory of Sassenheim' **new**	EPot
- 'Graecus'	EPot ERos
- 'Grand Maître'	LAma
- 'Haarlem Gem'	EPot
- 'Jeanne d'Arc'	CAvo CBro EPfP EPot LAma LPhx NBir NRog WShi
- 'King of the Blues'	NRog
- 'Negro Boy'	EPot
- 'Paulus Potter'	EPot
- 'Peter Pan'	NRog
- 'Pickwick'	EPfP EPot LAma NBir NRog WShi
§ - 'Purpureus Grandiflorus'	CBro EPot LAma NRog
- 'Queen of the Blues'	CAvo CBro EPot LPhx NRog
- 'Remembrance'	EPfP EPot LAma LPhx NBir NRog WShi
- 'Sky Blue'	NRog
- 'Snowstorm'	LAma
- 'Striped Beauty'	LAma NRog
- 'Twinborn' **new**	EPot
- 'Vanguard'	see *C.* 'Vanguard'
- subsp. *vernus*	see *C. vernus* 'Purpureus Grandiflorus'
'Grandiflorus'	Grandiflorus'
§ - - Heuffelianus Group	EPot GCrs WWst
- - var. *neapolitanus*	ERos
- - 'Oradea'	WWst
§ - - var. *scepusiensis*	EPot ERos
- 'White Christmas' **new**	EPot
* *versicolor*	EHyt
- 'Picturatus'	EPot ERos LAma LRHS WLin
'Yellow Mammoth'	see *C.* x *luteus* 'Golden Yellow'
'Zephyr' ♀H4	CBro EPot ERos LAma LRHS
zonatus	see *C. kotschyanus* subsp. *kotschyanus*

Croomia (Stemonaceae)

heterosepala	WCru

Crowea (Rutaceae)

exalata x *saligna*	CPLG

Crucianella (Rubiaceae)

maritima **new**	XPep
stylosa	see *Phuopsis stylosa*

Cruciata (Rubiaceae)

§ *laevipes*	CNat NMir

Cryptanthus (Bromeliaceae)

bivittatus ♀H1	CHal
- 'Roseus Pictus'	CHal
bromelioides	MBri

Cryptogramma (Adiantaceae)

crispa	SRms WHer

Cryptomeria (Cupressaceae)

fortunei	see *C. japonica* var. *sinensis*
japonica ♀H4	CDul CTho GKir ISea NBea STre WEve WNor
- Araucarioides Group	EHul IArd LCon NLar
- 'Bandai' **new**	LBuc
- 'Bandai-sugi' ♀H4	CDoC CKen CMac EHul EOrn EPfP LCon LLin LRHS MBar MGos MOne NDlv SLim STre WEve WGor WStI
- 'Barabits Gold'	GTSp MGos
- 'Compressa'	CDoC CFee CKen CSli EBre EHul EPfP ESis LBee LLin LRHS MAsh MBar MGos SLim
§ - 'Cristata'	CDoC CMac ECho ELan EOrn LCon MBar NPal
* - 'Cristata Compacta'	EOrn
- Elegans Group	CBcs CBrm CMac CSBt CTri EBre EHul ELan ENot EOrn EPfP GKir LCon LLin LPan MBar MGos MWat SHBN SKee SLim SPer WDin WFar
- 'Elegans Aurea'	CBcs CDoC CTri EHul LCon LLin MAsh MBar SPoG STre WDin WEve WStI
- 'Elegans Compacta' ♀H4	CBrm CDoC CSBt CWib EBre EHul EOrn GBin IMGH LBee LCon LRHS MAsh MBNS MBar MBri SLim SPoG WBVN WEve
- 'Elegans Nana'	EBre LBee LRHS SLim SRms
- 'Elegans Viridis'	EBre ELan LBuc LRHS SCoo SLim SPer
- 'Globosa'	EOrn
- 'Globosa Nana' ♀H4	CBrm ECho EHul ERom LBee LCon LLin LPan LRHS MAsh MBar NDlv SHBN SLim SPoG WFar WGor
- 'Golden Promise'	EBre EOrn MAsh MBri SCoo SLim WEve WGor
- 'Jindai-sugi'	CMac MBar NDlv NLar WEve
- 'Kilmacurragh'	CDoC CKen EHul MBar NWea SLim
- 'Knaptonensis' (v)	CDoC LLin
- 'Kohui Yatsubusa'	CKen ECho
* - 'Konijn Yatsubusa'	CKen
- 'Koshiji-yatsubusa'	EOrn MBar
- 'Koshyi'	CKen
- 'Little Champion'	CKen NLar SLim
- 'Little Diamond'	CKen
- 'Littleworth Dwarf'	see *C. japonica* 'Littleworth Gnom'
§ - 'Littleworth Gnom'	LLin
- 'Lobbii Nana' hort.	see *C. japonica* 'Nana'
§ - 'Mankichi-sugi'	NLar
- 'Monstrosa'	MBar
- 'Monstrosa Nana'	see *C. japonica* 'Mankichi-sugi'
§ - 'Nana'	CDoC CMac CTri EBre EGra EHul EOrn EPfP LCon LLin LRHS MOne SCoo WFar

- 'Pipo'	CKen
- 'Pygmaea'	LCon LLin MBar MGos SRms
- 'Rasen-sugi'	COtt LBuc LCon LLin NPal SCoo SLim SMad
- 'Sekkan-sugi'	CBcs CSli EBre EHul EOrn LBee LCon LLin LRHS MAsh MBar MGos NLar SCoo SLim WEve WFar
- 'Sekka-sugi'	see *C. japonica* 'Cristata'
§ - var. **sinensis**	CMCN NOGN WPGP
* - - 'Vilmoriniana Compacta'	EOrn
§ - 'Spiralis'	CDoC CKen CMac EBre EHul EOrn EPfP LBee LCon LLin LRHS MAsh MBar SCoo SLim SPer SPla SPoG WEve WFar
§ - 'Spiraliter Falcata'	CDoC LBuc MBar NLar
§ - 'Tansu'	CKen ECho EHul EOrn LCon LLin MBar
- 'Tenzan-sugi'	CKen LLin SOkd
- 'Tilford Cream'	MAsh
- 'Tilford Gold'	EHul EOrn LLin MBar MGos NDlv NHol WBcn WEve WFar
- 'Vilmorin Gold'	CKen EOrn WEve
- 'Vilmoriniana' ♀H4	CDoC CKen CMHG CNic CSli EBre EHul ENot EOrn EPfP EPot IMGH LBee LCon LLin LRHS MAsh MBar MGos NHol SAga SHBN SLim SPer WDin WEve WFar
- 'Viminalis'	NHol
- 'Winter Bronze'	CKen
- 'Yatsubusa'	see *C. japonica* 'Tansu'
- 'Yore-sugi'	see *C. japonica* 'Spiralis', 'Spiraliter Falcata'
- 'Yoshino'	CKen
sinensis	see *C. japonica* var. *sinensis*

Cryptotaenia (*Apiaceae*)

canadensis	EBee MRav
japonica	CAgr CPou MHer MSal WHer WJek
- f. **atropurpurea**	CFwr CHar CPla CSpe ECha ECoo EGle EHoe EMan EMon GCal GGar ITer LDai LPVe LPhx LRHS LSpr MFir MNrw MWrn NSti NVic SBla WCHb WCru WEas WFar WWhi

Ctenanthe (*Marantaceae*)

§ **amabilis** ♀H1	CHal
lubbersiana ♀H1	CHal
§ **oppenheimiana**	LRHS

Cucubalus (*Caryophyllaceae*)

baccifer	EBee GFlt GIBF NLar WPer

Cudrania see *Maclura*

cumin see *Cuminum cyminum*

Cuminum (*Apiaceae*)

cyminum	CArn SIde WHHs

Cunninghamia (*Cupressaceae*)

§ **lanceolata**	CBcs CDoC CDul CMCN CTho EBre IArd IDee LCon LLin LRHS MBlu MBro SAPC SArc SCoo SLim SMad SSta STre WEve WNor WPGP
§ - 'Bánó'	CMac MBro
- 'Compacta'	see *C. lanceolata* 'Bánó'
- 'Little Leo'	CKen
sinensis	see *C. lanceolata*
unicaniculata	see *C. lanceolata*

Cunonia (*Cunoniaceae*)

capensis	CTrC EShb

Cuphea (*Lythraceae*)

blepharophylla **new**	LRav
caeciliae	CHal MOak WBor
cyanaea	CMHG CPLG MLLN MOak SDix SIgm SOWG SSte
glutinosa	ITer
hirtella	LHop MOak SDys SOWG SSte
aff. **hookeriana** B&SWJ 9039 **new**	WCru
hyssopifolia ♀H1	CFee CHal CHll ESlt MBri MOak SOWG SRms STre SWvt
- 'Alba'	LIck MOak SOWG STre SWvt
- 'Riverdene Gold'	CHal EMan
- 'Rosea'	LIck SWvt
§ **ignea** ♀H1	CHal ELan EShb MBri MLLN MOak SOWG SRms
- 'Variegata' (v)	CHal MOak SOWG
§ **llavea** 'Georgia Scarlet'	EBee LAst LIck MOak NPri SSte SUsu
- 'Tiny Mice'	see *C. llavea* 'Georgia Scarlet'
macrophylla hort.	CHll MOak
melvilla	ERea
platycentra	see *C. ignea*

x *Cupressocyparis* ✿ (*Cupressaceae*)

§ **leylandii** ♀H4	CBcs CChe CDoC CDul CMac EBre EHul ENot EPfP GKir LBuc LPan LRHS MAsh MBar MBri MGos NBlu NWea SLim SPer SWvt WDin WEve WHar WMou WStI
§ - 'Castlewellan'	CBcs CChe CDoC CDul CMac EBre EHul ENot EPfP ERom GKir LBuc LPan LRHS MAsh MBar MBri MGos MWat NBlu NWea SLim SPer SWvt WDin WEve WFar WHar WMou WStI
- 'Galway Gold'	see x *C. leylandii* 'Castlewellan'
- 'Gold Rider' ♀H4	CDoC EHul LBee LPan MAsh MBar MBri MGos NMoo SCoo SLim SPer SWvt WDin WEve WHar
§ - 'Harlequin' (v)	LRHS MBar SLim SWvt
- 'Herculea'	CDoC LPan MAsh
- 'Hyde Hall'	CTri EOrn EPla LBee
- 'Naylor's Blue'	CMac SEND
- 'New Ornament'	SMad
- 'Olive's Green'	CDoC EHul LPan SCoo SWvt
- 'Robinson's Gold' ♀H4	CMac EHul GQui LBee MBar NWea SLim WEve WFar WHar WStI
- 'Silver Dust' (v)	MBri SRms WFar
- 'Variegata'	see x *C. leylandii* 'Harlequin'
- 'Winter Sun'	WCFE
notabilis	WCwm
ovensii	EHul WCwm

Cupressus (*Cupressaceae*)

arizonica	CDul ECrN
var. **arizonica**	
§ - - 'Arctic'	MBri
- 'Conica Glauca'	MBar
§ - var. **glabra** **new**	ECrN
- - 'Aurea'	EBre ECho EHul LCon LLin LPan MAsh MBar SLim WEve
- - 'Blue Ice' ♀H3	CBcs CDoC CDul CMHG CTho EBre EHul EOrn LCon LLin LRHS MAsh MBar MBri MGos SCoo SLim SPer WEve WGer
- - 'Blue Pyramid'	WEve
- - 'Compacta'	CKen
- - 'Conica'	CKen NBlu SBod
I - - 'Fastigiata'	CBcs CDoC EHul LCon LPan MBar
- - 'Glauca'	ECho MBlu
* - - 'Lutea'	EOrn
- 'Pyramidalis' ♀H3	CMac ECho EPfP LRHS MAsh SCoo WCwm WEve

I - 'Sulfurea' — CKen MAsh NLar WEve
cashmeriana ♀H2 — CBcs CDoC CTho EBre EPla ERea GTSp IDee LCon LLin LPan LRHS NPal SLim WEve WNor
duclouxiana — CMHG WCwm
dupreziana — WCwm
§ funebris — CMCN IDee
gigantea — CDoC
glabra 'Arctic' — see *C. arizonica* var. *arizonica* 'Arctic'
goveniana — MBar
- var. abramsiana — WCwm
guadalupensis — CMHG
- var. forbesii — WCwm
lusitanica — WCwm
- var. benthamii — WCwm
'Knightiana'
- 'Brice's Weeping' — CKen
- 'Glauca Pendula' — CKen EPfP LCon MBri WCwm WEve
- 'Pygmy' — CKen
macrocarpa — CDoC CDul CSBt CTrC EHul SEND
- 'Barnham Gold' — SBod SRms
- 'Compacta' — CKen
- 'Conybearii Aurea' new — WEve
- 'Donard Gold' — CMac CSBt ECho EOrn MBar
- 'Gold Spread' — CDoC EBre ECho EHul EOrn LBee LLin LRHS SCoo SLim SPoG WBcn WEve
- 'Goldcrest' ♀H3 — More than 30 suppliers
- 'Golden Cone' — CKen CMac CSBt ECho LRHS WEve
- 'Golden Pillar' ♀H3 — CDoC CMac CTrC EHul EOrn LBee LRHS MAsh MBar MBri MWat SLim WDin WGer
- 'Golden Spire' — SWvt
- 'Greenstead Magnificent' — EBre LCon LRHS SCoo SLim
- 'Horizontalis Aurea' — EHul MBar WBcn
- 'Lohbrunner' — CKen
- 'Lutea' — CDoC CMac CTrC ECho
- 'Pygmaea' — CKen
- 'Sulphur Cushion' — CKen
- 'Wilma' — EBre ECho EHul LBee LLin LRHS MAsh MGos SCoo SLim SWvt WBcn WEve WStI
- 'Woking' — CKen
sempervirens — CBcs CDul CMCN CTCP ECrN EHul ELan ERom ISea LLin STop WEve WFar
- 'Garda' — CDoC
- 'Green Pencil' — CKen EPfP LRHS
- 'Pyramidalis' — see *C. sempervirens* Stricta Group
- var. sempervirens — see *C. sempervirens* Stricta Group
§ - Stricta Group ♀H3 — CArn CMCN CSWP EHul EPfP LCon LLin LPan SAPC SArc SCoo WCFE WEve
- 'Swane's Gold' — CBcs CDoC CDul CFee CKen CMHG EBre ECho EHul EOrn EPfP LBee LCon LLin LRHS MAsh SCoo SLim WEve
- 'Totem Pole' — CDoC CKen CSBt CTho EBre EHul EOrn EPfP LBee LCon LLin LRHS MAsh MGos SCoo SEND SLim SPoG WBcn WEve WGor
torulosa — CDoC EGFP
- CC 3687 — WHCr

x *Cuprocyparis* (Cupressaceae)
leylandii — see x *Cupressocyparis leylandii*

Curculigo (Hypoxidaceae)
'Fireball' new — CKob

Curcuma (Zingiberaceae)
alismatifolia new — ECho
- 'Chiang Mai Dark Pink' new — CKob
- 'Chiang Mai Pink' new — CKob
- 'Chiang Mai White' new — CKob
- 'Lady of the Dawn' new — CKob
- 'Noi White-Pink' new — CKob
- 'Siam Violet' new — CKob
- 'Tropic Snow' new — CKob
amada — CKob EUJe LEur MOak
angustifolia — CKob EUJe LEur MOak
aromatica — CKob EAmu EUJe LEur MOak
aurantiaca — CKob MOak
'Blue Top' new — CKob
'Cobra' new — CKob
cordata — MOak
- 'Amethyst' new — CKob
elata — CKob
gracillima 'Chiang Mai Chocolate' — MOak
- 'Chiang Mai Chocolate Zebra' new — CKob
- 'Peacock' new — CKob
harmandii new — CKob
'Khmer Giant' new — CKob
leucorhiza new — EUJe
longa — CKob EUJe GPoy LEur MOak MSal
ornata — CKob
parviflora 'White Angel' new — CKob
petiolata 'Emperor' (v) — CKob
'Prachinburi' new — CKob
'Precious Patumma' new — CKob
'Red Fire' new — CKob
'Red Giant' new — CKob
'Ribbon' new — CKob
roscoeana — CKob MOak
'Ruby' new — CKob
'Siam Diamond' — MOak
'Siam Ruby' — CKob MOak
siamensis 'Chiang Mai Delight' new — CKob
- 'Dwarf Chiang Mai Delight' new — CKob
thorelii 'Chiang Mai Snow' — CKob MOak
- 'Dwarf Chiang Mai Snow' new — CKob
zedoaria — CKob EUJe GPoy LAma LEur LRHS MOak WMul

Curcumorpha (Zingiberaceae)
longiflora new — LEur

currant see *Ribes*

Curtonus see *Crocosmia*

Cuscuta (Convolvulaceae)
chinensis — MSal

Cussonia (Araliaceae)
paniculata — CKob SIgm WMul
spicata — CKob WMul
transvaalensis — CKob

custard apple see *Annona cherimola*, *A. reticulata*

Cyananthus (Campanulaceae)
integer misapplied — see *C. microphyllus*
integer Wallich — WOBN
'Sherriff's Variety'

lobatus ♀H4 — CPla ECho EHyt EMan GBuc NJOw NLAp NSla SBla SIng WOBN
- 'Albus' — EPot EWes GEdr SBla WAbe WPat
- dark — EWes WAbe
- giant — CNic EPot GCrs GEdr GTou SBla WAbe WCom
lobatus x **microphyllus** — EPot NWCA WAbe
macrocalyx — EMan GEdr SBla
§ **microphyllus** ♀H4 — CPla EPot GEdr NJOw NSla SBla WAbe WCom WPat
sherriffii — EHyt GEdr WAbe
spathulifolius CLD 1492 — EHyt

Cyanella (Tecophilaeaceae)
lutea new — ECho

Cyanotis (Commelinaceae)
somaliensis ♀H1 — CHal

Cyathea (Cyatheaceae)
from New Guinea — WRic
arborea — WRic
* **atrox** — WRic
australis — EAmu EFtx GQui LPal WFib WMul WRic
brownii — EAmu WMul WRic
cooperi — CBcs EAmu EFtx WFib WRic
* - 'Brentwood' — WRic
cunninghamii — LRav WRic
dealbata — CAbb CBcs CBrP CTrC EAmu EUJe GQui LPal MGos WMul WRic
dregei — SPlb WRic
incisoserrata — WRic
kermadecensis — WRic
medullaris — CAbb CBcs CTrC EAmu MGos WMul WRic
robusta — WRic
smithii — CTrC EAmu EFtx EUJe WMul WRic
spinulosa — WRic
tomentosissima — EFtx WRic

Cyathodes (Epacridaceae)
§ **colensoi** — EPot GCrs MBar MBri MGos NHol NJOw NLAp NLar NWCA SLon SSpi WAbe WBod WPat
empetrifolia — EPot
fasciculata — see *Leucopogon fasciculatus*
fraseri — see *Leucopogon fraseri*
juniperina — ECou SReu
§ **parviflora** — ECou
parvifolia — ECou

Cycas (Cycadaceae)
cairnsiana — CRoM
circinalis — CRoM LPal
media — CRoM
panzihihuaensis — LPal
platyphylla — CRoM
revoluta ♀H1 — CAbb CBrP CDoC CHEx CRoM CTrC CWSG EAmu EPfP ESlt LPal LRHS MBri MPRe NMoo NPal SAPC SArc SChr SEND WHPE WMul WNor
revoluta x **taitungensis** — CBrP
§ **rumphii** — CBrP EAmu LPal LRHS
siamensis — LPal
taitungensis — CBrP CRoM
thouarsii — see *C. rumphii*

Cyclamen ✿ (Primulaceae)
africanum — CBro CLCN CStu EBee EJWh GFlt ITim LAma LRHS MAsh STil WCom WPat

alpinum — CBro CLCN EJWh LAma LRHS MAsh NGar NRog STil
balearicum — CBro CLCN EJWh EPot LAma LRHS MAsh NMen STil
cilicium ♀H2-4 — CBri CBro CLAP CLCN CMea EBre ECtt EHyt EJWh EPot ERos GIBF ITim LAma LRHS MBri MS&S MTho NHol NMen SBla SDeJ SSpi STil WCom WCot WFar WIvy WNor WPat
- f. **album** — CBel CBro CLCN CWCL CWoo EBre EHyt EJWh EPot GCrs ITim LAma LRHS MAsh STil WAbe WLFP NBir
- patterned leaf — NBir
§ **coum** ♀H4 — More than 30 suppliers
- var. **abchasicum** — see *C. coum* subsp. *caucasicum*
§ - subsp. **caucasicum** — ERos ETow LAma SSpi STil
I - - 'Album' — NMen
- subsp. **coum** — CBro
- - f. **albissimum** — WLFP
- - - 'Golan Heights' — MAsh STil WLFP
- - - 'Atkinsii' — CBro MBro
- - f. **coum** 'Crimson King' — SDeJ
- - - 'Linnett Jewel' — WLFP
- - - 'Linnett Rose' — WLFP
- - - Nymans Group — CLAP CWCL MAsh SBla
- - - Pewter Group ♀H2-4 — CBel CWCL ECGP ERos MAsh MTho NGar NPar SSpi WCom WIvy
- - - - bicoloured — EJWh
- - - - 'Blush' — MAsh NGar STil
- - - - 'Maurice Dryden' — CAvo CBel CBro CLAP CPBP CWCL ECGP EHrv GBuc GCrs ITim LAma LRHS MAsh NGar SSpi STil WAbe WIvy WLFP
- - - - red — CLCN LAma WLFP WPat
- - - - 'Tilebarn Elizabeth' — CBel EHrv EHyt MAsh NGar STil WHoo
- - - - white — GBuc MAsh
- - - - plain-leaved red — STil
- - - 'Roseum' — CWCL GBuc LAma SDeJ STil
- - - Silver Group — CBro CWoo EHrv GCrs LRHS MAvo MBro NSla SSpi WAbe WLFP
- - - - bicolor — WLFP
- - - - red — CAvo EBre EPot MTho STil WHoo
- - - - 'Silver Star' — WLFP
- - - - 'Sterling Silver' — WLFP
- - magenta — CBri CWCL MBro
- - f. **pallidum** — GCrs
- - - 'Album' — CAvo CBel EPot ERos ITim LAma MAsh NGar SDeJ SIng STil WAbe WCot WHoo WNor WPat
- - - 'Marbled Moon' — MAsh STil WLFP
- dark pink — CAvo CLAP EDAr ITim WHoo
- from Turkey — ERos
- marbled leaf — CWCL EDAr ITim WCot WHoo
- 'Meaden's Crimson' — WLFP
- plain-leaved — CLAP EPot ITim WAbe WLFP
- red — CLAP CStu EDAr
- scented — ITim
creticum — CLCN CWCL EJWh ITim LAma MAsh STil
creticum x **repandum** — see *C.* x *meiklei*
cyprium — CBro CFwr CLCN CStu CWCL EHyt EJWh ITim LAma LRHS MAsh NJOw STil WCot WIvy
- 'E.S.' — CWCL MAsh STil
elegans — MAsh STil WLFP
europaeum — see *C. purpurascens*
fatrense — see *C. purpurascens* subsp. *purpurascens* from Fatra, Slovakia
graecum — CBro CFil CLCN CStu CWoo EJWh EPot ESis LAma LRHS MAsh NMen SIgm SRot SSpi STil WCot WIvy

- f. *album*	CBro CWCL EJWh EPot LAma LRHS MAsh STil
- subsp. *anatolicum*	STil
- subsp. *candicum*	MAsh
- subsp. *graecum*	STil
f. *graecum* 'Glyfada'	
§ *hederifolium* ♀H4	More than 30 suppliers
hederifolium	ECho EHyt ITim
x *africanum*	
- arrow-head	CLAP
- var. *confusum*	MAsh STil WCot WLFP
- var. *hederifolium*	More than 30 suppliers
f. *albiflorum*	
§ - - - 'Album' **new**	CBri
- - - 'Bowles'	CLCN SIgm WCom WLFP
Apollo Group	
§ - - - - 'Artemis'	CWCL STil
- - - - 'White Bowles'	see *C. hederifolium* var.
Apollo	*hederifolium* f. *albiflorum* (Bowles' Apollo Group) 'Artemis'
- - - 'Linnett Longbow'	WLFP
- - - 'Linnett Stargazer'	WLFP
- - - 'Nettleton Silver'	see *C. hederifolium* var. *hederifolium* f. *albiflorum* 'White Cloud'
- - - 'Perlenteppich'	EDAr WLFP
§ - - - 'White Cloud'	CLAP EHyt EPot ITim MAsh STil WIvy WLFP
- - f. *hederifolium*	CLAP CWCL ECGP MAsh SBla SSpi STil WCom
Bowles' Apollo Group	
- - - 'Daley Thompson'	WLFP
- - - 'Fairy Longbow'	WLFP
- - - 'Fairy Rings'	MAsh WLFP
- - - 'Oliver Twist'	WLFP
- - - 'Rosenteppich'	EDAr EShb GBuc MAsh NHol WLFP
- - - 'Ruby Glow'	CBel CWCL MAsh WCot WLFP WPat
- - - 'Silver Cloud'	CBel CBro CLAP CLCN GBuc MAsh NBir SSpi STil WAbe WIvy WLFP WTin
- - - 'Silver Foil'	WLFP
- - - 'Silver Shield'	WLFP
- island scented strain	WCot
- scented	CLCN STil
- silver-leaved	CBri ECGP EPot GCrs LHop LRHS MAsh NGar SBla SRot STil WLFP
x *hildebrandii*	WIvy
ibericum	see *C. coum* subsp. *caucasicum*
intaminatum	CBel CBro CLCN CPBP CSWP CWoo EJWh ERos LAma LRHS MAsh NHol NMen SChr STil WAbe WIvy WPat
- 'E.K. Balls'	CWCL
- patterned-leaved	CBel EJWh MAsh STil WLFP
- pink	CWCL MAsh NMen STil
- plain-leaved	MAsh STil
latifolium	see *C. persicum*
libanoticum	CAvo CBel CBro CLCN CWCL EJWh ERos LAma LRHS MAsh NMen SBla STil WAbe WCot WLFP
§ x *meiklei*	CBro CLCN
mirabile ♀H2-3	CBel CBro CLCN CWCL CWoo EJWh LAma LRHS MAsh NMen STil WAbe WIvy
- 'Tilebarn Anne'	MAsh STil
- 'Tilebarn Jan'	STil
- 'Tilebarn Nicholas'	EHyt MAsh STil WCot
neapolitanum	see *C. hederifolium*
orbiculatum	see *C. coum*
parviflorum	EJWh LAma MAsh STil
peloponnesiacum ♀H2-3	EJWh ERos MAsh WAbe WCot

* - subsp.	CBel CBro CLCN SSpi STil WLFP
peloponnesiacum	
* - subsp. *rhodense*	CLCN LAma MAsh SSpi STil WLFP
* - subsp. *vividum*	STil
- white-flowered	STil
§ *persicum*	CBro CFil CLCN EJWh LAma LRHS MAsh NMen SChr STil
- CSE 90560	STil
- var. *persicum*	STil
f. *puniceum*	
from Lebanon	
- - - 'Tilebarn Karpathos'	STil
pseudibericum ♀H2-3	CBel CBro CLCN CWCL CWoo EHyt EJWh GCrs LAma LRHS MAsh SBla SIng STil WLFP
- 'Roseum'	CLCN MAsh NMen STil WLFP
§ *purpurascens* ♀H4	CBro CFil CLCN EBee EBre EJWh GBuc LAma LRHS MAsh MBro MS&S NHol NMen SBla SSpi STil WHoo WIvy WPat
- f. *album*	SBla
- var. *fatrense*	see *C. purpurascens* subsp. *purpurascens* from Fatra, Slovakia
- 'Lake Garda'	CFil MAsh SSpi WPGP
§ - subsp. *purpurascens*	EHyt STil WAbe
from Fatra, Slovakia	
- silver-leaved	WLFP
- silver-leaved from	EHyt SBla SSpi
Limone, Italy	
repandum	CBro CFil CLCN CMea EHrv EHyt EJWh ERos LAma LRHS MAsh NMen SBla SSpi STil WCot WHer WLFP
- BS 961	WCot
- JCA 5157	SSpi
- subsp. *repandum*	CLAP CLCN EJWh MAsh SBla STil
f. *album*	WCot
rohlfsianum	CBro CFil CWCL EJWh LRHS MAsh STil
x *saundersii*	CLCN EJWh MAsh STil
trochopteranthum	see *C. alpinum*
x *wellensiekii*	MAsh STil

Cyclosorus (*Thelypteridaceae*)

pennigera **new**	CTrC

Cydonia ✿ (*Rosaceae*)

japonica	see *Chaenomeles speciosa*
oblonga 'Agvambari' (F)	SKee
- 'Aromatnya' **new**	ERea
- 'Champion' (F)	SKee
- 'Early Prolific'	ECrN
- 'Ekmek' (F)	SKee
- 'Isfahan' (F)	SKee
- 'Krymsk' (F)	ESim
- 'Leskovac' (F)	MGos
§ - 'Lusitanica' (F)	GTwe NRog SKee
- 'Meech's Prolific' (F)	CAgr CCVT CLnd CTho CTri ECrN EMui EPAt ERea GKir GTwe LRHS MBlu MGos MWat SDea SFam SKee SPer
- pear-shaped (F)	ECrN ENot NRog
- Portugal	see *C. oblonga* 'Lusitanica'
- 'Seibosa' (F)	SKee
- 'Shams' (F)	SKee
- 'Sobu' (F)	SKee
§ - 'Vranja' Nenadovic (F) ♀H4	CCVT CDoC CDul CEnd CLnd CMac CSBt CTho CTri EBee ECrN EMui EPfP ERea GTwe LBuc LRHS MBri MGos NRog SDea SFam SKee SPer WDin

Cymbalaria (*Scrophulariaceae*)

aequitriloba 'Alba'	GGar

§	**hepaticifolia**	EDAr LRHS NLar WCru WPer
	– 'Alba'	CNic
§	**muralis**	ECtt IHMH MBar MHer MWat NJOw NPri SECG WBVN WBri WGor WHer XPep
	– 'Albiflora'	see *C. muralis* 'Pallidior'
§	– 'Globosa Alba'	CHal EDAr MDHE NWCA
	– 'Kenilworth White'	WMoo
	– 'Len's Favourite'	MGas
	– 'Nana Alba'	EMlt MDHE NJOw NPri WPer
§	– 'Pallidior'	MAvo MBar NVic WWin
	– 'Rosea'	WFar
§	**pallida**	CMea LRHS NSla SBla SPlb WCru WFar WMoo WPer
§	**pilosa**	ECtt EMan NJOw NLar

Cymbopogon (Poaceae)
	citratus	CArn CBod COld CSev GPoy LRav MGol MSal NGHP NPri SHDw SIde SWal WCHb WHHs WHer WJek WLHH
	flexuosus	GWCH MGol MHer WBri
	martini	CArn GPoy MSal
	nardus	CArn GPoy MSal

Cymophyllus (Cyperaceae)
	fraserianus	CDes CHEx EPla GBin

Cymopterus (Apiaceae)
	terebinthinus	SIgm

Cynanchum (Asclepiadaceae)
	acuminatifolium	EMan GCal

Cynara (Asteraceae)
§	**baetica** subsp. **maroccana**	SIgm
§	**cardunculus** ♀H3-4	More than 30 suppliers
	– ACL 380/78	SWat
*	– 'Cardy'	EBee EChP EGoo EMan MSPs MWat NCGa SMrm SWat WWhi SMHy WWpP
	– dwarf	SMHy WWpP
*	– 'Florist Cardy'	COlW IGor NLar NPSI SRob WBry WWpP
§	– Scolymus Group	CAgr CBcs CHEx CKno EBee EBre EDAr EHoe ENot EPfP EWes GCal GPoy IGor ILis LRHS MBri MLan SDnm SMrm SPer WFar WHHs WHer WHil WHoo
	– – 'Gigante di Romagna'	WHer
	– – 'Green Globe'	CBod CPrp CSBt CSev EBee NPer NVic WBry
	– – 'Gros Camus de Bretagne'	MAvo WBar WCot
	– – 'Gros Vert de Lâon'	CBcs CElw CPrp EBee EBlw ECha ELan IBal MSPs NBhm WCot
	– – 'Large Green'	NLar
	– – 'Purple Globe'	CArn CSBt WBry
	– – 'Violetto di Chioggia'	CSev WHer
	– 'Vert de Vaux en Velin'	LPio
	hystrix	see *C. baetica* subsp. *maroccana*
	scolymus	see *C. cardunculus* Scolymus Group

Cynodon (Poaceae)
	aethiopicus	EHoe LPhx SMrm
	dactylon 'Santana' **new**	XPep

Cynoglossum (Boraginaceae)
	amabile ♀H4	CTCP MFOX NCGa WTMC
	– 'Firmament'	GFlt
	– f. **roseum**	WPGP
	'Mystery Rose'	

	dioscoridis	CBot EChP NLar WPer WWin
	nervosum	CArn CBot CTCP EBee EBre ECtt EFou ELan EMan EMil EPar EPfP GMac LHop LRHS MRav MTis MWgw NCHi NGdn SPer SWat WCHb WCot WMoo WTMC WWin SPet
	– **roseum**	
	officinale	CArn MHer MSal SECG WCHb WHer WWye

Cypella (Iridaceae)
	aquatilis	MSta
§	**coelestis**	EBee EMan WCot
	herbertii	CNic CPom EDif LAma
	peruviana	EMan
	plumbea	see *C. coelestis*

Cyperus (Cyperaceae)
	from South Africa **new**	EPPr
§	**albostriatus**	CHal MBri
	alternifolius misapplied	see *C. involucratus*
	– 'Compactus'	see *C. involucratus* 'Nanus'
	alternifolius L. **new**	LPBA
	'Chira'	EChP EWsh MBNS MWod SWal WWpP
§	**cyperoides**	MBri
	diffusus hort.	see *C. albostriatus*
§	**eragrostis**	CArn CBrm CElw CHad CHal CMea CMil CPLG CRow EBlw EHoe EPPr EPla EWsh GKir ITer MCCP NArg NOGN NSti SDix SPlb SWal SWat WAbb WMAq WMoo WWhi WWpP
	esculentus	CPLG IBlr LRav
	fuscus	EPPr MDKP NSti WFar WHal WMoo
§	**giganteus**	CDWL
	glaber	EMan EOMN EPGN EPza EShb EUJe MBar
	haspan misapplied	see *C. papyrus* 'Nanus'
§	**involucratus** ♀H1	CBen CHEx CHal CRow CWCL EBak EHon EMFW EPza ERea EShb EUJe EWsh LPBA MBri MSta NArg NBea SArc SSte SWal SWat SYvo WFar WMAq WMul WWpP WWye
	– 'Gracilis'	EBak MBri
§	– 'Nanus'	LPBA SWal
	longus	CFwr CHad CRow EHoe EHon EMFW EMon EPPr EPza LNCo LPBA MBar MSta NArg NPer NSti SWal SWat WFar WHal WMAq WMyn WPrP WWpP WWye
	nanus	CHEx
	papyrus ♀H1	CHEx CHad CHal CKno CMCo CPLG CTrC EAmu ERea EShb ESlt EUJe LPan MBri MSta SAPC SArc SLdr WHal WMul
	– 'Mexico'	see *C. giganteus*
§	– 'Nanus' ♀H1	CDWL ERea ESlt LPal WMul
	rotundus	CFwr CRow EChP EPGN GFlt MCCP MSPs SWal WWpP
	sumula hort.	see *C. cyperoides*
	ustulatus	CTrC EPPr MMoz
	vegetus	see *C. eragrostis*
	'Zumila' **new**	WMul

Cyphomandra (Solanaceae)
	betacea (F)	CHEx CPLG LRav WMul
	– 'Goldmine' (F)	ERea
	– 'Oratia Red' (F)	ERea

Cyphostemma (Vitaceae)
	juttae	CRoM

Cypripedium (Orchidaceae)

Aki g.	CHdy XFro
x *andrewsii*	XFro
calceolus	CHdy EBee EHrv WCot
californicum **new**	CHdy
debile	CHdy EFEx
Emil g.	CHdy XFro
§ *formosanum*	CHdy EFEx LAma SSpi
Gisela g.	CHdy GCrs XFro
- yellow	GCrs XFro
guttatum	see *C. yatabeanum*
var. *yatabeanum*	
Hank Small g.	CHdy
henryi	EFEx LAma
himalaicum	EFEx
§ *japonicum*	EFEx LAma
- var. *formosanum*	see *C. formosanum*
- var. *japonicum*	see *C. japonicum*
Karl Heinz g.	CHdy
kentuckiense	CHdy
kentuckiense x *reginae*	CHdy
macranthos	CFir CHdy EFEx
- green-flowered	EFEx
- var. *hotei-*	EFEx
atsumorianum	
- var. *rebunense*	EFEx
- var. *speciosum*	EFEx
margaritaceum	EFEx
montanum	EFEx LAma
parviflorum	CHdy
§ - var. *pubescens*	CHdy LAma
Philipp g.	XFro
pubescens	see *C. parviflorum* var. *pubescens*
Rascal g. **new**	CHdy
reginae	CHdy EBee EHrv LAma SSpi WCot
segawae	CHdy EFEx
tibeticum	CHdy EFEx
Ulla Silkens g. **new**	XFro
§ *yatabeanum*	EFEx

Cyrilla (Cyrillaceae)

parvifolia	SSpi
racemiflora	WBcn

Cyrtanthus (Amaryllidaceae)

'Alaska'PBR	CBro LRHS WCot
§ *brachyscyphus*	EBee EGrW GGar MTis SHFr WCot WSPU
breviflorus	CDes SIgm
contractus	CDes
'Edwina'	ECho
§ *elatus* ♀H1	CBro CHal CSev CSpe CStu EMan ERea LAma LRHS MCCP NCiC NRog SYvo WCot WHer
- 'Cream Beauty' **new**	WCot
- pink	CSpe
'Elizabeth'	ECho
flanaganii	CDes
loddigiesianus **new**	CDes
§ *luteus*	EBee
mackenii	CDes CPne EBee EGrW WCot
- var. *cooperi*	EBee EGrW WCot
montanus	EBee EGrW WCot
obliquus	WCot
* *ochroleucus*	WCot
'Stutterheim Variety'	
parviflorus	see *C. brachyscyphus*
* 'Pink Diamond'	CBro LRHS
purpureus	see *C. elatus*
sanguineus	ECho EGrW WCot WPGP
smithiae	CDes
speciosus	see *C. elatus*

Cyrtomium (Dryopteridaceae)

§ *caryotideum*	CLAP GQui NMar WRic
§ *falcatum* ♀H3	CFwr CHEx CHal CLAP CMHG CMil EBee EBlw EFtx ELan GCal LEur MDun NHol NMar NOrc NSti SEND SPla SRms SRot WFar WPnP WRic
* - 'Muricatum' **new**	ELan
- 'Rochfordianum'	WFib
§ *fortunei* ♀H4	More than 30 suppliers
- var. *clivicola*	CFwr EBee EChP LEur MAsh NDlv NLar SMac SRot WHil WRic
lonchitoides	CLAP
macrophyllum	CFil CLAP NMar WCru WRic

Cystopteris ✿ (Woodsiaceae)

bulbifera	CLAP EFer GQui NMar
diaphana	WRic
dickieana	CLAP EBee EMon LEur NMar NVic WCot WFib
fragilis	ECha EFer GQui LEur MAvo NBro NMar SRms WRic
- 'Cristata'	CLAP
- var. *sempervirens*	WRic
* *gracilis* **new**	WFib
tennesseensis	WRic

Cytisus (Papilionaceae)

albus misapplied	see *C. multiflorus*
albus Hacq.	see *Chamaecytisus albus*
'Amber Elf' **new**	COtt EBre LRHS MBri
'Andreanus'	see *C. scoparius* f. *andreanus*
'Apricot Gem'	MBar MGos WBcn
ardoinoi ♀H4	ECho
battandieri ♀H4	More than 30 suppliers
- 'Yellow Tail' ♀H4	CEnd LRHS WPGP WSPU
x *beanii* ♀H4	CPLG EBee ELan ENot EPfP GKir LRHS MAsh MBar SLon SRms SSto WDin
'Boskoop Ruby' ♀H4	CBrm CDoC CHar CSBt EBee EGra ENot EPfP GEil GKir LAst LRHS NBlu SPer SWvt WRHF
'Burkwoodii' ♀H4	CBcs CDoC CHar CSBt CWSG EBee EBre EGra ELan ENot EPfP GKir LAst LRHS MRav MSwo MWhi SPoG WFar WStI
canariensis	see *Genista canariensis*
'Compact Crimson'	CDoC EBee
'Cottage'	EPot
'Dainty'	EBee
'Dainty Maid'	CEnd
'Daisy Hill'	CSBt
§ *decumbens*	CLyd MAsh SSto WLin
demissus	see *Chamaecytisus polytrichus*
'Donard Gem'	CDoC LAst WWeb
'Dorothy Walpole'	WFar
'Dragonfly'	WBVN
'Dukaat'	EBee GKir SHBN WBcn
'Firefly'	CBcs CSBt NBlu
'Fulgens'	CSBt EPfP MAsh MBar NBlu WWeb
'Golden Cascade'	CBcs CBgR CDoC ELan LAst LRHS
'Golden Sunlight'	CSBt EBee ENot EPfP GEil SHBN WBVN WStI
'Goldfinch'	CBcs CDoC CHar CSBt CWSG EBee ELan ENot GKir MAsh MBri MRav MSwo MWat NBlu NPri WWpP
hirsutus	see *Chamaecytisus hirsutus*
'Hollandia' ♀H4	CBcs CDoC CHar CWSG EBee ENot EPAt EPfP EWTr GKir LRHS MBar MGos NPri SHBN SPer WDin WFar WStI WWin
x *kewensis* ♀H4	CBrm CSBt CWSG EBee EBre ELan ENot EPfP GKir LRHS MAsh MBar

MBri MGos MRav SHBN SPer SReu
SRms WDin WWeb WWin
- 'Niki' CDoC EBee EPfP LRHS MAsh
MGos SPer SPoG WGer
'Killiney Red' EBee ELan ENot GKir MBri MRav
'Killiney Salmon' CTri ENot GEil MAsh MRav NBlu
SSto WFar
'La Coquette' CDoC CMHG EBee EGra LRHS
MAsh MBar MWat SPlb
leiocarpus GEil
'Lena' ♀H4 CDoC EBee EBre EGra EPfP GKir
LAst LRHS MAsh MBar MBri MGos
MRav NBlu NPri SGar WFar WRHF
WStI WWeb
leucanthus see *Chamaecytisus albus*
'Luna' EBee LRHS NBlu
maderensis see *Genista maderensis*
'Maria Burkwood' EPfP NBlu SHBN
'Minstead' CDoC EBee ELan EPfP GGar SPer
SPoG
* 'Minstead Pink' GEil
monspessulanus see *Genista monspessulana*
'Moonlight' EWTr
'Moyclare Pink' CMHG
§ *multiflorus* ♀H4 GKir LRav SRms
nigrescens see *C. nigricans*
§ *nigricans* CFil CPle EBee ENot WPGP
- 'Cyni' ELan GEil IArd LAst LRHS MAsh
SPer SSpi
orientalis WCot
'Palette' EBee LAst LRHS MBar MSwo
'Porlock' see *Genista* 'Porlock'
x *praecox* CBrm CSBt EWTr LAst MRav SLon
WFar
- 'Albus' CDoC CHar EBee ELan ENot EPfP
EWTr GEil GKir LAst LRHS MAsh
MBar MGos MRav MWat NBlu
SEND SHBN SPer WBod WFar
WHCG WWeb
- 'Allgold' ♀H4 More than 30 suppliers
- 'Canary Bird' see *C.* x *praecox* 'Goldspeer'
- 'Frisia' CBcs MBar NBlu WBod
§ - 'Goldspeer' CSBt EBee ENot SEND
- 'Lilac Lady' EBre LRHS
§ - 'Warminster' ♀H4 EBee ENot EPfP GKir LAst LRHS
MAsh MBar MBri MGos MRav
MWat NBlu NWea SPer SRms
'Princess' LRHS WBcn
procumbens GEil LHop NBid
purpureus see *Chamaecytisus purpureus*
'Queen Mary' WBcn
racemosus hort. see *Genista* x *spachiana*
Red Favourite see *C.* 'Roter Favorit'
'Red Wings' GKir SPer WStI
§ 'Roter Favorit' EPfP MBar WGor
scoparius CArn CRWN ENot GWCH MCoo
NWea SECG SRms WDin
§ - f. *andreanus* ♀H4 CBgR CDoC EBee EGra ENot EPfP
GKir MGos MRav NWea SPer SPoG
- - 'Splendens' CBcs EWTr SSto WStI
- 'Cornish Cream' CBgR EBee ECot EPfP GKir SPer
WWeb
- 'Jessica' **new** NBlu
§ - subsp. *maritimus* GEil GSki MMHG MRav SLPl
- var. *prostratus* see *C. scoparius* subsp. *maritimus*
- 'Vanesse' ENot NBlu
x *spachianus* see *Genista* x *spachiana*
supinus see *Chamaecytisus supinus*
'Windlesham Ruby' CBrm CDoC CPLG EBee ELan EPfP
GKir LAst LRHS MAsh MBar NBlu
SPer WDin WFar WWpP
'Zeelandia' ♀H4 CBcs EBee ENot EPfP GKir LAst
LRHS MBar MRav MWat NBlu NPri
SEND SPer WFar WWeb

D

Daboecia ✿ (Ericaceae)

§ *cantabrica* f. *alba* CSBt MBar MBri NHol WStI
- 'Alba Globosa' EHea EPfP MBar MSwo
* - 'Arielle' EHea WBan
- 'Atropurpurea' CNCN CSBt EHea GKir NHol WStI
- subsp. *azorica* EHea
  'Arthur P. Dome'
- 'Barbara Phillips' EHea MBar
- 'Bellita' **new** EHea
- 'Bicolor' ♀H4 CNCN EHea
- 'Blueless' EHea EPfP
- f. *blumii* 'Pink Blum' EHea
- - 'White Blum' EHea
- 'Bubbles' EHea
- 'Celtic Star' EHea WBan
- 'Chaldon' EHea
- 'Charles Nelson' (d) EHea MBar
- 'Cherub' EHea
- 'Cinderella' CNCN EHea MBar
- 'Cleggan' EHea
- 'Covadonga' EHea MBar
- 'Creeping White' EHea
- 'Cupido' CNCN EHea
- 'David Moss' ♀H4 EHea MBar WBan
- 'Donard Pink' EHea MBar
- 'Early Bride' EHea
- 'Eskdale Baron' EHea
- 'Eskdale Blea' EHea
- 'Eskdale Blonde' EHea
- 'Glamour' EHea
- 'Globosa Pink' EHea
- 'Harlequin' EHea
- 'Heather Yates' EHea
- 'Herault' EHea
- 'Hookstone Purple' EHea MBar NHol
- 'Lilac Osmond' EHea MBar
- 'Pink' see *D. cantabrica* 'Donard Pink'
- 'Pink Lady' EHea MBar
- 'Polifolia' CNCN EHea SRms
- 'Porter's Variety' EHea MBar
- 'Praegerae' CNCN CTri EHea GKir MBar NHol
- 'Purpurea' EHea MBar
- 'Rainbow' (v) CNCN EHea MBar
- 'Rodeo' EHea
- 'Rosea' EHea MBar
- 'Rubra' EHea
- subsp. *scotica* EHea MBar
  'Bearsden'
- - 'Ben' EHea
- - 'Cora' CNCN EHea
- - 'Golden Imp' **new** EHea
- - 'Goscote' EHea MGos
- - 'Jack Drake' ♀H4 CNCN EHea MBar MBri NDlv
- - 'Red Imp' EHea
- - 'Robin' EHea
- - 'Silverwells' ♀H4 CBcs CNCN EHea MBar MBri NDlv
- - 'Tabramhill' CNCN EHea MBar
- - 'William Buchanan' CNCN EHea GKir MBar MBri NDlv
  ♀H4 NHol NMen
- - 'William Buchanan CNCN EHea MBar MBri
  Gold' (v)
- 'Snowdrift' EHea MBar
- 'Waley's Red' ♀H4 EHea GQui MBar
- 'White Carpet' EHea
- 'Wijnie' EHea

Dacrycarpus (Podocarpaceae)

§ *dacrydioides* ECou LEdu
- 'Dark Delight' ECou

Dacrydium (Podocarpaceae)

bidwillii	see *Halocarpus bidwillii*
cupressinum	CAbb CDoC CTrC LCon SMad
franklinii	see *Lagarostrobos franklinii*
laxifolium	see *Lepidothamnus laxifolius*

Dactylis (Poaceae)

glomerata 'Variegata' (v)	CBod CPen EBee ECGP EMan
	EMon ENot EPPr IBlr IHMH MBlu
	MCCP NBid NBro NGdn NHol NSti
	WFar

Dactylorhiza (Orchidaceae)

aristata	EFEx
x **braunii**	ECha IBlr
Calibra g.	CHdy
(*elata* x *majalis*)	
§ **elata** ♀H4	CDes CEnd CHdy CLAP EPar GCrs
	IBlr LAma LPhx MBri MDun SMHy
	SSpi WCot WGMN
- 'Lydia'	CLAP GCrs
Estella g. (*elata* x *foliosa*)	CHdy LEur
§ **foliosa** ♀H4	CBro CDes CElw CFir CLAP CRow
	ERos ETow GCrs GKir IBlr MDun
	MTho SBla WCot WFar WOld
foliosa x **saccifera**	CHdy
§ **fuchsii**	CHdy CMil EPot ERos GBuc GCrs
	GKev MGos MNrw NGar NMen
	NRya SCnR SSpi SUsu WHer WTin
- 'Bressingham Bonus'	GCrs
x **grandis**	CHdy SMHy
incarnata	CFir CHdy LAma SSpi
§ **maculata**	CHdy CHid EChP EHrv ELan EMan
	EPar LAma NGdn WCot WFar
	WHer
- 'Madam Butterfly'	CAvo CBro EPot GCrs LEur
maderensis	see *D. foliosa*
Madonna g.	CHdy
(*majalis* x *sambucina*)	
§ **majalis**	CHdy CLAP LAma SSpi WFar WHil
- subsp. **praetermissa**	see *D. praetermissa*
mascula	see *Orchis mascula*
§ **praetermissa**	CFir CHdy CLAP LEur SSpi WFar
purpurella	CHdy CLAP SSpi WCot WFar WSan
saccifera	CHdy
sambucina	CHdy

Dahlia ✿ (Asteraceae)

'A la Mode' (LD)	CWGr
'Abba' (SD)	CWGr
'Abridge Alex' (SD)	CWGr
'Abridge Ben' (MinD)	CWGr
'Abridge Florist' (SWL)	CWGr
'Abridge Fox' (MinD)	CWGr
'Abridge Primrose' (SWL)	CWGr
'Abridge Taffy' (MinD)	CWGr
'Adelaide Fontane' (LD)	CWGr
'Admiral Rawlings' **new**	CHad MAJR
'Aimie' (MinD)	CWGr
'Akita' (Misc)	WAba
'Alan Sparkes' (SWL)	CWGr
'Albert Schweitzer' (MS-c)	CWGr
'Alden Regal' (MinC)	CWGr
'Alfred C' (MS-c) **new**	CWGr
'Alfred Grille' (S-c)	CWGr LRHS
'Alf's Mascot' **new**	WAba
'Aljo' (MS-c)	CWGr
'All Triumph' (MinS-c)	CWGr
'Allan Snowfire' (MS-c)	NHal WAba
'Allan Sparkes' (SWL) ♀H3	LAyl
'Alloway Cottage' (MD)	CWGr NHal
'Alltami Apollo' (GS-c)	CWGr
'Alltami Classic' (MD)	CWGr NHal

'Alltami Corsair' (MS-c)	CWGr
'Alltami Cosmic' (LD)	CWGr
'Alltami Ruby' (MS-c)	CWGr
'Almand's Climax' (GD)	MTiv WAba
♀H3	
'Alpen Beauty' (Col)	CWGr
'Alpen Fern' (Fim)	CWGr
'Alpen Flame' (MinC)	CWGr
'Alpen Mildred' (SS-c)	CWGr
'Alpen Sun' (MinS-c)	CWGr
'Alva's Doris' (SS-c) ♀H3	CWGr LAyl
'Alva's Lilac' (SD)	CWGr
'Alva's Supreme' (GD)	CWGr MTiv NHal WAba
♀H3	
'Amanda Jarvis' (SC)	CWGr
'Amanjanca' (MinS-c)	CWGr
'Amaran Candyfloss' (SD)	CWGr
'Amaran Pentire' (SS-c)	CWGr
'Amaran Relish' (LD)	CWGr
'Amaran Royale' (MinD)	CWGr
'Amaran Troy' (SWL)	CWGr
'Amber Banker' (MC)	CWGr
'Amber Festival' (SD)	CWGr NHal
'Amber Vale' (MinD)	CWGr
'Amberglow' (MinBa)	CWGr LAyl MTiv
'Amberley Jean' (SD)	CWGr
'Amberley Joan' (SD)	CWGr
'Amberley Nicola' (SD)	CWGr
'Amberley Victoria' (MD)	CWGr
'Ambition' (SS-c)	CWGr NHal
'Amelia's Surprise' (LD)	CWGr
'American Copper' (GD)	CWGr
'Amethyst' (SD)	CWGr
'Amgard Coronet' (MinD)	CWGr WAba
'Amgard Rosie' (SD)	CWGr
'Amira' (SBa)	CWGr MTiv NHal WAba
'Amorangi Joy' (SC)	CWGr
'Amy Campbell' (MD)	NHal
'Ananta Patel' (SD)	CWGr
'Anchorite' (SD)	CWGr
'Andrea Clark' (MD)	LBut NHal
'Andrew Lockwood'	CWGr MTiv
(Pom)	
'Andrew Mitchell' (MS-c)	CWGr NHal WAba
* 'Andries' Amber' (MinS-c)	LBut
'Andries' Orange' (MinS-c)	CWGr LBut
'Anglian Water' (MinD)	NHal
'Anja Doc' (MS-c)	CWGr
'Anniversary Ball' (MinBa)	CWGr LAyl
'Apache' (MS-c/Fim)	CWGr
'Appenzell' (MS-c)	MTiv
'Appetizer' (SS-c)	CWGr
I 'Appleblossom' (Col) **new**	CWGr
'Apricot Beauty' (MS-c)	LAyl MTiv
'Apricot Honeymoon	CWGr WAba
Dress' (SD)	
'Apricot Jewel' (SD)	LAyl
'Apricot Parfait' (SS-c)	CWGr
'April Dawn' (MD)	CWGr
'Arab Queen' (GS-c)	CWGr
'Arabian Night' (SD)	CAvo CBcs CElw CPen CSam CSpe
	CWGr EBee EBlw EChP EHrv ELan
	EMan EPfP ERou EUJe LPio LRHS
	MMil MNrw MSte NPPs NPSI SDeJ
	WAba WCot WSpi WWeb
'Arc de Triomphe' (MD)	CWGr
'Arnhem' (SD)	CWGr
'Arthur Godfrey' (GD)	CWGr
'Arthur Hankin' (SD)	CWGr
'Arthur Hills' (SC)	CWGr
'Arthur's Delight' (GD)	CWGr
'Asahi Chohje' (Anem)	CWGr
♀H3	
'Aspen' (MS-c)	CWGr

'Athelston John' (SC)	CWGr	
'Atilla' (SD)	CWGr	
'Audacity' (MD)	CWGr LAyl	
'Audrey R' (SWL)	CWGr	
'Aurora's Kiss' (MinBa)	CWGr LBut NHal	
'Aurwen's Violet' (Pom)	CWGr LAyl NHal	
australis	CFil	
'Autumn Choice' (MD)	LAyl NHal	
'Autumn Lustre' (SWL) ♀H3	CWGr LAyl	
'Awaikoe' (Col)	CWGr	
'B.J. Beauty' (MD)	LAyl NHal WAba	
'Babette' (S-c)	LBut	
'Baby Fonteneau' (SS-c)	CWGr	
'Baby Royal' (SD)	CHad	
'Babylon' (GD)	EPfP	
'Bacchus' (MS-c)	CWGr	
'Bach' (MC)	CWGr LRHS	
'Balcombe' (SD)	CWGr	
'Ballego's Glory' (MD)	CWGr	
'Bambino' (Lil)	CWGr	
'Banker' (MC)	CWGr	
'Bantling' (MinBa)	CWGr	
'Barb' (LC)	CWGr	
'Barbara' (MinBa) **new**	CWGr	
'Barbara Schell' (GD)	CWGr	
'Barbara's Pastelle' (MS-c)	CWGr	
'Barbarossa' (LD)	CWGr	
'Barbarry Ball' (SBa)	CWGr	
'Barbarry Banker' (MinD)	CWGr LAyl	
'Barbarry Bluebird' (MinD)	NHal	
'Barbarry Cadet' (MinD)	CWGr	
'Barbarry Carousel' (SBa)	CWGr WAba	
'Barbarry Cascade' (SD) **new**	CWGr	
'Barbarry Challenger' (MinD) **new**	CWGr	
'Barbarry Chick' (MinD)	WAba	
'Barbarry Choice' (SD)	WAba	
'Barbarry Clover' (SB)	CWGr	
'Barbarry Coronet' (MinD) **new**	WAba	
'Barbarry Cosmos' (SD)	CWGr	
'Barbarry Dominion' (MinD)	CWGr	
'Barbarry Flag' (MinD)	CWGr NHal WAba	
'Barbarry Gem' (MinBa)	CWGr	
'Barbarry Ideal' (MinD)	CWGr	
'Barbarry Monitor' (MinBa) **new**	CWGr	
'Barbarry Noble' (MinD)	CWGr	
'Barbarry Olympic' (SBa)	CWGr MTiv	
'Barbarry Oracle' (SD)	CWGr WAba	
'Barbarry Orange' (SD)	WAba	
'Barbarry Pinky' (SD)	CWGr	
'Barbarry Red' (MinD)	CWGr	
'Barbarry Ticket' (SD)	WAba	
'Barbarry Token' (SD)	WAba	
'Barbarry Triumph' (MinD)	CWGr	
'Barbetta' (MinD)	CWGr	
'Barbette' (MinD)	CWGr	
'Baret Joy' (LS-c)	CWGr NHal WAba	
'Bargaly Blush' (MD)	NHal	
'Baron Ray' (SD)	CWGr	
'Barry Williams' (MD)	CWGr	
'Bart' (SD)	CWGr	
'Baseball' (MinBa)	CWGr	
'Bassingbourne Beauty' (SD)	CWGr	
'Bayswater Red' (Pom)	CWGr	
'Bea' (SWL)	WAba	
'Beach Boy' (SD)	CWGr	
'Beacon Light' (SD)	CWGr	
* 'Beatrice' (MinBa)	CWGr	
'Beatrice' (MinD)	MTiv	
'Bedford Sally' (MD)	CWGr	
'Bednall Beauty' (Misc/DwB) ♀H3	CBgR CBos CHll CSpe CWGr EBee ECtt EMan EMil ERou EShb EUJe EWes SChu SDys WAba WCot WDyG	
'Bell Boy' (MinBa)	CWGr	
'Bella S' (GD)	CWGr	
'Belle Epoque' (MC)	CWGr	
'Belle Moore' (SD)	CWGr	
'Bell's Boy' (MS-c)	WAba	
'Ben Huston' (GD)	WAba	
'Berger's Rekord' (S-c)	CSut CWGr LRHS	
'Berliner Kleene' (MinD/DwB)	CWGr LRHS MTiv	
'Bernice Sunset' (SS-c)	CWGr	
'Berolina' (MinD)	CWGr	
'Berwick Banker' (SBa)	CWGr	
'Berwick Wood' (MD)	CWGr MTiv NHal	
'Bess Painter' (SD)	CWGr	
'Betty Ann' (Pom)	CWGr	
'Betty Bowen' (SD)	CWGr	
'Biddenham Fairy' (MinD)	CWGr	
'Biddenham Strawberry' (SD)	CWGr	
'Bill Homberg' (GD)	MTiv	
'Bingley' (SD)	CWGr	
'Bingo' (MinD)	CWGr	
'Bishop of Llandaff' (Misc) ♀H3	More than 30 suppliers	
'Bitter Lemon' (SD)	CWGr	
'Black Fire' (SD)	CWGr LAyl	
'Black Monarch' (GD)	CWGr NHal	
'Black Narcissus' (MC)	CWGr	
'Black Spider' (SS-c)	CWGr	
'Black Tucker' (Pom)	CWGr	
'Blaze' (MD)	CWGr	
'Blewbury First' (SWL)	CWGr	
'Bliss' (SWL)	CWGr WAba	
'Bloemfontein' (SD)	LRHS	
'Bloodstone' (SD)	CWGr	
'Bloom's Amy' (MinD)	CWGr	
'Bloom's Graham' (SS-c)	CWGr	
'Bloom's Kenn' (MD)	CWGr	
I 'Blossom' (Pom)	CWGr	
'Blue Beard' (SS-c)	CWGr	
'Blue Diamond' (MC)	CWGr	
'Bluesette' (SD)	CWGr MTiv	
'Blyton Crystal' (SD) **new**	NHal	
'Bob Fitzjohn' (GS-c)	CWGr	
'Bonaventure' (GD)	NHal	
'Bonne Espérance' (Sin/Lil)	CWGr	
'Bonny Blue' (SBa)	CWGr	
'Bonny Brenda' (MinD)	CWGr	
'Boogie Woogie' (Anem) **new**	CWGr	
'Bora Bora' (SS-c) **new**	CWGr	
'Border Princess' (SC/DwB)	CWGr	
'Border Triumph' (DwB)	MTiv	
'Bracken Ballerina' (SWL)	LAyl NHal WAba	
'Brackenhill Flame' (SD)	CWGr WAba	
'Brackenridge Ballerina' (SWL)	CWGr WAba	
'Brandaris' (MS-c)	CWGr	
'Brandysnap' (SD)	CWGr	
'Brian R' (MD)	CWGr	
'Brian's Dream' (MinD)	NHal	
'Bride's Bouquet' (Col)	CWGr	
'Bridge View Aloha' (MS-c) ♀H3 **new**	CWGr	
'Bridgette' (SD)	CWGr	
'Bristol Petite' (MinD)	CWGr	
'Bronze Glints' (MS-c) **new**	WAba	

'Brookfield Delight' CWGr LBut
  (Sin/Lil) ♀H3
'Brookfield Dierdre' CWGr
  (MinBa)
'Brookfield Judith' (MinD) NHal
'Brookfield Rachel' CWGr
  (MinBa)
'Brookfield Rene' CWGr
  (Dwf MinD)
'Brookfield Snowball' CWGr
  (SBa)
'Brookfield Sweetie' CWGr
  (DwB/Lil) **new**
'Brookside Cheri' (SC) CWGr
'Bryce B. Morrison' (SD) CWGr
'Bud Flanagan' (MD) CWGr
* 'Buttercup' (Pom) CWGr MTiv
'Buttermere' (SD) CWGr
'By George' (GD) CWGr
'Caer Urfa' (MinBa) WAba
'Café au Lait' (LD) CWGr EBee
'Calgary' (SD) CWGr
'Camano Ariel' (MC) CWGr
'Camano Choice' (SD) CWGr
'Camano Passion' (MS-c) CWGr
'Camano Poppet' (SBa) CWGr
'Camano Regal' (MS-c) CWGr
'Cameo' (WL) CWGr LBut
'Campos Hush' (SS-c) CWGr
'Campos Philip M' (GD) CWGr
* 'Canary Fubuki' (MD) CWGr
'Candy' (MS-c) CWGr
'Candy Cane' (MinBa) CWGr
'Candy Cupid' (MinBa) ♀H3 CWGr LBut MTiv NHal WAba
'Candy Hamilton CWGr
  Lilian' (SD)
'Candy Keene' (LS-c) NHal
'Capulet' (SBa) CWGr
'Cara Tina' (Dwf O) CWGr
'Careless' (SD) CWGr
'Carolina Moon' (SD) CWGr LAyl NHal
'Carstone Cobblers' (SBa) WAba
'Carstone Ruby' (SD) NHal
'Carstone Sunbeam' (SD) CWGr
'Carstone Suntan' (MinC) CWGr MTiv NHal
'Castle Drive' (MD) CWGr
'Catherine Ireland' (MinD) CWGr
'Cerise Prefect' (MS-c) CWGr
'Cha Cha' (SS-c) CWGr
'Chanson d'Amour' (SD) CWGr
'Chantal' (MinBa) **new** CWGr
'Charles de Coster' (MD) CWGr
'Charlie Kenwood' (MinD) CWGr
'Charlie Two' (MD) CWGr LAyl LBut NHal WAba
'Charlotte Bateson' (MinBa) CWGr
'Chat Noir' (MS-c) CWGr
'Chee' (SWL) CWGr
'Cheerio' (SS-c) MTiv
'Cheerleader' (GS-c) CWGr
'Cherokee Beauty' (GD) CWGr
'Cherry Wine' (SD) CWGr
'Cherrywood Millfield' CWGr
  (MS-c)
'Cherrywood Stoddard' CWGr
  (MD)
'Cherrywood Turnpike' CWGr
  (SD)
'Cherrywood Wilderness' CWGr
  (MD)
'Cherubino' (Col) CWGr
'Cherwell Goldcrest' CWGr LAyl NHal WAba
  (SS-c)
'Cherwell Lapwing' NHal
  (SS-c) **new**

'Cherwell Skylark' (SS-c) NHal
'Chessy' (Sin/Lil) AGM CWGr LAyl LRHS WAba
'Chilson's Pride' (SD) CWGr
'Chiltern Amber' (SD) CWGr
'Chiltern Fantastic' (SC) CWGr
'Chiltern Herald' (MS-c) CWGr
'Chiltern Sylvia' (MinS-c) CWGr
'Chimacum Topaz' (MS-c) CWGr
'Chimborazo' (Col) CWGr LAyl SDix
'Chorus Girl' (MinD) CWGr
'Christine' (SD) CWGr
'Christmas Carol' (Col) NHal
'Christmas Star' (Col) CWGr
'Christopher Nickerson' CWGr
  (MS-c)
'Christopher Taylor' (SWL) CWGr NHal WAba
I 'Cindy' (MinD) WAba
'Clair de Lune' (Col) ♀H3 CWGr ERou NHal
'Claire Diane' (SD) CWGr
'Clara May' (MS-c/Fim) CWGr
'Clarence' (S-c) CWGr
'Classic A.1' (MC) CWGr LAyl
'Classic Elise' (Misc) **new** CWGr
'Classic Masquerade'PBR EBee EPfP
  (Misc) **new**
'Classic Poème'PBR EBee
  (Misc) **new**
'Classic Rosamunde'PBR EBee
  (Misc) **new**
'Classic Summertime' CWGr EBee
  (Misc) **new**
'Classic Swanlake'PBR EBee
  (Misc) **new**
'Clint's Climax' (LD) WAba
'Cloverdale' (SD) CWGr
coccinea (B) CBgR CElw CFil CHll CWGr EMan
  EOrc EUJe MSte SChu SDix WAba
  WCot WDyG WSHC
- B&SWJ 9126 WCru
- var. *palmeri* MCCP
coccinea x *merckii* (B) EBee EMan EWes
'Cocktail' (S-c) CWGr
'Colac' (LD) CWGr
'Color Spectacle' LS-c CWGr
'Coltness Gem' (Sin/DwB) CWGr
'Comet' (Misc Anem) CWGr
'Como Polly' (LD) CWGr
I 'Concordia' (SD) CWGr
'Connie Bartlam' (MD) CWGr NHal
'Connoisseur's Choice' CWGr
  (MinBa)
'Constance Bateson' (SD) CWGr
'Contraste' (Misc) CWGr
'Copper Queen' (MinD) NHal
* 'Coral Puff' LRHS
'Coral Relation' (SC) **new** CWGr
'Coral Strand' (SD) CWGr
'Cornel' (SBa) CWGr LAyl LBut MTiv NHal
'Corona' (SS-c/DwB) CWGr
'Coronella' (MD) CWGr
'Corrie Vigor' (SS-c) NHal
'Corrine' (SWL) WAba
'Cortez Silver' (MD) CWGr
'Cortez Sovereign' (SS-c) CWGr
'Corton Bess' (SD) CWGr
'Corton Olympic' (GD) CWGr
'Cottesmore' (MD) CWGr
'Country Boy' (MS-c) CWGr
'Crazy Legs' (MinD) CWGr
'Cream Alva's' (GD) ♀H3 CWGr MTiv
'Cream Beauty' (SWL) MTiv
'Cream Delight' (SS-c) CWGr
'Cream Klankstad' (SC) CWGr
'Cream Linda' (SD) CWGr

'Cream Moonlight' (MS-c)   CWGr WAba
'Cream Reliance' (SD)   CWGr
'Creve Coeur' (GD)   CWGr
'Crichton Cherry' (MinD)   CWGr
'Crichton Honey' (SBa)   CWGr
'Crossfield Allegro' (SS-c)   CWGr
'Crossfield Anne' (MinD)   CWGr
'Crossfield Ebony' (Pom)   CWGr
'Crossfield Festival' (LD)   CWGr
'Croydon Ace' (GD)   CWGr
'Croydon Jumbo' (GD)   CWGr
'Croydon Snotop' (GD)   CWGr
'Crushed Velvet' (MinD)   CWGr
'Cryfield Bryn' (SS-c)   NHal
'Cryfield Jane' (MinBa)   CWGr
'Cryfield Keene' (LS-c)   CWGr
'Cryfield Max' (SC)   CWGr
'Cryfield Rosie' (SBa)   CWGr
'Curate' (Misc)   CWGr
'Curiosity' (Col)   CWGr LAyl NHal
'Currant Cream' (SBa)   CWGr
'Cyclone' (MD)   CWGr
'Cycloop' (SS-c)   CWGr
'Cynthia Chalwin' (MinBa)   CWGr
'Cynthia Louise' (GD)   CWGr
'Czardas'   GCal
'Daddy's Choice' (SS-c)   CWGr
'Dad's Delight' (MinD)   CWGr
'Daleko Adonis' (GS-c)   CWGr
'Daleko Gold' (MD)   CWGr
'Daleko Jupiter' (GS-c)   CWGr MTiv NHal WAba
'Daleko Tangerine' (MD)   CWGr
'Dana Champ'   CWGr
    (MinS-c) **new**
'Dana Dream' (MinS-c)   CWGr
'Dana Iris' (SS-c)   CWGr
'Dana Sunset' (SC)   CWGr
'Dancing Queen' (S-c)   CWGr
'Danjo Doc' (SD)   CWGr
'Danum Cherry' (SD)   CWGr
'Danum Chippy' (SD)   CWGr
'Danum Fancy' (SD)   CWGr
'Danum Gail' (LD)   CWGr
'Danum Julie' (SBa)   CWGr
'Danum Meteor' (GS-c)   CWGr WAba
'Danum Rebel' (LS-c)   CWGr
'Danum Rhoda' (GD)   CWGr
'Danum Salmon' (MS-c)   CWGr
'Danum Torch' (Col)   CWGr
'Dark Desire' (Sin/DwB)   CAvo MBri
'Dark Stranger' (MC)   ♀H3 CWGr MTiv
'Darlington Diamond'   CWGr
    (MS-c)
'Darlington Jubilation'   CWGr
    (SS-c)
'Davar Hayley' (SC)   CWGr
'Davenport Anita' (MinD)   CWGr
'Davenport Honey'   CWGr WAba
    (MinD)
'Davenport Lesley' (MinD)   CWGr
'Davenport Sunlight'   CWGr NHal
    (MS-c)
'David Digweed' (SD)   CWGr NHal
'David Howard' (MinD)   More than 30 suppliers
    ♀H3
'David Shaw' (MD)   CWGr
'David's Choice' (MinD)   CWGr
'Dawn Chorus' (MinD)   CWGr
'Dawn Sky' (SD)   LAyl
'Daytona' (SD)   CWGr
'Deborah's Kiwi' (SC)   CWGr NHal WAba
'Debra Anne Craven'   CWGr NHal WAba
    (GS-c)
I 'Decorete Rose' **new**   CWGr

'Decorette'   CWGr
    (DwB/SD) **new**
'Decorette Bronze' **new**   CWGr
'Deepest Yellow' (MinBa)   CWGr
'Denise Willow' (Pom)   WAba
'Dentelle de Venise' (MC)   CWGr
'Deuil du Roi Albert' (MD)   CWGr
'Deutschland' (MD)   CWGr
'Devon Joy' (MinD)   CWGr
I 'Diamond Rose'   CWGr
    (Anem/DwB) **new**
'Diana Gregory' (Pom)   MTiv
'Dinah Shore' (LS-c)   CWGr
dissecta   CFil
'Doc van Horn' (LS-c)   CWGr
'Doctor Anne Dyson' (SC)   CWGr
'Doctor Arnett' (GS-c)   CWGr
'Doctor Caroline Rabbitt'   CWGr MTiv
    (SD)
'Doctor John Grainger'   CWGr
    (MinD)
'Doktor Hans Ricken' (SD)   WAba
'Don's Delight' (Pom)   CWGr
'Doris Bacon' (MinBa)   CWGr
'Doris Day' (SC)   CWGr LBut MTiv NHal WAba
'Doris Knight' (SC)   LBut
'Doris Rollins' (SC)   CWGr
'Dottie D.' (SBa)   CWGr
'Downham Royal' (MinBa)   CWGr
'Drummer Boy' (LD)   CWGr
'Duet' (MD)   CWGr LRHS
'Dusky Harmony' (SWL)   CWGr LBut
'Dutch Baby' (Pom)   CWGr WAba
'Dutch Boy' (SD)   CWGr
'Dutch Triumph' (LWL)   CWGr
'Earl Haig' (LD)   CWGr
'Earl Marc' (SC)   CWGr LBut
'Early Bird' (SD)   CWGr
'Easter Sunday' (Col)   CWGr
'Eastwood Moonlight'   CWGr MTiv NHal WAba
    (MS-c)
'Eastwood Star' (MS-c)   CWGr WAba
'Ebbw Vale Festival'   CWGr
    (MinD)
'Ebony Witch' (LD) **new**   CWGr
'Edge of Gold' (GD)   CWGr
'Edgeway Joyce' (MinBa)   CWGr
'Edinburgh' (SD)   CWGr WAba
'Edith Holmes' (SC)   CWGr
'Edith Mueller' (Pom)   CWGr
'Eileen Denny' (MS-c)   CWGr
'Eisprinzessin' **new**   CWGr
'El Cid' (SD)   CWGr
'El Paso' (SD)   CSut CWGr
'Eleanor Fiesta'   CWGr
    (MinS-c) **new**
'Elgico Leanne' (MC)   CWGr
'Elizabeth Hammett'   CWGr MTiv WAba
    (MinD)
'Elizabeth Snowden' (Col)   CWGr WAba
'Ella Britton' (MinD)   CPen EBee LRHS MWgw
'Ellen Huston' (Sin/DwB)   CWGr EBee LRHS MBri NHal SAga
    ♀H3
'Elma E' (LD)   CWGr NHal WAba
'Elmbrook Chieftain' (GD)   CWGr
'Elmbrook Rebel' (GS-c)   CWGr
'Emma's Coronet' (MinD)   CWGr WAba
'Emmie Lou' (MD)   CWGr
'Emory Paul' (LD)   CWGr
'Emperor' (MD)   CWGr
'Engadin' (MD)   CWGr
'Enid Adams' (SD)   CWGr
'Eric's Choice' (SD)   CWGr
'Ernie Pitt' (SD)   CWGr

'Esau' (GD) CWGr
'Esther' MBri
'Eunice Arrigo' (LS-c) **new** CWGr
'Eveline' (SD) CBgR CWGr LRHS
'Evelyn Foster' (MD) CWGr NHal
'Evelyn Rumbold' (GD) CWGr
'Evening Lady' (MinD) CWGr
excelsa (B) CHll
'Exotic Dwarf' (Sin/Lil) CWGr NHal WCot
'Explosion' (SS-c) CWGr
'Extase' (MD) CWGr LRHS
'Fabula' (Col) CWGr
'Facet' (Sin/Lil) WAba
'Fairway Pilot' (GD) CWGr
'Fairway Spur' (GD) CWGr LAyl NHal
'Fairy Queen' (MinC) CWGr
'Falcon's Future' (MS-c) CWGr
'Fascination' (SWL/DwB) CBgR CBos CHad CWGr LAyl
 ♀H3 MAJR NHal SChu
'Fascination Aus' (Col) **new** CWGr
'Fashion Monger' (Col) CWGr NHal
'Fata Morgana' **new** CWGr
'Fermain' (MinD) CWGr WAba
'Fern Irene' (MWL) CWGr
'Ferncliffe Illusion' **new** CWGr
'Fernhill Champion' (MD) CWGr
* 'Fernhill Suprise' (SD) CWGr LBut
'Festivo' (Dwf Col) CWGr
'Feu Céleste' (Col) CWGr
'Fidalgo Blacky' (MinD) CWGr
'Fidalgo Bounce' (SD) CWGr
'Fidalgo Climax' (LS-c/Fim) CWGr
'Fidalgo Magic' (MD) CWGr WAba
'Fidalgo Snowman' (GS-c) CWGr NHal
'Fidalgo Splash' (MD) CWGr
'Fidalgo Supreme' (MD) CWGr LAyl
'Figurine' (SWL) ♀H3 CWGr NHal WAba
'Fille du Diable' (LS-c) CWGr MTiv
'Finchcocks' (SWL) ♀H3 CWGr LAyl
'Fire Magic' (SS-c) **new** CWGr
* 'Fire Mountain' MTiv NHal
 (MinD/DwB)
'Firebird' (Sin) LRHS WAba
'Firebird' (MS-c) see *D.* 'Vuurvogel'
'First Lady' (MD) CWGr
'Flevohof' (MS-c) CWGr
'Floorimoor' **new** CWGr
'Flutterby' (SWL) CWGr
'Formby Supreme' (MD) MTiv
'Forncett Furnace' (B) GCal
'Forrestal' (MS-c) CWGr
'Frank Holmes' (Pom) CWGr WAba
'Frank Hornsey' (SD) CWGr
'Frank Lovell' (GS-c) CWGr WAba
'Franz Kafka' (Pom) CWGr
'Frau Louise Mayer' (SS-c) CWGr
'Fred Wallace' (SC) CWGr
'Freelancer' (LC) CWGr
'Freestyle' (SC) CWGr
'Freya's Paso Doble' CWGr LAyl
 (Anem) ♀H3
'Freya's Thalia' LAyl
 (Sin/Lil) ♀H3
'Friendship' (S-c) CWGr
'Fringed Star' (MS-c) LRHS
'Frits' (MinBa) CWGr
'Funny Face' (Misc) CWGr WAba
'Fusion' (MD) CWGr
'Gala Parade' (SD) CWGr NHal
'Gale Lane' (Pom) CWGr
'Gallery Art Deco'PBR NHal WWol
 (SD) ♀H3
'Gallery Art Fair'PBR WWol
 (MinD)

'Gallery Art Nouveau'PBR NHal WWol
 (MinD) ♀H3
'Gallery Cézanne'PBR WWol
 (MinD) **new**
'Gallery Leonardo'PBR WSpi WWol
 (SD) ♀H3
'Gallery Singer'PBR WWol
 (MinD) **new**
'Gamelan' (Dwf Anem) CWGr
'Garden Festival' (SWL) CWGr LAyl MTiv
'Garden Party' CWGr LAyl
 (MC/DwB) ♀H3
'Garden Princess' CWGr
 (SC/DwB)
'Garden Wonder' (SD) LPio LRHS WWol
'Gargantuan' (GS-c) CWGr
Gateshead Festival see *D.* 'Peach Melba'
'Gaudy' (GD) **new** CWGr
'Gay Mini' (MinD) CWGr
'Gay Princess' (SWL) CWGr LAyl
§ 'Geerlings' Indian MTiv NHal
 Summer' (MS-c) ♀H3
'Geerlings Jubilee' MTiv
 (SS-c) **new**
'Geerlings Yellow' (SS-c) CWGr
'Gemma Darling' (GD) CWGr WAba
'Gemma's Place' (Pom) CWGr
'Geneve' (MD) CWGr
'Geoffrey Kent' (MinD) NHal
 ♀H3
'Gerald Grace' (LS-c) CWGr
'Gerlos' (MD) CWGr
'Gerrie Hoek' (SWL) CWGr LBut LRHS MTiv
'GF Hemerick' CWGr
 (Sin/DwB) **new**
'Gill's Pastelle' (MS-c) CWGr WAba
'Gina Lombaert' (MS-c) CWGr LRHS WAba
* 'Ginger Willo' CWGr
'Giraffe' (Misc) CWGr
'Gitts Perfection' (GD) CWGr
'Gitty' (SBa) CWGr
'Glad Huston' (Dwf SS-c) CWGr
'Glenbank Honeycomb' CWGr
 (Pom) **new**
'Glenbank Paleface' CWGr
 (Pom)
'Glenbank Twinkle' CWGr
 (MinC)
'Glengarry' (SC) CWGr
'Globular' (MinBa) CWGr
'Gloria Romaine' (SD) CWGr MTiv
'Glorie van Heemstede' CWGr LAyl LBut LPio LRHS MTiv
 (SWL) ♀H3 NHal WWol
'Glorie van Naardwijk' CWGr
 (SD)
'Glory' (LD) CWGr
'Glow Orange' (MinBa) CWGr
'Go American' (GD) CWGr MTiv NHal
'Gold Ball' (MinBa) CWGr
'Gold Crown' (LS-c) CSut
'Gold Standard' (LD) CWGr
'Goldean' (GD) CWGr
'Golden Emblem' (MD) CWGr SDeJ
'Golden Fizz' (MinBa) CWGr
'Golden Glitter' (MS-c) CWGr
 new
'Golden Heart' (MS-c) CWGr
'Golden Horn' CWGr
 (MS-c) **new**
'Golden Impact' (MS-c) MTiv NHal
'Golden Jubilee' (D) **new** EPfP
'Golden Leader' (SD) CWGr
'Golden Sceptre WAba
 (Saphire)' (MinD)

'Golden Symbol' (MS-c) CWGr WAba
'Golden Turban' (MD) CWGr
'Golden Willo' (Pom) CWGr
'Goldilocks' (S-c) CWGr
'Goldorange' (SS-c) CWGr
'Good Earth' (MC) CWGr
'Good Hope' (MinD) CWGr
'Good Intent' (MinBa) CWGr
'Goshen Beauty' CWGr
(SWL) **new**
'Goya's Venus' (SS-c) CWGr
'Grace Nash' (SD) CWGr
'Grace Rushton' (SWL) CWGr
'Gracie S' (MinC) **new** NHal
'Grand Prix' (GD) CWGr
'Grand Willo' (Pom) WAba
'Grenadier' (SWL) CBgR EBee EMan ERou LPio SDix
SDys WAba WCot
'Grenidor Pastelle' (MS-c) CWGr LBut NHal WAba
'Gretchen Heine' (SD) CWGr
'Grock' (Pom) CWGr
'Gunyu' (GD) CWGr
'Gurtla Twilight' (Pom) CWGr NHal
'Gypsy Boy' (LD) CWGr LAyl MTiv
'Gypsy Girl' (SD) CWGr
'Halam Portia' (SWL) WAba
'Hallwood Asset' (MinD) CWGr
'Hallwood Coppernob' CWGr
(MD)
'Hallwood Satin' (MD) CWGr
'Hallwood Tiptop' (MinD) CWGr
'Hamari Accord' (LS-c) LAyl MTiv NHal WAba
♀H3
'Hamari Bride' (MS-c) CWGr LAyl
♀H3
'Hamari Girl' (GD) CWGr NHal
'Hamari Gold' (GD) ♀H3 CWGr NHal WAba
'Hamari Katrina' (LS-c) CWGr LRHS MTiv WAba
'Hamari Rosé' (MinBa) CWGr LAyl MTiv NHal
♀H3
'Hamari Sunshine' (LD) CWGr NHal
♀H3
'Hamilton Amanda' (SD) CWGr
'Hamilton Lillian' (SD) CWGr WAba
♀H3
'Hans Radi' (Misc) WAba
'Hans Ricken' (SD) CWGr
'Happy Caroline' CWGr LRHS
* 'Haresbrook' CBgR EBee EMan ERou MSte
NGdn SDys WAba WCot WSpi
'Harvest Amanda' (Sin/Lil) LBut
♀H3
'Harvest Brownie' (Sin/Lil) LBut
§ 'Harvest Imp' (Sin/Lil) LAyl
§ 'Harvest Inflammation' LBut
(Sin/Lil) ♀H3
§ 'Harvest Samantha' LAyl LBut
(Sin/Lil) ♀H3
'Haseley Bridal Wish' CWGr
(MC)
'Haseley Goldicote' (SD) CWGr
'Haseley Miranda' (SD) CWGr
'Haseley Triumph' (SD) CWGr
'Haseley Yellow Angora' CWGr
(SD)
'Hayley Jayne' (SC) CWGr WAba
'Helga' (MS-c) CWGr
'Helma Rost' (SS-c) CWGr
'Henri Lweii' (SC) CWGr
'Henriette' (MC) **new** CWGr
'Herbert Smith' (D) CWGr
'Hexton Copper' (SBa) CWGr
'Hi Ace' (LC) CWGr
'Hidi' (SS-c) **new** CWGr

'Higherfield Champion' CWGr
(SS-c)
'Highflyer' (MinD) **new** NHal
'Highness' (MinS-c) CWGr
'Hildepuppe' (Pom) CWGr
'Hillcrest Amour' (SD) CWGr
'Hillcrest Bobbin' (SBa) CWGr
'Hillcrest Camelot' (GS-c) CWGr
'Hillcrest Carmen' (SD) CWGr
'Hillcrest Contessa' CWGr
(MinBa)
'Hillcrest Delight' (MD) NHal
'Hillcrest Desire' (SC) CWGr LAyl WAba
♀H3
'Hillcrest Divine' (MinD) NHal WAba
'Hillcrest Fiesta' (MS-c) CWGr
'Hillcrest Hannah' **new** NHal
'Hillcrest Heights' (LS-c) CWGr WAba
'Hillcrest Kismet' (MD) NHal
'Hillcrest Margaret' **new** WAba
'Hillcrest Pearl' (MD) CWGr
'Hillcrest Regal' (Col) CWGr WAba
'Hillcrest Royal' (MC) NHal SDix
♀H3
'Hillcrest Suffusion' (SD) CWGr
'Hillcrest Ultra' (SD) CWGr
'Hill's Delight' (MS-c) CWGr
'Hindu Star' (MinBa) CWGr
'Hit Parade' (MS-c) CWGr
'Hockley Maroon' (SD) CWGr
'Hockley Nymph' CWGr
(SWL) **new**
'Holland Festival' (GD) MTiv
'Homer T' (LS-c) **new** CWGr
'Honey' (Anem/DwB) CWGr LRHS WAba
'Honeymoon Dress' (SD) CWGr
'Honka' (Misc) ♀H3 **new** CWGr
'Hot Chocolate' **new** CWGr ECho SChu
'Hugh Mather' (MWL) CWGr
'Hulin's Carnival' (MinD) CWGr
'Hy Clown' (SD) **new** CWGr
'Hy Fire' (MinBa) CWGr
'Ice Queen' (SWL) CWGr
'Ida Gayer' (LD) CWGr
'I-lyke-it' (SS-c) CWGr
'Imp' see *D.* 'Harvest Imp'
imperialis (B) CHEx CHll EMon EWes GCal LPio
MOak WBVN WDyG WHal WMul
I – 'Tasmania' (B) GCal
'Impression Famosa' **new** WWeb
'Impression WWeb
Fantastico' **new**
'Impression Flamenco' CWGr LRHS
'Impression Fortuna' CWGr
(Dwf Col)
'Impression Futuro' **new** WWeb
'In Green' **new** MBri
'Inca Concord' (MD) CWGr
'Inca Dambuster' (GS-c) CWGr MTiv NHal
'Inca Glamour' (LD) CWGr
'Inca Matchless' (MD) CWGr WAba
'Inca Metropolitan' (LD) CWGr
'Inca Panorama' (MD) CWGr
'Inca Royale' (LD) CWGr
'Inca Vanguard' (GD) CWGr
'Inca Vulcan' (GS-c) CWGr
'Indian Summer' (SC) CWGr
'Inflammation' see *D.* 'Harvest Inflammation'
'Inglebrook Jill' (Col) CWGr LAyl
'Inland Dynasty' (GS-c) CWGr
'Inn's Gerrie Hoek' (MD) CWGr
'Irene Ellen' (SD) **new** WAba
'Irene van der Zwet' (Sin) CWGr EPfP
'Iris' (Pom) MTiv WAba

'Irisel' (MS-c) — CWGr
'Islander' (LD) — CWGr
'Ivanetti' (MinBa) — NHal
'Jack Hood' (SD) **new** — CWGr
'Jackie Magson' (SS-c) — CWGr WAba
'Jackie's Baby' (MinD) — WAba
'Jacqueline Tivey' (SD) — CWGr MTiv
'Jaldec Jerry' (GS-c) — CWGr
'Jaldec John' (GD) — CWGr
'Jaldec Joker' (SC) — CWGr
'Jaldec Jolly' (SC) — CWGr
'Jamaica' (MinWL) — CWGr
'Jamie' (SS-c) — CWGr
'Jan van Schaffelaar' — CWGr
'Janal Amy' (GS-c) — NHal
'Jane Cowl' (LD) — CWGr
'Jane Horton' (Col) — CWGr
* 'Janet Becket' (LC) — CWGr
'Janet Clarke' (Pom) — CWGr
'Janet Jean' (SWL) — CWGr
'Japanese Waterlily' (SWL) — CWGr
'Jason' (SS-c) — WAba
'Jazzy' (Col) — CWGr
'Je Maintiendrai' (GD) — CWGr
'Jean Fairs' (MinWL) — CWGr LBut
'Jean Marie'PBR (MD) — CWGr LRHS
'Jean McMillan' (SC) — WAba
'Jean Melville' (MinD) — CWGr
'Jeanette Carter' (MinD) — CWGr
    ♀H3
'Jeanne d'Arc' (GC) — CSut CWGr
'Jeannie Leroux' — CWGr
    (SS-c/Fim)
'Jean's Carol' (Pom) — CWGr
'Jennie' (MC/Fim) — CWGr
'Jescot Buttercup' (SD) — CWGr
'Jescot India' (MinD) — CWGr
'Jescot Jess' (MinD) — CWGr LBut
'Jescot Jim' (SD) — CWGr
'Jescot Julie' (O) — CWGr LAyl
'Jescot Lingold' (MinD) — CWGr WAba
'Jescot Nubia' (SS-c) — CWGr
'Jescot Redun' (MinD) — CWGr
'Jessica' (S-c) — CWGr
'Jessie G' (SBa) — CWGr
'Jessie Ross' (MinD/DwB) — CWGr
'Jet' (SS-c) — CWGr
'Jill Day' (SC) — CWGr LBut
* 'Jill's Blush' (MS-c) — CWGr
'Jill's Delight' (MD) — CWGr
'Jim Branigan' (LS-c) — CWGr NHal WAba
'Jim's Jupiter' (LS-c) **new** — WAba
'Jive' **new** — CWGr
'Joan Beecham' (SWL) — CWGr
'Jocondo' (GD) — CWGr NHal
'Johann' (Pom) — CWGr NHal
'John Butterworth' (GD) — CWGr
'John Prior' (SD) — CWGr
'John Street' (SWL) ♀H3 — CWGr
'John's Champion' (MD) — CWGr
'Jomanda' (MinBa) ♀H3 — LBut NHal WAba
'Jorja' (MS-c) — CWGr NHal
'Jo's Choice' (MinD) — CWGr LBut
'Joy Donaldson' (MC) — CWGr
'Joyce Green' (GS-c) — CWGr
'Joyce Margaret Cunliffe' — CWGr
    (SD)
'Juanita' (MS-c) — CWGr
'Judy Tregidden' — NHal
    (MWL) **new**
'Julie One' (Misc Dbl O) — CWGr
'Julio' (MinBa) — CWGr
'Jura' (SS-c) — CWGr
'Just Jill' (MinD) — CWGr

'Kaftan' (MD) — CWGr
'Kaiserwalzer' (Col) — CWGr
'Karenglen' (MinD) ♀H3 — LBut NHal WAba
'Kari Quill' (SC) — CWGr
'Karma Amanda' (SD) **new** — WAba
'Karma Bon Biuni' — WAba
    (SC) **new**
'Karma Corona'PBR — WAba
    (SC) **new**
'Karma Lagoon'PBR **new** — WAba
'Karma Maarten — WAba
    Zwaan'PBR (SWL) **new**
'Karma Naomi'PBR **new** — WAba
'Karma Sangria'PBR **new** — WAba
'Karma Serena'PBR **new** — WAba
I 'Karma Thalia' **new** — WAba
'Karma Ventura' (SD) **new** — WAba
'Karma Yin-Yang' — WAba
    (SD) **new**
'Karras' (SS-c) — NHal
'Karras 150' (SS-c) — CWGr
'Kate's Pastelle' **new** — WAba
'Kathleen's Alliance' (SC) — NHal
    ♀H3
'Kathryn's Cupid' (MinBa) — CWGr SWal WAba
    ♀H3
'Kathy' (SC) — CWGr
'Katie Dahl' (MinD) — CWGr NHal
'Katisha' (MinD) — CWGr
'Kay Helen' (Pom) — CWGr
'Keith's Choice' (MD) — CWGr NHal WAba
'Kelsea Carla' (SS-c) — CWGr NHal WAba
* 'Keltie Jimmy Flood' — NHal
    (MinBa)
'Keltie Peach' (MD) — NHal
'Kelvin Floodlight' (GD) — CWGr
'Kenn Emerland' (MS-c) — CSut
'Kenora Canada' (MS-c) — CWGr WAba
'Kenora Challenger' (LS-c) — CWGr NHal WAba
'Kenora Christmas' (SBa) — CWGr
'Kenora Clyde' (GS-c) — CWGr
'Kenora Fireball' (MinBa) — NHal
'Kenora Jubilee' — NHal
    (LS-c) **new**
'Kenora Lisa' (MD) — CWGr WAba
'Kenora Moonbeam' (MD) — CWGr
'Kenora Ontario' — CWGr
    (LS-c) **new**
'Kenora Peace' (MinBa) — CWGr
'Kenora Sunset' (MS-c) — CWGr LAyl LBut NHal
    ♀H3
'Kenora Superb' (LS-c) — CWGr NHal WAba
'Kenora Valentine' (LD) — CWGr LAyl MTiv NHal
    ♀H3
'Kenora Wildfire' (LD) — CWGr
'Ken's Choice' (SBa) **new** — NHal
'Ken's Coral' (SWL) — CWGr NHal
'Ken's Flame' (SWL) — CWGr
'Ken's Rarity' (SWL) — NHal
'Keri Blue' (SWL) **new** — CWGr
'Kidd's Climax' (GD) — CWGr MTiv NHal WAba
    ♀H3
'Kilmorie' (SS-c) — NHal
'Kim Willo' (Pom) — CWGr
'Kimberley B' (MinD) — CWGr
'Kim's Marc' (SC) — LBut
* 'Kingston' (MinD) — CWGr
'Kismet' (SBa) — CWGr
'Kiss' (MinD) — CWGr
'Kiwi Brother' (SS-c) — CWGr
'Kiwi Cousin' (SC) — CWGr
'Kiwi Gloria' (SC) — MTiv NHal WAba
'Klondike' (MS-c) — CWGr WAba
* 'Kogano Fubuki' (MD) — CWGr

'Korgill Meadow' (MD) **new**	CWGr
'Kotare Jackpot' (SS-c)	CWGr
'Kung Fu' (SD)	CWGr MTiv
I 'Kyoto' (SWL)	CWGr WAba
'L.A.T.E.' (MinBa)	CWGr NHal WAba
'La Cierva' (Col)	CWGr
'La Gioconda' (Col)	CWGr
'Lady Kerkrade' (SC)	CWGr MTiv
'Lady Linda' (SD)	CWGr LBut MTiv NHal WAba
'Lady Orpah' (SD)	CWGr
'Lady Sunshine' (SS-c)	CWGr
'L'Ancresse' (MinBa)	CWGr LAyl NHal WAba
'Larkford' (SD)	CWGr
'Last Dance' (MD)	CWGr
* 'Latascn' **new**	WCot
'Laura Marie' (MinBa)	CWGr
* 'Laura's Choice' (SD)	CWGr
'Lauren's Moonlight' (MS-c)	CWGr NHal WAba
'Lavendale' (MinD)	CWGr
'Lavender Chiffon' (MS-c) **new**	CWGr
'Lavender Freestyle' (SC)	CWGr
'Lavender Leycett' (GD)	CWGr
'Lavender Line' (SC)	CWGr NHal
'Lavender Nunton Harvest' (SD)	CWGr
'Lavender Perfection' (GD)	CSut CWGr
'Lavender Prince' (MD)	CWGr
'Lavengro' (GD)	CWGr
'Le Castel' (D)	CWGr
'Le Patineur' (MD)	CWGr
'Leander' (GS-c)	CWGr
'Lecta' (MS-c)	CWGr
'Lemon' (Anem)	CWGr WAba
'Lemon Cane' (Misc)	CWGr WAba
'Lemon Elegans' (SS-c) ♀H3	CWGr LBut MTiv NHal WAba
'Lemon Meringue' (SD)	CWGr
* 'Lemon Puff' (Anem)	CWGr
'Lemon Symbol' (MS-c) **new**	CWGr
'Lemon Zing' (MinBa)	NHal WAba
* 'Lenny' (MinD)	CWGr
'Lexington' (Pom)	CWGr
'Leycett' (GD)	CWGr
'Libretto' (Col)	CWGr
* 'Life Force' (GD)	CWGr
'Life Size' (LD)	CWGr
'Light Music' (MS-c)	CWGr
'Lilac Athalie' (SC)	CWGr
'Lilac Shadow' (S-c)	CWGr
§ 'Lilac Taratahi' (SC) ♀H3	CWGr MTiv NHal
'Lilac Time' (MD)	EPfP LRHS SDeJ
'Lilac Willo' (Pom)	CWGr
'Lillianne Ballego' (MinD)	CWGr NHal
'Linda's Chester' (SC)	CWGr LBut
'Linda's Diane' (SD) **new**	CWGr
'Lisa'^PBR	CWGr
'Lismore Canary' (SWL)	NHal
'Lismore Carol' (Pom)	CWGr NHal
'Lismore Chaffinch' (MinD)	NHal
'Lismore Moonlight' (Pom)	CWGr LAyl NHal
'Lismore Peggy' (Pom)	CWGr
'Lismore Robin' (MinD)	NHal
'Lismore Sunset' (Pom)	CWGr WAba
'Lismore Willie' (SWL) ♀H3	LBut NHal WAba
'Little Dorrit' (Sin/Lil) ♀H3	CWGr LBut

'Little Glenfern' (MinC)	CWGr
'Little Jack' (MinS-c) **new**	CWGr
'Little John'	CWGr
'Little Laura' (MinBa)	CWGr
'Little Reggie' (SS-c)	CWGr
'Little Robert' (MinD)	CWGr
'Little Sally' (Pom)	CWGr
'Little Scottie' (Pom)	CWGr
'Little Shona' (MinD)	CWGr
'Little Snowdrop' (Pom)	CWGr
'Little Tiger'	CWGr
'Little Treasure' **new**	EPfP
'Liz' (MS-c)	CWGr
'Lois Walcher' (MD)	CWGr
'Lombada' (Misc)	CWGr
'Long Island Lil' (SD)	CWGr
'Longwood Dainty' (DwB)	CWGr NHal
'Loretta' (SBa)	CWGr
'Loud Applause' (SC)	CWGr
'Louis V' (LS-c)	CWGr
'Louise Bailey' (MinD)	CWGr
'Lucky Devil' (MD)	CWGr
'Lucky Number' (MD)	CWGr
'Ludwig Helfert' (S-c)	CWGr EPfP LRHS
'Lupin Dixie' (SC)	CWGr
'Lyn Mayo' (SD)	CWGr
'Lyndsey Murray' (MinD)	CWGr
'Lynn Clark' (SD)	WAba
'Mabel Ann' (GD)	CWGr
I 'Madame de Rosa' (LS-c) **new**	NHal
'Madame J. Snapper' **new**	WSpi
'Madame Simone Stappers' (WL)	CWGr EBee
'Madame Vera' (SD)	CWGr LBut
'Madelaine Ann' (GD)	CWGr
'Mafolie' (GS-c)	CWGr
'Magenta Magic' (Sin/DwB)	NHal
'Magic Moment' (MS-c)	CWGr
'Magnificat' (MinD)	CWGr
'Maisie Mooney' (GD)	CWGr
'Majestic Athalie' (SC)	CWGr
'Majestic Kerkrade' (SC)	CWGr
'Majjas Symbol' (MS-c)	CWGr
'Malham Honey' (SD)	CWGr
'Maltby Fanfare' (Col)	CWGr
'Maltby Whisper' (SC)	LAyl NHal
'Mandy' (MinD)	CWGr
'March Magic' (MinD) **new**	CWGr
'Margaret Ann' (MinD)	CWGr LAyl LBut MTiv
'Margaret Brookes' (LD)	CWGr
* 'Margaret Haggo' (SWL)	LAyl NHal
'Margie' (SD)	WAba
'Marie' (SD)	CWGr
'Marie Schnugg' (Misc) ♀H3	CWGr
'Mariposa' (Col)	CWGr WAba
'Mark Damp' (LS-c)	CWGr
'Mark Hardwick' (GD)	NHal
'Mark Lockwood' (Pom)	CWGr MTiv WAba
'Market Joy' (SD)	CWGr
'Marla Lu' (MC)	CWGr
'Marlene Joy' (MS-c/Fim)	CWGr NHal WAba
'Maroen'^PBR (Misc)	CWGr
'Mars' (Col)	CWGr
'Marshmello Sky' (Col)	CWGr
'Martin's Red' (Pom)	CWGr
'Martin's Yellow' (Pom)	NHal WAba
'Marvelous Sal' (MD) **new**	NHal
'Mary Eveline' (Col)	LAyl NHal
'Mary Hammett' (MinD)	WAba

'Mary Jennie' (MinS-c)	CWGr
'Mary Lunns' (Pom)	CWGr
'Mary Magson' (SS-c)	CWGr
'Mary Partridge' (SWL)	CWGr
'Mary Pitt' (MinD)	CWGr
'Mary Richards' (SD)	CWGr
'Mary's Jomanda' (SBa)	NHal
'Master David' (MinBa)	CWGr
'Master Michael' (Pom)	CWGr
'Match' (SS-c)	CWGr MTiv
'Matilda Huston' (SS-c)	CWGr NHal
'Matt Armour' (Sin)	CWGr
'Maureen Hardwick' (GD)	CWGr
'Maxine Bailey' (SD)	CWGr
'Maya' (SD)	CWGr
'Meiro' (SD)	CWGr MTiv
'Melanie Jane' (MS-c)	CWGr
'Melody Dixie'^{PBR} (MinD) **new**	CWGr
'Melody Dora'^{PBR} **new**	CWGr
'Melody Gipsy'^{PBR} (SS-c) **new**	WWeb
'Melody Swing'^{PBR} **new**	CWGr
'Melton' (MinD)	CWGr
merckii (B)	CBgR CHad CMdw CSpe EBre EGoo EOrc EWes GCal GEil GFlt GMac LRHS MNrw MSte SChu SMad WAba WCom WDyG WSHC WWin
- *alba* (B)	CFil CHad EBee MSte WCru WPGP
- compact (B)	CBos CFil EMan WPGP
- 'Edith Edelman' (B)	CFil
'Meredith's Marion Smith' (SD)	CWGr
'Mermaid of Zennor' (Sin)	CFir CPrp EBee EBlw EMan ERou NCot WCot
'Merriwell Topic' (MD)	CWGr
'Mi Wong' (Pom)	NHal
'Miami' (SD)	CWGr
'Michael J' (MinD)	CWGr
'Michigan' (MinD)	CWGr
'Mick' (SC)	CWGr
'Mick's Peppermint' (MS-c)	MTiv
'Midas' (SS-c)	CWGr
'Midnight' (Pom)	CWGr
'Midnight Sun' (MinD)	NHal
'Mies' (Sin)	CWGr
'Mignon Silver' (Dwf Sin) **new**	CWGr
'Minder' (GD)	MTiv
'Mingus Gregory' (LS-c)	CWGr
'Mingus Kyle D' (SD)	CWGr
'Mingus Nichole' (LD)	CWGr
'Mingus Tracy Lynn' (SS-c)	CWGr
'Mingus Whitney' (GS-c)	CWGr
'Mini' (Sin/Lil)	CWGr LBut
'Mini Red' (MinS-c)	CWGr
'Minley Carol' (Pom) ♀^{H3}	CWGr LAyl NHal WAba
'Minley Linda' (Pom)	CWGr MTiv
'Minnesota' (LD)	WAba
'Miramar' (SD)	CWGr
'Miss Blanc' (SD)	CWGr MTiv
'Miss Rose Fletcher' (SS-c)	CWGr
'Miss Swiss' (SD)	CWGr
'Misterton' (MD)	CWGr
'Mistill Beauty' (SC)	CWGr
'Mistill Delight' (MinD)	CWGr
'Mom's Special' (LD)	CWGr
'Monk Marc' (SC)	CWGr LBut
'Monkstown Diane' (SC)	CWGr
'Monrovia' (Pom)	CWGr
'Mon Tresor' (MS-c)	CWGr

'Moonfire' (Misc/DwB) ♀^{H3}	More than 30 suppliers
'Moonglow' (LS-c)	CWGr
'Moor Place' (Pom)	MTiv NHal WAba
'Moray Susan' (4) **new**	CWGr WAba
'Moret' (SS-c)	CWGr
'Morley Lady' (SD)	CWGr
'Morley Lass' (SS-c)	CWGr
'Morning Dew' (SC)	CWGr
'Mount Noddy' (Sin)	CWGr
'Mrs A. Woods' (MD)	CWGr
'Mrs Black' (Pom)	CWGr
'Mrs Geo Le Boutillier' (GD) **new**	CWGr
'Mrs H. Brown' (Col)	CWGr
'Mrs McDonald Quill' (LD)	CWGr NHal
'Mrs Silverston' (SD)	CWGr
'Mummies Favourite' (SD)	CWGr
'München' (MinD)	CWGr
'Murdoch'	CBgR CPen EBee ECtt EMan EPfP ERou SDys WAba WCot WSpi
'Muriel Gladwell' (SS-c)	CWGr
'Murillo'	MBri
'Murray May' (LD)	CWGr
'Musette' (MinD)	CWGr
'My Beverley' (MS-c)(Fim) **new**	NHal
'My Joy' (Pom)	CWGr
'My Love' (SS-c)	CSut LRHS
'My Valentine' (SWL)	CWGr
'Mystery Day' (MD)	CSut CWGr
'Nancy H' (MinBa)	CWGr
'Nankyoko'	CWGr
'Nargold' (MS-c/Fim)	CWGr LAyl
'Natal' (MinBa)	CWGr
'National Vulcan' (MinD)	CWGr
'Nationwide' (SD)	CWGr MTiv WAba
'Neal Gillson' (MD)	CWGr
'Nellie Birch' (MinBa)	CWGr
'Nellie Geerlings' (Sin)	CWGr
'Nenekazi' (MS-c/Fim)	CWGr LAyl
'Nepos' (SWL)	CWGr LBut
'Nescio' (Pom)	CWGr WAba
'Nettie' (MinBa)	CWGr
'New Baby' (MinBa)	CWGr LRHS
'New Dimension' (SS-c)	CWGr
'New Look' (LS-c)	CWGr
'Newsham Wonder' (SD)	CWGr
'Nicola' (SS-c)	CWGr
'Nicola Jane' (Pom) ♀^{H3}	NHal
'Nicolette' (MWL)	CWGr
'Night Life' (SC) **new**	CWGr
'Nijinsky' (SBa)	CWGr
'Nina Chester' (SD)	CWGr MTiv WAba
'Nonette' (SWL)	CWGr WAba WCot
'Norbeck Dusky' (SS-c)	CWGr
'Noreen' (Pom)	CWGr NHal
'North Sea' (MD)	CWGr
'Northland Primrose' (SC)	CWGr
* 'Nuit d'Eté' (MS-c)	CWGr EBee LPio
Nunton form (SD)	CWGr
'Nunton Harvest' (SD)	CWGr
'Nutley Sunrise' (MC)	CWGr
'Nymphenburg' (SD)	CWGr
'Oakwood Diamond' (SBa)	CWGr LBut
'Old Boy' (SBa)	CWGr
'Omo' (Sin/Lil) ♀^{H3}	LAyl LBut WAba
'Onesta' (SWL)	CWGr
'Only Love' (MS-c)	CWGr
'Onslow Michelle' (SD)	CWGr
'Onslow Renown' (LS-c)	CWGr
'Opal' (SBa)	CWGr
'Optic Illusion' (SD)	CWGr
'Opus' (SD)	CWGr

'Orange Berger's Record' (MS-c) — CWGr

'Orange Fire' (MS-c) — CWGr

'Orange Jewel' (SWL) — CWGr

'Orange Keith's Choice' (MD) — CWGr NHal

'Orange Mullett' (MinD/DwB) — CWGr

'Orange Nugget' (MinBa) — CWGr LRHS

I 'Orange Queen' (MC) — CWGr

'Orange Sun' (LD) — CWGr

'Oranjestad' (SWL) — CWGr

'Orel' (Col) — CWGr WAba

'Oreti Duke' (Pom) — NHal

'Oreti Fiesta' (SD) — NHal

'Orfeo' (MC) — CWGr

I 'Orion' (MD) — CWGr

'Ornamental Rays' (SC) — CWGr LBut

'Othello' (MS-c) — CWGr

'Pacific Argyle' (SD) — NHal

'Pacific Revival' (Pom) — NHal

'Paint Box' (MS-c) — CWGr

'Palomino' (MinD) — CWGr

'Pamela' (SD) — CWGr

'Park Princess' (SC/DwB) — CWGr LRHS NHal SDeJ

'Parkflamme' (MinD) — CWGr

'Paroa Gillian' (SC) — CWGr

'Party Girl' **new** — NHal

'Paso Doble' misapplied (Anem) — see *D.* 'Freya's Paso Doble'

'Pat Mark' (LS-c) — CWGr NHal

'Pat 'n' Dee' (SD) — CWGr

'Pat Seed' (MD) — CWGr

'Patricia' (Col) — NHal

'Paul Critchley' (SC) — CWGr

'Paul's Delight' (SD) — CWGr

'Peace Pact' (SWL) — CWGr WAba

'Peach Athalie' (SC) — CWGr

'Peach Cupid' (MinBa) ♀H3 — CWGr LBut NHal WAba

'Peach Melba' (SD) — NHal WAba

'Peaches and Cream' PBR **new** — CWGr

'Pearl Hornsey' (SD) — CWGr

'Pearl of Heemstede' (SD) ♀H3 — LAyl MTiv NHal

'Pearl Sharowean' (MS-c) — WAba

'Pearson's Ben' (SS-c) **new** — CWGr

'Pearson's Mellanie' (SC) **new** — CWGr

'Pembroke Pattie' (Pom) — CWGr

'Pennsclout' (GD) — CWGr

'Pennsgift' (GD) — CWGr

'Pensford Marion' (Pom) — WAba

'Perfectos' (MC) — CWGr

'Periton' (MinBa) — CWGr

'Peter' (MinD) **new** — CWGr

I 'Peter' (LD) — LRHS

'Peter Nelson' (SBa) — CWGr

'Petit Bôt' (SS-c) — CWGr

'Petit Byoux' — CWGr

'Philis Farmer' (SWL) — CWGr

I 'Phoenix' (MD) — CWGr WAba

'Pianella' (SS-c) — CWGr

'Pim's Moonlight' (MS-c) — CWGr

'Pineholt Princess' (LD) — CWGr

'Pinelands Pam' (MS-c) — CWGr LAyl NHal

'Pink Attraction' (MinD) — CWGr

'Pink Breckland Joy' (MD) — CWGr

'Pink Carol' (Pom) — CWGr

'Pink Giraffe' (O) — CWGr

'Pink Honeymoon Dress' (SD) — CWGr

'Pink Jupiter' (GS-c) — NHal

'Pink Katisha' (MinD) — CWGr MTiv

'Pink Kerkrade' (SC) — CWGr

'Pink Loveliness' (SWL) — CWGr

'Pink Newby' (MinD) — CWGr

'Pink Pastelle' (MS-c) ♀H3 — CWGr NHal WAba

'Pink Preference' (SS-c) — CWGr

'Pink Robin Hood' (SBa) — CWGr

'Pink Sensation' (SC) ♀H3 — LBut

'Pink Shirley Alliance' (SC) — LAyl

'Pink Suffusion' (SD) — WAba

'Pink Sylvia' (MinD) — CWGr

'Pink Worton Ann' (MinD) — CWGr

pinnata soft yellow — WAba

'Piperoo' (MC) — CWGr

'Piper's Pink' (SS-c/DwB) — CWGr LAyl MTiv

I 'Pippa' (MinWL) — LBut

'Playa Blanca' — LRHS

'Playboy' (GD) — CWGr

'Plum Surprise' (Pom) — CWGr

'Polar Sight' (GC) — CWGr

'Polly Bergen' (MD) — CWGr

'Polly Peachum' (SD) — CWGr

'Polventon Supreme' (SBa) — CWGr

'Polyand' (LD) — CWGr

'Pontiac' (SC) — CWGr LAyl

'Pooh' (Col) **new** — NHal

'Pop Willo' (Pom) — CWGr

I 'Poppet' (Pom) — CWGr WAba

'Popular Guest' (MS-c/Fim) — CWGr

'Porcelain' (SWL) ♀H3 — LBut NHal

'Potgieter' (MinBa) — CWGr

'Pot-Pourri' (MinD) — CWGr

'Prefect' (MS-c) — CWGr

'Prefere' — CWGr LRHS

'Preference' (SS-c) — CWGr

'Preston Park' (Sin/DwB) ♀H3 — CWGr LAyl MAJR NHal

Pride of Berlin — see *D.* 'Stolz von Berlin'

'Pride of Holland' (LC) — CWGr

'Prime Minister' (GD) — CWGr

'Primeur' (MS-c) **new** — CWGr

'Primrose Accord' (LS-c) — CWGr

'Primrose Diane' (SD) — NHal WAba

'Primrose Pastelle' (MS-c) **new** — NHal

'Primrose Rustig' (MD) — CWGr

'Prince Valiant' (SD) — CWGr

'Princess Beatrix' (LD) — CWGr

'Princess Marie José' (Dwf Sin) — CWGr

'Pristine' (Pom) — CWGr

'Procyon' (SD) — CSut CWGr LRHS

'Prom' (Pom) — CWGr

'Promise' (MS-c/Fim) — CWGr

'Punky' (Pom) — CWGr

'Purbeck Lydia' (LS-c) — CWGr

'Purbeck Princess' (MinD) — CWGr

'Purity (Dutch)' (SS-c) — CWGr

'Purpinca' (Dwf Anem) — CWGr WAba

'Purple Cottesmore' (MWL) — CWGr

'Purple Gem' — CSut CWGr LRHS

'Purple R 'O' Schen' — CWGr

'Purple Sensation' (SS-c) — CWGr

'Purple Tai Hei Jo' (GD) — CWGr

'Pussycat' (SD) — CWGr

'Quel Diable' (LS-c) — CWGr MTiv

'Quick Step' **new** — CWGr

'Rachel's Place' (Pom) — CWGr

'Radfo' (SS-c) — CWGr WAba

'Radiance' (MC) — CWGr

'Raffles' (SD) — CWGr LAyl

I 'Ragged Robin' (Misc) — CAvo MBri

sherffii	CHad CHal CWGr EOrc GEil	
	MCCP MNrw	
sherffii x *coccinea*	CHad	
'Sherwood Monarch'	CWGr MTiv	
(GS-c)		
'Sherwood Standard' (MD)	CWGr NHal WAba	
'Sherwood Sunrise' (SD)	CWGr	
'Sherwood Titan' (GD)	CWGr MTiv	
'Shiloh Noelle' (GD)	CWGr	
'Shining Star' (SC)	CWGr	
'Shirley Alliance' (SWL)	WAba	
'Shooting Star' (LS-c)	CWGr	
'Shy Princess' (MC)	CWGr	
'Siedlerstolz' (LD)	CWGr	
'Siemen Doorenbos'	WAba	
(Anem)		
'Silver City' (LD)	CWGr NHal	
'Silver Slipper' (SS-c)	CWGr	
'Silver Years'	CWGr	
'Sir Alf Ramsey' (GD)	NHal WAba	
'Sisa' (SD)	CWGr	
'Skipley Spot' (SD)	CWGr MTiv	
'Skipper Rock' (GD)	CWGr	
'Sky High' (SD)	CWGr MTiv	
'Small World' (Pom) ♀H3	LAyl MTiv NHal WAba	
'Smokey'	CWGr LRHS	
'Smoky O' (MS-c)	CWGr	
'Sneezy' (Sin)	CWGr LRHS	
'Snip' (MinS-c)	CWGr WAba	
'Snoho Barbara' (MS-c)	CWGr	
'Snoho Christmas' **new**	CWGr	
'Snoho Tammie' (MinBa)	CWGr	
'Snow Cap' (SS-c)	CWGr	
'Snow Fairy' (MinC)	CWGr	
'Snow White' (Dwf Sin)	CWGr	
'Snowflake' (SWL)	CWGr WAba	
'Snowstorm' (MD)	CSut SDeJ	
'Snowy' (MinBa)	CWGr	
'So Dainty' (MinS-c) ♀H3	CWGr LAyl WAba	
'Sondervig' (SD)	CWGr	
'Song of Olympia' (SWL)	CWGr	
'Sonia'	CWGr	
'Sorrento Fiesta' (SS-c)	WAba	
'Sorrento Girl' (SS-c)	WAba	
'Sorrento Style' (SD)	WAba	
'Soulman' **new**	CWGr	
'Sourire de Crozon' (SD)	CWGr	
'Souvenir d'Été' (MinD)	CWGr	
'Spartacus' (LD)	CSut MTiv	
'Spassmacher' (MS-c)	CWGr	
'Spectacular' (SD)	CWGr	
'Spencer' (SD)	CWGr	
'Spennythorn King' (SD)	CWGr	
'Spikey Symbol' (MS-c)	CWGr	
'Sprinter' **new**	CWGr	
'Star Child' (Misc)	CWGr WAba	
'Star Elite'	LRHS	
'Star Spectacle' (MS-c)	CWGr	
'Starry Night' (MinC)	CWGr	
'Star's Elite' (MS-c)	CWGr	
'Star's Favourite' (MS-c)	CWGr	
'Star's Lady' (SS-c)	CWGr	
'Star Surprise' (SC)	CWGr	
'Stefan Bergerhoff'	CWGr	
(Dwf D)		
'Stella J' (SWL)	CWGr	
'Stella's Delight' (SD)	CWGr	
'Stellyvonne' (LS-c/Fim)	CWGr	
'Stephanie' (SS-c)	CWGr	
§ 'Stolz von Berlin' (MinBa)	CWGr WAba	
'Stoneleigh Cherry' (Pom)	LAyl	
'Stoneleigh Joyce' (Pom)	CWGr	
'Storm Warning' (GD)	CWGr	
'Stylemaster' (MC)	CWGr	

'Sue Willo' (Pom)	CWGr	
'Suffolk Fantasy' (SWL)	CWGr	
'Suffolk Punch' (MD)	CWGr LAyl LBut	
'Suitzus Julie' (Lil)	CWGr	
'Summer Festival' (SD)	CWGr	
'Summer Night' (MC)	CHad CPlt ECGP	
'Summer Night' (SC)	LAyl NHal	
'Summer's End'	CWGr	
'Sungold' (MinBa)	CWGr	
'Sunlight Pastelle' (MS-c)	CWGr WAba	
* 'Sunny Boy' (MinBa)	CWGr LRHS WAba	
'Sunray Glint' (MS-c)	CWGr WAba	
'Sunray Silk' (MS-c)	CWGr	
I 'Sunshine' (Sin)	LAyl	
'Sunstruck' (MS-c)	CWGr	
'Super Rays' (MC)	CWGr	
'Super Trouper' (SD)	CWGr	
'Superfine' (SC)	CWGr MTiv WAba	
'Sure Thing' (MC)	CWGr	
'Susan Willo' (Pom)	CWGr	
'Susannah York' (SWL)	CWGr	
'Suzette' (Dwf SD)	CWGr	
'Swallow Falls' (SD)	CWGr	
'Swan Lake' (SD)	LPio MBri	
'Swanvale' (SD)	CWGr	
'Sweet Content' (SD)	CWGr	
'Sweet Sensation' (MS-c)	WAba	
'Sweetheart' (SD)	CBgR LRHS WAba	
'Swiss Miss'	CWGr	
(MinBa/O) **new**		
'Sylvia's Desire' (SC)	CWGr WAba	
'Symbol' (MS-c)	CWGr	
'Sympathy' (SWL)	WAba	
'Syston Harlequin' (SD)	CWGr	
'Syston Sophia' (MinBa)	CWGr	
'Tahiti Sunrise' (MS-c)	CWGr	
'Tally Ho' (Misc) ♀H3	CBgR CM&M CWGr EBee EMan	
	ERou LPio LRHS MBri MSph SDys	
	SPla WAba WBry WCot WWhi	
	WWol	
'Taratahi Lilac'	see *D.* 'Lilac Taratahi'	
'Taratahi Ruby'	CWGr LBut MTiv NHal	
(SWL) ♀H3		
'Tartan' (MD)	CWGr	
'Teesbrooke Audrey' (Col)	LAyl NHal	
'Temptress' (SC)	CWGr	
'Tender Moon' (SD)	CWGr	
'Thames Valley' (MD)	CWGr	
'That's It!' (SD)	CWGr	
'The Baron' (SD)	CWGr	
'Thelma Clements' (LD)	CWGr MTiv	
'Theo Sprengers' (SD)	CWGr	
'Thomas A. Edison' (MD)	CSut CWGr	
'Thoresby Jewel' (SD)	CWGr	
'Tiara' (SD)	CWGr	
'Tiffany Lynn' (Misc)	CWGr	
'Tiger Eye' (MD)	CWGr	
'Tiger Tiv' (MD)	CWGr MTiv	
'Tina B' (SBa)	CWGr WAba	
'Tinker's White' (SD)	CWGr	
'Tioga Spice' (MS-c/Fim)	CWGr	
'Toga' (SWL)	CWGr	
'Tohsuikyoh' (Misc)	CWGr WAba	
'Tommy Doc' (SS-c)	CWGr NHal WAba	
'Tommy Keith' (MinBa)	CWGr	
'Tomo' (SD)	LAyl NHal	
'Top Affair' (MS-c)	CWGr	
'Top Choice' (GS-c)	SDeJ	
* 'Topaz Puff'	LRHS	
* 'Toto' (DwB)	CWGr NHal	
I 'Tranquility' (Col)	NHal	
'Trelawny' (GD)	WAba	
'Trelyn Kiwi' (SC)	WAba	

'Trengrove Autumn' (MD) CWGr
'Trengrove d'Or' (MD) CWGr
'Trengrove Jill' (MD) CWGr LAyl MTiv
'Trengrove Summer' (MD) MTiv
'Trengrove Tauranga' (MD) CWGr
'Trengrove Terror' (GD) CWGr
'Trevelyn Kiwi' (S-c) NHal
'Trevor' (Col) CWGr
'Tropical Sunset' **new** CWGr
'Tsuki Yorine Shisha' (MC) CWGr WAba
'Tu Tu' (MS-c) CWGr
'Tui Avis' (MinC) **new** CWGr
'Tui Orange' (SS-c) CWGr NHal WAba
'Tui Ruth' (SS-c) CWGr
'Tujays Lemondrop' (SD) NHal
'Tula Rosa' (Pom) CWGr
'Tutankhamun' (Pom) CWGr
'Twiggy' (SWL) CWGr LRHS
'Twilight Time' (MD) CWGr LPio LRHS WWol
'Uchuu' (GD) CWGr
'Union Jack' (Sin) CWGr WAba
'United' (SD) CWGr
'Usugesho' (LD) CWGr
'Vader Abraham' (MinD) CWGr
'Vaguely Noble' (SBa) CWGr
'Valentine Lil' (SWL) CWGr
'Vancouver' (Misc) **new** CWGr
'Vanquisher' (LS-c) CWGr
'Variace' (MinBa) **new** CWGr
'Vera's Elma' (LD) NHal
'Vesuvius' (MD) CWGr
'Vicky Crutchfield' (SWL) LBut
'Vicky Jackson' (SWL) CWGr
'Victory Day' (LC) CWGr
'Vidal Rhapsody' (MS-c) CWGr
'Vigor' (SWL) CWGr
'Vinovium' (MinBa) CWGr
'Violet Davies' (MS-c) CWGr
'Vivex' (MinBa) CWGr
'Volkskanzler' (Sin) CWGr
'Vrouwe Jacoba' (SS-c) CWGr
'Vulcan' (LS-c) CWGr
'Vuurvogel' (MS-c) **new** CWGr
'Walter Hardisty' (GD) CWGr
'Walter James' (SD) CWGr
'Wanborough Gem' (SBa) CWGr
'Wanda's Aurora' (GD) **new** NHal
'Wanda's Capella' (GD) CWGr MTiv NHal WAba
'Wanda's Moonlight' (GD) CWGr
'Wandy' (Pom) ♀H3 CWGr WAba
I 'War of the Roses' **new** WHer
'Warkton Willo' (Pom) CWGr
'Warmunda' LRHS
'Washington' CWGr
'Waveney Pearl' (SWL) CWGr
'Welcome Guest' (MS-c) CWGr MTiv WAba
'Welsh Beauty' (SBa) CWGr
'Wendy' (MinBa) CWGr
'Wendy Spencer' (MinD) CWGr
'Wendy's Place' (Pom) CWGr
'Weston Aramac' (SS-c) CWGr
'Weston Forge' (SC) CWGr
'Weston Miss' (MinS-c) CWGr
'Weston Nugget' (MinC) CWGr WAba
'Weston Princekin' CWGr
  (MinS-c)
'Weston Spanish Dancer' CWGr LBut WAba
  (MinC) ♀H3
'Whale's Rhonda' (Pom) WAba
'Wheel' (Col) WAba
'White Alva's' (GD) ♀H3 CWGr LAyl MTiv NHal
'White Ballet' (SD) ♀H3 CWGr LAyl LBut NHal
'White Charlie Two' (MD) NHal
'White Hunter' (SD) CWGr

'White Klankstad' (SC) CWGr
'White Knight' (MinD) NHal
'White Linda' (SD) CWGr NHal
'White Mathilda' (Dwf) CWGr
'White Merriwell' (SD) CWGr
'White Moonlight' (MS-c) LAyl LBut NHal WAba
'White Nettie' (MinBa) CWGr
'White Pastelle' (MS-c) WAba
'White Perfection' (LD) CSut CWGr
'White Polventon' (SBa) CWGr NHal
'White Rustig' (MD) CWGr
'White Star' CWGr LRHS
'White Swallow' (SS-c) NHal
'Wicky Woo' (SD) CWGr
'Wildwood Marie' (SWL) CWGr
'Willemse Glory' CWGr
  (Misc Orch)
'William 'B'' (GD) CWGr
'Williamsburg' (MS-c) CWGr
'Willo's Borealis' (Pom) CWGr NHal
'Willo's Flecks' (Pom) MTiv WAba
'Willo's Night' (Pom) CWGr
'Willo's Surprise' (Pom) CWGr MTiv NHal
'Willo's Violet' (Pom) CWGr MTiv WAba
'Willowfield Kay' WAba
  (MS-c) **new**
'Willowfield Matthew' NHal
  (MinD)
'Willowfield Mick' (LD) CWGr LAyl NHal WAba
'Winholme Diane' (SD) NHal WAba
'Winkie Colonel' (GD) CWGr NHal
'Winnie' (Pom) CWGr
'Winsome' (SWL) CWGr
'Winston Churchill' (MinD) CWGr LBut
'Winter Dawn' (SWL) CWGr
'Wise Guy' (GD) CWGr
'Wisk' (Pom) CWGr
'Wittem' (MD) CWGr
'Wittemans Superba' CWGr LAyl NHal SDix
  (SS-c) ♀H3
'Wootton Cupid' CWGr LBut MTiv NHal WAba
  (MinBa) ♀H3
'Wootton Impact' NHal
  (MS-c) ♀H3
'Wootton Phebe' (SD) CWGr
'Wootton Tempest' (MS-c) CWGr
'Worton Bluestreak' (SS-c) CWGr
'Worton Revival' (MD) CWGr
'Worton Superb' (SD) CWGr
'Wundal Horizon' (LS-c) CWGr
'Yellow Abundance' (SD) CWGr
'Yellow Baby' (Pom) CWGr
'Yellow Bird' (Col) CWGr
'Yellow Frank Hornsey' WAba
  (SD)
'Yellow Galator' (MC) CWGr
'Yellow Hammer' CWGr LAyl NHal SChu
  (Sin/DwB) ♀H3
'Yellow Linda's Chester' CWGr
  (SC)
'Yellow Pages' (SD) CWGr
'Yellow Pet' (MinD) CWGr
'Yellow Snow' (MD) CWGr
'Yellow Spiky' (MS-c) CWGr
'Yellow Star' (MS-c) CWGr
'Yellow Symbol' (MS-c) CWGr LBut
'Yellow Twist' CHad
'Yelno Enchantment' CWGr LAyl
  (SWL)
'Yelno Firelight' (SWL) CWGr
'Yelno Harmony' (SD) CWGr LBut
  ♀H3
'Yelno Petite Glory' CWGr
  (MinD)

'York and Lancaster' (MD)	CWGr EMon IGor
'Yorkie' (MS-c)	CWGr MTiv WAba
'Yoro Kobi' (DwB)	NHal
'Yukino' (Col)	CWGr
I 'Yvonne' (MWL)	WAba
'Zagato' (MinD)	CWGr
* 'Zakuro Fubuki' (MD)	CWGr
'Zakuro-Hime' (SD)	CWGr
'Zelda' (LD)	CWGr
'Zest' (MD)	CWGr
'Zing' (LS-c)	CWGr
'Zorro' (GD) ♀H3	CWGr MTiv NHal WAba
'Zurich' (SS-c)	CWGr

Dais (Thymelaeaceae)
cotinifolia	CPle

Daiswa see *Paris*

Dalea (Papilionaceae)
candida **new**	SUsu
purpurea	SUsu

Dalechampia (Euphorbiaceae)
dioscoreifolia	ERea ESlt

Dampiera (Goodeniaceae)
diversifolia	CSpe ECou SScr
lanceolata	ECou
teres	ECou

damson see *Prunus insititia*

Danae (Ruscaceae)
§ racemosa	CBcs CFil EBee ELan EMon ENot EPfP EPla ETow GCal IDee LRHS MGos MRav SAPC SArc SDry SPer SRms SSpi SSta WCot WDin WPGP

Danthonia (Poaceae)
californica	CBig

Daphne ✿ (Thymelaeaceae)
acutiloba	CFil CPMA ERea GKir NABC SAga
albowiana	CFil CPMA CPle EPot EWes SAga SBla SSpi WCru WPGP
'Allison Carver' (v)	CPMA
alpina	CPMA EHyt EPot SBla
altaica	CPMA
arbuscula ♀H4	CPMA EPot NMen SBla SIgm
- subsp. **arbuscula** f. **albiflora**	SBla
- f. **radicans new**	CPMA
bholua	CAbP CHll CPMA ERea GEdr LHop LRHS MGos MWya NABC SAga SIng SReu SSpi SSta WAbe WCru WPat
I - 'Alba'	CBcs CFil CPMA GAbr GKir LTwo MGos MPRe NABC NLar SBla SSpi SSta WCru WPGP
- 'Darjeeling'	CFil CPLG CPMA EPfP LRHS MAsh SCoo SSpi SSta WPGP
- var. **glacialis**	WCru
- - 'Gurkha'	CFil CPMA NABC SBla
- 'Glendoick'	EPfP GGGa
- 'Jacqueline Postill' ♀H3	More than 30 suppliers
- 'Peter Smithers'	SBla SCoo SReu SSpi SSta
- 'Rupina La' SCH 2611 **new**	SBla
blagayana	CBcs CFil CPMA EPot GAbr GCrs GGGa GKir MDun NABC SBla SIgm SRms SSpi WBVN WFar WPat
- 'Brenda Anderson'	ITim
'Bramdean'	see *D.* x *napolitana* 'Bramdean'
x **burkwoodii** ♀H4	CBcs EBee ECho ECrN EPot GKir MWya SAga SHBN SLon WBrE WDin WGwG
- 'Albert Burkwood'	CBcs CPMA EPot GKir GLbr LTwo MDun NABC NLar NWea WBrE WGwG
- 'Astrid' (v)	CPMA CWib LHop LRHS MGos MLan NMen SAga SCoo SMrm SMur SSta WDin WStI WWes
- Briggs Moonlight = 'Brimoon' (v)	LRHS
§ - 'Carol Mackie' (v)	CPMA GAbr GGGa GKir LRHS LTwo MDun MGos NABC NLar SIgm SSta
- 'G.K. Argles' (v) ♀H4	CBcs CFil CPMA ERea GEdr GKir GLbr LAst LRHS MAsh MBri MDun MGos MLan NABC WBrE WFar WPGP WPat WWes
- 'Gold Strike' (v)	CPMA
- 'Lavenirei'	CPMA NLar
- 'Somerset'	More than 30 suppliers
§ - 'Somerset Gold Edge' (v)	CPMA SIng
§ - 'Somerset Variegated' (v)	LAst NABC SAga
I - 'Variegata' (v)	SAga WPat
- 'Variegata' broad cream edge	see *D.* x *burkwoodii* 'Somerset Variegated'
- 'Variegata' broad gold edge	see *D.* x *burkwoodii* 'Somerset Gold Edge'
- 'Variegata' narrow gold edge	see *D.* x *burkwoodii* 'Carol Mackie'
caucasica	CPMA SBla
circassica	SBla
cneorum	CBcs CFil CPMA ENot EPfP GKir LRHS MGos NBee NMen SBod SMur SPer SSpi WDin WPat WStI WWin
- f. **alba**	CPMA SBla
- 'Blackthorn Triumph'	CPMA SBla
- 'Eximia' ♀H4	CBcs CPMA EMil EPot GAbr GEdr GKir GLbr MDun MGos MLan MPRe NABC SBla SHBN SIng SMrm SPer SRms SSpi WAbe WCot WGwG WPat
- 'Grandiflora'	see *D.* x *napolitana* 'Maxima'
- 'Lac des Gloriettes'	CPMA
- 'Puszta'	CPMA SAga SIgm WCru
- var. **pygmaea**	CPMA EPot SBla
- - 'Alba'	CPMA SBla
- 'Rose Glow'	CPMA
- 'Stasek'	CPMA SAga SBla
- 'Variegata' (v)	CBcs CPMA ECho EPot GCrs LHop MGos MMil NABC NWCA SHBN SIng
- 'Velky Kosir'	CPMA
- var. **verlotii**	CPMA
x **arbuscula**	
collina	see *D. sericea* Collina Group
collina x petraea	SSta
x **eschmannii new**	SIng
'Fragrant Cloud' **new**	WBcn
'Fragrant Cloud' **new** (aff. *acutiloba*) CD&R 626	CPMA SBla
genkwa	LRHS SBla WCru
giraldii	CPMA EHyt MDun SIgm SSpi WCru
aff. **giraldii new**	GKir NMen
x **hendersonii**	CEnd CPMA EPot
- 'Appleblossom'	CPMA EPot SBla
- 'Aymon Correvon'	CPMA SBla
- 'Blackthorn Rose'	SBla
- 'Ernst Hauser'	CPMA EPot GAbr GKir GLbr LTwo MPRe NABC SBla SScr SSpi WAbe WPat

- 'Fritz Kummert' CPMA SBla
- 'Kath Dryden' SBla
- 'Marion White' **new** SBla
- 'Rosebud' SBla
x *houtteana* CBot CPMA NABC NBir
x *hybrida* CPMA ECho SBla
japonica 'Striata' see *D. odora* 'Aureomarginata'
jasminea CPMA ECho NMen SBla
jezoensis CPMA SBla SSta WCru
juliae CPMA SBla
laureola CFil CPMA CSWP EPfP GPoy MGos
  MSte NBir NPer WCFE WPGP WWye
- var. *cantabrica* SChu
- 'Margaret Mathew' CPMA EPot
- subsp. *philippi* CBcs CBgR CPMA CPle CWSG
  ELan EPfP GEdr GKir LHop LRHS
  MAsh MBro NABC NDlv NMen
  SChu SHBN SPer SSpi SSta WCot
  WCru WFar
'Leila Haines' SBla
'Leila Haines' x *arbuscula* CPMA
longilobata CPle
- 'Peter Moore' NABC
x *manteniana* MGos SSpi
- 'Manten' CPMA GEdr GGGa GLbr MDun
  MPRe SLon
x *mauerbachii* CPMA SBla
  'Perfume of Spring'
'Meon' see *D.* x *napolitana* 'Meon'
mezereum More than 30 suppliers
- f. *alba* CFil CPMA CPle CWib EPfP GIBF
  GKir LAst LHop LRHS MBar MDun
  MGos MPRe SBla SHBN SIng SPer
  SRms WAbe WCru WPat WSpi
  WTin
- - 'Bowles' Variety' CBot CPMA GAbr
- 'Rosea' SRms
- var. *rubra* CBcs CFil CPMA CSBt CWSG EBre
  ELan EPfP GKir MGos MSwo NBee
  NBlu SBod SPer WCru WDin WOrn
  WStI
- 'Variegata' (v) LHop
x *napolitana* ♀H4 CPMA ECho EMil EPot GAbr
  GGGa GKir GLbr MDun MGos
  MPRe NABC NBPC NLar NMen
  SHBN SPer SSpi WAbe WBrE WPat
§ - 'Bramdean' **new** EPot SBla
§ - 'Maxima' MGos
§ - 'Meon' CPMA EPot LTwo NMen SBla
  WAbe WPat
odora CPMA CPle CSBt ERea LRHS LSpr
  MGos MPRe MSwo NMen SChu
  SPer SSta WDin WStI
§ - f. *alba* CEnd CPMA ERea LRHS MGos
I - 'Aureamarginata Alba' (v) CPMA WLow
§ - 'Aureomarginata' More than 30 suppliers
  (v) ♀H3-4
- 'Clotted Cream' CPMA
- 'Geisha Girl' (v) ERea SBla
- var. *leucantha* see *D. odora* f. *alba*
- 'Marginata' see *D. odora* 'Aureomarginata'
- var. *rubra* LRHS NABC
- 'Sakiwaka' CPMA
- 'Walberton' (v) EBre GKir LRHS
oleoides CPMA SBla
petraea SBla WAbe
- 'Alba' see *D. petraea* 'Tremalzo'
- 'Grandiflora' GCrs NMen SBla WAbe
§ - 'Tremalzo' SBla
pontica ♀H4 CBcs CFil CPMA CPle EHyt EPfP
  EPla GKir MBro NLar SDix SSpi
  WCot WCru WPGP
pseudomezereum WCru
retusa see *D. tangutica* Retusa Group

'Richard's Choice' CPMA
x *rollsdorfii* CPMA EPot
  'Arnold Cihlarz'
- 'Wilhelm Schacht' CPMA EPot SBla
'Rosy Wave' CPMA EPot SAga SBla
x *schlyteri* CPMA SBla
§ *sericea* CPMA SBla
§ - Collina Group CPMA EPfP GGGa SBla SIgm SRms
  SSpi SSta WAbe
- Hidcote form EPot
x *susannae* 'Anton CPMA NLar
  Fahndrich' x *collina*
- 'Cheriton' CPMA EPot LTwo NLar SBla SSta
  WBcn
- 'Tichborne' CPMA SBla
tangutica ♀H4 More than 30 suppliers
§ - Retusa Group ♀H4 CPMA EPot GAbr GCrs GGGa
  GKir ITim LAst LHop MAsh MBri
  MGos NABC NLAp NMen NRya
  SHBN SIgm SReu SRms SSpi SSta
  WCru
x *thauma* EPot NMen SBla
x *transatlantica* SBla
  'Jim's Pride'
x *whiteorum* CPMA GKir GLbr NABC SBla SIgm
  'Beauworth' WAbe
- 'Kilmeston' CPMA GKir NABC NMen
- 'Warnford' CPMA

Daphniphyllum (Daphniphyllaceae)

calycinum NLar SSpi
glaucescens B&SWJ 4058 WCru
- var. *oldhamii* WCru
  B&SWJ 6872 **new**
- - B&SWJ 7056 WCru
§ *himalaense* subsp. CBcs CDoC CFil CHEx CMCN
  macropodum EBee EPfP NLar SAPC SArc SDix
  SLPl SSpi WCru WFar WPGP
- - B&SWJ 2898 WCru
- - B&SWJ 581 WCru
- - B&SWJ 6809 WCru
  from Taiwan
- - B&SWJ 8763 WCru
  from Cheju-Do
- subsp. *macropodum* WCru
  dwarf **new**
humile see *D. himalaense* subsp.
  macropodum
teijsmannii CBcs
- B&SWJ 3805 WCru

Darlingtonia (Sarraceniaceae)

californica ♀H1 CFil CSWC EFEx LHew MCCP
  SHmp WSSs

Darmera (Saxifragaceae)

§ *peltata* ♀H4 More than 30 suppliers
- 'Nana' CCol CHEx EBee ECha GBuc GKir
  MBri MFir MTed MTis NLar SWat
  WCot WFar WPnP

Darwinia (Myrtaceae)

collina SOWG
fascicularis SOWG
grandiflora SOWG
leyostyla SOWG
oxylepis SOWG
rhadinophylla SOWG
squarrosa SOWG
taxifolia SOWG

Dasylirion (Dracaenaceae)

from Coahuilla, EOas
  Mexico **new**

§ **acrotrichum**   SAPC SArc XPep
  glaucophyllum   EAmu MPRe WMul
  gracile Planchon   see *D. acrotrichum*
  leiophyllum   XPep
  longissimum   CAbb CBrP CTrC EAmu EOas EShb
                            SChr WMul XPep
  texanum   CTrC EOas XPep
  wheeleri ♀H1   CBrP CRoM CTrC EAmu EOas
                            EShb SChr XPep

date see *Phoenix dactylifera*

Datisca (Datiscaceae)
  cannabina   CArn EBee ECha EMan GCal GFlt
                            LPhx LPio MAvo MGol NBPC
                            SMrm WCot WMoo WPGP WPic

Datura (Solanaceae)
  arborea   see *Brugmansia arborea*
  chlorantha   see *Brugmansia chlorantha*
  cornigera   see *Brugmansia arborea*
§ **inoxia** ♀H3   EBak MGol MSal SVen
  metel   MGol
  – 'Belle Blanche'   MGol
  – 'Cherub' (d)   GQui
  meteloides   see *D. inoxia*
  rosea   see *Brugmansia* x *insignis* pink
  rosei   see *Brugmansia sanguinea*
  sanguinea   see *Brugmansia sanguinea*
  stramonium   CArn MGol MSal
  – var. **chalybaea**   MSal
  – var. **inermis**   MSal
  suaveolens   see *Brugmansia suaveolens*
  versicolor   see *Brugmansia versicolor* Lagerh.
  – 'Grand Marnier'   see *Brugmansia* x *candida*
                            'Grand Marnier'

Daucus (Apiaceae)
  carota   CArn CRWN GBBs MBow NSco
                            WHer
  – 'Jane's Lace'   CNat

Davallia (Davalliaceae)
  canariensis ♀H1   CFil
§ **mariesii** ♀H3   CFil NMar SMad WAbe WCot
  – var. **stenolepis**   NMar
  pyxidata   see *D. solida* var. *pyxidata*
§ **solida** var. **pyxidata**   NMar
  tasmanii   CFil
  trichomanoides   NMar
  – f. **barbata**   NMar
  – var. **lorrainei**   NMar

Davidia (Cornaceae)
  involucrata ♀H4   More than 30 suppliers
  – var. **vilmoriniana** ♀H4   CBcs CDoC ELan EPfP EWTr
                            IMGH LRHS MCCP MDun MGos
                            NBlu SPer SPoG WOrn

Daviesia (Papilionaceae)
  brevifolia   SPlb

Decaisnea (Lardizabalaceae)
  fargesii   CAbP CAgr CDoC CDul CMCN
                            CPLG CPne CWib EBee ECre ELan
                            EPfP EPla EWTr GGGa MBlu MCCP
                            MGos NHol NPal SDnm SMad SPer
                            WBor WDin WFar WHer WPGP
                            WPat
  – B&SWJ 8070   WCru
  insignis   WNor WPGP

Decodon (Lythraceae)
  verticillatus   EMon

Decumaria (Hydrangeaceae)
  barbara   CBcs CDoC CFil CFwr CMac CTrC
                            EBee EMil GEil LRHS NSti SBra
                            SHBN SLim SLon SPer SSta WCru
                            WFar WSHC
  sinensis   EPfP SBra SLon SSpi WCru WSHC

Degenia (Brassicaceae)
  velebitica   EHyt WLin

Deinanthe (Hydrangeaceae)
  bifida   CLAP EBee WCru
  – B&SWJ 5012   WCru
  – B&SWJ 5655   WCru
  bifida x **caerulea** **new**   CDes CLAP
  caerulea   CDes CLAP EBee GEdr LEur MHar
                            SBla WCru WPGP

Delairea (Asteraceae)
§ **odorata**   WMul

Delonix (Caesalpiniaceae)
  regia   MGol SMur SOWG XBlo

Delosperma (Aizoaceae)
  LEG 037   CStu
§ **aberdeenense** ♀H1   CHEx
* **album**   CHEx
  ashtonii   CStu EDAr WPer
  'Basutoland'   see *D. nubigenum*
  congestum   NJOw
  cooperi   CFai EBre EChP ECtt EDAr ETow
                            EWll GEdr ITim NJOw NLAp SChr
                            SIng SMad WBea WFar WPat WPer
                            WShp WWeb XPep
* **deschampsii**   WShp
  floribundum   CTrC
  lineare   NBir XPep
  lydenburgense   CHEx CTrC SChr
§ **nubigenum**   CHEx CHal CTrC EBre ECtt EDAr
                            ELan EMlt EPot GEdr GGar ITim
                            LRHS NBlu NJOw WPer WWin
  sutherlandii   EDAr EWll NJOw NLAp

Delphinium ✿ (Ranunculaceae)
  'Abendleuchten'   LPhx
  'After Midnight'   CNMi
  'Agnes Brookes'   ERou
  'Alice Artindale' (d)   CBos CDes CHad CPlt EBee EMon
                            IFro LPhx SAga SBla SMrm WPGP
                            WSan
  'Alie Duyvensteyn'   EBee ERou
  ambiguum   see *Consolida ajacis*
  'Amour'   GLbr
  'Ann Woodfield'   CNMi
  'Anne Page'   ERou
  Astolat Group   CBcs CBot COlW CSBt CWib
                            EBee EBre ELan EPfP EWTr
                            GKir LPVe LRHS MBri MRav
                            MWat MWgw NBPC NBir NFor
                            NLar NPri SMer SPer WFar WHoo
                            WWeb
  'Augenweide'   EFou
  'Baby Doll' **new**   CNMi
  Belladonna Group   EShb
  – 'Atlantis' ♀H4   EBee ECha EFou ERou LPhx
                            LRHS MBri SBla SBod SMrm SOkh
                            SWat
  – 'Ballkleid'   EBee ERou
  – 'Capri'   EBee
  – 'Casa Blanca'   CPlt EBee EFou EShb LRHS MAnH
                            NBrk NLar SBla SIgm SMrm SWat
                            WMnd WPer

- 'Cliveden Beauty'	CBot EBee EPyc GBri MAnH MRav MSte NChi NLar NPri SBla SIgm SWat WMnd WPer WShp
- 'Kleine Nachtmusik'	EBee
- 'Moerheimii'	EBee EBre ERou LRHS SBod SMrm
- 'Peace'	EBre LRHS
- 'Piccolo'	EBee EBre ECha ERou LRHS SMrm SWat
- 'Pink Sensation'	see *D.* x *ruysii* 'Pink Sensation'
- 'Völkerfrieden'	EBee EBre EFou ERou LRHS MBri MRav NPri NPro SBod
x *bellamosum*	CBot EBee EFou LRHS MAnH MWgw NLar SWat WPer WShp
'Berghimmel'	EBee EFou LRHS
'Beryl Burton'	CNMi ERou
Black Knight Group	CBcs COlW CSBt CTri CWib EBre ECtt ELan EPfP EWTr GKir LRHS MBow MBri MRav MWat MWgw NFor NGdn NLar NMir NPri NVic SMer SPer SPla SPlb WCAu WFar WShp
'Black Pearl' **new**	EBee
'Blackberry Ice' **new**	CNMi
'Blauwal'	EBee SWat
'Blondie' **new**	CNMi
Blue Bird Group	CBcs COlW CSBt CTri ELan EPfP GAbr GKir LRHS MBri MBro MRav MWgw NFor NLar NMir NPri SMer SPer SPla WCAu WFar WHoo
'Blue Butterfly'	see *D. grandiflorum* 'Blue Butterfly'
'Blue Dawn' ♀H4	CBla CNMi ERou
Blue Fountains Group	CSBt EPfP GKir LPVe LRHS MBri NBee SPer SPet SRms WBVN WStI
Blue Jade Group	CBla ERou
'Blue Jay'	CBcs CTri EBre ENot EWTr LRHS MBow MWgw NBir NLar NPri SPer WCAu
'Blue Lagoon'	CBla
'Blue Mirror'	SRms
'Blue Nile' ♀H4	CBla CNMi ERou
'Blue Oasis'	CNMi
'Blue Skies'	NLar
Blue Springs Group	NGdn NLar NOrc
'Blue Tit'	CBla CNMi ERou
'Blue Triumphator'	EBee
'Bruce' ♀H4	CNMi CPlt ERou WCFE
brunonianum	SBla WLin
bulleyanum	EBee
'Butterball'	CBla CNMi
Cameliard Group	CBcs CSBt EBre ECtt ELan LRHS MWgw NLar NPri SPer
'Can-can' ♀H4	CNMi ERou
cardinale	EHrv GEil
'Carl Topping'	ERou
cashmerianum	MTho WSHC
'Cassius' ♀H4	CBla CNMi ERou
'Chelsea Star'	CBla CNMi ERou
'Cher'	CNMi
'Cherry Blossom'	NLar
'Cherub' ♀H4	CBla ERou
chinense	see *D. grandiflorum*
'Christel'	EBee ERou
'Circe'	ERou
'Clack's Choice'	ERou
Clear Springs Series	LIck
'Clifford Pink'	CBla
Connecticut Yankees Group	MAnH SIgm SRms
'Conspicuous' ♀H4	CBla CNMi ERou
'Constance Rivett' ♀H4	ERou
'Cream Cracker'	CNMi
'Cressida'	ERou
'Cristella'	ERou

'Crown Jewel'	CBla ERou WCFE
'Cupid'	CBla CNMi ERou
'Darling Sue'	CNMi
'Darwin's Blue Indulgence'PBR **new**	EBee
'Darwin's Pink Indulgence'PBR	SPoG WCot
delavayi	GEil SBla WCot
- B&SWJ 7796	WCru
- 'Demavand'	CNMi
'Dolly Bird'	CBla ERou
'Dreaming Spires'	SRms
'Dunsden Green' **new**	CNMi
dwarf dark blue	LRHS
dwarf lavender	LRHS
dwarf pink	LRHS
dwarf sky blue	LRHS
'Eelkje'	EBee ERou
elatum	CArn GCal GEil MAnH SRms SSth
'Elizabeth Cook' ♀H4	CNMi
'Elmhimmel' **new**	EBee
'Emily Hawkins' ♀H4	CNMi ERou
'Eminence'	EBee
'Eva Gower'	ERou
'F.W. Smith'	EBee
'Fanfare'	CBla CNMi ERou
'Father Thames'	ERou
'Faust' ♀H4	CBla CNMi EBee ERou
'Fenella' ♀H4	CBla CNMi CTCP WCFE
'Filique Arrow'	CFir
'Finsteraarhorn'	EBee EFou ERou
flexuosum **new**	EBee
'Florestan'	CNMi
'Frühschein'	EFou
Galahad Group	More than 30 suppliers
'Galileo' ♀H4 **new**	CNMi
'Garden Party'	CBla
'Gemma'	CNMi
'Gillian Dallas' ♀H4	CBla CNMi ERou
'Giotto' ♀H4	CNMi
'Gletscherwasser'	EFou LPhx
'Gordon Forsyth'	CBla CNMi ERou
'Gossamer'	CNMi EBee
§ *grandiflorum*	SMrm
§ - 'Blauer Zwerg'	CWCL EBee EPfP IBal
§ - 'Blue Butterfly'	CBot CSpe CWCL EBee EBre EBur ENor LRHS MWgw NCot NOrc SBla SCoo SPer SPlb WPer WWeb WWin
- Blue Dwarf	see *D. grandiflorum* 'Blauer Zwerg'
* - 'Tom Pouce'	CBot NGdn
- 'White Butterfly'	CBot
Guinevere Group	CBcs CSBt CWib EBre ECtt GAbr LPVe LRHS MBow MBri MRav MWat NBPC NBir NFor NLar NPri SPer SPla WFar
'Guy Langdon'	CNMi ERou
'Harlekijn'	EBee ERou
'Harmony'	ERou
'Heavenly Blue'	LPVe NLar
'Holly Cookland Wilkins' **new**	CNMi
Ivory Towers Group	ECtt
'Jenny Agutter'	CNMi
'Jill Curley'	CNMi
'Joan Edwards' **new**	CNMi
'Joyce Roffey'	ERou
'Kasana' **new**	CNMi
'Kathleen Cooke'	CNMi
'Kennington Calypso'	CNMi
'Kennington Carnival' **new**	CNMi
'Kennington Classic' **new**	CNMi

'Kestrel'	CNMi ERou
King Arthur Group	CBcs CMHG CSBt ECtt EHol ELan ENot EPfP EWTr GAbr GKir MBri MOne MRav MWat MWgw NBPC NLar NPri SMer SPer WFar WHoo
'La Bohème' **new**	EBee WCot WSan
'Lady Guinevere'	EBee ERou
§ 'Langdon's Royal Flush' ♀H4	CBla CNMi
'Lanzenträger'	EFou
'Leonora'	CNMi ERou
likiangense	CTCP ETow
'Loch Leven' ♀H4	CBla CNMi ERou
'Loch Nevis'	CNMi
'Lord Butler' ♀H4	CBla CNMi WCot
'Lorna'	ERou
'Lucia Sahin' ♀H4	CNMi
§ *luteum*	SIgm WIvy
maackianum	GCal
Magic Fountains Series	CSam EBre GKir NPri SPlb WGor WHil WLow WRHF
- 'Magic Fountains Lavender'	WBVN WWeb
- 'Magic Fountains Dark Blue'	EPfP MBow NLar WBVN
- 'Magic Fountains Deep Blue'	CBrm NLar
- 'Magic Fountains Lilac Rose'	EChP NLar NVic WWeb
- 'Magic Fountains Pure White'	EChP EPfP MBow NLar WBVN WWeb
- 'Magic Fountains Sky Blue'	EChP LRHS NVic
'Margaret Farrand'	ERou
menziesii	CTCP ERos
'Mèrel'	EBee MBri
'Michael Ayres' ♀H4	CBla CNMi ERou
'Micky'	EBee
micropetalum CNDS 031	WCru
'Mighty Atom'	CBla CNMi CPlt EBee ERou WCot
'Min' ♀H4	CNMi ERou
'Molly Buchanan'	CBla CNMi ERou
'Moonbeam'	CBla CNMi
'Morning Cloud'	CNMi
'Mother Teresa'	ERou
'Mrs Newton Lees'	EBee ERou
'Mrs T. Carlile'	ERou
'Mystique'	CBla ERou
'Ned Rose'	ERou
'Ned Wit'	ERou
New Century hybrids	CBcs EBre LRHS
'Nicolas Woodfield' **new**	CNMi
'Nimrod'	CBla ERou
'Nobility'	CBla ERou
nudicaule	CPBP EBee EDAr EPfP LPVe MBNS SRot
- 'Laurin' **new**	EBre
- var. *luteum*	see *D. luteum*
'Olive Poppleton' ♀H4	CBla CNMi
'Oliver' ♀H4	CNMi
* *orfordii*	EBee
'Our Deb' ♀H4	CNMi
'Ouvertüre'	EBee
oxysepalum	CTCP
Pacific hybrids	ENot EPfP GAbr GKir LPVe LRHS MHer NBlu NLar SGar SPet SRms SWvt WLow
'Pandora'	CBla
'Parade'	ERou
'Parlemour'	EBee
'Patricia Johnson'	ERou
Percival Group	EBee LRHS NLar
'Pericles'	CBla CNMi
'Perlmutterbaum'	LPhx
'Petticoat'	EBee
'Pink Ruffles'	CBla CNMi CPlt
Princess Caroline = 'Odabar'PBR	CBcs
'Purity'	ERou
'Purple Ruffles'	ERou
'Purple Sky'	EBee
'Purple Triumph'	ERou
'Purple Velvet'	CBla CNMi
'Pyramus'	ERou
'Rakker'	EBee ERou
'Red Caroline' **new**	CBcs
requienii	CTCP GEil MTho MWgw NBir WCot WEas WOut
'Rona'	CNMi
'Rosemary Brock' ♀H4	CNMi ERou
'Royal Flush'	see *D.* 'Langdon's Royal Flush'
'Rubin'	LPhx
'Ruby'	CBla CPlt
§ x *ruysii* 'Pink Sensation'	CDes EBee EMon ERou EWTr GBri NLar NPri NPro SBod STes WFar WPGP WShp
'Sabrina'	CBla
'Samantha'	ERou
'Sandpiper' ♀H4	CNMi
'Schildknappe'	EBee
§ *semibarbatum*	NPri SIgm
'Sentinel'	CNMi
'Shimmer'	CBla ERou
siamense B&SWJ 7278	WCru
'Silver Jubilee'	CNMi ERou
'Silver Moon'	ERou
'Sir Harry Secombe'	CNMi
'Sky Beauty'	EBee
'Skyline'	CBla CNMi CWCL ERou
'Snowdon'	CNMi
'Solomon'	ERou
'Sommerabend'	LPhx
* 'Space Fantasy'	SBla
'Spindrift' ♀H4	CNMi
stapeliosmum B&SWJ 2954	WCru
staphisagria	CArn ECGP EOHP MGol MSal SSth
'Strawberry Fair'	CBla CNMi EBee ERou
'Summer Haze'	ERou
Summer Skies Group	CBcs CMHG CSBt ECtt ELan EPfP EWTr LHop LRHS MBri MWat MWgw NBir NLar NPri SMer SPer WBrE WCau WFar WHoo
'Summerfield Diana'	CNMi
'Summerfield Miranda' ♀H4	CNMi
'Summerfield Oberon'	CBos CNMi WCot
'Sungleam' ♀H4	CBla CFir CNMi CPlt EBee ERou EWTr
'Sunkissed' ♀H4	CNMi
sutchuenense B&SWJ 7867	WCru
tatsienense	SRms WCru
- 'Album'	EWes WCom
- 'Blue Ice'	EHyt
tenii B&SWJ 7693	WCru
'Tessa'	ERou
'Thundercloud'	ERou
'Tiddles' ♀H4	CBla
'Tiger Eye' **new**	CNMi
'Titania'	CBla
tricorne	CLAP
'Turkish Delight'	CBla ERou
'Vanessa Mae'	CNMi
'Venus Carmine'	LRHS
'Vespers'	CBla
vestitum	NBir
'Walton Beauty'	CNMi

'Walton Benjamin'	CNMi
'Walton Gemstone' ♀H4	CBla CNMi
'Watkin Samuel'	ERou
'West End Blue'PBR	EBee MBri WMnd
'White Ruffles'	CBla CNMi
'Wishful Thinking'PBR **new**	EBee
Woodfield strain	WHrl
'Yvonne'	ERou
zalil	see *D. semibarbatum*

Dendranthema ✿ (Asteraceae)

nankingense	see *Chrysanthemum nankingense*
pacificum	see *Ajania pacifica*

Dendriopoterium see *Sanguisorba*

Dendrobenthamia see *Cornus*

Dendromecon (Papaveraceae)

rigida	CBcs CFil EPfP LHop LRHS NLar SMad SMur SSpi WPGP

Dennstaedtia (Dennstaedtiaceae)

punctilobula	WCot WRic

Dentaria see *Cardamine*

microphylla	see *Cardamine microphylla*
pinnata	see *Cardamine heptaphylla*
polyphylla	see *Cardamine kitaibelii*

Deparia (Woodsiaceae)

pycnosora	WRic

Derwentia see *Parahebe*

Deschampsia (Poaceae)

caespitosa	GBin
'Schottland' **new**	
cespitosa	More than 30 suppliers
- subsp. *alpina*	EMon EPPr LRHS
- Bronze Veil	see *D. cespitosa* 'Bronzeschleier'
§ - 'Bronzeschleier'	CKno CTrC ECGN ECoo EFou EHoe ELan EPla EPza EWsh GBri GCal GKir LPhx MBnl MCLN MSte MWgw NGdn NHol NSti SMrm SPer SPla WCAu WCom WMoo
- 'Fairy's Joke'	see *D. cespitosa* var. *vivipara*
- Gold Dust	see *D. cespitosa* 'Goldstaub'
- Golden Dew	see *D. cespitosa* 'Goldtau'
- Golden Pendant	see *D. cespitosa* 'Goldgehänge'
- Golden Shower	see *D. cespitosa* 'Goldgehänge'
- Golden Veil	see *D. cespitosa* 'Goldschleier'
§ - 'Goldgehänge'	CSam ECtt EHoe EHul EMan EMon EPPr EPfP EPla MMHG NBir NHol NPro NSti SLPl
§ - 'Goldschleier'	CBrm CFwr EBlw EBre ECGN ECGP EChP ECha EFou EHoe EMon EPPr EPla EWsh GKir GOrn LPhx MCLN NGdn NJOw SPet SWal WCot WMoo WPGP
§ - 'Goldstaub'	EFou EPPr
§ - 'Goldtau'	CHar EBre ECGN EHoe EHul EMon EPGN EPPr EPla EPza EWTr EWsh GKir LPhx LRHS MBnl MMoz MRav MWgw MWhi NGdn NHol NOrc NSti SHel SLPl SPer SPla SUsu
- 'Morning Dew'	ECoo WFar
- 'Northern Lights' (v)	CBrm CFwr CMHG CMil CPen CSam CTrC EBee EBlw EBre ELan EMan ENot EPPr EPfP EPza GKir LBuc LHop MAvo MBnl MBri NOak SAsh SPer SPla SRms WLeb WPGP

- subsp. *paludosa*	EMon EPPr
§ - var. *vivipara*	CKno EBee EBlw ECtt EHoe EMon EPPr EPla LRHS MMHG NBid NBro NHol NOGN NSti SWal WCom WRos WWpP
- 'Willow Green'	GCal MRav WWeb
elongata	CBig
flexuosa	CBig CBrm COlW CPen EHoe EMon EPPr EWTr EWsh GIBF MBri MHar WEas WPer
- 'Tatra Gold'	More than 30 suppliers
holciformis	CBig

Desfontainia (Loganiaceae)

§ *spinosa* ♀H3	More than 30 suppliers
- 'Harold Comber'	CMac MDun WBod WCru WDin WGer
- *hookeri*	see *D. spinosa*

Desmanthus (Mimosaceae)

illinoensis	EBee MGol MSal

Desmodium (Papilionaceae)

callianthum	CDoC CMac EPfP LRHS WSHC
canadense	CPLG EBee EMan MGol MSPs NLar WCot
§ *elegans* ♀H4	CBcs CFil CHEx CHar CPle EBee EPfP GMac MGol SSpi WCru WHer WPGP WSHC WSPU
glutinosum	EBee
praestans	see *D. yunnanense*
tiliifolium	see *D. elegans*
§ *yunnanense*	CHEx CPle EPfP LRHS SSpi WSHC

Desmoschoenus (Cyperaceae)

spiralis	CTrC

Deutzia ✿ (Hydrangeaceae)

calycosa	CFil GQui
- B&SWJ 7742	WCru
- Farrer 846	SMHy
- 'Dali'	CFil
- - SBEC 417	SDys WPGP
chunii	see *D. ningpoensis*
compacta	CFil GEil SLon WBod WFar WPGP
- 'Lavender Time'	GSki MBNS MBro WCFE
cordatula	CFil WPGP
- B&SWJ 6917	WCru
coreana BWJ 8588 **new**	WCru
corymbosa	CDoC CFil
aff. *crenata*	WCru
BWJ 8879 **new**	
- 'Flore Pleno'	see *D. scabra* 'Plena'
- var. *heterotricha*	WCru
BWJ 8896 **new**	
- var. *nakaiana*	SIng WPat
- - 'Nikko'	see *D. gracilis* 'Nikko'
- 'Pride of Rochester' (d)	CBcs CTri CWib EHol ENot MBar MDun MRav SLon SMac WDin WHar
§ - var. *pubescens*	CFil WPGP
discolor 'Major'	CPLG GEil
x *elegantissima*	ENot MRav SReu SRms
- 'Fasciculata'	EPfP SPer WLeb WWin
- 'Roscalind' ♀H4	CBcs CTri EBee EBre ECrN ECtt ENot EPfP EWTr LHop LRHS MRav NBee NSti SReu SRms SSpi WBod WCom WKif WPGP WSHC
glabrata	WPGP
- B&SWJ 617	WCru
glauca L&S 979 **new**	WPGP
glomeruliflora	CFil WPGP
- B&SWJ 7748	WCru
gracilis	CDoC CHar CSBt EBee ELan EPfP EWTr GEil GQui MBar MBro MRav

	MSwo MWat NBee SPer SWal WBod WDin WFar WGwG WMoo WStI
- B&SWJ 5805	WCru
- 'Carminea'	see *D.* x *rosea* 'Carminea'
§ - 'Marmorata' (v)	SLon WCom WHCG
§ - 'Nikko'	CAbP CBcs CPBP EBee EHyt EWTr EWes GEil GKir LRHS MBar MBro MGos MHer NJOw NPro SPlb WDin WHCG WKif WSHC WWin
- 'Rosea'	see *D.* x *rosea*
- 'Variegata'	see *D. gracilis* 'Marmorata'
hookeriana	GGGa WFar
x *hybrida* 'Contraste'	SPer
- 'Joconde'	CPLG ECtt WFar WKif
- 'Magicien'	CBrm CDoC CHar CMHG CPLG CSBt CSam CWib EBee ENot EPfP GKir GQui MAsh MRav MSwo NHol SHBN SLon SMrm SPer SWvt WFar WHCG WHar WKif WPGP WPat
- 'Mont Rose' ♀H4	CBrm CDoC CDul CPLG EBee EBre ELan ENot EPfP GKir IMGH LAst LBuc LRHS MAsh MBar MGos MRav MSwo NBee SWvt WCFE WDin WFar WHCG WMoo WSHC WStI WWin
- 'Perle Rose'	CWSG
- 'Strawberry Fields' ♀H4	CBot CFai CFil CHar CPLG CTri EBee ELan EMil EPla GKir LAst LBuc LRHS MBar MBlu MBri MRav MTis NBee NPro SBod SLon WBod WGMN WKif WPGP
'Iris Alford' **new**	SLon
x *kalmiiflora*	CBcs CSBt CTri EBee EHol GKir GQui LRHS MBar MBri MDun MRav MWhi NFor NLRH SLPl SPer SRms WMoo
x *lemoinei*	CBot
longifolia	CFil WPGP
- 'Veitchii' ♀H4	CDul CPLG CPle CSBt GEil GQui MRav SMHy SMrm WCFE
§ - 'Vilmoriniae'	MRav
'Macrocephala'	GEil
x *magnifica*	CBcs CDul ECrN EHol ELan EPfP GEil GQui LRHS MBri SRms WCom WDin WHCG WHar WWin
- 'Nancy'	EWTr
- 'Rubra'	see *D.* x *hybrida* 'Strawberry Fields'
x *maliflora* 'Boule Rouge'	GEil
monbeigii	ENot WBcn WKif
§ *ningpoensis* ♀H4	CBcs CFil EBee EWTr NHol SLPl SPer SSta WBcn WPGP
parviflora var. *barbinervis* B&SWJ 8427 **new**	WCru
'Pink Pompon'	see *D.* 'Rosea Plena'
pubescens	see *D. crenata* var. *pubescens*
pulchra	CBot CFai CFil CHar CPom ECha EPfP GEil GKir NPro SLon SMHy SMac SMrm SPer SSpi WFar WHCG WPGP
- B&SWJ 3870	WCru
- B&SWJ 6908	WCru
aff. *purpurascens* BWJ 8007 **new**	WCru
§ x *rosea*	CBot CDul CPle CTrw CWSG CWib EBee EBre ENot EPfP LAst LRHS MBar MWat SHBN SMer SRms WFar WKif WStI WWin
- 'Campanulata'	CPLG ENot EPfP
§ - 'Carminea'	CChe EWTr MDun MRav MSwo SPlb SRms SSta WCom WDin WFar WMoo

§ - 'Rosea Plena' (d)	CBcs CBot CDoC CHar CPLG CSBt CWib EGra EPfP GKir LRHS MAsh MDun MGos NBlu SLim SSta WBod WCFE WCom WFar WGwG WPat
rubens	GEil
scabra	CDul GKir NPro
§ - 'Candidissima' (d)	CMHG ECrN GQui MRav SMer SPer WBod WCFE
- 'Codsall Pink'	MBri MRav
§ - 'Plena' (d)	CChe CPLG EBee ECtt ELan EPfP EWTr IMGH LRHS MDun MRav SHBN SPer WMoo
- 'Punctata' (v)	CFai EHoe SRms WFar
- 'Variegata' (v)	CDul NPro SLim WPGP WSHC
aff. *scabra* B&SWJ 8924 **new**	WCru
setchuenensis	CFil EPfP GGGa GQui SSpi WHCG WSHC
- var. *corymbiflora* ♀H4	CBcs CBot CDoC CDul CFil CTri EBee EPfP GEil SMrm SPoG WBcn WCom WFar WKif WPGP
staminea	CFil WPGP
taiwanensis	CFil NLar WPGP
- B&SWJ 6858	WCru
'Tourbillon Rouge'	GEil GKir WDin
x *wellsii*	see *D. scabra* 'Candidissima'
x *wilsonii*	SRms

Dianella ✿ (*Phormiaceae*)

brevipedunculata **new**	CWil
caerulea	CRez CWil EBla ECou ELan GBuc IGor NBir
- var. *petasmatodes*	EBee EMan WCot
- 'Variegata'	see *D. tasmanica* 'Variegata'
intermedia	CTrC IBlr SMad WCot
- 'Variegata' (v)	IBlr
nigra	CFil CFir CPou CWil ECou IFro LEdu WFar WHer
revoluta	CFir CWil ECou IBlr
tasmanica	CAbb CElw CFee CFil CFir CHEx CKno CPLG CPne CRow CSpe CStu CWil EBee ECou ECre EPfP GBuc GGar IBlr LEdu LHop MCCP NCGa SArc SIgm SMad SSpi WOld WSHC
§ - 'Variegata' (v)	CFir CSpe ECou ELan EMan EPfP GFlt GQui IBlr LHop MSte SMad WCot WCru WOld

Dianthus ✿ (*Caryophyllaceae*)

ACW 2116	CLyd LBee WPer
from Czechoslovakia	CStu
'Activa' (pf) **new**	SBai
'Admiral Lord Anson' (b)	WKin
'Alan Titchmarsh' (p)	EWll MMHG NLar SBai
'Albatross' (p)	SChu
'Albus'	MWgw
'Alegro' **new**	SHay
'Alice' (p)	EMFP EPfP SHay WKin
'Alice Forbes' (b)	SHay
'Alice Lever' (p)	MDHE WAbe
§ 'Allen's Huntsman' (p)	CBcs
'Alloway Star' (p)	EMFP WKin
'Allspice' (p)	CLyd MRav SChu SSvw WEas WHoo WKin WWye
'Allspice Sport' (p)	WKin
Allwoodii Alpinus Group (p)	ECho LPVe NJOw SRms
'Allwood's Crimson' (pf)	SHay
alpinus ♀H4	CLyd EHyt EMlt GKev GKir GTou ITim LBee LRHS MDHE NBlu NMen NWCA SIng SPet SRms WCom WHen WPer
- 'Albus'	CPBP EHyt LRHS WAbe

§ - 'Joan's Blood' ♀H4 — LHop MBro NHol NMen NWCA SBla WAbe WCom WHoo
- 'Millstream Salmon' — CLyd
amurensis — GCal LPhx LRHS NDov SIgm SSvw WPer
- 'Andrey' — GCal SHar
- 'Siberian Blue' — GBin
anatolicus — CElw CLyd CTri LBee LRHS MHer NDlv SSvw WCom WPer XPep
'Annabelle' (p) — EMFP EMil LAst LRHS SChu
'Annette' (pf) — EDAr LRHS MBNS NWoo
'Anniversay' (p) — CBcs SBai
'Apollo' (b) — GAbr
'Apricot Chace' (b) — SHay
'Apricot Sue' (pf) — SHay
'Arctic Star' (p) — CMea EBee EDAr MBNS NCGa NLar SPet WLin
arenarius — CNic EMlt LPVe MHer NJOw SPlb SSvw WPer
'Arevalo' (pf) — SHay
'Argus' — SChu WKin
armeria — WBWf WHer WOut WPer
arpadianus — MDHE NHol
- var. *pumilus* — NWCA
'Arthur' (p) — EMFP WKin
§ x *arvernensis* (p) ♀H4 — ECha EPot GAbr MBro
'Audrey's Frilly' — SChu WKin
'Aurora' (b) — SHay
'Auvergne' — see *D*. x *arvernensis*
'Avon Dasset' — EDAr LBuc
'Baby Treasure' (p) — CLyd ECho GAbr NHol SRot
'Badenia' (p) — CElw CLyd LBee LRHS MDHE SChu SIgm
'Bailey's Celebration' (p) — SBai
'Bailey's Festival' (p) — SBai
'Baltico'PBR (pf) **new** — SBai
barbatus **new** — GWCH
- 'Indian Carpet' **new** — NBlu
- Nigrescens Group — CBre CHad CHrt CMea CSpe LPhx (p,a) ♀H4
I - 'Sooty' — CBri EBee EChP ELan GBri MWrn NDlv WBry WCom WHer
'Barleyfield Rose' (p) — CLyd SBla
'Bath's Pink' — GMac LRHS
§ 'Bat's Double Red' (p) — EMFP SChu SWal WKin
'Beauty of Healey' (p) — EMFP WKin
'Becka Falls' (p) — SHay
'Becky Robinson' (p) ♀H4 — SHay
'Berlin Snow' — CLyd EPot ESis ITim
'Bet Gilroy' (b) — SHay
'Betty Buckle' (p) — SChu
'Betty Morton' (p) ♀H4 — COkL ECtt MSph SBla SSvw WKif WKin
'Betty Tucker' (b) — SHay
'Binsey Red' (p) — EMFP SSvw WKin
Black and White — CElw CLyd WKin
Minstrels Group
Blakeney seedling (p) — WKin
blandus — MDHE
* 'Blue Carpet' — WPer
'Blue Hills' (p) — CLyd ECho ELan GCrs MWat SChu
'Blue Ice' (b) — SHay
'Blush' — see *D*. 'Souvenir de la Malmaison'
'Bobby Ames' (b) — SHay
'Bookham Fancy' (b) — SHay
'Bookham Grand' (b) — SHay
'Bookham Perfume' (b) — SHay
'Bourboule' — see *D*. 'La Bourboule'
'Bovey Belle' (p) ♀H4 — CBcs LRHS MBNS SBai SHay
'Boydii' (p) — CLyd
'Bransgore' (p) — CLyd
'Bremen' — COkL
'Bressingham Pink' (p) — ECtt
'Bridal Veil' (p) — EMFP GAbr SChu SSvw WKin

'Brigadier' (p) — WWin
'Brilliance' (p) — MBow
'Brilliant' — see *D. deltoides* 'Brilliant'
'Brilliant Star' (p) ♀H4 — CPBP EDAr SPet
'Brimstone' (b) — SHay
'Brympton Red' (p) — ECha EMFP EOrc MRav SBla SChu WCom WEas WKif WKin
'Buckfast Abbey' (p) — CHll
§ 'Caesar's Mantle' (p) — WKin
caesius — see *D. gratianopolitanus*
callizonus — NSla
'Calypso Star' (p) ♀H4 — EBee ECtt EDAr GBuc MBNS NCGa NLar SPet
'Camelford' (p) — SChu WKin
'Camilla' (b) — CLyd EGoo EMFP SSvw WCom WKin
'Can-can' (pf) — ECtt
'Candy Clove' (b) — SHay
'Candy Spice' (p) — EBee WLin WWol
'Carinda' (p) — SHay
'Carlotta' (p) — SHay
'Carmen' (b) — SHay
'Carmine Letitia Wyatt'PBR (p) — EMFP
'Caroline Bone' (b) — SHay
'Caroline Clove' (b) — SHay
carthusianorum — CElw CHad CKno IGor LPhx MSte NDlv NDov SAga SCro SGar SScr SSvw SWat WCom WEas WOut WPer XPep
caryophyllus — CArn GBar GWCH WHHs WHer
- 'Balkonfeuer' **new** — WWol
- 'Casser's Pink' (p) — GBuc
* 'Catherine Tucker' — WEas
'Cecil Wyatt' (p) — CThr EBee EMFP EPfP MAvo NLar WMnd
§ 'Cedric's Oldest' (p) — SChu WKin
'Charcoal' — EBee WCot
'Charles Musgrave' — see *D*. 'Musgrave's Pink'
'Charm' (b) — SHay
'Chastity' (p) — MBro SBla SChu WHoo WKin
Cheddar pink — see *D. gratianopolitanus*
'Cheerio' (pf) — SBai SHay
'Cherry Moon' — LRHS
'Cherry Pie' (p) — WWol
'Cherryripe' (p) — SHay
'Cheryl' — see *D*. 'Houndspool Cheryl'
'Chetwyn Doris' (p) ♀H4 — SBai
'Chianti' (pf) — MBNS NGdn
'China Doll' (p) — SBai
chinensis (p,a) — WHer
'Chocolate Chip' (p) — EMFP
'Christopher' (p) — LRHS SHay
'Circular Saw' (p) — SChu
'Clare' (p) — SHay
'Claret Joy' (p) ♀H4 — CBcs CThr EBee EDAr EMFP EOMN EPfP LAst WGwG
'Clifford Pink' — WKin
'Clotted Cream' **new** — EBee
'Clunie' (b) — SHay
§ 'Cockenzie Pink' (p) — EMFP GAbr WEas WKin
'Constance Finnis' — see *D*. 'Fair Folly'
'Conwy Silver' — WAbe
'Conwy Star' — WAbe
'Copperhead' (b) — SHay
'Corleone' (pf) — SBai SHay
'Coronation Ruby' (p) ♀H4 — CBcs SBai SHay
corsicus **new** — XPep
'Coste Budde' (p) — CLyd WEas WKin WSHC
'Cotton Chace' (b) — SHay
'Cranborne Seedling' (p) — WKin
'Cranmere Pool' (p) ♀H4 — CBcs CMea CThr ECtt EDAr ELan LAst LRHS MBNS MBow SBai SHay SMrm WCra WLin WWol

'Cream Sue' (pf)	SHay
cretaceus	NWCA
'Crimson Ace' (p)	SHay
'Crimson Joy' (p) ♀H4	EDAr
'Crimson Tempo'PBR (pf)	SBai SHay WWol
'Crimson Velvet' (b)	SHay
crinitus	NJOw SHFr
cruentus	LPhx MSte
'Dad's Choice' (p)	CBcs SBai
'Dad's Favourite' (p)	CThr EMFP EOrc SChu SHay SRms
	SSvw WCom WEas WHer WKin
	WWhi
'Daily Mail' (p)	CBcs SBai SChu
'Dainty Dame' (p) ♀H4	CSpe CTri EBee EBre EDAr EMlt
	ESis GBuc LRHS MWgw NHol
	NJOw SAga SBla SChu SRot
'Damask Superb' (p)	WKin
'Dark Star' (p)	EMFP
'Dark Tempo' (pf)	SHay
'Dartington Laced'	WKin
'David' (p)	COkL SHay WShp
'Dawlish Charm' (p)	SBai
'Dawlish Joy' (p)	EDAr EMFP
'Dawn' (b)	SHay
'Daydream' (pf)	SBai SHay WWol
'Deep Purple' (pf)	SHay
'Delphi' (pf)	SHay WWol
deltoides ♀H4	CArn CElw CSev ECha ELau EPfP
	GBar GWCH MDKP NSco NWCA
	SIng SPlb SRms WBWf WFar WJck
	WRHF WSel
– 'Albus'	CNic EBre ECGP ECha EPfP GBar
	IHMH MBar NPri SWat WCom
	WHrl WMoo WPer WRos WSel
– 'Arctic Fire'	EBre NGdn WMoo
– 'Bright Eyes'	ECho
§ – 'Brilliant'	GTou LPVe MDKP MDun MFOX
	NPri NVic SRms SWat WGor WHrl
	WWpP
– 'Broughty Blaze'	NRya
– 'Dark Eyes'	EWes
– 'Erectus'	EPfP
– Flashing Light	see *D. deltoides* 'Leuchtfunk'
§ – 'Leuchtfunk'	CElw COkL EBre ECtt EPfP GGar
	GKir GTou LGro LRHS MOne
	NBPC NMir SWal WCom WEas
	WFar WHen WPer WRos
– 'Microchip'	NJOw SPet WFar
– 'Nelli' (p)	WMoo
– red	NBlu
– 'Shrimp'	NBlu
– *splendens*	WShp
'Denis' (p)	ELan
'Desmond'	WCom
'Devon Charm' (p)	LRHS
'Devon Cream'PBR (p)	CThr EBee EMFP LRHS WCra WLin
	WWol
'Devon Dove'PBR (p) ♀H4	CMea CThr EBee EGra EPfP LAst
	NPri
'Devon General'PBR (p)	CThr CTri EBee EBre ECtt EMFP
	LHop
'Devon Glow'PBR (p) ♀H4	CThr EBee EMFP EPfP LRHS WCAu
	WLin
'Devon Joy' (p)	LRHS
'Devon Maid'PBR (p) ♀H4	CThr EBee EPfP
'Devon Pearl'PBR (p)	CThr EMFP LHop WLin WWol
'Devon Velvet'PBR	NLar WLin
'Devon Wizard'PBR (p) ♀H4	CHar EMFP LRHS NPri WCAu
'Dewdrop' (p)	CMea CTri ECtt EDAr ESis LRHS
	MHer NBir NGdn WAbe WCom WFar WKin WPer
'Diana'	see *Dianthus* Dona = 'Brecas'
'Diane' (p) ♀H4	CThr EBee EDAr ELan EMFP SHay
	SPla WLin WMnd

'Dianne' (pf)	EDAr
'Doctor Archie	SHay
Cameron' (b)	
§ Dona = 'Brecas' (pf)	LRHS SBai SHay
'Donnet's Variety'	WEas
'Dora'	LRHS SChu
'Doris' (p) ♀H4	More than 30 suppliers
'Doris Allwood' (pf)	CSBt SHay WMal
'Doris Ruby'	see *D.* 'Houndspool Ruby'
'Doris Supreme' (p)	SHay
§ 'Dubarry' (p)	CTri ECtt WGor WPer
'Duchess of	WMal
Westminster' (M)	
'Duke of Norfolk' (pf) **new**	WMal
'Dusky' (p)	WKin
'Dwarf Vienna'	COkL
'E.J. Baldry' (b)	SHay
'Earl of Essex' (p)	EMFP SHay SSvw WKin
echiniformis	GKir
'Edenside Scarlet' (b)	SHay
'Eileen Lever' (p)	CPBP EPot MDHE SBla WAbe
'Eleanor's Old Irish' **new**	WCot WTin
'Elfin Star' (p)	EDAr SPet
'Elizabeth' (p)	WEas
'Elizabeth Pink'	SMrm
'Elizabethan' (p)	CFee GAbr GMac SBla WKin
* 'Elizabethan Pink' (p)	CCge CNic
'Emile Paré' (p)	SChu WCom WKin
'Emperor'	see *D.* 'Bat's Double Red'
'Empire' **new**	SHay
'Enid Anderson' (p)	SChu WKin
'Enid Burgoyne'	WKin
erinaceus	EHol EPot GTou LRHS MOne NJOw
	NWCA SRot WAbe WPer WWin
– var. *alpinus*	CLyd EPot GKir
'Ethel Hurford'	WHoo WKin
'Eva Humphries' (b)	SHay
'Evening Star' (p)	CPBP EDAr MWgw SPet
'Excelsior' (p)	CThr NFor SSvw
§ 'Fair Folly' (p)	SChu SSvw WEas WKin
'Falcon' (pf)	SBai SHay WWol
'Fanal' (p)	NBir WKin
'Fancy Schubert'PBR (pf)	SBai
'Farida'PBR (pf)	SBai SHay
'Farnham Rose' (p)	SChu
'Fenbow Nutmeg	SChu WKin WMnd
Clove' (b)	
ferrugineus	MDHE
'Fettes Mount' (p)	CLyd GAbr SChu WCot WKin
'Feuerhexe' (p)	EBre LRHS NPro
'Fiery Cross' (b)	SHay
'Fimbriatus' (p)	WHoo WKin
'Flame' (p)	SHay
'Fountain's Abbey' (p)	WIvy WKin
'Fragrans' (pf)	NJOw
'Fragrant Ann' (pf) ♀H1	SHay
* *fragrantissimus*	LRHS
'Frances Sellars' (b)	SHay
'Frank's Frilly' (p)	WKin
'Freckles' (p)	SHay
freynii	CLyd EWes MDHE NDlv NLAp SBla
	WAbe
N fringed pink	see *D. superbus*
'Fusilier' (p)	CElw CMea EBee EBre ECtt EDAr
	EMFP EPfP GKir LHop LRHS MBar
	MWgw NCGa NPri NWCA SChu
	SHay WBVN WFar WKin WPat
'G.W. Hayward' (b)	SHay
'Garland' (p)	CTri LRHS WGor
'Garnet' (p)	COkL SChu
giganteus	CSpe IBlr MBct MSte NJOw WKin
'Gingham Gown' (p)	NBir SBla
'Gipsy Clove' (b)	SHay
glacialis	GTou MDHE

'Gloriosa' (p) — WKin
'Gold Flake' (p) **new** — SHay
'Gold Fleck' — EMlt EPot LBee SChu
graniticus — WPer
'Gran's Favourite' — CBcs CMea CSBt CTri EBee EBre
(p) ♀H4 — ECtt EDAr EMFP EPfP LAst LRHS
— MBow MWat NPri SBai SBla SChu
— SHay SPlb SRms WCra WEas WKin
— WLin WWol
§ *gratianopolitanus* ♀H4 — CArn CElw CSLe CTri EPot GTou
— LRHS MBow MFOX MHer MNrw
— MRav MWgw NBid NJOw NWCA
— SPet SRms WAbe WBWf WKin
— WPer WWye
– 'Albus' — CLyd EPot
– 'Flore Pleno' (d) — EMFP MInt SSvw
– from Cheddar — CLyd
– 'Rosenfeder' (p) — WPer
– 'Splendens' (p) — WPer
§ – 'Tiny Rubies' (p) — ECho WKin
'Gravetye Gem' (b) — SRms
'Gravetye Gem' (p) — ECho ELan
'Grenadier' (p) — ECho ELan
* *greyii* **new** — CTCP
'Gwendolen Read' (p) — SHay
'Gypsy Star' (p) — CMea ECho EDAr MBNS NCGa
— WLin
haematocalyx — CPBP MDHE NWCA WAbe WCom
— WPer
– 'Alpinus' — see *D. haematocalyx* subsp.
— *pindicola*
§ – subsp. *pindicola* — CGra CLyd ITim MDHE NHol
— NLAp NMen WPat
'Harlequin' (p) — ECtt EMFP WPer
'Harmony' (b) — SHay
'Harry Oaks' (p) — WKin
'Havana' (pf) — SHay
'Haytor' — see *D.* 'Haytor White'
'Haytor Rock' (p) ♀H4 — EBre EPfP SHay WCra
§ 'Haytor White' (p) ♀H4 — CThr EBee EBre EDAr EMFP EPfP
— LAst LRHS SBai SChu SHay SRms
— WEas WLin WShp WWhi
I 'Heath' (b) — WKin
'Heidi' (p) — EPfP
'Helen' (p) — SHay
'Herbert's Pink' (p) — WKin
'Hereford Butter Market' — EBee SChu WKin
'Hidcote' (p) — CLyd CTri ELan EMlt LRHS MWat
— NMen SBla SHay WKin WLin WWin
'Hidcote Red' — ECho LBee LRHS
'Highland Fraser' (p) — MBro SChu SRms WEas WKif
— WWin
Highland hybrids — MWgw
'Highland Queen' (p) — WKin
'Hoo House' (p) — WKin
'Hope' (p) — EMFP SChu WKin
'Horsa' (b) — SHay
'Hot Spice' (p) ♀H4 — EBee EWll WHlf WLin WWol
§ 'Houndspool Cheryl' — COkL CSBt CTri EBee EMFP EPfP
(p) ♀H4 — LRHS SRms
§ 'Houndspool Ruby' — CThr EMFP EPfP MBNS MWat SBai
(p) ♀H4 — WCAu WEas
'Huntsman' — see *D.* 'Allen's Huntsman'
'Ian' (p) — CBcs CThr SBai SHay
'Ibis' (b) — SHay
'Icomb' (p) — CLyd MBro SRms WHoo WKin
— WPer
'Imperial Clove' (b) — SHay
'Impulse'PBR (pf) — SBai
'Ina' (p) — SRms
'Incas' (pf) ♀H1 — SHay
'Inchmery' (p) — EMFP NFor SChu SHay SSvw WEas
— WHoo WKin WTin WWhi
'India Star'PBR (p) ♀H4 — CPBP EDAr LAst SPet

'Indios' (pf) ♀H1 — SBai SHay
'Ine' (p) — COKL
'Inglestone' (p) — CTri NHol WLin WPer
'Inshriach Dazzler' — CLyd CMea CPBP EBre ECtt EDAr
(p) ♀H4 — GKir LBee MHer NDlv NHol NPri
— SBla SIng SMrm WAbe WCom
— WKin
'Inshriach Startler' (p) — CLyd CMea
'Ipswich Pink' (p) — CBri LGro LPVe LRHS WBro
'Itsy Bitsy' (p) **new** — EMFP
I 'Ivonne' (pf) — SHay
'Ivonne Orange' (pf) — SBai SHay
'James Michael — SHay
Hayward' (b)
'James Portman' (p) — WLin WWol
'Jane Austen' (p) — SChu WKin WPer
'Jane Coffey' (b) — SHay
japonicus — CSpe
'Jenny Wyatt' (p) — SHay
'Joan Schofield' (p) — CLyd EDAr EMlt NLRH SHel SRot
'Joan Siminson' (p) — WKin
'Joan's Blood' — see *D. alpinus* 'Joan's Blood'
'John Ball' (p) — EMFP WKin
'John Grey' (p) — WKin
'Joy' (p) ♀H4 — CBcs CThr EBee ECtt EDAr EMFP
— EPfP LAst LRHS SHay
'June Hammond' — SHay
'Kesteven Chambery' (p) — WPer
'Kesteven Chamonix' (p) — WPer
'Kesteven Kirkstead' — CSWP
(p) ♀H4
'King of the Blacks' (p,a) — ELan MRav
kitaibelii — see *D. petraeus* subsp. *petraeus*
knappii — ELan EPfP GAbr MLLN NVic SSvw
— WPer WWin XPep
– 'Yellow Harmony' (p,a) — EWsh LRHS MBNS WHer
'Komachi' (pf) **new** — SBai
§ 'La Bourboule' (p) ♀H4 — CMea CTri EBre EChP EDAr ELan
— EMlt EPot GAbr GKir LBee LRHS
— MBar MBro MWat NHol NMen
— NPri SBla SRms WFar WGwG WKin
— WLin WPat WWin
'La Bourboule Albus' (p) — EDAr EMlt EPot GCrs NHol SBla
— WFar WGor WWin
'Laced Hero' (p) — IGor SChu WKin
'Laced Joy' (p) — CElw EDAr EMFP SChu SHay
'Laced Monarch' (p) — CBcs CSBt CThr ECtt EDAr LRHS
— NLar SBai SChu SPlb WKin
'Laced Mrs Sinkins' (p) — CBcs SBai
'Laced Prudence' — see *D.* 'Prudence'
'Laced Romeo' (p) — EMFP SChu SHay WKin
'Lady Granville' (p) — IGor SSvw WKin
'Lady Salisbury' (p) — EMFP WKin
§ 'Lady Wharncliffe' (p) — EMFP IGor WKin
'Lancing Monarch' (b) — SHay
'Laura' (p) — SHay
'Lavastrom' — EMlt SOkd
'Lawley's Red' (p) — WKin
'Lemsii' (p) ♀H4 — CNic ECtt EMFP NMen NVic WPer
— WWye
'Leslie Rennison' (b) — SHay
'Letitia Wyatt' (p) ♀H4 — CMea CThr EDAr EMFP WCra
— WLin
'Leuchtkugel' — ECho
'Liberty' (pf) — SBai SHay
liboschitzianus — MDHE
'Lionheart' (p) — EBre LRHS WCra
'Lipstick' (pf) — SHay
'Lisboa' (pf) — SHay
'Little Gem' (pf) — WKin
'Little Jock' (p) — EBre EDAr ELan EPot GKir LBee
— LRHS MBar MHer MRav NHol NPri
— SBla SChu SHay SMrm SPlb SRms
— WEas WFar WKin WPat WWin

	'Little Miss Muffet' (p)	CHll
	'London Brocade' (p)	WKin
	'London Delight' (p)	EMFP SHay WKin
	'London Glow' (p)	WKin
	'London Lovely' (p)	SSvw WKin
	'London Poppet' (p)	NDlv SSvw WKin
	'Loveliness' (p)	CBre
	lumnitzeri	EHyt GCal LTwo MDHE WPer XPep
	'Lustre' (b)	SHay
	'Mab'	WKin
	'Mabel Appleby' (p)	SHel
	'Madame Dubarry'	see *D.* 'Dubarry'
	'Madonna' (pf)	SHay WKin
	'Malaga' (pf) ♀H1	SBai SHay
	'Mambo' (pf) ♀H4	SBai SHay WWol
	'Manningtree Pink'	see *D.* 'Cedric's Oldest'
	'Marmion' (M)	WMal
	'Mars' (p)	ECtt ELan GAbr NDlv SChu WAbe WFar
	'Marshmallow' (p)	NLar WLin
	'Marshwood Melody' (p)	SBai
	'Marshwood Mystery' (p)	WKin
*	'Mary's Gilliflower'	EMFP WKin
	'Matador' (b)	SHay
	'Maybole' (b)	SHay
	'Maythorne' (p)	SRms
	'Mendip Hills' (b)	SHay
	'Mendlesham Belle' (p) ♀H4	EMFP
	'Mendlesham Frilly' (p)	EMFP
	'Mendlesham Glow' (p)	EMFP
	'Mendlesham Maid' (p) ♀H4	EMFP ENor
	Mendlesham Minx = 'Russmin'PBR (p)	CLyd EDAr EMFP GBuc WLin
	'Mendlesham Miss' (p)	EMFP ENor
	'Mendlesham Moll' (p)	EMFP
	'Mendlesham Saint Helen's' (p)	EMFP
	'Mendlesham Spice' (p)	EMFP
	'Mendlesham Sweetheart' (p) **new**	EMFP
	'Merlin'	EBee ENot
	'Merlin Clove' (b)	SHay
	microlepis	CGra EHyt GCrs ITim NMen NWCA SBla WAbe
	- f. *albus*	CGra NSla WAbe
*	- var. *degenii*	CPBP
	- 'Leuchtkugel'	ECho EHyt ITim WAbe
	- var. *musalae*	CLyd CMea CPBP EHyt LTwo MDHE WAbe
	'Miniver'	SHay
	'Miss Sinkins' (p)	EDAr GKir SPet SPla
	'Mondriaan' (pf)	SCro
	'Monica Wyatt' (p) ♀H4	CThr EBee EMFP GKir LRHS SBai SChu SHay
	monspessulanus	NWCA WMoo WPer
	'Montrose Pink'	see *D.* 'Cockenzie Pink'
	'Moortown Plume'	WKin
	'Moulin Rouge' (p)	MBow SChu WLin WWol
	'Mountain Mist' (b)	EFou
	'Mrs Clark'	see *D.* 'Nellie Clark'
	'Mrs Gumbly' (p)	WKin
	'Mrs Holt' (p)	EMFP
	'Mrs Jackson' (p)	CLyd
	'Mrs Macbride' (p)	WKin
	'Mrs N. Clark'	see *D.* 'Nellie Clark'
	'Mrs Roxburgh'	CSam WKin
	'Mrs Sinkins' (p)	More than 30 suppliers
	'Munot'	WShp
	'Murray Douglas' (p) **new**	SSvw
	'Murray's Laced Pink' (p)	WKin WSPU
N	'Musgrave's Pink' (p)	CNic CSam ECha MRav SAga SBla SChu SHay SSvw WCom WEas WKin
	'Musgrave's White'	see *D.* 'Musgrave's Pink'

	myrtinervius	CLyd ECho EHyt NLar SRms WPer
	- subsp. *caespitosus*	EHyt
	- - MESE 433	WAbe
	'Nan Bailey' (p)	SBai
	'Nancy Lindsay' (p)	SSvw
	'Napoleon III' (p)	WCom WKif
	nardiformis	WPer
	'Nautilus' (b)	SHay
	neglectus	see *D. pavonius*
§	'Nellie Clark' (p)	CLyd SChu SRot
	'Nelson'PBR	SHay
	'Neon Star' (p)	EDAr EMFP
	'New Tempo' (pf)	SBai SHay
	'Night Star' (pf) ♀H4	EChP NCGa SChu SPet WLin
	nitidus	CLyd NBir NWCA WPer
	nivalis	NWCA
	noeanus	see *D. petraeus* subsp. *noeanus*
	'Nonsuch' (p)	WKin
	'Northland' (pf)	SHay
	'Nyewoods Cream' (p)	CMea CTri EBre EMFP EPot GAbr GKir LBee LRHS MBar MBro MHer MRav NHol NMen NPri SIng SRot WCom WPat WPer
§	'Oakington' (p)	CTri EBre LRHS MRav MWat NPri NWCA SChu WKin WTel
	'Oakington Rose'	see *D.* 'Oakington'
	'Oakwood Gillian Garforth' (p) ♀H4	SBai
	'Oakwood Splendour' (p) ♀H4	MBNS
	'Old Blush'	see *D.* 'Souvenir de la Malmaison'
	'Old Dutch Pink' (p)	SChu WKin
	'Old Fringed Pink' (p)	WKin
	'Old Fringed White' (p)	EMFP
	'Old Irish' (p)	WKin
	'Old Mother Hubbard' (p)	CFee CHll
	'Old Red Clove' (p)	WCot WEas
§	'Old Square Eyes' (p)	EBee EOrc MNrw SAga SBla SChu SHay SMrm SSvw WEas WKin
	'Old Velvet' (p)	GCal SChu WKin
	'Opera'	SHay
	'Osprey' (b)	SHay
	'Pacifico' (pf) **new**	SBai
	'Paddington' (p)	SChu WKin
	'Painted Beauty' (p)	EMFP NBir
	'Painted Lady' (p)	CLyd SChu WKin
	'Paisley Gem' (p)	SChu SSvw WKin
	'Patricia' (b)	SHay
	'Paul Hayward' (p)	SHay
§	*pavonius* ♀H4	CLyd EMlt EWes GTou NLar NWCA SBla SIgm WAbe WCom WPer
	- *roysii*	see *D.* 'Roysii'
	'Pax' (pf)	SBai SHay
	'Peach' (p)	SHay
	'Perfect Clove' (b) **new**	SHay
§	*petraeus*	EWes NWCA
§	- subsp. *noeanus*	CLyd LTwo WAbe WPer
	- - *albus*	GCrs WLin
§	- subsp. *petraeus*	NOak WPer
	'Petticoat Lace' (p)	SHay
	'Phantom' (b)	SHay
	'Pheasant's Eye' (p)	EMFP SSvw WHer WKin
	'Philip Archer' (b)	SHay
*	'Picton's Propeller' (p)	GBuc
	'Pike's Pink' (p) ♀H4	More than 30 suppliers
	pindicola	see *D. haematocalyx* subsp. *pindicola*
	'Pink Bizarre' (b)	SHay
*	'Pink Dona' (pf)	SHay
	'Pink Dover' (pf) **new**	SBai
	'Pink Jewel' (p)	CLyd CMea EDAr EMlt EPot LBee LRHS MHer NHol NMen SChu WEas WRHF

	'Pink Mist Sim' (pf)	EPot
	'Pink Mrs Sinkins' (p)	EMFP MHer SBai SChu WKin
	'Pink Pearl' (p)	CThr EDAr
	'Pixie' (b)	EBre EPot NHol
	'Pixie Star'PBR (p) ♀H4	EDAr WLin
	plumarius	NJOw NMir SECG SRms SSvw WGor WGwG WHHs WHer WMoo WPer WSSM
	- 'Albiflorus'	WPer
I	- 'Snowdonia'	WBry
	- 'Spring Charm'	LPVe
	pontederae	NDlv WPer
	'Portsdown Fancy' (b)	SHay
	'Prado' (pf) ♀H4	SHay
	'Prado Refit' (pf)	SBai
	'Pretty'	EBre LHop LRHS
	'Primero Dark' (pf) **new**	SBai
	'Prince Charming' (p)	CLyd ELan EPot NHol NMen NPri SRms WPer
	'Princess of Wales' (M)	WMal
§	'Prudence' (p)	CThr WKin
	'Pudsey Prize' (p)	CLyd CPBP EHyt EPot
	'Pummelchen' (p)	ITim WAbe
	'Purple Pacal' (pf)	SHay
	pygmaeus	CTCP LHop NBro SMac SScr
*	- 'Pink Frills'	WBro
*	*pyrenaicus* 'Cap Béar' **new**	XPep
	'Queen of Hearts' (p)	CTri LRHS NWCA SMrm WPer
§	'Queen of Henri' (p)	ECtt EDAr GEdr LBee LRHS MHer SBla SChu SHar WBVN WFar WKin
	'Queen of Sheba' (p)	SChu SSvw WKin
	'Rachel' (p)	ECtt WPat
	'Raggio di Sole' (pf)	SBai
	'Rainbow Loveliness' (p,a)	CTCP GAbr NBir WHil WRHF
	'Ralph Gould' (p)	ECho
	'Raspberry Parfait' **new**	CWCL
	'Red and White' (p)	WKin
	'Red Dwarf'	CWCL SPet
	'Red Velvet'	CLyd LRHS SAsh
	'Reine de Henri'	see *D.* 'Queen of Henri'
	'Rendez-vous'PBR (pf)	SBai
	'Renoir' (b)	SHay
	'Revell's Lady Wharncliffe'	see *D.* 'Lady Wharncliffe'
	'Richard Gibbs' (p)	MOne
	'Rivendell' (p)	CLyd CPBP NSla WAbe
	'Robert Baden-Powell' (b)	SHay
*	'Robin Ritchie'	WHoo WKin WWhi
	'Robin Thain' (b)	SHay
	'Robina's Daughter' **new**	GAbr
	'Roodkapje' (p)	WKin
	'Rose de Mai' (p)	CLyd CSam CSev EMFP SChu SSvw WHoo WKin
	'Rose Joy' (p) ♀H4	CThr EBee EMFP EPfP SHay
	'Rose Monica Wyatt'PBR (p) ♀H4	CThr
	'Rosealic' (p)	SHay
	'Royalty' (p)	SHay
§	'Roysii' (p)	NDlv WPer
	'Rubin' (pf)	WEas
	'Ruby'	see *D.* 'Houndspool Ruby'
	'Ruby Doris'	see *D.* 'Houndspool Ruby'
	'Saint Edith' (p)	WKin
	'Saint Nicholas' (p)	EMFP SChu WKin
	'Saint Winifred'	SChu WKin
	Salamanca = 'Kosalamana' (pf)	SBai SHay
	'Sally Anne Hayward' (b)	SHay
	'Sam Barlow' (p)	COkL EGoo EWTr SChu SHay WKin WWye
	'Santa Claus' (b)	SHay
	'Santorini'	SHay
	'Scania' (pf)	SHay
	'Scarlet Fragrance' (b)	SHay
	'Schubert' (pf) **new**	SBai
	scopulorum perplexans	EPot ETow
	seguieri	MNrw SSvw WAbe WMoo WPer
	serotinus	EPot WCot
	Shiplake seedling (p)	WKin
	'Show Portrait' (p)	NFor
	simulans	CLyd EHyt
	'Sir Cedric Morris'	see *D.* 'Cedric's Oldest'
	'Sir David Scott' (p)	WKin
*	'Six Hills'	NHol WCom WPat
	'Snowfire'	SChu
	'Snowshill Manor' (p)	WPer
	'Solar Chiaro' (p)	SBai
	'Solar Giallo Oro' (pf)	SBai
	'Solomon' (p)	SSvw WKin
	'Solomon's Hat' (p)	WKin
	'Sops-in-wine' (p)	EChP ECha EMFP GBuc GCal ITim MNrw SChu SHay SMrm WKin WSSM
	'Southmead' (p)	ECho
§	'Souvenir de la Malmaison' (M)	WMal
	'Spangled Star' (p)	MBNS
	'Spencer Bickham' (p)	EMFP EPot MNrw WKin
	'Spirit'PBR (pf)	SBai SHay
	'Spring Beauty' (p)	LPVe NBir WHer
	'Spring Star'	ECtt NLar
	'Square Eyes'	see *D.* 'Old Square Eyes'
	squarrosus	EPot GKir NWCA
*	- *alpinus*	ECho ITim
	- 'Nanus'	ELan EWes LRHS
	'Squeeks' (p)	SChu
	'Stan Stroud' (b)	SHay
	'Starry Eyes'	NCGa WLin
	'Storm' (pf)	WMal
	'Strathspey' (b)	SHay
	'Strawberries and Cream' (p)	CBcs CHar CThr EBee ECtt EMFP EOMN EWTr LAst LHop LRHS MAvo NOrc SHay SPla WLin WMnd WWol
*	*strictus* subsp. *pulchellus*	EHyt GCrs SOkd
§	*subacaulis*	NLar
	suendermannii	see *D. petraeus*
	'Sunray' (b)	SHay
	'Sunstar' (b)	SHay
§	*superbus*	EGoo EShb EWTr LPhx MSal MTho SSpi WCom WHer WKin WOut WPer WWye
	- 'Crimsonia'	WHrl WPer
	- 'Dwarf Snow Lady' **new**	NFla
	- var. *longicalycinus*	MNrw MSte WHer
I	- 'Primadonna'	WPer
*	- 'Rose'	WPer
	- 'Snowdonia'	WOut WPer
	- subsp. *speciosus* **new**	CTCP
	'Swanlake' (p)	SHay
	'Sway Belle' (p)	CBcs SBai
	'Sway Delight' (p)	SBai
	'Sway Melody' (p)	CBcs SBai
	'Sway Pearl' (p)	CBcs
	'Sway Ripple' (p)	CBcs
	'Sway Sorbet' (p)	SBai
	'Sway Sunset' (p)	CBcs
	'Sweet Sue' (b)	SHay
	'Sweetheart Abbey' (p)	CThr EMFP GBuc IGor SChu SSvw WKin
	sylvestris	EPot
	- subsp. *tergestinus*	MDHE
	'Syston Beauty' (p)	WKin
	'Tamsin' (p) ♀H4	SBla WKin
	'Tatra Blush'	GCal GMac

'Tatra Bull's-eye' (p)	GCal
'Tatra Fragrance'	CMdw GCal
'Tatra Ghost'	GCal
'Tayside Red' (M)	WMal
'Tempo' (pf) ♀H1	SBai SHay WWol
'Terranova'ᴾᴮᴿ **new**	SHay
'Terry Sutcliffe' (p)	WKin
the Bloodie pink	see *D.* 'Caesar's Mantle'
'Thomas' (p)	CSLe SChu SMrm WEas
'Thora' (M)	WMal
I 'Tickled Pink' **new**	COtt
'Tiny Rubies'	see *D. gratianopolitanus* 'Tiny Rubies'
'Toledo' (p)	EMFP WKin
'Treasure' (p)	SHay
'Tundra'ᴾᴮᴿ (pf)	SBai SHay
turkestanicus	NBir
'Tweedale Seedling'	GBuc
'Unique' (p)	EMFP SChu SSvw WHoo WKin
'Ursula Le Grove' (p)	EMFP IGor SChu SSvw WIvy WKin
'Valda Wyatt' (p) ♀H4	CBcs CThr EBee ELan EMFP EPfP GKir LAst LRHS MAvo MBow SBai SChu SHay SPla WGwG WLin WMnd
'Violet Clove' (b)	SHay
'W.A. Musgrave'	see *D.* 'Musgrave's Pink'
'Waithman Beauty' (p)	CTri ECtt GAbr MBar WKin WPer WTin WWye
'Waithman's Jubilee' (p)	SRms WLin
'Warden Hybrid' (p)	CMea CTri EBee EBre ECtt EDAr EPfP GEdr LBBr LRHS SHay WAbe WLin
'Weetwood Double' (p)	CFee
'Welcome' (b)	SHay
weyrichii	CLyd ECho NMen
'Whatfield Anona' (p)	ELan
'Whatfield Beauty'	EChP ECho ECtt EDAr ELan EMlt GAbr LRHS
'Whatfield Brilliant' (p)	GKir
'Whatfield Can-can' ♀H4	CLyd CMea COkL CPBP EBee EBre ECtt EDAr EMFP GKir LRHS NCGa NJOw NPri WAbe
'Whatfield Cerise'	CLyd
'Whatfield Cream Lace'	GAbr NWCA
'Whatfield Cyclops'	CLyd CPBP EDAr EMlt LRHS SChu WKin
'Whatfield Dawn'	CLyd ECho ELan
'Whatfield Dorothy Mann' (p)	ECho ELan
'Whatfield Fuchsia' (p)	CLyd
'Whatfield Gem' (p)	CLyd CPBP EBee EBre ECtt ELan EMFP EMlt ESis GCal LAst LRHS MRav MWgw NJOw NPri WFar WKin WPer
'Whatfield Joy' (p)	CLyd ECtt EDAr ELan EMlt EPfP EPot ESis GAbr LBBr LBee LRHS MHer NMen NPri WPat
'Whatfield Magenta' (p) ♀H4	CLyd EBre ELan EMlt ESis GAbr GEdr GKir LBee LRHS NJOw NWCA SChu WAbe WEas
'Whatfield Mini' (p)	EDAr SRms WPer
'Whatfield Misty Morn' (p)	CLyd ECho ELan
'Whatfield Pom Pom' (p)	CLyd
'Whatfield Pretty Lady' (p)	ECho ELan
'Whatfield Rose' (p)	ECho EPot
'Whatfield Ruby' (p)	CLyd ELan GKir LRHS NWCA WPer
'Whatfield Supergem'	CLyd ECho ECtt ELan EPot
'Whatfield White' (p)	CLyd ECho ECtt ELan EWTr LRHS SRms WGwG
'Whatfield White Moon' (p)	ECho

'Whatfield Wisp' (p)	CM&M CPBP CTri ELan ESis GAbr GEdr MRav NBir NMen NWCA WAbe WFar
'White Joy'ᴾᴮᴿ (p) ♀H4	EDAr EMFP
'White Ladies' (p)	ELan ENot EWTr WKin
'White Liberty'ᴾᴮᴿ (pf)	SHay
'Whitecliff' (b)	SHay
'Whitehill' (p) ♀H4	MBro MHer NHol NMen NWCA NWoo WLin WPat WWin
'Whitford Belle' (p)	SBai
'Widecombe Fair' (p) ♀H4	CMea CTri ECtt EDAr ELan LRHS NLar SRms WLin
* 'Wild Velvet' (p)	WKin
'William Brownhill' (p)	EMFP SChu WKin
'Winsome' (p)	SHay
'Yorkshireman' (b)	SHay
'Zebra' (b)	SHay
zederbaueri	NWCA
'Zoe's Choice' (p) ♀H4	COkL

Diapensia (*Diapensiaceae*)

lapponica var. *obovata*	WAbe

Diarrhena (*Poaceae*)

japonica	EPPr WDyG
* *mandschurica* **new**	EPPr

Diascia ✿ (*Scrophulariaceae*)

anastrepta	EOrc MHom
– HWEL 0219	NWCA
'Appleby Appleblossom'	EOrc GCal SChu WWeb
'Appleby Apricot'	NDov NGdn
'Apricot' hort.	see *D. barberae* 'Hopleys Apricot'
* 'Aquarius'	SChu
'Baby Bums'	WWol
barberae	ELan
– 'Belmore Beauty' (v)	CCge ECtt EMan EPyc EWes MHer NFla SChu SScr
– 'Blackthorn Apricot' ♀H3-4	EChP ECha ECtt EDAr EHyt ELan EPfP GBuc GKir GMac IHMH LAst LRHS MBow MHer MSte NRya SBla SChu SMrm SPer SPlb SWvt WCAu WCom WFar WPer WSHC WWeb
– 'Crûg Variegated' (v)	EMan EPot WCru
§ – 'Fisher's Flora' ♀H3-4	EPyc NBro NDov NMen WFar
– 'Fisher's Flora' x 'Lilac Belle'	ECtt EDAr SCoo SHFr
§ – 'Hopleys Apricot'	EPfP LHop
§ – 'Ruby Field' ♀H3-4	CBcs CMea EBre ECha ECtt EDAr ELan EPfP GKir LAst LHop LRHS MDun MHer NGdn NPPs NRya SBla SPer SPla SRms SWvt WCFE WFar
Blue Bonnet = 'Hecbon'	CElw EChP ECtt EMan EPot GMac MDKP SChu SGar SMrm SWvt WFar
'Blush'	see *D. integerrima* 'Blush'
'Coldham'	ECtt EMan LHop SDys SGar
Coral Belle = 'Hecbel'ᴾᴮᴿ ♀H3-4	CHar EBee ECtt EHyt EMan EOrc EPfP EPot EWes GMac LAst LHop LRHS MBow MDun MSte MTis SChu SIng SUsu WEas WFar WPer WWeb
cordata misapplied	see *D. barberae* 'Fisher's Flora'
cordifolia	see *D. barberae* 'Fisher's Flora'
'Dainty Duet'	SChu
'Dark Eyes' ♀H3-4	MSte SChu
Eclat = 'Heclat'ᴾᴮᴿ	ECtt EPot WFar
elegans misapplied	see *D. fetcaniensis*, *D. vigilis*
'Elizabeth' ♀H3-4	MMil WSPU
'Emma'	LHop SChu SUsu SWvt
felthamii	see *D. fetcaniensis*
§ *fetcaniensis*	CMHG EBee EPfP LHop MHom SBri SCro SIgm SScr WBVN WBrk WCFE WHal WSpi WWin

- 'Daydream'	LRHS WLin WShp WWeb
flanaganii misapplied	see *D. vigilis*
flanaganii Hiern	see *D. stachyoides*
'Frilly' ♀H3-4	ECtt MSte SChu
I 'Hazel'	SScr
'Hector Harrison'	see *D.* 'Salmon Supreme'
'Hector's Hardy' ♀H3-4	EMan MSte
Ice Cracker = 'Hecrack'	CElw CMea CSpe EChP ECtt EHyt
	ELan EMan EOrc EPot GMac LAst
	LHop MBow NFla NGdn SIng SScr
	WWol
Iceberg = 'Hecice'PBR	CHar CSpe SWvt
§ *integerrima* ♀H3-4	CSam ECha ELan EMan EOrc LLWP
	LPhx MHom SChu SGar SIgm
	SMrm SPla WCot
- 'Alba'	see *D. integerrima* 'Blush'
§ - 'Blush'	CElw CSam CSpe EGoo EMan
	GMac MHom MSte NPPs SAga
	SGar SMrm
- 'Ivory Angel'	see *D. integerrima* 'Blush'
integrifolia	see *D. integerrima*
'Jack Elliott'	see *D. vigilis* 'Jack Elliott'
'Jacqueline's Joy'	CMea EMan GMac MSte NFla
	NGdn NPer SChu SMrm WBar
	WFar
'Joyce's Choice' ♀H3-4	EOrc EWes LPhx MSte NDov
	NGdn SBri WFar
'Kate'	LRHS NDov SChu
'Katherine Sharman' (v)	ECtt EMan EWes LRHS MBNS
	MDKP NGdn SAga WCom WWol
'Lady Valerie' ♀H3-4	CElw EWes MSte WPer WWin
'Lilac Belle' ♀H3-4	CBcs CCge CMea EBre ECtt EHyt
	ELan EPfP ESis LAst LHop LRHS
	MBro MHar MHer NGdn SMrm
	SPla SPlb WFar WHoo WPer WWin
'Lilac Mist' ♀H3-4	NPer NWoo SChu WPen
lilacina	ESis
Little Dancer = 'Pendan'PBR	LAst SGar SIng WGor WLow
'Louise'	CSpe EOrc EPot GBuc
'Lucy'	EMan EPot
'Lucy' x *mollis*	SChu SDys SUsu
'Miro'	MBow WWol
patens	CHll EMan
Pink Panther = 'Penther'PBR	CSpe ECtt EMan SIng SWvt WGor
'Pink Queen'	ECtt SRms
* 'Pisces'	SChu
purpurea	SScr
Red Ace = 'Hecrace'PBR	EBee EChP EOrc EPfP NPer SIng
	SWvt
Redstart = 'Hecstart'	EBee ECtt EPfP LAst LHop NFla
	NGdn NPri SChu SPet SWvt WFar
	WWeb WWin WWol
rigescens ♀H3	More than 30 suppliers
§ - 'Anne Rennie'	EMan
- pale	see *D. rigescens* 'Anne Rennie'
rigescens x *lilacina*	CCge CElw SIgm
I 'Rosa'	WWol
'Ruby Field'	see *D. barberae* 'Ruby Field'
'Rupert Lambert' ♀H3-4	CElw CStr EMon EPot GBuc LLWP
	MHom NDov SBri SChu WPer
§ 'Salmon Supreme'	EBee EBre ECtt ELan LPhx NDov
	NGdn NPer NPri SChu SRms WFar
	WMoo WPer
'Selina's Choice'	GBuc SChu
§ *stachyoides*	ELan LHop
Sun Chimes Series	LIck NPri
ApricotDelight = 'Codicot' **new**	
- Blush Delight = 'Codiush' **new**	LIck
- Pink Delight = Codiink' **new**	LIck

Susan = 'Winsue'PBR	WFar
Sydney Olympics = 'Hecsyd'	EMan
tugelensis	WFar
'Twinkle' ♀H3-4	CPBP ECtt EDAr EPfP EPot EWes
	GCal LAst NBir NGdn NPer NPri
	SChu SIng SMrm SPet WFar WPer
	WWeb WWin
* 'Twins Gully'	GCal MTed SMrm
* *variegata* (v)	MBNS
§ *vigilis* ♀H3	CFee CMHG CPLG CSam EChP
	ECha EDAr EOrc EPfP EWTr GCal
	LPhx MTis NBro SAga SChu SDix
	SGar WCom
§ - 'Jack Elliott'	CWCL MDun SHel SPla WCFE
- - ex JE 8955	LHop
'White Cloud'	SChu WSPU

Diascia x *Linaria* see *Nemesia caerulea*

Dicentra ✿ (*Papaveraceae*)

'Adrian Bloom'	EBee EBre EChP ECtt EHrv EPla
	EWTr GSki LRHS MBNS MCLN
	MWgw NSti SCoo SWvt WFar
	WMnd WMoo
'Bacchanal' ♀H4	More than 30 suppliers
'Boothman's Variety'	see *D.* 'Stuart Boothman'
'Bountiful'	CMHG EBee EMan GKir GSki
	LRHS MBro MLLN MRav MWgw
	NArg NFor NGdn NSti SChu SPer
	SPet SPla SWvt WMnd WRHF
	WWeb
'Brownie'	GBuc
canadensis	EBee EPot GBuc GSki MTho NSti
	SSpi WCot WCru
'Coldham'	SMac WCru WSHC WTin
cucullaria	More than 30 suppliers
- 'Pittsburg'	CBos SSpi WCot
* 'Dark Stuart Boothman'	ECGN
eximia hort.	see *D.formosa*
eximia (Ker Gawl.) Torr.	EBee MTho MWat SWat
- 'Alba'	see *D. eximia* 'Snowdrift'
§ - 'Snowdrift'	CLAP CM&M EBee EBre EChP ECtt
	EHrv ELan EPfP EWTr GKir IHMH
	LRHS MBro MRav MTho NGdn
	SMrm SRms SSpi WBar WFar
	WHoo WMnd WMoo WPnP WPrP
	WShp
§ *formosa*	More than 30 suppliers
§ - *alba*	CPLG CRow CTri ECha MWrn
	NBir NCot NFor NMRc NSti NVic
	SChu SPer SPla SRms STes WCAu
	WCru WFar
* - 'Aurora'	CBct CBre EBee EBre EChP EMan
	EWTr GBin GFlt GSki LRHS MBri
	MCCP MCLN MRav NHol SWvt
	WBor WFar WMnd WSan WShp
- dark	WMoo
- 'Furse's Form' **new**	GBin
- subsp. *oregana*	CLAP CRow EBee EPPr EPar EPot
	GAbr GCal GKir NChi SBla SSpi
	WAbb WCru WWin
- - NNS 00-233	WCot
- - 'Rosea'	EPPr NPar SSpi
- - 'Spring Gold'	ECha WMoo
'King of Hearts'	More than 30 suppliers
'Langtrees' ♀H4	More than 30 suppliers
lichiangensis **new**	WCru
'Luxuriant' ♀H4	CBcs CSBt EBee EBre EChP ECtt
	ELan EPar EPfP EWTr GAbr GKir
	GSki LRHS MBri MCLN MLLN MTis
	SAga SRms SWat SWvt WBVN
	WCra WFar WLow WMnd WMoo
	WPnP WSan

macrantha	CBos CDes CFil CLAP CRow EBee ECha EPfP GBuc LAma LPhx MTho SBla SMad SSpi WCru WPGP WSHC
macrocapnos	CBcs CFir CRow CTCP EChP EMan EPfP GBuc GQui LRHS MDKP MSPs MTho NABC NSti WBor WBrE WCru WPrP WTre
'Paramount'	GBin
'Pearl Drops'	More than 30 suppliers
peregrina	GTou SOkd
§ *scandens*	CBrm CMHG CMil CRHN CRow CSpe EPfP EPot GCal IFro MCCP MTho NLar SGar SMac SSpi WHil WSHC WSPU WWhi
– B&SWJ 2427	WCru
– CC 3223	WRos
– CC 3806	WCot
– 'Shirley Clemo'	CPLG
'Silversmith'	CFil
Snowflakes = 'Fusd'	EBre EWes GKir LRHS MCCP MRav
spectabilis ♀H4	More than 30 suppliers
– 'Alba' ♀H4	More than 30 suppliers
– 'Gold Heart'PBR	CHad CPen EBee EHan EMan ENot EPfP GBri GKir NCGa NLar NSti SPer WFar WWeb
'Spring Morning'	CElw CMHG CMil CPLG CPrp CRow CSam EHrv EPPr EPfP IBlr NSti SChu SSpi WEas WRHF
§ 'Stuart Boothman' ♀H4	More than 30 suppliers
thalictrifolia	see *D. scandens*
torulosa B&SWJ 7814	WCru

Dichelostemma (*Alliaceae*)

§ *capitatum*	ETow
– NNS 95-213	WCot
congestum	CAvo EBee EMan EPot ERos LRHS WCot
– NNS 97-75	SIgm
§ *ida-maia*	CAvo CBro CStu EBee EPot LPhx LRHS
– 'Californian Firecrackers' **new**	MDKP
– 'Pink Diamond'	CBro EBee EPot MDKP
multiflorum	WCot
pulchellum	see *D. capitatum*
volubile NNS 95-220	WCot

Dichocarpum (*Ranunculaceae*)

dalzielii	EBee

Dichondra (*Convolvulaceae*)

micrantha	EShb
– 'Silver Falls' **new**	COtt EShb NPri
repens misapplied	see *D. micrantha*
repens ambig. **new**	XPep

Dichotomanthes (*Rosaceae*)

tristaniicarpa	CFil

Dichroa (*Hydrangeaceae*)

febrifuga	CAbb CBcs CDoC CFil CHll CKob CMil CPLG CWib EWes GBri GQui LRHS SLon SOWG WCot WCru WOVN WPGP
– B&SWJ 2367	WCru
– pink	CHEx
aff. *hirsuta* B&SWJ 8207 from Thailand **new**	WCru
– B&SWJ 8371 from Lao	WCru
versicolor B&SWJ 6565	WCru

Dichromena see *Rhynchospora*

Dicksonia ✿ (*Dicksoniaceae*)

antarctica ♀H3	More than 30 suppliers
fibrosa ♀H3	CAbb CBcs CTrC EAmu EUJe IDee LPan SChr WMul WRic
selloviana	WRic
squarrosa ♀H2	CAbb CBcs CBrP CHEx CTrC ERea EUJe LPan NBlu NMoo NPSI SAPC SArc WMul WRic
youngiae	WRic

Dicliptera (*Acanthaceae*)

§ *suberecta*	CBcs CHal CHll EHol EMan ERea LHop MOak SAga SHFr SIgm SOWG SUsu WCot WDyG XPep

Dictamnus ✿ (*Rutaceae*)

albus	CArn CBcs CTri EBlw ECha EFou EHrv ELan EPat EPfP ERou GCal LHop LPhx LRHS MBri MRav NCGa NSti SChu SECG SPer WCAu WCom WCot WHoo WSHC WWye
§ – var. *purpureus* ♀H4	More than 30 suppliers
caucasicus	EBee EBre
fraxinella	see *D. albus* var. *purpureus*

Dictyolimon (*Plumbaginaceae*)

macrorrhabdos	WCot

Dictyosperma (*Arecaceae*)

album	CRoM LPal

Didymochlaena (*Dryopteridaceae*)

lunulata	see *D. truncatula*
§ *truncatula*	CHal MBri

Dieffenbachia (*Araceae*)

'Camille' (v) ♀H1	LRHS
'Compacta' (v)	LRHS

Dierama ✿ (*Iridaceae*)

CD&R 192	CRow
ambiguum	ECGN ITim NPPs SHFr WPrP
argyreum	CFil CPla EBee IBlr
'Ariel'	IBlr
'Black Knight'	CPen IBlr
'Blush'	IBlr
'Candy Stripe'	CPla CRow GBri GSki MCCP STes
'Cherry Chimes' **new**	EBee LBuc WWeb
cooperi	CElw CPne CPrp GBri IBlr
– 'Edinburgh White'	WLFP
'Coral Bells' **new**	GCal
'Donard Legacy'	GBri IBlr
§ *dracomontanum*	More than 30 suppliers
– dwarf lilac	CM&M MAnH
– dwarf pale pink	CM&M
– dwarf pink	CBot CPne
dubium	IBlr
dubium x *robustum*	EBee
ensifolium	see *D. pendulum*
erectum	CLAP EBee IBlr MAnH WCot WGMN
'Fairy Bells' **new**	CPen
'Flamingo' **new**	IBlr
floriferum	CBro IBlr
galpinii	CFil CLAP CPla GSki MAnH MWrn STes WGMN
grandiflorum	IBlr
'Guinevere'	More than 30 suppliers
igneum	More than 30 suppliers
– CD&R 278	CPou
'Iris'	IBlr
jucundum	EPot GBri GBuc MLLN
'Knee-high Lavender'	CSpe SAga

'Lancelot' **new** — CFir CKno EBee GBuc IBlr LAst MBnl NCot SPla WCot

latifolium — CHid ECGN EChP GSki IBlr ITim MWrn SIgm SMad WCot WPrP WSan

luteoalbidum — CDes CLAP CStu EBee WPGP

'Mandarin' — IBlr

medium — CFil CMil CPen EBee GSki LPio SMrm SUsu SWat WCot WOBN WPGP

'Merlin' — More than 30 suppliers

'Milkmaid' — IBlr

mossii — EBee IBlr WGMN

nixonianum — IBlr

'Pamina' — IBlr

'Papagena' — IBlr

'Papageno' — IBlr

pauciflorum — More than 30 suppliers

- CD&R 197 — CPBP MDKP

§ *pendulum* — CAvo CBot CBro CFee CPne ELan ENot EPfP EPza ERou GGar GKir IBlr LAst LPio LRHS MFir MNrw MRav NCGa NHol NLAp SPer SWat SWvt WAbe WCot WGwG WPen

pictum **new** — IBlr

Plant World hybrids **new** — MWrn

'Pretty Flamingo' — IBlr

'Puck' — CDes CPen EBee GCal IBlr IGor MLLN WPGP

pulcherrimum — More than 30 suppliers

- var. *album* — CAbb CBot CFil CHar CHea CM&M EBee ECGN ECha GBuc GSki ITim LHop LPio MAnH MNrw MWrn NCGa SHar STes SUsu WHrl WLFP WWhi WWpP

- 'Angel Gabriel' — WWpP

- 'Blackbird' — More than 30 suppliers

- brick red — WHil

- dark pink **new** — WHil

- dwarf — GCal GSki LHop WWhi

- 'Falcon' **new** — IBlr

- lilac — LHop

- 'Pearly Queen' — CRow

- 'Peregrine' — WPGP

- pink — CDWL CTbh EPza GBBs NBPC NBid WBVN WWhi

- 'Red Orr' **new** — ITim

- Slieve Donard hybrids — CLAP CSam ECGN EChP ECtt EFou EMan GBri GCal ITim LHop LRHS MAnH MAvo MFOX MHer MTis MWrn WCot WHrl WPnP WRHF WSSM WSan

pumilum hort. — see *D. dracomontanum*

'Queen of the Night' — IBlr

'Redwing' **new** — IBlr

reynoldsii — CAbb CDes CFil CHid CPLG CPla EBee EMan GAbr GBuc GCal GSki IBlr ITim MAnH MCCP MHar MWrn NPPs SGar SMad SPlb STes WGMN WLFP WPrP

'Rich Pink' **new** — CPen

robustum — CFil CLAP CPou GBri IBlr WAbe WBVN

- SH 20 — CPLG

'Sarastro' — IBlr

'September Charm' — IBlr

sertum — CBro

'Snowballs' — CLAP CPen CWCL ELan MAnH SOkh WCAu

- B&SWJ 2827 — WCru

'Tamino' — IBlr

'Tiny Bells' **new** — GCal

'Titania' — CPen IBlr ITim

trichorhizum — CLAP CPla GBri GSki IBlr MNrw

MWrn NLar SAga SMad STes WGMN WPrP

'Tubular Bells' — IBlr

'Violet Ice' — IBlr

'Westminster Chimes' — CDes CKno EBee IBlr WPGP

Dierama ✿ (*Caprifoliaceae*)

lonicera — CHar SLon SMac WFar

middendorffiana — see *Weigela middendorffiana*

rivularis — CPle

§ *sessilifolia* — CBcs CHar CPle EBee ECrN EPar EPfP IMGH MRav SGar SLon WBVN WBod WCFE WCot WFar WSHC WTin WWin WWpP

- 'Butterfly' — GKir LRHS

x *splendens* — CAbP CCge CMHG CPle CWib EBee EHoe ELan EPfP GEil LAst LHop LRHS MBNS MBar MRav MSwo MTis NHol SGar SLPl SPer SPla SSta WBcn WDin

Dietes (*Iridaceae*)

bicolor — CAbb CDes CHEx EMan ERea LEdu LPio SDnm

grandiflora — CAbb CArn CFee CFwr EBee EDif EMan ERea LEdu LPio LRHS WAbe WWye

* - 'Reen Lelie' — CMdw

§ *iridioides* — CNic CSWP CTCP EBee GBin GGar LRHS MSte WPGP

Digitalis ✿ (*Scrophulariaceae*)

ambigua — see *D. grandiflora*

apricot hybrids — see *D. purpurea* 'Sutton's Apricot'

'Ashdon Glory' **new** — EBee

'Callisto' — LEur

cariensis — EBla WBry

ciliata — CFir EBee EChP ELan MLLN WBry WCom WCot

cream hybrids — EFou

davisiana — CBot CBri CPLG EBee EBla EChP GBuc MLwd NLar NOak SBla SDnm WCHb WMoo WPer

dubia — CBot EBee EBla EPfP EWTr NBir NLar SBla SDnm WAbe WCom

- 'Silver Anniversary' — WWeb

'Elsie Kelsey' — CFwr ITer MAnH MDKP SDnm WTMC

eriostachya — see *D. lutea*

ferruginea ♀[H4] — More than 30 suppliers

- 'Gelber Herold' — CBel CBot CBri EChP EMan EPfP ERou LPhx LRHS MSPs MSte NLar WGor WWeb

- 'Gigantea' — CBot EBee ECGN EMan ERou EWTr GCal LRHS MBNS MWgw NCGa NNor NPri NSti SSte SWat

- var. *schischkinii* — CDes CPLG CTCP EBee EBla EWTr GCal MBNS NLar SDnm WLin WPGP

'Flashing Spires' — see *D. lutea* 'Flashing Spires'

* *floribunda* — CTCP EBee SDnm

fontanesii — EBee EChP GBuc NBur WLin

'Foxley Primrose' **new** — MBri

'Frosty' — MCLN

x *fulva* — MLLN NBir

'Glory of Roundway' — CBot CDes CPom EBee MEHN MFOX MHer SSvw SWat WBro WFar

§ *grandiflora* ♀[H4] — More than 30 suppliers

- MESE 359 — EBee

- MESE 407 — EBee

- 'Carillon' — CBot CPom CSam EBee EChP EMan EMar EShb LDai LPVe LPhx MBNS MSte MTis NLar NPri WBro WGor WHil WPer

- 'Temple Bells'	EBla ECoo EMar SAga SWat WBry WPer
heywoodii	see *D. purpurea* subsp. *heywoodii*
'John Innes Tetra'	CBot CSam EBlw EChP ECoo LRHS MBNS NPPs SWal SWat WBry WPGP WPer WWin
kishinskyi	see *D. parviflora*
laevigata	More than 30 suppliers
- subsp. *graeca*	EBee WGor
- white-flowered **new**	GMac
lamarckii hort.	see *D. lanata*
lamarckii Ivanina	CTCP EBee SIgm WPer
§ *lanata*	More than 30 suppliers
leucophaea	EGoo EMar
§ *lutea*	More than 30 suppliers
§ - subsp. *australis*	CTCP EBla LDai SDnm SHFr WBry
§ - 'Flashing Spires' (v)	CPla EMan GBBs GBri MLwd MSPs SSte SWat WBry WHer
- 'Yellow Medley'	WCot
x *media*	ECGN
x *mertonensis* ♀H4	More than 30 suppliers
- 'Summer King'	CBot ECtt MBow NGHP WGor
micrantha	see *D. lutea* subsp. *australis*
nervosa	CPLG EBla
obscura	CBot CFir CPom EBee EBla EBlw ECGN EChP EHrv EMan EPPr ERou GEil LAst LRHS MLwd MWgw NGHP NPri SBla SDnm SIgm SSpi WCHb WCot WGor WHer WLin WPer WWeb
orientalis	see *D. grandiflora*
§ *parviflora*	More than 30 suppliers
- 'Milk Chocolate' **new**	SSvw
purpurea	CArn CHrt EBlw ECtt EDAr EFou ELau ENot EWTr GPoy MBow MHer NArg NFor NLRH NLan NMir NPri SIde SPlb WMoo WPer WWye
- f. *albiflora*	More than 30 suppliers
- - 'Anne Redetzky' **new**	EBee EChP LBuc SCoo SPer WWeb
- - unspotted	EMar
* - 'Campanulata Alba'	CBot
- 'Chedglow' (v)	CNat WCHb WHil
- dwarf red	MBNS WGor
- Excelsior Group	CBcs CBot CCge COlW CSBt CTri EBre EMan ENot EPfP ERou MBow MBri MWat NBlu NMir NVic SMer SPer SRms SWal SWvt WGor WLow
- - primrose	ERou SPer
- - (Suttons; Unwins) ♀H4	ECtt MRav
- - white	ERou
- Foxy Group	CBot CWib ECtt EHrv EMar ENor GKir MBNS NJOw SPet SRms WFar WHen WPer WSan
- - 'Foxy Apricot'	CBot COlW MTis NSti SPla SWvt
- - 'Foxy Pink'	EMan NSti SPla SSpi
- - 'Foxy Primrose'	CBot EChP
- Giant Spotted Group	CBot COtt EBlw ECoo ECtt EHrv EPfP GKir LHop LRHS SCoo WHil WPer
- Glittering Prizes Group	LRHS SWat WBry
- - white	WHPP
- Gloxinioides Group	CBot EBee ELan ENot EPfP SHFr WCot
- - 'Isabellina'	CBot WPer
- - 'The Shirley' ♀H4	ECtt WBry WGor
* - *heptandra*	CNat
§ - subsp. *heywoodii*	CBot CHrt CSam CTCP EBee EChP ELan ENot GBuc NPPs SDnm WCHb WGMN WHil WMoo WPer WWin
- - 'Pink Champagne'	EBre
- subsp. *mariana*	EBee
- subsp. *nevadensis*	CBot

- 'Pam's Choice'	CHad CSpe ECoo EDif EMar MAnH MWrn
- peloric	WCHb
- 'Primrose Carousel'	EBre ECoo ECtt ERou MBct MWrn SWal WBry WGwG WHHs
- 'Snow Thimble'	CBot CFwr CSam EBee EBre MAnH MSPs NLar NVic WHil
§ - 'Sutton's Apricot' ♀H4	More than 30 suppliers
* - 'Sutton's Giant Primrose'	CBot EMan EWll MWrn WBry WSSM WSpi
- 'Tinkerbell'	ECoo MDKP
'Saltwood' **new**	GKir
'Saltwood Summer'	COtt EBre MBri SCoo
sibirica	EBee EChP GBuc GMac LPhx WCHb WPer WTMC
* *spaniflora*	EChP LPhx
* *stewartii*	CHar CTCP EBee ECGN EChP ECtt ELan EMan EWes GAbr GBBs GIBF LDai MAnH MAvo MBNS MDKP MSPs NBur NCGa NChi SBod SDnm SPer SPoG WBry WCot WGMN WLin WMoo
thapsi	CBot CBri CTCP EBla EChP ECtt EDAr EMan EMlt MBNS MLLN MSPs NBur NPri SBla SBod SDnm WCHb WGMN WPer
- JCA 410.000	EBee
trojana	EBee ECGN ECtt GBuc LRHS MLLN MWod SGar WWin
* *tuberosa*	CBri
viridiflora	CPLG CPom EBee EBla EBlw ECtt EDAr EWTr MBNS MDKP MHer MLwd MWhi NBro NChi SDnm SGar WCHb WFar WHer WPer WWin

dill see *Anethum graveolens*

Dionaea (Droseraceae)

muscipula	CSWC LRHS MCCP NABC WSSs
- 'Akai Ryu' **new**	WSSs
- 'Royal Red'	CSWC

Dionysia (Primulaceae)

'Annielle'	EHyt
archibaldii	EHyt
aretioides ♀H2	WOBN
- SLIZE 035	EHyt
- 'Bevere' **new**	EHyt WAbe
- 'Gravetye'	ECho
- 'Phyllis Carter'	ECho SIng
- 'Susan Hale'	EHyt
- 'Susan Tucker'	EHyt
bryoides SLIZE 236 **new**	EHyt
'Charlson Drew'	EHyt
'Charlson Emma' **new**	EHyt
'Charlson Gem'	EHyt
'Charlson Jake'	EHyt
'Charlson Petite'	EHyt
'Charlson Stuart'	EHyt
'Charlson Terri' **new**	EHyt
'Charlson Thomas'	EHyt
'Cinderella' **new**	EHyt
curviflora	EHyt
- SLIZE 213	EHyt
curviflora x *tapetodes*	WOBN
'Emmely'	EHyt
'Eric Watson'	EHyt
'Ewesley Epsilon'	EHyt
'Ewesley Gamma'	EHyt
'Ewesley Iota'	EHyt
'Ewesley Kappa'	EHyt
'Ewesley Mu'	EHyt
'Ewesley Theta'	EHyt
'Francesca'	EHyt

freitagii	EHyt
freitagii × *viscidula*	EHyt
MK 91-1	
'Ina'	EHyt
iranshahrii	EHyt
SLIZE 213 **new**	
janthina	EHyt
– SLIZE 265	EHyt
lamingtonii	EHyt
'Markus'	EHyt
michauxii	EHyt
– SLIZE 254	EHyt
'Monika'	EHyt EPot WAbe
'Nan Watson'	EHyt
'Nocturne'	EHyt
'Orion' **new**	EHyt
'Rhapsodie'	EHyt
'Schneeball'	EHyt
tapetodes 'Brimstone'	EHyt WAbe
– farinose	ECho
– 'Peter Edwards'	EHyt
– 'Sulphur'	EHyt
viscidula GWH 1305 **new**	EHyt
zagrica SLIZE 176 **new**	EHyt

Dioon (*Zamiaceae*)

califanoi **new**	CBrP
caputoi **new**	CBrP
edule ♀H1	CBrP CRoM LPal WMul
– var. *angustifolium*	CBrP
mejiae	CBrP LPal
merolae	CBrP
rzedowskii	CBrP
spinulosum	CBrP EAmu LPal WMul

Dioscorea (*Dioscoreaceae*)

B&SWJ 1935	WCru
from Taiwan **new**	
batatas	LEdu MSal WCru
japonica	EBee ITer WBVN
nipponica	MSal
opposita **new**	EBee
pentaphylla **new**	EBee
quinqueloba	WCru
villosa	CArn MSal

Diosma (*Rutaceae*)

ericoides	LBuc
– 'Pink Fountain'	CWSG LBuc
– 'Sunset Gold'	LBuc SCoo
hirsuta 'Silver Flame' **new**	LBuc

Diosphaera (*Campanulaceae*)

asperuloides	see *Trachelium asperuloides*

Diospyros (*Ebenaceae*)

duclouxii	CFil SSpi
kaki (F)	CBcs CMCN EPfP ERom NLar SSpi WDin
lotus	CBcs CFil CLnd CMCN CTho ECre LEdu LPan NLar SSpi WFar WPGP
rhombifolia	CFil WPGP
virginiana (F)	CBcs CMCN CTho LEdu NLar SSpi

Dipcadi (*Hyacinthaceae*)

glaucum **new**	CDes
lividum	WPGP

Dipelta (*Caprifoliaceae*)

floribunda ♀H4	CBot CBrm CFil CMCN CPMA EBee ELan EMil EPfP GKir LRHS MBlu NLar SLon SSpi SSta WBod WPGP

ventricosa	CAbP CFil CMCN CPMA CPle EPfP GKir LRHS MBlu NLar SLon SSpi WFar WPGP
yunnanensis	CFil CPLG CPMA CTri ELan EMil EPfP IArd IDee LRHS NLar SSpi SSta WPGP WPat WWes

Diphylleia (*Berberidaceae*)

cymosa	CLAP EBee ECha EMan EPar LEur LPhx MSal SSpi WCot WCru WTin
grayi	CLAP EBee WCru
sinensis	CLAP EBee LEur WCru

Dipidax see *Onixotis*

Diplacus see *Mimulus*

Dipladenia see *Mandevilla*

Diplarrhena (*Iridaceae*)

Helen Dillon's form	EMan SUsu
§ *latifolia*	CFil CHar EMan GBBs GGar WAbe WCot
moraea	CAbP CBrm CDes CFil CMea CPLG CWCL EBee EBre EGle EMan GAbr GCal GSki IBlr ILis ITim LPio LRHS NCGa SSpi WAbe WBrE WCot WLin WPGP WSHC WWin
– *minor*	GBBs
– West Coast form	see *D. latifolia*

Diplazium (*Woodsiaceae*)

caudatum	WRic

Diplolaena (*Rutaceae*)

dampieri	SOWG

Diplotaxis (*Brassicaceae*)

muralis	CArn WJek

Dipsacus ❀ (*Dipsacaceae*)

asper	EBee
§ *fullonum*	CArn CHrt EPAt GBar MBow MHer NBid NBro NMir NPri NVic SECG SIde SYvo WBea WHer WWpP WWye
– subsp. *fullonum*	CPrp WJek
inermis	CPom EBee ECha EMon GBar LPhx NBid NLar WFar WHer
japonicus	EBee MSal
– HWJ 695	WCru
laciniatus	WMoo
pilosus	CPom EBee WBWf
sativus	NLar WHer
strigosus **new**	LPhx MLwd WHil
sylvestris	see *D. fullonum*

Dipteracanthus see *Ruellia*

Dipteronia (*Aceraceae*)

sinensis	CFil CMCN IArd LRHS NLar SSpi WBcn WNor WPGP

Disanthus (*Hamamelidaceae*)

cercidifolius ♀H4	CAbP CBcs CMCN EPfP GKir IDee IMGH LRHS MAsh MBlu MGos NLar SPer SSpi WBod

Discaria (*Rhamnaceae*)

chacaye	CFil LEdu WPGP

Diselma (*Cupressaceae*)

archeri	CDoC CKen CNic MBar SCoo

Disphyma (Aizoaceae)

crassifolium	SChr

Disporopsis (Convallariaceae)

B&SWJ 3891	EBee LEur WCru
from Philippines	
arisanensis	CDes CLAP LEdu LEur WFar
- B&SWJ 1490	EBee WCru WFar
* **aspera**	CDes CLAP EBee LEur WCru
fuscopicta	CLAP EBee EHrv EPPr LEur WCru WTin
longifolia	CLAP
- B&SWJ 5284	WCru
* **luzoniensis**	WCru
B&SWJ 3891 **new**	
'Min Shan' **new**	CBct
§ **pernyi**	More than 30 suppliers
- 'Bill Baker' **new**	MAvo
* **punctata new**	SBla

Disporum (Convallariaceae)

bodinieri	EBee LEur
calcaratum new	EBee
cantoniense	CDes CLAP EBee LEur WCru WPGP
- B&L 12512	CLAP SBla
- B&SWJ 1424	WCru
- DJHC 98485	CDes
I - 'Aureovariegata' **new**	WCot
- var. **cantoniense**	WCru
f. **brunneum**	
B&SWJ 5290	
- var. **kawakamii**	WCru
B&SWJ 350	
flavens	CBct CDes CFil CLAP CPom CStu EBee EBre EMan EPar EPfP GKir LEur LPhx MDun SBla SOkh SSpi SUsu WFar WPGP WSHC
- B&SWJ 872	WCru
* **flavum**	LRHS SOkd
hookeri	CLAP EPar GFlt GKir NMen WCot WCru
- var. **oreganum**	CBro GCrs GTou IBlr WCru
lanuginosum	CBro EBee GCrs WCot WCru
leucanthum	LEur SMHy
- B&SWJ 2389	WCru
lutescens	LEur WCru
maculatum	CBct CLAP EBee EPar LPhx NLar SMac WCru
megalanthum	CLAP EBee EHrv LEur SSpi WCru
- CD&R 2412b	EPPr
nantauense	CStu WPGP
- B&SWJ 359	CBct EBee WCot WCru
sessile	EBee EWTr LEur WCru
I - 'Aureovariegatum' (v)	WCru
I - 'Robustum Variegatum'	EBee
- 'Variegatum' (v)	CBro CFil CFwr CRow EBee ECha ELan EPPr EPar EPfP EPla EWTr GEdr LEdu LEur LRHS MRav SBla SMac SSpi WAul WCot WCru WFar WHil WPGP WPnP WWin WWye
- var. **yakushimense**	WCru
shimadae B&SWJ 399	WCru
smilacinum	EBee EPar LEur WCru
- B&SWJ 713	WCru
* - 'Aureovariegatum' (v)	WCot WCru
- 'Choyo'	WCru
- double	GCrs WCru
- pink	WCru
smithii	CBct CFil CStu EBee EPar EPot ERos GBuc GCrs GFlt GKir ITim LEur NBir NGar NMen SSpi WCot WCru WPGP

---

taiwanense B&SWJ 1513	LEur WCru
uniflorum	WCru
- B&SWJ 651	LEur WCot WCru
viridescens	EBee SSpi WCru
- B&SWJ 4598	WCru

Distylium (Hamamelidaceae)

myricoides	CFil CMCN WFar
racemosum	CBcs CFil CPLG EBee EPfP GSki IDee LRHS MBlu SHBN SMur SReu SSta WBVN WBcn WFar WSHC

Diuranthera see *Chlorophytum*

Dizygotheca see *Schefflera*

Dobinea (Podoaceae)

vulgaris B&SWJ 2532	WCru

Dodecatheon (Primulaceae)

alpinum	GEdr NLAp NRya SRms
- JCA 11744	SBla
- subsp. **majus**	NSla
amethystinum	see *D. pulchellum*
'Aphrodite'	EBee EMan NCGa NLar
austrofrigidum	GKev
clevelandii	ETow
- subsp. **insulare**	LRHS NWCA
- subsp. **patulum**	GBuc LRHS WCom
conjugens	CNic EBee
cusickii	see *D. pulchellum* subsp. *cusickii*
dentatum ♀H4	CElw CPBP CPLG EPar GBuc LRHS MDKP MTho NSla WAbe WFar
- subsp. **ellisiae**	GCrs
frigidum	WAbe
§ **hendersonii** ♀H4	CBro CNic EBee EPar EPot GBuc NMen NPar NSla SRms
integrifolium	see *D. hendersonii*
§ **jeffreyi**	CBri CFwr CMHG EBee EBlw GSki LRHS NBid NDlv NMen NWCA SBla WAbe WFar
- 'Rotlicht'	SRms WPer
* x **lemoinei**	WAbe
§ **meadia** ♀H4	More than 30 suppliers
- f. **album** ♀H4	CBcs CBro CMea CSWP CStu CTri EBee EBlw EChP EGle ELan EOrc EPar EPfP GFlt GSki LAma LHop LPhx LRHS MLLN MTho NMen SPer SRms SWvt WLin WPnP WPrP WWhi
- 'Aphrodite'	EChP
- from Cedar County	WAbe
* - 'Goliath'	GSki NLar WMoo
- membranaceous	WAbe
- Millard's clone	EPar
- 'Queen Victoria'	CFwr EBee GSki LPhx WFar WPnP
pauciflorum hort.	see *D. pulchellum*
pauciflorum	see *D. meadia*
(Dur.) E.Greene	
poeticum	ETow MDKP
§ **pulchellum** ♀H4	CBro CNic EBee EHyt EPar GCrs GKev GSki LHop LRHS MNrw NMen NRya
§ - subsp. **cusickii**	LRHS NWCA SRms
- subsp. **pulchellum**	CFwr CMea EBee GCrs GEdr LPhx
'Red Wings'	MBri MDKP NWCA WHoo WLin WSan
- **radicatum**	see *D. pulchellum*
- 'Sooke's Variety'	CStu WAbe
radicatum	see *D. pulchellum*
redolens	WAbe
tetrandrum	see *D. jeffreyi*

Dodonaea (Sapindaceae)

RCB/Eq P2-1 **new**   WCot
viscosa   CArn CTrC ECou SPlb XPep
- (f)   ECou
- (m)   ECou
- 'Picton' (f)   ECou
- 'Purpurea'   CAbb CBcs CBrm CDoC ECou ERea
   EShb IArd LRav WGer WSpi XPep
- 'Purpurea' (f)   ECou
- 'Purpurea' (m)   ECou
- 'Red Wings' (f)   ECou

Doellingeria (Asteraceae)

scabra   see _Aster scaber_

Dombeya (Sterculiaceae)

burgessiae   IDee LRHS SOWG

Dondia see _Hacquetia_

Doodia (Blechnaceae)

aspera   GQui NMar
§ _caudata_   EFtx NMar WRic
heterophylla   NMar
media   GQui NMar WRic
mollis   NMar
I   'Sonter's Linearis'   WRic
squarrosa   see _D. caudata_

Doronicum ❀ (Asteraceae)

austriacum   NBid
carpetanum   CSam
caucasicum   see _D. orientale_
§ _columnae_   NMen
cordatum   see _D. columnae_
§ x _excelsum_ 'Harpur   EBee ERou MCLN MRav NPer
   Crewe'   NVic WCAu WEas
   'Finesse'   EBee EOMN EPfP LRHS MWgw
   SRms WCot WMoo
§   'Frühlingspracht' (d)   WEas
glaciale   NMen
grandiflorum   EBee
   'Little Leo'   CMHG COIW EBee EBre ELan
   EMan EPyc ERou EShb LHop LRav
   MBow MBri MHer NBPC NCGa
   NChi NHol NLar NVic SPet WBrE
   WHil WWeb
   'Miss Mason' ♀H4   LRHS
§ _orientale_   CBri CPrp EChP ENot EPfP LRHS
   NBid NBlu NFla NJOw SPer STes
   SWat WShp WWpP
- 'Goldcut'   LPVe NGdn
- 'Magnificum'   CBri CHrt CSBt CSam EBee EPfP
   GKir LAst LPVe LRHS MHer MWrn
   NArg NMir NPri SECG SMer SPer
   SRms WBea WFar WMnd WWin
pardalianches   CMea ECha GGar IHMH NSco
   WRHF
plantagineum 'Excelsum' see _D._ x _excelsum_ 'Harpur Crewe'
   'Riedels Goldkranz'   MRav MWhi
   Spring Beauty   see _D._ 'Frühlingspracht'

Doryanthes (Doryanthaceae)

palmeri   CHEx

Dorycnium see _Lotus_

Doryopteris (Adiantaceae)

pedata   MBri

Douglasia see _Androsace_

idahoensis   see _Androsace idahoensis_
laevigata   see _Androsace laevigata_

montana   see _Androsace montana_
nivalis   see _Androsace nivalis_
vitaliana   see _Vitaliana primuliflora_

Dovyalis (Flacourtiaceae)

caffra (F)   XBlo

Doxantha see _Macfadyena_

Draba (Brassicaceae)

acaulis   EHyt
aizoides   ELan EMlt GKir LRHS MOne MWat
   NPri SIng SPlb SRms WWin
aizoon   see _D. lasiocarpa_
bertolonii Boiss.   see _D. loeseleurii_
bruniifolia   CGra EBre EBur EWes LRHS MTho
   NWCA
bryoides   see _D. rigida_ var. _bryoides_
cappadocica   EHyt
compacta   see _D. lasiocarpa_ Compacta
   Group
cretica   NMen
cuspidata   CNic
dedeana   ECho EHyt EWes WLin
§ _glabella_   NLAp
hispanica   NMen
- var. _segurensis_   WLin
§ _incana_   MOne
§ _lasiocarpa_   NArg NBlu NJOw WShp
§ - Compacta Group   CNic ECho NRya NWCA
lemmonii   CGra
§ _loeseleurii_   MMHG
longisiliqua ♀H2   EHyt SIng
- EMR 2551   EPot
mollissima   EPot GTou WAbe
oligosperma   NWCA
- subsp. _subsessilis_   WLin
ossetica   EHyt WLin
paysonii var. _treleasei_   WAbe
polytricha   EHyt GTou WLin
repens   see _D. sibirica_
rigida   MOne MTho
§ - var. _bryoides_   EHyt ITim NWCA SOkd WAbe
- var. _imbricata_   EPot
   f. _compacta_
rosularis   EHyt
sakuraii   EDAr
scardica   see _D. lasiocarpa_
§ _sibirica_   CNic WShp
ussuriensis   WPer
ventosa   GTou WAbe

Dracaena ❀ (Dracaenaceae)

congesta   see _Cordyline stricta_
draco ♀H1   CArn CTrC IDee
fragrans   MBri
- (Compacta Group)   MBri
   'Compacta Purpurea'
- - 'Compacta   MBri
   Variegata' (v)
- (Deremensis Group)   LRHS MBri
   'Lemon Lime' (v) ♀H1
- - 'Warneckei' (v) ♀H1   MBri
- - 'Yellow Stripe' (v) ♀H1   MBri
* - _glauca_   MBri
- 'Janet Craig'   MBri
- 'Massangeana' (v) ♀H1   MBri
indivisa   see _Cordyline indivisa_
marginata (v) ♀H1   LRHS MBri
- 'Colorama' (v)   MBri SMur
sanderiana (v) ♀H1   LRHS MBri
* _schrijveriana_   MBri
steudneri   MBri
stricta   see _Cordyline stricta_

Dracocephalum (Lamiaceae)

altaiense	see *D. imberbe*
argunense	CPBP CPlt EBee GEdr GKir LBee LPhx LRHS MBro MWgw MWrn NLAp SAga SBla SGar SRms SRot WCom WCru WPat WPer WWin
* – 'Album'	EBee SAga
– 'Fuji Blue'	CFwr EBee EPPr NLar WWeb
– 'Fuji White'	CPBP EBee EMan EPPr LPhx WPer WWeb
botryoides	CPBP EMan GFlt GSki NLar NWCA WMoo WPer
'Eminence Grise'	SUsu
forrestii	EPot WOut
grandiflorum	CBod CMHG CMdw CNic CPom EBre EChP EMFP GSki LPhx LTwo MMHG NLar SAga SBla WCAu WFar WMoo WWeb
hemsleyanum	EBee MBro NLAp WPat
§ *imberbe*	MLLN WOut
isabellae	GEil NLar WLin
moldavica	SIde
nutans	EBee MWrn NLar SLon WPer
palmatum	EBee
paulsenii **new**	WLin
peregrinum	SGar
prattii	see *Nepeta prattii*
rupestre	CFwr EPPr MBri MBro NLAp WPat
ruyschianum	CFwr CMdw EChP EMan GEdr LPhx LRHS MLLN MRav MWrn NFla NLAp NLar NWCA WPat WShp WWeb
sibiricum	see *Nepeta sibirica*
speciosum **new**	WLin
tanguticum	NLar
* *tataricum*	EBee
virginicum	see *Physostegia virginiana*
wallichii **new**	WLin
wendelboi	GEdr MLLN NBir NLAp NWCA WPat WWin

Dracophyllum (Epacridaceae)

longifolium **new**	CHEx
pronum	ITim
traversii **new**	GKev

Dracunculus (Araceae)

canariensis	CStu EBee ITer LEur WCot
muscivorus	see *Helicodiceros muscivorus*
§ *vulgaris*	CHid CMea CPom EBee EHrv EMan EMon EPar EPot EUJe ITer LEdu LRHS MAvo MCCP MRav NJOw SDix SEND SMad WCot WCru WHil WPnP
– 'Variegata' (v)	WCot

Dregea (Asclepiadaceae)

§ *sinensis*	CBcs CBot CHEx CSam ELan EPfP ERea EWes GQui LRHS MAsh SBra SOWG WCot WCru WFar WPGP WSHC
– 'Variegata' (v)	WCot

Drepanocladus (Amblystegiaceae)

revolvens	EMFW

Drepanostachyum (Poaceae)

§ *falcatum*	CAbb MGos WJun
falconeri hort.	see *Himalayacalamus falconeri*
hookerianum	see *Himalayacalamus hookerianus*
§ *khasianum*	CFil EBee WMul WPGP
§ *microphyllum*	SDry WJun
* *porcatus* **new**	WPGP

Drimiopsis (Hyacinthaceae)

maculata	CStu WCot

Drimys (Winteraceae)

aromatica	see *D. lanceolata*
colorata	see *Pseudowintera colorata*
granatensis	CFil WPGP
§ *lanceolata*	More than 30 suppliers
– (f)	CTrC ECou GEil GGar NCGa
– (m)	CDoC CTrC ECou GGar
– L 1737	CFil
– 'Mount Wellington'	GCal
* *latifolia*	CBcs CHEx
winteri ♀H4	CBcs CDoC CDul CFil CHEx CMac CSBt CSam CTrG CTrw ELan EPfP GGar IArd MRav SAPC SArc SHBN SLim SPer WBrE WCwm WDin WFar WGer WPic WSHC
– var. *andina*	CFil EBee EPfP GGGa SSpi WPGP
§ – var. *chilensis*	CFil CHEx CPLG EBee EPfP ISea MAsh SSpi WCru WPGP
– Latifolia Group	see *D. winteri* var. *chilensis*

Drosanthemum (Aizoaceae)

floribundum	CHEx
hispidum	CHEx CStu EBre ECtt EDAr ELan EMlt EPfP EPot ITim LRHS MBro MTho NMen NWCA SIng SPlb WBea WPat XPep

Drosera (Droseraceae)

admirabilis	LHew
aliciae	CSWC SHmp
andersoniana	EFEx
binata	SHmp
§ – subsp. *dichotoma*	CSWC
– 'Multifida'	MCCP
browniana	EFEx
bulbigena	EFEx
bulbosa subsp. *bulbosa*	EFEx
– subsp. *major*	EFEx
callistos	LHew
capensis	LRHS MCCP NABC SHmp
– 'Albino'	MCCP
citrina **new**	LHew
dichotoma	see *D. binata* subsp. *dichotoma*
dichrosepala	LHew
erythrorhiza	EFEx
– subsp. *collina*	EFEx
– subsp. *erythrorhiza*	EFEx LHew
– subsp. *magna*	EFEx
– subsp. *squamosa*	EFEx
gigantea	EFEx
graniticola	EFEx
heterophylla	EFEx
intermedia 'Carolina Giant' **new**	MCCP
loureiroi	EFEx
macrantha	EFEx
– subsp. *macrantha*	EFEx
macrophylla subsp. *macrophylla*	EFEx
marchantii subsp. *prophylla*	EFEx
menziesii subsp. *basifolia*	EFEx
– subsp. *menziesii*	EFEx
– subsp. *thysanosepala*	EFEx
modesta	EFEx
orbiculata	EFEx
peltata	CSWC EFEx
platypoda	EFEx
ramellosa	EFEx

rosulata	EFEx
rotundifolia	SHmp
salina	EFEx
scorpioides	CSWC
sewelliae	LHew
slackii	LHew
stelliflora .	LHew
stolonifera subsp. *compacta*	EFEx
- subsp. **humilis**	EFEx
- subsp. **porrecta**	EFEx
- subsp. **rupicola**	EFEx
- subsp. **stolonifera**	EFEx
tubaestylus	EFEx
zonaria	EFEx

Drosophyllum (Droseraceae)

lusitanicum	LHew

Dryandra (Proteaceae)

formosa	CTrC SPlb
praemorsa	CTrC

Dryas (Rosaceae)

drummondii	EPot SBla WAbe
§ **integrifolia**	CMea NMen
- 'Greenland Green'	WAbe
octopetala ♀H4	CMea CTri EDAr EPfP GIBF GKir GTou LHop MWat NChi NFor NLAp NRya NVic SBla SIng SRms WAbe WCom WCot WHoo WWin
- var. *lanata*	GIBF
- 'Minor' ♀H4	CLyd EDAr LBee LRHS NMen NWCA NWoo WAbe
x **suendermannii** ♀H4	EHol EPfP EPot GKir GTou LRHS MBro MCCP NLAp NMen NWCA SMrm WAbe WBVN
tenella Pursh	see *D. integrifolia*

Dryopteris ✿ (Dryopteridaceae)

from Emei Shan, China	WPGP
aemula	SRms
§ **affinis** ♀H4	CFil CLAP CRow EBee EBlw ECha EFou EMFW EMon ENot EPar EPfP LPBA MMoz NHol NMar SRms SSto WFib WRic
§ - subsp. **borreri**	EFer MBri
- subsp. **cambrensis**	EFer
- - 'Insubrica'	EFer
- 'Congesta'	CLAP EBee GKir
- 'Congesta Cristata'	CLAP CPrp CWCL EDAr EFer EPfP LPBA MBri MRav NHol NSti SPla SRot
- Crispa Group	CLAP CSBt EBlw ENot GBin LAst LRHS MMoz SMac
- 'Crispa Barnes'	WPGP
§ - 'Crispa Gracilis' ♀H4	CBos CLAP EFer ELan ENot EPPr GBin MAsh MBri MCCP MWgw NBir WRic
* - 'Crispa Gracilis Congesta' **new**	WFib
§ - 'Cristata' ♀H4	More than 30 suppliers
- 'Cristata Angustata' ♀H4	CFwr CLAP EFer ELan EMon GBin MAsh MFan MMoz MWgw NDlv NHol NMar SRms WFib WMoo WPGP WRic
- 'Cristata The King'	see *D. affinis* 'Cristata'
- 'Grandiceps Askew'	EFer NMar SRms WFib
- 'Pinderi'	CLAP CPrp EBee EFer EFou ELan GBin MBri NOrc SRms
- Polydactyla Group	CLAP EBee GQui MDun MRav NMar WFar
- 'Polydactyla Dadds'	CLAP EBee MBri
- 'Polydactyla Mapplebeck' ♀H4	CLAP CRow LPBA NHol SRms
- 'Revolvens'	CLAP EFer SRms
atrata misapplied	see *D. cycadina*
x **australis**	WRic
austriaca hort.	see *D. dilatata*
bissetiana	WRic
blanfordii	CFil WPGP
borreri	see *D. affinis* subsp. *borreri*
buschiana	CLAP
carthusiana	CBgR CFil CLAP EBee EFer GBin SRms WRic
celsa	WRic
championii	WRic
clintoniana	CFil CFwr CLAP EBee EFer LEur WPGP WRic
x **complexa** 'Ramosissima Wright' **new**	CLAP
- 'Stablerae'	CLAP GQui NMar WFib WPGP WRic
- 'Stablerae' crisped **new**	WFib
crassirhizoma	LEur
crispifolia	NVic
cristata	CFwr EBee EFer EMar EMon EPfP EPza LEur MAvo MLan WCru WMoo WRic
§ **cycadina** ♀H4	More than 30 suppliers
§ **dickinsii**	EBee EMon WRic
§ **dilatata** ♀H4	CRWN EBee ECha EFer EFtx ELan EMon EPfP MAsh MGas MSte MWgw NHol NMar SRms WFib WRic WShi WWye
- 'Crispa Whiteside' ♀H4	CFil CFwr CLAP CWCL EBee EFer EFtx EMon GEdr MAsh MBct MBri MWgw NHol NLar SPlb SRms WFib WPGP WRic
- 'Grandiceps'	CLAP CMHG CRow CWil EFer EMon NHol SChu WFib WRic
- 'Jimmy Dyce'	WRic
- 'Lepidota Crispa Cristata'	CLAP LRHS
- 'Lepidota Cristata' ♀H4	CFwr CLAP CMHG CWCL EBee EFer EFtx ELan EMon GBin IMGH MAsh MBct NHol NMar NVic SRms WCru WFib WMoo WPrP WRic
- 'Lepidota Grandiceps'	CLAP NMar
* - 'Recurvata'	CLAP MBct WRic
erythrosora ♀H4	More than 30 suppliers
I - 'Prolifera'	see *D. erythrosora* var. *prolifica*
§ - var. **prolifica** ♀H4	CFwr CLAP EChP EFtx GCal MAsh MAvo MBct MSte MWgw NBir NCiC NDlv NHol NRib NSti SPla WCot WFib WRic
expansa	EMon
filix-mas ♀H4	CSBt CTri CWCL EBee EBlw ECha EFou EMFW ENot EPfP EPza GKir LPBA LRHS MAsh MBow MCLN MFan MMoz MRav NHol SGar SMac SPer SRms SSto WShi WWye
- 'Barnesii'	CFwr CLAP EFer MAsh MSte NDlv NLar NMar SPlb WRic
- 'Bollandiae'	WRic
* - 'Corymbifera Crispa'	EFer
- 'Crispa'	EBee EHon NHol SMac WFib
- 'Crispa Congesta'	see *D. affinis* 'Crispa Gracilis'
- 'Crispa Cristata'	CFwr CLAP CPrp EGol ELan EMon LHop MAsh MBnl MBri MCLN MDun MWgw NHol NMar NSti SChu SMer SRms SWat WFib WGor WRic WWye
- 'Crispatissima'	NVic
- 'Cristata' ♀H4	CFil CFwr CLAP CRow EFer EHon ELan GKir MMoz NMar NOak NOrc SWat WFib WMoo WRic WWye

– Cristata Group	EBee EBlw EFer NMar WFib WRic
– – 'Fred Jackson'	CLAP NHol WFib
* – 'Cristata Grandiceps'	EFer
– 'Cristata Jackson'	CLAP SPlb
– 'Cristata Martindale'	CLAP CRow GQui NHol NMar
	SRms WFib WRic
– 'Depauperata'	CFil CLAP SChu WPGP
– 'Euxinensis'	CLAP
* – 'Furcans'	CLAP
– 'Grandiceps Wills' ♀H4	CRow EMon NHol NMar SChu
	WFib WRic
– 'Linearis'	CMHG CRow EBee EBlw EFer
	EHon ELan EMon LPBA MBri
	MGos SRms
– 'Linearis Congesta'	CFil WPGP
– 'Linearis Cristata'	NMar WRic
– 'Linearis Polydactyla'	CBrm CFwr CLAP CPrp CSBt
	CWCL EBee EFer EFtx GBin IMGH
	MAsh MAvo MBct MBri MMoz NHol
	NMar SLdr SMac STes WAbe WMoo
– 'Multicristata'	NMar
* – Polydactyla Group	MGos MRav NMar
– 'Rich Beauty'	WBor
formosana	EFer
goldieana	CFwr CLAP CMHG EBee EFer EFtx
	GBin NBir NLar NMar SSpi STes
	WCru WFar WGwG WMoo WPnP
	WRic WSpi
hirtipes	see *D. cycadina*
hondoensis	CFil WRic
'Imperial Wizard' **new**	CFir
marginalis	CFwr CLAP EBee GBin GCal
	MMoz NHol NLar NOGN WCru
	WMoo WRic
oreades	SRms WAbe
pacifica	WRic
paleacea	CLAP
polylepis	WRic
pseudofilix-mas	WRic
pseudomas	see *D. affinis*
pycnopteroides	WRic
x *remota*	SRms WRic
sieboldii	CFil CFwr CLAP EBee ELan EMon
	GCal GGar IMGH LEur MAsh MSte
	NDlv NHol NOGN SChu SMad
	SRms SSpi WCru WFib WMoo
	WPGP WRic WWye
stewartii	CLAP
tokyoensis	CFwr CLAP GBin GCal LEur NHol
	NLar SHar SMac WRic WSpi
uniformis	CLAP ELan EMon LPBA
– 'Cristata'	WRic
wallichiana ♀H4	More than 30 suppliers

Duchesnea (Rosaceae)

chrysantha	see *D. indica*
§ *indica*	CAgr CBgR CSWP GAbr IBlr IGor
	ITer MRav NHol NWCA WBor
	WMoo
§ – 'Harlequin' (v)	EMan GBar ITer MCCP MTho
	WCom
* – 'Snowflake' (v)	CRow EBee WMoo
– 'Taff's Silverline' (v) **new**	EMon
– 'Variegata'	see *D. indica* 'Harlequin'

Dudleya (Crassulaceae)

abramsii **new**	WLin
– subsp. *affinis*	WCot
NNS 01-156 **new**	
cymosa	ETow SIgm
– JCA 11777	CNic
– subsp. *paniculata*	WCot
NNS 98-221 **new**	
– subsp. *pumila*	WCot

farinosa	CHEx
lanceolata	EMan WCot
pulverulenta	SIgm
saxosa subsp. *aloides*	WCot
NNS 99-141	
verityi NNS 01-159 **new**	WCot

Dugaldia (Asteraceae)

hoopesii	CMHG CPrp EHrv EPfP EPza GKir
	GSki IHMH LHop LRHS MBNS
	MBow MNrw MRav NLRH NPri
	NSti SCro SPer SPet SRms SWvt
	WFar WMnd WMoo WPer WShp

Dunalia (Solanaceae)

australis	see *Iochroma australe*
– blue	see *Iochroma australe* 'Bill Evans'
– white	see *Iochroma australe* 'Andean Snow'

Duranta (Verbenaceae)

§ *erecta*	EShb LRHS
plumieri	see *D. erecta*
repens	see *D. erecta*

Dyckia (Bromeliaceae)

'Morris Hobbs'	EMan WCot
* *parviflora* **new**	EPem
remotiflora	SChr

Dymondia (Asteraceae)

margaretae	SBla WAbe
* *repens* **new**	XPep

Dypsis (Arecaceae)

§ *decaryi*	CBrP EAmu LPal WMul XBlo
decipiens	CBrP CRoM WMul
§ *lutescens* ♀H1	CRoM LPal LRHS MBri

Dyschoriste (Acanthaceae)

thunbergiiflora **new**	GFai

Dysosma see *Podophyllum*

E

Ebenus (Papilionaceae)

cretica	XPep

Ecballium (Cucurbitaceae)

elaterium	CArn LEdu MSal WHer

Eccremocarpus (Bignoniaceae)

scaber	CBcs CDul CRHN CTrG EBee ELan
	EMil ENot EPfP GAbr GKir LIck
	MBri MEHN MNrw NPPs NPer
	SGar SLim SPer SRms SYvo WBrE
– apricot	EMar
– 'Aureus'	EPfP MAsh NLar SHFr SLon
– 'Carmine Brilliant' **new**	SWal
– 'Carmineus'	CBri EPfP GGar MAsh MFOX NChi
	NLar SGar
– orange	MAsh MWgw
I – 'Roseus'	MAsh

Echeveria ✿ (Crassulaceae)

affinis	MBri
agavoides ♀H1	MRav WBrE
* – 'Metallica'	MBri
* 'Black Prince'	EMan NPer SRot WCom WCot
	WDyG

'Crûg Ice' **new**	WCru
derenbergii ♀H1	CHEx
x *derosa* 'Worfield Wonder' ♀H1	WEas
'Duchess of Nuremberg'	SRot
elegans ♀H1	CHEx CHal EBee EOas MBri SAPC WBrE WDyG WGwG
elegans x *elegans* var. *hernandonis*	EBla
§ *gibbiflora* var. *metallica* ♀H1	WEas
glauca Bak.	see *E. secunda* var. *glauca*
harmsii ♀H1	CHal CSWP
'Imbricata'	CHEx
'Mahogany'	MAvo SUsu
'Paul Bunyon'	CHal
peacockii	EBee EPfP SPet
'Perle d'Azur'	CHEx WCom WCot
'Perle von Nürnberg' ♀H1	EPem
pulvinata ♀H1	CHal
secunda	CAbb EMlt STre SWal
§ - var. *glauca* ♀H1	CHEx EBee ELan MAvo NBir SArc STre SUsu WCom WCot
* - - 'Gigantea'	NPer
setosa ♀H1	CHEx WCot
* *splendens* **new**	WCot

Echinacea ✿ *(Asteraceae)*

angustifolia	CArn CCge CFwr EBee EChP EHrv EMan EPPr EPfP GPoy LPio LRHS MBNS MHer MLLN MSal MWrn NGHP NSti WBri WHer WMnd WSel WWye
atrorubens	EBee
'Greenheart'	LPhx
laevigata	EBee
pallida	More than 30 suppliers
paradoxa	CBot CPou EChP EHrv EMan EMar EPPr GEil GSki LDai LPhx MSal MWrn NDov NGHP SDnm SDys SPlb SUsu SWal WBea WBro WHil WWhi WWpP
§ *purpurea*	More than 30 suppliers
- 'Alba'	CBot CCge EBre IHMH NBlu NDov
- 'Augustkönigin'	CBos EBee GBin MSph MSte NBir NDov NLar SAga SBla WCot WShp WWpP
- Bressingham hybrids	EBee EBre ELan EMar LRHS SChu SPer SPet WFar
- dark stemmed	GBBs LPhx MAnH SAga
- 'Forncett Parasol'	EFou
- 'Green Edge'	CFwr EBee
- 'Kim's Knee High'PBR	More than 30 suppliers
- 'Kim's Mop Head'	CFai CHar CKno EBee EBre EHrv ENor EWes GAbr GBin LAst LRHS MBNS MBnl NLar SAga SHar SPla SUsu WCot WShp WWhi
- 'Leuchtstern'	EBee ECGN EShb GSki NBir NCGa NGdn SMrm SWat WBea WPer
- 'Magnus'	More than 30 suppliers
- 'Maxima'	EBee LRHS MBnl WCot
- 'Monty Python' **new**	EBee
- 'Pink Flamingo'	WWhi
- 'Robert Bloom'	EBee EBre ECGN EHrv EMil LPhx MBNS MBnl MSph NSti SCro SVal SWat WCot WLin WShp WWhi
- 'Rubinglow'	CBos CKno CMil EBee EBlw EChP ECtt EGle EMar IBal LAst MBNS MBnl MCLN MMil MSph MSte NBir NDov NGHP NLar SPoG STes SWvt WCAu WCot
- 'Rubinstern'	More than 30 suppliers
- 'Ruby Giant' **new**	MSph SPla WHlf
- 'Verbesserter Leuchtstern'	NGHP NLar WHil

- 'White Lustre'	EBee EChP ECha EPfP GSki MBNS MSPs NCGa NDov NLar WCAu WCot WFar WLin WMnd WShp WWhi
- 'White Swan'	More than 30 suppliers
simulata	SUsu
tennesseensis	CArn EBee

Echinocereus ✿ *(Cactaceae)*

triglochidiatus **new**	CTrC

Echinops *(Asteraceae)*

RCB/TQ H-2	WCot
albus	see *E.* 'Nivalis'
§ *bannaticus*	CSBt EBee GSki NBid SMer WCot WFar WHil WShp WTel
* - 'Albus'	EPfP EWll LAst LRHS NGdn NSti SPoG
§ - 'Blue Globe'	CKno COIW EBee ECGN EChP EMan EPfP ERou EWTr GCal GSki IBal LAst LPVe LRHS MWrn NCGa NVic SCoo SIgm SMad WBrE WFar WHil WMnd WPer WWeb
- 'Blue Pearl' **new**	CM&M EBee EFou WHil
- 'Taplow Blue' ♀H4	More than 30 suppliers
commutatus	see *E. exaltatus*
§ *exaltatus*	EBee MWgw NBir WCot
maracandicus	GCal WCot
§ 'Nivalis'	CBre EBee ECha ERou GCal SEND
niveus	IFro
* *perringii*	GCal
ritro hort.	see *E. bannaticus*
§ *ritro* L. ♀H4	More than 30 suppliers
- 'Moonstone'	CRow
- subsp. *ruthenicus* ♀H4	CBrm EBee ECGP EFWa EGra ELan EWTr GBuc IGor MHar SIgm SPet WCot WPGP
- - 'Platinum Blue' **new**	EBee EMan MBNS MBri MWrn WMnd
- 'Veitch's Blue'	More than 30 suppliers
- 'Veitch's Blue' misapplied	see *E. ritro* L.
setifer B&SWJ 8416 **new**	WCru
sphaerocephalus	CPen EMan EWTr GFlt IBlr NBid NBur SBla SIgm SPlb WBea WPer WWpP
- 'Arctic Glow'	More than 30 suppliers
strigosus	EBee
tienschanicus	EFWa GIBF MHar MLwd NBPC NLar WCAu
tjanschanicus	EMan EWll WBVN
tschimganicus	EBee

Echinospartum see *Genista*

Echium *(Boraginaceae)*

albicans	CTCP EWll
amoenum	EBee
boissieri	CTCP ELan WOut
brevirame	CTCP
§ *candicans* ♀H2-3	CAbb CBcs CCtw CFir CHEx CTCP CTbh CTrC EBee ECre ESlt IDee MAnH NBur SAPC SArc SRob SSte WCHb WCot WFar WMul WSpi
decaisnei	CTCP
fastuosum	see *E. candicans*
giganteum	CTCP
italicum	CTCP MAnH NLar SIde
lusitanicum subsp. *polycaulon*	CTCP NLar WGMN WOut
nervosum	CTrC EBee
§ *pininana* ♀H2-3	More than 30 suppliers
- 'Pink Fountain' **new**	ELan SIde
- 'Snow Tower'	CPla ELan MAnH SIde

pininana x *wildpretii*	CTCP MAnH
pinnifolium	see *E. pininana*
rossicum	GIBF SPlb
russicum	CFir CTCP ECGN EChP EGoo EPyc EWll LPhx MAnH MSPs NBPC NChi NLar SDnm SIde SIgm SSte WAul WBVN WCHb WCot WHil WSan WWeb
x *scilloniense*	SYvo
simplex	CTCP WSpi
strictum	CTCP
sventenii	CTCP
tuberculatum	EBee EChP LPhx NBur SBod SIde
virescens	CTCP
vulgare	CArn ECGN EChP ELan EOHP MBow MHer MSal NLar NMir NSco SECG SIde WBrE WCHb WHHs WHer WJek WWye
– Drake's form	CCge MAnH SGar
webbii	CTCP
wildpretii ♀H2-3	CTrC EWll
– subsp. *wildpretii*	CTCP
wildprettii subsp. *trichosiphon*	CTCP

Eclipta (Asteraceae)

alba	see *E. prostrata*
§ *prostrata*	MSal

Edgeworthia (Thymelaeaceae)

§ *chrysantha*	CBcs CPLG CPMA EPfP LBuc LPan SMur SPer WSHC
– B&SWJ 1048	WCru
I – 'Grandiflora'	CPMA NLar
– 'Red Dragon'	CPMA NLar
– f. *rubra* hort.	see *E. chrysantha* 'Red Dragon'
gardneri new	NLar
papyrifera	see *E. chrysantha*

Edraianthus (Campanulaceae)

croaticus	see *E. graminifolius*
dalmaticus	ETow SBla
– *albus*	EPot
dinaricus	NSla WLin
§ *graminifolius*	CPBP ECho ECtt ETow NLAp NMen SPet WFar WPer
§ *pumilio* ♀H4	CGra CLyd GEdr LRHS NMen NSla NWCA SBla SRms WAbe WLin
§ *serpyllifolius*	NMen SScr
§ – 'Major'	EHyt NMen SBla WAbe
tenuifolius	CPBP ETow NJOw SScr

Egeria (Hydrocharitaceae)

§ *densa*	EPAt

Ehretia (Boraginaceae)

dicksonii	CFil CHEx WPGP

Ehrharta (Poaceae)

thunbergii	EPPr

Eichhornia (Pontederiaceae)

crassipes	CWat EMFW EPAt LPBA MSta NArg SCoo WPnP
– 'Major'	NPer

Elaeagnus ✿ (Elaeagnaceae)

angustifolia	CAgr CBot ECrN EPfP EWTr LPan LRHS MBar MBlu MCoo MRav SHBN SPer SRms WBVN WDin XPep
– Caspica Group	see *E.* 'Quicksilver'
argentea	see *E. commutata*
§ *commutata*	CBot CMCN ECrN EGra EHoe EPar

	EPfP IMGH LHop MBlu MWgw MWhi NFor SPer WDin
– 'Zempin' **new**	GKir
x *ebbingei*	More than 30 suppliers
– 'Coastal Gold' (v)	CAbP CBcs CDoC CDul COtt EBee EMil ENot LBuc LRHS MAsh MGos SLim SReu SRms WPat WStl WWes
– 'Gilt Edge' (v) ♀H4	More than 30 suppliers
– Gold Splash = 'Lannou' (v)	CDoC CDul CTrC CWSG EBee EGra ENot MAsh SArc SPoG SWvt
– 'Limelight' (v)	More than 30 suppliers
– 'Salcombe Seedling'	LRHS NLar
glabra	EPfP
– 'Reflexa'	see *E.* x *reflexa*
macrophylla	CSam EPfP NFor SDry SSpi
multiflora	CDul CFil SPer WPGP
parvifolia	ENot EPfP
pungens	ERom EWTr NBir
– 'Argenteovariegata'	see *E. pungens* 'Variegata'
– 'Aureovariegata'	see *E. pungens* 'Maculata'
– 'Dicksonii' (v)	CTrC CWib LRHS NLar SLon SPer SRms WBcn WFar
– 'Forest Gold' (v)	CAbP ELan EPfP LRHS MAsh
– 'Frederici' (v)	CBcs CDoC CDul CMHG CMac CTrC EBee EHoe ELan EPfP EPla MAsh MGos MRav SHBN SLim SPer WDin WHCG WPat WRHF WWeb
– 'Goldrim' (v) ♀H4	COtt EBee EPfP LRHS MGos SHBN SLim WDin
– 'Hosuba-fukurin' (v) **new**	MAsh SPoG
§ – 'Maculata' (v)	More than 30 suppliers
§ – 'Variegata' (v)	CBcs CMac CPLG EBee LRHS NBir SHBN SPer WGer WHCG
§ 'Quicksilver' ♀H4	More than 30 suppliers
x *reflexa*	CFil WBcn WHCG WPGP
x *submacrophylla*	see *E.* x *ebbingei*
umbellata	CPle CTho EBee ECrN EPfP EWTr MBlu SMad SPer WBcn WHCG WMou WRHF WSHC XPep

Elatostema (Urticaceae)

repens var. *pulchrum* ♀H1	CHal MBri
– var. *repens*	CHal

elderberry see *Sambucus nigra*

Elegia (Restionaceae)

capensis	CAbb CBig CCtw CFee CFir CFwr CHEx CPen CTrC CWil GGar SPlb WDyG WMul WNor
cuspidata	CBig CPLG LRav
equisetacea	CBig CFee WNor
filacea	CBig
fistulosa	CBig
grandis	CBig
grandispicata	CBig
persistens	CBig

Eleocharis (Cyperaceae)

acicularis	ELan EMFW EPza IHMH NArg WMAq WWpP
dulcis variegated (v)	CRow EPla WWpP
palustris	CRWN EMFW MSta
sphacelata	GGar

Elettaria (Zingiberaceae)

cardamomum	CArn EAmu EShb GPoy LEdu MBri MSal SHDw WJek WMul

Eleusine (Poaceae)

coracana 'Green Cat' **new**	GFlt

Eleutherococcus (*Araliaceae*)

hypoleucus B&SWJ 5532	WCru
nikaianus B&SWJ 5027	WCru
pictus	see *Kalopanax septemlobus*
sciadophylloides B&SWJ 4728	WCru
senticosus	GIBF GPoy LEdu
– B&SWJ 4528	WCru
septemlobus	see *Kalopanax septemlobus*
sessiliflorus	GIBF
§ **sieboldianus**	MRav WDin WFar
§ – 'Variegatus' (v)	CBot CFwr EBee EGra EHoe ELan EPfP LAst MBlu MGos MRav NPal WHer WSHC

Elingamita (*Myrsinaceae*)

johnsonii	ECou

Elisena (*Amaryllidaceae*)

longipetala	see *Hymenocallis longipetala*

Elliottia (*Ericaceae*)

bracteata	see *Tripetaleia bracteata*
* **paniculata latifolia** new	NLar
racemosa	CTrC

Ellisiophyllum (*Scrophulariaceae*)

pinnatum B&SWJ 197	WCru WPrP

Elodea (*Hydrocharitaceae*)

canadensis	EHon EMFW EPAt WMAq
crispa	see *Lagarosiphon major*
densa	see *Egeria densa*

Elsholtzia (*Lamiaceae*)

ciliata	CArn MSal
fruticosa	CArn WWye
stauntonii	CArn CBcs CBot CBrm EBee ECha ECre EMan EOHP GPoy MHer SLPl SPer WBor WMoo WWye XPep
– 'Alba'	CArn CBot LRav WWye

Elymus (*Poaceae*)

arenarius	see *Leymus arenarius*
'Blue Steel' new	EBee
californicus	CBig
canadensis	CRWN CWCL EHoe EPPr EWsh SWal WMoo
– f. **glaucifolius**	CFir GCal MTed SLim
cinereus from Washington State, USA	EPPr
fibrosus	EPPr
giganteus	see *Leymus racemosus*
glaucus hort.	see *E. hispidus*
glaucus Buckley	EPPr
§ **hispidus**	CBod CBri CFwr CHrt COIW CSLe CWCL EBlw EGle EGoo EHoe EPPr ESis EWsh LRHS MBlu MBri MFan MMoz NCGa NHol NSti SPer SPla SUsu WCFE WCot WPrP WRos
N **magellanicus**	More than 30 suppliers
– 'Blue Sword' new	NBPC
riparius	EPPr
§ **scabrus**	SMrm
sibiricus	EPPr SWal
solandri	CFwr GBin
– JCA 5.345.500	WPGP
tenuis	SMad
villosus	EPPr
– var. **arkansanus**	EPPr NOGN WWpP
virginicus	EPPr

Elytrigia (*Poaceae*)

campestris	EPPr

Embothrium ✿ (*Proteaceae*)

coccineum	CBrm CFil CHEx CPLG CPne CTrG EPfP IMGH LRHS MAsh MCCP MPRe SDry SReu WBrE WNor WPGP WPat
– Lanceolatum Group	CBrm CDoC CEnd CSBt CTbh ELan EPfP GGar GKir LRHS MDun MLan NPal SHBN SPer SSpi SSta WCot WDin WPat WPic
– – 'Inca Flame'	CBcs CDoC CDul COtt CPMA CSBt ELan EPfP ISea LRHS MDun NDlv NLar SHGC SMur SSta SWvt WPat
– – 'Norquinco' ♀H3	CBcs CDoC GGar LRHS SSpi WBod WCru
– Longifolium Group	IArd IBlr ISea
grandiflorum	CFil

Emmenopterys (*Rubiaceae*)

henryi	CFai CFil CMCN EBee EPfP IArd NLar SMad SSpi WPGP

Empetrum (*Empetraceae*)

luteum	MBar
nigrum	GPoy MBar
– 'Bernstein'	NHol
– var. **japonicum**	GTou
rubrum	WWes

Encelia (*Asteraceae*)

farinosa new	XPep

Encephalartos (*Zamiaceae*)

altensteinii	CBrP
cycadifolius	LPal
ghellinckii	LPal
kisambo	LPal
lebomboensis	CBrP
lehmannii	CBrP LPal
natalensis	CBrP LPal
senticosus	LPal
villosus	CBrP LPal

Encyclia (*Orchidaceae*)

cochleata new	WHlf

Endymion see *Hyacinthoides*

Engelmannia (*Asteraceae*)

pinnatifida	EBee

Enkianthus ✿ (*Ericaceae*)

campanulatus ♀H4	More than 30 suppliers
– var. **campanulatus** f. **albiflorus**	LRHS MAsh NLar SMur SSpi
– var. **palibinii**	EPfP GGGa GKir LRHS MAsh MGos NHol NLar SSpi SSta WBrE WNor
– 'Red Bells'	CDoC COtt EBee EPfP GKir LRHS MDun MGos NDlv SPer SSpi SSta SWvt
– var. **sikokianus**	GGGa LRHS MDun NLar SSpi
– 'Tokyo Masquerade' new	NLar
* – 'Variegatus' (v)	LRHS MAsh
– 'Wallaby'	NLar
cernuus	GKir
– f. **rubens** ♀H4	EPfP GGGa IMGH LRHS NBea SSpi WDin WNor WPic WSHC
chinensis	EPfP GGGa GKir LRHS MAsh NLar SSpi SSta WNor

deflexus CFil LRHS SReu SSpi SSta WPGP
perulatus ♀H4 CFil CRez EPfP GKir MBar SPoG SSpi WWes
sikokianus CAbP

Ensete (Musaceae)

glaucum CKob EAmu MJnS WHPE WMul
- from China **new** CKob
- from Thailand **new** CKob
- 'Vudu Vudu' CKob
superbum CKob WMul XBlo
- from Thailand **new** CKob
§ **ventricosum** ♀H1+3 CBot CDoC CHEx CKob CRoM EAmu ESlt EUJe LPal LPan MGol MJnS SAPC SArc WHPE WKif WMul XBlo
- B&SWJ 9070 WCru
§ - 'Maurelii' CBrP CHEx CKob EAmu MJnS MPRe MSPs SAPC SArc WMul WPGP
- 'Montbeliardii' **new** CKob
- 'Rubrum' see *E. ventricosum* 'Maurelii'

Entelea (Tiliaceae)
arborescens CHEx ECou

Eomecon (Papaveraceae)
chionantha More than 30 suppliers

Epacris (Epacridaceae)
longiflora SOWG
microphylla SOWG
paludosa GCrs GGGa SReu
petrophila GCrs GGGa

Ephedra (Ephedraceae)
distachya GPoy MSal NFor WWye
equisetina MSal
fragilis SDry
gerardiana IFro
- KR 0853 EPla
- var. **sikkimensis** CStu EPla NLar SDry WBod WOld WPer
§ **major** SDry WHer
minima NWCA
nebrodensis see *E. major*
nevadensis GPoy MSal
sinica MSal
viridis CArn ELau EShb MSal

Epidendrum (Orchidaceae)
§ **ibaguense** CHal

Epigaea (Ericaceae)
gaultherioides GGGa
repens GGGa

Epilobium (Onagraceae)
angustifolium see *Chamerion angustifolium*
californicum hort. see *Zauschneria californica*
canum see *Zauschneria californica* subsp. *cana*
§ **chlorifolium** EBee GEdr
- var. **kaikourense** see *E. chlorifolium*
crassum GBuc NWoo WMoo WWin
dodonaei see *Chamerion dodonaei*
fleischeri see *Chamerion fleischeri*
garrettii see *Zauschneria californica* subsp. *garrettii*
N **glabellum** hort. CHea CSpe EBre ECtt EMan GKir GMac LPhx LRHS MRav MWat NBir NPPs SAga SUsu WAbe WCom WCru WEas WWhi
hirsutum SWat

- 'Album' NSti
- **roseum** WRha
- 'Well Creek' (v) CHea CM&M EMan MLLN NBid WBar WCHb WCot WHrl
microphyllum see *Zauschneria californica* subsp. *cana*
obcordatum CPBP CStu
rigidum **new** SSpi
septentrionale see *Zauschneria septentrionalis*
tasmanicum CLyd
villosum see *Zauschneria californica* subsp. *mexicana*
wilsonii hort. see *E. chlorifolium*

Epimedium ✿ (Berberidaceae)
from Yunnan, China CPom LEur
acuminatum CDes CElw CFil CLAP EBee EFEx EHyt GLil LEur LPio SChu SMac WAbe WPGP
- L 1962 SBla
- L 575 EHrv MSte SBla SSpi WAbe WPnP
- 'Galaxy' L 1962 EBee SBla
'Akakage' GLil
'Akebono' CDes CLAP EBee GLil LEur NLar WPGP
alpinum CFis CMac EBee EMon EPPr EPar GBBs GBuc GKir LEur NHol SMer WMoo WSHC
'Amanagowa' CLAP CPMA LEur SBla
Asiatic hybrids CElw CLAP EBee LEur SChu WPnP
'Beni-chidori' EBee GLil LEur WPGP
'Beni-kujaku' EBee GBuc GLil LEur WPGP
brachyrrhizum CDes EBee LEur
- CPC 940477 SBla
brevicornu CLAP CPMA EBee LEur
- Og 88.010 SBla
- f. **rotundatum** CDes
- - Og 82.010 LEur SBla
'Buckland Spider' SBla
campanulatum CDes EBee
- Og 93087 SBla
x **cantabrigiense** CBro CPom EBee ECtt EMan EOrc EPPr EPla EWTr GKir GLil LEur LRHS MRav NHol SMac SPer
chlorandrum CDes LEur
- Og 94.003 SBla
cremeum see *E. grandiflorum* subsp. *koreanum*
davidii CDes CPMA CPom EBee ECha GBri LEur MBro MSte SMac SSpi WAbe WFar WHal WHoo WPGP WSHC
- EMR 4125 CElw CLAP EHrv LEur SBla
diphyllum CPom EHrv LEur NDov SAga WBVN WHal
- dwarf white GLil
dolichostemon CLAP EBee EGle MSte
- Og 81.010 LEur SBla
ecalcaratum CDes CLAP CPMA EBee LEur WPGP
- Og 93.082 SBla
elongatum EBee
'Enchantress' CDes CLAP CPom EBee EGle EHrv GBuc LEur MSte SSpi WAbe WHal
epsteinii CDes CLAP EBee
- CPC 940347 SBla
fangii SSpi
fargesii CDes EBee EHrv WPGP
- Og 93.053 LEur
- Og 93.057 SBla
- 'Pink Constellation' CLAP CPMA LEur
- - Og 93.023 SBla
flavum CLAP EBee EHrv
- Og 92.036 LEur SBla

franchetii — LEur
- 'Brimstone Butterfly' — CDes CLAP CPMA EBee SSpi
- - - Og 87.001 — LEur SBla WAbe
- 'Genpei' — GLil
§ **grandiflorum** ♀H4 — CBcs CElw CFis CPla CTri EBlw EBre EHrv ELan EPar EPfP GAbr GKir LEur MAvo MBro NBir NMen SAga SBla SPer WCru WFar WPnP
- 'Album' — CBos CLAP IMGH
- var. **coelestre** — GLil LEur
- 'Crimson Beauty' — CLAP CPMA ECha GBuc LEur MRav SAga SChu SMac SUsu WCru WHal WHoo WSHC
- 'Crimson Queen' — CDes EBee WPGP
- 'Elfenkönigin' — LEur WAbe
- 'Freya' — CBos EBee
- 'Jennie Maillard' — SUsu
- 'Koji' — EGle LEur
§ - subsp. **koreanum** — CFil CLAP CPla EBee ECha EFEx GLil WAbe
- - - 'La Rocaille' — CLAP EBee LEur SBla
- lilac — CLAP CPlt WFar
- 'Lilacinum' — EBee LEur SBla
- 'Lilafee' — More than 30 suppliers
- 'Mount Kitadake' — CLAP GLil LEur SOkh SSpi WAbe
- 'Nanum' ♀H4 — CBos CDes CLyd CPom EBee EHrv EHyt ETow NMen NWCA SBla SChu SSpi WAbe WCru WPGP
I - 'Nigrum' — LEur
- 'Pallidum' — CHid EBee
- pink — EHrv
- 'Purple Prince' — EBee SBla
- 'Queen Esta' — CDes SBla
- 'Red Beauty' — CLAP GAbr MSte
- 'Rose Queen' ♀H4 — CBos CM&M EBlw EChP EHrv EHyt ELan EPar EPfP EWTr GBuc GGar LEur LRHS MAvo MBri MRav NLar SAga SBla SChu SOkh SSpi SUsu SVil SWvt WAbe WPnP WSan
§ - 'Roseum' — CFwr CHid CLAP EBee EBlw GBri NMen WSHC
- 'Rubinkrone' — EBee GBin GLil LEur NHol NLar WOVN
- 'Saturn' — EBee SBla
- 'Shikinomai' — EBee EGle LEur WAbe
- 'Sirius' — CDes EBee SBla
- f. **violaceum** — CFir CLAP LEur SBla SChu SMac WAbe WSHC
- 'White Beauty' — EGle WSHC
- 'White Queen' ♀H4 — CFir CPMA EBee EChP EHrv LEur NOak SBla SOkh SSpi WAbe
- 'Yellow Princess' — SBla
higoense — EBee SIgm
ilicifolium — CDes
- Og 93020 — SBla
'Kaguyahime' — CDes CLAP EBee EHrv LEur MSte SBla WAbe
latisepalum — CDes CLAP CPMA EBee EHrv LEur SHar WPGP
leptorrhizum — CDes CLAP CPMA EBee EBlw EGle EHrv EMon GCrs GEil GLil LEur SWat WAbe WPGP WSHC
- Og Y 44 — EHyt SAga SDys SSpi
- 'Mariko' — SBla
  Og 93.009 **new**
liishihchenii — SBla
  Og 96.024 **new**
'Little Shrimp' — CLyd CTri EBee EGle EPPr GBuc LEur MBro NLar WPat
macranthum — see *E. grandiflorum*
membranaceum — CLAP CPMA CPom EBee LEur WAbe
- Og 93.047 — SBla
myrianthum — LEur
  large-flowered **new**

ogisui — CDes CLAP CPMA CPom EBee EGle EHrv MSte WHil WPGP
- Og 91.001 — LEur SSpi WAbe
x *omeiense* — LEur WBcn
- 'Akame' — CDes CLAP CPMA EBee WPGP
- - Og 82.001 — LEur SBla
- 'Emei Shan' — see *E.* x *omeiense* 'Akame'
- 'Pale Fire Sibling' **new** — CPom
- 'Stormcloud' — CDes CLAP CPMA SMac
- - Og 82.002 — LEur SBla
pauciflorum — CPMA EBee LEur
x *perralchicum* ♀H4 — CBro CPMA CTri EBee EMan EMon GBuc GKev GKir NPPs SGar SLPl SSpi WBVN WPnP WSHC
- 'Frohnleiten' — More than 30 suppliers
- 'Lichtenberg' **new** — CFwr
- 'Nachfolger' **new** — CFwr
- 'Wisley' — CElw CPMA CStu EHrv EWes LEur MTed SBla
perralderianum — CFil CHEx CSam CStu EBee EGle ELan EMan ENot EPar GKir LEur LGro MFir SRms SSpi WAbe WCru WHen WPGP WPnP WViv WWin MTed
- 'Weihenstephan' — MTed
'Pink Elf' **new** — SPla
pinnatum — EBee GLil LEur MDun WHal WRha
§ - subsp. **colchicum** ♀H4 — More than 30 suppliers
- - L 321 — LEur SBla
- - 'Black Sea' — CLAP EHrv GLil IBlr LEur LHop NLar
- elegans — see *E. pinnatum* subsp. *colchicum*
platypetalum — CLAP CPMA EBee
- Og 93.085 — EGle LEur SBla
- album — EBee
pubescens — CPMA EHrv LEur SAga WAbe
- Og 91.003 — CFwr CHid CPMA EBee ECha EGle EMan GAbr GBuc GKir GLil IMGH LEur NHol NPri WCAu WLin
pubigerum — CLAP CPom EBee LEur WPGP
rhizomatosum — CPMA SBla
- Og 92.114 — More than 30 suppliers
x *rubrum* ♀H4 — CLAP EBee EFEx GLil LEur
sagittatum — GBuc
'Sasaki' — CLAP CPom LEur
sempervirens — CFil CHEx ECha EHrv GAbr LEur MSte SMac SSpi WAbe WSPU
x *setosum* — EBee GLil LEur
'Shiho' — EBee
'Sohayaki' — CDes CLAP CPom EBee EHrv EHyt SMac WCot WPGP WSPU
stellulatum 'Wudang Star' — EWes LEur WAbe
- - L 1193 — GLil
'Sunset' — LEur
sutchuenense **new** — EBee LEur
'Tama-no-genpei' — CPLG LEur WMoo
x *versicolor* — LEur SMHy SMac SSpi
- 'Cupreum' — CBro CLAP CM&M EMon EPPr LEur SAga SBla SSpi WViv
- 'Neosulphureum' — More than 30 suppliers
- 'Sulphureum' ♀H4 — CLAP EHrv SAga SBla
- 'Versicolor' — CElw CFwr CKno CPMA EChP ECha EHyt ELan EPfP EWTr GAbr GBBs GKir GLil LEur LPhx LRHS MRav NHol SAga SBla SMac SUsu WAbe WFar WHal WPGP WViv WWhi WWin
x *warleyense* —
- 'Orangekönigin' — EBee EGle EPar GBuc LEur LPio MLwd MMil NDov NPPs NSti SAga SLPl SPla WAbe WBor WCAu WHil WMoo WPnP
wushanense — CLAP CPMA LEur
- Og 93.019 — SBla

– 'Caramel'	CDes CLAP CPMA EBee EHrv LEur WPGP
– – Og 92.009	SBla
x *youngianum*	CBcs EBee EGle LEur WCru
– blush	LEur
– 'Capella'	LEur
– 'Lilacinum'	see *E.* x *youngianum* 'Roseum'
– 'Merlin'	CBos CFir CLAP EBee ECha EHrv EHyt EPPr LEur SBla SChu SOkh WAbe
– 'Niveum' ♀H4	More than 30 suppliers
§ – 'Roseum'	More than 30 suppliers
– 'Tamabotan'	CDes GBuc GLil SBla
– 'Typicum'	CLAP EBee EGle EHyt LEur WAbe
– white	NMen WLin
– 'Yenomoto'	CLAP EBee LEur SBla
'Yubac' **new**	EBee
* *yunnanense* **new**	EBee
zhushanense **new**	EBee

Epipactis (*Orchidaceae*)

gigantea	CAvo CBct CBro CFil CHdy CMea EBee ECha ELan EMan EPar EPot ERos GCrs IBlr LEur LRHS MTho NGar NLAp NMen NWCA SBla SRot WAbe WCru WFar WPGP
– 'Enchantment'	CHdy
– 'Serpentine Night'	IBlr
* **Lowland Legacy g.** 'Edelstein'	CHdy LEur
* **Lowland Legacy g.** 'Frankfurt'	CHdy LEur
palustris	CHdy EHyt WHer
'Renate'	CHdy LEur
royleana **new**	SBla
Sabine g.	CHdy
* Sabine g. 'Frankfurt'	CHdy LEur NGar SBla
thunbergii	EFEx

Epiphyllum (*Cactaceae*)

oxypetalum **new**	ESlt

Epipremnum (*Araceae*)

§ *aureum* ♀H1	CHal EBak MBri
– 'Marble Queen' (v)	CHal LRHS
§ *pinnatum*	LRHS MBri

Episcia (*Gesneriaceae*)

'Country Kitten'	CHal
cupreata	CHal
§ *dianthiflora*	CHal SRms WDib
'Pink Panther'	CHal
* 'San Miguel'	CHal WDib

Equisetum ✿ (*Equisetaceae*)

arvense	CArn MSal
'Bandit'	CNat CRow EMon SMad
x *bowmanii*	CNat
* *camtschatcense*	CDes CMCo CNat CRow ITer SMad
x *dycei*	CNat
fluviatile	CNat EUJe NLar
hyemale	CBrm CDWL CKno CMCo CMil CNat CTrC EBla EPfP EPla EPza NPer SLon SPlb SSpi WCot WDyG WFar WHal WMAq WMoo WPrP WWhi
§ – var. *affine*	CNat CRow ELan EMan EMon EPla LEur MBlu NLar SMad WHal WOld WWye
– var. *robustum*	see *E. hyemale* var. *affine*
palustre	GWCH
ramosissimum var. *japonicum*	EMFW MCCP NArg NFor WWpP

scirpoides	CDWL CMCo CMil CNat CPen CTrC EFer EMFW EMon EPla EPza EUJe MCCP NPer SLon SPlb WMAq WMoo WPrP
sylvaticum	CNat
telmateia	CNat
variegatum	EBee NVic WCot

Eragrostis (*Poaceae*)

RCB/Arg S-7 **new**	WCot
abyssinica	see *E. tef*
airoides	CFwr CHar CKno CMea CSam CWCL EBee EChP EMan EWsh GAbr ITer LAst LPhx MAvo NOak NPro SAsh SMad WCot WHrl WMoo WPGP WPnP WRos WWeb WWpP
chloromelas	CDes CKno CMHG EBee EMan EPPr LPhx MSte WPGP
curvula	More than 30 suppliers
– S&SH 10	MSte WPGP
– 'Totnes Burgundy'	CDes CKno CStr CWCL EBee EPPr MAvo MMoz WPGP
elliottii	CBrm EMan EPPr
gummiflua	CBig EMan
'Silver Needles'	see *Agrostis canina* 'Silver Needles'
spectabilis	CBrm CFwr
§ *tef*	LIck
trichodes	CBig CBrm CPen CWCL EBee ECGP EGoo EMan EPPr EPza GBin WPer

Eranthis (*Ranunculaceae*)

§ *hyemalis* ♀H4	CBro CHar CMea ELan EMon EPar EPfP EPot LAma LRHS MBri MBro NRog WBVN WCot WFar WShi
§ – Cilicica Group	CBri CBro ELan EMon EPar EPot GEdr GFlt IBal LAma NGar NRog WCot WShi
– 'Flore Pleno' (d)	EPot NGar
– 'Orange Glow'	EHyt NGar
§ – Tubergenii Group	EPot
– – 'Guinea Gold' ♀H4	CBro EHyt GCrs SOkd WCom
pinnatifida	EFEx GCrs WCru
stellata	EBee

Ercilla (*Phytolaccaceae*)

volubilis	CAbb CFee CPLG CRHN EBee WCot WCru WPic WSHC

Eremaea (*Myrtaceae*)

beaufortioides	SOWG
pauciflora	SOWG

Eremophila (*Myoporaceae*)

bignoniiflora **new**	SOWG
debilis	ECou
glabra 'Burgundy'	SOWG
'Kilbara Carpet' **new**	SOWG
maculata	CPLG ECou
– var. *brevifolia*	SOWG
– pale pink-flowered	SOWG
– 'Peaches and Cream'	SOWG
* 'Summer Blue' **new**	SOWG
'Yellow Trumpet'	ECou

Eremurus (*Asphodelaceae*)

§ *aitchisonii*	EBee GIBF LAma NRog SIgm
* 'Brutus'	EBee ERou LAma MSte
bungei	see *E. stenophyllus* subsp. *stenophyllus*
comosus **new**	EBee
elwesii	see *E. aitchisonii*

'Emmy Ro'	EBee LAma LRHS NRog
'Harmony'	NRog
'Helena' **new**	LAma
himalaicus	CBot EBee EHrv ELan EMan EPar EPot ERou EWTr GIBF LAma LRHS MHer MSte NRog SPer WCot
'Image'	EBee MBNS NRog
x *isabellinus* 'Cleopatra'	CAvo CMea CSWP CSpe EBee EBlw EChP EHrv EMon ERou GAbr GFlt LAma LPhx LRHS MAnH MBNS MHer MLLN MMil MSph MSte MWgw NFor NRog SPer WCot WFar WPGP WViv
– 'Obelisk'	CMea CPen EBee ELan LAma LRHS NRog WCot
– 'Pinokkio'	EBee LAma MHer NFor NLar NRog WPGP WViv
– Ruiter hybrids	CMea CSWP EBee EBlw EChP ECot ELan EMon EPar EPfP LAma LAst LRHS MAnH MLLN MWgw NRog SPer WAul WFar WLow WViv WWol
– Shelford hybrids	CBcs CBro EBee EBlw ELan EMon EWsh LAma LPhx LRHS MFOX MLLN MNrw NOak SDeJ WFar
– 'Tropical Dream'	EBee EChP LAst WViv
'Jeanne-Claire'	EBee LAma NLar
'Joanne'	EBee LAma NLar
korshinskyi JJH 70 **new**	EBee
lactiflorus	SIgm
'Moneymaker'	EBee ERou LAma LRHS NRog WViv
'Oase'	CAvo CMea CPen EBee EBlw EChP EHrv ELan ERou LRHS MSte NLar NRog SPer WCot
olgae	GIBF
'Rexona'	EBee LAma NRog
robustus ♀H4	CAvo CBcs CBot CMea EBee EHrv ELan EMon EPar EPot ERou EWTr GFlt LAma LPio LRHS MHer MSte NLar NRog SIgm SMad SPer SPlb SWat WAul WBVN WCot WFar
'Roford'	CPen EBee LAma LAst NRog
'Romance'	CAvo CMea EBee EMon LAma LRHS MSte NRog WViv
spectabilis **new**	EBee
stenophyllus ♀H4	CBro EChP EPot LHop LPhx LRHS SMrm WCot WPGP WViv WWeb
* – *perfectus* **new**	GEil
§ – subsp. *stenophyllus*	CAvo CMea EBee EHrv EMon EPar ERou EWTr LAma MAnH MHer MLLN MNrw MRav NBPC NFor NOak NPer NPri NRog SPer WFar
'Yellow Giant'	EBee WCot

Erepsia (Aizoaceae)
inclaudens **new**	SChr

Erianthus see *Saccharum*

Erica ✿ (Ericaceae)
'African Fanfare' **new**	EHea
x *afroeuropaea*	EHea
arborea	CNCN CTrG SAPC SLon SPlb
§ – 'Albert's Gold' ♀H4	CBcs CBrm CNCN CSBt CTri CWCL EBre EHea ELan EPfP GKir LRHS MAsh MBar MBri MSwo NBlu NHol SPer SPla WBan WBod
– var. *alpina* ♀H4	CDoC CNCN CTri EBee EHea ENot EPfP GAbr GKir LRHS MBar NHol SPer SPoG
– 'Arbora Gold'	see *E. arborea* 'Albert's Gold'
– 'Arnold's Gold'	see *E. arborea* 'Albert's Gold'
– 'Estrella Gold' ♀H4	CDoC CNCN CSBt CTri EBre EHea

	ELan EPfP LRHS MAsh MBar MGos NHol SPer SPla SPoG WBan WStI
– 'Picos Pygmy'	EHea SDys
– 'Spanish Lime'	EHea SDys
– 'Spring Smile'	EHea
australis ♀H4	CBcs LRHS MBar
– 'Castellar Blush'	CNCN EHea
– 'Holehird'	EHea
– 'Mr Robert' ♀H3	CNCN EHea EPfP LRHS MBar
– 'Riverslea' ♀H4	CNCN CTri EHea LRHS MBar WBcn
caffra	CTrC EHea IDee SPlb
canaliculata ♀H3	CBcs EHea
carnea	ELan
– 'Accent'	EHea
– 'Adrienne Duncan' ♀H4	CNCN EHea GKir MBar MBri NDlv NHol WTel
– 'Alan Coates'	CNCN EHea MBar
– 'Alba'	EHea
– 'Altadena'	CNCN EHea MBar
– 'Amy Doncaster'	see *E. carnea* 'Treasure Trove'
– 'Ann Sparkes' ♀H4	CNCN CSBt CTri EBre EHea EPfP GKir LGro MBar MBri MSwo MWat NHol SPla
– 'Atrorubra'	CNCN EHea MBar NHol
– 'Aurea'	CNCN CSBt EHea LGro MBar MBri NDlv NHol
– 'Barry Sellers'	EHea LRHS NHol
– 'Bell's Extra Special'	EHea
– 'Beoley Pink'	CNCN EHea
– 'C.J. Backhouse'	EHea
– 'Carnea'	CNCN EHea MBar NHol
– 'Catherine Kolster'	EHea
– 'Cecilia M. Beale'	CNCN EHea MBar NHol
– 'Challenger' ♀H4	CNCN EBre EHea EPfP MBar MBri MGos NHol SCoo SPla
– 'Christine Fletcher'	EHea
– 'Clare Wilkinson'	CNCN EHea
– 'David's Seedling'	EHea
– 'December Red'	CBcs CNCN CSBt EBre EHea EPfP MBar MBri MSwo MWat NHol SPla WBan
– 'Dommesmoen'	EHea
– 'Dwingeloo Pride'	EHea
– 'Early Red'	EHea
– 'Eileen Porter'	CNCN EHea MBar WBcn
– 'Foxhollow' ♀H4	CNCN CSBt CTri EBre EHea EPfP GKir IArd LGro MBar MBri MGos MSwo MWat NHol SPla WBan WTel
– 'Foxhollow Fairy'	CBcs CBrm CNCN EHea MBar SRms
– 'Gelber Findling'	EHea
– 'Golden Starlet' ♀H4	CNCN CTri CWCL EHea EPfP LGro MBar MGos NBlu NHol SPla WBan
– 'Gracilis'	EHea MBar NDlv NHol
– 'Hamburg'	EHea
– 'Heathwood'	CNCN EHea MBar NHol SCoo SPla SRms
– 'Hilletje'	CNCN EHea NHol
– 'Ice Princess' ♀H4	CNCN EHea EPfP NHol SCoo SPla WBan WBcn
– 'Isabell' ♀H4	CNCN EBre EHea EPfP LRHS SCoo SPla WBan WBcn
– 'Jack Stitt'	EHea MBar
– 'James Backhouse'	CNCN CTri EHea NHol
– 'January Sun'	EHea NHol
– 'Jason Attwater'	EHea
– 'Jean'	CNCN EHea LRHS NHol
– 'Jennifer Anne'	CNCN EHea MBar
– 'John Kampa'	CNCN EHea MBar NHol
– 'John Pook'	EHea
– 'King George'	CNCN CSBt CTri EBre EHea GKir MBar MWat NHol WTel

- 'Kramer's Rubin'	EHea
- 'Lake Garda'	EHea NHol
- 'Late Pink'	EHea
- 'Lesley Sparkes'	CSBt EHea MBar
- 'Little Peter'	EHea
- 'Lohse's Rubin'	EHea NBlu NDlv
- 'Lohse's Rubinfeuer' **new**	EHea
- 'Lohse's Rubinschimmer'	EHea
- 'Loughrigg' ♀H4	CNCN CSBt CTri EBre EHea GKir MBar NBlu NHol SPla WStI WTel
- Madame Seedling	see *E. carnea* 'Weisse March Seedling'
- 'March Seedling'	CNCN EHea MBar MBri NHol WStI WTel
- 'Margery Frearson'	EHea
- 'Martin'	EHea
- 'Moonlight'	EHea
- 'Mrs Sam Doncaster'	CNCN EHea MBar
- 'Myretoun Ruby' ♀H4	CBcs CBrm CNCN CSBt CTri EBre EHea GKir LGro MBar MBri MGos NBlu NDlv NHol SPla WTel
- 'Nathalie' ♀H4	CNCN EHea LRHS MSwo NHol SCoo WBan WBcn
- 'Netherfield Orange'	EHea
- 'Orient'	EHea
- 'Pallida'	EHea
- 'Pink Beauty'	see *E. carnea* 'Pink Pearl'
- 'Pink Cloud'	CNCN EHea
- 'Pink Mist'	EHea LRHS
§ - 'Pink Pearl'	CNCN EHea MBar
- 'Pink Spangles' ♀H4	CBcs CNCN CSBt CTri EBre EHea GKir MBar MBri MGos MSwo NHol WTel
- 'Pirbright Rose'	CNCN EHea MGos
- 'Polden Pride'	EHea
- 'Porter's Red'	EHea LRHS MBar WBan
- 'Praecox Rubra' ♀H4	CBcs CNCN EHea GKir LGro MBar NHol
- 'Prince of Wales'	CNCN CSBt EHea NHol
- 'Queen Mary'	CNCN EHea
- 'Queen of Spain'	EHea MBri
- 'R.B. Cooke' ♀H4	CBrm CNCN EHea EPfP MBar MBri SCoo SPla
- 'Red Rover'	EHea
- 'Robert Jan'	EHea
- 'Romance'	EHea
- 'Rosalie' ♀H4	CBcs CNCN EHea IArd LRHS MSwo NHol SCoo SPla WBan WBcn
- 'Rosalinde Schorn'	EHea NHol
- 'Rosantha'	EHea NHol
- 'Rosea'	EHea SPlb
- 'Rosy Gem'	CNCN EHea MBar
- 'Rosy Morn'	EHea
- 'Rotes Juwel'	EHea LRHS
- 'Rubinteppich'	CNCN EHea
- 'Rubra'	EHea
- 'Ruby Glow'	CNCN CSBt EHea GKir MBar MSwo NDlv NHol SPla WTel
- 'Scatterley'	EHea
- 'Schatzalp'	EHea
- 'Schneekuppe'	EHea NHol
- 'Schneesturm'	EHea
§ - 'Sherwood Creeping'	EHea MBar
- 'Sherwoodii'	see *E. carnea* 'Sherwood Creeping'
- 'Smart's Heath'	CNCN EHea NHol
- 'Sneznik'	EHea
- 'Snow Prince'	EHea
- 'Snow Queen'	CNCN EHea MBar
- 'Snow White'	EHea
- 'Spring Cottage Crimson'	EHea MBar
- 'Spring Day'	EHea MSwo
- 'Springwood Pink'	CBcs CBrm CNCN CSBt CTri EHea MBar MBri MWat NHol WTel
- 'Springwood White' ♀H4	CBcs CBrm CNCN CSBt CTri EBre EHea EPfP GKir MBar MBri MGos MSwo MWat NHol SPla WTel
I - 'Startler'	EHea LRHS MBar NHol
- 'Sunshine Rambler' ♀H4	CNCN EHea MBar NHol
- 'Thomas Kingscote'	CNCN EHea MBar
§ - 'Treasure Trove'	EHea NBlu NHol
- 'Tybesta Gold'	CNCN EHea NHol
- 'Urville'	see *E. carnea* 'Vivellii'
- 'Viking'	CNCN EHea NHol
§ - 'Vivellii' ♀H4	CNCN CSBt CTri EBre EHea GKir MBar MBri MWat NBlu NDlv NHol WTel
- 'Vivellii Aurea'	EHea
- 'Walter Reisert'	CNCN EHea
- 'Wanda'	EHea MBar
- 'Weisse March Seedling'	EHea
- 'Wentwood Red'	EHea
- 'Westwood Yellow' ♀H4	CNCN CSBt CWCL EBre EHea GKir MBar MBri MGos NHol SPla
- Whisky	see *E. carnea* 'Bell's Extra Special'
- 'Whitehall'	CBrm EHea LRHS NHol
- 'Winter Beauty'	CNCN EHea GKir MGos NDlv NHol
- 'Winter Gold'	EHea
- 'Winter Melody'	EHea
- Winter Rubin	see *E. carnea* 'Kramer's Rubin'
- 'Winter Snow'	EHea SCoo
- 'Winter Sport'	EHea
- 'Winterfreude'	EHea NHol
- 'Wintersonne'	CBcs EHea EPfP LGro NHol
ciliaris alba	EHea
- 'Aurea'	CNCN EHea MBar SRms
- 'Bretagne' **new**	EHea
- 'Camla'	EHea MBar
- 'Corfe Castle'	CNCN EHea MBar
- 'David McClintock'	CNCN EHea MBar
- 'Globosa'	EHea
- 'Maweana'	EHea
- 'Mrs C.H. Gill' ♀H4	CNCN EHea
- 'Ram'	EHea
- 'Rotundiflora'	EHea
- 'Stapehill'	EHea
- 'Stoborough' ♀H4	CNCN EHea MBar
- 'White Wings'	CNCN EHea
- 'Wych'	EHea
cinerea f. *alba* 'Alba Major'	CNCN CSBt EHea MBar
- f. *alba* 'Alba Minor' ♀H4	CNCN EHea MBar MBri NBlu NHol
- - 'Celebration'	EHea
- - 'Doctor Small's Seedling'	EHea
- - 'Domino'	CNCN EHea MBar
- - 'Godrevy'	EHea
- - 'Hookstone White' ♀H4	CNCN EHea MBar NDlv
- - 'Jos' Honeymoon'	EHea
- - 'Marina'	EHea
- - 'Nell'	EHea MBar
- - 'Snow Cream'	EHea MBar
- - 'White Dale'	EHea MBar
- 'Alette'	EHea
- 'Alfred Bowerman'	EHea
- 'Alice Ann Davies'	EHea
- 'Angarrack'	EHea
- 'Anja Bakker'	EHea
- 'Anja Blum'	EHea
- 'Anja Slegers'	EHea
- 'Ann Berry'	CNCN EHea MBar
- 'Apple Blossom'	EHea
- 'Apricot Charm'	CNCN CSBt EHea MBar MSwo
- 'Aquarel'	EHea
- 'Ashdown Forest'	EHea
- 'Ashgarth Garnet'	EHea MBar

– 'Atropurpurea'	CNCN EHea MBar NDlv
– 'Atrorubens'	EHea GKir MBar SRms
– 'Atrorubens, Daisy Hill'	EHea
– 'Atrosanguinea'	CNCN MBar
– 'Atrosanguinea Reuthe's Variety'	EHea
– 'Atrosanguinea, Smith's Variety'	EHea
– 'Baylay's Variety'	EHea MBar
– 'Bemmel' **new**	EHea
– 'Blossom Time'	EHea MBar
– 'Brick'	EHea
– 'Bucklebury Red'	EHea
– 'C.D. Eason' ♀H4	CBcs CNCN CSBt CTri EHea EPfP GKir MBar MBri NHol
§ – 'C.G. Best' ♀H4	CNCN ECho EHea MBar
– 'Cairn Valley'	EHea
– 'Caldy Island'	EHea MBar
– 'Carnea'	EHea
– 'Carnea, Underwood's Variety'	EHea
– 'Cevennes'	CNCN EHea MBar
– 'Champs Hill'	EHea
– 'Cindy' ♀H4	CNCN EHea MBar NHol
– 'Coccinea'	CNCN EHea
– 'Colligan Bridge'	EHea MBar
– 'Constance'	EHea MBar
– 'Contrast'	EHea LRHS MBar
– 'Crimson Glow' **new**	EHea
– 'Daphne Maginess'	CNCN
– 'Discovery'	EHea
– 'Duncan Fraser'	CNCN EHea MBar
– 'Eden Valley' ♀H4	CNCN EHea GKir MBar NHol SRms
– 'Eline'	EHea
– 'England'	EHea
– 'Felthorpe'	EHea
– 'Fiddler's Gold' ♀H4	CNCN EHea MBar MBri NDlv NHol
– 'Flamingo'	EHea
– 'Foxhollow Mahogany'	EHea MBar
– 'Frances'	EHea
– 'Frankrijk'	EHea
– 'Fred Corston'	EHea
– 'G. Osmond'	EHea MBar
– 'Geke'	EHea
– 'Glasnevin Red'	EHea MBar
– 'Glencairn'	EHea MBar NHol
– 'Golden Charm'	CNCN EHea NHol
– 'Golden Drop'	CNCN CSBt EHea GKir MBar MBri MSwo NHol
– 'Golden Hue' ♀H4	CNCN EHea MBar NDlv NHol
– 'Golden Sport'	EHea
– 'Golden Tee'	EHea
– 'Goldilocks' **new**	EHea
– 'Graham Thomas'	see *E. cinerea* 'C.G. Best'
– 'Grandiflora'	EHea MBar
– 'Guernsey Lime'	EHea MBar
– 'Guernsey Pink'	EHea
– 'Guernsey Plum'	EHea
– 'Guernsey Purple'	EHea
– 'Hardwick's Rose'	CNCN EHea MBar
– 'Harry Fulcher'	CNCN EHea MBri
– 'Heatherbank'	EHea
– 'Heathfield'	EHea
– 'Heidebrand'	EHea MBar
– 'Hermann Dijkhuizen'	EHea
– 'Honeymoon'	EHea MBar
– 'Hookstone Lavender'	EHea
– 'Hutton's Seedling'	EHea
– 'Iberian Beauty'	EHea
– 'Jack London'	CNCN EHea
– 'Janet'	EHea MBar
– 'Jersey Wonder'	EHea
– 'Jiri'	EHea
– 'John Ardron'	EHea
– 'John Eason'	EHea
– 'Jos' Golden'	EHea
– 'Joseph Murphy'	CNCN EHea MBar
– 'Joseph Rock'	EHea
– 'Josephine Ross'	EHea MBar
– 'Joyce Burfitt'	CNCN EHea
– 'Katinka'	CNCN EHea MBar MSwo NHol
– 'Kerry Cherry'	EHea
– 'Knap Hill Pink' ♀H4	CNCN EHea MBar
– 'Lady Skelton'	EHea MBar
– 'Lavender Lady'	EHea
– 'Lilac Time'	EHea MBar
– 'Lilacina'	EHea MBar
– 'Lime Soda' ♀H4	CNCN CWCL EHea MBri
– 'Lorna Anne Hutton'	EHea
– 'Maginess Pink'	CNCN
– 'Michael Hugo'	CNCN EHea
– 'Miss Waters'	EHea MBar
– 'Mrs Dill'	EHea MBar
– 'Mrs E.A. Mitchell'	CNCN EHea LRHS NHol SPlb
– 'Mrs Ford'	EHea MBar
– 'My Love'	CNCN EHea MBar MBri
– 'Nellie Dawson'	EHea
– 'Newick Lilac'	EHea MBar
– 'Next Best'	EHea MBar
– 'Novar'	EHea
– 'Old Rose'	EHea
– 'P.S. Patrick' ♀H4	CNCN EHea GKir MBar
– 'Pallas'	EHea
– 'Pallida'	EHea
– 'Patricia Maginess'	CNCN
– 'Paul's Purple' **new**	EHea
– 'Peñaz'	EHea
– 'Pentreath' ♀H4	CNCN EHea MBar MBri
– 'Pink Foam'	EHea MBar
– 'Pink Ice' ♀H4	CNCN CTri EBre EHea EPfP GKir MBar MBri MSwo NDlv NHol
– 'Plummer's Seedling'	EHea MBar
– 'Promenade'	EHea
– 'Prostrate Lavender'	EHea
– 'Providence'	EHea LRHS
– 'Purple Beauty'	CNCN EHea MBar
– 'Purple Robe'	EHea LRHS
– 'Purple Spreader'	EHea
– 'Purpurea'	EHea
– 'Pygmaea'	EHea MBar
– 'Red Pentreath'	EHea
– 'Robert Michael'	EHea
– 'Rock Pool'	EHea MBar NHol
– 'Rock Ruth'	EHea
– 'Romiley'	EHea MBar MBri
– 'Rose Queen'	EHea
– 'Rosea'	EHea
* – 'Rosea Splendens'	EHea
– 'Rosy Chimes'	CNCN EHea MBar
– 'Rozanne Waterer'	EHea
– 'Ruby'	CNCN EHea MBar
– 'Sandpit Hill'	EHea MBar
– 'Schizopetala'	CNCN EHea MBar
– 'Screel'	EHea
– 'Sea Foam'	CNCN EHea MBar
– 'Sherry'	CNCN EHea MBar
– 'Smith's Lawn'	EHea
– 'Spicata'	EHea
– 'Splendens'	CNCN EHea
– 'Startler'	EHea MBri
– 'Stephen Davis' ♀H4	CNCN EHea GKir MBar MBri NHol
– 'Strawberry Bells'	EHea
– 'Sue Lloyd'	EHea
– 'Summer Gold'	CNCN EHea LRHS NDlv
– 'Summer Wonder' **new**	EHea
– 'Tilford'	EHea

	- 'Tom Waterer'	EHea MBar
	- 'Uschie Ziehmann'	EHea
	- 'Velvet Night' ♀H4	CNCN CSBt CWCL EHea GKir MBar MBri NHol SRms
	- 'Victoria'	EHea MBar
	- 'Violacea'	EHea
	- 'Violetta'	CNCN EHea
	- 'Vivienne Patricia'	EHea MBar NBlu
	- 'W.G. Notley'	EHea
	- 'West End'	EHea
	- 'Windlebrooke' ♀H4	CNCN EHea MBar NHol
	- 'Wine'	EHea
	- 'Yvonne'	EHea
	curviflora	EHea SPlb
	x *darleyensis*	WTel
	- 'Ada S. Collings'	CNCN EHea MBar
	- 'Alba'	see *E.* x *darleyensis* 'Silberschmelze'
	- 'Archie Graham'	EHea
	- 'Arthur Johnson' ♀H4	CBcs CNCN CSBt CTri EHea MBri NHol SRms
	- 'Aurélie Brégeon'	EHea
	- 'Cherry Stevens'	see *E.* x *darleyensis* 'Furzey'
§	- 'Darley Dale'	CBcs CNCN CSBt EBre EHea EPfP MBar MBri NBlu NHol SCoo
	- 'Dunreggan'	EHea
	- 'Dunwood Splendour'	MBar
	- 'Epe'	EHea
	- 'Erecta'	EHea
§	- 'Furzey' ♀H4	CNCN CSBt EHea GKir MBar MBri MGos NBlu NDlv NHol SCoo SRms WTel
	- 'George Rendall'	CNCN CSBt CTri CWCL EHea EPfP GKir NHol SCoo SPla
	- 'Ghost Hills' ♀H4	CBcs CBrm CNCN EHea EPfP MBar MSwo NHol SCoo
	- 'J.W. Porter' ♀H4	CBcs CNCN EHea EPfP MBar NDlv SCoo SPla WTel
§	- 'Jack H. Brummage'	CBrm CNCN CSBt CTri EBre EHea GKir IArd MBar MBri MGos MSwo NHol SPla WTel
	- 'James Smith'	EHea MBar
	- 'Jenny Porter' ♀H4	CNCN CSBt EHea EPfP MBar MBri NBlu WBan
	- 'Kramer's Rote' ♀H4	CBrm CNCN CTri EBre EHea EPfP GKir MBar MBri MGos NBlu NDlv NHol SPla WBan
	- 'Margaret Porter'	CBcs CNCN EHea EPfP SPla WTel
	- 'Mary Helen'	CBcs CBrm CNCN EHea EPfP LRHS NBlu NHol SCoo SPla WBan WBcn
	- Molten Silver	see *E.* x *darleyensis* 'Silberschmelze'
	- 'Mrs Parris' Red'	EHea
	- 'N.R.Webster'	CNCN EHea
	- 'Pink Perfection'	see *E.* x *darleyensis* 'Darley Dale'
§	- 'Silberschmelze'	CBcs CBrm CNCN CSBt CTri EHea EPfP GKir MBar MBri MGos MSwo NBlu NDlv NHol WTel
	- 'Spring Surprise'PBR	EHea EPfP
	- 'W.G. Pine'	EHea
	- 'White Fairy'	EHea
	- 'White Glow'	CNCN CSBt CTri EHea NHol SPla
	- 'White Perfection' ♀H4	CBcs CNCN EBre EHea EPfP IArd MBar MBri NHol SCoo SPla
	discolor	EHea
	erigena 'Alba'	EHea MBar
	- 'Brian Proudley'	CNCN EHea MBar
	- 'Brightness'	CBcs CNCN CSBt EHea EPfP GKir MBar MBri MSwo NDlv NHol SCoo WTel
	- 'Coccinea'	EHea
	- 'Ewan Jones'	CNCN EHea MBar
	- 'Glauca'	EHea

	- 'Golden Lady' ♀H4	CNCN CSBt EHea MBar MBri MSwo NHol SCoo
	- 'Hibernica'	EHea
	- 'Hibernica Alba'	EHea MBar
	- 'Irish Dusk' ♀H4	CNCN CSBt CTri EHea GKir MBar MBri MGos NHol SCoo SPla SRms
	- 'Irish Salmon'	CNCN CSBt EHea MBar NDlv
	- 'Irish Silver'	MBar MBri
	- 'Maxima'	EHea
	- 'Mrs Parris' Lavender'	EHea
	- 'Mrs Parris' White'	EHea
	- 'Nana'	EHea
	- 'Nana Alba'	CNCN EHea MBar
	- 'Nana Compacta'	EHea
	- 'Rosea'	EHea MBar
	- 'Rosslare'	EHea
	- 'Rubra'	EHea NDlv
	- 'Superba'	CNCN EHea MBar MGos
	- 'Thing Nee'	EHea
	- 'W.T. Rackliff' ♀H4	CBcs CNCN CSBt EHea EPfP GKir MBar MBri MGos MSwo NHol SCoo SPla
	- 'W.T. Rackliff Variegated' (v)	EHea
	x *garforthensis* 'Tracy Wilson'	EHea
	gracilis	EHea
	x *griffithsii*	NHol
	- 'Ashlea Gold'	EHea
	- 'Elegant Spike'	EHea
§	- 'Heaven Scent'	CNCN EHea LRHS WBan
	- 'Jaqueline'	EHea SPla WBan WBcn
§	- 'Valerie Griffiths'	CBrm EHea LRHS MBar NHol SCoo WBcn
	'Heaven Scent'	see *E.* x *griffithsii* 'Heaven Scent'
	'Helène'	EHea
	x *hyemalis* 'Ghislaine'	EHea
	x *krameri*	SDys
	- 'Otto' **new**	EHea
	- 'Rudi' **new**	EHea
	lusitanica ♀H3	CBcs CNCN CTrG EHea MBar
	- 'George Hunt'	CNCN EHea ELan LRHS SPer SPla WBcn
	- 'Sheffield Park'	EHea ELan LRHS SPer WBcn
	mackayana subsp. *andevalensis*	EHea
	- subsp. *andevalensis* f. *albiflora*	EHea
	- 'Ann D. Frearson' (d)	CNCN EHea
	- 'Doctor Ronald Gray'	CNCN EHea MBar MBri
	- 'Donegal'	EHea
	- 'Errigal Dusk'	EHea
	- 'Galicia'	CNCN EHea
	- 'Lawsoniana'	EHea
	- 'Maura' (d)	EHea
	- 'Plena' (d)	CNCN EHea MBar
	- 'Shining Light'	EHea SDys
	- 'William M'Calla'	EHea
	manipuliflora	MBar
	- 'Aldeburgh'	CNCN EHea
§	- 'Cascades'	EHea
	- 'Corfu'	EHea
	- 'Don Richards'	EHea
	- 'Ian Cooper'	EHea
	- 'Korčula'	EHea
	- 'Waterfall'	see *E. manipuliflora* 'Cascades'
	manipuliflora x *vagans*	see *E.* x *griffithsii*
	multiflora **new**	XPep
	- 'Formentor'	EHea
I	*oatesii* 'Winter Fire' **new**	EHea
	x *oldenburgensis* 'Ammerland'	EHea SDys
	- 'Oldenburg'	EHea
	pageana	EHea

patersonia	SPlb
x *praegeri*	see *E.* x *stuartii*
racemosa	EHea
scoparia subsp. *azorica*	EHea
- subsp. *maderincola*	EHea
'Madeira Gold'	
- subsp. *platycodon*	EHea
§ - subsp. *scoparia*	EHea MBar
'Minima'	
- - 'Pumila'	see *E. scoparia* subsp. *scoparia*
	'Minima'
sessiliflora	CTrC
sparsa	EHea
spiculifolia	EHea ITim MBar
- f. *albiflora*	EHea
- 'Balkan Rose'	EHea GCrs NHol
straussiana	SPlb
§ x *stuartii*	MBar
- 'Connemara'	EHea
- 'Irish Lemon' ♀H4	CNCN CSBt EHea EPfP MBar
	MSwo NHol
- 'Irish Orange'	CBcs CNCN CSBt EHea GKir MBar
	NBlu NHol
- 'Irish Rose'	EHea
- 'Nacung'	EHea
- 'Pat Turpin'	EHea
§ - 'Stuartii'	CNCN EHea
subdivaricata	EHea
§ *terminalis* ♀H4	CNCN EHea ENot MBar SRms
- 'Golden Oriole'	EHea
- *stricta*	see *E. terminalis*
- 'Thelma Woolner'	CNCN EHea MBar
tetralix	SRms
- 'Alba'	EHea
- 'Alba Mollis' ♀H4	CNCN CSBt EHea MBar MBri NHol
- 'Alba Praecox'	EHea
- 'Allendale Pink'	EHea
- 'Ardy'	EHea
- 'Bala'	CNCN EHea
- 'Bartinney' ♀H4	EHea MBar
- 'Con Underwood' ♀H4	CNCN CSBt EHea GKir MBar MBri
	MSwo NHol SRms
- 'Curled Roundstone'	EHea
- 'Dänemark'	EHea
- 'Daphne Underwood'	EHea
- 'Darleyensis'	EHea
- 'Dee'	EHea
- 'Delta'	EHea MBar
- 'Foxhome'	EHea MBar
- 'George Fraser'	EHea
- 'Gratis'	EHea
- 'Hailstones'	EHea MBar
- 'Helma'	EHea
- 'Helma Variegated' (v)	EHea
- 'Hookstone Pink'	CNCN EHea GKir MSwo
- 'Humoresque'	EHea
- 'Jos' Creeping'	EHea
- 'Ken Underwood'	CNCN EHea MBar
- 'L.E. Underwood'	EHea MBar NHol
- 'Mary Grace'	EHea
- 'Melbury White'	CNCN EHea MBar
- 'Morning Glow'	see *E.* x *watsonii* 'F.White'
- 'Pink Glow'	EHea
- 'Pink Pepper'	EHea NLAp
- 'Pink Star' ♀H4	CNCN EHea MBar NHol
- 'Renate'	EHea
- 'Riko'	EHea
- 'Rosea'	EHea
- 'Rubra'	EHea
§ - 'Ruby's Variety'	EHea MBar
- 'Ruby's Velvet'	see *E. tetralix* 'Ruby's Variety'
- 'Ruth's Gold'	CNCN EHea MBar NHol
- 'Salmon Seedling'	EHea
- 'Samtpfötchen'	EHea
- 'Silver Bells'	CSBt EHea MBar
- 'Stardome'	EHea
- 'Stikker'	EHea
- 'Swedish Yellow'	EHea
- 'Terschelling'	EHea
- 'Tina'	CNCN EHea
- 'Trixie'	EHea
- 'White House'	EHea
transparens	EHea
umbellata	CNCN EHea MBar
- 'Anne Small'	EHea
- 'David Small'	EHea
vagans 'Alba Nana'	see *E. vagans* 'Nana'
- f. *anandra*	EHea
- 'Bianca'	EHea
- 'Birch Glow' ♀H4	CNCN EHea EPfP GKir
- 'Carnea'	EHea
- 'Charm'	EHea
- 'Chittendenii'	EHea
- 'Cornish Cream' ♀H4	CNCN CWCL EHea EPfP MBar
	NHol
- 'Cream'	CNCN EHea
- 'Diana Hornibrook'	CNCN EHea MBar
- 'Diana's Gold'	EHea
- 'Fiddlestone'	CNCN EHea MBar
- 'French White'	CNCN EHea MBar
- 'George Underwood'	EHea MBar
- 'Golden Triumph'	EHea MBar NHol WBan
- 'Grandiflora'	CNCN EHea MBar
- 'Holden Pink'	CNCN EHea
- 'Hookstone Rosea'	EHea MBar
- 'Ida M. Britten'	EHea MBar
- 'J.C. Fletcher'	EHea
- 'Kevernensis Alba' ♀H4	EHea MBar
- 'Leucantha'	EHea
- 'Lilacina'	CNCN EHea MBar
- 'Lyonesse' ♀H4	CNCN CTri EHea MBar MBri MGos
	MSwo NHol SRms
- 'Miss Waterer'	EHea MBar
- 'Mrs D.F. Maxwell' ♀H4	CBcs CNCN CSBt CTri EHea GKir
	MBar MBri MGos MSwo NHol
	SRms WBan
- 'Mrs Donaldson'	EHea
§ - 'Nana'	EHea MBar
- 'Pallida'	CNCN EHea
- 'Peach Blossom'	EHea MBar
- 'Pyrenees Pink'	CNCN EHea MBar
- 'Rosea'	EHea
- 'Rubra'	CNCN EHea MBar
- 'Saint Keverne'	CNCN CSBt CTri EHea GKir IArd
	MBar NHol WBan
- 'Summertime'	CNCN EHea MBar
- 'Valerie Proudley' ♀H4	CBcs CNCN CSBt EHea GKir MBar
	MBri MGos MWat NBlu NHol
	SRms
- 'Valerie Smith'	EHea
- 'Viridiflora'	CNCN EHea MBar
- 'White Giant'	EHea
- 'White Lady'	EHea MBar NBlu
- 'White Rocket'	CNCN EHea MBar
- 'White Spire'	EHea
- 'Yellow John'	CNCN EHea MBar WBan
x *veitchii* 'Brockhill'	EHea
- 'Exeter' ♀H3	CNCN CSBt EHea ELan EPfP LRHS
	MBar NHol SPer SPoG WBcn
- 'Gold Tips' ♀H4	CNCN CSBt EHea EPfP MBar MBri
	NHol
- 'Pink Joy'	CNCN EHea MBri
ventricosa	EHea
verticillata	CTrC EHea
viridescens	EHea
x *watsonii* 'Cherry	EHea
Turpin'	
- 'Dawn' ♀H4	CNCN EHea MBar MBri

	- 'Dorothy Metheny'	EHea
	- 'Dorset Beauty'	EHea
§	- 'E White'	EHea MBar
	- 'Gwen'	CNCN EHea MBar
	- 'H. Maxwell'	CNCN EHea
	- 'Mary'	EHea
	- 'Morning Mist'	EHea
	- 'Pink Pacific'	EHea
	- 'Rachel'	EHea
	- 'Truro'	EHea
	x *williamsii* 'Cow-y-Jack'	EHea
	- 'Croft Pascoe'	EHea
	- 'David Coombe'	EHea
	- 'Gew Graze'	EHea
	- 'Gold Button'	EHea MBar
	- 'Gwavas'	CNCN EHea MBar
	- 'Jean Julian'	EHea
	- 'Ken Wilson'	EHea SDys
	- 'Lizard Downs'	EHea
	- 'Marion Hughes'	EHea
	- 'P.D. Williams' ♀H4	CNCN EHea MBar

Erigeron ✿ (Asteraceae)

	from Bald Mountains	NWCA
	from Big Horn **new**	NLAp WOBN
	acer	WHer
	- var. *debilis*	ESis
	'Adria'	EBee EChP GBuc LAst LRHS NGdn SPer WMnd
§	*alpinus*	EHol GKir GTou LRHS MOne NPPs
	aurantiacus	EDAr EHol EPfP LPVe MBNS MHer NBro NChi NJOw NOak SPet
§	*aureus*	NSla WAbe
§	- NNS 96-87	NWCA
§	- 'Canary Bird' ♀H4	CPBP EPfP EPot GEdr NBir NMen NPri SIng SPer WAbe WLin
*	'Azure Beauty'	EBee EPfP LRHS NFla NPro
	Azure Fairy	see *E.* 'Azurfee'
§	'Azurfee'	CBot CSBt EBee ELan ENot EPfP ERou EWTr GAbr GKir LPVe MBNS MHer NBir NOak SPer SPla SWvt WHen WMoo WPer WSSM WShp WWin
	Black Sea	see *E.* 'Schwarzes Meer'
	blue	WBar
	'Blue Beauty'	LRHS SRms
	'Charity'	ERou LRHS MRav WBrE
	chrysopsidis 'Grand Ridge'	CPBP EHyt EPfP EPot LHop LRHS LTwo NWCA SBla
	compositus	CPBP CTri ITim SRms WPer
§	- var. *discoideus*	EBur ESis GKir NMen SPlb WPer
	- 'Mount Adams Dwarf' **new**	EHyt WLin
	- 'Rocky'	ECho ECtt NMen
	Darkest of All	see *E.* 'Dunkelste Aller'
	deep pink	CHEx
	'Dignity'	EBee EFou EGle ELan EOMN ERou MCLN MWat NBro SPer SSpe SUsu WFar WPGP
	'Dimity'	CMea ECha EDAr MBri WAbe WBrk WFar WWin
§	'Dunkelste Aller' ♀H3	More than 30 suppliers
	'Felicity'	EBee EFou ERou
	flettii	EBee NJOw WPat WPer WWin
	'Foersters Liebling' ♀H4	CStr EBee EGle ENot EPfP GKir LAst LRHS MNrw MWat NFla NGdn SPet WCot
	'Four Winds'	EBre ECtt EDAr ELan EWes LHop LRHS MRav NGdn NJOw NMen NWCA WPer WWeb
	'Gaiety'	EBee EFou WWpP
	glaucus	CHrt COIW CSBt EBee EHol EMar EWll GAbr IHMH MWgw NWCA

		SMad SMrm WBea WBrk WCot WFar WHoo WWeb
	- 'Albus'	EGoo LHop LRHS SMad WBea WPer
	- 'Elstead Pink'	CTri EBee EChP SAga SPla WFar WSHC WWeb
	- pink	SPla
	- 'Roseus'	CBcs CHal ERou
	- 'Sea Breeze'	COIW MBNS NBlu NPri
	'Goat Rocks'	GCrs
	howellii	EBee
§	*karvinskianus* ♀H3	More than 30 suppliers
	leiomerus	EFou LBee LTwo
	linearis	NMen WAbe
*	*montanensis* **new**	CGra
	'Mrs F.H. Beale'	EFou
	mucronatus	see *E. karvinskianus*
	'Nachthimmel'	EBee EMan LAst NGdn SPet
	nanus	NWCA WPer
	oreades **new**	EHyt
§	*peregrinus*	NOak
	philadelphicus	CElw IGor NBir NBro WSHC
	'Pink Beauty'	ECtt
	Pink Jewel	see *E.* 'Rosa Juwel'
	Pink Triumph	see *E.* 'Rosa Triumph'
	pinnatisectus	WPer
	'Profusion'	see *E. karvinskianus*
	'Prosperity'	EBee
	pyrenaicus hort.	see *E. alpinus*
	'Quakeress'	CElw CSam EBre ECtt EFou EMan EPfP GAbr GKir GMac LAst LRHS MCLN MRav NBro NGar SMrm SSpe SUsu WCot WFar WRHF WTel
§	'Rosa Juwel'	CBri CSBt CTri EBee ECtt ENot EPfP GAbr GFlt GKir IBal LPVe LRHS MBNS MHer MTis NBir NOak SEND SPer SPla SRms SWvt WHen WMnd WMoo WPer WShp
§	'Rosa Triumph'	EBee EFou
	'Rotes Meer'	EBee EBre ELan LRHS MCLN
	rotundifolius	see *Bellis rotundifolia*
	'Caerulescens'	'Caerulescens'
	salsuginosus misapplied	see *Aster sibiricus, E. peregrinus* subsp. *callianthemus*
	salsuginosus (Richardson) A. Gray	see *E. peregrinus*
§	'Schneewittchen'	CM&M EBee EChP ECtt EFou ELan EMan EPfP LAst LHop MRav MWat MWgw NCGa NVic SPet SPla SPoG SWvt WCAu
§	'Schwarzes Meer'	EBee ERou GKir LRHS NGdn WCot WFar
	scopulinus	CGra CPBP EHyt ITim LRHS NJOw
	simplex	CPBP LRHS MWat NMen
	'Sincerity'	EBee EFou
	'Snow Queen'	WFar
	Snow White	see *E.* 'Schneewittchen'
	'Sommerabend'	EBee
	'Sommerneuschnee'	ECha WMnd
	speciosus	EBee SMer
	- var. *macranthus*	SIgm
	'Strahlenmeer'	EBee LRHS WBrk WMnd
	'The Jewel' **new**	CBot
	thunbergii var. *glabratus* B&SWJ 8790 **new**	WCru
	trifidus	see *E. compositus* var. *discoideus*
	tweedyi	NBro
	uncialis var. *conjugans*	CGra
	uniflorus	LTwo
	vagus	LTwo WWin
	'Wayne Roderick'	SMac
	'White Quakeress'	CElw CMea EGle ERou GBuc MAnH NGar WCot WRHF
	'Wuppertal'	EBee MRav NBro NGdn WMnd

Erinacea (Papilionaceae)

§ **anthyllis** ♀H4   SIng SOkd XPep
  pungens   see *E. anthyllis*

Erinus (Scrophulariaceae)

alpinus ♀H4   CMHG CMea CTri CWCL ECtt
     EMlt EPfP GAbr GFlt GKir GTou
     MBro MWat NBlu NFor NHol SIng
     SPet SRms WCom WEas WFar WPer
     WShp WWin
- var. **albus**   CBot CNic EMlt GTou MBro NHol
     NLar NMen SIng SRms WAbe
     WCom WHoo WPer
- 'Doktor Hähnle'   CNic EBre EDAr EMlt GKir LRHS
     NLAp NLar NMen SIng SRms
     WHoo
- 'Mrs Charles Boyle'   MBro

Eriobotrya (Rosaceae)

deflexa   CFil CHEx CKob WGer
japonica (F) ♀H3   CAbb CBcs CBot CFil CHEx CKob
     CMCN EPfP ERea ERom ESlt GQui
     IDee IFro LEdu LPan MRav NPSI
     NPal SArc SDry SPer SSta WHer
     WMul WNor WPGP WSHC XBlo

Eriocapitella see *Anemone*

Eriocephalus (Asteraceae)

africanus   SPlb WJek

Eriogonum (Polygonaceae)

cespitosum   CGra WLin
- subsp. **douglasii**   see *E. douglasii*
§ **douglasii**   WLin
flavum   GEdr WPer
jamesii   WPat
libertini new   WLin
ovalifolium   WLin
- var. **nivale**   WLin
thymoides   CGra
umbellatum   LRHS NLAp
- var. **humistratum**   SBla
- var. **porteri**   NWCA
- var. **torreyanum**   CMea EPot MBro NHol WPat
- var. **umbellatum**   LBee

Eriophorum (Cyperaceae)

angustifolium   CBen CBrm COlW CRWN CWat
     EGle EHoe EHon EMFW ENot EPAt
     EPla EPza GOrn LPBA MCCP MSta
     NArg SPlb SWat WHer WMAq
     WPer WPnP WWpP
latifolium   LPBA
vaginatum   CKno CRow EHoe MWrn WWpP

Eriophyllum (Asteraceae)

lanatum   CFis CHal EBee ECha EPfP MDKP
     MEHN MWat NArg NBid SAga SBla
     SCro WCom WWeb WWin
- 'Bella'   NLar
* - 'Pointe'   GSki

Eriostemon (Rutaceae)

'Cascade of Stars'   SOWG

Eritrichium (Boraginaceae)

rupestre var. **pectinatum** NSla

Erodium ✿ (Geraniaceae)

absinthoides   LRHS MDHE
- var. **amanum**   see *E. amanum*
- from Genoa   MDHE

§ **acaule**   EMan GSki NCiC NLar
'Almodovar'   MDHE
§ **alpinum**   MDHE
§ **amanum**   EBee LRHS MDHE WAbe
'Ardwick Redeye'   CElw MDHE SRot
balearicum   see *E.* x *variabile* 'Album'
- 'Bidderi'   CElw MDHE NChi WAbe
'Burnside Silver'   MDHE
'Carla'   MDHE
'Carmel'   MDHE WAbe
'Caroline'   CElw MBro MDHE WHoo
carvifolium   CElw EBee GKir LRHS MDHE
     NWCA WFar WLin WWpP
§ **castellanum**   CLyd EBee ETow GCrs GKir LTwo
     NBro NMen NSti SBla SRms
- 'Cupidon'   MDHE
- 'Dujardin'   LPhx MDHE
- 'La Féline'   MDHE
- 'Logroños Real'   MDHE SIgm
'Catherine Bunuel'   MDHE
celtibericum   MDHE
- 'Javalambre'   MDHE
- 'Peñagolosa'   MDHE SIgm
chamaedryoides   see *E. reichardii*
cheilanthifolium   EBee MDHE SHBN
- 'Bidderi'   see *E.* 'Bidderi'
- 'David Crocker'   EPot
chrysanthum   More than 30 suppliers
- pink   CSpe ECha LPhx NCot SBla SMrm
     SRot SUsu
- **sulphureum**   EFou
corsicum   CNic EBur EHyt ETow MDHE
     MTho NMen SRot WAbe XPep
- 'Album'   EHyt LAst LTwo MDHE SIng WAbe
§ 'County Park'   CLyd CMea CPlt EBee ECha ECou
     EDAr EMlt MOne NMen NRya SBla
     SChu SHBN SRms WAul WCom
crispum x **saxatile**   MDHE
daucoides hort.   see *E. castellanum*
'Eileen Emmett'   MDHE WAbe
§ **foetidum**   EGle ETow MDHE MTis MWat
     NMen NSla XPep
- 'County Park'   see *E.* 'County Park'
- 'Pallidum'   see *E.* 'Pallidum'
- 'Roseum'   GCal MWat
'Fran's Choice'   see *E.* 'Fran's Delight'
§ 'Fran's Delight'   CElw CMea CSpe MBro MDHE
     WHoo
'Fripetta'   MDHE
'Géant de Saint Cyr'   CElw EMan EMon
N **glandulosum** ♀H4   EBee EDAr EMlt EPfP GCal MBro
     MDHE MHer SBla SRms WCom
     WKif WPat WSHC
- 'Emma'   CMea MDHE
- 'Espiguette'   SIgm
- 'Marie Poligné'   MDHE
gruinum   LPhx MAnH SScr WPat WSan
     WWpP
guicciardii   EDAr MDHE
guttatum misapplied   see *E.* 'Katherine Joy'
N **guttatum**   EBee EChP EMan EPot ERou EWTr
     LPio MWat SAga SRms WCom
     WHal WPer WSHC WWeb
x **hybridum** misapplied   see *E.* 'Sara Francesca'
x **hybridum** Sünderm.   EGle WAbe WHal
hymenodes L'Hér.   see *E. trifolium*
jahandiezianum   MDHE
'Julie Ritchie'   CMea MDHE WHoo
'Katherine Joy'   CNic EWes MDHE MHer MOne
     NChi NDlv NLAp NRya SRot WAbe
x **kolbianum**   MBro MDHE NDlv SMrm WAbe
     WHoo
- 'Nadia'   MDHE
- 'Natasha'   CMHG CNic EMlt EPot EWes GKir

	LBee LRHS MAvo MDHE MHer NChi NHol NMen SChu SMrm SWat WAbe WFar WKif
'La Belette'	MDHE
'Las Meninas'	CPlt
'Lilac Wonder'	MDHE
x *lindavicum*	MDHE NChi
- 'Charter House'	LPio MDHE NChi
'Lograno Real'	SIgm
macradenum	see *E. glandulosum*
manescaui	More than 30 suppliers
'Maryla'	MDHE WAbe
'Merstham Pink'	MDHE NChi NLar SBla WLin
'Nunwood Pink'	MDHE
§ 'Pallidum'	CHal CSam
'Parma'	MDHE
pelargoniiflorum	CBri CBrm CHrt CSpe EBlw EPfP EWTr EWsh GFlt GSki MAnH MHer MTho NBro NChi NDov NLar SCro SRms STes SWal WEas WFar WHil WKif WPGP WPer WWin WWpP
'Pequenito'	MDHE
'Peter Vernon'	NWCA
petraeum subsp. *crispum* misapplied	see *E. cheilanthifolium*
- subsp. *glandulosum*	see *E. glandulosum*
- subsp. *petraeum*	MHer SBla
'Pickering Pink'	MDHE NMen SRot SWat
'Princesse Marion'	MDHE
* 'Purple Haze'	CSpe LIck MMil NPri SRot
§ *reichardii*	CElw ECtt EMlt GSki LBee LRHS MDHE MHer MTho NLar NPPs SBla SPet SRms SWat WAbe WTel
- ex coll	NWCA
- albino	EPot MDHE NJOw
- 'Album'	EHyt NWoo WHoo WShp
- 'Bianca'	EChP MLLN
- 'Pipsqueak'	MDHE WAbe
* - 'Rubrum'	CElw MDHE
'Robertino' **new**	MDHE
'Robespierre'	LPhx MDHE
'Robin'	MDHE
'Rock et Rocaille'	MDHE
rodiei	MDHE
rodiei x *glandulosum*	MDHE
romanum	see *E. acaule*
§ *rupestre*	ECho ECtt MDHE MOne NDlv SAsh SBla SRot
'Santamixa'	MDHE
§ 'Sara Francesca'	EPot MDHE NSla
'Sarck'	MDHE
'Sierra Celtica'	MDHE
'Spanish Eyes'	GKir MAvo MDHE NChi SAga SMrm SRot SScr WAbe WCot
'Stephanie'	CFis CLyd EGle EWes LBee LPio LRHS MAvo MDHE MHer NChi NDlv NHol SAsh SIgm SRot SWal
supracanum	see *E. rupestre*
'Tini Kyni'	MDHE
'Tiny Kyni'	WAbe
tordylioides	EBee
trichomanifolium misapplied	see *E. cheilanthifolium*, *E. saxatile*
trichomanifolium L'Hér.	EWes LBee LRHS MHer NJOw
§ *trifolium*	ELan EPfP NChi NGiC NSti SBri SGar SIng SSpi WBrk WCru WHal WHoo WTMC XPep
§ x *variabile*	CBrm ECtt EHyt MDHE SIng
§ - 'Album'	CMHG CNic EBee EDAr EPot GBuc LBee MBar MDHE MHer MTho NHol NPri NWCA SBla SHFr SRms WAbe WBrk WEas WPat WPer WTel WWin

I - 'Bishop's Form'	CBri CMHG EBee ECtt EDAr EHyt EMlt EPot ESis LAst LPio LRHS MBar MBro MDHE MHer NBro NHol NMen NPri NWCA SBla SRms WCom WHoo WPat WWeb
- 'Derek'	CGra ECho
- 'Flore Pleno' (d)	EBee ECtt EDAr EHyt ELan EMlt EOrc EWes MDHE MHer NHol NJOw NMen SHFr SIng SRms SUsu WAbe WBrk WFar WPer
- 'Red Rock'	EWes MDHE SIng
- 'Roseum' ♀H4	CBot CNic ECho ECtt EDAr ELan EOrc GSki LRHS MDHE MHer NLAp NWCA SRms WAbe WBrk WFar WPer WShp WWin
'Veinina'	MDHE
I 'Westacre Seedling'	EWes MDHE
'Whiteleaf'	MDHE
x *willkommianum*	MDHE NFla

Erpetion see *Viola*

Eruca (Brassicaceae)

vesicaria **new**	MBow
- subsp. *sativa*	CArn CSpe ELau GPoy MBow MHer MSal NGHP SIde WHHs WJek WLHH WSel

Eryngium ✿ (Apiaceae)

CD&R	EWes
CD&R 1227	EBee
CDPR 3076	CFil WPGP
PC&H 268	MAvo MSph NLar
RB 94054	MSph NChi
RCB/Arg R-5	WCot
RCB/TQ A-3	WCot
§ *agavifolium*	More than 30 suppliers
alpinum ♀H4	More than 30 suppliers
- 'Amethyst'	EBee EFou GBuc LPhx LRHS MAvo MBri MSte MTed NBro NLar SMrm WWeb
- 'Blue Jacket' **new**	NCGa
- 'Blue Star'	More than 30 suppliers
- 'Holden Blue'	CPlt GMac
- 'Slieve Donard'	see *E.* x *zabelii* 'Donard Variety'
- 'Superbum'	CBot CKno EBee EBlw ECtt EHrv EMar GBri GBuc GSki MBnl MNFA MNrw NBPC NDov NLar SBla SMad SPla SRms WCot WSan WViv
amethystinum	CBot CMdw ECGN EChP EGle EHrv EMan GSki LPhx LPio MAnH MNFA MNrw MWrn NPPs NSla SChu SIgm SPer SPla WBVN WBea WCAu WPer WSHC
biebersteinianum	see *E. caeruleum*
'Blue Jackpot' **new**	MTis SPoG SVil
bourgatii	More than 30 suppliers
- Graham Stuart Thomas's selection	More than 30 suppliers
- 'Oxford Blue' ♀H4	CBot COIW CPom EHrv EPar LPio MHer MMil NCGa SGar SPer SSpi SWvt WCom WEas WHoo WOld
- 'Picos Blue' PBR	CBot EHrv LPhx MBro SMrm WCom WHoo WPGP WWeb WWhi
bromeliifolium misapplied	see *E. agavifolium*
bromeliifolium F.Delaroche **new**	LRHS
§ *caeruleum*	GBuc MAvo MNrw SIng
campestre	CAgr CBot EWll MDKP MHer NChi NGby NLar SIgm WFar WPer
carlinae	LPhx MAnH NDov
caucasicum	see *E. caeruleum*
creticum	EBee MAvo NBir NBro NChi WTin

Delaroux — see *E. proteiflorum*
dichotomum — EMon EPPr GFlt NChi
ebracteatum — CFil CHad EBee GCal LPhx LPio SIgm WCot WPGP
- var. *poterioides* — CFil LPhx MAnH SMad
§ *eburneum* — CBot CFil CTCP EBee EBre ECha ECoo EPfP EWes GBuc LEdu LPio LRHS MAnH MWgw NBro NChi WCot WFar WPic

foetidum — CArn
§ *giganteum* ♀H4 — More than 30 suppliers
- 'Silver Ghost' ♀H4 — More than 30 suppliers
glaciale — NSla WAbe WLin
- JJA 461.000 — NWCA
horridum — CFil CFwr EBee EBre EFWa EWes GAbr LEdu LPhx LPio LRHS MAnH MEHN MFir MNrw NChi SAPC SArc SIgm WCAu WFar WHer WWhi WWin

- HCM 98048 — WCru
'Jos Eijking'PBR — EBre EMan ENot GKir GMac LRHS MRav NLar SPer WBro
maritimum — CArn CBot CPom CPou EGoo GPoy LPhx MAvo MHer NLar SIgm SPlb WCot WFar WSel

Miss Willmott's ghost — see *E. giganteum*
monocephalum — CFil WPGP WTin
x *oliverianum* ♀H4 — CHad CTri EBlw EBre EHrv ELan ENot GBuc GMac LRHS MAvo MBro SDix SIgm SPer SUsu WCAu WWhi

palmatum — EBee
§ *pandanifolium* — CBct CFil CFwr CHEx CHar CKno CMHG CRez CTCP CTrG EBee EMan EPfP EWes GCal IBlr MAnH MMil MWrn SAPC SMad SPer WBor WBrE WCot WPGP WShp

- purple — CFil LPhx SDix SMHy SPet
paniculatum — CFil WSPG
pectinatum — WCru
  B&SWJ 9109 new
petiolatum new — MNrw
planum — More than 30 suppliers
- 'Bethlehem' ♀H4 — EBee EMan GCal LRHS MBNS NBro WSpi
§ - 'Blauer Zwerg' — CKno EBee EFou LHop LRHS NFla SPla SWat WFar
- 'Blaukappe' — CBot CFir CHar COlW CWCL EBee EBlw ECGN ERou GBBs GBri GFlt GMac LDai LPhx LRHS MAnH MWrn NLar SMad SMrm WBea WCom WFar WHil WLin WViv WWhi WWpP
* - 'Blue Candle' — EBee WFar WSpi
- Blue Dwarf — see *E. planum* 'Blauer Zwerg'
- 'Blue Ribbon' — CSam EBee EMan GBBs LAst LRHS SWat WCAu
- 'Flüela' — CElw CM&M EBee ECtt EMan EPPr EWes GCal IPot LRHS MAvo MBnl MBow MNFA MWgw NBid NBro SPet SPla SWat WCAu WHoo WTin
- 'Seven Seas' — CFir CM&M EBee EOMN LHop LRHS MWgw NBro SChu SPla SWat WCAu WCom WCot WPer
- 'Silverstone' — EBee EOMN GCal GSki LDai LRHS MBnl MNFA NBro NCGa NOrc NPri WCAu
- 'Tetra Petra' — EBee LPio MAvo MCCP NBPC WPer
- violet blue — GCal
§ *proteiflorum* — CBot GCal LPhx LPio LRHS MAnH SWat WCru

serbicum new — GCal

serra — EBee EPyc EWes GBuc LDai LRHS NChi
- RB 90454 — MDKP
spinalba — CBot GSki LPio MAvo NChi SIgm
tricuspidatum — EBee EBre ECtt LRHS WPer
x *tripartitum* ♀H4 — More than 30 suppliers
* - 'Electric Blue' new — EBee
* *umbellatum* — EMon
variifolium — More than 30 suppliers
venustum — EBee LPhx MAnH SIgm
yuccifolium — CBct CBot CFil CHEx EBlw EBre ECGN EChP ECoo ERou EWes GCal GKir LEdu LPio MAnH NChi NLRH NSti SDix SDnm SIgm SPet SWvt WBrE WFar

- 'Green Sword' new — MBnl
x *zabelii* — EBee ELan ETow GCal GMac LPhx MAvo MFir NBir NDov SMrm WEas WPGP
- 'Donard Variety' — CDes EBee EBlw GCal GKir GMac IBlr ITim LAst LRHS MDKP SWat WHil
- 'Forncett Ultra' — CDes WPGP
- 'Jewel' — CMdw MNFA SUsu SWat
- 'Violetta' — CPlt ELan GBuc IGor MAvo MSte MTed NGby SWat WFar WHoo

Erysimum (Brassicaceae)
from Madeira — CPLG
alpinum hort. — see *E. hieraciifolium*
* *altaicum* — WLin
  var. *humillinum* new
'Anne Marie' — ELan SOkh
'Apricot Delight' — COtt SCoo
'Apricot Twist' — More than 30 suppliers
arenicola — see *E. torulosum*
  var. *torulosum*
arkansanum — see *E. helveticum*
§ *asperum* — IFro
'Aunt May' — SMrm
bicolor — WCot
'Bowles' Mauve' ♀H3 — More than 30 suppliers
'Bowles' Purple' — CBrm CWCL EChP LAst SRms SWvt WBVN WShp
'Bowles' Yellow' — ECtt ERou GBuc NLar
'Bredon' ♀H3 — CFis CHar COlW CWCL EBee EChP ECoo EMan EPfP GKir LRHS MAsh NPer NPri WHoo WKif
'Butterscotch' — CFee GKir MMHG WBry WEas WHoo WTin WWhi
'Butterscotch Variegated' (v) — GBri
candicum new — XPep
capitatum — CLyd NMen
cheiri — CArn GWCH MBow MHer NSco WHer
- 'Bloody Warrior' (d) — CBot CElw EChP ECtt ELan GBri GBuc NPer NSla WCAu WEas
- 'Harpur Crewe' (d) — CElw CFee CTri EBee EChP ELan EPfP ERou EShb GKir IFro LRHS MTho NPer SChu SIng SMrm SRms WCom WCot WHoo WPat WWin
- 'Jane's Derision' — CNat
'Chelsea Jacket' — EBee EChP EHol EPfP ERou EWTr GBri LDai MRav MSph NSti WEas WPer
'Chequers' — see *E. suffrutescens*
concinnum — see *E. suffrutescens*
'Constant Cheer' — CElw CPlt CSpe EBee EChP ECtt EGoo ELan EMan EPfP ERou GBuc GGar LRHS MEHN NFla NPer SUsu SWvt WCAu WCom WKif WMnd WPat WPer WRha WShp WWhi
'Cotswold Gem' (v) — CElw COtt EBee EBlw EChP EHoe EMan EPPr EPfP GBri LAst LDai MAvo MBnl MHer MSph NPPs

	NPer SAga SBri SMrm SPoG SWvt WCFE WCot WLin WShp
'Devon Gold'	see *E.* 'Plant World Gold'
'Devon Sunset'	CElw GBri MSte SAga SChu WHoo WWhi
'Dorothy Elmhirst'	see *E.* 'Mrs L.K. Elmhirst'
dwarf lemon	WHoo
'Ellen Willmott'	WBry
'Fragrant Sunshine'	MAsh
* *gelidum* var. *kotschyi*	NWCA
* 'Gingernut'	NPer
'Glowing Embers'	SOkh
'Golden Gem'	EMlt IHMH NDlv NPro WPer
'Golden Jubilee'	CHar EBre ECho LIck SIng
grandiflorum	MBow
'Hector Harrison' **new**	COtt
§ *helveticum*	ECoo EMlt GTou IFro NPri SRms WRHF
§ *hieraciifolium*	CNic EHol NBlu NFla NLAp
humile	WLin
'Jacob's Jacket'	CStu ECtt EWTr NPer SChu WEas WWin
'John Codrington'	CBel CElw CPlt GBri GBuc MHer MRav NFor NGdn NPer SAga SChu SUsu WKif
'Joseph's Coat'	CElw
'Jubilee Gold' **new**	EWll
'Julian Orchard'	CBel CElw CFis CSpe EBlw ECtt NCiC SAga SChu SSth WCom
kotschyanum	CGra CLyd CPBP ECtt EHyt ETow LBee MDHE MOne NMen NWCA SRms SScr WAbe WCom WPat
'Lady Roborough'	CFee GBuc
linifolium	EBur ECoo EWTr SRms WBVN WGor XPep
§ - 'Variegatum' (v)	CArn CBrm EBee EBlw ECtt ELan EOrc EPfP EPot ERou GGar LRHS NPer SAga SMrm SPer SRot WCom WHoo WPGP
'Miss Hopton'	ETow WEas WLin
'Moonlight'	ECtt EPot GBuc LBee MHer MTho NCGa NDov NFla NFor SAga SBla SChu SRms WBVN
§ 'Mrs L.K. Elmhirst'	NPer SOkh WCot
mutabile	CBgR CFwr CTri EBlw EGoo EOrc LPhx MRav NBir
- 'Variegatum' (v)	WEas
nivale	WLin
odoratum	MBow
'Orange Flame'	CMea CWCL EBre ECtt EPot LAst LBee MBar MHer NPer NWCA SIng SMrm WCom WPer
'Parish's'	CBgR CSpe EChP ECtt EWTr MRav SChu SMrm
perofskianum	WEas
Perry's hybrid	NPer
'Perry's Peculiar'	NPer
'Perry's Pumpkin'	NPer
'Plant World Antique'	WBry
§ 'Plant World Gold'	CElw
'Plant World Lemon'	CElw WCom
§ *pulchellum*	MWat
- 'Variegatum' (v)	EBee WBrE WShp
pumilum DC.	see *E. helveticum*
rupestre	see *E. pulchellum*
'Rushfield Sunrise'	CBgR CElw
* 'Rushfield Surprise'	NLar
'Sissinghurst Variegated'	see *E. linifolium* 'Variegatum'
'Sprite'	CLyd CMea CTri ECtt EDAr EPot IHMH NPer
§ *suffrutescens*	LPhx NPer XPep
'Sweet Sorbet'	CHar EBee EChP LAst MTis NPri WShp
§ *torulosum*	WLin

'Valerie Finnis'	WCom
'Variegatum' ambig. (v)	CBcs WWin
'Walberton's Fragrant Sunshine'	COtt EBre LRHS MBri SCoo
'Wenlock Beauty'	CBel LDai MTis NDov NFor NGdn NPPs SChu SRms WHoo WWhi
wheeleri	ECoo EWTr NBur NPer
witmannii	SSth

Erythraea see *Centaurium*

Erythrina (*Papilionaceae*)

× *bidwillii*	SSpi
caffra	WMul
crista-galli	CAbb CBcs CBot CFwr CHEx CSpe EBee ELan ERea GQui ITer LAst LRHS MLan SMur SOWG SPlb SSpi WCot WHPE WMul WPat
- 'Compacta'	SMad
flabelliformis	MGol
herbacea	EMan SSpi
- pink-flowered	SSpi
lysistemon	SOWG
vespertilio	SOWG

Erythronium ✿ (*Liliaceae*)

albidum	CBro CLAP EBee EPot GBuc GCrs GKev LAma SSpi
americanum	CArn CLAP CWoo EBee EPot GBuc GCrs GEdr IBlr LAma MLLN MS&S NMen NRog SSpi WCru
'Beechpark'	IBlr
'Blush'	GBuc IBlr
californicum ♀H4	CLAP CWoo EBee NRog SCnR WAbe WCru WWst
- J&JA 1.350.209	CWoo
- J&JA 13216	CLAP
- Plas Merdyn form	IBlr
§ - 'White Beauty' ♀H4	More than 30 suppliers
caucasicum	CLAP
citrinum	CWoo GBuc WLin
- J&JA 1.350.410	CWoo
- J&JA 13462	CLAP CWoo
'Citronella'	CBro CLAP EBee EChP EHrv ERos GBuc IBlr ITim LAma LRHS MMHG MS&S NDlv NJOw NMyG SSpi WAbe WCru WFar WPnP
cliftonii hort.	see *E. multiscapoideum* Cliftonii Group
dens-canis ♀H4	More than 30 suppliers
- JCA 470.001	CLAP
- WM 9615 from E Slovenia	MPhe
- 'Charmer'	EPot WWst
- 'Frans Hals'	CLAP EPar EPot ERos GBuc GCrs GEdr GGar LAma MNFA MTho NMen NRog WAbe WCru
- from Slovenia	CLAP
- 'Lilac Wonder'	EBee EPar EPot LAma LRHS MTho NRog WAbe WWst
* - 'Moerheimii' (d)	IBlr WWst
- var. *niveum*	ERos IBlr
- 'Old Aberdeen'	CLAP IBlr
- 'Pink Perfection'	EBee EPar ERos GCrs GGar LAma LRHS NRog WCru WOBN
- 'Purple King'	EBee EPot ERos GCrs GEdr LAma NRog WCru WGMN
- 'Rose Queen'	CAvo CBro EBee EBlw EPar EPot ERos GBuc GCrs GGar LAma LRHS MAvo MTho NJOw NRog SSpi WGMN WLin
* - 'Semi-plenum' (d)	IBlr
- 'Snowflake'	CAvo CLAP CMea EBee ECha EPar EPot ERos GCrs GEdr GGar LAma

<table>
<tr><td></td><td>MNFA NBir NMen NRog SSpi
WAbe WCru</td></tr>
</table>

- 'White Splendour'	CBro ERos IBlr WWst
elegans	EBee NMen SSpi WPGP
'Flash'	IBlr
§ *grandiflorum*	GBuc GCrs GEdr GKir NMen
- J&JA 11394	CLAP
- M&PS 007	CLAP SSpi
- M&PS 025	WWst
- M&PS 96/024	NMen
- subsp. *chrysandrum*	see *E. grandiflorum*
helenae	CLAP CWoo IBlr WPGP
- J&JA 11678	WWst
hendersonii	CLAP CWoo EBee LAma MS&S WAbe
- J&JA 1.351.301	CWoo
- J&JA 12945	CLAP CWoo SSpi
- JCA 11116	CLAP
howellii	CLAP GCrs SSpi WPGP
- J&JA 13441	CLAP
japonicum	EBee EFEx GBBs GBuc LAma MPhe NMen NRog SPer WCru
'Jeannine'	GBuc GEdr IBlr WCru
'Joanna'	CLAP IBlr LAma
'Kondo'	CBri EBee EHyt EPot ERos GBBs GBuc GCrs GEdr IBlr LAma LRHS MAvo MBro MS&S MTho NBir NJOw NMen NRog SPer WAbe WCru WFar WHil WPnP
'Margaret Mathew'	WAbe
mesochoreum	IBlr
§ *multiscapoideum*	CLAP CWoo MPhe WCot WLin
- J&JA 135.2000	WOBN
- JCA 12700	SSpi
§ - Cliftonii Group	CLAP MPhe
- J&JA 13525	CLAP SSpi
oregonum	CLAP CWoo ETow GBuc MS&S WCot WCru
- subsp. *leucandrum*	CLAP MPhe
- - J&JA 13494	CWoo SSpi
'Pagoda' ♀H4	More than 30 suppliers
purdyi	see *E. multiscapoideum*
revolutum ♀H4	CBro CFir CLAP CWoo EPot GBuc GCrs GGar IBlr ITim MS&S SBla SCnR SRot SSpi WAbe WCru
- 'Guincho Splendour'	IBlr
- Johnsonii Group	CNic CWoo ITim SSpi WAbe WCru
- 'Knightshayes Pink'	CLAP GBuc IBlr
- 'Pink Beauty'	WNor
- Plas Merdyn form	IBlr
- 'White Beauty'	see *E. californicum* 'White Beauty'
'Rippling Waters'	IBlr
'Rosalind'	IBlr
sibiricum	EBee GCrs GKev
- white	WWst
'Sundisc'	ECha IBlr MS&S MTho WAbe
tuolumnense ♀H4	CBro CLAP EBee EHrv EMon EPar EPot ERos GBuc GCrs GGar IBlr LAma MCCP MS&S NMen NRog WAbe WCot
- (EBA clone 2) **new**	WAbe
- (EBA clone 3) **new**	WAbe
- 'Spindlestone'	IBlr WWst
umbilicatum	GCrs IBlr

Escallonia ✿ (Escalloniaceae)

'Alice'	EBee SLPl SPer
'Apple Blossom' ♀H4	More than 30 suppliers
§ *bifida* ♀H3	CDoC CFee CPle WBcn WFar WSHC
'C.F. Ball'	CSBt CTri EBee EHol ELan GEil GGar LBuc MGos MSwo NBlu NWea SEND SLim SRms WAbe WBVN WBod WDin WFar WMoo WStI WTel

'Dart's Rosy Red'	NHol SLPl
'Donard Beauty'	CChe EBee SRms WFar
'Donard Brilliance'	MGos
'Donard Radiance' ♀H4	More than 30 suppliers
'Donard Seedling'	More than 30 suppliers
'Donard Star'	CDoC CSBt CWib EBee ENot EPfP LAst MGos MRav NWea SLPl WCFE WWeb
'Donard Surprise'	NFor
'Donard White'	COkL
'Edinensis'	EBee ECtt ENot EPfP MBar MRav SEND SLim WDin WFar WGer WMoo
'Erecta'	EPfP LAst
x *exoniensis*	SRms
'Glory of Donard'	ENot
'Gwendolyn Anley'	CMHG SLPl SPer WFar
'Hopleys Gold'	see *E. laevis* 'Gold Brian'
illinita	WPGP
'Iveyi' ♀H3	More than 30 suppliers
§ *laevis*	CDoC CTrw SDry WFar
§ - 'Gold Brian'^PBR	CDul CMHG CSBt EBre EHoe ELan ENot EPfP LRHS MAsh MGos MWat NScw SCoo SHop SMer SPer SWal WBod WFar WHar WStI
- 'Gold Ellen' (v)	CChe CTri CWSG EBee EBre EMil EPfP LRHS MAsh MCCP MGos MRav MSwo NHol SAga SCoo SEND SLim SPer SPla SWvt WCot WWeb
'Langleyensis' ♀H4	CPLG CSBt CTri CWib MWat NWea SPer WDin WFar WHar
leucantha	WKif
mexicana	CBot WFar WPGP
montevidensis	see *E. bifida*
'Newry'	SPer
organensis	see *E. laevis*
'Peach Blossom' ♀H4	CChe CDoC CDul CPle CSam EBee ECrN ELan EMil ENot EPfP GKir LRHS MAsh MBNS MBri MGos MSwo NBee NBlu SHBN SLPl SLim SPer WFar
'Pink Elf'	ECtt LRHS MSwo NHol
'Pride of Donard' ♀H4	CBcs CDoC CSBt EBee EPfP GGar LRHS MAsh NBlu NPri SRms SSto WBrE
'Red Dream'	CChe CWSG EBee EBre LRHS MAsh MBri MGos MSwo NBlu NPro NScw SCoo SRms SWvt WFar WGer WStI WWeb
'Red Dwarf'	SWvt
'Red Elf'	CBrm EBee EBre ECrN ECtt ELan ENot EPfP GKir LAst LHop LRHS MAsh MBar MBri MGos MRav MSwo MTis MWat NHol SGar SLPl SPer SPlb SRms SWvt WFar WHen WWeb
'Red Hedger'	CDoC CSBt CTrG CWib LRHS MGos MTis SCoo
resinosa	CBcs CPle IFro SAPC SArc SVen
revoluta	SDry WKif
rubra 'Crimson Spire' ♀H4	More than 30 suppliers
- 'Ingramii'	CChe CSBt CWib NWea SHBN
§ - var. *macrantha*	CBcs CChe CDoC CDul CSBt CWSG CWib EBee ECrN EPfP GGar GKir IArd LAst LRHS MBri MHer NBlu NWea SLim SMer SPer WDin WFar WGer WGwG WMoo WStI XPep
* - - *aurea* **new**	NScw
- 'Pygmaea'	see *E. rubra* 'Woodside'
- var. *uniflora*	SDry

§ – 'Woodside' ECrN EHol EPfP GEdr GEil NHol SRms SSto WHCG
'Silver Anniversary' MSwo WBcn
'Slieve Donard' EBee ECrN ENot EPfP MGos MRav NHol NWea SLPl SLim SLon SRms WFar

Eschscholzia (Papaveraceae)

californica ♀H4 XPep
– 'Jersey Cream' CSpe
– var. *maritima* XPep

Eucalyptus ✿ (Myrtaceae)

acaciiformis	LRav
aggregata	GTSp LRav SAPC SArc SPer WCel WMul
amygdalina	GGar
approximans subsp. *approximans*	LRav WCel
archeri	CBrm CCVT CDul EPfP GKir GQui GTSp LPan MBNS NHol WBod WCel WOVN WPGP
baeuerlenii	LRav
barberi	LRav
§ *bridgesiana*	LRav MHer
caesia	LRav SPlb
calycogona	LRav
camaldulensis	LRav SPlb
camphora	CTho LRav WCel
cinerea	CTrC GQui LRav SPlb WCel
citriodora	CPLG CWib GQui LRav MHer NGHP SPlb WCel WHHs WNor
coccifera	CCVT CDoC CHEx CSBt CTho ECrN ELan EPfP GGar GKir LRHS MCCP MLan NBea NHol NPri SEND SPlb SSpi WBVN WBod WCel WDin WMul WNor
cordata	CCVT CTrC LRav WCel
crenulata	CTrC GQui LRav WCel
crucis subsp. *crucis* **new**	SPlb
cypellocarpa	SPlb SVen
dalrympleana ♀H3	CAbb CBcs CCVT CDoC CDul CMHG ELan ENot EPfP EWTr EWes GKir LPan LRHS MGos MSwo NBea SKee SPer SRms WBod WBrE WCel WDin WMul WOrn WPGP WWeb
dalrympleana x *fraxinoides*	LRav
deanei	WCel
debeuzevillei	see *E. pauciflora* subsp. *debeuzevillei*
delegatensis	CMHG GTSp LRav WCel WMul
– subsp. *tasmaniensis*	GGar WNor
divaricata	see *E. gunnii divaricata*
dives	LRav
erythrocorys	SPlb
eximia	SPlb
* – *nana*	LRav WGwG WOut
ficifolia	MGol
fraxinoides	LRav SPlb WCel
gamophylla	SPlb
glaucescens	CCVT CDoC CMHG CTho EPfP EWes GKir GQui LPan LRHS NHol NPri SAPC SArc SPer WBVN WCel WGer WMul
globulus	CHEx ISea LRav MSal WCel WFar WMul
goniocalyx	EPfP WCel
§ *gregsoniana*	CCVT CDoC LRav SPlb WBVN WCel
grossa	SVen
gunnii ♀H3	More than 30 suppliers

I – *divaricata*	CCVT EPfP GQui LRHS MBri NHol WCel WGer
johnstonii	CDul GGar ISea LRav SKee SPer
kitsoniana	LRav WCel
kruseana	SPlb
kybeanensis	CCVT GQui GTSp LPan LRav WBod WCel
lacrimans	WCel
lehmannii	SOWG
leucoxylon	WCel
– subsp. *megalocarpa*	SPlb
ligustrina	LRav WCel
'Little Boy Blue' **new**	CWib
macarthurii	LRav WCel
macrocarpa	SMur SPlb
macroryncha	SPlb
mannifera subsp. *elliptica*	LRav WCel
– subsp. *praecox*	LRav
mitchelliana	LRav WCel WDin
moorei	WCel
* – *nana*	LRav MWat WNor
neglecta	EPfP LRav WCel
nicholii	CBrm CCVT CDul ECrN EPfP EWes GKir GQui GTSp MGos NHol SVen WBod WCel WGer WMul WOVN
niphophila	see *E. pauciflora* subsp. *niphophila*
nitens	CCVT CLnd GKir LRav SAPC SArc SPlb WBod WCel WMul
§ *nitida*	CMHG EPAt WCel WNor
nova-anglica	CMHG CTho LRav
obliqua	GGar
ovata	GGar
parviflora **new**	WHPE
parvifolia ♀H4	CBcs CCVT CDoC CLnd EPfP EShb EWTr GKir ISea LPan LRHS LRav NHol SDry SEND WBVN WBod WCel WMul WWeb
pauciflora	CCVT CDoC CSBt CTho CTrC EGra ELan EPfP MGos NHol SEND SPer WBod WBrE WCel WMul WNor
– subsp. *acerina*	WCel
§ – subsp. *debeuzevillei*	CCVT CDoC CLnd CMHG CTho EPfP EWTr EWes GKir GQui LPan LRHS MBlu MGos SAPC SArc WCel WMul WPGP WWeb
– subsp. *hedraia*	WCel
– var. *nana*	see *E. gregsoniana*
§ – subsp. *niphophila* ♀H4	More than 30 suppliers
– – 'Pendula'	CCVT GTSp LPan LRHS WCel WPGP
– subsp. *pauciflora* **new**	LRav
perriniana	CCVT CDul CLnd CMHG CSBt EBee ECrN ELan ENot EPfP GKir LRHS MBri MGos NHol SDry SKee SPer SPlb WBVN WBod WCel WDin WFar WMul WNor WOrn
phoenicea	SOWG
pulchella	LRav
pulverulenta	CDul CSLe GTSp IMGH LRHS LRav SPlb WGer WHer
– 'Baby Blue'	LRav WCel
regnans	GGar WMul
risdonii	GGar LRav WNor
rodwayi	GGar LRav
rubida	CMHG LRav WCel
scoparia	LRav
sideroxylon	SPlb
– 'Rosea'	SPlb
simmondsii	see *E. nitida*
spathulata	SVen
stellulata	LRav WCel

stricta	LRav
stuartiana	see *E. bridgesiana*
sturgissiana	LRav
subcrenulata	CCVT CMHG EPfP GKir GQui GTSp LPan LRav MBNS NHol WBod WCel WOrn
tenuiramis	LRav
torquata	SPlb
urnigera	CCVT GKir LHop LRHS MBNS WCel WDin
vernicosa	CBrm CCVT GGar WCel
- subsp. ***johnstonii***	CMHG WCel
viminalis	CArn CHEx EPAt GGar LRav WCel WDin
***youmanii* new**	LRav

Eucharidium see *Clarkia*

Eucharis (Amaryllidaceae)

§ ***amazonica*** ♀H1	EUJe LAma LRHS MLan MOak NRog SDeJ
grandiflora hort.	see *E. amazonica*

Eucodonia (Gesneriaceae)

'Adele'	WDib
andrieuxii 'Naomi'	WDib

Eucomis (Hyacinthaceae)

'African Bride' **new**	WWeb
§ ***autumnalis*** ♀H2-3	CAbb CAvo CBro CHEx CPou CRHN CSWP EBee EPot EUJe GBin GSki LAma LPio LRHS MCCP MDun SDnm SPer WPGP WTin
- subsp. ***amaryllidifolia***	CFil
- subsp. ***autumnalis***	CFil
- subsp. ***clavata***	CFil
- 'White Dwarf'	CStu EShb
bicolor ♀H2-3	More than 30 suppliers
- 'Alba'	CAvo CPLG EAmu EBee GSki LPio LRHS SDnm
- 'Stars and Stripes' **new**	WCru
§ ***comosa***	CAvo CBrm CBro CHEx CHll CPLG CRHN CRez EBee EChP GSki LAma LEdu LRHS MDun NRog SDnm SVen SYvo WCru WEas WHil
- 'First Red'	CPou
- purple-leaved	SBla SIgm
- 'Sparkling Burgundy'	More than 30 suppliers
hybrid	SDix WHil
'John Treasure'	SMHy
'Joy's Purple' **new**	CPen
montana	CCtw CFil
pallidiflora ♀H4	CFil CHEx EBee LEdu
pole-evansii	CFil CFir CHEx CPLG EBee EOrc EPza EUJe GBin GCal MMil NPSI SMrm WCot WCru WHil
- bronze	CPne
- 'Burgundy'	EBla
- 'Purpurea'	GCal
punctata	see *E. comosa*
- 'Cornwood'	CAvo
regia	CPLG WCot
* ***reichenbachii***	WCot
'Royal Burgundy' **new**	SPer
'Swazi Pride' **new**	WWeb
undulata	see *E. autumnalis*
zambesiaca	CPen CPne EBee GBin GCal LPio WWeb
'Zeal Bronze'	CDoC CFil CMHG CStu EBee EPfP GCal LPio MAsh MCCP NCGa NSti WCot WCru WPGP

Eucommia (Eucommiaceae)

ulmoides	CBcs CFil CMCN

Eucryphia ✿ (Eucryphiaceae)

'Castlewellan'	ISea
cordifolia	CAbP CFil CMac CPne CTho CTrw IDee ISea SSpi WBod WDin WPGP
- Crarae hardy form	GGGa
cordifolia x ***lucida***	CBcs CBrm CFai CPLG ELan ISea WDin WPat
glutinosa ♀H4	CBcs CDul CTho ELan EPfP GKir LHyd LRHS MAsh MBar MBri MDun NBea NBir SHBN SPer SSpi SSta WBod WDin WFar WNor WPat
- Plena Group (d)	WPat
x ***hillieri***	IDee
- 'Winton'	CMHG GQui ISea SSpi
x ***intermedia***	CDul CSam CTrC CTrG CWSG ELan EPfP GGGa LRHS NPal NPri SHBN SRms SSpi WDin WFar WPat
- 'Rostrevor' ♀H3	CBcs CDul CMHG CPMA CSBt ELan EPfP GQui IArd IMGH ISea LHyd LRHS MAsh MDun MGos NCGa NRib SLon SPer SReu SSta WBod WFar WPat WPic WSHC
lucida	CDoC CFil CTrC EBee ELan EPfP GGar GSki GTSp IArd IMGH ISea WBod WFar WNor WPGP
- 'Ballerina'	CPMA ISea LRHS SSpi WFar
- 'Gilt Edge' (v)	CFil ISea WPGP
- 'Leatherwood Cream' (v)	ISea
- 'Pink Cloud'	CBcs CDoC CEnd CFil CPLG CPMA CWSG ELan EPfP GQui IMGH ISea LPan LRHS MDun NPri SDnm SPer SSpi SSta SWvt WFar WPGP
- 'Pink Whisper' **new**	ISea
- 'Spring Glow' (v)	ISea
milliganii	CAbP CDoC CFil CMHG CPMA CTrC EBee EPfP GGar GQui ISea LHop MBlu MDun NPal SHBN SRms SSpi WAbe WBod WPGP WSHC
moorei	CBcs CFil ELan GQui ISea SSpi WPGP
x ***nymansensis***	CDul CFil CTrG EMil NBee SAPC SArc SDnm SReu SRms SSpi WBrE WFar WHCG WStI
- 'George Graham'	GGGa ISea
- 'Mount Usher'	ISea
- 'Nymansay' ♀H3	More than 30 suppliers
'Penwith' ambig.	CDoC CPMA GQui SSpi WBrE WDin WFar WGer
'Penwith' misapplied	see *E. cordifolia* x *E. lucida*

Eugenia (Myrtaceae)

myrtifolia	ERom
smithii	ECou

Eumorphia (Asteraceae)

prostrata	CTrC
sericea	CTrC

Eunomia see *Aethionema*

Euodia (Rutaceae)

daniellii	see *Tetradium daniellii*
hupehensis	see *Tetradium daniellii* Hupehense Group

Euonymus (Celastraceae)

B&L 12543	EPla EWes
alatus ♀H4	More than 30 suppliers
- var. ***apterus***	EPfP SHBN
- Chicago Fire	see *E. alatus* 'Timber Creek'
- 'Ciliodentatus'	see *E. alatus* 'Compactus'

§ – 'Compactus' ♀H4	CDoC CEnd CMCN CPMA EBee EPfP ESis EWTr GKir LHop LPan LRHS MAsh MBri MBro MGos MRav NCGa SLim SPer SPla SReu SSpi WCFE WDin WFar WPGP WPat
– 'Fire Ball'	EPfP
– 'Rudy Haag'	CPMA EPfP
– 'Select'	see *E. alatus* 'Fire Ball'
§ – 'Timber Creek'	CPMA EPfP GKir NLar
americanus	CBot EPfP GIBF NLar
– narrow-leaved	EPfP NLar
atropurpureus	EPfP
bungeanus	CMCN EPfP EPla NLar
– 'Dart's Pride'	CPMA EPfP NLar
* – var. *mongolicus*	EPfP
– 'Pendulus'	EPfP GKir
– var. *semipersistens*	CPMA EPla
carnosus	EPfP NLar
cornutus var.	CFil CPMA EPfP GKir MAsh MBlu
quinquecornutus	NBhm NLar WPat
'Den Haag'	EPfP
echinatus	EPfP EPla
– BL&M 306	SLon
europaeus	CArn CCVT CDoC CDul CLnd CRWN CSam CWib ECrN ELan EPfP EPla EWTr GIBF GKir LBuc LPan MHer MSwo NWea SKee SRms SWvt SYvo WBVN WDin WHar WHer WMou XPep
– f. *albus*	CBot CPMA EPfP LTwo
– 'Atropurpureus'	CMCN CTho EPfP GKir MBlu NLar
– 'Atrorubens'	CPMA
– 'Aucubifolius' (v)	CFil EPfP WBcn
* – 'Aureus'	CNat
* – f. *bulgaricus*	EPfP
– 'Chrysophyllus'	EPfP MBlu
– 'Howard'	EPfP
– var. *intermedius*	EBee ENot EPfP MBlu NLar WWes
– 'Miss Pinkie' **new**	CMCN
– 'Red Cascade' ♀H4	More than 30 suppliers
– 'Scarlet Wonder'	CPMA EPfP NLar
– 'Thornhayes'	CTho
farreri	see *E. nanus*
fimbriatus	CBcs EPfP
fortunei	CDul
– Blondy = 'Interbolwi'PBR (v)	More than 30 suppliers
– 'Canadale Gold' (v)	CDoC COkL EBee ENot EPla GEil LRHS MAsh MGos MRav MWhi NBee NHol SPer WCFE WDin
– 'Coloratus'	EBee EHol ENot EPfP MBar MSwo SHBN SLon SPer WDin
– 'Croftway'	SCro
– 'Dart's Blanket'	CDul ECrN ELan ENot EPla MRav MWhi NScw SLPl SSta WDin
– 'Emerald Cushion'	EBee ENot MRav SPer
– 'Emerald Gaiety' (v) ♀H4	More than 30 suppliers
– 'Emerald 'n' Gold' (v) ♀H4	More than 30 suppliers
– 'Emerald Surprise' (v) ♀H4	EBee ENot LRHS MBri NHol NPro
– 'Gold Spot'	see *E. fortunei* 'Sunspot'
– 'Gold Tip'	see *E. fortunei* Golden Prince
§ – 'Golden Pillar' (v)	EBee EHoe EHol EPla ESis NHol WCot WFar
§ – Golden Prince (v)	EBee ENot EPfP EPla LRHS MBar MRav MSwo NHol NPro SLim SPer SRms WFar WGor WGwG WStI
– 'Harlequin' (v)	CBcs COtt CSBt CWSG EBee EHoe ELan EPfP EPla LBuc LRHS MAsh MBar MGos MRav NPro SAga SHBN SLim SPer SPla SRms SWvt WBod WCot WFar WGMN
– 'Kewensis'	EBee ENot EPfP LAst MBar MRav MWat SAPC SArc SBod SLon WCru WFar
– 'Minimus'	CTri EPla ESis MGos NHol NPro SMrm WFar
* – 'Minimus Variegatus' (v)	ECho SPlb
§ – var. *radicans*	CRez WWpP
– 'Sheridan Gold'	COkL CTri EBee ECtt EHoe EPla MRav NHol SHBN
– 'Silver Gem'	see *E. fortunei* 'Variegatus'
– 'Silver Pillar' (v)	ECrN EHoe EMlt ENot LRHS MRav NHol WFar
– 'Silver Queen' (v)	More than 30 suppliers
– 'Sunshine' (v)	CAbP ELan EPla LRHS MAsh NHol
§ – 'Sunspot' (v)	CBcs CChe CMHG CWSG EBee ECrN ECtt EGra ELan ENot EPla IBal LRHS MBar MGos MRav MSwo NHol SLim SPer SRms WBrE WDin WFar WHar WTel
– 'Tustin' ♀H4	EBee EPla MRav SLPl
§ – 'Variegatus' (v)	CMHG ENot MBar NFor NSti SPer SRms STre WCot WDin
– var. *vegetus*	EPla
– 'Wolong Ghost' **new**	SSpi
frigidus	EPfP
grandiflorus	CPMA EPfP GIBF GKir MBlu NLar SSpi WFar
– 'Red Wine'	CPMA CTho EBee EPfP LRHS NLar SLim
– f. *salicifolius*	CPMA EPfP
hamiltonianus	CMCN GKir SSpi WFar
– subsp. *hians*	see *E. hamiltonianus* subsp. *sieboldianus*
– 'Indian Summer'	CPMA EBee EPfP GKir LRHS MBlu NLar SSpi SSta WBcn
– 'Koi Boy' **new**	GKir LRHS
– *maackii*	GIBF
– 'Miss Pinkie'	GKir LRHS MAsh MGos SCoo SKee SSpi SSta
– 'Pink Delight' **new**	CPMA
– 'Poort Bulten' **new**	NLar
– 'Rainbow' **new**	NLar
– 'Red Elf'	CPMA EPfP GKir
§ – subsp. *sieboldianus*	CDul CMCN CPMA CTho EPfP GIBF GKir MRav SLPl WFar
– – 'Calocarpus'	EPfP GKir NLar
– – 'Coral Charm'	CPMA EPfP NLar SMur
– – Semiexsertus Group	EPfP
* – – var. *yedoensis* f. *koehneanus*	EPfP
– 'Snow'	EPfP NLar
– 'Winter Glory'	CPMA EPfP GKir LRHS MBlu NLar WWes
– var. *yedoensis*	see *E. hamiltonianus* subsp. *sieboldianus*
hibarimisake	see *E. japonicus* 'Hibarimisake'
japonicus	CDoC CDul CTrC ECrN ENot EPfP LRHS MRav SAPC SArc SGar SPer STop WDin XPep
– 'Albomarginatus'	CBcs CTri MBar NBlu SEND SRms STop
* – 'Argentus Compactus'	LPan
– 'Aureopictus'	see *E. japonicus* 'Aureus'
– 'Aureovariegatus'	see *E. japonicus* 'Ovatus Aureus'
§ – 'Aureus' (v)	CBcs CBrm CDoC CMHG CSBt CWib EBee ECrN EGra ENot LPan LRHS MRav MSwo MWat SHBN SHFr SLon SPer SSto WDin WHar WTel
– 'Bravo'	CDoC EBee ECrN EGra EHoe EMil LAst LRHS MBri NLar WDin WFar WBcn
– 'Chedju' (v)	WBcn
– 'Chollipo' ♀H4	ELan EPla LRHS MAsh
– 'Compactus'	LPan SAPC SArc

- 'Duc d'Anjou' Carrière (v)   CBcs CHrt EHoe ELan EPla EWes LPan MRav SDry
- 'Duc d'Anjou' hort.   see *E. japonicus* 'Viridivariegatus'
- 'Golden Maiden'   ELan EPfP LRHS MAsh SLim
- 'Golden Pillar'   see *E. fortunei* 'Golden Pillar'
- 'Grey Beauty'   EBee NLar
§ - 'Hibarimisake'   EPla SBla
- 'Kathy'[PBR] **new**   NScw SPoG
§ - 'Latifolius Albomarginatus'   CDul EBee EHoe EHol EPfP EPla LRHS MRav MSwo SPer SPoG WDin WWeb
- 'Luna'   see *E. japonicus* 'Aureus'
- 'Macrophyllus' **new**   ECrN
- 'Macrophyllus Albus'   see *E. japonicus* 'Latifolius Albomarginatus'
- 'Maiden's Gold'   COtt CSBt
- 'Marieke'   see *E. japonicus* 'Ovatus Aureus'
- 'Microphyllus'   CDoC CMac EMil SAga STre WFar WGwG
§ - 'Microphyllus Albovariegatus' (v)   More than 30 suppliers
§ - 'Microphyllus Aureovariegatus' (v)   CDoC CSLe EGra EHyt EMil EPfP LPan MWhi NLRH NLar WCFE WPat
- 'Microphyllus Aureus'   see *E. japonicus* 'Microphyllus Pulchellus'
§ - 'Microphyllus Pulchellus' (v)   CBcs CDoC CMHG CSBt CWSG EBee ECrN ENot EPfP EPla LHop MBar MRav NDlv NHol NJOw SPoG SWvt WDin WHCG WWeb
- 'Microphyllus Variegatus'   see *E. japonicus* 'Microphyllus Albovariegatus'
§ - 'Ovatus Aureus' (v) ♀[H4]   More than 30 suppliers
- 'Président Gauthier' (v)   CDoC EBee ECrN LPan MGos SPer WBod WDin
- 'Pulchellus Aureovariegatus'   see *E. japonicus* 'Microphyllus Aureovariegatus'
- 'Robustus'   EPfP EPla
- 'Royal Gold'   WWeb
- 'Silver King'   EBee
- 'Silver Princess = 'Moness'   SHBN
- 'Susan'   EGra EPla
§ - 'Viridivariegatus' (v)   EBee GEil LRHS MAsh NHol
kiautschovicus   EPfP EPla GKir
- 'Berry Hill'   EPfP
latifolius   CMCN CPMA CTho EPfP NLar WDin
macropterus   EPfP EPla NLar
maximowiczianus   EPfP GIBF NLar
morrisonensis B&SWJ 3700   WCru
myrianthus   CPMA EPfP GKir NLar
§ *nanus*   CNic CWib EHol EPfP EPla NHol NLar SSpi WSHC
- var. *turkestanicus*   EPfP EPla SLon SRms WFar
obovatus   EPfP
occidentalis   EPfP
oresbius   CPMA EPfP WPGP
oxyphyllus   CMCN CPMA CTho EPfP GKir NLar WCru WDin WWes
pauciflorus   EPfP
§ *pendulus*   CHEx
phellomanus ♀[H4]   CDul CEnd CTho EBee EHol EPfP GIBF GKir LHop LRHS MAsh MBar MBlu MBri NLar SHBN SMac WDin WFar WPat
- 'Silver Surprise' (v)   CPMA EPfP GKir NLar
§ *planipes* ♀[H4]   More than 30 suppliers
radicans   see *E. fortunei* var. *radicans*
'Rokojô'   CLyd MBro NWCA
rosmarinifolius   see *E. nanus*
sachalinensis hort.   see *E. planipes*
sachalinensis (F.Schmidt) Maxim. from Ussuriland   GIBF

sacrosanctus   EPfP
sanguineus   CPMA CTho EPfP LRHS NLar SSpi
tanakae   GIBF
tingens   CFil EPfP GIBF GKir
vagans   EPfP EPla
- L 551   EPla SLon
velutinus   EPfP NLar
verrucosus   CPMA EPfP EPla NLar WWes
vidalii   EPfP
yedoensis   see *E. hamiltonianus* subsp. *sieboldianus*

Eupatorium (Asteraceae)

B&SWJ 9052 from Guatemala **new**   WCru
RCB/Arg L-2   WCot
RCB/Arg P-1   WCot
RCB/Arg Q-2   WCot
§ *album*   ERou NBid WPer
- 'Braunlaub'   EBee EChP EMan EMar EMon EPza EWTr GKir LPio LRHS NGdn NSti SSpi WCAu WHil WMnd
altissimum   CBot EPar MSal SRms
aromaticum   CRow CSev MLLN MRav MWgw NBro NSti SWat WCHb WPer WWye
atrorubens   EBee EMan ERea EShb GCal
cannabinum   CArn EBee EHon ELan EMFW EMar GBar GFlt GGar GPoy LPBA MBNS MBow MHer MRav MSal MSta NBir NGHP NMir NPer NSti SECG SRob SSpi SWat WHHs WPer WWpP WWye
- 'Album'   CSam EMon SMHy
- 'Flore Pleno' (d)   More than 30 suppliers
- 'Not Quite White'   LNCo
- 'Spraypaint'   CNat EPPr
* - 'Variegatum' (v) **new**   EBee
capillifolium   ERea LPio MLLN SAga SArc SDix SMrm WCAu WDyG WPGP
- 'Elegant Feather'   CFwr CSpe EMan EWes LHop LPhx SHar SLon SUsu
chinense   EBee
coelestinum   EBee EMan EShb EWes GCal LAst SMad WFar
* *cyclophyllum*   EMan
fistulosum   MGol
* - 'Atropurpureum'   CKno IBal WPer WSSM
forrestii **new**   EBee
fortunei   CArn EMon SSpi
* - 'Variegatum' (v)   EBee EMan WCot WPGP
hyssopifolium   EBee
§ *ligustrinum* ♀[H3]   CBcs CDoC CPLG CPle CRHN CSam CTbh CTri CWib EBee ECha ELan EMan GEil ISea LPhx LRHS NCGa SAga SDix SLim SMHy SMrm SPer WCHb WCot WFar WHCG WSHC
lindleyanum   EBee
maculatum   see *E. purpureum* subsp. *maculatum*
madrense   CSam
'Massive White'   GCal
micranthum   see *E. ligustrinum*
occidentale NNS 94-53   WCot
perfoliatum   CAgr CArn EBee GPoy MNrw MSal NLar WPer WWye
purpureum   More than 30 suppliers
- 'Album'   EPPr GKir LPhx
- 'Bartered Bride'   GKir
§ - subsp. *maculatum*   CSam ECGP EHrv EMon MDKP NGHP NGdn NLar SBri SSpi STes WFar WHil WHrl WOut WPer WWpP

– – 'Album'	EMFP EMon EWTr NBir NSti
– – 'Atropurpureum' ♀H4	More than 30 suppliers
– – 'Berggarten'	GCal
– – 'Gateway'	CRow ECtt EFou WTin
– – 'Glutball'	EBee GCal NChi SMad WWpP
– – 'Riesinschirm'	CKno EBee LPhx LRHS MSph MSte
	MTed SSvw SWat
– 'Purple Bush'	CHad CKno EBee ECha EFou LPhx
	NDov SSvw
rugosum	EBee ELan EMar EOrc EPfP GBar
	GKir LPhx MFir MGol MWgw
	NLar SDys SPer WCHb WTin
– *album*	see *E. album*
– 'Brunette'	EHrv
– 'Chocolate' ♀H4	More than 30 suppliers
* 'Snowball'	SMrm
triplinerve	MSte
* *variabile* 'Variegatum' (v)	EMan EWes WCot
weinmannianum	see *E. ligustrinum*

Euphorbia ✿ (*Euphorbiaceae*)

'Abbey Dore'	WCot
acanthothamnos	LPhx
altissima	MSte
amygdaloides	CRow EBee ECtt GKir NBlu NWit
	SSpi WShp
– 'Brithembottom'	CSam
– 'Craigieburn'	CDes CMdw CSam EBee EChP
	EGle EMan EWes GBri GCal MAvo
	NDov SUsu WCom WPGP
§ – 'Purpurea'	More than 30 suppliers
– 'Red Shank'	SBla
§ – var. *robbiae* ♀H4	More than 30 suppliers
– – dwarf	EPot GCal
– – 'Pom Pom'	CDes EMan
– – 'Redbud'	EBee EPla EWes
– var. *robbiae* x *characias*	WCot
– 'Rubra'	see *E. amygdaloides* 'Purpurea'
– 'Variegata' (v)	CBri GBuc SHBN SMad WWeb
– 'Welsh Dragon'	WCot
barrelieri	NWit WCot
baselicis	CPla EMan GBBs MAnH MAvo
	MGol NPro SIgm WGMN WLin
biglandulosa	see *E. rigida*
biumbellata	NWit
'Blue Haze'	SBla
brittingeri	NWit
– Baker's form	EPPr
broteroi	WCot
buschiana	WLin
capitata	CLyd
capitulata	ELan EPot EWes MBro MTho NWit
	SMrm
ceratocarpa	EBee EPPr EWes GBuc NWit SIgm
	SMad WCHb WCot WLun WSHC
characias	CBcs CBot CHEx COlW EBlw
	ECha ECtt EPfP GKir MBri MBro
	MDun MTis NOak NPer NPri NVic
	SPer SRms SSpi WAul WCot WFar
	WHen WMnd WPer XPep
– Ballyrogan hybrids	IBlr
– 'Black Pearl'	CBcs CBel CBri CFwr CHid CMHG
	EBee EChP EPfP GKir IPot LAst
	MAvo MBNS MCCP MDun MSte
	NCGa NSti SDnm SSpi SWvt WCra
	WFar WOVN WSpi WSpi
– 'Blue Wonder'	CM&M CSpe EBee EBlw EPfP GBin
	GCal LRHS MCCP MDun MSte
	NLar NWit SDnm SSpi SVil WCot
	WCra WGer WSpi WWeb
– subsp. *characias*	EBee EHrv GAbr MGos WCru
– – 'Blue Hills'	ECtt EGle EMan GBin GBuc GCal
	MSph NCGa NWit SMrm

– – 'Burrow Silver' (v)	CBcs CBot CBro CFai CFir CFwr
	CPen CSLe EBee ECtt ELan EMan
	EPyc LAst LDai MBNS MCCP
	MLLN MMHG NBPC NCGa SCoo
	SDnm SLim SSpi SWat WWhi
– – 'Green Mantle'	IBlr
– – 'H.E. Bates'	NBir
– – 'Humpty Dumpty'	More than 30 suppliers
– – 'Perry's Winter Blusher'	ECtt NWit
– dwarf	SMrm
– 'Forescate'	CSWP EBee EGle EMil EPfP LRHS
	MRav MSte NBPC NCGa NGdn
	NWit SDnm WFar WLun WMnd
	WShp
– 'Giant Green Turtle'	CMil
– 'Goldbrook'	CHad CSam EBee EGle EHoe EMan
	LAst LHop LRHS MRav MSph NPSI
	SHBN SSpi
– 'Portuguese Velvet' ♀H4	More than 30 suppliers
– Silver Swan = 'Wilcott'PBR (v)	ELan EMan ENot EPfP LBuc MGos
	NSti SHGC
– 'Sombre Melody'	IBlr
– 'Spring Splendour'	EBee EWes NWit
– 'Starbright'	NWit
– 'Whistleberry Gold'	CFwr EGle
– 'Whistleberry Jade'	CFwr EGle NWit
– subsp. *wulfenii* ♀H3-4	More than 30 suppliers
– – 'Bosahan' (v)	CBcs NWit
– – 'Emmer Green' (v)	CSpe EBee ECGP ECtt EHrv EMan
	EWes GBri GCal NWit SBla SHBN
	SUsu SWat WFoF
– – 'Jimmy Platt'	EGle SRms SRob WBrE WCot
	WGMN WHrl WWhi
§ – – 'John Tomlinson' ♀H3-4	CDes CHar CHea EBee ECha EHrv
	EWes GAbr GBin MBri MFOX
	SDnm SMrm SSth SUsu WCot WSpi
– – Kew form	see *E. characias* subsp. *wulfenii*
	'John Tomlinson'
– – 'Lambrook Gold' ♀H3-4	CFwr CSam EBee ECtt EGle ENot
	EPar EPfP LRHS MBri MRav MWat
	NPer SSth SVal WCom WCot WFar
	WGer
– – 'Lambrook Gold' seed-raised	see *E. characias* subsp. *wulfenii*
	Margery Fish Group
– – 'Lambrook Yellow'	EMon EWsh GBuc LPio SMur SVal
	WLun WSPU
§ – – Margery Fish Group	EBee EFou EGle EMan LRHS MLLN
	NBir NDov NPSI SMrm SPer
– – 'Perry's Tangerine'	EWes NPer NWit
§ – – 'Purple and Gold'	CFwr CM&M EBee EWes MAvo
	SHBN SWvt WBrE WCot WLun
– – 'Purpurea'	see *E. characias* subsp. *wulfenii*
	'Purple and Gold'
– – var. *sibthorpii*	ECGN SSth
– – 'Thelma's Giant'	NWit
clavarioides var. *truncata*	WCot
cognata	NWit
– CC&McK 607	EWes
– CC&McK 724	EBee GBin
conifera	CBos
'Copton Ash'	CSam CSpe EBee EFou NWit
corallioides	CBrm EBee ECha EMan EWTr IBlr
	LRHS MFOX NBPC NPer NSti SHFr
	SIgm SRms WBrE WGMN WHer
	WPnP WSHC WWin XPep
§ *cornigera* ♀H4	CElw CFil CHad EBre ECha EMar
	GBBs GBin GCal IBlr LPio LRHS
	MAvo MBri MCLN NCGa NDov
	NGdn NLar NSti SDix SSpi SWat
	WCom WCot WHoo WPGP WPen
	WPnP WSHC
– 'Goldener Turm'	CFwr EBee EChP GBin
corollata	WCot

cyparissias — CArn CBcs EChP ECha EDAr ELan GAbr GKir LRHS NBir NFor NGdn NJOw NMen NSti NVic NWCA SPer SRms WEas WFar WFoF WMoo WPer WTin WWin XPep
- 'Baby' — WFar
- 'Betten' — see *E.* x *gayeri* 'Betten'
- 'Bushman Boy' — GBri IBlr
- 'Clarice Howard' — see *E. cyparissias* 'Fens Ruby'
- clone 2 — WCot
§ - 'Fens Ruby' — More than 30 suppliers
- 'Orange Man' — CFwr EBee EChP EDAr EFou EMon EPPr EPfP ERou EWes GBin GBri GEil IBlr LRHS NBPC NBro NHol NSti SPla SWat SWvt WFar
- 'Purpurea' — see *E. cyparissias* 'Fens Ruby'
- 'Red Devil' — CBre IBlr NWit SChu
- 'Tall Boy' — EMon EWes GBri IBlr XPep
dendroides — SIgm SSpi
denticulata — SBla
§ **donii** — EGle EWes IBlr MAvo NWit SDix SVal WPer
- 'Amjilassa' **new** — WGMN
dulcis — CBre CStu ECtt EFou EPar NBro NOak NSti NWit WEas WHen
- 'Chameleon' — More than 30 suppliers
I - 'Nana' — NHol
epithymoides — see *E. polychroma*
esula Baker's form — NWit
Excalibur = — CBro CFwr CMil CTrC EBee EMan
'Froeup'PBR ♀H4 — GBin GBuc LHop LRHS MAvo MBNS MBri MCCP NBir NCGa NSti SHBN SPoG SSpi SVil WFar WSHC WWhi
fragifera — EBee NWit
'Garblesham Enchanter' — EPPr NWit
§ x **gayeri** 'Betten' — EMan GCal
glauca — CFee CFir WCot
'Golden Foam' — see *E. stricta*
griffithii — CHll GKir NBro SSpi SWat WAbb WGer WTel
- 'Dixter' ♀H4 — More than 30 suppliers
- 'Dixter Flame' — CFwr MBri NWit
- 'Fern Cottage' — CElw EBee EFou EHrv EWes GAbr SMHy SMrm SUsu WHal
- 'Fireglow' — More than 30 suppliers
- 'King's Caple' — CFwr NWit WCru
- 'Robert Poland' — MBri
- 'Wickstead' — EBee SMHy WBrE WLun WViv
'Hale Bop' — CFwr
hyberna — CFis GBri IBlr MLLN NMen NWit SChu SWat
jacquemontii — EMan LPio MNrw NChi NWit SBla SIgm
'Jade Dragon' — CSpe EFou MAvo
jolkinii new — GKev
x **keysii** — MBri
lathyris — CArn CBre CRow EBlw EMar MDun MHer NBid NLar NPer SRms WBrk WEas WHer WWye
longifolia hort. — see *E. cornigera*
longifolia D. Don — see *E. donii*
longifolia Lamarck — see *E. mellifera*
margalidiana new — EWes
x **martini** ♀H3 — More than 30 suppliers
- 'Baby Charm' **new** — CPen
- dwarf — CFir GCal WShp
- 'Red Dwarf' — CElw CMil CPlt MSph
§ **mellifera** ♀H3 — More than 30 suppliers
milii ♀H1 — CHal EBak SHFr SVal
- 'Koenigers Aalbäumle' — MBri SHFr
* - 'Variegata' (v) — CHal
- yellow-flowered — CHal ECtt
I 'Mini Martinii' **new** — EBee

myrsinites ♀H4 — More than 30 suppliers
nereidum — EWes NWit
nicaeensis — CDes CFil EBee EMan GCal LHop LPhx NWit SBla SMad SMrm SSpi WPGP XPep
- subsp. **glareosa** — NWit SUsu
oblongata — CFil EBee EMan ERou EWes GBuc IBlr LRHS NWit WCHb
palustris ♀H4 — More than 30 suppliers
- 'Walenburg's Glorie' — CMHG EBee EChP ECha ELan EWTr GBin LRHS NBir MCLN MNrw MRav NWit SMad SWat WCot WCra WLun WRHF
- 'Zauberflöte' — CHrt LPBA SRms WFar
x **paradoxa** — NWit
paralias — NWit WCot WHer XPep
pekinensis — MSal NWit
pilosa 'Major' — see *E. polychroma* 'Major'
pithyusa — CBot CBro CNic CSam CSpe EBee EChP ECha ECtt ELan EMan EPfP LAst MLLN MRav NGdn SChu SHBN SSvw WCom WLun WWeb XPep
§ **polychroma** ♀H4 — More than 30 suppliers
§ - 'Candy' — CBri CSam EBre EChP ECha ECtt EHrv ELan EPfP ERou GBin GCal LRHS MAvo MBro MCCP MDun MTis NHol NSti SBla SPla WCom WCot WFar WHoo WLin WMnd
- 'Emerald Jade' — EBee GBri IBlr NWit WPGP
§ - 'Lacy' (v) — CDoC CFwr CSpe EBee ECtt EGle EHoe EHrv EMan ERou EWes MAvo MCCP MCLN NBir NSti NWit SMad SPla WCAu WCom WCot WHer WHil WLin WSan
- 'Major' ♀H4 — CMHG CPLG ECha GCal LPhx LPio MBri SAga WCom WCot WEas
- 'Midas' — CFee EGle MNrw NLar NWit SMHy SMrm
- 'Orange Flush' — WHoo WTin
- 'Purpurea' — see *E. polychroma* 'Candy'
* - 'Senior' — EBee EMil GBin MCCP WMnd
- 'Sonnengold' — EWes GCal WSHC
- 'Variegata' — see *E. polychroma* 'Lacy'
portlandica — CNic MBri NWit SVen WHer
§ x **pseudovirgata** — EMan IBlr LHop NWit
pugniformis — MBri
pulcherrima — LRHS MBri
'Purple Preference' — EPPr NWit
Redwing = — EBee EBre ECtt ELan EMan ENot
'Charam'PBR ♀H4 — EPfP LPan LRHS MGos MRav NCGa NSti SCoo SHGC SPer SSpi
reflexa — see *E. seguieriana* subsp. *niciciana*
resinifera — EOas
§ **rigida** — CBot CBro CDes CFil EBee EChP EGle EGoo EHrv EMan EPfP EPyc EWes GCal LPhx MLLN NSti SBla SIgm SMrm SPet SSpi WCot WHoo WPGP WSHC
- 'Sardis' — NWit
robbiae — see *E. amygdaloides* var. *robbiae*
sarawschanica — EBee EMan GBin LPhx NWit SMHy WCot
schillingii ♀H4 — More than 30 suppliers
seguieriana — ECha EMan GBin NBir NLar WPer
§ - subsp. **niciciana** — EMan EMon MBro MRav NBir NPPs SBla SMrm SUsu WCra WHoo WPGP
serrata new — XPep
serrulata — see *E. stricta*
sikkimensis ♀H4 — CFee CFwr CMHG CPLG CSam CSpe CWCL EBre ECha EGra GBBs MAvo MBri SBla SIgm SMrm SRms

	WCHb WCom WCru WEas WFar WGMN WLun WWin WWye
soongarica	MSte NWit
spinosa	NWit SIgm SMad XPep
§ *stricta*	EMan EWsh GBri IBlr MCCP WBWf WBrk WTin
stygiana	CBot CFil LEdu LPhx MSte NWit SAga SSpi WCru WSHC
- 'Devil's Honey'	NWit
stygiana x *mellifera*	MAnH SIgm WMul WPGP
* *submammillaris*	MBri
'Variegata' (v)	
terracina	WCot
uralensis	see *E.* x *pseudovirgata*
villosa	GBin NWit
§ *virgata*	EMFP EWes NSti NWit WCHb WCot
x *waldsteinii*	see *E. virgata*
wallichii misapplied	see *E. donii*
wallichii Kohli	see *E. cornigera*
wallichii Hook.f.	CDes CPLG CSam EBee EBre EMan GEil GKir IBlr LRHS MBri NBid NOrc SMrm WAbb WHil WSHC
- 'Lemon and Lime' **new**	MWhi

Euphrasia (Scrophulariaceae)

officinalis **new**	SECG

Euptelea (Eupteleaceae)

franchetii	see *E. pleiosperma*
§ *pleiosperma*	CMCN EPfP IArd NLar SSpi
polyandra	CFil CMCN EPfP IArd NLar WPGP

Eurya (Theaceae)

japonica	CFil WPGP
- 'Variegata' misapplied	see *Cleyera japonica* 'Fortunei'

Euryops (Asteraceae)

abrotanifolius	GGar
§ *acraeus* ♀H4	CBot CHea CMea CPle CSBt ELan EPot GTou LHop LRHS MDun MWat NFor NLAp NMen NWCA SIng WAbe WCom WWin
candollei	CTrC WAbe
§ *chrysanthemoides*	CBcs CHEx CSam EBee ERea GGar MMil MSte SVen
- 'Sonnenschein'	CHal EBee SPet
decumbens	CNic NJOw NMen WLin
evansii	see *E. acraeus*
linearis	GGar
pectinatus ♀H2	CBcs CDoC CHEx CPLG CSLe CSam CTrC CTrG CTri CWCL EBee ERea EShb ESlt GEil GGar MMil MNrw MRav SDry SGar SHBN SMrm SOWG WCFE WHer WWye XPep
tysonii	CPle CStu CTrC GGar SPlb WCot
virgineus	CBcs CHEx CTrC GGar IDee LRav NWCA SVen WGer

Euscaphis (Staphyleaceae)

japonica	CPle NLar

Eustachys (Poaceae)

§ *distichophylla*	EPPr WCot

Eustoma (Gentianaceae)

§ *grandiflorum*	LRHS MBri
russellianum	see *E. grandiflorum*

Eustrephus (Philesiaceae)

latifolius	ECou

Eutaxia (Papilionaceae)

obovata **new**	ECou

Evolvulus (Convolvulaceae)

convolvuloides	ERea
§ *pilosus* 'Blue Daze'	ERea

Ewartia (Asteraceae)

planchonii	EPot ITim

Exacum (Gentianaceae)

affine ♀H1+3	LRHS MBri
- 'Rococo'	MBri

Exochorda (Rosaceae)

alberti	see *E. korolkowii*
giraldii	CFwr CPle
- var. *wilsonii*	CEnd CSam EBee EPfP GEil GKir LHop LRHS MAsh MBNS MBlu NLar SLim SSta SWvt
§ *korolkowii*	WBcn
x *macrantha*	More than 30 suppliers
'The Bride' ♀H4	
racemosa	EHol EPfP ISea LHop MGos NBlu NLar SGar SHBN SPer WDin WHCG
serratifolia	EPfP NLar
- 'Northern Pearls'	CPMA
- 'Snow White'	CPMA EBee MBlu MDun

F

Fabiana (Solanaceae)

imbricata	CAbP EBee EMil EPfP GGar GQui LRHS SBra SLon SPer SPoG
- 'Prostrata'	EPfP GCal LRHS SDry SPer SSpi WAbe WWin
- f. *violacea* ♀H3	CBcs CFee CPLG CSBt CTri EBee EHol EMil EPfP GQui LAst LRHS MBar SPer WKif WPGP WSHC XPep

Fagopyrum (Polygonaceae)

cymosum	see *F. dibotrys*
§ *dibotrys*	EBee ECha ELan EPPr LEdu MGol NSti

Fagus ✿ (Fagaceae)

§ *crenata*	CMCN CMen WDin WNor
- 'Mount Fuji'	SBir
engleriana	CMCN
grandifolia	CMCN LPan
- subsp. *mexicana*	SBir
japonica	CMCN LRHS
lucida	CMCN
orientalis	CMCN CTho ECrN LRHS
sieboldii	see *F. crenata*
sylvatica ♀H4	More than 30 suppliers
§ - 'Albomarginata' (v)	CLnd CMCN
- 'Albovariegata'	see *F. sylvatica* 'Albomarginata'
- 'Ansorgei'	CDul CEnd CLnd CMCN CTho GKir MBlu NLar
- 'Argenteomarmorata'	CDul
N - Atropurpurea Group	More than 30 suppliers
- - 'Swat Magret'	GKir LPan
- 'Aurea Pendula'	CDul CEnd CMCN EPla GKir MBlu SBLw SMad
- 'Bicolor Sartini' **new**	MBlu
- 'Birr Zebra'	CEnd
- 'Black Swan'	CEnd CMCN LPan MBlu SBLw SBir SMad WGor
- 'Bornyensis'	SBir
- 'Cochleata'	CMCN GKir LRHS

- 'Cockleshell' CDul CMCN CTho LRHS
- 'Comptoniifolia' see *F.sylvatica* var. *heterophylla*
  'Comptoniifolia'
- 'Cristata' CMCN MBlu
N - Cuprea Group NWea
§ - 'Dawyck' ♀H4 CBcs CDoC CDul CLnd CMCN
  COtt CSBt CTho EBee ECrN ELan
  EMil ENot EPfP GKir LPan LRHS
  MBar MGos MRav NWea SBLw
  SLim SPer WDin WOrn
- 'Dawyck Gold' ♀H4 More than 30 suppliers
- 'Dawyck Purple' ♀H4 More than 30 suppliers
- 'Fastigiata' misapplied see *F.sylvatica* 'Dawyck'
- 'Felderbach' LRHS MBlu
- 'Franken' (v) MBlu
- 'Frisio' CDul CEnd CMCN
- 'Grandidentata' CMCN LPan LRHS
- 'Greenwood' CDul CMCN MBlu
* - 'Haaren' CMCN GKir
- var. *heterophylla* CLnd CSBt CTho ISea NWea WOrn
- - 'Aspleniifolia' ♀H4 CDoC CDul CEnd CMCN COtt
  EBee ELan EMil ENot EPfP GKir
  IMGH LPan LRHS MAsh MBar MBri
  NPSI SBLw SBir SCoo SPer WDin
  WMou WNor
§ - - 'Comptoniifolia' GKir
- - f. *laciniata* CMCN GKir LRHS MBlu
- 'Horizontalis' CMCN
- f. *latifolia* SBLw
- 'Luteovariegata' (v) CEnd CMCN NLar
- 'Mercedes' CMCN GKir MBlu
- 'Miltonensis' CDul LPan LRHS
N - 'Pendula' ♀H4 CBcs CDoC CDul CEnd CLnd
  CMCN CSBt CTho EBee ECrN
  ELan ENot GKir ISea LPan MBar
  MRav MSwo NWea SBLw SBir SPer
  WDin WHar WMou WOrn WStI
- 'Prince George of Crete' CDul CEnd CMCN CTho LRHS
- 'Purple Fountain' ♀H4 CDoC CEnd CMCN COtt EBee
  ELan EMil GKir LPan LRHS MAsh
  MBar MBlu MBri MGos NBee
  SBLw SKee SLim SPoG WOrn
- Purple-leaved Group see *F.sylvatica* Atropurpurea
  Group
- 'Purpurea Nana' CMCN LRHS
- 'Purpurea Pendula' CDul CEnd CMCN CSBt CTho CTri
  CWib EBee ECrN ELan ENot EPfP
  LPan LRHS MBar MGos MSwo
  MWat NBee NBlu NWea SBLw
  SCoo SKee SLim SPer WDin WFar
  WHar WStI
§ - 'Purpurea Tricolor' (v) CDoC CEnd CMCN ECrN GKir
  LPan LRHS MBar MGos NBea NBee
  NBlu SBir SCoo SHBN SLim SPer
  WDin
- 'Quercifolia' CDul CMCN MBlu
I - 'Quercina' CMCN LRHS
- 'Red Obelisk' see *F.sylvatica* 'Rohan Obelisk'
- 'Riversii' ♀H4 More than 30 suppliers
- 'Rohan Gold' CDul CEnd CLnd CMCN EBee
  GKir LPan LRHS MBlu
- 'Rohan Obelisk' CEnd CMCN EBee ELan IArd LPan
  LRHS MBlu MGos SBir WOrn
I - 'Rohan Pyramidalis' CDul CEnd CMCN LRHS
- 'Rohan Trompenburg' CMCN LRHS MBlu
- 'Rohan Weeping' MBlu
- 'Rohanii' CAbP CBcs CDoC CDul CEnd
  CLnd CMCN COtt CTho CTri EBee
  ECrN ELan EMil EPfP IMGH LRHS
  MAsh NBee SHBN SPer WDin
  WOrn
- 'Roseomarginata' see *F.sylvatica* 'Purpurea Tricolor'
- 'Rotundifolia' CDoC CTho LPan MBlu
- 'Silver Wood' CMCN LRHS

- 'Spaethiana' CMCN LRHS
- 'Striata' CMCN GKir LRHS SBir
- 'Tortuosa Purpurea' CMCN CTho MBlu
- 'Tricolor' (v) CBcs CDul CLnd CSBt CWib EBee
  ELan MAsh SBLw SKee WDin
- 'Tricolor' misapplied see *F.sylvatica* 'Purpurea Tricolor'
- 'Viridivariegata' (v) CMCN
- 'Zlatia' CBcs CDoC CDul CLnd CMCN
  COtt CSBt CTho CWib ELan EPfP
  GKir LPan LRHS MAsh MBar MGos
  MSwo NBee NWea SBLw SBir
  SHBN SKee SPer WDin WOrn WStI

Falkia (Convolvulaceae)
repens CFir WCot

Fallopia (Polygonaceae)
aubertii see *F.baldschuanica*
§ **baldschuanica** More than 30 suppliers
- Summer Sunshine = MCCP
  'Acofal'PBR
x **bohemica** CRow EMon
  'Spectabilis' (v)
§ **japonica** var. **compacta** CRow NLar NPri WBea WFar
  WMoo WShp
- - 'Fuji Snow' see *F.japonica* var. *compacta* 'Milk
  Boy'
- - 'Midas' IBlr
§ - - 'Milk Boy' (v) CRow EMan EWes IBlr ITer SMad
- - 'Variegata' see *F.japonica* var. *compacta* 'Milk
  Boy'
- 'Crimson Beauty' CRow
§ **multiflora** CArn EOHP MSal
- var. **hypoleuca** WCru
  B&SWJ 120
sachalinensis CHEx CRow EWes NLar

Farfugium (Asteraceae)
formosanum WCru
  B&SWJ 7125
§ **japonicum** CHEx EUJe MTho
- B&SWJ 884 WCru
- 'Argenteum' (v) CFir SDnm WCot WFar WHal WSan
- 'Aureomaculatum' CAbb CFir CHEx CKob EBre EChP
  (v) ♀H1 EHoe EMan EPfP MBNS MCCP
  MTho SDnm SMad SPer SWat WFar
  WGMN WHal WHer WHil WMul
  WSan
- 'Crispatum' More than 30 suppliers
- var. **giganteum** CHEx
* - 'Kagami-jishi' (v) WCot
- 'Kinkan' (v) WCot
I - 'Nanum' CHEx
- 'Ryuto' WCot
- 'Tsuwa-ubki' **new** WCot
tussilagineum see *F.japonicum*

Fargesia (Poaceae)
from Jiuzhaigou, China **new** WJun
angustissima CFil EPla
contracta EPla
denudata CFil EPla WJun
- L 1575 MMoz WPGP
dracocephala CAbb CBrm CDoC CFil EBee EPfP
  EPla GBin GCal LEdu MAvo MBrN
  MMoz MWht NBlu NGdn SDry
  SEND SLPl WJun WMul WNor
  WPGP
ferox CFil EPla
frigida EPla WJun
fungosa CFil EPla WJun WPGP
§ **murielae** ♀H4 More than 30 suppliers
- 'Bimbo' CFil CTrC EPfP GBin MFan MWht
  MWod WJun WMul WPGP

	- 'Grüne Hecke'	MWht
	- 'Harewood'	CWSG EBee GBin MAsh MBri MCCP MMoz MWht SWvt WFar
	- 'Jumbo'	More than 30 suppliers
	- 'Kranich'	CFil MBri NLar
§	- 'Leda' (v)	SDry
	- 'Mae'	GBin
	- 'Novecento'	ELan MBri
	- 'Simba' ♀H4	More than 30 suppliers
I	- 'Willow'	EBee MBri MGos
§	**nitida**	More than 30 suppliers
	- 'Anceps'	EPla MWht NPri
	- 'Eisenach'	CAbb CFil EBee EPla LRHS MBri MMoz NGdn WCru WFar
*	- from Jiuzhaigou, China	CFil EPla WPGP
	- Gansu 2 **new**	WPGP
	- 'Nymphenburg' ♀H4	CFil CFwr CPMA EBee EBlw EBre EPla GKir LRHS MBri MMoz MWhi MWht NLar NPri WFar WMoo
	- 'Wakehurst'	EPla MWht NLar
	papyrifera new	WJun
	robusta	CAbb CBrm CEnd CFil EBee EFul EPfP EPla GBin LPal MBrN MBri MMoz MWht NGdn NLar NMoo SDry SLPl WJun WMul WNor
	- 'Pingwu' **new**	NLar
	- 'Red Sheath'	CFil EPla ERod MMoz MWht SEND WJun WPGP
	rufa	CAbb CBrm CFil CMCo EBee ENot EPfP EPla MAvo MBrN MBri MCCP MMoz MWht NLar WJun WNor WPGP
	scabrida new	WJun
	spathacea hort.	see *F. murielae*
	utilis	CAbb CFil EBee EPla ERod LEdu MAvo MMoz MWht NLar SDry SEND WJun WNor WPGP
	yulongshanensis	CFil EPla MWht
	aff. **yulongshanensis new**	WPGP

Farsetia (Brassicaceae)

	clypeata	see *Fibigia clypeata*

Fascicularia (Bromeliaceae)

	andina	see *F. bicolor*
§	**bicolor**	More than 30 suppliers
§	- subsp. **canaliculata**	CFil EOas IBlr LEdu WCot WPGP
	kirchhoffiana	see *F. bicolor* subsp. *canaliculata*
	pitcairniifolia (Verlot) Mez	see *Ochagavia* sp.
	pitcairniifolia misapplied	see *F. bicolor*

x *Fatshedera* (Araliaceae)

	lizei ♀H3	CBcs CBot CDoC CDul CHEx EBee EGra EPfP EPla GKir GQui LRHS MPRe MWat NPal SAPC SArc SBra SDix SDry SLon SMac SPer SPla SPlb SWvt WCFE WDin WFar
§	- 'Annemieke' (v) ♀H3	CFwr CHEx CSWP EPfP SBra SMac SMad SPer SPoG
§	- 'Aurea' (v)	EHoe ELan EPfP LRHS SBra SDry SEND
	- 'Aureopicta'	see x *F. lizei* 'Aurea'
	- 'Lemon and Lime'	see x *F. lizei* 'Annemieke'
	- 'Maculata'	see x *F. lizei* 'Annemieke'
	- 'Pia'	CSWP
*	- 'Silver Prusca'	EPla
	- 'Variegata' (v) ♀H3	CBcs ELan EPfP LAst LRHS MAsh MPRe SBra SDry SEND SMac SMer SPer SPla SWvt WCot WDin WFar

Fatsia (Araliaceae)

§	**japonica** ♀H4	More than 30 suppliers
	- 'Moseri'	CAbP CSam EChP ECtt GBin IBal

		LAst MNrw MSte NGdn NLar SWvt WCot WWhi
	- 'Murakumo-nishiki' (v)	NPal SPer
	- 'Variegata' (v) ♀H3	CBcs CHEx EBee ECrN LRHS MBri MGos NBlu NPal SArc SHBN SPer
	papyrifera	see *Tetrapanax papyrifer*
	polycarpa new	CHEx
	- B&SWJ 7144	WCru

Feijoa see *Acca*

Felicia (Asteraceae)

§	**amelloides**	CHal ERea LRHS MLan SChu SGar SPlb
	- 'Read's Blue'	CHal LIck SDnm SGar SPet XPep
	- 'Read's White'	CHal ERea MOak MSte SDnm SPet
§	- 'Santa Anita' ♀H3	CHal CTri CWCL ECtt ERea LIck MOak WEas
§	- variegated (v)	CHal ECtt ERea IHMH LIck MBNS MBri MOak MSte NBlu NPer NPri SHFr SPet SUsu WEas
	- variegated, white-flowered (v)	LIck
§	**amoena**	CHal CTri MOak SRms
	- 'Variegata' (v)	CTri CWCL SChu
	capensis	see *F. amelloides*
	- 'Variegata'	see *F. amelloides* variegated
	coelestis	see *F. amelloides*
	drakensbergensis	ETow
	erigeroides	CHal
	filifolia	XPep
	- blue	LAst
	natalensis	see *F. rosulata*
	pappei	see *F. amoena*
§	**petiolata**	EBee EMan MOak NSti SGar SSpi WCot WWin
§	**rosulata**	CStu EBre EHyt EMon GCrs GGar GKir MHer MTho NBro NJOw SRms SRot WCom WWin
	uliginosa	EDAr EWes GAbr GEdr GGar GTou IHMH LRHS MTho WOBN

fennel see *Foeniculum vulgare*

fenugreek see *Trigonella foenum-graecum*

Ferraria (Iridaceae)

§	**crispa**	EBee
	undulata	see *F. crispa*

Ferula (Apiaceae)

	from Spain **new**	WPGP
	assa-foetida	CArn EBee LDai MSal WJek
	chiliantha	see *F. communis* subsp. *glauca*
§	**communis**	CArn EBee ECGP ECha EWTr GKir LEdu MFir NBid NDov NLar SDix SDnm SMad SMrm SPlb WCAu WCot WJek WSHC
	- 'Gigantea'	see *F. communis*
§	- subsp. **glauca**	CSpe EBee EMan LPhx SDix SGar SIgm WCot WPGP XPep
	'Giant Bronze'	see *Foeniculum vulgare* 'Giant Bronze'
	tingitana	SIgm SMad
	- 'Cedric Morris'	ECha LPhx SIgm SMHy SMad WCot

Ferulago (Apiaceae)

	sylvatica	EBee

Festuca (Poaceae)

§	**actae**	CBig LEdu MAvo WHrl
	amethystina	CBig CBrm CHrt CKno CWCL EHoe EMon EPot EPza ESis EWsh

	IPot LRHS MBnl MNrw MWhi NBlu NCGa NCiC NGdn NHol NOak SPer WMoo WPer WRos WTin
- 'Aprilgrün'	EHoe EPPr
arundinacea	CRWN EWTr
'Banks Peninsula Blue'	see *F. actae*
californica	CBig EPPr
coxii **new**	WCot
curvula subsp. *crassifolia*	EPla EWsh NHol
'Eisvogel'	EBee
erecta	EHoe
eskia	CKno EBee EHoe EHul EPPr ESis GKir GOrn LRHS MWhi NHol SHel SPer SPla SVil WCot WDyG WPer
filiformis	EHoe EMon
'Fromefield Blue'	CSLe EBee EChP EHul
§ *gautieri*	CBrm EBee GBin GIBF LPVe MBar MBrN NGdn WFoF
- 'Pic Carlit'	EMon
gigantea	CBig EPza GBin
glacialis	EHoe
glauca	More than 30 suppliers
I - 'Auslese'	LPVe MWod NGdn WBar WSSM WWeb
- 'Azurit'	CBig EChP EHoe EMon EPPr EPla EPza EWes EWsh LAst MBnl NHol NLar WPrP
§ - 'Blaufuchs' ♀H4	More than 30 suppliers
§ - 'Blauglut'	CBig EBee EBre EHoe EHul EPGN EPfP EPla EPza GKir GSki LRHS MWgw NHol SHel WCra WGer
- Blue Fox	see *F. glauca* 'Blaufuchs'
- Blue Glow	see *F. glauca* 'Blauglut'
- 'Boulder Blue' **new**	CKno
- 'Elijah Blue'	More than 30 suppliers
- 'Golden Toupee'	More than 30 suppliers
- 'Harz'	CBrm EBee EBre EHoe EHul EMil EPla GKir LBuc MBNS MBar NBea NCGa WPnP
* - *minima*	EPPr IHMH WBcn WPGP
- 'Pallens'	see *F. longifolia*
- Sea Urchin	see *F. glauca* 'Seeigel'
§ - 'Seeigel'	CBig EBre EHoe GKir MBnl MMoz NHol NPro NSti
- 'Seven Seas'	see *F. valesiaca* 'Silbersee'
- 'Silberreiher'	EPPr
- 'Uchte'	CWCL
'Hogar'	EHoe
idahoensis	CBig
§ *longifolia*	EPPr
mairei	EHoe EMon EPPr LRHS SWal WDyG
novae-zelandiae	CPen CTrC CWCL EPPr EWsh NNor
ovina	CBrm EFWa EHoe NGdn WPer
- subsp. *coxii*	EHoe
- var. *duriuscula* **new**	CRWN
paniculata	EGle EHoe EPla GOrn
- subsp. *spadicea* **new**	EPPr
pulchella	CBig
punctoria	EBee EHoe EWsh MRav SIng WMoo
rubra	CBig CRWN
- var. *nankotaizanensis*	WCot
- - B&SWJ 3190	EBee WCru
scoparia	see *F. gautieri*
tatrae	CBrm GBin MSPs WCot
valesiaca	GOrn WFar
- var. *glaucantha*	CBig EWll GWCH MBri NGdn NLar XPep
§ - 'Silbersee'	CBig EBee ECha EHoe EPot ESis EWsh LRHS MBar MBnl MNrw MSte NHol NOak SIng SRms WCom WFar
- Silver Sea	see *F. valesiaca* 'Silbersee'

violacea	EChP EHoe EMan EPPr EPza GFlt MBNS NLar SWal WRos WWpP
vivipara	CNat EGoo EHoe EMon EPPr LEdu NBid NHol WRos WWhi
* 'Willow Green'	CBod MSte SLim SPlb

Fibigia (Brassicaceae)

§ *clypeata*	SGar
- 'Select'	CSpe

Ficus ✿ (Moraceae)

afghanistanica	ERea
australis hort.	see *F. rubiginosa* 'Australis'
benghalensis	MBri WMul
benjamina ♀H1	CHal LRHS MBri SRms
- 'Exotica'	CHal LRHS MBri
- 'Golden King'	LRHS MBri
- 'Starlight' (v) ♀H1	LRHS MBri SMur
capitola 'Long'	ERea
carica (F)	CWSG EGra LPan MBri SArc
- 'Abbey Slip' (F)	CHEx
* - 'Acanthifolia' **new**	XPep
- 'Adam' (F)	ERea
- 'Alma' (F)	ERea
- 'Angélique' (F)	ERea
- 'Beall' (F)	ERea
- 'Bellone' (F)	ERea
- 'Bifère' (F)	ERea
- 'Black Ischia' (F)	ERea
- 'Black Mission' (F)	ERea
- 'Boule d'Or' (F)	ERea
- 'Bourjassotte Grise' (F)	ERea SDea
- 'Brown Turkey' (F) ♀H3	More than 30 suppliers
- 'Brunswick' (F)	CWib EBee ERea GBon GTwe LRHS MCCP MCoo NGHP SLim WCot
- 'Castle Kennedy' (F)	ERea GTwe
- 'Col de Dame Blanc' (F)	ERea
- 'Conandria' (F)	ERea
§ - 'Desert King' (F)	ESim
- 'Figue d'Or' (F)	ERea
- 'Goutte d'Or' (F)	ERea SDea
- 'Grise de Saint Jean' (F)	ERea
- 'Grise Ronde' (F)	ERea
- 'Grosse Grise' (F)	ERea
- 'Kaape Bruin' (F)	ERea
- 'Kadota' (F)	ERea
- 'King'	see *F. carica* 'Desert King'
* - 'Laciniata' (F)	SMad
- 'Lisa' (F)	ERea
- 'Longue d'Août' (F)	ERea
- 'Malcolm's Giant' (F)	ERea
- 'Malta' (F)	ERea GTwe
- 'Marseillaise' (F)	ERea GTwe SDea
- 'Negro Largo' (F)	ERea
- 'Newlyn Harbour' (F)	CHEx
- 'Noir de Provence'	see *F. carica* 'Reculver'
- 'Osborn's Prolific' (F)	ERea SWvt
- 'Panachée' (F)	ERea
- 'Pastilière' (F)	ERea
- 'Peter's Honey' (F)	ERea
- 'Petite Grise' (F)	ERea
- 'Pied de Boeuf' (F)	ERea
- 'Pittaluse' (F)	ERea
- 'Précoce Ronde de Bordeaux' (F)	ERea
- 'Precose de Dalmatie' **new**	ERea
§ - 'Reculver' (F)	ERea
- 'Rouge de Bordeaux' (F)	ERea SDea
- 'Saint Johns' (F)	ERea
- 'San Pedro Miro' (F)	ERea
- 'Snowden' (F)	ERea
- 'Sollies Pont' (F)	ECrN ERea

- 'Sugar 12' (F)	ERea
- 'Sultane' (F)	ERea
- 'Tena' (F)	ERea
- 'Trojano' (F)	ERea
- 'Verte d'Argenteuil' (F)	ERea
- 'Violette Dauphine' (F)	ERea
- 'Violette de Sollies' (F)	ERea
- 'Violette Sepor' (F)	ERea
- 'White Genoa'	see *F. carica* 'White Marseilles'
- 'White Ischia' (F)	ERea
§ - 'White Marseilles' (F)	CWib ECrN EHol EPfP ERea LRHS
	MCoo NGHP SDea SKee
cyathistipula	MBri
deltoidea	MBri
var. ***diversifolia***	
elastica	LRHS SEND
- 'Doescheri' (v) ♀H1	NScw
- 'Robusta'	MBri
foveolata Wallich	see *F. sarmentosa*
lyrata ♀H1	MBri
microcarpa	STre
- 'Hawaii' (v)	CHal
pumila ♀H1	CHEx CHal EBak LRHS MBri SAPC
	SArc XPep
- 'Minima'	CFee
- 'Sonny' (v)	MBri
- 'Variegata' (v)	CHEx CHal MBri
radicans 'Variegata'	see *F. sagittata* 'Variegata'
***religiosa* new**	WMul
§ ***rubiginosa*** 'Australis'	MBri
- 'Variegata' (v) ♀H1	CHal
§ ***sagittata*** 'Variegata' (v)	MBri
§ ***sarmentosa***	MBri

fig see *Ficus carica*

filbert see *Corylus maxima*

Filipendula ✿ (Rosaceae)

alnifolia 'Variegata'	see *F. ulmaria* 'Variegata'
camtschatica	CFir CMCo CRow EBee ELan GIBF
	MTed NBid NLar NMir NPSI NPol
	WFar WMoo WPGP
- 'Rosea'	LHop SMad
digitata 'Nana'	see *F. multijuga*
formosa	WCru
B&SWJ 8707 **new**	
hexapetala	see *F. vulgaris*
'Kahome'	CMCo CRow EBee EBre EChP
	EMan EMon GBuc GGar GKir
	GMac IPot LAst LHop LRHS MBro
	NBir NGdn NLar NMir NOrc NSti
	SMac SPla SVil WCra WFar WHoo
	WMoo WWpP
kiraishiensis	EBee WCru
B&SWJ 1571	
§ ***multijuga***	CRow EBee GCal GGar GSki MBro
	WFar WHoo WMoo
palmata	ECha GCal GSki WFar WMoo
- 'Digitata Nana'	see *F. multijuga*
- dwarf	CLAP GSki
- 'Elegantissima'	see *F. purpurea* 'Elegans'
- 'Nana'	see *F. multijuga*
- ***purpurea***	see *F. purpurea*
- 'Rosea'	ERou IBlr NBir WCHb
- 'Rubra'	CTri GSki MRav NGdn WHHs
	WMyn
- ***rufinervis*** B&SWJ 8611	WCru
- - B&SWJ 941	WCru
§ ***purpurea*** ♀H4	CKno CRow CSBt EBee EPfP EWTr
	GGar GSki LRHS MBri MWrn
	WCru WFar WMoo WShp
- f. ***albiflora***	LPhx MBri NPri WMoo WPnP
	WWye

§ - 'Elegans'	CHVG CHea CRow EBee ECGN
	EChP ECha EMan EMil ERou
	EWsh GCal GGar GMac LAst MSte
	NBid NHol NPSI NSti SSpe SWat
	WBro WFar WLow WMoo WMyn
	WPnP
- 'Nephele' **new**	EBee SMHy
- 'Pink Dreamland'	EPPr LPhx
* - 'Plena' (d)	NLar
- 'White Dreamland' **new**	EBee
'Queen of the Prairies'	see *F. rubra*
§ ***rubra***	CRow GEil LAst NBid NWoo
	WBVN WCra WFar WWpP
§ - 'Venusta' ♀H4	More than 30 suppliers
- 'Venusta Magnifica'	see *F. rubra* 'Venusta'
§ ***ulmaria***	More than 30 suppliers
- 'Aurea'	More than 30 suppliers
- 'Flore Pleno' (d)	CBre CMil CRow EBee GKir GSki
	LAst LRHS NBid NGdn NHol NSti
	SIde SWat WCot WFar WPnP WTin
- 'Rosea'	CDes EBee IBlr WWpP
§ - 'Variegata' (v)	More than 30 suppliers
§ ***vulgaris***	CArn CFee CRWN CTri EBee ECtt
	GBar LAst LPBA MSal MWgw NArg
	NBro NMir NOrc SECG SWat
	WBWf WBea WPer WShp WWpP
	WWye
- 'Alba'	EBee
- 'Flore Pleno' (d)	see *F. vulgaris* 'Multiplex'
- 'Grandiflora'	EPPr WCot
§ - 'Multiplex' (d)	More than 30 suppliers
- 'Plena'	see *F. vulgaris* 'Multiplex'
- 'Rosea'	EBee

Fingerhuthia (Poaceae)
sesleriiformis	CWCL

Firmiana (Sterculiaceae)
simplex	CHEx LPan WMul

Fittonia (Acanthaceae)
albivenis Argyroneura	CHal LRHS
Group ♀H1	
- Verschaffeltii Group ♀H1	CHal
- - 'Pearcei' **new**	CHal

Fitzroya (Cupressaceae)
cupressoides	CDoC CMac CTho IArd IDee LCon
	LRHS MBar SCoo SLim WCwm

Foeniculum (Apiaceae)
vulgare	CAgr CArn CHby CPrp EChP ECha
	ELan ELau EPAt GBar GPoy MBow
	MHer MSal NGHP NPri SIde SPer
	SPlb WBrE WHHs WMoo WPer
	WSel WWye XPep
- 'Bronze'	see *F. vulgare* 'Purpureum'
- var. ***dulce***	CSev SIde
§ - 'Giant Bronze'	ELan GKir LPhx WBrE WHen
§ - 'Purpureum'	More than 30 suppliers
- 'Smokey'	ECha MRav

Fokienia (Cupressaceae)
hodginsii	SMad

Fontanesia (Oleaceae)
phillyreoides	CMCN

Fontinalis (Sphagnaceae)
antipyretica	WFar

Forestiera (Oleaceae)
neomexicana	see *F. pubescens*
§ ***pubescens***	CBcs CFil

Forsythia (*Oleaceae*)

'Arnold Dwarf'	CDul NLar SRms
'Beatrix Farrand' ambig.	CTri CWSG EBee ECtt GKir LRHS MGos MWat NFor NHol NWea SIng SPer SRms WBod WMoo WRHF WTel
§ Boucle d'Or	COtt ENot SLim WWeb
= 'Courtacour'PBR	
'Fiesta' (v)	CWSG EBee EBre ENot EPfP GKir LAst LRHS MAsh MBar MGos MRav MSwo MTis NPro NWea SHBN SLim SPer WCot WDin WFar WWpP
giraldiana	MSwo SLon SRms WBcn
Gold CurlPBR	see *F.* Boucle d'Or = 'Courtacour'
Gold TidePBR	see *F.* Marée d'Or = 'Courtasol'
'Golden Bells'	CDul EMil ENot LRHS
'Golden Nugget'	EBee ELan EPfP LRHS MAsh SLon SMer SPer WCFE
'Golden Times' (v)	EBee EHoe EWes LBuc LRHS MAsh MGos NHol NLar NPro SCoo SWal SWvt WBcn WBod WCot WDin
'Golden Times Allgold'	WBcn
x *intermedia*	MBlu WBod
'Arnold Giant'	
- 'Densiflora'	NWea
- 'Goldzauber'	NWea
- 'Karl Sax'	GEil
- 'Lynwood' ♀H4	More than 30 suppliers
- - LA 79	MLan SPoG
- 'Lynwood' variegated	CWib
- 'Minigold'	ECtt EPfP GEil LRHS MGos MSwo MWat NHol SRms WBVN WRHF WStl WTel
- 'Spectabilis'	CDul EPfP GKir LBuc MAsh MBar NWea SPer WDin WFar WLow WTel
- 'Spectabilis Variegated' (v)	LRHS MBNS NPro WCot
- 'Spring Glory'	EBee ECtt ENot LPan LRHS MHer NWea
- 'Variegata' (v)	GEil NSti NWea SPer
- Week-End	CWSG EBee ENot EPfP LPan MAsh MBri MGos NWea SLim SMer SPlb WDin WFar
= 'Courtalyn'PBR ♀H4	
japonica var. *saxatilis*	GEil
'Josefa'	WBcn
koreana 'Ilgwang' (v)	CPMA
§ Marée d'Or	COtt CWSG ENot LRHS MGos MRav NLar SMer SPer SPoG WDin
= 'Courtasol'PBR ♀H4	
Mêlée d'Or	ENot LRHS SPer
= 'Courtaneur'PBR	
Melissa = 'Courtadic'	NLar NWea
'Northern Gold'	EPfP
ovata 'Tetragold'	CBcs EBee MBar NBee NWea
'Paulina'	NLar
spectabilis 'Yosefa' **new**	ELan MAsh
* 'Spring Beauty'	GEil
suspensa	CBcs CTri CWib EBee ENot EPfP LRHS MBar MSal MWat MVic NWea SHBN SPer WStl WTel
- f. *atrocaulis*	CDul CPle
- 'Decipiens'	WBod
- 'Nymans'	EBee EPfP GEil GKir MBri MRav NSti NWea SLPl WMoo
§ - 'Taff's Arnold' (v)	CFai CPLG CPMA EBee GEdr WBcn WBod WSPU WWpP
- 'Variegata'	see *F.* suspensa 'Taff's Arnold'
'Swingtime' (v) **new**	EGra
'Tremonia'	NFor WGwG
viridissima	NFor NWea
- 'Bronxensis'	EHyt EPot GEdr NBir NLar NWea SMad SRot WAbe
- 'Weber's Bronx'	MBar NLar NWea

x *Fortucitrocirus* (*Rutaceae*)

- citrangequat	MJnS
'Thomasville' **new**	

Fortunella (*Rutaceae*)

x *crassifolia* (F)	SCit
- 'Meiwa' (F) ♀H1	ERea
- 'Fukushu' (F) ♀H1	ERea ESlt SCit
hindsii (F)	SCit
§ *japonica* (F)	SAPC SArc SCit
§ *margarita* (F)	CDoC CWSG LPan MBri SCit SPer
- 'Nagami' (F)	ERea ESlt

Fothergilla (*Hamamelidaceae*)

gardenii	CBcs CPMA ELan EPfP EWTr GKir MBlu MBri NLar SPer SSpi SSta WDin
- 'Blue Mist'	CAbP CDoC CEnd CPMA CWSG ELan EPfP LRHS MBri SLim SPer SPla SReu SSpi SSta WDin WFar WPat
- 'Suzanne' **new**	NLar
major ♀H4	CBcs CBrm CDul CEnd CPMA CWib EBee ELan EPfP EWTr GKir LRHS MBri MGos MLan NBee NBlu SHBN SPoG SReu SSpi WBVN WDin WFar WNor WPat WStl
- Monticola Group	CDoC CPMA CSBt CWSG EBee ELan ENot EPfP IMGH LRHS MBar MBri MDun NCGa NDlv NPal SChu SHBN SLim SPer SSpi SSta SWvt WBrE WFar
'Mount Airy'	CDoC CMCN CPMA EPfP IArd IMGH

Fragaria (*Rosaceae*)

from Taiwan	WHer
alpina	see *F.* vesca 'Semperflorens'
x *ananassa* 'Alice' (F)	CSut EMui NRog
- 'Aromel' (F) ♀H4	CSBt CWSG GTwe LRHS SDea
- 'Auchincruive Climax' (F)	EMui
- 'Bogota' (F)	LRHS
- 'Bolero'PBR (F)	CSBt CSut EMui MBri SKee
- 'Calypso'PBR (F)	CSBt EBre SDea
- 'Cambridge Favourite' (F) ♀H4	CMac CWSG EBre EMui GKir GTwe LRHS MBri NRog SDea SKee
- 'Cambridge Late Pine' (F)	CWSG EMui GTwe LRHS
- 'Cambridge Rival' (F)	LRHS
- 'Cambridge Sentry' (F)	EMui
- 'Cambridge Vigour' (F)	CWSG GKir GTwe LRHS NBee SDea
- 'Challenger' (F)	EMui
- 'Darselect'PBR (F)	CSBt EMui
- 'Elsanta'PBR (F)	CSBt CTri CWSG EBre EMui GKir GTwe IArd LRHS NPri NRog SDea SPer
- 'Elvira'PBR (F)	EMui
* - 'Emily' (F)	EMui GTwe LRHS NPri SPer
- 'Eros'PBR (F)	EMui GTwe NPri SKee
- 'Evita'PBR (F)	EMui
- 'Florence'PBR (F)	EMui GTwe LRHS SKee SPer
- 'Fraise des Bois'	see *F.* vesca
* - 'Franny Karan' (F)	WGor
- 'Gorella' (F)	LRHS
- 'Hapil'PBR (F) ♀H4	CSBt CTri EBre EMui GTwe LRHS NPri NRog
- 'Honeoye' (F) ♀H4	EBre EMui GTwe LRHS MBri SKee
- 'Kimberly'PBR **new**	CSBt
- 'Korona' (F)	CSut EMui
- 'Kouril' (F)	LRHS
- 'Laura' (F)	EMui LRHS

– 'Maraline' (F)	EMui
– Marastil' (F)	EMui
– 'Maxim' (F)	EMui
– 'Pantagruella' (F)	LRHS
– Pegasus'PBR (F) ♀H4	EBre EMui GTwe LRHS NRog
– pink-flowered	CFee
– 'Redgauntlet' (F)	EBre GTwe LRHS NRog
– 'Rhapsody'PBR (F) ♀H4	EMui GTwe LRHS
– 'Rosie'PBR (F)	EMui SDea
– 'Royal Sovereign' (F)	EMui GTwe LRHS
– 'Serenata' (F)	NBur
– 'Sophie'PBR (F)	CSBt EBre LRHS
– 'Symphony'PBR (F) ♀H4	EBre EMui NRog SKee
– 'Talisman' (F)	LRHS
– 'Tamella' (F)	EMui LRHS
– 'Tango' (F)	EMui
– 'Totem' (F)	GTwe
§ – 'Variegata' (v)	CArn CMea CSev EBee EMan
	EMon EPPr EPla EPza LBuc LDai
	LHop LRHS MCCP MHar MRav
	MWgw NHol NSti SPer WBea
	WCom WMoo WRha
– 'Viva Rosa' (F)	EMui MBNS SSte
'Bowles' Double'	see *F. vesca* 'Multiplex'
chiloensis (F)	CAgr EMon LEdu
– 'Chaval'	CHid ECha EGoo EHrv EMon EPPr
	MRav MWgw NWoo WMoo
* – 'Variegata' ambig. (v)	WEas
– 'Variegata' misapplied	see *F. x ananassa* 'Variegata'
indica	see *Duchesnea indica*
'Lipstick'	EBee ENot NLar NPro WRos
nubicola	GPoy
Pink Panda = 'Frel'PBR (F)	CTri EBee EBre EChP ECtt EGra
	ELan EWsh GKir LBuc LEdu LRHS
	NHol NLar SHFr SIng SPer SSto
	WCAu WEas WFar
Red Ruby = 'Samba'PBR	EBee EBre EChP EMan GKir LRHS
	MLwd MRav NGdn NLar SIng
	WCAu WMoo
'Variegata'	see *F. x ananassa* 'Variegata'
§ *vesca* (F)	CAgr CArn CRWN ECoo EPfP
	EWTr GPoy LPVe LRHS MBow
	MGas MHer NBlu NGHP NMir
	NPri SECG SIde SPet SPlb WHHs
	WJek WPer WShi WShp WWye
– 'Alexandra' (F)	CArn CBod CPrp ELau IHMH LPVe
	LRHS MBow NVic SIde WCHb
	WHer
– 'Flore Pleno'	see *F. vesca* 'Multiplex'
– 'Fructu Albo' (F)	CAgr CArn CBgR CBre CRow
	IHMH NLar SSte WMoo WPer
	WWpP
– 'Mara des Bois'PBR (F)	EMui GTwe MBri
– 'Monophylla' (F)	CRow EMon IGor LRHS NHol SIde
	WHer
§ – 'Multiplex' (d)	CNat CRow CSev EMon MInt
	MRav NGHP NHol NLar SMac SSte
	WCHb WHer WHer WWye
§ – 'Muricata'	CPou CRow GAbr IGor ITer LEdu
	WCom WHer WWye
* – 'Pineapple Crush'	WHer
– 'Plymouth Strawberry'	see *F. vesca* 'Muricata'
– 'Rügen' (F)	CHal IGor
§ – 'Semperflorens' (F)	ILis WHer WRHF
* – 'Variegata' ambig. (v)	EHoe EHrv EPar GAbr LAst MBct
	NGHP SMac WFar WHrl WPer WSel
– 'Variegata' misapplied	see *F. x ananassa* 'Variegata'
virginiana	CAgr

Francoa (Saxifragaceae)

appendiculata	CRez EBee EBla EMFP EMan GMac
	LPio SGar SMac SOkh SWal WCAu
	WFar WHer WPic WPnP
– red-flowered **new**	CKno

Ballyrogan strain	IBlr MAvo
'Confetti'	CDes CKno CPLG EBee EPPr LPhx
	LPio MAnH MAvo SWal WCot
	WPGP
'Purple Spike'	see *F. sonchifolia* Rogerson's form
§ *ramosa*	CMCo CPLG CTri EBee EChP EHrv
	EMan GBri GBuc IBlr LRHS MBct
	MLan MNrw MTis MWat MWrn
	NBro SAga SDix SWal WCom
	WCru WFar WMoo
* – 'Alba'	CSpe SIng
sonchifolia	More than 30 suppliers
– 'Alba'	CPlt EBee MDKP SHar SMrm SUsu
– 'Dr Tom Smith'	MAvo WCot
– 'Molly Anderson'	MAvo
§ – Rogerson's form	More than 30 suppliers

Frangula see *Rhamnus*

Frankenia (Frankeniaceae)

laevis	CHal CTri NFla SRms WRHF XPep
thymifolia	CBrm CHal CMHG EBre EPar EPot
	ESis LRHS MBar MHer MWat SPlb
	WFar WPer WTel WTin WWin
	XPep

Franklinia (Theaceae)

alatamaha	CBcs CPMA EPfP LHyd SSpi WBor
	WFar WNor

Fraxinus ✿ (Oleaceae)

americana	CDul CMCN EGFP EPfP SBLw
	SKee WDin
– 'Autumn Purple'	CDul CEnd CTho ECrN EPfP GKir
	LRHS MAsh MBlu SBLw SKee
– 'Rosehill'	CTho
§ *angustifolia*	CMCN CTho EGFP
– 'Elegantissima'	CTho
– var. *lentiscifolia*	CTho
§ – 'Monophylla'	CLnd CTho
§ – subsp. *oxycarpa*	GIBF
– 'Raywood' ♀H4	CBcs CCVT CDoC CDul CEnd
	CLnd CTho CTri CWib ECrN ELan
	ENot EPfP GKir LRHS MAsh MBlu
	MGos MSwo NBee NWea SBLw
	SMad SPer WDin WFar WOrn
* – 'Variegata' (v)	MGos
anomala	GIBF
bungeana	CMCN EGFP
chinensis	CDul CLnd CMCN CTho GIBF
– subsp. *rhyncophylla*	GIBF GKir
elonza	CLnd CTho
excelsior	CBcs CCVT CDoC CDul CLnd
	CRWN CSBt CTri CWib EBee ECrN
	ENot EPfP GKir LBuc LPan MBar
	MGos NBee NWea SBLw SHBN
	SHFr SKee STre WDin WMou
	WOrn WStI
– 'Allgold'	CEnd
– 'Aurea **new**	SBLw
– 'Aurea Pendula'	CDul CEnd CMCN CWib EBee
	ECrN EPfP LRHS MAsh MBlu SBLw
	SKee WGer
– 'Crispa'	NLar SBLw WCom
– f. *diversifolia*	CDul CLnd CTho WMou
– 'Geessink'	ENot
– 'Globosa' **new**	SBLw
– 'Jaspidea' ♀H4	More than 30 suppliers
– 'Nana'	EMon SBLw WPat
– 'Pendula' ♀H4	CCVT CDoC CDul CEnd CLnd
	CTho EBee ECrN ENot EPfP GKir
	LPan LRHS MBlu MBri NBee NWea
	SBLw SHBN SKee SLim SPer WDin
	WMou WOrn WStI

- 'R.E. Davey'	CDul CNat
- variegated (v)	CDul ECrN
- 'Westhof's Glorie' ♀H4	CCVT CDoC CLnd EBee ECrN ENot SBLw WDin WOrn
holotricha	CTho
insularis var. **henryana**	CFil CMCN WPGP
§ **latifolia**	EGFP GIBF
longicuspis	GIBF
mariesii	see *F. sieboldiana*
nigra	CFil CMCN
- 'Fallgold'	CEnd
ornus ♀H4	CCVT CDul CLnd CMCN EBee ECrN ELan ENot EPfP EWTr GKir LRHS MBri MSwo NWea SBLw SPer SSta WDin WFar WMoo WOrn
- 'Arie Peters'	CDul SBLw WStI
- 'Mecsek'	MBri
- 'Obelisk'	MBri
- 'Rotterdam' **new**	SBLw
oxycarpa	see *F. angustifolia* subsp. *oxycarpa*
pennsylvanica	CDul CLnd CMCN GIBF
- 'Aucubifolia' (v)	CTho
- 'Summit'	CTho
- 'Variegata' (v)	CLnd CTho EBee GKir LPan LRHS MAsh MBri SSta
quadrangulata	NWea WDin
§ **sieboldiana**	CDoC CDul CFil CLnd CMCN CPMA EPfP GKir MBlu NLar SSpi WPGP WPat
'Veltheimii'	see *F. angustifolia* 'Monophylla'
velutina	CDul CLnd CTho SLPl

Freesia (Iridaceae)

hybrids	CSut NRog
laxa	see *Anomatheca laxa*
Royal Series	EMui

Fremontodendron (Sterculiaceae)

'California Glory' ♀H3	More than 30 suppliers
californicum	CDul CSBt CTri EBee ELan EMil MBri MLan MWhi NBlu SHBN SLim SOWG SPlb WBod WCFE WDin WNor WStI
'Ken Taylor'	LRHS
mexicanum	XPep
'Pacific Sunset'	CPMA EBee EBre ENot EPfP LHop LRHS MGos MRav SBra SMur SPer
'Tequila Sunrise'	CPMA EBee EBre ENot MGos MRav NLar

Freylinia (Scrophulariaceae)

tropica	GFai

Fritillaria ✿ (Liliaceae)

acmopetala ♀H4	CAvo CBro CPom EHyt EPar EPot ERos GBuc GCrs GEdr GIBF ITim LAma LPhx LRHS MS&S MSte MTho NMen NRog SSpi WCot WCra WLin WSel
- subsp. **wendelboi**	EPot LAma LPhx WCot WDav
§ **affinis**	GCrs GKir LAma MS&S NMen SBla SSpi
§ - var. **gracilis**	LAma
- 'Sunray'	GCrs SSpi
§ - var. **tristulis**	ERos NMen
- 'Vancouver Island'	ECho EPot
* **albidiflora**	LAma
alburyana	EPot
arabica	see *F. persica*
assyriaca **new**	EPot NBPC NJOw
aurea	EPot GCrs MS&S NMen
- 'Golden Flag'	EPfP GEdr LTwo NMen WDav WWst

biflora	GCrs GIBF WCot
- 'Martha Roderick'	CBro GEdr LAma MS&S SBla WWst
§ **bithynica**	CBro EHyt GEdr ITim LAma MS&S SCnR WCot
bucharica	EHyt NMen
- 'Nurek Giant'	WWst
camschatcensis	CAvo CBro ECha EFEx EPar EPfP EPot GBBs GCrs GEdr GFlt GKir LAma LPhx MS&S MTho NBir NDov NMen NRog SSpi WAbe WCru WDav WHil WLin
- from Alaska	GCrs
I - **alpina aurea**	GCrs
- 'Aurea'	GBuc GKir NMen SSpi
- black	GBuc GKir SOkh
- f. **flavescens**	EFEx GEdr LAma
- green	WWst
I - **multiflora** (d)	CFir
carduchorum	see *F. minuta*
carica	EHyt EPot MS&S NMen
- brown-flowered	EPot
caucasica	EHyt LAma NMen
cirrhosa	EPot GKir WWst
- brown-flowered	GEdr GKir NMen
- green-flowered	GEdr GKir NMen
citrina	see *F. bithynica*
conica	EHyt EPot GCrs NMen WCot
crassifolia	GIBF LAma MS&S WCot
- subsp. **crassifolia**	CGra EHyt
§ - subsp. **kurdica**	CAvo EHyt EPot GCrs GEdr NMen SSpi WCot WLin
dagana	WWst
davisii	EHyt EPot GEdr GKev LAma LPhx NMen SSpi WCot WDav
delphinensis	see *F. tubiformis*
drenovskii	WCot
eduardii	WWst
ehrhartii	EPot SBla
elwesii	EHyt EPot GCrs GEdr NMen WCot
ferganensis	see *F. walujewii*
fleischeriana	WWst
fusca new	EBee
glauca	LAma MS&S NMen
* - 'Golden Flag'	NMen
- 'Goldilocks'	EPot LRHS NMen WDav
graeca	CAvo CBro EPot GBuc GCrs GEdr MTho NMen WCot WDav WLin
- subsp. **graeca**	EHyt
- subsp. **ionica**	see *F. thessala*
§ **grayana**	MS&S NMen
- tall	WCot
gussichiae	EHyt EPot GCrs MS&S NMen WWst
hermonis from Jebel esh Sharqui Mtns, Lebanon	WWst
- subsp. **amana**	CBro EHyt EPot GCrs GEdr ITim LAma LTwo NMen WCot WLin
- - 'Cambridge' ♀H4	WCot
- - yellow-flowered **new**	EPot
hispanica	see *F. lusitanica*
hupehensis	LAma
imperialis	ECGP GIBF MBri NRog
- 'Argenteovariegata' (v)	EBee LAma
- 'Aureomarginata' (v)	EBee EPar LAma LRHS MBri NRog
- 'Aurora'	EPar EPot GBBs LAma LRHS MBNS MWat NBPC NGHP NPer NRog WFar WPnP
- 'Crown upon Crown'	see *F. imperialis* 'Prolifera'
- 'Lutea'	CAvo CMea ELan EPfP LRHS MSte NBPC NFor WPnP
- 'Lutea Maxima'	see *F. imperialis* 'Maxima Lutea'
- 'Maxima'	see *F. imperialis* 'Rubra Maxima'
§ - 'Maxima Lutea' ♀H4	CBro EBee EMon EPar EPfP EPot LAma LRHS NRog

	– 'Orange Brilliant' **new**	EBee MSte
§	– 'Prolifera'	EPar LAma LRHS
	– 'Rubra'	CAvo EBee EMon EPar GBBs LAma NBPC NBir NRog WFar
§	– 'Rubra Maxima'	CBro CMea EPfP EPot LAma LRHS MSte
	– 'Slagzwaard'	EBee
	– 'Sulpherino'	EBee EMon LAma LRHS
	– 'The Premier'	EBee EPar EPot LAma LRHS
	– 'William Rex'	CMea EPot LAma
	involucrata	EHyt GKir LAma MS&S WCot
	ionica	see *F. thessala*
	japonica	EFEx
	var. **koidzumiana**	
	karadaghensis	see *F. crassifolia* subsp. *kurdica*
I	*karelinii*	WWst
	kotschyana	EPot GCrs NMen WCot WWst
	lanceolata	see *F. affinis* var. *tristulis*
	latakiensis	WWst
§	*latifolia*	GEdr LAma
	– var. **nobilis**	see *F. latifolia*
§	*lusitanica*	LAma MS&S NMen SBla
	meleagris	More than 30 suppliers
	– 'Aphrodite'	EPot GBuc NBir
	– var. **unicolor**	CAvo CBro CBro CFwr EPot GBri
	subvar. **alba** ♀H4	GBuc GFlt LAma LRHS MBri MBro MS&S NLAp NRya WLin WPnP WShi
§	*messanensis*	EHyt GCrs LAma MS&S SBla WCot WLin
	– subsp. **gracilis**	EHyt GCrs MS&S WLin WWst
	– subsp. **messanensis**	CBro
	michailovskyi ♀H2	More than 30 suppliers
§	*minuta*	EPot GCrs MS&S NMen
	montana	EHyt GEdr NMen
	nigra hort.	see *F. pyrenaica*
	obliqua	WCot
§	*olivieri*	GCrs
§	*orientalis*	WWst
§	*pallidiflora* ♀H4	CBro CLAP CMea CPom EBee EHyt EPar EPot ERos GEdr GFlt GIBF LAma LPhx MLLN MS&S MSte MTho NBir NMen NSla SSpi WCom WCot WCru WLin WPnP
§	*persica*	CBri EBee EBlw ECtt EHrv EMar EPar EPfP EPot GBBs GFlt GIBF LAma LPhx LRHS MBow MBri MLan MWgw NBPC NJOw NMen SGar WCra WSel
	– 'Adiyaman' ♀H4	CAvo CBro EBee ELan EMon LPhx NRog WDav
	phaeanthera	see *F. affinis* var. *gracilis*
	pinardii	EHyt EPot GCrs NMen WWst
	pontica	CAvo CBri CBro CFwr CLAP EHyt EPar EPot ERos GAbr GBuc GCrs GEdr GFlt GKir ITim LAma LPhx MLLN MS&S MTho NMen NSla SBla SSpi WCot WCru WLin
	– Prasil form	WWst
	przewalskii **new**	EPot
	pudica	GCrs GEdr GKir LAma MS&S MTho NMen SCnR WLin
*	– 'Fragrant'	EPot GCrs NMen
	– 'Giant' **new**	EPot
	– 'Richard Britten'	EHyt GCrs NMen
	puqiensis	LAma
	purdyi	GEdr GKir MS&S WDav
§	*pyrenaica* ♀H4	CBro CLAP CMea CNic EHyt EPot ERos ETow GCrs GEdr GFlt LAma MS&S NGar NMen NSla SBla SChu SSpi WCom WCot WCru WDav WTin WWst
	– 'Cedric Morris'	LPhx
	raddeana	EPot LAma

	recurva	GIBF
	– NNS 00-384	WCot
	– *coccinea*	SSpi
	– 'Sensational'	LAma
	rhodocanakis	NMen WWst
	subsp. **argolica**	
	roderickii	see *F. grayana*
	roylei	MS&S
	rubra major	see *F. imperialis* 'Rubra Maxima'
	ruthenica	ERos MS&S NMen SBla
	sewerzowii	GCrs WLin WWst
	sibthorpiana	CBro EHyt NMen
	sphaciotica	see *F. messanensis*
	stenanthera	CBro EPot LAma NMen WCot
	stribrnyi	WWst
	tachengensis	see *F. yuminensis*
	taipaiensis **new**	EBee
	tenella	see *F. orientalis*
§	*thessala*	EHyt GBuc MS&S MTho NMen WCot WDav WLin
	– SBEL 443	WCot
	thunbergii	EHyt EPar GCrs GEdr LPhx NMen WDav WWst
	tortifolia	LAma
§	*tubiformis*	GCrs GEdr GKir NMen WLin
	tuntasia	NMen
	usuriensis	LAma WWst
§	*uva-vulpis*	More than 30 suppliers
	verticillata	CBro CMea ECha EHrv EPar EPot GCrs GEdr LAma MS&S MTho NGHP NMen WCot WCru
§	*walujewii*	EPot LAma WWst
§	*whittallii*	EPot GCrs MS&S NMen
§	*yuminensis*	LAma
	– var. **roseoflora** **new**	EPot

Fuchsia ✿ (*Onagraceae*)

'A.M. Larwick'	CSil EBak EKMF
'A.W. Taylor'	EBak
'Aalt Groothuis'	WP&B
'Aat van Wijk' (d)	WP&B
'Abbé Farges' (d)	CDoC CLoc CSil CWVF EBak ECtt EKMF EPts MWhe NDlv SLBF SPet SWal WFFs
'Abbey Hill'	MWar
'Abigail'	CWVF EKMF MJac WFFs WP&B
'Abundance'	CSil
'Acclamation' (d)	WP&B
'Achievement' ♀H4	CDoC CLoc CSil EKMF LCla MJac NDlv SPet
'Ada Perry' (d)	ECtt
'Adagio' (d)	CLoc
'Ada's Love'	EKMF
'Adinda'	CDoC LCla MWar SLBF WP&B
'Admiration'	CSil EKMF
'Adrienne' **new**	GLbr LAst MJac SVil
'Ahehee' (d) **new**	WP&B
'Ailsa Garnett'	EBak
'Aintree'	CWVF
'Airedale'	CWVF MJac WP&B
'Alabama Improved'	WP&B
'Aladna's Sanders'	CWVF WP&B
'Alan Ayckbourn'	CWVF WP&B
'Alan Titchmarsh' (d)	CDoC EKMF EPts LCla MWar SLBF
'Alaska' (d)	CLoc EBak EKMF WGwG WP&B
'Albertus Schwab'	LCla WP&B
'Alde'	CSil CWVF
'Alderford' **new**	WP&B
'Alf Thornley' (d)	CWVF MWhe
'Alfred Rambaud' (d)	CDoC CSil
'Algerine'	SLBF
'Ali' (d) **new**	EKMF
'Alice Ashton' (d)	EBak EKMF
'Alice Blue Gown' (d) **new**	CWVF

'Alice Doran' CDoC EKMF LCla SLBF WP&B
'Alice Hoffman' (d) ♀H3-4 CDoC CLoc COkL COlW CSBt CSil
CWVF EBak EKMF EPts LAst LRHS
LVER MAsh MBar MGos MJac
MWat MWhe SIng SMac SPer SPet
SPla SSea SWal WFFs WGwG
WWeb
'Alice Mary' (d) EBak EMan
'Alice Stringer' ECtt
'Alice Sweetapple' CWVF
'Alice Travis' (d) EBak
'Alipat' **new** EBak
'Alipatti' EKMF
'Alison Ewart' CLoc CWVF EBak MJac MWhe
SPet
'Alison Patricia' ♀H3 CWVF EBak EKMF EMan LAst LCla
MJac MWar MWhe SLBF WFFs
WP&B
'Alison Reynolds' (d) CWVF LCla
'Alison Ruth Griffin' (d) MJac
'Alison Ryle' (d) EBak
'Alison Sweetman' ♀H1+3 CSil CWVF EKMF MJac MWhe
'Alison Woods' (d) MWar
'Allure' (d) CWVF EPts
'Alma Hulscher' CWVF
'Aloha' **new** SLBF
§ *alpestris* CDoC CSil EBak EKMF LCla
WGwG
'Alton Water' (d/v) MWar
'Alwin' (d) CSil CWVF GLbr MWhe
'Alyce Larson' (d) CWVF EBak MJac WGwG
'Amanda Bridgland' (d) EKMF
'Amanda Jones' EKMF MWhe
'Amazing Maisie' (d) MWar SLBF WP&B
'Ambassador' CWVF EBak SPet
'Ambriorix' **new** WP&B
'Amelie Aubin' CLoc CWVF EBak EKMF
'America' **new** CWVF EBak
'American Flaming WP&B
    Glory' (d)
'Amethyst Fire' (d) CSil
'Amigo' EBak
§ *ampliata* EKMF LCla
'Amy Lou' MWar SLBF WFFs
'Amy Lye' CLoc CSil EBak EKMF WGwG
'Amy Ruth' **new** CWVF
§ 'Andenken an CDoC CLoc CWVF EBak ECtt
    Heinrich Henkel' EKMF MOak MWhe
'André Le Nostre' (d) CWVF EBak
'Andreas Schwab' LCla
andrei CDoC EKMF LCla WP&B
'Andrew' EBak EKMF
'Andrew Carnegie' (d) CLoc
'Andrew George' MJac
'Andrew Hadfield' CWVF EKMF MWar SLBF WFFs
I 'Andromeda' De Groot CSil
'Andy Jordens' WP&B
'Angela Leslie' (d) CLoc CWVF EBak EKMF
'Angela Rippon' CWVF MJac
'Angel's Flight' (d) EBak
'Anita' (d) CLoc CSil CWVF EKMF EPts LAst
MJac MWar MWhe SLBF WFFs
WGor WP&B
'Anjo' (v) CWVF SSea
'Ann Adams' (d) MJac
'Ann Howard Tripp' CLoc CWVF MBri MJac MWhe
WP&B
'Ann Lee' (d) EBak
'Anna of Longleat' (d) CWVF EBak EMan MJac SPet
WP&B
'Anna Pauline' (d) WP&B
'Annabel' (d) ♀H3 CDoC CLoc CSil CTri CWVF EBak
EKMF EMan EPts GLbr LAst LCla
LVER MBri MJac MWar MWhe

SLBF SPet SSea WFFs WGwG
WP&B
'Annabelle Stubbs' (d) LAst
'Anneke de Keijzer' LCla WP&B
'Annie Earle' EKMF
'Anniek Geerlings' WP&B
'Anthea Day' (d) CLoc
'Anthony Heavens' SLBF WFFs WP&B
'Antigone' CDoC SLBF WP&B
'Anton Schreuder' (d) WP&B
'Aphrodite' (d) CLoc CWVF EBak
'Applause' (d) CLoc CWVF EBak ECtt EKMF EPts
LCla LVER SPet
'Apple Blossom' EKMF WP&B
aprica hort. see *F.* x *bacillaris*
aprica Lundell see *F. microphylla* subsp. *aprica*
'Aquarius' MWhe
'Aquillette' **new** WP&B
'Arabella' CWVF MWhe
'Arabella Improved' CWVF
arborea see *F. arborescens*
§ *arborescens* CDoC CLoc CSil CWVF EBak
EKMF EPts ERea EShb LCla LRHS
SHFr SYvo WGwG WP&B
 - f. *parva* IFro
'Arcadia Gold' (d) CWVF ECtt MWhe WGwG
'Arcadia Lady' MJac
'Arcady' CLoc CWVF
'Arend Moerman' (d) WP&B
'Arendsnestje' WP&B
'Ariel' CDoC CSil WCom
'Arlendon' CWVF
'Army Nurse' (d) ♀H4 CDoC CLoc CSil CWVF EKMF
LVER MWhe NBir NDlv SLBF SPet
SWal WFFs WWpP
'Art Deco' (d) WP&B
'Arthur Baxter' **new** EBak
'Ashley' CDoC LCla
'Ashley and Isobel' CWVF WP&B
'Ashtede' LCla SLBF
'Athela' EBak
'Ati' **new** WP&B
'Atlantic Star' CWVF EKMF MJac WGwG
'Atlantis' (d) CWVF MJac
'Atomic Glow' (d) EBak
'Aubergine' see *F.* 'Gerharda's Aubergine'
'Audrey Hepburn' CWVF EKMF
'Audrey Lamotte' WP&B
'August Cools' WP&B
'Augustin Thierry' (d) MWhe
'Aunt Juliana' (d) EBak
'Auntie Bertha' (d) EPts
'Auntie Jinks' CDoC CSil CWVF EBak ECtt LAst
LCla MJac MWar MWhe SPet WFFs
WGwG
'Aurora Superba' CLoc CSil CWVF EBak EKMF
'Australia Fair' (d) CWVF EBak
§ *austromontana* EBak
'Autumnale' ♀H1+3 CDoC CLoc CWVF EBak ECtt
EKMF EMan EPts LAst LCla LRHS
LVER MWhe NBlu NVic SLBF
SMrm SPet SPoG SSea
'Avalanche' (d) CLoc CSil EBak EKMF SLBF SWal
WP&B
'Avocet' CLoc EBak
'Avon Celebration' (d) CLoc
'Avon Gem' CLoc CSil
'Avon Glow' CLoc
'Avon Gold' CLoc
ayavacensis EKMF LCla
'Azure Sky' (d) EKMF MJac
'Babette' (d) EKMF
'Baby Blue Eyes' CDoC CSil CWVF EKMF SLBF WFFs

'Baby Bright' — CDoC CWVF EPts LCla SLBF WFFs WP&B
'Baby Chang' — CSil LCla MWhe
'Baby Girl' — EKMF
'Baby Pink' (d) — CWVF
'Baby Thumb' (d) — CSil EPts
§ x **bacillaris** — CAbb CDoC CDul EBak EWes ITim MBlu SLBF SRms
§ – 'Cottinghamii' — CDoC CSil EKMF IDee WGwG WSHC
– 'Oosje' — see *F.* 'Oosje'
§ – 'Reflexa' — CAbP CTrC GQui WGMN WPat
'Bagworthy Water' — CLoc
'Baker's Tri' — EBak
'Bali Hi' — WP&B
'Balkon' **new** — CWVF
'Balkonkönigin' — CLoc EBak ECtt
'Ballerina' — CDoC
'Ballerina Blue' **new** — LAst
'Ballet Girl' (d) ♀H1+3 — CLoc CSil CWVF EBak ECtt EKMF GLbr LCla SLBF SPet
'Bambini' — CWVF EPts WGwG
'Banks Peninsula' — GQui
'Barbara' — CLoc CSil CWVF EBak EKMF EPts MJac MWar MWhe SPet WEas WP&B
'Barbara Evans' — MWar
'Barbara Pountain' (d) — CWVF LVER
'Barbara Windsor' — CWVF EPts LAst MJac WP&B
'Barbara's Gem' (d) — SLBF
'Baron de Ketteler' (d) — CSil EKMF
'Barry M. Cox' — CSil WP&B
'Barry's Queen' — CSil EBak EKMF SPet
'Bashful' (d) — CDoC CSil EPts LCla LRHS NDlv SPet
'Beacon' — CDoC CLoc CSil CWVF EBak EKMF EMan EPts LAst LCla MBri MJac MWhe NDlv SPet SSea SWal WFFs WStl WTel WWeb
'Beacon Rosa' — CDoC CLoc CSil CWVF EKMF EMan EPts LCla MBri MJac MWar MWhe NDlv SLBF SPet SWal WP&B
'Beacon Superior' — CSil
'Bealings' (d) — CDoC CLoc CWVF ECtt EMan GLbr MBri WFFs
'Beatrice Burtoft' — EKMF
'Beau Nash' — CLoc
'Beautiful Bobbie' (d) — SLBF
'Beauty of Bath' (d) — CLoc EBak
'Beauty of Clyffe Hall' — CSil EBak EKMF
'Beauty of Exeter' (d) — COtt CWVF EBak EKMF
'Beauty of Prussia' (d) — CDoC CLoc CSil CWVF ECtt
'Beauty of Swanley' — EBak
'Beauty of Trowbridge' — CDoC CWVF LCla
'Becky' — LCla WP&B
'Becky Jane' — CSil
'Bel Cinette' **new** — WP&B
'Belijn' — WP&B
'Belinda Jane' — WP&B
'Bella Forbes' (d) ♀H1+3 — CLoc CSil EBak EKMF
'Bella Rosella' (d) — CSil CWVF ECtt EKMF EPts GLbr LAst MJac SCoo SLBF
'Belsay Beauty' (d) — CWVF MJac
'Belvoir Beauty' (d) — CLoc
'Belvoir Lakes' — ECtt
'Ben de Jong' — LCla MJac
'Ben Jammin' — CDoC CLoc CSil CWVF EPts LAst LCla MJac MWar WFFs WGor WP&B
'Béranger' ambig. — WP&B
I 'Béranger' Lemoine 1897 (d) — CSil EBak EKMF
'Berba's Coronation' (d) — EKMF WP&B
'Berba's Happiness' (d) — CWVF
'Berba's Inge Mariel' (d) — ECtt
'Berba's Trio' — WP&B
'Bergnimf' — WGwG
'Berliner Kind' (d) — CSil CWVF EBak EKMF
'Bermuda' (d) — CSil CWVF
'Bernadette' — CWVF
'Bernie's Big-un' (d) — MJac
'Bernisser Hardy' — CDoC CSil EKMF EPts LCla WFFs
'Bert de Jong' — WP&B
'Bertha Gadsby' — EKMF
'Beryl Shaffery' — WP&B
'Bessie Kimberley' **new** — LCla
'Beth Robley' (d) — CWVF
'Betsy Ross' (d) — EBak
'Betty Jean' (d) — MWar WP&B
'Betty' (Shadowdancer Series) **new** — LAst
'Betzi' — SLBF
'Beverley' — CSil CWVF EBak EKMF EPts SPet WFFs
'Bewitched' (d) — EBak
'Bianca' (d) — CWVF WP&B
'Bicentennial' (d) — CDoC CLoc CSil CWVF EBak EKMF EPts LAst LCla LVER MJac MWar MWhe SPet SSea WP&B
'Big Slim' — WP&B
'Billy Green' ♀H1+3 — CDoC CLoc CWVF EBak ECtt EPts LCla LRHS MJac MWar MWhe SLBF SPet SWal WFFs
'Bishop's Bells' (d) — CWVF
'Bittersweet' (d) — CDoC ECtt
'Black Beauty' (d) — CSil CWVF
'Black Prince' — CDoC CSil CWVF MWar
'Blackmore Vale' (d) — CWVF
I 'Blanche Regina' (d) — CWVF MJac MWhe
'Bland's New Striped' — EBak EKMF EPts SLBF
'Blauer Engel' — WP&B
'Blaze Away' (d) — MBri MJac MWar
'Blood Donor' (d) — EKMF MJac
'Blowick' — CDoC CWVF EMan MBri MJac MWhe SPet WFFs
'Blue Beauty' (d) — CSil EBak EKMF
'Blue Bush' — CSil CWVF EKMF MJac NDlv
'Blue Butterfly' (d) — CWVF EBak
'Blue Eyes' (d) — CDoC GLbr
'Blue Gown' (d) — CDoC CLoc CSil CWVF EBak EKMF LRHS LVER MWhe NDlv SPet SWal WGwG WP&B
'Blue Halo' (d) — WP&B
'Blue Hawaii' **new** — WP&B
'Blue Ice' — CSil MWhe
'Blue Jacket' **new** — WP&B
'Blue Lace' (d) — CSil
'Blue Lagoon' ambig. (d) — CWVF
'Blue Lake' (d) — CSil CWVF ECtt LVER
'Blue Mink' — EBak
'Blue Mirage' (d) — CWVF EKMF GLbr MJac WGwG WP&B
'Blue Mist' (d) — EBak
'Blue Pearl' (d) — CWVF EBak
'Blue Petticoat' (d) — CLoc
'Blue Pinwheel' — EBak
'Blue Satin' (d) — COtt MWhe
'Blue Tit' — CSil
'Blue Veil' (d) — CLoc CSil CWVF EKMF LVER MJac MWar SCoo SLBF
'Blue Waves' (d) — CDoC CLoc CSBt CSil CWVF EBak MJac MWar MWhe SPet WGwG
'Blush o' Dawn' (d) — CLoc CWVF EBak EKMF EPts LVER SPet WGwG WP&B
'Blythe' (d) — EPts SLBF
'Bob Pacey' — CWVF
'Bobby Boy' (d) — EBak

'Bobby Dazzler' (d)   CWVF ECtt EKMF
'Bobby Shaftoe' (d)   EBak MWhe
'Bobby Wingrove'   EBak
'Bobby's Girl'   EPts
'Bobolink' (d)   EBak
'Bob's Best' (d)   CWVF EPts LVER MJac
'Boerhaave'   EBak
'Boke' **new**   WP&B
boliviana Britton   see *F. sanctae-rosae*
§ *boliviana* Carrière   CAbb CDoC CHEx CLoc CSil CWVF EBak EKMF LCla MOak SHFr SYvo
§ – var. *alba* ♀H1+3   CDoC CLoc CSil EBak EKMF EPts LCla MOak
  – var. *boliviana*   LRHS WGwG
  – var. *luxurians*   see *F. boliviana* Carrière var. *alba*
  – f. *puberulenta*   see *F. boliviana* Carrière
'Boliviana Tipica' **new**   WP&B
'Bon Accorde'   CLoc CSil CWVF EBak EKMF EPts MJac SSea
'Bon Bon' (d)   CWVF EBak
'Bonita' (d)   CWVF MJac WP&B
'Bonnie Lass' (d)   EBak
'Bonny' (d)   CLoc
'Bora Bora' (d)   CWVF EBak EKMF WP&B
'Borde Hill'   EPts SLBF
'Border Princess'   EBak
'Border Queen' ♀H3-4   CBgR CDoC CLoc CSil CWVF EBak EKMF EMan EPts LCla MBNS MJac MWar SPet WFFs WP&B WSpi
'Border Raider'   MWar SLBF WP&B
'Border Reiver'   EBak
'Börnemann's Beste'   see *F. 'Georg Börnemann'*
'Bouffant'   CLoc
I 'Bountiful' Munkner (d)   CLoc CWVF EKMF MWhe SPet
'Bountiful' ambig. **new**   WP&B
'Bouquet' (d)   CSil EKMF LCla
'Bow Bells'   CDoC CLoc CWVF MJac MWhe SPet
'Boy Marc'   LCla WP&B
'Braamt's Glorie'   WP&B
bracelinae   EKMF
'Brandt's Five Hundred Club'   CDoC CLoc EBak SPet
'Brechtje'   WP&B
'Breckland'   EBak
'Breeders' Delight'   CSil CWVF MBri
'Breeder's Dream' (d)   EBak WP&B
'Breevis Blauwtje'   WP&B
I 'Breevis Iris' **new**   WP&B
I 'Breevis Jordani'   WP&B
'Breevis Karna'   WP&B
I 'Breevis Lowi'   WP&B
'Brenda' (d)   CLoc CSil CWVF EBak
'Brenda Pritchard' (d)   ECtt LVER
'Brenda White'   CDoC CLoc CWVF EBak EPts
'Brentwood' (d)   EBak
brevilobis   CSil EKMF WP&B
'Brian A. McDonald' (d)   CWVF
'Brian C. Morrison'   LCla WP&B
'Brian G. Soanes'   EBak
'Brian Hilton'   MWar
'Brian Kimberley'   LCla MWar
'Bridal Veil' (d)   EBak
'Bridesmaid' (d)   CWVF EBak SPet
'Brigadoon' (d)   CLoc EBak
'Brightling'   WP&B
'Brighton Belle'   CDoC CSil CWVF EWll WGwG
I 'Brilliant' Bull   CDoC CLoc CSil EBak EKMF LCla MGos MWhe SWal
'Brilliant' ambig.   CWVF NDlv
'Briony Caunt'   CSil EKMF
'British Jubilee' (d)   CDoC CWVF EKMF
'Brixham Orpheus' **new**   CWVF

'Brodsworth'   CSil EKMF NDlv
'Bronze Banks Peninsula'   CSil EKMF
'Brookwood Belle' (d)   CWVF EPts LCla MJac SLBF WFFs
'Brookwood Dale'   MWhe
'Brookwood Joy' (d)   CWVF MJac
'Brookwood Lady'   MWhe
'Brutus' ♀H4   CDoC CLoc CSil CWVF EBak EKMF EMan EPts LAst LCla LRHS MWat MWhe NDlv SPet SWal WBod WGwG WP&B WStI
'Bryan Breary'   LCla SLBF
'Buddha' (d)   EBak
'Bugle Boy'   EPts LCla MWar SLBF
'Bunny' (d)   CWVF EBak SLBF
'Burnt Hill' **new**   SLBF
'Burton Brew'   MJac
'Buster' (d) **new**   EKMF LCla SLBF WP&B
I 'Buttercup'   CLoc CWVF EBak
'C.J. Howlett'   CSil EBak EKMF
'Caballero' (d)   EBak
'Caesar' (d)   CWVF EBak
'Caitlin Isabelle'   WP&B
'Caledonia'   CSil EBak EKMF
'California'   WP&B
'Callaly Pink'   CWVF
'Cambridge Louie'   CSil CWVF EBak MBri MWar MWhe SPet WFFs
'Cameron Ryle'   WP&B
campii   EKMF LCla
campos-portoi   CDoC CSil EKMF LCla
'Cancun' (d)   MJac
'Candlelight' (d)   CLoc EBak
'Candy Bells' (d)   SCoo
'Candy Stripe'   CLoc
canescens Munz   see *F. ampliata*
'Cannenburch Floriant'   WP&B
'Canny Bob'   MJac
'Canopy' (d)   CWVF WP&B
'Capri' (d)   CSil CWVF EBak
'Caprice' **new**   WP&B
'Cara Mia' (d)   CLoc CSil CWVF SPet
'Caradela'   CLoc EKMF MJac
'Cardinal'   CLoc EKMF
'Cardinal Farges' (d)   CLoc CSil CWVF EKMF SLBF SPet SSea WFFs WP&B
'Carillon van Amsterdam'   MWhe
'Carioca'   EBak
'Carisbrooke Castle' (d)   EKMF
'Carl Drude' (d)   CSil
'Carl Wallace' (d)   EKMF MJac
'Carla Johnston' ♀H1+3   CDoC CLoc CWVF EKMF EPts LCla LVER MBri MJac MWar MWhe SSea SWal WFFs WP&B
'Carleton George' **new**   MWar
'Carlisle Bells'   WP&B
'Carmel Blue'   CDoC CLoc CSil EKMF LAst LCla MWar MWhe SPet WFFs WGor WGwG WLow
'Carmen' Lemoine (d)   CDoC CSil EKMF
'Carmine Bell'   CSil EKMF
'Carnea'   CSil
'Carnival' (d)   CWVF
'Carnoustie' (d)   EBak
'Carol Grace' (d)   CLoc
'Carol Lynn Whittemore' (d)   SLBF WP&B
'Carol Nash' (d)   CLoc
'Carol Roe'   EKMF
'Caroline'   CLoc CWVF EBak EPts MWhe WP&B
'Caroline's Joy'   MJac MWhe SVil
'Caron Keating' **new**   WP&B
'Cascade'   CDoC CLoc CSil CWVF ECtt EKMF EMan EPts MBri MJac MWar

	MWhe SPet SSea WBVN WGwG WP&B
'Caspar Hauser' (d)	CDoC CSil CWVF SLBF WP&B
'Catharina'	LCla
'Catherine Bartlett'	CWVF EKMF
'Cathie MacDougall' (d)	EBak
'Cecil Glass'	EKMF
'Cecile' (d)	CDoC CWVF ECtt EKMF EPts GLbr LAst LCla LVER MJac MWar MWhe SLBF WGwG WP&B
'Celadore' (d)	CWVF LVER MJac
'Celebration' (d)	CLoc CWVF MWar
'Celebrette' **new**	WP&B
'Celia Smedley' ♀H3	CDoC CLoc CSil CWVF EBak EKMF EPts LAst LCla LVER MBri MJac MWar MWhe SLBF SPet WFFs WP&B
'Celine'	MWar WP&B
'Centerpiece' (d)	EBak
'Ceri'	CLoc
'Chameleon'	CDoC SPet WGwG
'Champagne Celebration'	CLoc
'Chancellor'	CWVF
'Chandleri'	CWVF EKMF SLBF
'Chang' ♀H1+3	CDoC CLoc CSil CWVF EBak EKMF LCla LRHS MWar MWhe SLBF WFFs
'Chantry Park'	CDoC LCla
'Charles Edward'	CSil EKMF
Charlie Dimmock = 'Foncha'	LAst MWhe SWal WP&B
'Charlie Gardiner'	CWVF EBak MWhe
'Charlie Girl' (d)	EBak
'Charlotte Clyne'	MJac
'Charming'	CDoC CLoc CSil CWVF EBak EKMF MJac MWar NDlv SPet
'Chase Delight' (v)	CDoC
'Checkerboard' ♀H3	CLoc CSil CWVF EBak ECtt EKMF EPts LCla LVER MJac MWar MWhe SLBF SPet SSea SVil WFFs WGwG
'Cheeky Chantelle' (d)	SLBF WP&B
'Cheers' (d)	CWVF EKMF MWhe
'Chelsea Louise'	EPts
'Chenois Godelieve'	WP&B
I 'Cherry' Götz	LAst WP&B
'Cheryl'	MJac
'Chessboard'	CLoc
'Cheviot Princess' **new**	WP&B
'Chillerton Beauty' ♀H3	CDoC CLoc CSil CTri CWVF ECtt EKMF LCla LRHS MJac MWhe SLBF SPer WBod WGwG
'China Doll' (d)	CWVF EBak MWhe
'China Lantern'	CLoc CSil CWVF EBak WFFs
'Chor Echo' **new**	WP&B
'Chris Nicholls'	CSil EKMF
'Christine Bamford'	CDoC CSil CWVF
'Christine Shaffery' (d)	WP&B
'Churchtown'	CWVF
cinerea	EKMF LCla
'Cinnabarina'	CLoc SLBF
* 'Cinnamon'	WP&B
'Cinque Port Liberty' (d)	SLBF
'Cinvulca'	LCla
'Circe' (d)	CWVF EBak EKMF
'Circus'	EBak
'Circus Spangles' (d)	CDoC COtt ECtt EKMF LAst MWar WGwG WP&B
'Citation'	CDoC CLoc CSil CWVF EBak SSea
'City of Adelaide' (d)	CLoc MWhe
'City of Leicester'	CSil CWVF LCla SPet
'Claire de Lune'	CDoC CWVF EBak WP&B
'Claire Evans' (d)	CLoc CWVF
'Claire Oram'	CLoc SSea
'Clare Frisby'	EKMF WP&B
'Claudia' (d)	GLbr LAst MJac MWar
'Cliantha' (d)	LCla MJac MWar MWhe
'Clifford Gadsby' (d)	EBak
'Cliff's Hardy'	CSil EKMF LCla SPet
'Cliff's Unique' (d)	CWVF EPts
'Clifton Beauty' (d)	CWVF MJac
'Clifton Belle'	CWVF
'Clifton Charm'	CSil EKMF EPts LCla MJac
'Clipper'	CSil CWVF
'Cloth of Gold'	CLoc CWVF EBak MJac MWhe SPet SSea
'Cloverdale Jewel' (d)	CDoC CWVF EBak ECtt LCla MWhe SPet
'Cloverdale Joy'	EBak
'Cloverdale Pearl'	CWVF EBak EKMF EMan ENot EPfP MJac MWhe SPet WFFs
'Cloverdale Star' **new**	WP&B
'Coachman' ♀H4	CLoc CSil CWVF EBak EKMF EMan EPts LCla MWar MWhe SLBF SPet WBVN WGwG
coccinea	CDoC CSil EKMF EPts LCla WP&B
x *colensoi*	CDoC CSil ECou EKMF LCla SHFr
'Collingwood' (d)	CLoc CWVF EBak
'Colne Fantasy' (v)	CDoC EKMF EPts
'Come Dancing' (d)	CDoC CWVF ECtt LCla SPet
I 'Comet' (d)	CLoc EBak SPet
'Comet' Banks **new**	CWVF
'Conchilla'	EBak
'Condor' **new**	WP&B
'Connie' (d)	CSil EBak EKMF
'Conspicua'	CSil CWVF EBak EKMF WP&B
'Constable Country' (d)	CWVF
'Constance' (d)	CDoC CLoc CSil CWVF EKMF EPts LCla MJac MWar MWhe NDlv SLBF SPet SWal WFFs
'Constance Comer'	MJac
I 'Constellation' Schnabel (d)	CLoc EBak
'Constellation' ambig.	CWVF
'Contamine'	WP&B
'Coombe Park'	MJac MWar
'Copycat'	CSil
'Coq Au Vin' (d)	WP&B
'Coquet Bell'	CWVF EBak
'Coquet Dale' (d)	CWVF EBak
'Coquet Gold' (d/v)	ECtt
'Coral Baby'	LCla SLBF
'Coral Rose'	CSil
'Coral Seas' **new**	EBak
§ 'Coralle'	CDoC CLoc CWVF EBak EKMF EMan EPts LCla MJac MWar MWhe SLBF SWal WFFs
'Corallina'	CDoC CLoc CSil EBak EHol EKMF LVER MWhe SPet SSea WFar WGwG WP&B WWpP
I 'Corallina Variegata' (v)	CSil
cordifolia hort.	see *F. splendens*
cordifolia Benth.	CBcs EBak EKMF MOak WP&B
'Core'ngrato' (d)	CLoc CWVF EBak
coriacifolia	EKMF LCla
'Cornelia Smith'	WP&B
'Cornwall Calls' (d)	EBak
'Corsage' (d)	CWVF
'Corsair' (d)	EBak EKMF
corymbiflora misapplied	see *F. boliviana*
- alba	see *F. boliviana* var. *alba*
§ *corymbiflora* Ruíz & Pav.	CDoC EBak EKMF EPts
'Cosmopolitan' (d)	EBak
'Costa Brava'	CLoc EBak
'Cotta 2000'	EKMF LCla
'Cotta Bella' (d)	EKMF
'Cotta Bright Star'	CWVF EKMF LCla
'Cotta Carousel'	EKMF LCla

'Cotta Christmas Tree'   EKMF LCla SLBF
'Cotta Fairy'   CWVF EKMF
'Cotta Princess' (d)   EKMF
'Cotta Vino'   EKMF SLBF
Cottinghamii   see *F.* x *bacillaris* 'Cottinghamii'
'Cotton Candy' (d)   CLoc CWVF ECtt EPts LCla MWhe
'Countdown Carol' (d)   EPts WP&B
'Countess of Aberdeen'   CLoc CSil CWVF EBak EKMF SLBF
'Countess of Maritza' (d)   CLoc CWVF
'County Park'   ECou EWes
'Court Jester' (d)   CLoc EBak
'Cover Girl' (d)   EBak EPts LAst MWhe SPet WP&B
'Coxeen'   EBak
'Crackerjack'   CLoc EBak
crassistipula   EKMF LCla
'Crescendo' (d)   CLoc CWVF
'Crinkley Bottom' (d)   EPts LVER MJac SLBF WP&B
'Crinoline' (d)   EBak
'Crosby Serendipity'   CLoc
'Crosby Soroptimist'   CWVF MWar MWhe
'Cross Check'   CWVF EMan MBri MJac
'Crusader' (d)   CWVF
'Crystal Aniversary' (d)   CWVF
'Crystal Blue'   EBak
'Cupid'   CSil EBak
'Curly Q'   CDoC EBak SPet
'Curtain Call' (d)   CLoc CWVF EBak
x *cuzco*   EKMF LCla
cylindracea Lindl.   CSil EKMF LCla WP&B
cylindracea misapplied   see *F.* x *bacillaris*
'Cymon' (d)   CWVF MWhe
'Cyndy Robyn'   WP&B
cyrtandroides   CSil EKMF
'Dainty'   EBak
'Dainty Lady' (d)   EBak
'Daisy Bell'   CDoC CLoc CSil CWVF EBak ECtt
    EKMF LCla MJac SPet SSea WGwG
    WP&B
'Dalton'   EBak
'Dana Samantha'   EPts
'Dancing Bloom'   EPts
'Dancing Flame' (d)   CLoc CWVF EBak EKMF EMan
    ♀H1+3   EPts LAst LCla LVER MBri MJac
    MWar MWhe SLBF SPet WGwG
    WLow WP&B
'Daniel Austin' (d)   MJac
'Danielle'   LAst
'Danielle Frijstein'   WP&B
'Danielle's Dream' (d)   SLBF WP&B
'Danish Pastry'   CWVF SPet
'Danny Boy' (d)   CLoc CWVF EBak EKMF MWhe
    WP&B
'Danny Kaye' (d)   WP&B
'Daphne Arlene'   CSil WP&B
'Dark Eyes' (d) ♀H4   CLoc CSil CWVF EBak EKMF EMan
    GLbr LAst LVER MBri MJac MWhe
    SLBF SPet SSea WFFs WGwG
    WP&B
'Dark Lady'   MWhe
'Dark Mystery' (d)   SLBF WP&B
'Dark Night' (d)   CSil
'Dark Secret' (d)   EBak
'Dark Treasure' (d)   CDoC EKMF SWal
'Daryn John Woods' **new**   WP&B
'Dave's Delight' **new**   EKMF
'David'   CDoC CLoc CSil CWVF EKMF
    EOHP EPts LAst LCla MWhe NDlv
    SIng SLBF WFFs WGor WGwG
    WP&B WSPU
'David Alston' (d)   CLoc CWVF EBak
'David Lockyer' (d)   CLoc CWVF
'David Savage' (d)   LCla
'Dawn'   EBak
'Dawn Carless' (d)   WP&B

'Dawn Fantasia' (v)   CLoc EKMF EPts MWar WP&B
'Dawn Redfern'   CWVF
'Dawn Sky' (d)   EBak SVil
'Dawn Star' (d)   CWVF GLbr LAst LVER MJac MWhe
'Day by Day'   CSil
'Day Star'   EBak
'De Groot's Beauty' (d)   WP&B
'De Groot's Happiness'   WP&B
'De Groot's Moonlight'   WP&B
'De Groot's Parade'   WP&B
'De Groot's Pipes'   WP&B
'De Groot's Queen'   WP&B
'De Groot's Regenboog'   WP&B
'De Vondeling' **new**   WP&B
'Debby' (d)   EBak
'Deben Petite'   EWll LCla
'Deben Rose'   WGwG
'Deborah Mitchell'   WGwG
'Deborah Street'   CLoc
§ *decussata* Ruíz & Pav.   CDoC EBak EKMF LCla
'Dee Copley' (d)   EBak
'Dee Star' (d)   WP&B
'Deep Purple' (d)   CDoC CLoc CWVF ECtt EKMF
    GLbr LAst MJac SCoo SLBF WP&B
'Delilah' (d)   CWVF MJac
'Delta's Angelique'   LCla SLBF WP&B
'Delta's Bride'   SLBF WP&B
'Delta's Delight'   WP&B
'Delta's Dream'   CWVF LCla WGwG WP&B
'Delta's Emperor'   WP&B
'Delta's Groom'   LCla WP&B
'Delta's K.O.' (d)   WP&B
'Delta's Matador'   LAst MJac
'Delta's Night'   WP&B
'Delta's Paljas'   WP&B
'Delta's Parade' (d)   EPts LCla MWar WP&B
'Delta's Robijn'   WP&B
'Delta's Song'   WP&B
'Delta's Symphonie' (d)   CWVF WP&B
'Delta's Trick'   WP&B
'Delta's Wonder'   CSil WP&B
'Demi van Roovert'   WP&B
§ *denticulata*   CDoC CLoc CSil CWVF EBak
    EKMF EPts LCla MOak SLBF
    WGwG WP&B
dependens   see *F. corymbiflora* Ruíz & Pav.
'Derby Imp'   CDoC CWVF
'Desire' **new**   WP&B
'Desperate Daniel'   EKMF EPts LCla
'Devonshire   CDoC CLoc CSil CWVF EBak ECtt
    Dumpling' (d)   EKMF EMan EPts LAst LCla LVER
    MBri MJac MWar MWhe SLBF SPet
    WGwG WLow
'Diablo' (d)   EBak
'Diamond Celebration' (d)   EKMF MWar WP&B
'Diana' (d)   CDoC EBak
'Diana Brown'   CWVF EKMF MWhe SSea
'Diana Wills' (d)   CWVF MWhe
'Diana Wright'   CSil EKMF WSPU
'Diane Marie' **new**   SLBF
§ 'Die Schöne Wilhelmine'   WP&B
'Dilly-Dilly' (d)   CWVF ECtt
'Dimples' (d)   CSil MBri
'Dipton Dainty' (d)   CLoc EBak LCla
'Dirk van Delen'   MWhe
'Display' ♀H4   CDoC CLoc CSil CWVF EBak ECtt
    EKMF EMan EPts LAst LCla LVER
    MBri MJac MWhe NDlv NPer SLBF
    SPet SSea WFFs WGwG WP&B
    WStl
'Doc'   CDoC CSil NDlv SPet
'Doctor'   see *F.* 'The Doctor'
'Doctor Foster' ♀H4   CDoC CLoc CSil CTri EBak EKMF
    ENot EPts NDlv WEas

'Doctor Judith' (d) **new** — CWVF
'Doctor Mason' **new** — CWVF
'Doctor Olson' (d) — CLoc EBak
'Doctor Robert' — CWVF EPts MBri MJac MWhe
'Dodo' — WP&B
§ 'Dollar Princess' (d) ♀H4 — CDoC CLoc CSil CWVF EBak ECtt EKMF EMan EPts GLbr LAst LCla MBri MJac MWar MWhe NDlv NPer SChu SLBF SPet SPlb SWal WFFs WFar WGwG WLow WStI WWeb
'Dolly Daydream' (d) — EKMF
'Dominique' (d) — EKMF
'Dominyana' — EBak EKMF LCla WP&B
'Don Peralta' — EBak
'Dopey' (d) — CDoC CSil SPet
'Doreen Redfern' — CLoc CWVF MJac MWhe SPet
'Doreen Stroud' — CWVF
'Doris Coleman' (d) — EMan
'Doris Deaves' — SLBF
'Doris Joan' — SLBF
'Dorothea Flower' — CLoc CSil CWVF EBak EKMF
'Dorothy' — CSil EKMF LCla SLBF SPet
'Dorothy Ann' — SLBF WP&B
'Dorothy Cheal' **new** — CWVF
'Dorothy Day' (d) — CLoc
'Dorothy Hanley' (d) — CSil EKMF EPts LAst MAsh MJac MWhe SLBF WFFs WGor WP&B
'Dorothy Shields' (d) — CWVF MJac WP&B
'Dorrian Brogdale' — LCla WP&B
'Dorset Delight' (d) — CWVF WP&B
'Dot Woodage' **new** — WP&B
'Dove House' — EKMF
'Dr Topinard' — CLoc EBak EKMF WP&B
'Drake 400' (d) — CLoc
'Drama Girl' — CWVF
'Drame' (d) — CDoC CSil CWVF EBak EKMF LCla NDlv SPet SSea
'Drum Major' (d) — EBak
'Du Barry' (d) — EBak
'Duchess of Albany' — CLoc CSil EBak
'Duchess of Cornwall' (d) — CSil
I 'Duke of Wellington' Haag (d) — CLoc
'Dulcie Elizabeth' (d) — CWVF EBak MJac SPet
'Dunrobin Bedder' — CSil
'Dusky Beauty' — CWVF
'Dusky Rose' (d) — CDoC CLoc CWVF EBak MJac MWhe WGwG
'Dusted Pink' (d) **new** — CWVF
'Dutch Kingsize' — WP&B
'Dutch Mill' — CLoc CWVF EBak
'Duyfken' — CWVF
'Dying Embers' — CLoc
'Dymph Werker van Groenland' **new** — LCla
'East Anglian' — CLoc EBak
'Easter Bonnet' (d) — CLoc CWVF
'Ebanflo' **new** — EBak MWar
'Ebbtide' (d) — CLoc EBak WP&B
'Echo' — CLoc CWVF LRHS
'Ectors Nursery' — WP&B
'Ed Largarde' (d) — CWVF EBak EKMF
'Edale' — EKMF
'Eden Lady' — CDoC CLoc SPet
'Eden Princess' — CWVF MJac MWhe
'Edith' Brown' (d) — CSil EKMF LCla SLBF
'Edith' ambig. — NDlv
'Edith Emery' (d) — CDoC SPet
'Edna May' — CWVF
'Edna W. Smith' — CWVF ECtt
'Eileen Raffill' — EBak
'Eileen Saunders' — CSil EBak
'Eileen Storey' — EKMF WP&B

'Eisvogel' — WP&B
'El Camino' (d) — CWVF WBVN
'El Cid' — CLoc CSil EBak EKMF
'Elaine Ann' — EPts MJac
'Eleanor Leytham' — CDoC CWVF EBak EKMF LCla
'Eleanor Rawlins' — CSil EBak EKMF
'Elf' — CSil
'Elfin Glade' — CLoc CSil CWVF EBak EKMF
'Elfrida' (d) — CSil EKMF NDlv
'Elfriede Ott' — CLoc EBak MWhe WP&B
'Eline Brantz' — WP&B
I 'Elizabeth' Whiteman — EBak EKMF
'Elizabeth Broughton' — EKMF
'Elizabeth Tompkins' (d) — MJac
'Elizabeth Travis' — EBak
'Ellen Morgan' (d) — CWVF EBak
'Ellie Jane' **new** — EPts
'Elma' — CSil LCla
'Elsa' (d) — CWVF ECtt LRHS SPet
'Elsie Maude' (d) **new** — CWVF
'Elsie Mitchell' (d) — CWVF MWhe SPet
'Elsie Vert' (d) — WP&B
'Elsstar' — WP&B
'Elysée' — CSil EKMF
§ 'Emile de Wildeman' (d) — CSil CWVF EBak EKMF LVER SPet
'Emily' **new** — MJac
'Emily Austen' — CWVF EKMF MJac
'Emma Alice' (d) **new** — CWVF
'Emma Louise' (d) — CWVF
'Empress of Prussia' ♀H4 — CDoC CLoc CSil CWVF EBak ECtt EKMF EMan GLbr LAst LRHS NDlv SLBF SPet SSea SWal WP&B
'Enchanted' (d) — CWVF EBak MWar
encliandra — CDoC EKMF LCla
  subsp. **encliandra**
* - var. **gris** — LCla
§ - subsp. **tetradactyla** — EKMF
§ 'Enfant Prodigue' (d) — CDoC CLoc CSil EKMF SDix SMrm
'English Rose' (d) — CWVF
'Enid Joyce' — SLBF
'Enstone' — see *F. magellanica* var. *molinae* 'Enstone'
'Erecta' — MBNS NPri
'Erica Julie' (d) — MWhe SLBF
'Eric's Everest' (d) — EKMF WP&B
'Eric's Hardy' (d) — CSil
'Eric's Majestic' (d) — EKMF MJac
'Erika Frohmann' (d) — WP&B
'Erika Köth' — LCla
'Ernest Rankin' — CSil
'Ernie Bromley' — CSil CWVF SLBF
'Errol' — CLoc
'Estelle Marie' — CLoc CSil CWVF EBak MBri MWar MWhe SLBF SPet SSea WP&B
'Eternal Flame' (d) — CSil CWVF EBak EPts MBri MWhe
'Ethel May' **new** — MJac
'Ethel Wilson' — CSil
'Eureka Red' (d) — CWVF LAst WGwG
'Eurydice' (d) — CLoc
'Eusebia' (d) — MJac
'Eva Boerg' — CLoc CSil CTri CWVF EBak ECtt EKMF EMan LAst LCla MBri MWar SPet WFFs WGwG WKif
'Eva Dayes' — EKMF
'Evanson's Choice' — CDoC
'Evelyn Stanley' (d) — CWVF
§ 'Evelyn Steele Little' — EBak
'Evening Sky' (d) — EBak
'Evensong' — CLoc CWVF EBak MWhe
I 'Excordi' — WP&B
excorticata — CBcs CDoC CHEx CPLG CPle CRHN CSil CTrw EKMF LCla WPGP WPat WSHC
'Exmoor Woods' — CSil

'Fabian Franck' CDoC LCla
'Fairytales' (d) WP&B
'Falklands' (d) CSil EKMF
'Falling Stars' CLoc CWVF EBak ECtt MWhe
'Fan Dancer' (d) EBak
'Fancy Free' (d) MBri
'Fancy Pants' (d) CLoc CWVF EBak
'Fanfare' CDoC EBak EKMF EWll LCla
'Fascination' see *F.* 'Emile de Wildeman'
'Fashion' (d) EBak
'Favourite' EBak
'Felicke' **new** WP&B
'Feltham's Pride' CWVF
'Fenman' CWVF EPts
'Fergie' (d) LCla
'Festival' (d) MWhe WP&B
'Festival Lights' SLBF
'Festoon' EBak
'Fey' (d) CWVF EKMF WP&B
'Ffion' EPts
'Fiery Spider' EBak
'Finn' CWVF EPts WP&B
'Fiona' CLoc CWVF EBak SPet
'Fiona Jane' EKMF
'Fire Mountain' (d) CLoc CSil ECtt SSea
Firecracker = 'John CHEx EBre MJac SCoo WGwG
 Ridding'[PBR] (v)
'Firelite' (d) EBak
'Firenza' (d) CWVF
'First Kiss' CWVF
'First Lady' (d) CWVF
'First Lord' CWVF
'First Success' CDoC CWVF EKMF LCla LHop
  WGwG
'Flair' (d) CLoc CWVF
'Flame' EBak
'Flamenco Dancer' (d) CLoc CWVF ECtt LAst
'Flash' ♀[H3-4] CDoC CLoc CSil CTri CWVF EBak
  EKMF EPts LCla MAsh MJac MWhe
  NDlv SLBF SPet WGwG WStI
'Flashlight' CDoC CSil CWVF LAst NDlv WFFs
'Flashlight Amélioré' CSil
'Flat Jack o' Lancashire' CSil ECtt EKMF SLBF
 (d)
'Flavia' (d) EBak
'Fleur de Picardie' WP&B
'Flirt' WP&B
'Flirtation Waltz' (d) CLoc CSil CWVF EBak EKMF EMan
  EPts LCla LVER MJac MWhe SPet
  SSea
'Flocon de Neige' CSil EBak EKMF
'Floral City' (d) CLoc EBak
'Florence Mary Abbott' EMan WP&B
'Florence Taylor' CWVF
'Florence Turner' CSil EBak EKMF MWhe
'Florentina' (d) CLoc CWVF EBak EKMF
'Florrie's Gem' (d) SLBF
'Flowerdream' CWVF
'Flyaway' (d) EBak
'Fly-by-night' (d) CWVF
'Flying Cloud' (d) CLoc CSil CWVF EBak EKMF MBri
'Flying Scotsman' (d) CLoc CWVF EBak EKMF EPts LVER
  MJac
'Fohnhimmel' (d) WP&B
'Folies Bergères' (d) EBak
'Foolke' CSil EBak EPts
'Forfar's Pride' (d) CSil MWar
'Forget-me-not' CLoc CSil CWVF EBak EKMF
'Fort Bragg' (d) CWVF EBak
'Forward Look' CDoC MWhe WP&B
'Fountains Abbey' (d) CWVF EMan
'Four Farthings' (d) EKMF WP&B
'Foxgrove Wood' ♀[H3-4] CSil CWVF EBak EKMF EPts SLBF
  WFFs

'Foxtrot' CWVF
'Foxy Lady' (d) CWVF EKMF WP&B
'Frances Haskins' CSil MWhe
'Frank Lawrence' LCla
'Frank Saunders' CWVF LCla WP&B
'Frank Unsworth' (d) CWVF ECtt EKMF EPts MJac SPet
'Frankie's Magnificent EPts
 Seven' (d)
'Frau Hilde Rademacher' CDoC CSil CWVF EBak EKMF
 (d) EMan LVER SLBF SWal WP&B
'Fred Hansford' CSil CWVF SLBF
'Fred's First' (d) CDoC CSil EKMF SWal
'Freefall' EBak
'Friendly Fire' (d) CLoc
'Frosted Flame' CDoC CLoc CSil CWVF EBak
  EKMF LCla MJac MWar MWhe
  SPet SSea WP&B
'Frozen Tears' WP&B
'Frühling' (d) CSil EBak EKMF
'Fuchsiade '88' CLoc CSil CWVF EBak EKMF
  MWhe WP&B
'Fuchsiarama '91' CWVF WP&B
'Fuji-San' CDoC EPts LCla WP&B
'Fuksie Foetsie' CDoC CSil WGwG
fulgens ♀[H1+3] CDoC EKMF GCal IFro LCla MOak
  MWhe
 – 'Gesneriana' see *F.* 'Gesneriana'
* – var. *minuata* EKMF
 – 'Rubra Grandiflora' see *F.* 'Rubra Grandiflora'
* – 'Variegata' (v) CDoC CLoc CSil EKMF EPts LCla
  WCom WP&B
'Fulpila' LCla
'Für Elise' (d) EBak
furfuracea EKMF
'Gala' (d) EBak
'Garden News' (d) ♀[H3-4] CDoC CLoc CSil CWVF ECtt EKMF
  EPts GLbr LAst LCla LRHS LVER
  MGos MJac MWar MWhe NDlv
  SLBF SPet SWal WFFs WFar WGwG
  WP&B
'Garden Week' (d) CWVF MWhe WP&B
'Gartenmeister Bonstedt' CDoC CLoc CWVF EBak EKMF
 ♀[H1+3] EPts LCla LRHS SPet SSea WGwG
  WP&B
'Gay Anne' (d) EKMF
'Gay Fandango' (d) CLoc CWVF EBak ECtt LCla SPet
  WFFs
'Gay Future' EKMF
'Gay Parasol' (d) CLoc LAst MJac
'Gay Paree' (d) EBak WP&B
'Gay Senorita' EBak
'Gay Spinner' (d) CLoc
'Gazenhof' **new** WP&B
gehrigeri EBak EKMF LCla
'Gelre' WP&B
'Gemma Fisher' (d) EPts
Gene = 'Goetzgene'[PBR] WGor
 (Shadowdancer
 Series) **new**
'Général Monk' (d) CDoC CSil CWVF EBak ECtt EKMF
  EMan EPts LAst LVER MBri SWal
  WP&B
'Général Voyron' CSil
'General Wavell' (d) WGwG
'Genii' ♀[H4] More than 30 suppliers
'Geoffrey Smith' (d) CSil ECtt EKMF
§ 'Georg Börnemann' CDoC CLoc CWVF EBak WGwG
  WP&B
'Georgana' (d) MWhe WP&B
'George Barr' CDoC EKMF LRHS WFFs
'George Bartlett' CLoc WFFs
'George Johnson' CDoC SPet WGwG
'George Travis' (d) EBak
'Georges Remy' WP&B

'Gerald Drewitt' CSil
§ 'Gerharda's Aubergine' CLoc CSil CWVF EKMF SSea WP&B
'Gerharda's Kiekeboe' EKMF WP&B
§ 'Gesneriana' CDoC CLoc EBak WGwG
'Ghislaine' (d) WP&B
'Giant Pink Enchanted' (d) CLoc EBak
'Gilda' CWVF MJac
'Gillian Althea' (d) CDoC CWVF
'Gillian's Gem' (d) **new** SLBF
'Gilt Edge' (v) CLoc
Ginger = 'Goetzginger'[PBR] WGor
  (Shadowdancer
  Series) **new**
'Gingham Girl' (d) MJac
'Gipsy Princess' (d) CLoc
'Girls Brigade' CWVF EKMF
'Gitana' WP&B
'Gladiator' (d) EBak EKMF LCla
'Gladys Cecilia' (d) **new** SLBF
'Gladys Godfrey' **new** EBak
'Gladys Lorimer' CWVF EPts
'Gladys Miller' CLoc
glazioviana CDoC CSil CWVF EKMF LCla SLBF SWal WP&B
'Glenby' (d) CWVF
'Glendale' CWVF
'Glitters' CWVF EBak EKMF EPts
§ 'Globosa' CAgr CSil EBak EKMF
'Gloria Johnson' EKMF
'Glow' CSil EBak EKMF
'Glowing Embers' EBak
Glowing Lilac (d) CSil ECtt EMan EPts
'Glyn Jones' (d) EKMF
'Gold Brocade' CSil SPet
'Gold Crest' EBak WP&B
'Gold Leaf' CWVF
'Gold Reitze' **new** WP&B
'Golden Anniversary' (d) CLoc CWVF EBak EKMF EMan LVER MJac WP&B
'Golden Arrow' CDoC CWVF LCla
'Golden Border Queen' CLoc
'Golden Dawn' CLoc CWVF EBak ECtt SPet
'Golden Eden Lady' (v) MWhe
'Golden Girl' **new** SLBF
'Golden Herald' CSil SLBF SSea
'Golden La Campanella' CLoc ECtt MBri (d/v)
'Golden Lena' (d/v) CSil CWVF EMan
'Golden Margaret Roe' (v) CSil
'Golden Marinka' (v) ♀H3 CLoc EBak ECtt EKMF LAst LRHS MBri SPet WFFs
'Golden Melody' (d) CSil
'Golden Swingtime' (d) CSil ECtt EPts LAst MBri MJac SPet SSea WGwG WP&B
'Golden Treasure' (v) CLoc CSil CWVF ECtt EKMF MBri MWar
'Golden Vergeer' (v) EKMF MWar SLBF
'Golden Wedding' EKMF
'Goldsworth Beauty' CSil LCla
'Golondrina' CSil CWVF EBak
'Goody Goody' CDoC EBak
'Gooseberry Hill' **new** WP&B
'Gordon Boy' (d) CSil
'Gordon Thorley' CSil EKMF MWhe
'Gordon's China Rose' LCla
'Gorgeous Gemma' (d) SLBF WP&B
'Gottingen' EBak EKMF WP&B
'Governor 'Pat' Brown' (d) EBak
'Grace Darling' CWVF EBak MWhe
gracilis see *F. magellanica* var. *gracilis*
'Graf Witte' CDoC CSil CWVF EKMF EPts NDlv SPet WGwG
'Grand Duke' (d) CWVF

'Grandad Hobbs' (d) LCla
'Grandma Hobbs' LCla
'Grandma Sinton' (d) CLoc CWVF EMan MBri MWhe
'Grandpa George' (d) CSil LCla
'Grandpa Jack' (d) SLBF WP&B
'Grayrigg' CDoC CSil EKMF LCla NDlv
'Great Ouse' (d) EPts
'Great Scott' (d) CLoc
'Green 'n' Gold' EBak
'Greenpeace' EKMF SLBF WP&B
'Grenzland' **new** WP&B
'Greta' CDoC
'Gretna Chase' MBri MWhe
'Grey Lady' (d) CSil
'Grietje' WP&B
'Grobo '60' (d) WP&B
'Groene Boelvaar' (d) WP&B
'Groene Kan's Glorie' CDoC
'Grumpy' CDoC CSil CWVF EHol EPts LRHS MBri MLan MWhe SPet
'Gruss aus dem Bodethal' CLoc CWVF EBak EKMF EPts WP&B
'Guinevere' CWVF EBak
'Gustave Doré' (d) CSil EBak EKMF
'Guy Dauphine' (d) EBak
'Gwen Burralls' (d) EKMF
'Gwen Dodge' LCla WP&B
'Gypsy Girl' (d) CWVF
* 'H.C. Brown' **new** LCla
'H.G. Brown' CSil EBak EKMF MWhe
'Halsall Beauty' (d) MBri
'Halsall Belle' (d) MBri
'Halsall Pride' (d) MBri
'Hampshire Beauty' (d) MJac
'Hampshire Blue' CDoC CWVF SSea
'Hampshire Pride' WGwG
'Hampshire Prince' (d) LVER
'Hampshire Treasure' (d) CSil CWVF
'Hanau' **new** WP&B
'Hannah Gwen' (d) EKMF
'Hannah Louise' (d) EPts
'Hannah Rogers' **new** MWar
'Hans Callaars' WP&B
'Happy' CDoC CSil CWVF EPts LCla MWhe SPet
'Happy Anniversary' CLoc
I 'Happy Anniversary' (d/v) EKMF
'Happy Fellow' CDoC CLoc CSil EBak EKMF NDlv
'Happy Wedding Day' (d) CDoC CLoc CWVF ECtt EKMF EPts GLbr LAst MJac MWhe SCoo WGwG WP&B
'Hapsburgh' **new** EBak
'Harlow Car' CWVF EKMF EPts WGwG
'Harlow Perfection' EKMF
I 'Harmony' Niederholzer EBak
'Harnser's Flight' CSil
'Harrow Pride' (d) CSil
'Harry Cawood' (d) SLBF
'Harry Dunnett' EBak
'Harry Gray' (d) CLoc CSil CWVF EBak ECtt EMan EPts GLbr LAst LCla MBri MJac MWhe SPet SSea WGwG
'Harry Pullen' **new** EBak
'Harry Taylor' (d) EPts
hartwegii CDoC CSil EKMF LCla
'Hathersage' (d) EBak
Hathor WP&B
hatschbachii CDoC CSil EKMF EPts LCla
'Haute Cuisine' (d) CLoc EMan LVER MWhe
'Hawaiian Princess' (d) ECtt
'Hawaiian Sunset' (d) CWVF LCla SLBF WBVN
'Hawkshead' ♀H3-4 CDoC CLoc CSil CWVF ECha EKMF ELan EPfP EPts GCal GQui LCla LRHS MBri MGos MJac MWhe

NChi SChu SGar SLBF SMrm SPet WBcn WCom WP&B WWpP

I 'Hazel' (d) — CWVF GLbr MJac MWhe WP&B
'Heart Throb' (d) — EBak
'Heavenly Hayley' (d) — SLBF WP&B
'Hebe' — EBak MWhe
I 'Hedens Montana' — WP&B
'Heidi Ann' (d) ♀H3 — CDoC CLoc CSil CWVF EBak EKMF EMan EPts LAst LCla MBri MWhe NDlv SLBF SPet SSea SWal WFFs WGwG
'Heidi Blue' (d) **new** — SLBF
§ 'Heidi Weiss' (d) — CDoC CLoc CSil CWVF MBri SPet WGwG
'Heinrich Henkel' — see *F.* 'Andenken an Heinrich Henkel'
'Heinzelmannchen' **new** — WP&B
'Heirloom' (d) — ECtt EKMF
'Helen Clare' (d) — CLoc CWVF EBak
'Helen Gair' (d) **new** — CWVF WP&B
'Helen Nicholls' (d) — EKMF WP&B
'Hellen Devine' — CWVF
'Hello Dolly' — CLoc
'Hemsleyana' — see *F. microphylla* subsp. *hemsleyana*
'Henkelly's Elegantie' — WP&B
'Henkelly's Stippelke' — WP&B
'Hennie Bouman' (d) **new** — WP&B
'Henning Becker' — CWVF WP&B
'Henri Poincaré' — CDoC EBak EKMF
'Herald' ♀H4 — CDoC CSil CWVF EBak EKMF NDlv SLBF SWal WGwG
'Herbé de Jacques' — see *Fuchsia* 'Mr West'
'Heritage' (d) — CLoc CSil EBak EKMF
'Herman de Graaff' (d) — EKMF WP&B
'Hermiena' — CLoc CSil CWVF LCla MWar MWhe SLBF WFFs WGwG WP&B
'Heron' — CSil EBak EKMF
'Hertogin van Brabant' (d) **new** — WP&B
'Hessett Festival' (d) — CDoC CWVF EBak MWhe
'Heston Blue' (d) — CWVF EKMF
'Het Halens Helmpje' **new** — WP&B
'Hettenheuvel' — WP&B
'Hetty Blok' (d) — WP&B
'Heydon' — CWVF
'Hi Jinks' (d) — EBak
hidalgensis — see *F. microphylla* subsp. *hidalgensis*
'Hidcote Beauty' — CDoC CLoc CSil CWVF EBak MWhe SLBF SPet SSea WFFs WGwG
'Hidden Treasure' — LCla MWar WP&B
'Hie Zenne Kik' **new** — WP&B
'Hier Ben Ik' — LCla
'Highland Pipes' — CSil EKMF LCla
'Hilda May Salmon' — CWVF
'Hindu Belle' — EBak
'Hinnerike' — CSil CWVF EPts LCla WP&B
'Hiroshige' — LCla
hirtella — WP&B
'His Excellency' (d) — EBak
'Hobo' (d) — CSil MWar WP&B
'Hobson's Choice' (d) — CWVF SLBF
'Hokusai' — WP&B
'Holly Hobit' — NMRc
'Holly's Beauty' (d) — CDoC EKMF EPts LAst MWar WGwG WP&B
'Hollywood Park' (d) — EBak
'Horatio' — ECtt MJac
'Hot Coals' — CLoc CSil CWVF ECtt EKMF EPts LCla MJac MWar MWhe WP&B
'Howlett's Hardy' — CDoC CLoc CSil CWVF EBak ECtt EKMF EPts LRHS MBri NLar SWal WP&B

'Hula Girl' (d) — CWVF EBak EKMF MJac MWar MWhe SLBF SPet WP&B
'Humboldt Holiday' (d) — EKMF
'Huntsman' (d) — CDoC ECtt EKMF LAst MWhe WGwG
'Ian Brazewell' (d) — CLoc
'Ian Leedham' (d) — EBak
'Ice Cream Soda' (d) — EBak
'Ice Maiden' ambig. (d) — WP&B
'Iceberg' — CWVF EBak
'Icecap' — CWVF EKMF MBri
'Iced Champagne' — CLoc CWVF EBak GLbr MJac
'Ichiban' (d) — CLoc WP&B
'Icicle' (d) — WP&B
'Ida' (d) — EBak EKMF
'Igloo Maid' (d) — CLoc CWVF EBak EKMF MWhe SPet SSea
'Illusion' **new** — WP&B
'Impala' (d) — CWVF
'Imperial Fantasy' (d) — CWVF
'Impudence' — CLoc EBak SPet SSea
'Impulse' (d) — CLoc EKMF
'Indian Maid' (d) — CDoC CWVF EBak LVER WGwG WP&B
inflata — EKMF
'Inge Frazer' **new** — WP&B
'Insulinde' — CDoC CFee CWVF EPts LCla MWar SLBF WFFs WP&B
'Interlude' (d) — EBak
'Iolanthe' — CWVF
'Irene L. Peartree' (d) — CWVF LCla
'Iris Amer' (d) — CLoc CWVF EBak
'Irish Dawn' — MWar
'Irving Alexander' (d) **new** — WP&B
'Isabel Erkamp' **new** — WP&B
'Isabel Ryan' — CSil
'Isis' ambig. — WP&B
'Isis' Lemoine — CSil
'Isle of Mull' — CDoC CSil SPet WP&B
'Italiano' (d) — CWVF MJac
'Ivy Grace' — CSil
'Jack Acland' — CWVF ECtt
'Jack Shahan' ♀H3 — CDoC CLoc CSil CWVF EBak EKMF EMan LAst LCla MBri MJac MWar MWhe NBlu SPet SSea WFFs WGwG
'Jack Stanway' (v) — CSil CWVF EKMF EPts MWar
'Jack Wilson' — CSil
'Jackie Bull' (d) — CWVF EBak
'Jackpot' (d) — EBak
'Jackqueline' — CSil CWVF
'Jadas Mam' **new** — WP&B
'Jam Roll' (d) — LVER
'Jamboree' (d) — EBak
'James Lye' (d) — CWVF EBak EKMF SWal
'James Savage' — LCla
'James Travis' (d) — CDoC CSil EBak EKMF LCla
'Jan' ambig. — WP&B
'Jan Lokhorst' **new** — WP&B
'Jan van Erp' — WP&B
'Jandel' — CWVF
'Jane Humber' (d) — CWVF EKMF LCla MJac
'Jane Lye' — EBak
'Janet Williams' (d) — CSil
'Janice Ann' — EKMF LCla MWar WFFs WP&B
'Janice Perry's Gold' (v) — CLoc MJac
'Janie' (d) — MAsh WWeb
'Janneke Brinkman-Salentijn' — WP&B
'Jap Vantveer' — LCla
'Jaunty Jack' — SLBF
'Javelin' — WP&B
'Jean Baker' — CSil
'Jean Campbell' — EBak

'Jean Clark' — WP&B
'Jean Frisby' — CLoc
'Jeane' — EKMF
'Jeangil' **new** — WP&B
'Jennifer' — EBak
'Jennifer Hampson' (d) — CSil
'Jennifer Lister' (d) — CSil EKMF
'Jenny Brinson' (d) **new** — SLBF WP&B
'Jenny May' — EPts WP&B
'Jenny Sorensen' — CWVF EKMF LCla
'Jess' — LCla SLBF WP&B
'Jessica Reynolds' — SLBF
'Jessie Pearson' — CWVF
'Jessimae' — CWVF SPet
'Jester' Holmes (d) — CLoc CSil
'Jet Fire' (d) — EBak
'Jezebel' — WP&B
'Jiddles' — LCla SLBF
'Jill Harris' — SLBF WP&B
'Jill Whitworth' — CDoC
'Jim Coleman' — CWVF
'Jim Dodge' (d) — EPts
'Jim Hawkins' **new** — EBak
'Jim Muncaster' — CWVF EKMF
jimenezii — EKMF LCla WP&B
– hybrid — EKMF
'Jimmy Carr' (d) — EKMF
'Jimmy Cricket' — LCla
'Jingle Bells' — MWhe
'Jinlye' — EKMF WP&B
'Joan Barnes' (d) — CSil CWVF
'Joan Cooper' — CLoc CSil CWVF EBak EKMF SLBF
'Joan Goy' — CWVF EKMF EPts MJac MWhe
'Joan Knight' — CLoc
'Joan Leach' — CSil
'Joan Margaret' (d) — MJac
'Joan Morris' — SLBF
'Joan Pacey' — CWVF EBak EKMF
'Joan Paxton' (d) — LCla
'Joan Smith' — EBak
'Joan Waters' (d) **new** — CWVF
'Jo-Anne Fisher' (d) — EPts
'Joe Kusber' (d) — CSil CWVF EBak MJac WP&B
'Joe Nicholls' (d) — EKMF
'Joel' — CLoc SLBF WP&B
'John Bartlett' **new** — CLoc
'John E. Caunt' — CSil EKMF
'John Grooms' (d) — CLoc MJac
'John Lockyer' — CLoc CWVF EBak
'John Maynard Scales' — CDoC CWVF LCla MJac MWhe WP&B
'John Quirk' (d) **new** — SLBF
'John Stephens' — EPts
'John Suckley' (d) — EBak
'John Wright' — CSil LCla
'Johnny' (d) — CLoc SSea
'Jomam' ♀H3 — CLoc CWVF MWar WP&B
'Jon Oram' — CLoc CWVF
'Jopie' (d) — WP&B
'Jose's Joan' (d) — CWVF
'Joy Bielby' — EKMF
'Joy Patmore' — CLoc CSil CWVF EBak EKMF EPts LCla MBri MWar MWhe SLBF SPet WP&B
'Joyce' **new** — WP&B
'Joyce Adey' (d) — CWVF
'Joyce Maynard' (d) — MJac
'Joyce Sinton' — CWVF EMan MBri
'Joyce Storey' — EKMF
'Joyce Wilson' (d) — EPts LCla
'Jubie-Lin' (d) — WP&B
'Jubilee Quest' — EKMF LCla MWar
'Judith Coupland' — CWVF
'Jülchen' — CWVF WP&B

'Jules Daloges' (d) — EBak EKMF
'Julia' (d) — EKMF WP&B
'Julie Ann' — MWar
'Julie Horton' (d) — WP&B
'Julie Marie' (d) — CSil CWVF MJac
'June Gardner' — EKMF
'Jungle' — LCla WP&B
I   'Juno' Kennett — EBak
juntasensis — EKMF WP&B
'Jupiter' **new** — WP&B
'Jupiter Seventy' — EBak
'Just a Tad' (d) — SLBF
'Justin's Pride' — CDoC CSil EKMF
'Kaboutertje' — EKMF
'Kaleidoscope' (d) — EBak
'Kallinga' **new** — WP&B
'Kapsalon Styling' **new** — WP&B
'Karen Bielby' — EKMF
'Karen Bradley' — MJac
'Karen Isles' — LCla SLBF
'Karen Louise' (d) — CLoc
'Karin de Groot' — EKMF
'Karin Siegers' — CSil
'Kate Harriet' (d) — WGwG
'Kate Wylie' — MWar
'Kath van Hanegem' — CSil EPts LCla SLBF WP&B
'Kathleen Muncaster' (d) — EKMF WP&B
'Kathleen Smith' (d) — ECtt EKMF
'Kathleen van Hanegan' — CLoc
'Kathy Louise' (d) — EMan WP&B
'Kathy's Pipes' — EKMF
'Kathy's Prince' — ECtt EKMF WP&B
'Kathy's Sparkler' (d) — EKMF
'Katie Elizabeth Ann' (d) — MWar SLBF
'Katie Rogers' **new** — EPts
'Katinka' — CWVF EPts LCla
'Katjan' — EKMF SLBF
'Katrien Michiels' **new** — WP&B
'Katrina' (d) — CLoc EBak
'Katrina Thompsen' — CLoc CWVF EKMF EPts LCla MWar SLBF SSea
'Katy James' — EKMF MWar
'Katy M' **new** — WP&B
'Keepsake' (d) — CLoc EBak
'Kegworth Carnival' (d) — CWVF
'Kegworth Supreme' — MJac
'Kelly's Dream' (d) — SLBF WP&B
'Ken Goldsmith' — CWVF EPts
'Ken Jennings' — CWVF MJac
'Ken Shelton' — SLBF
'Kenny Dalglish' (d) — CSil EKMF
'Kenny Holmes' **new** — CWVF
'Kenny Walkling' **new** — SLBF
'Kernan Robson' (d) — CLoc CWVF EBak
'Kerry Anne' — EPts
'Kevin R. Peake' (d) — MWar
'Keystone' — EBak
'Khada' — MWhe
'Kim Wright' (d) — MWhe
'Kimberly' (d) — EBak
'King of Bath' (d) — EBak
'King of Hearts' (d) — EBak
'King's Ransom' (d) — CLoc CSil CWVF EBak LRHS MWhe SPet
'Kiss 'n' Tell' — CWVF MJac MWhe
'Kit Oxtoby' (d) — CWVF ECtt EKMF EMan GLbr LCla LVER MJac SVil WFFs WP&B
'Kiwi' (d) — EBak
'Klassic' — LCla SLBF
'Kleine Sandra' — LCla
'Knight Errant' — SSea
'Knockout' (d) — CWVF EKMF
'Kolding Perle' — CDoC CWVF EKMF SPet
'Königin der Frühe' — WGwG

'Königin der Nacht'   WP&B
'Kon-Tiki' (d)   CLoc EKMF SPet
'Koralle'   see F. 'Coralle'
'Krimar' **new**   WP&B
'Krommenie' **new**   WP&B
'Kwintet'   CWVF EBak LCla MJac SPet
'Kyoto'   CWVF
'La Bianca'   EBak
'La Campanella' (d) ♀H3 CDoC CLoc CSil CWVF EBak ECtt
                        EKMF EMan EPts LAst LCla MBri
                        MJac MWar MWhe NVic SPet WFFs
                        WGwG
'La Fiesta' (d)   EBak
'La France' (d)   EBak EKMF
'La Neige' ambig.   CWVF
'La Neige' Lemoine (d) EBak EKMF
'La Porte' (d)   CLoc CWVF
'La Rosita' (d)   EBak SLBF
'La Traviata' ambig.   WP&B
I 'La Traviata' Blackwell (d) EBak
'La Violetta' (d)   MWhe
'Lace Petticoats' (d)   EBak EKMF
'Lady Boothby'   CDoC CHEx CSil CWVF EBak
                        EKMF LRHS SLBF SMrm SPet
                        WP&B WWeb
'Lady Framlingham' (d) EPts
'Lady Heytesbury'   EKMF MJac
'Lady in Grey' (d)   EKMF LAst MJac
'Lady Isobel Barnett'   CDoC CLoc CSil CWVF EBak
                        EKMF MBri MJac MWar MWhe
                        SPet WP&B
'Lady Kathleen Spence' CWVF EBak MWhe SPet
'Lady Patricia   CWVF EKMF EMan MJac MWhe
  Mountbatten'   WGwG
'Lady Ramsey'   EBak
'Lady Rebecca' (d)   CLoc
'Lady Thumb' (d) ♀H3   More than 30 suppliers
'Lady's Smock'   EKMF
§ 'Laing's Hybrid'   CWVF EBak
'Lakeland Princess'   EBak
'Lakeside'   CWVF EBak
'Laleham Lass'   EKMF
'Lambada'   LAst MJac MWhe WFFs WP&B
'Lancambe'   MWar
'Lancashire Lad' (d)   LAst MWar
'Lancashire Lass'   CWVF MBri
'Lancelot'   EBak WP&B
'Land van Beveren'   MWar SLBF WFFs WP&B
'Lark'   CWVF EPts WP&B
'L'Arlésienne' (d)   CLoc
'Lassie' (d)   CDoC CLoc CWVF EBak
I 'Laura' (Dutch)   CLoc CSil EPts LCla MWar SLBF
I 'Laura' Martin (d)   EKMF MWhe
'Laura' ambig.   CWVF
'Laura Amanda' (d)   EPts
'Laure Buelens' **new** WP&B
'Lavaglut'   WP&B
'Lavender Kate' (d)   CLoc CWVF EBak
'Lavender Lace'   MWhe
'Lazy Lady' (d)   CWVF EBak
'Le Postier'   WP&B
'Lea's Aubergine' **new** WP&B
'Lechlade Apache'   LCla MWar
'Lechlade Chinaman'   CDoC EKMF WFFs WGwG
'Lechlade Debutante'   LCla
'Lechlade Fire-eater'   LCla WP&B
'Lechlade Gordon'   WGwG
'Lechlade Gorgon'   CDoC CWVF EKMF LCla SLBF
                        WGwG
'Lechlade Magician'   CDoC CSil EKMF LCla WFFs
                        WGwG WSPU
'Lechlade Maiden'   CWVF LCla
'Lechlade Martianess'   LCla
'Lechlade Potentate'   LCla

'Lechlade Tinkerbell'   LCla
'Lechlade Violet'   CDoC CSil EKMF WGwG
lehmanii **new**   LCla
'Leica' (d)   EKMF
'Leicestershire Silver' (d) MJac
'Leila' (d) **new**   WP&B
'Len Bielby'   CDoC CWVF LCla
'Lena' (d) ♀H3   CDoC CLoc CSil CTri CWVF EBak
                        EKMF EPts LAst LVER MBri MJac
                        MWhe NDlv SPer SPet SSea WEas
                        WGwG WP&B WWol
'Lena Dalton' (d)   CLoc CWVF EBak MWhe
'Leonhart von Fuchs'   WP&B
'Leonora'   CDoC CLoc CSil CWVF EBak
                        EKMF LCla MBri MWhe SLBF SPet
                        WGwG WP&B
'Lesley'   CWVF
'Lett's Delight' (d)   CWVF EPts
'Letty Lye'   EBak
'Leverhulme'   see F. 'Leverkusen'
§ 'Leverkusen'   CDoC CLoc EBak LCla MJac
                        MWhe WGwG
'Li Kai Lin'   CSil
I 'Liebesträume'   EBak
  Blackwell (d)
'Liebesträume' ambig.   WP&B
'Liebriez' (d) ♀H3-4   CSil EBak EKMF EPts NDlv SPet
                        SWal
'Liemers Lantaern'   CWVF
'Lieze Brantze' **new** WP&B
'Likalin' **new**   CWVF
'Lilac'   CSil EBak
'Lilac Dainty' (d)   CSil
'Lilac Lustre' (d)   CLoc CWVF EBak SPet
'Lilac Princess'   MJac
'Lilac Queen' (d)   EBak
'Lilian'   EKMF WP&B
'Lillian Annetts' (d)   CDoC CWVF EKMF LAst LCla
                        MJac SLBF WFFs WP&B
'Lillibet' (d)   CLoc CWVF EBak WGwG
'Lilo Vogt'   WGwG
'Lime Lite' (d)   MJac
'Linda Goulding'   CWVF EBak MWhe SSea
'Linda Grace'   EKMF EPts MJac MWar
'Linda Mary Nutt' **new** MWar
'Linda Rosling' (d) **new** EKMF
'Lindisfarne' (d)   CLoc CWVF EBak EKMF MJac SPet
'L'Ingénue'   WP&B
'Linlithgow Lass' **new** MWar
'Lionel'   CSil
'Lisa' (d)   CDoC EPts WP&B
'Lisa Jane'   MWhe
'Lisa Rowe' (d)   WP&B
'Lisi'   WP&B
'Little Annie Gee' **new** MWar
'Little Baby'   EKMF
'Little Beauty'   CDoC CSil CWVF EKMF MWhe
                        WP&B
'Little Boy Blue' **new** EPts
'Little Brook Gem'   SLBF
'Little Catbells' **new** SLBF
'Little Gene'   EBak
'Little Jewel'   SPet
'Little Orphan Annie'   LCla WP&B
'Little Ouse' (d)   CWVF MWhe
'Little Snow Queen' **new** WP&B
'Little Witch'   EKMF LCla SLBF
'Liz' (d)   CSil EBak EKMF
Liza = 'Goetzliza'PBR   LAst
  (Shadowdancer
  Series) **new**
'Lochinver' (d)   CWVF
'Loeke's Marie-Lou'   WP&B
'Loeky'   CLoc CWVF EBak SPet SSea

'Logan Garden' — see *F. magellanica* 'Logan Woods'
'Lolita' (d) — CWVF EBak
'London 2000' — LCla MJac SLBF WP&B
'London in Bloom' **new** — SLBF
'Lonely Ballerina' (d) — CLoc CWVF
'Long Wings' — EKMF LCla
'Lonneke' — WP&B
'Lord Byron' — CLoc EBak EKMF
'Lord Derby' — CSil
'Lord Jim' — LCla
'Lord Lonsdale' — CWVF EBak EPts LCla MWhe WP&B
'Lord Roberts' — CLoc CSil CWVF
'Lorelei' — EPts
'Lorna Fairclough' — MJac
'Lorna Swinbank' — CLoc CWVF
'Lottie Hobby' ♀H1+3 — CDoC CLoc CSil CWVF ECtt EKMF EPfP EPts LCla LRHS MAvo MHar MOak MWhe SGar SPet WBod WCom WFFs WGwG WP&B
'Louise Emershaw' (d) — CWVF EBak MJac
'Louise Nicholls' — EKMF
'Lovable' (d) — EBak
'Lovable Rascal' (d) — SLBF
'Loveliness' — CLoc CWVF EBak EKMF MWhe
'Lovely Blue' (d) **new** — WP&B
'Lovely Chipi' **new** — WP&B
'Lovely Les' (d) — LCla
'Lovely Linda' — SLBF
'Lovely Nouchka' **new** — WP&B
'Love's Reward' ♀H1+3 — CLoc CWVF EKMF EPts LCla MJac MWar MWhe SLBF SVil WP&B
'Lower Raydon' **new** — EBak
I 'Loxensis' — CDoC CWVF EBak EKMF LCla
loxensis misapplied — see *F.* 'Speciosa', *F.* 'Loxensis'
'Loxhore Calypso' — EKMF
'Loxhore Fairy Dancer' — CSil LCla
'Loxhore Herald' — CSil
'Loxhore Lullaby' — CSil SLBF
'Loxhore Mazurka' — CSil WFFs WP&B
'Loxhore Minuet' — CDoC CSil LCla
'Loxhore Operetta' — CSil
'Loxhore Posthorn' — CSil LCla
'Lucinda' — CWVF
'Lucky Strike' (d) — CLoc EBak
Lucy = 'Goetzlucy' — EBak
'Lucy Locket' — MJac
'Lukas' **new** — WP&B
'Lunter's Trots' (d) — WP&B
'Lustre' — CWVF EBak
'Lutz Bogemann' **new** — WP&B
§ *lycioides* Andrews — EBak EKMF
I 'Lycioides' — LCla
'Lye's Elegance' — CSil EKMF
'Lye's Excelsior' — EBak
'Lye's Own' — EBak SPet
'Lye's Perfection' — EKMF
'Lye's Unique' ♀H1+3 — CDoC CLoc CSil CWVF EBak EKMF EPts LCla MJac MWar MWhe SLBF SPet
'Lynette' (d) — CLoc
'Lynn Ellen' (d) — CWVF EBak
'Lynne Marshall' — CSil
'Lyric' **new** — WP&B
'Maartje' **new** — WP&B
'Mabel Greaves' (d) — CWVF WP&B
'Machu Picchu' — CLoc CWVF EKMF EPts LCla WP&B
macrophylla — EKMF
macrostigma — EKMF LCla
'Madame Aubin' — EKMF
'Madame Butterfly' (d) — CLoc
'Madame Cornélissen' (d) ♀H3 — More than 30 suppliers

'Madame Eva Boye' — EBak EKMF
'Madeleine Sweeney' (d) — MBri
'Maes-y-Groes' — CSil EKMF
magdalenae — EKMF
magellanica — CDoC CDul COld CWib EKMF EMil MWgw NFor NPer NWea SPer WFar WGwG WP&B WPnn WRha WSSM
– 'Alba' — see *F. magellanica* var. *molinae*
I – 'Alba Aureovariegata' (v) — CDoC EPfP LAst SPer WBcn WGwG
– 'Alba Variegata' (v) — CSil NPol WEas WMoo
– 'Americana Elegans' — CDoC CSil
– var. *conica* — CDoC CSil EKMF
– 'Derek Cook' **new** — WBcn
– var. *discolor* — CSil
– 'Exmoor Gold' (v) — CSil WBcn
– 'Fire Gold' — LRHS
– 'Globosa' — see *F.* 'Globosa'
§ – var. *gracilis* ♀H3 — CDoC CHEx CLoc CSil CTri CWVF EKMF LRHS MWhe WBod WPic WPnn
– – 'Aurea' — CDoC CSil CWVF EBee EHoe EKMF ELan ENot EPfP GQui LAst LCla LRHS MRav MWhe SAga SDix SLBF SPer SPet SPla WCom WFar WGwG WHen WPnn
§ – – 'Tricolor' (v) — CDoC CSLe CSil EHol EKMF EPts EWes LCla LRHS SLBF SRms SSea WCFE WP&B WPnn WWpP
– – 'Variegata' (v) ♀H3 — CSil EBak EBee ENot EPfP LCla LRHS MGos MRav SAga SChu SDix SIng SPer SPet SPoG WBVN WCom WPnn
– 'Lady Bacon' **new** — EKMF MSte
§ – 'Logan Woods' — CDoC CSil EKMF GCal SMrm WBcn WSPU
– 'Longipedunculata' — CDoC CSil EKMF
– var. *macrostema* — CSil EKMF
§ – var. *molinae* — More than 30 suppliers
§ – – 'Enstone' (v) — CBrm CSBt EHoe EKMF EPts
– – 'Enstone Gold' — EKMF
– – 'Golden Sharpitor' (v) — MDKP WCom WHen
– – 'Mr Knight's Blush' — SAga
§ – – 'Sharpitor' (v) — CBcs CDoC CElw CSLe CSil EBak ECha EKMF ELan EPfP EPts GGar IFro LRHS MAsh MBar MRav MWat NPer SGar SPer WCom WEas WFFs WFar WKif WSHC
– var. *myrtifolia* — CDoC CSil EKMF GEil
* – var. *prostrata* — CSil
– var. *pumila* — CBgR CDoC CSil ETow EWes GCal GEil LAst NLar SAga SBla SIng SPer SRot
– 'Riccartonii' — see *F.* 'Riccartonii'
§ – 'Thompsonii' — CDoC CSil ECGP EKMF GCal NDlv SMHy
§ – 'Versicolor' (v) — More than 30 suppliers
'Magenta Flush' — CWVF
'Magic Flute' — CLoc CWVF MJac
'Maharaja' (d) — EBak
'Major Heaphy' — CWVF EBak EKMF MAsh MWhe WCot
'Malibu Mist' (d) — CWVF EKMF LVER WP&B
'Mama Bleuss' (d) — EBak
'Mancunian' (d) — CSil CWVF LCla MWar
I 'Mandarin' Schnabel — EBak
'Mandi' — EWll LCla MWar
'Mantilla' — CDoC CLoc CSil CWVF EBak EKMF MJac MWhe WP&B
'Maori Maid' **new** — WP&B
'Maori Pipes' — CSil
'Marcia'^{PBR} **new** — LAst

'Marcus Graham' (d) — CLoc CWVF EBak EKMF MWar MWhe SCoo WP&B
'Marcus Hanton' (d) — CWVF LCla
'Mardi Gras' (d) — EBak WGwG
'Margam Park' **new** — LCla
'Margaret' (d) ♀H4 — CDoC CDul CLoc CSil CTri CWVF EBak EKMF ENot EPts ISea LCla LVER MWar MWhe NDlv SLBF SPet SSea SWal WGwG WP&B WStI
'Margaret Berger' (d) **new** — SLBF
'Margaret Brown' ♀H4 — CDoC CLoc CSil CTri CWVF EBak EKMF LCla MWhe NDlv SLBF SPet SWal WStI
'Margaret Davidson' (d) — CLoc
'Margaret Ellen' — WP&B
'Margaret Hazelwood' — EKMF
'Margaret Pilkington' — CWVF MJac MWar SSea
'Margaret Roe' — CDoC CSil CWVF EBak EKMF MJac SPet SWal WP&B
'Margaret Rose' — MJac
'Margaret Susan' — EBak
'Margaret Tebbit' — LAst MJac WGor
'Margarite Dawson' (d) — CSil
'Margery Blake' — CSil EBak
'Margrit Willimann' **new** — WP&B
'Maria Landy' — CWVF EKMF EMan LCla MJac MWar WFFs
'Maria Merrills' (d) — EKMF EMan
'Marie Elizabeth' (d) **new** — WP&B
'Marie Helene Meus' **new** — WP&B
'Mariken' **new** — WP&B
'Marilyn Olsen' — CWVF EPts LCla
'Marin Belle' — EBak
'Marin Glow' ♀H3 — CLoc CSil CWVF EBak MWhe SLBF SPet
'Marinka' ♀H3 — CLoc CSil CWVF EBak ECtt EKMF EMan EPts GLbr LAst LCla LVER MBri MJac MWar MWhe NBlu SLBF SPet SSea WFFs WGwG
'Marion Hilton' — MWar
'Mark Kirby' (d) — CWVF EBak EKMF WP&B
'Marlea's Rittepetiet' **new** — WP&B
'Marlea's Schouwpijpke' **new** — WP&B
'Marlies de Keijzer' — LCla
'Martin's Inspiration' — LCla MWar
'Martin's Umbrella' **new** — WP&B
'Martin's Yellow Surprise' — CLoc LCla SLBF
'Martinus' (d) **new** — WP&B
'Marton Smith' — MWhe
'Marty' (d) — EBak
'Mary' ♀H1+3 — CDoC CLoc CSil CWVF EKMF EPts LCla LRHS MLan MWar MWhe SLBF SSea WGwG WP&B
'Mary Ellen Guffey' (d) — SLBF
'Mary Jones' (d) — EKMF
'Mary Lockyer' (d) — CLoc EBak
'Mary Poppins' — CWVF
'Mary Reynolds' (d) — CWVF
'Mary Shead' (d) — MWar
'Mary Thorne' — CSil EBak EKMF
'Mary Wright' (d) — MWhe
'Mary's Millennium' **new** — CWVF
'Masquerade' (d) — CWVF EBak EMan
'Matador' — CSil
mathewsii **new** — EKMF
'Maureen Ward' — EKMF
'Mauve Beauty' (d) — CSil CWVF EKMF NDlv
'Mauve Lace' (d) — CSil
'Max Jaffa' — CSil CWVF
I   'Maxima' **new** — WP&B
'Maybe Baby' **new** — LAst
'Mayblossom' (d) — CWVF ECtt SPet
'Mayfayre' (d) — CLoc

'Mayfield' — CWVF MWhe
'Mazda' — CWVF
'Meadowlark' (d) — CWVF EBak ECtt EKMF
'Mechtildis de Lechy' **new** — WP&B
'Meditation' (d) — CLoc CSil
'Melanie' — CDoC WP&B
'Melissa Heavens' — CWVF
'Melody' — EBak MWhe SPet
'Melody Ann' (d) — EBak
'Melting Moments' (d) — EKMF MJac WP&B
'Menna' — WP&B
'Mephisto' — CSil CWVF
'Mercurius' — CSil
'Merlin' — CSil EKMF LCla
'Merry Mary' (d) — CWVF EBak EKMF WP&B
I   'Mexicali Rose' Machado — CLoc
'Mia Goedman' **new** — WP&B
'Michael' (d) — CWVF EPts WP&B
'Michelle C. Struck' **new** — WP&B
michoacanensis — see *F. microphylla* subsp. *aprica*
  misapplied
michoacanensis — WP&B
  Sessé & Moç.
 – B&SWJ 8982 — WCru
'Micky Goult' ♀H1+3 — CLoc CWVF EKMF EPts LCla MJac MWhe SPet SSea WFFs WP&B
'Microchip' — CSil LCla
microphylla — CBrd CDoC CElw CLoc CPLG CSil CWCL CWVF EBak GCal GGar MLan MWhe SLon SSea STre WCru WEas WGwG
 – B&SWJ 9101 — WCru
§ – subsp. *aprica* — EKMF LCla
§ – subsp. *hemsleyana* — CDoC CPLG CSil EKMF LCla MWhe SWal WGwG WOut
§ – subsp. *hidalgensis* — CSil CTbh EKMF LCla
 – subsp. *microphylla* — CSil EKMF
§ – subsp. *minimiflora* **new** — WP&B
 – subsp. *quercetorum* — CDoC CSil EKMF LCla
 – 'Sparkle' **new** — WCot
'Midas' — CWVF MBri
'Midnight Sun' (d) — CSil CWVF EBak EPts
'Midwinter' — LAst
'Mieke Alferink' — WP&B
'Mieke Meursing' ♀H1+3 — CDoC CLoc CWVF EBak ECtt EKMF MJac MWhe SPet WP&B
'Mien Kuypers' **new** — WP&B
'Mien van Oirschot' (d) **new** — WP&B
'Miep Aalhuizen' — LCla WGwG WP&B
'Mike Foxton' **new** — EKMF
'Mike Oxtoby' — CWVF EKMF
'Mildred Wagg' — MWar
'Millie Butler' — CWVF
'Ming' — CLoc
'Mini Skirt' — WP&B
'Miniature Jewels' — LCla SLBF
minimiflora Hemsley — see *F. microphylla* subsp. *minimiflora*
'Minirose' — CDoC CSil CWVF EPts MJac MWar MWhe
'Minnesota' (d) — EBak
'Mipan' — SLBF
'Mischief' — CSil
'Miss California' (d) — CDoC CLoc CWVF EBak ECtt MBri MWhe WFFs
'Miss Great Britain' — CWVF
'Miss Lye' — CSil EKMF
'Miss Muffett' (d) — CSil
'Miss Vallejo' (d) — EBak
'Mission Bells' — CDoC CLoc CSil CWVF EBak EKMF EPts SPet WGwG
'Misty Blue' (d) — CSil

'Misty Haze' (d) — CWVF LVER
'Moira Ann' — ECtt
'Molesworth' (d) — CSil CWVF EBak EKMF MJac MWhe SPet
'Mollie Beaulah' (d) — CSil CWVF ECtt EKMF WP&B
'Money Spinner' — CLoc EBak
'Monsieur Thibaut' ♀H4 — CSil EKMF ENot LCla SPet
'Monte Rosa' (d) — CLoc CWVF
'Monterey' — MWhe
'Montevideo' (d) — CWVF
'Monument' (d) — CSil
'Mood Indigo' (d) — CSil CWVF LVER WGwG WP&B
'Moon Glow' — LAst MJac WP&B
'Moonbeam' (d) — CLoc MWhe
'Moonlight Sonata' — CLoc CWVF EBak SPet
'Moonraker' (d) — CWVF
'More Applause' (d) — CLoc EKMF LVER MWhe WP&B
'Morecott' (d) **new** — CWVF
'Morning Light' (d) — CLoc CWVF EBak SPet
'Morning Mist' — EBak
'Morning Star' — MBri
'Morrells' (d) — EBak
'Moth Blue' (d) — CSil CWVF EBak SPet
'Mountain Mist' (d) — CWVF EKMF
'Moyra' (d) — CWVF EKMF
'Mr A. Huggett' — CLoc CSil CWVF EKMF EPts LCla MWhe SPet
'Mr P.D. Lee' — MWhe
'Mr W. Rundle' — EBak WP&B
§ 'Mr West' (v) — CSil EHoe EKMF SPet WFFs WP&B
'Mrs Churchill' — CLoc
'Mrs John D. Fredericks' — CSil
'Mrs Lawrence Lyon' (d) — EBak
'Mrs Lovell Swisher' ♀H4 — CDoC CSil CWVF EBak EPts LCla MJac MWhe SPet WP&B
'Mrs Marshall' — CSil CWVF EBak SLBF SPet
'Mrs Popple' ♀H3 — More than 30 suppliers
'Mrs W. Castle' — CSil EKMF WGwG
'Mrs W.P. Wood' ♀H3 — CDoC CLoc CSil CWVF EKMF MBri WP&B
'Mrs W. Rundle' — CLoc CSil CWVF EBak EKMF LRHS MWhe SLBF SPet WP&B
'Multa' — LAst MJac WFFs
'Muriel' (d) — CLoc CWVF EBak ECtt EKMF
'My Delight' **new** — CWVF
'My Dingaling' **new** — WP&B
'My Fair Lady' (d) — CLoc CWVF EBak SPet
'My Honey' — CSil
'My Mum' — LCla SLBF WP&B
'My Reward' (d) **new** — CWVF
'Naaldwijk 800' **new** — WP&B
'Nancy Darnley' (d) — EKMF
'Nancy Lou' (d) — CDoC CLoc CWVF EPts LAst LCla LVER MJac MWhe SLBF SPet WFFs
'Nanny Ed' (d) — CWVF MBri
'Natasha Sinton' (d) — CLoc CSil CWVF ECtt EKMF EMan LAst LVER MBri MJac MWar MWhe NBlu SLBF SPet WFFs WGwG WP&B
'Native Dancer' (d) — CWVF EBak WP&B
'Naughty Nicole' (d) — LCla SLBF WP&B
'Nautilus' (d) — EBak EKMF
'Navy Blue' — CSil
'Neapolitan' (d) — CDoC EPts MWhe SLBF
'Neil Clyne' — MWhe
'Nell Gwyn' — CLoc CWVF EBak
'Nellie Nuttall' ♀H3 — CDoC CLoc CSil CWVF EBak EKMF EPts MWar MWhe SLBF SPet SSea WFFs WP&B
'Neopolitan' — CLoc CSil WGwG
'Nettala' — CDoC WP&B
'Neue Welt' — CSil CWVF EBak EKMF
'New Fascination' (d) — EBak
'New Millennium' **new** — LVER

'Newmel' **new** — MWar
'Nice 'n' Easy' (d) — LVER MBri MJac
'Nicki's Findling' — CDoC CSil CWVF EPts LCla WFFs WP&B
'Nicky Veerman' — WP&B
'Nicola' — CLoc EBak
'Nicola Jane' (d) — CDoC CSil CWVF EBak EKMF EPts LCla MBri MJac MWhe SLBF SPet SWal WP&B
'Nicolette' — CWVF MJac
'Nightingale' (d) — CLoc CWVF EBak
§ **nigricans** — CDoC EKMF LCla
nigricans × gehrigeri — EKMF
'Nina Wills' — EBak
'Niobe' (d) — EBak
'Niula' — EKMF LCla
'No Name' (d) — EBak
'Nonchalance' **new** — LCla
'Nora' (d) **new** — WP&B
'Norcross' **new** — MJac
'Norfolk Ivor' (d) — WP&B
'Normandy Bell' — CWVF EBak SPet
'North Cascades' (d) — WP&B
'Northern Dancer' (d) — EKMF WP&B
'Northumbrian Belle' — EBak WGwG
'Northumbrian Pipes' **new** — LCla WP&B
'Northway' — CLoc CWVF MJac MWhe SPet
'Norvell Gillespie' (d) — EBak
'Novato' — EBak EPts
'Novella' (d) — CWVF EBak
'Nuance' **new** — WP&B
'Nunthorpe Gem' (d) — CDoC CSil
obconica — CSil EKMF LCla
'Obcylin' — EKMF LCla SLBF
'Obergärtner Koch' — EKMF LCla SLBF
'Ocean Beach' — EPts
'Oetnang' (d) — CTri SCoo
'Old Somerset' (v) — LCla WP&B
'Olive Moon' (d) — WP&B
'Olive Smith' — CWVF EPts LCla MJac MWar MWhe WP&B
'Olympia' — EKMF MWhe
'Olympic Lass' (d) — EBak WP&B
'Onward' — CSil EKMF WFFs WP&B
§ 'Oosje' — CDoC CSil LCla SLBF
'Opalescent' (d) — CLoc CWVF
'Orange Crush' — CLoc CWVF EBak MJac MWhe SPet SVil
'Orange Crystal' — CWVF EBak EKMF MJac MWhe SPet
'Orange Drops' — CLoc CSil CWVF EBak EKMF EPts MWhe SPet
'Orange Flare' — CLoc CWVF EBak MWhe SLBF SSea
'Orange King' (d) — CLoc CSil CWVF EMan SSea
'Orange Mirage' — CLoc CSil CWVF EBak LAst LVER MWhe SPet
'Orangeblossom' — CDoC SLBF WP&B
'Oranje van Os' — CWVF MJac MWhe
'Orchid Flame' **new** — WP&B
'Orient Express' — CDoC CWVF LAst MJac MWar MWhe WFFs WGor WGwG WP&B
'Oriental Flame' — EKMF
'Oriental Sunrise' — CWVF MWhe
'Ornamental Pearl' — CLoc CWVF EBak
'Orwell' (d) — CWVF WP&B
'Oso Sweet' — CWVF
'Other Fellow' — CDoC CSil CWVF EBak EKMF EPts LCla MJac MWhe SLBF SPet
'Oulton Empress' — SLBF
'Oulton Fairy' **new** — SLBF
'Oulton Red Imp' — LCla SLBF
'Oulton Travellers Rest' — SLBF

'Our Darling'   CWVF MWhe
'Our Nan' (d)   MJac
'Our Ted'   EKMF EPts WP&B
'Our William' **new** SLBF
'Overbecks'   see *F. magellanica* var. *molinae*
                       'Sharpitor'
'Overbecks Ruby'   GBuc
'Pabbe's Torreldöve' **new** WP&B
'Pacemaker' **new**   MGos
pachyrrhiza   EKMF
'Pacific Grove' Greene see *Fuchsia* 'Evelyn Steele Little'
'Pacific Grove'   EBak
   Niederholzer (d)
'Pacific Queen' (d)   CLoc EBak
'Pacquesa' (d)   CDoC CWVF EBak EPts MWhe
                       SPet
'Padre Pio' (d)   CWVF EBak MJac
'Pallas'   CSil
pallescens   EKMF LCla
'Paloma' **PBR new**   LAst
'Pam Plack'   CSil EKMF LCla
'Pamela Knights' (d)   EBak
'Pamela Wallace' **new** SLBF
'Pam's People'   LCla
'Pan'   MWar WP&B
'Pan America' (d)   EBak
'Panache' (d)   LCla
'Pangea'   LCla WP&B
paniculata ♀H1+3 CDoC CEnd CRHN CTbh CWVF
                       EBak EGra EKMF EPts LCla SHFr
                       SLBF WCru
'Panique'   CSil LCla
'Pantaloons' (d)   EBak
'Pantomine Dame'   CWVF
   (d) **new**
'Panylla Prince'   CDoC EPts LCla
'Papa Bleuss' (d)   CLoc CWVF EBak
'Papoose' (d)   CDoC CSil EBak EKMF LCla WP&B
'Papua' (d) **new**   SLBF WP&B
'Parasol' **new**   WP&B
'Parkstone Centenary' CWVF
   (d) **new**
'Party Frock'   CLoc CWVF EBak LVER SPet
'Party Time' (d) **new** CWVF
parviflora hort.   see *F.* x *bacillaris*
§ **parviflora** Lindley EBak
'Pastel'   EBak
'Pat Meara'   CLoc EBak
'Patatin Pataton' (d) **new** WP&B
'Pathétique' (d)   CLoc
'Patience' (d)   CWVF EBak MJac SWal
'Patio King'   EKMF
'Patio Princess' (d)   CWVF EPts LAst LCla MBri MJac
                       MWhe SSea WFFs WGor
'Patricia' Wood   CSil EBak
'Patricia Bervoets' (d) **new** WP&B
'Patricia Joan Yates' WP&B
'Patty Evans' (d)   CWVF EBak
'Patty Sue' (d)   MBri
'Paul Berry'   CSil EKMF LCla WP&B
'Paul Cambon' (d)   EBak EKMF
'Paul Roe' (d)   MJac
'Paul Storey'   EKMF WP&B
'Paula Jane' (d)   CLoc CWVF LAst LCla MBri MJac
                       MWar MWhe SLBF WFFs WGor
                       WP&B
'Pauline Rawlins' (d) CLoc EBak
'Paulus'   WP&B
'Peace' (d)   EBak
'Peaches 'n' Cream'   LCla
'Peachy' (d)   CDoC EKMF LAst MJac SCoo
                       WP&B
'Peachy Keen' (d)   EBak WP&B
'Peacock' (d)   CLoc

'Pearly Gates'   CWVF
'Pearly King' (d) **new** CWVF
'Pee Wee Rose'   CSil EBak EKMF MAsh
'Peggy Cole'   EPts
'Peggy King'   CDoC CSil EBak EKMF LCla MWhe
                       SPet
'Peggy' (Shadowdancer LAst
   Series) **new**
'Peloria' (d)   CLoc EBak
'Pennine'   MBri MWar
'People's Princess'   MJac WP&B
'Peper Harow'   EBak
'Pepi' (d)   CLoc CWVF EBak SPet
'Peppermint Candy' (d) CWVF EPts LAst WGwG
'Peppermint Stick' (d) CDoC CLoc CSil CWVF EBak
                       EKMF EMan LRHS LVER MBri MJac
                       MWhe SPet SSea
'Perky Pink' (d)   CWVF EBak EPts MWhe SPet
'Perry Park'   CWVF EBak MBri MJac
'Perry's Jumbo'   NBir NPer
perscandens   CSil EKMF LCla MWhe WGwG
'Personality' (d)   EBak
'Peter Bellerby' (d)   EKMF
'Peter Bielby' (d)   CWVF EKMF LCla MWar
'Peter Crookes'   CWVF
'Peter Grange' **new** EBak
'Peter James' (d)   CSil EKMF
'Peter Pan'   CSil CWVF SIng SPer
'Peter Sanderson'   MJac
petiolaris   CDoC EKMF LCla
'Petit Four'   CWVF WP&B
'Petite' (d)   EBak
'Phaidra'   LCla
'Pharaoh'   CLoc
'Phénoménal' (d)   CSil CWVF EBak EKMF EPts LRHS
                       WP&B
'Phillip Taylor'   MJac
'Phyllis' (d) ♀H4   CDoC CLoc CSil CWVF EBak
                       EKMF EPts LCla MJac MWhe NDlv
                       SLBF SPet WFFs WGwG WP&B
                       WTel
'Phyrne' (d)   CSil EBak EKMF SWal
'Piet G. Vergeer'   WP&B
'Piet van der Sande' **new** LCla
pilaloensis   EKMF
x **pilcopata**   LCla
'Pinch Me' (d)   CWVF EBak EKMF LVER SPet
'Pink Aurora'   CLoc
'Pink Ballet Girl' (d) CLoc EBak ECtt
'Pink Bon Accorde'   CLoc CWVF WGwG
'Pink Cloud'   CLoc EBak
'Pink Cornet'   LCla
'Pink Darling'   CLoc EBak MWhe
'Pink Dessert'   EBak
'Pink Domino' (d)   EKMF
'Pink Fairy' (d)   CWVF EBak SPet
'Pink Fandango' (d)   CLoc
'Pink Fantasia'   CDoC CLoc CSil CWVF EBak
                       EKMF EPts LAst LCla MJac MWar
                       MWhe SSea WP&B
'Pink Flamingo' (d)   CLoc EBak
'Pink Galore' (d)   CLoc CSil CWVF EBak EKMF EMan
                       GLbr LAst LCla LVER MBri MJac
                       MWhe SPet SSea WGwG WP&B
'Pink Goon' (d)   CDoC CSil EKMF LCla LRHS NDlv
                       SLBF SWal
'Pink Jade'   CWVF EBak WP&B
'Pink la Campanella'   EBak EMan LAst MBri MWar
                       MWhe WBVN WGor
'Pink Lace' (d)   CSil SPet
'Pink Lady' Ryle-Atkinson MWhe
'Pink Marshmallow'   CLoc CSil CWVF EBak EKMF EMan
   (d) ♀H1+3   GLbr LAst LCla LVER MJac MWar
                       SLBF SPet SSea WGwG

'Pink Panther' (d) — EKMF MJac WFFs
'Pink Pearl' Bright (d) — CSil EBak EKMF LVER
'Pink Picotee' — MJac
'Pink Profusion' — EBak
'Pink Quartet' (d) — CLoc CWVF EBak SPet
'Pink Rain' — CSil CWVF EKMF EPts MJac WFFs WP&B
'Pink Slippers' — CLoc
'Pink Spangles' — CWVF EMan MBri SSea WGwG
'Pink Surprise' (d) — MJac
'Pink Temptation' — CLoc CWVF EBak
'Pink Trumpet' **new** — WP&B
'Pinkmost' (d) — ECtt EKMF
'Pinocchio' **new** — WP&B
'Pinto de Blue' (d) — EKMF LCla MWar WP&B
'Pinwheel' (d) — CLoc EBak
'Piper' (d) — CDoC CSil CWVF
'Piper's Vale' — LCla MJac SLBF SWal WFFs
'Pippa Rolt' — EKMF EPts
'Pirbright' — CWVF EKMF
'Pixie' — CDoC CLoc CSil CWVF EBak EKMF MJac NDlv SLBF SPet
'Playford' — CWVF EBak
'Plenty' — CSil EBak
'Plumb Bob' (d) **new** — CWVF
'Poermenneke' **new** — WP&B
'Pole Star' — CSil
'Polmont Pride' — EKMF
'Pop Whitlock' (v) — CWVF EKMF SPet SSea WP&B
'Popely Pride' (d) — WP&B
'Poppet' — CWVF
'Popsie Girl' — MWar SLBF
'Port Arthur' (d) — CSil EBak
'Postiljon' — CWVF EBak SPet WFFs
'Powder Puff' Hodges (d) — CLoc LVER
I 'Powder Puff' Tabraham (d) — CSil
'Powder Puff' ambig. — CWVF ECtt MBri SPet
I 'Prelude' Kennett (d) — EBak EKMF
'Prelude' Blackwell — CLoc CSil
'President' — CDoC CSil EBak EKMF LCla WFFs
'President B.W. Rawlins' — EBak
§ 'President Elliot' — CSil EKMF MWhe
'President George Bartlett' (d) — CSil EKMF EPts LAst LCla MAsh MJac MWar SLBF WFFs
'President Joan Morris' (d) — EKMF SLBF
'President Leo Boullemier' — CDoC CSil CWVF EBak ECtt EKMF LCla MJac SPet WFFs WGwG WP&B
'President Margaret Slater' — CDoC CLoc CSil CWVF EBak EMan LCla MJac MWhe SPet
'President Moir' (d) — SLBF WP&B
'President Norman Hobbs' — CWVF EKMF MWar
'President Roosevelt' (d) — CDoC ECtt
'President Stanley Wilson' — CWVF EBak ECtt EPts SPet
'Preston Guild' ♀H1+3 — CDoC CLoc CSil CWVF EBak EKMF LRHS MWar MWhe NPer SLBF SPet WFFs
'Pride of the West' — CSil EBak EKMF
'Prince of Orange' — CLoc CSil CWVF EBak EKMF
'Princess Dollar' — see *F.* 'Dollar Princess'
'Princess of Bath' (d) — CLoc
'Princess Pamela' (d) — SLBF
'Princessita' — CSil CWVF EBak ECtt EMan MJac MWhe SPet
procumbens — More than 30 suppliers
- 'Argentea' — see *F.* *procumbens* 'Wirral'
- 'Variegata' — see *F.* *procumbens* 'Wirral'
- 'Wirral' (v) — CDoC CLoc CSil CStu EKMF GCal WCom WCot
'Prodigy' — see *F.* 'Enfant Prodigue'
'Profusion' ambig. — EKMF MWhe
'Prosperity' (d) ♀H3 — CDoC CLoc CSil CWVF EBak EBee EKMF ENot EPfP EPts LCla LRHS LVER MJac MWar MWhe NDlv SPet SWal

'Pumila' — CWib ECha EKMF ELan EPfP EPts ITim SPet SWal
'Purbeck Mist' (d) — CWVF EKMF
'Purperklokje' — CDoC CSil CWVF EBak LCla WP&B
'Purple Ann' — EKMF
'Purple Emperor' (d) — CLoc
'Purple Heart' (d) — CLoc EBak
'Purple Lace' — CSil
'Purple Patch' — MBri
'Purple Pride' — MBri
'Purple Rain' — CLoc CSil EKMF
'Purple Splendour' (d) — CDoC CSil
'Pussy Cat' — CLoc CWVF EBak WP&B
'Putney Pride' — EPts
'Put's Folly' — CWVF EBak MJac WFFs
putumayensis — CSil EBak
'Quasar' (d) — CDoC CLoc CSil CWVF EKMF EPts LAst LCla LRHS LVER MJac MWhe SLBF SPet WBVN WGwG WP&B
'Queen Elizabeth II' **new** — EKMF LCla
'Queen Mabs' — EBak
'Queen Mary' — CLoc CSil EBak EKMF
'Queen of Bath' (d) — EBak
'Queen of Derby' (d) — CWVF LCla
'Queen Victoria' Smith (d) — EKMF
'Queen's Park' (d) — EBak
'Query' — CSil EBak WP&B
'R.A.F.' (d) — CLoc CSil CWVF EBak ECtt EKMF EPts GLbr LCla MWar SLBF SPet SSea WP&B
'Rachel Craig' (d) — MWar
'Rachel Sinton' (d) — EMan LAst MBri MJac
'Radcliffe Beauty' — MWhe
'Radcliffe Bedder' (d) — CDoC CSil EKMF
'Radings Gerda' — LCla
'Radings Karin' — CDoC WP&B
'Radings Magma' — WP&B
'Radings Mia' — LCla SLBF
'Radings Michelle' — CSil CWVF LCla
'Rahnee' — CWVF
'Rainbow' — CWVF
'Ralph Oliver' (d) — WP&B
'Ralph's Delight' (d) — CWVF LAst MJac WP&B
'Rambling Rose' (d) — CLoc CWVF EBak ECtt MJac
'Rams Royal' (d) — CDoC LVER MJac
'Rascal' (d) — MWar
I 'Raspberry' (d) — CLoc CWVF EBak LCla MWhe
'Raspberry Sweet' (d) **new** — CWVF
'Ratae Beauty' — CWVF
'Ratatouille' (d) — EKMF WP&B
ravenii — CSil LCla
'Ravensbarrow' — CSil WP&B
'Ravenslaw' — CSil EKMF
'Ray Redfern' — CWVF
'Razzle Dazzle' (d) — EBak
'Reading Show' (d) — CSil CWVF EKMF EPts LCla SLBF
'Rebecca Williamson' (d) — CWVF MJac MWhe WP&B
'Rebeka Sinton' — CLoc EBak MBri MWar
'Red Ace' (d) — CSil
'Red Imp' (d) — CDoC CSil
'Red Jacket' (d) — CWVF EBak
'Red Petticoat' **new** — CWVF
'Red Rain' — CWVF LCla WP&B
'Red Ribbons' (d) — EBak
'Red Rover' — MWar SLBF
'Red Rum' (d) — CSil SPet
'Red Shadows' (d) — CLoc CSil CWVF EBak MJac WGwG
'Red Spider' — CLoc CSil CWVF EBak EKMF EMan LAst MWar MWhe SCoo SPet SSea WGor WGwG WP&B
'Red Sunlight' — EPts WP&B

'Red Wing'	CLoc	
'Reflexa'	see *F.* x *bacillaris* 'Reflexa'	
'Reg Gubler'	SLBF	
'Regal'	CLoc	
regia	CSil	
– var. *alpestris*	see *F. alpestris*	
– subsp. *regia*	CDoC CSil EKMF EPts LCla	
– subsp. *reitzii*	CDoC CSil EKMF LCla WGwG	
– subsp. *serrae*	CSil EKMF	
'Remember Eric'	EKMF LCla WP&B	
'Remembrance' (d)	CSil EKMF EPts LCla SLBF SSea	
'Remus' (d)	CSil	
'Remy Kind' (d) **new**	WP&B	
'Rene Schwab'	LCla	
'Renee' **new**	WP&B	
'Renee-Madeleine' **new**	WP&B	
'Rensina' **new**	WP&B	
'Requiem'	CLoc	
'Reverend Doctor Brown' (d)	EBak	
'Reverend Elliott'	see *F.* 'President Elliot'	
I 'Rhapsody' Blackwell (d)	CLoc	
'Rhombifolia'	CSil	
'Rianne Foks'	WP&B	
§ 'Riccartonii' ♀H3	More than 30 suppliers	
'Richard John Carrington'	CSil	
'Ridestar' (d)	CLoc CWVF EBak EMan MJac MWhe	
'Rijs 2001' **new**	MWar	
'Rina Felix'	WP&B	
'Ringwood Market' (d)	CSil CWVF ECtt EKMF EPts LCla MJac MWhe SPet	
'Robbie'	EKMF WP&B	
'Robbie's Reward' (d)	SLBF	
'Robert J. Pierce'	MWar	
'Robin Hood' (d)	CDoC CSil EKMF NDlv	
'Rocket' **new**	WP&B	
'Rocket Fire' (d)	CWVF EPts LAst	
'Rodeo'	WP&B	
'Roesse Esli' **new**	WP&B	
'Roesse Femke' **new**	WP&B	
'Roesse Marie' **new**	WP&B	
'Roesse Tricolor' **new**	WP&B	
'Roger de Cooker'	CLoc WP&B	
'Rohees Alchita'	WP&B	
'Rohees Alioth' (d) **new**	WP&B	
'Rohees Azha' **new**	WP&B	
'Rohees Canopus' **new**	WP&B	
'Rohees Izar' **new**	WP&B	
'Rohees King' **new**	WP&B	
'Rohees Ksora' (d) **new**	WP&B	
'Rohees Maasym' **new**	WP&B	
'Rohees Menkar' **new**	WP&B	
'Rohees Merope' **new**	WP&B	
'Rohees Metallah' **new**	WP&B	
'Rohees Minkar' **new**	WP&B	
'Rohees Mintaka' (d) **new**	WP&B	
'Rohees Mira' **new**	WP&B	
'Rohees Naos' **new**	WP&B	
'Rohees Nekkar' **new**	WP&B	
'Rohees New Millennium' (d)	LCla WP&B	
'Rohees Queen'	WP&B	
'Rohees Rana' **new**	WP&B	
'Rohees Reda' (d) **new**	WP&B	
'Rohees Rotanev' **new**	WP&B	
'Rohees Sadir' **new**	WP&B	
'Rohees Segin' **new**	WP&B	
'Rolla' (d)	CWVF EBak EKMF	
'Rolt's Bride' (d)	EKMF	
'Rolt's Ruby' (d)	CSil EKMF EPts	
'Roman City' (d)	CLoc WP&B	
'Romance' (d)	CWVF	
'Romany Rose'	CLoc	
'Ron Chambers Love'	MWar	
'Ron Ewart'	EKMF MWhe	
'Ronald L. Lockerbie' (d)	CLoc CWVF	
'Ron's Ruby'	LCla MWhe WP&B	
'Roos Breytenbach'	CDoC EKMF LAst LCla MJac WFFs WP&B	
'Rosamunda'	CLoc	
'Rose Aylett' (d)	EBak	
'Rose Bradwardine' (d)	EBak	
'Rose Churchill' (d)	MBri MJac	
'Rose Fantasia'	CDoC CLoc CSil CWVF EKMF EPts LAst LCla MJac MWar MWhe SLBF SSea WFFs WP&B	
'Rose Marie' (d)	CLoc	
'Rose of Castile'	CDoC CLoc CSil EBak EKMF LCla LRHS MJac MWhe WFFs	
'Rose of Castile Improved' ♀H4	CSil CWVF EBak EKMF LCla MJac MWar SPet WP&B	
'Rose of Denmark'	CLoc CSil CWVF EBak LAst MBri MJac MWar MWhe SPet WGor WGwG WP&B	
'Rose Reverie' (d)	EBak	
'Rose Winston' (d)	LAst MWhe	
rosea Ruíz & Pav.	see *F. lycioides* Andrews	
rosea hort.	see *F.* 'Globosa'	
'Rosebud' (d)	EBak WP&B	
'Rosecroft Beauty' (d)	CSil CWVF EBak MWhe	
'Rosella' **new**	WP&B	
'Rosemarie Higham'	MJac WP&B	
'Rosemary Day'	CLoc	
'Roslyn Lowe' (d)	CDoC	
'Ross Lea' (d)	CSil	
'Roswitha'	SLBF	
'Rosy Bows'	CWVF	
'Rosy Frills' (d)	CWVF LCla MJac MWhe	
'Rosy Morn' (d)	CLoc EBak	
'Rosy Ruffles' (d)	EKMF	
'Rough Silk'	CLoc CSil CWVF EBak	
'Roy Castle' (d) **new**	CWVF	
'Roy Sinton' **new**	LAst WP&B	
'Roy Walker' (d)	CLoc CWVF LVER MJac	
'Royal and Ancient'	CWVF	
'Royal Mosaic' (d)	CDoC CWVF LAst MJac WP&B	
'Royal Orchid'	EBak	
'Royal Purple' (d)	CSil EBak EKMF MBri SLBF WP&B	
'Royal Serenade' (d) **new**	CWVF	
'Royal Touch' (d)	EBak WP&B	
'Royal Velvet' (d) ♀H3	CLoc CSil CWVF EBak EKMF EMan EPts LAst LCla LVER MJac MWar MWhe SLBF SPet SWal WGwG	
'Royal Wedding'	LCla	
§ 'Rubra Grandiflora'	CWVF EBak EKMF LCla SLBF	
'Ruby Wedding' (d)	CSil CWVF EKMF SLBF WP&B	
'Ruddigore'	CWVF WP&B	
'Ruffles' (d)	CWVF EBak	
§ 'Rufus' ♀H3-4	CDoC CLoc CSil CTri CWVF EBak EHol EKMF EPts LCla LRHS MJac MWar MWhe NDlv SLBF SPet WGwG WP&B	
'Rufus the Red'	see *F.* 'Rufus'	
'Rummens Trots' **new**	WP&B	
'Ruth'	CSil	
'Ruth Brazewell' (d)	CLoc	
'Ruth King' (d)	CDoC CWVF EBak ECtt WGwG	
'Sailor'	EPts MJac WFFs	
'Sally Bell'	CSil	
'Salmon Cascade'	CSil CWVF EBak ECtt EKMF EMan EPts LCla MJac MWhe SLBF SSea WP&B	
'Salmon Glow'	CWVF MJac MWhe	
'Samantha Reynolds' **new**	WP&B	
'Samba' **new**	LAst	
'Sam's Song' (d)	MJac	
'Samson' (d/v)	EBak	
'San Diego' (d)	CSil CWVF	

'San Francisco'	EBak
'San Leandro' (d)	EBak
'San Mateo' (d)	EBak
§ *sanctae-rosae*	EBak EKMF EPts LCla WP&B
'Sandboy'	CWVF EBak
'Sandra Kim' **new**	WP&B
'Sanguinea'	CSil EKMF WP&B
'Sanrina'	EKMF
'Santa Cruz' (d)	CSil CWVF EBak EKMF LCla
	MWhe NDlv SLBF SWal WP&B
'Santa Lucia' (d)	CLoc EBak
'Santa Monica' (d)	EBak
'Sapphire' (d)	CSil EBak
'Sara Helen' (d)	CLoc EBak
'Sarah Eliza' (d)	SCoo
'Sarah Elizabeth' **new**	GLbr
'Sarah Greensmith'	EKMF
'Sarah Jane' (d)	CSil EBak
'Sarah Louise'	CWVF
'Sarong' (d)	EBak
'Satellite'	CLoc CWVF EBak EKMF SPet
	WP&B
'Saturnus'	CSil CWVF EBak SPet
scabriuscula	CDoC EKMF LCla
scandens	see *F. decussata*
'Scarborough	WP&B
Starshine' **new**	
'Scarcity'	CDoC CSil CWVF EBak EKMF
	MWhe SPet SWal WFFs
'Scarlet Cascade'	EKMF
'Schiller' ambig.	EKMF
'Schimpens Glorie'	WP&B
(d) **new**	
'Schlosz Bentheim' **new**	WP&B
'Schneckerl' (d)	SLBF
'Schneeball' (d)	CSil EBak EKMF
'Schneewitcher' **new**	EPts
'Schneewittchen' Hoech	CSil EKMF
'Schneewittchen' Klein	CSil EBak
'Schönbrunner	EBak
Schuljubiläum'	
I 'Schöne Wilhelmine'	see *Fuchsia* 'Die Schöne
	Wilhelmine'
'Scotch Heather' (d)	CWVF
'Sea Shell' (d)	CWVF EBak
'Seaforth'	EBak EKMF
'Sealand Prince'	CDoC CWVF ECtt EKMF LCla
'Sebastopol' (d)	CLoc
'Serendipity'	WP&B
serratifolia Hook.	see *F. austromontana*
serratifolia Ruíz & Pav.	see *F. denticulata*
sessilifolia	EKMF LCla
'Seventh Heaven' (d)	CLoc CWVF GLbr LAst MJac
'Severn Queen'	CWVF
'Shady Blue' **new**	CWVF
'Shangri-La' (d)	EBak WP&B
'Shanley'	CWVF WP&B
'Sharon Allsop' (d)	CWVF MWhe WGwG
'Sharon Caunt' (d)	CSil EKMF
'Sharon Elle'	EKMF
'Sharpitor'	see *F. magellanica* var. *molinae*
	'Sharpitor'
'Shauna Lindsay' **new**	WP&B
'Sheila Crooks' (d)	CWVF EBak EMan MJac MWhe
	WP&B
'Sheila Kirby'	CWVF MJac
'Sheila Mary' (d)	EKMF
'Sheila Steele' (d) **new**	CWVF
'Sheila's Love'	MJac
'Sheila's Surprise' (d) **new**	SLBF
'Shekirb' (d) **new**	MJac
'Shelford'	CDoC CLoc CWVF EBak EKMF
	EMan EPts LCla MJac MWar MWhe
	SLBF SSea WFFs WP&B

'Shell Pink'	CSil
'Shirley'^PBR	LAst
'Shirley Halladay' (d)	EKMF LCla
'Shooting Star' (d)	EBak
'Showfire' **new**	EBak
'Showtime' (d)	CWVF
'Shy Lady' (d)	MWhe SPet WP&B
'Siberoet' **new**	WP&B
'Sierra Blue' (d)	CLoc CWVF EBak EKMF
'Silver Anniversary' (d)	EKMF
'Silver Dawn' (d)	CSil CWVF EKMF EPts SLBF
'Silver Dollar'	MWhe WGwG
'Silver King' **new**	WP&B
'Silver Pink'	CSil
'Silverdale'	CDoC CSil EKMF MWhe
'Simmari' **new**	WP&B
'Simon J. Rowell'	LCla
'Simone	WP&B
Delhommeau' **new**	
'Simple Simon'	CSil
simplicicaulis	EBak EKMF LCla
'Sincerity' (d)	CLoc
'Sint Bartholomeus'	WP&B
(d) **new**	
'Sinton's Standard'	MBri
'Siobhan'	CWVF
'Sir Alfred Ramsey'	CWVF EBak MWhe
'Sir Matt Busby' (d)	EKMF EPts GLbr LAst MJac MWar
	WP&B
'Siren' Baker (d)	EBak
'Sissy Sue' **new**	WP&B
'Sister Ann Haley'	EKMF EPts
'Sister Sister' (d)	SLBF WP&B
'Six Squadron'	EKMF
skutchiana	CPLG SMrm
'Sleepy'	CSil MBri SPet WFFs WP&B
'Sleigh Bells'	CLoc CSil CWVF EBak EKMF
	MWhe SPet WGwG
'Small Pipes'	CWVF EKMF LCla WP&B
'Smokey Mountain' (d)	MJac MWar
'Smoky' (d)	WP&B
'Smouldering Fires' **new**	WP&B
'Sneezy'	CSil MWhe
'Snow Burner' (d)	CDoC CWVF LAst MJac WGwG
	WP&B
'Snow White' (d)	CSil SPet WGwG WP&B
'Snowbird' (d)	MWar SLBF WP&B
§ 'Snowcap' (d) ♀^H3-4	CDoC CLoc CSil CWVF EBak
	EKMF EPts GKir GLbr LAst LCla
	LVER MBNS MBri MGos MJac
	MWar MWhe NDlv NPer SLBF SPet
	SPla SSea WFFs WFar WGwG
	WLow WP&B WStI
'Snowdon' (d)	CWVF
'Snowdrift' Colville (d)	CLoc
'Snowdrift' Kennett (d)	EBak
'Snowfall'	CWVF
'Snowfire' (d)	CLoc CSil CWVF ECtt EKMF MJac
	MWhe SCoo WGwG WP&B
'Snowflake'	EKMF LCla SLBF WBor
'Snowstorm' (d)	ECtt SPet
'Snowy Summit' (d)	WGwG
'So Big' (d)	EKMF
'Softpink Jubelteen' **new**	WP&B
'Son of Thumb' ♀^H4	CDoC CLoc COkL CSil CWVF
	EKMF EMan EPfP EPts LAst MAsh
	MBar MBri MGos MJac MWhe
	NDlv SIng SLBF SPet SSea WFFs
	WFar WP&B
'Sonata' (d)	CLoc CWVF EBak
'Sophie Louise'	EKMF EPts MWar WP&B
'Sophie's Silver	MJac SVil
Lining' **new**	
'Sophie's Surprise'	WP&B

'Sophisticated Lady' (d)   CLoc CWVF EBak ECtt EKMF EPts LVER MWar SPet
'Soroptimist International'   MWar
'South Gate' (d)   CLoc CWVF EBak EKMF EMan EPts GLbr LAst MBri MJac MWar MWhe SPet WFFs WGwG WP&B
'South Lakeland'   CSil
'South Seas' (d)   EBak
'Southern Pride' **new**   SLBF
'Southlanders'   EBak
'Southwell Minster'   EKMF
'Space Shuttle'   CLoc EKMF LCla MWhe SLBF
'Sparky'   CDoC CWVF EPts LCla MWar MWhe WP&B
§ 'Speciosa'   EBak EKMF LCla MWhe
'Spice of Life' (d) **new**   CWVF
'Spion Kop' (d)   CDoC CWVF EBak EKMF GLbr LAst MJac MWar MWhe SPet WGor
§ **splendens** ♀H1+3   CDoC CLoc EBak EKMF EPts LCla NPer WGwG
– 'Karl Hartweg'   CDoC
'Sporty'   MJac
'Spring Bells' (d)   MWhe
'Spring Classic'   WP&B
'Squadron Leader' (d)   CWVF EBak EPts LCla LVER
'Stanley Cash' (d)   CLoc CSil CWVF EKMF LVER MWar SPet WP&B
'Stan's Choice'   WP&B
'Star Wars'   MBri MJac MWar MWhe SVil
'Stardust'   CWVF EBak MJac MWhe
'Steeley' (d)   MWhe
'Steirerblut'   WP&B
'Stella Ann'   CSil CWVF EBak EPts LCla WP&B
'Stella Didden' (d) **new**   WP&B
'Stella Marina' (d)   CLoc EBak
I 'Stephanie Wheat' **new**   MWar
'Stewart Taylor'   MJac
steyermarkii   EKMF
'Straat Magelhaen'   LCla
'Straat Malakka'   EPts LCla
'Straat Napier'   WP&B
'Strawberry Delight' (d)   CLoc CWVF EBak ECtt EKMF LVER MJac MWhe SPet
'Strawberry Mousse' (d)   LVER
'Strawberry Sundae' (d)   CLoc CWVF EBak
'Strawberry Supreme' (d)   CSil EKMF
'String of Pearls'   CLoc CWVF EKMF MJac SLBF SPet SSea WP&B
'Stuart Joe'   CWVF EKMF
'Student Prince'   CWVF
'Sue' **new**   SLBF
'Sugar Almond' (d)   CWVF
'Sugar Blues' (d)   CDoC EBak
'Summerdaffodil'   SLBF WP&B
'Sunkissed' (d)   COtt EBak WGwG
'Sunningdale'   CWVF LCla
'Sunny'   COtt
'Sunny Smiles'   CSil CWVF EKMF SPet
'Sunray' (v)   CLoc CWVF EBak EHoe EKMF LAst LRHS MAsh MBNS MWar MWhe NMRc NSti SPla SWal WCot WP&B
'Sunset'   CLoc CSil CWVF EBak MWhe SPer
'Sunset Boulevard' (d)   CDoC
'Supersport' (d)   CDoC WP&B
'Superstar'   CWVF EPts WP&B
'Surrey Symphony'   WP&B
'Susan' (d)   COtt LAst
'Susan Drew' **new**   SLBF
'Susan Ford' (d)   CWVF SPet WGwG
'Susan Green'   CDoC CSil CWVF EBak EKMF EMan MJac MWar MWhe SPet WGwG
'Susan McMaster'   CLoc

'Susan Olcese' (d)   CWVF EBak
'Susan Skeen'   MJac WP&B
'Susan Travis'   CLoc CSil CWVF EBak EKMF MWhe SPet
'Swanley Gem' ♀H3   CLoc CWVF EBak EKMF MWhe SLBF SPet SSea
'Swanley Pendula'   CLoc
'Swanley Yellow'   CWVF EBak
'Sweet Leilani' (d)   CLoc EBak
'Sweet Sarah' **new**   SLBF
'Sweet Sixteen' (d)   CLoc
I 'Sweetheart' van Wieringen   EBak
'Sweetheart' ambig.   CWVF
'Swingtime' (d) ♀H3   CLoc CSil CWVF EBak EKMF EMan EPts GLbr LAst LCla LVER MGos MJac MWar MWhe NBlu SLBF SPet WGwG WP&B
'S'Wonderful' (d)   CLoc EBak
sylvatica Munz   see *F. nigricans*
sylvatica Benth.   EKMF LCla
'Sylvia Barker'   CWVF LCla MJac MWar WFFs
'Sylvia Noad' **new**   MWar SLBF
'Sylvia Rose' (d) **new**   CWVF
'Sylvia's Choice' **new**   EBak
'Sylvy'   MWhe
'Symphony'   CLoc CWVF EBak
'T.S.J.' **new**   LCla SLBF
'Taatje' **new**   WP&B
'Taco'   LCla WP&B
'Taddle'   CWVF EMan MJac SLBF SPet WGwG
'Taffeta Bow' (d)   CLoc EKMF LVER
'Taffy'   EBak WP&B
'Tahoe'   WP&B
'Tamworth'   CLoc CWVF EBak MJac SSea
'Tangerine'   CLoc CSil CWVF EBak MWhe SSea
'Tantalising Tracy' (d)   SLBF WP&B
'Tanya'   CLoc EKMF SPet
'Tanya Bridger' (d)   EBak
'Tarra Valley'   LCla MWhe WP&B
'Task Force'   CWVF
'Taudens Heil' (d) **new**   WP&B
'Tausendschön' (d)   CLoc ECtt
'Ted Perry' (d)   CWVF
'Temptation' ambig.   CWVF ECtt SPet
'Temptation' Peterson   CLoc EBak
'Tenderlight' **new**   WP&B
'Tennessee Waltz' (d) ♀H3   CDoC CLoc CSil CWVF EBak EKMF EMan EPts LCla LRHS LVER MJac MWar MWhe SChu SLBF SPer SPet SWal WEas WGwG WP&B
'Terri's Treasure' (d)   SLBF
'Tessa Jane'   CSil
tetradactyla   see *F. encliandra* subsp. *tetradactyla*
tetradactyla misapplied   see *F.* x *bacillaris*
'Texas Longhorn' (d)   CLoc CSil CWVF EBak EKMF WP&B
'Texas Star'   WP&B
'Thalia' ♀H1+3   CDoC CHrt CLoc CSil CWVF EBak ECtt EKMF EPts LAst LCla LRHS LVER MBri MJac MOak MWar MWhe NBlu SGar SLBF SPet SPla SWal WBod WCom WEas WFFs WGwG WP&B
'Thamar'   CDoC CLoc CSil CWVF EPts MWar MWhe WFFs WP&B
'That's It' (d)   EBak WP&B
'The Aristocrat' (d)   CLoc EBak WGwG
'The Boys'   SLBF
§ 'The Doctor'   CLoc CSil CWVF EBak EKMF MWhe
'The Jester' (d)   EBak
'The Madame' (d)   CWVF EBak

'The Tarns'	CSil CWVF EBak EKMF NCiC	
'Theresa Drew'	SLBF	
'Therese Dupois'	CSil	
'Théroigne de Méricourt'	EBak EKMF	
'Thilco'	CSil EKMF	
'Think Pink'	WGwG	
'Thistle Hill' (d)	CSil EKMF	
'Thompsonii'	see *F. magellanica* 'Thompsonii'	
'Thornley's Hardy'	CDoC CSil EMan SPet	
'Three Cheers'	CLoc EBak	
'Three Counties'	EBak	
'Thunderbird' (d)	CLoc CWVF EBak	
thymifolia	CWVF GQui LHop SHFr SIng SMrm WKif	
- subsp. *minimiflora*	CSil EKMF LCla	
- subsp. *thymifolia*	CDoC CSil EKMF LCla WKif	
'Tiara' (d)	EBak	
'Tiffany' Reedstrom (d)	EBak	
'Tijl Uilenspiegel' **new**	WP&B	
'Tilla Dohmen' **new**	WP&B	
tillettiana	EKMF	
'Tillingbourne' (d)	CSil EKMF LCla	
'Tillmouth Lass'	EKMF	
'Tilly' (Shadowdancer Series) **new**	LAst	
'Timlin Brened'	CSil CWVF EBak MWhe	
'Timothy Titus'	LCla MWar SLBF	
'Tina's Teardrops' (d)	WP&B	
'Ting-a-ling'	CDoC CLoc CSil CWVF EBak EKMF MWhe SLBF SPet SSea WP&B	
'Tinker Bell' Hodges	EBak WP&B	
'Tinker Bell' ambig.	CDoC NDlv	
'Tinker Bell' Tabraham	CSil EKMF WP&B	
'Tintern Abbey'	CWVF	
'Tjinegara'	LCla	
'Toby Bridger' (d)	CLoc EBak	
'Tolling Bell'	CWVF EBak MJac MWhe SPet WGwG WP&B	
'Tom Goedeman' **new**	LCla	
'Tom H. Oliver' (d)	EBak	
'Tom Knights'	CDoC EBak MWhe SPet WGwG	
'Tom Silcock'	WP&B	
'Tom Thorne'	EBak	
'Tom Thumb' ♀H3	More than 30 suppliers	
'Tom West' Meillez (v)	More than 30 suppliers	
'Tom West' misapplied	see *Fuchsia* 'Mr West'	
'Tom Woods'	CDoC CWVF MWhe	
'Tony Porter' (d)	MJac	
'Tony's Treat' (d)	EPts	
'Topaz' (d)	CLoc EBak	
'Topper' (d)	CWVF EMan	
'Torch' (d)	CLoc CWVF EBak	
'Torchlight'	CWVF EPts LCla	
'Torvill and Dean' (d)	CLoc CWVF EKMF EPts LAst LRHS LVER MJac MWar MWhe SPet WGor	
'Tosca'	CWVF	
'Towen' **new**	WP&B	
'Trabant'	WP&B	
'Tracid' (d)	CLoc CSil	
'Tracie Ann' (d)	EKMF	
'Trail Blazer' (d)	CLoc CSil CWVF EBak MJac SPet	
'Trailing King' **new**	WP&B	
'Trailing Queen'	CSil EBak EKMF MJac WP&B	
'Tranquility'	WP&B	
'Trase' (d)	CDoC CSil CWVF CWib EBak EKMF EPts LVER SWal WP&B	
'Traudchen Bonstedt'	CDoC CLoc CSil CWVF EBak EKMF EPts LCla MWhe SLBF SPet WFFs WP&B	
'Traviata'	see *Fuchsia* 'La Traviata' Blackwell	
'Treasure' (d)	EBak	
'Tresco'	CSil WBcn	
'Treslong'	WP&B	
'Triantha' **new**	WP&B	
'Tricolor'	see *F. magellanica* var. *gracilis* 'Tricolor'	
'Tricolorii'	see *F. magellanica* var. *gracilis* 'Tricolor'	
'Trientje'	LCla	
'Trimley Bells' **new**	EBak	
'Trio' (d)	CLoc	
triphylla	EBak EKMF LCla LRHS	
- 'Dominica' **new**	WP&B	
'Tristesse' (d)	CLoc CWVF EBak	
'Troika' (d)	EBak EKMF	
'Troon'	CWVF	
'Tropic Sunset' (d)	MBri MWhe	
'Tropicana' (d)	CLoc CWVF EBak	
'Troubador' Waltz (d)	CLoc	
'Troutbeck'	CSil	
'Trudi Davro'	GLbr LAst MJac	
'Trudy'	CSil CWVF EBak EKMF SPet SWal	
'True Love' **new**	WP&B	
'Truly Treena' (d)	SLBF	
'Trumpeter' ambig.	CDoC CWVF WP&B	
'Trumpeter' Reiter	CLoc EBak EKMF EPts LAst LCla MJac MWhe	
'Tsjiep'	CDoC	
'Tubular Bells'	EKMF LCla WP&B	
'Tumbling Waters' (d)	LVER	
'Tuonela' (d)	CLoc CWVF EBak MWhe WP&B	
'Turandot' **new**	WP&B	
'Turkish Delight' **new**	LAst MJac MWar SVil WP&B	
'Tutti-frutti' (d)	CLoc	
'Twinkletoes'	EPts	
'Twinkling Stars'	CSil CWVF EKMF MJac WP&B	
'Twinney' **new**	CWVF	
'Twinny'	EKMF EPts MWar SLBF	
'Twirling Square Dancer' (d)	WP&B	
'Twist of Fate' (d)	CSil EKMF	
'Two Tiers' (d)	CSil CWVF EKMF LCla WGwG WP&B	
'U.F.O.'	CWVF	
'Ullswater' (d)	CWVF EBak LVER	
'Ulrika' (d)	MWar	
'Ultramar' (d)	EBak	
'Uncle Charley' (d)	CDoC CLoc CSil EBak EKMF WEas	
'Uncle Jinks'	SPet	
'Uncle Steve' (d)	EBak	
'University of Liverpool'	MJac	
'Upward Look'	EBak EKMF SSea	
'Valda May' (d) **new**	CWVF	
'Valentine' (d)	EBak	
'Valerie Ann' (d)	EBak SPet WFFs	
'Valerie Hobbs' (d)	LCla	
'Valerie Tooke' (d)	LCla	
'Valiant'	EBak	
'Vanessa' (d)	CLoc	
'Vanessa Jackson'	CLoc CWVF MJac MWhe WGwG	
'Vanity Fair' (d)	CLoc EBak WP&B	
vargasiana	CDoC	
'Variegated Brenda White' (v) **new**	EKMF	
'Variegated la Campanella' (d/v)	MWhe	
'Variegated Lottie Hobby' (v)	CSil EKMF EPts LCla	
'Variegated Pixie'	CSil EKMF	
'Variegated Procumbens'	see *F. procumbens* 'Wirral'	
'Variegated Snowcap' (d/v)	MWhe	
'Variegated Superstar' (v)	MBri	
'Variegated Swingtime' (v)	EBak	
'Variegated Vivienne Thompson' (d/v)	MBri	

Note: "I" markers appear to the left of 'Tinker Bell' Tabraham and 'Triantha' **new**.

'Variegated Waveney Sunrise' (v) — MBri
'Variegated White Joy' (v) — EKMF
'Veenlust' — LAst MJac WP&B
'Vendeta' — LCla
'Venus Victrix' — CSil EBak EKMF MWhe SLBF
venusta — CDoC EBak EKMF LCla
'Versicolor' — see *F. magellanica* 'Versicolor'
'Vesuvio' — EKMF
'Vicky' **new** — EKMF
'Victoria Smith' **new** — EKMF
'Victorian' (d) — CSil
'Victory' Reiter (d) — EBak
'Vielliebchen' — CDoC CSil
'Vienna Waltz' (d) — MJac
'Vincent van Gogh' — WP&B
'Violet Bassett-Burr' (d) — CLoc EBak
'Violet Gem' (d) — CLoc
'Violet Lace' (d) — CSil
'Violet Rosette' (d) — CWVF EBak
'Violette' (Shadowdancer Series) **new** — LAst
'Viva Ireland' — EBak ECtt
'Vivian Miller' **new** — CWVF
'Vivien Colville' — CLoc EKMF SSea
'Vobeglo' — CWVF EKMF
'Vogue' (d) — EBak
'Voltaire' — CSil EBak EKMF
'Voodoo' (d) — CDoC CLoc CSil CWVF EBak EKMF EMan EPts GLbr LAst MWar SLBF SPet SSea WGwG
vulcanica André — see *F. ampliata*
vulcanica Berry — CDoC EKMF LCla WP&B
– subsp. *hitchcockii* — EKMF
'Vyvian Miller' — MJac
'W.P. Wood' — CSil
§ 'Wagtails White Pixie' — CSil EBak
'Waldfee' — CDoC CSil EKMF LCla MWhe WGwG
'Waldis Geisha' (d) — SLBF
'Waldis Lea' **new** — WP&B
'Waldis Lydia' (d) — SLBF
'Waldis Ovambo' — SLBF
'Waldis Simon' **new** — SLBF
'Wally Yendell' (v) — WFFs
'Walsingham' (d) — CWVF EBak WP&B
'Walton Jewel' — EBak
'Walz Banjo' **new** — WP&B
'Walz Beiaard' **new** — WP&B
'Walz Bella' — LCla WP&B
'Walz Blauwkous' (d) — CWVF
'Walz Cello' **new** — WP&B
'Walz Epicurist' **new** — WP&B
'Walz Fanclub' — LCla WP&B
'Walz Floreat' **new** — WP&B
'Walz Fluit' — LAst MJac WGor WP&B
'Walz Freule' — CWVF EKMF MJac
'Walz Gitaar' — WP&B
'Walz Gong' — WP&B
'Walz Harp' — CDoC CWVF LCla WP&B
'Walz Hoorn' **new** — WP&B
'Walz Jubelteen' — CDoC CLoc CSil CWVF EKMF EMan EPts LCla MJac MWar MWhe SLBF SSea WP&B
'Walz Kattesnoor' — WP&B
'Walz Klarinet' **new** — WP&B
'Walz Lucifer' — LCla SLBF WFFs WP&B
'Walz Luit' — CDoC
'Walz Mandoline' (d) — CWVF WP&B
'Walz Nugget' **new** — WP&B
'Walz Panfluit' **new** — LCla
'Walz Parasol' — WP&B
'Walz Pauk' (d) **new** — WP&B
'Walz Piano' **new** — WP&B

'Walz Piston' **new** — WP&B
'Walz Polka' — LCla WP&B
'Walz Spinet' **new** — WP&B
'Walz Sprietje' **new** — WP&B
'Walz Tamtam' (d) — CDoC
'Walz Telescope' **new** — WP&B
'Walz Triangel' (d) — CSil EKMF WP&B
'Walz Trombone' **new** — WP&B
'Walz Trommel' (d) — WP&B
'Walz Tuba' **new** — WP&B
'Walz Waterval' — WP&B
'Walz Wipneus' — WP&B
'Wapenveld's Bloei' — CDoC LCla SLBF WFFs WP&B
'War Dance' (d) — MWhe
'War Paint' (d) — CLoc EBak
'War Pipes' **new** — LCla
'Warton Crag' — CWVF
'Water Nymph' — CLoc SLBF SSea WP&B
'Wave of Life' — CWVF EKMF MWhe
'Waveney Gem' — CDoC CSil CWVF EBak EKMF EMan LCla MJac MWar SLBF SPet WFFs
'Waveney Queen' — CWVF
'Waveney Sunrise' — CWVF MJac MWar MWhe SPet
'Waveney Unique' — CWVF
'Waveney Valley' — EBak MJac
'Waveney Waltz' — CWVF EBak MJac MWar
'Welsh Dragon' (d) — CLoc EBak WGwG WP&B
'Wendy' Catt — see *F.* 'Snowcap'
'Wendy Atkinson' (d) — EKMF
'Wendy Harris' (d) — MJac
'Wendy Leedham' (d) — ECtt EKMF
'Wendy van Wanten' — EPts WP&B
'Wendy's Beauty' (d) — CLoc EPts MJac WP&B
'Wentworth' — CWVF
'Wessex Belle' (d/v) — CWVF
'Wessex Hardy' — CSil EKMF
'Westham' — LCla
'Westminster Chimes' (d) — CLoc CWVF MWhe SPet WP&B
'Wharfedale' — CSil MJac SLBF
'Whickham Blue' — CWVF
'Whirlaway' (d) — CLoc CSil CWVF EBak EKMF
'White Ann' (d) — see *F.* 'Heidi Weiss'
'White Clove' — CDoC CSil LCla WGwG
'White Fairy' — WP&B
'White Galore' (d) — CWVF EBak EKMF EMan LVER SPet
'White General Monk' (d) — CDoC CSil LAst
'White Gold' (v) — EBak WP&B
'White Heidi Ann' (d) — CSil MWhe SSea WGwG
'White Joy' — EBak
'White King' (d) — CLoc CSil CWVF EBak EKMF EMan LVER MJac MWhe SPet WP&B
'White Lace' — CSil
'White Lady Patricia Mountbatten' — EMan
'White Pixie' ♀H3-4 — CDoC CSil EKMF EPts LCla LVER MJac NDlv SPer SPet WP&B
'White Pixie Wagtail' — see *Fuchsia* 'Wagtails White Pixie'
'White Queen' Doyle — EBak MWhe
'White Queen' ambig. — CWVF
'White Spider' — CLoc CWVF EBak MWhe SPet SSea
'White Veil' (d) **new** — CWVF
'White Water' — WP&B
'Whiteknights Amethyst' — CDoC CSil EKMF WBcn WGwG
'Whiteknights Blush' — CDoC CMdw CSil CStr GCal GQui SMrm WBcn WP&B
'Whiteknights Cheeky' — CWVF EBak EPts LCla WGwG WP&B
'Whiteknights Green Glister' — CDoC CSil EKMF
'Whiteknights Pearl' ♀H1+3 — CBot CDoC CSil CWVF ECha ECtt EKMF EPts LCla MAsh SLBF SMHy SPet WFFs WGwG
'Whiteknights Ruby' — CSil EKMF LCla
'Whitton Starburst' — LCla
'Wicked Queen' (d) — CDoC CSil

'Widow Twanky' (d) **new** — CWVF WP&B
'Wigan Pier' (d) — LCla MWar SLBF WFFs
'Wight Magic' (d) — MJac
'Wild and Beautiful' (d) — CWVF EKMF SPet
'Wilf Langton' — MWar
'Wilfred C. Dodson' — WP&B
'Wilhelm Tell' **new** — WP&B
'Wilhelmina Schwab' — LCla
'Will van Brakel' — WP&B
'William Caunt' — EKMF
'Willie Tamerus' **new** — WP&B
'Willy Winky' — CSil
'Wilma van Druten' **new** — WP&B
'Wilma Versloot' — WP&B
'Wilson's Colours' — EPts
'Wilson's Joy' — MJac WFFs WP&B
'Wilson's Pearls' (d) — SLBF SPet WGwG
'Wilson's Sugar Pink' — EPts LCla MJac MWhe
'Win Oxtoby' (d) — CWVF EKMF
'Windmill' **new** — CWVF
'Wine and Roses' (d) — EBak
'Wings of Song' (d) — CWVF EBak
'Winston Churchill' (d) ♀H3 — CLoc CSil CWVF EBak EKMF EMan EPts GLbr LAst LVER MBri MJac MWhe NVic SPet SPlb SSea SWal WFFs WLow WP&B
'Winter's Touch' — EKMF
'Woodnook' (d) — CWVF
'Woodside' (d) — CSil
wurdackii — EKMF
'Ymkje' — EBak
'Yolanda Franck' — CDoC CSil
'Youth' **new** — EKMF
'Yuletide' (d) — CSil
'Yvonne Schwab' — LCla
'Zara' — MWhe WP&B
'Zellertal' — WP&B
'Zets Bravo' — CDoC WGwG
'Ziegfield Girl' (d) — EBak WP&B
'Zulu King' — CDoC CSil
'Zwarte Dit' — WP&B
'Zwarte Snor' (d) — CWVF WP&B

Fumana (Cistaceae)
ericoides **new** — XPep
thymifolia — XPep

Fumaria (Papaveraceae)
lutea — see *Corydalis lutea*
officinalis — CArn MSal

Furcraea (Agavaceae)
bedinghausii — CBct CFil CHll CTrC EOas WMul WPGP
longaeva — CAbb CCtw CHEx CPne CTrC EAmu EBee EOas MOak SAPC SArc SChr SDix WCot WPGP
selloa var. *marginata* (v) — CDoC CHEx EOas

G

Gagea (Liliaceae)
lutea — EPot
pratensis — EPot

Gahnia (Cyperaceae)
filum — GGar

Gaillardia (Asteraceae)
aristata 'Maxima Aurea' — CWCL WCAu WWeb
'Bijou' — EBee EBre NVic SWvt WWeb

'Bremen' — EBee LRHS MAvo NNor NPri WShp
'Burgunder' — More than 30 suppliers
'Dazzler' ♀H4 — CSBt CWCL EBee ECtt ELan ENot EPfP ERou GKir LRHS MBri MWgw NLar NVic SPer WCAu WGor WPer WStI
'Dwarf Goblin' — SPet
§ 'Fackelschein' — SRms WHer XPep
'Fanfare' **new** — COtt EBre MBri SCoo SPer WWeb
Goblin — see *G.* 'Kobold'
§ 'Goldkobold' — ELan EPar ERou MBri MHer
x *grandiflora* 'Aurea' — LRHS
– 'Aurea Plena' (d) — EBee
§ 'Kobold' — More than 30 suppliers
'Mandarin' — LRHS SRms
* new giant hybrids — WFar WLow
'Tokajer' — EBee EPfP NLar WCAu
Torchlight — see *G.* 'Fackelschein'
'Wirral Flame' — EPar
Yellow Goblin — see *G.* 'Goldkobold'

Galactites (Asteraceae)
tomentosa — CHrt CPom CSpe EHrv ELan EMan EMar GBBs LDai LPhx LRHS MBct MBri NBPC NBur NDov SDnm SGar SPer WCot WEas WHrl WWeb
– white — CPla NBur

Galanthus ✿ (Amaryllidaceae)
x *allenii* — CAvo CBro EHyt ENGS WIvy
alpinus — CLAP LAma
§ – var. *alpinus* — CAvo CBro EHyt ENGS LAma MBri MTho NGar WIin
– – late-flowering — LRHS
§ *angustifolius* — CBro
'Anne of Geierstein' — ENGS
'Armine' — CAvo ENGS
'Atkinsii' ♀H4 — CAvo CBel CBro CElw CLAP EMon ENGS EOrc EPar EPot ETow GAbr GCrs LAma MRav NBir NGar SChr WPGP WShi WTin WWye
'Barbara's Double' (d) — CLAP ENGS NGar
'Benhall Beauty' — CAvo ENGS
'Benton Magnet' — ENGS
'Bertram Anderson' — ENGS NGar
'Brenda Troyle' — CAvo CBel CBro CLAP EPar EPot GCrs NGar NPol WIvy
byzantinus — see *G. plicatus* subsp. *byzantinus*
'Castlegar' **new** — CAvo
caucasicus misapplied — see *G. elwesii* var. *monostictus*
caucasicus (Bak.) Grossh. — see *G. alpinus* var. *alpinus*
– 'Comet' — see *G. elwesii* 'Comet'
– var. *hiemalis* — see *G. elwesii* var. *monostictus* Hiemalis Group
– 'John Tomlinson' — see *G. elwesii* 'John Tomlinson'
– late-flowering — see *G. alpinus* var. *alpinus* late-flowering
– 'Mrs McNamara' — see *G. elwesii* 'Mrs McNamara'
'Charmer Flore Pleno' — see *G. nivalisi* 'Doncaster's Double Charmer'
'Clare Blakeway-Phillips' — CLAP EHyt ENGS NGar
'Colesborne' — ENGS
corcyrensis spring-flowering — see *G. reginae-olgae* subsp. *vernalis*
– winter-flowering — see *G. reginae-olgae* subsp. *reginae-olgae* Winter-flowering Group
'Cordelia' (d) — CLAP EMon ENGS EPot
'Curly' — ENGS
'Desdemona' (d) — CLAP EPot WCot WIvy
'Dionysus' (d) — CAvo CBgR CBro CLAP EHyt ENGS EOrc EPot ERos MHom NBir NGar
§ *elwesii* ♀H4 — CAvo CBel CBro CFwr ELan EMon ENGS EOrc EPfP EPot ERos GFlt

	LAma LRHS NBir NGar NMen NPol NRog SRms WCot WIvy WShi
– 'Athenae'	CBro GCrs
§ – 'Comet'	EMon ENGS NGar
– 'Daphne's Scissors'	CBel WIvy
– 'David Shackleton'	ENGS
– Edward Whittall Group	CLAP
– var. *elwesii*	NGar
'Fenstead End'	
– – 'Kite'	CBro ENGS NPol
– – 'Magnus'	CLAP
– – 'Maidwell L'	CAvo ENGS
– – 'Paradise Giant'	EPar
– 'Flore Pleno' (d)	CAvo
– Hiemalis Group **new**	CBel
– 'J. Haydn'	LAma
§ – 'John Tomlinson'	ENGS
– 'Kyre Park'	EMon
§ – var. *monostictus* ♀H4	CAvo EMon GFlt
– – 'G. Handel'	LAma
* – – 'Green Tips'	NGar NPol
– – 'H. Purcell'	LAma
§ – – Hiemalis Group	CBro ECha EMon ENGS LAma WCot
§ – 'Mrs McNamara'	CBel ENGS
§ – 'Ransom's Dwarf'	ENGS
– 'Selborne Green Tips'	EMon
– 'Washfield Colesbourne'	see *G.* 'Washfield Colesbourne'
– 'Zwanenburg'	EMon NGar
'Falkland House'	ENGS
'Fieldgate Superb'	ENGS
fosteri	CBro EHyt LAma LRHS
– PD 256830	ENGS
'Foxton'	ENGS
'G71' (d)	CAvo
'Galatea'	CAvo CLAP EMon ENGS LRHS MHom NGar WIvy
'Ginns'	CLAP ENGS
§ *gracilis*	CBro CLAP ENGS EPar ERos MTho NPol WIvy
– 'Corkscrew'	ENGS
– 'Highdown'	CLAP EHyt
graecus misapplied	see *G. gracilis*
graecus Orph. ex Boiss.	see *G. elwesii*
'Grayling'	see *G. plicatus* 'Percy Picton'
Greatorex double (d)	CLAP SSvw
'Heffalump' (d)	ENGS
'Hill Poë' (d)	CAvo CBel CBro ENGS EPar NGar
'Hippolyta' (d)	CAvo CBro CElw CLAP ECha ENGS EPar EPot WIvy
x *hybridus* 'Merlin'	CAvo CBel CBro EOrc IGor MHom NGar NPol WIvy
– 'Robin Hood'	CFee CLAP EHyt ENGS ERos GCrs NGar SBla
'Icicle'	ENGS
ikariae misapplied	see *G. woronowii*
§ *ikariae* Baker	CElw EHyt EOrc EPar EPot ERos GKev LAma WFar
– Butt's form	ENGS NPol
– Latifolius Group	see *G. platyphyllus*
– subsp. *snogerupii*	see *G. ikariae*
'Imbolc'	ENGS
'Jacquenetta' (d)	CBro CLAP ENGS MHom WPGP
'John Gray'	CBel CBro EMon ENGS GCrs NGar NPol
'Ketton'	CAvo CBro CElw ENGS LRHS WIvy
'Kingston Double' (d)	CLAP
'Lady Beatrix Stanley' (d)	CBro CLAP ECha EMon ENGS EPar EPot ERos LAma LRHS MTho NGar
latifolius misapplied	see *G. woronowii*
latifolius Rupr.	see *G. platyphyllus*
'Lavinia' (d)	CAvo CElw CLAP
'Limetree'	CBel CLAP NPol
'Little Ben' **new**	GFlt
'Little Dorrit'	ENGS
lutescens	see *G. nivalis* 'Sandersii'
'Magnet' ♀H4	CAvo CBel CBro CFee CLAP ECha ENGS EPot GAbr ITim LAma NGar NPol WCot WPGP
'Mighty Atom'	CBel CFee ENGS
'Modern Art'	ENGS
'Mrs Thompson'	ENGS NGar WIvy
'Mrs Wrightson's Double' (d)	ENGS
nivalis ♀H4	CBro CNic CTri ELan ENGS EPar EPfP EPot GFlt ITim LAma LRHS MAvo MBow MBri NGar NJOw NRog NRya SHFr SRms WCot WFar WShi
– JRM 3139	ENGS
– 'Anglesey Abbey'	EMon ENGS NGar
– var. *angustifolius*	see *G. angustifolius*
– 'April Fool'	MHom
– 'Bitton'	CBro CLAP EHyt NGar NPol
– 'Blonde Inge'	ENGS
– 'Doncaster's Double Charmer'	ENGS
– 'Dreycott Greentip'	NGar
– 'Greenish'	ENGS
– subsp. *imperati*	EHyt
– 'Lutescens'	see *G. nivalis* 'Sandersii'
– 'Maximus'	CFwr
– 'Melvillei'	EMon
– 'Pewsey Vale'	ENGS
– f. *pleniflorus*	CLAP
'Blewbury Tart' (d)	
– – 'Flore Pleno' (d)	CBro CFwr CStu CTri EPar EPfP EPla EPot GAbr GFlt LAma LRHS NGar NRog NRya SRms WCot WFar WGwG WHen WShi WWye
– – 'Hambutt's Orchard' (d)	ENGS
– – 'Lady Elphinstone' (d)	CAvo CBel CBgR CBro CLAP CRow ENGS EPar GCrs LAma MRav MTho NGar NPol WIvy
– – 'Pusey Green Tip' (d)	CAvo CBro CElw CLAP EHyt ENGS EPar EPot GCrs NGar SIgm WPGP WTin
– – 'Walrus' (d)	ENGS NGar
§ – – 'Wonston Double' (d)	ENGS
– Poculiformis Group	CLAP EMon NGar
– 'Sandhill Gate'	ENGS NGar
§ – 'Sandersii'	CBro ENGS EPot NGar NPol SSpi
– (Sandersii Group) 'Savill Gold'	ENGS
§ – Scharlockii Group	CAvo CBel CBro EHyt EMon ENGS EOrc LAma NGar SBla
– 'Sibbertoft White'	ENGS
– 'Tiny'	EPot NGar
– 'Tiny Tim'	NPar NRya
§ – 'Virescens'	CLAP ENGS SBla
– 'Viridapice'	CAvo CBro CFwr ECha EHyt EMon ENGS EPar EPot GCrs GEdr LAma LRHS NGar NMen NPol SIgm WCot WIvy WPGP WShi
– 'Warei'	ENGS NGar
'Ophelia' (d)	CAvo CBel CBro ENGS EOrc EPar GAbr NGar NPar
* 'Paradise Double'	EPar
'Peg Sharples'	ENGS
§ *platyphyllus*	CBro ENGS EOrc LAma NGar WTin
plicatus ♀H4	CFee EMon EPot GAbr GFlt NGar NMen SScr WShi
– 'Augustus'	CAvo CBel CFee EHyt ENGS ERos WIvy
– 'Baxendale's Late'	ENGS
– 'Bowles' Large'	ERos MHom

§ - subsp. **byzantinus**	CAvo CBro EHyt ENGS EOrc EPar ERos
- - LP 17	ENGS
- - 'Ron Ginns'	NGar
- 'Colossus'	CAvo CBel
- 'Edinburgh Ketton'	ENGS
- 'Gerard Parker'	ENGS
- large	EOrc NPol
- 'Maidwell C'	ENGS
§ - 'Percy Picton'	ENGS
- 'Sally Passmore'	CAvo
- 'Sophie North'	CLAP GCrs
- 'Three Ships'	ENGS
- 'Trym'	ENGS
- 'Warham'	CAvo CBro ENGS EPot WPGP
- 'Warley Belles'	NGar
- 'Washfield Warham'	ECha EMon EOrc LRHS
- 'Wendy's Gold'	EMon ENGS GCrs
'Primrose Warburg'	ENGS
'Ransom's Dwarf'	see *G. elwesii* 'Ransom's Dwarf'
reginae-olgae	CBro EHyt ENGS ERos LAma MRav NGar SSpi WCom WCot
- WM 9901	MPhe
- WM 9908	MPhe
- subsp. **reginae-olgae** 'Cambridge'	ENGS NGar
§ - - Winter-flowering Group	CBro ENGS LAma
§ - subsp. **vernalis**	EMon ENGS LRHS
- - AJM 75	ENGS
rizehensis	EPot WIvy
'Rushmere Green'	ENGS
'S. Arnott' ♀H4	CAvo CBel CBro CElw CFir CFwr CLAP ECha EHyt ELan ENGS EPar EPot GBuc LAma NBir NGar NMen NRya SBla SIgm WCom WCot WLin WPGP WTin
'Saint Anne's'	CAvo WIvy
'Scharlockii'	see *G. nivalis* Scharlockii Group
'Shaggy'	EHyt
§ 'Straffan'	CAvo CBel CBro EHyt ENGS EOrc EPar EPot IGor LAma LRHS MHom NGar NPol SBla
'The Linns'	GCrs
'The O'Mahoney'	see *Galanthus* 'Straffan'
'The Pearl' misapplied	ENGS
'Three Leaves'	ENGS
'Titania' (d)	CBro ENGS EPot NGar
'Trotter's Merlin'	CAvo ENGS
'Tubby Merlin'	ENGS WIvy
* 'Warley Duo'	NGar
'Warley Longbow'	NGar
§ 'Washfield Colesbourne'	ECha ENGS
'William Thomson'	EMon
'Winifrede Mathias'	CLAP ENGS
'Wonston Double'	see *G. nivalis* 'Wonston Double'
§ **woronowii** ♀H4	CAvo CBel CBro CFwr CLAP EMon ETow LAma

Galax (Diapensiaceae)

aphylla	see *G. urceolata*
§ **urceolata**	CMac IBlr SOkd SSpi

Galega (Papilionaceae)

* **aurea new**	WWeb
bicolor	IBlr MLLN NBir NBrk SRms SSth STes SWat WFar
'Duchess of Bedford'	CFir CFwr MTis SWat
x **hartlandii**	IBlr MRav WHoo WWhi
- 'Alba' ♀H4	CFwr EGle EHrv EMar EMon EWes GBar GBri GCal IBlr LPhx NBrk NDov SAga SMHy SOkh SWat WCom WCot WHoo WPrP WSHC WWhi

- 'Lady Wilson' ♀H4	CPlt CPom CStr EBee ECtt EGle EMan EWes MRav NBrk NDov WCom WCot WFoF WHoo WPen
- 'Spring Light' (v)	ECtt EMan EWes
'Her Majesty'	see *G.* 'His Majesty'
§ 'His Majesty'	CBos CKno EBee ECtt EGle EMan GBri MBro MRav NBrk NGby SAga SWat WBea WBry WCot WFar WHoo WPGP
officinalis	More than 30 suppliers
- 'Alba' ♀H4	CMdw COlW CPom CPrp CStr EBee ECtt ELan ELau EMan EPfP ITer MBrN MHer SWal WBea WCHb WFar WHer WHil WHrl WMoo WWye
- Coconut Ice = 'Kelgal'PBR (v) **new**	EBee MBri SPer WWeb
orientalis	CDes EBee ECtt GCal LPhx LRHS MLLN MRav SMac SWat WAbb WCom WCot WMoo WPGP WSHC

Galeobdolon see *Lamium*

Galium (Rubiaceae)

aristatum	EMan MLLN
cruciata	see *Cruciata laevipes*
mollugo	CArn CRWN MSal NSco SIde WCHb
§ **odoratum**	More than 30 suppliers
verum	CAgr CArn CRWN GPoy GWCH MBow MGas MHer MSal NLan NMir NSco SECG SIde WCHb WHbs WHer

Galtonia (Hyacinthaceae)

§ **candicans** ♀H4	More than 30 suppliers
princeps	CAvo CBri CBro EBee ECha ERos ERou GBuc LPio SMHy SMac WBro
regalis	CBri EBee GCal GEdr LPio
viridiflora	More than 30 suppliers

Galvezia (Scrophulariaceae)

speciosa new	XPep

Gardenia (Rubiaceae)

augusta	see *G. jasminoides*
florida L.	see *G. jasminoides*
globosa	see *Rothmannia globosa*
grandiflora	see *G. jasminoides*
jasminoides ♀H1	EBak ELau LRHS MBri
- 'Kleim's Hardy' **new**	ELan LRHS MAsh
- 'Star'	SOWG
thunbergia	EShb

garlic see *Allium sativum*

Garrya ✿ (Garryaceae)

elliptica	CBcs CDul EBee EBre EMui ENot GKir ISea LPan LRHS MBri MGos NFor NHol NPSI NWea SPet SPlb SReu WCru WFar WHar WPat WStI WWeb
- (f)	ECrt LAst MSwo SWvt WPat
- (m)	CDoC CSBt EHol MAsh NBlu SLim WBod WFar
- 'James Roof' (m) ♀H4	More than 30 suppliers
fremontii	NLar SMer WBVN
x **issaquahensis**	CAbP CDoC CFai CPMA EBee
'Glasnevin Wine'	ELan EPfP IMGH ISea LRHS MAsh MBlu MBri NHol NLar NSti SMur SPer SSta WFar
- 'Pat Ballard' (m)	CPMA EPfP LRHS NHol NLar SPer
x **thuretii**	MGos NLar WFar

Garuleum (Asteraceae)

woodii JCA 324000	CPBP

Gasteria ✿ (Aloaceae)

liliputana	EPem WCot
* **multipluncata**	EPem
verrucosa	EOas EPem

x *Gaulnettya* see *Gaultheria*

Gaultheria ✿ (Ericaceae)

SF 276	ISea
cardiosepala	GEdr
cumingiana B&SWJ 1542	WCru
cuneata ♀H4	GEdr LRHS MAsh MBar NDlv
	NLAp SPer SPoG
- 'Pinkie'	GKir LRHS
§ **eriophylla**	SReu
furiens	see *G. insana*
glomerata var. **petraea**	SSta
hookeri	IBlr
§ **insana**	WPic
itoana	GEdr MBar NDlv NLAp
'Jingle Bells'	MGos
miqueliana	MGos MMHG
mucronata	EBee EPfP MBar NWea WDin
- (m)	CDoC CSBt CTri CWSG ENot EPfP
	GKir LAst MAsh MBar MBri MGos
	MRav NBlu NHol SPer SPoG SRms
- RB 94095	GTou
- 'Alba' (f)	MBar MGos MRav SLon
- 'Bell's Seedling'	CDoC CDul CTri CWSG EPfP GGar
(f/m) ♀H4	GKir LRHS MAsh MGos NLRH
	SHBN SPer SPoG SReu SSta
- 'Cherry Ripe' (f)	GKir SHBN
- 'Crimsonia' (f) ♀H4	CBcs CChe EPfP GKir LRHS MBar
	MDun MGos SHBN SPer SReu SRms
- 'Indian Lake'	NHol
- 'Lilacina' (f)	MGos WGwG
- 'Lilian' (f)	CSBt CWSG ENot EPfP GKir GSki
	LAst SHBN SPer
- Mother of Pearl	see *G. mucronata* 'Parelmoer'
- 'Mulberry Wine' (f) ♀H4	CTri EPfP GKir LRHS NHol SPoG
- 'October Red' (f)	NHol
§ - 'Parelmoer' (f)	CBcs ENot GKir LAst SPer SPoG
- 'Pink Pearl' (f) ♀H4	SRms
- pink-berried (f) **new**	NBlu
- 'Rosea' (f)	MBar MGos
- 'Rosie' (f)	SBod
§ - 'Signaal' (f)	CBrm CDoC EBee ENot EPfP GKir
	GWCH LAst LRHS MGos SPer
- Signal	see *G. mucronata* 'Signaal'
§ - 'Sneeuwwitje' (f)	CChe CWSG EBee ENot EPfP GKir
	GSki LAst LRHS SHBN SPer
- Snow White	see *G. mucronata* 'Sneeuwwitje'
- 'Stag River' (f)	MGos
- 'Thymifolia' (m)	CChe EPfP SHBN
- 'White Pearl' (f)	GKir
- white-berried (f) **new**	NBlu
- 'Wintertime' (f) ♀H4	CBrm MGos SRms
* **mucronifolia** dwarf **new**	NWCA
nana Colenso	see *G. parvula*
nummularioides	GEdr NHol SReu
- **minor**	ITim
§ **parvula**	GCrs
'Pearls'	GCrs WOBN
phillyreifolia	CMHG WPic
'Pink Champagne'	SSta
poeppigii	ITim
* - **racemosa**	SSta
procumbens ♀H4	More than 30 suppliers
pumila	GAbr GCrs LEdu MBar MGos NHol
	NMen
- 'E.K. Balls'	NHol
pyroloides	GCrs
shallon	CBcs CDoC CSBt EBee ENot EWTr
	GBar GKir MBar MDun MGos
	SHBN SPer SRms SWvt WDin WFar
- 'Snowqualmi Pass' **new**	NLar
tasmanica	ECou GAbr MBar WAbe
tetramera **new**	IDee
thymifolia	LAst
willisiana	see *G. eriophylla*
x **wisleyensis**	LRHS SLon SRms SSta
- 'Glenroy Maureen'	MAsh
- 'Pink Pixie'	CMHG GKir LRHS MAsh MBar
	MGos SPer SSta
- 'Wisley Pearl'	CBcs CDoC GKir IBlr IDee LAst
	MBar MGos SReu WFar
yunnanensis	SReu

Gaura (Onagraceae)

lindheimeri ♀H4	More than 30 suppliers
- 'Cherry Brandy' **new**	EBee GBin
- compact red	CSpe
- 'Corrie's Gold' (v)	CBcs CWSG EChP ECha ECtt EDAr
	EHoe ELan ENot EPfP ERou LAst
	LHop LPhx LPio LRHS MBri MHer
	MLLN NBlu NVic SAga SPer SPet
	WMnd WWin XPep
- 'Crimson Butterfly'	CHea COtt EBre ENor LAst MTis
	NCGa SPoG WShp WWeb
- 'Jo Adela' (v)	EBee ELan EMan EPfP
- 'Madonna'	EBee
- 'My Melody' **new**	EBee
- short	CSpe SGar
- 'Siskiyou Pink'	More than 30 suppliers
- 'The Bride'	CTri EBee EFou LRHS MAnH
	NGdn SCoo SMrm SPla STes SWal
	SWvt WHil WMnd
- 'Val's Pink'	WHoo WSPU
- 'Whirling Butterflies'	CKno CSpe CWCL EBee ECtt ELan
	EMan EMil ENot EPfP IBal LAst
	LPio MBri MLLN MTis NPri SAsh
	SBod SIng SMad SMrm SWat
	WMnd XPep
- 'White Heron' **new**	EBee EChP IBal MNrw
longiflora	EShb
I - 'Variegata' (v) **new**	CBrm

Gaussia (Arecaceae)

maya	LPal

Gaylussacia (Ericaceae)

baccata **new**	NLar
brachycera	GGGa

Gazania (Asteraceae)

'Aztec' ♀H1+3	CHal SUsu
'Bicton Cream'	CHal
'Blackberry Ripple'	COIW LAst NCiC SAga SCoo
'Christopher'	CHal MOak MSte SAga SCoo
I 'Christopher Lloyd'	COIW LAst
'Cookei' ♀H1+3	CSpe MSte SAga WCot
'Cornish Pixie'	CHal
cream	CHal NCiC
'Cream Beauty'	MSte
'Cream Dream'	LAst MOak
Daybreak Series	LPVe
- 'Daybreak Bronze'	MLan
double bronze	CHal
'Dwarf Orange'	SScr
'Flash'	WEas
'Freddie'	SMrm
'Garden Sun'	MLan
* **grayi**	CHal
* 'Hazel'	MSte

Kiss Series 'Kiss Bronze Star' LIck SGar
I   - 'Kiss Pomegranate'   LIck
- 'Kiss Rose'   CBrm SGar
- 'Kiss Yellow'   LIck SGar
krebsiana   XPep
linearis RMRP 95-0283   ETow
- 'Colorado Gold'   CFir
'Magic'   LAst NPri SCoo
'Northbourne' ♀H1+3   GGar MSte
'Orange Beauty'   ELan
pectinata **new**   CPBP
'Red Velvet'   CSpe MSte SAga
§ *rigens*   LRHS
- 'Aureovariegata' (v)   SAga
- var. *uniflora* ♀H1+3   MSte XPep
- 'Variegata' (v) ♀H1+3   ELan LAst MOak SPoG
'Silverbrite'   CHal
splendens   see *G. rigens*
'Talent'   CBrm CHal

Geissorhiza (Iridaceae)
imbricata   CStu

Gelasine (Iridaceae)
azurea   see *G. coerulea*
§ *coerulea*   EBee EMan WCot

Gelidocalamus (Poaceae)
fangianus   see *Drepanostachyum microphyllum*

Gelsemium (Loganiaceae)
sempervirens ♀H1-2   CArn CFwr CMCN ERea EShb
   IDee MSal SOWG
- 'Flore Pleno' (d)   ERea
- 'Pride of Augusta'   CMCN

Genista (Papilionaceae)
aetnensis ♀H4   More than 30 suppliers
§ *canariensis*   CPLG CSBt CWib ERea WBrE
carinalis **new**   WLin
cinerea   WCFE
decumbens   see *Cytisus decumbens*
delphinensis   see *G. sagittalis* subsp. *delphinensis*
'Emerald Spreader'   see *G. pilosa* 'Yellow Spreader'
fragrans   see *G. canariensis*
hispanica   CBcs CSBt CTri EBee EBre ECrN
   ELan ENot EPfP GKir LRHS MBar
   MGos MWat SHBN SLim SPer
   SRms SWvt WCFE WDin WFar
   WHar WStI WTel XPep
humifusa   see *G. pulchella*
lydia ♀H4   More than 30 suppliers
maderensis   WPic
monosperma   see *Retama monosperma*
§ *monspessulana*   XPep
pilosa   CTri ENot EPot ISea MBar MDun
   MWhi NMen WBVN WWin
- 'Lemon Spreader'   see *G. pilosa* 'Yellow Spreader'
* - *major*   NMen
- var. *minor*   GKir GTou NLar NMen WAbe
- 'Procumbens'   CMea MDKP WPat
- 'Vancouver Gold'   CBcs CSBt CTrC EBee ELan ENot
   EPfP LRHS MAsh MGos MRav
   SMad SPer SRms WDin WFar WGor
§ - 'Yellow Spreader'   CBcs CMHG CSBt EHol GEdr IArd
   MSwo NJOw WBod WWeb
§ 'Porlock' ♀H3   CBcs CDoC CSPN CWCL CWSG
   MRav SEND WDin WStI WWeb
§ *pulchella*   CTri SBla
sagittalis   CTri EPfP GEil LHop MDKP NBir
   NFor NWoo SBla SLon SPer WBVN
   WTin

§ - subsp. *delphinensis*   CStu NMen
   ♀H4
- *minor*   see *G. sagittalis* subsp. *delphinensis*
§ x *spachiana* ♀H1   CTri GEil
tenera 'Golden Shower'   CPLG SLPl
tinctoria   CAgr CArn GBar GPoy GWCH ILis
   MGol MHer MSal NFor SIde WHer
   WWye
- 'Flore Pleno' (d) ♀H4   CLyd MGos NMen NPro SRot
   WWeb
- 'Humifusa'   EPot GEdr
- 'Moesiaca'   ITim
- var. *prostrata*   LBee
- 'Royal Gold' ♀H4   CWSG CWib EBee ENot EPfP
   MGos MRav MSwo SHBN SPer
   SPlb WBod WWeb
villarsii   see *G. pulchella*

Gentiana ✿ (Gentianaceae)
§ *acaulis* ♀H4   More than 30 suppliers
- 'Alboviolacea'   NLar
- 'Belvedere'   GCrs NMen WAbe
- 'Coelestina'   EPot GCrs
- 'Dinarica'   see *G. dinarica*
- 'Krumrey'   EHyt EPot
- 'Max Frei'   GCrs
- *occidentalis*   see *G. occidentalis*
- 'Rannoch'   EPot NMen
- 'Stumpy' **new**   EPot
- 'Trotter's Variety'   EPot
- 'Undulatifolia'   EPot
- 'Velkokvensis'   EHyt
'Alex Duguid' **new**   GEdr
'Amethyst'   CWrd EPot GCrs NLAp SIng WAbe
   WLin
angustifolia   GCrs
- Frei hybrid   WLin
- 'Rannoch' **new**   GKev
'Ann's Special'   CWrd GCrs GKir
asclepiadea ♀H4   More than 30 suppliers
- var. *alba*   CFil CHea CTCP EBee GAbr GBuc
   GMac LRHS MDKP MTho NChi
   NLAp SPer SRms WCom WCru
   WHoo WTin
- 'Hoo House'   WHoo
- 'Knightshayes'   EBee NLAp WCom WHoo
- pale blue-flowered   CFil WPGP
- 'Phyllis'   GBuc WCom WHoo
- 'Pink Cascade'   SIgm
- 'Pink Swallow'   GBuc
- 'Rosea'   CDes EBee GAbr GBuc MDKP
   MNrw NChi WHoo WPGP
- 'Turquoise' **new**   NLAp
- yellow-flowered   ELan
atuntsiensis   GKev
'Barbara Lyle'   CWrd WAbe
bavarica   SPlb
   var. *subacaulis*
bellidifolia   GTou
x *bernardii*   see *G.* x *stevenagensis* 'Bernardii'
bisetaea   SRms
'Blauer Diamant'   GCrs
'Blue Flame'   GCrs WAbe
'Blue Heaven'   WAbe
'Blue Sea'   CWrd
'Blue Shell'   CWrd
'Blue Silk'   CWrd EWes GCrs NLAp SBla WAbe
* *buglossoides* **new**   SLon
burseri   SSpi
- var. *villarsii*   GIBF
cachemirica ambig.   EBee GTou NLAp WPat
'Cairngorm'   CWCL CWrd EWes GAbr GCrs
   GEdr GKir NDlv
Cambrian hybrids **new**   CWrd

x **caroli**	SBla WAbe	
'Christine Jean'	CWrd GCrs GTou NDlv SIng	
clausa	GIBF	
clusii	EPot GCrs NLAp WAbe	
- **alba**	WAbe	
- subsp. **costei**	WAbe	
- purple	CNic	
'Compact Gem'	GCrs NLAp WAbe WOld	
corymbifera	GCrs	
§ **cruciata**	EBee GAbr GTou MTho	
- subsp. **phlogifolia**	GIBF	
§ **dahurica**	EBee EPfP GCal LRHS SBla SSto WShp	
'Dark Hedgehog'	GEdr	
decumbens	GAbr GCal	
depressa	MTho WAbe	
'Devonhall'	GEdr	
§ **dinarica**	CLyd MTho WAbe	
divisa new	GKev	
Drake's strain	CWrd GEdr GKir LRHS	
'Dumpy'	CPBP CWrd EPot GEdr WAbe WOBN WPat	
'Dusk'	CWrd GCrs	
'Eleanor'	GCrs	
'Elizabeth'	CWrd EWes GCrs GEdr NDlv	
'Ettrick' **new**	GEdr	
'Eugen's Allerbester' **new**	CWrd	
farreri	EWes GKir NSla WAbe	
- 'Duguid'	GEdr	
- hybrids	WAbe	
'Fasta Highlands'	NBir	
fetissowii	see *G. macrophylla* var. *fetissowii*	
freyniana	SOkd	
gelida	WLin	
Glamis strain	GCrs GEdr NDlv	
'Glen Isla'	EWes	
§ **gracilipes**	ECho LRHS MWat SPlb SRms	
- 'Yuatensis'	see *G. macrophylla* var. *fetissowii*	
grossheimii	GAbr GIBF WWin	
x **hascombensis**	see *G. septemfida* var. *lagodechiana*	
'Hascombensis'		
'Henry'	WAbe	
x **hexafarreri**	CWCL CWrd GCrs	
Inshriach hybrids	CWrd GCrs	
'Inverleith' ♀H4	CWCL CWrd EDAr EWes GCrs GEdr GKir IHMH MBro NHol SPlb WGor WOld WPat	
'Joan Ward' **new**	CWrd	
'John Ward' **new**	CWrd	
'Kirriemuir'	CWrd EWes GCrs NDlv	
kochiana	see *G. acaulis*	
kurroo	NLAp WPat	
- var. **brevidens**	see *G. dahurica*	
lagodechiana	see *G. septemfida* var. *lagodechiana*	
ligustica new	GCrs	
lucerna	CWCL CWrd GCrs GEdr GKir	
lutea	EBee EWTr GAbr GCal GIBF GKir GPoy NBid NChi SDix SRms WAul WHil WWye	
x **macaulayi** ♀H4	CPla CWrd EDAr GCrs GEdr GKir MBro SIng SRms WHoo WOld	
- 'Edinburgh' ♀H4	GEdr	
- 'Elata'	CWrd GCrs NDlv NHol	
- 'Kidbrooke Seedling'	CTri CWCL CWrd EDAr EWes GCrs GEdr GKir GTou NLAp NRya WAbe	
- 'Kingfisher'	CPla CTri CWCL CWrd EDAr GEdr GKir NBir NFor NLAp NMen SBla SBod SIng WAbe	
§ - 'Praecox'	CWCL CWrd EDAr GCrs GEdr GKir GTou NDlv NLAp WOBN	
§ - 'Wells's Variety'	CWrd GCrs GEdr	
§ **macrophylla**	ECho GAbr	
var. **fetissowii**		

makinoi 'Royal Blue'	CFai CWCL	
'Margaret'	WAbe	
'Maryfield'	GEdr	
melandriifolia	WAbe	
'Merlin'	GCrs	
'Multiflora'	CWCL CWrd GCrs GEdr	
* **nepaulensis**	GIBF	
nipponica	EBee GIBF	
§ **nubigena**	CBrm GIBF WWin	
nummulariifolia new	EPot	
§ **occidentalis**	EPot NLAp	
Olga's pale	GCrs	
orbicularis	SOkd	
oreodoxa	CWrd GCrs GTou	
paradoxa	CLyd GAbr GEdr NDlv NLAp NSla SBla SIgm SOkd WPat	
- 'Blauer Herold'	NCGa	
phlogifolia	see *G. cruciata*	
platypetala	SOkd	
pneumonanthe	GIBF SPlb SSpi	
prolata	GCrs SOkd WAbe	
- CC 2650	WOBN	
przewalskii	see *G. nubigena*	
pumila	WAbe	
subsp. **delphinensis**	ITim NLAp	
punctata	see *G. gracilipes*	
purdomii	see *G. gracilipes*	
purpurea	GCal GIBF	
robusta	GAbr	
'Robyn Lyle'	WAbe	
'Royal Highlander'	CWrd GEdr	
'Saphir Select'	CWCL EDAr GEdr	
saxosa	CLyd CPBP CWCL EHyt EPot GCrs GEdr GKir GTou ITim NBir NLAp NMen SIgm SIng WAbe	
scabra	EDAr WWye	
- 'Ishusuki'	SBla	
- 'Zuikorindo' **new**	NLar	
'Sensation'	CStu GEdr	
septemfida ♀H4	CWCL EHyt ELan GCrs GEdr GKir LBee LHop LRHS MBri MBro MHer MTho MWat NBir NLAp NRya SBla SIng SPlb SRms WCom WHoo WKif WPat	
- 'Alba'	NBir NLAp WPat	
§ - var. **lagodechiana** ♀H4	CSam CTCP EDAr EHyt EWTr GAbr GCal LPVe NLAp SRms WBVN	
- - 'Doeringiana'	ECho NMen	
§ - - 'Hascombensis'	ECho	
'Serenity'	CWrd GEdr WAbe	
setigera	GKir	
'Shot Silk'	CWCL CWrd EDAr EWes GCrs GEdr NHol SUsu WAbe WWin	
sikkimensis	GEdr	
'Silken Giant' **new**	WAbe	
'Silken Seas' **new**	WAbe	
'Silken Skies'	GBuc WAbe	
sino-ornata ♀H4	CPla CTri CWCL EDAr GCrs GEdr GGar GKir LRHS MBri NLAp NMen SBla SIng SPer SRms WAbe WBVN WCom WFar WOld WShp	
- 'Alba'	CPla CWrd GKir WFar	
- 'Angel's Wings'	CWCL CWrd EDAr GCrs GEdr GKir GTou	
- 'Anna' **new**	CWCL	
- 'Bellatrix'	CWrd	
- 'Blautopf'	CWrd	
- 'Brin Form'	CWrd SBod SIng SRms WAbe	
- 'Denvie' **new**	CWCL	
- 'Downfield'	CWrd GCrs NDlv NHol	
- 'Edith Sarah'	GCrs GEdr NHol SBla SRms WPat WWin	
- 'Mary Lyle'	CWrd GEdr WAbe	

- 'Praecox' — see *G.* x *macaulayi* 'Praecox'
- 'Trogg's Form' — CWrd EWes NDlv NRya
- 'Weisser Traum' — CWrd
- 'White Wings' — CWrd EWes GCrs LRHS NDlv
'Soutra' **new** — GEdr
x *stevenagensis* ♀H4 — CLyd CPla CTri CWCL CWrd LRHS SIng
§ - 'Bernardii' — CWrd EDAr GCrs GEdr SIng WAbe
- dark — CWrd MBro WAbe WPat
- 'Frank Barker' — CWrd WAbe
stragulata — GCrs GKev WAbe
straminea — GAbr MDKP WCot
'Strathmore' ♀H4 — CStu CTri CWCL EDAr EHyt EWes GAbr GCrs GEdr GKir LRHS NHol NLAp NRya SIng SPlb WAbe WOld WWin
'Susan Jane' — GTou
ternifolia — EDAr GCrs
- 'Cangshan' — GCrs GEdr WAbe
- 'Dali' — GEdr NBir
tibetica — CArn CPla EBee GAbr GCal GIBF GPoy MAnH MNrw NBid SOkd WCAu WEas WTin WWye
aff. *tibetica* 3935 **new** — MGol
trichotoma — WAbe
triflora — CDes EPot GBuc GCrs WFar WPGP
- 'Alba' — GBuc GKir
- var. *japonica* — GBuc GCal
- 'Royal Blue' — GCal NGby
Tweeddale strain — GCrs GEdr
verna — CPBP CTCP CWCL EBre EHyt EPfP EWes GKir LHop LRHS MBro MTho NMen NRya NSla SBla SIng WAbe WBWf WCom WPat
- 'Alba' — CGra CPBP GCrs MBro NLAp WAbe WCom WPat
§ - subsp. *balcanica* — CLyd ELan GCrs GTou MBro MTho NLAp SRms WHoo WPat
- subsp. *oschtenica* — GCrs WAbe
- slate blue — MBro NLAp WPat
§ - subsp. *tergestina* — EDAr
'Violette' — CWrd GCrs GEdr
waltonii — ECho EWes
wellsii — see *G.* x *macaulayi* 'Wells's Variety'
wutaiensis — see *G. macrophylla* var. *fetissowii*

Gentianella (Gentianaceae)
amarella **new** — WBWf

Gentianopsis (Gentianaceae)
grandis — GKev

Geranium (Geraniaceae)
from Pamirs, Tadzhikistan — EBee EOrc EPPr WPnP
from Sikkim — NWCA
aconitifolium misapplied — see *G. palmatum*
aconitifolium L'Hér. — see *G. rivulare*
'Alan Mayes' — CSev EPPr NSti SCou
'Alaska' **new** — CBgR
albanum — CElw COIW EBee EChP EGra EMan EMar EOrc EPAt EPPr EWsh GAbr GSki LLWP MNrw MTis NCot NSti SCou SDix SWal WCru WMoo WTMC WWpP
- 'Pink and Stripes' **new** — CDes
albiflorum — CBri CCge CMCo EBee EChP EPPr IMGH LRHS MNFA MWhe SCou WCru WMoo WWpP
anemonifolium — see *G. palmatum*
'Ann Folkard' ♀H4 — More than 30 suppliers
'Anne Thomson' — More than 30 suppliers

x *antipodeum* — CBos CMHG SRms SWat
(*G. sessiliflorum* subsp. *novae-zelandiae* 'Nigricans' x *G. traversii* var. *elegans*)
x *antipodeum* 'Chocolate Candy'PBR — CFai EPfP GBri LAst NCot WFoF WWeb
§ - Crûg strain — CHid CSpe EHrv EMan EPAt EPot GKir GSki LRHS MCCP MDKP MDun MLLN NBPC SHBN STes WCru WGwG WShp
- 'Crûg's Dark Delight' — WCru
- 'Elizabeth Wood' — CCge EMan NBro WCra
- 'Persian Carpet' — NLar
- 'Sea Spray' — CCge ECtt EFou EMar EPPr EWes GBuc GGar GSki LAst LPio MNrw MSte MWgw NGdn SWat WCru WMnd WTMC WWpP
- 'Stanhoe' — CCge CSpe ECtt GBin LRHS MWgw SHar WFar
argenteum — WCru
aristatum — CDes CPou EBee EBla EChP EMar EOrc EPPr EWes MLwd MNFA MNrw MRav MSph MTis NBir NCot SBri SCou SCro STes WCra WCru WMoo WPnP WTMC WWpP
- NS 649 — NWCA
armenum — see *G. psilostemon*
asphodeloides — More than 30 suppliers
- subsp. *asphodeloides* 'Prince Regent' — CHid CStr EMan EPPr MNFA SBri WCra WLin
§ - - white — CCge EBla EMan EOrc EPPr WFar WHen WMoo WWpP
- subsp. *crenophilum* — CElw WWpP
- 'Starlight' — NBid SHel
atlanticum Hook. f. — see *G. malviflorum*
'Aussie Gem' — CCge MSte
'Aya' — LPio
'Baby Blue' — see *G. himalayense* 'Baby Blue'
'Bertie Crûg' — More than 30 suppliers
biuncinatum — IFro MLwd WPnP
Black Beauty = 'Nodbeauty' — CCge CHad CPen ELan LBuc SCoo SDnm SPer WWeb
'Black Ice' — GBuc SHel WCru
'Blue Boy' **new** — EBee
'Blue Cloud' — CBos CElw CMea CSpe EBee ECGP EGra EPPr LPhx MAvo MBri MTed MTis NBir NChi NCot NMRc SCou SHel SMrm SSvw SUsu WCra WMoo WPnP WTMC WWpP
'Blue Pearl' — CCge EBee EPPr MMil NBir NCot NSti SCou SHel SUsu SVil WCra WPnP WWpP
§ 'Blue Sunrise' — CCge CFwr EBee EBre EMan GKir LAst LPio LRHS MCCP MSte MWhe NLar NSti SAga SCou SPla WCra WFar WWpP
'Bob's Blunder' — CCge CElw ECtt EMan EMar MAvo MBNS MBnl MEHN NCot NSti SPla SWvt WCot WCru WGor WHlf
bohemicum — CCge EBee EMan GSki MAnH MLwd NCot NSti NWCA WBrk WCru WHen WHer WPnP WWpP
- 'Orchid Blue' — CCge CFwr EPfP GBBs LRHS SWvt WFar
'Bright Stranger' **new** — EBee
'Brookside' — More than 30 suppliers
brutium — MLwd
brycei — MNrw
'Buckland Beauty' — CDes CElw EPPr SBla SSpi
'Buxton's Blue' — see *G. wallichianum* 'Buxton's Variety'
caeruleatum — EBee EBla EMon EPPr SHel SUsu

	Name	Suppliers
	caffrum	CCge CMCo CPla EMan GBuc GSki MNrw NChi NCot NPPs NWCA WBea WCru WEas WLin WOut WWpP
	californicum	CElw GBuc WCru
	candicans hort.	see *G. lambertii*
§	x *cantabrigiense*	More than 30 suppliers
	- 'Berggarten'	CElw EBee EPPr SCro SHel WWpP
	- 'Biokovo'	More than 30 suppliers
	- 'Cambridge'	More than 30 suppliers
	- 'Karmina'	CBri CElw CMCo EBee EChP EGle EPPr EPla GKir IHMH MBnl MBro MNrw SCou WHoo WMoo WPnP WShp WTMC WTin WWpP
	- 'Show Time'	CMCo SCro WHal
	- 'St Ola'	More than 30 suppliers
	- 'Westray'PBR	CCge CHid EBee EBre EChP EPPr GAbr GBin GKir GLbr MCCP MSte NBlu NGdn NPro SCro SMac SSpi STes SVil SWvt WSSM WShp WWeb WWpP
	cataractarum	CCge MLLN MNrw WCru
	'Chantilly'	CElw CMCo CSam EBee EBla EGra EMan EPPr GBuc MAvo MLwd MNrw NBir NPro SCou SCro SUsu WBea WCru WMoo WPGP WPnP WTMC WWpP
	'Chocolate Pot'	NArg
	christensenianum	EPPr
	- B&SWJ 8022	WCru
	cinereum	CCge EBee ENot GKir NSla WBrE WLin
	- 'Album'	WCru
	- 'Apple Blossom'	see *G.* x *lindavicum* 'Apple Blossom'
	- 'Ballerina'	see *Geranium* (Cinereum Group) 'Ballerina'
I	- 'Heather'	CCge EBee EChP EMan EPPr LRHS MAvo NBro NGdn NSti SVil
	- hybrids	WCru
	- 'Janette'PBR	COtt EBee GKir LAst LRHS MCLN
	- subsp. *nanum*	see *G. nanum*
	- 'Purple Pillow'	EBee MBNS MBri MCLN NBro NCot STes
	- 'Rothbury Gem' **new**	EBre WCra
	- subsp. *subcaulescens*	More than 30 suppliers
	var. *subcaulescens* ♀H4	
§	(Cinereum Group) 'Ballerina' ♀H4	More than 30 suppliers
	- 'Carol'	CCge EBee EBre EChP EMan EMar EPPr EWes GKir MAvo MCLN NBro NGdn NLar NSti SCou SLon SVil SWvt WPnP
	- 'Laurence Flatman'	More than 30 suppliers
	- 'Sugar Babe'PBR	CCge
	'Claridge Druce'	see *G.* x *oxonianum* 'Claridge Druce'
	clarkei 'Kashmir Green'	CFwr EBee EPPr MAvo
	- 'Kashmir Pink'	More than 30 suppliers
§	- 'Kashmir Purple'	More than 30 suppliers
§	- 'Kashmir White' ♀H4	More than 30 suppliers
	- 'Mount Stewart' **new**	WCru
	'Coffee Time'	SCro
	collinum	EPPr GAbr GBuc LLWP MLwd MNrw NBir NCot SCou SCro WBrk WCru WHen WPnP WTMC WWpP
	'Coombland White'	CBri CCge EBee EBla EFou EOrc EPPr GMac IFro LPio MBri MBro MNrw NCot NSti SCou SCro SVil WCra WCru WHoo WMoo WPnP WWeb WWpP
	Crûg strain	see *Geranium* x *antipodeum* Crûg strain
	'Cyril's Fancy'	EBee EBla EChP EPPr MAvo MNFA SCro SHel SUsu WWpP
	dahuricum	EBee WCru
	dalmaticum ♀H4	More than 30 suppliers
	- 'Album'	EBre ECtt EDAr EHyt ELan EMlt EPPr EPot GKir MBro MHer MRav MTho MWhe NChi SCou SIng SRms SRot WAbe WCom WCra WCru WFar WHCG WPat WWin
	- 'Bridal Bouquet'	EBee GBri NChi NMen SBla WAbe WHer
	dalmaticum x *macrorrhizum*	see *G.* x *cantabrigiense*
	delavayi hort.	CDes EBee WCru
	delavayi Franch.	WCru
	- B&SWJ 7582	WCru
	'Derek Cooke' **new**	CElw CStr EChP EGle EGra EPPr LPio MNrw MSte NBir NGdn NSti SBla SCou SHel SUsu WBea WCra WCru WFar WHal WHen WMoo WPnP WTMC WWpP
	'Dilys'	CHll MSal SCou
	dissectum	EBee EPPr
	'Distant Hills'	CCge CElw CMCo CSam EBee EBla EPPr GBBs MAvo MCLN MMil MNrw NSti SCou SCro SVil WCra WCru WPnP WTMC WWpP
	'Diva'	
	donianum HWJCM 311	WCru
	drakensbergense	CCge SCou
	'Dusky Crûg'	CElw MNrw NPPs WCom WCru
	'Dusky Gem' **new**	SUsu
	'Dusky Rose'	CFai ELan EMan EPfP GKir LRHS
*	'Eleanor Fisher' **new**	SUsu
	'Elizabeth Ross'	CElw EPPr LRHS MAvo MNrw WCra WCru WMoo WOBN WRha WTMC WWhi WWpP
	'Elworthy Dusky'	CCge
	endressii ♀H4	More than 30 suppliers
	- 'Album'	see *Geranium* 'Mary Mottram'
	- 'Beholder's Eye'	CCge CHid COlW EBee EBla EPPr GAbr MBnl MSte NCot NSti WPnP WShp WTMC WWpP
	- 'Betty Catchpole'	EPPr
	- 'Castle Drogo'	ECtt EPPr WBea WCra WTMC WWpP
	- dark	GBBs
	- 'Prestbury White'	see *G. oxonianum* 'Prestbury Blush'
	- 'Priestling's Red'	CElw CMCo EGra EMar NCot SMrm
I	- 'Rose'	WPer WWpP
	- white-flowered	SSpi
	erianthum	CCge EMan EPAt GAbr GBuc GMac LLWP MSte MWhe NLar WBrk WCru WWpP
	- 'Calm Sea'	CCge CDes GBuc SUsu WCru WMoo WTMC
	- 'Neptune'	EPPr SChu SCou SUsu WCra WCru
	eriostemon Fischer	see *G. platyanthum*
§	*farreri*	CCge CLyd EBee EGle EHyt ETow GBri GBuc GCal LHop LRHS MNrw NBir SBla WCru WEas MTPN
	'Flamingo'	WCru
	glaberrimum	SSpi
	goldmannii	CBri EBee EChP EOrc EPla GBuc MNrw NBPC NBir SCou SCro WBrk WCra WCru WHal WMoo WPnP WTMC WWpP
	gracile	CElw EBee EPPr SCou WWpP
	- 'Blanche'	CElw CMCo EBee EMan EPPr WWpP
	- 'Blush'	
	grandiflorum	see *G. himalayense*

	- var. *alpinum*	see *G. himalayense* 'Gravetye'
	'Grasmere' **new**	EGra
	'Gwen Thompson'	WOut
	gymnocaulon	CCge CElw CM&M CMCo CMHG EBee EBla EMan EMar EPPr LRHS NSti SCou STes WCru WMnd WWpP
	gymnocaulon x *platypetalum*	EBee
	'Harmony'	EPPr
	harveyi	CBrm CElw CMea EBee EMan EPPr EWes GSki LGro LPhx MBro MNrw NWCA SScr WAbe WCom WCra WCru WKif WPGP WPat WPnn
	hayatanum	NCot WTMC
	- B&SWJ 164	CBod EBee WCru WMoo WWpP
§	*himalayense*	More than 30 suppliers
	- from Tibetan border **new**	EPPr
	- *alpinum*	see *G. himalayense* 'Gravetye'
§	- 'Baby Blue'	CBos CElw CSpe EBee EBla EFou EGle EPPr GBuc GCal GKir MAvo MBri MCLN MNrw NCot NSti SCou SCro WCra WCru WEas WHen WMoo WTMC WWpP
	- 'Birch Double'	see *G. himalayense* 'Plenum'
	- 'Devil's Blue'	SCro
	- 'Frances Perry'	CCge SMur
§	- 'Gravetye' ♀H4	More than 30 suppliers
	- 'Irish Blue'	CElw CMCo EChP ECtt EFou EGle EGra EPPr GBuc GCal GMac MBri MCLN MSte NPPs NPol NSti SCou SCro WAbb WCAu WCra WCru WHal WHen WMoo WTMC WTin WWpP
	- *meeboldii*	see *G. himalayense*
	- 'Pale Irish Blue'	GCal
§	- 'Plenum' (d)	More than 30 suppliers
	hispidissimum	CFee
	ibericum misapplied	see *G.* x *magnificum*
	ibericum	CCge CNic CSBt CTri NLar SMac STes WFar WWpP
	- 'Blue Springs' **new**	EGra
	- subsp. *ibericum*	EBee EPPr MTis
	- subsp. *jubatum*	CElw EBee EPPr GCal GKir GMac MNFA MNrw NCot SCou SCro SRms WCru WMoo WTMC WWpP
	- subsp. *jubatum* x *renardii*	GCal SWvt
	- - 'White Zigana' **new**	CFwr
	- var. *platypetalum* Boissier	see *G. platypetalum* Fisch. & C.A. Mey.
	- var. *platypetalum* Fisch. & C.A. Mey	see *G.* x *magnificum*
	ibericum x *renardii* **new**	NSti
	incanum	CCge CHll CPLG CSev ECoo EMan EPAt ETow EWes IFro MLwd MNrw NBir SGar SMrm SScr WAbe WCot WLin WWpP XPep
	- var. *multifidum*	GGar SUsu WCru WFar
	'Ivan'	CCge CElw CMCo EBee EMan EPPr GBuc LPhx LRHS MBNS SCou SCro SIgm WCot WCru WMoo WPGP WPnP WWpP WCru WTMC
	'Jean Armour'	WCru WTMC
	'Jean's Lilac'	see *G.* x *oxonianum* 'Jean's Lilac'
	'Johnson's Blue' ♀H4	More than 30 suppliers
	'Jolly Bee' **new**	CFai EBee EChP EHrv EMan EPAt MBNS MBnl MCLN MTis NCot NPro NSti STes SUsu WCot WCra WPnP WTMC
	'Joy'	More than 30 suppliers
	'Kahlua'	CFai EBee EHrv EMan EPfP MAvo MBNS NCot

§	'Kashmir Blue'	CCge CHar EBee EChP EGra EPPr ERou EWsh GKir MAvo MBnl MNFA NCot NSti SCou SCro SHel WCAu WMoo WPnP
I	'Kashmir Lilac'	WHen
§	'Kate'	CElw EBla EGle EPPr WCru WPnn
	'Kate Folkard'	see *G.* 'Kate'
§	'Khan'	CBos CMil EBee EBla EPPr IFro MNrw NCot NPro SCou SDys SMHy WCra WCru WPnP WWpP
	kishtvariense	CMCo EBee EBla EBre ECoo EMan EOrc EPPr GCal LPio LRHS MNrw MRav NCot NHol SSpi WCru WOVN WPnP WWpP
	koraiense	CBod CCge EMan MLwd NSti WMoo WWpP
	- B&SWJ 797	WCru
	- B&SWJ 878	EBee WCru
	koreanum	CCge CFil CPla GBuc GFlt GKir LRHS MNFA NCot SSpi SUsu WBea WFar WMoo WPGP WTMC
	- B&SWJ 602	WCru
§	*kotschyi* var. *charlesii*	EBee
	krameri	EMan
	- B&SWJ 1142	EBee EBla WCru
§	*lambertii*	CCge EWes GBuc LPio MNrw NBir WTMC WWpP
	- 'Swansdown'	CBos EChP EMan GBuc MAvo MNrw WCra WCru WSHC
	lanuginosum	EChP
	libani	CDes EBee EBre EPPr GBuc GCal LLWP MTho MWhe NCot NSti SCou SCro WCot WCra WCru WEas WPnP WTMC WTin WWpP
	libani x *ibericum* **new**	GCal
	libani x *peloponnesiacum*	CCge CDes
	'Libretto'	CElw EBee EPPr SScr WCru
§	x *lindavicum* 'Alanah'	WLin
§	- 'Apple Blossom'	CCge CElw CLyd CMil CNic EDAr EPPr GBuc GKir GSki LRHS MSte MTis NChi NMen NPPs SAsh SBla SRot WAbe WCom WHCG WLin WWin
	- 'Gypsy' **new**	SBla
	- 'Lissadell'	SBla
	linearilobum subsp. *transversale*	EPPr SRot WCru
§	'Little David'	EPPr SUsu WWpP
	'Little Devil'	see *G.* 'Little David'
	'Little Gem'	CBrm CCge CMea EBee EBre EFou EMan GKir LHop LRHS MRav NChi NDov SCro SUsu WCra WCru WFar WTMC WWpP
	lucidum	EPAt EPPr MSal NSti NVic
	'Lydia'	WWpP
§	*macrorrhizum*	More than 30 suppliers
	- AL & JS 90179YU	CHid EPPr
	- JJH 7003/95	EBee
	- 'Album' ♀H4	More than 30 suppliers
	- 'Bevan's Variety'	More than 30 suppliers
	- 'Bulgaria'	EPPr WTMC WWpP
	- 'Czakor'	More than 30 suppliers
I	- 'De Bilt'	CFwr EBee WOut
	- 'Freundorf' **new**	GCal
	- 'Ingwersen's Variety' ♀H4	More than 30 suppliers
	- 'Lohfelden'	CDes EGle EPPr GBuc MBro MNFA NChi SHel WCra WMoo WRHF WWpP
	- 'Mount Olympus'	see *G. macrorrhizum* 'White-Ness'
	- 'Mount Olympus White'	see *G. macrorrhizum* 'White-Ness'
	- 'Pindus'	CPrp EBee EBre EPPr GAbr MBro MNFA NCot NMRc NSti SCou SHel

	SUsu WCru WFar WMoo WPnP WTMC WWpP
– 'Ridsko'	CElw CFee CMCo EBee EOrc EPPr GBuc GCal MNFA NBro SCou SCro WCru WHen WWpP
– *roseum*	see *G. macrorrhizum*
– 'Sandwijck'	CFwr EPPr WWpP
– 'Snow Sprite'	CCge CMea COlW CPla EBee EPPr EPyc GSki MAnH MCCP NCot NPro SPoG STes WHrl
– 'Spessart'	CCge EBee EChP ELan ENot EPPr EPfP GKir LAst NBee SCou WBVN WCra WCru WFar WOVN WRHF WShp WTMC WWpP
– 'Variegatum' (v)	More than 30 suppliers
– 'Velebit'	CBel CBri CCge EBee EPPr MSte WCru WMoo WTMC WWpP
§ – 'White-Ness'	CBel CCge CElw CLAP CPrp EBee EGoo EMon EPPr EPfP MWhi NBPC NDov NGar NPro SHel SRms SUsu WBrk WCot WCru WFar WHal WHen WMoo WPGP WShp WTMC WWeb WWpP
macrostylum	CDes CPou EBee LHop MBro WBVN WCot WCru WPGP WPer WPnP
– *see G. tuberosum* 'Leonidas'
maculatum	CArn CElw CSev ECha EFou EGra EPfP GCal GPoy LRHS MBro MRav MSal NSti SCou SMac WCAu WCra WCru WHal WHen WHoo WPnP WWpP WWye
– f. *albiflorum*	CElw CMea EGle EMan EMon EPPr GCal LPhx MBro MNrw NBid NSti SCou SSpi SUsu WBrk WCra WCru WMoo WPen WPnP WTMC WWpP
– 'Beth Chatto'	More than 30 suppliers
– 'Espresso'	CDes CElw CFai CKno EBee EBla EChP EHrv EMan EMar EPPr GBuc IBal LRHS MAvo MBNS MSph NCot NGdn NSti SMHy WCAu WCot WTMC
– purple	EPPr SCro WWpP
– 'Shameface'	EBee EPPr MSte NBrk SDys SGar SHel SOkh
– 'Vickie Lynn'	CFwr
maderense ♀H2	More than 30 suppliers
§ x *magnificum* ♀H4	More than 30 suppliers
– 'Peter Yeo'	EPPr NSti WLin
– 'Rosemoor'	CCge CFwr CHid CSpe EBee EChP EFou ELan EPPr EPfP IPot LBBr MSte NCot NPro NSti WCra WMnd WTMC WWpP
magniflorum	IFro MRav NBid WCru WSHC
§ *malviflorum*	More than 30 suppliers
– pink	CDes CMil EBee SBla SCro WCru WMoo WPnP
– Spanish form	EPPr EWes WSHC
§ 'Mary Mottram'	CMCo EBee EPPr MAvo MCLN NBir NCot NSti SCro WCot WEas WWpP
maximowiczii	CCge CElw EBee
'Maxwelton'	WTMC
'Menna Bach' **new**	WCru
microphyllum	*see G. potentilloides*
molle	MSal NLRH
§ x *monacense*	CMCo EBee EFWa ELan EMar EPAt EPla GGar GKir GSki LRHS MWgw MWhe NSti SBri SCou SCro SMac SSea SWat WBea WBrk WCru WHer WMnd WMoo WPnP WWpP
– var. *anglicum*	CCge EBla EChP ECtt EOrc EPPr GKir MBro MNFA MRav MWhe NSti SCou SCro WCra WMoo WPnP
– 'Breckland Fever'	EPPr

– 'Claudine Dupont'	EPPr
– dark	CBri WMoo
– var. *monacense*	WFar WHen
§ – 'Muldoon'	CHar CSev EBlw EBre EChP ECoo EPPr EPla GKir GMac GSki LRHS MBow MRav NBPC NBir NBrk NOak STes WFar WHCG WHen WMoo WPer WPnP WTMC
moupinense	EBee
'Mourning Widow'	*see G. phaeum* var. *phaeum* black-flowered
multisectum	WCru WTMC
§ *nanum*	NWCA
napuligerum misapplied	*see G. farreri*
napuligerum Franch.	NSla WCot
'Natalie'	EBee MAvo NChi NCot
nepalense	CMCo EPAt ITim NCot SCou SHel SRms WMoo WWpP
nervosum	*see G. viscosissimum* var. *incisum*
'Nicola'	CCge CElw EBee EGle EPPr MNFA SAga WCra WTMC WWpP
'Nimbus'	More than 30 suppliers
nodosum	More than 30 suppliers
– dark	*see G. nodosum* 'Swish Purple'
– 'Julie's Velvet'	CDes MSte MTed WCra WHoo WWhi WWpP
– pale	*see G. nodosum* 'Svelte Lilac'
– 'Pascal' **new**	EBee
– 'Saucy Charlie' **new**	SHel
§ – 'Svelte Lilac'	CElw EBee EBla ECGP EGle EMan EMon EPPr EPfP GCal MAvo MSte NBrk NFor SCou SHel SWat WBea WCAu WCot WCru WFar WMoo WPnP WWpP
§ – 'Swish Purple'	CElw CHar EBee EPPr MNFA MSte NCiC SCro SHel SWat WCru WFar WHen WMoo WPGP WPnP WWpP
– 'Whiteleaf'	CBos CElw EBee EBla ECoo EGle EPPr MAvo NBrk NPro SAga SBla SUsu SWat WBea WCru WFar WMoo WPnP WTMC WWpP
– 'Whiteleaf' seedling	EMan EMar SHel
'Nora Bremner'	SUsu
'Nunnykirk Pink' **new**	EMan GCal
'Nunwood Purple'	EPPr NCot WTMC
ocellatum	CBre CCge MLwd WMoo
oreganum	CCge CMCo ECGP EOrc NBrk SCou SCro
§ *orientalitibeticum*	More than 30 suppliers
'Orion'	CCge CElw EBee ECGP EChP EPPr GBuc MBnl MNFA MSte NCot NGby SCou SSvw STes SUsu WCru WPnP WWpP
'Orkney Blue' **new**	WCru
'Orkney Dawn' **new**	WCru
'Orkney Pink'	More than 30 suppliers
ornithopodon	CDes IFro NCot
'Out of the Blue'	WOut
x *oxonianum*	EPAt MHer NCot NPPs SCou WCru WMoo
– 'A.T. Johnson' ♀H4	More than 30 suppliers
– 'Breckland Brownie'	CElw EPPr WWpP
– 'Breckland Sunset'	EBee EPPr SCou SHel WPnP WTMC WWpP
– 'Bregover Pearl'	CBre CElw CMCo EBee EChP EPPr MNFA SCou WMoo WTMC WWpP
– 'Bressingham's Delight'	CMCo EBee EBre ECtt EWsh GKir LRHS MCLN MWhe NCot SCou SHel WCra WTMC WWpP
I – 'Buttercup'	EMan EPPr WWpP
I – 'Cally Seedling'	EBee EPPr EWes GCal NCot NPro
§ – 'Claridge Druce'	More than 30 suppliers
– 'Coronet'	CCge EBee EPPr MNFA NBrk SHel WBea WBrk WMoo WWpP

- 'David McClintock'	CCge CElw EBee EMan EPPr MAvo MNFA NSti SCou SHel WFar WMoo WTMC WWpP	
- 'Dawn Time'	SCro WPnP	
- 'Dirk Gunst'	CElw	
- 'Elsbeth Blush'	EBee	
- 'Elworthy Misty'	CElw EPPr WWpP	
- 'Frank Lawley'	CElw CFis CMCo CPrp EBee EBla EChP EPPr GBuc GMac LLWP MNFA NBid NCot NPro NSti SCou SCro SHel SMrm WBea WBrk WCra WMoo WPnP WTMC WWpP	
§ - 'Fran's Star' (d)	EBla WBrk WCru	
- 'Hexham Pink'	CCge NPro SCou WTMC WWpP	
- 'Hollywood'	CCge CElw CMCo EBee EChP ELan EOrc EPPr GBBs GBuc GMac LRHS MBri MSte MTho NCot NPer SBri SCro SMrm SSpe WBea WBor WBrk WCra WFar WMoo WPnP WTMC WWpP	
I - 'Jean's Lilac'	NCot	
- 'Julie Brennan'	CElw EPPr GAbr GBin GCal GMac MNFA NGdn NSti SHel WBea WCra WMoo WPnP WWpP	
- 'Kate Moss'	EPPr GKir MBnl MNFA NSti WBar WCra WTMC WWpP	
§ - 'Kingston'	EPPr	
- 'Königshof'	EPPr	
- 'Kurt's Variegated' (v)	see *G.* x *oxonianum* 'Spring Fling'	
- 'Lace Time'	CBre CElw CMCo CSev EBee EBla EPPr GBBs GMac MCLN MNFA MNrw MWhe NCot NHol NOak NPPs SCro WBea WMoo WPnP WSSM WTMC	
- 'Lady Moore'	CElw CMCo CPrp EBee EPPr EPla GBuc MNrw MWhe NBro NCot SCou SCro WBea WBor WCra WHen WMoo WPnP WTMC WWpP	
- 'Lambrook Gillian'	CCge CElw CFis EBee EPPr MNFA NCot SBri SCou WBea WBrk WPnP WTMC WWpP	
- 'Lasting Impression'	EPPr WWpP	
- 'Miriam Rundle'	CElw EBee EOrc EPPr MNFA MNrw NCot WBea WBrk WCru WMoo WPnP WTMC WWpP	
- 'Moorland Jenny'	WMoo WOut	
- 'Moorland Star' **new**	WMoo	
- 'Mrs Charles Perrin'	CCge CPrp	
- 'Old Rose'	CBrm EBee EGle EPPr GCal GKir LRHS MNFA MTis NCot NPro SCou WBea WCru WMoo WPnP WTMC WWpP	
- 'Pat Smallacombe'	CElw EPPr NCot WBea WCru WMoo WTMC	
- 'Phoebe Noble'	CBel CBre CBri CElw CMCo CMil CPrp EBla EChP EGle EMar EPPr GKir IFro LRHS MNrw MWgw NCot NSti SAga SCou SCro SHel SUsu WBea WCAu WCra WMoo WTMC WWpP	
- 'Phoebe's Blush'	EPPr GFlt GMac MNFA SHel WBea WTMC WWpP	
- 'Pink Lace'	CCge NCot	
§ - 'Prestbury Blush'	CBre CElw EBee EGle EOrc EPPr SCou WBea WCot WCru WMoo WTMC WWin WWpP	
- 'Prestbury White'	see *G.* x *oxonianum* 'Prestbury Blush'	
- 'Rebecca Moss'	CMil CPrp CSev EBee EChP EMar EMon EPPr GBuc GKir GMac LRHS MCLN MLwd MSte NCot NSti SCou SHBN SSpe WCra WCru WFar WPnP WTMC WWpP	
- 'Red Sputnik'	EPPr WWpP	
- 'Rose Clair'	CElw CHid CMCo CPrp EGle GKir LRHS MWhe NBir NCot NSti SChu SCou SGar SHel SPet WBea WBrk WCom WCra WCru WEas WHen WMnd WMoo WPer WTMC WWpP	
I - 'Rosemary'	SCou WWpP	
- 'Rosemary Verey'	SHel	
- 'Rosenlicht'	CBos CElw CSev EBee EFou EMon EPPr LRHS MCLN MRav NLar SChu SCou SHel SSpi WBea WCAu WCra WCru WMnd WMoo WPGP WPnP WWpP	
- x *sessiliflorum* subsp. *novae-zelandiae* 'Nigricans'	EHrv	
- 'Sherwood'	EChP ECtt EOrc EPPr GCal GKir MCLN MLwd MTho MWgw NBro NCot NPro NVic SCou SCro SGar SHel WBea WCAu WCra WFar WLin WMoo WPnP WWpP	
- 'Spring Fling' (v)	CBct CElw CFai EChP EHrv EPPr MBnl MHar NBPC NCot NSti SPla WCot	
- 'Stillingfleet'	see *G.* x *oxonianum* 'Stillingfleet Keira'	
§ - 'Stillingfleet Keira'	NSti	
§ - 'Summer Surprise'	CElw CFwr EBee EPPr EWes SCou SCro SHel SUsu WCru WPnP WTMC	
- 'Susan'	EBla EPPr EWes	
- 'Susie White'	CElw EPPr MAvo WWpP	
* - f. *thurstonianum*	More than 30 suppliers	
- - 'Armitageae'	CElw EPPr MNFA NCot SCou SHel WTMC WWpP	
- - 'Crûg Star'	CCge CElw	
- - 'Southcombe Double' (d)	CBel CElw CMCo CPla CSev CStr EGle EMar EMon EPPr GBBs GMac IFro IPot MAvo MCLN MFir MLwd NCot NGdn SUsu WBea WCru WFar WHen WMoo WTMC WWhi WWin	
§ - - 'Southcombe Star'	CMCo EOrc EPPr GAbr GCal IPot MFir MNFA NBrk NBro NGdn NSti SHel WBea WBrk WCru WFar WHen WMoo WPer WPnP WTMC WWpP	
- 'Trevor's White'	EBee EBla EChP EGle EPPr MBnl MNFA MNrw NCot WCAu WCru WTMC WWpP	
- 'Wageningen'	CBre CElw CMCo EBee EGle EMar GCal GKir GMac LRHS MAvo NCot NGdn NPro SAga SCou WBea WBrk WCra WCru WHen WHer WMoo WTMC WWpP	
- 'Walter's Gift'	More than 30 suppliers	
- 'Wargrave Pink' ♀H4	More than 30 suppliers	
- 'Waystrode'	CMCo EBee EBla EPPr SCou WTMC WWpP	
- 'Whitehaven'	NCot	
- 'Winscombe'	CElw CMCo EChP EFou GCal LGro LLWP LRHS MBow MLwd MRav MTho MWgw NCot NSti SCro WBea WCru WGwG WHen WMnd WMoo WWpP	
'Pagoda'	CCge EOrc MNrw NCot	
§ *palmatum* ♀H3	More than 30 suppliers	
palustre	CBri CElw EBee EChP EMar EOrc EPAt EPPr LLWP MLwd MNFA MNrw NBro NCot NHol NSti SCou STes WCra WCru WFar WHen WMoo WPnP WTMC WWpP	
- 'Tidmarsh'	EBee	
papuanum	SBla WCru	
'Pastel Clouds'	EBee	

	'Patricia'	More than 30 suppliers
	peloponnesiacum	CDes CStr EBee EPPr GGar WCru WFar
	– NS 660	CElw
	'Peter Hale'	CMea
	phaeum	More than 30 suppliers
	– 'Album'	More than 30 suppliers
	– 'Alec's Pink'	EBla LLWP WOut
	– 'All Saints'	CElw EBee EMon SUsu WTMC
	– 'Aureum'	see *G. phaeum* 'Golden Spring'
	– black	see *G. phaeum* var. *phaeum* black-flowered
	– 'Blauwvoet' **new**	CFwr
	– 'Blue Shadow'	CElw EPPr WTMC WWpP
	– 'Calligrapher'	CElw EBee EChP EGle EPPr NBrk SCou SHel SUsu WCra WMoo WTMC WWpP
	– 'Charles Perrin'	CBgR CElw CHid EBee STes
	– 'Chocolate Chip'	CFwr
	– dark	CBri CElw SCou
	– 'David Bromley'	EMon WPrP WTMC
*	– 'Geele Samobor' **new**	WTMC
§	– 'Golden Spring'	CCge CElw EPPr GBBs NChi NCot NPro
	– 'Hannah Perry'	CBel CBri CElw CHad EBee EPPr LLWP MBnl WBea WBro
	– var. *hungaricum*	EPPr SCou WCru WTMC WWpP
	– 'Klepper' **new**	CFwr
§	– 'Lily Lovell'	More than 30 suppliers
	– 'Little Boy'	CElw EMon EPPr WTMC
	– var. *lividum*	More than 30 suppliers
	– – 'Joan Baker'	More than 30 suppliers
	– – 'Majus'	CCge CElw ECtt EMon EPPr EPfP GKir LLWP LPhx MNFA MWgw NSti SCou SCro SWat WFar WMoo WPnP WTMC
	– 'Marchant's Ghost' **new**	SMHy
	– 'Margaret Wilson' (v)	CBos CElw EBee EBla EChP EMan EPPr LPio MBNS NCot NSti SCou SCro SUsu WTMC
	– 'Mierhausen'	CElw EPPr
	– 'Moorland Dylan' **new**	WMoo
	– 'Mourning Widow'	see *G. phaeum* var. *phaeum* black-flowered
	– 'Night Time'	EPPr LLWP SCro WBea
§	– var. *phaeum* black-flowered	CMil EChP EGle EPPr GBin GCal IBlr MWhe NCot NDov SCou SCro SGar SRms WBea WCra WCru WHen WMoo WPGP WWpP
	– – 'Langthorns Blue'	CCge CElw CMCo CMea CSev EBee ELan EPPr MNFA MNrw NCot SCro WBar WCra WHen WTMC WWpP
I	– 'Ploeger de Bilt'	EPPr WTMC
	– purple-flowered	MDun
	– 'Rachel's Rhapsody' **new**	EPPr
	– 'Raven'	CFwr
	– red	MRav MTed
I	– 'Rise Top Lilac'	EBee NCot WPGP
	– 'Rose Air'	EBee EChP EGoo EPPr MNFA NBrk WCra WMoo WPnP WTMC WWpP
	– 'Rose Madder'	CBel CCge CElw CHad CM&M EBee EGle EPPr GBuc GCal LHop LLWP LPhx MNFA MNrw MSte NChi NCot SCou SHBN WMoo WPnP WWpP
	– 'Samobor'	More than 30 suppliers
	– 'Saturn'	EBee
	– 'Silver Fox'	WRha
I	– 'Small Grey'	EPPr WTMC
	– 'Springtime' PBR **new**	EBee EChP MCLN WTMC
	– 'Stillingfleet Ghost'	CElw EBee EBre EPPr LRHS NCot NPro NSti SCou WTMC
	– 'Taff's Jester' (v)	CCge CElw EWes NHol NSti WCot WHer WTMC WWpP
	– 'Thorn's Blue' **new**	LRHS
	– 'Tom Stone' **new**	EPPr
	– 'Variegatum' (v)	More than 30 suppliers
	– 'Walküre'	EPPr
	– 'Zit Factory'	WTMC
	'Philippe Vapelle'	More than 30 suppliers
	'Pink Delight'	CElw LPio WWpP
	'Pink Spice' PBR	CCge ECtt MRav MWhe NSti WWeb
§	***platyanthum***	CCge EBee EChP EPPr GCal GGar GKir MAnH MNrw NBPC WBrk WCru WHCG WHen WMoo WPer
	– giant	SGar
	– var. *reinii*	WCru
	– – f. *onoei*	EBee WCru
	platypetalum misapplied	see *G. x magnificum*
	platypetalum Franch.	see *G. sinense*
§	***platypetalum*** Fisch. & C.A. Mey.	EChP ENot EPPr EWsh GKir LRHS MAvo NBir NSti SCou SRms SWat WCru WMoo WTMC WWpP
	– 'Georgia Blue'	CFil EBee MSte SSpi WCru WFar WMoo
	– 'Turco' **new**	GBin
§	***pogonanthum***	CDes EBee EOrc GBuc GCal IFro MNrw NBir WCru WMoo
	polyanthes	CMCo EBee GBuc GTou MSph WTMC
	– CC 2721	WOBN
	– CC 3329	WRos
	– HWJCM 276	WCru
	aff. ***polyanthes*** **new**	SOkd
§	***potentilloides***	CCge EBee EPAt GSki NBir WBrk WMoo
	pratense	More than 30 suppliers
	– CC&McK 442	CMCo GTou
I	– 'Bittersweet'	CHar EBee EChP EMon EPPr NBrk NCot WOut
	– 'Cluden Sapphire'	CAbP EFou GKir MWhi NCot NHol NPro WCru WFar
	– 'Flore Pleno'	see *G. pratense* 'Plenum Violaceum'
	– 'Gay Hellyer'	SCro
*	– 'Himalayanum'	LGro NLar
	– 'Hocus Pocus' **new**	CFai EBee EChP EHrv EPfP MBNS MBnl MCLN MTis NCot WCot WCra WTMC
	– 'Janet's Special'	WHoo
	– 'Lilac Lullaby' **new**	EBee
	– Midnight Reiter strain	CBAn CBos CCol CElw CHar CSpe EBee EChP EMan GBin GBri LRHS MBNS MCLN MDun MSte NCGa NChi SCoo SSpi SUsu WCAu WCot WCru WFar WPnP WTMC
	– 'Mount Stewart'	IBlr WCru
	– 'Mrs Kendall Clark' ♀H4	More than 30 suppliers
	– 'New Dimension' **new**	EFou GBin NSti SCou
	– pale form	EBee NPPs
§	– 'Plenum Caeruleum' (d)	More than 30 suppliers
	– 'Plenum Purpureum'	see *G. pratense* 'Plenum Violaceum'
§	– 'Plenum Violaceum' (d) ♀H4	More than 30 suppliers
	– var. *pratense* f. *albiflorum*	CBot CElw CSpe EPPr IFro MAnH MBow MCLN MHer MNrw NBid NCot NOrc NPPs NSti SCou SCro WBea WCom WCra WCru WHCG WHen WMnd WMoo WPnP WTMC WWin WWpP
	– – – 'Galactic'	CCge EBee EChP EPPr GKir NBir WCra WCru WHen WMoo
	– – 'Plenum Album' (d)	CDes EBee CStr
	– – – 'Silver Queen'	CBre CHar EBee EChP ECtt EOrc EPPr MAnH MBow MNrw MWhe NBir NBrk NCot NMRc NPPs SCou

– – – 'Whimble White'	WBea WFar WHen WLin WMoo WPGP WPnP WSSM WTMC WWpP WWhi
– 'Purple Heron'	More than 30 suppliers
– 'Purple-haze'	CCge CPla ECoo GBuc GSki MAnH MCCP MWhi NLar NPPs WHoo WHrl WOut
– 'Rectum Album'	see *G. clarkei* 'Kashmir White'
§ – 'Rose Queen'	CBri EBee EOrc MAnH MNrw MRav NBir NHol NLar NSti SSpi WBea WCom WCra WCru WHen WPnP WTMC WWpP
– 'Roseum'	see *G. pratense* 'Rose Queen'
– 'Spinners'	see *G.* 'Spinners'
– 'Splish-splash'	More than 30 suppliers
– 'Stanton Mill'	NBid
– var. *stewartianum*	EBee MRav WPnP
– – 'Elizabeth Yeo'	CCge EBee EBla EPPr SCou SCro SUsu WCra WTMC WWpP
– 'Striatum'	More than 30 suppliers
– 'Striatum' dwarf **new**	WCru
– 'Striatum' pale	CBre
– Victor Reiter Junior strain	More than 30 suppliers
– 'Wisley Blue'	CMCo EBee EBla EPPr MSte SCou SCro SHel WHal WMnd
– 'Yorkshire Queen'	EBee EPPr NGdn SCou WCra
'Prelude'	CElw EBee EPPr NBir NPro WBea WCra WTMC
'Priestley's Pink'	EBee
procurrens	More than 30 suppliers
– 'Trick or Treat' (v) **new**	EWes
pseudosibiricum	EBee
§ *psilostemon* ♀H4	More than 30 suppliers
– 'Bressingham Flair'	CMCo EChP ECtt EGle EGra EPfP GAbr GCal GKir GSki LHop LRHS MCLN MMil MRav MWhe NBid NGdn NLar NOrc SChu SCou SPer SRms WCAu WCru WFar WMoo WSHC WTMC
– 'Gold Leaf'	WCot
– 'Goliath' **new**	EPPr
– hybrid	CElw
pulchrum	CElw CHid CMCo CSev CSpe EMan EOrc EPAt EPPr LPio MNrw MWhi NBPC SGar SIgm SSpi STes SWat WCot WCru WPer WRos WWpP
punctatum hort.	see *G.* x *monacense* 'Muldoon'
– 'Variegatum'	see *G. phaeum* 'Variegatum'
pusillum	MSal
pylzowianum	CCge EPAt GGar MBro MRav NBid NJOw NRya SBla WBea WCra WCru WFar WHen WMoo WPnP WTel
pyrenaicum	CCge CElw CRWN CSev EBee EPAt GAbr MBow NCot NSti SCou WBea WHen WTMC WWpP
– f. *albiflorum*	CElw CPrp EBee EChP EGra EPAt GAbr GBBs LLWP MNrw MTho NBir NCot NSti SBri SCou SCro WBea WBrk WCra WHen WPer WWin WWpP
– 'Bill Wallis'	More than 30 suppliers
– 'Isparta'	CElw EChP EPPr IFro LPhx LPio SUsu WBrk
– 'Summer Sky'	CCge NCot WWpP
– 'Summer Snow'	EBee NCot NLar SPoG WWpP
'Rambling Robin'	CCge EBee EMan EPPr WCot WCru WPGP WWpP XPep
'Ray's Pink'	CCge CPla EBee MAnH NPro WWpP
rectum	EBee EPPr NCot SCou WCra
– 'Album'	see *G. clarkei* 'Kashmir White'
'Red Admiral'	NPro

'Red Dwarf'	CElw EPPr WMoo
reflexum	CHid CSev EBee EBla EChP EMan EPPr NHol SCou SCro WFar WHCG WOut WPnP WTMC WWpP
refractoides	EBee
refractum	EBee
regelii	CBos CCge CElw CMCo CSam EBee EOrc EPPr GMac NCot SAga SChu WCra WCru WMoo WPnP WWpP
renardii ♀H4	More than 30 suppliers
– 'Beldo' **new**	EBee
– blue	see *G. renardii* 'Whiteknights'
– 'Heidi Morris'	SCro
– 'Tcschelda'	CFai CMil EBee EChP EFou EMan EMil GBBs LPio MAnH MCLN NCot SBod SPla SUsu SWat WCra WPnP WViv WWhi WWpP
§ – 'Whiteknights'	CElw CFee EGra GBuc GSki MAnH MAvo MBro NBir NPro WBea WCru WEas WIvy WWin
– 'Zetterlund'	CElw CMCo CSpe EBee EBre EGle EHrv EPPr GKir LLWP MAvo MLLN SCou SUsu SWat WBea WCAu WCru WFar WMoo WTMC WWeb
retrorsum	CCge
reuteri	CBod CCge CPla CSpe EBee EMan EMar EWes LDai LPhx LPio SBod SChr SCou SGar SRob WCru WPnP WWpP
'Richard John'	CCge
richardsonii	CCge EBee EChP EMan EPPr GCal GMac MLwd MNrw NBir NCot SCro SRms WCra WCru WPnP WTMC WWpP
x *riversleaianum*	WCru
– 'Mavis Simpson'	More than 30 suppliers
– 'Russell Prichard' ♀H4	More than 30 suppliers
§ *rivulare*	CBri CCge CMCo EBee EMan GKir GSki MNFA NCot NSti STes WBea WHCG WMnd WPnP
robertianum	CArn EPAt EPPr GWCH MHer SCou SECG SRms WHbs WHen WWpP
§ – 'Album'	CBgR EPPr NSti SCou SRms
– f. *bernettii*	see *G. robertianum* 'Album'
– 'Celtic White'	CBgR CBod CBre CCge ECoo EMon EPPr GCal GSki MHer WBrk WHen WPnP WWpP
robustum	CBod EBee EOrc EPAt EPPr GSki IFro MNrw MSph NBPC NBro NChi NCot SIgm SMad STes WBea WCot WCra WCru WFar WHal WHer WPGP WSHC WWin WWpP XPep
– S&SH 14	WBea
– Hannays' form	CCge CKno CSev CSpe WPGP
– 'Norman Warrington'	WHer
robustum x *incanum*	CCge CMea CSpe MAnH MSph WCom WCru
'Rosie Crûg'	CCge CDes CHid EBee EChP EMan MDun NLar SAga SWvt WCot WCru WWhi
rosthornii	WCru
rotundifolium	SCou
Rozanne = 'Gerwat'PBR	CCge EBre GKir SCou SPer WCra WFar
rubifolium	CBod EMan GGar MLwd NBrk NHol SSpi WCru WTMC
ruprechtii	CBel CElw EBee EBre ECoo EMar EPAt EPPr GMac MAvo MLwd MNrw NCot WBea WPer WPnP WWin WWye
'Salome'	More than 30 suppliers

sanguineum	More than 30 suppliers	
- Alan Bloom	EBre ECtt GKir LRHS SCou SIng	
= 'Bloger'PBR	SMer WCra WTMC	
- 'Album' ♀H4	More than 30 suppliers	
- 'Alpenglow'	SHel	
- 'Ankum's Pride'	More than 30 suppliers	
- 'Apfelblüte' **new**	EBee SCou SSvw	
- 'Aviemore'	EBee EPPr SCou SHel	
- 'Barnsley'	CElw EBee NBro NPro SCou SHel	
	WTMC WWpP	
- 'Belle of Herterton'	CMCo EPPr MSte NPro SCou SUsu	
	WCru WTMC WWpP	
- 'Bloody Graham'	EGle EPPr MWhe SCou SHel	
	WMoo	
- 'Canon Miles' **new**	EBee	
- 'Catforth Carnival'	EPPr	
- 'Cedric Morris'	CElw CFil EChP ECha EFou	
	EGle EGra EPPr LPio MAvo	
	MTho NBid SAga SCou SCro SHel	
	SUsu WCru WHen WPnP WTMC	
	WWpP	
§ - 'Droplet'	SCou SUsu WPnP WWpP	
- 'Elliott's Variety'	SIng	
- 'Elsbeth'	CBri CCge CElw CMCo CMil EBee	
	EChP ECtt EGra EMar EPPr EWes	
	GBuc MCLN NCot NGdn NHol	
	NSti SCou SHel WCra WCru WFar	
	WHal WMoo WPnP WShp WTMC	
	WWpP	
- 'Feu d'Automne'	NPro	
- 'Fran's Star'	see *G. x oxonianum* 'Fran's Star'	
- 'Glenluce'	More than 30 suppliers	
- 'Hampshire Purple'	see *G. sanguineum* 'New	
	Hampshire Purple'	
- 'Holden'	CElw EPPr SCou SHel WCra	
- 'Joanna'	SCou SHel	
- 'John Elsley'	CElw CMCo CPrp EBre EChP ECtt	
	EFou EHoe EPPr GKir LLWP LRHS	
	MMil MWhe NBro NCot NGdn	
	NLar SHel SSpe SSpi SWat WBVN	
	WCAu WCra WMnd WPer WPnP	
	WTMC WWpP	
- 'Jubilee Pink'	CElw EBla EPPr GCal SBla WCra	
	WCru WTMC	
- var. *lancastrense*	see *G. sanguineum* var. *striatum*	
- 'Leeds Variety'	see *G. sanguineum* 'Rod Leeds'	
§ - 'Little Bead'	EPar NHol NMen WCru WPnP	
	WWpP	
- 'Max Frei'	More than 30 suppliers	
- 'Minutum'	see *G. sanguineum* 'Droplet'	
- 'Nanum'	see *G. sanguineum* 'Little Bead'	
§ - 'New Hampshire Purple'	CBgR EBee EChP EFou EPPr NBro	
	NGdn NLar NSti SSvw WCAu	
	WTMC WWpP	
- 'Nyewood'	ECGP EMon EPPr IMGH MLLN	
	SCou SEND WCra WCru	
I - 'Plenum' (d)	EPPr	
- var. *prostratum*	see *G. sanguineum* var. *striatum*	
§ - 'Rod Leeds'	CBel CBgR EBee LPio MSte NCot	
	NPro NSti SCou WCAu WHal	
	WPnP WTMC	
- 'Sara'	NSti WHen WPnP	
- 'Shepherd's Warning'	CMea CSev EBre ECtt EDAr EPPr	
♀H4	GKir LRHS MBro MLLN MRav	
	MWhe NBir NLar SCou SWat WBea	
	WCra WCru WHCG WHoo WIvy	
	WTel WTin WWpP	
- 'Shepherd's Warning'	GCal	
seedlings		
- 'South Nutfield'	SCou	
§ - var. *striatum* ♀H4	More than 30 suppliers	
- - deep pink	CSBt CWCL GBBs MSwo SCro	
	SWvt WShp	
- - 'Reginald Farrer'	GBuc WCra	

- - 'Splendens'	CBri CElw CSev EBre ECha ELan	
	ENot EPPr LBee LHop MRav MWat	
	NBid NChi NCot WCru WEas WTin	
	WWhi WWpP	
- x **swatense**	WMoo	
- 'Vision'	CCge EBla LRHS NCot WPnP	
	WWpP	
- 'Westacre Poppet'	EWes	
'Sarah Louisa'	NPar	
'Sea Fire'	CCge CElw CWCL MNrw SCro	
'Sea Pink'	CElw MNrw WHal	
'Sellindge Blue'	CElw WCra	
sessiliflorum	ECou EPar	
- subsp. *novae-*	SWat	
zelandiae green-leaved		
I - - 'Nigricans'	CBrm CCge CHar CMea ECha ELan	
	EOrc EPat EPPr EWTr GAbr LGro	
	LLWP MBow MHer MLwd MRav	
	NBid NHol NPPs WCom WCra	
	WCru WEas WFar WHCG WPnP	
	WTMC WWpP	
§ - - 'Porter's Pass'	CMea CWib EHoe EWes GBuc	
	MBro MCCP MNrw NBir SPlb SWat	
	WCom WCra WCru WFar WHoo	
	WPnP WTMC WWpP	
- - red-leaved	see *G. sessiliflorum* subsp. *novae-*	
	zelandiae 'Porter's Pass'	
- 'Rubrum'	CCge EBee GSki	
'Sheilah Hannay'	CSpe CStr	
shensianum new	EBee	
shikokianum	EBee EChP GMac NLar SPer	
	WWpP	
- var. *kaimontanum*	EBee WCru	
- var. *quelpaertense*	CDes EBee WHal WPGP	
- - B&SWJ 1234	WCru	
- var. *yoshiianum*	CElw EBee GBuc WCru WMoo	
	WPat WTMC	
- - B&SWJ 6147	WCru	
sibiricum	EBla	
'Silver Cloak'	ECre MCCP WCot WCra WWpP	
'Silver Shadow'	CCge LDai NDlv	
§ **sinense**	CElw EBee EChP EMar EPAt GCal	
	ITer NCot NLar SCou WCra WCru	
	WHCG WHer WMnd WMoo WPer	
	WTMC WWhi WWpP	
- B&SWJ 7870	WCru	
'Sirak'	CBos CElw CLAP EBla EChP EGle	
	EPPr GBin GCal GMac MAnH	
	MAvo MBro MMil MNFA NCot NSti	
	SAga SCou SMac SUsu WCra WCru	
	WFar WHoo WMoo WPnP WTMC	
	WTin WWpP	
soboliferum	CBod CBos EBee EBre ELan EMan	
	EPPr GCal GMac LRHS MAvo	
	MHar NBir NCot NDlv NSti SCou	
	SCro SMac SPla WCra WCru WHal	
	WMoo WWpP	
- Cally strain	GCal MSte	
'Southcombe Star'	see *G. x oxonianum* 'Southcombe	
	Star'	
§ 'Spinners'	More than 30 suppliers	
stapfianum var. *roseum*	see *G. orientalitibeticum*	
'Stephanie'	CDes CElw EBee EPPr NPPs WCra	
	WWpP	
'Strawberry Frost'	CElw EBee EChP EMan LTwo	
	MBNS MBnl MDun NSti SCou	
	WCAu	
subcaulescens	CTbh EBre EChP ECtt EFou EPPr	
'Guiseppii'	GKir LGro MNrw MRav MWhe	
	NBro NCot NGdn NHol SCou SPla	
	WBea WCra WFar WPnP WWeb	
- 'Splendens' ♀H4	CSpe EBre ECtt EDAr EFou EPPr	
	EPfP GLbr LHop LRHS MBNS	
	MDun MTis MWhe NSla NSti	

	SHBN SPla SRms SWat WCra WFar WIvy WPat WPnP WWpP
* - 'Violaceum'	EPPr
'Sue Crûg'	More than 30 suppliers
'Summer Cloud'	EPPr SHel WCra WHrl
Summer Skies	CCge CStr EBre EMan LRHS LSpr
= 'Gernic'PBR (d)	MBnl NLar SCou WBor WCra WHil WTMC
suzukii	IFro
- B&SWJ 016	WCru
swatense	MLLN SWat WCru
sylvaticum	CBri CM&M CRWN EPAt EWTr GKir MBow MSal NBid SCou SSpi WBVN WBrk WHal WHen WMoo WOut WPer WShi WTMC
- f. *albiflorum*	CBel CBre CCge CElw CMil EBee ELan EMar MBro MWhe NSti SSpi WCru WTin WWin
- 'Album' ♀H4	More than 30 suppliers
- 'Amy Doncaster'	More than 30 suppliers
- 'Angulatum'	CElw CPlt EBee EPPr LPhx MNFA WMoo WWpP
- 'Birch Lilac'	CBel CElw EBee EChP EPPr EPfP EWTr GBuc GCal GKir LRHS MAvo NPPs NSti SWal WBea WCra WFar WMoo WPnP WTMC WWpP
- 'Blue Ice'	EBee EPPr
- 'Cyril's Fancy'	see G. 'Cyril's Fancy'
- 'Heron'	CCge
- 'Immaculée'	MRav
- 'Kanzlersgrund'	CElw
- 'Lilac Time'	EPPr
- 'Mayflower' ♀H4	More than 30 suppliers
- 'Meran'	CCge EBre
- f. *roseum*	CCge EBee GGar GKir NLar SCro
- - 'Baker's Pink'	CBos CCge CElw CFil CMCo CMil EBee EGle EPPr MRav NCot SBla SCou SSpi WCom WCra WCru WFar WHCG WMoo WPnP WTMC WTin WWpP
I - 'Silva'	CCol CElw EBee ECtt EMan EPPr MAvo MRav NBrk SCou SCro SWat WCru
- subsp. *sylvaticum* var. *wanneri*	CCge EBee EPPr MRav WCru WTMC WWpP
'Terre Franche'	EBee EFou EPPr GBin NGby NLar NSti SCou SSpi SSvw
§ *thunbergii*	CBri CCge CHid CMCo EBee EPAt GFlt GGar GSki LAst LGro MBow MNrw MRav NBid NJOw NOak NSti WBrk WHen WPer WWpP
- dark	CSev EMar
- 'Jester's Jacket' (v)	CCge CMil CPla EMan ITer MAvo MCCP NPro SPoG WBrk WCru WGMN WMoo WOut WTMC WWpP
- pink	EPPr SCou WCru WTMC
- white	EPPr WTMC
thurstonianum	see G. x *oxonianum* f. *thurstonianum*
'Tinpenny Mauve'	WHoo WTin
'Tiny Monster'	CDes CFwr EBee MAvo
transbaicalicum	CCge EBee EMan EPPr MBow MLwd MNrw SCro
traversii	CCge CLyd CPBP EGle MDKP MLwd SMrm WRos
- 'Big White'	WPnP
- var. *elegans*	CFee CSpe ECtt EPAt GEdr GGar IGor LPhx MLwd MNrw NCot WCru WEas WHCG WKif WPGP WPnP WSSM WWpP
tuberosum	More than 30 suppliers
- var. *charlesii*	see G. *kotschyi* var. *charlesii*
§ - 'Leonidas'	CFwr CPou LPhx LRHS WPnP
- subsp. *linearifolium*	WCru

- pink	WCru WHoo WPnP
'Vera May'	SUsu
'Verguld Saffier'	see G. 'Blue Sunrise'
versicolor	More than 30 suppliers
- 'Kingston'	see G. x *oxonianum* 'Kingston'
- 'Knighton'	EBee
§ - 'Snow White'	CCge CElw CMCo EBee EChP EGoo EOrc EPPr GMac MGas MNrw MWhe NBrk NCot NDov WBea WCra WCru WMoo WPnP WTMC WWpP
- 'The Bride'	CMea EGra EMan EMar
- 'White Lady'	see G. *versicolor* 'Snow White'
'Victor Reiter'	see G. *pratense* Victor Reiter Junior Strain
violareum	see *Pelargonium* 'Splendide'
viscosissimum	EBee EBla GCal GSki STes WCra WMnd WPnP
§ - var. *incisum*	CMCo EBee EWsh MCCP NPro SCou STes WPnP WTMC WWpP
- rose pink	NBir
wallichianum	CBod CBot CCge CMCo CPou CStr EBee ECGP IFro LRHS NBir NChi NSti SBla WBea WFar WHen WMoo WTMC
- CC 3648	ITer
§ - 'Buxton's Variety' ♀H4	More than 30 suppliers
- 'Chadwell's Pink'	CCge
- 'Martha' **new**	EBee
- pale blue	CElw
- pink	EBla EFou EMan EPPr GBuc GKir LPio MTed NCot WBrk WCra WCru
- RBGE form	EBee EPPr SUsu
- 'Silvery Blue' **new**	CFwr
- 'Syabru'	CBri CCge CElw CMea EBee EBla EMar EMil GBuc GSki MLwd MNrw NCot NLar NPro SAga SSpi WBVN WFar WMoo
'Wednesday's Child'	WFar
'Welsh Guiness'	WCru WTMC
wilfordii misapplied	see G. *thunbergii*
wilfordii Maxim.	CCge
- *variegated*	WCru
Wisley hybrid	see G. 'Khan'
wlassovianum	More than 30 suppliers
- 'Blue Star'	CCge GKir MBri MRav NPro WCra WTMC WWpP
yeoi	CCge CSpe EMar EPAt EPPr GGar MNrw NBir NBro NSti SUsu WCru WHal WOut WTMC
yesoense	EBee EBla EPPr GBin GGar MDKP MLwd NBir NSti SWat WCru WFar WOut WPnP
- var. *nipponicum*	WCru
- white	EBee NWCA
yoshinoi	CMCo EBee EBla EMan EPAt EPot EWes GAbr GBuc GMac GSki LLWP MSte MWhi NCot NLar NPro SHel SWal SWat WMoo WPGP WTMC WWpP
yunnanense misapplied	see G. *pogonanthum*
yunnanense Franchet	CFir EBee GGar MNrw
- BWJ 7543	WCru

Gerbera (Asteraceae)

gossypina	EBee
jamesonii	CBrm
nivea	EMan

Gesneria (Gesneriaceae)

cardinalis	see *Sinningia cardinalis*
x *cardosa*	see *Sinningia* x *cardosa*
* *macrantha*	EShb
'Compacta' **new**	

Geum ✿ (*Rosaceae*)

'Abendsonne'	CElw
aleppicum	CFee EBee EPPr WBea WMoo
alpinum	see *G. montanum*
'Apricot Beauty'	EBee LPVe
'Beech House Apricot'	CBre CDes CElw CSev EBre ECtt GBri GKir LHop LPhx MAvo MBri MNrw MRav NChi NDov NPro SBri SMac SOkh WAbe WCAu WMoo WPGP WPnP WPrP WTMC WTin WWeb WWye
'Bell Bank'	GBri MAvo MRav NChi NDov NPPs NPro WHil
'Birkhead's Cream'	NBir
'Birkhead's Creamy Lemon'	MAvo
'Blazing Sunset' (d)	CElw EBee ECtt MDKP MSph MWrn NArg NDlv NPPs SBri SOkh WHil
N 'Borisii'	More than 30 suppliers
'Borisii' x *montanum*	LHop
bulgaricum	CBri EBee GKir LRHS MAvo MNrw MRav NBir NLar NPro NRya WPnP WPrP WSSM WTMC WTin
calthifolium	EBee EPPr GKir MCCP MLLN MRav NBro
capense	MAvo NPro WCot
- JJ&JH 9401271	EBee EWes
§ *chiloense*	EBee NArg NPPs
- P&W 6513	GBri MSte NWCA
coccineum hort.	see *G. chiloense*
coccineum ambig.	CPlt WRha
coccineum Sibth. & Sm. MESE 374	EBee
- 'Werner Arends'	CBos CMHG CSev EBee GCal MAvo MBnl MRav NBro SBri WCot WFar
'Coppertone'	CElw CPla EBee ECha ECtt EHrv ELan EMon GCal MAvo MBro MNrw MRav NBir NBro NChi NCot NRya SBla SBri SUsu WBea WCom WHoo WMoo WPGP WTMC WTin WWhi WWpP
'Dingle Apricot'	ECtt EMan GCal MAvo MNrw MRav MTed MWgw NBir
'Dolly North'	CFir CHea EBee EFou EMan ERou GBri GGar LRHS MAvo MBNS MBri MNrw MRav NBro SBri WAul WCAu WHal WPrP WTMC WTin
I 'Elaine's Variety'	MAvo
elatum	EBee
I 'Farmer John Cross'	CBre CBri CDes CElw EBee ECtt MAvo MHar MNrw NCot SBri WCra WHal WPGP
fauriei x *kamtschatica*	EBee
'Feuermeer'	MSte NPro SBri
'Fire Opal' ♀H4	CDes CPlt EBee MAvo MNrw MSph NBir WPGP
'Flames of Passion'PBR	CElw EChP GBin IPot MAvo MBNS MBnl MBri MCLN NDov NLar NPro STes WAul WCAu WCot WHil
'Georgeham'	CPla WWhi
'Georgenburg'	More than 30 suppliers
glaciale album	EBee
'Herterton Primrose'	ECtt MAvo
* *hybridum luteum*	NSti
x *intermedium*	CBre EBee EGle EMan EMon EPPr GBri LRHS MAvo MNrw NLar NPro SBri SChu SCro WBWf WBea WFar WMoo WTMC WWin
- 'Diane' **new**	MAvo
japonicum	EBee
'Karlskaer'	CElw EBee EChP ECtt EGle EPfP EWes GBin GCal LPVe LPio MAvo

	MBri MHar MNrw SAga SBri SMrm SOkh SUsu WCot WHil WMoo WPGP WPnP WTin WViv
'Kashmir' **new**	EBre MAvo
'Lady Stratheden' ♀H4	More than 30 suppliers
'Lemon Drops'	CBri CElw CPrp EBee ECha ECtt EMan GBri GMac MAvo MHar MNrw MRav MSte NChi NDov NPro SBla SBri SChu SOkh SWal WBea WFar WHil WMoo WPGP WTMC WViv WWhi
'Lionel Cox'	More than 30 suppliers
macrophyllum	EBee EMan GBar MNrw WMoo
magellanicum	EBee WCot
- *perincisum*	EBee
'Mandarin'	CBos CFir CMdw GCal MTed WViv
'Marika'	CBos CBre CHid CRow EBee LRHS MNrw NBrk SBri SChu WCot WMoo
'Marmalade'	CPlt EBee EChP ECtt LPhx MAvo MBnl MHar MNrw NPPs NPro SAga SDys SMHy SUsu WBea WCot WCra
§ *montanum* ♀H4	CElw GKir GTou ITim MBro NArg NBid NBir NBro NDlv NPri NRya SPet SRms WBea WBrk WMoo WPat WPer
- 'Maximum'	MNrw
'Moorland Sorbet' **new**	WMoo
'Mrs J. Bradshaw' ♀H4	More than 30 suppliers
'Mrs W. Moore'	CDes EBee ECtt GBri GFlt MAvo MBnl MLLN MNrw NBir NChi NCot NPPs NPro WBea WCot WPGP WTMC
'Nordek'	EBee EMan GMac MAvo NBrk NCot SBri WWhi
* 'Orangeman'	MNrw
parviflorum	GGar LEdu MLLN MNrw NBro
'Paso Doble'	NCot NPro WRos WSan
§ *pentapetalum*	GEdr MNrw WAbe
- 'Flore Pleno' (d)	WAbe
'Pink Frills'	CElw ECha SMHy
'Present'	EBee SBri WPGP
I 'Primrose'	NPro WTMC
'Prince of Orange'	CElw GAbr IGor MNrw WFar WMoo WRha
'Prinses Juliana'	More than 30 suppliers
pyrenaicum	EBee MNrw NWCA
quellyon	see *G. chiloense*
I 'Rearsby Hybrid' **new**	MAvo
'Red Wings'	CBre CM&M EBee EFou EMan ERou GCal MBNS MRav NBro SUsu WCra
x *rhaeticum*	EBee ECtt ETow MNrw WMoo WPic
rhodopeum	EBee MNrw
'Rijnstroom'	EBee EChP ELan EWTr MBnl NBro SBri SUsu WAul WCra WHil
rivale	More than 30 suppliers
- 'Album'	More than 30 suppliers
- apricot	LGro WWin
- 'Barbra Lawton' **new**	MDKP
- 'Cream Drop'	NChi NGby NPro NWoo SBri
- cream, from Tien Shan, China	CFee
- 'Deep Rose' **new**	SBri
* - *islandicum*	EBee
- lemon	EMan NPPs
- 'Leonard's Double' (d)	CPrp WMoo WTMC
- 'Leonard's Variety'	More than 30 suppliers
- 'Marmalade'	MSph NBPC NChi SOkh
- 'Oxford Marmalade'	CElw
- 'Snowflake' **new**	NChi
roylei	EBee SBri

'Rubin' — EBee EFou MAvo MBNS MCLN MNrw NBro NDov NGdn SChu SCro SSpe WAul WCot WTMC

'Sigiswang' — CDes EFou GAbr GMac MAvo MFir MNrw MRav MSte NCot NPro SBri

I 'Starker's Magnificum' **new** — WCot

'Tangerine' — GGar MAvo MNrw MRav MWrn NPro WCot

'Tinpenny Orange' **new** — WTin

x *tirolense* — EBee SBri

triflorum — CPBP EBee EChP EHrv EMan EPla GKir GTou LPhx LPio LRHS MCCP MNrw MRav MTis MWrn NCot NLar SRot WFar WPnP WTin WWhi

- var. *campanulatum* — EDAr EHyt ETow GBri NChi NGar NPro NRya

urbanum — CArn ELau GBar GWCH IHMH MBow MGas NLan NSco SWat WBWf WHbs WHer WMoo WPic

- from Patagonia — MDKP

- 'Checkmate' (v) — EMon ITer WBea

'Werner Arends' — see *G. coccineum* 'Werner Arends'

Gevuina (Proteaceae)
avellana — CBcs CHEx CTrG CTrw SSpi

Gilia (Polemoniaceae)
aggregata — see *Ipomopsis aggregata*
californica — see *Leptodactylon californicum*
'Red Dwarf' **new** — NPol
tricolor **new** — NPol

Gillenia (Rosaceae)
stipulata — CHea CPlt CWCL EBee EGle EMon GCal LPhx NLar SVal
trifoliata ♀H4 — More than 30 suppliers
- 'Pixie' — CFil EBee WPGP

Gingidia (Apiaceae)
montana — NWCA

Ginkgo ✿ (Ginkgoaceae)
biloba ♀H4 — More than 30 suppliers
- B&SWJ 8753 — WCru
- 'Anny's Dwarf' — MBlu MBri
- 'Autumn Gold' (m) — CBcs CEnd CMCN EPfP MBlu MGos SKee SMad WPGP
I - 'Barabits Nana' — CMCN SMad
- 'Barabits Sztráda' — MBlu SMad
- 'Chotek' — MBlu
- 'Fairmount' (m) — CMCN MBlu
- 'Fastigiata' (m) — CMCN MGos NLar SBLw
- 'Hekt Leiden' — CMCN
- 'Horizontalis' — CMCN EPfP MBlu
- 'Jade Butterflies' **new** — MPkF
- 'King of Dongting' (f) — CMCN GKir MBlu WMou
- 'Mariken' **new** — MPkF SLim
- Pendula Group — CBcs CEnd CMCN CTho EPfP LPan NPal
- 'Princeton Sentry' (m) — MBlu SMad
I - 'Prostrata' — CPMA
- 'Saratoga' (m) — CEnd CMCN CPMA CTho EMil MGos WPGP
- 'Tit' — CMCN EPfP MGos
- 'Tremonia' — CMCN LRHS MBlu
- 'Tubifolia' — CMCN MBlu
- 'Umbrella' — CMCN
- Variegata Group (v) — CMCN CPMA MBlu NLar

Gladiolus (Iridaceae)
acuminatus — EGrW WCot
'Advantage' PBR (L) — EGrW MSGs
alatus — EGrW

'Alex Hall' (G) — EGrW
'Alexandra' (P) — EGrW
'Allosius' (S) — EGrW
'Amanda Mahy' (N) — CBro
'Ambiance' (L) — EGrW
'Amsterdam' (G) — EGrW MSGs
'Anchorage' (L) — MSGs
'Andre Viette' — EBee EMan MSph WCot
angustus — EGrW WCot
'Anna Leorah' (L) — EGrW MSGs
antakiensis — CPou
'Antique Rose' (M) — EGrW MSGs WCot
'Apricot Perfection' (P) — EGrW MSGs
'Arabella' (P) — EGrW WCot
'Arctic Day' (M/E) — EGrW MSGs
'Atom' (S/P) — CBro EBee MSph
atroviolaceus — WCot WPGP
'Aubrey Lane' (M) — EGrW MSGs
'August Days' (L) — EGrW MSGs
aureus — EGrW
Barnard hybrids — EGrW
'Beau Rivage' (G) — MSGs
'Beautiful Angel' — MSGs
'Beauty Bride' (L) **new** — MSGs
'Beauty of Holland' PBR (L) — EGrW MSGs
'Bell Tower' (G) — EGrW
'Ben Venuto' (L) — EGrW
'Bizar' **new** — EPfP
'Black Lash' (S) — MSGs
'Black Pearls' (S) **new** — MSGs
blandus var. *carneus* — see *G. carneus*
'Blue Clouds' (L) — EGrW
'Blue Conqueror' (L) — LRHS
'Blue Sky' (L) — EGrW
'Blue Tit' (P) — EGrW
'Blueberry Ice' (M) **new** — MSGs
'Blueberry Wine' (L/E) — EGrW
bonaespei — CDes
'Bono's Memory' — LRHS
'Bradley W' — MSGs
'Bronze Tiger' (M/E) — EGrW
'Brooke M' (S) — EGrW
'Burgundy Queen' — EGrW MSGs
byzantinus — see *G. communis* subsp. *byzantinus*
caeruleus — CPou EGrW
'Calimero' (M/E) — EGrW
callianthus — CBri CSWP EBla EOrc EPfP EPyc GFlt LPio MSte SVen WFar WWhi
'Calliope' (L/E) — EGrW
'Candy Cane' (L) — EGrW
cardinalis — CDes CFil CMea CPne EBee EBla EGrW EMan GCal IBlr LPio SAga SIgm SSpi WCot WPGP
carinatus — EBee EGrW WCot
carinatus x *orchidiflorus* **new** — EBee
'Carine' (N) — EGrW
'Carla Gabor' (L) — EGrW
carmineus — CFil EGrW
§ *carneus* — CPou EBee EGrW EMan GCal LPhx LRHS NRog
- 'Georgina' — EGrW
'Carquirenne' (G) — EGrW MSGs
'Carrara' (L) **new** — MSGs
'Cartago' (L) — EGrW
'Carved Ivory' (M) — MSGs
caryophyllaceus — CFil CPou EGrW
'CGS 75th Anniversary' (L) — MSGs
'Cha Cha' PBR (L) — EGrW
'Charm' (N/Tub) — CAvo CBro EBee EBla EGrW
'Charming Beauty' (Tub) — ECho NRog
'Charming Lady' (Tub) — ECho
'Chloe' (M) — MSGs

'Chocolate Ripple' (L) **new** MSGs
'Christabel' (L)   EGrW ERos
'Cindy' (B)   ECho
citrinus   see *G. trichonemifolius*
'Clarence's Choice' (L)   MSGs
'Columbine' (P)   NRog
x *colvillei*   IBlr
- 'Albus'   WHil
'Comet' (N)   EGrW LPio
communis   LAma
§ - subsp. *byzantinus* ♀H4 More than 30 suppliers
- subsp. *communis*   EBee
'Coral Butterfly' (L) **new**   MSGs
'Coral Dream' (L)   EGrW
'Côte d'Azur' (G)   EGrW MSGs
crassifolius   CFir GBuc LPio
'Crimson Fire' (G)   EGrW
§ *dalenii*   CPou CSam EGrW ERos GCal IBlr
    LPio SSpi WCot
- hybrids   SDeJ
- orange-flowered **new**   CDes
* - f. *rubra*   CFil
- yellow-flowered   CDes CFil EBee
'Darlin' Clementine'   MSGs
    (L) **new**
'Daydreamer' (L)   EGrW MSGs
'Desirée' (B)   MSGs SPet
'Dominick C' (S) **new**   MSGs
'Doris Darling' (L)   MSGs
'Drama' (L)   EGrW MSGs
'Dream's End' (G)   EGrW
'Dynamic'   MSGs
'Early Little Lilac' (S)   EGrW MSGs
ecklonii   CFil
'Egret' (L/E)   EGrW
'El Diablo' (L/E)   EGrW
'Elegance' (G)   EGrW MSGs
'Elin' (M)   EGrW
'Elvira' (N)   EBee EBla ECho EGrW GFlt LAma
    WPGP
'Emerald Spring' (S)   EGrW WCot
'Emir' (S)   MSGs
equitans   EGrW
'Esperanto' (M)   MSGs
'Essex' (P)   EGrW
'Esta Bonita' (G)   EGrW MSGs
'Estonia' (G)   EGrW
'Eunice Ann'   MSGs
'Fashion Romance'   MSGs
'Fidelio' (L)   LAma
'Finishing Touch'PBR (L)   EGrW
'Fireball II' (L)   MSGs
'Firesprite' (Min)   EGrW
'Flamenco' (L)   MSGs
'Flamingo Dawn' (L/E)   EGrW
flanaganii **new**   GKir
'Flevo Amico' (S)   EGrW
'Flevo Bambino'   EGrW MSGs
'Flevo Candy'   EGrW MSGs
'Flevo Clown' (S)   EGrW MSGs
'Flevo Cosmic' (Min)   EGrW GBri LPio MSGs WCot
'Flevo Eclips'PBR (G)   EGrW MSGs
'Flevo Eyes'PBR (L) **new**   MSGs
'Flevo Fire'PBR (M)   EGrW MSGs
'Flevo Jive' (S)   EGrW MSGs
'Flevo Junior' (S)   EGrW WCot
'Flevo Maitre' (L)   EGrW MSGs
'Flevo Option'   EGrW
'Flevo Party'   EGrW MSGs
'Flevo Smile' (S)   EGrW MSGs WCot
'Flevo Souvenir'PBR (L)   EGrW
'Flevo Sunset'PBR (L) **new**   MSGs
'Flevo Vision' (L) **new**   MSGs
'Florence C' (M)   EGrW MSGs

floribundus   CFil EGrW
'Flower's Sculpture' (L/E)   EGrW
'Flowersong' (L)   LAma
'French Silk' (L)   EGrW
'Friendship' (L)   LRHS
'Frost Fawn' (G) **new**   MSGs
garnieri   EGrW SSpi
geardii   WCot
'General Patton' (G)   MSGs
'Gladiris' (L)   MSGs
'Golden Melody' (M)   MSGs
'Golden Sunset' (L)   EGrW MSGs
'Good Luck' (N)   CBro
gracilis   EGrW
grandis   see *G. liliaceus*
'Green Star' (L)   MSGs
'Green with Envy' (L)   MSGs
'Green Woodpecker' (M)   LAma LRHS NRog
'Greyfriars' (P)   EGrW
gueinzii **new**   CFil
'Guernsey Glory' (N)   EGrW
§ *guthriei*   EGrW
'Halley' (N)   CBro ECho
'Heidi' (S)   EGrW
'Henriette' (P)   EGrW
'High Hopes' (S)   EGrW
'High Style' (L)   EGrW
hirsutus   EGrW
'Hunting Song' (L)   LAma
'Huron Darkness'   MSGs
'Huron Glow' (L) **new**   MSGs
'Huron Heaven' (L) **new**   MSGs
'Huron Lady'   MSGs
'Huron Silk'   MSGs
huttonii   EGrW
huttonii x *tristis* **new**   CPou
- x - var. *concolor* **new**   WCot
hyalinus   EGrW WCot
'Ice Cap' (L)   EGrW MSGs
'Ice Follies' (L)   MSGs
illyricus   CBrm CFil CNat CSam EGrW GBuc
    WPGP
- 'Mallorca'   EGrW
imbricatus   EBee EGrW EPot ERos GBuc GCrs
'Impressive' (N)   NRog SPet
'Intrigue' (G) **new**   MSGs
§ *italicus*   CFil EBee EGrW ELan GKir LPhx
    LPio
'Ivory Priscilla'PBR   MSGs
    (L) **new**
'Ivory Tower' (G)   EGrW
'Jayvee' (S) **new**   MSGs
'Jim S'   MSGs
'Julianna' (L)   EGrW
'Jupiter' (B)   LRHS
'Kathy's Choice' (M) **new**   MSGs
§ *kotschyanus*   GCrs GKir
'Krakatoa' (G)   EGrW
'Kristin' (L)   EGrW MSGs
'Kytice' (L) **new**   MSGs
'Lady Anne' (P) **new**   MSGs
'Lady Barbara' (P) **new**   MSGs
'Lady Caroline' (P) **new**   MSGs
'Lady Eleanor' (P)   WCot
'Lady Godiva' (P/S)   NRog
'Lady in Red' (L)   MSGs
'Lady Lucille' (M)   EGrW MSGs
'Lavender Flare' (S)   EGrW
'Lavender Masterpiece' (L)   EGrW MSGs
'Lavender Reflections'   MSGs
    (L) **new**
'Lemon Slice' (S) **new**   MSGs
lewisiae   SSpi
§ *liliaceus*   EGrW WCot

'Lime Green' (P)	LRHS
'Little Jude' (P)	EGrW MSGs WCot
'Little Wiggy' (P)	MSGs
'Loretta Fay' (S) **new**	MSGs
'Loulou' (G) **new**	MSGs
'Lowland Queen' (L)	EGrW MSGs
'Maggie' (S) **new**	EPfP MSGs
'Margaret' (P)	EGrW
'Marj S' (L)	EGrW MSGs
marlothii	EGrW
'Meersen' (L)	EGrW
'Mileesh' (L)	EGrW MSGs
'Mirella' (N)	EGrW MRav NRog
'Miss America' (M)	MSGs
'Mondiale' (G)	EGrW MSGs
'Moon Kist' (S)	EGrW
mortonius	CFil SIgm
'Mother Theresa'	MSGs
'Mother's Day' (G)	MSGs
'Mountain Meadow' (L)	EGrW
'Mr Chris' (S)	EGrW MSGs
'Mr Fox' (S)	MSGs
'Mrs Rowley' (P)	EGrW GBri
§ *murielae* ♀H3	CAvo CBro CFwr EBee EGrW LAma LPhx NRog SDeJ STes WBea WCFE WHoo WRHF
'Murieliae'	see *G. murielae*
'My Girl' (L)	EGrW MSGs
'My Love' (L)	LAma
natalensis	see *G. dalenii*
'Nathalie' (N)	EGrW LPio MBow WHil
'New Parfait' (L) **new**	MSGs
'New Wave'PBR	MSGs
'Nicholas' (S)	MSGs
'Nola' (S) **new**	MSGs
'Northern Messenger' (S)	EGrW
'Nova Lux' (L)	CSut LAma LRHS
'Nymph' (N)	CAvo EBla EChP EGrW ITim LAma LDai LPhx LPio MBow MSph NRog WHil
'Oasis'PBR (G)	EGrW
'Ocean Breeze' (S) **new**	MSGs
ochroleucus	EGrW
'Of Singular Beauty' (L)	EGrW MSGs
'Olympic Torch' (L) **new**	MSGs
§ *oppositiflorus*	CFil CPou EGrW SIgm
- subsp. *salmoneus*	see *G. oppositiflorus*
'Orchid Lace' (S/E)	EGrW
orchidiflorus	CSWP EGrW
'Orlando'PBR	MSGs
'Oscar' (G)	CSut LAma LRHS NRog
palustris	ERos
'Paparcio Ziedas' (L/E)	EGrW
papilio	More than 30 suppliers
- 'David Hills'	EGrW
§ - Purpureoauratus Group	CBro CSam EBee EMan ERos GKir IBlr MFir SRms
- yellow-flowered	SMad SUsu
pappei	CDes CFil EBee EGrW WPGP
'Parade' (G)	EGrW
'Patricia' (L)	MSGs
'Peach Royale' (L) **new**	MSGs
'Penelope' (P)	EGrW
'Perth Ivory' (M) **new**	MSGs
'Perth Pearl'	MSGs
'Peter Pears' (L)	CSut LAma LRHS NRog
'Phenom' (G)	EGrW
'Phyllis M' (L)	EGrW MSGs
Pilbeam hybrids	EGrW
'Pink Elegance' (L) **new**	MSGs
'Pink Elf' (S)	MSGs
'Pink Lady' (L)	EGrW MSGs
'Pink Phantom' (L)	EGrW
'Pinnacle' (L) **new**	MSGs

'Plum Tart' (L)	LRHS
'Pop Art'	LRHS
'Praha' (L)	LAma
'Pretty Woman' (L)	EGrW MSGs
primulinus	see *G. dalenii*
'Prince Indigo' (L)	MSGs
'Princess Margaret Rose' (Min)	LAma
'Prins Claus' (N)	CBro EBee EBla EGrW LAma LRHS NRog SPet
priorii	EGrW
'Priscilla' (L)	LAma
'Pulchritude' (M)	EGrW MSGs
punctulatus	ERos
var. *punctulatus*	
'Purple Prince' (M)	WCot
'Purple Velvet' (M)	EGrW
purpureoauratus	see *G. papilio* Purpureoauratus Group
quadrangularis	SSpi
'Rasmin' (L)	MSGs
'Red Beauty'	LRHS MSGs
'Red Ruffles'	MSGs
'Robinetta' (*recurvus* hybrid) ♀H3	CBri EBla EChP ECho EGrW EPfP LAma LDai
rogersii	CDes EGrW
'Rose Elf' (S)	EGrW MSGs
'Route One' (L)	EGrW
'Roxborough' (P)	EGrW
'Royal Canadian' (S)	MSGs
'Royal Dutch' (L)	EGrW
'Royal Mounted' (Min)	EGrW
'Sabu'	LRHS
saccatus	EGrW
'Sailor's Delight' (L)	EGrW MSGs
'Sally's Orange' (P)	EGrW
'Salmon Sorbet'	EGrW
'Samson' (L) **new**	MSGs
'San Remo'PBR (L)	EGrW MSGs
'Sarah Catherine' (L) **new**	MSGs
saundersii	CFil EGrW SIgm WCot WPGP
'Scarlet Lady' (P)	EGrW
scullyi	EGrW
segetum	see *G. italicus*
'Serafin' (Min)	LRHS
sericeovillosus	EGrW IBlr
'Sharkey' (G)	MSGs
'Shawna' (Min)	MSGs
'Show Chairman' (L) **new**	MSGs
'Showstar' (L) **new**	MSGs
'Silver Shadow'PBR (S)	EGrW EPfP
'Sirael' (L/E)	EGrW
'Smokey Joe' (L)	EGrW
'Souvenir'	MSGs
splendens	CDes CFil EGrW WCot
'Spring Green' **new**	EPfP
'Starry Night' (L) **new**	MSGs
stefaniae	EGrW
'Stromboli' (L)	EGrW MSGs
'Summer Trumpet' (L) **new**	MSGs
'Sun Valley'	MSGs
'Sunglo'	MSGs
'Sunset Fire' (L)	EGrW MSGs
'Sunsport' (M)	EGrW
'Super High Brow' (G)	EGrW MSGs
'Tan Royale' (P)	MSGs
'Tantastic' (S)	MSGs
tenellus	EGrW
'The Bride' (x *colvillei*) ♀H3	CAvo CBos CBro CHad CMil EBee EBla ECho EGrW EPyc GFlt ITim LAma LDai NRog
'Three Musketeers' (M/E)	EGrW
'Tickatoo' (P)	EGrW

'Tiger Eyes' (S) — MSGs
'Top o' the Marque' (M/E) — EGrW
'Topaz' (L) — EGrW MSGs
'Torch' (L/E) — EGrW
'Trader Horn' (G) — LAma
§ *trichonemifolius* — EGrW SSpi
tristis — CBro CElw CFil CPLG CPne CPou ECha EGrW ELan EMan EPot LPio NCGa SAga SSpi SUsu WAbe WHal WPGP WPrP WWhi
— var. *concolor* — CFil CPLG EBee EGrW EMan ERos WCot WHer
'Tuscany' — MSGs
'Ultimate' (S) **new** — MSGs
undulatus — CDes CSWP EGrW ERos SSpi WCot
'Upper Crust' (L) **new** — MSGs
usyiae **new** — WCot
'Victoria' (M) — EGrW LRHS
'Video' (L) — EGrW
'Vienna' (L) — EGrW
'Violetta' (M) — ECho EGrW EMan MSGs
virescens — EGrW SSpi WCot
watsonioides — CPou ERos SSpi WCot
'Whistle Stop' (S) **new** — MSGs
'White City' (P/S) — LRHS
'White Darling' — MSGs
'White Friendship' (L) — LAma NRog
'White Prosperity' (L) — CSut LRHS

Glandularia see *Verbena*

Glaucidium (*Glaucidiaceae*)
palmatum ♀H4 — EBee EFEx EHyt ETow GCrs GEdr GIBF ITer NSla WAbe WCru
— 'Album' — see *G. palmatum* var. *leucanthum*
§ — var. *leucanthum* — CBri EFEx GCrs ITer

Glaucium (*Papaveraceae*)
§ *corniculatum* — CHar EBre EChP LPhx MLLN MSPs NLar SEND WCot WEas WHil WMoo
flavum — CSpe ECha EGoo ELan EMFP GKir LRHS MHer MWgw NLar WHer WWin XPep
— *aurantiacum* — see *G. flavum* f. *fulvum*
§ — f. *fulvum* — ECha EMFP EMan SChu SDix SMHy WHil
— orange — see *G. flavum* f. *fulvum*
— red — see *G. corniculatum*
grandiflorum — WWin
phoenicium — see *G. corniculatum*

Glaux (*Primulaceae*)
maritima — WPer

Glechoma (*Lamiaceae*)
hederacea — CAgr CArn GBar GPoy MHer NMir NSco WHbs WHer WShp WWye XPep
— 'Barry Yinger Variegated' (v) — CRow EBee WCot
— 'Rosea' — GBar WWye
— 'Variegata' (v) — CHal IHMH ILis LRHS MBri MRav SPet WShp

Gleditsia (*Caesalpiniaceae*)
japonica — EPfP
macrantha **new** — EGFP
sinensis — EGFP NLar SMad
triacanthos — CAgr CDul CWib ECrN ENot LEdu LPan MGol SBLw SPlb WBVN WNor
— 'Bujotii' — SBLw
— 'Emerald Cascade' — CDul CEnd CLnd CPMA LRHS

— f. *inermis* — CAgr SBLw WNor
— 'Rubylace' — CBcs CDul CEnd CLnd CMCN COtt CTri EBee ECrN ELan EPfP EWTr LBuc LPan LRHS MAsh MBar MBlu MBri MDun MGos MRav MSwo NHol SHBN SKee SPer SSpi WDin WOrn
— 'Shademaster' — EBee ENot MRav SBLw
— 'Skyline' — LPan SBLw
— 'Sunburst' ♀H4 — More than 30 suppliers

Gleichenia (*Gleicheniaceae*)
microphylla — WRic

Globba (*Zingiberaceae*)
andersonii — CKob LEur MOak
* *cathcartii* — CKob LEur MOak
'Compact Golden' **new** — CKob
'Emerald Isle' — LRHS
marantina — CKob EUJe LEur MOak
'Pink Superior Compact' **new** — CKob
'Purple Compact' **new** — CKob
'White Rain' **new** — CKob
'White Superior Compact' **new** — CKob
winitii — LRHS
— 'Burmese White' **new** — CKob
— 'Golden Dragon' — MOak
— 'Mauve Dancing Girl' — MOak
— 'Pink Dancing Girl' **new** — CKob
— 'Purple Dancing Girl' **new** — CKob
— 'Red Leaf' — MOak
— 'Violett' — MOak
— 'White Dancing Girl' **new** — CKob
— 'White Dragon' — MOak
— 'Yellow Rain' **new** — CKob

Globularia (*Globulariaceae*)
alypum **new** — XPep
bellidifolia — see *G. meridionalis*
bisnagarica — GEdr WLin
cordifolia ♀H4 — CBrm CNic CTri EBre EDAr EPot GEdr IMGH LBee LRHS MBro MTho NMen SAga SBla SIng WFar WHoo WPat
— NS 696 — NWCA
incanescens — LBee LRHS WWin
§ *meridionalis* — CFee CLyd CPBP EPot EWes GEdr MBro MWat NLAp NMen NWCA SAga SBla WPat
* — 'Alba' **new** — NMen
— 'Hort's Variety' — CTri NMen WAbe
nana — see *G. repens*
nudicaulis — MBro NLAp SBla
— 'Alba' — WIvy
§ *punctata* — LRHS NJOw NWCA SOkh SRms
pygmaea — see *G. meridionalis*
§ *repens* — CLyd CNic EPot MTho NLAp NMen WPat
spinosa — NMen
stygia — NMen NSla
trichosantha — CFee EDAr NRya SRms WCom WPer

Gloriosa (*Colchicaceae*)
lutea — see *G. superba* 'Lutea'
rothschildiana — see *G. superba* 'Rothschildiana'
§ *superba* ♀H1 — LAma MBri NRog
§ — 'Lutea' — CHal LAma LRHS NRog
§ — 'Rothschildiana' — CBcs CHal CRHN CStu LAma LRHS MOak SOWG SRms

Gloxinia (*Gesneriaceae*)
'Medusa'	WDib
sylvatica	CHal CSpe WDib

Glumicalyx (*Scrophulariaceae*)
flanaganii	CStu GEdr NGar WAbe WHil
- HWEL 0325	NWCA
goseloides	ECre
montanus	CFee CTrC EBee EMan IDee MAvo
	NWCA
nutans	CStu

Glyceria (*Poaceae*)
aquatica variegata	see *G. maxima* var. *variegata*
maxima	CRWN EMFW LNCo NPer SPlb
§ - var. *variegata* (v)	More than 30 suppliers
spectabilis 'Variegata'	see *G. maxima* var. *variegata*

Glycyrrhiza (*Papilionaceae*)
echinata	CAgr CArn MSal NLar
§ *glabra*	CAgr CArn ELau EShb GWCH
	LPhx MHer MSal NBPC NLar SECG
	SIde WHer WJek WWye XPep
- 'Poznan'	GPoy
glandulifera	see *G. glabra*
uralensis	CArn ELau GPoy MHer MSal
yunnanensis	LPhx

Glyptostrobus (*Cupressaceae*)
§ *pensilis*	CFil WPGP

Gnaphalium (*Asteraceae*)
'Fairy Gold'	see *Helichrysum thianschanicum*
	'Goldkind'

Godetia see *Clarkia*

Gomphocarpus (*Asclepiadaceae*)
§ *fruticosus*	SSte
§ *physocarpus*	CArn EWll NLar

Gomphostigma (*Buddlejaceae*)
virgatum	CDes CPle CPlt CTrC EBee EMan
	EPPr LPio LRHS MLLN MSte SPlb
	SSvw WCot WHrl WSHC WWeb
- 'White Candy'	EBee MAvo

Gonatanthus (*Araceae*)
pumilus **new**	EBee LEur

Goniolimon (*Plumbaginaceae*)
§ *incanum*	EBee XPep
- 'Blue Diamond'	CM&M
§ *tataricum*	EMan LAst MWrn NLar
§ - var. *angustifolium*	EBee NBlu SRms WPer
- 'Woodcreek'	MWgw NLar

Goodyera (*Orchidaceae*)
biflora	EFEx
pubescens	EFEx LRHS WCru
schlechtendaliana	EFEx

gooseberry see *Ribes uva-crispa* var. *reclinatum*

Gordonia (*Theaceae*)
axillaris	CDoC CHEx CHll

Gossypium (*Malvaceae*)
herbaceum	MSal

granadilla see *Passiflora quadrangularis*

granadilla, purple see *Passiflora edulis*

granadilla, sweet see *Passiflora ligularis*

granadilla, yellow see *Passiflora laurifolia*

grape see *Vitis*

grapefruit see *Citrus* x *paradisi*

Graptopetalum (*Crassulaceae*)
bellum ♀H1	CStu SChr
§ *paraguayense*	CHal EOas SVen

Gratiola (*Scrophulariaceae*)
officinalis	CArn EHon EMFW EMan MHer
	MSal WSel WWpP WWye

Greenovia (*Crassulaceae*)
aizoon	ETow

Grevillea ✿ (*Proteaceae*)
alpina	CFee CPLG CPle EBee GQui SMur
	SOWG
- 'Goldfields'	SOWG
- 'Olympic Flame'	CBcs CDoC CFwr CPLG CSBt
	CTrw SOWG
aquifolium	SOWG
arenaria	SOWG
- subsp. *canescens*	SOWG
aspleniifolia	SOWG
'Robyn Gordon'	
'Austraflora Copper Crest'	see *Grevillea* 'Copper Crest'
australis var. *brevifolia*	CPLG
banksii	CPLG
- 'Canberra Hybrid'	see *G.* 'Canberra Gem'
- var. *forsteri*	SOWG SPlb
banyabba **new**	SOWG
barklyana	SOWG
baueri	SOWG
beadleana	SOWG
bedggoodiana	SOWG
bipinnatifida	SOWG
'Bonnie Prince Charlie'	CPLG SOWG
'Bronze Rambler'	SOWG
§ 'Canberra Gem' ♀H3-4	CDoC CDul CHEx CPLG CPMA
	CPle CTrG CWSG EBee ECou LHop
	LRHS MAsh MBri MBro SCoo SDix
	SDry SIgm SOWG SPoG SSpi SWvt
	WBrE WCru WFar WGer WPat
'Clearview David'	ESlt LRHS SOWG
confertifolia	SOWG
§ 'Copper Crest'	SOWG
'Cranbrook Yellow'	CDoC CPLG SOWG
crithmifolia	CPLG SOWG
curviloba	CPLG
diffusa subsp. *evansiana*	SOWG
drummondii subsp.	SOWG
pimeleoides **new**	
endlicheriana **new**	SOWG
'Evelyn's Coronet'	SOWG
'Fanfare'	SOWG
fulgens **new**	SOWG
x *gaudichaudii*	SOWG
* 'Honey Eater	SOWG
Heaven' **new**	
'Honey Gem'	SOWG
involucrata **new**	SOWG
johnsonii	ESlt SOWG
juniperina	CPLG GGar
- subsp. *amphitricha*	CPLG
- 'Molonglo'	CPLG
- f. *sulphurea*	CBcs CDoC CFil CHll COtt CPLG
	CSBt CTrG CTrw EPfP GQui SIgm
	SOWG SPer WBod WPat

lanigera	CPLG
I - 'Lutea' **new**	SOWG
- 'Mount Tamboritha'	CMHG CPLG CTrC
- prostrate	SIgm SOWG
* *laspicalla* **new**	SOWG
levis	SOWG
longistyla	SOWG SPlb
'Majestic' **new**	SOWG
'Mason's Hybrid'	SOWG
monticola	CPLG
'Moonlight'	SOWG
nudiflora **new**	SOWG
obtusifolia 'Gingin Gem'	SOWG
olivacea 'Apricot Glow'	SOWG
'Orange Marmalade'	SOWG
paniculata	SOWG SPlb
'Pink Lady'	SOWG
'Pink Surprise'	SOWG
'Poorinda Elegance' **new**	SOWG
'Poorinda Peter'	CPLG SOWG
quercifolia **new**	SOWG
repens **new**	SOWG
rhyolitica **new**	SOWG
robusta ♀H1+3	CHal CTrC IDee MGol SMur SOWG SPlb
'Robyn Gordon'	ESlt
'Rondeau'	ESlt
rosmarinifolia ♀H3	More than 30 suppliers
- 'Desert Flame'	CPLG
- 'Jenkinsii'	CPLG
'Sandra Gordon'	SOWG
'Scarlet Sprite'	SOWG
§ x *semperflorens*	CAbb CDoC CEnd CPLG CRez CWib SOWG
sericea	SOWG
shiressii	SOWG
'Sid Reynolds'	CPLG
'Spider Man'	ESlt
'Splendour'	SOWG
thelemanniana	CPLG ECou ESlt
- Spriggs' form	SOWG
thyrsoides	CBcs CPLG SDry
tolminsis	see *G.* x *semperflorens*
tridentifera	CPLG
victoriae	CPLG SOWG SSpi
williamsonii	ECou SIgm SOWG

Grewia (*Tiliaceae*)

§ *biloba*	EGFP
flavicans	SSte
lasiocarpa	SSte
occidentalis	SSte
robusta	SSte

Greyia (*Greyiaceae*)

sutherlandii	CKob CTrC SGar SOWG SPlb

Grindelia (*Asteraceae*)

§ *camporum*	EChP EMan GBar MSal NLar SPlb WCot WPer
chiloensis	CAbb SDry SIgm SMad WPat
robusta	see *G. camporum*
'Setting Sun' **new**	WCru
squarrosa	GBar
stricta	CArn

Griselinia (*Griseliniaceae*)

* 'Crinkles'	SDry SLon
littoralis ♀H3	More than 30 suppliers
- 'Bantry Bay' (v)	CAbP CDoC CWSG EBee EHoe ELan GGar LRHS MSwo SAga SEND SLim SPer SSto SWvt WCru WFar
- 'Brodick Gold'	CPLG GGar GTSp

- 'Dixon's Cream' (v)	CBcs CSBt EPfP GQui IArd SAga SDry SLon WCru
- 'Green Jewel' (v)	CBcs CPMA CPne EBee SDry SPla WLeb
- 'Luscombe's Gold'	CPne
- 'Variegata' (v) ♀H3	More than 30 suppliers
ruscifolia	WPGP
scandens	WSHC

guava, common see *Psidium guajava*

guava, purple or strawberry see *Psidium littorale*

Gueldenstaedtia (*Papilionaceae*)

himalaica B&SWJ 2631	WCru

Gundelia (*Asteraceae*)

tournefortii	EBee

Gunnera (*Gunneraceae*)

arenaria	GGar
chilensis	see *G. tinctoria*
dentata	CPla
flavida	CPla CRow EBee EMan EPAt GGar GSki
hamiltonii	CFwr CPla CRow CStu EBee EBla ECha ECou EMan GEil GFlt GGar NBir
magellanica	More than 30 suppliers
- 'Munoz Gamero' **new**	WShi
- 'Osorno'	EBee SSpi WPGP
manicata ♀H3-4	More than 30 suppliers
monoica	CRow GAbr GGar GSki IBlr
prorepens	CFee CPla CStu EBee EBla ECha EMan EPAt EPza GSki IBlr LEdu NBir SSpi WWye
scabra	see *G. tinctoria*
§ *tinctoria*	More than 30 suppliers
- 'Nana'	IBlr

Guzmania (*Bromeliaceae*)

'Gran Prix'	MBri
* 'Surprise'	see x *Niduregelia* 'Surprise'
'Vulkan'	MBri

Gymnadenia (*Orchidaceae*)

conopsea	EFEx

Gymnocarpium (*Woodsiaceae*)

dryopteris ♀H4	CLAP EFer EFtx EMar EMon EPar GGar LEur MBri MMoz NLar NMar NWCA SDix SRms WFib WNor WRic
- 'Plumosum' ♀H4	CFil CFwr CLAP EFtx GBin GQui LEur MWgw NHol NMar NVic SChu SPoG WFib WHal
oyamense	CLAP EFer
robertianum	CLAP EFer EFtx

Gymnocladus (*Caesalpiniaceae*)

chinensis	WNor
dioica	CAgr CBcs CDul CFil CMCN CTho ELan EPfP LEdu MBlu MBri SPer SSpi WDin WGer WNor WPGP

Gymnospermium (*Berberidaceae*)

§ *albertii*	WCot
altaicum	GCrs

Gynandriris (*Iridaceae*)

sisyrinchium	EBee EMan

Gynerium (*Poaceae*)

argenteum	see *Cortaderia selloana*

Gynostemma (Cucurbitaceae)
pentaphyllum B&SWJ 570 WCru

Gynura (Asteraceae)
§ **aurantiaca** 'Purple ⏤ MBri
⏤ Passion' ♀H1
⏤ **sarmentosa** hort. ⏤ see *G. aurantiaca* 'Purple Passion'

Gypsophila (Caryophyllaceae)
⏤ **acutifolia** ⏤ ELan EMon LPio
⏤ **aretioides** ⏤ EPot LRHS NJOw NMen NSla
⏤ ⏤ NWCA WRos
§ ⏤ 'Caucasica' ⏤ CPBP EBur EHyt EPot LTwo NDlv
⏤ ⏤ SIng WAbe
⏤ ⏤ 'Compacta' ⏤ see *G. aretioides* 'Caucasica'
⏤ **briquetiana** ⏤ NLAp WPat
⏤ **cerastioides** ⏤ CTri EBre ECtt EMan EWTr GAbr
⏤ ⏤ GBBs GGar GTou ITim LHop LPVe
⏤ ⏤ LRHS MRav NDlv NLAp NMen
⏤ ⏤ NWCA SPlb WAbe WMoo WPer
⏤ ⏤ WPnn WShp WWin
⏤ **dubia** ⏤ see *G. repens* 'Dubia'
⏤ **fastigiata** ⏤ EBee EMan ITim WPer
⏤ Festival Series 'Festival'PBR ⏤ EBre
⏤ ⏤ 'Festival Pink' ⏤ GKir GMac LRHS SMrm WFar
⏤ ⏤ WViv
⏤ ⏤ 'Happy Festival' ⏤ LRHS WViv
⏤ ⏤ 'Royal Festival' ⏤ WViv
⏤ ⏤ 'White Festival'PBR ⏤ NLar WFar WViv
⏤ **gracilescens** ⏤ see *G. tenuifolia*
⏤ 'Jolien' **new** ⏤ EBee WHil
⏤ **muralis** 'Garden Bride' ⏤ LIck
⏤ ⏤ 'Gypsy Pink' (d) ⏤ LIck
⏤ **nana** 'Compacta' ⏤ CLyd
⏤ **oldhamiana** ⏤ EBee MLLN
⏤ **pacifica** ⏤ EBee ECtt MWgw NBro NLar WPer
§ **paniculata** ⏤ EBee GKir GWCH LAst MWgw
⏤ ⏤ NFor NMir SECG SRms SWat
⏤ ⏤ WBod WShp
⏤ ⏤ 'Bristol Fairy' (d) ♀H4 ⏤ CSBt CWCL EBee EFou ELan EMan
⏤ ⏤ ENot EPfP ERou GKir LRHS MAvo
⏤ ⏤ MBow MBri MDun NBlu NLar
⏤ ⏤ NOrc SSto SWvt WBrE WCAu WHil
⏤ ⏤ WShp WWol
⏤ ⏤ 'Compacta Plena' (d) ⏤ EBee EChP ECtt EFou EGle ELan
⏤ ⏤ EPfP GCal GMac LHop MRav NLar
⏤ ⏤ NVic SMrm SPet SPla SRms WCom
⏤ ⏤ WPer
⏤ ⏤ double pink (d) ⏤ GKir
⏤ ⏤ double white (d) ⏤ GKir
⏤ ⏤ 'Fairy Perfect' ⏤ EBee
⏤ ⏤ 'Flamingo' (d) ⏤ CBcs CWCL EBee ECha ECot EFou
⏤ ⏤ ERou MBri NLar SPer WShp WWol
⏤ ⏤ 'Magic Gilboa'PBR ⏤ COtt
⏤ ⏤ 'Magic Golan'PBR ⏤ COtt
⏤ ⏤ 'Pacific Pink' **new** ⏤ LAst
⏤ ⏤ 'Perfekta' ⏤ CBcs EBee SCoo SPer
§ ⏤ 'Schneeflocke' (d) ⏤ EBee GKir MWat NLar NPri SRms
⏤ ⏤ SSto WPer
⏤ ⏤ 'Snow White' ⏤ LPVe NOrc
⏤ ⏤ Snowflake ⏤ see *G. paniculata* 'Schneeflocke'
§ **petraea** ⏤ EPot
⏤ **repens** ♀H4 ⏤ ECtt EMil GKir GTou LBee LPVe
⏤ ⏤ MHer MOne MWat MWrn NJOw
⏤ ⏤ SPlb WFar WPer
⏤ ⏤ 'Dorothy Teacher' ⏤ CLyd CMea ECtt SIng WEas WGor
§ ⏤ 'Dubia' ⏤ CLyd ECha ECtt EDAr EHol ELan
⏤ ⏤ EPot ESis MHer SIgm SRms WLin
⏤ ⏤ WPer WWin
⏤ ⏤ 'Fratensis' ⏤ ECtt ELan ESis ITim NMen
⏤ ⏤ Pink Beauty ⏤ see *G. repens* 'Rosa Schönheit'
§ ⏤ 'Rosa Schönheit' ⏤ EBee ECha EPot LRHS NLar SIgm
⏤ ⏤ 'Rose Fountain' ⏤ WPat

⏤ ⏤ 'Rosea' ⏤ CMea CTri CWib ECtt EFou EMlt
⏤ ⏤ EPfP GKir LPVe MWat MWrn NFor
⏤ ⏤ NOak NWCA SAga SBla SPet SRms
⏤ ⏤ SWvt WBrE WCom WFar WHal
⏤ ⏤ WHoo WShp WTin
⏤ ⏤ white ⏤ CM&M CWib EBre EFou ELan EPfP
⏤ ⏤ ESis NFla NFor SPet SWvt WPer
⏤ ⏤ WShp
§ ⏤ 'Rosenschleier' (d) ♀H4 ⏤ CMea CWCL EBee EChP ECha
⏤ ⏤ ECtt EFou EGoo ELan ENot EPfP
⏤ ⏤ GKir MRav NDov NJOw SIgm
⏤ ⏤ SMrm SRms SUsu SWat SWvt
⏤ ⏤ WCAu WEas WHoo WOld WShp
⏤ ⏤ WTin
⏤ 'Rosy Veil' ⏤ see *G.* 'Rosenschleier'
⏤ 'Summer Snow' **new** ⏤ ENor
§ **tenuifolia** ⏤ CLyd EHyt EPot ITim LBee MBro
⏤ ⏤ MWat NDlv NHol NMen SBla
⏤ **transylvanica** ⏤ see *G. petraea*
⏤ Veil of Roses ⏤ see *G.* 'Rosenschleier'

H

Haastia (Asteraceae)
⏤ **sinclairii new** ⏤ EBre

Habenaria (Orchidaceae)
⏤ **radiata** ⏤ see *Pecteilis radiata*

Haberlea (Gesneriaceae)
⏤ **ferdinandi-coburgii** ⏤ CLAP CStu EPot SIgm
⏤ **rhodopensis** ♀H4 ⏤ CDes CElw CNic CStu EBee EHyt
⏤ ⏤ EPar GCrs GEdr GFlt GGar MBro
⏤ ⏤ MSte MWat NGar NLAp NMen
⏤ ⏤ NRya NSla NWCA SBla SIng SRms
⏤ ⏤ SSpi WAbe WPGP WPat WTin
⏤ ⏤ 'Virginalis' ⏤ CElw CLAP CStu EBee SBla SOkd

Habranthus ✿ (Amaryllidaceae)
⏤ **andersonii** ⏤ see *H. tubispathus*
⏤ **brachyandrus** ⏤ CBro SRms
⏤ **gracilifolius** ⏤ CBro ERos
⏤ **martinezii** ⏤ CBro EHyt
§ **robustus** ♀H1 ⏤ CBro CDes EBee EPot LAma LRHS
⏤ ⏤ NRog NWCA SIgm WCot
⏤ **texanus** ⏤ CBro ERos WAbe
§ **tubispathus** ♀H1 ⏤ CBro CStu EBee ERos NWCA SVen
⏤ ⏤ WCot WOBN WPrP

Hacquetia (Apiaceae)
§ **epipactis** ♀H4 ⏤ More than 30 suppliers
§ ⏤ 'Thor' (v) ⏤ CDes EMon SBla SRot
⏤ ⏤ 'Variegata' ⏤ see *H. epipactis* 'Thor'

Haemanthus (Amaryllidaceae)
⏤ **albiflos** ♀H1 ⏤ CHEx CHal CStu LAma SRms WCot
⏤ **amarylloides** subsp. ⏤ ECho
⏤ ⏤ **polyanthes new**
⏤ **barkerae new** ⏤ ECho
⏤ **coccineus** ♀H1 ⏤ ECho
⏤ **humilis new** ⏤ ECho
⏤ **katherinae** ⏤ see *Scadoxus multiflorus* subsp.
⏤ ⏤ *katherinae*
⏤ **natalensis** ⏤ see *Scadoxus puniceus*
⏤ **pauculifolius new** ⏤ ECho
⏤ **pubescens** ⏤ ECho
⏤ ⏤ subsp. **leipoldtii new**
⏤ **sanguineus** ⏤ ERea

Hakea (Proteaceae)
⏤ **bucculenta** ⏤ LRHS

§ *drupacea*	CTrC
elliptica **new**	CTrC
epiglottis	CTrC ECou
lissocarpha	CTrC
§ *lissosperma*	CDoC CFil CTrC ECou EPla SPlb WPGP
microcarpa	SLon
nodosa	CTrC
§ *salicifolia*	CBcs IMGH LRHS SPlb
- 'Gold Medal' (v) **new**	CBcs CTrC SPoG
saligna	see *H. salicifolia*
sericea hort.	see *H. lissosperma*
- pink **new**	CTrC
suaveolens	see *H. drupacea*
teretifolia	CTrC IDee

Hakonechloa (*Poaceae*)

macra	CFil CPla EBee EBlw EBre EHoe EMon EPar EPla LPhx MAvo MMoz MRav MSPs NOGN SMad WCot WPGP
§ - 'Alboaurea' ♀H4	More than 30 suppliers
* - 'Albolineata'	CDes CKno EBee EBlw EMon LEdu
- 'Aureola' ♀H4	More than 30 suppliers
- 'Beni-kaze'	EBee
* - 'Mediovariegata' (v)	CFil EPPr EPla SAsh SSpi WPGP
- 'Variegata'	see *H. macra* 'Alboaurea'

Halenia (*Gentianaceae*)

elliptica	GKev

Halesia (*Styracaceae*)

§ *carolina*	More than 30 suppliers
diptera	CMCN MBlu
- var. *magniflora*	MBlu
monticola	CBcs CLnd CMCN ELan EPfP LRHS SPer SReu SSpi WFar WNor
- var. *vestita* ♀H4	CAbP CDoC CPMA CTho EBee EPfP GKir IMGH LRHS MBlu NLar SHBN SPer SSpi WDin WFar WHCG WPat
- - f. *rosea*	CBcs CPLG EPfP MBlu
tetraptera	see *H. carolina*

x *Halimiocistus* (*Cistaceae*)

algarvensis	see *Halimium ocymoides*
§ 'Ingwersenii'	CBcs CDoC EBee ELan EWes MAsh MWhi SPer SRms WAbe WBod WCom
revolii misapplied.	see x *H. sahucii*
revolii (Coste & Soulié) Dansereau **new**	XPep
§ *sahucii* ♀H4	CDoC CSBt EBee EBre ECha ELan EMlt EPfP EWTr LAst MAsh MBNS MRav MSwo MWat NBlu SDys SGar SHBN SPer SWvt WAbe WCFE WDin WFar WKif WWeb WWin XPep
- 'Ice Dancer' (v)	CDoC EBee EPfP LAst MAsh NLar SPer SWvt
'Susan'	see *Halimium* 'Susan'
§ *wintonensis* ♀H3	CBcs CChe CDoC CSBt EBee EBre ECrN ELan EPfP LRHS MAsh MRav MWat SHBN SPer SPla SRms SSpi WAbe WCFE WHar WSHC WWeb XPep
§ - 'Merrist Wood Cream' ♀H3	CBcs CDoC CSBt EBee ECrN ELan ENot EPfP GEil LAst LHop LRHS MAsh MSwo MWgw NBir NSti SChu SPer SPla SSpi SSta SWvt WAbe WDin WFar WPat WSHC WStI XPep

Halimione (*Chenopodiaceae*)

§ *portulacoides*	XPep

Halimium ✿ (*Cistaceae*)

§ *atriplicifolium*	EWTr LRav SUsu XPep
§ *calycinum*	EBee ELan EPfP GEil LRHS MAsh MSwo MWgw SCoo SLim SPer SSpi SWvt WAbe WBrE WDin WWeb XPep
commutatum	see *H. calycinum*
formosum	see *H. lasianthum* subsp. *formosum*
halimifolium misapplied	see *H.* x *pauanum*, *H.* x *santae*
halimifolium Willk.	WBrE WSHC XPep
§ *lasianthum* ♀H3	CBcs CHar CPLG CSBt CWib EBee EChP ELan ENot EPfP LPhx LRHS MAsh MRav MTis SLim WBod WBrE WCFE WEas WWin
- 'Concolor'	CWib EBee MSwo SDry SWvt WDin WWin
§ - subsp. *formosum*	CHar GEil WSHC XPep
- - 'Sandling'	EGoo ELan EPfP LRHS WAbe
- 'Hannay Silver' **new**	WAbe
libanotis	see *H. calycinum*
§ *ocymoides* ♀H3	CBcs CChe CDoC CTrC CWib EBee EGoo ELan EPfP LPhx LRHS MAsh MMHG MSwo MWat MWgw SLon SPer WBod WBrE WHar XPep
x *pauanum*	EBee LPhx LRHS SUsu WSPU XPep
x *santae*	LPhx XPep
'Sarah' **new**	XPep
§ 'Susan' ♀H3	CDoC EBee ELan EPfP LRHS MBro MMHG SLim SPer WAbe
§ *umbellatum*	LPhx LRHS NLar SPer WDin WHCG WKif WPat
verticillatum **new**	XPep
wintonense	see x *Halimiocistus wintonensis*

Halimodendron (*Papilionaceae*)

halodendron	EPfP MBlu NBlu SPer WDin

Halleria (*Scrophulariaceae*)

lucida	CTCP

Halocarpus (*Podocarpaceae*)

§ *bidwillii*	CDoC ECou

Haloragis (*Haloragaceae*)

erecta	CPle CSev
- 'Rubra'	CBrm WCot WPer
- 'Wellington Bronze'	CPLG CSpe EBee ECtt EMan GBBs GGar GSki ITer LEdu LRHS MBNS MCCP SBod SDys SMad SOkh SWal WEas WHer WMoo WSHC WWpP

Hamamelis ✿ (*Hamamelidaceae*)

§ 'Brevipetala'	CBcs CEnd GKir MBri NHol
x *intermedia* 'Allgold'	MBri
- 'Angelly'	MBlu MBri SSta
- 'Aphrodite'	EPfP LRHS MBlu MBri MGos NBhm SSpi SSta
- 'Arnold Promise' ♀H4	More than 30 suppliers
- 'Aurora'	MBri SSpi
- 'Barmstedt Gold' ♀H4	CWib EPfP GKir LRHS MAsh MBlu MBri MGos NHol SReu SSpi SSta
- 'Carmine Red'	MGos WNor
- 'Copper Beauty'	see *H.* x *intermedia* 'Jelena'
- 'Diane' ♀H4	More than 30 suppliers
- 'Doerak'	NLar
§ - 'Feuerzauber'	CDul CMac GKir LBuc MGos MSwo NBlu SPer WDin WOrn
* - 'Fire Cracker'	CSBt
- 'Girard's Orange'	EPfP
- 'Harry'	LRHS MBri
- 'Hiltingbury'	LRHS MAsh SSpi
§ - 'Jelena' ♀H4	More than 30 suppliers

- Magic Fire	see *H.* x *intermedia* 'Feuerzauber'
- 'Moonlight'	CDul
- 'Nina'	WOrn
- 'Orange Beauty'	CBcs ENot EPfP MGos NLar
- 'Orange Peel'	EPfP LRHS MAsh MBri NLar SSpi
- 'Pallida' ♀H4	More than 30 suppliers
- 'Primavera'	CWSG EBee EPfP MLan NHol SPla
- 'Ripe Corn'	EPfP LRHS MBri SSpi
- 'Robert'	MBri
- 'Rubin'	LRHS
- 'Ruby Glow'	CBcs ECho GKir MGos NLar SPer
	SPoG WDin
- 'Strawberries	EPfP NLar
and Cream'	
- 'Sunburst'	EPfP MBri SSta
- 'Vesna'	EPfP LRHS MBlu MBri NLar SSpi
§ - 'Westerstede'	COtt CWSG EBee ENot LBuc LPan
	LRHS MGos MRav NBlu NHol NLar
	NWea SLim WDin WHar
japonica	WFar
- 'Arborea'	WNor
- 'Robin'	NLar
mollis ♀H4	CBcs CEnd CSBt CWSG EBee ELan
	ENot EPfP GKir MBar MBri MGos
	MSwo NBea NHol NWea SHBN
	SLim SPer SReu SSpi SSta WBVN
	WDin WFar WPGP WPat WStI
- 'Boskoop'	SSta
- 'Brevipetala'	see *H.* 'Brevipetala'
- 'Coombe Wood'	MBri
- 'Jermyns Gold'	EPfP
- 'Select'	see *H.* x *intermedia* 'Westerstede'
- 'Superba'	LRHS MAsh
- 'Wisley Supreme'	LRHS MBri SSpi
vernalis	GIBF WDin
- 'Lombart's Weeping'	NLar
- purple	MBlu NLar
- 'Purpurea'	CBcs
- 'Sandra' ♀H4	CMCN EPfP GIBF GKir LBuc LRHS
	MBri MGos SHBN SPer SPoG SReu
	SSpi SSta
virginiana	CBcs ECrN GIBF GPoy MDun
	WDin WFar

Hanabusaya (Campanulaceae)

§ *asiatica*	CHar CPom WFar

Haplocarpha (Asteraceae)

rueppellii	NBro NGar SRms SRot WPer

Haplopappus (Asteraceae)

RB 94063	EBee
brandegeei	see *Erigeron aureus*
coronopifolius	see *H. glutinosus*
§ *glutinosus*	CMHG ECha ECtt EPot GEdr MMil
	MTho NWCA SAga SPlb SRms
	WCom XPep
lanceolatus	see *Pyrrocoma lanceolata*
lyallii	see *Tonestus lyallii*
microcephalus	WPer
prunelloides	GEdr
- var. *mustersii*	CPBP EBee
- - F&W 9384	WCot
pygmaeus	see *Tonestus pygmaeus*
rehderi	EBee NJOw SPet WFar

Hardenbergia (Papilionaceae)

comptoniana ♀H1	CSpe
- 'Rosea'	CSpe ERea
violacea ♀H1	CAbb CHll CRHN CSPN CSpe
	CTrC ELan EMil ERea ESlt GKir
	GQui LRHS SLim SMur SPer WCot
	EShb
- f. *alba* **new**	
§ - - 'White Crystal'	EBee ERea ESlt SPer

- 'Happy Wanderer'	EBee EMil ERea LRHS SOWG
- f. *rosea*	CBcs EBee ESlt SPer WWeb

Harpephyllum (Anacardiaceae)

caffrum (F)	XBlo

Harrimanella see *Cassiope*

Hastingsia (Hyacinthaceae)

alba	GBuc
- NNS 98-310	WCot
- NNS 98-311	WCot

Haworthia ✿ (Aloaceae)

cymbiformis	EPem
var. *umbraticola*	
reinwardtii ♀H1	CHal
tortusa	EPem

hazelnut see *Corylus*

Hebe ✿ (Scrophulariaceae)

albicans ♀H4	More than 30 suppliers
- 'Cobb'	ECou
- 'Cranleigh Gem'	ECou
- 'Pewter Dome'	see *H.* 'Pewter Dome'
- prostrate	see *H. albicans* 'Snow Cover'
- 'Red Edge'	see *H.* 'Red Edge'
§ - 'Snow Cover'	EBee ECou EWes
- 'Snow Drift'	see *H. albicans* 'Snow Cover'
- 'Snow Mound'	ECou
- 'Sussex Carpet'	ECou ESis
§ 'Alicia Amherst'	EHol SPer SRms SSto
allanii	see *H. amplexicaulis* f. *hirta*
'Amanda Cook' (v)	EHoe ESis MCCP NPer SDry
amplexicaulis	CNic
- clone 4	STre
- f. *hirta*	NDlv NHol
§ 'Amy'	EBre ESis MAsh NBur NPer SHBN
	SPer WCom WSHC
x *andersonii*	COkL
- 'Argenteovariegata'	see *H.* x *andersonii* 'Variegata'
§ - 'Aurea' (v)	SDry
- 'Aureovariegata'	see *H.* x *andersonii* 'Aurea'
§ - 'Variegata' (v)	CSpe NBur NSti SDry SRms
anomala misapplied	see *H.* 'Imposter'
anomala (Armstr.)	see *H. odora*
Cockayne	
'Aoira'	see *H. recurva* 'Aoira'
§ *armstrongii*	CMHG EHoe EOrn GGar GKir
	MBar NFor WDin WPer
'Arthur'	ECou
'Autumn Beauty'	COkL WBrE
'Autumn Glory'	More than 30 suppliers
'Azurea'	see *H. venustula*
'Azurens'	see *H.* 'Maori Gem'
'Baby Blush'PBR	CAbP EBre ELan MAsh MBri
	WWeb
'Baby Marie'	CAbP CDoC CLyd COtt CSBt EBee
	ECot ECou EHoe ELan EPfP ESis
	GKir LRHS MAsh MGos MSwo
	NBee NBlu NHol NJOw NMen
	NPer SLim SPla SRms SSto SWvt
	WGwG WWin
'Balfouriana'	WHCG
barkeri	ECou
'Beatrice'	ECou NDlv
'Beverley Hills'PBR	LRHS MAsh SCoo
bishopiana	EBee ECou ELan EOMN ESis LRHS
	MAsh SBod SCoo SSto SWal
- 'Champagne'	see *H. bishopiana*
'Blue Clouds' ♀H3	ECou ESis LAst MBNS MSwo MWat
	NDlv SAga SPer SWal WCFE
'Blue Star'	LRHS MAsh SPoG

bollonsii	GGar MSte
'Boscawenii'	CTrG EOMN MGos
'Bowles' Variety'	see *H.* 'Bowles's Hybrid'
§ 'Bowles' Hybrid'	COkL CSBt EBee ECou ESis LRHS
	MRav MSwo NBee NFor SRms
	WAbe
brachysiphon	CTrC ECrN ENot EPfP GWCH
	MGos MWhi SMer SPer SWal WDin
	WHCG
- 'White Gem'	see *H.* 'White Gem'
brevifolia	ECou
breviracemosa	ECou
* 'Brill Blue'	ELan MBNS NMen WWin
buchananii	EBee ECou ESis GGar GKir GTou
	MBar MDHE MGos MHer MTho
	NBur NDlv NFor NHol NPer WPer
- 'Christchurch'	ECou
§ - 'Minor'	CLyd EPot GCrs MBar NBir NDlv
	NMen NWCA SIng
- 'Nana'	see *H. buchananii* 'Minor'
- 'Ohau'	ECou
§ - 'Sir George Fenwick'	MBro WHoo
buxifolia misapplied.	see *H. odora*
buxifolia (Benth.)	ENot GGar GLbr NBlu NHol NSti
Ckn. & Allan	NWea WDin WStI
- 'Champagne'	see *H. bishopiana*
N 'C.P. Raffill'	ECou
§ 'Caledonia' ♀H3	CSBt EBee EBre ECou EPfP ESis
	GGar GLbr LRHS MAsh MBri
	MGos MSte MWhi NBlu NDlv
	NHol NJOw NPer SCoo SPer SWal
	WCom WFar WPat WTin WWeb
'Candy'	ECou
§ *canterburiensis*	ECou ECrN GGar
N 'Carl Teschner'	see *H.* 'Youngii'
'Carnea'	CElw
'Carnea Variegata' (v)	SBod SPer WOut
carnosula	EHoe ESis GEil GGar GTSp LRHS
	MBrN MGos NBir NFor SPer
	WCom WPer
catarractae	see *Parahebe catarractae*
I 'Chalk's Buchananii'	SBla WCom
* 'Charming White'	EBee EPfP LRHS MBNS SWal
chathamica	CNic ECou GGar MHer NRya SDry
	SVen
'Christabel'	ECou ESis
ciliolata x *odora*	GGar
'Clear Skies'	ECou
colensoi	ESis
- 'Glauca'	see *H.* 'Leonard Cockayne'
'Colwall'	ECho ESis WHen
'County Park'	ECou ECtt ESis EWes NHol NMen
'Cranleighensis'	SSto
'Cupins'	see *H. propinqua* 'Cupins'
cupressoides	CFis CMHG ECrN GKir MBar NDlv
	SEND WDin
- 'Boughton Dome'	EBee ECou EHoe EPfP ESis GTou
	MAsh MBro MGos MTho NLAp
	NMen WAbe WCom WEas WHoo
	WPer WSHC
- 'Golden Dome'	ESis
- 'Nana'	ECou NJOw
darwiniana	see *H. glaucophylla*
'David Hughes'	ENot
'Dazzler'PBR (v)	CAbP CSBt ELan LRHS MAsh
	MBNS NBlu SPer SPoG WWeb
* 'Deans Fya'	ESis
decumbens	CLyd CNic ECou ESis EWes GGar
	NHol
'Diana'	ECou
dieffenbachii	GGar SVen
diosmifolia	CAbP CBot CDoC CPle EBee ECou
	ELan SMrm WAbe
- 'Marie'	ECou ESis

divaricata	ECou
- 'Marlborough'	ECou
- 'Nelson'	ECou
x *divergens*	NDlv
'Dorothy Peach'	see *H.* 'Watson's Pink'
'E.A. Bowles'	ECou ECrN
'E.B. Anderson'	see *H.* 'Caledonia'
'Early Blue'	CSpe NBir
'Edinensis'	CNic COkL EBee ECou GEil GKir
	NJOw WSHC WSPU
'Edington'	CElw CHal ECou LRHS SPer WCFE
elliptica	CDul COkL ECou
- 'Anatoki'	ECou
- 'Charleston'	ECou
- 'Kapiti'	ECou
- 'Variegata'	see *H.* x *franciscana* 'Variegata'
'Emerald Dome'	MSwo
'Emerald Gem'	see *H.* 'Emerald Green'
§ 'Emerald Green' ♀H3	More than 30 suppliers
epacridea	EWes GTou NHol
'Ettrick Shepherd' **new**	ECrN
'Eveline'	see *H.* 'Gauntlettii'
evenosa	LRHS NDlv
'Eversley Seedling'	see *H.* 'Bowles's Hybrid'
'Fairfieldii'	CPLG EHol MMil NMen SScr WTin
'First Light'PBR	NPro SPoG
'Fragrant Jewel' **new**	CPle SEND
x *franciscana*	ECou LRHS
§ - 'Blue Gem'	CDul COkL ECrN ENot ESis GGar
	GLbr LPVe LRHS MGos MWgw
	NBir NPer NWea SPer SPlb SRms
	SSto WBod WGer WHar XPep
- 'Purple Tips' misapplied	see *H. speciosa* 'Variegata'
§ - 'Variegata' (v) ♀H2	CSBt CSpe CWSG EBee EBre ECou
	ECrN EGra ELan ENot EPfP ESis
	GGar LRHS MAsh MBar MGos
	NJOw NPer NSti SPer SSto WBod
	WHar WStI
- 'White Gem'	SRms
'Franjo'	ECou
§ 'Gauntlettii'	COkL CSBt EBee EHol ELan LRHS
	NBir SPer
'Gibby'	ECou
N *glaucophylla*	ECou GLbr SBod
- 'Clarence'	ECou
'Glaucophylla	CNic CTri ECou ESis GLbr MHer
Variegata' (v)	NBir NDlv NSti SPer SWal WCom
	WKif
'Glengarriff'	NHol
'Godefroyana'	see *H. pinguifolia* 'Godefroyana'
'Great Orme' ♀H3	More than 30 suppliers
'Green Globe'	see *H.* 'Emerald Green'
'Greensleeves'	EBee ECou ESis GGar LRHS MBar
	MGos NDlv
'Gruninard's Seedling'	GGar
haastii	EPfP NFor NLar
'Hagley Park'	CSBt EHol EPfP ESis LRHS MAsh
	MMil SAga SOkh WCot WHCG
§ 'Hartii'	MRav SPer
'Heartbreaker' **new**	MAsh
hectorii	ESis GTou
'Heidi'	ESis
'Highdownensis'	COkL
'Hinderwell'	NPer
'Hinerua'	ECou GGar NJOw NNor
'Holywell' **new**	SBod
hookeriana	see *Parahebe hookeriana*
hulkeana ♀H3	CBot CStr EOrc MHer MMil MTis
	NBir SIgm SSpi WCom WEas
	WHCG WHoo WKif WTin
- 'Alba' **new**	CPle
§ 'Imposter'	CNic SRms SWal
'Inspiration'	MRav
insularis	ECou

'James Platt'	ESis	
'James Stirling'	see *H. ochracea* 'James Stirling'	
'Jane Holden'	WCom WSHC	
'Janet'	COkL SGar	
'Jannas Blue'	EPfP	
'Jasper'	ECou ESis	
'Joan Lewis'	ECou ESis	
'Joanna'	ECou	
§ 'Johny Day'	CDul MBNS	
'Joyce Parker'	NDlv	
'Judy'	ECou	
'June Small'	CNic	
'Karo Golden Esk'	ECou	
'Kirkii'	EBee EMil EPfP SCoo SPer	
'Knightshayes'	see *H.* 'Caledonia'	
'La Séduisante'	see *H. speciosa* 'La Séduisante'	
'Lady Ardilaun'	see *H.* 'Amy'	
laevis	see *H. venustula*	
laingii	CNic	
latifolia	see *H.* x *franciscana* 'Blue Gem'	
'Lavender Spray'	see *H.* 'Hartii'	
§ 'Leonard Cockayne'	WSHC	
'Lindsayi'	CLyd ECou NDlv NJOw	
§ 'Loganioides'	CFai ESis GGar MHer NFor	
'Lopen' (v)	ECou EGra EWes	
'Louise'	COkL SGar	
lyallii	see *Parahebe lyallii*	
lycopodioides	EWes	
- 'Aurea'	see *H. armstrongii*	
§ 'Macewanii'	ECou NDlv	
mackenii	see *H.* 'Emerald Green'	
macrantha ♀H3	EBee EPfP GCrs GGar ITim LRHS	
	NFor NMen SIng SPer SRms WWin	
macrocarpa	ECou LRHS	
- var. *latisepala*	ECou	
§ 'Maori Gem'	CTrC EBee EWes SCoo SMrm SSto	
	WCom	
'Margery Fish'	see *H.* 'Primley Gem'	
'Margret'PBR ♀H4	COtt CSBt EBee EBre EMil EPfP	
	ESis GKir LAst LRHS MAsh MBNS	
	MGos MSwo NBlu NMen SCoo	
	SHBN SMrm SPer SSto WStI WWeb	
'Marie Antoinette'	WWeb	
'Marjorie'	CDul CSBt CTrC EBee ECrN ECtt	
	ENot EPfP GLbr LRHS MGos MRav	
	MSwo NDlv NFor NPer NWea	
	SBod SPer SSto WDin WTel	
matthewsii	ECou	
'Mauve Queen'	EHol	
'Mauvena'	SPer	
'McCabe' **new**	NJOw	
'McEwanii'	see *H.* 'Macewanii'	
'McKean'	ECou ESis	
'Megan'	ECou	
'Mercury'	see *H. pimeleoides* 'Mercury'	
'Midsummer Beauty' ♀H3	CTrC ECou ECrN ENot EPfP GGar	
	GKir LRHS MGos MRav NBir NFor	
	SBod SHBN SPer SPlb SSto SWvt	
	WDin WFar WGwG WStI	
'Milmont Emerald'	see *H.* 'Emerald Green'	
'Miss E. Fittall'	ECou	
'Monica'	ECou NDlv NHol	
* 'Moppets Hardy'	SPer	
'Mount Nimrod'	GEil	
§ 'Mrs Winder' ♀H4	More than 30 suppliers	
'Mystery'	ECou ELan SWal	
'Mystery Red'	MAsh MBNS	
'Nantyderry'	CHal GHal MWgw	
'Neil's Choice' ♀H4	ECou MBNS MSte SCoo STre SWal	
'Netta Dick'	ECou	
'Nicola's Blush' ♀H4	More than 30 suppliers	
obtusata	ECou SCoo	
ochracea	MGos WCom	
§ - 'James Stirling' ♀H4	More than 30 suppliers	

'Oddity'	ECou	
§ *odora*	EBee ECou EPfP ESis ITim MRav	
	MWhi WBrE WCFE	
I - 'Nana' **new**	EPfP	
- 'New Zealand Gold'	CNic EBee ECou ESis GKir LRHS	
	MBNS NDlv SEND SLon SSto SWal	
	SWvt WStI	
* - *patens*	MGos WHCG	
- prostrate	ECou	
- 'Stewart'	ECou	
- 'Summer Frost'	CRez EBee MBNS NPri SCoo	
- 'Wintergreen'	MRav	
'Oratia Beauty' ♀H4	EBre EOMN MAsh MRav WWeb	
'Orphan Annie'PBR (v)	CSBt MAsh MBri SCoo SPer SPoG	
	WGwG WWeb	
'Oswego'	ECou	
'Otari Delight'	CMHG	
parviflora hort.	see *H.* 'Bowles's Hybrid'	
§ *parviflora* (Vahl)	GGar	
Cockayne & Allan		
- 'Holdsworth'	SDys	
- 'Palmerston'	ECou	
- var. *angustifolia*	see *H. stenophylla*	
- var. *arborea*	see *H. parviflora* (Vahl) Cockayne	
	& Allan	
'Pascal' ♀H4	COkL EBre ECou ELan EPfP MAsh	
	MBNS MBri MRav SPoG WWeb	
'Pascale' **new**	NPri	
pauciramosa	ESis SRms SWal	
'Paula'	ECtt	
'Pearl of Paradise'PBR	SPoG	
perfoliata	see *Parahebe perfoliata*	
'Perry's Rubyleaf'	NPer	
'Petra's Pink'	EOrc ESis LRHS MAsh SIgm WWeb	
§ 'Pewter Dome' ♀H4	CDoC CSBt EBee ECou ECtt EHoe	
	ENot EPfP MGos MRav NBee NDlv	
	NFor NHol SBod SDix SRms STre	
	WBrE WCom WHen	
'Pimeba'	NHol WCom	
pimeleoides	ECou MWhi NHol SScr	
- 'Glauca'	NPer SWal	
- 'Glaucocaerulea'	ECou NDlv SPer WMoo	
§ - 'Mercury'	ECou	
- 'Quicksilver' ♀H4	CSBt CSLe EBee ECou EHoe ELan	
	ENot EPfP ESis GGar GKir LHop	
	LRHS MBar MGos MRav MSwo	
	NBir NHol NPPs NPer SPer SWal	
	WBrE WCom WCot WEas WFar	
	WGwG WPat	
- var. *rupestris*	ECou	
pinguifolia	ECou NDlv SPlb WFar	
§ - 'Godefroyana'	SWal	
- 'Hutt'	ECou WGwG	
- 'Mount Dobson'	NHol	
- 'Pagei' ♀H4	More than 30 suppliers	
- 'Sutherlandii'	CDoC CNic GEil GLbr LEdu LRHS	
	MBar MWhi NBee NDlv SSto WFar	
§ - 'Wardiensis'	CMHG	
'Pink Elephant' (v) ♀H3	CAbP CDoC CSBt EBre ELan ENor	
	ENot EPfP ESis LAst LRHS MAsh	
	SCoo SPer SPla SWvt WWeb	
'Pink Fantasy'	LRHS MRav	
'Pink Goddess'	CAbP MAsh MBNS WWeb	
'Pink Paradise'PBR	ELan EPfP LAst LRHS MBNS NBlu	
	NPri SBod SSto	
'Pink Payne'	see *H.* 'Gauntlettii'	
'Pink Pixie'	MBri SCoo WWeb	
'Pink Wand'	LPVe	
poppelwellii	ITim	
'Porlock Purple'	see *Parahebe cataractae* 'Delight'	
§ 'Primley Gem'	ESis LRHS	
propinqua	MHer NLAp NMen SWal	
- 'Cupins'	CLyd SWal	
- 'Minor'	NDlv	

'Prostrata' — CNic CSBt NDlv
'Purple Emperor' — see *H*. 'Neil's Choice'
'Purple Paradise'[PBR] — EPfP MBNS MBri
'Purple Picture' — ECtt SDry
Purple Pixie — COtt MBri MGos SCoo WWeb
　= 'Mohawk'[PBR]
'Purple Princess' — MBNS
'Purple Queen' — CPLG CSBt EBee ECrN ELan EPfP GGar GLbr MAsh MBNS SHFr SPla WWeb
Purple Shamrock — CSBt EPfP MAsh MBNS MBri SCoo SPer SPoG WGwG WWeb
　= 'Neprock'[PBR] (v)
'Purple Tips' misapplied — see *H. speciosa* 'Variegata'
'Rachel' — WWeb
rakaiensis ♀[H4] — More than 30 suppliers
ramosissima — EPot GTou WAbe
raoulii — GBri NWCA WAbe WHoo
 - 'Mount Hutt' — GTou
§ *recurva* — CNic CSam CTri EBee ECou EPfP ESis GGar GKir LAst LRHS MTis NBee NFor NHol SHFr SRms WBrE WCom WCot WDin
§ - 'Aoira' — COkL ECou NDlv
 - 'Boughton Silver' ♀[H3] — ELan EPfP LRHS MAsh MBNS SDry
 - 'White Torrent' — ECou
§ 'Red Edge' ♀[H4] — More than 30 suppliers
'Red Ruth' — see *H*. 'Gauntlettii'
rigidula — ECou ESis NHol SWal
'Ronda' — ECou
'Rosie'[PBR] — EOMN EPfP MBNS MMHG NBee NMen SCoo SPer
'Royal Purple' — see *H*. 'Alicia Amherst'
salicifolia — CChe CNic COkL ECou ECrN ELan ENot EPfP GAbr GGar LAst LGro MRav SHBN SPer SPlb SRms SWal WFar WHCG WTel
 - BR 30 — GGar
'Sapphire' ♀[H4] — CDoC COkL ECou ESis GGar GKir MAsh MBNS MBar MGos NBlu SCoo SMrm SPer SSto WGer
'Sarana' — ECou
'Seksti' — SWal
selaginoides hort. — see *H*. 'Loganioides'
'Shiraz' **new** — MBNS SCoo
'Silver Dollar' (v) — CAbP CM&M CSBt EHoe ELan ENot EPfP ESis MAsh MBNS MBri NBlu NPri SIng SPer SPoG SSto SWvt WWeb
'Simon Delaux' — CPLG CSBt ECou LRHS NCiC SPer SSto WWeb
'Snow Mass' — GLbr
'Snow Wreath' (v) — WCom
§ *speciosa* 'La Séduisante' — CDul CElw CSBt ECou ENot GKir MRav SEND SGar WKif WSHC
 - 'Rangatira' — ECou EWes
 - 'Ruddigore' — see *H. speciosa* 'La Séduisante'
§ - 'Variegata' (v) — CHal IBlr NPer SDry SSto WEas WRHF
'Spender's Seedling' — ECou EPfP LRHS NBee SEND SRms STre
'Spender's Seedling' misapplied — see *H. stenophylla*
'Spring Glory' — LRHS
stenophylla — ECou EShb EWes GAbr MTed SAPC SArc SDix SHFr SMac
 - 'White Lady' **new** — GGar
stricta — ECou
 - var. *egmontiana* — ECou
 - var. *macroura* — ECou SDry
subalpina — CSBt EBee ECou ESis MOne MTis
subsimilis — SBla
'Summer Blue' — EBee NBlu WWeb
'Summer Snow' — NBir
'Super Red' **new** — MBri

'Susan' — ECou
'Sussex Carpet' — see *H. albicans* 'Sussex Carpet'
'Sweet Kim' (v) — COtt MBri WWeb
tetrasticha — CNic
'Tina' — ECou
'Tiny Tot' — CLyd EHyt MTho
'Tom Marshall' — see *H. canterburiensis*
topiaria ♀[H4] — CAbP CSBt EBee ECou EMil EPfP ESis GEil GGar GKir GLbr LAst LHop MBrN MBri MSwo MTis MWgw NBee NFor NHol SAga SMrm SPer SPla STre WAbe WEas WLow WStI
townsonii — ECou SAga
traversii — EBee ECou MSte NHol SRms
 - 'Mason' — ECou
 - 'Woodside' — ECou
'Tricolor' — see *H. speciosa* 'Variegata'
'Trixie' — CNic ECou
'Twisty' **new** — MAsh MBNS SPoG
urvilleana — ECou
'Veitchii' — see *H*. 'Alicia Amherst'
§ *venustula* — ECou ESis GGar IArd SMrm WPer
 - 'Blue Skies' — ECou
 - 'Patricia Davies' — ECou
vernicosa ♀[H3] — CNic EBee ECou ECrN EPfP ESis GLbr MBar MBri MGos MHer NBee NBlu NDlv NFor NHol NJOw NPro SIgm SPer SPlb SRot STre SWvt WAbe WCom WGwG WHCG WRHF
'Vogue' — COkL EPfP MAsh
'Waikiki' — see *H*. 'Mrs Winder'
'Wardiensis' — see *H. pinguifolia* 'Wardiensis'
'Warleyensis' — see *H*. 'Mrs Winder'
§ 'Watson's Pink' — COkL ECou GGar SPer WKif
'White Diamond' — SPer
§ 'White Gem' — ECou ECrN ESis GEil MGos NBee NDlv NFor NPer SPer WBVN WFar WStI
　(*brachysiphon* hybrid) ♀[H4]
* 'White Grape' — CM&M
'White Heather' — EBee ESis GEil LRHS NBir
'Willcoxii' — see *H. buchananii* 'Sir George Fenwick'
'Wingletye' ♀[H3] — EBee ECou EGoo ESis GEil GGar LRHS MBri MGos MWhi NDlv NNor WAbe WCom WGwG WPer WTel
'Winter Glow' — CLyd COtt SWal
'Wiri Blush' — SWvt
'Wiri Charm' — CAbP CBcs CDoC COtt CSBt EBee ECrN ENot EPfP ESis GLbr MLan MRav MTis SHBN SSto SVil WBVN WGer WGwG WOut
'Wiri Cloud' ♀[H3] — CAbP CSBt EBee ECrN EOMN EPfP ESis GGar MSwo MTis NBee NBlu SSto WGwG
'Wiri Dawn' ♀[H3] — CAbP CBcs COtt CSBt EBee ELan EPfP ESis EWes GGar MWgw SHBN SSto SVil SWvt WHrl
'Wiri Gem' — LRHS MRav
'Wiri Image' — CBcs CDoC COtt CSBt EBee EOMN LRHS MRav SWal
'Wiri Joy' — LRHS
'Wiri Mist' — CBcs COtt CTrC EBee EOMN ESis GGar LRHS
'Wiri Prince' — EBee ECrN EOMN
'Wiri Splash' — CDoC COtt CSBt CTrC EOMN LRHS SHBN SSto WGwG
'Wiri Vision' — COtt CSBt LRHS
§ 'Youngii' ♀[H3-4] — More than 30 suppliers

Hebenstretia (*Scrophulariaceae*)

dura — CPBP SScr

Hedera ✿ *(Araliaceae)*

	algeriensis	see *H. canariensis* hort.
	'Anita'	CHal
§	*azorica*	CWhi WFar WFib
	- 'Pico'	WFib
§	*canariensis* hort.	CDoC CDul CWhi SAPC SArc WFib
	- 'Algeriensis'	see *H. canariensis* hort.
	- var. *azorica*	see *H. azorica*
	- 'Cantabrian'	see *H. maroccana* 'Spanish Canary'
*	- 'Casablanca'	CWhi
*	- 'Etna'	CWhi
§	- 'Gloire de Marengo' (v) ♀H3	More than 30 suppliers
	- 'Marginomaculata' ♀H3	CDoC EBee EPfP EShb LRHS MAsh SPoG WFib WWeb
	- 'Montgomery'	MWht
	- 'Nevada'	see *H. hibernica* 'Nevada'
	- 'Ravensholst' ♀H3	CMac NSti WFib
	- 'Variegata'	see *H. canariensis* hort. 'Gloire de Marengo'
	chinensis	see *H. nepalensis* var. *sinensis*
	- typica	see *H. nepalensis* var. *sinensis*
§	*colchica* ♀H4	CWhi ENot EPfP LRHS SPer WCFE WDin WFar WFib
	- 'Arborescens'	see *H. colchica* 'Dendroides'
	- 'Batumi'	CWhi MBNS
	- 'Dendroides'	ECrN
	- 'Dentata' ♀H4	CWhi EPla MRav WFib
	- 'Dentata Aurea'	see *H. colchica* 'Dentata Variegata'
§	- 'Dentata Variegata' (v) ♀H4	More than 30 suppliers
	- 'My Heart'	see *H. colchica*
	- 'Paddy's Pride'	see *H. colchica* 'Sulphur Heart'
§	- 'Sulphur Heart' (v) ♀H4	More than 30 suppliers
	- 'Variegata'	see *H. colchica* 'Dentata Variegata'
	cristata	see *H. helix* 'Parsley Crested'
§	*cypria*	WFib
	'Dixie' **new**	NLar
	helix	CDul CRWN CTri MBar MGos NWea SHFr WDin WHer XPep
	- 'Abundance'	see *H. helix* 'California'
	- 'Adam' (v)	COkL CWhi CWib ECrN LAst MBri MTho WFib
I	- 'Ahorn'	CWhi
	- 'Alpha'	CWhi
	- 'Alte Heidelberg'	CWhi
	- 'Amberwaves'	CWhi WFib
I	- 'Ambrosia' (v)	CWhi
	- 'Anchor'	CWhi
§	- 'Angularis'	CWhi ECot
	- 'Angularis Aurea' ♀H4	CWhi EBee EHoe EPfP MWht NBir NHol SHBN WFib
	- 'Anita'	CBgR ECrN GBin NLRH WFib
§	- 'Anna Marie' (v)	CMac COkL CWhi EBee ECrN LRHS MBri WFib
	- 'Anne Borch'	see *H. helix* 'Anna Marie'
	- 'Annette'	see *H. helix* 'California'
	- 'Arapahoe'	CWhi
	- 'Arborescens'	CNat NPal WCot WDin
	- 'Ardingly' (v)	CWhi MWhi WFib
	- 'Asterisk'	CWhi NBrk WFib
	- 'Astin'	CWhi
	- 'Atropurpurea'	CNat CWhi EPPr EPla GBin MBar WDin WFib
	- 'Aurea Densa'	see *H. helix* 'Aureovariegata'
§	- 'Aureovariegata' (v)	CMac CNic CWhi
	- 'Avon' (v)	CWhi
	- 'Baby Face'	CWhi WFib
	- 'Baccifera'	CWhi
	- 'Baden-Baden'	CWhi
	- var. *baltica*	WFib
	- 'Barabits' Silver' (v)	EGoo EPla

	- 'Big Deal'	CWhi
	- 'Bill Archer'	CWhi WFib
	- 'Bird's Foot'	see *H. helix* 'Pedata'
	- 'Blue Moon' **new**	WFib
	- 'Bodil' (v)	CWhi SHFr
	- 'Boskoop'	CWhi WFib
	- 'Bowles Ox Heart'	CWhi WFib
	- 'Bowles Shield'	CNic
	- 'Bredon'	ECrN
	- 'Brigette'	see *H. helix* 'California'
§	- 'Brokamp'	CWhi MWht SLPl WFib
	- 'Bruder Ingobert' (v)	CWhi WHrl
	- 'Buttercup'	More than 30 suppliers
	- 'Buttercup' arborescent	MAsh
§	- 'Caecilia' (v) ♀H4	CBcs CMac CWhi EBee ECrN ELan EPfP LRHS MAsh MGos MSwo NLar NSti SLim SPer WCot WFar WFib
N	- 'Caenwoodiana'	see *H. helix* 'Pedata'
	- 'Caenwoodiana Aurea'	CWhi WFib
	- 'Calico'	see *H. helix* 'Schäfer Three'
§	- 'California'	CWhi MBri NSti
	- 'California Fan'	CWhi
	- 'California Gold' (v)	CWhi NPro WFib
	- 'Calypso' **new**	WFib
	- 'Carolina Crinkle'	CBgR CWhi ECrN MWhi NBrk WFib
	- 'Cathedral Wall'	WFib
§	- 'Cavendishii' (v)	CWhi NBrk SRms WFib
§	- 'Ceridwen' (v) ♀H4	CRHN CWhi MBri SPlb WFib WWeb
	- 'Chalice' **new**	WFib
	- 'Chedglow Fasciated'	CNat WFar
	- 'Cheeky' **new**	WFib
	- 'Cheltenham Blizzard' (v)	CNat
	- 'Chester' (v)	CWhi MAsh MBri WFar WFib
	- 'Chicago'	CWhi CWib WFib
	- 'Chicago Variegated'	see *H. helix* 'Harald'
	- 'Christian'	see *H. helix* 'Direktor Badke'
	- 'Chrysophylla'	CWhi EPla MSwo
	- 'Clotted Cream'	see *H. helix* 'Caecilia'
	- 'Cockle Shell'	CWhi EPot WFib
	- 'Colin'	GBin
	- 'Congesta' ♀H4	CWhi ECrN EPla MTho SRms STre WFib
	- 'Conglomerata'	CWhi ELan EPla MBar MBri MBro NBir NFor SPer SRms WDin WFib WTel WTin
	- 'Conglomerata Erecta'	CSWP SLon SRms WCFE WFib
	- 'Corage' **new**	WFib
	- 'Crenata'	CWhi WFib
	- 'Crispa'	MRav NFor
	- 'Cristata'	see *H. helix* 'Parsley Crested'
	- 'Cristata Melanie'	see *H. helix* 'Melanie'
	- 'Curleylocks'	see *H. helix* 'Manda's Crested'
	- 'Curley-Q'	see *H. helix* 'Dragon Claw'
	- 'Curvaceous' (v)	CWhi WCot WFib
	- 'Cuspidata Major'	see *H. hibernica* 'Cuspidata Major'
	- 'Cuspidata Minor'	see *H. hibernica* 'Cuspidata Minor'
	- 'Cyprus'	see *H. cypria*
	- 'Dainty Bess'	CWib
	- 'Dead Again'	WCot
	- 'Dealbata' (v)	CMac CWhi WFib
	- 'Deltoidea'	see *H. hibernica* 'Deltoidea'
	- 'Denticulata'	CWhi
	- 'Diana'	CWhi
	- 'Dicke von Stauss'	CWhi
§	- 'Direktor Badke'	CWhi
	- 'Discolor'	see *H. helix* 'Minor Marmorata', *H. helix* 'Dealbata'
	- 'Dolly'	CWhi
	- 'Domino' (v)	CWhi EWes
§	- 'Donerailensis'	CBgR CWhi MBlu WFib WPer
	- 'Don's Papillon'	CBgR CNat

	- 'Dovers'	WFib
§	- 'Dragon Claw'	CWhi ECrN EPla NBrk WCru WFib
	- 'Duckfoot' ♀H4	CBgR CDoC CHal CSWP CWhi
		ECrN MTho MWhi NSti WFar WFib
		WOut
	- 'Dunloe Gap'	see *H. hibernica* 'Dunloe Gap'
	- 'Edison'	CWhi
	- 'Egret' **new**	WFib
	- 'Eileen' (v) **new**	WFib
	- 'Elegance'	CWhi
	- 'Elfenbein' (v)	CWhi WFib
	- 'Emerald Gem'	see *H. belix* 'Angularis'
	- 'Emerald Globe'	CWhi
	- 'Emerald Jewel'	see *H. belix* 'Pittsburgh'
	- 'Erecta' ♀H4	CMac CWhi EMFP EPfP EPla GEil
		MBar MGos MTho MWhi NBlu
		NGHP NHol SMac SPer SPlb WCot
		WDin WFar WFib WPat WPrP
		WWye XPep
	- 'Ester'	see *H. belix* 'Harald'
	- 'Eugen Hahn' (v)	CWhi
§	- 'Eva' (v)	CMac CWhi ECrN MBri MGos NBir
		WDin WFib
	- 'Fallen Angel'	CWhi
	- 'Fan'	CWhi
	- 'Fanfare' **new**	WFib
	- 'Fantasia' (v)	CWhi ECrN WFib
	- 'Feenfinger'	WFib
	- 'Ferney'	WFib
	- 'Filigran'	CWhi ECrN NLar SMad WFib
		WHer
	- 'Flamenco'	CWhi
	- 'Flashback' (v) **new**	WFib
	- 'Flava' (v)	CWhi
	- 'Flavescens' **new**	WFib
	- 'Fleur de Lis'	CNat CWhi ECrN
	- 'Fluffy Ruffles'	CWhi ECrN EPla WFib
*	- 'Francis'	MBri
I	- 'Francis Ivy' **new**	WFib
	- 'Fringette'	see *H. belix* 'Manda Fringette'
	- 'Frizzle' **new**	WFib
	- 'Frosty' (v)	CWhi WFib
	- 'Garland'	CWhi
	- 'Gavotte'	CWhi EPPr MTho MWht WFib
	- 'Gertrud Stauss' (v)	CWhi MBri
	- 'Ghost' **new**	WFib
	- 'Gilded Hawke' **new**	WFib
	- 'Glache' (v)	SHFr WFib
	- 'Glacier' (v) ♀H4	More than 30 suppliers
	- 'Glymii'	CWhi EPla SBra SLPl WFib
	- 'Gold Harald'	see *H. belix* 'Goldchild'
	- 'Gold Nugget'	CWhi
	- 'Gold Ripple'	EHoe
§	- 'Goldchild' (v) ♀H3-4	More than 30 suppliers
	- 'Goldcraft' (v)	CWhi WFib
	- 'Golden Ann'	see *H. belix* 'Ceridwen'
*	- 'Golden Arrow'	ELan LRHS MAsh
	- 'Golden Curl' (v)	EPfP
	- 'Golden Ester'	see *H. belix* 'Ceridwen'
	- 'Golden Gate' (v)	CWhi ECrN LAst MBri WFib
	- 'Golden Gem'	NPro
	- 'Golden Girl' **new**	WFib
	- 'Golden Ingot' (v) ♀H4	COkL CWhi ECrN ELan EPla MBar
		MGos MWhi WFib
	- 'Golden Kolibri'	see *H. belix* 'Midas Touch'
	- 'Golden Mathilde' (v)	CHal COkL EBee
	- 'Golden Pittsburgh'	WFib
	(v) **new**	
	- 'Golden Snow' (v)	MBri WFib
	- 'Goldfinch' **new**	WFib
	- 'Goldfinger'	see *H. belix* 'Goldstern'
	- 'Goldheart'	see *H. belix* 'Oro di Bogliasco'
§	- 'Goldstern' (v)	CBgR CWhi EHoe MWhi MWht
		WFib

	- 'Goldwolke' (v)	CWhi SLPl
	- 'Gracilis'	see *H. hibernica* 'Gracilis'
§	- 'Green Feather'	CWhi EGoo ESis
	- 'Green Finger'	see *H. belix* 'Très Coupé'
	- 'Green Heart'	CBrm
§	- 'Green Ripple'	CBcs CMac CSBt CTri CWhi CWib
		EBee ECrN ENot GKir LRHS MAsh
		MBar MGos MRav MSwo MWht
		NBro NCiC NPro SEND SLim SPer
		SPlb WDin WFib WHen
	- 'Green Spear'	see *H. belix* 'Spear Point'
	- 'Greenman' **new**	WFib
	- 'Hahn's Green Ripple'	see *H. hibernica* 'Hamilton'
	- 'Hamilton'	see *H. hibernica* 'Hamilton'
§	- 'Harald' (v)	CDoC CWhi CWib LAst MBri NSti
		WDin WFib
	- 'Harlequin' (v)	COkL WFib
	- 'Harrison'	CWhi
*	- 'Hazel' (v)	WFib
	- 'Hebron'	CWhi
	- 'Hedge Hog' **new**	WFib
	- 'Heise' (v)	CWhi WFib
	- 'Heise Denmark' (v)	WFib
	- 'Helvetica'	CWhi
	- 'Helvig'	see *H. belix* 'White Knight'
	- 'Henrietta'	CStr WFib
	- 'Hester' **new**	WFib
	- subsp. *hibernica*	see *H. hibernica*
	- 'Hispanica'	see *H. maderensis* subsp. *iberica*
	- 'Hite's Miniature'	see *H. belix* 'Merion Beauty'
	- 'Holly'	see *H. belix* 'Parsley Crested'
	- 'Hullavington'	CNat
	- 'Humpty Dumpty'	CPLG MBar
	- 'Ideal'	see *H. belix* 'California'
	- 'Imp'	see *H. belix* 'Brokamp'
	- 'Ingelise'	see *H. belix* 'Sagittifolia Variegata'
	- 'Ingrid'	see *H. belix* 'Harald'
	- 'Irish Lace'	WFar
	- 'Ivalace' ♀H4	CBcs CNat CRHN CWhi EBee
		ECha ECrN EPfP EPla MAsh MNrw
		MRav MSwo MWhi MWht NBid
		NSti SRms WDin WFib WTin
	- 'Jack Frost' (v)	CWhi
	- 'Jake'	CHal NLRH WFib
	- 'Jake's Gold'	WBcn
	- 'Jane's Findling' (v)	CNat
	- 'Jasper'	WFib
	- 'Jersey Doris' (v)	CWhi WFib
	- 'Jerusalem'	see *H. belix* 'Schäfer Three'
	- 'Jester's Gold'	ELan ENot EPfP EPla LRHS MBri
		MGos MRav
	- 'Jubilee' (v)	COkL CWhi ECrN WCFE WFar
		WFib
	- 'Kaleidoscope' **new**	WFib
	- 'Kevin' **new**	WFib
	- 'Knülch'	CWhi EPla MWat WFib
	- 'Kolibri' (v)	CDoC CHal CMac COkL CRHN
		CWhi EBee EMil EPfP LAst MBar
		MBri MWht NPro WFib
§	- 'Königer's Auslese'	CRHN CWhi SLPl WFib
	- 'Kurios'	CNat CWhi
	- 'La Plata'	CWhi
§	- 'Lady Kay'	CWhi
	- 'Lalla Rookh'	CWhi MWgw NBrk WBcn WFib
		WHrl
	- 'Lemon Swirl' (v)	CWhi WFib
	- 'Leo Swicegood'	CBgR CSWP CWhi MWhi WFib
	- 'Light Fingers'	MAsh WBod WFib WHrl
*	- 'Lime Regis'	CWhi
	- 'Limey'	CWhi WFib
	- 'Little Diamond' (v)	CDoC CTri CWhi EBee EHoe ELan
		EPfP EPla LHop LRHS MAsh MBar
		MBri MGos MWgw MWht SAga
		SHBN SLon SWvt WDin WFib WHrl

	- 'Little Gem'	CWhi
	- 'Little Luzii' (v)	WFib
	- 'Little Picture'	CWhi
	- 'Little Witch'	CWhi EPla
	- 'Liz'	see *H. helix* 'Eva'
	- 'Lucille' **new**	WFib
	- 'Lucy Kay'	see *H. helix* 'Lady Kay'
§	- 'Luzii' (v)	ECrN EHoe MBar MGos NSti SHBN WFib
	- 'Maculata'	see *H. helix* 'Minor Marmorata'
§	- 'Manda Fringette'	CWhi MTho
§	- 'Manda's Crested' ♀H4	CSWP CWhi ECrN NCiC NLar WFib
	- 'Maple Leaf' ♀H4	CWhi WFib
	- 'Maple Queen'	MBri
	- 'Marginata' (v)	SRms
	- 'Marginata Elegantissima'	see *H. helix* 'Tricolor'
	- 'Marginata Major' (v)	CWhi
	- 'Marginata Minor'	see *H. helix* 'Cavendishii'
	- 'Marilyn' (v)	CWhi
	- 'Marmorata'	see *H. helix* 'Luzii'
	- 'Masquerade' (v)	WGor
	- 'Mathilde' (v)	CWhi LRHS MWht WFib
	- 'Meagheri'	see *H. helix* 'Green Feather'
§	- 'Melanie' ♀H4	ECha ECrN EPla LRHS NBrk WCot WCru WFib
	- 'Meon'	WFib
§	- 'Merion Beauty'	CWhi WFib
§	- 'Midas Touch' (v) ♀H3-4	CChe COtt CWhi CWib EPfP MBri NLar WFib
	- 'Midget'	CRow
	- 'Mini Ester' (v)	CWhi EPfP MBri
	- 'Mini Heron'	LAst MBri
	- 'Mini Pittsburgh'	COkL LAst
	- 'Minikin' (v) **new**	WFib
	- 'Minima'	see *H. helix* 'Donerailensis'
§	- 'Minor Marmorata' (v) ♀H4	CHal CWhi EBee MTho WFib WSHC
	- 'Mint Kolibri'	EHoe MBri WBcn
	- 'Minty' (v)	CWhi EPla LRHS MWht WFib
*	- 'Minutissima'	EPla WBcn
	- 'Miss Maroc'	see *H. helix* 'Manda Fringette'
	- 'Misty' (v)	CWhi EPot WFib
	- 'Mrs Pollock'	see *H. hibernica* 'Mrs Pollock'
	- 'Needlepoint'	EHoe
	- 'Neilson'	CWhi
	- 'Neptune'	CWhi
	- 'New Ripples'	CWhi ECrN MWht NBrk
	- 'Nigra'	CWhi
	- 'Nigra Aurea' (v)	CWhi WFib
	- 'Norfolk Lace'	EWes
	- 'Northington Gold'	CWhi WBcn
	- 'Obovata'	CWhi WFib
	- 'Olive Rose'	CStr CWhi MTho
N	- 'Oro di Bogliasco' (v)	More than 30 suppliers
	- 'Ovata' **new**	WFib
	- 'Paper Doll' (v)	CWhi
§	- 'Parsley Crested' ♀H4	CMac CSBt CWhi EBee ECrN EPfP MBar NLRH NSti SGar SPer SRms WBVN WCru WFar WFib
	- 'Patent Leather' **new**	WFib
N	- 'Pedata'	CSWP CWhi ECrN EPfP MSwo WFib
	- 'Pedata Heron'	CWhi
	- 'Pencil Point'	CWhi
	- 'Pennsylvanian'	CWhi
	- 'Perkeo'	CHal CWhi EGoo WFib
	- 'Perle' (v)	CWhi NBir
	- 'Persian Carpet'	CWhi WFib
	- 'Peter' (v)	CWhi NBrk WFib
	- 'Peter Pan' **new**	WFib
*	- 'Pin Oak'	EBee EHoe LBuc WCru WFar
I	- 'Pink 'n' Very Curly'	WCom WCot
	- 'Pirouette'	CWhi

§	- 'Pittsburgh'	WFib
	- 'Plume d'Or'	CHal MTho WFib
§	- f. *poetarum*	CNat EPla MBlu WBcn WFib
	- - 'Poetica Arborea'	ECha SDix
	- 'Poetica'	see *H. helix* f. *poetarum*
	- 'Preston Tiny'	NBir
	- 'Professor Friedrich Tobler'	CWhi EBee
	- 'Quatermas'	CWhi
	- 'Raleigh Delight' (v)	WCot
	- 'Ralf'	CWhi
	- 'Rambler'	NBir
	- 'Rauschgold' (v)	CWhi
	- 'Ray's Supreme'	see *H. helix* 'Pittsburgh'
	- 'Regency' (v)	CWhi
	- subsp. *rhizomatifera*	WFib
	- 'Ritterkreuz'	CWhi WFib
	- 'Romanze' (v)	CWhi WFib
	- 'Rüsche'	CWhi EGoo
	- 'Russelliana' **new**	WFib
	- 'Sagittifolia' Hibberd	see *H. hibernica* 'Sagittifolia'
	- 'Sagittifolia' misapplied	see *H. helix* 'Königers Auslese'
§	- 'Sagittifolia Variegata' (v)	COkL CWhi EBee ECrN LRHS MAsh MBri NBea WFib WRHF
	- 'Sally' (v)	CWhi WFib
	- 'Salt and Pepper'	see *H. helix* 'Minor Marmorata'
§	- 'Schäfer Three' (v)	CWib WFib
	- 'Shadow' **new**	WFib
	- 'Shamrock'	COkL CWhi EBee EPfP MBri MWht WFib
	- 'Shannon'	CWhi
	- 'Silver Butterflies' (v) **new**	WFib
	- 'Silver Ferny'	EPot NLRH
	- 'Silver King' (v)	EBee MRav MWht NBir WFib
	- 'Silver Queen'	see *H. helix* 'Tricolor'
	- 'Small Deal'	CWhi
§	- 'Spear Point'	CWhi ECrN
	- 'Spectre' (v)	CWhi MTho WHer
	- 'Spetchley' ♀H4	CHal CNic CSWP CWhi EPla EPot ESis GCal MBar MRav MTho MWhi NPer SMad WBcn WCFE WCot WFib WPat WPrP WTin
	- 'Spinosa'	CWhi EPla
	- 'Spiriusa'	WFib
	- 'Staghorn'	CWhi
	- 'Stuttgart'	CWhi CWil WFib
	- 'Sunrise'	CWhi ECrN WFib
	- 'Suzanne'	see *H. nepalensis* var. *nepalensis* 'Suzanne'
	- 'Symmetry'	CWhi
	- 'Tango'	ECrN
	- 'Tanja' **new**	WFib
	- 'Teardrop'	ECrN
	- 'Telecurl'	CBgR CWhi WFib
	- 'Tenerife'	EPla WFib
	- 'Tiger Eyes'	CBcs CWhi WFib
	- 'Tony'	COkL
	- 'Topazolite' (v) **new**	WFib
*	- 'Touch of Class'	CWhi
§	- 'Très Coupé'	CBcs CDoC CSWP CWhi EBee ECrN EGoo ISea LRHS MAsh MTho SAPC SArc WDin
§	- 'Tricolor' (v)	CBcs CTri CWhi EPfP LRHS MAsh MGos MWht NBlu SBra SHBN SMer WCFE WFib WTel
	- 'Trinity' (v)	WFib
	- 'Tripod' **new**	WFib
	- 'Tristram' (v)	CWhi
	- 'Triton'	CWhi MBar MTho WFib
	- 'Troll'	CWhi WFib
	- 'Trustee'	CWhi
	- 'Tussie Mussie' (v)	ECrN WFib
	- 'Ursula' (v)	CSWP EShb LPBA WFib

- 'Ustler'	CWhi
* - 'Verity'	CWhi
- 'Very Merry'	CBgR LPBA
- 'White Heart'	EBee MGos
§ - 'White Knight' (v) ♀H4	CWhi MBri WFib
- 'White Kolibri'	MBri
- 'White Mein Herz' (v)	GBin WFib
- 'Wichtel'	CWhi
- 'William Kennedy' (v)	CWhi WFib
- 'Williamsiana' (v)	WFib
- 'Woeneri'	CWhi MWht SLPl WFib
- 'Wonder' **new**	WFib
- 'Yab Yum' (v)	WBcn
- 'Yellow Ripple'	COkL CWhi LPBA WBcn
- 'Zebra' (v)	WFib
§ *hibernica* ♀H4	CBcs CNat CSBt EBee ENot GKir
	LBuc LRHS MBar MRav MSwo
	NBea NBlu NFor NWea SBra SPer
	SRms WDin WStI
- 'Anna Marie'	see *H. helix* 'Anna Marie'
- 'Aracena'	EPla SLPl
- 'Betty Allen' **new**	WFib
§ - 'Cuspidata Major'	CWhi
§ - 'Cuspidata Minor'	CWhi
§ - 'Deltoidea' ♀H4	CWhi EPla MBri MWht WFib
§ - 'Digitata'	CWhi
I - 'Digitata Crûg Gold'	WCru
- 'Dunloe Gap'	EPla
§ - 'Gracilis'	CWhi WFib
§ - 'Hamilton'	WFib
- 'Helena' (v)	CWhi
- 'Helford River'	CWhi
* - 'Lactimaculata'	CWhi
- 'Lobata Major'	SRms
- 'Maculata' (v)	EPla SLPl WBcn WSHC
- 'Mrs Pollock' (v)	CWhi WHPP
- 'Nevada'	CWhi
- 'Palmata'	CWhi WFib
- 'Rona'	CWhi WFib
§ - 'Sagittifolia'	COkL CTri CWhi EPfP GBin LRHS
	MAsh MBar SHFr SRms WFar
	WGwG
- 'Sulphurea' (v)	CWhi WFib
- 'Tess'	CWhi EPla
- 'Variegata' (v)	COkL CWhi MBar
maderensis	WFib
§ - subsp. *iberica*	WFib
maroccana 'Morocco'	WFib
§ - 'Spanish Canary'	CWhi WFib
nepalensis	WBcn WFib
§ - var. *nepalensis*	MBar WFib
'Suzanne'	
§ - var. *sinensis*	CWhi MWht WFib
- - L 555	EPla
pastuchovii	CWhi WBcn WFib
- from Troódos, Cyprus	see *H. cypria*
- 'Ann Ala' **new**	WFib
* - 'Volga'	CWhi
§ *rhombea*	CWhi WCot WFib
- 'Eastern Dawn' **new**	WFib
- 'Japonica'	see *H. rhombea*
I - f. *pedunculata*	CWib
'Maculata'	
- var. *rhombea*	WFib
'Variegata' (v)	

Hedychium ❀ (*Zingiberaceae*)

B&SWJ 3110	WPGP
B&SWJ 3110	WPGP
'Anne Bishop'	CFil MJnS
aurantiacum	CFil CPne EAmu EBee EUJe LEdu
	MJnS WMul WPnP
'Ayo'	LEur
'Beni-oran'	LEur

'Betty Ho'	LEur
'Carnival'	LEur
chrysoleucum	CTrC LAma LEur LPio MJnS
- B&SWJ 8116	WCru
coccineum ♀H1	CBcs CFil CKob EAmu EShb EUJe
	LAma LRHS MJnS MNrw MOak
	WHPE WMul
- var. *angustifolium*	CFil LEur WPGP
I - - 'Peach'	LEur
- var. *aurantiacum*	CBct CHEx LAma LEur
- 'Orange Brush'	LEur
- 'Tara' ♀H3	CBct CDes CDoC CFil CHEx CKob
	CTrC EBee EPfP ERea IBlr LEdu
	LEur LPJP LPio MJnS MNrw MSte
	SAPC SArc SChr SDix SSpi SUsu
	WCot WCru WHPE WMul WPGP
coronarium	CAvo CBct CDes CHEx CKob
	EAmu EBee EUJe LRHS MJnS
	MOak MSte SYvo WHPE WMul
- 'Andromeda'	LEur WMul
- var. *coronarium*	LEur
- var. *flavescens*	see *H. flavescens*
- gold-spotted	CKob EUJe LEur WHPE
- var. *maximum*	CFir
- 'Orange Spot'	EAmu
coronarium	WMul
x *gardnerianum* **new**	
'Daniel Weeks'	LEur
'Dave Case'	CKob
densiflorum	CBct CBrd CDes CFil CHEx CHll
	CKob CPne EAmu EBee ECha EUJe
	IBlr LEur MOak SDix SSpi WCru
	WHPE WMul WPGP
- 'Assam Orange'	CAvo CBct CBrm CDoC CFil CHEx
	CKob CPlt CPne CSam EBee GCal
	LEdu LEur LPio MJnS MNrw MOak
	MSte SChr SDix WBVN WCru
	WMul WPGP
- 'Stephen'	CBct CBrd CDes CFil CHEx CKob
	EBee LEur LPio MNrw MSte WMul
	WPGP
'Doctor Moy'	CKob LEur
'Double Eagle'	CFil CKob LEur
'Elizabeth'	CDes CFil LEur MJnS WMul
ellipticum	CKob EAmu EBee EUJe LAma
	LEdu LEur MNrw MOak WCru
	WHPE WMul
- B&SWJ 7171	WCru
'Filigree'	CDes CFir CKob LEur
§ *flavescens*	CBct CFil CKob EAmu EBee EUJe
	LAma LEdu LEur LRHS MJnS
	MNrw MOak SChr WCru WHPE
	WMul WPGP WPnP
- B&SWJ 7900	WCru
forrestii	CBrm CFil CKob EAmu EBee GCal
	IBlr ITer LEur LPJP LPio MJnS
	MNrw MOak MSte SAPC SArc SSpi
	WCru WKif WMul WPGP
gardnerianum ♀H1	More than 30 suppliers
- B&SWJ 7155	WCru
- var. *pallidum*	CKob
'Giant Yellow'	LEur
'Gold Flame'	CDes CFil CFir CKob EBee LEur
	MNrw MOak WPGP
'Golden Butterfly'	LEur
'Golden Glow'	LEur
gracile	CFil CKob EAmu EUJe LEur MOak
	WHPE
greenii	CBct CDoC CFil CFir CHEx CKob
	CSam EBee EUJe LEdu LEur LPio
	LRHS MJnS MNrw MOak MSte
	NPal SArc SChr SDix SYvo WBor
	WCot WCru WHPE WMul WPGP
	WPnP

griffithianum	EBee LEur MNrw
'Hardy Exotics 1'	CHEx
hasseltii **new**	CDes
horsfieldii	CKob
hybrid from Great Dixter	CKob
§ 'Kinkaku'	CFil CKob LEur WPGP
'Lemon Beauty'	LEur
'Lemon Sherbet'	CFir CKob LEur
longicornutum	MSte
'Luna Moth'	CFil CKob EBee LEur WMul
maximum	WMul
'Mutant'	LEur
'Orange Brush'	CKob
'Oto-himi'	LEur
pink **new**	CDes
'Pink Flame'	CKob
'Pink Sparks'	CFil CKob LEur
'Pink V'	CFil CKob EAmu LEur
'Pradhan'	CFir CHEx EBee LEur
x *raffillii*	CKob MNrw
'Shamshiri'	see *Hedychium* 'Kinkaku'
spicatum	CDes CFil CFir CHEx CKob CMdw
	CPLG CPne EBee EChP EMan EUJe
	GPoy LEdu LEur MNrw MOak
	MSte SSpi WCFE WHPE WMul
- B&SWJ 2303	WCru WPGP
- CC 1705	CKob
- CC 3249	WCot
- CC 3611	GKev
- CC 3650	ITer
- PF 218	LEur
'Telstar 4'	CHEx
thyrsiforme	CFil CKob EAmu EBee EUJe LEur
	MOak WMul
'Tropic Bird'	LEur
'Twengwainran'	MOak
villosum	EBee LAma WMul
- var. *tenuiflorum*	LEur
- var. *villosum*	LEur
'White Starburst'	LEur
yunnanense	CDes CFil CHEx CKob EAmu LEur
	MNrw WCot WCru WPGP
- L 633	CKob

Hedysarum (Papilionaceae)

coronarium	CArn CBri CFwr CPle CSpe CWCL
	EBee EHrv ELan EMan EPfP LHop
	MAnH MBrN SPet SSpi SWal SYvo
	WCom WCra WKif
hedysaroides	EMan LPVe WCot
multijugum	CBcs IDee MBlu SPer WSHC

Heimia (Lythraceae)

myrtifolia	GEil
salicifolia	CArn CBrm CPle EMan GEil LRav
	MBlu MGol MSal SGar WSHC
	WWye

Helenium ✿ (Asteraceae)

'Autumn Lollipop'	CKno GFlt SDnm SMac WMnd
	WWpP
autumnale	CSam CTri EBee EBlw LDai MBNS
	MSal NChi NJOw SMac SPet SSvw
	SWvt WBVN WBea WFar WMoo
- 'All Gold'	SWvt
- 'Praecox'	CSam MWrn
'Baronin Linden' **new**	CSam
'Baudirektor Linne' ♀H4	CSam GKir LRHS SCro WSpi
'Biedermeier'	CSam CWCL EBee ECtt EFou MTis
	NGdn SPer SPla SUsu
'Blütentisch' ♀H4	CPrp CSam EBee EChP EFou EMan
	MBnl MMil MNFA MWgw NCGa
	SPoG SUsu WHal WMnd WWpP
'Bressingham Gold'	CElw CSam
'Bruno'	CFwr CHar CWCL EFou EGle ELan
	ERou GKir GSki LRHS MMil SChu
	SHop SOkh WWpP
'Butterpat' ♀H4	CHad EBee EBre EChP ECtt EFou
	EHrv EPfP ERou GKir LRHS MBnl
	MCLN MMil MRav NBPC NCGa
	NPPs NPri NSti SBla SChu SCro
	SHop WSam
'Chipperfield Orange'	CElw CHad CPlt CSam ERou GBri
	LHop MMil MRav NGdn NVic
	WOld
'Coppelia'	EBre GKir NGdn SMrm WOld WTel
Copper Spray	see *H.* 'Kupfersprudel'
'Crimson Beauty'	CPlt CSam EBee EBre ECtt ELan
	LRHS MLLN MRav NBlu NGdn
	SPer WSpi
'Croftway Variety'	GKir SCro
Dark Beauty	see *H.* 'Dunkelpracht'
'Die Blonde'	EGle LPhx NDov SAga SCro SMHy
	WCot
§ 'Dunkelpracht'	More than 30 suppliers
'Feuersiegel' ♀H4	CSam EBee LPhx NDov NPPs SAga
	SMrm WOld
'Fiesta' **new**	CSam
'Flammendes Käthchen'	CSam EBre LPhx LRHS NDov SAga
	WWpP
'Flammenspiel'	CFwr CSam EBee EChP ECtt LRHS
	MRav
flexuosum	CSam EBee MSPs MWrn NChi
'Gartensonne' ♀H4	CSam EFou MAvo WOut
'Gay-go-round'	CSam
'Gold Fox'	see *H.* 'Goldfuchs'
'Gold Intoxication'	see *H.* 'Goldrausch'
Golden Youth	see *H.* 'Goldene Jugend'
§ 'Goldene Jugend'	CElw CMea CSam ELan MRav SSpe
	WCot WEas WWpP
§ 'Goldfuchs'	CElw CSam WCot
§ 'Goldlackzwerg'	EBee
§ 'Goldrausch'	CBel CHar CSam EBee EFou MDKP
	MWat SCro WSpi WWpP
hoopesii	see *Dugaldia hoopesii*
'Indianersommer'	CBri CFwr CSam CWCL EBee
	EChP ECtt EGle EHrv EMan LDai
	MAvo MBNS MBnl MLLN MOne
	MSph MTis NBPC NFla NLar NOrc
	SMHy SUsu WBea WFar WHil
'July Sun'	NBir SSpe
'Kanaria'	CBre CElw CPrp EBee EBre EMar
	EMil ERou EWll LRHS MNFA MRav
	NGby WHil WMnd WOld WWpP
'Karneol'	CSam LHop LRHS SOkh WWpP
'Kleiner Fuchs'	CSam EBee EChP MRav NLar SCro
'Kokarde' **new**	CSam
'Königstiger'	CFwr CSam EBee EBre EFou LRHS
	MBri WWpP
'Kugelsonne'	EFou
§ 'Kupfersprudel'	CFwr EBre
'Kupferzwerg'	CBel CSam CWCL LPhx NDov
	SAga SCro SOkh WEas
'Mahogany'	see *H.* 'Goldlackzwerg'
'Margot'	CDes CSam EFou WCAu
'Meranti' **new**	CSam
'Mexican Hat'	EFou
'Moerheim Beauty' ♀H4	More than 30 suppliers
Pipsqueak = 'Blopip'	CHea CWCL EBre ECtt EMan GBri
	LRHS
'Potter's Wheel'	CDes CSam
'Pumilum Magnificum'	CDes CPrp CSam EHol EPar EPfP
	GSki LEdu LHop LRHS MBri MNFA
	MWat SCro SPer WFar WShp WTel
'Rauchtopas' **new**	CSam
Red and Gold	see *H.* 'Rotgold'
'Ring of Fire' ♀H4	CSam
'Riverton Beauty'	CSam CStr EBee ERou

'Riverton Gem'   CSam ECtt
§ 'Rotgold'   CBri CFwr CM&M ECGN ECtt
                 ENot MHer MWrn NArg NOak
                 NPri SGar SRms STes WFar WMoo
                 WPer WWeb
'Rubinkuppel'   CSam LPhx NDov SChu SUsu
'Rubinzwerg' ♀H4 More than 30 suppliers
'Sahin's Early Flowerer' More than 30 suppliers
   ♀H4
'Septemberfuchs' EBee EFou SCro WWpP
'Septembergold' CSam
'Sonnenwunder'   CSam ECha GKir WOld WWpP
'Summer Circle' ♀H4 CBel
'Sunshine'   CBrm WBrk WSan
The Bishop'   More than 30 suppliers
'Vivace' **new** CSam
'Waldhorn' **new** LRHS
'Waldtraut' ♀H4 More than 30 suppliers
'Wesergold' ♀H4 EBee EChP EFou MRav
'Wonnadonga'   CFwr
'Wyndley'   More than 30 suppliers
'Zimbelstern'   CDes CElw CFwr CMdw CMil
                 CSam EBee ECha ERou GKir LPhx
                 LRHS MRav NDov SAga SOkh
                 WAul WFar WWpP

Heliamphora (Sarraceniaceae)
   nutans   SHmp

Helianthella (Asteraceae)
   parryi **new** EBee
§ *quinquenervis* CStr EMan GCal GFlt NLar WFar

Helianthemum ✿ (Cistaceae)
'Alice Howarth' CFul MDHE
alpestre serpyllifolium see *H. nummularium* subsp.
                 glabrum
'Amabile Plenum' (d) CFul EPfP GCal MBNS NLar SIgm
                 WShp
'Amber'   CFul
'Amy Baring' ♀H4 CFul GKir LRHS MOne WCom
                 WPer
'Annabel'   CFul COkL EBre ECha EPfP GAbr
                 GKir IGor MWya SBla SChu SMer
                 WBVN WCom WPer WTel
apenninum   CFul MDHE SRms XPep
'Apricot'   CFul SBla SBod WBcn
'Apricot Blush' CFul WAbe
'Baby Buttercup' CFul CLyd CMea GAbr MBro WPat
'Banwy Copper'   WBVN
'Beech Park Red' CFul ECtt ESis LBee LRHS MBro
                 MDHE MHer MWat MWgw SAga
                 SChu SHel SIgm WHoo WKif
'Ben Afflick'   CFul COkL EBre EMlt GKir LBee
                 LRHS MBNS MDHE SIgm SRms
'Ben Alder'   CFul COkL GAbr MDHE MHer
'Ben Attow' **new** CFul
'Ben Dearg'   CFul CMea COkL ECtt GAbr
                 MDHE SRms
'Ben Fhada'   CBcs CFul CMea COkL COIW
                 CPBP ECtt EMlt ENot EPfP GAbr
                 GKir LBee LRHS MDHE MHer
                 NHol NPri SBla SBod SRms WAbe
                 WBrE WPer WRHF WWin
'Ben Heckla'   CFul COkL CSam CTri EBre ECtt
                 EMlt EPfP GAbr GKir IHMH ITim
                 LRHS MDHE MSte SBla WPer WTel
'Ben Hope'   CFul COkL ECGP ECtt EPfP GAbr
                 MDHE NPPs SGar WShp WWin
'Ben Ledi'   CBcs CBrm CFul COkL ECtt EMlt
                 ENot EPfP GAbr IHMH LRHS MBar
                 MDHE MHer MWgw NChi NHol
                 NPri NSla NVic SBod SRms WAbe
                 WCFE WHoo WPer WWin

'Ben Lomond'   CFul COkL GAbr
'Ben Macdhui'   CFul COkL GAbr
'Ben More'   CBcs CFul COkL COIW ECtt GAbr
                 GKir GTou LRHS MDHE MSwo
                 MWat NBir NPri SBod SIng SRms
                 WBrE WWin
'Ben Nevis'   CFul COkL CTri ECha GAbr MDHE
                 SBla SRms WTel WWin
'Ben Vane'   CFul COkL COIW GAbr LRHS
                 MDHE
'Bentley'   CFul
'Birch White'   CFul MDHE
'Bishopsthorpe' CFul
'Boughton Double CFul EBre ELan EWes GKir LRHS
   Primrose' (d) MBro SBla SChu SIgm SMer WEas
                 WHoo WSHC WSel WTin
'Brilliant'   NBir
'Broughty Beacon' CFul COkL GAbr MDHE WGor
'Broughty Orange' **new** WSel
'Broughty Sunset' CFul COkL CSam MBro MDHE
                 NBir SIgm WHoo WSel
'Bunbury'   CFul CMea COIW GAbr IHMH
                 MBrN MDHE MWhi NBir SRms
'Butterball' (d) CFul MDHE
canum   SBla
'Captivation'   CFul COkL EGoo GAbr
caput-felis **new** XPep
'Cerise Queen' (d) CFul CTri EBre ECha EWTr GAbr
                 GKir LRHS MSwo SDix SIgm SRms
                 WBVN WCom WHoo
chamaecistus   see *H. nummularium*
'Cheviot'   CFul CMea ECha GAbr MBro
                 MDHE NBir WEas WHoo WPer
                 WSHC
'Chichester'   CFul
'Chocolate Blotch' CFul COIW ECtt GKir LHop LRHS
                 MHer NChi NHol SChu SEND
                 SRms WPer
'Coppernob'   CFul
'Cornish Cream' CFul EMlt GAbr LBee LRHS
croceum   LTwo
cupreum   CFul GAbr
'David'   CFul EGoo
'Diana' **new**   CMea
'Die Braut' **new** CFul
double apricot (d) GAbr
double cream (d) ECha MDHE WFar
double pale pink (d) SIgm
double pale yellow (d) NWoo
double pink (d) MWat NWoo WFar
double primrose (d) EMlt GAbr MDHE
double red (d)   NChi
'Elisabeth'   CFul EGoo
'Ellen' (d) **new** CMea
'Etna'   CFul STre
'Fairy'   CFul GAbr LTwo MDHE
§ 'Fire Dragon' ♀H4 CFul CMea ECha EPfP GAbr
                 GKir LRHS MDHE MWhi NBir
                 NWCA SBla SChu SIgm SRms
                 WAbe WCom XPep
'Fireball'   see *H.* 'Mrs C.W. Earle'
'Firegold'   WAbe
'Flame'   CFul COkL
'Georgeham'   CFul EBre ECtt EPfP GAbr GKir
                 LBee LRHS MDHE NBir SBla SMer
                 SRms WEas WGor WHoo WPer
'Gloiriette'   CFul
§ 'Golden Queen' CFul COkL ECtt EPfP GAbr ITim
                 LRHS MAvo MBNS MSwo MWhi
                 NLar SChu WFar WPer WSan WShp
'Henfield Brilliant' ♀H4 CBrm CFul COkL CPBP CPLG
                 CSpe EBre EPfP GAbr GKir LAst
                 LHop LRHS MBro MDHE NBir
                 NHol NPPs NVic SBla SMad SMer

	SRms WEas WHoo WLin WPer WSHC WSel WTel
'Hidcote Apricot'	CFul GAbr MDHE SGar
'Highdown'	CFul GAbr SRms
'Highdown Apricot'	ENot MDHE NPPs
'Highdown Peach'	GAbr
'Honeymoon'	CFul MDHE SBla WHil WRHF WSel
'John Lanyon'	CFul MDHE
'Jubilee' (d) ♀H4	CFul COkL COlW CRez ECtt ELan EMlt ENot GAbr LAst MDHE NBir NChi NFor NHol SBla SDix SRms WAbe WEas WSel WTel
I 'Jubilee Variegatum' (v)	CFul GAbr
'Karen's Silver'	CFul WAbe
'Kathleen Druce' (d)	CFul COkL EWes GAbr MWat WHoo WHrl
'Kathleen Mary' **new**	CMea
'Lawrenson's Pink'	CFul ECha GAbr WSan WShp
I 'Linton Rose'	NBir
'Lucy Elizabeth'	CFul COkL GAbr
lunulatum	CLyd CMea ECtt ESis LBee LRHS MBro MDHE NHol NMen SIgm WAbe WPat WWin
'Magnificum'	CFul EHol MDHE MWat
§ 'Mrs C.W. Earle' (d) ♀H4	CFul COkL COlW CTri ECtt ELan EMlt ESis GAbr MBow MDHE MWya NPri SBla SDix SGar SRms WAbe WHil WHoo WSel WWin
'Mrs Clay'	see *H.* 'Fire Dragon'
'Mrs Croft'	WPer
'Mrs Hays'	CFul MDHE
'Mrs Jenkinson'	CFul WTel
'Mrs Lake'	CFul GAbr
'Mrs Moules'	CFul SRms
mutabile	SPlb
§ *nummularium*	EBre GPoy LPVe MBow MDHE MHer NMir NSco WPat WWye XPep
§ – subsp. *glabrum*	CFul CNic EHyt GAbr MBro MDHE NHol NJOw NLAp WCom WPat
– subsp. *grandiflorum* 'Variegatum' (v)	MWat
* – 'Lemon Queen'	WBcn
§ – subsp. *tomentosum*	CFul GAbr MDHE MWat
oelandicum	NWCA
– subsp. *alpestre*	CLyd MBro NJOw NMen WPer
– subsp. *piloselloides*	CLyd WWin
'Old Gold'	CFul EBre GAbr GKir LRHS MDHE SIgm SRms WAbe WPer WSel WTel
'Ovum Supreme'	CFul GAbr
pilosum	SIgm
'Pink Beauty'	WHil
'Pink Glow'	CFul WPer
'Praecox'	CFul CMea CTri GAbr LBee LRHS SIgm SMer SRms WHoo WPer WTel
'Prima Donna'	CFul NBir
'Prostrate Orange'	SRms
'Raspberry Ripple'	CFul CHar EBre ELan EPfP EPot EWTr GAbr GKir LHop LRHS MAvo NHol SIng SRms WAbe WBVN WHoo WShp WWin
'Razzle Dazzle' (v)	LAst
'Red Dragon'	GKir WAbe
'Red Orient'	see *H.* 'Supreme'
'Regenbogen' (d)	GCal
§ 'Rhodanthe Carneum' ♀H4	More than 30 suppliers
§ 'Rosa Königin'	EBre ECtt GAbr GKir MDHE MHer WAbe
'Rose of Leeswood' (d)	CBrm CFul CMea CPBP CTri LBee LRHS MBro MDHE SIgm SRms STre WEas WHoo WKif WSHC WSel WWin
Rose Queen	see *H.* 'Rosa Königin'

'Rosenburg'	GAbr
'Roxburgh Gold'	CFul SRms
'Rushfield's White'	CFul WBcn
'Saint John's College Yellow'	CFul COlW CSam GAbr LRHS MDHE WFar
'Salmon Beauty' **new**	CFul
'Salmon Bee'	CFul
'Salmon Queen'	CElw CFul COkL EBre ECtt EWTr GAbr GKir LBee LRHS MDHE NHol NPri SRms WHrl WPer WRHF WSel WWin
* *scardicum*	CFul CMea
'Schnee' (d)	CFul EGoo
serpyllifolium	see *H. nummularium* subsp. *glabrum*
'Shot Silk'	CFul COkL EWes MDHE
'Silvery Salmon' (v)	WAbe
'Snow Queen'	see *H.* 'The Bride'
'Southmead'	CFul COkL GAbr
'Sterntaler'	CFul ESis GAbr MDHE SRms
'Sudbury Gem'	CFul COkL COlW EBre EChP ECha GAbr GKir LRHS NHol NSla SMer WTel
'Sulphureum Plenum' (d)	CFul ECtt EPfP
'Summertime' **new**	CFul
'Sunbeam'	CSam GAbr MDHE SRms
'Sunburst'	CFul GAbr
§ 'Supreme'	CFul ECGP ELan EPfP EWes LBee LRHS MWat SDix SIgm SRms WSel WWeb
'Tangerine'	CFul GAbr
'Terracotta'	CRez
§ 'The Bride' ♀H4	CFul CMea EBre ECha ELan EPfP GAbr GKir LHop LRHS MBow MBro MDHE MHer MSte MWat NHol SBla SChu SDix SIng SRms WAbe WCom WEas WHoo WLin WSel WShp
'Tigrinum Plenum' (d)	CFul CPBP ESis EWes LRHS MDHE WWin
'Tomato Red'	CFul ECha NSla
tomentosum	see *H. nummularium*
umbellatum	see *Halimium umbellatum*
'Venustum Plenum' (d)	WEas
'Voltaire'	CFul COkL ECtt EPfP GAbr MDHE MOne NPri SWal WWin
'Watergate Rose'	CFul MWat NBir
'Welsh Flame'	WAbe
'Windermere'	SIgm
'Windmill Gold'	CFul COkL LBee
'Wisley Pink'	see *H.* 'Rhodanthe Carneum'
'Wisley Primrose' ♀H4	More than 30 suppliers
'Wisley White'	CFul COkL CTri ECha ECtt EGoo EPfP MBro WCom WHoo
'Wisley Yellow'	CBrm GKir
'Yellow Queen'	see *H.* 'Golden Queen'

Helianthus ✿ (*Asteraceae*)

angustifolius	CFwr WPer
atrorubens	EBee LRHS MAvo MRav WFar
'Capenoch Star' ♀H4	CElw CPrp CRez CStr EBee ECha ECtt EFou EMan ERou EWTr GBuc LRHS MBri MFir MLLN MRav NBro NCGa NLar SDix SMac SMrm WFar WOld WWpP
'Capenoch Supreme'	EBee EMan
cusickii	EBee
decapetalus	CStr MDKP NFla WWye
– 'Maximus'	SRms
– Morning Sun	see *Helianthus* 'Morgensonne'
divaricatus	EBee
x *doronicoides*	SRms
giganteus 'Sheila's Sunshine'	CBre CElw CStr EBee GBri MHar MSte WCot WOld

	'Golden Pyramid' **new**	WCot
	gracilentus	EBee
	grosseserratus	LPhx WCot
	'Gullick's Variety' ♀H4	CBre CHea CStr EBee ECtt EFou EPfP IBlr LLWP LPhx MAvo MBnl NBro NChi NPSI NSti STes WBrk WOld WShp WWpP
	'Hazel's Gold'	EBee
	hirsutus	EBee
	x *kellermanii*	CStr EBee EFou EMon LPhx MTed MWgw NDov SAga
§	x *laetiflorus*	EBee ELan EMan MDKP NLar NOrc
	– 'Miss Mellish'	WCot
	– var. *rigidus*	see *H. pauciflorus*
*	– 'Superbus'	IBlr NPSI
§	'Lemon Queen' ♀H4	More than 30 suppliers
	'Limelight'	see *H.* 'Lemon Queen'
§	'Loddon Gold' ♀H4	CElw EFou ELan EMan EPfP ERou IBlr LPhx LRHS MAvo MBnl MBow MBri MRav MTis NVic SAga SMrm WBVN WBrE WBrk WCot WCra WFar WMoo WWye
	'Low Down'	ENor LRHS
§	*maximiliani*	EBee ECGN LRHS MDKP MSte WBea XPep
	microcephalus	EBee
	mollis	EBee WPer
	'Monarch' ♀H4	CElw CFwr CStr EBee EMan ERou LPhx MAvo MFir MRav MWgw SAga SDix SVal WCot WOld
	'Morgensonne'	EHrv ERou MAvo MDKP MLLN WCot
	x *multiflorus* 'Meteor'	EBee NChi
	nuttallii	EBee
	occidentalis	IBlr LRHS WPer
	orgyalis	see *H. salicifolius*
§	*pauciflorus*	EMon
	quinquenervis	see *Helianthella quinquenervis*
	rigidus misapplied	see *H.* x *laetiflorus*
	rigidus (Cass.) Desf.	see *H. pauciflorus*
§	*salicifolius*	CFwr CStr EBee ECGN EMan EMon EPPr EWTr LPhx LRHS MSte MWat NCGa NSti SDix SMad SMrm SSpe WAul WCot WFar WHrl WMnd WOld WTin WWye XPep
	scaberrimus	see *H.* x *laetiflorus*
	'Soleil d'Or'	EBee ECtt WCAu WOld
	strumosus	WCot
	'Triomphe de Gand'	CHea CRez CStr GBri LPhx MFir MRav MWat WFar WOld
	tuberosus	EBee GPoy WOld
	– 'Fuseau'	LEdu
	– 'Garnet'	LEdu
	– 'Sugarball'	LEdu

Helichrysum (Asteraceae)

	from Drakensberg Mountains, South Africa	CNic NWCA
	acutatum	GCal
	alveolatum	see *H. splendidum*
	ambiguum	CFis CStu SIgm WBcn WCom
	angustifolium	see *H. italicum*
	– from Crete	see *H. microphyllum* (Willd.) Cambess.
	arenarium	ECho
§	*arwae*	EHyt LBee NLAp WAbe
	aureum	WLin
	var. *scopulosum*	
	bellidioides	CTri EBre ECha GAbr GGar LRHS NLAp SMer WCru
	bellum	NWCA
	bracteatum	see *Xerochrysum bracteatum*
	chionophilum	NWCA

	'Coco'	see *Xerochrysum bracteatum* 'Coco'
§	*conglobatum*	XPep
	coralloides	see *Ozothamnus coralloides*
	'County Park Silver'	see *Ozothamnus* 'County Park Silver'
	'Dargan Hill Monarch'	see *Xerochrysum bracteatum* 'Dargan Hill Monarch'
	doerfleri	XPep
	'Elmstead'	see *H. stoechas* 'White Barn'
	fontanesii	SPer WHer XPep
	frigidum	CPBP EHyt ITim LRHS NLAp WAbe
	heldreichii	EPot SMrm
	– NS 127	NWCA
	hookeri	see *Ozothamnus hookeri*
	hypoleucum	GGar
§	*italicum* ♀H3	CArn CBod CSLe EChP ECha EGra ELau EShb ESis GPoy IHMH LGro MBar MBow MBri MHer MWgw NGHP SECG SPer SPet SRms WDin WEas WGwG WHCG WHHs WWye XPep
	– from Crete	NWCA
	– 'Dartington'	CBod EOHP MHer NGHP SIde WJek WSel
I	– 'Glaucum'	CWib
	– 'Korma'PBR	CAbP EBee ELan ENot EPfP EWTr MAsh MBNS NGHP WJek
	– subsp. *microphyllum*	see *H. microphyllum* (Willd.) Cambess.
	– 'Nanum'	see *H. microphyllum* (Willd.) Cambess.
§	– subsp. *serotinum*	CChe EBee EGoo EPfP GGar GPoy MRav SLim SMer SPer SPla SRms STre SWal SWvt WDin WPer WSel WTel XPep
	lanatum	see *H. thianschanicum*
	ledifolium	see *Ozothamnus ledifolius*
	marginatum misapplied	see *H. milfordiae*
	marginatum DC.	CPBP
	– JJ&JH 9401733	NWCA
	microphyllum misapplied	see *Plecostachys serpyllifolia*
	microphyllum Benth. & Hooker	see *Ozothamnus microphyllus*
§	*microphyllum* (Willd.) Cambess.	CFis ETow GBar MHer NBlu NWoo SIde SIgm WJek WSel XPep
§	*milfordiae* ♀H2-3	EDAr EPot GEdr NLAp NWCA SIng SRms WAbe WLin WPat
	montanum	NWCA
	orientale	EPot SMer XPep
	pagophilum	CPBP EPot ITim WAbe WLin
	– JJ&JH 9401304	NWCA
§	*petiolare* ♀H2	CHrt CSLe EBak ECtt LPVe MOak MRav NBlu SGar
	– 'Aureum'	see *H. petiolare* 'Limelight'
§	– 'Goring Silver' ♀H2-3	CHal MOak NPri SPet
§	– 'Limelight' ♀H2	CHal CHrt ECtt MOak MRav NBlu NPri SPet
	– 'Roundabout' (v)	CHrt MOak
	– 'Variegatum' (v) ♀H2	CHal ECtt MRav NPri SPet SPoG
	petiolatum	see *H. petiolare*
	plicatum	MWrn
	plumeum	EPot WAbe
	populifolium	WHer
	rosmarinifolium	see *Ozothamnus rosmarinifolius*
	Ruby Cluster = 'Blorub'	EBre SPer WFar
	rupestre **new**	XPep
§	'Schwefellicht'	CSLe EBee ECha EFou EGle EPfP ERou LRHS MBri MWgw NVic SChu SMer SPer SPet SWat WCAu WEas WKif WSHC
	selago	see *Ozothamnus selago*
	– var. *tumidum*	NSla

	serotinum	see *H. italicum* subsp. *serotinum*
	serpyllifolium	see *Plecostachys serpyllifolia*
	sessile	see *H. sessilioides*
§	*sessilioides*	EPot ITim NLAp NSla NWCA WAbe
§	*sibthorpii*	CSev LRHS NWCA
	'Skynet'	see *Xerochrysum bracteatum* 'Skynet'
§	*splendidum* ♀H3	CStu EHoe EPfP GEil NBro NFor SLon SPer WBrE WCom WDin WPer XPep
	aff. *splendidum* JJ&JH 9401783	NWCA
	stoechas	CArn XPep
§	- 'White Barn'	WCot
	Sulphur Light	see *H.* 'Schwefellicht'
§	*thianschanicum*	ENot SRms XPep
	- Golden Baby	see *H. thianschanicum* 'Goldkind'
§	- 'Goldkind'	EPfP GKir IHMH NBir NPri WMoo
	thyrsoideum	see *Ozothamnus thyrsoideus*
	trilineatum	see *H. splendidum*
	tumidum	see *Ozothamnus selago* var. *tumidus*
	virgineum	see *H. sibthorpii*
	woodii	see *H. arwae*

Helicodiceros (Araceae)

§	*muscivorus*	CDes CFir CHid EBee EUJe ITer WCot

Heliconia (Heliconiaceae)

bihai	WMul
bourgaeana	LPal
caribaea 'Purpurea' **new**	XBlo
'Fire and Ice' **new**	WMul
latispatha 'Orange Gyro' **new**	XBlo
lingulata 'Fan'	LPal
metallica **new**	XBlo
rostrata	LPal XBlo

Helictotrichon (Poaceae)

	pratense	EHoe EMon MAvo
§	*sempervirens* ♀H4	More than 30 suppliers
	- var. *pendulum*	EMon EPPr MAvo
	- 'Saphirsprudel'	CKno EBee EPPr WCot WPGP

Heliophila (Brassicaceae)

carnosa	SPla
longifolia	CSpe

Heliopsis ✿ (Asteraceae)

	helianthoides	CFwr CStr EMon LRHS
	- 'Limelight'	see *Helianthus* 'Lemon Queen'
	- var. *scabra*	EBee EPfP LPVe MDKP WMnd WWeb
	- - Ballerina	see *H. helianthoides* var. *scabra* 'Spitzentänzerin'
	- - 'Benzinggold' ♀H4	MRav SMrm
	- - Golden Plume	see *H. helianthoides* var. *scabra* 'Goldgefieder'
§	- - 'Goldgefieder' ♀H4	EBee EMan EPfP LRHS MBnl NBrk NFla
	- - Goldgreenheart	see *H. helianthoides* var. *scabra* 'Goldgrünherz'
§	- - 'Goldgrünherz'	CFwr EBee MBri WAul
	- - 'Hohlspiegel'	EBee EMan
	- - 'Incomparabilis'	MWgw WCAu
	- - 'Light of Loddon' ♀H4	MWat SVal
§	- - 'Sommersonne'	CFwr CSBt EBre ECtt EFou ERou MRav MWrn NArg NLRH NMir NPer SAga SPer SRms STes WCAu WFar WHil WMnd WWeb WWin WWpP

§	- - 'Spitzentänzerin' ♀H4	CFwr EBee MBri
	- - Summer Sun	see *H. helianthoides* var. *scabra* 'Sommersonne'
	- - 'Venus'	CFwr EBee LAst MBnl MTis NGdn NVic SSpe WCAu WHil
	Loraine Sunshine = 'Helhan' 'PBR (v)	EBre EMan LRHS
	orientalis	EWTr

Heliotropium ✿ (Boraginaceae)

§	*arborescens*	CArn EPfP MHom MOak
	- 'Chatsworth' ♀H1	CHad CPle CSev EHol EMan ERea EShb MAJR MHom MOak MSte SDnm WFar WPen
	- 'Dame Alice de Hales'	CHal ERea MHom MOak
	- 'Gatton Park'	ERea MHom MOak MRav SMrm
	- 'Lord Roberts'	ERea MHom MOak
	- 'Marine'	LIck SGar SUsu WGor
	- 'Mrs J.W. Lowther'	MAJR MOak
	- 'Netherhall White'	ERea
	- 'P.K. Lowther'	ERea WEas
	- 'President Garfield'	MOak WFar
	- 'Princess Marina' ♀H1	CHal CSev EMan ERea LAst LRHS MSte WEas
*	- 'The Queen'	ERea
	- 'The Speaker'	MHom MOak
	- 'White Lady'	CHal CPLG CSev EHol ERea MHom MOak
	- 'White Queen'	MAJR MHom
	peruvianum	see *H. arborescens*

Helipterum (Asteraceae)

anthemoides	see *Rhodanthe anthemoides*
'Paper Cascade' 'PBR	see *Rhodanthe anthemoides* 'Paper Cascade'

Helleborus ✿ (Ranunculaceae)

	abschasicus	EBee ITim
§	*argutifolius* ♀H4	More than 30 suppliers
	- from Italy	EHrv MGos
	- 'Janet Starnes' (v) **new**	MAsh
	- 'Little 'Erbert'	MAsh
	- mottled-leaved	see *H. argutifolius* 'Pacific Frost'
§	- 'Pacific Frost' (v)	CLAP CMil CPla MCCP NPro SSth WBVN
	- 'Silver Lace'	CBcs CFir CHid CMil CWCL EBee ELan EPfP EPyc EWTr GKir MAvo MCCP MGos NBir NSti SPer SSth WPGP
	atrorubens misapplied	see *H. orientalis* Lam. subsp. *abchasicus* Early Purple Group
	atrorubens Waldst. & Kit.	CBel CLCN EBee MHom NBlu WAbe WStI
	- WM 9028 from Slovenia	MPhe NRar
	- WM 9216 from Slovenia	MPhe WCru
	- WM 9319	NRar
	- WM 9617 from Slovenia	SSth
	- WM 9805 from Croatia	MPhe
	- from Slovenia	GBuc
	x *ballardiae*	LEur MAsh MPhe WAbe WFar
	bocconei	see *H. multifidus* subsp. *bocconei*
	subsp. *bocconei*	
	colchicus	see *H. orientalis* Lam. subsp. *abchasicus*
	corsicus	see *H. argutifolius*
	croaticus	CBel CLCN LBuc SSth
	- WM 9313	MPhe
	- WM 9416	MPhe
	- WM 9810 from Croatia	MPhe
	- from Croatia	GBuc
	cyclophyllus	EBee EMar EPfP GBuc GEdr GKir LRHS MHom MPhe NDov NHol SSpi WFar
	- JCA 560.625	CLCN SSpi

dumetorum — CBel CLCN EBee GBuc MAsh MHom NHol NLar NSla WCru WFar WPGP
- WM 9209 from Hungary — MPhe
- WM 9209 from Slovenia — MPhe
- WM 9627 from Croatia — MPhe
§ x *ericsmithii* — CLAP CPMA EChP EHrv LHop LRHS LTwo MAsh SBla SVil WAbe WCot WFar

foetidus ♀H4 — More than 30 suppliers
- from Andorra — MAsh
- from Italy — GBin MAsh WCot
- 'Chedglow' — CNat
- 'Chedglow Variegated' (v) — CNat
- compact **new** — ITer
- 'Curio' (v) — CNat
- 'Gold Bullion' — CPla EBee MCCP
- 'Green Giant' — CBel MAsh MTho WCru
- 'Miss Jekyll's Scented' — LBuc
- 'Ruth' — MAsh MPhe SSth
- scented — MHom
- 'Sienna' — LBuc
- 'Sopron' — EBee MAsh NLar WCru WLin
- Wester Flisk Group — More than 30 suppliers
N x *hybridus* — More than 30 suppliers
- 'Agnes Brook' — WFib
- 'Alys Collins' **new** — WFib
- Anderson's red hybrids — CLCN
- anemone-centred — CLAP EHrv NRar WFar WLFP
- 'Angela Tandy' — WFib
- 'Apple Blossom' — EHrv WFar
- apricot — CLAP CLCN EHrv GBuc SPla WFar WLFP WTin
- 'Aquarius' — CLCN
- Ashwood Garden hybrids — EHrv ENot EPPr GKir LRHS MAsh MGos MRav SCoo WCra WSpi
- Ashwood Garden hybrids, anemone-centred — EPfP MAsh
- Ashwood Garden hybrids, double (d) — MAsh
- 'Baby Black' — ECot
- Ballard's Group — CLAP EBee EBre EChP GEdr GKir MBnl MBri NRar WCot WCru WFar WPnP
- black — CBel CLAP CLCN EHrv EPPr GBuc NRar WCru WFar WHoo WTin
- 'Blowsy' seedlings — CLCN
- 'Blue Lady' — CBot CBrm EBee EBre EChP EPfP LAst MBNS MGos MNrw WLow WWeb
- 'Blue Wisp' — WLFP
- blue-grey — CLCN EHrv GKir
- Bradfield hybrids — EHrv
- Bradfield hybrids, anemone-centred — EHrv
- Bradfield Star Group — EHrv
- 'Button' — WLFP
- Caborn hybrids — LLWP
- 'Cally Double White' **new** — GCal
- 'Carlton Hall' — WFib
- 'Cheerful' — GKir NBir WCru WLFP
- 'Cherry Davis' **new** — WFib
- 'Citron' — CLAP WLFP
* - 'Compact Cream' — NRar
I - 'Cosmos' **new** — MTed
- cream — CLAP CPMA MCCP NHol NPSI WFar WTin
- 'David's Star' (d) **new** — CFir
- deep red — CLAP GKir WFar WTin WViv
- double (d) — CBel CLAP NRar WFar WHoo WLFP
- 'Dove Cottage Double Pink' **new** — NDov

- Draco strain — CLCN
- 'Dusk' — WCru WLFP
- 'Elizabeth Coburn' — WFib
- 'Fibrex Black' **new** — WFib
- 'Fred Whitsey' — WFib
- Galaxy Group — NPar
- 'Garnet' — WFar WLFP
- 'Gertrude Raithby' — WFib
- 'Gladys Burrow' — WFib
- green — CLCN MBNS WCru WFar
- 'Greencups' — WLFP
- 'Hades' — WLFP
- 'Hades' seedling — WCru
- Hadspen hybrids — CHad
- 'Harvington Pink' — GKir LRHS MHer WBry
- 'Harvington Red' — GKir LRHS MHer WBry
- 'Harvington Shades of the Night' — MHer SLon WBry
- 'Harvington Speckled' — GKir LRHS MHer SPoG
- 'Harvington White' — GKir LRHS MHer
- 'Harvington Yellow' — GKir LRHS MHer
- 'Harvington Yellow Speckled' — MHer SPoG
- 'Hazel Key' **new** — WFib
- 'Helen Ballard' — WLFP
- 'Helena Hall' **new** — WFib
- 'Ian Raithby' — WFib
- 'Ingot' — WLFP
- ivory — CLCN WFar
- 'John Raithby' — WFib
- Joy hybrids **new** — EChP GFlt
- Kaye's garden hybrids — EBre EOMN EPfP LAst MWgw NBPC WMnd WShp
- Kochii Group — ECha GKir NBrk WCru
- 'Lady Charlotte Bonham-Carter' — WFib
- 'Lady Macbeth' — EWes
- Lady Series **new** — COtt
- large-flowered pink **new** — WTin
- 'Leo' — MTed
- 'Le Max Creme' **new** — EBee EChP
- 'Limelight' — ECha
- 'Little Black' — ECho ELan EWes
- 'Lynne' — WLFP
- 'Maia' — WLFP
- maroon — EBre NRar SPla WFar
- 'Mary Petit' — WFib
- 'Massive White' — NPar
- 'Maureen Key' — WFib
- 'Metallic Blue' — CFai CMil EBee MBNS MNrw
- 'Mystery' — WCru
- 'Orion' — WLFP
- 'Pamina' — EHrv WLFP
- Party Dress Group (d) — EHrv NDov SBla WFar
- 'Pebworth White' — WFib
- 'Peggy Ballard' **new** — MAsh
- 'Petsamo' — NRar
- 'Philip Ballard' — MAsh SSth WCru WLFP
- 'Philip Wilson' — MAsh
- 'Picotee' — CLAP EHrv GBuc GKir MBro NDov NRar SPla SPoG WCru WFar WHoo WLFP
- pink — CBel CLAP CLCN CPMA EGra GBuc MBNS MBro MCCP NRar SPla SSth WAbe WCru WFar WHoo WTin WViv
- 'Pink Lady' **new** — WWeb
- plum — CLAP CLCN EGra EHrv SSth WFar WTin
- 'Plum Stippled' — ECha
- 'Pluto' — WLFP
- primrose — CBel CLAP EBre GBuc GKir MBNS NHol NRar SPla WAbe WCru WFar WTin

torquatus — CBel CBro CLCN EBee EHrv LBuc MHom MPhe MTho NHol SSth WFar WTin
- WM 9106 from Montenegro — GBuc MPhe WCru
- WM 9820 from Bosnia — MPhe
- Caborn hybrids — LLWP
- 'Dido' (d) — WFar
- double-flowered hybrids (d) — CBos WFar
- double-flowered, from Montenegro (d) — WFar
- hybrids — CBel ECGP EHrv SBla WFar
- Party Dress Group — see *Helleborus* x *hybridus* Party Dress Group
- semi-double (d) — WFar
- Wolverton hybrids — SBla WFar
vesicarius — EBee EHrv SSpi
viridis — EBee ECha EHrv EMar EPfP GKir LRHS SRms WBWf WCAu WCru WFar WTin
- subsp. *occidentalis* — CBel CBro LBuc MHom
- - WM 9401 — MPhe
- - WM 9502 from Germany — MPhe
- subsp. *viridis* — LBuc SSth
- - WM 9723 from Italy — MPhe
'Winter Joy Bouquet' — EBre

Helonias (Liliaceae)
bullata — EBee GEdr WCot

Heloniopsis (Melanthiaceae)
acutifolia B&SWJ 218 — WCru
japonica — see *H. orientalis*
kawanoi — CLAP NGar NMen SOkd WAbe WCru
§ *orientalis* — CBro CLAP CPLG EBee GBuc GCal GEdr LRHS NGar NMen SIng SOkd SSpi WCot WCru
- B&SWJ 956 from Korea — WCru
§ - var. *breviscapa* — CFil NGar WCru WPGP
orientalis variegated (v) — WCru
- var. *yakusimensis* — see *H. kawanoi*
umbellata — CLAP
- B&SWJ 1839 — WCru

Helwingia (Helwingiaceae)
* *asiatica* — CFil WPGP
chinensis — CPle CSam NLar SSpi
himalaica — CFil WPGP
japonica — EFEx WFar

Helxine see *Soleirolia*

Hemerocallis ✿ (Hemerocallidaceae)
'Aabachee' — CCol
'Absolute Zero' — SDay
'Adah' — SDay
'Addie Branch Smith' — EGol SDay
'Admiral' — WCAu
'Aglow' — MTed
'Alan' — EBre EChP MNFA MRav SCro WFar
'Alan Adair' — MAnH
'Alaqua' — CFir CMil EGle MBNS MNrw SPer WCAu WSan
'Albany' — CCol SAga
'Alborado' **new** — EBee
'Alec Allen' — SRos
'Alien Encounter' **new** — SPol
'All American Baby' — EBee MBNS SPol
'All Fired Up' — CCol
'Almandine' — EFou
altissima — CHEx EMon EPla LPhx MNFA SDix

'Always Afternoon' — CAbx EBee EChP EMar GBri MBNS NLar SDay WAul WCAu
'Amadeus' — SDay
'Amazon Amethyst' — WCAu
'Amber Star' — LPBA
'American Revolution' — CPar CPen CSpe EBee ECtt EFou EHrv EMan EWll MBNS MCCP MSte SDnm SRos WCAu WCot WGer WPnP WSpi WTin WWhi
'Amersham' — EBee EGle GSki MNFA
'Amy' **new** — EBee
'Andrea Nicole' **new** — CCol
'Andrew Christian' **new** — SPol
'Angel Artistry' — SDay
'Angel Curls' — EGol
'Angel Unawares' — WTin
'Ann Kelley' — MSte SDay
'Anna Warner' — EBee
'Annie Welch' — CFai EBee ECGP EPla MBNS MMil
'Antique Rose' — CKel SDay
'Anzac' — EBre ECha ECtt EHrv EPla ERou GKir GMac LRHS MLwd MNFA NGdn NHol NPri SAga SDnm SWvt WFar WTMC
'Apache Uprising' — SDay
'Apres Moi' — EMar LAst LPVe MBNS MLLN NLar WCAu
'Apricot Beauty' — EBee EMar EWTr LBuc NPri WSpi
'Apricotta' — WBro WCot WPnP
'Arctic Snow' — CCol EBee EBre EChP EGle EHoe EMar EPfP EWoo MAvo MLan MNrw NLar SDnm SRos SUsu WAul WSan WShp
'Ariadne' — SBla
'Arriba' — MNFA NBro
'Artistic Gold' — WTin
'Artist's Brush' — LBuc
'Asiatic Pheasant' — CCol
'Aten' — CCol LPVe MNFA NPri WAul
'Atlanta Bouquet' — SRos
'Atlanta Full House' — SDay
'August Orange' **new** — MNFA
aurantiaca — MWrn
'Autumn Lace' — SCro
'Autumn Minaret' — CCol
'Autumn Red' — EBee EMar MBNS NBir NOak
'Ava Michelle' — SDay
'Avante Garde' — SPol
'Awakening Dream' **new** — SRos
'Awesome Blossom' — CPen EBre ENot
'Baby Darling' — SDay
'Baby Julia' — MTed
'Baby Moon Café' — CAbx
'Baby Talk' — CFir LRHS SVil
'Baja' — MNFA WFar
'Bald Eagle' — CMCo EGle SChu
§ 'Bali Hai' — EBee EMar LRHS MBNS NGdn WHrl WShp
'Ballerina Girl' — SRos
'Ballet Dancer' — ERou
'Bandolero' (d) — EBee
'Bangkok Belle' — SDay
'Barbara Mitchell' — CCol EBee EChP MBNS SDay WAul
'Barbary Corsair' — SDay
'Baronet's Badge' **new** — SPol
'Baroni' — ECha
'Battle Hymn' — WCAu
'Bayou Ribbons' — MAvo MBNS
'Beat the Barons' — SPol SRos
'Beautiful Edgings' — SRos
'Beauty Bright' — WCAu
'Beauty to Behold' — SDay SRos
'Becky Lynn' — CCol EBee MBNS WAul WHoo
'Bed of Roses' — MNFA

'Bedarra Island' SDay
'Beige Ruffles' **new** EBee
'Bejewelled' EBee EGol EPla NMoo
'Bela Lugosi' CPar EBee EChP EMar MBNS MMil
  NCot SDnm WBVN WCot WHlf
'Beloved Returns' ♀H4 WCau
'Benchmark' MNFA SRos
'Berlin Lemon' ♀H4 MNFA
'Berlin Oxblood' EFou MNFA
'Berlin Red' ♀H4 CPrp EBee ECha EGle EMar EOMN
  EPla MMil MNFA NGdn SChu
'Berlin Red Velvet' ♀H4 MNFA
'Berlin Yellow' EFou
'Berliner Premiere' MNFA
'Bernard Thompson' EMar MNFA
'Bertie Ferris' LBuc
'Bess Ross' CMHG MNFA WCau
'Bess Vestale' ENot MNFA MWat NHol
'Best of Friends' GKir
'Bette Davis Eyes' SPol SRos
'Betty Woods' (d) SRos
'Bibury' SCro
'Big Bird' CPar EChP EFou MBNS SHBN SHar
'Big Smile' IPot MBNS
'Big Snowbird' SRos
'Big World' MNFA
'Bill Norris' SRos
'Bird Bath Pink' **new** SPol
'Bitsy' EBee EGle EGol MNFA MOne MSte
  MTed SPet SSpe WCot WMnd
'Black Emmanuella' EBee EMar
'Black Eyed Stella' CKel EBee ENot MBNS
'Black Knight' SRms
'Black Magic' CBro CHad CHar CTri EBee EGol
  ELan EPla ERou LRHS MNFA MRav
  MWgw NBir NGdn NHol SChu
  SPer WCau WHer WMoo
'Black Plush' CCol SRos
'Black Prince' EBee EWll MBNS SMrm SOkh
  WAul WCau
'Black Spot' **new** CCol
'Blackberry Candy' GBri MBNS WAul WCau
'Blaze of Fire' WCau
'Blessing' SRos
'Blonde Is Beautiful' SRos
'Bloodspot' **new** SDay
'Blue Happiness' SDay
'Blue Sheen' CCol CFir EBee ECtt EGle EGol
  EMar EWoo LAst LRHS MBNS
  MCCP NGdn NOrc NPri SDnm
  WCau WMoo WWeb
'Blueberry Candy' MBNS WAul WSan
'Blushing Belle' CFai CMil EBee ECGP EChP EMar
  LRHS MAnH MBNS MNFA WWin
  WCau
'Bold Courtier' WCau
'Bold One' CAbx SRos
'Bold Tiger' SDay
'Bonanza' More than 30 suppliers
'Booger' SRos
'Boulderbrook Serenity' SDay
'Bourbon Kings' CMHG EBee EGol EMar ERou
  MBNS SDay WCau
'Bowl of Roses' WCau
'Brass Buckles' see *H*. 'Puddin'
'Brenda Newbold' **new** SPol
'Bridget' ELan
'Bright Banner' WCau
'Bright Spangles' SDay SRos WEas
'Brocaded Gown' SDay SRos
'Brunette' MHar SAga
'Bruno Müller' MNFA
'Bubbly' SDay
'Buffy's Doll' EBee MBNS MNFA SDay SRos
'Bumble Bee' EMar GKir MBNS

'Buried Treasure' MNFA
'Burning Daylight' ♀H4 EBre EHrv EMar EPfP EPla ERou
  GSki LRHS MBow MCLN MNFA
  MNrw MRav NFla NHol SPer SRms
  WCot WFar WWol
'Bus Stop' **new** SPol
'Buttercup Parade' **new** EBee
'Butterfly Ballet' SDay
'Butterpat' EFou
'Button Box' NBPC
'Buzz Bomb' CWat EBee EBre ECGP EGle EHrv
  EMar GSki LRHS MHar MNFA
  NGdn NPPs SChu SPer SRos WCau
'Caballero' **new** CAbx
'California Sunshine' SRos
'Call to
  Remembrance' **new** EFou
'Camden Gold Dollar' EGol
'Cameroons' SDay
'Canadian Border Patrol' EBee EPfP MBNS SPol
'Canadian Goose' EFou
'Canary Glow' CSBt CTri EBre ERou SRos SSpe
  WFar
'Capernaum
  Cocktail' **new** SPol
'Captive Audience' SRos
'Caramea' EMar WFar
'Caroline' **new** WHrl
'Cartwheels' ♀H4 EBre EGra EHrv EMFW EMar EPfP
  EPla ERou EWTr LRHS MBNS MMil
  MNFA NBro SPer SRos WCau WFar
  WMoo WTin
'Casino Gold' SRos
'Catherine Neal' **new** SRos
'Catherine Woodbery' More than 30 suppliers
'Cathy's Sunset' CSam EBee EBre EMar MBNS
  MWgw NBro NGdn NHol
'Cedar Waxwing' CHea EGol SCro
'Chance Encounter' CCol MBNS SDay
'Chantilly Lace' CMHG NGdn
'Charbonier' MNFA
'Charles Johnston' CKel EBee EChP GMac SDay SRos
  WAul WTMC
'Charlie Brown' SDay
'Charlie Pierce Memorial' SRos
'Chartreuse Magic' EGol EPla ERou NHol SChu SPer
'Cherry Cheeks' ECtt EGol ELan EPfP ERou GKir
  LRHS MBNS MBri MRav NHol SRos
  SVil WAul WCau WCot WCra WFar
  WWeb
'Cherry Eyed Pumpkin' SRos
'Cherry Kiss' SRos
'Chesiere's Lunar
  Moth' **new** SPol
'Chic Bonnet' SPer
'Chicago Apache' CFir COtt EBee EBre EChP EGle
  EMar ENot EPfP LPan MBNS NBir
  NCGa SDay SRos SUsu SVil WAul
  WSpi
'Chicago Arnie's Choice' WSan
'Chicago Blackout' CFir COtt CSpe EBee EChP EGol
  EPfP NHol WAul WCau
'Chicago Cattleya' CFir EChP EFou EGle EGol EWoo
  LAst MRav WAul
'Chicago Cherry' GEil WWpP
'Chicago Fire' EBee EFou EGol EPfP MBNS WWye
'Chicago Firecracker' CAbx
'Chicago Heirloom' CFir COtt EChP EGle EGol SVil
  WAul WCAu
'Chicago Jewel' CFir EBee EGle EGol NSti SCro
  WAul WWpP
'Chicago Knobby' EMar LPan MBNS
'Chicago Knockout' CFir COtt EGle EGol EPfP EWoo
  MBNS SPer WAul WCAu WHil

'Chicago Peach'	EChP EFou IPot NBir WCAu
'Chicago Peach Parfait' **new**	WSan
'Chicago Petticoats'	EGol NHol WAul
'Chicago Picotee Lace'	EBee EChP EGle EGol EPfP GKir NGdn WAul WCAu
'Chicago Picotee Memories'	EBee EGle MBNS
'Chicago Picotee Queen'	MNFA
'Chicago Princess'	EGle EGol
'Chicago Rainbow'	EWoo IPot MBNS WAul WSan
'Chicago Rosy'	EFou EGol
'Chicago Royal Robe'	CWat EBee EBre EFou EGol EPla ERou GKir LLWP MBNS MNFA MRav MSte NBid NCGa SCro SPer SWal WCot WTin WWhi WWin
'Chicago Silver'	CFir COtt EGle EGol IPot MBNS WCAu
'Chicago Star' **new**	SRos
'Chicago Sunrise'	CHad EBee EGol EMar EPla IBlr LPVe LRHS MBNS MBri MNFA MRav MSta NCGa NGdn NHol NMoo NOrc SAga SRos SUsu SVil SWvt WPer WShp
'Chicago Violet'	WCAu
'Chief Sarcoxie' ♀H4	SRos WCAu
'Children's Festival'	More than 30 suppliers
'China Bride' **new**	SDay
'Chinese Autumn'	SRos
'Chinese Cloisonne'	CKel
'Chinese Coral'	WBcn
'Chloe's Child'	SCro
'Chorus Line'	SDay SRos
'Christmas Is'	CCol EBee EFou EGol EMar MBNS MNFA SDay SDnm WAul WCAu
'Christmas Island' **new**	NCGa
'Churchill Downs'	MNFA
citrina	ELan EWTr LRHS MNFA MSte MWgw NFla NGdn SSte WTin XPep
'Civil Rights'	SRos
'Classic Simplicity'	WCAu
'Classy Lassie'	MTed
'Claudine'	CAbx
'Cleopatra'	CPar
'Cloth of Gold' **new**	WCot
'Clothed in Glory' **new**	MBNS
'Coburg Fright Wig'	CAbx
'Colonial Dame'	WTin
'Coming up Roses'	SRos
'Constitutional Island'	WCAu
'Contessa'	CBro EBre EHon SCro WWpP
'Cool It'	EBee EGle EMar LPio LRHS MBNS NCGa
'Cool Jazz'	EMar SRos
'Coral Dawn'	CKel
'Coral Lace' **new**	EBee
'Coral Mist'	CCol CSBt EFou MBNS WWeb
coreana **new**	CCol
'Corky' ♀H4	More than 30 suppliers
'Corsican Bandit'	CM&M SDay
'Cosmic Hummingbird'	SDay
'Country Club'	EBee EChP EGle EGol EWoo LAst LHop MBNS NHol WCAu WSan WWpP
'Country Fair Winds' **new**	CCol
'Country Melody'	SDay
'Court Concubine'	CAbx
'Court Magician'	SRos
'Cranberry Baby'	EGle SDay SRos WHoo WTin
'Crazy Pierre'	SPol
'Cream Drop'	CPrp EBre EChP ECtt EFou EGle EGol EMar LRHS MBri MCLN MRav MTis MWat NBro NCiC

	NOrc SChu SDnm SPer SSpe WAul WCAu WCot WCra WMoo WTMC WTel WTin
'Creative Art' **new**	SRos
'Creative Edge'	ERou MBNS SDnm
'Crimson Icon'	MSte SDay WTin
'Crimson Pirate'	CBre CCol EBee EBre EMil EPPr ERou GKir LRHS MBNS MLan MNFA MSph NBir NCGa NHol NOrc NPro SPlb WCAu WHrl WShp WTin
'Croesus'	NHol SCro SRms WCAu
'Croftway'	SCro
'Cupid's Bow'	EGol
'Cupid's Gold'	SDay SRos
'Custard Candy'	EChP MBNS NBir SRos SUsu WAul WCAu
'Cynthia Mary'	EBee EGle EMar MBNS MNFA
'Dad's Best White'	EMar SCro
'Daily Dollar'	GKir LRHS NGdn
'Dainty Pink'	EGol
'Dallas Spider Time'	MNFA
'Dallas Star'	SPol
'Dan Tau'	CKel
'Dance Ballerina Dance'	SDay SRos
'Dancing Dwarf'	SDay
'Dancing Shiva'	SDay
'Dancing Summerbird'	SPol
'Daring Deception'	CKel CRez MBNS WAul WCAu
'Dark Elf'	SDay
'Darrell'	SDay
'David Kirchhoff'	WAul WCAu
'Decatur Imp'	EGol
'Delightsome'	SDay SRos
'Demetrius'	EBee MBri MNFA
'Destined to see'	CFir CPar EBee EMar MBNS NCot WBVN WCot WGMN WHlf
'Devil's Footprint' **new**	SDay SPol
'Devon Cream'	SChu
'Devonshire'	SRos
'Diamond Dust'	CCol EBee EChP EGle EMar EOMN EPla LPhx LRHS MBNS MNFA MTed NLar SChu SLon SPer WTin
'Dido'	CTri ERou GBuc MSte
'Divertissment'	CAbx CCol
'Dominic'	COIW CPar SRos
'Dorethe Louise'	SDay SRos
'Dorothy McDade'	EGol ENot
'Double Cream' (d)	EBee WCot
'Double Cutie' (d)	CCol CHVG EBee EOMN MBNS NLar SChu SDay WAul
'Double Daffodil' (d)	WCAu
'Double Dream' (d)	EMar WWin
'Double Firecracker' (d)	CBcs EBee EMar MBNS WWin
'Double Oh' (d)	MTed
'Double Pompom' (d)	WCAu
'Double River Wye' (d)	CCol CFir COIW EBee EChP EGol EMar EMil IPot LPan MBNS MBro MNrw MTed NPri SCro SHBN SHar SRos WCot WHoo WMnd WTin WWye
'Dragon King'	SPol
'Dragon Mouth'	EGol
'Dragon's Eye'	CCol SDay
'Dragon's Orb'	CKel
'Dream Baby' **new**	EOMN
'Dream Legacy'	WAul
'Dreamy Cream' **new**	SRos
'Dresden Doll'	SPer
§ 'Dubloon'	ENot ERou GBuc NHol WCAu
dumortieri	More than 30 suppliers
'Dutch Beauty'	EBre EMar EPla WFar WTMC
'Dutch Gold'	CFai MNrw NBro
'Earlianna' **new**	SPol

'Easy Ned'	SDay SRos
'Ed Murray'	EBee MNFA SRos WAul WCAu
'Edelweiss'	EWTr SDay WBcn
'Edgar Brown' **new**	MBNS
'Edge Ahead' **new**	CCol MBNS
'Edge of Darkness'	EBee EChP EGle EPfP MBNS SDnm
	STes WCAu
'Edna Spalding'	SDay SRos
'Eenie Allegro'	CBro CCol EChP EGle EGol EMan
	IBal MBNS SOkh SPla WMnd
'Eenie Fanfare'	COtt EBre EGle EGol GKir LRHS
	MBNS MNFA WAul WCra
'Eenie Gold'	LRHS
'Eenie Weenie'	CBro CFee EBla ECtt EGle EGol
	EPla ERos GKir IBal LRHS MBNS
	MBri MSwo NBro NBur SAga SChu
	SHBN SPer SRms SPer WTMC
	WWye
'Eenie Weenie Non-stop'	ECha EPPr
'Eggplant Escapade' **new**	CAbx SPol
'Egyptian Ibis'	MBNS
'El Desperado'	CPar ECtt EMar MBNS MLLN
	MNrw NCGa NCot SDnm SUsu
	WBVN WCAu WCot WHlf
'Elaine Strutt'	EGol MBNS MNFA SDay SRos
	SWvt WSpi
'Eleanor Marcotte'	SDay
'Elegant Candy'	CCol CKel CPen EBee ENot LBuc
	MBNS WSan WShp
'Elegant Greeting'	CCol EBee ERou LBuc MBNS
	NOak
'Elizabeth Ann Hudson'	MNFA SDay
'Elizabeth Salter'	EBee MBNS MCLN SRos SUsu
	WCAu
'Elizabeth Yancey'	EGol
'Elva White Glow' **new**	SDay
'Emperor's Dragon' **new**	CCol
'Enchanting Blessing'	SDay
'Erin Prairie'	CAbx
esculenta	SMad
'Esther Walker'	WBcn
'Eternal Blessing'	SRos
'Evelyn Claar'	EChP SCro
'Ever So Ruffled'	SRos
exaltata	GIBF
'Exotic Love' **new**	SDay
'Eye Yi Yi' **new**	SPol
'Fabulous Prize' **new**	SRos
'Fairest Love'	EBee EMar MBNS
'Fairy Jester'	SDay
'Fairy Tale Pink'	MNFA SDay SRos
'Faith Nabor'	CAbx EMar SRos
'Fan Dancer'	EGol
'Fandango' **new**	MNFA SPer
'Farmer's Daughter'	SRos
'Fashion Model' **new**	WPer
'Femme Osage'	SRos
'Festive Art' **new**	MBNS MCLN SRos
'Finlandia'	MNFA
'Fire Dance'	SCro SRos
'Fire Tree' **new**	SPol
'First Formal'	SPer
'Flamboyant Show'	EBee LBuc
'Flames of Fantasy'	MTed SRos
'Flaming Sword'	EBee GBuc LRHS NBlu NHol NPPs
flava	see *H. lilioasphodelus*
'Fleeting Fancy'	SRos
'Fly Catcher'	CAbx EMar SRos
'Fooled Me' **new**	SRos
forrestii	EBee
- 'Perry's Variety'	CCol EMon
'Forsyth Lemon Drop'	SDay
'Forty Second Street'	CFir MBNS MLLN
'Fragrant Bouquet'	SRos

'Fragrant Pastel Cheer'	SDay
'Frances Fay'	SRos WAul WCAu
'Frandean' **new**	MNFA
'Frank Gladney'	MNFA SRos
'Frans Hals'	More than 30 suppliers
'French Porcelain'	SDay
'Fritz Schroer'	CAbx
'Frozen Jade' **new**	SRos
'Full Reward'	WCAu
fulva	EGra ELan IBlr LRHS MHar NBir
	SHBN SRms WBVN WBrk WPnP
	WWin WWpP
- 'Flore Pleno' (d)	CAvo CFee CHar CMHG CStu
	EChP ECtt EGol EHon ELan EMon
	EPfP IBlr LHop MCLN MFOX MFir
	MRav NBir NBro NGdn NSti SHBN
	SPer SRms SWat WCAu WEas
	WMoo WWin
- 'Green Kwanso' (d)	CHar CPLG CRow CSWP EBlw
	ECGP ECha ECtt EMon EPla GFlt
	IBlr MCLN MHer MMHG NVic
	SMad SPla WAul WBrk WFar WPnP
	WRha WTin WWpP
- 'Kwanso'	see *H. fulva* 'Flore Pleno', *H. fulva*
	'Green Kwanso, *H. fulva* 'Kwanso
	Variegata'
- 'Kwanso' ambig. (d)	NOrc
- 'Kwanso Variegata' (d/v)	CBot CRow EBee EGle ELan EMon
	EPPr IBlr LHop MRav MTed MTho
	NBir SBla WBcn WCot WFar WHer
- var. *littorea*	SSpi
- var. *rosea*	EMon MNFA SMHy
I 'Funky Fuchsia' **new**	SPol
'Gadsden Goliath'	CAbx SPol
'Gadsden Light' **new**	CCol
'Garden Plants'	SRos
'Gaucho' **new**	MNFA
'Gay Music' **new**	CCol
'Gay Rapture'	SPer
'Gemini'	SRos
'Gene Foster' **new**	CAbx
'Gentle Country Breeze'	SRos
'Gentle Shepherd'	More than 30 suppliers
'George Cunningham'	CSev ECtt EGle EGol EHrv ELan
	EPla ERou MNFA MRav NBir SChu
	SRos SUsu WCAu WFar
'Georgette Belden'	MBri
'Georgia Cream' (d)	MBNS
'German Ballerina' **new**	SPol
'Giant Moon'	CMHG EBre ELan EPla ERou LRHS
	SChu SRms WFar
'Glittering Treasure' **new**	EBre
'Glory's Legacy' **new**	SRos
'Glowing Gold'	ENot WCAu
'Gold Crest'	MNFA
'Gold Imperial'	EWll
'Golden Bell'	NGdn NHol
'Golden Chance'	WCAu
'Golden Chimes' ♀H4	More than 30 suppliers
'Golden Ginkgo'	LRHS MBri MNFA
'Golden Nugget'	MBNS
'Golden Orchid'	see *H.* 'Dubloon'
'Golden Peace'	SRos
'Golden Prize'	EBre EFou EPla MNFA NGdn NPri
	SDay SRos WCot WFar
'Golden Scroll'	SDay SRos
'Golden Zebra' (v)	EBre ENot EPfP NSti SHGC WSpi
	WWeb
'Good Looking'	EGol
'Grace and Favour' **new**	SPol
'Graceful Eye'	SRos
'Graceland' **new**	SDay
'Grand Masterpiece'	CM&M CSpe EBee EChP IPot
	NGdn

'Grand Palais' SRos
'Grape Magic' EGol WTin
'Grape Velvet' CHar CPar CSpe EBee EGle EGol
MBNS MCCP MCLN MNFA NSti
SHar SOkh WAul WCAu WMnd
WWye
'Green Dragon' **new** SDay
'Green Drop' WFar
'Green Eyed Giant' MNFA
'Green Flutter' ♀H4 CSev EBee EChP EPfP EWTr GCal
LPhx LPio LRHS MBNS MNFA NBir
NCGa NGdn SAsh SRos SVil WSpi
'Green Glitter' MNFA
'Green Gold' CMHG MNFA
'Green Puff' NBir SDay
'Green Spider' CAbx
'Green Valley' **new** MNFA
'Grumbly' EBee ELan WPnP
'Guardian Angel' WTin
'Gusto' WCAu
'Halo Light' MNFA
'Hamlet' **new** SDay
'Happy Returns' CHid COtt EBee EBre ECha EGol
ELan EMar EWoo IBal IFro LAst
MAnH MBNS MBri MHar MNFA
NBlu NGdn SDay SRos SSpe WAul
WCAu
'Harbor Blue' CCol SAga
'Hawaian Punch' EGol
'Hawaiian Purple' EGol
'Hawk' **new** SPol
'Hazel Monette' EGol
'Heartthrob' WCAu
'Heavenly Treasure' EBre MTed SRos
'Heidi Edelweiss' CPLG EBee
'Heirloom Lace' WBcn WCAu WFar
'Helle Berlinerin' ♀H4 EFou MNFA
'Helter Skelter' CAbx
'Her Majesty's SPol
    Wizard' **new**
'Hey There' CAbx SDay SRos
'High Tor' GCal GQui MNFA SHar
'Highland Lord' (d) SDay
'Holiday Mood' ELan ERou
'Holly Dancer' **new** SPol
'Honey Jubilee' **new** SPol
'Hope Diamond' CCol SDay WCAu
'Hornby Castle' CBro LRHS NHol WPer
'Hot Ticket' SRos
'Hot Wire' **new** SRos
'Houdini' EChP EGle EGol WCAu WMnd
WWye
'House of Orange' **new** SPol
'Howard Goodson' **new** MNFA
'Humdinger' SRos
'Hyperion' CPrp CSev EBre ECha ECtt EGol
EPfP GKir LAst LPVe LPio MLan
MNFA MRav NGdn NHol SChu
SHBN SPer SUsu WCAu WTMC
WWye
'Ice Cap' EBee SChu WFar WPnP WWpP
'Ice Carnival' CKel EBee EFou EGle EPfP ERou
LPVe LRHS MBNS MNFA NGdn
NOrc SVil WSpi
'Ice Castles' SDay
'Ice Cool' SRos
'Icy Lemon' SRos
'Ida Duke Miles' SDay SRos
'Ida Munson' EGol
'Ida's Magic' WAul
'Imperator' EPla LPBA NHol NPPs
'In Depth' (d) EGle EPfP MBNS NCGa NLar WCot
'Indian Paintbrush' EBee EChP EGle EWoo GKir LHop
MBri NBir SPol SVil WCAu

'Inner View' EChP ECtt LHop LPVe MBNS NLar
STes WAul WMnd
'Inspired Edge' **new** MBNS
'Inspired Word' SRos
'Invictus' SRos
'Iridescent Jewel' SDay
'Irish Elf' GBuc GMac WTin
'Iron Gate Glacier' MBNS
'Isle of Dreams' CAbx
'Jake Russell' MNFA
'James Marsh' CCol CPar EChP EGle EWes MBNS
MBri MNFA MNrw NSti SRos SSpe
WAul WCAu WHil WMnd
'Janet Gordon' SPol
'Janice Brown' CCol CKel EChP EMar MBNS
MNFA SDay SRos WCAu
'Jason Salter' EBee SDay WAul
'Java Sea' **new** EBee
'Jean' **new** SDay
'Jedi Dot Pierce' SRos
'Jenny Wren' EMar EPPr GSki LRHS MBNS
MNFA SSpe SUsu WAul WCAu
'Jingling Geordie' **new** CAbx
'Jo Jo' WCAu WWin
'Joan Senior' More than 30 suppliers
'Jock Randall' MNFA
'Jockey Club' (d) MBNS
'John Bierman' SRos
'Journey's End' SDay
'Jovial' SDay
'Joylene Nichole' SRos
'Judah' SDay SRos
'June Wine' SDay
'Justin June' CCol
'Kate Carpenter' SRos
'Kathleen Salter' **new** SRos
'Katie Elizabeth Miller' SRos
'Kecia' MNFA
'Kelly's Girl' SRos
'Killer Purple' SDay
'Kindly Light' CAbx MNFA SRos WCAu
'King Haiglar' CCol EGol SRos
N 'Kwanso Flore Pleno' see *H. fulva* 'Green Kwanso'
N 'Kwanso Flore Pleno' see *H. fulva* 'Kwanso Variegata'
    Variegata'
'Lady Cynthia' CSBt
'Lady F. Hesketh' **new** SMHy
'Lady Fingers' CCol SAga
'Lady Neva' CCol
'Ladykin' SRos
'Lark Song' EBre EGol EOrc WBcn WFar
'Lavender Bonanza' WCAu WCFE
'Lavender Deal' EBee EMar
'Lavender Memories' SDay
'Lavender Silver SPol
    Chords' **new**
'Lemon Bells' ♀H4 EBee EBre ECha EFou EGle EMFW
EMar EPPr EPfP GSki MBNS MNFA
MWgw NBro NCGa NGdn SChu
SDay SMrm SRos SVil WCAu
'Lemon Fellow' **new** CAbx
'Lemon Mint' EGol MTed SRos
'Lenox' SDay SRos
'Light the Way' ECha
'Lilac Wine' ECha
§ *lilioasphodelus* ♀H4 More than 30 suppliers
 - 'Rowden Golden CRow
    Jubilee' (v) **new**
'Lillian Frye' EGol
'Lilting Belle' CCol
'Lilting Lady' SDay
'Lilting Lavender' SDay
'Lime Frost' SRos
'Linda' ERou EWll MLwd MRav NHol SRos

* 'Liners Moon'	EGol
'Little Audrey'	EGle
'Little Bee'	EFou MBNS
'Little Beige Magic'	EGol
'Little Big Man'	SDay
'Little Bugger'	MBNS NGby NLar
'Little Bumble Bee'	CFir COIW EGle EGol EMar MBNS MNFA WCAu WTin
'Little Business'	EFou MBNS MNFA SDay
'Little Cadet'	MNFA
'Little Cameo'	EGol
'Little Carnation'	SCro
'Little Carpet' **new**	MBNS SPer
'Little Carrot Top'	WCAu
'Little Cranberry Cove'	EGol
'Little Dandy'	EGol
'Little Deeke'	MNFA SDay SRos
'Little Fantastic'	EGol
'Little Fat Dazzler'	SDay
'Little Fellow' **new**	MBNS
'Little Grapette'	CHad CPlt CPrp EBee EGle EGol EMar MBNS MNFA NLar NSti SBod SCro SRos SVil WAul WBcn WCAu WHrl WTin
'Little Greenie'	SDay
'Little Gypsy Vagabond'	SDay SRos
'Little Lassie'	MBNS
'Little Lavender Princess'	EGol
'Little Maggie'	MHar MSte SDay
'Little Missy'	EMar EMil MBNS WHoo WSan
'Little Monica'	SDay
'Little Pumpkin Face'	EGol
'Little Rainbow'	EGol
'Little Red Hen'	EBre EMar GBuc LRHS MBNS MNFA NBro NGdn SDay WCAu
'Little Sweet Sue'	MNFA
'Little Tawny'	WCAu
'Little Violet Lace'	GSki SDay
'Little Wart'	EGol SDay
'Little Wine Cup'	More than 30 suppliers
'Little Woman'	SDay
'Little Zinger'	SDay
'Lochinvar'	CAbx EBee ENot GBuc MRav SRos
'Long Stocking' **new**	SPol
'Longfield Purple Edge'	EBee MBNS
'Longfield's Bandit' **new**	EBee
'Longfield's Beauty'	EGle MBNS
'Longfield's Glory'	CCol MBNS
'Longfield's Mandy' **new**	EBee
'Longfield's Pride'	MBNS WBor
'Longfield's Purple Eye' **new**	MBNS
'Longfield's Twins' **new**	MBNS
longituba	CPLG WCot
- B&SWJ 4576	WCru
'Love Glow'	CFir
'Lucretius' **new**	MNFA
'Lullaby Baby'	CCol EGle EGol LPVe MBNS NOrc SDay SRos STes
luna	NOak
'Lupine'	MTed
'Lusty Leland'	CHea CPar EBee EGle EGol EMar MBNS SCro SRos
x *luteola*	SDay
'Luxury Lace'	More than 30 suppliers
'Lynn Hall'	EBee EGol WSpi
'Mabel Fuller'	MRav SCro SPer
'Mad Max'	CAbx
'Magic Carpet Ride'	SPol
'Magical Merriment' **new**	CCol
'Mahogany Magic'	SRos
'Mallard'	CWat EBre ECtt EGol EHrv EMar EPla LLWP LRHS MBri MRav MTis SRos WBcn WCra WPer WTMC

'Manchurian Apricot'	SRos
'Marathon Dancer'	CAbx
'Marble Faun'	SRos
'Margaret Perry'	CFee WAul
'Marion Vaughn' ♀[H4]	CSev ECot EFou EGle EGol EHrv ELan EMan EPfP EPla GSki LRHS MMil MNFA MWat NPPs NSti SChu SDix SPer SSpi
'Mariska'	SDay SRos
'Marse Connell' **new**	SRos
'Martha Adams' **new**	SDay
'Mary Todd'	EBee EGle EGol LPan MBNS MNFA NBlu SCro WCAu
'Mary's Gold'	SRos
'Matt'	SRos SWal
'Mauna Loa'	CCol EBee EFou EOMN MBNS MNFA WAul WCAu WCot
'Mavoureen Nesmith'	SCro
'May Colvin'	EBre
'Meadow Mist'	EBee EGle EGol
'Meadow Sprite'	SDay SRos
'Melody Lane'	EGol MNFA
'Meno'	EGol
'Merlot Rouge'	WAul
'Metaphor'	SDay
'Michele Coe'	CM&M EBee EBre EGol EHrv EMar LRHS MBNS MNFA MTed NBro NCGa NGdn SChu SRos WCAu WMoo
middendorffii	CAvo EBee EMon EWTr GCal NFla NGdn NSti WCAu WFar WPnP WShp WWpP
- 'Elfin' **new**	EMon
- var. *esculenta*	EMon
- 'Major'	CFee
'Mikado'	LRHS
'Milady Greensleeves'	CCol SDay SRos
'Millie Schlumpf'	SRos
'Mimosa Umbrella'	CAbx
'Ming Porcelain'	SDay SRos
'Mini Pearl'	CSpe EChP EGol EPfP GKir LRHS MBri SChu SDay SPer SRos SVil WPer WWye
'Mini Stella'	CBro ECtt IBal LPVe MBNS NOrc SMac WAul WBcn WFar WPnP
miniature hybrids	SRms WPer
minor	CBro EGol EMon GCal NGdn SRms
'Miressa Purple' **new**	EBee
'Missenden' ♀[H4]	MNrw SRos
'Mission Moonlight'	COtt EGol WCAu
'Missouri Beauty'	CCol CPar EBee ERou LPVe LRHS MBNS NOrc NPri SOkh WWeb
'Mokan Cindy'	EMar
'Moment of Truth'	MBNS
'Monica Marie'	SRos
'Moon Witch'	SDay SRos
'Moonlight Mist'	CCol SRos
'Moonlit Caress'	EBee EWoo MBNS WAul
'Moonlit Crystal'	CSpe
'Moonlit Masquerade'	CPen EBee EChP EGle EMar ENot ERou LPio MBNS MBri MCCP MLLN MTed NCGa NOrc SDnm SPer SRos WAul WCAu WSan
'Moontraveller' **new**	WCot
'Mormon'	CAbx
'Morning Dawn'	EFou EGle
'Morning Sun'	EMar MBNS WCot
'Morocco Red'	CBro CTri EBee ELan GSki MMil NGdn
'Mountain Laurel'	LRHS MNFA MRav WFar
'Mountain Sprite' **new**	SCro
'Mrs B.F. Bonner'	WAul
'Mrs David Hall'	CMdw SCro

'Mrs Hugh Johnson'   CHad CPlt CSev ECGN ECot MSte
                     NHol SHBN WWpP
'Mrs Joan Cook'   EGle
'Mrs John J. Tigert' ERou
'Mrs Lester'   SDay
multiflora   EMon MNFA NHol SMHy WCot
'My Darling Clementine' SDay
'My Melinda'   SDay
'Mynelle's Starfish' SPol
'Mysterious Veil'   EGol
'Nacogdoches Lady' **new**   CCol
nana   EBee EPot
'Nanuq'   SDay SRos
'Naomi Ruth'   EGle EGol LAst MBNS WCAu WTin
'Nashville'   CBro EBee ELan ERou IBlr MMil
                     WGMN
'Nashville Lights'   CAbx
'Neal Berrey'   SRos
'Nefertiti'   CM&M EBee EChP LAst LHop NBir
                     SPer WCAu WSan
'Netsuke'   EFou
'Neyron Rose' ♀H4   CHea EGol EOMN EPfP EPla ERou
                     GSki MBNS MNFA NGdn SChu
                     SRos WCAu WMoo
'Night Beacon'   EBee ECtt EGol EMar EWes EWoo
                     IBal MBNS MBri MNrw NLar SDay
                     SRos WCAu WHrl
'Night Raider' **new**   SDay SRos
'Nigrette'   LPBA MTed NHol WWpP
'Nile Crane'   ERou MBNS MNrw SPer WAul
'Nob Hill'   CMdw EGol EPla MNFA SRos
'Nordic Night' **new**   CCol
'North Star'   MTed
'Norton Orange'   MNFA WFar
'Nova' ♀H4   CPrp EBee MNFA
'Oachita Beauty'   CAbx
'Ocean Rain'   SRos
x *ochroleuca*   SSpi
'Old-fashioned   CAbx
   Maiden' **new**
'Olive Bailey Langdon'   EGol SRos
'Olive's Odd One' **new**   CAbx
'Olympic Showcase' **new**   SRos
'Omomuki'   SRos
'Oom-pa-pa'   ECha
'Open Hearth'   CAbx CCol SRos
'Optic Elegance'   SAsh
'Orange Dream'   SDay
'Orange Velvet'   SRos
'Orange Vols'   CAbx
'Orangeman' hort.   EMar EPla GSki LRHS MBNS
'Orchid Beauty'   ECha
'Orchid Candy'   MBNS NBir WHil
'Orchid Corsage'   SDay
'Orford'   WWin
'Oriental Ruby'   EGol MNFA
'Outrageous'   SRos
'Paige Parker'   EGol
'Paige's Pinata' **new**   EBee MBNS
'Paintbrush' **new**   CRez
'Painted Lady'   MNFA
'Palace Guard' **new**   MNFA
'Pandora's Box'   More than 30 suppliers
'Paper Butterfly'   CKel SRos
'Parade of Peacocks' **new**   CCol
'Paradise Pink'   NPri
'Paradise Prince' **new**   EGol
'Pardon Me'   CM&M CMHG EBee EGle EGol
                     ELan IBal LPVe LPio MBNS NGdn
                     NHol SRos WAul WBor WCAu
'Pastel Ballerina'   SRos
'Pastel Classic'   SRos
'Pastilline' **new**   SPol
'Patchwork Puzzle'   SRos

'Patsy Bickers'   CCol
'Peach Petticoats'   SRos
'Peacock Maiden'   SDay
'Pear Ornament'   SRos
'Pearl Lewis'   SDay
'Penelope Vestey'   EBee EBla EGle EMar EOMN GBuc
                     LRHS MBNS MNFA NCGa NGdn
                     SRos
'Penny's Worth'   EBre EFou EGol GKir LPVe MBNS
                     NOrc WAul WCot
'Permaquid Light'   CMHG
'Persian Princess'   WBcn
'Persian Ruby' **new**   SPol
'Persimmone' **new**   CAbx
'Petite Ballerina'   SDay
'Piccadilly Princess' SRos
'Pink Attraction'   EFou
'Pink Ballerina'   EGol
'Pink Charm'   COlW EBee EChP ECha EMar ENot
                     GBBs LPBA LRHS MLwd MNFA
                     MWgw NBro NGdn NHol NOrc
                     SChu SHBN SRos WCAu WCra
'Pink Cotton Candy' SRos
'Pink Damask' ♀H4   More than 30 suppliers
'Pink Dream'   EBee EMar IPot LRHS MBNS MNFA
                     NBir NHol WCAu
'Pink Glow'   CM&M
'Pink Grace'   CAbx
'Pink Heaven'   EGol
'Pink Lady'   ERou MBrN MNrw MRav NBur
                     SHBN SRms
'Pink Lavender Appeal'   EGol WCAu
'Pink Prelude'   CCol EBee EChP EMar EWll LRHS
                     MBNS MNFA NBro SChu
'Pink Puff'   ERou MAvo MBNS NBir NLar SDay
'Pink Salute'   SRos
'Pink Sundae'   ECha
'Pink Super Spider' MNFA SRos
'Pinocchio'   MBNS
'Piquante'   EBee
'Pirate's Patch'   SPol SRos
'Pixie Parasol' **new**   WSpi
'Pixie Pipestone'   CCol
'Plum Beauty' **new**   EBee
'Pompeian Purple'   EGol
'Poneytail Pink'   EGol
'Pony'   EGol SDay
'Prague Spring'   MNFA
'Prairie Bells'   CSWP EWTr MBNS MBro STes
                     WBar WCAu WFar WHoo WWhi
'Prairie Blue Eyes' CCol EBee EChP EGle EGol LRHS
                     MBNS MNFA NCGa NPri SCro SPlb
                     WAul WBcn WCAu WCot WMnd
                     WTMC
'Prairie Charmer'   EBee IPot
'Prairie Moonlight' EBee SRos
'Prairie Queen'   IPot
'Prairie Sunset'   WCAu
'Prelude to Love'   EMar
'Pretty Mist'   GKir MBri
'Pretty Peggy'   MNFA
'Prima Donna'   SCro
'Primrose Mascotte' MTed NBir WWin
'Prince Redbird'   SDay
'Princess Ellen' **new**   CCol
'Prize Picotee Deluxe'   SRos
'Prize Picotee Elite'   SRos WTin
'Protocol'   SDay
§ 'Puddin'   CM&M NHol SDay WAul
'Pumpkin Kid'   SRos
'Puppet Show'   SDay
'Pure and Simple'   SDay SPol
'Purple Bicolor' **new**   EBee
'Purple Pinwheel' **new**   SPol

'Purple Rain' CHea MBNS SWvt
'Purple Waters' CCol EPfP EWll LPVe LRHS MBNS
MLwd MWgw NOrc NPri WAul
'Pursuit of Excellence' SRos
'Queen Beatrice' EBee
'Queen of May' WCot
'Quick Results' SRos
'Radiant Ruffles' WCAu
'Raging Tiger' SDay
'Rainbow Candy' MBNS WGMN
'Raindrop' EGol SSpe
'Rajah' EGra EMar NBro
'Raspberry Candy' CBro EChP EMar MAvo MBNS
NOrc WAul WCAu WHrl
'Raspberry Pixie' EGol MNFA MTed
'Raspberry Wine' WBro
'Real Wind' CCol MNFA
'Red Flag' **new** CCol
'Red Precious' ♀H4 EGol MNFA MNrw SAsh SRos
'Red Ribbons' CCol SDay SPol SRos
'Red Rum' EFou EWll MBNS SMrm WPnP
WWhi
'Red Twister' CAbx
'Red Volunteer' SRos
'Regal Finale' **new** CAbx
'Ringlets' **new** EBre MNFA
'Robin Coleman' MNFA
'Rocket City' ELan
'Roger Grounds' CCol
'Romantic Rose' EMar MBNS
'Romany' LPBA
'Root Beer' SRos WBcn WCAu WTin
'Rose Emily' SDay SRos
'Rose Festival' WCAu
'Rosella Sheridan' SRos
'Royal Braid' CPen EBee EChP EGle EPfP MBNS
MCLN MNrw NCGa NLar NOrc
SPer WAul WCot WSan
'Royal Charm' SRos
'Royal Corduroy' SRos
'Royal Robe' EBlw
'Royal Saracen' SDay
'Royalty' NGdn WWpP
'Ruby Spider' CCol SDay
'Rudolf Seyer' MBNS
I 'Ruffled Antique WCAu
Lavender' **new**
'Ruffled Apricot' CKel LPVe MBNS SDay SRos WCAu
'Ruffles and Lace' **new** CCol
'Russell Prichard' ERou
'Russian Easter' **new** SRos
'Russian Rhapsody' CKel SRos
'Rutilans' CFee
'Sabina Bauer' **new** IPot
'Sabra Salina' SDay SRos
'Salmon Sheen' MNFA SDay SRos
'Sammy Russell' More than 30 suppliers
'Sandra Walker' EGol
'Satin Clouds' EGol
'Satin Glass' MNFA
'Satin Glow' ECha
'Satin Silk' EBre
'Scarlet Flame' ECha
* 'Scarlet Oak' LRHS MBri MNFA
'Scarlet Orbit' SRos
'Scarlet Ribbons' **new** CAbx SPol
'Scarlock' **new** MNFA
'Scatterbrain' CKel
'Schoolgirl' EBre
'Scorpio' CCol MNFA
'Scotland' IBal
'Searcy Marsh' EGol
'Sebastian' SRos
'Secret Splendor' SPol

'Semiramide' **new** CAbx
'Serena Madonna' CFir
'Serena Sunburst' CAbx SRos
'Shaman' SRos
'Sherry Lane Carr' SPol
'Shooting Star' SPla
'Shopinger Anfang' **new** EBee
'Show Amber' SRos
'Showgirl' GKir
'Silken Fairy' EGol SDay
'Siloam Angel Blush' SDay
'Siloam Baby Talk' CM&M EChP EGle EGol EMar LAst
NBir SCro SRos WAul WHoo WPnP
WTin
'Siloam Bo Peep' EGol MNFA WAul WTMC
'Siloam Brian Henke' SRos
'Siloam Button Box' EBee EChP EGol EWoo SPer WAul
WSan
'Siloam Byelo' EGol SDay
'Siloam Cinderella' EGol SDay SRos
'Siloam David Kirchhoff' EBee MBNS SDay SRos
'Siloam Doodlebug' EGol SRos
'Siloam Double Classic' (d) EGol SRos
'Siloam Dream Baby' EPPr EPza GBri MBNS
'Siloam Edith Scholar' EGol
'Siloam Ethel Smith' EGol SCro SDay SRos
'Siloam Fairy Tale' EChP EGol
'Siloam Flower Girl' SDay
'Siloam French Doll' CCol MBNS
'Siloam Gold Coin' SDay
'Siloam Grace Stamile' CFir SRos
'Siloam Harold Flickinger' SRos
'Siloam Joan Senior' ECtt EGol MBNS SDay
'Siloam John Yonski' SDay
'Siloam June Bug' EGle EGol ELan MNFA WCAu
'Siloam Justin Lee' MBNS
'Siloam Kewpie Doll' EGol
'Siloam Little Angel' EGol
'Siloam Little Girl' EGol SDay SRos
'Siloam Mama' SDay
'Siloam Merle Kent' SDay SRos
'Siloam New Toy' EGol
'Siloam Orchid Jewel' EGol
'Siloam Pee Wee' EGol WCAu
'Siloam Pink' LAst
'Siloam Pink Glow' EGle EGol WAul
'Siloam Pink Petite' EGol
'Siloam Plum Tree' EGol
'Siloam Pocket Size' EGol MSte
'Siloam Prissy' EGol
'Siloam Purple Plum' EGol
'Siloam Red Ruby' EGol
'Siloam Red Toy' EGol MNFA SDay
'Siloam Red Velvet' EGol
'Siloam Ribbon Candy' EGol SDay
'Siloam Rose Dawn' SRos
'Siloam Rose Queen' SDay
'Siloam Royal Prince' CM&M EChP EGle EGol EPfP
MNFA NHol SCro SDay
'Siloam Ruffled Infant' SDay
'Siloam Shocker' CAbx EGol
'Siloam Show Girl' CCol CRez EGle EGol GKir MBNS
MBri NCGa WAul WGMN
'Siloam Sugar Time' EGol
'Siloam Tee Tiny' EGle EGol
'Siloam Tinker Toy' EGol
'Siloam Tiny Mite' EGol SDay
'Siloam Toddler' EGol
'Siloam Tom Thumb' EGol EMar MBNS WCAu
'Siloam Ury Winniford' CBro EGol MBNS MCCP MNFA
SDay SPer WAul WHoo WPnP WTin
'Siloam Virginia Henson' COtt EBee EGol MNFA SOkh SRos
WCAu
'Silver Ice' SRos

'Silver Trumpet' EGle EGol SCro
'Silver Veil' WFar
'Sir Modred' MAnH
'Sirius' NHol
'Sirocco' EChP WTin
'Slender Lady' SRos
'Smoky Mountain Autumn' SDay SRos
'Snappy Rhythm' MNFA
'Snowed In' **new** SRos
'Snowy Apparition' EWTr EWll MBri MNFA MSte SMrm
'Snowy Eyes' CHid EBee EGle EGol EMar GBuc IPot MBNS NHol WCAu WWin
'Someone Special' SRos
'Song Sparrow' EBre GKir GMac LRHS MBri WPer WWye
'Sovereign Queen' EGol
'Spacecoast Starburst' EBee MBNS WCAu
'Spider Breeder' CAbx
'Spider Miracle' MNFA
'Spiderman' SRos WCAu
'Spilled Milk' **new** SPol
'Spinneret' CAbx
'Stafford' More than 30 suppliers
'Starling' CFir CPar EBee EChP EGle EGol MNFA MSte WAul WCAu WSpi
'Stars and Stripes' MNFA
'Stella de Oro' More than 30 suppliers
'Stineette' WCot
'Stoke Poges' ♀H4 CBro CSev EBee EChP EGle EGoo EMFW EMar EPPr EPfP EPla LAst LHop LRHS MBNS MMil MNFA NGdn SChu SDay SPer SRos STes WCAu
'Stoplight' CAbx CCol SDay SRos
'Strawberry Candy' CM&M EBee EBre EChP EMar EPfP EWoo LAst LPan MBNS MBri MCLN NCGa NGdn NOrc SOkh SPer SRos SVil WAul WCAu WHoo WShp
'Strawberry Fields Forever' MBNS MCLN
'Strawberry Swirl' **new** MNFA
I 'Streaker' B. Brown (v) WCot
'Streaker' McKinney MNFA
'Strutter's Ball' CPar EChP EGle EWoo IPot LHop MNFA NGdn SDay SPer SRos SVil WAul WCAu WCot WHoo WMnd
'Sugar Cookie' **new** SDay SRos
'Summer Interlude' WCAu WMoo
'Summer Jubilee' SDay
'Summer Wine' More than 30 suppliers
* 'Summertime' WBcn
'Sun Pixie' SCro
'Sunday Gloves' CAbx EGol
'Sunstar' **new** CCol
'Super Purple' CKel
'Superlative' SRos
'Sure Thing' **new** CAbx
'Suzie Wong' MNFA SChu
'Svengali' SDay SPol
'Sweet Harmony' **new** CCol
'Sweet Pea' EGol
'Swirling Spider' CAbx
'Taj Mahal' WFar
'Tang' EBee MAvo MBNS MNFA NOrc WCAu
'Tango Noturno' **new** SPol
'Techny Peach Lace' SRos
'Techny Spider' SRos
'Tejas' CElw EBee EMil MBNS
'Tender Shepherd' EGol WCAu
'Tetraploid Stella de Oro' SDay
'Tetrina's Daughter' ♀H4 EPfP NHol SRos
'Texas Sunlight' EWTr WAul

'Thumbelina' ECha MNFA
§ *thunbergii* EBee ECha EMon MNFA MNrw SMac SSpi WCAu
'Tigerling' **new** SRos
'Time Lord' SDay
'Timeless Fire' SRos
'Tinker Bell' MSte SRos
'Tom Collins' SRos
'Tom Wise' SRos
'Tonia Gay' SRos
'Tootsie' SDay
'Tootsie Rose' SRos
'Torpoint' EMar LRHS MBNS MNFA
'Towhead' EBee EGol ENot MRav MTed
'Toyland' CSev EBee EChP EGol EPPr EPfP GSki MBNS NBir NGdn NPri SSpe SUsu WWeb
'Trahlyta' CPar SPol SRos
'Tropical Toy' SDay
'Tuolumne Fairy Tale' **new** SPol
'Tuscawilla Blackout' **new** SRos
'Tuscawilla Tigress' EBee EMar MTed
'Twenty Third Psalm' WTin
'Twiggy' **new** CAbx
'Uniquely Different' **new** SPol
'Upper Class Peach' SRos
'Uptown Girl' SRos
'Valiant' **new** EMar
'Varsity' EBre EGol NBir SPer SRos WCAu
'Veiled Beauty' WCAu
'Vera Biaglow' SDay
'Vespers' EBre WCra WFar WPnP
vespertina see *H. thunbergii*
'Victoria Aden' CBro IBal LBuc
'Victorian Ribbons' **new** SPol
'Victorian Violet' SDay
'Vino di Notte' **new** SRos
'Vintage Bordeaux' ELan
'Violet Explosion' CAbx
'Violet Hour' SDay
'Violet Light' **new** EOMN
'Virgin's Blush' SPer
* 'Vohann' CMdw
'Wajang' **new** EFou
'Walking on Sunshine' SRos
'Wally Nance' SDay
'Water Witch' EGol
'Waxwing' WPer
'Wayside Green Imp' EBee EFou EGol SCro SOkh
'Wayside Green Lamp' EGle MNrw MSte
'Wee Chalice' EGol
'Welchkins' EBee WAul
'Whichford' ♀H4 CBro CHad EBre ECtt EGol ELan ETow LAst LPhx LRHS MNFA SChu SPla WCAu WWin
'White Coral' EBre EMar LRHS MNFA NBro WCAu
'White Dish' EGol
'White Edged Madonna' EBee EMar GFlt
'White Temptation' CFir CM&M CSpe EBee EChP EGol EPfP EWoo MNFA NGdn SDay SRos WAul WCAu
'Whooperie' SRos
'Wide Eyed' EPla MNFA
'Wild About Sherry' **new** SPol
'Wild Mustang' CCol EBee MBNS
'Wild Welcome' WCAu
'Wind Frills' CCol SDay
'Window Dressing' COlW EGol GMac
'Windsor Tan' WCAu WCFE
'Wine Bubbles' EGol
'Wine Merchant' **new** MNFA
'Wineberry Candy' CPar EGle EPfP MBNS MCLN WCAu WGMN

	'Winnetka'	WCAu
	'Winnie the Pooh'	SDay
	'Winsome Lady'	ECha WHrl
	'Winter Olympics'	SDay
	'Wishing Well'	SChu
*	'Witch Hazel'	COtt WCAu
	'Witch Stitchery'	CAbx
	'Witches Brew' **new**	CAbx
	'Wood Duck'	COtt EGle LBuc
	'Wren'	COtt
	'Xia Xiang'	SDay
	'Yabba Dabba Doo'	CAbx SPol
	'Yellow Lollipop'	MNFA SDay SRos
	'Yellow Mantle'	MNFA
	'Yellow Petticoats'	MTed
	'Yellow Rain'	SAsh
	'Yesterday Memories'	SRos
	'Zagora' **new**	WCAu
	'Zampa'	CAbx SDay
	'Zara'	CAbx SPer

Hemiorchis (Zingiberaceae)

pantlingii	CKob MOak

Hemiphragma (Scrophulariaceae)

heterophyllum	NLAp

Hepatica ✿ (Ranunculaceae)

	acutiloba	CArn CBro CLAP EBee EPot GAbr GBuc GCrs GFlt GKir LAma LEur MAsh NBir NGar NLar SIgm WCru WPnP
	'Akane'	LHop
	americana	EBee EHrv GBuc GCrs MAsh NBir NLar SBla WCru WPnP
	angulosa	see *H. transsilvanica*
	'Baien'	LHop
	'Gyousei' **new**	EBee
	'Hatsane'	LHop
	henryi	EBee LAma MAsh WCru
	insularis	SBla
	- B&SWJ 859	WCru
	maxima	EBee
	- B&SWJ 4344	WCru
	x *media*	WCom
	- 'Ballardii'	GKir IBlr
	- 'Harvington Beauty'	CBAn CLAP GBuc IBlr MAsh NBir NGar WCot
	'Miyoshino'	LHop
	'Miyuki' (d) **new**	EBee
	'Mocharu' **new**	EBee
§	*nobilis* ♀H4	More than 30 suppliers
	- blue	CDes GAbr GBuc GEdr LPio MAsh MS&S NGar NSla SBla SRot WAbe WCru
	- 'Cobalt'	NMyG NSla WAbe
	- dark blue	CLAP NGar
	- double pink	see *H. nobilis* 'Rubra Plena'
	- var. *japonica*	CArn CBro EBee GBuc GCrs LAma MAsh NBir NGar SBla SIgm WCru
	- lilac	MTho SBla
	- mottled leaf	EHrv LEur MTho
	- 'Pearl Grey'	NPar
	- Picos strain	SBla
	- pink	CLAP EHyt EPot ETow GCrs GFlt LEur MAsh MS&S NGar NWCA SBla SIng SRot
	- var. *pubescens* **new**	MAsh
*	- var. *pyrenaica*	EBee GBuc MAsh
*	- - 'Apple Blossom'	GCrs NBir
*	- 'Pyrenean Marbles'	CLAP
*	- red	NGar WAbe
	- 'Roger's Silver'	NPar
	- var. *rubra*	CLAP NMen NSla
§	- 'Rubra Plena' (d)	ECha GCrs NGar
	- violet	SBla
	- white	CLAP CNic EBee EHyt GCrs LPio MAsh MAvo MS&S NGar NMen NSla SBla SIng SRot WCru WIvy
	'Noubeni' **new**	EBee
	'Noumurasaki'	LHop
	'Oboroyo'	LHop
	'Ô-murasaki'	LHop
	'Ryokka'	LHop
*	'Ryoustsu'	LHop
	'Sakaya'	LHop
	'Sakuragari'	LHop
	'Sougetsu'	LHop
	'Syungyou' **new**	EBee
	'Syunsai' **new**	EBee
	'Tenshin Ume'	LHop
§	*transsilvanica* ♀H4	CBro CLAP EBee EHyt EPot GCrs GKir LAma LHop LRHS MAsh MS&S MWat NGar NMen SBla SCro WAbe WAul WCot WCru WTin
	- 'Ada Scott' **new**	WSHC
*	- *alba*	MAsh NGar SBla
	- 'Blue Jewel'	CFir CLAP CRez EBee GCrs GEdr WPnP
	- 'De Buis'	CFwr CLAP EBee EPot GCrs GEdr LPhx LPio MDun NLar WPnP
	- deep blue	IBlr
	- 'Eisvogel'	CBro CLAP EPot NGar NMen NPar
	- 'Elison Spence' (d)	EBee ECha IBlr NGar NPar SBla
	- 'Lilacina'	ECha MAsh NGar NPar
	- 'Loddon Blue'	IBlr NGar NPar
	- pink	CLAP EPot SBla
	- semi-double **new**	ECha
	triloba	see *H. nobilis*
	'Umezono' **new**	EBee
	'Wakana'	LHop
	yamatutai	LEur MAsh SBla
	aff. *yamatutai*	EBee

Heptacodium (Caprifoliaceae)

	jasminoides	see *H. miconioides*
§	*miconioides*	CABp CBot CBrm CFil CMCN CPMA CPle ELan EOrc EPAt EPfP GEil GIBF GQui IArd MBlu MCCP MGos SMac SMad SSpi WBVN WCot WMou WPGP WSHC

Heptapleurum see *Schefflera*

Heracleum (Apiaceae)

candicans	EMan
- BWJ 8157	WCru
dulce	EBee
lanatum 'Washington Limes' (v)	EBee EMan EPPr ITer WCot
lehmannianum	EBee EMan SDix WCot
minimum 'Roseum'	CPom NLAp WPat
moellendorfii	EBee
sphondylium pink	CNat

Herbertia (Iridaceae)

§ *lahue*	CDes LRHS WCot

Hereroa (Aizoaceae)

odorata	EShb

Hermannia (Sterculiaceae)

althaeoides **new**	CPBP
candicans	see *H. incana*
erodioides JCA 15523	CPBP
flammea	CPBP
§ *incana*	CHal MOak
stricta	CPBP SIgm SScr WAbe

Hermodactylus (Iridaceae)

§ **tuberosus** CAvo CBro CMea CTri EBee ECGP
ECha EMan EPar EWTr GFlt LAma
LPhx LPio LRHS NRog STes WCot
WTin
– MS 821 WCot

Herniaria (Illecebraceae)

glabra CArn EOHP EPAt GBar GPoy MSal
NJOw SIde WHer WLHH WWye

Herpolirion (Anthericaceae)

novae-zealandiae ECou

Hertia see *Othonna*

Hesperaloe (Agavaceae)

funifera EOas XPep
parviflora CTrC EMan EOas LPio SChr SIgm
WCot WMul XPep

Hesperantha (Iridaceae)

§ **baurii** CLyd CNic CPBP CStu EBee EMan
EPot GBuc GFlt NMen SSpi WAbe
coccinea see *Schizostylis coccinea*
cucullata EBee GFlt
* – 'Rubra' NWCA
huttonii EBee EMan GMac MFir MWrn NBir
NCGa
mossii see *H. baurii*
petitiana GCal
radiata new EBee
woodii CDes CFir

Hesperis (Brassicaceae)

lutea see *Sisymbrium luteum*
matronalis More than 30 suppliers
§ – var. **albiflora** CCge CHrt CPrp CSpe CTri EBee
EFou ELau EMar EPfP ERou LRHS
MBow MWrn NDov NGHP NPri
SIde SPer SSvw WBrk WCAu WFar
WMnd WMoo WPer WWye
– – 'Alba Plena' (d) CAbP CCge CElw CMea CPne
EBee ECtt ELan EMan LRHS MCLN
MNrw NBir NPri SBla SPoG WBrk
WCAu WCot WFar
– double (d) EChP GKir MBri SMrm
– 'Frogswell Doris' EOrc IFro
– 'Lilacina Flore Pleno' (d) CBos CElw EMon MCLN NDov
NPri SMrm
steveniana ECoo SMrm

Heterocentron (Melastomataceae)

§ **elegans** EMan

Heterolepis (Asteraceae)

aliena GFai SGar

Heteromeles (Rosaceae)

arbutifolia see *H. salicifolia*
salicifolia EShb

Heteromorpha (Apiaceae)

arborescens CTrC SIgm SPlb

Heteropappus (Asteraceae)

altaicus WPer

Heteropyxis (Myrtaceae)

natalensis new EShb

Heterotheca (Asteraceae)

jonesii new WLin

---

mariana see *Chrysopsis mariana*
pumila NWCA
§ **villosa** EMan
– 'Golden Sunshine' EBee

Heuchera ✿ (Saxifragaceae)

abramsii WLin
'Amber Waves' More than 30 suppliers
§ **americana** EBee ECha GBar MHar MMil MRav
NBir NSti
– Dale's strain CBct ECGN ECha EMan GKir IBal
LRHS MNrw NGdn NLar SPlb
SWvt WGor WHrl WMnd WPnP
WTMC WWeb
– 'Harry Hay' EPPr MSte
– 'Ring of Fire' CBcs COtt EBee EBre EGle EHan
EPfP GBri IArd IBal LRHS MAvo
MBow MDun MSPs MSte NCGa
NMyG NPri NSti SDnm SPla SWvt
WBea WCot WFar WGMN WPnP
WShp
'Amethyst Myst' CFai COIW EBee EBre EMan EPfP
GAbr GBBs LRHS MBNS MBnl
NLar NMyG NPri SDnm SRot
WBea WCot WFar WGor WShp
argutifolia 'Temple MCCP
Bells' **new**
'Beauty Colour' CFee CFwr EBee EBre EChP EDAr
EFou EMan EMar EPfP GKir IBal
IHMH MAvo MBri MRav NGdn
NPPs SCoo WBea WCot WCra
WFar WOVN WSSM WShp
'Black Beauty' **new** IBal
* 'Black Velvet' EBee EFou EPfP EPyc MCCP
'Blackbird' ♀H4 CFai EBee EBre EDAr MBNS NPro
SDnm SSto STes WMnd
'Blood Vein' EWll ITer ITim MWrn
Bressingham hybrids CWib EBre ENot GKir LAst LRHS
NArg NBir NBlu NMir SPer SPet
SRms WFar WMoo WPer WSSM
x **brizoides** IHMH
'Burgundy Frost' WCot
♀H4 **new**
Cally hybrids GCal
'Can-can' ♀H4 More than 30 suppliers
'Canyon Chimes' COtt
'Canyon Duet' COtt
'Canyon Pink' NSti WCot
'Cappuccino' CBct CHar EBee EChP ECtt EMan
IBal MBNS MBnl MBow MDHE
NBro NPri SDnm SWvt WFar WLin
WWeb WWol WWpP
'Cascade Dawn' CMHG EBee EMan GBuc IBal LAst
LHop LRHS MFan MRav MSte NBir
NHol NLar NPri SMrm SPer WBea
WBrk WCot WFar WShp
'Champagne Bubbles'PBR SHar
Charles Bloom = 'Chablo' EBre
'Cherries Jubilee'PBR CBAn EBee MBNS MBnl MLLN
MSph NCGa SHar WBea WCot
WCra WGor WShp WWol
'Chiqui' SUsu
chlorantha EBee GBin GCal
'Chocolate Ruffles'PBR More than 30 suppliers
'Chocolate Veil' ♀H4 EBee MAvo SHar WWeb
coral bells see *H. sanguinea*
'Coral Bouquet' EBee EMan MBNS MLLN SHar
WCot
'Coral Cloud' EBee MRav
'Crimson Curls' EBee LRHS
'Crispy Curly' COIW EMan EWll ITim MBNS
MWrn NBur WBVN
cylindrica MBNS MRav MSte MWgw WPer
– var. **alpina** NWCA

- 'Greenfinch'   CFee COlW EBre ECha ELan ENot EPfP ERou EWTr GCal GKir GTou IHMH LRHS MTis NBir NDov NOrc WBea WPer WSSM
- 'Hyperion'   ECtt
'Dainty Bells'   WCot
'Dennis Davidson'   see *H.* 'Huntsman'
'Diana Clare'   ECtt
'Dingle Mint Chocolate'   ECtt
'Ebony and Ivory'   CAbP CM&M CPen EBee EBre EChP EHrv EMan ENor EPPr EPfP MBnl MBri MDHE MLLN NDov NGdn NLar NSti SAsh SHar SRot SSto SUsu SWvt WCot WSan WShp
I   'Eco Magnifiolia'   CLAP CLAP
'Eden's Aurora'   EChP WMnd
'Eden's Joy'   EBee EChP EFou MBNS
'Eden's Mystery'   EBee EBre ECtt EFou
'Eden's Shine'   EBee
elegans   NMen
'Emperor's Cloak'   CBri CHar ECtt EMil ENot ITim MWrn NBur NDlv NLar NPro STes SWal WMoo WSan
'Firebird'   NBir NVic
Firefly   see *H.* 'Leuchtkäfer'
'Fireworks'[PBR] ♀[H4]   EBee GBBs GBin MBNS MBnl SHar SPla WCot WHoo WShp
'Florist's Choice'   CAbP EBee EMan IBal MBNS NDov SHar WCot WHoo
glabra   EBee
glauca   see *H. americana*
'Green Ivory'   CSam EBee EBre EMan LRHS MRav NGdn NSti
'Green Spice'   GBin MAvo MBNS SAsh WLow
'Green Spire' **new**   CFai
'Greenfinch'   EGle GKir IBal MHer NHol SPer WFar WGwG WMnd WShp
grossulariifolia   EBee MBNS WPer
hallii   EBee ETow
'Helen Dillon' (v)   CHid EBla ECtt EGle EMan GBri IBal LAst MLLN MRav NBir NPri SDnm SPer SPla SWvt WCom WCot WFar WPnP WWhi WWpP
'Hercules'[PBR]   EBee EChP ECtt MBNS
hispida   EMan MSte WPer
§   'Huntsman'   EBee EChP ECha ELan EMan GBri GBuc IBal MBNS MRav WBcn WFar WMnd
'Ibis'   EBee
'Jubilee'   EBee
'Lady in Red'   EBee EFou MBNS
'Lady Romney'   GCal
§   'Leuchtkäfer'   More than 30 suppliers
'Magic Wand'[PBR] ♀[H4]   CAbP EBee MBNS NGdn SHar WCot WShp
'Mars' **new**   EBee MBNS MBnl
maxima   EMon
'Mercury' **new**   EBee EChP MBNS
'Metallica'   MWrn NLar
micans   see *H. rubescens*
micrantha   EBee GCal SRms
- var. *diversifolia*   EBee EBre EGle EPla LRHS MBri
Bressingham Bronze   SPla SVil WCAu WFar
= 'Absi'[PBR]
N   - - 'Palace Purple'   More than 30 suppliers
§   - 'Ruffles'   LRHS
'Mini Mouse'   EBee GKir
'Mint Frost'[PBR]   More than 30 suppliers
'Monet'   see *H. sanguinea* 'Monet'
'Montrose Ruby'   EBee
'Mother of Pearl'   ECtt
'Neptune' **new**   EBee EChP EPfP IPot MBNS MBnl SPoG
'Northern Fire'   CRez EBee MBNS

'Oakington Jewel'   CRez EBee EBre ELan EMan LRHS
'Painted Lady'   GBuc
'Palace Passion'   WBrE
*   'Palace Purple Select'   CWib EDAr IBal LAst NJOw SWvt WShp
parishii NNS 93-384   NWCA
'Party Bells'   NGar
parvifolia var. *nivalis*   EBee
'Persian Carpet'   EBee EBlw ECha ECtt EMan EMar EPza GKir LRHS MAvo MDun MFan MLLN NBir NGdn NPri SDnm SPer SSpi SWvt WBea WCom WCot WFar WLin WShp
'Petite Marbled Burgundy'   CMdw COtt CStr EBee ECtt EDAr EGle GBri IBal LAst LTwo MCLN MDHE MSte NDov NLar NSti SUsu SWvt WBea WCot WFar WLin WShp WWhi
'Petite Pearl Fairy'   CBct CHid CM&M COtt CSpe EBee EGle EHoe GBin MBri MDHE MSte NGdn NLar NPro SOkh SPla SSte STes WAul WBea WCom WCot WGor WLin WWhi
'Petite Pink Bouquet'   EBee EBre EChP ECtt EMan GAbr IBal MBNS MBnl NBPC NPro SPla WCot WShp
'Pewter Moon'   CBro CHEx CSBt CSpe EBee ELan EMil ENot EPfP EUJe GKir IHMH LRHS MGos MRav NBir NPri SChu SDnm SPer SSto WBrk WFar WMnd WPnP WTin
'Pewter Veil'[PBR]   EBee EMan ENot EPfP EPyc MBnl NCGa SPer WEas WFar WPnP WShp
§   'Pluie de Feu'   CFir CWCL EBee EChP ECtt EPfP EWsh GBri IBal MBNS MBri MRav SSto WShp
'Plum Fairy'   CM&M
'Plum Pudding'[PBR]   More than 30 suppliers
'Prince'   CPen EBee EBre EPfP MBNS
'Prince of Silver' **new**   EBee MBNS
pringlei   see *H. rubescens*
*   x *pruhonicana* Doctor   SRms
    Sitar's hybrids
*   'Pruhonicana'   EBee
pubescens   GBri
pulchella   CPBP CSam EBee EBre EDAr EMar GFlt IBal ITim MHer MWrn NCGa NJOw SMac SRms SUsu
- JCA 9508   NMen NWoo
'Purple Petticoats' ♀[H4]   CBcs EFou EPfP IBal MLLN NCGa NDlv NFla NGdn SHar SPer SRot WCot WShp
'Quick Silver' **new**   MDHE
'Quilter's Joy' ♀[H4]   EFou
'Rachel'   More than 30 suppliers
Rain of Fire   see *H.* 'Pluie de Feu'
'Raspberry Regal' ♀[H4]   CMHG EBee ECtt EFou EGle EMan GAbr MLLN MRav MSph NBir NHol NSti SWvt WAul WCom WCot WSSM
'Red Spangles'   EBee EBre EPfP LRHS MBNS NBir WCAu
'Regina' ♀[H4]   CAbP CBri CSpe EBee ECtt EFou GKir IBal MBNS MBri MDHE MFan NBro NCGa WFar WShp
richardsonii   MNrw
'Robert'   EBee LAst MBNS SChu WCAu
Rosemary Bloom   EBre LRHS
= 'Heuros'[PBR]
§   *rubescens*   CAbP EDAr EHyt MTho NBro NMen SIng WPer WTin WWin
rubra 'Redstart'   ECtt
'Ruby Veil'   EBee EBre EFou GKir SMrm WGor

	'Ruffles'	see *H. micrantha* 'Ruffles'
	'Sancyl'	SRms
§	*sanguinea*	CAgr CSBt EBee EDAr LRHS NBir NFor SECG WPer
	– 'Alba' ♀H4	EMon WBcn
	– 'Geisha's Fan'	EBee EDAr IBal MAvo MTis NBhm NGdn SHar SPer
§	– 'Monet' (v)	EBee EBre EChP EMan ENot GKir MBNS NSti
	– 'Sioux Falls'	EBee EChP EWes LAst MWrn WPnP
§	– 'Snow Storm' (v)	EBee ECtt ELan ENot EPfP GKir IBal MBar MGos MHer MRav SPer SPlb WAul WFar WMnd
	– 'Splendens'	WShp
	– 'Taff's Joy' (v)	CRow EMon EWes MNrw
	– 'Vivid Crimson'	MWrn
	– 'White Cloud' (v)	CFwr EBee LAst SRms WPnP
	'Saturn'	EBee EChP MBnl NOrc
	'Schneewittchen'	EBee EMan EOMN EPfP EWTr LRHS MRav
	'Scintillation' ♀H4	EBee EBre ECtt LRHS SRms
	'Silver Indiana'PBR	EBee LBuc SMrm SPoG WShp
	'Silver Scrolls'	More than 30 suppliers
	'Silver Shadows'	SHar
	'Silver Streak'	see x *Heucherella* 'Silver Streak'
	'Sioux Falls' **new**	MSPs NCGa
	'Smokey Rose' ♀H4	EBee
	'Snow Storm' (v)	see *H. sanguinea* 'Snow Storm'
	'Stormy Seas'	More than 30 suppliers
	'Strawberries and Cream' (v)	EBee EHrv NPPs
	'Strawberry Candy'	EBee EBre GAbr GBBs NCGa SPer WLin WShp
	'Strawberry Spangles' **new**	WCra
	'Strawberry Swirl'	CBcs CHar CMHG EBee ECtt EGle GMac LAst MLLN MMil MRav MSte NBir NDov NHol NLar NPri NSti SSpi SWat SWvt WAul WCAu WCot WFar WLin WOVN WShp WWhi
	'Swirling Fantasy'	EBee EChP EPfP MBnl
	'Titania'	EBee
	'Van Gogh'	EBee MBNS
	'Veil of Passion'	SHar
	'Velvet Cloak'	EBre EHan
	'Velvet Night'	EBee EBre EMan LRHS MAvo MBNS NBir SHar SSte SVil WFar WSan
	'Venus' **new**	EBee MBNS
	'Vesuvius'	SHar WShp
	villosa	ECGN ECha MRav
	– 'Autumn Bride'	MWrn
	– var. *macrorhiza*	ECGN GCal
	– 'Royal Red'	ECha GBuc
	– 'White Marble'	SHar
	– 'Winter Red'	EBee EBre NOrc WCAu
	– 'Yeti'	EBee WPnP
	'Zabelliana'	GBri GCal

x *Heucherella* (Saxifragaceae)

	alba 'Bridget Bloom'	CHVG EBre EChP ECha ELan GKir LGro MBro MRav NOrc NPri SPer SRms WCAu WFar WHoo WMnd WPnP
§	– 'Rosalie'	CElw CFee CMHG EBre ECha EMar EWsh LRHS MAvo MBNS MBri MRav MSte MTis NBir NBro NDov NJOw NPro SPlb WBrk WPar WHoo WMnd WMoo WPnP WTin
	'Burnished Bronze'	CSpe EBee EMan MBnl MLLN MSte NBro NCGa NGdn NLar SDnm SHar SRot SUsu SWvt WFar WGor WMoo
	'Chocolate Lace'	MLLN SHar

	'Cinnamon Bear'	SHar
	'Dayglow Pink'	EBee NBro NCGa SHar SRot WFar WGor WMoo WSan WShp WSpi
	'Kimono' ♀H4	EBee ECtt EMan LAst MBri NBro NCGa NGdn NPri SHar SRot WCot WShp
	'Ninja'	see *Tiarella* 'Ninja'
	'Pearl Kohl' (v)	CCol
	'Quicksilver'	CBcs CBct EBee EBre ECGN EChP GAbr LAst MSte NDov NGdn NPSI NSti SPer SSpi SWvt WBea WCAu WCot WFar WLin WMoo WPnP WShp WWhi
	'Ring of Fire' **new**	CHar
§	'Silver Streak'	CMHG EBre EChP EFou GKir LHop MSte NBro NCGa NPSI NPri SPla SSpi SWvt WCot WCra WFar WMoo WShp WWpP
	'Sunspot' **new**	MAvo SHar
	tiarelloides ♀H4	EBee EMan EMil EPfP LRHS MWgw NSti SPer SVal WMnd
	'Viking Ship'PBR	More than 30 suppliers

Hexastylis see *Asarum*

Hibanobambusa (Poaceae)

	tranquillans	CMCo EFul EPla LPan MBrN MMoz SDry WJun
	– 'Kimmei'	EBee
	– 'Shiroshima' (v) ♀H4	CAbb CDoC CFil CFwr EBee EBlw EBre EPla ERod IFro LPal MBrN MCCP MMoz MWhi MWht NMoo NVic SDry WHPE WJun WNor WPGP

Hibbertia (Dilleniaceae)

	aspera	CPLG CPle CRHN WBcn WFar WSHC
§	*cuneiformis*	CPle ERea MAsh WPat
	pedunculata	ECou
	procumbens	ITim NLAp
§	*scandens* ♀H1	CHEx CRHN ECou ELan ERea GQui LRHS SOWG WMul
	stricta	ECou
	tetrandra	see *H. cuneiformis*
*	*venustula*	ECou
	volubilis	see *H. scandens*

Hibiscus ✿ (Malvaceae)

	cannabinus	SIde
	coccineus	MSte SOWG SSpi
	fallax	CHll
	hamabo	CWSG
	huegelii	see *Alyogyne huegelii*
	leopoldii	SPer SRms
*	*moesiana*	MBri
	moscheutos	CArn CFir MSte SMad
	– 'Galaxy'	LPVe
	– subsp. *palustris* **new**	SMad
	mutabilis	SOWG
	paramutabilis	SMad
	radiatus **new**	EShb
	rosa-sinensis	EBak LRHS MBri SOWG
	– 'All Aglow' **new**	SOWG
	– 'Bimbo' **new**	SOWG
	– 'Casablanca'	MBri
	– 'Cockatoo' **new**	SOWG
	– 'Cooperi' (v) ♀H1	CHal SOWG
	– Full Moon = 'Moonon' (d)	SOWG
	– 'Gina Marie' **new**	SOWG
	– 'Great White' **new**	SOWG
	– 'Hawaiian Sunset' **new**	SOWG
	– 'Holiday'	MBri
	– 'Jewel of India' **new**	SOWG

- 'Kardinal' MBri
- 'Kim Ellen' **new** SOWG
- 'Kinchen's Yellow' **new** SOWG
- 'Koeniger' MBri
- 'Lady Flo' **new** SOWG
- 'Molly Cummings' **new** SOWG
- 'Mrs Andreasen' **new** SOWG
- 'Norman Lee' **new** SOWG
- 'Pink Mist' **new** SOWG
- 'Sprinkle Rain' **new** SOWG
- 'Tarantella' **new** SOWG
- 'Ten Thirty Seven' **new** SOWG
- 'Thelma Bennell' SOWG
- 'Tivoli' MBri
- 'Wings Away' **new** SOWG
sabdariffa MSal
schizopetalus ♀H1 SOWG
sinosyriacus EPfP LRHS
- 'Lilac Queen' LRHS WBcn
- 'Ruby Glow' MGos WPGP
syriacus SPet WFar WLow WNor
- 'Admiral Dewey' (d) MGos SPla
- 'Aphrodite' CPMA EBee ENot MRav
- 'Ardens' (d) CEnd CSBt CWSG EBee EMui EPfP
   LRHS MGos SPer
- Blue Bird see *H. syriacus* 'Oiseau Bleu'
- 'Boule de Feu' (d) ELan
- 'Bredon Springs' ♀H4 WBcn
- 'Coelestis' SPer
- 'Diana' CDoC CDul EBee EMil ENot EPfP
   LRHS MBNS MRav SLon WBcn
- 'Dorothy Crane' CEnd EBee ENot LRHS MGos
   MRav WWes
- 'Duc de Brabant' (d) CDoC CSBt EMil EMui LRHS SHBN
   SPer WBcn
- 'Elegantissimus' see *H. syriacus* 'Lady Stanley'
- 'Hamabo' ♀H4 CBcs CDul CSBt EBee EMil ENot
   EPAt EPfP LAst LPan LRHS MBri
   MGos MRav MSwo MWat NBlu
   NLar NPri SHBN SLim SPer SPla
   SPlb SWvt WDin WFar WStI
- 'Helene' EBee ELan LRHS MBri MRav WBcn
- 'Jeanne d'Arc' (d) SLon
§ - 'Lady Stanley' (d) CSBt EBee LRHS SPer
- Lavender Chiffon EBee ENot EPfP LRHS MGos MRav
   = 'Notwoodone'PBR NPri SPer
- 'Lenny' ♀H4 EBee ENot MGos MRav
- 'Leopoldii' NBlu
- 'Marina' EMui
§ - 'Meehanii' (v) ♀H4 CDul CEnd EBee ENot EPfP LRHS
   MAsh MBri MGos SCoo SLim SPer
   SPla SPoG SSta WBcn
§ - 'Oiseau Bleu' ♀H4 More than 30 suppliers
- Pink Giant = 'Flogi' CBcs CDoC CDul CMHG EBee
   EBre ELan EPfP LPan LRHS MBri
   MGos SLon SPer WDin
- 'Purpureus Plenus' (d) SLim
- 'Purpureus Variegatus' (v) SLim
- 'Red Heart' ♀H4 CEnd CSBt ELan EPfP LAst LRHS
   MAsh MBNS MBri NBlu NLar NPri
   SPer SPla SPoG SRms SWvt WDin
   WStI
- 'Rosalbane' MBri
- 'Roseus Plenus' (d) SLim WBcn WDin
- Russian Violet = 'Floru' CEnd COtt EBee ELan EMil EPfP
   LRHS MBri MGos MRav
- 'Speciosus' EMui ENot MRav SLon SPer
- 'Stadt Erlenbach' **new** MGos
- 'Totus Albus' CSBt EMil WSHC
- 'Variegatus' see *H. syriacus* 'Purpureus
   Variegatus'
- White Chiffon EBee ENot EPfP LRHS MGos MRav
   = 'Notwoodtwo'PBR SPer
   ♀H4

- 'William R. Smith' ♀H4 CWSG EBee ELan ENot LAst LPan
   LRHS MGos MRav MSwo SHBN
   SPer SSta WDin WWes
- 'Woodbridge' ♀H4 More than 30 suppliers
trionum CSpe WKif
- 'Sunny Day' ELan

hickory, shagbark see *Carya ovata*

Hieracium (Asteraceae)
aurantiacum see *Pilosella aurantiaca*
brunneocroceum see *Pilosella aurantiaca* subsp.
   carpathicola
§ *glaucum* WEas WWin
§ *lanatum* CSpe EHol GFlt MDKP NBir WEas
   WPer WRos WWin
maculatum see *H. spilophaeum*
pannosum MESE 409 EBee
pilosella see *Pilosella officinarum*
praecox see *H. glaucum*
§ *spilophaeum* CRow ECoo EGra EHoe EMar
   GGar GKir LRHS MWod NBid
   NGHP NPer NWCA SIng WMoo
   WPer WRos
- 'Leopard' (v) EFWa EMan MSPs NJOw SCro
   SGar
umbellatum WOut
villosum CSpe EBee EHoe LRHS MDun
   NBro NPri WCot WHer WOut
   WPer WRos WWin
waldsteinii MBro MDKP
welwitschii see *H. lanatum*

Hierochloe (Poaceae)
occidentalis CBig
odorata CBig CPen ELau EMan EMon EPPr
   GPoy LPVe MGol SSvw WPnP WSSM
redolens GAbr GOrn

Himalayacalamus (Poaceae)
asper CFil EPla ERod WPGP
§ *falconeri* CBrm CFil EBee EFul EPfP EPla
   MAsh MMoz SDix SDys WPGP
§ - 'Damarapa' CFil EPla MMoz SDix WDyG WJun
   WPGP
§ *hookerianus* CAbb CFil WJun
§ *porcatus* CFil

Hippeastrum ✿ (Amaryllidaceae)
x *acramannii* GCal WCot
advenum see *Rhodophiala advena*
'Apple Blossom' LAma MBri NRog
'Beautiful Lady' LAma
'Bestseller' ♀H1 LAma
bifidum see *Rhodophiala bifida*
'Christmas Gift' LRHS
'Dutch Belle' LAma
elwesii SBla
'Fairy Tale' MBri
'Fantastica' LAma
'Hercules' **new** MBri
'Inca' LAma
'Jewel' (d) LRHS MBri
'Lady Jane' MBri
'Lemon Lime' LAma LRHS
'Lima' LAma
'Ludwig's Goliath' LAma
'Mary Lou' (d) LAma
papilio ♀H1 LAma
* - 'Butterfly' LRHS
'Papillon' LAma
'Pasadena' LRHS
'Picotee' LAma LRHS
* 'San Antonio Rose' **new** WCot

striatum **new**	WPGP
'Toughie' **new**	EMan WCot
'White Dazzler'	LAma
'Yellow Pioneer'	LAma

Hippocrepis (*Papilionaceae*)

§	*comosa*	CRWN SSpi XPep
§	*emerus*	CBcs CMHG CTri ELan EPfP ERea
		GEil LAst LHop MGos MMil STre
		WHCG WSHC XPep

Hippolytia (*Asteraceae*)

§	*herderi*	EMan SMrm WCot

Hippophae (*Elaeagnaceae*)

rhamnoides ♀H4		CArn CBcs CCVT CDul CLnd
		CRWN CSBt EBee ELan ENot EPfP
		GIBF GKir GPoy LBuc MBar MBlu
		MCoo MRav MWat NWea SPer
		SPlb WDin WFar WHCG WMou
		WStI XPep
- 'Askola' (f)		MGos
- 'Hergo' (f)		EWTr
- 'Leikora' (f)		ELan ESim MBlu MGos SPer
- 'Pollmix' (m)		ELan ESim EWTr MBlu MGos SPer
salicifolia		LEdu

Hippuris (*Hippuridaceae*)

vulgaris	CBen EHon EMFW IHMH NArg
	NPer WFar WMAq WWpP

Hirpicium (*Asteraceae*)

armerioides	NWCA

Histiopteris (*Dennstaedtiaceae*)

incisa	CFil

Hoheria ✿ (*Malvaceae*)

§	*angustifolia*	CFil CTho ECou
	'Borde Hill'	CPMA EPfP SSpi SSta WHCG
	glabrata	CBcs CFil ECou EPfP GGar IMGH
		NPal WPGP
	- 'Silver Stars'	EPfP
	'Glory of Amlwch' ♀H3	CFil CPMA CSam EPfP GCal LRHS
		SMad SSpi WCru WKif WPGP
	'Hill House'	CHll
§	*lyallii* ♀H4	CBcs CDoC CDul CPLG ECou
		ELan EPfP IDee NPSI SHBN SPer
		SSpi SSta WDin
	microphylla	see *H. angustifolia*
	populnea	CBcs CBot CPle
	- 'Alba Variegata' (v)	CDoC CTrC SMad
	sexstylosa	CAbb CBot CDoC CDul CHEx
		CHid CMHG CTri ELan EPfP IMGH
		ISea LAst MDun SLon SPer SSta
		SWvt WGer
	- 'Pendula'	CBcs WDin
	- 'Stardust' ♀H4	CAbP CDul CFil CMCN CPLG
		CPMA ELan EPfP LRHS MAsh MBri
		MGos NLar NPal SKee SMad SMur
		SPer SPoG SReu SSpi WFar WPGP
		WPat WSHC WSpi
*	- 'Starshine'	ERea

Holboellia (*Lardizabalaceae*)

coriacea	CBcs CBot CHEx CHll CRHN CRez
	CSam EBee EPfP LRHS MDun
	MGos SAPC SArc SBra SOWG SSta
	WCFE WCot WCru
fargesii DJHC 506	WCru
aff. *grandiflora*	WCru
B&SWJ 8223 **new**	
latifolia	CHEx COtt CRHN CSBt CSam
	CTrG CTri EBee EPfP ERea LRHS

	MTPN SAPC SArc SBra SEND SLim
	SOWG SPer WFar
- SF 95134	ISea

Holcus (*Poaceae*)

mollis 'Albovariegatus' (v)	More than 30 suppliers
- 'White Fog' (v)	CChe CPen EBee EHul MBlu MBri
	NHol WFar WLeb

Holodiscus (*Rosaceae*)

discolor	CAgr CDul CFil CPLG CPle EBee
	ELan EWes GKir LRHS MBlu MBri
	MBro MTis NBlu NSti SHBN SLon
	SMad SPer SSpi SSta WBVN WDin
	WHCG WPat
- NJM 94044	WPGP
- var. *ariifolius*	EPfP WPGP
- var. *discolor*	CBcs
dumosus	WPat

Homalocladium (*Polygonaceae*)

§	*platycladum*	CHal CPle LEdu

Homeria (*Iridaceae*)

	breyniana	see *H. collina*
	- var. *aurantiaca*	see *H. flaccida*
§	*collina*	CPLG EMui ERos
§	*flaccida*	LAma NRog
	ochroleuca	LAma NRog

Homoglossum see *Gladiolus*

Homoranthus (*Myrtaceae*)

flavescens	SOWG

Honckenya (*Caryophyllaceae*)

peploides	MLwd

Hordeum (*Poaceae*)

brachyantherum	CBig
chilense	EBee EPPr
jubatum	CBig CBri CKno CSpe CWCL
	EChP EGoo EHoe EPla EPza EUJe
	EWes EWsh LHop LIck LRHS
	MAvo MFan NChi NDov NGdn
	NHol NPPs NSti SIng SUsu WRos
	WWeb WWye

Horkelia (*Rosaceae*)

fusca subsp. *capitata*	EBee

Horkeliella (*Rosaceae*)

purpurascens	WCot
NNS 98-323 **new**	

Horminum (*Lamiaceae*)

pyrenaicum	CMHG CPlt EBee ELan EMan GAbr
	MAvo MBro NGar NJOw SBla
	SRms WBVN WBea WCom WFar
	WGMN WMoo WPer WTin WWin
- pale blue	MAvo MDKP MSte

horseradish see *Armoracia rusticana*

Hosta ✿ (*Hostaceae*)

AGSJ 302	CDes
'Abba Dabba Do' (v)	CBdn EBee EGol EMic EPGN LRHS
	NMyG
'Abby' (v)	CBdn EGol EMic EPGN
'Abiqua Ariel'	CBdn EMic
'Abiqua Blue Crinkles'	CBdn EMic NBir
'Abiqua Drinking Gourd'	CBdn EBee EFou EGol EMic EOMN
	EOrc EPGN GKir GSki LRHS
	MHom NMyG

'Abiqua Ground Cover' EGol
'Abiqua Moonbeam' (v) CBdn CRez CWin EBee EMic
EPGN IBal MSwo NMyG
'Abiqua Recluse' EGol LRHS
'Abiqua Trumpet' CBdn EGol IBal NMyG
'Abiqua Zodiac' CBdn
aequinoctiiantha EGol
albomarginata see H. 'Paxton's Original'
(*sieboldii*)
§ 'Albomarginata' CBcs CBdn CBri CHar EBee EGol
(*fortunei*) (v) EMic EPGN GKir MBar MNrw NBir
NMyG SHBN SPer SWvt
'Alex Summers' **new** IBal
'Allan P. McConnell' (v) CBdn EGol EMic EPGN LBuc
'Allegan Fog' (v) **new** EGol IBal
'Alligator Shoes' (v) **new** EGol
'Alpine Aire' EMic
'Alvatine Taylor' (v) CBdn EBee EGol
'Amanuma' EGol EMic MHom
'Amber Maiden' (v) EGol
'Amber Tiara' EMic
'American Dream' (v) CBdn EGol EMic EPGN IBal
'Amy Elizabeth' (v) CBdn EGol EMic
'Angel Feathers' (v) EGol
'Ann Kulpa' (v) **new** CBdn EMic EPGN
'Anne' (v) CBdn EBee EGol IBal
'Anne Arett' (*sieboldii*) (v) EPGN
'Antioch' (*fortunei*) (v) CBdn EBee EGol EMic GAbr IBal
IHMH MIDC MRav MSte NMyG
WFar
'Aoki' (*fortunei*) EMic EPGN NHol
'Aphrodite' CFir CWin EBee EGol EMic EPGN
(*plantaginea*) (d) IBal MBNS MBri MHom MSte NLar
WCot
'Apple Green' EMic
'Aqua Velva' EGol LRHS
'Archangel' EGol
'Argentea Variegata' see H. *undulata* var. *undulata*
(*undulata*)
'Aristocrat' (Tardiana CBdn EGol EPGN IBal
Group) (v)
'August Beauty' CBdn EMic
'August Moon' More than 30 suppliers
aureafolia see H. 'Starker Yellow Leaf'
'Aureoalba' (*fortunei*) see H. 'Spinners'
'Aureomaculata' (*fortunei*) see H. *fortunei* var. *albopicta*
* 'Aureomarginata' CPrp CSBt EGra GAbr GKir LPVe
ambig. (v)
§ 'Aureomarginata' CBdn CBos CBri CSBt EBre EGol
(*montana*) (v) EHoe EMic EPGN EWsh GCal IBal
MBri NHol NLar NMyG SCro SPla
SSpi SUsu WBVN WTin
§ 'Aureomarginata' CBdn CBro EBre ECha EGol EMic
(*ventricosa*) (v) ♀H4 EPfP IBal LRHS MBri MIDC NGdn
NVic WBVN WTin WWye
'Aureostriata' (*tardiva*) see H. 'Inaho'
'Aurora Borealis' EGol EPGN
(*sieboldiana*) (v)
'Austin Dickinson' (v) EGol EMic IBal
'Azure Snow' CBdn EGol LRHS WBcn
'Babbling Brook' EGol
'Baby Bunting' CBdn EGol EMic EPGN MBNS
MIDC NBro NMyG NPro
'Ballerina' EGol
'Banana Boat' (v) **new** EGol IBal
'Banyai's Dancing Girl' EGol EMic
'Barbara Ann' (v) CBdn EMic EPGN MBri NMyG
'Barbara White' EGol
'Beauty Substance' CBdn EBee EGle EGol EMic EPGN
NMyG
bella see H. *fortunei* var. *obscura*
'Bennie McRae' EGol
'Betcher's Blue' EGol
'Betsy King' EBee EGol MRav NHol NMyG

'Bette Davis Eyes' EGol
'Betty' EGol EPGN
'Big Boy' (*montana*) EGol GKir
'Big Daddy' (*sieboldiana* More than 30 suppliers
hybrid) (v)
'Big Mama' EBee EGol EPGN EUJe LRHS MBNS
NLar
'Bigfoot' EGol
'Bill Brinka' (v) EGol
'Birchwood Blue' EGol
'Birchwood Elegance' CBdn
§ 'Birchwood Parky's Gold' CBdn CMHG EGol EMic EPGN
EPfP EWTr GKir IHMH LPVe LRHS
MBNS MIDC MTed NHol NOak
SHBN SMrm SSpi WShp WWeb
'Birchwood Ruffled EGol EMic
Queen'
'Bitsy Gold' EGol
'Bitsy Green' EGol
'Black Beauty' EGol EPGN
'Black Hills' CBdn EGol EPGN LRHS NMyG
WMul
'Blaue Venus' EGol
§ 'Blonde Elf' EGol EMic EOMN EPGN IBal
NGdn NMyG WShp
'Blue Angel' misapplied see H. *sieboldiana* var. *elegans*
'Blue Angel' More than 30 suppliers
(*sieboldiana*) ♀H4
'Blue Arrow' CBdn EGol EPGN
'Blue Belle' (Tardiana CBdn EBee EGol EMic EPGN MBro
Group) MSte NGdn NLar NPro WHoo
WTin
'Blue Blazes' LRHS
'Blue Blush' (Tardiana CBdn EGol EPGN WTMC
Group)
'Blue Boy' CBdn EBee EGol EMic EPGN EWes
NHol NMyG
'Blue Cadet' CBcs CBdn EBee EGol EMic GEdr
GKir GSki IHMH LAst LPBA LPVe
MBar NBee NBir NLar NMyG
NOak SBod WCAu WCra WFar
WMnd WShp WStl WWeb WWpP
'Blue Cup' (*sieboldiana*) CBdn ENot MRav
'Blue Danube' (Tardiana CBdn EGol EMic MHom
Group)
'Blue Diamond' (Tardiana CBdn CMHG CWin EBee EGol
Group) EMic EPGN WFar
'Blue Dimples' (Tardiana CBdn CWin EGol IPot LRHS MBNS
Group)
'Blue Edger' CBdn NBir
'Blue Heart' (*sieboldiana*) ECha EMic LPio
'Blue Ice' (Tardiana CBdn EGol
Group)
'Blue Impression' EMic
'Blue Jay' (Tardiana CBdn EGol
Group)
'Blue Lady' CBdn EMic
'Blue Mammoth' CBdn EBee EGol EMic EPGN LRHS
(*sieboldiana*)
'Blue Moon' (Tardiana CBdn EBee EFou EGol EOMN
Group) EOrc EPGN EPfP ERos IPot LPBA
LPhx MBNS MHom MIDC NHol
NMyG
'Blue Seer' (*sieboldiana*) CBdn
'Blue Shadows' CBdn CWin EBee EPGN IBal LPio
(*tokudama*) (v) LRHS MIDC NMyG SHBN WMul
'Blue Skies' (Tardiana CBdn EGol EPGN MHom
Group)
§ 'Blue Umbrellas' CBdn EBee EGol EHan ELan EMic
(*sieboldiana* hybrid) EOrc EPGN EPfP GSki IPot LRHS
MBri MHom MIDC NGdn NHol
NLar NMyG WMul
'Blue Velvet' CBdn
'Blue Vision' EPGN LRHS

'Blue Wedgwood' (Tardiana Group) — CBdn CBro CPrp CRow EBee EGol ELan EMic EOrc GKir IBal LAst LPBA MIDC NHol NMyG SChu SPla WCFE WHil WTMC WWpP

'Bold Edger' (v) — CBdn EGol EPGN
'Bold Ribbons' (v) — CBdn EGol EMic GAbr WTin
'Bold Ruffles' (*sieboldiana*) — EGol LRHS
'Bonanza' — EMic
'Border Bandit' (v) — EGol
'Borsch 1' — CBdn
'Borwick Beauty' (*sieboldiana*) (v) — CBdn EMic NGdn NLar NMyG
'Bountiful' — EGol EMic
'Bouquet' — EGol
'Bressingham Blue' — CBdn CHVG CPrp CWin EBee EBre ECtt EGol LPVe LRHS MIDC MRav NMyG SWvt WCAu WFar WMnd WTMC WWpP
'Brigadier' — EGol
'Bright Glow' (Tardiana Group) — EGol
'Bright Lights' (*tokudama*) (v) — CBdn CRez CWin EGol EMic EPGN GBBs IBal LAst NMyG WTMC
'Brim Cup' (v) — CBdn CWin EBee EGol EMic EPGN GKir IBal MBNS MBri MIDC NBro NGdn NOrc
'Brooke' — EGol EMic EPGN NMyG
'Brother Ronald' (Tardiana Group) — CBdn EGol EMic LRHS
'Bruce's Blue' — EGol GSki
'Buckshaw Blue' — CBdn EFou EGol EPGN ETow MDKP NBir NGdn NPro SSpi WBcn WTMC
'Butter Rim' (*sieboldii*) (v) — EGol
'Cadillac' (v) — CBdn MIDC
I 'Calypso' (v) — CBdn EGol EMic EPGN
'Camelot' (Tardiana Group) — CBdn EGol EMic LRHS NGdn
'Canadian Blue' — EBee EFou WTMC
'Candy Hearts' — CBdn CMHG CSam EGle EGol EMic EPGN MHom WTin
capitata B&SWJ 588 — WCru
 - MSF 850 — CFil
caput-avis — see *H. kikutii* var. *caput-avis*
'Carnival' (v) — CBdn EBee EGol EMic EPGN IBal MIDC
'Carol' (*fortunei*) (v) — CBdn CLAP CWin EBee EGol EMic EWsh IBal LAst MSte NMyG WHal
'Carousel' (v) — EGol
'Carrie Ann' (v) — see *H.* 'Carrie'
§ 'Carrie' (*sieboldii*) (v) — EGol
'Cascades' (v) — CBdn EGol EMic
'Celebration' (v) — EBre EGol ELan EMic EPGN LRHS MDKP
'Challenger' — EMic
'Change of Tradition' (*lancifolia*) (v) — CBdn EMic
'Chantilly Lace' (v) — CBdn EGol EMic EPGN IBal WTin
'Chartreuse Waves' — EGol
'Chartreuse Wiggles' (*sieboldii*) — EPGN LRHS
'Cheatin Heart' — EGol
'Chelsea Babe' (*fortunei*) (v) — EGol
'Chelsea Ore' (*plantaginea* hybrid) (v) — CHad
'Cherry Berry' (v) — CBdn CMHG CPen CRez CWin EBee EGol EMic EPGN IBal MBNS MCLN MIDC NBro NGdn NMyG NPro SVil WBor
'Cherub' (v) — EGol
* 'China' (*plantaginea*) — EMic

'Chinese Sunrise' (v) — CBdn EBee EChP EGol EMic EOrc EPGN IPot MBNS MHom NHol NMyG SCro
'Chiquita' — EGol
§ 'Chôkô Nishiki' (*montana*) (v) — CBdn CFir EGle EGol EMic EPGN IBal IPot MIDC NABC NGdn NMyG SChu
'Christmas Tree' (v) — CBdn CM&M CWin EBee EGle EGol EMic EPGN GBri IPot LRHS MIDC NBPC NGdn NMyG SVil WTMC
'Citation' (v) — EGol LRHS
'City Lights' — EGol
clausa var. *normalis* — CBdn EBee EGol GQui LRHS NBir NGdn NLar NMyG
'Collectors Choice' — EGol
'Color Glory' (v) — CWin EBee EChP EGle EGol EPGN GAbr GBin IBal LAst NGdn NLar NMyG WBcn WTMC
'Colossal' — EGol EMic
'Columbus Circle' (v) — CBdn EGol
'Coquette' (v) — CBdn EGol EMic
'Cotillion' (v) — CBdn EGol
'County Park' — CBdn EGol EMic
'Craig's Temptation' — CBdn
'Cream Cheese' (v) — EGol
'Cream Delight' (*undulata*) — see *H. undulata* var. *undulata*
'Cream Edge' — see *H.* 'Fisher Cream Edge'
'Crepe Suzette' (v) — CBdn EGol EPGN LRHS
'Crested Reef' — CBdn EGol EMic NMyG
'Crested Surf' (v) — EGol EMic
§ *crispula* (v) ♀H4 — CBdn CHad CRow EFou EGol EHon EMic EPGN EPar GMac LGro MBar MHom NChi NMyG SChu SHBN WWpP
'Crown Jewel' (v) — EPGN
'Crown Prince' (v) — CBdn EGol EPGN
§ 'Crowned Imperial' (*fortunei*) (v) — CBdn EMic NHol
'Crusader' (v) — CBdn EBee EGol EMic EPGN LRHS NMyG
'Cupid's Dart' (v) — EGol
'Curlew' (Tardiana Group) — CBdn EGol
'Dark Star' (v) — CBdn EGol EPGN
'Dartmoor Forest' — CBdn
'Darwin's Standard' (v) — CBdn
'Dawn' — CBdn EGol EPar
'Daybreak' — CBdn CWin EBee EGol EMic EPGN LAst LRHS MBri NBro SVil WTMC WWye
'Day's End' (v) — EGol
decorata — CBdn EGol EMic EMil MBar MLwd
'Delia' (v) — EPGN
'Delta Dawn' **new** — IBal
'Devon Blue' (Tardiana Group) — CBdn CPrp EGol
'Devon Desire' (*montana*) — CBdn
'Devon Discovery' — CBdn
'Devon Giant' — CBdn
'Devon Gold' — CBdn
'Devon Green' — CBdn CLAP EBee EHan EPGN GBri IBal IPot MIDC MLLN MSte NBro NGdn NLar NMyG NPPs NPro WAul WFar
'Devon Hills' — CBdn
'Devon Mist' — CBdn LPVe
'Devon Tor' — CBdn EPGN
'Dew Drop' (v) — CBdn EGol EMic NMyG
'Diamond Tiara' (v) — CBdn EGol EMic EPGN GAbr IBal LAst LRHS MIDC NMyG SChu
'Diana Remembered' **new** — CBdn EMic
'Dick Ward' **new** — IBal
'Domaine de Courson' — CBdn EMic GBin WFar
'Don Stevens' (v) — CBdn EGol

'Donahue Piecrust'	CBdn EGol
'Dorset Blue' (Tardiana Group)	CBdn EGol EPGN GSki LRHS
'Dorset Charm' (Tardiana Group)	CBdn EGol
'Dorset Flair' (Tardiana Group)	EGol EMic
'Doubloons'	EGol
'Dream Weaver' (v) **new**	EGol EMic IBal
'Drummer Boy'	CBdn EGol EMic
'Duchess' (*nakaiana*) (v)	EGol
'DuPage Delight' (*sieboldiana*) (v)	CBdn EGol NLar
'Dust Devil' (*fortunei*) (v)	EGol IBal
'Edge of Night'	CBdn EGol
'Edwin Bibby' **new**	EPGN
'El Capitan' (v)	CBdn EGol EMic EPGN LRHS
'El Niño' (Tardiana Group) (v) **new**	CWin IBal MIDC NBro
§ *elata*	EBee EGol EGra EMic
'Elatior' (*nigrescens*)	CBdn EMic
'Eldorado'	see *H.* 'Frances Williams'
'Eleanor Lachman' (v) **new**	EGol IBal
'Electrum Stater' (v)	CBdn
'Elegans'	see *H. sieboldiana* var. *elegans*
'Elfin Power' (*sieboldii*) (v)	EGol
'Elisabeth'	CBdn EBee LBuc NMyG
'Elizabeth Campbell' (*fortunei*) (v)	CBdn CLAP EBee EGol EMic MSte SSpi
'Ellen'	EMic
'Ellerbroek' (*fortunei*) (v)	EMic EMic GSki
'Elsley Runner'	EGol
'Elvis Lives'	CBdn EGol IBal IPot LAst LRHS MCCP NGdn NMyG NPPs NPro WShp
'Emerald Carpet'	EGol
'Emerald Necklace' (v)	EGol
'Emerald Skies'	EGol
'Emerald Tiara' (v)	CBdn EGol EMic EPGN LRHS MIDC NMyG SVil WTin
'Emeralds and Rubies'	EGol
'Emily Dickinson' (v)	CBdn EBee EGol IBal LRHS
'Eric Smith' (Tardiana Group)	CBdn EGol EMic EPGN LPhx MHom NMyG SChu WFar
'Evelyn McCafferty' (*tokudama* hybrid)	EGol
'Evening Magic' (v)	EGol EPGN
'Eventide' (v) **new**	EGol
'Everlasting Love' (v)	EGol
'Excitation'	CBdn EGol LPio
'Fair Maiden' (v)	CBdn EGol EPGN
'Fall Bouquet' (*longipes* var. *hypoglauca*)	EGol
'Fall Emerald'	CBdn EMic
'Falling Waters' (v) **new**	EGol IBal
'Fan Dance' (v)	EGol
'Fantastic' (*sieboldiana* hybrid)	EGol LRHS
'Fascination' (v) **new**	EPGN
'Feather Boa'	EGol EPGN
'Fenman's Fascination'	EMic
'Fire and Ice' (v)	More than 30 suppliers
§ 'Fisher Cream Edge' (*fortunei*) (v)	CBdn
'Flame Stitch' (*ventricosa*) (v)	EGol
'Floradora'	CBdn EGol EMic EPGN IBal NMyG
'Flower Power'	CBdn EGol
fluctuans	GBBs GIBF
'Fond Hope'	CBdn
'Fool's Gold' (*fortunei*)	CBdn EMic
'Forest Shadows' **new**	IBal
'Formal Attire' (*sieboldiana* hybrid) (v)	CBdn EGol EMic IBal LRHS

'Forncett Frances' (v)	EGol
'Fortis'	see *H. undulata* var. *erromena*
fortunei	CBdn CM&M CRow EGol EMic IBal MIDC NHol SChu SPer WCAu WEas WFar WPnP WWye
§ - var. *albopicta* ♀H4	More than 30 suppliers
- - f. *aurea* ♀H4	CBdn CHad CMHG CRow EBee ECha EFou EGol EHoe ELan EPla GKir LRHS MBar NLar NMyG SChu SCro SPer SPla SRms WFar
- - - dwarf	EMic
§ - var. *aureomarginata* ♀H4	More than 30 suppliers
- var. *gigantea*	see *H. montana*
§ - var. *hyacinthina* ♀H4	CBdn EBee EGol EMic EOrc EPfP GCal LRHS MBar MRav NMyG NOrc SSpi WFar WMyn WWeb WWin
- - variegated	see *H.* 'Crowned Imperial' (*fortunei*)
§ - var. *obscura*	CBdn EBee ECho EGol EMic WLin
- var. *rugosa*	EMic
'Fountain'	NHol
'Fourth of July'	EGol
'Fragrant Blue'	CBdn EBee EGol EMic EOMN GBBs LRHS MFan NMyG WRHF
'Fragrant Bouquet' (v)	CBdn CMHG CWin EBee EFou EGol EMic EPGN IBal LRHS NGdn NHol NLar NMyG SChu SVil
'Fragrant Dream'	CBdn EMic
'Fragrant Gold'	EGol
'Francee' (*fortunei*) (v) ♀H4	More than 30 suppliers
'Frances Williams Improved' (*sieboldiana*) (v)	EGol EPfP MWat WShp
'Frances Williams' seedlings	NSti
§ 'Frances Williams' (*sieboldiana*) (v) ♀H4	More than 30 suppliers
'Freising' (*fortunei*)	EBee
'Fresh' (v)	EGol EPGN
'Fried Bananas'	CBdn EGol EMic
'Fried Green Tomatoes'	CBdn EBee EGol EMic EPGN LRHS MIDC NLar NMyG NOrc
'Fringe Benefit' (v)	CWin EBee EGol EMic GAbr GKir
'Frosted Jade' (v)	CBdn EBee EGol EPGN LRHS NMyG WTin
'Fulda'	EGol
'Gaiety' (v)	EGol EPGN
'Gaijin' (v)	CBdn
'Gala' (*tardiflora*) (v)	CBdn EPGN NMyG
'Gay Blade' (v)	EGol
'Gay Feather' (v)	EBee LAst NMyG SPoG
'Gay Search' (v)	EPGN
'Geisha' (v)	CBdn EGol EPGN GBin IBal MBNS MCCP NMyG NPro WBcn
'Gene's Joy'	EPGN
'Gigantea' (*sieboldiana*)	see *H. elata*
'Gilt Edge' (*sieboldiana*) (v)	EMic NMyG
'Ginko Craig' (v)	More than 30 suppliers
glauca	see *H. sieboldiana* var. *elegans*
'Glockenspiel'	CBdn EGol
I 'Gloriosa' (*fortunei*) (v)	EGol
'Glory'	CBdn EGol
'Goddess of Athena' (*decorata*) (v)	EGol
'Gold Drop' (*venusta* hybrid)	CBdn EBee ECho EGol EMic EOrc LPhx LRHS NHol
'Gold Edger'	More than 30 suppliers
§ 'Gold Haze' (*fortunei*)	CBdn EGol EMic EOrc EPGN MHom NBir NCGa NHol NMyG
'Gold High Fat Cream'	EPGN
'Gold Leaf' (*fortunei*)	EGol

'Gold Regal'	CBdn CWin EBee EGol EMic EPGN MHom MSte NMyG SMrm WMnd
'Gold Rush'PBR	CBdn EPGN
* 'Gold Splash'	MBro WHoo
'Gold Standard' (*fortunei*) (v)	More than 30 suppliers
'Goldbrook' (v)	EGol WBcn WTin
'Goldbrook Genie'	EGol
'Goldbrook Ghost' (v) **new**	EGol
'Goldbrook Girl'	EGol
'Goldbrook Glamour' (v)	EGol
'Goldbrook Glimmer' (Tardiana Group) (v)	EGol
'Goldbrook Gold'	EGol
'Goldbrook Grace'	EGol
'Goldbrook Gratis' (v)	EGol
'Goldbrook Grayling'	EGol
'Goldbrook Grebe'	EGol
'Golden Age'	see *H.* 'Gold Haze'
'Golden Anniversary'	CBdn EBee NHol WTMC
'Golden Ben'	ITim
'Golden Bullion' (*tokudama*)	CBdn EGol EPGN GBri LRHS
'Golden Decade'	EGol
'Golden Fascination'	EGol
'Golden Friendship' **new**	EGol
'Golden Guernsey' (v)	EMic
'Golden Isle'	EGol
'Golden Jubilee' **new**	EPGN
'Golden Medallion' (*tokudama*)	CBdn CMHG EBee EGol ELan EOrc GKir IBal MBNS NGdn NHol NMyG WFar
'Golden Nakaiana'	see *H.* 'Birchwood Parky's Gold'
'Golden' (*nakaiana*)	see *H.* 'Birchwood Parky's Gold'
'Golden Oriole'	CBdn
'Golden Prayers'	CBdn EGle EGol EHan ELan ENot EPGN ERos GSki LPhx LRHS MIDC MRav NBir NBro NGdn NHol NMyG NOrc SChu SPer SPla
'Golden Scepter'	CBdn CMHG EGol EMic EPGN NHol NMyG WFar
'Golden Sculpture' (*sieboldiana*)	CBdn EGol LRHS
'Golden Spider'	EGol EMic
'Golden Sunburst' (*sieboldiana*)	CBdn CPrp EBee EGol EGra ELan EMic GSki IBal NBid NGdn NHol SMrm WFar
'Golden Tiara' (v) ♀H4	More than 30 suppliers
'Golden Waffles'	CMHG EBee
'Goldpfeil'	EMic
'Goldsmith'	EGol
'Good as Gold'	EMic EPGN NMyG
'Gosan' (*takahashii*)	EGol
gracillima	CRow EPGN EPar NRya
'Granary Gold' (*fortunei*)	CBdn EGol EPGN LRHS NABC SChu
'Grand Master'	EGol EPGN IBal MDKP
'Grand Tiara' (v)	CBdn EGol EPGN NMyG
'Gray Cole' (*sieboldiana*)	CBdn EGol EMic EPGN
'Great Expectations' (*sieboldiana*) (v)	More than 30 suppliers
'Green Acres' (*montana*)	EGle EPGN LPhx MSte SChu WFar
'Green Angel' (*sieboldiana*)	EGol
'Green Eyes' (*sieboldii*) (v)	EGol
'Green Fountain' (*kikutii*)	CBdn EFou EGol EMic EPGN LRHS MIDC MSte
'Green Gold' (*fortunei*) (v)	CBdn EBee EMic
'Green Piecrust'	CBdn EGol EPGN LRHS
'Green Ripples'	CHid
'Green Sheen'	EGol EPGN NMyG
'Green Summer Fragrance'	CBdn
'Green Velveteen'	CBdn EGol
'Green with Envy' (v)	CBdn EGol
'Grey Piecrust'	EGol

'Ground Master' (v)	CBdn CMHG COIW COtt ECha ECtt EGol ELan EOrc EPGN EPfP GSki IBal LPBA LRHS MBri MRav MSwo NBro NHol NMyG NSti SPer WFar WShp WWeb
'Ground Sulphur'	EGol EPGN
'Guacamole' (v)	CBdn EBee EGle EGol EMic EPGN IBal IPot MIDC NLar NMyG SUsu SVil WTin
'Guardian Angel' (*sieboldiana*)	CBdn EBee EGol EPGN IBal WMul
'Gum Drop'	CBdn EMic EPGN
'Gun Metal Blue'	EGol
'Hadspen Blue' (Tardiana Group)	More than 30 suppliers
'Hadspen Hawk' (Tardiana Group)	EGol LPhx NMyG
'Hadspen Heron' (Tardiana Group)	CBdn EGol MHom NMyG SChu
I 'Hadspen Nymphaea'	EGol
'Hadspen Rainbow'	CBdn IBal
I 'Hadspen Samphire'	EGol EMic EPGN LRHS MHom NBir
'Hadspen White' (*fortunei*)	EBee EGol EMic
'Haku-chu-han' (*sieboldii*) (v)	CBdn
'Hakujima' (*sieboldii*)	EGol LPhx
§ 'Halcyon' (Tardiana Group) ♀H4	More than 30 suppliers
'Halo' **new**	EGol
'Happiness' (Tardiana Group)	CBdn CWin EGol EHoe EMic MHom MRav NMyG
'Happy Hearts'	EGol EMic
'Harmony' (Tardiana Group)	CBdn EGol EMic
'Harvest Glow'	EGol
'Harvest Moon'	GKir
'Heart Ache'	EGol
'Heart and Soul' (v) **new**	EGol
'Heartleaf'	EMic
'Heart's Content' (v)	CBdn EGol
'Heartsong' (v)	EGol EPGN NMyG
'Helen Doriot' (*sieboldiana*)	EGol EMic
helonioides hort. f. *albopicta*	see *H. rohdeifolia*
'Herifu' (v)	CBdn EGol
'Hidden Cove' (v) **new**	EGol
'Hilda Wassman' (v)	EGol
'Hirao Majesty'	CBdn EGol
'Hirao Splendor'	EGol NMyG
'Hirao Supreme'	CBdn EGol
'Hirao Tetra'	CBdn
'Holstein'	see *H.* 'Halcyon'
'Honey Moon'	CBdn EGol
§ 'Honeybells' ♀H4	More than 30 suppliers
'Honeysong' (v)	CBdn EMic EPGN
'Hoosier Harmony' (v)	CBdn EGol EMic LRHS
'Hoosier Homecoming'	CBdn
'Hope' (v)	EGol
§ 'Hyacintha Variegata' (*fortunei*) (v)	CMHG GBri IHMH LPVe WShp
'Hydon Gleam'	EMic EPGN
'Hydon Sunset' (*nakaiana*)	CBdn CM&M CMHG EBre EGol EMic EOrc EPGN GKir LHyd MIDC NHol NMyG NOak NSti WMnd WTin
hypoleuca	EGol WLin
'Ice Cream' (*cathayana*) (v)	EGol
'Ilona' (v)	EGol
§ 'Inaho'	CBdn EGol EPGN
'Inca Gold'	EGol
'Independence Day' (v) **new**	EPGN

'Inniswood' (v) — CBdn CLAP CWin EBee EFou EGle EGol EPGN IBal IPot LRHS MBNS NGdn NMyG NSti WMnd WPnP

'Invincible' — CBdn CLAP EBee EFou EGle EGol EMic EPGN IBal LPhx LRHS MBNS MIDC NLar NMyG SVil WLow WTin WWye

'Iona' (*fortunei*) — CBdn EBee EGol EMic EPGN NMyG SSpi

'Irische see' (Tardiana Group) — EGol

'Iron Gate Delight' (v) — CBdn

'Iron Gate Glamour' (v) — EGol WBcn

'Iron Gate Special' (v) — EMic

'Island Charm' (v) — CBdn EGol EMic EPGN IBal

'Iwa Soules' — EGol

'Jade Beauty' — CBdn

'Jade Cascade' — CBdn CLAP EBee EFou EGol ELan EMic LRHS MSte NBir NHol NLar NMyG SMrm WCot WLin WOVN

'Jade Scepter' — EGol EMic

'Jadette' (v) — EGol EPGN SChu

'Janet' (*fortunei*) (v) — CBdn CMil EBee EGol EOrc LRHS NGdn NHol NMyG WBar

'Japan Girl' — see *H.* 'Mount Royal'

'Jimmy Crack Corn' — EGol

'Joker' (*fortunei*) (v) — CBdn EBee GKir

'Jolly Green Giant' — EMic

'Joseph' **new** — EGol

'Journeyman' — EGol EMic LRHS

'Julia' (*fortunei*) (v) — EGol EMic IBal

'Julie Morss' — CBdn CWin EBee EGol EMic EPGN MHom WWpP

'Jumbo' (*sieboldiana* hybrid) — EMic

'June' (Tardiana Group) [PBR] (v) — CBdn EBee EBre EGol EHan EMic ENot EPGN EPfP GAbr GBin GBuc GSki IBal MCLN MIDC MRav NCGa NGdn NMyG SHBN SMrm SPer SUsu WAul WCAu WShp WTMC WWeb WWye

'Just So' (v) — CBdn EGol EMic EPGN IBal LRHS

'Kabitan' — see *H. sieboldii* var. *sieboldii* f. *kabitan*

'Karin' [PBR] — CBdn EBee EMic

'Katherine Lewis' (Tardiana Group) (v) — CBdn

'Kelsey' — EGol EMic

'Kifukurin' (*kikutii*) — see 'Kifukurin Hyuga'

'Kifukurin Hyuga' (v) — CBdn

'Kifukurin Ko Mame' (*gracillima*) (v) — CBdn

I 'Kifukurin' (*pulchella*) (v) — CBdn EGol EMic

'Kifukurin Ubatake' (*pulchella*) — CBdn EPGN

§ *kikutii* — EGol EMic EOrc WTin
§ - var. *caput-avis* — EGol EMic
- var. *polyneuron* — CLAP EGol
- var. *tosana* — EGol
§ - var. *yakusimensis* — CBdn EGol EMic ETow SMad

'Kingfisher' (Tardiana Group) — EGol

§ 'Kirishima' — CBdn EPGN

'Kiwi Black Magic' **new** — SSpi

'Kiwi Cream Edge' (v) — EMic

'Kiwi Spearmint' **new** — IBal

'Kiwi Treasure Trove' **new** — IBal

kiyosumiensis — NHol

'Klopping Variegated' (v) — EGol

'Knave's Green' — EPGN

'Knockout' (v) — CBdn CWin EBee EGol EOMN EPGN IBal MBNS MNrw NBro NGdn NLar NMyG WShp

'Koriyama' (*sieboldiana*) (v) — CBdn EMic IBal

'Krossa Regal' ♀[H4] — More than 30 suppliers

* *laciniata* — WSSM

'Lacy Belle' (v) — CBdn CWin EGol EMic IBal LRHS NBro NGdn NPro

'Lady Helen' — EMic

'Lady Isobel Barnett' (v) — CBdn EMic NMyG

laevigata — EGol

'Lakeside Black Satin' — CBdn EMic EPGN

'Lakeside Cha Cha' (v) — CBdn EGol EMic

'Lakeside Kaleidoscope' **new** — CBdn EMic IBal

'Lakeside Looking Glass' **new** — CBdn EMic

'Lakeside Neat Petite' — EGol

'Lakeside Ninita' (v) — EGol EMic

'Lakeside Premier' **new** — CBdn EMic

'Lakeside Symphony' (v) — EGol

§ *lancifolia* ♀[H4] — CBdn CBro CMHG CRow ECha EGol EHrv ELan EMic EPGN EPar GKir LGro LPVe MRav NGdn NHol NMyG NSti SBod SRms SSpi WAul WCot WGwG WPGP WShp WTin

'Leather Sheen' — EGol EMic EPGN

'Lee Armiger' (*tokudama* hybrid) — EGol

'Lemon Delight' — CBdn EGol EMic EPGN

'Lemon Lime' — CBdn EGol EMic IBal LRHS MHom MNrw NMyG NPro WBrk WIvy WPat WTin WWhi WWye

'Lemon Twist' — LRHS

'Leola Fraim' (v) — CBdn EBee EGol EMic EPGN IBal LRHS NMyG WBcn

'Leviathan' — EMic

'Liberty' (v) **new** — EGol

* *lilacina* — SCro WFar

'Lily Pad' — EPGN

'Lime Piecrust' — EGol

'Limey Lisa' — EMic

'Little Aurora' (*tokudama* hybrid) — EGol EMic EPGN

'Little Black Scape' — CFwr CMHG CPen EBee EGol EMic EPGN EWTr IBal MHom NGdn NHol NLar NMyG NPro

'Little Blue' (*ventricosa*) — EGol

'Little Bo Beep' (v) — EGol

'Little Caesar' (v) — CBdn EGol EMic EPGN

'Little Doll' (v) — EGol

'Little Razor' — EGol

'Little Sunspot' (v) — CBdn EGol IBal

'Little White Lines' (v) — CBdn EGol EPGN

'Little Wonder' (v) — CBdn EGol SChu

longipes — EGol LPhx

longissima — CMHG EGol WCru

'Louisa' (v) — ECha EGol MSte

'Love Pat' ♀[H4] — CBdn CFir CWin EBee EGol EMic EPGN EPfP EWsh GAbr GBin GSki IBal LAst MCCP MIDC MRav NMyG SPla SVil WCAu

'Loyalist' (v) — CBdn EMic EPGN NLar NMyG WCra

'Lucky Charm' — EMic

'Lucy Vitols' (v) — CBdn EGol EMic

'Lunar Eclipse' (v) — CWin EBee EGol LPhx

'Lunar Orbit' (v) — CBdn

'Mack the Knife' **new** — IBal

'Maekawa' — EGol

'Mama Mia' (v) — EBee EGol EMic EPGN GAbr MBNS

'Maraschino Cherry' — EBee EGol EMic EPGN IBal

'Margin of Error' (v) — EPGN

'Marginata Alba' (*fortunei*) ambig. (v) — CBot CHad ECha GKir LPBA WWin

'Marilyn' — EGol LRHS

'Marquis' (*nakaiana* hybrid) — EGol

'Maruba Iwa' (*longipes* var. *latifolia*) — CBdn

'Maruba' (*longipes* var. *latifolia*) — EGol

'Mary Joe' — EMic

'Mary Marie Ann' (*fortunei*) (v) — CBdn EGol EMic EPGN NCGa NMyG

§ 'Masquerade' (v) — CBdn EGol EMic EPGN NABC WFar

'Mediovariegata' (*undulata*) — see *H. undulata* var. *undulata*

'Medusa' (v) — EGol WCot

'Mentor Gold' — EGol

'Mesa Fringe' (*montana*) — CBdn

'Metallic Sheen' — CBdn LRHS

I 'Metallica' — CBdn

'Midas Touch' — CBdn EGol EOrc NHol NLar NMyG

'Middle Ridge' — EBee NHol

§ 'Midwest Gold' — MHom

'Midwest Magic' (v) — CBdn EBee EGol EMic IBal LRHS WBcn

'Mildred Seaver' (v) — CBdn CWin EGol EMic EPGN IBal LRHS MWat

'Millie's Memoirs' (v) — EGol

'Minnie Klopping' — EMic EPGN

minor hort. f. *alba* — see *H. sieboldii* var. *alba*

§ *minor* — CBdn CBro EBee EBre EGol EMic EPGN ERos EWTr GEdr GFlt GGar GSki MTho NHol NMyG SSpi WCot WFar

- from Korea — EGol
- Goldbrook form — EGol

'Minor' (*ventricosa*) — see *H. minor*

'Minuteman' (*fortunei*) (v) — CBdn CBri CWin EBee EGle EMic EPGN EPfP GAbr GBin IBal IPot LAst LPVe LRHS MBNS MIDC MSte NCGa NGdn NMyG NOrc SPla WGor WShp WTMC WTin

'Moerheim' (*fortunei*) (v) — CBdn EGol EMic EPGN EPar GBin LRHS MBar MBri MIDC NHol SChu WHal WLin WTMC

N *montana* — CBdn CHad ECha EGol EMic NHol

- B&SWJ 4796 — WCru
- B&SWJ 5585 — WCru
- 'Aureomarginata' — see *H. 'Aureomarginata' (montana)*
- f. *macrophylla* — EGol

'Moon Glow' (v) — EGol EPGN NMyG

'Moon River' (v) — CBdn EGol EMic EPGN LRHS

'Moon Shadow' (v) — EGol

'Moon Waves' — EGol

'Moonbeam' — CBdn WTMC

'Moonlight' (*fortunei*) (v) — CBdn EChP EGol EMic EPGN LRHS NABC NMyG WBcn

'Moonlight Sonata' — CBdn EGol

'Moonstruck' **new** — CBdn

'Morning Light' — CBdn EBee EGol EMic EPGN MBNS MBri NCGa WBor

'Moscow Blue' — EGol LRHS

'Mount Everest' **new** — CBdn EMic

'Mount Fuji' (*montana*) — EGol

'Mount Hope' (v) — EGol

'Mount Kirishima' (*sieboldii*) — see *H. 'Kirishima'*

§ 'Mount Royal' — NHol

'Mountain Snow' (*montana*) (v) — CBdn CWin EBee EGol EMic EPGN LRHS NMyG WTMC

'Mountain Sunrise' (*montana*) — EGol

'Mr Big' — MBNS WCot

'Munchkin' (*sieboldii*) — CBdn

'Myerscough Magic' (v) — CBdn MSte NMyG

nakaiana — EBee EMic GCal NDlv

'Nakaimo' — CBdn GBin NHol

'Nameoki' — NHol

'Nana' (*ventricosa*) — see *H. minor*

§ 'Nancy Lindsay' (*fortunei*) — CBdn CTri EBee EGol EMic NGdn SChu WTMC

'Nancy Minks' **new** — CBdn EMic

'Neat Splash' (v) — CBdn EChP NBir NHol

'Neat Splash Rim' (v) — EPGN

'New Wave' — EGol

'Niagara Falls' **new** — CBdn

'Nicola' — EGol EMic EPGN MHom NMyG

'Night before Christmas' (v) — CBdn CFir COtt CWin EBee EGle EGol EPGN EWsh GBin IBal IPot LAst MBri MCLN MIDC MNrw NBro NCGa NGdn NHol SHBN SPla WSan WShp WTMC WWpP WWye

nigrescens — CBdn CWin EBee EGol EPGN GCal MTed WShp

'Nokogiryama' — EGol EMic

'North Hills' (*fortunei*) (v) — CBdn EGol EMic LPio LRHS NBir NGdn SChu SMrm SWvt

'Northern Exposure' (*sieboldiana*) (v) — CFir CWin EBee EGol EMic IBal NGdn NMyG

'Northern Halo' (*sieboldiana*) — EGol EMic

'Northern Lights' (*sieboldiana*) — EGol

'Obscura Marginata' (*fortunei*) — see *H. fortunei* var. *aureomarginata*

'Obsession' — EGol

'Okazuki Special' — CBdn EGol

'Old Faithful' — CBdn EGol

'Olga's Shiny Leaf' — EGol EMic

'Olive Bailey Langdon' (*sieboldiana*) (v) — CBdn EBee EMic IBal

'Olive Branch' (v) — EGol

'Olympic Edger' **new** — IBal

'Ophir' **new** — IBal

'Oriana' (*fortunei*) — EGol

'Osprey' (Tardiana Group) — EGol LRHS

'Oxheart' — EMic

pachyscapa — EMic

'Pacific Blue Edger' — CBdn CFir CM&M CWin EFou EGle EGol EMic EPGN LAst MBri WWye

'Pandora's Box' (v) — CBdn EBee EGol EMic IBal WCot

'Paradigm' (v) — CBdn EBee EGol EMic EPGN IBal

'Paradise Joyce'[PBR] — CBdn EBee EGol EMic EPGN MCLN MIDC

'Paradise Power'[PBR] — CBdn EGol EMic

'Paradise Puppet' (*venusta*) — CBdn EPGN

'Paradise Red Delight' (*pycnophylla*) — CBdn EMic

'Paradise Standard' (d) — CBdn

'Pastures Green' — EGol

'Pastures New' — EFou EGol EMic EPGN LPhx MHom NHol NMyG

'Pathfinder' (v) **new** — EGol IBal

'Patrician' (v) — EMic EPGN

'Patriot' (v) — More than 30 suppliers

'Paul's Glory' (v) — CBdn CWin EGle EGol EMic EPGN GBin GMac IBal LAst LRHS MBri MCLN NGdn NMyG SUsu SVil WTMC WWye

§ 'Paxton's Original' (*sieboldii*) (v) ♀H4 — CHar EGol EHrv GKir IHMH MBar NLar SRms WMyn

'Peace' — EGol EMic EPGN

'Pearl Lake' — CBdn EBee EGol EMic EPGN IHMH LPhx LRHS MHom MSte MWat NBir NHol NLar NMyG SVil WTin

'Peedee Gold Flash' (v) — CBdn EPGN NMyG

'Pelham Blue Tump' — EGol EMic

'Peppermint Ice' (v) **new** — EGol

'Permanent Wave' — EFou EGol

'Perry's True Blue' — CBdn

'Peter Pan'	CBdn EGol EMic
'Phoenix'	EGol GBin
'Photo Finish' (v)	CBdn EGle EPGN
'Phyllis Campbell' (*fortunei*)	see *H.* 'Sharmon'
'Picta' (*fortunei*)	see *H. fortunei* var. *albopicta*
'Piecrust Power'	CBdn EGol
'Piedmont Gold'	CBdn EGol EMic EOrc EPGN IBal LPhx MSte WTMC
'Pilgrim' (v)	CBdn EBee EGol EMic EPGN IBal
'Pineapple Poll'	CBdn EMic EPGN MIDC NMyG WTin
'Pineapple Upside Down Cake' (v)	EPGN IBal
'Pizzazz' (v)	CBdn CWin EBee EGle EGol EMic EPGN LAst MHom MIDC NGdn NHol NLar NMyG WHil WTMC
plantaginea	CBdn EGol EMic EPar EUJe LEdu LPhx MHom MIDC NMyG SSpi WCFE WCru
- var. *grandiflora*	see *H. plantaginea* var. *japonica*
§ - var. *japonica* ♀H4	CBot CHad CLAP CStu ECha EHrv EMic EPGN EPar GSki SChu SMHy WCAu
'Platinum Tiara' (v)	CBdn EMic EPGN IBal NBir
'Pooh Bear' (v)	CBdn EGol
'Popo'	CBdn EGol
'Potomac Pride'	CBdn EPGN LRHS NMyG
'Praying Hands' (v) **new**	EGol EMic
'Pretty Flamingo'	EMic
'Prince of Wales' **new**	CBdn
'Puck'	EGol
'Purple and Gold'	CBdn
'Purple Dwarf'	CBdn EGol EMic GKir LRHS NGdn NHol NLar WCra
'Purple Profusion'	EGol EMic
pycnophylla	EGol SIgm
'Queen Josephine' (v)	CBdn COtt CWin EBee EGol EMic EPGN IBal IPot LAst MBNS MBri MHom NCGa NGdn NMyG NPro WTMC WWye
'Queen of Islip' (*sieboldiana*) (v)	CBdn
'Quilting Bee'	EGol
'Radiant Edger' (v)	CBdn CWin EBee EGol EMic EPGN IBal LRHS NHol
'Raleigh Remembrance'	EGol
'Rascal' (v)	CBdn EGol EMic LRHS
'Raspberry Sorbet'	CBdn EGol EPGN LRHS
rectifolia	NHol
'Red Neck Heaven' (*kikutii* var. *caput-avis*)	CBdn WTin
'Red October'	CBdn CMHG CRez EBee EChP EGol EMic EPAt EPGN EPfP IBal MBri MCCP NMyG
'Red Salamander' **new**	EGol
'Regal Splendor' (v)	CBdn CWin EBee EGol EMFW EMic EPGN GSki IBal LRHS MBri MHom NBro NCGa NDov NHol NMyG NPSI SMrm SPla SVil WMnd WSSM WWpP
'Remember Me' **new**	CBdn EBee EDAr EGol EMic EPGN IBal LAst MCCP NCGa NGdn NHol NLar NMyG WGor
'Resonance' (v)	EPGN MBri NGdn NLar NPro WTMC
'Reversed' (v)	CBdn CLAP CWin EBee EGol ELan EMic EPGN EPfP EWsh MDKP MIDC MSte NBro NDov NGdn NHol NMyG WTMC
'Revolution'PBR (v)	CBdn CPen CWin EBee EGle EGol EMic IBal IPot MBNS MBri MIDC NBro NCGa NLar NMyG NOrc
'Rhapsody' (*fortunei*) (v)	EGol

'Rhapsody in Blue' **new**	EGol
'Richland Gold' (*fortunei*)	CBdn EBee EGol EMic EPGN LPhx NMyG
'Rippled Honey'	CBdn CPen EPGN IBal NMyG NPro
'Rippling Waves'	EGol EMic
'Riptide' **new**	CBdn
'Rising Sun'	EGol
'Robert Frost' (v)	CBdn EGol EMic IBal WTin
'Robusta' (*fortunei*)	see *H. sieboldiana* var. *elegans*
§ *rohdeifolia* (v)	CLAP EGol LBuc LRHS WHal
§ - f. *albopicta*	CBdn EGol ELan EPar NHol SChu
'Rosemoor'	CBdn EGol
§ 'Royal Standard' ♀H4	More than 30 suppliers
'Royalty'	EGol
rupifraga	EGol
§ 'Sagae' (v) ♀H3-4	CBdn CHid CLAP CWin EBre EChP EGle EGol EMic EPGN EPfP IBal IPot LPan LRHS MBri MHom MIDC MNrw MSte NGdn NMyG SMrm SPla WAul WFar WTMC
'Saint Elmo's Fire' (v)	CBdn CHid EGol EMic IBal MCCP NCGa SPla
'Saint Fiacre' **new**	CBdn
§ 'Saishu Jima' (*sieboldii* f. *spathulata*)	EPla NHol WCru
'Saishu Yahite Site' (v) **new**	EGol
'Salute' (Tardiana Group)	CBdn EGol
'Samurai' (*sieboldiana*) (v)	CBdn CWin EBee EGol IBal IPot LAst MRav NBir NBro NGdn
'Sarah Kennedy' (v)	EPGN
'Savannah'	EGol LRHS
'Sazanami' (*crispula*)	see *H. crispula*
'Scooter' (v)	CBdn EGol EMic EPGN NMyG
'Sea Bunny'	EGol
'Sea Dream' (v)	CBdn EGol EMic EPGN NMyG WBcn
'Sea Drift'	EGol
'Sea Fire'	EGol LRHS
'Sea Gold Star'	CBdn EGol EPGN NMyG
'Sea Gulf Stream' **new**	IBal
'Sea Hero'	EGol
'Sea Lotus Leaf'	CBdn EGol EMic EPGN NLar
'Sea Mist' (v)	CBdn
'Sea Monster'	EGol
'Sea Octopus'	EGol
'Sea Sapphire'	EGol LRHS
'Sea Sprite' (v)	EPGN LBuc LRHS
'Sea Sunrise' **new**	EPGN
'Sea Thunder' (v)	CBdn EGol EMic EPGN IBal
'Sea Yellow Sunrise'	CBdn EGol EMic IBal
'Second Wind' (*fortunei*) (v)	CBdn EMic EPGN LRHS NMyG
'See Saw' (*undulata*)	EGol WPnP
'Semperaurea' (*sieboldiana*)	GFlt GSki
'September Sun' (v)	CBdn EGol EPGN LRHS NMyG
'Serendipity'	CBdn EGol EMic EPGN MHom
'Shade Beauty' (v)	CBdn EMic
'Shade Fanfare' (v) ♀H4	CBdn EBre EGol ELan EMic ENot EOrc EPGN EPar EPfP GKir LRHS MBNS MBri MIDC MRav NBir NGdn NLar NMyG NSti SCro WCAu WFar WMnd WTin
'Shade Master'	CBdn EBre EGol GKir LAst NHol SMer SVil
§ 'Sharmon' (*fortunei*) (v)	CBdn CWin EBee EGol EMic EOMN EPGN IPot LPVe MBNS NHol NMyG SChu
'Sheila West'	CBdn
'Shelleys' (v)	EGol
'Sherborne Profusion' (Tardiana Group)	CBdn EMic

'Sherborne Swift'   CBdn EGol
    (Tardiana Group)
'Shining Tot'   CBdn EGol
'Shirley Vaughn' (v)   EGol
'Shogun' (v)   EGol
'Showboat' (v)   CBdn EBee EGol EPGN
sieboldiana   CMHG CRow CSBt EBee EFou
    EGol ELan EMic EPar EPfP LPVe
    MRav NChi NFor NHol NJOw SPer
    SPlb SRms WBVN WCru WFar
    WGwG WShp WTin WWpP
§   - var. *elegans* ♀H4   More than 30 suppliers
  - 'George Smith' **new**   IBal
sieboldii **new**   MLwd
§   - var. *alba*   CHad EGol SSpi
§   - var. *sieboldii*   CBdn CLAP EGol EPGN MIDC
    f. *kabitan* (v)   NABC NMyG NSti SChu WGwG
    WTin
  - - f. *shiro-kabitan* (v)   EGol EMic EPGN
'Silk Kimono' (v) **new**   EGol
'Silver Bowl'   EGol
'Silver Crown'   see *H.* 'Albomarginata'
'Silver Lance' (v)   CBdn EGol EMic EPGN NMyG
'Silver Spray' (v) **new**   EGol
'Silvery Slugproof'   CBdn NMyG
    (Tardiana Group)
'Sitting Pretty' (v)   EGol EPGN
'Slick Willie'   EGol
'Slim Polly'   CBdn
'Snow Cap' (v)   CBdn CWin EGle EGol EMic EPGN
    IBal ITim MBri MIDC NMyG NPro
'Snow Crust' (v)   CBdn EGol EMic LRHS
'Snow Flakes' (*sieboldii*)   CBdn EBee EGol EPGN EPfP EWTr
    GCal GKir LPio LRHS MBar MBri
    NBro NGdn NHol NMyG NPro
    SBod SPer WFar WGwG WSSM
    WShp WTMC WTin
'Snow White' (*undulata*) (v)   EGol
'Snowden'   CBdn CHad CMHG EBee ECha
    EFou EGol EMic EOrc EPGN MBro
    MLwd NBir NGdn NHol NMyG
    NPar SCro SMrm SSpi WHoo WPnP
'Snowstorm' (*sieboldii*)   CBdn NHol
'So Sweet' (v)   CBdn CLAP CWin EBee EGol EHan
    EMFW EMic EMil EOrc EPGN GSki
    IBal LPBA MBri MHom MIDC MSte
    MSwo NBPC NBro NGdn NHol
    NMyG SMrm WLow
'Solar Flare'   EGol
'Something Blue'   CBdn
'Something Different'   EPGN
    (*fortunei*) (v)
'Sparkling Burgundy'   CBdn EGol
'Sparky' (v)   EGol
'Special Gift'   CBdn EBee EGol EMic LBuc LRHS
'Spilt Milk' (*tokudama*) (v)   CBdn EGol EMic EPGN
§ 'Spinners' (*fortunei*) (v)   CBdn EBre ECha EGol EMic SChu
    SSpi
'Spinning Wheel' (v)   EGol
'Spritzer' (v)   CBdn EGol EMic EPGN NMyG
    WBcn
'Squash Casserole'   EGol
'Squiggles' (v)   EGol
'Starburst' (v) **new**   EGol
§ 'Starker Yellow Leaf'   EMic
'Stenantha' (*fortunei*)   EMic
'Stenantha Variegated'   NHol
    (*fortunei*)
'Stetson' (v)   EGol
'Stiletto' (v)   CBdn EBee EGol EMic EOMN
    EPGN IBal IHMH IPot LAst MBNS
    MHom MIDC NBro NFla NGdn
    NLar NMyG NPro NSti SDnm WAul
    WShp

'Striptease' (*fortunei*) (v)   CBdn CWin EBee EBre EGol EMic
    EPGN GBin GKir IBal LAst LPio
    MBNS MIDC NGdn NHol NLar
    NOrc SHBN SVil WTMC
'Sugar and Cream' (v)   CM&M CRez CWin EBee EGol
    EMic EOrc EPGN LAst LPio LRHS
    NGdn SChu WTMC
'Sugar Plum Fairy'   EGol
    (*gracillima*)
'Sultana' (v)   EMic IBal
'Sum and Substance' ♀H4   More than 30 suppliers
'Summer Breeze' (v)   EGol IBal
'Summer Fragrance'   CBdn EGol EMic EPGN LRHS
'Summer Music' (v)   CBdn CWin EBee EGle EGol EMic
    EPGN IBal LAst MBNS MBri
'Summer Serenade' (v)   CBdn EGol EMic
'Summer Snow' (v)   EPGN
'Sun Glow'   EGol
'Sun Power'   CBdn CPen CWin EBee EGol EMic
    EOrc EPGN EPar LRHS MBNS
    MCLN NBro NLar NMyG NSti
'Sundance' (*fortunei*) (v)   EGol
* 'Sunflower'   NOak
'Super Bowl'   EGol
'Super Nova' (v)   CBdn EBee EGol EMic EPGN IBal
    LRHS
'Sweet Bo Beep'   EGol
'Sweet Home Chicago' (v)   EGol IBal
'Sweet Marjorie'   EGol
'Sweet Susan'   EBre EGol EMic EOrc LRHS MBNS
    WWpP
'Sweet Tater Pie'   CBdn EGol EPGN
'Sweetheart'   EMic
'Sweetie' (v)   CBdn EGol EMic IBal LRHS
'Swirling Hearts'   EGol LRHS
'Tall Boy'   CBdn CSev EBee ECha EGol EPla
    GCal MWgw NBir SSpi
'Tamborine' (v)   CBdn EGol EPGN LRHS
Tardiana Group   CBdn CBro EGol ELan MHom
    NGdn NHol SPer
tardiflora   CBdn CFil EGol ERos WCot WPGP
tardiva   CBdn LRHS
'Tattoo' (v)   CBdn EBee EDAr EGol EHan EMic
    EPGN MBNS MIDC NCGa NMyG
'Tea and Crumpets' (v)   CBdn EPGN
'Temple Bells'   EGol LRHS
'Tenryu'   EGol EPGN
'The Twister'   EGol EMic
'Thomas Hogg'   see *H. undulata* var.
    albomarginata
'Thumb Nail'   CBdn ECha EGol GSki
'Thumbelina' **new**   IBal
'Thunderbolt'   CBdn EBee EPGN IBal MBNS
    (*sieboldiana*)
tibae   CBdn
'Timpany's Own'   ITim
    (*sieboldiana*) **new**
'Tiny Tears'   CBdn EGol LRHS
'Titanic' **new**   IBal
tokudama   EGol LRHS MHom NBir NGdn
    NHol NSti SChu
§   - f. *aureonebulosa*   CBdn CWin EGol EMic EPGN IBal
    IPot LPhx LRHS MSte NGdn NMyG
    NSti WMnd
  - f. *flavocircinalis* (v)   CBdn CPrp CWin EBee EGol EMic
    EPGN IBal LRHS NBPC NBro SSpe
    WFar WHoo WMnd WWye
'Torchlight' (v)   CBdn EGol EMic LRHS
'Tot Tot'   EGol
'Touchstone' (v)   CBdn EBee MBri NMyG SWvt
'Trail's End'   EMic
'True Blue'   CBdn CWin EBee EGol EMic GAbr
    IBal LAst
'Tutu'   EGol MIDC

'Twilight' *(fortunei)* (v)	CBdn CWin EBee EGol EMic EPGN IBal MBNS NLar SWvt WRHF	
'Twinkle Toes'	EGol	
'Twist of Lime' (v)	CBdn EGol	
'Ultraviolet Light'	EGol	
§	*undulata*	CHar MIDC WBrE WFar WWpP
§	- var. *albomarginata*	More than 30 suppliers
§	- var. *erromena* ♀H4	CBdn EHon EMic EPfP LPBA MBro MWgw NBid NFla NHol SPer WWpP
§	- var. *undulata* (v) ♀H4	More than 30 suppliers
§	- var. *univittata* (v) ♀H4	CBro CRow ECha EGol EPGN EPfP IBal MHom NBir NPro WBrk WFar WKif WMoo
	'Urajiro Hachijo'	EGol WBcn
	'Urajiro' *(hypoleuca)*	EGol
	'Valentine Lace'	CBdn EBee EGol EMic LRHS
	'Van Wade' (v)	CBdn EGol EMic EPGN
	'Vanilla Cream' *(cathayana)*	EGol EPGN LRHS NMyG
	'Variegata' *(gracillima)*	see *H.* 'Vera Verde'
	'Variegata' *(tokudama)*	see *H. tokudama* f. *aureonebulosa*
	'Variegata' *(undulata)*	see *H. undulata* var. *undulata*
	'Variegata' *(ventricosa)*	see *H.* 'Aureomarginata' *(ventricosa)*
	'Variegated' *(fluctuans)*	see *H.* 'Sagae'
	ventricosa ♀H4	CBcs CBdn CBro CHid EBre EGol EGoo EMic EPfP EUJe GBBs LPBA MHer MNrw MRav NHol SGar WBVN WBrk WCFE WFar WShp WWye
	- BWJ 8160 from Sichuan	WCru
	- var. *aureomaculata*	CBdn EBee EGol EPGN NBir NSti SPer
	- 'Aureomarginata'	see *H.* 'Aureomarginata' *(ventricosa)*
I	'Venucosa'	EGol EMic WFar
	'Venus Star'	EPGN GSki NMyG
	venusta ♀H4	More than 30 suppliers
	- B&SWJ 4389	WCru
	- dwarf	CSWP LPhx
	- *yakusimensis*	see *H. kikutii* var. *yakusimensis*
§	'Vera Verde' (v)	CBdn EBee EPGN ERos GQui MHom NBir NMyG
	'Verna Jean' (v)	CBdn EGol
	'Veronica Lake' (v)	CBdn EGol EMic LRHS
	'Vilmoriniana'	EGol EMic
	'Viridis Marginata'	see *H. sieboldii* var. *sieboldii* f. *kabitan*
	'Wagtail' (Tardiana Group)	CBdn EMic
	'Wahoo' *(tokudama)* (v)	EGol
	'Warwick Choice' (v)	CBdn
	'Warwick Curtsey' (v)	EGol
	'Warwick Delight' (v)	CBdn EGol
	'Warwick Edge' (v)	CBdn EGol
	'Warwick Essence'	EGol EMic
	'Warwick Sheen' **new**	IBal
	'Waving Winds' (v)	EGol
	'Waving Wuffles'	EMic
	'Wayside Blue'	EMic
	'Wayside Perfection'	see *H.* 'Royal Standard'
	'Weihenstephan' *(sieboldii)*	EGol EMic
	'Weser'	EGol
	'Wheaton Blue'	CBdn EMic LRHS
	'Whirlwind' *(fortunei)* (v)	CBdn CRez CWin EBee EGol EOrc EPGN GBBs GBin IBal IPot MBri MIDC MNrw NBro NGdn NMyG SVil WAul WMnd WTMC WWye
	'Whirlwind Tour' (v)	EGol
	'White Christmas' *(undulata)* (v)	CBdn EBee EGle EGol EPGN LRHS
	'White Fairy' *(plantaginea)* (d)	CBdn EBee EPGN IBal NMyG

	'White Feather' *(undulata)*	CBdn EMic
	'White Gold'	CBdn EGol EPGN
	'White Tacchi'	EMon
	'White Triumphator' *(rectifolia)*	CBdn EGol EPGN MBri
	'White Vision' **new**	EGol
	'Whoopee' (v) **new**	EPGN
	'Wide Brim' (v) ♀H4	More than 30 suppliers
	'Wind River Gold'	EGol
	'Windsor Gold'	see *H.* 'Nancy Lindsay'
	'Winfield Blue'	CMHG EGol LRHS
	'Winfield Gold'	CBdn EGol
	'Wogon Giboshi'	see *H.* 'Wogon' *(sieboldii)*
§	'Wogon' *(sieboldii)*	CBdn CM&M CRow EPGN NDlv NHol NMen NSti
	'Wogon's Boy'	CBdn EGol EPGN
	'Wolverine' (v)	EBee EGol EPGN IBal MBNS MHom MIDC NMyG WCot WLin
	'Wrinkles and Crinkles'	EGol EPGN
	'Yakushima-mizu' *(gracillima)*	CBdn EGol
*	*yakushimana*	GCrs NMen
	'Yellow Boa'	EGol
	'Yellow Edge' *(fortunei)*	see *H. fortunei* var. *aureomarginata*
	'Yellow Edge' *(sieboldiana)*	see *H.* 'Frances Williams'
	'Yellow River'	CBdn EGol EMic EPGN IBal LRHS NGdn NMyG
	'Yellow Splash' (v)	CBdn EBee ECha EPGN LRHS MBNS MHom NMyG SChu
	'Yellow Splash Rim' (v)	EGol MBri WBcn
	'Yellow Splashed Edged' (v)	EMic
	'Yellow Waves'	CBdn
	yingeri	EGol
	- B&SWJ 546	WCru
	'Zager Blue'	EMic
	'Zager Green'	EMic
	'Zager White Edge' *(fortunei)* (v)	CLAP EGol EMic EPGN NMyG WTin
	'Zounds'	CBdn CBot CMHG EBre EChP EFou EGol EHoe ELan ENot EOrc EPGN EPfP GFlt GKir IBal IHMH LRHS MDun MIDC MRav NHol NMyG NOak NOrc NSti SCro SHBN SPla WFar

Hottonia (Primulaceae)

palustris	ECoo EHon ELan EMFW LPBA MSta NArg NBlu NVic SWat

Houstonia (Rubiaceae)

caerulea L.	ECho NLAp WWin
- var. *alba*	IHMH WPer
michauxii 'Fred Mullard'	EWes WShp

Houttuynia (Saururaceae)

	cordata	GBar IBlr LNCo NArg SWat WBrE WFar
§	- 'Boo-Boo' (v)	EChP EMan EOMN EPfP EPla LHop MCLN
§	- 'Chameleon' (v)	More than 30 suppliers
	- 'Flame' (v)	NCGa
	- 'Flore Pleno' (d)	More than 30 suppliers
	- 'Joker's Gold'	EBee EMan EOMN EPPr EPfP MBNS NBro NVic SLon SMrm WWpP
*	- 'Pied Piper'	CDoC EBee ENot LRHS SAga
	- 'Tequila Sunrise'	CHEx
	- 'Terry Clarke' (v)	see *H. cordata* 'Boo-Boo'
	- 'Tricolor'	see *H. cordata* 'Chameleon'
	- Variegata Group (v)	EBla GBar IBlr LPBA NArg NBro SIng WWpP

Hovenia (*Rhamnaceae*)

acerba	CFil
dulcis	CAgr CBcs CMCN CPle EPfP IArd ITer LEdu MBlu WBVN

Howea (*Arecaceae*)

forsteriana ♀H1	LPal LRHS MBri WMul

Hoya (*Asclepiadaceae*)

§ **australis**	LRHS SOWG
bella	see *H. lanceolata* subsp. *bella*
carnosa ♀H1	CBcs CRHN EBak ELan EOHP ESlt GQui MGol SRms
- 'Compacta'	CHal ESlt
* - 'Hindu Rope'	NPer
* - 'Krinkle'	NPer
- 'Red Princess'	MBri
- 'Rubra'	SYvo
- 'Tricolor'	NPer
- 'Variegata' (v)	MBri SMur
cinnamomifolia	SOWG
* **compacta** 'Tricolor'	NPer
darwinii hort.	see *H. australis*
lacunosa	LRHS
§ **lanceolata**	CHal EShb GQui SRms
subsp. **bella** ♀H1	
linearis	SOWG
multiflora	ESlt SOWG

Hugueninia (*Brassicaceae*)

tanacetifolia	MWod
subsp. **suffruticosa**	

Humata (*Davalliaceae*)

pyxidata	see *Davallia solida* var. *pyxidata*
tyermannii	NMar WFib

Humea (*Asteraceae*)

elegans	see *Calomeria amaranthoides*

Humulus (*Cannabaceae*)

japonicus	ECoo MSal
lupulus	CArn CBcs CDul CRWN ECoo ELau EPfP GBar GPoy ILis MHer MSal SIde WDin WHer WSel WStI WWye
- (f)	NGHP
- 'Aureus' ♀H4	More than 30 suppliers
- 'Aureus' (f)	CFwr CRHN GBar MAnH MCCP MPRe SPla WCot
- 'Aureus' (m)	MCCP
* - **compactus**	GPoy
- 'Fuggle'	CAgr GPoy SDea
- (Goldings Group) 'Cobbs'	SDea
- - 'Mathons'	CAgr SDea
- 'Hallertauer'	SDea
- 'Hip-hop'	EMon EWes
- 'Prima Donna'	CBcs CBct CFwr GBin MBNS NGHP SIde SPoG SWvt
- 'Taff's Variegated' (v)	EMon EWes WBcn WHil
- 'Wye Challenger'	CAgr GPoy
- 'Wye Northdown'	SDea

Hunnemannia (*Papaveraceae*)

fumariifolia 'Sunlite'	WCot

Huodendron (*Styracaceae*)

tibeticum **new**	CFil

Hutchinsia see *Pritzelago*

Hyacinthella (*Hyacinthaceae*)

dalmatica	ECho WWst
'Grandiflora' **new**	

heldreichii **new**	ERos
lazuliria **new**	ERos
leucophaea **new**	ERos
millingenii	EHyt ERos

Hyacinthoides (*Hyacinthaceae*)

§ **hispanica**	CBro CHid EPot IBlr MBri NBir SPer WFar WWye
- 'Alba'	EPot SPer
- 'Excelsior'	LRHS
- 'La Grandesse'	CBro
- 'Rosabella'	CBro
- 'Rose'	CMea EPot
- 'Rosea'	CPom
§ **italica**	WShi
§ **non-scripta**	CArn CAvo CBro CTri EPar EPfP EPot GAbr IBlr LAma LRHS MBow MHer NMir NRog SHFr SPer WBVN WHer WShi
- pink	CBgR WShi
- 'Wavertree' **new**	CBgR
- white **new**	CBgR
reverchonii **new**	WWst
§ **vicentina**	ERos

Hyacinthus ✿ (*Hyacinthaceae*)

amethystinus	see *Brimeura amethystina*
azureus	see *Muscari azureum*
comosus 'Plumosus'	see *Muscari comosum* 'Plumosum'
fastigiatus	see *Brimeura fastigiata*
orientalis	WShi
- 'Amethyst'	LAma
- 'Amsterdam'	LAma
- 'Anna Marie' ♀H4	CAvo CBro LAma MBri NRog
- 'Ben Nevis' (d)	LAma MBri
- 'Bismarck'	LAma
- 'Blue Giant'	LAma
- 'Blue Jacket' ♀H4	CBro LAma NRog
- 'Blue Magic'	LAma
- 'Blue Orchid' (d)	LAma
- 'Blue Star'	LAma
- 'Borah' ♀H4	LAma
- 'Carnegie'	CAvo CBro LAma NRog SPer
- 'City of Haarlem' ♀H4	CBro LAma NRog SPer
- 'Colosseum'	LAma
- 'Crystal Palace' (d) **new**	LAma
- 'Delft Blue' ♀H4	CAvo CBro LAma MBri NRog SPer
- 'Fondant'	LAma SPer
- 'General Köhler' (d)	LAma
- 'Gipsy Princess' **new**	LAma
- 'Gipsy Queen' ♀H4	LAma MBri NRog SPer
- 'Hollyhock' (d)	LAma MBri
- 'Jan Bos'	EPfP LAma NRog
- 'King Codro' (d)	LAma MBri
- 'King of the Blues'	LAma
- 'La Victoire'	LAma
- 'Lady Derby'	CBro LAma
- 'L'Innocence' ♀H4	CBro EPfP LAma SPer
- 'Marconi' (d)	LAma
- 'Marie'	LAma
- 'Mulberry Rose'	LAma
- 'Myosotis'	LAma
- 'Odysseus' **new**	LAma
§ - 'Oranje Boven'	LAma
- 'Ostara' ♀H4	CBro EPfP LAma MBri NRog
- 'Peter Stuyvesant'	LAma
- 'Pink Pearl' ♀H4	CBro EPfP LAma NRog
- 'Pink Royal' (d)	LAma
- 'Princess Margaret'	LAma
- 'Queen of the Pinks'	LAma
- 'Red Magic' **new**	LAma
- 'Rosette' (d)	LAma
- 'Salmonetta'	see *H. orientalis* 'Oranje Boven'

§ - 'Sneeuwwitje' | LAma
- Snow White | see *H. orientalis* 'Sneeuwwitje'
- 'Violet Pearl' | CBro LAma
- 'Vuurbaak' | LAma
- 'White Pearl' | CAvo LAma
- 'Woodstock' | LAma MBri SPer

Hydrangea ✿ (*Hydrangeaceae*)

angustipetala | CFil CSam
- B&SWJ 3454 | WCru
- B&SWJ 3814 | WCru
- B&SWJ 6038 from Yakushima | WCru
- B&SWJ 7121 | WCru
* - f. **formosa** B&SWJ 7097 **new** | WCru
* - f. **macrosepala** B&SWJ 3476 | WCru
* - f. **obovatifolia** B&SWJ 3487b **new** | WCru
anomala | SSpi WBcn
　subsp. **anomala**
- - B&SWJ 2411 | WCru
- subsp. **anomala** 'Winter Glow' **new** | WCru
- subsp. **glabra** B&SWJ 3117 | WCru
§ - subsp. **petiolaris** ♀H4 | More than 30 suppliers
- - B&SWJ 6337 | WCru
§ - - var. **cordifolia** | CFil MBNS NLar
- - - 'Brookside Littleleaf' | NLar
- - - dwarf | see *H. anomala* subsp. *petiolaris* var. *cordifolia*
- - B&SWJ 6081 from Yakushima | WCru
- - - 'Furuaziai' **new** | WCru
* - - var. **tiliifolia** | EBee EPfP GCal SNut WFar
- - B&SWJ 8497 | WCru
- - 'Yakushima' | CFil WCru WPGP
* - subsp. **quelpartensis** B&SWJ 8799 **new** | WCru
§ **arborescens** | CArn CFil CPLG MRav WFar WPGP
- 'Annabelle' ♀H4 | More than 30 suppliers
§ - subsp. **discolor** | GEil WCru WPat
- - 'Sterilis' | CFil GEil SPla SSpi WCru WPGP
- 'Grandiflora' ♀H4 | CBcs CBot CFil ELan EPfP MRav SPer WBod WCru WDin WHCG WPGP WSHC WWin
- subsp. **radiata** | CAbP CFil CMil GEil GIBF LRHS SSpi WBcn WCru WFar WPGP
aspera | CFil GKir SLon SSpi SSta WCru WKif
- 'Anthony Bullivant' | SSpi SWvt
- Kawakamii Group | CFil CMil CSpe EPla SSpi WCru WPGP
- - B&SWJ 1420 | WCru
- - B&SWJ 3462 | WCru
- - B&SWJ 6827 | WCru
- - B&SWJ 7025 | WCru
- - B&SWJ 7101 | WCru
- - 'August Abundance' **new** | WCru
- - 'September Splendour' **new** | WCru
- 'Kawakamii' | NLar
§ - 'Macrophylla' ♀H3 | CFil CMil CWib EPfP EWTr LRHS NBee NBlu NPal SMad SPer SPoG SSpi WCru WPGP
- 'Mauvette' | CBcs CFil CMil MBlu NPal SPer SSpi SSta WBcn WCru WGer WPGP
- 'Peter Chappell' | NLar SSpi WPGP
§ - subsp. **robusta** | CFil WCru WPGP
- 'Rocklon' | CFil CMil NLar SSpi WCru WGMN WPGP

- 'Rosthornii' | see *H. aspera* subsp. *robusta*
- 'Sam MacDonald' | CFil LRHS NLar SSpi WBcn WPGP
§ - subsp. **sargentiana** ♀H3 | More than 30 suppliers
- - large-leaved | WCot WPGP
- 'Spinners' | SSpi
- subsp. **strigosa** | CFil CMil CPLG EPfP WCru WPGP
- - B&SWJ 8201 | WCru
- 'Taiwan' | LRHS SSpi
- 'Taiwan Pink' | EPfP NLar
§ - Villosa Group ♀H3 | More than 30 suppliers
- 'Brilliant' | GEil
cinerea | see *H. arborescens* subsp. *discolor*
- 'Diabolo' | GEil
glandulosa B&SWJ 4031 | WCru
'Hallasan' (L) | CBcs
§ **heteromalla** | CFai CFil CMHG CTrG EPfP SSpi WPGP
- B&SWJ 2142 from India | WCru
- BWJ 7657 from China | WCru
- HWJCM 180 | WCru
- SF 338 | ISea
- B&SWJ 2602 from Sikkim | WCru
- Bretschneideri Group | EPfP GQui MBlu NLar WBod WBor WCru WFar
- 'Fan Si Pan' **new** | WCru
- 'Morrey's Form' | WCru
- 'Snowcap' | GQui IArd SLdr WBcn WCru
- f. **xanthoneura** | CFil SSpi
- - 'Wilsonii' | WCru WKif WSHC
- 'Yalung Ridge' | WCru
* **heterophylla** | MGos
hirta | CFil
- B&SWJ 5000 | WCru
indochinensis B&SWJ 8307 | WCru
integerrima | see *H. serratifolia*
integrifolia | CFil GGGa WCot
- B&SWJ 022 | WCru
- B&SWJ 6967 | WCru
involucrata | CFil CPLG EPfP GEil LRHS SSpi WBcn WCru WDin
- dwarf | CFil GEil WCru
- 'Hortensis' (d) ♀H3-4 | CDul CElw CFil CMil CPLG CPle EPfP MRav SPer SSpi WAbe WBod WCru WKif WPGP WSHC
* - 'Plena' (d) | CLAP WCot WCru WTMC
* - 'Sterilis' | EPfP SSpi
- 'Viridescens' | SSpi
'Korale Red' | WBcn
lobbii | WPGP
- B&SWJ 3214 | WCru
longipes | CFil CMil WCru WPGP
- BWJ 8188 | WCru
'Love You Kiss' (L) | WBcn
luteovenosa | CFil IDee WCru
- B&SWJ 5602 | WCru
* **macrocephala** | SSpi WPGP
macrophylla | LRHS
- Alpen Glow | see *H. macrophylla* 'Alpenglühen'
§ - 'Alpenglühen' (H) | CBcs CPLG CSBt ELan SHBN SRms WPGP
- 'Altona' (H) ♀H3-4 | CBcs CFil CWSG EPfP IArd ISea LRHS MGos MRav NPri SBod SPer WPGP WStI
- 'Amethyst' (H/d) | CFil WPGP
- 'Ami Pasquier' (H) ♀H3-4 | CBcs CDoC CFil CMac CSBt EBee EPfP GKir LRHS MRav MSwo SCoo SGar SLim SPla SSpi SWvt WBcn WGer WPGP WWeb
* - 'Aureomarginata' (v) | EPfP WCot
- 'Aureovariegata' (v) | CFil ELan LRHS SNut WBcn WPGP
- 'Ayesha' (H) | More than 30 suppliers
- 'Ayesha Blue' (H) | CPLG ENot LAst SWvt
- 'Bachstelze' (L) **new** | SSpi

– 'Beauté Vendômoise' (L)	CFil SSpi WPGP
– 'Benelux' (H)	CBcs CWSG
§ – 'Blauer Prinz' (H)	CFil CSBt CSam LRHS SHBN
§ – 'Blauling' (L)	CDoC SLdr WBVN
§ – 'Blaumeise' (L)	CFil MAsh MBri MRav NBlu SLdr SLon SSpi WGer WPGP
– 'Blue Bonnet' (H)	CFil COtt CSBt EPfP IBal SPer WHen WPGP
– Blue Butterfly	see *H. macrophylla* 'Blauling'
– Blue Prince	see *H. macrophylla* 'Blauer Prinz'
– Blue Sky	see *H. macrophylla* 'Blaumeise'
– Blue Tit	see *H. macrophylla* 'Blaumeise'
– 'Blue Wave'	see *H. macrophylla* 'Mariesii Perfecta'
– 'Bluebird' misapplied	see *H. serrata* 'Bluebird'
– 'Bodensee' (H)	CBcs EGra ENot GKir LRHS SBod SPla WBVN WStI
– 'Bouquet Rose' (H)	CWib ECtt GEil MRav WBod
– 'Bridal Bouquet' (H)	CDoC
– 'Brunette' (H)	CFil CMil
– 'Buchfink' (L)	CFil SSpi WPGP
– 'Cordata'	see *H. arborescens*
– 'Deutschland' (H)	CTri
– 'Domotoi' (H/d)	CFai CFil CMil GEil SNut
– Dragonfly	see *H. macrophylla* 'Hobella', 'Libelle'
* – 'Dwaag Pink'	MRav
– Early Sensation' **new**	SPoG WHil
– 'Eldorado' (H)	EHol
§ – 'Enziandom' (H)	CBcs CFil CSBt SSpi WPGP
– 'Europa' (H) ♀H3-4	CBcs CMac CTrw CWSG GKir LRHS MGos NPri SBod SEND WStI
§ – 'Fasan' (L)	CFil WPGP WSPU
– Firelight	see *H. macrophylla* 'Leuchtfeuer'
– Fireworks Blue	see *H. macrophylla* 'Jogosaki'
– Fireworks Pink	see *H. macrophylla* 'Jogosaki'
– Fireworks White	see *H. macrophylla* 'Hanabi'
– 'Fischer's Silberblau' (H)	CFil
– 'Forever Pink'	MAsh WGer
§ – 'Frau Fujiyo' (H)	CPLG LRHS
§ – 'Frau Katsuko'	LRHS SPer
§ – 'Frau Mariko' (H)	LRHS
§ – 'Frau Nobuko' (H)	LRHS WGMN
– 'Freudenstein' **new**	EOMN
– 'Frillibet' (H)	CAbP CDoC CFil EPfP LRHS WBcn WPGP
– 'Gartenbaudirektor Kuhnert' (H)	SMer
§ – 'Générale Vicomtesse de Vibraye' (H) ♀H3-4	CBcs CDoC CEnd CFil CMHG CTri CWSG EBee EPfP GKir LRHS MBar NCGa SHBN SLim SNut SPer SSpi WPGP WWin
– Gentian Dome	see *H. macrophylla* 'Enziandom'
– 'Geoffrey Chadbund'	see *H. macrophylla* 'Möwe'
– 'Gerda Steiniger'	CBcs SLdr
– 'Gertrud Glahn' (H)	CBcs EOMN SLdr SNut WFar
– 'Glowing Embers'	CFil IArd MBNS SEND WPGP
– Gold Dust' (v)	CFil WPGP
– 'Goliath' (H)	CFil EPfP LRHS WPGP
– 'Hamburg' (H)	CBcs CEnd CFil CTri CWSG EBee ECtt ENot EPfP LPVe LPan LRHS MGos MRav NBlu SDix SLdr WBrE WFar WStI WWeb
– 'Hanabi' (L/d)	CBcs CDoC CFee CMil MBlu WBcn WPGP
– 'Harlequin'	CFil CMil WPGP
– 'Harry's Pink Topper' (H)	MAsh
– 'Hatfield Rose' (H)	CBcs
– 'Hatsushimo' **new**	NLar
– 'Heinrich Seidel' (H)	CBcs CFil WBrE WMoo WPGP
– 'Hobergine'PBR (H)	CBcs
– 'Holstein' (H)	CFil MAsh MDun WPGP
§ – 'Hörnli' (H)	CFil LPan WPGP
– 'Izu-no-hana' (L/d)	CBcs CFil CMil MBlu SMHy SSpi SUsu WPGP

– 'Jogosaki' (L/d)	CBcs MBlu NLar WPGP
§ – 'Joseph Banks' (H)	CBcs
§ – 'Kardinal' (L)	CFil WPGP
– 'King George' (H)	CBcs CDoC CFil CSBt CTbh CWSG EBee EBre GEil GKir LAst LRHS MBar MGos MRav MWat SLdr SLim SPer SWvt WFar WMoo WPGP WStI WTel
– 'Kluis Superba' (H)	CBcs CFil CTri MRav WPGP
§ – 'Koningin Wilhelmina' (H)	CFil WBcn WPGP WTel
– 'Kuro-hime' (L)	CBcs
– 'La France' (H)	COtt CTri CWSG LRHS MBar MRav SLdr SMer WFar
– 'Lady Fujiyo'	see *H. macrophylla* 'Frau Fujiyo'
– Lady Katsuko' (H)	see *H. macrophylla* 'Frau Katsuko'
– 'Lady Mariko'	see *H. macrophylla* 'Frau Mariko'
– 'Lady Nobuko'	see *H. macrophylla* 'Frau Nobuko'
– 'Lady Taiko Blue'	see *H. macrophylla* 'Taiko' blue
– 'Lady Taiko Pink'	see *H. macrophylla* 'Taiko' pink
– 'Lanarth White' (L) ♀H3-4	CBcs CDoC CFil CSBt CTbh CTri EBee ELan EPfP MRav MSwo SHBN SLdr SLim SPer SReu SRms SSpi WBod WCru WPGP WPnP
– 'Leuchtfeuer' (H)	ENot EOMN LRHS WBcn WGer
§ – 'Libelle' (L)	CBcs CDoC CFil CSBt EBee EPfP MAsh SLim SNut SPer SPoG SSpi WBVN WKif WPGP WWeb
– 'Lilacina'	see *H. macrophylla* 'Mariesii Lilacina'
§ – 'Maculata' (L/v)	CSBt EHol ELan GEil GQui SGar WGwG
– 'Madame A. Riverain' (H)	CFil CWSG LRHS SBod
§ – 'Madame Emile Mouillère' (H) ♀H3-4	CBcs CBot CBrm CDoC CEnd CFil CPLG CSBt ENot EPfP GEil GKir LRHS MRav SBod SDix SHBN SLim SMer SNut SPer SPla SRms SSpi SSta WBod WCFE WGwG WPGP WWeb
– 'Maréchal Foch' (H)	CFil CTri WPGP
– 'Mariesii' (L)	CFil CMHG CSBt CTri EBee ELan ENot ISea LHop LRHS MSwo SDix SPer WGwG WKif WPnP WStI
§ – 'Mariesii Grandiflora' (L) ♀H3-4	CDul CFil EBee ENot EPfP LRHS MBar NBlu NCGa NPri SBod SEND SHBN SLdr SNut SPer SRms SSpi WBod WDin WFar WPGP WStI
§ – 'Mariesii Lilacina' (L) ♀H3-4	CFil EPfP MWhi SPer SSpi WKif WMoo WPGP
§ – 'Mariesii Perfecta' (L) ♀H3-4	More than 30 suppliers
– 'Mariesii Variegata' (L/v)	CWib
– 'Masja' (H)	CBcs COtt EGra IArd LRHS MGos MSwo NBee NBlu SHBN SLdr WWeb
– 'Mathilda Gutges' (H)	CDoC CFil CTbh SSpi WPGP WStI WWeb
– 'Merveille Sanguine'	IArd MAsh WBcn WPGP WPat
– 'Mini Hörnli'	see *H. macrophylla* 'Hörnli'
– 'Miss Belgium' (H)	CFil CTri
– 'Miss Hepburn'	CSBt SPer
– 'Mousmée'	CFil IArd SSpi
– 'Mousseline' (H)	LPan
§ – 'Möwe' (L) ♀H3-4	CBcs CDoC CEnd CFil CPLG EBee ECtt ENot LHop NPri SChu SCoo SDix SGar SLdr SNut SPer SRms SSpi SSta WPGP
§ – 'Nachtigall' (L)	SNut SSpi
– 'Niedersachsen' (H)	CDoC CFil MRav SMer WPGP
– Nightingale	see *H. macrophylla* 'Nachtigall'
– 'Nigra' (H) ♀H3-4	CBcs CChe CFil CPLG CWib EBee ELan EPfP EPla MGos SDix SHBN SNut SPer WCru WFar WGwG WPGP WStI

- 'Nikko Blue' (H)	CBcs CFil CWSG EBee EPfP MBar MDun NBlu SEND WBod WPGP	
§ - 'Nymphe' (H)	ENot LRHS	
- 'Otaksa' (H)	CFil	
- 'Parzifal' (H) ♀H3-4	CBcs CFil CTrw EPfP WPGP	
- 'Pax'	see *H. macrophylla* 'Nymphe'	
- 'Pfau' (L)	SSpi	
- Pheasant	see *H. macrophylla* 'Fasan'	
- 'Pia' (H)	CBcs CDoC CFil CPLG CPla CStu EHyt ELan ENor GKir IArd MAsh MBNS MRav MTho NWCA SBod SLim SMad SPer SPla SPoG SRms WAbe WCru WFar WPGP WPat WPnP WWeb	
- Pigeon	see *H. macrophylla* 'Taube'	
- 'Prinses Beatrix'	CBcs CChe CFil WPGP	
- 'Quadricolor' (L/v)	CAbb CFil CMil CPLG CTbh EBee EHoe EPfP LRHS MRav SDix SGar SHBN SLdr SLim SNut SPer SPla SPlb SRms WCot WGMN WHCG WPGP WSHC WWeb	
- Queen Wilhelmina	see *H. macrophylla* 'Koningin Wilhelmina'	
- 'R.F. Felton'	CBcs	
- 'Ramis Pietis' (L)	CBcs	
- 'Red Baron'	ENot	
- 'Red Masja' **new**	WWeb	
- Redbreast	see *H. macrophylla* 'Rotkehlchen'	
- 'Regula' (H)	CTrw	
- 'Renate Steiniger' (H)	CFai ENot SLdr WBcn WBod WGwG	
- 'Rosita' (H)	ENot LPan LRHS MAsh WFar	
§ - 'Rotkehlchen' (L)	CFai CFil SSpi WPGP	
- 'Rotschwanz' (L)	CFil CMil SSpi	
- 'Saint Claire'	CBcs CPLG	
- 'Sanguinea'	NPPs	
- 'Schwabenland'	NPri	
- 'Sea Foam' (L)	EBee NBlu WBan	
* - 'Shower'	LRHS	
- 'Sibylla' (H)	CBcs CFil WPGP	
- Sister Therese	see *H. macrophylla* 'Soeur Thérèse'	
§ - 'Soeur Thérèse' (H)	CBcs CFil CSBt ENot LPan LRHS MAsh MGos SWvt WGwG WPGP WStI	
§ - 'Taiko' blue (H)	LRHS SPer	
§ - 'Taiko' pink (H)	LRHS	
§ - 'Taube' (L)	CBcs CFil CPLG GQui NBlu	
N - Teller Blau (L)	CDoC COtt CSBt EBee ENot EPfP MAsh SCoo SLim SPoG SWvt WDin WWeb	
N - Teller Rosa (L)	CDoC EBee ENot EPfP MAsh NBlu SCoo SWvt WWeb	
N - Teller Rot (L)	CDoC EBee ENot EPfP MAsh SCoo SPlb SWvt WDin WWeb	
N - Teller variegated	see *H. macrophylla* 'Tricolor'	
N - Teller Weiss	see *H. macrophylla* 'Libelle'	
- 'Tokyo Delight' (L) ♀H3-4	CBrd CChe CDoC CFil CPLG EBee SLdr SSpi WBcn WPGP	
- 'Tovelit'	IArd LRHS	
- 'Tricolor' (L/v)	CBcs CBot CDoC CFil LAst LRHS MAsh MGos MTis NBee SBod SLon SPer WFar WKif WMoo WPGP WPnP	
- 'Val de Loire'	CWSG	
- 'Variegata'	see *H. macrophylla* 'Maculata'	
- 'Veitchii' (L) ♀H3-4	CBcs CBot CFil CMHG CPLG CSBt ENot EPfP MRav MSwo SBod SDix SGar SPer SPoG SSpi WPGP	
- 'Vicomte de Vibraye'	see *H. macrophylla* 'Générale Vicomtesse de Vibraye'	
- 'Westfalen' (H) ♀H3-4	IArd LRHS SDix SPla	
- 'White Lace' (L)	ELan	
- 'White Mop' **new**	CWib	

- 'White Wave'	see *H. macrophylla* 'Mariesii Grandiflora'	
'Messaline' **new**	SNut	
'Midori' (L)	CBcs	
paniculata	CFil CMCN CPne CTrw GIBF GKir LAst	
- B&SWJ 5413 from Japan	WCru	
- B&SWJ 3556 from Taiwan	WCru	
- 'Brussels Lace'	CAbP CFil LRHS MAsh NLar SNut SPla SSpi	
- 'Burgundy Lace'	CBcs MBlu	
- 'Everest'	CAbP LRHS MAsh SNut	
- 'Floribunda'	CFil EPfP EWTr LRHS MAsh SPer SSpi WPGP	
- 'Grandiflora' ♀H4	More than 30 suppliers	
- 'Greenspire'	CBcs LBuc LRHS MBlu WBcn	
- 'Kyushu' ♀H4	More than 30 suppliers	
- 'Limelight' PBR	CBcs MBlu WOVN	
- 'Mount Aso' **new**	CFil WPGP	
- 'Mount Everest' **new**	SLdr	
- 'Phantom'	WPat	
- Pink Diamond = 'Interhydia' ♀H4	CAbP CDoC CTbh CTri EBee EBre ENot LAst LRHS MAsh MBlu MBri MRav NPri SLim SMad SPla SSpi SSta WBod WCru WFar WPat	
- 'Pink Jewel'	CWib	
- 'Praecox'	SLon WCru WWin	
- 'Tardiva'	CBcs CBot CDoC GEil LPan LRHS MGos MRav NHol SDix SPer SRms WBan WBod WFar WHCG WKif WPGP WPat WWeb	
- 'Unique' ♀H4	CBcs CDoC CFil CHad CMil EBee ENot EPfP LRHS MAsh MBri MRav NBee SNut SPer SPla SSpi WBan WBod WCru WDin WFar WPGP WPat	
- 'White Lace'	MBlu WWes	
- 'White Moth'	CBcs CFil NLar SLdr SNut WBod SSpi	
peruviana		
× *serratifolia*		
petiolaris	see *H. anomala* subsp. *petiolaris*	
§ - 'Preziosa' ♀H3-4	More than 30 suppliers	
quelpartensis	CBcs CRHN GQui SSpi	
- B&SWJ 4400	WCru	
quercifolia ♀H3-4	More than 30 suppliers	
- 'Burgundy'	EPfP NLar	
- 'Flore Pleno'	see *H. quercifolia* 'Snow Flake'	
- 'Harmony'	CEnd CFil IArd SSta WHCG WPGP WPat	
- 'Pee Wee'	EPfP GEil LRHS MAsh SReu WBcn WPat	
- 'Sike's Dwarf'	CEnd CFil GCal NLar SSpi WPGP WPat	
§ - 'Snow Flake' (d)	CAbP CBcs CDoC CDul CEnd CFil CMil CPle CSPN ELan EMil EPfP GKir LRHS MAsh SLon SMur SPer SPla SSpi SSta WHCG WPGP	
- Snow Queen = 'Flemygea'	CBcs CDoC CKno CPMA CSBt CWSG EBee EPfP ISea MGos MRav MSte MWgw NLar SLim SPer SPla SWvt WFar WHCG WPGP	
- 'Tennessee Clone'	CFil WPGP	
robusta	SLPl	
sargentiana	see *H. aspera* subsp. *sargentiana*	
scandens	CFil	
- B&SWJ 5523	WCru	
- B&SWJ 5893	WCru	
§ - subsp. *chinensis*	WFar	
- - B&SWJ 1488	WCru	
- - B&SWJ 3420	WCru	
- - B&SWJ 3423 from Taiwan	WCru	
- - BWJ 8000 from Sichuan	WCru	
- subsp. *liukiuensis*	WCru	

– – B&SWJ 6022 — WCru
seemannii — More than 30 suppliers
serrata — CDul CTrw CWib WDin WKif
– B&SWJ 4817 — WCru
– B&SWJ 6241 — WCru
– 'Acuminata' — see *H. serrata* 'Bluebird'
– 'Aigaku' — CLAP WPGP
– 'Amacha' — CFil CMil WPGP
– 'Amagayana' — CMil CPLG WPGP
– 'Belle Deckle' — see *H. serrata* 'Blue Deckle'
– 'Beni-gaku' — CFil CLAP CMil CPLG CTbh EBee
  NLar SMer WPGP
– 'Beni-yama' — CFil WPGP
– 'Blue Deckle' (L) — CFil CMHG MAsh MRav SLdr SNut
  SPla SSpi WBcn WPGP
§ – 'Bluebird' ♀H3-4 — More than 30 suppliers
– 'Diadem' ♀H3-4 — CFil CMil CPLG SDix WPGP WSHC
– dwarf white — WCru
– 'Fuji Snowstorm' — CMil
– 'Golden Showers' **new** — CMil
– 'Golden Sunlight'PBR — LRHS MAsh SLon SPoG SWvt
– 'Graciosa' **new** — CFil CMil WPGP
– 'Grayswood' ♀H3-4 — CBcs CEnd CFil CSBt CWSG GKir
  GQui LRHS MBri MRav SDix SGar
  SPer SSpi WKif WPGP
– 'Hime-benigaku' **new** — CMil
– 'Intermedia' — CFil WPGP
– 'Jogasaki' — CFil
§ – 'Kiyosumi' (L) — CBcs CDoC CEnd CFil CLAP CMil
  CPLG SSpi WCru WPGP
– 'Klaveren' **new** — CMil
– 'Koreana' (L) — CMil
– 'Kurenai' (L) — SSpi
– 'Macrosepala' — CFil CMil
– 'Maiko' — CBcs CMil
– 'Miranda' (L) ♀H3-4 — CBrd CFil CPLG CSam SSpi WFar
  WPGP
– 'Miyama-yae-murasaki' — CFil CLAP CMil WPGP
  (d)
– 'Preziosa' — see *H.* 'Preziosa'
– 'Professeur Iida' **new** — CFil WPGP
– f. *prolifera* **new** — CFil CMil WPGP
– 'Ramis Pictis' **new** — CFil WPGP
– 'Red Brocade' — WCot
– 'Rosalba' ♀H3-4 — CFil CLAP CPLG EPfP MRav SPer
  SPla WFar WPGP WSHC
– 'Shichidanka-nishiki' — CBcs CFil
  (d/v)
– 'Shinonome' — CFil CLAP CMil WPGP
– 'Shirofugi' — CFil CMil WPGP
– 'Shirotae' (d) — CBcs CFil CMil WPGP
– 'Spreading Beauty' **new** — CMil
– var. *thunbergii* — CBcs CFil CMHG GQui WFar
  WPGP
* – – 'Plena' (d) — WCru
– 'Tiara' ♀H3-4 — CFil CMil EBee SSpi WBcn WPGP
  WWes
– 'Uzu Azisai' — CFil WPGP
– 'Yae-no-amacha' **new** — CFil WPGP
– subsp. *yezoensis* — CFil WPGP
  'Wryneck' (H)
§ *serratifolia* — CFil CHEx EPfP EPla SBra SSpi SSta
  WCru WGer WPGP
sikokiana — CLAP
– B&SWJ 5035 — WCru
– B&SWJ 5855 — WCru
'Sunset' (L) — CBcs
tiliifolia — see *H. anomala* subsp. *petiolaris*
villosa — see *H. aspera* Villosa Group
xanthoneura — see *H. heteromalla*
'Ya-no-amacha' — CBcs

Hydrastis (Ranunculaceae)
canadensis — CArn EBee GBuc GPoy LEur WCru

Hydrocharis (Hydrocharitaceae)
morsus-ranae — CDWL CRow EHon EMFW EPAt
  LNCo LPBA MSta NPer SWat

Hydrocotyle (Apiaceae)
asiatica — see *Centella asiatica*
nepalensis **new** — EBee
* *sibthorpioides* — CDes CPLG EBee EMan EMon
  'Variegata' (v) — EPPr GAbr GCal GMac WCHb
  WHil WPer
vulgaris — EMFW MSta NArg

Hydrophyllum (Hydrophyllaceae)
canadense — EBee EMar WCru
virginianum — EBee MSal

Hylomecon (Papaveraceae)
erectum — EBee
§ *japonica* — CPom EChP EGra EPar ERos ETow
  GCrs GEdr GKir MSte NBir NDov
  NGar NMen NRya SIng WAbe
  WCru WFar WHil WTin

Hylotelephium see *Sedum*

Hymenanthera see *Melicytus*

Hymenocallis (Amaryllidaceae)
'Advance' — LAma LRHS
§ *caroliniana* — LAma
x *festalis* ♀H1 — ERea EWTr LAma LRHS MBri NRog
  SDeJ SYvo WCot
harrisiana — LRHS WCot
§ *longipetala* — LRHS WCot
occidentalis — see *H. caroliniana*
'Sulphur Queen' ♀H1 — LRHS NRog SDeJ WCot

Hymenolepis (Asteraceae)
parviflora — see *Athanasia parviflora*

Hymenosporum (Pittosporaceae)
flavum — CPLG LRHS SOWG

Hymenoxys (Asteraceae)
brandegeei — see *Tetraneuris brandegeei*

Hyophorbe (Arecaceae)
indica — CRoM
§ *lagenicaulis* — CRoM LPal
verschaffeltii — CRoM LPal

Hyoscyamus (Solanaceae)
albus — GBar MGol MSal
niger — CArn EMFP GPoy MGol MSal
  WWye

Hyparrhenia (Poaceae)
hirta **new** — XPep

Hypericum ✿ (Clusiaceae)
ACE 2467 — WOBN
acmosepalum — CFil GEil GIBF WPGP WPat
§ *addingtonii* — EPla
aegypticum — CIyd CPBP EDAr EHyt EMlt EPot
  LBee LRHS MHer NJOw NMen
  NWCA NWoo SBla SIgm SRot SUsu
  WCom WFar WOld WPat WPer
  XPep
amblycalyx — SIgm
androsaemum — CAgr CArn CRWN ECha EGoo
  ELan ELau ENot GKir ISea MHer
  MRav MSal MSwo NPer NSco SHFr
  WDin WMoo WWpP

§ - 'Albury Purple' — CElw GBuc GEil GKir LDai MHer MRav WHrl
- 'Autumn Blaze' — MGos
§ - 'Dart's Golden Penny' — SPer WBcn
- 'Excellent Flair' — MGos NLar
- 'Orange Flair' — WWpP
§ - f. *variegatum* 'Mrs Gladis Brabazon' (v) — MWgw NBir NSti SBod SLon WBcn WCom WCot WHrl WWpP
§ *annulatum* — EMon
ascyron — EBee GIBF
athoum — CLyd EHyt MBro NBir NLAp SScr WPat
atomarium — EBee WPGP
attenuatum — GIBF
balearicum — CFil CLyd EHrv IFro MTho SDry SIgm WAbe WCom WPGP XPep
barbatum — NRya
- MESE 371 — EBee
§ *beanii* — WBod
bellum — CPle GCal SLon
buckleyi — WPat
calycinum — CBcs CChe CDul ELan ENot EPfP GKir IHMH LBuc LGro MBar MGos MRav MWat NBlu NWea SHBN SPer SWvt WDin WGwG WMoo WShp WTel WWpP
§ *cerastioides* — CTri CWib EDAr GKir LBee LRHS SIgm SIng SRms SScr WAbe WPer WWin
coris — CLyd EWes LRHS MBro MTho MWat SRms
cuneatum — see *H. pallens*
x *cyathiflorum* — CDoC CMac
'Gold Cup'
densiflorum — CBcs
'Goldball' **new**
x *dummeri* — EMil NHol
'Peter Dummer'
'Eastleigh Gold' — SLon
elatum — see *H.* x *inodorum*
elodeoides — MSta
elodes — EMFW
empetrifolium — XPep
- 'Prostatum' — see *H. empetrifolium* subsp. *tortuosum*
§ - subsp. *tortuosum* — CLyd EWes
§ *forrestii* ♀H4 — CFil EBee EPfP LRHS NWea WFar WPGP
- B&L 12469 — WPGP
- Hird 54 — WPGP
N *fragile* hort. — see *H. olympicum* f. *minus*
frondosum 'Buttercup' — NLar
- 'Sunburst' — EBee EPfP LRHS MGos MWgw WFar
N 'Gemo' — MGos
'Gold Penny' — see *H. androsaemum* 'Dart's Golden Penny'
'Golden Beacon' **new** — GBin LAst SPoG WBcn WCot
grandiflorum — see *H. kouytchense*
henryi L 753 — SRms
'Hidcote' ♀H4 — More than 30 suppliers
'Hidcote Silver Ghost' — WBcn
'Hidcote Variegated' (v) — EBee GEil MAsh MCCP SLim SPer SRms WBrE WFar WWeb
hircinum — EOHP
- subsp. *cambessedesii* — LRHS
humifusum — EHyt
§ x *inodorum* — GGar NBir
- 'Albury Purple' — see *H. androsaemum* 'Albury Purple'
- 'Elstead' — ECtt ELan EWTr GKir MBar MGos MRav MWat NBid NBlu NLRH SHBN SRms WBan WDin WHCG WWin

- 'Summergold' (v) — WBod
- 'Ysella' — EHoe EWes MRav MSwo MTPN SDry SPer
japonicum — EWes
kalmianum — EWes
kelleri — EHyt ITim
§ *kiusianum* — MBar MTho
var. *yakusimense*
§ *kouytchense* ♀H4 — CBcs EPfP EWes GQui LRHS MAsh MRav NLRH SDry WBVN WCFE WCwm WPat WSpi
lancasteri — EPfP LRHS WBcn
leschenaultii hort. — see *H. addingtonii*, *H.* 'Rowallane'
linarioides — CLyd GTou
'Locke' — LAst
maclarenii — GCal WPGP
'Milkmaid' — GEil
x *moserianum* ♀H4 — EBee ENot EPfP MBar MRav NPer SHBN SPer SRms WDin WStI
§ - 'Tricolor' (v) — More than 30 suppliers
- 'Variegatum' — see *H.* x *moserianum* 'Tricolor'
'Mrs Brabazon' — see *H. androsaemum* f. *variegatum* 'Mrs Gladis Brabazon'
nummularium — NBir WAbe
olympicum ♀H4 — CNic CTri ECha ELan EMlt EPfP GKir LGro LRHS MBrN MHer MWat MWgw NFor SBla SIng SPer SRms WDin WHen WShp XPep
I - 'Calypso' — MWgw
- 'Eden Star' — NPro
- 'Grandiflorum' — see *H. olympicum* f. *uniflorum*
§ - f. *minus* — CNic CTri ECtt EGoo GCal LRHS MOne MWhi NBlu SPlb SRms WCom WPer WStI WWin
§ - - 'Sulphureum' — CBot ESis EWes MLLN NBir SPer SRms WCFE WSHC WWin
§ - - 'Variegatum' (v) — EHyt EWes LBee NBir NLAp WPat
- f. *uniflorum* — CM&M EBre EDAr IHMH LIck MBar MBro NBro NPri NVic SEND
- - 'Citrinum' ♀H4 — CLyd CMea ECha ECtt EDAr EHyt LBee LRHS MBro MWat NBro NDlv NLAp SBla SIgm SUsu WAbe WCom WCot WEas WHoo WKif WPGP WPat
orientale — EBee EWes SScr
§ *pallens* — ECho NMen
patulum var. *forrestii* — see *H. forrestii*
- var. *henryi* Rehder & hort. — see *H. pseudohenryi*
- var. *henryi* Veitch ex Bean — see *H. beanii*
perforatum — CAgr CArn CHby EBee ELau EOHP EPfP GBar GPoy MGas MHer NMir SIde WHer WJek WMoo WSel WWye
- 'Crusader' (v) — WHer
polyphyllum — see *H. olympicum* f. *minus*
- 'Citrinum' — see *H. olympicum* f. *minus* 'Sulphureum'
- 'Grandiflorum' — see *H. olympicum* f. *uniflorum*
- 'Sulphureum' — see *H. olympicum* f. *minus* 'Sulphureum'
- 'Variegatum' — see *H. olympicum* f. *minus* 'Variegatum'
prolificum — CFai ECtt MMHG
§ *pseudohenryi* L 1029 — GBuc
pseudopetiolatum — GTou
- var. *yakusimense* — see *H. kiusianum* var. *yakusimense*
quadrangulum L. — see *H. tetrapterum*
reptans hort. — see *H. olympicum* f. *minus*
reptans Dyer — CMea CNic CPBP ECha EWes
§ 'Rowallane' ♀H3 — CDul CTrC CTrw EPfP EPla ISea SDix SHBN SMrm SSpi WBod

stellatum	WBcn WCFE WFar
'Sungold'	see *H. kouytchense*
tenuicaule KR 743	ISea
§ ***tetrapterum***	CArn MSal NSco
tomentosum	XPep
trichocaulon	CLyd EHol EWes GFlt MBro NLАp
	WPat WWin
uralum HWJ 520	WCru
xylosteifolium	SLon
yakusimense	see *H. kiusianum* var.
	yakusimense
yezoense	WBrE

Hypocalymma (*Myrtaceae*)
angustifolium	SOWG

Hypocalyptus (*Papilionaceae*)
sophoroides	SPlb

Hypochaeris (*Asteraceae*)
maculata	WHer
radicata	NMir

Hypocyrta see *Nematanthus*

Hypoestes (*Acanthaceae*)
aristata	CPLG ERea EShb
§ ***phyllostachya*** (v) ♀H1	MBri
- 'Bettina' (v)	MBri
- 'Carmina' (v)	MBri
- 'Purpuriana' (v)	MBri
- 'Wit' (v)	MBri
sanguinolenta	see *H. phyllostachya*
misapplied	

Hypolepis (*Dennstaedtiaceae*)
***alpina* new**	EAmu
millefolium	GGar WCot
punctata	EFer

Hypoxis (*Hypoxidaceae*)
hirsuta	EWes
hygrometrica	ECou NMen WAbe WOBN
krebsii	LTwo
parvula	ITim NMen SBla
- var. ***albiflora***	EPot
§ - - 'Hebron Farm Biscuit'	CBro CWrd EWes GEdr SAga SBla
	WAbe
- pink-flowered	EPot
* ***tasmanica***	EMan

Hypoxis x *Rhodohypoxis* see x *Rhodoxis*
H. parvula x *R. baurii* see x *Rhodoxis hybrida*

Hypsela (*Campanulaceae*)
RB 94066	MNrw
longiflora	see *H. reniformis*
§ ***reniformis***	EBre EDAr EMan EMlt GKir LBee
	LRHS MOne MRav NHol NJOw
	NLAp NRya NWCA SIng WFar
	WWin
- 'Greencourt White' **new**	GBuc

Hyssopus (*Lamiaceae*)
***ambiguus* new**	XPep
officinalis	More than 30 suppliers
- f. ***albus***	CBod CSev ECha EGoo ELau EPfP
	GPoy MBow MHer NBlu NGHP
	SIde SPlb WBry WCHb WHHs
	WHer WJek WPer WSel WWye
§ - subsp. ***aristatus***	CArn CBod CHrt EBee EBre EDAr
	ELau GPoy LLWP MHer NBlu
	NLRH SWal WCHb WEas WJek
	WSSM WSel WWin WWye

- - white	WEas
- subsp. ***canescens* new**	XPep
- 'Roseus'	CBod CBrm CSev EBee ECha EGoo
	ELau EPPr EPfP GPoy LLWP MBNS
	MBow MHer NFor NGHP SIde
	WCHb WHHs WHer WJek WKif
	WPer WWye
* ***schugnanicus***	EBee LLWP MHar
* - ***albus***	EBee
seravschanicus	EOHP
tianschanicus	LLWP

Hystrix (*Poaceae*)
patula	More than 30 suppliers

I

Iberis (*Brassicaceae*)
amara	WBWf
aurosica 'Sweetheart'	EBre LPVe NMen
'Betty Swainson'	GBri SMrm WCot
candolleana	see *I. pruitii* Candolleana Group
commutata	see *I. sempervirens*
'Correvoniana'	WEas
'Dick Self'	EBre LRHS
gibraltarica	LRav NFor NPri SECG SRms WBVN
	WGor
'Golden Candy'	EBre ENot WWeb
§ ***pruitii*** Candolleana	EHyt
Group	
saxatilis	EDAr XPep
- ***candolleana***	see *I. pruitii* Candolleana Group
semperflorens	WCFE WCom WCot WSPU XPep
§ ***sempervirens*** ♀H4	CBcs CHrt CTri EBre ELan EPfP
	LAst LGro MHer MWat NArg NBid
	NBlu NBro NFor NOrc NVic SEND
	SRms STre WBrE WCFE WFar WPer
	WShp
- 'Compacta'	MWrn SBod
- 'Little Gem'	see *I. sempervirens* 'Weisser
	Zwerg'
- 'Plena' (d)	WCom
- 'Pygmaea'	CNic ECtt MWat NMen SBla WHil
§ - 'Schneeflocke' ♀H4	COIW CWCL EBre EMlt ENot GKir
	LPVe LRHS LRav MBro NHol
	NJOw SIng SPer SWvt WHoo
	WShp
- Snowflake	see *I. sempervirens* 'Schneeflocke'
- 'Variegata' (v)	WCom
§ - 'Weisser Zwerg'	CMea ECha ECtt ELan LAst LBee
	LRHS MBro MHer MRav NMen
	SBla SRms WAbe WHoo WShp
	WWin

Idesia (*Flacourtiaceae*)
polycarpa	CAbP CAgr CBcs CFil CMCN CTho
	EPfP IDee LHop LRHS SSpi SSta
	WBVN WDin WFar WPGP WPat

Ilex ✿ (*Aquifoliaceae*)
N x ***altaclerensis***	GKir SHHo STop
- 'Atkinsonii' (m)	SHHo
- 'Belgica' (f)	SHHo
§ - 'Belgica Aurea' (f/v)	CBcs CDoC CSBt CTho EBee EPfP
♀H4	GKir LPan MBar MBri MGos MWat
	NBee NHol NWea SEND SHBN
	SHHo SKee WBcn WFar WWHy
- 'Camelliifolia' (f) ♀H4	CSBt CTho EBee ELan EPfP GKir
	LPan MBlu MBri MRav MWat
	NWea SHHo SPer STop WBcn WFar
- 'Golden King' (f/v) ♀H4	More than 30 suppliers

- 'Hendersonii' (f)
- 'Hodginsii' (m) ♀H4 — ECot MBar MRav NWea SEND SHHo WFar
- 'Howick' (f/v) — SHHo WBcn
- 'James G. Esson' (f) — SBir SHHo
- 'Lady Valerie' (f/v) — IArd SHHo
- 'Lawsoniana' (f/v) ♀H4 — More than 30 suppliers
- 'Maderensis' — NRib
- 'Maderensis Variegata' — see *I. aquifolium* 'Maderensis Variegata'
- 'Marnockii' (f) — SHHo WBcn
- 'Moorei' (m) — SHHo
- 'Mundyi' (m) — SHHo
- 'Purple Shaft' (f) — GKir MAsh MRav SHHo
- 'Ripley Gold' (f/v) — EBee GKir MAsh NHol SAga SCoo SHHo STop
- 'Silver Sentinel' — see *I.* x *altaclerensis* 'Belgica Aurea'
- 'W.J. Bean' (f) — SHHo
- 'Wilsonii' (f) — LPan MWat NWea SHHo
aquifolium ♀H4 — More than 30 suppliers
- 'Alaska' (f) — CDoC CDul CMCN CTho EBee EBre EMil ENot GKir LAst LBuc MAsh NBlu NSti SBir SHHo STop SWvt WFar WWHy
- 'Amber' (f) ♀H4 — CTri MWat SHHo SMad WBcn
- 'Angustifolia' (f) — EPla WFar
- 'Angustifolia' (m or f) — EPfP MBar MWat NHol SHHo WBVN WBcn WFar
§ - 'Argentea Marginata' (f/v) ♀H4 — More than 30 suppliers
§ - 'Argentea Marginata Pendula' (f/v) — CDoC CDul CTri CWib ELan ENot EPfP GKir LPan LRHS MAsh NHol NWea SHHo SLim SRms WFar WPat
- 'Argentea Pendula' — see *I. aquifolium* 'Argentea Marginata Pendula'
- 'Argentea Variegata' — see *I. aquifolium* 'Argentea Marginata'
- 'Atlas' (m) — CBcs CDoC LBuc
- 'Aurea Marginata' (f/v) — CMHG CTho EBee EHoe GKir LPan MGos NBlu NHol NWea SBod SHBN SHHo SKee WCFE WDin WFar WPat WRHF
- 'Aurea Marginata Pendula' (f/v) — CDoC NHol SLim SPer WPat
- 'Aurea Ovata' — see *I. aquifolium* 'Ovata Aurea'
- 'Aurea Regina' — see *I. aquifolium* 'Golden Queen'
- 'Aureovariegata Pendula' — see *I. aquifolium* 'Weeping Golden Milkmaid'
- 'Aurifodina' (f) — GKir IMGH SHHo WBcn
§ - 'Bacciflava' (f) — CBcs CDoC CDul CSBt CTho CTri EBee ELan EPfP EWTr GKir LRHS MBar MBlu MBri MGos MRav MWat NBee NBlu NFor NHol NWea SHHo SLim SPer SRms SWvt WCFE WDin
- 'Bowland' (f/v) — NHol SHHo
- 'Cookii' (f) — SHHo
- 'Copper' — WBcn
- 'Crassifolia' (f) — EPla SHHo SMad
- 'Crispa' (m) — CDul CPle EBee MBlu NHol SBir SHHo
- 'Crispa Aureomaculata' — see *I. aquifolium* 'Crispa Aureopicta'
§ - 'Crispa Aureopicta' (m/v) — SHHo WBcn WPat
- 'Elegantissima' (m/v) — SHHo WWHy
- 'Ferox' (m) — CDul ELan EPfP GKir LRHS NLRH SHHo SPer STop WBcn WDin WGwG WWHy
- 'Ferox Argentea' (m/v) ♀H4 — More than 30 suppliers
* - 'Ferox Argentea Picta' (m/v) — LRHS WWHy

- 'Ferox Aurea' (m/v) — CDoC CPle CSBt EBee ELan EPfP EPla GKir LAst MAsh NHol SHHo SPer WWHy
§ - 'Flavescens' (f) — CBot EBee EPfP NHol SHHo WBcn
* - 'Forest Weeping' — LRHS
- 'Foxii' (m) — SHHo
- 'Fructo Aurantiaco' (f) — EBee
- 'Fructu Luteo' — see *I. aquifolium* 'Bacciflava'
- 'Gold Flash' (f/v) — EBee GKir LRHS MBri MGos NBee NBlu NHol SHHo SLim WBcn WDin
- 'Golden Hedgehog' — EPfP GKir WWHy
- 'Golden Milkboy' (m/v) — EBee ELan EMil EPfP GKir MBlu MGos SHHo WCFE WDin WPat WWHy
- 'Golden Milkmaid' (f/v) — EHol
§ - 'Golden Queen' (m/v) ♀H4 — CDoC CWSG CWib EBee ENot GKir LRHS MGos NBir NHol NWea SHHo SPer SReu SRms WPat
- 'Golden Tears' — SHHo WBcn
- 'Golden van Tol' (f/v) — CBcs CDoC CLnd CSBt CTri EBee EBre ELan ENot GKir IMGH LAst LPan LRHS MBar MBlu MGos MSwo NBee NHol NSti SHBN SHHo SRms WDin WStI WWeb
- 'Green Pillar' (f) — EPfP LBuc SHHo WWHy
- 'Handsworth New Silver' (f/v) ♀H4 — More than 30 suppliers
- 'Harpune' (f) — SHHo WWHy
§ - 'Hascombensis' — EHol LHop LPhx MBro MGos NHol NMen WFar
- 'Hastata' (m) — CWib IArd
- 'Ingramii' (m/v) — SBir SHHo WBcn
- 'J.C. van Tol' (f) ♀H4 — More than 30 suppliers
- 'Latispina' (f) — SHHo
- 'Laurifolia Aurea' (m/v) — SHHo
- 'Lichtenthalii' (f) — IArd SHHo
- 'Madame Briot' (f/v) ♀H4 — CDoC CMHG CSBt CTri CWib EBee ELan ENot EPfP GKir IMGH LAst LRHS MAsh MBar MBri MSwo NBlu NHol NWea SHHo SPer SRms SWvt WBVN WDin WFar WMoo WTel WWHy
§ - 'Maderensis Variegata' (m/v) — SHHo
- 'Monstrosa' (m) — SHHo
- moonlight holly — see *I. aquifolium* 'Flavescens'
- 'Myrtifolia' (m) — CDoC ELan EPfP GKir MBar MBlu MGos MRav MTed NBlu WFar WWHy
- 'Myrtifolia Aurea' (m/v) — SBir WBcn
§ - 'Myrtifolia Aurea Maculata' (m/v) ♀H4 — CBrm CDoC CSam EBee EHoe ELan EPfP GKir IMGH LAst LRHS MAsh MBri MRav NHol NSti NWea SHHo SLim SPer SWvt WBVN WFar WPat
- 'Myrtifolia Aureovariegata' — see *I. aquifolium* 'Myrtifolia Aurea Maculata'
§ - 'Ovata Aurea' (m/v) — SHHo
- 'Pendula' (f) — EPfP MWat SHHo
- 'Pendula Mediopicta' — see *I. aquifolium* 'Weeping Golden Milkmaid'
- 'Purple Lady' — WBcn
- 'Purple Lord' — WBcn
§ - 'Pyramidalis' (f) ♀H4 — CDoC CDul CEnd CSBt CTho CTri EBee ELan ENot GKir LRHS MAsh MBar MBri MGos MLan MRav NBee NBlu NFor NHol NWea SHHo SRms WDin WWHy
- 'Pyramidalis Aureomarginata' (f/v) — CDoC LRHS MGos MLan SHHo WBcn
- 'Pyramidalis Fructu Luteo' (f) ♀H4 — GKir MBar NWea SHHo WBcn
- 'Rubricaulis Aurea' (f/v) — NHol SHHo STop WBcn

- 'Sharpy' (f)	SBir
- Siberia = 'Limsi'[PBR] (f)	EBee SHHo
- 'Silver King'	see *I. aquifolium* 'Silver Queen'
- 'Silver Lining' (f/v)	SHHo STop
- 'Silver Milkboy' (f/v)	CTho EHoe ELan EMil LRHS MBNS
	MBlu MGos SBir WFar WWHy
- 'Silver Milkmaid' (f/v)	CDoC CWSG EBee EPfP GKir LAst
	LRHS MBar MRav NHol SHBN
	SHHo SLim SPer SWvt WBVN
	WMoo WRHF WWHy
§ - 'Silver Queen' (m/v) ♀H4	More than 30 suppliers
- 'Silver Sentinel'	see *I. x altaclerensis* 'Belgica Aurea'
- 'Silver van Tol' (f/v)	CDoC EBee ELan ENot IMGH LAst
	LRHS NHol NPer NWea SHHo SPer
	SPoG WBcn WFar WStl WWHy
	WWeb
- 'Victoria' (m)	WBcn
§ - 'Watereriana' (m/v)	EHol LRHS MAsh SMur WBcn
- 'Waterer's Gold'	see *I. aquifolium* 'Watereriana'
§ - 'Weeping Golden Milkmaid' (f/v)	SHHo WPat
x *aquipernyi*	
- Dragon Lady = 'Meschick' (f)	COtt LPan SHHo WWHy
- 'San Jose' (f)	CMCN SHHo
x *attenuata*	WFar
- 'Sunny Foster' (f/v)	CDul CMCN ENot EPla MGos
	SHHo WBcn WFar
§ *bioritsensis*	CMCN CTri NWea SBir WBcn
buergeri	CMCN
cassine	CMCN
§ - var. *angustifolia*	MAsh STop
chinensis misapplied	see *I. purpurea*
ciliospinosa	CFil CMCN WPGP
colchica	CMCN SBir SHHo
corallina	CBcs CMCN
cornuta	ERom LPan SHHo WBcn WFar
* - 'Aurea'	SHHo
- 'Burfordii' (f)	SHHo
§ - 'Dazzler' (f)	LPan SHHo
- 'Fine Line' (f)	SHHo
- 'Ira S. Nelson' (f/v)	SHHo
- 'O. Spring' (f/v)	CMHG EPla SHHo WBcn
- 'Rotunda' (f)	SHHo
I - 'Willowleaf' (f)	SHHo
crenata	CMCN CTri ERom ESis GKir LPan
	MBar SHHo WDin WFar WNor
- 'Akagi'	WFar
- 'Aureovariegata'	see *I. crenata* 'Variegata'
- 'Braddock Heights' (f)	SHHo
- 'Cape Fear' (m)	SHHo
- 'Carolina Upright' (m)	SHHo
- 'Cole's Hardy' (f)	SHHo
- 'Convexa' (f) ♀H4	CBcs EBee ENot EPfP EGil GKir
	IMGH LPan LRHS MBar MBri NHol
	NWea SHHo WFar WPat
- 'Convexed Gold'	MBri
- 'Fastigiata' (f)	CChe CDoC CEnd EBee EPfP EPla
	GKir LAst LPan LRHS MAsh MBNS
	MBar MBri MGos NBlu SCoo SHHo
	SPer WFar WWes
- 'Fructo Luteo'	see *I. crenata* f. *watanabeana*
- 'Fukarin'	see *I. crenata* 'Shiro-fukurin'
* - 'Glory Gem' (f)	SHHo
- 'Gold Tips'	MGos
- 'Golden Gem' (f) ♀H4	CBrm CDoC CDul CSBt ELan ENot
	EPfP GEil GKir LPan LRHS MAsh
	MBar MBri MGos MLan MRav
	MWat NBee NBlu NHol NWea
	SHHo SLim SPer WDin WFar
	WGwG WHar WPat
- 'Green Dragon' (m)	EPla WWes
- 'Green Hedge'	LBuc
- 'Green Island' (m)	SHHo

- 'Green Lustre' (f)	SHHo
- 'Helleri' (f)	CMCN EPfP EPla MBar MBro SBla
	SHHo WPat
- 'Hetzii' (f)	SHHo
- 'Ivory Hall' (f)	EPla SHHo
- 'Ivory Tower' (f)	SHHo
* - 'Kobold'	SHHo
- 'Korean Gem'	EPla SHHo
- var. *latifolia* (m)	SHHo
- 'Luteovariegata'	see *I. crenata* 'Variegata'
- 'Mariesii' (f)	ESis IMGH MBlu MBro SBla SHHo
	WPat
- 'Mount Halla' (f)	CMCN
- 'Nakada' (m)	SHHo
- var. *paludosa*	CFil EBee WPGP
- 'Pride's Tiny'	SHHo
I - 'Pyramidalis' (f)	CMil NHol NWea WPat
§ - 'Shiro-fukurin' (f/v)	CMCN CMHG ELan EPfP GKir
	LAst LRHS MAsh NHol SHHo
- 'Sky Pencil' (f)	CMCN
- 'Snowflake'	see *I. crenata* 'Shiro-fukurin'
- 'Stokes' (m)	LRHS NLRH NLar SHHo
§ - 'Variegata' (v)	CMCN EPla GKir LRHS MBar NHol
	SHHo
§ - f. *watanabeana* (f)	SHHo
'Dazzler'	see *I. cornuta* 'Dazzler'
decidua	CMCN CPle
dimorphophylla	CBcs CDoC CMCN SHHo
- 'Somerset Pixie'	SHHo
dipyrena	CFil
'Doctor Kassab' (f)	CMCN SHHo
'Drace' (f)	SHHo
'Elegance' (f)	WFar
fargesii	CPne CTho
ficoidea	CMCN
glabra	SHHo
'Good Taste' (f)	SHHo WFar
hascombensis	see *I. aquifolium* 'Hascombensis'
hookeri	SHHo
'Indian Chief' (f)	MBlu SMad WFar
insignis	see *I. kingiana*
integra	CFil
'John T. Morris' (m)	SHHo
§ *kingiana*	CFil EPla WFar WPGP
x *koehneana*	CBot CFil
- 'Chestnut Leaf' (f) ♀H4	CDoC CFil CLnd CMCN MRav
	SHHo SMad WBcn WFar WLeb
	WPGP WWeb
latifolia	CFil CHEx CMCN SHHo SMad
	WPGP
'Lydia Morris' (f)	CSam SHHo WFar
'Mary Nell' (f)	SBir SHHo
x *meserveae*	SHHo
- Blue Angel (f)	More than 30 suppliers
- Blue Maid = 'Mesid' (f)	EMil
- Blue Prince (m)	CBcs CBrm CDoC CDul COtt EBee
	GKir LBuc MBar MBlu NBlu NHol
	NWea SBir SHBN SHHo SLim SPer
	WDin WFar WStl WWHy
- Blue Princess (f)	CBcs CBrm COtt ENot EPfP GKir
	LBuc LPan MBar MBlu MRav NBlu
	NHol NSti NWea SHBN SHHo SLim
	SPer WStl WWHy
- Golden Girl = 'Mesgolg' (f)	EMil
* - Red Darling' (f)	CDul
muchagara	CBcs CMCN
myrtifolia	CMCN ECot MLan MRav NPri
	WCFE
'Nellie R. Stevens' (f)	CDoC LPan NWea SBir WBcn
nothofagifolia	WAbe
opaca	CMCN
pedunculosa	CMCN SHHo
perado latifolia	see *I. perado* subsp. *platyphylla*

§ – subsp. **platyphylla** — CBcs CHEx CMCN EPla MBlu SAPC SArc SHHo WPGP

pernyi — CMCN CTrG GKir SHHo SLon WBVN WBcn WFar WPic

– var. **veitchii** — see *I. bioritsensis*

§ **purpurea** — CMCN

'Pyramidalis' — see *I. aquifolium* 'Pyramidalis'

rugosa — CMCN

'September Gem' (f) — CMCN

serrata — CMen

'Sparkleberry' (f) — LRHS

suaveolens — CMCN

verticillata — CMCN CPne EPla GKir IMGH LPan NWea WDin WFar

– (f) — EPfP NWea WFar

– (m) — CDoC EPfP

– 'Christmas Cheer' (f) — WFar

– 'Maryland Beauty' (f) **new** — CPMA

– 'Southern Gentleman' (m) — CPMA

– 'Winter Red' (f) — CMCN CPMA GKir MMHG

vomitoria — CMCN

x **wandoensis** — CMCN SBir SHHo

'Washington' (f) — CPle SBir

yunnanensis — CMCN

Iliamna see *Sphaeralcea*

Illicium (Illiciaceae)

anisatum — CArn CBcs CFil CPle EPfP SSpi WFar WPGP WPat WSHC

floridanum — CFil EPfP NLar SSpi WPGP

– 'Halley's Comet' — NLar

– variegated (v) — SSpi

henryi — CFil CMCN CMHG EPfP NLar SSpi WPGP WSHC

aff. **henryi** BWJ 8024 **new** — WCru

parviflorum — SSpi

'Woodland Ruby' — SSpi

Impatiens ✿ (Balsaminaceae)

from China — CLAP CPom CSpe EBee EMan GCal MCCP WCot WPGP

apiculata — CPLG GCal WHil

arguta — CPLG CPom CSpe EMan GCal WCru

auricoma — EBak SHFr

balfourii — EHrv EMan EMon NBir WCot

'Cardinal Red' — CHal

congolensis — EPfP

cristata — CPLG WCot

'Diamond Rose' — CHal

double-flowered (d) — EBak

falcifer — CSpe

Fiesta Series 'Burgundy Rose' PBR (d) — WWol

– Fiesta Appleblossom = 'Balfieplos' (d) — LAst NPri SVil WWol

– Fiesta Blush = 'Balfieblus' (d) — NPri

– Fiesta Coral Bells = 'Balfiecobl' (d) — NPri

– 'Fiesta White' PBR (d) — NPri WWol

– Fiesta Olé Cherry = 'Balolecher' (d) — NPri

– Fiesta Olé Frost = 'Balolefro' (d) — NPri

– Fiesta Olé Peppermint = 'Balolepep' (d) **new** — SVil

– Fiesta Olé Salmon = 'Balolesal' (d) **new** — NPri SVil

– Fiesta Olé Stardust = 'Balolestop' (d) — NPri

– Fiesta Orange Spice = 'Balficorce' PBR (d) — WWol

– Fiesta Sparkler Cherry = 'Balfiespary' (d) **new** — SVil

– Fiesta Stardust Lavender = 'Balfiesala' — LIck

– 'Lavender Orchid' PBR (d) — NPri

– 'Pink Ruffle' PBR (d) — LAst NPri

– 'Salsa Red' PBR (d) — LAst NPri WWol

– 'Sparkler Rose' PBR (d) — NPri SVil

glandulifera 'Candida' — CBre EMon

Harmony Series Harmony Light Pink = 'Danharltpk' **new** — LAst

– Harmony Purple Eye = 'Danharpley' **new** — LAst

– Margenta = 'Danharmgta' **new** — LAst

hawkeri — see *I. schlechteri*

hians — SHFr

aff. **kerriae** B&SWJ 7219 — WCru

kilimanjari — CSpe GCal

x **pseudoviola**

longiloba B&SWJ 6623 — WCru

'Madame Pompadour' — CHal

New Guinea Group — see *I. schlechteri*

niamniamensis — CHll EBak ERea SSte

– 'Congo Cockatoo' — CHal EOHP ESlt LIck SHFr SRms

– 'Golden Cockatoo' (v) — CHal EBak ESlt IFro MCCP

omeiana — CHEx CLAP CPom CSpe EBee EMan EPPr GCal ITer MCCP MNrw SAga SSpi SSte WBor WCot WCru WDyG WPGP

pink-flowered, from China **new** — CPom

pseudoviola — SDix SHFr

'Raspberry Ripple' — CHal

§ **schlecteri** — CHal EBak MBri

sodenii — CSpe SDys SHFr

sulcata — SHFr

sultani — see *I. walleriana*

tinctoria — CDoC CFil CFir CHEx CHll CPLG CPlt CPom CSpe GCal ITer MNrw SBla SIgm SSpi SSte WCot WCru WMul WPGP WPrP

– subsp. **elegantissima** — CFee

– subsp. **tinctoria** — IFro

ugandensis — CFil SSpi

uniflora new — GCal

Velvetea = 'Secret Love' PBR — CSpe

violeta B&SWJ 6608 — WCru

walkeri — CFee WCot

§ **walleriana** — EBak MBri

– 'Dapper Dan' (Duet Series) (d/v) — CHal

– Summer Ice Series 'Blackberry Ice' PBR (d/v) — CHal WWol

– – 'Cherry Ice' PBR (d/v) — CHal WWol

– – 'Orange Ice' PBR (d/v) — WWol

– – 'Peach Ice' (d/v) — CHal WWol

– – 'Pink Ice' PBR (d/v) — WWol

– – 'Raspberry Ice' (d/v) — WWol

– Tempo Series 'Meloblue' **new** — LAst

– – 'Meloda' **new** — LAst

– – 'Melody' **new** — LAst

– – 'Shocking Pink' **new** — LAst

* – 'Variegata' (v) — CHal

zombensis — SHFr

Imperata (Poaceae)

brevifolia	CBrm CFwr
cylindrica	CMen EPar MSal
- 'Red Baron'	see *I. cylindrica* 'Rubra'
§ - 'Rubra'	More than 30 suppliers

Incarvillea (Bignoniaceae)

BWJ 7692 from China **new**	WCru
§ arguta	CBot CPLG EBee LPio SBla WAbe WWin
brevipes	see *I. mairei*
compacta	MDKP NSla
- ACE 1455	EBee
- BWJ 7620	WCru
delavayi	More than 30 suppliers
- 'Alba'	see *I. delavayi* 'Snowtop'
- 'Bees' Pink'	EBee GBuc GCal
§ - 'Snowtop'	COtt EBee EChP ELan ENot EPfP EPot ERou GBBs GBuc GCal LAst MCCP MDun MLLN MMil NBid NLar SBla SPer SPet SPla SWvt WBrE WCot WFar WPGP WShp
diffusa	SBla
forrestii	EBee LPio NSla
- KGB 43	EHyt
grandiflora	EBee EHyt ELan GCrs SBla
himalayensis 'Frank Ludlow'	GBuc SIgm
- 'Nyoto Sama'	GBuc
§ mairei	EBee EGoo EHyt EMan GCrs GSki LHop LRHS MLLN NLar SIgm WPer WWin
- ACE 2420	EBee
- var. *mairei*	EPot GBuc
- - CLD 101	GCrs
- - f. *multifoliata*	see *I. zhongdianensis*
- pink	EHyt SBla
§ olgae	CBri EMan ESis GFlt GSki LPVe MDKP NLar NWCA
przewalskii	WAbe
younghusbandii	EBee
§ zhongdianensis	EBee EPot GBri GBuc GCrs GEdr MDKP NSla SBla SMrm
- BWJ 7978	WCru
- CLD 233	EHyt

Indigofera (Papilionaceae)

amblyantha ♀H4	CHar EPfP GCal IDee MBlu NLar SDry SPoG SSpi WBVN WDin WPat WSHC WSpi
articulata	CFil
australis	LRav SOWG
balfouriana	WCru
BWJ 7851 **new**	
cytisoides	GFai
decora f. *alba*	EPfP GEil IArd IDee
dielsiana	CBcs EPfP SSpi WKif
'Dosua'	NPSI
frutescens	CPLG
gerardiana	see *I. heterantha*
hebepetala	CPLG WCru WDin WSHC
heterantha ♀H4	More than 30 suppliers
kirilowii	CFil EPfP IArd SOWG WSHC
pendula	EPfP WPGP
- B&SWJ 7741	WCru
potaninii	EPfP SHBN WCru WHer
pseudotinctoria	CFil EBee EGFP EPfP LRav SRms WFar
tinctoria	CArn MSal

Indocalamus (Poaceae)

latifolius	EPPr EPla ERod LPal MMoz MWht SDry SEND WJun

- 'Hopei'	EPla
longiauritus	EPla SDry
solidus	see *Bonia solida*
tesselatus f. hamadae	EPla ERod MWht SDry WJun
§ tessellatus ♀H4	CAbb CDoC CFil CHEx CMCo EBee EFul EPfP EPla ERod IFro MCCP MMoz MWht NGdn NMoo SMad WDyG WFar WJun WMoo WMul WPGP WPnP

Inula (Asteraceae)

acaulis	MLLN NJOw WCot WWeb
barbata	LHop MLLN
candida	XPep
cappa	EBee
conyzae	ITim
crithmoides	WCFE WHer XPep
dysenterica	see *Pulicaria dysenterica*
ensifolia	CHrt ELan EPfP GBBs GKir MLLN MSte MTho NBro SAga SLPl SMac WBea WCAu WFar WOld WPnP WShp WWpP
- 'Compacta'	EFou
- 'Gold Star'	EBee EMan EPfP LPVe MHer MLLN MWgw NBid NBir NFor NJOw SBla SPet WFar WHHs WLow WMnd WPer WRHF
glandulosa	see *I. orientalis*
* harassii	CHll
helenium	CAgr CArn CSev EFWa ELau GBBs GBar GPoy ILis LPBA LRHS MBct MBow MHer MLLN MSal NArg NBid NGHP NMir SECG SRms SYvo WCAu WHbs WHer WMoo WPer WWye
- 'Goliath'	ELau MLLN
helianthus-aquatilis	MLLN
hirta	MLLN SLPl WPer
hookeri	More than 30 suppliers
macrocephala misapplied	see *I. royleana*
macrocephala Boiss. & Kotschy ex Boiss.	MLLN
magnifica	More than 30 suppliers
- 'Sonnenstrahl' ♀H4	LPhx
oculus-christi	EBee EWes MLLN
- MESE 437	EPPr
* 'Oriental Star'	WHil
§ orientalis	COIW EBee EChP EFWa EPPr EPfP EWTr EWsh GBBs GIBF IHMH LRHS MBri NBPC NVic SBri SMac SMad SPer SPet WCAu WFar WLin WMnd WOld WPGP WPer WWeb
racemosa	EBee EMon EPla EWes GBin GCal IBlr MNrw MSte NBid NSti SPlb SRms WFar WTin WWpP
- 'Sonnenspeer'	ECGN EMan NLar SLPl SMad WPer
rhizocephala	CSam MLLN NJOw WPer
§ royleana	GBuc GCal GFlt GMac MNrw MRav MSte NChi SBla
salicina	EBee
verbascifolia	ECho

Iochroma (Solanaceae)

§ australe	CBcs CHEx CHll CKob CPle CSpe LHop LRav MOak SGar SHFr SOWG SSte SVen WCom WCot
§ - 'Andean Snow'	CHll CPLG MOak
§ - 'Bill Evans'	EWll
cyaneum	CKob CPLG ERea SHFr SOWG SSte SYvo
- purple	CHll
§ - 'Trebah'	CBcs ERea MOak SYvo
gesnerioides 'Coccineum'	CHll

§ ***grandiflorum*** CHEx CHll CSev SOWG SVen SYvo
   violaceum hort. see *I. cyaneum* 'Trebah'
   warscewiczii see *I. grandiflorum*

Ipheion (*Alliaceae*)
  'Alberto Castillo' CAvo CBro CDes CMea CPlt CPom
        EBee EGrW EHyt ELan EMan EPot
        ERos EWes LAma LTwo MAsh
        MBro MTho SBla SIgm SIng WAbe
        WCom WCot WHoo WIvy WPGP
        WTin
  dialystemon SBla SOkd WAbe
  'Rolf Fiedler' ♀H2-3 More than 30 suppliers
  sellowianum MAsh NWCA WCot
  uniflorum More than 30 suppliers
  - 'Album' CBro CMea ECha EHyt ELan EPar
        EPot ERos EWes LPio LRHS MAsh
        MRav MTho SBla SIng WCot WPnP
  - 'Charlotte Bishop' More than 30 suppliers
  - 'Froyle Mill' ♀H4 More than 30 suppliers
  - 'Wisley Blue' ♀H4 More than 30 suppliers

Ipomoea (*Convolvulaceae*)
  acuminata see *I. indica*
  alba CSpe
  batatas 'Blackie' ESlt WCot WFar
  carnea LRHS SOWG
§ ***indica*** ♀H1 CBcs CHEx CHal CHll ERea EShb
        ESlt MJnS MPRe SOWG SYvo
        WMul
  learii see *I. indica*
§ ***lobata*** CSpe LRHS SGar SHFr SUsu SYvo
  purpurea 'Kniola's CSpe
    Purple-black'
  - red-flowered, double CSpe
    (d) **new**
  tuberosa see *Merremia tuberosa*
  versicolor see *I. lobata*

Ipomopsis (*Polemoniaceae*)
§ ***aggregata*** EBee LTwo NPol
  rubra EBee NPol
  tenuituba RMRP 1-01 **new** EBee

Iresine (*Amaranthaceae*)
  herbstii CHal EBak ERea SMur
  - 'Aureoreticulata' CHal MOak
  - 'Brilliantissima' CHal MOak SMrm
  lindenii ♀H1 CHal MOak

Iris ✿ (*Iridaceae*)
  AGSJ 431 EWoo
  CLD 1399 NHol
  'Abridged Version' (MTB) NZep
  'Ace of Clubs' (SDB) NZep
  'Acoma' (TB) EWoo
  'Action Front' (TB) CM&M COtt EBee EBre ECGP
        EChP EHrv ERou EWTr MWgw
        NGdn SCoo SDnm SLon WWeb
  'Actress' (TB) EBee EChP EFou
  'Adobe Rose' (TB) ESgI
  'Afternoon Delight' (TB) ESgI WCAu
  'Agatha Christie' (IB) **new** WCAu
  'Agatha Dawson' EMon
    (Reticulata/v)
  'Agnes James' (CH) ♀H3 CBro
  'Ahead of Times' (TB) EFam
  'Ain't She Sweet' (IB) SCro
  'Albatross' (TB) CKel SMrm
  albicans ♀H4 SCro WHal
§ ***albomarginata*** WWst
  'Alcazar' (TB) EBee EPfP EWTr NMoo SWat WEas
        WFar WMnd WShp
  'Aldo Ratti' (TB) **new** ESgI

  'Alenette' (TB) WCAu
  'Alice Harding' (TB) ESgI
  'Alien Mist' (TB) LIri
  'Alizes' (TB) ♀H4 ESgI EWoo LIri
  'All Right' (IB) NZep
  'Allegiance' (TB) WEas
  'Alpine Journey' (TB) **new** ESgI
  'Alpine Lake' (MDB) NZep
  'Alpine Twilight' (TB) EFam
  'Alsterquelle' (SDB) WTin
  'Altruist' (TB) SCro
  'Amadora' (TB) CKel
  'Amas' (TB) WCAu
  'Ambassadeur' (TB) EBee ERou EWTr
  'Amber Blaze' (SDB) NZep
  'Amber Queen' (DB) EBee ECtt ELan ERos MSte NBir
        NMen SPer SPet WWeb
  'Ambroisie' (TB) ESgI LIri
  'Amethyst Flame' (TB) EBee EBre ENot ERou ESgI SRms
        WCAu
  'Amigo' (TB) ESgI SCro
  'Amphora' (SDB) CBro ERos GBuc
  'Andalou' (TB) ESgI LIri
  'Angel Unawares' (TB) WCAu
  'Angelic Wings' (TB) EFam
  'Angel's Tears' see *I. histrioides* 'Angel's Tears'
  anglica see *I. latifolia*
  'Anna Belle Babson' (TB) ESgI WCAu
  'Anna Marie' (TB) EFam
  'Annabel Jane' (TB) CKel SCro WCAu
  'Anne Elizabeth' (SDB) CBro ERos
  'Annikins' (IB) ♀H4 CKel
  'Anniversary CKel
    Celebration' (TB)
  'Antarctique' (IB) **new** ESgI
  'Antigone' ESgI
  'Anvil of Darkness' (TB) LIri
  aphylla GIBF NOrc
  'Apollo' (Dut) CFwr CRez MBow MSph
  'Apollo's Touch' (IB) NZep
  'Appledore' (SDB) CBro ERos MBro
  'Appointer' CRow
  'Apricorange' (TB) ♀H4 CKel
  'Apricot Frosty' (BB) LIri
  'Apricot Skies' (BB) NZep
  'Arab Chief' (TB) CKel
  'Arabi Pasha' (TB) SCro WCAu
* 'Arabic Night' (IB) WCAu
  'Arctic Fancy' (IB) ♀H4 CKel
  'Arctic Snow' (TB) WCAu
  'Arctic Star' (TB) CKel
  'Arnold Sunrise' (CH) WWst
    ♀H3
  'Around Midnight' (TB) SCro
  'Art School Angel' (TB) LIri
  'Artistic Gold' (TB) EFam
  'Artist's Whim' (TB) EFam
  'Ask Alma' (IB) EFou ESgI NZep SCro
  'Astrid Cayeux' (TB) ESgI EWoo
* 'Atlantique' (TB) CKel
  'Attention Please' (TB) CKel
§ ***attica*** CBro CPBP EHyt EPPr EPot ERos
        LBee LRHS LTwo NJOw NWCA
        WAbe WHal WLin
  - lemon GCrs
§ ***aucheri*** ♀H2 CBro GKev LAma WWst
  'Audacious' (BB) NZep
  'Aunt Martha' (BB) MBri WCAu
  'Austrian Sky' (SDB) CSam EBee ENot MBro NSti WPGP
  'Autumn Clouds' (TB) EFam
  'Autumn Leaves' (TB) WCAu
  'Autumn Mists' (TB) EFam
  'Autumn Orangelite' (TB) EFam
  'Autumn Tryst' (TB) **new** WCAu

'Avalon Sunset' (TB) **new**　ESgI
'Avanelle' (IB)　EFou ERou
'Az Ap' (IB)　EBee NZep SCro WCAu
'Azurea' (MDB)　WShp
'Babbling Brook' (TB)　EBee MRav WShp
'Baboon Bottom' (BB)　LIri
'Baby Bibs' (MTB)　NZep
'Baby Blessed' (SDB)　CBro EFam NZep WCAu
'Baby Prince' (SDB)　EFam
'Baccarat' (TB)　WCAu
'Back in Black' (TB)　CKel
'Back Street Affair' (TB)　LIri
bakeriana　LAma
'Bal Masque' (TB)　ESgI LIri
baldschuanica　WWst
'Ballerina'　NBir
'Ballerina Blue' (TB)　ERou
'Ballet Lesson' (SDB)　♀H4　LIri
'Ballyhoo' (TB)　WCAu
'Banbury Beauty' (CH)　CLAP CPlt
　♀H3
'Banbury Fair' (CH)　WWst
'Banbury Melody' (CH)　CFee GMac
'Banbury Ruffles' (SDB)　ESgI NMen WCAu
'Banbury Welcome' (CH)　IBlr
'Bang' (TB)　CKel
'Bar de Nuit' (TB)　ESgI
'Baria' (IB)　NFla
barnumae　EPot
'Baroque Prelude' (TB)　CKel
'Barrymore Charmer' (TB)　CKel
'Basso' (IB)　SCro
'Batik' (BB)　LIri SCro WCot
'Batsford' (SDB)　CBro EHyt
'Battle Royal' (TB)　LIri
'Bayberry Candle' (TB)　LIri WAul
'Be Dazzled' (SDB)　EFou
'Be Happy' (SDB)　NZep
'Beachgirl' (TB)　LIri
'Beauty Mark' (SDB)　NZep
'Bedford Lilac' (SDB)　♀H4　LIri NZep
'Bedtime Story' (IB)　WShp
'Bee Wings' (MDB)　NZep WEas
'Before the Storm' (TB)　CKel ESgI LIri SCro
'Beguine' (TB)　ESgI
'Being Busy' (SDB) **new**　ESgI
'Bel Azur' (IB)　ESgI SCro
'Bellboy' (MTB)　NZep
'Belvi Cloud' (TB)　EFam
'Belvi Queen' (TB)　EFam MNrw
* 'Ben Hasel'　ECha
N 'Benton Arundel' (TB)　SCro
'Benton Dierdre' (TB)　SCro SRms
'Benton Evora' (TB)　ENot
N 'Benton Lorna' (TB)　SCro
'Benton Sheila' (TB)　SCro
'Berkeley Gold' (TB)　CMea COtt CPrp CSBt EBee EBre
　ECtt ELan EPfP EWes EWsh GMac
　NGdn NOrc NVic SCoo SHBN SPer
'Berlin Tiger'　♀H4　CRow EPPr
'Best Bet' (TB)　EFam EWoo WCAu
'Best Man' (TB)　EFam
'Bethany Claire' (TB)　ESgI
'Betty Chatten' (TB)　EPot NMen
'Betty my Love' (Spuria)　LIri
'Betty Simon' (TB)　CKel ESgI EWoo
'Beverly Sills' (TB)　ESgI LIri WCAu
'Bewilderbeast' (TB)　LIri
'Bibury' (SDB)　♀H4　EGle
N 'Big Day' (TB)　GFlt
'Big Dipper' (TB)　EWoo
'Big Money' (CH)　♀H3　GBuc WWst
'Big Wheel' (CH)　GMac
biglumis　see *I. lactea*

biliottii　CBro
'Bionic Comet' (AB)　SCro
'Bishop's Robe' (TB) **new**　SSvw
'Black as Night' (TB)　WShp
'Black Beauty' (TB) **new**　CBri WHil
'Black Dragon' (TB)　SCro WBrE
'Black Gamecock' (La)　SSpi WMAq
'Black Hills' (TB)　WCAu
'Black Ink' (TB)　COIW
'Black Knight' (TB)　CSBt EBee EHol ENor MBow MRav
　NGdn WShp
'Black Swan' (TB)　CHad COtt EBee EBre ECGP EChP
　ECha ECtt EMan ESgI MCLN MMil
　MSte NGdn SDnm SHBN WCot
　WEas WWeb
'Black Taffeta' (TB)　CKel
'Black Tie Affair' (TB)　ESgI EWoo WCAu
'Black Watch' (IB)　WAul
'Blackbeard' (BB)　♀H4　CKel WCAu
'Blackout' (TB) **new**　ESgI
'Blatant' (TB) **new**　WCAu
'Blazing Saddles' (TB)　NZep
'Blenheim Royal' (TB)　ESgI SCro WCAu
'Blessed Again' (IB) **new**　EBee
'Blessed Assurance' (IB)　EFam
'Blitz' (SDB)　NZep
'Blood Covenant' (SDB)　NZep
'Blue Ballerina' (CH)　♀H3　GBuc WLin
'Blue Crusader' (TB)　LIri
'Blue Denim' (SDB)　CBro CM&M EBee EBre ECtt EGle
　EHyt ENot GFlt MBNS MRav NBir
　NBro NCot SIri SMrm WHoo WLin
　WTin
'Blue Doll' (MDB)　NZep SIng
'Blue Duchess' (TB)　SMrm
'Blue Eyed Blond' (IB)　SCro
'Blue Hendred' (SDB)　NBir WCAu
'Blue Horizon' (TB)　ERos NMen
'Blue Icing' (IB)　EFou
'Blue Line' (SDB)　♀H4　NZep
'Blue Luster' (TB)　♀H4　CKel ESgI SCro
'Blue Moonlight' (TB)　EFam
'Blue Pigmy' (SDB)　EBee EBre ERos LBBr MBNS NMen
　SIri SPet
'Blue Pools' (SDB)　EFou EGle EHyt MBri NBir NZep
　WTin
'Blue Rhythm' (TB)　CKel CM&M EBee EChP ELan
　ERou EWTr GMac MRav MSte
　MWgw NMoo SChu SCoo SCro
　WCAu WMnd
'Blue Sapphire' (TB)　CHad SHBN
'Blue Shimmer' (TB)　COtt CSBt EBee ECGN ELan ENot
　EPfP MRav NGdn SCoo SCro SWat
　WBVN WCAu
'Blue Staccato' (TB)　ESgI SCro SMrm
'Blue Velvet' (TB)　WMoo
'Blue Warlsind'　GKev
'Bluebeard' (TB)　EHyt
'Bluebird Wine' (TB)　WCAu
'Blushes' (IB)　SCro
'Blushing Pink' (TB)　SCro
'Bodacious' (TB)　ESgI
'Bohemian' (TB)　ESgI
'Boisterous' (BB)　LIri
'Bold Lassie' (SDB)　WHer
'Bold Look' (TB)　LIri
'Bold Print' (IB)　SCro WCAu WWin
'Bollinger'　see *Iris* 'Hornpipe'
'Bonnie Davenport' (TB)　LIri
'Bonny' (MDB)　CBro
'Boo' (SDB)　NZep WAul WCAu WDav WWin
'Bourne Graceful'　CBct CPLG EPPr SSpi
'Bouzy Bouzy' (TB)　ESgI
bracteata　CFil GBuc NWoo WPer

- JCA 13427 — CLAP
'Braithwaite' (TB) — CKel EBee EBre ELan ENot ERou MSte NGdn SCro SRms SWat WCAu
'Brandy' (TB) — LIri
'Brannigan' (SDB) — CBro EBee EHyt GKir MBri NBir NSti
'Brasilia' (TB) — EBee NBir
'Brass Tacks' (SDB) — NZep
'Brassie' (SDB) — CBro CKel EOMN ERos IHMH MBNS NBro SMrm WShp
'Breakers' (TB) ♀H4 — CKel ESgI EWoo
'Bridal Crown' (TB) — SCro
§ 'Bride' (DB) — MBro WMnd
'Bride's Halo' (TB) — EWoo SCro
'Brigantino' (BB) **new** — ESgI
'Bright Button' (SDB) — CKel ESgI EWoo WDav
'Bright Chic' (SDB) **new** — ESgI
'Bright Fire' (TB) **new** — EWoo
'Bright Herald' (TB) **new** — SGar
'Bright Vision' (SDB) — ESgI NZep
'Bright White' (MDB) — CBro EHyt ERos MBNS MBri NFla NMen WDav
'Bright Yellow' (DB) — EBre MRav
'Brighteyes' (IB) — ESis GKir MBro SCro SRms
'Brilliant Excuse' (TB) — NZep
'Brindisi' (TB) — ESgI WCAu
'Bristo Magic' (TB) — SCro
'Bristol Gem' (TB) — SCro
'Broadleigh Ann' (CH) — CBro WWst
'Broadleigh Carolyn' (CH) ♀H3 — CBro
'Broadleigh Charlotte' — CBro WWst
'Broadleigh Clare' (CH) — CBro
'Broadleigh Dorothy' (CH) — CBro GGar WWst
'Broadleigh Elizabeth' (CH) — CBro
N 'Broadleigh Emily' (CH) — CBro WWst
N 'Broadleigh Florence' (CH) — CBro
'Broadleigh Jean' — CBro WWst
'Broadleigh Joan' (CH) — CBro
'Broadleigh Joyce' (CH) — CBro WWst
'Broadleigh Lavinia' (CH) — CBro EPPr MAvo MRav WWst
'Broadleigh Mitre' (CH) — CBro CPBP
'Broadleigh Nancy' (CH) — CBro MAvo
'Broadleigh Peacock' (CH) — CBro CNic EBla IBal IBlr MAvo MMil MRav
N 'Broadleigh Rose' (CH) — CBos CBro CElw CHad CHid CPlt EBla EBre EHrv EPPr GBuc GKir IBlr MBrN MRav SAga SIri SMrm SWal WLin WSHC
'Broadleigh Sybil' (CH) — CBro
'Broadleigh Victoria' (CH) — CBro GBuc
'Broadway' (TB) — EBee NZep SCro
'Broadway Baby' (IB) — ESgI
'Broadway Doll' (BB) — EFam
'Broadway Star' **new** — CSBt
'Brom Bones' (SDB) — EFam
'Bromyard' (SDB) ♀H4 — CBro
'Bronzaire' (IB) ♀H4 — WCAu
'Bronze Beauty' (*boogiana* hybrid) — GBBs NBir
'Bronze Perfection' (Dut) — CRez
'Bronze Queen' (Dut) — LRHS
N 'Brown Chocolate' **new** — WCAu
'Brown Lasso' (BB) ♀H4 — EFou LIri SCro
'Brown Trout' (TB) — NBir
'Brummit's Mauve' — WCAu
'Bruno' (TB) **new** — EBee
'Bubbling Over' (TB) — SCro
bucharica hort. — see *I. orchioides* Carrière
§ *bucharica* Foster ♀H3-4 — CBro CPom CSam EPar EPfP EPot GFlt GIBF LAma NRog SIng

bucharica ambig. — WBor
- 'Yellow Dushanbe' — EBee WWst
'Buisson de Roses' (TB) **new** — ESgI
bulleyana — GBBs GCrs GIBF GKev NWoo SIgm SRms WAbe
- ACE 2296 — EBee EHyt GBuc
- black — GKev
aff. *bulleyana* — GBBs
'Bumblebee Deelite' (MTB) ♀H4 — NZep WDav
'Burgundy Brown' (TB) — NZep
'Burgundy Bubbles' (TB) — LIri
'Burnt Toffee' (TB) — ESgI
'Butter Pecan' (IB) — SCro
'Buttercup Bower' (TB) — WCAu
'Buttercup Charm' (MDB) — NZep
'Buttered Popcorn' **new** — EBee MBow
'Buttermere' (TB) — SRms
'Butterpat' (IB) — ESgI NZep
'Butterscotch Kiss' (TB) — EBee EBre ECGP EChP ELan ERou MRav MWgw NBir ECoo SCro SDnm SHBN
'Button Box' (SDB) — NZep
'Cabaret Royale' (TB) — ESgI
'Cable Car' (TB) — CKel EWoo
'Caliente' (TB) — EBee EPfP MRav WCAu WShp
'California Style' (IB) — NZep
§ Californian hybrids — CElw CPBP CWCL EBre ECGP EPot GFlt MRav NBir SSpi WCFE WCot WWhi
'Calypso Mood' (TB) — SCro
'Cambridge Blue' — see *I.* 'Monspur Cambridge Blue'
'Camelot Rose' (TB) — WCAu
'Cameo Blush' (BB) — EFam
'Cameroun' (TB) — ESgI
'Campbellii' — see *I. lutescens* 'Campbellii'
canadensis — see *I. hookeri*
'Candyland' (BB) — EFam
'Cannington Ochre' (SDB) — CBro
'Cannington Skies' (IB) — MMil
'Cantab' (Reticulata) — CAvo CBro EHyt EPar EPot LAma NRog WLin
'Cantina' (TB) — EFam
capnoides — WWst
'Capricious' (TB) — ESgI SCro
'Caption' (TB) — ESgI
'Caramba' (TB) — SCro WCAu
'Carilla' (SDB) — ERos
'Carnaby' (TB) — EFou ESgI MBri WCAu
'Carnival Time' (TB) — EBee EChP EFou
'Carnton' (TB) — WEas
'Carolina Gold' (TB) — SCro
'Carolyn' (CH) — CFir
'Carolyn Rose' (MTB) ♀H4 — NZep
'Caronte' (IB) **new** — ESgI
'Carved Pink' (TB) — SCro
'Cascade Sprite' (SDB) — SRms
'Cascadian Skies' (TB) — ERou
caucasica subsp. *turcica* — WWst
* 'Cedric Morris' — EWes
'Cee Jay' (IB) ♀H4 — EWoo LIri
'Celebration Song' (TB) — ESgI WCAu
'Centre Court' (TB) — SCro
'Certainly Certainly' (TB) — EFam
chamaeiris — see *I. lutescens*
'Champagne Elegance' (TB) — ESgI MMil NBir WCAu
'Champagne Encore' (IB) **new** — ESgI
'Champagne Waltz' (TB) — LIri
'Change of Pace' (TB) — SCro
'Chanted' (SDB) — ESgI
'Chanteuse' (TB) — SCro

'Chantilly' (TB)	CM&M COtt CPrp EBee EBre EChP ELan EPfP MRav MTis NBir NGdn NOrc SCro SDnm SPer WCra WFoF
'Charger' (TB)	MMil
'Chartreuse Ruffles' (TB)	EBre EWoo SCro
'Chasing Rainbows' (TB)	LIri
'Chaste White' (TB)	EFam
'Cheers' (IB)	NZep
'Cherished' **new**	CSBt EBee
'Cherokee Lace' (Spuria)	WTin
'Cherry Garden' (SDB)	CBro CFwr CKel EBee ECtt EGoo EHrv ELan EWes GKir IPot MBNS MBri MBro MMil MRav NBPC NBir NSti NWCA SIng SMrm WEas
'Cherry Glen' (TB)	LIri
'Cherry Orchard' (TB)	NFor
'Cherry Ripe' (TB)	SGar
'Cherry Smoke' (TB)	SCro
'Cherub Tears' (SDB)	EHyt NZep
'Cherub's Smile' (TB)	ESgI SCro
'Chickee' (MTB) ♀H4	CKel NZep
'Chicken Little' (MDB)	CBro EBee NMoo
'Chief Quinaby' (TB)	SCro
I 'Chieftain' (SDB)	MRav WWin
'China Dragon' (TB)	SCro
'Chivalry' (TB)	WTin
'Chocolate Vanilla' (TB)	LIri
'Chorus Girl' (TB)	CKel
'Christmas Angel' (TB)	ERou
chrysographes ♀H4	CHid CPrp CWCL EBre GKir GMac LPVe LRHS MBnl MCCP MCLN MRav MWrn NMRc NSti SMac SRms SScr SWal WAul WCAu WHil WPnP WRHF WWeb WWhi
- *alba*	NBir
- black	More than 30 suppliers
I - 'Black Beauty'	CFir GBBs
I - 'Black Knight'	CBot CHid CMdw EPfP EWsh GBuc GCal MDun MHer MSte NBid NChi NFor NLar SWat WCom WMnd WViv WWin
- crimson	IBlr NWoo
N - 'Inshriach'	CFai EHyt GBuc IBlr WAbe
- 'Kew Black'	CDes NBir NChi NHol NWCA WHer WHil
- 'Mandarin Purple'	EBee GBuc GCal SPer SWat WCot WMoo
- purple	MBro
§ - 'Rubella'	CPlt CRow GMac MMil MRav MSte WFar WPrP
* - var. *rubella* 'Wine'	CHad
- 'Rubra'	see *I. chrysographes* 'Rubella'
chrysographes x *forrestii*	NBir WViv
chrysophylla	GBuc
- JCA 13233	CLAP
'Chuck Waltermire' (TB)	EFam
N 'Cider Haze' (TB)	CKel
'Cimarron Rose' (SDB)	ESgI NZep
'City Lights' (TB)	WCAu
'City of David' (TB)	SCro
'Clairette' (Reticulata)	CBro EPar LAma
'Clarence' (TB)	ESgI LIri
clarkei	EPot GIBF WFar
- CC 3408	WCot
- purple-flowered **new**	GFlt
'Classic Bordeaux' (TB)	LIri
'Classic Look' (TB)	ESgI LIri
'Clay's Caper' (SDB)	EFou
'Clear Morning Sky' (TB) ♀H4	LIri
N 'Cleo' (TB)	CKel NBir NSti
'Cleo Murrell' (TB) **new**	ESgI

'Cliffs of Dover' (TB)	SGar SIri SRms
'Cloud Mistress' (IB) **new**	ESgI
'Cloudcap' (TB)	SRms
'Cloudless Sunrise' (TB)	ERou
'Coalignition' (TB)	LIri WCAu
'Cobalt Mesa' (Spuria)	LIri
'Codicil' (TB)	ESgI EWoo
'Colchesterensis'	CBen CDWL CLAP CRow CWat EGol EMFW LPBA MSta NPer SLon SWat WCra WHrl WMAq WTMC
'Colette Thurillet' (TB)	ESgI WCAu
collettii	EBee
'Colonial Gold' (TB)	WCAu
'Color Brite' (BB)	SCro
'Color Splash' (TB)	SCro
'Columbia Blue' (TB)	SCro
'Comandante' (TB) **new**	ESgI
'Combo' (SDB)	CKel
confusa ♀H3	CAbP CHEx CPla CSev EPla IFro SAPC SArc SChr SEND SSpi SSte WBor WBrk WDyG WFar WMul WPic WWst
§ - 'Martyn Rix'	CBct CDes CFwr CHad CHid CLAP CPou CRez CSev CSpe EBee EMan GCal LPio MBct MHer SChr SSpi WCot WDyG WFar WHrl WMnd WOld WPGP WPer WPrP WSHC
'Conjuration' (TB)	ESgI EWoo LIri
'Conspiracy' (TB)	LIri
'Constant Wattez' (IB)	CKel EBee ESgI EWTr LBuc NLar WMnd
'Consummation' (MTB)	NZep
'Cool Treat' (BB) ♀H4	LIri
'Copatonic' (TB)	LIri
'Copper Classic' (TB)	ESgI NZep SCro SIri
'Cops' (SDB)	NZep
'Coquetterie' (TB)	ESgI
'Coral Chalice' (TB)	ERou
'Coral Point' (TB) **new**	WCAu
'Coral Wings' (SDB)	NZep
'Cordoba' (TB)	LIri
'Corn Harvest' (TB)	EFam NZep
'Corrida' (TB)	LBuc
'Côte d'Or' (TB)	SCro
'Cozy Calico' (TB)	ESgI SCro
'Cracklin Burgundy' (TB)	SCro
'Cranapple' (BB) ♀H4	LIri
'Cranberry Ice' (TB)	EWoo SCro
'Cream Cake' (SDB)	NZep
'Cream Soda' (TB) ♀H4	CKel
'Creative Stitchery' (TB)	SCro
'Creme d'Or' (TB)	ESgI
cretensis	see *I. unguicularis* subsp. *cretensis*
'Cricket Lane' (SDB)	NZep
'Crimson Fire' (TB)	SCro
'Crimson Tiger' (TB)	EFam LIri
'Crinoline' (TB)	CKel
'Crispette' (TB)	WCAu
cristata ♀H4	EBla EPot GBuc MDHE NPro SRms WCru
- 'Alba'	EBee ERos LBee LRHS NWCA WAbe
cristata x *lacustris*	ETow NMen
crocea ♀H4	CPLG GKev SCro
'Croftway Lemon' (TB)	SCro
'Cross Stitch' (TB)	MMil NZep
'Crown Sterling' (TB)	SCro
'Crowned Heads' (TB)	LIri
'Crushed Velvet' (TB)	WCAu
'Crystal Glitters' (TB)	ESgI
'Cum Laude' (IB)	SCro
cuniculiformis ACE 2224	GBuc
'Cup Race' (TB)	GFlt WCAu

'Cupid's Cup' (SDB) — ESgl
'Curtain Up' (TB) — EFam
'Cutie' (IB) — EBee ESgl NZep
'Cyanea' (DB) — EBee EFam SMrm
cycloglossa — CFwr EBee EPot LRHS SSpi WWst
'Dale Dennis' (DB) — CFwr
'Dance Away' (TB) — ESgl
'Dancers Veil' (TB) — CHar ECtt EFou ERou GKir MRav NVic SCro SIri SMer
'Dancin'' (IB) — NZep
'Dancing Gold' (MTB) — NZep
danfordiae — CAvo CBcs CBro EPar EPfP EPot EWTr LAma LRHS NJOw NRog SPet WLin
'Danger' (TB) **new** — ESgl
'Dardanus' (AB) — CFwr EPot
'Dark Blizzard' (IB) — NZep
'Dark Crystal' (SDB) — ESgl
'Dark Spark' (SDB) — WCAu
'Dark Vader' (SDB) — ESgl
'Darkside' (TB) — SCro
'Dash Away' (SDB) — ESgl
'Dauntless' (TB) — ESgl
'Dawning' (TB) — ESgl LIri
'Dazzling Gold' (TB) — ESgl SCro
§ *decora* — CBro EBee GIBF LEdu MNrw
- B&SWJ 2122 — WCru
'Deep Black' (TB) — COtt EBee EBre EChP ELan EMan EPfP MBNS MWgw NOrc SChu SCro SDnm SHBN SWat WCAu
'Deep Caress' (TB) — ESgl
'Deep Dark Secret' (TB) — LIri
'Deep Fire' (TB) — SCro
'Deep Pacific' (TB) — MBri
'Deft Touch' (CH) — WCAu
delavayi ♀H4 — EBee EWes GIBF IBlr MLLN WCot
- SDR 50 — GKev
'Delicate Lady' (IB) ♀H4 — CKel
'Delta Blues' (TB) — EWoo
'Delta Butterfly' (La) — WMAq
'Demon' (SDB) — CKel CMil EFou EHyt WDav
'Denys Humphry' (TB) — CKel
'Deputé Nomblot' (TB) — ESgl
'Derwentwater' (TB) — SRms
'Desert Dream' (AB) — GAbr GGar
'Desert Echo' (TB) — EFou
'Desert Song' (TB) — CKel WCAu
'Designer Gown' (TB) — ERou
'Devilry' (SDB) — EHyt
'Dew Point' (IB) — SCro
'Diabolique' (TB) — LIri
dichotoma — EBee
'Dilly Green' (TB) — LIri
'Ditto' (MDB) — EFam
'Divine' (TB) **new** — CKel
'Dixie Darling' (TB) — ESgl
'Dixie Pixie' (SDB) — EGle ESis WCAu WTin
'Doll' (IB) — EWoo
'Dolly Madison' (TB) — ESgl
'Don't Be Cruel' (TB) — LIri
'Dorcas Lives Again' (TB) — EFam
'Dorothy Robbins' (CH) — WWst
'Double Espoir' (TB) **new** — ESgl
'Double Lament' (SDB) — CBro ERos WOut
'Double Time' (TB) — EFam
douglasiana ♀H4 — CAvo EChP EPar GBBs GKev IBlr MLLN SMac SSpi WAbe WFar WOut WTin
- 'Amiguita' (CH) — CFir WCom WWst
* - Bandon strain — SSpi
'Dover Beach' (TB) **new** — SGar
'Doxa' (IB) — SCro
'Draco' (TB) — ESgl
'Dream Indigo' (IB) — WCAu

'Dreamsicle' (TB) — SCro
'Dress Circle' (Spuria) — LIri
'Dualtone' (TB) — CKel
'Duke of Earl' (TB) — EFam
'Dundee' (TB) — SCro
'Dunlin' (MDB) — CBro EHyt ERos NBir NMen
'Dusky Challenger' (TB) — CKel ESgl EWoo LIri SCoo SCro WCAu
'Dutch Chocolate' (TB) — ESgl SIri WCAu
dykesii — CRow EBee
'Dynamite' (TB) — LIri
'Eardisland' (IB) ♀H4 — MMil
'Earl of Essex' (TB) — EFam SCro WCAu
'Early Edition' (IB) — EBre EFou
'Early Frost' (IB) — CKel SCro WAul
'Early Light' (TB) ♀H4 — LIri WCAu
'Echo de France' (TB) — ESgl EWoo
'Ecstatic Echo' (TB) — ESgl
'Edith Wolford' (TB) — EBee ESgl EWoo LIri WCAu WSan
'Ed's Blue' (DB) — ELan
'Edward' (Reticulata) — EPot LAma
'Edward Windsor' (TB) — CMil EBee ELan ERou NBir NOrc SCoo SDnm WMnd
'Eileen Louise' (TB) — WCAu
♀H4 **new**
'Elainealope' (TB) — EFam LIri
'Eleanor's Pride' (TB) — CKel ESgl WCAu
elegantissima — see *I. iberica* subsp. *elegantissima*
'Elizabeth of England' (TB) — EBee
'Elizabeth Poldark' (TB) — ESgl LIri WCAu
'Elvinhall' — CBro
'Empress of India' (TB) — EBee
'Enchanted Gold' (SDB) — NZep
'Encircle' (CH) — GBuc WWst
'Encre Bleue' (IB) **new** — ESgl
'English Charm' (TB) — EFam
'English Cottage' (TB) — GCal MMil MWat SCro WCAu WIvy WShp
'English Knight' (TB) — EFam
'Ennerdale' (TB) — SRms
§ *ensata* ♀H4 — CBen CMHG COIW CSBt EBee EBre ECGP ELan EMFW ENot EPfP GFlt GMac LPBA LRHS MNrw MSta NBro NGdn NLar SPlb SRms SWal SWat WFar WMyn WPer WWin WWpP
- 'Activity' — CLAP CRow CSBt NBro SHar SMrm WFar WOBN WPrP WSan
- 'Alba' — ECha
- 'Aldridge Prelude' — WAul
- 'Apollo' — CBen CRow EWTr
- 'Artist' — NBro
- 'Azuma-kagami' **new** — CWrd
I - 'Azure' **new** — CWrd
- 'Barnhawk Sybil' — SSpi
- 'Barr Purple East' ♀H4 — CRow NBrk
- 'Beni-Tsubaki' — WAul WOBN
I - 'Blue King' — CLAP NBrk NBro
I - 'Blue Peter' — CBen CRow
- 'Blush' — NBro
- 'Butterflies in Flight' — CRow
- 'Caprician Butterfly' — EBee EPfP NLar WCAu WHil
♀H4
- 'Carnival Prince' — CFir CLAP NBro SBod SMrm WFar WMoo WPnP
- 'Cascade Crest' **new** — WAul
- 'Cascade Spice' **new** — WAul
- 'Chitose-no-tomo' — CRow
- 'Cry of Rejoice' — EBee GBri NBPC NBro SWat WAul WCAu WFar
- 'Crystal Halo' — NBrk
- 'Dace' **new** — CWrd
- 'Dancing Waves' — CRow NBrk

– 'Darling'	CLAP CPen CRow CSam EBee IBlr LRHS MBNS NBrk NBro NLar SIri SMrm WAul WCAu WMoo WTMC WWin
– 'Dramatic Moment' **new**	CLAP CWrd EBee
– 'Dresden China'	CRow NBrk
– 'Eden's Artist'	EBee
– 'Eden's Blue Pearl'	CHid EBee EChP EGle IPot NBro SMrm SSpe WHil
– 'Eden's Blush'	CMil EBee SSpe WAul WHil WSan
– 'Eden's Charm'	CMil EChP EGle ELan NBro NHol SHar SPet SVil WAul WHil WWeb WWye
– 'Eden's Delight'	EBee NHol SMrm
– 'Eden's Harmony'	CRez EBee EChP NBro SCou SMrm WAul WHil WSan WTMC
– 'Eden's Paintbrush'	CM&M CMil EBee EChP EGle ELan EPfP NBro NGdn NPSI SCou SVil WHil WTMC
– 'Eden's Picasso'	CFir EBee EGle ELan EPfP IPot NBro NGdn NPSI SCou SVil WSan WTMC
– 'Eden's Purple Glory'	CHid EBee EGle NBro SCou SSpe WCot WHil WTin
– 'Eden's Starship'	CFir EBee NGdn WHil WSan
– 'Electric Rays' **new**	CWrd WAul
I – 'Emotion'	CLAP EBee EWTr LRHS NBrk NBro SMrm WAul WFar WPnP
– 'Enkaishu' **new**	CWrd
– 'Flashing Koi'	NBrk
– 'Fortune'	CLAP EBee EHrv WAul
– 'Frilled Enchantment'	WAul
– 'Frosted Pyramid'	NBrk
* – 'Galathea'	SMrm
– 'Garnet Royalty'	WOBN
– 'Gipsy'	CLAP CSpe EBee EWTr LRHS SMrm WAul
– 'Glitter and Gayety'	NBrk
– 'Good Omen'	CWrd
– 'Gracieuse'	CLAP CPrp CSev EBee EGle EPPr MCLN NBPC NBro NLar SWat WAul WFar WHil WMoo WPnP
– 'Hana-aoi'	IBlr
– 'Hatsu-shimo'	IBlr
– 'Hercule'	CHad CRow EGle GAbr NBir NBrk NGdn SMrm WTMC
– Higo hybrids	EBre IBlr LPBA MSta
– Higo white	SPer
N – 'Hokkaido'	CRow IBlr NBrk
– 'Hue and Cry' ♀H4	WAul WOBN
* – 'Innocence'	CLAP EHrv LRHS NLar WAul WMoo
– 'Iso-no-nami'	CLAP EWll NBro WAul WPrP WTMC
– 'Jodlesong'	CLAP EBee
– 'Kalamazoo'	WFar
– 'Katy Mendez' ♀H4	WAul
– 'Kogesho'	EBee EPfP NBro NLar WAul
– 'Koh Dom'	SPer
– 'Koh Shan'	CLAP
– 'Kongo San' **new**	CWrd
– 'Kuma-funjin'	CRow IBlr
– 'Kumo-no-obi'	CLAP EBee EWTr EWll NBro SWat WAul
– 'Laced'	SPer
– 'Landscape at Dawn'	CRow
– 'Lasting Pleasure' ♀H4 **new**	CWrd
– 'Laughing Lion'	CLAP COtt CRez EWTr NBro WAul WFar WMoo WPnP
– 'l'Ideal' **new**	CPen
– 'Light at Dawn'	EBee EGle IPot NBro WAul WGMN WHil WMoo
– 'Lilac Blotch'	SPer
– 'Loyalty' **new**	CLAP CWrd EBee

– 'Manadzuru'	IBlr
I – 'Mandarin'	CRow NBrk
– 'Midnight Stars'	WAul
– 'Midnight Whispers'	WAul
– 'Midsummer Reverie'	CRow
– 'Momozomo' **new**	CWrd
§ – 'Moonlight Waves'	CHad CMHG CPrp CRow EBee EBre EGle ELan EPfP EWll GBuc GMac MBri MFir MSte NBrk NBro NGdn SChu SSpi SVil SWat WAul WFar WOBN WTMC
– 'Narihira'	IBlr
– 'Ocean Mist'	CLAP CWrd EBee NBro
– 'Oku-banri'	CPrp IBlr
– 'Oriental Eyes'	NGdn WAul WCAu
– pale mauve	NBir SPer
– 'Peacock'	EBee SMrm
– 'Pin Stripe'	EBee MBri NBro WAul
– 'Pink Frost'	CLAP CRow EBre EGle GKir WFar WTMC WTin
– 'Pleasant Earlybird' **new**	WAul
– 'Pleasant Journey'	CLAP
– 'Prairie Frost'	EPfP
– 'Prairie Noble'	EBee NBro WHil
– 'Prairie Twilight'	NBrk
– purple-flowered	ITim SPer WWye
– 'Purple Glory'	ELan
– 'Ranpo'	CRow
– 'Rebecca Johns'	CRow
– 'Reign of Glory'	WAul
I – 'Reveille'	CLAP EPPr MTis NBro WAul
– 'Ridge Ruby'	WOBN
§ – 'Rose Queen' ♀H4	More than 30 suppliers
– 'Rowden Amir'	CRow
– 'Rowden Autocrat'	CRow
– 'Rowden Begum'	CRow
– 'Rowden Dauphin'	CRow
– 'Rowden Emperor'	CRow
– 'Rowden King'	CRow
– 'Rowden Knave'	CRow
– 'Rowden Knight'	CRow
– 'Rowden Mikado'	CRow
– 'Rowden Nuncio'	CRow
– 'Rowden Paladin'	CRow
– 'Rowden Pasha'	CRow
– 'Rowden Prince'	CRow
– 'Rowden Queen'	CRow
– 'Rowden Shah'	CRow
– 'Rowden Sultana'	CRow
I – 'Royal Banner'	EBee NBro WAul WFar
– 'Royal Crown'	NBrk
I – 'Ruby King'	CLAP WAul
I – 'Sensation'	CLAP EBee GAbr NBPC NLar SMrm SWat WAul WCAu WPrP
N – 'Shihainami'	IBlr
– 'Signal' **new**	EBee
– 'Silverband'	NBrk
– 'Snowy Hills' **new**	WAul
– 'Sorcerer's Triumph'	WOBN
– var. **spontanea**	GIBF WAbe
– – B&SWJ 1103	WCru
– 'Springtime Melody' **new**	WAul
– 'Stippled Ripples' **new**	EBee
– 'Strut and Flourish' **new**	WCAu
– 'Summer Storm' ♀H4	SPer
– 'Sylvia's Masquerade' **new**	EBee GBin
– 'Taga-sode'	NBrk
– 'Teleyoshi'	SHar
– 'The Great Mogul' ♀H4	CRow
– 'Tsumabeni' **new**	CWrd
– 'Variegata' (v) ♀H4	More than 30 suppliers
– 'Veinette' **new**	CWrd
– 'Velvety Queen'	WAul

	- 'Waka-murasaki'	CLAP EBee EGle EWTr EWll GKir MBNS NBro WAul
	- 'White Ladies' **new**	CLAP CSBt CWrd
I	- 'White Pearl'	CRow NBrk
	- white-flowered **new**	WMyn
	- 'Wine Ruffles'	MCLN
	- 'Yako-no-tama'	CRow WMoo
	- 'Yedo-yeman'	CLAP WFar
	- 'Yezo-nishiki'	CLAP EBee SBod WAul
	- 'Yoake Mae'	WOBN
	- 'Yu Nagi' **new**	SPer
	'Erect' (IB)	LIri
	'Escalona' (CH) **new**	WWst
	'Esoteric' (SDB)	ESgl
	'Eternal Bliss' (TB)	EFam
	'Evening Magic' (TB)	SCro
	'Ever After' (TB)	ESgl
	'Everything Plus' (TB)	ERou ESgl
	'Exclusivity' (TB)	LIri
	'Exotic Gem' (TB)	WCAu
	'Exotic Isle' (TB)	ESgl NZep
	'Extravagant' (TB)	SCro
	'Eyebright' (SDB) ♀H4	CBro WPGP WWin
	'Fakir's Fire' (MTB)	NZep
	'Falcon's Crest' (Spuria)	LIri
	'Fall Fiesta' (TB)	ESgl
	'Fall Primrose' (TB)	EFam
	'Falstaff Cottage' (CH)	WWst
	'Fancy Woman' (TB)	LIri
	'Fanfaron' (TB)	ESgl SCro
	'Fantaisie' (TB)	CKel
	'Fashion Lady' (MDB)	CBro EHyt
	'Fashion Statement' (TB)	LIri
	'Favorite Angel' (SDB)	NZep
	'Feature Attraction' (TB)	LIri
	'Feed Back' (TB)	EFam
	'Feminine Charm' (TB)	WCAu
	'Feminist' (TB)	SCro
	'Festive Skirt' (TB)	CKel WCAu
	'Feu du Ciel' (TB)	ESgl LIri
	'Fierce Fire' (IB) ♀H4	CKel
	'Fiesta Time' (TB) **new**	EWoo
	filifolia	CBro
	- J&JA 0.586.410	EBee
	- var. *latifolia*	SSpi
	'Film Festival' (TB)	ESgl
N	'Fire and Flame' (TB)	NBir
	'Firebug' (IB) **new**	ESgl
	'Firecracker' (TB)	ERou MRav
	'First Interstate' (TB)	ESgl LIri SCro
	'First Step' (SDB)	NZep
	'Five Star Admiral' (TB)	SCro
	'Flaming Dragon' (TB)	CKel EBee
	'Flapjack' (SDB)	NZep
	'Flash' (Fulva)	NHol
	'Flashing Beacon' (MTB)	NZep
	'Flea Circus' (MDB)	NZep
	'Flirty Mary' (SDB)	EGle
§	'Florentina' (IB/TB) ♀H4	CArn CBro EMFP ESgl EWoo GPoy IBlr ILis MHer MRav NBid NBir SCro Slde WCAu WCot WPic WWye
	'Flower Shower' (SDB)	EFam
	'Flumadiddle' (IB)	CBro CKel
	'Focal Point' (TB)	LBuc
	'Focus' (TB)	SCro
§	*foetidissima* ♀H4	More than 30 suppliers
	- 'Aurea' **new**	WCot
	- *chinensis*	see *I. foetidissima* var. *citrina*
§	- var. *citrina*	CFil CFir CRow EBee EGle EPPr EPla GAbr GCal GKir IBlr LPio MBro MRav SSpi STes SUsu WAbe WCom WCot WEas WHoo WSSM WWin WWye

	- 'Fructu Albo'	CNat EBee EChP LPio MBNS NLar WCot WTin
	- var. *lutescens*	CHid EMon EPPr IBlr MTed
	- 'Moonshy Seedling'	CSWP EGol
	- 'Variegata' (v) ♀H4	CBro CElw CFil CRow EBee ECtt EGle EHrv EOrc EPPr EPfP EPla EWsh MBri MCCP MRav NBir NLar NPar NPer SSpi WBVN WCot WWhi WCot WTin
	- yellow-seeded	EFou MTed SMHy WCot WTin
	'Foggy Dew' (TB)	GKir
	'Folkwang' (TB)	EBee EWTr
	'Fondation Van Gogh' (TB)	ESgl LIri
	'Forest Light' (SDB)	CBro EHyt ESgl MBro
	'Forever Yours' (TB)	EFam
	'Forge Fire' (TB)	ESgl
	'Forgotten Dreams' (CH)	WWst
	formosana B&SWJ 3076	WCru WPrP
	forrestii ♀H4	CHid CRow EChP EPar EPfP GAbr GBBs GBin GCal GGar GIBF GKir IBlr LPBA LRHS MBri MHer NBir NBro NCGa NChi NGdn NHol NSti SMac SRot SSpi WAbe WHer
	- hybrids	IBlr
	'Fort Apache' (TB)	ESgl EWoo SCro
	fosteriana	WWst
	'Foxy Lady' (TB)	ESgl
	'Frank Elder' (Reticulata)	CBro EHyt EPot ERos LAma LPio LRHS MRav MTho NMen
	'Frans Hals' (Dut)	EWTr MNrw
	'French Fashion' (TB)	LIri
	'Fresno Calypso' (TB)	ESgl WCAu
	'Fresno Flash' (TB)	SCro
	'Fringe of Gold' (TB)	EBee SCro
	'Frison-roche' (TB)	ESgl
	'Fritillary Flight' (IB) ♀H4	CKel
	'Frontier Marshall' (TB)	NMoo
	'Frost and Flame' (TB)	CM&M EBee EBre EChP ECtt ELan ENot EPfP ERou EWll GKir MBri MRav MSte NGdn NMoo NOrc SChu SCro SPer SWat
	'Frosted Angel' (SDB)	LAst WDav
	'Frosted Velvet'	EFam
	'Frosty Jewels' (TB) **new**	ESgl
	'Full Tide' (TB)	SCro
	fulva	CDes CRow EBee GCal IBlr LPio NBir NBro NPPs NSti SIri SMrm SSpi WCot WEas WPGP WTin
	- 'Marvell Gold' (La)	CRow EBee
	x *fulvala* ♀H4	CDes CFir CSam EBee EMon EWes IBlr NBir NSti SCro
	- 'Violacea'	EBee
	'Furnaceman' (SDB)	CBro EHyt ERos MBri MBro
	'Fuzzy' (MDB)	ERos
	'Fuzzy Face' (SDB)	NZep
	'Gala Gown' (TB)	WCAu
§	*galatica*	WWst
	'Galleon Gold' (SDB)	NZep
§	'Gelbe Mantel' (Sino-Sib)	CBgR CHid CLAP EBee EBla EChP LHop MBri NBir NBro NGdn NHol NSti WFar
	'Gentius' (TB)	EBee WMnd
	'Gentle Grace' (SDB)	ESgl
	'George' (Reticulata) ♀H4	CAvo CBro EPar EPot ERos GAbr GCrs LRHS WCot
	'Gerald Darby'	see *I.* x *robusta* 'Gerald Darby'
	germanica ♀H4	EHol NFor WCAu
	- var. *florentina*	see *I.* 'Florentina'
*	- 'Mel Jopc'	NBir
	- 'Nepalensis'	EGoo
*	- 'The King'	WCAu
	'Gingerbread Man' (SDB)	CBro CHad CMea EFou EGle EHrv ERos ESgl LPio MBrN MBro NMen SMrm SWal WCAu WHoo WIvy WWin

'Glacier King' (TB)	EFam
'Glad Rags' (TB)	ESgI NZep
'Glenwillow' (MDB)	NZep
'Gnu' (TB)	LIri
'Gnus Flash' (TB)	LIri
'Godfrey Owen' (TB)	CKel WCAu
'Godsend' (TB)	LIri
'Going My Way' (TB)	EBee EOMN ESgI EWoo SIri STes
	WCAu
'Gold Burst' (TB)	SCro
'Gold Galore' (TB)	SCro
'Gold Mania' (Spuria)	LIri
'Gold of Autumn' (TB)	CKel SMrm
'Golden Alps' (TB)	ENot SRms
'Golden Child' (SDB)	EFam
'Golden Encore' (TB)	CKel EFam MWat WCAu
'Golden Fair' (SDB)	NBir
'Golden Giant' (Dut)	CFwr LRHS
'Golden Inmortal' (TB)	EFam
'Golden Muffin' (IB)	NZep
'Golden Opportunity' (TB)	LIri
'Golden Planet' (TB)	CKel

N 'Golden Surprise' (TB) WShp
'Golden Violet' (SDB) **new** ESgI
'Golden Waves' CBro
  (Cal-Sib) ♀H3

goniocarpa EBee
- var. *grossa* EBee
'Good and True' (IB) SCro
'Good Looking' (TB) LIri WCAu
'Good Show' (TB) EWoo SCro
'Goodbye Heart' (TB) **new** ESgI
'Gordon' (Reticulata) EPot LAma LRHS
'Goring Ace' (CH) ♀H3 WWst
'Goring Steeple' (CH) WWst
  ♀H4

gormanii see *I. tenax*
'Gossip' (SDB) CBro ESgI
gracilipes GEdr
- 'Alba' GEdr
gracilipes x *lacustris* GEdr WAbe
graeberiana EPot
- white fall LRHS WWst
- yellow fall EPot LRHS WWst
graminea ♀H4 More than 30 suppliers
- 'Hort's Variety' GCal
- var. *pseudocyperus* CRow NSti SDys
graminifolia see *I. kerneriana*
'Granada Gold' (TB) ENot MLwd SRms
'Grand Baroque' (TB) EFam
'Grandma's Hat' (SDB) EBee
'Grape Reprise' (TB) EFam
'Grapelet' (MDB) ERos NZep
'Grapesicle' (SDB) NZep
'Great Lakes' ESgI
'Grecian Goddess' (TB) EFam
'Green Halo' (DB) EGle
'Green Prophecy' (TB) LIri
'Green Spot' (SDB) ♀H4 CBro CHad EBee ECtt EHrv EHyt
  ELan EPfP ESis GKir LHop MRav
  NBir NHol NMen NSti NWCA SAga
  SBla SChu SPer SPet WCFE WEas
  WHoo WWeb
'Green Streak' (TB) LIri
'Gringo' (TB) WCAu
'Gypsy Beauty' (Dut) CFwr MSph WHil
'Gypsy Boy' (SDB) NZep
'Gypsy Caravan' (TB) SCro
'Gypsy Jewels' (TB) CKel ESgI
'Gypsy Romance' (TB) ESgI LIri
* 'Haizon Bleu' EWoo
'Hallowed Thought' (TB) MMil MWat
halophila see *I. spuria* subsp. *halophila*
'Hand Painted' (TB) EFam

'Handshake' (TB) LIri
'Happening' (SDB) NZep
'Happy Birthday' (TB) ESgI
* 'Happy Border' WCAu
'Happy Mood' (IB) ♀H4 EFou SIri WCAu
'Happy Pal' (TB) EFam
'Harbor Blue' (TB) CKel EBee MWat SCro WCAu
'Harlow Gold' (IB) EFou ESgI NZep
'Harmony' (Reticulata) CAvo CBro EPfP EPot GBBs LAma
  LRHS MBri NJOw NRog SPet
  WRHF
'Harriette Halloway' (TB) CPrp EBee SMrm
'Harvest King' (TB) ESgI LIri
'Heavenly Days' (TB) WCAu
'Heaven's Bounty' (BB) EFam
'Helen Boehm' (TB) SCro
'Helen Proctor' (IB) ESgI NZep SCro
'Helen Traubel' (TB) WCAu
'Helge' (IB) COIW EBee EPfP SWat
'Hellcat' (IB) NZep WAul
'Hello Darkness' (TB) ESgI LIri
'Hell's Fire' (TB) SCro
'Hercules' (Reticulata) LAma
'Hers' (IB) SCro
'Heure Bleue' (TB) **new** EWoo
'High Command' (TB) CKel SCro SMrm
'High Energy' (TB) EFam
'High Life' (TB) SCro
'Hildegarde' (Dut) CFwr
'His' (IB) SCro
histrio EHyt EPot LAma
- subsp. *aintabensis* EPot LAma
histrioides GCrs WAbe WLin
§ - 'Angel's Tears' CLAP ERos
- 'Lady Beatrice Stanley' CLAP EPot NMen
N - 'Major' CBro CDes CLAP GCrs LAma
- 'Reine Immaculée' ERos
- var. *sophenensis* CLAP
'Hocus Pocus' (SDB) EFou EHyt EPPr EWoo
'Holden Clough' CBot CHad CHar CKel CM&M
  (SpecHybrid) ♀H4 CRow EFou ELan EMFW EPfP EPla
  GBuc LRHS MFir MMil MRav
  MWgw NBir NGdn NSti WAul
  WCAu WEas WFar WLin WPrP
  WTin WWin
'Honey Glazed' (IB) ESgI NZep WAul WCAu
'Honey Scoop' (TB) EFam
'Honington' (SDB) WCAu
'Honky Tonk Blues' (TB) ESgI LIri
'Honorabile' (MTB) SMrm WCAu
hoogiana ♀H3 EBee GKev LRHS MBow
- 'Alba' WWst
- 'Purpurea' LRHS
§ *hookeri* CSam EBre EDAr EHyt ELan EMlt
  EPPr GBBs GEdr GIBF NJOw
  NWoo SAga SOkd WAbe WWeb
hookeriana WCot
'Hopscotch' (BB) SCro
§ 'Hornpipe' (TB) **new** WCAu
'Hot Chocolate' (TB) LIri
'Hot Fudge' (IB) WAul
'Hot Spice' (IB) NZep WCAu
'Hubbub' (IB) SCro
'Hula Doll' (MDB) EGle NMen
'Hula Honey' (TB) EFam
hyrcana CBro EBee EHyt LAma LRHS
'I Bless' (IB) EFam
'I Do' (TB) NZep
§ *iberica* EHyt EPot
  subsp. *elegantissima*
- subsp. *iberica* EPot WWst
'Ice Dancer' (TB) ♀H4 CKel
'Iced Tea' (TB) LIri
'Iced Vanilla' (IB) CKel

'Ida' (Reticulata)		EPot LAma
illyrica		see *I. pallida*
'Imbue' (SDB) **new**		ESgl
'Immortality' (TB)		CKel EBee SCro WCAu
'Imperator' (TB)		EBee EWTr
'Imperial Bronze' (Spuria)		EFou NFor
'Impetuous' (BB) ♀H4		EFou
'Imprimis' (TB)		ESgl LIri
'In Depth' (Spuria)		LIri
'In Town' (TB)		ESgl EWoo
inconspicua		WWst
'Incoscente' (SDB) **new**		ESgl
'Indeed' (IB)		EBre
'Indian Chief' (TB)		EBee EMil WCAu WShp
'Indian Jewel' (SDB)		EGle
'Indian Pow Wow' (SDB)		CSev
'Indigo Flight' (IB)		EFou
'Infernal Fire' (TB)		LIri
'Infinite Grace' (TB)		ESgl SCro
'Innocent Heart' (IB) ♀H4		SCro
innominata		CFil CWCL EBee ECha IBlr LHop LRHS MLwd MNrw NBir NBro SRms SWal WBVN WCom WShp
– JCA 13225		CLAP SSpi
– JCA 13227		SSpi
– apricot		IBlr NWoo
– Ballyrogan hybrids		IBlr
– rose		CNic ERos
N – 'Spinners'		SSpi
– yellow		CAvo NRya
'Inscription' (SDB)		EGle EHyt
'Interpol' (TB)		ESgl EWoo WCAu WWhi
'Invitation' (TB)		ESgl
'Irish Doll' (MDB)		EGle
'Irish Tune' (TB)		ESgl
'Ishmael' (SDB)		EGle
'Isolinc' (TB) **new**		ESgl
'Istanbul' (TB)		EFam
'It's Magic' (TB)		LIri
'J.S. Dijt' (Reticulata)		CAvo CBro EPar EPot LAma LRHS MBow MBri NRog
'Jade Mist' (SDB)		EGle GKir
'Jan Reagan' (SDB)		NZep
'Jane Phillips' (TB) ♀H4		More than 30 suppliers
'Jane Taylor' (SDB)		CBro EGle
'Janet Lane' (BB)		CKel
'Janice Chesnik' (Spuria)		LIri
japonica ♀H3		CHEx CPLG EHrv LPio NPer WFar
– L 638		SCro
– 'Aphrodite' (v)		WPnP WTin
– 'Ledger'		CAvo CBro CHll CKel CPrp CSpe EBee ECha EHrv ELan EPar EPfP EPla IGor MRav SChr SIri SMad
– *pallescens*		EBee
– 'Variegata' (v) ♀H3		CAvo CBot CHEx CHad CKel CSpe ECha EHrv EPar GGar LRHS NBro NOrc NPer SAPC SAga SArc SMad SSpi WCFE WEas WFar WHer WHil WMyn WPic
'Jasper Gem' (MDB)		EBre EGle ERos GKir NBir
'Jazz Festival' (TB)		WCAu
'Jazzamatazz' (SDB)		ESgl
'Jazzebel' (TB)		SCro
'Jean Cayeux' (TB)		ESgl
'Jean Guymer' (TB)		EFam NBir WCAu
'Jeanne Price' (TB)		SCoo WCAu
'Jeannine' (Reticulata)		LAma
'Jephthah's Daughter' (TB)		EFam
'Jeremy Brian' (SDB) ♀H4		WCAu
'Jersey Lilli' (SDB)		WCAu
'Jesse's Song' (TB)		ESgl NZep SCro
'Jewel Baby' (SDB)		CBro NZep
'Jewel Bright' (SDB)		EFou

'Jeweler's Art' (SDB)		EWoo
'Jiansada' (SDB)		CBro
'Jitterbug' (TB)		EHrv WCAu
'Joanna' (TB)		EBee NLar
'Joanna Taylor' (MDB)		EHyt ERos NMen NZep WCAu
N 'Joe Elliott' (CH)		EGle
'John' (IB)		CKel SCro
'Joy Boy' (SDB) **new**		ESgl
'Joyce' (Reticulata)		CBro EPar EPot LAma LRHS MBri NRog SPet
'Joyce Terry' (TB)		ESgl GKir
'Joyful' (SDB)		ESgl
'Jubilee Gem' (TB)		CKel
'July Sunshine' (TB)		EFam
'June Prom' (IB)		SCro
'Jungle Shadows' (BB)		MRav NBir SMrm WCAu
'Jurassic Park' (TB)		LIri
'Juris Prudence' (TB) **new**		ESgl
'Just Dance' (IB)		ESgl
'Just Jennifer' (BB)		WCAu
kaempferi		see *I. ensata*
'Kaibab Trail' (Spuria)		LIri
'Kangchenjunga' (TB)		ESgl
'Karen Christine' (TB)		SCro
kashmiriana		CBcs
'Katharine Hodgkin' (Reticulata) ♀H4		More than 30 suppliers
'Katie-Koo' (IB) ♀H4		CKel WDav
'Katinka' (CH)		WWst
'Katy Petts' (SDB)		EFou NZep
'Kayo' (SDB)		EFou EGle EHyt NZep
'Kelway Renaissance' (TB)		CKel
kemaonensis		EBee
'Ken's Choice' (TB) ♀H4 **new**		CKel
'Kent Pride' (TB)		CHad CMil EBee EBre ECGP EChP EFou EPPr EPfP ERou GKir MMil MRav MSte MWat SChu SCro SGar SWat WBVN WCAu WTin WWin
'Kentucky Bluegrass' (SDB)		EFou MMil WWin
'Kentucky Derby' (TB)		SCro
'Kermit' (IB)		SCro
§ *kerneriana* ♀H4		CBro CPom EBee ERos GBuc LRHS MLLN MNrw NBir SIgm SMHy SScr SUsu WOBN WPen
'Kevin's Theme' (TB)		LIri
'Kildonan' (TB)		WCAu
'Kissing Circle' (TB)		ESgl EWoo
'Kitt Peak' (Spuria) ♀H4		LIri
'Kiwi Capers' (SDB)		NZep
'Kiwi Slices' (SDB)		ESgl
klattii		see *I. spuria* subsp. *musulmanica*
'Knick Knack' (MDB)		CBro EBee EBre EHyt ERos ESis GCrs LBee LPio LRHS MLwd MRav NMen SDnm SMrm WHil WOBN WWeb WWin
kochii		GCal
kolpakowskiana		WWst
'Kona Nights' (BB) **new**		ESgl
'Korea' (TB) **new**		CRow
korolkowii		GIBF
– 'Violacea'		EBee WWst
kuschakewiczii		WWst
'La Nina Rosa' (BB)		WCAu
'La Senda' (Spuria)		GFlt WCot
'La Vie en Rose' (TB) **new**		ESgl
'Laced Cotton' (TB)		SCoo
'Laced Lemonade' (SDB)		EBre EFou GKir MBri
§ *lactea* ♀H4		SCro
lacustris ♀H4		CBro ERos NBro NMen NWCA WAbe
'Lady Emma' (MTB)		EFam
'Lady Essex' (TB)		EFam

'Lady Friend' (TB) — ERou ESgI EWoo WCAu
'Lady Ilse' (TB) — WCAu
'Lady in Red' (SDB) **new** — ESgI
'Lady Mohr' (AB) — WTin
'Lady of Fatima' (TB) — ESgI
'Lady R' (SDB) — EHyt
laeuinea — EBee
§ *laevigata* ♀H4 — CDWL CRow CWat ECha EGle EGol EHon ELan EMFW EPfP LNCo LPBA MRav MSta NBrk NBro NGdn NPer SGar SPer SWat WFar WMAq WMyn WPnP WShi WTin WWpP
– var. *alba* — CBen CRow ECha EGol EHon ELan EPfP LPBA NArg SSpi SWat WAbe WFar WWpP
– 'Albopurpurea' — CDWL CLAP EMFW SLon WTMC
– 'Atropurpurea' — CRow EGol IBlr LPBA
– 'Dark Pettale' — CLAP
I – 'Dorothy' — LPBA MSta NGdn
– 'Dorothy Robinson' — LNCo SWat
– 'Elegant' — see *I. laevigata* 'Weymouth Elegant'
I – 'Elegante' — SWat
– 'Elgar' — WMAq
– 'Liam Johns' — CRow
– 'Midnight' — see *I. laevigata* 'Weymouth Midnight'
– 'Mottled Beauty' — CRow MSta
N – 'Plum Purple' — EGle
– 'Rashomon' **new** — CRow
– 'Regal' — CDWL
I – 'Reveille' — EGle
– 'Richard Greaney' — CRow
– 'Rose Queen' — see *I. ensata* 'Rose Queen'
– 'Shirasagi' — CRow
I – 'Snowdrift' — CBen CLAP CRow CWat EHon EMFW EPla LNCo LPBA MSta NBir NGdn NPer SCro SLon SPer SWat WFar WMAq WTMC WWpP
– 'Variegata' (v) ♀H4 — More than 30 suppliers
– 'Violet Garth' — CRow
– 'Weymouth' — see *I. laevigata* 'Weymouth Blue'
§ – 'Weymouth Blue' — CRow
§ – 'Weymouth Elegant' — CBen CFir CRow
§ – 'Weymouth Midnight' — CBen CFir CRow ECGP EGol EHon LPBA SWat WOBN
'Lake Placid' (TB) — SCro
'Land o' Lakes' (TB) — SCro
N 'Langport Chapter' (IB) — CKel
N 'Langport Chief' (IB) — CKel
N 'Langport Claret' (IB) — CKel
N 'Langport Curlew' (IB) — CKel
N 'Langport Duchess' (IB) — WDav
N 'Langport Finch' (IB) — NBir WIvy
N 'Langport Flame' (IB) — CKel WTin
N 'Langport Flush' (IB) — SCro
N 'Langport Haze' (IB) — CKel
N 'Langport Hope' (IB) — CKel
N 'Langport Jane' (IB) — CKel
N 'Langport Lord' (IB) — CKel
'Langport Midnight' — SMrm
'Langport Minstrel' (IB) — CKel
N 'Langport Robe' (IB) — CKel
N 'Langport Snow' (IB) — CKel
N 'Langport Star' (IB) — CKel
'Langport Storm' (IB) — CHad EBee EBre EChP EFou EMil NGdn SChu WDav WIvy WTin
N 'Langport Sun' (IB) — CKel SMrm
N 'Langport Swift' (IB) — CKel
'Langport Sylvia' (IB) — CKel
N 'Langport Tartan' (IB) — CKel
'Langport Vista' (IB) — CKel

'Langport Wren' (IB) ♀H4 — CBro CKel CMil EBre GKir MBri NBir SMrm WEas WTin
'Lark Rise' (TB) ♀H4 — CKel
'Larry Gaulter' (TB) — WCAu
'Lascivious Dreams' (TB) — EFam
§ *latifolia* ♀H4 — GIBF
– 'Duchess of York' — EPot
– 'Isabella' — EBee EPot
– 'King of the Blues' — EPot WCot
– 'Mansfield' — EPot
– 'Montblanc' — EBee EPot
– 'Queen of the Blues' (Eng) — EBee EPot
'Latin Rock' (TB) — SCro WCAu
latiphilum — GIBF
§ *lazica* ♀H4 — CAbP CBro CMea CRow CSpe EBee ECre EHyt EMan EPPr EPot EWsh GGar GMac IBlr MAvo MRav MSte NBir NSti SChu SCro SMHy SSpi SUsu WCot WEas WPGP WSpi
– deep blue — WCom
– 'Joy Bishop' — WCot
– 'Turkish Blue' **new** — IBlr
'Leah Traded' (BB) — EFam
'Leda's Lover' (TB) — ESgI SCro
'Lemon Beauty' (TB) **new** — EBee
'Lemon Brocade' (TB) — EBre ESgI EWoo GKir MBri WCAu
'Lemon Dilemma' (Spuria) — LIri
I 'Lemon Drop' (TB) — CKel
'Lemon Flare' (SDB) — ECtt MRav SRms WCAu
'Lemon Glitter' (TB) — EFou
'Lemon Mist' (TB) — ESgI
'Lemon Puff' (MDB) — CBro WCAu
'Lemon Whip' (IB) — EWoo
N 'Lena' (SDB) — CBro EBee
'Lenora Pearl' (BB) — ESgI
'Lent A. Williamson' (TB) — SCro
'Lenten Prayer' (TB) — LIri
'Lenzschnee' (TB) — EBee
'Let's Elope' (IB) — ESgI
'Light Cavalry' (IB) — ESgI EWoo NZep
'Light Laughter' (IB) — WCAu
'Lighten Up' (SDB) — NZep
'Lilac and Lavender' (SDB) — NZep
'Lilac Stitchery' (TB) — EFam
'Lilli-white' (SDB) — EBee EGle ELan ENot MBNS MRav SIri WCAu
'Lima Colada' (SDB) — SMrm
'Limbo' (SpecHybrid) **new** — CRow
'Limelight' (TB) — SRms
'Lincoln Imp' (CH) ♀H3 — WWst
'Linesman' (SDB) — NZep
linifolia — WWst
'Lion's Share' (TB) — LIri
'Little Amigo' (SDB) — NZep
N 'Little Amoena' — ERos NMen
'Little Annie' (SDB) — NZep
'Little Bill' (SDB) — EFou EGle
'Little Black Belt' (SDB) — EFou NZep SIri SMrm
'Little Blackfoot' (SDB) — ESgI WCAu WHoo WWin
'Little Chestnut' (SDB) — WWin
'Little Dandy' (SDB) — EGle WIvy
'Little Dogie' (SDB) — EGle EHyt
'Little Dream' (SDB) — EGle NZep WCAu
'Little Episode' (SDB) — NZep
'Little Pearl' (MDB) — NZep
'Little Rosy Wings' (SDB) — CBro ERos
'Little Shadow' (SDB) — ENot MRav SRms
'Little Snow Lemon' (IB) — EFam NZep
'Little Tilgates' (CH) ♀H3 — WWst
'Live Coals' (SDB) — LIri
'Live Jazz' (SDB) — NZep
loczyi — EBee
'Lodore' (TB) — SRms WCAu

'Lois Parrish' (TB)   LIri
'Lollipop' (SDB)   ESgI
'London Pride' (TB)   MMil
longipetala   GIBF NBir
'Lookin' Good' (IB)   NZep
'Loop the Loop' (TB)   CFwr EBee EGle EPfP EWoo SWat WShp
'Lord Baltimore' (TB)   SCro
'Lord Warden' (TB)   EBee EChP EFou
'Loreley' (TB)   ESgI
'Lorenzaccio de Medecis' (TB)   ESgI
'Lorilee' (TB)   ESgI SCro
'Lothario' (TB)   WFoF
'Louis d'Or' (TB) **new**   LIri
'Louvois' (TB)   ESgI
'Love Chant' (TB)   CKel
'Love for Leila' (Spuria) ♀H4   LIri
'Love the Sun' (TB)   ESgI
'Lovely Again' (TB)   MWat WCAu
'Lovely Dawn' (TB)   LIri
'Lovely Fran' (TB)   EFam
'Lovely Kay' (TB)   SCro
'Lovely Light' (TB)   MBri
'Love's Tune' (IB)   SCro
'Loveshine' (SDB)   MMil MRav NZep
'Low Ho Silver' (IB)   EFam
'Low Snow' (SDB)   NZep
'Lugano' (TB)   ESgI
'Luli-Ann' (SDB) ♀H4 **new**   CKel
'Lumiere d'Automne' (TB)   ESgI
'Luminosity' (TB)   EFam
§ *lutescens* ♀H4   ERos GEdr GFlt GKev WAbe XPep
§ - 'Campbellii'   CBro EHyt ERos MBro NMen
I - 'Goldcrest'   MBro
- subsp. *lutescens*   WLin
'Lyme Tyme' (TB)   LIri
'Ma Mie' (IB)   ESgI
macrosiphon   GKev
'Madame Maurice Lassailly' (TB) **new**   ESgI
'Madeira Belle' (TB)   EWoo WCAu
'Magharee' (TB)   ESgI
'Magic Bubbles' (IB) ♀H4   LIri
'Magic Flute' (MDB)   EGle
'Magic Man' (TB)   EBee
magnifica ♀H3-4   CBro EBee EHyt GKev
- 'Agalik'   CMea LRHS WWst
- 'Alba'   LRHS
'Mahogany Snow' (SDB)   NZep
'Maisie Lowe' (TB) **new**   ESgI
'Making Eyes' (SDB)   ESgI EWoo WCAu
I 'Mandarin' (TB)   ESgI
'Mandarin Purple' (Sino-Sib)   CDes EBee GGar IBlr NGdn NHol
mandshurica   GIBF
'Mango Entree' (TB)   LIri
'Many Moons Tales' (TB)   EFam
'Maple Treat' (TB)   LIri
'Marcel Turbat' (TB)   ESgI
'Marche Turque' (TB)   ESgI
'Marco Polo' (TB) **new**   ESgI
'Margaret Inez' (TB)   LIri
'Margot Holmes' (Cal-Sib)   EBee GCal IBlr SChu
'Marhaba' (MDB)   CBro ERos
'Mariposa Skies' (TB)   LIri
'Marmalade Skies' (BB)   NZep WCAu
'Marshlander' (TB)   EFou SCro
'Martyn Rix'   see *I. confusa* 'Martyn Rix'
'Mary Constance' (IB) ♀H4   CKel LIri

'Mary Frances' (TB)   SCro WCAu
'Mary McIlroy' (SDB) ♀H4   CBro WTin
'Mary Vernon' (TB) **new**   GFlt
'Master Touch' (TB)   SCro
'Matinata' (TB)   CKel EBre
'Maui Moonlight' (IB) ♀H4   CKel EFou LIri MMil NZep
'May Melody' (TB)   WCAu
'Meadow Court' (SDB)   CBro CFwr CKel CM&M CRez EBee ERos NBro NZep WCAu WDav WWin
'Media Luz' (Spuria)   WCAu
'Meg's Mantle' (TB) ♀H4   CKel
'Melissa Sue' (TB)   SCro
mellita   see *I. suaveolens*
- var. *rubromarginata*   see *I. suaveolens*
'Melon Honey' (SDB)   CKel EGle EHyt MMil NZep WCAu WDav WHrl WWin
'Memphis Blues' (TB)   EWoo
'Mer du Sud' (TB)   ESgI SCoo
'Merseyside' (SDB)   EGle
'Mesmerizer' (TB)   LIri
'Metaphor' (TB)   MMil WCAu
'Mezza Cartuccia' (IB)   ESgI
'Michael Paul' (SDB) ♀H4   ESgI
'Midday Blues' (IB)   NZep
'Midnight Caller' (TB)   EFam
'Midnight Fire' (TB)   ERou
'Midnight Oil' (TB)   LIri
'Midnight Pacific' (TB)   EFam
'Mil Byers' (TB)   EFam
milesii ♀H4   CDes CPou EBee EMon GBuc GIBF IGor MSph NBir WPer WPic
'Mind Reader' (TB)   LIri
'Mini-Agnes' (SDB)   CBro
'Minnesota Glitters' (TB)   SCro
'Minnie Colquitt' (TB)   SCro
'Miss Carla' (IB)   CKel MMil SCro
'Miss Scarlett' (BB)   EFam
'Mission Ridge' (TB)   EBee WShp
'Mission Sunset' (TB)   EHrv WCAu
'Missouri Lakes' (Spuria)   LIri
'Missouri Rivers' (Spuria)   LIri
missouriensis ♀H4   IBlr IGor NBid SSpi
'Mister Roberts' (SDB)   ESgI NZep
'Mme Chereau' (TB)   ESgI WCAu
'Mme Louis Aureau' (TB)   ESgI
'Modern Classic' (TB)   EWoo
'Mogul' (TB)   LIri
* 'Mohogang Mountain' (TB)   EFam
'Monaco' (TB)   EFou
'Money' (TB)   SCro
monnieri   IBlr NLar SDix SMHy
Monspur Group   EBee GCal SSpi WCot WPic
§ 'Monspur Cambridge Blue' (Spuria) ♀H4   WCAu WPic
'Moon Pearl' (CH)   WWst
'Moon Sparkle' (IB)   CKel SIri
'Moonbeam' (TB)   CKel
'Moonlight' (TB)   NFor WCot
'Moonlight Waves'   see *I. ensata* 'Moonlight Waves'
'Moonstruck' (TB)   EWoo
'Morning Hymn' (TB)   SCro
'Morning Show' (IB)   SCro WShp
'Morning's Blush' (SDB) ♀H4   LIri
'Morocco' (TB)   SCro
'Morwenna' (TB) ♀H4   CKel
* 'Mount Stewart Black'   GCal
'Mrs Horace Darwin' (TB)   CFir EBee SWat WMnd
'Mrs Nate Rudolph' (SDB)   EBee EFou EGle ESis MBri SMrm
'Mrs Tait' (Spuria)   GCal NChi
'Mulled Wine' (TB)   ESgI
'Music Box' (SDB)   NZep
'My Friend Jonathan' (TB)   EFam

'My Impulse' (Spuria)	LIri	
N	'My Seedling' (MDB)	CBro ERos NMen WIvy
'Mystique' (TB)	SCro	
'Naivasha' (TB)	CKel	
'Nancy Hardy' (MDB)	CBro ERos NMen	
narbutii	WWst	
narcissiflora	CFir EBee	
narynensis	WWst	
I	'Natascha' (Reticulata)	EHyt EPot LAma WLin
'Navajo Jewel' (TB)	ESgI EWoo	
'Nectar' (IB)	ESgI	
'Needlecraft' (TB)	MMil	
'Needlepoint' (TB)	ESgI SCro	
'Neige de Mai' (TB) **new**	ESgI	
* 'Nel Jupe' (TB)	WShp	
'Neon Pixie' (SDB)	NZep	
nepalensis	see *I. decora*	
nertschinskia	see *I. sanguinea*	
'New Idea' (MTB)	ESgI WCAu	
'New Snow' (TB)	WCAu	
'Nibelungen' (TB)	EBee EPfP MLwd WFar WShp	
'Nice n' Nifty' (IB)	NZep WTin	
'Nicola Jane' (TB)	CKel	
♀H4 **new**		
nicolai	WWst	
'Nigerian Raspberry' (TB)	LIri	
'Night Game' (TB)	LIri	
'Night Owl' (TB)	CKel EBee SCro	
'Night Ruler' (TB)	ESgI	
'Nightfall' (TB)	EBee	
'Nights of Gladness' (TB)	ESgI	
'Noces Blanches' (IB)	ESgI	
'Noon Siesta' (TB)	ESgI	
'Northern Flame' (TB)	EFam	
'Northwest Pride'	WCAu	
(TB) **new**		
'Northwest Progress' (TB)	LIri	
'Nova'	WCot	
'O Shenandoah' (TB)	EFam	
'Ochraurea' (Spuria)	GCal NGdn	
ochroleuca	see *I. orientalis* Mill.	
'October' (TB)	EFam	
odaesanensis **new**	EBee	
'Oklahoma Crude' (TB)	LIri	
'Oktoberfest' (TB)	ESgI	
'Ola Kalá' (TB)	CM&M EBee ERou ESgI EWTr	
	MSte SCro SPer WCAu WShp	
'Old Black Magic' (TB)	LIri	
'Olympiad' (TB)	ESgI	
'Olympic Challenge' (TB)	ESgI	
'Olympic Torch' (TB)	WCAu	
'One Desire' (TB)	NZep	
'Open Sky' (SDB)	NZep	
'Orageux' (IB)	ESgI	
'Orange Blaze' (SDB)	CBro	
'Orange Caper' (SDB)	EBee EBre EGoo ESgI GBuc MBri	
	MRav NLar NZep SIri SPet	
'Orange Harvest' (TB)	EFam EWoo	
'Orange Order' (TB) **new**	WCAu	
'Orange Petals' (IB)	LIri	
N	'Orange Plaza' (TB)	NMen WIvy
'Orange Tiger' (SDB)	NZep	
'Orchardist' (TB)	CKel	
'Orchid Cloud' (TB)	EFam	
'Orchidea Selvaggia'	ESgI	
(TB) **new**		
orchioides hort.	see *I. bucharica* Foster	
§	*orchioides* Carrière	CBri CMea EBee EChP EHyt ELan
	ERos ETow GBBs MBow NBPC	
	NWCA WAul WLin	
- 'Urungachsai' **new**	WWst	
'Oregold' (SDB)	NZep	
'Oregon Skies' (TB)	EWoo SCro	
'Oriental Baby' (IB)	EWoo	

'Oriental Blush' (SDB)	EHyt	
'Oriental Glory' (TB)	WCAu	
'Oriental Touch'	CRow	
(SpecHybrid)		
orientalis Thunb.	see *I. sanguinea*	
§	*orientalis* Mill. ♀H4	EBee EPPr GIBF IFro LPBA MNrw
	MSte MWgw SChu SGar SPer SSpi	
	WPic WWin WWst	
- 'Alba'	see *I. sanguinea* 'Alba'	
'Orinoco Flow' (BB) ♀H4	CHar CKel ESgI LIri WCAu	
'Out Yonder' (TB)	WCAu	
'Ovation' (IB)	ESgI SCro	
'Overnight Sensation' (TB)	SCro	
'O'What' (SDB)	ESgI	
'Owyhee Desert' (TB)	LIri	
'Ozone Alert' (TB)	LIri	
'Pacer' (IB)	NZep	
Pacific Coast hybrids	see *I. Californian hybrids*	
'Pacific Gambler' (TB)	EFou	
'Pacific Mist' (TB)	SCro WCAu	
'Pacific Panorama' (TB)	EBee ESgI	
'Pagan Princess' (TB)	WCAu	
'Pageant' (TB)	WTin	
'Paint It Black' (TB)	EWoo	
'Pajaro Dunes' (CH) ♀H3	WWst	
'Pale Primrose' (TB)	WBar	
'Pale Shades' (IB) ♀H4	CBro CKel ERos	
§	*pallida*	CHad CPrp EFou ESis GKir MCCP
	MRav MSte WBrE WCAu WMnd	
- 'Argentea Variegata' (v)	CHad CPrp EBee EChP EHoe EHrv	
	EPfP GGar GKir LAst LHop LPio	
	LRHS MBrN MLLN MRav MTis	
	NBir NCiC NMir NSti SCro SSpi	
	SUsu WCot WHoo WViv	
- 'Aurea'	see *I. pallida* 'Variegata' Hort.	
- 'Aurea Variegata'	see *I. pallida* 'Variegata' Hort.	
- var. *dalmatica*	see *I. pallida* subsp. *pallida*	
§	- subsp. *pallida* ♀H4	CBot CKel CWCL EBee EBre EChP
	ECha ELan MBri SCro SDix SMrm	
	SPer WCot	
N	- 'Variegata' Hort. (v) ♀H4	More than 30 suppliers
'Palomino' (TB)	WCAu	
'Paltec' (IB)	CPou EBee LPhx	
'Pandora's Purple' (TB)	SCro	
'Pane e Vino' (TB) **new**	ESgI	
'Paradise' (TB)	EPfP SCro WShp	
'Paradise Bird' (TB) ♀H4	WCAu	
paradoxa	WWst	
- f. *choschab*	EHyt EPot SBla SOkd	
'Paricutin' (SDB)	CBro EGle	
'Party Dress' (TB)	CM&M EBee EBre ENot ERou	
	EWTr LAst MRav NBir NGdn NOrc	
	SPer SRms WBVN WShp WWeb	
parvula **new**	WWst	
'Pastel Charm' (SDB)	CM&M CRez EBee NSti SIri WMnd	
'Pastel Delight' (SDB)	NZep	
'Patches' (TB)	ESgI	
'Path of Gold' (DB)	CBro	
'Patina' (TB)	EWoo WCAu	
'Patterdale' (TB)	NBir	
'Pauline' (Reticulata)	CBro EPfP EPot GBBs LAma LRHS	
	NRog SPet	
'Peace and Harmony' (TB)	LIri	
'Peaceful Warden'	EWoo	
(TB) **new**		
'Peach Band' (TB)	ERou	
'Peach Eyes' (SDB)	CBro NZep	
'Peach Float' (TB)	WCAu	
'Peach Melba' (TB)	ESgI	
'Peach Petals' (BB)	NZep	
'Peach Picotee' (TB)	ESgI SCro	
'Peach Spot' (TB)	WCAu	
'Peacock'	see *I. ensata* 'Peacock', *I. unguicularis* 'Peacock'	

'Pearly Dawn' (TB)	EBee EChP ECha MSte MWat SChu SCoo SCro SPer SSvw	
'Pegasus' (TB)	SCro	
'Peggy Chambers' (IB) ♀H4	EFou MMil SMrm	
'Peking Summer' (TB)	SCro	
'Pele' (SDB) **new**	WCAu	
'Pennies' (MDB)	NZep	
'Penny Pinch' (TB) **new**	EBee	
'Pennyworth' (IB)	SCro	
'People Pleaser' (SDB)	NZep	
'Peppermint Twist' (SDB)	NZep	
'Perfume Counter' (TB)	EFam	
'Persian Doll' (MDB)	NZep	
'Pet' (SDB)	NZep	
'Phaeton' (TB)	LIri	
'Pharaoh's Daughter' (IB) **new**	WAul	
'Pheasant Feathers' (TB)	LIri	
'Phil Keen' (TB) ♀H4	CKel	
'Phillida' (CH)	WWst	
'Picacho Peak' (Spuria)	LIri	
'Picadee'	EBee EPfP GBuc	
'Piero Bargellini' (TB)	ESgI LIri	
'Pigeon' (SDB)	NZep	
'Pigmy Gold' (IB)	ENot ERos	
'Pinewood Amethyst' (CH)	CPlt WWst	
'Pinewood Delight' (CH)	CPlt	
'Pinewood Prelude' (CH)	WWst	
'Pinewood Sunshine' (CH)	CPlt	
'Pink Angel' (TB)	EWoo SCro	
'Pink Attraction' (TB)	EFam ESgI	
'Pink Bubbles' (BB)	EFou NZep	
'Pink Charm' (TB)	EChP	
'Pink Charming' (TB)	LIri	
'Pink Confetti' (TB)	ESgI SCro	
'Pink Fawn' (SDB)	LIri	
'Pink Formal' (TB) **new**	ESgI	
'Pink Horizon' (TB)	CSBt EBee EPfP SCro WShp	
'Pink Kitten' (IB)	NZep WCAu	
N 'Pink Lavender' (TB)	SCro	
'Pink Light'	EBee	
'Pink Pussycat' (TB)	MBri	
N 'Pink Randall' (TB)	SCro	
'Pink Ruffles' (IB)	CHar	
'Pink Swan' (TB)	ESgI	
'Pink Taffeta' (TB)	ESgI	
'Pinkness' (TB)	EFam	
'Pinnacle' (TB)	CKel EBee SWat WShp	
'Pioneer' (TB) **new**	EBee	
'Piper's Tune' (IB)	SIri SMrm	
'Pipes of Pan' (TB) **new**	MRav WCAu	
'Piquant Lass' (MTB)	NZep	
'Pirate's Patch' (SDB)	ESgI	
'Piroska' (TB)	ESgI LIri	
'Piu Blue' (TB) **new**	ESgI	
I 'Pixie' (Reticulata)	EPot	
'Pixie Flirt' (MDB)	ERos	
planifolia	WWst	
'Playgirl' (TB)	SCro	
'Pleased as Punch' (IB)	EFam	
'Pledge Allegiance' (TB)	SCro	
plicata	WCAu	
'Plickadee' (SDB)	CBro EPot	
'Pluie d'Or' (TB) **new**	ESgI	
'Pogo' (SDB)	EBee EChP ECtt EGle EHyt ENot EWoo GBuc GKir MMil MRav NBir NWCA SRms	
'Point Made' (TB)	LIri	
'Pond Lily' (TB)	LIri	
'Port of Call' (Spuria)	CWrd	
'Post Time' (TB)	SCro	
'Power Surge' (TB)	EWoo LIri	
'Prancing Pony' (TB)	SCro	

'Precious Heather' (TB) ♀H4	CKel	
'Pretender' (TB)	LRHS WCAu	
'Prettie Print' (TB)	SCro	
'Pretty Please' (TB)	ESgI	
'Priceless Pearl' (TB)	SCro	
'Prince' (SDB)	EFou EGle	
'Prince Indigo' (TB)	ENot	
'Prince of Burgundy' (IB) ♀H4	LIri	
'Prince of Earl' (TB)	EFam	
'Princess Beatrice' (TB)	WCAu	
'Princess Pittypat' (TB)	EFam	
'Princess Sabra' (TB) ♀H4	CKel	
'Princesse Caroline de Monaco' (TB)	LIri	
prismatica	WTin	
'Professor Blaauw' (Dut) ♀H4	CFwr LRHS MSph	
'Progressive Attitude' (TB)	LIri	
'Prophetic Message' (AB)	EFou	
'Prosper Laugier' (IB)	SCro	
'Proud Tradition' (TB)	SCro	
'Provencal' (TB)	ESgI WCAu	
'Prudy' (BB) ♀H4	CKel	
pseudacorus ♀H4	More than 30 suppliers	
- 'Alba'	CRow SSpi	
- var. *bastardii*	CBgR CRow CWat ECGP ECha EGol EMFP EMFW LPBA NPer SLon SMHy SPer SSpi WFar WTin WWpP	
- 'Beuron'	CRow	
- cream	EGol MTed NBir NBrk WAul	
- 'Esk'	GCal MTed SMHy	
N - 'Flore Pleno' (d)	CBgR CBot CRow EBee EMFW EPPr MInt NLar NPer WCot WFar	
- 'Golden Daggers'	CRow	
I - 'Golden Fleece'	SPer	
- 'Golden Queen'	CRow MSta WWpP	
- 'Ilgengold'	CRow	
N - 'Ivory'	CRow	
- 'Lime Sorbet' (v)	WCot	
* - *nana*	CRow LPBA	
- 'Roy Davidson' ♀H4	CBgR CDWL CKel CLAP CRow EMFW IBlr LPBA SLon WTin	
* - 'Sulphur Queen'	WCot	
- 'Sun Cascade'	CRow	
- 'Tiggah'	CRow	
- 'Turnipseed'	EBee WTin	
- 'Variegata' (v) ♀H4	More than 30 suppliers	
pseudacorus x versicolor	SCro	
'Pulse Rate' (SDB)	CBro	
pumila	EBre EPla EPot LRHS MBro MHer NFor NMen NWCA WLin WRHF WWin	
- *atroviolacea*	CKel NFla SMrm WMnd	
- subsp. *attica*	see *I. attica*	
- 'Aurea'	WMnd	
- blue	SWal	
* - 'Gelber Mantel'	NBir	
- 'Jackanapes'	WEas	
- 'Lavendel Plicata'	EBee EWTr NBro	
- 'Purpurea' (DB)	EHyt	
- 'Violacea' (DB)	MBro SRms	
- yellow	NFla SWal	
'Pumpin' Iron' (SDB)	CKel ESgI WDav	
'Pumpkin Center' (SDB)	NZep	
'Puppet' (SDB)	EGle	
'Puppet Baby' (MDB)	NZep	
'Puppy Love' (MTB)	NZep	
purdyi	GBuc	
'Pure Allure' (SDB)	NZep	
'Purple Duet' (TB)	EFam	

'Purple Gem' (Reticulata)	CBro EPot LAma	
'Purple Sensation' (Dut)	CFwr CRez MSph	
'Purple Streaker' (TB)	SCro	
purpurea	see *I. galatica*	
'Pussycat' (MDB)	GKir	
'Quaker Lady' (TB)	ESgI	
'Quark' (SDB)	CBro CKel NZep	
'Quechee' (TB)	EBee ECGP EChP EMan EPfP ERou	
	EWTr MBow MRav MSte MWat	
	NGdn SChu SCro SWat	
'Queen in Calico' (TB)	ESgI SCro WCAu	
'Queen of Hearts' (TB)	SCro	
'Queen of May' (TB)	ESgI	
'Queen's Circle' (TB)	LIri	
'Queen's Ivory' (SDB)	WCAu	
'Queen's Pawn' (SDB) **new**	NZep	
'Quietly' (SDB)	EFam	
'Quintana' (CH)	WWst	
'Radiant Apogee' (TB)	ESgI	
'Radiant Summer' (TB)	SCro	
'Rain Dance' (SDB) ♀H4	ESgI NZep	
'Rajah' (TB)	CSBt EBee EChP EPfP ERou MRav	
	MSte NGdn NOrc SChu SCoo SLon	
	WMnd	
'Rameses' (TB)	ESgI	
'Rancho Rose' (TB)	SCro	
'Rapture in Blue' (TB)	EWoo	
'Rare Edition' (IB)	CKel EBre EFou EWoo GKir MBri	
	NZep SCro WAul	
'Rare Treat' (TB)	NZep	
'Raspberry Acres' (IB)	WCAu	
'Raspberry Blush'	CHad CKel CPar EBee EFou EOMN	
(IB) ♀H4	EPfP LAst NZep SCro SWat	
'Raspberry Jam' (SDB)	EGle EHyt NZep	
'Raspberry Sundae' (BB)	NZep	
'Rebecca Perret'	EWoo LIri	
(TB) **new**		
'Red Duet' (TB)	EFam	
I 'Red Flash' (TB)	SMrm	
'Red Hawk' (TB)	LIri	
'Red Heart' (SDB)	EBee ESgI LIri MRav	
'Red Lion' (TB)	EFou NZep	
'Red Orchid' (IB)	EBee ELan EWTr	
'Red Revival' (TB)	MWat SCro WCAu	
N 'Red Rum' (TB)	CKel	
'Red Tornado' (TB)	ESgI	
'Red Zinger' (IB)	ESgI NZep SCro WAul	
'Redelta' (TB)	EFam	
'Redwood Supreme'	CWrd	
(Spuria)		
'Regal Surprise'	CRow	
(SpecHybrid)		
'Regards' (SDB)	CBro EGle	
§ *reichenbachii*	EBee ERos LBee LTwo NWCA	
– NS 700	CPou	
'Repartee' (TB)	ESgI EWoo SCro	
'Response' (Spuria) **new**	CWrd	
§ *reticulata* ♀H4	CBcs CBro EPar LRHS MBNS	
	NJOw NRog SPet	
* – 'Violet Queen'	EPot	
'Returning Chameleon'	EFam	
(TB)		
'Returning Peace' (TB)	EFam	
'Riches' (SDB)	NZep	
'Ride the Wind' (TB)	SCro	
'Right Royal' (TB)	ENot	
'Rime Frost' (TB)	WCAu	
'Rimfire' (TB)	EBee	
'Ringo' (TB)	CKel ESgI LIri WCAu	
'Ripple Chip' (SDB)	NZep WTin	
'Rippling Waters' (TB)	ESgI	
'Rising Moon' (TB)	SCro	
'Rive Gauche' (TB)	ESgI	
'River Avon' (TB) ♀H4	LIri	

'River Hawk' (TB)	SCro	
'River Pearl' (TB)	LIri	
§ x *robusta* 'Dark Aura'	WCot	
§ – 'Gerald Darby' ♀H4	More than 30 suppliers	
– 'Mountain Brook'	CRow	
– 'Nutfield Blue'	NSti	
§ – 'Rocket' (TB)	EBee ECGN EChP IPot MRav NBir	
	NGdn SCoo SCro	
'Rogue' (TB)	LIri	
'Roman Rhythm'	EWoo WCAu	
(TB) **new**		
'Romance' (TB)	ERou	
'Romano' (Dut)	CFwr CRez MNrw MSph	
'Ron' (TB)	EWoo	
'Roney's Encore' (TB)	EFam	
'Rosalie Figge' (TB)	EFam	
'Rose Queen'	see *I. ensata* 'Rose Queen'	
'Rosemary's Dream'	CKel	
(MTB)		
rosenbachiana	WWst	
– 'Harangon' **new**	WWst	
I – 'Sina' **new**	WWst	
– 'Varzob' **new**	WWst	
'Roseplic' (TB)	ESgI	
'Rosette Wine' (TB)	ESgI LIri	
'Rosy Veil' (TB)	ESgI	
'Rosy Wings' (TB)	EHyt ESgI	
'Roulette' (TB) **new**	MBri	
'Roustabout' (SDB)	EGle	
N 'Roy Elliott'	LHop NHol NMen SIng	
'Royal Cadet' (Spuria)	LIri	
'Royal Contrast' (SDB)	NZep	
♀H4		
'Royal Elegance' (TB)	EWoo	
'Royal Intrigue' (TB)	SCro	
'Royal Magician' (SDB)	WHoo WTin	
'Royal Satin' (TB) **new**	EWoo	
'Royal Summer' (TB)	EFam	
'Royal Touch' (TB)	EBee EFou	
'Royal Yellow' (Dut)	CFwr CRez	
'Ruban Bleu' (TB)	ESgI EWoo	
'Rubistar' (TB)	ESgI	
'Ruby Chimes' (IB)	SCro WCAu	
'Ruby Contrast' (TB)	CHad WCAu	
rudskyi	see *I. variegata*	
'Ruffled Copper Sunset'	LIri	
(TB)		
'Ruffles and Lace' (TB)	SCro	
'Rustic Cedar' (TB)	ESgI	
'Rustic Royalty' (TB)	LIri	
'Rustler' (TB)	LIri SCro	
'Rusty Dusty' (SDB)	NZep	
ruthenica	ERos GIBF NMen	
– *leucantha*	EBee	
– var. *nana*	GKev	
– – ACE 1665	EPot	
– – L 1280	EPot	
'Sable' (TB)	CHad CPrp EBee EBre EChP ELan	
	EMan EPPr ESgI MCLN MRav MSte	
	MWat MWgw NGdn NOrc SCoo	
	SCro SPer WCAu	
'Sable Night' (TB)	CHar CKel ERou	
'Sager Cedric' (TB)	WCAu	
'Saharan Sun' (TB)	LIri	
'Saint Crispin' (TB)	CM&M EBee ERou ESgI MRav	
	MSte MWat SChu SCro SPer WWeb	
'Sally Jane' (TB)	WCAu	
'Salonique' (TB)	ESgI NBlu WCAu WFar	
* 'Saltbox' (SDB)	WIvy	
'Saltwood' (SDB)	CBro	
'Sam Carne' (TB)	WCAu	
'San Francisco' (TB)	ESgI	
'San Leandro' (TB)	MBri	
'Sand Princess' (MTB)	EFou SMrm	

'Sandstone Sentinel' (BB)	LIri
'Sandy Caper' (IB)	WCAu
'Sangone' (IB) **new**	ESgI
'Sangreal' (IB)	EBee
§ *sanguinea* ♀H4	GFlt GIBF
§ - 'Alba'	IBlr
§ - 'Snow Queen'	More than 30 suppliers
sanguinea x *laevigata*	SCro
'Santana' (TB)	SCro
'Sapphire Gem' (SDB)	CKel SMrm WCAu WDav
'Sapphire Hills' (TB)	SCro WCAu
'Sapphire Jewel' (SDB)	NZep
'Sarah Taylor' (SDB) ♀H4	CBro EFou EHyt EWoo WCAu
sari	SBla
'Sass with Class' (SDB)	WTin
'Satin Gown' (TB)	GKir WCAu
'Saturday Night Live' (TB)	LIri
'Saxon' (TB)	EFam
'Scented Bubbles' (TB)	EFam
schachtii purple	SBla
'Scintillation' (TB)	SCro
'Scribe' (MDB)	CBro EBee EGle GKir NBir
'Scrimmage' (SDB)	NZep
'Sea Fret' (SDB)	CBro
'Sea of Joy' (TB)	SCro
'Second Opinion' (MTB)	NZep
'Semola' (SDB) **new**	ESgI
'Seneca Rebound' (SDB)	EFam
'Senlac' (TB)	EBee EWTr WBro WMnd
'September Frost' (TB)	EFam
serbica	see *I. reichenbachii*
'Serengeti Spaghetti' (TB)	LIri
'Serenity Prayer' (SDB)	WCAu
setosa ♀H4	CBro CFwr EBee EBre EGle EMFW
	EPfP ERos GAbr GBBs GFlt GKev
	LRHS MFir MNrw MOne MSta
	NArg NDlv NGdn NLAp SCro
- *alba*	MSte NLar SIng WLin
- var. *arctica*	EMon EPot GBuc MBro NHol
	NMen NWCA SBla WHoo WPer
- subsp. *canadensis*	see *I. hookeri*
- dwarf	see *I. hookeri*
§ - 'Hondoensis'	MSte
- 'Hookeri'	see *I. hookeri*
- 'Kasho En'	CHad
- 'Kirigamini'	see *I. setosa* 'Hondoensis'
- var. *nana*	see *I. hookeri*
- *tricuspis*	GEdr
* 'Sevenly Seven' (TB)	EFam
'Shampoo' (IB)	EFou WCAu
'Sheer Ecstasy' (TB)	LIri
'Sheila Ann Germaney' (Reticulata)	EHyt EPot NMen
'Shelford Giant' (Spuria) ♀H4	EWTr LIri NBir
'Shepherd's Delight' (TB)	GKir MBri
'Sherbet Lemon' (IB) ♀H4	WCAu
'Short Distance' (IB)	EWoo
'Show Me Yellow' (SDB)	NZep
'Showman' (TB)	ERou
shrevei	see *I. virginica* var. *shrevei*
'Shurton Inn' (TB)	CKel WCAu
'Shy Violet' (SDB)	NZep
'Si Senor' (TB)	EFou
sibirica ♀H4	More than 30 suppliers
- 'Alba'	see *I.* 'Sibirica Alba'
- 'Ann Dasch'	EBee EFou WLin
- 'Annemarie Troeger' ♀H4	EBee EFou WLin
- 'Annick'	LPhx
- 'Anniversary'	CDes CLAP CMdw EBee LRHS
	MBNS SCro
- 'Baby Sister'	CMHG EBee EBre EFou EGle GAbr
	LRHS MBri NBro WAul WHil

- 'Baxteri'	see *I.* 'Sibirica Baxteri'
- 'Berlin Bluebird'	LPhx
- 'Berlin Sky'	CAbx
- 'Bickley Cape'	EBee
- 'Blue Brilliant' **new**	WLin
- 'Blue Burgee'	ECha SCro
* - 'Blue Emperor'	EBee WBrE
- 'Blue King'	CHid CKel COtt EBee EChP EGle
	EPfP EPyc LPve LRHS MBNS MBro
	MRav NGdn NMoo SMrm WLin
	WMnd WMoo WShp
- 'Blue Meadow Fly'	CLAP EBee EGle
- 'Blue Mere'	WLin
- 'Blue Moon' **new**	CRez
- 'Blue Pennant' **new**	CWrd
- 'Blue Reverie'	CPen EPPr
- 'Borbeleta'	LPhx
- 'Bournemouth Beauty' ♀H4 **new**	WLin
- 'Bracknell'	LPhx
- 'Bridal Jig' **new**	CWrd
- 'Brynmawr'	CAbx WLin
- 'Butter and Sugar' ♀H4	More than 30 suppliers
- 'Caesar's Brother'	CHid CPrp EBee EChP EGle ELan
	EMil IBlr LPVe LRHS MBnl MOne
	MSta NArg SMer SPer SWal SWat
	WCAu WLin WWhi WWin
- 'Caezar'	CRow GFlt GKir SDys SRms WLin
- 'Camberley'	WLin
- 'Cambridge' ♀H4	EBla EBre MTed NHol SWat WCAu
	WFar
- 'Canonbury Belle'	WLin
- 'Charming Darlene' **new**	CWrd
- 'Chartreuse Bounty'	EBee EBre ECGP EChP EGle ERou
	EWes GAbr LAst MAvo MBNS
	MBnl MLLN NLar STes
- 'Chateuse Belle' **new**	CWrd
- 'Circle Round'	EPPr LPhx
- 'Clee Hills'	CAbx WLin
- 'Cleedownton' ♀H4 **new**	WLin
- 'Clouded Moon'	see *I. sibirica* 'Forncett Moon'
- 'Colin's Pale Blue' **new**	SMHy
- 'Cool Spring'	WLin
- 'Coquet Waters'	WLin
- 'Coronation Anthem' **new**	WLin
- cream	see *I. sibirica* 'Primrose Cream'
- 'Crème Chantilly' ♀H4	SCro WLin
- 'Dance Ballerina Dance'	CFwr CRow EBee EChP ERou
	MAvo MCLN MHar MLLN MNFA
	NBrk STes SUsu SWat WFar
- 'Dancing Moon' **new**	CWrd
- 'Dancing Nanou'	EBee SWat
- 'Dark Circle' **new**	CWrd
- 'Dark Desire'	MRav SCro
- 'Dear Delight'	EBee EPPr
- 'Dear Dianne'	CKel ECha EFou GMac
- 'Dewful'	WFar WLin
- 'Dragonfly'	GMac WWhi
- 'Dreaming Green'	EBee GBin
- 'Dreaming Spires' ♀H4	GBin GKir WLin
- 'Dreaming Yellow' ♀H4	CBre CFee EBee EBre ECha EFou
	EGle EPfP MCLN MNFA MRav
	NArg NBro NChi NGdn SCro
	SHBN SMrm SPer SSpe WCAu
	WMoo
- 'Ego'	CHid COtt CSpe EBee ECha GFlt
	GKir LBBr LRHS MCLN NBro
	NGby NHol SWat WLin WPrP
- 'Ellesmere'	NGdn WLin
- 'Emperor'	CRow CWat EBee ERou LPBA
	LPhx MSte MWgw NBur NHol
	NSti SMrm SWat WLin

-	'Eric the Red'	IBlr NBur
-	'Ever Again' **new**	CWrd
-	'Ewen'	CHid CLAP CMdw CPou CRow
		CSam EBee EFou EGle GBuc IBlr
		MNrw MTed NGdn SCro SWat
		WCot WFar WLin WPrP
-	'Exuberant Encore' ♀H4	WLin
-	'Flight of Butterflies'	More than 30 suppliers
§	'Forncett Moon'	GMac
-	'Fourfold Lavender'	EBee NBrk
-	'Fourfold White'	EBee GMac LPhx LRHS
-	'Gatineau'	CDes CLAP EBee GBuc NHol WLin
-	'Gerbel Mantel'	GBin SHBN WHil
-	'Glanusk' ♀H4 **new**	WLin
-	'Glaslyn' ♀H4	CAbx WLin
-	'Granaat'	EBee
-	'Gull's Wings' **new**	EBee
-	'Harpswell Hallelujah'	EBee SCro
-	'Harpswell Happiness'	CHVG CLAP CPrp EBee EGle EPfP
	♀H4	LPio MBnl MBri SWat WAul WMoo
-	'Harpswell Haze'	ECha WMoo
-	'Harpswell Velvet' **new**	CWrd
-	'Heavenly Blue'	EHon LPBA MWat SSpe WWpP
-	'Helen Astor'	CBos CDes CLAP CMea CRow
		CSam CTri EBee EGle EWTr LRHS
		MBNS MHar MRav MTed NHol
		SMrm SWat WTin
-	'High Standards' **new**	CWrd
-	'Himmel von Komi' **new**	GBin
-	'Hoar Edge'	CAbx WLin
-	'Hubbard'	CPen EBee NHol SCro
-	'Illini Charm'	CHid EBee EChP NBro SSpe SSvw
		WMoo
-	'Indy' **new**	WCot
-	'Isla Serle' ♀H4	WLin
-	'Kingfisher'	WLin
-	'Lady of Quality'	SCro
-	'Lady Vanessa'	CPou CWrd EGle MRav SCro
-	'Langthorns Pink'	CMdw EGle ELan MRav
-	'Laurenbuhl'	CPLG SCro WLin
-	'Lavender Bounty'	CHid EBee EFou EGle MBnl NBro
		NSti SCro SPet WCAu WHil
-	'Lavender Light'	WLin
-	'Limeheart'	CPou CSev EGle ELan ERou WLin
N	'Limelight'	EGle LRHS
-	'Little Blue'	EBee EBre LRHS SCro
-	'Little Twinkle Star'	CHid EBee GBin NPro
-	'Little White' **new**	SMHy
-	'Looks Mohrish'	SCro
-	'Maranatha'	EFou SMrm
-	'Marcus Perry'	CRow MSte
-	'Marilyn Holmes'	EBee EGle NFor WCot
-	'Marlene Ahlburg'	CAbx WLin
-	'Marshmallow Frosting'	WFar
§	'Melton Red Flare'	CMHG CPen EBee EHon ELan
		EPPr MBNS MNFA SDys SLon
		SOkh WHer
-	'Moon Moth' **new**	WLin
-	'Mountain Lake'	CPen EPPr GBin MBnl SLon SWat
-	'Mrs Rowe'	CDes CFee CPou CRow EBee EFou
		EGle EGra EPPr LLWP MNFA MRav
		MSte MWat SWat WCAu WLin
		WTin
-	'Mrs Saunders'	CAbx WLin
-	'My Love'	WLin
-	'Navy Brass'	EGle GBuc
-	'Nottingham Lace'	EBee EGle NBrk SWat WBcn
-	'Oban' ♀H4	CAbx
-	'Orville Fay'	EChP EFou EGle GMac SCro WCot
		WGMN
-	'Ottawa'	CBot CPou CRow EBee ELan ERou
		GMac LRHS MBNS SCro SWat
		WFar
-	'Outset'	EBee SCro SSvw

-	'Painted Desert' **new**	EBee
-	'Pansy Purple' **new**	SCro
-	'Papillon'	CTri EBee ECGN EChP ECtt EGle
		ELan EPPr ERou GIBF GKir MAvo
		MCLN MWat NBir NBro NGdn
		NHol NLar NPri NSti SChu WFar
		WHil WLin WPer WPnP
N	'Pearl Queen'	MTPN WFar
-	'Peg Edwards' **new**	EBee
-	'Perry's Blue'	More than 30 suppliers
I	'Perry's Favourite'	CFee CRow
-	'Perry's Pigmy'	GBuc WLin
-	'Persimmon'	CFir CHid EBee ECtt EGle EMFW
		EMan ERou GKir LRHS MWat
		NMoo SAga SWat WMoo
*	'Phosphor Flame'	WLin
-	'Pink Haze'	CHar CRow EBee EGle MBnl MBri
		MNFA MTis NBro NSti SCro WHil
		WHrl
-	'Pirate Prince'	CAbx MBro NPer WHoo
-	'Pirouette'	WLin
-	'Placid Waters'	EGle SCro
-	Plant World hybrids	MDKP SWal
§	'Primrose Cream'	MTed WCot
-	'Purple Cloak'	MSte WBcn
-	'Purple Mere'	CAbx WLin
-	'Reddy Maid'	NBrk SCro
-	'Redflare'	see *I. sibirica* 'Melton Red Flare'
-	'Regency Buck' **new**	CWrd
-	'Rejoice Always'	GMac
-	'Rimouski'	WLin
-	'Roanoke's Choice' **new**	CFwr CWrd EBee GBin
N	'Roger Perry'	CFee
-	'Roisin' **new**	WLin
-	'Rosselline' ♀H4 **new**	WLin
-	'Rowden Aurelius'	CRow
I	'Royal Blue'	ECha GBuc SWat
-	'Ruffled Velvet' ♀H4	More than 30 suppliers
-	'Ruffles Plus'	CWrd
-	'Sally Kerlin'	SCro
-	'Savoir Faire'	ECha EGle SPer
-	'Sea Horse'	GBuc WLin
-	'Sea Shadows'	MBri NBir SIri WLin
-	'Seren Wib' **new**	WLin
-	'Shaker's Prayer' **new**	CWrd
-	'Shall We Dance'	WLin
	♀H4 **new**	
-	'Shirley Pope' ♀H4	CDes EBee EBre EGle GKir LPhx
		LRHS MBri MNFA NSti SSpi WAul
		WCot WLin WMoo
-	'Showdown'	EBee ECtt EGle LRHS SAga SCro
		WCAu WFar WGMN
-	'Shrawley'	CAbx
-	'Silver Edge' ♀H4	More than 30 suppliers
-	'Siobhan' ♀H4 **new**	WLin
-	'Sky Wings'	CRow ECha EGle
-	'Snow Prince' **new**	CWrd
-	'Snow Queen'	see *I. sanguinea* 'Snow Queen'
-	'Snowcrest'	CBre NBrk WLin
-	'Soft Blue' ♀H4	CDes EBee SCro WLin WTin
N	'Southcombe White'	COlW CRow GBuc GCal LPio
		MHar NGdn SIri SMHy
-	'Sparkling Rosé'	More than 30 suppliers
-	'Splashdown' (Sino-Sib)	SWat
-	'Steve'	CHVG CPar EBee EChP EPPr LPio
		MBnl MNFA MTis NBPC NBro
		NCGa STes SUsu SWat WAul
-	'Steve Varner'	SCro WLin
-	'Summer Sky'	CAbx CBre EBla SCro SSpi SWat
		WCAu WCot WLin WTin
-	'Super Ego'	WTin
-	'Superba'	WLin
-	'Taldra'	WLin

	- 'Tal-y-Bont'	WLin
	- 'Teal Velvet'	EBee ECha WFar
	- 'Tealwood'	WLin
	- 'Temper Tantrum'	CKel
	- 'Towanda Redflare'	EGle
	- 'Trim the Velvet' ♀H4 **new**	WLin
	- 'Tropic Night'	More than 30 suppliers
	- 'Tycoon'	CHid EBee GBuc IBlr LRHS MNFA NChi SPer WLin
	- 'Valda' **new**	EBee WLin
	- 'Vee One'	WLin
	- 'Velvet Night'	WLin
	- 'Vi Luihn'	CBcs ECha EGle EPPr
	- 'Violet Joy' **new**	EBre
	- 'Violetmere'	WLin
	- 'Weisse Etagen'	WLin
	- 'Welcome Return'	CHVG EBee GBin MBnl WMoo
	- 'Welfenfurstin' **new**	GBin
	- 'Welfenprinz' ♀H4 **new**	WLin
	- white	EGle WOut
I	- 'White Swan'	LAst
	- 'White Swirl' ♀H4	More than 30 suppliers
	- 'Winscombe'	CHid
	- 'Wisley White'	EGle EGlt MWgw WLin
	- 'Yankee Consul' **new**	CWrd
	- 'Yellow Court'	CRow
§	'Sibirica Alba'	CBrm CRow ECha EHon EPfP EShb GAbr GBBs GFlt LLWP MHer NChi SWat WBrk WFar WWpP WWye
§	'Sibirica Baxteri'	CFee
	sichuanensis	EBee
	sieboldii	see *I. sanguinea*
	'Sierra Blue' (TB)	ESgI
	'Sierra Grande' (TB)	EWoo
	'Sierra Nevada' (Spuria)	EFou
	'Sign of Leo' (TB)	EFam
	sikkimensis	GIBF
	'Silent Strings' (IB)	MBri
	'Silicon Prairie' (TB)	ESgI
	'Silver Dividends' (TB)	EFam
	'Silver Tide' (TB)	WEas
	'Silverado' (TB)	ESgI LIri MMil SCro WCAu
	'Silvery Beauty' (Dut)	GBBs NBir
	'Silvery Moon' (TB)	SCro
	sindjarensis	see *I. aucheri*
	'Sindpers' (Juno) ♀H3	SBla WWst
	sintenisii ♀H4	CBro CHid EBee EHyt
	'Sir Michael' (TB)	ESgI
	'Sissinghurst' (SDB)	WHoo WIvy
	'Sister Helen' (TB)	EFam
	'Siva Siva' (TB)	EBee ENot ERou MRav WCAu
	'Skating Party' (TB)	CKel ESgI EWoo
	'Skiers' Delight' (TB)	LIri WCAu
	'Skip Stitch' (SDB)	EHyt
	'Sky Hooks' (TB)	LIri SCro
	'Skyfire' (TB)	ESgI
	'Skywalker' (TB)	LIri
	'Slap Bang' (SDB)	NZep
	'Sleepy Time' (MDB)	NZep
	'Small Sky' (SDB)	CBro
N	'Smart Girl' (TB)	CKel SMrm
	'Smell the Roses' (SDB)	EFam NZep
	'Smoke Rings' (TB)	SCro
	'Smoked Salmon' (TB)	CKel
	'Smokey Dream' (TB)	CKel
	'Snow Cloud' (TB)	EWoo
	'Snow Festival' (IB)	NZep
	'Snow Fiddler' (MTB)	NZep
	'Snow Tracery' (TB)	ENot MBri
	'Snow Tree' (SDB)	NZep
	'Snow Troll' (SDB)	WCAu WWin
	'Snowbrook' (TB)	SCro

	'Snowcone' (IB)	ESgI
	'Snowmound' (TB)	CKel SCro
	'Snowy Owl' (TB) ♀H4	CKel WCAu
	'Snowy River' (MDB)	NZep
	'Social Event' (TB)	ESgI
	'Soft Breeze' (SDB)	NZep
	'Solid Mahogany' (TB)	MRav WCAu
	'Solonique' (TB)	EBee
	'Solstice' (TB)	EFam
	'Somerset Blue' (TB) ♀H4	CKel
N	'Somerset Vale' (TB)	SMrm
	'Somerton Brocade' (SDB)	CKel WDav
	'Somerton Dance' (SDB) **new**	CKel
	'Song of Norway' (TB)	ESgI NZep SCoo WCAu
	songarica	EBee
	'Sonoran Señorita' (Spuria) ♀H4	LIri
	'Sopra il Vulcano' (BB)	ESgI
	'Sostenique' (TB)	ESgI WCAu
	'Soul Power' (TB)	ERou
	'Southern Clipper' (SDB)	EHyt MBri
	'Southern Spy' (TB)	EFam
	'Spanish Coins' (MTB)	NZep
	'Sparkling Cloud' (SDB)	EGle WWin
	'Sparkling Eyes' (DB)	EFou
	'Spartan'	CKel
	speculatrix	EBee
	'Spellbreaker' (TB)	ESgI EWoo
	'Spiced Custard' (TB)	ESgI SCro
	'Spiced Tiger' (TB)	LIri
	'Spin-off' (TB)	SCro
	'Splash of Red' (SDB)	NZep
	'Split Decision' (SDB)	NZep
	'Spreckles' (TB)	ESgI
	sprengeri	EHyt WWst
	'Spring Bells' (SDB)	EFou
	'Spring Dancer' (IB)	SCro
	'Spring Festival' (TB)	WCAu
	'Springtime' (Reticulata)	LAma LRHS NRog
	'Spun Gold' (TB)	ESgI
	spuria	CPou ELan
	- subsp. *carthaliniae*	EBee WPer
§	- subsp. *halophila*	GIBF
	- 'Jubilant Spirit' **new**	CWrd EBee
	- 'Just Reward' **new**	CWrd
	- subsp. *maritima*	EMan
§	- subsp. *musulmanica*	ETow GIBF
	- subsp. *notha* CC 1550	WCot
	- subsp. *ochroleuca*	see *I. orientalis* Mill.
	- subsp. *spuria*	GBuc GIBF
	- var. *subbarbata*	GIBF
	'Stairway to Heaven' (TB)	LIri WCAu
	'Stapleford' (SDB)	CBro EGle
	'Star Performer' (TB)	EFam
	'Star Sailor' (TB)	SCro
	'Star Shine' (TB)	WCAu
	'Starcrest' (TB)	ESgI
	'Starry Eyed' (SDB)	EGle
	'Starship' (TB)	EFam ESgI
	'Staten Island' (TB)	ENot GKir MBri SRms WCAu WTin
	'Stella Polaris' (TB)	SCro
	'Stellar Lights' (TB)	EWoo
§	*stenophylla*	WWst
	'Stepping Out' (TB) ♀H4	EBee EFou ESgI GBin MBri MCLN SCro WCAu WShp
	'Stinger' (SDB) ♀H4	LIri
	'Stitch in Time' (TB)	EWoo SCro WCAu
	'Stockholm' (SDB)	CKel NZep WDav
	stolonifera 'George Barr'	EBee
	- 'Vera'	WWst
	'Stormy Night' (TB)	EFam
N	'Storrington' (TB)	SCro
	'Strange Child' (SDB)	NZep

'Strawberry Ice' (IB) — EFou
'Strawberry Love' (IB) ♀H4 — MMil
'Strawberry Sensation' (TB) — NZep
'Striking' (TB) — EWoo
'Study In Black' (TB) **new** — WCAu
stylosa — see *I. unguicularis*
'Suave' (TB) — SCro
§ *suaveolens* — CBro CPou EPot LPio NMen SRot SScr WBor WDav WIvy
* – var. *flavescens* — WWst
* – *rubra nana* **new** — GKev
– 'Rubromarginata' — ERos NJOw
* – var. *violacea* — EBee NMen NWCA WWst
subdichotoma **new** — EBee
'Sugar' (IB) — NSti WCAu
'Sugar Candy' (CH) — WWst
'Sugar Snaps' (IB) — EFam
'Sultan's Palace' (TB) — ESgI SCro
'Sumatra' (TB) **new** — ESgI
'Summer Green Shadows' (TB) — EFam
'Summer Holidays' (TB) — EFam
'Summer Luxury' (TB) — NZep
'Summer's Smile' (TB) — ESgI
'Sun Dappled' (TB) — ERou
'Sun Doll' (SDB) ♀H4 — CKel NZep
'Sundown Red' (IB) — NBir
'Sunny Dawn' (IB) ♀H4 — CKel WDav
'Sunny Honey' (IB) — NZep
'Sunny Tyke' (MDB) — EFam
'Sunrise in Sonora' (Spuria) ♀H4 — LIri
'Sunset Colors' (Spuria) ♀H4 — LIri
'Sunshine Isle' (SDB) — NZep
'Superlation' (TB) — SCro
'Superstition' (TB) ♀H4 — EFou ESgI GBin MMil SCro SIri SMrm WAul WCAu
'Supreme Sultan' (TB) — ESgI EWoo LIri SCro WAul WCAu
'Surprise Orange' (MDB) — NZep
'Susan Bliss' (TB) — CKel EBee ELan EPfP ESgI MBNS SIri SMrm WCAu
susiana — LAma
'Swaledale' (TB) — WCAu
'Swazi Princess' (TB) — CKel ESgI SCro WCAu
'Sweet Musette' (TB) — SCro WCAu
'Sweeter than Wine' (TB) — LIri SCro WCAu
'Swingtown' (TB) — LIri
'Sybil' — GBin
'Sylvia Murray' (TB) — WCAu
'Symphony' (Dut) — LRHS NBir
tadshikorum — WWst
'Tall Chief' (TB) — EBre MLwd MTis NBrk SCro WCAu
'Tan Tingo' (IB) — EFou
'Tangerine Sky' (TB) — WCAu
'Tangfu' (IB) **new** — ESgI
'Tantara' (SDB) — WTin
'Tanzanian Tangerine' (TB) — LIri
'Tarheel Elf' (SDB) — ESgI WTin
'Tarn Hows' (TB) — SIri SRms WCAu
'Tea Leaves' (TB) — EFam
tectorum — CSWP EHol ERos GAbr GIBF GSki ITer MNrw NWCA SGar WHil WOut
– 'Alba' — CPBP CPou EPPr
– 'Variegata' (v) — CHid CPrp EPPr MRav SVil WBor WWpP
'Tell Fibs' (SDB) — CBro EGle
'Temple Gold' (TB) — CKel
'Temple Meads' (IB) — WCAu
'Templecloud' (IB) ♀H4 — CHar CKel
'Tempting Fate' (TB) **new** — EWoo
'Temptone' (TB) — LIri

'Ten' (SDB) — NZep
§ *tenax* — CLAP CNic CPBP ECho ETow GBuc GEdr GKir GSki
'Tender Years' (IB) — WAul
'Tennessee Vol' (TB) — LIri
tenuifolia — EBee
tenuis — GBin
tenuissima — GBuc SSpi
'Terra Rosa' (TB) — LIri
'Thais' (TB) — ESgI
'The Bride' — see *I.* 'Bride'
'The Citadel' (TB) — SCro
'The Rocket' — see *I.* 'Rocket'
'Theatre' (TB) — ESgI SCro
'Theda Clark' (IB) — SCro
'Theseus' (Aril) — EHyt
'Third Charm' (SDB) — CBro EFam
'Third World' (SDB) — CBro
'Thornbird' (TB) ♀H4 — ESgI LIri WCAu
'Thousand Lakes' (SDB) — NZep
'Three Cherries' (MDB) — CBro EGle
'Thriller' (TB) — ESgI MMil WCAu
'Throb' (TB) — LIri
thunbergii — see *I. sanguinea*
'Thunder Echo' (TB) — ESgI
'Tide's In' (TB) — ERou EWoo SCro
'Tiffany' (TB) **new** — WTin
'Tiger Blues' (Spuria) — LIri
'Tiger Butter' (TB) — ESgI
'Tiger Honey' (TB) — LIri
tigridia — EBee
'Timeless Moment' (TB) — SCro
timofejewii — WCot
tingitana var. *fontanesii* — SSpi WPGP
'Tinkerbell' (SDB) — CPBP EBee EGle ESis MSte NBir SChu SPet WWin
'Tintinara' (TB) ♀H4 — CKel
'Tiny Freckles' (MDB) — NZep
'Tiny Lou' (Spuria) — LIri
'Titan's Glory' (TB) ♀H4 — ESgI LIri MRav SCro WCAu WCot
'To the Point' (TB) — LIri
'Tol-long' ♀H4 — MSte
'Tom Johnson' (TB) — LIri
'Tom Tit' (TB) — WCAu
'Tomingo' (SDB) — WCAu
'Tomorrow's Child' (TB) — ESgI SCro
'Toni Lynn' (MDB) — EHyt
'Toots' (SDB) — EGle EHyt WTin
'Top Flight' (TB) — EBee EChP ELan ENot ERou LAst SCoo SPer SRms
N 'Topolino' (TB) — CKel SGar SIri SMrm
'Total Eclipse' — SRms
'Tracy Tyrene' (TB) — ESgI
transylvanica — GIBF
tridentata — WOBN
'Trillion' (TB) — LIri
'Triple Whammy' (TB) — ESgI
'Tu Tu Turquoise' (SDB) — NZep
tuberosa — see *Hermodactylus tuberosus*
'Tumbleweeds' (SDB) — NZep
'Tumultueux' (TB) — ESgI
N 'Tuscan' (TB) — CKel CMil
'Tut's Gold' (TB) — ESgI WCAu
'Tuxedo' (TB) **new** — EBee
'Twist of Fate' (TB) — SCro
'Two Rubies' (SDB) — NZep
'Tyke' (MTB) — NZep
typhifolia — WLin
§ *unguicularis* ♀H4 — More than 30 suppliers
– 'Abington Purple' — CBro WCot
– 'Alba' — CBro ECha WAbe WMnd
N – 'Bob Thompson' — CBro SAga
– broken form — MAvo MLwd

– subsp. *carica*	IBlr WCot	
var. *angustifolia*		
§ – subsp. *cretensis*	EBee EPot NMen WAbe	
– – MS 860	WCot	
– – white	SBla	
– 'Diana Clare' **new**	WCot	
– var. *lazica*	see *I. lazica*	
– 'Marondera'	CAvo	
– 'Mary Barnard' ♀H4	CAvo CBro CFee CHar CMea CPou	
	CSam ECGP ECha EHrv GFlt IBlr	
	MAvo NBir NMen SBla SIng WCot	
	WGwG WMnd	
N – 'Oxford Dwarf'	CBro ECho	
– 'Palette'	ELan	
– 'Peacock'	WWst	
§ – 'Walter Butt'	CAvo ECGP ECha NBir SRot WFar	
	WMnd	
uniflora var. *caricina*	MNrw	
uromovii	GBuc	
'Vague a l'Ame' (TB)	ESgI	
'Vanity' (TB) ♀H4	ESgI SCro WCAu	
'Vanity's Child' (TB)	ERou	
§ *variegata* ♀H4	CPou EGoo EPar GCal SUsu WCAu	
	WCot WWst	
'Vegas Showgirl' (SDB)	NZep	
'Velvet Caper' (SDB)	WTin	
'Velvet Robe' (TB)	EBee	
* *venaidae*	WWst	
'Veneer' (TB)	LIri	
'Verity Blamey' (TB)	CKel	
verna	EBee EPot ERos NHol	
versicolor ♀H4	CArn CBen CDWL CElw CRow	
	EGol EHon EMFW EPPr EPar GBin	
	GFlt IBlr LNCo LPBA LRHS MNrw	
	MSal MSta NGdn SPlb SRms SWat	
	WAbe WFar WMAq WShi WWpP	
– 'Between the Lines'	CRow	
– 'China West Lake'	CRow	
– 'Claret Cup' **new**	CPou	
– 'Dottie's Double'	CRow	
– 'Georgia Bay' **new**	CRow	
N – 'Goldbrook'	EGol	
– 'Kermesina'	CDWL CRow CWat EBee ECha	
	EGol EHon ELan EMFW EPar GBuc	
	GCal GGar IBlr LPBA MSta NArg	
	NPer NSti SLon SRms SWat WEas	
	WFar WMoo WTin	
– 'Mysterious Monique'	CMdw CRow	
– 'Party Line'	CRow	
– var. *rosea*	CRow	
– 'Rowden Allegro'	CRow	
– 'Rowden Aria'	CRow	
– 'Rowden Cadenza'	CRow	
– 'Rowden Cantata' **new**	CRow	
– 'Rowden Concerto'	CRow	
– 'Rowden Fugue'	CRow	
– 'Rowden Lyric'	CRow	
– 'Rowden Mazurka'	CRow	
– 'Rowden Nocturne'	CRow	
– 'Rowden Prelude' **new**	CRow	
– 'Rowden Refrain' **new**	CRow	
– 'Rowden Rondo'	CRow	
– 'Rowdeni Sonata'	CRow	
– 'Rowden Symphony'	CRow	
– 'Rowden Waltz'	CRow	
– 'Silvington'	CRow	
– 'Whodunit'	CRow	
'Vert Gallant' (TB)	ESgI	
vicaria	EPot WWst	
I – 'Sina' **new**	WWst	
'Victor Herbert' (TB)	SCro	
'Victoria Falls' (TB)	ESgI SCro WCAu	
'Vigilante' (TB)	LIri	
'Vinho Verde' (IB) ♀H4	CKel	

'Vino Rosso' (SDB) **new**	ESgI	
'Vintage Press' (IB) **new**	WCAu	
'Vintage Year' (Spuria)	EFou	
violacea	see *I. spuria* subsp. *musulmanica*	
'Violet Beauty' (Reticulata)	EPot LAma LPhx LRHS MBow	
'Violet Classic' (TB)	EFou	
'Violet Icing' (TB) ♀H4	CKel EFou	
'Violet Lass' (SDB)	NZep	
'Violet Rings' (TB) **new**	WCAu	
virginica 'De Luxe'	see *I.* x *robusta* 'Dark Aura'	
– 'Pond Crown Point'	CRow	
– 'Pond Lilac Dream'	CRow	
N – 'Purple Fan'	CRow	
§ – var. *shrevei*	CRow	
'Vita Fire' **new**	EBee	
'Vitality' (IB)	ESgI SCro	
'Vive la France' (TB)	ESgI EWoo	
'Vivien' (TB)	SCro	
'Voila' (IB)	EFou NZep	
'Voltage' (TB)	LIri	
'Volute' (TB)	ESgI	
'Voyage' (SDB)	EWoo	
'W.R. Dykes' (TB)	WTin	
'Wabash' (TB)	EBee ERou ESgI MBow WCAu WTin	
'Walter Butt'	see *I. unguicularis* 'Walter Butt'	
'War Chief' (TB)	ESgI WCAu	
'War Sails' (TB)	WCAu	
warleyensis	WWst	
'Warl-sind' (Juno)	EBee EPot WWst	
'Warrior King' (TB)	WCAu	
'Waterboy' (SDB)	NZep	
'Watercolor' (SDB)	NZep	
wattii	EBee GCal	
'Webelos' (SDB)	EGle EHyt MBri	
'Wedding Candles' (TB)	SCro	
'Well Suited' (SDB)	EWoo	
'Westar' (SDB) ♀H4	NZep	
'Westwell' (SDB)	WCAu WWin	
'What Again' (SDB)	SCro SUsu	
'Wheels' (SDB)	WTin	
'White Bridge' (Dut)	MSph	
'White City' (TB)	CHad CPrp EBee ECGP EOrc EPfP	
	MMil MRav MWat NGdn NPer	
	SChu SCoo SDnm SIri SPer SRms	
	SWat WCAu WMnd	
'White Excelsior' (Dut)	LAma LRHS	
'White Gem' (SDB)	WWin	
'White Knight' (TB)	EBee ELan EPfP SCoo WMnd WShp	
'White Shimmer' (Spuria)	LIri	
'White Superior' (Dut)	NBir	
'White van Vliet' (Dut)	CFwr	
'White Wedgwood' (Dut)	CFwr CRez	
'Whoop 'em Up' (BB)	NZep	
'Why Not' (IB)	NZep	
'Widdershins' (TB)	LIri	
'Widecombe Fair' (SDB)	EHyt WIvy WWin	
'Wild Thing' (TB)	SCro	
'Wild West' (TB)	CKel	
willmottiana	WWst	
– 'Alba'	EBee	
'Willow Ware' (IB)	SCro	
'Willowmist' (SDB)	NZep	
wilsonii ♀H4	EBee GBBs GBuc GIBF SSpi WOBN	
– 'Gelbe Mantel'	see *I.* 'Gelbe Mantel'	
'Windsor Rose' (TB)	CHar	
'Winemaster' (TB) **new**	EWoo	
winogradowii ♀H4	CAvo CBro EHyt EPot ERos GCrs	
	GKir LAma MTho SDix WAbe	
'Winter Olympics' (TB)	EFou ESgI	
'Wise Gift' (Cal-Sib) ♀H4	WWst	
'Wisteria Sachet' (IB)	WCAu	
'Witch of Endor' (TB)	MMil	
'Witching' (TB) **new**	WCAu	
'Wizard of Id' (SDB)	EGle NZep WTin	

'Wondrous' (TB)	ESgI
'World News' (TB)	SCro
'Wow' (SDB)	EGle EHyt
'Wyoming Cowboys' (Spuria) ♀H4	LIri
xiphioides	see *I. latifolia*
xiphium	GIBF SSpi
'Yaquina Blue' (TB)	EWoo LIri
'Yellow Girl' (SDB)	NZep
'Yo-yo' (SDB)	NZep
'Yvonne Pelletier' (TB)	WCAu
'Zantha' (TB)	WCAu
'Zinc Pink' (BB)	SCro
'Zowie' (SDB)	NZep

Isatis (Brassicaceae)

tinctoria	CAgr CArn CBri COld CRWN CSev EOHP GPoy ILis LRHS MHer MSal NVic SDnm SECG SIde WAul WBWf WBri WCHb WHHs WHer WJek WSel WWye

Ischyrolepis (Restionaceae)

ocreata	CTrC WNor
§ *subverticillata*	CHEx CTrC WMul

Ismene see *Hymenocallis*

Isodon (Lamiaceae)

serra 'Korean Zest' ex B&SWJ 735	EBee EGoo EMan WCru WWeb

Isolepis (Cyperaceae)

§ *cernua*	CBrm CHal EMFW EMan EPfP MAvo MBri NArg NBlu NPri WDyG WFar WMAq WPrP

Isoloma see *Kobleria*

Isoplexis (Scrophulariaceae)

canariensis	CAbb CBot CFil CHEx CHrt CRHN CSpe CTCP CTrC EBee ECre EMan EWll SHFr SPlb WCFE WSPU
isabelliana	CFil EBee EDif LDai MGol SSte WCot WEas
sceptrum	CBcs CBot CFil CHEx CPLG CSpe ECre EMan SAPC SArc SDnm SHFr SSpi
- pink	CDes CSpe

Isopogon (Proteaceae)

anethifolius	SPlb

Isopyrum (Ranunculaceae)

biternatum	GBuc LEur NLar
nipponicum	CLAP WCru
thalictroides	EBee EPot WAbe

Isotoma (Campanulaceae)

§ *axillaris*	EBre LIck LRHS MOak SCoo SHFr SMrm SPet WWin
- 'Fairy Carpet'	CWCL EBre EMan MBNS
fluviatilis	CBrm ECou WCru
- white	ECou

Itea (Escalloniaceae)

ilicifolia ♀H3	More than 30 suppliers
japonica 'Beppu'	MGos SLPl
virginica	CAbP CBcs CMCN CMHG CPle ELan EPfP EWTr MBlu MGos MRav SLon SPer WBVN WFar
§ - 'Henry's Garnet'	CDoC CEnd CFai CMCN CPMA CWSG EBee EPfP LAst MBlu
	MWgw NLar NPSl NPri SLim SSpi SWvt WDin WGwG
- 'Long Spire'	CPMA
- 'Merlot'	CPMA NLar
- 'Sarah Eve'	CMCN CPMA
- 'Shirley's Compact' **new**	SSpi
- Swarthmore form	see *I. virginica* 'Henry's Garnet'
yunnanensis	CPLG

Itoa (Flacourtiaceae)

orientalis SF 92300	ISea

Ixia (Iridaceae)

Bird of Paradise	see *I.* 'Paradijsvogel'
'Blue Bird'	GFlt LAma
'Castor'	ECho WHil
dubia	EGrW
flexuosa	WCot
'Giant' **new**	ECho WHil
'Hogarth'	GFlt LAma
'Holland Glory' **new**	ECho
hybrids	SDeJ
lutea **new**	WCot
'Mabel'	NRog
maculata	SSpi WCot
'Marquette' **new**	GFlt NRog
monadelpha	EGrW WCot
paniculata	EGrW
'Panorama' **new**	ECho
§ 'Paradijsvogel'	LAma
pumilio	EGrW WCot
purpureorosea	ECho
'Saldanha' **new**	
rapunculoides	EGrW
'Rose Emperor'	LAma
'Spotlight' **new**	ECho
thomasiae	WCot
'Venus'	LAma
viridiflora	WCot
'Vulcan' **new**	ECho
'Yellow Emperor'	WCot WHil

Ixiolirion (Ixioliriaceae)

pallasii	see *I. tataricum*
§ *tataricum*	EBee EMan GFlt LAma LPhx MBow MBri WHil
- Ledebourii Group	CAvo LAma

Ixora (Rubiaceae)

chinensis 'Apricot Queen'	SOWG
'Golden Ball'	SOWG
'Pink Malay'	SOWG

J

Jaborosa (Solanaceae)

integrifolia	CFir CPLG CStu EBee ELan GCal MNrw WAul WBor WCot WCru WDyG WPGP WPnP WPrP XPep

Jacaranda (Bignoniaceae)

acutifolia hort.	see *J. mimosifolia*
acutifolia Kunth	MBri
§ *mimosifolia*	ELan ERea ESlt GQui ITer MGol MPRe SMur SOWG SPlb WMul

Jacobinia see *Justicia*

Jamesbrittenia (Scrophulariaceae)

§ *jurassica*	EHyt
'Pink Pearl'	COtt

pristisepala 'Sani' SScr

Jamesia (Hydrangeaceae)
americana CPle NLar WWin

x *Jancaemonda* (Gesneriaceae)
vandedemii SOkd

Jasione (Campanulaceae)
§ *crispa* MWrn
§ *heldreichii* CTCP GAbr LRHS MWrn SBla
  SRms WWin
  jankae see *J. heldreichii*
§ *laevis* ECot GAbr IHMH LRHS MDKP
  SRms WGwG WShp
§ - 'Blaulicht' More than 30 suppliers
  - Blue Light see *J. laevis* 'Blaulicht'
  montana EDAr GKir MBow MDKP NLAp
  SECG WHer
  perennis see *J. laevis*

Jasminum (Oleaceae)
angulare ♀H1 EHol ERea LRHS SOWG
azoricum ♀H1 CRHN ELan EPfP ERea EShb ESlt
  GQui NPal WMul XPep
beesianum More than 30 suppliers
bignoniaceum WSHC
dispermum CRHN
floridum EBee EWes XPep
fruticans CMac CPle EBee EPla WBcn WCru
  XPep
grandiflorum L. **new** XPep
- 'De Grasse' ♀H1 CRHN EBee ERea LRHS SOWG
humile CPle EHol GSki IMGH MHer MRav
  SHFr WBod WFar WKif
- f. *farreri* WCru
§ - 'Revolutum' ♀H4 More than 30 suppliers
- f. *wallichianum* CPle
- - B&SWJ 2559 WCru
§ *laurifolium* f. *nitidum* ERea
§ *mesnyi* ♀H2-3 CFRD CMac CRHN CSBt CTri
  CWib EBak EBee ELan EPfP ERea
  IGor SBra SLim SOWG SPer SSte
  STre SYvo WBcn WCot WEas
  WSHC XPep
multipartitum bushy CSpe
nitidum see *J. laurifolium* f. *nitidum*
nudiflorum ♀H4 More than 30 suppliers
- 'Argenteum' see *J. nudiflorum* 'Mystique'
- 'Aureum' CRow EBee ELan EPfP EPla GQui
  LRHS MAsh MBro MCCP MRav
  NSti SLim SPer SPla WCot WHCG
  WPat WTel
§ - 'Mystique' (v) ELan EWes NLar SLon SMur SPer
  WCot WPat
odoratissimum ERea LRHS SOWG
officinale ♀H4 More than 30 suppliers
- CC 1709 WCot WHCr
§ - f. *affine* CBcs CRHN CSPN CSam CTri
  CWSG CWib EBee EBre ELan ENor
  ENot EOrc EPfP ERea MAsh MRav
  MWgw NHol SDix SLim SMad
  SRms WCru WFar WWeb
§ - 'Argenteovariegatum' More than 30 suppliers
  (v) ♀H4
- 'Aureovariegatum' see *J. officinale* 'Aureum'
§ - 'Aureum' (v) CBrm CChe CDoC CMac CWSG
  CWib EBee ECtt ELan EPfP EPla
  LRHS MBri MHer MLan MWat
  MWgw NBir NHol SHBN SLim
  SLon SPer SRms WGwG WHCG
  WPat WSHC WWeb
- 'Crûg's Collection' WCru
  ex B&SWJ 2987

- Fiona Sunrise More than 30 suppliers
  = 'Frojas'PBR
- 'Grandiflorum' see *J. officinale* f. *affine*
- 'Inverleith' ♀H4 CDoC CWSG EBee ELan EPfP GCal
  IArd LAst LHop LRHS MAsh MBNS
  MBri MCCP MLan MRav SBra SCoo
  SLim SMac SMad SPer SVil WFar
  WGwG WPat WWeb
- 'Variegatum' see *J. officinale*
  'Argenteovariegatum'
parkeri CBcs CFee CMea CTri EBee EHyt
  EPfP ESis IMGH ITim LHop MBNS
  MBro NRya NWCA SHGC SIgm
  SIng SPla SRot WAbe WCru WFar
  WPat XPep
polyanthum ♀H1-2 CArn CBcs CPLG CRHN CSBt CTri
  CTrw EBak EBee ELan EPfP ERea
  ERom EShb GQui LPan LRHS MBri
  NBlu NPal SLim SOWG SRms
  WCFE XPep
primulinum see *J. mesnyi*
reevesii hort. see *J. humile* 'Revolutum'
sambac ♀H1 CHll CRHN EHol ELan EPfP ESlt
  LPan LRHS NPal SOWG SYvo
  WMul XPep
- 'Grand Duke of ERea LRHS SOWG
  Tuscany' (d)
- 'Maid of Orleans' LRHS SOWG
  (d) ♀H1
x *stephanense* More than 30 suppliers

Jatropha (Euphorbiaceae)
integerrima ESlt SOWG
podagrica ♀H1 ESlt EUJe MOak

Jeffersonia (Berberidaceae)
diphylla More than 30 suppliers
dubia CBos CFir EBee EHyt EWes GBuc
  GCrs GKir IBlr LEur LRHS NBir
  NGar NMen NRog SBla SIgm SRot
  WAbe WCot WCru
- B&SWJ 984 WCru
- 'Alba' LEur SBla

jostaberry see *Ribes* x *culverwellii* Jostaberry

Jovellana (Scrophulariaceae)
procumbens CPne
punctata CDoC CPLG CPle CSpe EBee IBlr
  MBlu WBor
repens CFir EBee IBlr WCot WCru
sinclairii CHll CPLG ECou EHyt IBlr SSpi
  WCru
violacea ♀H3 CAbP CAbb CBcs CDoC CPLG
  CPle CSpe CTrC EBee EMil ERea
  GCal GGGa IBlr IDee ISea ITim
  LAst SAPC SArc SDry SSpi SVen
  WBor WCru WPic WSHC

Jovibarba ✿ (Crassulaceae)
§ *allionii* CMea CTri CWil EHol EMlt EPot
  GAbr LBee LRHS MBro MHer
  MOne NHol SBla SIng WAbe
  WCom WCot WIvy WPer WTin
  WWin
- 'Oki' CWil MOne
allionii x *hirta* CWil GAbr MBro MOne NHol
  NJOw NMen SDys
§ *arenaria* CWil EHol ESis GAbr MBro MDHE
  NMen SIng
- from Murtal, Austria MDHE
- from Passo Monte CWil
  Crocecar Nico
'Emerald Spring' CWil NMen

§ **heuffelii**	CWil LRHS NHol NMen NPri SIng WPer
- 'Aga'	NHol WIvy
- 'Aiolos'	NHol
- 'Alemene' **new**	NHol
- 'Almkroon'	NHol
- 'Angel Wings'	CWil NHol NMen
- 'Aquarius'	CWil
- 'Artemis'	NHol
- 'Aurora' **new**	NHol
- 'Be Mine'	CWil
- 'Beacon Hill'	CWil MBro
- 'Belcore'	CWil WIvy
- 'Benjamin'	NHol
- 'Bermuda'	CMea
- 'Bermuda Sunset'	NHol
- 'Big Red'	NHol
- 'Brandaris'	NHol SDys
- 'Brocade'	NHol
- 'Bronze Ingot'	CWil
§ - 'Cherry Glow'	CWil NHol
- 'Chocoleto'	WTin
- 'Cleopatra'	NHol
- 'Copper King'	CWil
- 'Dunbar Red'	NHol
- 'Fandango'	CWil MHom WIvy
- 'Gento'	CWil NHol
- 'Geronimo'	NHol
- 'Giuseppi Spiny'	CWil MHom NHol WTin
- var. **glabra**	MBro WHoo
§ - - 'Cameo'	NHol
- - from Anabakanak	CWil MHom NHol WTin
- - from Anthoborio	CWil NMen WTin
- - from Backovo	NHol
- - from Galicica	NHol
- - from Haila, Montenegro/Kosovo	CWil NHol NMen
- - from Jakupica, Macedonia	CWil WIvy
- - from Koprovnik, Kosovo	CWil WTin
- - from Ljuboten	CWil NHol NMen WTin
- - from Pasina Glava	CWil
- - from Rhodope	CWil MHom NHol
- - from Treska Gorge, Macedonia	CWil MBro NMen WTin
- - from Vitse, Greece	CWil
- 'Gold Rand'	NHol
- 'Green Land'	CWil
- 'Greenstone'	CMea CWil MBro MHom NHol NMen WIvy WTin
- 'Harmony'	CWil
- 'Henry Correvon'	CWil
- 'Inferno'	CWil MHom NHol
- 'Inge'	CWil
- 'Ithaca'	NHol
- 'Iuno'	CWil
- 'Jade'	CWil NMen
- var. **kopaonikensis**	CWil MHom NMen
- 'Mary Ann'	MHom
- 'Miller's Violet'	CWil WTin
- 'Minuta'	CWil NHol NMen WIvy WTin
- 'Mystique'	CMea CWil MBro NMen
- 'Nannette'	CWil
- 'Opele'	NHol
- 'Orion'	CMea CWil NHol NMen
- 'Pink Skies'	MBro
- 'Prisma'	CWil WTin
- 'Purple Haze'	MBro
- 'Sungold'	NHol
- 'Suntan'	CWil NHol
- 'Sylvan Memory'	CWil
- 'Tan'	CWil MBro NHol WTin
- 'Torrid Zone'	WTin
- 'Tuxedo'	CWil
- 'Vesta' **new**	CWil
- 'Violet'	CWil SDys
§ **hirta**	CHal CWil GAbr GCrs MDHE MOne NHol NMen NWCA SBla STre WPer
- subsp. **borealis**	CWil MBro MOne NDlv NHol
- from Wintergraben	SIng SPlb
- subsp. **glabrescens**	EPot ESis
- - from Belansky Tatra	CWil LBee MDHE MOne NDlv
- - from High Tatra **new**	MDHE
- - from Smeryouka	CWil MBro SIng
- - var. **neilreichii**	LRHS
- 'Lowe's 66'	MOne
- var. **neilreichii**	MHom WBVN
- 'Preissiana'	CWil GEdr LBee MBro MOne NDlv NHol NMen SIng WTin
§ **sobolifera**	CHEx CWil ELau EPot GEdr MBro MOne NFla NHol NJOw NMen SIng SPlb WAbe WPer
- 'August Cream'	CWil LBee
- 'Green Globe'	CWil ELau MDHE SDys WTin
- 'Miss Lorraine'	CWil

Juanulloa (Solanaceae)

aurantiaca	see *J. mexicana*
§ **mexicana**	ESlt SOWG

Jubaea (Arecaceae)

§ **chilensis**	CBrP CDoC CPHo CRoM EAmu LPJP LPal SChr WHPE WMul
spectabilis	see *J. chilensis*

Juglans ✿ (Juglandaceae)

§ **ailanthifolia**	CDul CMCN CTho WPGP
- var. **cordiformis**	CAgr
'Brock' (F) **new**	
- - 'Campbell CW1' (F) **new**	CAgr
- - 'Fodermaier' seedling **new**	CAgr
cathayensis (F)	WGWT
- B&SWJ 6778	WCru
cinerea (F)	CMCN EGFP
- 'Booth' seedlings (F)	CAgr
§ **elaeopyren**	EGFP WGWT
hindsii	CMCN EGFP
x **intermedia**	SKee WGWT
mandschurica	EGFP WGWT
microcarpa	WGWT
- subsp. **major**	see *J. elaeopyren*
nigra (F) ♀H4	More than 30 suppliers
- 'Laciniata'	CMCN CTho GKir MBlu WGWT
- 'Purpurea'	MBlu
- 'Thomas' (F)	ESim
- 'Weschke' (F)	CAgr
'Paradox'	WGWT
'Red Danube' (F)	WGWT
regia (F) ♀H4	More than 30 suppliers
- 'Axel' (F)	WGWT
- 'Broadview' (F)	CAgr CDoC CDul CEnd CTho EMui ERea ESim GTwe LRHS MBlu MBri MCoo MGos SCoo SDea SKee WGWT
- 'Buccaneer' (F)	CAgr CDul CTho ERea ESim GTwe LRHS SDea SKee WGWT
- 'Cascade' (F)	ESim
- 'Coenen' (F)	WGWT
- 'Ferjean' (F) **new**	CAgr
- 'Fernette'PBR	CAgr SKee
- 'Fernor'PBR	CAgr SKee
- 'Franquette' (F)	CAgr CDoC CTho ENot GTwe LRHS MCoo SKee WDin
- 'Hansen' (F)	WGWT

	- 'Laciniata'	CMCN GKir WGWT
	- 'Lara'	GTwe SKee WGWT
	- 'Leopold'	WGWT
	- 'Lu Guang' **new**	WGWT
	- 'Mayette' (F)	SKee WDin
	- 'Metcalfe' (F)	WGWT
	- 'Meylannaise' (F)	CAgr SKee
	- number 139 (f)	ESim
	- number 16 (F)	WGWT
	- number 26 (f)	ESim
	- 'Parisienne' (F)	SKee
	- 'Pedro' **new**	WGWT
	- 'Pendula'	WGWT
	- 'Plovdivski' (F)	CAgr WGWT
	- 'Proslavski' (F)	CAgr WGWT
	- 'Purpurea'	CMCN WGWT
	- 'Rita'	WGWT
	- 'Ronde de Montignac' (F)	SKee
	- 'Soleze' (F)	WGWT
	- 'Tremlett's Giant' **new**	WGWT
	- 'Zhong Lin' **new**	WGWT
	sieboldiana	see *J. ailanthifolia*

jujube see *Ziziphus jujuba*

Juncus (*Juncaceae*)

	acutus	CPen WRos WWye XPep
*	*balticus* 'Spiralis'	CTrC ECho WBea WBrk WCot
	bulbosus	CRWN
	conglomeratus	EHoe
	- 'Spiralis'	NGdn
§	*decipiens* 'Curly-wurly'	More than 30 suppliers
	- 'Spiralis'	see *J. decipiens* 'Curly-wurly'
§	*effusus*	CHEx CRWN EMFW LNCo
		LPBA NArg NPer NSti SWat
		WMAq WWpP
	- 'Gold Strike' (v)	CRow CWCL EMan EPPr EPla EUJe
		LIck MAvo WBcn WWpP
§	- f. *spiralis*	More than 30 suppliers
	- 'Yellow Line' (v) **new**	CPen EBee NHol
	ensifolius	CDWL CPen CRow CWat EHoe
		EMFW EPza EWes LIck LNCo LPBA
		MAvo MSta NArg NPer SWal WFar
		WRos
	filiformis 'Spiralis'	CBgR CBig CBrm GEil GIBF LBBr
		LPVe MAvo WCot WWeb
	inflexus	CAgr CRWN EHon EPza NArg
		SWat WWpP
	- 'Afro'	CBig CKno CMea EBee EMan
		EMon LRHS MAvo MBrN MCCP
		NBro SPlb SWal WCot
	membranaceus	NRya
	HLMS 94.0541	
	pallidus	EBee EPPr GCal GGar LIck NBid
	patens 'Carman's Gray'	CFee CFil CKno EBee EMan EPPr
		EPla GCal LRHS MAvo MCCP
		MMoz MTed NGdn NOak NSti
		WCot WPGP WWpP
	- 'Elk Blue'	CKno
	'Silver Spears'	EBee EMan EWTr MCCP SWal
		WWpP
	'Unicorn'PBR **new**	CPen
	xiphioides	EHoe EPla GCal LRHS NOGN SWal
	- JLS 8609LACA	EPPr

Junellia (*Verbenaceae*)

	odonnellii	EBee
	thymifolia F&W 9341	EBee
	toninii F&W 9332 **new**	CPBP
	wilczekii	WFar
	- F&W 7770	NWCA

Juniperus ✿ (*Cupressaceae*)

	chinensis	CMac CMen SEND

	- 'Aurea' ♀H4	CBcs CKen CMac EHul EOrn LCon
		MBar MGos WEve
§	- 'Blaauw' ♀H4	CDoC CMac CMen EHul ENot
		EOrn GKir LLin MBar MGos SCoo
		SHBN SLim STre WStI
	- 'Blue Alps'	CDoC CSli EBre EHul EOrn GKir
		IMGH LCon LPan MBar MBri
		MGos NBee NHol SEND SLim
		WDin WFar WOrn
	- 'Blue Point'	ENot MBar MGos
	- 'Densa Spartan'	see *J. chinensis* 'Spartan'
	- 'Echiniformis'	CKen CMac EOrn
	- 'Expansa	CDoC CKen CMac EBre EHul
	Aureospicata' (v)	EOrn EPfP LCon LLin MBar MGos
		SLim SRms
§	- 'Expansa Variegata' (v)	CDoC CMac CWib EBre EGra EHul
		EOrn EPfP GKir IMGH LCon LLin
		MAsh MBar MGos SLim SMer
		SRms WDin WFar WMoo WStI
		WTel
	- 'Globosa Cinerea'	MBar
	- 'Japonica'	EOrn MBar SMer
	- 'Japonica Variegata' (v)	EBre SLim
	- 'Kaizuka' ♀H4	CDoC CMac EBre EHul EOrn GKir
		LBee LCon LRHS MAsh MBar SLim
		SMad SMer SPoG STre XPep
	- 'Kaizuka Variegata'	see *J. chinensis* 'Variegated
		Kaizuka'
	- 'Keteleeri'	MBar WCwm
	- 'Kuriwao Gold'	see *J.* x *pfitzeriana* 'Kuriwao Gold'
	- 'Obelisk' ♀H4	EHul LCon LRHS MBar MGos SBod
	- 'Oblonga'	EHul MAsh MBar SMer STre
§	- 'Parsonsii'	CMac MBar SHBN STre WCFE
	- 'Plumosa' **new**	MBar
	- 'Plumosa	EOrn MBar
	Albovariegata' (v)	
	- 'Plumosa Aurea' ♀H4	EBre EHul ENot EOrn LCon MBar
		WDin WFar
	- 'Plumosa	CKen EOrn LCon MBar SLim
	Aureovariegata' (v)	
	- 'Pyramidalis' ♀H4	CBrm CDoC EBre EHul ENot EPfP
		GKir IMGH LCon LLin MGos
		MOne SBod SRms WDin WFar
	- 'Pyramidalis Variegata'	see *J. chinensis* 'Variegata'
	- 'Robust Green'	EOrn GKir MBar SLim
	- 'San José'	CDoC CMen EBre EHul EOrn LLin
		MAsh MBar SCoo SLim WDin
§	- var. *sargentii*	STre
	- 'Shimpaku'	CKen CMen EOrn LLin MBar NLar
§	- 'Spartan'	EHul
	- 'Stricta'	CKen CSBt EHul ENot GKir LBee
		LRHS MAsh MBar MGos NBee
		NBlu SLim SPla WDin WStI
	- 'Stricta Variegata'	see *J. chinensis* 'Variegata'
	- 'Sulphur Spray'	see *J.* x *pfitzeriana* 'Sulphur Spray'
	- 'Torulosa'	see *J. chinensis* 'Kaizuka'
§	- 'Variegata' (v)	EBre MBar
§	- 'Variegated Kaizuka' (v)	CBrm EBre EHul EOrn GKir LCon
		LLin MAsh MBar SPoG WEve WFar
	- 'Wilson's Weeping'	LLin WBcn
	communis	CArn CRWN CTrG EHul GPoy
		MHer MSal NWea SIde WBWf
	- (f)	SIde
	- 'Arnold'	LCon MBar MGos
	- 'Arnold Sentinel'	CKen
	- 'Atholl'	CKen
I	- 'Aureopicta' (v)	MBar WBcn
	- 'Barton'	MBar NHol WBcn
	- 'Berkshire'	CKen
	- 'Brien'	CDoC CKen
	- 'Brynhyfryd Gold'	CKen WBcn
	- var. *communis*	ECho EPot MBar NDlv
	- 'Compressa' ♀H4	More than 30 suppliers
§	- 'Constance Franklin' (v)	ECho EHul LLin MBar STre WBcn

– 'Corielagan'	CKen CNic MBar NLar	
– 'Cracovia'	CKen EHul	
– var. **depressa**	GPoy MBar	
– 'Depressa Aurea'	CKen CMac CSBt EBre EHul ENot	
	GKir LBee LCon LLin LPan LRHS	
	MBar MGos NDlv SHBN SMer	
	WFar WTel	
– 'Depressed Star'	EHul MBar	
– 'Derrynane'	EHul	
– 'Effusa'	CKen	
– 'Gelb'	see *J. communis* 'Schneverdingen	
	Goldmachangel'	
§ – 'Gold Cone'	CKen CSli EBre EHul ENot GKir	
	LBee LCon LLin LRHS MAsh MBar	
	MBri MGos NDlv NHol SLim SMer	
	WDin WEve WFar	
– 'Golden Showers'	see *J. communis* 'Schneverdingen	
	Goldmachangel'	
– 'Green Carpet' ♀H4	CAgr CDoC CKen EBre EHul EOrn	
	EPfP EPla GKir IMGH LBee LBuc	
	LCon LLin LRHS MAsh MBar NHol	
	SLim SMer WCFE WDin WEve	
– 'Haverbeck'	CKen	
– var. **hemispherica**	see *J. communis* var. *communis*	
– 'Hibernica' ♀H4	More than 30 suppliers	
– 'Hibernica Variegata'	see *J. communis* 'Constance	
	Franklin'	
– 'Hornibrookii' ♀H4	CMac EHul ENot EOrn LLin MBar	
	MGos SBod SHBN SMer SRms STre	
	WDin	
– 'Horstmann'	EBre EPla MBar SLim	
I – 'Horstmann's Pendula'	CDoC LCon LLin WBcn	
– 'Kenwith Castle'	CKen	
§ – 'Minima'	SBod	
– 'Pendula' **new**	NPSI	
– 'Prostrata'	WFar	
– 'Pyramidalis'	SPlb	
– 'Repanda' ♀H4	CAgr CBcs CDoC CMac CSBt	
	CWib EBre EHul ENot EPfP GKir	
	LCon LLin MAsh MBar MGos NBee	
	NBlu NDlv NWea SLim SMer SPer	
	SPla SRms WCFE WDin WEve WFar	
§ – 'Schneverdingen	EBre EOrn GKir LLin MAsh MOne	
Goldmachangel'	NHol SLim SMer SPoG	
– 'Sentinel'	EBre EHul EPfP LCon LRHS MBar	
	NBee NBlu NHol SLim WCFE	
	WDin WEve WStI	
– 'Sieben Steinhauser'	CKen	
– 'Silver Mist'	CKen	
– 'Spotty Spreader' (v)	EBre GKir SCoo SLim	
– Suecica Group	EHul ENot MBar NWea	
– 'Suecica Aurea'	EHul EOrn	
– 'Zeal'	CKen	
conferta	see *J. rigida* subsp. *conferta*	
– 'Blue Tosho'	EBre SLim SPoG	
– var. **maritima**	see *J. taxifolia*	
– 'Silver Mist'	CKen	
davurica	EHul	
– 'Expansa'	see *J. chinensis* 'Parsonsii'	
– 'Expansa Albopicta'	see *J. chinensis* 'Expansa Variegata'	
– 'Expansa Variegata'	see *J. chinensis* 'Expansa Variegata'	
deppeana 'Silver Spire'	EGra MBar MGos	
x **gracilis** 'Blaauw'	see *J. chinensis* 'Blaauw'	
horizontalis	ENot NWea	
§ – 'Andorra Compact'	CNic EMil MAsh MBar SCoo	
– 'Bar Harbor'	CKen CMac EHul GKir MBar MGos	
	SBod WGor	
§ – 'Blue Chip'	CKen CMac EBre EHul ENot EOrn	
	EPfP GKir LBee LLin LRHS MAsh	
	MBar MGos SBod SLim SPer WDin	
	XPep	
– 'Blue Moon'	see *J. horizontalis* 'Blue Chip'	
– 'Blue Pygmy'	CKen	
– 'Blue Rug'	see *J. horizontalis* 'Wiltonii'	

– 'Douglasii'	CKen CMac EHol EHul MBar WGor	
– 'Emerald Spreader'	CKen EHul ENot GKir MBar MGos	
– 'Glacier'	CKen WEve	
– Glauca Group	CMac CSBt EHul ENot GKir LLin	
	MBar MGos SMer SPer WDin	
– 'Glomerata'	CKen MBar	
– 'Golden Carpet'	EBre EOrn GKir IMGH LBee LBuc	
	MAsh NHol NPro SCoo SLim SPer	
	WEve	
– 'Golden Spreader'	CDoC GKir WBcn	
– 'Grey Pearl'	CKen EBre EHul GKir SBod SLim	
– 'Hughes'	CMac EBre EHul ENot GKir LBee	
	LLin LRHS MAsh MBar MGos NDlv	
	SBod SLim SPla	
– 'Jade River'	CKen EBre EHul GKir LRHS MGos	
	SCoo SLim SPer	
– 'Limeglow'	CKen SLim	
– 'Mother Lode'	CKen	
– 'Neumänn'	CKen	
– 'Plumosa'	NDlv	
– 'Plumosa Compacta'	see *J. horizontalis* 'Andorra	
	Compact'	
– 'Prince of Wales'	CKen EBre EHul GKir LLin LRHS	
	MAsh MGos MOne SLim XPep	
– var. **saxatalis** E.Murray	see *J. communis* var. *communis*	
– 'Turquoise Spreader'	CKen CSBt EBre EHul GKir MBar	
	SCoo	
– 'Variegata' (v)	MBar	
– 'Venusta'	see *J. virginiana* 'Venusta'	
– 'Villa Marie'	CKen	
– 'Webber'	MBar	
§ – 'Wiltonii' ♀H4	CKen CSli EHul ENot EOrn MGos	
– 'Winter Blue'	EBre LBee LCon LRHS SLim SPer	
– 'Youngstown'	CMac CSWP EBre GKir LLin MBar	
	MGos SBod WGor	
– 'Yukon Belle'	CKen	
N x **media**	see *J. x pfitzeriana*	
§ x **pfitzeriana**	CDul	
– 'Armstrongii'	EHul	
– 'Blaauw'	see *J. chinensis* 'Blaauw'	
– 'Blue and Gold' (v)	CKen EHul EOrn LLin MBar SHBN	
	SLim	
– 'Blue Cloud'	see *J. virginiana* 'Blue Cloud'	
§ – 'Carbery Gold'	CDoC CMac CSBt CSam CSli EBre	
	EGra EHul EOrn GKir LBee LCon	
	LLin LRHS MAsh MBar MGos SLim	
	SPoG WBVN WEve	
– 'Gold Coast'	CDoC CKen CMac CSBt EBre EHul	
	ENot EPfP GKir LBee LRHS MAsh	
	MBar MBri MGos MWat SLim SPer	
	SPla WDin WEve	
– Gold Sovereign	EBre EOrn GKir LBee MAsh MGos	
= 'Blound'PBR	NHol SMer	
– 'Gold Star'	EOrn WBcn	
* – 'Golden Joy'	SLim	
– 'Golden Saucer'	MAsh MBar MBri NBlu SCoo	
– 'Goldkissen'	MBri	
§ – 'Kuriwao Gold'	CMac EBre EHul ENot EPfP GKir	
	LBee MAsh MBar MGos NHol SBod	
	SLim SMer STre WFar WOrn WStI	
– 'Milky Way' (v)	EBre SLim	
– 'Mint Julep'	CMac CSBt EBre EHul ENot GKir	
	IMGH LBee LCon LLin LPan LRHS	
	MAsh MBar MGos NBlu SLim SPer	
	WBrE WDin WEve WFar WMoo	
	WOrn	
– 'Mordigan Gold'	LBee LPan	
– 'Old Gold' ♀H4	CKen CMac EBre EHul ENot EOrn	
	EPfP GKir IMGH LBee LCon LLin	
	LRHS MAsh MBar MGos NBlu	
	NDlv NHol NWea SBod SLim SMer	
	SPlb SRms WDin WEve WFar WTel	
– 'Old Gold Carbery'	see *J. x pfitzeriana* 'Carbery Gold'	
– 'Pfitzeriana'	see *J. x pfitzeriana* 'Wilhelm Pfitzer'	

- 'Pfitzeriana Aurea'	CBcs CBrm CDoC CDul CMac CSBt CTri EHul ENot EPfP GKir LCon LRHS MBar MBri MGos MWat NBlu NWea SHBN WCFE WDin WEve WFar
- 'Pfitzeriana Compacta' ♀H4	CMac ECho EHul MBar SLim
- 'Pfitzeriana Glauca'	EHul ENot IMGH LPan LRHS MBar SCoo SLim WGor
- 'Richeson'	MBar
- 'Saybrook Gold'	LPan
- 'Silver Cascade'	EHul
§ - 'Sulphur Spray' ♀H4	More than 30 suppliers
§ - 'Wilhelm Pfitzer'	CMac EHul ENot EPfP MBar NWea WStI
- 'Winter Surprise' (v)	MGos
phoenicea new	XPep
§ **pingii** 'Glassell'	CDoC ECho MBar MGos
§ - 'Pygmaea'	EOrn MBar
§ - var. **wilsonii**	CDoC CKen ECho EHul EOrn MBar
procumbens 'Bonin Isles'	EBre LLin MGos SLim
- 'Nana' ♀H4	CDoC CKen CMac CSBt EBre EHul ENot EOrn EPfP GKir IMGH LBee LCon LLin LRHS MAsh MBar MGos MWat NHol SHBN SLim SPla WCFE WDin WEve WFar
recurva 'Castlewellan'	EOrn LCon MGos WCwm WEve
- var. **coxii**	CDoC CMac EHul EOrn GGGa GKir ISea LCon LLin MBar MGos SRms WCFE WCwm WEve WPic
§ - 'Densa'	CDoC CKen EHul EOrn MBar NHol SHBN
- 'Embley Park'	EHul MAsh MBar
- 'Nana'	see *J. recurva* 'Densa'
rigida	CMen EHul LBee LLin MBar MWat NLar
§ - subsp. **conferta**	EBre LCon SLim SPer STre WEve WStI
* - - 'Blue Ice'	CKen EOrn LLin
- - 'Blue Pacific'	CMac COtt EHul GKir MBar SLim SPoG WFar
- - 'Emerald Sea'	EHul
sabina	NWea
§ - 'Blaue Donau'	CSBt EHul MBar MGos WEve
- Blue Danube	see *J. sabina* 'Blaue Donau'
- 'Broadmoor'	EHul
- 'Buffalo'	EHul
- Cupressifolia Group	MBar
- 'Hicksii'	CBcs CMac MBar NWea
- 'Knap Hill'	see *J.* x *pfitzeriana* 'Wilhelm Pfitzer'
- 'Mountaineer'	see *J. scopulorum* 'Mountaineer'
- 'Rockery Gem'	EBre EHul EOrn MGos SLim SPla WEve WGor
- 'Skandia'	CKen
- 'Tamariscifolia'	More than 30 suppliers
- 'Tripartita'	see *J. virginiana* 'Tripartita'
- 'Variegata' (v)	CMac EHul MAsh MBar NWea WBcn
sargentii	see *J. chinensis* var. *sargentii*
scopulorum	CKen MBar
§ - 'Banff'	CSBt
- 'Blue Arrow'	More than 30 suppliers
- 'Blue Banff'	CKen
- 'Blue Heaven'	EHul LCon MAsh MBar NLar SRms
- 'Blue Pyramid'	EHul
- 'Boothman'	EHul
- 'Moonglow'	EHul MBar
§ - 'Mountaineer'	EHul
- 'Mrs Marriage'	CKen
- 'Repens'	MBar MGos
- 'Silver Star' (v)	EHul MBar MGos WEve
- 'Skyrocket'	More than 30 suppliers
- 'Springbank'	CMac EHul LBee LRHS MBar
- 'Tabletop'	MBar WBcn
- 'Wichita Blue'	EBre EHul EPfP LCon LPan SEND WEve WGor
§ **squamata**	WBVN
- 'Blue Carpet' ♀H4	More than 30 suppliers
- 'Blue Spider'	CKen LRHS MBar SCoo SLim WGor
- 'Blue Star' ♀H4	More than 30 suppliers
- 'Blue Star Variegated'	see *J. squamata* 'Golden Flame'
- 'Blue Swede'	see *J. squamata* 'Hunnetorp'
- 'Chinese Silver'	EHul LCon MBar SLim WBcn
- 'Dream Joy'	CKen SLim
- var. **fargesii**	see *J. squamata*
- 'Filborna'	CKen EBre GTSp LBee MBar MWat SLim SMer
- 'Glassell'	see *J. pingii* 'Glassell'
§ - 'Golden Flame' (v)	CKen
- 'Holger' ♀H4	CDoC CKen CMac CSBt EBre EGra EHul EOrn EPfP EPla GKir LBee LCon LLin LRHS MAsh MBar MBri MGos SBod SLim WCFE WEve WStI
§ - 'Hunnetorp'	EOrn GKir MBar MGos WEve WGor
- 'Loderi'	see *J. pingii* var. *wilsonii*
- 'Meyeri'	CTri EBre EHul ENot EOrn GKir IMGH MBar NWea SBod SCoo SMer STre WDin WFar WStI WTel
- 'Pygmaea'	see *J. pingii* 'Pygmaea'
- 'Wilsonii'	see *J. pingii* var. *wilsonii*
- 'Yellow Tip'	WBcn
§ **taxifolia**	EOrn IMGH LBee
virginiana	CAgr CPne
§ - 'Blue Cloud'	EBre EHul MBar SLim WEve WGor
- 'Burkii'	CDoC EHul LCon
- 'Frosty Morn'	CKen ECho EHul MAsh MBar SCoo WFar
- 'Glauca'	CSWP EHul NWea
- 'Golden Spring'	CKen
- 'Grey Owl' ♀H4	CMac EBre EHul ELan ENot EPfP GKir MBar MGos NWea SLim SLon SMer SRms STre WDin WFar WGor WTel
- 'Helle'	see *J. chinensis* 'Spartan'
- 'Hetzii'	CBcs CMac ECho EHul MBar NBlu NWea WDin WFar
- 'Hillii'	MBar
- 'Hillspire'	EHul
- 'Nana Compacta'	MBar
- Silver Spreader	CKen CSBt EHul MGos SCoo
= 'Mona'	WBcn WEve
- 'Staver'	EHul
- 'Sulphur Spray'	see *J.* x *pfitzeriana* 'Sulphur Spray'
§ - 'Tripartita'	MBar
§ - 'Venusta'	CKen

Jurinea (Asteraceae)

alata	EMan
cyanoides	EMan
glycacantha new	LRHS
mollis	GBuc

Jurinella see *Jurinea*

Jussiaea see *Ludwigia*

Justicia (Acanthaceae)

§ **brandegeeana** ♀H1	CHal EShb MBri SOWG
- 'Lutea'	see *J. brandegeeana* 'Yellow Queen'
§ - 'Yellow Queen'	CHal
§ **carnea**	CHEx CHal CSev EBak EHol ERea GCal LRHS MBri MTis SLdr SMad SOWG WMul

guttata	see *J. brandegeeana*
'Norgaard's Favourite'	MBri
ovata	SMad
'Penrhosiensis' L.H. Bailey	EShb
pohliana	see *J. carnea*
rizzinii ♀H1	CHal CHll CPle CSev ERea EShb
	SOWG
spicigera	ERea
suberecta	see *Dicliptera suberecta*

K

Kadsura (*Schisandraceae*)

japonica	CBcs CMen EMil
- B&SWJ 1027	WCru
- 'Shiromi'	EMil EPfP SBra
- 'Variegata' (v)	EPfP SBra SSpi WSHC

Kaempferia (*Zingiberaceae*)

galanga	CKob LEur
linearis	CKob
rotunda	CKob LAma LEur MOak

kaffir plum see *Harpephyllum caffrum*

Kageneckia (*Rosaceae*)

oblonga	IFro

Kalanchoe (*Crassulaceae*)

beharensis ♀H1	CHal EShb MBri
- 'Rusty' **new**	CSpe
blossfeldiana	EOHP LRHS
- 'Variegata' (v)	CHal
daigremontiana	CHal EShb SRms
§ *delagoensis*	CHal EShb SMur STre
fedtschenkoi	CHal STre
manginii ♀H1	CDoC EOHP
pumila ♀H1	CHal EMan ERea EWoo SPet STre
	WEas
'Tessa' ♀H1	MBri MLan SPet SRms STre
tomentosa ♀H1	CHal SHFr SMur SPet WEas
tubiflora	see *K. delagoensis*
'Wendy' ♀H1	WGwG

Kalimeris (*Asteraceae*)

§ *incisa*	EWll GMac IHMH WFar WMoo
	WTin
- 'Alba'	EBee EFou NLar SHel SSvw WFar
- 'Blue Star'	EBee EFou LHop NLar WFar
- 'Charlotte' **new**	EWes NDov
* - 'Variegata' (v)	EBee
integrifolia	ECha WTin
intricifolia	EBee
§ *mongolica*	EBee ECha MAnH WFar WPGP
	WPer
§ *pinnatifida*	EBee EChP EMan EPPr WCot
- 'Hortensis' **new**	NSti WHil
§ *yomena* 'Shogun' (v)	EBee ECha EHoe ELan EMon EPPr
	GBri GBuc GEdr GKir MAvo MLLN
	NBid NBir NPri SAga SCro SPer
	SPlb WCot WCra WFar WSHC
	WShp
- 'Variegata'	see *K. yomena* 'Shogun'

Kalmia ✿ (*Ericaceae*)

angustifolia ♀H4	MBar NLAp SRms WDin WFar
- var. *angustifolia*	WAbe
f. *candida*	
- var. *pumila*	SReu WAbe
- f. *rubra* ♀H4	CBcs CDoC CMHG CSBt EBre
	ELan EPfP GKir ISea ITim LRHS

	MAsh MGos NBlu NDlv NHol
	SHBN SPer SReu SSta WFar WHar
	WPat
latifolia ♀H4	CBcs CEnd CTrG ELan EMil EPfP
	MBar MDun MGos MLan NBee
	NBlu NWea SPer SReu SSpi SSta
	WBrE WDin WFar WGer WNor
	WStI
- 'Alpine Pink'	CBrm NLar
- 'Carousel'	CAbP EPfP GGGa GKir LRHS
	MGos MLea
- 'Elf'	GEdr LRHS MGos MLea NLar
- 'Freckles' ♀H4	ELan EPfP GEdr GGGa GKir LRHS
	MDun MGos NDlv WGwG
- 'Fresca'	LRHS MDun
- 'Galaxy'	GGGa
- 'Heart of Fire'	CAbP GGGa GKir LRHS NDlv
- 'Keepsake'	GGGa
- 'Little Linda' ♀H4	GGGa GKir IMGH LRHS MAsh
	MBri NDlv
- 'Minuet'	CAbP CDoC CWSG EPfP EPot
	GEdr GGGa GKir IMGH ISea LRHS
	MAsh MDun MLan MLea NDlv
	SPoG SSpi SWvt WBrE
- f. *myrtifolia*	GEdr LPan MLea
- 'Olympic Fire' ♀H4	CEnd ELan EPfP GGGa GKir LPan
	LRHS MGos NDlv NHol SSpi
- 'Ostbo Red'	CBcs CDoC CSBt EMil EPfP EPot
	GEdr GGGa GKir IMGH ISea MBri
	MGos MLea NDlv NHol SHBN SPer
	SReu SSpi SSta SWvt WBod WGwG
- 'Peppermint'	GGGa
- 'Pink Charm' ♀H4	CAbP ELan GGGa GKir GWCH
	LPan MAsh NDlv SMer SPer WBan
- 'Pink Frost'	CBcs GEdr GGGa NDlv NHol SPer
- 'Pristine'	GGGa
- 'Quinnipiac'	NHol
- 'Raspberry Glow'	GGGa
- 'Richard Jaynes'	EPot GEdr LRHS MAsh WBrE
- 'Sarah'	GGGa MBri NLar SSpi
- 'Silver Dollar'	GGGa NHol
- 'Snowdrift'	GGGa LRHS SSpi
§ *microphylla*	GGGa
polifolia	CBcs MBar MBro NHol NLAp WPat
- var. *compacta*	WAbe WSHC
- 'Glauca'	see *K. microphylla*
- f. *leucantha*	GGGa NLAp WAbe WPat

Kalmia x *Rhododendron* (*Ericaceae*)

§ *K. latifolia* x	SReu
R. williamsianum,	
'Everlasting'	

Kalmiopsis (*Ericaceae*)

leachiana ♀H4	CStu EPot GCrs SOkd SSta WAbe
- 'Glendoick'	GGGa LTwo MBro MDun WPat
- 'Hiawatha'	SReu
* - 'Shooting Star'	ITim LTwo NLAp WPat

x *Kalmiothamnus* (*Ericaceae*)

ornithomma 'Cosdon'	WAbe
- 'Haytor'	WAbe
'Sindleberg' **new**	ITim

Kalopanax (*Araliaceae*)

pictus	see *K. septemlobus*
§ *septemlobus*	CBcs CFil CHEx CLnd ELan EWTr
	GIBF NPal WBVN WOVN
- var. *lutchuensis*	WCru
B&SWJ 5947	
- var. *maximowiczii*	CDoC CDul EPfP MBlu NBee

Keckiella (*Scrophulariaceae*)

§ *cordifolia*	EMan

Kelseya (Rosaceae)

uniflora CGra WAbe

Kennedia (Papilionaceae)

beckxiana LRHS SOWG
coccinea CBcs LRHS
nigricans ESlt SOWG
prostrata SPlb
rubicunda CHal CRHN

Kentranthus see *Centranthus*

Kerria (Rosaceae)

japonica misapplied (single) see *K. japonica* 'Simplex'
japonica (d) see *K. japonica* 'Pleniflora'
- 'Albescens' CBot CFai NPro WFar
- 'Golden Guinea' ♀H4 CChe CPLG CPom CWSG EBee EBre ECtt ELan EPfP GKir LRHS MAsh MGos MNrw MSwo NPro SCoo SPer SPoG SSte SWal SWvt WDin WFar WWeb WWpP
§ - 'Picta' (v) CDul CWib EBee EBre EHoe ENot EPAt EPfP LAst MBar MBri MGos MRav MSwo SGar SLim SLon SPer SRms WDin WFar WHil WSHC WTel WWeb WWpP
§ - 'Pleniflora' (d) ♀H4 More than 30 suppliers
§ - 'Simplex' CDul CSBt ENot EWTr GKir NWea WDin WFar WTel
- 'Variegata' see *K. japonica* 'Picta'

Khadia (Aizoaceae)

sp. CStu CTrC

khat see *Catha edulis*

Kickxia (Scrophulariaceae)

spuria MSal

Kirengeshoma (Hydrangeaceae)

palmata ♀H4 More than 30 suppliers
- dwarf WCot
§ - Koreana Group CHid CLAP EBee EChP ECha EGle EHrv ELan EMan EPar EPfP GKir GSki IPot LAst LPhx MBri MRav MWrn NBPC NBir SCro SMad SPer WCot WFar WHil WOVN WTMC

Kitagawia (Apiaceae)

§ **litoralis** EBee

Kitaibela (Malvaceae)

vitifolia CFee CPLG CSpe EBee ELan EMon EWTr GCal GEil IFro NBid SDnm SGar SPlb WHer WPer WPic WRos WTMC WWin
- 'Chalice' CStr

Kitchingia see *Kalanchoe*

kiwi fruit see *Actinidia deliciosa*

Kleinia (Asteraceae)

articulata see *Senecio articulatus*
grantii ERea
repens see *Senecio serpens*
senecioides WEas
stapeliiformis ♀H1 EShb
new

Knautia (Dipsacaceae)

§ **arvensis** CArn CBgR CHll CRWN ECoo

MBow MGas MHer MLLN MSwo MWya NLan NLar NMir NPri NSco WFar WHer WMoo WSHC WSSM
- 'Rachel' **new** CPLG
dipsacifolia SHar
godetii EBee
* **jankiae** WHer
§ **macedonica** More than 30 suppliers
- 'Crimson Cushion' NCot SOkh
- 'Macedonia Lilac' EBlw
- 'Mars Midget' CBgR CBrm CFwr CHll CSam CSpe EBee EChP EGoo MSPs MWrn NCGa NLar SLon SPla SWvt WCot WWeb
- Melton pastels EChP EMar ENot EPfP EShb GKir IBal MWgw MWrn SCro SPet SRot SWal SWat SWvt WBar WFar WMnd WWeb
- pink CMil CSam
- red **new** CWib
- 'Red Dress' EBee
- short **new** NCot
- tall, pale LPhx
sarajevensis EBee MAvo
§ **tatarica** EBee

Knightia (Proteaceae)

excelsa CTrC

Kniphofia ❀ (Asphodelaceae)

'Ada' EBre ECGP ERou EWes LRHS MLLN MRav
'Alcazar' More than 30 suppliers
'Amsterdam' MWat
angustifolia WHil
'Apple Court' NBir
'Apricot' CMdw
'Apricot Souffle' EMan GBri MLLN WCot WPrP
'Atlanta' CFil CPne EMon GCal LRHS WCot
'Barton Fever' WCot
baurii WCot
'Beauty of Wexford' **new** SCro
'Bees' Flame' EBee
'Bee's Gold' **new** ERou
'Bees' Lemon' More than 30 suppliers
'Bees' Sunset' ♀H4 CDes EBee EGle GBri GBuc MRav MWgw NBir SHBN SMrm SOkh SUsu WCAu WCot WPGP WPrP WTMC
* **bicolor** NSti WCot WPrP
'Border Ballet' CBrm EBre ECtt EMan ERou LRHS MRav MWgw NBir NBro NLar SWat WFar
brachystachya CPou EBee GCal SIgm SPlb WCot
'Bressingham Comet' CRez EBee EBre ECtt EMan EPfP GKir LRHS MBri MRav NBir SBla WPGP
'Bressingham Gleam' WCot
Bressingham hybrids EBre NBir
Bressingham Sunbeam = 'Bresun' CPen EBee GSki MBri WCot
'Brimstone' ♀H4 More than 30 suppliers
buchananii EBee
'Buttercup' ♀H4 CMHG CMdw GAbr SBri SOkh WSHC WTin
'C.M. Prichard' hort. see *K. rooperi*
'C.M. Prichard' Prichard WCot
'Candlelight' CDes CPlt EBee EMan SChu SCro SDys SUsu WCot WPGP
* 'Candlemass' LPio
caulescens ♀H3-4 More than 30 suppliers
- 'Coral Breakers' WCot WTMC
- from John May **new** WCot
- short SMrm

citrina — CBri CFir EBee EBre ECGN EMan EPfP LAst LRHS NLar WCot

'Cobra' — CDes CStr EBee EBre LRHS SCro WCot WPGP

'Comet' — ECtt

'Corallina' — EBee NPri WCot WFar WPnP

'Dingaan' — CAbb CPou CPrp EBee EChP EMan EPPr GBin GCal GSki MNrw SAga SDnm WCot WFar WLin WShp

'Doctor E.M. Mills' — CPrp CSam

'Dorset Sentry' — CAbP CHea CMdw CPrp CSam EBee EChP EGle EMan EMar GBuc GCal GSki LAst MAnH MLLN MNrw MSte NLar NMyG NSti WCot WShp

* 'Dropmore Apricot' — CM&M

'Drummore Apricot' — CMHG CPrp CSam CTrC EBee EChP ECha EGle ELan EMan EWll LAst MSte NBir NDov NPPs NSti SDnm SMrm WCot WFar WHrl WPGP WPrP WTMC WWhi WWye

'E.C. Mills' — WCot

'Earliest of All' — COtt EBee EBre EMan EOMN EWll GSki LRHS MBNS

'Early Buttercup' — CPrp ECot EPfP GBri MRav WCot WFar

§ *ensifolia* — CPne CPou ECtt EGra NGdn SIgm SRms WBcn

'Ernest Mitchell' — EGle MRav SMrm WCot

Express hybrids — EBee NLar

'Fairyland' — EMan LPio MNrw WBrk WBro WTin

'False Maid' **new** — SMHy

* 'Fat Yellow' — EMar MWgw

fibrosa — CFir WCot

'Fiery Fred' — CMil EBre ELan EMan LRHS MRav WCot WEas

'Flamenco' — WSSM WWeb

'Flaming Torch' **new** — ECha

fluviatilis — EBee

foliosa — CPne EBee EMan EWsh LRHS SChr SMrm

'Forncett Harvest' — EFou

'Frances Victoria' — WCot

galpinii hort. — see *K. triangularis* subsp. *triangularis*

galpinii Baker ♀H4 — CStu EBee EMar GBri MRav SAga SPer SRms WTMC

* 'Géant' **new** — XPep

'Gilt Bronze' — SMrm WCot

'Gladness' — ECtt MRav NBir NSti SChu WCot WPrP

'Goldelse' — NBir

'Goldfinch' — CMdw EBee MRav SMHy SUsu

gracilis — WCot

'Green and Cream' — MNrw

'Green Jade' — CDes CFir CMdw COtt CRow EChP ECha EPar EPfP GBri GKir MCLN MRav NBir SChu SCro SEND SGar SIgm SMrm SOkh WAul WBro WCot WFar WHoo WPGP WTMC WTin

'H.E. Beale' — GCal MRav SMrm WCot

hirsuta — CPne EBee EBre ELan EMan LPio MSte WCot

– JCA 3.461.900 — WCot

– JCA 346 900 — SSpi

– 'Traffic Lights' **new** — GFlt

'Hollard's Gold' — WCot

'Ice Queen' — CBri CFir CPar CSam CSev EBee EBre ECGP EGle EOrc EPPr ERou GBri GCal LPhx MBri MMil MRav NChi SMrm SWvt WCot WPnP WTin

ichopensis — CDes CFil EBee GBuc

'Ingénue' — EMan LPio WCot

'Innocence' — EBre

'Jenny Bloom' — More than 30 suppliers

'John Benary' — More than 30 suppliers

'Johnathan' — MWat WCot

laxiflora — CDes CFil CPou EBee LPio SSpi WCot

'Lemon Ice' — WCot

'Light of the World' — see *K. triangularis* subsp. *triangularis* 'Light of the World'

'Limelight' — EMar

linearifolia — CFil CPou CTrC EBee GGar MNrw SPlb WCot

'Little Elf' — LPio MWat SBla SDys WSHC

'Little Maid' — More than 30 suppliers

'Lord Roberts' — CPen EBee ECha EMan ENot SMad WCot

'Luna' — WCot

'Lye End' — EBee SMrm

macowanii — see *K. triangularis* subsp. *triangularis*

'Maid of Orleans' — CRow GBri GKir WCot

'Mermaiden' — CMHG CPrp CRow EBee EChP ECtt EMan GFlt GSki LAst MNrw WCot

'Minister Verschuur' — EBee EMar GSki LRHS NFla SAga WFar WMnd WWol

'Modesta' — EBee GBri SBla WPGP WSHC

'Mount Etna' — WCot

'Mrs Henry' **new** — CDes

'Nancy's Red' — More than 30 suppliers

nelsonii hort. — see *K. triangularis* subsp. *triangularis* 'Light of the World'

'Nobilis' — see *K. uvaria* 'Nobilis'

northiae — CBot CFil CFir CHEx CPou EMan GBin GCal LEdu MNrw SAPC SArc SIgm SPlb SSpi WCot WCru

'November Glory' **new** — WCot

I 'Old Court Seedling' — WCot WPrP

'Orange Torch' **new** — CPou

'Painted Lady' — CTri GCal MAnH MBro MRav SMrm WHoo

parviflora — CPou

pauciflora — CBro CStr EMan LHop SDys SIgm WCot

'Peaches and Cream' **new** — ECha

'Percy's Pride' — More than 30 suppliers

'Perry's White' — SOkh WViv

'Pfitzeri' — SRms

porphyrantha — WCot

x *praecox* — CFil EBee WCFE WCot

'Primulina' hort. — CPou EBre EGra EMan LRHS

'Prince Igor' — CFir CPne EBre ECha EMan MRav NBir SChu SIgm SMad WCot

pumila — EBee ITer MNrw

'Ralph Idden' **new** — EChP

'Ranelagh Gardens' — SArc

ritualis — CFil EBee WCot

§ *rooperi* — CBot CFil CHEx CMdw CMil EMan GBri GCal GGar GSki IGor LPhx LPio MHer MMil MNrw NRib SCro SDnm SMac SMrm WCot WPic WViv WWye

– 'Torchlight' — CFwr CPne CPrp WViv

'Ross Sunshine' — EOrc

'Rougham Beauty' — ERou

'Royal Caste' — CFwr EBee MMil MRav NBir NOrc NPri WFar WShp

'Royal Standard' ♀H4 — CBcs COtt EBee ELan EMan ENot EPfP ERou GBri GSki LRHS MNrw MRav SCro SPer SRms SWvt WCAu WCot WFar WMoo WShp WWeb

rufa — CPou EBee WCot

aff. *rufa* — SSpi

'Safranvogel'	SUsu WCot
'Samuel's Sensation' ♀H4	CFir CSam EBee EBre EChP EMan GBri GSki LRHS MBnl MBri MCLN MNFA MRav NSti SHBN WCot WShp
sarmentosa	CFil CPne CPou EBee SIgm WCot WPGP XPep
'September Sunshine'	MRav
'Shining Sceptre'	CFwr CSam EBee EBre ECGN ECha ECtt ERou GSki LIck LPio LRHS MLLN MRav MWat NCGa SGar SIgm SMad SSvw SWvt WAul WCot WEas WHil
'Springtime'	WCot
'Star of Baden-Baden'	ECGN NBir WCot
'Strawberries and Cream'	EBee ECha EMan EPfP GSki LPhx LPio MSte SAga SOkh SUsu
stricta	SIgm WCot
'Sunbeam'	NBir
'Sunningdale Yellow' ♀H4	CDes CMdw COlW CPou EBee EBre ECha EHrv EMan ENot ERou MCLN MFir MWat SChu SMHy SOkh SPer SRms WCot WEas WPGP
'Tawny King'	More than 30 suppliers
'Tetbury Torch'PBR	EBre LRHS WWeb
thodei	CPou
thomsonii	GCal
- var. *snowdenii* ambig.	CHEx CPou EBee WHrl WPGP WSHC
- var. *snowdenii* misapplied	see *K. thomsonii* var. *thomsonii*
§ - var. *thomsonii*	CBot CDes CFir EMan EMar EOrc ETow GBri MNrw SCro SMHy SMrm WCot WHal WPrP
- - triploid variety	GSki
- yellow	GCal
'Timothy'	More than 30 suppliers
'Toasted Corn'	ECha
'Toffee Nosed' ♀H4	More than 30 suppliers
'Torchbearer'	WCot WFar
triangularis	CHad CMHG EBee ECGN EPfP GCal GSki LRHS NPPs SAga WFar
§ - subsp. *triangularis*	CBri CBro CHad CKno COlW CPrp EChP EMar ENot GBuc ITer LAst LRHS MRav MTis NBro NPri SCoo SLon SMrm SRms SWat WBrE WCAu WPrP WShp
§ - - 'Light of the World'	More than 30 suppliers
'Tubergeniana'	WCot
I 'Tuckii'	CStu EMan EWll MNrw SRms
tuckii Baker	see *K. ensifolia*
typhoides	GCal SPlb SSpi WCot WHal
tysonii	SPlb
uvaria	CPou CSBt CTrC EBee GSki ITer LPio LRHS MHer NBir NPri NVic SRms SSpi WCot WHoo WHrl WMnd WTMC
* - Fairyland hybrids	LIck WFar
- 'Flamenco'	CFwr EWll LPVe NGdn SMac WHil WTMC
§ - 'Nobilis' ♀H4	CFir CKno CSam EBee EChP EMan ERou GAbr GBin GBri GSki MAvo MLLN MNFA MNrw SAPC SArc SDnm SMad SPoG SSpi SWvt WCAu WCot WShp
'Vanilla'	CFir CPen EBee EChP EFou EMan GSki LAst LPio MBNS MRav SMrm WHil WTMC
'Wrexham Buttercup'	CDes CKno CPne CPrp CSam EBee EChP ECtt EMan GBri GCal GMac GSki MAvo MBnl MCLN MLLN MNFA MRav SSpi WBVN WCot WHal WTMC

'Yellow Cheer'	CPen EBee LRHS
'Yellow Hammer'	EBee EBre ECha WFar WPrP
'Zululandiae'	WCot

Kochia see *Bassia*

Koeleria (*Poaceae*)
cristata	see *K. macrantha*, *K. pyramidata*
glauca	More than 30 suppliers
§ *macrantha*	CBig EMan NHol NLar NNor NOGN
vallesiana	EHoe EMon ESis LRHS MNrw

Koelreuteria (*Sapindaceae*)
bipinnata	CMCN
* - var. *integrifoliola*	CFil WPGP
paniculata ♀H4	More than 30 suppliers
- var. *apiculata*	CMHG
- 'Fastigiata'	EBee EPfP LRHS MBlu NPal SKee
- 'Rosseels'	MBlu NLar NPal

Kohleria (*Gesneriaceae*)
'Clytie'	MBri
'Dark Velvet'	CHal WDib
eriantha ♀H1	CHal EShb MBri WDib
'Jester' ♀H1	CHal WDib
* - 'Linda'	CHal
'Strawberry Fields' ♀H1	MBri
§ *warscewiczii* ♀H1	CHal LRHS WDib

Kolkwitzia (*Caprifoliaceae*)
amabilis	CBcs CPLG CSBt CTrw EBee ELan EMil EPfP GIBF LPan MGos NFor NWea SPlb SRms WCFE WDin WGwG WHCG WHar WMoo WNor WStI WTel
- 'Maradco'	CPMA EBee EPfP LRHS MAsh NPro WPat
- 'Pink Cloud' ♀H4	More than 30 suppliers

Kosteletzkya (*Malvaceae*)
virginica	EMan SPlb

Krascheninnikovia (*Chenopodiaceae*)
§ *lanata* new	XPep

Kunzea (*Myrtaceae*)
ambigua	CPLG CTrC ECou SOWG SPlb
baxteri	CTrC ECou SOWG
capitata	SOWG
ericifolia	SPlb
§ *ericoides*	CTrC ECou GGar SOWG
- 'Auckland'	ECou
- 'Bemm'	ECou
parvifolia	CPLG ECou SOWG
pomifera	ECou

L

Lablab (*Caesalpiniaceae*)
§ *purpureus*	SMur
'Ruby Moon' new	CSpe

+ *Laburnocytisus* (*Papilionaceae*)
'Adamii'	CDul CLnd COtt EBee EPfP GKir LBuc LPan LRHS MBlu MGos SMad SPer SSpi

Laburnum ✿ (*Papilionaceae*)
alpinum	CNic EPfP NWea SPlb SSpi WDin
- 'Pendulum'	CBcs CDoC CLnd ELan EPfP GKir

		LPan LRHS MAsh MBar MBri MGos MRav MWat NBee NBlu SBLw SKee SLim SPer WDin WOrn WStI
§	*anagyroides*	CDul CWib ECrN ISea NWea SBLw SEND SRms WBVN WDin
	- 'Aureum'	GKir
	vulgare	see *L. anagyroides*
	x *watereri* 'Alford's Weeping'	CBcs
I	- 'Fastigata' **new**	CBcs
	- 'Vossii' ♀H4	More than 30 suppliers

Lachenalia (Hyacinthaceae)

§	*aloides*	CStu EPot MBri WCom
	- var. *aurea* ♀H1	LRHS MSte
*	- var. *bicolor*	WCot
	- 'Nelsonii'	LRHS
	- 'Pearsonii'	LDai LRHS
	- var. *quadricolor* ♀H1	LDai LRHS WCot
§	*bulbifera* ♀H1	MBri
	contaminata ♀H1	LRHS WCot
	mutabilis	LRHS WCot
	namaquensis **new**	WCot
	neilii **new**	WCot
	orchioides var. *glaucina* **new**	WCot
	orthopetala **new**	WCot
	pendula	see *L. bulbifera*
	purpureocoerulea	WCot
	pustulata ♀H1	LRHS WCot
	reflexa	WCot
	'Rolina' **new**	ECho
	'Romelia'PBR **new**	WCot
	'Ronina' **new**	ECho
	splendida	WCot
	tricolor	see *L. aloides*
	unicolor	WCot
	unifolia	ECho
	violacea	WCot
	viridiflora ♀H1	LRHS WCot

Lactuca (Asteraceae)

alpina	see *Cicerbita alpina*
perennis	CElw CPrp EBee ECoo EMan LHop MBNS MTho SPla WCot WHer
virosa	CArn MSal

Lagarosiphon (Hydrocharitaceae)

§	*major*	CBen CDWL CRow EHon EMFW EPAt EPfP LNCo NBlu WFar WMAq

Lagarostrobos (Podocarpaceae)

§	*franklinii*	CBcs CDoC CTrG LCon LLin WPic

Lagerstroemia (Lythraceae)

indica ♀H1	EShb LPan SEND SMur SPlb WCom
- 'Rosea'	CBcs LPan SEND

Lagunaria (Malvaceae)

patersonii	CPLG WPGP XPep
- 'Royal Purple'	ERea

Lagurus (Poaceae)

ovatus ♀H3	CHrt EPza SAdn

Lamiastrum see *Lamium*

'Golden Anniversary' **new**	SSto

Lamium ✿ (Lamiaceae)

from Turkey **new**	CStu
album	CArn GWCH
- 'Aureovariegatum'	see *L. album* 'Goldflake'
- 'Brightstone Gem' (v)	WCHb
- 'Friday' (v)	CBgR EHoe EMan MTho WCHb WHer WWye
- 'Goldflake' (v)	WCHb
barbatum	EBee
§ *galeobdolon*	CArn CHEx CNat CTri CWib EWTr LGro MHar MHer MSal MWat NCot NSco SRms WBrE WWpP
- 'Hermann's Pride'	More than 30 suppliers
- 'Kirkcudbright Dwarf' **new**	EBee EWes
- subsp. *montanum* 'Canfold Wood'	WCHb WWpP
§ - - 'Florentinum'	CHal CRow CSBt EBee EChP ECha EHoe ELan EMan EPar EPfP GKir MRav NBlu NVic SHel SPer WBrk WCAu WFar WPer
§ - 'Silberteppich'	CRow ECha EFou ELan EMan EMar LRHS MRav MTho WCot
- 'Silver Angel'	EMan NSti
- Silver Carpet	see *L. galeobdolon* 'Silberteppich'
- 'Variegatum'	see *L. galeobdolon* subsp. *montanum* 'Florentinum'
garganicum	WTMC
- subsp. *garganicum*	CDes CPom EWes GBri GEil WPer WWpP
- subsp. *pictum*	see *L. garganicum* subsp. *striatum*
- subsp. *reniforme*	see *L. garganicum* subsp. *striatum*
§ - subsp. *striatum*	SBla
- - DS&T 89011T	EPPr
luteum	see *L. galeobdolon*
maculatum	CArn EGoo IHMH NArg SEND SHFr SRms WSSM
- 'Album'	EBee ELan EPfP LGro SAga SPer SRms WShp
- 'Anne Greenaway' (v)	CBgR EOMN GBri SChu SPet WBea WCAu WCHb WCot WEas WGMN MInt WWye
- 'Annecy'	MInt WWye
§ - 'Aureum'	CArn COlW EBre ECha EHoe ELan GKir IHMH LAst LGro MTho SPer SPet SUsu SWvt WBVN WCHb WEas WFar WGMN WPer
- 'Beacon Silver'	More than 30 suppliers
- 'Beedham's White'	NBir NSti WCot
- 'Brightstone Pearl'	EGoo EPPr EWes
- 'Cannon's Gold'	EBee ECha ECtt EHoe ELan ERou EWes GBuc IHMH NBlu SWvt WShp
- 'Chequers' ambig.	CBgR EBee EOMN LRHS SPer SPla WCAu WWpP
- 'Dingle Candy'	CBgR CMdw
- 'Elaine Franks'	CSam
- 'Elisabeth de Haas' (v)	CHal EWes WCHb WWpP
- 'Forncett Lustre'	CBgR EBee
- 'Gold Leaf'	see *L. maculatum* 'Aureum'
- Golden Anniversary = 'Dellam'PBR (v)	EBee ELan ERou ESis GAbr LAst LRHS MBow NArg NBro NGdn SPla WFar WShp
- 'Golden Nuggets'	see *L. maculatum* 'Aureum'
- 'Golden Wedding'	COtt
- 'Hatfield'	EBee GAbr GBuc
- 'Ickwell Beauty' (v)	EWes GBri
- 'Immaculate'	EBee
- 'James Boyd Parselle'	CBgR EGle GEil MLLN SCro WCAu WCHb WCot WRHF
- 'Margery Fish'	SRms WEas
- 'Pink Nancy'	CBot EGoo GAbr GKir MTho SWvt WFar
- 'Pink Pearls'	CHrt COlW CSBt LRHS NCiC NCot SPet WMoo
- 'Pink Pewter'	CHrt ECGP ECha ECtt EFou EHoe ELan EPla EWTr GKir IHMH LGro LRHS NChi NGdn NSti SCro SPer SPla SPlb SUsu WBrE WCHb WShp LRHS
- 'Purple Winter'	LRHS
- 'Red Nancy'	EBee EMar GCal NChi
§ - 'Roseum'	CWib EBee EFer ELan EMar EPar EPfP GKir LGro LHop MRav MWat

	MWgw NArg NFor NSti SGar SPer WCAu WGwG WPer WShp WWpP
- 'Shell Pink'	see *L. maculatum* 'Roseum'
- 'Silver Shield'	EWes
- 'Sterling Silver'	EBee WPer
- 'White Nancy' ♀H4	More than 30 suppliers
- 'Wootton Pink'	CBos GBuc GCal LRHS MBri MHer NBir NLar SSvw SWvt WBro WCra WEas
microphyllum	EHyt
orvala	More than 30 suppliers
- 'Album'	CBot CPle EBee EBre EChP ELan EMon EOrc EPPr EWTr LRHS MSte SGar SHar SIng SMrm SUsu WHer WTin
- 'Silva'	EMan WCot WSHC
sandrasicum	CPBP CStu EHyt SBla WPat
'Silberlicht'	CHEx

Lampranthus (Aizoaceae)

aberdeenensis	see *Delosperma aberdeenense*
aurantiacus	CBcs CHEx SPet
aureus	CTrC
'Bagdad'	CHEx
blandus	CBcs CHEx
§ *brownii*	CBcs CHal ECho ELan EMlt NBir SChr SEND SPet
coccineus	SPet
coralliflorus	CTrC
deltoides	see *Oscularia deltoides*
edulis	see *Carpobrotus edulis*
glaucus	SEND
haworthii	CHal
multiradiatus	CTrC SEND
oscularis	see *Oscularia deltoides*
roseus	EMlt SPet
scaber	CTrC
spectabilis	CBcs CHal CStu CWCL SAPC SArc SMur SPet WBrE
- 'Tresco Apricot'	CBcs
- 'Tresco Brilliant'	CBcs CHEx SPet
- 'Tresco Fire'	CDoC CHal
- 'Tresco Peach'	CHEx CHal CStu EMlt
- 'Tresco Red'	CBcs

Lamprothyrsus (Poaceae)
| CDPR 3096 | WPGP |

Lantana (Verbenaceae)
'Aloha' (v)	CHal SSte SWal WWol
camara	ELan EPfP MBri MOak SRms SYvo XPep
- 'Firebrand'	SYvo
- orange-flowered	SWal WWol
- pink-flowered	NPri SWal WWol
- 'Radiation'	SGar
- red-flowered	SWal WWol
- 'Snow White'	LAst MOak
- 'Sonja'	LAst
- white-flowered	SWal WWol
- yellow-flowered	NPri WWol
§ *montevidensis*	CHal MOak SPet XPep
- 'Boston Gold'	CHal
sellowiana	see *L. montevidensis*
'Spreading Sunset'	SOWG

Lapageria (Philesiaceae)
rosea ♀H3	CBcs CPLG CRHN CTCP EPfP GEil GQui IDee MDun NRib NSla SAdn SHBN WNor
- var. *albiflora*	ITim
- 'Flesh Pink'	CPLG CRHN
- 'Nash Court'	ECot EMil

Lapeirousia (Iridaceae)
cruenta	see *Anomatheca laxa*
laxa	see *Anomatheca laxa*
* *viridis*	WPGP

Lapsana (Asteraceae)
| *communis* 'Inky' | CNat |

Lardizabala (Lardizabalaceae)
| *biternata* | see *L. funaria* |
| *funaria* | CTrG |

Larix (Pinaceae)
decidua ♀H4	CAgr CBcs CCVT CDoC CDul CRWN CSBt ECrN ELan ENot EPfP EWTr GKir LCon LPan MBar NWea SHBN SPer WDin WEve WFar WHar WMou WStI
- 'Autumn Gold Weeping'	GKir
- 'Corley'	CKen LLin MBlu
- 'Croxby Broom'	CKen
- 'Globus'	NHol SLim
- 'Horstmann Recurved'	EBre NLar SCoo SLim
- 'Little Bogle'	CKen MAsh NHol
- 'Oberförster Karsten'	CKen
- 'Pendula'	CBcs GKir WEve
- 'Puli'	CEnd COtt GKir LLin MAsh MBlu NHol SCoo SLim SPer SPoG WEve
x *eurolepis*	see *L.* x *marschlinsii*
europaea Middend.	see *L. sibirica*
gmelinii	GIBF
- var. *olgensis*	NLar
- var. *principis-rupprechtii*	GIBF GTSp LCon
- 'Tharandt'	CKen
§ *kaempferi* ♀H4	CDoC CDul CLnd CSBt CTri ECrN ELan EMil ENot GKir LBuc LCon MAsh MBar NWea SLim SPer STre WDin WEve WFar WMou WNor WStI
- 'Bambino'	CKen
- 'Bingman'	CKen
- 'Blue Ball'	CKen LLin NLar WEve
- 'Blue Dwarf'	CKen COtt EBre GKir LCon LLin MAsh MGos NBlu SLim WEve WOrn
- 'Blue Haze'	CKen
- 'Blue Rabbit'	CKen CTho SKee WEve
- 'Blue Rabbit Weeping'	COtt GKir LCon LLin MGos NHol SCoo SLim WDin WEve WOrn
- 'Cruwys Morchard'	CKen
- 'Cupido'	LLin NHol
- 'Diane'	CEnd CKen EBre GKir LCon LLin LRHS MAsh MBlu MBri MGos NHol NLar SBLw SLim SPoG
- 'Elizabeth Rehder'	CKen
- 'Grant Haddow'	CKen
- 'Grey Green Dwarf'	MAsh NHol
- 'Grey Pearl'	CKen LLin NLar
- 'Hobbit'	CKen
- 'Jakobsen'	LCon
* - 'Jakobsen's Pyramid'	CEnd LLin MAsh NHol SCoo
- 'Nana'	CKen LLin MAsh NLar WWes
I - 'Nana Prostrata'	CKen
- 'Pendula'	CDul CEnd ECrN EPfP GKir LLin MAsh MBar MBlu MGos NHol SBLw SKee SPer WEve
- 'Pulii' **new**	SBLw
- 'Stiff Weeping'	GKir MAsh NLar SLim
- 'Swallow Falls'	CKen
- 'Varley'	CKen
- 'Wehlen'	CKen
- 'Wolterdingen'	CKen MBlu NLar

- 'Yanus Olieslagers'	CKen
laricina	SMad
- 'Arethusa Bog'	CKen
- 'Bear Swamp'	CKen
- 'Bingman'	CKen
- 'Hartwig Pine'	CKen
- 'Newport Beauty'	CKen
leptolepis	see *L. kaempferi*
§ x **marschlinsii**	CSBt ECrN ENot GKir NWea WMou
- 'Domino'	CKen LLin NLar
- 'Gail'	CKen
- 'Julie'	CKen
* x **pendula** 'Pendulina'	ECrN
potaninii var. *himalaica*	ISea
SF 95206	
russica	see *L. sibirica*
§ **sibirica**	ISea MBar

Larrea (Zygophyllaceae)

tridentata	CArn

Laserpitium (Apiaceae)

gallicum new	EBee
halleri new	EBee
latifolium	EBee
siler	CArn EBee MAvo NLar SIgm SMHy SPlb

Lasiagrostis see *Stipa*

Lastreopsis (Dryopteridaceae)

glabella new	CTrC

Latania (Arecaceae)

loddigesii	EAmu LPal
verschaffeltii	LPal

Lathyrus ❀ (Papilionaceae)

albus	CEnd
amphicarpos	EBee
angulatus	CTCP
§ **articulatus**	ELan WCHb
§ **aureus**	CBos CDes CHEx CHad CPom CTCP EBee EBre EMon GBuc GCal GFlt LPhx MAnH MAvo MTho NBir NChi SBla SUsu WCom WCru WEas WHal WHil WPGP WPat WSan WViv
azureus hort.	see *L. sativus*
chloranthus	WViv
cicera	CTCP
cirrhosus	CDes EBee EMon WPGP
clymenum articulatus	see *L. articulatus*
cyaneus hort.	see *L. vernus*
* - 'Alboroseus'	MTho SWat
davidii	EMon
fremontii hort.	see *L. laxiflorus*
§ **gmelinii**	NLar WSan
- 'Aureus'	see *L. aureus*
grandiflorus	CSev CStr CTCP EBee EChP EMon LPhx NLar SBla SMac SMrm SWat WCom WCot
heterophyllus	EBee EMon EWsh MNrw SHel
inconspicuus	CTCP
inermis	see *L. laxiflorus*
japonicus	WHer
- subsp. *maritimus*	EBee
laevigatus	NLar
latifolius ♀H4	More than 30 suppliers
§ - 'Albus' ♀H4	CBot EBee ECGP ELan EMan GKir LPhx MNrw SRms SSpi WBry
- 'Blushing Bride'	WCot
- deep pink	MHer NSti
- pale pink	NSti
- Pink Pearl	see *L. latifolius* 'Rosa Perle'
- 'Red Pearl'	EChP ECtt EFou ELan ERou GAbr MBri MTis NPri SMrm SPer SPlb SSvw WFar WPer WShp WViv WWeb
§ - 'Rosa Perle' ♀H4	CChe COlW CTri EBee EChP ECtt EFou EMan ERou GKir LHop MBri MSte NLar NPer NPri SBla SBra SMrm SPer SSvw WCAu WViv WWeb
I - 'Rubra'	EPfP
- Weisse Perle	see *L. latifolius* 'White Pearl'
§ - 'White Pearl' ♀H4	CBcs COlW EChP ECha EFou EMon EOrc EPfP ERou MBNS MBri MHer MSte MTis NLar NPer NPri NSti SBra SMad SPer SSvw WBro WCAu WFar WHrl WPer WShp WViv WWeb
- 'White Pearl' misapplied	see *L. latifolius* 'Albus'
§ **laxiflorus**	CTCP EBee ECoo ETow MCCP MHar MNrw MTho NLar WCom WViv WWin
linifolius	CDes NLar
- var. *montanus*	EBee WViv
luteus (L.) Peterm.	see *L. gmelinii*
- 'Aureus'	see *L. aureus*
magellanicus F&W 10225	CPBP
montanus	EBee SSpi
§ **nervosus**	CPou CSpe MTho SBla SRms
neurolobus	CNic CTCP ITer MOne
niger	CFee CPom EBee EMon LHop MAnH MLLN MSph NLar SHFr SUsu WFar WHil
nissolia	CTCP ELan
odoratus	CHar EWll
- 'Bicolor'	ELan
- 'Black Knight' **new**	MSph
- 'Blanche Ferry' **new**	MSph
- 'Cupani'	SUsu
- 'Kingsize Navy Blue' **new**	MSph
- 'Matucana'	CSpe EBee MAnH
- 'Painted Lady'	MAnH SMrm WBry
- 'Wiltshire Ripple' **new**	MSph
palustris	CTCP NLar
polyphyllus	WCot
pratensis	MBow MGol NSco
pubescens	CRHN GBuc WCot WSPU
roseus	WSHC WViv
rotundifolius ♀H4	CHad EBee ECoo EMon GCal LPhx MNrw MTho WCom WCot WFar WHoo WViv
- hybrids	LPhx
- 'Tillyperone'	EMon WWpP
§ **sativus**	CHid CSpe CTCP ELan WCHb WLFP
- var. *azureus*	see *L. sativus*
- **caeruleus**	SAga
sphaericus	CTCP WCHb
sylvestris	CAgr CNat CPLG EBee EMon MHer MLLN MNrw MSte SPet SSpi WBWf WViv
- 'Wagneri'	EBee
tingitanus	CRHN WCHb
- 'Roseus'	CRHN
transsilvanicus	WViv
tuberosus	CTCP EBee EMon MNrw SSpi WBWf WCot
'Tubro'	EMon
undulatus	SSpi
venetus	CDes MNrw WSHC
§ **vernus** ♀H4	More than 30 suppliers
- 'Alboroseus' ♀H4	More than 30 suppliers

– var. **albus**	CDes EWes WLFP
– **aurantiacus**	see *L. aureus*
– 'Caeruleus'	CBos CDes EBee EMon LHop LPhx SMrm SUsu WPGP
* – 'Cyaneus'	SAga SOkh SWat WCot WSan
– 'Flaccidus'	EBee EChP EGle EMon WCom WCot WKif WSHC WTin
* – 'Gracilis'	WViv
– 'Indigo Eyes'	WCom
– 'Rainbow'	EBre WHil
– 'Rosenelfe'	CBot CDes EMan SCro SOkh WHil WPGP WSan WViv
– f. **roseus**	ECGN ECha MRav NBir SRms WCot
– 'Spring Beauty'	WViv
– 'Spring Melody'	EBee MRav SOkh WCot WPat
– 'Subtle Hints'	EMon

Laurelia (Monimiaceae)

§ **sempervirens**	CBcs CFil CTrw WPGP
serrata	see *L. sempervirens*

Laurentia see *Isotoma*

Laurus (Lauraceae)

§ **azorica**	CBcs WFar
canariensis	see *L. azorica*
nobilis ♀H4	More than 30 suppliers
– f. **angustifolia**	CMCN CSWP EBee EPla GQui MBlu MRav NGHP SAPC SArc SDry WBcn WCHb WPGP WSel
– 'Aurea' ♀H4	CBcs CBrm CDul CMHG CSBt EBee ELan ELau EMil EPfP EPla ERea GQui LHop LRHS MAsh MBlu MBro SLim SLon SMad SPer SWvt WCHb WCot WDin WFar WJek WPat WSel
– clipped pyramid **new**	NBlu
– 'Crispa'	MRav
– 'Sunspot' (v)	WCot

Lavandula ✿ (Lamiaceae)

'Alba'	see *L. angustifolia* 'Alba', *L.* x *intermedia* 'Alba'
'Alba' ambig.	CArn CBcs CBot CSev CWib EGra MHrb SAdn SIde SPer SWat WEas WPer
§ x **allardii**	CArn CPLG CPrp CSev EBee EShb GBar MBNS MHer NGHP NLLv WBad WJek WLav WOut WSel XPep
– 'African Pride'	GBar SDow XPep
§ **angustifolia**	More than 30 suppliers
– 'Alba'	CChe EBee EDAr EHoe ELau EPfP GPoy LBuc MBNS MHer MRav MSwo NMen SLon SPlb SSto WBry WDin WFar WHHs WSel XPep
– 'Alba Nana'	see *L. angustifolia* 'Nana Alba'
– 'Arctic Snow'	CFai ENor MHrb NBPC NGHP SDnm SPer SPoG WLav WShp
– 'Ashdown Forest'	CSev EBee ELau GBar MHer NGHP SAdn SDow SIde SMrm WBad WHHs WHoo WJek WLav WSpi
– 'Beechwood Blue' ♀H4	MHrb SDow WBad WLav
– Blue Cushion = 'Lavandula Schola'PBR	EBre ENot EPfP GKir MAsh MBNS NPri SDow WLav
– 'Blue Ice' **new**	SDow
– 'Blue Mountain'	GBar MHer MHrb SDow
– 'Blue Mountain White'	SDow
§ – 'Bowles' Early'	CSam GBar NGHP SAdn SDow WBad WHHs WLav XPep
– 'Bowles' Grey'	see *L. angustifolia* 'Bowles' Early'
– 'Bowles' Variety'	see *L. angustifolia* 'Bowles' Early'
– 'Buena Vista' **new**	SDow

– 'Cedar Blue'	CSev EGoo ELau GBar MHer NBur NGHP SDow SHDw SIde SMrm SPla WBad WBar WFar WHHs WLav
– 'Compacta'	MHrb WBad
– 'Dwarf Blue'	WBad WFar WShp XPep
I – 'Eastgrove Nana'	WEas
* – 'Erbalunga' **new**	XPep
– 'Folgate'	CArn CBcs CWCL ELau GBar LAst MHer MHrb NBur NGHP NHHG SDow SIde WBad WFar WHoo WLav WMnd WSel WTel XPep
– 'Fring Favourite'	SDow
§ – 'Hidcote' ♀H4	More than 30 suppliers
– 'Hidcote Pink'	CArn CWib EDAr GBar MHer MRav MWat NFor SDow SPer WBad WFar WHHs WHen WHrl WKif WMnd WPer WSel XPep
– 'Hidcote Superior'	EWTr LPVe WShp WWeb
– 'Imperial Gem' ♀H4	More than 30 suppliers
§ – 'Jean Davis'	EBee GBar MAsh MHrb NGHP NHHG NPri SAdn SIde WBad WFar WHHs WLav WSel
– 'Lady'	CBrm NOrc SEND SHDw WBad
– 'Lady Anne'	ENor WBad WLav
N – 'Lavender Lady'	ELau NPer SAdn SSto SWal WPer
– 'Lavenite Petite'	ENor EPfP LRHS LTwo MAsh MHrb NCGa SDow WLav WShp WWeb
– Little Lady = 'Batlad'PBR	ENor MAsh MHer MHrb NLLv SSto SVil WBad WLav WShp
– Little Lottie = 'Clarmo' ♀H4	EBee ECGP EMil ENot EPfP LRHS MAvo MHer MHrb SCoo SDow SIde SLim SPer SSto SWvt WBad WLav WShp
– 'Loddon Blue' ♀H4	CBcs ELau GBar NHHG SAdn SDow SIde WBad WHoo WLav
§ – 'Loddon Pink' ♀H4	CSLe EBee ENot EPfP ERea GBar GKir LRHS MAsh MRav NGHP NPri SAdn SDow SSto WBad WEas WFar WHHs WHoo WLav WPGP
* – 'Lumière des Alpes' **new**	XPep
– 'Maillette'	MHrb SDow SIde WHHs XPep
* – 'Matheronne' **new**	XPep
– 'Mellisa Lilac' **new**	SDow
– 'Miss Donnington'	see *L. angustifolia* 'Bowles' Early'
– 'Miss Katherine'PBR ♀H4	CSBt ELan ENor EPfP LRHS MAsh MHrb NBPC NCGa NGHP SDow SPoG SVil WBad WLav WShp
– Miss Muffet = 'Scholmis' ♀H4	EBee EMil ENor LTwo MHrb NLLv SDow SPer WBad WLav WShp
– 'Munstead'	More than 30 suppliers
§ – 'Nana Alba' ♀H4	More than 30 suppliers
– 'Nana Atropurpurea'	SDow WBad WSel
– 'Nana Rosea'	ITim
– No. 9	MHrb SDow
– 'Peter Pan'	MHrb MLan SDow WLav WShp
– 'Princess Blue'	CSBt CWCL EBee ELan ELau ENor ENot GBar LRHS MAsh MBNS NPri SAga SDow SIde SSto WBad WFar WLav WPer WShp WWeb WWpP XPep
* – 'Rêve de Jean-Claude' **new**	XPep
§ – 'Rosea'	More than 30 suppliers
– 'Royal Purple'	CArn CBcs CSLe EBee ELau ENor EWes GBar LRHS MAsh MBNS MHer NGHP NHHG NPri SAdn SDow SIde SMur SSto SWvt WBad WLav WSSM WShp WWpP XPep
N – 'Twickel Purple'	CSBt CWCL CWSG EBee ENot EPfP GKir LHop LRHS MAsh MHer MRav NGHP NHHG NPri SDix SIde SPer SPla SWvt WBad WCom WFar WHHs WLav WSel XPep
aristibractea	MHer WLav

'Avonview'	CBcs GBar MHer MHrb NGHP SDow WLav
'Ballerina' **new**	SDow
'Blue River' PBR	WLav
'Blue Star'	MAvo NBlu NGHP WHHs
'Bowers Beauty'	WBad WLav
buchii var. *buchii*	SDow XPep
- var. *gracilis*	SDow
N 'Cambridge Lady'	WLav
canariensis	CSev ERea MHer MHrb NHHG SDow SHDw WBad WCHb WJek WLav XPep
X *christiana*	CWCL EBee ELau GBar MAsh MHer MHrb NGHP SDow SHDw WBad WJek WLav WShp WWpP XPep
'Cornard Blue'	see *L.* 'Sawyers'
dentata	CArn CPrp CSev CWCL EBee ELau ERea GBar MHer NGHP NHHG SAdn SDry WBad WHHs WHer WPat WPic WWpP WWye XPep
§ - var. *candicans*	CSev CSpe EBee ELau GBar LHop MHer MHrb NHHG NLLv SDow SMrm WBad WCHb WLav WWye XPep
- 'Dusky Maiden'	CWCL MHrb SDow WLav
- 'Linda Ligon' (v)	EBee EOHP ESis GBar MHrb SDow WBad WHHs WJek WLav XPep
- 'Ploughman's Blue'	CWCL MHrb SDow WBad
- 'Pure Harmony' **new**	SDow
- f. *rosea* **new**	SDow
- 'Royal Crown' ♀H2-3	GBar MHer SDow WBad WFar WLav XPep
- 'Royal Standard'	SHBN
- silver	see *L. dentata* var. *candicans*
- 'Silver Queen'	WLav
'Devantville Cuche'	ELau MHrb WJek WLav XPep
I 'Edelweiss'	EBee NBur NGHP NLLv SVil WLav
'Fathead'	CElw COtt CSBt CWCL EBee EBre ELan ENor EPfP EWTr GBar LAst LRHS MAsh MHer MHrb MLan NBPC NGHP SAdn SDow SLim SMrm WBad WBrE WHHs WJek WWpP
'Fragrant Memories'	CSLe EBee ELau ERea GBar MAsh MHrb NPri SDow SIde WBad WLav
Goldburg = 'Burgoldeen' (v)	CSBt EBre ELan ENot EPfP LAst MAsh MBNS MBri MCCP MGos MHer MTis NBur NGHP NLLv NPri SCoo SDnm SLim SPer SPla SSto WBad WLav WShp WWeb
'Goodwin Creek Grey'	CWCL GBar MAsh MHrb NLLv SDow WBad WHHs WLav XPep
'Gorgeous' **new**	SDow
I 'Hazel' **new**	WLav
'Helmsdale' PBR	More than 30 suppliers
heterophylla hort.	see *L.* x *allardii*
'Hidcote Blue'	see *L. angustifolia* 'Hidcote'
§ x *intermedia*	SPla
- 'Abrialii'	NLLv SDow WLav XPep
- 'Alba' ♀H4	CPrp GBar NHHG SDow SGar WBad XPep
N - 'Arabian Night' ♀H4	COtt ELau SDow WBad WHHs WLav WPat WWeb XPep
- 'Badsey Blue' **new**	WBad
- 'Bogong'	WLav
- 'Chaix'	GBar
§ - Dutch Group	CArn CWCL EDAr ENot EPfP EWTr GBar GKir MAsh MBar MBri MRav MSwo SCoo SDow SGar SLim SPer SWat WBad WCom WHHs WHen WJek WPer WSel WShp XPep
§ - - Walberton's Silver Edge = 'Walvera' (v)	CWCL EBre ENor ESis LRHS MAsh MGos SCoo SDow SIde
* - 'Futura' **new**	XPep
- 'Grappenhall'	CArn CEnd CPrp CSBt CSLe CSam CTri CWSG EBee ELau EMil GBar GKir MHer MRav MWgw NGHP NVic SDow SMrm SPer WBad WFar WMnd WPer WPnn WSel XPep
- 'Grey Hedge'	CSLe WBad WHHs WLav
- 'Gros Bleu' **new**	SDow
- 'Grosso'	CChe COkL COtt CSLe CSam CSev CTri EBee ELau EPfP GBar MHer MHrb MRav NBPC NGHP SAdn SDow SMrm SSto SSvw SWvt WBad WDin WFar WJek WSSM WSel WShp XPep
- 'Hidcote Giant' ♀H4	CSLe EBee GBar LRHS MHrb NPer SDow WBad WKif WLav WSel WShp XPep
* - 'Hidcote White'	MHer NLLv WBad WLav XPep
- 'Impress Purple'	GBar SDow WLav XPep
* - 'Jaubert' **new**	XPep
* - 'Julien' **new**	XPep
- 'Lullingstone Castle'	CBod CPrp CSLe ELau GBar LHop SDow WBad WHHs WJek WLav WSPU
- 'Old English'	CSLe MHrb SDow WCFE
- Old English Group	CArn CBod ECGP ELau MBow WBad WHoo WJek WLav WSel
- 'Seal'	CArn CPrp CSLe ELau GBar MBow MHer MHrb NGHP NHHG SDow SMrm WBad WHCG WHHs WMnd WPer WSel XPep
* - 'Sumian' **new**	XPep
* - 'Super'	XPep
- 'Sussex'	GBar MHrb SDow WLav
N - 'Twickel Purple'	CArn CMHG CSev CWib ECGP ELau ENot EWes NHHG SMrm SWat WHoo WJek WMnd
'Jean Davis'	see *L. angustifolia* 'Jean Davis'
lanata ♀H3	CArn CBot ECha EOHP GBar GPoy MBro MHer MWat NHHG NWCA SDow SDry SHFr WBad WEas WLav WWye XPep
lanata x *angustifolia*	GBar NHHG WBad
§ *latifolia*	CArn LPVe SDow WBad WSSM XPep
'Loddon Pink'	see *L. angustifolia* 'Loddon Pink'
mairei **new**	XPep
mairei x *intermedia*	WBad
'Marshwood' PBR	CBri CSLe CTri EBee ENot EPfP LBuc LRHS MAsh MHer MHrb MRav SCoo SDow SIde SLim SPer SPla WBad WSpi
'Midnight' **new**	WSpi
minutolii	MHer MHrb SDow WBad XPep
multifida	CArn CSev EHol ERea MHer NLLv SDow WBad WBry WCHb WHer WLav XPep
- 'Blue Wonder'	NGHP WBad
* - 'Tizi-n-Test' **new**	XPep
officinalis	see *L. angustifolia*
§ *pinnata*	CArn CSev CWCL EBee GBar MHer MHrb NHHG NPri SDow SDry SRob WBad WCHb WEas WHHs XPep
'Pippa White' **new**	NLLv
pterostoechas pinnata	see *L. pinnata*
pubescens	SDow XPep
'Quicksilver' **new**	SPoG
'Regal Splendour'	CWCL ELan ENor EPfP MAsh MBri MHrb NCGa NGHP NLLv NPri SDow WLav

'Richard Gray' ♀H3-4	CCge CSLe EBee ECGP EMon GBar LRHS MAsh MHer NCGa NGHP NPri SDnm SDow SSvw SVil WAbe WBad WBcn WHen WLav WMnd XPep
'Rosea'	see *L. angustifolia* 'Rosea'
rotundifolia	EBee MHer SDow XPep
'Roxlea Park'	EBee ENor MHrb SVil WLav
'Saint Brelade'	EBee EPfP GBar MAsh MHrb NGHP NLLv SDow WBad WLav
§ 'Sawyers' ♀H4	More than 30 suppliers
'Silver Edge'	see *L. x intermedia* (Dutch Group) Walberton's Silver Edge = 'Walvera'
'Silver Frost' **new**	XPep
N *spica*	see *L. angustifolia*, *L. latifolia*, *L. x intermedia*
- 'Hidcote Purple'	see *L. angustifolia* 'Hidcote'
stoechas ♀H3-4	More than 30 suppliers
- var. *albiflora*	see *L. stoechas* f. *leucantha*
- 'Aphrodite'	LRHS MAsh SDow WLav
- subsp. *atlantica*	SDow WBad
- 'Avenue Bellevue' **new**	ITim
- 'Badsey Starlite' **new**	WBad
- subsp. *cariensis*	SDow
- dark	WBad
- 'Devonshire'	CSBt CWCL MHer WBad WHHs WJek
- 'Evelyn Cadzow'	WBry
- 'Kew Red'	More than 30 suppliers
§ - f. *leucantha*	CArn CBot CMHG CSBt CSev CWib ECha ELan ELau EPfP GBar LAst MBri MSwo NWoo SChu SDow SPla WAbe WBad WCHb WEas WFar
- 'Lilac Wings' **new**	LRHS
- subsp. *luisieri*	GBar SDow WBri WOut
- subsp. *lusitanica*	MHer WBad WLav
- 'Madrid' **new**	CWCL
- 'Madrid Blue' **new**	WLav
- 'Madrid Purple' **new**	WLav
- 'Madrid White' **new**	CWCL NGHP WLav
- 'Papillon'	see *L. stoechas* subsp. *pedunculata*
§ - subsp. *pedunculata* ♀H3-4	More than 30 suppliers
- - dark-flowered **new**	WLav
- - 'James Compton'	CWib EBee ECha LRHS MAsh SLim WBad WLav WTel
- - 'Purple Ribbon' **new**	WLav
- 'Pippa'	WBad
- 'Pukehou'	ENor EPfP LRHS MAsh MHrb NBPC SDow WBad WLav WPat
- 'Rocky Red'	CBcs
- 'Rocky Road'	ENor LBuc LRHS MHrb NGHP SPer WLav WShp WWeb
* - var. *rosea* **new**	NChi
- subsp. *sampaioana*	SDow WBad WLav
- - 'Purple Emperor' **new**	WLav
- 'Snowman'	CSBt EBee ENor EPPr EPfP LAst LRHS MBNS MHer MHrb MSPs MTPN MWat NPri SAdn SDow SLim SPer SSto SVil SWvt WBad WFar WHHs WShp WWeb
- subsp. *stoechas*	CSLe WShp
- - 'Liberty'	ENor LRHS MHrb NGHP SDow
- 'Sugar Plum'	WBad WLav
- 'Summerset Mist'	WBad MHrb WLav
- 'Willow Vale' ♀H3-4	More than 30 suppliers
- 'Willowbridge Calico'	NGHP NPro WLav
* - 'Wine Red'	WBad WBcn WHHs WKif WLav
subnuda	WBad
'Tickled Pink'	CWCL ELan ENor MAsh MBri MHrb NGHP SDnm WLav
'Van Gogh' **new**	SDow
vera hort.	see *L. x intermedia* Dutch Group
vera DC.	see *L. angustifolia*
viridis	CArn CPla CSev EBee EGoo ELan ELau EPfP GBar LRHS MHer MSwo MWgw NChi NGHP NHHG NLLv NPer SDow SGar SPer SPla WBad WCHb WHHs WHer WKif WWye XPep
'Willy's Purple' **new**	CWCL

Lavatera (Malvaceae)

arborea	SChr WHer
- 'Rosea'	see *L. x clementii* 'Rosea'
- 'Variegata' (v)	CBcs ELan EMan NPer NSti SBod SDix SEND WCHb WCot WEas WHer WHil
assurgentiflora	CPLG EPfP
bicolor	see *L. maritima*
cachemiriana	GBuc GCal MWgw NBur NPer NSti WPer
x *clementii* 'Baby Barnsley' **new**	LRHS NPri
- 'Barnsley'	More than 30 suppliers
- 'Blushing Bride'	CDoC CDul EPfP LRHS MBri NLar NPri SBod SDix SMrm SPer SPla WBcn WHar
- 'Bredon Springs' ♀H3-4	CDoC CWSG EBee ECha ECtt EMil ENot EPfP GBri GKir LHop LRHS MAsh MBri MNrw MRav MSwo SBod SLim SMer SMrm SPer SPla SWvt WFar WStI WWeb
- 'Burgundy Wine' ♀H3-4	More than 30 suppliers
- 'Candy Floss' ♀H3-4	EBee EPfP LRHS MBNS MBar MGos NPer SAdn SMrm WDin WStI
- 'Eye Catcher'	CFai GKir LRHS MBNS MSwo NLar
- 'Kew Rose'	CDoC CTri EBee EMil EPfP LRHS MSwo NPer SLim SPla WGwG WWeb
- 'Lavender Lady'	EBee ECtt GKir NCot
- 'Lilac Lady'	CElw CFai CFwr ECha ELan LRHS MBNS MCCP NBPC NCGa NLar SPer WFar WWeb
- 'Lisanne'	EBee EOrc GEil LRHS MCCP MNrw MSwo NPri SMrm
- 'Mary Hope'	CFai LRHS MAsh
- Memories = 'Stelav'PBR	CFai CHid EBee ELan ENor ENot EPfP LRHS MAsh MLan NBlu NLar NPer NPri NPro SLim
- 'Pavlova'	CDoC EBee EPfP LRHS SMrm
- 'Poynton Lady'	MGos
- 'Rosea' ♀H3-4	More than 30 suppliers
- 'Shorty'	WFar
- 'Wembdon Variegated' (v)	NPer
'Linda'	WBcn
§ *maritima* ♀H2-3	CBot CDoC CHrt CMHG CRHN EBee ECtt ELan EPfP LHop NCot NPri SDry SHBN SPer SUsu SWvt WCFE WEas WFar WHCG WKif XPep
- *bicolor*	see *L. maritima*
- 'Princesse de Lignes' **new**	MBri XPep
mauritanica **new**	CTCP
'Moody Blue' **new**	WWeb
oblongifolia	CBot
N *olbia*	CTri GKir LAst MTis MWat SPlb SRms XPep
- 'Pink Frills'	CBot EBee LHop LRHS MBar MNrw MRav NPri SDry SHBN SMrm SPla WCot WStI
'Peppermint Ice'	see *L. thuringiaca* 'Ice Cool'

'Pink Frills'   see *L. olbia* 'Pink Frills'
plebeia   EBee EChP
'Rosea'   see *L.* x *clementii* 'Rosea'
'Shadyvale Star'   NPro
'Summer Kisses'^PBR **new**   MBri NCGa
'Sweet Dreams'^PBR   LRHS MBri
tauricensis   EMan NLar
N *thuringiaca*   MWhi NPri WFar
§ – 'Ice Cool'   CBot CElw ECha ECtt GCal LRHS
                          MAsh MBar MGos NBee NPer SBla
                          SMrm SPer WCot WFar WShp
                          WWeb
'White Angel'^PBR   LRHS WShp
'White Satin'^PBR   CFai MBri NCGa NPri SSvw

Lawsonia (Lythraceae)
inermis   MSal

Ledebouria (Hyacinthaceae)
adlamii   see *L. cooperi*
§ *cooperi*   CDes CHal CStu EBla EHyt ELan
                          EMan ERos GCal ITim NCGa SRot
                          WPGP WPrP
§ *socialis*   CHEx CHal CSWP CSev CSpe CStu
                          EPem ERos EShb MBro
violacea   see *L. socialis*

x *Ledodendron* (Ericaceae)
§ 'Arctic Tern' ♀^H4   CDoC CSBt GGGa GKev GKir LMil
                          LRHS MAsh MBar MDun MGos
                          MLea NHol NWCA SLdr SReu
                          WBrE WPic

Ledum (Ericaceae)
§ x *columbianum*   GGGa NLar
groenlandicum   GEil GGGa MBar MLea SPer WAbe
                          WDin WFar WGer WSHC
– 'Compactum'   MAsh NLar WFar
macrophyllum   CFir
palustre   GGGa GPoy NLar
– subsp. *decumbens*   GCrs GGGa SOkd

Leea (Leeaceae)
coccinea   see *L. guineensis*
§ *guineensis*   MBri

Leersia (Poaceae)
oryzoides   EBee

Legousia (Campanulaceae)
'Devon Sky'   EMan

Leibnitzia (Asteraceae)
anandria   EBee NWCA
nepalensis   EBee
pusilla   EBee

Leiophyllum (Ericaceae)
buxifolium ♀^H4   EPfP GCrs GKir ITim LRHS MBro
                          NHol SSpi WPat

Lembotropis see *Cytisus*

Lemna (Lemnaceae)
gibba   CWat LPBA NPer
minor   CWat EHon EMFW LPBA MSta
                          NPer SWat
polyrhiza   see *Spirodela polyrhiza*
trisulca   CWat EHon EMFW LPBA MSta
                          NPer SWat

lemon balm see *Melissa officinalis*

lemon grass see *Cymbopogon citratus*

lemon see *Citrus limon*

lemon verbena see *Aloysia triphylla*

Leonotis (Lamiaceae)
leonitis   see *L. ocymifolia*
leonurus   CHEx CHll CTCP CTbh CTrC
                          GGar MAnH MGol SMad
– var. *albiflora*   EShb LRav
nepetifolia   EMan MGol
§ *ocymifolia*   CFee CPLG NSti WWye
– var. *ocymifolia*   EMan GGar WCot
– var. *raineriana*   CHll
'Staircase'   SDnm WRos

Leontice (Berberidaceae)
albertii   see *Gymnospermium albertii*

Leontodon (Asteraceae)
crispus asper MESE 307 EBee
hispidus   MGas NMir
§ *rigens*   EMan GBri GBuc GFlt GKir ITer
                          MFOX NBid NSti SBri SDix SGar
                          SMad SMrm WFar WMoo WPrP
– 'Girandole'   CMCo EBee LIck MNrw WRos

Leontopodium (Asteraceae)
alpinum   CTri CWib EBre GAbr GKir GTou
                          IHMH LRHS NBlu NFor NJOw
                          NMen SIng SPlb SRms WMoo WPer
                          WShp WWin
– 'Mignon'   CMea EWes GTou NMen WAbe
                          WHoo
– subsp. *nivale*   WPat
coreanum   GKev
§ *discolor*   WAbe
himalayanum   WLin
monocephalum **new**   WLin
§ *ochroleucum*   MDKP NLar NSla WPer
   var. *campestre*
palibinianum   see *L. ochroleucum* var. *campestre*

Leonurus (Lamiaceae)
artemisia   see *L. japonicus*
cardiaca   CAgr CArn EBee EGoo EMan
                          EMon GBar GPoy MHer MSal
                          SECG SIde WBri WHbs WHer
                          WMoo WSel WWye
– 'Crispa'   EMon
– subsp. *villosus*   EBee
§ *japonicus*   CTCP MSal
macranthus   EFEx
– var. *alba*   EFEx
sibiricus L.   MGol MSal WMoo

Leopoldia (Hyacinthaceae)
comosa   see *Muscari comosum*
spreitzenhoferi   see *Muscari spreitzenhoferi*
tenuiflora   see *Muscari tenuiflorum*

Lepechinia (Lamiaceae)
§ *chamaedryoides*   CHll CPLG CSpe WOut
floribunda   CPle CSev
hastata   CBrd XPep
salviae   CTCP EBee EMan
                          WCot

Lepidium (Brassicaceae)
campestre   CArn
nanum   EHyt
peruvianum **new**   MSal
ruderale   MSal
virginicum   MSal

Lepidothamnus (Podocarpaceae)
§ *laxifolius* CMHG

Lepidozamia (Zamiaceae)
hopei LPal NRog
peroffskyana CBrP CRoM LPal NRog

Leptinella (Asteraceae)
§ *albida* CStu GCrs LGro
* *alpina* **new** LGro
§ *atrata* IHMH
  - subsp. *luteola* NWCA SChu SDys
  'County Park' **new** ECou
§ *dendyi* ECou EDAr EWes GGar LBee MHer
    NLAp NMen WMAq
dioica **new** CTrC
filicula ECou
hispida see *Cotula hispida*
§ *minor* ECou MOne WMoo
pectinata var. *sericea* see *L. albida*
  - subsp. *villosa* CC 475 NWCA
§ *potentillina* CTri EBee ECha EHoe ESis MBNS
    MWgw NJOw NRya SChu SIng
    SRms WCru WPer WRHF WShp
    WWin
§ *pusilla* SDys
§ *pyrethrifolia* EBee GKev NMen SIng
  - 'Macabe' **new** ECou
§ *rotundata* ECou WPer
§ *serrulata* MBar WCru
§ *squalida* CNic ECha ESis GGar IHMH MBar
    NRya NSti STre WPer WRHF WShp
§ 'Platt's Black' EBee EBre ECGP EDAr EMan EWes
    GCrs GEdr GGar LRHS NSti SDys
    SIng WBea WHoo WMoo WPer
    WPrP WRHF
traillii GGar

Leptocarpus (Restionaceae)
similis **new** CTrC

Leptodactylon (Polemoniaceae)
§ *californicum* CPBP NPol
  - subsp. *californicum* CPBP
    new

Leptospermum ✿ (Myrtaceae)
citratum see *L. petersonii*
* *compactum* CPLG
'Confetti' ECou
'County Park Blush' ECou
cunninghamii see *L. myrtifolium*
ericoides see *Kunzea ericoides*
flavescens misapplied see *L. glaucescens*
flavescens Sm. see *L. polygalifolium*
§ *glaucescens* CMHG ECou GGar
§ *grandiflorum* CFil CTrG ELan EPfP GGar ISea
    LRHS SOWG SSpi WSHC
grandifolium **new** ECou
  - 'Silver Sheen' see *L.* 'Silver Sheen'
'Green Eyes' (*minutifolium* ECou
  x *scoparium*)
'Havering Hardy' ECou
humifusum see *L. rupestre*
juniperinum SPlb
laevigatum 'Yarrum' ECou
§ *lanigerum* CMHG CMac CTrC CTri ECou EPfP
    GGar SLim SOWG WAbe WBVN
  - 'Cunninghamii' see *L. myrtifolium*
  - 'Silver Sheen' see *L.* 'Silver Sheen'
  - 'Wellington' ECou
macrocarpum SOWG
micromyrtus **new** NVne

minutifolium ECou
morrisonii **new** ECou
§ *myrtifolium* CTri ECou EPla EWes GGar SDry
    SOWG SPer SSta WPat WPic
  - 'Newnes Forest' ECou
  - 'Silver Sheen' see *L.* 'Silver Sheen'
myrtifolium ECou
  x *scoparium*
nitidum CTrC ECou GGar SOWG SPlb
  - 'Cradle' ECou
obovatum CMHG
§ *petersonii* CArn ECou EOHP MHer SOWG
  - 'Chlorinda' **new** ECou
phylicoides see *Kunzea ericoides*
'Pink Surprise' ECou SOWG
  (*minutifolium*
  x *scoparium*)
§ *polygalifolium* CTrC ECou GGar SPlb SRms
prostratum see *L. rupestre*
pubescens see *L. lanigerum*
'Red Cascade' MGos SWvt
rodwayanum see *L. grandiflorum*
rotundifolium CTrC ECou
§ *rupestre* ♀H4 CDoC CPne CTri ECou EPot GGar
    GTou MBar MGos SDry SPlb SRms
    WFar WSHC
rupestre x *scoparium* ECou
scoparium CArn CTrC ECou ELau ERom SPlb
    WDin
  - 'Adrianne' ELan MAsh
  - 'Autumn Glory' CSBt CWSG EBee EHoe SLim
  - 'Avocet' ECou
  - 'Black Robin' LRHS SOWG
  - 'Blossom' (d) CBcs ECou SOWG WGer
  - 'Boscawenii' SHGC
  - 'Burgundy Queen' (d) CBcs CSBt ECou
  - 'Chapmanii' CMHG CPen CTrG EBee GGar
  - 'Coral Candy' CBcs SOWG
  - 'County Park Pink' ECou
  - 'County Park Red' ECou
  - 'Crimson Glory' (d) **new** CBrm
  - 'Elizabeth Jane' GGar GQui
  - 'Essex' ECou
  - 'Fred's Red' NLAp WPat
  - 'Gaiety Girl' (d) CBrm CSBt
  - 'Grandiflorum' WGer
  - var. *incanum* ECou MGos SOWG
    'Keatleyi' ♀H3
  - - 'Wairere' ECou
  - 'Jubilee' (d) CBcs CSBt ISea
  - 'Kerry' MAsh
  - 'Leonard Wilson' (d) CTri ECou EWes
  - 'Lyndon' ECou
  - 'Martini' CDoC CSBt CTrG LRHS MGos
    SOWG WCot WWeb
  - 'McLean' ECou
  - (Nanum Group) 'Huia' CBcs ENot WOBN
  - 'Kea' CSBt ECou GQui MGos WGer
  - - 'Kiwi' ♀H3 CBcs CBrm CDoC CDul CSBt
    CTbh CTrC EBee ECou ELan ENot
    EPfP EWes GQui ISea LRHS MAsh
    MDun MGos SLim SPla WFar WGer
    WPat WWeb
  - - 'Kompakt' EPot
  - - 'Nanum' ECou EPot NJOw NMen SBod
    SHBN SIng
  - - 'Pipit' EPot EWes ITim WAbe
  - - 'Tui' CSBt CTrC
  - 'Nichollsii' ♀H3 CTrC CTri GQui SOWG WHar
    WSHC
  - 'Nichollsii CDoC CMea EPot ITim NLAp NSla
    Nanum' ♀H2-3 SIng SRms WAbe WPat
  - 'Pink Cascade' CBcs CSBt CTri IMGH SLim
  - 'Pink Damask' SWvt

- 'Pink Frills' **new** — ECou
- 'Pink Pearl' (d) — SAga
- 'Pink Splash' — ECou
- var. **prostratum** hort. — see *L. rupestre*
- 'Red Damask' (d) ♀H3 — More than 30 suppliers
- 'Red Falls' — CDoC CPLG ECou SOWG
- 'Redpoll' — ECou
- 'Roseum' — MTPN WBrE
- 'Rosy Morn' — ISea
- 'Ruby Glow' (d) — CTri LRHS
* - 'Ruby Wedding' — ELan LRHS SPla
- var. **scoparium** — GGar
* - 'Silver Spire' — SOWG
- 'Snow Flurry' — CBcs CTbh CTrC EBee SLim SSte
- 'Sunraysia' — CSBt CTrw
- 'Winter Cheer' — CBcs WWeb
- 'Wiri Joan' (d) — MGos
- 'Zeehan' — ECou
sericeum — SOWG
§ 'Silver Sheen' ♀H3 — CEnd EBee ECou ELan EPfP LRHS SLon SPoG WGer WPGP
'Snow Column' **new** — ECou
spectabile — SOWG
sphaerocarpum — ECou
squarrosum — CTrC
'Wellington Dwarf' — ECou

Leschenaultia (Goodeniaceae)

'Angels Kiss' **new** — ECou
biloba — ECou
- 'Big Blue' — SOWG
- 'Sky Blue' **new** — ECou
'Blue Moon' **new** — ECou
'Carnival' **new** — ECou
* 'Eldorado' — SOWG
formosa red — ECou
- 'Scarlett O'Hara' — SOWG
- yellow — ECou
hirsuta — SOWG
pink — ECou
'Prima' **new** — ECou

Lespedeza (Papilionaceae)

bicolor — CAgr CBcs EDif LAst MGol SEND WDin WFar WHCG
- 'Yakushima' **new** — NLar
buergeri — NLar SMur WSHC
capitata — MSal SUsu
japonica **new** — CPLG
thunbergii ♀H4 — CBcs CDul EBee EChP ELan EMil EPfP IDee IMGH LRHS MAsh MBlu NBPC NBlu SHGC SLon SOWG SOkh SPer SSpi SSta WDin WFar WHCG WSHC
- 'Summer Beauty' — EPfP MGos
* - 'Variegata' (v) — LRHS
- 'White Fountain' **new** — WBcn
tiliifolia — see *Desmodium elegans*
virginica — EBee

Lesquerella (Brassicaceae)

arctica var. **purshii** — WPat

Leucadendron (Proteaceae)

argenteum — CDoC CHEx CTrC SIgm
'Bell's Supreme' — CTrC
daphnoides — SPlb
discolor — CTrC
eucalyptifolium — CTrC SPlb
galpinii — CTrC
'Inca Gold' **new** — CTrC
laureolum — CTrC
'Maui Sunset' — CTrC
'Mrs Stanley' **new** — CTrC

pubescens **new** — CTrC
'Safari Sunset' — CAbb CBcs CTrC IDee WGer
salicifolium — CTrC IDee
salignum — CTrC
- 'Early Yellow' — CTrC
- 'Fireglow' — CAbb CDoC CTrC
strobilinum — CDoC CTrC
tinctum — CTrC
uliginosum — CTrC

Leucanthemella (Asteraceae)

§ *serotina* ♀H4 — More than 30 suppliers

Leucanthemopsis (Asteraceae)

§ *alpina* — LRHS
hosmariensis — see *Rhodanthemum hosmariense*
§ *pectinata* — LBee NSla
radicans — see *L. pectinata*

Leucanthemum ✿ (Asteraceae)

* *angustifolium* — CHar
var. *album* **new**
atlanticum — see *Rhodanthemum atlanticum*
catananche — see *Rhodanthemum catananche*
'Fringe Benefit' — EMon
graminifolium **new** — WPer
hosmariense — see *Rhodanthemum hosmariense*
mawii — see *Rhodanthemum gayanum*
maximum hort. — see *L.* × *superbum*
§ *maximum* (Ramond) DC. — NBro NPer WBea
* - *nanus* **new** — WWeb
- *uliginosum* — see *Leucanthemella serotina*
nipponicum — see *Nipponanthemum nipponicum*
§ × *superbum* — CWCL EHol EWsh MBow MHer MNrw MGgw NSti NVic SMac WFar
- 'Aglaia' (d) ♀H4 — More than 30 suppliers
- 'Alaska' — EBee EBla EFou LAst LRHS NGdn NLRH NOak NPri SPer SWal SWvt WBor WPer WWpP
- 'Amelia' — EBee NLar
- 'Anita Allen' (d) — CElw CFee CPou EFou MAvo MSPs WCot WFar WPer WWpP
- 'Antwerp Star' — NLar WBrk WWpP
- 'Barbara Bush' (v/d) — CFai EBee EChP ECtt EGle EMan ERou MBNS MBnl MCLN MLLN MSph MTis NBir SPla SPoG SWvt WCot
- 'Beauté Nivelloise' — EBee MAvo SUsu WCot WFar WPer WRHF WRha WSpi
- 'Becky' — CElw EBee EChP ECha EPfP MBNS NPro WHil
- 'Bishopstone' — CBos ELan EMan ERou SChu WEas WPer
- 'Christine Hagemann' — CFwr CPlt EBee EFou LRHS MAvo MBri MDKP MRav WHoo WWpP
- 'Cobham Gold' (d) — CElw CStr EBee ECtt EMan ERea NFla NOrc SOkh WWpP
- 'Coconut Ice' — WPer
I - 'Crazy Daisy' — CM&M CTri ECGP GFlt NLar WWpP
- 'Droitwich Beauty' — EBee MAvo MBct MNrw WHoo WSPU WTel
- 'Duchess of Abercorn' — CStr
- 'Edgebrook Giant' **new** — MAvo
- 'Eisstern' **new** — MAvo
- 'Esther Read' (d) — CElw CHar CM&M CPrp EBee ECtt EGle EHol ELan EMan ERea ERou LAst MAvo MBri MFir NChi NFla NPri SHel SRms STes SWat SWvt WCot WFar WViv WWol
- 'Etoile d'Anvers' **new** — CFwr XPep
- 'Everest' — NOak SHar SRms

- 'Fiona Coghill' (d)   CElw CHar CHea CMil CStr EBee
ECGP ECtt EGle GBri IBlr MAvo
MBnl MDKP MFir MHer MLLN NBrk
NChi NPri WBro WCot WHil WHoo
- 'Firnglanz' **new**   CFwr GBin
- 'Grupenstolz' **new**   GBin
- 'H. Seibert'   CElw CMil EBla
- 'Highland White   WFar WWeb
Dream'PBR
- 'Horace Read' (d)   CElw CHar CHea CMdw CMea
CMil EBee ELan ERea MGas NBir
SAga WEas WPer
- 'Jennifer Read'   ERea WCot
- 'John Murray'   NBir WAbb
- 'Little Miss Muffet'   LRHS MBri NPro
- 'Little Princess'   see *L.* x *superbum*
'Silberprinzesschen'
- 'Manhattan'   CFwr CMdw EBee EBre EFou
EWes GBuc LRHS MBri MTed
- 'Margaretchen' **new**   MAvo
- 'Mayfield Giant'   CTri ERou MWgw WPer
- 'Mount Everest'   WCot
- 'Northern Lights'   SMac
- 'Octopus' **new**   MAvo
- 'Old Court' **new**   CFwr EBee EChP MAvo MBnl MBri
MTis
- 'Phyllis Smith'   CFwr CHea COlW EBee EFou EGle
EMan GMac LRHS MAvo MCLN
MHer MTis MWrn NGdn NSti SAga
SHel SMad STes WAbb WBVN
WBea WBro WCot WFar WMoo
WPrP WWpP
- 'Polaris'   CFwr LRHS NOak WMoo WShp
- 'Rags and Tatters'   MAvo
* - 'Schneehurken'   CElw CFwr EBee MAvo SUsu
WLFP
- 'Shaggy'   EChP ECtt MLLN NFla SWat WPrP
§ - 'Silberprinzesschen'   COlW CPrp EBee EChP EFou EPfP
GGar GKir IHMH LRHS NBlu NMir
NOak NPri SPlb SRms WBea WFar
WHen WMoo WPer WShp WWpP
- 'Silver Spoon' **new**   WPer
- 'Snow Lady'   EBee IHMH LRHS NMir NPer SPet
SRms WFar WHen WTel WWeb
WWpP
- 'Snowcap'   EBee EBre ECha EGle ENot EPfP
LRHS MBri MRav NGdn SBla SLon
SPer SPla SWvt WTin WWpP
- 'Snowdrift'   CFwr CM&M MAvo MSPs NPri
WCot WHil WWeb
§ - 'Sonnenschein'   More than 30 suppliers
- 'Starburst' (d)   SHel SRms WHen
- 'Stina' **new**   CFwr GBin
- 'Summer Snowball' (d)   CElw EGle EWes LRHS MAvo SHel
SUsu WCot WFar WTel WWpP
- 'Sunny Killin' **new**   WTin
- 'Sunny Side Up'   CElw EChP ECtt EWes MBNS MBri
- Sunshine   see *L.* x *superbum* 'Sonnenschein'
- 'T.E. Killin' (d) ♀H4   CElw CHea CKno CPrp CSam
EBee EBla EBre ECha ECtt EGle
EMan EMar EPfP LRHS MBnl
MCLN NChi WCAu WCot WFar
WSpi
- 'White Iceberg' (d)   WPer
- 'White Knight'   LRHS WBrk
- 'Wirral Pride'   CHar EBee MBnl NPri WCra WWol
§ - 'Wirral Supreme'   More than 30 suppliers
(d) ♀H4
'Tizi-n-Test'   see *Rhodanthemum catananche*
'Tizi-n-Test'
§ *vulgare*   CArn CKno CRWN ECoo EFWa EPar
GBar GWCH IHMH MBow MHer
NLRH NLan NMir NSco SIde WBrk
WHen WHer WJek WShi WWye

- 'Avondale' (v)   NGdn
- 'Filigran'   CKno SIde WWeb
§ - 'Maikönigin'   CBgR EBee GCal IHMH NSti WHrl
WRHF WShp WWpP
- May Queen   see *L. vulgare* 'Maikönigin'
- 'Sunny'   CBgR CBre

Leucheria (Asteraceae)
RCB/Arg C-9 **new**   WCot

Leucochrysum (Asteraceae)
albicans subsp. *alpinum* CStu
new

Leucocoryne (Alliaceae)
hybrids **new**   WHil
odorata   WCot
purpurea ♀H1   LRHS WCot

Leucogenes (Asteraceae)
grandiceps   GCrs GTou NSla
leontopodium   EPot GCrs GEdr GGar GTou
MDKP NLAp NSla WAbe
tarahaoa   WAbe

Leucojum (Amaryllidaceae)
aestivum   CBcs CBri CFee EBee EChP EPAt
EPfP EWTr GBBs GCrs GFlt LAma
LRHS MAvo MLwd MWgw NHol
NRog SRms WAbe WBVN WBea
WBod WCot WCra WEas WFar
WShi WTin WWye
- 'Gravetye Giant' ♀H4   More than 30 suppliers
autumnale ♀H4   More than 30 suppliers
- 'Cobb's Variety'   WCot
- var. *oporanthum*   EPot ERos NRog
- var. *pulchellum*   CBro EPot ERos
longifolium **new**   ERos
nicaeense ♀H2-3   CGra CLyd CPBP CStu EBur EHyt
EPot ERos MTho NGar SSpi WCom
WCot WIvy
roseum   CLyd EBur EHyt EPot ERos LAma
NRya SIgm
tingitanum   CBro EHyt EPot SSpi WCot
trichophyllum   CBro ERos
valentinum   CBro EPot SCnR SRot SSpi
vernum ♀H4   CAvo CBro EHrv ELan EPar EPfP
EPot GCrs GFlt LAma LPio LRHS
MBow MLwd MNrw MRav NGar
NMen SRms WAbe WFar WHer
WPnP WShi
- var. *carpathicum*   CLAP ECha EHrv GEdr LAma
MRav NMen
- var. *vagneri*   CLAP ECha EHrv EMon GEdr
LHop NHol WTin

Leucophyllum (Scrophulariaceae)
frutescens   SOWG XPep
minus **new**   XPep

Leucophyta (Asteraceae)
§ *brownii*   ECou EMan MRav SVen XPep

Leucopogon (Epacridaceae)
ericoides   MBar WPat
§ *fasciculatus*   ECou
§ *fraseri*   ECou GCrs
parviflorus   see *Cyathodes parviflora*

x *Leucoraoulia* (Asteraceae)
§ hybrid (*Raoulia hectorii* EPot GTou NSla SIng WAbe
x *Leucogenes*
grandiceps)
§ *loganii*   EPot GCrs ITim NWCA WAbe

Leucosceptrum (*Lamiaceae*)

canum	CPLG CTrG
stellipilum	SSpi
var. *formosanum*	
- - B&SWJ 1804	EBee WCru

Leucospermum (*Proteaceae*)

cordifolium	SOWG
'Scarlet Ribbon' **new**	CTrC

Leucothoe (*Ericaceae*)

Carinella = 'Zebekot'	MBri MGos
davisiae	NLar
§ *fontanesiana* ♀H4	LRHS NBea SPer STre WBrE WStI
- 'Lovita'	CEnd EBee GCal LRHS MBri MRav
	NLar SCoo SSta
- 'Nana'	LRHS MAsh
- 'Rainbow' (v)	CBcs CSBt CTrG CTri CWSG
	EMil ENot EPfP GKir LRHS MAsh
	MBar MGos MRav NBlu SHBN
	SLim SPer SPla SPlb SReu SRms
	SSta SWvt WBVN WDin WFar
	WGwG WWeb
- 'Rollissonii' ♀H4	MBar MRav SRms WBod
keiskei	EPfP LRHS MAsh
- 'Minor'	SSta
- 'Royal Ruby'	CWSG EBee NHol NLar WDin
	WFar
populifolia	see *Agarista populifolia*
racemosa	NLar
Red Lips = 'Lipsbolwi'PBR	MGos
Scarletta = 'Zeblid'	More than 30 suppliers
walteri	see *L. fontanesiana*

Leuzea (*Asteraceae*)

centauroides	see *Stemmacantha centauriodes*
* *conifera major* **new**	SScr

Levisticum (*Apiaceae*)

officinale	CAgr CArn CHby CSev ELau GAbr
	GBar GPoy MBar MBow MHer
	NBid NBlu NGHP SDix SECG SIde
	SPlb SWat WBVN WBri WBrk
	WGwG WHHs WHbs WHer WPer
	WSel WWye

Lewisia ✿ (*Portulacaceae*)

'Archangel'	NRya
Ashwood Carousel hybrids	CGra EDAr ENot GCrs MAsh
	MDHE
'Ashwood Pearl'	MAsh
'Ben Chace'	MAsh WAbe
Birch strain	CBcs ECho ELan
brachycalyx ♀H2	EWes GTou ITim MAsh MTho
cantelovii	MAsh
columbiana	EHyt GTou ITim MAsh MDHE
	WAbe
- 'Alba'	MAsh WAbe
- subsp. *columbiana*	CGra
- 'Rosea'	GCrs MAsh NSla WAbe WGor
- subsp. *rupicola*	LTwo MAsh MMHG NWCA WGor
	WOBN
- subsp. *wallowensis*	MAsh MDHE NMen WGor
congdonii	MAsh
cotyledon ♀H4	LRHS LTwo MNrw MOne NWCA
	SPet WBrE WFar WPat
- J&JA 12959	NWCA
- f. *alba*	GTou LHop MAsh NWCA
- 'Ashwood Ruby'	MAsh
- Ashwood strain	CTri CWCL EBre ENot EPfP ESis
	EWes LBee LRHS MAsh MBri
	MOne NRya SRms WBod WGor
- Crags hybrids	SRms

- 'Fransi'	NLar
- var. *heckneri* ♀H4	WGor
- var. *howellii*	LTwo SRms WGor
- hybrids	CBrm CStu EDAr EPot GTou ITim
	LHop MBro NBlu NMen SIng
	WAbe WBVN WBod WGor WLin
	WWin
- 'John's Special'	GCrs
- magenta	MAsh WGor
§ - 'Regenbogen' mixed	LAst LPVe SSto WGor WPer
- Rose Splendour'	WGor
- Sunset Group ♀H4	EMlt GAbr GKir MBri MHer NHol
	NJOw NLar NWCA SRms WPer
- 'White Splendour'	SIng WGor
'George Henley'	EPfP EWes MAsh NMen NRya SIng
	WAbe
* 'Holly'	MDHE
'Joyce Halley'	GCrs
leeana	EHyt MAsh
'Little Plum'	CMea CPBP EDAr GEdr ITim LPVe
	MAsh MDKP MSte NCGa NDlv
	NHol NLap NLar NSla NWCA SIng
	WGor
§ *longipetala*	GTou MAsh MOne NWCA
longipetala x *cotyledon*	GTou
§ *nevadensis*	ERos ESis GEdr GFlt GTou ITim
	MAsh MBri MNrw MTho NJOw
	NLAp NMen NRya NWCA SRms
	SRot WLin WPer
- *bernardina*	see *L. nevadensis*
- 'Rosea'	CGra EPot GCrs MAsh NWCA
oppositifolia	GCrs MAsh NLAp
- 'Richeyi'	EHyt MAsh
'Phyllellia'	MAsh
'Pinkie'	CPBP EDAr GCrs GEdr IHMH
	ITim LTwo MAsh MDHE NLAp
	NMen
pygmaea	CGra EHyt EWes GCrs GEdr GTou
	ITim LAst LRHS MAsh MBri NBir
	NHol NJOw NLAp NMen NWCA
	WPer
- *alba*	ITim
- subsp. *longipetala*	see *L. longipetala*
Rainbow mixture	see *L. cotyledon* 'Regenbogen'
	mixed
'Rawreth'	LTwo WAbe
rediviva	CGra CPBP ETow EWes GCrs
	GTou ITim MAsh NMen NSla
	NWCA SIgm WAbe WLin
- Jolon strain	WGor
- var. *rediviva*	EHyt
- white	MAsh NMen
serrata	MAsh
sierrae	MAsh NMen WPer
'Trevosia'	EHyt EPot MAsh MDHE
tweedyi ♀H2	EBre EHyt GCrs GTou ITim LHop
	LRHS MAsh MOne NBir NWCA
	SIgm SIng WAbe WGor
- 'Alba'	GCrs ITim LRHS MAsh NWCA
	WAbe
- 'Elliott's Variety'	MAsh WGor
- 'Rosea'	EBre EHyt LHop LRHS MAsh
	NMen SIng WGor

Leycesteria (*Caprifoliaceae*)

crocothyrsos	CArn CBcs CBrm CCge CHar CPle
	CWib GEil GQui IFro MMil MWrn
	NBid SLon SMad WBod WFar
	WMoo WPic WWpP
formosa ♀H4	More than 30 suppliers
- Golden Lanterns	CPLG EBre ENot MGos NPri SCoo
= 'Notbruce'PBR	SHGC WWeb
- 'Golden Pheasant' (v)	CPMA MRav
- 'Purple Rain'	NLar WBcn

Leymus (Poaceae)

from Falkland Islands	EPPr
§ *arenarius*	More than 30 suppliers
condensatus 'Canyon Prince' **new**	CKno
hispidus	see *Elymus hispidus*
'Niveus'	EHul
§ *racemosus*	CHrt MMHG

Lhotzkya see *Calytrix*

Liatris (Asteraceae)

aspera	EBee EMan NLar SIgm WPer
cylindracea	EBee
elegans	EShb NLar SPlb WPer
lancifolia	EBee
ligulistylis	EBee EMan SIgm WMoo
punctata	EBee WWeb
pycnostachya	CRWN EMan MLLN NLar SRms WMoo WPer
– 'Alba'	EBee
– 'Alexandra'	EBee
scariosa 'Gracious'	EWll
– 'Magnifica'	CBcs
§ *spicata*	More than 30 suppliers
– 'Alba'	CBri CPrp CSBt EBee ECha ECtt EFou ELan EMlt EPfP GKir IHMH LAma LAst LPio MNrw MTis SDeJ SPer SPlb WBea WBrE WHoo WLow WPer WShp
– 'Blue Bird'	WViv
– *callilepis*	see *L. spicata*
– 'Floristan Violett'	CBrm CFwr CHar CWCL EBee EChP EMar EPPr EPfP LAst LPVe LRHS MHer MTis MWgw NLRH SCoo SPlb SWvt WBar WFar WMnd WMoo WPer WWeb
– 'Floristan Weiss'	CArn CBrm CFwr CHar COIW ECGN EChP ELau EPPr EPfP GBuc LAst LPVe LRHS MHer MRav MWgw NBPC NLRH NPri SPla SWvt WFar WHHs WHil WMnd WMoo WPer WWeb WWin
– Goblin	see *L. spicata* 'Kobold'
§ – 'Kobold'	More than 30 suppliers
squarrosa	EBee

Libertia ✿ (Iridaceae)

'Amazing Grace'	CDes CPne EBee EPPr IBlr SUsu WCot WPGP
'Ballyrogan Blue'	IBlr
Ballyrogan hybrid	IBlr
* *breunioides*	CPLG IBlr
caerulescens	CFil CPLG EBee EChP EGoo EMan ERos GSki IBlr LHop LPio NBPC NBir NLar SCro SMrm WCot WFar WHer WPGP WPic WSHC WSan WWin
chilensis	see *L. formosa*
elegans	CPLG GBuc IBlr
§ *formosa*	More than 30 suppliers
– brown-stemmed	IBlr
grandiflora ♀H4	More than 30 suppliers
– Cally strain	GCal
ixioides	CElw CWil ECou EMan GMac GSki IBlr MFir NSti WCFE WLeb WPGP WPic WPrP WRHF
– hybrid	SDix
– 'Tricolor'	GGar IBlr
'Nelson Dwarf'	IBlr
paniculata	CPLG
peregrinans	More than 30 suppliers
– East Cape form	IBlr

– 'Gold Leaf'	CBcs CElw CPrp CWil EHrv IBlr LAst LPio SMad SOkh WCot WCru WDyG WPic WViv
* *procera*	CFil EBee IBlr WPGP
pulchella	EMan IBlr
sessiliflora	CFee EBee IBlr NBir WCot WFar WPic
– RB 94073	MNrw SMad
Shackleton hybrid	IBlr
tricolor	EBee GBuc
* *umbellata*	IBlr

Libocedrus (Cupressaceae)

bidwillii	CDoC
chilensis	see *Austrocedrus chilensis*
decurrens	see *Calocedrus decurrens*
plumosa	CBcs CDoC

Libonia see *Justicia*

Licuala (Arecaceae)

grandis	MBri
ramsayi	CBrP
spinosa	LPal

Ligularia ✿ (Asteraceae)

B&SWJ 2977	WCru	
BWJ 7686 small, from China	WCru	
B&SWJ 1158 from Korea		WCru
alatipes	GBin	
amplexicaulis	EBee IBlr	
calthifolia	CRow EBee	
clivorum	see *L. dentata*	
§ *dentata*	CRow EBee ECtt GFlt GIBF GKir NArg NBro NGby SRms SWat WFar WWeb	
– 'Britt-Marie Crawford'	More than 30 suppliers	
– 'Dark Beauty'	EMan ERou GSki IBal	
– 'Desdemona' ♀H4	More than 30 suppliers	
– 'Megamona'	EBee	
– 'Orange Princess'	EBee NPer WPer	
– 'Othello'	More than 30 suppliers	
– 'Ox-eye'	WGer	
– 'Sommergold'	ECha GSki IBlr SPer WFar	
§ *fischeri*	EBee ECha GSki LEdu MLLN NFor WCot WPer	
– B&SWJ 1158	WFar	
– B&SWJ 2570	WCru	
– B&SWJ 4478	WCru	
– B&SWJ 5540	WCru	
– B&SWJ 5841	WCru	
glabrescens	CRow	
§ 'Gregynog Gold' ♀H4	CRow EBee EBlw ECha EGle EMFW EMan EPfP EPza ERou GAbr GKir GSki IBlr LRHS MWgw NBro NGdn NOrc SChu SCro SDnm WCru WFar WHil WMul	
x *hessei*	EBee GKir GSki NLar SWat WFar WPnP	
hodgsonii	CRow EBre EMan GKir GSki IBlr LEdu MBri MNrw WFar WPer	
intermedia	WFar	
– B&SWJ 4383	WCru	
– B&SWJ 606a	WCru	
japonica	CHar CRez CRow EBee ECha GSki ITer LEdu NLar WFar WShp	
– B&SWJ 2883	WCru	
– 'Rising Sun' **new**	WCru	
aff. *kaialpina* B&SWJ 5806	WCru	
– B&SWJ 6185	EBee	
kanaitzensis ACE 1968	WCru	
– BWJ 7758	WCru	
macrophylla	CRow MWhi WCot WFar	

nelumbifolia	WCru
BWJ 7608 **new**	
x **palmatiloba**	see *L.* x *yoshizoeana* 'Palmatiloba'
§ **przewalskii** ♀H4	More than 30 suppliers
- variegated (v)	EBlw
sachalinensis	EBee GCal
sibirica	EBee EChP GSki NLar WCAu WFar
	WLin WMoo WPer WPnP
- 'Hietala'	EBee
- var. **speciosa**	see *L. fischeri*
smithii	see *Senecio smithii*
speciosa	see *L. fischeri*
stenocephala	EBee EMil GKir IBlr NBro NLar
	SWat WFar WShp
- B&SWJ 283	WCru
'Sungold'	CSam EBre WPnP
tangutica	see *Sinacalia tangutica*
'The Rocket' ♀H4	More than 30 suppliers
tussilaginea	see *Farfugium japonicum*
veitchiana	CHEx CRow EBee EMan EMar
	EPfP EPza GCal GGar GKir IBlr
	LEdu MBri MSte NGdn NSti SDnm
	SWat WCAu WCot WFar WTMC
vorobievii	EBee GSki
'Weihenstephan'	GKir IBlr LRHS MBri
wilsoniana	CBct CHEx CRow EBee ECtt EMan
	MLLN MRav SDnm SWat WCAu
	WFar
§ x **yoshizoeana**	More than 30 suppliers
'Palmatiloba'	
'Zepter'	EBee GBuc GCal MBri MTed NLar

Ligusticum (*Apiaceae*)

jeholense	EBee
lucidum	CDul CMCN EHol EPfP EWTr LPhx
	MSal SIgm WFar
porteri	MSal
scoticum	CArn EOHP EWes GBar GPoy ILis
	MSal WDyG
striatum B&SWJ 7259	WCru

Ligustrum ✿ (*Oleaceae*)

chenaultii	see *L. compactum*
§ **compactum**	CLnd NLar
§ **delavayanum**	CBcs ERom LPan LRHS MBar SAPC
	SArc WFar WSpi
ionandrum	see *L. delavayanum*
japonicum	ENot LPan NPSI SEND SMur SPer
	WDin WFar XPep
I - 'Aureum' **new**	NPSI
- 'Coriaceum'	see *L. japonicum* 'Rotundifolium'
- 'Macrophyllum'	EPfP LRHS MAsh
§ - 'Rotundifolium'	CAbP CDoC CHEx CPLG CPle
	EBee EMil EPfP EPla GEil LRHS
	MAsh MRav SBod SLim SMad
	WAbe WBcn WFar
- 'Texanum'	LPan LRHS NPSI
* - 'Texanum Argenteum'	LPan
lucidum ♀H4	CDoC CSBt CTho EBee ELan ENot
	EWTr LAst LPan MBar MGos MRav
	MSwo NLar NWea SAPC SArc
	SMad SPer SSpi WBVN WDin WFar
	XPep
- 'Excelsum	CAbP CLnd CPMA ELan ENot EPfP
Superbum' (v) ♀H4	LAst LPan LRHS MAsh MBar MGos
	SPer SSpi WBcn WCot
- 'Golden Wax'	CAbP CPMA EBee ENot LRHS
	MRav WBcn
- 'Latifolium'	CDul
- 'Tricolor' (v)	CPMA EBee ELan ENot EPfP LRHS
	SHBN SLim SPer SPla SSpi SSta
	SWvt WDin WFar
obtusifolium 'Darts	SLPl
Perfecta'	

- var. **regelianum**	SEND WFar
ovalifolium	CBcs CCVT CChe CDoC CLnd
	CSBt CTri EPfP GKir IHMH LBuc
	LPan LRHS MAsh MBar MBri MGos
	MSwo NBee NBlu NWea SLim SPer
	WDin WGwG WMou
§ - 'Argenteum' (v)	CBcs CDoC CDul CTri EBee EHoe
	GKir IHMH LBuc LRHS MAsh
	MBar MBri NBlu NHol SLim SPer
	SPla SWvt WDin WFar WTel WWin
- 'Aureomarginatum'	see *L. ovalifolium* 'Aureum'
§ - 'Aureum' (v) ♀H4	More than 30 suppliers
* - 'Lemon and Lime' (v)	EMil
- 'Taff's Indecision' (v)	CPMA
- 'Variegatum'	see *L. ovalifolium* 'Argenteum'
quihoui ♀H4	ECre ELan EPfP MBri SDix SMad
	SPer SSpi SSta WBcn WFar WHCG
	WPat
§ **sempervirens**	EPfP SLon SMad SSta
sinense	CHEx CMCN EPfP MRav WFar
	WPGP
- 'Multiflorum'	CWib WFar
- 'Pendulum'	CFil CLnd EPla WPGP
- 'Variegatum' (v)	CLnd CMHG CPMA EPla LAst
	LHop MRav SPer
- 'Wimbei'	EPla NPro SSpi WBcn WFar
strongylophyllum	WFar
texanum	see *L. japonicum* 'Texanum'
tschonoskii	SLPl
undulatum 'Lemon	NLar
Lime and Clippers'	
'Vicaryi'	CDul CMHG CPMA EBee ELan
	EPfP EPla IArd LRHS MAsh MBar
	MGos NPro SDix SPer SPla WFar
	WWeb
vulgare	CCVT CDul CRWN CTri ENot EPfP
	GKir LBuc MSwo NBlu NWea SHFr
	SKee WBVN WDin WMou XPep
- 'Lodense'	MBar SLPl

Lilium (*Liliaceae*)

from China (IX)	CLAP
'Acapulco' (VIId)	LAma MCLN
African Queen Group	CAvo ECot GBuc LAma MBNS
(VIa) ♀H4	MLwd NRog SCoo SDeJ SPer WFar
- 'African Queen'	CSut ECri
(VIa) **new**	
albanicum	see *L. pyrenaicum* subsp.
	carniolicum var. *albanicum*
amabile (IX)	CLAP EBee LRHS WDav WWst
- 'Luteum' (IX)	CLAP EBee LRHS WDav
'Amber Gold' (Ic)	CLAP
America = 'Holean' (Ia)	WDav
amoenum (IX)	EBee EPot LAma LEur
'Angela North' (Ic)	CLAP
'Apeldoorn' (Ic)	ECri LRHS
'Aphrodite' (Ia/d)	EPot NBir
'Apollo' (Ia) ♀H4	CBro EPot GBuc LAma LRHS
	MBNS MBri SDeJ
'Arena' (VIIb)	LRHS SCoo SPer
'Ariadne' (Ic)	CLAP
* Asiatic hybrids (VI/VII)	LAma NGdn SDeJ SGar
auratum (IX)	EBee EFEx EPfP GBuc
- 'Classic' (IX)	CLAP
- 'Gold Band'	see *L. auratum* var. *platyphyllum*
§ - var. **platyphyllum** (IX)	ECri WDav WWst
- Red Band Group (IX)	WFar
- var. **virginale** (IX)	LAma LRHS WDav
Aurelian hybrids (VI)	SMrm
'Avignon' (Ia)	ECri LAma LRHS
Backhouse hybrids (II)	CLAP EBee
bakerianum (IX)	LAma LEur
- var. **aureum**	EBee GKev
- var. **delavayi** (IX)	EBee LAma

- var. **rubrum**	EBee LAma LEur WDav
- var. **yunnaense**	EBee GKev
'Barbara North' (Ic)	CLAP
'Barbaresco' (VII)	SCoo SPer
'Barcelona' (Ia)	MNrw
'Batist' (Ia)	ECri LAma
Bellingham Group (IV)	CLAP EBee GBuc SSpi
'Bergamo' (VIId)	SCoo
'Bianco Uno' **new**	MBri
'Black Beauty' (VIId)	CAvo CBrm CLAP GBuc LAma
	LRHS SSpi WBor
'Black Bird' **new**	IBal
'Black Dragon' (VIa)	CHar ECri SGar
'Blazing Dwarf' (Ia)	MBri
bolanderi (IX)	EBee WAbe
'Bonfire' (VIIb)	SDeJ
* **brasilia new**	WWeb
'Bright Pixie'	IBal
'Bright Star' (VIb)	LAma SDeJ
'Brocade' (II)	CLAP
'Bronwen North' (Ic) **new**	CLAP
brownii (IX)	EBee LAma LEur
- var. **australe** (IX)	WCru
B&SWJ 4082	
'Buff Pixie'^PBR (Ia)	LAma
bulbiferum	CLAP GBuc
- var. **croceum** (IX)	EBee GIBF
Bullwood hybrids (IV)	CLAP
'Bums' (Ia/d)	EMon
'Butter Pixie'^PBR (Ia)	LAma MCLN WGor
callosum	EBee
- var. **luteum**	WWst
'Cameleon' **new**	IBal
camtschatcense	GIBF
§ **canadense** (IX)	EBee GBuc GGGa LAma LPio SDeJ
	SSpi
- var. **coccineum** (IX)	CLAP WWst
- var. **editorum** (IX)	LAma
- var. **flavum**	see *L. canadense*
'Cancum'	ECri EPot LRHS
candidum (IX) ♀H4	CArn CAvo CBcs CBrm CBro CHar
	CMea CTri ECha EHrv ELan EPfP
	GIBF LAma LPhx LRHS MAvo MBri
	MHer MRav NGHP NRog SDeJ
	SIgm SPer WBrE WCot WHil WPnP
- 'Plenum' (IX/d)	EMon
- var. **salonikae**	GIBF
carniolicum	see *L. pyrenaicum* subsp.
	carniolicum
'Casa Blanca' (VIIb) ♀H4	CAvo CBro ECri EPfP GBuc GFlt
	IBal LAma MBNS MLLN NRog
	SCoo SDeJ WFar
§ 'Casa Rosa' (V)	CSWP MDKP NBir SWat
cernuum (IX)	CLAP EBee GEdr LAma MBow
	WCot WPrP
'Chardonnay' **new**	MBri
'Cherry Joy' **new**	WWeb
'Chinook' (Ia)	NRog
'Chippendale' (Ic)	CLAP
'Chris North'	CLAP
'Cinnabar' (Ia)	ECri
Citronella Group (Ic)	ECri LAma LRHS NRog WFar WHil
'Colibri'	WWeb
columbianum (IX)	CBro GBuc GCrs NMen SSpi WCot
- dwarf (IX)	NMen
'Con Amore' (VIIb)	LRHS SCoo
concolor (IX)	EBee WDav WWst
- var. **coridion**	WWst
- var. **stictum**	GIBF
'Connecticut King' (Ia)	ECri LAma NRog SDeJ SVen
'Coral Butterflies'	CLAP
cordatum	CBri
'Corina' (Ia)	ECri GBuc MBNS SGar WGor
'Côte d'Azur' (Ia)	CBro EPot GFlt LAma SDeJ WGor

'Crimson Pixie' (Ia)	CBro IBal WWol
x **dalhansonii** (IX)	CLAP WCot
§ - 'Marhan' (II)	CLAP SSpi
'Dame Blanche' (VII)	LAma
§ **dauricum** (IX)	EBee GCrs GEdr LEur
davidii (IX)	EBee GEdr GIBF LAma SSpi WCru
	WDav WWst
- var. **unicolor**	CLAP EBee
§ - var. **willmottiae** (IX)	CLAP GIBF WViv
debile	GIBF
distichum	EBee GIBF
- B&SWJ 794	WCru
'Doeskin' (Ic)	CLAP
duchartrei (IX)	CLAP EBee GBuc GCrs GEdr LAma
	LEur NSla SMac SSpi WAbe WCru
	WDav
- white (IX)	WDav
§ 'Ed' (VII)	EPot LAma SPer WWol
'Eileen North' (Ic)	CLAP
'Electric' (Ia)	ECri LAma
'Elfin Sun'	LAma
'Ellen Willmott' (II)	CLAP
'Enchantment' (Ia)	ECri LAma MBNS MBri MCLN
	NRog SDeJ
'Eros'	CLAP
'Eurydike' (Ic)	CLAP
'Evelina'	LRHS
'Everest' (VIId)	MLwd SGar WDav
'Exception' (Ib/d)	LAma
'Fairest' (Ib-c/d)	CLAP
'Fancy Joy' **new**	MBri
fargesii (IX)	EBee LAma
'Farolito' **new**	MBri
'Fata Morgana'	EPfP LRHS SCoo
(Ia/d) ♀H4	
'Festival' (Ia)	LAma
'Fire King' (Ib)	CBro CLAP CSut ECGP ECri LAma
	NBir NRog SCoo SDeJ WDav WFar
formosanum (IX)	EBee EBre EPyc GKir IBal MWrn
	SEND WCot WLFP WViv
- B&SWJ 1589	WCru
- var. **pricei** (IX)	CMea CSam EBee EBre EDAr ELan
	EPfP EPot ESis GEdr LBee LEur
	LHop LRHS MHer MNrw MTho
	NJOw NLAp NMen NWCA SBla
	SBri SCoo SRot WBVN WFar WHer
	WPer
- 'Snow Queen' (IX)	EBee ECri MDKP
- 'White Swan' (IX)	GBuc
'Garden Party' (VII) ♀H4	CSut LRHS MTis WFar
'George Slate' (Ic/d)	CLAP
§ 'Gibraltar' (Ia)	ECri
'Golden Joy' **new**	MBri WWeb
'Golden Melody' (Ia)	ECri
Golden Splendor Group	ECri LAma MBNS NRog SCoo
(VIa) ♀H4	SWat WHil
'Gran Paradiso' (Ia)	ECri LAma
'Grand Cru' (Ia) ♀H4	ECri LAma SDeJ
grayi (IX)	CLAP NSla SSpi
'Green Magic' (VIa)	CAvo CHid ECri
'Hannah North' (Ic)	CLAP
hansonii (IX)	CLAP EBee IBlr LAma NRog WDav
- B&SWJ 4756	WCru
henryi (IX) ♀H4	CAvo CLAP CSWP EBee ECri EPot
	GIBF LAma LPhx LRHS MLLN
	NRog SDeJ WCru WDav WPrP
- 'Carlton Yerex'	WWst
- var. **citrinum**	CLAP WCot WWst
henryi x Pink Perfection	CLAP
Group	
'Hit Parade' (VII)	LAma
x **hollandicum new**	ECri
'Honeymoon' **new**	WWeb
'Hotlips' **new**	EPfP

humboldtii (IX)	WWst
- var. *humboldtii*	SIgm
Imperial Silver Group (VIIc)	LAma
'Inzell' (Ia)	WDav
'Iona' (Ic)	CLAP
'Ivory Pixie' (Ia) **new**	CBro
'Jacqueline'	WDav
§ 'Jacques S. Dijt' (II)	CLAP
japonicum (IX)	EFEx WCru
'Jetfire' (Ia)	SDeJ
'Journey's End' (VIId)	GBuc LAma LRHS MBNS NRog
§ 'Joy' (VIIb) ♀H4	ECri LAma
'Karen North' (Ic)	CLAP
§ *kelleyanum* (IX)	CLAP GBuc GGGa
- NNS 98-373	WCot
kesselringianum **new**	EBee
'King Pete' (Ib) ♀H4	SDeJ
'Kiss Proof' (VIIb)	LRHS
'Kiwi Fanfare'	CBrm
'Kyoto' (VIId)	LAma
'Lady Alice' (VI)	CLAP
'Ladykiller' (Ia)	NRog
§ *lancifolium* (IX)	CArn EMFP GIBF LAma SDeJ SSpi WBrk WFar
- B&SWJ 539	WCru
* - *album* **new**	EBee
- Farrer's Form **new**	WCot
- var. *flaviflorum* (IX)	CLAP EBee ECri GBuc
- 'Flore Pleno' (IX/d)	CLAP CMil CSWP CSam EBre EMFP EMon EPPr EUJe GAbr GBuc GCal GSki IBlr ITer LRHS NBir NSti SMrm SOkd WCom WCot WCru WDav WFar WGMN WTin
- Forrest's form (IX)	CLAP GKir IBlr
§ - var. *splendens* (IX) ♀H4	CBro EBee ECri LAma LPhx LRHS MLLN MWgw SDeJ SGar WBor WCot
* - *viridulum* **new**	EBee
lankongense (IX)	CLAP GEdr GIBF LAma WCot WDav WWst
'Last Dance' (Ic)	CLAP
'Le Rêve'	see *L.* 'Joy'
leichtlinii	CLAP ECri WDav
- var. *maximowiczii*	CLAP EBee WWst
'Lemon Pixie'PBR (Ia)	CSut GKir LAma WWol
leucanthum (IX)	EBee GIBF LAma LEur SSpi
- var. *centifolium* (IX)	CLAP WCru WWst
'Liberation' (I)	NBir
'Little John' **new**	MBri
'Lollypop' (Ia)	CFwr EPfP IBal LRHS MDKP MLLN MNrw SCoo WWol
longiflorum (IX) ♀H2-3	EBee ECri LAma LRHS NRog SCoo WCru
- B&SWJ 4885	WCru
- 'Casa Rosa'	see *L.* 'Casa Rosa'
- 'Gelria' (IX)	SDeJ
- 'Memories' **new**	MBri WWeb
- Mount Carmel = 'Carmel' **new**	IBal
§ - 'White American' (IX)	CBro CSWP LRHS MLLN SPer
- 'White Elegance' **new**	WWol
lophophorum (IX)	EBee EPot GIBF LAma WCru WDav
- var. *linearifolium* **new**	LEur
'Lovely Girl' (VIIb)	WDav
'Luxor' (Ib)	ECri EPfP LRHS NBir
mackliniae (IX)	CLAP EChP GBuc GCal GCrs GEdr GGGa GKir GTou IBlr ITim SBla SIgm SSpi WAbe
x *maculatum* var. *davuricum*	see *L. dauricum*
- Japanese double (IX)	EMon
'Marco Polo' (Ia)	LAma SCoo
'Marhan'	see *L.* x *dalhansonii* 'Marhan'
'Marie North' (Ic)	CLAP

martagon (IX) ♀H4	More than 30 suppliers
- var. *album* (IX) ♀H4	More than 30 suppliers
- var. *bukozanense* **new**	WWst
- 'Inshriach' (IX)	WCot
- var. *pilosiusculum* (IX)	EBee
- pink-flowered (IX)	CLAP
- 'Plenum' (IX/d)	EMon
'Maxwill' (Ic)	EBee
'Medaillon' (Ia) ♀H4	LAma
medeoloides (IX)	EBee EFEx EHyt GBuc GCrs GGGa NMen SSpi WDav
'Mediterrannee' (VIIb/d)	ECri
'Menton' (Ia)	ECri
michiganense (IX)	CSWP GBuc GCrs
'Milano' (Ia)	ECri
minima	GIBF
'Mirabella' **new**	MBri
'Miss Rio' (VII)	LRHS SCoo SPer
'Mona Lisa' (VIIb/d)	EPfP EPot IBal LAma LAst LRHS MBri MCLN MLLN MTis SPer WBVN WFar WHil WWeb WWol
§ *monadelphum* (IX)	CBro CLAP EBee ETow GBuc GCrs LAma NRog SIgm SSpi WDav
'Mont Blanc' (Ia)	LAma MLLN NBir SDeJ
'Montana'	LRHS
'Monte Negro' (Ia)	ECri WDav WHil
'Montreux' (Ia)	LAma
'Mr Ed'	see *L.* 'Ed'
'Mr Ruud'	see *L.* 'Ruud'
'Mrs R.O. Backhouse' (II)	CLAP
'Muscadet'PBR (VII)	CSut LRHS WWol
§ *nanum* (IX)	EBee EHyt EPot GBuc GCrs GEdr GGGa GKev LAma LEur NMen NRog NSla WCru
- var. *flavidum* (IX)	EPot GEdr NMen WCru
- from Bhutan (IX)	EHyt GBuc GCrs GEdr WCru
- 'Len's Lilac' (IX)	WCru
- McBeath's form (IX)	WCru
neilgherrense (IX)	CFil WPGP
nepalense (IX)	CBro CLAP CMil CPLG CSWP EBee EBla EPot GCrs GEdr GIBF GKir LAma LEur LRHS MDun NCot SBla SDeJ SSpi WCot WCru WFar WGMN WHlf WPnP
- B&SWJ 2985	WCru
nobilissimum (IX)	EFEx
'Noblesse' (VII)	LRHS
'Novo Cento' ♀H4 **new**	ECri
'Odeon' **new**	ECri
'Olivia' (Ia)	ECri LAma MLLN WDav WHil
Olympic Group (VIa)	ECri LAma
'Omega' (VII)	LAma
'Orange Pixie' (Ia)	CSut ECri EPfP GKir IBal LAma SCoo WGor
'Orange Triumph' (Ia)	EPfP EPot LAma
'Orestes' (Ib)	CLAP
* Oriental Superb Group	NGdn
§ *oxypetalum* (IX)	GCrs GGGa
- var. *insigne* (IX)	CLAP EPot ETow GBuc GCrs GEdr GFlt GGGa GIBF LAma NMen NSla SSpi WCru WDav
'Painted Pixie' (Ia) **new**	WWol
'Pan' (Ic)	CLAP
papilliferum	EBee LAma
pardalinum (IX) ♀H4	CAvo CLAP EBee IBlr LRHS MSte NSla WCot WCru WDav WGMN WWhi
- var. *giganteum* (IX)	CBro CLAP ECri MNrw WDav WTin
- subsp. *shastense*	CLAP GCrs NMen SSpi
- subsp. *shastense* x *vollmeri* NNS 00-490 **new**	WCot
parryi (IX)	GBuc

– NNS 93-452	WCot
parvum (IX)	GBuc
'Passion' **new**	WWeb
'Peach Butterflies' (Ic/d)	CLAP
'Peach Pixie' (Ia)	LAma NBir SCoo WWol
'Peggy North' (Ic)	CLAP
'Perugia' (VIId)	LAma
Petit Pink = 'Hobozi' (Ia)	MBri
'Petit Pintura' **new**	MBri
philippinense (IX)	CBrm CFwr EBee ETow NSla SIgm
– B&SWJ 4000	WCru
Pink Perfection Group	CAvo CBro ECri EPfP LAma MBNS
(VIa) ♀H4	NRog SCoo SPer SWat WFar
'Pink Pixie'PBR (Ia)	CSut ECri IBal SGar
'Pink Tiger' (Ib)	CBro CLAP ECri LRHS WGor
pitkinense (IX)	SOkd WWst
polyphyllum **new**	EBee
primulinum (IX)	WWst
– var. *burmanicum* **new**	LEur
– var. *ochraceum*	LAma WWst
§ *pumilum* (IX) ♀H4	CBro CLAP EBee ECri EPot GBuc
	GCal GEdr GFlt GIBF LAma LRHS
	MLLN MSte MTho SDeJ WAul
	WCru WDav WPrP WViv
– 'Golden Gleam' (IX)	WWst
pyrenaicum (IX)	CBro CLAP IBlr LPio LTwo WCot
	WDav WPGP WRha WShi WViv
§ – subsp. *carniolicum*	NMen NSla SSpi
(IX)	
§ – – var. *albanicum* (IX)	SSpi
– subsp. *pyrenaicum*	CLAP SSpi WCot
var. *rubrum* (IX)	
'Quinta'PBR **new**	MBri
'Raspberry Butterflies'	CLAP
(Ic/d)	
'Red Carpet' (Ia)	CBrm ECri LRHS NBir WGor
'Red Dwarf' (Ia)	CSut IBal
Red Jewels Group	LAma
(Ic) **new**	
'Red Night' (I)	EGoo LRHS
'Red Rum' **new**	MBri
'Red Star' **new**	WWeb
'Red Tiger' (Ib)	CLAP
'Red Velvet' (Ib)	CLAP
'Red Wine' **new**	MBri
regale (IX) ♀H4	More than 30 suppliers
– 'Album' (IX)	CAvo CBri CSWP EBee EBre ECri
	LAma LRHS MCLN NRog SCoo
	SDeJ SGar WCot WFar WHil
§ – 'Royal Gold' (IX)	ECri MBNS MWgw SDeJ WDav
'Reinesse' (Ia)	MBri
'Roma' (Ia)	LAma LRHS MBNS NBir
'Rosefire' (Ia)	ECri
'Rosemary North' (I)	CLAP
Rosepoint Lace	CLAP
Group (Ic)	
'Rosita' (Ia)	ECri
rosthornii	CLAP EBee LEur SSpi WCot WCru
'Rosy Joy' **new**	MBri
'Royal Gold'	see *L. regale* 'Royal Gold'
rubellum (IX)	EFEx GBuc
§ 'Ruud' (VII)	EPfP EPot LAma LRHS SPer
sachalinense	WWst
'Sam' (VII) ♀H4	EPot GBuc LAma LRHS SCoo
	WWol
sargentiae (IX)	CLAP EBee GCrs GGGa LEur
	NMen WCot WCru
'Scentwood' (IV)	CLAP
sempervivoideum (IX)	EBee EPot LAma LEur WDav
'Serrada'PBR **new**	MBri
shastense	see *L. kelleyanum*
'Showbiz' (VIII)	LAma
'Shuksan' (IV)	CLAP ·
'Silly Girl' (Ia)	ECri

'Snow Princess'	LAma
'Snow Trumpet' (V)	CSam
speciosum (IX)	NSla
– var. *album* (IX)	EBee ECri EPot GBuc LAma LPio
	LRHS NBir SDeJ
– 'Coral Queen' (IX)	CSut
– var. *gloriosoides* (IX)	EBee EPot LAma LEur SSpi
– var. *roseum* (IX)	ECri GBuc
– var. *rubrum* (IX)	CAvo CHar CLAP ECha ECri EPot
	GBuc GFlt LAma LRHS MLLN NBir
	NRog SDeJ SPer WPrP
§ – 'Uchida' (IX)	ECri SDeJ SGar WDav
'Star Gazer' (VIIc)	CBro CSut ECot ECri EPfP IBal
	LAma LPhx LRHS MBNS NRog
	SCoo SDeJ SPer WFar WGor
'Starfighter' (VIId)	IBal LRHS
'Sterling Star' (Ia)	CLAP ECri EPfP LAma NRog
stewartianum (IX)	LAma
sulphureum	EBee LAma LEur
'Sun Ray' (Ia)	CBro LRHS NRog
'Sunburst' **new**	WWeb
superbum (IX)	CLAP EBee LAma NRog WCru
	WDav
'Sutton Court' (II)	CLAP
'Sweet Surrender' (I)	ECri LRHS
szovitsianum	see *L. monadelphum*
taliense (IX)	EBee GEdr GIBF LAma LEur WCru
'Tamara' (Ib)	MBNS
tenuifolium	see *L. pumilum*
x *testaceum* (IX) ♀H4	LAma
'Theseus' (Ic)	CLAP
tianschanica	EBee LEur
'Tiger White' (Ic)	CLAP
tigrinum	see *L. lancifolium*
'Time Out'PBR	WWol
'Tinkerbell' (Ic)	CLAP
tsingtauense (IX)	CLAP GIBF LEur WDav
– B&SWJ 519	WCru
'Turandot'PBR **new**	MBri
'Uchida Kanoka'	see *L. speciosum* 'Uchida'
'Viva' (Ic)	CLAP
vollmeri (IX)	CLAP GCrs SSpi
wallichianum (IX)	EBee LAma NRog SDeJ
wardii (IX)	WWst
wenshanense	EBee LEur
'White American'	see *L. longiflorum* 'White American'
'White Butterflies' (Ic/d)	CLAP
'White Happiness' (Ia)	LAma
'White Henryi' (VId)	CLAP
'White Kiss' (Ia/d)	LAma LRHS
I 'White Lace' (Ic/d)	CLAP
'White Paradise' (V)	SCoo
White Pixie = 'Snow Crystal' (I)	EPfP MBNS
'White Tiger' (Ib)	CLAP
wigginsii (IX)	CLAP EHyt GCrs GGGa SSpi
willmottiae	see *L. davidii* var. *willmottiae*
xanthellum	GEdr WWst
var. *luteum* **new**	
Yellow Blaze Group (Ia)	ECri EPfP LAma NRog
'Yellow Bunting' (I)	WWst
'Yellow Star' (Ib)	LRHS
yunnanense **new**	EBee

lime see *Citrus aurantiifolia*

lime, djeruk see *Citrus amblycarpa*

lime, Philippine see x *Citrofortunella microcarpa*

Limnanthes (Limnanthaceae)

douglasii ♀H4	CArn EPAt EPfP

Limnophila (Scrophulariaceae)
aromatica   MSal

Limoniastrum (Plumbaginaceae)
monopetalum new   XPep

Limonium (Plumbaginaceae)
bellidifolium   EBee ECha EDAr ESis ETow ITer
NJOw SBla SIng WEas WHoo WPer
XPep
- 'Dazzling Blue'   EChP
binervosum   EBee
caspium new   EDif
cosyrense   CMea MHer NMen WPer WWin
dumosum   see *Goniolimon tataricum* var.
angustifolium
globulariifolium   see *L. ramosissimum*
gmelinii   MLLN SPlb WPer
* - subsp. **hungaricum**   ECGN NLar
- 'Perestrojka'   EBee
gougetianum   ETow WPer
latifolium   see *L platyphyllum*
minutum   CNic NJOw
'Misty Blue'[PBR]   EMui
'Misty Pink'   EMui
'Misty White'   EMui
otolepis   MAvo
paradoxum   MOne
perezii   EDAr WPer
§ **platyphyllum**   More than 30 suppliers
- 'Robert Butler'   EBre EMan GCal LRHS MRav
- 'Violetta'   CTri EBee EBre ECGP ECha ELan
EMan ERou GKir GMac LRHS MBri
MMHG MRav MTis NCGa NLar
SPer SUsu WHoo
pruinosum new   XPep
§ **ramosissimum**   EBee
sinense   EShb
speciosum   see *Goniolimon incanum*
'Stardust'   MWgw
tataricum   see *Goniolimon tataricum*
vulgare   SECG WHer XPep

Linanthastrum see *Linanthus*

Linanthus (Polemoniaceae)
nuttallii subsp.   CPBP
floribundus

Linaria (Scrophulariaceae)
aeruginea   CSpe EChP EMlt
aeruginosa subsp.   LRHS
nevadensis
'Gemstones'
alpina   CMea CSpe ECtt EMlt GFlt GTou
LPVe MTho NWCA SRms SScr
WEas WPer
'Anstey'   CElw
anticaria 'Antique Silver'   CHea EBee ECha EMan EOMN
GBuc LAst LRHS MSte NLar SSvw
WPGP WWeb
Blue Lace = 'Yalin'   EBee LAst NPri
* 'Blue Pygmy'   SScr
capraria   CPBP
cymbalaria   see *Cymbalaria muralis*
§ **dalmatica**   EBee EChP ECha ELan ERou GBBs
LPhx MFOX MHar MWhi NBid
NBro NChi NPri SChu WCAu
WCot WKif WMoo WPer
x **dominii** 'Carnforth'   CMdw CPom EBee ECGP MBrN
NBro WBry WCot WWpP
- 'Yuppie Surprise'   CHid EBee ECGP EChP ECtt EMan
EMon LDai LPio NBir NDov NGdn

SWvt WCot WCra WPGP WSpi
genistifolia   CSpe ECtt MDKP
- subsp. **dalmatica**   see *L. dalmatica*
'Globosa Alba'   see *Cymbalaria muralis* 'Globosa
Alba'
hepaticifolia   see *Cymbalaria hepaticifolia*
japonica new   GKev
* **lobata alba**   SPlb
maroccana new   CTCP
'Natalie'   SBla
origanifolia   see *Chaenorhinum origanifolium*
pallida   see *Cymbalaria pallida*
pilosa   see *Cymbalaria pilosa*
purpurea   COIW EBee EFWa EGra EHrv ELan
EMlt EWTr MFir MHer MWgw
NBPC NBro NPPs NPer NPri SRms
WCAu WHen WMoo WPer WWye
- 'Alba'   see *L. purpurea* 'Springside White'
- 'Canon Went'   More than 30 suppliers
- 'Charlton White'   CNat
- pink   MBow
- 'Radcliffe Innocence'   see *L. purpurea* 'Springside White'
§ - 'Springside White'   CElw EBee ECha ECtt EMan EMlt
ERou GBuc LPhx MAnH MBow
MSte MWrn NBid NBir NPri SBla
SSvw WBea WCAu WMoo WPer
WRha
- 'Thurgarton Beauty'   MDKP
- 'Vainglorious'   CNat
repens   CPom CTCP MNrw WBWf WCot
WHbs WHer
'Sue'   EBee
'Toni Aldiss'   CSpe EBee
triornithophora   CBot CFir CSpe EBee ECha EMan
EMar GBuc GFlt IGor MAnH
MWgw MWrn WBea WCot WMoo
WOut WPer WRha WWye
- purple   ELan MHar STes WBea WMoo
vulgaris   CArn ELau GWCH LDai MBow
MGas MHer NMir NSco WHer
WJek WLHH
- hemipeloric **new**   CNat
- 'Peloria'   CNat EBee EMon WCot
'Winifrid's Delight'   CHea EBee EOMN EPfP
LAst

Lindelofia (Boraginaceae)
anchusoides hort.   see *L. longiflora*
§ **anchusoides** (Lindl.)   EPPr GBri NBid WLin
Lehm.
§ **longiflora**   CFir ECGN EMan GBin GBuc GCal
LRHS MLLN NLar WBro WPGP
WPer

Lindera (Lauraceae)
aggregata   CBcs
angustifolia   CFil
benzoin   CFil CMCN CPLG EPfP GIBF MSal
SSpi WDin WPGP
communis new   CFil WPGP
erythrocarpa   CFil CMCN EPfP SSpi
WPGP
- B&SWJ 6271   WCru
megaphylla   CBcs CFil
obtusiloba   ♀H4   CAbP CFil EPfP IArd LRHS NLar
SSpi WNor WPGP
praecox   CFil EPfP WPGP
praetermissa   CFil EPfP WPGP
reflexa   CBcs CMCN EPfP WPGP
strychnifolia   CMCN EPfP
triloba   CFil WPGP
umbellata var.   WCru
membranaceae
B&SWJ 6227

Lindernia (Scrophulariaceae)
grandiflora blue ECou SSpi

Linnaea (Caprifoliaceae)
borealis ILis MHar NSla WAbe
- subsp. **americana** NWCA

Linum ✿ (Linaceae)
arboreum ♀H4 MBro SBla SIgm WAbe WKif WPat
- NS 529 NWCA
austriacum EBee
capitatum EBee EBre NMen NSla WHoo
cariense new WLin
dolomiticum WPat
empetrifolium new WLin
flavum CTri EPfP GTou XPep
- 'Compactum' GAbr LHop NPri SBla SMrm SRms
  WCot WHrl WShp WWin
'Gemmell's Hybrid' ♀H4 CLyd CMea EPot EWes LRHS MBro
  MDKP NBir NMen NRya NWCA
  SBla SScr WAbe WLin WPat
kingii var. *sedoides* LTwo WLin
leonii LRHS WCom WKif
monogynum CDes EBee ECou WPGP
§ - var. *diffusum* ECou
- dwarf GTou
- 'Nelson' see *L. monogynum* var. *diffusum*
narbonense CSam CSpe EBee ECGP LDai LGro
  LPhx LRHS MBri MBro NLar NOak
  SIgm SMrm SRms WHoo WKif
- 'Heavenly Blue' ERou SVal WEas WHen
§ *perenne* More than 30 suppliers
- 'Album' EBee ECha ELan EPfP ERou NLar
  SPer WBro WCAu WHen WPer
  WShp
- subsp. *alpinum* SIng
- - 'Alice Blue' CPBP LBee NMen SBla WWin
§ - 'Blau Saphir' CBgR CBod CTri EBee LPVe LRHS
  MLLN NLar NPri SRms WBVN
  WHen WMoo WWeb
- Blue Sapphire see *L. perenne* 'Blau Saphir'
- 'Diamant' CBod EBee LPVe LRHS NPri WMoo
- 'Himmelszelt' NLar
- subsp. *lewisii* EBee NBir SAga
- 'Nanum Diamond' NLar
- 'White Diamond' NPri WHer
rubrum CSpe
sibiricum see *L. perenne*
suffruticosum CPBP
- subsp. *salsoloides* SBla WPat
  'Nanum'
- - 'Prostratum' GBuc SIgm
usitatissimum CRWN MHer

Liparia (Papilionaceae)
splendens **new** CPLG SGar

Liparis (Orchidaceae)
coelogynoides ECou
cordifolia EFEx
fujisanensis EFEx
krameri var. *krameri* EFEx
kumokiri EFEx
makinoana EFEx
nigra EFEx
sootenzanensis EFEx

Lippia (Verbenaceae)
alba MSal
canescens see *Phyla nodiflora* var.
  canescens
chamaedrifolia see *Verbena peruviana*
citriodora see *Aloysia triphylla*

dulcis CArn CFir EOHP EShb LRav MSal
nodiflora see *Phyla nodiflora*
repens see *Phyla nodiflora*

Liquidambar ✿ (Hamamelidaceae)
acalycina CPMA LRHS MGos SBir SSpi SSta
  WNor WPGP WPat
'Elstead Mill' LPan
formosana CDul CEnd CMCN CPle EBee
  ECrN EPfP IMGH LPan MBlu MGos
  SBir SPer SSta WNor WPGP
- B&SWJ 6855 WCru
- Monticola Group CPMA EPfP SBir SSta
orientalis CDul CLnd CMCN CPMA EPfP
  LPan SBir SSta
styraciflua More than 30 suppliers
- 'Andrew Hewson' CLnd CPMA LRHS MAsh SBir SSpi
  SSta
- 'Anja' CPMA MBlu SBir SSta
- 'Anneke' CLnd CPMA LRHS SBir SSta
* - 'Argenta' CLnd
- 'Aurea' see *L. styraciflua* 'Variegata'
- 'Aurea Variegata' see *L. styraciflua* 'Variegata'
- 'Aurora' CPMA EBre SBir SCoo SLim
- 'Burgundy' CLnd CPMA CTho NHol SBir SSta
  WPat
- 'Fastigiata' MBlu
- 'Festeri' CEnd SBir SSta WPat
- 'Festival' CPMA SBLw SSta
- 'Globe' CPMA
- 'Golden Treasure' (v) CMCN CPMA LRHS MAsh NLar
  SMad SSpi WPat
- 'Gum Ball' CEnd CLnd CMCN CPMA EBee
  EPfP EWes LTwo MAsh MGos NLar
  SMad SSta WPat
- 'Happidaze' WPat
- 'Jennifer Carol' CPMA
- 'Kia' CEnd CPMA WPat
- 'Kirsten' CPMA
- 'Lane Roberts' ♀H4 CDoC CDul CLnd CMCN CTho
  EBee EBre EPfP LPan LRHS MAsh
  MBlu MBri MGos NLar SBir SKee
  SLim SReu SSta WDin WPGP WPat
- 'Manon' (v) CDoC CEnd CPMA NBhm
  SLim
- 'Midwest Sunset' WPat
- 'Moonbeam' (v) CEnd CMCN CPMA CTho EBre
  NHol NLar SBir SCoo SLim SSta
  WPat
- 'Moraine' CMCN CPMA SBLw
- 'Naree' CMCN CPMA
- 'Oconee' WPat
- 'Paarl' **new** CMCN
- 'Palo Alto' CEnd CPMA LTwo MAsh NHol
  SBLw SBir SSta WPGP WPat
- 'Parasol' CEnd CPMA SBir SSta
- 'Pendula' CLnd CMCN CPMA LRHS SBir SSta
- 'Penwood' CPMA SSpi SSta
- 'Rotundiloba' CLnd CMCN CPMA EPfP SSpi
  SSta
- 'Silver King' (v) CDul CMCN CPMA EBee EBre
  ECrN EHoe EPfP IMGH LRHS
  MAsh MGos SCoo SKee SLim SPer
  SPoG SSta WOrn WPat
- 'Stared' CLnd CPMA SBir WPat
- 'Stella' CLnd WPat
- 'Thea' CPMA LRHS MAsh MBlu SBir SSta
§ - 'Variegata' (v) CBcs CBot CDul CLnd COtt
  CPMA CTho ECrN ELan EPfP
  LPan LRHS MAsh MDun MGos
  NBee NHol SHBN SKee SLim
  SPer SSpi SSta WDin
  WPat
- 'Worplesdon' ♀H4 More than 30 suppliers

Liriodendron ✿ (*Magnoliaceae*)

chinense	CBcs CMCN CTho EPfP MBlu SSpi WPGP
'T. Jackson'	NLar
tulipifera ♀H4	More than 30 suppliers
– 'Ardis'	CMCN SSpi
– 'Arnold'	CMCN
– 'Aureomarginatum' (v) ♀H4	More than 30 suppliers
– 'Aureum'	CMCN
– 'Crispum'	CMCN
– 'Fastigiatum'	CBcs CDoC CEnd CLnd CMCN COtt CTho EBee ECrN ELan ENot EPfP IArd LPan LRHS MAsh MBlu MBri MGos NPal SBLw SKee SPer SSpi SSta WOrn
– 'Glen Gold'	CEnd CMCN MBlu MGos SMad
– 'Mediopictum' (v)	CMCN CTho MBlu

Liriope ✿ (*Convallariaceae*)

'Big Blue'	see *L. muscari* 'Big Blue'
§ **exiliflora**	CEnd CLAP EBee EGle EMan EPar GCal NLar WCAu WFar
§ – 'Ariaka-janshige' (v)	EMan SWat
§ **gigantea**	CLAP EBee GSki SWat
graminifolia misapplied	see *L. muscari*
hyacinthifolia	see *Reineckea carnea*
kansuensis	ERos
koreana	GCal
'Majestic'	CBct EGle ENot ERou GSki MBri SPla WCot WFar WSpi
§ **muscari** ♀H4	More than 30 suppliers
– B&SWJ 561	WCru
– 'Alba'	see *L. muscari* 'Monroe White'
§ – 'Big Blue'	CBct CKno CLAP CM&M COlW CPrp EBee EMan EPfP EWll GSki LHop LRHS MRav NArg NLar WCAu WCFE WMoo WSpi
– 'Christmas Tree'	CBct CPrp EBee SMac WBor
– 'Evergreen Giant'	see *L. gigantea*
– 'Gold-banded' (v)	CHea CPrp EGle EMan EPfP GCal LRHS NRib SHBN SPer SWat WFar WSpi WViv
– 'Ingwersen'	CPrp EBee EDAr GBin GFlt LPhx MSph WShp
– 'John Burch' (v)	CBct CLAP COlW CPrp EBee EMan ENot GBin LHop MCCP NLar SMac SUsu WBor WSpi
– 'Majestic' misapplied	see *L. exiliflora*
§ – 'Monroe White'	More than 30 suppliers
– 'Okina' **new**	EMon
– 'Paul Aden'	CFil EPfP WPGP
– 'Pee Dee Ingot' **new**	EBee
– 'Royal Purple'	CBct CLAP CPrp EBee EMan ENot EPfP GSki NBPC NFla NGdn NLar NOrc SMac SPla WShp
– 'Silver Ribbon'	CLAP CPrp EBee EMan EPfP GSki NSti WPGP
– 'Silvery Midget' (v)	CPrp SUsu WMoo
– 'Superba'	WCot
§ – 'Variegata' (v)	CDes CFir CLAP CPrp ECot ELan ENot EPPr EPar EPfP EPla EPza ERou EWes GSki LAst LHop LRHS MCCP MRav MTho NBir NSti SCro SMad SPer SWvt WCot WFar WPGP
* – 'Variegated Alba' (v)	CFir
– 'Webster Wideleaf'	GSki WCot
platyphylla	see *L. muscari*
'Samantha'	CBct CKno CPrp EBee ECha LRHS SMac
§ **spicata**	CBro EBee ERos LPio MBro SSpi SWat WAul WWeb
– 'Alba'	CRow EBee GCal MRav MTed MTho SWal WTin WWin
§ – 'Gin-ryu' (v)	CBct CCge CElw CFir CKno CLAP COlW EBee EPPr EWes GSki LEdu LPio MCCP MRav MSte SLPl SPer SUsu WCot WPGP WViv
– 'Silver Dragon'	see *L. spicata* 'Gin-ryu'
– 'Small Green'	EBee

Lisianthius (*Gentianaceae*)

russelianus	see *Eustoma grandiflorum*

Listera (*Orchidaceae*)

ovata	WHer

Lithocarpus ✿ (*Fagaceae*)

densiflorus var. **echinoides** NNS 00-504	WCot
edulis	CHEx SArc
pachyphyllus	CBcs CHEx
* **pathisapsis** SF 96178	ISea

Lithodora (*Boraginaceae*)

§ **diffusa**	MAsh SGar
– 'Alba'	ECtt EMil EPfP GKir LBee LRHS MBri MGos NLAp SGar SPer WFar
– 'Cambridge Blue'	LRHS NFla SLdr SPer WShp
– 'Compacta'	CLyd EWes NWCA
– 'Grace Ward' ♀H4	GKev MAsh MBro MGos MWya NHol SBod WAbe WPat
– 'Heavenly Blue' ♀H4	More than 30 suppliers
– 'Inverleith'	EWes WFar
– 'Pete's Favourite'	WAbe WShp
– 'Picos'	CMea EDAr EHyt EPot GCrs GTou MBro NMen SIgm WAbe WPat
– 'Star'PBR	CBcs CLyd CMHG CWCL ECtt EPfP GKir LRHS NLar SBod SCoo SIng SPer SPoG WBod WLin WShp
fruticosa new	CArn XPep
graminifolia	see *Moltkia suffruticosa*
hispidula	SAga SIgm WAbe WLin
x **intermedia**	see *Moltkia* x *intermedia*
§ **oleifolia** ♀H4	MBro MWat NBir NMen NSla SBla WAbe WPat
rosmarinifolia	CSpe EHyt GKir LRHS
zahnii	CLyd CStu EBee EPot SIgm WAbe WPat

Lithophragma (*Saxifragaceae*)

parviflorum	CPom EBee EHyt EMan MSte MTho NBir NMen NRya NWCA SSpi WCru WFar WPnP

Lithospermum (*Boraginaceae*)

diffusum	see *Lithodora diffusa*
doerfleri	see *Moltkia doerfleri*
erythrorhizon	MSal WWye
officinale	CArn GBar GPoy MGol MSal
oleifolium	see *Lithodora oleifolia*
purpureocaeruleum	see *Buglossoides purpurocaerulea*

Litsea (*Lauraceae*)

glauca	see *Neolitsea sericea*

Littonia (*Colchicaceae*)

modesta	CRHN ITer

Livistona (*Arecaceae*)

australis	CBrP CRoM CTrC EAmu LPal WMul
chinensis ♀H1	CAbb CBrP CPHo CRoM EAmu EUJe LPJP LPal MPRe WMul
decipiens	CRoM CTrC LPal MPRe WMul
mariae	LPal

Lloydia (Liliaceae)

flavonutans	EBee
ixiolirioides	EBee
oxycarpa	EBee
serotina	EBee
tibetica	EBee
yunnanensis	EBee EPot

Loasa (Loasaceae)

triphylla var. *volcanica*	EMan EWes GCal WSHC

Lobelia (Campanulaceae)

B&SWJ 9006 from Guatemala **new**	WCru
RCB/Arg K2-5	WCot
RCB/Arg S-4	WCot
'Alice'	WCot WFar WOut
anatina	CFai CFir LRHS WDyG
angulata	see *Pratia angulata*
'Bees' Flame'	CFir EBee EBre EMan EMar EPza ERou MLLN MSchu SLon SVil SWat LAst
Big Blue = 'Weslobigblue'^{PBR}	
Blue Star = 'Wesstar'^{PBR}	ECtt LAst
bridgesii	CPLG CSpe EChP EMan GCal GGar IFro SSte WCom
'Butterfly Blue'	CBcs EBee EChP EGle GBuc MTis SPla
'Butterfly Rose'	EGle GBuc SRot WCHb
cardinalis ♀^{H3}	More than 30 suppliers
- subsp. *graminea* var. *multiflora*	CFir
'Cherry Ripe'	CM&M ECoo EMan EPfP LHop LRHS NHol SMrm WCHb WEas WMoo
'Cinnabar Deep Red'	see *L.* 'Fan Tiefrot'
'Cinnabar Rose'	see *L.* 'Fan Zinnoberrosa'
'Complexion'	LRHS
Compliment Blue	see *L.* 'Kompliment Blau'
Compliment Deep Red	see *L.* 'Kompliment Tiefrot'
Compliment Purple	see *L.* 'Kompliment Purpur'
Compliment Scarlet	see *L.* 'Kompliment Scharlach'
coronopifolia	EShb
'Cotton Candy'	EFou NSti
'Dark Crusader'	CPrp EBee EBlw ECtt ELan EMan EMar EPza LRHS MBri NGdn NPro SAga SChu SMrm SPla WCHb WCru WEas WMnd WSan
dortmanna	EMFW
erecta	MGol
erinus 'Kathleen Mallard' (d)	ECtt LAst SWvt WBVN
- 'Richardii'	see *L. richardsonii*
'Eulalia Berridge'	CSam EBee EChP EGle GBuc MBri MMil SAga SMrm WCru WDyG WMoo WSHC
excelsa	CPle CTbh GFlt LTwo MAvo MGol MWrn NCGa SDnm SIgm SSte WCot WFar WGMN WPic
Fan Deep Red	see *L.* 'Fan Tiefrot'
'Fan Deep Rose'	see *L.* 'Fan Orchidrosa'
§ 'Fan Orchidrosa' ♀^{H3-4}	CFwr EBee EShb MWgw NGdn SRot WWeb
'Fan Scharlach' ♀^{H3-4}	EBee EShb IBal LPVe MAvo MWgw NCGa NLar SGar SRot SWvt WHil WWeb
§ 'Fan Tiefrot' ♀^{H3-4}	CBrm CDWL EBee ERou LPVe MWgw NCGa NGdn SBla SHel SMHy SRms SSpi SWat SWvt WCHb WHil WPer WWeb
§ 'Fan Zinnoberrosa' ♀^{H3-4}	CBcs CBrm CFir CM&M EBee ERou LAst LRHS MFOX MHar

	SRms SRot SWvt WCHb WMoo WPer WWin
'Flamingo'	see *L.* 'Pink Flamingo'
fulgens	EPfP IHMH LNCo NPer WEas WFar
§ - 'Elmfeuer'	CFai CMHG EBee EChP EMar ERou LPVe MAnH MWgw NLar SMrm SPlb SWvt WFar
- 'Illumination'	GBuc
- Saint Elmo's Fire	see *L fulgens* 'Elmfeuer'
x *gerardii*	CBri CSam EBee EWll SSte WBor WGMN WMoo WSHC WWpP
- 'Eastgrove Pink'	WEas
- 'Hadspen Purple'	CBAn CFwr CHad CPen EBee MAnH MBri NCGa
- 'Rosencavalier'	CBre EBee EMar LRHS MMil WFar WOut
§ - 'Vedrariensis'	More than 30 suppliers
gibberoa	CHEx
'Grape Knee-High' **new**	CFai SVil
'Hadspen Purple'	see *L.* x *gerardii* 'Hadspen Purple'
imperialis	WCom
inflata	CArn GPoy MSal SECG WCHb WWye
'Jack McMaster'	SUsu
kalmii	CFwr
'Kimbridge Beet'	CMac SLon
§ 'Kompliment Blau'	CFir ERou LRHS NArg SWvt WPer
§ 'Kompliment Purpur'	ERou MNrw SWvt
§ 'Kompliment Scharlach' ♀^{H3-4}	CBri CSWP EBee EBre EPfP ERou LRHS MBNS MNrw MWrn NCGa NHol NPer SSpi SWvt WCHb WFar WMnd WPer
§ 'Kompliment Tiefrot'	ERou MAnH MNrw NArg SWvt WAul WPer
laxiflora	CBot EGra MTho SAga SIgm SPet
- B&SWJ 9064	WCru
- var. *angustifolia*	CHEx CPrp CSam CTbh CWCL EMan ERea GCal MOak MSte SDnm SHFr SMrm SRms SSte WHil WPrP WWye XPep
'Lena'	SWat
lindblomii	CFee CStu
linnaeoides	EMan SPlb WEas
longifolia from Chile	CFee
§ *lutea*	EDif LRHS LRav
'Martha' **new**	EBee
'Monet Moment' **new**	EBee
pedunculata	see *Pratia pedunculata*
perpusilla	see *Pratia perpusilla*
'Pink Elephant' ♀^{H4}	CHar CSWP EBee GMac MAnH MDKP NBrk SBla SChu SHar WFar WPGP WRha WWeb
§ 'Pink Flamingo'	CM&M EBee EBlw EBre EPar LRHS SMrm SOkh SWat WCHb WFar WSHC WShi WWeb WWye
polyphylla	GFlt LTwo MGol MHar MWrn NCGa SIgm SSte WGMN WWin
preslii **new**	CPBP
puberula	CFir
'Purple Towers'	EBee
'Queen Victoria' ♀^{H3}	More than 30 suppliers
'Red Chester' **new**	CWCL
regalis	WCHb WHal
§ *richardsonii* ♀^{H1+3}	ECtt LAst LIck SWvt
'Rosenkavalier' **new**	CPen
roughii	EMan
'Royal Purple' **new**	SMHy
'Ruby Slippers'	CBcs CFai EBee EBre EFou ELan EMan ENor LAst MTis NCGa NLar WShp
I 'Russian Princess' misapplied, purple-flowered	CMHG CPrp CSam EBee EBlw EBre EChP ECtt ELan EMan EMar EWTr LAst LPBA LRHS MAnH MBri MHer MMil NBrk NCGa NHol

	SChu SMad SPer SUsu WCAu
	WCHb WFar WWeb
sessilifolia	CPLG CTCP CWat EBee EGle
	GBuc GCal LPBA MWrn WBVN
	WCot WOut WPer WWye
- B&L 12396	EMon
siphilitica	More than 30 suppliers
- 'Alba'	CSam EBee EPfP GBBs GFlt LPBA
	LPVe LRHS MLLN SRms SWal SWvt
	WCHb WFar WHoo WHrl WMoo
	WPGP WPer WSan WWpP WWye
- Blue selection	LPVe NLar SWvt WSan
- 'Rosea'	MNrw
'Sparkle DeVine'	EFou WCot WWpP
x *speciosa*	EFou GMac MNrw WMoo WWeb
- dark	CMHG EGle SMrm
'Tania'	More than 30 suppliers
treadwellii	see *Pratia angulata* 'Treadwellii'
Tresahor Series	CHEx
tupa	More than 30 suppliers
- JCA 12527	EBlw LAst MBnl MTPN WCot
- Archibald's form	CPLG MCCP
- dark orange	SMrm
urens	CFil SSpi WPGP
valida	CPBP EMan GQui SGar SPet SWvt
	WOut
- 'South Seas'	WBar
vedrariensis	see *L.* x *gerardii* 'Vedrariensis'
'Wildwood Splendour'	EFou
'Will Scarlet'	LRHS
'Zinnoberrosa'	see *L.* 'Fan Zinnoberrosa'

Lobularia (Brassicaceae)

maritima **new**	XPep

Loeselia (Polemoniaceae)

mexicana	EMan

loganberry see *Rubus* x *loganobaccus*

Loiseleuria (Ericaceae)

procumbens from Japan	GCrs WAbe

Lomandra (Lomandraceae)

hystrix	WCot
longifolia	ECou GCal WCot

Lomaria see *Blechnum*

Lomatia (Proteaceae)

dentata	WPGP
ferruginea	CAbb CBcs CDoC CFil CHEx CPne
	CTrG EPfP ISea SAPC SArc WCru
	WPGP
fraseri	SSpi WPGP
hirsuta	CFil
longifolia	see *L. myricoides*
§ *myricoides*	CAbb CDoC CFil CTrG CTrw EPfP
	LRHS SAPC SArc SLon SPer SSpi
	WPGP
polymorpha	WPGP
silaifolia	CDoC EPfP WGMN
§ *tinctoria*	CDoC CTrC CTrw EPfP IDee LRHS
	SArc SSpi

Lomatium (Apiaceae)

brandegeei	SIgm
columbianum	SIgm
dissectum	EBee
- var. *multifidum*	SIgm
grayi	SIgm
- NNS 00-522	EPPr
hallii NNS 00-526	SIgm
macrocarpum	SIgm

martindalei	SIgm
nudicaule	SIgm
utriculatum	MSal SIgm

Lonicera ✿ (Caprifoliaceae)

KR 291	EPla
PC&H 17A	SBra
from China	WCru
from Sikkim B&SWJ 2654	WCru
§ *acuminata*	GIBF IArd LAst LRHS SLim WGwG
	WPnP WSHC
- B&SWJ 3480	WCru
alberti	CFai MBNS MRav SLon WGwG
	WHCG WSHC
albiflora	WSHC
- var. *albiflora*	SBra
alpigena	GIBF
alseuosmoides	CTrC GBin IArd SAga SBra SLon
	WBcn WCru WSHC WWeb
x *americana* misapplied	see *L.* x *italica*
§ x *americana* (Miller)	CHad CRHN EPfP LAst LFol LHop
K. Koch	LRHS MAsh MGos NBea NPer
	NWea SBra SEND SLPl SLim SPla
	SReu SSta WBod WCru
x *brownii*	CMac SGar
§ - 'Dropmore Scarlet'	More than 30 suppliers
- 'Fuchsioides'	EPfP MBro NBrk NSti WSHC
- 'Fuchsioides' misapplied	see *L.* x *brownii* 'Dropmore
	Scarlet'
caerulea	CMCN GEil MRav WHCG
- var. *edulis*	CAgr ESim LEdu
- subsp. *kamtschatica*	CAgr CMCN
new	
canadensis	SBra
§ *caprifolium* ♀H4	CBcs CDoC CRHN EBee ECtt ELan
	EOrc EPfP LBuc LRHS MAsh MBar
	MBri MLan NBea SBra SHBN WCot
- 'Anna Fletcher'	CRHN CSPN EBee MBNS SBra
	SCoo SLim WCFE WCru
- 'Inga'	SBra
- f. *pauciflora*	see *L.* x *italica*
chaetocarpa	CMHG CPle GEil WBcn WPat
chamissoi	GIBF
§ *chrysantha*	CMCN GEil GIBF NRya
ciliosa	CBrm NBea
'Clavey's Dwarf'	see *L.* x *xylosteoides* 'Clavey's
	Dwarf'
deflexicalyx	EPfP GIBF
demissa	GIBF
dioica	SBra
'Early Cream'	see *L. caprifolium*
edulis	GIBF
etrusca	GIBF LAst MRav SHel WCom
	WWeb XPep
- 'Donald Waterer' ♀H4	CBgR EBee EPfP LRHS MAsh SBra
	SCoo SPla WFar WGor
- 'Michael Rosse'	EBee ELan IArd LRHS MBNS MSte
	SBra SRms
- 'Superba' ♀H4	CRHN EBee ECtt ELan EPfP LRHS
	MAsh MLLN NBrk SBra SEND SLim
	SPer SPla WCru WFar WPen WSHC
ferdinandii	GIBF WWes
flexuosa	see *L. japonica* var. *repens*
fragrantissima	More than 30 suppliers
gibbiflora Maxim.	see *L. chrysantha*
x *gibbiflora* Dippel	NRya
giraldii hort.	see *L. acuminata*
giraldii Rehder	CBot CFRD EBee EPfP LBuc MAsh
	NHol SBra SLim WCot WCru
glabrata	EBee GEil LBuc SBra SCoo SLPl
	SLim
- B&SWJ 2150	SBra WCru
gracilipes	GIBF
gracilis	MBlu

grata	see *L. x americana* (Miller) K. Koch
x heckrottii	CDoC CFRD CMac CRHN CSBt EBee ECtt LRHS MBar NBea NBee NSti WDin WStI
- 'Gold Flame'	More than 30 suppliers
- 'Gold Flame' misapplied	see *L. x beckrottii* 'American Beauty'
§ *henryi*	More than 30 suppliers
- B&SWJ 8109	WCru
- 'Copper Beauty' **new**	COtt MBlu WWeb
- var. *subcoriacea*	see *L. henryi*
hildebrandiana	ERea EShb LRHS SBra SOWG SSpi WPGP XPep
'Hill House'	CHll
hirsuta	NBea SBra
'Honey Baby' PBR	MBlu MGos MRav NBlu NCGa NHol SPoG WPat WRHF
implexa	EHol EPla MAsh NPro SBra WCru WSHC XPep
infundibulum var. *rockii*	EPfP
insularis	see *L. morrowii*
involucrata	CFee CMCN CMHG CPLG CPMA CPle CWib LHop MBNS MBar MBlu MRav NChi NHol SMac SPer WCFE WCom WDin WFar
- var. *ledebourii*	CBgR CPle EBee ELan EPfP GKir LAst MTis NHol SDys WTel WWin
§ **x italica** ♀H4	CMac COIW CRHN CSam CWSG EBee ECtt ELan ENot GEil LAst LRHS MBri MRav MWgw NCGa NPer NSti SBra SDix SLim SMer SPer SSpi WBod WCru WDin WFar WTel WWeb
- Harlequin = 'Sherlite' PBR (v)	CBot CSPN EBee ECtt ELan EMil ENot EPfP GKir LAst LHop LRHS MAsh MAvo MGos MRav MTis MWat NBea NSti SBra SLim SMad SPer SPlb SVil SWvt WGwG WPGP
§ *japonica*	More than 30 suppliers
'Aureoreticulata' (v)	
- 'Cream Cascade'	EBee LBuc MLLN
- 'Dart's World'	CFRD EBee NHol SPla SVil WBcn WFar WStI
- 'Halliana' ♀H4	More than 30 suppliers
- 'Hall's Prolific'	CDoC CSBt CSam CWSG EBre ECtt ELan ENot EWll GEil GKir LBuc LRHS MAsh MBar MBlu MBri MGos MRav MWgw NBea NHol SBra SLim SMer SPet SPla SWvt WFar WWeb
§ - 'Horwood Gem' (v)	EBee ECtt LFol MGos NHol NPro SBra SCoo WBcn WFar WWeb
- 'Mint Crisp' PBR (v)	CFwr CSBt ELan ENor EPfP LAst LRHS MAsh MBri MGos NPro SHGC SMur SPer SWvt WWeb
- 'Peter Adams'	see *L. japonica* 'Horwood Gem'
- 'Red World'	NBrk
§ - var. *repens* ♀H4	More than 30 suppliers
- 'Variegata'	see *L. japonica* 'Aureoreticulata'
korolkowii	CBot CPMA EBee EPfP GEil LRHS MBNS MBri NBir SLon SPla WBcn WCom WHCG WLeb WSHC WWin
- var. *zabelii* misapplied	see *L. tatarica* 'Zabelii'
- var. *zabelii* Rehder	ELan
lanceolata AC 3120	GGar
maackii	CHll CMCN EPfP WHCG
* *macgregorii*	CMCN
'Mandarin' PBR	CDoC CWSG EBee ELan ENot EPfP GKir LRHS MAsh MBNS MBlu MGos MRav MWgw SBra SCoo SWvt WSpi
maximowiczii	GEil GIBF
§ *morrowii*	CMCN GIBF MBlu
x muscaviensis	GEil
nervosa	GIBF
nitida	CBcs CCVT CDul CTri EBee ENot EPfP MRav NBlu NWea SHBN SKee SPer STre WBVN WDin WFar WHar WHen WStI
- 'Baggesen's Gold' ♀H4	More than 30 suppliers
- 'Cumbrian Calypso'	NPro
- 'Eden Spring'	NPro
- Edmée Gold = 'Briloni' **new**	MBri
- 'Elegant'	LBuc
- 'Ernest Wilson'	MBar
- 'Fertilis'	ENot SPer
- 'Hohenheimer Findling'	WDin
- 'Lemon Beauty' (v)	More than 30 suppliers
- 'Lemon Queen'	CWib ELan MSwo
- 'Lemon Spreader'	LBuc
§ - 'Maigrün'	CBcs EBee EGra EMil ENot LBuc LRHS MBri MSwo NPro SPer WDin WFar WGwG
- Maygreen	see *L. nitida* 'Maigrün'
- 'Red Tips'	EBee EHoe EPla GEil LRHS MBNS MGos MLLN NHol WDin WFar WPnP WWeb
- 'Silver Beauty' (v)	More than 30 suppliers
* - 'Silver Cloud'	NHol
- 'Silver Lining'	see *L. pileata* 'Silver Lining'
- 'Silver Queen'	WEas
- 'Twiggy' (v)	EMil LBuc LHop LRHS MBri MGos NPro
nummulariifolia	XPep
periclymenum	CArn CDul CRWN CTri ELau GPoy MDun MHer NBea NFor NSco NWea SECG SHFr SPlb WDin WHCG WWye
§ - 'Belgica'	More than 30 suppliers
- 'Belgica' misapplied	see *L. x italica*
* - 'Cream Cascade'	GKir
- 'Cream Cloud'	SBra
- 'Florida'	see *L. periclymenum* 'Serotina'
- 'Graham Thomas' ♀H4	More than 30 suppliers
- 'Heaven Scent'	EMil SBra
- 'Honeybush'	CSPN EBee SCoo WWeb
- 'La Gasnaérie'	EBee SBra SLim
- 'Liden'	SBra
- 'Llyn Brianne'	WBcn
- 'Munster'	CFRD EBee MBri NBrk SBra WBcn WSHC
- 'Red Gables'	CFRD CSam EBee GEil MBNS MBri MGos MRav MSte NHol SBra SEND SLim SPla SVil WCot WGor WKif WPat
N - 'Serotina' ♀H4	More than 30 suppliers
- - EM '85	ENot
- 'Serpentine'	EBee NBrk SBra
* - *sulphurea*	EWll WFar
- 'Sweet Sue'	CRHN CSPN EBee ECtt ELan EPfP GCal LAst LRHS MAsh MBNS MGos MLan MSte MTis NCGa NSti SBra SCoo SWvt WBcn WFar WPnP WWeb
- 'Winchester'	EBee LBuc WWeb
pileata	More than 30 suppliers
- 'Moss Green'	CDoC EBee EWTr MGos WHCG
- 'Pilot'	SLPl
§ - 'Silver Lining' (v)	EPla GBuc WCot
- 'Stockholm'	SLPl
pilosa Willd. CD&R 1216	SBra
praeflorens	CPle
x purpusii	CDoC CPle CTri CWSG CWib EBee ENot EPfP EWTr LAst MBNS MBar MGos MSwo MWat NBea SLim SPer SPla SRms

	WBod WFar WHCG WHar WSHC WTel WWin
- 'Spring Romance'	SLon
- 'Winter Beauty' ♀H4	More than 30 suppliers
pyrenaica	CPle
quinquelocularis	GIBF MBlu
f. *translucens*	
rupicola var.	see *L. syringantha*
syringantha	
ruprechtiana	GEil
saccata	CPMA EPfP
sempervirens ♀H4	CBot CSBt EBee EPar EPfP MBNS MCCP MRav NBea SBra WFar WSHC
- 'Dropmore Scarlet'	see *L.* x *brownii* 'Dropmore Scarlet'
- 'Leo'	CSPN
N - f. *sulphurea*	EBee EPfP LRHS NBea SBra SPer WSHC WWeb
- - 'John Clayton'	SBra
serotina 'Honeybush'	CDoC CPle MAsh MBlu MTis NHol NPri SBra SLim
setifera	CPle
- 'Daphnis'	EPfP
similis var.	CBot CRHN CSPN CSam EBee
delavayi ♀H4	EBre ELan EPfP GEil IArd LRHS MAsh MLan MRav NBea NSti SBra SDix SEND SLPl SPla WCru WFar WGwG WPGP WPen WSHC
'Simonet'	SBra
splendida	SBra WSHC
standishii	CBcs CTri EBee EHol ENor MGos MRav SPer WDin WFar WHCG WRha WWin
- 'Budapest'	MBlu MGos
stenantha **new**	NLar
'Stone Green'	MGos NLRH NPro
subequalis	CFil
§ *syringantha*	CBrm CDul CHar CSBt CSam EBee ELan EPfP EWTr GEil GKir LAst MBlu MGos MTis MWhi NBea NPro SHBN SPer SPla WCFE WCru WDin WFar WHCG WSHC WTel WWin XPep
- 'Grandiflora'	GQui
tatarica	CMCN CWib MRav MWhi SLon WBVN WFar WHCG WTel WWin MTed
- 'Alba'	MTed
- 'Arnold Red'	CBcs EBee ELan EPfP EWTr GEil MBlu MHer NBlu SGar WDin WTel XPep
- 'Hack's Red'	CBcs EBee EPfP MRav SPer SWvt WCot WDin WFar WGMN WHCG
§ - 'Zabelii'	EBee EPfP EWTr MGos
x *tellmanniana*	More than 30 suppliers
- 'Joan Sayer'	MBNS MBri MGos NBrk SBra SLim WBcn WCFE WCru WWeb
thibetica	GIBF MBlu SPer WBcn WFar
tragophylla ♀H4	CBcs CDoC CPLG CSBt EBee ELan EPfP GCal GIBF LHop LRHS MBNS MBlu MBri NSti SBra SDnm SLim SPer SSpi SWvt WCru WDin WSHC WWeb
- 'Maurice Foster'	EBee GCal SBra SMad
* - 'Pharoah's Trumpet'	ERea LRHS MAsh SSpi WBcn
trichosantha	GIBF
var. *acutiuscula*	
vesicaria	CPle
webbiana	ELan
x *xylosteoides*	MRav WFar
- 'Clavey's Dwarf'	MBlu MGos NBrk SLPl
- 'Miniglobe'	NPro
xylosteum	CArn

Lopezia (Onagraceae)

racemosa	CSpe SHFr

Lophatherum (Poaceae)

gracile **new**	CPLG EMan EShb MAvo WDyG

Lophomyrtus (Myrtaceae)

§ *bullata*	CAbP CHEx CTrC EBee ECou GQui IDee SPer WCHb WFar
- 'Matai Bay'	CBcs CTrC EBee
'Gloriosa' (v)	CAbP CDoC CPle LAst WCHb WGer
§ *obcordata*	SSpi
§ x *ralphii*	IDee LAst MHer WCHb WPic
§ - 'Kathryn'	CBcs CDoC CPLG CPen CPle EBee IArd ISea SSpi WCHb WSHC
- 'Little Star' (v)	CBcs CDoC CTrC GBri LRHS WPat
I - 'Multicolor' (v)	CTrC EBee
- 'Pixie'	CAbP CDoC CTrC WPat
- 'Red Dragon'	CTrC EBee GBri IArd WPat
§ - 'Traversii' (v)	LRHS SMur
- 'Wild Cherry'	CTrC
'Tricolor' (v)	CPle CTrC WCot

Lophosoria (Dicksoniaceae)

quadripinnata	CFil

Lophospermum (Scrophulariaceae)

§ *erubescens* ♀H2-3	CBot CBri CHEx CHal CRHN MSte MTis SGar SHFr SMur
- 'Bridal Bouquet'	CPla
'Magic Dragon' **new**	MCCP
§ 'Red Dragon'	CPla CSpe CTCP SGar
§ *scandens*	CBcs CRHN ELan SMur
§ - 'Pink Ice'	LRHS SOWG

loquat see *Eriobotrya japonica*

Loropetalum (Hamamelidaceae)

chinense	CFil CMCN CPen SSpi
- 'Daybreak's Flame' **new**	CPen
- 'Ming Dynasty'	CPen
- 'Pippa's Red' **new**	CPen
- f. *rubrum*	CFil SLon
- - 'Blush'	CFil
- - 'Fire Dance'	CDoC CFai CPMA CPen EMil IDee SSpi SWvt
I - - 'Zhuzhou Fuchsia'	CMCN
- 'Tang Dynasty' **new**	CPen

Lotononis (Papilionaceae)

pulchella	SPlb

Lotus (Papilionaceae)

berthelotii	CFee CHEx CHal ECtt ELan ERea ESlt MOak SChu SPet SPoG
- deep red ♀H1+3	LIck SWvt
berthelotii x *maculatus* ♀H1+3	WIvy
- x - 'Fire Vine' **new**	LAst
corniculatus	CArn GWCH MBow MCoo MHer NLan NSco NTHB SECG SIde SPet WBri WShp XPep
- 'Plenus' (d)	EPot MTho NLar WPer
creticus	SHFr
cytisoides **new**	XPep
§ *hirsutus* ♀H3-4	More than 30 suppliers
- 'Brimstone' (v)	CEnd ECtt EGoo EPPr LHop LRHS MCCP SPer SVil SWvt WBro
- dwarf	LHop
- 'Fréjorgues' **new**	XPep
- 'Lois'	EBee MDKP WSPU
maculatus	ESlt NPri SHFr SOWG SPet WIvy

maritimus	EBee EWll LPhx MOne MWgw MWrn SHFr SRot SScr WWin
mascaensis hort.	see *L. sessilifolius*
pedunculatus	see *L. uliginosus*
pentaphyllus **new**	XPep
- subsp. *herbaceus*	XPep
§ - subsp. *pentaphyllus*	EChP
§ *sessilifolius*	CHal ERea
suffruticosus	see *L. pentaphyllus* subsp. *pentaphyllus*
tetragonolobus	SRot WHer
§ *uliginosus*	MGas NMir NSco

lovage see *Levisticum officinale*

Luculia (Rubiaceae)

grandifolia	LRHS SOWG
gratissima 'Rosea'	LRHS

Ludwigia (Onagraceae)

grandiflora	WDyG WMAq WWpP
uruguayensis	LPBA MCCP

Luetkea (Rosaceae)

pectinata	NRya WAbe

Luma (Myrtaceae)

§ *apiculata* ♀H3	More than 30 suppliers
§ - 'Glanleam Gold' (v) ♀H3	More than 30 suppliers
- 'Penwith' (v)	CTrC
- 'Variegata' (v)	CMHG CTri ISea SAga SLim WCru WWye
§ *chequen*	CBcs CFee GGar IDee MHer NLar WCHb WCwm WFar WJek WMoo XPep

Lunaria (Brassicaceae)

§ *annua*	GWCH MBow MWgw SIde SWat WHer
- var. *albiflora* ♀H4	MWgw NBir SWat
I - - 'Alba Variegata' (v)	CCge CSpe EBla MAnH MFir MHer WCom WTin
- 'Munstead Purple'	EBla
* - 'Stella'	WHen
- 'Variegata' (v)	CHar EBla GFlt IBlr MAvo MCCP MTho NBid NBir SWat WEas WHer WSan
- violet	NBir WFar
biennis	see *L. annua*
rediviva	CSpe EBee ECGP ECha EMon EPPr EPla GAbr GCal GGar GKir GLil IBlr LPhx LRHS MBct NBid NChi NPer NSti SBla SBre SSpi SUsu WCot WEas WFar WHen WHer WPGP

Lupinus ✿ (Papilionaceae)

'African Sunset'	CWCL
albifrons	MWgw SIgm XPep
'Amber Glow'	CWCL
'Approaching Storm'	SMrm
'Apricot Spire'	CWCL
arboreus ♀H4	More than 30 suppliers
- *albus*	CSpe CWib WBry WCom
- 'Barton-on-Sea'	CFwr CNat MAvo NLar
- blue	CBri CBrm CHar CMea EBre ECGN ECGP ERou GBBs MAvo MCCP MPRe MWrn NLar SPer SPlb SWvt WBVN WBry WFar WHer WMoo WWeb
- blue and white **new**	WOut
- 'Blue Boy'	CFwr SPla
- cream	ECGP MWgw
- 'Mauve Queen'	CBri CHEx CHar MWrn NLar SUsu
- mixed	CArn SMac SPet
- prostrate	CFwr MMHG
- 'Snow Queen'	CBrm CTCP MAvo MCCP MWrn NBur NLar
- 'Sulphur Yellow'	CBri ERou SWvt
- white	WOut
arboreus x *variicolor*	CHid
arcticus	CDes EBee
'Aston Villa'	CWCL
'Avalon' **new**	CWCL
'Baby Doll'	CWCL
Band of Nobles Series ♀H4	CBri ECtt SSth WFar
bicolor	CHar CTCP
'Bishop's Tipple'	CWCL EWes
'Blue Moon'	CWCL
'Blue Streak'	CWCL
'Blueberry Pie'	CWCL
'Bubblegum' **new**	CWCL
'Cashmere Cream'	CWCL
chamissonis	CAbb CFwr CPla CSpe CStr CTCP EBee EChP EHrv EMan EWes GEil LHop LRHS MTho MTis SDry SGar SPer WCom WFar WGMN
'Chandelier'	More than 30 suppliers
'Cherry Belle'	CWCL
'Copperlight'	CWCL
'Desert Sun'	CWCL
'Dolly Mixture'	CWCL
'Dreaming Spires' **new**	CWCL
Dwarf Gallery hybrids	ENot GKir LIck
'Dwarf Lulu'	see *L.* 'Lulu'
elegans 'Dwarf Pink Fairy' **new**	CSpe
Gallery Series	COIW CSBt EBre SCoo SPlb WBVN WFar WHil
- 'Gallery Blue'	ECtt EPfP MBow NBlu NCGa NLar NNor NPri NVic SCoo WHil
- 'Gallery Pink'	EPfP LRHS NBlu NCGa NLar NPri NVic SCoo SPla WBry WHil
- 'Gallery Red'	ECtt EPfP LRHS NBlu NCGa NLar NPri NVic SCoo SPla WBry
- 'Gallery Rose'	MBow
- 'Gallery White'	EPfP LPVe LRHS NLar NPri NVic SCoo SPla WHil
- 'Gallery Yellow'	ECtt EPfP LRHS MBow NBlu NCGa NLar NPri NVic SCoo SPla WHil
'Garden Gnome'	LRav WPer
'Lady Penelope'	CWCL
lepidus	EMan
- var. *lobbii*	SIgm
- var. *sellulus*	SIgm
littoralis	CTCP EMan SIgm
'Lollipop'	CWCL
§ 'Lulu'	CBri COtt EBre ECtt ENot LRHS MFOX MRav NPPs SPer SWvt WFar WMnd WMoo
'Manhattan Lights' **new**	CWCL
Minarette Group	CTri ECtt MBri NBlu SGar SPet SRms WFar WGor WHil
'My Castle'	More than 30 suppliers
'Noble Maiden' (Band of Nobles Series)	CSBt CTri EBre EChP ECtt ELan EPfP ERou EWTr GAbr GKir GLil LRHS MBri MWgw NBPC NBlu NBrk NMir SMer SPer SWal SWvt WCAu WFar WHen WPer WShp WWeb
nootkatensis	EBee
'Pagoda Prince'	CWCL
perennis	CAgr EBee ECGN
'Pink Cadillac'	CWCL
'Plum Duff'	CWCL
'Plummy Blue'	EMan MCCP SMac
'Poached Salmon'	SMrm
'Polar Princess'	CWCL ERou EWes SWat

polyphyllus	CTCP EBee SECG WOut
propinquus	CTCP
'Queen of Hearts'	CWCL
'Red Arrow'	CWCL
x *regalis* 'Morello Cherry'	CWib EWTr MWrn
rivularis **new**	EMan
'Rote Flamme'	EWes
'Ruby Lantern' **new**	CWCL
Russell hybrids	COIW CSBt ELan ENot EPfP GKir
	LHop MHer NBlu SPet SPlb SRms
	SWvt WFar WMnd WSSM
'Saint George' **new**	CWCL
'Sand Pink'	EWes
sericeus	EMan
'Sherbert Dip'	CWCL
'Silk Rain'	CWCL
'Snowgoose'	CWCL
'Storm'	CWCL
'Terracotta'	CWCL
texensis	CSpe
'The Chatelaine' (Band of	More than 30 suppliers
Nobles Series)	
'The Governor' (Band of	More than 30 suppliers
Nobles Series)	
'The Page' (Band of	CBri ELan EPfP ERou LRHS MBri
Nobles Series)	MRav MWgw NBPC NBrk NMir
	SECG SMer SPer SWal SWvt WBVN
	WFar WMoo WPer WWol
'Thundercloud'	CHad CPlt SMrm
variicolor	CHid CSpe SIgm SSpi
versicolor	CArn CFwr CTCP EBee EMan
	GBBs GFlt LDai LGro LRav MBri
	MCCP MEHN MHer MLLN SGar
	WBVN WBrk WBry WHoo
– 'Dumpty' **new**	CWCL

Lutzia (Brassicaceae)
cretica **new**	XPep

Luzula (Juncaceae)
from New Guinea	EBee EWes
alpinopilosa	CBig EPPr GBin
x *borreri*	EPPr
– 'Botany Bay' (v)	ECtt EPla GBin
canariensis	CFwr WDyG WWye
forsteri	CBgR CBrm EPPr
lactea	EMon EPPr LRHS
luzuloides	CBig WDyG WPer
– 'Schneehäschen'	EBee EMan EMon EPPr GBin GCal
	MWgw WPrP WWpP
maxima	see *L. sylvatica*
multiflora	EBee
nivea	More than 30 suppliers
pilosa	CBgR EPla GCal IBlr
– 'Igel' **new**	GBin SLPl
purpureosplendens	CElw
'Ruby Stiletto'	MAvo
rufa	CTrC ECou
§ *sylvatica*	CRWN CRow CSWP CTrC EFou
	ELan EPPr EPfP EPla EPza GKir
	GOrn MBow MFir MLLN MMoz
	MRav NBro NOrc WDin WFar
	WHer WPGP WShi
– from Tatra Mountains,	EPPr
Czechoslovakia **new**	
– 'A. Rutherford'	see *L. sylvatica* 'Taggart's Cream'
– 'Aurea'	More than 30 suppliers
– 'Aureomarginata'	see *L. sylvatica* 'Marginata'
I – 'Auslese'	CBig EBee EPPr GBin LRHS WMoo
– 'Bromel'	CRez
– 'Hohe Tatra'	More than 30 suppliers
§ – 'Marginata' (v)	More than 30 suppliers
* – f. *nova*	EPPr
– 'Select'	CTrC

§ – 'Taggart's Cream' (v)	CElw CRez CRow EBee EGra EHoe
	EMar EMon EPla MAvo NBid WBea
	WDyG WLeb WMoo WPrP
– 'Tauernpass'	CBgR EBee EHoe EMon EPPr EPla
	GCal NBid NHol SMac
– 'Wäldler'	EHoe EPPr MBNS NHol
– 'Waulkmill Bay'	SLPl
ulophylla	CBig CFir EBee ECou EGoo EMan
	ESis GBin GEdr NWCA

Luzuriaga (Philesiaceae)
radicans	CFee EBee ERos IBlr WCot WCru
	WFar WSHC
– MK 92	SSpi

x *Lycene* (Caryophyllaceae)
§ *kubotae*	EBee

Lychnis (Caryophyllaceae)
alpina	CMHG EBee EMlt EPfP GIBF GKir
	GTou IHMH NArg NBlu NJOw
	NPri NVic WBea WPer WShp
– 'Alba'	GTou NBir
– compact	GTou
– 'Rosea'	NBir
– var. *serpentinicola*	GKev
new	
– 'Snow Flurry'	CPBP EMlt GFlt NLar
§ x *arkwrightii*	EBee EBre ECha ELan NNor SRot
	WBea WFar
– 'Orange Zwerg'	EBee LAst NBPC WWeb
– 'Vesuvius'	CBcs ENot EPfP GFlt GKir LAst
	LPVe LRHS MNrw MRav MTis NBir
	NBlu SPer SRms STes WPer WShp
* 'Blushing Bride'	WRHF
chalcedonica ♀H4	More than 30 suppliers
– var. *albiflora*	EBee ECha IBlr LAst LRHS MBri
	MWgw NArg NBid NBro NSti SPer
	WFar WHen WMoo WPer
– apricot	MBro NBid WBry WHrl
– 'Carnea'	EOMN EWsh GCal LPVe LRHS
	MFir WBea WHil
– 'Dusky Pink' **new**	NBPC
– 'Dusky Salmon'	ITer MDKP MWrn NBPC WGMN
	WWpP
– 'Flore Pleno' (d)	CBot EBee ECha ELan ERou GCal
	GKir IFro MCCP MLLN MOne
	NLar NPri NSti WCot WFar
– 'Morgenrot'	EChP MCCP NLar WBea
– 'Pinkie'	EBee ELan NLar SBod WGMN
– 'Rauhreif'	EChP WBea
– 'Rosea'	EBee EBre EPfP GKir LIck LRHS
	NBir WFar WHen WHrl WMoo
	WPer
* – 'Salmonea'	EBee EBre ECtt GBri LAst LPio
	MBri MTis NBir SRms WCAu
– salmon-pink	COIW WWhi
– 'Summer Sparkle	SWal
Pink' **new**	
– 'Summer Sparkle	SWal
Red' **new**	
– 'Summer Sparkle	SWal
White' **new**	
cognata	CDes EBee MAvo MDKP WCot
	WCru
– B&SWJ 4234	WCru
§ *coronaria* ♀H4	More than 30 suppliers
– MESE 356	EBee
– 'Abbotswood Rose'	see *L.* x *walkeri* 'Abbotswood
	Rose'
– 'Alba' ♀H4	More than 30 suppliers
– 'Angel's Blush'	CBri EBee GAbr LHop LRHS MBnl
	MDKP MRav NBir SPer WGMN
	WPer WRha
– Atrosanguinea Group	CBre EBee EBre EFou ERou EShb

	IBlr LHop LPio LRHS MBnl MRav MTis NCot NPri SPer WBVN WPer
- 'Cerise'	MDKP NBir WBry
- 'Dancing Ladies'	WMnd
- 'Flottbek'	MOne NLar
- 'Hutchinson's Cream' (v)	EMan GFlt NPro WCHb WCot
- Oculata Group	CSpe EBee ECtt EGoo ERou GAbr GKir IBlr MFir MTho NOak NPPs NPri SPlb SWal WFar WHen WHer WPer
coronata	SBla
§ - var. *sieboldii*	EBee WBar WSan
dioica	see *Silene dioica*
flos-cuculi	CArn CNic CRWN CSam EBee EHon EMFW EPfP LNco LPBA MBow MHer MSal MSta NArg NLan NMir NPri SECG SGar WBVN WCAu WHen WHer WMAq WMoo WWpP
- var. *albiflora*	CBre ECoo EMFW EPar LPBA MBow MLLN NBro NLar WCHb WHer WMoo WOut
- 'Jenny' **new**	EBre SPer
* - 'Little Robin'	NHol
- 'Nana'	CSpe EDAr EMar EMlt GAbr NLar NRya SIng WBea WPat WPer WWeb WWin
flos-jovis ♀H4	CTCP EBee EOMN EPfP EWTr IGor LPVe NArg SMer SRms WOut WPer
- 'Hort's Variety'	EBre ERou GKir MRav NSti SBla SUsu WBea
- 'Minor'	see *L. flos-jovis* 'Nana'
§ - 'Nana'	CBrm NBid NWCA WCom
- 'Peggy'	CM&M EBee EGoo ERou MAvo MCCP NLar WWeb
fulgens	EBee
gracillima **new**	CTCP
x *haageana*	EBee LAst LRHS NWCA SAga SIng SRms WSpi
kubotae	see x *Lycene kubotae*
lagascae	see *Petrocoptis pyrenaica* subsp. *glaucifolia*
miqueliana	WMoo
- 'Variegated Lacy Red' (v)	WCot
'Molten Lava'	CFir EBee LPVe LRHS MHer NArg NOrc NPro SGar WMoo WPer WWeb
nutans	MSal
preslii minor	EBee
sibirica	EBee
sieboldii 'Matsu Moto' **new**	WGMN
* *sikkimensis*	EBee
'Terry's Pink'	EBee MLLN NCGa NLar WFar
§ *viscaria*	CArn CElw ECha GIBF IHMH LDai MSal NCiC NFor SECG SGar WBVN WBea WFar WHer WMoo WTin WWeb
- 'Alba'	EBee ECha GCal MLLN NBro WRha WWeb
- *alpina*	see *L. viscaria*
- subsp. *atropurpurea*	CBri EBee EChP SRms WBea WCAu WGMN
- 'Feuer'	CBrm CMea EBee NLar WCot WMoo
- 'Firebird'	EWes NBur
- 'Plena' (d)	EChP MDun MInt SUsu WBor WSan WTin
- 'Schnee'	EMar EWTr WCAu
- 'Snowbird'	WOut
- 'Splendens'	EPfP IHMH WShp
- 'Splendens Plena' (d) ♀H4	CHar EBee GMac MBri MWgw NBro SBla WBea WEas WFar
- 'White Cloud'	MSph
§ x *walkeri* 'Abbotswood Rose' ♀H4	GBuc GFlt IBlr
wilfordii	CFir EBee MLLN MTis SHar
§ *yunnanensis*	CSam EBee GKev MSte NBid NHol SIng WBea WMoo WPer
- *alba*	see *L. yunnanensis*

Lycianthes (Solanaceae)
rantonnetii	see *Solanum rantonnetii*

Lycium (Solanaceae)
barbarum	NBlu SMad
chinense	CArn
europaeum	XPep

Lycopodium (Lycopodiaceae)
clavatum	GPoy

Lycopsis see *Anchusa*

Lycopus (Lamiaceae)
americanus	EBee GPoy MSal
europaeus	CArn ELau EPAt GBar GPoy MHer MSal SECG WBri WGwG WHer WJek WWye
* *hirtus* **new**	EBee
lucidus	MSal
virginicus	CFwr COld MSal SDys WWye

Lycoris (Amaryllidaceae)
aurea	EBee LPhx LRHS
chinensis	EBee
haywardii	WCot
incarnata **new**	EBee
longituba	EBee
radiata	CStu EBee GSki LPhx LRHS
sanguinea	EBee

Lygodium (Schizaeaceae)
japonicum	WFib WRic
§ *microphyllum*	NMar
scandens	see *L. microphyllum*

Lygos (Papilionaceae)
sphaerocarpa	see *Retama sphaerocarpa*

Lyonia (Ericaceae)
ligustrina	LRHS NLar SMur
mariana **new**	NLar

Lyonothamnus (Rosaceae)
floribundus subsp. *aspleniifolius*	CAbb SAPC SArc SGar SIgm SSpi WFar WPGP

Lysichiton (Araceae)
americanus ♀H4	More than 30 suppliers
camtschatcensis ♀H4	More than 30 suppliers
camtschatcensis x *americanus*	SSpi

Lysimachia ✿ (Primulaceae)
acroadenia **new**	CPLG
§ *atropurpurea*	More than 30 suppliers
- 'Beaujolais'	CBod EWll MSPs MWrn NBPC SWal WSan WWeb WWpP
- 'Geronimo'	CSpe
barystachys	CHea CRow EBee EBlw GMac MAnH MRav MWrn SHar SMac SMer WCot WFar WOut
candida	EBee
ciliata	CMHG CRow EBee ECha EHoe ELan EMar EPar GFlt GMac MBri MFir MNrw NArg NFor NGdn NSti

	SChu WBea WCAu WCot WEas WFar WMnd WPer WTin WWin
§ - 'Firecracker' ♀H4	More than 30 suppliers
- 'Purpurea'	see *L. ciliata* 'Firecracker'
clethroides ♀H4	More than 30 suppliers
- 'Geisha' (v)	CDes EBee EMan MBNS MBnl MSph WCot
- 'Lady Jane'	CBrm NBur SRms
§ **congestiflora**	LPVe NPer SHFr SPet
- 'Outback Sunset'PBR (v)	ECtt LAst LRHS NBlu
decurrens	CDes EBee
- JCA 4.542.500	WCot
ephemerum	More than 30 suppliers
fortunei	EBee IHMH SHel SMac WCot
henryi	EWes
hybrida	EBee WCot
japonica var.	CRow MTho NLar SIng SRot
minutissima	
lichiangensis	CBri CFir EMFP EMan GKir GSki MLLN NArg SHFr WMoo WPer WPnP
lyssii	see *L. congestiflora*
mauritiana	EBee EMan GEil WWpP
aff. **mauritiana**	WCru
B&SWJ 8815 **new**	
melampyroides	EBee
minoricensis	CArn CBrm EBee EHrv ELan EMan IHMH MAnH SWat WHer WPer WWin WWpP
nemorum	EFer WPer WRHF
- 'Pale Star'	CBgR CBre WWye
nummularia	CHal COlW CSBt CTri CWat ECtt EHon EPfP GPoy IHMH LNCo LPBA MBar MBow MBri NArg NFor SHFr SWat WBrk WCot WGwG WShp WWpP WWye
- 'Aurea' ♀H4	More than 30 suppliers
paridiformis	EBee
- var. **stenophylla**	CDes
DJHC 704 **new**	
pseudohenryi	EBee
punctata misapplied	see *L. verticillaris*
punctata L.	More than 30 suppliers
§ - 'Alexander' (v)	More than 30 suppliers
- 'Gaulthier Brousse'	WCot
- 'Golden Alexander' **new**	EChP MBNS MBnl NPro
- 'Golden Glory' (v)	WCot
- 'Ivy Maclean' (v)	EBee EChP EMan LBBr MAvo SSvw SWvt WCot
- 'Senior'	EMil
- 'Sunspot'	EBee WCot
- 'Variegata'	see *L. punctata* 'Alexander'
- **verticillata**	see *L. verticillaris*
serpyllifolia	ECtt SHFr
thyrsiflora	EBee EHon EMFW IHMH LNCo MCCP MSta NBlu NLar NPer SWat WCot WHer WMAq WWpP
§ **verticillaris**	WBea WCot
vulgaris	CArn CRWN LPBA MBow SIde WBWf WFar WMoo WPer WShi WWpP WWye
- subsp. **davurica**	WCot
yunnanensis	CElw EBee EMan EPPr EWTr GBBs GFlt GIBF MAnH MDKP MSPs MTis MWrn NBPC SBri SMac WCot WPer WWpP

Lysionotus (Gesneriaceae)

gamosepalus	WCru
B&SWJ 7241 **new**	
pauciflorus	CDes ETow GCrs
- B&SWJ 189	WCru
- B&SWJ 303	WCru
- B&SWJ 335	WCru

aff. **kwangsiensis**	WCru
HWJ 643 **new**	

Lythrum (Lythraceae)

alatum	EBee MGol WSan
anceps	MWrn NLar
salicaria	More than 30 suppliers
- 'Blush' ♀H4	More than 30 suppliers
- 'Brightness'	CDWL NArg
§ - 'Feuerkerze' ♀H4	More than 30 suppliers
- Firecandle	see *L. salicaria* 'Feuerkerze'
- 'Happy'	EBee SChu SCro SMrm
- 'Lady Sackville'	CBos CDWL EBee GBuc LRHS MBNS NDov SSvw SUsu WCAu WTMC WTel
- 'Morden Pink'	CDWL EBee EChP EGle LPhx MBri MSte NGby WBry WFar
- 'Prichard's Variety'	EBee
- 'Robert'	More than 30 suppliers
- 'Rose'	ELan MWgw NBir SWvt
- 'Rosencaule'	EBee EBre
- 'Swirl'	EFou
- 'The Beacon'	CDWL CMHG EBee EMan GCal NPro SRms
- Ulverscroft form	MTed
- 'Zigeunerblut'	CMHG CPlt EBee EGle EMan LPhx MRav MSte NDov NGby NLar SAga SMrm SOkh SWat WAul
virgatum	CMHG LPhx SMHy SMrm SOkh
- 'Dropmore Purple'	CHar CSBt EBee EChP EFou EPPr ERou LHop LPhx LRHS MBri MDKP MSte NDov NFla SOkh WCAu WFar WWpP
- 'Rose Queen'	ECha EMan MRav WFar WPer
- 'Rosy Gem'	CM&M EBee EBlw ECtt EPfP GKir GMac MBNS MWat MWgw NBid NBro NOak SMer SRms SWal SWvt WBea WFar WHil WHoo WLow WPer WViv WWpP
- 'The Rocket'	CM&M CTri EBee EChP EGle EPfP ERou LAst LRHS NBro NDov NSti SMer SPer SWvt WWin

Lytocaryum (Arecaceae)

§ **weddellianum** ♀H1	LPal MBri

M

Maackia (Papilionaceae)

amurensis	CBcs CMCN CPle EBee ELan EPfP IDee IMGH LRav WBVN WNor WSHC
- var. **buergeri**	CLnd GBin
chinensis	CMCN MBlu
fauriei	CPle

Macbridea (Lamiaceae)

caroliniana	CDes EBee WPGP

Macfadyena (Bignoniaceae)

uncata	SOWG
§ **unguis-cati**	CRHN CTCP XPep

Machaeranthera (Asteraceae)

§ **bigelovii**	EBee
shastensis	EBee

Machaerina (Cyperaceae)

rubiginosa 'Variegata' (v)	CDWL

Machilus see *Persea*

Mackaya (Acanthaceae)

§ *bella* ♀H1   CHll ERea EShb SOWG SYvo

Macleania (Ericaceae)

ericae   WCot

Macleaya (Papaveraceae)

cordata misapplied   see *M. x kewensis*
§ *cordata* (Willd.)   More than 30 suppliers
   R. Br. ♀H4
   - 'Celadon Ruffles' **new**   GBin
§ x *kewensis*   EBee GFlt MBro WCom WHoo
     WPGP
   - 'Flamingo' ♀H4   EBee ECha GCal MCLN MRav
     SChu SMrm SWvt WCAu WWye
§ *microcarpa*   MAnH MFOX MGol NPSI SGar
     SWat WHer WSel
   - 'Kelway's Coral   More than 30 suppliers
     Plume' ♀H4
   - 'Spetchley Ruby'   EMan LPhx MRav NBir NDov
     WCot

Maclura (Moraceae)

pomifera   CBcs CFil CMCN EPAt IDee MGol
     WDin WFar WPGP XPep
   - 'Pretty Woman' **new**   NLar
tricuspidata   EGFP

Macrodiervilla see *Weigela*

Macropiper (Piperaceae)

§ *excelsum*   CHEx ECou

Macrozamia (Zamiaceae)

communis   CBrP CRoM LPal WNor
diplomera   CBrP
dyeri   see *M. riedlei*
glaucophylla **new**   CBrP
johnsonii   CBrP
lucida   CBrP
miquelii   CBrP
moorei   CBrP CRoM LPal
mountperiensis   CBrP
§ *riedlei*   CBrP CRoM
spiralis   CRoM

Maddenia (Rosaceae)

hypocleuca **new**   NLar

Madia (Asteraceae)

elegans   EMan NBur

Maesa (Myrsinaceae)

montana **new**   CFil CPLG WPGP

Magnolia ✿ (Magnoliaceae)

acuminata   CBcs CDul CMCN EPfP IDee
     NBhm NPal
   - 'Golden Glow'   CMHG
* - 'Kinju'   CEnd WPGP
   - 'Koban Dori'   CBcs CPMA CTho NPSI
§ - var. *subcordata*   LBuc NLar WPGP
§ - - 'Miss Honeybee'   LRHS SSpi
   'Advance'   CBcs CPMA
   'Albatross'   CBcs CDoC CEnd CTho LRHS
     SSpi
amoena   CBcs CTho WNor
   - 'Multiogeca'   CBcs
   'Ann' ♀H4   CPLG CSdC CTrh SSpi
   'Apollo'   CBcs CEnd CPMA NPSI SSpi
ashei   see *M. macrophylla* subsp. *ashei*
   'Athene'   CBcs CDoC CMHG CPMA LRHS
     SSpi

'Atlas'   CBcs CEnd CMHG CPMA CTho
     EMil LMil LRHS MGos SSpi WPGP
'Betty' ♀H4   CBcs CDoC CSdC LPan MGos NLar
     SSta WBod WDin WFar
'Big Dude'   CFil IArd SSpi WPGP
biondii   CBcs CFil CTho NLar SSpi WNor
     WPGP
I 'Black Tulip'   ENot LRHS MGos NPri SSpi
x *brooklynensis*   CTho
   'Evamaria'
   - 'Hattie Carthan'   WPGP
   - 'Woodsman'   LBuc NLar SSta
   - 'Yellow Bird'   CEnd CMCN COtt CPMA CTho
     ENot EPfP LRHS MBlu MDun
     MGos NLar SLim SSpi SSta
'Butterflies'   CBcs CDoC CEnd CFai CFil CMHG
     CPMA CTho ELan EPfP ISea LHyd
     LRHS MDun NLar SHBN SSpi SSta
     WFar WPGP
'Caerhays Belle'   CBcs CPMA SSpi
'Caerhays Surprise'   CBcs CPMA SSpi
campbellii   CBcs CDul CFil CMCN CPMA
     CTho ELan EPfP ISea LRHS MDun
     SHBN SSpi WFar WPGP WPic
   - Alba Group   CBcs CEnd CTho MGos WFar
     WPGP
I - - 'Trelissick Alba' **new**   CTho
   - 'Betty Jessel'   CBcs CPMA CTho
   - 'Darjeeling'   CBcs EMil
   - 'Lamellan Pink'   CTho
   - 'Lamellan White'   CTho
   - subsp. *mollicomata*   CBcs CEnd CHEx CSam CTrw EPfP
     ISea SSpi WFar WPGP
   - - 'Lanarth'   CBcs CEnd SSpi WBod
   - - 'Maharanee'   CBcs NPSI
   - - 'Peter Borlase'   CDoC CTho LRHS
   - (Raffillii Group)   CAbP CBcs CLnd ELan EMil EPfP
     'Charles Raffill'   MDun MGos MLan SHBN SLim
     SPer SPoG WDin
   - - 'Kew's Surprise'   CBcs CPMA
'Candy Cane'   SSpi
'Cecil Nice'   WPGP
Chameleon   see *M.* 'Chang Hua'
§ 'Chang Hua'   MDun NLar
'Charles Coates'   MDun NLar
China Town   MDun
   = 'Jing Ning' **new**
* *chingii* **new**   CBcs
'Columbus'   CFil CPMA SSpi WPGP
'Coral Lake'   MDun
cordata   see *M. acuminata* var. *subcordata*
   - 'Miss Honeybee'   see *M. acuminata* var. *subcordata*
     'Miss Honeybee'
cylindrica hort.   see *M.* 'Pegasus'
cylindrica Wilson   CMCN CPMA EPfP IArd LRHS SSpi
* 'Dan Quing'   LPan MDun NLar
'Dark Shadow'   WPGP
§ 'Darrell Dean'   CTho WPGP
'David Clulow'   CBcs CPMA CTho LRHS SSpi
dawsoniana   CBcs CMCN EPfP NLar SSpi
   - 'Chyverton Red'   CTho SSpi
'Daybreak'   SSpi
delavayi   CBcs CBrP CFil CHEx EPfP GGGa
     LRHS SAPC SArc SSpi WMul WPGP
§ *denudata* ♀H3-4   CBcs CMCN CPMA CTho CTrw
     EMil EPfP LMil LPan LRHS NPSI
     SMur SReu SSpi SSta WBod WDin
     WFar WNor WPGP
   - 'Dubbel'   CBcs MDun
   - 'Forrest's Pink'   CBcs
   - 'Yellow River'   CEnd LPan MDun NLar SPoG
   'Elisa Odenwald'   SSpi WPGP
   'Elizabeth' ♀H4   CDoC CEnd CFil CMCN CPMA
     CTho ELan EPfP GGGa IMGH ISea

	LAst LMil LRHS MBri MDun MGos
	NHol SHBN SKee SPer SSpi SSta
	WPGP
'Fei Huang' **new**	CDoC
'Fireglow'	CTho
'Frank Gladney'	CPMA CTho
'Frank's Masterpiece'	MDun
fraseri AM	SSpi
'Full Eclipse'	CFil WPGP
'Galaxy' ♀H4	CBcs CDoC CEnd CFil CMCN
	CSdC CTho EPfP IArd IMGH ISea
	LPan LRHS MBar MBri MGos MSte
	NBhm SKee SLdr SLim SSpi SSta
	WBVN WBrE WDin WPGP
'George Henry Kern'	CBcs CDoC COtt EBee IArd ISea
	LRHS MBri MSte NBlu SSpi SSta
	WDin WFar
globosa	CFil GGGa WFar WPGP
– from India	SSpi
'Gold Crown'	SSpi
'Gold Star'	CBcs CFil CMCN CPMA CTho
	EBee LRHS MBlu MGos SSpi WBcn
	WPGP
'Golden Endeavour'	MDun
'Golden Gift'	SSpi
grandiflora	CDul CMCN EBee EBre EPfP LAst
	LRHS MRav MWya NBlu NLar
	SAPC SArc SHBN WBVN WDin
	WFar WMul WNor WOrn
– 'Blanchard' **new**	CBcs
– 'Edith Bogue'	CPMA ENot MGos MRav NLar
	WBVN
– 'Exmouth' ♀H3-4	More than 30 suppliers
– 'Ferruginea'	CBcs EBee SLim
– 'Francois Treyve' **new**	WGer
– 'Galissonnière'	CBcs COtt EBee IMGH LPan LRHS
	MGos MRav NPSI SLim SSpi SWvt
	WDin WPGP
I – 'Gallissonnière Nana'	LPan
– 'Goliath'	CBcs CEnd CFil CHEx EBee ELan
	EPfP SPoG SSpi WPGP
– 'Harold Poole' **new**	CBcs
– 'Little Gem'	CDoC CPMA LRHS SSpi WBcn
	WGer WStI
– 'Mainstreet' **new**	CBcs
– 'Nannetensis'	CPMA EBee
– 'Overton' **new**	CBcs
– 'Russet'	CBcs CPMA
– 'Saint Mary'	CPMA
– 'Samuel Sommer'	CPMA SAPC SArc WPGP
– 'Symmes Select' **new**	CBcs
– 'Undulata'	WGer
– 'Victoria' ♀H3-4	CBcs CDoC CPMA CTho EBee
	ELan EPfP ISea LAst LHyd LRHS
	MBlu SLim SReu SSpi SSta WFar
	WPGP
'Hawk'	WPGP
'Heaven Scent' ♀H4	More than 30 suppliers
'Helen Fogg'	WPGP
heptapeta	see *M. denudata*
'Honeyliz' **new**	SSpi
§ 'Hong Yur'	CEnd CPMA MDun
'Hot Lips'	WPGP
hypoleuca	see *M. obovata* Thunb.
'Iolanthe'	CBcs CEnd CFil CMCN CMHG
	CPMA CSdC CTho ELan GKir
	LRHS MGos NBhm NHol SPer SSpi
	SSta WFar WPGP
'J.C.Williams'	CDoC CTho LRHS
'Jane' ♀H4	CDoC COtt CSdC ELan EPfP LRHS
	MAsh MBri MGos NHol SHBN SLdr
	SSta
'Jersey Belle' **new**	CBcs CPMA
§ 'Joe McDaniel'	CDoC MBri SKee SSpi WBVN

'Jon Jon'	CPMA
'Judy'	COtt
x *kewensis* 'Windsor Beauty' **new**	SSpi
kobus	CBcs CLnd CMCN CSBt CTho
	ENot EWTr IMGH LPan MDun
	NMoo SBLw SHBN SPer WBod
	WDin WFar WNor
– var. *borealis*	CPMA CTho
– 'Norman Gould'	see *M. stellata* 'Norman Gould'
'Lamellan Surprise'	CTho LRHS
'Leda'	CMCN SSpi
§ *liliiflora*	CTrw MBar
§ – 'Nigra' ♀H4	CBcs CDoC CWib EBre ELan ENot
	EPfP EWTr LPan LRHS MAsh MGos
	MLan MRav MSwo NBlu SHBN
	SLdr SLim SPer SPla SReu SSpi SSta
	WBVN WBod WDin WFar WOrn
	WStI
– 'Oldfield'	WPGP
* 'Limelight'	SSpi
x *loebneri*	CBcs LRHS WNor
– 'Ballerina'	CDoC COtt SSta
– 'Donna'	NLar SSpi WGer
– 'Leonard Messel' ♀H4	More than 30 suppliers
– 'Merrill' ♀H4	CBcs CMCN CMHG CTho CTrh
	ELan EPfP ISea LPan LRHS MAsh
	MBri MGos NHol SPer SReu SSpi
	SSta WBVN WBod WDin WPGP
– 'Snowdrift'	SSta
§ *lotungensis*	SSpi
I 'Lotus' **new**	LMil
macrophylla	CBrP CFil CHEx CMCN EPfP IDee
	MBlu SAPC SArc SSpi WNor WPGP
§ – subsp. *ashei*	SSpi WNor
'Manchu Fan'	CBcs CDoC CMCN CPMA CSdC
	EMil IArd MDun SMur SSpi SSta
'Margaret Helen'	CBcs CPMA
'Marj Gossler'	SSpi
'Maryland'	CFil CPMA SSpi SSta WPGP
'Milky Way' ♀H4	CBcs CMHG CPMA CTho LRHS
	MGos NPSI SMur SSpi
'Nimbus'	CPMA SSpi
obovata Diels	see *M. officinalis*
§ *obovata* Thunb. ♀H4	CFil CHEx CMCN CPMA CTho
	EPfP IDee IMGH MDun MLan NLar
	SHBN SPer SSpi SSta WDin WPGP
§ *officinalis*	CFil CMCN EPfP NLar WFar WPGP
– var. *biloba*	EPfP NLar
§ 'Pegasus'	CEnd ISea SSpi
'Peppermint Stick'	CBcs CSdC MGos SSta
'Peter Smithers'	CPMA CTho WFar
'Phelan Bright'	WPGP
'Phillip Tregunna'	CTho LRHS
'Pickard's Sundew'	see *M.* 'Sundew'
'Pinkie' ♀H4	LRHS MBri NLar SSpi SSta WGer
'Pirouette'	SSpi
'Princess Margaret'	CPMA SSpi
x *proctoriana*	CAbP CDoC CFil EBee EPfP LRHS
	WPGP
– 'Slavin's Snowy'	LRHS
quinquepeta	see *M. liliiflora*
'Randy'	EPfP
'Raspberry Ice'	CDoC CEnd CMHG COtt CPLG
	CSdC CTho CTrw EPfP ISea LRHS
	NLar WFar
'Ricki'	COtt CSdC EMil LBuc MBlu MGos
	NBlu NLar WFar
rostrata	CFil
'Rouged Alabaster'	LRHS
'Royal Crown'	CDoC CSdC EMil NBhm SLim
	WGer
'Ruby'	CBcs CPMA MGos
'Ruth' **new**	CBcs

salicifolia ♀H3-4	CFil CMCN EPfP ISea LRHS SSpi SSta
- 'Jermyns'	SSpi
- 'Wada's Memory' ♀H4	CBcs CDoC CFil CMCN CMHG CPMA CTho ELan EPfP GKir ISea LRHS MAsh MBri MSte SPer SSpi SSta WDin WFar
sargentiana var. **robusta**	CBcs CBrd CEnd CMCN CTho ELan EPfP IMGH ISea MDun MGos SPer SSpi SSta WDin WFar WPGP
- - 'Blood Moon'	SSpi
- - 'Multipetal'	CBrd
'Sayonara' ♀H4	CPMA EPfP SSpi WDin
'Schmetterling'	see *M.* x *soulangeana* 'Pickard's Schmetterling'
'Serene'	CBcs CMHG CPMA LMil SSpi SSta
'Shirazz'	CBcs CPMA
sieboldii	More than 30 suppliers
- B&SWJ 4127	WCru
- hardy selection from Korea	GGGa
- 'Colossus'	SSpi
- 'Genesis'	SSpi
- 'Michiko Renge'	NLar
- subsp. **sinensis**	CBcs CDoC CMCN CPMA CSam CTho ELan EPfP GGGa GGar IMGH LRHS MBlu MDun MWya SKee SPer SSpi SSta WCwm WDin WGer
x **soulangeana**	More than 30 suppliers
§ - 'Alba'	CBcs CDoC CEnd CSBt ENot EPfP LRHS MGos NBlu SLim SPer SSpi WBVN WFar
- 'Alba Superba'	see *M.* x *soulangeana* 'Alba'
- 'Alexandrina'	CBcs EPfP LRHS MGos NLar
- 'Amabilis'	COtt
- 'Brozzonii' ♀H3-4	CDoC CMHG EPfP LRHS NLar SSpi
- 'Burgundy'	CBcs CBot CDoC CTbh LRHS WFar
- 'Darrell Dean'	see *M.*'Darrell Dean'
- 'Joe McDaniel'	see *M.*'Joe McDaniel'
- 'Lennei' ♀H3-4	CBcs CDoC CEnd CMCN CMHG CSBt EPfP EWTr IMGH LPan LRHS MAsh MGos MSwo NHol NPri SHBN SLim SRms WBVN WFar WNor WOrn WPGP WStI
- 'Lennei Alba' ♀H3-4	CDoC CMCN CSdC MMHG SLdr WFar
- 'Nigra'	see *M. liliiflora* 'Nigra'
- 'Pickard's Ruby'	CBcs MDun
§ - 'Pickard's Schmetterling'	CDoC CSdC LMil SSta
- 'Pickard's Snow Queen' **new**	WGer
- 'Pickard's Sundew'	see *M.* 'Sundew'
- 'Picture'	CBcs CDoC WDin
- Red Lucky	see *M.* 'Hong Yur'
- 'Rubra' misapplied	see *M.* x *soulangeana* 'Rustica Rubra'
§ - 'Rustica Rubra' ♀H3-4	CBcs CDoC CMCN CPMA CSBt EBee EBre ELan EMui ENot EPfP IMGH LAst LMil LPan LRHS MAsh MBri MDun SHBN SReu SSpi SSta WBVN WDin WFar WPGP
- 'San José'	CBcs LMil LRHS MAsh MBri MDun NLar SSpi SSta
- 'Sweet Sixteen'	see *M.*'Sweet Sixteen'
- 'Verbanica'	EBre LMil LRHS MAsh NLar SSpi
'Spectrum'	CBcs CEnd CFil CPMA CSdC IArd LMil MGos NLar SSpi WPGP
sprengeri	WNor WWes
- 'Copeland Court'	CBcs CTho LRHS
- var. **diva**	CBcs CEnd CFil SSpi WPGP
- - 'Burncoose'	CBcs CDoC
- - 'Claret Cup'	SSpi WBod WPGP
- - 'Lanhydrock'	CFil CTho LRHS SSpi WPGP
- var. **elongata**	COtt
- 'Eric Savill'	CTho LRHS SSpi
- 'Marwood Spring'	CBcs CMHG CTho LRHS
'Star Wars' ♀H4	CBcs CDoC CEnd CFil CPMA CSdC CTho EMil EPfP LMil MAsh MBri NLar SMur SSpi SSta WBVN WPGP
'Stellar Acclaim'	MDun
§ **stellata** ♀H4	More than 30 suppliers
- 'Centennial'	CBcs CDoC MBri WFar
- 'Chrysanthemiflora'	LMil SSpi
- 'Jane Platt'	MDun SSpi
- f. **keiskei**	CEnd COtt CSdC
- 'King Rose'	CBcs CDoC COtt CSdC EPfP ISea LAst LRHS MAsh MBri MSte SPer SPla WBod
§ - 'Norman Gould'	CDoC EPfP GTSp MBri NLar SSta WDin WGer
- 'Pink Perfection'	MDun
- 'Rosea'	CMCN COtt ELan LRHS MDun MGos MSwo NBlu NLar SHBN WBod WDin
I - 'Rosea Massey'	WFar
- 'Royal Star'	CBcs CBrm CDoC CEnd CMCN CSam CTri ENot EPfP ISea LMil LPan LRHS MAsh MBri MGos MRav NBlu NHol NLar NPri SPer SSpi SSta WBrE WDin WHar WOrn WStI
- 'Waterlily' ♀H4	CBcs CMCN CTbh ELan EMil EPfP GKir LAst LRHS SLim SPer SPla SPoG SSpi SSta WDin
'Summer Solstice'	CPMA SSpi
'Sunburst'	MDun SSpi
'Sundance'	CFil CPMA EMil MDun MGos NLar NPSI WPGP
I 'Sundew'	CBcs CDoC CMCN EBee EPfP IArd MGos SHBN SMrm WBVN WPGP
'Susan' ♀H4	More than 30 suppliers
'Susanna van Veen'	CBcs
§ 'Sweet Sixteen'	WPGP
x **thompsoniana** AM	CMCN EPfP SSpi
- 'Olmenhof'	SSpi
'Thousand Butterflies' **new**	CPMA
'Tiffany'	WPGP
'Tina Durio'	CDoC
'Todd Gresham'	CPMA WPGP
'Tranquility'	MDun
'Treve Holman'	CSdC
'Trewidden Belle'	CEnd
tripetala	CBcs CHEx CLnd CMCN CPne CTho EPfP IMGH LPan MBlu MDun MLan NWea SHBN SMad SSpi SSta WCwm WDin WOrn WPGP
x **veitchii**	CDoC CDul CSBt EPfP SSpi SSta WBVN
- 'Isca'	CTho
- 'Peter Veitch'	CTho SSta
virginiana	CMCN CPMA CPne CTho EBee EPfP LRHS SSpi WDin WPGP
- 'Havener'	IArd
- 'Henry Hicks'	SSpi
- 'Moonglow' **new**	CPMA
- 'Vulcan'	CBcs CEnd CMCN CMHG CPMA CTho MBlu MDun
x **watsonii**	see *M.* x *wieseneri*
§ x **wieseneri**	CBcs CFil CMCN CPMA ELan EPfP GKir LMil LRHS MBlu SSpi SSta WFar
- 'Aashild Kalleberg'	SSpi
wilsonii ♀H4	More than 30 suppliers
- 'Gwen Baker'	CEnd

'Yellow Fever'	CBcs CMCN CMHG CPMA CTho EMil MDun SMur SSta
'Yellow Lantern'	CAbP CBcs CEnd CMCN EPfP LMil LRHS MAsh MBlu NLar SSpi SSta WPGP
zenii **new**	CMCN

x *Mahoberberis* (*Berberidaceae*)

aquisargentii	ENot EPfP GBin GEil GKir MRav SHGC SLon WBor WDin WFar WPat
'Dart's Treasure'	EPla WFar
'Magic'	MGos
miethkeana	MBar SRms

Mahonia ✿ (*Berberidaceae*)

§ *aquifolium*	CAgr CBcs CDul CTrG EBee ENot GKir LAst MBar MBri MGos MRav MWat NBlu NWea SHBN SPer SPlb SReu WCFE WDin WFar WStI
- 'Apollo' ♀H4	CMac EBee ELan EMil ENot EPfP GKir LRHS MAsh MBar MBow MBri MGos MRav NBee NBlu NPri SCoo SHBN SMer SPer SReu SSta WDin
- 'Atropurpurea'	CBcs ELan ENot EPfP EPla GKir LRHS MAsh NBee NLar SHBN SPer SPla WDin
* - 'Cosmo Crawl'	MGos
- 'Fascicularis'	see *M.* x *wagneri* 'Pinnacle'
- 'Green Ripple'	EPfP MBri MGos NLar WBcn WFar
- 'Mirena'	MGos
- 'Orange Flame'	EPfP MBlu NLar
- 'Smaragd'	CBcs CDoC CMac EBee EBre ELan ENot EPfP LRHS MAsh MBlu MGos MRav WHCG
- 'Versicolor'	MBlu
bealei	see *M. japonica* Bealei Group
confusa	CDoC CFil EPla NLar SSpi WBcn WCru WFar WPGP
eutriphylla	see *M. trifolia*
fortunei	EPla NLar WBcn WSHC
fremontii	GCal SIgm
gracilipes	CFil MDun NLar WSPU
haematocarpa	SIgm
japonica ♀H4	More than 30 suppliers
§ - Bealei Group	CBcs CDul CSBt EBee EBre ELan EPfP EPla GKir LAst LRHS MAsh MBar MGos MRav MSwo NBlu NPer SLim SMer SWvt WDin WFar WGwG WWeb
- 'Hiemalis'	see *M. japonica* 'Hivernant'
§ - 'Hivernant'	EPla MGos NBlu
lomariifolia ♀H3	CBcs CBot ENot EPfP LRHS MFan SAPC SArc SDry SSpi WBor
x *media* 'Arthur Menzies'	EPla
- 'Buckland' ♀H4	CAbP CBcs CDul CMac CSBt CSam CTrw CWSG EPfP ISea LAst LRHS MDun NHol SPer SRms WPat WStI
- 'Charity'	More than 30 suppliers
- 'Charity's Sister'	EBee EPla
- 'Faith'	EPla
- 'Lionel Fortescue' ♀H4	CBcs CBrm CEnd CMac CSBt CTrw CWSG EBee EBre ELan ENot EPfP EPla ISea LHop LRHS MAsh MRav SLon SMad SPer SReu SSpi SSta WFar WHCG
- 'Underway' ♀H4	EBee EPfP EPla LRHS SMur WWes
- 'Winter Sun' ♀H4	More than 30 suppliers
nervosa	CBcs COtt EPfP EPla MBlu NBee SPer WBcn WCru WPat
pallida	CFil EBee EPla SIgm WCot WPGP
pinnata misapplied	see *M.* x *wagneri* 'Pinnacle'
pinnata ambig.	EBee ENot EPfP EPla MBar

pumila	SSpi WCru
repens	EPla MWhi
- 'Rotundifolia'	EPla
russellii	CFil
x *savilliana*	CFil EPla WCru
- 'Commissioner' **new**	CWib
§ *trifolia*	EPla
trifoliolata	EPfP
- var. *glauca*	CEnd NLar
x *wagneri* 'Fireflame'	EPla
- 'Hastings Elegant'	NLar
- 'Moseri'	EMil NLar SSpi WPat
§ - 'Pinnacle' ♀H4	ELan ENot EPfP EPla EWTr LRHS MAsh MGos MLan NFor SMur SPer
- 'Sunset'	MBlu NLar
- 'Undulata'	ENot EPfP MBlu NLar SDix SPer SRms SWvt WHCG

Maianthemum (*Convallariaceae*)

bifolium	CAvo CBct CDes CHid CPLG CRow EBee EMan EPot GBuc GFlt LEur MDun MNrw MTho NBro NMen SRms WCru WPGP WPnP WPrP WTin WWye
- from Yakushima	EBee SOkd
§ - subsp. *kamtschaticum*	CAvo CCol CLAP CRow EBee EPar GKir LBuc LEur SMac WCot WTin
- - B&SWJ 4360	WCru WPrP
* - - var. *minimum*	WCru
canadense	EBee GKir NBid NMen
* *chasmanthum* **new**	LRHS
dilatatum	see *M. bifolium* subsp. *kamtschaticum*
racemosum	see *Smilacina racemosa*

Maihuenia (*Cactaceae*)

poeppigii	SPlb
- JCA 2.575.600	WCot

Maireana (*Chenopodiaceae*)

georgei	SPlb

Malacothamnus (*Malvaceae*)

fremontii	EMan
marrubioides	EMan

Malcolmia (*Brassicaceae*)

littorea **new**	XPep

Malephora (*Aizoaceae*)

crassa	CTrC
crocea var.	XPep
purpureocrocea **new**	

Mallotus (*Euphorbiaceae*)

japonicus	CPLG
- B&SWJ 6852	WCru

Malpighia (*Malpighiaceae*)

coccigera	ESlt

Malus ✿ (*Rosaceae*)

§ 'Adirondack'	CDoC EPfP LRHS MAsh MBri MGos
'Admiration'	see *M.* 'Adirondack'
x *adstringens* 'Almey'	ECrN
- 'Hopa'	CDul CLnd SCrf
- 'Simcoe'	CLnd MGos
'Aldenhamensis'	see *M.* x *purpurea* 'Aldenhamensis'
'Amberina'	CLnd
* *arborescens*	CLnd CTho
x *atrosanguinea*	CTho
- 'Gorgeous'	CCAT CDul CLnd COtt CTho CWSG EBee ECrN GKir GTwe

	LRHS MAsh MGos MSwo NBlu SCoo SCrf SKee SLim SPer WDin WOrn
baccata	CFil CLnd CMCN CTho GTwe NWea SEND WNor
- W 264	GIBF
- - MF 96038	SSpi
- 'Dolgo'	CCAT CDoC LRHS SKee
- 'Gracilis'	CWSG SBLw
- 'Lady Northcliffe'	CLnd SFam
- var. *mandshurica*	CTho EPfP
- 'Street Parade'	MBri
aff. *baccata*	MAsh NWea
§ *bhutanica*	CDul CTho EPfP GIBF WNor
brevipes	CLnd CTho
'Butterball'	CLnd CTho ECrN EPfP GKir LRHS MBlu SCoo SKee WDin
* 'Cheal's Weeping'	ECrN LAst NBea
Coccinella	WDin
= 'Courtarou'PBR	
'Coralburst'	MBri
coronaria var. *dasycalyx*	CDoC CDul CLnd EBee ENot EPfP LRHS MBri SCrf SFam SPer
'Charlottae' (d)	
- 'Elk River'	LRHS MAsh
- 'Nieuwlandiana'	GIBF
'Crimson Brilliant'	CLnd
'Crittenden'	EBee ECrN ENot MRav
denticulata	GIBF
* 'Directeur Moerlands'	CDoC ECrN EPfP GKir LRHS MBri MGos WDin
domestica (F)	MGos
- 'Acklam Russet' (D) **new**	SKee
- 'Acme' (D)	SDea SKee
- 'Adams's Pearmain' (D)	CCAT CTho GKir GTwe LRHS MBri SDea SFam SKee
- 'Advance' (D)	SKee
- 'Akane' (D)	SDea
§ - 'Alexander' (C)	SKee
- 'Alfriston' (C)	SKee
- 'Alkmene' (D) ♀H4	GTwe SDea SKee
- 'All Doer' (D/C/Cider) **new**	CTho
- 'All Red Gravenstein' (D)	NRog
- 'Allen's Everlasting' (D)	GTwe SDea SKee
- 'Allington Pippin' (D)	CSBt CTho CTri ECrN LRHS NRog SDea SKee
- 'American Golden Russet' (D)	CTho
- 'American Mother'	see *M. domestica* 'Mother'
- 'Ananas Reinette' (D)	SKee
- 'Anna Boelens' (D)	SDea
- 'Annie Elizabeth' (C)	CCAT CTho CWib ECrN GKir GTwe LRHS MBri SDea SFam SKee
- 'Anniversary' (D)	SDea
- 'Api Rose' (D)	SKee
- 'Ard Cairn Russet' (D)	GTwe SDea SKee
- 'Aromatic Russet' (D)	SKee
- 'Arthur Turner' (C) ♀H4	CCVT CDoC CTri EMui ENot GKir GTwe LBuc LRHS MGos NRog SCrf SDea SFam SKee
- 'Ashmead's Kernel' (D) ♀H4	CCAT CSBt CTho CTri CWib ECrN EMui EPfP ERea GKir GTwe LBuc LRHS MRav MWat NRog NWea SCrf SDea SFam SKee WHar WOrn
- 'Ashton Bitter' (Cider)	CCAT CTho GTwe SFam
- 'Ashton Brown Jersey' (Cider)	CCAT CTho
- 'Autumn Pearmain' (D)	CTho SDea
- 'Backwell Red' (Cider)	CCAT
- 'Baker's Delicious' (D)	ECrN SDea SKee
- 'Ball's Bittersweet' (Cider)	CCAT CTho
- 'Ballyfatten' (C)	CTho

- 'Balsam'	see *M. domestica* 'Green Balsam'
- 'Banns' (D)	SKee
- 'Barnack Beauty' (D)	CTho SKee
- 'Barnack Orange' (D)	SKee
- 'Barnhill Beauty'	CTho
- 'Baron Wood' (C)	SKee
- 'Baumann's Reinette' (D)	SKee
- 'Baxter's Pearmain' (D)	SDea SKee
- 'Beauty of Bath' (D)	CCAT CCVT CDoC CTho CTri CWib ECrN GKir GTwe LBuc LRHS NRog SCrf SDea SFam SKee
- 'Beauty of Bedford' (D)	SKee
- 'Beauty of Hants' (D)	ECrN SKee
- 'Beauty of Kent' (C)	SDea SKee
- 'Beauty of Moray' (C)	SKee
- 'Bedwyn Beauty' (C)	CTho
- 'Beeley Pippin' (D)	GTwe SDea SKee
- 'Belfleur Kitaika' (D)	SKee
- 'Bell Apple' (Cider/C)	CCAT CTho
- 'Belle de Boskoop' (C/D) ♀H4	CCAT GTwe NRog SDea SKee
- 'Belle Flavoise'	SKee
- 'Bembridge Beauty' (F)	SDea
- 'Ben's Red' (D)	CCAT CEnd CTho SKee
- 'Bess Pool' (D)	SDea SFam
- 'Bewley Down Pippin'	see *M. domestica* 'Crimson King'
- 'Bickington Grey' (Cider)	CTho
- 'Billy Down Pippin' (F)	CTho
- 'Bismarck' (C)	CCAT NRog SKee
- 'Black Dabinett' (Cider)	CCAT CTho
- 'Black Tom Putt' (C/D)	CTho
- 'Blackamore Red' (C)	CTho
- 'Blenheim Orange' (C/D) ♀H4	CCAT CCVT CDoC CSBt CTho CTri CWib ECrN EMui ENot EPfP GKir GTwe LBuc LRHS MBri MWat NRog SCrf SDea SFam SKee SPer WOrn
- 'Blenheim Red' (C/D)	see *M. domestica* 'Red Blenheim'
- 'Bloody Butcher' (C)	CTho
- 'Bloody Ploughman' (D)	GKir SKee
- 'Blue Pearmain' (D)	SDea SKee
- 'Blue Sweet' (Cider)	CTho
- Bolero = 'Tuscan'PBR (D/Ball)	ENot LRHS MGos SDea
- 'Bonum' (D/C)	CTho
- 'Boston Russet'	see *M. domestica* 'Roxbury Russet'
- 'Bountiful' (C)	CAgr CDoC COtt CSBt CTri CWib ECrN EMui GKir GTwe LBuc LRHS MBri MGos SDea SKee WHar WStI
- 'Bow Hill Pippin' (D)	SKee
- 'Box Apple' (D)	SKee
- 'Braddick Nonpareil' (D)	SKee
- 'Braeburn' (D)	ECrN EMui SDea SKee
- 'Bramley's Seedling' (C) ♀H4	More than 30 suppliers
- 'Bramley's Seedling' clone 20	CDoC MBri SCoo SDea
- 'Bramshott Rectory' (D/C)	SKee
- 'Bread Fruit' (C/D)	CEnd CTho
- 'Breakwell's Seedling' (Cider)	CCAT CTho
- 'Breitling' (D)	SKee
- 'Bridgwater Pippin' (C)	CCAT CTho
- 'Broad-eyed Pippin' (C)	SKee
- 'Brown Snout' (Cider)	CCAT CTho
- 'Brownlees Russet' (D)	CCAT CTho EMui GTwe NRog NWea SDea SFam SKee
- 'Brown's Apple' (Cider)	CCAT GTwe
- 'Broxwood Foxwhelp' (Cider)	CCAT CTho
- 'Bulmer's Norman' (Cider)	CCAT
- 'Burn's Seedling' (D)	CTho

- 'Burr Knot' (C) SKee
- 'Burrowhill Early' (Cider) CTho
- 'Bushey Grove' (C) SDea SKee
- 'Buttery Do' CTho
- 'Caledon' CTho
- 'Calville Blanc d'Hiver' SKee
  (D)
- 'Cambusnethan Pippin' SKee
  (D)
- 'Camelot' (Cider/C) CCAT CTho
- 'Cap of Liberty' (Cider) CCAT
- 'Captain Broad' CCAT CEnd CTho
  (D/Cider)
- 'Captain Kidd' (D) SKee
- 'Captain Smith' (F) CEnd
- 'Carlisle Codlin' (C) GKir GTwe SDea
- 'Catshead' (C) CCAT GKir GQui SDea SKee
- 'Cellini' (C/D) SDea SKee
- 'Charles Ross' CAgr CCAT CDoC CMac CSBt
  (C/D) ♀H4 CTho CTri ECrN EMui GBon GKir
  GTwe LBuc LRHS MBri MRav
  MWat NBlu NRog NWea SCoo
  SDea SFam SKee WHar WOrn
- 'Charlotte'PBR (C/Ball) ENot LRHS MGos SDea
- 'Chaxhill Red' (Cider/D) CCAT CTho
- 'Cheddar Cross' (D) CTri SKee
- 'Chelmsford Wonder' (C) SKee
- 'Chips' **new** SKee
- 'Chisel Jersey' (Cider) CCAT CTri
- 'Chivers Delight' (D) CAgr CCAT CSBt ECrN EMui
  GTwe LRHS SCrf SDea SKee
- 'Chorister Boy' (D) CTho
- 'Christmas Pearmain' (D) CTho GTwe SDea SFam SKee
- 'Cider Lady's Finger' CCAT CTho
  (Cider)
- 'Cistecké' (D) SKee
- 'Claygate Pearmain' CCAT CTho GTwe SDea SFam
  (D) ♀H4 SKee
- 'Clopton Red' (D) SKee
- 'Coat Jersey' (Cider) CCAT
- 'Cockle Pippin' (D) CTho GTwe SDea
- 'Coeur de Boeuf' (C/D) SKee
- 'Coleman's Seedling' CTho
  (Cider)
- 'Collogett Pippin' CCAT CEnd CTho
  (C/Cider)
- 'Colonel Vaughan' CTho SKee
  (C/D) **new**
- 'Cooper's Seedling' (C) SCrf
- 'Cornish Aromatic' (D) CCAT CTho EMui GTwe SCrf SDea
  SFam SKee
- 'Cornish Crimson GTwe
  Queen' (F)
- 'Cornish Gilliflower' (D) CCAT CTho ECrN SDea SFam SKee
- 'Cornish Honeypin' (D) CTho SKee
- 'Cornish Longstem' (D) CEnd CTho
- 'Cornish Mother' (D) CEnd CTho
- 'Cornish Pine' (D) CEnd CTho SDea SKee
- 'Coronation' (D) SDea SKee
- 'Corse Hill' (D) **new** CTho
- 'Costard' (C) GTwe SKee
- 'Cottenham Seedling' (C) SKee
- 'Coul Blush' (D) SKee
- 'Court of Wick' (D) CCAT CTho SKee
- 'Court Pendu Plat' (D) CCAT CTho GKir LBuc MWat
  NRog NWea SDea SFam SKee
  WOrn
§ - 'Court Royal' (Cider) CCAT CTho
- 'Cow Apple' (C) CTho
- 'Cox's Orange CBcs CCAT CCVT CMac CSBt CTri
  Pippin' (D) CWib EBre ECrN ENot GTwe LBuc
  LRHS MWat NPri NRog NWea SCrf
  SDea SFam SKee SPer WOrn
- 'Cox's Pomona' (C/D) CTho SDea SKee

- 'Cox's Rouge de SKee
  Flandres' (D)
- 'Cox's Selfing' (D) CDoC CWSG CWib EMui EPfP
  ERea GTwe LBuc MBri MGos NBlu
  SCrf SDea SKee WHar
- 'Crawley Beauty' (C) CCAT GTwe SDea SFam SKee
- 'Crimson Bramley' (C) CCAT
- 'Crimson Cox' (D) SDea
§ - 'Crimson King' CCAT CTho
  (Cider/C)
- 'Crimson Peasgood' (C) GKir
- 'Crimson Queening' (D) SKee
- 'Crimson Victoria' CTho
  (Cider)
- Crispin see *M. domestica* 'Mutsu'
§ - 'Crowngold'PBR (D) EMui GTwe
- 'Cummy Norman' CCAT
  (Cider)
- 'Curl Tail' (D) SKee
- 'Cutler Grieve' (D) SDea
- 'Dabinett' (Cider) CCAT CTho CTri EMui GTwe LBuc
  SCrf SDea SKee WOrn
- 'D'Arcy Spice' (D) CCAT CLnd EPfP GKir SDea SFam
  SKee
- 'Dawn' (D) SKee
- 'De Boutteville' (Cider) CTho
- 'Deacon's Blushing SDea
  Beauty' (C/D)
- 'Deacon's Millennium' SDea
- 'Decio' (D) SKee
- 'Delprim' (D) **new** SKee
- 'Devon Crimson CTho
  Queen' (D)
- 'Devonshire CEnd CTho
  Buckland' (C)
- 'Devonshire Crimson SDea
  Queen' (D)
- 'Devonshire CCAT CEnd CTho EMui SDea
  Quarrenden' (D) SFam SKee
- 'Devonshire Red' (D/C) CTho
- 'Dewdney's Seedling' (C) GTwe
- 'Diamond Jubilee' (D) SKee
- 'Discovery' (D) ♀H4 CAgr CBcs CCAT CDoC CSBt CTri
  CWib EBre EMui ENot EPfP EWTr
  GBon GKir GTwe LBuc LRHS MBri
  MRav MWat NBee NBlu NRog
  NWea SDea SFam SKee SPer WOrn
  WStI
- 'Doctor Hare's' (C) MCoo
- 'Doctor Harvey' (C) ECrN SFam
- 'Doctor Kidd's see *M. domestica* 'Kidd's Orange
  Orange Red' Red'
- 'Dog's Snout' (C/D) NRog
- 'Doll's Eye' CTho
- 'Domino' (C) SKee
- 'Don's Delight' (C) CTho
- 'Dove' (Cider) CTho
- 'Dredge's Fame' (D) CTho SKee
- 'Duchess of Oldenburg' SKee
  (C/D)
- 'Duchess's Favourite' (D) SKee
- 'Dufflin' (Cider) CCAT CTho
- 'Duke of Cornwall' CTho
  (C) **new**
- 'Duke of Devonshire' (D) CSam CTho SDea SFam SKee
N - 'Dumeller's Seedling' see *M. domestica* 'Dummellor's
  Seedling'
§ - 'Dummellor's Seedling' CCAT CTho SDea SKee
  (C) ♀H4
- 'Dunkerton Late Sweet' CCAT CTho
  (Cider)
- 'Dunn's Seedling' (D) SDea
§ - 'Dutch Mignonne' (D) SKee
- 'Dymock Red' (Cider) CCAT

- 'Early Blenheim' (D/C) — CEnd CTho
- 'Early Bower' (D) — CEnd
- 'Early Julyan' (C) — SKee
- 'Early Victoria' — see *M. domestica* 'Emneth Early'
- 'Early Worcester' — see *M. domestica* 'Tydeman's Early Worcester'
- 'Easter Orange' (D) — GTwe SCrf SKee
- 'Ecklinville' (C) — SDea SKee
- 'Edward VII' (C) ♀H4 — CDoC GTwe SCrf SDea SFam SKee
- 'Egremont Russet' (D) ♀H4 — More than 30 suppliers
- 'Ellis' Bitter' (Cider) — CCAT CTho GTwe
- 'Ellison's Orange' (D) ♀H4 — CCAT CSBt CTri CWib ECrN ENot GBon GKir GTwe LBuc LRHS NRog NWea SDea SFam SKee WHar WStI
- 'Elstar' (D) ♀H4 — ECrN EMui GTwe MRav SDea SKee
- 'Elton Beauty' (D) — SDea SKee
§ - 'Emneth Early' (C) ♀H4 — EMui GTwe NRog SDea SFam SKee WOrn
- 'Emperor Alexander' (C/D) — see *M. domestica* 'Alexander'
- 'Empire' (D) — SKee
- 'Encore' (C) — SDea
- 'English Codling' (C) — CTho
- 'Epicure' (D) — see *M. domestica* 'Laxton's Epicure'
- 'Ernie's Russet' (D) — SDea
- 'Evening Gold' (C) — SDea
- 'Eve's Delight' (D) — SDea
- 'Exeter Cross' (D) — CCAT SDea SFam
- 'Fair Maid of Devon' (Cider) — CCAT CTho
- 'Fairfield' (D) — CTho
- 'Fall Russet' (D) — GTwe
- 'Falstaff' PBR (D) ♀H4 — CCAT CDoC ECrN EMui EPfP GKir GTwe MGos SDea SKee
- 'Fameuse' (D) **new** — SKee
- 'Fearn's Pippin' (D) — SKee
- 'Fiesta' PBR (D) ♀H4 — CCAT CDoC CSBt CTri CWSG CWib EBre ECrN EMui ENot EPfP GBon GTwe LBuc LRHS MBri MGos NBlu NPri NRog SDea SFam SKee WHar WOrn
- 'Fillbarrel' (Cider) — CCAT CTho
- 'Fillingham Pippin' (C) **new** — SKee
- 'Firmgold' (D) — SDea
- 'Five Crowns' (D) — SKee
- 'Flamenco' (D) — ENot MGos SDea
§ - 'Flower of Kent' (C) — CCAT SCrf SDea SKee
- 'Flower of the Town' (D) — SKee
- 'Forfar' — see *M. domestica* 'Dutch Mignonne'
- 'Forge' (D) — SDea SKee
- 'Fortune' (D) — see *M. domestica* 'Laxton's Fortune'
- 'Foster's Seedling' (D) — SKee
- 'Foulden Pearmain' (D) — SKee
- 'Francis' (D) — SKee
- 'Frederick' (Cider) — CCAT CTho
- 'French Crab' (C) — CTho SDea
- 'Freyberg' (D) — SKee
- 'Fuji' (D) — SDea SKee
- 'Gala' (D) — CSBt GBon GTwe NBlu NPri SCrf SDea SFam SKee
I - 'Gala Royal' — see *M. domestica* 'Royal Gala'
- 'Galloway Pippin' (C) — GKir GTwe SKee
- 'Gascoyne's Scarlet' (D) — CCAT NRog SDea SFam SKee
- 'Gavin' (D) — SDea SKee
- 'Genesis II' (D/C) — SDea
- 'Genet Moyle' (C/Cider) — CCAT CTho
- 'George Carpenter' (D) — CTho SDea SKee

- 'George Cave' (D) — CTho ECrN GTwe NRog SCrf SDea SFam SKee
- 'George Neal' (C) ♀H4 — CTho SDea SFam SKee
- 'Gilliflower of Gloucester' (D) — CTho
- 'Ginny Lin' (D) — CTho
- 'Gladstone' (D) — CTho SKee
- 'Glasbury' (C) — SKee
§ - 'Glass Apple' (C/D) — CEnd CTho
- 'Gloria Mundi' (C) — SDea SKee
- 'Gloster '69' (D) — GTwe SDea SKee
- 'Gloucester Cross' (D) — SKee
- 'Gloucester Royal' (D) — CTho
- 'Gloucester Underleaf' — CTho
- 'Golden Ball' — CTho
- 'Golden Bittersweet' (D) — CTho
- 'Golden Delicious' (D) ♀H4 — CSBt CWib EBre ECrN EMui ENot GBon NRog NWea SCrf SDea SKee SPer WHar WOrn WStI
- 'Golden Glow' (C) — SDea
- 'Golden Harvey' (D) — CCAT CTho
- 'Golden Knob' (D) — CCAT CTho SKee
- 'Golden Noble' (C) ♀H4 — CCAT CDoC CSam CTho ECrN EMui GKir GTwe SDea SFam SKee WOrn
- 'Golden Nugget' (D) — SKee
- 'Golden Pippin' (C) — CCAT CTho SKee
- 'Golden Reinette' (D) — GTwe SKee
- 'Golden Russet' (D) — GTwe SDea SKee
- 'Golden Spire' (C) — NRog SDea SKee
- 'Gooseberry' (C) — SKee
- 'Goring' (Cider) — CCAT CTho
- 'Grand Sultan' (D) — CCAT CTho
- 'Grandpa Buxton' (C) — NRog
- 'Granny Smith' (D) — CLnd CWib ECrN GTwe NBlu NPri SCrf SDea SKee SPer
- 'Gravenstein' (D) — CCAT GQui SDea SFam SKee
- 'Greasy Butcher' — CTho
- 'Greasy Pippin' (D/C) — CTho
§ - 'Green Balsam' (C) — CTri NRog
- 'Green Roland' — SKee
- 'Greensleeves' PBR (D) ♀H4 — CCAT CDoC CSBt CTri CWSG CWib EBre ECrN EMui GKir GTwe LRHS MBri MGos NBlu NRog NWea SDea SKee WBVN WHar WOrn
- 'Grenadier' (C) ♀H4 — CDoC CSBt CTri ECrN GKir GTwe LRHS MGos NBee NRog SCrf SDea SKee WBVN WOrn WStI
- 'Halstow Natural' (Cider) — CTho
- 'Hambledon Deux Ans' (C) — SDea SKee
- 'Hangy Down' (Cider) — CCAT CTho
- 'Harragan Payne' (D) **new** — CTho
§ - 'Harry Master's Jersey' (Cider) — CCAT CTho CTri SDea
- 'Harvester' (D) — CTho
- 'Harvey' (C) — SDea SKee
- 'Hawthornden' (C) — SKee
- 'Hereford Cross' (D) — SKee
- 'Herefordshire Beefing' (C) — SKee WOrn
- 'Herefordshire Pippin' (D) — CTho
- 'Herring's Pippin' (D) — CTri GTwe SDea SKee
- 'Heusgen's Golden Reinette' (D) — CCAT SKee
- 'Hibb's Seedling' (C) — SKee
- 'Hibernal' (C) — SKee
- 'High View Pippin' (D) — SKee
- 'Hoary Morning' (C) — CCAT CTho SDea SKee
- 'Hocking's Green' (C/D) — CCAT CEnd CTho
- 'Holland Pippin' (C) — SKee

- 'Hollow Core' (C)	CTho
- 'Holstein' (D)	COtt CSam CTho GTwe SDea SKee
- 'Horneburger Pfannkuchen' (C)	SKee
- 'Horsford Prolific' (D)	SKee
- 'Horsham Russet' (D)	SKee
- 'Howgate Wonder' (C)	CAgr CCAT CCVT CDoC CSBt CWib ECrN EMui GBon GKir GTwe LBuc LRHS NBee NPri NRog SCrf SDea SFam SKee WBVN
- 'Hubbard's Pearmain' (D)	SKee
- 'Hunt's Duke of Gloucester' (D) **new**	CTho
- 'Idared' (D) ♀H4	CWib ECrN GBon GKir MGos SDea SKee
- 'Improved Cockpit' (D)	NRog
- 'Improved Dove' (Cider)	CCAT
- 'Improved Keswick' (C/D)	CEnd
- 'Improved Lambrook Pippin' (Cider)	CCAT CTho CTri
- 'Improved Redstreak' (Cider)	CTho
- 'Ingall's Pippin' (D) **new**	SKee
- 'Ingrid Marie' (D)	NRog SCrf SDea SKee
- 'Irish Johnnies'	CTho
- 'Irish Peach' (D)	CCAT ECrN GTwe LBuc LRHS NRog SDea SFam SKee
- 'Isaac Newton's Tree'	see *M. domestica* 'Flower of Kent'
- 'Isle of Wight Pippin' (D)	SDea
- 'Isle of Wight Russet' (D)	SDea
- 'Jackson's' (Cider)	see *M. domestica* 'Crimson King'
- 'Jacques Lebel' (C)	SKee
- 'James Grieve' (D) ♀H4	CBcs CCAT CCVT CDoC CMac CSBt CTri CWSG CWib EMui ENot EPfP GBon GKir GTwe LBuc LRHS MBri MRav MWat NBee NBlu NRog SDea SFam SKee SPer WHar WOrn
- 'Jefferies'	SKee
- 'Jerseymac' (D)	SDea
- 'Jester' (D)	ECrN GTwe NRog SDea SKee
- 'John Apple' (C)	SKee
- 'John Standish' (D)	CCAT CTri GTwe NRog SCrf SDea
- 'John Toucher's'	see *M. domestica* 'Crimson King'
- 'Johnny Andrews' (Cider)	CCAT CTho
- 'Johnny Voun' (D)	CEnd CTho
- 'Jonagold' (D) ♀H4	CTri CWib ECrN EWTr GTwe NWea SCrf SDea SFam SKee SPer
- 'Jonagold Crowngold'PBR	see *M. domestica* 'Crowngold'
§ - 'Jonagored'PBR (D)	NRog SDea SKee
- 'Jonared' (D)	GTwe
- 'Jonathan' (D)	SDea SKee
- 'Jordan's Weeping' (C)	GTwe SDea
- 'Josephine' (D)	SDea
- 'Joybells' (D)	SKee
- 'Jubilee'	see *M. domestica* 'Royal Jubilee'
- 'Jupiter'PBR (D) ♀H4	CCAT CDoC CSBt CTri CWib ECrN EWTr GBon GKir GTwe MGos NRog SDea SKee WOrn
- 'Kapai Red Jonathan' (D)	SDea
- 'Karmijn de Sonnaville' (D)	SDea SKee
§ - 'Katja' (D)	CCAT CCVT CDoC CTri CWib ECrN EMui EPfP EWTr GBon GKir GTwe LBuc LRHS NBee NRog SCrf SDea SKee SPer WHar WOrn
- Katy	see *M. domestica* 'Katja'
- 'Keegan'	CTho
- 'Kent' (D)	GTwe SCrf SDea SKee
- 'Kentish Fillbasket' (C)	SKee
- 'Kentish Pippin' (C/Cider/D)	SKee

- 'Kentish Quarrenden' (D) **new**	SKee
- 'Kerry Pippin' (D)	SKee
- 'Keswick Codlin' (C)	CTho ECrN GKir GTwe NRog NWea SDea SKee
§ - 'Kidd's Orange Red' (D) ♀H4	CCAT CTri EBre EMui GQui GTwe LBuc LRHS NRog SCrf SDea SFam SKee
- 'Kilkenny Pippin' (F)	GTwe
- 'Kill Boy'	CTho
- 'Killerton Sharp' (Cider)	CTho
- 'Killerton Sweet' (Cider)	CTho
- 'King Byerd' (C/D)	CEnd CTho
- 'King Charles' Pearmain' (D)	CTho SKee
- 'King George V' (D)	SKee
- 'King Luscious' (D)	SDea
§ - 'King of the Pippins' (D) ♀H4	CCAT CTho CTri GTwe LBuc SCrf SDea SFam SKee WOrn
- 'King of Tompkins County' (D)	NRog
- 'King Russet' (D) ♀H4	SDea
- 'King's Acre Bountiful' (C)	SKee
- 'King's Acre Pippin' (D)	CCAT SDea SFam SKee
- 'Kingston Bitter' (Cider)	CTho
- 'Kingston Black' (Cider/D)	CCAT CTho CTri GTwe SDea SKee
- 'Kirton Fair' (D)	CTho
- 'Knobby Russet' (D)	GTwe SKee
- 'Lady Henniker' (D)	CCAT CTho ECrN GTwe NRog SDea SKee
- 'Lady of the Wemyss' (C)	SKee
- 'Lady Sudeley' (D)	CTho SDea SKee
- 'Lady's Finger' (C/D)	CEnd GKir
- 'Lady's Finger of Lancaster' (C/D)	NRog SKee
- 'Lady's Finger of Offaly' (D)	SDea
- 'Lakeland' (D)	SKee
- 'Lake's Kernel' (D) **new**	CTho
- 'Lamb Abbey Pearmain' (D)	SKee
- 'Landsberger Reinette' (D)	SKee
- 'Lane's Prince Albert' (C) ♀H4	CCAT CSBt ECrN EMui ENot GBon GKir GTwe LRHS MGos MRav MWat NRog NWea SCrf SDea SFam SKee WOrn
- 'Langley Pippin' (D)	SDea SKee
§ - 'Langworthy' (Cider)	CCAT CTho
§ - 'Lass o' Gowrie' (C)	CTho
§ - 'Laxton's Epicure' (D) ♀H4	CAgr CDoC ECrN GBon GTwe NRog SCrf SDea SFam SKee
- 'Laxton's Favourite' (D)	ECrN
§ - 'Laxton's Fortune' (D) ♀H4	CCAT CDoC CMac CSBt CTri CWib EMui GKir GTwe MGos NPri NRog NWea SCrf SDea SFam SKee WHar
- 'Laxton's Rearguard' (D)	SKee
- 'Laxton's Royalty' (D)	SDea SFam
§ - 'Laxton's Superb' (D)	CBcs CCAT CCVT CDoC CSBt CTri CWib ECrN EMui ENot GBon GKir GTwe LBuc LRHS MBri NBlu NPri NRog SCrf SDea SKee SPer WHar WOrn
- 'Leathercoat Russet' (D)	CTho SKee
- 'Lemon Pippin' (C)	CCAT CTho SDea SKee
- 'Lemon Pippin of Gloucestershire' (D) **new**	CTho
- 'Lewis's Incomparable' (C)	SKee
- 'Liberty' (D)	SDea

- 'Limberland' (C) — CTho
- 'Limelight' (D) — MBri SCoo SKee
- 'Linda' (D) — SKee
- 'Listener' (Cider/D) — CTho
- 'Lobo' (D) — SCrf
§ - 'Loddington' (C) — SKee
- 'Lodi' (C) — SDea
- 'London Pearmain' (D) — SKee
- 'London Pippin' (C) — CTho SKee
- 'Longkeeper' (D) — CEnd CTho
- 'Longstem' (Cider) — CTho
- 'Lord Burghley' (D) — GTwe SDea SKee
- 'Lord Derby' (C) — CCAT CMac CTho CWib ECrN EMui GKir GTwe MBri NRog SCrf SDea SFam SKee
- 'Lord Grosvenor' (C) — GTwe SKee
- 'Lord Hindlip' (D) — GTwe SDea SFam SKee
- 'Lord Lambourne' (D) ♀H4 — CAgr CCAT CDoC CSBt CTri CWib EBre ECrN EMui EPfP GKir GTwe LRHS MWat NRog SCrf SDea SFam SKee SPer WBVN WHar WOrn
- 'Lord Nelson' (C) — SKee
- 'Lord of the Isles' (F) — CCAT
- 'Lord Rosebery' (D) — SKee
- 'Lord Stradbroke' (C) — SKee
- 'Lord Suffield' (C) — CTri SKee
- 'Lucombe's Pine' (D) — CEnd CTho
- 'Lucombe's Seedling' (D) — CTho SKee
- 'Lynn's Pippin' (D) **new** — SKee
- 'Mabbott's Pearmain' (D) — SDea
- 'Madresfield Court' (D) — SDea SKee
- 'Major' (Cider) — CCAT CTho
- 'Malling Kent' (D) — EMui SDea SFam
- 'Maltster' (D) — SKee
- 'Manaccan Primrose' (C/D) — CEnd CLnd
- 'Margil' (D) — CCAT GTwe SDea SFam SKee
- 'Mary Golds' — CTho
- 'May Queen' (D) — SDea SFam
- 'Maypole'PBR (D/Ball) — LRHS MAsh MGos SDea
- 'Maypole 2000' (C/Ball) — ENot
- 'McIntosh' (D) — SKee
- 'Measday's Favourite' (C) — SKee
- 'Médaille d'Or' (Cider) — CCAT
- 'Medina' (D) — GTwe
- 'Melba' (D) — SKee
- 'Melcombe Russet' (D) — CTho
- 'Melon' (D) — SDea
- 'Melrose' (D) — ECrN GTwe SKee
- 'Merchant Apple' (D) — CCAT
- 'Merchant Apple of Illminster' (D) — CCAT CTho
- 'Mère de Ménage' (C) — SFam
- 'Meridian' (D) — EMui MBri SDea SKee
- 'Merton Charm' (D) ♀H4 — SKee
- 'Merton Knave' (D) — GTwe MGos SDea SFam
- 'Merton Russet' (D) — SDea SKee
- 'Merton Worcester' (D) — ECrN SDea SKee
- 'Michaelmas Red' (D) — GTwe NRog SKee
- 'Michelin' (Cider) — CCAT CTri EMui GTwe SDea SKee WOrn
- 'Miller's Seedling' (D) — GTwe SKee
- 'Millicent Barnes' (D) — SDea
- 'Mollie's Delicious' (D) — SKee
- 'Monarch' (C) — CCAT CTri ECrN GTwe NRog SDea SFam SKee
- 'Monidel'PBR — SKee
- 'Morgan's Sweet' (C/Cider) — CCAT CTho CTri SDea SKee
- 'Moss's Seedling' (D) — SDea
§ - 'Mother' (D) ♀H4 — CCAT CDoC CSBt CTri GTwe SCrf SDea SFam SKee
- 'Munster Tulip' (D/C) — CTho

- 'Muscadet de Dieppe' (Cider) — CCAT
§ - 'Mutsu' (D) — CCAT CTri ECrN GTwe NRog SCrf SDea SKee
- 'Nemes Szercsika Alma' (C) — SKee
- 'Nettlestone Pippin' (D) — SDea
- 'Newton Wonder' (D/C) ♀H4 — CCAT CDoC CMac CSBt CTho CTri CWib ECrN GTwe LRHS NRog SCrf SDea SFam SKee
- 'Newtown Pippin' (D) — SDea
- 'Nine Square' (D) — CTho
- 'Nittany Red' (D) — SDea
- 'No Pip' (C) — CTho
- 'Nonpareil' (D) — SKee
- 'Norfolk Beauty' (C) — SKee
- 'Norfolk Beefing' (C) — SDea SFam SKee
- 'Norfolk Royal' (D) — CDoC ECrN GTwe SDea SKee
- 'Norfolk Summer Broadend' (C) — SKee
- 'Norfolk Winter Coleman' (C) — SKee
- 'Northcott Superb' (D) — CTho
- 'Northern Greening' (C) — GTwe SKee
§ - 'Northwood' (Cider) — CCAT CTho
- 'Nutmeg Pippin' (D) — ECrN SDea SKee
- 'Oaken Pin' (C) — CCAT CTho
- 'Old Pearmain' (D) — CTho SDea SKee
- 'Old Somerset Russet' (D) — CTho
- 'Opalescent' (D) — SKee
- 'Orange Goff' (D) — SKee
- 'Orin' (D) **new** — SKee
- 'Orkney Apple' (F) — SKee
- 'Orleans Reinette' (D) — CAgr CCAT CTho CTri CWib ECrN EMui GTwe LRHS MWat NRog SCrf SDea SFam SKee
- 'Osier' (Cider) — CCAT
- 'Oslin' (D) — SKee
- 'Owen Thomas' (D) — CTri SKee
- 'Oxford Conquest' (D) — SKee
- 'Paignton Marigold' (Cider) — CTho
- 'Palmer's Rosey' (D) — SKee
- 'Pascoe's Pippin' (D/C) — CTho
- 'Payhembury' (C/Cider) — CTho
- 'Peacemaker' (D) — SKee
- 'Pear Apple' (D) — CEnd CTho
- 'Pearl' (D) — SDea
- 'Peasgood's Nonsuch' (C) ♀H4 — CCAT ECrN GKir GTwe LBuc LRHS MBri NRog SCrf SDea SFam SKee WOrn
- 'Peck's Pleasant' (D) — SKee
- 'Pendragon' (D) — CTho
- 'Penhallow Pippin' (D) — CTho
- 'Pennard Bitter' (Cider) — CCAT
- 'Peter Lock' (C/D) — CEnd CTho
- 'Peter's Pippin' (D) — SDea
- 'Peter's Seedling' (D) — SDea
- 'Pickering's Seedling' (D) — SKee
- 'Pigeonette de Rouen' (D) — SKee
- 'Pig's Nose Pippin' (D) — CEnd SKee
- 'Pig's Nose Pippin Type III (D) — CTho
- 'Pig's Snout' (Cider/C/D) — CCAT CEnd CTho
- 'Pine Golden Pippin' (D) — SKee
- 'Pitmaston Pine Apple' (D) — CCAT CTho CTri ECrN LRHS NRog SCrf SDea SFam SKee WOrn
- 'Pitmaston Russet Nonpareil' (D) — SKee
- 'Pixie' (D) ♀H4 — CCAT CSam GTwe SDea SFam SKee
- 'Plum Vite' (D) — CTho CTri

- 'Plympton Pippin' (C)   CEnd CTho
- Polka = 'Trajan'^PBR   ENot LRHS MGos SDea
  (D/Ball)
- 'Polly' (C/D)   CEnd
- 'Polly Prosser' (D)   SKee
- 'Polly Whitehair' (C/D)   CTho SDea SKee
- 'Pomeroy of Somerset'   CCAT CTho SKee
  (D)
- 'Ponsford' (C)   CCAT CTho
- 'Pónyik Alma' (c)   SKee
- 'Port Wine'   see *M. domestica* 'Harry Master's
     Jersey'
- 'Porter's Perfection'   CCAT CTho
  (Cider)
- 'Pott's Seedling' (C)   SKee
- 'Princesse'   GKir SDea SKee WBVN
- 'Purpurroter Cousinot'   SKee
  (D)
- 'Quarry Apple' (C)   CTho
- 'Queen' (C)   CCAT CTho SKee
- 'Queen Cox' (D)   EMui GBon MRav SDea SKee
- – self-fertile   SDea
- 'Queens' (D)   CTho
- 'Quench' (D/Cider)   CTho
- 'Radford Beauty' **new**   MCoo
- 'Red Alkmene' (D)   MBri
§ - 'Red Blenheim' (C/D)   SKee
- 'Red Bramley' (C)   CWib
- 'Red Charles Ross' (C/D)   SDea
- 'Red Delicious' (D)   SCrf
- 'Red Devil' (D)   CAgr COtt CTri CWSG ECrN EMui
     GKir GTwe LRHS MBri NBee SCoo
     SDea SKee SPoG
- 'Red Ellison' (D)   CCAT CTho CTri GTwe NRog SCrf
     SDea
- 'Red Elstar' (D)   SCrf
- 'Red Falstaff'^PBR (D)   CAgr GKir LBuc LRHS MBri MCoo
     SKee WBVN
- 'Red Fuji' (D)   SDea
- 'Red Gravenstein' (D)   NRog
- 'Red Jersey' (Cider)   CCAT
- 'Red Joaneting' (D)   SKee
- 'Red Jonagold'^PBR   see *M. domestica*
     'Jonagored'
- 'Red Jonathan' (D)   SDea
- 'Red Miller's Seedling'   SCrf SDea
  (D)
- 'Red Rattler' (D)   CTho
- 'Red Robin' (F)   CEnd
- 'Red Roller' (D) **new**   CTho
- 'Red Ruby' (F)   CTho
- 'Red Victoria' (C)   GTwe
- 'Red Windsor'   EMui SCoo SKee
- 'Redcoat Grieve' (D)   GKir SDea
- 'Redsleeves' (D)   CAgr GTwe SDea SKee
- 'Redstrake' (Cider)   CCAT
- 'Reine des Reinettes'   see *M. domestica* 'King of the
     Pippins'
- 'Reinette d'Obry' (Cider)   CCAT
- 'Reinette Dorée de   GTwe
  Boediker' (D)
- 'Reinette du Canada' (D)   SKee
- 'Reinette Rouge Etoilée'   CCAT SDea
  (D)
- 'Reverend Greeves' (C)   SDea
- 'Reverend W. Wilks' (C)   CCAT CCVT CDoC COtt CTri
     ECrN EMui GKir LBuc LRHS MWat
     NRog SCrf SDea SFam SKee
- 'Ribston Pippin' (D) ♀H4   CCAT CTho CWib ECrN EMui
     GTwe LBuc LRHS MWat NRog
     SCrf SDea SFam SKee
- 'Rival' (D)   SDea
- 'Robin Pippin' (D)   GTwe
- 'Rome Beauty' (D)   SDea

- 'Rosemary Russet'   CCAT CTho GTwe MCoo NRog
  (D) ♀H4   SCrf SDea SFam SKee
- 'Rosmarina Bianca' (D/C)   SKee
- 'Ross Nonpareil' (D)   GTwe SDea SKee
- 'Roter Ananas' (D)   SKee
- 'Roter Eiserapfel' (D)   SKee
- 'Rough Pippin' (D)   CEnd CTho
- 'Roundway Magnum   CCAT CTho SDea SFam SKee
  Bonum' (D)
§ - 'Roxbury Russet' (D)   SKee
§ - 'Royal Gala' (D) ♀H4   ECrN EMui LRHS SDea SKee
§ - 'Royal Jubilee' (C)   CCAT SKee
- 'Royal Russet' (C)   SDea
- 'Royal Snow' (D)   SKee
- 'Royal Somerset'   CCAT CTho
  (C/Cider)
- 'Rubens' (D)   SKee
- 'Rubinette' (D)   CDoC COtt ECrN GTwe MGos
     SDea SKee WBVN
- 'Sabaros' (C)   SKee
- 'Saint Albans Pippin' (D)   SKee
- 'Saint Augustine's   SKee
  Orange' (D)
- 'Saint Cecilia' (D)   SDea SKee
§ - 'Saint Edmund's Pippin'   CTho ECrN GTwe LBuc SCrf SDea
  (D) ♀H4   SFam SKee
- 'Saint Edmund's Russet'   see *M. domestica* 'Saint Edmund's
     Pippin'
- 'Saint Magdalen' (D)   SKee
- 'Saltcote Pippin' (D)   SKee
- 'Sam Young' (D)   SKee
- 'Sandlands' (D)   SDea
- 'Sandringham' (C)   ECrN SKee
- 'Sanspareil' (D)   SKee
- 'Saturn'^PBR   CDoC CTri EMui GTwe SDea SKee
- 'Saw Pits' (F)   CEnd SKee
- 'Scarlet Nonpareil' (D)   SDea SKee
- 'Scarlet Pimpernel' (D)   SCrf
- 'Scotch Bridget' (C)   GKir SKee WOrn
- 'Scotch Dumpling' (C)   GKir GTwe LRHS MCoo
- 'Scrumptious' (D)   CAgr CDoC GKir LBuc MBri SCoo
     SKee SPer
- 'Sercombe's Natural'   CCAT CTho
  (Cider)
- 'Severn Bank' (C)   CCAT CTho
- 'Sharleston Pippin' (D)   SKee
- 'Sheep's Nose' (C)   CCAT SDea SKee
- 'Shenandoah' (C)   SKee
- 'Sidney Strake' (C)   CEnd
- 'Sikulai Alma' (D)   SKee
- 'Sir Isaac Newton's'   see *M. domestica* 'Flower of Kent'
- 'Sir John Thornycroft' (D)   SDea
- 'Sisson's Worksop   SKee
  Newtown' (D)
- 'Slack Ma Girdle' (Cider)   CCAT CTho
- 'Smart's Prince Arthur'   SDea
  (C)
- 'Snell's Glass Apple'   see *M. domestica* 'Glass Apple'
- 'Somerset Lasting' (C)   CTho
- 'Somerset Redstreak'   CCAT CTho GTwe
  (Cider)
- 'Sops in Wine' (C/Cider)   CCAT CTho NLar
- 'Sour Bay' (Cider)   CTho
- 'Sour Natural'   see *M. domestica* 'Langworthy'
- 'Spartan' (D)   CCAT CDoC CSBt CTri CWib EBre
     ECrN EMui ENot EPfP EWTr GBon
     GKir GTwe LBuc LRHS MGos
     NBlu NPri NRog SCrf SDea SFam
     SKee SPer WOrn WStI
- 'Spencer' (D)   CTri ECrN SKee
- 'Spotted Dick' (Cider)   CTho
- 'Stable Jersey' (Cider)   CCAT
- 'Stamford Pippin' (D)   SDea
- 'Star of Devon' (D)   CCAT SDea

- 'Stark' (D) — SDea
- 'Starking' (D) — ECrN
- 'Starkrimson' (D) — SKee
- 'Starkspur Golden Delicious' (D) — SKee
- 'Stembridge Cluster' (Cider) — CCAT
- 'Stembridge Jersey' (Cider) — CCAT
- 'Steyne Seedling' (D) — SDea
- 'Stirling Castle' (C) — CAgr GKir GQui GTwe SKee
- 'Stobo Castle' (C) — SKee
- 'Stockbearer' (C) — CTho
- 'Stoke Edith Pippin' (D) — WOrn
- 'Stoke Red' (Cider) — CCAT CTho
- 'Stone's' — see *M. domestica* 'Loddington'
- 'Stoup Leadington' (C) — SKee
- 'Strawberry Pippin' (D) — CTho
- 'Striped Beefing' (C) — SKee
- 'Strippy' (C) — CTho
- 'Stub Nose' (F) — SKee
- 'Sturmer Pippin' (D) — CSBt ECrN GTwe LRHS MWat NRog SCrf SDea SFam SKee
- 'Sugar Bush' (C/D) — CTho
- 'Summer Golden Pippin' (D) — SKee
- 'Summerred' (D) — ECrN
- 'Sunnydale' (D/C) — SDea
I - 'Sunrise' (D) — EMui LRHS SKee
- 'Sunset' (D) ♀H4 — CCAT CCVT CDoC CSBt CSam CTho CTri CWib EMui EPfP EWTr GKir GTwe LBuc LRHS MBri NBee NBlu NPri NRog NWea SCrf SDea SFam SKee SPer WHar WOrn
- 'Suntan' (D) ♀H4 — CCAT CWib ECrN GBon GTwe MWat NBee SDea SKee
- 'Superb' — see *M. domestica* 'Laxton's Superb'
- 'Surprise' (D) — GTwe
- 'Sweet Alford' (Cider) — CCAT CTho
- 'Sweet Bay' (Cider) — CTho
- 'Sweet Cleave' (Cider) — CCAT CTho
- 'Sweet Coppin' (Cider) — CTho CTri
- 'Tale Sweet' (Cider) — CCAT CTho
- 'Tamar Beauty' (F) — CEnd
- 'Tan Harvey' (Cider) — CCAT CEnd CTho
- 'Taunton Cross' (D) — SKee
- 'Taunton Fair Maid' (Cider) — CCAT CTho
- 'Taylor's' (Cider) — CCAT SDea
- 'Ten Commandments' (D/Cider) — CCAT SDea
- 'Téton de Demoiselle' (D) — SKee
- 'Tewkesbury Baron' (D) **new** — CTho
- 'The Rattler' (F) — CEnd
- 'Thomas Rivers' (C) — SDea
- 'Thorle Pippin' (D) — SKee
- 'Tidicombe Seedling' (D) — CTho
- 'Tom Putt' (C) — CCAT CCVT CTho CTri CWib ECrN GKir GTwe LBuc LRHS SDea SKee WOrn
- 'Tommy Knight' (D) — CCAT CEnd CTho
- 'Totnes Apple' (D) **new** — CTho
- 'Tower of Glamis' (C) — GQui GTwe SKee
- 'Town Farm Number 59' (Cider) — CTho
- 'Transparente de Croncels' (C) — CTho
- 'Tregoana King' (C/D) — CCAT CEnd CTho
- 'Tremlett's Bitter' (Cider) — CCAT CTho SDea
- 'Trumpington' (D) — CTho
- 'Twenty Ounce' (C) — CCAT GTwe SKee
- 'Twinings Pippin' (D) — SKee

§ - 'Tydeman's Early Worcester' (D) — CAgr CLnd CWib ECrN GTwe LRHS NBee NRog SDea SKee
- 'Tydeman's Late Orange' (D) — CTri ECrN GTwe NRog SDea SFam SKee
- 'Tyler's Kernel' (C) — SKee
- 'Underleaf' (D) — CCAT
- 'Upton Pyne' (D) — CCAT CSam CTho SCrf SDea SKee
- 'Veitch's Perfection' (C/D) — CTho
- 'Venus Pippin' (C/D) — CEnd
- 'Vernade' **new** — SKee
- 'Vicar of Beighton' (D) — SKee
- 'Vickey's Delight' (D) — SDea
- 'Vileberie' (Cider) — CCAT
- 'Vista-bella' (D) — ECrN GTwe NBee SDea SKee
- 'Vitgylling' (D/C) — SKee
- 'Wagener' (D) — NRog SDea SKee
- 'Waltz = 'Telamon'PBR (D/Ball) — LRHS MGos SDea
- 'Wanstall Pippin' (D) — SKee
- 'Warner's King' (C) ♀H4 — CTho CTri NRog SCrf SDea SKee
- 'Warrior' — CTho
- 'Wealthy' (D) — SDea SKee
- 'Wellington' (C) — see *M. domestica* 'Dummellor's Seedling'
- 'Wellington' (Cider) — CTho
§ - 'Wellspur' (D) — GTwe
- 'Wellspur Red Delicious' — see *M. domestica* 'Wellspur'
- 'Welsh Russet' (D) — SDea
- 'White Alphington' (Cider) — CTho
- 'White Close Pippin' (Cider) — CTho
- 'White Jersey' (Cider) — CCAT
- 'White Joaneting' (D) — GTwe SKee
- 'White Melrose' (C) — GTwe SDea SKee
- 'White Paradise' (C) — SKee
- 'White Transparent' (C/D) — SDea SKee
- 'William Crump' (D) — CCAT CTho ECrN SDea SFam SKee
- 'Winston' (D) ♀H4 — CCAT CCVT CSBt CTri ECrN GTwe NRog NWea SCrf SDea SFam
- 'Winter Banana' (D) — ECrN NRog SDea SKee
- 'Winter Gem' (D) — COtt ECrN EMui GKir LBuc LRHS MBri MGos SDea SKee WBVN
- 'Winter Peach' (D/C) — CEnd CTho
- 'Winter Pearmain' (D) — SKee
- 'Winter Quarrenden' (D) — SDea
- 'Winter Queening' (D/C) — SDea
- 'Winter Stubbard' (C) — CTho
- 'Woodbine' — see *M. domestica* 'Northwood'
- 'Woolbrook Pippin' (D) — CCAT CTho
- 'Woolbrook Russet' (C) — CCAT CTho SKee
- 'Worcester Pearmain' (D) ♀H4 — CBcs CCAT CCVT CSBt CTho CTri CWib ECrN EMui ENot GBon GKir GTwe LBuc LRHS MWat NPri NRog NWea SDea SFam SKee SPer WHar WOrn WStI
- 'Wormsley Pippin' (D) — ECrN SKee
- 'Wyatt's Seedling' — see *M. domestica* 'Langworthy'
- 'Wyken Pippin' (D) — CCAT ECrN GTwe SDea SFam SKee
- 'Yarlington Mill' (Cider) — CCAT CTho CTri SDea SKee
- 'Yellow Bellflower' (D/C) — SKee
- 'Yellow Ingestrie' (D) — SFam SKee
- 'Yellow Styre' (Cider) **new** — CTho
- 'Zabergäu Renette' (D) — SKee
- 'Donald Wyman' — SKee
- 'Echtermeyer' — see *M. x gloriosa* 'Oekonomierat Echtermeyer'
§ 'Evereste' ♀H4 — More than 30 suppliers

florentina	CMCN CTho EPfP GIBF LTwo MRav
floribunda ♀H4	More than 30 suppliers
'Gardener's Gold'	CEnd CTho
§ x *gloriosa* 'Oekonomierat Echtermeyer'	CCAT EBee GKir GQui MAsh SCrf SDea WDin
'Golden Gem'	CCAT CRez EPfP GTwe LRHS MAsh MDun SCoo SKee
'Golden Hornet'	see *M.* x *zumi* 'Golden Hornet'
'Goldsworth Red' **new**	CCAT
'Harry Baker'	ERea LRHS
'Hillieri'	see *M.* x *schiedeckeri* 'Hillieri'
hupehensis ♀H4	CCAT CEnd CLnd CMCN CSBt CTho EBee ENot EPfP GKir GTwe LRHS MBlu MRav SCrf SFam SHBN SLPl SPer WMou
'John Downie' (C) ♀H4	More than 30 suppliers
'Kaido'	see *M.* x *micromalus*
kansuensis	CLnd EBee GIBF WCwm
'Laura' PBR	COtt EMui ENot EPfP GKir LRHS MAsh MBlu MGos SCoo SKee
'Louisa'	MAsh
x *magdeburgensis*	CLnd CSBt
'Mandarin' **new**	LRHS
'Marshal Ôyama'	CTho
§ x *micromalus*	CLnd
x *moerlandsii*	CLnd
- 'Liset'	CDul CEnd CLnd COtt CWib EBee ECrN ENot MAsh MRav SFam SKee WFar WStI
§ - 'Profusion'	CDul CLnd CTri EBee EBre ECrN ELan ENot GKir LPan LRHS MBri MGos MRav MSwo NWea SCrf SHBN SKee SPer SSta WDin WStI
- 'Profusion Improved'	CCAT CEnd COtt CSBt CWSG GKir MAsh MWat NBee SCoo SKee SLim WOrn
niedzwetzkyana	see *M. pumila* 'Niedzwetzkyana'
orthocarpa	CLnd
Perpetu	see *M.* 'Evereste'
'Pink Glow'	LRHS MAsh SCoo SLim SPoG
'Pink Perfection'	CDoC CLnd EBee ENot LRHS MDun SHBN SKee SPer
Pom'Zaï = 'Courtabri'	CDoC
'Prairie Fire'	MBri SKee
prattii	CLnd CTho
'Profusion'	see *M.* x *moerlandsii* 'Profusion'
prunifolia 'Cheal's Crimson'	NRog
- 'Fastigiata'	GIBF
- var. *prunifolia*	GIBF
- var. *rinkii*	GIBF
pumila 'Cowichan'	GKir LRHS MBri
- 'Dartmouth'	CCAT CDul CLnd CSBt CSam CTho CTri ECrN NRog SFam
- 'Montreal Beauty'	GKir LRHS MBri SKee WOrn
§ - 'Niedzwetzkyana'	CLnd
§ x *purpurea* 'Aldenhamensis'	CCAT CLnd NRog SCrf SDea WDin WOrn
- 'Eleyi'	CLnd ECrN ENot MAsh MRav NWea SCrf WDin WStI
- 'Lemoinei'	CLnd ECrN EMui EWTr
- 'Neville Copeman'	CDoC CDul CLnd CTri EBee ECrN EWTr LPan LRHS MGos WOrn
- 'Pendula'	see *M.* x *gloriosa* 'Oekonomierat Echtermeyer'
'R.J. Fulcher'	CLnd CTho
'Ralph Shay'	CLnd
'Red Barron'	CLnd
'Red Glow'	CDoC CLnd COtt EBee ECrN GQui MAsh SCrf
'Red Jade'	see *M.* x *schiedeckeri* 'Red Jade'
§ x *robusta*	CDoC CLnd CTri EBee GTwe LPan LRHS NWea SCrf SLon
- 'Red Sentinel' ♀H4	More than 30 suppliers
- 'Red Siberian'	ECrN SDea SHBN SPer
- 'Yellow Siberian'	CLnd SPer
rockii	GIBF
'Royal Beauty' ♀H4	CDoC CLnd CWib EBee EBre ENot EPfP GKir GTwe LPan LRHS MAsh MBri MGos MRav MSwo SCoo SCrf SKee WDin WHar WOrn
'Royalty'	More than 30 suppliers
'Rudolph'	CCAT CCVT CDul CLnd EBee ECrN ENot EWTr LPan LRHS MAsh MRav SCoo SLim
'Ruth Ann'	CLnd
sargentii	see *M. toringo* subsp. *sargentii*
'Satin Cloud'	CLnd
§ x *scheideckeri* 'Hillieri'	CCAT CDul CLnd ECrN MAsh SCrf SFam
§ - 'Red Jade'	More than 30 suppliers
Siberian crab	see *M.* x *robusta*
sieboldii	see *M. toringo*
sikkimensis	GIBF WHCr
- B&SWJ 2431	WCru
'Silver Drift'	CLnd
'Snowcloud'	CCAT CDul CEnd CLnd EBee ECrN ENot EPfP LRHS MAsh MBlu MBri SHBN SPer WOrn
spectabilis	CLnd
'Street Parade'	CLnd
'Sun Rival'	CCAT CDoC CDul CEnd COtt CSBt CWSG EBee EMui EPfP GKir GTwe LRHS MAsh MBri MDun MGos SCoo SFam SKee SLim WHar
sylvestris	CArn CCVT CDul CLnd CRWN CTri ECrN EPfP GKir LBuc MRav NBee NRog NWea WDin WOrn
§ *toringo*	CLnd ECrN GIBF SSpi WSHC
- var. *arborescens*	GIBF
§ - subsp. *sargentii*	CDul CLnd CMCN CTho EBee ECrN ENot GKir LRHS MBri MGos MRav NWea SFam SPer SPoG WNor
- - 'Tina'	CLnd
toringoides	see *M. bhutanica*
transitoria ♀H4	CCAT CDoC CDul CEnd CFil CLnd CTho EBee ECrN EMil EPfP GIBF GKir LRHS MAsh MBlu MRav NWea SCoo SPer SSpi WPGP
- 'Thornhayes Tansy'	CTho LRHS MBri
trilobata	CCAT CLnd CTho EPfP MAsh MGos SCoo SKee WMou
- 'Guardsman'	MBri
tschonoskii ♀H4	More than 30 suppliers
- 'White Star'	see *M.* 'White Star'
'Van Eseltine'	CCAT CDul CLnd CSBt CWSG CWib EBee EMui GKir GTwe LRHS MAsh MBri MWat SFam SKee SPer
'Veitch's Scarlet'	CDul CLnd CSBt CTho GQui GTwe NRog SFam
§ 'White Star'	CCAT CDoC CDul CSBt CWSG ECrN LRHS SCoo SKee SLim
'Winter Gold'	CDoC CDul CLnd CSam SCrf WStI
'Wisley Crab'	CLnd EBee EMil GTwe SDea SFam SKee
yunnanensis var. *veitchii*	CTho GIBF
x *zumi* var. *calocarpa*	CLnd CTho
§ - 'Golden Hornet' ♀H4	More than 30 suppliers
- 'Professor Sprenger'	CLnd CSam

Malva (Malvaceae)

alcea	CAgr EPfP
- 'Alba'	WShp
- var. *fastigiata*	CArn EMan ERou LRHS MBow NBid NBro NBur SAga SPer SRms WPer WShp

bicolor	see *Lavatera maritima*
'Gibbortello'	CCge MCLN NBur
moschata	More than 30 suppliers
- f. *alba* ♀H4	More than 30 suppliers
- - 'Pirouette'	WHen
- 'Pink Perfection'	EFWa
- 'Romney Marsh'	see *Althaea officinalis* 'Romney Marsh'
- *rosea*	ECha EPfP NCot NPer SWvt WPnP
'Park Allee'	EBee EChP EMan LDai MCCP MMHG NCot SUsu
sylvestris	CAgr CArn GWCH MBow NBro NSco SMad SWat WHHs WHer WJek WMoo WRos WWin WWye
- 'Alba'	CArn CNat
- 'Brave Heart'	CM&M GBri NBur NLar SWvt WGwG WHHs
- 'Knockout'	EWes
I - 'Magic Hollyhock' (d)	SGar
- Marina = 'Dema'PBR	EBee ELan NCot NLar WShp
- subsp. *mauritanica*	CHea EBee ECoo EMar EPfP GBri NPer SSvw WHil WMoo
- - 'Bibor Fehlo'	CSpe MAnH NBur NGdn WCFE WHil
- 'Mystic Merlin'	CBgR CM&M EWll WCAu WGwG WHHs
- 'Perry's Blue'	NPer
- 'Primley Blue'	CBot CElw EBee EChP ECha ECtt ELan EMan EPfP GBri MRav MTho NBPC NBlu NBrk NCot NGdn NPer NPri NSti SMad SPer WFar WHHs WSan WShp WWin
- 'Richard Perry'	NPer
- 'Windsor Castle' **new**	WHil
- 'Zebrina'	CM&M EBee EMar GBri LDai MCLN NBrk NBur NGdn NPri SPer SWvt WHil WMoo WRha

Malvastrum (Malvaceae)

x *hypomadarum*	see *Anisodontea* x *hypomadara* (Sprague) Bates
lateritium	More than 30 suppliers
* *latifolium*	SOkh

Malvaviscus (Malvaceae)

arboreus	CHll CKob XPep
- var. *mexicanus*	ERea SYvo
- pink	CKob

mandarin see *Citrus reticulata*

mandarin, Cleopatra see *Citrus reshni*

Mandevilla (Apocynaceae)

x *amabilis* 'Alice du Pont' ♀H1	CBcs CRHN ELan EMil ERea ESlt LRHS SMur SOWG
boliviensis ♀H1	ELan ESlt LRHS SOWG
§ *laxa* ♀H2	CHEx CHll ELan ERea ESlt SHFr SOWG WCot WCru WHrl WSHC
sanderi	MBri
- 'Rosea'	CSpe ERea
splendens ♀H1	EBak LRHS SOWG
suaveolens	see *M. laxa*

Mandragora (Solanaceae)

autumnalis	EBee GCal MGol MSal NLar WCot
caulescens	EBee
§ *officinarum*	CFwr EBee GCal GPoy LEdu MGol MSal

Manettia (Rubiaceae)

inflata	see *M. luteorubra*
§ *luteorubra*	ELan

Manfreda see *Agave*

Manglietia (Magnoliaceae)

conifera **new**	CFil WPGP
insignis	CFil CHEx SSpi WPGP

Manihot (Euphorbiaceae)

esculenta	CKob
- 'Variegata'	CKob EAmu

Maranta (Marantaceae)

leuconeura var. *kerchoveana* ♀H1	CHal LRHS MBri XBlo

Margyricarpus (Rosaceae)

§ *pinnatus*	CFee CPle GEdr GEil GGar NWCA WCom WPer
setosus	see *M. pinnatus*

Mariscus see *Cyperus*

marjoram, pot see *Origanum onites*

marjoram, sweet see *Origanum majorana*

marjoram, wild, or oregano see *Origanum vulgare*

Marrubium (Lamiaceae)

candidissimum	see *M. incanum*
cylleneum	EBlw ECha
* - 'Velvetissimum'	SBla WCHb
friwaldskyanum **new**	XPep
'Gold Leaf'	ECha
§ *incanum*	CBot EBee EChP EMan IFro MBri NCGa SMrm WEas
libanoticum	ECha MSte WPer
pestalloziae	EBee WCot
supinum	CArn CStr NWoo XPep
vulgare	CArn ELau GBar GPoy GWCH MHer NOrc SIde WCHb WHer WPer WSel WWye
- 'Green Pompon'	ELau NLar

Marshallia (Asteraceae)

grandiflora	CDes EBee NLar SIgm
trinerva	EBee SUsu WCot

Marsilea (Marsileaceae)

quadrifolia	IHMH WWpP

Mascarena see *Hyophorbe*

Massonia (Hyacinthaceae)

depressa **new**	CStu
echinata	CStu
pustulata	CStu

Mathiasella (Apiaceae)

from Mexico	SIgm
bupleuroides **new**	WCot

Matricaria (Asteraceae)

chamomilla	see *M. recutita*
parthenium	see *Tanacetum parthenium*
§ *recutita*	GPoy
tchihatchewii **new**	XPep

Matteuccia (Woodsiaceae)

intermedia	see *Onoclea intermedia*
orientalis	CFil CLAP GCal LEur MAsh NLar NMar NOrc WFar WRic

pensylvanica	CLAP EBee EMon NHol SMrm
struthiopteris ♀H4	More than 30 suppliers
- 'Bedraggled Feathers'	EMon
* - 'Depauperata' **new**	CLAP

Matthiola (Brassicaceae)

* **arborescens alba**	CHrt CWCL WBVN
§ **fruticulosa**	EBee
- 'Alba'	CDes EBee WPGP
- subsp. *perennis*	EBee NWCA
incana	CBgR CWCL WCot WPer WRHF
- *alba*	CBot ELan GBBs NBir
thessala	see *M. fruticulosa*
white perennial	CArn CHad CMea CMil CSev CSpe ERou ETow LPhx LRav MBct MSte MWgw NBrk NPer SEND SSth SWal WCAu WCom WEas WHoo

Maurandella (Scrophulariaceae)

§ *antirrhiniflora*	LRHS

Maurandya (Scrophulariaceae)

§ *barclayana*	CBot CHll CRHN CSpe MBri SGar
- *alba*	CBot
erubescens	see *Lophospermum erubescens*
lophantha	see *Lophospermum scandens*
lophospermum	see *Lophospermum scandens*
'Pink Ice'	see *Lophospermum scandens* 'Pink Ice'
'Red Dragon'	see *Lophospermum* 'Red Dragon'
§ 'Victoria Falls'	LRHS SOWG

Maytenus (Celastraceae)

boaria	CMCN EPfP GEil LEdu NLar SAPC SArc SLon WFar WPGP WPic
- 'Worplesdon Fastigiate'	CFil
chubutensis **new**	LEdu
magellanica	CFil WFar

Mazus (Scrophulariaceae)

radicans	CStu WCru
reptans	EBee EBre EDAr EMan EMlt EPAt EPfP GEdr NFla NHol NWCA SIng WOut WPer
- 'Albus'	CNic EBee EBre EDAr EMFW EMlt MDKP NHol SIng SPlb WOut WPer
surculosus	CPom

Meconopsis ✿ (Papaveraceae)

CC 3315	WRos
aculeata	EBee GGGa GTou
baileyi	see *M. betonicifolia*
Ballyrogan form	GEdr IBlr
x *beamishii*	GBuc
§ *betonicifolia* ♀H4	More than 30 suppliers
- var. *alba*	EBee EDAr ELan GBuc GGGa GGar IMGH ITim LHop MBri NBlu NChi NLar SLon SPer SRms WCAu WCru
- 'Glacier Blue'	GAbr
- 'Hensol Violet'	EBee EChP GBuc GCal GCrs GFle GGGa GMac ITim LHop NLar WViv
- var. *pratensis*	GCrs
cambrica	CHrt CTri EBee EHrv ELan EMar GGar GTou MBow NCot NHol NPri SChu SGar SIng WAbe WBea WBrk WCru WFar WHen WHer WPnP WWye
- 'Anne Greenaway' (d)	ELan LHop
- var. *aurantiaca*	SWal
- *flore-pleno* (d)	CHar EPar GBuc MTho NBid
- - orange (d)	NBid NBir NPol WAbe WCot WCru WHen
- - yellow (d)	WCot WCru

§ - 'Frances Perry'	CBgR ETow GBuc GCal IBlr WCru WFar WPnP WRos
- 'Muriel Brown' (d)	NCot WCru WPnP
- 'Rubra'	see *M. cambrica* 'Frances Perry'
chelidoniifolia	CFil GCal GKir IBlr NBid SSpi WCru WFar
delavayi	GGGa
dhwojii	GBri GFle GKev LRHS
(Fertile Blue Group) 'Blue Ice'	see *Meconopsis* (Fertile Blue Group) 'Lingholm'
N - 'Lingholm'	CLAP EBee EPza GBBs GBuc GCal GCrs GEdr GFle GGar GMac GTou IPot NCGa NGdn SSpi WBVN WLin WViv
N George Sherriff Group	CLAP GBuc GCal GEdr IBlr NBir GCrs
- 'Ascreavie'	GCrs
- 'Branklyn'	CDes CFil GAbr GBri IBlr WPGP
- 'Huntfield'	GCrs
- 'Jimmy Bayne'	GBuc GCrs GEdr GGGa
- 'Keillour' **new**	GKev
- 'Spring Hill'	GBuc IBlr
grandis misapplied	see *M. George Sherriff Group*
N *grandis* ambig.	CHar CPla CSam EBee EDAr EGle ENot GEdr GGGa GIBF ITim LRHS MNrw NChi NSla SBla SLon SRms WAbe WBVN WCom WHen WHlf WLin WPnP WViv
- Balruddery form	GGGa
- GS 600	see *M. George Sherriff Group*
henrici	GGGa
horridula	EBee GFle GGGa GKev LRHS MTho NLar
- B&SWJ 7983	WCru
- var. *racemosa*	see *M. racemosa* var. *racemosa*
- Rudis Group	EBee
impedita **new**	GCrs
N (Infertile Blue Group) 'Bobby Masterton'	GBuc GCrs
N - 'Crewdson Hybrid'	CLAP EChP GBuc GCrs NLar
N - 'Cruickshank'	GCrs
N - 'Dawyck'	GCrs
N - 'Mrs Jebb'	GBuc GCrs
N - 'Slieve Donard' ♀H4	CDes CFil CLAP EBee GBri GBuc GCrs GMac IBlr WPGP
integrifolia	EBee GFle GGGa WAbe
- ACE 1798	GTou
§ - subsp. *integrifolia* 'Wolong'	GCrs
Kingsbarns hybrids	GCrs GGGa
lancifolia	EBee GGGa
latifolia	GGGa
'Mrs McMurtrie'	IBlr
napaulensis	CFil CSam EBee EBre EDAr ENot GCrs GEdr GFle GFlt GGGa GGar GKir IBlr IMGH ITer ITim LHop LRHS MBri NChi NLar SLon WHlf WLin WMoo WRos
- pink-flowered	EBee GKev NGdn WShp
- red-flowered	EBee GBuc GKev ITer ITim WCru
- Wallich's form	see *M. wallichii*
- white-flowered **new**	GKev
nudicaulis	see *Papaver nudicaule*
'Ormswell' ambig.	GBuc IBlr
paniculata	GFle GGGa IBlr ITim LRHS NBir WAbe WLin
- CC&McK 296	GTou
- from Ghunsa, Nepal	CDes CLAP EGle
pseudointegrifolia	GGGa GKir WLin
- B&SWJ 7595	WCru
punicea	GCrs GGGa GIBF
quintuplinervia ♀H4	CLAP GBri GCrs GEdr GFle GFlt GGGa GKev GTou IBlr MLLN NBid NBir NGar NRya NSla
- 'Kaye's Compact'	GBuc GEdr IBlr

§ **racemosa** var. **racemosa** GKev WLin
  regia EBee EDAr GFle GIBF LHop LRHS
    NBPC NLar WBar WMoo
  regia x **grandis** GBuc
  robusta EBee ITim
  x **sarsonsii** GFle GKev
  x **sheldonii** misapplied see *M.* Fertile Blue Group
    (fertile)
  x **sheldonii** misapplied see *M.* Infertile Blue Group
    (sterile)
N x **sheldonii** ambig. CBcs CWCL EBee EDAr ENot EPfP
    GBin GBuc GGGa GKir ITer LAst
    LHop MBri MDun MFir NBPC NBir
    NBlu SLon SRms WCra WCru WFar
    WPGP WPnP WViv
  simplicifolia GGGa GKev
  superba GBuc GGGa
  villosa GBuc GCal GFle GGGa GKev
    GTou IBlr ITim WBVN WCru
  wallichii misapplied see *M. napaulensis* Wallich's form
  wallichii ambig. EBee ITim
  wallichii Hook. GGGa ITim
  – white-flowered GKev

Medeola (Convallariaceae)
  virginica LAma WCru

Medicago (Papilionaceae)
  arborea IBlr SEND XPep
  sativa WHer WMoo
  – subsp. **sativa** IBlr

Medinilla (Melastomataceae)
  magnifica ♀H1 LRHS MBri SMur

medlar see *Mespilus germanica*

Meehania (Lamiaceae)
  cordata CDes EBee NLar
* **pedunculata new** EBee
  urticifolia CDes EBee EPPr MHar MSte WSHC
    WTMC
  – B&SWJ 1210 WCru
  – 'Wandering Minstrel' (v) CDes EBee EMan EMon

Megacodon (Gentianaceae)
  stylophorus new EBee

Melaleuca (Myrtaceae)
  acerosa SOWG
  acuminata SPlb
  alternifolia CArn ECou ELau EOHP EShb GPoy
    IDee MGol MHer MSal NTHB
    SOWG SSte WHer
  armillaris CDoC CTrC SGar SOWG SPlb SSte
  – pink SOWG
  bracteata CTrC ECou
  citrina SOWG
  coccinea SOWG
  cuticularis SPlb
  decora SOWG
  decussata CTrC ECou SOWG SPlb
  elliptica SOWG SSte
  ericifolia CTri SOWG SPlb
  filifolia SOWG
  fulgens SOWG SPlb SSte
  – apricot SOWG
* – 'Hot Pink' SOWG
  – purple-flowered SOWG
  gibbosa CPLG EBee ECou IArd IDee SOWG
    SSte WSHC
  holosericea hort. see *M.smartiorum*
  huegelii SOWG SSte
  hypericifolia CPLG CTrC ECou SOWG SPlb SSte

  incana CTrC SOWG SSte
  lateritia ECou SOWG SSte
  leucadendra MSal
  linariifolia CTrC ECou SPlb SSte
  nesophila CTrC ECou IDee SOWG SPlb SSte
  platycalyx SOWG
  pulchella EShb SOWG SSte
  pungens SPlb
  pustulata ECou SOWG SSte
  radula SOWG
* **rosmarinifolia** SOWG
§ **smartiorum** SOWG
  spathulata SOWG
  squamea CTrC EBee IDee SSte WPic
* **squarmania new** SOWG
  squarrosa CPLG CTrC ECou GKir SOWG
    SPlb SSte
  thymifolia ECou MSal SOWG SPlb SSte
  viridiflora GQui
  wilsonii ECou IDee SOWG

Melandrium see *Vaccaria*
  rubrum see *Silene dioica*

Melanoselinum (Apiaceae)
§ **decipiens** CArn CHEx LPhx SIgm

Melasphaerula (Iridaceae)
  graminea see *M. ramosa*
§ **ramosa** CBre CPLG ERos WPrP

Melia (Meliaceae)
  azadirachta GPoy
§ **azedarach** CArn CBcs CHEx ELau LPan LRav
    NPSI WPGP
  – var. **japonica** see *M. azedarach*

Melianthus (Melianthaceae)
  comosus EWes GGar LPio SPlb SSte WCot
  elongatus new EShb
  major ♀H3 More than 30 suppliers
  minor CFir LPio SIgm
  villosus CFir CPle CTrC GFlt LPio MCCP
    SGar SIgm SPlb SSte WCot WLin

Melica (Poaceae)
  altissima 'Alba' EHoe
  – 'Atropurpurea' More than 30 suppliers
  ciliata CBig CBrm COlW EBee EHoe
    EWsh GBin MMoz NHol NNor
    WHil WRos WWeb WWpP
  – subsp. **taurica** EPPr
  macra EBee EHoe EPPr
  nutans CBig CBrm CWCL EHoe EPPr EPla
    EPza EWsh GBin GWCH NHol
    NPPs NWCA SYvo WHal WRos
    WWeb WWye
  penicillaris EBee EPPr WPer WWpP
  persica EBee EPPr
  torreyana EPPr
  transsilvanica NNor
  – 'Atropurpurea' EBee EChP EWll NHol
    SPer
  – 'Red Spire' CBig IBal LRav MWhi NGHP
    WWpP
  uniflora CBrm
  – f. **albida** CFil EBee EHoe EMan MBct SLPl
    SUsu WCot
  – 'Variegata' (v) CBre CFil EBee ECha EHoe EMan
    EPPr EPla GCal MBrN MBri MMoz
    NGdn WCot WTin

Melicope (Rutaceae)
  ternata ECou

Melicytus (Violaceae)

alpinus	ECou
angustifolius	ECou
crassifolius	CPle ECou EPla WHCG
dentatus (f) **new**	WAbe
- (m) **new**	WAbe
obovatus	ECou EMan
ramiflorus	ECou

Melilotus (Papilionaceae)

officinalis	CArn CWCL GPoy MGol NSco
	SIde WHer WSel WWye
- subsp. *albus*	WHer

Melinis (Poaceae)

nerviglumis	EBee
repens	CFwr WCot
roseus	EBee EHul MCCP SMad
* *rubrum*	WSpi

Meliosma (Meliosmaceae)

parviflora B&SWJ 8408	WCru

Melissa (Lamiaceae)

officinalis	CAgr CArn CHal CPrp CTri EDAr
	EFer ELau GPoy IHMH MBar
	MBow MBri MHer NArg NPri
	SECG SIde SPlb SWal WBea WBrk
	WHHs WPer WSSM WWpP WWye
	XPep
- 'All Gold'	CArn CBre CHal CPrp CSev ECha
	EDAr EHoe ELan ELau GBar MBri
	NBid NSti NVic WMoo WSSM
	WWye
§ - 'Aurea' (v)	More than 30 suppliers
* - 'Compacta'	GPoy MHer
- 'Quedlinburger	CArn
Niederliegende'	
N - 'Variegata' misapplied	see *M. officinalis* 'Aurea'

Melittis (Lamiaceae)

melissophyllum	CBrm CFir CPlt EBee EMan EPAt
	LPio MHar MTis NSti SCro SIgm
	SIng SRms SSpi SSvw WAbb WCAu
	WWye
- subsp. *albida*	CPom EBee SSpi
- pink	EMon SOkh
- 'Royal Velvet	CPen MBri
Distinction'PBR	

Melliodendron (Styracaceae)

xylocarpum	IArd

Menispermum (Menispermaceae)

canadense	CTri GPoy MSal SHBN
davuricum	MSal

Menstruocalamus (Poaceae)

sichuanensis	CFil WPGP

Mentha ✿ (Lamiaceae)

angustifolia Corb.	see *Mentha* x *villosa*
angustifolia Host	see *M. arvensis*
angustifolia ambig.	EOHP SIde
aquatica	More than 30 suppliers
§ - var. *crispa*	IHMH SIde
- krause minze	see *M. aquatica* var. *crispa*
- 'Mandeliensis'	EOHP IHMH
§ *arvensis*	CArn ELau EOHP GIBF IHMH
	MHer MSal NSco SIde WHer WJek
- 'Banana'	EOHP MHer
- var. *piperascens*	EOHP MSal SAga SIde
§ - - 'Sayakaze'	CArn ELau

asiatica	ELau MHer SIde WHer
Bowles' mint	see *M.* x *villosa* var. *alopecuroides*
	Bowles' mint
* *brevifolia*	EOHP IHMH SIde WHer
§ *cervina*	CBen CDWL CWat EMFW EOHP
	IHMH LPBA MHer MSta NArg SIde
	SLon SWat WBar WJek WMoo
* - *alba*	CDWL EOHP IHMH LPBA MHer
	SLon WMAq WMoo WWpP
citrata	see *M.* x *piperita* f. *citrata*
'Clarissa's Millennium'	EOHP SIde
cordifolia	see *M.* x *villosa*
corsica	see *M. requienii*
crispa L. (1753)	see *M. spicata* var. *crispa*
crispa L. (1763)	see *M. aquatica* var. *crispa*
crispa x *piperita*	EDAr GBar
'Dionysus'	EOHP IHMH SIde
x *dumetorum*	IHMH
'Eau de Cologne'	see *M.* x *piperita* f. *citrata*
eucalyptus mint	ELau EOHP GBar MHer WBea
	WHHs WRha
gattefossei	CArn ELau
x *gentilis*	see *M.* x *gracilis*
§ x *gracilis*	CArn CHby ELau EOHP GBar
	GWCH IHMH MBow NPri SIde
	WBea WJek WWye
- 'Aurea'	see *M.* x *gracilis* 'Variegata'
§ - 'Variegata' (v)	CAgr CBrm CHrt CPrp CSev ECha
	EHoe ELau EMar GGar GPoy ILis
	MBar MHer MRav NArg NBlu
	NGHP NPri NVic SPlb SWal WFar
	WHHs WHer WPer WSel
haplocalyx	CArn ELau EOHP MSal SIde
* 'Hillary's Sweet Lemon'	ELau EOHP MHer SIde
'Julia's Sweet Citrus'	EOHP MHer SIde
* *lacerata*	IHMH SIde
lavender mint	CBod CPrp ELau EMan ESis GBar
	GPoy MHer MRav NGHP NTHB
	WBea WBry WJek WRha
§ *longifolia*	CAgr CPrp ECoo ELau EMar GBar
	MBow MRav NSti SIde SPlb WEas
	WHer WJek WPer WSel WWye
- Buddleia Mint Group	CArn EBee ELau EMan ESis GAbr
	GGar GKir IHMH MHer MRav
	NGHP SIde WBea WBry WHHs
	WRha WSel
- subsp. *capensis*	GGar
- subsp. *schimperi*	WJek
- silver	CArn ELau ESis GWCH MHer NBlu
	WBea
* - 'Variegata' (v)	CBod CPrp ELau NSti WJek
Nile Valley mint	CArn CBod CPrp ELau EOHP
	SHDw SIde WCHb
x *piperita*	CArn CHby COkL CSev ECha EDAr
	EHoe ELau GBar GGar GPoy ILis
	MBow MBri MHer NArg NBlu
	NFor NGHP NPri NVic SPlb SWal
	WBea WHHs WHbs WPer WWye
- 'After Eight'	IHMH
* - alba	CArn GBar MHer WHHs
- 'Black Mitcham'	CArn EOHP GBar
- black peppermint	CAgr CHby ESis GWCH IHMH
	NGHP NHol NTHB WHHs WSSM
§ - f. *citrata*	CArn CHby CPrp ECha EDAr ELau
	ESis GAbr GBar GGar GKir GPoy
	MBar MBow MBri MHer MRav
	NBir NBlu NGHP SHDw SIde SPlb
	STre WBea WHHs WPer WSel
	WWye
* - - 'Basil'	CBod CHrt CPrp ELau EOHP GBar
	IHMH LLWP MHer MRav NBlu
	NGHP NTHB SHDw SIde WBea
	WBry WHHs WJek WRha
- - 'Bergamot'	EOHP IHMH

- - 'Chocolate'	CAgr CArn CBod CPrp ELau EMan EOHP ESis GBar GGar GKir IHMH ILis MHer NArg NGHP NPri SHDw SIde WBea WBry WHHs WJek WMoo WPer
- - 'Grapefruit'	EOHP GBar ILis LFol NGHP NTHB WJek
- - 'Lemon'	CPrp ELau EMan EOHP GAbr GBar IHMH MBow MBri MHer NGHP SHDw SIde WBea WCHb WHHs WJek WPer WRha WSel
- - 'Lime'	CHrt COkL CPrp EMan EOHP GBar ILis MHer NGHP SHDw SIde SPlb WBea WCHb WHHs WJek WSSM
- - orange	EOHP GBar MHer
- - 'Swiss Ricola'	EOHP MHer SIde
* - 'Extra Strong'	IHMH
- 'Logee's' (v)	EBee EMan EOHP EWes GBar MHer NGHP NHol NPri NTHB SIde WBea WBry WCHb WCot WHHs WHer WJek WRha
§ - 'Multimentha'	EOHP
- f. *officinalis*	ELau IHMH SIde
- var. *ouweneellii*	IHMH SIde
Belgian mint	
- 'Reine Rouge'	EOHP IHMH SIde
- 'Reverchonii'	IHMH SIde
I - Swiss mint	CArn CPrp NGHP WHHs
pulegium	CArn CHby CPrp CRWN CSev CTri EDAr ELau GBar GPoy IHMH MHer NArg NGHP NLRH NVic SECG SIde SPlb SRms WCHb WHHs WHbs WHer WJek WPer WWpP WWye
- 'Upright'	CArn CBod CPrp EOHP GBar GPoy MHer NTHB SHDw SIde WBry WCHb WHHs WJek WPer WSel
§ *requienii*	More than 30 suppliers
rotundifolia misapplied	see *M. suaveolens*
rotundifolia (L.) Hudson	see *M.* x *villosa*
rubra var. *raripila*	see *M.* x *smithiana*
'Sayakarze'	see *M. arvensis* var. *piperascens* 'Sayakaze'
§ x *smithiana*	CAgr CArn CPrp ELau EOHP GAbr GBar GPoy IHMH ILis MHer NBir NBlu NGHP NPri WBea WBry WHer WPer WRha WWye
- 'Capel Ulo' (v)	ELau WHer
§ *spicata*	More than 30 suppliers
- Algerian fruity	EOHP IHMH
* - 'Brundall'	ELau EOHP ILis
- 'Canaries'	EOHP IHMH
* - var. *crispa*	CArn CPrp ECha EDAr ELau EOHP GAbr GBar GGar IHMH LHop MHer NArg NGHP NHol NPri SIde SPlb WCHb WCot WPer WRha WSel WWye
- - large-leaved	IHMH
- - 'Moroccan'	More than 30 suppliers
- 'Persian'	IHMH
- 'Guernsey'	EOHP SHDw
- 'Mexican' **new**	CArn
- 'Newbourne'	ELau ESis
- 'Rhodos'	IHMH
- 'Russian'	NHol NTHB WHHs
- 'Small Dole' (v)	SHDw
- 'Spanish Furry'	EOHP MHer
- 'Spanish Pointed'	ELau EOHP
- 'Tashkent'	CArn CHby ELau EOHP GWCH MHer SHDw SIde WBea WBry WCHb WHHs WJek WWpP

- subsp. *tomentosa*	IHMH
* - 'Variegata' (v)	SHDw WHer
- 'Verte Blanche'	IHMH
§ *suaveolens*	CAgr CArn CHby ELau GBar GPoy GWCH IHMH ILis MBow MBri MHer NGHP NLRH NPri SIde SPlb SWal WBea WBrk WHHs WLHH WPer WSSM
* - 'Grapefruit'	CPrp ESis IHMH NPri WHHs
- 'Jokka'	EBee
* - 'Mobillei'	EOHP WJek
* - 'Pineapple'	COkL ESis NArg NLRH WHHs
- subsp. *timija*	ELau WJek
§ - 'Variegata' (v)	More than 30 suppliers
I 'Sweet Pear'	EOHP
sylvestris L.	see *M. longifolia*
Thüringer minze	see *M.* x *piperita* 'Multimentha'
§ x *villosa*	CArn EOHP IHMH SIde
§ - var. *alopecuroides*	CAgr CBre CHrt CPrp ELau EMan GBar GGar GPoy IHMH ILis MHer NGHP NSti SIde STre SWat WHHs WHer WJek WWye
Bowles' mint	
viridis	see *M. spicata*

Menyanthes (*Menyanthaceae*)

trifoliata	CBen CRow CWat ECoo EHon ELau EMFW EPAt GBar GPoy LNCo LPBA MCCP MSta NPer NVic SLon WBVN WFar WMAq WPnP WShi WWpP WWye

Menziesia (*Ericaceae*)

alba	see *Daboecia cantabrica* f. *alba*
ciliicalyx	SSpi
- dwarf	SReu SSta
- 'Glendoick Glaucous' **new**	GGGa
- *lasiophylla*	see *M. ciliicalyx* var. *purpurea*
- var. *multiflora*	CPLG GGGa MDun
- var. *purpurea*	CPLG GGGa
ferruginea	SReu SSta
'Spring Morning'	WAbe

Mercurialis (*Euphorbiaceae*)

perennis	GPoy MGol NSco WHer WShi
- 'Cae Rhos Lligwy'	WHer

Merendera (*Colchicaceae*)

§ *montana*	ERos WIvy WOBN
pyrenaica	see *M. montana*
sobolifera	EHyt EPot WFar

Merremia (*Convolvulaceae*)

pinnata	MSal
§ *tuberosa*	MGol SOWG

Mertensia (*Boraginaceae*)

ciliata	CMdw CPom EBre GKir LRHS MBri MNrw NChi SWat
echioides	EBee
franciscana	EBee GCal
lanceolata var. *nivalis*	EBee
maritima	EWll GPoy MSal NGby WWin
- subsp. *asiatica*	see *M. simplicissima*
primuloides	GEdr
pterocarpa	see *M. sibirica*
pulmonarioides	see *M. virginica*
§ *sibirica*	CLAP CSpe EBee ETow GKir LPhx NChi NDlv NLAp NLar NPri SMrm SPlb WBVN WPnP WWin
§ *simplicissima*	CBot CFir CMea EBre ECho EHyt EMan GEil GKev GKir ITim LPhx MBro MNrw NBir NWCA SBla SCro SPlb WCom WFar WHoo

virginica ♀H4   CBot CBro CFwr CLAP EBre ELan
EPfP EPot EWTr GBBs GFlt GGar
GKir LAma NBPC NLar SMac
SMrm SRms WCru WFar WPnP
viridis   LPhx

Meryta (*Araliaceae*)
sinclairii   CHEx CTrC WMul

Mesembryanthemum (*Aizoaceae*)
'Basutoland'   see *Delosperma nubigenum*
brownii   see *Lampranthus brownii*

Mespilus (*Rosaceae*)
germanica (F)   CBcs CDul CLnd CTri ECrN ELan
EWTr GTSp IDee LPan MWat NFor
SDnm SHBN WDin WFar WMou
WOrn
- 'Bredase Reus' (F)   SKee
- 'Dutch' (F)   SDea SFam SKee
- 'Large Russian' (F)   ERea ESim GTwe
- 'Macrocarpa'   SKee
- 'Monstrous' (F)   SDea
- 'Nottingham' (F)   CAgr CCVT CEnd CTho CWib
EBee ECrN EMui ENot EPfP ERea
GKir GTwe LBuc LPan LRHS MAsh
MBlu MGos MLan NBee SCoo
SDea SFam SKee SPer WMou WSpi
- 'Royal' (F)   CAgr SKee
- 'Westerveld' (F)   SKee

Metapanax see *Pseudopanax*

Metaplexis (*Asclepiadaceae*)
japonica B&SWJ 8459   WCru
new

Metasequoia (*Cupressaceae*)
glyptostroboides ♀H4   More than 30 suppliers
- 'Gold Rush'   CDoC CEnd CMCN CTho CTri
CWSG EBre EPfP GKir LCon LLin
LRHS MAsh MBlu MBri MGos NLar
NPal SCoo SKee SLim SPer SWvt
WEve
- 'Green Mantle'   EHul
- 'Sheridan Spire'   CEnd CTho WPGP
- 'Spring Cream'   EBre SLim
- 'White Spot' (v)   EBre LLin SLim SPoG

Metrosideros (*Myrtaceae*)
carminea   CHEx CTrC
- 'Carousel' (v)   ERea
- 'Ferris Wheel'   ERea
excelsa   CHEx CTrC CTrG EBak ECou SHFr
- 'Aureus'   ECou
- 'Fire Mountain'   CTrC
- 'Parnell'   CBcs CTrC
- 'Scarlet Pimpernel'   ERea SOWG
- 'Spring Fire'   CBcs
- 'Upper Hut' (v)   CTrC
- 'Vibrance'   CTrC
'Goldfinger' (v)   ERea
gold-flowered **new**   MCCP
kermadecensis   CTrC ECou
- 'Radiant' (v) **new**   CPLG
- 'Variegatus' (v)   CBcs CDoC CTrC ECou ERea
lucida   see *M. umbellata*
'Mistral'   ECou
'Moon Maiden'   SOWG
'Pink Lady'   CTrC
red-flowered **new**   MCCP
robusta   CTrC
rugosus **new**   CTrC
'Thomasii'   EShb ESlt LRHS SOWG

tomentosa   see *M. excelsa*
§ *umbellata*   CAbb CHEx CPne CTrC ECou
GGar IDee
villosa   SOWG
- 'Tahiti'   CBcs IDee

Meum (*Apiaceae*)
athamanticum   CRez CSev EBee EBre EFou EGle
EHrv EMan GBri GCal GPoy LRHS
MAvo MRav MSal MTho NBid
NCGa NSti SBla SIgm WFar WHil
WPer WPrP WTin

Michauxia (*Campanulaceae*)
campanuloides   WSan
tchihatchewii   CSpe

Michelia (*Magnoliaceae*)
cavalierieri **new**   CFil WPGP
chapensis   WPGP
- HWJ 621   WCru
compressa   EPfP
doltsopa   CBcs CFil CHEx EMil GQui SSpi
- 'Silver Cloud'   CBcs SSpi
figo   CFil EPfP ERea GQui SSpi WPGP
- var. *crassipes*   WPGP
foveolata **new**   CFil WPGP
lacei HWJ 533 **new**   WCru
macclurei **new**   CFil
martinii   SSpi
maudiae   CFil ISea SSpi WPGP
sinensis   see *M. wilsonii*
§ *wilsonii*   CFil SSpi
yunnanensis   CFil SSpi

Microbiota (*Cupressaceae*)
decussata ♀H4   CBcs CDoC CKen CMac CSBt EBre
EHul EOrn EPla GKir LBee LCon
LLin LRHS MBar MBri MGos MWat
NHol SLim WFar
- 'Gold Spot' **new**   NLar
- 'Jakobsen'   CKen
- 'Trompenburg'   CKen

Microcachrys (*Podocarpaceae*)
tetragona   CDoC ECho ECou EHul EOrn
IMGH LCon LLin MBri SCoo SIng

Microcoelum see *Lytocaryum*

Microglossa (*Asteraceae*)
albescens   see *Aster albescens*

Microlaena see *Ehrharta*

Microlepia (*Dennstaedtiaceae*)
speluncae   MBri

Micromeria (*Lamiaceae*)
corsica   see *Acinos corsicus*
croatica   CPBP EHyt ETow SScr
dalmatica   XPep
fruticosa **new**   XPep
graeca **new**   XPep
rupestris   see *M. thymifolia*
§ *thymifolia*   EMan GPoy NMen
SPlb

Microseris (*Asteraceae*)
ringens hort.   see *Leontodon*
rigens

Microsorum (*Polypodiaceae*)
diversifolium   see *Phymatosorus diversifolius*

Microstrobos (Podocarpaceae)
fitzgeraldii CKen
niphophilus ECou WGor

Microtropis (Celastraceae)
petelotii HWJ 719 **new** WCru

Mikania (Asteraceae)
§ *dentata* MBri
ternata see *M. dentata*

Milium (Poaceae)
effusum COld
- 'Aureum' ♀H4 More than 30 suppliers
- var. *esthonicum* EBee EPPr NHol WWpP
- 'Yaffle' (v) CBgR CFir CFwr EBee EBlw ECha
EFou EGle EMan EPPr GCal MAnH
MCCP SSvw SUsu WCot WLeb
WWeb

Milligania (Asteliaceae)
densiflora IBlr

Mimosa (Mimosaceae)
pudica LRHS MLan SMur

Mimulus (Scrophulariaceae)
'A.T. Johnson' NVic
'Andean Nymph' see *M. naiandinus*
§ *aurantiacus* ♀H2-3 CElw CFee CHal CPle CSpe EBak
ECtt EOrc EPot ERea LHop MOak
NBir NPer SAga SDnm SDry SGar
SHFr SMrm SPlb SUsu SWal WAbe
WCom WEas
§ - var. *puniceus* CHal CSpe CTri EBee EDif EMan
LHop MHar MOak SAga SDry
SMrm SUsu WCom
- 'Pure Gold' EDif
- 'Tangerine' EDif
'Aztec Trumpet' EDAr
× *bartonianus* see *M.* × *harrisonii*
'Bees' Scarlet' WShp
bifidus EBee MHar
- subsp. *fasciculatus* EBee
- 'Tapestry' CSpe
§ - 'Verity Buff' CSpe EDif LIck MOak WEas
- Verity hybrids ERea
§ - 'Verity Purple' CSpe EDif LIck SAga SOWG
- 'Wine' see *M. bifidus* 'Verity Purple'
× *burnetii* EMan LPBA SRms
cardinalis ♀H3 CDWL EBee EChP EHon ELan
IHMH LPBA MFir MNrw MTho
SHFr SPer WBor WCom WCot WFar
WHal WMoo WPer WWin WWpP
- NNS 95-344 EMan
- 'Dark Throat' SGar
cupreus 'Minor' ECho
- 'Whitecroft Scarlet' ♀H4 ECtt EDAr ELan EPfP LPBA LRHS
MDKP MHer SRms WPer WWin
WWpP
DK hybrid MDKP
'Eleanor' SAga SMrm SPet SUsu
flemingii **new** CSpe
glutinosus see *M. aurantiacus*
- *atrosanguineus* see *M. aurantiacus* var. *puniceus*
- *luteus* see *M. aurantiacus*
§ *guttatus* CBen CRow EMFW GPoy MGas
NPer NSco SRms WMAq WMoo
WPer WWpP
§ - 'Richard Bish' (v) CWat EBee EMFW EMan LHop
MCCP
× *harrisonii* CDes EBee EMan EPfP EWes GMac
WDyG

'Highland Orange' EBre EDAr EMlt EPfP GGar GKir
IHMH MHer NBlu NHol NJOw
SPlb WGor WMoo WPer
'Highland Pink' EDAr EMan EPfP GGar GKir NBlu
NHol NJOw SIng SPlb WCom
WGor WPer
I 'Highland Pink Rose' SWal
'Highland Red' ♀H4 EBre ECtt EDAr EMar EMlt EPfP
GGar GKev GKir IHMH LPBA
NArg NBlu NHol NJOw NPri SIng
SPlb SRms WCom WHen WPer
WWin
'Highland Yellow' ECtt EDAr EMlt GGar GKir LPBA
MHer NBlu SIng SPlb WHen WPer
hose-in-hose (d) CDWL EBee EMFW NPer
'Inca Sunset' EDAr EWes
langsdorffii see *M. guttatus*
lewisii ♀H3 CHll CTCP EBee EMan GGar GTou
MBrN MTho SLon SPer SRms WPer
WRha
- JCA 1.624.009 CDes
- f. *albus* SGar
longiflorus 'Santa Barbara' LIck
'Lothian Fire' WMAq WWpP
luteus CBen CRow CWat EHon ENot
EPfP GAbr IHMH LNCo LPBA
MHer MSta NPer NSco SHFr SWal
WBrk WFar WMAq WShp WWpP
- 'Gaby' (v) **new** MTho
- 'Variegatus' ambig. (v) CRow NGdn NPer
- 'Variegatus' misapplied see *M. guttatus* 'Richard Bish' (v)
* 'Major Bees' EPfP
'Malibu Ivory' MDKP
'Malibu Pink' MDKP
'Malibu Red' MDKP
minimus EMlt
moschatus CRow SIng
naiandinus ♀H3 CM&M CPBP EBee GKir LRHS
SPlb SRms WFar
- C&W 5257 EBre SRot SWat WRos
'Old Rose' EBee
'Orange Glow' EPfP IHMH WHal WShp
orange hose-in-hose (d) NBir
§ 'Orkney Gold' (d) EBee
'Orkney Lemon' **new** GCal
'Popacatapetl' CHal CHll CSpe EBee EDif EMan
LHop LIck MHar MOak MSte SAga
SChu SMrm SOWG SUsu
primuloides NMen NWCA SIng SPlb
'Puck' EBre GKir GMac LRHS
'Purple Mazz' SAga
'Quetzalcoatl' LIck MOak SAga SMrm
Red Emperor see *M.* 'Roter Kaiser'
ringens CBen CRow CWat EBee EHon
EMFW EPfP GBri LNCo LPBA MSta
NBir NPer SPer SPlb SRms WFar
WHil WMAq WMoo WPer WWpP
§ 'Roter Kaiser' LPVe WBar
'Royal Velvet' SAga
'Tawny' CSpe SAga
'Threave Variegated' (v) EBee EMan GBuc GCal MBri
MDKP MRav NBir WCom WFar
tilingii CHal ECho GTou
'Trish' CSpe
'Western Hills' MLLN
'Wine Red' see *M. bifidus* 'Verity
Purple'
'Wisley Red' ECot ELan SRms
yellow hose-in-hose (d) see *M.* 'Orkney Gold'

Mina see *Ipomoea*

mint, Bowles' see *Mentha* × *villosa* var.
alopecuroides

mint, curly see *Mentha spicata* var. *crispa*

mint, eau-de-Cologne see *Mentha* x *piperita* f. *citrata*

mint, ginger see *Mentha* x *gracilis*

mint, horse or long-leaved see *Mentha longifolia*

mint, pennyroyal see *Mentha pulegium*

mint, peppermint see *Mentha* x *piperita*

mint, round-leaved see *Mentha suaveolens*

mint, spearmint see *Mentha spicata*

Minuartia (*Caryophyllaceae*)

caucasica	see *M. circassica*
§ *circassica*	CLyd ETow NWCA WPer
juniperina	ESis
– *laricifolia*	CLyd LRHS
parnassica	see *M. stellata*
§ *stellata*	EPot ETow NDlv NJOw NMen SIng
– NS 758	NWCA
§ *verna*	NMen
– subsp. *caespitosa*	see *Sagina subulata* var. *glabrata*
'Aurea'	'Aurea'

Mirabilis (*Nyctaginaceae*)

jalapa	CArn CBrm CHrt ELan EUJe LAma LRHS MBri MGol MSal SEND SHFr SRms SYvo
multiflora	MGol

Miscanthus ✿ (*Poaceae*)

B&SWJ 6482 from Thailand **new**	WCru
CC 3619	CPLG
flavidus B&SWJ 3697	WCru
floridulus misapplied	see *M.* x *giganteus*
floridulus ambig.	MAvo MBrN MSPs NOak WPrP
–HWJ 522	WCru
x *giganteus*	CFir CHEx CKno CSev EBee EFou EHoe EPPr EWsh GCal LBBr LRHS MCCP MMoz MWgw NBea NPSI NVic SDix SEND SMad SPlb WCot WFar
nepalensis	CAbb CBrm CKno CPLG ECre EHoe EWes LEdu MAnH MAvo SMrm WCot
oligostachyus	CBig GCal NGdn
§ – 'Afrika'	CFwr LPhx
I – 'Nanus Variegatus' (v)	CBrm CKno CRow EBee EHoe EMan EMon EWes MMoz WCot WPGP
– 'Purpurascens'	see *M.* 'Purpurascens'
§ 'Purpurascens'	CBrm CFwr CKno EBee EBlw EBre ECGN ECha EHoe EHrv EHul EMan EPPr EPla EUJe EWsh GSki LAst LRHS MAvo MBrN MMoz MWgw NGdn SMad SPer SSte WBro WCot WTin
sacchariflorus	More than 30 suppliers
'Silver Spider' **new**	EBre
sinensis	CAgr CBig CHEx CHrt EBee EPfP GBin GKir MFan MMoz NOak WDin WMoo WRos XPep
– B&SWJ 6749	WCru
– 'Adagio'	CAbb CFwr CKno EBee EGle EMan EPPr LEdu LPhx SMHy WCot

– 'Afrika'	see *M. oligostachyus* 'Afrika'
– 'Arabesque'	CFwr EBee EBre EFou EGle EPPr IPot LPan MMoz
– 'Augustfeder'	CFwr EBee EGle LRHS
– 'Autumn Light'	CFwr EPPr IPot
– 'Blütenwunder'	CKno
– 'China'	CBig CBrm CDes CFir CFwr CHar CKno CWCL EBee ECGN EFou EHoe EMan EPGN EPPr EPla EWes EWsh GBin IPot LEdu LRHS NHol NOrc SAga SChu SMad SWat WPGP
– var. *condensatus*	EPPr
– – 'Cabaret' (v)	CKno CWCL EBee EFou EHoe EMan EPPr EUJe IPot LAst NCot NGdn SRos SSte WCot WHal
– – 'Central Park'	see *M. sinensis* var. *condensatus* 'Cosmo Revert'
– – 'Cosmo Revert'	CBig CKno CPen EBee EMil MMoz
– – 'Cosmopolitan' (v) ♀H4	More than 30 suppliers
– – 'Emerald Giant'	see *M. sinensis* var. *condensatus* 'Cosmo Revert'
– 'Dixieland' (v)	CBig EFou EGle EHoe EPPr IPot LEdu MMoz SMHy WHil
– dwarf form	SMad
– 'Ferner Osten'	More than 30 suppliers
– 'Feuergold' **new**	MSte
– 'Flamingo' ♀H4	More than 30 suppliers
– 'Flammenmeer' **new**	EBee
– 'Gearmella'	CBig CFwr EBee EBre EGle EPPr EWsh GKir LEdu LRHS
– 'Gewitterwolke' ♀H4	CFwr LPhx SMHy
– 'Ghana'	CFwr EBee LHop LPhx SMHy
– 'Giraffe'	CDes CFwr EBee EFou GKir LPhx WPGP
– 'Goldfeder' (v)	CFwr EBee EHoe EPla WBcn
– 'Goliath'	CBig CFwr CKno EBee EHoe EPPr IPot
– 'Gracillimus'	More than 30 suppliers
– 'Graziella'	More than 30 suppliers
– 'Grosse Fontäne' ♀H4	CBrm EBee EBre EFou EGle EHoe EPGN EPPr EPla EWsh GKir LEdu LRHS NHol SMHy WAul WMoo
– 'Haiku'	CFwr CKno LPhx
– 'Helga Reich'	CBig
– 'Hercules'	CBig EPPr MAvo MMoz
– 'Hermann Müssel'	CFwr EBee LPhx SMHy
– 'Hinjo' (v)	CDes CKno EBee WCot WPGP
– 'Juli'	IPot
– 'Kaskade' ♀H4	CBig CKno CWCL EBee EBre EGle EHoe EPGN EPPr EPla GKir LPhx LRHS MAvo MBri MMoz MSte NDov NOGN SMrm WBcn WFar WMoo
– 'Kleine Fontäne' ♀H4	More than 30 suppliers
– 'Kleine Silberspinne' ♀H4	More than 30 suppliers
– 'Krater'	CFwr EBee LEdu MBrN SWat
– 'Kupferberg' **new**	CFwr
§ – 'Little Kitten'	CDes CFwr CKno EBee EGle EPPr EPla EWsh LEdu MBar SMad WPGP
– 'Malepartus'	More than 30 suppliers
– 'Morning Light' (v) ♀H4	More than 30 suppliers
– new hybrids	CPen EChP EHul LRav
– 'Nippon'	CAbb CElw CKno CPrp EBee EGle EHoe EPPr EPla EPza LEdu LHop LRHS MAvo MCCP MCLN MMoz NDov NGdn NHol NOrc NPPs SChu SCro SDys SPer WCAu WPGP
– 'Nishidake'	CFwr EBee
– 'November Sunset'	EGle EPPr EWes IPot MMoz
– 'Poseidon'	EPPr SDys
– 'Positano'	CBig CKno EBee MMoz WPGP

- 'Professor Richard Hansen'	CFwr
- 'Pünktchen' (v)	CBrm CElw CFwr CKno CPen EBee EBre ECha EFou EGle EPPr EPla LEdu LPan LPhx SMHy SMad SMrm
- var. **purpurascens** misapplied	see *M.* 'Purpurascens'
- 'Rigoletto' (v)	EPPr
- 'Roland'	CBig CFwr CKno EBee GBin LBBr LPhx SAga
- 'Roterpfeil'	EBee LPhx
- 'Rotfuchs'	CFwr EBee GKir LPhx MGos SAga WFar
- 'Rotsilber'	More than 30 suppliers
- 'Samurai'	EBee EFou
- 'Sarabande'	CBig CBrm CFwr CKno EBee EBre ECGN EFou EGle EHoe EHul EPPr EWsh GKir IPot LPan LRHS SMHy WFar
- 'Septemberrot' ♀H4	CFwr
§ - 'Silberfeder' ♀H4	More than 30 suppliers
- 'Silberpfeil' (v)	MSte
- 'Silberspinne' AGM	CBig CMdw EBee EBre EFou EGle EPla GKir LEdu LPhx LRHS MCCP NGdn SAga SMHy SPlb WAul WDin
- 'Silberturm'	CFwr EBee LBBr
- Silver Feather	see *M. sinensis* 'Silberfeder'
- 'Sioux'	CBig CFwr EBee EBre EGle EHoe EPPr EPla EPza EWsh GKir LRHS MMoz SDnm SLon WBcn WTin
- 'Sirene'	CBig CFwr EBee EBre ECGP EGle EHoe EMan EPGN EPPr EPla GKir LPan LRHS MBNS MBlu NHol WCAu WFar WPrP
- 'Slavopour'	EPla
- 'Spätgrün'	EPla
- 'Strictus' (v) ♀H4	More than 30 suppliers
- 'Tiger Cub' (v)	CBig CWCL
- 'Undine' ♀H4	CFwr CKno CMea ECha EFou EGle EHoe EHrv ELan EPGN EPPr EPla EPza EWsh LEdu LPhx LRHS MCLN MMoz NDov NHol SChu SDix SHFr SPla WCAu
- 'Variegatus' (v) ♀H4	More than 30 suppliers
- 'Vorläufer'	CBrm CFwr CKno EBre EFou EHoe EPPr EPla EWsh GKir LPhx
- 'Wetterfahne'	CFwr EGle
§ - 'Yaku-jima'	EBee ECha EGle XPep
- 'Yakushima Dwarf'	More than 30 suppliers
- 'Zebrinus' (v) ♀H4	More than 30 suppliers
- 'Zwergelefant'	CBig CFwr EBee EBre MMoz SMHy
tinctorius 'Nanus Variegatus' misapplied	see *M. oligostachyus* 'Nanus Variegatus'
transmorrisonensis	CBig CBod CFwr CHid CHrt CKno EHoe EMan EPPr EWsh GBin LEdu LRav MAnH MMoz NHol NOak SMad SWal WHil WSSM
yakushimensis	see *M. sinensis* 'Yaku-jima', *M. sinensis* 'Little Kitten'

Mitchella (Rubiaceae)

repens	GBBs WCru
undulata B&SWJ 4402	WCru

Mitella (Saxifragaceae)

breweri	CHal CNic CSam EBee GBin GGar MAvo MRav MSte NHol NSti SHFr SHel SMac SRms SSpi WBea WEas WFar WMoo WPnP WTin WWye
caulescens	EBee ECha MRav NBro NHol WMoo WPnP
diphylla	EBee
formosana B&SWJ 125	EBee WCru

japonica B&SWJ 4971	WCru
kiusiana	CLAP
- B&SWJ 5888	GEdr WCru
makinoi	CLAP
- B&SWJ 4992	WCru
ovalis	EBee
pauciflora B&SWJ 6361	WCru
stauropetala	EBee NWoo
stylosa B&SWJ 5669	WCru
yoshinagae	EBee WMoo
- B&SWJ 4893	WCru WPnP

Mitraria (Gesneriaceae)

coccinea	CAbb CBcs CMac CNic CPLG CPle CTrG CTrw CWib ELan ERea EShb GEil GGGa IDee MBlu MDun SArc SLon SPer SSpi WBod WBor WCot WGwG WPat
- Clark's form	CSam CTrC GGar LAst MDun
- from Lake Puyehue	CDoC CFee CFwr ERea GQui LRHS MAsh MGos SBra SSta WCru WCwm WFar WPGP WSHC
- 'Lake Caburga'	GCal GGar IArd NSti WCot

Molinia (Poaceae)

altissima	see *M. caerulea* subsp. *arundinacea*
caerulea	CBig CFwr COtt CRWN EBee EHul EPPr LAst LPhx MBlu MWod WWpP
§ - subsp. **arundinacea**	CBig CBrm CWCL EBre ECGN ECha EFou EPPr GBin GKir MBNS NChi SLPl WPer
- - 'Bergfreund'	CSam EBee ECGN EHoe EMon EPPr EWsh GCal LPhx MAnH MAvo SCou SDys SHel SMHy SUsu WDyG WMoo WPrP WTin WWye
- - 'Cordoba'	EBee LPhx
- - 'Fontäne'	CBig CPen CSam EBee EFou EHoe EPPr LPan LPhx MSte SMHy
- - 'Karl Foerster'	More than 30 suppliers
- - 'Skyracer'	CBig CFwr COlW CPrp EBee EBre EFou EGle EHoe EPPr GBri LBBr LIck LPan LPhx MAnH MAvo MMoz SMHy SMad SWal WCot WFar WMoo WWpP
- - 'Staefa'	EHoe
- - 'Transparent'	CFwr CHad CKno CMea CWCL EBre ECha EFou EGle EHoe EPGN EPPr GBri GCal IGor LPan LPhx MAnH MBri MMoz MSte SMHy SMrm WHal WHoo WPrP
- - 'Windsaule'	EBee EPPr LPhx
- - 'Windspiel'	CKno CRow CSam CWCL EBee EBre ECGN ECha EFou EGle EHoe EMan EMil EMon EPGN EPPr EWsh GCal LEdu LPan LPhx MAnH MWgw NSti SMrm SWal WBro WCot WMoo WPGP
- - 'Zuneigung'	CBig CKno CSam EBee EHoe EPPr LPhx
- subsp. **caerulea**	CMdw
- - 'Carmarthen' (v)	CElw CNat EBee EPPr IPot MAvo SUsu WPrP
- - 'Claerwen' (v)	ECha EMan EPPr GBuc GCal SMHy
- - 'Dauerstrahl'	EPPr GBin MAvo NHol
- - 'Edith Dudszus'	CBod CEnd CFwr CHar CKno CM&M CWCL EBlw ECGN ECha EGle EHoe EPPr LPhx LRHS MAnH MBrN MMoz NGdn NHol NOGN SMHy SPer SVil WMoo WPGP WWeb
- - 'Heidebraut'	CBig CElw CFwr EBee ECGN ECGP ECha EGle EHoe EHul EMon

	EPPr GBin LPhx LRHS MBri MWgw NBro NCGa NDov SVil WFar WPnP
- - 'Moorflamme'	CBig CKno EPPr LPan LPhx
- - 'Moorhexe'	More than 30 suppliers
- - 'Strahlenquelle'	CElw CKno CSam EBee EGle ELan EMan EMon EPGN EPPr EPla GBin GCal LRHS MAvo MMoz NBro NCGa NOGN WPGP
- - 'Variegata' (v) ♀H4	More than 30 suppliers
- 'Winterfreude' **new**	GBin
litoralis	see *M. caerulea* subsp. *arundinacea*

Molopospermum (Apiaceae)

| *peloponnesiacum* | CFwr EBee EMan GCal ITer LEdu LPhx MLLN NChi NLar SIgm SMrm WCot WCru |

Moltkia (Boraginaceae)

aurea **new**	WLin
coerulea **new**	WLin
§ *doerfleri*	CPle NChi
graminifolia	see *M. suffruticosa*
§ x *intermedia* ♀H4	CMea CNic SLon SOkd SPet WAbe WCom WWin
petraea	SIgm WLin WPat
§ *suffruticosa*	NBir

Momordica (Cucurbitaceae)

| *balsamina* | MSal |
| *charantia* | MSal |

Monadenium (Euphorbiaceae)

| *lugardae* | MBri |
| 'Variegatum' (v) | MBri |

Monarda ❀ (Lamiaceae)

'Adam'	EBee GAbr GCal LRHS MLLN MSte WCAu WSHC
'Amethyst'	EBee EWes SIde SOkh
'Aquarius'	CBri CElw EChP EFou EPfP EPza ERou GKir LAst LRHS MBri MCLN MSte MWgw NPro NSti SChu SCro SPla WAul WCAu WCHb WFar WShp WWeb
austromontana	see *M. citriodora* subsp. *austromontana*
'Baby Spice'	EBee EBre ENot LRHS
§ 'Balance'	CSam EBee EChP ECtt EFou EMan EPPr LRHS NBro NDov NHol NPPs NSti SOkh SPla WCHb WFar WPGP WSHC
'Beauty of Cobham' ♀H4	CPrp EBre ECha ELan EOrc EPfP ERou GAbr GKir LHop LPhx LRHS MAnH MBow MBri MHer MSte NDov NGHP NLar NSti SChu SMad SPer WCHb WHil WSan WShp
'Blaukranz'	SChu SMrm
§ 'Blaustrumpf'	CElw EBee ECtt EMan EWTr GBri MSte NLar NOrc SPer WLin
Blue Stocking	see *M.* 'Blaustrumpf'
Bowman	see *M.* 'Sagittarius'
bradburyana	EBee MWrn WCHb
'Cambridge Scarlet' ♀H4	More than 30 suppliers
'Capricorn'	CStr EFou EMan EMar ERou GBuc LRHS MSte SChu SOkh WCHb
'Cherokee'	GBar GBri MRav WCHb WFar
citriodora	CArn EBre ECtt GPoy LRHS MHer MSal NSti SIde SPlb SRms SWat WHHs WJek WLHH WPer WSel
§ - subsp. *austromontana*	CArn EBee ECoo EMan MDKP NBir NJOw SIde WCot WFar WPer

'Comanche'	CFwr CStr EBee EFou EHrv EPfP EWes NDov SAga WCHb WFar
'Croftway Pink' ♀H4	CBcs COlW CPrp CSBt CStr ECha ECtt EFou ELan ELau EPfP ERou EWTr GBar GKir LRHS MHer NGHP NOrc NPPs NSti SCro SIde SPer SRms SWvt WCAu WCHb WFar WSHC
didyma	CAgr CArn CHar EDAr EPfP GKir MFir MSal MWrn NArg NBlu NBro NGHP SECG SWat WBrE WBri WHbs WJek
- 'Alba'	MGol WBea
- 'Duddiscombe'	CSam
- 'Goldmelise'	NGHP WBea WMoo
'Donnerwolke'	SChu
'Elsie's Lavender'	CStr EBee EFou EGle GBri GBuc LPhx MAnH NBro NDov WAul WCHb
§ 'Feuerschopf'	WOut
'Fireball'	EBee ERou WHil
Firecrown	see *M.* 'Feuerschopf'
§ 'Fishes'	CSam EBee EChP ECtt EHrv ELan EMar EWes MCLN MRav MSte MWrn NDov NLar NPPs SAga SChu SPla WCAu WCHb WFar WMnd WSHC
fistulosa	CArn CHby EBee EWTr GPoy MBow MSal MWrn WHHs WHer WJek WLHH WMoo WPer
'Gardenview'	CMdw EWes GCal MAnH NBrk NSti SMrm WRHF
'Gardenview Scarlet'	EBee EBre ECtt EFou EOMN EOrc GBri GKir LPhx LRHS MBri MDKP NCGa NChi NGby WCHb WPer WSan
Gemini	see *M.* 'Twins'
'Hartswood Wine'	SMad
'Jacob Cline'	EFou
'Kardinal'	EBee
'Lambada'	LRHS
Libra	see *M.* 'Balance'
'Loddon Crown'	CBos CHar CHea EBee ECtt EMar LRHS MBri MDKP NChi NGHP SCro SIde WCHb WFar WRha WWeb WWpP
I 'Mahogany'	CElw CHar CStr ECGN EChP EGle EMar ENor ERou EWTr GBri GKir LRHS MBow MHer MRav NCGa NChi NDov NGHP NPPs NSti SMad SPer WCHb WSHC WSan
'Marshall's Delight'	CElw EBee EBre EChP GKir MCLN SMrm WCAu WGwG WHHs WHil
media	EBee
'Melissa'	EBee EFou EGle WOut WSan
menthifolia	CArn EWTr GCal LRHS MCCP SAga SMrm
'Mohawk'	EBee EChP ECtt EFou EHrv EMan EPPr ERou LRHS MAnH MWgw NDov WCAu WCHb
'Mrs Perry'	EWes MHer
'Ou Charm'	CElw CFwr CStr EBre EChP EPPr ERou EWes GBri LRHS MCLN MLLN MMil MWrn NCiC NDov NGHP NPPs SAga SMad STes WAul WCHb WCom WCot WFar WSan
'Panorama'	ECtt MSal SPlb WMoo WPer
'Panorama Red Shades' (Panorama Series)	CWib NGHP
'Pawnee'	SChu WCHb
'Petite Delight'	CRez EBee ECtt EMar LHop LRHS MBnl MSph MWgw NCot NGby NLar SOkh SPla WAul WCot WFar
'Petite Pink Supreme'	EBee MBnl MBri MTis WHil

'Pink Tourmaline' — EBee EChP ERou LPhx MCLN NDov NGby SMad SMrm WCAu WCHb WFar

Pisces — see *M.* 'Fishes'

'Poyntzfield Pink' — GPoy

Prairie Glow — see *M.* 'Prärieglut'

Prairie Night — see *M.* 'Prärienacht'

'Präriebrand' — MBri

§ 'Prärieglut' — MBri

§ 'Prärienacht' — More than 30 suppliers

punctata — CArn EBee ELan EMan GSki LRHS MLLN MMHG MSPs MSal MWrn NJOw SDnm SGar SLon SMrm SWat WBrk WCHb WJek WMoo

'Purple Ann' — CFwr NCGa NDov SAga SMrm

'Raspberry Wine' — GBri

'Ruby Glow' — CHad EBee ECGN EChP EHrv EMan LPhx LRHS MBri MCLN NCGa NChi NDov NPPs SChu SMad SOkh WCHb WFar

§ 'Sagittarius' — EBee EChP EGle EMan GKir LRHS MCLN MMil MWgw NGdn SChu SPla WCAu WCHb WWeb

'Sahin's Mildew-free' — WCHb

§ 'Schneewittchen' — More than 30 suppliers

§ 'Scorpion' — More than 30 suppliers

'Sioux' — EHrv EWes GBar GBuc GKir LRHS SMrm WCHb WFar WHil WRha

'Snow Maiden' — see *M.* 'Schneewittchen'

'Snow Queen' — CSam EBee ECtt EFou GKir LRHS NHol NPro SLon SPla WMnd

Snow White — see *M.* 'Schneewittchen'

'Squaw' — More than 30 suppliers

§ 'Twins' — CMil CPrp EBee EChP EFou EMar ERou EWTr GAbr LRHS MBri MLLN SWat SWvt WCAu WCHb WLin WSan WShp

'Velvet Queen' — SMrm

'Vintage Wine' — ECtt EFou EGle GBri SMrm WCHb WCot WFar WWye

'Violacea' — WCHb WWpP

'Violet Queen' — EBee EBre EChP EFou EMan EMar EPza EWes LRHS NHol NPro WCAu

Monardella (Lamiaceae)

macrantha — CPBP CStu SBla

nana subsp. *arida* — CPBP CStu

odoratissima — CArn ECoo EMan LRav SBla WJek

villosa subsp. *globosa* — WCot NNS 95-355

Monochoria (Pontederiaceae)

hastata — SLon

Monopsis (Campanulaceae)

lutea — see *Lobelia lutea*

Midnight = 'Yagemon'[PBR] — LAst

unidentata — EMan

Monstera (Araceae)

deliciosa (F) ♀[H1] — MBri SRms XBlo

- 'Variegata' (v) ♀[H1] — MBri SRms

Montbretia see *Crocosmia*

Montia (Portulacaceae)

australasica — see *Neopaxia australasica*

californica — see *Claytonia nevadensis*

parvifolia — see *Naiocrene parvifolia*

perfoliata — see *Claytonia perfoliata*

sibirica — see *Claytonia sibirica*

Moraea (Iridaceae)

alpina — GCrs

---

alticola CDL 181 **new** — CStu

§ *bellendenii* — WCot

bipartita — WCot

dracomontana — CPBP

elegans **new** — WCot

§ *fugax* — IBlr WCot

gawleri — WCot

huttonii — CDes CFir EBee GSki SBla SMad WBVN WCot WCru WSHC

iridioides — see *Dietes iridioides*

longifolia Sweet — see *M. fugax*

lurida — WCot

natalensis — SBla

papilionacea — EBee

pavonia var. *lutea* — see *M. bellendenii*

polyanthos — WCot

polystachya — EBee LRHS

robusta — SIgm

spathacea — see *M. spathulata*

§ *spathulata* — CBro CPLG CStu EBee EMan ERos GCal GMac LPio WCot WSHC

thomsonii — LPio

vegeta — CPBP WCot

versicolor **new** — CStu

villosa — SIgm WCot

Moricandia (Brassicaceae)

moricandioides — CSpe

Morina (Morinaceae)

alba — EBee GKev NChi

longifolia — More than 30 suppliers

persica — EBee EChP GBBs GBuc LPio MBro SIgm WHoo

polyphylla — EBee GPoy

Morisia (Brassicaceae)

hypogaea — see *M. monanthos*

§ *monanthos* — CPla IHMM MBar NHol NLAp NWCA WLin

- 'Fred Hemingway' — EBre EHyt GCrs ITim LRHS NMen NSla SBla SIng WAbe WPat

Morus ✿ (Moraceae)

§ *alba* — CArn CBcs CDul CLnd CMCN CMen CTho EBee ECrN ELan EPfP ERea EWTr GKir GTwe LBuc MGos NPSI SBLw SHBN WBVN WDin WFar

- 'Laciniata' — IDee

- 'Macrophylla' — CMCN SMad

- var. *multicaulis* — ERea

- 'Pendula' — CBcs CDoC CEnd CLnd CTri ECrN ELan EPfP ERea GTwe LPan LRHS MAsh MBlu MBri MLan MWat NBee NPSI SBLw SHBN SLim WDin WOrn

- 'Platanifolia' — LPan MBlu NPSI

- var. *tatarica* — LEdu

§ *bombycis* — LPan SBLw

- 'Atomic Blast' — WBcn

- 'Illinois Everbearing' (F) — ECrN ESim

kagayamae — see *M. bombycis*

latifolia 'Spirata' **new** — NLar

nigra (F) ♀[H4] — More than 30 suppliers

§ - 'Chelsea' (F) — CEnd COtt CTho CTri ECrN EMui EPfP ERea GTwe MBri MGos MLan NWea SKee SLim SPer SPoG

- 'King James' — see *M. nigra* 'Chelsea'

- 'Large Black' (F) — EMui

- 'Wellington' (F) — CEnd

Mosla (Lamiaceae)

dianthera — EMan GCal

Muehlenbeckia (*Polygonaceae*)

astonii	ECou
axillaris misapplied	see *M. complexa*
§ **axillaris** Walp.	CTri ECou GCal GGar SDry WGMN
- 'Mount Cook' (f)	ECou
- 'Ohau' (m)	ECou
§ **complexa**	CBcs CDoC CHEx CHal CPLG CTrC CTri CWib EBee ECou EPla ESlt GEil GQui IBlr LRHS MCCP NSti SAPC SArc SBra SDry SLim SLon SMac SWvt WCFE WSHC XPep
- (f)	ECou
- 'Nana'	see *M. axillaris* Walp.
- var. **trilobata**	EPla IBlr WCru XPep
- 'Ward' (m)	ECou
ephedroides	ECou
- 'Clarence Pass'	ECou
- var. **muricatula**	ECou
gunnii	ECou
platyclados	see *Homalocladium platycladum*

Muhlenbergia (*Poaceae*)

capillaris	CKno
emersleyi	CBrm
japonica 'Cream Delight' (v)	CBod CFwr CPen EBee EHoe EMan EMon EPPr MCCP WWpP
mexicana	CBig CBod CPen EBee EPPr EPza WWpP
rigens	CBig CKno XPep

Mukdenia (*Saxifragaceae*)

acanthifolia	WCru
§ **rossii**	EBee EMan EMon EPla GCal MSte MTed NGar NLar SHar SMac SMad SSpi WCot WCru WTMC WTin
- dwarf	GCal
* - 'Ögon'	WCru
- variegated	EMon

mulberry see *Morus*

Mundulea (*Papilionaceae*)

sericea **new**	SGar

Murraya (*Rutaceae*)

* **elliptica**	SOWG
exotica	see *M. paniculata*
koenigii	EOHP GPoy
§ **paniculata**	CArn EOHP ERea SMur

Musa (*Musaceae*)

from Yunnan, China	CKob EAmu ITer MJnS WHPE WMul WPGP XBlo
§ **acuminata**	MBri
- 'Bordelon' **new**	CKob
- 'Buitenzorg' **new**	CKob
- 'Double' (AAA+ Group) (F)	CKob
§ - 'Dwarf Cavendish' (AAA Group) (F) ♀H1	CKob EAmu ELan EPfP ESlt EUJe MJnS NScw WMul XBlo
- 'Dwarf Red' (AAA Group) (F)	CKob XBlo
- 'Dwarf Red Jamaican' (AAA Group) (F)	CKob
- 'Igitsiri' (AAA Group) (F) **new**	CKob
- 'Iholena Ula'ula" (AAA Group) (F) **new**	CKob
- 'Kru' (AA Group) (F) **new**	CKob
- 'Mai'a oa' **new**	CKob
- 'Malaysian Blood' (AA Group) (F) **new**	CKob
- 'Monyet' **new**	CKob
- 'Pink Striped' (AA Group) (F) **new**	CKob
- 'Pisang Berlin' (AA Group) (F)	CKob
- 'Pisang Jari Buaya' (AA Group) (F) **new**	CKob
- 'Pisang Lidi' (AA Group) (F)	CKob
- 'Red Iholena' (AAA Group) (F)	CKob XBlo
* - 'Rose' (AA Group) (F)	CKob
- 'Tapo' (AA Group) (F)	CKob
- 'Tuu Ghia' (AA Group) (F) **new**	CKob
- 'White Iholena' (AAA Group) (F) **new**	CKob
- 'Williams' (AAA Group) (F)	EAmu
- 'Zebrina' ♀H1+3	CKob EAmu MJnS XBlo
acuminata 'Zebrina' x **acuminata** 'Grand Nain'	EAmu
balbisiana	CKob EAmu EUJe WMul XBlo
- 'Cardaba' (BBB Group) (F)	CKob
- 'Tani' (BB Group) (F)	CKob
basjoo ♀H3-4	More than 30 suppliers
- 'Sakhalin'	CKob WMul
beccarii	CKob
'Burmese Blue'	CKob
'Butuhan' (**balbisiana** x **textilis**)	CKob
'Cavendish Super Dwarf' **new**	MJnS
'Cavendish Zan Moreno' **new**	MJnS
cavendishii	see *M. acuminata* 'Dwarf Cavendish'
§ **coccinea** ♀H1	CKob WMul XBlo
ensete	see *Ensete ventricosum*
(Fe'i Group) 'Utafan' (F)	CKob
hookeri	see *M. sikkimensis*
itinerans 'Yunnan' **new**	CKob
* 'Kru'	XBlo
§ **lasiocarpa**	CAbb CDWL CDoC CHEx CKob CTrC EAmu ESlt LRHS MBri MJnS WHPE WMul WPGP
laterita	CKob EUJe
mannii	CKob WMul
nana Lour.	see *M. acuminata*
nana auct.	see *M. acuminata* 'Dwarf Cavendish'
ornata ♀H1	LPal WMul XBlo
- 'African Red'	CKob
- 'Macro'	CKob
- 'Purple'	CKob
- 'Royal Red Salmon'	EAmu
x **paradisiaca** (AAB Group)	XBlo
- 'Belle' (AAB Group) (F) **new**	CKob
- 'Dwarf Orinoco' (ABB Group) (F)	CKob
- 'Ele-ele' (AAB Group) (F)	CKob
- Goldfinger = 'FHIA-01' (AAAB Group) (F)	CKob
- 'Hajaré' (ABB Group) (F)	CKob
- 'Hua Moa' (AAB Group) (F) **new**	CKob
- 'Malbhog' (AAB Group) (F)	CKob
- 'Monthan' (ABB Group) (F)	CKob

– 'Mysore' (AAB Group) (F)	CKob	
– 'Ney Mannan' (AAB Group) (F) **new**	CKob	
– 'Ney Poovan' (AB Group) (F)	CKob EAmu EUJe	
– 'Orinoco' (ABB Group) (F)	CKob EAmu WMul	
– 'Pisang Awak' (AAB Group) (F)	CKob	
– 'Pisang Seribu' **new** (AAB Group) (F)	CKob	
– 'Popoulu' (AAB Group) (F) **new**	CKob	
– 'Rajapuri' (AAB Group) (F)	CKob EAmu MJnS	
– 'Safet Velchi' (AB Group) (F)	CKob	
– 'Silk' (AAB Group) (F)	CKob	
– 'Yawa Dwarf' (ABB Group) (F)	CKob	
'Royal Pink' (*ornata* hybrid)	CKob	
'Royal Purple' (*ornata* hybrid)	CKob	
'Royal Red' (*ornata* hybrid)	CKob	
'Saba' ambig. (F)	CKob	
sanguinea **new**	CKob	
§ *sikkimensis*	CDoC CHid CKob EAmu ELan ESlt EUJe EWes LPJP MJnS SChr WHPE WMul WPGP XBlo	
textilis	CKob	
'Tropicana' **new**	SMer SSto	
uranoscopus misapplied	see *M. coccinea*	
velutina ♀H1+3	CKob EAmu EUJe MJnS SSte WHPE WMul WPGP XBlo	
* 'Violacea' (*ornata* hybrid)	LPal	
'Wompa' (AS Group) (F) **new**	CKob	

Muscari ❀ (Hyacinthaceae)

ambrosiacum	see *M. muscarimi*	
armeniacum ♀H4	CBro EPar EPfP ERos GFlt IHMH LRHS MBri NJOw NRog SChr SRms WCot WShi	
– 'Argaei Album'	EPot LAma	
– 'Babies Breath'	see *M. neglectum* 'Baby's Breath'	
– 'Blue Pearl'	LRHS	
– 'Blue Spike' (d)	CBro EPar EPfP LAma LRHS MBri NBir NBlu NRog SChr WCot	
– 'Christmas Pearl'	WCot	
– 'Early Giant'	LAma	
– 'Fantasy Creation'	CFwr EChP EPot LRHS MLwd WCot	
– 'Heavenly Blue'	LAma	
– 'Saffier'	LAma LRHS	
– 'Valerie Finnis'	CAvo CBre CBro CFwr CMea CRez EPPr EPot GCrs ITim LPhx LRHS MSte WAbe WAul WCot WPen	
§ *aucheri* ♀H4	EPar LAma NRog NRya WHoo	
– 'Blue Magic' **new**	EPot	
– 'Mount Hood' **new**	CFwr	
§ *azureum* ♀H4	CAvo CBro CNic EPar EPfP ERos LAma LRHS NJOw NMen NRog WCot	
– 'Album'	CBro EPar ERos LAma LRHS MAvo NJOw NRog WBry	
botryoides	LAma NRog	
– 'Album'	CAvo CBro CMea CStu EChP EPfP GFlt LAma LRHS MBri NRog SRms WShi	
caucasicum	WCot	
chalusicum	see *M. pseudomuscari*	
§ *comosum*	CBro EPar EPfP LRHS	
– 'Monstrosum'	see *M. comosum* 'Plumosum'	
– 'Pinard' **new**	ERos	
§ – 'Plumosum'	CAvo CBro EMan EMon EPar EPot GFlt ITim LAma LPhx LRHS MAvo MBri WCot	
dionysicum HOA 8965	WCot	
grandifolium	EHyt	
– JCA 689.450	WCot	
latifolium	CAvo CBro CFwr CMea EHyt EPar GFlt GGar ITim LAma LPhx LRHS MLLN NChi NRog WBry WCot WHil WHoo WTin	
* – 'Blue Angels'	NBir	
§ *macrocarpum*	CAvo CBro CMea ECha EHyt EPot ERos LAma WAbe WCot	
mirum	EHyt	
moschatum	see *M. muscarimi*	
§ *muscarimi*	CBro EPar LAma WCot	
– var. *flavum*	see *M. macrocarpum*	
§ *neglectum*	CBgR CMea CSWP ERos LAma SEND WShi WWst	
§ – 'Baby's Breath'	CMil EHrv SMad SMrm WCot	
pallens	EHyt NWCA	
paradoxum	see *Bellevalia paradoxa*	
§ *pseudomuscari*	EHyt	
♀H4 BSBE 842		
racemosum	see *M. neglectum*	
'Sky Blue'	EPot	
§ *spreitzenhoferi*	ERos	
§ *tenuiflorum*	WCot	
weissii **new**	ERos .	
'White Beauty'	EPot LRHS	

Muscarimia (Hyacinthaceae)

ambrosiacum	see *Muscari muscarimi*
macrocarpum	see *Muscari macrocarpum*

Musella (Musaceae)

lasiocarpa	see *Musa lasiocarpa*

Musschia (Campanulaceae)

wollastonii	CHEx CPla EMan

Mutisia (Asteraceae)

clematis	CRHN
coccinea	CBcs
'Glendoick' **new**	GGGa
ilicifolia	IBlr LRHS MTPN SIgm WLin WSHC
latifolia	CBcs
oligodon	IBlr
retusa	see *M. spinosa* var. *pulchella*
§ *spinosa* var. *pulchella*	SSpi
subulata f. *rosea*	CFil

Myoporum (Myoporaceae)

debile	see *Eremophila debilis*
laetum	CDoC CHEx CPLG CTbh CTrC XPep
parvifolium **new**	XPep

Myosotidium (Boraginaceae)

§ *hortensia*	More than 30 suppliers
– white	CBos CPla NCot WNor
nobile	see *M. hortensia*

Myosotis (Boraginaceae)

§ *alpestris*	SECG
– 'Ruth Fischer'	NBir NMen
arvensis	GWCH MBow
australis	EShb GCal MMHG MSPs
'Bill Baker'	CPLG EMon
capitata **new**	GCrs
colensoi	ECou EDAr NMen NWCA
explanata	NMen
palustris	see *M. scorpioides*
pulvinaris	CPBP SIng WAbe

rakiura	GCrs GTou MAvo NLAp
rupicola	see *M. alpestris*
§ *scorpioides*	CBen CRow CWat EHon EMFW EPfP LNCo LPBA MBow MSta NBlu NGdn SCoo SLon SPlb SRms SWat WEas WMAq WMoo WMyn WPnP WWpP
– 'Alba' **new**	LPBA
– Maytime = 'Blaqua' (v)	CDWL EMan EMon LPBA NBir NGdn WWpP
– 'Mermaid'	CBen CRow CWat ECha EHon EPfP GAbr GMac LPBA LRHS MSta NDov SDix SWat WFar WPer WWpP
– 'Pinkie'	CDWL CRow CWat EMFW GMac LPBA NGdn SWat WWpP
– 'Snowflakes'	CRow CWat WWpP
sylvatica	CRWN
– alba	see *M. sylvatica* f. *lactea*
§ – f. *lactea*	CRow

Myrceugenia (*Myrtaceae*)

ovata	CTrG
planipes	CTrG

Myrcia (*Myrtaceae*)

tomentosa	GIBF

Myrica (*Myricaceae*)

californica	CFil CPle WPGP
cerifera	CAgr CArn LEdu
gale	CAgr CRWN GPoy MGos SWat WDin WWye
pensylvanica	GIBF GTSp IFro IMGH NBlu

Myriophyllum (*Haloragaceae*)

propinquum	EMFW NArg
* 'Red Stem'	LPBA
spicatum	EHon EMFW
verticillatum	EHon SCoo

Myrrhidendron (*Apiaceae*)

donnellsmithii	WCru
B&SWJ 9099 **new**	

Myrrhis (*Apiaceae*)

odorata	More than 30 suppliers
– 'Forncett Chevron'	EFou

Myrsine (*Myrsinaceae*)

africana	CPle XPep
divaricata	CTrC IDee
nummularia	GGar

Myrteola (*Myrtaceae*)

§ *nummularia*	ISea NMen WAbe

Myrtus (*Myrtaceae*)

apiculata	see *Luma apiculata*
bullata	see *Lophomyrtus bullata*
chequen	see *Luma chequen*
communis ♀H3	More than 30 suppliers
* – 'Alhambra' **new**	XPep
– 'Baetica' **new**	XPep
* – 'Cascade' **new**	XPep
– 'Flore Pleno' (d)	GQui XPep
– 'Jenny Reitenbach'	see *M. communis* subsp. *tarentina*
* – 'La Clape' **new**	XPep
* – 'La Clape Blanc' **new**	XPep
– 'Merion'	WJek
– 'Microphylla'	see *M. communis* subsp. *tarentina*
– 'Nana'	see *M. communis* subsp. *tarentina*
§ – subsp. *tarentina* ♀H3	More than 30 suppliers
– – 'Compacta'	CStu WSel
* – – 'Granada' **new**	XPep
§ – – 'Microphylla' Variegata' (v)	CPle GBar MHer NGHP SAga SPer STre WBrE WHHs WJek WSHC WSel
– – pink-flowered **new**	XPep
I – – 'Variegata' **new**	XPep
* – – 'Vieussan' **new**	XPep
– 'Tricolor'	see *M. communis* 'Variegata'
§ – 'Variegata' (v)	More than 30 suppliers
dulcis	see *Austromyrtus dulcis*
'Glanleam Gold'	see *Luma apiculata* 'Glanleam Gold'
lechleriana	see *Amomyrtus luma*
luma	see *Luma apiculata*
nummularia	see *Myrteola nummularia*
obcordata	see *Lophomyrtus obcordata*
* *paraguayensis*	CTrC
x *ralphii*	see *Lophomyrtus* x *ralphii*
'Traversii'	see *Lophomyrtus* x *ralphii* 'Traversii'
ugni	see *Ugni molinae*
* *variegata* 'Penlee' (v)	CTrG

N

Nabalus (*Asteraceae*)

albus	see *Prenanthes alba*

Naiocrene (*Portulacaceae*)

§ *parvifolia*	CNic

Nandina (*Berberidaceae*)

domestica ♀H3	More than 30 suppliers
– B&SWJ 4923	WCru
– 'Fire Power' ♀H3	More than 30 suppliers
– 'Harbor Dwarf'	LRHS WFar
– var. *leucocarpa*	EPla MBlu
– 'Little Princess'	EPla
– 'Nana'	see *N. domestica* 'Pygmaea'
– 'Nana Purpurea'	CDul EPla
§ – 'Pygmaea'	WBod WDin
– 'Richmond'	CBcs CSBt ECrN ELan EPfP LRHS MAsh MGos NLar SBod SHBN SPer SPla WBrE WFar

Nannorrhops (*Arecaceae*)

ritchieana	CBrP LPal WMul

Napaea (*Malvaceae*)

dioica	EBee EMan

Narcissus ✿ (*Amaryllidaceae*)

'Aberfoyle' (2) ♀H4	GEve
'Abstract' (11a) **new**	CQua
'Accent' (2) ♀H4	CQua
'Achduart' (3)	CQua GEve
'Achentoul' (4)	CQua
'Achnasheen' (3)	CQua GEve
'Acropolis' (4)	CQua LAma LRHS
'Actaea' (9) ♀H4	LRHS MBri NRog
'Admiration' (8)	CQua
'Advocat' (3)	CQua
'Aflame' (3)	LAma
'Ahwahnee' (2)	IRhd
'Aintree' (3)	CQua
'Aircastle' (3)	CQua
'Akepa' (5)	CQua
I *albidus* subsp. *occidentalis* (13)	ERos
'Albus Plenus Odoratus'	see *N. poeticus* 'Plenus'
'Alpine Glow' (1) **new**	CQua

'Alston' (2) — IRhd
'Alto' (2) — IRhd
'Altruist' (3) — CQua
'Altun Ha' (2) — CQua EHof IRhd
'Amazing Grace' — IRhd
'Amber Castle' (2) — CQua
'Ambergate' (2) — GEve LAma NRog
'American Heritage' (1) — CQua IRhd
'American Robin' (6) **new** — CQua
'American Shores' (1) — CQua IRhd
'Amor' (3) — NRog
'Amstel' (4) — CQua
'Andalusia' (6) — ERos
'Angel Face' (3) — EHof IRhd
'Angelito' (2) — IRhd
'Angkor' (4) — CQua
'An-gof' (7) — CQua
'Annalong' (3) — IRhd
'Apotheose' (4) — MBri NRog
'Applins' (2) — IRhd
'Apricot' (1) — CBro
'Apricot Blush' (2) **new** — CQua
'April Love' (1) — CQua
'April Snow' (2) — CBro CQua
'Aranjuez' (2) — CQua
'Arctic Gold' (1) ♀H4 — CQua
'Ardglass' (3) — GEve IRhd
'Ardress' (2) — CQua
'Ardview' (3) — IRhd
'Areley Kings' (2) — CQua
'Arid Plains' (3) **new** — IRhd
'Arish Mell' (5) — CQua
'Arkle' (1) ♀H4 — CQua GEve
'Arleston' (2) — IRhd
'Armidale' (3) — IRhd
'Arndilly' (2) — CQua
'Arpege' (2) — CQua
'Arran Isle' (2) — IRhd
'Arthurian' (1) — IRhd
'Arwenack' (11a) — CQua
'Ashmore' (2) — CQua IRhd
'Ashton Wold' (2) — EHof
'Asila' (2) — IRhd
'Assertion' (2) — IRhd
§ **assoanus** (13) — CBro CLAP EPar EPot ERos GKir LAma
§ **asturiensis** (13) ♀H3-4 — CSam EPar EPot IBlr LPhx MNrw NGar
asturiensis × cyclamineus
atlanticus (13) — CLAP
'Atricilla' — IRhd
'Audubon' (2) — CQua
'Auntie Eileen' (2) — CQua
§ **aureus** (13) — CQua
'Auspicious' (2) — IRhd
'Avalanche' (8) ♀H3 — CQua LRHS
'Avalon' (2) — CQua
'Azocor' (1) — IRhd
'Baby Moon' (7) — CQua EPar EPot GFlt LAma LRHS MBri NRog SPer
'Badanloch' (3) — CQua
'Badbury Rings' (3) ♀H4 — CQua
'Balalaika' (2) — CQua
'Baldock' (4) — CQua
'Ballinamallard' (3) — IRhd
'Ballygarvey' (1) — CQua
'Ballygowan' (3) — IRhd
'Ballykinler' (3) — IRhd
'Ballymorran' (1) — IRhd
'Ballynahinch' (3) — IRhd
'Ballynichol' (3) — IRhd
'Ballyrobert' (1) — CQua
'Baltic Shore' (3) — IRhd
'Balvenie' (2) — CQua

'Bambi' (1) — ERos
'Banbridge' (1) — IRhd
'Bandesara' (3) — IRhd
'Bandit' (2) — CQua
'Banstead Village' (2) — CQua
'Bantam' (2) ♀H4 — CBro CQua ERos MBri
'Barleywine' (2) — IRhd
'Barlow' (6) — CQua
'Barnesgold' (1) — IRhd
'Barnsdale Wood' (2) — CQua
'Barnum' (1) ♀H4 — IRhd
'Barr Hall' (9) — IRhd
'Barrett Browning' (3) — MBri NRog
'Bartley' (6) — CQua
'Bath's Flame' (3) **new** — CQua
'Bear Springs' (4) — IRhd
'Bebop' (7) — CBro
'Bedruthan' (2) — CQua
'Belbroughton' (2) — CQua
'Belcanto' (11a) — CQua
'Belisana' (2) — LAma
'Bell Rock' (1) — CQua
'Bell Song' (7) — CAvo CBro CQua EPfP ERos GFlt LRHS MBri SPer
'Belzone' (2) **new** — CQua
'Ben Aligin' (1) — CQua
'Ben Armine' (2) — GEve
'Ben Avon' (1) — GEve
'Ben Hee' (2) ♀H4 — CQua
'Ben Loyal' (2) — GEve
'Ben Vorlich' (2) — GEve
'Benbane Head' (9) — IRhd
'Berceuse' (2) — IRhd
'Bere Ferrers' (4) — CQua
'Bergerac' (11a) — CQua
'Berlin' (2) — ERos
'Beryl' (6) — CBro CQua ERos LAma LRHS
'Best of Luck' (3) — IRhd
'Bethal' (3) **new** — CQua
'Betsy MacDonald' (6) — CQua
'Biffo' (4) — CQua
'Big John' (1) — GEve
'Bilbo' (6) — CBro CQua
'Binkie' (2) — CBro CQua LAma NRog
'Birdsong' (3) — CQua
'Birkdale' (2) — GEve
'Birma' (3) — EFam LAma NRog
'Birthday Girl' (2) — IRhd
'Bishops Light' (2) — CQua
'Blarney' (3) — CQua
'Blisland' (9) — CQua
'Blossom' (4) — CQua
'Blue Danube' (1) — IRhd
'Blushing Maiden' (4) — CQua
'Bob Minor' (1) — CQua
'Bob Spotts' (2) **new** — EHof
'Bobbysoxer' (7) — CBro CQua ERos LAma MTho
'Bobolink' (2) — CQua
'Bodwannick' (2) — CQua
'Bolton' (7) — CBro
'Bon Viveur' (11a) **new** — IRhd
'Bosbigal' (11a) — CQua
'Boscastle' (7) — CQua
'Boscoppa' (11a) **new** — CQua
'Boslowick' (11a) ♀H4 — CQua
'Bosmeor' (2) — CQua
'Bossa Nova' (3) — CQua
'Bossiney' (11a) — CQua
'Bosvale' (11a) — CQua
'Bouzouki' (2) — IRhd
'Bowles' Early Sulphur' (1) — CRow
'Boyne Bridge' (1) — IRhd
'Brandaris' (11a) — CQua GEve
'Bravoure' (1) ♀H4 — CQua NRog

'Brentswood' (8) CQua
'Bridal Crown' (4) EPfP LAma LRHS NRog
'Bright Flame' (2) CQua
'Brindle Pink' (2) IRhd
'Broadland' (2) CQua
'Broadway Star' (11b) LAma LRHS NRog
'Brodick' (3) GEve IRhd
'Broomhill' (2) ♀H4 CQua
broussonetii (13) CFil
'Budock Bells' (5) CQua
'Bugle Major' (2) EHof
bulbocodium (13) ♀H3-4 CBro CFil CNic EHyt LBee LPhx
 LRHS NGar NRya NWCA SRms
 WCom WPGP
§ - subsp. *bulbocodium* CBro
 (13)
§ - - var. *citrinus* (13) EHyt SSpi
 - - var. *conspicuus* (13) CArn CAvo CBro CNic CPMA
 CQua CSam EHyt EPar EPot ERos
 GCrs GEdr IFro ITim LAma MS&S
 NJOw NRog NRya SGar
* - - *filifolius* (13) CBro
 - - var. *genuinus* EHyt
 x 'Jessamy'
§ - - var. *graellsii* (13) NSla
 - - var. *nivalis* (13) ERos
§ - - var. *tenuifolius* (13) CNic EHyt EPot MNrw
 - - var. *tenuifolius* EHyt NGar
 x *triandrus* (13)
§ - 'Golden Bells' (10) CAvo CBro CFwr CPom CQua
 EPot GEdr GFlt LRHS MAvo MBri
 NJOw WAbe WHil
 - var. *mesatlanticus* see *N. romieuxii* subsp. *romieuxii*
 var. *mesatlanticus*
 - subsp. *praecox* CAvo
 var. *paucinervis* (13)
 - subsp. *romieuxii* see *N. romieuxii*
I - subsp. *viriditubus* EHyt ERos
 (13)
 - subsp. *vulgaris* see *N. bulbocodium* subsp.
 bulbocodium
'Bunchie' (5) **new** CQua
'Bunclody' (2) CQua
'Bunting' (7) ♀H4 CQua
'Burning Bush' (3) IRhd
'Burntollet' (1) CQua
'Busselton' (3) IRhd
'Buttercup' (7) CBro
'Butterscotch' (2) CQua
'Cabernet' (2) IRhd
'Cacatua' (11a) IRhd
'Cadgwith' (2) CQua
'Caedmon' (9) CQua
'Cairntoul' (3) CQua
'Calamansack' (2) CQua
'California Rose' (4) IRhd
'Camellia' (4) EFam
'Camelot' (2) ♀H4 EPfP
'Cameo King' (2) CQua
'Camoro' (10) **new** EHyt
'Campernelli Plenus' see *N.* x *odorus* 'Double
 Campernelle'
'Campion' (9) CQua IRhd
'Canaliculatus' (8) CArn CBro CQua EHyt EPar ERos
 GFlt LAma LRHS MBri
canaliculatus Gussone see *N. tazetta* subsp. *lacticolor*
'Canary' (7) **new** CQua
'Canarybird' (8) CBro
'Canasta' (11a) CQua
'Canisp' (2) CQua
'Cantabile' (9) ♀H4 CBro CQua IRhd
cantabricus (13) CFil LPhx SSpi WPGP
 - subsp. *cantabricus* CLAP EHyt ERos
 (13)

- - var. *foliosus* EPot SCnR
 (13) ♀H2
- - var. *petunioides* (13) LAma SOkd
'Cantatrice' (1) **new** CQua
'Capax Plenus' see *N.* 'Eystettensis'
'Cape Cornwall' (2) CQua
'Cape Helles' (3) IRhd
'Cape Point' (2) IRhd
'Capisco' (3) CQua IRhd
'Caramba' (2) CQua
'Carbineer' (2) EFam LAma NRog
'Carclew' (6) CQua
'Cargreen' (9) CQua
'Cariad' (5) CQua
'Carib Gipsy' (2) ♀H4 CQua EHof IRhd
'Caribbean Snow' (2) EHof
'Carlton' (2) ♀H4 EFam LAma MBri NRog
'Carnearny' (3) CQua GEve
'Carnkief' (2) CQua
'Carnyorth' (11a) CQua
'Carole Lombard' (3) CQua IRhd
'Cassata' (11) EFam LAma LRHS NBir NRog
'Castanets' (8) IRhd
'Casterbridge' (2) CQua IRhd
'Castlehill' (3) IRhd
'Catalyst' (2) IRhd
'Catherine MacKenzie' GEve
 (3) **new**
'Catistock' (2) CQua
'Causeway Sunset' IRhd
 (2) **new**
'Cavalryman' (3) IRhd
'Cavendish' (4) IRhd
'Caye Chapel' (3) EHof
'Cazique' (6) CQua
'Ceasefire' (2) IRhd
'Cedar Hills' (3) **new** CQua
'Cedric Morris' (1) CBro CDes CElw CHid CLAP ECha
 NDov SMrm SSpi WCot
'Celestial Fire' (2) EHof
'Celtic Gold' (2) CQua
'Centrefold' (3) CQua
'Cha-cha' (6) CBro CQua
'Chanson' (1) IRhd
'Chanterelle' (11a) LAma NRog
'Chapman's Peak' (2) IRhd
'Charity May' (6) ♀H4 CBro CQua IRhd LAma MBri
'Charleston' (2) CQua
'Chaste' (1) CQua IRhd
'Chat' (7) CQua
'Cheer Leader' (3) CQua GEve
'Cheerfulness' (4) ♀H4 CAvo CQua ITim LAma LRHS MBri
 NRog
'Cheesewring' (3) **new** CQua
'Cheetah' (1) IRhd
'Chelsea Girl' (2) CQua GEve
'Cheltenham' (2) CQua
'Chérie' (7) CBro CQua
'Cherrygardens' (2) CQua IRhd
'Chesapeake Bay' (1) EHof
'Chesterton' (9) ♀H4 CQua
'Chickadee' (6) CBro CQua
'Chickerell' (3) CQua
'Chief Inspector' (1) CQua IRhd
'Chilmark' (3) IRhd
'Chiloquin' (1) CQua
'China Doll' (2) CQua
'Chinchilla' (2) CQua IRhd
'Chingah' (1) **new** IRhd
'Chinita' (8) CBro CQua
'Chit Chat' (7) ♀H4 CBro ERos LAma
'Chobe River' (1) IRhd
'Chorus Line' (8) IRhd
'Chukar' (4) IRhd

'Churchman' (2)	IRhd	
'Churston Ferrers' (4)	CQua	
'Cisticola' (3)	IRhd	
citrinus	see *N. bulbocodium* subsp. *bulbocodium* var. *citrinus*	
'Citron' (3) **new**	CQua	
'Citronita' (3)	CQua	
'Clare' (7)	CBro CQua	
'Clashmore' (2)	GEve	
'Clearbrook' (2)	CQua	
'Close Harmony' (4)	IRhd	
'Cloud Nine' (2)	CBro	
'Clouded Yellow' (2)	EHof IRhd	
'Clouds Rest' (2)	IRhd	
'Codlins and Cream'	see *N.* 'Sulphur Phoenix'	
'Colin's Joy' (2) **new**	CQua	
'Colleen Bawn'**new**	CAvo	
'Colley Gate' (3)	CQua	
'Colliford' (2) **new**	CQua	
'Colorama' (11a)	CQua	
'Colour Sergeant' (2)	IRhd	
'Colourful' (2)	IRhd	
'Columbus' (2)	CQua	
'Colville' (9)	CQua	
'Comal' (1)	CQua	
'Compton Court' (3)	IRhd	
concolor (Haworth) Link	see *N. triandrus* subsp. *triandrus* var. *concolor*	
'Conestoga' (2)	IRhd	
'Confuoco' (2)	EFam	
'Congress' (11a)	CQua	
* 'Connie Number 1'	EHyt	
* 'Connie Number 2'	EHyt	
'Cool Crystal' (3)	CQua IRhd	
'Cool Evening' (11a)	CQua IRhd	
'Cool Pink' (2)	CQua	
'Cool Shades' (2)	EHof	
'Coombe Creek' (6)	CQua	
'Copper Nob' (2)	IRhd	
'Cora Ann' (7)	CBro	
'Corbiere' (1)	CQua IRhd	
cordubensis (13)	EHyt EPot SSpi	
'Cornet' (6)	CQua	
'Cornish Chuckles' (12)	CQua	
'Corofin' (3)	CQua	
'Coromandel' (2)	IRhd	
'Corozal' (3)	EHof	
'Cosmic Dance' (3)	IRhd	
'Cotinga' (6)	CQua	
'Countdown' (2) **new**	CQua	
'Crackington' (4) ♀H4	CQua IRhd	
'Cragford' (8)	LAma	
'Craig Stiel' (2)	CQua	
'Craigarusky' (2)	IRhd	
'Creag Dubh' (2)	CQua GEve	
'Crenver' (3)	CQua	
'Crevenagh' (2)	IRhd	
'Crimson Chalice' (3)	CQua IRhd	
'Cristobal' (1)	CQua	
'Crock of Gold' (1)	CQua	
'Croesus' (2) **new**	CQua	
'Crofty' (6)	CQua	
'Croila' (2)	CQua	
'Crown Royalist' (2)	IRhd	
'Crowndale' (4)	IRhd	
'Cryptic' (1)	IRhd	
'Crystal Star' (2) **new**	CQua	
'Cuan Gold' (4)	IRhd	
cuatrecasasii (13)	EPot ERos	
'Cul Beag' (3)	CQua	
'Culmination' (2)	CQua	
'Cultured Pearl' (2) **new**	CQua	
'Cupid's Eye' (3)	CQua IRhd	
'Curlew' (7)	CQua	

cyclamineus (13) ♀H4	CBro CDes CFil CPom CStu CWoo EPar LAma MS&S NRog SBla SCnR SIgm SRms SScr SSpi WAbe WCru WLFP WPGP	
'Cyclope' (1)	CQua	
cypri (8)	CQua	
'Cyros' (1)	CQua	
'Dailmanach' (2) **new**	CQua IRhd	
'Dailmystic' (2)	IRhd	
'Dallas' (3)	CQua	
'Damson' (2) **new**	CQua	
'Dan du Plessis' (8)	CQua	
'Dancing Queen' (2)	IRhd	
'Dardanelles' (2)	IRhd	
'Dateline' (3)	CQua	
'David Alexander' (1)	CQua	
'Davochfin Lass' (1)	GEve	
'Dawn' (5)	CBro	
'Dawn Run' (2)	IRhd	
'Dawn Sky' (2)	EHof	
'Daydream' (2) ♀H3	CQua LAma NRog	
'Debutante' (2)	CQua	
'December Bride' (11a) **new**	CQua	
'Decoy' (2)	IRhd	
'Delia' (6)	IRhd	
'Delibes' (2)	LAma NRog	
'Dell Chapel' (3)	CQua	
'Delnashaugh' (4)	CQua	
'Delos' (3)	CQua	
'Delphin Hill' (4)	IRhd	
'Delta Flight' (6)	IRhd	
'Demand' (2)	CQua	
'Denali' (1)	IRhd	
'Derryboy' (3)	IRhd	
'Descant' (1)	IRhd	
'Desdemona' (2) ♀H4	NRog	
'Desert Bells' (7)	CQua	
'Desert Orchid' (2)	CQua	
'Diatone' (4)	GEve	
'Dick Wilden' (4)	LAma	
'Dickcissel' (7) ♀H4	CBro CQua ERos NRog	
'Dimity' (3)	CQua	
'Dimple' (9)	CQua	
'Dinkie' (3)	CBro	
'Diversity' (11a)	IRhd	
'Doctor Hugh' (3) ♀H4	CQua GEve IRhd	
'Doctor Jazz' (2)	EHof	
'Dolly Mollinger' (11b)	NRog	
'Doombar' (1)	CQua	
'Dora Allum' (2) **new**	CQua	
'Dorchester' (4)	IRhd	
'Double Campernelle'	see *N.* x *odorus* 'Double Campernelle'	
'Double Fashion' (4)	NRog	
double pheasant eye	see *N. poeticus* 'Plenus'	
double Roman	see *N.* 'Romanus'	
'Double White' (4) **new**	CQua	
'Doubleday' (4)	IRhd	
'Doublet' (4)	CQua	
'Doubtful' (3)	CQua	
'Dove Wings' (6) ♀H4	CBro CQua LAma	
'Dover Cliffs' (2)	CQua	
'Downpatrick' (1)	CQua	
'Dragon Run' (2)	CQua	
'Drama Queen' (11a)	IRhd	
'Drumbeg' (2)	IRhd	
'Drumlin' (1) ♀H4	IRhd	
dubius (13)	CBro	
'Duiker' (6)	IRhd	
'Duke of Windsor' (2)	EFam	
'Dulcimer' (9)	CQua	
'Dunadry Inn' (4)	IRhd	
'Dunkeld' (2) **new**	CQua	

'Dunkery' (4) — CQua IRhd
'Dunley Hall' (3) — CQua IRhd
'Dunmurry' (1) — CQua
'Dunskey' (3) — CQua
'Dusky Lad' (2) — IRhd
'Dusky Maiden' (2) — IRhd
'Dutch Delight' (2) — IRhd
'Dutch Master' (1) ♀H4 — CQua LAma MBri NRog
'Early Splendour' (8) — CQua LAma
'Easter Bonnet' (2) — LAma MBri
'Eaton Song' (12) ♀H4 — CBro CQua
'Eddy Canzony' (2) — CQua
'Edenderry' (1) — IRhd
'Edgbaston' (2) — CQua EHof
'Edge Grove' (2) — CQua
'Edna Earl' (3) — NRog
'Edward Buxton' (3) — LAma MBri
'Egard' (11a) — CQua
'Eland' (7) — CQua
'Electrus' (11a) — IRhd
'Elf' (2) — CBro CQua
'Elfin Gold' (6) — CQua IRhd
'Elizabeth Ann' (6) — CQua
'Elka' (1) — CQua IRhd
'Elphin' (4) — CQua GEve
'Elrond' (2) — CQua
'Elven Lady' (2) — CQua
'Elvira' (8) — CBro CQua
'Embo' (2) — GEve
'Emily' (2) — CQua
'Emperor's Waltz' (6) — CQua IRhd
'Empress of Ireland' (1) ♀H4 — CQua IRhd
'Englander' (6) — EPot
'English Caye' (1) — EHof
'Ensemble' (4) — CQua
'Eribol' (2) — GEve
'Eriskay' (4) — GEve
'Erlicheer' (4) — CQua
'Escapee' (3) — IRhd
'Ethereal Beauty' (2) — IRhd
'Ethos' (1) — IRhd
'Euryalus' (1) — CQua
'Eve Robertson' (2) **new** — EHof
'Evelix' (2) — GEve
'Evening' (2) — CQua
'Evesham' (3) — IRhd
'Eye Level' (9) — IRhd
'Eyeglass' (3) — IRhd
'Eyelet' (3) — IRhd
'Eype' (4) — IRhd
'Eyrie' (3) — IRhd
§ 'Eystettensis' (4) — CBro ECha ERos GCrs IBlr
'Fair Head' (9) — CQua
'Fair Prospect' (2) — CQua
'Fair William' (2) **new** — CQua
'Fairgreen' (3) — CQua
'Fairlawns' (3) — CQua
'Fairsel' (3) — IRhd
'Fairy Chimes' (5) — CBro CQua
'Fairy Footsteps' (3) — IRhd
'Fairy Gold' (6) — CAvo
'Fairy Island' (3) — CQua
'Fairy Magic' (2) — IRhd
'Fairy Spell' (3) — IRhd
'Falconet' (8) ♀H4 — CBro CQua ERos
'Falmouth Bay' (3) — CQua
'Falstaff' (2) — CQua
'Famecheck Giant' — EFam
'Famecheck Luck' (2) — EFam
'Famecheck Silver' (11b) — EFam
'Fanad Head' (9) — IRhd
'Far Country' (2) — GEve
'Faro' (1) — IRhd

'Farranfad' (2) — IRhd
'Fastidious' (2) — CQua
'Favor Royal' (3) — IRhd
'February Gold' (6) ♀H4 — CAvo CBro EPar EPfP EPot ERos LAma LRHS MBri NBir NRog SPer SRms WShi
'February Silver' (6) — CBro EPar EPot LAma LRHS NRog
'Felindre' (9) — CQua IRhd
'Feline Queen' (1) **new** — IRhd
'Fellowship' (2) — GEve
'Feock' (3) — CQua
fernandesii (13) — CBro SCnR
'Ferndown' (3) — CQua IRhd
'Ffitch's Ffolly' (2) — CQua
'Filoli' (1) — IRhd
'Fine Gold' (1) — CQua
'Fine Romance' (2) — CQua EHof
'Fiona MacKillop' (2) — IRhd
'Fionn' (2) **new** — GEve
'Firebrand' (2) — CQua WShi
'First Formal' (3) — CQua
'Flirt' (6) — CQua
'Flomay' (7) — CBro
'Florida Manor' (3) — IRhd
'Flower Drift' (4) — LAma NRog
'Flower Record' (2) — LAma NRog
'Flycatcher' (7) — CQua IRhd
'Flying Colours' (4) — IRhd
'Foresight' (1) — EFam NRog
'Forge Mill' (2) — CQua
'Fortune' (2) — CQua EFam LAma MBri NRog
'Foundling' (6) ♀H4 — CBro CQua GEve IRhd
'Fragrant Rose' (2) — CQua IRhd
'Francolin' (1) — IRhd
'Frank's Fancy' (9) — IRhd
'Freedom Rings' (2) — CQua
'Fresco' (11a) — IRhd
'Fresh Lime' (1) — EHof
'Fresno' (3) — IRhd
'Frogmore' (6) — CQua
'Front Royal' (2) — CQua
'Frosted Pink' (2) — IRhd
'Frostkist' (6) **new** — CBro CQua
'Frou-frou' (4) — CQua
'Frozen Jade' (1) **new** — EHof
'Fruit Cup' (7) — CQua
'Furnace Creek' (2) — IRhd
'Fynbos' (3) — IRhd
'Gabriël Kleiberg' (11a) — NRog
gaditanus (13) — CBro ERos
'Galilee' (3) **new** — GFlt
'Garden News' (3) — IRhd
'Garden Princess' (6) — CBro
'Gay Cavalier' (4) — CQua
'Gay Kybo' (4) ♀H4 — CQua
'Gay Song' (4) — CQua
§ *gayi* (13) — CBro CQua
'Geevor' (4) — CQua
'Gemini Girl' (2) — CQua
'George Leak' (2) — CQua
'Georgie Girl' (6) — CQua
'Geranium' (8) ♀H4 — CBro CQua LAma LRHS MBri NRog
'Gettysburg' (2) — CQua
'Gigantic Star' (2) — LAma MBri NRog
'Gilda' (2) — IRhd
'Gillan' (11a) — CQua
'Gin and Lime' (1) ♀H4 — CQua
'Gipsy Moon' (2) — EHof
'Gipsy Queen' (1) — CQua EHyt
'Gironde' (11) — CQua
'Glen Cassley' (3) — CQua GEve
'Glen Clova' (2) — CQua GEve
'Glen Lorne' (2) — GEve

'Glencalvie' (2)	GEve
'Glenfarclas' (1) ♀H4	GEve
'Glenmorangie' (2)	GEve
'Glenside' (2)	CQua
'Glissando' (2)	CQua
'Gloriosus' (8)	CQua
'Glover's Reef' (1) **new**	EHof
'Glowing Pheonix' (4) **new**	CQua
'Glowing Red' (4)	CQua
'Goff's Caye' (2)	CQua EHof IRhd
'Gold Bond' (2)	CQua IRhd
'Gold Charm' (2)	CQua
'Gold Convention' (2) ♀H4	CQua IRhd
'Gold Ingot' (2)	IRhd
'Gold Medal' (1)	LAma NRog
'Gold Mine' (2)	IRhd
'Gold Strike' (1)	GEve
'Golden Amber' (2)	CQua IRhd
'Golden Aura' (2) ♀H4	CQua IRhd
'Golden Bear' (4)	CQua
'Golden Bells'	see *N. bulbocodium* 'Golden Bells'
'Golden Cheer' (2)	CQua
'Golden Cycle' (6)	CQua
'Golden Dawn' (8) ♀H3	CQua
'Golden Ducat' (4)	CQua LAma MBri NBir NRog
'Golden Halo' (2)	CQua IRhd
'Golden Harvest' (1)	LAma LRHS MBri NRog
'Golden Incense' (7)	CQua
'Golden Jewel' (2) ♀H4	CQua GEve
'Golden Joy' (2)	CQua
'Golden Orbit' (4)	CQua
'Golden Quince' (12)	CBro CQua
'Golden Radiance' (1)	IRhd
'Golden Rain' (4) **new**	CQua
'Golden Rapture' (1) ♀H4	CQua
'Golden Sceptre' (7) **new**	CBro
'Golden Sheen' (2)	CQua
'Golden Sovereign' (1)	IRhd
'Golden Spur' (1) **new**	CQua
'Golden Strand' (2)	IRhd
'Golden Topaz' (2)	IRhd
'Golden Vale' (1) ♀H4	CQua
'Golden Wings' (6)	IRhd
'Goldfinger' (1) ♀H4	CQua IRhd
'Goldhanger' (2)	EHof
'Goldsithney' (2)	CBro
'Golitha Falls' (2)	CQua
'Good Measure' (2)	CQua
'Goose Green' (3)	IRhd
'Gorran' (3)	CQua
'Gossmoor' (4) **new**	CQua
'Grace Note' (3)	CQua
graellsii	see *N. bulbocodium* subsp. *bulbocodium* var. *graellsii*
'Grand Monarque'	see *N. tazetta* subsp. *lacticolor* 'Grand Monarque'
'Grand Opening' (4)	IRhd
'Grand Primo Citronière' (8)	CQua
'Grand Prospect' (2)	CQua
'Grand Soleil d'Or' (8)	CQua EPfP LAma NRog
'Grapillon' (11a)	GEve
'Grasmere' (1) ♀H4	GEve
'Great Expectations' (2)	CQua
'Greatwood' (1)	CQua
'Green Chartreuse' (2)	EHof
'Green Lodge' (9)	IRhd
'Greenlet' (6)	CBro CQua LRHS MSte
'Greenodd' (3)	CQua
'Greenpark' (9)	IRhd
'Gresham' (4)	CQua IRhd
'Gribben Head' (4)	CQua

'Groundkeeper' (3) **new**	IRhd
'Grullemans Senior' (2)	EFam
'Gulliver' (3)	CQua
'Gunwalloe' (11a)	CQua
'Guy Wilson' (2)	EHof
'Gwennap' (1)	CQua
'Gwinear' (2)	CQua
'Halley's Comet' (3)	CQua IRhd
'Halvose' (8)	CBro
'Hambledon' (2) ♀H4	CQua
'Happy Dreams' (2) **new**	IRhd
'Happy Fellow' (2)	CQua EHof
'Harbour View' (2)	IRhd
'Harmony Bells' (5)	CQua
'Harp Music' (2) **new**	IRhd
'Harpers Ferry' (1)	CQua
'Hartlebury' (3)	CQua
* 'Hat' (10)	EHyt
'Hawangi' (3)	IRhd
'Hawera' (5) ♀H4	CAvo CBri CBro CQua EPar EPfP EPot GFlt LAma LRHS MBri MLwd NJOw NRog WHil
'Hazel Rutherford' (2)	GEve
'Heamoor' (4)	CQua
hedraeanthus (13) SG 13	WCot
'Helford Dawn' (2)	CQua
'Helios' (2) **new**	CQua
hellenicus	see *N. poeticus* var. *hellenicus*
henriquesii	see *N. jonquilla* var. *henriquesii*
'Hero' (1)	CQua
'Hesla' (7)	CBro
'Hexameter' (9)	CQua
'High Society' (2) ♀H4	CQua IRhd
'Highfield Beauty' (8) ♀H4	CQua
'Highgrove' (1)	EHof
'Highlite' (2)	CQua
'Hilford' (2)	IRhd
'Hill Head' (9)	IRhd
'Hillstar' (7)	CQua IRhd
'Hocus Pocus' (3) **new**	IRhd
'Holland Sensation' (1)	LAma
'Holly Berry' (2)	CQua
'Hollypark' (3)	IRhd
'Holme Fen' (2)	EHof
'Honey Pink' (2) **new**	CQua
'Honeybird' (1)	CQua
'Honeyorange' (2)	IRhd
'Honolulu' (4)	CQua
'Hoopoe' (8) ♀H4	CBro CQua
'Horace' (9)	CQua
'Horn of Plenty' (5)	CBro CQua
'Hornpipe' (1)	IRhd
'Hors d'Oeuvre' (8)	CBro
'Hospodar' (2) **new**	CQua
'Hot Gossip' (2)	CQua EHof
'Hotspur' (2)	CQua
'Hugh Town' (8)	CQua
'Hullabaloo' (2) **new**	IRhd
'Hunting Caye' (2)	CQua EHof
'Huntley Down' (1)	CQua
'Ice Diamond' (4)	CQua
'Ice Follies' (2) ♀H4	CQua EFam LAma MBri NBir NBlu NRog
'Ice King' (4)	NBir NRog
'Ice Wings' (5) ♀H4	CAvo CBro CQua EPot ERos LRHS MSte WShi
'Idless' (1)	CQua
'Immaculate' (2)	CQua
'Inara' (4)	CQua
'Inca' (6)	CQua
x *incomparabilis*	GIBF
'Independence Day' (4) **new**	CQua

'Indian Chief' (4) EFam
'Indian Maid' (7) CQua
'Indora' (4) CQua
'Inner Glow' (2) IRhd
'Innovator' (4) IRhd
'Inny River' (1) IRhd
'Interim' (2) CQua
§ x *intermedius* (13) CBro CQua ERos
§ - 'Compressus' (8) CQua
'Intrigue' (7) ♀H4 **new** CQua IRhd
'Invercassley' (3) **new** GEve
'Inverpolly' (2) GEve
'Ipi Tombi' (2) ERos
'Ireland's Eye' (9) CQua IRhd
'Irene Copeland' (4) NRog
'Irish Light' (2) CQua
'Irish Linen' (3) CQua
'Isambard' (4) CQua
'Islander' (4) CQua
'Islandhill' (3) IRhd
'Ita' (2) IRhd
'Itzim' (6) ♀H4 CBro CQua ERos
'Jack Snipe' (6) ♀H4 CAvo CBro CNic CQua EPfP EPot
  ERos LAma LRHS MBNS MBri MSte
  NRog WShi
'Jack Wood' (11a) CQua
'Jackadee' (2) IRhd
'Jake' (3) IRhd
'Jamage' (8) CQua
'Jamaica Inn' (4) CQua
'Jambo' (2) IRhd
'Jamestown' (3) IRhd
'Jane Frances' (1) GEve
'Jane MacLennan' (4) GEve
'Janelle' (2) **new** CQua
'Jantje' (11a) CQua
'January Moon' **new** MBri
jeanmonodii (13) WCot
  JCA 701.870
'Jenny' (6) ♀H4 CAvo CBro CQua EPar EPot ERos
  LAma LRHS NBir NRog WShi
'Jersey Pride' **new** MBri
'Jessamy' (10) EHyt
'Jetage' (6) CBro
'Jetfire' (6) ♀H4 CBro CQua EPfP EPot ERos GEve
  GKir LAma LRHS NRog
'Jezebel' (3) CBro
'Johanna' (5) CBro
'John Ballance' (1) IRhd
'John Daniel' (4) CQua
'John's Delight' (3) CQua
jonquilla (13) ♀H4 CAvo CBro CQua EPar EPot ERos
  LAma LPhx LRHS NGar NJOw
  NRog NSla WPGP WShi
§ - var. *henriquesii* (13) CBro CFil CQua LAma SCnR WPGP
'Joppa' (7) CQua
'Joy Bishop' see *N. romieuxii* 'Joy Bishop'
'Joybell' (6) CQua
'Juanita' (2) EPfP
'Jules Verne' (2) CQua
'Julia Jane' see *N. romieuxii* 'Julia Jane'
'Jumblie' (12) ♀H4 CBro CQua EPfP EPot ERos ITim
  LAma LRHS MBri NRog SPer WShi
juncifolius see *N. assoanus*
'June Lake' (2) CQua IRhd
'Kabani' (9) CQua
'Kalimna' (1) **new** CQua
'Kamau' (9) IRhd
'Kamms' (1) **new** CQua
'Kamura' (2) **new** CQua
'Kathleen Munro' (2) GEve
'Kathy's Clown' (6) CQua
'Kaydee' (6) ♀H4 CQua IRhd
'Kea' (6) CQua

'Keats' (4) CBro
'Kebaya' (2) CQua
'Kehelland' (4) CBro
'Kenbane Head' (9) IRhd
'Kenellis' (10) CBro CQua GEdr
'Kernow' (2) CQua
'Kidling' (7) CQua
'Killara' (8) CQua
'Killearnan' (9) CQua
'Killeen' (2) IRhd
'Killigrew' (2) **new** CQua
'Killyleagh' (3) IRhd
'Kilmood' (2) IRhd
'Kiltarn' (2) IRhd
'Kiltonga' (2) IRhd
'Kilworth' (2) CQua EFam LAma
'Kimmeridge' (3) CQua
'King Alfred' (1) CQua EPfP
'King Size' (11a) GEve
'Kinglet' (7) CQua
'King's Grove' (1) ♀H4 CQua IRhd
'Kings Pipe' (2) CQua
'Kingscourt' (1) ♀H4 CQua
'Kirkcubbin' (3) IRhd
'Kissproof' (2) NRog
'Kit Hill' (7) CQua
'Kitten' (6) CQua
'Kitty' (6) CBro ERos
'Kiwi Magic' (4) CQua IRhd
'Kiwi Solstice' (4) **new** CQua
'Kiwi Sunset' (4) CQua
'Kokopelli' (7) CBro
'Korora Bay' (1) IRhd
'Kuantan' (3) EHof
'La Argentina' (2) EFam
'La Riante' (2) CQua
'Ladies' Choice' (7) IRhd
'Lady Ann' (2) IRhd
'Lady Be Good' (2) EHof
'Lady Emily' (2) IRhd
'Lady Eve' (11a) IRhd
'Lady Margaret
  Boscawen' (2) **new** CQua
'Lady Serena' (9) CQua
'Lady's Maid' (2) **new** IRhd
'Lake Tahoe' (2) IRhd
'Lalique' (3) CQua
'Lamanva' (2) CQua
'Lamlash' (2) **new** IRhd
'Lanarth' (7) CBro
'Lancaster' (3) IRhd
'Lapwing' (5) CBro ERos IRhd
'Larkelly' (6) CBro ERos
'Larkhill' (2) CQua
'Larkwhistle' (6) ♀H4 CBro ERos
'Lauren' (3) IRhd
'Lavender Lass' (6) CQua
'Lee Moor' (1) CQua
'Lemon Beauty' (11b) CQua LRHS NRog
'Lemon Drops' (5) ♀H4 CBro ERos MSte
'Lemon Grey' (3) IRhd
'Lemon Heart' (5) CBro
'Lemon Silk' (6) CQua
'Lemon Snow' (2) IRhd
'Lemonade' (3) CQua
'Lennymore' (2) CQua IRhd
'Lewis George' (1) CQua
'Libby' (2) IRhd
'Liberty Bells' (5) CBro CQua EPot LAma LRHS MBri
  NRog
'Life' (7) CQua
'Light Star' (11b) **new** NRog
'Lighthouse' (3) CQua GEve
'Lighthouse Reef' (1) EHof IRhd

'Lilac Charm' (6) — CQua IRhd
'Lilac Hue' (6) — CBro
'Lilac Mist' (2) — EHof
'Limbo' (2) — CQua IRhd
'Limehurst' (2) — CQua
'Limpopo' (3) — IRhd
'Lindsay Joy' (2) — CQua
'Lingerie' (4) ♀H4 — NZep
'Lintie' (7) — CBro CQua ERos LRHS MBri
'Lisbarnett' (3) — IRhd
'Lisnamulligan' (3) — IRhd
'Lisnaruddy' (3) — IRhd
'Little Beauty' (1) ♀H4 — CAvo CBro CQua EPot ERos GFlt
  LAma
'Little Dancer' (1) — CBro CQua
'Little Gem' (1) ♀H4 — CAvo CBro CMea CQua EPot LAma
  NRog
'Little Karoo' (3) — IRhd
'Little Rosie' (2) **new** — IRhd
'Little Sentry' (7) — CBro CQua
'Little Soldier' (10) — CQua
'Little Spell' (1) — CBro LAma
'Little Witch' (6) — CAvo CBro CQua EPot ERos ITim
  LAma LRHS MBri NJOw NRog
  WShi
'Liverpool Festival' (2) — CQua
lobularis — see *N. pseudonarcissus* 'Lobularis'
'Loch Alsh' (3) — IRhd
'Loch Assynt' (3) — CQua GEve
'Loch Brora' (2) — CQua GEve
'Loch Coire' (3) — CQua
'Loch Fada' (2) — CQua
'Loch Hope' (2) — CQua GEve
'Loch Leven' (2) — CQua GEve
'Loch Lundie' (2) — CQua
'Loch Maberry' (2) — CQua
'Loch Naver' (2) — CQua GEve
'Loch Stac' (2) — CQua
'Logan Rock' (7) — CQua
longispathus (13) — SSpi
  MS 546
'Lorikeet' (1) — CQua NZep
'Lothario' (2) — LAma MBri
'Lough Bawn' (2) — GEve
'Lough Gowna' (1) — IRhd
'Lough Ryan' (1) — IRhd
'Loughanisland' (1) — IRhd
'Loveny' (2) — CQua
'Lubaantun' (1) — EHof
'Lucifer' (2) **new** — CQua WShi
'Lucky Chance' (11a) — IRhd
'Lundy Light' (2) — CQua
'Lyrebird' (3) — CQua
'Lyric' (9) — CQua
'Lysander' (2) — CQua
x *macleayi* (13) — CQua
'Madam Speaker' (4) — CQua
'Magician' (2) — IRhd NZep
'Magnet' (1) — LAma MBri NRog
'Magnificence' (1) — LAma
'Majarde' (2) — EFam
'Majestic Star' (1) — CQua
'Malin Head' (5) — IRhd
'Mallee' (11a) — IRhd
'Manaccan' (1) — CQua
'Mangaweka' (6) **new** — CQua
'Manly' (4) ♀H4 — CQua
'Mantle' (2) — CQua
'March Sunshine' (6) — CBro LAma
'Marilyn Anne' (2) **new** — CQua
'Marjorie Treveal' (4) — CQua
'Marlborough' (2) — CQua
'Marlborough Freya' — CQua
  (2) **new**

'Martha Washington' (8) — CBro CQua
'Martinette' (8) — CQua LRHS MBri NRog
marvieri — see *N. rupicola* subsp. *marvieri*
'Mary Copeland' (4) — LAma NRog
'Mary Kate' (2) — CQua IRhd
'Mary Lou' (6) — IRhd
'Mary Schouten' (2) — GEve
'Marzo' (7) — IRhd
'Matador' (8) — CQua IRhd
'Max' (11a) — CQua LAma
'Maya Dynasty' (2) — CQua
'Mayan Gold' (1) — IRhd
'Mazzard' (4) — CQua
'Media Girl' (2) — IRhd
x *medioluteus* (13) — CBro CQua
'Medusa' (8) — CBro
'Melbury' (2) — CQua
'Meldrum' (1) — CQua
'Memento' (1) **new** — CQua
'Menabilly' (4) — CQua
'Men-an-Tol' (2) — CQua
'Menehay' (11a) ♀H4 — CQua IRhd
'Mentor' (2) — GEve
'Mercato' (2) — LAma
'Merida' (2) — IRhd
'Merlin' (3) ♀H4 — CQua GEve LAma
'Merry Bells' (5) — CQua
'Merrymeet' (4) — CQua
'Mexico City' (2) — IRhd
'Michaels Gold' (2) — EHof
'Midas Touch' (1) — CQua
'Midget' — CAvo CBro CMea EPot ERos GEdr
'Mike Pollock' (8) **new** — CQua
'Milan' (9) — CQua
'Millennium' (1) — CBro
'Millennium Sunrise' (2) — CQua
'Millennium Sunset' (2) — CQua
'Minicycla' (6) — CAvo CBro
'minimus* hort. — see *N. asturiensis*
'Minnow' (8) ♀H3 — CAvo CBro CMea CQua EPot ERos
  GFlt LAma LRHS MBri NJOw NRog
  SPer WHil
§ *minor* (13) ♀H4 — CBro CQua ECha LAma WShi
  - 'Douglasbank' (1) — GCrs
  - var. *pumilus* 'Plenus' — see *N.* 'Rip van Winkle'
  - Ulster form — IBlr
'Minute Waltz' (6) — CQua
'Mission Bells' (5) ♀H4 — CQua IRhd
'Mistral' (11) — NRog
'Misty Dawn' (3) — IRhd
'Misty Glen' (2) ♀H4 — CQua GEve
'Mite' (6) ♀H4 — CAvo CBro CMea CQua EPot ERos
  GEdr
'Mitylene' (2) — CQua
'Mockingbird' (7) — IRhd
'Modern Art' (2) — NRog
'Mondragon' (11a) — CQua EFam MBri NRog
'Mongleath' (2) — CQua
'Monks Wood' (1) — EHof
'Monksilver' (3) — CQua
'Montclair' (2) — CQua
'Montego' (3) — CQua
'Monza' (4) — IRhd
'Moon Dream' (1) **new** — CQua
'Moon Ranger' (3) — IRhd
'Moon Rhythm' (4) — IRhd
'Moon Shadow' (3) — IRhd
'Moon Tide' (3) — IRhd
'Moon Valley' (2) — GEve IRhd
'Moonspell' (2) — IRhd
'Moralee' (4) — IRhd
§ *moschatus* (13) ♀H4 — CBro CQua EPot GEdr LAma WCot
'Mother Catherine — EFam
  Grullemans' (2)

'Mount Fuji' (2)	CQua
'Mount Hood' (1) ♀H4	EPfP LAma MBri NBir NRog SPer
'Mount Oriel' (2)	IRhd
'Mount Royal' (2)	IRhd
'Mourneview' (1)	IRhd
'Movie Star' (2)	IRhd
'Mowser' (7)	CQua
'Moyle' (9)	IRhd
'Mrs Langtry' (3)	CQua WShi
'Mrs R.O. Backhouse' (2)	LAma MBri NMyG NRog WShi
'Muirfield' (1)	GEve
'Mullion' (3)	CQua
'Mulroy Bay' (1)	IRhd
'Murlough' (9)	CQua IRhd
'Muscadet' (2)	CQua
'My Sunshine' (2)	EHof
'Naivasha' (2)	IRhd
'Namraj' (2)	CQua
'Nancegollan' (7)	CBro CQua
'Nangiles' (4)	CQua
'Nanpee' (7)	CQua
'Nansidwell' (2)	CQua
'Nanstallon' (1)	CQua
nanus	SGar
'Nederburg' (1)	IRhd
§ *nevadensis* (13)	SBla SSpi
'New Hope' (3)	CQua
'New Life' (3) **new**	CQua
'New-baby' (7)	CQua
'Newcastle' (1)	CQua
'Night Music' (4)	CQua
'Nightcap' (1)	CQua
'Nirvana' (7)	CBro
'Niveth' (5)	CQua
nobilis var. *nobilis* (13)	EPot
'Nonchalant' (3)	CQua IRhd
'Norma Jean' (2)	CQua
'Nor-nor' (2)	CBro ERos
'Northern Sceptre' (2)	IRhd
'Noss Mayo' (6)	CBro CQua
'Notre Dame' (2) ♀H4	IRhd
'Nouvelle' (3)	IRhd
'Numen Rose' (2)	IRhd
Nylon Group (10)	CBro CLAP CNic EPot SSpi WCom
'Obdam' (4)	NRog
'Obelisk' (11a)	CQua
obesus (13)	CLAP EHyt ERos
obvallaris (13) ♀H4	CArn CAvo CBro CQua EPar EPot ERos GBin NJOw NRog SGar WBWf WHer WPnP WShi
'Ocarino' (4)	CQua
'Ocean Blue' (2)	IRhd
x *odorus* (13)	WShi
§ - 'Double Campernelle' (4) WShi	CQua EPar LAma NRog WCot WHil
- 'Rugulosus'	see *N.* 'Rugulosus'
'Odyssey' (4)	IRhd
'Oecumene' (11a)	CQua
old pheasant's eye	see *N. poeticus* var. *recurvus*
'Omaha' (3)	IRhd
'Orange Monarch' (2)	EFam
'Orange Walk' (3)	EHof IRhd
'Orangery' (11a)	EFam LAma LRHS MBri NRog
'Oregon Pioneer' (2)	IRhd
'Ormeau' (2) ♀H4	CQua
'Oryx' (7) ♀H4	CQua IRhd
'Osmington' (2)	CQua
'Ottoman Gold' (2)	IRhd
'Ouma' (1)	CQua
'Outline' (2)	IRhd
'Ouzel' (6)	CQua
'Oykel' (3)	CQua GEve
'Oz' (12)	CBro CQua ERos

'Pacific Rim' (2)	IRhd
'Painted Desert' (3)	CQua
'Pale Sunlight' (2) **new**	CQua
§ *pallidiflorus* (13)	ECha
'Palmares' (11a)	CQua NRog
'Pamela Hubble' (2) **new**	CQua
'Panache' (1)	CQua GEve
'Paper White'	see *N. papyraceus*
'Paper White Grandiflorus' (8)	SPer
'Papillon Blanc' (11b)	LAma NRog
'Papua' (4) ♀H4	CQua
papyraceus (13)	CQua EPfP LAma MBri
'Paradigm' (4)	IRhd
'Parcpat' (7)	CBro
'Parisienne' (11a)	LAma NRog
'Park Springs' (3)	CQua
'Parkdene' (2) **new**	CQua
'Party Time' (2)	IRhd
'Passionale' (2) ♀H4	CQua LAma NBir NRog SPer
'Pastiche' (2)	CQua
'Patabundy' (2)	CQua
'Patois' (9)	IRhd
'Paula Cottell' (3)	CBro
'Pay Day' (1)	CQua
'Peach Prince' (4)	CQua
'Pearlshell' (11a)	CQua GEve
'Peeping Tom' (6) ♀H4	CBro EPar ERos LAma MBri NRog SRms
'Peggy's Gift' (3)	IRhd
'Pencrebar' (4)	CBro CQua EPot ERos LAma LRHS MBri WShi
'Pend Oreille' (3) **new**	CQua
'Pengarth' (2)	CQua
'Penjerrick' (9)	CQua
'Penkivel' (2)	CQua
'Pennance Mill' (2)	CQua
'Pennine Way' (1)	CQua
'Pennyghael' (2)	GEve
'Penpol' (7)	CBro CQua
'Penril' (6)	CQua ERos
'Pentille' (1)	CQua
'Pepper' (2)	CBro
'Pequenita' (7)	CBro
'Percuil' (6)	CQua
'Perdredda' (3)	CQua
'Perimeter' (3)	CQua
'Peripheral Pink' (2)	CQua
§ 'Perlax' (11a)	CQua
'Permissive' (2)	IRhd
'Perseus' (1)	GEve
'Petit Four' (4)	LAma NRog
'Petrel' (5)	CBro CQua EPot LRHS MSte NJOw
'Phalarope' (6)	CQua
'Phantom' (11a)	CQua
'Phil's Gift' (1) **new**	CQua
'Phinda' (2)	IRhd
'Picoblanco' (2)	CBro CQua
'Pink Angel' (7)	CQua
'Pink Champagne' (4)	CQua
'Pink Charm' (2)	NRog
'Pink Flush' (2)	IRhd
'Pink Holly' (11a)	CQua
'Pink Pageant' (4)	CQua IRhd
'Pink Paradise' (4)	CQua IRhd
'Pink Perry' (2)	IRhd
'Pink Silk' (1)	CQua IRhd NZep
'Pink Tango' (11a)	CQua
'Pipe Major' (2)	CQua
'Pipers Barn' (7)	CBro CQua
'Pipestone' (2) **new**	CQua
'Pipit' (7) ♀H4	CAvo CBro CMea CQua EPfP EPot ERos LAma LRHS MNrw NBir NJOw NRog SPer WHil WShi

'Piraeus' (4) — IRhd
'Pismo Beach' (2) — CQua GEve
'Pitchroy' (2) — CQua
poeticus (13) — CAvo LAma LRHS WBWf WHer
§ - var. **hellenicus** (13) — CBro CQua
- old pheasant's eye — see *N. poeticus* var. *recurvus*
- var. **physaloides** (13) — CQua
N - 'Plenus' (4) — CBro CQua EPot GQui WCot WShi
- 'Praecox' (9) — CQua
§ - var. **recurvus** (13) ♀H4 — CArn CBro CQua EPar EPfP EPot LAma NBir SPer WShi
'Poet's Way' (9) — CQua
'Pol Crocan' (2) — CQua IRhd
'Pol Dornie' (2) — CQua
'Pol Voulin' (2) — CQua IRhd
'Polglase' (8) — CBro
'Polly's Pearl' (8) — CQua
'Polnesk' (7) — CBro
'Polwheveral' (2) — CQua
'Pooka' (3) — IRhd
'Poppy's Choice' (4) **new** — CQua
'Pops Legacy' (1) — CQua IRhd
'Port Logan' (3) — IRhd
'Port Patrick' (3) — IRhd
'Port Salon' (3) — IRhd
'Port William' (3) — IRhd
'Portfolio' (1) — IRhd
'Porthchapel' (7) — CQua
'Portrush' (3) — CQua
'Portstewart' (3) — IRhd
'Potential' (1) **new** — CQua
'Powerstock' (2) — IRhd
'Prairie Fire' (3) — CQua IRhd
'Preamble' (1) — CQua IRhd
I 'Precocious' (2) ♀H4 — CQua
'Premiere' (2) — CQua
'Presidential Pink' (2) **new** — CQua
'Pretty Baby' (3) — EHof
'Pride of Cornwall' (8) — CBro
'Primrose Beauty' (4) — CQua
'Princeps' (1) — CQua
'Princess Zaide' (3) — CQua
'Princeton' (3) **new** — CQua
'Prism' (2) — CQua
'Probus' (1) — CQua
'Professor Einstein' (2) — LAma NRog
'Prologue' (1) — CQua
'Prototype' (6) — IRhd
pseudonarcissus (13) ♀H4 — CBro CQua CRow LAma MBow SSpi WBWf WHer WShi
- subsp. **gayi** — see *N. gayi*
§ - 'Lobularis' — CAvo CBro CQua EPar EPot ERos LRHS NRog SPer
- subsp. **moschatus** — see *N. moschatus*
- subsp. **nevadensis** — see *N. nevadensis*
- subsp. **pallidiflorus** — see *N. pallidiflorus*
'Ptolemy' (1) — LRHS
'Pueblo' (7) — CAvo ERos LRHS WShi
pulchellus — see *N. triandrus* subsp. *triandrus* var. *pulchellus*
'Pulsar' (2) — IRhd
pumilus (13) — EPot ERos LRHS
'Punchline' (7) **new** — CQua
'Puppet' (5) — CQua
'Purbeck' (3) ♀H4 — CQua IRhd
'Quail' (7) ♀H4 — CBro CQua EPot ERos LAma LRHS MBri NRog SPer
'Quasar' (2) — CQua GEve NZep
Queen Anne's double daffodil — see *N.* 'Eystettensis'
'Queen's Guard' (1) — IRhd
'Quetzal' (9) — CQua
'Quick Step' (7) — CQua IRhd
'Quiet Hero' (3) — IRhd

'Quiet Waters' (1) — CQua EHof
'Quince' (12) — CBro CQua CSam EPot MSte NRog SPer
'Quirinus' (2) — LAma
radiiflorus var. **poetarum** (13) — CBro
'Radjel' (4) — CQua
'Rainbow' (2) ♀H4 — CQua NRog
'Rame Head' (1) — CQua
'Rameses' (2) — CQua
'Ramore Head' (9) — IRhd
'Rapture' (6) ♀H4 — CQua IRhd
'Raspberry Ring' (2) — CQua
'Ravenhill' (3) — CQua
'Recital' (2) — CQua
'Red Devon' (2) ♀H4 — MBri
'Red Goblet' (2) — LAma
'Red Socks' (6) **new** — CQua
'Reference Point' (2) **new** — GEve
'Refrain' (2) — CQua
'Regal Bliss' (2) — CQua
'Reggae' (6) ♀H4 — CBro CQua IRhd
'Rembrandt' (1) — LAma MBri
'Rendezvous Caye' (2) — EHof
'Replete' (4) — CQua
requienii — see *N. assoanus*
'Ribald' (2) **new** — IRhd
'Ridgecrest' (3) — IRhd
rifanus — see *N. romieuxii* subsp. *romieuxii* var. *rifanus*
'Rijnveld's Early Sensation' (1) ♀H4 — CAvo CBro CMea CQua ERos MBri
'Rikki' (7) — CBro CQua ERos
'Rima' (1) — CQua
'Rimmon' (3) — CQua
'Ring Fence' (3) — IRhd
'Ringhaddy' (3) — IRhd
'Ringing Bells' (5) — CQua
'Ringleader' (2) — CQua
'Ringmaster' (2) — CQua
'Rio Bravo' (2) — IRhd
'Rio Gusto' (2) — IRhd
'Rio Lobo' (2) — IRhd
'Rio Rondo' (2) — IRhd
'Rio Rouge' (2) — IRhd
§ 'Rip van Winkle' (4) — CBro CQua CSWP EPar EPot ERos LAma LRHS MBri MLwd NRog WShi
'Rippling Waters' (5) ♀H4 — CBro CQua EPot ERos LAma LRHS
'Rising Star' (7) — IRhd
'Ristin' (1) — CQua
'Rival' (6) — CQua
'River Dance' (2) — IRhd
'River Queen' (2) — IRhd
'Rockall' (3) — CQua
'Roger' (6) — CBro
'Romance' (2) ♀H4 — LAma
§ 'Romanus' (4) — CQua
§ *romieuxii* (13) ♀H2-3 — CAvo CBro CFil EHyt EPot ERos ITim LRHS NGar SCnR SSpi WAbe WPGP
- JCA 805 — EPot
- subsp. **albidus** (13) — EPot
- - SF 15 — EHyt
- - SF 110 — EHyt
§ - - var. **zaianicus** (13) SB&L 82 — WCot
§ - - - f. **lutescens** (13) — EHyt
- 'Atlas Gold' — EHyt
- 'Joy Bishop' ex JCA 805 (10) — EPot ERos SCnR
§ - 'Julia Jane' ex JCA 805 (10) — EPot ERos GEdr SCnR
- subsp. **romieuxii** var. **mesatlanticus** (13) — CStu EHyt EPot ERos LPhx NGar

– – var. **mesatlanticus**	NGar
x **bulbocodium**	
filifolius	
§ – – var. **rifanus** (13)	SSpi
– 'Treble Chance' (10)	EPot
ex JCA 805	
'Rosannor Gold' (11a)	CQua
'Roscarrick' (6)	CQua
'Rose Gold' (1)	IRhd
'Rose Royale' (2)	CQua
'Rose Umber' (2)	IRhd
'Rosedown' (5)	CBro
'Rosemerryn' (2)	CQua
'Rosevine' (3)	EHof
'Roseworthy' (2)	ERos NRog
'Rossferry' (2)	IRhd
'Rosy Trumpet' (1)	CBro
'Roxton' (4)	IRhd
'Royal Ballet' (2)	CQua
'Royal Connection'	CQua
(8) **new**	
'Royal Dornoch' (1)	GEve
'Royal Marine' (2) **new**	CQua
'Royal Orange' (2)	EFam
'Royal Princess' (3)	CQua
'Royal Regiment' (2)	CQua
'Rubh Mor' (2)	CQua
'Ruby Rose' (4)	IRhd
'Ruby Wedding' (2)	IRhd
'Rubythroat' (2)	CQua
'Rugulosus' (7) ♀H4	CBro EPar ERos LAma NRog
* 'Rugulosus Flore Pleno'	CRez
(d) **new**	
rupicola (13)	CAvo CBro CLAP CWoo ERos GCrs
	MS&S NSla SSpi
§ – subsp. **marvieri**	ERos SSpi
(13) ♀H2	
§ – subsp. **watieri** (13)	CBro EHyt ERos GCrs LPhx MTho
	SCnR
– – AB&S 4518	SSpi
'Rustom Pasha' (2)	CQua
'Rytha' (2)	CQua
'Saberwing' (5)	CQua
'Sabine Hay' (3)	CQua IRhd NRog
'Saint Agnes' (8) **new**	CQua
'Saint Budock' (1)	CQua
'Saint Day' (5)	CQua
'Saint Dilpe' (2)	CQua
'Saint Duthus' (1)	GEve
'Saint Keverne' (2)	CQua LAma NRog
♀H4	
'Saint Keyne' (8)	CQua
'Saint Magnus' (1)	GEve
'Saint Patrick's Day' (2)	CQua LAma NRog SPer
'Saint Piran' (7)	CQua MBri
'Salakee' (2)	CQua
'Salcey Forest' (1) **new**	EHof
'Salome' (2) ♀H4	LAma LRHS MBri NBir NRog
'Salute' (2) **new**	CQua
'Samantha' (4)	CQua
'Samaria' (3)	CBro
'Samba' (5)	ERos
'Sancerre' (11a)	CQua
'Sandycove' (2)	IRhd
'Sandymount' (2) **new**	IRhd
'Sarah' (2)	MBri
'Sargeant's Caye' (1)	EHof
'Satin Pink' (2)	MBri
'Saturn' (3)	CQua
'Savoir Faire' (2)	IRhd
scaberulus (13)	CBro CStu ERos
'Scarlet Chord' (2) **new**	CQua
'Scarlet Elegance' (2)	LAma
'Scarlet Gem' (8)	LAma

'Scarlet Tanager' (2) **new**	CQua
'Scarlett O'Hara' (2)	CQua LAma
'Scented Breeze' (2)	IRhd
'Scrumpy' (2) **new**	EHof
'Sea Dream' (3)	CQua
'Sea Gift' (7)	CBro
'Sea Green' (9)	CQua
'Sea Shanty' (2) **new**	IRhd
'Seagull' (3)	CQua
'Sealing Wax' (2)	CQua
'Segovia' (3) ♀H4	CBro CQua EPot ERos SPer
'Selma Lagerlöf' (2)	EFam
'Sempre Avanti' (2)	LAma MBri NRog
'Sennocke' (5)	CBro
'Seraglio' (3)	CQua
'Serena Beach' (4)	IRhd
'Serena Lodge' (4) ♀H4	IRhd
serotinus (13)	EPot GIBF
'Sextant' (6)	CQua
'Shangani' (2)	IRhd
'Sheelagh Rowan' (2)	CQua EHof IRhd
'Sheer Joy' (6)	IRhd
'Shepherd's Hey' (7)	CQua
'Sherborne' (4)	CQua
'Sherpa' (1)	CQua IRhd
'Sheviock' (2)	CQua
'Shin Falls' (1) **new**	GEve
'Shindig' (2)	IRhd
'Shining Light' (2)	CQua
'Siam' (2)	EFam
'Sidley' (3)	CQua IRhd
'Signorina' (2)	IRhd
'Silent Valley' (1) ♀H4	CQua
'Silk Cut' (2)	CQua
'Silkwood' (3) **new**	CQua
'Silver Bells' (5)	CQua IRhd
'Silver Chimes' (8)	CBro CQua EPfP ERos LAma NBir
	NRog
'Silver Crystal' (3)	IRhd
'Silver Plate' (11a)	CQua
'Silver Sabre' (2)	IRhd
'Silver Shell' (11a) **new**	CQua
'Silver Standard' (2)	CQua
'Silver Surf' (2)	CQua IRhd
'Silversmith' (2)	CQua
'Silverthorne' (3)	CQua
'Silverwood' (3)	CQua IRhd
'Singing Pub' (3)	IRhd
'Sinopel' (3)	LAma
'Sir Watkin' (2)	CQua
'Sir Winston Churchill'	CQua EPfP LAma LRHS NRog SPer
(4) ♀H4	
'Skibo' (2)	GEve
'Skilliwidden' (2)	CQua
'Skywalker' (2)	IRhd
'Slieveboy' (1) **new**	CQua
'Sligachan' (1)	GEve
'Slipstream' (6)	IRhd
'Small Fry' (1)	CQua
'Small Talk' (1)	CAvo CQua
'Smokey Bear' (4)	CQua
'Snoopie' (6)	CQua
'Snow Bunting' (7)	CBro
'Snowcrest' (3)	CQua
'Snowshill' (2)	CQua
'Soft Focus' (2)	IRhd
'Solar System' (3)	IRhd
'Solar Tan' (3)	CQua IRhd
'Soleil d'Or' (8)	MBri
'Soloist' (2) **new**	IRhd
'Solveig's Song'	EHyt EPot
'Sonata' (9)	CQua
'Songket' (2)	CQua
'Soprano' (2)	IRhd

'Trigonometry' (11a)	IRhd
'Tripartite' (11a) ♀H4	CQua GEve NZep
'Triple Crown' (3) ♀H4	CQua IRhd
'Tropic Isle' (4)	CQua
'Tropical Heat' (2)	IRhd
'Trousseau' (1)	CQua
'Troutbeck' (3)	CQua
'Trueblood' (3)	IRhd
'Trumpet Warrior' (4)	CQua IRhd
'Tudor Minstrel' (2)	CQua
'Tuesday's Child' (5) ♀H4	CQua ERos
'Tullynagee' (3)	IRhd
'Turncoat' (6)	CQua
'Tutankhamun' (2)	CQua
'Twink' (4)	CQua
'Tyee' (2)	CQua
'Tyrian Rose' (2)	IRhd
'Tyrone Gold' (1) ♀H4	IRhd
'Tyrree' (1) **new**	IRhd
'Tywara' (1)	EHof
'Ulster Bank' (3)	CQua
'Ulster Bride' (4)	CQua
'Ulster Bullion' (2)	IRhd
'Una Bremner' (2)	GEve
'Uncle Duncan' (1)	CQua EHof IRhd
'Unique' (4) ♀H4	CQua LAma NRog
'Unsurpassable' (1)	LAma NRog
'Urchin' (2)	IRhd
'Utiku' (6)	CQua
'Val d'Incles' (3)	IRhd
'Valdrome' (11a)	CQua MBri
'Valinor' (2)	CQua
'Van Sion'	see *N.* 'Telamonius Plenus'
'Vandyke' (2)	IRhd
'Vanellus' (11a)	IRhd
'Veneration' (1)	CQua
'Verdin' (7)	CQua
'Verger' (3)	LAma MBri
'Vernal Prince' (3) ♀H4	CQua GEve
'Verona' (3) ♀H4	CQua
'Verran Rose' (2)	IRhd
'Vers Libre' (9)	CQua
'Vice-President' (2)	CQua
'Vickie Linn' (6)	IRhd
'Victorious' (2)	CQua
'Vigil' (1) ♀H4	CQua
'Vigilante' (1)	GEve
'Viking' (1) ♀H4	CQua GEve
'Violetta' (2)	CQua
viridiflorus (13)	SSpi
- MS 500	SSpi
'Vulcan' (2) ♀H4	CQua
'W.P. Milner' (1)	CAvo CBro EPot LAma LRHS MBri NMyG NRog WShi
'Wadavers' (2)	CQua
'Waif' (6)	CQua
'Waldorf Astoria' (4)	CQua IRhd
'Walton' (7) **new**	CQua
'War Dance' (3)	IRhd
'Warbler' (6)	CQua LAma
'Watamu' (3)	IRhd
'Waterperry' (7)	CBro LAma NJOw NRog SPer
watieri	see *N. rupicola* subsp. *watieri*
'Wavelength' (3)	IRhd
'Waxwing' (5)	CQua
'Wee Bee' (1)	CQua
'Welcome' (2)	CQua
'Westward' (4)	CQua
'Whang-hi' (6)	CQua ERos
'Wheal Bush' (4) **new**	CQua
'Wheal Coates' (7) ♀H4	CQua
'Wheal Honey' (1)	CQua
'Wheal Jane' (2)	CQua
'Wheal Kitty' (7)	CQua ERos

'Wheatear' (6)	IRhd
'Whetstone' (1)	CQua
'Whipcord' (7)	IRhd
'Whisky Galore' (2)	EHof
'Whisky Mac' (2)	EHof
'White Emperor' (1) **new**	CQua
'White Hill' (2)	IRhd
'White Lady' (3)	CAvo CQua WShi
'White Lion' (4) ♀H4	CQua EFam LAma NRog
'White Marvel' (4)	CQua LRHS
'White Nile' (2)	CQua
'White Star' (1)	CQua IRhd
'Wicklow Hills' (3)	CQua
willkommii (13)	CBro
'Winged Victory' (6)	CQua
'Winholm Jenni' (3)	CQua
'Winifred van Graven' (3) **new**	CQua
'Winter Waltz' (6) **new**	CQua
'Witch Doctor' (3)	IRhd
'Witch Hunt' (4)	IRhd
'Wodan' (2)	EFam
'Woodcock' (6)	CBro CQua
'Woodland Prince' (3)	CQua
'Woodland Star' (3)	CQua
'Woodley Vale' (2)	CQua
'Woolsthorpe' (2)	CQua
'Xit' (3)	CAvo CBro CQua EHyt GCrs SCnR
'Xunantunich' (2)	EHof IRhd
'Yellow Cheerfulness' (4) ♀H4	LAma LRHS MBri NRog
'Yellow Minnow' (8) **new**	CQua
'Yellow Xit' (3)	CQua
'York Minster' (1)	CQua IRhd
'Young American' (1)	CQua
'Young Blood' (2)	CQua IRhd
'Your Grace' (2)	EHof
'Yum-Yum' (3)	IRhd
zaianicus	see *N. romieuxii* subsp. *albidus* var. *zaianicus*
- *lutescens*	see *N. romieuxii* subsp. *albidus* var. *zaianicus* f. *lutescens*
'Zekiah' (1)	CQua

Nardophyllum (Asteraceae)
bryoides	GTou

Nardostachys (Valerianaceae)
grandiflora	CArn GPoy

Nardus (Poaceae)
stricta **new**	CRWN

Narthecium (Melanthiaceae)
ossifragum	WShi

Nassella (Poaceae)
cernua	CBig CBrm EBee EPPr EWsh SWal WRos
lepida	CBig
pulchra	CBig
trichotoma	CBrm CFwr CHrt CMea EBee EBre EHoe EMan EMon EPPr EPla EWsh GFlt LRHS MBNS MCCP SAsh SLim SMac SMrm WDyG WPGP WRos

Nasturtium (Brassicaceae)
officinale	CPrp EMFW SWat WHer

Natal plum see *Carissa macrocarpa*

Nautilocalyx (Gesneriaceae)
pemphidius	WDib

nectarine see *Prunus persica* var. *nectarina*

Nectaroscordum (*Alliaceae*)

bivalve	ERos
§ *siculum*	CArn CAvo CBre CBro CMea CMil EChP ELan EOrc EPar GBBs GFlt LLWP LPhx MBro MLwd NBir NChi NJOw SSvw WBVN WFar WHil WHoo WLin WRHF
- subsp. *bulgaricum*	CBri CBro CFwr CHad ECha EMar EPar EPfP EPot ERos GSki IBlr LPhx LPio LRHS MAvo MDun MNrw MWgw NBid NGHP SAga SSpi WAbb WBrE WCom WCot WCra WTin WWhi
tripedale	CLAP CMea WCot

Neillia (*Rosaceae*)

affinis	ENot GEil LTwo MTis NBid NLar NPro SSpi WBVN WDin WHCG
longiracemosa	see *N. thibetica*
sinensis	CMCN CPle MRav
§ *thibetica*	More than 30 suppliers

Nelumbo (*Nelumbonaceae*)

'Baby Doll' **new**	CDWL
'Chawan Basu' **new**	CDWL
'Debbie Gibson' **new**	CDWL
'Momo Botan' **new**	CDWL
'Mrs Perry D. Slocum' **new**	CDWL
nucifera 'Shiroman' **new**	CDWL

Nematanthus (*Gesneriaceae*)

'Apres'	WDib
'Black Magic'	CHal WDib
'Christmas Holly'	WDib
'Freckles'	WDib
§ *gregarius* ♀H1	CHal EBak WDib
- 'Golden West' (v)	CHal WDib
- 'Variegatus'	see *N. gregarius* 'Golden West'
radicans	see *N. gregarius*
'Tropicana' ♀H1	CHal WDib

Nemesia (*Scrophulariaceae*)

'Amélie' **new**	COtt EBre SPer SPoG
Aromatica Series	LIck
Aromatica Deep Blue = 'Balardeblu' **new**	
- Aromatica Light Pink = 'Balarlipi' **new**	LIck
- Aromatica Rose Pink = 'Balarropi' **new**	LIck
- Aromatica White = 'Balarwhit' **new**	LIck NPri
Blue Cloud = 'Penblu' ♀H3	SAga
Blue Lagoon = 'Pengoon' PBR (Maritana Series)	ENor LAst SCoo WShp
Bluebird = 'Hubbird' PBR	CHll NPri
§ *caerulea*	ECtt MTho WPer
- 'Joan Wilder' (clonal)	ECtt EMan WEas WSPU
N - 'Joan Wilder' (seed raised)	see *N. caerulea* lilac/blue
§ - lilac/blue	WPer
Candy Girl = 'Pencand' PBR (Maritana Series)	SCoo
'Delphi'	EOrc
§ *denticulata* ♀H3-4	CElw CHal CHar CWCL ECtt EOrc EPfP IHMM LAst LHop LRHS MAvo MBNS MTis NBlu SAga SCoo SGar SMrm SRms SRob WBrE WFar WFoF WGwG WWeb

- 'Confetti'	see *N. denticulata*
foetens	see *N. caerulea*
'Fragrant Cloud' PBR	CChe EBee EChP ELan EOrc EPfP LRHS MCCP MNrw SPla WShp
fruticans misapplied	see *N. caerulea*
Honey Girl = 'Penhon' PBR (Maritana Series)	SCoo
'Innocence' ♀H3	CHal COIW EBee EMan EOrc LAst LHop MAvo WCot WGwG
Karoo Blue = 'Innkablue'	CSpe SCoo
Karoo Pink = 'Innkapink'	NPri
Melanie = 'Fleuron' PBR ♀H3	EPfP LRHS
'Orchard Blue'	EBee EOrc EPfP MAvo
'Pippa Manby' **new**	LAst
'Rose Wings'	EPfP
Sugar Girl = 'Pensug' PBR (Maritana Series)	WShp
sylvatica	CSpe
'Tanith's Treasure' **new**	EMan
umbonata hort.	see *N. caerulea* lilac/blue
'Vanilla Mist'	ENor EPfP MAsh
'White Wings' PBR	EPfP

Nemopanthus (*Aquifoliaceae*)

mucronatus	CPle

Nemophila (*Hydrophyllaceae*)

menziesii 'Penny Black' **new**	CSpe

Neodypsis (*Arecaceae*)

decaryi	see *Dypsis decaryi*

Neolitsea (*Lauraceae*)

glauca	see *N. sericea*
§ *sericea*	CBcs CHEx SSpi

Neomarica (*Iridaceae*)

caerulea **new**	CDes
gracilis	WCot WPGP

Neopanax see *Pseudopanax*

Neopaxia (*Portulacaceae*)

§ *australasica*	ECou
- 'Kosciusko'	GGar
- 'Lyndon'	ECou
- 'Ohau'	ECou

Neoregelia (*Bromeliaceae*)

carolinae	MBri
§ - - 'Flandria' (v)	MBri
- - 'Meyendorffii'	MBri
- f. *tricolor* (v) ♀H1	CHal MBri
§ Claret Group	MBri
marmorata ♀H1	ESlt

Neotinea (*Orchidaceae*)

maculata	WCot

Neottianthe (*Orchidaceae*)

cucullata	EFEx

Nepenthes (*Nepenthaceae*)

alata	CSWC
alata x *ventricosa*	SHmp
ampullaria **new**	CSWC
bicalcarata **new**	CSWC
x *coccinea*	MBri
fusca **new**	CSWC
fusca x *maxima*	SHmp
§ x *hookeriana*	CSWC

	khasiana	SHmp
	maxima x *mixta*	SHmp
	rafflesiana	CSWC
	sanguinea	SHmp
	spectabilis	SHmp
	stenophylla	SHmp

Nepeta (*Lamiaceae*)

	RCB/TQ H-6	WCot
§	*argolica*	EBee MSte
	'Bide-a-wee Variegated' (v)	NBid
	'Blue Beauty'	see *N. sibirica* 'Souvenir d'André Chaudron'
	bucharica	GBuc GFlt WOut
*	*buddlejifolium*	NLar
	camphorata	GBar GTou MLLN MNrw MSte SAga SGar SIde WOut
	cataria	CArn CPrp CSev EBee ELau GBar GPoy MBow MHer MSal MWrn NBro NGHP NPri SCro SECG SIde WHer WMoo WPer WSel WWye XPep
§	– 'Citriodora'	CArn CBri CHar CPrp EBee ELan ELau EWTr GBBs GBar GPoy MBow MHer MSal NVic SChu SIde WBar WBea WCHb WCom WHHs WHer WHil WSSM WSel
	citriodora Dum.	see *N. cataria* 'Citriodora'
	clarkei	CBri CStr EBee EFou EMan EPPr GEil LPhx MDKP MMHG MNrw MSte MWrn NBPC NCGa SAga SBla SBod SIde SMac SWat WCom WCot WPer WSSM WWhi
	'Dropmore'	EBee XPep
§	x *faassenii* ♀H4	More than 30 suppliers
	– 'Alba'	CBri COlW CStr EBee ECtt EPfP NGHP NLar WBea WHil WMnd
	glechoma 'Variegata'	see *Glechoma hederacea* 'Variegata'
	'Gottfried Kühn'	GBar
	govaniana	More than 30 suppliers
	grandiflora	EBee EFou EWsh MRav SBla SIde WFar WHer WOut
	– 'Blue Danube' **new**	NDov
	– 'Bramdean'	CMea CPrp CSam CStr EBee EMan LPhx MBri NDov SAga SCro SUsu WKif WOut
	– 'Dawn to Dusk'	More than 30 suppliers
	– 'Pool Bank'	CStr EBee ECtt EGoo EMan NCGa SChu SCro SGar SIde SUsu
	hederacea 'Variegata'	see *Glechoma hederacea* 'Variegata'
	italica	CBri EBee MAnH SBla SHar SIde
*	*kubabiana*	EBee
	kubanica	EMan LPhx
	laevigata	EBee
	lanceolata	see *N. nepetella*
	latifolia	EBee LPhx MLLN SIde
	'Lilac Cloud'	NBir
*	*longipes* hort.	More than 30 suppliers
	macrantha	see *N. sibirica*
	melissifolia	EBee MHer WCHb WOut WPer WWye XPep
	mussinii Spreng.	see *N. racemosa*
	mussinii hort.	see *N.* x *faassenii*
§	*nepetella*	EBee GBri NBir NChi WFar WOut WPer
	nervosa	More than 30 suppliers
	– 'Blue Carpet'	GCal
	– 'Forncett Select'	CSam EBee EFou EMan NDov NGar SDys SMrm
§	*nuda*	CBri CSam EBee EChP ECha ECtt EMan LDai MDKP MLLN SIde WCAu WFar WMnd XPep
	– subsp. *albiflora*	CBri ECha
*	– 'Anne's Choice'	EBee MSte
*	– 'Grandiflora'	NLar WMoo WPic
	– 'Isis'	EBee EFou
	– subsp. *nuda*	CBre
	pannonica	see *N. nuda*
	parnassica	CBri CSam CStr EBee EChP ECoo EMan EPPr EWTr GBBs GBar LRHS MAnH MWgw MWrn NBPC NCGa NLar SAga SIde SMad SPet WBri WCot WHer WMoo WPic WWhi XPep
	phyllochlamys	CPBP EBee
	'Porzellan'	CPrp CStr EBee EBre ECGP EChP EFou EMan LAst MMil MSte NCGa SAga SMrm SVil
§	*prattii*	CBri CM&M EBee EChP ECoo ERou MSPs NBPC NCGa SBod SIde SMrm SPoG STes WPer
	– SBQE 903	EPPr
§	*racemosa* ♀H4	CArn CBot COlW CSBt CSev EBee EBre ELau EPfP GBar GKir LRHS MRav NBlu SIde WMoo WWin WWye XPep
	– *alba*	WFar
	– 'Blue Ice'	GBuc SIde
	– 'Grog'	CBri CStr EBee EOMN SIde
	– 'Leporello' (v) **new**	EPPr
	– 'Little Titch'	CBri CPrp EBee EBre EFou EMan EPPr EWTr GCal LAst LRHS MSte NLar SAga SChu SIde SMrm SPla SSpe SWat WFar WHil WOut WRHF WSHC WWeb
	– 'Snowflake'	CBri CMea CPrp EBre EFou ELan EPfP GCal GKir LRHS MAnH MHer MSte NBir NBrk SChu SIde SPer SPla STes SUsu SWvt WCAu WCom WFar WGwG WHHs WSel WShp XPep
§	– 'Superba'	EFou EMon GBuc WHoo
	– 'Walker's Low'	More than 30 suppliers
	reichenbachiana	see *N. racemosa*
§	*sibirica*	CBri EBlw ECGN ECha EFou ELan ELau EPfP EWTr GBBs GKir LRHS MAnH MHer MNrw MRav MWrn NBid NDov NPri SChu SCro SIgm WCot WFar WHal WPer
	– 'Souvenir d'André Chaudron'	More than 30 suppliers
	sibthorpii	see *N. argolica*
	sintenisii	CSWP IFro
	'Six Hills Giant'	More than 30 suppliers
	stewartiana	CBri CPom CStr EChP EPPr GBuc LDai MLLN MWrn NLar STes WHoo WMoo WOut WSan
	– ACE 1611	EBee GBuc SMrm
	– BWJ 7999	WCru
	– CLD 551	EMan
	subsessilis	More than 30 suppliers
	– pink	CSam CStr EBre ECha EGle GBuc GEil MAnH MAvo MLLN MSte SAga SBla
	– 'Sweet Dreams'	CBri CHar EBee ECGP EChP EOMN GBri MDKP NGby NLar SHar SSvw WFar WOut WWeb
	– var. *yesoensis*	CPlt
	tenuifolia	EBee MSal
	transcaucasica	CArn CStr EBee WOut
	– 'Blue Infinity'	EFou EWTr NArg NPPs SMac
	troodii	CBri EMan SIde
	tuberosa	CBri CSam CSpe CStr EBee EChP ECha ECoo EMan GBri LRHS MAnH MHer MRav MWrn NBPC

	SBla SChu SIde STes WCot WPic WWye XPep
yunnanensis	EBee EMan MAnH SOkh

Nephrolepis (*Oleandraceae*)

cordifolia	GQui MBri NMar
exaltata ♀H2	EFtx ERea LRHS
- 'Bostoniensis'	MBri
- 'Smithii'	MBri
- 'Smithii Linda'	MBri
- 'Teddy Junior'	MBri
- 'Todeoides'	NMar
- 'Whitmanii Improved'	NMar

Nephrophyllidium (*Menyanthaceae*)

crista-galli	IBlr

Nerine ✿ (*Amaryllidaceae*)

from Lime Close	LPhx
'Administrator'	SSpr
'Afterglow'	LAma MBNS SSpr
'Airies'	SSpr
'Albivetta' **new**	EBee
'Alexandra'	SSpr
'Amalfi'	SSpr
'Angelico'	SSpr
'Atlanta'	SSpr
'Audrey'	WCot
'Baghdad'	SSpr
'Belladonna'	SSpr
'Berlioz'	SSpr
'Blanchefleur'	SSpr
bowdenii ♀H3-4	More than 30 suppliers
- 'Alba'	CBro ECha ELan LRHS SCoo
- 'Codora' **new**	SPer
- 'E.B.Anderson' **new**	WCot
- 'Manina'	EBee SSpr WCot
- 'Mark Fenwick'	CAvo CBcs CBro EBee ECha WCot WOld
- 'Marnie Rogerson'	CBro WCot
§ - 'Mollie Cowie' (v)	EMon GCal IBlr MAvo MTed WCot WCru
- 'Pink Triumph'	CAbP CBcs CFwr CLyd EBee EBla EMan EPAt EPyc GBuc GQui IBlr LAma LRHS MSte NRog SChr SDeJ SPer SPla WCot WDav WHoo
- 'Quinton Wells'	LPhx
- 'Regina' **new**	SSpr
- 'Variegata'	see *N. bowdenii* 'Mollie Cowie'
- 'Wellsii'	CDes CMil EBee EMan WCot WLFP
'Brahms'	SSpr
'Branstone'	SSpr
'Canasta'	SSpr
'Cardinal'	SSpr
'Carisbrooke'	SSpr
'Carnival'	SSpr
'Caroline'	SSpr
'Catherine'	SSpr
'Clarabel'	SSpr
'Clarissa'	SSpr
'Clent Charm'	SSpr
corusca 'Major'	see *N. sarniensis* var. *corusca*
crispa	see *N. undulata*
'Curiosity'	SSpr
'Cynthia Chance'	SSpr
'Dame Alice Godman'	SSpr
'Darius'	SSpr
'Drucilla'	SSpr
'Dunkirk'	SSpr
'Elspeth'	SSpr
'Eve'	SSpr
'Ffiske'	SSpr
filamentosa	CBro

filifolia	CPen EBee EHyt EPot ERos GCal ITim MNrw WCot
flexuosa	GSki MRav SSpr WViv
- 'Alba'	CBro CPne EBee ECha EPot EWTr GSki LAma LPhx LRHS MRav SDeJ SSpr WCot WViv
'Fortune'	SSpr
'Fucine'	CDes
'Gaby Deslys'	SSpr
'Glensavage Gem'	SSpr
'Gloaming'	SSpr
'Goya'	SSpr
'Hamlet'	SSpr
'Harlequin'	SSpr
'Harry Dalton'	SSpr
'Hawaii'	SSpr
'Helen Smith'	SSpr
'Helena'	SSpr
'Hera'	CBro EMon LPhx MBri MSte
humilis	CStu WCot
'Inchmery Kate'	SSpr
innominata	SSpr
'Janet'	SSpr
'Jenny Wren'	SSpr
'Jill'	SSpr
'Joan'	SSpr
'Judith'	SSpr
'Juliet Berkeley'	SSpr
'Kasmir'	SSpr
'Kilwa'	SSpr
'King Leopold'	SSpr
'King of the Belgians'	GAbr LAma WCot
'Kingship'	SSpr
'Kola'	SSpr
'Konak'	SSpr
'Koriba'	SSpr
'Kymina'	SSpr
'Kyoto'	SSpr
'Kyrie'	SSpr
'Lady Cynthia Colville'	SSpr
'Lady Eleanor Keane'	SSpr
'Lambourne'	SSpr
laticoma	WCot
'Latu'	SSpr
'Lawlord'	SSpr
'Leila Hughes'	SSpr
'Locharber'	SSpr
'Lord Grenfell'	IBlr
'Lucinda'	SSpr
'Lyndhurst Salmon'	SSpr
'Mandarin'	SSpr
'Mansellii'	CBro SSpr
'Maria'	SSpr WCot
masoniorum	CBro CStu EBee EHyt ERos MTho NMen SChr WCot
'Meadowbankii'	SSpr
'Miss Cator' **new**	WCot
'Miss Edith Godman'	SSpr
'Monet'	SSpr
'Mrs Goldsmith'	SSpr
'Natasha'	SSpr
'Noreen'	SSpr
'Oberon'	SSpr
'Orange Queen'	SSpr
'Osborne'	SSpr
peersii	WCot
'Penelope'	SSpr
'Pink Galore'	SSpr
'Plain Jane'	SSpr
'Plymouth'	SChr SSpr
pudica	WCot
'Quarr'	SSpr
'Red Pimpernel'	GAbr LAma MBNS
'Rembrandt'	SSpr

'Rose Godman'   SSpr
'Rushmere Star'   SChr SSpr
'Salmonia'   SSpr
sarniensis ♀H2-3   CBro CFwr ECha LRHS MSte NRog
                               WDav
* - 'Alba'   WCot
§ - var. *corusca*   CStu LAma
  - - 'Major'   SChr SSpr WCot
  - var. *curvifolia*   SSpr WCot
    f. *fothergillii*
  - 'Mottistone'   SSpr
'Smokey Special'   SSpr
'Snowflake'   SSpr
'Solent Swan'   SSpr
'Springbank Alice'   SSpr
'Springbank Matthew'   SSpr
'Stephanie'   EShb LAma LRHS SPer SSpr WDav
'Stephanie' x 'Moscow'   SSpr
§ *undulata*   CBgR CBro CFwr CSut ECha EPot
                               ERos LAma LPhx LRHS MBri MSte
                               WCot WHil WViv
'Vestal'   SSpr
'White Swan'   LAma MBNS SSpr
'Wolsey'   SSpr
'Yaverland'   SSpr
'Zeal Candy Stripe' **new**   CFir
'Zeal Giant' ♀H3-4   CAvo CBro CFir GCal LPhx NGby
'Zeal Silver Stripe' **new**   CFir

Nerium ✿ (*Apocynaceae*)

oleander   CAbb CArn CHEx CMdw CTri
                               EBak ELan LPan LRHS MJnS MTis
                               SArc SRms WMul
  - 'Agnes Campbell' **new**   XPep
* - 'Alassio' **new**   XPep
  - 'Album Maximum' **new**   XPep
  - 'Album Plenum' (d)   SGar XPep
* - 'Almodovar' **new**   XPep
  - 'Alsace'   XPep
  - 'Altini'   XPep
  - 'Angiolo Pucci'   XPep
* - 'Apache' **new**   XPep
* - 'Aquarelle' **new**   XPep
* - 'Arad' **new**   XPep
* - 'Aramis' (d) **new**   XPep
* - 'Argunista' **new**   XPep
* - 'Arizona' **new**   XPep
* - 'Art Déco' **new**   XPep
* - 'Atlas' **new**   XPep
* - 'Barcelona' **new**   XPep
  - 'Belle Hélène'   XPep
  - 'Calypso' **new**   XPep
* - 'Campane' **new**   XPep
  - 'Cap Saint Vincent' **new** XPep
§ - 'Carneum Plenum' (d)   XPep
* - 'Caro' **new**   XPep
  - 'Cavalaire' (d)   XPep
* - 'Cheyenne' **new**   XPep
* - 'Christine' **new**   XPep
  - 'Clare'   SOWG
* - 'Claudia' **new**   XPep
  - 'Commandant   XPep
    Barthélemy' **new**
  - 'Cornouailles'   XPep
* - 'Dimona' **new**   XPep
  - 'Dottore Attilio   XPep
    Ragionieri' **new**
  - 'East End Pink' **new**   XPep
  - 'Ed Barr' **new**   XPep
* - 'Elat' **new**   XPep
  - 'Emile Sahut'   XPep
* - 'Eole' **new**   XPep
  - 'Eugenia Fowler'   XPep
    (d) **new**

* - 'Feuille d'Eucalyptus'   XPep
    new
* - 'Fiesta Pienk' **new**   XPep
* - 'Fiesta Rodi' **new**   XPep
  - 'Flavescens Plenum' (d)   XPep
  - 'Framboise'   XPep
* - 'Galipette' (d) **new**   XPep
* - 'Garlaban' **new**   XPep
  - 'Géant des Batailles' (d) SOWG
  - 'General Pershing'   XPep
    (d) **new**
  - 'Grandiflorum' **new**   XPep
* - 'Haïfa' **new**   XPep
  - 'Hardy Red'   XPep
* - 'Harriet Newding' **new** XPep
  - 'Hawaii'   XPep
* - 'Icare' **new**   XPep
* - subsp. *indicum* **new**   XPep
  - 'Isle of Capri'   SOWG XPep
  - 'Italia'   XPep
  - 'J.R.'   XPep
* - 'Jack'line' **new**   XPep
  - 'Jannoch'   XPep
* - 'Jardin du Luxembourg'   XPep
    new
* - 'Jordan Valley' **new**   XPep
* - 'La Fontaine' **new**   XPep
  - 'Lady Kate' **new**   XPep
  - 'Lane Taylor Sealy' **new** XPep
* - 'Lisou' **new**   XPep
  - 'Louis Pouget' (d)   XPep
  - 'Madame Allen' (d)   XPep
* - 'Madame de Billy' **new** XPep
  - 'Magaly'   XPep
  - 'Maguelone' **new**   XPep
* - 'Mainate' **new**   XPep
  - 'Maresciallo Graziani'   XPep
  - 'Margaritha'   XPep
  - 'Marie Gambetta'   XPep
  - 'Marie Mauron' **new**   XPep
  - subsp. *mascatense*   XPep
* - 'Massif de l'Etoile' **new** XPep
* - 'Maurin des Maures' **new** XPep
* - 'Mer Egée' **new**   XPep
  - 'Minouche' **new**   XPep
* - 'Mishna' **new**   XPep
  - 'Mont Blanc'   XPep
  - 'Mont Rose' **new**   XPep
* - 'Monts Saint Cyr' **new** XPep
  - 'Moshav' **new**   XPep
  - 'Mrs Burton' (d) **new**   XPep
  - 'Mrs Magnolia Willis   XPep
    Sealy' (d) **new**
  - 'Mrs Roeding'   see *N. oleander* 'Carneum Plenum'
  - 'Mrs Swanson' (d) **new** XPep
  - 'Mrs Trueheart' **new**   XPep
  - 'Mrs Willard Cooke' **new** XPep
  - 'Nana Rosso'   XPep
* - 'Natou' **new**   XPep
  - 'Navajo'   XPep
* - 'Neguev' **new**   XPep
* - 'Nomade' **new**   XPep
  - 'Oasis'   XPep
  - subsp. *oleander*   XPep
* - 'Osiris' **new**   XPep
  - 'Papa Gambetta'   XPep
* - 'Pasadena' **new**   XPep
  - 'Petite Pink'   XPep
  - 'Petite Red'   XPep
  - 'Petite Salmon'   XPep
* - 'Petite White' **new**   XPep
* - 'Pietra Ligure' **new**   XPep
  - 'Pink Beauty' **new**   XPep
* - 'Pirate Des Caraïbes' **new** XPep

- 'Porto' **new** — XPep
- 'Professeur Granel' (d) — XPep
- 'Professeur Parlatore' **new** — XPep
- 'Provence' (d) — SOWG XPep
* - 'Rivage' **new** — XPep
- 'Rosa Bartolini' **new** — XPep
- 'Rosario' (d) — XPep
- 'Rose des Borrels' — XPep
* - 'Rose des Vents' (d) **new** — XPep
- 'Rosée du Ventoux' (d) — SOWG
- 'Roscum Plenum' (d) — CRHN XPep
- 'Rosita' — XPep
* - 'Rossignol' **new** — XPep
* - 'Rubis' (d) **new** — XPep
* - 'Sabra' **new** — XPep
* - 'Sainte Beaume' **new** — XPep
* - 'Sainte Victoire' **new** — XPep
* - 'Santa Fe' **new** — XPep
* - 'Sausalito' **new** — XPep
- 'Scarlet Beauty' **new** — XPep
- 'Sealy Pink' — XPep
* - 'Simie' **new** — XPep
* - 'Snowflake' — SOWG
- 'Soeur Agnès' (d) — XPep
- 'Soeur Elisabeth' (d) **new** — XPep
- 'Soleil Levant' — XPep
* - 'Solfège' **new** — XPep
* - 'Sophie' **new** — XPep
- 'Souvenir d'Emma Schneider' — XPep
- 'Souvenir des Iles Canaries' — XPep
- 'Splendens' (d) — SOWG
- 'Splendens Foliis Variegatis' (d) **new** — XPep
- 'Splendens Giganteum' (d) — XPep
* - 'Tamouré' (d) **new** — XPep
* - 'Tavira' **new** — XPep
- 'Tiberias' **new** — XPep
- 'Tito Poggi' — XPep
* - 'Toulouse' **new** — XPep
- 'Variegatum' (v) ♀H1+3 — CBot
- 'Variegatum Plenum' (d/v) — WCot
* - 'Vénus' **new** — XPep
- 'Villa Romaine' — XPep
* - 'Ville d'Aubagne' **new** — XPep
- 'Ville de Carpentras' (d) — XPep
- 'Virginie' **new** — XPep
* - 'Zoulou' **new** — XPep

Nertera (Rubiaceae)
- **balfouriana** — ECou
- **granadensis** — MBri

Neviusia (Rosaceae)
- **alabamensis** — NLar WWes

Nicandra (Solanaceae)
- **physalodes** — CArn EMan EWll MGol MSal SYvo WRos
* - 'Blacky' — SMrm
- 'Splash of Cream' (v) — EMan EWll WWpP
- 'Violacea' — CSpe GGar SRms SWvt

Nicotiana (Solanaceae)
- **alata** 'Grandiflora' **new** — LRav
- **glauca** — CHll CPLG EBee EMan LRav MGol MOak MSte SDnm SSte
- **knightiana** — CSpe CTCP WEas
- **langsdorffii** ♀H3 — CBcs CBri CHad CHrt EBee EBla EMan EMon GBri LPio MGol SDnm SMrm SPet SUsu WEas

- 'Cream Splash' (v) — CPla EBee EChP EMon WBar
- 'Lime Green' ♀H3 — CSpe
- **longiflora** — CStr
* **mutabilis** — CHll CSpe EBee WPGP
- **quadrivalvis** var. **bigelovii** — MGol
- **rustica** — MGol
- **suaveolens** — CBre
- **sylvestris** ♀H3 — CBri CHad CSpe CStr EBee EIan EMan EPfP EWTr LPVe MAnH MGol MOak SDnm SEND SMrm SWvt WEas WHer WWhi WWye
- **tabacum** — CArn MGol

Nidorella (Asteraceae)
- **auriculata** — CTrC

Nidularium (Bromeliaceae)
- **flandria** — see *Neoregelia carolinae* (Meyendorffii Group) 'Flandria'

x *Niduregelia* (Bromeliaceae)
§ 'Surprise' — MBri

Nierembergia (Solanaceae)
- **caerulea** — see *N. linariifolia*
- **frutescens** — see *N. scoparia*
- **hippomanica** — see *N. linariifolia*
§ **linariifolia** ♀H1 — CAbP EBee ECha EHrv EMan
§ **repens** — CFee EBre ECGP EDAr EMlt EPot GKir LRHS NLAp NLar WWin
- **rivularis** — see *N. repens*
§ **scoparia** — LPhx NFla SScr XPep
- 'Mont Blanc' — LRHS
- 'Purple Robe' — LRHS

Nigella (Ranunculaceae)
- **sativa** — WJek

Nipponanthemum (Asteraceae)
§ **nipponicum** — CDes CNic EBee GCal GMac LAst LPio MNrw NJOw NSti SMrm SRms WCot WTin

Noccaea see *Thlaspi*

Nolina (Dracaenaceae)
- **beldingii** — SIgm
- **bigelowii** — CBrP
- **brevifolia** — SIgm
- **greenii** — SIgm
- **longifolia** — EOas
- **microcarpa** — XPep
- **palmeri** — SIgm
§ **recurvata** ♀H1 — CTrC EOas EUJe LPal MBri
- **stricta** — EOas
- **texana** — CTrC NWCA SIgm

Nomocharis (Liliaceae)
- **aperta** — EBee EHyt EPot GBuc GCrs GEdr GFlt GKev GKir ITim LAma SSpi WCru WLin
- CLD 229 — GBuc GKir
- **basilissa** — EBee
- **farreri** — EBee EPot GCrs GEdr GKir WCru
- **mairei** — see *N. pardanthina*
- **meleagrina** — EBee EPot GBuc GEdr LAma
- **nana** — see *Lilium nanum*
- **oxypetala** — see *Lilium oxypetalum*
§ **pardanthina** — EMan GBuc GGGa GMac LAma NSla WAbe WCru
- f. **punctulata** — GBuc GGGa GKir WCru
- **saluenensis** — EBee GGGa GTou ITim WAbe WCru

Nonea (Boraginaceae)

intermedia **new**	CTCP
lutea	CBri EChP ECoo GFlt MFir MLLN NOrc NSti WCHb WHal WRos WSSM WWye

Nothochelone see *Penstemon*

Nothofagus ✿ (Fagaceae)

§ x *alpina*	CLnd CMCN GKir NWea WMou WNor
antarctica	CBcs CCVT CLnd CMCN CTho ECrN ELan EPfP EWTr IArd ISea LBuc LPan LRHS MBar MBlu MBri MGos NBee NPal NWea SBLw SKee SPer STre WDin WFar WNor WPGP
cunninghamii	GGGa IArd IDee ISea STre WNor
dombeyi	CDoC CDul CLnd CTho IDee ISea LHyd LRHS SAPC SArc SSpi WNor
fusca	CAbb CBcs CDoC CTrC MGos
menziesii	CAbb CBcs CDul CTrC WPGP
§ nervosa	CDul GTSp IDee LRHS SKee WDin
obliqua	CBcs CDoC CDul CLnd CMCN ECrN GTSp NBee NWea WDin WMou WNor
procera misapplied	see *N.* x *alpina*
procera Oerst.	see *N. nervosa*
solanderi	CAbb CTrC
- var. *cliffortioides*	CBcs WCwm

Notholaena see *Cheilanthes*

Notholirion (Liliaceae)

bulbuliferum	EBee GKir WAbe WCot
campanulatum	EBee LPhx
macrophyllum	EBee EPot GBuc GEdr NLar
thomsonianum	GCrs

Nothopanax see *Polyscias*

Nothoscordum (Alliaceae)

bivalve	CStu
gracile	CFir EBee
inodorum	GBuc
neriniflorum	see *Caloscordum neriniflorum*

Notobuxus (Buxaceae)

natalensis	SLan

Notospartium (Papilionaceae)

carmichaeliae	ECou
- 'Hodder'	ECou
- 'Seymour'	ECou
glabrescens	ECou
- 'Ben More'	ECou
- 'Woodside'	ECou
'Joy'	ECou
torulosum	ECou
- 'Blue Butterfly'	ECou
- 'Malvern Hills'	ECou
torulosum x glabrescens	ECou

Nuphar (Nymphaeaceae)

advenum **new**	LPBA
japonica	CDWL
- var. *variegata* (v)	CRow
lutea	CDWL CRow EHon EMFW EPAt LNCo LPBA MSta NArg SCoo SLon SWat WFar
- subsp. *advena*	EMFW
pumila	MSta
* - *variegata* (v)	MSta

Nuxia (Buddlejaceae)

floribunda **new**	EShb

Nylandtia (Polygalaceae)

spinosa	SPlb

Nymphaea ✿ (Nymphaeaceae)

'Afterglow' (T/D)	CDWL
alba (H)	CBen CRWN CRow CWat EHon EMFW EPAt EPfP LNCo LPBA MSta NArg NBlu SCoo SWat WFar WMAq WStl
§ - subsp. *occidentalis* (H)	MSta
'Alba Plenissima' (H)	MSta
alba var. *rubra* (H)	MSta
'Albatros' Latour-Marliac (H)	CDWL EPAt LNCo LPBA MSta SWat WBcn
'Albatros' misapplied	see *N.* 'Hermine'
* 'Albida' **new**	CDWL
'Amabilis' (H)	CBen CDWL CRow EMFW LPBA MSta SWat WBcn WMAq
'American Star' (H)	CWat EMFW MSta SWat WMAq
'Andreana' (H)	CDWL CWat LPBA MSta SWat
'Arabian Nights' (T/D) **new**	CDWL
'Arc-en-ciel' (H)	CDWL LPBA MSta SCoo SWat WMAq
'Arethusa' (H)	LPBA MSta
'Atropurpurea' (H)	CBen CDWL EMFW LPBA MSta SWat WBcn WMAq
'Attraction' (H)	CBen CDWL CRow EHon EMFW EPAt LNCo LPBA MCCP MSta NBlu NPer SCoo SWat WMAq
'Aurora' (H)	CDWL EMFW EPAt LPBA MSta SWat WMAq
'Barbara Davies' (H) **new**	MSta
'Barbara Dobbins' (H)	CDWL MSta
'Baroness Orczy' (H)	MSta
'Bateau' (H)	MSta
'Berit Strawn' (H)	CDWL EMFW
'Berthold' (H)	CBen MSta
'Blue Beauty' (T/D)	CBen
'Blue Horizon' (T/D) **new**	CDWL
'Bory de Saint-Vincent' (H)	MSta
'Brakeleyi Rosea' (H)	LPBA MSta
'Burgundy Princess' (H)	CDWL
candida (H)	CBen EHon EMFW LPBA MSta WMAq
- var. *rubra* (H)	MSta
'Candidissima' (H)	CDWL EPAt MSta SWat
'Candidissima Rosea' (H)	MSta
§ capensis (T/D)	MSta
'Caroliniana' (H)	CDWL CWat MSta
'Caroliniana Nivea' (H)	CBen CDWL EMFW MSta
'Caroliniana Perfecta' (H)	CBen LPBA MSta SWat
'Caroliniana Rosea' (H)	MSta
'Celebration' (H)	MSta
§ 'Charlene Strawn' (H)	CWat EMFW MSta SWat WBcn WMAq
'Charles de Meurville' (H)	CBen CDWL CRow EMFW EPAt LNCo LPBA MSta NArg NPer WMAq
'Château le Rouge' (H)	MSta
'Chrysantha' (H)	MSta
'Chubby' (H)	EMFW MSta
'Colonel A.J. Welch' (H)	CBen CDWL CRow EHon EMFW EPAt LNCo LPBA MSta NArg NPer SCoo SWat WFar WMAq WMyn
'Colorado' (H)	CDWL
colorata	see *N. capensis*
'Colossea' (H)	CBen CWat EHon EMFW LNCo LPBA MSta NBlu

'Comanche' (H) — CBen EMFW MSta NPer WMAq

'Comte de Bouchaud' (H) — MSta

'Conqueror' (H) — EMFW IArd LNCo LPBA MSta SCoo SWat WFar

'Danieda' — SWat

§ 'Darwin' (H) — CBen CDWL CWat EMFW MSta SWat WMAq

'David' (H) — CWat MSta

'Deva' (H) — MSta

'Director George T. Moore' (T/D) — CDWL

'Ellisiana' (H) — CBen CDWL CWat EMFW LPBA MSta SLon SWat

'Elysée' (H) — MSta

'Escarboucle' (H) ♀H4 — CBen CDWL CRow CWat EHon EMFW EPAt LNCo LPBA MSta NPer SCoo SWat WBcn WMAq

'Esmeralda' (H) — MSta SWat

'Eucharis' (H) — MSta

'Eugénia de Land' (H) — MSta

'Evelyn Randig' (T/D) — CDWL MSta

'Excalibur' **new** — CDWL

'Exquisita' — see *N.* 'Odorata Exquisita'

§ 'Fabiola' (H) — CBen CDWL CRow EHon EMFW EPfP LPBA MSta NArg SCoo WBcn WFar WMAq

'Fire Crest' (H) — CBen EHon EMFW EPAt LNCo LPBA MCCP MSta NBlu SCoo SLon SWat WBcn WFar WMAq

'Formosa' (H) — MSta

'France' (H) — MSta

'Fritz Junge' (H) — MSta

'Froebelii' (H) — CBen CDWL CRow CWat EHon EMFW EPAt LNCo LPBA MSta NArg SWat WBcn WFar WMAq

'Fulva' (H) — MSta

'Galatée' (H) — CDWL MSta

'Geisha Girl' **new** — CDWL

'General Pershing' (T/D) — CDWL

'Georgia Peach' (H) **new** — CDWL

gigantea (T/D) — MSta

'Gladstoneana' (H) ♀H4 — CBen CRow CWat EHon EMFW EPAt LNCo LPBA MSta NArg NPer SCoo SWat WMAq WMyn

'Gloire du Temple-sur-Lot' (H) — CBen CDWL EMFW MSta SWat WMAq

'Gloriosa' (H) — CBen CDWL LPBA MSta SCoo SWat WFar

'Gold Medal' (H) — CBen

'Golden West' (T/D) — CDWL

'Goliath' (H) — MSta

'Gonnère' (H) ♀H4 — CBen CDWL CRow CWat EHon EMFW EPAt EPfP LNCo LPBA MSta NArg SWat WBcn WMAq

'Graziella' (H) — EPAt LPBA MSta NArg SWat WBcn WMAq

'Green Smoke' (T/D) — CDWL

'Grésilias' (H) — MSta

'H.C. Haarstick' (T/N) — CDWL

'Hal Miller' (H) — MSta

'Helen Fowler' (H) — CDWL EMFW MSta SLon SWat WMAq

x *helvola* — see *N.* 'Pygmaea Helvola'

§ 'Hermine' (H) — CBen CDWL EMFW MSta SWat WMAq

'Hever White' (H) — MSta

'Hollandia' Koster (H) — SWat

'Hollandia' misapplied — see *N.* 'Darwin'

'Indiana' (H) — CBen CDWL EMFW LPBA MSta WMAq

'Irene Heritage' (H) — CBen

'J.C.N. Forestier' — MSta

'James Brydon' (H) ♀H4 — CBen CDWL CRow CWat EHon EMFW EPAt EPfP LNCo LPBA MSta NArg NPer SCoo SWat WBcn WFar WMAq WPnP

'James Hudson' (H) — MSta

'Jean de Lamarsalle' (H) — MSta

'Jean Laydeker' (H) — MSta

§ 'Joanne Pring' (H) — MSta SWat

'Joey Tomocik' (H) — CDWL CWat LNCo LPBA SCoo SLon WMAq

'June Alison' (T/D) **new** — CDWL

'Lactea' (H) — CDWL MSta

'Laydekeri Alba' — CDWL

'Laydekeri Fulgens' (H) — CBen CDWL EMFW LPBA MSta SWat WMAq

'Laydekeri Liliacea' (H) — CBen CDWL CRow EMFW EPAt LNCo LPBA MSta SWat WMAq

'Laydekeri Purpurata' (H) — CDWL EMFW EPAt LPBA MSta SWat WBcn WMAq

'Laydekeri Rosea' misapplied — see *N.* 'Laydekeri Rosea Prolifera'

§ 'Laydekeri Rosea Prolifera' (H) — CBen EMFW LPBA MSta

'Lemon Chiffon' (H) — CDWL

'Leviathan' (H) — MSta

'Limelight' — SWat

'Little Sue' (H) **new** — CDWL

'Livingstone' (H) — CWat MSta

'Luciana' — see *N.* 'Odorata Luciana'

'Lucida' (H) — CBen CDWL CWat EMFW LPBA MSta SWat WMAq

'Lusitania' (H) — MSta

'Madame Bory Latour-Marliac' (H) — MSta

'Madame de Bonseigneur' (H) — CDWL MSta

'Madame Ganna Walska' (T/D) **new** — CDWL

'Madame Julien Chifflot' (H) — MSta

'Madame Maurice Laydeker' (H) — MSta

'Madame Wilfon Gonnère' (H) — CBen CDWL CWat EHon EMFW EPAt LNCo LPBA MSta SWat WBcn WMAq

'Marliacea Albida' (H) — CBen CWat EHon EMFW EPAt LNCo LPBA MCCP MSta SWat WFar WMAq WPnP

'Marliacea Carnea' (H) — CBen CDWL CRow EHon EMFW EPAt EPfP LNCo LPBA MSta NArg NBlu NPer SCoo SWat WBcn WFar WMAq WMyn

§ 'Marliacea Chromatella' (H) ♀H4 — CBen CDWL CRow CWat EHon EMFW EPAt EPfP LNCo LPBA MCCP MSta NArg SCoo SLon SWat WBcn WFar WMAq WPnP

'Marliacea Flammea' (H) — MSta

'Marliacea Ignea' (H) — MSta

'Marliacea Rosea' (H) — EMFW EPAt MSta NArg SWat WMAq

'Marliacea Rubra Punctata' (H) — LPBA MSta

'Martin E. Randig' — CDWL

'Mary Exquisita' (H) — MSta

'Mary Patricia' (H) — MSta

'Masaniello' (H) — CBen CDWL CRow EHon EMFW EPAt LPBA MSta NArg SWat WBcn WMAq

'Maurice Laydeker' (H) — CDWL EPAt MSta

'Mayla' — EPAt

§ 'Météor' (H) — CBen CWat EMFW MSta WBcn WMAq

mexicana — MSta NArg

'Millennium Pink' **new** — CDWL

'Moorei' (H) — CBen CDWL EHon EMFW LPBA MSta SLon SWat WMAq

'Mrs C.W.Thomas' (H)   MSta
'Mrs George C. Hitchcock'   CDWL
  (TN) **new**
'Mrs Richmond'   SWat
  Latour-Marliac (H)
'Mrs Richmond'   see *N.* 'Fabiola'
  misapplied
'Murillo' (H)   MSta
'Neptune' (H)   MSta
'Newchapel Beauty'   WMAq
'Newton' (H)   CDWL MSta SWat WMAq
'Nigel' (H)   MSta SWat
'Nobilissima' (H)   MSta
'Norma Gedye' (H)   CBen LPBA MSta SWat WMAq
'Occidentalis'   see *N. alba* subsp. *occidentalis*
'Odalisque' (H)   CWat EMFW MSta
§ *odorata* (H)   CBen CRow EHon EPAt LPBA MSta
                       NArg SCoo WBcn WMAq
  - var. *gigantea* (H)   MSta
§ - var. *minor* (H)   CBen CDWL CRow EMFW EPAt
                       LPBA MSta SWat WFar WMAq
  - 'Pumila'   see *N. odorata* var. *minor*
  - var. *rosea* (H)   MSta
  - f. *rubra* (H)   MSta
  - subsp.*tuberosa* (H)   CBen LPBA MSta WMAq
'Odorata Alba'   see *N. odorata*
§ 'Odorata Exquisita' (H)   MSta
'Odorata Juliana' (H)   MSta
§ 'Odorata Luciana' (H)   EMFW MSta
'Odorata Sulphurea' (H)   CDWL EPAt LNCo MSta NArg SLon
                       SWat WBcn WFar
§ 'Odorata Sulphurea   CBen CDWL CRow CWat EMFW
  Grandiflora' (H)   LPBA MSta SCoo SLon SWat WBcn
  'Maxima' (H)
§ 'Odorata Turicensis' (H)   LPBA MSta
'Odorata William B. Shaw'   see *N.* 'W.B. Shaw'
'Orange   CDWL
  Commanche' **new**
'Pam Bennett' (H)   CBen MSta
'Pamela' (T/D)   CBen
'Patio Joe'   CDWL
'Paul Hariot' (H)   CDWL CWat EHon EMFW LPBA
                       MSta SWat WBcn WMAq
'Peaches and Cream' (H)   CDWL
Pearl of the Pool (H)   MSta SWat
'Perry's Baby Red' (H)   CBen CDWL CWat EPAt SCoo
                       WMAq
'Perry's Double White' (H)   CBen
'Perry's Fire Opal' (H)   CDWL
'Perry's Pink' (H)   MSta SWat WMAq
'Perry's Viviparous   CBen
  Pink' (H)
'Perry's Yellow Sensation'   see *Nymphaea* 'Yellow Sensation'
'Peter Slocum' (H)   CDWL EMFW MSta SWat
'Philippe Laydeker' (H)   MSta
'Phoebus' (H)   CDWL MSta SWat WBcn
'Phoenix' (H)   MSta
'Picciola' (H)   MSta
pink hybrid **new**   CDWL
'Pink Opal' (H)   CBen CDWL CWat EMFW LPBA
                       MSta SLon
'Pink Platter' (T/D)   CBen
'Pink Sensation' (H)   CBen CDWL EMFW MSta NArg
                       SWat WMAq
'Pink Sunrise' (H)   MSta
'Pöstlingberg' (H)   LPBA MSta
'Président Viger' (H)   MSta
'Princess Elizabeth' (H)   EHon LPBA MSta
'Pygmaea Alba'   see *N. tetragona*
§ 'Pygmaea Helvola' (H)   CBen CDWL CRow CWat EHon
  ♀H4   EMFW EPAt LNCo LPBA MSta NPer
                       SCoo SWat WMAq WPnP
'Pygmaea Rubis' (H)   CRow EHon LPBA MSta SWat
                       WMAq

'Pygmaea Rubra' (H)   CBen CDWL CWat EMFW EPAt
                       LNCo MSta NBlu NPer SCoo
                       WMAq WPnP
'Ray Davies' (H)   EMFW MSta
'Red Spider' (H)   LPBA
'Rembrandt' Koster (H)   CDWL EPAt
'Rembrandt' misapplied   see *N.* 'Météor'
'René Gérard' (H)   CBen CDWL CWat EHon EMFW
                       EPAt LNCo LPBA MSta NArg SWat
                       WBcn WFar WMAq WPnP
'Robinsonii' (H)   MSta
'Rosanna Supreme' (H)   MSta SWat
'Rose Arey' (H)   CBen CDWL CRow CWat EMFW
                       EPAt LPBA MSta NArg SCoo SWat
                       WBcn WMAq
'Rose Magnolia' (H)   CDWL MSta SLon SWat
§ 'Rosea' (H)   CBen LPBA MSta WMAq
'Rosennymphe' (H)   CBen LPBA MSta SWat WFar
                       WMAq
'Rosita' (H)   MSta
'Rosy Morn' (H)   MSta
'Saint Louis Gold' (T/D)   CDWL
'Sanguinea' (H)   MSta
'Seignouretti' (H)   EMFW MSta WBcn WMAq
'Senegal' (H)   MSta
'Sioux' (H)   CBen CDWL EHon EMFW EPAt
                       LPBA MSta NArg NBlu NPer SLon
                       SWat WBcn WMAq
'Sir Galahad' (T/N)   CDWL
'Sirius' (H)   CBen CDWL EMFW MSta SWat
'Snow Princess' **new**   LPBA WPnP
'Solfatare' (H)   MSta
'Somptuosa' (H)   MSta WMAq
'Souvenir de Jules   MSta
  Jacquier' (H)
'Speciosa' (H)   MSta
'Spectabilis' (H)   MSta
'Splendida' (H)   MSta WMAq
'Suavissima' (H)   MSta
'Sultan' (H)   EPAt MSta
'Sunny Pink'   CDWL
'Sunrise'   see 'Odorata Sulphurea
                       Grandiflora'
'Superba' (H)   MSta
'Sylphida' (H)   MSta
'Temple Fire' (H)   MSta
§ *tetragona* (H)   CBen CDWL CRow CWat EHon
                       EMFW LNCo LPBA MSta NArg
                       SLon WFar WMAq
  - 'Alba'   see *N. tetragona*
  - 'Johann Pring'   see *N.* 'Joanne Pring'
§ - var. *rubra* (H)   MSta
'Texas Dawn' (H)   CDWL MSta SLon WMAq
'Tina' (TD) **new**   CDWL
'Tuberosa Flavescens'   see *N.* 'Marliacea Chromatella'
'Tuberosa Richardsonii'   EHon EMFW LNCo MSta WFar
  (H)
tuberosa 'Rosea'   see *N.* 'Rosea'
'Tulipiformis' (H)   MSta
'Turicensis'   see *N.* 'Odorata Turicensis'
'Venusta' (H)   MSta
'Vera Louise' (H)   MSta
'Vésuve' (H)   CDWL EMFW MSta SLon SWat
'Virginalis' (H)   LPBA MSta SWat
'Virginia' (H)   MSta
§ 'W.B. Shaw' (H)   CBen EHon EMFW EPAt LNCo
                       LPBA MSta NArg SWat WMAq
'Walter Pagels' (H)   CDWL EMFW MSta SLon WMAq
'Weymouth Red' (H)   CBen
'White Delight' (TD) **new** CDWL
'William Doogue' (H)   MSta WBcn
'William Falconer' (H)   CBen CDWL CWat EMFW LPBA
                       MSta SLon SWat
'Wow' (H)   CDWL SLon

'Yellow Commanche'**new** CDWL
'Yellow Dazzler' (T/D) CDWL
'Yellow Princess' (H) CDWL
§ 'Yellow Sensation' (H) CBen
'Yul Ling' SWat
'Zeus'**new** CDWL

Nymphoides (*Menyanthaceae*)

peltata CWat EMFW EPfP LNCo NArg
NPer SCoo SLon SWat WFar WMAq
WWpP
§ - 'Bennettii' EHon LPBA MSta

Nyssa (*Cornaceae*)

aquatica CLnd CTho IArd IDee LRHS SSpi
SSta
sinensis ♀H4 CAbP CBcs CDoC CDul CEnd
CLnd CMCN CPMA CTho ELan
EPfP GKir LRHS MBlu MBri NHol
SPer SReu SSpi SSta WCwm WNor
WPGP
- Nymans form EPfP LRHS
sylvatica ♀H4 More than 30 suppliers
- 'Autumn Cascades' EPfP IArd MBlu
- var. *biflora* CMCN
- 'Jermyns Flame' CAbP EPfP LRHS MAsh SSpi
- 'Red Red Wine' EPfP MBlu
- 'Sheffield Park' CAbP CMCN EPfP LRHS SSpi
- 'Windsor' EPfP LRHS SSpi
- 'Wisley Bonfire' EPfP LRHS MAsh SSpi

O

Oakesiella see *Uvularia*

Ochagavia (*Bromeliaceae*)

carnea CPne EOas
rosea CHEx CPne

Ocimum (*Lamiaceae*)

'African Blue' CArn ELau EMan EOHP GPoy
MHer WHHs
§ **americanum** WHer
- 'Meng Luk' see *O. americanum*
basilicum CArn CHrt CSev GPoy LRHS
MBow MBri NPri SECG SIde SWat
WHer WPer WSel
- 'Anise' see *O. basilicum* 'Horapha'
- 'Ararat' WHHs
* - 'Cinnamon' CHrt EMan LRHS MBow MHer
MSal NGHP NPri SHDw WHHs
WHer WJek WSel
- 'Fine Verde' WHHs
- 'Genovese' CHrt ELau MHer NGHP NVic
WHHs
- 'Glycyrrhiza' see *O. basilicum* 'Horapha'
- 'Green Globe' WHHs
- 'Green Ruffles' LRHS WJek WSel
- 'Holy' see *O. tenuiflorum*
§ - 'Horapha' CArn CSev EOHP MBow MHer
MSal NGHP SIde WHHs WJek
* - 'Horapha Nanum' NGHP WJek
- 'Napolitano' CBod MHer NGHP SIde SWat
WHHs WJek
- var. *purpurascens* CArn CSev MBri SIde WHer
- - 'Dark Opal' CBod NGHP SHDw WJek WSel
- - 'Purple Ruffles' EOHP MBow SIde SWat WHHs
WJek WSel
- - 'Red Rubin' EOHP MHer WJek
- 'Thai' see *O. basilicum* 'Horapha'
canum see *O. americanum*

× *citriodorum* CArn LRHS MBow MHer MSal
NGHP SHDw SIde WJek WSel
- 'Lime' CHrt NGHP WHHs WJek
- 'Siam Queen' CHrt LRHS MHer WJek
gratissimum ELau MHer
kilimandscharicum GPoy
× *basilicum* var.
purpurascens
minimum CArn CBod CHrt CSev ELau GPoy
LRHS MBri MHer NPri SIde WHHs
WHer WJek WPer WSel
sanctum see *O. tenuiflorum*
'Spicy Globe' WHHs WJek
§ **tenuiflorum** CArn CSev GPoy LRHS MSal NGHP
SHDw SIde WHHs WHer WJek

Odontonema (*Acanthaceae*)

strictum WMul

Oemleria (*Rosaceae*)

§ **cerasiformis** CBcs CFwr CPLG CPle EPfP EPla
MWat SSpi WCot WEas WHCG
WSHC WWin

Oenanthe (*Apiaceae*)

aquatica IHMH
- 'Variegata' (v) EMFW
* **javanica** 'Atropurpurea' EHoe
- 'Flamingo' (v) CRow EChP EGra ELan EMan
EMon EPfP GGar IHMH LPBA
LRHS MBNS NArg NBro NJOw
SGar SLon WCom WFar WHer
WMAq WPer WWpP

Oenothera ✿ (*Onagraceae*)

from South America MTho
§ **acaulis** CBot CSpe EBee GCal MNrw SBri
SGar WRos
- *alba* MDKP
§ - 'Aurea' SRot WPer
- 'Lutea' see *O. acaulis* 'Aurea'
'Apricot Delight' CBri EBre EChP ECoo EFWa EMan
GBBs LRHS MAnH MCCP MGol
MHer MWgw MWrn NBur NPPs
STes WMoo
§ **biennis** CArn CRow CSev EHoe ELan
EWTr GPoy MBow MHer NBro
NGHP SECG SGar SIde WBrk WEas
WFar WHer WJek WPer
brachycarpa EBee
caespitosa CHrt EMan MTho NRib
- subsp. *caespitosa* NWCA
NNS 93-505
* **campylocalyx** EBee EChP ECoo LDai NBur
childsii see *O. speciosa*
cinaeus see *O. fruticosa* subsp. *glauca*
'Colin Porter' CCge EBee EBur EDAr MNrw NBur
NGHP NWCA SGar WPer
coryi EBee
'Crown Imperial' COlW EBee EBre EOMN GKir
MCCP SHar SLon SPer SSpi SSto
SVil WShp
deltoides var. *howellii* SMrm
drummondii new XPep
§ **elata** subsp. *hookeri* EBee EMan WPer
erythrosepala see *O. glazioviana*
'Finlay's Fancy' **new** WCru
flava EBee EFWa
- subsp. *taraxacoides* CGra
new
§ **fruticosa** CSam EChP EFWa NLar SPlb
WWpP
- 'African Sun' PBR EBee ECtt EFWa EMan EWes SBod
SRot

- 'Camel' (v) — CBct CPlt EBee EFWa EGle EMan EMon LDai LHop MAvo MHar NPro SAga SUsu WHrl WMoo WWeb
- Fireworks — see *O. fruticosa* 'Fyrverkeri'
- subsp. **fruticosa** — EBee
§ - 'Fyrverkeri' ♀H4 — More than 30 suppliers
§ - subsp. **glauca** ♀H4 — CElw CHrt COIW EFWa EPfP ERou GBBs GSki LPVe MDKP MNrw MTho MWgw MWhi NBlu NGar NPro SPet SRms SYvo WEas WHil WPer
- - 'Erica Robin' (v) — More than 30 suppliers
- - 'Frühlingsgold' (v) — CBct EBee SUsu
- - narrow grey-leaved — SUsu
- - Solstice — see *O. fruticosa* subsp. *glauca* 'Sonnenwende'
§ - - 'Sonnenwende' — CBre CElw EBee EBre EMon LPVe LRHS MAvo MLLN NGHP NLar NPro SGar WMoo WTel
- - 'Sunspot' (v) — GBuc GFlt SScr
- Highlight — see *O. fruticosa* 'Hoheslicht'
§ - 'Hoheslicht' — EBee
- 'Lady Brookeborough' — MRav NGar
- 'Michelle Ploeger' — EBee EBre EGle EMan
- 'Silberblatt' — EBee EMan EPPr
- 'W. Cuthbertson' — EBee
- 'Yellow River' — CElw EBee LRHS MHar WBrk WWeb
- 'Youngii' — EBee EFWa EPfP ERou Llck MCCP MLLN SSto WPer
glabra Miller — see *O. biennis*
glabra misapplied — ECha NSti SIgm SIng SUsu WCom
glazioviana — EBee EChP ECoo EFWa GBBs NBir WFar WHrl WPer WWpP WWye
hookeri — see *O. elata* subsp. *hookeri*
kunthiana — CBri CStr EBee ECoo EDAr EFWa EGoo EMan ERou GCal IFro MDKP NWCA SBri SCro SPet WGMN WMoo WPer
lamarckiana — see *O. glazioviana*
'Lemon Sunset' — EBre ECoo EFWa LHop MCCP MTis NBur NGHP SSvw SWal SWat WMoo
linearis — see *O. fruticosa*
'Longest Day' — EFou EPfP LRHS MBrN SAsh
§ **macrocarpa** ♀H4 — More than 30 suppliers
- 'Greencourt Lemon' — LPhx
- subsp. **incana** — CMea EBre EMan LPVe NGHP SMad WCot WWin
macrosceles — EBee
* **minima** — EBee MDKP
missouriensis — see *O. macrocarpa*
* **mollis** — EBee
muricata — EBee EFWa
oakesiana — EBee
odorata misapplied — see *O. stricta*
odorata Hook. & Arn. — see *O. biennis*
odorata Jacquin — CArn EFWa GCal IBlr NOrc
- 'Sulphurea' — see *O. stricta* 'Sulphurea'
organensis — CDes EBee EFWa MLLN WPGP
pallida — MBri NGHP SWat
- 'Innocence' — CBot ECtt LRHS MBNS MGol SRot WPer
- 'Wedding Bells' — EFWa NPer
'Penelope Hobhouse' — CBct EBee GBuc SAga SUsu SWat
§ **perennis** — CNic CStr EBee GKir MTho NPro SRms SWat WBVN WEas WPer
pumila — see *O. perennis*
rosea — NBur
serrulata — see *Calylophus serrulatus*
speciosa — CMHG CRWN EBee EMon GBBs LPVe MRav SAga SEND SPer SWat WCot WPer XPep

* - 'Alba' **new** — XPep
- 'Ballerina' — EMan LHop WCFE
- var. **childsii** — see *O. speciosa*
- 'Pink Petticoats' — ECha ECoo ECtt EFWa EMlt GBBs LAst MAvo MCCP NGHP NPer SWat WSan
§ - 'Rosea' — CBot CFir CNic CPrp EBee ECoo LAst Llck LRHS MNrw SGar SPlb SWat WPer WWin
- 'Siskiyou' — CFis CHrt COtt CPrp CSpe EBee EMlt ENot EPfP GBuc LRHS SBod SCoo SGar SHar SIng SLon SMad SMrm SPer SRot SUsu SWat WHer WShp
- 'Woodside White' — SMrm
§ **stricta** — CHar CHrt CMea CSam EBee ECGP EFWa EGoo MBri NPro SCro SIng WBrk WBry WCom WPer WWye
* - 'Moonlight' — SGar
§ - 'Sulphurea' — CHad CHar CMHG CMil EBee EChP ECoo EGoo ELan EMan GCal IBlr IFro MWgw NPer SChu SCro SGar SMrm SUsu WAbb WCot WPer
'Summer Sun' — EBee EBre LRHS MCLN SLon SPoG SSpe
'Sunburst' (v) — EMan
taraxacifolia — see *O. acaulis*
tetragona — see *O. fruticosa* subsp. *glauca*
- var. **fraseri** — see *O. fruticosa* subsp. *glauca*
- 'Sonnenwende' — see *O. fruticosa* subsp. *glauca* 'Sonnenwende'
tetraptera — NWCA
texensis — SWat
- 'Early Rise' — EMan LHop
versicolor 'Sunset Boulevard' — CHad CM&M CMea CSpe EChP ECtt EFWa EWTr GBuc LDai LPVe MAnH MBri MHer MWrn NBPC NGHP NPPs SBod SGar SMrm SPer WBar WHer WMoo WPer WSan WWeb WWin

Olea (Oleaceae)

europaea (F) — More than 30 suppliers
- subsp. **africana** — CTrC XPep
- 'Aglandau' (F) — ERea
- 'Amygdalolia' (F) — ERea
- 'Bouteillan' (F) — ERea
- 'Cailletier' (F) — ERea
- 'Chelsea Physic Garden' — WPGP
§ - 'Cipressino' (F) — ERea LPan XPep
- 'El Greco' (F) — CBcs ERea
- subsp. **europaea** var. **sylvestris new** — XPep
- 'Manzanillo' (F) — ERea
- 'Picholine' (F) — ERea
- 'Pyramidalis' — see *O. europaea* 'Cipressino'
* - 'Sativa' (F) — EMui

Olearia ✿ (Asteraceae)

albida misapplied — see *O.* 'Talbot de Malahide'
albida Hook. f. — GGar
- var. **angulata** — CBcs CTrC
algida — ECou GGar
arborescens — GEil GGar GSki
* - 'Variegata' (v) — NPro
argophylla — ECou GGar
avicenniifolia — CBcs CHEx CTrC ECou GGar WBcn WGer WSHC
capillaris — CDoC CPle ECou GGar SDry SIgm WCwm
chathamica — CPLG GGar IDee
§ **cheesemanii** — CDoC CMHG CPLG CPle CTrC EBee GGar IDee SPer

coriacea	ECou GGar
'County Park'	ECou
erubescens	CDoC CPle
floribunda	CPle GGar
forsteri from Tresco	CDoC
furfuracea	CDoC CPle
glandulosa	ECou GGar
gunniana	see *O. phlogopappa*
x *haastii*	More than 30 suppliers
- 'McKenzie'	ECou
hectorii	ECou
§ 'Henry Travers'	CDoC CPLG CPle EPfP GEil GGar GQui IBlr MDun NLar
§ *ilicifolia*	CDoC CFil CPle GGar GSki LRHS MDun SDry SSpi
§ *ilicifolia* x *moschata*	GGar IDee LRHS WKif
insignis	see *Pachystegia insignis*
lacunosa	MDun
ledifolia **new**	GGar
lepidophylla	ECou
- silver	ECou
lirata	ECou GGar
macrodonta ♀H3	More than 30 suppliers
- 'Intermedia'	GGar
- 'Major'	GGar SHBN
- 'Minor'	CBcs CDoC CTrC ELan EPfP GGar GQui NLar SPlb WBcn WFar WStI
x *mollis* hort.	see *O. ilicifolia* x *O. moschata*
x *mollis* (Kirk) Cockayne	CPle GQui SSpi WBcn WSHC
- 'Zennorensis' ♀H3	CBcs CDoC CPLG CPle GGar IArd IDee ISea MDun SDry SOWG WBcn WCru WDin WEas WGer
moschata	CPle GGar
myrsinoides	CFai CPle
§ *nummulariifolia*	CDoC CPle CTrC CTri ECou EPfP EPla GGar SDry SEND SPer SSto WBod WDin WFar WKif WSHC WTel
- var. *cymbifolia*	CNic ECou WGer
- hybrids	ECou
- 'Little Lou'	ECou
odorata	CPle ECou GGar ISea NLar WFar WHCG
oleifolia	see *O.* 'Waikariensis'
paniculata	CMHG CPle CTrC CTri EPfP GEil GGar GSki IDee ISea SDry WGer WPic
§ *phlogopappa*	CSBt CTri EBee ECou GGar SVen WBrE WPic
- 'Comber's Blue'	CBcs EBee EPfP GGar IBlr LRHS NCGa NPer SSta WBod
- 'Comber's Pink'	CBcs CDoC CPLG EBee EPfP GGar IBlr LRHS MPRe NCGa NPer SPer WBod WEas WHil WKif
- pink	CBrm CTrG
- 'Rosea'	see *O. phlogopappa* 'Comber's Pink'
- Splendens Group	CAbb WFar
- var. *subrepanda*	CPle CTrC GGar LEdu SEND WAbe WBod
§ *ramulosa*	CDoC CPLG CPle WKif WSHC
- 'Blue Stars'	ECou GGar LRHS
- var. *ramulosa*	ECou
- 'White Stars'	ECou
rani hort.	see *O. cheesemanii*
rani Druce	ISea
x *scilloniensis* hort.	see *O. stellulata* DC.
x *scilloniensis* Dorrien-Smith ♀H3	CBrm CWCL GGar XPep
- 'Master Michael'	CBot CDoC EBee EPfP MPRe NLar SOWG SPer WBea WKif WSHC WWeb
semidentata misapplied	see *O.* 'Henry Travers'
solandri	CDoC CFwr CHEx CPle CSam

	CTrC EBee ECou EPla GGar SDix SDry SHFr SPer STre XPep
- 'Aurea'	CBcs GQui
stellulata hort.	see *O. phlogopappa*
§ *stellulata* DC.	CBot CChe CPLG CSBt CSLe CTrG CWSG CWib ECou ECrN ELan ENot EPfP ISea MWat MWgw SAga SDix SOWG SPer SPla WBrE WDin WEas WFar WHCG WKif WPic WSHC WStI
- 'Michael's Pride'	CPLG
§ 'Talbot de Malahide'	EHol GGar
traversii	CAbb CBcs CDoC CHEx CMHG CSBt CTrC EBee GGar NBlu SEND SVen WGer WHer XPep
§ - 'Tweedledum' (v)	CDoC CTrC ECou EHoe GGar MOak SSto WGer
virgata	ECou GGar GSki WCot XPep
- var. *laxiflora*	WHer
- var. *lineata*	CDoC CPle ECou GEil GGar NLar SEND WDin WPic WSHC
- - 'Dartonii'	CBcs EBee ECou EHol GGar MBlu SLPl WSHC
viscosa	CPle GGar
§ 'Waikariensis'	CBot CMHG CPLG CPle CSam CTrC ECou GEil GGar IDee LRHS SChu SEND SLon WCFE WDin WGer WPat

Oligostachyum (Poaceae)

lubricum	see *Semiarundinaria lubrica*

olive see *Olea europaea*

Olsynium (Iridaceae)

§ *biflorum*	WCot
§ *douglasii* ♀H4	CBro CMea EDAr EHyt ELan EPar EPot ETow GCrs GEdr LTwo NGar NMen NRya SIng WAbe WCot
- 'Album'	CMea EHyt EPar EPot GCrs GEdr NMen NRya NSla WCot
- var. *inflatum*	EWes
§ *filifolium*	CStu MNrw NMen
§ *junceum*	CBri CFil MDKP SBla WCot
- JCA 12289	MTho
- JCA 14211	CFir

Omphalodes (Boraginaceae)

cappadocica ♀H4	CElw CRow ECGN ECha EOrc EPar EPot EWTr GFlt GKir LLWP LPio LRHS MBro NBrk NBro NCGa NFor NPer SGar SPer SRms SSpi SWat WBrk WPat WSSM
- 'Alba'	GKir LLWP
- 'Anthea Bloom'	GBuc IBlr
- 'Blue Rug'	IHMH
- 'Cherry Ingram' ♀H4	More than 30 suppliers
- 'Kathryn' **new**	EBee
- 'Lilac Mist'	CElw CLAP CPom EBee EMan ENot LLWP MAvo MLwd MRav NLar SMrm SRms SSvw SWat SWvt WPnP WTin
- 'Parisian Skies'	CLAP
- 'Starry Eyes'	More than 30 suppliers
§ *linifolia* ♀H4	CMea CSpe ECoo NMen WWeb
- alba	see *O. linifolia*
lojkae	NSla SOkd
luciliae	CLAP WHoo
nitida	CPom EMon GGar NRya SSpi WCot
verna	More than 30 suppliers
- 'Alba'	CBot CBre CDes EBee EChP ECha EGle ELan EMon GAbr GBBs LAst LHop MHar MTho NCGa NChi

	NCot NHol NLar SAga SPer SRms
	SSvw SWat SWvt WBea WEas WFar
	WWpP
- 'Elfenauge'	CElw CMil EBee EGle EMon EPPr
	NBir NCot NDov NRya
- *grandiflora*	WCot

Omphalogramma (*Primulaceae*)

| *delavayi* | GFle |
| *forrestii* **new** | EBee |

Oncostema see *Scilla*

onion see *Allium cepa*

Onixotis (*Colchicaceae*)

| *stricta* **new** | CPLG |
| *triquetra* | WCot |

Onobrychis (*Papilionaceae*)

tournefortii	EBee
viciifolia	EBee EMan MGol MSal SECG SHar
	WBWf

Onoclea (*Woodsiaceae*)

§ *intermedia*	EMon
sensibilis ♀H4	More than 30 suppliers
- copper	CFil CRow SBla WPGP

Ononis (*Papilionaceae*)

repens	CArn CNic MSal NMir
rotundifolia	CWCL MSal
spinosa	CPom EBee EWll LRav MHer MSal
	WFar WPer XPep

Onopordum (*Asteraceae*)

acanthium	More than 30 suppliers
arabicum	see *O. nervosum*
bracteatum	WPer
§ *nervosum* ♀H4	CArn CSpe EBee NBro NBur SRms
	WCot WFar

Onosma (*Boraginaceae*)

alborosea	CMdw CPom CSev ECha EGoo
	EOrc GBri GCal GEdr NLAp NMRc
	SAga SChu WEas WKif WPGP WPat
arenaria	EGoo
conferta BWJ 7735 **new**	WCru
helvetica	EMan MBro WPat
nana	CStu GFlt
stellulata	EGoo SSpi
taurica ♀H4	ETow MOne NBir WWin

Onychium (*Adiantaceae*)

contiguum	WAbe
japonicum	CFil EBee EFer EFtx GQui SBla
	SChu WAbe
- 'Dali' L 1649	SBla
lucidum **new**	WCot

Ophiopogon ❀ (*Convallariaceae*)

BWJ 8244 from Vietnam **new**	WCru
'Black Dragon'	see *O. planiscapus* 'Nigrescens'
bodinieri	CBct ERos EWes LEdu LEur SMac
	WRHF
- B&L 12505	CLAP EBee EPPr EPla MTed
aff. *caulescens* HWJ 590 **new**	WCru
chingii	EMon GCal LEdu
- 'Chinese Whisper' **new**	EMon
formosanus	CPrp
- B&SWJ 3659	EBee WCru
'Gin-ryu'	see *Liriope spicata* 'Gin-ryu'

graminifolius	see *Liriope muscari*
intermedius	CBct EBee EPla ERos ESis LEur
	MSte WCot WPGP
§ - 'Argenteomarginatus'	ERos EWes WPGP
- *parviflorus*	NSti
- 'Variegatus'	see *O. intermedius*
	'Argenteomarginatus'
§ *jaburan*	CHid EBee EShb LAma LEdu MSte
	NHol WPnP
- 'Variegatus'	see *O. jaburan* 'Vittatus'
§ - 'Vittatus' (v)	CMHG CPrp CSBt EBee EHoe ELan
	EMan EPfP EWes GSki ITer LEur
	LRHS MCCP MGos SAga SPer SYvo
	WCot WFar WSpi
japonicus	CBro CRow EPPr EPfP EPla GSki
	LEdu NSti SSte XPep
- B&SWJ 1842	WCru
- 'Albus'	CLAP NHol
- 'Compactus'	CDoC CFil CStu EBee LRHS SMac
	SPla SSpi WPGP WWye
- 'Kigimafukiduma'	CBrm CFwr EBee MRav NLar
	WGwG WSpi
- 'Kyoto' **new**	GSki
- 'Minor'	CBct CSBt EPfP EPla NLar SMac
	WPGP
- 'Nanus Variegatus' (v)	CDes EBee EMon
- 'Nippon'	CM&M CPrp EBee EHoe EPza LAst
	LPio LRHS
- 'Tama-ryu'	EHyt
* - 'Tama-ryu Number Two'	ECho SIng
- 'Torafu' (v)	EPPr
* - 'Variegatus' (v)	EPla SLPl
malcolmsonii	WCru
B&SWJ 5264	
planiscapus	CFee CHEx CKno CMHG CPLG
	CSWP CSev CStu EBee EPar EPla
	EWTr GAbr GCal GOrn MSte
	MTho MWod NBro SAga SPla SSte
	STre WBVN WMoo
* - 'Albovariegatus'	EBee SPoG
- 'Green Dragon' **new**	ELan
- *leucanthus*	EPPr WCot
- 'Little Tabby' (v)	CDes CLAP CSpe EBee ESis MDKP
	MMoz MWrn NPro SAga SSte
	WCot WDyG WPGP WTin
* - *minimus*	ERos
§ - 'Nigrescens' ♀H4	More than 30 suppliers
- 'Silver Ribbon'	MDKP SGar SWat
scaber B&SWJ 1871	WCru
'Spring Gold'	EMon
'Tama-hime-nishiki' (v) **new**	EMon
wallichianus	EPPr EPla GIBF LEur NLar SGar
	SSpi WCom WCot WPGP

Ophiorrhiza (*Rubiaceae*)

intermedius	EBee
japonicus	EBee
mairei	EBee

Ophrys (*Orchidaceae*)

| *apifera* | CHdy WHer |

Oplismenus (*Poaceae*)

| § *africanus* 'Variegatus' (v) ♀H1 | CHal |
| *undulatifolius* | EBee NBro |

Oplopanax (*Araliaceae*)

| *horridus* **new** | MBlu |

Opuntia ❀ (*Cactaceae*)

| *cantabrigiensis* | EOas SChr |
| *compressa* | SChr |

cyclodes **new**	CTrC
cymochila **new**	CTrC
engelmannii	SChr
erinacea var. *utahensis*	WCot
x *polycantha*	
NNS 99-263	
grahamii	SChr
grandiflora	see *O. macrorhiza*
humifusa	ELau SChr SMad WMul
§ *macrorhiza*	SChr
polyacantha	SChr SPlb
rhodantha	EOas SChr
santa-rita	EOas SChr
stenopetala	CAbb CTrC

orange, sour or Seville see *Citrus aurantium*

orange, sweet see *Citrus sinensis*

Orchis (*Orchidaceae*)

elata	see *Dactylorhiza elata*
foliosa	see *Dactylorhiza foliosa*
fuchsii	see *Dactylorhiza fuchsii*
§ *laxiflora*	CHdy
maculata	see *Dactylorhiza maculata*
maderensis	see *Dactylorhiza foliosa*
majalis	see *Dactylorhiza majalis*
§ *mascula*	CHdy GPoy WHer

oregano see *Origanum vulgare*

Oreomyrrhis (*Apiaceae*)

argentea	CStu

Oreopanax (*Araliaceae*)

dactylifolius	LEdu

Oreopteris (*Thelypteridaceae*)

§ *limbosperma*	SRms

Oreoxis (*Apiaceae*)

alpina	EBee

Oresitrophe (*Saxifragaceae*)

rupifraga	EBee WCru

Origanum ❀ (*Lamiaceae*)

from Santa Cruz	CArn
from Yunnan, China	NWoo
acutidens	EHyt NWCA WCHb XPep
amanum ♀H2-3	CPBP CStu EBee EGle EHyt ETow
	EWes LRHS MBro NBir NMen SBla
	SChu SIgm SIng WAbe WCom
	WHoo WLin WPat WWye
- var. *album*	EBee ECho SBla WAbe WPat
x *applii*	EDAr ELau
'Barbara Tingey'	CBot CSpe CWCL EBee EChP EGle
	EHyt ELan ETow EWes LBee LPhx
	LRHS MBro MHer MNrw MSte
	MTho NWCA SAga SBla SChu
	SUsu WAbe WCFE WCru WHoo
	WPat
I 'Bristol Cross'	CFwr CNic CStr ECha GBar WPat
'Buckland'	CHea CPlt EBee EDAr EHyt EPot
	ESis LPhx LRHS MHer MSte NWCA
	SBla WCom WPat
caespitosum	see *O. vulgare* 'Nanum'
§ *calcaratum*	EBee EMan ETow LRHS MTho SBla
	SMrm WAbe WPat
creticum	see *O. vulgare* subsp. *hirtum*
dictamnus	CArn EHyt GPoy LRHS LTwo SBla
	SHDw WAbe WJek XPep
'Dingle Fairy'	CM&M EBee EGoo ELan EMan
	EWes GBar MHer MLLN MMHG

	MNrw MTho NBir NWCA SIde
	SIng WBry WMoo WWye
'Erntedank'	EBee
'Frank Tingey'	CPBP ECho EHyt ELan LTwo SUsu
	WAbe
'Gold Splash'	EDAr GBar SIde WHHs
'Goudgeel'	CStr
heracleoticum L.	see *O. vulgare* subsp. *hirtum*
§ x *hybridinum*	SAga SBla WLin WPat WWin
'Ingolstadt'	EBee SAga SCro WWye
'Kent Beauty'	More than 30 suppliers
kopetdaghense **new**	XPep
laevigatum ♀H3	CArn CLyd CMHG CStr ELan EPfP
	MBro MHar MHer NBro NGHP
	NMir NPer NWCA SAga SBla SGar
	SIde SMer WCom WMoo WPer
	WSHC WWhi WWin XPep
- 'Herrenhausen' ♀H4	More than 30 suppliers
- 'Hopleys'	More than 30 suppliers
- 'Purple Charm'	EBee ELau WCot
- 'Springwood'	WWye
majorana	CArn CSev ELan ELau GWCH
	MBow MHer MSal SECG SIde SWat
	WHHs WJek WPer WSel WWye
	XPep
I - 'Aureum' **new**	SWal
microphyllum	CArn CFee CMHG EDAr EGle EHyt
	GBar LPhx LRHS MTho NMen SBla
	SChu WAbe WCru WPat WWye
	XPep
minutiflorum	ECho EPot LTwo SIng
'Norton Gold'	CBre CElw EBee EBre ECha EPot
	GBar GBuc LRHS NPer SIde
'Nymphenburg'	CFee CSam EBee EChP EMan MSte
	SAga SChu SIde SMrm WCru WHer
	WWhi
onites	CArn CHby ELau GBar GPoy
	IHMH ILis MHer MSal MWat NBlu
	SIde SPlb WBrk WHHs WHer WJek
	WPer WSel WWpP WWye XPep
'Pilgrim'	EBre WMoo
'Pink Cloud'	EDAr
* *prismaticum*	GBar
pulchellum	see *O.* x *hybridinum*
'Purple Cloud'	EDAr NBir
'Rosenkuppel'	More than 30 suppliers
'Rotkugel'	CPrp EBee EChP EGle EMan LPhx
	MSte WCru
rotundifolium ♀H4	CArn CMea EBee EDAr ELan LEdu
	MDKP MHer NBir SBla SChu WAbe
- hybrid	MDKP
- 'Pagoda Bells'	EBee EDAr SIng
scabrum	CArn WWye
- subsp. *pulchrum*	CStu XPep
- - 'Newleaze'	LHoo
sipyleum	EBee EHyt NWCA SBla WAbe
syriacum **new**	XPep
'Thundercloud'	WWeb
'Tinpenny Pink' **new**	WTin
tournefortii	see *O. calcaratum*
tytthanthum **new**	WLin XPep
virens	CArn GBar ILis MCCP
vulgare	CAgr CArn CHrt CRWN CSev
	ECoo EDAr GBar GKir GPoy IHMH
	MBar MBow MHer NBro NLan
	NMir NPri SGar SIde SPlb SWal
	WHHs WHer WPer WWpP WWye
	XPep
- from Israel	ELau
- 'Acorn Bank'	CArn CBod CPrp EBee EGoo EGra
	ELau EOMN EWes MHer SAga SIde
	WBry WCHb WHHs WHer WJek
- var. *album*	CElw MHer WHer WJek
- - 'Aureum Album'	MCLN WHer

	– 'Aureum' ♀H4	More than 30 suppliers
	– 'Aureum Crispum'	CPrp ECha EDAr EGoo ELau GAbr GBar GPoy IHMH ILis NBid NBlu NGHP SIde SWat WHHs WJek WRha WSel WWpP WWye
	– 'Compactum'	More than 30 suppliers
	– 'Corinne Tremaine' (v)	NBir SAga WHer
	– 'Country Cream' (v)	More than 30 suppliers
	– 'Curly Gold'	CPrp
	– *formosanum*	WCru
	B&SWJ 3180	
§	– 'Gold Tip' (v)	CMea CSev CStr EBee EDAr EHoe ELau GBar IHMH ILis MHer NArg NGHP NHol NPri SIde SPlb SWat WCAu WCHb WHer WWpP WWye
	– 'Golden Shine'	CM&M EBee EWes MWat NGHP WRha
§	– subsp. *hirtum*	CArn CHby EOHP GPoy LEdu MSal NWoo SPlb WBri WJek WPer WWpP XPep
	– – 'Greek'	CBod CPrp ELau GWCH MBow MHer NGHP NPri SECG WHHs
§	– 'Nanum'	GBar LRHS WJek
	– 'Nyamba' **new**	GPoy
	– 'Polyphant' (v)	CMHG CSev EBee EChP EDAr EGle EMan EOHP GBar LHop LPio MLLN NBir WBea WBrE WCHb WHHs WHer WJek WMoo WSel WWye
	– 'Thumble's Variety'	CBod CElw CMea CPrp EBre ECGP ECha ECoo EGle EGoo EHoe GBar GKir IHMH LHop LPhx LRHS MBri MHer MRav NHol SIde SLon SSvw SWat WEas WMnd WMoo WWpP XPep
	– 'Tomintoul' **new**	GPoy
	– 'Variegatum'	see *O. vulgare* 'Gold Tip'
	– 'Webb's White'	GBar
	– yellow, long-leaved	ECha
	'White Cloud'	EDAr
	'Z'Attar'	MHer

Orites (Proteaceae)

myrtoidea	CFil

Orixa (Rutaceae)

japonica	CBot EPfP SSpi WFar WPGP
– 'Variegata' (v)	EPfP LRHS

Orlaya (Apiaceae)

grandiflora	CSpe WCot WFar

Ornithogalum (Hyacinthaceae)

	arabicum	CBro EChP LAma LPhx LRHS MBri MLLN SPet WCot WDav
	arcuatum	WCot
	balansae	see *O. oligophyllum*
	caudatum	see *O. longibracteatum*
	chionophilum	CFwr EBee
	ciliiferum	EBee
	collinum **new**	WWst
	conicum **new**	WHil
	dubium ♀H1	WBor WCot
	fimbriatum	EBee EPot WCot
	lanceolatum	CAvo EHyt WCot
§	*longibracteatum*	CHEx CPLG CStu EBee EPem SChr SYvo WGwG WHer
	magnum	CAvo CMea EBee EChP WPnP
	– 'Saguramo'	WCot
	montanum	WWst
	nanum	see *O. sigmoideum*
	narbonense	CFwr EBee GBuc LPhx LRHS WCot WDav
	nutans ♀H4	CAvo CBro CFwr CMea EChP

		EMan EMon EPar EPfP EPot LAma LPhx MAvo MEHN MLLN MMil MNrw NMen NRog WAul WBea WCot WPer
§	*oligophyllum*	CBro CStu EBee EPot LPhx MNrw WCot WDav
	oreoides **new**	WWst
	orthophyllum	CStu WCot
	platyphyllum	EBee
	ponticum	ERos
	pyramidale	CDes CFwr CSpe EBee EChP EPot MNrw WCot
	pyrenaicum	CAvo CStu EBee ECha ERos WCot WShi
	– Flavescens Group	EBee
	reverchonii	CDes EBee WCot
	saundersiae	EBee
	schmalhausenii **new**	WWst
	sibthorpii	see *O. sigmoideum*
§	*sigmoideum*	CStu EPot WAbe
	sintenisii	EBee WWst
	tenuifolium	see *O. orthophyllum*
	thyrsoides ♀H1	LAma LRHS MBri SPet WBea
	umbellatum	CBro CNic ELan EMon EPar EPfP GPoy LAma LRHS MBri MNrw NMen NRog SRms WBVN WBea WCot WFar WHil WPer WShi WWye

Orontium (Araceae)

aquaticum	CBen CDWL CWat EHon EMFW EPAt LNCo LPBA MSta NArg NLar SWat WMAq WMyn WPnP WWpP

Orostachys (Crassulaceae)

§	*aggregata*	SChr
	furusei	EBee EMan GAbr LHop WCot WFar WShp WWhi
	iwarenge	CStu
	malacophylla	see *O. aggregata*
§	*spinosa*	EMan ETow NMen WCot WFar

Orphium (Gentianaceae)

frutescens	CPLG

Orthrosanthus (Iridaceae)

	chimboracensis	CDes CFir EMan MAnH WCot WFar WPGP WPer WPic
	– JCA 13743	CPou
	laxus	CFir CPle EBee ERos GBuc GFlt MAnH SMad WOut WWin
	multiflorus	CDes CElw EBee ETow WPGP
	polystachyus	CPle CPom CRez CSpe EChP EMan ERos MAvo MLwd WSHC

Oryzopsis (Poaceae)

lessoniana	see *Stipa arundinacea*
miliacea	CBig CHrt EBee ECha EHoe EMan EPPr WCot WDyG WPGP WSPU
paradoxa	EBee EPPr

Osbeckia (Melastomataceae)

CC 4089	CPLG
stellata var. *crinita*	EBee

Oscularia (Aizoaceae)

§	*deltoides* ♀H1-2	CHEx CStu MRav SPet WCot WEas

Osmanthus (Oleaceae)

	americanus	WBcn
	armatus	CAbP CFil CTri EPfP LPan WFar
§	x *burkwoodii* ♀H4	More than 30 suppliers
§	*decorus*	CBcs CDul CSBt CTri ELan EPfP EWTr GKir MGos MRav NWea SPer SSta WBcn WDin WFar

- 'Angustifolius'	MGos WBcn
delavayi ♀H4	More than 30 suppliers
- 'Latifolius'	EPfP GKir LRHS SLon WBcn WFar
forrestii	see *O. yunnanensis*
x *fortunei*	CPle EBee EPfP LPan LRHS SLPl WFar WPGP
fragrans	LAst LPan
- f. *thunbergii*	SSpi
§ *heterophyllus*	CBcs CDul EMil ENot EPfP LPan MBar MWya NFor SPer SReu SRms SSpi SSta WDin WFar WGwG WStI XPep
§ - all gold	CAbP CDoC EGra EOMN LAst MBlu SMer SPer SPla WSHC
- 'Argenteomarginatus'	see *O. heterophyllus* 'Variegatus'
§ - 'Aureomarginatus' (v)	CBcs CBrm CDoC CFil CHar CMHG CSBt EBee EHoe EMil EPfP LRHS MWya SHBN SLon SPer
- 'Aureus' misapplied	see *O. heterophyllus* all gold
- 'Aureus' Rehder	see *O. heterophyllus* 'Aureomarginatus'
§ - 'Goshiki' (v)	More than 30 suppliers
N - 'Gulftide' ♀H4	CDoC EBee ECrN EMil EPfP LRHS MGos MWht NLar WFar WRHF WStI
- 'Purple Shaft'	CAbP ELan EPfP LRHS MAsh
- 'Purpureus'	CAbP CBcs CBot CDoC CDul CMHG CWib ECrN EHoe EPfP LRHS MBri MDun MGos MRav MSph NDlv SDry SLim SLon SSpi SWal WDin WRHF WStI WWeb
- 'Rotundifolius'	CBcs CFil
- Tricolor	see *O. heterophyllus* 'Goshiki'
§ - 'Variegatus' (v) ♀H4	CBcs CBot CBrm CSBt CWib EBee ECrN EGra ELan EMil ENot EPfP LAst LRHS MAsh MBar MGos MRav MWat SLim SPer SPla SReu SSta WBVN WDin WFar WHar WPat WWeb
ilicifolius	see *O. heterophyllus*
serrulatus	CBot CFil NLar WPGP
suavis	CFil EPfP GKir LRHS NLar SSpi
§ *yunnanensis*	CMHG EPfP LRHS MBlu SAPC SArc SSpi WBcn WFar WPGP

x *Osmarea* (Oleaceae)

burkwoodii	see *Osmanthus* x *burkwoodii*

Osmaronia see *Oemleria*

Osmorhiza (Apiaceae)

aristata B&SWJ 1607	WCru

Osmunda ✿ (Osmundaceae)

cinnamomea ♀H4	CFil CLAP CPLG EBee GBin LEur MAsh NBPC SSpi WPGP WRic
claytoniana ♀H4	CFil CLAP CPLG EBee EPfP GCal LEur MAsh NHol NLar NOGN WCru WMoo WRic
japonica	EBee
lancea **new**	NLar
regalis ♀H4	More than 30 suppliers
§ - 'Cristata' ♀H4	CBcs CFil CFwr CLAP CPLG EBee ELan GBin GCal LPBA MBri NHol SLon WFib WPGP WRic
- 'Purpurascens'	More than 30 suppliers
- var. *spectabilis*	WRic
§ - 'Undulata'	ELan GBin LPBA NHol NMar WFib WRic

Osteomeles (Rosaceae)

schweriniae	EMan
- B&L 12360	CPle SAga

Osteospermum ✿ (Asteraceae)

'African Queen'	see *O.* 'Nairobi Purple'
'Antares'PBR (Springstar Series)	LAst LHop
'Arctur'PBR	CBcs SMrm
barberae hort.	see *O. jucundum*
'Blackthorn Seedling'	see *O. jucundum* 'Blackthorn Seedling'
'Blue Streak'	NBur SMrm
'Brickell's Hybrid'	see *O.* 'Chris Brickell'
'Brightside'PBR (Side Series)	WWol
'Buttermilk' ♀H1+3	CHal ELan LRHS MBri SMrm
'Campo' **new**	Llck
'Cannington Katrina'	MOak
'Cannington Roy'	CMHG CSam CTbh ECtt EPfP MBri NBur WAbe
caulescens hort.	see *O.* 'White Pim'
§ 'Chris Brickell'	CHal GCal MOak MSte NBur WHen
'Countryside' (Side Series)	WWol
Cream Symphony = 'Seidacre'PBR	LAst SMrm
'Darkside' (Side Series)	WWol
ecklonis	CHea CHll CTbh EChP GGar IBlr ISea MHer NBro NGdn SMrm WBar WFar WMoo WPer WWin
- var. *prostratum*	see *O.* 'White Pim'
'Edna Bond'	WEas
fruticosum **new**	XPep
I - 'Album' **new**	XPep
'Gemma'PBR (Springstar Series)	MBNS WGor
'Giles Gilbey' (v)	CHEx CHal CPLG CTbh MBNS MOak NBur SVen WOut
'Gold Sparkler' (v)	LRHS SMrm
'Gweek Variegated' (v)	CBcs
'Helen Dimond'	COtt WWeb
'Hopleys' ♀H3-4	MBNS MHer MWrn SEND
'Irish'	EPot MWrn
'James Elliman'	MOak
'Jewel' (v)	COtt
§ *jucundum* ♀H3-4	CMHG CMea CWCL EBlw EChP ECha EPfP EWTr LRHS MBow MNrw MTis MWat MWgw NBrk NChi NGdn NPer SAga SEND SIng SPlb SRms WCom WCra WHen WHil WPat WWeb WWpP
§ - 'Blackthorn Seedling' ♀H3-4	CPlt ECha MBri MSph NFla NGdn SAga SBla
- var. *compactum*	CHEx CLyd CPBP MBro MHar NPer WAbe WCom WHen WHoo MBri
- 'Elliott's Form'	MBri
- 'Jackarandum'	MDKP
§ - 'Killerton Pink'	CMHG WPer
§ - 'Langtrees' ♀H3-4	ECtt EOrc LHop SMrm
'Killerton Pink'	see *O. jucundum* 'Killerton Pink'
§ - 'Lady Leitrim' ♀H3-4	CBri CHEx CHrt EBlw ECha EOrc EPfP GBri GGar IBlr LHop MBNS MBnl MBow MCLN MOak MWrn NBrk NPer SAga SChu SSvw WAbe WCAu WCom WWeb WWpP
'Langtrees'	see *O. jucundum* 'Langtrees'
'Lemon Symphony'PBR	CBcs LAst Llck MBNS SMrm
'Lubango'PBR	CBcs
'Mira'PBR	SMrm
'Nairobi Purple'	CDoC CFee CHEx CHal CPLG ELan GGar MOak NBur SAga SVen
Nasinga Series	CBcs CElw
Orange Symphony = 'Seimora'PBR	CBcs CTbh LAst Llck MBNS SMrm
Orania Terracotta = 'Akterra' **new**	Llck

'Pale Face'   see *O.* 'Lady Leitrim'
'Peach Symphony' **new**   LAst MBNS
'Peggyi'   see *O.* 'Nairobi Purple'
'Penny Pink'   ECtt
'Pink Whirls' ♀H1+3   CBot CHal CWCL LRHS MBri NBur
'Pollux'PBR (Springstar   MBNS SMrm
  Series)
'Port Wine'   see *O.* 'Nairobi Purple'
'Seaside'PBR (Side Series)   WWol
'Seaspray'   COtt
'Silver Sparkler' (v) ♀H1+3   CSLe ELan EShb LRHS MBNS MHer
                                     MOak NBur SChu SSto SVen
                                     WBrE
'Sirius'PBR   SMrm
'Snow White'   CHal
'Sparkler'   CHEx MSte
'Stardust'PBR   COtt LRHS NPer SCoo
'Stringston Gemma'   CHal
'Sunny Alex'PBR   LRHS
'Sunny Amelia' **new**   LAst
'Sunny Dark   LAst
  Martha'PBR **new**
'Sunny Martha'PBR   LAst LRHS
'Sunny Serena' **new**   LAst
* 'Superbum'   CHEx
'Svelte'   MSte
'Tauranga'   see *O.* 'Whirlygig'
'Tresco Peggy'   see *O.* 'Nairobi Purple'
'Tresco Pink'   IBlr
'Tresco Purple'   see *O.* 'Nairobi Purple'
'Vega'   LAst LHop WGor
'Weetwood' ♀H3-4   CMHG CPLG EBlw ECtt EPot EShb
                                     LHop MBNS MBri MHar MHer
                                     MSte NBrk SAga SBla SMrm WAbe
                                     WEas WWeb
'Westside' (Side Series)   WWol
§ 'Whirlygig' ♀H1+3   CHal MBri MHer MOak
§ 'White Pim' ♀H3-4   CHll CMHG ELan LPhx LRHS
                                     MWrn NPer SChu SDix SPer SUsu
                                     XPep
'Wildside'PBR (Side Series)   WWol
'Wine Purple'   see *O.* 'Nairobi Purple'
Wisley hybrids   GGar WEas
'Wisley Pink'   EPyc
'Zambesi'   LRHS
'Zimba'PBR   ELan LRHS
'Zulu'PBR   LRHS MHer

Ostrowskia (*Campanulaceae*)
magnifica   MTho

Ostrya (*Corylaceae*)
carpinifolia   CAgr CBcs CDul CLnd CMCN
                                     CTho EPAt IMGH LRHS MBar
                                     MBlu NLar SBLw WDin WNor
                                     WOrn
japonica   CFil CMCN
virginiana   CFil CMCN ECrN EPfP IMGH
                                     WNor

Otanthus (*Asteraceae*)
maritimus **new**   XPep

Otatea (*Poaceae*)
aztecorum   CFil

Othonna (*Asteraceae*)
capensis   CHal
§ *cheirifolia*   CBot CMea CSam CSev EGoo ELan
                                     EMan NBir NFor SDry SIgm SMac
                                     SPer WCom WCot WEas WPer
                                     XPep

Othonnopsis see *Othonna*

Ourisia (*Scrophulariaceae*)
caespitosa   GCrs IBlr NGar NMen NRya
- var. *gracilis*   GEdr GGar GTou IBlr NMen
§ *coccinea*   EMan GAbr GBuc GEdr GGar
                                     GKev GMac IBlr LRHS NBir NGar
                                     NGby NRya SSpi WAbe
crosbyi   GEdr GGar IBlr
crosbyi x *macrocarpa*   IBlr
elegans   see *O. coccinea*
lactea   IBlr
'Loch Ewe'   CPLG CPla GAbr GBuc GCrs GEdr
                                     GGar IBlr MDun NCGa NGar
                                     WCru WPGP
macrocarpa   IBlr
macrophylla   EBee GBuc GGar IBlr IGor NBPC
                                     WAbe
macrophylla   IBlr
  x *modesta*
microphylla   EHyt NWCA WAbe
* - f. *alba*   EHyt WAbe
modesta   IBlr
polyantha F&W 8487   WAbe
'Snowflake' ♀H4   EMan EPot GAbr GCrs GEdr GFlt
                                     GKev IBlr MDun MOne NBir NGar
                                     NMen WAbe

Oxalis ✿ (*Oxalidaceae*)
F&W 8673   CPBP
from Mount Stewart   ECha
acetosella   CHid CNat CRWN ERos MBow
                                     MHer NMir NSco WHer WShi
- var. *subpurpurascens*   SScr WCot
adenophylla ♀H4   More than 30 suppliers
- 'Brenda Anderson' **new**   SBla
- dark   MTho
anomala   EBee EMan WCot
arborescens   CHEx
§ *articulata*   EMan LGro MTho NPer SEND
                                     WCot WWin
- 'Alba'   ETow LRHS
- 'Aureoreticulata'   MTho
- 'Festival'   CFwr EBee
'Beatrice Anderson'   EHyt GCrs MBro MTho NHol
                                     NJOw NMen SBla WAbe
bowiei   EPot
- 'Amarantha'   EBee EMan
'Bowles' White'   MTho
brasiliensis   CStu EMlt EPot MTho NJOw
                                     NMen WOBN
brick-orange   WCot
chrysantha   EMlt IHMH SIng WAbe
compacta F&W 8011   CPBP
corniculata var.   MTho
  atropurpurea
'Dark Eye' **new**   GCrs
debilis 'Aureoreticulata'   WCot
deppei   see *O. tetraphylla*
§ *depressa*   CStu CTri EBee EPot EWes GEdr
                                     GSki LTwo MTho NBir NHol
                                     NJOw NMen NRya NSla SIng SRms
                                     WBea WBrE WCot WFar
- 'Irish Mist' **new**   EBee
* *eckloniana* var.   WCot
  sonderi **new**
enneaphylla ♀H4   EMan EPot GCrs GGar LRHS MTho
                                     NHol NMen NRya
enneaphylla x   see *O.* 'Matthew Forrest'
  adenophylla
- 'Alba'   CGra EHyt ERos ETow GBuc ITim
                                     MBro NHol NMen NSla WAbe
                                     WCom WIvy
I - 'Hythe Seedling'   EHyt
- 'Lady Elizabeth'   SBla

	- 'Minutifolia'	ERos GCrs LRHS LTwo MTho NHol NMen NRya NSla WCom WIvy
*	- 'Minutifolia Rosea'	CGra
	- 'Rosea'	CBro EHyt EPot ERos MTho NHol NRya NSla SBla
	- 'Ruth Tweedie'	ETow NSla
	- 'Sheffield Swan'	CGra EHyt NMen SBla SOkd WAbe
	europaea	GWCH
	falcatula	WCot
	'Fanny' **new**	EBee
	flava	LAma NJOw
	floribunda hort.	see *O. articulata*
	fourcadii **new**	WCot
	geminata	NBir
	'Gwen McBride'	GCrs SBla WAbe
	'Hemswell Knight'	ETow NMen WAbe
	hirta	CBro CDes MTho NJOw
	- 'Gothenburg'	CPBP EMan ERos MTho NMen
	imbricata	EPot LTwo
	inops	see *O. depressa*
	'Ione Hecker' ♀H4	CBro CGra CLyd EHyt EPot ERos GCrs GEdr GGar GTou ITim MTho NHol NMen NRya NSla NWCA NWoo SBla SIgm WAbe WCom WIvy WLin
*	*karroica* **new**	WCot
§	*laciniata*	CGra EHyt ERos GCrs MTho NHol NMen NSla SBla
	- dark	EHyt ITim
	- 'Seven Bells'	CGra SBla
	lactea double	see *O. magellanica* 'Nelson'
	lasiandra	CFwr EBee EPot ERos
	lobata	CBro CNic CPBP CStu EHyt EMan EPot ERos ETow EWes LHop LRHS MTho NJOw WAbe WCom
	magellanica	CFee CHal CMHG CPom CRow CSpe CTri EBla EMlt ESis GGar LBee MTho NHol SIng SPlb WBea WFar WHrl WPer
	- 'Flore Pleno'	see *O. magellanica* 'Nelson'
§	- 'Nelson' (d)	CElw CHal CNic CPLG CRow CSpe CStu EBee EMan EMlt EPot EWes GCal GGar GMac LBee LRHS MTho NBir NBro NJOw NPer NWoo SSvw WCru WPer WPnP WPrP
	massoniana	SIng
§	'Matthew Forrest'	NJOw WAbe
	megalorrhiza **new**	CPLG
	nahuelhuapiensis F&W 8469	CPBP
	namaquana	WCot
	obtusa	CLyd CSpe CStu EMan EPot ESis ETow MTho SCnR WCot
	- apricot	SOkd WCom WCot
	oregana	CDes CNic CRow GBuc GGar GMac WCru WPGP WSHC
	- f. *smalliana*	EBee EWes WCru WHal
	palmifrons	CPBP CStu EPot LTwo MTho NJOw
	patagonica	EPot ERos GCrs NMen
*	*pulchra*	CSpe
§	*purpurea*	CSpe IHMH WAbe
	- 'Ken Aslet'	CBro CFee CLyd CNic CStu EHyt EMan EPot GCrs GFlt LTwo NJOw WAbe WOBN
	regnellii	see *O. triangularis* subsp. *papilionacea*
	rosea hort.	see *O. rubra*
§	*rubra*	EBee
	semiloba	EBee EMan GCal WCot
	speciosa	see *O. purpurea*
	squamata **new**	NLAp WPat

	squamosoradicosa	see *O. laciniata*
	stipularis	CNic
	succulenta Barnéoud	CFwr CHll CSpe
	'Sunny'	CFwr EBee
	'Superstar'	WAbe
§	*tetraphylla*	CAgr CM&M EBee EPot GSki LAma LRHS MBri MTho NOrc NPer NRog SWal WRha
	- *alba*	EBee
	- 'Iron Cross'	CHEx EBee EMan EPot ESis GCrs GFlt GSki LAma MMHG NBir NJOw SWal WBVN WBea WBrE WBro WHal
	triangularis	CHEx CStu EOHP LAma NBir NJOw NPer WBrE WFar
	- 'Cupido'	WPer WWin
	- 'Mijke' **new**	EBee
§	- subsp. *papilionacea* ♀H1	EBee EMan GSki LAma LRHS MMHG NJOw NRog WWin
	- - 'Atropurpurea'	EBee WBVN WCot
*	- - *rosea*	EMan WCot
	- subsp. *triangularis*	EBee
	tuberosa	GPoy ILis LEdu WHer
	- 'Fat Red'	EOHP
	- 'Fat White'	EOHP
	'Ute'	CGra GEdr
	valdiviensis	EMan MDKP NBur
	versicolor ♀H1	CPBP CSpe CStu EHyt EMan EPot ERos ITim MTho NMen SBla SCnR SOkd SUsu WAbe WCom WCot
	vulcanicola	CStu SDix
	zeekoevleyensis	WCot

Oxycoccus see *Vaccinium*

Oxydendrum (Ericaceae)

arboreum	CAbP CBcs CDoC CEnd CMCN ECrN EPfP GKir IDee LEdu LPan MBri MGos NLar SPer SSpi SSta WCru WDin WFar WNor
- 'Chameleon'	EPfP LRHS SSpi SSta

Oxygraphis (Ranunculaceae)

polypetala **new**	EBee

Oxylobium (Papilionaceae)

ellipticum	ECou

Oxypetalum (Asclepiadaceae)

caeruleum	see *Tweedia caerulea*

Oxyria (Polygonaceae)

digyna	CAgr EMan GGar NBro NLar WHer

Oxytropis (Papilionaceae)

deflexa var.	LTwo
deflexa **new**	
hailarensis var. *chankaensis*	CPBP
lambertii	LTwo
megalantha	EMan NWCA
purpurea	EMan LTwo
shokanbetsuensis	EMan LTwo SOkd
uralensis	LTwo

Ozothamnus (Asteraceae)

	antennaria	WSHC
§	*coralloides* ♀H2-3	EPot GCrs GGar ITim NJOw NLAp NRya NWCA SIng
§	'County Park Silver'	EWes GEdr ITim NDlv NLAp NLar NWCA SBla WCom WPat
§	*hookeri*	CAbb CDoC ECou GGar NLar NWCA SChu WPat
§	*ledifolius* ♀H4	CBcs CDoC CMHG CPle CSam

		ELan EPfP GGar GTou LRHS MBri
		NBir SChu SLon SPer SSpi WDin
		WHCG WHar WPat WSHC
§	**microphyllus**	ITim
§	**rosmarinifolius**	CBcs CDoC CMHG CPLG CTrG
		EBee ELan EPfP GGar LRHS MSwo
		SChu SPer WBod WBrE WDin WEas
		WFar WHCG WPic XPep
	- 'Kiandra'	ECou
	- 'Silver Jubilee' ♀H3	CBcs CDoC CEnd CHEx CPLG
		CSBt CSam CTrC CTrG EBee ECrN
		ELan EPfP LRHS MAsh MSwo
		SHBN SLon SPer SSpi WDin WFar
		WHCG WKif XPep
	scutellifolius	ECou
§	**selago**	EBee ECou EPot ITim NRya WCot
	- var. **intermedium**	GGar
	- 'Minor'	NWCA
§	- var. **tumidus**	SIng
	'Sussex Silver'	NBlu
	'Threave Seedling'	CDoC CSam LRHS SPer SSpi
§	**thyrsoideus**	CPLG WFar

P

Pachyphragma (Brassicaceae)

§	**macrophyllum**	CPom CSev ECGP ECha EGle EHrv
		ELan EMon EPPr GCal GFlt IBlr
		LRHS MRav MTed NCiC NLar
		NMRc NSti SSpi WCot WCru WEas
		WPGP WSHC WWin

Pachypodium (Apocynaceae)

	bispinosum	CRoM
	geayi ♀H1	CRoM
	horombense	CRoM
	lamerei ♀H1	CRoM EAmu MBri SMur
	lealii subsp. **saundersii**	CRoM
	rosulatum var. **gracilius**	CRoM
	succulentum	CRoM

Pachysandra (Buxaceae)

	axillaris	CLAP GCal
	procumbens	CLAP EBee EPla NLar SSpi WCot
		WCru
	stylosa	CBct CDoC EPla MRav NLar SMad
	terminalis	More than 30 suppliers
	- 'Green Carpet' ♀H4	CBcs CDoC CSam EBee EBre ECot
		EGol EPfP EWTr GKir IHMH LRHS
		MAsh MBar MBri MGos MSwo
		NBlu NHol NPro SCoo SMac SPer
		SPla SWvt WCAu
		WShp
	- 'Variegata' (v) ♀H4	More than 30 suppliers

Pachystachys (Acanthaceae)

	lutea ♀H1	CHal ERea EShb LRHS MBri

Pachystegia (Asteraceae)

	insignis	CTrC GGar
	minor	WCru

Pachystima see *Paxistima*

Packera (Asteraceae)

§	**aurea**	ECha EMan MSal SSpi

Paederia (Rubiaceae)

	scandens	CPLG WCru
		WSHC
	- var. **mairei** B&SWJ 989	WCru

Paederota (Scrophulariaceae)

§	**bonarota**	CLyd NWCA
	lutea	CDes NWCA

Paeonia ✿ (Paeoniaceae)

	albiflora	see *P. lactiflora*
	'Angel Cobb Freeborn'	WCAu
	'Angelet' **new**	CKel
	anomala	CFir EPot MHom MPhe NSla SSpi
	- var. **intermedia new**	GCal
	- subsp. **veitchii**	see *P. veitchii*
	arietina	see *P. mascula* subsp. *arietina*
	'Avant Garde'	WKif
	bakeri	EBee
	banatica	see *P. officinalis* subsp. *banatica*
	'Black Pirate'	CKel
	'Blaze' **new**	WCAu
	Blue and Purple Giant	see *P. suffruticosa* 'Zi Lan Kui'
	'Bridal Icing' **new**	WCAu
	broteroi	CLAP SSpi
	brownii	EPot
	'Buckeye Belle'	CKel EBee EFou GKir LPio MBri
		MHom MPhe MSte SHar WCAu
	'Burma Ruby'	WCot
	cambessedesii ♀H2-3	CBrd CBro CFil EBre EGle EHyt
		EPot ETow LRHS MTho NBir
		NMen NSla SAga SBla SIgm SRot
		SSpi WCot WPGP
	'Carol'	WCAu
	caucasica	see *P. mascula* subsp. *mascula*
	'China Pink'	MBri
	'Chinese Dragon'	CKel
	'Claire de Lune'	MBri WCAu WCot
	'Claudia'	WCAu
	'Coral Charm'	WCot
	'Coral Fay'	MSte WCAu
	corallina	see *P. mascula* subsp. *mascula*
	coriacea var. **atlantica**	CBro
	Crimson Red	see *P. suffruticosa* 'Hu Hong'
	'Cytherea'	WCAu
	'Dancing Butterflies'	EBee EBre ENot WCAu WWeb
	daurica	see *P. mascula* subsp. *triternata*
	decomposita	EBee MPhe
	decora	see *P. peregrina*
	'Defender'	WCAu
	delavayi (S) ♀H4	CBcs CHad CKel CSam EBre EChP
		EOrc EPfP EPla GAbr GCal GKir
		IBlr LHop LRHS MAsh MDun MTis
		NBir NCGa NSti SLPl SMad SPer
		SRms SSpi WBrE WCAu
	- BWJ 7775	WCru
§	- var. **angustiloba**	SSpi
	f. **angustiloba**	
	- - - ACE 1047	EPot
	- - - white-flowered **new**	EBee
	- var. **atropurpurea**	NFor
	- from China (S)	MPhe
	- hybrid (S)	ENot
§	- var. **ludlowii** (S) ♀H4	CBcs CKel CSam EBee EChP ELan
		EOrc EPfP EWTr GGGa GKir ISea
		ITer LRHS MAvo MDun MPhe NBir
		NBrk NCGa NPer SLPl SPer SPlb
		SSpi WCAu WCot WDin
		WEas WFar
§	- var. **lutea** (S)	CDul CHad ENot EPfP LRHS MAsh
		MBro MLan SAga SHBN SLon SRms
		STre WAul WBrE WHar WHoo
		WPnP WTin
	- 'Mrs Sarson'	MCCP SLPl SWat
	- Potaninii Group (S)	see *P. delavayi* var. *angustiloba* f.
		angustiloba
	- Trollioides Group	EBee WCAu
	(S) **new**	

delavayi × *delavayi* var. *lutea*	ELan GKir
Drizzling Rain Cloud	see *P. suffruticosa* 'Shiguregumo'
'Early Bird'	GKir
'Eastgrove Ruby Lace'	WEas
'Ellen Cowley'	WCAu
emodi	CLAP LPio WCot
'Fairy Princess'	MBri WCAu
'Flame'	EBee MNrw MSte NLar SPer WCAu WHil
Fragrance and Beauty	see *P. suffruticosa* 'Lan Tian Yu'
Gansu Mudan Group (S)	CKel MPhe
- 'Bing Shan Xue Lian' (S)	MPhe
- 'Bai Bi Fen Xia' (S)	MPhe
- 'Bai Bi Lan Xia' (S)	MPhe
- 'Cheng Xin' (S) **new**	MPhe
- 'Fen He' (S)	MPhe
- 'Feng Xian' (S) **new**	MPhe
- 'Hei Xuan Feng' (S) **new**	MPhe
- 'He Ping Lian' (S)	MPhe
- 'Hong Lian' (S)	MPhe
- 'Huang He' (S) **new**	MPhe
- 'Hui He' (S)	MPhe
- 'Lan Hai Yiu Bo' (S) **new**	MPhe
- 'Lan He' (S)	MPhe
- 'Lian Chun' (S) **new**	MPhe
- 'Li Xiang' (S)	MPhe
- 'Shu Sheng Peng Mo' (S)	MPhe
- 'Xue Lian' (S) **new**	MPhe
- 'Zi Die Ying Feng' (S)	MPhe
- 'Zie Pie' (S) **new**	MPhe
'Golden Bowl'	CKel
'Golden Isles' **new**	CKel
Green Dragon Lying on a Chinese Inkstone	see *P. suffruticosa* 'Qing Long Wo Mo Chi'
'Hei Hua Kui'	see *P. suffruticosa* 'Hei Hua Kui'
'High Noon'	CKel ENot MPhe NBlu
'Hoki' **new**	CKel
'Honor'	WCAu
§ 'Huang Hua Kui' (S)	MPhe
humilis	see *P. officinalis* subsp. *microcarpa*
'Illini Warrior'	WCAu
japonica misapplied	see *P. lactiflora*
jishanensis	MPhe
'Joseph Rock'	see *P. rockii*
'Joyce Ellen'	WCAu
kavachensis	EBee GCal GIBF
kevachensis	see *P. mascula* subsp. *mascula*
'Kinkaku'	see *P.* × *lemoinei* 'Souvenir de Maxime Cornu'
'Kinko'	see *P.* × *lemoinei* 'Alice Harding'
'Kinshi'	see *P.* × *lemoinei* 'Chromatella'
'Kintei'	see *P.* × *lemoinei* 'L'Espérance'
'Kokkou-Tsukasa'	CKel
'Kun Shan Ye Guang'	CKel
§ *lactiflora*	EHrv MPhe SSpi
- 'A.F.W. Hayward'	CKel
* - 'Afterglow'	CKel
- 'Agida'	EBee
- 'Agnes Mary Kelway' **new**	CKel
- 'Albert Crousse'	CBcs CKel GKir NBir NBlu WCAu
I - 'Albertii' **new**	EBee
- 'Alexander Fleming'	EBee EChP ECot GKir NBir WCAu WWeb
- 'Algae Adamson'	CKel
- 'Alice Balfour'	CKel
- 'Alice Harding'	WCot
- 'Amibilis'	WCAu
- 'Angel Cheeks'	WCAu
- 'Anna Pavlova'	CKel
- 'Antwerpen'	ERou MBri WCAu

- 'Arabian Prince'	CKel
- 'Argentine'	WCAu
- 'Artist'	CKel
- 'Asa Gray'	CKel
- 'Auguste Dessert'	CKel EBee WCAu
§ - 'Augustin d'Hour'	CKel EBee ERou
- 'Aureole'	CKel
- 'Avalanche' **new**	EBee
- 'Ballerina'	CKel
- 'Barbara'	CKel WCAu
- 'Baroness Schröder'	EBee ELan
- 'Barrington Belle'	EBee EMan GKir MBri MSte NBPC WAul WCAu
- 'Barrymore'	CKel
- 'Beacon'	CKel
- 'Beatrice Kelway'	CKel
- 'Belle Center'	WCAu
- 'Best Man' **new**	WCAu
- 'Bethcar'	CKel
- 'Better Times'	WCAu
- 'Big Ben'	EBee NBPC SVil
- 'Blaze of Beauty'	CKel EBee
- 'Blenheim'	CKel
- 'Blush Queen'	EBee ELan SMrm WCAu
- 'Border Gem'	GKir
- 'Bouchela'	EBee
- 'Boulanger'	EBee
- 'Bower of Roses'	CKel
- 'Bowl of Beauty' ♀H4	More than 30 suppliers
- 'Bowl of Cream'	EBee EMan SWvt WCAu
- 'Bracken'	CKel
- 'Break o' Day'	WCAu
- 'Bridal Veil'	CKel
- 'Bridesmaid'	CKel
- 'British Beauty'	CKel
- 'British Empire'	NPar
- 'Bunker Hill'	CKel EBee EWTr GKir SMur SPer SVil SWvt WCAu
- 'Butter Bowl'	WCAu
- 'Calypso'	CKel
- 'Canarie'	CKel MBri
- 'Candeur'	CKel EBee
- 'Cang Long'	CKel
- 'Captivation'	CKel
- 'Carnival'	CKel EBee
- 'Caroline Allain'	CKel
- 'Cascade'	CKel
- 'Catherine Fontijn'	CKel EBee LBuc WCAu WHil
- 'Challenger'	CKel
- 'Charlemagne'	CKel
- 'Charles' White'	EBee EGle LPVe LPio MAvo WCAu
- 'Cheddar Charm'	GKir WCAu
- 'Cheddar Cheese'	GKir MBri
- 'Cheddar Gold' ♀H4	GKir MBri
- 'Cherry Hill'	WCAu
- 'Chestine Gowdy'	CKel
- 'Christine Kelway'	CKel
- 'Chun Xiao'	CKel
- 'Claire Dubois'	CKel ERou GKir WCAu
- 'Colonel Heneage'	CKel
- 'Cornelia Shaylor'	WCAu
- 'Coronation'	CKel
- 'Country Girl'	CKel
- 'Crimson Glory'	CKel
- 'Crimson Velvet'	CKel
- 'Cringley White'	SBod
- 'Da Fu Gui'	CKel
- 'Dark Vintage'	CKel
- 'Dawn Crest'	CKel
- 'Dayspring'	CKel
- 'Delachei'	CKel
- 'Desire'	CKel
- 'Diana Drinkwater'	CKel
- 'Dinner Plate'	EBee MBri SPer WCAu WCot

- 'Display'	CKel
- 'Do Tell'	EBee NBPC SVil
- 'Docteur H. Barnsby'	CKel
- 'Doctor Alexander Fleming'	CKel EBre SWvt
- 'Dominion'	CKel
- 'Doreen'	EBee NBPC WCAu
- 'Dorothy Welsh'	CKel
- 'Dresden'	CKel
- 'Duchess of Bedford'	CKel
- 'Duchess of Somerset'	CKel
- 'Duchesse de Nemours' ♀H4	CKel COtt EBee EChP EFou ELan ENot EPfP GKir LAst LHop LPVe MBri MBro MSte NBir NLar SMrm SPer SRms SWvt WAul WCAu WCot WHil WHoo WShp WViv WWeb
- 'Duchesse d'Orléans'	WCAu
- 'Duke of Devonshire'	CKel
- 'Eden's Temptation'	EBee SPer SVil
- 'Edmund Spencer'	CKel
- 'Edulis Superba'	CKel EBee EBre EChP EGle ELan ENot GKir LPVe LRHS MBNS NPer SMrm SPer WCAu
- 'Elaine' **new**	CKel
- 'Elizabeth Stone'	CKel
- 'Ella Christine Kelway'	CKel
- 'Elma'	CKel
- 'Elsa Sass'	WCAu
- 'Emma Klehm'	EBee WCAu
- 'Emperor of India'	CKel
- 'Enchantment'	CKel
- 'English Princess'	CKel
- 'Ethelreda'	CKel
- 'Ethereal'	CKel
- 'Eugénie Verdier'	MTed
- 'Evening Glow'	CKel
- 'Evening World'	CKel MRav
- 'Faire Rosamond'	CKel
- 'Fashion Show' **new**	CKel
- 'Felicity'	CKel
- 'Félix Crousse' ♀H4	CKel CTri EBee EBre ELan EMil ENot EPfP ERou GKir LAst LPVe MBNS NBir SPer SRms SWat WCAu WWeb
- 'Fen Chi Jin Yu'	CKel
- 'Fen Mian Tao Hua'	CKel
- 'Festiva Maxima' ♀H4	CKel CSBt CTri EBee EChP ECot ELan EPfP ERou GKir LPVe LRHS MBri MBro MSte NLar SPer SPla SRms SWvt WAul WCAu WHil WHoo WViv
- 'Florence Ellis'	WCAu
- 'France'	CKel
- 'Gainsborough'	CKel
- 'Gardenia'	EBee
- 'Gay Paree'	EBee WCAu
- 'Gayborder June'	CKel EBee MBri WCAu
- 'Général MacMahon'	see *P. lactiflora* 'Augustin d'Hour'
- 'General Wolfe'	CKel
- 'Germaine Bigot'	CKel WCAu
- 'Gilbert Barthelot'	WCAu
- 'Gleam of Light'	CKel MBri
- 'Gloriana'	WCAu
- 'Glory Hallelujah'	WCAu
- 'Glowing Candles' **new**	WCAu
- 'Gold Mine'	CKel
- 'Golden Fleece'	WCAu
- 'Goodform'	CKel
- 'Grover Cleveland'	CKel
- 'Guidon'	WCAu
- 'Gypsy Girl'	CKel
- 'Hakodate'	CKel
- 'Heartbeat'	CKel
- 'Hei Hai Bo Tao'	CKel
- 'Helen Hayes'	WCAu
- 'Henri Potin'	CKel
- 'Henry Woodward' **new**	CKel
- 'Her Grace'	CKel
- 'Her Majesty'	NBir
- 'Herbert Oliver'	CKel
- 'Hiawatha'	WCAu
- 'Hit Parade'	WCAu
- 'Honey Gold'	EBee ELan EMan NBPC SVil WAul WCAu
- 'Huang Jin Lun'	CKel
- 'Hyperion'	CKel
- 'Immaculée'	EBee ENot NLar WHil
- 'Ingenieur Doriat'	CKel
- 'Inspecteur Lavergne'	CKel CM&M EBee LRHS WAul WCAu WCot
- 'Instituteur Doriat'	CKel EBee MPhe WCAu
- 'Israel'	CKel
- 'Jacques Doriat'	CKel
- 'Jadwigha' **new**	EBee
- 'James Kelway'	CKel
- 'James William Kelway'	CKel
- 'Jan van Leeuwen'	CPen EBee EPfP ERou GKir WCAu
- 'Jeanne d'Arc'	CKel
- 'Jewel'	CKel
- 'Jin Chi Yu'	CKel
- 'Jin Dai Wei'	CKel
- 'Joan Kelway'	CKel
- 'John Howard Wigell'	WCAu
- 'Joseph Plagne'	CKel
- 'Joy of Life'	CKel
- 'June Morning'	CKel
- 'June Rose'	WCAu
- 'Kansas'	CKel EBee ELan ERou MPhe WCAu WFar
- 'Karen Gray'	WCAu
- 'Karl Rosenfield'	CKel CSBt EBee EChP ECot EGle ENot EPfP GKir LAst LRHS MBri MBro MSte NBee SPer SPla SRms STes SWvt WFar WHil WHoo WShp WViv WWeb
- 'Kathleen Mavoureen'	CKel EBee
- 'Kelway's Betty'	CKel
- 'Kelway's Brilliant'	CKel
- 'Kelway's Circe'	CKel
- 'Kelway's Daystar'	CKel
- 'Kelway's Exquisite'	CKel
- 'Kelway's Fairy Queen'	CKel
- 'Kelway's Glorious'	CKel EBee EChP ERou EWTr GKir LPVe MTed SMrm WHil
- 'Kelway's Gorgeous'	EBee
- 'Kelway's Lovely'	CKel
- 'Kelway's Lovely Lady'	CKel
- 'Kelway's Majestic'	CKel
- 'Kelway's Queen'	CKel
- 'Kelway's Scented Rose'	CKel
- 'Kelway's Silvo' **new**	CKel
- 'Kelway's Supreme'	CKel SWat
- 'King of England'	CKel
- 'Knighthood'	CKel
- 'Kocho-jishi' **new**	CKel
- 'Konigin Wilhelmina'	EBee
- 'Krinkled White'	EBee GBin LPio MBri MPhe NLar WAul WCAu
- 'La Belle Hélène'	CKel
- 'La Lorraine'	CKel
- 'La Perle'	CKel
- 'Lady Alexandra Duff' ♀H4	CKel COtt EBee EChP EPfP EWTr GKir LPVe MRav MTis NFla SCoo SRms SWvt WCAu WHil
- 'Lady Ann' **new**	EBee
- 'Lady Bramwell' **new**	EBee
- 'Lady Kate' **new**	WCAu
- 'Lady Ley'	CKel

	- 'Lady Mayoress'	CKel
	- 'Lady Orchid'	WCAu
I	- 'Langport Cross'	CKel
	- 'Langport Triumph'	CKel
	- 'Laura Dessert' ♀H4	EBee EBre EPfP ERou EWTr EWll GKir WCAu
	- 'Leading Lady'	CKel
	- 'L'Eclatante'	CKel EBee WViv
	- 'Legion of Honor'	CKel
	- 'Lemon Ice'	CKel
	- 'Lemon Queen'	CKel
	- 'Letitia'	CKel
	- 'Lillian Wild'	WCAu
	- 'Lois Kelsey'	WCAu
	- 'Longfellow'	CKel
	- 'Lord Calvin'	WCAu
	- 'Lord Derby'	CKel
	- 'Lord Kitchener'	CKel
	- 'Lorna Doone'	CKel
	- 'Lotus Queen'	WCAu
	- 'Louis Barthelot'	WCAu
	- 'Louis Joliet'	EBee EChP MSte
	- 'Louis van Houtte'	EBee
	- 'Lowell Thomas'	WCAu
	- 'Lyric'	CKel
	- 'M. Millet'	CKel
	- 'Madame Calot'	EBee MSph SRms WCAu WHil
	- 'Madame Claude Tain'	NBlu WCot
	- 'Madame de Verneville'	CKel
	- 'Madame Ducel'	CKel WCAu
	- 'Madame Edouard Doriat'	CKel
	- 'Madame Emile Debatène'	CKel EBee WCAu
	- 'Madame Jules Dessert'	WCAu
	- 'Madelon'	CKel
	- 'Magic Melody'	CKel
	- 'Magic Orb'	CKel
	- 'Margaret Truman'	CKel EBee NLar WCAu
	- 'Marie Clutton'	CKel
	- 'Marie Lemoine'	CKel EBee SMur WCAu
	- 'Marquisite'	CKel
	- 'Mary Brand'	WCAu
	- 'Masterpiece'	CKel
	- 'Meteor Flag'	CKel
	- 'Midnight Sun' **new**	MBri WCAu
	- 'Mikado'	GKir
	- 'Mischief'	CKel WCAu
	- 'Miss America'	WCAu
	- 'Miss Eckhart'	CKel EBee ERou WCAu
	- 'Mister Ed'	WCAu
	- 'Mistral'	MBri
	- 'Mo Zi Ling' **new**	WCAu
	- 'Monsieur Jules Elie' ♀H4	CKel CM&M EBee EChP EMan EPfP ERou EWTr GKir LAst LPVe MBri MPhe SPla SVil WAul WCAu WViv
	- 'Monsieur Martin Cahuzac'	CFir EBee EMan WCAu
	- 'Moon of Nippon'	MPhe
	- 'Moon River'	EBee EMan SVil
	- 'Moonglow'	WCAu
	- 'Mother's Choice'	EBee WCAu
	- 'Mr G.F. Hemerik'	CKel EBee GKir MBri MPhe WCAu WHil
	- 'Mrs Edward Harding'	WCAu
	- 'Mrs F.J. Hemerik'	WCAu
	- 'Mrs Franklin D. Roosevelt'	WCAu
	- 'Mrs J.V. Edlund'	WCAu
	- 'Mrs Livingston Farrand'	WCAu
	- 'My Pal Rudy'	WCAu
	- 'Nancy Nicholls'	WCAu
	- 'Nancy Nora'	EBee SVil

I	- 'Nellie'	CKel
	- 'Newfoundland'	CKel
	- 'Nick Shaylor'	GKir WCAu
	- 'Nippon Beauty'	CPen EBee EGle MBri
	- 'Nobility'	CKel
	- 'Ornament'	CKel
	- 'Orpen'	CKel
	- 'Othello'	CKel
	- 'Paola'	CKel
	- 'Paul M. Wild'	EBee EChP NBPC WCAu
	- 'Peche'	CPen EBee LPVe WHil
*	- 'Pecher' **new**	NPer STes
	- 'Peregrine'	CKel
	- 'Persier'	EBee
	- 'Peter Brand'	CKel EBee
	- 'Philomèle'	WCAu
	- 'Pico' **new**	WCAu
	- 'Pillow Talk'	EBee WCAu
	- 'Pink Cameo'	EBee WCAu WCot
	- 'Pink Jazz'	EBee
	- 'Pink Parfait'	CKel WCAu
	- 'Pink Princess'	MBri WCAu
	- 'Polar King'	WCAu
	- 'Port Royale' **new**	CKel
	- 'President Franklin D. Roosevelt'	GKir SWat
	- 'Président Poincaré'	CKel GKir SMur SWat
	- 'President Taft'	see *P.lactiflora* 'Reine Hortense'
	- 'Primevere'	EBee EPfP EWll MBNS WCAu
	- 'Princess Beatrice'	CKel
	- 'Qi Hua Lu Shuang'	CKel
	- 'Qing Wen'	CKel
	- 'Queen of Sheba'	WCAu
	- 'Raoul Dessert'	WCAu
	- 'Raspberry Sundae'	EBee ERou NLar WCAu WCot
	- 'Red Charm'	EBee MPhe
	- 'Red Dwarf'	CKel
	- 'Red Emperor' **new**	WCAu
	- 'Red King'	CKel
	- 'Red Sarah Bernhardt' **new**	MBri
§	- 'Reine Hortense'	CKel EBee WCAu
	- 'Renato'	EBee EFou SVil
	- 'Rose of Delight'	CKel
	- 'Ruth Cobb'	WCAu
	- 'Sante Fe'	WCAu
	- 'Santorb'	CKel
	- 'Sarah Bernhardt' ♀H4	More than 30 suppliers
	- 'Shen Tao Hua'	CKel
	- 'Shimmering Velvet'	CKel
	- 'Shi-pen Kue' **new**	MBri
	- 'Shirley Temple'	CKel EBee ELan EWTr GKir LPVe MAvo MBri MBro MRav MSte NBPC SHar SMrm WCAu WCot WHil WHoo WViv WWeb
	- 'Silver Flare'	CKel
	- 'Sir Edward Elgar'	CKel
	- 'Snow Swan'	CKel
	- 'Solange'	CKel EBee EChP LPVe LPio STes WCAu
	- 'Sorbet'	COtt CPen EBee EChP EMan EPfP LRHS MPhe NBPC NPer WHil
	- 'Spearmint'	CKel
	- 'Strephon'	CKel
	- 'Surugu'	MBri
	- 'Suzanne Dessert' **new**	CKel
	- 'Sweet Sixteen'	WCAu
	- 'Sword Dance'	EBee EGle GBin MPhe WHil WSpi
	- 'Taff' **new**	EBee
	- 'Tamate-boko'	WCAu
	- 'The Nymph'	CPen
	- 'Thérèse'	WCAu
	- 'Top Brass'	EBee MPhe MRav WCAu
	- 'Toro-no-maki'	WCAu

- 'Translucent'	CKel
- var. *trichocarpa*	EBee
- 'Victoire de la Marne'	EBee EBre EWTr SMur WHil
- 'Vogue'	CKel EBee MBri SMur SWvt WCAu
- 'Westerner'	WCAu
- 'White Angel' **new**	EBee
- 'White Ivory' **new**	WCAu
- 'White Rose of Sharon' **new**	CKel
- 'White Wings'	CBcs CKel COtt CPen EBee EGle ELan EPfP GKir MBri MSte NBee SPer SSpi SWvt WAul WCAu WCot
- 'Whitleyi Major' ♀H4	GKir WCot
- 'Wiesbaden'	WCAu
- 'Wilbur Wright'	WCAu
- 'Wladyslawa'	EBee NLar
- 'Xuan Li Duo Cai'	CKel
- 'Xue Feng'	CKel
- 'Yan Fei Chu Yu'	CKel
- 'Yan Zi Dian Yu'	CKel
- 'Zhu Sha Dian Yu'	CKel
- 'Zus Braun'	EBee
§ x *lemoinei* 'Alice Harding' (S)	CKel ENot LBuc SPer WCAu
§ - 'Chromatella' (S)	CKel ENot LAma
§ - 'L'Espérance' (S)	LAma
§ - 'Souvenir de Maxime Cornu' (S)	CKel ENot LAma LRHS MGos MPhe SPer WCAu
lithophila	see *P. tenuifolia* subsp. *lithophila*
lobata 'Fire King'	see *P. peregrina*
'Lois Arleen'	WCAu
ludlowii	see *P. delavayi* var. *ludlowii*
lutea	see *P. delavayi* var. *lutea*
- var. *ludlowii*	see *P. delavayi* var. *ludlowii*
macrophylla	MPhe
'Mai Fleuri'	GKir
mairei	MPhe
§ *mascula*	CAvo CBro EPfP GIBF LRHS NBir
- from Sicily	MPhe
§ - subsp. *arietina*	ECha Slgm WEas WKif
- - 'Northern Glory'	GKir LSpr WCAu WCot
- subsp. *hellenica*	EBee
- - from Sicily	MPhe
§ - subsp. *mascula*	CBro EBee EGle EPot GIBF MAvo WCot
- - from Georgia	MPhe
- - from SE Georgia	WPGP
§ - subsp. *russoi*	GIBF Slgm SSpi WCot
- - from Sardinia **new**	MPhe
§ - subsp. *triternata*	CLAP EBee MPhe SSpi
- - from Crimea	WPGP
'Mikuhino Akebono' **new**	CKel
mlokosewitschii ♀H4	More than 30 suppliers
mollis	see *P. officinalis* subsp. *villosa*
'Moonrise'	WCAu
'Nymphe'	CKel EBee EChP LRHS MBNS MBri MRav WAul WCAu WHil
obovata ♀H4	CFir CLAP GIBF GKir MPhe MSal SSpi WCot
- var. *alba* ♀H4	GCrs NSla WCot WEas
- 'Grandiflora'	GKir
- var. *willmottiae*	MPhe
officinalis	CMil EWsh GPoy NBrk SBla
- 'Alba Plena'	CKel CPou EBee EWTr GKir MBri MRav SMrm SWvt WAul WCAu
- 'Anemoniflora Rosea' ♀H4	CKel EBee EChP EGle EPfP GKir LRHS MBri MHom SWvt WCAu
§ - subsp. *banatica*	MHom MPhe SSpi WCAu
- 'China Rose'	GKir
- WM 9821 from Slovenia	MPhe
- subsp. *humilis*	see *P. officinalis* subsp. *microcarpa*
- 'James Crawford Weguelin'	WCot
- 'Lize van Veen'	GKir WCAu
§ - subsp. *microcarpa*	SSpi
- 'Mutabilis Plena'	EBee IBlr WCAu
- 'Rosea Plena' ♀H4	CKel EBee ECtt EPfP GBin GKir LAst LHop LPVe MRav NBPC SMrm SPer SWat SWvt WCAu
- 'Rosea Superba Plena'	EBee EFou EWTr WCAu
- 'Rubra Plena' ♀H4	CKel CPou EBee ECtt EMil EPfP GBin GKir LAst LHop LPVe MHom NGdn SMrm SPer SRms SWat SWvt WAul WCAu WFar WHil
- subsp. *villosa*	CKel EBee ELan LPio MBri MTis WCAu
'Oriental Gold'	CKel
ostii (S)	CKel MPhe SSpi
- dark-flowered (S)	CKel
papaveracea	see *P. suffruticosa*
paradoxa	see *P. officinalis* subsp. *microcarpa*
'Paula Fay'	EChP MPhe MRav WCAu
Peony with the Purple Roots	see *P. suffruticosa* 'Shou An Hong'
§ *peregrina*	CFil CLAP ECho GCal MHom MPhe NSla SBla Slgm SSpi WCAu WPGP
- from Macedonia	MPhe
§ - 'Otto Froebel' ♀H4	GKir MBri WCAu WCot
- 'Sunshine'	see *P. peregrina* 'Otto Froebel'
'Phoenix White' (S)	MBlu
'Postilion'	MBri
potaninii	see *P. delavayi* var. *angustiloba* f. *angustiloba*
'Red Charm'	MBri WCAu
'Red Magic'	NLar WHil
'Requiem'	WCAu
'Robert W. Auten' **new**	WCAu
§ *rockii* (S)	EPfP MPhe SSpi WViv
- hybrid	see *P.* Gansu Mudan Group
- subsp. *linyanshani* (S) **new**	MPhe
'Roman Gold'	CKel
romanica	see *P. peregrina*
'Rose Garland'	WCAu
Rouge Red	see *P. suffruticosa* 'Zhi Hong'
ruprechtiana **new**	WCot
russoi	see *P. mascula* subsp. *russoi*
'Scarlett O'Hara'	WCAu
'Shi-pen-kue'	MBri
sinensis	see *P. lactiflora*
'Smouthii'	GKir MBri WCot
sterniana **new**	EBee
steveniana	MHom MPhe
§ *suffruticosa* (S)	CWib EBee ELan LPan MGos MPhe SSpi WStI
- 'Akashigata' (S)	CKel
- 'Alice Palmer' (S)	CKel
- 'Bai Yu' (S)	CBcs
- 'Bai Yuan Hong Xia'	WCAu
- 'Bai Yulan' **new**	NBlu
- Best-shaped Red	see *P. suffruticosa* 'Zhuan Yuan Hong'
- Bird of Rimpo	see *P. suffruticosa* 'Rimpo'
- Black Dragon Brocade	see *P. suffruticosa* 'Kokuryû-nishiki'
- Black Flower Chief	see *P. suffruticosa* 'Hei Hua Kui'
- 'Cang Zhi Hong' (S)	WViv
- 'Cardinal Vaughan' (S)	CKel
- 'Chojuraku'	MPhe
- 'Da Hong Ye'	MPhe
- 'Da Hu Hong'	MPhe
- 'Dou Lu' (S)	CBcs CKel MPhe
- Double Cherry	see *P. suffruticosa* 'Yae-zakura'
- 'Duchess of Kent'(S) **new**	CKel
- 'Duchess of Marlborough' (S)	CKel

- 'Er Qiao' (S)	CBcs CKel MPhe
- Eternal Camellias	see *P. suffruticosa* 'Yachiyo-tsubaki'
- 'Fen Qiao' (S)	CBcs
§ - 'Feng Dan Bai' (S)	CKel MPhe NBlu WCAu WViv
- 'Feng Zhong Guan' (S)	CKel
- Flight of Cranes	see *P. suffruticosa* 'Renkaku'
- Floral Rivalry	see *P. suffruticosa* 'Hana-kisoi'
- 'Fuji Zome Goromo'	CKel
* - 'Glory of Huish' (S)	CKel
- 'Godaishu' (S)	CKel LAma LRHS MPhe SPer
- 'Guan Qun Fang' **new**	MPhe
- 'Guan Shi Mo Yu' (S)	MPhe
§ - 'Hakuojisi' (S)	CKel EBee ENot WCAu
§ - 'Hana-daijin' (S)	LAma LRHS NBlu SPer WCAu
§ - 'Hana-kisoi' (S)	CKel LAma MPhe NBlu SPer WCAu
- 'Haru-no-akebono' (S)	CKel
§ - 'Hei Hua Kui' (S)	CKel MPhe
§ - 'Higurashi' (S)	EBee ENot LBuc
§ - 'Hu Hong' (S)	NBlu WBrE
- Jewel in the Lotus	see *P. suffruticosa* 'Tama-fuyo'
- Jewelled Screen	see *P. suffruticosa* 'Tama-sudare'
- 'Jia Ge Jin Zi' (S)	CKel WViv
- 'Jin Xing Xiu Lang' **new**	MPhe
§ - 'Jitsugetsu-nishiki' (S)	CKel
- 'Joseph Rock'	see *P. rockii*
- Kamada Brocade	see *P. suffruticosa* 'Kamada-nishiki'
§ - 'Kamada-fuji' (S)	CKel LAma WCAu
§ - 'Kamada-nishiki' (S)	CKel
§ - 'Kaow' (S)	CKel WCAu
- King of Flowers	see *P. suffruticosa* 'Kaow'
- King of White Lions	see *P. suffruticosa* 'Hakuojisi'
* - 'Kingdom of the Moon' (s)	LRHS
- 'Kinkaku'	see *P. x lemoinei* 'Souvenir de Maxime Cornu'
- 'Kinshi'	see *P. x lemoinei* 'Alice Harding'
§ - 'Kokuryû-nishiki' (S)	CKel LAma SPoG
- 'Koshi-no-yuki' (S)	CKel
- 'Lan Fu Rong'	CBcs MPhe
§ - 'Lan Tian Yu' (S)	CKel MPhe
- 'Luo Han Hong' (S)	WViv
- Magnificent Flower	see *P. suffruticosa* 'Hana-daijin'
- 'Mikasayama'	MPhe
- 'Montrose' (S)	CKel
* - 'Mrs Shirley Fry' (S)	CKel
- 'Mrs William Kelway' (S)	CKel
- 'Nigata Akashigata' (S)	CKel
- 'Nishoo' **new**	CKel
- Pride of Taisho	see *P. suffruticosa* 'Taisho-no-hokori'
- 'Qie Lan Dan Sha' **new**	MPhe
§ - 'Qing Long Wo Mo Chi' (S)	CKel WCAu
- 'Qing Shan Guan Xue' (S)	WViv
- 'Raphael' (S)	CKel
- 'Reine Elisabeth' (S)	CKel
§ - 'Renkaku' (S)	CKel LRHS MPhe SPer
§ - 'Rimpo' (S)	CKel EBee ENot LAma LBuc MPhe SPer
- subsp. *rockii* (S)	see *P. rockii*
- 'Rou Fu Rong' (S)	MPhe WCAu
- 'Ruan Zhi Lan' (S)	MPhe WViv
§ - 'San Bian Sai Yu' (S)	WViv
- 'Sheng Hei Zi'	CBcs
§ - 'Shiguregumo' (S)	CKel
- 'Shimadaigin'	CKel MPhe
- 'Shimane-chojuraku' (S)	CKel
- 'Shimane-hakugan' (S)	CKel
- 'Shimane-seidai' (S)	CKel
- 'Shin Shima Kagayaki' (S)	CKel
- 'Shintoyen' (S)	CKel
- 'Shirotae' (S)	CKel

§ - 'Shou An Hong' (S)	MPhe
- 'Si He Lian' (S)	MPhe
- 'Sumi-no-ichi' (S)	CKel
- 'Superb' (S)	CKel
§ - 'Taisho-no-hokori' (S)	LRHS WCAu
§ - 'Taiyo' (S)	CKel ENot LAma LRHS MPhe
§ - 'Tama-fuyo' (S)	CKel LAma
§ - 'Tama-sudare' (S)	CKel NBlu
- The Sun	see *P. suffruticosa* 'Taiyo'
- 'Tian Xiang'	MPhe
- Twilight	see *P. suffruticosa* 'Higurashi'
- Wisteria at Kamada	see *P. suffruticosa* 'Kamada-fuji'
- 'Wu Jin Yao Hui' (S)	CBcs MPhe
- 'Wu Long Peng Sheng'	CKel MPhe
- 'Xiao Tao Hong'	CBcs
- 'Xue Ta' (S)	CKel
- 'Xue Ying Tao Hua' **new**	MPhe
§ - 'Yachiyo-tsubaki' (S)	CKel ENot LAma LBuc
§ - 'Yae-zakura' (S)	LAma
- 'Yan Long Zi Zhu Pan' (S)	CKel
- 'Yin Hong Qiao Dui' (S)	CKel
§ - 'Ying Luo Bao Zhu' (S)	WViv
- 'Yomo-zakura' (S)	LRHS
- 'Yoshinogawa' (S)	CKel EBee ENot LBuc LRHS
- 'Yu Lu Dian Cui' (S)	WViv
- 'Yu Xi Ying Xue' (S)	MPhe
- 'Zhao Fen' (S)	MPhe NPer
§ - 'Zhi Hong' (S)	CKel
- 'Zhu Sha Lei' (S)	CKel MPhe NBlu
* - 'Zhuan Yuan Hong' (S)	NBlu
- 'Zi Er Qiao' (S)	CKel MPhe
- 'Zi Jin Pan' (S)	WViv
- 'Zi Lan Kui' (S)	CKel
'Sunshine'	see *P. peregrina* 'Otto Froebel'
tenuifolia	CBot CLAP EBee GCal GIBF LPio MDun MHom NMen NSla SIgm SSpi WCot
- subsp. *carthalinica*	MHom MPhe
§ - subsp. *lithophila*	GKir MHom MPhe
- 'Plena'	GKir LPio MPhe
Three-sided Jade	see *P. suffruticosa* 'San Bian Sai Yu'
tomentosa	CMil MPhe WWst
veitchii	CLAP EBee GIBF MTho MWgw NDlv NMen SIgm SSpi WAbe WCAu
- dwarf from China	MPhe
- var. *leiocarpa*	EBee
- var. *woodwardii*	CLyd CMil CPne ERos GCrs MTho NGar NSla NWCA SIgm SSpi WCAu WCot WHoo
'Vesuvian' **new**	CKel
White Phoenix	see *P. suffruticosa* 'Feng Dan Bai'
wittmanniana	CBro CLAP GKir MDun WCot
§ - 'Yao Huang' (S)	CBcs MPhe WCAu
Yao's Yellow	see *P.* 'Yao Huang'
'Yellow Dream'	WCot
'Yellow Emperor'	WCot
Yellow Flower of Summer	see *P.* 'Huang Hua Kui'

Paesia (Dennstaedtiaceae)

scaberula	CFil CWil GCal NBir SSpi WAbe WCot

Paliurus (Rhamnaceae)

spina-christi	CArn CBcs CLnd CPle EBee EGFP SLon SMad WSPU XPep

Pallenis (Asteraceae)

maritima	LIck SPet XPep
- 'Golden Dollar'	NPri

Panax (Araliaceae)

ginseng	EBee GPoy

japonicus	GPoy WCru
- BWJ 7932	WCru
quinquefolius	GPoy MSal

Pancratium (Amaryllidaceae)

maritimum	EBee LRHS NJOw
	WCot

Pandanus (Pandanaceae)

furcatus **new**	CBrP
utilis	EAmu

Pandorea (Bignoniaceae)

jasminoides	CFwr CHal CRHN CSpe EBak ECot
	LRHS MRav SOWG
§ - 'Charisma' (v)	CBcs EHol EMil EPfP EShb SOWG
	WCot
§ - 'Lady Di'	ERea LRHS SOWG SYvo WCot
- 'Rosea'	MCCP MJnS
- 'Rosea Superba' ♀H1	CBcs CFwr CHEx CRHN EBee
	EHol EMil ERea LRHS WCot
- 'Variegata'	see *P. jasminoides* 'Charisma'
lindleyana	see *Clytostoma calystegioides*
pandorana	CRHN ERea SLim SYvo WCot
- 'Golden Rain'	CBcs CMdw CRHN EBee ERea
	SLim SOWG

Panicum (Poaceae)

bulbosum	EHoe EPPr EPla
clandestinum	CFwr EBee EHoe EPPr EPla EWes
	LEdu MCCP NPro
miliaceum	EBre EGle MSal
- 'Violaceum'	CSpe EMan SWal WGMN
'Squaw'	LRHS
virgatum	CBig CRWN CTri EPza LRav WPer
	XPep
- 'Blue Tower'	LPhx MAnH
- 'Cloud Nine'	CBig CKno CPen EBee EFou EPPr
	LHop LPhx MAnH
- 'Dallas Blues'	CKno CPen EBee EFou EMan
	EPPr
- 'Hänse Herms'	CBig CBrm CFwr CKno CMil EGle
	EHoe EPPr IPot LPhx SCou SPla
	WFar WWpP
- 'Heavy Metal'	More than 30 suppliers
- 'Northwind'	CKno CPen EFou EPPr SMHy
- 'Prairie Sky'	CKno CStr EBee EMan EPPr LPhx
	MAnH MAvo WPGP
- 'Red Cloud'	CKno
- 'Rehbraun'	CBrm CFwr CSBt EBee ECGN EGle
	EHoe EPPr EPfP EWTr EWsh IPot
	LEdu LPhx MWgw NGdn NOak
	NPPs SWal WCAu WFar
- 'Rotstrahlbusch'	CFwr CKno CPrp EBee ECGN
	EFou EGle EHoe EMan EPPr MAvo
	MSte MWhi NBea STes SWal WCot
	WPGP
- 'Rubrum'	CKno COlW CSBt EBlw EBre EChP
	ECha ECot EHoe ELan ENot EPPr
	EPfP EPza EWsh LRHS MAvo MRav
	NBPC NSti SChu SDix SHBN SPer
	SPla WMoo WPrP
- 'Shenandoah'	CAbb CBig CFwr CKno CPen EBee
	IPot MAvo MBri
- 'Squaw'	CFwr CHar CKno CWCL EBee
	EBlw EBre EGle EHoe EPPr EWsh
	GKir IPot MAnH MSte MWgw
	NPPs NPro SHBN SMad WCAu
	WCot WDyG WFar WLin WPnP
	WPrP WWeb WWye
- 'Strictum'	CBig EBee EHoe EHul EMan EMil
	EPPr EWes LPhx NLar SHel
- 'Warrior'	More than 30 suppliers
- 'Wood's Variegated' (v)	EPPr LEdu

Papaver ✿ (Papaveraceae)

alboroseum	EDAr EHyt GTou
'Alpha Centauri' (Super	SWat
Poppy Series)	
§ *alpinum* L.	CSpe EBre EDAr EMlt GKir GTou
	LRHS MMHG NBlu SIng SRms
	SWat WFar WWin
- 'Flore Pleno' (d)	NBir
amurense	EBee GCal MFOX SWat
anomalum	CBri
- *album*	CBri CSpe EBee NArg
apokrinomenon	ELan
§ *atlanticum*	CTCP EBee ECoo EMar EOMN
	GBuc LDai MLan NBro SBri SPlb
- 'Flore Pleno' (d)	CSpe EBee MCCP NBro WBrk
	WFar WOld
'Aurora' (Super Poppy	SWat
Series)	
'Beyond Red' (Super	SWat
Poppy Series) **new**	
bracteatum	see *P. orientale* var. *bracteatum*
'Brooklyn' **new**	EBee
burseri	SRot
'Cathay' (Super Poppy	SWat
Series)	
'Celebration' (Super	SWat
Poppy Series)	
commutatum ♀H4	CSpe ELan SWat WBry WEas
corona-sancti-stephani	CTCP SWat
'Eccentric Silk' (Super	SWat
Poppy Series) **new**	
fauriei	EBee
§ 'Fireball'	CMHG CPlt CRow EChP ECha
	EGle ETow GCal IGor LHop MLLN
	MTis MWat SScr WBry WMnd
	WRHF
'Harlequin' (Super	SWat
Poppy Series)	
'Heartbeat' (Super	SWat
Poppy Series) **new**	
heldreichii	see *P. spicatum*
x *hybridum* 'Flore	EBee NBrk SWat
Pleno' (d)	
'Jacinth' (Super Poppy	SWat
Series)	
lateritium	CPou MBow MLLN SRms WWpP
- 'Flore Pleno' (d)	EBee EGle NLar
'Lauffeuer' **new**	EMon
macounii subsp.	EBee
discolor	
'Matador' **new**	MBri
'Medallion' (Super Poppy	SWat
Series)	
§ *miyabeanum*	CSpe CTCP EBre EDAr ELan GAbr
	GKir GTou LRHS NWCA WFar
	WPer WTMC WWin
- *album* **new**	ECho
- 'Pacino'	CBAn EBre EChP EDAr EMil EMlt
	EWll GBuc LRHS NLar WWeb
- *tatewakii*	see *P. miyabeanum*
nanum 'Flore Pleno'	see *P.* 'Fireball'
§ *nudicaule*	CTCP CWCL ELan NBlu WPer
- Champagne Bubbles	EBre GWCH LRHS SWat WFar
Group	WLow WWeb
- Constance Finnis	EMon GBuc LRHS
Group	
- var. *croceum*	ERou LRHS
'Flamenco'	
- Garden Gnome Group	see *P. nudicaule* Gartenzwerg Series
§ - Gartenzwerg Series	COlW CSpe EMil GAbr GBBs MBri
	NJOw NLar NPri SPlb WGor WShp
	WWeb
- 'Kelmscott Giant' **new**	MWgw

- 'Meadow Pastels' **new**	MWgw
- 'Pacino'	SPet SRms WFar
- 'San Remo'	WWeb
- 'Solar Fire Orange'	EBre EMar EWll WWeb
- 'Summer Breeze Orange'	NPri
- 'Summer Breeze Yellow'	NPri
- Wonderland Series	EHrv GFlt
- - 'Wonderland Gold'	WWeb
- - 'Wonderland Orange'	NPri
- - 'Wonderland Pink Shades'	NPri
- - 'Wonderland White'	NPri
- - 'Wonderland Yellow'	NPri
orientale	CBcs EPfP GFlt IHMH MBow MBro SRms SWal SWat WBrE WCFE WFar WPer
- 'Abu Hassan'	SWat
- 'Aglaja' ♀H4	CMil EBee EChP EMan EMil GBin LAst LPhx MAnH MNFA MSph MSte NCot NDov NGdn NSti SPoG SUsu SWat WCot WHoo WWhi
- 'Aladin'	SWat WWeb
- 'Ali Baba'	SWat WWeb
- 'Alison' **new**	SWat
- 'Allegro'	CPrp CSBt CSam EBre ECtt EGle GKir IBal LAst LRHS MBNS MBct MBri MHer MRav NBlu NBrk NCGa NVic SPer SPlb SWat SWvt WCAu WLow WWeb
- 'Arwide'	CMil SWat WGMN
- 'Aslahan'	ECha SWat WBro
- 'Atrosanguineum'	SWat
- 'Avebury Crimson'	LPhx MBct MWat SWat
- 'Ballkleid'	ECha SWat WBro
- 'Beauty Queen'	EBee EBre ECha ECot EGle EMan GKir GMac LRHS MAnH MNFA MRav MWgw NBrk NGdn SDix SWat
- 'Bergermeister Rot'	SWat
- 'Big Jim'	EBee SPla SWat
- 'Black and White' ♀H4	More than 30 suppliers
- 'Blackberry Queen'	EMan LPio MBow SWat
- 'Blickfang'	SWat
- 'Bloomsbury'	EChP
- 'Blue Moon'	LPhx NCGa WHal
- 'Bonfire'	CM&M CSam EHrv SOkh
- 'Bonfire Red'	CStr EBee LRHS SWat WCAu
§ - var. *bracteatum* ♀H4	EChP ECha EWll MLwd NBir NBur SMHy SWat
- 'Brilliant'	EBee EOMN LRHS NBur NLar WFar WMoo
* - 'Carneum'	EBee EChP LRHS NLar WHil
- 'Carnival'	CMil EBee EFou NLar SWat
- 'Catherina'	EBee SWat
- 'Cedar Hill'	EBee EWes GMac LRHS MMil SMrm SWat
- 'Cedric Morris' ♀H4	CMil CSpe ECha EFou EGle ELan ERou GCal GMac LPhx MAnH MRav MSte MWat MWgw NSti SChu SMrm SWat WCAu WCot WEas WMnd WWhi WWin
- 'Charming'	CHad CPar EBee EChP EGle EMan LPhx LRHS MMil MNFA NDov NGdn SAga SWat
- 'Checkers' **new**	CFwr EBee EOMN LRav
- 'China Boy'	CMil EBee SWat WWeb
- 'Choir Boy'	CM&M EBee ECtt EGle NBrk NBur NCot NLar SGar STes WBry WGMN WHrl WRHF
- 'Coral Reef'	CFwr EBee EGra EOMN EWll GBBs MHer NBur SAga SWat WBry WCra WGMN WHer WHrl WPen

- 'Coralie' **new**	CMil
- 'Corrina'	EBee SWat
- 'Curlilocks'	CPar EBre EChP ECtt ELan EPfP ERou LAst LRHS MAnH MBow MCLN MRav NBPC NBrk NPSl SAga SPer SRms SWat SWvt WHoo WSan WWin
- 'Derwisch'	SWat
* - 'Diana'	SMrm SWat
- 'Distinction' **new**	CHad
- double orange (d)	IBal
- 'Double Pleasure' (d)	EBee MCLN NCot
- 'Doubloon'	EBee EBre ERou GKir NBrk NGdn SWat WFar
- 'Dwarf Allegro'	GBuc MFir MSPs NFor WMnd
- 'Effendi' ♀H4	CHea CMil EFou IPot LPhx MAvo MBct SBla SDys SMHy SUsu SWat WBro WGMN
- 'Elam Pink'	CMil EBee EGle LPhx MLLN MSph MTis SWat WCot
- 'Erste Zuneigung'	EBee EGle LPhx SWat WBro
- 'Eskimo Pie'	SWat
- 'Eyecatcher' **new**	EBee
- 'Fatima'	CHad CMil EBee MAnH SMrm SWat WWeb
- 'Feuerriese'	SWat
- 'Feuerwerk' **new**	EBee
- 'Feuerzwerg'	IBal SWat
- 'Fiesta'	CMil SWat
- 'Flamenco'	ECtt SWat
- 'Forncett Summer'	EBee EChP EFou EMan EMar GMac LPio MBnl MSph NGdn SChu SWat WCAu WCot
- 'Garden Glory'	CPar CPlt EBee EBre EChP ECtt EFou EMan LAst LRHS MBri NBrk NBro SMrm SWat WCAu WTMC
- 'Garden Gnome'	ENot GKir SPet
- 'Glowing Embers'	EBre ERou GKir LRHS SMrm SWat
- 'Glowing Rose'	SWat
- Goliath Group	CElw CMil EBee EBre ECha ELan EMan GKir LHop LRHS MAvo MCLN MRav NBrk NBro NPri NVic SDix SPer SRms SWat WCra WEas WFar WMnd WPen
- - 'Beauty of Livermere'	More than 30 suppliers
- 'Graue Witwe'	CMil EBee EFou EGle GBuc MBow NCot SMHy SWat WPGP WTin
- 'Halima'	SWat
- 'Harvest Moon'	CMHG EBee EBre EChP EHol ERou EWTr GKir LPio LRHS MBow NPer NPri SWat WHil WShp
- 'Heidi' **new**	SWat
- 'Helen Elisabeth'	CMHG COlW CSpe EBre EChP ECtt EFou EGle EMar ERou GCal GKir LAst LPio MBow MCLN MLLN MSte NBPC NBrk NGdn NPri SWat WCAu WCom WFar WShp WTMC
- 'Hula Hula'	ECha SWat
- 'Indian Chief'	CM&M CMHG COlW CPrp EBee EChP EGle EMan ENor EPfP ERou GBin GMac LPio LRHS MAnH MRav MSte NBro NGdn NPer NPri WBar WCAu WHil WMnd WShp
- 'Joanne'	NLar
- 'John III' ♀H4	EBee LPhx MSph SMHy SWat
- 'John Metcalf'	CMil EBee EFou EGle LPio LRHS MAvo MLLN NSti SChu SMrm SWat WCAu WCot WSpi
- 'Juliane'	CPlt EBee ECha EGle GMac LHop LPhx MBct MRav MWgw NDov NSti SAga SWat WBro WCot WTin WWhi
- 'Karine' ♀H4	More than 30 suppliers

- 'Khedive' ♀H4 — SWat
- 'King George' — GBuc SWat
- 'Kleine Tänzerin' — CMil CSam EBee EBre EChP EGle EMan EMar GBin GBri LPhx LRHS MBnl MCLN MLLN MWgw NCot NDov NGdn NSti SAga SBla STes SUsu SWat WCAu WCot WHil WWeb
- 'Kollebloem' — SWat
- 'Lady Frederick Moore' — EBee LPio LRHS MBow MLLN SWat WCra
- 'Lady Roscoe' — SWat
- 'Ladybird' — EBee ENot ERou GKir LRHS MSte NBrk SCro
- 'Laffeuer' **new** — EBee
- 'Lambada' — SWat

I — 'Lauren's Lilac' — CBos CMil LPhx MAnH SWat
- 'Lavender Girl' — CFir
- 'Leuchtfeuer' ♀H4 — EBee ECha LPhx MSph SMHy SWat
- 'Lighthouse' ♀H4 — SWat
- 'Lilac Girl' — More than 30 suppliers
- 'Little Dancer' — GMac
- 'Maiden's Blush' — CMil EBee NSti SWat
- 'Marcus Perry' — CStr EBee ENot EPfP ERou EWes LRHS NPri SCro SPer SWat WCAu WFar WShp
- 'Mary Finnan' — EBee EGle LPio SWat
- 'Master Richard' — SWat
- 'May Queen' (d) — EBee EChP EWes IBlr LAst LRHS MRav NBro NCGa NSti SLon SMrm WCot WPen
- 'May Sadler' — COIW EBee ENot SWat
- 'Midnight' — EBee ERou SCro
- 'Mrs H.G. Stobart' — MBow SWat
- 'Mrs Marrow's Plum' — see *P. orientale* 'Patty's Plum'
- 'Mrs Perry' — More than 30 suppliers
- 'Nanum Flore Pleno' — see *P.* 'Fireball'
- 'Noema' — SWat
- 'Orange Glow' — EBee NCot NPri SWat WMoo
- 'Orangeade Maison' — CStr EBee LPio SWat WBro
- 'Oriana' — EBee EHol LRHS MMil NGdn SLon SWat
- 'Oriental' — SWat
- 'Pale Face' — ERou SWat
§ - 'Patty's Plum' — More than 30 suppliers
- 'Perry's White' — More than 30 suppliers
- 'Peter Pan' — EBee MLLN SWat
- 'Petticoat' — EBee EChP ECtt EFou ELan EMan IPot LAst MAvo SWat
- 'Picotée' — More than 30 suppliers
- 'Pink Lassie' — SWat
- 'Pink Panda' — SWat
- 'Pink Ruffles'PBR — EBee EMan MBri MCLN NCot SWat WShp
- 'Pinnacle' — CM&M CMil CSWP EBee ERou EWTr GLil LRHS MBri NBPC NGdn NPri SMrm SWat WFar WSan
- 'Pizzicato' — CM&M CPar CWib EBre EChP EHrv ERou EShb GBBs ITer LHop LPhx LRHS MBri NArg NPer SGar SPet SWal SWat WFar WGwG WLow WMoo WWeb
- 'Pizzicato White' **new** — CM&M
- 'Polka' — SWat
- 'Prince of Orange' — EBee SWat WHil
- 'Princess Victoria Louise' — see *P. orientale* 'Prinzessin Victoria Louise'
- 'Prinz Eugen' — CMil EBee ECGP EFou MAnH SLon SWat
§ - 'Prinzessin Victoria Louise' — CBot CSWP EBee EChP EMan GBBs GFlt GKir IBal LAst LPVe LRHS MLLN MMil NBro NCGa NPri SIde SSvw SWat WBVN WCAu WFar WGMN WPer WShp

- 'Prospero' — EBee
- 'Queen Alexandra' — CBot EBee EHrv NLar
- 'Raspberry Queen' — More than 30 suppliers
- 'Raspberry Ruffles' — CMil LPhx SWat
- 'Rembrandt' — EBee ECot EHrv ERou LRHS MMil NMoo NPri SWat WBar WPer
- 'Rosenpokal' — CM&M CMil EBee EChP EOMN LRHS NGdn SWat WBro
- 'Roter Zwerg' — ECha
- 'Royal Chocolate Distinction' — EBee EChP EMan MAnH MCLN NCot STes SWat WCAu WHil WSan
- 'Royal Wedding' — CBot EBre EChP EGle ERou EWTr GKir IBal ITim LAst LPVe LPio LRHS MBri MHer MMil NGdn NLar NPri SChu SMad SMrm SPer SPla SSvw SWat WCot WMoo WWeb
* - 'Saffron' — CHad CMil MAnH SAga SWat
- 'Salmon Glow' — CBcs EBee EChP EWTr GKir GLil LAst MHer SSvw SWat WFar WPer
- 'Salome' — SWat
- scarlet — MWgw NCot
- 'Scarlet King' — EBee EMan EWll LRHS MMil SWat
- 'Showgirl' — EBee MBow MLLN MSPs SOkh SWat
* - 'Silberosa' — ECha
- 'Sindbad' — EBee EFou GMac LPhx LRHS NLar SLon SWat
- 'Snow Goose' — CMil CPlt LPhx MAnH SWat WHoo
- 'Spätzünder' — SWat
- 'Springtime' — CSpe EBee EChP EFou EGle EMan EWes LRHS MRav NGdn NLar SWat WCAu WHoo WSan WTMC WTin WWhi
- 'Stokesby Belle' — MWgw
- Stormtorch — see *P. orientale* 'Sturmfackel'
§ - 'Sturmfackel' — EBee EGle ERou SWat
- 'Suleika' — SWat
- 'Sultana' — EBee ECha EGle ERou GMac LPhx MAnH MWat SWat WBro WCAu
- 'The Promise' — SWat
- 'Türkenlouis' — CHar CMHG COIW CSBt EBre ECtt EFou EGle ENot EPfP ERou GAbr GFlt GKir GLil GMac LAst LRHS MAnH NBPC SCro SMrm STes SWat WCAu WFar WHoo WShp WTin
- 'Turkish Delight' — EBee EBre EPfP ERou GKir LRHS MBow MMil MRav MTis NBid NBir NBro NPri SMer SWat SWvt WCAu WFar
- 'Tutu' — EBee IBal SWat
- 'Victoria Dreyfuss' — SWat
- 'Viola' — SWat
- 'Water Babies' — SWat
- 'Watermelon' — CMil COtt EBre EChP ECtt ERou GKir LAst LRHS MAnH MAvo MBri MCLN MLLN MRav NCot NGdn NPri NSti SCro SWat WBro WCAu WCom WFar WHoo WTMC
- 'Wild Salmon' — WRHF
- 'Wisley Beacon' — SWat
- 'Wunderkind' — CM&M EBee EChP ECtt EGle EMan IBal LAst SWat WCAu
'Party Fun' — WWeb
pilosum — CHrt EMan GBuc SRms SWat WCot WTin
'Pink Lightning' (Super Poppy Series) — SWat
rhaeticum — EHyt
rhoeas — CArn GPoy MBow WJek
- Angels' Choir (d) — ERou SWat
- 'Mother of Pearl' — SWat
- Shirley — MBow
rupifragum — CBri CFir CHar CHrt CMCo CPLG CTCP EBee EChP ECha ECtt GAbr

	LPio MFir MLLN NPPs NPol SGar
	SWal WCot WEas WFar WHrl WPer
	WRha WTMC
- 'Double Tangerine	CPen WCFE
Gem' (d)	
- 'Flore Pleno' (d)	CSWP CSam CSpe EBee EMan
	LPio LRHS MBri MFOX NChi SScr
	STes WCru WHen WHer WMoo
	WWhi
- 'Orange Bubbles'	EWsh
- 'Tangerine Dream'	MCCP
sendtneri	CTCP MHer
'Serena' (Super Poppy	SWat
Series)	
'Shasta' (Super Poppy	SWat
Series)	
somniferum	CArn GPoy MSal SWat
- 'Black Beauty' (d)	CBot CSpe SWat
- 'Chedglow Variegated'	CPla EMan
(v)	
- 'Flemish Antique'	SWat
- var. *paeoniiflorum*	SWat
(d) **new**	
- 'Pink Chiffon'	SWat WEas
- 'Swansdown' **new**	CSpe
- 'White Cloud' (d)	SWat
§ *spicatum*	CMea CSpe EBee ECGP ECha EGle
	EGoo EMan GCal MSte MWgw
	NBir NChi SGar SIgm SMrm SUsu
	WCot WMoo WWeb
'Tequila Sunrise' (Super	SWat
Poppy Series)	
'The Cardinal'	WRHF
triniifolium	CTCP EMan SIgm WMoo
'Vesuvius' **new**	SWat
'Viva' (Super Poppy Series)	SWat
* 'Witchery'	NCot WWeb

papaya (paw paw) see *Carica papaya*

Parabenzoin see *Lindera*

Parachampionella see *Strobilanthes*

Paradisea (Asphodelaceae)

liliastrum ♀H4	CHid CMdw CPrp EBee EMan EPPr
	ERos GIBF ITer LPio NBPC NChi
	NWoo SRms WBVN WCFE WCot
- 'Major'	GSki
lusitanica	CAvo CBrm CDes CHid CMHG
	EBee EChP ERos GFlt LPio MWgw
	MWrn SSpi WCot WGMN WLin
	WPGP WTin WWeb

Parahebe (Scrophulariaceae)

'Arabella'	LRHS
'Betty'	GGar
x *bidwillii*	MHer NDlv NWCA SRms SRot
- 'Kea'	CFee ECou ECtt GEdr MDKP SBla
	SRot WPer
- 'Rosea'	WCom
canescens	ECou
§ *catarractae*	CHar CMHG CPLG EBee ECou
	EMlt GGar GKir MFir MNrw MTis
	MWat NBee NBro NLAp NPri SAga
	SBri SUsu WBrE WCom WCru WFar
	WHen WKif WPer WWhi
- 'Baby Blue'	CAbP EPfP MAsh SReu SSta
- blue	CHar EPfP GKir MWgw NBee SPer
- 'County Park'	ECou
- 'Cuckoo'	ECou NHol
§ - 'Delight' ♀H3	CNic ECou ESis EWes GGar LRHS
	MHer NHol NPer SDix SHFr SIgm
	SMrm SRot STre WEas WFar WHen

- subsp. *diffusa*	ECou LRHS MHer NPer NVic
	WCom
- - 'Annie'	ECou NHol NJOw
- - 'Pinkie'	ECou
- from Chatham Island	EWes
- garden form	ECha LLWP NLAp SBla
- subsp. *martinii*	ECou NJOw
- 'Miss Willmott'	NLAp NPri NVic SPer SPlb SVen
	WBVN WBea WBod WCom WPer
- 'Porlock Purple'	see *P. catarractae* 'Delight'
- 'Rosea'	COkL ESis SSto WBrE
- 'Tinycat'	ITim
- white	CPom ECha ESis IBlr LHop MFir
	MWgw SUsu WBVN WEas WPer
	WWhi WWpP
densifolia	see *Chionohebe densifolia*
§ *formosa*	CPle ECou WHCG
- erect	ECou GGar
'Gillian'	ECtt WPer
'Greencourt'	see *P. catarractae* 'Delight'
§ *hookeriana*	GGar SAga
§ - var. *olsenii*	ECou GGar
'Joy'	ECou EWes
'Julia'	GGar
'June'	GGar
'Lesley'	GGar
linifolia **new**	CTri
- 'Blue Skies'	ECou EDAr
§ *lyallii*	CHar COkL ECou EDAr EMlt ESis
	LAst MBar MHer MSwo MWat
	NChi NDlv NHol NJOw NPol
	NWCA SBla SPlb SRms WBVN
	WCom WKif WWin
- 'Baby Pink'	EPfP MAsh
- 'Clarence'	CLyd ECou EHol
- 'Glacier'	ECou
- 'Julie-Anne' ♀H3	CAbP COkL ECou EPfP ESis GCal
	LRHS MAsh
- 'Rosea'	CTri GGar WPer
- 'Summer Snow'	ECou
'Mervyn'	CLyd CTri ECtt EDAr MDKP NDlv
	NLRH WHen WPer
olsenii	see *P. hookeriana* var. *olsenii*
§ *perfoliata* ♀H3-4	More than 30 suppliers
- dark blue	GBuc GCal MBro SMad SMrm
- 'Pringle'	CAbP EPfP LRHS MAsh SMrm
'Snowcap'	CDoC EPfP LRHS MAsh SPlb

Parajubaea (Arecaceae)

cocoides	LPJP

Parakmeria (Magnoliaceae)

lotungensis	see *Magnolia lotungensis*

Paraquilegia (Ranunculaceae)

adoxoides	see *Semiaquilegia adoxoides*
§ *anemonoides*	GCrs GGGa GTou SBla WAbe
grandiflora	see *P. anemonoides*

Paraserianthes (Mimosaceae)

distachya	see *P. lophantha*
§ *lophantha* ♀H1	CHEx CRHN CTCP CTbh CTrC
	EBak ERea IDee SAPC SArc
	SOWG

Parasyringa see *Ligustrum*

x *Pardancanda* (Iridaceae)

norrisii	CFir EBee EChP EMan EWes GSki
	LIck LRHS WAul WFoF
- 'Dazzler'	EShb

Pardanthopsis (Iridaceae)

dichotoma	EBee

Parietaria (Urticaceae)

§ *judaica* GEil GPoy MSal WHer

Paris ✿ (Trilliaceae)

axialis var. *rubra* LEur
bashanensis EBee LEur SSpi WCru
chinensis EBee LEur WCru
- B&SWJ 265 from Taiwan WCru
cronquistii CLAP EBee
- var. *cronquistii* LEur
delavayi EBee LEur WCru
- var. *petiolata* EBee
fargesii EBee LAma LEur WCru
- var. *brevipetalata* **new** EBee WCru
- var. *petiolata* EBee SSpi WCru
forrestii WCru
incompleta CAvo CLAP EPot GCrs LEur SSpi WCot
japonica SOkd WCru
lancifolia B&SWJ 3044 from Taiwan WCru
luquanensis LEur
mairei EBee LAma LEur WCru
marmorata EBee WCru
§ *polyphylla* CBro CFir CLAP EBee EMar EUJe GFlt LAma LEur WCot WCru WPnP
- B&SWJ 2125 WCru
- F 5945 **new** GCal
- F 5947 ITim
- HWJCM 475 WCru
- var. *stenophylla* CLAP EBee LAma WCru
- var. *yunnanensis* CFir EBee
* - - *alba* EBee LEur
quadrifolia CFil CFir CLAP EBee GPoy LPhx MDun SSpi WCot WCru WHer WPnP WShi WTin
tetraphylla WCru
thibetica CLAP EBee LEur WCru
- var. *apetala* LEur
- var. *thibetica* GEdr SSpi
verticillata CLAP EBee LAma LEur WCru

Parnassia (Parnassiaceae)

palustris WHer

Parochetus (Papilionaceae)

§ *africanus* ♀H2 CHid EWes GBuc
communis misapplied see *P. africanus*
communis ambig. CBcs CFee CPLG GKev IFro MMHG MRav NPer WBea WBor WRha WWhi
- B&SWJ 7215 Golden Triangle WCru
- from Himalaya CWCL IBlr
- - HWJCM 526 EBee WCru
* - 'Blue Gem' IHMH
- dark GCal

Paronychia (Illecebraceae)

argentea CLyd NHol NLap WPat WPer
§ *capitata* CHal Clyd CNic CTri EBre IFro SRms WPer WWin
§ *kapela* EMan ETow SMad SPlb WPer
- 'Binsted Gold' (v) EMan LRHS MBro WPer
§ - subsp. *serpyllifolia* ESis NRya XPep
nivea see *P. capitata*
serpyllifolia see *P. kapela* subsp. *serpyllifolia*

Parrotia (Hamamelidaceae)

persica ♀H4 More than 30 suppliers
- 'Burgundy' CPMA
- 'Jodrell Bank' **new** MBlu

§ - 'Lamplighter' (v) CPMA
- 'Pendula' CMCN CPMA EPfP
- 'Vanessa' CEnd CMCN CPMA EWes GKir IArd LBuc LPan MBlu MBri NLar SKee WOrn
- 'Variegata' see *P. persica* 'Lamplighter'

Parrotiopsis (Hamamelidaceae)

jacquemontiana CBcs IDee NLar NPal

Parrya (Brassicaceae)

albida EBee
menziesii see *Phoenicaulis cheiranthoides*

parsley see *Petroselinum crispum*

Parsonsia (Apocynaceae)

capsularis CPLG ECou
heterophylla ECou

Parthenium (Asteraceae)

integrifolium CArn GPoy MSal

Parthenocissus (Vitaceae)

§ *henryana* ♀H4 More than 30 suppliers
heptaphylla WWes
himalayana CPLG
- 'Purpurea' see *P. himalayana* var. *rubrifolia*
§ - var. *rubrifolia* EBee ELan EPfP LRHS MAsh MRav SLim SLon SPoG WCru WFar
§ *quinquefolia* ♀H4 More than 30 suppliers
- var. *engelmannii* EBee LAst LBuc MGos WCFE
- 'Guy's Garnet' **new** WCru
semicordata WCru
    B&SWJ 6551
striata see *Cissus striata*
§ *tricuspidata* ♀H4 CAgr CDul CHEx CWib EBee ECtt EHoe EPAt EPfP GKir LAst MGos NFor SMer SPer SReu WDin WFar WWeb
- 'Beverley Brook' CMac EBee LBuc MBri SBra SPer SPla SRms
- 'Crûg Compact' B&SWJ 1162 WCru
- 'Fenway Park' **new** MBlu
- 'Green Spring' EBee IArd MBri MGos NBrk
- 'Lowii' CMac EBee ECot EPfP EPla LBuc LRHS MBlu MGos MRav SLon SPer WBcn
- 'Minutifolia' SPer
- 'Purpurea' MBlu
- 'Robusta' EBee LPan MBNS XPep
§ - 'Veitchii' More than 30 suppliers

Pasithea (Anthericaceae)

caerulea EMan WCot
- F&W 8766 EBee

Paspalum (Poaceae)

glaucifolium LEdu WDyG
quadrifarium EMan EPPr WCot

Passiflora ✿ (Passifloraceae)

RCB/Arg P-12 **new** WCot
RCB/Arg R-7 WCot
actinia CPas CRHN CSPN SLim SSte
adenopoda CPas
'Adularia' CPas SSte
alata (F) ♀H1 CAbb CPas CSPN EBak ERea LRHS SSte
- 'Shannon' (F) CPas SSte
x *alatocaerulea* see *P.* x *belotii*
allantophylla CPas
'Allardii' CPas

amalocarpa	CPas SSte	
ambigua	CPas	
§ 'Amethyst' ♀H1	CPas CRHN CSPN EMil LHop	
	LRHS MJnS SBra SHGC SPet WFar	
	WPGP WPat	
amethystina misapplied	see *P.* 'Amethyst'	
§ *amethystina* Mikan	CBcs CDoC CPas ECre EHol ERea	
	LRHS SSte	
amoena	CPas	
ampullacea (F)	CPas	
'Andy'	CPas	
'Anemona'	SSte	
anfracta	CPas	
'Angelo Blu' **new**	CPas	
'Anna'	CSPN	
'Anna Christine'	CSPN	
antioquiensis misapplied	see *P.* x *exoniensis*	
antioquiensis ambig.	CBcs CHEx CPas CRHN CTbh	
	EBee EHol ERea GQui LRHS MJnS	
	MTis SAga SMur SOWG SVen	
	WOld	
apetala	CPas SSte	
arbelaezii **new**	CPas	
x *atropurpurea*	CPas SSte	
§ *aurantia*	CPas	
auriculata	CPas	
banksii	see *P. aurantia*	
'Barborea' **new**	CPas	
§ x *belotii*	CPas ECre EHol LRHS SSte	
- 'Impératrice Eugénie'	see *P.* x *belotii*	
biflora Lamarck	CPas SSte	
'Blue Bird' **new**	CPas	
'Blue Carnival'	CSPN	
'Blue Moon'	CPas CSPN	
boenderi	CPas	
'Byron Beauty'	CPas CSPN	
§ *caerulea* ♀H3	More than 30 suppliers	
- 'Constance Elliot'	CBcs CBot CDoC CMac CPas	
	CRHN CSBt CSPN CWSG EBee	
	ELan EMil ENot EOrc EPfP LRHS	
	MAsh SBra SHGC SLim SOWG SPer	
	SPla SSte SWal SWvt WFar WGwG	
	WLow WWeb	
- *rubra*	LRHS WFar	
x *caponii*	ERea	
capsularis	CHll CPas SSte	
cerasina	CPas	
chinensis	see *P. caerulea*	
cincinnata	CPas	
cinnabarina	CPas	
cirrhiflora	CPas	
citrifolia **new**	CPas	
citrina	CPas ERea ESlt LRHS SOWG SSte	
coccinea (F)	CPas LRHS	
colinvauxii	CPas	
x *colvillii*	CHll CPas	
conzattiana	CPas	
§ *coriacea*	CPas CSPN LRHS SSte	
costaricensis	CPas	
crenata	CPas	
cuneata	CPas	
§ - 'Miguel Molinari'	CPas SSte	
cuprea	CPas SSte	
I 'Curiosa'	CPas	
cuspidifolia	CPas	
§ *cyanea*	CPas	
'Debby'	CPas CSPN	
x *decaisneana* (F)	CPas EAmu	
dioscoreifolia	CPas	
discophora	CPas	
'Eclipse'	CSPN	
'Eden' **new**	COtt LRHS MBri	
edulis (F)	CAgr CPas CSPN LRHS MJnS SHFr	
	SSte	

- 'Crackerjack' (F)	ERea	
- f. *flavicarpa* (F)	CPas ESlt SSte	
* - 'Golden Nuggett' (F)	CPas	
elegans	CPas	
'Elizabeth' (F)	CPas	
'Empress Eugenie'	see *P.* x *belotii*	
'Erik' **new**	CPas	
* 'Evatoria'	CSPN	
'Excel' **new**	CPas	
§ x *exoniensis* ♀H1	CHll CPas CRHN ECre	
exura	CPas	
filipes	CPas	
'Fledermouse'	CPas CSPN	
foetida	CPas LRHS SOWG SSte	
- var. *galapagensis*	CPas	
- var. *hirsuta* (F)	CPas	
- var. *hirsutissima*	CPas	
- var. *orinocensis*	CPas	
garckei	CPas	
gibertii	CPas	
gilbertiana	CPas WFar	
glandulosa	CPas	
gracilis	CPas	
gracillima	CPas	
gritensis	CPas SSte	
guatemalensis	CPas	
hahnii	CPas	
helleri	CPas	
herbertiana (F)	CPas SSte SVen	
hirtiflora	CPas	
holosericea	CPas SSte	
incana	see *P. seemannii*	
incarnata (F)	CArn CPas ITer MSal SPlb SSte	
'Incense' (F) ♀H1	CPas EBak ENor LRHS SLim SPlb	
indecora	CPas	
jatunsachensis	CPas	
'Jeanette'	CPas	
'Jelly Joker'	CPas CSPN SSte	
jorullensis	CPas	
juliana	CPas	
kalbreyeri	CPas	
karwinskii	CPas	
'Kate Adie' **new**	CPas	
x *kewensis*	CPas SSte	
lancearia	CPas	
lancetellesis	CPas SSte	
laurifolia (F)	CPas SLim	
§ *ligularis* (F)	CPas LRHS SSte	
'Lilac Lady'	see *P.* x *violacea* 'Tresederi'	
lindeniana	CPas	
lobata	CPas	
lourdesae	see *P. cuneata* 'Miguel Molinari'	
lowei	see *P. ligularis*	
lutea	CPas	
macrophylla	CPas	
maliformis (F)	CHll CPas	
manicata (F)	CPas EShb	
matthewsii	CPas SSte	
'Mavis Mastics'	see *P.* x *violacea* 'Tresederi'	
mayana	see *P. caerulea*	
mayarum	CPas	
membranacea (F)	CPas SSte	
* *menispermifolia*	SSte	
rosea **new**		
microstipula	CPas	
'Miranda'	CSPN	
misera	CPas	
mixta (F)	CSPN ERea SBra	
* - var. *pinanga*	CPas	
mixta x *antioquiensis*	CDoC CTrC	
mollissima (F) ♀H1	CBcs CPas CRHN CTCP EBak EBee	
	EPfP ERea EShb LRHS SMrm	
	SOWG SPlb SSte	
mooreana	CPas	

morifolia		CPas SSte
mucronata		CPas
multiflora		CPas
murucuja		CPas SSte
naviculata		CPas
nephrodes		CPas
'New Incense' **new**		CPas
nitida (F)		CPas
oblongata		CPas
obtusifolia		see *P. coriacea*
oerstedii		CPas
- var. *choconhiana*		CPas
onychina		see *P. amethystina*
organensis		CPas SSte
palmeri		CPas SSte
penduliflora		CPas
perfoliata		CPas SSte
* 'Perfume'		CPas
pergrandis		CPas
phoenicea		CPas SSte
pilosicorona		CPas
'Pink Jewel'		CPas
'Pink Nightmare' **new**		SSte
pinnatistipula (F)		CPas
x *piresiae*		CPas
pittieri		CPas
platyloba		CPas
* *pseudo-oerstedii* **new**		CPas
punctata		CPas
'Pura Vida'		CPas SSte
'Purple Haze'		CPas CRHN NScw SBra WWeb
'Purple Rain'		CSPN NScw
quadrangularis L. (F) ♀H1		CBcs CHll CPas CTbh CWSG EBak ERea EShb LPan LRHS MJnS SMur WMul
quadrifaria		CPas
quinquangularis		CPas
racemosa ♀H2		CPas EBee ERea IBlr LAst LRHS SOWG
'Red Inca'		CPas
reflexiflora		CPas
resticulata		CPas
retipetala		see *P. cyanea*
rovirosae		CPas LRHS SSte
rubra		CPas SLim WBod WStl
- round-fruited **new**		SSte
* *rufa*		CPas
sagastegui **new**		SSte
'Saint Rule'		CPas
sanguinolenta		CPas LRHS SSte
'Sapphire'		CPas
'Sarah Aimee'		CPas
§ *seemannii*		CPas
serrata		see *P. serratodigitata*
serratifolia		CPas SSte
§ *serratodigitata*		CPas
serrulata		CPas
sexflora		CPas LRHS
'Simply Red'		CPas
'Smythiana'		CPas
sprucei		CPas
standleyi		CPas
'Star of Bristol' ♀H2		CHEx CPas EBee SBra SLim
'Star of Clevedon'		CPas
'Star of Kingston'		CPas
stipulata		CPas
suberosa		CPas SSte
subpeltata		CPas SSte
subpurpurea		CPas
'Sunburst'		CHEx CPas LRHS SOWG SSte
'Susan Brigham'		SSte
talamancensis		CPas SSte
tenuifila		CPas
§ *tetrandra*		CPas ECou

x *tresederi*		see *P.* x *violacea* 'Tresederi'
trialata		CPas
tricuspis		CPas SSte
tridactylites		CPas
trifasciata		CPas CSPN SSte
tripartita		CPas
trisecta		CPas
tryphostemmatoides		CPas
tuberosa		CPas
tulae		CPas SSte
umbilicata		CPas WCru
urbaniana		CPas
variolata **new**		CPas
vespertilio		CPas
§ x *violacea* ♀H1		CPas CRHN ERea EShb ESlt MBri MJnS
- 'Eynsford Gem'		CPas
- 'Lilac Lady'		see *P.* x *violacea* 'Tresederi'
§ - 'Tresederi'		CPas ELan MAsh SAga WFar
- 'Victoria'		CPas SLim WOld
viridescens		CPas
viridiflora		CPas
vitifolia (F)		CPas ERea ESlt LRHS SMur SOWG
- 'Scarlet Flame' (F)		CPas
wurdackii		CPas
xiikzodz		CPas
yucatanensis		CPas
zamorana		CPas

passion fruit see *Passiflora*

passion fruit, banana see *Passiflora mollissima*

Patrinia (Valerianaceae)

gibbosa		CBAn CLyd EBee EMan EOrc IFro LRHS MWrn NLAp SMac SScr SWal WCru WFar WMoo WPat WPnP
rupestris		EBee
* *sambucifolia*		NCGa
saniculifolia		WCru
scabiosifolia		CTCP EBee EChP ECha EGle GAbr GBuc GFlt GSki IFro LPio MLLN NBPC NBir NChi NLar SEND SIgm SMac SMrm SSvw SUsu WBVN WBca WCom WFar WHer WMoo WPic WWin
- 'Nagoya'		MNrw
triloba		CLyd CPla EBre EDAr GBuc GCrs GKir LRHS MRav MWrn NWoo SMac SSpi SUsu WBVN WMoo
* - 'Minor'		ECho
- var. *palmata*		EBee WDyG WFar WMoo
- var. *triloba*		ETow GCal WWin
villosa		EBee NLar

Paulownia (Scrophulariaceae)

catalpifolia		CFil EPla WPGP
elongata **new**		NLar WPGP
fargesii Osborn		see *P. tomentosa* 'Lilacina'
fargesii Franch.		SLPl SMad
fortunei		MBlu NPal WBVN WNor WPGP
kawakamii		CFil WPGP
- B&SWJ 6784		WCru
tomentosa ♀H3		More than 30 suppliers
- 'Coreana'		CHll
- - B&SWJ 8503 from Ullŭngdo		WCru
§ - 'Lilacina'		CFil

Pavonia (Malvaceae)

missionum		EShb
multiflora Jussieu ♀H1		ERea
praemorsa		CBot

paw paw (false banana) see *Asimina triloba*

Paxistima (*Celastraceae*)
canbyi	EHyt NLar NPro WWes
myrsinites	see *P. myrtifolia*
§ **myrtifolia**	EPla ESis

peach see *Prunus persica*

pear see *Pyrus communis*

pear, Asian see *Pyrus pyrifolia*

pecan see *Carya illinoinensis*

Pecteilis (*Orchidaceae*)
* **dentata**	EFEx
§ **radiata**	EBee EFEx
* – 'Albomarginata' (v)	EFEx
* – 'Aureomarginata' (v)	EFEx

Pedicularis (*Scrophulariaceae*)
longiflora var. **tubiformis**	GKev
rhinanthoides subsp. **tibetica**	GKev
tricolor new	GKev

Pegaeophyton (*Brassicaceae*)
scapiflorum new	EBee

Peganum (*Zygophyllaceae*)
harmala	CArn EMan MGol MHer MSal WWye

Pelargonium ✿ (*Geraniaceae*)
B&SWJ 6497 from Thailand	WCru
'A Happy Thought'	see *P.* 'Happy Thought'
'A.M. Mayne' (Z/d)	CWDa SPet WFib
'Abba' (Z/d)	CWDa WFib
'Abel Carrière' (I/d)	SKen SPet
abrotanifolium (Sc)	CRHN CSev EWoo MBPg MHer SSea WFib XPep
'Abundance' (Sc)	LDea
'Acapulco' (I)	WWol
acerifolium hort.	see *P. vitifolium*
acetosum	CSpe GCal LPio MSte SHFr SMrm
* – 'Variegatum' (v)	MSte
'Acushla by Brian' (Sc)	MBPg MWhe
'Ada Green' (R)	LDea
'Ada Sutterby' (Dw/d)	SKen
'Adagio' (Dw)	ESul
'Adam's Quilt' (Z/C)	SKen WEas
'Adele' (Min/d)	ESul
'Ade's Elf' (Z/St)	NFir SSea
'Aerosol' (Min)	ESul
'African Belle' (R)	SAga
'Ailsa' (Min/d)	ESul SKen
'Ainsdale Angel' (A)	LDea
'Ainsdale Eyeful' (Z)	WFib
'Akela' (Min)	ESul
'Alberta' (Z)	SKen
album	CWDa
alchemilloides	CRHN NCiC
'Alcyone' (Dw/d)	ESul SKen WFib
'Alde' (Min)	ESul MWhe NFir WFib
'Aldenham' (Z)	WFib
'Aldham' (Min)	ESul WFib
'Aldwyck' (R)	ESul LDea WFib
'Alex' (Z)	CWDa SKen
'Alex Kitson' (Z) new	WFib
'Alex Mary' (R)	SSea
'Algenon' (Min/d)	ESul WFib
I 'Alice' (Min) new	WFib
'Alice Greenfield' (Z)	NFir
'Alison' (Dw)	ESul
'Alison Jill' (Z/d)	CWDa
'Alison Wheeler' (Min/d)	MWhe
'All My Love' (R)	LDea
'Allicia' (R)	ESul
'Alma' (Dw/C)	ESul
'Almond' (Sc) new	MBPg
'Almost Heaven' (Dw/Z/v)	MWhe
'Alpine Glow' (Z/d)	MWhe
'Alpine Orange' (Z/d)	CWDa
'Altair' (Min/d)	ESul
alternans	CSev
'Amari' (R)	LDea WFib
'Ambrose' (Min/d)	ESul WFib
'American Prince of Orange' (Sc)	MBPg
'Amethyst' (R)	ESul LDea SCoo SKen SPet WFib
§ Amethyst = 'Fisdel'PBR (I/d) ♀H1+3	ECtt LDea LVER MWhe NPri
I 'Amy' (Dw) new	WFib
'Andersonii' (Sc)	MBPg MHer
'Andrew Salvidge' (R)	LDea
'Androcles' (A)	NFir
'Angel Eyes' new	LAst
'Angela' (R)	LDea
'Angela Brook'	CWDa
'Angela Read' (Dw)	ESul
'Angela Tandy'	LPio NFir
'Angela Woodberry' (I/d)	CWDa
'Angela Woodberry' (Z) new	WFib
'Angelique' (Dw/d)	ESul LVER NFir WFib
'Angel's Wings' new	NWoo
'Anglia' (Dw)	ESul
'Ann Field' (Dw/d)	ESul
'Ann Hoystead' (R) ♀H1+3	ESul WFib
'Ann Redington' (R)	LDea
'Anna' (Min)	ESul
'Anna Scheen' (Min)	ESul
'Anne' (I/d) new	WFib
'Annsbrook Aquarius' (St)	ESul NFir
'Annsbrook Beauty' (A/C)	ESul LDea MBPg NFir WFib
'Annsbrook Capricorn' (St/d)	ESul
'Annsbrook Jupitor' (Z/St)	ESul NFir
'Annsbrook Mars' (St/C)	ESul
'Annsbrook Peaches' (Min) new	ESul
'Annsbrook Pluto' (Z/St)	ESul NFir
'Annsbrook Rowan' (Min) new	ESul
'Annsbrook Squirrel' (Min)	ESul
'Annsbrook Venus' (Z/St)	ESul
'Antigua' (R)	LDea
'Antoine Crozy' (ZxI/d)	WFib
'Antoinette' (Min)	ESul
'Apache' (Z/d) ♀H1+3	CHal CWDa WFib
'Aphrodite' (Z)	CWDa ECtt
'Apollo' (R)	CWDa
'Apple Betty' (Sc)	EWoo LDea MBPg MHer WFib
'Apple Blossom Rosebud' (Z/d) ♀H1+3	ECtt EShb ESul LAst LRHS LVER MBri MWhe SKen SMrm SPet SSea WBrk WGwG WWol
'Appledram' (R)	ESul LDea
'Apri Parmer' (Min)	ESul
'Apricot' (Z/St)	ESul LAst SAga SKen WGor
'Apricot Queen' (I/d)	LDea
'Apricot Star'	CSpe MSte MWhe WHPP
'April Hamilton' (I)	LDea WFib
'April Showers' (A)	LDea WFib
Arcona 2000 = 'Klecona'PBR new	LAst

'Arctic Frost'	WFib
§	'Arctic Star' (Z/St)	CSpe ESul LRHS LVER NFir SAga SKen SSea WBrk WFib WHPP
'Ardens'	CSpe ESul EWoo IBal LPio NFir SAga SMrm SSea SUsu SWvt WCot WEas WFib
'Ardwick Cinnamon' (Sc)	ESul EWoo LDea LVER MBPg NFir WFib
'Aries' (Min)	MWhe
'Arizona' (Min/d)	ESul SKen
'Arnside Fringed Aztec' (R)	LDea WFib
'Aroma' (Sc)	EWoo LIck MBPg
'Arron Dixon' (A)	NFir
'Arthington Slam' (R)	LDea
'Arthur Biggin' (Z)	MWhe SKen
'Ashby' (U/Sc)	LVER MBPg NFir
'Ashfield Blaze' (Z/d)	LVER
'Ashfield Jubilee' (Z/C)	NFir SKen
'Ashfield Monarch' (Z/d) ♀H1+3	LVER MWhe NFir
'Ashfield Serenade' (Z) ♀H1+3	SKen WFib
'Ashley Stephenson' (R)	WFib
'Askham Fringed Aztec' (R) ♀H1+3	ESul LDea LVER WFib
'Askham Slam' (R)	LDea
asperum Ehr. ex Willd.	see *P.* 'Graveolens'
'Asperum' **new**	MBPg
'Athabasca' (Min)	ESul
§	'Atomic Snowflake' (Sc/v)	CArn CHal ESul GBar LDea LVER MBPg MHer MSte MWhe SDnm SKen SPet SSea WBrk WFib
'Atrium' (U) **new**	WFib
'Attar of Roses' (Sc) ♀H1+3	CArn CHal CHby CRHN ESul GBar LDea LVER MBPg MHer MSte MWhe NFir NHHG SDnm SIde SKen SSea WBrk WFib WGwG WWye
'Attraction' (Z/Ca/d)	SSea
'Audrey Baghurst' (I)	CWDa
'Audrey Clifton' (I/d)	SKen
'Augusta'	SAga SMrm
auritum subsp. *auritum* **new**	NFir
'Aurora' (Z/d)	MWhe SKen
'Aurore' (U)	see *P.* 'Unique Aurore'
australe	CFir CRHN EWoo LPio SSpi WFib
'Australian Bute' (R)	ESul LVER
'Australian Mystery' (R/Dec)	CSpe ESul MSte NFir SAga WFib WHPP
'Autumn' (Z/d)	MWhe
'Autumn Colours' (Min)	ESul
'Avril'	ESul
'Aztec' (R) ♀H1+3	ESul LDea LVER MSte NFir WFib
'Baby Bird's Egg' (Min)	ESul WFib
'Baby Brocade' (Min/d)	ESul WFib
'Baby Face' (Dw)	EWoo
'Baby Harry' (Dw/v) **new**	WFib
'Baby Helen' (Min)	ESul
'Baby James' (Min)	ESul
'Baby Snooks' (A)	ESul LDea MWhe
'Babylon' (R)	EWoo NFir
'Badley' (Dw)	ESul
Balcon Imperial	see *P.* 'Roi des Balcons Impérial'
'Balcon Lilas'	see *P.* 'Roi des Balcons Lilas'
'Balcon Rose'	see *P.* 'Hederinum'
'Balcon Rouge'	see *P.* 'Roi des Balcons Impérial'
'Balcon Royale'	see *P.* 'Roi des Balcons Impérial'
I	'Ballerina' (Min) **new**	WFib
'Ballerina' (Z/d)	MWhe
'Ballerina' (R)	see *P.* 'Carisbrooke'
'Bandit' (Min)	ESul

'Banstead Village' (Z)	LVER
'Bantam' (Min/d)	ESul WFib
§	'Barbe Bleu' (I/d)	ECtt EWoo LDea LVER MWhe NFir SKen SSea WFib
'Barham' (Min/d)	ESul
'Barking' (Min)	ESul NFir
'Barnston Dale' (Dw/d)	ESul NFir
'Barock '96'	NPri
'Bath Beauty' (Dw)	SKen WEas
'Baylham' (Min)	ESul
Beach = 'Fisbea' (I/d)	NPri
'Beacon Hill' (Min)	ESul
'Beatrice Cottington' (I/d)	SKen WFib
'Beatrix' (Z/d)	LVER SKen
'Beau Geste' (R)	ESul
'Beauty of Diane' (I/d)	LDea
'Beauty of Eastbourne' misapplied	see *P.* 'Lachskönigin'
'Beauty of El Segundo' (Z/d)	SKen
'Beckwith's Pink' (Z)	SKen
'Belinda Adams' (Min/d) ♀H1+3	MWhe NFir
§	Belladonna = 'Fisopa' (I/d)	ECtt NPri SCoo
'Belvedere' (R)	ESul
'Bembridge' (Z/St/d)	LVER SSea WFib
'Ben Franklin' (Z/d/v) ♀H1+3	ESul LVER MWhe NFir SPet
'Ben Matt' (R)	LDea WFib
'Ben Nevis' (Dw/d)	ESul LVER
'Ben Picton' (Z/d) **new**	WFib
'Bentley' (Dw)	ESul
'Berkswell Dainty' (A) **new**	LDea
'Berliner Balkon' (I)	SKen
Bernardo = 'Guiber'PBR (I/d)	LAst NBlu WHPP
'Beromünster' (Dec)	CSpe ESul EWoo LDea MSte NFir WFib
'Bert Pearce' (R)	LDea WFib
'Beryl Gibbons' (Z/d)	LVER MWhe
'Beryl Read' (Dw)	ESul
'Beryl Reid' (R)	ESul LDea WFib
'Berylette' (Min/d)	ESul SKen
'Bess' (Z/d)	ESul SKen
'Bette Shellard' (Z/d/v)	MWhe NFir
'Betty' (Z/d)	LVER
'Betty Hulsman' (A)	ESul LDea NFir
'Betty Merry' (R) **new**	LDea
'Betty Read' (Dw)	ESul
'Betty West' (Min/d)	ESul
betulinum	EWoo SSea WFib
'Betwixt' (Z/v)	SKen SSea
'Bianca' (Min/d)	ESul
'Bi-coloured Startel' (Z/St/d)	MWhe
I	'Big Apple' (Sc) **new**	MBPg
'Bildeston' (Dw/C)	ESul NFir WFib
'Bill Holdaway' (Z)	LVER
'Bill West' (I)	WFib
'Billie Read' (Dw/d)	ESul
'Bingo' (Min)	ESul
'Bird Dancer' (Dw/St) ♀H1+3	CHal CPlt CSpe ESul LVER MSte MWhe NFir SAga SHFr SKen SSea WBrk
'Birdbush Blush' (Sc) **new**	MBPg
'Birdbush Bold and Beautiful'(Sc) **new**	MBPg
'Birdbush Bramley' (Sc) **new**	MBPg
'Birdbush Chloe' (St) **new**	MBPg
'Birdbush Eleanor' (Z) **new**	MBPg

'Birdbush Lemon and Lime' (Sc) **new**   MBPg
'Birdbush Matty' **new**   MBPg
'Birdbush Nutty' (Sc) **new**   MBPg
'Birdbush Sweetness' (Sc) **new**   MBPg
'Birdbush Velvet' (Sc) **new**   MBPg
'Birthday Girl' (R)   WFib
'Bitter Lemon' (Sc)   ESul MBPg
'Black Butterfly'   see *P.* 'Brown's Butterfly'
'Black Country Bugle' (Z/d)   CWDa
'Black Knight' (R)   CElw CSpe EWoo LDea LVER MSte SAga
'Black Knight' Lea (Dw/d/c)   ESul MSte NFir WHPP
'Black Magic' (R)   NPri WWol
'Black Night' (A)   ESul MBPg
'Black Pearl' (Z/d)   LVER
'Black Prince' (R)   CElw ESul NFir WFib
'Black Velvet' (R)   LDea
'Black Vesuvius'   see *P.* 'Red Black Vesuvius'
'Blakesdorf' (Dw)   ESul MWhe
Blanca = 'Penwei'PBR (Z/d)   LAst LVER
Blanche Roche = 'Guitoblanc' (I/d)   EWoo LAst SCoo
§ 'Blandfordianum' (Sc)   EWoo LDea MHer MSte
'Blandfordianum Roseum' (Sc)   LDea
§ 'Blauer Frühling' (I x Z/d)   LVER WFib
'Blaze Away'   SSea
'Blazonry' (Z/v)   MWhe SKen SSea WFib
'Blendworth' (R)   LDea
'Blooming Gem' (Min/I/d)   LDea
'Blue Beard'   see *P.* 'Barbe Bleu'
'Blue Fox' (Z)   CWDa
'Blue Peter' (I/d)   SKen
Blue Spring   see *P.* 'Blauer Frühling'
'Blue Sybil' (I) **new**   LAst
'Bluebeard'   see *P.* 'Barbe Bleu'
Blue-Blizzard = 'Fisrain'PBR (I)   SCoo WWol
§ Blues = 'Fisblu'PBR (Z/d)   CWDa
'Blush Petit Pierre' (Min)   ESul
'Blushing Bride' (I/d)   LDea SKen
'Blushing Emma' (Dw/d)   ESul
'Bobberstone' (Z/St) **new**   LVER WFib
'Bode's Trina' (I)   CWDa
'Bold Candy' (R)   LDea WHPP
'Bold Carmine' (Z/d)   NFir
'Bold Dawn' (Z)   NFir
'Bold Flame' (Z/d)   WFib
'Bold Gypsy' (R)   LDea
'Bold Sunrise' (Z/d)   LVER NFir
'Bold Sunset' (Z/d)   LVER NFir WFib
'Bold White' (Z)   NFir
'Bolero' (U) ♀H1+3   EWoo LVER MSte NFir SSea WFib WHPP
'Bon Bon' (Min/St) **new**   WFib
'Bonito' (I/d)   LVER
'Bosham' (R)   ESul LDea WFib
'Both's Snowflake' (Sc/v)   EWoo MBPg
'Botley Beauty' (R)   ESul LDea
bowkeri   WFib
'Brackenwood' (Dw/d) ♀H1+3   ESul LVER NFir
'Bramford' (Dw)   ESul
'Braque' (R)   LDea
Bravo = 'Fisbravo'PBR (Z/d)   LAst MWhe WFib

'Break o' Day' (R)   LDea WEas
'Bredon' (R) ♀H1+3   ESul
'Brenda' (Min/d)   ESul WFib
'Brenda Hyatt' (Dw/d)   ESul WFib
'Brenda Kitson' (Z/d)   LVER MWhe
'Brettenham' (Min)   ESul
'Briarlyn Beauty' (A)   LDea MBPg MWhe NFir WHPP
'Briarlyn Moonglow' (A)   ESul LDea LVER SSea
'Bridesmaid' (Dw/d)   ESul NFir WFib
'Bright Eyes' (Dw) **new**   WFib
'Brightstone'   WFib
'Brightwell' (Min/d)   ESul
'Brilliant' (Dec)   MBPg MHer WFib
'Brilliantine' (Sc)   ESul EWoo MBPg MHer WFib
'Bristol' (Z/v)   SKen SMrm SSea
'Britannia' (R)   LDea
'Brixworth Boquet' (Min/C/d)   MWhe
'Brixworth Charmer' (Z/v)   MWhe
'Brixworth Melody' (Z/v)   MWhe
'Brixworth Pearl' (Z)   MWhe WFib
'Brixworth Rhapsody' (Z/v)   MWhe
'Brixworth Starlight' (I/v)   MWhe
'Brockbury Scarlet' (Ca)   WFib
'Bronze Corinne' (Z/C/d)   SKen SPet
'Bronze Nuhulumby' (R)   ESul
'Bronze Queen' (Z/C)   MWhe
'Bronze Velvet' (R)   LDea
'Brook's Purple'   see *P.* 'Royal Purple'
'Brookside Betty' (Dw/C/d)   ESul
'Brookside Bolero' (Z)   ESul
'Brookside Candy' (Dw/d)   ESul
'Brookside Champagne' (Min/d)   ESul
'Brookside Flamenco' (Dw/d)   ESul MWhe WFib
'Brookside Primrose' (Min/d)   ESul MWhe NFir WFib
'Brookside Rosita' (Min)   ESul
'Brookside Serenade' (Dw)   ESul WFib
'Brookside Spitfire' (Dw/d)   ESul
§ 'Brown's Butterfly' (R)   ECtt LDea NFir SMrm WFib
§ 'Bruni' (Z/d)   CHal MWhe
'Brunswick' (Sc)   ESul EWoo LDea LPio LVER MBPg MHer MSte SSea WFib
'Brutus' (Z)   CWDa
'Bucklesham' (Dw)   ESul
'Bumblebee' (Dw)   ESul
'Burgenlandmädel' (Z/d)   LVER SKen
'Burgundy' (R)   LVER WHPP
'Burstall' (Min/d)   ESul
'Bushfire' (R) ♀H1+3   ESul EWoo LDea WFib
'Butley' (Min)   ESul
'Butterfly' (Min/v)   ECtt NPri
§ Butterfly = 'Fisam'PBR (I)   SCoo
'Button 'n' Bows' (I/d) **new**   WFib
'Cal'   see *P.* 'Salmon Irene'
'Caledonia' (Z)   SKen
'California Brilliant' (U)   MBPg
'Cameo' (Dw/d)   MWhe
'Camisole' (Dw/d)   LVER
'Camphor Rose' (Sc)   ESul EWoo LDea MBPg MHer NFir SSea
'Can-can' (I/d)   WFib
candicans   LPio
'Candy' (Min/d)   ESul
'Candy Kisses' (D)   ESul
canescens   see *P.* 'Blandfordianum'

'Capel' (Dw/d) ESul
capitatum EWoo MBPg MHer WFib
'Capri' (Sc) WFib
'Caprice' (R) EWoo
'Capricorn' (Min/d) ESul
'Captain Starlight' (A) CRHN ESul EWoo LDea LVER
MBPg MHer NFir NWoo SKen SSea
WFib WHPP
'Caravan' (A) LDea
'Cardinal' see *P.* 'Kardinal'
'Cardinal Pink' (Z/d) CWDa
'Carefree' (U) EWoo LPio MSte NFir WFib
'Cariboo Gold' ESul
(Min/C) ♥H1+3
§ 'Carisbrooke' (R) ♥H1+3 LDea SKen SSea WEas WFib
'Carl Gaffney' **new** LDea
'Carmel' (Z) EWoo WFib
'Carnival' (R) see *P.* 'Marie Vogel'
'Carol' (R) ESul
'Carol Gibbons' (Z/d) LVER MWhe NFir WFib
'Carol Helyar' (Z/d) **new** WFib
'Carole Munroe' (Z/d) LVER
'Caroline Plumridge' ESul
(Dw)
'Caroline Schmidt' CHal ESul LAst LRHS LVER MSte
(Z/d/v) MWhe NFir NWoo SKen SPet SSea
WBrk WFib
'Carolyn' (Dw) ESul
'Carolyn Hardy' (Z/d) WFib
new
'Carousel' (Z/d) CWDa
Cascade Lilac see *P.* 'Roi des Balcons Lilas'
Cascade Pink see *P.* 'Hederinum'
Cascade Red see *P.* 'Red Cascade'
'Catford Belle' (A) ♥H1+3 CHal CSpe ESul LDea MWhe SAga
SSea WFib WHPP
'Cathay' (Z/St) ESul MWhe NFir SSea
'Catherine Wheels' LVER
(Z/St) **new**
'Cathy' (R) NFir
caucalifolium subsp. WFib
convolvulifolium
'Celebration' (Z/d) ESul
'Cézanne' (R) LDea LVER WFib
§ 'Champagne' (Z) CWDa
'Chantilly Claret' (R) LDea
'Chantilly Lace' (R) ESul LDea
'Charity' (Sc) ♥H1+3 CHal ESul EWoo LDea LIck LVER
MBPg MHer MSte MWhe NFir SSea
WBrk WFib WHPP
'Charlie Boy' (R) LDea
'Charlotte Amy' (R) LDea
'Charlotte Bidwell' (Min) ESul
'Charlotte Bronte' WFib
(Dw/v) **new**
'Charm' (Min) ESul
'Charmant' CWDa
'Charmay Alf' (A) LDea
'Charmay Marjorie' LDea
(A) **new**
'Charmay Snowflake' ESul MBPg WHer
(Sc/v)
'Charmer' (R) LDea
'Chattisham' (Dw/C) ESul
'Chelmondiston' (Min/d) ESul MWhe
'Chelsea Diane' (Min) LVER
new
§ 'Chelsea Gem' LRHS LVER NFir SKen SSea WFib
(Z/d/v) ♥H1+3
'Chelsea Morning' (Z/d) WFib
'Chelsworth' (Min/d) ESul
'Chelvey' (R) LDea
'Cherie' (R) ESul LDea
'Cherie Bidwell' (Dw/d/v) ESul

'Cherie Maid' (Z/v) ESul SSea
'Cherry' (Min) LVER WFib
'Cherry Baby' (Dec) LPio NFir
'Cherry Cocktail' (Z/d/v) MWhe NFir
'Cherry Hazel Ruffled' (R) LDea
'Cherry Orchard' (R) LDea LVER SSea
'Cherry Sundae' (Z/d/v) ESul
'Cheryldene' (R) LDea
'Chew Magna' (R) WFib
'Chi-Chi' (Min) **new** ESul
'Chieko' (Min/d) ESul MWhe WFib
'Chime' (Min/d) ESul
'China Doll' (Dw/d) WFib
'Chinz' (R) CSpe NFir SAga
'Chocolate Drops' (Z) LVER
§ 'Chocolate CHal CHrt CSev ESul GBar LDea
Peppermint' (Sc) MBPg MHer MWhe NBur NFir
NHHG SSea SYvo WBrk WFib
WHPP WHer
'Chocolate Tomentosum' see *P.* 'Chocolate Peppermint'
'Chrissie' (R) ESul WFib
'Christina Beere' (R) LDea
'Christopher Ley' (Z) LVER SKen
'Cindy' (Dw/d) ESul WFib
'Circus Day' (R) LDea
'Citriodorum' (Sc) ♥H1+3 CArn LDea MBPg MHer NHHG
WFib
'Citronella' (Sc) CRHN LDea MBPg MHer MSte
WFib
citronellum (Sc) MBPg
'Clara Read' (Dw) ESul
'Claret Cruz' (I) CWDa
'Claret Rock Unique' (U) EWoo LDea MHer MSte SKen WFib
'Clarissa' (Min) ESul
'Clatterbridge' (Dw/d) ESul LVER NFir
'Claude Read' (Dw) ESul
'Claudette' (Min) ESul
'Claudius' (Min) ESul
'Claydon' (Dw/d) ESul NFir
'Claydon Firebird' (R) ESul
'Clorinda' (U/Sc) CHal CRHN ESul EWoo GBar LVER
MBPg MHer MSte NBur SKen SSea
WFib WHer
'Clorinda Variegated' see *P.* 'Variegated Clorinda'
'Coconut Ice' (Dw) ESul
§ Coco-Rico (I) SKen
'Coddenham' (Dw/d) WFib
§ 'Colonel Baden-Powell' LDea WFib
(I/d)
Comedy WGwG
= 'Fiscomedy'[PBR] (I)
'Conner' (Min) **new** ESul
'Conspicuous' (R) EWoo
'Constance Spry' (Z) WEas
'Contrast' (Z/d/C/v) LAst LRHS MBri MWhe SCoo SKen
SPoG SSea WFib
'Cook's Peachblossom' WFib
new
'Copdock' (Min/d) ESul
'Copthorne' CRHN ESul LDea LVER MBPg
(U/Sc) ♥H1+3 MHer MSte SKen SSea WBrk WFib
WHPP
'Coral Frills' (Min/d) ESul
'Coral Sunset' (d) CWDa
cordifolium CRHN EWoo WFib
coriandrifolium see *P. myrrhifolium* var.
coriandrifolium
'Cornell' (I/d) ECtt WFib
'Coronia' (Z/Ca) CWDa
'Corsair' (Z/d) ♥H1+3 MWhe
'Corvina' (R) WFib
'Cotta Lilac Queen' (I/d) LVER
'Cottenham Beauty' (A) ESul EWoo LDea NFir
'Cottenham Charm' (A) ESul

'Cottenham Delight' (A) ESul LDea NFir
'Cottenham Gem' (A) ESul
'Cottenham Glamour' ESul
  (A) **new**
'Cottenham Harmony' (A) ESul
'Cottenham Jubilee' ESul
  (A) **new**
'Cottenham Surprise' (A) ESul LDea MBPg MSte MWhe NFir
'Cottenham Treasure' (A) ESul
'Cotton Candy' (Min/d) ESul
'Cottontail' (Min/d) ESul WFib
cotyledonis WFib
'Countess Mariza' see *P.* 'Gräfin Mariza'
'Countess of Scarborough' see *P.* 'Lady Scarborough'
'Country Girl' (R) SPet
'Cover Girl' (Z/d) WFib
'Cramdon Red' (Dw) SKen WFib
'Crampel's Master' (Z) LVER SKen
'Cranbrook Black' EWoo
'Cranbrooks Unique' EWoo
'Cransley Blends' (R) ESul LDea
'Cransley Star' (A) LDea MWhe WFib
'Cream 'n' Green' (R/v) NFir
'Creamery' (d) WFib
§ 'Creamy Nutmeg' (Sc/v) CArn CHal CHrt ESul GBar LDea
  LVER MHer MWhe NBur NFir
  SRob SSea
'Creeting St Mary' (Min) ESul
'Creeting St Peter' (Min) ESul
'Crescendo' (I/d) ECtt
'Crimson Crampel' (Z) CWDa
'Crimson Fire' (Z) MBri MWhe SKen
'Crimson Unique' CRHN CSpe EWoo MBPg MHer
  (U) ♀H1+3 SAga SKen SSea WFib
§ *crispum* (Sc) CHrt GBar GPoy LDea LPhx MBPg
  NHHG WRha
- 'Golden Well MBPg NFir WFib
  Sweep' (Sc/v)
- 'Major' (Sc) ESul MBPg SKen WFib
- 'Minor' (Sc) MBPg MHer
- 'Peach Cream' (Sc/v) CHal ESul MBPg MWhe WFib
- 'Variegatum' CHal CRHN CSev GBar GPoy LDea
  (Sc/v) ♀H1+3 LVER MBPg MHer MWhe NFir SPet
  SSea WFib
crithmifolium MHer
'Crock O Day' (I/d) LVER
'Crocketta' (I/d/v) LVER NFir SSea
'Crocodile' (I/C/d) ECtt EShb LDea LVER MWhe NFir
  SKen SSea WFib
'Crowfield' (Min/d) ESul WFib
'Crown Jewels' (R) LDea
'Crystal Palace Gem' (Z/v) LAst LRHS LVER MWhe SKen
  SMrm SSea WFib WHPP
cucullatum ESul EWoo MHer SSea SVen WFib
  WHPP
- 'Flore Pleno' **new** WFib
'Culpho' (Min/C/d) ESul
'Cupid' (Min/Dw/d) ESul WFib
'Cyril Read' (Dw) ESul
'Dainty Lassie' (Dw/v) ESul
'Dainty Maid' (Sc) ESul EWoo LVER MBPg NFir SAga
  SSea
'Dale Queen' (Z) WFib
'Dallimore' (Dw) **new** ESul
'Dame Anna Neagle' LVER
  (Dw/d) ♀H1+3
'Danielle Marie' (A) LDea
I 'Daphne' (A) **new** LAst
'Dark Ascot' (Dec) ESul
'Dark Lady' (Sc) MBPg
'Dark Red Irene' (Z/d) LVER MWhe SKen WFib
'Dark Secret' (R) CSpe ESul EWoo LDea MSte SKen
  WFib WHPP
'Dark Venus' (R) LDea WFib

Dark-Red-Blizzard NPri WWol
  = 'Fisblizdark' (I)
'Darmsden' (A) ♀H1+3 ESul EWoo LDea NFir
'David John' (Dw/d) ESul
'David Mitchell' ESul
  (Min/Ca/d)
'Davina' (Min/d) ESul MWhe WFib
'Dawn Star' (Z/St) ESul NFir
'Deacon Arlon' (Dw/d) ESul LVER MWhe SKen
'Deacon Avalon' (Dw/d) WFib
'Deacon Barbecue' (Z/d) ESul MWhe SKen WFib
'Deacon Birthday' (Z/d) ESul LVER MWhe WFib
'Deacon Bonanza' (Z/d) ESul MWhe SKen WFib
'Deacon Clarion' (Z/d) ESul SKen WFib
'Deacon Constancy' (Z/d) ESul LVER MWhe
'Deacon Coral Reef' (Z/d) ESul MWhe SKen WFib
'Deacon Delight' EWoo
'Deacon Finale' (Z/d) ESul LVER
'Deacon Fireball' (Z/d) ESul LVER MWhe SKen WFib
'Deacon Flamingo' (Z/d) ESul MWhe WBrk
'Deacon Gala' (Z/d) ESul MWhe WFib
'Deacon Golden ESul WFib
  Bonanza' (Z/C/d)
'Deacon Golden Gala' ESul SKen
  (Z/C/d)
'Deacon Golden Lilac ESul SKen WFib
  Mist' (Z/C/d)
'Deacon Golden Mist' see *P.* 'Golden Mist'
'Deacon Jubilant' (Z/d) ESul MWhe SKen
'Deacon Lilac Mist' (Z/d) ESul LVER MWhe SKen WFib
'Deacon Mandarin' (Z/d) ESul MWhe SKen WFib
'Deacon Minuet' (Z/d) ESul LVER MWhe NFir SKen WFib
'Deacon Moonlight' (Z/d) ESul LVER MWhe
'Deacon Peacock' (Z/C/d) ESul MWhe SKen WFib
'Deacon Picotee' (Z/d) ESul MWhe SKen WFib
'Deacon Regalia' (Z/d) ESul MWhe SKen WFib
'Deacon Romance' (Z/d) ESul LVER MWhe SKen
§ 'Deacon Summertime' ESul LVER MWhe WFib
  (Z/d)
'Deacon Sunburst' (Z/d) ESul LVER MWhe SKen
'Deacon Suntan' (Z/d) ESul LVER MWhe SKen
'Deacon Trousseau' (Z/d) ESul MWhe WFib
'Dean's Delight' (Sc) LDea MBPg
'Debbie Parmer' (Dw/d) ESul
'Debbie Thrower' (Dw) ESul
'Decora Impérial' (I) LAst LVER
'Decora Lavender' see *P.* 'Decora Lilas'
§ 'Decora Lilas' (I) ECtt LAst LVER SPet
'Decora Mauve' see *P.* 'Decora Lilas'
I 'Decora Pink' **new** LAst
I 'Decora Red' **new** LAst
§ 'Decora Rose' (I) CWDa ECtt LAst SPet
'Decora Rouge' (I) ECtt SPet
'Deerwood Darling' WFib
  (Min/v/d) **new**
'Deerwood Don MWhe
  Quixote' (A)
'Deerwood Lavender ESul EWoo LDea MBPg MHer WFib
  Lad' (Sc)
'Deerwood Lavender ESul LDea MBPg MHer
  Lass'
'Deerwood Pink WFib
  Puff' (St/d) **new**
'Delhi' (R) NPer WFib
'Delightful' (R) WFib
'Delilah' (R) LDea
'Delta' (Min/d) ESul
'Denebola' (Min/d) ESul
denticulatum EWoo GBar MHer NHHG SKen
  SSea
§ - 'Filicifolium' (Sc) CHal CRHN EShb ESul EWoo
  MBPg MHer NHHG SSea WFib
'Diana Hull' **new** MBPg
'Diana Palmer' (Z/d) SKen

'Diane' (Min/d) — ESul
'Dibbinsdale' (Z) — ESul NFir
dichondrifolium (Sc) — EWoo LVER MBPg MHer NCiC NFir WFib WHPP
dichondrifolium × ***reniforme*** (Sc) — NFir
'Diddi-Di' (Min/d) — ESul
'Didi' (Min) — ESul SKen
'Dinky' (Min/d) — ESul
§ Disco = 'Fisdis' (Z/d) — CWDa
'Display' (Dw/v) **new** — WFib
'Distinction' (Z) — ESul LAst MWhe NFir SAga SKen SSea WFib WHPP
'Doctor A. Chipault' (I/d) — LDea
'Doctor A. Vialettes' (Z/d) — CWDa
'Dodd's Super Double' (Z/d) — CHal SMrm
'Dollar Bute' (R) — ESul LDea
'Dollar Princess' (Z/C) — SKen
'Dolly Read' (Dw) — ESul
'Dolly Varden' (Z/v) ♀H1+3 — ESul LDea LVER MWhe NFir SKen SPet SSea WFib
'Don Quixote' (A) — LDea
'Don's Barbra Leonard' (Dw/B) — NFir
'Don's Helen Bainbridge' (Z/C) — NFir
'Don's Jubilee' (Dw/C) — NFir
'Don's Mona Noble' (Z/C/v) — NFir SKen
'Don's Richard A. Costain' (Z/C) — NFir
'Don's Seagold' — NFir
'Don's Shiela Jane' (Z/C/d) — NFir
'Don's Silva Perle' (Dw/v) — SKen
'Don's Southport' (Z/v) — NFir
'Don's Stokesley Gem' (Z/C) — NFir
'Don's Swanland Girl' (Min) — ESul
'Don's Whirlygig' (Z/C) — NFir
'Dorcas Brigham Lime' (Sc) — EWoo
'Dorcus Bingham' (Sc) **new** — MBPg
'Doreen' (Z/d) — LVER
'Doris Frith' (R) — LDea
'Dorothy May' (A) — LDea
'Double Bird's Egg' (Z/d) — CWDa SKen
'Double Grace Wells' (Min/d) — ESul
'Double Lilac White' (I/d) — SKen
'Double New Life' (Z/d) — CHal CWDa
'Double Orange' (Z/d) — SKen
'Dovedale' (Dw/C) — ESul NFir WFib
'Downlands' (Z/d) — WFib
'Dragon's Breath' (Z/St) — LVER
'Dream' (Z) — CWDa
'Dresden China' (R) — EWoo LDea
'Dresden Pippa Rosa' (Z) — SKen
'Dresden White' (Dw) — WFib
'Dresdner Amethyst' **new** — LAst
Dresdner Coralit = 'Coralit' (I/d) — LVER
Dresdner Purpalit (I) — LVER
'Dresdner Red Sybil' (I) — LAst
Dresdner Rosalit = 'Rosalit'PBR (I/d) — LVER
'Drummer Boy' (Z) — CWDa SKen
'Dryden' (Z) — SKen
'Dubonnet' (R) — LDea
'Duchess of Devonshire' (Z) — WFib

'Duke of Buckingham' (Z/d) — LVER
'Duke of Devonshire' (Z/d) — LVER
'Duke of Edinburgh' — see *P.* 'Hederinum Variegatum'
'Dulcie' (Min) — ESul
'Dunkery Beacon' (R) — WFib
'Dusty Rose' (Min) — ESul
§ 'Dwarf Miriam Baisey' (Min) — LVER
'Dwarf Miriam Read' — see *P.* 'Dwarf Miriam Baisey'
'E. Dabner' (Z/d) — CWDa SKen WFib
'Earl of Chester' (Min/d) ♀H1+3 — WFib
'Earliana' (Dec) — ESul LDea SKen
'Earlsfour' (R) — LDea MSte
'Easter Morn' (Z/St) — SSea
echinatum — CSpe EWoo MBPg MHer SAga WHPP
- 'Album' — WFib
- 'Miss Stapleton' — see *P.* 'Miss Stapleton'
'Eclipse' (I/d) — MWhe SKen
'Eden Gem' (Min/d) — WFib
'Edith Stern' (Dw/d) — ESul LVER
'Edmond Lachenal' (Z/d) — WFib
'Edward Humphris' (Z) — EWoo SKen
'Eileen' (Min/d) — ESul NFir
'Eileen Postle' (R) ♀H1+3 — WFib
'Eileen Stanley' (R) — LDea
'Elaine' (R) — LDea
Elbe Silver = 'Pensil'PBR (I) — NFir SCoo
'Electra' (Z/d) — CWDa LVER SKen
'Elizabeth Angus' (Z) — SKen WFib
'Elizabeth Read' (Dw) — ESul
'Elmsett' (Dw/C/d) — ESul LVER NFir WFib
'Elna' (Min) — ESul
'Els' (Dw/St) — ESul LVER SKen WBrk
'Elsi' (I × Z/d/v) — LVER WFib
'Elsie Hickman' (R) — LDea
'Elsie Portas' (Z/C/d) — ESul SKen
'Embassy' (Min) — ESul WFib
'Emerald' (I) — SKen
'Emilia Joy' (A) — MHer
'Emma Bannister' (R) — ESul
'Emma Hössle' — see *P.* 'Frau Emma Hössle'
'Emma Jane Read' (Dw/d) — ESul MWhe NFir WFib
'Emma Louise' (Z) — SKen
'Emmy Sensation' (R) — LDea
'Emperor Nicholas' (Z/d) — MWhe SKen
'Empress' (Z) — SKen
'Ena' (Min) — ESul
'Enchantress' (I) — SKen
'Encore' (Z/d/v) — LRHS LVER MWhe NFir
endlicherianum — NBhm NWCA SIgm WCot WHPP
'Endsleigh' (Sc) — MBPg MHer
'Enid Blackaby' (R) — WHPP
* 'Eric Lee' — CWDa
'Eroica 2000' **new** — LAst
'Erwarton' (Min/d) — ESul NFir
'Escapade' (Min/d) — ESul
'Evelyn' (Min) — ESul
Evening Glow = 'Bergpalais'PBR — LAst
'Evka'PBR (I/v) — LAst LVER NBlu NFir SCoo SSea
'Excalibur' (Z/Min/v) **new** — LVER
'Explosive' (I) — NPri
exstipulatum — EWoo WEas XPep
'Eyes Randy' (A) **new** — LAst
§ 'Fair Dinkum' (Z/v) — ESul MWhe NFir
§ 'Fair Ellen' (Sc) — ESul EWoo LDea MBPg MHer SKen WFib
'Fairlee' (DwI) — WFib

'Fairy Lights' (Dw/St)   ESul NFir
'Fairy Orchid' (A)   ESul LDea LVER SSea WFib
'Fairy Princess' (R)   LDea
'Fairy Queen'   LDea MHer
'Falkenham' (Min)   ESul
'Falkland Brother' (Z/C/v)   ESul WFib
'Falkland Hero' (Z/v)   LVER NFir
'Fandango' (Z/St)   ESul MWhe NFir WFib
* 'Fanfare'   CWDa
'Fanny Eden' (R)   WFib
'Fantasia' white   ESul MWhe WFib
   (Dw/d) ♀H1+3
'Fareham' (R) ♀H1+3   LDea MSte WFib
'Faye Brawner'   LVER
   (Z/St) **new**
'Feneela' (Dw/d)   ESul
'Fenton Farm' (Dw/C)   ESul NFir WFib
I 'Fern Mint' (Sc) **new**   MBPg
'Festal' (Min/d)   ESul
'Feuerriese' (Z)   LVER SKen
'Fiat' (Z/d)   CWDa SKen
'Fiat Queen' (Z/d)   SKen WFib
'Fiat Supreme' (Z/d)   SKen
'Fiery Sunrise' (R)   ESul EWoo LDea
'Fiesta' (I/d)   LDea
'Fifth Avenue' (R)   CSpe EWoo MSte WFib WHPP
'Filicifolium'   see *P. denticulatum* 'Filicifolium'
'Fir Trees Audrey B' (St)   NFir
'Fir Trees Big Show'   NFir
   (I) (v) **new**
'Fir Trees Echoes of   EWoo NFir
   Pink' (A)
'Fir Trees Eileen' (St)   NFir
'Fir Trees Ele' (A/v) **new**   NFir
'Fir Trees Flamingo' (Dw)   NFir
'Fir Trees Jack' (Z/Dw)   NFir
'Fir Trees John Grainger'   NFir
   (Z) (v) **new**
'Fir Trees Roseberry   NFir
   Topping' (Dw)
'Fir Trees Ruby Wedding'   NFir
'Fir Trees Silver Wedding'   NFir
   (Z/C/d)
'Fir Trees Sparkler'   NFir
'Fire Dragon' (Z/St/d)   SKen SSea
'Firebrand' (Z/d)   LVER
'Firefly' (Min/d)   ESul
'Firestone' (Dw)   ESul
'Fireworks Light Pink'   LAst
   new
'Fireworks White' **new**   LAst
'First Blush' (R)   WFib
'First Love' (Z)   LVER NFir
'Flakey' (I/d/v) ♀H1+3   CSpe ESul LDea NFir SKen
'Flarepath' (Z/C/v)   NFir
'Flesh Pink' (Z/d)   CWDa
'Fleurette' (Min/d)   CHal ESul MWhe SKen SPet
'Fleurisse' (Z) **new**   WFib
'Flirt' (Min) **new**   ESul
§ Flirt (Min)   WFib
'Floria Moore' (Dec)   ESul EWoo NFir
'Flower Basket' (R/d)   LDea NFir
'Flower of Spring'   CHal LVER MWhe SKen SSea
   (Z/v) ♀H1+3
'Flowton' (Dw/d)   ESul
* 'Forever' (d)   CWDa
'Foxhall' (Dw)   ESul
Fragrans Group (Sc)   CHal CRHN CSev ESul EWoo GBar
     GPoy LPio MBPg MHer MWhe
     NHHG SDnm SKen SPet WBrk
     WFib WHer WWye XPep
 - 'Creamy Nutmeg'   see *P.* 'Creamy Nutmeg'
§ - 'Fragrans Variegatum'   CSev ESul Llck MBPg MWhe NFir
   (Sc/v)   SKen WBrk WFib WHPP

 - 'Snowy Nutmeg'   see *P.* (Fragrans Group) 'Fragrans
     Variegatum'
'Fraiche Beauté' (Z/d)   CWDa WFib
'Francis Gibbon'   WFib
   (Z/d) **new**
'Francis James' (Z)   EWoo WFib
'Francis Parmenter'   SSea
   (MinI/v)
'Francis Parrett'   ESul MWhe SKen WFib
   (Min/d) ♀H1+3
'Francis Read' (Dw/d)   ESul SPet
'Frank Headley'   CHal CSpe ESul LAst LRHS LVER
   (Z/v) ♀H1+3   MSte MWhe NPer NVic SCoo
     SDnm SKen SMrm SPet SSea WBrk
     WFib WHPP
§ 'Frau Emma Hössle'   ESul MWhe WFib
   (Dw/d)
'Frau Käthe Neubronner'   CWDa
   (Z/d)
'Freak of Nature' (Z/v)   ESul MWhe NFir SKen SSea WFib
'Frensham' (Sc)   ESul EWoo MBPg MHer SSea WFib
'Freshfields Suki' (Dw)   NFir
'Freshwater' (St/C)   ESul MWhe
'Freston' (Dw)   ESul
'Friary Wood' (Z/C/d)   ESul NFir WFib
'Friesdorf' (Dw/Fr)   ESul LVER MHer MWhe NFir SKen
     WBrk WFib
'Frills' (Min/d)   ESul MWhe NFir
'Fringed Angel' (A)   CFee LDea
'Fringed Apple' (Sc)   LDea MBPg NBur
§ 'Fringed Aztec' (R)   ESul LDea LVER NFir SPet WFib
   ♀H1+3   WHPP
'Fringed Jer'Ray' (A)   LDea
'Fringed Rouletta' (I)   LDea
'Frosty' misapplied   see *P.* 'Variegated Kleine Liebling'
'Frosty Petit Pierre'   see *P.* 'Variegated Kleine Liebling'
'Frühlingszauber Lila' (R)   ESul
'Fruity' (Sc) **new**   MBPg
frutetorum   MBPg MHer
fruticosum   EShb EWoo LPio WFib
'Fuji' (R)   NFir
fulgidum   EWoo MHer WFib
'Fynn' (Dw)   ESul
'Gabriel' (A)   ESul EWoo LDea MBPg NFir
'Galilee' (Z/d) ♀H1+3   LDea LVER SKen
Galleria Sunrise   ESul LDea LVER SKen WEas WFib
   = 'Purple Rose'
'Galway Girl' (Sc) **new**   MBPg
'Galway Star'   MBPg MHer SKen WBrk WFib
   (Sc/v) ♀H1+3
'Garibaldi' (Z/d)   CWDa
'Garland' (Dw/d)   ESul LVER
'Garnet' (Z/d)   ESul LVER
'Garnet Rosebud' (Min/d)   ESul WFib
'Gartendirektor   ESul EWoo NFir WFib WHPP
   Herman' (Dec)
'Gary Salvidge' (R)   LDea
'Gaudy' (Z)   WFib
'Gay Baby' (DwI)   ESul LDea MWhe
'Gay Baby Supreme'   ESul
   (DwI)
§ 'Gemini' (Z/St/d)   ESul MWhe NFir SSea WFib
'Gemma' (R)   LVER NFir SAga
'Gemma Finito' (R)   LDea
'Gemma Jewel'   ESul
   (R) ♀H1+3
'Gemma Rose' (R)   LDea
'Gemma Sweetheart' (R)   LDea
I 'Gemstone' (Min) **new**   ESul
'Gemstone' (Sc) ♀H1+3   EWoo LDea MBPg MHer NFir
     WBrk
'Genie' (Z/d)   LVER MWhe SKen WFib
'Gentle Georgia' (R)   WFib
'Geoff May' (Min)   ESul

'Georgia' (R)	WFib WHPP	
'Georgia Mai Read' **new**	ERea	
'Georgia Peach' (R)	ESul WFib	
'Georgie' (R)	LDea	
'Georgina Blythe' (R) ♀H1+3	WFib	
'Geo's Pink' (Z/v)	MWhe	
'Geosta' **new**	LAst	
'Gerald Portas' (Dw/C)	ESul	
'Gerald Wells' (Min)	ESul	
'Geraldine' (Min)	ESul	
'Gess Portas' (Z/v)	ESul	
'Ghost Storey' (Z/C)	NFir	
'Giant Butterfly' (R)	LDea	
'Giant Oak' (Sc)	ESul MBPg MHer MSte	
§ *gibbosum*	EWoo MHer WFib	
'Gilbert West' (Z)	SKen	
'Gilda' (R/v)	LDea NFir	
'Gill' (Min/Ca)	ESul	
'Ginger Frost' (Sc/v) **new**	MBPg WFib	
'Ginger Rogers' (Z)	NFir	
'Glacier Claret' (Z)	WFib	
'Glacier Crimson' (Z)	SKen	
'Glacis'^PBR (Z/d)	LAst	
'Gladys Evelyn' (Z/d)	WFib	
'Gladys Stevens' (Min/d)	ESul	
'Gleam' (Z/d)	LVER	
'Gloria Pearce' (R)	LDea	
'Glowing Embers' (R)	LDea	
§ *glutinosum*	MBPg MHer WFib	
'Goblin' (Min/d)	ESul SKen WFib	
'Godshill' (R)	LDea	
'Gold Star' (Z/St/C)	ESul	
'Golden Baby' (Dwl/C)	ESul LDea MWhe NFir WFib WHPP	
'Golden Brilliantissimum' (Z/v)	ESul LRHS LVER MWhe SKen SSea WFib	
'Golden Butterfly' (Z/C)	ESul	
'Golden Chalice' (Min/v)	ESul MWhe WFib	
'Golden Charity' (Sc) **new**	MBPg	
'Golden Clorinda' (U/Sc/C)	CRHN EWoo LDea MBPg MHer NFir WBrk WEas	
'Golden Crest' (Z/C)	SKen SMrm	
'Golden Ears' (Dw/St/C)	ESul MWhe NFir NPer WFib	
'Golden Edinburgh' (I/v) **new**	WFib	
'Golden Everaarts' (Dw/C)	ESul	
'Golden Fleece' (Dw/C/d)	ESul	
'Golden Gates' (Z/C)	ESul SKen	
'Golden Harry Hieover' (Z/C) ♀H1+3	ESul MBri MHer	
'Golden Lilac Gem' (I/d) **new**	WFib	
'Golden Little Darling' (Min/v)	LVER	
§ 'Golden Mist' (Dw/C/d)	LVER	
'Golden Petit Pierre' (Min/C)	ESul	
'Golden Princess' (Min/C)	WFib	
'Golden Roc' (Min/C)	ESul	
'Golden Staphs' (Z/St/C)	ESul LVER NFir SSea WFib	
'Golden Stardust' (Z/St)	ESul	
'Golden Wedding' (Z/d/v)	LRHS LVER MWhe NFir	
'Golden Well Sweep'	see *P.crispum* 'Golden Well Sweep'	
'Goldilocks' (A)	ESul LDea	
'Gooseberry Leaf'	see *P.grossularioides*	
'Gordano Midnight' (R)	EWoo LDea	
'Gosbeck' (A)	LDea SSea WFib	
'Gossamer Carnival' (Z/d)	NFir	
'Gothenburg' (R)	ESul	
'Grace' (A)	LDea	
'Grace Thomas' (Sc) ♀H1+3	EWoo LDea MBPg MHer WFib	
'Grace Wells' (Min)	ESul WFib	

§ 'Gräfin Mariza' (Z/d)	SKen	
'Grand Duchess' (R)	LDea	
'Grand Slam' (R)	ESul LDea LVER NFir WFib	
'Grandad Mac' (Dw/St)	ESul NFir	
grandiflorum	WFib	
'Grandma Fischer'	see *P.* 'Grossmutter Fischer'	
'Grandma Ross' (R)	ESul LDea	
'Granny Hewitt' (Min/d)	ESul	
graveolens	EWoo WBrk	
§ 'Graveolens' (Sc)	CHal ESul GBar GPoy LVER MBPg MHer MWhe SSea WFib WGwG	
'Great Bricett' (Dw/d)	ESul LVER	
'Green Ears' (Z/St)	ESul	
'Green Eyes' (I/d)	SKen	
'Green Goddess' (I/d)	LDea SKen	
'Green Gold Petit Pierre' (Min)	ESul	
'Green Lady' (Sc)	MBPg	
'Green Woodpecker' (R)	LDea SSea	
§ 'Greengold Kleine Liebling' (Min/C/v)	ESul SKen	
'Greengold Petit Pierre'	see *P.* 'Greengold Kleine Liebling'	
'Greetings' (Min/v)	ESul MBri WFib	
§ 'Grenadier' (Z)	CWDa	
'Grey Lady Plymouth' (Sc/v)	ESul EWoo LDea MBPg MHer NFir WFib WHPP	
'Grey Sprite' (Min/v)	ESul WFib	
* 'Groombridge Success' (d)	CWDa	
§ 'Grossmutter Fischer' (R)	LDea	
§ *grossularioides*	EOHP IFro MBPg MHer	
I - 'Coconut' **new**	MBPg	
'Grozser Garten' (Dw)	ESul	
'Grozser Garten Weiss' (Dw)	ESul	
'Guardsman' (Dw)	ESul	
Guido = 'Kleugudo' (Z/d)	LAst LRHS	
'Gwen' (Min/v)	MWhe NFir	
'H. Rigler' (Z)	SKen	
'Hadleigh' (Min)	ESul	
'Hamble Lass' (R)	LDea	
§ 'Hannaford Star' (Z/St)	ESul NFir WFib	
'Hansen's Pinkie' (R)	LDea	
'Hansen's Wild Spice' (Sc) **new**	MBPg	
'Happy Appleblossom' (Z/v/d)	NFir SKen	
'Happy Birthday' (Z/T)	LVER	
§ 'Happy Thought' (Z/v) ♀H1+3	CHal ESul LAst LVER MBri MWhe NFir NVic SCoo SKen SSea WFib	
'Happy Valley' (R)	ESul	
'Harbour Lights' (R)	LDea WFib WHPP	
'Harewood Slam' (R)	ESul EWoo LDea MSte WFib	
'Harkstead' (Dw)	ESul	
'Harlequin' (Dw)	ESul	
'Harlequin Alpine Glow' (I/d)	LVER MWhe	
'Harlequin Candy Floss' (I/d)	CWDa	
'Harlequin Mahogany' (I/d)	LDea LVER MWhe SKen	
§ 'Harlequin Miss Liver Bird' (I)	SKen	
'Harlequin Picotee' (I/d)	LDea LVER SKen	
'Harlequin Pretty Girl' (I x Z/d)	LVER MWhe WFib	
'Harlequin Rosie O'Day' (I)	LDea MWhe SKen WFib	
'Harlequin Ted Day' (I/d)	LDea LVER	
'Harmony' (Z/Dw) **new**	LVER	
'Harriet Le Hair' (Z)	SKen	

'Harvard' (I/d) — LVER WFib
'Harvey' (Z) — MWhe
'Havenstreet' (Dw/St) **new** — ESul
'Hayley Charlotte' (Z/v) — MWhe
'Hazel' (R) — LVER WFib
'Hazel Anson' (R) — LDea
'Hazel Barolo' (R) — LDea
'Hazel Birkby' (R) — ESul LDea
'Hazel Burtoff' (R) — ESul LDea
'Hazel Carey' (R) — LDea
'Hazel Cerise' (R) — LDea
'Hazel Cherry' (R) — LDea MSte WFib
'Hazel Choice' (R) — ESul LDea NFir
'Hazel Dean' (R) — NFir
'Hazel Glory' (R) — LDea
'Hazel Gowland' (R) — LDea
'Hazel Gypsy' (R) — ESul LDea
'Hazel Harmony' (R) — LDea
'Hazel Henderson' (R) — LDea
'Hazel Herald' (R) — ESul LDea
'Hazel Perfection' (R) — LDea NFir
'Hazel Rose' (R) — LDea
'Hazel Saga' (R) — ESul
'Hazel Satin' (R) — LDea
'Hazel Shiraz' (R) — LDea
'Hazel Star' (R) — ESul
'Hazel Stardust' (R) — NFir WHPP
'Hazel Wright' (R) — LDea
§ 'Hederinum' (I) — LVER SKen WFib
§ 'Hederinum Variegatum' (I/v) — CHal NFir SPet WFib
'Heidi' (Min/d) — ESul
* 'Helen Bowie' — CWDa
'Helen Christine' (Z/St) — ESul MWhe NFir WFib
'Helena' (I/d) — LDea MWhe SKen
'Hemingstone' (A) — LDea
'Hemley' (Sc) — LDea MBPg
'Henhurst Gleam' (Dw/d) — ESul
'Henry Weller' (A) — ESul MBPg NFir
'Hermanus Show' (Sc) **new** — MBPg
'Hermione' (Z/d) — CHal MWhe WFib
'High Tor' (Dw/C/d) — SKen
'Highfields Appleblossom' (Z) — LVER NFir SKen
'Highfields Attracta' (Z/d) — LVER SKen WFib
'Highfields Ballerina' (Z/d) — LVER
'Highfields Candy Floss' (Z/d) — LVER NFir
'Highfields Charisma' (Z/d) — LVER
'Highfields Choice' (Z) — LVER SKen
'Highfields Comet' (Z) — SKen
'Highfields Contessa' (Z/d) — LVER SKen WFib
'Highfields Dazzler' (Z) — LVER
'Highfields Delight' (Z) — LVER
'Highfields Fancy' (Z/d) — LVER NFir SKen
'Highfields Fashion' (Z) **new** — LVER
'Highfields Festival' (Z/d) — LVER MWhe NFir SKen WFib
'Highfields Flair' (Z/d) — LVER
'Highfields Melody' (Z/d) — WFib
'Highfields Orange' (Z) — LVER MWhe
'Highfields Paramount' (Z) — SKen
'Highfields Pearl' (Z) **new** — LVER
'Highfields Perfecta' (Z) — CWDa
'Highfields Pride' (Z) — LVER SKen WFib
'Highfields Prima Donna' (Z/d) — LVER MWhe SKen
'Highfields Promise' (Z) — SKen

'Highfields Serenade' (Z) — LVER
'Highfields Snowdrift' (Z) — LVER SKen
'Highfields Sugar Candy' (Z/d) — WFib
'Highfields Supreme' (Z) — LVER
'Highfields Symphony' (Z) — LVER
'Highfields Vogue' (Z) — LVER
'Hilbre Island' (Z/C/d) — NFir
'Hildegard' (Z/d) — CHal SKen
'Hills of Snow' (Z/v) — CHal LVER MBri MHer SKen SSea WFib
'Hillscheider Amethyst' — see *P.* Amethyst = 'Fisdel'
'Hindoo' (RxU) — EWoo LVER NFir SSea WFib
I 'Hindoo Rose' (U) **new** — NFir
'Hintlesham' (Min) — ESul
hispidum — MBPg MHer
'Hitcham' (Min/d) — ESul WFib
'Holbrook' (Dw/C/d) — ESul NFir WFib
'Holmes C. Miller' (Z/d) — ESul
'Honeywood Lindy' (R) — ESul
'Honeywood Margaret' (R) — ESul
'Honeywood Matthew' (Dw) — ESul
'Honeywood Suzanne' (Min/Fr) — ESul LVER NFir SKen
'Honne Frühling' (Z) — SKen
'Honneas' (Dw) — ESul
'Honnestolz' (Dw) — ESul SKen
'Hope Valley' (Dw/C/d) ♀H1+3 — ESul MWhe NFir SKen
'Horace Parsons' (R) — WFib
'Horace Read' (Dw) — ESul
'Horning Ferry' (Dw) — ESul
'House and Garden' (R) — NFir
'Howard's Orange' (R) — LDea
'Hugo de Vries' (Dw/d) — CWDa
'Hula' (U x R) — EWoo MHer
'Hulda Conn' (Z/Ca/d) — WFib
'Hulverstone' (Dw/St) **new** — ESul
'Hunter's Moon' (Z/C) — NFir
'Hurdy-gurdy' (Z/d/v) — ESul MWhe
'Ian Read' (Min/d) — ESul SPet
'Icecrystal'PBR (Z/d) — CWDa LAst
'Icing Sugar' (I/d) — ESul LDea SSea WFib
ignescens **new** — MBPg
* 'Ilse Fisher' — CWDa
'Immaculatum' (Z) — WFib
'Imperial' **new** — LAst
'Imperial Butterfly' (A/Sc) — ESul LDea LVER MBPg MSte MWhe NFir SKen WFib
incrassatum — NBur
iocastum — NFir
ionidiflorum — CSpe EShb EWoo LPio MBPg MHer SAga WCom XPep
'Ipswich Town' (Dw/d) — ESul
'Irene' (Z/d) ♀H1+3 — SKen WFib
'Irene Cal' (Z/d) ♀H1+3 — SKen
'Irene Collet' (R) — LDea
'Irene Picardy' (Z/d) — SKen
'Irene Toyon' (Z) ♀H1+3 — SKen WFib
* 'Iris Monroe' — CWDa
§ 'Isabell' (Z/d) — LAst WGor
'Isidel' (I/d) ♀H1+3 — SKen WFib
I 'Islington Peppermint' (Sc) — LVER MBPg SSea WFib
'Isobel Eden' (Sc) **new** — LDea MBPg
'Italian Gem' (I) — SKen
'Ivalo' (Z/d) — MWhe SKen WFib
'Ivory Snow' (Z/d/v) — ESul EWoo LVER MWhe NFir WFib
'Jacey' (Z/d) — LVER SKen
'Jack of Hearts' (I x Z/d) — WFib
'Jack Wood' (Z/d) — NFir WFib

§	'Jackie' (I/d)	EWoo LVER MBri SKen WFib
	'Jackie Davies' (R)	LDea
	'Jackie Gall'	see *P.* 'Jackie'
	'Jackie's Gem' (I/d)	MWhe
	'Jacko' (I/d)	EWoo
I	'Jackpot Wild Rose' (Z/d) **new**	WFib
	'Jacqueline' (Z/d)	SKen
	'Jane Biggin' (Dw/C/d)	ESul MWhe SKen
	'Janet Dean' (R)	LDea
	'Janet Hofman' (Z/d)	WFib
	'Janet Kerrigan' (Min/d)	ESul MWhe WEas
	'Janet Scott' (Z)	CWDa
	'Jasmin' (R)	ESul LDea
	'Jaunty' (Min/d)	ESul
	'Jayne' (Min/d)	ESul
	'Jayne Eyre' (Min/d)	CHal ESul MWhe NFir SKen WFib
§	'Jazz'	CWDa
	'Jean Bart' (I)	CWDa LVER
	'Jean Beatty' (Dw/d)	LVER
	'Jean Oberle' (Z/d)	SKen
	'Jeanetta' (R)	LDea
§	'Jeanne d'Arc' (I/d)	SKen WFib
	'Jenifer Read' (Dw)	ESul
	'Jennifer' (Min)	ESul
	'Jer'Ray' (A)	ESul LDea MHer WFib
	'Jessel's Unique' (U)	LDea MHer MSte SPet SSea
*	'Jetfire' (d)	CWDa
	'Jewel' (Z/d)	LAst
	'Jewel' (R)	ESul
	'Jey-Rey' (A) **new**	NFir
	'Jinny Reeves' (R)	ESul LDea
	'Joan Cashmere' (Z/d)	ESul
	'Joan Fontaine' (Z)	WFib
	'Joan Hayward' (Min)	ESul
	'Joan Morf' (R)	ESul EWoo LDea LVER NFir SSea WFib
	'Joan of Arc'	see *P.* 'Jeanne d'Arc'
	'Joan Sharman' (Min)	ESul
	'Joanna Pearce' (R)	ESul LDea SKen
	'John Thorp' (R)	LDea
	'John's Angela'	LVER
	'John's Pride'	MBri
	'Joseph Haydn' (R)	ESul LDea MSte
	'Joseph Wheeler' (A)	ESul LDea MWhe
	'Joy' (R) ♀H1+3	ESul LDea LRHS LVER NFir WFib
	'Joy' (I)	SPet
I	'Joy' (Z/d)	SKen
	Joy = 'Fiseye'PBR	CSpe WHPP
	'Joy Lucille' (Sc)	CSev ESul EWoo LDea MBPg MHer
	'Joyden'	CWDa
	'Joyful' (Min)	ESul
	'Jubel Parr' (Z/d)	CWDa
	'Judy Read' (Dw)	ESul
	'Julia' (R) ♀H1+3	ESul LDea
	'Juliana' (R)	LDea
	'Julie' (A)	ESul
	'Julie Bannister' (R)	ESul
	'Julie Smith' (R)	LDea WFib
	'Jungle Night' (R)	ESul EWoo
	'Juniper' (Sc)	EWoo MBPg MHer WFib
	'Jupiter' (Min/d)	SKen
	'Jupiter' (R)	ESul NFir
	'Just Rita' (A)	SSea
	'Just William' (Min/C/d)	ESul WFib
	'Kamahl' (R)	WFib
§	'Kardinal' (Z/d)	SPet
	'Karl Hagele' (Z/d)	LVER SKen SYvo WFib
	'Karmin Ball'	CWDa WFib
	karrooense	see *P. quercifolium*
	'Kathleen' (Min) **new**	ESul
	'Kathleen Gamble' (Z)	WFib
	'Kathryn' (Min)	ESul
	'Kathryn Portas' (Z/v)	ESul SKen

	'Katie' (R)	EWoo
	'Kayleigh West' (Min)	ESul
	'Keepsake' (Min/d)	ESul WFib
	'Keith Vernon' (Z)	NFir
	'Kelvedon Beauty' (Min)	WEas
	'Ken Lea' (Z/v) **new**	LVER
	'Ken Salmon' (Dw/d)	ESul
	'Kennard Castle' (Z)	CWDa
	'Kenny's Double' (Z/d)	WFib
	'Kensington' (A)	LDea
	'Kerensa' (Min/d)	ESul SKen WFib
	'Kershy' (Min)	ESul
	'Kesgrave' (Min/d)	ESul WFib
	'Kettlebaston' (A)	ESul LDea WFib
	'Kewense' (Z)	EShb
	'Key's Unique' (U) **new**	EWoo
	'Kimono' (R)	ESul EWoo LDea NFir
	'Kinder Gaisha' (R)	NFir
	'King Edmund' (R)	LDea
	'King of Balcon'	see *P.* 'Hederinum'
	'King of Denmark' (Z/d)	LVER WFib
	'King Solomon' (R)	LDea
	'King's Ransom' (R)	LDea
	'Kirton' (Min/d)	ESul
§	'Kleine Liebling' (Min)	ESul MWhe WFib
I	'Korcicum' (Sc) **new**	MBPg
	'Krista' (Min/d)	ESul WBrk WFib
	'Kyoto' (R)	NFir
	'Kyra' (Min/d)	ESul WFib
	'L.E.Wharton' (Z)	SKen
	'La France' (I/d) ♀H1+3	LDea LVER MWhe SKen WFib
	'La Paloma' (R)	WFib
	'Laced Mini Rose Cascade' (I)	NFir
	Laced Red Mini Cascade = 'Achspen' (I)	NFir
	'Lachsball' (Z/d)	SKen
§	'Lachskönigin' (I/d)	LVER SKen SPet WFib
	'Lady Alice of Valencia'	see *P.* 'Grenadier' (Z)
	'Lady Cullum' (Z/C/v)	MWhe
	'Lady Ilchester' (Z/d)	SKen WFib
	'Lady Love Song' (R)	ESul NFir
	'Lady Mary' (Sc)	ESul EWoo LVER MBPg MHer
	'Lady Mavis Pilkington' (Z/d)	WFib
	'Lady Plymouth' (Sc/v) ♀H1+3	CHal CHrt CRHN CSpe ESul GBar LDea LPio LRHS LVER MBPg MHer MSte MWhe NFir NHHG SKen SMrm SPet SSea WBrk WFib WHPP WWye
	'Lady Ramona' **new**	LAst
§	'Lady Scarborough' (Sc)	ESul EWoo LDea LPio MBPg WFib
	'Lady Scott' (Sc) **new**	MBPg
	'Lady Woods' (Z)	SSea
	'Lakeland' (I)	ESul
	'Lakis' (R)	LDea
	'Lamorna' (R)	LDea SKen
	'Land of Song' (A)	NFir
	'Langley' (R)	LDea
	'Lanham Lane' (I)	LDea MWhe
	'Lanham Royal' (Dw/d)	ESul
	'Lara Aladin' (A)	LDea MBPg
	'Lara Candy Dancer' (Sc) ♀H1+3	CRHN ESul LDea MBPg MHer WFib
	'Lara Jester' (Sc)	EWoo MBPg MHer WFib
	'Lara Maid' (A) ♀H1+3	CHrt MWhe WEas WFib
	'Lara Nomad' (Sc)	EWoo LDea MBPg
	'Lara Starshine' (Sc) ♀H1+3	CHal ESul EWoo LPio MBPg MHer NFir SSea WFib WHPP
	'Lara Susan'	EWoo NFir
	'Lara Waltz' (R/d) **new**	WFib
	'Lark' (Min/d)	ESul
	'Larkfield' (Z/v)	SSea

N 'Lass o' Gowrie' (Z/v)   ESul LRHS LVER MSte MWhe NFir SKen

'Lass o' Gowrie' (American) (Z/v)   SMrm

'Laura Parmer' (Dw/St)   ESul

'Laura Wheeler' (A)   ESul LDea MWhe

'Laurel Hayward' (R)   WFib

'Lauretta' (Sweetheart Series) **new**   LAst

'Lavenda' **new**   LAst

'Lavender Grand Slam' (R) ♀H1+3   ESul LDea LVER NFir

'Lavender Harewood Slam' (R)   ESul LDea

'Lavender Mini Cascade'PBR   see *P.* Lilac Mini Cascade = 'Lilamica'

'Lavender Sensation' (R)   WFib

'Lavender Wings' (I)   LDea

'Lawrenceanum' **new**   ESul WFib

'Layham' (Dw/d)   ESul

'Layton's White' (Z/d)   CWDa

'Le Lutin' (Z/d)   CWDa

'L'Elégante' (I/v) ♀H1+3   CHal EWoo LAst LDea LVER MWhe NFir SKen SSea WEas WFib WGwG

'Lemon Air' (Sc)   ESul MBPg

'Lemon Crisp'   see *P. crispum*

'Lemon Fancy' (Sc)   CHby EWoo LDea LVER MBPg MHer MWhe NFir WFib

'Lemon Kiss' (Sc) **new**   MBPg

'Lemon Toby' (Sc) **new**   MBPg

'Len Chandler' (Min)   ESul

'Lenore' (Min/d)   ESul

'Leo' (Min)   ESul

'Leonie Holbrow' (Min)   ESul

'Leopard' (I/d)   CWDa

'Leslie Salmon' (Dw/C)   ESul MWhe

Lila Compakt-Cascade   see *P.* 'Decora Lilas'

Lilac Cascade   see *P.* 'Roi des Balcons Lilas'

'Lilac Domino'   see *P.* 'Telston's Prima'

'Lilac Elaine' (R)   LDea

'Lilac Gem' (Min/I/d)   LDea LVER MWhe NFir

'Lilac Jewel' (R)   ESul

'Lilac Joy' (R) **new**   LVER

§ Lilac Mini Cascade = 'Lilamica'PBR (I)   ESul LDea LVER NFir

'Lili Marlene' (I)   LVER SPet

'Lilian' (Min)   ESul LAst

'Lilian Pottinger' (Sc)   CArn CHal CRHN ESul GBar LDea MBPg MHer MWhe NFir SKen SSea

'Lilo Cascade'   MBPg

'Limelight' (Z/v)   SSea

'Limoneum' (Sc)   CSev LDea MBPg MHer NBur SKen

'Linda' (R)   ESul LDea

'Lindsey' (Min)   ESul

'Lindy Portas' (I/d)   SKen

'Lipstick' (St) **new**   WFib

'Lisa' (Min/C)   ESul WFib

'Lisa Jo' (St/v/Dw/d) **new**   WFib

'Little Alice' (Dw/d) ♀H1+3   ESul MWhe NFir WFib

'Little Blakenham' (A)   ESul LDea

'Little Fi-fine' (Dw/C)   ESul NFir

'Little Gem' (Sc)   EWoo LDea LVER MBPg MHer SSea WFib WHPP

'Little Jip' (Z/d/v)   LVER NFir WFib

'Little Margaret' (Min/v)   ESul

'Little Perky' (MinI)   ESul

'Little Primular' (Min)   ESul

'Lively Lady' (Dw/C)   ESul

'Liverbird'   see *P.* 'Harlequin Miss Liver Bird'

longicaule **new**   MBPg

'Lord Baden-Powell'   see *P.* 'Colonel Baden-Powell'

'Lord Bute' (R) ♀H1+3   CElw CSpe ECtt EShb ESul EWoo LAst LDea LIck LPio LRHS LVER MHer MSte NCiC NFir NPer NWoo SDnm SKen SMer SMrm SPet SUsu WEas WFib WHPP WPen

'Lord Constantine' (R)   LDea

'Lord de Ramsey'   see *P.* 'Tip Top Duet'

'Lord Roberts' (Z)   WFib

'Lorelei' (Z/d)   CWDa

'Lorena' **new**   LAst

'Loretta' (Dw)   ESul

'Lorna' (Dw/d)   ESul

'Lorraine' (Dw) **new**   ESul

'Lotusland' (Dw/St/C)   ESul LAst LVER NFir WFib

'Louise' (Min)   ESul

I 'Louise' (R) **new**   ESul

'Love Song' (R/v)   ESul LDea LVER NFir SSea WFib

'Love Story' (Z/v)   ESul

'Loveliness' (Z)   WFib

* 'Loverly' (Min/d)   ESul

'Lovesdown' (Dw/St) **new**   ESul

'Lucilla' (Min)   ESul

'Lucinda' (Min)   ESul

'Lucy' (Min)   ESul

'Lucy Gunnett' (Z/d/v)   ESul MWhe NFir

'Lucy Jane' (R)   LDea

'Lulu' (I/d)   NPri

Luna = 'Fisuna' (I/d)   NPri

'Luscious' (Min) **new**   ESul

'Lustre' (R)   ESul

'Lyewood Bonanza' (R)   ESul LDea LVER

'Lynne Valerie' (A)   LDea

'Lyric' (Min/d)   ESul WFib

'Mabel Grey' (Sc) ♀H1+3   CHal CRHN CSev CSpe EShb ESul EWoo LIck LVER MBPg MHer MSte MWhe NBur NFir NHHG SKen WFib WHPP

§ 'Madame Auguste Nonin' (U/Sc)   CHal ESul EWoo LVER MBPg MHer NFir NWoo SKen WFib

'Madame Butterfly' (Z/d/v)   ESul MWhe NFir SKen

'Madame Crousse' (I/d) ♀H1+3   WFib

'Madame Fournier' (Dw/C)   ESul

'Madame Hibbault' (Z)   SKen

'Madame Layal' (A)   EWoo LDea LIck MSte NFir SAga SKen WFib

'Madame Margot'   see *P.* 'Hederinum Variegatum'

'Madame Salleron' (Min/v) ♀H1+3   LDea LRHS LVER MSte SKen SPet

'Madame Thibaut' (R)   LDea MSte

'Madge Taylor' (R)   NFir

'Magaluf' (I/C/d)   SSea

'Magda' (Z/d)   ESul LVER

'Magic Lantern' (Z/C)   NFir

'Magnum' (R)   WFib

'Maid of Honour' (Min)   ESul

'Maiden Petticoat' **new**   LAst

'Maiden Rosepink' (R) **new**   WGor

'Mairi' (A)   LDea WFib

'Maloya' (Z)   SKen

'Mamie' (Z/d)   SKen

'Mandarin' (R)   ESul

'Mangles' Variegated' (Z/v)   SPet SSea WFib

'Mantilla' (Min)   ESul SKen

'Manx Maid' (A)   ESul LDea NFir SKen

'Maple Leaf' (Sc)   EWoo MBPg

'Marble Sunset'   see *P.* 'Wood's Surprise'

'Marchioness of Bute' (R)   EMan LDea LVER MSte NFir NPer WFib

'Maréchal MacMahon' (Z/C)   SKen SPet

'Margaret Parmenter' (I/C)	ESul	
'Margaret Pearce' (R)	LDea	
'Margaret Salvidge' (R)	LDea	
'Margaret Soley' (R) ♀H1+3	LDea	
'Margaret Stimpson' (R)	LDea	
'Margaret Thorp'	LVER	
'Margaret Waite' (R)	WFib	
'Margery Stimpson' (Min/d)	ESul WFib	
'Maria Thomas' (Sc) **new**	MBPg	
'Maria Wilkes' (Z/d)	WFib	
'Marie Rober' (R)	SKen	
'Marie Rudlin' (R) **new**	LVER	
'Marie Thomas' (Sc)	LDea MHer SSea	
§ 'Marie Vogel' (R)	MSte	
'Marilyn' (Dw/d)	ESul	
Marimba = 'Fisrimba'PBR	NPri SCoo	
'Marion' (Min)	ESul	
'Mariquita' (R)	WFib	
'Marja' (R)	LDea	
'Marmalade' (Min/d)	ESul MWhe WFib	
'Marquis of Bute' (R/v)	ESul LVER	
'Martha Parmer' (Min)	ESul	
'Martin Parrett' (Min/d)	WFib	
'Martin's Splendour' (Min)	ESul	
'Martlesham' (Dw)	ESul	
'Mary Ellen Tanner' (Min/d)	ESul	
'Mary Read' (Min)	ESul	
'Mary Rose' (R)	LDea	
'Mary Webster' (Min)	ESul	
'Masquerade' (R)	SPet	
'Masquerade' (Min) **new**	ESul	
'Master Paul' (Z/v)	ESul	
'Masterpiece' (Z/C/d)	ESul	
'Matthew Salvidge' (R)	ESul	
'Maureen' (Min)	ESul NFir	
'Mauve Beauty' (I/d)	SKen WFib	
'Maxime Kovalevski' (Z)	WFib	
'Maxine' (Z/C)	NFir	
'Maxine Colley' (Z/d/v)	LVER	
'May Day' (R)	LDea	
'May Magic' (R)	NFir WFib	
'Mayor of Seville' (Z/d)	WFib	
I 'Meadowside Dark and Dainty' (St)	NFir WFib	
'Meadowside Fancy' (Z/d/C)	LVER	
'Meadowside Harvest' (Z/St/C)	ESul NFir WFib	
'Meadowside Julie Colley' (Dw)	NFir	
I 'Meadowside Mahogany' (Z/C)	LVER	
'Meadowside Mardi Gras' (Dw/d)	NFir	
'Meadowside Midnight' (St/C)	MHer MWhe SHFr WFib	
'Meadowside Orange' (Z/d)	LVER	
'Medallion' (Z/C)	MHer SSea	
'Meditation' (Min)	ESul	
'Medley' (Min/d)	MWhe WFib	
'Melanie' (R)	LDea	
'Melanie' (Min) **new**	ESul	
* 'Melissa' (Min)	ESul	
'Melosilver' **new**	LAst SPoG	
'Memento' (Min/d)	ESul SKen WFib	
'Mendip' (R)	WFib	
'Mendip Anne' (R) **new**	NFir	
'Mendip Barbie' (R) **new**	NFir	
'Mendip Blanch' (R) **new**	NFir	

'Mendip Candy Floss' (R) **new**	ESul	
'Mendip Sentire' (R) **new**	NFir	
'Meon Maid' (R)	ESul LDea WFib WHPP	
'Mere Caribbean' (R)	NFir	
'Mere Casino' (Z)	WFib	
'Mere Greeting' (Z/d)	MWhe WFib	
'Mere Sunglow' (R)	LDea	
'Merle Seville' (Z/d)	SKen	
'Merlin' (Sc) **new**	MBPg	
'Merry-go-round' (Z/C/v)	LVER MWhe	
'Mexica Katrine' **new**	LAst	
'Mexica Tom'	LAst WGor	
'Mexican Beauty' (I)	CHal MWhe WFib	
'Mexicana' **new**	LAst	
'Mexicanerin'	see *P.* 'Rouletta'	
'Michael' (A)	ESul LDea	
'Michelle' (Min/C)	LDea	
'Michelle West' (Min)	ESul WFib	
'Midas Touch' (Dw/C/d)	ESul	
'Milden' (Dw/Z/C)	ESul NFir	
'Millbern Choice' (Z)	MWhe	
'Millbern Clover' (Min/d)	ESul MWhe SAga	
'Millbern Engagement' (Min/d)	MWhe	
'Millbern Peach' (Z)	MWhe	
'Millbern Serenade'	MWhe	
'Millbern Sharna' (Min/d)	ESul MWhe	
'Millbern Skye' (A)	MWhe	
Millennium Dawn (Dw)	LVER	
'Miller's Valentine' (Z/v)	ESul LVER WFib	
'Millfield Gem' (I/d)	LVER SKen WFib	
'Millfield Rose' (I/d)	LVER MWhe	
'Millie' (Z/d)	CWDa	
'Mimi' (Dw/C/d)	ESul SSea	
'Minah's Cascade' (Z/d)	LVER	
'Mini-Czech' (Min/St)	ESul	
'Minnie' (Z/d/St)	ESul LVER	
'Minstrel Boy' (R)	ESul LDea NFir WFib	
'Minx' (Min/d)	WFib	
* 'Mirage'	CWDa	
'Miranda' (Dw)	ESul	
'Miriam Basey'	see *P.* 'Dwarf Miriam Baisey'	
'Miss Australia' (R/v)	LDea MBPg	
'Miss Burdett Coutts' (Z/v)	ESul LVER MWhe SKen SPet SSea WFib	
'Miss Flora' (I)	CWDa MWhe	
'Miss Liverbird' (I/d)	ECtt	
'Miss McKinsey' (Z/St/d)	LVER NFir	
§ 'Miss Stapleton'	EWoo LPio MHer WFib	
'Miss Wackles' (Min/d)	ESul	
'Mistress' (Z/C)	NFir	
'Misty' (Z)	ESul	
'Modesty' (Z/d)	SKen WFib	
'Mohawk' (R)	ESul NFir WFib WHPP	
Molina = 'Fismoli'PBR (I/d)	NPri	
'Mollie' (R)	CSpe	
'Molly' (A)	NFir WHPP	
'Mona Lisa'PBR	ESul	
'Monarch' (Dw/v)	ESul	
'Monica Bennett' (Dw)	ESul SKen WEas	
'Monks Eleigh' (Dw)	ESul	
'Monkwood Charm' (R)	LDea	
'Monkwood Rose' (A)	LDea NFir	
'Monkwood Sprite' (R)	LDea SMrm	
'Monsal Dale' (Dw/C/d)	ESul SKen	
'Monsieur Ninon' hort.	see *P.* 'Madame Auguste Nonin'	
§ 'Monsieur Ninon' (U)	CRHN EWoo MSte WFib	
'Mont Blanc' (Z/v)	ESul LVER MWhe SKen WFib	
'Montague Garabaldi Smith' (R) **new**	WFib	
'Moon Maiden' (A)	ESul WFib	

'Moor' (Min/d)	ESul	
'Moppet' (Min/d)	ESul	
'More's Victory' (U/Sc)	SSea	
'Morning Cloud' (Min/d)	ESul	
'Morse' (Z)	SKen	
'Morval' (Dw/C/d) ♀H1+3	ESul LVER MWhe SKen WFib	
'Morwenna' (R)	ESul EWoo LDea LPio LVER MSte NFir SKen WFib	
'Mosaic Gay Baby' (I/v/d) **new**	WFib	
'Mosaic Silky' (Z/C/d/v)	LVER	
'Mountie' (Dw)	ESul	
'Mr Everaarts' (Dw/d)	ESul MWhe	
'Mr Henry Apps' (Dw/C/d)	MWhe	
'Mr Henry Cox' (Z/v) ♀H1+3	ESul MHer MWhe NFir SKen WFib	
'Mr Wren' (Z)	CHal LVER MWhe SKen WFib	
'Mrs A.M. Mayne' (Z)	SKen	
'Mrs Cannell' (Z)	SKen WFib	
'Mrs Dumbrill' (A)	ESul LDea LIck	
'Mrs E.G. Hill' (Z)	CWDa	
'Mrs Farren' (Z/v)	MWhe SKen SSea	
'Mrs G.H. Smith' (A)	ESul LDea MBPg MSte MWhe NFir WFib WHPP	
'Mrs G. Morf' (R)	ESul SSea	
§ 'Mrs H.J. Jones' (I)	WFib	
'Mrs J.C. Mappin' (Z/v) ♀H1+3	SAga SKen SSea	
'Mrs Kingsbury' (U)	WEas WFib	
'Mrs Langtry' (R)	LDea	
'Mrs Lawrence' (Z/d)	SKen	
'Mrs Martin' (I/d)	WFib	
'Mrs McKenzie' (Z/St)	WFib	
'Mrs Morf' (R)	LDea NFir	
'Mrs Parker' (Z/d/v)	ESul LRHS LVER MWhe NFir SKen WFib	
'Mrs Pat' (Dw/St/C)	ESul MWhe NFir	
'Mrs Pollock' (Z/v)	LAst LRHS LVER MWhe NVic SCoo SPet SSea WBrk WFib	
'Mrs Quilter' (Z/C) ♀H1+3	LVER MBri MHer MWhe NVic SAga SKen SMrm SSea WFib	
'Mrs Salter Bevis' (Z/Ca/d)	ESul LVER WFib	
'Mrs Strang' (Z/d/v)	LVER MWhe SKen SSea	
'Mrs Tarrant' (Z/d)	CHal	
'Mrs Taylor' (Sc) **new**	MBPg	
'Mrs W.A.R. Clifton' (I/d)	LDea SKen WFib	
mutans	WFib WHPP	
'Müttertag' (R)	ESul LDea MSte	
§ 'Mutzel' (I/v)	LVER NFir	
'My Chance'	EWoo NFir	
'My Choice' (R)	LDea	
§ *myrrhifolium* var. *coriandrifolium*	SAga	
'Mystery' (U) ♀H1+3	EWoo LVER MBPg NFir SAga SSea WFib	
'Nacton' (Min)	ESul	
'Nadine' (Dw/d)	ESul	
'Nancy Grey' (Min)	ESul NFir	
'Naomi' (R)	LDea	
'Narina' (I)	NPri SCoo	
'Natalie' (Dw)	ESul	
'Naughton' (Min)	ESul	
'Naunton Windmill' (R)	WHPP	
'Needham Market' (A)	ESul LDea MSte WFib	
'Neene' (Dw)	ESul	
'Neil Clemenson' (Sc)	MBPg WFib	
'Neil Jameson' (Z/v)	SKen	
'Nell Smith' (Z/d)	WFib	
'Nellie' (R)	LDea	
'Nellie Nuttall' (Z)	WFib	
'Nervosum' (Sc)	ESul MBPg MOak	
'Nervous Mabel' (Sc) ♀H1+3	ESul EWoo LDea MBPg MHer NFir WBrk WFib	
'Nettlecombe' (Min/St)	ESul	
'Nettlestead' (Dw/d)	ESul LVER	
'Neville West' (Z)	SSea	
'New Day' (A)	LDea	
'New Life' (Z)	ESul MWhe NFir	
'Nicola Buck' (R)	LDea	
'Nicor Star' (Min)	ESul WFib	
'Nikki' (A)	LDea	
'Nimrod' (R)	LDea	
'Noche' (Z)	LDea SKen SMrm	
'Noel' (Z/Ca/d)	LVER WFib	
'Noele Gordon' (Z/d)	LVER WFib	
'Nomad' (R)	NFir	
'Nomad's Sweetheart' (A)	LVER	
'Nono' (I)	WFib	
'Norrland' (Z/d) **new**	LVER	
* 'Norvic' (d)	CWDa	
'Nostra' **new**	LAst	
'Notting Hill Beauty' (Z)	SKen	
'Occold Embers' (Dw/C/d)	ESul NFir	
'Occold Lagoon' (Dw/d)	ESul	
'Occold Orange Tip' (Min/d)	ESul	
'Occold Profusion' (Dw/d)	ESul NFir	
'Occold Ruby' (Dw/C)	CWDa	
'Occold Shield' (Dw/C/d)	ESul LAst LRHS NFir SDnm SMrm WBrk WFib	
'Occold Tangerine' (Dw)	WFib	
'Occold Volcano' (Dw/C/d)	WFib	
odoratissimum (Sc)	CHal ESul GBar GPoy LDea LVER MBPg MHer NFir NHHG SKen WFib	
'Offton' (Dw)	ESul	
'Old Orchard' (A)	LDea SSea	
'Old Rose' (Z/d)	WFib	
'Old Spice' (Sc/v)	ESul GBar MBPg MHer NFir WFib	
'Oldbury Duet' (A/v)	LDea LVER NFir	
'Olga Shipstone' (Sc)	EWoo MBPg WHPP	
'Olivia' (R)	ESul WHPP	
'Olympia' (Z/d)	CWDa	
'Onnalee' (Dw)	ESul WFib	
'Opera House' (R)	WFib	
'Orange' (Z/St)	MBPg	
'Orange Fizz' (Sc)	ESul SDnm WHPP	
'Orange Fizz' (Z/d)	LDea	
'Orange Imp' (Dw/d)	ESul	
'Orange Parfait' (R)	WFib	
I 'Orange Princeanum' (Sc) **new**	MBPg	
'Orange Ricard' (Z/d)	MWhe SKen	
'Orange River' (Min/d)	ESul	
'Orange Ruffy' (Min)	ESul	
'Orange Splash' (Z)	LVER SKen	
'Orangeade' (Dw/d)	ESul LVER SKen WFib	
'Orangesonne' (Z/d)	LVER	
'Orchid Clorinda' (Sc) **new**	MBPg WFib	
'Orchid Paloma' (Dw/d)	ESul SKen	
'Oregon Hostess' (Dw)	ESul	
'Orion' (Min/d)	ESul MWhe SKen WFib	
'Orsett' (Sc) ♀H1+3	EWoo LDea LVER MBPg	
'Oscar' (Z/d)	CWDa	
'Osna' (Z)	LAst SKen	
'Otto's Red' (R)	NFir	
'Our Gynette' (R)	NFir	
ovale subsp. *ovale*	EShb	
'Oyster' (Dw)	ESul	
'Paddie' (Min)	ESul	
'Pagoda' (Z/St/d)	ESul LVER MSte MWhe SKen WFib WHPP	

'Ritchie' (R) — ESul
'Robe'^PBR (Z/d) — LAst LRHS LVER WGor
I 'Rober's Lavender' (Dw) — ESul
I 'Rober's Lemon Rose' (Sc) — CRHN ESul EWoo GBar LDea MBPg MHer SKen SSea WWye
'Rober's Salmon Coral' (Dw/d) — ESul
'Robert Fish' (Z/C) — ESul LRHS
'Robert McElwain' — WFib
'Robin' (Sc) — LDea MBPg
'Robin' (R) — LDea
'Robin's Unique' (U) — EWoo NFir WFib
Rocky Mountain White = 'Fisrowi'^PBR (Z/d) **new** — WWol
'Roger's Delight' (R/Sc) — EWoo LDea MBPg
'Rogue' (R) — ESul EWoo LDea MSte WFib
'Roi des Balcons' — see P. 'Hederinum'
§ 'Roi des Balcons Impérial' (I) ♀H1+3 — MWhe
§ 'Roi des Balcons Lilas' (I) ♀H1+3 — MWhe SKen WFib
'Roi des Balcons Rose' — see P. 'Hederinum'
§ Rokoko = 'Fisfid'^PBR (Z) — CWDa
'Roller's David' (I/d) — CWDa
'Roller's Echo' (A) — ESul LDea LIck MWhe WFib
'Roller's Gabriella' (A) — LDea
'Roller's Pathfinder' (I/d/v) — LDea LVER
'Roller's Pioneer' (I/v) — EWoo LDea LVER SAga SKen
'Roller's Satinique' (U) ♀H1+3 — EWoo LIck MBPg MHer SSea WHPP
'Roller's Shadow' (A) **new** — LDea
'Rollisson's Unique' (U) — MBPg MHer MSte NBur WFib
'Romeo' (R) — EWoo LVER WHPP
§ Romy (I) — LDea
§ 'Rosa Mini-cascade' (I) — ESul LAst LVER MWhe NFir
'Rosaleen' (Min) — ESul
'Rosalie' (R) — ESul
'Rose Bengal' (A) — CRHN ESul LDea MWhe WFib
Rose Evka (Dw/I/v) = 'Penevro'^PBR — LAst NFir
'Rose Irene' (Z/d) — MWhe
'Rose Jewel' (R) — ESul
'Rose of Amsterdam' (Min/d) — ESul
'Rose Paton's Unique' (U/Sc) **new** — LDea
'Rose Silver Cascade' (I) — LDea LVER
'Rosebud Supreme' (Z/d) — ESul WFib
'Rosecrystal'^PBR (Z/d) — LVER
* 'Roselo' — CWDa
'Rosemarie' (Z/d) — MWhe
'Rosina Read' (Dw/d) — ESul LVER
'Rosmaroy' (R) — ESul LDea LVER NFir WFib
§ 'Rospen' (Z/d) — SKen
'Rosy Dawn' (Min) — WFib
'Rosy Morn' (R) — NFir
'Rote Mini-cascade' — see P. Red-Mini-Cascade = 'Rotemica'
§ 'Rouletta' (I/d) — CHrt ECtt LDea LVER MWhe NPri SKen WFib
'Rousillon' (R) — LDea
'Rousseau' (Min/C) — ESul
'Royal Ascot' (R) — CHal CSpe ESul EWoo LDea MSte NFir SAga SMrm SPet WHPP
'Royal Carpet' (Min/d) — WFib
'Royal Court' (R) — LDea
'Royal Decree' (R) — LDea
'Royal Norfolk' (Min/d) — ESul MWhe NFir SKen
'Royal Oak' (Sc) ♀H1+3 — CElw CSev ESul EWoo GBar LDea MBPg MHer MWhe NBur SGar SPet SSea WFib WRha

'Royal Opera' (R) **new** — LDea
§ 'Royal Purple' (Z/d) — CHal LVER WFib
* 'Royal Salmon' — CWDa
'Royal Sovereign' (Z/C/d) — LDea
'Royal Star' (R) — LDea
'Royal Surprise' (R) — ESul LDea NFir
'Royal Wedding' (R) — LDea
'Rubi Lee' (A) — MWhe
* 'Rubican' — CWDa
'Rubin Improved' (Z/d) — SKen
'Ruby' (Min/d) — ESul WFib
'Ruby Orchid' (A) — LDea NFir WHPP
'Ruffled Velvet' (R) — EWoo SSea
'Rushmere' (Dw/d) — ESul WFib
'Rusty' (Dw/C/d) — ESul
'Sabine'^PBR (Z/d) — LVER
Saint Malo = 'Guisaint'^PBR (I) — LAst
'Sally Munro' (R) — LDea
'Sally Read' (Dw/d) — ESul
'Salmon Beauty' (Min/d) — WFib
'Salmon Black Vesuvius' (Min/d) — ESul
§ 'Salmon Irene' (Z/d) — WFib
'Salmon Queen' — see P. 'Lachskönigin'
'Salmon Startel' (Z/St/d) — ESul MWhe
'Samantha' (R) — ESul WFib
'Samantha Stamp' (Dw/d/C) — SAga WFib
'Samelia' **new** — LAst
'Sancho Panza' (Dec) ♀H1+3 — CSpe ESul EWoo LDea LVER MBPg MHer MSte SAga SKen SSea WFib WHPP
'Sandford' (Dw/St) **new** — ESul
'Sandown' (Dw/d) **new** — ESul
'Sandra Lorraine' (I/d) **new** — WFib
'Sanguineum' — CSpe SAga WHPP
'Santa Fé' (Z) **new** — LVER
'Santa Maria' (Z/d) — LVER SKen
'Santa Marie' (R) — LDea
'Santa Paula' (I/d) — ECtt LDea MWhe SKen
'Sarah Jane' (Sc) **new** — MBPg
'Sassa'^PBR (Z/d) — CWDa LAst WGor
'Satsuki' (R) — ESul LDea NFir
§ *scabrum* — MBPg
'Scarlet Gem' (Z/St) — WFib
* 'Scarlet Kewense' (Dw) — ESul
'Scarlet Nosegay' — CHal WHPP
'Scarlet Pet' (U) — CFee CRHN ESul MBPg MHer NFir
'Scarlet Pimpernel' (Z/C/d) — ESul
'Scarlet Rambler' (Z/d) — EShb EWoo LVER SKen SMrm WFib
'Scarlet Unique' (U) — CRHN EWoo LDea MHer MSte NFir SKen SSea WFib
'Scatterbrain' (Z) — CWDa
schizopetalum — WFib
§ 'Schneekönigin' (I/d) — ECtt LDea LVER MSte SKen
§ 'Schöne Helena'^PBR (Z/d) — CWDa
'Schottii' **new** — NFir WFib
x *schottii* — see P. 'Schottii'
'Secret Love' (Sc) — LDea MBPg
'Seeley's Pansy' (A) — CSpe EWoo LDea MHer SAga WFib WHPP
'Sefton' (R) ♀H1+3 — ESul LDea WFib WHPP
'Selena' (Min) — ESul
'Semer' (Min) — ESul SKen
* 'Serre de la Madone' (Sc) — WEas
'Shalimar' (St) — CSpe MSte NFir SAga WHPP
'Shanklin' (Dw/St) — ESul
'Shanks' (Z) — NFir
'Shannon' **new** — WFib
'Sharon' (Min/d) — ESul

'Sheila' (Dw)	ESul	
'Shelley' (Dw)	ESul SKen	
'Sheraton' (Min/d)	MWhe	
'Shimmer' (Z/d)	LVER MWhe	
'Shirley Ash' (A)	LDea WFib	
'Shirley Maureen' (R)	LDea	
'Shocking Pink' (Z/d)	LAst	
'Shogan' (R)	NFir	
'Shottesham Pet' (Sc)	CRHN ESul EWoo MBPg MHer NFir WHPP	
'Shrubland Pet' (U/Sc)	EWoo MHer	
'Shrubland Rose' (Sc)	WHPP	
'Sid' (R)	LDea	
sidoides	CSpe CTrC EPyc EShb IFro LPhx LPio MBPg MHer NFir SAga SMrm SScr SSea WCom WCot WEas WFib	
– black	CSpe SUsu	
– raspberry	CSpe SAga	
'Sienna' (R)	LDea NFir	
* 'Sils'	CWDa	
'Silver Anne' (R/v)	ESul NFir	
'Silver Delight' (v/d) **new**	WFib	
'Silver Kewense' (Dw/v)	ESul WFib	
I 'Silver Leaf Rose' (Sc) **new**	MBPg	
* 'Silver Lights'	CWDa	
'Silver Monarch' (Dw/v)	ESul	
'Silver Wings' (Z/v)	ESul LRHS MWhe SSea	
'Silvia' (R)	ESul	
'Simon Portas' (I/d)	SKen	
'Simon Read' (Dw)	ESul	
'Simplicity' (Z)	LVER	
'Single New Life' (Z)	LVER	
'Sir Colin' (Z)	SSea	
'Skelly's Pride' (Z)	LVER SKen WEas WFib	
'Skies of Italy' (Z/C/d)	CHal MBri MHer SKen SSea WFib	
'Small Fortune' (Min/d)	ESul SKen	
'Smuggler' (R)	LDea	
'Snape' (Min)	ESul	
'Sneezy' (Min)	ESul NFir	
'Snow Cap' (MinI)	NFir	
Snow Queen	see *P.* 'Schneekönigin'	
'Snow White' (Min)	ESul	
'Snowbaby' (Min/d)	ESul	
'Snowberry' (R)	ESul	
'Snowdrift' (I/d)	LVER WFib	
'Snowflake' (Min)	see *P.* 'Atomic Snowflake' (Sc/v)	
'Snowmass' (Z/d)	CHal MWhe	
'Snowstorm' (Z)	WFib	
'Snowy Baby' (Min/d)	WFib	
'Sofie'	see *P.* 'Decora Rose'	
'Solent Waves' (R)	ESul LDea	
'Solferino' (A)	ESul LDea SKen	
§ Solidor (I/d) ♀H1+3	LDea NFir	
Solo = 'Guillio' (Z/I)	LVER	
'Somersham' (Min)	ESul WFib	
'Something Special' (Z/d)	LVER MWhe NFir WFib	
'Sonata' (Dw/d)	ESul	
Sophie Casade	see *P.* 'Decora Rose'	
'Sophie Dumaresque' (Z/v)	LVER MBri MWhe NFir SKen SSea WFib	
'Sorcery' (Dw/C)	ESul MWhe SKen	
'Sound Appeal' (A)	ESul LDea MBPg	
'South African Sun' (Z/d) **new**	LVER	
'South American Bronze' (R) ♀H1+3	LDea SKen SMrm WFib	
'South American Delight' (R)	LVER	
'South Walsham Broad' (Dw)	ESul	
'Southern Belle' (A)	LDea	
'Southern Belle' (Z/d)	WFib	
'Southern Charm' (Z/v)	LVER	
'Southern Cherub' (A)	LDea	
'Southern Gem' (Min/d)	ESul	
'Southern Peach' (Min/d)	ESul	
'Souvenir' (R)	CHal LDea SSea	
'Spanish Angel' (A) ♀H1+3	ESul LDea NFir NWoo SSea WFib	
'Sparkler' (Z)	LVER	
'Spellbound' (R)	WFib	
'Spital Dam' (Dw/d)	ESul NFir	
'Spitfire' (Z/Ca/d/v)	ESul LVER SSea WFib WHPP	
'Spithead Cherry' (R)	LDea	
§ 'Splendide'	CSpe EShb ESul LPio MBPg MHer NFir SAga SScr SSea SWvt WCot WEas WFib WPen	
'Splendide' white-flowered **new**	MBPg	
'Spotlite Hotline' (I)	LDea	
'Spotlite Winner' (I)	LDea	
'Spot-on-bonanza' (R)	ESul LDea NFir WFib	
'Spring Bride' (R)	LDea	
'Spring Park' (A)	ESul LVER WFib	
'Springfield Ann' (R)	ESul	
'Springfield Black' (R)	ESul LDea LVER SSea	
'Springfield Charm' (R)	ESul	
'Springfield Mary Parfitt' (R)	ESul	
'Springfield Moonbeam' (R)	ESul	
'Springfield Pearl' (R)	LDea	
'Springfield Purple' (R)	ESul	
'Springfield Unique' (R)	LDea	
'Springtime' (Z/d)	MWhe SKen WFib	
'Sprite' (Min/v)	MWhe	
'Sproughton' (Dw)	ESul	
'St. Elmos Fire' (St/Min/d) **new**	WFib	
'St Helen's Favourite' (Min)	ESul	
'Stacey' (R)	LDea	
'Stadt Bern' (Z/C)	LRHS LVER MBri MSte MWhe NFir SKen	
x *stapletoniae*	see *P.* 'Miss Stapleton'	
'Star Flecks'	NFir	
'Star of Persia' (Z/Ca/d)	WFib WHPP	
'Starburst' (Z)	NFir	
'Starflecks' (St)	LVER	
'Starlet' (Ca)	WFib	
'Starlight' (R)	WFib	
'Starlight Magic' (A) ♀H1+3	ESul LDea	
'Starry Eyes' (Dw)	ESul	
'Stella Read' (Dw/d)	ESul	
'Stellar Arctic Star'	see *P.* 'Arctic Star'	
'Stellar Cathay' (Z/St/d)	LRHS	
'Stellar Hannaford Star'	see *P.* 'Hannaford Star'	
* 'Stellar Orange Pixie' (St/d)	CWDa	
'Stephen Read' (Min)	ESul	
'Stewart Meehan' (R)	LDea	
'Stirling Stent' (Z)	CWDa	
'Strawberries and Cream' (Z/St)	NFir	
'Strawberry Fayre' (Dw/St)	LVER	
'Strawberry Sundae' (R)	ESul LDea LVER MSte NFir WFib	
'Stringer's Delight' (Dw/v)	ESul LVER	
'Stuart Mark' (R)	LDea	
'Stutton' (Min)	ESul	
suburbanum	EShb	
'Suffolk Agate' (R)	ESul	
'Suffolk Amethyst' (A)	ESul	
'Suffolk Coral' (R)	ESul	
'Suffolk Emerald' (A)	ESul	

	'Turkish Delight' (Dw/C)	ESul MWhe NFir WFib
	'Turtle's Surprise' (Z/d/v)	SKen
	'Turtle's White' (R)	LDea
	'Tuyo' (R)	WFib
	'Tweedle-Dum' (Dw)	CSpe ESul MWhe
	'Twinkle' (Min/d)	ESul WFib
	'Tyabb Princess' (R)	LDea
	'Ullswater' (Dw/C)	ESul
§	'Unique Aurore' (U)	EWoo LPio LVER MBPg MHer MSte SKen
	'Unique Mons Ninon'	see *P.* 'Monsieur Ninon'
	'Unity' (Dw)	LVER
	'Urchin' (Min)	ESul MWhe NFir SHFr WFib
	'Ursula Key' (Z/c)	SKen WFib
	'Valanza' (A)	ESul
	'Valentina' (Min/d)	ESul
	'Valentine' (R)	ESul
	'Vancouver Centennial' (Dw/St/C) ♀H1+3	CSpe ESul LAst LRHS LVER MBri MHer MWhe NFir SAga SCoo SDnm SHFr SKen Smrm SPet SPoG SSea WFib
	'Vandersea'	EWoo
I	'Variegated Attar of Roses' (Sc/v) **new**	MBPg
§	'Variegated Clorinda' (Sc/v)	EWoo WFib
	'Variegated Fragrans'	see *P.* (Fragrans Group) 'Fragrans Variegatum'
	'Variegated Joy Lucille' (Sc/v) **new**	MBPg
§	'Variegated Kleine Liebling' (Min/v)	ESul SSea WFib
	'Variegated Madame Layal' (A/v) ♀H1+3	WFib
	'Variegated Petit Pierre' (Min/v)	WFib
	'Vasco da Gama' (Dw/d)	ESul
	'Vectis Allure' (Z/St) **new**	LVER
	'Vectis Blaze' (I)	EWoo
	'Vectis Cascade'	EWoo
	'Vectis Glitter' (Z/St)	CSpe LVER MWhe NFir WFib
	'Vectis Sparkler' (Dw/St) **new**	ESul
	'Velvet' (Z)	CWDa LVER
	'Velvet Duet' (A) ♀H1+3	CHal EWoo LAst LDea LIck LPio LRHS LVER MBPg MWhe NFir SKen SSea WGor
	'Venus' (Min/d)	ESul LRHS
	'Verdale' (A)	LDea WFib
	'Verity Palace' (R)	EWoo LDea WFib
	'Verona' (Z/C)	CHal MBri SKen
	'Verona Contreras' (A)	ESul LDea MWhe NFir WFib
I	'Veronica' (Z/d)	MWhe SKen
	'Vicki Town' (R)	WFib
	'Vicky Claire' (R)	ESul LDea NFir SKen Smrm WFib
	'Victor' (Z) **new**	LAst
	'Victoria' (Z/d)	LAst SKen
	'Victoria Regina' (R)	LDea
	'Viking' (Min/d)	SKen
	'Viking Red' (Z)	MWhe
	'Village Hill Oak' (Sc)	ESul LDea LVER MBPg MHer
	'Ville de Paris'	see *P.* 'Hederinum'
	'Vina' (Dw/C/d)	ESul MWhe SKen WFib
	'Vincent Gerris' (A)	ESul LDea MWhe
	Vinco = 'Guivin'PBR (I/d)	CWDa WHPP
	violareum hort.	see *P.* 'Splendide'
	'Violet Lambton' (Z/v)	WFib
	'Violet Unique' (U)	MHer
	'Violetta' (R)	LDea WFib
	'Virginia' (R)	LDea SPet
	'Viscossisimum' (Sc)	MHer SKen
	viscosum	see *P. glutinosum*
§	*vitifolium*	MBPg MHer SVen
	'Viva' (R)	ESul

	'Vivat Regina' (Z/d)	WFib
	'Voo Doo' (Dec)	ESul LPio
	'Voodoo' (U) ♀H1+3	CBrm CSpe EWoo MBPg MHer MSte NCiC NFir SAga SSea SUsu WCot WFib WHPP
	'Wallace Fairman' (R)	LDea
	'Wallis Friesdorf' (Dw/C/d)	ESul MWhe
	'Wantirna' (Z/v)	CSpe ECtt LIck LVER MHer NFir
	'Warrenorth Coral' (Z/C/d)	LVER
	'Warrenorth Rubellite' (Z/v) **new**	LVER
	'Warrion' (Z/d)	LVER
	'Washbrook' (Min/d)	ESul NFir
	'Watersmeet' (R)	LDea
	'Wattisham' (Dec)	LDea
	'Waveney' (Min)	ESul
	'Wayward Angel' (A) ♀H1+3	ESul LDea LVER WFib
	'Wedding Royale' (Dw/d)	ESul LVER WFib
	'Welcome' (Z/d)	WFib
	'Welling' (Sc)	ESul GBar LDea LVER MBPg NFir
	'Wellington' (R)	LDea
	'Wendy' (Min)	LAst
	'Wendy Anne'	SKen
	'Wendy Jane' (Dw/d) **new**	WFib
	'Wendy Read' (Dw/d)	ESul LVER MWhe SPet WFib
	'Wensum' (Min/d)	ESul
	'Westdale Appleblossom' (Z/d/C)	ESul LVER WFib
*	'Westdale Beauty' (d)	CWDa
	'Whisper' (R)	WFib
	'White Bird's Egg' (Z)	WFib
	'White Boar' (Fr)	EWoo MSte WFib
	'White Bonanza' (R)	ESul WFib
	'White Charm' (R)	ESul LDea
	'White Chiffon' (R)	LVER
	'White Duet' (A)	LDea MWhe
	'White Eggshell' (Min)	ESul LVER WFib
	'White Feather' (Z/St)	MHer
	'White Glory' (R) ♀H1+3	ESul LDea NFir
	'White Lively Lady' (Dw/C)	ESul
§	'White Mesh' (I/v)	ECtt MBri MWhe SKen
	'White Prince of Orange' (Sc) **new**	MBPg
	'White Queen' (Z/d)	CWDa
	'White Roc' (Min/d)	ESul
	'White Truffle' **new**	LAst
	'White Unique' (U)	CHal EWoo LDea MBPg MHer MSte NBur SPet SSea WFib WHPP
	'White Velvet Duet' (A)	ESul
	White-Blizzard = 'Fisbliz'PBR	NPri SCoo WWol
	'Wickham Lad' (R)	LDea
	Wico = 'Guimongol'PBR (I/d)	LAst NBlu
	'Wild Spice' (Sc)	LDea LPio LVER
	'Wildmalva' (Sc) **new**	MBPg
	'Wilf Vernon' (Min/d)	ESul
	'Wilhelm Kolle' (Z)	WFib
	'Wilhelm Langath'	SCoo SDnm WHPP
	'Winford Festival'	LVER
	'Winnie Read' (Dw/d)	ESul
	'Winston Churchill' (R)	LDea
	'Wirral Target' (Z/d/v)	ESul MWhe
	'Wishing Star' (Min/St)	ESul
	'Wispy' (Dw/St/C)	ESul
	'Witnesham' (Min/d)	ESul
§	'Wood's Surprise' (MinI/d/v)	ESul LDea MWhe NFir SAga SKen SWal
	'Wooton's Unique' **new**	CSpe

'Wordsworth'	MBPg
'Wroxham' (Dw)	ESul
'Wychwood' (A/Sc)	EWoo LDea MBPg
'Wyck Beacon' (I/d)	SKen
'Yale' (I/d) ♥H1+3	CHal LDea LVER MBri MSte MWhe
	SKen WFib
'Yhu' (R)	ESul LDea NFir SAga WFib
'Yolanda' (Dw/C)	ESul
'York Florist' (Z/d/v)	LVER
'York Minster' (Dw/v)	SKen
'Yvonne' (Z)	WFib
'Zama' (R)	ESul NFir
'Zemmies' (MinI)	ESul
'Zena' (Dw)	ESul
'Zinc' (Z/d)	WFib
'Zoe' (A)	LDea WHPP
zonale	EWoo WFib
'Zulu King' (R)	WFib
'Zulu Warrior' (R)	WFib

Peliosanthes (Convallariaceae)
monticola B&SWJ 5183	WCru

Pellaea (Adiantaceae)
atropurpurea	CLAP EFer WFib
cordifolia	WRic
falcata	MBri
rotundifolia ♥H2	CHal CTrC MBri NMar SMur
sagittata	NMar

Pellionia see *Elatostema*

Peltandra (Araceae)
alba	see *P. sagittifolia*
§ *sagittifolia*	CRow
undulata	see *P. virginica*
virginica	CDWL CRow EMFW LPBA MSta
	NPer SLon SWat
- 'Snow Splash' (v) **new**	CRow

Peltaria (Brassicaceae)
alliacea	CSpe EBee EPPr
	LEdu
turkmena	EMan

Peltiphyllum see *Darmera*

Peltoboykinia (Saxifragaceae)
§ *tellimoides*	CCol CLAP EBee GCal NBir NHol
	SMac WBVN WFar WMoo
watanabei	CDes CLAP EBee GIBF GTou SMac
	WCru WFar WMoo WPGP

Pennantia (Icacinaceae)
baylisiana **new**	ECou
corymbosa	ECou
- 'Akoroa'	ECou
- 'Woodside'	ECou

Pennellianthus see *Penstemon*

Pennisetum (Poaceae)
B&SWJ 3854	WCru
§ *alopecuroides*	More than 30 suppliers
- Autumn Wizard	see *P. alopecuroides*
	'Herbstzauber'
- 'Bruno Ears'	EHoe
- 'Cassian's Choice'	CBrm CKno EFou EHoe SMrm
	SUsu
- 'Caudatum'	CKno CPen CRez
- f. *erythrochaetum*	WCru
	'Ferris' **new**
- 'Hameln'	More than 30 suppliers
§ - 'Herbstzauber'	CFir CFwr CPen EBee EGle EHoe

	EPfP GCal LHop LPan SMHy SMrm
	WPnP
- 'Little Bunny'	CBAn CBrm CFwr CHar CKno
	COIW CPen EBee EBre EChP EHoe
	EMan ENot EPPr EPla GCal GKir
	LAst LPan LRHS NGdn NPro WBea
	WDin WPGP
- 'Little Honey' (v)	CBrm CKno CPrp EBee EMan EPPr
	NLar SMer SPla WCot WLeb WPGP
- 'Moudry'	CBig CBrm CKno CPen EFou EHoe
	EPPr SMrm
- 'National Arboretum'	CPen EHoe
- var. *purpurascens*	CBig CWCL
- - B&SWJ 5822	WCru
- f. *viridescens*	CBri CBrm CFwr CKno CStr EBee
	ECha EGle EHoe ELan EMan EPfP
	EPza EWsh LPan LRHS MAvo
	MLLN MMoz NSti SMHy WBea
- 'Weserbergland'	CBig CFir CKno EBee EHoe EPPr
- 'Woodside'	CBig CKno CMea CPen CSam
	CWCL EBee EHoe EMan EPPr LBBr
	MBNS SHel SPla
compressum	see *P. alopecuroides*
flaccidum	EBee EHul EMan EMon EPPr
	WWpP
incomptum	CSam EBre EHoe GKir LRHS SMrm
	XPep
- purple	CKno CStr EBee MMoz
longistylum hort.	see *P. villosum*
macrostachyum	CKno MAnH
'Burgundy Giant' **new**	
macrourum	CBrm CFil CFwr CHea CHrt CKno
	CMea CSam EBee ECha EGle EHoe
	EPGN EPla EWsh LHop MAnH
	SMHy SMrm SUsu SWal WBea
	WPGP
massaicum 'Red	CKno CPen
Buttons'	
orientale ♥H3	More than 30 suppliers
I - 'Karley Rose'	CFwr CKno CPen CRez EBee IPot
	LPhx
* - 'Shogun'	LPhx MAvo
- 'Tall Tails'	CBig CFwr CKno CPen EBee EHoe
	EMan EPPr LPhx MAvo WCot
rueppellii	see *P. setaceum*
§ *setaceum* ♥H3	CBig CHrt CKno CPen CWCL
	EBlw EMan EPPr MAnH MGol
	MNrw MWat SIde SWal WWpP
	XPep
- 'Eaton Canyon'	CKno CPen
- 'Rubrum'	CAbb CBig CFwr CKno CPen SDix
	SGar SMad SUsu SWvt WBcn
spatheolatum	CKno
'Malibu' **new**	
§ *villosum* ♥H3	More than 30 suppliers

pennyroyal see *Mentha pulegium*

Penstemon ✿ (Scrophulariaceae)
P&C 150	CFee
PC&H 148	GBri
'Abberley'	WPer
'Abbotsmerry'	CEIw EBee LPhx SAga SGar WEll
	WPPR WSPU
'Agnes Laing'	CWCL LPen LRHS MBNS SPlb
albertinus	see *P. humilis*
albidus	NLAp
§ 'Alice Hindley' ♥H3	More than 30 suppliers
alpinus	CLyd CNic CTCP GAbr GTou
	MHar NLAp NOak WEll
ambiguus	EBee
§ 'Andenken an Friedrich	More than 30 suppliers
Hahn' ♥H4	
§ *angustifolius*	MNrw SRms

'Apple Blossom' ♀H3-4 — More than 30 suppliers
'Apple Blossom' — see *P.* 'Thorn'
  misapplied
aridus — CNic NSla
arizonicus — see *P. whippleanus*
arkansanus — NLAp
'Ashton' — CElw EBee LPen WEll WSPU
'Aston' **new** — SLon
attenuatus NNS 96-176 — WCot
'Audrey Cooper' — EBee WPPR
auriberbis — EBee
'Axe Valley Penny — CStr
  Mitchell' **new**
'Axe Valley Suzie' **new** — CStr
azureus — CPBP GEil
'Barbara Barker' — see *P.* 'Beech Park'
§ *barbatus* — CBot CFee ECha EHrv ELan ERou
  LPhx MLan MWat NLAp SChu
  SECG SMrm SRms WHCG WLin
  WWin XPep
§ - 'Blue Spring' — ECtt
  - 'Cambridge Mixed' — EDAr ERou EWll LRHS LRav
  - subsp. *coccineus* — CWCL EBee EWTr LPen LPhx
  LRHS MBNS MBri MCCP NBPC
  NDlv NLar WCAu
  - 'Iron Maiden' **new** — EBee NWCA SSvw
  - 'Jingle Bells' — CWCL EBee GKir LPen STes
  - orange-flowered — SAga SMrm
  - 'Peter Catt' **new** — SCro
  - var. *praecox* — MBNS NJOw NLAp WCom WPer
  - - f. *nanus* — CBot EMan LRHS MSte SRms
  - - - 'Rondo' — NLar NWCA
barrettiae — NLAp
'Beckford' — EBee WCFE WEll WSPU
§ 'Beech Park' ♀H3 — EBee ECtt ELan ERou EWes LAst
  LPen LRHS MBNS NBir SAga SBri
  WCot WHCG WSPU
§ *berryi* — EPot GKev SMrm
'Bisham Seedling' — see *P.* 'White Bedder'
'Blackbird' — More than 30 suppliers
'Blue Spring' misapplied — see *P. heterophyllus* 'Blue Springs'
'Bodnant' — EBee MHar WBan WPer
bradburii — see *P. grandiflorus*
'Bredon' — CElw CHea EBee WEll WSPU
breviculus — LTwo
bridgesii — see *P. rostriflorus*
'Burford Purple' — see *P.* 'Burgundy'
'Burford Seedling' — see *P.* 'Burgundy'
'Burford White' — see *P.* 'White Bedder'
§ 'Burgundy' — More than 30 suppliers
caeruleus — see *P. angustifolius*
caespitosus — CTCP SBri
  - subsp. *suffruticosus* — see *P. tusharensis*
§ *californicus* — CGra WAbe WLin
calycosus — EBee
§ *campanulatus* — CMHG EBee ECtt EPfP EPot EWes
  GBBs GEdr LPen MAsh MLLN
  NHol NMen SRms WBea WEll
  WGwG WHCG WPer WSPU
  - PC&H 148 — EMan MSPs NOak STes WPPR
  - *pulchellus* — see *P. campanulatus*
  - *roseus* misapplied — see *P. kunthii*
'Candy Pink' — see *P.* 'Old Candy Pink'
cardwellii — EWes GTou MDKP SRms
'Carolyn Orr' (v) — EBee EMan MHar WCot
'Castle Forbes' — EPyc GMac LAst LPen MBNS MHar
  MLLN NBur WBan WEll WHCG
  WPer WSSM
'Catherine de la Mare' — see *P. heterophyllus* 'Catherine de
  la Mare'
* 'Centra' — EBee LPen MLLN WEll WPPR
centranthifolius — SIgm
  JJA 13106
'Charles Rudd' — EBee ERou GEil GMac LLWP LPen

LRHS MBNS MCLN MLLN SAga
  SBai SChu SGar SUsu SWal SWvt
  SYvo WEll WHCG WLow WPPR
  WSSM
§ 'Cherry' ♀H3 — EBee EOrc GMac LPen MBNS
  MHer MLLN NBur SAga SBri SCro
  SMrm SPla SPlb WGMN WHCG
  WHil WPPR WPer WSPU WWhi
'Cherry Ripe' misapplied — see *P.* 'Cherry'
§ 'Chester Scarlet' ♀H3 — CBri CElw CMCo CWCL EBlw
  ENot GBri GMac LPen MNrw
  MOak MRav MSte NBrk SDix SGar
  SLon SMrm WCFE WEll WHCG
  WPPR WPer WSPU WWye
clutei — EBee EWTr
cobaea — CTCP EBee GKev SUsu
'Comberton' — CHea EBee MAnH SAga WSPU
confertus — CMHG CNic CTCP CTri EBee EGra
  EHyt EPot GAbr LPen LPio MBNS
  MHer NChi NLAp NMen NWCA
  SRms WBVN WHCG WPPR WPer
  WRHF WSPU
'Connie's Pink' ♀H3 — EBee ENot LPen MBNS MLLN MSte
  NBur WEll WHCG WPPR WSPU
* 'Coral Pink' — CStr SLon
cordifolius — see *Keckiella cordifolia*
'Cottage Garden Red' — see *P.* 'Windsor Red'
§ 'Countess of Dalkeith' — More than 30 suppliers
crandallii — CPBP
  - subsp. *glabrescens* — WHCG WLin
§ - subsp. *taosensis* — NWCA SMrm
cristatus — see *P. eriantherus*
davidsonii — EWes NLAp SRms WAbe WPat
  - var. *davidsonii* — CGra CPBP
§ - var. *menziesii* ♀H4 — EBee GEil GTou MDun NWCA
  SRms
  - - 'Broken Top Mountain' — CLyd CStu
  - - 'Microphyllus' — EPot LTwo NMen NSla WAbe WLin
  - var. *praeteritus* — CNic EPot MDKP
'Dazzler' — CBod CM&M CWCL EBee ERou
  LPen NChi SWvt WEll WPPR WPer
  WSPU
§ *deaveri* — WSPU
'Devonshire Cream' — CElw CStr CWCL LPen LRHS
  MBNS SAga WHCG
diffusus — see *P. serrulatus*
digitalis — CBri CNic CRWN EBre ECha EMan
  EWTr LPen LPhx MBNS NLAp
  WFar WHCG WPer
§ - 'Husker Red' — More than 30 suppliers
  - 'Purpureus' — see *P. digitalis* 'Husker Red'
  - 'Ruby Tuesday' — CDes EBee
  - white-flowered — GBBs LPhx SRms
discolor pale — NBir WFar
  lavender-flowered
dissectus — NLAp
'Dorothy Wilson' — MLLN
§ 'Drinkstone' — EGoo EHol ERou LPen LRHS NChi
  SAga SDix SOkh WHCG WPPR
  WPer WSPU
'Drinkwater Red' — see *P.* 'Drinkstone'
eatonii — EBee
  - subsp. *undosus* — WCot
  NNS 95-381
'Edithae' — LPen SChu SRms WEas WHCG
  WIvy WKif
'Elmley' — EBee MLLN SAga SGar WEll WSPU
§ *eriantherus* — CGra WHCG
'Etna' — EBee ECtt GKir LRHS MBri MMil
  SWal WEll WGMN
euglaucus — CNic EBee LTwo SAga SGar
§ 'Evelyn' ♀H4 — More than 30 suppliers
'Firebird' — see *P.* 'Schoenholzeri'
'Flame' — CBri EMan LHop LPen LRHS NBur

		SLon WEll WHCG WPPR WPer WSPU
'Flamingo'		CBri CWCL EBee EChP ECtt EPfP ERou EWes LAst LPen LRHS MAsh MBNS MSte NCGa SAga SBai SGar SWal SWvt WCFE WEll WFar WHil WPPR WSPU WShp
fremontii **new**		WLin
frutescens		GTou WSPU
fruticosus		CTCP NNrw NWCA WAbe
§ - var. *scouleri* ♀H4		MOne NLAp SRms WBVN WCFE WPPR WSPU
- - f. *albus* ♀H4		LPen NLAp SChu SIng WAbe WIvy WKif
- - 'Amethyst'		NLAp WAbe WBod WLin
- var. *serratus*		LPen NLAp
- - 'Holly'		NMen SBla
Fujiyama = 'Yayama'PBR		ECtt LRHS MBow MBri MMil NGdn WFar
'Gaff's Pink'		SChu
'Gaiety'		CM&M
'Garden Red'		see *P.* 'Windsor Red'
'Garnet'		see *P.* 'Andenken an Friedrich Hahn'
gentianoides		MNrw NBro
'Geoff Hamilton'		CElw LHop LPen MBNS SAga
'George Elrick'		LPen MBNS
§ 'George Home' ♀H3		CBri CWCL EBee ECGP ECtt EWes LPen LRHS MBNS MLLN MNrw MSte NBur SAga SChu SMrm SOkh SSvw WBVN WHCG
'Ghent Purple'		CFee
'Gilchrist' **new**		SGar SLon
glaber		CBri CMHG CMea GMac LHop LLWP LPen LRHS MBNS MBri MEHN MLLN MRav NBro NGdn NLAp SBai SECG SHFr SMrm WBVN WEas WEll WHCG WHoo WKif WPPR WPer WSPU
- 'Roundway Snowflake'		CMea CStr
- white-flowered **new**		SGar
'Gloire de Quatre Rue'		CWCL LPen
gormanii		CStr CTCP
gracilis		EBee GCal WPer
§ *grandiflorus*		CTCP EBee EMan EWTr NLAp SMrm WCAu WLin
- 'Prairie Snow'		EBee
'Greencourt Purple'		WShp
hallii		CGra CNic EBee EPot EWes GTou LRHS WLin WPPR WPat
hartwegii ♀H3-4		CBrm CNic EPyc GMac LHop LPen SChu WBan WHCG WLin WPPR WPer WSPU
- 'Albus'		EBee GEil LHop LPen LRHS MSte SAga SGar WCom WEll WHCG WPPR WSPU
I - 'Tubular Bells Rose'		CWCL NPri SPet
heterodoxus		CNic SGar
§ *heterophyllus*		CHea CWCL EBee ETow LGro LPen MNrw NBir SAga SBri SChu SMer SRms STes SWal WCFE WEas WHCG WPPR WPer WSPU
- 'Blue Eye'		WSPU
- 'Blue Fountain'		LPen WEll WPPR WSPU
- 'Blue Gem'		CBod CElw CTri EBre ECtt EOrc LRHS NChi SCro SIng SPla WPGP WSPU
§ - 'Blue Springs'		CBot CBrm EBee LPen LRHS MAnH MSte NLAp SAga SBla WAbe
§ - 'Catherine de la Mare' ♀H4		CHad CHar CStr EBre ELan GKir LHop LPen LRHS MBow MHer MWat NBir NBro NLAp SAga SChu SMrm SPla SWvt WEas WFar WKif WPPR WSPU
- 'Heavenly Blue'		CWCL EBee ECtt EPfP ERou GEil LAst LPen LRHS MBNS MCLN NDov NLAp NPPs SBai SOkh SWal SWat SWvt WCFE WCra WEll WLin WMnd WPPR WWhi
- 'Hergest Croft'		CElw SChu WPPR
- 'Jeanette'		EBee WCot WHoo
- subsp. *purdyi*		EPyc WHCG
- 'Roehrsier'		LPen
- 'True Blue'		see *P. heterophyllus*
- 'Züriblau'		CFai CMdw EBee LPen MSPs WWeb
'Hewell Pink Bedder' ♀H3		More than 30 suppliers
'Hewitt's Pink'		ECtt SAga WEll
§ 'Hidcote Pink' ♀H3-4		More than 30 suppliers
'Hidcote Purple'		CElw CM&M NBrk NGdn SAga SChu
* 'Hidcote White'		CM&M CWCL EOrc MHer SWvt WEll
'Hillview Pink'		WHil
'Hillview Red'		SAga WHil
§ *hirsutus*		CNic CTCP EBee LBBr LPen MDKP MNrw NLAp SECG SGar SIng WBVN WPer WSan
- f. *albiflorus*		EBee LPen NLAp NWCA WAbe
- var. *minimus*		NLAp
- var. *pygmaeus*		CLyd CMea CNic EBee EDAr EWTr GTou LBee LPen MBro MHer NJOw NMen NWCA SBla SGar SIng SPlb SRms SRot SWal WAbe WCom WHoo WLin WPer WWin
- - f. *albus*		WPer
- - 'Purpureus'		WLin
'Hopleys Variegated' (v)		EBee EMan MHar MHer MNrw NBir SAga SBai SGar SWvt WCot WPPR WSPU WWeb
§ *humilis*		CNic EBee MLLN NLAp SRms WBar WLin
- 'Pulchellus'		NLAp NWCA
idahoensis **new**		WLin
isophyllus ♀H3-4		CTri CWCL EChP EPfP ERou GEil ITim LPen LRHS MAsh MMil SChu WCom WEll WFar WHCG WPPR WPer WSPU
jamesii		CBrm CGra CTCP EBee EChP EHyt WHrl
janishiae		CGra NWCA WLin
Jean Grace = 'Penbow'		CHar EBre GKir LRHS SIng
'Jill Lucas'		SCro
'John Booth'		MSte WEas
'John Nash'		MHer MTPN SAga SChu SIgm WEll
'John Nash' misapplied		see *P.* 'Alice Hindley'
'John Spedan Lewis'		SLon
'Joy'		EBee EPyc LPen MLLN MSte WPPR WPer
'June'		see *P.* 'Pennington Gem'
Kilimanjaro = 'Yajaro'		EBee EBre WEll
'King George V'		More than 30 suppliers
'Knight's Purple'		CElw LPen WEll WHCG
'Knightwick'		CElw LPen SAga SGar WEll WPPR WPer WSPU
§ *kunthii*		CBri CStr CWCL EBee EPPr GEdr LPen MDKP NBur NLAp SAga SCro SScr WEll WHrl WPPR WSPU SGar WLin
- upright		SGar WLin
§ *laetus* subsp. *roezlii*		EHyt EPot GCrs GEdr LRHS MBar MDun MLan NLAp NSla NWCA SRms WBVN WWin
laricifolius		CNic NWCA
§ 'Le Phare'		CBod LPen LRHS MBNS MHar WEll WHCG WPPR WPer WSPU
leonensis		CTCP
'Lilac and Burgundy'		CHar CHea CPlt EBee EChP ERou

	EWTr LPen LRHS MBNS SBai SWal SWvt WEll WFar WLin WPPR
linarioides	CStr LPen NHol NLAp WPat
- subsp. *sileri* **new**	WLin
'Little Witley'	LPen SAga WEll WHCG WPer
'Lord Home'	see *P.* 'George Home'
lyallii	EBee EHrv ELan EMan LPen MCCP MLLN MNrw NLAp NMRc SRms WGMN WPPR WSPU WSan
'Lynette'	LPen LRHS MBNS SAga SPlb WCot WEll WHCG WHil WPPR WPer
'Macpenny's Pink'	EBee EPyc LPen SBri SChu WEll
§ 'Madame Golding'	EBee GMac LPen LRHS MBNS MNrw SGar WEll WHCG WPPR WPer WSPU
'Margery Fish' ♀H3	CElw CStr ERou EWes LPen LRHS MAvo MMil MNrw MSte SBai WEll WGMN WPPR WPer WSPU
'Maurice Gibbs' ♀H3	CBcs CBri CHar CM&M COlW EBee ECtt EPyc ERou EWes LPen LRHS MBNS MLLN MWgw NBPC NGdn SAga SBai SIgm SWal WEll WFoF WHCG WMnd WPPR WSPU WWeb
mensarum	EBee
menziesii	see *P. davidsonii* var. *menziesii*
Mexicali hybrids	EBee LPen MLLN WPPR
mexicanus	WLin
'Midnight'	CBcs CHar EChP ELan EPfP GBri LLWP LPen MAnH MAvo MOak MRav MSte NBrk SGar SIgm SWvt WBVN WCFE WCom WHCG WHoo WPPR WPer WSPU WWeb WWin
'Mint Pink'	SGar SScr WPPR
'Modesty'	EBee LPen LRHS MBNS NBur WEll WHCG WLow WPPR WPer WSPU
montanus	CNic EBee NLAp SAga
'Mother of Pearl'	More than 30 suppliers
'Mrs Miller'	LPen MBNS NBur
'Mrs Morse'	see *P.* 'Chester Scarlet'
multiflorus	EBee LPen
§ 'Myddelton Gem'	CHar LPen LRHS MBNS MNrw WEll WFoF WHCG WPPR WSPU
'Myddelton Red'	see *P.* 'Myddelton Gem'
nanus **new**	CGra
neomexicanus	EBee
neotericus	CGra NWCA SIgm
newberryi ♀H4	CMea CTCP GKev GKir SRot WCom WKif WPat WWin
- subsp. *berryi*	see *P. berryi*
- f. *humilior*	EPot WLin
§ - subsp. *sonomensis*	EPot NWCA WAbe
'Newbury Gem'	MBNS NBur SBai SWvt WEll WFar WPPR
§ *nitidus*	MNrw
'Oaklea Red'	ECtt EPyc ERou LPen SWal SWat
§ 'Old Candy Pink'	CFee EBee LLWP LPen MSte SBai SWvt WEll WPPR WPer WSPU
'Old Silk'	WCot
'Osprey' ♀H3	More than 30 suppliers
ovatus	CTCP EBee GBBs GFlt LPen LPhx LPio MAnH MLLN NDlv NLAp SBla SGar SIgm SMrm SRms WCot WHCG WKif WLin WSan
'Overbury'	EBee LPen WSPU
pachyphyllus	WLin
pallidus **new**	EBee
palmeri	ECtt EMan MSPs SAga WLin
'Papal Purple'	CBri CMHG CMea CWCL ERou LLWP LPen LRHS MBNS MSte NBir NBrk NChi SAga SBai SChu SLon SMrm SRms SWal WCom WEll WFar WHCG WPPR WSPU WWhi
'Papal Purple' x 'Evelyn'	CBri CMHG LPen SAga SCro SGar

'Patio Pink'	ERou LPen MLLN WEll
'Patio Red'	CWCL
'Patio Shell'	GKir LRHS
'Patio Wine'	GKir
payettensis	LTwo WLin
paysoniorum	WLin
'Peace'	EBlw LPen LRHS MBNS SLon WEll WHCG WPPR WSPU
'Pearl'	EPyc
§ 'Pennington Gem' ♀H3	CElw EBre ECtt EGra ELan GBri GKir GMac LLWP LPen LRHS MHer MLLN MNrw MSte MWgw NBrk NGdn SBai SGar SIng SPer SWal SWvt WEas WHCG WPPR WPer WSPU
'Pensham Arctic Fox' **new**	EBee MBri
'Pensham Arctic Sunset'	SAga WEll WPPR
'Pensham Avonbelle'	WEll WPPR
'Pensham Barbara Dixon'	WPPR
'Pensham Bilberry Ice' **new**	CHar WWol
'Pensham Blackberry Ice' **new**	WWol
'Pensham Blueberry Ice'	CHar CSpe EBee MAvo MBnl MBri WCra WWol
'Pensham Bow Bells'	SAga WPPR
'Pensham Capricorn Moon'	EBee SAga WEll WPPR
'Pensham Cardinal'	WPPR
'Pensham Cassis Royale' **new**	CStr
'Pensham Celebration'	WPPR
'Pensham Charles Romer'	WEll WPPR
'Pensham Choir Boy' **new**	CStr
'Pensham Claret'	WEll WPPR
'Pensham Daybreak'	WEll WPPR
'Pensham Dorothy Wilson'	EBee MBnl WEll WPPR
'Pensham Edith Biggs'	EBee MBnl WPPR
'Pensham Fields'	WPPR
'Pensham Freshwater Pearl'	CElw CStr SAga WEll WPPR
'Pensham Great Expectations'	EBee SAga SOkh WEll WPPR
'Pensham Just Jayne'	CElw MBnl SLon SOkh WEll WPPR WWol
'Pensham Marjorie Lewis'	WEll WPPR
'Pensham Mischief'	WPPR
'Pensham Miss Wilson'	CStr WEll WPPR
'Pensham Petticoat'	EBee MAvo MBnl MBri SOkh WEll WPPR
'Pensham Plum Dandy'	CStr WEll WPPR
'Pensham Plum Jerkum'	EBee MBnl MBri WCra WPPR
'Pensham Prolific'	WPPR
'Pensham Raspberry Ice' **new**	MAvo WWol
'Pensham Saint James's'	WEll WPPR
'Pensham Son of Raven'	WEll WPPR
'Pensham Tayberry Ice' **new**	EBee MBnl WWol
'Pensham The Dean's Damson'	WPPR
'Pensham Tiger Belle Coral'	WPPR
I 'Pensham Tiger Belle Rose'	SAga WEll WPPR
'Pensham Twilight'	CStr WPPR
'Pensham Victoria Plum'	CStr WEll WPPR
'Pensham Wedding Bells' **new**	EBee MBri
perfoliatus **new**	WLin
'Pershore Carnival'	NPro WSPU WSSM
'Pershore Fanfare'	CElw LPen WEll WHrl WSPU

'Pershore Pink Necklace' LPen MLLN SAga SBai SMrm SWvt
WBan WCot WEll WHCG WPPR
WSPU WSan
'Phare' see *P.* 'Le Phare'
'Phyllis' see *P.* 'Evelyn'
pinifolius ♀H4 More than 30 suppliers
- 'Mersea Yellow' More than 30 suppliers
- 'Wisley Flame' ♀H4 EPfP EPot ESis GEdr NJOw SIgm
'Pink Bedder' see *P.* 'Hewell Pink Bedder', *P.*
'Sutton's Pink Bedder'
'Pink Dragon' CLyd WHCG
'Pink Endurance' CBri CMea EBee ERou LPen MCLN
MSte WEll WHCG WHal WHoo
WPPR WPer WSPU
'Pink Ice' WHil
'Pink Profusion' MRav SIgm
'Port Wine' ♀H3 CHar CSam CTri CWCL EBee GAbr
LLWP LPen LRHS MBow MHar
MLLN NBir NPPs SAga SBai SBri
SPer SPla WCot WHCG WHoo
WPPR WPer WSPU
potosinus EWes
'Powis Castle' EBee EWes MHar WBan WEll
WPPR WPer WWye
'Prairie Dusk' LPen
'Prairie Fire' EBee ERou LPen SAga WPPR WSPU
* 'Prairie Pride' LPen
'Priory Purple' WEll WHCG WPer
procerus EBee EChP GBri LPen MDHE
MLLN SRms WPer
- var. *brachyanthus* CNic EBee
§ - var. *formosus* EPot GAbr WAbe
- var. *procerus* new EHyt
§ - 'Roy Davidson' ♀H4 CMea CPBP ETow LBee LRHS
NHol NLAp SBla SOkd WAbe WFar
WLin WPPR
- var. *tolmiei* EBee EPot GCal GEdr LBee LPen
NChi NHol NSla WLin
- - white GEil
pruinosus EBee
pubescens see *P. hirsutus*
pulchellus Greene see *P. procerus* var. *formosus*
pulchellus Lindl. see *P. campanulatus*
* *pulcherrimus* NBro
pumilus SRms
'Purple and White' see *P.* 'Countess of Dalkeith'
'Purple Bedder' More than 30 suppliers
'Purple Passion' EBee EBre EChP EHrv EPfP EWes
LPen LRHS SCro WEll
'Purpureus Albus' see *P.* 'Countess of Dalkeith'
purpusii SIgm WLin
'Rajah' EBee LPen
'Raven' ♀H3 More than 30 suppliers
'Razzle Dazzle' CWCL LPen LRHS MBNS SOkh
SPlb WEll WPPR WPer
'Red Ace' MNrw
'Red Emperor' CStr ECtt LPen MBNS MHar SPlb
WEas WEll WHCG WPer WSPU
'Red Knight' CWCL LPen LRHS MBNS
'Red Sea' CStr
'Rich Purple' EPyc LLWP LRHS MBNS SPlb
'Rich Ruby' More than 30 suppliers
richardsonii EHyt MDKP MNrw SIgm SRms
WEll WGwG
'Ridgeway Red' EBee WEll WPPR WSPU
roezlii Regel see *P. laetus* subsp. *roezlii*
§ *rostriflorus* NNS 95-407 WCot
- 'Rosy Gem' new WSSM
'Rosy Blush' CBri EBee LPen LRHS MBNS SMrm
SPlb WHCG
'Roundhay' CFee
'Roy Davidson' see *P. procerus* 'Roy Davidson'
'Royal White' see *P.* 'White Bedder'
'Rubicundus' ♀H3 EBee EBre ECtt EHrv ELan EPfP

ERou GEil LHop LPen LRHS MAsh
MBNS MBri SAga SBai SCro SMrm
SPla SWvt WCot WCra WEll WFar
WHCG WMnd WPPR WSPU WWeb
'Ruby' see *P.* 'Schoenholzeri'
'Ruby Field' EBee EOrc EPyc MWgw WEll
WHCG WPPR
'Ruby Gem' LPen LRHS MBNS
rupicola ♀H4 EHyt GCrs GKev GTou LHop LRHS
NSla NWCA SIgm WAbe WLin
WWin
- 'Albus' NSla WAbe
- 'Conwy Lilac' WAbe
- 'Conwy Rose' WAbe
- 'Diamond Lake' CMea NLAp WPat
- 'Russian River' EBee EWes LAst LLWP LPen LRHS
MCLN NBur SGar SMrm SOkh SPlb
SWal WHCG WPPR WPer WSPU
rydbergii CTCP EPot NLAp
* Saskatoon hybrids EBee
§ 'Schoenholzeri' ♀H4 More than 30 suppliers
scouleri see *P. fruticosus* var. *scouleri*
secundiflorus EBee
§ *serrulatus* CNic CTCP EBee EPot EWes GTou
LPen MSte MWgw NLAp SBri SGar
SHFr SMad WBVN WHrl WKif WSPU
- 'Albus' EBee LPen MSte SIgm WPPR WSPU
'Shell Pink' LPen WPPR WPer
* 'Sherbourne Blue' GBuc SLon WEll WPer
* 'Shrawley' WPer
'Sissinghurst Pink' see *P.* 'Evelyn'
'Six Hills' NLAp SRms WAbe WHCG WLin
WPat WSPU
'Skyline' COkL EPfP
smallii CMHG EBee EDAr EMan EWTr
EWes LPVe LPen LPhx MHar MSPs
NLAp NWCA SCro SGar SIgm SIng
WHoo WWeb
'Snow Storm' see *P.* 'White Bedder'
'Snowflake' see *P.* 'White Bedder'
sonomensis see *P. newberryi* subsp.
sonomensis
'Sour Grapes' hort. see *P.* 'Stapleford Gem'
§ 'Sour Grapes' ♀H3-4 More than 30 suppliers
'Southcombe Pink' CWCL LPen MLLN WEll WHCG
WPPR
'Southgate Gem' GKir LPen LRHS MNrw MWat
SCro SWvt WEll WHCG WPPR
'Souvenir d'Adrian CBri LPen
Regnier'
'Souvenir d'André Torres' LLWP LPen WEll WPPR
'Souvenir d'André see *P.* 'Chester Scarlet'
Torres' misapplied
§ 'Stapleford Gem' ♀H3 More than 30 suppliers
'Strawberry Fizz' CWCL LPen MBNS
strictus EBee EGoo EMan EWTr LPVe LPen
LPio MBNS MHar MLLN NLAp
SCro SGar SIgm SRms WPer WSPU
'Stromboli = 'Yaboli' EBee MBri
subglaber EBee
'Sutton's Pink Bedder' CWCL EBee LRHS MBNS SPlb WEll
WSPU
'Sylvia Buss' LPen
tall pink see *P.* 'Welsh Dawn'
N 'Taoensis' EWes SGar WEll
taosensis see *P. crandallii* subsp. *taosensis*
teucrioides EPot NLAp NWCA WLin
- JCA 1717050 CPBP
'The Juggler'PBR EPfP LPen LRHS MBNS WFar WWol
thompsoniae new WLin
§ 'Thorn' More than 30 suppliers
'Threave Pink' CWCL ERou LLWP SMrm SPoG
SWvt WCom WEll WLin WMoo
WPPR

*	'Threave White'	WPen
	'Torquay Gem'	CWCL GBuc LPen SDys SOkh
		WHCG WPer
	tracyi	CPBP
	'True Sour Grapes'	see *P.* 'Sour Grapes'
	'Tubular Bells Red' **new**	NPri
§	*tusharensis*	CPBP EBee SBla
	'Twinkle Toes' **new**	SECG
§	*unilateralis*	CMHG
	utahensis	CBot CMHG EBee GBri SAga
	venustus	CFir EBee GBuc GKev MHar
		MNrw SGar SRms SRot WHCG
		WRos WWye
	Vesuvius = 'Yasius'	CBel CStr EBee EBre EPyc GKir
		LPen MBri SGar WEll WFar
	virens	CNic NLAp WPat WPer
*	- *albus*	MDKP WWin
	virgatus subsp.	see *P. deaveri*
	arizonicus	
	- subsp. *asa-grayi*	see *P. unilateralis*
	- 'Blue Buckle' **new**	CPBP EBee EShb WWeb
	- subsp. *virgatus*	CMHG NLAp
	'Volcano Fujiyama' **new**	CBri
	'Volcano Vesuvius' **new**	CBri
	watsonii	CStr CTCP EBee EMan MLLN SRms
		WHCG WHoo
	'Wedding Bells'	CStr
§	'Welsh Dawn'	LPen WEll WPPR WSPU
§	*whippleanus*	CBri EBee EWTr LPen MSte NChi
		SAga WAbb WBea
	- 'Chocolate Drop'	CBgR WGMN
§	'White Bedder' ♀H3	More than 30 suppliers
	'Whitethroat'	LLWP LPen LRHS MBNS SAga SLon
		WEll WHCG WPPR WPer WSPU
		WWin
	wilcoxii	EBee
	'Willy's Purple'	SLon WPPR
§	'Windsor Red'	CBod EBee EBre ECtt EPfP ERou
		LPen LRHS MAsh MBNS MSPs
		MSte SBai SGar SUsu SWal SWvt
		WCot WGor WHCG WPPR WSPU
		WSSM
§	*wislizeni*	EBee EPfP MLan MNrw MOne
		SRms

Pentaglottis (Boraginaceae)

§	*sempervirens*	CArn EPfP MHer MSal WHen
		WWye
	- 'Ballydowling' **new**	CNat

Pentapterygium see *Agapetes*

Pentas (Rubiaceae)

	lanceolata	CHal ELan LRHS MBri

Peperomia (Piperaceae)

§	*argyreia* ♀H1	MBri
	arifolia	CHal
	caperata	LRHS MBri
	clusiifolia	CHal
	- 'Variegata' (v)	CHal
	glabella	CHal
	- 'Variegata' (v)	CHal
	obtusifolia 'Jamaica'	MBri
	- (Magnoliifolia Group)	MBri
	'Golden Gate' (v)	
	- - 'Greengold'	CHal MBri
	- - 'USA' (v)	MBri
	- 'Tricolor' (v)	MBri
	orba 'Pixie'	MBri
I	- 'Pixie Variegata' (v)	MBri
	pulchella	see *P. verticillata*
	sandersii	see *P. argyreia*
	scandens ♀H1	MBri

	- 'Variegata' (v)	CHal MBri
§	*verticillata*	CHal

pepino see *Solanum muricatum*

peppermint see *Mentha piperita*

Perezia (Asteraceae)

linearis	GBuc
recurvata	GTou

Pericallis (Asteraceae)

§	*lanata* (L'Hér.) B. Nord.	CHll ELan MBlu SAga WDyG
	- Kew form	CRHN CSpe SAga SMrm
	multiflora	LHop SAga

Perilla (Lamiaceae)

§	*frutescens* var.	CArn WJek
	crispa ♀H2	
	- green-leaved	EOHP
	- var. *nankinensis*	see *P. frutescens* var. *crispa*
	- var. *purpurascens*	CArn CSpe EOHP WJek

Periploca (Asclepiadaceae)

	graeca	CArn CBcs CMac CRHN GQui ITer
		SLon SYvo WSHC
	purpurea B&SWJ 7235	WCru
	sepium	CPLG

Peristrophe (Acanthaceae)

speciosa	ECre ERea

Pernettya see *Gaultheria*

Perovskia (Lamiaceae)

	abrotanoides **new**	XPep
	atriplicifolia	CArn CBot CDul CMea GPoy
		MHer WHCG WPer
	- 'Little Spire' PBR	ENot MAsh MBri NPro WShp
	'Blue Haze'	GCal
	'Blue Spire' ♀H4	More than 30 suppliers
	'Filigran'	ECGP EFou GBuc LAst LRHS NSti
		SChu SMHy SPet WSpi XPep
	'Longin' **new**	XPep
	scrophulariifolia	WCom

Persea (Lauraceae)

	ichangensis	CPLG
	indica	CFil CPLG WPGP
	lingue	LEdu
	thunbergii	CFil CHEx

Persicaria (Polygonaceae)

§	*affinis*	CBcs CSBt EBlw GAbr GKir MBar
		MTho MWhi NBro NVic SMer
		SWat WBVN WBrE WCFE WFar
		WMoo
	- 'Darjeeling Red' ♀H4	More than 30 suppliers
	- 'Dimity'	see *P. affinis* 'Superba'
	- 'Donald Lowndes' ♀H4	More than 30 suppliers
	- 'Kabouter'	LBuc
	- 'Ron McBeath'	CRow
§	- 'Superba' ♀H4	More than 30 suppliers
	alata	see *P. nepalensis*
	alpina	CRow
	amphibia	CRow
§	*amplexicaulis*	CBre COld CRow ELan EMar LGro
		MBro MHer MWat MWgw NChi
		NFor NOrc SChu SEND WFar
		WHoo WMoo WRHF WTel WTin
		WWpP
	- 'Alba'	CBos CElw CHar CRow EBee
		ECGN ECha EFou EMan EPla ERou
		LHop LPhx MLLN SHar SMrm

SWat WBea WCAu WCot WFar WMoo WPnP WTin

- 'Atrosanguinea' CNic CRow CTri EBee ECha EGra EMFW EMan EPla ERou GGar LPhx LRHS MFir MRav MWgw NBir NDov NVic SPer SRms SWvt WFar WOld WWin WWpP
- 'Baron' **new** CRow
- 'Border Beauty' **new** EBee
- 'Clent Charm' WSPU
- 'Cottesbrooke Gold' CRow WCot
- 'Dikke Floskes' **new** CRow
- 'Firedance' LPhx NDov SMHy SMrm SWat WCot
- 'Firetail' ♀H4 More than 30 suppliers
- 'High Society' **new** EBee
- 'Inverleith' CBre CDes CHar CKno CRow EBee ECha ECtt EPla WBVN WMoo WOld WPGP
- 'Orange Crest' **new** EBee
- * var. *pendula* CRow EBee ECha NBir SBla WBea WCot WFar WMoo
- 'Pink Lady' **new** CRow
- 'Rosea' CBos CRow EBee ECGN ECha ELan EMan EPPr EPla EWTr LPhx MBri MRav NBro NDov NSti SDys SWat WBea WCAu WCot WFar WMoo WPGP WSpi
- 'Rowden Gem' CRow EPla WMoo
- 'Rowden Jewel' CRow EPla
- 'Rowden Rose Quartz' CRow
- 'Summer Dance' EBee EFou NDov
- Taurus = 'Blotau' CElw CRow EBee EGle EPla ERou MLLN SMHy WFar WPGP WTin

§ *bistorta* CAgr CArn CHar CRow ELau GBar GPoy MHer MSal MWhi NBir NGHP NSco SWat WCra WHHs WSel WWpP WWye

- subsp. *carnea* CRow EBee ECha EMan EWsh NBir NDov SLon WFar WMoo
- 'Hohe Tatra' CRow EBre EMan GKir LPhx MTed WFar WTMC
- 'Superba' ♀H4 More than 30 suppliers

bistortoides MSal

* 'Blush Clent' WSPU WTin

campanulata CElw CRow EChP ECha ECtt EMar EWTr GAbr GBuc GCal GGar MHar MWgw NBid NBro NFor NGdn SPer WBcn WBea WCom WFar WMoo WOld WWin WWye

- Alba Group CElw CRow EWTr GCal GGar GKir MWgw NBro NGdn NSti WHer WLin WMoo WWye
- 'Madame Figard' CRow
- 'Rosenrot' CBre CKno CRow EMan EPPr GBuc GCal NBir NGdn NHol NLar SSpi SWat WBea WCot WFar WWpP
- 'Southcombe White' CRow EPPr EPla GBri WBea

capitata CHal CPLG CRow EMan SHFr SIng SRms WBea WCom WEas WMoo

- CC 3693 WCot
- from Afghanistan WBea
- 'Pink Bubbles' ECtt SPet SWvt

conspicua EBee

coriacea CRow

* *dschawachiswillii* **new** SMHy

elata CRez EBee EMan EMar EMon GBuc GGar NBur

emodi CRow

longiseta MSal

§ *macrophylla* CRow EBee LDai MTed WFar

microcephala CRow EWes MHer SAga SMac

- 'Red Dragon' More than 30 suppliers

- var. *wallichii* CRow
- * *milletii* CRow EBee EBre EWes GBuc GKir MBri MTho SMac WCAu WCru WFar WMoo WTin
- § *mollis* CRow EBee WPGP
- * var. *frondosa* EBee
- *nakaii* EBee
- *neofiliformis* EBee
- § *nepalensis* CRow EPPr SMad
- § *odorata* CArn ELau EOHP EPza GPoy LRav MHer MSal NGHP SHDw SIde WJek
- *orientalis* MSal SMrm
- * *paleaceum* **new** EBee
- *polymorpha* CBct CDes CFwr CKno CRow EBee EBre ECGN ECha EFou EGle EHrv ELan EMan EMon LHop LPhx MTed NCGa NDov SMad SMrm SSpe WCom WCot WFar WLow WMoo WTin
- *polystachya* see *P. wallichii*
- * *regeliana* EBee LRHS
- § *runcinata* CPLG CRow EBee ECtt EMar GGar NBid NBir NLar WBar WFar WHer WMoo WPer
- Needham's form CDes CRow NBid
- *scoparia* see *Polygonum scoparium*
- *sphaerostachya* Meisn. see *P. macrophylla*
- *tenuicaulis* CBre CLyd CRow EBee EHrv EMon EPPr EPar EPla GGar MFir NGar SBla WCot WCru WFar WMoo
- § *tinctoria* EBee EOHP
- *vacciniifolia* ♀H4 More than 30 suppliers
- 'Ron McBeath' CRow
- § *virginiana* CMHG CRow ECtt EMan MSal NLar WMoo WTMC
- Compton's form CBct CRow EBee ECha EMan EPPr LDai MAvo WCot WMoo WTMC WWpP
- 'Filiformis' ECtt MAvo WCot
- 'Lance Corporal' CFwr CRow EBee EFou SMrm WMnd WMoo
- Variegata Group CBot CM&M CRez CRow EBee EChP ECha EMan ERou GCal MBNS NLar WAul WCot WMoo WOld
- § - 'Painter's Palette' (v) More than 30 suppliers
- white-flowered EPPr GCal
- *vivipara* CRow NLar
- § *wallichii* CRow EBee ECha GBri NLar NSti SDix WCot WMoo WOld
- § *weyrichii* EMan EMon EPPr GCal MTed NBir NBro NLar SMrm WBea WCot WMoo

persimmon see *Diospyros virginiana*

persimmon, Japanese see *Diospyros kaki*

Petalostemon see *Dalea*

Petamenes see *Gladiolus*

Petasites (Asteraceae)

- *albus* EBee GGar GPoy GSki NLar
- *formosanus* LEdu
- B&SWJ 3025 WCru
- *fragrans* CNat ELan EMon EPar MGas MHer MSta NLar SWat WFar WHer
- § *frigidus* var. *palmatus* CRow EBee EPla LEdu MWgw NLar NSti WCru
- JLS 86317CLOR SMad WCot
- var. *palmatus* EFou NSti SSpi
- 'Golden Palms'

hybridus	EMFW LEdu SECG WHer	
japonicus	EBee	
- var. *giganteus*	CArn CHEx CRow ECha ELan	
	EMon EPar EPfP EUJe LEdu NVic	
	WCra WCru WMoo WShp WTMC	
§ - - 'Nishiki-buki' (v)	CHEx CMCo CRow EBee ECoo	
	EMan EMon EPPr EPla EUJe IBlr	
	ITer MFOX NSti SMad WCHb WCot	
	WCru WFar WMoo WPGP WPnP	
	WTMC	
- - 'Variegatus'	see *P. japonicus* var. *giganteus*	
	'Nishiki-buki'	
- f. *purpureus*	CDes EBee EMan EPPr WCot WCru	
	WPGP WPnP	
palmatus	see *P. frigidus* var. *palmatus*	
paradoxus	CDes CLAP EBee LEdu MRav NLar	
	SMad WCot	

Petrea (Verbenaceae)
volubilis	LRHS SOWG WMul	

Petrocallis (Brassicaceae)
lagascae	see *P. pyrenaica*	
§ *pyrenaica*	NWCA WLin	

Petrocoptis (Caryophyllaceae)
pardoi **new**	WLin	
pseudoviscosa	EHyt WAbe	
pyrenaica	EBur SBla SRms	
§ - subsp. *glaucifolia*	CNic EDAr EMan GTou NBir NLar	

Petrocosmea (Gesneriaceae)
new	LAma	
- B&SWJ 7249 from	WCru	
Thailand		
kerrii B&SWJ 6634	WCru	

Petrophytum (Rosaceae)
caespitosum	CGra CMea GTou NSla	
cinerascens	NWCA SIng	
§ *hendersonii*	GGar NHol NWCA WAbe	

Petrorhagia (Caryophyllaceae)
illyrica subsp.	SPet	
haynaldiana		
'Pink Starlets' **new**	LRav	
§ *saxifraga* ♀H4	CNic EBre EBur EPAt MBow NJOw	
	NPri SAga SGar SRms WBea WMoo	
	WPer WWhi	
§ - 'Rosette'	MTho WWin	

Petroselinum (Apiaceae)
§ *crispum*	CArn CSev EDAr EPAt GPoy	
	GWCH ILis LRHS MBar MDun	
	NBlu NGHP SECG SIde SWal	
	WLHH WPer WSel WWye	
- 'Bravour' ♀H4	ELau MBow MHer	
- 'Darki'	CSev NGHP NPri	
- French	CArn EDAr ELau MBow MHer	
	NBlu NPri NVic WJek WLHH	
	WWye	
- 'Greek'	ELau	
- 'Italian'	see *P. crispum* var. *neapolitanum*	
§ - var. *neapolitanum*	ELau GWCH MHer SIde WLHH	
- 'Super Moss Curled'	NVic	
§ - var. *tuberosum*	MHer SIde WHer	
hortense	see *P. crispum*	
tuberosum	see *P. crispum* var. *tuberosum*	

Petteria (Papilionaceae)
ramentacea	EGFP EPfP NLar SLPl WBVN	

Petunia (Solanaceae)
* 'Angels Blue' **new**	LAst	

Blue Spark	LAst	
= 'Dancasblue'[PBR]		
(Cascadias Series) **new**		
Carillon Series	see *Calibrachoa* Carillon Series	
Cascadias Yellow Eye	LAst	
= 'Dancasye' [PBR]		
(Cascadias Series)		
♀H3 **new**		
'Charlie's Angels Pink'	LAst	
(Charlie's Angel		
Series) **new**		
Conchita Doble Series	LAst	
'Conchita Doble		
Dark Blue'		
I - 'Conchita Doble	LAst	
Lavender'		
- 'Conchita Doble	LAst	
Orchid Lace' **new**		
- 'Conchita Doble Pink'	LAst	
- 'Conchita Doble Velvet'	LAst	
new		
- 'Conchita Doble White'	LAst	
Doubloon Series Doubloon	LAst	
Blue Star = 'Dandbblst'		
(d) **new**		
- Doubloon Pink Star	LAst	
= 'Dandpkst' (d) **new**		
Million Bells Series	see *Calibrachoa* Million Bells Series	
Pink Spark	LAst	
= 'Dancaspink'[PBR]		
new		
Priscilla = 'Kerpril'[PBR]	LAst NPri	
(Tumbelina Series)		
'Purple Surprise' **new**	LAst	
Rosella = 'Kerros'	LAst	
(Tumbelina Series)		
Superbells Magenta **new**	NPri	
Superbells Royal	NPri	
Blue **new**		
Surfinia Baby Pink	LAst	
Morn **new**		
Surfinia Baby Red **new**	WHlf	
Surfinia Blue Spark **new**	LAst	
Surfinia Blue = 'Sunblue'	LAst NPri	
Surfinia Blue Vein	LAst NPri	
= 'Sunsolos'[PBR]		
Surfinia Double Purple	LAst	
= 'Keidopuel'[PBR] (d)		
Surfinia Hot Pink	LAst NBlu NPri	
= 'Marrose'[PBR]		
Surfinia Lime	LAst NBlu NPri WWol	
= 'Keiyeul'[PBR]		
Surfinia Pastel 2000	NPri	
= 'Sunpapi'		
Surfinia Patio Blue	LAst WWol	
= 'Keipabukas' **new**		
Surfinia Pink Ice	LAst NBlu NPri	
= 'Hakice'[PBR] (v)		
Surfinia Pink Vein	GKir NPri	
= 'Suntosol'[PBR] ♀H3		
Surfinia Purple	NPri	
= 'Shihi Brilliant' ♀H3		
Surfinia Purple	LAst	
Sunrise **new**		
Surfinia Purple Vein	WWol	
= 'Sunpurve'[PBR] ♀H3		
Surfinia Red	LAst NPri WWol	
= 'Keirekul' **new**		
Surfinia Rose Pink	WWol	
= 'Sunrospi'[PBR] **new**		
Surfinia Rose Vein	LAst	
= 'Sunrove' **new**		
Surfinia Sky Blue	LAst NPri	
= 'Keilavbu'[PBR] ♀H3		

Surfinia White GKir LAst WWol
= 'Kesupite'
Tumbelina Series LAst NPri
Tumbelina Candyfloss
- Tumbelina Julia LAst NPri
= 'Kerjul'[PBR]
- Tumbelina Margarita LAst
- Tumbelina Rosella LAst
Improved

Peucedanum (*Apiaceae*)

aegopodioides EGle
formosanum WCru
B&SWJ 3647
japonicum CSpe
litorale see *Kitagawia litoralis*
ostruthium GPoy
- 'Daphnis' (v) CDes CElw CSpe EBee EGle EMan
EMon EPPr LEdu MTed NChi
NGby NPro SMHy WCom WCot
WHrl WPGP
siamicum B&SWJ 264 WCru
verticillare CArn CSpe CTCP EBee EMan LPhx
MDun MWgw NBid NChi NDov
NLar SDix SIgm SMad SSpi WCom
WCot WMoo

Phacelia (*Hydrophyllaceae*)

bolanderi SPet
sericea new EMan NWCA WLin
tanacetifolia EWTr

Phaedranassa (*Amaryllidaceae*)

carmiolii WCot
dubia WCot
* **montana** LRHS
viridiflora WCot

Phaenocoma (*Asteraceae*)

prolifera SPlb

Phaenosperma (*Poaceae*)

globosa CHar CKno EBee EGle EHoe
EPPr EPla EPza EWes EWsh
LEdu LRHS NHol WBor WDyG
WPGP WPrP

Phaiophleps (*Iridaceae*)

nigricans see *Sisyrinchium striatum*

Phaius (*Orchidaceae*)

minor EFEx

Phalaris (*Poaceae*)

§ **aquatica** MGol
arundinacea CWCL EGra EMFW EPla LPVe MBNS
MGol MLan SPlb SWat WBan WTin
- 'Elegantissima' see *P.arundinacea* var. *picta*
'Picta'
- var. **picta** CBri CHEx CHrt CWib EMFW
GKir LRHS NArg NBid NBur NPer
SHel SLon SYvo WDin WFar
- - 'Aureovariegata' (v) CBcs CSWP MRav NGdn NPer
SWat WMoo
- - 'Feesey' (v) More than 30 suppliers
- - 'Luteopicta' (v) EBee EHoe EMan EPPr EPfP EPla
MMoz WLeb WTin WWpP
- - 'Luteovariegata' (v) EMon NGdn
§ - - 'Picta' (v) ♀[H4] COlW CRow EBre EHon ELan
ENot EPfP EPla GWCH IHMH LEdu
LGro LPBA LRHS MBar MWgw
MWod NBlu NFor NHol NSti SPer
SWal SWat WEas WMoo WWin
WWpP WWye

- - 'Streamlined' (v) EBee EMon EPla EWsh SLPl WFar
- - 'Tricolor' (v) CPen EBee EHoe EMon EOMN
EPla MBar WBea
canariensis LIck SWal
tuberosa stenoptera see *P. aquatica*

Phanerophlebia (*Dryopteridaceae*)

caryotidea see *Cyrtomium caryotideum*
falcata see *Cyrtomium falcatum*
fortunei see *Cyrtomium fortunei*

Pharbitis see *Ipomoea*

Phaseolus (*Papilionaceae*)

caracalla see *Vigna caracalla*

Phegopteris (*Thelypteridaceae*)

§ **connectilis** EFer EMon NMar NVic SRms
decursive-pinnata CFwr CLAP EMon GBri LEur NHol
NMar SPoG WRic WSpi
hexagonoptera LEur

Phellodendron (*Rutaceae*)

amurense CBcs CDul CFil CMCN ECre EPfP
EWTr GIBF LEdu LPan NLar SBLw
SPer SSpi WDin WNor WPic
- var. **sachalinense** CBcs GIBF LRHS WPGP
chinense CMCN
lavalleei EPfP WPGP

Phenakospermum (*Strelitziaceae*)

guianense XBlo

Philadelphus ✿ (*Hydrangeaceae*)

'Albâtre' (d) LRHS
'Atlas' (v) WCom
'Avalanche' CMHG EBee EBre GKir LRHS NLar
NPro SRms WDin WFar WHCG
'Beauclerk' ♀[H4] CDoC CDul CMHG CSBt CTri
EBee EBre ECrN ENot EPfP EWTr
GKir LRHS MGos MRav NBee
NHol NWea SLim SPer SReu SRms
SSpi SWal SWvt WHCG WKif
WWin
'Belle Etoile' ♀[H4] More than 30 suppliers
'Bicolore' MWya
'Boule d'Argent' (d) CMHG
'Bouquet Blanc' GKir GQui MRav NLar SPer SRms
brachybotrys CFil EPfP MRav NHol WHCG WPGP
'Buckley's Quill' (d) EPfP MRav MWya WBcn
'Burfordensis' EPfP SPer WCom
'Burkwoodii' LRHS SMer
aff. **calvescens** WCru
BWJ 8005 **new**
caucasicus GEil
coronarius CDul ENot EPfP LBuc LRHS MWat
MWhi NFor SGar SHBN SMer SPer
WBVN WDin XPep
- 'Aureus' ♀[H4] More than 30 suppliers
- 'Bowles' Variety' see *P. coronarius* 'Variegatus'
- 'Gold Mound' MGos MRav
§ - 'Variegatus' (v) ♀[H4] More than 30 suppliers
'Cotswold' **new** WBcn
'Coupe d'Argent' CPLG MRav
'Dame Blanche' (d) EWTr LRHS MAsh MRav NPro
delavayi CFil CPle EBee EPfP NWea SGar
SSpi WCru WHCG WPGP
- AC 1648 GGar
- EDHCH 97170 EPPr
- var. **calvescens** see *P. purpurascens*
'Enchantement' (d) MRav SDix
§ 'Erectus' CSBt CWib EBee EHol ENot EPfP
ISea MRav SMac SPla WCom WDin
WHCG WPat WTel

fragrans	CFil WPGP
'Frosty Morn' (d)	CBcs LBuc LRHS MGos SMac SPer SPla WCom WGwG
henryi	WPGP
incanus B&SWJ 8616	WCru
§ 'Innocence' (v)	More than 30 suppliers
'Innocence Variegatus'	see *P.* 'Innocence'
§ *insignis*	MRav WBod
keteleeri	GEil
x *lemoinei*	CTri EBee EWTr GEil GKir MGos NFor SHBN SMer WDin WFar WGwG WStI
- 'Erectus'	see *P.* 'Erectus'
- 'Lemoinei'	NWea
'Lemon Hill'	WBcn
lewisii	CFil ECre GKir LPhx
- L 1896	WPGP
- 'Waterton'	LBuc
madrensis	CFil LHop WPGP
- CD&R 1226	WPGP
'Manteau d'Hermine' (d) ♀H4	More than 30 suppliers
'Marjorie'	CHar
mexicanus	CFil MWya
- 'Rose Syringa'	CFil WPGP
microphyllus	CBot CDul CFil CMHG EBee ELan EPfP GEil GKir LAst LPhx LRHS MBro MRav MWhi NHol SLon SPer SReu SSpi WBVN WHCG WPat WSHC
- var. *occidentalis*	CFil NLar
'Miniature Snowflake' (d) **new**	WPat
'Minnesota Snowflake' (d)	CBcs EBee ECtt EWes LBuc LRHS MRav NHol NLar NPro WFar WRHF
'Mont Blanc'	CBcs WFar
'Mrs E.L. Robinson' (d)	EBee ECtt LAst LRHS
'Natchez' (d)	ECtt GKir MBNS SVil WBcn WTel
'Norma'	WBcn
'Oeil de Pourpre'	MRav WBcn
palmeri	CFil WPGP
pekinensis	CPLG ECre
pubescens	GEil
§ *purpurascens*	CFil EWes GIBF GKir MRav SSpi WBcn WPat
- BWJ 7540	WCru
x *purpureomaculatus*	WPat
'Russalka'	MWya
schrenkii	CFil WPGP
- B&SWJ 8465	WCru
§ 'Silberregen'	CDoC CFwr EBee ECtt EPfP EWTr LAst LRHS MBar MGos MRav NCGa NPro SHBN SPoG SRms SWvt WBod WFar WPat
Silver Showers	see *P.* 'Silberregen'
'Snow Velvet'	LRHS
'Snowflake'	CWSG EMil LAst NMoo
'Souvenir de Billiard'	see *P. insignis*
subcanus	MRav
'Sybille' ♀H4	CMHG ECrN ENot EPfP GKir LRHS MBri MRav SPer SPoG SRms SSpi WBcn WHCG WKif WPat WSHC
tenuifolius	CMCN GIBF NLar
tomentosus	CFil CPLG GEil WHCG WPGP
- B&SWJ 2707	WCru
'Velléda'	CFil
'Virginal' (d)	More than 30 suppliers
'Voie Lactée'	CFil GEil MRav
White Icicle	MBri
= 'Bialy Sopel' **new**	
White Rock = 'Pekphil'	CDoC COtt CWSG EBee LAst LRHS LTwo MAsh NMoo SPer WPat

Philesia (Philesiaceae)

buxifolia	see *P. magellanica*
§ *magellanica*	EMil GGGa GSki ITim SOkd SSpi WBod WCru WSHC
- 'Rosea'	CPLG

Phillyrea (Oleaceae)

angustifolia	CDul CFil CMCN CTri EBee EHol EPfP ERom MGos NPSI SEND SLPl SPer SSpi WBVN WBcn WDin WPGP WSHC XPep
- from Mallorca **new**	SSpi
- f. *rosmarinifolia*	CFil EPla LAst WPGP XPep
decora	see *Osmanthus decorus*
§ *latifolia*	CFil CHEx CPLG EBee EPfP LRHS SAPC SArc SLPl SSpi WBcn WDin WPGP XPep
media	see *P. latifolia*
I - 'Rodrigueziensis'	WCFE

Philodendron (Araceae)

epipremnum	see *Epipremnum pinnatum*
erubescens	LRHS
'Burgundy' ♀H1	
- 'Red Emerald'	CHal
scandens ♀H1 **new**	CHal XBlo
selloum	EAmu WMul
'Xanadu' **new**	XBlo

Phlebodium see *Polypodium*

Phleum (Poaceae)

bertolonii **new**	CRWN
pratense	CBig EFWa EHoe

Phlomis ✿ (Lamiaceae)

alpina	EBee
* *anatolica*	XPep
* - 'Lloyd's Variety'	CAbP CSam EBee ELan GCal LRHS MAsh MBri MSte SPer SSvw WCom WCot WPen
aff. *anisodonta*	WPhl
armeniaca	WPhl
atropurpurea	EBee GBin WPGP WPhl
betonicoides B&L 12600	EPPr
bourgaei 'Whirling Dervish' JMT 271	WPhl
bovei subsp. *maroccana*	CBot EBee GCal IFro LPio WOut WPhl XPep
breviflora	WPhl
capitata **new**	WLin
cashmeriana	CBot ECha LDai MGol NLar WCFE WPhl
chrysophylla ♀H3	CAbP CBot CStr EBee ECha ELan EMan EPfP LAst LRHS SBla SDix SDry SIgm SPer WCFE WCom WCot WPhl XPep
cretica	WPhl
* *cristata*	CCge
cypria **new**	WPhl XPep
- var. *occidentalis*	WPhl
§ 'Edward Bowles'	CBot SDry SIgm SLPl SLon SWvt WCom WCot WPhl XPep
* 'Elliot's Variety'	CPLG
fruticosa ♀H4	More than 30 suppliers
- 'Butterfly' **new**	XPep
grandiflora	CBot EBee SEND XPep
- JMT 256	WPhl
herba-venti **new**	XPep
italica	More than 30 suppliers
- 'Pink Glory'	WPhl
jeholensis	EBee
lanata ♀H3-4	CAbP CCge CStr EBee ELan EMan

	EPfP GEil LRHS MSte NCGa NPro SBla SDry SPer SPoG SSpi WEas WGer WKif WPhl WWye XPep
- 'Pygmy'	NPro SLon WPhl XPep
'Le Sud' **new**	XPep
leucophracta	EBee XPep
- 'Golden Janissary'	CFil EBee WPGP XPep
longifolia	CBgR CBot CHad EBee EPfP LHop LRHS SIgm SPer WGer XPep
- var. *bailanica*	LRHS SMac WFar WSPU
- var. *longifolia*	WPhl
lunariifolia	XPep
- JMT 258	WPhl
lychnitis	MWrn XPep
lycia	CStr LRHS SIgm WPhl XPep
megalantha	EBee
milingensis	EBee
monocephala	WPhl XPep
platystegia	WPhl
purpurea	CAbP CSam ELan EPfP GFlt LRHS MAsh MGol MHer NBir WCot WOVN WPhl WSHC XPep
- *alba*	CBot EPfP LHop WSHC XPep
- subsp. *almeriensis*	CPom CStr WPhl XPep
- subsp. *caballeroi* **new**	XPep
- 'Compact'	WPhl
rigida	EBee WCru
rotata	EBee
§ *russeliana* ♀[H4]	More than 30 suppliers
samia Boiss.	see *P. russeliana*
samia L.	CPom EBee EMar LDai MAvo MGol NChi NGdn NLar WCot WFar XPep
- JMT 285	LRHS WPhl
'Sunningdale Gold'	WPhl
tatsienensis var. *tatsienensis*	EBee
tuberosa	More than 30 suppliers
- 'Amazone'	CFir CHVG CKno EBee EBlw EChP ECha EFou EHrv EMan EPfP LAst LPhx MBri MCLN MTis NSti SAga SMad SMrm SUsu WCAu WCot WFar WTMC
viscosa misapplied	see *P. russeliana*
viscosa Poiret	WPhl XPep

Phlox ✿ (Polemoniaceae)

adsurgens ♀[H4]	EDAr ITim WAbe
- 'Alba'	NSla SBla WAbe
- 'Red Buttes'	CLyd EPot LPio SBla
- 'Wagon Wheel'	CLyd CWCL EBre ECtt EDAr EHyt EPot EWes GEdr GGar ITim LRHS NLAp NSla SIng SMrm SPlb SRms WAbe WCFE WCom WFar WLin WWin
alyssifolia **new**	CPBP
x *arendsii* 'Anja'	EBee WCot
- 'Early Star'	EBee
- 'Hilda'	CStr EBee
- 'Lilac Star'	CFir EFou LAst WHil
§ - 'Luc's Lilac'	CMHG CPrp EBee EMan EMar GBin LPhx LTwo NBro NDov NGdn NVic STes SVil
- 'Ping Pong'	EBee EFou LDai MBnl MTis NBPC NPro STes WSan
- 'Purple Star' **new**	MBnl
- 'Rosa Star'	CFir EBee LAst
- 'Sabine'	CFir EBee EFou
§ - Spring Pearl Series	CCol CHea CM&M EBee EChP EFou EGle NHol SBla WCot WTin
'Miss Jill'	
§ - - 'Miss Jo-Ellen'	EFou EGle GBri
§ - - 'Miss Karen'	CCol EChP EGle ERou NBro
§ - - 'Miss Margie'	CBos EBee EChP EFou EGle ERou GBri LAst NBir WHil
§ - - 'Miss Mary'	CCol CM&M EBee EChP EFou

	EGle GBri MDKP NHol NPro STes WHoo
§ - - 'Miss Wilma'	CCol WBar
- 'Suzanne'	EBee
austromontana	EPot ITim NWCA
bifida 'Alba'	LTwo WAbe
- blue	LRHS SBla SUsu
- 'Colvin's White'	CLyd EDAr SAga SBla
- 'Minima Colvin'	ECtt EPot
- 'Petticoat'	CLyd CMea CPBP EPot GEdr LRHS SBla SUsu WLin
- 'Ralph Haywood'	CLyd GBuc ITim NLAp WAbe WOBN
- 'Starbrite'	CLyd LRHS SHar WFar
- 'Thefi'	EWes LTwo
borealis	see *P. sibirica* subsp. *borealis*
* - *arctica*	EPot
bryoides	see *P. hoodii* subsp. *muscoides*
buckleyi	EFou
caespitosa	EWes ITim NDlv NMen NWCA
- subsp. *condensata*	see *P. condensata*
- subsp. *pulvinata*	see *P. pulvinata*
canadensis	see *P. divaricata*
carolina subsp. *angusta* **new**	EFou
- 'Bill Baker' ♀[H4]	More than 30 suppliers
- 'Magnificence'	CM&M CPrp EChP EGle EWes GBuc GMac LAst MSte SOkh SSvw WLow WSHC WTin
- 'Miss Lingard' ♀[H4]	CHea CMea CPrp CSam EChP EFou EGle EPfP GBuc GCal GMac LAst LRHS MBnl MRav MSte NBir NGdn NSti SAga SBla SChu SCro SPla WAul WCot WHil WLow WSHC WWin
* 'Chanel'	MLan
'Charles Ricardo'	CElw EBee ETow EWes GBuc MBro MCLN SAga SBri SMrm SUsu SVil WHoo
'Chattahoochee'	see *P. divaricata* subsp. *laphamii* 'Chattahoochee'
§ *condensata*	NLAp NWCA WAbe WPat
covillei	see *P. condensata*
'Daniel's Cushion'	see *P. subulata* 'McDaniel's Cushion'
diffusa	NMen
§ *divaricata* ♀[H4]	EHol EWTr GKir MRav MSte SBod SHBN SPlb WPer WWin
- f. *albiflora*	ELan
- 'Blue Dreams'	CElw CFir CHea CMHG EBre EChP EHrv EPPr GBuc GKir LRHS MNrw MSte MTis NDov NGdn NPPs SChu SMrm SOkh SPla SUsu WCAu WCom WCra WFar WHal WPGP WSan
- 'Blue Perfume'	CM&M CMHG EChP EFou ENor LPVe NBrk NBro NCGa NGdn NLar NMyG NSti WShp
- 'Clouds of Perfume'	CHea CM&M EBee EChP EMan GBri GEdr LAst LPVe LRHS MWgw NCGa NPPs NSti SBla SBod SMer SMrm SOkh STes SWat WAul WFar WLin WLow WSan WShp
- 'Dirigo Ice'	CLyd CPlt EBee EBre EHrv EMan GBri LHop NBrk NLar SAga SBla WFar WRHF
- 'Eco Texas Purple'	CPlt CRez EBee EChP ECtt EMan EPPr MHar NBrk SAga SIgm SMrm WFar WPGP
- 'Fuller's White'	CLyd
§ - subsp. *laphamii*	EGle EWes NSti SOkh SUsu WCru WFar WFoF
§ - - 'Chattahoochee' ♀[H4]	CBot CPBP CSpe CWCL EBre EChP ECtt EDAr EHyt ELan EPfP

EWes GBuc GMac LHop LRHS
MBow MBro MWgw NPPs SBla
SIng SMrm SOkh WCFE WCom
WHoo WSHC WWin
- - 'Chattahoochee   EDAr LRHS
  Variegated' (v)
§ - 'Louisiana Purple'   EBee SVil WSHC
- 'May Breeze'   CLyd EBre EGle EHrv GKir LAst
LHop LRHS MBow MCLN MNrw
MSte MWgw NBrk NCGa NGdn
SCro SMrm SPla WCAu WCom
WFar WIvy WPGP WSHC WShp
- 'Plum Perfect'   NLar SHar
* - 'White Perfume'   CM&M CMHG EBee EChP EFou
EMil EWes GBri LAst LPVe MBrN
MDKP MTis NBro NLar NSti SChu
SMrm
douglasii   NPol NWCA SRms
- 'Apollo'   CLyd CTri EDAr LRHS NHol NMen
SBla WWin
- 'Boothman's   CLyd CMea CWCL ECha EDAr
  Variety' ♀H4   ELan EPar EPfP EPot GKir LRHS
MWat NMen SRms WCom WEas
WWin
- 'Crackerjack' ♀H4   CLyd CMea CWCL ECtt EDAr ELan
EMlt EPfP GAbr GEdr GKev GKir
ITim LRHS MBow MHer NMen
NPro SBod SIng WFar WLin WShp
- 'Eva'   CLyd CM&M CWCL EBre EDAr
ELan EPot GKir GTou ITim LRHS
NBir NHol NMen NWCA SMrm
WLin WWin
- 'Galaxy'   CLyd EWes
- 'Ice Mountain'   ECho EDAr ELan EMlt ITim NMen
NWCA SRot WLin WRHF
- 'Iceberg' ♀H4   CLyd EPot ITim NMen WRHF
WWin
- 'Lilac Cloud'   NPro WShp
- Lilac Queen   see *P. douglasii* 'Lilakönigin'
§ - 'Lilakönigin'   EDAr WRHF
- 'Napoleon'   CPBP ITim LTwo NMen
- 'Ochsenblut'   EPot GEdr MDHE MHer
- 'Red Admiral' ♀H4   CNic CWCL EBre EWes GKir LRHS
NHol NMen SBod SMrm WCFE
WFar
- 'Rose Cushion'   EDAr EWes ITim LRHS MDHE
MHer NMen
- 'Rose Queen'   CLyd
- 'Rosea'   EBre EDAr ELan EPar LRHS NMen
NPol SBod SMer WFar
- 'Silver Rose'   GTou NWCA
- 'Sprite'   SRms
- 'Tycoon'   see *P. subulata* 'Tamaongalei'
- 'Violet Queen'   EWes WFar WPat
- 'Waterloo'   CLyd EPot ITim LRHS NMen SChu
I - 'White Admiral'   NPro SIng WBVN
'Geddington Cross'   MWgw
hendersonii   CGra
* 'Herfstsering'   EFou
hoodii   CLyd CPBP ECho
§ - subsp. *muscoides*   EWes
'Kelly's Eye' ♀H4   CLyd CM&M CPBP CSam EDAr
ELan EPot LRHS NHol NMen WFar
WLin WRHF
kelseyi   NWCA WAbe
- 'Lemhi Purple'   CGra CPBP SOkd
- 'Rosette'   CLyd EPot ESis LRHS MDKP NHol
NMen WPer
§ *latifolia*   EMan SAga
longifolia subsp.   CPBP SOkd
  brevifolia
'Louisiana'   see *P. divaricata* 'Louisiana Purple'
maculata   NOrc WBVN WPer
- 'Alba'   CMea WShp WTin

- 'Alpha' ♀H4   More than 30 suppliers
- Avalanche   see *P. maculata* 'Schneelawine'
- 'Delta'   CHea EBee EChP EMan GBuc
LRHS NBPC NFla NHol NSti SMad
SOkh SPer SWvt WCAu WFar
WPnP
- 'Natascha'   More than 30 suppliers
- 'Omega' ♀H4   More than 30 suppliers
- 'Princess Sturdza' ♀H4   CBos SDix
- 'Reine du Jour'   CPlt EBee EFou GMac LPhx MSte
NDov SAga SDys SMrm SOkh SUsu
WSHC
- 'Rosalinde'   EBee EBre EChP EMan EMar GBuc
LBBr LRHS MRav MSte MWgw
NBPC NFla NHol NLar SBla SChu
SPla SVil SWvt WCAu WHil WSHC
§ - 'Schneelawine'   EFou SChu
'Matineus'   LPhx
- 'Millstream'   see *P.* x *procumbens* 'Millstream'
muscoides   see *P. hoodii* subsp. *muscoides*
nana 'Mary Maslin'   SScr
nivalis   NMen
- 'Camlaensis'   CLyd
- 'Jill Alexander'   CMea
- 'Nivea'   EPot LRHS WAbe
ovata misapplied   see *P. latifolia*
paniculata   CBos CHad EBee GFlt LPhx NBid
NDov NFor SDix WCot WOld
WTin
- 'A.E. Amos'   ERou
- 'Aida'   CBcs EBee MWat
- var. *alba*   EBee GCal NDov SDix WCot WTin
- 'Alba Grandiflora' ♀H4   EHrv SBla WEas
- 'Amethyst' Foerster   CFir CFwr CSam CWCL EBee EGle
EHrv EPfP ERou GKir MCLN MTis
NBir NBlu NOrc SBod SMer WCAu
WFar WHrl WShp WWye
- 'Amethyst' misapplied   see *P. paniculata* 'Lilac Time'
- 'Ann' **new**   CFwr
- 'Anthony Six'   EBee
- 'Antoinette Six'   CFwr EBee MDKP
- 'Balmoral'   CFwr EBee ECtt GKir LLWP LRHS
MRav MSte NHol NPri NSti SMer
SWat SWvt
- 'Barnwell'   EFou
- 'Becky Towe'[PBR] (v)   COtt EBee EBre EGle ENor LRHS
- 'Betty Symons-Jeune'   CFwr
- 'Bill Green'   EBre LRHS
- 'Blue Boy'   CBri CElw CFwr EBee EGle ENot
ERou LRHS MBnl MDKP NBir
NBro WFar WHil WMoo WViv
- 'Blue Evening'   LPhx SMrm
- 'Blue Ice' ♀H4   EBee EBre EFou ELan EMar LPhx
LRHS MMHG MRav MWat SChu
SLon SMrm SPla
- 'Blue Mist'   EFou
- 'Blue Paradise'   CDes CElw CFwr CHar CSpe EChP
EFou EGle EMon LPVe LPhx LRHS
MAnH NCGa NGdn NSti SAga SBla
SMrm SVil SWat WFar WHil WPGP
WSHC WWye
- 'Blushing Bride'   SRms
- 'Border Gem'   CBcs CFwr EBee EBre ECtt EFou
ENot ERou GKir MSte MWgw
NChi NLRH NLar SMer SWat SWvt
WCot
- 'Branklyn'   EBee EBre GKir LRHS SMer WFar
- 'Bressingham White'   NBrk
- 'Brigadier' ♀H4   CBla CFwr CSam EBee EBre ECtt
ELan ENot EWTr GBin GKir LRHS
MDKP MFir MWat NFla NVic SPer
SPla SRms WCAu
- 'Bright Eyes' ♀H4   CBla CBri CFwr COtt EBee EBre
ECtt ENot ERou GKir LRHS MDKP

		NCGa SBod SMer STes SUsu SWvt
		WCAu WShp WTel
- 'Burgi'		CBos SDix
- 'Caroline van den Berg'		GKir SMer SRms
- 'Cecil Hanbury'		CFwr EBee ERou NBlu NLar SRms
- 'Charlotte' **new**		EFou
- 'Chintz'		EFou MRav SRms
- 'Cinderella'		CFwr EBee EFou ERou
§ - 'Cool of the Evening'		CBos CFwr LPhx
- Count Zeppelin		see *P. paniculata* 'Graf Zeppelin'
- 'Crème de Menthe' (v)		CFwr EBee MDKP
- 'Daisy Field' **new**		EFou
- 'Danielle'		CFwr
- 'Darwin's Choice'		see *P. paniculata* 'Norah Leigh'
- 'David'		EBee EBre EChP ECha EGle ERou
		IPot LAst LPVe LRHS MBnl MCLN
		NBid NCGa NChi NGby NOrc
		SLon SUsu WAul WBor WCAu
		WCot
- 'Discovery'		EBee ECGP EMar EOMN EWes SPla
		STes SWat
- 'Dodo		EHol
Hanbury-Forbes' ♥H4		
- 'Dresden China'		EBee SWat
- 'Duchess of York'		CBos
§ - 'Duesterlohe'		CElw CSam EBee EFou EGle ERou
		GBuc GMac MCLN NBPC NBir
		NLar NSti SMrm SPer WCAu WFar
		WHil WHoo
- 'Early Flower' **new**		CFwr
- 'Eclaireur' Lemoine		CFwr EBee SWat
- 'Eclaireur' misapplied		see *P. paniculata* 'Duesterlohe'
- 'Eden's Crush'		CM&M EBee EChP EFou NVic
- 'Eden's Flash'		EGle ERou WHil
- 'Eden's Glory'		EChP EGle
- 'Eden's Glow'		EChP WHil
- 'Eden's Smile'		CFwr EBee EChP EFou ERou SHar
- 'Elizabeth Arden'		CFwr EBee EFou ERou MSte NLar
		SWat
- 'Empty Feelings'PBR		EBee EChP EGle NBPC NSti WHil
- 'Etoile de Paris'		see *P. paniculata* 'Toits de Paris'
- 'Europa'		CBcs COlW EBee EBre ELan EPfP
		ERou LRHS MBri MFir MWat NBir
		NGdn NLar SBod SChu SPer SPla
		WCAu WFar WShp
- 'Eva Cullum'		EBee EBre ECtt EFou EGle GKir
		LRHS MBnl MCLN MRav MTis
		NBPC NPps SMer SPer SPet SWat
		WCot WHil WMoo
- 'Eventide' ♥H4		EBee EBre ECtt EFou ENot EPfP
		GKir LAst LRHS MCLN MWgw
		NLar SChu SMer SPer SPet SWat
		WCAu WCot
- 'Excelsior'		EBre MRav
- 'Fairy's Petticoat'		MWat
- 'Flamingo'		CFwr EBee EBre ERou LRHS MBrN
		NLar SWvt
- 'Franz Schubert'		CHrt CRez EBee EBre ECGP EFou
		EGle GKir GMac LRHS MAnH
		MRav NBir NChi NLar NSti SChu
		SMer STes SWat SWvt WCot WTel
§ - 'Frau Alfred von		COlW EBee MBri SMrm
Mauthner'		
- 'Frosted Elegance' (v)		EBee EChP EPPr MBnl WHil
- 'Fujiyama'		see *P. paniculata* 'Mount Fuji'
- 'Glamis'		MWat
- 'Gnoom' **new**		CFwr
- 'Goldmine'PBR (v)		CFai MCCP MLLN WCot
§ - 'Graf Zeppelin'		CBla CFwr ELan EWll LRHS MWat
		SRms
- 'Hampton Court'		NBrk
- 'Harlequin' (v)		CBos CElw CMil EBee EBre ECha
		EHoe ERou GBuc GFlt GKir MCCP
		MCLN NBPC NBid NLar NSti SPer

		SPla SUsu WCAu WCom WCot
		WFar WLin WTel
I - 'Hesperis'		LPhx MAnH SMHy SMrm SUsu
- 'Iceberg'		MFir
- 'Iris'		CDes EGle GBuc LPio SRms
- 'Jubilee'		CFwr
- 'Judy'		EBee NBro
- 'Jules Sandeau'		CFwr EBee EBre LRHS MBri SMrm
§ - 'Juliglut'		CBri EBee EChP ERou MBnl MWat
		NCGa SWat WCot
- July Glow		see *P. paniculata* 'Juliglut'
- 'Katarina'		CElw CFwr EBee EChP ECtt EPfP
		MBnl MCLN NCGa SUsu WBor
- 'Katherine' **new**		CFwr
- 'Kirchenfuerst'		CFwr EBee MBri NBir NFla SMrm
- 'Kirmeslaendler'		CBcs EBee ERou LRHS MLLN NLar
		SVil WHil
- 'Lady Clare'		SRms
- 'Landhochzeit' **new**		EBee SLon
* - 'Laura'		CM&M COtt EBee EFou EGle ERou
		IPot NBPC NBro NVic SMrm STes
		WFar WHil WHoo WLow WShp
		WWol
§ - 'Lavendelwolke'		CFwr EBee GCal NBir NLar SWat
		WAul
- Lavender Cloud		see *P. paniculata* 'Lavendelwolke'
- 'Le Mahdi' ♥H4		CFwr EBee ELan GBin MBrN MRav
		MWat SRms
- 'Lichtspel'		EFou LPhx
§ - 'Lilac Time'		CBla CFwr EBee EHrv EOMN EWll
		MBnl MDKP MSte MTis NFla SWvt
- 'Little Boy'		CElw EBee EChP EGle ERou LRHS
		MDKP NFla NLar STes WFar WHil
- 'Little Laura'		CMHG MBnl NCGa NLar
- 'Little Princess'		CFwr EGle MBnl NCGa NLar
		WWol
- 'Lizzy'PBR		ERou MBri NCGa
- 'Look Again'		CFwr
- 'Manoir d'Hézèques'		WCot
- 'Mary Christine' (v)		EBee
- 'Mary Fox'		CSam
- 'Mia Ruys'		EBee ERou GMac MBri MLLN
		SMrm
- 'Mies Copijn'		CFwr EBee WFar
- 'Milly van Hoboken'		CBos SCro
- 'Miss Elie'		CHea CM&M EBee EGle ERou
		WFar WHil WHoo
- 'Miss Holland'		CHea EBee EChP EGle WHoo
		WLow WSan
- 'Miss Jessica'		EBee ERou LAst WHil
- 'Miss Jill'		see *Phlox* x *arendsii* Spring Pearl
		Series 'Miss Jill'
- 'Miss Jo-Ellen'		see *Phlox* x *arendsii* Spring Pearl
		Series Miss Jo-Ellen'
- 'Miss Karen'		see *Phlox* x *arendsii* Spring Pearl
		Series 'Miss Karen'
- 'Miss Kelly'		CM&M COtt EBee WHoo
- 'Miss Margie'		see *Phlox* x *arendsii* Spring Pearl
		Series 'Miss Margie'
- 'Miss Mary'		see *Phlox* x *arendsii* Spring Pearl
		Series 'Miss Mary'
- 'Miss Pepper'		EBee EFou EMil ERou EWll IPot
		LRHS MBnl MCLN NLar SMrm
		WCAu WFar WHil
- 'Miss Universe'		CM&M CRez EBee EGle MCCP
		WHil WHoo WSan
- 'Miss Wilma'		see *Phlox* x *arendsii* Spring Pearl
		Series 'Miss Wilma'
- 'Monica Lynden-Bell'		CBos CDes CFai CM&M CMdw
		CSam EBee EChP GBri LAst MAvo
		MBnl MCLN MEHN MMil MNrw
		NBPC NChi NDov NLar SMrm SPla
		STes WAul WCot WFar WPGP
- 'Mother of Pearl' ♥H4		EBee EBre ELan EMar EOMN LRHS

		MCLN MWat NVic SBla SPer SPet SVil
§	– 'Mount Fuji' ♀H4	More than 30 suppliers
	– 'Mount Fujiyama'	see *P. paniculata* 'Mount Fuji'
	– 'Mrs A.E. Jeans'	SRms
	– 'Natural Feelings' **new**	CSpe EBee MCLN NBro SPoG WCot WHil WSan WTMC
	– 'Newbird'	CSBt EBee SRms
	– 'Nicky'	see *P. paniculata* 'Duesterlohe'
§	– 'Norah Leigh' (v)	More than 30 suppliers
	– 'Orange Perfection'	see *P. paniculata* 'Prince of Orange'
	– 'Othello'	EBee EMar MCLN NSti SLon
	– 'Otley Choice'	EBee LAst LRHS MRav MSte MWat NLar NSti SChu SCoo SPet SVil
	– 'P.D. Williams'	WCot
	– 'Pastorale'	MWat WCot WTel
	– 'Pat Coleman'	EFou
	– 'Pax'	EBee EMon ERou LPhx
	– 'Petite Chérie' **new**	WCot
	– 'Pink Posie' PBR (v)	MBri WFar WWeb
	– 'Popeye'	CFwr EBee ECtt MBri NLar
§	– 'Prince of Orange' ♀H4	More than 30 suppliers
	– 'Prospero' ♀H4	CHar CSam EBee EHrv EOrc GFlt NBid SChu SMer SUsu SVil WCAu WTel
	– 'Rainbow'	CFwr EBee EGle LPVe
	– 'Rapture'	MWat
	– 'Red Feelings' PBR **new**	EBee NBro WHil WSan
	– 'Red Indian'	MWat SMer
	– 'Red Riding Hood'	CFwr EBee LAst WCot WHil
I	– 'Reddish Hesperis' **new**	SMHy
	– 'Rembrandt'	EBee EBre ERou GBri LRHS NBlu SBla WCot
	– 'Rijnstroom'	CBcs CSBt EBee EBre ECot ERou LRHS MBnl MBow WFar WShp WTel
	– 'Robert Poore' **new**	EFou
	– 'Rosa Pastell'	CBos CFwr EBee EFou EGle EHrv EMon LPhx SAga SCro
	– 'Rosa Spier'	CFwr EBee
	– 'Rosy Veil' **new**	CFwr
	– 'Rubymine' PBR (v)	CFai EChP ERou MBnl
	– 'Russian Violet'	MWat
	– 'San Antonio'	CFwr EBre WFar
	– 'Sandringham'	EBee EBre EHrv EPfP GKir LRHS MNrw MRav MSte NBir NHol SBla SMer SPer SWvt WCAu
§	– 'Schneerausch'	GKir LPhx
	– 'Septemberglut'	CFwr EBee NLar
	– 'Shortwood' **new**	EFou
	– 'Silvermine' (v)	CFai EBee EChP MCCP SDnm
	– 'Sir Malcolm Campbell'	CFwr EBee
	– 'Skylight'	MWat NVic SPer
	– 'Snow White'	NVic
	– Snowdrift	see *P. paniculata* 'Schneerausch'
	– 'Speed Limit' **new**	CFwr
	– 'Speed Limit 45' **new**	WCot
	– 'Spitfire'	see *P. paniculata* 'Frau Alfred von Mauthner'
	– 'Starburst'	CRez EBee NGdn
	– 'Starfire' ♀H4	More than 30 suppliers
	– 'Steeple Bumpstead'	EGle WCot
	– 'Sweetheart'	GFlt
	– 'Tenor'	CFir EBee EBre EChP EFou ERou GKir LRHS MDKP MSte NGdn NPri SAga SBla SChu SPet SPla SWvt WCAu WCot WFar WHrl WLow WMoo WShp
	– 'The King'	EBee EChP EGle EWll GBri LRHS MBnl MDKP NBro SUsu SWat WBor WCot WHil WTel
	– 'Toits de Paris'	see *P. paniculata* 'Cool of the Evening'
	misapplied	

	– 'Toits de Paris' ambig.	SMHy
§	– 'Toits de Paris' Symons-Jeune	LPhx MWat WSHC
	– 'Uspekh'	CFwr EBee EBre EFou EMar EOMN EPPr EWes MCLN MDKP MSte MTis SChu SPer SVil WFar
	– 'Utopia'	LPhx SMHy SUsu
	– 'Van Gogh'	CFwr EBee EHrv
	– 'Vintage Wine'	ENot MSte
	– 'Violetta Gloriosa'	CBos EFou LPhx
	– 'Visions'	EBee WHil
	– 'We Du' **new**	EFou
	– 'Wennschondennschon' **new**	GBin
	– 'White Admiral' ♀H4	More than 30 suppliers
	– 'Wilhelm Kesselring'	CFai CFwr GBin NFla WBor
	– 'Windsor' ♀H4	CBla CBri CFwr EBee EBre EFou EPfP ERou GBri GKir LRHS MCLN MLLN NDov NHol SCoo SRms SWvt WCAu
I	– 'Zurstock Rose' **new**	CFwr
pilosa		ECha EMan GMac NPro WFar
	– subsp. *ozarkana*	SSpi
§	x *procumbens* 'Millstream' ♀H4	EBee EDAr GAbr SAga SBla SHar
	– 'Variegata' (v)	EBee ECha EDAr EMlt EPot LRHS MDKP NHol NWCA SBla SPlb WCom WFar WLin WPat WWin
§	*pulvinata*	CPBP
	'Sandra' **new**	LRHS
	'Scented Pillow'	LRHS
§	*sibirica* subsp. *borealis*	EDAr
	stansburyi	EHyt
	stolonifera	CBcs EPar GKir MNrw
I	– 'Alba' **new**	SMac
	– 'Ariane'	EBee ECha EDAr EPar GEdr MNrw SBla SCro SMrm WFar WWin
I	– 'Atropurpurea'	CBcs WShp
	– 'Blue Ridge' ♀H4	CFir EBee EBre ECha EDAr EMan EPar EPfP GBuc GEil GKir IMGH LAst MBri MRav SMac SMer SMrm SRms WFar WRHF WSan WShp WWin
	– 'Bob's Motley' (v)	EMan WCot
	– compact	EPot
	– 'Compact Pink'	WFar
	– 'Fran's Purple'	CLyd EBee EMan GMac NBro SCro WCFE WFar WPGP WSPU WViv
	– 'Home Fires'	EBee EDAr GAbr MDKP MFir MNrw NBro NLar SAga SBla SCro SMrm SPlb WShp
	– 'Mary Belle Frey'	EMan GKir MSte WFar WWin
	– 'Montrose Tricolor' (v) **new**	EMan NBro
	– 'Pink Ridge'	CWCL EWll MBri MNrw NBir
	– 'Purpurea'	EBee MDKP SMac WShp
	– 'Sherwood Purple'	IFro
	– variegated (v)	MNrw WCot
	– 'Violet Vere'	CLyd EDAr GBuc MNrw SMrm WCom WFar
subulata		EPar GKir NWCA WBrE
	– 'Alexander's Surprise'	CMHG CMea CWCL ECtt EDAr EPfP LBee LRHS MDKP NBir NFla SChu SPlb
	– 'Amazing Grace'	CWCL EBre EDAr ELan ESis EWes GKir LBee LHop LRHS MHer NHol NSla NWCA SChu SIng WBVN WWin
	– 'Apple Blossom'	EDAr NPro SRms
	– 'Atropurpurea'	EBre LRHS NFor NJOw NPro WShp WWin
	– 'Beauty of Ronsdorf'	see *P. subulata* 'Ronsdorfer Schöne'
	– 'Betty'	ECtt MBNS MDHE NJOw

- 'Blue Eyes'	see *P. subulata* 'Oakington Blue Eyes'
- 'Blue Saucer'	MDHE
- 'Bonita'	CPBP CWCL EBre EHyt GKir LBee LRHS SMer WWin
- 'Bressingham Blue Eyes'	see *P. subulata* 'Oakington Blue Eyes'
- 'Brightness'	CNic EBre GKir GTou LRHS NHol
- 'Candy Stripe'	see *P. subulata* 'Tamaongalei'
- 'Cavaldes White'	MDKP WShp
- 'Christine Bishop'	LRHS
- 'Coral Eye'	EPfP
- 'Drumm'	see *P. subulata* 'Tamaongalei'
- 'Emerald Cushion'	CSam CTri ECtt EDAr EMan MDKP MHer NFor WCFE WRHF
- 'Emerald Cushion Blue'	CNic EBre EMlt EPfP EWTr GKir GTou MBow NMen NPri NPro SBla SMrm SPlb WPer WShp
- 'Fairy'	WPer
- 'G.F.Wilson'	see *P. subulata* 'Lilacina'
- 'Greencourt Purple'	EDAr NBur
* - 'Holly'	EPot ITim MDHE NMen
- 'Jupiter'	SChu
- 'Kimono'	see *P. subulata* 'Tamaongalei'
§ - 'Lilacina'	CLyd CMea EDAr ELan GEdr GTou LGro LRHS MWat NFor NHol NJOw SBla SChu WWin
§ - 'Maischnee'	CLyd CMea ECtt EDAr EPfP EPot GAbr GKir LGro LRHS MHer MWat NFor NHol SIng SPlb WEas WWin
- 'Marjorie'	CLyd CMHG CWCL ECtt LBee MDKP MHer NPri NWCA SMer
- May Snow	see *P. subulata* 'Maischnee'
§ - 'McDaniel's Cushion' ♀H4	CLyd CNic CWCL EBre ECha EDAr ELan EMlt EPfP EPot GKir GTou ITim LBee LRHS NFor NHol NJOw NMen NWCA SPlb WBVN WCFE WFar WRHF WShp WTel WWin
- 'Mikado'	see *P. subulata* 'Tamaongalei'
- 'Model'	LGro NSla
- 'Moonlight'	CLyd ECtt
- 'Nettleton Variation' (v)	EBre EDAr EPot EWes GKir ITim LBee LHop LRHS MBro MDKP MHer NFla NPri SAga SIng SPlb WCom WPat
§ - 'Oakington Blue Eyes'	CNic CWCL EBre EPar GKir LRHS SMrm SRms
- 'Pink Pearl'	EWes
- 'Purple Beauty' **new**	WLin
- 'Red Wings' ♀H4	CWCL EBre ECtt EPfP GKir LRHS NMen SRms WFar
§ - 'Ronsdorfer Schöne'	EPot ITim LBee LRHS NJOw
- 'Rose Mabel'	EDAr
- 'Samson'	GTou LRHS SMer WWin
- 'Scarlet Flame'	CMea CSam ECha ECtt EDAr ELan EMlt EPfP LGro MHer MWat NFla NHol NPri SAga WWin
- 'Schneewittchen'	CLyd
- 'Sensation'	GTou SBla
- 'Snow Queen'	see *P. subulata* 'Maischnee'
- 'Starglow'	GTou
§ - 'Tamaongalei'	CLyd CMea CPBP CWCL EBre EDAr EHyt EMlt EPfP EPot EWes GKir IMGH LRHS MHer SBla SChu SCoo SIng SRms WBVN WBor WCFE WFar WShp WWin
- 'Temiskaming'	ECha EDAr ELan ENot EWes LBee LGro LRHS NMen SBla SChu SRms WCom
- violet seedling	CLyd
- 'White Delight'	CLyd ECtt ELan GTou LBee NMen
- 'Woodside'	CNic
'Tiny Bugles'	SBla
'Vivid'	EDAr MDHE SIgm

Phoebe (Lauraceae)

sheareri	CFil WPGP

Phoenicaulis (Brassicaceae)

§ *cheiranthoides*	LTwo NWCA

Phoenix (Arecaceae)

canariensis ♀H1+3	More than 30 suppliers
dactylifera (F)	CRoM EAmu LPal MPRe WHPE WMul
reclinata	CKob CRoM LPJP NPal WMul
roebelenii ♀H1+3	CBrP CDoC CRoM EPfP ESlt EUJe LPal MBri NPal WMul
rupicola	CRoM LPal
sylvestris	EAmu LPal WMul
theophrasti	CFil CPHo EAmu LEdu LPJP LPal WMul

Phormium ✿ (Phormiaceae)

'Alison Blackman' **new**	CPen CTrC CWil IBal MPRe
'Amazing Red'	CWil IBlr
'Apricot Queen' (v)	CAbb CBcs CBrm CDoC CHEx CSBt CTrC CWil EBee EBre EPfP GQui IBal IBlr LRHS MAsh MCCP MDun MFan MPRe NMoo NPal NPri SLim SPer SSto WBcn WBod WFar
Ballyrogan variegated (v)	IBlr
* 'Black Edge'	CWil IBlr MRav NPri
'Bronze Baby'	More than 30 suppliers
'Buckland Ruby' **new**	CWil MAsh
colensoi	see *P. cookianum*
§ *cookianum*	CHEx CTrC CWil EBee ECre EMil EPfP IBlr MGos SAPC SArc SEND SMad WFar WMul
- 'Alpinum Purpureum'	see *P. tenax* 'Nanum Purpureum'
- dwarf	IBlr SLPl
- 'Flamingo'	CTrC CWil EBee ECre EPfP MAsh MBri SLim SSto
- 'Golden Wonder'	IBlr
- subsp. *hookeri*	More than 30 suppliers
'Cream Delight' (v) ♀H3-4	
- - 'Tricolor' ♀H3-4	More than 30 suppliers
* 'Copper Beauty'	COtt CWil NMoo SMer WDyG
* 'Crimson Devil' **new**	CBcs CPen
'Dark Delight'	IBlr
'Dazzler' (v)	IBlr MGos MRav WCot
'Duet' (v) ♀H3	CBcs CDoC COtt CSBt CTrC CWil EHoe EPfP IBal IBlr LRHS MFan SPla SWvt WBcn WFar
'Dusky Chief'	CSBt CWil LRHS MAsh WPat
'Dusky Princess' **new**	MFan
'Emerald Isle'	CWil ECrN MAsh
* 'Emerald Pink'	COtt
'Evening Glow' (v)	CPen CTrC CWil EBee ELan EPfP IBal IBlr LRHS MAsh MPRe MRav SAga SWvt WBor WCot WGer WPat WWeb
'Firebird'	IBlr SAga SLon SWvt
'Flamingo' (v)	CMHG CSBt CWil LRHS SLim SPer WCot WPat WWeb
'Fortescue's Bronze' **new**	CWil
'Glowing Embers' **new**	CTrC
'Gold Ray' **new**	CBcs
'Gold Sword' (v)	CBcs CMHG COtt CTrC CWil EBee ENot IBlr LRHS MAsh MFan SAga SSto
'Guardsman' (v)	IBlr
'Jack Spratt' (v)	CBcs CBrm CFwr CMHG COtt CPen CWil EBee ECou EHoe IBal IBlr LRHS MAsh MBrN MSwo SWvt WLeb WPrP

	'Jester' (v)	More than 30 suppliers
	'Limelight'	CWil SWvt
	'Mahogany' **new**	CWil
§	'Maori Chief' (v)	CFil CSBt CWil EPfP GQui IBal IBlr
		LRHS NMoo SHBN SWvt WCot
		WLeb WPGP WPat
	'Maori Eclipse'	CWil
	'Maori Elegance'	CWil
	'Maori Maiden' (v)	CBcs CBrm CDoC CDul CMHG
		CSBt CTrC CTri EBee ECre EHoe
		ENot GKir GQui IBal LRHS MAsh
		MFan MGos MPRe MRav SMad
		SWvt WCot WFar WLeb WWeb
§	'Maori Queen' (v)	CBcs CDoC CMHG CSBt CTrC
		CWil EBee ENot EPfP GQui IBal
		IBlr LRHS MAsh MFan MGos MPRe
		MRav MSwo NMoo SPer SSto SWal
		SWvt WCot WFar WPat WWeb
§	'Maori Sunrise' (v)	More than 30 suppliers
	'Margaret Jones' **new**	CWil
	'Merlot' **new**	CPen CWil
	'Pink Panther' (v)	More than 30 suppliers
	'Pink Stripe' (v)	CSBt CWil EBee EBre ECrN ENot
		IBlr LRHS MAsh MRav NPal SWvt
		WCot WGer WPat
	'Platt's Black'	CBcs CBrm CKno CMHG CPen
		CSpe CWil EAmu ELan EPfP EWes
		GGar GKir IBal LHop LRHS MAsh
		MCCP MGos MPRe MSwo SSto
		WGer WLeb WPGP
		WPat
	'Rainbow Chief'	see *P.* 'Maori Chief'
	Rainbow hybrids	ECrN
	'Rainbow Maiden'	see *P.* 'Maori Maiden'
	'Rainbow Queen'	see *P.* 'Maori Queen'
	'Rainbow Sunrise'	see *P.* 'Maori Sunrise'
I	'Rubrum'	CWil
	'Sea Jade'	IBlr
	'Stormy Dawn'	WCot
	'Sundowner' (v) ♀H3	More than 30 suppliers
	'Sunset' (v)	CSBt IBlr SWvt WCot
	'Surfer' (v)	COtt CTrC CWil EHoe IBlr LPan
		MCCP SMad WBcn WLeb WPat
		WWhi
	'Surfer Boy'	CWil SMer
	'Surfer Bronze'	CPen CWil EAmu MGos NPal
		WGer WWeb
	'Surfer Green'	MGos NPal
	tenax ♀H4	More than 30 suppliers
	- 'Bronze'	CBrm CWil ECrN SWvt
	- 'Co-ordination'	CWil EBee EPfP IBal IBlr LRHS
		WBcn
	- 'Darkside'	EWes
*	- dwarf	IBlr SLPl
*	- *lineatum*	NBlu SEND WMul
§	- 'Nanum Purpureum'	CPLG IBlr MSte SEND SMad
	- 'Platinum'	IBlr
	- Purpureum	More than 30 suppliers
	Group ♀H3-4	
	- 'Radiance' (v)	CWil IBlr
	- 'Rainbow Queen'	see *P.* 'Maori Queen'
	- 'Rainbow Sunrise'	see *P.* 'Maori Sunrise'
	- 'Variegatum' (v) ♀H3-4	CBrm CFil CHEx CSBt ENot EPfP
		IBlr LPal LPan LRHS MFan NMoo
		SAPC SArc SEND SRms WBrE WFar
		WMul WPGP WPat
	- 'Veitchianum' (v)	CHEx CWil IBlr LRHS SPer
		WPGP
	- 'Yellow Queen'	MRav
	'Thumbelina'	CBcs CTri CWil EBee EHoe IBal
		LRHS MDKP MSte SSto WPat
	'Tom Thumb'	CBrm CWil LPan WDin WDyG
		WPrP
	'Yellow Wave' (v) ♀H3	More than 30 suppliers

Photinia ✿ (Rosaceae)

	arbutifolia	see *Heteromeles salicifolia*
	beauverdiana	CSam CTho SRms WFar
	- var. *notabilis*	EPfP NLar
	'Branpara'PBR	WWeb
§	*davidiana*	CDul CSam EBee ELan EPfP GIBF
		ISea MBar MRav NLar SPer SRms
		WDin WFar WNor
	- 'Palette' (v)	More than 30 suppliers
	- var. *undulata*	CMHG LRHS WBcn
	- - 'Fructu Luteo'	CMHG CSam CTrG EBee EPfP EPla
		LRHS MBri MRav NLar SPer WFar
	- - 'Prostrata'	ELan EPfP MBar MRav SPer WDin
		WFar
	x *fraseri*	CMCN
	- 'Birmingham'	EBee EHoe GKir LPVe LPan LRHS
		MAsh LRHS SRms WDin WWeb
	- 'Purple Peter'	LRHS SKee
	- 'Red Robin' ♀H4	More than 30 suppliers
	- 'Robusta'	CTrC EBee EPfP LRHS SLim SWvt
	- 'Super Hedger' **new**	LBuc
	glabra	SArc
	- B&SWJ 8903	WCru
§	- 'Parfait' (v)	CAbP ELan LRHS MAsh MRav SDry
		SHBN SPer SPla SPoG WFar
	- 'Pink Lady'	see *P. glabra* 'Parfait'
	- 'Rubens'	ELan EPfP LRHS MAsh MBri NHol
		SDry SPer SPla SSta WPat
	- 'Variegata'	see *P. glabra* 'Parfait'
	glomerata misapplied	see *P. prionophylla*
	lasiogyna	CMCN WWes
	niitakayamensis	GIBF
	nussia	CDoC
	parvifolia	EPfP
	prionophylla	CHEx
§	'Redstart'	CEnd EBee EPfP LRHS MGos NPro
		SLon SPer SSta SWvt WMoo
§	*serratifolia*	CBot CDul CHEx CMHG EBee EPfP
		LRHS SAPC SArc SDry SPer SSpi
		SSta WRav WFar WPGP WSHC XPep
	serrulata	see *P. serratifolia*
	villosa ♀H4	CAbP CDul CTho GIBF MBar NPal
	- B&SWJ 8877	WCru
	- var. *laevis*	EPfP EWTr LBuc LPan
	- f. *maximowicziana*	EPfP GIBF

Phragmites (Poaceae)

	from Sichuan, China	EPPr
§	*australis*	CRWN EMFW EPAt LPBA MGol
		NArg SWat WDyG WFar WMAq
		XPep
	- subsp. *australis*	EMon EPPr MTed
	var. *striatopictus*	
	- - 'Variegatus' (v)	More than 30 suppliers
	- subsp. *pseudodonax*	EMon EPPr
	communis	see *P. australis*
	karka	EPPr
	- 'Candy Stripe' (v)	CDWL EPPr
	- 'Variegatus' (v)	LRav

Phrynium (Marantaceae)

pubinerve	CKob

Phuopsis (Rubiaceae)

§	*stylosa*	More than 30 suppliers
	- 'Purpurea'	CElw CWCL EBee ELan MNrw
		MRav NBrk NChi SChu WCom
		WHal

Phygelius ✿ (Scrophulariaceae)

aequalis	CFee CHEx CSev MNrw MWgw
	SChu SHom SMac SPla WMoo
	WPer WSHC WSan

- albus	see *P. aequalis* 'Yellow Trumpet'
- 'Aureus'	see *P. aequalis* 'Yellow Trumpet'
- Cedric Morris form	SHom
- 'Cream Trumpet'	see *P. aequalis* 'Yellow Trumpet'
- 'Indian Chief'	see *P.* x *rectus* 'African Queen'
* - 'Pink Trumpet'	CDoC EWTr GCal LRHS SCoo
	SMac SMrm SOkh SPer WRha
- Sensation	CFwr CSpe EBee EBlw EChP ECtt
= 'Sani Pass'PBR	EGra EPfP GBri LRHS MAsh MCCP
	MOak NCGa NPri SCoo SMac SPer
	SSvw SWvt
- 'Trewidden Pink' ♀H4	More than 30 suppliers
§ - 'Yellow Trumpet' ♀H3-4	More than 30 suppliers
aequalis x *capensis*	see *P.* x *rectus*
'Bridgetown Beauty'	GCal
§ *capensis* ♀H3-4	CChe CWib EChP ELan ENot EOrc
	EPfP LSpr MAsh MBNS MHer NLar
	SGar SHom SMac SPer SPet SRms
	WBod WFar WMnd WMoo WPer
	WWpP WWye
- CD&R	EWes
- S&SH 50	SMac
- 'Caborn Flame' (v)	EBee
- coccineus	see *P. capensis*
- 'Janet's Jewel' (v)	SHom
- orange-flowered	LHop SHom
- pink-flowered	WLow
'Golden Gate'	see *P. aequalis* 'Yellow Trumpet'
Logan form	EBee EBlw MCCP WWpP
New Sensation	COtt EBre LAst SBla
= 'Blaphy'	
§ x *rectus*	EOMN MDKP SYvo
§ - 'African Queen' ♀H3-4	More than 30 suppliers
- 'Aylesham's Pride'	SHom
- 'Bridgetown Beauty'	SHom
- 'Devil's Tears' ♀H4	More than 30 suppliers
- Logan form	EBlw SHom
* - 'Logan's Pink'	NGdn
- 'Moonraker'	More than 30 suppliers
- 'Pink Elf'	ELan SHom SLon SMac
- 'Raspberry Swirl'	EPfP SHom
- 'Salmon Leap' ♀H4	More than 30 suppliers
- 'Sunshine'	CFwr COtt EBee EGra EHoe ELan
	EMan EPza EWes LAst LHop LRHS
	MAsh MDKP MSph SPoG SSte
	SWal WCom WGwG WWpP
§ - 'Winchester Fanfare'	More than 30 suppliers
- 'Winton Fanfare'	see *P.* x *rectus* 'Winchester Fanfare'

Phyla (Verbenaceae)

§ *nodiflora*	CNic EBre ECha GKir NFla NWCA
	SEND SIng WMoo WPer XPep
- 'Alba'	CNic
- var. *canescens*	WCru

Phylica (Rhamnaceae)

arborea 'Superba'	CBcs CPLG
ericoides	CPLG

x *Phylliopsis* (Ericaceae)

'Coppelia' ♀H4	EPot GCrs GGGa ITim LTwo SReu
	SSta WAbe WPat
hillieri 'Askival'	GCrs GGGa WAbe
- 'Pinocchio'	CMHG GCrs GGGa GTou ITim
	LRHS MDun NLAp NLar WAbe
	WPat
'Hobgoblin'	SReu SSta WAbe WPat
'Mermaid'	GGGa ITim SReu WAbe
'Puck'	WAbe
'Sprite'	GCrs SReu WAbe WPat
'Sugar Plum'	CWSG IDee ITim MDun SSpi SSta
	SWvt WAbe

Phyllitis see *Asplenium*

Phyllocladus (Phyllocladaceae)

trichomanoides	CDoC CTrC LCon NLar
var. *alpinus*	

Phyllodoce (Ericaceae)

aleutica	CTCP EPot GCrs GGGa GKir MBar
	NDlv NMen SRms WAbe
§ - subsp. *glanduliflora*	CMHG
'Flora Slack'	
- - white-flowered	see *P. aleutica* subsp.
	glanduliflora 'Flora Slack'
aleutica x *caerulea*	GCrs GKir
breweri	GKir WAbe
caerulea ♀H4	GEdr GKir NDlv
- *japonica*	see *P. nipponica*
- 'Viking'	GCrs
empetriformis	MBar NSla SRms
x *intermedia*	CMHG GKir
'Drummondii'	
- 'Fred Stoker'	CMHG
§ *nipponica* ♀H4	GCrs WAbe
- var. *oblongo-ovata*	GCrs GKir
tsugifolia	GCrs

Phyllostachys ✿ (Poaceae)

angusta	CFil EPla SDry WJun WPGP
arcana	EPla GKir SDry WJun
- 'Luteosulcata'	CBcs CFil EPla GKir LPal MMoz
	MWht NPal SDry WJun WNor
§ *atrovaginata*	EPla ERod SDry WJun
aurea ♀H4	More than 30 suppliers
- 'Albovariegata' (v)	EFul MPRe SDry
- 'Flavescens Inversa'	EPla ERod SDry WJun
- 'Holochrysa'	CBrP EFul EPla ERod SDry WJun
- 'Koi'	CFil EFul EPla ERod LPal MMoz
	NMoo SDry WPGP
aureocaulis	see *P. aureosulcata* f. *aureocaulis*,
	P. vivax f. *aureocaulis*
aureosulcata	CWib EBee EFul EPfP EPla ERod
	GKir LRHS MAsh MMoz NMoo
	SDry WBVN WHPE WJun WMoo
- f. *alata*	see *P. aureosulcata* f. *pekinensis*
- 'Argus'	EPla
- f. *aureocaulis* ♀H4	More than 30 suppliers
- 'Harbin'	EPla ERod SDry
- 'Harbin Inversa'	EPla ERod
- 'Lama Temple'	CFil EPla
§ - f. *pekinensis*	CFil EPla NLar SDry WPGP
- f. *spectabilis* ♀H4	More than 30 suppliers
bambusoides	CBcs EPla GKir SDix SDry WJun
- 'Allgold'	see *P. bambusoides* 'Holochrysa'
- 'Castilloni'	CAbb CBcs CFil EAmu EBee EFul
	EPla ERod EWes GKir LEdu LPal
	MMoz MWht NBea NMoo NPal
	SDix SDry SEND WJun WMul WPGP
- 'Castilloni Inversa'	CFil EPla ERod LPal MMoz SDry
	WJun WMul WPGP
§ - 'Holochrysa'	CFil CPen EPla ERod GKir NMoo
	NPal SDry SEND WJun
- 'Katashibo' **new**	EPla
- 'Kawadana'	EPla ERod SDry
- f. *lacrima-deae*	CFil EPla
- 'Marliacea'	EPla ERod WJun
- 'Subvariegata'	CFil EPla SDry WPGP
- 'Sulphurea'	see *P. bambusoides* 'Holochrysa'
- 'Tanakae'	MMoz MSwo NLar NMoo SDry
- 'Violascens'	NMoo
bissetii	More than 30 suppliers
circumpilis	EPla
congesta hort.	see *P. atrovaginata*
decora	CAbb EAmu EBee EPla ERod MBri
	MMoz MWht NMoo NPal SDry
	SEND WJun WPGP

dulcis	EPfP EPla ERod LEdu LPJP WJun
§ *edulis*	CBcs EFul EHoe ERod IFro MMoz
	SDry WJun WMul WPGP
- 'Bicolor'	SDry WMul
- 'Heterocycla'	SDry
- f. *pubescens*	see *P. edulis*
flexuosa	CFil CPen EFul EPfP EPla IMGH
	MWht SDry WJun WMul WPGP
glauca	CAbb EBee EPla ERod MMoz
	MWht NLar NMoo NPal
- f. *yunzhu*	EPla ERod SDry WJun
heteroclada	NMoo SDry WJun
- 'Solid Stem' misapplied	see *P. purpurata* 'Straight Stem'
heterocycla	see *P. edulis* 'Heterocycla'
- f. *pubescens*	see *P. edulis*
humilis	CBcs CDul EBee EPla ERod LAst
	LPan MCCP MGos MMoz MWht
	NLar NMoo NPal SDry WJun
iridescens	EPla MSwo NLar SDry WJun
lofushanensis	CFil EPla WPGP
makinoi	ERod
mannii	CPen EPla SDry
meyeri	CPen EPla SDry
nidularia	EPla ERod MMoz SDry WJun
- f. *farcta*	CFil EPla
§ - f. *glabrovagina*	EPla
- smooth sheath	see *P. nidularia* f. *glabrovagina*
nigella	EPla
nigra ♀H4	More than 30 suppliers
- 'Boryana'	CAbb CBig CBrm CDoC CFil
	EAmu EBee EFul EPfP EPla GKir
	LAst MAsh MGos MMoz MWht
	NMoo SArc SDry SWvt WFar WJun
	WMoo WMul WPGP
- 'Fulva'	EPla
- 'Hale'	EPla
- f. *henonis* ♀H4	CAbb CBcs CFil EAmu EBee EFul
	EMil ERod LPal MMoz MWht
	NBea NLar NMoo SDry WJun
	WMul WPGP
- 'Megurochiku'	EPla ERod SDry WJun
- f. *nigra*	EPla SPer
- f. *punctata*	CBrm CDoC CFil EBee EPfP EPla
	ERod MAvo MWht NGdn SDry
	SEND WDyG WJun WPGP
- 'Tosaensis'	EPla
- 'Wisley'	EPla
nuda	EAmu EBee EPla ERod GKir MGos
	MMoz MWht NPal SDry WJun
- f. *localis*	MWht SDry
parvifolia	EPla ERod WJun
platyglossa	CFil EPla ERod WPGP
praecox	EPla NMoo WJun
propinqua	CBig CDoC CDul EPla ERod MCCP
	MMoz MWht SArc WJun WMul
* - 'Bicolor'	WJun
- 'Li Yu Gan'	CFil EPla WPGP
* *pubescens* 'Mazel'	NMoo
§ *purpurata*	EPla MWht SDry
'Straight Stem'	
rubicunda	CFil EPla WJun
rubromarginata	CFil CPen EPla ERod MWht NLar
	SDry WJun
stimulosa	EPla ERod WJun
§ *sulphurea*	NMoo
- 'Houzeau'	EPla ERod SDry
- 'Robert Young'	EPla SDry
- 'Sulphurea'	see *P. sulphurea*
- f. *viridis*	EPla ERod GKir LPal LPan MAsh
	MWht NMoo SDry
violascens	CFil EFul EPla ERod LPal MMoz
	SDry WJun WPGP
virella	CFil EPla WPGP
viridiglaucescens	CAbb CBcs CFil CHEx EAmu EBee

	EFul EPfP EPla GKir LPan MBrN
	MFir MMoz MWht SArc SDry
	SEND SPla WCot WJun WMul
viridis	see *P. sulphurea* f. *viridis*
vivax	EFul EPfP EPla ERod LEdu MMoz
	MWht SDry WJun WMul WNor
- f. *aureocaulis* ♀H4	CAbb CBcs CDoC CDul CFil CHEx
	EBee EFul EPfP EPla ERod GKir
	LEdu LPJP LPal LRHS MMoz MWht
	NGdn NPal SAPC SDry SPla WHPE
	WJun WMul WNor WPGP
* - f. *huanvenzhu*	CFil EFul EPla ERod MMoz NMoo
	WJun WMul
- 'Katrin'	LEdu

x *Phyllothamnus* (Ericaceae)

erectus	GCrs GGGa SReu SSta WAbe WPat

Phymatosorus (Polypodiaceae)

§ *diversifolius*	CFil

Phymosia (Malvaceae)

§ *umbellata*	CBot CRHN ERea LRHS SOWG

Phyodina see *Callisia*

Physalis (Solanaceae)

alkekengi ♀H4	EBee EPAt EPfP EWTr GKir MLan
	NBir SWvt
- var. *franchetii*	More than 30 suppliers
- - dwarf	LPVe NLar WHil
- - 'Gigantea'	ECGP GBuc NLar SPlb
- - 'Gnome' **new**	EBee
- - 'Variegata' (v)	EBee ECha ECtt EMan EPla EWes
	IBlr MAvo NPro WOld
angulata B&SWJ 7016	WCru
edulis (F)	see *P. peruviana*
§ *peruviana* (F)	LRav SHDw

Physocarpus (Rosaceae)

malvaceus **new**	EWes
opulifolius	GIBF IFro MSal
- 'Dart's Gold' ♀H4	More than 30 suppliers
- 'Diabolo'PBR ♀H4	More than 30 suppliers
§ - 'Luteus'	CBot CDoC CMHG CSam CWib
	EBee EPfP GEil GKir IMGH ISea
	MBar MDun MRav MWhi SPer
	SRms WBod WDin WFar WMoo
ribesifolius **new**	GEil
ribesifolius 'Aureus'	see *P. opulifolius* 'Luteus'

Physochlaina (Solanaceae)

orientalis	CPom EMan MSal NChi WAul

Physoplexis (Campanulaceae)

§ *comosa* ♀H2-3	ETow EWes LRHS NSla SBla WHoo

Physostegia (Lamiaceae)

angustifolia	CSam EBee
§ *virginiana*	CKno CSBt CWCL EBee EGra
	EWTr GBar GKir LAst MBNS NBlu
	NGar NSti SGar SWat WBrk WFar
	WRHF
- 'Alba'	CBot CSBt EBee EBre EChP EGra
	EPfP EShb GBar GBri GKir LRHS
	MSte MTis NLar NOrc SPet SPlb
	WEas WHrl WRHF WRha
§ - 'Crown of Snow'	CBri CDWL CFir CM&M EBee ECtt
	ERou EWTr GKir LPVe MBNS
	MBow MHer MRav MWrn NArg
	STes SWal SWvt WHil WMoo WPer
- 'Grandiflora'	CFir SECG
- 'Grandiflora Rose'	NArg NPri SWal SWvt
- 'Miss Manners'	EBee WCot

- 'Olympic Gold' (v)	EBee EMan ENot EPPr WMoo
- pale pink-flowered	EFou SWat
- 'Red Beauty'	CFir EBee ERou LRHS MDKP SPla WHil WWin
- 'Rose Queen'	LPVe MFOX WTin
- 'Rosea'	CBcs CBot EBee EChP ERou GKir IGor MBow MDKP NBPC WFar WHrl WPer
- Schneekrone	see *P. virginiana* 'Crown of Snow'
- 'Snow Queen'	see *P. virginiana* 'Summer Snow'
- var. *speciosa*	EMon WFar
§ - - 'Bouquet Rose'	CDWL EBee EBre ECha EMan EPfP LRHS MFir MHer MRav MSte NBir NBlu NGar NHol NOak SChu SCro SMac SPer SWvt WAul WCAu WFar WMoo WRos WShp WTel WWeb
- - Rose Bouquet	see *P. virginiana* subsp. *speciosa* 'Bouquet Rose'
§ - - 'Variegata' (v)	More than 30 suppliers
§ - 'Summer Snow' ♀H4	CBcs EBee ECha EFou ELan ENot EPfP IBal LAst LHop LRHS MBri MFir MWat MWgw NCGa NHol SChu SPer SPla SRms WBea WBrk WCAu WCot WFar WHoo WMnd WShp WWin
- 'Summer Spire'	EBee ECha EHrv ELan EMan MSte NHol SPer WBea WFar
- 'Vivid' ♀H4	More than 30 suppliers
- 'Wassenhove'	EBee EMon

Phyteuma (*Campanulaceae*)

balbisii	see *P. cordatum*
comosum	see *Physoplexis comosa*
§ *cordatum*	MWrn
hemisphaericum	WPat
humile	EDAr WAbe
nigrum	CDes GCal GFlt LRHS MNrw NBid WLin
orbiculare	WAbe
scheuchzeri	CMea CNic EBee EBre EMan EPfP GTou MHer MTis NChi NJOw NPri NWCA SBla SCro SPet SRms SRot WAbe WCom WWin
sieberi	CPBP NBir WAbe
spicatum	CDes EPat NBro

Phytolacca (*Phytolaccaceae*)

acinosa	GPoy MGol MSal NLar SWat WHer
- HWJ 647	WCru
§ *americana*	CAgr CArn CHEx CSev ECha ELan ELau EMar EPfP GPoy ITer MBNS MHer MSal MWat SEND SIde SRms SWat WCru WEas WFar WHer WHil WJek WMoo WWye
- 'Silberstein' (v)	ITer WCru
clavigera	see *P. polyandra*
decandra	see *P. americana*
dioica	CHEx CPLG
esculenta	CHid EBee LEdu LHop
icosandra B&SWJ 8988	WCru
japonica B&SWJ 4897	WCru
octandra	ITer
§ *polyandra*	EBee ECha NBid NBro SGar SRms WBan WWye

Picea ✿ (*Pinaceae*)

§ *abies*	CCVT CDul CLnd CSBt CTri CWib EHul ENot EPfP GKir LBuc LRHS MBar MBri MGos NBlu NWea WBVN WDin WEve WMou
- 'Acrocona'	CDoC ECho EHul EOrn GKir LCon LLin LRHS MAsh MBar MBlu MBri MGos SCoo WEve
- 'Archer'	CKen
- 'Argenteospica' (v)	NHol WEve
- 'Aurea'	ECho EOrn IMGH LLin WEve
- 'Capitata'	CKen GTSp MBar NLar
- 'Clanbrassiliana'	CDoC CKen IMGH LCon MAsh MBar WEve
- Compacta Group	LBee LRHS
I - 'Congesta'	CKen
- 'Crippsii'	CKen
I - 'Cruenta'	CKen
- 'Cupressina'	CKen
- 'Diffusa'	CKen LCon MBar
- 'Dumpy'	LCon
- 'Elegans'	MBar
- 'Ellwangeriana'	NLar
- 'Excelsa'	see *P. abies*
- 'Fahndrich'	CKen
- 'Finedonensis'	LCon NLar
- 'Formanek'	CDoC CKen LCon LLin NLar
- 'Four Winds'	CAbP CKen
- 'Frohburg'	CDoC COtt GKir LRHS MBar MGos SCoo
- 'Globosa'	MBar
- 'Globosa Nana'	MGos
- 'Gregoryana'	CKen CMac GKir IMGH MBar NDlv NHol
- 'Heartland Gem' **new**	CKen
- 'Horace Wilson' **new**	CKen
- 'Humilis'	CKen LCon
- 'Hystrix'	LCon NLar
- 'Inversa'	EBre EHul EOrn LCon LLin LPan MBar MBlu MGos SCoo WEve
- 'J.W. Daisy's White'	see *P. glauca* 'J.W. Daisy's White'
- 'Jana'	CKen
- 'Kral'	CKen
- 'Little Gem' ♀H4	CDoC CFee CKen CMac EBre EHul ENot EOrn GBin GKir IMGH LBee LCon LLin LRHS MAsh MBar MGos NBee SLim SPer WEve
- 'Maxwellii'	EHul GKir MBar MGos
- 'Mikulasovice' **new**	NLar
- 'Nana'	MBar
- 'Nana Compacta'	CKen EHul IMGH LBee MAsh MBar MOne WFar
- 'Nidiformis' ♀H4	CDoC CKen CMac CSBt CTri EBre EHul ENot EOrn GBin GKir LLin LPan LRHS MAsh MBar NBlu NWea SLim SRms WDin WEve WFar WStl
- 'Norrkoping'	CKen
- 'Ohlendorffii'	CKen EHul LCon MBar NLar SCoo WStl
- 'Pachyphylla'	CKen
- 'Pendula Major'	SHBN
- 'Procumbens'	MBar
- 'Pumila'	EOrn
- 'Pumila Nigra'	CMac EHul LLin MBar MGos SCoo SLim
- 'Pusch'	CKen
- 'Pygmaea'	CKen GTSp MBar MGos
- 'Reflexa'	EHul GBin IMGH MAsh WEve
- 'Repens'	LRHS MBar MBlu MGos NBee
- 'Rydal'	LCon MAsh
- 'Saint James'	CKen
- 'Tabuliformis'	MBar
- 'Tufty'	EOrn
- 'Vermont Gold'	CKen NLar
- 'Waldbrunn'	MAsh
- 'Walter Bron'	CKen
- 'Waugh'	MBar
- 'Will's Dwarf'	see *P. abies* 'Wills Zwerg'
§ - 'Wills Zwerg'	LPan LRHS MAsh
ajanensis	GIBF
alcoquiana	GKir LCon
- var. *alcoquiana*	MAsh
I - 'Prostrata'	MBar

	- var. *reflexa* **new**	MPkF
	breweriana ♀H4	More than 30 suppliers
	engelmannii	GKir GTSp MBar
	- subsp. *engelmannii*	LCon MBar
	glauca	CDul CTri WEve
	- 'Alberta Blue'	CDoC CKen CSBt EBre EOrn GKir LCon LLin LPan LRHS MAsh SCoo SLim WEve WFar
	- var. *albertiana* 'Alberta Globe'	CDoC CSBt EHul EOrn EPot GKir IMGH LBee LCon LLin MAsh MBar MBri MGos NBee NDlv NHol SAga SLim SPoG WEve WFar
	- - 'Conica'	More than 30 suppliers
	- - 'Gnome'	CKen WEve
	- - 'Laurin'	CDoC CKen EBre EOrn GKir LBee LCon LRHS MAsh MBar SCoo WEve
	- - 'Tiny'	CDoC CKen ENot EOrn LCon LLin MBar
	- 'Arneson's Blue Variegated' (v)	CKen MAsh MBri SLim WEve
	- 'Blue Planet'	CKen NLar
	- 'Coerulea'	LCon MBar
I	- 'Coerulea Nana'	NLar
	- 'Cy's Wonder'	CKen
	- 'Echiniformis' ♀H4	CKen GKir LBee LRHS MBar MBri
	- var. *glauca*	GIBF
	- 'Goldilocks'	CKen
§	- 'J.W. Daisy's White'	CDoC CKen EBre EOrn GKir LCon LLin LRHS MAsh MGos SCoo SLim SMur SPer WEve WFar WGor
	- 'Lilliput'	EHul EOrn LCon MBar MGos NLar WEve
	- 'Nana'	CKen
	- 'Piccolo'	CKen GKir LRHS MAsh SLim
	- 'Pixie'	CKen
	- 'Rainbow's End' (v)	CKen EBre SLim
	- 'Sander's Blue'	CKen EOrn LBee SCoo SLim SPoG WEve
	- 'Zucherhut'	LRHS MBar MBri
	glehnii	LCon
	- 'Sasanosei'	CKen
	- 'Shimezusei'	CKen
	jezoensis	MGos
	- subsp. *hondoensis*	WNor
	- 'Yatsabusa'	CKen CMen
	koraiensis	GIBF GKir
	kosteri 'Glauca'	see *P. pungens* 'Koster'
	likiangensis	CMCN GTSp ISea LCon
	- var. *balfouriana*	see *P. likiangensis* var. *rubescens*
	- var. *purpurea*	see *P. purpurea*
§	- var. *rubescens*	CDoC CKen IDee MBri NHol WWes
	mariana	GTSp NWea
	- 'Aureovariegata' (v)	LCon
	- 'Doumetii'	EOrn
	- 'Fastigiata'	CKen EOrn
	- 'Nana' ♀H4	CDoC CKen CMac EBre EHul ENot EPfP GKir IMGH LCon LLin LRHS MAsh MBar MBri MGos MNrw MWat NBee NBlu NDlv NHol NWea SLim WBrE WDin WEve WFar
I	- 'Pygmaea'	CKen
	x *mariorika*	MBar
	obovata var. *coerulea*	GIBF NLar
	omorika ♀H4	CBcs CDoC CMCN ENot GKir LBuc LCon MBar MGos NWea SPer WBrE WCFE WDin WFar WMou
	- 'Frohnleiten'	CKen
	- 'Frondenberg' **new**	CKen
	- 'Karel'	CKen NLar
	- 'Nana' ♀H4	CMac EHul LBee LCon LPan MAsh MBar SCoo SLim WEve
	- 'Pendula' ♀H4	CDoC GKir GTSp LCon LRHS MBar MBlu NLar SHBN SSta
	- 'Pimoko'	CKen GKir LCon LRHS MAsh NLar
	- 'Schneverdingen'	CKen
	- 'Tijn'	CKen
	- 'Treblitsch'	CDoC CKen
	orientalis ♀H4	CDul CLnd LCon LPan LRav NWea
§	- 'Aurea' (v) ♀H4	CMac EBre ECrN EHul ELan ENot GKir LCon LLin LPan MBar MBri MLan NHol SHBN SLim WDin
	- 'Aureospicata'	CDoC CTho ECho MAsh MBlu WEve
	- 'Bergman's Gem'	CKen
	- 'Early Gold' (v)	IArd
	- 'Gowdy'	MBar NLar
	- 'Jewel' **new**	CKen
	- 'Kenwith'	CKen
	- 'Mount Vernon' **new**	CKen
	- Pendula Group	MGos
	- 'Professor Langner'	CKen
	- 'Skylands'	CDoC CKen EBre LCon LLin MAsh MBri MGos SCoo SLim
*	- 'Wittbold Compact'	EBre LBee SCoo
	pungens	MBar NWea WDin WNor
	- 'Baby Blueeyes' **new**	MPkF
	- 'Blaukissen'	CKen
	- 'Blue Mountain' **new**	MPkF
	- 'Drayer'	MPkF
	- 'Edith' **new**	MPkF
	- 'Endtz'	MPkF
	- 'Erich Frahm'	CTri EBre GKir LCon LRHS MAsh MBar MBri MGos MPkF NBee NBlu SCoo SKee SLim WFar WOrn
	- 'Fat Albert'	CWib GKir LBee SCoo WFar
	- Glauca Group	CBrm CLnd ECrN EWTr GKir GWCH LBee MBar NWea WBVN WDin WEve WFar WMou WOrn WStI
N	- 'Glauca Pendula'	GKir
	- 'Glauca Procumbens'	MAsh
§	- 'Glauca Prostrata'	EHul GKir MBar
	- 'Globe'	CKen CMen
I	- 'Globosa' ♀H4	CBcs CDoC CKen EBre EHul EOrn GKir LBee LCon LLin LPan MAsh MBar MBri MGos MWat NBee SHBN SLim SRms WEve
	- 'Gloria'	CKen
	- 'Hoopsii' ♀H4	CBcs CDoC CMac CSBt EBre ECrN EHul ENot EOrn EPfP GKir IMGH LCon LPan LRHS MAsh MBar MGos MWat NBee NBlu NPSI SHBN SKee SLim SPer SWvt WDin WEve
	- 'Hoto'	EHul EOrn MBar SCoo
	- 'Hunnewelliana'	EOrn
	- 'Iseli Fastigiate'	CDoC COtt GKir LCon LLin MAsh MBri WEve
§	- 'Koster' ♀H4	CDoC CMac CSBt EHul EOrn EPfP GKir LLin LPan MAsh MBar MGos NWea SLim SPer SPoG SRms WDin WEve WFar
	- 'Lucky Strike'	CDoC CKen LCon LLin MGos NLar
	- 'Maigold' (v)	CKen LCon MAsh NLar
	- 'Moerheimii'	EHul EOrn LCon MBar MGos NLar WEve
	- 'Montgomery'	CKen LCon LLin MBar NLar
	- 'Mrs Cesarini'	CKen
	- 'Nimety'	CKen NLar
	- 'Oldenburg'	ENot MBar NBee
	- 'Omega'	GKir
	- 'Procumbens'	CKen
	- 'Prostrata'	see *P. pungens* 'Glauca Prostrata'
	- 'Prostrate Blue Mist'	WEve
	- 'Rovelli's Monument'	NLar
	- 'Saint Mary's Broom'	CKen
	- 'Schovenhorst'	EHul EOrn LPan

- 'Snowkiss' **new**	MPkF
- 'Spek'	MPkF
- 'Thomsen'	CKen EHul EOrn LCon MAsh
- 'Thuem'	EHul EOrn LLin MGos NDlv NLar
	WEve WFar
- 'Wendy'	CKen
§ *purpurea*	GKir LCon WEve
rubens	LCon
sitchensis	CDul GKir NWea WMou
- 'Nana'	CDoC LLin NHol
- 'Papoose'	see *P. sitchensis* 'Tenas'
- 'Silberzwerg'	CKen NLar
- 'Strypemonde'	CKen
§ - 'Tenas'	CDoC CKen LCon MAsh NHol
	NLar WEve
- 'Trinket' **new**	NLar
smithiana	CDoC GKir GTSp ISea LCon NLar
	SBir
- 'Sunray' **new**	LCon
wilsonii	LCon

Picrasma (Simaroubaceae)

ailanthoides	see *P. quassioides*
§ *quassioides*	CFil CMCN EPfP WPGP

Picris (Asteraceae)

echioides	WHer

Picrorhiza (Scrophulariaceae)

kurrooa	GPoy

Pieris ✿ (Ericaceae)

'Bert Chandler'	GKir LRHS SPer SSpi
'Brouwer's Beauty'	MGos SLim
'Firecrest' ♀H4	CBcs CDoC CMHG CTrG CTrh
	ENot SSpi WBod
'Flaming Silver' (v) ♀H4	More than 30 suppliers
floribunda	MBar SPer
'Forest Flame' ♀H4	More than 30 suppliers
formosa B&SWJ 2257	WCru
- var. *forrestii*	CDoC CTrw CWib ISea NWea
- - 'Ball of Fire'	SSpi
- - 'Fota Pink'	WHar
- - 'Jermyns'	SHBN
- - 'Wakehurst' ♀H3	CAbP CBcs CDul CTrG CWSG
	EPfP LHyd LRHS MAsh MRav NHol
	NWea SPer SPoG SReu SSpi SSta
	WBod WFar
Havila = 'Mouwsvila' (v)	CDoC MAsh MBri MGos NLar WFar
japonica	CBcs CTrw GIBF MBar MGos
	NWea SArc SReu WDin
- 'Bisbee Dwarf'	ITim MBar NHol
- 'Blush' ♀H4	GKir LRHS MAsh MBri NHol SBod
	SHBN
- 'Bonfire'	CEnd MBri MGos WWeb
- 'Brookside Miniature'	NHol
- 'Buchanan's Dwarf'	SReu SSta
- 'Carnaval' (v)	CEnd CSBt CWib EBee ELan ENot
	EPfP LRHS MAsh MGos NLar NPri
	SWvt WFar
- 'Cavatine' ♀H4	CMHG LRHS SBod
§ - 'Christmas Cheer'	MGos NHol NLar SSto WMoo
- 'Compacta'	NHol WAbe
- 'Cupido'	CDoC EMil LRHS MAsh MBar MBri
	MGos NHol WFar
- 'Daisen'	CTrw
§ - 'Debutante' ♀H4	CDoC CWSG CWib ELan ENot
	EPfP GKir LRHS MAsh MBri MDun
	MOne NHol SSpi SWvt WFar WStI
- 'Don'	see *P. japonica* 'Pygmaea'
- 'Dorothy Wyckoff'	CBcs CMHG CPLG CSBt CTrG
	CWSG GKir LRHS MAsh MBri
	MDun NDlv NHol SHBN SSta
	WCwm

- 'Flaming Star'	ECot SWvt WBrE
- 'Flamingo'	CTrw ENot LRHS MAsh MBar
	MGos NDlv NHol WBod WPat
- 'Geisha'	NHol WPat
- 'Grayswood' ♀H4	CMHG EPfP LRHS MBri NHol WFar
* - 'Katsura' **new**	LBuc LRHS MAsh SSpi WWeb
- 'Little Heath' (v) ♀H4	More than 30 suppliers
- 'Little Heath	CChe CDoC CMHG CSBt CTrG
Green' ♀H4	GKir LHyd LRHS MAsh MBar
	MGos NDlv SSta SSto SWvt WBrE
	WFar WPic WWeb
- 'Minor'	ITim MBar NHol
- 'Mountain Fire' ♀H4	More than 30 suppliers
- 'Pink Delight' ♀H4	CAbP CBcs CDoC GKir LRHS
	MAsh MBar MGos MRav NHol
	SHBN SPer SPoG SRms SSto WBod
	WGwG WPat
- 'Prelude' ♀H4	CTrG CWSG GKir LRHS MAsh
	MBri MRav NHol WAbe WBod
	WFar WPat
- 'Purity' ♀H4	CBcs CDoC CMHG CWSG EBre
	EPfP LRHS MBar MGos MLan NHol
	SMer SReu SSta SSto SWvt WBod
	WDin WFar WStI
§ - 'Pygmaea'	CMHG NHol WAbe
- 'Red Mill'	CEnd CWSG ENot EPfP GKir LRHS
	MAsh NBee NHol SPer SSpi WBod
	WFar
- 'Robinswood'	WBcn
- 'Rokujo's Dwarf'	SReu SSta
- 'Rosalinda'	NLar WFar
- 'Rosea'	LHyd WBVN
- 'Sarabande' ♀H4	COtt LRHS MBar MBri MGos
	MOne NHol SPoG SSta WPat
- 'Scarlett O'Hara'	CSBt MGos NLar
- 'Select'	MGos
- 'Silver Mills'	MGos
- 'Snowdrift'	LRHS
- 'Spring Candy'	MGos
- 'Spring Snow'	LRHS
- Taiwanensis Group	CMHG EPfP GGar LRHS MAsh
	MBar MDun MRav NWea SRms
	SSta WFar WPat
- 'Temple Bells'	CPLG CSBt ENot SMer
- 'Tickled Pink'	NHol
- 'Valley Rose'	COtt CSBt ELan ENot EPfP GKir
	MGos NBee SPer SSpi WFar WStI
- 'Valley Valentine' ♀H4	More than 30 suppliers
- 'Variegata' hort.	see *P. japonica* 'White Rim'
§ - 'Variegata' (Carrière)	CDul CMHG EPfP EPot GKir LHyd
Bean (v)	MAsh MBar MGos NBee NDlv
	NHol SHBN SLdr SPer SReu SSta
	WBod WDin WHar WPat WSHC
- 'Wada's Pink'	see *P. japonica* 'Christmas Cheer'
- 'White Pearl'	CAbP MAsh MGos NBee SPer
§ - 'White Rim' (v) ♀H4	CBcs ENot EPfP GKir MAsh MGos
	SPlb WBVN WFar
- 'William Buchanan'	GCrs MBar NHol NLAp WAbe
- var. *yakushimensis*	WBod
koidzumiana	SSta
nana	MBar
- 'Redshank'	SOkd
'Tilford'	LRHS MBri NHol

Pilea (Urticaceae)

* 'Anette'	MBri
cadierei ♀H1	CHal MBri
depressa	CHal
involucrata 'Norfolk' ♀H1	CHal
§ *microphylla*	CHal EBak
muscosa	see *P. microphylla*
nummulariifolia	CHal
peperomioides ♀H1	CHal CSev EPem
repens	MBri

Pileostegia (Hydrangeaceae)

viburnoides ♀[H4]	More than 30 suppliers
- B&SWJ 3565	WCru

Pilosella (Asteraceae)

§ *aurantiaca*	CArn CHrt CMCo CNic CRWN EGra ELan MBow MHer MWgw NArg NBid NBlu NOrc NPri NSti SBri SECG SIde SPet WBVN WCAu WHer WMoo WShp WWye
§ - subsp. *carpathicola*	GGar
§ *officinarum*	MGas NRya

Pilularia (Marsileaceae)

globulifera	CBgR CNat EFer

Pimelea (Thymelaeaceae)

coarctata	see *P. prostrata*
drupacea	ECou
ferruginea 'Magenta Mist'	SOWG
filiformis	ECou
ligustrina	GGar
§ *prostrata*	CLyd CTri ECou EPot GCrs MBar NHol NJOw SRot SScr WPat WPer
- f. *parvifolia*	ECou
- Tennyson's form	SBla
tomentosa	ECou

Pimpinella (Apiaceae)

anisum	CArn MSal SIde WHHs WHer WSel
bicknellii	CDes EBee SIgm WCot WPGP
flahaultii	EBee
major 'Rosea'	CDes CHad EBee EMon LHop LPhx MAvo SBla SMrm WCot WEas WFar WHal WPGP
niitakayamensis B&SWJ 6942	WCru
saxifraga	CAgr EBee WBVN

pineapple guava see *Acca sellowiana*

pineapple see *Ananas comosus*

Pinellia (Araceae)

cordata	CPom EBee EMan LEdu MDKP MSte NMen SBla SOkd WAbe WCot WCru
- variegated	EBee
pedatisecta	CDes CRow EBee EMan ERos ITer LEur LPio WCot WCru WPnP
pinnatisecta	see *P. tripartita*
ternata	CRow CStu EBee EPar ERos LEur MSal NMen WCot WCru WWye
- B&SWJ 3532	LEur WCru
§ *tripartita*	CPom CStu EBee ITer MDKP WAbe WBVN WCot WCru WPnP
- B&SWJ 1102	WCru
- 'Purple Face' B&SWJ 4850	ITer WCru

Pinguicula ✿ (Lentibulariaceae)

acuminata	SHmp
crassifolia	LHew
crassifolia x *emarginata*	SHmp
cyclosecta	LHew SHmp
ehlersiae	EFEx
esseriana	EFEx
gigantea	SHmp
gracilis	LHew
grandiflora	CSWC EFEx GCrs GEdr IFro LRHS MCCP NMen NRya WAbe WHer WPGP

heterophylla	SHmp
jaumavensis	LHew
lauana	LHew
longifolia subsp. *longifolia*	EFEx WPGP
macrophylla	LHew SHmp
moctezumae	SHmp
moranensis var. *caudata*	EFEx
- *moreana*	EFEx
- *superba*	EFEx
* *pilosa*	SHmp
primuliflora	CSWC
rotundiflora	LHew SHmp
vallisneriifolia small	LHew
vulgaris	EFEx
'Weser'	CSWC
zecheri x *macrophylla*	SHmp

pinkcurrant see *Ribes rubrum* (P)

Pinus ✿ (Pinaceae)

albicaulis	WNor
- 'Flinck'	CKen
- 'Nana'	see *P. albicaulis* 'Noble's Dwarf'
§ - 'Noble's Dwarf'	CKen
aristata	CAbP CDul CFil CLnd CMCN EHul EOrn GKir LCon LLin MAsh MBar MGos NBee SIng SSpi STre WDin WEve
- 'Cecilia'	CKen
- 'Sherwood Compact'	CKen
armandii	CDul GKir IDee LCon WEve
- 'Gold Tip'	CKen
austriaca	see *P. nigra* subsp. *nigra*
N *ayacahuite*	LCon
banksiana	CDul CLnd GKir IDee LCon
- 'Arctis' **new**	NLar
- 'Chippewa'	CKen LLin
I - 'Compacta'	CKen
- 'H.J. Welch'	CKen
- 'Manomet'	CKen
- 'Neponset'	CKen
- 'Schneverdingen' **new**	CKen
- 'Schoodic'	LLin SLim
- 'Uncle Fogy'	WEve
- 'Wisconsin'	CKen
bungeana	CDoC CLnd CMCN CTho EPfP GKir IDee LCon LLin MBlu SLPl SSpi WEve WNor
- 'Diamant'	CKen
canariensis	CDul EHul IDee ISea
cembra	CDul CLnd EHul GIBF GKir LCon LPan MBar NLar NWea STre WEve
- 'Aurea'	see *P. cembra* 'Aureovariegata'
§ - 'Aureovariegata' (v)	CKen EBre GKir LLin LRHS MAsh NDlv WEve
- 'Barnhourie'	CKen
- 'Blue Mound'	CKen
- 'Chalet'	CKen
- 'Compacta Glauca'	CDoC LCon MBri
* - 'Griffithii'	WDin
- 'Inverleith'	CKen
- 'Jermyns'	CKen
- 'King's Dwarf'	CKen
- 'Roughills'	CKen
- 'Stricta'	CKen
- witches' broom	CKen
contorta	CBcs CDoC CDul CTrC GKir MBar MGos NWea WDin WMou
- 'Asher'	CKen
- 'Frisian Gold'	CKen EBre SLim
- var. *latifolia*	CLnd LRav WDin
- 'Spaan's Dwarf'	CDoC CKen EBre GKir LLin MAsh

		MBar MBri MGos NLar SCoo SLim WEve
	coulteri ♀H4	CMCN GKir GTSp LCon LLin SMad SSpi WNor WPGP
	densiflora	CDul CMCN LEdu WNor
	– SF 99088	ISea
	– 'Alice Verkade'	CDoC EBre EHul GKir LBee LCon LLin LRHS MAsh MBri NDlv SCoo SLim WEve WFar
	– 'Aurea'	MBar MGos SLim
	– 'Jane Kluis'	CDoC CKen COtt EBre EHul GKir LBee LLin LRHS MAsh MBri NDlv NLar SCoo SLim WEve
I	– 'Jim Cross'	CKen SLim
	– 'Low Glow'	CKen
	– 'Oculus-draconis' (v)	GKir LLin MBar MGos SCoo SLim WEve
	– 'Pendula'	CKen GKir LLin MBri SLim WFar
*	– 'Pyramidalis'	ECho
	– 'Umbraculifera'	CDoC GKir IMGH LCon LLin MAsh MBar MGos MOne NLar SCoo SSta WEve WFar
I	– 'Umbraculifera Nana'	LLin
§	*devoniana*	LCon
	edulis 'Juno'	CKen
	flexilis	LCon
	– 'Firmament'	LLin SLim
	– 'Glenmore Dwarf'	CKen
	– 'Nana'	CKen
	– 'Pendula'	LLin
I	– 'Pygmaea'	NLar
	– 'Vanderwolf's Pyramid'	EPfP GKir MAsh MBri NLar
	– WB No. 1	CKen
	– WB No. 2	CKen
	gerardiana	GKir LCon
	greggii	EPfP
	griffithii	see *P. wallichiana*
	halepensis	CDul ECrN
§	*heldreichii* ♀H4	CDoC CDul CMac GKir LRav MBar SCoo WNor
	– 'Aureospicata'	LLin MBar NDlv NLar
	– 'Groen'	CKen
	– var. *leucodermis*	see *P. heldreichii*
	– – 'Compact Gem'	CDoC CKen EBre GKir LBee LCon LLin LRHS MAsh MBar MBri MGos SCoo SLim SSta WEve
	– 'Malink'	CKen
	– 'Ottocek'	CKen
	– 'Pygmy'	CKen
	– 'Satellit'	CDoC CTri EBre EHul EOrn GKir LCon LLin LRHS MAsh MGos NLar SCoo SLim WEve
§	– 'Smidtii' ♀H4	CDoC CKen EBre LCon LLin MAsh MBar NLar SLim
	– 'Zwerg Schneverdingen'	CKen
	jeffreyi ♀H4	CLnd CMCN CTrC GKir GTSp ISea LCon LRav MBar NWea
	– 'Joppi'	CKen
	koraiensis	GKir WNor
	– 'Bergman'	CKen
	– 'Dragon Eye'	CKen
	– 'Jack Corbit'	CKen
	– 'Shibamichi' (v)	CKen
	– 'Silver Lining'	MAsh
	– 'Silveray'	CDoC GKir NLar
	– 'Silvergrey'	CKen
	– 'Winton'	CKen
	lambertiana	GKir
	leucodermis	see *P. heldreichii*
	longaeva	EPfP
	magnifica	see *P. devoniana*
	massoniana	ISea WNor
	monophylla	LLin
	montezumae ambig.	CDul SAPC SArc WNor

	monticola 'Pendula'	CKen MBar
	– 'Pygmy'	see *P. monticola* 'Raraflora'
§	– 'Raraflora'	CKen
	– 'Skyline'	LCon MBar
	– 'Strobicola'	LCon
	– 'Windsor Dwarf'	CKen
	mugo	CBcs CDul CSBt CTri EHul ENot GKir MBar MGos NWea WBrE WDin WEve WFar WStI
	– 'Benjamin'	CKen
	– 'Bisley Green'	LLin WEve
	– 'Brownie'	CKen
	– 'Carsten'	CKen EBre LLin SLim WEve
	– 'Carsten's Wintergold'	MAsh MBri WEve
	– 'Corley's Mat'	CKen EBre GKir LLin MAsh NHol SCoo SLim WEve
	– 'Gnom'	CDoC CDul CKen CMac EBre EHul ENot EOrn GKir IMGH LCon LLin LRHS MAsh MBar MBri MGos MOne NBee SCoo WDin WEve WFar
	– 'Golden Glow' **new**	LLin MBri
	– 'Hoersholm'	CKen
	– 'Humpy'	CDoC CKen CMen EBre EOrn GKir IMGH LBee LCon LLin LRHS MAsh MBar MBri MGos MOne SLim WEve WFar
	– 'Jacobsen'	CKen NLar
	– 'Janovsky'	CKen
	– 'Kissen'	CKen LCon LLin MGos NLar WEve
	– 'Klosterkotter'	CDoC MGos NLar
	– 'Kobold'	NDlv NHol WFar
	– 'Krauskopf'	CKen
	– 'Laarheide'	GKir MGos WEve
	– 'Laurin'	CKen
	– 'Marand' **new**	LLin
	– 'March'	CKen EHul LLin
	– 'Mini Mops'	CKen CMen
	– 'Minikin'	CKen
	– 'Mops' ♀H4	CDoC CDul EBre EHul EPfP EPla GKir LBee LCon LLin LPan LRHS MAsh MBar MBlu MGos NBee SLim SPer SSta WDin WFar
	– 'Mops Midget'	EBre GKir LBee LCon LLin MAsh MBri SCoo WEve
	– var. *mughus*	see *P. mugo* subsp. *mugo*
§	– subsp. *mugo*	EOrn GKir LBuc LPan MAsh MBar NBlu NWea WEve WFar
	– 'Mumpitz'	CKen
	– 'Ophir'	CDoC CDul CKen EBre EHul EOrn EPfP EPla GKir IMGH LBee LCon LLin LRHS MAsh MBar MBri MGos SLim SPer SPla SSta WDin WEve WFar
	– 'Pal Maleter' (v)	EBre GKir LCon LLin MAsh NLar SCoo SLim WEve
	– 'Piggelmee'	CKen
	– Pumilio Group ♀H4	CDoC CDul CLnd CMac EGra EHul ENot EOrn GBin GKir LBee LCon LLin LPan MBar MBro MGos MLan NBlu NPal NWea SCoo SHBN STre WBVN WDin WFar WNor
	– 'Pygmy'	NDlv
	– var. *rostrata*	see *P. mugo* subsp. *uncinata*
	– 'Rushmore'	CKen
	– 'Spaan'	CKen WEve
	– 'Sunshine' (v)	CKen GKir NLar
§	– subsp. *uncinata*	GIBF GKir NWea WFar
	– – 'Grüne Welle'	CKen
	– – 'Paradekissen'	CKen NLar
	– – 'White Tip'	CKen MAsh
	– 'Winter Gold'	CKen EBre EHul EOrn EPfP GKir LCon LLin LPan MAsh NLar SCoo SSta WEve WFar

- 'Winter Sun'	MAsh	
- 'Winzig'	CKen	
- 'Yellow Tip' (v)	MAsh	
- 'Zundert'	CDoC CKen EHul GKir LLin MAsh	
	MBar MGos NLar WEve	
- 'Zwergkugel'	CKen	
muricata ♀H4	CDoC CDul CLnd GKir GTSp	
	LCon LRav MGos NWea	
nigra ♀H4	CBcs CDoC CLnd CSBt CTri	
	ECrN GKir LCon MBar MGos NPSI	
	SAPC SArc SHBN WBrE WDin	
	WMou	
- var. **austriaca**	see *P. nigra* subsp. *nigra*	
- 'Black Prince'	CDul CFee CKen EBre EOrn GKir	
	IMGH LBee LCon LLin LRHS MAsh	
	NLar SCoo SLim WEve WGor	
N - 'Cebennensis Nana'	CKen	
- var. **corsicana**	see *P. nigra* subsp. *laricio*	
- 'Frank'	CKen NLar	
- 'Hornibrookiana'	CKen LLin MAsh	
§ - subsp. **laricio** ♀H4	CAgr CDoC CDul CKen CSBt EMil	
	ENot GWCH LBuc LCon LRav	
	MBar MGos NWea WMou	
- - 'Bobby McGregor'	CKen GKir LLin SCoo SLim	
- - 'Globosa Viridis'	GKir IMGH LLin NHol SLim WEve	
- - 'Goldfingers'	CKen LLin WEve	
§ - - 'Moseri'	CKen EBre LLin SLim SSta	
- - 'Pygmaea'	CKen ECho NDlv WFar	
- - 'Spingarn'	CKen	
- - 'Talland Bay'	CKen	
- - 'Wurstle'	CKen	
- subsp. **maritima**	see *P. nigra* subsp. *laricio*	
- 'Nana'	CDoC LBee LPan	
§ - subsp. **nigra**	CAgr CCVT CDoC CLnd EWTr	
	LBuc LPan MGos NWea SPer WEve	
	WFar WStI	
- - 'Bright Eyes'	CFee CKen EBre ECho EOrn GKir	
	IMGH LBee LCon LLin LRHS MAsh	
	NLar SCoo SPoG WEve	
- - 'Helga'	CKen	
- - 'Schovenhorst'	CKen	
- - 'Strypemonde'	CKen	
- - 'Yaffle Hill'	CKen	
- 'Obelisk'	CKen NLar	
- subsp. **pallasiana**	CDul LCon NLar WPGP	
- 'Richard' **new**	CKen	
- 'Uelzen'	CKen	
palustris	LCon LLin MAsh SSpi	
parviflora	CTri STre WDin WNor	
- 'Adcock's Dwarf' ♀H4	CKen EBre GKir LCon LLin MBar	
	MGos NLar SLim	
- Aizu-goyo Group	LLin	
- 'Al Fordham'	CKen	
- 'Aoi'	CKen CMen	
- 'Ara-kawa'	CKen CMen	
- Azuma-goyo Group	CKen	
I - 'Baasch's Form'	CKen	
- 'Bergman'	LCon MAsh MBar NLar	
- 'Blue Giant'	ECho NLar	
- 'Bonnie Bergman'	CKen LLin WEve	
- 'Dai-ho'	CKen	
- 'Daisetsusan'	CKen	
- 'Doctor Landis Gold'	CKen	
- 'Fukai' (v)	CKen NLar	
- 'Fukiju'	CKen	
- Fukushima-goyo Group	CKen CMen WEve	
- 'Fuku-zu-mi'	CKen LLin	
- 'Fu-shiro'	CKen	
- 'Gin-sho-chuba' **new**	CKen	
- Glauca Group	CMac EHul LCon LLin LPan MAsh	
	MBar MBri MGos NBlu WEve WFar	
I - 'Glauca Nana'	CKen	
I - 'Goldilocks'	CKen	
- 'Gyok-ke-sen'	CKen	

- 'Gyo-ko-haku'	CKen	
- 'Gyokuei'	CKen	
- 'Gyokusen Sämling'	CKen NLar	
- 'Gyo-ku-sui'	CKen LLin	
- 'Hagaromo Seedling'	CKen LLin MAsh NLar	
- 'Hakko'	CKen	
- 'Hatchichi'	CKen	
- 'Ibo-can'	CKen CMen	
- 'Ichi-no-se'	CKen	
- 'Iri-fune'	CKen	
- Ishizuchi-goyo Group	CKen	
- 'Ka-ho'	CKen LLin	
- 'Kanzan'	CKen	
- 'Kiyomatsu'	CKen	
- 'Kobe'	CKen LLin	
- 'Kokonoe'	CKen CMen LLin	
- 'Kokuho'	CKen	
- 'Koraku'	CKen	
- 'Kusu-dama'	CKen	
- 'Meiko'	CKen	
- 'Michinoku'	CKen	
- 'Momo-yama' **new**	CKen	
- 'Myo-jo'	CKen	
- Nasu-goyo Group	CKen	
- 'Negishi'	CDoC CKen CMen LCon LLin LPan	
	LRHS MAsh MBri NLar WEve	
- 'Ogon-janome'	CKen	
- 'Ossorio Dwarf'	CKen	
- 'Regenhold' **new**	CKen	
- 'Richard Lee'	CKen	
- 'Ryo-ku-ho'	CKen	
- 'Ryu-ju'	CKen	
- 'San-bo'	CDoC CKen MBar	
§ - 'Saphir' **new**	CKen ECho	
- 'Setsugekka'	CKen	
- 'Shika-shima'	CKen	
- Shiobara-goyo Group	CKen	
- 'Shizukagoten'	CKen	
- 'Shu-re'	CKen	
- 'Sieryoden'	CKen	
- 'Tani-mano-uki'	CKen	
- 'Tempelhof'	COtt CTho GKir LPan LRHS MBar	
	SLim	
- 'Templeflora'	MLan	
- 'Tenysu-kazu'	CKen	
I - 'Torulosa'	LLin	
- 'Venus'	NDlv	
I - 'Zelkova'	CMen LLin	
- 'Zui-sho'	CKen	
patula ♀H2-3	CAbb CDoC CDul CLnd CTrC	
	ECre EGra GKir LAst LCon LRav	
	MBlu SAPC SArc SBir SCoo SLim	
	WEve	
peuce	CDoC EHoe GKir LCon LRav MBar	
	NWea STre	
- 'Arnold Dwarf'	CKen	
- 'Cesarini'	CKen	
pinaster ♀H4	CBcs CDoC CLnd EHul GKir LCon	
	WBVN	
pinea ♀H4	CDoC CFil CKen CLnd CMac	
	CTho ECrN EPfP GKir LCon LEdu	
	LPan LRHS MGos NPSI SAPC SArc	
	SEND WEve WNor	
- 'Queensway'	CKen	
ponderosa ♀H4	CLnd CMCN GTSp LCon LRav	
	WPGP	
pumila 'Buchanan'	CKen	
- 'Draijer's Dwarf'	CDoC EBre EOrn GKir LLin SCoo	
	SLim	
- 'Dwarf Blue'	MAsh NDlv	
§ - 'Glauca' ♀H4	CKen LCon LLin LRHS MAsh MBar	
	MBri	
- 'Globe'	GKir LBee LLin MAsh MBri	
- 'Jeddeloh'	CKen	

	- 'Knightshayes'	CKen
	- 'Säntis'	CKen
	- 'Saphir'	see *P. parviflora* 'Saphir'
*	*pungens* 'Glauca'	EWTr
	radiata ♀H3-4	CAgr CBcs CDoC CDul CSBt CTrC CTri CTrw ECrN ELan ENot EWTr GBin GKir LCon LRHS LRav NWea SAPC SArc SHBN SKee STre WDin WEve
	- Aurea Group	CDoC CDul CKen EBre GKir LBee LCon LLin LRHS MAsh MBri SBir SCoo SLim SMur WEve WFar
	- 'Bodnant'	CKen
	- 'Isca'	CKen
	- 'Marshwood' (v)	CKen EBre LCon SCoo SLim
	- var. *radiata*	NPal
	resinosa	GIBF
	- 'Don Smith'	CKen
	- 'Joel's Broom'	CKen
	- 'Quinobequin'	CKen
	roxburghii	LCon SSpi
	x *schwerinii*	CDoC GKir LRHS
	- 'Wiethorst'	CKen
	sibirica	GIBF
	strobiformis	ISea
	strobus	CTho EMil GKir ISea LPan MBar NWea SLim STre WDin WEve WNor
§	- 'Alba'	MGos
	- 'Amelia's Dwarf'	CKen
	- 'Anna Fiele'	CKen
	- 'Bergman's Mini'	CKen NLar
	- 'Bergman's Pendula Broom'	CKen
I	- 'Bergman's Sport of Prostrata'	CKen
	- 'Bloomer's Dark Globe'	CKen
	- 'Blue Shag'	CKen COtt EBre EMil GKir LBee LLin MGos NLar SCoo SLim SPoG WEve
	- 'Cesarini'	CKen
	- 'Densa'	CKen
	- 'Dove's Dwarf'	CKen
	- 'Ed's Broom'	CKen
	- 'Elkins Dwarf'	CKen
	- 'Fastigiata'	CKen GBin GKir IMGH LLin MBri
	- 'Greg'	CKen
	- 'Hillside Gem'	CKen
	- 'Himmelblau' **new**	NLar
	- 'Horsford'	CKen LLin MBlu
	- 'Jericho'	CKen NDlv
	- 'Krügers Lilliput'	EBre LCon LLin LRHS MBri NLar SCoo SLim
	- 'Louie' **new**	NLar
	- 'Macopin'	LLin MGos NLar
	- 'Mary Butler'	CKen
	- 'Merrimack'	CKen NLar
	- 'Minima'	CKen EBre LBee LCon LLin LRHS MBar MBlu MBri SCoo SLim WGor
	- 'Minuta'	CKen
	- 'Nana'	see *P. strobus* Nana Group
	- Nana Group	LLin
	- 'Nivea'	see *P. strobus* 'Alba'
	- 'Northway Broom'	CKen EBre LCon LLin SLim
	- 'Ontario'	MBlu
	- 'Pendula'	CKen GKir SMad
§	- 'Radiata'	CTri EHul EPla GKir LCon MBar NBee NLar SLim
I	- 'Radiata Aurea'	WEve
	- 'Reinshaus'	CKen LLin
	- 'Sayville'	CKen
	- 'Sea Urchin'	CKen
	- 'Uncatena'	CKen
	- 'Verkade's Broom'	CKen

	sylvestris ♀H4	More than 30 suppliers
	- 'Abergeldie'	CKen
	- 'Alderly Edge'	WEve
	- 'Andorra'	CKen
§	- 'Argentea'	CMen
§	- Aurea Group ♀H4	CDul CKen CMac CMen EBre EHul EPfP GBin GKir IMGH LBee LCon LLin LRHS MAsh MBar SHBN SLim SPer SSta WEve
	- 'Aurea'	see *P. sylvestris* Aurea Group
	- 'Avondene'	CKen
	- 'Bergfield'	NLar
	- 'Beuvronensis' ♀H4	CDul CKen CLnd CMac CMen EBre EOrn GKir IMGH LBee LLin LRHS MAsh MGos NHol SCoo SLim SSta WEve
	- 'Bonna'	EBre GKir SCoo
	- 'Brevifolia'	MBar
	- 'Buchanan's Gold'	CKen
	- 'Burghfield'	CKen LLin WEve
	- 'Chantry Blue'	CDoC CDul EBre EHul EOrn GKir IMGH LBee LCon LLin LRHS MAsh MBar MGos NLar SCoo SLim WEve WFar
	- 'Clumber Blue'	CKen
	- 'Compressa'	LLin
	- 'Corley'	GKir LLin
	- 'Dereham'	CKen LLin
	- 'Doone Valley'	CKen GKir LLin WEve
	- 'Edwin Hillier'	see *P. sylvestris* 'Argentea'
	- Fastigiata Group	CDoC CEnd CKen CMen EBre EOrn GKir IMGH LBee LCon LLin LPan LRHS MAsh MBar MGos NDlv SCoo SLim WEve WFar
	- 'Frensham'	CDoC CKen EOrn IMGH LBee LLin MAsh MGos MOne WEve WFar
	- 'Globosa'	LRHS MBri
	- 'Gold Coin'	CDoC CKen EBre EOrn EPfP GKir LBee LLin MAsh MBri MGos NDlv NLar SCoo SLim SPoG WFar
	- 'Gold Medal'	CKen GKir LLin WEve
	- 'Grand Rapids'	CKen
	- 'Gwydyr Castle' **new**	CKen
	- 'Hillside Creeper'	CKen GKir LCon LLin NLar SLim WEve
	- 'Inverleith' (v)	EHul GKir LBuc LCon LLin MBar MGos NHol SCoo SLim SPoG WEve
	- 'Jeremy'	CKen EBre LCon LLin SCoo SLim WEve
	- 'John Boy'	CMen LLin
	- 'Kelpie'	LLin
	- 'Kenwith'	CKen
	- 'Lakeside Dwarf'	LLin WEve
	- 'Lodge Hill'	CMen EBre EOrn GKir IMGH LBee LLin LRHS MAsh MOne SCoo SLim
	- 'Longmoor'	CKen NLar
	- 'Martham'	CKen LLin WEve
	- var. *mongolica*	GIBF
*	- 'Moseri'	ECho GKir LBee LRHS MAsh MBri WEve
	- 'Munches Blue' **new**	CKen
	- 'Nana Compacta'	CMen GKir LLin
	- 'Nana' misapplied	see *P. sylvestris* 'Watereri'
§	- 'Nisbet's Gem'	CKen LLin NLar
	- 'Padworth'	CKen CMen NLar
	- 'Pixie'	CKen LLin NLar
I	- 'Prostrata'	GKir SCoo
	- 'Pulham'	LLin WEve
	- 'Pygmaea'	EBre GKir SCoo SLim
	- 'Reedham'	LLin WEve
	- 'Repens'	CKen
	- 'Saint George'	CKen

- 'Sandringham'	LLin WEve
- 'Saxatilis'	CKen EOrn GKir LBee LLin MAsh WEve
- subsp. *scotica*	GIBF
- 'Scott's Dwarf'	see *P. sylvestris* 'Nisbet's Gem'
- 'Scrubby'	LLin NLar
- 'Sentinel'	CKen
- 'Skjak I'	CKen
- 'Skjak II'	CKen
- 'Spaan's Slow Column'	CKen
- 'Tabuliformis'	LLin
- 'Tage'	CKen LLin WEve
- 'Tanya'	CKen
- 'Tilhead'	CKen
- 'Treasure'	CKen LLin
- 'Variegata' (v)	WEve
- 'Viridis Compacta' **new**	CMen
§ - 'Watereri'	CMac EBre EHul ENot GKir IMGH LBee LCon LLin LPan LRHS MAsh MBar MBri MGos NHol SCoo SLim SPer WDin WEve WFar
- 'Westonbirt'	CKen CMen EHul LLin MAsh WEve
- 'Wishmoor'	LLin WEve
- 'Wolf Gold'	CKen
* - 'Yaff Hill'	LLin
tabuliformis	CDul CMCN GIBF GTSp IDee LCon MBlu
thunbergii	CDul CLnd EHul LCon LLin MGos STre WNor
- 'Akame'	CKen CMen
- 'Akame Yatsabusa'	CMen
- 'Aocha-matsu' (v)	CKen CMen NLar
- 'Arakawa-sho'	CKen CMen
- 'Banshosho'	CKen CMen NLar
- 'Beni-kujaku'	CKen CMen
- 'Compacta'	CKen CMen
- 'Dainagon'	CKen CMen
- 'Iwai'	CMen
- 'Katsuga' **new**	CMen
- 'Kotobuki'	CKen CMen NLar
- 'Koyosho'	CMen GKir
- 'Kujaku'	CKen CMen
- 'Kyushu'	CKen CMen
- 'Miyajuna'	CKen CMen NLar
- 'Nishiki-ne'	CKen CMen
- 'Nishiki-tsusaka' **new**	CMen
- 'Oculus-draconis' (v)	CMen GKir LBuc LLin
- 'Ogon'	CKen CMen NLar
- 'Porky'	CKen CMen
§ - 'Sayonara'	CKen CMen EBre LLin MAsh NHol NLar SLim
- 'Senryu'	CKen CMen
- 'Shinsho'	CKen CMen
- 'Shio-guro'	CKen CMen
- 'Suchiro Yatabusa'	CKen CMen
- 'Sunsho'	CKen CMen
- 'Taihei'	CKen CMen
I - 'Thunderhead'	CKen CMen NLar
- 'Yatsubusa'	see *P. thunbergii* 'Sayonara'
- 'Yumaki'	CKen CMen
uncinata	see *P. mugo* subsp. *uncinata*
- 'Jezek' **new**	CKen
- 'Susse Perle' **new**	CKen
virginiana 'Wate's Golden'	CKen
§ *wallichiana* ♀H4	CDoC CDul CKen CMCN CTho EBre EHul ENot EPfP EPla GKir LCon LLin LPan MBar MBlu MGos NBee NPSI NWea SBir SLim SSpi STre WDin WEve WFar WGer WNor WOrn
- SF 00001	ISea
- 'Densa'	MBri

- 'Nana'	CKen EHul LCon LLin MBar NLar SLim WEve
- 'Umbraculifera'	LRHS MBri
- 'Zebrina' (v)	CDoC GKir LBee MBar MGos NLar SMad WEve
yunnanensis	GKir SSpi WEve WNor

Piper (Piperaceae)

betle	MSal
excelsum	see *Macropiper excelsum*
nigrum	MSal

Piptanthus (Papilionaceae)

forrestii	see *P. nepalensis*
laburnifolius	see *P. nepalensis*
§ *nepalensis*	More than 30 suppliers
- B&SWJ 2241	WCru
aff. *nepalensis*	GIBF
tomentosus	CFil SDry WPGP

Pistacia (Anacardiaceae)

atlantica	EGFP
chinensis	CBrd CMCN CPMA EPfP SSpi WPic XPep
lentiscus	CBcs XPep
terebinthus	XPep

Pistia (Araceae)

stratiotes	LPBA MSta NArg NPer SCoo

Pittosporum ❀ (Pittosporaceae)

anomalum	ECou SDry
- (f)	ECou
- (m)	ECou
- 'Falcon'	ECou
- 'Raven' (f)	ECou
- 'Starling' (m)	ECou
'Arundel Green'	CDoC CWSG EBee EPfP LRHS SDry SLim SWvt WWeb
bicolor	CFil CPle ECou EShb GQui IDee SAPC SArc WBor WPGP
- 'Cradle' (f) **new**	ECou
- 'Mount Field' (f) **new**	ECou
buchananii	SGar SVen
colensoi	ECou
- 'Cobb' (f)	ECou
- 'Wanaka' (m)	ECou
crassifolium	CFil CPle CTrC ECou ERea WPGP XPep
- 'Compactum' **new**	XPep
- 'Havering Dwarf' (f)	ECou
- 'Napier' (f)	ECou
- 'Variegatum' (v)	CPne WBcn WSPU
crassifolium x *tenuifolium*	CWib ECou SWvt
'Craxten' (f)	ECou
'Crinkles' (f)	ECou
daphniphylloides B&SWJ 6789	WCru
- ETE 275	WPGP
- var. *adaphniphylloides*	CFil
'Dark Delight' (m)	ECou
divaricatum	ECou
'Essex' (f/v)	ECou
eugenioides	CBcs CHEx CMHG CTrC CTrG GGar SLon
- 'Platinum' (v)	CBcs MGos
- 'Variegatum' (v) ♀H3	CAbb CBcs CBrm CDoC EBee EMil EPfP GGar GQui IArd LRHS NPSI NPal SAga SLim SSpi SSto WGer WPGP WSPU WWeb
'Garnettii' (v) ♀H3	More than 30 suppliers
heterophyllum	ECou XPep

- variegated (v)	ECou SLim SSpi
'Humpty Dumpty'	ECou
illicioides var.	WCru
illicioides	
B&SWJ 6712	
'Limelight' (v)	CBcs CPLG CSBt CSPN CTrC EBee
	EMil ENot LRHS WWeb WWes
lineare	ECou
§ 'Margaret Turnbull' (v)	CBcs CMHG CTrC ECou EMil
	EWes IArd LRHS MGos WBcn
michiei	ECou
- (f)	ECou
- (m)	ECou
- 'Jack' (m)	ECou
- 'Jill' (f)	ECou
'Nanum Variegatum'	see *P. tobira* 'Variegatum'
obcordatum	ECou
- var. *kaitaiaense*	ECou
omeiense	CFil ECou ECre WPGP
phillyreoides	CFil XPep
pimeleoides var.	ECou
reflexum (m) **new**	
'Purple Princess'	ECou
ralphii	EBee ECou
- 'Green Globe'	ECou XPep
- 'Variegatum' (v)	SSpi
* *robustum* **new**	EWes
'Saundersii' (v)	ECrN ENot
'Tadina Gold' **new**	CDul
tenuifolium ♀H3	More than 30 suppliers
- 'Abbotsbury Gold' (f/v)	CAbb CBcs CChe CDoC CSam
	CTri CWSG EBee ECou LRHS ELan
	EMil EWes GBri LAst LRHS MPRe
	SAga SDry SEND SHBN SLim SPer
	SSto WSHC
- 'Atropurpureum'	CBcs WBcn
- 'County Park Dwarf'	ECou WCru
- 'Deborah' (v)	ECou EHol LRHS WBcn
- 'Dixie'	ECou
§ - 'Eila Keightley' (v)	CMHG SAga
- 'Elizabeth' (m/v)	CDoC CTrC EBee ECou LRHS NPSI
	WBcn
* - 'French Lace'	CBcs ECou NLar WFar
- 'Gold Star'	CBcs CDoC CTrC ECou EMil LRHS
	NPal SLim
- 'Golden King'	CDoC CMHG CSBt EBee LRHS
	MRav NScw SLim SRms SSto
	WWeb
- 'Golden Princess' (f)	ECou
- 'Green Elf'	CTrC ECou
- 'Green Thumb'	CWSG LRHS
- 'Irene Paterson'	CAbb CBcs CBrm CDoC CSBt
(m/v) ♀H3	CSam CWSG ECou ELan ENot EPfP
	LAst LHop LRHS MGos NBea SAga
	SDry SLim SLon SPer SPla SRms
	SSpi SSta WAbe WDin WSHC XPep
- 'James Stirling'	EBee ECou EPfP LRHS SSto
- 'John Flanagan'	see *P.* 'Margaret Turnbull'
- 'Loxhill Gold'	EBee LRHS SSto
- 'Marjory Channon' (v)	CBcs LRHS SSpi
- 'Mellow Yellow'	CAbP LRHS WBcn
- 'Moonlight' (v)	CTrC EBee NPSI
- 'Purpureum' (m)	CBrm CDul CPle CSBt CSam CTri
	CTrw ECou EPfP LAst LRHS LSpr
	MPRe SAga SDry SHBN SPer SPla
	SRms SSto WGer WSHC
- 'Silver Magic' (v)	CBcs CPen CSBt EMil MGos
- 'Silver 'n' Gold'	EBee LRHS
- 'Silver Princess' (f)	ECou
- 'Silver Queen'	More than 30 suppliers
(f/v) ♀H3	
- 'Silver Sheen'	CBcs ECou LRHS
- 'Stirling Gold' (f/v)	ECou EPfP EWes
- 'Sunburst'	see *P. tenuifolium* 'Eila Keightley'

- 'Tandara Gold' (v)	CAbb CBrm CDoC CTrC EBee ECou
	EMil ENot LPVe SLim SPla WFar
- 'Tiki'	CBcs CTrC ECou
- 'Tom Thumb' ♀H3	More than 30 suppliers
- 'Tresederi' (f/m)	CTrC CTrw ECou LRHS
- 'Variegatum' (m/v)	CBcs CDoC ECou EMil GBri LAst
	LRHS SWvt
- 'Victoria' (v)	CDoC CTrC EMil
- 'Warnham Gold'	CBrm COtt CSBt CTrw CWSG
(m) ♀H3	CWib EBee ECou ECrN ELan EPfP
	GBri LAst LRHS MCCP MPRe SDry
	SLim SSpi WAbe WDin
- 'Wendle Channon'	CBcs CMHG CSam CTrC EBee
(m/v)	ECot ECou EPfP LRHS NBlu SLim
	SPer SSto WBcn
- 'Winter Sunshine'	LRHS SSta
tobira ♀H3	More than 30 suppliers
- B&SWJ 4362	WCru
* - 'Cuneatum'	LHop SAga
* - 'Nanum'	CBcs CDoC EBee ECou ELan EPfP
	ERea LPan MGos MPRe SAPC SArc
	SLim WBcn WDin WGer XPep
§ - 'Variegatum' (v) ♀H2-3	CBcs CBot CPle CSam ECou ECrN
	ELan EPfP GQui LHop LRHS NPal
	SAga SDnm SLon SPer SPla SSta
	SSto WBcn WCru WDin WGer
	WPGP WSHC WWeb XPep
truncatum	ECre EWes XPep
* - 'Variegatum' **new**	XPep
undulatum	CHEx ECou
viridiflorum	ECou

Plagianthus (Malvaceae)

betulinus	see *P. regius*
divaricatus	CFil CTrC ECou GEil WPGP
lyallii	see *Hoheria lyallii*
§ *regius*	CTrC ECou GGar GQui LRHS

Plagiorhegma see *Jeffersonia*

Plantago (Plantaginaceae)

asiatica	MSal
- 'Ki Fu' (v)	ITer MAvo
- 'Variegata' (v)	CRow EBee EMan GBuc MBNS
	NBro NLar WHer WMoo WRos
	WWye
cynops	MTho XPep
holosteum **new**	EHyt
lanceolata	CNat EBee EChP
'Ballydowling	
Variegated' (v)	
- 'Blond Bomi-noka'	CNat
- 'Bomi-noka'	CNat
- 'Burren Rose'	CBgR CNat CRow
- 'Golden Spears'	CBgR CBre CPla EBee EChP
- 'Keer's Pride' (v)	WCot
- 'Pink Bomi-noka'	CNat
- 'Streaker' (v)	CRow EBee MTed WCot WHal
major	WHbs
- 'Atropurpurea'	see *P. major* 'Rubrifolia'
- 'Bowles' Variety'	see *P. major* 'Rosularis'
- 'Frills'	CBre CNat CRow EBee WHer
* - 'Karmozijn'	EMan
§ - 'Rosularis'	CArn CFwr CNat CRow CSpe
	EBee EChP ILis ITer MAnH MHer
	MTho MWgw NBid NBro NChi
	NSti NWCA SUsu WBVN WBea
	WEas WHer WPer WWye
§ - 'Rubrifolia'	CArn CFwr CHid CPom CRow
	CSpe EBee EChP ECoo IHMH ITer
	LDai MFir MHer MWgw NBid
	NBro NChi NSti WBVN WBar
	WBea WCAu WHer WMoo WPer
	WRos WWye

- 'Tony Lewis'	CNat
maritima	WHer
media	CBgR MHer WBWf
nivalis	EBee GEdr MBro SMad WWin
psyllium L.	CArn MSal
raoulii	WCot
rosea	see *P. major* 'Rosularis'
uniflora Hook. f.	WCot

Platanthera (Orchidaceae)

chlorantha **new**	CHdy
hologlottis	EFEx
metabifolia	EFEx

Platanus ✿ (Platanaceae)

x *acerifolia*	see *P.* x *hispanica*
§ x *hispanica* ♀H4	CBcs CCVT CDul CLnd CMCN CTho EBee ECrN EMil ENot EPfP EWTr LBuc LPan LRHS MGos NWea SBLw SEND SHBN SKee SPer WDin WFar WMou
- 'Bloodgood'	SBLw
- 'Dakvorm' **new**	SBLw
- 'Dortmund' **new**	SBLw
- 'Pyramidalis'	CTho SBLw WOrn
- 'Suttneri' (v)	CEnd CLnd CTho SBLw SMad WBcn WMou
- 'Tremonia'	LRHS
orientalis ♀H4	CDul CLnd CMCN CTho ECrN EPfP LEdu LPan NWea SBLw SKee SLPl SMad WDin WMou WPGP
- MSF 0028 from Sfendili, Crete	WPGP
- 'Cuneata'	CDoC GKir LRHS MBri
§ - f. *digitata* ♀H4	CDoC CDul CLnd CMCN EPfP ERod SBLw SLPl SMad WMou
- var. *insularis*	CEnd WPGP
- 'Laciniata'	see *P. orientalis* f. *digitata*
- 'Minaret'	EMil WMou
- 'Mirkovec'	CDoC LRHS MBri SMad SPer WMou

Platycarya (Juglandaceae)

strobilacea	EPfP IDee

Platycerium (Polypodiaceae)

alcicorne hort.	see *P. bifurcatum*
§ *bifurcatum* ♀H1	LRHS MBri

Platycladus (Cupressaceae)

orientalis 'Aurea Nana' ♀H4	More than 30 suppliers
- 'Autumn Glow'	CKen LBee LRHS SCoo WGor
- 'Beverleyensis'	LLin NLar WEve
- 'Blue Cone'	MBar
- 'Caribbean Holiday'	MAsh
- 'Collen's Gold'	CTri EHul EOrn MAsh MBar WBcn
- 'Conspicua'	CKen CWib EHul LBee LCon LRHS MAsh MBar
- 'Elegantissima' ♀H4	CMac EHul EOrn LBee LRHS MAsh MBar SCoo
- 'Golden Minaret'	WBcn
- 'Golden Pillar'	EOrn
- 'Golden Pygmy'	CKen EOrn MAsh WBcn
- 'Juniperoides'	EHul LCon MAsh MBar
- 'Kenwith'	CKen
- 'Lemon 'n Lime' **new**	SPoG
- 'Madurodam'	LLin MBar
- 'Magnifica'	EHul
- 'Meldensis'	CDoC CTri EBre EHul MBar WTel
- 'Minima'	EHul WGor
- 'Minima Glauca'	CKen MBar
- 'Mint Chocolate'	LLin
- 'Purple King'	EBre LRHS SCoo SLim

I - 'Pyramidalis Aurea'	LBee LCon LPan LRHS
- 'Rosedalis'	CKen CMac CSBt EBre EHul EOrn EPfP LBee LLin LRHS MAsh MBar MBri MWat SLim SMer SPla WEve WFar WTel
- 'Sanderi'	MBar WCFE
- 'Semperaurea'	CMac IMGH
- 'Shirley Chilcott'	MAsh
- 'Sieboldii'	EHul
- 'Southport'	LBee LCon LLin LRHS MAsh
- 'Summer Cream'	CKen EHul MBar
- 'Westmont' (v)	CKen CSBt EOrn WBcn

Platycodon ✿ (Campanulaceae)

grandiflorus ♀H4	CArn CBot CMea COlW CTri EBee ECha ELau EPot LHop MBro MHer MNrw MSal SGar SIng SRms SWal WBrE WCom WHoo WWye
- 'Albus'	CBro EBee EChP EPfP LAst LHop MBri SPer SPla SWvt WCom WHoo WPer
- 'Apoyama' ♀H4	CLyd CStu EBee GMac LBee LRHS NMen WHoo WPer WWin
- *apoyama albus*	WEas WHoo
- - 'Fairy Snow'	EMar ITim SLon WHil WHoo WSel
- 'Astra Blue' (Astra Series)	EBee
- 'Blue Haze'	EBee
- 'Blue Pearl'	WHoo
- 'Blue Pygmy'	SMac
- 'Florist Rose'	WWye
- 'Florist Snow'	WWye
- 'Fuji Blue'	ERou EWll ITim LAst LLck NBro NCGa NLar SPet WGwG WHHs WMnd WSel
- 'Fuji Pink'	CBro EBee ELan EMar EPfP ERou LAst LHop MRav MTis NBro NCGa NLar SMrm SPer SPet SPoG SWvt WCAu WMnd WSel
- 'Fuji White'	ELan ERou LAst NBro NLar SMrm SPet WMnd WSel
- 'Hakone'	EMan LHop MBro MRav SMrm WHoo
- 'Hakone Blue'	ERou ITim NCGa NLar
* - 'Hakone Double Blue' (d)	EBee ECGP ELan EMar LRHS MTis SLon SRms WCAu
- 'Hakone White'	CBot CBrm EBee ECGP ERou ITim MBro NChi NGby NLar NMen SChu SLon SPet SPoG WCAu WHoo
- 'Mariesii' ♀H4	More than 30 suppliers
- *mariesii albus*	EBee WHoo
- 'Misato Purple'	NCGa WCom WSel
- Mother of Pearl	see *P. grandiflorus* 'Perlmutterschale'
- 'Park's Double Blue' (d)	WHoo
§ - 'Perlmutterschale'	CBot CBrm EBee EChP EMar EPPr EPfP EWTr MBri SLon SPet WCAu WHoo
- *pumilus*	EBee MBro NChi NWCA WHoo
- *roseus*	CNic MNrw WHoo
- 'Sentimental Blue'	CWib EBee LPVe NJOw NLar SMrm
- 'Shell Pink'	see *P. grandiflorus* 'Perlmutterschale'
- white-flowered, double **new**	CBro
- 'Zwerg'	EBee

Platycrater (Hydrangeaceae)

arguta	WCru
- B&SWJ 6266	WCru

Plecostachys (Asteraceae)

§ *serpyllifolia*	CHal MOak SPet

Plectranthus (*Lamiaceae*)

from Puerto Rico	CArn
ambiguus	EOHP
- 'Manchzuko' **new**	EOHP
- 'Umigoye'	EOHP
amboinicus	CArn CHal EOHP EShb MOak NHor
* - 'Variegatus' (v)	EOHP
- 'Well Sweep Wedgewood' **new**	EOHP
argentatus ♀H2	CAbb CDoC CHad CHrt CMdw CPLG CSev CSpe EBee EBlw EMan EShb MOak MSte SAga SDix SGar SHFr SMrm SUsu WCom WDyG WKif
- 'Hill House' (v)	CHll CPne EMan EOHP EShb LDai MOak
australis misapplied	see *P. verticillatus*
behrii	see *P. fruticosus*
ciliatus	CPne EOHP MOak SUsu WEas
- 'All Gold' **new**	CPne
- 'Easy Gold' **new**	CPne EOHP MOak
- 'Sasha'	CDoC CHll
coleoides 'Marginatus'	see *P. forsteri* 'Marginatus'
- 'Variegatus'	see *P. madagascariensis* 'Variegated Mintleaf'
crassus	EOHP
Cuban oregano	EOHP WJek
ecklonii	EOHP
- 'Medley-Wood' **new**	EOHP
ernstii	EOHP MOak
excisus	EMon
§ *forsteri* 'Marginatus'	CHal ERea MOak SGar
fredericii	see *P. welwitschii*
§ *fruticosus*	CHal CPne EOHP GBri MOak
- 'Frills' **new**	CPne EOHP
- 'James'	CPne EOHP
hadiensis var. *tomentosus*	EOHP MOak
- - 'Carnegie' **new**	EOHP
- - green-leaved **new**	EOHP
I - 'Variegata' **new**	CPne
hilliardiae **new**	CPne
hirtellus gold	MOak
- variegated (v)	MOak
madagascariensis	CPne EOHP
- gold-leaved **new**	EOHP
§ - 'Variegated Mintleaf' (v)	CHal EOHP MRav SHFr SPet SRms SVen
menthol-scented, large-leaved	EOHP
menthol-scented, small-leaved	EOHP
§ *oertendahlii* ♀H1	CHal CPne EBak EOHP MOak SMur
- silver-leaved	EOHP
- 'Uvongo' **new**	CPne
§ *ornatus*	EOHP EShb MOak NScw
parviflorus	SMur
rehmannii	EOHP
saccatus	CPne EOHP GFai
spicatus	EOHP
- 'Nelspruit'	EOHP
- 'Ubombo' **new**	EOHP
Swedish ivy	see *P. verticillatus*, *P. oertendablii*
§ *thyrsoideus*	CHal EOHP SVen
§ *verticillatus*	CHal EOHP
Vick's plant	EOHP
§ *welwitschii*	NHor
zatarhendii	CPne EMan EOHP
zuluensis	CFee CFwr CHal CMdw CPne EOHP MOak WBor
- dark-leaved	EOHP
- light-leaved	EOHP

Pleioblastus ✿ (*Poaceae*)

akebono	see *P. argenteostriatus* 'Akebono'
§ *argenteostriatus* 'Akebono'	SDry
- 'Okinadake' (v)	EBee EPla WViv
§ - f. *glaber* (v)	MAsh SDry
§ - f. *pumilus*	CDoC CRow CSam EBee EHoe ENot EPar EPfP GKir LAst LRHS MBlu MMoz NHol SDry SPla SPlb WFar WJun WNor WPat WPer WViv
auricomus	see *P. viridistriatus*
- 'Vagans'	see *Sasaella ramosa*
§ *chino*	CHEx EPla SDry
- f. *angustifolius*	see *P. chino* 'Murakamianus'
- var. *argenteostriatus*	see *P. argenteostriatus* 'Okinadake'
* - f. *aureostriatus* (v)	EPla MMoz SDry
- f. *elegantissimus*	CDoC CEnd CFir COtt EBee EPla EPza ERod LAst MGos MMoz MWhi NMoo SDry SEND WJun WMoo WPGP
- 'Kimmei'	SDry
- 'Murakamianus'	SDry
* *funghomii* **new**	SEND
'Gauntlettii'	see *P. humilis*
glaber 'Albostriatus'	see *Sasaella masamuneana* 'Albostriata'
gramineus	EPla SDry WJun
§ *hindsii*	EPla ERod LPan MMoz NMoo SArc SDry SEND
§ *humilis*	ELan EPza SSto
- var. *pumilus*	see *P. argenteostriatus* f. *pumilus*
kongosanensis 'Aureostriatus' (v)	EPla SDry
linearis	CAbb EAmu EBee EFul EPla ERod LAst LPal MMoz NMoo SDry WJun
longifimbriatus	see *Sinobambusa intermedia*
oleosus	EPla SDry WJun
§ *pygmaeus*	More than 30 suppliers
§ - 'Distichus'	EBee EBlw EFul EHul EPPr EPla LAst LRHS MAsh MGos MMoz MWht NDlv NGdn NMoo SSto WJun WWin
* - 'Mini'	WCot WWpP
* - 'Mirrezuzume'	CPLG WFar
§ *simonii*	CAgr CBcs EAmu EBee EBlw EFul ENot EPla GBin GCal LAst LPan LRHS MBNS MMoz MWhi SArc SDry
§ - 'Variegatus' (v)	CFil EPla MBar MBlu NGdn SDry SPer WJun WPGP
§ *variegatus* (v) ♀H4	More than 30 suppliers
- 'Tsuboii' (v)	CAbb CBig CBrm CDoC CEnd COtt EBee EPPr EPla ERod IFro LAst LPJP LPal LRHS MBNS MBrN MBri MMoz MWhi MWht NMoo SDry WFar WJun WMul WPGP WPnP WWin
- var. *viridis* (v)	see *P. argenteostriatus* f. *glaber*
§ *viridistriatus* (v) ♀H4	More than 30 suppliers
- 'Bracken Hill'	SDry
- var. *chrysophyllus*	EPla MMoz SDry WJun
- *variegatus* (v)	CHar EPza SAga SWvt WMoo

Pleione ✿ (*Orchidaceae*)

albiflora	CHdy
Alishan g.	CHdy CNic EPot GCrs LBut
- 'Foxhill'	NSpr
- 'Merlin'	LBut NSpr
- 'Mount Fuji'	LBut
- 'Soldier Blue'	LBut
Asama g.	CHdy
- 'Bittern' **new**	LBut
- 'Red Grouse'	LBut

aurita **new**	LBut
Bandai-san g.	LBut
x *barbarae* **new**	LBut NSpr
Barcena g.	CHdy LBut
Berapi g.	CHdy EPot LBut
Brigadoon g.	CHdy GCrs LBut NSpr
- 'Stonechat'	LBut
Britannia g.	CHdy LBut
- 'Doreen'	LBut NSpr
§ *bulbocodioides*	EPot ERos MBro NSpr WOBN
- Limprichtii Group	see *P. limprichtii*
- Pricei Group	see *P. formosana* Pricei Group
§ - 'Yunnan'	NSpr
Burnsall g.	NSpr
Captain Hook g.	LBut NSpr
Chinese Dragon g.	NSpr
§ *chunii*	EFEx LAma NSpr
x *confusa*	CHdy LBut
Danan g.	LBut
Deriba g.	LBut
Eiger g.	CHdy EPot ERos LBut NSpr
- cream	ERos LBut
- 'Pinchbeck Diamond'	EPot GCrs
El Pico g.	GCrs
- 'Pheasant'	EPot LBut NSpr
- 'Starling'	LBut
Erebus g.	CHdy
- 'Quail'	LBut
Erh Hai g.	NSpr
Etna g.	CHdy EPot GCrs LBut
Follifoot g. 'Princess	NSpr
Tiger' **new**	
formosana ♀H2	CBri CKob EFEx EPot ETow GBuc
	GCrs LAma NCGa SAga SDeJ WFar
	WPnP
- 'Achievement'	LBut
I - 'Alba'	GCrs
- 'Avalanche'	LBut
- 'Blush of Dawn'	CHdy GCrs LBut NSpr
- 'C.P. Diamond'	EPot
- 'Cairngorm'	NSpr
- 'Chen'	CHdy EPot
- 'Christine Anne'	CHdy NSpr
- 'Clare'	CHdy EPot ERos GCrs LBut NSpr
- 'Eugenie'	CHdy EPot
- 'Greenhill'	LBut
I - 'Iris'	CHdy EPot
- 'Lilac Jubilee' **new**	CHdy
- 'Little Winnie'	EPot
- 'Lucy Diamond'	EPot
- 'Lulu'	CHdy EPot
- 'Pitlochry'	LBut
- 'Polar Sun'	CHdy EPot
§ - Pricei Group	EPot ERos ETow
- - 'Oriental Grace'	CHdy LBut MFir
- - 'Oriental Splendour'	CHdy EPot LBut
- 'Red Spot'	EPot
- 'Roydon'	EPot
- 'Snow Bunting'	LBut
- 'Snow White'	GCrs LBut
forrestii	EFEx LAma
Fu Manchu g.	NSpr
Fuego g.	CHdy NSpr
- 'Wren'	LBut
Gerry Mundey g.	LBut NSpr
Giacomo Leopardi g.	NSpr
§ *grandiflora*	NSpr
Heathfield g.	NSpr
Hekla g.	CHdy EPot ERos GCrs NSpr
- 'Partridge'	LBut
Helgafell g.	LBut
hookeriana	GCrs
humilis	NSpr
Irazu g.	GCrs LBut NSpr

- 'Irazu Violet'	GCrs
Jorullo g.	CHdy LBut NSpr
- 'Long-tailed Tit'	LBut
Katla g.	CHdy NSpr
Katmai g.	LBut
Keith Rattray g.	LBut
'Kelty' **new**	
Kenya g. **new**	LBut
Kilauea g.	EPot LBut
- 'Curlew'	LBut
Kituro g.	LBut
Kohala g.	LBut
§ *limprichtii* ♀H2	EFEx EPot ETow LBut
	WPnP
- 'Primrose Peach'	GCrs
maculata	EFEx
Marco Polo g.	LBut NSpr
Masaya g. **new**	LBut
Matupi g.	LBut NSpr
Mazama g.	LBut
Myojin g.	CHdy LBut
Novarupta g.	LBut
Orinoco g.	CHdy LBut
- 'Gemini'	LBut
Orizaba g.	LBut
Paricutin g.	LBut
Pavlof g.	LBut
pinkepankii	see *P. grandiflora*
Piton g.	CHdy EPot LAma LBut
pleionoides	LBut
- 'Blakeway Phillips'	CHdy
pogonioides hort.	see *P. pleionoides*
pogonioides (Rolfe)	see *P. bulbocodioides*
Rolfe	
Rainier g.	LBut
Rakata g.	CHdy EPot LBut
- 'Blackbird'	LBut
- 'Redwing'	LBut
- 'Shot Silk'	LBut NSpr
- 'Skylark'	LBut
Ruby Wedding g. **new**	LBut
San Salvador g.	LBut
Santorini g.	LBut
scopulorum	EFEx
Shantung g.	CHdy EPot GCrs ITim LAma LBut
	NSpr
- 'Candy Floss'	NSpr
- 'Ducat'	EPot GCrs LAma LBut NSpr
- 'Gerry Mundey'	LBut
- 'Golden Jubilee'	NSpr
- 'Golden Plover'	LBut
- 'Gwen'	EPot
- 'Miki'	NSpr
- 'Muriel Harberd' ♀H2	EPot NSpr
- 'R6.7'	NSpr
- 'Ridgeway'	CHdy EPot GCrs LBut NSpr
- 'Silver Anniversary' **new**	LBut
Shepherd's Warning g.	NSpr
'Gillian Clare' **new**	
- 'Mary Buchanan' **new**	NSpr
Sorea g.	LBut
Soufrière g.	LBut NSpr
- 'Sunrise' **new**	NSpr
speciosa Ames & Schltr.	see *P. pleionoides*
Starbotton g. **new**	NSpr
Stromboli g.	CHdy EPot GCrs NSpr
- 'Fireball'	EPot GCrs LBut NSpr
- 'Robin'	LBut
Surtsey g.	LBut
- 'Stephanie Rose'	NSpr
x *taliensis*	LBut
Tarawera g.	LBut
Tolima g.	CHdy CNic EPot LBut
- 'Moorhen'	EPot

Tongariro g. CHdy CPBP EPot ERos GCrs LBut NSpr
- 'Jackdaw' CHdy LBut
Versailles g. CHdy EPot ERos LBut
- 'Bucklebury' ♀H2 CNic EPot GCrs LBut NSpr
- 'Heron' CHdy LBut
- 'Muriel Turner' EPot NSpr
Vesuvius g. CHdy EPot LBut
- 'Aphrodite' EPot
- 'Grey Wagtail' LBut
- 'Leopard' LBut NSpr
* - 'Phoenix' EPot LBut NSpr
- 'Tawny Owl' LBut
Volcanello g. CHdy GCrs LBut NSpr
- 'Honey Buzzard' LBut
- 'Song Thrush' LBut
Wunzen g. LBut
yunnanensis hort. see *P. bulbocodioides* 'Yunnan'
yunnanensis (Rolfe) CHdy LAma
   Rolfe
Zeus Weinstein g. EPot LBut NSpr
- 'Desert Sands' LBut

Pleomele see *Dracaena*

Pleurospermum (Apiaceae)
aff. *amabile* WCru
   BWJ 7886 **new**
benthamii WCru
   B&SWJ 2988 **new**
brunonis EBee
calcareum B&SWJ 8008 WCru

plum see *Prunus domestica*

Plumbago (Plumbaginaceae)
§ *auriculata* ♀H1-2 CBcs CBrm CDoC CEnd CHEx
   CRHN CSBt CTri CWSG EBak ELan
   EPfP ERea EShb ISea MBri MLan
   MOak MRav MTis NPal SOWG
   SPer SRms SYvo WBod XPep
- var. *alba* ♀H1-2 CBcs CHEx CHal CRHN CSev EBak
   EBee EMil EPfP ERea MLan MOak
   SEND SOWG SPer SYvo XPep
* - *aurea* LIck
- 'Crystal Waters' ELan
- dark blue-flowered MJnS XPep
- 'Escapade Blue' EShb
   (Escapade Series)
capensis see *P. auriculata*
§ *indica* ♀H1 CHal LRHS SOWG
- *rosea* see *P. indica*
larpentiae see *Ceratostigma*
   plumbaginoides

Plumeria (Apocynaceae)
rubra ♀H1 ESlt LRHS SOWG
- f. *acutifolia* LRHS SOWG

Pneumatopteris see *Cyclosorus*

Poa (Poaceae)
alpina CBig NGdn NJOw NLar
- *nodosa* CBig EMan SWal
chaixii CBig CBod EHoe EMan EMon EPPr
   EPza GKir NHol NNor SLPl SWal
   WFoF WWpP
cita CTrC EMan EPPr LRav
colensoi CBod EHoe EMan EPPr MAvo NFor
   WPnP WWeb
eminens from EMan EPPr
   Magadan, Siberia **new**
x *jemtlandica* EHoe EPPr NHol
labillardierei CBrm CKno CMea CSam CWCL

ECGP ECha EGle EHoe EMan EPPr
EPza GGar GKir MAvo MFan NBid
SUsu WDyG WMoo WPrP XPep
trivialis CRWN

Podalyria (Papilionaceae)
calyptrata SPlb
canescens SPlb

Podocarpus (Podocarpaceae)
acutifolius CBcs CDoC ECou EPla GEil GGar
   MBar STre
- (f) ECou
- (m) ECou
alpinus R. Br. Ex Hook f. see *P. lawrencei*
andinus see *Prumnopitys andina*
'Autumn Shades' (m) ECou
'Blaze' (f) CBcs EBre ECou EPla LBuc LCon
   LLin MBrN SCoo SLim WEve
chilinus see *P. salignus*
'Chocolate Box' (f) ECou
'County Park Fire'PBR (f) CDoC CKen CWSG EBre ECou
   EOrn EPfP LCon LLin MGos MOne
   NPal SCoo SLim WEve WFar WGor
cunninghamii CBcs CTrC ECou WCwm
- 'Kiwi' (f) CBcs ECou
- 'Roro' (m) CBcs ECou LLin
cunninghamii x ECou
   nivalis (f)
dacrydioides see *Dacrycarpus dacrydioides*
elongatus CTrC
'Flame' CDoC ECou EPla
'Havering' (f) ECou
henkelii CHEx CTrC GGar IDee WMul
'Jill' (f) **new** ECou
latifolius ECou
lawrencei ECho EHul
- (f) ECou MBar
- 'Alpine Lass' (f) ECou
- 'Blue Gem' (f) CDoC EBre ECou EOrn EPla IArd
   IDee LCon LLin LRHS MAsh MBar
   MBri MGos MOne NDlv NHol
   SCoo SLim SPoG WBcn WFar
- 'Kiandra' ECou
- 'Red Tip' CDoC EBre LLin MAsh SCoo SLim
'Macho' (m) **new** ECou
macrophyllus CHEx CTrC EOrn LPan NLar SAPC
   SArc SMad STre WFar
- (m) ECou
'Maori Prince' (m) ECou EPla LLin
nivalis CBcs CMac CPLG CTrC EBre ECou
   EOrn EPla GGar LLin MBar SRms
- 'Arthur' (m) ECou
- 'Bronze' EPla
- 'Christmas Lights' ECou
   (f) **new**
- 'Clarence' (m) ECou LLin
- 'Green Queen' (f) ECou
- 'Jack's Pass' (m) ECou
- 'Kaweka' (m) ECou
- 'Kilworth Cream' (v) CBcs CDoC EBre ECou EPla GTSp
   LBuc LCon LLin MGos SCoo WEve
- 'Little Lady' (f) ECou
- 'Livingstone' (f) ECou
- 'Lodestone' (m) ECou
- 'Moffatt' (f) CBcs ECou LLin
- 'Otari' (m) CBcs ECou LLin
- 'Park Cover' ECou
- 'Princess' (f) ECou MBrN
- 'Ruapehu' (m) ECou EPla
- 'Trompenburg' **new** NLar
'Orangeade' (f) **new** CBcs NLar
* - 'Redtip' LBuc SLim
'Rough Creek' LLin

§ **salignus** ♀H3 — CAbb CBcs CBrd CDoC CDul CHEx EPla IDee ISea SAPC SArc WFar WSHC
- (f) — ECou
- (m) — ECou
spicatus — see *Prumnopitys taxifolia*
'Spring Sunshine' (f) — CBcs ECou EPla LLin NLar
totara — CBcs CHEx CTrC ECou GGar LEdu STre WFar WPic
- 'Albany Gold' — CTrC IDee LCon
- 'Aureus' — CBcs CDoC ECou EPla LLin MBar SHBN WBcn WEve
- 'Pendulus' — CDoC ECou
'Young Rusty' (f) — CBcs CDoC ECou EPla GTSp LCon LLin MGos WEve

Podophyllum (Berberidaceae)

§ **delavayi** — CLAP EBee LEur WCru
difforme — CLAP EBee LEur WCru
emodi — see *P. hexandrum*
- var. **chinense** — see *P. hexandrum* 'Chinense'
§ **hexandrum** — More than 30 suppliers
- 'Chinense' — CBro CLAP CRow EBee EMan GBuc GEdr IBlr LEdu LEur SMad WCru WPnP
- - BWJ 7908 — WCru
- - CT 232 — CFwr
- 'Chinese White' CT 232 **new** — WCot
- 'Majus' — CFir CLAP EBee WCot WHal
peltatum — CArn CBro CLAP CRow EBee EBla ECGN GBBs GFlt GPoy IBlr LAma LPhx MSal NMyG NSti SSpi WCru WFar WPGP
pleianthum — CLAP EBee LEur MMil SSpi WCru
- short — WCru
veitchii — see *P. delavayi*
versipelle — CLAP EBee LEur SSpi WCru

Podranea (Bignoniaceae)

brycei — EShb
§ **ricasoliana** — CRHN CTCP ERea SOWG XPep
- 'Comtesse Sarah' **new** — XPep

Pogonatherum (Poaceae)

§ **paniceum** — LRHS MBri
saccharoideum — see *P. paniceum*

Pogonia (Orchidaceae)

ophioglossoides — CHdy SSpi

Pogostemon (Lamiaceae)

§ **cablin** — GPoy MGol MSal
from An Veleniki Herb Farm, Pennsylvania — CArn
heyneanus — MSal
patchouly — see *P. cablin*

Polemonium (Polemoniaceae)

acutiflorum — see *P. caeruleum* subsp. *villosum*
acutifolium var. **nipponicum** — see *P. caeruleum* subsp. *nipponicum*
ambervicsii — see *P. pauciflorum* subsp. *hinckleyi*
'Apricot Beauty' — see *P. carneum* 'Apricot Delight'
N **archibaldiae** ♀H4 — EBee MBro NBir SRms
§ **boreale** — EMan GCal GKir IGor MBow MNrw MOne NArg NLRH NPol SBla SPet SWvt WFar WMoo
* - **album** — WBrE
- 'Heavenly Habit' — EBee LPVe MAnH NPro WWeb
§ **brandegeei** Greene — NArg NBro NCGa SAga SHop WPer
- subsp. **mellitum** — see *P. brandegeei* Greene
'Bressingham Purple' — EBre SPer WFar

caeruleum misapplied, Himalayan — see *P. cashmerianum*
§ **caeruleum** — More than 30 suppliers
- subsp. **amygdalinum** — see *P. occidentale*
- 'Bambino Blue' — EBee IBal LRHS SMac SWvt WHil WPer
- 'Blue Bell' — ELau
- Brise d'Anjou = 'Blanjou'PBR (v) — More than 30 suppliers
- subsp. **caeruleum** f. **album** — More than 30 suppliers
I - f. **dissectum** — NPol
- 'Golden Showers' (v) — CCge NPro
- var. **grandiflorum** — see *P. caeruleum* subsp. *himalayanum*
§ - subsp. **himalayanum** — EBee EPPr NChi WPer
- 'Humile' — see *P.* 'Northern Lights'
- 'Idylle' — EMan EMon GMac MAnH NPol
- 'Larch Cottage' (v) — NLar NPol
- 'Newark Park' — EPPr NPol
§ - subsp. **nipponicum** — EBee GBin NPol WPer
- 'Snow and Sapphires' (v) — EBee EPfP LAst MBNS MBnl MBri NCGa NCot NPer NPri SVil WCot WSan
- 'Southern Skies' — CStr
§ - subsp. **villosum** — CStr EBee NPol
- subsp. **vulgare new** — NPol
californicum — NPol
carneum — CTri ECha EGle EMan EOrc GFlt GKir LAst MCCP MNrw MTho MWgw NJOw NPol SCro SPer SSpi STes WAul WBea WCAu WFar WLin WMoo WPer WSan WWin
§ - 'Apricot Delight' — More than 30 suppliers
- 'Rachael' **new** — NPol
§ **cashmerianum** — EBee EPPr LPVe LRHS MBro MHar NBur SPet WFar WHen WHoo WSan
chartaceum — NPol
'Churchills' — CBre CLAP EBee EChP NPol WPGP WPrP
confertum — NPol
§ 'Dawn Flight' — NPol WFar
delicatum — see *P. pulcherrimum* subsp. *delicatum*
'Eastbury Purple' — CElw CStr MAnH MBct NPol
elegans — NPol
'Elworthy Amethyst' — CElw EBee EMan MAvo NCot NPol WPGP
eximium — NPol
flavum — see *P. foliosissimum* var. *flavum*
foliosissimum hort. — see *P. archibaldiae*
foliosissimum A. Gray — CTCP IGor MBct MNrw WLin WPer
- var. **albiflorum** — see *P. foliosissimum* var. *alpinum*
§ - var. **alpinum** — EBee NBir NPol
- 'Bressingham' **new** — NPol
- 'Cottage Cream' — CBre CStr NPol
§ - var. **flavum** — NPol
- var. **foliosissimum** — EWes NPol
- - NNS 99-422 — EPPr
- 'Scottish Garden' **new** — NPol
- 'White Spirit' **new** — NPol
'Glebe Cottage Lilac' — CCge CElw CHar CMil CStr EBee LPio MAvo NBir WPGP
'Glebe Cottage Violet' — NPol
grandiflorum new — NPol
'Hannah Billcliffe' — CDes CLAP MAnH MAvo NCot NPol
§ 'Hopleys' — CLAP CStr EChP EMan GBar GBri GCal IFro NBrk NCot NGdn NPol WFar
x **jacobaea** — CDes EBee EMan EPPr NPol WCot
'Katie Daley' — see *P.* 'Hopleys'

kiushianum	EBee	
'Lace Towers'	NSti SHar	
§ 'Lambrook Mauve' ♀H4	More than 30 suppliers	
'Mary Mottram'	NPol	
mellitum	see *P. brandegeei* Greene	
'North Tyne'	MAvo NBid NChi NPol	
'Northern Lights'	CBos CDes CSev CStr EBee ECGP	
	EGle EMan EMon EPPr EWes GBri	
	GMac MAnH MAvo MBri MMil	
	MNrw NCot NPol NSti SAga SMrm	
	STes WCot WFar WMoo WPGP	
'Norwell Mauve'	MNrw NPol	
§ *occidentale*	EBee	
- subsp. *occidentale* **new**	NPol	
'Pam' (v)	NPol	
§ *pauciflorum*	CBri ECtt EHrv EOrc GBBs GKir	
	GTou LAst LPio LRHS MAnH	
	MNrw MTho MTis NBid NBir	
	NGHP NPPs SHFr SMac SYvo	
	WBea WFar WHHs WHer WMoo	
	WPer WWeb WWhi WWin	
§ - subsp. *hinckleyi*	EPPr NCot NGar NPol SGar WOut	
§ - subsp. *pauciflorum*	LRHS MAnH NPol SGar SMac	
	WSan	
- silver-leaved	see *P. pauciflorum* subsp.	
	pauciflorum	
- 'Sulphur Trumpets'	MAnH SWvt WGwG WHHs	
- subsp. *typicum*	see *P. pauciflorum* subsp.	
	pauciflorum	
§ 'Pink Beauty'	CBre EBee EFou ELan EMar EPfP	
	LRHS NCot NPol SLon SUsu WWhi	
pulchellum Salisb.	see *P. reptans*	
pulchellum Turcz.	see *P. caeruleum*	
- 'Tricolor'	see *P. boreale*	
pulcherrimum hort.	see *P. boreale*	
pulcherrimum Hook.	EBee GAbr GTou NBro WHen	
	WLin WPer WWeb	
§ - subsp. *delicatum*	MTho NPol	
§ - subsp. *pulcherrimum*	EHyt LTwo NPol	
§ *reptans*	CAgr CArn CHea CTCP ECoo GBar	
	GBri GPoy MHer MSal NBro NPol	
	SIng WFar WMoo WPer WWeb	
	WWye	
- 'Album'	see *P. reptans* 'Virginia White'	
- 'Blue Ice' **new**	NPol	
- 'Blue Pearl'	CElw CMea COlW EBee EChP	
	EMan EPar EPfP LRHS MLLN	
	MNrw NBro NChi NFor NGdn	
	NHol NPol SGar SMrm SPer SPla	
	SUsu SWal WCom WFar WHen	
	WSan WShp WWeb	
- 'Dawn Flight'	see *P.* 'Dawn Flight'	
- 'Firmament'	CDes EBee WPGP	
- 'Lambrook Manor'	see *P.* 'Lambrook Mauve'	
- 'Pink Beauty'	see *P.* 'Pink Beauty'	
- 'Pink Dawn'	EChP EMil EPfP MLLN NCot NGdn	
	SPla WHil	
* - 'Sky Blue'	NBro	
§ - 'Virginia White'	CBcs CBre CDes CElw CMea CStr	
	EBee LRHS MAvo MBnl NChi NGar	
	NPol SUsu WFar	
- 'White Pearl'	COlW IGor WBVN	
'Ribby' **new**	NPol	
richardsonii hort.	see *P.* 'Northern Lights'	
richardsonii Graham	see *P. boreale*	
'Sapphire'	CBre CStr ELan EMan EMon MBrN	
	NPol	
scopulinum	see *P. pulcherrimum* subsp.	
	delicatum	
I 'Sonia's Bluebell'	CDes CElw CKno CLAP CMil CStr	
	EBee ECGP EMan EPPr EWes	
	MAvo MBnl MDKP MNrw MSte	
	NCot NPol SUsu WPGP	

'Theddingworth'	NPol WBar WFar	
vanbruntiae	EBee NPol	
viscosum	GBuc MBrN NPol SGar SYvo	
	WHen	
- 'Blue Whirl' **new**	MGol	
- f. *leucanthum* **new**	NPol	
yezoense	CBre CStr GBri MNrw NCot NPol	
	WFar	
- *hidakanum*	CStr EBee NPol	
- 'Purple Rain'	CHar CStr EBee EHrv EMan ENor	
	EPfP EWes GBuc GFlt MAnH MBnl	
	MCCP MLLN MNrw NPol SSpi	
	WFar WRha WWhi	

Polianthes (Agavaceae)

nelsonii	CFir	
tuberosa ♀H1-2	CBcs CSpe LRHS NRog	
- 'The Pearl' (d)	LAma	

Poliomintha (Lamiaceae)

bustamanta	LPhx NBir SAga SScr	

Poliothyrsis (Flacourtiaceae)

sinensis ♀H4	CAbP CFil CPne CTho EPfP GIBF	
	LAst LRHS MBri NLar SMad WBor	
	WWes	

Pollia (Commelinaceae)

japonica	EBee EMan IFro	
- B&SWJ 8884	WCru	
minor B&SWJ 6843	WCru	

Polygala (Polygalaceae)

alpicola	SOkd	
amoenissima	SOkd	
calcarea	LTwo MBro NLAp WAbe WPat	
- Bulley's form	EPot LRHS	
- 'Lillet' ♀H4	CPBP EHyt EPot LHop LRHS LTwo	
	MBro NLAp NLar NMen NSla SScr	
	SSte WFar WPat WWin	
chamaebuxus ♀H4	CBcs CWCL GCrs MDKP MGos	
	MLLN NLAp NLar NSla SRms	
	WBVN WTin WWin	
- *alba*	EHyt LBee LRHS NLar WAbe	
§ - var. *grandiflora* ♀H4	CBcs EPot GAbr GEdr GGar GKir	
	LBee LHop MAsh MBar MBro	
	MDun MGos NHol NLAp NMen	
	NSla NWCA SBla SChu WAbe	
	WBVN WBod WFar WPat WSHC	
	WWin	
- 'Kamniski'	CMHG EPot LBuc	
- 'Loibl'	EPot SBla	
- 'Purpurea'	see *P. chamaebuxus* var.	
	grandiflora	
- 'Rhodoptera'	see *P. chamaebuxus* var.	
	grandiflora	
§ × *dalmaisiana* ♀H1	CAbb CHEx CHll CRHN CSpe	
	EBee ERea GQui LHop SBla SGar	
	SMur WAbe WBor WCFE	
myrtifolia	CPLG CTrC IDee SGar SHFr SIgm	
	SMrm SPlb WOBN WWye XPep	
- 'Grandiflora'	see *P.* × *dalmaisiana*	
pauciflora	SOkd	
'Rosengarten'	SBla	
vayredae	GEdr	
virgata	ERea EShb ESlt SSte	

Polygonatum (Convallariaceae)

acuminatifolium	EBee LEur	
altelobatum B&SWJ 286	WCru	
§ *biflorum*	More than 30 suppliers	
- dwarf	EPla IBlr LEur WCot	
- polyploid	LEur	
canaliculatum	see *P. biflorum*	

cathcartii	EBee LEur
cirrhifolium	CDes CLAP CPom EBee EBla ELan GKir LEur MDun NPar WCot WCru WPGP
commutatum	see *P. biflorum*
cryptanthum	WCru
curvistylum	CAvo CBct CLAP CPom CStu EBee EBla ECha EGle EHrv IBlr LEur LPhx MFir NLar NRya WAbe WCru WFar WViv
cyrtonema hort.	see *Disporopsis pernyi*
cyrtonema Hua	EBee LEur
– B&SWJ 271	WCru
falcatum hort.	see *P. humile*
§ *falcatum* A. Gray	CLyd EBee EGle EPla GGar IBlr LEur NOak SIng WHer WWin
– B&SWJ 1077	WCru
– 'Variegatum'	see *P. odoratum* var. *pluriflorum* 'Variegatum'
'Falcon'	see *P. humile*
filipes	EBee WCru
fuscum	LEur WCru
geminiflorum	EBee IBlr SOkd WFar
– McB 2448	GEdr
giganteum	see *P. biflorum*
glaberrimum	WCot
§ *graminifolium*	CBct CLAP EBee EPot ERos GEdr LEur MSte NCGa SCnR SScr WCot WCru
– G-W&P 803	WPnP
§ *hirtum*	CBct CHid CLAP CPom EMon EPla EPot IBlr LEur WCru WFar
– BM 7012	EBee LEur
hookeri	More than 30 suppliers
– McB 1413	GEdr
§ *humile*	CBct CLAP EBee EBla EHrv EHyt ELan EMan EPla ERos GBri GCal IBlr NJOw NMen SBla SMac SSpi SUsu WAbe WAul WCot WCru WFar WPnP
§ x *hybridum* ♀H4	More than 30 suppliers
– 'Betberg'	CBct CRow EBee ECha EHrv LEur NBPC NBir WCot
– 'Flore Pleno' (d)	WHer
– 'Nanum'	CHid LEur
§ – 'Striatum' (v)	More than 30 suppliers
– 'Variegatum'	see *P. x hybridum* 'Striatum'
– 'Wakehurst'	EBla EHrv
inflatum	EBee LEur WCru
– B&SWJ 922	WCru
involucratum	EBee LEur WCru
japonicum	see *P. odoratum*
kingianum	CBct EBee LEur
– yellow-flowered B&SWJ 6562	WCru
'Langthorns Variegated' (v)	ELan LEur
lasianthum	WCru
latifolium	see *P. hirtum*
maximowiczii	GCal GSki
multiflorum hort.	see *P. x hybridum*
multiflorum L.	CDes CElw CRow CSBt EBee EBre ECha EFou EPla EPza EWTr EWsh GAbr GKir LRHS NVic SAga SPlb SRms SWal WShp
– *giganteum* hort.	see *P. biflorum*
nodosum	EBee LEur WCru
obtusifolium	EBee
§ *odoratum* ♀H4	CAvo CBct CBro CRow CSWP EBee EHrv ELau EPar EPfP EPla GEdr GIBF IBlr LEur MSal NBid NLar NRya SAga SSpi WCru WPnP
§ – dwarf	IBlr
– 'Flore Pleno' (d) ♀H4	CAvo CDes CLAP CRow EBee

	ECha EHrv IBlr LEur SBla SCnR WCot WHoo WPGP WPnP
– 'Grace Barker'	see *P. x hybridum* 'Striatum'
– var. *pluriflorum*	GBuc IBlr SSpi
§ – – 'Variegatum' (v) ♀H4	More than 30 suppliers
– 'Red Stem'	WCru
– 'Silver Wings' (v)	CLAP EBla ECha EHrv ERou LEur NBir NLar NPar
officinale	see *P. odoratum*
oppositifolium	LEur WFar
– B&SWJ 2537	EBee WCru
§ *orientale*	CHid CLAP EBee EBla WCot
pluriflorum	see *P. graminifolium*
polyanthemum	see *P. orientale*
prattii	EBee LEur SOkd
pubescens	EBee WCru
pumilum	see *P. odoratum* dwarf
punctatum	LEdu LEur WFar
– B&SWJ 2395	CBct EBla WCru
racemosum	SIng
roseum	CDes EBee WHer WPnP
sewerzowii	EBee EPla
sibiricum	CAvo EBee GEdr IBlr WCru
– ACE 1753	EPot
stenophyllum	CAvo LEur
stewartianum	CLAP EPPr EPar IBlr LEur
tonkinense HWJ 551 **new**	WCru
verticillatum	CAvo CBct CBro CHid CLyd CRow EBee EBla EBre ECha EPla GKir IBlr LEur MTho SMad WCot WCru WFar WPGP
– CC 1324	CPLG
– 'Himalayan Giant'	CHid EBee LEur
* – *rubrum*	CArn CBct CRow EBla EGle EHrv EPPr EPar IBlr LEur LPhx MTho MTho NGby WCot WPrP
– 'Serbian Dwarf'	CHid EBee LEur
aff. *verticillatum*	LEur
zanlanscianense	EBee LEur WCru

Polygonum ✿ (Polygonaceae)

affine	see *Persicaria affinis*
amplexicaule	see *Persicaria amplexicaulis*
aubertii	see *Fallopia baldschuanica*
aviculare	CArn
baldschuanicum	see *Fallopia baldschuanica*
bistorta	see *Persicaria bistorta*
capitatum **new**	XPep
compactum	see *Fallopia japonica* var. *compacta*
equisetiforme hort.	see *P. scoparium*
filiforme	see *Persicaria virginiana*
forrestii **new**	WLin
longisetum	see *Persicaria longiseta*
molle	see *Persicaria mollis*
multiflorum	see *Fallopia multiflora*
odoratum	see *Persicaria odorata*
polystachyum	see *Persicaria wallichii*
runciforme	see *Persicaria runcinata*
§ *scoparium*	CBrm CRow EMan EPPr EPla GEil MFir SDry SDys SIng SMad WCot WTin
tinctorium	see *Persicaria tinctoria*
weyrichii	see *Persicaria weyrichii*

Polylepis (Rosaceae)

australis	CFil LEdu SMad SSpi WCot WCru

Polymnia (Asteraceae)

sonchifolia	LEdu
uvedalia	see *Smallanthus uvedalius*

Polypodium ✿ (Polypodiaceae)

australe	see *P. cambricum*

§ **cambricum** — EFer NMar WCot WFib WRic
§ - 'Barrowii' — CLAP NMar WFib WRic
- 'Cambricum' ♀H4 — WRic WWye
- 'Cristatum' — CLAP WFib WRic
- (Cristatum Group) — WRic
  'Grandiceps Forster'
- - 'Grandiceps — WFib WRic
  Fox' ♀H4
- 'Hornet' — WFib
- 'Macrostachyon' — CLAP EFer WFib
- 'Oakleyae' — SMHy WPGP
- 'Omnilacerum Oxford' — CLAP WRic WWye
- 'Prestonii' — WFib WRic
- Pulcherrimum Group — CBgR CLAP EGol WAbe
- 'Pulcherrimum Addison' — WAbe WWye
- Pulcherrimum — WRic
  Group bifid
- 'Richard Kayse' — CDes WFib WRic WWye
- Semilacerum Group — NMar WRic
- - 'Carew Lane' — WFib WRic
- - 'Falcatum O'Kelly' — WAbe WRic
- - 'Jubilee' — NMar
- - 'Robustum' — NMar WFib WRic
- 'Whilharris' ♀H4 — CLAP SMHy WPGP WRic
I x **coughlinii** — WRic
  'Bifidograndiceps'
glycyrrhiza — GPoy LEur WFib WRic
- Grandiceps Group — WRic
- 'Longicaudatum' ♀H4 — CLAP EBee EMon NMar WCot
  WFib WRic WSPU WWye
- 'Malahatense' — CLAP NMar
- 'Malahatense' (sterile) — WAbe WRic
interjectum — CLAP CWCL EBee EFer NMar
  NOrc NVic WRic
- 'Acutum' — NMar
- 'Cornubiense' ♀H4 — CFil CLAP EFer EMon GCal NBir
  NBro NHol NMar NVic SSpi WAbe
  WFib WPGP WRic WTin
- 'Ramosum Hillman' — WRic
x **mantoniae** — LEur WFib
- 'Bifidograndiceps' — SIng WFib WPGP WRic
scouleri — CLAP NBro
vulgare — More than 30 suppliers
- 'Bifidocristatum' — see *P. vulgare* 'Bifidomultifidum'
- 'Bifidomultifidum' — CBgR CLAP CWCL EBee EMon
  GBin GEdr MAsh MCCP NHol
  NMar SIng SMac SPla SSpi WCot
  SRms WRic
- 'Cornubiense
  Grandiceps'
* - 'Cornubiense — EBee WCot
  Multifidum'
- Ramosum Group — NMar
- 'Trichomanoides — CLAP WAbe WFib
  Backhouse'

Polypompholyx see *Utricularia*

Polyscias (Araliaceae)
'Elegans' — MBri
fruticosa — MBri
scutellaria — MBri
  'Pennockii' (v)

Polystichum ❀ (Dryopteridaceae)
acrostichoides — CFwr CLAP CMHG CPrp EBee
  EFtx GCal GEdr GQui LEur NGby
  NLar SMac SNut SSpi WRic
aculeatum ♀H4 — More than 30 suppliers
I - Densum Group — EFer
- Grandiceps Group — EFer NMar
andersonii — CLAP CWCL NHol
braunii — CBcs CMHG CPrp CWCL EBee
  EFtx EGol GBin LEur MLan MMoz
  NOGN WFib WPnP

caryotideum — see *Cyrtomium caryotideum*
deltodon — EBee LEur
falcatum — see *Cyrtomium falcatum*
fortunei — see *Cyrtomium fortunei*
imbricans — CLAP SArc
lonchitis — NWoo
luctuosum — WRic
makinoi — CLAP NHol WFib WRic
mohrioides — CLAP
munitum ♀H4 — More than 30 suppliers
- 'Incisum' — GCal
neolobatum — WFib
ovatopaleaceum — WRic
polyblepharum ♀H4 — More than 30 suppliers
proliferum (R. Br.) — CFwr EAmu EFtx GCal WFib WRic
  C. Presl
* - **plumosum** — CFwr NOak
retrorsopaleaceum — LEur NMar WRic
richardii — WAbe
rigens — CElw CFwr CLAP EBee EFer GCal
  NDlv NHol NMar NOGN SNut
  SRms WCru WFib
§ **setiferum** ♀H4 — More than 30 suppliers
§ - Acutilobum Group — CBcs CFil CFwr CLAP CMHG
  CWCL EBee ECha EFtx ENot
  MBow NHol SDix SMad SPer SSpi
  STes WCru WMoo WPGP WPnP
  WPrP
- Congestum Group — GBin MBri MMoz NHol NMar
  SChu SRms WFib WRic
- 'Congestum' — CFwr CLAP CPrp EBee EFtx ELan
  ENot EPfP GCal LRHS MAsh MBct
  MDun NBir NBlu NFor NSti SMer
  SMrm SNut SPla SSto WGor WMoo
  WPrP
- 'Cristatopinnulum' — CFil CLAP WPGP
- Cristatum Group — CLAP SRms
- Cruciatum Group — CLAP
- Divisilobum Group — More than 30 suppliers
- - 'Dahlem' — CDoC CFwr CLAP CPen ECha EFer
  EFtx ELan EMon GKir MDun
  MMoz MSte NFor NHol SMac SMer
  SNut SSto WAbe WMoo WPnP
  WRic
- - 'Herrenhausen' — CFwr CLAP EBee EBlw ECha EFtx
  ELan EPfP GKir LPBA LRHS MAvo
  MBri MCCP MDun MWgw NBPC
  NFor NMar NOGN NOrc NSti SPer
  WAbe WFar WFib WMoo WPnP
  WRic
- - 'Madame Patti' — GBin
- 'Divisilobum — CLAP ENot EPfP NBir NOrc SNut
  Densum' ♀H4 — SSpi
- 'Divisilobum — CLAP GBin NHol SRms WFib
  Iveryanum' ♀H4
- 'Divisilobum Laxum' — CLAP EPar SChu
- 'Foliosum' — CLAP GBin
- 'Gracile' — NBir
- 'Grandiceps' — CLAP EFer ELan
- Green Lace — GBin
  = 'Gracillimum' **new**
- 'Hamlet' — GBin
- 'Helena' — GBin
- 'Hirondelle' — SRms
- Lineare Group — CFil CLAP NHol WFib
- Multilobum Group — CLAP WFib WRic
- 'Nantes' **new** — GBin
- Perserratum Group — WFib
- 'Plumo-Densum' — see *P. setiferum*
  'Plumosomultilobum'
- 'Plumosodensum' — see *P. setiferum*
  'Plumosomultilobum'
- Plumosodivisilobum — CLAP CMil CRow ECha EGol NBid
  Group — SPla WAbe WCru WFib

- - 'Baldwinii'	CLAP
§ - 'Plumosomultilobum'	CFwr CLAP CPrp EBee EFtx ENot EPfP GBin LAst LRHS MAsh MBnl MCLN MWgw NSti SMer SMrm SNut SPla WAbe WFib WMoo WPnP WRic
- Plumosum Group	CLAP CMHG CSam CSpe EBlw EChP EFtx LEur NOrc SAPC SArc SBla SChu WStl
- - dwarf	CBos CSBt WCot
* - *plumosum grande* 'Moly'	CLAP SRms
- Proliferum Group	see *P. setiferum* Acutilobum Group
* - 'Proliferum Wollaston'	CFwr ENot NRib SNut SSto WWeb
- 'Pulcherrimum Bevis' ♀H4	CLAP SHFr WFib WPGP
* - 'Ramopinnatum'	CLAP
- 'Ray Smith'	GBin WFib
- Revolvens Group	EFer
- Rotundatum Group	CLAP
- - 'Cristatum'	CLAP
- 'Wakeleyanum'	SRms
- 'Wollaston' ambig.	CFwr CLAP GBin MAsh MFan NHol WAbe
tagawanum	WRic
triangulum	NMar
tripteron	WRic
tsussimense ♀H4	More than 30 suppliers
vestitum	CLAP CTrC
xiphophyllum	WRic

Polyxena (*Hyacinthaceae*)

corymbosa	CStu
§ *ensifolia*	ERos
odorata	CLyd CStu WCot
pygmaea	see *P. ensifolia*

Pomaderris (*Rhamnaceae*)

apetala	CPLG
elliptica	CPLG ECou

pomegranate see *Punica granatum*

Poncirus (*Rutaceae*)

§ *trifoliata*	CArn CBcs CDoC CFil EBee ELan ENot EPfP ERea IDee LAst LRHS MBlu MJnS MRav NWea SAPC SArc SKee SLon SMad SPer WBVN WDin WFar WPGP WPat WSHC WTel

Pontederia (*Pontederiaceae*)

'Blue Spires' **new**	CDWL
cordata ♀H4	CBen CDWL CHEx CRow CWat ECha EHon ELan EMFW ENot EPfP LNCo LPBA MCCP MSta NArg NPer SCoo SLon SPlb SWat WFar WMAq WPnP WWpP
- f. *albiflora*	CRow CWat EMFW EPfP LPBA MCCP NLar SLon WDyG WMAq
§ - var. *lancifolia*	CRow ECha EMFW LPBA MCCP MSta NPer SWat WDyG WTin WWpP
- 'Pink Pons'	CRow NLar
lanceolata	see *P. cordata* var. *lancifolia*

Populus ✿ (*Salicaceae*)

x *acuminata*	WMou
alba	CCVT CDoC CDul CLnd CSBt CTri CWib EBee ECrN ENot GKir LBuc MBar NBee NWea SBLw SHBN SPer WBVN WDin WMou WOrn WStl
- 'Bolleana'	see *P. alba* f. *pyramidalis*
- 'Nivea'	EWTr SBLw
§ - f. *pyramidalis*	CBcs SRms WMou
§ - 'Raket'	CLnd CTho ECrN ELan ENot MGos NWea SBLw SPer
- 'Richardii'	CDul CLnd CTho ECtt GKir MBar SPer WCot WFar WMou
- Rocket	see *P. alba* 'Raket'
alba x *grandidentata*	WMou
§ 'Balsam Spire' (f) ♀H4	CDoC CDul CTho EBee ENot GKir NWea WDin WMou
§ *balsamifera*	CCVT CDoC CTho CTri EBee ECrN GKir MGos NWea SBLw SHBN SPer SRms WCot WDin WFar
x *berolinensis*	CDoC
x *canadensis*	ECrN SBLw
- 'Aurea' ♀H4	CDoC CDul CLnd CTho CWib EBee ENot LPan MDun MRav SKee SPer WDin WFar WMou
- 'Aurea' x *jackii* 'Aurora'	MRav WBVN WDin
- 'Eugenei' (m)	CTho
- 'Robusta' (m)	CDoC CDul CLnd CTri EBee EMil ENot LBuc NWea WDin WMou
- 'Serotina' (m)	CDoC ECrN WDin WMou
x *candicans* misapplied	see *P.* x *jackii*
x *canescens*	CDoC ECrN GKir MBri SBLw WDin WMou
- 'De Moffart' (m)	ENot SBLw
- 'Tower'	WMou
x *generosa* 'Beaupré'	CTho GKir LBuc WDin WMou
§ x *jackii* (f)	WDin
- 'Aurora' (f/v)	CBcs CDul CLnd CSBt CTrw ELan ENot GKir LBuc LRHS MBar MBri MGos MRav MWat NBee NBlu NWea SBLw SHBN SPer SRms WDin WFar WHar
lasiocarpa ♀H4	CDoC CFil CLnd CTho EBee EPfP MBlu MRav SBLw SLPl SMad WMou WPGP
- var. *tibetica*	WMou
maximowiczii	WMou
nigra	CDul EPfP NWea WDin
- (f)	ECrN SLPl
- (m)	SLPl
- subsp. *betulifolia*	CCVT CDul CTho EBee ENot LBuc MGos NWea WDin WMou WOrn
- - (f)	WMou
- - (m)	WMou
- 'Italica' ambig.	CCVT CDoC CDul CLnd CSBt CTho CTri CWib EBee ECrN ELan ENot GKir LBuc LRHS MBri MGos NBee NWea SBLw SHBN SPer SRms WDin WOrn
- 'Italica Aurea'	see *P. nigra* 'Lombardy Gold'
- 'Italica Aurea'	see *P. nigra* 'Lombardy Gold'
§ - 'Lombardy Gold' (m)	CEnd CTho MBlu
- 'Pyramidalis'	see *P. nigra* 'Italica'
simonii 'Fastigiata'	WMou
- 'Obtusata'	WMou
szechuanica	WMou
- var. *tibetica*	CDul CFil WPGP
tacamahaca	see *P. balsamifera*
'Tacatricho 32'	see *P.* 'Balsam Spire'
tomentosa	WMou
tremula ♀H4	CCVT CDoC CDul CLnd CRWN CSBt CTho CWib EBee ECrN ELan ENot GKir LBuc LRHS NBee NWea SBLw SHBN SKee SPer WDin WMoo WMou WOrn
§ - 'Erecta'	CDul CEnd CLnd CTho EBee GKir LRHS MBlu MBri SMad SPoG WFar WMou
- 'Fastigiata'	see *P. tremula* 'Erecta'
- 'Pendula' (m)	CDul CEnd CLnd CTho ECrN GKir SBLw WCFE WDin WMou
trichocarpa	CDul CTho ECrN SPer
- 'Columbia River'	GKir

- 'Fritzi Pauley' (f)	CDul CTho WMou
violascens	see *P. lasiocarpa* var. *tibetica*
yunnanensis	CFil CLnd CMHG WMou WPGP

Porophyllum (Asteraceae)

ruderale	MSal

Portulaca (Portulacaceae)

grandiflora	MBri
oleracea	CArn MHer SECG SIde WJek WLHH
- var. *aurea*	WJek WLHH

Potamogeton (Potamogetonaceae)

crispus	EHon EMFW EPat NArg WMAq

Potentilla ✿ (Rosaceae)

alba	CPLG CSev CTri EBee ECha EFou ELan EMar GBuc LGro MWgw NChi NFla SCro SPer SUsu WAul WCot WPer
alchemilloides	MNrw SMer WPer
alpicola	WPer
ambigua	see *P. cuneata*
andicola	EBee
anserina	CArn GBar MGas MHer WHbs WHer XPep
- 'Golden Treasure' (v)	EBee EPPr ITer MLLN WCot WHer WShp
- 'Shine'	EMan WCot
anserinoides	EBee EGoo EMan GCal WCot WDyG WMoo WPer
arbuscula hort.	see *P. fruticosa* 'Elizabeth'
'Arc-en-Ciel'	CFwr CHid CRez EBee EBre EChP EMan EMar GSki LAst MBNS MBri NLar SBri SHar SUsu WCAu WFar WHil WMoo
argentea	CRWN CSWP CSev LIck LPVe MBNS MWgw NNor SBri SPlb SSte WBea WFar WPer
arguta	EBee
argyrophylla	see *P. atrosanguinea* var. *argyrophylla*
* - *insignis rubra*	NChi
astracanica **new**	CStr
atrosanguinea	More than 30 suppliers
§ - var. *argyrophylla*	EChP ECha ELan GCal GTou MRav MWat MWgw NBir NBro NCot NJOw NMir NOak SBri SCro SOkh SRms SWal WBea WFar WHil WMoo WPer WWhi WWin
- - SS&W 7768	MSte
- var. *leucochroa*	see *P. atrosanguinea* var. *argyrophylla*
aucheriana	EHyt
aurea	EBee EBre ECtt EDAr EPfP IHMH MTho NArg NBlu NLAp NMen NMir NWCA SHFr WBVN WBrk WPat WShp
- 'Aurantiaca'	EDAr EWes NLar SRot
§ - subsp. *chrysocraspeda*	GCrs NMen STre
§ - 'Goldklumpen'	ECtt MRav NPro SLon
- 'Plena' (d)	EBre GTou MBro NSla SRot
'Blazeaway'	EBee EBre EChP EMan LRHS MBNS MBri MNFA NGdn NHol SLon WBea WCAu WFar
burmiensis	EBee
calabra	CMea ECha EDAr EMan SMer SSvw WHer WWin
§ *cinerea*	CTri LBee SBla WRHF
§ *collina*	CNic EBee SBri
§ *crantzii*	CMea EBee GCrs GTou MBar MSte SRms

- 'Nana'	see *P. crantzii* 'Pygmaea'
§ - 'Pygmaea'	CNic ECtt EPfP MOne NBir NJOw NMen WBea
§ *cuneata* ♀H4	CLyd EDAr GAbr GTou IHMH MTho NLAp NRya NWCA SIng WPer WWin
'Custard and Cream'	EChP
delavayi	GEil GlBF MNrw
detommasii	MHar WPer
- MESE 400	EBee
dickinsii	CNic ETow NMen SOkd
'Emilie'	CMea EBee EChP EFou EGle EMan EMar GCal LPVe MBNS MBri NLar NPro NSti SUsu SWvt WFar WHil
§ *erecta*	CArn CRWN EGle EOHP GBar GPoy GWCH MHer MSal WBri WHbs WWye
eriocarpa	CLyd ECtt EHol EMlt GEdr IMGH MWat NJOw NLAp NMen SBri WAbe WPat
'Etna'	More than 30 suppliers
'Everest'	see *P. fruticosa* 'Mount Everest'
'Fireflame'	EBee ECha NLar SBri WMoo
fissa	CTCP EBee MNrw MSte NBir WBar
'Flambeau' (d)	CHad EBee EChP EMan MNFA MRav NDov NGdn NHol NLar SLon
'Flamenco'	CSam CTri EBee EBre EChP ECtt EFou EMil ERou GKir MBri MNrw MRav NBir NFor SAga SUsu WAbb WFar WLow WPGP
fragariiformis	see *P. megalantha*
fruticosa	CPLG LBuc NMen NWea
- 'Abbotswood' ♀H4	More than 30 suppliers
- 'Abbotswood Silver' (v)	EBee ECtt LAst MBNS MSwo SLim WFar WMoo
- 'Alice' **new**	WWeb
- 'Annette'	LRHS NPro WBod WWeb
- 'Apple Blossom'	CWib
- var. *arbuscula* hort.	see *P. fruticosa* 'Elizabeth'
- - 'Kingdon Ward'	WWeb
- 'Argentea Nana'	see *P. fruticosa* 'Beesii'
- 'Barnbarroch' **new**	WWeb
- 'Beanii'	WWeb
§ - 'Beesii'	EBee ELan EPfP GKir LRHS MAsh MBNS MBar SIgm SPla WHCG WTel WWeb WWin
- 'Bewerley Surprise'	EHol GEil NBir WHCG WWeb
- 'Cascade'	WBcn
- 'Charlotte'	WBcn
* - 'Chelsea Star' ♀H4	WWeb
- 'Chilo' (v)	MGos WBcn WMoo WWeb
- 'Clotted Cream'	MBar
- var. *dahurica* 'Farrer's White'	WFar
- - 'Hersii'	see *P. fruticosa* 'Snowflake'
- - 'Rhodocalyx'	CPle WFar
- 'Dart's Cream'	LRHS
- 'Dart's Golddigger'	CTri EBee ECtt ENot WWeb
- 'Daydawn'	More than 30 suppliers
- 'Elizabeth'	CBcs CDoC CSam CTri CWib EBee ENot EPfP GKir LGro LHop LRHS MBar MGos MRav NBee NWea SHBN SPer SRms SWvt WBVN WBod WCFE WDin WFar WMoo WTel
- 'Farreri'	see *P. fruticosa* 'Gold Drop'
- 'Floppy Disc'	EPfP LRHS MAsh MGos NHol NWoo SHBN SPer SPla
- 'Frances, Lady Daresbury'	GKir WWeb
- 'Glenroy Pinkie'	CSam EBee EPfP LRHS MTis NPro SLon WWeb
§ - 'Gold Drop'	WHCG WTel

- 'Gold Parade' **new** WWeb
- 'Golden Charm' **new** WWeb
- 'Golden Dwarf' LRHS MGos
- 'Golden Spreader' GKir NPro WWeb
- 'Goldfinger' CChe CDoC CSBt EBee ELan ENot
EPfP GEil GKir LHop LRHS MGos
MRav MSwo MWat NHol SLim
SMer SPer SPlb WDin WHar WStI
WTel WWeb
- Goldkugel see *P. fruticosa* 'Gold Drop'
- 'Goldstar' EBee ENot GKir IArd LRHS MBNS
MBri NHol WFar WHCG WWeb
- 'Goldteppich' LBuc MBar SHBN
- Goscote MGos
- 'Grace Darling' CAbP EPfP EWes GGar NBir SWvt
WBVN WBod WGwG WHCG
WMoo WWeb
- 'Groneland' ♀H4 WWeb
- 'Haytor's Orange' CWib
- 'Honey' LHop WHCG WWeb
- 'Hopleys Orange' ♀H4 CChe EPfP EWes GKir LHop LRHS
MAsh MBri MWat NPri WBod WFar
WGor WHCG WWeb WWin
- 'Hopleys Pink' WWeb
- 'Hunter's Moon' WWeb
- 'Hurstbourne' NPro
- 'Jackman's Variety' ♀H4 CSam CWib ECtt ENot SRms WStI
WWeb
- 'Janet' **new** WWeb
- 'Jolina' WWeb
- 'Katherine Dykes' CChe CDoC CDul CSBt CWib
EBee ENot EPfP GEil GKir LRHS
MAsh MBar MDun MRav NWea
SLim SLon SPer SRms WBod WDin
WFar WGwG WHar WMoo WStI
WTel WWeb
* - 'King Cup' ♀H4 WWeb
- 'Klondike' CBcs CSBt EMil EPfP GKir NWea
§ - 'Knap Hill' EBee ENot GEil MRav WWeb
- 'Knap Hill Buttercup' see *P. fruticosa* 'Knap Hill'
- 'Kobold' GEil MBar
* - 'Lemon and Lime' MBlu NBir NPro WWeb
- 'Limelight' ♀H4 CSBt EBee EBre ELan GKir LRHS
MAsh MBri MRav MSwo MWgw
NPri SPla SPoG WBcn WFar WHCG
WWeb
- 'Longacre Variety' CTri ENot GKir MBar MSwo NWea
WBod WFar WTel
- Lovely Pink CDoC COtt CSBt EBee EBre ENot
= 'Pink Beauty'PBR LRHS MAsh MBNS MRav NBlu
♀H4 NPri SCoo SPer SWvt WWeb
§ - 'Maanelys' CSBt CTrw ECtt MWat NWea SPer
SRms WDin WFar WHCG WMoo
§ - 'Manchu' CDoC CTri ENot GEil MBar MRav
MWat NPro SChu SHBN SPer SRms
WCFE WTel WWin
- Marian Red Robin CDoC CSBt CWib EBee EBre ELan
= 'Marrob'PBR ♀H4 ENot EPfP GKir LAst LRHS MAsh
MBri MRav MSwo MTis MWat
NWea SCoo SLim SPer SWvt WDin
WStI WWeb
- 'Maybe' **new** WWeb
- 'McKay's White' **new** WWeb
- 'Medicine Wheel EBee ELan EWes GEil LRHS MAsh
Mountain' ♀H4 MBri MRav NLar NPro SLim SPer
WHCG WWeb
- Moonlight see *P. fruticosa* 'Maanelys'
§ - 'Mount Everest' EHol MBar NHol NWea SLon SRms
WWeb
- 'Nana Argentea' see *P. fruticosa* 'Beesii'
- 'New Dawn' CDoC GKir LRHS MAsh MBNS
MBri SPer WBcn WFar WWeb
- 'Orange Star' NHol WHCG WWeb
- 'Orangeade' LRHS MAsh SMur WWeb

- 'Peaches and Cream' WEas WHCG WWeb
* - 'Peachy Proud' NPro
- 'Pink Pearl' GKir WBcn WMoo WWin
- 'Pink Queen' EMil MBri
- 'Pink Whisper' **new** WWeb
- 'Pretty Polly' CChe CSBt CTri CWSG EBee ENot
EPfP GKir LAst LRHS MAsh MBar
MGos MSwo SHBN SPer SPla SSta
WBod WDin WFar WHCG WHar
WMoo WStI WWeb
- 'Primrose Beauty' ♀H4 CDoC CDul EBee EBre EGra ELan
ENot EPfP GEil GKir LAst LRHS
MBar MGos MRav MSwo MWgw
NBlu NJOw SLim SMer SPlb WDin
WFar WGwG WHar WMoo WStI
WWeb
- Princess = 'Blink'PBR CSBt CTri CWSG EBee EBre ELan
ENot GKir LRHS MAsh MBNS
MBar MRav MSwo NBlu SLim SPer
SReu SRms WDin WFar WHar WStI
WWeb
- 'Prostrate Copper' NJOw
- var. **pumila** MBro WPat
- 'Red Ace' More than 30 suppliers
- var. **rigida** WBcn
- 'Royal Flush' MBar WStI
- 'Silver Schilling' NPro
- 'Snowbird' EBee EPfP LRHS MBNS MGos NPro
SLim WFar WWeb
§ - 'Snowflake' CBcs WMoo
- 'Sommerflor' ♀H4 EBee ENot MRav
- 'Sophie's Blush' CChe LAst MRav NHol NWea
WDin WHCG WSHC WWeb
- 'Summer Sorbet' **new** MAsh
- 'Sunset' CBcs CBrm CSBt CSam CWSG
CWib EBee ELan ENot EPfP GKir
LRHS MBar MGos MRav NBir NPPs
NWea SAga SLim SPer SReu SRms
SSta WBVN WBod WFar WStI
WWeb
- 'Tangerine' More than 30 suppliers
- 'Tilford Cream' CDoC CSBt CSam EBee ELan ENot
EPfP EWTr LAst LRHS MAsh MBar
MRav MSwo MWgw NBir NBlu
NHol SHBN SPer SReu SRms
WBVN WCFE WDin WFar WHCG
WMoo WStI WWeb
- 'Tom Conway' WHCG WWeb
- 'Tropicana' WBcn
- 'Valley Gold' **new** WWeb
§ - var. **veitchii** CSBt SHBN WStI
- 'Vilmoriniana' CBot CTri ELan EPfP LRHS MAsh
MRav NPro SIgm SLon SMac SPer
SSpi WAbe WCFE WGwG WHCG
WSHC WTel WTin WWeb
- 'Wessex Silver' CFai WHCG
- 'Whirligig' CFai WHCG
- 'White Rain' GKir WWeb
- 'Wickwar Beauty' CWib
- 'Wickwar Trailer' CLyd WHoo
- 'William Purdom' WHCG
- 'Wychbold White' **new** WWeb
- 'Yellow Bird' ♀H4 LRHS MGos
- 'Yellow Carpet' WHCG WWeb
- 'Yellow Giant' WWeb
gelida EHyt
'Gibson's Scarlet' ♀H4 More than 30 suppliers
glandulosa EBee MNrw
'Gloire de Nancy' (d) CKno CSpe EBee EBre ERou GCal
LHop LRHS MRav NBir WCot
WPGP WWhi
'Gold Clogs' see *P. aurea* 'Goldklumpen'
'Gold Sovereign' EBee ENot EPfP
gracilis CTCP EBee SBri

- var. **glabrata**	EBee EPPr
- subsp. **nuttallii**	see *P. gracilis* var. *glabrata*
'Harlow Cream'	NBid
'Helen Jane'	EBee EBre EWTr GBuc GFlt GKir
	LPio LRHS MBri MHer NBir NGdn
	NJOw NLar NPro STes WBea WCot
	WFar WMnd WPer
heptaphylla **new**	GSki
'Herzblut'	EBee EPfP GBuc MNrw NLar
x **hopwoodiana**	CBos CFwr CHad CSpe EBee EChP
	EFou EGle EPPr EPfP GCal LPVe
	LPhx MBri MCLN MNrw MTis
	NBir NDov SAga SCro STes SUsu
	WAbb WCAu WHil WLin WPnP
	WSan WWeb
* x **hybrida** 'Jean Jabber'	EBee EWll GBuc GMac MRav NBur
	NLar
hyparctica	MDKP
- **nana**	CLyd LBee LRHS MBro NHol WPat
'Jack Elliot'	WWeb
'Mandshurica'	see *P. fruticosa* 'Manchu'
§ **megalantha** ♀H4	More than 30 suppliers
- 'Gold Sovereign'	EBre NGdn NPro
'Melton'	EBee ECoo MNrw NBir NOak
	WHen
* 'Melton Fire'	ECtt EGra GFlt GKir MBri MFOX
	MWrn NArg NBir NBur NCot
	NJOw NPPs SBri SGar SUsu SWal
	WBea WCot WMnd WMoo
'Monarch's Velvet'	see *P. thurberi* 'Monarch's Velvet'
'Monsieur Rouillard' (d)	CSam EBee EMan EMar GKir
	MCLN MHer MNrw MRav MWat
	NCot NDov NFor NGdn SBri SHop
	SUsu SWal WHoo WSan WWhi
'Mont d'Or'	MBri MRav
montana	NHol WHer WPer
nepalensis	CTCP EBee ECha EDAr GKir IMGH
	LAst MFir NBro NFor NPro NSti
	SBri SHFr SHel WBrk WHoo
- 'Flammenspiel'	WFar
- 'Master Floris'	SAga WFar WHer
§ - 'Miss Willmott' ♀H4	More than 30 suppliers
- 'Ron McBeath'	CBri CBrm CHea CPlt EBee EChP
	ECtt EFou EMan EMar GBin GBuc
	GSki LPVe LRav MBNS MBri MBro
	MSPs NHol NSti SBri SIng SWvt
	WBro WCra WHoo WMoo WWeb
- 'Roxana'	EBee ECGP ELan ERou GBuc GKir
	GSki LAst LPVe MBNS MDKP
	MRav NBro NPPs WAbb WBea
	WFar WMoo WPer WRos
- 'Shogran'	EBee EBre EChP EMlt GAbr GBuc
	NGby NLar SBri WBea WHil WWeb
§ **neumanniana**	EMlt NBir NPri WFar XPep
- 'Goldrausch'	ECha MRav SBla
§ - 'Nana'	CNic EPot LBee LRHS MBro MHer
	MWat NJOw NLAp NLar NMen
	SPlb SRms WEas WFar WWin
nevadensis	CLyd CTri ECho GEdr SRms WPer
nitida	GEdr NMen SRms WAbe WLin
- 'Alba'	EPot NLAp
- 'Lissadell'	CPBP
- 'Rubra'	CFir CMea EDAr GCrs GEdr GTou
	IMGH MBro MHer MWat NBir
	NHol NLAp NWCA SAga SBla
	SRms WAbe WPat
nivea	GTou SRot
- 'Nunk'	GSki LRHS MBar MWgw
* 'Olympic Mountains'	WPer
ovina	WPer
palustris	EBee MSta NLar WBea WMoo
pamiroalaica **new**	EHyt
pedata	LLWP
'Pink Orleans'	WWeb

aff. **polyphylla**	GKev
CHP&W 314 **new**	
recta	CStr ELau EMan EOMN ERou
	GTou NPri SScr WRos
- 'Alba'	EGoo LPVe NBur WPer WWhi
- 'Citrina'	see *P. recta* var. *sulphurea*
- 'Macrantha'	see *P. recta* 'Warrenii'
§ - var. **sulphurea**	More than 30 suppliers
§ - 'Warrenii'	CHea CSBt EChP EFou EMlt EPla
	LAst LRHS MBNS MCLN MRav
	MTis MWat NBir NDov NJOw
	NMir NOrc SIng SPer SRms SWal
	WBea WCAu WFar WHal WMoo
	WPer
reptans	CRWN XPep
- 'Pleniflora' (d)	MInt
'Roxanne' (d)	MHer
rupestris	CM&M CPom EBee EChP ECha
	EMan EPPr LAst MCLN MFir MLLN
	MNrw NChi NDlv NSti SBri SGar
	WBea WCAu WFar WHal WMoo
	WPer WWin
salesoviana	WLin
speciosa	EMan EWes IGor MDKP WMoo
sterilis	CHid IHMH
'Sungold'	ECho WHCG
tabernaemontani	see *P. neumanniana*
ternata	see *P. aurea* subsp.
	chrysocraspeda
thurberi	CHid CStr EBee EGle EGra EMan
	EPPr GCal LPhx LPio MNrw MRav
	NLar WMoo
§ - 'Monarch's Velvet'	More than 30 suppliers
- 'White Queen'	see *P.* 'White Queen'
tommasiniana	see *P. cinerea*
x **tonguei** ♀H4	More than 30 suppliers
tormentilla	see *P. erecta*
tridentata	see *Sibbaldiopsis tridentata*
verna	see *P. neumanniana*
- 'Pygmaea'	see *P. neumanniana* 'Nana'
'Versicolor Plena' (d)	CMea
villosa	see *P. crantzii*
'Volcan'	CBos CKno CMea CMil CPlt EBee
	EWes GCal LPhx MBNS MBri NChi
	WAbb WCra WFar WPGP
§ 'White Queen'	CBAn EBee EWTr EWll GKir
	MNrw MWrn NBur NPri SHar SRot
	SWal WMnd
'William Rollison' ♀H4	More than 30 suppliers
willmottiae	see *P. nepalensis* 'Miss Willmott'
'Yellow Queen'	CBcs CBos CTri EBre EMil ENot
	EPfP ERou GSki MBNS MNrw
	MRav NHol SPer SWat WCAu WFar

Poterium see *Sanguisorba*

sanguisorba	see *Sanguisorba minor*

Prasium (*Lamiaceae*)

majus **new**	XPep

Pratia (*Campanulaceae*)

§ **angulata**	EWll GGar
- 'Tim Rees'	IHMH
§ - 'Treadwellii'	EBre ECha EDAr EMan ESis GMac
	LBee LRHS MBNS SPlb WHal
	WHen
- 'Woodside'	ECou
angulata x	GGar
pedunculata	
'Celestial Spice'	ECou
macrodon	WCru
§ **pedunculata**	More than 30 suppliers
- 'County Park'	More than 30 suppliers
- 'Kiandra'	ECou

- 'Tom Stone' MBNS
- 'White Stars' WLFP
§ ***perpusilla*** ECou
- 'Fragrant Carpet' ECou
- 'Summer Meadows' ECou WPer

Prenanthes (Asteraceae)
§ *alba* EBee

Preslia see Mentha

Primula ✿ (Primulaceae)

Lismore 79-26 EHyt
acaulis see *P. vulgaris*
'Adrian Jones' (2) EHyt ITim WAbe
agleniana **new** EBee
'Aire Mist' (*allionii* CGra CPBP EPot GKev GNor ITim
hybrid) (2) MFie NHol NLAp NRya WAbe WLin
'Alan Robb' (dPrim) (30) MBri NCGa NHol WFar
'Alexina' (*allionii* EHyt ITim MFie NHol WLin
hybrid) (2)
algida (11) ECho GFle MWrn NWCA
§ *allionii* (2) ♀H2 EHyt GTou ITim MFie NHol NLAp
NWCA WAbe WCom
- Hartside 383/3 NHol
- KRW 56/380 EPot
- KRW 56/392 EPot
- KRW 60/394 EPot
- KRW 65/338 EPot
- KRW 67/412 EPot
- KRW 74/481 EPot
- KRW 75/504 CNic
- KRW 76/504 EPot
- Lismore 81/19/3 MFie
- 'A.K. Wells' (2) EPot WAbe
- 'Agnes' (2) EHyt ITim
- 'Aire Waves' see *Primula* x *loiseleurii* 'Aire
Waves'
- var. *alba* (2) EHyt NHol
* - 'Alexander' (2) CGra
- 'Amy' **new** ITim
- 'Anna Griffith' (2) EHyt GCrs ITim LRHS MFie NHol
NRya NWCA WAbe WLin
- 'Anne' (2) EHyt EPot GCrs ITim NDlv
§ - 'Apple Blossom' (2) GAbr MDHE NLAp
- 'Archer' (2) EHyt ITim NDlv NHol WLin
- x *auricula* 'Blairside GNor
Yellow' (2)
- x *auricula* 'Old Red GCrs MFie NHol WLin
Dusty Miller' hort. (2)
- 'Austen' (2) ITim NDlv NHol
- 'Avalanche' (2) ITim NHol WAbe
- 'Beryl' **new** EHyt
- 'Bill Martin' (2) EPot ITim
- 'Brilliant' (2) WAbe
- Burnley form (2) NHol
- 'Candy' (2) **new** EHyt
- 'Chivalry' (2) CGra
- 'Clarence Elliott' see *P.* 'Clarence Elliott' (2)
- 'Claude Flight' (2) EHyt
- 'Confection' (2) EHyt
- 'Crowsley Variety' (2) CNic LRHS NHol NSla NWCA
WAbe
- 'Crusader' (2) EHyt ITim
- 'Crystal' (2) EHyt
- 'Duncan' (2) CNic ITim
* - 'E.G. Watson' (2) EHyt
§ - 'Edinburgh' (2) CNic EHyt EPot GKir ITim MFie
NHol NJOw WAbe
- 'Edrom' (2) ITim NHol
- 'Elizabeth Baker' (2) GNor ITim MFie WAbe
- 'Elizabeth Burrow' (2) EHyt
- 'Elizabeth Earle' (2) EHyt EPot ITim NHol WAbe
- 'Elliott's Large' see *P. allionii* 'Edinburgh'

- 'Elliott's Variety' see *P. allionii* 'Edinburgh'
- 'Eureka' **new** CGra
- 'Fanfare' (2) CGra EHyt EPot ITim LRHS NHol
WGwG WHHs
- 'Flute' (2) EHyt
- 'Frank Barker' (2) EPot NHol
- GFS 1984 (2) CGra
§ - 'Gilderdale Glow' (2) CGra NRya
- 'Giuseppi's Form' see *P. allionii* 'Mrs Dyas'
- 'Grandiflora' (2) ITim
- 'Hemswell Blush' see *P.* 'Hemswell Blush'
- 'Hemswell Ember' see *P.* 'Hemswell Ember'
- x *hirsuta* (2) ITim MFie
- 'Hocker Edge' (2) ITim NHol
- 'Horwood' (2) EHyt
- 'Huntsman' (2) MFie
- 'Imp' **new** EHyt
- Ingwersen's form (2) GTou
- 'Isobel' **new** EHyt
- 'Jenny' (2) JCA 4161/22 CGra EHyt EPot
- 'Joseph Collins' **new** CGra
- K R W see *P. allionii* 'Ken's Seedling'
- 'Kath Dryden' (2) CNic EHyt
§ - 'Ken's Seedling' (2) CNic EPot NHol NJOw
- 'Lindum Prima' **new** EHyt
- x 'Lismore Treasure' (2) CGra CPBP NWCA
- 'Louise' (2) EHyt
- 'Malcolm' (2) EHyt
- 'Margaret Earle' (2) NHol WAbe
- 'Marion' (2) EPot GNor ITim NHol
- 'Marjorie Wooster' (2) EHyt ITim MFie NWCA WAbe
- 'Martin' (2) ITim NHol
- 'Mary Anne' GCrs
- 'Mary Berry' (2) ITim MFie WAbe
- 'Maurice Dryden' (2) EHyt
§ - 'Mrs Dyas' (2) EHyt ITim NHol WAbe
- 'New Dawn' (2) EHyt
I - 'Paula' (2) EHyt
- 'Peace' (2) EPot
- - KRW 147-47 EHyt
- x *pedemontana* see *P.* x *sendtneri*
- 'Peggy Wilson' (2) EPot EWes NHol
- 'Pennine Pink' (2) ITim NHol
- 'Perkie' (2) EHyt
- 'Picton's Variety' (2) NDlv NHol
- 'Pink Aire' see *P.* 'Pink Aire'
- 'Pinkie' (2) CGra
- 'Praecox' (2) NHol NSla
- x *pubescens* 'Harlow CLyd GMac ITim
Car' (2)
- 'Raymond Wooster' (2) EHyt ITim LRHS NHol
- 'Robert' (2) CGra
I - 'Roy' (2) EHyt
- x *rubra* (2) ITim NHol
- 'Scimitar' (2) EHyt NHol
- 'Serendipity' (2) EHyt
- x 'Snow Ruffles' (2) ITim
- 'Snowflake' (2) CGra CPBP EHyt ITim LRHS
NWCA WAbe
- 'Stanton House' (2) MFie NDlv NHol
- 'Stephen' (2) EHyt ITim
- 'Superba' EHyt
- 'Sylvia Martinelli' **new** EHyt
- 'Tranquillity' (2) EHyt ITim MFie NHol
§ - 'Travellers' (2) EHyt EPot
- 'Viscountess Byng' (2) ITim WLin
- x 'White Linda Pope' (2) ITim MFie NHol WLin
- 'William Earle' (2) EHyt GCrs ITim LRHS MFie NDlv
NHol NWCA WAbe

alpicola (26) ♀H4 CFee CRow CSWP EBre EPfP GCrs
GEdr GFle GGar GIBF GKir LPBA
LRHS MCLN MFOX MFie NBid
NBro NDlv NLAp SPer WAbe
WBVN WLin

- var. **alba** (26)	CPla CRow CSWP GBuc GEdr GGar ITim MBow MNrw SLon SWat
§ - var. **alpicola** (26)	CSWP EBee GBuc GEdr GFle MNrw WAbe
- var. **luna**	see *P. alpicola* var. *alpicola*
- var. **violacea** (26)	CDWL CPla CRow CSWP GGar LRHS MBow MBri MCLN MFie MNrw NBid SLon SWat WAbe WWhi
'Altaica'	see *P. elatior* subsp. *meyeri*
altaica grandiflora	see *P. elatior* subsp. *meyeri*
amethystina new	GKev
amoena	see *P. elatior* subsp. *meyeri*
angustifolia (20)	GFle
anisodora	see *P. wilsonii* var. *anisodora*
§ x **anisodoxa**	GKev WHil
'Annemijne' **new**	EMon
'April Rose' (dPrim) (30)	ENot MRav NBid
x **arctotis**	see *P.* x *pubescens*
atrodentata (9)	WAbe
aurantiaca (4)	CFir CPla GBar GCrs GEdr GFle MSta SRms WHil
aureata (21)	GCrs GGGa ITim NLAp WAbe
- subsp. **fimbriata** (21)	GCrs ITim
§ **auricula** L. (2) ♀H4	EDAr ELan GCrs GFlt GKir GNor GTou LRHS MFie MHer NBro NSla SIng SPer SPet SPlb SWal WAbe WCom WMAq
- var. **albocincta** (2)	NWCA
- subsp. **auricula** (2)	GTou
- subsp. **balbisii**	see *P. auricula* L. subsp. *ciliata*
- subsp. **bauhinii** (2)	WLin
§ - subsp. **ciliata** (2)	GFle NLAp
auricula ambig. (2)	NBlu WRHF
auricula hort. '2nd Vic' **new**	SPop
- A74 (A)	WBrE
- 'Abundance' (A)	MAln
- 'Achates' (A)	MAln
- 'Admiral' (A)	MAln MCre
- 'Adrian' (A)	GAbr ITim MCre MFie NBro NLAp SPop WLin
- 'Adrienne Ruan' (A)	MAln
- 'Aga Khan' (A)	MAln
- 'Agamemnon' (A)	MAln MCre
- 'Alamo' (A)	MCre SPop
- 'Alan Ravenscroft' (A)	MAln MFie
- 'Alansford' (A)	MAln
- 'Albert Bailey' (S/d)	GNor ITim MAln MCre SPop
- 'Alexandra Georgina' (A)	MAln
- 'Alf' (A)	MAln
- 'Alfred Charles' (A) **new**	MAln
- 'Alfred Niblett' (S)	WLin
- 'Alice Haysom' (S)	CNic EBee ELan MCre MFie NJOw SDnm SPop WHil WLin
- 'Alicia' (A)	MCre SDnm SPop
- 'Alison Jane' (A)	CLyd MCre MFie NOak SUsu
- 'Allensford' (A)	MCre
- 'Almondbury' (S)	GNor
- alpine mixed (A)	CNic EBre EMlt MBow SRms
- 'Amber Light' (S)	MAln
- 'Amicable' (A)	MCre SPop WHil
- 'Ancient Order' (A)	MAln
- 'Ancient Society' (A) **new**	SPop
- 'Andrea Julie' (A)	GAbr ITim MCre MFie MOne NRya SPop WLin
- 'Andrew Hunter' (A)	MAln SPop
- 'Andy Cole' (A)	MAln
- 'Angelo' (A)	MAln
- 'Angie' (d)	MAln
- 'Ann Taylor' (A)	MAln MCre
- 'Anne Hyatt' (d)	MAln
- 'Anne Swithinbank' (d)	MAln
- 'Antoc' (S)	MFie
- 'Anwar Sadat' (A)	GAbr MCre MFie SPop
- 'Applecross' (A)	ITim MCre MFie WLin
- 'April Moon' (S)	MAln SPop
- 'April Tiger' (S)	MAln
- 'Arabian Night' (A)	MAln
- 'Arapaho' (A)	MAln
- 'Arctic Fox'	MAln
- 'Argus' (A)	CLyd MCre MFie NBir SPop SUsu WLin
- 'Arlene' (A) **new**	MAln
- 'Aromanches' (A)	MAln
- 'Arthur Delbridge' (A)	MCre MFie
- 'Arundel Star'	NLAp
- 'Arundell' (S/St)	GAbr ITim MCre NJOw NLAp SPop WHil WLin
- 'Ashcliffe Gem' (A)	MAln
- 'Ashcliffe Gold' (A) **new**	MAln
- 'Astolat' (S)	ITim MCre MFie NLAp NOak NRya SDnm SPop SUsu WHil WLin
- 'Athene' (S)	MAln
- 'Aurora' (A)	MFie
- 'Austin' (A)	MAln
- 'Avril' (A) **new**	MAln
- 'Avril Hunter' (A)	MCre MFie SPop WLin
- 'Aztec' (d) **new**	MAln
- 'Bacchante' (d) **new**	MAln
- 'Bacchus' (S)	ITim MCre MFie
- 'Balbithan' (B)	GAbr
- 'Ballet' (S)	MFie
- 'Barbara Mason'	MAln
- 'Barbarella' (S)	MCre MFie SPop WLin
- Barnhaven doubles (d)	CSWP GAbr MAnH WLin
- 'Basilio' (S) **new**	MAln
- 'Basuto' (A)	MCre MFie SPop WHil
- 'Beatrice' (A)	CLyd GAbr GNor ITim MCre MFie SPop WHil WLin
- 'Beauty of Bath' (S)	MAln
- 'Beckminster' (A)	MAln
- 'Bedford Lad' (A)	MAln MCre
- 'Beechen Green' (S)	GAbr ITim MCre NJOw SPop WLin
- 'Belle Zana' (S)	MAln SPop
- 'Bellezana'	MFie
- 'Ben Lawers' (S)	WLin
- 'Ben Wyves' (S)	MCre
- 'Bendigo' (S)	MAln
- 'Bewitched' (A)	MAln
- 'Bilbao' (A)	MAln
- 'Bilbo Baggins' (A)	MAln
- 'Bill Bailey' **new**	MOne
- 'Bilton' (S)	CLyd NLAp
- 'Black Ice' (S)	MAln
- 'Black Jack'	COtt MAln WWeb
- 'Black Knight' (d)	MAln
- 'Blackfield' (S)	MFie
- 'Blackpool Rock' (St)	MAln
- 'Blairside Yellow' (B)	EWes NSla
- 'Blakeney' (d)	MAln NLAp
- 'Blossom' (S)	MFie WLin
- 'Blue Bonnet' (d)	MAln
- 'Blue Bonnet' (A/d)	GAbr GNor MCre NLAp SPop
- 'Blue Chips' (S)	MAln
- 'Blue Cliffs' (S)	MAln
- 'Blue Denim' (S)	MAln
- 'Blue Frills'	MAln
- 'Blue Heaven'	GAbr MOne
- 'Blue Jean' (S)	GNor MFie NLAp SPop
- 'Blue Miller' (B) **new**	GAbr
- 'Blue Mist' (B)	GNor
- 'Blue Moon' (S)	MAln

	- 'Blue Nile' (S)	MCre MFie SPop
	- 'Blue Steel' (S)	MAln
	- 'Blue Velvet' (B)	GNor MFie NBro SPop WLin
	- 'Blue Wave' (d)	WLin
	- 'Bob Dingley' (A)	MCre
	- 'Bob Lancashire' (S)	GNor ITim MCre MFie SPop SUsu
		WHil WLin
	- 'Bold Tartan' (St)	MAln
	- 'Bolero' (A)	MAln SPop
	- 'Bollin Tiger' (St)	MAln
	- 'Bonanza' (S)	MAln
	- 'Bookham Firefly' (A)	GNor ITim MCre MFie NRya SPop
		WHil WLin
	- 'Boromir' (A)	MAln
	- 'Boy Blue' (S)	MAln
	- 'Bradford City' (A)	MAln SDnm
	- 'Branno' (S) **new**	MAln
	- 'Brasso'	MAln
	- 'Brazil' (S)	GAbr GNor ITim LRHS MCre MFie
		NLAp NOak SDnm SPop WHil
		WLin
	- 'Brazos River' (A)	MAln
	- 'Brenda's Choice' (A)	MCre MFie
	- 'Brentford Bees'	MAln
	(St) **new**	
	- 'Bright Eyes' (A)	MCre MFie
	- 'Broad Gold' (A)	MAln MCre SPop
	- 'Broadwell Gold' (B)	CLyd GAbr WLin
	- 'Brocade' (St) **new**	MAln
	- 'Brompton' (S)	MAln
	- 'Brookfield' (S)	GNor ITim MCre MFie SPop WHil
	- 'Broughton' (S)	MFie WLin
	- 'Brown Ben'	MFie
	- 'Brown Bess' (A)	GNor ITim MCre MFie MOne SPop
		WLin
	- 'Brownie' (B)	NBir SDnm
	- 'Bubbles' (A)	MAln
	- 'Buccaneer'	MAln
	- 'Bucks Green' (S)	SPop
	- 'Bunty' (A)	MFie
	- 'Butterwick' (A)	GAbr LRHS MBNS MCre MFie
		SPop WLin
	- 'C.F Hill' (A)	MAln
	- 'C.G. Haysom' (S)	GAbr GNor MCre MFie SPop
	- 'C.W. Needham' (A)	ITim MCre MFie NLAp WLin
I	- 'Calypso' (A)	MAln
	- 'Cambodunum' (A)	MCre MFie SPop
	- 'Camelot' (d)	CLyd ELan GCrs GNor MCre MFie
		MOne NBro NPri SPop SUsu WFar
	- 'Cameo' (A)	MAln MCre
	- 'Camilla' (A)	MAln
I	- 'Candida' (d)	MAln MCre SPop
	- 'Caramel' (A)	MAln
	- 'Carioca' (A)	MAln
	- 'Carol Anne' (d) **new**	MAln
	- 'Carole' (A)	MFie WLin
	- 'Cartouche' (A)	MAln
	- 'Catherine Redding' (d)	MAln
	- 'Catherine Wheel'	MAln
	(St) **new**	
	- 'Chaffinch' (S)	GNor NLAp
	- 'Chamois' (B)	GAbr
	- 'Channel' (S)	MAln
	- 'Chantilly Cream' (d)	MAln MCre
	- 'Charles Bronson' (d)	MAln
	- 'Charles Rennie' (B)	MAln
	- 'Charlie's Aunt' (A)	MAln
	- 'Checkmate'	MAln
	- 'Chelsea Bridge' (A)	ITim MCre MFie NLAp SPop
	- 'Chelsea Girl' (d)	MOne
	- 'Cherry'	GAbr ITim
	- 'Cherry Picker' (A)	MCre
	- 'Cheyenne' (S)	GAbr ITim MCre MFie WLin
	- 'Chiffon' (S)	MAln

	- 'Chirichua' (S)	MAln
	- 'Chloë' (S)	MOne
	- 'Chloris' (S)	MAln NBir
	- 'Chocolate Soldier' (A)	MAln
	- 'Chorister' (S)	CLyd EBee ELan GAbr GNor ITim
		MCre MFie MOne NBir NLAp
		NOak NPri SUsu WHil WLin
	- 'Cicero' (A)	MAln
I	- 'Cinnamon' (d)	MCre SPop WLin
	- 'Ciribiribin' (A)	MAln
	- 'Clare' (S)	MCre NRya
	- 'Clatter-Ha' (d)	GCrs
	- 'Claudia Taylor'	WLin
	- 'Clouded Yellow' (S)	MAln
	- 'Clunie' (S)	GNor ITim MCre
	- 'Clunie II' (S)	GCrs ITim NLAp WLin
	- 'Cobden Meadows' (A)	MAln
I	- 'Coffee' (S)	MCre MFie NLAp SUsu WLin
	- 'Colbury' (S)	MCre MFie SPop WLin
	- 'Colonel Champney' (S)	GNor ITim MCre MFie NJOw SPop
		WLin
	- 'Confederate' (S)	MAln
	- 'Connaught Court' (A)	MAln
	- 'Conservative' (S)	GAbr MFie SUsu WLin
	- 'Consett' (S)	ITim MFie WHil
	- 'Coppi' (A)	MAln SPop
	- 'Coral' (S)	MFie
	- 'Coral Sea' (S)	MAln
	- 'Cornmeal' (S)	MAln MFie
	- 'Corntime' (S)	MAln
	- 'Corporal Kate'	MAln
	(St) **new**	
	- 'Corrie Files' (d)	MAln
	- 'Cortez Silver' (S) **new**	MAln
	- 'Cortina' (S)	EBee ECGP GNor ITim MCre
		MOne NOak NRya SDnm SPop
		SUsu WHil WLin
	- 'County Park Red' (B)	ECou
	- 'Craig Vaughan' (A)	MFie WHil WLin
	- 'Cranbourne' (A)	MAln
	- 'Crecy' (A)	MAln
	- 'Crimple' (S)	MAln
	- 'Crimson Glow' (d)	MAln
	- 'Cuckoo Fair'	SPop
	- 'Cuckoo Fare' (S)	MAln
	- 'Cuddles' (A)	MAln
	- 'Curry Blend' (B) **new**	GAbr
	- 'D.S.J.' (S)	WLin
	- 'Daftie Green' (S)	GAbr ITim MCre NLAp WHil
	- 'Dales Red' (B)	MAln SDnm WHil WLin
	- 'Dan Tiger' (St)	MAln
	- 'Daniel' (A)	MAln
	- 'Daphnis' (S)	MAln MCre
	- 'Dark Eyes' (d)	MAln NLAp WLin
	- 'Dark Lady' (A)	MAln
	- 'David Beckham'	MAln
	(d) **new**	
	- 'Decaff' (St) **new**	MAln
	- 'Delilah' (d)	GAbr GNor MCre MFie WLin
	- 'Denise' (S)	MAln
	- 'Denna Snuffer' (d)	GAbr GNor ITim NLAp
	- 'Devon Cream' (d)	GNor MCre MFie WFar
	- 'Diamond' (d)	MAln
	- 'Diane' (A)	MFie
	- 'Digit' (d)	MAln
	- 'Digsby' (d)	MAln
*	- 'Dilemma' (A)	MAln
*	- 'Dill' (A)	MAln
	- 'Dilly Dilly' (A)	MAln
	- 'Divint Dunch' (A)	MCre SPop
	- 'Doctor Duthie' (S)	MAln
	- 'Doctor Jones' (d) **new**	MAln
	- 'Doctor Lennon's	MCre MFie SPop
	White' (B)	

- 'Dolly Viney' (d) — MAln
- 'Donhead' (A) — MCre MFie
- 'Donna Clancy' (S) — MFie
- 'Dorado' (d) **new** — MAln
- 'Doreen Stevens' (A) — MAln
- 'Doris Jean' (A) — MFie
- 'Dorothy' (S) — MAln
- 'Doublet' (d) — CLyd GAbr GNor ITim MCre MFie NLAp NOak NRya SPop WHil WLin
- 'Doublure' (d) — GAbr GNor MCre
- 'Douglas Bader' (A) — MCre
- 'Douglas Black' (S) — GAbr MCre NLAp SPop WLin
- 'Douglas Blue' (S) — MAln
- 'Douglas Gold' — WLin
- 'Douglas Green' (S) — MFie SPop
- 'Douglas Red' (S) — WLin
- 'Douglas White' (S) — MFie
- 'Dovedale' (S) — MAln
- 'Dowager' (A) — MFie
- 'Doyen' (d) — MAln
- 'Drax' (A) — MAln
- 'Dubarii' (A) — MAln
- 'Duchess of Malfi' (S) — SPop
- 'Duchess of York' (2) — GBuc WBro
* - 'Dusky' — WLin
- 'Dusky Girl' (A) **new** — MAln
- 'Dusky Maiden' (A) — GNor MCre MFie SPop WLin
- 'Dusty Miller' (B) — MRav NBid NBir
- 'Eastern Promise' (A) — MAln MFie SPop
- 'Ed Spivey' (A) — MCre
- 'Eddy Gordon' (A) — MAln
- 'Eden Carmine' (B) — MFie
- 'Eden David' (B) — MFie
- 'Eden Peach' (B) — MFie
- 'Eden Picotee' (B) — MAln MFie
- 'Edith Allen' (A) — MAln
- 'Edward Sweeney' (S) **new** — MAln
- 'Eli Jenkins' **new** — MAln
- 'Elizabeth Ann' (A) — GAbr MCre
- 'Ellen Thompson' (A) — MCre MFie WLin
- 'Elsie' (A) — GNor MCre
- 'Elsie May' (A) — GNor MCre MFie NLAp SPop WLin
- 'Elsinore' (S) — MCre
- 'Emberglow' (d) **new** — MAln
- 'Embley' (S) — CLyd GNor NLAp SPop
- 'Emery Down' (S) — NLAp
- 'Emma Louise' — MFie
- 'Emmett Smith' (A) — MAln
- 'Enigma' (S) — MAln
- 'Envy' (S) — MAln
I - 'Erica' (A) — MCre MFie SUsu WHil WLin
- 'Erjon' (S) — MAln
- 'Error' (S) — MAln
- 'Ethel' — WHil
- 'Etna' (S) **new** — MAln
- 'Ettrick' (S) — MAln
- 'Eventide' (S) — SPop
- 'Everest Blue' (S) — SPop SUsu
- 'Excalibur' (d) — MAln WLin
- 'Exhibition Series 'Exhibition Blau' (B) — MFie
- - 'Exhibition Gelb' (B) — MFie
- - 'Exhibition Rot' (B) — MFie
- 'Eyeopener' (A) — MAln MCre SPop
- 'Fairy' (A) — MAln
- 'Fairy Moon' (S) **new** — MAln
- 'Falaraki' (A) — MAln
- 'Falstaff' (d) — MAln
- 'Fanciful' (S) — CLyd MFie WLin
- 'Fandancer' (A) — MAln
- 'Fanfare' (S) — MAln SPop
- 'Fanny Meerbeck' (S) — GAbr GNor ITim MFie NOak SPop WLin

- 'Faro' (S) — MAln
- 'Favourite' (S) — MCre MFie NJOw SPop WHil
- 'Fen Tiger' (St) — MAln
- 'Fennay' (S) — MAln
- 'Figaro' (S) — MAln MFie SPop WLin
- 'Finavon' — GCrs
- 'Finchfield' (A) — MCre SUsu
- 'Firecracker' — MAln
- 'Firenze' (A) — SPop
- 'Firsby' (d) — MAln
- 'Fishtoft' (d) — MAln
- 'Flame' (A) — ITim MAln
- 'Fleminghouse' (S) — GNor
- 'Florence Brown' (S) — ITim
- 'Forest Pines' (S) — MAln
- 'Fradley' (A) — MAln
- 'Francis Bacon' (A) **new** — MAln
- 'Frank Bailey' (d) — MAln
- 'Frank Crosland' (A) — MFie
- 'Frank Faulkner' (A) — MFie
- 'Frank Jenning' (A) — MAln
- 'Fred Booley' (d) — SPop WHil WLin
- 'Fred Livesley' (A) — MAln
- 'Fresco' (A) — MAln
- 'Friskney' (d) — MAln
- 'Frittenden Yellow' (B) — WLin
- 'Fuller's Red' (S) — CLyd MFie SPop
- 'Fuzzy' (St) **new** — MAln
- 'Gaia' (d) — MAln
- 'Galatea' (S) **new** — MAln
- 'Galen' (A) — MCre MFie WLin
- 'Ganymede' (d) — MAln
- 'Gary Pallister' (A) — MAln
- 'Gavin Ward' (S) — MAln
- 'Gay Crusader' (A) — GNor ITim MCre MFie SPop
- 'Gazza' (A) — MAln
- 'Gee Cross' (A) — GNor MCre MFie SPop
§ - 'Geldersome Green' (S) — GNor MCre MFie SPop WLin
- 'Generosity' (A) — MAln MCre SPop
- 'Geordie' (A) — MAln
- 'George Harrison' (B) — GAbr
- 'George Jennings' (A) — MAln
- 'George Stephens' (A) — MAln
- 'Geronimo' (S) — GNor MFie SPop
- 'Girl Guide' (S) — MAln
- 'Gizaboon' **new** — GNor
- 'Gizabroon' (S) — CLyd MCre MFie SDnm WLin
- 'Glasnost' (S) **new** — MAln
- 'Gleam' (S) — GCrs GNor LTwo MCre MFie NJOw NLAp SPop WHil WLin
- 'Gleneagles' (S) — ITim MAln MCre NLAp SPop
- 'Glenelg' (S) — GAbr GCrs ITim MCre MFie SPop WCot WLin
- 'Glenluce' (S) — WHil
- 'Glenna Goodwin' (d) **new** — MAln
- 'Gnome' (B) — GAbr
- 'Gold Seam' (A) — MAln
- 'Golden Boy' (A) — MAln
- 'Golden Chartreuse' (d) — GAbr MCre
- 'Golden Eagle' (A) — MAln
- 'Golden Eye' (S) — MAln
- 'Golden Fleece' (S) — GAbr GNor SPop
- 'Golden Girl' (A) — MAln
- 'Golden Glory' (A) — MAln
- 'Golden Hind' (d) — SPop WLin
- 'Golden Splendour' (d) — MCre MFie SPop WLin
- 'Golden Wedding' (A) — MAln SPop
- 'Goldthorn' (A) — MCre
- 'Goldwin' (A) — MAln MCre
- 'Gollum' (A) — MAln
- 'Good Report' (A) — SPop
- 'Gordon Douglas' (A) — MCre MFie
- 'Grabley' (S) — MAln

- 'Grandad's Favourite' SPop
  (B) **new**
- 'Green Finger' (S) SPop
- 'Green Frill' ITim
- 'Green Goddess' MAln
  (St) **new**
- 'Green Isle' (S) GAbr MCre MFie NBir SPop WLin
- 'Green Jacket' (S) GNor MCre
- 'Green Magic' (S) **new** MAln
- 'Green Meadows' (S) MAln SPop
- 'Green Mouse' (S) MFie
- 'Green Parrot' (S) CLyd ITim MCre WLin
- 'Green Shank' (S) GNor ITim MFie SPop WHil WLin
- 'Greenfinger' (S) MAln
- 'Greenheart' (S) GNor ITim
- 'Greenpeace' (S) LRHS
- 'Greensleeves' (S) GNor
- 'Greenways' (S) MAln
- 'Greta' (S) ELan GNor MCre NLAp NOak
  SPop WLin
- 'Gretna Green' (S) MFie SPop
- 'Grey Dawn' (S) MAln
- 'Grey Edge' ITim SUsu
- 'Grey Friar' (S) MAln
- 'Grey Lady' (S) MAln
- 'Grey Lag' (S) GNor MFie
- 'Grey Monarch' (S) GNor ITim MCre MFie WLin
- 'Grey Owl' (S) MAln
- 'Grey Shrike' (S) MAln
- 'Grizedale' (S) MAln
- 'Guildersome Green' see *P. auricula* 'Geldersome
  Green'
- 'Guinea' (S) GAbr MFie SPop WLin
- 'Gwen' (A) MAln MCre
- 'Gwen Baker' (d) MAln
- 'Gwen Gaulthiers' (S) MAln
- 'Gwenda' (A) MAln
- 'Gypsy Rose Lee' (A) MAln
- 'Habanera' (A) MCre SPop
- 'Hadrian's Shooting MAln
  Star' (d) **new**
- 'Haffner' (S) MAln
- 'Hallmark' (A) MAln
- 'Hardley' (S) MAln
- 'Harmony' (B) MFie NBro
- 'Harry Hotspur' (A) SPop
- 'Harry 'O'' (S) ITim MCre NLAp SPop
- 'Haughmond' (A) MCre
- 'Hawkwood' (S) GNor ITim MCre NJOw SDnm
  SPop SUsu WHil
- 'Hawkwood Fancy' (S) MFie WLin
* - 'Hazel' (A) MCre MFie
- 'Headdress' (S) GAbr MCre MFie SPop
- 'Heady' (A) SPop
- 'Heart of Gold' (A) MAln SPop
- 'Hebers' MAln
- 'Helen Barter' (S) SPop
- 'Helen Ruane' (d) MAln SPop WLin
- 'Helena' (S) ITim MCre MFie NLAp NOak WHil
- 'Helena Dean' (d) MAln
- 'Heliocentre' (A) MAln
- 'Helmswell Blush' **new** MOne
- 'Helmswell Ember' **new** MOne
- 'Henry Hall' **new** MOne
- 'Hetty Woolf' (S) GAbr GNor MCre
- 'High Hopes' **new** MAln
- 'Hillhouse' (A) MCre
- 'Hinton Admiral' (A) ITim MAln NLAp WLin
- 'Hinton Fields' (S) EBee ECGP GNor MCre MFie
  SDnm SMrm SPop WHil WLin
- 'Hinton Green GAbr
  Fields' **new**
- 'Hobby Horse' **new** WLin
- 'Hogton Gem' (d) MAln

- 'Holyrood' (S) GAbr MFie
- 'Honey' (d) MAln SPop
- 'Honeymoon' (S) MAln
- 'Hopleys Coffee' (d) GNor MAln SPop
- 'Howard Telford' (A) MCre
- 'Hurstwood Midnight' MFie
* - 'Hyacinth' (S) LRHS NWCA
- 'Iago' (S) MAln
- 'Ian Greville' (A) MAln
- 'Ibis' (S) MAln MCre MFie
- 'Ice Maiden' MAln SPop
- 'Idmiston' (S) MCre SPop WLin
- 'Immaculate' (A) MAln SPop
- 'Impassioned' (A) MAln MFie SPop
- 'Impeccable' (A) MAln
- 'Imperturbable' (A) MAln
- 'Indian Love Call' (A) MCre SPop WHil
- 'Isabel' (S) MAln
- 'Isabella' **new** MAln
- 'Jack Dean' (A) MAln MCre MFie SPop WHil
- 'James Arnot' (S) GNor MFie NOak NRya SPop
- 'Jane' (S) MAln
- 'Jane Myers' (d) MAln MFie
- 'Janie Hill' (A) MAln MCre MFie
- 'Jean Fielder' (A) **new** MAln
- 'Jean Jacques' (A) **new** MAln
- 'Jeannie Telford' (A) MCre MFie SPop
- 'Jenny' (A) EBee ITim LHop MBNS MCre MFie
  NLAp SPop WHil
- 'Jersey Bounce' (A) MAln
- 'Jesmond' (S) MAln
- 'Jessica' (S) MAln
- 'Jessie' (d) MAln
- 'Joan Elliott' (A) CLyd GAbr
- 'Joanne' (A) MCre
- 'Joe Perks' (A) MAln MFie NRya WHil
- 'Joel' (S) MAln MCre MFie NLAp SPop WLin
- 'Johann Bach' (B) MFie
- 'John Gledhill' (A) MCre
- 'John Stewart' (A) MCre MFie
- 'John Wayne' (A) MCre MFie
- 'Jonathon' (A) MAln
- 'Joy' (A) CLyd GNor ITim LTwo MCre MFie
  NLAp SPop WHil
- 'Joyce' (A) GAbr MCre MFie NBir SPop WLin
- 'Julia' (S) MAln
- 'July Sky' (A) MCre
- 'June' (A) MAln
- 'Jungfrau' (d) MAln
- 'Jupiter' (S) MAln
- 'Jura' (S) MAln
- 'Just Steven' (A) **new** MAln
- 'Karen Cordrey' (S) GAbr GNor ITim MCre SDnm
  SPop WHil WLin
- 'Karen McDonald' (A) SPop
- 'Kath Dryden' see *P. allionii* 'Kath Dryden'
- 'Kelso' (A) MFie
- 'Ken Chilton' (A) MAln MFie WHil
- 'Kercup' (A) MFie
- 'Kevin Keegan' (A) SPop
- 'Key West' (A) MAln
- 'Khachaturian' (A) MAln
- 'Kim' (A) MCre MFie WLin
- 'Kingcup' (A) MCre MFie SPop
- 'Kingfisher' (A) SPop
- 'Kiowa' (S) SPop
- 'Kirklands' (d) MFie SPop
- 'Klondyke' (d) MAln
- 'Königin der Nacht' (St) MAln
- 'Kustard' (d) MAln
- 'Lady Daresbury' (A) MCre MFie NRya SPop
- 'Lady Diana' (S) MAln
- 'Lady Emma Monson' (S) CHad
- 'Lady Joyful' (S) MCre

- 'Lady of the Vale' (A) — MAln
- 'Lady Penelope' (S) — MAln
- 'Lady Zoë' (S) — MAln MCre MFie SPop
- 'Lancelot' (d) — MAln SPop
- 'Landy' (A) — GCrs MCre MFie SPop
- 'Langley Park' (A) — MCre MFie SPop
- 'Lara' (A) — MAln
- 'Laredo' (A) — MAln
- 'Larry' (A) — MAln MCre MFie SPop
- 'Lavenham' (S) — MAln
- 'Laverock' (S) — MCre NBir NBro
- 'Laverock Fancy' (S) — GNor ITim MFie SUsu WLin
- 'Lazy River' (A) **new** — MAln
- 'Leather Jacket' — GAbr
- 'Lechistan' (S) — ITim MCre MFie SPop WHil WLin
- 'Lee' (A) — MAln MCre
- 'Lee Clark' (A) — MAln MCre
- 'Lee Paul' (A) — GNor ITim MCre MFie NLAp NRya SPop WLin
- 'Lee Sharpe' (A) — MAln
- 'Lemon Drop' (S) — MCre NBro NLAp SPop
- 'Lemon Sherbet' (B) — MFie
- 'Lepton Jubilee' (S) — MAln
- 'Leroy Brown' (A) **new** — MAln
- 'Letty' (S) — MAln
- 'Leverton' (d) — MAln
- 'Lewis Telford' (A) — MAln
- 'Lichfield' (A/d) — MAln MCre
- 'Light Hearted' — MFie NLAp
- 'Lila' (A) — MAln
- 'Lilac Domino' (S) — MCre MFie SPop WHil WLin
- 'Lilac Domino' (A) — ITim MAln NRya SPop
- 'Lillian Hill' (A) — MAln
- 'Lima' (d) — MAln
- 'Limelight' (A) — MAln SPop
- 'Limelight' (S) — MAln
- 'Lindsey Moreno' (S) — MAln
- 'Ling' (A) — ITim MCre MFie SPop
- 'Lisa' (A) — CLyd MCre MFie SPop WLin
- 'Lisa Clara' (S) — GNor ITim WLin
- 'Lisa's Smile' (S) — MFie NLAp WHil
- 'Little Rosetta' (d) — MAln WHil
- 'Lord Saye and Sele' (St) — GAbr GNor ITim MCre MFie NLAp SPop WLin
- 'Lothlorien' (A) **new** — MAln
- 'Louisa Woolhead' (d) — SPop
- 'Lovebird' (S) — GAbr GNor MCre MFie SPop SUsu
- 'Lucky Strike' **new** — MAln
- 'Ludlow' (S) — GAbr MAln
- 'Lune Tiger' (St) — MAln
- 'Lupy Minstrel' (S) — MAln
- 'Lynn' (A) — MAln
- 'Madame Gina' (S) — MAln MFie
- 'Maggie' (S) — GNor ITim MCre
- 'Magnolia' (B) — MFie
- 'Maid Marion' (d) — MCre
- 'Maizie' (S) — MAln
- 'Mandarin' (A) — MCre MFie SPop
- 'Mansell's Green' (S) — MAln WHil
- 'Margaret Dee' (d) **new** — MAln
- 'Margaret Faulkner' (A) — GNor ITim MCre MFie WLin
- 'Margaret Irene' (A) — MAln SPop
- 'Margaret Martin' (S) — MAln WLin
- 'Margot Fonteyn' (A) — GAbr MAln SPop
- 'Marie Crousse' (d) — CPBP NLAp WLin
- 'Marigold' (d) — CLyd WFar
- 'Marion Howard Spring' (A) — MAln MCre MFie
- 'Marion Tiger' (St) — MAln
- 'Mark' (A) — ITim MCre MFie NBro SPop WLin
- 'Marmion' (S) — MAln NLAp SPop WHil
- 'Martha Livesley' (A) — MAln
- 'Martha's Choice' (A) **new** — MAln

- 'Martin Luther King' (S) — MFie
- 'Mary' (d) — GAbr GNor MCre
- 'Mary Taylor' (S) — MAln
- 'Mary Zach' (S) — WHil
- 'Matthew Yates' (d) — CHad LHop MCre MFie MOne NPri SDnm SPop SUsu WCot WHil WLin WRha
- 'Maureen Millward' (A) — MCre MFie SPop
- 'May' (A) — MAln MCre
- 'Mazetta Stripe' (S/St) — GAbr ITim NLAp SPop WLin
- 'McWatt's Blue' (B) — GAbr GNor IGor WLin
- 'Meadowlark' (A) — MAln MCre
- 'Mease Tiger' (St) — GAbr MAln
- 'Megan' (d) — MAln
- 'Mehta' (A) — MAln
- 'Mellifluous' — MAln MCre
- 'Mere Green' (S) — MAln
- 'Merlin' (A) — WLin
- 'Merlin' (S) — MAln
- 'Merlin Stripe' (St) — MCre SPop WHil
- 'Mermaid' (d) — GAbr GNor MCre
- 'Merridale' (A) — MCre MFie
- 'Mersey Tiger' (S) — GAbr GNor ITim NLAp SPop
- 'Mesquite' (A) — MAln
- 'Mexicano' (A) — MAln
- 'Michael' (S) — MAln
- 'Michael Watham' (S) — MAln
- 'Michael Wattam' (S) **new** — MAln
- 'Mick' (A) — MAln
- 'Midnight' (S) — CLyd
- 'Midnight' (A) — ITim MAln
- 'Mikado' (A) — MCre MFie SPop WLin
- 'Milkmaid' (A) — MAln
- 'Millicent' (A) — MAln MFie
- 'Mink' (A) — MFie WHil
- 'Minley' (S) — GNor ITim MCre MFie NBir NBro SPop WHil WLin
- 'Minsmere' (S) — MAln
- 'Mirabella Bay' (A) — MAln
- 'Mirandinha' (A) — MAln MCre
- 'Miriam' (A) — MAln
- 'Miss Bluey' (d) **new** — MAln
- 'Miss Newman' (A) — MAln
- 'Mohawk' (S) — MCre
- 'Mojave' (S) — GNor ITim MCre MFie NLAp NRya SPop WHil WLin
- 'Mollie Langford' (A) — MAln MCre SPop
- 'Monet' (S) — MAln
- 'Moneymoon' (S) — MFie
- 'Monica' (A) — MFie
- 'Monk' (S) — MCre MFie WHil
- 'Monk's Eleigh' (A) — MAln
- 'Moonglow' (S) — MFie
- 'Moonlight' (S) — GAbr MAln
- 'Moonrise' (S) — MFie
- 'Moonriver' (A) — MAln MCre SPop
- 'Moonshadow' (d) — MAln
- 'Moonstone' (d) — MAln MFie WLin
- 'Moselle' (S) — MAln
- 'Mr 'A'' (S) — CLyd MCre SPop WLin
- 'Mrs A. Bolton' (A) — MCre
- 'Mrs L. Hearn' (A) — MCre MFie SPop
- 'Mrs R. Bolton' (A) — WRha
- 'Murray Lanes' (A) — MAln
- 'My Fair Lady' (A) — MAln
- 'Myrtle Park' (A) — MAln
- 'Nankenan' (S) — MAln MFie
- 'Neat and Tidy' (S) — LRHS MCre MFie NLAp NOak NRya SPop WHil WLin
- 'Nefertiti' (A) — MAln SPop
- 'Nessundorma' (A) — MAln
- 'Neville Telford' (S) — GNor ITim MCre MFie WLin
- 'Nickity' (A) — GAbr MCre MFie SPop WLin

- 'Nicola Jane' (A)	MAln
- 'Nigel' (d)	GAbr ITim NLAp WLin
- 'Night and Day' (S)	MFie NLAp
- 'Nightwick' (S) **new**	MAln
- 'Nightwink' (S)	MAln
- 'Nina' (A)	MAln
- 'Nita' (d)	MAln
- 'Nocturne' (S)	GNor MCre MFie NBro NLAp SPop WLin
- 'Noelle' (S)	ITim
- 'Nonchalance' (A)	MCre MFie
- 'Norma' (A)	MFie WLin
- 'Notability' (A)	MAln
- 'Notable' (A) **new**	MAln
- 'Nureyev' (A)	MAln
- 'Oakie' (S) **new**	MAln
- 'Ol' Blue Eyes' (St) **new**	MAln
- 'Old England' (S)	MFie SPop
- 'Old Gold' (S)	GAbr SUsu WLin
- 'Old Irish Blue' (B)	CLyd IGor MFie
- 'Old Irish Scented' (B)	GAbr IGor NBro WLin
- 'Old Mustard' (B)	SMHy
- 'Old Red Dusty Miller' (B)	ECha LTwo MFie NBir NJOw
- 'Old Red Elvet' (S)	GNor MAln NLAp SPop
- 'Old Smokey' (A)	MAln SPop
- 'Old Suffolk Bronze' (B)	GAbr MFie
- 'Old Wine' (A)	CLyd
- 'Old Yellow Dusty Miller' (B)	CLyd EWes GAbr MFie MSte NBro NRya WLin WWin
- 'Olton' (A)	MCre MFie
- 'Opus One' (A)	MAln
- 'Orb' (S)	CLyd MCre MFie NLAp SPop
- 'Ordvic' (S)	MAln NRya WLin
- 'Orlando' (S)	MAln
- 'Orwell Tiger' (St)	SPop
- 'Osbourne Green' (B)	GAbr GNor MCre MFie NJOw NLAp SPop SUsu WHil WLin
- 'Otto Dix' (A) **new**	MAln
- 'Overdale' (A)	MAln MCre
- 'Paddlin Madeleine' (A)	MAln
- 'Pagoda Belle' (A)	MAln
- 'Paleface' (A)	MAln MCre WHil
- 'Pam Tiger' (St)	MAln
- 'Panache' (S) **new**	MAln
- 'Papageno' (St)	MAln
- 'Paradise Yellow' (B)	GNor MFie SPop
- 'Paragon' (A)	MAln MCre
- 'Paris' (S)	MAln
- 'Party Time' (S)	MAln
- 'Pastiche' (A)	MCre MFie
- 'Pat' (S)	MFie SPop
- 'Pat Mooney' (d)	MAln
- 'Patience' (S)	NJOw SPop WHil
- 'Patricia Barras' (S)	MAln
- 'Pauline' (A)	MFie
- 'Pauline Taylor' (d)	MAln
- 'Pear Drops'	GAbr
- 'Pegasus'	MAln
- 'Peggy' (A)	WHil WLin
- 'Peggy's Lad' (A)	MAln
- 'Pequod' (A)	MAln
- 'Peruvian' (S)	MAln
- 'Peter Beardsley' (A)	MAln
- 'Peter Hall' (d)	MAln
- 'Phantom'	MAln
- 'Pharaoh' (A)	MAln MFie NLAp SPop
- 'Phyllis Douglas' (A)	ITim MCre MFie NLAp SPop
- 'Pierot' (S)	MCre MFie SPop
- 'Piers Telford'	GNor MCre MFie SDnm SPop WHil
- 'Pink Fondant' (A)	MAln
- 'Pink Lady' (A)	MFie NBro
I - 'Pink Lilac'	GNor
- 'Pink Panther' (S) **new**	MAln
- 'Pinkie' (A)	MAln
- 'Pioneer Stripe' (S)	NJOw WHil
- 'Pippin' (A)	MCre MFie NBro SPop WLin
- 'Pixie' (A)	MAln MCre
- 'Playboy' (A)	MAln
- 'Plush Royal' (S)	MAln MFie
- 'Polestar' (A)	MCre SPop WLin
- 'Pop's Blue' (S/d)	MAln SPop
- 'Portree' (S)	GAbr
- 'Pot o' Gold' (S)	GNor ITim MCre MFie NLAp NOak SPop WHil
- 'Prague' (S)	GAbr GNor MCre MFie NBir SPop SUsu
- 'Pretender' (A)	MAln SPop
- 'Prima'	MAln
- 'Prince Bishop' (S)	MAln
- 'Prince Charming' (S)	ITim MFie SPop SUsu WLin
- 'Prince Igor' (A)	MAln
- 'Prince John' (A)	ITim MCre MFie NBro SPop WHil WLin
- 'Prince Regent' (B)	NBro
- 'Prometheus' (d)	MAln
- 'Purple Glow' (d)	MAln WLin
- 'Purple Sage' (S)	GNor
- 'Purple Velvet' (S)	SPop
- 'Quality Chase' (A)	MAln MCre
- 'Quatro' (d)	MAln
- 'Queen Alexander'	GAbr
- 'Queen Bee' (S)	GAbr GNor ITim
- 'Queen of Sheba' (S)	MAln NLAp
- 'Quintessence' (A)	MAln MCre
- 'Rab C. Nesbitt' (A) **new**	MAln
- 'Rabley Heath' (A)	CLyd MCre MFie SPop WLin
- 'Rachel' (A)	MAln
- 'Radiant' (A)	MFie
- 'Rajah' (S)	ELan GNor ITim MFie NRya SDnm SPop WHil WLin
- 'Raleigh Stripe' (S)	MAln SPop
- 'Ralenzano' (A)	MAln
- 'Rameses' (A)	MAln MCre
- 'Rebecca Hyatt' (d) **new**	MAln
- 'Red Admiral'	MAln
- 'Red Arrows' **new**	MAln
- 'Red Beret' (S)	MFie NLAp
- 'Red Denna' (d)	MAln
- 'Red Embers' (S)	MAln
- 'Red Gauntlet' (S)	EBee EDAr ITim MBri MFie MRav MSte NLAp SPop WCot WHil WLin
- 'Red Mark' (A)	MCre MFie
- 'Red Raddle' **new**	MAln
- 'Red Rum' (S)	GAbr MFie
- 'Redcar' (A)	MAln MCre
- 'Regency' (A)	MAln
- 'Remus' (S)	ELan GAbr GNor LTwo MCre MFie SPop SUsu WHil WLin
- 'Rene' (A)	GAbr MCre
- 'Respectable' (A) **new**	MAln
- 'Reverie' (d)	MAln
- 'Riatty' (d)	GAbr MAln MFie
- 'Richard Shaw' (A)	MFie WHil WLin
- 'Ring of Bells' (S)	MAln
- 'Rita' (S) **new**	MAln
- 'Robert Lee' (A)	MAln
- 'Roberto' (S)	MAln
- 'Robin Hood' (A)	MAln
- 'Rock Sand' (S)	GNor MFie NLAp WHil WLin
- 'Rodeo' (A)	GAbr MCre MFie NLAp WPat
- 'Rolts' (S)	CLyd ELan GAbr GNor ITim MCre MFie NBir NBro NHol NLAp NOak SDnm SPop WHil
- 'Ronald Ward' (B)	MAln
- 'Rondy' (S)	MAln
- 'Ronnie Johnson'	MAln
- 'Ronny Simpson'	MCre

- 'Rosalie' **new**	SPop
- 'Rosalie Edwards' (S)	ITim MFie
- 'Rose Conjou' (d)	GAbr MAln
- 'Rose Kaye' (A)	GNor MAln SPop
- 'Rosebud' (S)	GAbr
- 'Rosemary' (S)	MCre MFie SUsu WHil
- 'Rothesay Robin' (A)	MAln
- 'Rowena' (A)	CLyd MCre MFie NBro SDnm SPop WLin
- 'Roxborough' (A)	MAln
- 'Roxburgh' (A)	MCre MFie SPop
- 'Roy Keane' (A)	MAln SPop
- 'Royal Mail' (S) **new**	MAln
- 'Royal Marine' (S) **new**	MAln
- 'Royal Purple' (S)	NBir
- 'Royal Velvet' (S)	GAbr
- 'Ruby Hyde' (B)	GAbr
- 'Rusty Dusty'	IGor
- 'Ryecroft' (A)	MAln
- 'Saginaw' (A)	MAln
- 'Sailor Boy' (S)	MFie NLAp
- 'Saint Boswells' (S)	GNor MAln MCre MFie NLAp SPop
- 'Saint Elmo' (A)	MFie
- 'Saint Gerrans' White' (B)	MFie
- 'Saint Quentin' (S)	MAln
- 'Salad' (S)	GCrs MFie
- 'Sale Green' (S)	MFie
- 'Sally' (A)	MAln MCre
- 'Sam Gamgee' (A)	MAln
- 'Sam Hunter' (A)	MAln SPop
- 'San Antonio' (A)	MAln
- 'Sandhills' (A)	MAln MCre
- 'Sandmartin' (S)	MFie
- 'Sandra' (A)	ELan GAbr MCre MFie SPop WLin
- 'Sandra's Lass' (A)	MAln
- 'Sandwood Bay' (A)	CLyd GAbr GNor LRHS MCre MFie NBro SPop WHil
- 'Sarah Humphries' (d)	MAln
- 'Sarah Lodge' (d)	GAbr ITim MFie WLin
- 'Sarah Woodhead' (D)	MAln
- 'Satchmo' (S)	NLAp
- 'Scipio' (S)	MAln
- 'Scorcher' (S)	MAln
- 'Sea Mist' (d)	MAln
- 'Serenity' (S)	GNor MCre MFie
- 'Sergeant Wilson'	MAln
- 'Shako' (A)	MAln
- 'Shalford' (d)	MFie SPop WLin
- 'Sharman's Cross' (S)	MAln
- 'Sharon Louise' (S)	MCre
- 'Sheila' (S)	MAln MCre MFie NJOw SPop WHil WLin
- 'Sherbet Lemon' (S)	MAln
- 'Shere' (S)	MCre MFie NLAp SPop WLin
- 'Shergold' (A)	MCre MFie
- 'Sherwood' (S)	ITim MCre MFie SPop WLin
- 'Shirley' (S)	MAln
- 'Shotley' (A)	MCre
- 'Showman' (S)	MAln
- 'Sibsey' (d)	MAln SPop
- 'Sidney' (A)	MAln
- 'Silmaril'	MAln
- 'Silverway' (S)	MCre NABC SPop WHil WLin
- 'Simply Red' **new**	MAln
- 'Sir John' (A)	MAln
- 'Sir John Hall'	MAln
- 'Sir Robert' (d)	MAln
- 'Sirbol' (A)	MAln MCre MFie
- 'Sirius' (A)	CLyd GAbr GNor ITim LRHS MCre MFie MOne NLAp SPop WLin
- 'Sister Josephine' (d)	MAln
- 'Skipper' (d)	SPop
- 'Skylark' (A)	MAln MCre SPop

- 'Skyliner' (A)	MAln
- 'Slioch' (S)	GAbr GNor ITim MCre MFie NLAp SPop
- 'Slip Anchor' (A)	MAln
- 'Smart Tar' (S) **new**	MAln
- 'Snooty Fox' (A)	GAbr MFie NJOw
- 'Snooty Fox II' (A)	GNor MCre SPop
- 'Snowy Owl' (S)	GNor MCre MFie NLAp SPop
- 'Somersby' (d)	MAln SPop
- 'Soncy Face' (A)	MAln
- 'Song of India' (A)	MAln
- 'Sonny Boy' (A)	MAln
- 'Sonya' (A)	ITim WLin
- 'Sophie' (d) **new**	MAln
- 'South Barrow' (d)	GAbr ITim MCre SPop SUsu
- 'Sparky' (A)	MAln
- 'Spartan' **new**	MAln
- 'Spring Meadows' (S)	GAbr MCre MFie MOne NChi NLAp NPri SPop SUsu
- 'Springtime' (A)	MAln SPop
- 'Standish' (d)	GAbr
- 'Stant's Blue' (S)	GNor ITim MCre MFie NBro
- 'Star Wars' (S)	ITim MAln MFie SPop
- 'Starburst' (S)	MAln
- 'Stella Coop' (d)	MAln
- 'Stetson' (A)	MAln
- 'Stoke Poges' (A)	MAln
- 'Stonnal' (A)	MCre MFie SPop
- 'Stormin Norman' (A)	MAln
- 'Stripey' (d)	MAln
- 'Stuart West' (A)	MAln MCre
- 'Subliminal' (A)	MAln MCre
- 'Sue' (A)	MCre MFie
- 'Sugar Plum Fairy' (S)	GAbr
- 'Sultan' (A) **new**	MAln
- 'Summer Sky' (A)	MCre SPop
- 'Summer Wine' (A)	MAln
- 'Sumo' (A)	MAln MCre SPop WLin
I - 'Sunflower' (S)	GAbr MCre MFie NLAp SPop WLin
- 'Sunstar' (S)	MFie
- 'Super Para' (S)	GNor MCre MFie NLAp SPop WLin
- 'Superb' (A)	MAln
- 'Susan' (A)	ITim MCre MFie
- 'Susannah' (d)	GAbr GNor LRHS MFie MOne NHol NPri SDnm SPop WLin
* - 'Sweet Chestnut' (S)	MAln WLin
- 'Sweet Georgia Brown' (A)	MAln
- 'Sweet Pastures' (S)	GNor ITim MCre MFie NHol SPop
- 'Swift' (S)	MFie
- 'Sword' (d)	GAbr GCrs GNor MAln MCre MFie MOne SPop WHil WLin
- 'Symphony' (A)	MFie SUsu
- 'Taffeta' (S)	MAln SDnm
- 'Tall Purple Dusty Miller' (B)	SPop
- 'Tally-ho' (A)	MAln
- 'Tamino' (S)	MAln
- 'Tandem' (St) **new**	MAln
- 'Tarantella' (A)	GAbr GNor MCre MFie WLin
- 'Tawny Owl' (B)	GAbr NBro
- 'Tay Tiger' (St)	SPop
- 'Ted Gibbs' (A)	MAln MCre MFie
- 'Ted Roberts' (A)	MCre MFie SPop SUsu WLin
- 'Teem' (S)	GNor MCre MFie NRya SPop WLin
- 'Temeraire' (A)	MAln
- 'Tenby Grey' (S)	MCre MFie WLin
- 'Tender Trap' (A)	MAln
- 'Terpo' (S)	MAln
- 'Tess' (A)	MAln
- 'The Baron' (S)	GNor ITim MCre MFie MOne SPop WHil WLin
- 'The Bishop' (S)	MFie WHil
- 'The Bride' (S)	NLAp

- 'The Cardinal' (d) — MAln SUsu
- 'The Egyptian' (A) — MAln SPop WHil
- 'The Hobbit' (A) **new** — MAln
- 'The Raven' (S) — MFie NLAp SPop
- 'The Sneep' (A) — MCre SPop WHil
- 'The Snods' (S) — GNor MFie NLAp
- 'The Wrekin' (S) **new** — MAln
- 'Thebes' (A) — MAln
- 'Thetis' (A) — MCre MFie SPop
- 'Thirlmere' (d) — MAln
- 'Three Way Stripe' (St) — MCre
- 'Thutmoses' (A) — MAln
- 'Tiger Tim' — MAln
- 'Tinker' (S) — MAln
- 'Tinkerbell' (S) — MCre MFie SPop WLin
- 'Toddington Green' (S) **new** — MAln
- 'Toffee Crisp' (A) — MAln
- 'Tomboy' (S) — MFie SDnm SPop
- 'Toolyn' (S) — MAln
- 'Top Affair' (d) — MAln
- 'Tosca' (S) — GCrs GNor ITim MCre NRya SPop WHil WLin
- 'Trish' — GAbr
- 'Trouble' (d) — GAbr LHop LPio LRHS MBNS MCre MFie MOne SDnm SMrm SPop
- 'Troy Aykman' (A) — MAln
- 'Trudy' (S) — GAbr GNor ITim MCre MFie MOne SPop
- 'True Briton' (S) — MCre MFie SPop
- 'Trumpet Blue' (S) — MAln MFie
- 'Tumbledown' (A) — MFie
- 'Tummel' — MAln SPop
- 'Twiggy' (S) — MAln
- 'Tye Lea' (S) — MAln MCre
- 'Typhoon' (A) — MCre MFie SPop
- 'Uncle Arthur' (A) — MAln
- 'Unforgettable' (A) — MAln MCre
- 'Upton Belle' (S) — MAln
- 'Valerie' (A) — ITim MCre NLAp SPop
- 'Valerie Clare' — MAln
- 'Vee Too' (A) — MCre MFie SPop
- 'Vega' (A) — MAln
- 'Vein' (St) **new** — MAln
- 'Velvet Moon' (A) — MAln
- 'Venetian' (A) — MAln MFie SPop
- 'Venus' (A) — MAln
- 'Vera Eden' — MFie
- 'Vera Hill' (A) — MAln
- 'Verdi' (A) — ITim MAln MCre
- 'Victoria' (S) — MAln
- 'Victoria de Wemyss' (A) — MCre MFie
- 'Victoria Park' (A) **new** — MAln
- 'Virginia Belle' (St) — MAln
- 'Vivian' (S) — MAln
- 'Vulcan' (A) — MFie NBro SPop WLin
- 'Waincliffe Red' (S) — MFie
- 'Walter Lomas' (S) — MAln
- 'Walton' (A) — MCre MFie SPop
- 'Walton Heath' (d) — MCre MFie SPop WLin
- 'Waltz Time' (A) — MAln
- 'Watchett' (S) — MAln
- 'Waterfall' (A) — MAln
- 'Wayward' (S) — MAln
- 'Wedding Day' (S) — MAln MFie
- 'Wentworth' (A) — MAln
- 'Whistle Jacket' (S) — MAln
- 'White Ensign' (S) — GAbr GNor ITim MCre MFie NLAp NOak SPop WLin
- 'White Water' (A) — MAln SPop
- 'White Wings' (S) — MCre MFie NLAp SPop
- 'Whitecap' (S) — MAln
- 'Whoopee' (A) — MAln

- 'Wichita Falls' (A) — MAln
- 'Wide Awake' (A) — MCre MFie
- 'Wilf Booth' (A) — MAln SPop
- 'Wincha' (S) — MFie SPop
- 'Windways Mystery' (B) — MFie
- 'Windways Pisces' (d) — MAln
- 'Winifrid' (A) — CLyd GAbr GNor LRHS MCre MFie SPop
- 'Winlation' (A) — MAln
- 'Winnifred' (B) — SPop
- 'Woodmill' (A) — MAln SPop
- 'Wookey Hole' (A) — MAln
- 'Wycliffe Midnight' — GAbr GNor
- 'Wye Hen' (St) **new** — MAln
- 'Y.I. Hinney' (A) — MCre MFie
- 'Yellow Hammer' (S) — MAln
- 'Yellow Isle' (S) — MAln
- 'Yelverton' (S) — MAln MFie
- 'Yitzhak Rabin' (A) — MAln
- 'Yorkshire Grey' (S) — MFie NBro
- 'Zambia' (d) — CLyd GAbr ITim MCre MFie SPop SUsu
- 'Zircon' (S) — MAln
- 'Zodiac' (S) — MAln
- 'Zoe' (A) — MAln
- 'Zoe Ann' (S) — MAln
- I 'Zona' (A) — MAln
- 'Zorro' (St) **new** — MAln
- *auriculata* (11) — SBla
- 'Barbara Midwinter' (6x30) — CMea NGar WAbe
- Barnhaven Blues Group (Prim)(30) ♀H4 — CSWP GAbr MAnH
- Barnhaven doubles (dPoly)(30) — CSWP
- Barnhaven Gold-laced Group — see *P.* Gold-laced Group Barnhaven
- Barnhaven hybrids — CStu MAnH NCot WHrl
- Barnhaven Traditional Group — CSWP MAnH MAvo
- 'Beamish Foam' (Poly)(30) — NDov
- 'Beatrice Wooster' (2) — CLyd CNic GAbr ITim LRHS MFie NDlv NHol NJOw NLAp
- 'Bee' x 'Jo-Jo' — EHyt GCrs
- 'Beeches' Pink' — GAbr
- *beesiana* (4) — More than 30 suppliers
- *bella* — GKev
- 'Bellamy's Pride' — CLyd WAbe
- *bellidifolia* (17) — CPla GEdr GFle
- aff. *bellidifolia* **new** — GKev
- *beluensis* — see *P.* x *pubescens* 'Freedom'
- Bergfrühling Julianas Group (Prim)(30) — MFie
- § x *berninae* 'Windrush' (2) — CLyd WAbe
- 'Bewerley White' — see *P.* x *pubescens* 'Bewerley White'
- *bhutanica* — see *P. whitei* 'Sherriff's Variety'
- x *biflora* (2) **new** — WAbe
- 'Big Red Giant' (dPrim)(30) — MBNS MDKP MOne NGHP WCot
- *bileckii* — see *P.* x *forsteri* 'Bileckii'
- 'Blue Riband' (Prim)(30) — CBgR EDAr ENot EOMN EPfP MRav SBla WAbe WFar
- 'Blue Sapphire' (dPrim)(30) — CMil EPfP GAbr LRHS MBNS MFie MOne NCGa SIng SPer
- Blue Striped Victorians Group (Poly)(30) — GAbr
- 'Blutenkissen' (Prim)(30) — GAbr
- 'Bon Accord Purple' (dPoly)(30) — WFar
- *boothii alba* (21) — GCrs GFle GGGa LTwo

- subsp. *autumnalis* (21)	GGGa	
- subsp. *repens* (21)	MNrw	
'Boothman's Ruby'	see *P.* x *pubescens* 'Boothman's Variety'	
boveana (12)	MFie	
bracteata **new**	GKev	
§ *bracteosa* (21)	GCrs GFle ITim NLAp	
Bressingham (4)	WFar	
brevicaula	see *P. chionantha* subsp. *brevicaula*	
brigantia	GIBF	
'Broadwell Pink' (2)	EHyt ITim	
'Broadwell Ruby' (2)	EHyt WAbe WLin	
'Bronwyn' (Prim)(30)	NBir	
'Broxbourne'	CLyd ITim NLAp	
'Buckland Wine' (Prim)(30)	ITim	
x *bulleesiana* (4)	CM&M EBee EChP EMFW GFlt IBal LRHS MBri MTis NBro NChi NLAp NLar SMrm SPer SRms STes SWat WFar WMnd WMoo WPer	
- Moerheim hybrids (4)	WFar	
bulleyana (4) ♀H4	More than 30 suppliers	
- ACE 2484	WAbe	
burmanica (4)	CPla GBuc GEdr GFle GGar GIBF MSta SIng SLon SRms SWat WFar WGwG WHHs	
'Butter's Bronze' (Prim)	WOut	
'Butterscotch' (Prim)(30)	CSWP	
'Caerulea Plena' (dPrim)(30)	GCal	
calderiana (21)	EBee GFle	
candelabra hybrids (4)	CBre CBro CHar COIW EChP GFlt GGar ITim NBir NPPs SPet SWal SWat WRos	
Candy Pinks Group (Prim)(30)	CSWP WHil	
capitata (5)	CM&M CPla CSWP EBee EDAr GFle GTou IFro ITim MFie NLAp WAbe WBea WCom WFar WGwG WHHs WMoo WPer	
- subsp. *crispata* (5)	WLin	
- subsp. *mooreana* (5)	CFir CTCP EChP EWTr GFle ITim LPBA NDlv SPlb WBVN WPnP	
- subsp. *sphaerocephala* (5)	GKev	
'Captain Blood' (dPrim)(30)	EPfP MBow MFie NLar NSti NWCA SIng WFar WLin WRha	
'Carmen' (Prim)(30)	CLyd ITim	
Carnation Victorians Group (Poly)(30)	MFie	
carniolica (2)	GFle MFie	
Casquet mixture (Prim)(30)	CSWP	
cernua (17)	EBee GFle MFie NArg WLin	
Chartreuse Group (Poly)(30)	CSWP MFie WRha	
'Chevithorne Pink' (Poly)(30)	NPar	
§ *chionantha* (18) ♀H4	EBee EDAr GCrs GFle GGar GKir GTou ITim LRHS MFie MNrw NBir NLAp SPer SWat WAbe WFar WGwG WHHs	
- subsp. *brevicaula*	GKev	
§ - subsp. *melanops* (18)	EBee GFle GIBF GMac LRHS	
§ - subsp. *sinopurpurea* (18)	EBee EChP GFle GGar GIBF GTou NLar SWat WAbe WCom WFar WHil WPer	
chungensis (4)	CBcs CWCL EBee EDAr GEdr GFle GGar GIBF GKir GTou MLLN NDlv SRms SUsu SWvt WAbe WMoo	
§ *chungensis* x *pulverulenta* (4)	CWCL EBee EChP GBuc GEdr MFie NHol NLar SMrm WAbe WFar	

x *chunglenta*	see *P. chungensis* x *pulverulenta* (4)	
§ 'Clarence Elliott' (2)	CGra CLyd EHyt GCrs ITim WAbe WCom WLin	
clarkei (11)	CLyd GEdr GFle GTou NWCA WAbe	
clusiana (2)	EBee NSla	
- 'Murray-Lyon' (2)	GCrs NSla	
cockburniana (4) ♀H4	CBcs CRow CTCP EChP GEdr GFle GGar GIBF GTou MFie NWCA SRms WAbe WFar WHil SWat	
- hybrids (4)	SWat	
- yellow-flowered	GGar GKev	
concholoba (17)	CPla GFle GFlt GKev GTou MFie NLAp WAbe	
'Corporal Baxter' (dPrim)(30)	ENot EPfP MBNS MNrw MOne NCGa NGHP WRha WWol	
cortusoides (7)	CPla EWTr GFle MNrw NLar SRms	
Cowichan (Poly)(30)	GAbr WMyn	
Cowichan Amethyst Group (Poly)(30)	CSWP GAbr MAnH	
Cowichan Blue Group (Poly)(30)	CSWP GAbr MAnH	
Cowichan Garnet Group (Poly)(30)MFie	CSWP EWoo GAbr GBuc MAnH	
Cowichan Red Group (Poly)(30)	MAnH WFar	
Cowichan Venetian Group (Poly)(30)	CSWP GAbr MAnH WFar	
Cowichan Yellow Group (Poly)(30)	GAbr WCot	
'Coy' **new**	EHyt	
'Craddock White' (Prim) (30)	CBos	
'Craven Gem' (Poly)(30)	GBuc	
Crescendo Series (Poly)(30)	GAbr	
'Crimson Velvet' (2)	GAbr GNor ITim NHol NLAp WLin	
crispa	see *P. glomerata*	
* *cuneata*	GTou	
cuneifolia (8)	CTCP GFle GNor	
daonensis (2)	GFle	
darialica (11)	CNic	
davidii **new**	EBee	
'Dawn Ansell' (dPrim)(30)	CHad CRow CSpe EPfP GAbr ITer LRHS MBNS MBri MCLN MFie MOne NBir NDov NGHP NWCA SBla SPer SSte SUsu WHer WLin	
Daybreak Group (Poly)(30)	CSWP MFie	
deflexa (17)	GCrs GFle LRHS WLin	
- BWJ 7877	WCru	
denticulata (9) ♀H4	More than 30 suppliers	
- var. *alba* (9)	More than 30 suppliers	
- blue (9)	GKir NLar WMyn	
- 'Bressingham Beauty' (9)	EBre	
- var. *cachemiriana* hort. (9)	EPfP NCot NFla WShp	
- 'Glenroy Crimson' (9)	CLAP EBee SRms SWvt WCom	
- 'Karryann' (9/v)	EMon WCot	
- lilac (9)	EHon GKir GTou MFie NCot NLAp NPri WMyn WWeb	
- purple (9)	GKir IBlr WMoo WMyn	
- red (9)	EPar EPfP GGar GKir MWgw NLAp NOrc WMoo WMyn	
- 'Robinson's Red' (9)	GBuc	
- 'Ronsdorf' (9)	LRHS	
- 'Rubin'	CWat EBee EHon EPfP GAbr GTou IHMH MBrN MBri MFie NBro NOak SRms WHen WHil WPer WShp WWeb	
- 'Rubin Auslese' **new**	CSam	
- 'Rubinball' (9)	EBre EPfP GCrs GKir NHol WCot	

- 'Snowball' (9)	MCLN NOak WHen
deorum (2)	GKev
x *deschmannii*	see *P.* x *vochinensis*
'Desert Sunset' (Poly)(30)	CSWP MFie
'Devon Cream' (Prim)(30)	GBuc WFar
'Dianne'	see *P.* x *forsteri* 'Dianne'
'Dorothy' (Poly)(30)	MRav
'Double Lilac'	see *P. vulgaris* 'Lilacina Plena'
dryadifolia **new**	GKev
'Duckyls Red' (Prim)(30)	GBuc
'Dusky Lady'	MBri WBar WFar
'Easter Bonnet' (dPrim)(30)	LRHS MOne NBid SPer
edelbergii (12)	CNic
edgeworthii	see *P. nana*
elatior (30) ♀H4	More than 30 suppliers
- hose-in-hose (30)(d)	NBid
- hybrids (30)	WHHs
- subsp. *intricata* (30)	NRya
- subsp. *leucophylla* (30)	EBee ECho
- subsp. *meyeri* (30)	GCrs GFle GNor NSla NWCA
- subsp. *pallasii* (30)	GCrs GEdr
'Elizabeth Killelay' (dPoly)(30)	CBct CBgR CBos CElw CMil ELan GBuc GMac LDai LHop MAvo MBri MFie MSph NBir NChi NCot NGdn NLar NSti SPer SUsu WCom WCot WHrl WLin WSan WWhi
'Ellen Page' (2)	MFie
'Ellenbank Pink Candelabra' **new**	GMac
ellisiae (21)	GFle SOkd
'Ethel Barker' (2)	CGra ITim LRHS NDlv NHol
'Eugénie' (dPrim)(30)	CHid GAbr MBNS MFie MOne NCGa NGHP SIng
'Fairy Rose' KRW 180/48 (2)	EHyt ITim WAbe
farinosa (11)	CLyd EBee GFle MFie NMen NRya WAbe WBWf WPer
fasciculata (11)	EHyt GEdr NLAp NSla SBla WHHs
- CLD 345	WAbe
- ex CLD 345	GFle
'Fife Yellow' (dPoly)(30)	GBuc
'Fire Dance' (Poly)(30)	MFie
firmipes (26)	EBee GIBF WCot
§ *flaccida* (28)	EBee GFle GGGa MHar WAbe
Flamingo Group (Poly)(30)	CSWP MFie
§ x *floerkeana* (2)	GCrs
- f. *biflora* 'Alba' (2)	SBla
florida (29)	WHHs
I - 'Pectinata' **new**	GCrs
florindae (26) ♀H4	More than 30 suppliers
- bronze (26)	GQui MFie NBir SWat WHHs
I - 'Butterscotch' (26)	WHrl
- hybrids (26)	CDWL EChP EHrv GAbr GEdr GGar ITim MFie MWrn
- orange (26)	CSam GMac IBlr MNrw WCru WFar WMoo WWpP
- 'Ray's Ruby' (26)	CHar GBBs GBuc GMac MCLN MFOX MNrw NBir SWat WHrl WWhi WWpP
- red (26)	EBee GBuc GCal GGar ITim MFie MSta NBid NChi NLar NPPs WBVN WCom WFar WLin
- terracotta (26)	CSWP
Footlight Parade Group (Prim)(30)	CSWP
forrestii (3)	EHyt GGGa MFie NLAp SSpi WAbe
- ACE 2474	GFle
- ACE 2480	EPot
§ x *forsteri* (2)	GFle MFie WAbe

§ - 'Bileckii' (2)	EPar GCrs GFle ITim LRHS NBir NLAp NWCA SRms WAbe WOBN
§ - 'Dianne' (2)	EHyt GAbr GBuc NBro NLAp NRya WAbe WGwG
- 'Dianne' hybrids (2)	MFie
'Francisca' (Poly) **new**	WCot
'Freckles' (dPrim)(30)	MBNS MBri MDun NHol SPer SWat
'Freedom'	see *P.* x *pubescens* 'Freedom'
frondosa (11) ♀H4	CLyd EBee GFle GIBF LRHS MBro MDKP MFie NLAp NMen NWCA WAbe WBVN WLin
Fuchsia Victorians Group (Poly)(30)	MFie
'Garnet' (*allionii* hybrid) (2)	MFie
'Garryard Guinevere'	see *P.* 'Guinevere'
'Garryarde Crimson'	WCot
gaubana (12)	MFie
gemmifera (11)	GFle GGGa
- var. *monantha* **new**	EBee
- var. *zambalensis* (11)	GCrs GFle WAbe
geraniifolia (7)	SOkd
'Gigha' (Prim)(30)	CSWP NGar
glabra	WAbe
glaucescens (2)	CGra CLyd EHyt GFle MFie NSla WLin
§ *glomerata* (5)	GBuc GFle GGGa WLin
- CC 3321	WRos
'Gloria Johnson' **new**	EHyt
'Glowing Embers' (4)	CSpe LRHS MFie NBir WHil
glutinosa All.	see *P. allionii*
Gold-laced Group (Poly)(30)	More than 30 suppliers
§ - Barnhaven (Poly)(30)	GAbr LPio MFie NBPC NBir
- Beeches strain (Poly)(30)	MAnH SSth
'Gordon'	NGar
gracilipes (21)	CDes GFle GGGa GGar ITim SRms WAbe
- L&S 1166	WAbe
- early-flowering (21)	WAbe
- 'Major'	see *P. bracteosa*
- 'Minor'	see *P. petiolaris*
Grand Canyon Group (Poly)(30)	MFie
grandis	GFle
griffithii (21)	GGGa
'Groenekan's Glorie' (Prim)(30)	EWTr GAbr GEdr LRHS MBri MRav NBir NBro SHar WFar WViv
§ 'Guinevere' (Poly) (30) ♀H4	More than 30 suppliers
'Hall Barn Blue'	GAbr WBod
§ *halleri* (11)	EBee GFle GTou MFie NDlv NMen NWCA WAbe
- 'Longiflora'	see *P. halleri*
Harbinger Group (Prim)(30)	CSWP GAbr LLWP
Harbour Lights mixture (Poly)(30)	CSWP MFie
Harlow Carr hybrids (4)	CSWP GQui MLLN NDlv NGar NWCA WEas
Harvest Yellows Group (Poly)(30)	MFie
helodoxa	see *P. prolifera*
§ 'Hemswell Blush' (2)	GNor ITim NHol NLAp
§ 'Hemswell Ember' (2)	CNic EPot GCrs MFie NDlv NLAp NRya WLin
heucherifolia (7)	CPla GFle
hidakana (24)	NSla SOkd
'High Point' (2)	CGra
hirsuta (2)	CNic EHyt GCrs GEdr GFle GIBF GTou ITim MFie WPat
- var. *exscapa* (2)	GFle
- 'Lismore Snow' (2)	ITim NLAp

hongshanensis <u>new</u>	GKev	
hose-in-hose (Poly)(30)(d)	CSWP GFlt ITer MHer MNrw	
§ 'Hyacinthia' (2)	CLyd EPot GIBF MFie	
ianthina	see *P. prolifera*	
iljinskyi	NWCA WLin	
incana <u>new</u>	GKev	
Indian Reds Group (Poly)(30)	CSWP MFie	
'Ingram's Blue' (Poly)(30)	LRHS WPen	
Inshriach hybrids (4)	CMHG CSWP EBre MBri MFie NLar WFar	
integrifolia (2)	GCrs GEdr GFle WAbe	
§ 'Inverewe' (4) ♀H4	ECGP GBin GCal GKev NBir SUsu	
involucrata (11)	see *P. munroi*	
ioessa (26)	CBrm EBee EWes GGGa NChi WAbe	
- hybrids (26)	NLAp WPen	
'Iris Mainwaring' (Prim)(30)	GAbr GEdr MDHE MFie NHol NWCA	
irregularis (21)	GCrs GGGa	
issiori	GIBF	
Jack in the Green Group (Poly)(30)	CSWP ITer MCre MNrw MRav MWgw NCot WBVN WFar WRha	
'Jackie Richards' (2)	EHyt MFie WLin	
jaffreyana (11)	NGar WAbe	
japonica (4)	CMHG CRow CSam ECha EWTr GFle GGar GIBF GKir GLil GTou ITim LPBA LRHS MFir NBid NBro NChi NFor NHol SWat WAbe WCra WCru WFar WHil WMoo WMyn WPer	
- 'Alba' (4)	EBee EHrv EWTr NArg NDlv NHol NPri SIng WAbe WCAu WFar WHil WMnd	
- 'Apple Blossom' (4)	GKev LHop SWvt	
* - 'Carminea' (4)	EBee EWTr GBuc NBro NHol NLar WFar	
- 'Fuji' (4)	CSWP GMac MSta NBro	
- 'Fuji' hybrids (4)	NLar	
- 'Merve's Red' (4)	CDes	
- 'Miller's Crimson' (4) ♀H4	More than 30 suppliers	
- 'Oriental Sunrise' (4)	CMil CSWP	
- 'Postford White' (4) ♀H4	More than 30 suppliers	
- red (4)	WAbe	
- 'Valley Red' (4)	GBuc GGar GMac ITim LHop WHil	
jesoana (7)	GFle LTwo	
- B&SWJ 618	WCru	
'Joan Hughes' (*allionii* hybrid) (2)	CLyd ITim SBla WAbe WLin	
'Joanna'	ECou EHyt	
'Johanna' (11)	GAbr GBuc GEdr GFle NGar NPro NWCA SOkd WAbe	
'John Fielding' (6x30)	CBgR CBro GEdr WCot	
'Jo-Jo' (2)	CLyd WAbe WLin	
juliae (30)	CPla EHyt ETow GFle GIBF LLWP LRHS SPlb WAbe WCom WCot WEas	
I - 'Millicent' (3O)	WCot	
'Kate Haywood'	CLyd WLin	
'Ken Dearman' (dPrim)(30)	CSpe ENot EPfP MBNS MBri MFie MOne MRav NBid NBir NGHP NHol NPPs SIng SPer WFar WWol	
kewensis (12) ♀H2	EShb GGar GKev MFie	
'Kinlough Beauty' (Poly)(30)	EMon EPar GEdr LRHS NRya NSti NWCA WEas	
'Kirk Ings' (2)	NGar	
§ *kisoana* (7)	CPla EBee MTho NLAp SBla WCru	
- var. *alba* (7)	CLAP CPla GGGa MTho	
- var. **shikokiana**	see *P. kisoana* (7)	
'Lady Greer' (Poly)(30) ♀H4	CSam EBee ECGN EDAr ETow GAbr GBuc LLWP MBri MFie MRav	
		NBir NChi NLAp NRya NSti NWCA SMac SUsu WCom WViv
'Lambrook Lilac' (Poly)(30)	CElw	
§ *latifolia* (2)	GFle GIBF SOkd	
latifolia x *pedemontana* (2)	GFle	
latisecta (7)	SOkd	
§ *laurentiana* (11)	EBee GFle NWCA WAbe	
'Lea Gardens' (*allionii* hybrid) (2)	EHyt ITim MFie NHol	
'Lee Myers' (*allionii* hybrid) (2)	EPot GNor ITim MFie NDlv	
'Lilac Domino' (2)	ITim NGar	
'Lilac Fairy'	CNic ITim NGar WLin	
'Lilian Harvey' (dPrim)(30)	CElw EPfP LRHS MFie MOne MRav NBir NHol WWol	
Limelight Group (Poly)(30)	MFie	
'Lindum Moonlight'	EHyt	
'Lingwood Beauty' (Prim)(30)	GAbr	
'Linnet' (21)	ITim	
'Lismore' (2)	WLin	
'Lismore Pink Ice'	WLin	
'Lismore Yellow' (2)	EHyt EPot GKev GTou NLAp WAbe WLin	
Lissadel hybrids (4)	GFle GMac	
littoniana	see *P. vialii*	
§ x *loiseleurii* 'Aire Waves' (2)	EHyt GNor ITim NLAp	
longiflora	see *P. halleri*	
luteola (11)	GFle GGar LTwo MNrw NHol NLar WFar	
macrophylla (18)	GFle GTou	
magellanica (11)	GFle WAbe	
- subsp. *magellanica* J&JA 2.749.900	NWCA	
malacoides (3)	MBri	
malvacea <u>new</u>	EBee GKev	
mandarin red (4)	CSWP	
marginata (2) ♀H4	EBre EPot GAbr GCrs GFle LHop LRHS MBro NDlv NHol NJOw NLAp WAbe WFar WPat	
- 'Adrian Evans' (2)	EHyt ITim	
- *alba* (2)	LRHS MBro NBro NDlv NGar NHol NLAp	
- 'Barbara Clough' (2)	CLyd ITim MFie NGar NSla WLin	
- 'Beamish' (2) ♀H4	CLyd EPot NBro NGar NRya NSla WCom	
- 'Beatrice Lascaris' (2)	EPot GCrs ITim MFie MOne NHol WAbe	
- 'Beverley Reid' (2)	ITim NGar	
- 'Boothman's Variety' (2)	ITim NGar NLAp	
- 'Caerulea' (2)	CLyd EPot ITim MOne NLAp WAbe	
- 'Clear's Variety' (2)	ITim	
- 'Correvon's Variety' (2)	CLyd NGar	
- cut-leaved (2)	ITim NHol	
- dark (2)	NGar	
- 'Doctor Jenkins' (2)	ITim NHol NLar	
- 'Drake's Form' (2)	ITim NHol NLAp NLar SOkd	
- dwarf (2)	LRHS MFie	
I - 'Earl L. Bolton'	see *P. marginata* 'El Bolton'	
- 'El Bolton' (2)	NGar NHol WAbe	
- 'Elizabeth Fry' (2)	CLyd NGar	
- from the Dolomites (2)	NHol NLAp	
- 'Gold Plate' (2)	NGar	
- 'Grandiflora' (2)	MBro NHol	
- 'Highland Twilight' (2)	NSla	
- 'Holden Clough' (2)	NJOw NRya WCom	
- 'Holden Variety' (2)	EPot ITim MBro NDlv NHol WAbe	
- 'Hyacinthia'	see *P.* 'Hyacinthia'	
- 'Ivy Agee' (2)	CLyd EPot ITim NLAp	
- 'Janet' (2)	CLyd EPot NLAp WCom	

- 'Jenkins Variety' (2) — CLyd EPot
- 'Kesselring's Variety' (2) — CLyd CM&M CMea ELan EPot GNor MBro MOne NDlv NJOw NLAp WAbe WTin WWin
- 'Laciniata' — NGar SBla WCom
- lilac-flowered — MFie
- 'Linda Pope' (2) ♀H4 — CLyd EPot ITim NBir NDlv NHol NSla SUsu WAbe
- maritime form (2) — NJOw
- 'Millard's Variety' (2) — CLyd ITim
- 'Mrs Carter Walmsley' (2) — NGar
- 'Nancy Lucy' (2) — WAbe
- 'Napoleon' (2) — ITim NGar NHol NLAp
- 'Oxember' (2) — NGar
I 'Peter's Variety' (2) — NGar
- 'Prichard's Variety' (2) ♀H4 — CLyd ELan EMlt EPot ITim LBee MBro MFie NDlv NGar NJOw NLAp NMyG NRya NWCA WAbe WEas WFar
- 'Rheniana' — see *Primula* 'Rheniana'
- 'Rosea' (2) — NHol
- 'Sheila Denby' (2) — ITim NGar NLAp
- 'Shipton' (2) — NGar
- 'The President' (2) — ITim
- 'Waithman's Variety' (2) — GCrs GTou ITim NLAp NRya
- wild-collected (2) — ITim MFie
'Maria Talbot' (*allionii* hybrid) (2) — EHyt NJOw
'Marianne Davey' (dPrim)(30) — MRav NBir
'Marie Crousse' (dPrim)(30) — CBgR ENot LRHS MBNS MFie MOne MWgw NHol SIng WCot WRha
Marine Blues Group (Poly)(30) — CSWP MAnH MFie
'Maris Tabbard' **new** — EHyt
'Mars' (*allionii* hybrid) (2) WLin — GNor ITim NDlv NHol NLAp NRya
'Marven' (2) — CLyd EPot NGar NHol NJOw
'Mary Anne' — GAbr
'Mauve Mist' (2) — NGar
Mauve Victorians Group (Poly)(30) — CSWP MFie
'McWatt's Claret' (Poly)(30) — LLWP NPar
'McWatt's Cream' (Poly)(30) — CSWP EBee EBre EDAr GEdr GFle GGar LHop NChi NHol NMen WCom
megaseifolia (6) — GKev
melanops — see *P. chionantha* subsp. *melanops*
x *meridiana* (2) — MFie
§ - 'Miniera' (2) — CLyd ITim
- 'Mexico' — MFie
Midnight Group — CSWP GEdr MAnH MFie
'Miniera' — see *P.* x *meridiana* 'Miniera'
minima (2) — CLyd GFle GTou MFie NBro NLAr NSla WAbe
- var. *alba* (2) — GCrs GFle GGGa MFie NRya NSla
minima x *hirsuta* (2) — see *P.* x *forsteri*
minima x *wulfeniana* (2) — see *P.* x *vochinensis*
'Miss Indigo' (dPrim)(30) — ENot EPfP GAbr LRHS MBNS MBri MCLN MFie MOne MRav NCGa NGHP NHol NWCA SIng SPer WCAu WEas WGwG WLin
mistassinica var. *macropoda* — see *P. laurentiana*
miyabeana (4) — GFle
- B&SWJ 3407 — WCru
modesta alba (11) — GFle
- var. *faurieae* (11) — MFie NWCA
- var. *matsumurae* (11) — GFle

mollis (7) — GEdr GIBF
'Mother's Day' — CElw
moupinensis (21) — CDes GCrs GGGa GKir ITim WAbe
- C&H 7038 — GFle GGGa
* 'Mrs Eagland' — GAbr
'Mrs Frank Neave' (Prim) — GEdr
§ *munroi* (11) — GFle NWCA SWat WAbe
§ - subsp. *yargongensis* (11) — EBee GFle GGar GTou LRHS MFie NLAp SWat WAbe WDyG WFar
muscarioides (17) — GFle GTou MFie WAbe WLin
Muted Victorians Group (Poly)(30) — CSWP MFie
§ *nana* (21) — GFle GKev ITim WAbe
- 'Alba' (21) — GCrs
'Netta Dennis' — ITim
nevadensis **new** — GFle
New Pinks Group (Poly)(30) — CSWP MFie
'Nightingale' — ITim
nivalis Pallas — see *P. chionantha*
nutans Delavay ex Franch. — see *P. flaccida*
nutans Georgi. — GKev
obconica (19) — LRHS MBri MFie WGwG
obliqua **new** — GKev
'Old Port' (Poly)(30) — CElw GEdr LLWP NHol NLAp WPat
Old Rose Victorians Group (Poly)(30) — CSWP MFie
'Olive Wyatt' (dPrim)(30) — NBir
orbicularis **new** — EBee GCrs
'Oriental Sunrise' (4) — CSWP MFie
Osiered Amber Group (Prim)(30) — CSWP
'Our Pat' (dPoly)(30) — WPnP
oxygraphidifolia **new** — GKev
* 'Page' — EHyt
palinuri (2) — GIBF WCom
palmata (7) — GCrs GEdr GFle GGGa WAbe
'Paris '90' (Poly)(30) — CSWP GAbr MFie
parryi (20) — GCrs GFle GIBF WFar
'Pat Cottle' (d) (Poly) (30) — CBos
'Peardrop' (2) — CGra GAbr NHol NLAp
pedemontana (2) — GFle MSte NWCA WAbe
- 'Alba' (2) — EHyt
'Perle von Bottrop' (Prim)(30) — GAbr
'Peter Klein' (11) — CElw GBuc GEdr GFle LTwo NLAp NLar NWCA WAbe WTin
petiolaris misapplied — see *P.* 'Redpoll'
§ *petiolaris* (21) — EHyt EPar GCrs GFle GGGa GNor ITim MDun WAbe
- Sherriff's form — see *P.* 'Redpoll'
'Petticoat' — NCGa WCot
§ 'Pink Aire' (2) — EHyt ITim MFie NGar
'Pink Fairy' — EHyt ITim
'Pink Ice' (*allionii* hybrid) (2) — CGra CLyd CPBP ITim MFie NHol NRya
pinnatifida (17) — GGGa
poissonii (4) — CDWL CHar CMHG CPla CTri EChP ELan GCrs GFle GGar GIBF GMac LPBA MFie MNrw NGby NLar WAbe WBVN WShi
- ACE 1946 — NWCA
- B&SWJ 7525 — WCru
polyanthus (30) — WFar
polyneura (7) — CPla ECha EDAr GEdr GFle GGar GIBF GNor MFie MNrw NBid NVic SRms
'Port Wine' (30) — EWTr MBct
praenitens — see *P. sinensis*
prenantha (4) — GGGa WAbe
'Prince Silverwings' (dPoly)(30) — WEas

§ **prolifera** (4) ♀H4	CBcs CMHG CTrw EBee ECha EHon GFle GGar GIBF GMac ISea ITer LPBA MFir MLLN MNrw MRav NBPC SLon SPer SRms SSpi SWat WAbe WFar WGwG WPer
– double-flowered (d) **new**	CFir
§ x **pubescens** (2) ♀H4	EMan MBro NLAp WPer
– 'Alba' (2)	WAbe
– 'Alison Gibbs' (2)	MOne
– 'Apple Blossom' (2)	CLyd ITim MFie
– 'Balfouriana' (2)	CNic NHol
§ – 'Bewerley White' (2)	EBee EDAr MBro MOne NDlv NHol NJOw NLAp WLin WWin
– 'Blue Wave' (2)	MFie
§ – 'Boothman's Variety' (2)	CLyd ITim LRHS MBro MFie MSte NDlv NHol NLAp NMyG NWCA WCom WFar WHoo WTin WWin
– 'Carmen'	see *P.* x *pubescens* 'Boothman's Variety'
– 'Chamois' (2)	MFie
– 'Christine' (2)	CLyd CMea MBro MFie NBir NDlv NHol NLAp
– 'Cream Viscosa' (2)	ITim MFie NDlv NHol NLAp WCom
– 'Deep Mrs Wilson' (2)	EHyt SUsu
– 'Ellen Page'	see *Primula* 'Ellen Page'
– 'Faldonside' (2)	CLyd CNic MBro NDlv NHol WCom WWin
§ – 'Freedom' (2)	CLyd CTri GTou ITim LRHS MFie NBir NDlv NHol NLAp SIng SRms WCom WEas WWin
– 'George Harrison' (2)	MFie
– 'Harlow Car' (2)	CLyd GMac ITim MFie NDlv NLAp WFar WLin
– 'Henry Hall' (2)	CLyd EWes
– 'Herbert Beresford' (2)	EHyt GCrs
– 'Joan Danger' (2)	CLyd CNic ITim MFie NHol
– 'Joan Gibbs' (2)	CLyd ITim MFie MOne NLAp
– 'Kath Dryden' (2)	ITim
– 'Lilac Fairy' (2)	ITim NDlv
– 'Mrs J.H. Wilson' (2)	CGra CLyd EHyt ITim LRHS MFie NDlv NHol NRya WPat
– 'Pat Barwick' (2)	CNic GCrs ITim MFie NDlv NHol NLAp
– 'Peggy' (2)	MFie
– 'Peggy Fell' (2)	GCrs MDHE
– 'Rufus' (2)	CLyd CNic ETow GCrs NHol WTin
– 'Snowcap' (2)	GCrs WLin
– 'Sonya' (2)	ITim
– 'The General' (2)	CLyd ITim MOne SPop WLin WWin
§ – 'Wedgwood' (2)	GNor
– x 'White Linda Pope' (2)	ITim
– 'Winifred' (2)	NHol
pulchella (11)	WAbe
pulchra (21)	GCrs GEdr GKir
pulverulenta (4) ♀H4	More than 30 suppliers
– 'Bartley'	SWat
– Bartley hybrids (4) ♀H4	CBot EBee GBuc GGar SMur SSpi
– 'Bartley Pink' (4)	CHar CPla CPlt GBuc SSpi WEas
pusilla new	GCrs
'Quaker's Bonnet'	see *P. vulgaris* 'Lilacina Plena'
'Rachel Kinnen' (2)	EHyt ITim MFie
'Ramona' (Poly)(30)	MAnH MFie
'Ravenglass Vermilion'	see *P.* 'Inverewe'
'Red Velvet' (dPrim)(30)	CMil ECGP MOne NGHP NPPs
§ 'Redpoll' (21)	EPar GCrs ITim WAbe
reidii (28)	GFle
– var. **williamsii** (28)	GEdr GFle GGGa GNor GTou WLin
– – **alba** (28)	GFle
reptans (16)	GCrs
'Reverie' (Poly)(30)	CSWP MAnH MFie

'Rheniana' (2)	EPot ITim NGar
'Rose O'Day' (dPrim)(30)	MNrw MOne NBir NHol
rosea (11) ♀H4	CPla CRow EBee EDAr EPar EPfP GEdr GFle GGGa GGar GKir GTou MFie MWgw NBid NBir NLAp NSti NVic SSpi WFar
– 'Delight'	see *P. rosea* 'Micia Visser-de Geer'
– 'Gigas' (11)	EBre GAbr MSta NHol
– 'Grandiflora' (11)	EBre EHon EPar EPfP EWTr GBar GCrs GFle GKev IHMH LPBA MBow MBri MRav NDlv NWCA SIng SRms SWat WFar WMyn WPer WWpP
– 'Micia Visser-de Geer' (11)	EBre LRHS
'Rowallane Rose' (4)	CBro EBre GBuc
'Roy Cope' (dPrim)(30)	EWTr MFie NBid NBir NCGa WBor WFar
'Roydon Ruby'	WCot WViv
rusbyi (20)	GFle GIBF
Rustic Reds Group (Poly)(30)	CSWP MFie
'Sapphire'	EHyt
saxatilis (7)	GCrs MFie
scandinavica (11)	GIBF MFie
x **scapeosa** (21)	GFle GGGa
scapigera (21)	GGGa
§ 'Schneekissen' (Prim)(30)	CBre CHid EBre MBri MHer NBir NBro NChi NGHP NMyG NPro SBla WBod WHil WViv
scotica (11)	CTCP GCrs GFle GIBF GPoy GTou MFie NLAp NSla NWCA WAbe WBWf WGwG WHHs
secundiflora (26)	More than 30 suppliers
– B&SWJ 7547	WCru
§ x **sendtneri** (2)	MFie
septemloba (7)	GFle WAbe
x **serrata**	see *P.* x *vochinensis*
serratifolia (4)	GGGa GGar GKev
sibthorpii	see *P. vulgaris* subsp. *sibthorpii*
sieboldii (7) ♀H4	CRow EHyt EPar GFle MNrw NMen NRya NWCA SIng SMac SRms SSpi SUsu WAbe WFar WLin
– **alba** (7)	CDes CLAP EBee NBro NMen SRot WCru WFar WPGP WTin
– blue-flowered (7)	CLAP NMen
– 'Blush' **new**	CLAP
– 'Carefree' (7)	CLAP LTwo NBro NLar NMen WOBN
– 'Cherubim' (7)	EBre WCra
– 'Dancing Ladies' (7)	CLAP CMil CSWP MFie NBro
– 'Galaxy' (7)	NBro
– 'Geisha Girl' (7)	CFir CLAP MRav NLar WAbe WFar
– 'Lilac Sunbonnet' (7)	ENot EPfP LRHS LTwo NHol
– 'Manakoora' (7)	CLAP CSWP MFie NBro
– 'Mikado' (7)	CFir CLAP MFie MRav
– 'Pago-Pago' (7)	CLAP MFie NBro NHol
– 'Purple Back' (7) **new**	EBee
– 'Purple Spider' (7) **new**	EBee
– 'Seraphim' (7)	CLAP EBre GMac WCra
– 'Snowflake' (7)	CLAP EBre NGar NLar NSla SBla WAbe WCra
– 'Tah-ni' (7)	NBro
– 'Winter Dreams' (7)	CLAP CSWP MFie NBid NBro
§ **sikkimensis** (26) ♀H4	CRow CWCL EBee GCrs GEdr GFle GGGa GGar GKir ITim LPBA MBri MBro MNrw MSta WAbe WHil WLin WRos
– ACE 1422	GBuc WCru
– B&SWJ 4808	WCru
– CC 3409	WRos
– CC&McK 1022	GTou
– DJHC 01051	WCru
– var. **hopeana** (26)	GCrs GFle WLin

– var. **pudibunda** (26)	GEdr
– 'Tilman Number 2' (26)	GAbr SPer
aff. **sikkimensis** (26)	ITim NArg WGwG WHHs
– ACE 2176	GBuc
Silver-laced Group (Poly) (30)	EPar SWvt
– 'Silver Lining' (Poly)(30)	LRHS
'Silverwells' (4)	GEdr
simensis new	GKev
§ **sinensis** (27)	GEdr
sinopurpurea	see *P. chionantha* subsp. *sinopurpurea*
'Sir Bedivere' (Prim)(30)	GBuc NGar NLar
smithiana	see *P. prolifera*
'Snow Carpet'	see *P.* 'Schneekissen'
'Snow Cushion'	see *P.* 'Schneekissen'
'Snow White' (Poly)(30)	GEdr MRav
Snowcushion	see *P.* 'Schneekissen'
'Snowruffles'	ITim
sonchifolia (21)	CFir GGGa ITim MDun
– from Tibet (21)	ITim MDun
sorachiana	see *P. yuparensis*
spectabilis (2)	EHyt GFle
specuicola (11)	GIBF
Spice Shades Group (Poly)(30)	CSWP GAbr MFie WCot
× **steinii**	see *P.* × *forsteri*
'Stradbrook Charm' (2) **new**	EPot WLin
'Stradbrook Dainty' (2)	EHyt ITim MFie NHol WLin
'Stradbrook Dream' (2)	CNic EHyt EPot ITim MFie NHol NLAp
'Stradbrook Gem' (2)	WAbe WPat
'Stradbrook Lilac Lustre' (2)	CGra MFie
'Stradbrook Lucy' (2)	EHyt ITim NHol NLAp WAbe WLin
'Stradbrook Mauve Magic' (2)	MFie
stricta (11)	GFle
Striped Victorians Group (Poly)(30)	CSWP EBre MFie
'Sue' **new**	EHyt
'Sue Jervis' (dPrim)(30)	GAbr NBir NCGa NGHP NLar NSti SBla WBar WCAu WGwG WHal WLin WRha WWol
suffrutescens (8)	NSla WAbe WLin
'Sunrise' (2)	ITim
'Sunshine Susie' (dPrim)(30)	ENot EPfP GAbr LRHS MBNS MFie MOne MRav NCGa NHol SIng WCAu WCot WWol
takedana (24)	GGGa
tangutica new	EBee
* – **alba new**	EBee
tanneri (21)	GFle
'Tantallon' (21)	CStu GCrs GGGa GGar ITim NLAp
§ Tartan Reds Group (Prim)(30)	CSWP MAnH
'Tawny Port' (Poly)(30)	GAbr NBro SRms
tibetica (11)	GFle GGGa
'Tie Dye' (Prim)(30)	WCot
'Tinney's Moonlight'	EHyt
'Tipperary Purple' (Prim)(30)	GEdr WGwG WPnP
'Tomato Red' (Prim)(30)	WCot
'Tony' (2)	WAbe WLin
tosaensis var. **brachycarpa** (24)	GFle
'Tournaig Pink' (4)	GGar
tournefortii new	GFle
'Tye Dye' **new**	GBri
'Val Horncastle' (dPrim)(30)	LRHS MBNS MBow MBri MDKP MFie MNrw MOne NBid NCGa NGHP NLar NWCA SIng SPer WLin

Valentine Victorians Group (Poly)(30)	MFie
veris (30) ♀H4	More than 30 suppliers
– hybrids (30)	SGar WLin
– 'Katy McSparron' (30/d)	CBgR CMea EBre MTed NCot WCot
§ – subsp. **macrocalyx** (30) **new**	NWCA
– orange-flowered **new**	WMoo
– red-flowered (30)	CM&M GFle NBid
– 'Sunset Shades' (30)	GCal NChi NGHP NJOw NLar WBea
vernalis	see *P. vulgaris*
verticillata (12)	MFie
§ **vialii** (17) ♀H4	More than 30 suppliers
Victorian shades (Poly)(30)	NPPs
§ **villosa** (2)	GCrs GFle GTou
– var. **cottica**	see *P. villosa*
Violet Victorians Group (Poly)(30)	CSWP MFie
viscosa All.	see *P. latifolia*
§ × **vochinensis** (2)	CFee CLyd EPot ITim NWCA SUsu
§ **vulgaris** (Prim) (30) ♀H4	More than 30 suppliers
– **alba** (30)	CRow NSla WAbe WBrk
– 'Alba Plena' (Prim)(30)	CRow GAbr GBuc GGar IBlr IGor
– 'Alex Brenton' (d)	LHop
– green-flowered	see *P. vulgaris* 'Viridis'
– 'Greyshot' **new**	NBir
§ – 'Lilacina Plena' (dPrim)(30)	ECGP ENot EPfP GAbr IBlr ITim MBNS MBow MNrw MRav NCGa NCot NHol SPer WCAu WCom WGwG
§ – subsp. **sibthorpii** (Prim)(30) ♀H4	CMHG CSam ENot ETow GAbr GTou ITim LLWP LRHS MBro MHer MRav MWgw NBro NChi NGHP NMyG NPPs NWCA SBla SRms WAbe WCom WEas WHil WOut
– – HH&K 337	GFle
§ – 'Viridis' (Prim)(30)	CRow IBlr NPar
walshii new	WLin
waltonii (26)	CPla EBee GCrs GEdr GFle GMac MNrw NHol
'Wanda' (Prim)(30) ♀H4	CBcs CRow CStu CTri GAbr LLWP LRHS NBid NSti NVic SBla SMer SPer SRms WBrk WCFE WCom WCot WEas WFar WTin
Wanda Group (Prim)(30)	CNic EBre NGar NJOw WGwG
– pale mauve (30)	WGwG
'Wanda Hose-in-hose' (Prim)(30)(d)	EMon GAbr MMHG NBir NChi NGar WCot WHer
'Wanda Jack in the Green' (Prim)(30)	CBgR CRow MLLN WCot WFar
wardii	see *P. munroi*
warshenewskiana (11)	CNic GEdr MDKP NHol NLAp NRya NWCA SIng WAbe WFar WGwG WHHs WPat
watsonii (17)	GCrs GGGa GTou NLAp SWat WAbe
'Wedgwood'	see *P.* × *pubescens* 'Wedgwood'
'Wharfedale Ballerina' (2) **new**	EHyt
'Wharfedale Bluebell' (2)	CLyd NBir WGwG
'Wharfedale Buttercup' (2)	NABC
'Wharfedale Butterfly' (2)	EHyt ITim NABC NHol
'Wharfedale Crusader' (2)	ITim NHol
'Wharfedale Gem' (*allionii* hybrid) (2)	GNor ITim MFie NGar NHol NLAp NRya WAbe
'Wharfedale Ling' (*allionii* hybrid) (2)	CGra CPBP CStu EHyt EPot MFie NHol NRya WLin
'Wharfedale Sunshine' (2) **new**	EHyt MFie

'Wharfedale Superb'   ITim MFie NHol NLAp WLin
  (*allionii* hybrid) (2)
'Wharfedale Village' (2)   CLyd GNor ITim NABC NHol
  WGwG
'White Linda Pope' (2)   CLyd NGar
'White Wanda' (Prim)(30)   CRow NCGa
'White Waves' (*allionii*   EHyt ITim
  hybrid) (2)
whitei (21)   GCrs MDun
§ - 'Sherriff's Variety' (21)   GCrs IBlr
wigramiana (28)   WAbe
wilsonii (4)   CHid CMHG CPla CTri EBee EChP
  EPot GBuc GFle LDai MNrw MOne
  NDlv NWCA SWat WAbe WBVN
  WHer WHoo WLin
§ - var. *anisodora* (4)   CNic CPla EBee GCrs GFle ITim
  MFie NLAp WGwG
- var. *anisodora*   see *P.* x *anisodoxa*
  x *prolifera*
'Windrush'   see *P.* x *berninae* 'Windrush'
'Windward Blue'   SBla
'Winter White'   see *P.* 'Gigha'
'Wisley Crimson'   see *P.* 'Wisley Red'
§ 'Wisley Red' (Prim)(30)   CElw
wollastonii (28)   GCrs WAbe
'Woodland Blue'   NWoo
wulfeniana (2)   CGra GCrs GFle MFie WAbe
xanthobasis (18)   GIBF
yargongensis   see *P. munroi* subsp. *yargongensis*
§ *yuparensis* (11)   EBee GFle WAbe

Prinsepia (Rosaceae)

sinensis   CBcs CFee CMCN ESim GBin GEil
  MBlu WBVN WBcn WPic WSHC
utilis   CTrG

Pritchardia (Arecaceae)

hillebrandii **new**   WMul

Pritzelago (Brassicaceae)

alpina   CNic NJOw NWCA WPat

Prostanthera (Lamiaceae)

aspalathoides   EBee ECou EWes SOWG WCot
'Badja Peak'   CPom WAbe
baxteri   ECou
chlorantha   SOWG
cuneata ♀H4   More than 30 suppliers
- 'Alpine Gold'   CMHG CWSG EBee WFar
- Kew form   CDul CPLG
§ *incisa*   CPLG CTbh CTrC CTrw SHDw
  WLeb
lasianthos   CBcs CDoC CHll ECou EWes LRHS
  SAga SHDw SOWG
- var. *subcoriacea*   CPLG CPle CRHN
magnifica **new**   SOWG
'Mauve Mantle'   SOWG
melissifolia   CArn CPLG ECre ESlt WSel
§ - var. *parvifolia*   CTrw EBee ECre LPhx WAbe WSHC
nivea   ECou
ovalifolia ♀H2   ECou NPPs
'Poorinda Ballerina'   CDoC CFwr CPLG CTbh CWSG
  EBee ECou EMan EOrc ESlt GKir
  LHop LRHS MCCP MDun MGos
  SMur SOWG SPer WFar WGwG
  WLeb
rotundifolia ♀H2   CAbb CBcs CBrm CDul CFwr
  CHEx CPle CSBt CSev CTrG CTri
  CWSG EBee EOHP ERea MWgw
  NGHP SEND SOWG SPer WLeb
- 'Chelsea Girl'   see *P. rotundifolia* 'Rosea'
§ - 'Rosea' ♀H2   CSBt CTrC CTrG EBee ECou ERea
  GGar LHop MLan NGHP SLon
  WGwG

* *scheelii*   SOWG
scutellarioides   ECou
  'Lavender Lady'
walteri   CBrm CDoC ECou

Protea ✿ (Proteaceae)

aurea   CHEx EShb
burchellii   SPlb
caffra **new**   CTrC IDee
coronata   CTrC SPlb
cynaroides   CBcs CCtw CHEx CTrC IDee
  SOWG SPlb
dracomontana   SPlb
effusa **new**   SPlb
eximia   CDoC CTrC
grandiceps   SPlb
lacticolor   SPlb
laurifolia   CDoC CTrC SPlb
magnifica **new**   CTrC
neriifolia   CTrC
  'Snowcrest' **new**
obtusifolia   SPlb
'Pink Ice'   CTrC
subvestita   CTrC SIgm
susannae   CDoC CTrC SPlb
venusta **new**   CTrC

Prumnopitys (Podocarpaceae)

§ *andina*   WFar
elegans   see *P. andina*
§ *taxifolia*   CTrC ECou

Prunella (Lamiaceae)

§ *grandiflora*   CArn EBee ECha EFer GBar GKir
  MWat SMac SPet SWat WBrE
  WCHb WFar WMoo WPGP WShp
  WWpP WWye
- 'Alba'   CElw CSBt EBee ECha EPfP EPyc
  GKir LPio LSpr MRav MWgw NBid
  NGHP NGdn NLar NOrc SPer SPla
  WCAu WCHb WMnd WShp WTin
  WWpP
- 'Blue Loveliness'   EMan GAbr GTou WCHb WCom
- 'Carminea'   EBee MNrw SPer
- light blue-flowered   NLar WMoo
- 'Little Red Riding Hood'   see *P. grandiflora* 'Rotkäppchen'
- 'Loveliness' ♀H4   CDoC EBee EBre ECha ECtt EGra
  EPar GKir LAst LSpr MRav MTis
  MWgw NBro NGdn NSti NVic
  SCro SOkh SPer SPla SPlb SPoG
  WCAu WFar WMnd WTin WWin
  Llck NLar SMac SWal WCHb
- 'Pagoda'   WMoo WSSM
- 'Pink Loveliness'   CElw CMCo CSBt EBre ENot EPar
  GTou LRHS MWgw NArg SRms
  WCHb WCom WFar WWin WWpP
- *rosea*   CSBt EBee EPfP MWat NFla WOut
§ - 'Rotkäppchen'   ECtt MNrw WMoo
- 'Rubra'   NGHP NLar WMoo WPer
- 'Senior' **new**   EBee
- 'White Loveliness'   CElw CTri EBee EBre EPar LRHS
  WCom WFar WPer WRHF WWin
  WWye
hispida **new**   WOut
hyssopifolia   EBee XPep
incisa   see *P. vulgaris*
* 'Inshriach Ruby'   NBir WCHb
laciniata   CMCo WCHb
x *pinnatifida* **new**   EBee
§ *vulgaris*   CAgr CArn CRWN GAbr GBar
  GPoy MBow MGol MHer MSal
  NLan NMir NSco NSti SECG WCHb
  WHbs WHer WWye
- 'Gleam' (v)   EBee EPPr WCot

- var. **leucantha** — GBar WHer
- var. **rubrifolia** — WRha
- 'Ruth Wainwright' (v) — WCHb
x **webbiana** — see *P. grandiflora*

Prunus ✿ (*Rosaceae*)

'Accolade' ♀H4 — More than 30 suppliers
§ 'Amanogawa' ♀H4 — More than 30 suppliers
x **amygdalopersica** — ESim
 'Ingrid' (F)
- 'Pollardii' — EBee ENot MAsh
- 'Robijn' (F) — LBuc
- 'Spring Glow' — CDoC CDul LRHS MBri
amygdalus — see *P. dulcis*
armeniaca 'Alfred' (F) — CTho EMui ERea GTwe SDea SKee SPer
- 'Blenheim' (F) — ERea
- 'Bredase' (F) — SDea
- 'Early Moorpark' (F) — CAgr CTri EPfP ERea GBon GTwe LRHS MBri SDea SFam
- 'Farmingdale' (F) — ERea SDea
- 'Garden Aprigold' (F) — EMui ENot
- 'Goldcot' (F) — ERea SDea
- 'Golden Glow' (F) — CTri GTwe LRHS MCoo SKee
- 'Harglow' (F) **new** — ERea
- 'Hemskirke' (F) — ERea SKee
- 'Hongaarse' (F) — SDea
- 'Isabella' (F) **new** — MBri SPoG
- 'Moorpark' (F) ♀H3 — CEnd CSBt CWib EMui ENot ERea GKir GTwe LBuc MGos NRog SDea SHBN SKee SPer WStI
- 'New Large Early' (F) — ERea GTwe SDea SEND SKee WBVN
- 'Tomcot' (F) **new** — MBri SPoG
- 'Tross Orange' (F) — SDea
'Asano' — see *P.* 'Geraldinae'
avium ♀H4 — CBcs CCVT CDul CLnd CRWN CSBt CWib EBee ECrN ENot EPfP GIBF GKir LBuc LPan MBar MGos MRav MSwo NBee NWea SFam SHBN SKee SPer WDin WHar WMoo WMou WOrn
- 'Amber Heart' (F) — SKee
- 'Bigarreau Gaucher' (F) — SHBN SKee
§ - 'Bigarreau Napoléon' (F) — GTwe MGos SFam SHBN SKee
- 'Birchenhayes' — see *P. avium* 'Early Birchenhayes'
- 'Black Eagle' (F) — CTho
- 'Black Glory' (F) — SKee
- 'Black Tartarian' (F) — SKee
- 'Bottlers' — see *P. avium* 'Preserving'
- 'Bradbourne Black' (F) — SKee
- 'Bullion' (F) — CEnd CTho
- 'Burcombe' (F) — CEnd CTho
- Celeste — COtt CWib GTwe LRHS MBri SDea
 = 'Sumpaca'PBR — (D)SKee
- 'Cherokee' — see *P. avium* 'Lapins'
- 'Colney' (F) — GTwe SFam SKee
- 'Dun' (F) — CTho
§ - 'Early Birchenhayes' (F) — CEnd CTho
- 'Early Rivers' (F) — CSBt CWib ENot GTwe LRHS SDea SHBN SKee
- 'Elton Heart' (F) — CTho
- 'Fice' (F) — CEnd CTho
- 'Florence' (F) — SKee
- 'Governor Wood' (F) — CWib GTwe
- 'Grandiflora' — see *P. avium* 'Plena'
- 'Greenstem Black' (F) — CTho
- 'Hannaford' (D/C) — CTho
- 'Hertford' (F) — SFam
- 'Inga' (F) — SFam SKee
- 'Ironsides' (F) — SKee
- 'Kentish Red' (F) — CTho
§ - 'Lapins' (F) — CAgr CTho EMui GTwe LRHS SDea SFam SKee WHar WOrn

- 'May Duke' — see *P.* x *gondouinii* 'May Duke'
- 'Merchant' (F) ♀H4 — GTwe SKee
- 'Merpet' (F) — GTwe
- 'Merton Crane' (F) — SKee
- 'Merton Favourite' (F) — SKee
- 'Merton Glory' (F) — CSBt EMui ENot GTwe MGos SFam SKee
- 'Merton Late' (F) — SKee
- 'Merton Marvel' (F) — SKee
- 'Merton Premier' (F) — SKee
- 'Merton Reward' — see *P.* x *gondouinii* 'Merton Reward'
- 'Napoléon' — see *P. avium* 'Bigarreau Napoléon'
- 'Newstar' (F) — EMui
- 'Noble' (F) **new** — SKee
- 'Noir de Guben' (F) — GTwe SKee
- 'Noir de Meched' (D) — SKee
- 'Nutberry Black' (F) — SKee
- 'Old Black Heart' (F) — SKee
§ - 'Plena' (d) ♀H4 — CBcs CCVT CDul CLnd CSBt CTho CWSG EBee ECrN ELan ENot EPfP GKir LBuc LPan LRHS MGos MRav MSwo NWea SFam SKee SPer WDin WFar WHar WOrn
§ - 'Preserving' (F) — CTho
- 'Ronald's Heart' (F) — SKee
- 'Roundel Heart' (F) — SKee
- 'Sasha' (F) — GTwe
- 'Small Black' (F) — CTho
- 'Starkrimson' (F) — GTwe
- 'Stella' (F) ♀H4 — CEnd CMac CTri CWSG CWib EMui EPfP ERea EWTr GBon GKir GTwe LBuc LRHS MBri MGos MRav NBee NRog SDea SFam SHBN SKee SPer WHar WOrn WStI
- 'Stella Compact' (F) — COtt CWib ENot MBri SDea SKee WHar
- 'Summer Sun' (D) — CTho CTri EMui GTwe MBri MCoo SCoo SDea SKee
- 'Summit' (F) — SHBN SKee
- 'Sunburst' (F) — CCVT CEnd CTho CTri EMui GTwe LBuc LRHS MBri SCoo SDea SFam SKee WOrn
- 'Sylvia' (F) — SKee
- 'Turkish Black' (F) — SKee
- 'Upright' (F) — CTho
- 'Van' (F) — ENot GTwe SKee
- 'Vega' (F) — EMui GTwe SFam
- 'Waterloo' (F) — CTho SKee
- 'White Heart' (F) — CTho CWib SKee
- 'Wildstar' **new** — CEnd
* 'Beni-no-dora' — SMur
* 'Beni-yutaka' — CEnd LBuc LRHS MAsh SKee SLim
 'Blaze ' — see *P. cerasifera* 'Nigra'
x **blireana** (d) ♀H4 — CDoC CDul CEnd CTri EBee ENot EPfP LPan LRHS MBar MBri MRav MWat NPSI SBLw SCoo SKee SPer WHar
- 'Moseri' (d) **new** — SBLw
 'Blushing Bride' — see *P.* 'Shôgetsu'
cerasifera — CAgr CRWN CTri ECrN GKir LBuc NWea SKee SPer WDin WMou
- 'Cherry Plum' (F) — CTri EMui SDea SKee
- 'Crimson Dwarf' — GKir LPan
- 'Hessei' (v) — CEnd EBee LRHS MAsh MBri MDun MGos MRav SLim
§ - Mýrobalan Group (F) — MRav SDea SKee
§ - 'Nigra' ♀H4 — More than 30 suppliers
§ - 'Pendula' — CTho ECrN
§ - 'Pissardii' — CWib EBre ECrN GKir LPan MAsh MBar MRav NBea NFor NWea SFam SLim WFar
* - 'Princess' — CEnd CWSG EBee EMui SKee SLim
- 'Rosea' — LRHS MBri

– 'Spring Glow'	CDul CEnd EBee EGra EPfP LRHS MAsh SKee WOrn
§ – 'Woodii'	SBLw
cerasus	SKee
'Montmorency' (F)	
– 'Morello' (C) ♀H4	CAgr CCVT CMac CSBt CTho CTri CWSG CWib EBee EBre EMui ENot EPfP GBon GKir GTwe LBuc LRHS MBri MGos NBee NRog SDea SFam SHBN SKee SPer WOrn
– 'Nabella' (F)	SKee
– 'Rhexii' (d)	CDul ECrN GKir MAsh MGos SPer
– 'Wye Morello' (F)	SKee
'Cheal's Weeping'	see *P.* 'Kiku-shidare-zakura'
'Chocolate Ice' **new**	LRHS
§ 'Chôshû-hizakura'	GKir SPer
§ × **cistena** ♀H4	CBcs CSBt CWSG EBee EBre ELan ENot EPfP GKir LRHS MBri MDun MGos NBee NBlu SBLw SHBN SLim SPer SPla WBVN WDin
'Crimson Dwarf'	see *P.* × *cistena*
'Collingwood Ingram'	GKir LRHS SKee
conradinae	see *P. hirtipes*
davidiana	CTho SPlb
domestica 'Allgroves Superb' (D)	ERea
– 'Angelina Burdett' (D)	ERea GTwe NRog SDea SKee
– 'Anna Späth' (C/D)	SKee
– 'Ariel' (C/D) **new**	SDea SKee
– 'Autumn Compote' (C)	SKee
– 'Avalon' (D)	CCVT ECrN EMui GTwe SDea SKee
– 'Belgian Purple' (C)	SKee
– 'Belle de Louvain' (C)	CTho CTri ECrN ERea GTwe NRog SDea SKee
– 'Birchenhayes' (F)	CEnd
– 'Black Diamond'	see *P. salicina* 'Black Diamond'
– 'Blaisdon Red' (C)	CTho
– 'Blue Tit' (C/D) ♀H4	CTho EMui ERea GTwe SDea SKee
– 'Bonne de Bry' (D)	SKee
§ – 'Bountiful' (C)	ERea
– 'Brandy Gage' (C/D)	SKee
– 'Bryanston Gage' (D)	CTho SKee
– 'Burbank's Giant'	see *P. domestica* 'Giant Prune'
– 'Burcombe'	CEnd
– 'Bush' (C)	SKee
– 'Cambridge Gage' (D) ♀H4	CDoC CTho CTri CWib EMui EPfP ERea GBon GKir GTwe LRHS MBri MGos MWat NRog SCrf SDea SFam SHBN SKee SPer WOrn WStI
– 'Chrislin' (F)	CTho
– 'Coe's Golden Drop' (D)	CDoC CTho ECrN EMui ERea GKir GTwe LRHS MGos MRav SCoo SDea SFam SKee
– 'Count Althann's Gage' (D)	ERea GTwe NRog SDea SFam SKee
– 'Cox's Emperor' (C)	SKee
– 'Crimson Drop' (D)	ERea SKee
– 'Cropper'	see *P. domestica* 'Laxton's Cropper'
– 'Curlew' (C)	SDea
– 'Czar' (C) ♀H4	CAgr CDoC CSBt CTri CWib EBre ECrN EMui EPfP GKir GTwe LBuc LRHS MGos NPri NRog NWea SDea SFam SKee SPer WOrn
– 'Delicious'	see *P. domestica* 'Laxton's Delicious'
– 'Denniston's Superb'	see *P. domestica* 'Imperial Gage'
– 'Diamond' (C)	SKee
– 'Dittisham Black' (C)	CTho
– 'Dittisham Ploughman' (C)	CTho SKee
– 'Dunster Plum' (F)	CTho CTri CWSG CWib
– 'Early Laxton' (C/D) ♀H4	ERea GTwe SDea SFam SKee

– 'Early Prolific'	see *P. domestica* 'Rivers's Early Prolific'
– 'Early Rivers'	see *P. domestica* 'Rivers's Early Prolific'
– 'Early Transparent Gage' (C/D)	CSBt CTho CTri EMui ERea GTwe LBuc MCoo SDea SFam SKee SPer
– 'Early Victoria' (C/D)	SDea
– 'Edwards' (C/D) ♀H4	CTri CWib ECrN GTwe NRog SDea SFam SKee
– 'Excalibur' (D)	ECrN GTwe SDea SKee
§ – 'German Prune Group' (C)	CTho SKee
§ – 'Giant Prune' (C)	CWib ECrN GTwe NRog SDea SKee
I – 'Godshill Big Sloe' (F)	SDea
– 'Godshill Blue' (C)	SDea
– 'Godshill Minigage' (F)	SDea
– 'Golden Transparent' (D)	CTho ERea GTwe NRog SFam SKee
– 'Goldfinch' (D)	GTwe NRog SKee
– Green Gage Group	see *P. domestica* Reine-Claude Group
– – 'Old Green Gage'	see *P. domestica* (Reine-Claude Group) 'Reine-Claude Vraie'
– 'Grey Plum' (F)	CTho
– 'Grove's Late Victoria' (C/D)	SKee
– 'Guthrie's Late Green' (D)	SKee
– 'Herman' (C/D)	ECrN GTwe LBuc LRHS MBri SDea SKee
– 'Heron' (F)	ECrN GTwe SKee
– 'Impérial Epineuse' (D)	SKee
§ – 'Imperial Gage' (C/D) ♀H4	CSBt CTho CTri CWib EMui ERea GTwe SDea SFam SKee SPoG WBVN WOrn
– 'Jan James' (F)	CEnd
– 'Jefferson' (D) ♀H4	CAgr ECrN EMui ERea GTwe NRog SDea SFam SKee
* – 'Jubilaeum' (D)	EMui GTwe MBri SKee
– 'Kea' (C)	CTho SKee
– 'Kirke's' (D)	CTho CTri ECrN ERea GTwe SDea SFam SKee WOrn
– 'Landkey Yellow' (F)	CTho
– 'Langley Gage' **new**	SDea
– 'Late Muscatelle' (D)	ERea SKee
– 'Laxton's Bountiful'	see *P. domestica* 'Bountiful'
§ – 'Laxton's Cropper' (C)	CTri GTwe NRog SKee
§ – 'Laxton's Delicious' (D)	GTwe SKee
– 'Laxton's Delight' (D) ♀H4	GTwe
– 'Laxton's Gage' (D)	SDea
– 'Manaccan' (C)	CTho
– 'Marjorie's Seedling' (C) ♀H4	CAgr CDoC CSBt CTho CTri CWib EBre ECrN EMui ERea EWTr GBon GTwe LBuc LRHS MGos MWat NPri SDea SEND SFam SKee SPer WOrn
– 'McLaughlin' (D)	SKee
– 'Merton Gem' (C/D)	GTwe SFam SKee
– 'Monarch' (C)	GTwe SKee
– 'Olympia' (C/D)	SKee
– 'Ontario' (C/D)	SKee
– 'Opal' (D) ♀H4	CAgr CDoC CWSG CWib ECrN EMui EPfP ERea GTwe LBuc MBri MGos MLan MWat NWea SDea SEND SFam SKee WOrn
– 'Orleans' (C)	SKee
– 'Oullins Gage' (C/D) ♀H4	CAgr CDoC CSBt CTri CWib ECrN EMui ENot EPfP ERea GBon GKir GTwe LBuc MBri MRav NRog SDea SFam SKee SPer WOrn
– 'Pershore' (C) ♀H4	CTho CWib ECrN ERea GTwe MBri NRog SDea SFam SKee WOrn WStI

'Kursar' ♀H4	CDul CLnd COtt CSBt CTho CTri EBee EMui EPfP GKir LRHS MAsh MBri NRog NWea SCoo SFam SKee SLim WOrn
laurocerasus ♀H4	CBcs CCVT CChe CDul CWSG EBee EBre ECrN ELan EPfP GKir LPan MRav MWat NBea NFor NPSI NWea SEND SPer SReu WFar WMoo WMou WStI WWeb
I – 'Albomaculata'	WBcn
– 'Angustifolia'	WDin
– 'Aureovariegata'	see *P. laurocerasus* 'Taff's Golden Gleam'
– 'Camelliifolia'	CTri EPla MBlu WBcn WCFE WDin WHCG WPGP
§ – 'Castlewellan' (v)	CBot CDoC CPLG CTri CTrw CWib EBee EGra EPfP EPla ISea LAst MBar MGos MSwo NBea NPro SDix SEND SPer SSta WDin WFar WHar WLeb WMoo
– 'Caucasica'	MGos
– 'Cherry Brandy'	ENot MRav SPer WBcn WCot WDin WStI
– Etna = 'Anbri'PBR	EBee ENot EPfP LRHS MBri MGos MRav NPri
– 'Golden Splash'	WBcn
– 'Green Marble' (v)	CTri EBee EPAt WSHC
– 'Herbergii'	ECrN WWeb
§ – 'Latifolia'	CHEx EPla GKir SArc SLPl SMad
§ – Low 'n' Green = 'Interlo'	EBee ENot MRav
– 'Magnoliifolia'	see *P. laurocerasus* 'Latifolia'
– 'Mano'	EMil MGos NBlu
– 'Marbled White'	see *P. laurocerasus* 'Castlewellan'
– 'Mischeana'	SLPl
– 'Mount Vernon'	EBee MBar MGos WBcn WDin
– 'Novita' **new**	EMil
– 'Otinii'	CHEx
– 'Otto Luyken' ♀H4	More than 30 suppliers
– Renault Ace = 'Renlau'	EBee ENot MGos MRav
– 'Reynvaanii'	LRHS MBri WBcn
– 'Rotundifolia'	CDoC CSBt CTri CWib EBee ELan EMil ENot GKir LBuc LPan LRHS MBNS MBar MBri MGos MSwo NBea NBee NBlu NWea SLim SRms STop SWvt WDin WHar WMoo WTel
– 'Schipkaensis'	SLPl SPer
§ – 'Taff's Golden Gleam' (v)	SMad WBcn WCot
– 'Van Nes'	EBee EMil WDin
– 'Variegata' misapplied	see *P. laurocerasus* 'Castlewellan' (v)
– 'Variegata' ambig. (v)	CWib EPla MBNS MGos SRms
– 'Zabeliana'	CDoC CDul CTri EBee ECrN ENot EPfP GKir IBal MBar MGos MSwo NWea SHBN SPer SRms WDin WFar WTel WWin
litigiosa	LRHS MBri SKee
* *longipedunculata*	LRHS
lusitanica ♀H4	More than 30 suppliers
– subsp. *azorica*	CDoC MRav WFar WPGP
– 'Myrtifolia'	EBee EPfP EPla GKir LAst LRHS MBri MLLN MRav SMad SWvt WCFE WDin WGer WPGP
– 'Variegata' (v)	More than 30 suppliers
maackii	CTho ECrN EPfP GIBF GKir MDun SBLw SEND SSpi WDin
– 'Amber Beauty'	CDoC CDul CEnd EPfP GKir LRHS MRav SBLw WDin
mahaleb	CTho
mandshurica	GIBF
'Matsumae-beni-murasaki'	GKir
'Matsumae-hana-gasa'	MBri

maximowiczii	GIBF
'Mount Fuji'	see *P.* 'Shirotae'
mume	CMCN WDin WNor
– 'Alboplena'	CChe
§ – 'Beni-chidori'	CWib ECrN EPfP LBuc LRHS MAsh MBlu MBri MGos NBea SHBN SLim SPoG SSpi SSta WPGP
I – 'Beni-shidori'	see *P. mume* 'Beni-chidori'
* – 'Ken Kyo'	LRHS
* – 'Kyo Koh'	LRHS
§ – 'Omoi-no-mama' (d)	CEnd LRHS MMHG
– 'Omoi-no-wac'	see *P. mume* 'Omoi-no-mama'
– 'Pendula'	LRHS
– 'Yae-kankobane' (d)	LRHS
myrobalana	see *P. cerasifera* Myrobalan Group
nipponica var.	CBcs
– *kurilensis*	GKir LPan MAsh MBri MGos
'Brilliant'	
– – 'Ruby'	CEnd GKir LRHS MAsh MBri MGos NBee NBlu SMur WFar
– – 'Spring Joy'	LRHS
'Okame' ♀H4	CLnd CSam CTho EBee EBre ENot EPfP GKir LRHS MAsh MBri MGos MRav NBlu NWea SCoo SKee SLim SPer WFar WOrn
* 'Okame Harlequin' **new**	SPoG
'Okumiyako' misapplied	see *Prunus* 'Shôgetsu'
padus	CCVT CDul CLnd CRWN CSBt CTri ECrN GIBF GKir LBuc MDun MGos MSwo NBea NBee NWea SBLw SSpi WDin WMou WOrn
– 'Albertii'	CTho LPan
– 'Colorata' ♀H4	CDoC CDul CEnd CMHG CSam CTho ECrN ELan GKir LBuc LPan MBri MDun MGos NBee SBLw SHBN SPer SSpi WDin WFar
– 'Dropmore'	EBee
– 'Grandiflora'	see *P. padus* 'Watereri'
– 'Plena' (d)	CTho
– 'Purple Queen'	CEnd CTho EBee ECrN ENot WStI
§ – 'Watereri' ♀H4	CBcs CCVT CDoC CDul CLnd CMCN CTho CTri CWib EBee ECrN ELan ENot EPfP EWTr GKir LPan LRHS MAsh MBri MGos NWea SBLw SCoo SHBN SKee SPer WDin WOrn
'Pandora' ♀H4	CBcs CLnd EBee ECrN ENot EPfP GKir LPan LRHS MAsh MBri MDun MRav MGos MWat NBea NBee NWea SBLw SCrf SEND SHBN SKee SPer WFar WOrn
§ *pendula* 'Pendula Rosea' ♀H4	CDoC CEnd CSBt CTri CWib ENot EPfP GKir LPan LRHS MAsh SBLw SPer WFar WOrn
§ – 'Pendula Rubra' ♀H4	CDoC CEnd CLnd COtt CSBt CWib EBee ECrN ENot EPfP GKir LRHS MBri MGos MSwo SCoo SFam SHBN SLim SPer SPoG SFam SHBN SLim SPer
§ – 'Stellata'	LRHS MBri SPer
persica 'Amsden June' (F)	ERea GTwe SDea SFam SKee
– 'Bellegarde' (F)	ERea GTwe SDea SFam SKee
– 'Bonanza' (F)	EMil EMui ERea
– 'Doctor Hogg' (F)	SDea
– 'Duke of York' (F) ♀H3	CTri ERea GTwe LRHS SDea SFam SKee WOrn
– 'Dymond' (F)	ERea
– 'Flat China' (F)	ERea
– 'Foliis Rubris' (F)	CDul WPGP
– 'Francis' (F)	SKee
– 'Garden Anny' (F)	EMil ERea LRHS
– 'Garden Lady' (F)	EMui ERea GTwe SKee
– 'Hale's Early' (F)	ENot ERea GTwe SEND SFam SKee SPer

– 'Hylands' (F)	SDea
– 'Melred'	MGos
– 'Melred Weeping' **new**	SBLw
– 'Natalia' (F)	SDea
– var. *nectarina* Crimson Gold (F)	SDea
– – 'Early Gem' (F)	ERea SDea
– – 'Early Rivers' (F) ♀H3	CMac EMui ERea GTwe NRog SDea SFam
– – 'Elruge' (F)	ERea GTwe SDea SEND SFam
– – 'Fantasia' (F)	ERea SDea
– – 'Fire Gold' (F)	SDea
– – 'Garden Beauty' (F/d)	EMui ENot
– – 'Humboldt' (F)	ERea GTwe SDea SKee
– – 'John Rivers' (F)	ERea GTwe SDea SKee
– – 'Lord Napier' (F) ♀H3	CAgr CDoC CSBt CWSG CWib EMui ERea GKir LBuc LRHS MGos SDea SEND SFam SKee SPer WBVN WStI
– – 'Nectared' (F)	CWib GTwe
– – 'Nectarella' (F)	EMui ERea GTwe LRHS SKee
– – 'Pineapple' (F)	CTri ERea GTwe LRHS SDea SFam SKee
– – 'Ruby Gold' (F)	GKir SDea
– – 'Terrace Ruby' (F)	ENot GKir
– – 'Peregrine' (F) ♀H3	CAgr CMac CSBt CTri CWSG CWib EMui ENot EPfP ERea GBon GKir GTwe LBuc LRHS MBri MGos NRog SDea SFam SHBN SKee SPer WOrn WStI
– 'Purpurea'	EMui
– 'Red Haven' (F)	GTwe SDea SKee
– 'Reliance' (F)	SDea
– 'Robin Redbreast' (F)	SDea
– 'Rochester' (F) ♀H3	CAgr CWSG EMui ENot ERea GBon GKir GTwe LRHS MBri SDea SFam SKee SPer SPoG WStI
– 'Royal George' (F)	GTwe NRog SFam
– 'Sagami-shidare'	LRHS
– 'Saturne' (F)	EMui LRHS SKee
– 'Springtime' (F)	ERea SDea
– 'Terrace Amber'	EMui ENot
– 'Terrace Garnet'	ENot
– 'Weeping Flame' (F)	LRHS
– 'White Cascade'	LRHS
'Pink Perfection' ♀H4	CBcs CDoC CDul CLnd CSBt CWSG CWib EBee EBre ECrN ENot EPfP LPan LRHS MBri NBee SFam SHBN SKee SPer WDin WFar WOrn
'Pink Shell' ♀H4	CLnd CTho EBee EPfP LRHS MAsh MBri NRog SFam SKee WOrn WStI
pissardii	see *P. cerasifera* 'Pissardii'
'Pissardii Nigra'	see *P. cerasifera* 'Nigra'
prostrata	WPat
* – 'Anita Kistler'	ECho
* – var. *discolor*	WNor
pseudocerasus 'Cantabrigiensis'	ECrN
pumila var. *depressa*	EMil MBar MBlu MRav NLar NPro
'Royal Burgundy'	CEnd CWSG EBee EMil GKir LRHS MAsh MBri MDun MGos MWat NBee SCoo SKee SLim SPer WGer WOrn
rufa	CLnd CPMA CTho MDun SCoo SSpi
sachalinensis	GIBF
salicina	GIBF
– 'Beauty' **new**	ERea
§ – 'Black Diamond' (F)	SDea
– 'Methley' (D)	ECrN ERea ESim
– 'Satsuma' (F)	ERea
– 'Shiro' (D)	ERea
sargentii ♀H4	More than 30 suppliers
– 'Charles Sargent'	GKir
– 'Columnaris'	GKir LRHS
– 'Rancho'	CLnd ENot SLPl WOrn
schmittii	CLnd EBee ECrN ENot MAsh SKee SPer
'Sekiyama'	see *P.* 'Kanzan'
serotina	CDul SBLw
§ *serrula* ♀H4	More than 30 suppliers
– Branklyn form	GKir MBri
– Dorothy Clive form	GKir LRHS MDun
§ – 'Mahogany Lustre'	CLnd
– var. *tibetica*	see *P. serrula*
serrula x *serrulata*	CBcs CTho
serrulata	ENot
– 'Erecta'	see *P.* 'Amanogawa'
– 'Grandiflora'	see *P.* 'Ukon'
– 'Longipes'	see *Prunus* 'Shôgetsu'
– 'Miyako' misapplied	see *Prunus* 'Shôgetsu'
N – var. *pubescens*	see *P. verecunda*
– 'Rosea'	see *P.* 'Kiku-shidare-zakura'
– var. *spontanea*	see *P. jamasakura*
'Shidare-zakura'	see *P.* 'Kiku-shidare-zakura'
'Shimizu-zakura'	see *Prunus* 'Shôgetsu'
'Shirofugen' ♀H4	CBcs CDoC CDul CLnd CMCN CSBt CTho CWib EBee ECrN EMil ENot EPfP GKir LBuc LPan LRHS MAsh MBri MRav MWat NBee SCrf SFam SKee SPer WDin WOrn
§ 'Shirotae' ♀H4	More than 30 suppliers
§ 'Shôgetsu' ♀H4	CBcs CDul CEnd CLnd CSBt CTho ECrN ELan EPfP GKir LPan LRHS MAsh MBri SFam SHBN SKee SLim SPer WDin
'Shosar'	CEnd CLnd CWib ECrN GKir LRHS MAsh MBri SKee SPer
'Snow Goose'	CDoC EBee GKir LRHS
'Snow Showers'	CEnd CWSG EMui GKir LRHS MAsh MBri MDun NWea SKee SPer WGer WGor
spinosa	CCVT CDoC CDul CRWN CTri ECrN ENot EPfP LBuc LRHS MBar MBlu MBri NBee NWea SPer WDin WFar WMou WNor XPep
– 'Plena' (d)	CEnd CTho MBlu
– 'Purpurea'	MBlu WBcn WDin WHCG WMou WPat
§ 'Spire' ♀H4	CDoC CDul CLnd CMCN CSBt CTho CWib EBee ECrN ENot EPfP GKir LBuc LPan LRHS MAsh MGos MRav MSwo NWea SHBN SKee SPer WDin WFar WOrn
x *subhirtella*	WNor
– 'Autumnalis' ♀H4	More than 30 suppliers
– 'Autumnalis Rosea' ♀H4	More than 30 suppliers
§ – 'Dahlem'	LRHS
– 'Fukubana'	CLnd CTho EBee GKir LPan LRHS MAsh MBri SBLw SCoo
– 'Pendula' hort.	see *P. pendula* 'Pendula Rosea'
– 'Pendula Plena Rosea' (d) **new**	SBLw
– 'Pendula Rubra'	see *P. pendula* 'Pendula Rubra'
– 'Plena'	see *P.* x *subhirtella* 'Dahlem'
N – 'Rosea'	CLnd GKir MRav WBVN
– 'Stellata'	see *P. pendula* 'Stellata'
'Sunset Boulevard'	GKir LRHS
'Taihaku' ♀H4	More than 30 suppliers
'Taki-nioi'	ECrN NWea
'Taoyame'	CLnd LRHS
tenella	CBcs ECrN ELan WCot
– 'Fire Hill'	CPMA CSBt ELan EPfP GKir LRHS MBar MBri MGos NBlu SBLw SHBN SKee SPer SSpi WCot WDin WOrn WPat
tibetica	see *P. serrula*

tomentosa	CRez ECrN WBVN
§ 'Trailblazer' (C/D)	CEnd CLnd CSBt CTho ECrN LPan MGos NWea SBLw SKee WStI
triloba	CBcs CSBt CTri ECrN EMil GIBF LBuc LPan LRHS NBee NBlu NWea SBLw SHBN SKee WDin
- 'Multiplex' (d)	EBre ENot LRHS MGos MRav NPri SPer SRms
- Rosemund = 'Korros'	LRHS MGos
§ 'Ukon' ♀H4	CBcs CDoC CDul CLnd CMCN CTho CTri ECrN ENot EPfP GKir LBuc LRHS MAsh MBar MBri MGos MRav NBee NWea SFam SHBN SKee SPer WDin WFar WOrn WStI
'Umineko'	CDoC CLnd EBee ECrN ENot GKir MGos SPer WDin WMoo
§ *verecunda*	CDoC CLnd NWea
- 'Autumn Glory'	CTho NBea
virginiana 'Schubert'	CDoC CDul CLnd EBee ECrN ENot LPan SBLw WFar WOrn
'White Cloud' **new**	CTho
yamadae	see *P. incisa* f. *yamadae*
§ x *yedoensis* ♀H4	CLnd CMCN CSBt CSam CTho CTri EBee ECrN ENot EPfP NWea SBLw SFam SKee SLim SPer WDin WLow WOrn
- 'Ivensii'	CBcs CDul CSBt CTri CWib GKir LRHS MAsh MDun MGos NBee NRog SCoo SFam SHBN SKee WDin WStI
- 'Pendula'	see *P.* x *yedoensis* 'Shidare-yoshino'
- 'Perpendens'	see *P.* x *yedoensis* 'Shidare-yoshino'
- 'Shidare-yoshino'	CEnd CLnd EBee ECrN EPfP GKir LRHS MAsh MBar MBri MGos MRav MSwo MWat NWea SBLw SKee SLim SPer WOrn
- 'Tsubame'	LRHS
'Yoshino'	see *P.* x *yedoensis*
'Yoshino Pendula'	see *P.* x *yedoensis* 'Shidare-yoshino'

Pseuderanthemum (Acanthaceae)

seticalyx	ESlt

Pseudocydonia (Rosaceae)

§ *sinensis*	CBcs ECre

Pseudofumaria see *Corydalis*

Pseudolarix (Pinaceae)

§ *amabilis* ♀H4	CDoC CEnd CFil CMCN CTho EBre EHul EPfP GBin LCon MBar MBlu MBri NBlu SCoo SLim SPoG STre WNor
kaempferi	see *P. amabilis*

Pseudomuscari see *Muscari*

Pseudopanax ✿ (Araliaceae)

(Adiantifolius Group) 'Adiantifolius'	CBcs CHEx CTrC GQui IDee SMad
- 'Cyril Watson' ♀H1	CBcs CDoC CHEx
arboreus	CAbb CBcs CDoC CHEx CTrC LEdu
'Black Ruby' **new**	CBcs
chathamicus	CDoC CHEx SAPC SArc
crassifolius	CAbb CBcs CBot CBrP CTrC EAmu SAPC SArc SMad
- var. *trifoliolatus*	CHEx
davidii	CHEx SLon
discolor	ECou
ferox	CAbb CBcs CBrP CHEx EAmu IDee ITer LEdu SAPC SArc SMad SSpi
laetus	CAbb CHEx CTrC ECou IDee LEdu SAPC SArc

lessonii	CBcs CHEx ECou
- 'Gold Splash' (v) ♀H1	CBcs CHEx SEND
- hybrids	CHEx
'Linearifolius'	CHEx CTrC IDee LEdu
'Purpureus' ♀H1	CHEx
'Sabre'	CHEx SMad
'Trident'	CDoC CHEx CTrC LEdu

Pseudophegopteris (Thelypteridaceae)

levingei	EFer EMon

Pseudophoenix (Arecaceae)

* *nativo*	MBri

Pseudosasa (Poaceae)

amabilis misapplied	see *Arundinaria gigantea*
§ *amabilis* (McClure)	LPal SDry WFar
Keng f.	
§ *japonica* ♀H4	More than 30 suppliers
- 'Akebonosuji' (v)	EFul EPla MMoz MWht NMoo SDry WJun WNor WPGP
§ - var. *pleioblastoides*	EPla MWht SDry
- 'Tsutsumiana'	CDoC CFwr CHEx CPen EBee EPla ERod MMoz MWht NLar NMoo SDry WJun
orthotropa	see *Sinobambusa orthotropa*
owatarii	SDry
pleioblastoides	see *P. japonica* var. *pleioblastoides*
usawai	EPla WJun
viridula	NMoo

Pseudotsuga (Pinaceae)

§ *menziesii* ♀H4	CBcs CDoC CDul CLnd ECrN EPfP GKir LBuc LCon LLin LRHS MBar MBlu NWea WDin WMou
- 'Bhiela Lhota'	CKen
- 'Blue Wonder'	CKen
- 'Densa'	CKen
- 'Fastigiata'	CKen LCon
- 'Fletcheri'	CKen MBar SCoo
- var. *glauca*	LCon MBar
- 'Glauca Pendula'	MBar MBlu MGos
I - 'Gotelli's Pendula'	CKen
- 'Graceful Grace'	CKen
- 'Idaho Gem' **new**	CKen
- 'Julie'	CKen
- 'Knaphill'	NLar
- 'Little Jamie'	CKen MBar
- 'Little Jon'	SCoo
- 'Lohbrunner'	CKen
- 'McKenzie'	CKen
- 'Nana'	CKen
- 'Stairii'	CKen
taxifolia	see *P. menziesii*

Pseudowintera (Winteraceae)

§ *colorata*	CBcs CDoC CPLG CPla CTrw GCal GGar GKir IDee IMGH ISea MAsh MDun NRib SLon WCru WFar WFoF WPic
- 'Mount Congreve'	LRHS SSpi WGer

Psidium (Myrtaceae)

cattleyanum	see *P. littorale* var. *longipes*
guajava (F)	XBlo
littorale (F)	ERea
§ - var. *longipes* (F)	XBlo

Psilotum (Psilotaceae)

nudum	ECou

Psoralea (Papilionaceae)

bituminosa	WSHC XPep
- HH&K 174	CStr

glabra **new** — SPlb
glandulosa — CArn CFil LRav WDyG WPGP WSHC
oligophylla — SPlb
pinnata — CHEx CPLG CTrC CTrG IDee SSte

Psychotria (Rubiaceae)

capensis — EShb
carthagenensis — MGol
viridis — MGol

Ptelea (Rutaceae)

trifoliata — CBcs CDul CFil CLnd CMCN CTho CWib EBee ECrN EPfP EWTr GIBF IMGH MBlu SBLw SPer SRms SSpi WBVN WDin WFar WHCG WNor WOrn
- 'Aurea' ♀H4 — More than 30 suppliers

Pteracanthus see Strobilanthes

Pteridophyllum (Papaveraceae)

racemosum — EFEx GCrs WCru

Pteris (Pteridaceae)

angustipinna B&SWJ 6738 **new** — WCru
argyraea — MBri NMar
cretica ♀H1+3 — CHEx MBri SAPC SArc
- var. *albolineata* ♀H1 — GQui MBri SRms
- 'Childsii' — NMar
- 'Cristata' — MBri
- 'Gautheri' — MBri
- 'Parkeri' — MBri NMar
- 'Rivertoniana' — MBri
- 'Rowei' — MBri
- 'Wimsettii' — MBri
ensiformis — MBri
* - 'Arguta' — MBri
- 'Victoriae' — MBri
gallinopes — WAbe
tremula — GQui MBri SRms
umbrosa — MBri WRic
vittata — SRms
wallichiana — CFil CHEx

Pterocarya (Juglandaceae)

fraxinifolia ♀H4 — CAgr CBcs CDul CLnd CMCN CTrG ECrN ENot EPfP EWTr MBlu NBee NPSI SBLw WDin
- var. *dumosa* — CDul
x *rehderiana* — CTho MBlu WMou
stenoptera — CBcs CFil CLnd CMCN CTho SLPl
- 'Fern Leaf' — CFil WMou WPGP

Pteroceltis (Ulmaceae)

tatarinowii — CMCN WHCr

Pterocephalus (Dipsacaceae)

depressus — WPat
parnassi — see *P.perennis*
§ *perennis* — CMea EDAr LRHS MHer NBir NJOw NLar NMen NWCA SBla SMer SRms WAbe WEas WHoo WWin XPep
- subsp. *perennis* — WHrl
pinardii — NWCA

Pterostylis (Orchidaceae)

acuminata ingens — EPot
coccinea — SSpi
curta — CStu LEur SCnR WIvy
Nodding Grace g. — CDes
truncata — SSpi

Pterostyrax (Styracaceae)

corymbosa — CBcs CMCN CPMA IArd IDee MBlu NLar SSpi WFar
hispida ♀H4 — CBcs CDul CFil CHEx CLnd CMCN CPMA CPne CSam EPfP EPla GKir IArd LAst LRHS MBlu MRav NLar SSpi WBVN WDin WFar WMul WPGP WWin
psilophylla — CMCN

Ptilostemon (Asteraceae)

afer — CPom EHrv EMan MWgw
§ *diacantha* — EBee NLar NSti WHil
* *psilophylla* **new** — EWll

Ptilotrichum see Alyssum

Puccinellia (Poaceae)

distans **new** — CRWN

Pueraria (Papilionaceae)

montana var. *lobata* — CAgr CArn LRav MSal

Pulicaria (Asteraceae)

§ *dysenterica* — CAgr CArn IHMM MHer MSal NMir SIde WBri WCHb WDyG WJek WLHH WWye

Pulmonaria ❀ (Boraginaceae)

'Abbey Dore Pink' — EBee WAbb
affinis — CElw CLAP EMon LRHS
* *altaica* **new** — GBin
angustifolia ♀H4 — CWCL EBee EPfP EWTr GKev GKir LRHS MBro MSal NBrk NOrc SChu SMer SRms WEas WFar WGMN WTin WWin
- subsp. *azurea* — More than 30 suppliers
- 'Blaues Meer' — CFir CSBt CSam EBee EGle EPfP GBuc GKir LPio MBNS MNFA SBod WCru
- 'Munstead Blue' — CElw CHea CLAP EBee EBre ECha EFou EGle EHrv ENot EPar IBlr LPio LSpr MRav MTho MWgw NBrk NHol NRya NSti SRms WCru
- 'Rubra' — see *P.rubra*
'Apple Frost' — EBee ECtt MBnl NBhm NSti WCra
'Barfield Regalia' — CLAP CMHG EBee EMon IGor MAvo MBct NSti SDys
'Benediction' — EBee LPhx NSti SAga
'Berries and Cream' — NSti
§ 'Beth's Blue' — ECha EMon WCAu WCru
'Beth's Pink' — ECha GAbr WCru WFar WWpP
'Blauer Hügel' — CBct CElw EMon GKir NSti
§ 'Blauhimmel' — CLAP EBre EGle EMon LRHS MBro
'Blue Buttons' — CFir CHea EBee GBin MBnl NSti SVil
'Blue Crown' — CElw CLAP CSev EBee EFou EHrv EMon EWes LRHS MBri NDov SAga SChu SSpe WCAu WCru WEas WHal WWeb
'Blue Ensign' — More than 30 suppliers
'Blue Haze' — EBee
'Blue Moon' — see *P.officinalis* 'Blue Mist'
'Blue Pearl' — EMon NSti
'Blueberry Muffin' — CSpe
'Bonnie' **new** — CMea
'Botanic Hybrid' — WCru
'British Sterling' — CLAP EBee
Cally hybrid — CElw CLAP EBee EMon GCal NSti WCot WCru
'Cedric Morris' — CElw NSti
'Chintz' — CLAP CSam EBee GBuc MAvo MMil SVil WCru WHal

'Cleeton Red'　EMon NSti WCru
'Coral Springs'　EBee EBre GKir NSti
'Corsage'　EBee ECtt
'Cotton Cool'　CBel CElw CFil CLAP EBee ECGP
　ECtt EMan EMon MAvo MBNS
　MBnl MBri MMHG MNFA NCGa
　NDov NSti SLon SSpi SUsu WCau
　WCot WCru WMoo WPGP
'Crawshay Chance'　WCru
'Dark Vader'　NSti
'De Vroomen's Pride' (v)　CBct CHid CLAP CSam EBee EChP
　EGle EMan LAst MOne MSte NSti
　WMnd
'Diana Clare'　More than 30 suppliers
'Duke's Silver'　CLAP
'Elworthy Rubies'　CElw MAvo
'Emerald Isles'　NSti
'Esther'　GSki NSti WCru
'Excalibur'　CBct CElw CHid CLAP EBee EBre
　EHrv EMan ENot GBin GBuc GKir
　ITer LAst MBct MBri MMil NSti
　SHar WCot
'Fiona'　CBct WCAu
'Gavin Compton' (v) **new**　EMon
'Glacier'　CBel CBro CElw CStr ECGP EMon
　EOrc EWTr LPio LRHS MMil MSte
　NChi NSti SAga SMHy SVil WCot
　WHal WWhi
'Hazel Kaye's Red'　CBel CElw LPio NSti WCru
'High Contrast'　NSti
'Highdown'　see *P.* 'Lewis Palmer'
'Ice Ballet'　EBre
　(Classic Series) **new**
'Joan's Red'　CElw WCot WTin
§ 'Lewis Palmer'　♀H4　More than 30 suppliers
'Lime Close'　LPhx SAga
'Little Blue'　NSti
'Little Star'　EBee EFou EGoo EMon GBuc
　NDov NSti SChu SUsu WCru
longifolia　More than 30 suppliers
§ – 'Ankum'　CBct CElw CLAP CMea CSam
　EBli EGle EPfP EPla GBuc GKir
　IBlr ITer LPio LRHS MBrN MRav
　MSte NBir NPPs NSti SMrm SSpe
　SVil WCot WMoo WSHC
– 'Ballyrogan Blue'　IBlr
– 'Bertram Anderson'　CLAP EChP ECtt EGle GGar GKir
　LAst LRHS MBow MLLN NBir
　NCGa NOrc NVic SBla SIng SPer
　SWvt WBrk WCAu WCot WCra
　WCru WMnd WPnP
– subsp. *cevennensis*　CBgR CLAP EBee EChP EMan ENot
　EPfP GKir LAst MBnl MBri MSte
　NSti SHar SSpe SSpi WBor
– 'Coen Jansen'　see *P. longifolia* 'Ankum'
– 'Coral Spring'　EMan MBNS MBnl WCAu
– 'Dordogne'　CBct CLAP EBee EBre EGle EMan
　GBuc GKir LRHS MAvo MRav NBir
　NOrc SBla WCAu WCru
– from France　EBee
– 'Howard Eggins'　EBee WSPU
– wild-collected　WCot
'Lovell Blue'　CElw NCot
'Mado' **new**　EBee
'Majesté'　More than 30 suppliers
§ 'Margery Fish'　♀H4　More than 30 suppliers
'Mary Mottram'　CElw CLAP CMea EBee EChP ECtt
　EFou ELan EMan GMac LAst MLLN
　MNFA NBir NPPs NPol NSti SAga
　SBla SMrm SSpe WCot WCru WHal
　WMnd WMoo WWhi
'Matese Blue' **new**　SBla
'Mawson's Blue'　CLAP CMea EBee EBre ECha EMon
　GKir LPio LRHS MBri MRav MWat

NBir NSti SWvt WCru WEas WMoo
　WRHF WSHC WWhi WWye
'May Bouquet'　NSti
'Melancholia'　IBlr
'Merlin'　CLAP EBee EMon LRHS NSti SSpi
'Middleton Red'　CElw
§ 'Milchstrasse'　CLAP NSti
Milky Way　see *P.* 'Milchstrasse'
mollis　CLAP CSWP EBee ECGP EGoo
　EMon EOrc GCal IBlr LRHS MBri
　NBrk NSti SMrm SSpi WCot WCru
– WM 9206　SBla
– 'Royal Blue'　EBee MRav
– 'Samobor'　CBct CLAP WCot
'Monksilver'　CBel EMon NSti
'Moonshine' **new**　NSti
'Moonstone'　CElw CLAP LAst LPhx LPio
'Moorland Mist' **new**　MCLN
'Mountain Magic' **new**　NSti
'Mournful Purple'　CElw CLAP ECoo EHrv NBrk SWat
　WCru
'Mrs Kittle'　CBct CElw CM&M EBee EChP
　EMan EWTr GBri MBro MCLN
　MNFA MRav NBir NSti SDys SSpi
　WBrk WCru WFar WHal WLin
　WMnd
'Netta Statham'　ECha
'Northern Lights'　SHar
'Nürnberg'　EMon LRHS MAvo WHal
obscura　LRHS
officinalis　CAgr CArn CBro CHby EHon
　EMon EOrc EPar GBBs GBar GPoy
　ITer LLWP LRHS MHer NBrk NVic
　SIde WBrk WCru WFar WHal WHbs
　WSSM WWpP WWye
– 'Alba'　EBee ELan GBBs WBrk WCru
§ – 'Blue Mist'　CBel CBro CElw CLAP CMea ECha
　EGle ELan EMon EOrc GBri GBuc
　GMac MAvo MBro NBir NPar
　SMrm SSpi WAbb WBrk WCot
　WCru WHal WHoo WMnd WMoo
　WTin
– 'Bowles' Blue'　see *P. officinalis* 'Blue Mist'
– Cambridge Blue Group　CPrp EBee ECGN EChP EFou EMar
　EMon LAst LRHS MBNS MRav NBir
　NLar NPPs NSti SLon WCAu WCot
　WCru WEas WHal
– 'Marjorie Lawley'　NPar
– 'Plas Merdyn'　IBlr
– *rubra*　see *P. rubra*
– 'Stillingfleet Gran'　EBee LPio NSti
– 'White Wings'　CElw CHea CLAP EBre EPla GKir
　LPio LRHS MBNS MBro NDov NPri
　NSti SIde WEas WFar WMoo
'Oliver Wyatt's White'　CLAP EBee WPGP
Opal = 'Ocupol'　More than 30 suppliers
'Pewter'　LPio
'Pink Haze'　EBee
'Polar Splash'　CBct EBee EPyc MBnl NSti SIde
　SRot WCra WFar
'Purple Haze'　NSti SHar
'Raspberry Ice'　NSti
'Raspberry Splash'　CBct CLAP CPom EMan NLar NSti
　SHar SRot
* 'Rowlatt Choules'　SSpi
'Roy Davidson'　More than 30 suppliers
§ *rubra*　♀H4　CElw COIW CSWP CStr ECha ELan
　EMar EOrc EWTr GKir IBlr LLWP
　NBid NOrc NSti SBla SChu SMac
　SRms WCAu WFar WTin
– var. *alba*　see *P. rubra* var.
　albocorollata
§ – var. *albocorollata*　CBct CBel CBre CElw CMHG EBee
　ECha ECtt EGle EHrv EMar EMon

	GAbr GKir LRHS MBro MSte NSti WCAu WCru WFar
- 'Ann'	CBct CElw CLAP EBee EChP EMon IBlr LRHS MBNS MBct MBnl NSti SVil WCru WFar WTin
- 'Barfield Pink'	CBro CElw CMea CPom EBee EChP ECtt EGle ELan EMon GBar GCal GKir GMac LAst LRHS MAvo MBro NBir NLar NSti SChu WBrk WCru WHal WPnP
- 'Barfield Ruby'	CLAP EMon GBuc LRHS MAvo
- 'Bowles' Red'	CBel EBee EBlw ECtt EHrv ENot GKir LRHS MRav NBir NCGa NGdn SCro SPer WFar WHal WMnd
- 'David Ward' (v)	More than 30 suppliers
- 'Prestbury Pink'	LRHS
- 'Rachel Vernie' (v)	CLAP CPou EMon MAvo WCot
- 'Redstart'	More than 30 suppliers
- 'Warburg's Red'	CElw EMon
§ *saccharata*	EBee ECha EHrv ELan EWTr GFlt IHMH LGro MBro MFir SChu SPet SRms WCAu WCru WFar WWin
- 'Alba'	CBro CElw ECha GBuc SRms
- Argentea Group ♀H4	CBro CSev EBee EBlw ECha ECoo ELan EOrc EPfP EWTr LAst LRHS MRav MTho NBro NGdn SBla SPet SSpi SWvt WCAu WCot WSan
- 'Blauhimmel'	see *P.* 'Blauhimmel'
- 'Brentor'	EBee WWpP
- 'Clent Skysilver'	EBee WSPU
- 'Dora Bielefeld'	More than 30 suppliers
- 'Frühlingshimmel'	CBro CElw CMea EBee EBre EFou GBBs GKir LPhx LPio MAvo MRav SChu SMrm WFar WHal WLin
- 'Glebe Cottage Blue'	CElw ECGP LPio NSti WCru WWpP
- 'Jill Richardson'	ELan
- 'Lady Lou's Pink'	WCru
- 'Leopard'	CBct CElw CLAP CMea CSam EChP ECtt GBuc GKir GSki LAst LRHS MBro NBir NSti SBla SMrm SUsu WBrk WCot WCru WFar WHoo WMnd WWol
- 'Mrs Moon'	EBee ECtt EMar ENot EPfP GKir LRHS MBNS MHer MWgw NBlu NBrk NOrc NPri SChu SIng SPer SWvt WGMN WHen WMnd WPnP WShp WWeb
- 'Old Rectory Silver'	CLAP NBir
- 'Picta'	see *P. saccharata*
- 'Pink Dawn'	CMHG CMea EBee EMan LRHS WCru WMnd
- pink-flowered **new**	WCru
- 'Reginald Kaye'	CElw ECha EWes GMac MBro NBrk NDov SCro SHBN
- 'Silverado'	CBct CHid EBee EBre MBNS MBnl NCGa NCot NLar NOrc NSti
- 'South Hayes'	CLAP
- 'Stanhoe' **new**	EWes
- 'White Barn'	see *P.* 'Beth's Blue'
'Saint Ann's'	CBct CElw EMon LRHS NSti
'Silver Maid'	WCAu WCot
'Silver Mist'	MAvo
'Silver Sabre'	IBlr
'Silver Shimmers'	MBri SHar
'Silver Streamers'PBR	NSti
'Silver Surprise'	WCot
'Sissinghurst White' ♀H4	More than 30 suppliers
'Skylight'	CElw
'Smoky Blue'	CHid CLAP EBee ECtt EMan EMon ENot EPfP LRHS MBro MRav NSti SMer SWat WFar WHal WMnd WMoo WWeb

'Spilled Milk'	CBct EBee EMan MBri NLar NSti
'Tim's Silver'	NBrk NPar WBcn
'Trevi Brooch'	EBee
'Trevi Fountain'	CBct CLAP EMan NSti SHar SRot
'Ultramarine'	EBee SCro
vallarsae 'Margery Fish'	see *P.* 'Margery Fish'
'Vera May'	EBee MAvo
'Victorian Brooch'PBR	CBct CLAP EBee GAbr LRHS NLar NSti SRot WFar WSpi
'Weetwood Blue'	CElw CLAP EBee EPfP EPla MSte WCru
'Wendy Perry'	CElw CLAP SHar
'Wisley White'	CElw

Pulsatilla (Ranunculaceae)

alba	CBro NSla NWCA WCra WShp WWol
albana	EHyt GCrs LHop LRHS SBla
- 'Lutea'	GKev WAbe
- white-flowering	SOkd
alpina	CBot EChP SRms WPat
§ - subsp. *apiifolia* ♀H4	EBee EHyt ELan GFlt GKev GTou WCom WCot WPat
- 'Reinesaat'	WWin
- subsp. *sulphurea*	see *P. alpina* subsp. *apiifolia*
ambigua	EBee SIgm
aurea JJH 199	SBla
campanella	GAbr WAbe
- JJH 196	EBee
caucasica	LRHS
cernua	CBro CPom EBee GBuc LHop LRHS SIgm
chinensis	EBee
dahurica	CTCP EBee
x *gayeri*	EBee NBir
georgica	EBee EHyt NSla SIgm
halleri ♀H4	EBee EMan GAbr GKev GKir NSla SIgm
- subsp. *slavica* ♀H4	CLyd GCrs LRHS NSla NWCA WCom WWin
- subsp. *taurica*	MSte SScr WCot
lutea	see *P. alpina* subsp. *apiifolia*
millefolium	EBee
montana	GBuc SIgm SPlb
multifida	GIBF
patens var. *multifida*	GBuc
- - NNS 96221	SIgm
pratensis	GPoy GTou SRms
- subsp. *nigricans*	CBro CTCP LHop LRHS
rubra	EBee GKir WWol
turczaninovii	EBee GBuc SIgm
§ *vernalis* ♀H2	GBuc GCrs GTou NSla SBla WPat
§ *vulgaris* ♀H4	More than 30 suppliers
- 'Alba' ♀H4	More than 30 suppliers
- 'Barton's Pink'	CBro EBre EWes EWll GKir LHop LRHS SBla WCom
- 'Blaue Glocke'	CBrm GSki NLar SWvt WHil WWeb
- Czech fringed hybrids	CNic
- double, fringed (d) **new**	SScr
- 'Eva Constance'	CBro EBee EBre EHyt GKir LHop LRHS NBir SIng WAbe
- 'Flore Pleno' (d)	CNic EHyt
- 'Gotlandica'	CLyd SIgm
- subsp. *grandis*	WCot
- - 'Budapest Seedling'	GCrs
- - 'Papageno'	CBot CFwr CSpe EBee EChP EDAr EMan EMar LHop LRHS MAvo NChi NLar NWCA SAga SIgm SMrm WHil
- Heiler hybrids	EBre ECGP EMan EMar
- pale pink-flowered	GKir
- Red Clock	see *P. vulgaris* 'Röde Klokke'
§ - 'Röde Klokke'	CBrm COIW EBee EChP ENot EWTr GEdr IBal LRHS NBPC NChi

NHol NJOw NLar NWCA SCro
SWvt WCot WHil WSel WSpi
WWeb

- *rosea*	WShp
- Rote Glocke	see *P. vulgaris* 'Röde Klokke'
- var. *rubra*	More than 30 suppliers
- violet blue-flowered	ITim
§ - 'Weisse Schwan'	CFwr GAbr NMen WWeb
- White Swan	see *P. vulgaris* 'Weisse Schwan'

pummelo see *Citrus maxima*

Punica (*Lythraceae*)

granatum	ERea ERom ESlt LPan LRHS MPRe
	SDnm SLim SOWG STre WSHC
	XPep
- 'Chico' **new**	XPep
- 'Fina Tendral'	ERea
- 'Fruits Violets' **new**	XPep
- 'Legrelleae' (d)	XPep
- 'Maxima Rubra' **new**	XPep
- 'Mollar de Elche' **new**	XPep
- var. *nana* ♀H3	CArn CHal CPle EPfP ERea EShb
	ESlt LPan MPRe SMrm SRms
	WPat
- 'Nana Racemosa'	CBcs
- f. *plena* (d)	CBcs MRav WCFE
- - 'Flore Pleno Luteo' (d)	XPep
- - 'Rubrum Flore	LPan
Pleno' (d) ♀H3	
- - 'Provence' **new**	XPep
* - 'Striata'	SOWG

Puschkinia (*Hyacinthaceae*)

scilloides	LRHS
§ - var. *libanotica*	CBro EPar EPfP EPot LAma LPhx
	LRHS NRog WPer WShi
- - 'Alba'	EPar EPot LAma LPhx LRHS
	NRog

Putoria (*Rubiaceae*)

calabrica	CLyd NWCA

Puya (*Bromeliaceae*)

RCB/Arg L-3	WCot
alpestris	CBrP CHEx CTbh CTrC EOas
	SAPC SChr SSpi WMul
chilensis	CAbb CBcs CBrd CCtw CDoC
	CHEx CKob CPne CTbh EBee
	EOas MFOX SAPC SArc SChr
	SPlb
coerulea	CFir EAmu LEdu MSPs SIgm SPlb
	WMul
ferruginea	EOas
gilmartiniae	CTrC IDee
laxa	SChr
laxa x *mirabilis* **new**	CFir
mirabilis	CAbb CHEx CKob CTrC EOas
	WMul WSPU

Pycnanthemum (*Lamiaceae*)

californicum	EBee
pilosum	CAgr CArn CHal EBee ELau EMan
	GPoy MHer MSal NLar NPri SIde
	WBri WGwG WHHs WHer WPer
	WPic WWye
tenuifolium	EBee EMan NLar
virginianum	EBee

Pycnostachys (*Lamiaceae*)

reticulata	CPLG EShb
urticifolia	ECre EWes

Pygmea see *Chionohebe*

Pyracantha ✿ (*Rosaceae*)

Alexander Pendula	EHol MRav MSwo SRms WFar
= 'Renolex'	WHar
angustifolia	WCFE
- DWD 67	WCot
§ *atalantioides*	CMac SPlb WCFE
§ - 'Aurea'	WWin
'Brilliant'	EPfP
'Buttercup'	EPla WBcn
§ *coccinea* 'Lalandei'	NFor SMer SPer WGwG XPep
- 'Red Column'	CChe CMac EBee ECtt ELan EPfP
	EWTr GKir LAst LBuc LHop LRHS
	MAsh MBNS MBar MGos MRav
	MSwo MWat NBee NWea SCoo
	SWvt WBod WDin WFar WGwG
	WHar WLow WWeb
- 'Red Cushion'	EBee ENot LRHS MGos MRav
	SRms
crenulata	WCFE
Dart's Red = 'Interrada'	CSBt EBee LRHS MRav WBod
gibbsii	see *P. atalantioides*
- 'Flava'	see *P. atalantioides* 'Aurea'
'Gold Rush'	EBee WSPU
'Golden Charmer' ♀H4	EBee EBre ECtt ENot EPfP GKir
	LRHS MAsh MGos MRav MSwo
	NBlu NWea SHBN SPer SRms SWvt
	WBod WDin WFar WGwG WHar
'Golden Dome'	LRHS
'Golden Glow'	LRHS
'Golden Sun'	see *P.* 'Soleil d'Or'
'Harlequin' (v)	ECtt EHoe EHol NPro SHBN SReu
	WCot
'Knap Hill Lemon'	CChe EBee MBlu WSPU
'Mohave'	CBrm CChe CMac EBee EBre
	ECrN ELan GKir LRHS MBar MGos
	MWat NDlv NWea SHBN SPer
	SRms SWvt WDin WGwG WStI
'Mohave Silver' (v)	CWSG EBee ECrN EHoe LAst LRHS
	MBNS MGos MWat WBod
'Molten Lava'	MBri
'Monrovia'	see *P. coccinea* 'Lalandei'
'Mozart'	WWeb
'Navaho'	EBee EPfP WBcn WBrE
'Orange Charmer'	CBcs CBrm CTri EBee ELan ENot
	EPfP EWTr GKir MGos MRav
	MWat NBee NBlu NWea SHBN
	SMer SPer SPlb WFar WStI WTel
'Orange Glow' ♀H4	More than 30 suppliers
'Orangeade'	MBri
* 'Red Pillar'	GKir
'Renault d'Or'	SLPl
rogersiana ♀H4	EBee ECrN ENot EPfP GKir MRav
	WFar WTel
- 'Flava' ♀H4	CBrm CSBt CTri EBee ECrN EHol
	ENot EPfP MAsh MBar MRav
	MWhi NWea SMer SPoG WBVN
	WGwG WTel
'Rosedale'	WSPU
Saphyr Jaune	CDoC CEnd CSBt CWSG EBee
= 'Cadaune'PBR	ENot EPfP GKir MBNS MGos MRav
	SMer SPer SPoG WRHF WStI
Saphyr Orange	CDoC CEnd COtt CSBt CWSG
= 'Cadange'PBR ♀H4	EBee EMil ENot EPfP EPla GKir
	LRHS MBri MGos MRav NPri SPer
	WRHF WStI
Saphyr Rouge	CDoC CEnd COtt CSBt CWSG
= 'Cadrou'PBR ♀H4	EBee ENot EPfP GKir LRHS MBri
	MGos MRav SPer SPoG WRHF
'Shawnee'	CMac CSBt EBee ECot EPfP MRav
	MSwo MWat NDlv WWeb
§ 'Soleil d'Or'	CMac CSBt CSam EBee EBre ECrN
	ECtt ELan ENot EPfP GKir LBuc
	LRHS MAsh MBar MRav NFor SLPl

SLon SPer SPlb SReu SWvt WBod
WDin WFar WGwG WHar WStI
WTel

'Sparkler' (v)   CDoC CMac EHoe LAst LRHS
MGos SPer WFar WHar

'Teton' ♀H4   CMac CWSG EBee ECrN ELan
ENot EPfP EPla GKir LAst LHop
LRHS MAsh MBar MBri MRav
MSwo NBlu NDlv SMac SRms
WBVN WDin WFar WLow WStl
WWeb

'Watereri'   ECrN SLPl SPer WTel
'Yellow Sun'   see *P.* 'Soleil d'Or'

Pyrenaria (*Theaceae*)
  spectabilis   see *Tutcheria spectabilis*

Pyrethropsis see *Rhodanthemum*

Pyrethrum see *Tanacetum*
  karelinii new   WLin

Pyrola (*Ericaceae*)
  decorata   EBee
  rotundifolia   SSpi WHer

Pyrostegia (*Bignoniaceae*)
  venusta   ESlt LRHS SOWG

Pyrrhopappus (*Asteraceae*)
  carolinianus   SSpi

Pyrrocoma (*Asteraceae*)
  clementis   EBee
  § **lanceolata**   EBee

Pyrrosia (*Polypodiaceae*)
  * **heterophylla**   NMar

Pyrus ✿ (*Rosaceae*)
  amygdaliformis   CTho
  - var. **cuneifolia**   CLnd CTho
  calleryana 'Bradford'   CLnd
  - 'Chanticleer' ♀H4   More than 30 suppliers
  x **canescens**   CTho
  communis (F)   CCVT CDul CTri GIBF LBuc SBLw
SKee SPer STre WMou
  - 'Abbé Fétel' (D)   SKee
  - 'Autumn Bergamot' (D)   CTho SKee
  - 'Barnet' (Perry)   CTho
  - 'Baronne de Mello' (D)   CTho SFam
  - 'Beech Hill' (F)   CDul CLnd CTho EBee ECrN EMil
ENot EPfP SBLw SPer
  - 'Belle Guérandaise' (D)   SKee
  - 'Belle Julie' (D)   SKee
  - 'Bergamotte d'Automne' (D)   SKee
  - 'Bergamotte Esperen' (D)   SKee
  - 'Beth' (D) ♀H4   CDoC CSBt CTri CWib ECrN EMui
EPfP GBon GTwe LBuc LRHS MBri
MGos NBee NPri NRog SDea SFam
SKee SPer WHar
  - 'Beurré Alexandre Lucas' (D)   SKee
  - 'Beurré Bedford' (D)   SKee
  - 'Beurré Bosc' (D)   SKee
  - 'Beurré Clairgeau' (C/D)   SKee
  - 'Beurré d'Amanlis' (D)   SKee
  - 'Beurré d'Avalon' (D)   SKee
  - 'Beurré de Beugny' (D)   SKee
  - 'Beurré de Naghin' (C/D)   SKee
  - 'Beurré Diel' (D)   SKee
  - 'Beurré Dubuisson' **new**   SKee

  - 'Beurré Dumont' (D)   SFam
  - 'Beurré Gris d'Hiver' (D) **new**   SKee
  - 'Beurré Hardy' (D) ♀H4   CAgr CCAT CDoC CSBt CTho CTri
CWib ECrN EMui ENot ERea EWTr
GKir GTwe LRHS MRav MWat
NRog SDea SFam SKee SPer WOrn
  - 'Beurré Mortillet' (D)   SKee
  - 'Beurré Six' (D)   SKee
  - 'Beurré Superfin' (D)   ECrN GTwe SFam SKee
  - 'Bianchettone' (D)   SKee
  - 'Bishop's Thumb' (D)   SDea SKee
  - 'Black Worcester' (C)   ECrN GTwe SDea SFam SKee
WSPU
  - 'Blakeney Red' (Perry)   CTho SDea
  - 'Blickling' (D)   SKee
  - 'Brandy' (Perry)   CTho SDea SKee
  - 'Bristol Cross' (D)   GTwe SKee
  § - 'Butirra Precoce Morettini' (D)   SDea
  - 'Catillac' (C) ♀H4   CAgr CTho GTwe NRog SFam
SKee
  - 'Chalk'   see *P. communis* 'Crawford'
  - 'Chaumontel' (D)   SKee
  - 'Clapp's Favourite' (D)   CTho ECrN GTwe SKee
  - 'Colmar d'Eté' (D)   CTho
  - 'Comte de Lamy' (D)   SKee
  - 'Concorde'PBR (D) ♀H4   CCVT CDoC CSBt CSam CTho
CTri CWib ECrN EMui ENot EPfP
ERea GTwe LBuc LRHS MBri MGos
MLan NBlu NRog NWea SDea
SFam SKee SPer WHar WOrn
  - 'Conference' (D) ♀H4   More than 30 suppliers
  - 'Crassane'   CTho
  § - 'Crawford' (D)   SKee
  - 'Cromwell' (D)   ESim
  - 'Deacon's Pear' (D)   SDea
  - 'Devoe' (D)   SDea
  - 'Docteur Jules Guyot' (D)   ECrN SDea SKee
  - 'Double de Guerre' (C/D)   SKee
  - 'Doyenné Blanc' (F)   SKee
  - 'Doyenné Boussoch' (D)   SKee
  - 'Doyenné d'Eté' (D)   ERea SFam SKee
  - 'Doyenné du Comice' (D) ♀H4   CCVT CDoC CMac CSBt CTho
CTri CWSG CWib EBre ECrN EMui
ENot EPfP ERea GBon LBuc LRHS
MBri MRav MWat NRog NWea
SDea SFam SKee SPer WHar WOrn
  - 'Doyenné Georges Boucher' (D)   SKee
  - 'Duchesse d'Angoulême' (D)   SKee
  - 'Durondeau' (D)   CTho GTwe NRog SDea SFam SKee
  - 'Easter Beurré' (D)   SKee
  - 'Emile d'Heyst' (D)   CTho GTwe
  - 'English Caillot Rosat' (D) **new**   SKee
  - 'Eva Baltet' (D)   SKee
  - 'Fair Maid' (D) **new**   SKee
  - 'Fertility' (D)   SKee
  - 'Fertility Improved'   see *P. communis* 'Improved Fertility'
  - 'Fondante d'Automne' (D)   CTho SKee
  - 'Forelle' (D)   ERea SKee
  - 'Gansel's Bergamot' (D)   SKee
  - 'Gin' (Perry)   CTho
  - 'Glou Morceau' (D)   CTho ECrN EMui GTwe LRHS
MWat NRog SDea SFam SKee
  - 'Glow Red Williams' (D)   SFam
  - 'Gorham' (D)   CAgr CTho ECrN GTwe MCoo
SFam SKee

- 'Gratiole de Jersey' (D) CTho
- 'Green Horse' (Perry) CTho
- 'Green Pear of Yair' (D) SKee
- 'Hacon's SKee
  Imcomparable' (D)
- 'Harrow Delight' (D) SDea
- 'Harvest Queen' (D/C) SDea
- 'Hessle' (D) GTwe NRog SDea SFam SKee
- 'Highland' (D) SKee
§ - 'Improved Fertility' (D) CAgr CDoC GBon GTwe SDea
  SKee
- 'Jack Green' CTho
- 'Jargonelle' (D) CAgr CTho GTwe NRog SDea
  SFam SKee
- 'Joséphine de Malines' CTho GTwe LRHS SDea SFam
  (D) ♀H4 SKee
- 'Laxton's Foremost' (D) SKee
- 'Laxton's Satisfaction' SFam
  (D)
- 'Le Lectier' (D) **new** SKee
- 'Louise Bonne CAgr CDoC CTho CTri ECrN EMui
  of Jersey' (D) GTwe LRHS MGos NRog SDea
  SFam SKee
- 'Marguérite Marillat' (D) SDea SKee
- 'Marie-Louise' (D) SKee
- 'Max Red Bartlett' MCoo
- 'Merton Pride' (D) CTho ECrN GTwe MWat SDea
  SFam SKee
- 'Merton Star' (D) SKee
- 'Monarch' (D) CLnd
- 'Moonglow' (D/C) CAgr MCoo SDea SKee
- 'Morettini' see *P. communis* 'Butirra Precoce
  Morettini'
- 'Nouveau Poiteau' (C/D) CAgr CTho ECrN GTwe LRHS
  SKee
- 'Olivier de Serres' (D) SFam SKee
- 'Onward' (D) ♀H4 CAgr CLnd CTri CWib ECrN EMui
  GTwe MBri MGos NRog NWea
  SDea SFam SKee WHar
§ - 'Packham's Triumph' (D) CDoC CTri CWib ECrN GTwe
  NRog SDea SKee
- 'Passe Colmar' (D) CTho
- 'Passe Crassane' (D) SKee
- 'Pear Apple' (D) SDea
- 'Pero Nobile' **new** SKee
- 'Pitmaston Duchess' ECrN GTwe SDea SKee
  (C/D) ♀H4
- 'Président Barabé' **new** SKee
- 'Red Comice' (D/C) GTwe SKee
- 'Red Sensation EMui GTwe MBri SKee
  Bartlett' (D/C)
- 'Robin' (C/D) ERea SDea SKee
- 'Roosevelt' (D) SKee
- 'Santa Claus' (D) SDea SFam SKee
- 'Seckel' (D) SFam SKee
- 'Soleil d'Automne' (F) SKee
- 'Swan's Egg' (D) CTho SKee
- 'Terrace Pearl' EMui ENot
- 'Thompson's' (D) GTwe SFam SKee
- 'Thorn' (Perry) CTho SKee
- 'Triomphe de Vienne' SFam SKee
  (D)
- 'Triumph' see *P. communis* 'Packham's
  Triumph'
- 'Uvedale's CTho SKee
  St Germain' (C)
- 'Verbelu' **new** SKee
- 'Vicar of GTwe SDea SKee
  Winkfield' (C/D)
- 'Williams' Bon Chrétien' CCVT CMac CSBt CTho CTri
  (D/C) ♀H4 CWSG CWib ECrN EMui ENot
  ERea GBon GKir LBuc LRHS MBri
  MGos MWat NRog SDea SFam
  SKee SPer WHar WOrn WStI

- 'Williams Red' (D/C) GTwe SKee
- 'Winnal's Longdon' CTho
  (Perry)
- 'Winter Nelis' (D) CTho CTri CWib ECrN GTwe MBri
  SDea SFam SKee
cordata CDul CTho SKee
cossonii CTho
elaeagnifolia CTho CWSG LRHS
- var. *kotschyana* CDul CEnd CLnd GIBF GKir LRHS
  MRav SLim WOrn
- 'Silver Sails' LRHS MAsh MBlu MGos SCoo
korshinskyi GIBF
nivalis CDul CLnd CTho EBee ENot EPfP
  GIBF SBLw SHBN SLPl SPer
- 'Catalia' **new** LRHS MBri
pyrifolia '20th Century' see *P. pyrifolia* 'Nijisseiki'
- 'Chojuro' (F) ERea ESim
- 'Kumoi' (F) SDea
* - 'Nashi Kumoi' LPan
§ - 'Nijisseiki' (F) ERea ESim
- 'Shinseiki' (F) EMui ERea ESim LBuc LRHS SDea
  SKee SLim
- 'Shinsui' (F) SDea SKee
salicifolia 'Pendula' ♀H4 More than 30 suppliers
ussuriensis GIBF

Qiongzhuea see *Chimonobambusa*

Quercus ✿ (*Fagaceae*)

§ *acuta* CBcs CHEx MBlu
§ *acutissima* CDul CMCN ECrN EPfP SBir WDin
  WNor
aegilops see *Q. ithaburensis* subsp.
  macrolepis
affinis CMCN
agrifolia CDul CMCN SBir
alba CDul CMCN ECrN WDin
- f. *elongata* EPfP LRHS
aliena CBcs CMCN SBir
- var. *acutiserrata* CMCN
alnifolia CDul
arkansana CMCN SBir
austrina CMCN
x *beadlei* see *Q. x saulii*
bicolor CDul CMCN ECrN IArd LRHS SBir
  WDin WNor
borealis see *Q. rubra*
breweri see *Q. garryana* var. *breweri*
buckleyi SBir
x *bushii* CMCN EPfP MBlu
x *byarsii* SBir
canariensis ♀H4 CDul CMCN CTho CTrG EPfP IArd
  IDee LRHS
castaneifolia CMCN ECrN EPfP LPan SBLw
  WDin
- 'Green Spire' ♀H4 CDoC CMCN CTho EPfP GKir
  IArd LRHS MBlu MBri SMad SPer
cerris CBcs CDoC CDul CLnd CMCN
  EBee ECrN EMil ENot EPfP GKir
  IArd LPan LRHS MGos MLan NWea
  SBLw SBir SEND SPer SSta WDin
  WMou
§ - 'Argenteovariegata' (v) CDul CEnd CLnd CMCN CRez
  CTho EBee ELan EPfP GKir IArd
  LRHS MAsh MBlu MBri MGos SBir
  SKee SMad SPoG
* - 'Marmorata' EPfP SBir
- 'Variegata' see *Q. cerris* 'Argenteovariegata'
- 'Wodan' CDul CMCN EPfP GKir LRHS MBlu

chapmanii	CMCN
chrysolepis	CBcs CMCN
coccifera	CDul CFil CMCN SSpi WDin WPGP WWes
- subsp. *calliprinos*	CMCN
coccinea	CBcs CDul CLnd CMCN CWSG ECrN EPfP GIBF GKir LRHS MWht NBea NWea SBLw SBir SPer SSta STre WDin WNor WOrn
- 'Splendens' ♀H4	CDoC CDul CEnd CMCN COtt CTho CTri EBee ELan EPfP EWTr GKir LPan LRHS MBlu MBri SBLw SHBN SMad SPer WDin
dentata	CMCN EPfP LRHS WDin
- 'Carl Ferris Miller'	CMCN EPfP IArd LRHS MBlu SBir SMad
- 'Pinnatifida'	CMCN EPfP IArd LRHS MBlu SMad
- 'Sir Harold Hillier'	EPfP
- subsp. *yunnanensis*	CMCN
douglasii	CLnd CMCN
dumosa	CMCN WNor
ellipsoidalis	CDul CMCN GKir LRHS SBir WNor
- 'Hemelrijk'	CDoC EPfP GKir LRHS MBlu
emoryi	SBir
fabrei	SBir
faginea	CLnd CMCN
falcata	CMCN EPfP
- var. *pagodifolia*	see *Q. pagoda*
x *fernaldii*	CMCN
frainetto	CDoC CDul CLnd CMCN CTho EBee ECrN ENot EPfP EWTr GKir ISea LPan LRHS MAsh MBri SBLw SEND SPer WDin WMou WNor
- 'Hungarian Crown' ♀H4	CMCN EPfP LRHS MBlu SMad
- 'Trump' **new**	CMCN MBlu
fruticosa	see *Q. lusitanica* Lamarck
gambelii	CMCN
garryana	CMCN SBir
§ - var. *breweri*	SBir
- var. *fruticosa*	see *Q. garryana* var. *breweri*
georgiana	CMCN SBir
glandulifera	see *Q. serrata*
§ *glauca*	CDul CFai CMCN EPfP SAPC SArc SBir WNor
gravesii	SBir
grisea	CMCN SBir
x *hastingsii*	CMCN EPfP
hemisphaerica	CDul CMCN EPfP SBir
x *heterophylla*	CDul CMCN SBir
x *hickelii*	CMCN LRHS
- 'Gieszelhorst'	MBlu
hinckleyi	WDin
§ x *hispanica*	CLnd WPic
- 'Ambrozyana'	CDul CMCN EPfP LRHS SBir SMad WDin
- 'Diversifolia'	CMCN EPfP MBlu
- 'Fulhamensis'	CMCN SEND
§ - 'Lucombeana' ♀H4	CBcs CDul CMCN CSBt CTho EPfP IArd MBlu SBir SPer
- 'Pseudoturneri'	CBcs CDul EPfP LPan MBlu
- 'Suberosa'	CTho
- 'Wageningen'	CMCN EPfP IArd SBir
ilex ♀H4	More than 30 suppliers
- 'Fordii' **new**	CTho
ilicifolia	CDul CMCN LRHS SBir WNor
imbricaria	CDul CLnd CMCN ECrN LRHS MBlu SBir WDin
incana Roxb.	see *Q. leucotrichophora*
§ *incana* Bartram	CMCN
infectoria	CDul
ithaburensis	CMCN EPfP
§ - subsp. *macrolepis*	CMCN GKir LEdu SBir
kelloggii	CMCN LRHS
x *kewensis*	CMCN
laevigata	see *Q. acuta*
laevis	CMCN EPfP SBir
§ *laurifolia*	CDul CMCN MBlu SBir
§ *leucotrichophora*	CMCN
liaotungensis	see *Q. wutaishanica*
x *libanerris*	CDul IArd SBir
- 'Rotterdam'	CMCN
libani	CDul CMCN EPfP WDin
lobata	CMCN LEdu
x *lucombeana*	see *Q.* x *hispanica*
- 'William Lucombe'	see *Q.* x *hispanica* 'Lucombeana'
x *ludoviciana*	CMCN EPfP SBir
§ *lusitanica* Lamarck	CMCN
lyrata	CMCN
'Macon'	LRHS
macranthera	CLnd CMCN EPfP GKir
macrocarpa	CLnd CMCN EPfP LRHS SBir WDin WNor
macrocarpa x *turbinella*	CMCN
macrolepis	see *Q. ithaburensis* subsp. *macrolepis*
margarettiae	CMCN
marilandica	CDul CEnd CMCN EPfP IArd LRHS SBir
mexicana	CMCN SBir
michauxii	CMCN LRHS
mongolica subsp. *crispula* var. *grosseserrata*	CMCN
§ *montana*	CMCN
muehlenbergii	CDul CMCN EPfP LRHS MBlu SBir
myrsinifolia	see *Q. glauca*
myrtifolia	CMCN EPfP
nigra	CDul CMCN CMHG SBir WNor
nuttallii	see *Q. texana*
obtusa	see *Q. laurifolia*
oglethorpensis	SBir
§ *pagoda*	CMCN MBlu SBir
palustris ♀H4	CDoC CDul CLnd CMCN CTho ECrN EPfP EWTr GKir LPan LRHS MAsh MBlu MBri MLan NWea SBLw SBir SKee SPer WDin WNor WOrn
* - 'Compacta'	EPfP
- 'Green Dwarf'	CMCN
- 'Pendula'	CEnd CMCN WPGP
- 'Swamp Pygmy'	CMCN MBlu
pedunculata	see *Q. robur*
pedunculiflora	see *Q. robur* subsp. *pedunculiflora*
§ *petraea* ♀H4	CDoC CDul CLnd CSBt ECrN EPfP GKir IMGH LBuc MBlu NBee NWea SBLw SPer WDin WMou
§ - 'Insecata'	CDoC CEnd CMCN LRHS WPGP
- 'Laciniata'	see *Q. petraea* 'Insecata'
- 'Mespilifolia'	CTho
§ - 'Purpurea'	CLnd CMCN GKir LRHS MBlu
- 'Rubicunda'	see *Q. petraea* 'Purpurea'
- 'Westcolumn'	IArd
§ *phellos*	CLnd CMCN CTho EBee ECrN EPfP LRHS MBlu SLPl SLdr WDin WNor
phillyreoides	CBcs CDul CLnd CMCN EPfP IDee SBir SLPl WDin WNor
polymorpha	CMCN
'Pondaim'	CMCN LRHS SBir
pontica	CMCN EPfP LRHS MBlu NWea
prinoides	CMCN
prinus Engelm.	see *Q. montana*
* *prinus* L.	CMCN SBir
pubescens	CFil CMCN GKir SBir
pumila Michx.	see *Q. montana*
pumila Walt.	see *Q. phellos*

pyrenaica	CLnd CMCN CTho
- 'Pendula'	CMCN WDin
rhysophylla	CDul EPfP MBlu SBir
§ **robur** ♀H4	More than 30 suppliers
- 'Argenteomarginata' (v)	CDul CMCN MBlu SMad SSta
- 'Atropurpurea'	CDul MGos WDin
* - 'Compacta'	MBlu
- 'Concordia'	CBcs CDoC CDul CEnd CFil CLnd
	CMCN COtt EBee EPfP GKir LRHS
	MBlu MBri SMad WDin
- 'Contorta'	CMCN LRHS
- 'Cristata'	CDul CMCN MBlu
- 'Cucullata'	CMCN
* - **dissecta**	CMCN
- 'Facrist'	CDul CEnd
- f. **fastigiata**	CDoC CDul CLnd CTho EBee
	ECrN ENot EPfP GKir LBuc LPan
	LRHS MBar MGos NBee NWea
	SBLw SCoo SKee SLPl SPer WDin
	WFar WOrn
- - 'Koster' ♀H4	CDoC CDul CMCN COtt EPfP
	GKir LPan MBlu NBee SSta
- 'Fennesseyi'	CMCN LRHS
- 'Filicifolia'	see *Q.* x *rosacea* 'Filicifolia'
- 'Filicifolia' misapplied	see *Q. robur* 'Pectinata'
- 'Hentzei'	CMCN
- 'Hungaria'	LRHS
- 'Irtha'	EPfP
§ - 'Pectinata'	CTho EPfP MBlu WDin
§ - subsp. **pedunculiflora**	CLnd CMCN
- 'Pendula'	CDul CEnd CMCN CTho MBlu
	MGos
- 'Purpurascens'	CEnd CMCN GKir MBlu
- 'Raba'	CMCN
§ - 'Salfast'	MBlu
- 'Salicifolia Fastigiata'	see *Q. robur* 'Salfast'
- 'Strypemonde'	CMCN
- 'Totem' **new**	MBlu SMad
- f. **variegata** (v)	LRHS MGos
- - 'Fürst	CMCN MBlu
Schwarzenburg' (v)	
robur x **turbinella**	CMCN
§ x **rosacea** 'Filicifolia'	CEnd CLnd GTSp NBea WMou
	WWes
§ **rubra** ♀H4	More than 30 suppliers
- 'Aurea'	CDul CEnd CFil CMCN EPfP GKir
	LRHS MBlu SPer SSpi WPGP
- 'Boltes Gold'	MBlu
- 'Magic Fire'	MBlu SMad
* - 'Sunshine'	CMCN LRHS MBlu SMad
rugosa	CMCN SBir
x **runcinata**	SBir
sadleriana	CMCN
sartorii	SBir
§ x **saulii**	CMCN SBir
x **schochiana**	EPfP
schottkyana	SBir
x **schuettei**	SBir
§ **serrata**	CDoC CMCN SBir
sessiliflora	see *Q. petraea*
shumardii	CDul CMCN EPfP LRHS SBir WDin
	WNor
stellata	CMCN SBir
suber	CBcs CDoC CDul CFil CLnd
	CMCN CTho ECrN EPfP IArd IDee
	ISea LEdu LRHS SAPC SArc SEND
	SSpi WDin WPGP
- 'Cambridge'	EPfP
§ **texana**	CMCN EPfP SBir
trojana	CMCN
turbinella	CMCN
x **turneri**	CDoC CLnd CMCN CTho WDin
	WMou
- 'Pseudoturneri'	see *Q.* x *bispanica* 'Pseudoturneri'
vacciniifolia	CMCN
variabilis	CMCN EPfP SBir
velutina	CDul CLnd CMCN CTho EPfP
	LRHS SBir
- 'Albertsii'	MBlu
- 'Rubrifolia'	CMCN EPfP
'Vilmoriana'	CMCN MBlu
virginiana	CMCN
'Warburgii'	EPfP
x **warei**	SBir
wislizeni	CBcs CMCN SBir
§ **wutaishanica**	CMCN SBir

Quillaja (Rosaceae)

saponaria	CPle CTrG

quince see *Cydonia oblonga*

Quisqualis (Combretaceae)

indica	SOWG

R

Racosperma see *Acacia*

Ramonda (Gesneriaceae)

§ **myconi** ♀H4	CLAP CPBP EHyt ITim LTwo
	MMHG NBPC NLar NMen NSla
	NWoo SBla SIgm SIng SRms
- var. **alba**	MTho WKif
- 'Jim's Shadow'	WAbe
- 'Rosea'	CLAP SBla
nathaliae ♀H4	CLAP CPBP NGar NWCA SIgm
- 'Alba'	CLAP SBla SOkd
pyrenaica	see *R. myconi*
serbica	SBla SIgm

Ranunculus ❀ (Ranunculaceae)

abnormis	GCrs NRya SCnR SIng
aconitifolius	EBee EChP ECha EPar NLar NSti
	SHar SMrm SWat WMnd
- 'Flore Pleno' (d) ♀H4	More than 30 suppliers
acris	NBir NLan NPer
* - **citrinus**	CBgR CElw CMdw EChP ECoo
	ECtt EGle EPar EWoo EWsh GFlt
	LRHS MFOX MHar MSte NCGa
	NRya SBri SMrm WBVN WCAu
	WMoo WRha
- 'Farrer's Yellow'	CRow LHop
- 'Flore Pleno' (d) ♀H4	More than 30 suppliers
- 'Hedgehog'	CDes EPPr NDov
- 'Stevenii'	CFee CRow EPPr IGor SDix
- 'Sulphureus'	CBre ECha WEas WFar WHal
alpestris	NMen NRya
alpestris x **bilobus**	NMen
amplexicaulis	ERos GCrs GTou MRav NLar NMen
	NSla SBla WAbe WCot
aquatilis	EHon EMFW NArg NBlu SWat
x **arendsii** 'Moonlight'	CElw SBla SRot
asiaticus	EPot WCot
- var. **albus**	SBla
- var. **flavus**	SBla
- var. **sanguineus**	SBla
- Tecolote hybrids	LAma
baurii	SSpi
bulbosus	NSco WBWf
§ - 'F.M. Burton'	CBos EBee ECtt EGle EHrv ETow
	GCal NRya NSti SCro WHal WTMC
- **farreri**	see *R. bulbosus* 'F.M. Burton'
- 'Speciosus Plenus'	see *R. constantinopolitanus*
	'Plenus'

calandrinioides ♀H2-3 CAvo EHyt EWes NBir SBla SIng
 SVal WAbe WCom WCot
 – SF 137 WCot
 chinensis EBee
§ *constantinopolitanus* CElw CRow EBee ECha GCal GKir
 'Plenus' (d) GMac MBri MInt MLLN MRav NBid
 NBro NRya WCot WEas WFar
 WMoo
 cortusifolius CFir CMHG EBee EMan MDKP
 MTed SBla SHar SWat WCot WCru
 crenatus CLyd EBee EHyt GEdr GTou LEur
 NMen NRya SOkd WHal
 ficaria CArn CNat CRow ELau GBar
 MBow MGas MHer MSal NSco
 WFar WHbs WHer WShi WWye
 – 'Aglow in the Dark' CHid CNat EBee
 – var. *albus* CElw CHid CRow EMon ERos
 LRHS NRya SIng WOut
 – anemone-centred see *R. ficaria* 'Collarette'
 – 'Art Nouveau' CNat
 – 'Ashen Primrose' **new** CRow EBee
§ – var. *aurantiacus* CNic CRow EBee ECha EMon EPar
 ERos EWsh LEur LPhx LRHS MBro
 MRav NGar NJOw NRya SIng
 SRms WAbe WCom WFar
 – 'Bantam Egg' CRow EBee
 – 'Binsted Woods' SCro
 – 'Blackadder' CRow
 – 'Bowles' Double' see *R. ficaria* 'Double Bronze',
 'Picton's Double'
 – 'Brambling' CBre CHea CLAP CNic CRow EBee
 ECGP EMon LEur LRHS MRav
 NGar NRya SIgm SSvw WCom
 – 'Brazen Child' CRow EBee
 – 'Brazen Daughter' CRow
 – 'Brazen Hussy' More than 30 suppliers
 – 'Bregover White' CRow EBee LEur
 – 'Broadleas Black' CNat
 – 'Budgerigar' CRow
 – subsp. *bulbilifer* CRow LEur MDKP
 'Chedglow'
 – 'Bunch' (d) CRow
 – 'Camouflage' (v) CNat
 – 'Cartwheel' (d) CRow
 – 'Champernowne Giant' CRow
 – 'Chocolate Cream' CRow
§ – subsp. *chrysocephalus* CRow ECha EMon NGar NRya
 SIng SSvw WCot WFar WHer
 – 'Clouded Yellow' (v) CRow
 – 'Coffee Cream' CRow EBee LEur
 – 'Coker Cream' CRow
§ – 'Collarette' (d) CHid CRow CStu EBee EHyt EMon
 EPar EPot ERos GBar GBuc GGar
 LEur LPhx LRHS MAvo MRav
 MTho NBir NGar NJOw NMen
 NRya SBla SIng SMac WAbe WCom
 WFar
 – 'Coppernob' CBre CElw CHid CRow EBee
 ECGP ECha GAbr LEur LPio MAvo
 NGar SBla WCot WFar WPnP
 WWpP
 – 'Corinne Tremaine' WHer
 – 'Coy Hussy' (v) CNat LEur
 – 'Crawshay Cream' CElw CRow EBee LPhx
 – 'Cupreus' see *R. ficaria* var. *aurantiacus*
 – 'Custard Tart' NGar
 – 'Damerham' (d) CHid CRow EMon LRHS NGar
 – 'Deborah Jope' CRow
 – 'Diane Rowe' EMon
 – 'Dimpsey' CRow
§ – 'Double Bronze' (d) CHid CRow CStu EBee ECGP
 EMon EPar ERos LEur LRHS MDKP
 MTho NBir NGar NLar NRya SIng
 WCot

 – double cream (d) see *R. ficaria* 'Double Mud'
 – double green eye (d) CHid CRow
§ – 'Double Mud' (d) CHid CLAP CRow CStu ECGP
 EMon ERos EWsh GAbr GBuc LEur
 LPhx LRHS MBro MTho NJOw
 NRya SBla SIng WAbe WCom WCot
 WFar WHal WWpP
 – double yellow (d) see *R. ficaria* flore-pleno
 – 'Dusky Maiden' CRow EMon LEur LRHS NGar SIng
 WFar
 – 'E.A. Bowles' see *R. ficaria* 'Collarette'
 – 'Elan' (d) CDes CRow
 – subsp. *ficariiformis* EMon NGar
§ – *flore-pleno* (d) CFee CHid CRow CStu EBee ECha
 ELan EMar EMon EPPr EPar ERos
 GAbr GGar LEur LRHS NGar
 NJOw NRya NSti SIng SRms WAbe
 WCot WFar WWin
 – 'Fried Egg' CRow
 – 'Green Mantle' NGar
 – 'Green Petal' CElw CHid CRow CStu EBee
 EMon EPar LEur LPhx MDKP
 MRav MTho NBir NJOw NLar
 NRya SIng SSvw WAbe WHal WHer
 WHil WWpP
 – 'Greencourt Gold' (d) CRow
 – 'Holly' see *R. ficaria* 'Holly Green'
 – 'Holly Bronze' CRow
§ – 'Holly Green' CRow
 – 'Hoskin's Miniature' CRow
 – 'Hoskin's Variegated' (v) CRow
 – 'Hyde Hall' EMon LEur LRHS NGar NLar SIng
 WFar
 – 'Inky' CNat LEur
 – 'Jake Perry' CBos CDes
 – 'Jane's Dress' CHid CNat CRow LEur
 – 'Ken Aslet Double' (d) CDes CRow EBee EMon LEur
 LRHS WHal WOut
 – 'Lambrook Black' WHer
 – 'Laysh On' (d) CRow
 – 'Lemon Queen' CHid
 – 'Leo' EMon
 – 'Limelight' CRow
 – 'Little Southey' CRow EBee
 – subsp. *major* see *R. ficaria* subsp.
 chrysocephalus
 – 'Martin Gibbs' CNat
 – 'Mimsey' (d) CRow
 – 'Mobled Jade' CHid CNat CRow EBee LEur
 – 'Newton Abbot' CBre CRow
I – 'Nigrifolia' NGar
 – 'Oakenden Cream' CRow
 – 'Old Master' MAvo NGar WCot
 – 'Orange Sorbet' CRow EMon LEur NGar NLar
§ – 'Picton's Double' (d) CRow CStu EBee ECGP EHyt GBar
 MTho NGar NJOw NRya WAbe
 – 'Primrose' CHid CRow EMon GGar LRHS
 MRav MTho NLar NRya WCot
 – 'Primrose Elf' CRow
 – 'Quantock Brown' CBgR
 – 'Quillet' (d) CRow EMon
§ – 'Ragamuffin' (d) CDes CRow EBee EMon
 – 'Randall's White' CRow CSWP CStu EBee ECha LEur
 LPhx MRav MTho SIgm WCom
 WCot WFar WWpP
 – 'Rowden Magna' CRow
 – 'Salad Bowl' (d) CRow
 – 'Salmon's White' CBre CFee CRow EBee ELan EMar
 EPPr EPar EPot LEur LPhx MRav
 NBir NJOw NRya SIng SSvw WAbe
 WFar WHal WHer WHrl WLin
 – 'Samidor' CRow
 – 'Sheldon' CRow
 – 'Sheldon Night' CNat

- 'Sheldon Silver'	CHid CNat CRow LEur
- 'Silver Collar'	EMon
- single cream	EMon NGar
- 'South Downs'	CNat
- 'Suffusion'	CNat CRow
- 'Sutherland's Double' (d)	CRow
- 'Sweet Chocolate'	CRow
- 'Torquay Elf'	CRow
- 'Tortoiseshell'	CHid CRow EBee LEur MAvo MRav NGar WCom WFar
- 'Trenwheal' (d)	CRow
- 'Winkworth'	EMon LEur
- 'Wisley White'	NSti
- 'Yaffle'	CBre CHid CRow EBee EChP EMon LRHS MRav NGar SIng WCot
flammula	CRow EHon EMFW LNco LPBA MSta SWat WWpP
- subsp. *minimus*	CRow WWpP
gouanii	ETow NRya
gramineus ♀H4	CMea CSam CStu EHyt EPot ERos GBuc GCrs LBee LPhx LRHS MNrw MRav MSPs MTho MWat NMen NRya SIgm SMad SRms WCAu WCom WCot WFar WLin WPer
- 'Pardal'	SBla WFar
illyricus	CDes EBee ECha NRya SRot WCru WHal
lanuginosus	EPPr
lapponicus	GIBF
lingua	CFir COld ECoo EMFW MCCP SLon SPlb
- 'Grandiflorus'	CBen CRow EHon LNco LPBA MSta NPer NRya SWat WHal WMAq WWpP WWye
lyallii	CPla EBee GGar ITim LEur SBla WAbe WSan
macauleyi	GCrs
millefoliatus	CDes EBee EHyt ERos ETow GBuc MTho NGar NMen NRya WPGP
montanus double (d)	EBee EBre SBla WCot
- 'Molten Gold' ♀H4	CStu ECtt GAbr GCrs MRav MTho NRya SBla SRot
parnassiifolius	CPBP EBee ETow GAbr GTou NMen SBla WAbe
platanifolius	LPhx MTed
pyrenaeus	NMen NSla
repens 'Boraston O.S.'	WCHb
* - 'Buttered Popcorn'	CRow EBee EPPr
- 'Cat's Eyes' (v)	CNat EMan WCot
- 'Gloria Spale'	CBre CRow EMon
- 'Joe's Golden'	EHoe NSti
- var. *pleniflorus* (d)	CBgR CBre CRow EBee EChP ECha GGar GKir NSti WEas WFar WCot
- 'Snowdrift' (v)	WCot
- 'Timothy Clark' (d)	CBre EMon MInt WHil
sceleratus	WHer
serbicus	EBee EPPr GCal
sieboldii	EBee
speciosus 'Flore Pleno'	see *R. constantinopolitanus* 'Plenus'
xinningensis	EBee

Ranzania (Berberidaceae)

japonica	WCru

Raoulia (Asteraceae)

australis misapplied	see *R. hookeri*
australis Hook.	CLyd EBre EDAr EPAt EPot GEdr GGar ITim MBar MHer MWat NBro NFla NRya NWCA SIng WDyG WHoo WShp
- 'Calf'	ITim
§ - Lutescens Group	ECha EPot ITim WLin

grandiflora	SOkd
haastii	CLyd ECou WBrE
§ *hookeri*	CLyd ECha ECou EDAr EPot GEdr GKir ITim MLan NWCA SIng SPlb SRms WBrE WCom WFar WPat
- var. *apice-nigra*	WAbe
- var. *laxa*	EPot EWes
x *loganii*	see x *Leucoraoulia loganii*
lutescens	see *R. australis* Lutescens Group
monroi	ITim
petriensis	GCrs
x *petrimia*	CGra EHyt ITim WAbe
'Margaret Pringle'	
subsericea	CLyd ECou EWes GCrs NMen WBrE
tenuicaulis	ECha ECou SPlb

Raoulia x *Leucogenes* see x *Leucoraoulia*

raspberry see *Rubus idaeus*

Ratibida (Asteraceae)

columnifera	CRWN EBee EMan GFlt LRHS MGol
- f. *pulcherrima*	EGoo EMan MBNS MLwd
- red	EDif LRav
- 'Red Midget' **new**	GFlt MDKP
pinnata	CRWN EBee EBre LRHS SCro SUsu WCAu
tagetes	EBee

Rauvolfia (Apocynaceae)

serpentina	MGol

Ravenala (Strelitziaceae)

madagascariensis	EAmu LPal WMul XBlo

Ravenea (Arecaceae)

rivularis	EAmu LPal WMul

Rechsteineria see *Sinningia*

redcurrant see *Ribes rubrum* (R)

Regelia (Myrtaceae)

velutina	SOWG

Rehderodendron (Styracaceae)

indochinense **new**	CFil
macrocarpum	CBcs

Rehmannia (Scrophulariaceae)

angulata hort.	see *R. elata*
§ *elata* ♀H2	CBot CBri CSev CSpe EBee EChP ELan EMan LAst LHop LPio LRHS MCLN MFOX MHer SAga SGar SIng SMrm SPet SYvo WCAu WCru WFar WMoo WPer WWin WWye
glutinosa ♀H3	WWye
'White Dragon'	CSpe

Reichardia (Asteraceae)

picroides	CAgr

Reineckea (Convallariaceae)

§ *carnea*	More than 30 suppliers
- B&SWJ 4808	WCru
- 'Alba'	SSpi
- 'Variegata' (v)	EMan WCot WCru

Reinwardtia (Linaceae)

elata	SMrm
§ *indica*	CHll
trigyna	see *R. indica*

Remusatia (*Araceae*)

hookeriana new	CKob EAmu EUJe
pumila new	CKob EAmu EUJe LEur
vivipara	CKob EBee EUJe LEur WMul

Reseda (*Resedaceae*)

alba	MHer
lutea	MSal SECG SIde
luteola	GBar GPoy MHer MSal NSco SECG WBri WCHb WHer WWye

Restio (*Restionaceae*)

bifarius	CTrC
quadratus	WMul WNor
subverticillatus	see *Ischyrolepis subverticillata*
tetraphyllus	CAbb CBod CBrm CFir CKno CPen CTrC EBee GGar LAst MBNS WCot

Retama (*Papilionaceae*)

§ **monosperma**	EShb XPep
raetam new	XPep
§ **sphaerocarpa**	SSpi

Reynoutria see *Fallopia*

Rhagodia (*Chenopodiaceae*)

triandra	ECou

Rhamnus (*Rhamnaceae*)

alaternus	XPep
- var. **angustifolia**	CFil WFar WPGP
§ - 'Argenteovariegata' (v) ♀H4	More than 30 suppliers
- 'Variegata'	see *R. alaternus* 'Argenteovariegata'
cathartica	CCVT CDul CLnd CTri ECrN GIBF LBuc NWea WDin WMou WTel
dahurica	GIBF
frangula	CArn CBgR CCVT CDul CLnd CRWN ECrN ENot LBuc MBlu MBow NWea STre WDin WFar WMou
- 'Aspleniifolia'	CFai EBee ENot EPfP IDee LBuc MBlu MBri MRav NLar SMur WBcn WDin WFar WPat
- 'Columnaris'	EMil SLPl
pumila new	NLar
purshiana	MSal

Rhaphiolepis (*Rosaceae*)

B&SWJ 4901	WPGP

Rhaphiolepis (*Rosaceae*)

x **delacourii**	CMHG CWSG CWib EBee EPfP GQui LAst LRHS SMur WBcn WBod WHCG
- 'Coates' Crimson'	CDoC EMil EPfP GQui IArd LHop SBra SHBN SLon SOWG WDin WLow WSHC
- Enchantress = 'Moness'	CBrm CMHG SMur
- 'Spring Song'	SLon
indica	ERom
- B&SWJ 8405	WCru
- Springtime = 'Monme'	SPer WDin XPep
umbellata ♀H2-3	CBcs CBot CHEx CTri CWib EBee EPfP GQui IDee LAst LHop LRHS MRav SBra SEND SLon SOWG WFar WHCG WPic WSHC
- f. **ovata**	CRez
- - B&SWJ 4706	WCru

Rhaphithamnus (*Verbenaceae*)

cyanocarpus	see *R. spinosus*
§ **spinosus**	CPle ERea WBod

Rhapidophyllum (*Arecaceae*)

hystrix	CBrP CRoM LPal NPal

Rhapis (*Arecaceae*)

§ **excelsa** ♀H1	CBrP CRoM CTrC EAmu LPal NPal WMul

Rhazya (*Apocynaceae*)

orientalis	see *Amsonia orientalis*

Rheum ✿ (*Polygonaceae*)

§ 'Ace of Hearts'	More than 30 suppliers
'Ace of Spades'	see *R.* 'Ace of Hearts'
acuminatum	CRow EBee GBin SBla
- HWJCM 252	WCru
alexandrae	CAgr CFir GCal GKir IBlr MTed
- BWJ 7670	WCru
'Andrew's Red'	GTwe
§ **australe**	CAgr CArn CRow EBee GCal LEdu LPBA LRHS MBro MLLN NBro NLar SMad WCot WFar WHoo
delavayi	EBee
- BWJ 7592	WCru
- SDR 1668	GKev
emodi	see *R. australe*
forrestii	CAgr
x **hybridum** 'Appleton's Forcing'	GTwe
- 'Baker's All Season'	GTwe
- 'Canada Red'	GTwe
- 'Cawood Delight'	GTwe NGHP SEND
- 'Champagne'	GTwe WSpi
- 'Daw's Champion'	GTwe
- 'Early Albert'	NGHP
- 'Early Cherry'	GTwe
- 'Fenton's Special'	GTwe
- 'German Wine'	GTwe
- 'Glaskins Perpetual' **new**	LBuc
- 'Goliath'	GTwe
- 'Grandad's Favorite'	EBre
- 'Greengage'	GTwe
- 'Hammond's Early'	GTwe SEND
- 'Harbinger'	GTwe
- 'Hawke's Champagne'	EBre GTwe
- 'Holsteiner Blut'	EBee WCot
- 'Mac Red'	GTwe
- 'Prince Albert'	GTwe
- 'Red Prolific'	GTwe
- 'Reed's Early Superb'	GTwe
- 'Stein's Champagne'	GTwe
- 'Stockbridge Arrow'	CSut GTwe NGHP
- 'Stockbridge Bingo'	GTwe
- 'Stockbridge Emerald'	GTwe
- 'Stockbridge Guardsman'	GTwe
* - 'Strawberry'	EMui GTwe MAsh
- 'Sutton's Cherry Red'	GTwe
- 'The Sutton'	GTwe
- 'Timperley Early'	CDoC CMac CTri EBre EMui ENot EPfP GTwe LRHS MAsh NBlu NGHP SCoo SDea SKee SPer
- 'Tingley Cherry'	GTwe
- 'Valentine'	GTwe
- 'Victoria'	EBre GKir GTwe LBuc LRHS MHer NGHP WTel
- 'Zwolle Seedling'	GTwe
kialense	CBct CDes EBee EGle GCal NBid NMRc NSti
moorcroftianum new	GCal
nobile	GKev WCru

– HWJK 2290 WCru
officinale CAgr CBct CHEx EPla GCal GKir
LRHS MBri SIde SWat
palmatum CArn CBcs CDWL EBee ECha ELan
EMFW ENot EPfP EPza GIBF GKir
LAst LPBA LRHS MRav MSal NGdn
SPer SSpi SWat WCAu WCot WFar
WMul WStI WWeb WWpP
– 'Atropurpureum' see *R. palmatum*
'Atrosanguineum'
§ – 'Atrosanguineum' ♀H4 CBct CBot CMea CRow EBre EChP
ECha ELan EPar EPla GBuc GFlt
GKir LPBA LRHS LRav MBri MRav
MWgw NBid NBro NFor SMad
SPer SPlb SWat WCom WCot WCru
WWin
– 'Bowles' Crimson' CBct CHad GKir LRHS MBri SAga
– 'Hadspen Crimson' CBct CHad WCot
– 'Red Herald' CBct SBla WCot
– *rubrum* COtt EBre GKir LRHS MCCP NArg
NBir WFar WMyn
– 'Saville' CBct GKir LRHS MBri MLLN MRav
– var. *tanguticum* More than 30 suppliers
I – – 'Rosa Auslese' LPhx WHil
rhabarbarum CRow
rhaponticum NLar
ribes WCot
subacaule **new** GKev
tataricum EBee LEdu

Rhigozum (Bignoniaceae)
obovatum **new** CTCP

Rhinanthus (Scrophulariaceae)
minor NSco

Rhodanthe (Asteraceae)
§ *anthemoides* ECou
– 'Paper Cascade'PBR GTwe LRHS

Rhodanthemum (Asteraceae)
from High Atlas, Morocco SIng
'African Eyes' EBee EBre EMan EPfP
§ *atlanticum* ECho EWes SScr
§ *catananche* ECho EPot ETow EWes MBNS
XPep
– 'Tizi-n-Test' LBee LRHS SBla
– 'Tizi-n-Tichka' CPBP CStu ETow EWes LBee LRHS
NBir SBla
§ *gayanum* EBee ECtt EWes LRHS SAga WCot
WHen XPep
– 'Flamingo' see *R. gayanum*
§ *hosmariense* ♀H4 CMHG EBee EBre ECha EDAr ELan
EPfP LHop LRHS MTis SAga SBla
SCoo SIng SPer SRms WAbe WCom
WEas XPep

Rhodiola (Crassulaceae)
bupleuroides CLD 1196 EMon
coccinea GCal WLin
crassipes see *R. wallichiana*
crenulata **new** EBee
dumulosa **new** EBee
§ *fastigiata* EMon GCal NMen
§ *heterodonta* ECha EGle ELan EMon LPio MRav
NPPs
himalensis (D. Don) Fu EMon
§ *ishidae* CTri
§ *kirilovii* EMon GBin GKir GTou
– var. *rubra* EBre WFar
linearifolia EMon GCal
pachyclados More than 30 suppliers
aff. *purpureoviridis* WCru
BWJ 7544 **new**

rhodantha NNS 99-454 NWCA
§ *rosea* CPrp EBre ECha EHoe ELan EMan
EPfP EPla GCal MHer NBid NBir
NFor NGdn NPPs NSla NSti SCro
SRms STre WAbb WCAu WCot
WDyG WEas WFar WTin WWhi
semenovii MHar NLar
§ *trollii* CNic CStu GCrs
§ *wallichiana* GCrs NBid WCot WDyG

Rhodochiton (Scrophulariaceae)
§ *atrosanguineus* ♀H1-2 CArn CBcs CEnd CPLG CRHN
CSpe CTCP ELan EPfP ERea GGar
LRHS MAsh NPPs SGar SHFr
SOWG WBVN
volubilis see *R. atrosanguineus*

Rhodocoma (Restionaceae)
arida WMul
capensis CAbb CBig CFir CPen CTrC ITer
WGer WMul
foliosa WMul
fruticosa CTrC
gigantea CAbb CBig CCtw CFir CTrC ITer
WMul WNor

Rhododendron ✿ (Ericaceae)
'A.J. Ivens' see *R*. 'Arthur J. Ivens'
'Abegail' MGos NPen SLdr
aberconwayi CWri LMil NLar NPen SLdr SReu
– 'His Lordship' GGGa LHyd
– pink NPen
acrophilum (V) GGGa
Argent 2768
'Actress' ISea NPen WCwm
'Ada Brunieres' (K) CSdC
'Addy Wery' (EA) ♀H3-4 CDoC ENot LKna MBar MGos
NPen SCam SLdr SPoG WBod WStI
adenogynum GGGa LMil NPen SLdr
– CLD 795 LMil
– Cox 6502 GGGa
§ – Adenophorum Group EMui
– – F 20444 SLdr
– – R 11471 NPen
– – 'Kirsty' NPen
– white NPen
adenophorum see *R. adenogynum*
Adenophorum Group
adenopodum GGGa NPen SLdr SReu
adenosum NHol NPen
– R 18228 GGGa
– Kuluense Group NPen
'Admiral Piet Hein' SReu
'Adonis' (EA/d) CMac MBar NLar SCam SLdr
'Adriaan Koster' (M) SLdr
adroserum see *R. lukiangense*
'Advance' (O) LRHS NPen SLdr
aeruginosum see *R. campanulatum* subsp.
aeruginosum
aganniphum GGGa LMil NPen SReu
– CN&W 1174 LMil
– EGM 284 LMil
– pink, KR 3528 from Pe, LMil
Doshang La
– var. *aganniphum* NPen
F 16472
§ – – Doshongense Group GGGa NPen
– – – KR 4979 LMil
– – – KW 5863 NPen
– – Glaucopeplum Group GGGa
– – Schizopeplum Group GGGa
– var. *flavorufum* GGGa MDun NPen
– – EGM 160 LMil
– 'Rusty' NPen

agapetum	see *R. kyawii* Agapetum Group
x **agastum**	NPen SLdr
- PW 98	LMil
'Ahren's Favourite'	MAsh
'Aida' (R/d)	CSBt SReu
'Aksel Olsen'	CTri ECho GEdr GKir MAsh MBar MDun NHol
'Aladdin' (EA)	CDoC ECho SLdr WFar WGwG
Aladdin Group	SReu
'Aladdin' (*auriculatum* hybrid)	GGGa
Albatross Group	IDee LKna LMil SLdr SReu SSta WGer
'Albatross Townhill Pink'	LMil
'Albert Schweitzer' ♀H4	CWri EMil GGGa LMil MBar MDun NBlu SLdr SPoG WFar
albiflorum (A)	GGGa
albrechtii (A)	GGGa LHyd LMil SReu SSpi WBod
- Whitney form (A)	LMil
'Alena'	GGGa
'Alexander' (EA) ♀H4	CDoC GQui LMil MGos SHBN SReu
'Alfred'	LRHS
'Alice' (EA)	LHyd LKna SPer
'Alice' (hybrid) ♀H4	CSBt LHyd LKna LMil NPen SLdr SReu
'Alice de Stuers' (M)	SLdr
'Alisa Nicole' (V)	SFai
Alison Johnstone Group	GGGa MDun MLea NPen ISea SLdr SReu WPic
'Alix'	LHyd
'Aloha'	MBar NBlu NDlv SHBN
Alpine Gem Group	GQui NHol SLdr
'Alpine Glow'	NPen
alutaceum	NPen
- var. **alutaceum**	GGGa
§ - - Globigerum Group	LMil
§ - - - R 11100	GGGa NPen
§ - var. **iodes**	GGGa LMil NPen SLdr
§ - var. **russotinctum**	GGGa MDun
- - R 158	SLdr
§ - - Triplonaevium Group USDAPI 59442/ R10923	GGGa
amagianum (A)	GGGa LMil SReu
ambiguum	LMil SLdr SReu WBod
- KR 185 select*	GGGa
I - 'Crosswater' **new**	LMil
- 'Jane Banks'	GTSp LMil
'Ambrosia' (EA)	CSBt
'America'	CBcs MAsh MBar MDun MGos WFar
amesiae	GGGa NPen
§ 'Amethystinum' (EA)	LKna
'Amity'	CDoC CWri ECho MAsh MLea SLdr WOrn
§ 'Amoenum' (EA/d)	CDoC CMac CSBt CTrG CTrw LHyd LKna LRHS MBar MGos NBlu NPen SCam SLdr SPer SPoG WAbe WBod WFar WPic
'Amoenum Coccineum' (EA/d)	SCam SReu WPat
Amor Group	LHyd
'Anah Kruschke'	MAsh SLdr
'Analin'	see *R.* 'Anuschka'
'Anchorite' (EA)	GQui LMil SLdr
'Andre'	NPen
* 'Andrea'	NPen
'Angelo'	LHyd
Angelo Group	CWri LHyd LMil SLdr SReu
'Ann Callingham' (K)	CSdC
'Ann Lindsay'	SReu
'Anna Baldsiefen'	ENot GLbr LMil MOne NHol SReu SSta
'Anna H. Hall'	MAsh SLdr
'Anna Rose Whitney'	CBcs CWri GGGa GKir LHyd LKna LMil LPan LRHS MAsh MBar MBri MDun MGos MLea NPen NPri SHBN SLdr SPer SReu SSta WBVN WBod
'Annabella' (K) ♀H4	CSdC MAsh MBri SLdr SReu
annae	GGGa LMil NPen SLdr
aff. **annae** C&H 7185	LMil
§ - Hardingii Group	NPen
'Anne Frank' (EA)	COtt MGos SReu WBod
'Anne George'	LHyd
'Anne Rothwell'	LHyd
'Anne Teese'	IDee LMil SLdr
'Annegret Hansmann'	GGGa
'Anneke' (A)	MBar MDun NDlv SLdr SReu SSta WBod
'Anny' (EA)	LKna SLdr
anthopogon	GCrs LMil
- from Marpha Meadow, Nepal	WAbe
- 'Betty Graham'	GGGa LMil
I - 'Crosswater **new**	LMil
§ - subsp. **hypenanthum**	LMil MDun
- - 'Annapurna'	GGGa NHol WAbe
§ **anthosphaerum**	GGGa NPen SLdr SReu
- KW 5684	NPen
- Gymnogynum Group	NPen
§ - Heptamerum Group	NPen
'Antilope' (Vs)	CWri LMil MDun SReu SSta
'Antje'	MAsh
'Antonio'	LMil WGer
Antonio Group	ELan
§ 'Anuschka'	GKir LRHS MAsh
§ **anwheiense**	CWri LHyd LMil NPen SReu
aperantum	GGGa
- F 27022	GGGa
- JN 498	GGGa
'Aphrodite' (EA)	GQui
apodectum	see *R. dichroanthum* subsp. *apodectum*
'Apotheose' (EA)	NBlu
'Apotrophia'	SLdr
'Apple Blossom' Wezelenburg (M)	NBlu SLdr
'Apple Blossom' ambig.	CMac CTrh SReu
N 'Appleblossom'	see *R.* 'Ho-o'
'Apricot Fantasy'	LMil
'Apricot Surprise'	GKir LRHS
'Apricot Top Garden'	SLdr
'April Dawn'	GGGa
'April Gem'	MAsh
§ 'April Glow'	LHyd
'April Showers' (A)	ENot LMil
'Arabesk' (EA)	SLdr
araiophyllum	GGGa
- BASEX 9698	GGGa
- KR 4029	LMil
§ **arborescens** (A)	GGGa LHyd LKna LMil NPen SLdr SReu
- pink (A)	LMil
arboreum	CHEx GGGa IDee ISea LMil MDun NPen SReu
- AC 4299	WAbe
- B&SWJ 2244	WCru
- C&S 1651	NPen
- C&S 1695	NPen
- subsp. **arboreum** KR 966	NPen
- 'Blood Red'	NPen SLdr
- subsp. **cinnamomeum**	GGGa LMil NPen SLdr SReu
- - var. **album**	LHyd SLdr SReu
- - var. **cinnamomeum** Campbelliae Group	NLar NPen SLdr

– – var. *roseum*	GGGa NPen
– – – BB 151*	NPen
* – – – *crispum*	SLdr
– – – 'Tony Schilling'	LHyd LMil NPen SLdr SReu
§ – subsp. *delavayi*	GGGa ISea NPen SLdr
– – C&H 7178	GGGa
– – C&S 1515	NPen
– – CN&W 994	LMil
– – EGM 360	LMil
– – KW 21796	NPen
– 'Heligan'	CWri SReu
– mid-pink	SLdr
§ – subsp. *nilagiricum*	GGGa SLdr
– var. *roseum*	SLdr
§ – subsp. *zeylanicum*	NPen SLdr
– – 'Rubaiyat'	NPen
'Arcadia' (EA)	LKna
'Arctic Fox' (EA)	GGGa
'Arctic Regent' (K)	CSdC GQui MAsh
'Arctic Tern'	see × *Ledodendron* 'Arctic Tern'
§ *argipeplum*	CWri GGGa LMil NPen SLdr
'Argosy' ♀H4	LMil NPen SLdr SReu
argyrophyllum	CWri IDee NPen SLdr
– subsp. *argyrophyllum*	SLdr
W/A 1210	
§ – subsp. *hypoglaucum*	NPen
– – 'Heane Wood'	GGGa
– subsp. *nankingense*	GGGa LMil NPen
– – 'Chinese Silver' ♀H4	LHyd LMil LRHS MDun NPen SReu
	WGer
§ *arizelum*	GGGa LHyd LMil LRHS MDun
	NPen SLdr
– BASEX 9580	GGGa
– R 25	GGGa
– SF 96228	ISea
– subsp. *arizelum*	LMil LRHS MDun NPen
Rubicosum Group	
'Armantine'	LKna
armitii (V) Woods 2518	GGGa
'Arneson Gem' (M)	CDoC CSam GGGa LMil MAsh
	NDlv NLar SLdr
'Arneson Ruby' (K)	CDoC
'Arpege' (Vs)	LMil NLar SReu
'Arthur Bedford'	CSBt LHyd LKna LMil SLdr SReu
§ 'Arthur J. Ivens'	SLdr
'Arthur Osborn'	GGGa SLdr
'Arthur Stevens'	SLdr
'Arthur Warren'	LKna
'Arthur's Choice' (V)	SFai
'Asa-gasumi' (EA)	LHyd SCam SLdr
asterochnoum	LMil
– C&H 7051	GGGa
– EGM 314	LMil
Asteroid Group	SLdr
'Astrid'	ENot NBlu
atlanticum (A)	GGGa LMil NPen SSpi
– 'Seaboard' (A)	LMil SLdr
'Audrey Wynniatt' (EA)	MAsh
Augfast Group	CTrw ISea SLdr WBod
'August Lamken'	MBri MDun
augustinii	CTrG CTrw CWri GGGa ISea LHyd
	LMil LRHS MLea NPen SLdr SPer
	SSpi SSta WAbe WBod
– subsp. *augustinii*	GGGa
C&H 7048	
§ – subsp. *chasmanthum*	GGGa LMil MDun SLdr WBod
– – C&Cu 9407 white	GGGa
– compact EGM 293 **new**	LMil
§ – Electra Group	GGGa IDee LHyd LMil MDun
	NPen SLdr
– Exbury best form	LHyd LMil SReu
§ – subsp. *hardyi*	GGGa SLdr
– pale lilac	SLdr
§ – subsp. *rubrum*	GGGa

– – 'Papillon'	NPen
* – 'Trewithen'	LMil
I – 'Werrington'	SReu WBor
§ *aureum*	GGGa GPoy LMil NPen SLdr
auriculatum	CWri GGGa LMil LRHS MDun
	NLar NPen SLdr SReu SSpi SSta
– PW 50	GGGa
– Reuthe's form	SReu
auriculatum	GGGa
× *hemsleyanum* **new**	
auritum	GGGa NPen SLdr WPic
'Aurora' (K)	NPen SLdr
'Aurore de Rooighem'	SLdr
(A) **new**	
§ *austrinum* (A)	LMil
– yellow (A)	LMil
'Autumn Gold'	LMil SLdr
'Avalanche' ♀H4	LMil SLdr SReu
Avocet Group	LMil SLdr
'Award'	LMil
'Aya-kammuri' (EA)	LHyd SLdr
Azamia Group	LHyd
Azor Group	LHyd NPen SReu
'Azorazie'	NPen
Azrie Group	SLdr
§ 'Azuma-kagami' (EA)	CDoC LHyd LKna LMil WBod
'Azurika'	NHol
'Azurro'	GGGa MBri
'Azurwolke'	LMil
'Babylon'	SReu
'Baden-Baden'	CDoC EBee GCrs GEdr LHyd LKna
	MAsh MBar MDun MGos NHol
	NPen NWea SBod SHBN SLdr SSta
	WBod WBrE WFar
'Bagshot Ruby'	ENot LKna NWea SReu
baileyi	GGGa NPen SLdr WAbe
– LS&H 17359	NPen
bainbridgeanum	NPen
USDAPI 59184/R11190	
'Balalaika' **new**	MDun
balangense EN 3530	GGGa
balfourianum	GGGa LMil NPen SLdr
– AC 1575 from	LMil
Xian Rindong	
– SSNY 224	GGGa
– var. *aganniphoides*	NPen
'Ballerina' (K)	SReu
'Balsaminiflorum'	see *R. indicum* 'Balsaminiflorum'
'Baltic Amber' (A)	GGGa
'Balzac' (K)	LHyd LMil MGos MLea SLdr WBVN
'Bambi'	CWri NPen SLdr SReu
'Bandoola'	SReu
'Barbara Coates' (EA)	SLdr
'Barbara Reuthe'	SReu
barbatum	CWri GGGa GGar IDee LHyd LMil
	MDun NPen SLdr
– B&SWJ 2237	WCru
– BL&M 325	NPen
I – 'Meteor' **new**	SReu
'Barbecue' (K)	LMil
'Barclayi Helen Fox'	NPen SLdr
'Barclayi Robert Fox'	NPen SLdr
'Bariton'	LMil
'Barmstedt'	CWri
'Barnaby Sunset'	GGGa GKir LMil LRHS MAsh NHol
'Barry Rodgers'	GGGa
'Bashful' ♀H4	CSBt EMui EPfP GKir LHyd LRHS
	MAsh MGos NPen SLdr SReu
§ *basilicum*	GGGa IDee LMil LRHS NPen
	SLdr
– AC 3009	WCwm
– AC 616	NPen
× *bathyphyllum*	NPen
– Cox 6542	GGGa

bauhiniiflorum — see *R. triflorum* var. *bauhiniiflorum*

beanianum — GGGa NPen SLdr
- KC 122 — GGGa
- KW 6805 — NPen
- compact — see *R. piercei*

'Beatrice Keir' — LMil NPen SLdr SReu
'Beattie' (EA) — MAsh SLdr
Beau Brummel Group — ELan LMil
'Beaulieu Manor' — GQui
'Beauty of Littleworth' — LHyd LKna NPen SLdr SPer SReu

beesianum — GGGa LMil NPen SLdr
- CN&W 1316 — ISea
- F 10195 — NPen
- F 16375 — SLdr
- JN 300 — GGGa
- KR 4114 — LMil
- KR 4150 — LMil
- red bud — SLdr

'Beethoven' (EA)   ♀H3-4 — CTrG LHyd NPen SCam SLdr SReu WGor WMoo WPic
'Belkanto' — ENot LMil
'Belle Heller' — SLdr
Bellerophon Group — NPen
'Ben Morrison' (EA) — SReu
'Bengal' — GEdr GKir MAsh MBar MDun NDlv NHol SReu WLow
'Bengal Beauty' (EA) — GQui SLdr
'Bengal Fire' (EA) — CMac
'Beni-giri' (EA) — CMac
'Bergie Larson' — CBcs CDoC LMil MAsh MBri MDun MLea SLdr

bergii — see *R. augustinii* subsp. *rubrum*
'Berg's Yellow' — CWri ISea MAsh MBri MDun MLea
'Bernard Shaw' — SReu
'Bernstein' — EMil NBlu WFar
'Berryrose' (K)   ♀H4 — CBcs CSBt CWri ENot EPfP GKir LHyd LKna LMil MAsh MBar MGos NBlu NPen SLdr SReu WBod
Berryrose Group — CDoC MDun
'Bert's Own' — CBcs SLdr
'Beryl Taylor' — GGGa NPen
'Betty' (EA) — CTrG LHyd SLdr WBod
'Betty Anne Voss' (EA) — GKir LHyd LMil LRHS MAsh NPri SCam SCoo SLdr SReu WGwG
'Betty Wormald' — CSBt CWri GKir LHyd LKna LMil MBri MGos MLea NPen SHBN SLdr SReu WBVN WOrn

bhutanense — LMil
- AC 119 — NPen
- AC 124 — NPen
- CH&M — GGGa
'Big Punkin' — LMil
'Billy Budd' — LHyd SLdr
'Birthday Girl' — CBcs COtt CWri LMil MDun MLea
'Birthday Greeting' — NPen
'Biscuit Box' — NPen
Biskra Group — GGGa LMil NPen
'Blaauw's Pink' (EA)   ♀H3-4 — CDoC CMac CSBt CTrh ENot EPfP GKir GQui LHyd LKna LMil LRHS MAsh MBar MBri MGos NPen SCam SLdr SPer SPlb SReu SRms WFar
'Black Hawk' (EA) — CBcs CTrG
'Black Knight' (A) — SLdr
'Black Magic' — CWri LMil
'Black Satin' — LMil
'Black Sport' — MLea
'Blatgold' — GGGa
Blaue Donau — see *R.* 'Blue Danube'
'Blazecheck' — LRHS MGos SCoo
'Blewbury'   ♀H4 — CDoC LHyd LMil LRHS MDun NPen SLdr SReu SSta
'Blue Beard' — SLdr

'Blue Bell' — LKna
'Blue Boy' — LMil
'Blue Chip' — LHyd NPen SLdr
§ 'Blue Danube' (EA)   ♀H3-4 — CDoC CMac CSBt CTrG CTrh CTri ENot GKir LHyd LKna LMil LRHS MAsh MBar MBri MDun NPen NPri SCam SLdr SPer SReu SSta WBod WPic WFar WOrn WStI
Blue Diamond Group — CBcs CBrm CChe CMHG CTrh ENot EPfP LKna LRHS MAsh MBar MDun MGos NHol NPen NWea SHBN SLdr SReu SRms WBod WPic
'Blue Diamond' — CSBt MLea WMoo
'Blue Gown' — LKna
'Blue Monday' — SLdr WBod
'Blue Moon' — MBar
'Blue Mountain' — NWea
'Blue Peter'   ♀H4 — CDoC CSBt CWri EMil ENot EPfP GGGa LHyd LKna LMil MAsh MBar MBri MDun MGos NBlu NPen SHBN SLdr SReu SSta
'Blue Pool' — LMil MBar WBod
Blue Ribbon Group — CMHG CTrw ISea
'Blue Silver' — GGGa LMil MAsh
'Blue Star' — GKir LHyd LRHS MAsh MDun MLea NMen
'Blue Steel' — see *R. fastigiatum* 'Blue Steel'
Blue Tit Group — CBcs CSBt CTrG GKir LHyd LKna LRHS MAsh MBar NPen SHBN SLdr SReu SSta WBod
Bluebird Group — CSBt ECho ENot LKna MBar MDun MGos NBlu NDlv NWCA SLdr SRms WBod
Bluestone Group — WBod
'Bluette' — MDun MLea NDlv
'Blurettia' — CWri LMil NLar
'Blutopia' **new** — WGer
'Bob Bovee' **new** — NLar
'Bobbie' — SReu
'Bob's Blue' — MDun
'Boddaertianum' — LHyd SReu
bodinieri — WBod
- USDAPI 59585/R11281 — NPen
'Bodnant Yellow' — CSam LMil
'Bold Janus' (V) — SFai
'Bonfire' — SReu
***boothii* new** — GGGa
'Bo-peep' — LHyd LRHS SReu
Bo-peep Group — CBcs LMil NPen SLdr
'Boskoop Ostara' — LMil
'Boule de Neige' — MDun
'Bouquet de Flore' (G)   ♀H4 — CDoC CSdC LMil MBar SLdr SPer SReu
Bow Bells Group — CSam ISea LHyd LKna LMil MAsh MBar MDun MGos MLea SHBN
'Bow Bells'   ♀H4 — EPfP GEdr GKir LRHS NBlu NLar NPen NPri SLdr WBod WFar
'Bow Street' — LHyd
brachyanthum — GGGa NPen
- subsp. ***hypolepidotum*** — GGGa LMil NPen
- - KW 7038 — NPen
brachycarpum — GGGa NPen SLdr
- from Japan — CStu
- subsp. ***brachycarpum*** Tigerstedtii Group — LMil SReu
§ - subsp. ***fauriei*** — NPen
- pink — NPen
- 'Roseum Dwarf' — GGGa NPen
brachysiphon — see *R. maddenii* subsp. *maddenii*
'Brazier' (EA) — CTrh LHyd LRHS NPen SCam SLdr
'Brazil' (K) — CSBt LKna SReu
Break of Day Group — CWri
'Bremen' — LMil SLdr
'Brets Own' — NPen

Bric-a-brac Group	CBcs CTrw NPen SLdr
'Bric-a-brac'	LHyd MDun
'Bride's Bouquet' (EA/d)	SReu
'Bridesmaid' (O)	ENot EPfP SLdr
'Brigadoon'	LMil MBri
'Bright Forecast' (K)	CWri MAsh SLdr WGor
'Brigitte'	CDoC CWri GGGa LMil LRHS MAsh SLdr
'Brilliant' (EA)	MGos WBod
'Brilliant' (hybrid)	MGos NHol
'Brilliant Blue'	MAsh
'Brilliant Crimson' (EA)	SLdr
'Britannia'	CSBt CSam CWri EPfP GKir ISea LHyd LKna MAsh MBar MGos NPen NWea SHBN SLdr SPer SReu WFar
'Britannia' x *griersonianum*	SLdr
'Brocade'	CSam LHyd LKna LMil MDun NPen SLdr
'Bronze Fire' (A)	SLdr SReu
'Broughtonii'	CWri NPen SLdr
'Brown Eyes'	MDun MLea SLdr
'Bruce Brechtbill' ♀H4	CDoC CWri GGGa GKir ISea LMil LRHS MAsh MBri MDun MGos NBlu NHol SLdr SReu SSta WOrn
§ 'Bruns Elfenbein'	NLar
'Bruns Gloria'	LMil
'Buccaneer' (EA)	LHyd SLdr
'Bud Flanagan'	LMil MDun NPen
'Buketta'	GGGa MDun
bullatum	see *R. edgeworthii*
bulu C&V 9503	GGGa
'Bungo-nishiki' (EA/d)	CMac
bureavii ♀H4	CABP GGGa LHyd LMil MDun NPen SLdr SReu SSta
- C&H 7158	GGGa
- F 15609	NPen
- R 25439	NPen
- SEH 211	LMil
- SF 517	ISea
- 'Ardrishaig'	GGGa
* - *cruentum*	LMil
I - 'Lem's Variety'	NLar
bureavii x Elizabeth Group	SReu
bureavioides	MDun NPen SReu
- Cox 5076	GGGa
'Burletta'	GGGa
burmanicum	GGGa LMil MDun NPen SLdr WBod
'Burning Love' **new**	NLar
'Butter Brickle'	MLea
'Butter Yellow'	ECho GEdr MDun WBod
'Buttercup' (K)	MBar
'Butterfly'	LKna MDun NPen SLdr
'Buttermilk' (V)	ISea
'Buttermint'	MAsh MBri MDun MGos MLea NPen SHBN SLdr WBVN WGwG
'Buttons and Bows' (K)	GGGa LMil
'Buzzard' (K)	CSdC LKna LMil
'C.I.S.'	NPen
'Caerhays Lavender'	CBcs
caesium	GGGa
calendulaceum (A)	LMil SReu
- red (A)	LMil
- yellow	LMil
Calfort Group	NPen SLdr
'Calico' (K)	CSdC
caliginis (V)	GGGa
callimorphum	GGGa LMil NPen
- var. *myiagrum* F 21821a	NPen SLdr
- - KW 6962	NPen
calophytum ♀H4	CHEx CWri GGGa IDee LHyd LMil LRHS NPen SLdr
- EGM 343	LMil
- Knott 151	NPen
- var. *openshawianum* C&H 7055	GGGa
- - EGM 318	LMil
calophytum x *praevernum*	WCwm
calostrotum	CBrm CWri WAbe
- SF 357	ISea
- 'Gigha' ♀H4	CDoC GGGa GKir LMil LRHS LTwo MDun MGos MOne SLdr WGwG
§ - subsp. *keleticum* ♀H4	CTrG GEdr LHyd MBar MDun MGos NHol WAbe
- - F 19915	NHol
- - F 21756	NPen
- - R 58	LMil
§ - - Radicans Group	GCrs GEdr LHyd LMil MBar MBro MDun MLea NHol WAbe WBod WPat
- - - USDAPI 59182/R11188	MLea
- - - mound form	NHol
- subsp. *riparium*	LMil
- - SF 95089	ISea
- - Calciphilum Group	GGGa MDun
§ - - Nitens Group	CDoC GGGa IDee LMil MAsh NDlv NMen WAbe WPGP
§ - - Rock's form R 178	GGGa NHol WAbe
caloxanthum	see *R. campylocarpum* subsp. *caloxanthum*
'Calsap'	GGGa
Calstocker Group	LMil
calvescens var. *duseimatum*	NPen
camelliiflorum	GGGa MDun
'Cameronian' (Ad)	LKna
campanulatum	COtt LHyd LKna MDun NPen SLdr SReu WAbe
- HWJCM 195	WCru
- SS&W 9107	SLdr
- TSS 11	NPen
§ - subsp. *aeruginosum*	GGGa LMil MDun NLar NPen SLdr SReu
- - Airth 10	GGGa
- *album*	NPen SLdr
- subsp. *campanulatum* BL&M 283	NPen
- - 'Roland Cooper'	NPen SLdr
- - 'Knap Hill'	LHyd NPen SLdr
- - 'Waxen Bell'	LHyd NPen
§ - 'Campfire' (EA)	SLdr
Campirr Group	LHyd
campylocarpum	GGGa LHyd LMil MDun NPen SLdr SReu
- LS&H 16495*	NPen
§ - subsp. *caloxanthum*	GGGa MDun NPen
- - KR 3516 from Pe, Doshang La	LMil
- - KR 6152	LMil
- - Telopeum Group	NPen
- - - KW 5718B	NPen
- subsp. *campylocarpum* TSS 12	NPen
- - Elatum Group	NPen
- East Nepal	MDun
campylogynum ♀H4	GCrs MGos MLea NMen SSpi WAbe
- Cox 6051	GGGa
- Cox 6096	GGGa
- SF 95181	ISea

	- 'Album'	see R. 'Leucanthum'
I	- 'Bramble'	MDun
	- Castle Hill form	LMil
	- Charopoeum Group	GCrs GGGa LMil MBar MDun MGos NHol WBod
	- - 'Patricia'	ECho GBin MDun WAbe WLow
	- claret	ECho GGGa MDun WAbe
§	- Cremastum Group	CTrG GGGa LHyd NHol NPen WAbe
	- - 'Bodnant Red'	GGGa LHyd MDun NPen WBod
	- var. **leucanthum**	see R. 'Leucanthum'
	- Myrtilloides Group	CDoC CTrw EPot GGGa GQui IDee LHyd LMil LRHS MAsh MDun NLAp NMen NPen SLdr SReu WAbe WBod
	- - Farrer 1046	GGGa
	- pink	MBar WAbe
	- plum	WAbe
	- salmon pink	ECho EPot GEdr MDun WBod
	camtschaticum	GGGa SReu WAbe
	- from Hokkaido, Japan	GCrs NMen
	- from Rishiri	GCrs
	- var. **albiflorum**	GGGa NMen
	- red	GGGa
	canadense (A)	GGGa NHol SLdr SReu
	- f. **albiflorum** (A)	GGGa LMil
	- dark-flowered (A)	LMil
	- 'Deer Lake' (A)	SReu
	'Canary'	LKna SLdr SReu
§	x **candelabrum**	NPen
	canescens (A)	LMil
	'Cannon's Double' (K/d) ♀H4	CWri GGGa LHyd LMil MAsh MBri MGos MLea NLar SLdr
	'Cannon's Purple'	GLbr
	'Canzonetta' (EA) ♀H4	GGGa LMil MGos SLdr
	'Capistrano'	GGGa
	capitatum	GGGa
	'Caprice' (EA)	SReu
	'Captain Jack'	GGGa SLdr
	'Caractacus'	EMil MBar NBlu WFar
	'Carat'	SLdr SReu
	'Cardinal'	SLdr
	cardiobasis	see R. orbiculare subsp. cardiobasis
	Carita Group	LKna SReu
	'Carita Golden Dream'	LKna LMil NPen
	'Carita Inchmery'	LHyd LKna NPen SLdr
	'Carmen'	CBrm GGGa GKir ISea LHyd LKna LMil LRHS MAsh MBar MDun MLea NHol NMen NPen NWea SHBN SLdr SReu SRms
	carneum	GGGa LMil
	'Caroline Allbrook' ♀H4	CDoC CSam CWri EMui GGGa GLbr ISea LHyd LMil MAsh MBri MDun MGos MLea NDlv NHol NPen SLdr SReu WBVN
	'Caroline de Zoete'	LHyd
	carolinianum	see R. minus var. minus
	'Cary Ann'	CBcs CSam CWri GKir LRHS MAsh NPen SReu WFar
	'Casablanca' (EA) **new**	SLdr
	'Cassley' (Vs)	LMil SLdr
	'Castle of Mey'	SLdr
	catacosmum	GGGa
§	'Catalode'	GGGa
	catawbiense	GGGa LHyd NPen SLdr
	'Catawbiense Album'	CWri GGGa GKir LRHS MAsh NBlu NWea WFar
	'Catawbiense Boursault'	MAsh
	'Catawbiense Grandiflorum'	GKir LRHS MAsh WFar
	'Catherine Hopwood'	NPen SLdr
	caucasicum	NPen
	- ex AC&H	NPen
§	- 'Cunningham's Sulphur'	MDun
	'Caucasicum Pictum'	GGGa LHyd LMil MBar SLdr
	'Cayenne' (EA)	SLdr
	'Cecile' (K) ♀H4	CBcs CWri GKir GLbr LHyd LKna LMil MAsh MBar MBri MDun MGos MLea NBlu NPen SLdr SReu
	'Celestial' (EA)	CMac
	'Centennial'	see R. 'Washington State Centennial'
	cephalanthum	GGGa LMil
	- subsp. **cephalanthum** SBEC 0751	GGGa WAbe
	- - Crebreflorum Group	GGGa LMil LRHS WAbe
	- - Nmaiense Group C&V 9513	GGGa
	- subsp. **platyphyllum**	GGGa LMil
	- - CN&W 835	LMil
	cerasinum	GGGa ISea LMil NPen SLdr
	- C&V 9504	GGGa
	- KR 3460	LMil
	- KR 3490 from Pe, Doshang La	LMil
	- KW 11011	NPen
	- SF 95067	ISea
	- 'Cherry Brandy'	LHyd NPen
	- 'Coals of Fire'	NPen
	- deep pink-flowered	NPen
	'Cetewayo' ♀H4	SReu
	chaetomallum	see R. haematodes subsp. chaetomallum
	'Chaffinch' (K)	LKna
	chamaethomsonii	GGGa LMil NPen
	- CCH&H 8195	GGGa
	- SF 95084	ISea
	- var. **chamaethauma** KR 3506 from Pe, Doshang La	LMil
	- - KW 5847	LMil
	- var. **chamaethomsonii** F 21723	NPen
	chameunum	see R. saluenense subsp. chameunum
§	'Champagne' ♀H3-4	CSBt GKir LHyd LKna LMil LRHS MAsh MDun MGos MLea NLar NPen SLdr SReu
	championiae	GGGa
	'Chanel' (Vs)	LMil MDun SLdr SReu SSta
	'Chanticleer' (EA)	CTrh SCam SLdr SReu
	chapaense	see R. maddenii subsp. crassum
	'Chapeau'	LMil
	charitopes	GGGa LMil NPen SLdr
	- subsp. **charitopes** F 25570	SReu
§	- subsp. **tsangpoense**	GGGa GQui LMil NHol
	- - C&V 9575*	GGGa
	'Charlemagne' (G) **new**	SLdr
*	'Charles Puddle'	WBod
	'Charlotte de Rothschild' (hybrid)	LMil NPen SLdr
	Charmaine Group	GGGa NHol SReu WBod
	'Charme La'	GGGa
	'Charming Valentino' (V)	SFai
	chasmanthum	see R. augustinii subsp. chasmanthum
	'Cheer'	COtt CWri LPan MAsh MBar NBlu SLdr SReu WFar WGor
	'Cheerful Giant' (K)	GKir LMil LRHS MGos
	'Chelsea Reach' (K/d)	CSdC LKna
	'Chelsea Seventy'	COtt ENot GKir LRHS MAsh NLar NPen SLdr
	'Chenille' (K/d)	LKna
	'Cherokee'	SCam SLdr
	'Cherries and Cream'	LMil
	'Cherry Drop' (EA) **new**	MAsh
	'Chetco' (K)	CDoC LMil

'Chevalier Félix
    de Sauvage' ♀H4   EMil LMil MGos NPen SReu
'Cheyenne'   SLdr
'Chicago' (M)   LKna
'Chiffchaff'   LHyd NMen
'Chikor'   CSBt CTrG GGGa GKir LKna MAsh
                        MBar MBri MDun MGos NHol
                        NPen SLdr SReu WBVN WBod
                        WFar
China Group   LKna SReu
'China A'   LKna SLdr
'Chinchilla' (EA)   GQui WGor
'Chink'   CBcs ENot MBar MDun NPen SLdr
                        WBod
'Chintz'   WBod
'Chionoides'   GGGa LKna NBlu SLdr
'Chipmunk' (EA/d)   LMil LRHS MAsh
'Chippewa' (EA)   GGGa GKir LMil LRHS
'Chocolate Ice' (K/d)   LKna SLdr
'Chopin' (EA)   WBod
'Choremia' ♀H3   LHyd LMil NPen SReu WBod
'Chorister' (K)   LKna
'Chris' (EA)   SLdr
christi (V)   GGGa
'Christina' (EA/d)   CMac SLdr SReu WBod WGor
'Christmas Cheer' (EA/d) see *R.* 'Ima-shojo'
'Christmas Cheer' (hybrid) CBcs CMac CWri GGGa ISea LHyd
                        LKna LMil MAsh MGos MLea NBlu
                        NPen SHBN SLdr SPer SReu WPic
§ 'Christopher Wren' (K) SLdr
chrysanthum   see *R. aureum*
chryseum   see *R. rupicola* var. *chryseum*
chrysodoron   GGGa LMil NPen
'Chrysomanicum'   NPen
ciliatum   CBcs GGGa LHyd LMil NPen SLdr
                        WAbe
- 'Multiflorum'   see *R.* 'Multiflorum'
ciliicalyx SF 535   ISea
- subsp. *lyi*   see *R. lyi*
- 'Walter Maynard' **new** LMil
Cilpinense Group   CBcs ENot GKir LKna LMil LRHS
                        MAsh MBar MDun NPen SLdr
                        WBod WFar
'Cilpinense' ♀H3-4   CSBt EBee EMil EPfP GGGa LHyd
                        LRHS NPri SPoG SReu WBrE
cinnabarinum   LMil MDun NPen SLdr
- B&SWJ 2633   WCru
- 'Caerhays Lawrence'   NPen SLdr
- subsp. *cinnabarinum* MDun SLdr
- - BL&M 234   LMil
- - 'Aestivale'   LMil
- - Blandfordiiflorum   GGGa IDee LMil NPen SLdr
    Group
§ - - 'Conroy'   GGGa LMil LRHS MDun MLea
                        SReu
- - from Ghunsa, Nepal MDun
- - 'Nepal'   LHyd
- - ex LS&M 21283   LMil
- - Roylei Group   GGGa LMil MDun MLea NPen SLdr
                        SReu
- - - 'Vin Rosé'   LMil MDun
§ - subsp. *tamaense*   GGGa NPen
- - KW 21003   NPen
- - KW 21021   GGGa NPen
§ - subsp. *xanthocodon* IDee LMil MDun MLea NPen SLdr
- - KW 8239   NPen
§ - - Concatenans Group CBcs GGGa MDun MLea NPen
                        SLdr
- - - C&V 9523   GGGa
- - - KW 5874   LMil
- - - LS&T 6560   NPen
- - - 'Amber'   LMil MDun MLea
- - - 'Copper'   SLdr
- - Purpurellum Group   GGGa MDun NPen SLdr WBod

Cinnkeys Group   GGGa MDun
Cinzan Group   LMil SReu
citriniflorum   NPen
- R 108   GGGa LMil
- var. *citriniflorum* LMil
- var. *horaeum*   NPen
- - F 21850*   GGGa
- - F 25901   NPen
'Citronella' **new**   SLdr
'Claydian Variegated' (v) GGGa
clementinae   GGGa LMil MDun NPen SLdr SReu
- F 25705   LMil NPen
- JN 352   GGGa
- JN 722   GGGa
- JN 723   GGGa
- JN 729   GGGa
clementinae x *pronum* GGGa
'Cliff Garland'   GQui LMil
Clio Group   NPen
'Coccineum Speciosum'   CSBt CSdC GGGa LMil MBar SReu
    (G) ♀H4
'Cockade' (EA)   LKna
'Cockatoo' (K)   LKna
§ *coelicum* F 25625   GGGa
- KW 21075   NPen
- KW 21077   NPen
coeloneuron   CBcs GGGa LMil MDun
- EGM 334   LMil
'Colin Kenrick' (K/d)   LKna SLdr
collettianum H&W 8975 GGGa
'Colonel Coen'   CWri GGGa GLbr LRHS MAsh
                        MBri MGos MLea NPri SHBN SLdr
Colonel Rogers Group   LHyd NPen SLdr SReu
x *columbianum*   see *Ledum* x *columbianum*
'Colyer' (EA)   SLdr
Comely Group   LHyd NPen SLdr
- 'Golden Orfe'   SLdr
complexum F 15392   GGGa
'Comte de Gomer' (hybrid) CBcs
concatenans   see *R. cinnabarinum* subsp.
                        xanthocodon Concatenans Group
concinnum   CTrw CWri LHyd MDun MLea
                        NPen SLdr
- Pseudoyanthinum   GGGa GQui LMil MDun NPen
    Group   SReu
'Conroy'   see *R. cinnabarinum* subsp.
                        cinnabarinum 'Conroy'
'Constable'   LHyd NPen SLdr
'Constant Nymph'   LKna
'Contina'   GGGa
Conyan Group   LHyd
cookeanum   see *R. sikangense* var. *cookeanum*
                        Cookeanum Group
'Coral Flare' (V)   SFai
'Coral Mist'   GGGa LMil
'Coral Reef'   NPen SLdr SReu
'Coral Sea' (EA)   SLdr SReu
'Coral Seas' (V) **new** SFai
'Coralie' (EA/d) **new** SLdr
'Cordial Orange' (V)   SFai
coriaceum   GGGa LMil LRHS NPen WCwm
- R 120   NPen
'Corneille' (G/d) ♀H4   CSBt LKna LMil SLdr SPer SReu
'Cornish Cracker'   NPen SLdr
Cornish Cross Group   LHyd NPen SLdr SReu
Cornish Early Red Group see *R.* Smithii Group
'Cornish Red'   see *R.* Smithii Group
Cornubia Group   NPen SLdr
'Corona'   LKna
'Coronation Day'   SLdr SReu
'Coronation Lady' (K)   ENot LKna
'Corringe' (K)   LMil
'Corry Koster'   LKna
coryanum   GGGa NPen

– – angel form	SLdr	
– – 'Ho Emma'	LMil MDun	
– – var. *kyomaruense* **new**	LMil	
– – 'Oki Island'	LMil	
– 'Rae's Delight'	LMil	
dekatanum	GGGa	
deleiense	see *R. tephropeplum*	
'Delicatissimum' (O)	CWri GGGa GQui LHyd MLea NLar SLdr WBVN WGwG	
'Delp's Cupcake'	NLar	
dendricola	SLdr	
– KW 20981	GGGa	
dendrocharis	GGGa	
– CC&H 4012	GGGa	
– Cox 5016	GGGa NHol WAbe	
– 'Glendoick Gem'	GGGa	
– 'Glendoick Jewel'	GGGa	
* 'Denny's Rose' (A)	LMil SLdr SReu	
'Denny's Scarlet'	SReu	
'Denny's White'	LMil SLdr SReu	
denudatum C&H 7118	GGGa	
– C&H 70102	GGGa	
– EGM 294	LMil	
– SEH 334	LMil	
'Desert Orchid'	LHyd	
'Desert Pink' (K)	LKna	
desquamatum	see *R. rubiginosum* Desquamatum Group	
x *detonsum*	LMil NPen SLdr	
– F13784	SLdr	
'Devisiperbile' (EA)	SLdr	
'Devonshire Cream'	SLdr	
'Diabolo' (K)	LKna	
Diamant Group (EA)	GGGa	
– lilac (EA)	GGGa LMil MBri MLea	
– pink (EA)	ECho MDun MGos MLea NBlu SReu WAbe WLow	
§ – purple (EA)	ECho MDun MGos MLea WAbe	
§ – red (EA)	MDun MLea NBlu WAbe	
– rosy red (EA)	ECho MBri	
– white (EA)	ECho LRHS MDun MLea NBlu SLdr WAbe	
'Diamant Purpur'	see *R.* Diamant Group purple	
'Diamant Rot'	see *R.* Diamant Group red	
'Diana Pearson'	LHyd NPen	
'Diane'	LKna NPen SLdr	
diaprepes	see *R. decorum* subsp. *diaprepes*	
dichroanthum	GGGa LHyd LMil MDun NPen SLdr SReu	
– CCH&H 8198	GGGa	
§ – subsp. *apodectum*	GGGa LMil NPen	
– subsp. *dichroanthum*	LMil	
– – F 6781	NPen	
– – SBEC 545	GGGa	
§ – subsp. *scyphocalyx*	GGGa LMil NPen SLdr	
– – F 24546	GGGa	
– – F 27115	GGGa	
– – F 27137	NPen	
– – Farrer 1024	GGGa	
– subsp. *septentroniale*	GGGa	
– – JN 575	GGGa	
dictyotum	see *R. traillianum* var. *dictyotum*	
'Dido'	LHyd	
didymum	see *R. sanguineum* subsp. *didymum*	
'Dietrich'	WFar	
dignabile C&V 9569	GGGa	
– KR 5385	LMil	
dilatatum	LMil	
dimitrum	MDun	
'Diny Dee'	MGos	
'Diorama' (Vs)	SLdr SReu SSta	
diphrocalyx	NPen	

§ 'Directeur Moerlands' (M)	SLdr	
discolor	see *R. fortunei* subsp. *discolor*	
'Doc'	EBee EMui ENot EPfP GKir LHyd LMil LRHS MAsh MBar MDun MGos NBlu NDlv NPen SLdr SReu WFar WStI	
'Doctor A. Blok' **new**	SLdr	
'Doctor Arnold W. Endtz'	NPen	
'Doctor Chas Baumann' (G) **new**	SLdr	
'Doctor Ernst Schäle'	GGGa	
'Doctor H.C. Dresselhuys'	MBar SHBN	
'Doctor Herman Sleumer' (V)	GGGa	
'Doctor M. Oosthoek' (M) ♀H4 **new**	CSBt SReu	
'Doctor Stocker'	NPen	
'Doctor Tjebbes'	ISea	
'Doctor V.H. Rutgers'	MBar WFar	
'Don Giovanni' **new**	NLar	
'Don Quixote' (K)	CSdC MAsh	
'Doncaster'	ENot GKir LKna MBar MGos NPen NWea SHBN SLdr WFar	
'Dopey' ♀H4	CDoC CSBt CWri EBre EMui ENot EPfP GGGa GKir LHyd LMil LRHS MAsh MBar MDun MGos MLea NBlu NDlv NHol NPen SHBN SLdr SReu	
'Dora Amateis' ♀H4	CBcs COtt GGGa GKir IDee ISea LHyd LMil LRHS MAsh MBar MBri MGos NHol NPen NPri SLdr SPer SReu WGwG WPic	
Dormouse Group	CDoC GGGa LMil SLdr SReu WBVN	
'Dorothea'	SLdr	
'Dorothy Corston' (K)	LKna	
'Dorothy Hayden' (EA)	SLdr	
'Dorset Sandy' (EA) **new**	MAsh	
'Dörte Reich'	GGGa	
doshongense	see *R. aganniphum* var. *aganniphum* Doshongense Group	
'Double Beauty' (EA/d)	LKna SReu SSta	
'Double Damask' (K/d) ♀H4	LHyd LKna SLdr SReu	
'Double Date' (d)	CDoC SLdr	
'Doubloons'	NPen SLdr	
'Douglas McEwan'	MDun SLdr	
'Dracula' (K)	GGGa	
Dragonfly Group	SReu	
Dragonfly Group x *serotinum*	SLdr	
'Drake's Mountain'	ECho MBar MDun	
'Dreamland' ♀H4	COtt CSBt CWri EBee ENot LHyd LMil MAsh MDun MGos MLea NPri SLdr SReu WFar WOrn	
'Dresden Doll' (V)	SFai	
'Driven Snow' (EA)	ENot SLdr	
drumonium	see *R. telmateium*	
'Drury Lane' (K)	GQui LMil LRHS	
dryophyllum hort.	see *R. phaeochrysum* var. *levistratum*	
'Duchess of Portland'	SReu	
'Duchess of Rothesay'	NPen	
'Duchess of Teck'	SReu	
'Dusky Dawn'	NPen SLdr	
'Dusky Orange'	SReu	
'Dusty' **new**	MDun	
'Dusty Miller'	COtt EBee GKir ISea LRHS MAsh MBar MDun MGos NBlu NDlv SHBN SLdr	
'Earl of Athlone'	LHyd SReu	
'Earl of Donoughmore'	LHyd LKna NBlu SReu SSta	
'Early Beni' (EA)	LHyd	
Early Brilliant Group	LKna	

'Ebony Pearl'　CWri GGGa MGos MLea SLdr
eclecteum　LMil MDun NPen SLdr
　- Cox 6054　GGGa
　- 'Rowallane Yellow'　NPen SLdr
'Eddy' (EA)　LKna NPen
§ *edgeworthii* ♀H2-3　GGGa ISea LMil NPen SLdr WAbe
　- AC 666　NPen
　- KC 0106　GGGa
edgeworthii x *leucaspis* CBcs
'Edith Bosley'　GGGa
'Edith Mackworth Praed'　SReu
'Edna Bee' (EA)　GQui LMil SLdr
'Effner'　LMil
'Egret' ♀H4　EPot GGGa GKir MAsh MBar MBri
　　MDun MGos MLea NHol SLdr
　　SReu WAbe
'Ehrengold'　LMil
'Eider'　GGGa ISea MAsh NPen SLdr SReu
　　WFar
'Eileen'　LMil SReu
'El Camino'　COtt MBri MLea NPen SHBN SLdr
'El Greco'　NPen SLdr
Eldorado Group　GQui
'Eleanor' (EA)　WBod
'Eleanor Habgood'　SLdr
Electra Group　see *R. augustinii* Electra Group
elegantulum　GGGa LHyd LMil MDun NPen SLdr
'Elfenbein'　see *R.* 'Bruns Elfenbein'
'Elfin Gold'　SReu
'Elisabeth Hobbie' ♀H4　GGGa LKna LMil MBar MDun
　　MGos SLdr WLow
Elizabeth Group　CBcs CDoC CTrh CTrw CWri
　　GGGa GLbr IMGH LHyd LKna LMil
　　LRHS MAsh MBar MGos NHol
　　NPen NWea SHBN SLdr SPer SReu
　　WBod WFar
'Elizabeth' **new**　MGos WOrn
N 'Elizabeth' (EA)　CSBt CSam ENot EPfP GKir MGos
　　NWCA WBod
'Elizabeth de Rothschild'　LMil MDun NPen SLdr
'Elizabeth Jenny'　see *R.* 'Creeping Jenny'
'Elizabeth Lockhart'　GEdr GGGa GKir GQui MBar
　　MDun MGos MLea WBod
'Elizabeth of Glamis'　GGGa
'Elizabeth Red Foliage'　CDoC CTri GGGa GKir LHyd LMil
　　LRHS MAsh MDun SPer SReu
elliottii　GGGa NPen SLdr SReu
　- KW 7725　NPen
Elsae Group　NPen SLdr SReu
'Else Frye'　GGGa
'Elsie Lee' (EA/d) ♀H3-4　CDoC CTrh GGGa LMil MAsh SLdr
　　SReu SSta
'Elsie Pratt' (A)　MBar SReu
'Elsie Straver'　NHol SHBN SLdr SReu
'Elsie Watson'　GGGa LMil
'Elspeth' **new**　LHyd LKna
§ *Emasculum*　COtt LKna SLdr SReu
'Ember Glow'　NPen
Emerald Isle Group　SReu
'Empire Day'　LKna SLdr
'Enborne'　NPen
'English Roseum'　NBlu SLdr
'Erato'　ENot GGGa LMil
eriocarpum 'Jitsugetsuse' LHyd
eriogynum　see *R. facetum*
eritimum　see *R. anthosphaerum*
'Ernest Inman'　LHyd Nmin SLdr
erosum　GGGa NPen SLdr
erubescens　see *R. oreodoxa* var. *fargesii*
　　Erubescens Group
§ x *erythrocalyx*　NPen
　　Panteumorphum Group
N 'Esmeralda'　CMac CTrG
Ethel Group　SLdr

'Etna' (EA)　SCam SLdr
'Etta Burrows'　CWri GGGa MDun
'Euan Cox'　GGGa NHol NMen
euchaites　see *R. neriiflorum* subsp.
　　neriiflorum Euchaites Group
euchroum　NPen
eudoxum　GGGa NPen
　- KW 5879*　NPen
　- var. *eudoxum* R 6c　NPen
'Eunice Updike' (EA)　LHyd
'Europa'　SReu
eurysiphon　NPen
　- KW 21557*　NPen
　- Arduaine form　GGGa
'Eva Goude' (K)　LKna
'Evelyn Hyde' (EA)　SLdr
'Evening Fragrance' (A)　SReu
'Evensong' (EA)　LKna
'Everbloom' (EA)　NPen SLdr
'Everest' (EA)　ENot LHyd LMil MAsh SLdr WBod
'Everestianum'　GGGa LKna MBar
'Everitt Hershey' (A) **new**　SLdr
'Everlasting'　see *Kalmia latifolia*
　　x *R. williamsianum*, 'Everlasting'
exasperatum　NPen
　- KC 0116　GGGa
　- KC 0126　GGGa
　- KW 8250　GGGa
'Exbury Albatross'　LKna
'Exbury Calstocker'　LMil
'Exbury May Day'　SReu
'Exbury Naomi'　LHyd LKna LMil NPen SLdr
'Exbury White' (K)　EPfP GQui
'Excalibur'　GGGa
excellens　LMil
　- AC 146　GGGa
　- SF 92074　ISea
　- SF 92079　ISea
　- SF 92303　ISea
eximium　see *R. falconeri* subsp. *eximium*
'Exquisitum' (O) ♀H4　CDoC CWri EPfP GGGa LMil MAsh
　　MBri MLea NLar SLdr SSpi WBVN
exquisitum　see *R. oreotrephes* Exquisitum
　　Group
§ *faberi*　GGGa LMil NPen SLdr
　- subsp. *prattii*　see *R. prattii*
'Fabia' ♀H3　GGGa LHyd LMil
Fabia Group　LKna MDun NPen SLdr
'Fabia' x *bureavii*　SLdr
'Fabia Roman Pottery'　MDun
§ 'Fabia Tangerine'　LHyd MDun MLea SReu WBod
'Fabia Waterer'　LMil
§ *facetum*　GGGa LMil MDun NPen SLdr
　- AC 3049　LMil
　- Farrer 1022　NPen
　- SF 612　ISea
'Faggetter's
　　Favourite' ♀H4　LKna LMil MDun NPen SLdr SPoG
　　SReu SSta
Fairy Light Group　CSam LMil SLdr
'Falcon'　see *R.* (Hawk Group) 'Hawk
　　Falcon'
falconeri ♀H3-4　CHEx GGGa IDee ISea LHyd LMil
　　LRHS MDun NPen SLdr SReu
　　WGer
　- B&SWJ 2437　WCru
§ - subsp. *eximium*　GGGa LMil MDun SLdr
　- subsp. *falconeri*　CWri
'Fanal' (K)　CDul SLdr
'Fanny'　see *R.* 'Pucella'
'Fantastica' ♀H4　CDoC ELan GGGa LHyd LMil LRHS
　　MAsh MBri MDun NLar SPoG SReu
fargesii　see *R. oreodoxa* var. *fargesii*
'Fashion'　CTrG
fastigiatum　GCrs LMil MBar NLAp NPen SLdr

– C&H 7159	GGGa
– SBEC 804/4869	GGGa MDun NHol
– SF 518	ISea
§ – 'Blue Steel' ♀H4	CBcs CDoC COtt CWri EBre GGGa
	GKir GLbr IMGH LMil LRHS MAsh
	MBri MBro MDun MGos NHol
	NPen SPlb SReu WAbe WPat
'Fastuosum Flore Pleno'	CSBt CWri GBin GGGa GKir ISea
(d) ♀H4	LHyd LKna LMil MBar MBri MDun
	MGos MLea NPen NWea SLdr
	SPoG SReu SSta WFar
§ *faucium*	GGGa LMil NPen
– C&V 9508	GGGa
– KR 3465 from	LMil
Pe, Doshang La	
– KR 3771	LMil
– KR 5024	GGGa
– KR 5040	LMil
– KR 6229	LMil
– KW 6401	NPen
– SF 95098	ISea
aff. *faucium* KW 5732	NPen
fauriei	see *R. brachycarpum* subsp.
	fauriei
'Favorite' (EA)	CMac CTrw LHyd LKna LRHS
	NPen SCam SLdr
'Fedora' (EA)	CBcs LHyd LKna SLdr
'Fernanda Sarmento' (A)	SReu
ferrugineum	GGGa LHyd LKna LMil MBar MGos
	NPen SLdr SReu WBod
* – *compactum*	ECho
– 'Plenum' (d)	MDun
– 'Festive'	LHyd
'Feuerwerk' (K)	SLdr
fictolacteum	see *R. rex* subsp. *fictolacteum*
Fire Bird Group	LHyd SLdr
'Fire Rim'	GGGa
'Fireball' (K) ♀H4	CBcs CDoC CTri CWri GGGa GLbr
	LHyd LMil LRHS MAsh MLea NBlu
	NDlv WOrn
'Fireball' (hybrid)	GKir LRHS NPri SLdr
Firedrake Group	SReu
'Firefly' (K)	ENot
'Firefly' (EA)	see *R.* 'Hexe'
'Fireglow'	CSBt CSdC SLdr WFar
'First Light' (V)	SFai
'Flamenco Dancer' (V)	SFai
'Flaming Bronze'	SReu
'Flaming June' (K)	LKna
§ *flammeum* (A)	LMil
'Flanagan's Daughter'	LMil LRHS MAsh
I Flava Group	see *R.* Volker Group
flavidum	GGGa LMil SLdr WAbe WBod
– Cox 6143	GGGa
– 'Album'	LMil LRHS SReu
§ 'Flavour'	LKna
fletcherianum	NPen WAbe
– R 22302	NPen
– 'Yellow Bunting'	GGGa
fleuryi KR 3286	GGGa
§ *flinckii*	GGGa LMil LRHS MDun NPen
– CH&M 3080	GGGa
floccigerum	GGGa LMil NPen SLdr
– AC 1898 from Da Po Shan	LMil
– bicolored	NPen
'Flora Lockblott'	SLdr
'Floradora' (M)	SReu
'Floriade'	LKna
floribundum	LMil LRHS NPen SLdr
– EGM 294	LMil
– 'Swinhoe'	SReu
'Florida' (EA/d) ♀H3-4	CMac LKna LMil NBlu SPoG SReu
	WBod WFar WMoo
'Flower Arranger' (EA)	LMil MAsh NPri SCoo

formosanum	GGGa
formosum	CBcs GGGa GQui NPen
§ – var. *formosum*	GGGa LMil NLar SLdr
Iteaphyllum Group	
– – 'Khasia' C&H 320	GGGa
– var. *inaequale* C&H 301	GGGa
forrestii	GGGa NPen
– subsp. *forrestii*	LMil
– – LS&T 5582	NPen
– – Repens Group	GGGa LMil NPen SLdr
– – – 'Scinghku'	GGGa
– Tumescens Group	GGGa NHol NPen SLdr
– – C&V 9517	GGGa
Fortorb Group	NPen
Fortune Group	NPen SLdr
fortunei	CBcs CWri GGGa ISea LHyd LKna
	LMil MDun NPen SLdr SReu
§ – subsp. *discolor* ♀H4	GGGa LMil NPen SLdr WGer
– – PW 34	GGGa
– – 'Hilliers Best'	SLdr
§ – – Houlstonii Group	LMil NPen
– – – 'John R. Elcock'	LMil
fortunei subsp. *discolor*	SLdr
x 'Lodauric Iceberg'	
– 'Foxy'	NPen SLdr
– 'Lu-Shan'	MDun
– 'Mrs Butler'	see *R. fortunei* 'Sir Charles Butler'
§ – 'Sir Charles Butler'	LMil LRHS
'Fox Hunter'	LKna SLdr
fragariiflorum	GGGa
C&V 9519	
– LS&E 15828	GGGa
'Fragrant Star' (A) **new**	GGGa
'Fragrantissimum' ♀H2-3	CBcs CDoC CTrG CTrw CWri
	GGGa ISea LHyd LMil MDun MRav
	NLar NPen WAbe WBod
'Francesca'	GGGa
Francis Hanger	NPen SLdr SReu
(Reuthe's) Group	
'Frank Baum'	NPen SReu
'Frank Galsworthy' ♀H4	LKna LMil NLar SReu
'Frans van der Bom' (M)	LMil SLdr
'Fraseri' (M)	GGGa
'Fred Hamilton **new**	CWri
'Fred Nutbeam' (EA)	LMil MGos
'Fred Peste'	LMil MAsh MDun MGos MLea
	SReu WBVN
'Fred Wynniatt'	CWri LHyd LMil NPen SLdr SReu
'Fred Wynniatt Stanway'	see *R.* 'Stanway'
'Frere Organ' (G)	SLdr
'Freya' (R/d)	LMil SLdr
'Fridoline' (EA)	GGGa
'Frilled Petticoats'	NPen SLdr SReu
'Frilly Lemon' (K/d)	CDoC LMil MDun NLar SLdr
'Frome' (K)	LKna
'Frosted Orange' (EA)	LMil MAsh SLdr
'Frosthexe'	GGGa WAbe
§ 'Frühlingstraum'	LHyd
'Fuko-hiko' (EA)	NPen
'Fulbrook'	NPen
fulgens	GGGa LHyd LMil MDun NPen
	SReu
fulvum ♀H4	CDoC GGGa IDee LHyd LMil LRHS
	MDun NPen SLdr SReu SSta
– AC 3083	LMil
– subsp. *fulvoides*	LMil NPen SLdr
– – Cox 6532	GGGa
– – R 143	NPen
– – R 180	NPen
'Fumiko' (EA)	SLdr
Furnivall's	CSBt CWri ENot EPfP GGGa LHyd
Daughter' ♀H4	LKna LMil LRHS MBar MBri MDun
	MGos NPen SLdr SReu SSta WFar
'Fusilier'	LHyd SReu

'Gabriele' (EA)	GQui SSpi
'Gabrielle Hill' (EA)	CDoC COtt LMil MAsh SLdr
'Gaiety' (EA)	LMil SReu
'Galactic'	NPen SLdr
galactinum	LMil MDun NPen SLdr
- EN 3537	GGGa
- W/A 4254	NPen
'Galathea' (EA)	CDoC
'Gandy Dancer'	CWri MBri MDun SLdr WBVN
'Garden State Glow' (EA/d)	SLdr
'Gartendirektor Glocker'	CWri GGGa MDun MLea SLdr SReu
'Gartendirektor Rieger' ♀H4	CWri GGGa IDee LMil MDun NHol SReu
'Gauche' (A)	GQui SLdr
'Gaugin'	GQui
Gaul Group	SLdr
'Gauntlettii' x *thomsonii*	SLdr
'Gay Lady' **new**	SLdr
'Geisha' (EA)	MBar
'Geisha Lilac' (EA)	COtt ECho GKir LMil LRHS MAsh MBar MBri MDun MLea NDlv
§ 'Geisha Orange' (EA) ♀H4	COtt CTrh EGra GGGa GKir LMil LRHS MAsh MBar MBri MDun MGos MLea NDlv NPri SLdr WAbe WLow
'Geisha Purple' (EA)	COtt LMil MAsh MBar MDun MLea NBlu WFar
'Geisha Red' (EA)	COtt EPfP LMil MBar MBri MDun MLea NDlv WAbe WFar
Geisha White = 'Hisako' (EA) **new**	MDun MLea NDlv
'Gekkeikan' (EA)	CBcs
'Gena Mae' (A/d)	GGGa LMil SLdr
'General Eisenhower'	CSBt SReu
'General Eric Harrison'	LHyd NPen SLdr
'General Practitioner'	ENot NPen SLdr
'General Sir John du Cane'	NPen
'General Wavell' (EA)	CMac LKna SLdr
'Gene's Favourite'	SReu
genestierianum	GGGa
CC&H 8080	
'Genghis Khan'	NPen
'Geoffroy Millais'	LMil
'Georg Arends' (EA)	NPri SLdr
'George Haslam'	SLdr
'George Hyde' (EA)	LMil MAsh NPri SCoo
'George Reynolds' (K)	GKir MAsh
'George's Delight'	CWri GGGa MAsh MLea SLdr
'Georgette'	LHyd NPen SLdr
§ x *geraldii*	SLdr
'Germania'	LMil MAsh MBar
Gertrud Schäle Group	CTri MBar MDun NHol SReu
Gibraltar Group	CTri
'Gibraltar' (K) ♀H4	CBcs CDoC CSBt CWri ENot EPfP GGGa GKir LHyd LKna LMil LRHS MAsh MBar MBri MGos MLea NPri SLdr SReu SSta WBod
giganteum	see *R. protistum* var. *giganteum*
'Gilbert Mullier'	MBri NBlu
'Ginger' (K)	CSBt EPfP LMil LRHS MAsh NPen SLdr
'Ginny Gee' ♀H4	CDoC COtt CSBt CTrh CWri EPfP GGGa GKir GLbr LHyd LMil LRHS MAsh MBar MBri MDun MGos MLea NHol NMen NPen NPri SLdr SReu SSta WAbe WBod WFar WOrn
§ 'Girard's Hot Shot' (EA)	CTrh ECho GQui MAsh MGos SLdr SReu
'Girard's Hot Shot' variegated (EA/v)	GGGa
'Glacier' (EA)	MGos SLdr
'Glamora' (EA)	SLdr

glanduliferum	LRHS SLdr
- C&H 7131	GGGa
- EGM 347	LMil
- PW 044 from Miao Miao Shan	LMil
glaucophyllum	GGGa LHyd LMil MDun NPen SLdr WAbe WBod
- B&SWJ 2638	WCru
- var. *album*	GGGa
- Borde Hill form	LMil
§ - subsp. *tubiforme*	NPen SReu
'Glendoick Butterscotch'	GGGa
'Glendoick Crimson' (EA)	GGGa
'Glendoick Dream' (EA)	GGGa
'Glendoick Ermine' (EA)	GGGa
'Glendoick Garnet' (EA)	GGGa
'Glendoick Glacier'	GGGa MGos
'Glendoick Goblin' (EA) **new**	GGGa
'Glendoick Gold'	GGGa
'Glendoick Ruby'	GGGa
'Glendoick Vanilla' **new**	GGGa
'Glendoick Velvet'	GGGa
'Glenroy Carpet'	SReu
'Glen's Orange'	CWri
'Gletschernacht'	CWri LMil
glischroides	see *R. glischrum* subsp. *glishchroides*
glischrum	GGGa NPen SReu
- subsp. *glischroides*	GGGa LMil NPen
- subsp. *glischrum*	GGGa LMil
§ - subsp. *rude*	GGGa LMil NPen
- - C&V 9524	GGGa
globigerum	see *R. alutaceum* var. *alutaceum* Globigerum Group
'Glockenspiel' (K/d)	LKna SLdr
'Gloria'	see *R.* 'Bruns Gloria'
'Gloria Mundi' (G)	SReu
'Glory of Leonardslee'	SLdr
'Glory of Littleworth' (Ad)	LMil
'Glory of Penjerrick'	NPen SLdr
'Glowing Embers' (K)	CDoC CTri CWri GKir LMil LRHS MAsh MBri MDun MLea SLdr SReu WBVN WFar WOrn
Goblin Group	SLdr
'Gog' (K)	CSBt LHyd LKna
'Gold Crest' (K)	LKna
'Gold Dust' (K)	SLdr
'Gold Mohur'	SLdr SReu
'Goldball'	see *R.* 'Christopher Wren'
'Goldbukett'	GGGa LHyd MGos SReu
'Golden Bee'	GGGa NHol
'Golden Belle'	CWri
'Golden Bouquet'	LRHS MAsh
'Golden Charm' (V)	SFai
'Golden Clipper'	LHyd
'Golden Coach'	COtt CWri MDun MGos MLea NPen SLdr WBVN
'Golden Eagle' (K)	CDoC CDul COtt GKir LMil MAsh MDun MGos SCoo SLdr WBVN WOrn
'Golden Eye' (K)	LKna SLdr
'Golden Flare' (K)	CBcs CDoC LHyd MAsh NBlu SLdr SPer SReu WBrE WMoo
'Golden Fleece'	LKna SReu
'Golden Gate'	CDoC MDun NPen SLdr WGor WGwG WOrn
'Golden Horn' (K)	GQui SLdr WGor
Golden Horn Group	NPen SLdr
'Golden Horn Persimmon'	see *R.* 'Persimmon'
'Golden Lights' (A)	CDoC CWri GKir LMil LRHS MAsh MBri MDun NPri WBVN WOrn
Golden Oriole Group	CBcs NHol NPen
§ - 'Talavera'	CBcs

'Golden Oriole'	LKna SReu
'Golden Princess'	COtt LMil MDun NHol
'Golden Ruby'	MBri
'Golden Splendour'	LMil
'Golden Sunset' (K)	COtt CSdC GLbr LMil MBar MBri MDun MGos MLea SLdr
'Golden Torch' ♀H4	CAbP CBcs CMHG COtt CSBt CWri EBee ENot EPfP GGGa GKir LHyd LMil LRHS MAsh MDun MGos MLea NBlu NDlv NPen SHBN SLdr SPer SReu SSta WBVN WOrn
'Golden Wedding'	CBcs CSBt CWri LHyd LMil MAsh MDun MGos MLea SLdr WBVN
'Golden Wit'	ECho MDun SLdr
'Goldfinch' (K)	LKna
'Goldfinger'	MDun
'Goldflamme'	SLdr
'Goldflimmer' (v)	EBee EMil ENot GGGa GKir LMil LRHS MAsh MGos MLan NBlu NPri SLdr SReu WFar
'Goldfort'	CWri LKna SReu
'Goldika'	LMil
'Goldkrone' ♀H4	CDoC CWri ENot GGGa ISea LHyd LMil MAsh MBri MDun MGos MLea NLar NPen SLdr SReu WBVN WOrn
Goldschatz = 'Goldprinz'	GGGa
'Goldstrike'	LMil SLdr
'Goldsworth Crimson'	LHyd
'Goldsworth Orange'	CSBt GGGa LKna MGos NPen SLdr SReu
'Goldsworth Pink'	LKna SReu
'Goldsworth Yellow'	CSBt CSam LKna MGos SLdr SReu
'Golfer'	GGGa LMil
'Gomer Waterer' ♀H4	CDoC CSBt CSam CWri EPfP GGGa GKir GLbr LHyd LKna LMil MAsh MBar MBri MDun MGos MLea NPen NWea SLdr SPer SReu SSta WBVN WFar WOrn
'Good News'	SLdr
'Gordon Jones'	GGGa
'Govenianum' (Ad)	LKna SLdr
'Grace Seabrook'	CDoC COtt CSam CTri CWri GGGa GKir GLbr LHyd LMil LRHS MAsh MDun MGos NPri SLdr SPer SReu WBVN WOrn
gracilentum (V)	GGGa
'Graciosum' (O)	LKna SReu
'Graf Lennart'	LMil MAsh
'Graham Thomas'	LMil SReu
'Grand Slam'	MDun SLdr
grande	GGGa NPen SLdr
- TSS 37	NPen
- pink	NPen
aff. *grande* KC 0105	GGGa
- KR 13649	NPen
'Grandeur Triomphante' (G)	CSdC SReu
gratum	see R. basilicum
'Graziella'	GGGa
'Greensleeves'	LKna LMil
'Greenway' (EA)	CBcs SLdr
'Gretia'	LHyd
'Gretzel'	NLar NPen SReu
griersonianum	CBcs GGGa LHyd LMil MDun NPen SLdr
- F 24116	NPen
griffithianum	CWri GGGa NPen SLdr WPic
- B&SWJ 2425	WCru
'Gristede' ♀H4	CDoC GGGa IDee LMil MAsh MDun NHol SLdr SReu
groenlandicum	see Ledum groenlandicum
'Grosclaude'	NPen SLdr
'Grouse' x *keiskei* var. ozawae 'Yaku Fairy'	ECho
'Grumpy'	CDoC CSBt CWri EMui ENot GGGa GKir LHyd LMil LRHS MBar MGos NDlv NPen SHBN SLdr SReu WOrn
'Guelder Rose'	SLdr
'Gumpo' (EA)	CMac EPot SLdr
'Gumpo Pink' (EA)	SLdr WBod
'Gumpo White' (EA)	MAsh WAbe WBod
'Gwenevere' (V)	SFai
'Gwillt-king'	WCwm
'H.H. Hume' (EA)	CDoC IMGH SLdr
'H.O. Carre' (EA)	CMac
'H. Whitner'	NPen
habrotrichum	GGGa NPen
- F 15778	NPen
'Hachmann's Bananaflip'	LHyd
'Hachmann's Brasilia'	MAsh MBri
'Hachmann's Charmant'	GGGa LMil MBri
'Hachmann's Diadem'	LMil
'Hachmann's Feuerschein'	ENot LMil
'Hachmann's Kabarett'	LMil
'Hachmann's Marlis' ♀H4	ENot LHyd LMil MAsh SReu
§ 'Hachmann's Polaris' ♀H4	LMil MBri MDun
'Hachmann's Porzellan'	LMil
§ 'Hachmann's Rokoko' (EA)	ECho GGGa LMil
haematodes	GGGa MDun NPen SRms
- AC 710	NPen
- CLD 1283	LMil
- 'Blood Red'	SLdr
§ - subsp. *chaetomallum*	GGGa LMil NPen SLdr
- - F 25601	NPen
- - JN 493	GGGa
- - R 18359	NPen
- - R 41	NPen
- subsp. *haemotodes* F 6773	NPen
- - McLaren S124A	NPen
- - SBEC 585	GGGa
'Haida Gold'	MGos MLea NPen SLdr SReu
'Halfdan Lem'	CBcs CDoC GGGa MAsh MBri MDun MGos MLea NPen SHBN SLdr SPer SReu SSta WOrn
'Hallelujah'	MAsh
'Halton'	NPen
'Hamlet' (M)	LMil
'Hammondii' (Ad)	LKna WOrn
'Hana-asobi' (EA)	LHyd LRHS SCam SLdr
hanceanum	NPen SLdr WBod
- 'Canton Consul'	GGGa LHyd
- Nanum Group	GGGa WBod
hanceanum x *lutescens*	WBod
'Handsworth Scarlet'	SLdr
'Hansel'	CWri MAsh MDun NLar SLdr
§ *haofui* Guiz 75	GGGa
Happy Group	GLbr SHBN
§ 'Hardijzer Beauty' (Ad)	LKna LRHS SLdr SReu WAbe
hardingii	see R. annae Hardingii Group
hardyi	see R. augustinii subsp. hardyi
'Harkwood Premiere'	GGGa MGos
'Harkwood Red' (EA)	CTrh GQui LHyd SCam SLdr
Harmony Group **new**	SLdr
'Harry Tagg'	CTrG SLdr
'Harumiji' (EA)	SLdr
'Harvest Moon' (K)	LMil MDun SCoo SReu
'Harvest Moon' (hybrid)	MBar MGos SLdr SReu
'Hatsugiri' (EA)	CMac ENot EPfP LHyd LKna LMil MBar SCam SLdr SReu
(Hawk Group) 'Crest'	see R. 'Crest'
- 'Hawk Buzzard'	SLdr
§ - 'Hawk Falcon'	SReu
- 'Jervis Bay'	see R. 'Jervis Bay'
'Haze'	SLdr

'Heather Macleod' (EA)	LHyd SLdr
heatheriae KR 6150 **new**	GGGa
- KR 6158	GGGa
- SF 99068	ISea
heftii	NPen
'Helen Close' (EA)	CTrh SCam SLdr
'Helen Curtis' (EA)	SReu
'Helen Martin' **new**	NLar
'Helena Pratt' (Vs) **new**	LMil
'Helene Schiffner' ♀H4	GGGa LMil NPen SReu
heliolepis	GGGa LMil
- AC 759	NPen
- SF 489	ISea
- SF 516	ISea
- var. **fumidum**	see *R. heliolepis* var. *heliolepis*
§ - var. **heliolepis**	LMil
- - CN&W 1038	ISea
- - F 6762	NPen
- - SSNY 66	NPen
x **hemigynum**	NPen SLdr
hemitrichotum	NPen
- F 30940	NPen
- KW 4050	NPen
hemsleyanum	GGGa LMil MDun NPen SLdr
hemsleyanum x **ungernii**	GGGa
heptamerum	see *R. degronianum* subsp. *heptamerum*
'Herbert' (EA)	CMac
'Heureuse Surprise' (G) **new**	SLdr
§ 'Hexe' (EA)	WBod
'High Summer'	LMil WGer
'Hilda Margaret'	SReu
'Hille'PBR	LMil
'Hino-crimson' (EA) ♀H3-4	CDoC CMac CSBt CTrG CTrh CTri LKna LMil LRHS MAsh MBar MBri MGos SCam SLdr SPer SReu SSta WFar WStI
'Hinode-giri' (EA)	CBcs CDoC CMac CTrw ENot LHyd LKna NPen SCam SLdr SReu WPic
'Hinode-no-kumo' (EA)	NPen SLdr
N 'Hinomayo' (EA) ♀H3-4	CMac CSBt CTrG EPfP GQui LHyd LKna LMil LRHS MAsh MBar NPen SCam SLdr SReu SSta WBod WPic WStI
'Hino-scarlet'	see *R.* 'Campfire'
'Hino-tsukasa' (EA)	NPen SLdr
hippophaeoides	CDoC EPfP LMil MDun NMen NPen SLdr WFar
- F 22197a	SLdr
- Yu 13845	GGGa LMil MDun
- 'Bei-ma-shan'	see *R. hippophaeoides* 'Haba Shan'
- 'Glendoick Iceberg' **new**	GGGa
§ - 'Haba Shan' ♀H4	GGGa LMil MDun
hirsutum	GGGa LHyd LMil SReu
- f. **albiflorum**	GGGa SReu
- 'Flore Pleno' (d)	ECho EPot GCrs GGGa MBar MDun MLea WBod
hirtipes	GGGa LMil
- AC 3257	SLdr
- C&V 9546	GGGa
- KR 5059	LMil
- KR 5219	LMil
- KW 6223	NPen
- LS&T 3624	NPen
x **hodconeri**	NPen
- 'pink'	NPen
hodgsonii	GGGa IDee LHyd LMil LRHS MDun NHol NPen SLdr SReu
- B&SWJ 2656	WCru
- LS&H 21296	NPen
- TSS 42A	NPen SLdr
- TSS 9	NPen SLdr
- 'Poet's Lawn'	NPen
'Hojo-no-odorikarako' (EA)	NPen
'Hollandia' (hybrid)	SHBN
'Homebush' (K/d) ♀H4	CBcs CDoC CDul CMHG CWri ENot EPfP GGGa GKir GLbr LHyd LKna LMil MAsh MBar MBri MDun MLea SLdr SReu SSta WBVN
'Honey'	LKna NPen
'Honey Star' (V)	SFai
'Honeymoon'	MAsh NPen
'Honeysuckle' (K)	MBar SLdr SReu WBod
'Hong Kong'	MAsh
hongkongense	GGGa NPen
§ 'Ho-o' (EA)	CBcs SLdr
hookeri	CTrG LMil NPen SReu
- KW 13859	NPen
- Tigh-na-Rudha form	GGGa
'Hope Findlay'	LHyd
'Hoppy'	CDoC CSBt CWri ENot GKir GWCH LMil LRHS MAsh MDun MLea NBlu NPen SLdr SReu WBVN WCwm WOrn
'Horizon Lakeside'	GGGa LMil
'Horizon Monarch' ♀H3-4	CWri GGGa LMil LRHS MDun SLdr
horlickianum	GGGa NPen
- KW 9403	NPen
'Hortulanus H. Witte' (M)	CSBt SLdr SReu WFar
'Hot Shot'	see *R.* 'Girard's Hot Shot'
'Hotei' ♀H4	CBcs CDoC CSBt CSam CTri CWri GEdr GGGa GKir IDee LHyd LMil LRHS MAsh MBar MDun MGos NPen NPri SHBN SLdr SReu SSta WBod
Hotspur Group (K)	GGGa LHyd SCoo
'Hotspur' (K)	CSBt CWri GKir MGos SLdr
'Hotspur Red' (K) ♀H4	CDoC GKir LKna LMil SReu WOrn
'Hotspur Yellow' (K)	SReu
houlstonii	see *R. fortunei* subsp. *discolor* Houlstonii Group
huanum	LMil
- C&H 7073	GGGa
- EGM 316	LMil
'Hugh Koster'	CSBt LKna MGos NPen SLdr
'Humboldt'	MAsh WFar
Humming Bird Group	CMHG CSam EPot GGGa ISea LHyd LKna MBar MDun MGos MLea NBlu NHol NPen SHBN SLdr SReu SRms WBod
hunnewellianum 'Crane'	GGGa SLdr
'Hurricane'	COtt MDun SLdr
'Hussar'	CWri
'Hyde and Seek'	GQui
'Hydie' (EA/d)	LMil MAsh MGos NPri SCoo
'Hydon Amethyst'	LHyd
'Hydon Ball'	LHyd
'Hydon Ben'	LHyd
'Hydon Comet'	LHyd
'Hydon Dawn' ♀H4	CDoC COtt CWri GGGa GKir LHyd LMil LRHS MDun MGos MLea NDlv NPen SLdr SReu SSta
'Hydon Glow'	LHyd NPen SLdr
'Hydon Gold'	LHyd
'Hydon Haley'	LHyd
'Hydon Hunter' ♀H4	COtt ISea LHyd LMil MAsh NDlv NPen SLdr SPer SReu SSta
'Hydon Juliet'	LHyd
'Hydon Mist'	LHyd
'Hydon Pearl'	LHyd
'Hydon Primrose'	LHyd
'Hydon Rodney'	LHyd
'Hydon Salmon'	LHyd NPen
'Hydon Velvet'	LHyd SReu
hylaeum	NPen

– BASEX 9659	GGGa	
– KW 6833	NPen	
Hyperion Group	LKna LMil SReu SSta WFar	
hyperythrum	GGGa LHyd LMil MDun NHol NPen SLdr SSpi	
– ETOT 196	MDun	
* – *album*	NPen	
– pink-flowered	NPen	
hypoglaucum	see *R. argyrophyllum* subsp. *hypoglaucum*	
Ibex Group	NPen	
'Ice Cream'	LKna	
'Ice Cube'	ISea MDun MGos MLea SLdr WOrn	
'Ice Maiden'	SReu	
'Iceberg'	see *R.* 'Lodauric Iceberg'	
'Icecream Flavour'	see *R.* 'Flavour'	
'Icecream Vanilla'	see *R.* 'Vanilla'	
Idealist Group	NPen	
'Idealist'	SReu	
'Ightham Gold'	SReu	
'Ightham Peach'	SReu	
'Ightham Purple'	SReu	
'Ightham Yellow'	NPen SLdr SReu	
'Igneum Novum' (G)	SReu	
§ 'Ilam Melford Lemon' (A)	LMil	
§ 'Ilam Ming' (A)	LMil	
§ 'Ilam Red Velvet'	SLdr	
'Ilam Violet'	LKna LMil	
Imago (K/d)	CSdC LKna MBri SLdr	
§ 'Ima-shojo' (EA/d)	CSBt LHyd LMil SCam SLdr WBod	
'Impala' (K)	LKna	
impeditum	CBcs CDoC CSBt CWib EBee ENot GGGa GLbr ISea LHyd LKna MAsh MBar MDun MGos MLea NHol NLAp NMen NPen NWea SLdr SPer SReu SSta WBVN WFar	
– F 29268	GGGa NPen	
– 'Blue Steel'	see *R. fastigiatum* 'Blue Steel'	
– dark, compact	LKna	
– 'Indigo'	CMHG MAsh MBri MDun WAbe WBod	
– 'Johnston's Impeditum'	LKna	
– 'Moerheim'	see *R.* 'Moerheim'	
– 'Pygmaeum'	MBro WAbe WPat	
– Reuthe's form	SReu	
– 'Williams'	SLdr	
imperator	see *R. uniflorum* var. *imperator*	
'Impi' **new**	SReu	
Impi Group	LKna MDun NLar NPen	
'Inamorata' **new**	SLdr	
'Independence Day'	MAsh	
Indiana Group	CWri	
§ *indicum*	CMac SLdr WAbe	
'Balsaminiflorum' (EA/d)		
– orange (EA)	SLdr	
x *inopinum*	GGGa NPen	
insigne ♀H4	GGGa GTSp IDee LHyd LMil MDun NPen SLdr WGer	
– hybrid	SLdr	
– Reuthe's form	SReu	
insigne x *yakushimanum*	SReu	
x *intermedium* white	GGGa	
Intrepid Group	SReu	
intricatum	GGGa WAbe	
– KW 4184	NPen	
Intrifast Group	GGGa LHyd NHol NMen SLdr WBod	
iodes	see *R. alutaceum* var. *iodes*	
'Irene Koster' (O) ♀H4	CMHG CSBt CWri EPfP GGGa GLbr LHyd LKna LMil MBri MDun NLar SLdr SReu	

'Irohayama' (EA) ♀H3-4	CMac CTrw GQui LHyd LKna LMil SCam SLdr SPoG SReu SSta	
irroratum	LMil NPen SLdr	
– C&H 7185	GGGa	
– CN&W 392	WCwm	
– CN&W 395	WCwm	
– SF 384	ISea	
– SF 92304	ISea	
– subsp. *irroratum* C&H 7100	GGGa	
* – subsp. *kontumense* var. *ningyuenense* EGM 339	LMil	
– 'Langbianense' KR 3295	LMil	
– pale pink	NPen	
§ – subsp. *pogonostylum*	NPen SLdr	
– 'Polka Dot'	GGGa LHyd LMil NPen SLdr	
'Isabel Pierce'	CWri LMil	
'Isabella Mangles'	LHyd	
'Isola Bella'	GGGa	
iteaphyllum	see *R. formosum* var. *formosum* Iteaphyllum Group	
'Ivette' (EA)	CMac LHyd LKna	
Iviza Group	SReu	
'Ivory Coast'	LMil	
'Iwato-kagami' (EA)	NPen	
'Izayoi' (EA)	WBod	
'J.C. Williams'	CBcs	
'J.M. de Montague'	see *R.* 'The Hon. Jean Marie de Montague'	
'J.R.R. Tolkien'	SLdr	
'Jabberwocky'	LHyd	
'Jack Skelton'	LHyd	
'Jack Skilton'	SLdr	
'Jacksonii'	ISea LKna MBar NPen SLdr SReu	
Jacques Group	NPen	
Jalisco Group	NPen SLdr	
'Jalisco Eclipse'	LKna SLdr	
'Jalisco Elect'	CDoC CWri LKna LMil NPen SLdr SPer WCwm	
'Jalisco Goshawk'	SLdr	
'Jalisco Janet'	NPen	
'James Barto'	LHyd NPen SLdr	
'James Burchett' ♀H4	LKna LMil NLar SLdr SReu	
'James Gable' (EA)	SLdr	
'Jan Bee'	SLdr	
'Jan Dekens'	SReu	
'Jan Steen' (M)	SLdr	
Jan Steen Group	NPen	
'Jane Abbott' (A)	GGGa	
'Janet Blair'	CDoC CWri GLbr ISea MAsh MDun SLdr WBVN	
'Janet Ward'	LHyd LKna SReu	
'Janine Alexandre Debray'	NPen SLdr	
japonicum (A. Gray) Valcken	see *R. molle* subsp. *japonicum*	
japonicum Schneider var. *japonicum*	see *R. degronianum* subsp. *heptamerum*	
– var. *pentamerum*	see *R. degronianum* subsp. *degronianum*	
jasminiflorum (V)	SFai	
'Jason'	SLdr	
'Java Light' (V)	SFai	
javanicum (V)	GGGa	
'Jazz Band' (V)	GGGa	
'Jean Marie Montague'	see *R.* 'The Hon. Jean Marie de Montague'	
'Jeanette' (EA)	LKna	
'Jeff Hill' (EA)	ECho LRHS SLdr SReu	
'Jennie Dosser'	LMil	
'Jenny'	see *R.* 'Creeping Jenny'	
'Jeremy Davies' **new**	SReu	
§ 'Jervis Bay' **new**	SReu	
I 'Jiminy Cricket' (V)	SFai	

'Jingle Bells'   GGGa NLar
'Joan Paton' (A) **new**   SLdr
Jock Group   CBcs CMHG CTrw
'Jock Brydon' (O)   GGGa LMil SLdr
'Jock Coutts' (K)   CSdC LKna
'Johann Sebastian   WBod
    Bach' (EA)
'Johann Strauss' (EA)   WBod
'Johanna' (EA) ♀H4   CDoC CTri GGGa GKir LMil LRHS
                                   MAsh MBar MBri NPri SLdr SPer
                                   SPoG SReu WBod
'John Barr Stevenson'   LHyd NPen
'John Cairns' (EA)   CMac LHyd LKna MBar SCam SLdr
                                   WBod
'John Walter'   MBar MGos SLdr
'John Waterer'   CSBt LKna WFar
'Johnny Bender'   SLdr
johnstoneanum   CBcs GGGa LMil NPen SLdr WBod
- 'Double Diamond' (d)   CBcs LMil
- 'Rubeotinctum' KW 7732   NPen
'Jolie Madame' (Vs)   CWri LMil SLdr SReu
'Jonathan Shaw'   GGGa LMil
'Josefa Blue'   GGGa
'Joseph Baumann' (G)   CSdC SLdr
'Joseph Haydn' (EA)   WBod
'Joseph Hill' (EA)   ECho NHol SReu SSpi WPat
'Josephine Klinger' (G)   CSdC SReu
'Joy's Delight' (Ad)   LKna
'Jubilant'   NPen SLdr
'Jubilee'   LKna SLdr
Jubilee Queen Group   SLdr
'Julischka'   MGos
'July Giant'   SLdr
'June Bee'   GGGa
'June Fire' (A)   SReu
'June Yellow'   GGGa
'Jungfrau'   CWri
'Just Peachy' (V)   SFai
'Juwel'   MGos
K56 (A) **new**   SLdr
kaempferi (EA)   GGGa LMil SLdr
- 'Damio'   see *R. kaempferi* 'Mikado'
- 'Firefly'   see *R.* 'Hexe'
§ - 'Mikado' (EA)   LMil SReu
'Kalinka'   GKir LMil LRHS MAsh MDun
                                   MGos NHol
'Kaponga'   MGos
'Karen Triplett'   LMil
'Karin'   COtt MDun SHBN SLdr
'Karin Seleger'   GGGa
'Kasane-kagaribi' (EA)   LHyd SLdr
'Kate Waterer' ♀H4   CWri LKna MBar MGos MLan
                                   NPen SReu WFar
'Katharine Fortescue'   CWri
N 'Kathleen' (A)   LHyd SLdr
'Kathleen' rosy red (EA)   LKna
* 'Katinka' (hybrid)   GGGa
'Katisha' (EA)   LHyd SLdr
'Katrina'   SLdr
'Katy Watson'   SReu
kawakamii (V)   GGGa
'Keija'   SReu
'Keinohana' (EA)   NPen
keiskei   LHyd NPen
- compact   SLdr
- Cordifolium Group   NHol WAbe
- 'Ebino'   GGGa NHol
- var. *ozawae* 'Yaku   GGGa ITim LMil LRHS MDun
    Fairy' ♀H4   WAbe
- - 'Yaku Fairy'   NHol
        x *campylogynum*
        var. *leucanthum*
keleticum   see *R. calostrotum* subsp.
                                   keleticum

§ 'Ken Janeck'   GGGa NLar
§ *kendrickii*   GGGa MDun NPen
- MH 62   GGGa
'Kentucky Colonel'   SLdr
'Kentucky Minstrel' (K)   SLdr
'Kermesinum' (EA)   COtt CTri GGGa LMil MAsh MBar
                                   SLdr SPlb SReu WPat
I 'Kermesinum Album' (EA)   MBar MGos SReu
I 'Kermesinum Rosé' (EA)   GGGa LMil MBar MBri MDun NBlu
                                   SLdr SReu
kesangiae   MDun
- AC 110   NPen SLdr
- CH&M 3058   GGGa
- CH&M 3099   GGGa
aff. *kesangiae* KR 1640   MDun NPen
- var. *kesangiae* KR 1136   NPen
Kewense Group **new**   LHyd
keysii   CBcs GGGa LHyd LMil MDun
                                   NPen
- CER 9906   GGGa
- EGM 064   LMil
- KC 0112   GGGa
- KC 0115   GGGa
- KR 974   NPen
- KW 8101*   NPen
- 'Unicolor'   NPen
'Kilimanjaro'   GGGa LMil SReu
Kilimanjaro Group   LMil NPen SSta
'Kimberly'   GGGa
'Kimbeth'   GGGa
'Kimigayo' (EA)   LHyd
'King Fisher'   NPen
'King George' Loder   see *R.* 'Loderi King George'
'King George' Van Nes   SReu
'King of Shrubs'   NLar SLdr
kingianum   see *R. arboreum* subsp.
                                   zeylanicum
'King's Buff'   CWri
'Kings Ride' **new**   LHyd
'Kingston'   MDun
§ 'Kirin' (EA/d)   CMac CSBt CTrw LHyd LKna LRHS
                                   SLdr WBod WPat
'Kirishima' (EA)   LKna SRms
'Kiritsubo' (EA)   LHyd SLdr
'Kisses' (V)   SFai
'Kitty Cole'   SLdr
kiusianum (EA) ♀H4   GGGa LHyd MAsh NPen SReu
                                   SRms WAbe
- 'Album' (EA)   LHyd LMil SReu WAbe
- 'Amoenum'   see *R.* 'Amoenum'
- 'Ekubo' (EA)   SReu
- 'Hillier's Pink' (EA)   LMil
- var. *kiusianum*   LRHS
    'Mountain Gem' (EA)
'Kiwi Majic'   LMil MAsh MBri MDun
'Klondyke' (K) ♀H4   CBcs CSBt CTri ENot EPfP GGGa
                                   GKir LMil LRHS MAsh MBri MDun
                                   MGos NPri SLdr SReu
'Kluis Sensation' ♀H4   CBcs CSBt EBee ENot LHyd LKna
                                   MDun MGos NPen NWea SHBN
                                   SLdr SReu
'Kluis Triumph'   LKna SReu
'Knap Hill Apricot' (K)   LKna LMil
'Knap Hill Red' (K)   CDoC LKna LMil SLdr WMoo
'Knap Hill White' (K)   CSdC
'Kobold' (EA)   NPen SLdr
'Koichiro Wada'   see *R. yakushimanum* 'Koichiro
                                   Wada'
'Kokardia'   CDoC MAsh SLdr
'Komurasaki' (EA)   NPen
kongboense   GGGa LMil
- C&V 9540   GGGa
- KR 5689   LMil
aff. *kongboense* KR 3725   LMil

§	'Koningin Emma' (M)	LMil NLar SLdr
§	'Koningin Wilhelmina' (M)	SLdr WBod
	konori	GGGa
	var. *phaeopeplum* (V)	
	'Koster's Brilliant Red' (M)	CSBt ENot LMil SLdr SReu
	kotschyi	see *R. myrtifolium*
	'Kralingen' **new**	NLar
§	'Kumo-no-ito' (EA)	SLdr
	'Kupferberg'	GGGa
§	'Kure-no-yuki' (EA/d)	CMac CSBt CTrG EPfP LHyd LKna LMil MAsh SCam
	kyawii	NPen WPic
§	- Agapetum Group	NPen
	lacteum	LMil MDun NPen SLdr
	- AC 928	LMil
	- CN&W 936	LMil
	- EGM 356 from Wumenshan	LMil
	- KR 2760	GGGa
	- SBEC 345	GGGa
	- SF 374	ISea
	- bright yellow-flowered	NPen
	'Lady Adam Gordon'	SLdr
	'Lady Alice Fitzwilliam' ♀H2-3	CBcs CDoC CMHG CTrG GGGa IDee ISea LHyd LMil NPen SLdr WBod WGer
	'Lady Annette de Trafford'	LKna
	'Lady Armstrong'	CSBt
	Lady Bessborough Group	SLdr
	'Lady Bowes Lyon'	LHyd NPen SLdr
	Lady Chamberlain Group	GGGa NPen SLdr
	'Lady Chamberlain Salmon Trout'	see *R.* 'Salmon Trout'
	'Lady Clementine Mitford' ♀H4	CDoC CSBt CWri EPfP GGGa IDee LHyd LKna LMil MBri MGos MLea NPen NWea SHBN SLdr SReu
	'Lady Decies'	SReu
	'Lady Digby'	CWri
	'Lady Eleanor Cathcart'	EPfP LKna MAsh NPen SLdr
	'Lady Elphinstone' (EA)	SLdr
	'Lady Grey Egerton'	LKna
	'Lady Horlick'	SLdr
	'Lady Longman'	LHyd
	'Lady Louise' (EA)	SLdr
	'Lady Primrose'	SReu
	'Lady Robin' (EA)	SLdr
	'Lady Romsey'	LMil
	'Lady Rosebery' (K)	CSdC MBri MDun
	Lady Rosebery Group	CSam MLea NPen
	Ladybird Group	LMil SReu
	laetum (V)	GGGa
	Lamellen Group	LHyd SLdr
	'Lampion'	ENot GGGa
	'Lamplighter'	SReu
	lanatoides	LMil NPen
	- C&C 7548	GGGa
	- C&C 7574	GGGa
	- C&C 7577	GGGa
	- KR 6385	LMil
	- KW 5971	NPen
	lanatum	LMil NPen
	- B&SWJ 2464	WCru
	- BB 185B	NPen
	- dwarf, cream-flowered	GGGa
	- Flinckii Group	see *R. flinckii*
	'Langmans' (EA)	LKna
	'Langworth'	CWri ECho LKna LMil MLea SReu WOrn
	lanigerum	MDun NPen SReu
	- C&V 9530	GGGa
	- KW 8251	GGGa
	- pink-flowered	NPen
	- red-flowered	NPen
	- 'Round Wood'	LHyd

	lapidosum **new**	GGGa
	lapponicum	GGGa
	Confertissimum Group	
	- Parvifolium Group from Siberia	GGGa WAbe
	'Lapwing' (K)	LKna MBri SLdr
	'Lascaux'	SReu
	'Late Love' (EA)	CDoC MGos SSpi
*	*laterifolium* **new**	GGGa
§	*latoucheae* (EA)	SSpi
	- PW 86	GGGa
	laudandum	GGGa
	var. *temoense*	
	Laura Aberconway Group	SLdr WBod
	'Laura Morland' (EA)	LHyd
	'Lava Flow'	LHyd NHol
	'Lavender Girl' ♀H4	GGGa LHyd LKna LMil MGos NLar NPen SLdr SReu SSta
	'Lavender Lady' (EA)	CTrG
	'Lavender Queen'	CWri NPen SLdr
	'Lavendula'	GGGa LMil
	'Le Progrès'	LMil MAsh SReu WGer
	'Lea Rainbow'	MLea
	'Ledifolium'	see *R.* x *mucronatum*
	'Ledifolium Album'	see *R.* x *mucronatum*
	'Lee's Dark Purple'	CDoC CSBt CWri LMil MBar NBlu NPen NPri NWea WFar
	'Lee's Scarlet'	LKna LMil SLdr
*	'Lemon Drop' (A)	GGGa
	'Lemon Lights' (A)	LMil MAsh
	'Lemonora' (M)	LMil SLdr
	'Lem's 45'	CWri MDun MLea SLdr
	'Lem's Cameo' ♀H3	GGGa LHyd LMil NPen SReu SSta WGer
	'Lem's Monarch' ♀H4	CBcs CDoC CWri GGGa LHyd LMil MBri MDun MGos MLea SLdr SReu SSta WGer
	'Lem's Tangerine'	LMil
	'Lemur' (EA)	GGGa MAsh MDun MLea NHol NLar SReu WPat
	'Leni'	GKir LRHS MAsh
	'Leny' (EA)	NHol
	'Leo' (EA)	GQui LHyd LKna LRHS NPen SCam SLdr
	'Leo' (hybrid)	EPfP LRHS NPen
	'Leonardslee Giles'	SLdr
	'Leonardslee Primrose'	SLdr
	Leonore Group	NPen SReu
	lepidostylum	CDoC CWri GGGa LHyd LMil LRHS MBar MDun NHol NLAp NPen SLdr SReu WAbe WFar
	lepidotum	GGGa MDun NPen WAbe
	- Elaeagnoides Group	GGGa
	- purple-flowered EN 6280 **new**	LMil
	- 'Reuthe's Purple'	see *R.* 'Reuthe's Purple'
	- yellow-flowered	ITim NPen
§	*leptocarpum*	GGGa LMil
	- C&H 420	NPen
	leptothrium	GGGa NPen WAbe
	Letty Edwards Group	CSBt LKna NPen SLdr SReu
§	'Leucanthum'	GGGa
	leucaspis	GGGa LHyd MDun NPen SLdr SReu
	- KW 7171	NPen
	'Leverett Richards'	SReu
	levinei	GGGa
	'Lila Pedigo'	COtt CWri GGGa ISea MAsh MDun MLea SLdr WBVN
	'Lilac Time' (EA)	MBar SLdr
	'Lilacinum' (EA)	WPic
	liliiflorum Guiz 163	GGGa
	'Lilliput' (EA)	MAsh
	'Lily Marleen' (EA)	CTri LRHS SCoo SLdr SReu

'Linda' ♀H4		CSam CTri GGGa LMil LRHS MBar MDun MGos SLdr SReu
'Linda Lee'		SLdr
'Linda R' (EA)		MGos
lindleyi		GQui LHyd LMil NPen
- L&S		GGGa
- 'Dame Edith Sitwell'		LMil
'Linearifolium'		see *R. stenopetalum* 'Linearifolium'
'Linnet' (K/d)		LKna
Lionel's Triumph Group		LMil NPen SLdr
'Little Beauty' (EA)		SCam SLdr
'Little Ben'		ECho MBar MDun NDlv
'Littlest Angel' (V)		SFai
'Loch Earn'		GGGa
'Loch Leven'		GGGa
'Loch o' the Lowes'		GGGa LHyd LMil MBri MDun MGos MLea SLdr WBVN
'Loch Rannoch'		GGGa GKir LMil MAsh MGos NPri WOrn
'Loch Tummel'		GGGa
lochiae (V)		GGGa
'Lochinch Spinbur'		GQui
x *lochmium*		GGGa
Lodauric Group		SReu
§ 'Lodauric Iceberg' ♀H3-4		LKna LMil SLdr SReu
'Lodbrit'		SReu
§ Loderi Group		SLdr
'Loderi Fairy Queen'		NPen SLdr
'Loderi Fairyland'		LHyd NPen
§ 'Loderi Game Chick' ♀H3-4		LHyd MLea NPen SLdr SReu
'Loderi Georgette'		NPen SLdr
'Loderi Helen'		NPen SLdr
§ 'Loderi Julie'		NPen SReu
§ 'Loderi King George' ♀H3-4		CBcs CWri GGGa IDee ISea LHyd LKna LMil MDun MLea NPen SHBN SLdr SPoG SReu SSta
'Loderi Patience'		LHyd NPen SLdr
'Loderi Pink Coral' **new**		SLdr
'Loderi Pink Diamond' ♀H3-4		CWri LMil SLdr
'Loderi Pink Topaz' ♀H3-4		LHyd LMil NPen SLdr
'Loderi Pretty Polly'		CWri NPen
'Loderi Princess Marina'		NPen SLdr
'Loderi Sir Edmund'		LHyd NPen SLdr
'Loderi Sir Joseph Hooker'		LHyd NPen SLdr
'Loderi Titan'		SReu
§ 'Loderi Venus' ♀H3-4		CDoC GGGa LHyd LKna LMil LRHS MDun MLea NPen SHBN SLdr SReu SSta
'Loderi White Diamond'		LHyd NPen SLdr
'Loder's White' ♀H3-4		CWri ENot GGGa LHyd LKna LMil LRHS MDun MLea NPen SLdr SReu SSta
§ 'Logan Damaris'		LHyd NPen SLdr SReu
longesquamatum		GGGa LMil NPen SLdr
longipes		SLdr
- EGM 336		LMil
- EGM 337		LMil
- var. *chienianum*		LMil
- var. *longipes* C&H 7072		GGGa
- - C&H 7113		GGGa
longistylum		GGGa NPen
'Longworth'		NPen
'Looking Glass'		LRHS MDun SHBN
lopsangianum LS&T 5651		NPen
'Lord Roberts' ♀H4		CBcs CTri CWri ENot GGGa GKir LKna LMil MAsh MBar MGos MLea NPen SHBN SLdr SReu WBVN WFar WMoo WOrn
'Lord Swaythling'		LHyd SLdr
'Lori Eichelser'		CSam MDun MLea NDlv
'Lorna' (EA)		ENot GQui LMil

'Louis Hellebuyck' (G) **new**		SLdr
'Louis Pasteur'		SReu
'Louisa' (EA)		SSpi
'Louise' (EA)		SLdr
'Louise Dowdle' (EA)		LMil SCam SLdr
'Love Song' (EA)		LRHS
'Lovely William'		LMil SLdr
lowndesii		WAbe
luciferum CER 9935 **new**		GGGa
- PIC 8535		GGGa
'Lucy Lou'		GGGa
ludlowii		GGGa
ludlowii x *viridescens*		NHol
ludwigianum		GGGa
§ *lukiangense*		NPen
- R 11275		NPen
- R 72		NPen
'Lullaby' (EA)		LKna SLdr
'Lunar Queen'		LHyd NPen SLdr
Luscombei Group		LHyd SLdr
'Luscombei Splendens'		SLdr
luteiflorum		LMil SLdr
- KW 21040		NPen
- KW 21556		GGGa
lutescens		CBcs CWri ISea LMil MDun NPen SLdr SLon SReu SSta WAbe
- C&H 7124		GGGa
- Cox 5092		NHol
- Cox 5100		NHol
- 'Bagshot Sands' ♀H3-4		CDoC GGGa IDee LHyd LMil LRHS SReu
§ *luteum* (A) ♀H4		More than 30 suppliers
§ *lyi*		NPen
- KR 2962		GGGa
* 'Mac Ovata'		CMac
macabeanum ♀H3-4		CBcs CDoC EPfP GGGa GTSp IDee LHyd LMil LRHS MDun NPen SLdr SReu SSpi SSta WFar WHer
- KW 7724		NPen
- deep cream-flowered		CWri SLdr
- Reuthe's form		SReu
macabeanum x *sinogrande*		SReu
macgregoriae (V) Woods 2646		GGGa
'Macranthum Roseum' (EA)		SReu
macrophyllum		GGGa
macrosmithii		see *R. argipeplum*
'Macrostemon'		see *R.* (Obtusum Group) 'Macrostemon'
maculiferum		GGGa NPen SLdr
- subsp. *anwheiense*		see *R. anwheiense*
'Madame Albert Moser'		LKna
'Madame de Bruin'		LKna SLdr
'Madame Knutz' (A)		SLdr
'Madame Masson'		CSam CTri CWri GGGa GKir GWCH LMil LRHS MAsh MBri MDun MGos MLea NPen NPri SHBN SLdr SReu SSta WBVN WFar
'Madame van Hecke' (EA)		CDoC COtt CTri EPfP GKir LMil LRHS MAsh MBri NBlu SLdr SReu WFar WGor
maddenii		IDee LMil NPen SLdr
§ - subsp. *crassum*		CTrw GGGa LMil NPen SLdr WBod WPic
- - AC 708		NPen SLdr
§ - - Obtusifolium Group		NPen SLdr
§ - subsp. *maddenii*		NPen WAbe
- - KR 2978		LMil
§ - - Polyandrum Group		CBcs GQui ISea NPen SLdr
'Madeline's Yellow'		SLdr
'Mademoiselle Masson'		WFar

'Maestro'	LHyd	
'Magic Flute' (EA) **new**	MAsh	
I 'Magic Flute' (V)	LMil NPri SCoo	
'Magnificum' (O)	LMil SLdr	
magnificum	NPen SLdr SReu	
'Maharani'	GGGa LRHS MAsh	
'Maja' (G)	SLdr	
§ *makinoi* ♀H4	CWri GGGa LHyd LMil LRHS	
	MDun NLar NPen SLdr SReu SSpi	
	SSta	
- 'Fuju-kaku-no-matsu'	MGos NLar	
mallotum	CWri GGGa IDee LHyd LMil	
	MDun NPen SLdr SReu	
- BASEX 9672	GGGa	
- Farrer 815	GGGa	
'Manda Sue'	SLdr WGor	
Mandalay Group	SLdr	
'Mandarin Lights' (A)	LMil LRHS MAsh MBri NPri	
'Manderley'	LMil	
manipurense	see *R. maddenii* subsp. *crassum*	
	Obtusifolium Group	
'Manor Hill'	SLdr	
'Marcel Ménard'	LMil NLar SReu WFar	
'Marchioness	CSBt	
of Lansdowne'		
'Marcia'	SLdr	
'Mardi Gras'	GGGa LMil MBri	
Margaret Dunn Group	CWri	
'Margaret Falmouth'	SReu	
'Margaret George' (EA)	LHyd	
'Maria Derby' (EA)	SLdr	
'Maricee'	GGGa SLdr	
'Marie' (EA)	CMac	
'Marie Curie'	SReu	
'Marie Verschaffelt'	SLdr	
(G) **new**		
'Marilee' (EA)	CDoC GKir LRHS MGos NLar SLdr	
Mariloo Group	NPen SLdr	
'Marinus Koster'	LKna SLdr	
'Marion'	LMil	
'Marion Merriman' (K)	LKna	
'Marion Street' ♀H4	LHyd LMil NPen SLdr SReu	
'Mark Turner'	SReu	
'Markeeta's Flame'	MDun	
'Markeeta's Prize' ♀H4	CDoC CSam CWri GGGa IDee	
	LMil LRHS MAsh MBri MDun	
	MGos MLea NPen SLdr SPoG	
	WOrn	
'Marley Hedges'	GGGa LMil MAsh	
'Marlies' (A)	SLdr	
'Marmot' (EA)	MBar MDun MLea	
'Mars'	GGGa SLdr SReu	
'Martha Hitchcock' (EA)	LKna SRms	
'Martha Isaacson'	MGos SReu WCwm	
(Ad) ♀H4		
'Martine' (Ad)	LKna MGos WBod	
martinianum	LMil NPen SLdr	
aff. *martinianum*	GGGa	
KW 21557		
'Mary Drennen'	LMil	
'Mary Fleming'	MDun NPen SLdr	
'Mary Helen' (EA)	GKir LHyd LRHS MAsh SCoo SReu	
	WPat	
'Mary Meredith' (EA)	LHyd	
'Mary Poppins' (K)	GKir LMil LRHS MAsh MBri NPri	
	SCoo	
'Maryke'	LMil	
Matador Group	NPen SReu WBod	
'Matador'	LHyd WBod	
'Mauna Loa' (K)	LKna	
'Maurice Skipworth'	CBcs	
maximum	GGGa NPen SLdr	
'Maxine Childers'	LMil	
§ 'Maxwellii' (EA)	CMac SLdr WBod	

'May Day' ♀H3-4	CDoC LHyd SReu	
May Day Group	CBcs CTrw CWri CWri ISea LKna MDun	
	MGos NPen SHBN SLdr SSta WBod	
'May Glow'	MGos	
May Morn Group	SReu	
'Mayor Johnstone'	CTri GKir LRHS MAsh NPri	
'Mazurka' (K)	LKna	
meddianum	GGGa NPen	
- var. *atrokermesinum*	NPen	
- - KW 2100a	GGGa	
- Harry White's form	SLdr	
Medea Group	SLdr	
Medusa Group	GGGa SReu	
megacalyx	CBcs GGGa ISea	
'Megan' (EA)	GGGa MAsh SLdr SReu WGwG	
megaphyllum	see *R. basilicum*	
megeratum	GGGa NPen SReu	
- R 18861	SLdr	
- 'Bodnant'	WAbe	
mekongense	GGGa	
- KR 5044	LMil	
- var. *mekongense*	SReu	
- - KW 5829	NPen	
- - Rubroluteum Group	see *R. viridescens* Rubroluteum	
	Group	
§ - var. *melinanthum*	NPen SReu	
- var. *rubrolineatum*	LMil NPen	
'Melford Lemon'	see *R.* 'Ilam Melford Lemon'	
'Melidioso'	LMil	
'Melina' (EA/d)	GGGa	
melinanthum	see *R. mekongense*	
	var. *melinanthum*	
'Merganser' ♀H4	GGGa LMil MDun MLea NDlv	
	NHol SReu WAbe	
'Merlin' (EA)	SLdr	
metternichii	see *R. degronianum* subsp.	
	heptamerum	
- var. *pentamerum*	see *R. degronianum* subsp.	
	degronianum	
'Mi Amor'	LMil	
'Miami' (A)	SLdr	
'Michael Hill' (EA)	CBcs CDoC COtt CTrh LHyd LMil	
	MAsh SLdr SSpi	
'Michael Waterer'	MDun NPen SLdr	
'Michael's Pride'	CBcs GQui NPen	
micranthum	GGGa MDun NPen SLdr	
microgynum	LMil NPen	
- F 21242	GGGa NPen	
microleucum	see *R. orthocladum* var.	
	microleucum	
micromeres	see *R. leptocarpum*	
microphyton	ISea	
'Midnight Mystique'	GGGa	
'Midori' (EA)	SLdr	
'Mikado' (EA)	see *R. kaempferi* 'Mikado'	
'Milton' (R) **new**	SLdr	
mimetes	NPen SLdr	
§ - var. *simulans*	NPen	
- - F 20428	GGGa NPen	
'Mimi' (EA)	CMac LHyd	
'Mimra' (A)	SLdr	
'Mindy's Love'	LMil	
'Ming'	see *R.* 'Ilam Ming'	
'Minterne Cinnkeys'	MDun	
minus	GQui	
- var. *chapmanii*	SSpi	
§ - var. *minus*	SLdr	
§ - - Carolinianum Group	LMil	
- - - 'Epoch' **new**	LMil	
§ - - Punctatum Group	MBar	
'Miss Muffet' (EA)	SLdr	
'Moerheim' ♀H4	CWri EMil GKir LRHS MAsh MBar	
	MGos MOne NHol NPri SReu SSta	
	WBVN WStI	

§ 'Moerheim's Pink'	LHyd LKna LMil MDun NHol SLdr SPer
'Moerheim's Scarlet'	LKna
'Moffat'	SReu
'Moidart' (Vs)	LMil
'Moira Salmon' (EA)	LHyd SLdr
'Molalla Red' (K)	LMil
§ *molle* subsp. *japonicum* (A)	GGGa SLdr
– – JR 871	GGGa
– subsp. *molle* (A) C&H 7181	GGGa
mollicomum	NPen
– F 10347	NPen
– F 30940	SLdr
'Mollie Coker'	CWri SLdr
Mollis orange (M)	MBar NBlu SRms
Mollis pink (M)	GGGa MBar NBlu SRms
Mollis red (M)	MBar NBlu SRms
Mollis salmon (M)	GGGa GQui
Mollis yellow (M)	GQui MBar NBlu SRms
'Molly Ann'	GGGa LRHS MDun SLdr SReu WGor
'Molten Gold' (v)	LRHS MAsh
monanthum	GGGa
CCH&H 8133	
monosematum	see *R. pachytrichum* var. *monosematum*
montiganum	ISea
– AC 2060	LMil
montroseanum	LMil LRHS MDun NPen SLdr SSpi WCru
* – 'Baravalla'	GGGa
– 'Benmore'	NPen
'Moon Maiden' (EA)	GQui SLdr WOrn
Moonbeam Group	LKna
Moonshine Group	SLdr
'Moonshine'	SReu
'Moonshine Bright'	LHyd MDun
'Moonshine Supreme'	LKna
Moonstone Group	MBar MDun MLea NPen SLdr WBod
– pink-tipped	NHol
'Moonstone Yellow'	GGGa
'Moonwax'	CSam CWri SLdr
§ 'Morgenrot'	EMui GGGa LMil LRHS MAsh MGos NBlu SReu WFar
morii	GGGa LHyd LMil MDun NPen
'Morning Cloud' YH4	CAbP GKir LHyd LMil LRHS MBar NDlv NPen SReu
'Morning Magic'	CWri LHyd NPen SLdr
Morning Red	see *R.* 'Morgenrot'
'Moser's Maroon'	CWri LKna MGos NLar NPen SLdr WBVN
'Moser's Strawberry'	LKna
'Motet' (K/d)	CSdC LKna SLdr
'Moth'	NHol
'Mother Greer'	GGGa
'Mother of Pearl'	LKna SReu
'Mother Theresa'	LKna
'Mother's Day' (EA) YH4	More than 30 suppliers
'Moulten Gold' new	GGGa
'Mount Everest'	GGGa LHyd LMil SReu SSta
'Mount Rainier' (K)	LMil MBri SReu
'Mount Saint Helens'	GGGa LMil MLea SLdr
'Mount Seven Star'	see *R. nakaharae* 'Mount Seven Star'
'Mountain Star'	SLdr
moupinense	CBcs GGGa IDee LHyd LMil NPen SLdr SReu
– pink-flowered	LMil
'Mozart' (EA)	WBod
'Mrs A.T. de la Mare' YH4	CSBt CWri ENot GGGa LHyd LKna LMil MDun NPen SLdr SReu SSta WGer
'Mrs Anthony Waterer' (O)	LKna
'Mrs Anthony Waterer' (hybrid)	LKna
'Mrs Betty Robertson'	CWri GWCH MDun MGos MLea SLdr SReu
'Mrs C.B. van Nes'	SReu
Mrs C. Whitner Group	NPen SLdr
'Mrs Charles E. Pearson' YH4	CBcs CSBt CWri ENot LHyd LKna LMil NPen SHBN SLdr SReu
'Mrs Davies Evans' YH4	CWri LHyd LKna MBar SReu SSta
'Mrs Dick Thompson'	SReu
'Mrs Donald Graham'	SReu
'Mrs Doorenbos'	CMac
'Mrs E.C. Stirling'	LHyd LKna SRms
'Mrs Emil Hager' (EA)	LHyd SLdr
'Mrs Furnivall' YH4	CBcs CWri EPfP GBin GGGa ISea LHyd LKna MDun MGos MLea SLdr SReu WOrn
'Mrs G.W. Leak'	CSBt CSam CWri ENot EPfP GGGa ISea LHyd LKna LMil MDun MLea NPen SHBN SLdr SPer SReu
'Mrs Helen Koster'	LKna
'Mrs Henry Agnew'	NPen
'Mrs J.C. Williams' YH4	LKna LMil NPen SLdr
'Mrs J.G. Millais'	LKna LMil MDun NPen SLdr
'Mrs James Horlick'	NPen
'Mrs Lindsay Smith'	LKna
'Mrs Lionel de Rothschild' YH4	MDun NPen SReu
Mrs Lionel de Rothschild Group	CWri LKna
'Mrs P.D. Williams'	LKna SReu
'Mrs Pamela Robinson' new	LHyd
'Mrs Peter Koster' (M)	SLdr WFar
'Mrs Philip Martineau'	LKna
'Mrs R.S. Holford' YH4	LKna NPen SLdr
'Mrs T.H. Lowinsky' YH4	CSBt EPfP GGGa LKna LMil MAsh MBri MDun MGos MLea NPen NWea SLdr SPer SReu SSta WBVN
'Mrs W.C. Slocock'	LHyd LKna MDun NPen SReu
'Mrs William Agnew'	LKna
'Mucronatum'	see *R.* x *mucronatum*
§ x *mucronatum* (EA)	NPen SLdr SRms WPic
'Mucronatum Amethystinum'	see *R.* 'Amethystinum'
mucronulatum	GGGa NPen
– B&SWJ 786	WCru
– pink-flowered	WPGP
– var. *chejuense*	see *R. mucronulatum* var. *taquetii*
– 'Cornell Pink' YH4	GGGa LMil WFar
§ – var. *taquetii*	GGGa
§ 'Multiflorum'	SReu
'Muncaster Bells'	NPen
'Muncaster Hybrid'	NPen
'Muncaster Mist'	LHyd NPen
§ *myrtifolium*	LMil
nakaharae (EA)	NPen SLdr SReu
§ – 'Mariko' (EA)	GGGa LHyd MBar MBro MGos NHol NLAp SLdr WAbe WPat
§ – 'Mount Seven Star' (EA) YH4	CDoC ECho GGGa LHyd LMil LRHS MAsh MBro NHol NLAp SLdr SReu WAbe WPat
§ – orange-flowered (EA)	GKir LMil LRHS MGos MOne NPri SHBN SReu SSta
– pink-flowered (EA)	GKir LHyd LMil LRHS MAsh MGos NPri SLdr SPer SReu SSta
– red-flowered (EA)	MGos SLdr
– 'Scree' (EA)	SReu
'Nakahari Orange'	see *R. nakaharae* orange-flowered
'Nakahari-mariko'	see *R. nakaharae* 'Mariko'
nakotiltum	NPen SLdr

'Nancy Evans' ♀H3-4 — CDoC COtt CSBt CWri GGGa GKir LHyd LMil LRHS MAsh MDun MLea NPri SLdr SReu SSpi WGer WOrn

'Nancy Waterer' (G) ♀H4 — LMil NLar SLdr SReu

'Nanki Poo' (EA) — LHyd SLdr

Naomi Group — CSam CWri LHyd LKna MLea SReu

N – 'Paris' — see *R.* 'Paris'

'Naomi' (EA) — GQui LHyd LKna LMil SCam SHBN SLdr

'Naomi Astarte' — LKna MDun SLdr

'Naomi Early Dawn' — NPen

'Naomi Hope' — SLdr

'Naomi Stella Maris' — LHyd SLdr

'Narcissiflorum' — CDoC CSBt ENot EPfP IDee LHyd (G/d) ♀H4 — LKna LMil LRHS NLar SPer SReu

'Naselle' — GGGa LMil

'Ne Plus Ultra' (V) — SFai

neriiflorum — GGGa ISea LMil MDun NPen SReu

– Bu 287 — GGGa

– SF 366 — ISea

§ – subsp. *neriiflorum* — GGGa
   L&S 1352

§ – – Euchaites Group — NPen

§ – – Phoenicodum Group — NPen
      Farrer 877

§ – subsp. *phaedropum* — MDun NPen

– – C&H 422 — NPen

– – CCH&H 8125 — GGGa

– – KR 5593 — LMil

– – KW 6845* — NPen

Neriihaem Group — NPen

nervulosum Sleumer (V) — GGGa

'Nestor' — SReu

'Netty Koster' — SLdr

'New Comet' — LHyd NPen SLdr

'New Moon' — SReu

'Newcomb's Sweetheart' — LMil MDun

'Niagara' (EA) ♀H3-4 — CTrh ENot EPfP GQui LHyd LMil NMen SLdr WBod

'Nichola' (EA) — SReu

'Nico' (EA) — CDoC CMac GKir LRHS MAsh WBod WPat

'Nicoletta' — LMil MBri

'Night Sky' — CDoC COtt GGGa LHyd LMil LRHS MAsh MBri MDun MGos MLea NHol SLdr WBVN WOrn

'Nightingale' — SReu

nigroglandulosum — GGGa

x *nikomontanum* — LMil

nilagiricum — see *R. arboreum* subsp. *nilagiricum*

'Nimbus' — LKna LMil SLdr

Nimrod Group — NPen SLdr

'Nippon' **new** — SLdr

nipponicum **new** — SReu

'Nishiki' (EA) — CMac

nitens — see *R. calostrotum* subsp. *riparium* Nitens Group

nitidulum — NPen WAbe

– var. *omeiense* KR 185 — GGGa LMil NHol

nivale subsp. *boreale* — GGGa
   Ramosissimum Group

§ – – Stictophyllum Group — GGGa WAbe

niveum ♀H4 — GGGa IDee LMil LRHS MDun NPen SLdr SReu WGer

– B&SWJ 2675 — WCru

– 'Nepal' — LHyd

'Noble Mountain' — LMil

§ Nobleanum Group — GGGa LHyd LKna LMil NPen SLdr SSta WBod

'Nobleanum Album' — LHyd LKna LMil NPen SLdr SReu SSta WBod

'Nobleanum Coccineum' — NPen SReu

'Nobleanum Venustum' — CSBt CWri IDee LHyd LKna LMil SLdr SReu SSta WBod

'Nofretete' — GGGa

'Nora' — WPic

'Nordlicht' (EA) — SLdr

'Noriko' (EA) — SLdr

N 'Norma' (R/d) ♀H4 — ENot LMil SReu

Norman Shaw Group — LHyd

'Northern Hi-Lights' (A) — GKir LMil LRHS MAsh MLea SLdr

'Northern Star' — LHyd

'Northern Starburst' — LMil

'Nova Zembla' — EPfP GGGa GLbr ISea MAsh MBar MGos NBlu NPri NWea SHBN SLdr SPer SReu SSta WBVN WStI

nudiflorum — see *R. periclymenoides*

nudipes — LMil

nuttallii — CBrd GGGa ISea LMil SLdr

'Oban' — GGGa LMil LRHS MDun MLea NHol NLap NMen WAbe

obtusum f. *amoenum* — see *R.* 'Amoenum'

Obtusum Group (EA) — LHyd

§ – 'Macrostemon' (EA) — WBod

occidentale (A) ♀H4 — GGGa LMil LRHS MDun SLdr SSpi

– 'Crescent City Double' — GGGa
   SM 28-2 **new**

ochraceum — LMil

– C&H 7052 — GGGa

– EGM 312 — LMil

'Odee Wright' — CDoC CTri CWri GGGa LRHS MAsh MLea NLar NPen SLdr SPer SReu

'Odoratum' (Ad) — MLea

'Oi-no-mezame' (EA) — LHyd

'Old Copper' — CWri SLdr

'Old Gold' (K) — MLea SLdr SReu

'Old Port' ♀H4 — LHyd LMil MAsh SHBN SReu

Oldenburgh Group — SLdr

oldhamii (EA) — NPen

– B&SWJ 3742 — WCru

– ETOT 601 — GGGa

'Olga' ♀H4 — LHyd LKna LMil NPen SLdr SReu SSta

'Olga Mezitt' — LHyd NHol

'Olga Niblett' (EA) — LMil SLdr

oligocarpum — GGGa

– Guiz 148* — GGGa

'Olive' — LHyd LKna LMil WBod

'Oliver Cromwell' — SReu

Olympic Lady Group — LHyd SLdr

Omar Group — MBar

§ 'One Thousand Butterflies' — COtt GGGa MDun MLea SLdr

N 'Ophelia' — SCam SLdr

'Oporto' — SLdr

'Orange Beauty' — CDoC CMac CSBt CTrh GGGa (EA) ♀H3-4 — LHyd LKna LMil MAsh MBar MGos NPen SCam SLdr SReu SSta WBVN WBod WFar WOrn WPic

I 'Orange Queen' (V) — SFai

'Orange Scout' — SLdr WGor WMoo

'Orange Splendour' (A) — LRHS

'Orange Sunset' **new** — MDun

'Orangengold' — MDun

orbiculare ♀H3-4 — GGGa IDee LHyd LMil MDun NPen SLdr SSta WBod

– C&K 230 — GGGa

§ – subsp. *cardiobasis* — LMil MDun NPen SLdr

– subsp. *orbiculare* — NPen
   W/V 1519

– Sandling Park form — SReu

'Orchid Lights' — GKir LRHS MAsh SLdr

'Oregon' (EA) — SLdr

oreodoxa ♀H4 — LMil NPen SLdr SReu

§ – var. *fargesii* ♀H4 — GGGa LHyd LMil NPen

– – Knott 348 — NPen

§ – – Erubescens Group | NPen
- var. **oreodoxa** | LMil
– – EN 4212 | GGGa
– – W/A 4245 | NPen
- var. **shensiense** | GGGa
oreotrephes | CDoC LHyd LMil LRHS MDun NPen SLdr SReu
- F 20489 | NPen
- F 20629 | NPen
- KW 9509 | NPen
- SF 640 | ISea
§ - Exquisitum Group | ISea SReu WGwG
- 'Pentland' **new** | LMil
- Timeteum Group | SReu
Orestes Group | SLdr
orthocladum | LMil MDun
§ - var. **microleucum** | GGGa ISea LMil NHol NPen WAbe
- var. **orthocladum** | GGGa NHol
  F 20488
'Oryx' (O) | CSdC LKna
'Osmar' ♀H4 | CBcs GGGa MGos SReu
'Ostara' | CBcs COtt MGos
'Ostbo's Low Yellow' | SLdr
'Ouchiyama' | LKna
'Oudijk's Sensation' | CBcs CWri LKna MAsh MGos MOne
ovatum CN&W 548 | ISea
ovatum (EA) | CBcs NPen WBod
- W/A 1391 | NPen
§ **pachypodum** | GGGa
pachysanthum ♀H4 | CDoC GTSp IDee LHyd LMil MDun NPen SLdr SReu SSpi
- RV 72/001 | GGGa NPen SLdr
- 'Crosswater' | LMil LRHS MDun
pachytrichum | GGGa NPen SLdr
§ - var. **monosematum** | ISea SLdr SReu
– – CN&W 953 | LMil
– – W/V 1522 | NPen
- var. **pachytrichum** | NPen
  W/A 1203
– – 'Sesame' | LMil
'Palestrina' (EA) ♀H3-4 | CBcs CMac CSBt CTrh EPfP EPot LHyd LKna LMil LRHS MGos NPen SCam SLdr SPer SReu SSta WBod WFar WGwG WMoo
'Pallas' (G) | SLdr SReu
'Pamela Miles' (EA) | LHyd
'Pamela-Louise' | LHyd
'Pancake' | CMac
'Panda' (EA) ♀H4 | CDoC CMac CTri GGGa LHyd LMil LRHS MAsh MBar MBri MDun MLea NDlv NPri SCoo SLdr SPoG SReu
panteumorphum | see *R.* x *erythrocalyx* Panteumorphum Group
'Papageno' **new** | NLar
'Papaya Punch' | LMil MDun
papillatum | NPen
'Paprika Spiced' | CDoC COtt CWri LMil MBri MDun MGos MLea SLdr WBVN WOrn
'Parade' (A) | LMil
'Paradise Pink' (EA) | ENot LMil
paradoxum | GGGa
'Paramount' (K/d) | LKna
'Paris' | LHyd
§ 'Parkfeuer' (A) | SLdr
parmulatum | LMil MDun NPen SLdr
- C&C 7538 | GGGa
- KW 5875 | NPen
- mauve-flowered | NPen
- 'Ocelot' | GGGa LHyd MDun NPen SLdr
- pink-flowered | GGGa NPen
parryae | GGGa
'Party Pink' | LMil

'Patty Bee' ♀H4 | More than 30 suppliers
patulum | see *R. pemakoense* Patulum Group
'Pavane' (K) | LKna
'Peace' | GGGa NPen
'Peach Blossom' | see *R.* 'Saotome'
'Peach Lady' | SLdr
'Peaches and Cream' | SLdr
'Peep-bo' (EA) | LHyd SLdr
'Peeping Tom' | CDoC GKir LMil MDun NPen SHBN SReu
pemakoense | CDoC CSBt CTrG GGGa IDee MAsh MBar MGos NHol NPen SLdr SReu WAbe
§ - Patulum Group | MBar NHol NPen SLdr
'Pemakofairy' | WAbe
pendulum LS&T 6660 | GGGa
Penelope Group | SReu
'Penheale Blue' ♀H4 | CDoC CTrh GBin GGGa LMil MAsh NDlv NHol SLdr
'Penjerrick Cream' | LHyd NPen SLdr
'Penjerrick Pink' | LHyd NPen
pennivenium | see *R. tanastylum* var. *pennivenium*
pentaphyllum (A) | LMil
'Percy Wiseman' ♀H4 | CBcs CDoC CSBt CSam CWri EBee EPfP GGGa GKir LHyd LMil LRHS MAsh MBar MBri MDun MGos MLea NBlu NDlv NHol NPen NPri SLdr SPer SReu SSta WFar WOrn
peregrinum | NPen
'Perfect Lady' | LMil
§ **periclymenoides** (A) | GGGa LMil LRHS SLdr
'Persil' (K) ♀H4 | CBcs CSBt CWri ENot EPfP GGGa LHyd LKna LMil MAsh MBar MBri MDun MGos MLea NBlu SCoo SLdr SPer SReu WBVN WBod WBrE WMoo WOrn
§ 'Persimmon' | LKna NPen
'Peste's Fire Light' | GGGa
'Peter Alan' | CWri
'Peter Berg' | MGos
'Peter Gable' (EA) | SLdr
'Peter John Mezitt' | see *R.* (PJM Group) 'Peter John Mezitt'
'Peter Koster' (hybrid) | CWri NPen SHBN SLdr WStI
petrocharis Guiz 120 | GGGa
'Petrouchka' (K) | LKna MBri MDun
phaedropum | see *R. neriiflorum* subsp. *phaedropum*
phaeochrysum | GGGa NPen SLdr
- USDAPI 59029/R11323 | NPen
- var. **agglutinatum** | GGGa NPen
- var. **levistratum** | NPen SLdr SReu
– – AC 1757 | WCwm
- McLaren cup winner | NPen
- var. **phaeochrysum** | NPen
  'Greenmantle'
'Phalarope' | CSam GGGa MAsh MBar NHol SReu WBod
'Pheasant Tail' | NPen SLdr
'Phoebe' (R/d) | SReu
phoenicodum | see *R. neriiflorum* subsp. *neriiflorum* Phoenicodum Group
'Phyllis Korn' | CDoC CWri LHyd MDun MLea NLar SLdr SPer WBVN
'Piccolo' (K/d) | CSdC LKna
§ **piercei** | GGGa LMil MDun NPen
- KW 11040 | GGGa NPen
Pilgrim Group | LKna LMil NPen
pingianum | NPen SLdr
- EGM 304 | LMil
- KR 150 | NPen
- KR 184 | GGGa
'Pink and Sweet' (A) | CDoC LMil

'Pink Bedspread'　SReu
'Pink Bountiful'　LKna
'Pink Bride'　SLdr
'Pink Cameo'　CWri
'Pink Cherub'　♀H4　EBee EMui ENot GLbr LRHS MAsh
　　　MBar MDun NBlu NPen SLdr SReu
　　　WOrn
'Pink Delight'　GLbr LHyd LKna WBod
'Pink Delight' (V)　SFai
I　'Pink Delight' (A) **new**　MAsh
'Pink Drift'　CDoC CSBt ENot LKna LMil MAsh
　　　MBar MDun MGos MOne NHol
　　　NPen NWea SHBN SLdr SPer
'Pink Ghost'　NPen SLdr
'Pink Gin'　LMil
'Pink Glory'　NPen SLdr
'Pink Lady' (A) **new**　NBlu
'Pink Leopard'　LMil MAsh MLea NPen SLdr
'Pink Mimosa' (Vs)　SLdr
'Pink Pancake' (EA)　♀H4　CBcs CTrh GQui LMil LRHS MAsh
　　　MGos SLdr SPoG SReu SSpi WGer
'Pink Pearl' (EA)　see R. 'Azuma-kagami' (EA)
'Pink Pearl' (hybrid)　CBcs CSBt CTri ENot EPfP GGGa
　　　GKir ISea LKna LMil LRHS MAsh
　　　MBar MDun MGos NBlu NPen
　　　NPri NWea SLdr SPer SReu SSta
　　　WBVN WBod WFar WMoo WOrn
'Pink Pebble'　♀H3-4　CTrw LHyd MAsh MDun MOne
　　　NPen SLdr WBVN WBod WOrn
'Pink Perfection'　MBar MGos NPen SLdr SReu WFar
'Pink Photo'　SLdr
'Pink Pillow'　SReu
'Pink Rosette'　LKna
N　'Pink Ruffles'　ENot WBod
'Pink Sensation'　MDun
'Pinkerton'　LKna
'Pintail'　GGGa IDee LMil WAbe
'Pipaluk'　NPen
'Pipit'　GGGa WAbe
'Pippa' (EA)　CMac CTrG
'PJM Elite'　GGGa LHyd LMil
PJM Group　MBri MDun MLea
§　- 'Peter John Mezitt'　♀H4　LHyd LMil MAsh NPen SLdr SReu
　　　WBod
planetum　LMil
'Pleasant White' (EA)　NBlu
pocophorum　GGGa NPen SLdr
§　- var. *hemidartum*　GGGa NPen SLdr
- var. *pocophorum*　NPen
　　USDAPI 59190/R11201
pogonostylum　see R. irroratum subsp.
　　　pogonostylum
'Point Defiance'　CWri GGGa LMil MDun NBlu SLdr
　　　WGer
'Polar Bear' (EA)　LRHS MBar MDun MGos SLdr
'Polar Bear'　♀H3-4　GLbr IDee LHyd LMil LRHS MAsh
　　　MGos MLan SReu SSpi WBVN
Polar Bear Group　CDoC COtt CWri GGGa GKir ISea
　　　LMil MLea NPen SLdr
'Polar Haven' (EA)　LKna
'Polaris'　see R. 'Hachmann's Polaris'
'Polaris' (EA)　ENot MGos SReu
§　*poluninii*　GGGa
polyandrum　see R. maddenii subsp. maddenii
　　　Polyandrum Group
§　*polycladum*　LMil
- Scintillans Group　LHyd MBar MDun MLea NHol
　　　NPen SLdr WPic
- - 'Policy'　♀H4　GGGa SReu
polylepis　GGGa LMil NPen
- AC 3810　SLdr
- C&K 284　GGGa
§　*ponticum*　CDoC CSBt CTri GGGa IDee LMil
　　　MBar MGos NWea SLdr WFar

- AC&H 205　GGGa
- 'Cheiranthifolium'　NPen
- 'Foliis Purpureis'　CWri SReu
§　- 'Silver Edge' (v)　CDoC CSBt LMil SLdr SMur
- 'Variegatum' (v)　CBcs CDoC CTri EBee ENot GGGa
　　　GKir ISea LRHS MAsh MBar MBri
　　　MDun MGos NBlu NPen NPri
　　　SReu SRms SSta WFar
'Pooh-Bah' (EA)　LHyd
'Pook'　LHyd
'Popcorn' (V)　GGGa SFai
'Popocatapetl'　SLdr SReu
'Port Knap' (EA)　LKna
'Port Wine' (EA)　LKna
'Potlatch'　GGGa
poukhanense　see R. yedoense var. poukhanense
§　'Praecox'　♀H4　CBcs CSBt CSam CTrw EBee ENot
　　　EPfP GGGa ISea LHyd LKna LMil
　　　LRHS MAsh MBar MDun MGos
　　　NBlu NHol NPen NPri SHBN SLdr
　　　SReu SSta WBod WFar
x *praecox* 'Emasculum'　see R. 'Emasculum'
praestans　GGGa IDee LMil MDun NPen SLdr
- KW 13369　NPen
praevernum　GGGa LMil NPen SLdr
§　*prattii*　NPen SLdr
- 'Perry Wood'　LMil
'Prawn'　LKna SReu
Prelude Group　SLdr
preptum　GGGa SLdr
'President Roosevelt' (v)　CSBt GKir LKna LMil LRHS MAsh
　　　MDun MGos NPen NPri SHBN
　　　SLdr SReu SSta WFar
'Pretty Girl'　LKna
'Pretty Woman'　GGGa LMil
'Pride of Leonardslee'　SLdr
'Pridenjoy'　LMil
'Prima Donna'　LMil SLdr
primuliflorum　GGGa SLdr WAbe
- CN&W 1237　ISea
- KW 4160　NPen
- 'Doker-La'　LMil LRHS WAbe
- white-flowered　WAbe
'Prince Camille de Rohan'　LMil
'Prince Henri de　CSdC LMil SLdr
　　Pays Bas' (G)
'Princess Alexandra' (V)　SFai
'Princess Alice'　CBcs LHyd NPen SLdr WAbe WBod
　　　WPic
'Princess Anne'　♀H4　CMHG CSam EBee ENot GGGa
　　　GKir LHyd LMil LRHS MAsh MBar
　　　MDun MGos MLea NPen SHBN
　　　SLdr SReu SSta WBod
'Princess Galadriel'　SLdr
'Princess Ida' (EA)　LHyd SLdr
'Princess Juliana'　LMil WGor
'Princess Margaret of　GQui LMil MAsh
　　Windsor' (K)
'Princess Margaret Toth'　CSdC
principis　LMil NPen SLdr
- C&V 9547　GGGa
- KR 3336 from　LMil
　　Potrang Gyala
- KR 3844 from Pasum Tzo　LMil
- LS&E 15831　NPen
- SF 95085　ISea
- 'Lost Horizon' KW 5656　LMil
§　- Vellereum Group　NPen SLdr
- - KW 5656　NPen
§　*prinophyllum* (A)　LMil LRHS
'Prins Bernhard' (EA)　LKna SCam SLdr
'Prinses Juliana' (EA)　SLdr SReu WFar
'Professor Hugo de　LHyd LKna MGos SReu
　　Vries'　♀H4

'Professor J.H. Zaayer' — MGos
pronum — GGGa
– R 151* — NPen
– R.B. Cooke form — GGGa
– Towercourt form — GGGa
'Prostigiatum' — MGos
prostratum — see *R. saluenense* subsp. *chameunum* Prostratum Group
proteoides — GGGa
– EGM 281 — LMil
– R 151 — NPen
* – 'Ascreavie' — GGGa
protistum — NPen SLdr
– KR 1986 — GGGa
– KW 8069 — NPen
§ – var. ***giganteum*** — NPen SReu
pruniflorum — GGGa NPen
prunifolium (A) — GGGa LMil LRHS SLdr
– 'Summer Sunset' (A) — NPen
przewalskii — GGGa LHyd NPen SLdr
– subsp. ***dabanshanense*** — GGGa
pseudochrysanthum ♀H4 — CDoC GGGa LHyd LMil LRHS NLar NPen SLdr SReu SSta
– ETE 442 — GGGa
– ETE 443 — GGGa
– dwarf — WAbe
Psyche Group — see *R.* Wega Group
'Psyche' (EA) — MDun
'Ptarmigan' ♀H3-4 — CBcs CDoC EPfP GGGa GLbr IDee LHyd LMil MAsh MBar MGos MLea NHol NLAp NMen NPen SLdr SReu SSta WBVN WBod WFar
pubescens — LMil SLdr
– KW 3953 — GGGa
pubicostatum — LMil SLdr
– AC 2051 — LMil
– CN&W 906 — ISea
§ 'Pucella' (G) ♀H4 — CWri LMil MAsh NLar SLdr SReu
pudorosum — NPen
– L&S 2752 — GGGa
'Pulchrum Maxwellii' — see *R.* 'Maxwellii'
pumilum — GGGa MDun NPen WAbe
'Puncta' — GGGa NHol
punctatum — see *R. minus* var. *minus* Punctatum Group
purdomii — GGGa SLdr
'Purple Diamond' — see *R.* Diamant Group purple
'Purple Emperor' — LKna
'Purple Gem' — NHol
purple Glenn Dale (EA) — SLdr
'Purple Heart' — ENot LMil
'Purple Queen' (EA/d) — MAsh
'Purple Splendor' (EA) — CMac LKna MGos SCam SLdr
'Purple Splendour' ♀H4 — CBcs CSBt CWri ENot EPfP GLbr IDee LHyd LKna LMil LRHS MAsh MBar MBri MDun MGos MLea NPen NWea SHBN SLdr SPer SReu SSta WBVN WFar WGwG
'Purple Triumph' (EA) ♀H3 — CBcs LKna LMil NPen SCam SLdr SReu SSta WBod
'Purpurtraum' (EA) ♀H4 — GGGa
'Quail' — GGGa
Quaver Group — SRms
'Queen Alice' — LRHS MAsh MDun
'Queen Elizabeth II' ♀H4 — LHyd LMil SPer
Queen Emma — see *R.* 'Koningin Emma'
'Queen Mary' — MBar
'Queen Mother' — see *R.* 'The Queen Mother'
'Queen of England' (G) — CSdC
Queen of Hearts Group — CWri NPen
'Queen of Hearts' — LHyd
'Queen Souriya' — SLdr SReu
Queen Wilhelmina — see *R.* 'Königin Wilhelmina'
'Queenswood Centenary' — LMil

'Quentin Metsys' (R) **new** — LMil SLdr
quinquefolium (A) — GGGa LMil NPen SLdr
racemosum ♀H4 — LMil MBar MDun NPen SLdr SSpi WAbe
– AC 719 — NPen
– ACE 1367 — WAbe
– SF 365 — ISea
– SSNY 47 — GGGa
– 'Glendoick' — GGGa
– 'Rock Rose' ex R 11265 ♀H3-4 — EPfP GGGa LHyd LMil NPen WGer
racemosum x ***tephropeplum*** — MBar
racemosum x ***trichocladum*** SBEC — NHol
'Racil' — LKna MBar MDun MGos MLea
'Racine' (G) **new** — SLdr
'Racoon' (EA) ♀H4 — GGGa
'Radiant' (M) — SLdr
radicans — see *R. calostrotum* subsp. *keleticum* Radicans Group
'Rainbow' — LKna NPen SLdr
'Ramapo' ♀H4 — GGGa GKir GLbr LMil LRHS MAsh MBar MDun MGos MLea NHol NMen NPri SPer SReu SSta WBod
ramsdenianum — GGGa LMil NPen SLdr
– KR 5619 — LMil
'Rangoon' — MBri NBlu
'Raphael de Smet' (G/d) — LMil SReu
'Rashomon' (EA) — LHyd SLdr SReu WBod
'Raspberry Ripple' — LKna SReu
ravum — see *R. cuneatum* Ravum Group
'Razorbill' ♀H4 — CDoC GGGa LHyd LMil LRHS MGos MLea SReu WAbe WBod
recurvoides — GGGa LHyd LMil MDun NPen SReu
– KW 7184 — NPen SLdr
– Keillour form — GGGa
recurvum — see *R. roxieanum* var. *roxieanum*
Red Admiral Group — NPen
Red Argenteum Group — NPen
'Red Arrow' — LHyd
'Red Carpet' — LMil NPen SLdr
'Red Delicious' — CWri GGGa ISea LMil
'Red Diamond' — see *R.* Diamant Group red
'Red Fountain' (EA) — LMil MAsh SLdr WPat
'Red Glow' — LHyd NPen
'Red Jack' — LMil
'Red Riding Hood' — CWri LKna
I 'Red Rover' (V) — SFai
'Red Sunset' (EA/d) — LRHS
'Red Velvet' — see *R.* 'Ilam Red Velvet'
'Red Wood' — GGGa
'Redpoll' — LHyd
'Redwing' (EA) — CDoC MAsh SLdr
Remo Group — SLdr
'Rendezvous' ♀H4 — ENot LMil SLdr SPoG SReu
'Rennie' (EA) — MAsh MGos
'Renoir' ♀H4 — CSBt LHyd LMil SLdr SReu
'Replique' (Vs) **new** — SLdr
reticulatum (A) — CBcs GGGa LMil NPen SLdr SReu
* – ***leucanthum*** (A) — GGGa
retusum (V) — GGGa
§ 'Reuthe's Purple' — GGGa NHol NPen SReu
'Rêve d'Amour' (Vs) — MDun SLdr SReu SSta
'Rex' (EA) — MAsh SLdr
rex — CDoC COtt GGGa IDee LHyd LMil LRHS MDun NPen SLdr
– EGM 295 — LMil
– subsp. ***arizelum*** — see *R. arizelum*
§ – subsp. ***fictolacteum*** ♀H3-4 — CDoC GGGa LHyd LMil MDun NPen SLdr SReu
– – SF 649 — ISea
– – USDAPI 59104/R11043 — NPen

- - 'Cherry Tip' R 11385 | NPen
- - Miniforme Group | LMil MDun
- subsp. *gratum* | LMil
- - AC 3009 from Zibenshan | LMil
- yellow-flowered | IDee
- - AC 901 | MDun
- - AC 2079 | LMil
rex X Sincerity Group | NPen
rhabdotum | see *R. dalhousieae* var. *rhabdotum*
'Ria Hardijzer' | LKna
'Ribera' (R) **new** | SLdr
rigidum | ISea LHyd NPen WAbe
* - *album* | NPen WBod
'Ring of Fire' | CDoC CWri LMil MAsh MBri MDun MGos MLea SLdr SReu
'Ripe Corn' | LHyd LKna NPen SLdr SReu
ripense (EA) | LHyd
'Riplet' | GEdr GGGa MDun MLea NDlv
'Ripples' (EA) | CTrh
ririei | CBcs GGGa LHyd NPen SLdr SReu WCwm
- AC 2036 | LMil
- W/V 1808 | NPen
- W/V 5139 | NPen
'Robert Croux' | SLdr
'Robert Keir' | NPen SLdr
'Robert Korn' | LMil MDun
'Robert Seleger' | GGGa LMil LRHS MAsh SReu WAbe
'Robert Whelan' (A) | MDun NLar SReu
'Robin Hill Frosty' (EA) | SLdr
Robin Hood Group | NPen
'Robin Redbreast' | NPen
'Robinette' | CBcs CWri MBri SLdr
'Rob's Favourite' (V) | SFai
'Rocket' | CTri GKir LMil MAsh MDun MLea NPen SLdr WBVN
'Rokoko' | see *R.* 'Hachmann's Rokoko'
Romany Chai Group | LHyd SLdr
Romany Chal Group **new** | LHyd
'Romy' | NPen
'Rosa Marie' | SLdr
'Rosa Mundi' | CSBt EBee ENot
Rosalind Group | LHyd SLdr
'Rosata' (Vs) ♀H4 | MBri MDun SReu SSta
'Rose Bud' | CSBt CTri MDun
'Rose de Flandre' (G) **new** | SLdr
'Rose Elf' | ECho MDun NDlv NHol WLow
'Rose Glow' (A) | SReu
'Rose Gown' | SReu
'Rose Greeley' (EA) | CDoC CTrh GQui LRHS SCam SLdr SPoG SReu WFar
'Rose Haze' (A) | SReu
'Rose Torch' (A) | SReu
roseatum F 17227 | GGGa
'Rosebud' (EA/d) ♀H3-4 | CBcs CMac CTrh CTrw ECho LHyd LKna MAsh MBar MGos NPen SCam SLdr SReu WBod
'Rosemary Hyde' (EA) | MAsh SCoo SLdr
'Rosenkavalier' | LHyd
roseotinctum | see *R. sanguineum* subsp. *sanguineum* var. *didymoides* Roseotinctum Group
roseum | see *R. prinophyllum*
'Roseum Elegans' | CTri ECho LRHS MAsh MBar NBlu NPen NPri SLdr WFar
'Rosiflorum' | see *R. indicum* 'Balsaminiflorum'
'Rosy Bell' | LKna
'Rosy Dream' | CAbP COtt CWri LMil MAsh MDun MLea SLdr
'Rosy Fire' (A) | SReu
'Rosy Lea' | MLea
'Rosy Lights' (A) | CTri MBri

'Rothenburg' | CSam CWri LHyd MDun SLdr
rothschildii | GGGa LMil LRHS NPen
- AC 1868 | LMil
- C&Cu 9312 | GGGa
rousei (V) **new** | GGGa
roxieanum | LHyd LMil NPen SLdr SReu
- R 25422 | NPen
§ - var. *cucullatum* | ISea LRHS MDun NPen
- - CN&W 680 | GGGa
- - CN&W 690 | LMil
- - CN&W 695 | LMil
- - R 10920 | NPen
- - SBEC 350 | GGGa
- - SBEC 0345 | NPen
- var. *oreonastes* ♀H4 | CDoC GGGa LHyd LMil LRHS MDun NPen SSta
- - USDAPI 59222/R11312 | GGGa NPen
- Nymans form | SReu
- var. *parvum* | GGGa
- var. *recurvum* | LMil
§ - var. *roxieanum* | NPen
- - F 16508 | NPen
'Royal Blood' | LHyd SLdr
'Royal Command' (K) | COtt CWri GKir MAsh MBar SLdr
Royal Flush Group | ISea
'Royal Lodge' (K) | SLdr
'Royal Purple' | WBod
'Royal Ruby' (K) | CWri GLbr MBri SLdr WOrn
'Roza Stevenson' | LHyd NPen SLdr
'Rozanne Waterer' (K)/d | LKna SLdr
'Rubicon' | CWri LHyd MAsh MLea SLdr WBVN
rubiginosum | GGGa GTSp LHyd LMil NPen SLdr SReu
- SF 368 | ISea
§ - Desquamatum Group | CBcs LHyd NPen SLdr
- pink-flowered | LMil
- white-flowered | LMil
rubineiflorum **new** | GGGa
'Rubinetta' (EA) | LMil LRHS SLdr WFar
rubroluteum | see *R. viridescens* Rubroluteum Group
'Ruby F. Bowman' | MGos NPen SLdr SReu
'Ruby Hart' | CBcs GGGa MAsh MDun NHol SReu
Ruddigore Group | LHyd WBod
rude | see *R. glischrum* subsp. *rude*
'Ruffles and Frills' | ECho MDun SLdr
rufum | GGGa NPen SLdr
- AC 4110 | LMil
- Sich 155 | GGGa
'Rumba' (K) | LKna
rupicola | LMil NMen NPen SLdr
§ - var. *chryseum* | GGGa LHyd NPen
- var. *muliense* | NPen
- - Yu 14042 | GGGa
russatum ♀H4 | CBcs EBee ENot EPot GGGa LHyd LMil MDun NPen SLdr WAbe WFar WPic
- C&Cu 9315 | GGGa
- blue-black-flowered | LMil LRHS
- 'Purple Pillow' | CSBt
* - 'Tower Court' | NPen
russotinctum | see *R. alutaceum* var. *russotinctum*
'Sabina' | SLdr
'Sacko' | CWri ECho GGGa GLbr LMil LTwo MAsh MDun MOne NHol SLdr WOrn
'Saffrano' | NBlu NLar
'Saffron Queen' | CBcs CTrG CTrw ISea WBod
'Sahara' (K) | CSdC LKna LMil SLdr
'Saint Breward' | CTrG GGGa LHyd MDun MLea NHol SLdr

'Saint Keverne'	SLdr
'Saint Kew'	SLdr
'Saint Merryn' ♀H4	CTrG ENot GGGa LHyd MDun NHol NPen SLdr WBod
'Saint Michael'	SReu
'Saint Minver'	LHyd SLdr
'Saint Tudy'	CDoC EPfP LHyd LKna MDun NPen SLdr
'Saint Valentine' (V)	SFai
'Sakata Red' (EA)	WBod
'Sakon' (EA)	NPen SLdr
'Salmon Bedspread'	SReu
'Salmon Sander' (EA)	SLdr
§ 'Salmon Trout'	LMil
'Salmon's Leap' (EA/v)	CBcs COtt CSBt GQui LMil LRHS NPri SHBN SLdr SReu WAbe WFar
saluenense	GGGa LMil NPen SLdr WAbe
– JN 260	GGGa
§ – subsp. *chameunum*	GGGa LMil NPen SLdr WAbe
– – ACE 2143	WAbe
§ – – Prostratum Group	GGGa LMil WAbe
§ – subsp. *riparioides*	see *R. calostrotum* subsp. *riparium* Rock's form
– subsp. *saluenense* F 19479	NPen
– – Exbury form R 11005	LMil
'Sammetglut'	CWri SReu
'Samoa'	NBlu
'Sang de Gentbrugge' (G)	CSdC GGGa LMil SReu
sanguineum	GGGa LMil MDun NPen SLdr SReu
§ – subsp. *didymum*	GGGa MDun NPen
– subsp. *sanguineum* var. *cloiophorum* R 10899	NPen
– – USDAPI 59553/R11212	NPen
– – var. *didymoides* Consanguineum Group	NPen
§ – – – Roseotinctum Group USDAPI 59038/ R10903	GGGa NPen
– – var. *haemaleum*	GGGa LMil NPen
– – F 21732	NPen
– – F 21735	GGGa NPen
– – USDAPI 59303/R10895	NPen
– – USDAPI 59453/R10938	NPen
– – var. *sanguineum* F 25521	LMil
– – – R 10893	NPen
– – USDAPI 59096/R11029	NPen
'Santa Maria'	COtt LRHS SLdr SReu SSta WBVN
§ 'Saotome' (EA)	LHyd SLdr
'Sapphire'	CSBt CTrG LKna MAsh MBar MDun NDlv SLdr SRms
'Sappho'	CBcs CSBt CWri EBee ENot EPfP GBin GGGa GLbr LHyd LKna LMil LRHS MBar MDun MGos MLea NPen SHBN SLdr SPer SReu SSta WBVN WFar WGer WMoo WOrn
'Sapporo'	GGGa LMil MBri
'Sarah Boscawen'	SReu
sargentianum	GGGa LMil MLea NMen NPen WAbe
– 'Whitebait'	GGGa NPen WAbe
'Sarita Loder' **new**	LHyd
'Sarled' ♀H4	GGGa LMil NLAp NMen SReu
Sarled Group	NPen SRms WAbe WBod
'Saroi' (EA)	NPen SLdr
'Sarsen' (K)	CSdC
'Saskia' (K)	LKna
'Satan' (K) ♀H4	CSBt LKna SLdr SReu
'Satschiko'	see *R.* 'Geisha Orange'
'Satsop Surprise'	GGGa
'Satsuki' (EA)	ECho
'Saturne' (G)	SLdr

'Saturnus' (M)	MAsh SLdr
'Saxon Bonnie Belle' (V) **new**	SFai
'Saxon Dwarf' (V)	SFai
scabrifolium	CTrG NPen
§ – var. *spiciferum*	GGGa NPen SLdr WPic
– – SF 502	ISea
– – SF 534	ISea
* *scallaforum* SF 99037 **new**	ISea
'Scandinavia'	LHyd
'Scarlet Romance' **new**	MBri
'Scarlet Wonder' ♀H4	More than 30 suppliers
'Schlaraffia' **new**	NLar
schlippenbachii (A)	GGGa GIBF LMil NPen SLdr SPer SReu SSpi WAbe
– 'Sid's Royal Pink' (A)	LMil MDun
'Schneeflöckchen'	GGGa
'Schneekrone'	GGGa MBri MDun NBlu NHol
'Schneespiegel'	ENot
'Schneewolke'	LMil
'Schubert' (EA)	MBar MGos SLdr WBod
scintillans	see *R. polycladum* Scintillans Group
'Scintillation'	CWri GGGa LMil MAsh MBar MDun MLea NPen SHBN SLdr WMoo WOrn
scopulorum	SLdr
– C&C 7571	GGGa
– KR 5770	LMil
– KW 6354	GGGa
scottianum	see *R. pachypodum*
scyphocalyx	see *R. dichroanthum* subsp. *scyphocalyx*
Seagull Group	NPen SLdr
searsiae	LMil NPen SLdr
'Sea-shell'	SLdr
'Seb'	SLdr
'Second Honeymoon'	CDoC CWri ISea MLea SLdr SReu
'Seikai' (EA)	SLdr
seinghkuense CCH&H 8106	GGGa
– KW 9254	GGGa
selense	GGGa LMil NPen SLdr
§ – subsp. *dasycladum*	LMil NPen
– – F 11312	NPen
– – KW 7189	NPen
– – R 11269	NPen
– subsp. *jucundum*	GGGa LMil MDun NPen
– – KR 4051B	LMil
– – SF 660	ISea
– subsp. *selense* F 14458	NPen
§ – subsp. *setiferum*	NPen SLdr
semnoides	GGGa NPen SLdr
– F 21870	NPen
– F 25639	NPen
– R 25388	NPen
'Senator Henry Jackson'	GGGa LMil
'Sennocke'	LHyd
'September Song'	COtt CWri GGGa LMil MAsh MBri MDun MGos MLea SLdr WBVN
'Serendipity'	GGGa
serotinum	LMil NPen SLdr SReu
– C&H 7189	GGGa
– KR 4653	LMil
– SEH 242	LMil
serpyllifolium (A)	CBcs GGGa NPen SLdr
sesostris (G)	CSdC
'Sesterianum'	CMHG SLdr
Seta Group	CBcs NPen SLdr SReu
setiferum	see *R. selense* subsp. *setiferum*
setosum	GGGa LMil MDun NPen SReu
'Seven Stars'	CSBt NPen SLdr SReu
'Seville'	SLdr

'Shamrock'   CDoC EPfP GCrs GEdr GKir ISea
LRHS MAsh MBar MDun MGos
MLea NHol SLdr SReu WBod WFar
'Shantung Rose' (V)   SFai
'Shanty' (K/d)   LKna
'Sheila' (EA)   CSBt NPri
shepherdii   see *R. kendrickii*
sherriffii   GGGa MDun NPen SLdr
– L&S 2751   NPen
'Shiko' (EA)   MAsh

I 'Shiko Lavender' (A)   LMil
Shilsonii Group   LHyd NPen SLdr SReu
'Shinimiagagino' (EA)   NPen
'Shi-no-noe' (EA)   NPen
'Shintoki-no-hagasane'   LHyd
(EA)
'Shintsune' (EA)   NPen
'Shira-fuji' (EA/v)   SLdr
Shot Silk Group   NPen SLdr
'Show Stopper' (V)   SFai
'Shrimp Girl'   EBee ENot LHyd LRHS MAsh
MDun MGos NPen SLdr SReu
'Shukishima' (EA)   NPen
shweliense   GGGa SReu
sichotense   GGGa
sidereum   GGGa NPen SLdr
– AC 3056   WCwm
– KW 6792   NPen
– SF 314   ISea
– SF 318   ISea
siderophyllum   LMil SLdr
sikangense   NPen SLdr
– EGM 108   LMil
– R 18142   NPen
§ – var. *cookeanum*   NPen
Cookeanum Group
– var. *exquisitum*   GGGa MDun
– – EGM 349   LMil
from Wumenshan
– var. *sikangense*   LMil
– – Cox 5105   NHol
'Silberglanz' **new**   LHyd
§ 'Silberwolke'   COtt EBee ENot LMil SReu
'Silver Anniversary'   MGos
Silver Cloud   see *R.* 'Silberwolke'
'Silver Edge'   see *R. ponticum* 'Silver Edge'
'Silver Fountain' (EA)   LMil LRHS MAsh
'Silver Glow' (EA)   CMac
'Silver Jubilee'   CWri LHyd LMil LRHS SLdr
'Silver Moon' (EA)   NPen SCam SLdr
'Silver Queen' (A)   ECho MGos
'Silver Sixpence'   EBee ENot EPfP GKir LRHS MAsh
MBar MDun MGos NPen NWea
SHBN SLdr SReu WOrn
'Silver Skies'   LMil
'Silver Slipper' (K) ♀H4   CDoC GKir LHyd LKna LMil LRHS
MAsh MBar MBri MLea SLdr SPer
SReu SSta WGor
'Silver Thimbles' (V)   GGGa
'Silverwood' (K)   LMil
'Silvester' (EA)   COtt MBri SCam SLdr
'Simona'   CWri LMil LRHS SPoG SReu
simsii (EA)   CMac SLdr
– SF 431   ISea
simulans   see *R. mimetes* var. *simulans*
sinofalconeri C&H 7183   GGGa
– SEH 229   LMil
sinogrande ♀H3   CBcs CDoC CHEx EPfP GGGa
IDee LHyd LMil LRHS MDun NPen
SLdr SPer SPoG SSpi WBod WFar
WGer WPic
– AC 1888   WCwm
– KR 4027   LMil
– KW 21111   NPen SLdr

– SF 350   ISea
'Sir Charles Lemon' ♀H3-4   CDoC CWri LMil LRHS MDun
MLea NPen SLdr SReu
* 'Sir G.E. Simpson'   NPen
'Sir George Sansom'   SLdr
'Sir Robert' (EA)   SLdr
'Sir William   LKna SReu
Lawrence' (EA)
'Skookum'   ECho GLbr MGos SLdr WBVN
WOrn
'Sleeping Beauty'   WAbe
'Sleepy'   ENot GLbr MAsh MGos NDlv
NPen SLdr WOrn
smirnowii   GGGa LMil LRHS NPen SLdr SReu
smithii   see *R. argipeplum*
§ Smithii Group   CWri SReu
'Sneezy'   CBcs CSBt CWri ENot EPfP GGGa
GKir LHyd LMil LRHS MAsh MBar
MGos NHol NPen SLdr WFar WOrn
'Snipe'   CBcs CDoC ENot GGGa GKir
GLbr LHyd LMil LRHS MAsh MBar
MDun MGos NHol NPri NWea
SReu WBod WLow WOrn
'Snow' (EA)   CMac CSBt LRHS MBar SCam SLdr
'Snow Crown'   MAsh SLdr
(*lindleyi* hybrid)
'Snow Hill' (EA)   GQui LHyd LMil SLdr
'Snow Lady'   CBcs EBee ENot EPfP GCrs GEdr
GLbr LMil MAsh MBar MDun
MGos MOne NHol NLAp SLdr
SReu WGwG WLow WOrn
'Snow Queen'   SLdr
Snow Queen Group   LKna LMil SReu
'Snowbird' (A)   GGGa LMil LRHS MAsh NLar NPri
'Snowdrift'   GGGa
'Snowflake' (EA/d)   see *R.* 'Kure-no-yuki'
'Snowhite' (EA)   NPri
'Snowstorm'   ECho SLdr WBVN
'Soho' (EA)   CSdC GQui SLdr
'Soir de Paris' (Vs)   CDoC GGGa LHyd MBar MBri
MDun MLea NPen SLdr SReu SSta
WBVN WBod
'Soldier Sam'   SReu SSta
'Solidarity'   ECho GLbr MAsh MDun MLea
SLdr WBVN
'Solway' (Vs)   CSdC LMil
'Sonata'   CWri GGGa MDun SReu WBod
'Sonatine'   LMil
'Songbird'   LHyd LKna LMil LRHS MBar MDun
NPen SLdr SReu WBod
'Sophie Hedges' (K/d)   LKna
sororium (V) KR 3080   GGGa
– KR 3085   LMil
– var. *wumengense*   LMil
CN&W 990
Souldis Group   LMil SLdr
souliei   LMil NPen SLdr
– deep-pink-flowered   GGGa
– white-flowered   GGGa
'Southern Cross'   CSam MLea NPen SLdr
'Souvenir de D.A. Koster'   SLdr
'Souvenir de   CSBt LKna MBar SLdr
Doctor S. Endtz' ♀H4
'Souvenir du   LKna
Président Carnot' (G/d)
'Souvenir of Anthony   LKna MDun SReu
Waterer' ♀H4
'Souvenir of W.C. Slocock'   LKna NPen SHBN SLdr SReu SSta
'Sparkler' (Vs)   GGGa
'Sparkler' (hybrid)   LRHS MGos
speciosum   see *R. flammeum*
'Spek's Brilliant' (M)   SReu
'Spek's Orange' (M) ♀H4   MGos SReu
sperabile   NPen

- var. *weihsiense*	GGGa LMil NPen
- - AC 1915	LMil
sperabiloides	GGGa NPen
- R 125	NPen
sphaeranthum	see *R. trichostomum*
sphaeroblastum	GGGa LMil SLdr
- KR 1481*	NPen
- var. *wumengense*	MDun
- - CN&W 510	ISea
- - CN&W 962	LMil
- - CN&W 968	GGGa
- - CN&W 1051	LMil
- - EGM 350	LMil
- - EGM 359	LMil
spiciferum	see *R. scabrifolium* var. *spiciferum*
spilotum	GGGa LMil NPen SLdr
spinuliferum	GGGa NPen WBod
- SF 247	ISea
'Spitfire'	MGos SReu
'Splendens' (G)	CSdC
'Spoonbill' (K)	LKna
'Spring Beauty' (EA)	CMac NBlu SCam SLdr SReu
'Spring Magic'	LMil NPen SLdr
'Spring Pearl'	see *R.* 'Moerheim's Pink'
'Spring Rose'	NPen SLdr
'Spring Sunshine'	LMil
'Springbok'	LHyd
'Squirrel' (EA) ♀H4	CDoC COtt GGGa GKir LHyd LMil LRHS MAsh MBri MDun MGos MLea NDlv SLdr SReu WBod WGer
'Squirrel' tall (EA)	SLdr
'Staccato'	GGGa
Stadt Essen Group	CDoC LMil SLdr
stamineum	GGGa LMil NPen
- SF 417	ISea
- W/V 887	NPen
'Standishii'	SLdr
'Stanley Rivlin'	LHyd
§ 'Stanway'	LMil NPen
'Starbright Champagne'	LMil
'Starcross'	LHyd
'Starfish'	SReu
'Stella'	NPen
§ *stenopetalum*	CMac ISea LHyd LMil NPen SLdr
'Linearifolium' (A)	SReu WAbe WPic
stenophyllum	see *R. makinoi*
stewartianum	GGGa MDun NPen SLdr
- SF 370	ISea
'Stewartstonian' (EA)	CMac LHyd MBar MBri SReu SSta WBod WFar
stictophyllum	see *R. nivale* subsp. *boreale* Stictophyllum Group
'Stoat' (EA)	GQui MDun
'Stopham Girl' (A)	LMil
'Stopham Lad' (A)	LMil
'Stranraer'	MDun
'Strawberry Cream'	GGGa NHol
'Strawberry Ice' (K) ♀H4	CBcs CDoC CMHG CSBt CWri ENot EPfP GGGa GKir LHyd LKna LMil LRHS MAsh MBar MBri MDun MGos MLea MMHG NBlu SLdr SPer SReu
strigillosum	GGGa MDun NPen SLdr
- C&H 7035	GGGa
- EGM 305	LMil
- EGM 338	LMil
- Reuthe's form	SReu
'Suave'	WBod
subansiriense C&H 418	GGGa NPen
suberosum	see *R. yunnanense* Suberosum Group
succothii	LHyd MDun
- BB 185a	NPen
- EGM 086	LMil

- LS&H 21295	NPen SLdr
'Suede'	MDun
'Sugar Pink'	LMil
'Sugared Almond' (K)	LMil
sulfureum	NPen
- SBEC 249	GGGa
'Sulphamer'	SLdr
'Summer Blaze' (A)	SReu
'Summer Flame'	SReu
'Summer Fragrance' (O) ♀H4	LMil SReu SSta
'Sun Chariot' (K)	CBcs LKna MAsh MBri SLdr SReu
'Sunbeam' (hybrid)	LKna SReu
'Sunny' (V)	GGGa
(Sunrise Group) 'Sunrise'	SLdr
'Sunset Pink' (K)	LHyd SLdr
'Sunte Nectarine' (K) ♀H4	GQui LHyd LMil MDun SCoo
superbum (V)	GGGa
'Superbum' (O)	SLdr
'Surprise' (EA)	CDoC CTrh CTri LRHS NPen SCam SCoo SLdr
'Surrey Heath'	CBcs COtt CWri EBee ENot EPfP GKir LMil LRHS MAsh MBar MDun MGos MLea NBlu NDlv NPen SLdr SReu WOrn
'Susan' ♀H4	CDoC CSBt CSam CWri GGGa LHyd LKna LMil MDun MLea NPen SLdr SPoG SReu
'Susannah Hill' (EA)	CDoC CTrh MGos SLdr SReu
'Sussex Bonfire'	NPen SLdr
sutchuenense	GGGa IDee LMil MDun NPen SLdr
- var. *geraldii*	see *R.* x *geraldii*
'Swamp Beauty'	CWri LMil MDun
'Swansong' (EA)	CMac
'Sweet Simplicity'	CSBt LKna
'Sweet Sixteen'	NPen SLdr
'Sweet Sue'	NBlu NPen SLdr SReu
'Swift'	CDoC GGGa GQui LMil LRHS LTwo MAsh NHol SLdr SReu WGer
'Sword of State' (K)	MAsh
'Sylphides' (K)	LKna MBri
'Sylvester'	CDoC MGos NBlu NMen SReu
'T.S. Black' (EA)	SLdr
taggianum 'Cliff Hanger' ex KW 8546	LMil
'Taka' (A)	SLdr
'Taka-no-tsukasa' (EA) **new**	SLdr
'Takasago' (EA/d)	LHyd LMil
'Talavera'	see *R.* (Golden Oriole Group) 'Talavera'
taliense	GGGa LHyd LMil MDun NPen SLdr
- F 6772	NPen SLdr
- JN 782	GGGa
- KR 2765	GGGa
- KR 4056 from Cangshan	LMil
- SSNY 352	GGGa
'Tally Ho'	LHyd SLdr
Tally Ho Group	NPen SLdr
tamaense	see *R. cinnabarinum* subsp. *tamaense*
'Tama-no-utena' (EA)	LHyd SLdr
'Tamarindos'	LMil
'Tanager' (EA)	CDoC CTrh LKna
§ *tanastylum* var. *pennivenium*	NPen SLdr
- - SF 593	ISea
'Tangerine'	see *R.* 'Fabia Tangerine'
tapetiforme	GGGa WAbe
'Tarantella'	ENot LMil
Tasco Group	SLdr
tashiroi (EA)	NPen SLdr
'Tatjana' ♀H4	ENot IDee LMil LRHS MAsh
tatsienense	GGGa

'Taurus' ♀H4   CDoC COtt CWri GGGa LMil
MAsh MDun MLea WBVN WGer
taxifolium (V) **new**   GGGa
'Tay' (K)   SLdr
'Teal'   MBar MDun MGos MLea NHol
NPen WLow
'Teddy Bear'   CDoC CWri GGGa LMil LRHS
MDun SLdr WAbe
§ *telmateium*   NPen SLdr
temenium   MDun
 - Cox 6037B   GGGa
 - R 10909   NPen
 - var. *dealbatum*   NPen
  Glaphyrum Group
  F 21902
 - var. *gilvum*   GGGa LMil NPen
  'Cruachan' R 22272
§ - var. *mesopolium*   NPen
  R 10950
 - var. *temenium* F 21734   NPen
 - - F 21809   NPen
'Temple Belle'   MDun WBod
Temple Belle Group   CSam LHyd LKna MLea NDlv
NPen SLdr
'Tender Heart' (K)   SLdr
'Tensing'   SLdr
§ *tephropeplum*   GGGa LHyd MDun NPen SLdr
 - KW 6303   NPen
 - SF 92069   ISea
 - USDAPQ 3914/R18408   GGGa
 - Deleiense Group   see *R. tephropeplum*
'Tequila Sunrise'   LHyd LMil NPen
'Terra-cotta'   LKna LMil
'Terra-cotta Beauty' (EA)   CTrG WPat
'Tessa'   CBcs MAsh SLdr
Tessa Group   CDoC LKna LMil LRHS MGos
'Tessa Bianca'   GGGa
'Tessa Roza' ♀H4   GGGa GQui LHyd NBlu
'Thai Gold' (V)   SFai
thayerianum   GGGa NPen SLdr
'The Dowager'   SLdr
'The Freak'   SLdr
§ 'The Hon. Jean Marie   CAbP CWri EPfP LKna LMil MAsh
  de Montague' ♀H4   MBri MDun MGos MLea NPen
SLdr SPer SReu WBVN
'The Master' ♀H4   LHyd LKna LMil NPen SLdr
SReu
§ 'The Queen Mother'   LHyd
thomsonii   GGGa IDee LHyd LMil LRHS
MDun NHol SLdr SReu
 - AC 113   NPen
 - B&SWJ 2638   WCru
 - var. *candelabrum*   see *R.* x *candelabrum*
§ - subsp. *lopsangianum*   GGGa
 - - LS&T 6561   NPen
 - subsp. *thomsonii*   NPen
  BL&M 228
 - - L&S 2847   GGGa
Thor Group   GGGa SReu
'Thousand Butterflies'   see *R.* 'One Thousand Butterflies'
'Thunderstorm'   LHyd LKna SReu
thymifolium   GGGa
'Tiana'   GGGa
'Tibet' ♀H3-4   GQui LMil MBar MDun SHBN
SLdr
'Tidbit' ♀H4   GGGa LHyd LKna LMil MGos
MLea NPen SLdr
'Tilford Seedling'   LKna
I 'Tilgates Peach'   CWri
'Timothy James'   LRHS MAsh SReu
'Tinkerbird'   GGGa
'Tinsmith' (K)   SLdr
'Tit Willow' (EA)   GKir LHyd LMil LRHS NPri SCoo
SLdr

'Titian Beauty'   CBcs COtt CSBt CWri EBee EPfP
GBin GGGa GKir LHyd LMil LRHS
MDun MGos NBlu NDlv NPen
NPri SLdr SPer WBVN WBrE WFar
WOrn
'Titipu' (EA)   LHyd SLdr
'Titness Park' **new**   LHyd
'Tolkien'   SReu
'Tom Hyde' (EA) **new**   MAsh
'Tom Williams'   NPen SLdr
'Too Bee'   NHol WAbe
'Top Banana'   LRHS MDun SLdr
'Topsvoort Pearl'   SReu
'Torch'   LKna MGos
'Toreador' (EA)   CTrG SCam SLdr
'Torero'   GGGa LMil
'Torridon' (Vs)   LMil
'Tortoiseshell Champagne'   see *R.* 'Champagne'
'Tortoiseshell   CDoC CSBt LHyd LKna LMil MBri
  Orange' ♀H3-4   MDun SHBN SLdr SPoG SReu SSta
'Tortoiseshell Salome'   LKna SReu
'Tortoiseshell Scarlet'   MDun NBlu SReu
'Tortoiseshell   LKna LMil MAsh MGos NPen NPri
  Wonder' ♀H3-4   SLdr SPoG SReu
'Totally Awesome' (K)   MBri MLea
'Toucan' (K)   CSBt MDun SLdr
'Tower Beauty' (A)   LHyd
'Tower Dainty' (A)   LHyd
'Tower Daring' (A)   LHyd SLdr
'Tower Dexter' (A)   LHyd
'Tower Dragon' (A)   LHyd LMil SLdr
'Trail Blazer'   GGGa
traillianum   GGGa LMil NPen SLdr
 - CN&W 746   ISea
 - F 5881   NPen
§ - var. *dictyotum*   NPen
 - - 'Kathmandu'   NPen SLdr
Treasure Group   LHyd SLdr
'Trebah Gem'   NPen SLdr
'Tregedna'   NPen SLdr
'Tregedna Red'   SReu
'Trewithen Orange'   MBar MDun NPen SHBN SLdr
'Trewithen Purple'   CTrw
'Trianon'   NPen
trichanthum   CPne GGGa LMil NPen
 - 'Honey Wood'   LHyd LMil SLdr
 - white-flowered **new**   LMil
trichocladum   NPen
 - CN&W 880   ISea
 - SF 661   ISea
 - SF 96179   ISea
§ *trichostomum*   GGGa LRHS NPen WAbe WBod
 - KW 4465   NPen
 - Ledoides Group   MLea NPen SReu
 - - 'Collingwood   LMil SLdr SReu
  Ingram' ♀H4
triflorum   GGGa ISea LMil MDun NPen
 - C&V 9573   GGGa
 - SF 95149   ISea
§ - var. *bauhiniiflorum*   CBcs NPen SLdr
 - var. *triflorum*   NPen
  Mahogani Group
'Trilby'   SReu
trilectorum **new**   GGGa
'Trinidad'   MDun
triplonaevium   see *R. alutaceum* var.
russotinctum Triplonaevium
Group
'Troll' (EA)   SReu
'Tromba'   GGGa
'Troupial' (K)   LKna
'Trude Webster'   GGGa MLea SReu
tsangpoense   see *R. charitopes* subsp.
tsangpoense

tsariense	GGGa LMil NHol NPen SLdr
- var. *magnum*	NPen
- Poluninii Group	see *R. poluninii*
- var. *trimoense*	GGGa LMil MDun NPen
- 'Yum Yum'	GGGa NPen SLdr
tsariense x *proteoides*	GGGa
§ *tsusiophyllum*	GGGa
'Tsuta-momiji' (EA)	LHyd
tubiforme	see *R. glaucophyllum* subsp.
	tubiforme
'Tuffet'	SReu
'Tulyar'	LKna
'Tunis' (K)	ECho
N 'Twilight' (EA)	MBri
'Twilight Pink'	NPen
'Twilight Sky' (A)	ENot SLdr
'Tyermannii'	LMil
'Ukamuse' (EA/d)	LHyd SLdr
'Umpqua Queen' (K)	MBri MLea
Ungerio Group	NPen
ungernii	GGGa LMil NPen SLdr
uniflorum	NHol NPen
§ - var. *imperator*	LMil
- - KW 6884	GGGa
- var. *uniflorum*	NPen
KW 5876	
'Unique' (G)	EPfP ISea LKna LRHS SPer
'Unique' (*campylocarpum*	CBcs CDoC CSam GGGa GKir
hybrid) ♀H4	LHyd LKna LMil LRHS MAsh MBri
	MDun NPen NPri SHBN SLdr SReu
	SSta WMoo
'Unique Marmalade'	LMil MAsh SLdr WBVN WOrn
uvariifolium	GGGa NPen SLdr
- CN&W 127	ISea
- CN&W 1275	ISea
- Cox 6519	GGGa
- KR 4158 from Napa	LMil
Hai, Zhongdian	
- var. *griseum*	IDee SLdr
- - C&C 7506	GGGa
- - KR 3423	LMil
- - KR 3428	LMil
- - KR 3774	LMil
- - KR 3782	LMil
- - SF 95184	ISea
- 'Reginald Childs'	LMil LRHS SLdr
- var. *uvariifolium*	NPen
USDAPI 59623/R11391	
- 'Yangtze Bend'	GGGa
vaccinioides	GGGa
(V) CCH&H 8051	
'Valentine' (EA)	GGGa
valentinianum	CBcs GGGa IDee NPen SLdr WAbe
- F 24347	NPen
- var. *oblongilobatum*	LMil
C&H 7186	
'Van'	LMil WGer
'Van Houttei Flore	SLdr
Pleno' **new**	
'Van Nes Sensation'	LMil
'Van Weerden Poelman'	EMil
Vanessa Group	LMil SReu WBod
'Vanessa Pastel' ♀H3-4	GGGa LHyd LMil MDun MLea
	NPen SLdr SReu WBod WGer
§ 'Vanilla'	LKna
vaseyi (A) ♀H3-4	GGGa LMil SLdr
- 'White Find' **new**	GGGa
- white-flowered (A)	LMil
veitchianum	GGGa
§ - Cubittii Group	GGGa NPen SLdr
- - 'Ashcombe'	LHyd
- KNE Cox 9001	GGGa
'Veldtstar'	LHyd
vellereum	see *R. principis* Vellereum Group

'Velvet Gown' (EA)	ENot SReu
venator	GGGa MDun NPen
'Venetia' (K)	MBri
'Venetian Chimes'	EBee ENot ISea MDun NLar NPen
	SLdr SReu
vernicosum	GGGa LMil NPen
- F 5881	NPen
- JN 180	GGGa
- McLaren T 71	NPen
- SF 416	ISea
- Yu 13961	SLdr
- Yu 14694	SLdr
- Euanthum Group F 5880	NPen
'Veryan Bay'	CBcs
vesiculiferum	NPen
'Vespers' (EA)	MAsh
vialii (A)	GGGa
'Victoria Hallett'	SLdr SReu
'Victory' x 'Idealist' **new**	SLdr
'Vida Brown' (EA/d)	CMac ENot LKna MAsh SLdr SReu
	WPat
'Viennese Waltz'	GGGa
'Viking' (EA)	LHyd WBod
'Vincent van Gogh'	GGGa MBri
'Vincourt Duke' (R/d)	CWri ECho GLbr MDun SLdr
'Vincourt	CDoC ECho MDun SLdr
Troubador' (K/d)	
'Vineland Dream' (K/d)	CWri ECho LRHS MAsh SLdr
'Vineland Fragrance'	MDun SLdr
I 'Vinestar'	SLdr
'Vintage Rosé' ♀H4	LMil NPen SLdr SReu
'Violet Longhurst' (EA)	LHyd SLdr
'Violetta' (EA)	GGGa LRHS NMen SLdr
Virginia Richards Group	CWri GKir LRHS MAsh MGos NBlu
	NPen SLdr SReu SSta
viridescens 'Doshong La'	LMil
§ - Rubroluteum Group	GGGa LMil
viscidifolium	GGGa NPen
'Viscosepalum' (G)	CSdC
viscosum (A) ♀H4	GGGa GIBF GQui IDee LHyd LKna
	LMil LRHS MAsh MDun SLdr SPer
	SPoG SReu WBrE WMoo
- 'Grey Leaf' (Vs)	LMil
- var. *montanum* (A)	IBlr
- f. *rhodanthum* (A)	LMil
- 'Roseum' (Vs)	LMil
'Viscount Powerscourt'	ENot LMil SLdr
'Viscy' ♀H4	CDoC CWri ECho GGGa
	GQui ISea LHyd LMil MBri MDun
	MGos MLea NLar SLdr WBVN
	WOrn
§ Volker Group	CWri LMil LRHS MAsh MBar NDlv
	SReu SSta WFar
- 'Babette'	LMil MBri MLea
- 'Lackblatt'	CDoC LMil MBri MGos MLea SLdr
'Vulcan' ♀H4	CBcs ENot EPfP GGGa LMil MLea
	SHBN SLdr
'Vulcan'	SReu
x *yakushimanum*	
'Vuyk's Rosyred' (EA) ♀H4	CDoC CDul CMac CSBt CTri ENot
	GQui LHyd LKna LMil LRHS MAsh
	MBar MBri MGos SCam SLdr SPer
	SReu WBod WFar WStI
'Vuyk's Scarlet' (EA) ♀H4	More than 30 suppliers
'W.E. Gumbleton' (M)	SReu
'W.F.H.' ♀H4	CWri LMil NPen SLdr
'W. Leith'	SLdr
'Wagtail'	NHol
wallichii	GGGa LHyd MDun SLdr
- B&SWJ 2633	WCru
- DM 21	LMil
- LS&H 17527	NPen
Walloper Group	NPen SReu
'Wallowa Red' (K)	ECho LHyd MBri MLea SLdr

'Wally Miller'	LMil MAsh MBri MDun MLea SReu SSta WBVN
walongense	NPen
aff. *walongense* C&H 373	GGGa
'War Dance'	GGGa
wardii	GGGa IDee ISea LHyd LMil LRHS MDun NPen SLdr
- C&V 9558	GGGa
- C&V 9606	GGGa
- KR 3684	LMil
- KR 4913	LMil
- KR 5268	LMil
- L&S	SReu
- SHEG 5672	NPen
- var. *puralbum*	GGGa NPen
- - F 10616	NPen
- 'Vibrant'	SLdr
- var. *wardii*	LMil
- - C&V 9548	GGGa
- - F 21551	NPen
- - KW 5736	NPen
- - LS&E 15764	NPen
- - LS&T 5679	NPen
- - LS&T 5686	NPen
- - LS&T 6591	NPen
§ - - Litiense Group	NPen SLdr
- - - CN&W 1079	ISea
'Ward's Ruby' (EA)	CTrh CTrw SLdr
§ 'Washington State Centennial' (A)	GGGa MBri
wasonii	GGGa LHyd LMil NPen
- f. *rhododactylum*	NPen
- - KW 1876	GGGa
- var. *wenchuanense*	GGGa NHol
- - C 5046	GGGa
- white-flowered	SReu
'Waterfall'	WBod
watsonii	GGGa NPen SLdr SReu
- Cox 5075	GGGa
'Waxbill'	GGGa
'Waxwing'	LKna MBri
websterianum Cox 5123	GGGa
- EGM 146	LMil
'Wee Bee' ♀H4	CDoC EPot GCrs GGGa GKir LMil LTwo MAsh MDun MLea NDlv NHol SReu WAbe WBod
§ Wega Group	LHyd
'Welkin'	WBod
'Werei'	NPen
'Westminster' (O)	LKna LMil
'Weston's Pink Diamond'	GGGa LMil NHol
'Weybridge'	NPen SLdr
weyrichii (A)	GGGa
'Wheatear'	GGGa
'Whidbey Island'	LMil
'Whisperingrose'	LMil MDun MGos MLea NDlv WLow
'White Frills' (EA)	GLbr LHyd
White Glory Group	NPen SLdr
'White Gold'	GGGa MDun
'White Grandeur' (EA)	CTrh
'White Jade' (EA)	SLdr
'White Lady' (EA)	LKna MBar SCam SLdr WGor
'White Lights' (A) ♀H4	LMil LRHS MAsh MBri SLdr
'White Olympic Lady'	LKna
'White Perfume'	MDun SReu
'White Peter'	GGGa
'White Swan' (hybrid)	ENot LKna SReu
'White Wings'	GQui SLdr WPic
'Whitethroat' (K/d) ♀H4	CSdC CWri EPfP GKir GLbr GQui LKna LMil MAsh MBri MDun SLdr SPer WBVN
'Whitney's Dwarf Red'	SLdr
'Wigeon'	GGGa GKir LMil LRHS NHol
wightii	GGGa MDun NPen SLdr
'Wild Affair'	MDun
'Wilgen's Ruby'	CDoC CSBt LKna MBar MGos NWea SHBN SLdr SPer WFar WStI
'Will Silent' (V)	SFai
'Willbrit'	CDoC CWri ECho LHyd MAsh MGos SLdr WGor WOrn
'William III' (G) **new**	SLdr
williamsianum ♀H4	CBcs CDoC CTrG CWri EPot GBin GGGa LHyd LMil LRHS MAsh MBar MDun MGos MLea NPen NWea SLdr SReu SRms SSpi WBod WPic
- Caerhays form	LMil MDun SLdr
- 'Special'	GGGa
- white-flowered	NPen
'Willy' (EA)	CTrh SCam SLdr
wilsoniae	see *R. latoucheae*
Wilsonii Group	CTrG LKna
wiltonii ♀H4	GGGa LMil MDun NPen SLdr
- CC&H 3906	GGGa
'Windlesham Scarlet'	EBee ENot LHyd SLdr
'Windsor Lad'	LKna SReu
'Windsor Peach Glow' (K)	LMil
'Windsor Sunbeam' (K)	CWri
'Winsome' (hybrid) ♀H3	CDoC GGGa LHyd LMil NPri SPoG SReu
Winsome Group	CBcs CTrw CWri GKir LKna LRHS MAsh MBar MDun NPen SLdr SSta WBod
'Winston Churchill' (M)	MBar SReu
I 'Wintergreen' (EA)	COtt CTrh
'Wishmoor'	NPen SLdr SReu
'Witch Doctor'	ECho LMil MDun MGos MLea SLdr WBVN
'Witchery'	GGGa
'Wojnar's Purple'	LMil MBri
'Wombat' (EA) ♀H4	CDoC COtt CTri EPot GGGa GKir LHyd LMil LRHS MAsh MGos NHol SLdr SReu
'Wonderland'	LKna
wongii	GGGa GQui LMil NPen SLdr
'Woodcock'	LHyd
'Wren'	CSam GCrs GEdr GGGa LRHS MAsh MBar MBri MDun MLea NHol SLdr SPer SReu WAbe WBod
'Wryneck' (K)	CSdC LHyd LMil SLdr SReu
'Wye' (K)	SLdr
x *xanthanthum*	MLea
xanthocodon	see *R. cinnabarinum* subsp. *xanthocodon*
xanthostephanum	NPen
- CCH&H 8070	GGGa
- KR 3095	LMil
- KR 4462	LMil
'Yaku Angel'	MDun
'Yaku Duke' **new**	LHyd
'Yaku Incense'	MAsh MDun WBVN
'Yaku Prince'	MDun MGos
'Yaku Princess'	MAsh
yakushimanum	CBcs CDoC CMHG CSam CWri EPfP GGGa IDee LHyd LKna LMil LPan LRHS MAsh MBar MBri MDun MGos MLea NPen NWea SLdr SPer SPlb SReu SSta WGer
I - 'Beefeater'	SLdr
- 'Berg'	MBri MDun
- 'Edelweiss'	GGGa
- Exbury form	SReu
- Exbury form	SReu
x *roxieanum* var. *oreonastes* **new**	
- FCC form	see *R. yakushimanum* 'Koichiro Wada'

§ - 'Koichiro Wada' ♀H4 | CAbP EBee EPfP GGGa GGar LHyd LMil LRHS MAsh MDun MGos NPen SLdr SPoG SReu WGer
- subsp. *makinoi* | see *R. makinoi*
- 'Snow Mountain' | SReu
I - 'Torch' | WBrE
yakushimanum | SReu
   x *bureavii*
- x 'Coronation Day' | SLdr
- x *decorum* | GGGa SLdr SReu
- x 'Elizabeth' | GGGa
- x 'Floriade' | SLdr
- x *griersonianum* | SLdr
- x *lanatum* | GGGa
- x *pachysanthum* | GGGa SLdr SReu
- x *proteoides* | GGGa
- x *rex* | SReu
- x *tsariense* | GGGa
'Yaye' (EA) | CDoC SLdr
§ *yedoense* | SLdr SReu
   var. *poukhanense*
'Yellow Cloud' (K) | CDoC ECho LMil MBri MDun
'Yellow Hammer' ♀H4 | CDoC CTrG EPfP EPot ISea MDun NWea WBVN WBrE
Yellow Hammer Group | CBcs CWri GGGa LKna LMil MBar MGos NPen SHBN SLdr SPer SReu SSta WBod
'Yellow Petticoats' | MLea
'Yellow Rolls Royce' | MDun
'Yoga' (K) | LKna
'Yol' | SLdr
I 'Yolanta' | WAbe
'Youthful Sin' | ISea
'Yo-zakura' (EA) | NPen
yungningense | LMil MDun NPen
yunnanense | GGGa IDee ISea LHyd LMil MDun NPen SLdr SSpi WPic
- AC 751 | MDun NPen
- C&H 7145 | GGGa
- KGB 551 | SReu
- KGB 559 | SReu
- SF 379 | ISea
- SF 400 | ISea
- SF 96102 | ISea
- 'Openwood' ♀H3-4 | GGGa LMil
- pink-flowered | GGGa
- 'Red Throat' | SLdr
- red-blotched **new** | LMil
§ - Suberosum Group | NPen
- white-flowered | GGGa LMil
'Yvonne Dawn' | NPen
zaleucum | LMil MDun
- AC 685 | MDun NPen
- F 15688 | GGGa
- F 27603 | NPen
- KR 2687 | GGGa
- KR 3979 | LMil
- SF 347 | ISea
- SF 578 | ISea
- Flaviflorum Group KW 20837 | NPen
Zelia Plumecocq Group | NPen SLdr SReu
zeylanicum | see *R. arboreum* subsp. *zeylanicum*
Zuiderzee Group | SLdr

Rhodohypoxis (Hypoxidaceae)

'Albrighton' | EPot ERos EWes GEdr IBal ITim LAma NHol NMen SAga SBla SIng WAbe WPat
I 'Andromeda' **new** | EWes
'Appleblossom' | CWrd EPot ERos EWes ITim LBee NLAp NMen SCnR SIng WAbe WOBN

baurii ♀H4 | CElw CMea CNic CPBP GCrs GEdr IBal IMGH ITim LRHS MBro MTho NMen NSla SAga SRms WAbe WWin
- 'Alba' | CMea EDAr ITim MLLN NMen
- var. *baurii* | CWrd EWes LBee NJOw SIng
- 'Coconut Ice' **new** | EPot
- var. *confecta* | EWes ITim SAga SBla SIng
- 'Daphne Mary' **new** | EWes
- 'Dulcie' | EWes ITim SCnR SIng SOkd
- 'Lily Jean' (d) | CStu CWrd ENot EWes GEdr LRHS NLAp SIng
- 'Mars' **new** | EWes
- 'Pearl' | ITim
- 'Perle' | EPot ERos EWes GEdr NJOw NMen SCnR SIng WAbe
- 'Pictus' | ITim
- 'Pink Pearl' | EPot EWes ITim NHol
- pink-flowered | ITim NLAp WCru
- var. *platypetala* | CWrd EPot EWes ITim NHol NLAp NMen SIng WAbe
- - Burtt 6981 | EWes
- var. *platypetala* | LTwo
   x *milloides*
- 'Rebecca' **new** | EWes
- 'Red King' | EWes
- red-flowered | NLAp SPlb
- 'Susan Garnett-Botfield' | CWrd EPot EWes IBal ITim NMen SIng WAbe
- white-flowered | EPot ITim NLAp NMen WCru
'Betsy Carmine' | GEdr
'Burgundy' | SIng
'Candy Stripe' | EWes GEdr LPan SIng
'Carina' | EWes
'Confusion' | CWrd EWes WAbe
'Dawn' | CNic CWrd EPot EWes ITim LAma NHol NLAp NMen SAga SBla SIng WAbe
deflexa | CGra CLyd CWrd EWes GCrs IMGH ITim NLAp SAga SBla SCnR SIng WAbe WFar WOBN
'Donald Mann' | EWes ITim NMen
double, red-flowered (d) | CStu
'Douglas' | CWrd EPot GFlt IBal ITim LAma NHol NMen SAga SBla SIng WAbe WPat
'Dusky' | CWrd
'E.A. Bowles' | EWes GCrs IBal ITim NMen SIng WAbe
'Emily Peel' | CWrd EWes WAbe
'Eva-Kate' | CWrd ERos EWes ITim LAma NHol SAga SBla SIng WPat
'Fred Broome' | CWrd EPot EWes ITim LAma NHol NMen SAga SBla SIng WAbe WPat
'Garnett' | CWrd EDAr EWes ITim NMen SBla WAbe WPat
'Great Scott' | CWrd ECho ERos EWes ITim SCnR SIng
'Harlequin' | CWrd EPot EWes IBal ITim LAma NHol NMen SIng WAbe
'Hebron Farm Biscuit' | see *Hypoxis parvula* var. *albiflora* 'Hebron Farm Biscuit'
'Hebron Farm Cerise' | see x *Rhodoxis* 'Hebron Farm Cerise'
'Hebron Farm Pink' | see x *Rhodoxis hybrida* 'Hebron Farm Pink'
§ 'Helen' | EPot EWes ITim NHol SBla SIng WAbe
hybrids | ELan WOBN
'Kiwi Joy' (d) | CStu SBla
'Knockdolian Red' | NHol
'Maddie's Blush' | WOBN

'Margaret Rose'	CWrd EPot EWes GCrs NMen SIng WAbe
milloides	CPla EMlt EPot EWes GEdr GGar IBal IMGH ITim LBee LRHS NHol NLAp NMen NWCA SAga SBla SCnR SIng SSpi WAbe WFar
- 'Claret'	CSam CWrd EWes LTwo SAga SBla SIng WAbe WFar WOBN WPat
- 'Damask'	EWes SAga SBla
- 'Drakensberg Snow' **new**	EWes
'Monty'	EPot EWes GEdr SIng
'New Look'	ERos EWes IBal ITim LTwo NMen SIng WAbe
'Picta' (v)	CWrd EPot EWes GCrs GEdr LAma NHol SAga SBla SSpi WAbe WOBN WPat
'Pink Ice' **new**	GEdr
'Pinkeen'	EPot EWes GEdr ITim LTwo SIng WAbe WFar
'Pintado'	EWes SBla
'Rosie Glow'	WOBN
'Ruth'	EWes GFlt LAma NHol SBla SIng WAbe
'Shell Pink'	EWes ITim
'Starlett' **new**	EWes
'Starry Eyes' (d)	CStu SBla
'Stella'	EPot ERos EWes GEdr IBal ITim NHol NMen SAga SBla SIng WAbe WOBN
tetra	ITim
'Tetra Pink'	EWes SIng WAbe
'Tetra Red'	CWrd EPot EWes GFlt ITim NHol NMen SIng WAbe WOBN WWin
'Tetra White'	see *R.* 'Helen'
thodiana	CWrd ERos EWes GEdr NLAp NMen SBla SCnR SIng SSpi WAbe
'Venetia'	CMea SIng

Rhodophiala (*Amaryllidaceae*)

§ *advena*	WCot
bagnoldii	EBee
- F&W 8695	WCot
§ *bifida*	WCot
chilensis	CLAP WCot
montana	NWoo
pratensis **new**	EBee

Rhodora see *Rhododendron*

Rhodothamnus (*Ericaceae*)

chamaecistus	GCrs WAbe

Rhodotypos (*Rosaceae*)

kerrioides	see *R. scandens*
§ *scandens*	CBcs CBot CPle CTri EBee EPfP EWTr EGil IMGH LHop MMHG SLon SMac SSpi WBVN WBod WCru WSHC WSPU WWin

x *Rhodoxis* (*Hypoxidaceae*)

'Aurora'	EWes
'Hebron Farm Biscuit'	see *Hypoxis parvula* var. *albiflora* 'Hebron Farm Biscuit'
§ 'Hebron Farm Cerise'	CWrd EWes GEdr NMen SAga
§ *hybrida*	EWes NMen SIng WAbe
- 'Aya San'	EWes
§ - 'Hebron Farm Pink'	CBro CWrd EWes GEdr NMen SAga SBla SCnR SIng SScr WAbe WFar WOBN
- 'Hebron Farm Red Eye'	CWrd EWes GEdr SBla SCnR SIng SScr WAbe
'Old Barn Pink'	WOBN

Rhoeo see *Tradescantia*

Rhopalostylis (*Arecaceae*)

baueri	CBrP EAmu LPal WMul
sapida	CAbb CBrP CTrC LPal MPRe WMul
- 'Chatham Island'	CBrP

rhubarb see *Rheum* x *hybridum*

Rhus (*Anacardiaceae*)

ambigua B&SWJ 3656	WCru
§ *aromatica*	CAgr CArn CFil CPle ELau EPfP IArd IDee WPGP
chinensis	CDoC CMCN EGFP EPfP
copallina	ELan EPfP GIBF LRHS SMur
- red-leaved **new**	WPat
coriaria	EPfP
cotinus	see *Cotinus coggygria*
glabra	CArn CBcs CDoC EPfP MGos SPer WDin
- 'Laciniata' Carrière **new**	NLar
- 'Laciniata' misapplied	see *R.* x *pulvinata* Autumn Lace Group
glauca **new**	EShb
N *hirta*	see *R. typhina*
incisa	SPlb
integrifolia	CArn CPle LRav
magalismontana	EShb
potaninii	EPfP SSpi
§ x *pulvinata* Autumn Lace Group	CDoC ENot EPfP GKir MGos SDix SHBN WPat
- - 'Red Autumn Lace' ♀H4	GKir LRHS MBlu MBri SPer
punjabensis var. *sinica*	CFee WPic
§ *radicans*	CArn COld GPoy
sylvestris	EPfP
toxicodendron	see *R. radicans*
trichocarpa	EPfP SSpi
trilobata	see *R. aromatica*
N *typhina* ♀H4	CBcs CDoC CLnd EBee ECrN ECtt ELan ENot EPfP GKir LRHS MAsh MBar MGos NBea NBee NBlu NFor NWea SHBN SPer SSta WBrE WDin WFar WStI WTel WWin
§ - 'Dissecta' ♀H4	CBcs CDoC CLnd CSBt EBee ECrN ELan ENot EPfP GKir MAsh MBar MBri MGos MWat NBea NBlu SEND SPer WDin WFar WOrn WTel
- 'Laciniata' hort.	see *R. typhina* 'Dissecta'
§ *verniciflua*	CFil CLnd CMCN EPfP GIBF IArd SSpi

Rhynchelytrum see *Melinis*

Rhynchospora (*Cyperaceae*)

§ *colorata*	CRow NPer WDyG
latifolia **new**	WCot

Ribes ✿ (*Grossulariaceae*)

alpinum	CPLG ECrN ENot LBuc MRav MWht NSti NWea SPer SRms WDin WGwG
- 'Aureum'	CMHG CSBt EHoe EPla GEil NFor NPro WCot WDin WSHC
- 'Schmidt'	LBuc MBar
americanum	EHoe ELan EPla MRav NHol SPer
'Variegatum' (v)	WPat
aureum hort.	see *R. odoratum*
* - 'Roxby Red'	MCoo
'Black Velvet' (D)	LRHS MCoo

x *culverwellii*   CAgr EMui GTwe LBuc LEdu LRHS
  Jostaberry (F)   SDea
diacanthum   CFil
divaricatum   CAgr LEdu
- 'Worcesterberry'   see *Ribes* 'Worcesterberry'
gayanum   CPMA CPle ECrN NLar SLPl
x *gordonianum*   CDoC CMHG CPLG CPMA EBee
   ELan EPfP EPla GBin GEil GKir
   LAst LHop LRHS MRav NHol NSti
   SEND SLim SLon SPer SSpi WBVN
   WCot WFar WHCG
laurifolium   CBcs CBot CDul CFil CPLG CPla
   ELan GEil SLim SPer WBor WCru
   WDin WHCG WSHC WWin
- (f)   CPMA EPfP GKir
- (m)   CHar CPMA EPfP GKir WCFE
   WPat
- 'Mrs Amy Doncaster'   EPla
- Rosemoor form   CSam EPfP SSpi WHCG WPGP
lobbii   EWes
nigrum 'Baldwin' (B)   CDoC CMac CTri CWSG EPfP
   GBon LRHS SDea SKee WStI
- 'Ben Alder'^{PBR} (B)   LRHS MAsh SDea
- 'Ben Connan'^{PBR}   CAgr CDoC COtt EMui EPfP GTwe
  (B) ♀H4   LRHS MBri MGos NBlu SCoo SDea
   SKee SPoG
- 'Ben Lomond'^{PBR}   CSBt CTri EMui ENot GBon GKir
  (B) ♀H4   GTwe LBuc LRHS MGos MRav
   NBee NGHP NRog SDea SPer WStI
- 'Ben Loyal' (B)   GTwe
- 'Ben More' (B)   CAgr CSBt GKir GTwe LRHS MBri
   NBee SDea WStI
- 'Ben Nevis' (B)   CSBt CTri GTwe SDea SKee
- 'Ben Sarek'^{PBR} (B) ♀H4   CAgr CDoC CSBt CSut CTri CWSG
   EMui ENot GKir GTwe LBuc LRHS
   MGos MRav NGHP NRog SDea
   SKee SPer
- 'Ben Tirran'^{PBR} (B)   CAgr CDoC LBuc LRHS MBri
   MGos SKee
- 'Black Reward' (B)   LRHS
- 'Blacksmith' (B)   MCoo
- 'Boskoop Giant' (B)   CAgr CMac GTwe LRHS NRog
   SPer
- 'Daniel's September' (B)   GTwe MCoo
- 'Farleigh' (B)   EMui
- 'Foxendown' (B)   EMui
- 'Jet' (B)   ENot GTwe LRHS NRog SPer
- 'Laciniatum'   EMon
- 'Laxton's Giant' (B)   GTwe
- 'Mendip Cross' (B)   GTwe
- 'Seabrook's' (B)   CAgr
- 'Wellington XXX' (B)   CAgr CSBt CTri ENot GTwe LBuc
   LRHS NBee NBlu NGHP NRog
   SPer WStI
- 'Westwick Choice' (B)   GTwe
§ *odoratum*   More than 30 suppliers
- 'Crandall'   ESim
praecox   CBcs SEND
rubrum 'Blanka' (W)   CSut
- 'Cherry' (R) **new**   CAgr
- 'Fay's New Prolific' (R)   GTwe
- 'Hollande Rose' (P)   GTwe
- 'Jonkheer van   CAgr CSBt CWSG EMui EPfP GKir
  Tets' (R) ♀H4   GTwe IArd LRHS MCoo NBlu SDea
   SKee SPoG
- 'Junifer' (R)   EMui GTwe MAsh
- 'Laxton's Number   CAgr CTri EMui ENot GBon GTwe
  One' (R)   LRHS MAsh MRav NGHP NRog
   SDea SPer
- 'Laxton's Perfection' (R)   MCoo
- 'October Currant' (P)   GTwe
- 'Raby Castle' (R)   GTwe
- 'Red Lake' (R) ♀H4   CAgr CMac CWSG EPfP ERea
   GBon GTwe LBuc LRHS MGos

   NBee NBlu NRog SDea SKee SPer
   WStI
- 'Redstart'^{PBR} (R)   CAgr COtt CSBt GTwe LBuc LRHS
   MBri SDea SKee
- 'Rondom' (R)   SDea
- 'Rovada' (R)   CAgr CSut EMui GTwe MAsh
- 'Roxby Red' (R)   NGHP NRog
- 'Stanza' (R) ♀H4   CAgr GTwe SDea
- 'Transparent' (W)   GTwe
§ - 'Versailles Blanche' (W)   CAgr CMac CSBt CTri EMui ENot
   EPfP GKir GTwe LBuc MBri MGos
   SDea SKee SPer
- 'White Dutch' (W)   MCoo
- 'White Grape' (W) ♀H4   GTwe NRog
- 'White Pearl' (W)   CBcs SDea
- White Versailles   see *R. rubrum* 'Versailles Blanche'
- 'Wilson's Long   GTwe
  Bunch' (R)
sanguineum   CDul GKir MBar WBVN WFar
   WMoo WStI
- 'Albescens'   MWat SPer WBcn
I - 'Atrorubens Select' **new**   MBri
- 'Brocklebankii'   CAbP CPLG EBee EPar EPfP EPla
   GKir LRHS MGos MRav MWat NPri
   NSti SHBN SLim SLon SPer SPla
   WAbe WEas WGwG WPen WSHC
- double   see *R. sanguineum* 'Plenum'
- 'Elk River Red'   GKir LRHS
- 'Flore Pleno'   see *R. sanguineum* 'Plenum'
- var. *glutinosum*   SChu
  'Albidum'
- 'King Edward VII'   More than 30 suppliers
- 'Koja'   EBee LAst LRHS MAsh WBcn WPat
   WWeb
- 'Lombartsii'   MRav
§ - 'Plenum'.(d)   CBot MTed
- 'Poky's Pink'   GKir GSki MGos MRav
- 'Pulborough   CBcs CChe CDoC CTri CWSG
  Scarlet' ♀H4   EBee EBre ECrN ELan ENot EPfP
   GKir LRHS MAsh MGos MRav
   MWat NBee NBir SLim SMer SPer
   SPla SPlb SRms SWvt WFar WLow
   WMoo WWeb
- 'Red Pimpernel'   CDoC CSBt EBee LAst MAsh MBNS
   MBri SCoo SWvt WBcn WFar
- 'Taff's Kim' (v)   EPla SMad
- 'Tydeman's White'   CChe CDul CPLG CSBt ECtt ELan
   EPfP LAst MBar NLar NPri SDnm
   SSpi WPat
- White Icicle   CBot CDoC CTri CWSG CWib
  = 'Ubric' ♀H4   ECrN ENot EPfP GKir GSki LAst
   LRHS MAsh MBri MGos MRav NBir
   NPri NSti SDnm SLim SPer SPla
   SPoG SWvt WFar WGwG
speciosum ♀H3   More than 30 suppliers
trilobum **new**   LEdu
uva-crispa   GTwe
  var. *reclinatum*
  'Achilles' (C/D)
- - 'Admiral Beattie' (F)   GTwe NRog
- - 'Alma' (D)   NRog
- - 'Annelii' (F)   SDea
- - 'Aston Red'   see *R. uva-crispa* var. *reclinatum*
   'Warrington'
- - 'Australia' (F)   NRog
- - 'Bedford Red' (D)   GTwe NRog
- - 'Bedford Yellow' (D)   GTwe
- - 'Beech Tree   GTwe
  Nestling' (F)
- - 'Bellona' (C)   NRog
- - 'Blucher' (D)   GTwe NRog
- - 'Bright Venus' (D)   GTwe
- - 'Broom Girl' (D)   GTwe NRog
- - 'Captivator' (F)   GTwe SDea

- - 'Careless' (C) ♀H4 — CMac CSBt EMui ENot GBon GKir GTwe LRHS MBri MGos MRav NBee NGHP NRog SDea SPer WStI
- - 'Catherine' **new** — SDea
- - 'Champagne Red' (F) — GTwe
- - 'Clayton' (F) — NRog
- - 'Cook's Eagle' (C) — GTwe
- - 'Cousen's Seedling' (F) — GTwe
- - 'Criterion' (C) — GTwe NRog
- - 'Crown Bob' (C/D) — GTwe LRHS NRog
- - 'Dan's Mistake' (D) — GTwe LRHS NRog
- - 'Drill' (F) — GTwe
- - 'Early Sulphur' (D/C) — GTwe LRHS NGHP NRog SDea WStI
- - 'Edith Cavell' (F) — GTwe
- - 'Firbob' (D) — GTwe NRog
- - 'Forester' (D) — GTwe
- - 'Freedom' (C) — GTwe NRog
- - 'Gipsey Queen' (F) — GTwe
- - 'Glenton Green' (D) — GTwe
- - 'Golden Ball' (D) — SDea
- - 'Golden Drop' (D) — GTwe LRHS
- - 'Green Gem' (C/D) — GTwe NRog
- - 'Green Ocean' (F) — GTwe NRog
- - 'Greenfinch'PBR (F) ♀H4 — CAgr EMui GTwe LRHS SDea
- - 'Greengage' (D) — NRog
- - 'Gretna Green' (F) — GTwe
- - 'Guido' (F) — GTwe NRog
- - 'Gunner' (D) — GTwe NRog
- - 'Heart of Oak' (F) — GTwe NRog
- - 'Hebburn Prolific' (D) — GTwe
- - 'Hedgehog' (D) — GTwe
- - 'Hero of the Nile' (C) — GTwe NRog
- - 'High Sheriff' (D) — GTwe NRog
- - 'Hinnonmäki Gul' (F) — ENot SDea
- - 'Hinnonmäki Röd' (F) — ENot GTwe MCoo SDea
- - 'Howard's Lancer' (C/D) — GTwe NRog SDea
- - 'Invicta'PBR (C) ♀H4 — CAgr CDoC CMac CSBt CSut CTri CWSG EBre EMui ENot EPfP GBon GKir LBuc LRHS MBri MGos SCoo SDea SKee SPer WBVN WStI
- - 'Ironmonger' (D) — GTwe LRHS NRog
- - 'Jubilee' (C/D) — COtt LBuc MBri MGos NRog
- - 'Keen's Seedling' (D) — GTwe
- - 'Keepsake' (C/D) — GTwe LRHS MRav NRog SDea
- - 'Kim' **new** — ESim
- - 'King of Trumps' (F) — GTwe LRHS NRog
- - 'Lancashire Lad' (C/D) — GTwe LRHS NGHP NRog
- - 'Langley Gage' (D) — GTwe LRHS NRog
- - 'Laxton's Amber' (D) — GTwe
- - 'Leveller' (D) ♀H4 — CMac CSBt CSut CTri EBre EMui ENot GBon GKir GTwe LBuc LRHS MGos MRav NGHP NRog SDea SKee SPer WStI
- - 'London' (C/D) — GTwe LRHS NRog
- - 'Lord Derby' (C/D) — GTwe NRog
- - 'Lord Kitchener' (F) — NRog
- - 'Macherauch's Seedling' (F) — NRog
- - 'Marigold' (F) — NRog
- - 'Martlet'PBR (F) — GTwe
- - 'Matchless' (D) — NRog
- - 'May Duke' (C/D) — LRHS NRog SDea
- - 'Mitre' (C) — GTwe
- - 'Pax'PBR (F) — CAgr CDoC CSBt EMui EPfP GTwe LBuc MBri SDea SKee
- - 'Peru' (F) — GTwe
- - 'Pitmaston Green Gage' (D) — GTwe
- - 'Plunder' (F) — GTwe NRog
- - 'Prince Charles' (F) — GTwe
- - 'Queen of Hearts' (F) — NRog
- - 'Queen of Trumps' (D) — GTwe NRog
- - 'Rifleman' (D) — GTwe
- - 'Rokula'PBR (D) — CDoC EMui GTwe SDea SKee
- - 'Rosebery' (D) — GTwe
- - 'Scotch Red Rough' (D) — GTwe
- - 'Scottish Chieftan' (D) — GTwe
- - 'Sir George Brown' (D) — NRog
- - 'Snowdrop' (D) — GTwe
- - 'Speedwell' (F) — NRog
- - 'Spinefree' (F) — GTwe
- - 'Sultan Juror' (F) — NRog
- - 'Surprise' (C) — GTwe NRog
- - 'Suter Johnny' (F) — NRog
- - 'Telegraph' (F) — GTwe
- - 'The Leader' (F) — NRog
- - 'Tom Joiner' (F) — GTwe
- - 'Trumpeter' (C) — NRog
§ - - 'Victoria' (C/D) — GTwe NRog
- - 'Warrington' (D) — GTwe NRog
- - 'Whinham's Industry' (C/D) ♀H4 — CMac CSBt CSut CTri EMui ENot GBon GKir GTwe LBuc MBri MGos MRav NBee NGHP NRog SDea SPer WStI
- - 'White Eagle' (C) — NRog
- - 'White Lion' (C/D) — GTwe NRog
- - 'White Transparent' (C) — GTwe
- - 'Whitesmith' (C/D) — GTwe LRHS NBlu NGHP NRog SDea WStI
- - 'Woodpecker' (D) — GTwe LRHS NRog
- - 'Yellow Champagne' (D) — GTwe LRHS NRog
- *viburnifolium* — CPle CSam LEdu WPGP
§ 'Worcesterberry' (F) — EMui LRHS MBri MGos NRog SDea SPer

Richea (Epacridaceae)

- *dracophylla* — GGar SAPC
- *scoparia* — GGar
- *sprengelioides* **new** — SSpi

Ricinocarpos (Euphorbiaceae)

- *pinifolius* — ECou

Ricinus (Euphorbiaceae)

- *communis* — CHEx SYvo
- - 'Carmencita' ♀H3 — LRav
- - 'Gibsonii' — WMul
- - 'Impala' — CSpe SYvo
- - 'Zanzibariensis' — EShb WMul

Riocreuxia (Asclepiadaceae)

- *torulosa* — SPlb

Robinia (Papilionaceae)

- x *ambigua* — SSpi
- *fertilis* — EBee NPSI SIgm SSpi
§ *hispida* — CDul CEnd CLnd CWib ECrN ELan EPfP EWTr MAsh MBlu SBLw SHBN SPer SSpi WDin WOrn WSHC WSPU
- - 'Macrophylla' — CEnd SSpi WPGP
- - 'Rosea' misapplied — see *R. boyntonii*, *R. elliottii*, *R. hispida*
- - 'Rosea' ambig. — CBcs CBot EBee ENot SBLw WPGP
- *kelseyi* — CDul MAsh SPer
- x *margaretta* Casque Rouge — see *R. x margaretta* 'Pink Cascade'
§ - 'Pink Cascade' — CDoC CDul CEnd CLnd EBee ECrN EPfP EWTr LPan LRHS MAsh MBlu MBri MGos MSwo SBLw SHBN SKee SLim SPer SSpi WDin
- *neomexicana* — CLnd

pseudoacacia	CAgr CCVT CDul CLnd ECrN ELan ENot EPfP LBuc LPan MCoo SBLw SPlb WBVN WDin WFar WNor
	NMyG NOrc SWvt WAul WCot WHil WLow WPnP WWin
- 'Bessoniana'	EBee ECrN ENot SBLw WDin
- 'Fastigiata'	see *R. pseudoacacia* 'Pyramidalis'
- 'Frisia' ♀H4	More than 30 suppliers
- 'Inermis' hort.	see *R. pseudoacacia* 'Umbraculifera'
* - 'Mimosifolia'	MBri
- 'Myrtifolia' **new**	SBLw
§ - 'Pyramidalis'	SBLw
- 'Red Cascade' **new**	SBLw
- 'Rozynskiana'	CDul LRHS SFam
- 'Tortuosa'	CDul CEnd CLnd EBee ECrN ELan EMil EPfP LPan LRHS MBlu MBri SBLw SLdr SPer WPGP
- Twisty Baby = 'Lace Lady'PBR	EBee EBre ELan ENot EPfP LRHS MAsh MBri MGos MRav NLar SCoo SLim WWeb WWes
§ - 'Umbraculifera'	CDul CLnd EBee ECrN EMil ENot LPan LRHS MGos SBLw SFam
- 'Unifoliola'	SBLw
x ***slavinii*** 'Hillieri' ♀H4	CDoC CDul CEnd CLnd ECrN ELan EPfP EWTr LRHS MAsh MBlu MGos SKee SPer SPoG SSpi WOrn WPGP

Rochea see *Crassula*

Rodgersia ✿ (*Saxifragaceae*)

ACE 2303	GBuc
CLD 1329	NHol
CLD 1432	NHol
aesculifolia ♀H4	More than 30 suppliers
- green bud	IBlr
- pink-flowered	IBlr SSpi
- 'Red Dawn'	IBlr
aff. ***aesculifolia*** petaloid	IBlr
'Blickfang'	IBlr
'Die Anmutige'	CRow
'Die Schöne'	CLAP
'Elfenbeinturm'	EBee IBlr
henrici	CBct CLAP CRow EGle GKir IBlr LBuc MBri NBro SLon SPer SWat WMoo WPnP WTin
- 'Buckshaw White'	IBlr
- 'Castlewellan' **new**	IBlr
- hybrid	EBee EMan GBuc ITim NHol NLar WAul WHil
'Herkules'	CBct EBee EMan GCal MBNS NLar SSpi WMul
'Ideal' **new**	WCot
'Irish Bronze' ♀H4	CLAP EBee EBlw EBre EMan EPla GBin GKir IBlr LPio LRHS SSpi WCAu WMoo WPnP
'Koriata'	IBlr
'Kupfermond'	CRow IBlr
'Maigrün'	IBlr
nepalensis	CFil CLAP IBlr MDun
- EMAK 713	WCot
'Panache'	IBlr
'Parasol'	CBct CFil CHad CLAP GBuc IBlr NHol SSpi WPnP
pinnata	More than 30 suppliers
- B&SWJ 7741A	WCru
- L 1670	CLAP SSpi
- 'Alba'	EBee GKir IBlr MBri MLLN NHol WPnP
- 'Buckland Beauty'	CLAP IBlr SBla SSpi
- 'Cally Salmon'	EGle GCal WCot
- 'Crûg Cardinal'	WCru
- 'Elegans'	CBct CHEx CHad EBee EBre EChP ELan EMan ENot EPar EPfP EPla GKir IBlr LAst LRHS MRav NHol

- from S W China	GIBF
- 'Maurice Mason'	SDix SMHy
- 'Mont Blanc'	IBlr
- Mount Stewart form	IBlr
- 'Perthshire Bronze'	IBlr
- 'Rosea'	IBlr
- 'Superba' ♀H4	More than 30 suppliers
- white-flowered	GAbr GCal
podophylla ♀H4	More than 30 suppliers
- 'Bronceblad'	IBlr
- Donard form	CFil IBlr MBri
- 'Rotlaub'	CDes CLAP CRow EGle GCal IBlr LRHS MBri WCot WMoo WPGP
- 'Smaragd'	CDes CLAP CRow EBee EBre EGle GCal IBlr LRHS NLar
purdomii hort.	CDes CLAP EBee GCal GKir LRHS SSpi WCot WPGP
§ 'Reinecke Fuchs'	IBlr
'Rosenlicht'	CRow MTed
'Rosenzipfel'	IBlr
sambucifolia	CBcs CLAP CRow EWTr GBBs GFlt GKir ITim MBri MFir NLar NSti SMac SMrm SPer SSpi WCAu WCru WFar WGwG WMoo WPnP WTin
- B&SWJ 7899	WCru
- dwarf pink-flowered	GKir IBlr
- dwarf white-flowered	IBlr
- large green-stemmed	IBlr
- large red-stemmed	IBlr
- 'Mountain Select'	WFar
- white-flowered **new**	ITim
sambucifolia x ***pinnata***	IBlr
tabularis	see *Astilboides tabularis*

Rohdea (*Convallariaceae*)

japonica	CFil LEur WCot WPGP
- B&SWJ 4853	WCru
- 'Godaishu' (v)	WCot
- 'Gunjaku' (v)	EMon WCot
- 'Lance Leaf'	EPla
- long-leaved	WCru WFar
- 'Talbot Manor' (v)	CFil EBee EBla EPla WCot WPGP
- 'Tama-jishi' (v)	WCot
- 'Tuneshige Rokujo' (v)	WCot
- variegated (v)	EBee WCot
watanabei B&SWJ 1911	WCru

Romanzoffia (*Hydrophyllaceae*)

§ ***sitchensis***	CTri MAvo
suksdorfii E. Greene	see *R. sitchensis*
tracyi	CDes EBee GGar NRya WBor WCru
unalaschcensis	CNic GTou NWCA SGar SRms WBVN WPer

Romneya (*Papaveraceae*)

coulteri ♀H4	More than 30 suppliers
§ - var. ***trichocalyx***	CFir EPla GMac IBlr SSpi WPGP
§ - 'White Cloud' ♀H4	EHol ENot ERea IBlr SMad WSpi
- 'White Sails'	IBlr
x ***hybrida***	see *R. coulteri* 'White Cloud'
trichocalyx	see *R. coulteri* var. *trichocalyx*

Romulea (*Iridaceae*)

amoena	ECho
'Niewoodville' **new**	
autumnalis **new**	ECho
barkerae	ECho
'Paternoster' **new**	
bulbocodium	CBro CNic ESis
- var. ***clusiana*** MS 239	EHyt
* - 'Knightshayes'	EHyt

- var. **leichtliniana** EHyt
  MS 784
columnae CNic
dichotoma new ECho
engleri WPGP
gigantea CStu
kamisensis new ECho
leipoldtii new ECho
linaresii CNic EHyt
longituba see *R. macowanii*
§ **macowanii** CPBP
- var. **alticola** EHyt WAbe
namaquensis new ECho
nivalis EHyt
obscura var. **blanda new** ECho
- var. **obscura new** ECho
* - var. **subslacea new** ECho
ramiflora EHyt
  subsp. **gaditana**
requienii CNic NMen
- L 65 EHyt
rosea CPBP
saldanhensis new EHyt
tempskyana EHyt
* **zahnii** CNic

Rondeletia (Rubiaceae)
amoena SOWG

Rorippa (Brassicaceae)
nasturtium-aquaticum EMFW MBow NArg WMAq

Rosa ❀ (Rosaceae)
ACE 241 CFee
A Shropshire Lad CSam ESty LRHS MAsh MAus MBri
= 'Ausled'PBR (S) SWCr
Abbeyfield Rose ENot GCoc GGre MMat MRav SPer
= 'Cocbrose'PBR SWCr
(HT) ♥H4
§ 'Abbotswood' EBls MAus
  (*canina* hybrid)
Abigaile NBat
= 'Tanelaigib'PBR (F)
Abraham Darby CGro CTri EBre EPfP ESty GGre
= 'Auscot'PBR (S) GKir LRHS LStr MAus MRav
MWgw SMad SPer SSea SWCr
WAct WHCG WStI
Acapulco IDic
= 'Dicblender'PBR (HT)
Ace of Hearts MBur SWCr
= 'Korred' (HT)
acicularis GIBF
- var. **nipponensis** EBls
'Adam' (ClT) EBls
'Adam Messerich' (Bb) EBee EBls MAus WHCG
'Adélaïde d'Orléans' CRHN EBls LRHS MAus MBri MRav
(Ra) ♥H4 SFam SPer SWCr WAct WHCG
'Admiral Rodney' (HT) NRog
Adriana = 'Frydesire' (HT) MBri
'Agatha' (G) see *R. x francofurtana* 'Agatha'
Agatha Christie ENot GGre MBri MMat MRav
= 'Kormeita'PBR (ClF) SWCr
'Aglaia' (Ra) MAus WHCG
'Agnes' (Ru) ♥H4 EBls ECnt EMFP ENot EPfP EWTr
GCoc IArd LRHS MAus MMat
MRav NBPC SPer SSea SWCr WAct
WHCG WOVN
'Aimée Vibert' (Ra) CSam EBee EBls MAus MRav SPer
SWCr WAct WHCG
'Alain Blanchard' (G) EBls MAus SWCr WHCG
x **alba** (A) EBls NRog
§ - 'Alba Maxima' (A) EBls EMFP ENot EWTr GCoc GGre
LRHS MAus MMat MRav NBPC
SFam SPer SSea SWCr WAct WHCG

§ - 'Alba Semiplena' CHad EBls EMFP LRHS MAus SPer
(A) ♥H4 SWCr WAct WHCG
- Celestial see *R.* 'Céleste'
- 'Maxima' see *R. x alba* 'Alba Maxima'
Alba Meidiland CBrm WOVN
= 'Meiflopan'PBR (S/GC)
'Albéric Barbier' (Ra) ♥H4 CHad CRHN CSBt CSam CWSG
EBee EBls ECnt ELan ENot EPfP
GKir LRHS LStr MAus MBNS MBri
MMat MRav NBir NPri NRog NWea
SPer SSea SWCr WAct WHCG WKif
WWeb
'Albertine' (Ra) ♥H4 More than 30 suppliers
'Alchymist' (S/Cl) CHad CPou EBee EBls ENot EPfP
LRHS MAsh MAus MBNS MBri
MMat MRav SFam SPer SWCr WAct
WHCG WKif WLow
Alec's Red = 'Cored' (HT) CBcs CGro CSBt CTri CWSG EBls
ENot GCoc GGre GKir LRHS LStr
MAsh MAus MMat MRav NPri
NRog SPer SWCr WWeb
Alexander = 'Harlex' CGro CSBt EBls ENot GCoc GGre
(HT) ♥H4 LGod LStr MAus MMat MRav NRog
SPer SSea SWCr
'Alexander Hill Gray' (T) EBls
'Alexandre Girault' (Ra) CRHN EBls EMFP LRHS MAsh
MAus MBri SPer SWCr WAct
WHCG
§ 'Alfred Colomb' (HP) EBls
'Alfred de Dalmas' see *R.* 'Mousseline'
misapplied
'Alfresco'PBR (ClHT) CSBt LGod SSea SWCr
'Alida Lovett' (Ra) EBls MAus
Alison = 'Coclibee'PBR (F) GCoc SWCr
'Alison Wheatcroft' (F) EBls
§ 'Alister Stella Gray' (N) EBee EBls EWTr LRHS MAus MRav
SPer SSea SWCr WAct WHCG
'Allen Chandler' (ClHT) EBls MAus
'Allgold' (F) CBcs CGro EBls ENot GKir SWCr
WStI
Alnwick Castle MAus SWCr
= 'Ausgrab' (S)
'Aloha' (ClHT) ♥H4 CBcs CGro CSam EBee EBls ENot
EPfP ESty GKir LAst LRHS LStr
MAsh MAus MBri MBur MRav NBat
NRog SChu SPer SSea SWCr WAct
WHCG
alpina see *R. pendulina*
'Alpine Sunset' (HT) CTri EBls ECnt ENot ESty GGre
GKir MAsh MRav SPer SWCr
altaica hort. see *R. pimpinellifolia* 'Grandiflora'
Altissimo = 'Delmur' (Cl) CHad EBee EBls EMFP ENot MAus
SPer SSea SWCr WAct
'Amadis' (Bs) EBls MAus WHCG
Amanda MBri
= 'Beesian'PBR (F)
'Amazing Grace' (HT) GCoc GGre SWCr
Amber Abundance SWCr
= 'Harfizz'PBR (S)
Amber Cover ECnt ESty MAsh
= 'Poulbambe'PBR (GC)
Amber Hit ECnt SWCr
= 'Poultrav'PBR (Patio)
Amber Queen CGro CSBt CTri EBee EBls ECnt
= 'Harroony'PBR EPfP ESty GCoc GGre GKir IArd
(F) ♥H4 LGod LStr MAsh MAus MBri MBur
MRav NPri NRog SMad SPer SSea
SWCr
Amber Star NBat
= 'Manstar' (Min)
Amber Sunset NBat
= 'Manamsun' (Min)
Ambridge Rose LRHS MAus MBri SPer SWCr
= 'Auswonder' (S)

'Amélia'	see *R.* 'Celsiana'
Amelia = 'Poulen011' (S) **new**	ECnt
'American Pillar' (Ra)	CGro CRHN CSBt CSam CTri CWSG EBls ECnt ELan ENot EWTr GKir ISea LRHS LStr MAsh MAus MMat MRav NRog SPer SSea SWCr WAct WHCG WWeb
'Amy Robsart' (RH)	EBls EMFP MAus SWCr
Anabell = 'Korbell' (F)	NBat
'Anaïs Ségalas' (G)	MAus
§ 'Andersonii' (*canina* hybrid)	EBls ISea MAus SWCr
§ 'Anemone' (Cl)	EBls MAus
anemoniflora	see *R.* x *beanii*
anemonoides	see *R.* 'Anemone'
- 'Ramona'	see *R.* 'Ramona'
'Angel Gates'	WAct
Angela Rippon = 'Ocaru' (Min)	CSBt MBur SPer SSea
'Angela's Choice' (F)	SWCr
'Angèle Pernet' (HT)	EBls
'Angelina' (S)	EBls
Anisley Dickson = 'Dickimono'[PBR] (F) ♀[H4]	IDic LGod NBat SPer SWCr
Ann = 'Ausfete'[PBR]	LRHS MAus SWCr
'Anna de Diesbach' (HP)	EBls
Anna Ford = 'Harpiccolo'[PBR] (Min/Patio) ♀[H4]	CWSG LStr MAus SPer SWCr WWeb
Anna Livia = 'Kormetter'[PBR] (F) ♀[H4]	ECnt ENot MBri MMat MRav
'Anna Olivier' (T)	EBls
'Anna Pavlova' (HT)	EBls SSea
Anne Boleyn = 'Ausecret' (S)	MAus SWCr
'Anne Cocker' (F)	GCoc
'Anne Dakin' (ClHT)	MAus
Anne Harkness = 'Harkaramel'[PBR] (F)	MAus SPer SSea
Anne Marie Laing = 'Jospink' (F)	EBls
'Anne of Geierstein' (RH)	EBls MAus SWCr
'Anne Watkins' (HT)	EBls
Anneka = 'Harronver' (F/HT)	ENot
'Anthony' (S)	EBls
Antique '89 = 'Kordalen'[PBR] (ClF)	EBee EBls ENot MBri MMat MRav WGer
'Antoine Rivoire' (HT)	EBls
'Antonia d'Ormois' (G)	EBls
'Anytime' (Min)	MBur
Aperitif = 'Macwaira'[PBR] (HT)	GCoc
apothecary's rose	see *R. gallica* var. *officinalis*
'Apple Blossom' (Ra)	EBls SWCr WHCG
'Applejack' (S)	EBls
Apricot Ice = 'Dicyeti' (Poly/F)	ESty IDic
'Apricot Nectar' (F)	MAus MBur SPer
'Apricot Silk' (HT)	CBcs CTri EBls GKir MAus MRav NRog SPer SWCr
Apricot Spice = 'Sanspic' (HT)	MBur
Apricot Summer = 'Korpapiro'[PBR] (Patio)WGer	ENot MAsh MBri MMat SWCr
Apricot Sunblaze = 'Savamark'[PBR] (Min)	CSBt EBls
'April Hamer' (HT)	NBat
Arcadian = 'Macnewye' (F)	MBur
'Archiduc Joseph' misapplied	see *R.* 'Général Schablikine'
'Archiduchesse Elisabeth d'Autriche' (HP)	EBls
'Ardoisée de Lyon' (HP)	EBls
Ards Beauty = 'Dicjoy' (F)	SPer
'Ards Rover' (ClHP)	EBls
'Arethusa' (Ch)	EBls SPla SWCr
'Aristide Briand' (Ra) **new**	EBls
'Arizona Sunset' (Min)	NBat
§ *arkansana* var. *suffulta*	EBls WHCG
Armada = 'Haruseful'[PBR] (S)	SSea SWCr
'Arrillaga' (HP)	MAus
Artful Dodger = 'Sabbelief' (Patio)	MBur
'Arthur Bell' (F) ♀[H4]	CSBt CWSG EBls EBre ENot EPfP ESty GGre GKir IArd LAst LStr MAsh MAus MBur MMat MRav NPri NRog SPer SSea SWCr WWeb
'Arthur de Sansal' (DPo)	EBls MAus WHCG
Arthur Merril = 'Hormerry' (F)	NBat
arvensis	CCVT CRWN EBls LBuc MAus NWea WAct
§ 'Aschermittwoch' (Cl)	EBls
Ash Wednesday	see *R.* 'Aschermittwoch'
'Assemblage des Beautés' (G)	EBls MAus
'Astra Desmond' (Ra)	WTin
'Astrid Späth Striped' (F)	EBls
Atlantis Palace = 'Poulsiana'[PBR] (F) **new**	MAsh
Audrey Hepburn = 'Twodore' (HT)	MBur SWCr
Audrey Wilcox = 'Frywilrey' (HT)	CSBt
'August Seebauer' (F)	EBls
'Auguste Gervais' (Ra)	EBls LRHS MAus SPer SWCr WHCG
'Augustine Guinoisseau' (HT)	EBls
'Augustine Halem' (HT)	EBls
Austrian copper rose	see *R. foetida* 'Bicolor'
Austrian yellow	see *R. foetida*
'Autumn' (HT)	NRog
'Autumn Delight' (HM)	EBls MAus WHCG
Autumn Fire	see *R.* 'Herbstfeuer'
'Autumn Sunlight' (ClF)	MBur SPer SWCr
'Autumn Sunset' (S)	EBls
'Autumnalis'	see *R.* 'Princesse de Nassau'
'Aviateur Blériot' (Ra)	EBls MAus
'Avignon' (F)	ECnt
Avocet = 'Harpluto' (F)	GGre SWCr
Avon = 'Poulmulti'[PBR] (GC) ♀[H4]	EBee ECnt ELan ENot GCoc LGod MMat MRav SPer SSea SWCr WHCG
Awakening = 'Probuzini' (Cl)	CHad EBee EBls SWCr WHCG
'Ayrshire Splendens'	see *R.* 'Splendens'
'Baby Bio' (F/Patio)	CBcs ESty MBri NRog SWCr
'Baby Darling' (Min)	SSea
'Baby Faurax' (Poly)	MAus
Baby Gold Star (Min)	see *R.* 'Estrellita de Oro'
'Baby Katie' (Min)	NBat
Baby Love = 'Scrivluv' (yellow) [PBR] (Min/Patio) ♀[H4]	MAsh MAus SWCr
Baby Masquerade = 'Tanba' (Min)	ENot MBur MMat NRog SPer SWCr WStl WWeb
'Ballerina' (HM/Poly) ♀[H4]	More than 30 suppliers
Ballindalloch Castle = 'Cocneel'[PBR] (F)	GCoc
'Baltimore Belle' (Ra)	CRHN EBls MAus SWCr WHCG

banksiae (Ra) — CPou GQui LPan SRms
- SF 96051 — ISea
§ - *alba* — see *R. banksiae* var. *banksiae*
§ - var. *banksiae* (Ra/d) — CBot CPou CSBt CTri EBee ELan EPfP ERea LStr MAus SBra SSea WBcn WGer XPep
- 'Lutea' (Ra/d) ♀H3 — More than 30 suppliers
- 'Lutescens' (Ra) — CSBt XPep
- var. *normalis* (Ra) — CBot CSBt LPhx MAus NSti SLon SWCr WHer WOut XPep
'Bantry Bay' (ClHT) — CSBt EBls ELan LStr MMat MRav SPer SPla SSea SWCr
Barbara Austin = 'Austop'PBR (S) — LRHS MAus SWCr
'Barbara Carrera' (F) — EBls
Barkarole = 'Tanelorak'PBR (HT) — CSBt LStr SSea
'Baron de Bonstetten' (HP) — EBls
'Baron de Wassenaer' (CeMo) — EBls SWCr
'Baron Girod de l'Ain' (HP) — EBls MAus MRav SPla SSea SWCr WGer WHCG WLow
'Baroness Rothschild' (HP) — see *R.* 'Baronne Adolph de Rothschild'
§ 'Baronne Adolph de Rothschild' (HP) — EMFP MRav SWCr WHCG
Baronne Edmond de Rothschild = 'Meigriso' (HT) — MAus SSea SWCr WAct
Baronne Edmond de Rothschild, Climbing = 'Meigrisosar' (Cl/HT) **new** — CSBt
'Baronne Henriette de Snoy' (T) — EBls
'Baronne Prévost' (HP) — EBls MAus SFam WAct WHCG
Baroque = 'Harbaroque'PBR (GC/F/S) — SWCr
Barry Fearn = 'Korschwama'PBR (HT) — ENot MRav
§ x *beanii* (Ra) — EPla SMad
'Beau Narcisse' (G) — MAus
'Beauté' (HT) — EBls
Beautiful Britain = 'Dicfire'PBR (F) — CWSG EBls IDic LStr MRav NRog SWCr
Beautiful Sunrise = 'Bostimebide' (Cl/Patio) — ESty MBri SWCr
'Beauty of Rosemawr' (ClT) — EBls
Beauty StarPBR — see *Rosa* Liverpool Remembers
Behold = 'Savahold' (Min) — NBat
bella — LRHS
Bella = 'Pouljill'PBR (S) — MAsh SWCr
'Belle Amour' (AxD) — EBls MAus SWCr WHCG
'Belle Blonde' (HT) — SPer
'Belle de Crécy' (G) ♀H4 — CPou CSam EBls ENot EWTr GKir LStr MAsh MAus SFam SPer SSea SWCr WAct WHCG WLow
'Belle des Jardins' misapplied — see *R.* 'Centifolia Variegata'
Belle Epoque = 'Fryyaboo'PBR (HT) — ENot GCoc LStr MAus MBur SWCr
'Belle Isis' (G) — EBls MAus MRav SPer SWCr
'Belle Lyonnaise' (ClT) — EBls
'Belle Poitevine' (Ru) — EBls MAus
'Belle Portugaise' (ClT) — EBls MAus
§ 'Belvedere' (Ra) — EBls MAus MBri SPer SWCr WHCG
* 'Bengal Beauty' — WCot
Benita = 'Dicquarrel'PBR (HT) — IDic

Benjamin Britten = 'Ausencart' (S) — CSBt MAus MBri SWCr
§ 'Bennett's Seedling' (Ra) — EBls
Benson and Hedges Gold = 'Macgem'PBR (HT) — CWSG
Benson and Hedges Special = 'Macshana'PBR (Min) — ELan ENot ESty
Berkshire = 'Korpinka'PBR (GC) ♀H4 — ENot LStr MMat MRav SSea SWCr
Best of Friends = 'Pouldunk' (HT) — ECnt
Best Wishes = 'Chessnut'PBR (Cl/v) — COtt ENot GGre MBri SSea SWCr
Bettina = 'Mepal' (HT) — SWCr
Betty Boop = 'Wekplapic'PBR (F) — GCoc SWCr
Betty Driver = 'Gandri'PBR (F) — SPer SWCr
Betty Harkness = 'Harette'PBR (F) — GCoc LStr
'Betty Prior' (F) — GCoc SWCr
'Betty Uprichard' (HT) — EBls
Bewitched = 'Poulbella'PBR (F) — ECnt SWCr
Bianco = 'Cocblanco'PBR (Patio/Min) — GCoc GGre MAus SWCr
§ *biebersteinii* — EBls
'Big Chief' (HT) — NRog
Big Purple = 'Stebigpu'PBR (HT) — ECnt GGre SWCr
Birthday Girl = 'Meilasso'PBR (F)WWeb — GGre LAst MBur MRav SWCr
Birthday Wishes = 'Guesdelay' (HT) — ENot
Bishop Elphinstone = 'Cocjolly' (F) — GCoc
'Bit o' Sunshine' (Min) — SWCr
'Black Beauty' (HT) — MAus
'Black Ice' (F) — SWCr
'Black Jack' (Ce) — see *R.* 'Tour de Malakoff'
Black Jack = 'Minkco' (Min/Patio) — NBat
Black Jade = 'Benblack' (Min/Patio) — MBur
'Black Prince' (HP) — EBls
'Blairii Number One' (Bb) — EBls
'Blairii Number Two' (ClBb) ♀H4 — EBls LRHS MAus MRav SFam SPer SWCr WAct WHCG
'Blanche de Vibert' (DPo) — EBls MAus
'Blanche Double de Coubert' (Ru) ♀H4 — CSam EBee EBls ECnt ELan ENot EPfP GCoc LBuc LRHS LStr MAus MMat MWgw NRog SFam SPer SSea SWCr WAct WHCG WOVN
'Blanche Moreau' (CeMo) — EBls GGre MAus SPer WAct
'Blanchefleur' (CexG) — EBls MAus MRav SSea
blanda — EBls
Blenheim = 'Tanmurse'PBR (GC) — MRav
'Blessings' (HT) ♀H4 — CBcs CGro CSBt EBls EBre ENot ESty GGre LAst LStr MAsh MAus MBri MBur MMat MRav NRog SPer SSea SWCr
'Bleu Magenta' (Ra) ♀H4 — EBee EBls IArd MAus MRav SWCr WAct WHCG WKif
'Bliss' (S) — EBls
'Blonde Bombshell' (F) **new** — ESty
'Bloomfield Abundance' (Poly) — CPou EBls MAus MRav SPer SWCr WHCG WHer
'Bloomfield Dainty' (HM) — EBls
Blooming Marvellous — GGre SWCr
'Blossomtime' (Cl) — NRog SMad SPer

'Blue Diamond' (HT) — SWCr
Blue Moon — CGro CTri EBls ELan ENot EPfP
= 'Tannacht' (HT) — GCoc GGre GKir LAst LGod MAsh
MBur NBlu NPri NRog SPer SWCr
WLow WWeb
Blue Parfum — SWCr
= 'Tanfifum'[PBR]
Blue Peter — ESty SSea SWCr WWeb
= 'Ruiblun'[PBR] (Min)
'Blush Boursault' (Bs) — EBls
'Blush Damask' (D) — EBls SSea SWCr WHCG
'Blush Hip' (A) — MAus
'Blush Noisette' — see *R.* 'Noisette Carnée'
'Blush Rambler' (Ra) — CSBt EBee EBls EWTr MAus SPer
SPla SWCr WHCG
'Blushing Lucy' (Ra) — LRHS MTPN SMrm WAct
WHCG
Blythe Spirit — MAus MBNS SWCr
= 'Auschool'[PBR] (S)
'Bob Woolley' (HT) — NBat
'Bobbie James' (Ra) ♀H4 — CHad EBee EBls ENot LRHS LStr
MAus MBri MBur MRav NBat SFam
SPer SSea SWCr WAct WBVN
WHCG
'Bobby Charlton' (HT) — NRog
'Bobolink' (Min) — SWCr
'Bon Silène' (T) — EBls
Bonbon Hit — ECnt SWCr
= 'Poulbon'[PBR] (Patio)
'Bonfire Night' (F) — CGro ENot MBur MMat MRav
SWCr
Bonica — CBrm CSam CTri EBee EBls ECnt
= 'Meidomonac'[PBR] — ELan ENot EPfP ESty GCoc LGod
(GC) ♀H4 — LRHS LStr MAsh MAus MBur MMat
MRav MWgw SPer SSea SWCr
WAct WHCG WOVN
Bonita = 'Poulen009' — ECnt
(S) **new**
'Bonn' (HM/S) — CBcs NRog
'Bonnie Scotland' (HT) — MBur
Boogie-Woogie — ECnt
= 'Poulyc006' (Cl) **new**
'Botzaris' (D) — EBls SFam
'Boule de Nanteuil' (G) — EBls
'Boule de Neige' (Bb) — EBee EBls ECnt ELan ENot EPfP
EWTr GCoc LGod LRHS LStr MAsh
MAus MMat MRav SFam SPer SPla
SSea SWCr WAct WHCG WOVN
'Bouquet d'Or' (N) — EBls MAus SWCr
'Bouquet Tout Fait' (N) — WHCG
'Bouquet Tout Fait' — see *R.* 'Nastarana' (N)
misapplied
'Bourbon Queen' (Bb) — EBls EMFP MAus SSea SWCr
WHCG
'Bournville' (Cl) **new** — MAsh
Bow Bells = 'Ausbells' (S) — MAus
Bowled Over — ESty
= 'Tandolgnil'[PBR]
(F) **new**
Boy O Boy — IDic SWCr
= 'Dicuniform'[PBR] (GC)
Boys' Brigade — GCoc SWCr
= 'Cocdinkum'[PBR]
(Patio)
§ *bracteata* — CHll CRHN EHol GQui MAus WAct
WHCG
'Brandysnap' (F) — GKir
Brass Ring[PBR] — see *R.* Peek-a-boo
Brave Heart — GGre MAsh MAus MRav NBat
= 'Horbondsmile' (F) — SCoo SWCr
Breath of Life — CGro CSBt CTri CWSG EBls ELan
= 'Harquanne'[PBR] — ENot EPfP ESty GGre GKir LGod
(ClHT) — LRHS LStr MAsh MAus MBri MRav
SPer SSea SWCr WLow

Breathtaking — ESty MBur
= 'Hargalore' (HT) **new**
Bredon = 'Ausbred' (S) — MAus MBri
'Breeze Hill' (Ra) — EBls
§ 'Brenda Colvin' (Ra) — ISea MAus
'Brennus' (China hybrid) — EBls
Brian Rix — GGre SWCr
= 'Harflipper'[PBR] (S)
'Briarcliff' (HT) — EBls
Bride — GCoc LStr MRav SWCr
= 'Fryyearn'[PBR] (HT)
Bridge of Sighs — ECnt GGre LStr MAsh MBri SWCr
= 'Harglow' (Cl)
Bright Day — ESty
= 'Chewvermillion'
(Min) (Cl) **new**
Bright Fire — MBri SWCr
= 'Peaxi'[PBR] (Cl)
'Bright Ideas' (Cl) **new** — EBls
Bright Smile — IDic MAus MRav SPer SSea SWCr
= 'Dicdance'[PBR]
(F/Patio)
Bright Spot — see *R.* Simply Sunblaze
Britannia — ECnt ESty MAsh SWCr
= 'Frycalm'[PBR] (HT)
Broadlands — CTri LGod MRav SChu SWCr
= 'Tanmirsch'[PBR] (GC)
Brother Cadfael — LRHS MAus MBri SPer SWCr
= 'Ausglobe'[PBR] (S)
Brown Velvet — SWCr
= 'Maccultra'[PBR] (F)
'Brownie' (F) — MBur SWCr
§ *brunonii* (Ra) — CDoC EBls EWes MAus
- 'Betty Sherriff' (Ra) — CDoC SSpi
§ - 'La Mortola' (Ra) — EBee EHol MAus MRav SPer
SWCr
Bubbles — SWCr
= 'Frybubbly'[PBR] (GC)
Buck's Fizz — SWCr
= 'Poulgav'[PBR] (F)
'Buff Beauty' (HM) ♀H4 — More than 30 suppliers
'Bullata' — see *R.* x *centifolia* 'Bullata'
§ 'Burgundiaca' (G) — EBee EBls LRHS MAus SSea SWCr
WAct
Burgundian rose — see *R.* 'Burgundiaca'
'Burma Star' (F) — MBur SWCr
burnet, double pink — see *R. pimpinellifolia* double pink
burnet, double white — see *R. pimpinellifolia* double
white
Bush Baby — LGod LStr SPer SSea SWCr
= 'Peanob'[PBR] (Min)
Buttercup — LRHS MAus MBri SWCr WWeb
= 'Ausband'[PBR] (S)
Buxom Beauty — ECnt ENot ESty GCoc MBri MMat
= 'Korbilant'[PBR] (HT) — NBat
'C.F. Meyer' — see *R.* 'Conrad Ferdinand Meyer'
'Café' (F) — WBcn
'Caledonian' (HT) — NBat
californica (S) — GIBF MAus SSea
- 'Plena' — see *R. nutkana* 'Plena'
Calliope — GGre SWCr
= 'Harfracas'[PBR] (F)
'Callisto' (HM) — EMFP MAus WHCG
Calypso — EBee ECnt GGre MBri SSea SWCr
= 'Poulclimb'[PBR] (Cl)
'Camaïeux' (G) — CPou EBee EBls LRHS MAus SPer
SSea SWCr WAct WHCG
Cambridgeshire — ENot LGod LStr MAus MMat MRav
= 'Korhaugen'[PBR] (GC) — SPer SSea SWCr
'Camélia Rose' (Ch) — EBls WHCG
'Cameo' (Poly) — EBls MAus
Camille Pisarro — ESty
 ' = 'Destricol' (F)
'Canary Bird' — see *R. xanthina* 'Canary Bird'

Candle in the Wind   MAsh SWCr
= 'Mackincat' (S)
Candy Rose   GGre
= 'Meiranovi' (S)
canina (S)   CArn CCVT CDul CGro CLnd
    CRWN CTri ENot EPfP GIBF GKir
    LBuc MAus MMat MRav NWea
    SKee WMou
    XPep
- 'Abbotswood'   see R. 'Abbotswood'
- 'Andersonii'   see R. 'Andersonii'
'Cantabrigiensis' (S) ♀H4   CSam EBee EBls ENot MAus NRog
    SFam SPer SSea SWCr WAct WFar
    WHCG WOVN
Canterbury   MAus
= 'Ausbury' (S)
'Capitaine Basroger'   EBls MAus
(CeMo)
'Capitaine John Ingram'   EBls MAus SPer SSea WHCG
(CeMo) ♀H4
'Captain Christy' (ClHT)   see R. 'Climbing Captain Christy'
'Captain Hayward' (HP)   EBls
'Cardinal de Richelieu'   CPou EBls ENot EPfP GCoc LRHS
(G) ♀H4   LStr MAsh MAus MRav SFam SPer
    SSea SWCr WAct WHCG
Cardinal Hume   EBls SPer SWCr
= 'Harregale' (S)
'Care 2000' (S)   EBls
Carefree Days   MAsh SWCr
= 'Meirivouri' (Patio)
§ Carefree Wonder   SWCr
= 'Meipitac' (S) **new**
'Caring' (Patio)   GGre SWCr
Caring for You   GCoc GGre SWCr
= 'Coclust'ᴾᴮᴿ (HT)
'Carmen' (Ru)   EBls
§ 'Carmenetta' (S)   EBls MAus SWCr WAct
'Carol' (Gn)   see R. 'Carol Amling'
§ 'Carol Amling' (Gn)   SWCr
carolina   LHop SLPl WHCG
'Caroline Testout'   see R. 'Madame Caroline Testout'
Cascade = 'Poulskab'ᴾᴮᴿ   MAsh SWCr
Casino = 'Macca' (ClHT)   CTri EBls ESty GCoc GKir MAsh
    MBur MRav NBlu SPer SWCr
Castle Apricot (F) **new**   MAsh
Castle Fuchsia Pink   MAsh
(F) **new**
Castle of Mey   GCoc GGre SWCr
= 'Coclucid' (F)
Castle Peach (F) **new**   MAsh
Castle Red (F) **new**   MAsh
Castle Yellow (F) **new**   MAsh
Catherine Cookson   ENot
= 'Noscook' (HT)
'Catherine Mermet' (T)   EBls MAus
'Catherine Seyton' (RH)   EBls
§ 'Cécile Brünner'   CTri EBls ECnt ELan EMFP ENot
(Poly) ♀H4   GCoc LStr MAus MMat MRav NRog
    SMad SPer SPla SSea SWCr WAct
    WHCG WLow WOVN
'Cécile Brünner, White'   see R. 'White Cécile Brünner'
'Celebration' (F)   GGre
Celebration 2000   MAus
= 'Horcoffitup'ᴾᴮᴿ (S)
§ 'Céleste' (A) ♀H4   EBee EBls EMFP ENot EWTr GCoc
    LGod LStr MRav SFam SPer SSea
    SWCr WAct WHCG WLow WOVN
'Célina' (CeMo)   EBls
'Céline Forestier' (N) ♀H3   EBee EBls EMFP MAus MRav NBPC
    SFam SPer SWCr WHCG
§ 'Celsiana' (D)   EBls LRHS MAus SFam SPer SSea
    SWCr WAct WHCG
Centenaire de Lourdes   EBls ESty
= 'Delge' (F)

Centenary   ENot MMat MRav SPer
= 'Koreledas'ᴾᴮᴿ
(F) ♀H4
§ x *centifolia* (Ce)   EBls MAus MRav NBPC NRog SSea
    SWCr WAct WHCG
§ - 'Bullata' (Ce)   EBls MAus
§ - 'Cristata' (Ce) ♀H4   CSam EBls ECnt EMFP ENot
    EPfP EWTr LStr MRav NRog SFam
    SPer SSea SWCr WAct WHCG
    WLow
- 'Muscosa' (CeMo)   EBls ENot GCoc LRHS MAus MRav
    MWgw NRog SFam SSea SWCr
    WAct
- 'Muscosa Alba'   WAct
- 'Parvifolia'   see R. 'Burgundiaca'
§ 'Centifolia Variegata' (Ce)   EBls MAus WLow
Centre Stage   SWCr
= 'Chewcreepy' (S/GC)
Century Sunset   SWCr
= 'Tansaras'ᴾᴮᴿ (HT)
'Cerise Bouquet' (S) ♀H4   EBee EBls LRHS MAus MRav SPer
    SWCr WAct WHCG
Champagne Cocktail   GGre SPer SPoG SWCr
= 'Horflash'ᴾᴮᴿ (F) ♀H4
'Champneys' Pink Cluster'   EBls MAus SFam
(China hybrid)
Champs Elysées   SWCr
= 'Meicarl' (HT)
'Chanelle' (F)   EBls GCoc MAus NRog SPer SSea
    SWCr
Chapeau de Napoléon   see R. x *centifolia* 'Cristata'
'Chaplin's Pink   EBls SWCr
Climber' (Cl)
Charity = 'Auschar' (S)   LRHS MAsh MAus SWCr
Charles Austin   MAus MRav WHCG
= 'Ausles' (S)
Charles Aznavour   SWCr
= 'Meibeausai' (F)
'Charles de Mills' (G) ♀H4   CHad EBee EBls ECnt ELan EMFP
    ENot EPfP EWTr GGre LGod LRHS
    LStr MAsh MAus MMat MRav
    NBPC SFam SPer SSea SWCr WAct
    WHCG WLow
'Charles Gater' (HP)   EBls
'Charles Lefèbvre' (HP)   EBls
'Charles Mallerin' (HT)   EBls
Charles Notcutt   ENot MMat SWCr
= 'Korhassi' (S)
Charles Rennie   CSBt LRHS MAsh MAus MBNS
Mackintosh   SWCr
= 'Ausren'ᴾᴮᴿ (S)
Charlie's Rose   SWCr
= 'Tanellepa' (HT)
Charlotte = 'Auspoly'ᴾᴮᴿ   CAbP ESty LRHS MAsh MAus SPer
(S) ♀H4   SSea SWCr WAct
Charmian = 'Ausmian' (S)   MAus
Charming Cover   MAsh
= 'Poulharmu'ᴾᴮᴿ
(GC/S) **new**
'Château de   IArd
Clos-Vougeot' (HT)
Chatsworth   MRav SCoo SPer SSea SWCr
= 'Tanotax'ᴾᴮᴿ (Patio/F)
§ Chaucer = 'Auscer' (S)   MAus
Chelsea Belle   NBat
= 'Talchelsea' (Min)
§ Cherry Brandy '85   CSBt MBur MRav SWCr
= 'Tanryrandy'ᴾᴮᴿ (HT)
Cheshire = 'Fryelise' (HT)   GCoc
Cheshire = 'Korkonopi'   ENot MAus MMat NPri
(County Rose Series) ᴾᴮᴿ
(S)
'Cheshire Life' (HT)   MAus MBur MRav NPri SWCr WStI
Chianti = 'Auswine' (S)   EBls MAus SWCr WAct WHCG

Chicago Peace   EBls ESty GGre GKir NBlu NRog
   = 'Johnago' (HT)   SWCr WStI
Childhood Memories   SPla SWCr
   = 'Ferho' (HM/Cl)
Child's Play   NBat
   = 'Savachild' (Min)
Chilterns   ENot MMat MRav SWCr
   = 'Kortemma'PBR (GC)
'Chinatown' (F/S) ♀H4   CBcs CGro CSBt CTri EBls
   ENot EPfP GGre GKir LStr MAsh
   MAus MMat MRav NRog SPer SSea
   SWCr
chinensis misapplied   see *R.* x *odorata*
chinensis Jacq. **new**   EBls
I - 'Angel Rose' (Min) **new**   NJOw
   - 'Minima' sensu stricto   see *R.* 'Pompon de Paris' (MinCh)
   hort.
   - 'Mutabilis'   see *R.* x *odorata* 'Mutabilis'
   - 'Old Blush'   see *R.* x *odorata* 'Pallida'
Chivalry   SWCr
   = 'Macpow' (HT) **new**
Chloe = 'Poulen003' (S)   CHad CPou ECnt SWCr
'Chloris' (A)   CPou EBls SWCr
'Chorus Girl' (F)   SWCr
Chris = 'Kirsan'PBR (Cl)   EBee ECnt ENot ESty LStr SSea
   SWCr WGor
Christian Dior   EBls
   = 'Meilie' (HT)
'Christine Gandy' (F)   SWCr
Christopher   GCoc
   = 'Cocpher' (HT)
Christopher Columbus   ENot IArd MBri MRav
   = 'Meinronsse' (HT)
Christopher Marlowe   MAus
   = 'Ausjump' (S) **new**
§ 'Chromatella' (N)   EBls
'Chrysler Imperial' (HT)   EBls
Cider Cup   ENot EPfP ESty GGre GKir IDic
   = 'Dicladida'PBR   LGod LStr MAsh MAus NBat SWCr
   (Min/Patio) ♀H4
'Cinderella' (Min)   CSBt
cinnamomea   see *R. majalis*
'Circus' (F)   SWCr
City Lights   CSBt MMat MRav
   = 'Poulgan'PBR (Patio)
City of Belfast   EBls ENot MAus
   = 'Macci' (F)
'City of Leeds' (F)   CWSG ENot GGre GKir MAsh
   NRog WStI
City of London   CSBt EBls GGre LStr SPer SWCr
   = 'Harukfore'PBR (F)
'City of Oelde' (S) **new**   EBls
'City of Portsmouth' (F)   CBcs
City of York   EBls
   = 'Direktör Benschop'
   (Cl)
Clair Matin = 'Meimont'   CPou EBls MAus SPer SWCr WAct
   (ClS)
'Claire Jacquier' (N)   EBee EBls MAus SFam SPer SWCr
   WHCG
Claire Rose   CGro EBee ESty GGre GKir LRHS
   = 'Auslight'PBR (S)   MAus MRav SPer SWCr
Clara = 'Poulen004' (S)   ECnt SWCr
'Clarence House' (Cl)   EBls
Clarinda   GCoc GGre
   = 'Cocsummery' (F)
'Clementina   EBls
   Carbonieri' (T)
§ Cleopatra   ENot MMat MRav
   = 'Korverpea'PBR (HT)
'Cliff Richard' (F)   ESty MBur SWCr
'Climbing Alec's Red'   SPer SWCr
   (ClHT)
'Climbing Allgold' (ClF)   EBls SSea SWCr

'Climbing Arthur Bell'PBR   CSBt CTri GGre LGod MAsh NRog
   (ClF) ♀H4   SPer SPoG SSea SWCr WWeb
'Climbing Ballerina' (Ra)   CSBt SWCr
Climbing Bettina   EBls SWCr
   = 'Mepalsar' (ClHT)
'Climbing Blessings' (ClHT)   EBls
'Climbing Blue Moon'   CFee NPri SWCr
   (ClHT)
§ 'Climbing Captain   EBls MAus
   Christy' (ClHT)
'Climbing Cécile   CSBt EBee EBls ECnt EPfP LGod
   Brünner' (ClPoly) ♀H4   LRHS LStr MAus MBur MRav
   MWgw NBPC SFam SPer SSea
   SWCr WAct WHCG
'Climbing Château de   EBls MAus
   Clos-Vougeot' (ClHT)
'Climbing Christine'   MAus
   (ClHT)
§ 'Climbing Columbia'   ERea NRog SPer WHCG
   (ClHT)
'Climbing Comtesse   EBls
   Vandal' (ClHT)
'Climbing Crimson   EBls EMFP MAus NRog SWCr WStI
   Glory' (ClHT)
§ 'Climbing Devoniensis'   CPou EBls
   (ClT)
'Climbing Ena Harkness'   CBcs CSam EBls GCoc GGre MAus
   (ClHT)   MBur MRav NRog SPer SPla SWCr
   WWeb
'Climbing Etoile de   CSBt CTri CWSG EBls EBre EMFP
   Hollande' (ClHT) ♀H4   EPfP GCoc GGre GKir LRHS LStr
   MAus MRav MWgw NBPC NRog
   SMad SPer SSea SWCr WOVN
   WWeb
'Climbing Fashion' (ClF)   EBls
Climbing Fragrant   CBcs ELan
   Cloud = 'Colfragrasar'
   (ClHT)
§ 'Climbing Frau Karl   EBls
   Druschki' (ClHP)
'Climbing General   EBls
   MacArthur' (ClHT)
'Climbing Grand-mère   EBls
   Jenny' (ClHT)
'Climbing Iceberg'   CGro CSBt EBee EBls EBre ELan
   (ClF) ♀H4   ENot EPfP ESty GGre GKir IArd
   LStr MAsh MAus MBri MMat MRav
   NRog SPer SPla SSea SWCr WHCG
   WWeb
'Climbing Josephine   LRHS SWCr
   Bruce' (ClHT)
'Climbing la France'   MAus MRav
   (ClHT)
§ 'Climbing Lady   EBee EBls EBre EMFP EPfP LRHS
   Hillingdon' (ClT) ♀H3   MAus MRav MWgw SFam SPer
   SSea SWCr WAct WHCG
'Climbing Lady Sylvia'   CSBt EBls EPfP LRHS MAsh MAus
   (ClHT)   NRog SPer SWCr
'Climbing Little   see *R.* 'Félicité Perpétue'
   White Pet'
'Climbing Madame Abel   EBls MAus
   Chatenay' (ClHT)
'Climbing Madame   CPou EBls EPfP LRHS MAus SPer
   Butterfly' (ClHT)   SWCr
'Climbing Madame   CPou EBls MAsh MAus NRog SPer
   Caroline Testout'   SWCr WBcn
   (ClHT)
§ 'Climbing Madame   EBls MAus SWCr
   Edouard Herriot'
   (ClHT)
'Climbing Madame Henri   EBls MAus
   Guillot' (ClHT)
'Climbing Maman   EBls MAus
   Cochet' (ClT)

'Climbing Masquerade' (ClF)	EBls GGre GKir MAus MRav NRog SPer SSea SWCr WStI WWeb
§ 'Climbing Mevrouw G.A. van Rossem' (ClHT)	EBls MAus
'Climbing Mrs Aaron Ward' (ClHT)	EBls MAus
'Climbing Mrs G.A. van Rossem'	see R. 'Climbing Mevrouw G.A. van Rossem'
'Climbing Mrs Herbert Stevens' (ClHT)	CPou EBee EBls LRHS MAus MRav NRog SPer SWCr WHCG WLow
'Climbing Mrs Sam McGredy' (ClHT)	CGro CSBt EBls MAus MBri NRog SWCr
'Climbing Niphetos' (ClT)	EBls MAus
'Climbing Ophelia' (ClHT)	CPou EBee EBls MAus SPer
Climbing Orange Sunblaze = 'Meiji Katarsar'PBR (ClMin)	ENot MBri SPer SWCr
'Climbing Pascali' (ClHT)	CBcs
§ 'Climbing Paul Lédé' (ClT)	EBee EBls LRHS MAus SWCr
'Climbing Peace' (ClHT)	CSBt SWCr
'Climbing Piccadilly' **new**	SWCr
'Climbing Picture' (ClHT)	EBls MAus
'Climbing Pompon de Paris' (ClMinCh)	CBot CTri EBls EMFP LHop LRHS MAus MRav SPer SWCr WHCG
'Climbing Regensberg' (ClF)	GGre SWCr
'Climbing Richmond' (ClHT)	EBls
'Climbing Roundelay' (Cl)	EBls
'Climbing Ruby Wedding' **new**	SWCr
'Climbing Shot Silk' (ClHT) ♀H4	CSBt EBee EBls EMFP SPer SWCr
§ 'Climbing Souvenir de la Malmaison' (ClBb)	CPou EBee EBls MAus SPer WAct WHCG
Climbing Super Star = 'Tangostar' (ClHT)	MAus
'Climbing Talisman' (ClHT)	EBls
'Climbing The Queen Elizabeth' (ClF)	EBls SWCr
'Climbing Trumpeter' (ClF)	MAsh
Clodagh McGredy = 'Macswanle' (F)	ESty
'Cloth of Gold'	see R. 'Chromatella'
Cocktail = 'Meimick' (S)	EBls
Colchester Beauty = 'Cansend' (F)	ECnt
§ Colibri = 'Meimal' (Min)	SPer
§ 'Colonel Fabvier'	EBls MAus SWCr XPep
colonial white	see R. 'Sombreuil'
'Columbian' (ClHT)	see R. 'Climbing Columbia'
'Commandant Beaurepaire' (Bb)	EBls LRHS MAus
common moss	see R. x centifolia 'Muscosa'
Commonwealth Glory = 'Harclue'PBR (HT)	ESty GGre SWCr
'Compassion' (ClHT) ♀H4	More than 30 suppliers
§ 'Complicata' (G) ♀H4	CAbP EBls ENot EPfP LRHS LStr MAus MRav MWgw NRog SFam SPer SSea SSpi SWCr WAct WHCG WOVN
N 'Comte de Chambord' misapplied	see R. 'Madame Knorr'
Comtes de Champagne = 'Ausufo' (S)	MAus SWCr
'Comtesse Cécile de Chabrillant' (HP)	EBls MAus
'Comtesse de Lacépède' misapplied	see R. 'Du Maître d'Ecole'
§ 'Comtesse de Murinais' (DMo)	EBls MAus SFam
'Comtesse du Caÿla' (Ch)	MAus SSea
'Condesa de Sástago' (HT)	EBls
§ 'Conditorum' (G)	EBls SFam SSea WAct
Congratulations = 'Korlift'PBR (HT)	CSBt CTri EBee ECnt ENot GCoc IArd LGod LStr MAus MMat MRav NPri SPer SSea SWCr WWeb
Conquest i= 'Harbrill'PBR (F)	MRav SWCr
'Conrad Ferdinand Meyer' (Ru)	CSBt EBls MAus SPer
Conservation = 'Cocdimple'PBR (Min/Patio)	GCoc GGre LAst MBri SSea SWCr
Constance Finn = 'Hareden'PBR (F) **new**	SWCr
Constance Spry = 'Austance' (Cl/S) ♀H4	CGro EBee EBls EBre ECnt ELan ENot EPfP LRHS LStr MAus MMat MRav NPri SFam SPer SSea SWCr WAct WGer WHCG
§ 'Cooperi' (Ra)	EBls MAus SLon SPer SSea WAct WHCG
Cooper's Burmese	see R. 'Cooperi'
'Copenhagen' (ClHT)	EBls LRHS MAus MBri
'Copper Delight' (F) **new**	NRog
Copper Pot = 'Dicpe' (F)	SPer SWCr
'Coral Cluster' (Poly)	EBls MAus
'Coral Creeper' (ClHT)	EBls
'Coral Dawn' (ClHT)	EBls
Coral Reef = 'Cocdarlee'PBR (Min/Patio)	ESty GGre MBri SWCr
'Coralie' (D)	EBls
'Coralin' (Min)	SWCr
Cordelia = 'Ausbottle' (S)	MAus MRav SWCr
Cordon Bleu = 'Harubasil' (HT)	MBur
'Cornelia' (HM) ♀H4	CBcs CSBt CSam EBee EBls ECnt ENot EPfP EWTr GBin GCoc GGre GKir IArd LStr MAsh MAus MBri MMat MRav NRog SFam SPer SSea SWCr WAct WHCG WOVN WWeb
'Coronet' (F)	WHCG
Corvedale = 'Ausnetting' (S)	MAsh MAus SWCr
'Coryana'	EBls
corymbifera	EBls
corymbulosa	EBls
'Cosimo Ridolfi' (G)	EBls
cottage maid	see R. 'Centifolia Variegata'
Cottage Rose = 'Ausglisten'PBR (S)	MAus MRav SWCr
Country Lady = 'Hartsam' (HT)	MBur
Country Living = 'Auscountry'PBR (S)	EBls LRHS
'Coupe d'Hébé' (Bb)	EBls MAus MBri
§ Courage = 'Poulduf'PBR (HT)	EBee ECnt
Courvoisier = 'Macsee' (HT)	CSBt
'Cramoisi Picotée' (G)	EBls MAus
'Cramoisi Supérieur' (Ch)	EBls MAus WHCG
Crathes Castle = 'Cocathes' **new**	GCoc
Crazy for You = 'Wekroalt'PBR (F)	ESty LGod MBur SWCr
Cream Abundance = 'Harflax'PBR (F)	GGre MAsh SWCr
Crème de la Crème = 'Gancre'PBR (Cl)	CSBt ECnt GCoc MBri MBur SSea SWCr
'Crépuscule' (N)	EBls SSea WHCG
Cressida = 'Auscress' (S)	MAus
crested moss	see R. x centifolia 'Cristata'
Cricri = 'Meicri' (Min)	MAus SWCr

Crimson Cascade | CSam ESty GKir MAsh MAus MBri
= 'Fryclimbdown'PBR | MRav NBat SSea SWCr WHCG
(Cl) | WWeb
'Crimson Conquest' | EBls
(ClHT)
crimson damask | see *R. gallica* var. *officinalis*
'Crimson Descant' (Cl) | EBee ECnt SSea
Crimson Floorshow | SWCr
= 'Harglamour'PBR (GC)
'Crimson Glory' (HT) | EBls MBur SWCr
'Crimson Rambler' (Ra) | WBcn
'Crimson Shower' | EBls EBre EMFP LRHS MAsh MAus
(Ra) ♀H4 | MBur MRav NRog SPer SWCr
| WGer WHCG WHer WStI
'Cristata' | see *R. x centifolia* 'Cristata'
Crocus Rose | ECnt MAus SWCr
= 'Ausquest'PBR (S)
Crown Princess | ECnt MAsh MAus MBri SCoo SPer
  Margareta | SWCr
= 'Auswinter' (S)
Crowning Glory | IDic MAsh SWCr
= 'Dicyardstick'PBR (S)
Crystal Palace | EBee ENot MMat SWCr
= 'Poulrek'PBR (F/Patio)
cuisse de nymphe | see *R.* 'Great Maiden's Blush'
'Cupid' (ClHT) | EBls MAus SPer
Curiosity = 'Cocty' (HT/v) | GGre SWCr
§ Cymbeline = 'Auslean' (S) | SPer
'Cynthia Brooke' (HT) | EBls
D.H. Lawrence | MBur
= 'Roslaw' (HT) **new**
'D'Aguesseau' (G) | EBls MAus
'Daily Mail' | see *R.* 'Climbing Madame Edouard
| Herriot'
Daily Sketch = 'Macai' (F) | SWCr
'Dainty Bess' (HT) | EBls MAus SSea
'Dainty Maid' (F) | EBls MAus
'Daisy Hill' | EBls
  ('Macrantha' hybrid)
x *damascena* var. *bifera* | see *R. x damascena* var.
| *semperflorens*
§ – var. *semperflorens* (D) | CBgR EBls EMFP EWTr MAus
| MRav SSea SWCr WAct WHCG
| WLow
N – 'Trigintipetala' | see *R.* 'Professeur Emile Perrot'
  misapplied
§ – var. *versicolor* (D) | EBls ENot SFam SPer SSea SWCr
| WAct WHCG
§ 'Dame de Coeur' (HT) | ENot SWCr
'Dame Edith Helen' (HT) | EBls
Dame Wendy | MAus SWCr
= 'Canson' (F)
'Danaë' (HM) | CHad EBls EMFP MAus SWCr
| WHCG
Dancing Pink | NBat
= 'Hendan' (F)
Danny Boy | IDic WGor
= 'Dicxcon'PBR (Patio)
§ Danse des Sylphes | EBls SWCr
= 'Malcair' (Cl)
'Danse du Feu' (Cl) | CBcs CGro CSBt CTri CWSG EBee
| EBls ELan ENot GCoc GGre GKir
| LGod LRHS LStr MAsh MAus MRav
| NPri NRog SPer SSea SWCr WBVN
| WWeb
'Daphne Gandy' (F) | SWCr
Dapple Dawn | MAus SPer SWCr
= 'Ausapple' (S)
Darling Flame | MRav SWCr
= 'Meilucca' (Min)
'Dart's Defender' | SLPl
David Whitfield | SWCr
= 'Gana'PBR (F)
davidii | EBls MAus SWCr

Dawn Chorus | CGro CSBt CWSG EBee ECnt ENot
= 'Dicquasar'PBR | EPfP ESty GCoc GGre IDic LGod
(HT) ♀H4 | LStr MAsh MAus MBri MMat MRav
| SPer SSea SWCr WWeb
'Day Dream' (HT) | SWCr
'Daybreak' (HM) | EBls MAus NRog SWCr WAct
| WHCG WLow
'Daydream' (F) | GGre
§ 'De Meaux' (Ce) | EBls ENot MAus MRav SPer SPla
| SSea SWCr WAct WHCG
'De Meaux, White' | see *R.* 'White de Meaux'
§ 'De Rescht' (DPo) ♀H4 | CPou EBee EBls ENot EPfP ESty
| LRHS MAsh MAus MBri MMat
| MRav MWgw SPer SPla SWCr
| WAct WGer WHCG
'Dearest' (F) | CBcs CSBt GGre MRav NRog SPer
| SWCr WStI
§ Deborah Devonshire | GGre SWCr
= 'Boscherrydrift'PBR
(F)
Deb's Delight | ELan
= 'Legsweet'PBR (F)
'Debutante' (Ra) | CSam EBee EBls LRHS MAus SFam
| WHCG
'Deep Red Patio' (Patio) | SWCr
'Deep Secret' (HT) ♀H4 | CGro CTri CWSG EBee ECnt EPfP
| ESty GCoc GGre GKir LAst MAsh
| MBur MRav NRog SPer SSea SWCr
| WWeb
'Delambre' (DPo) | EBls MAus MRav
'Delicata' (Ru) | MAus
Della Balfour | GGre
= 'Harblend'PBR (Cl)
'Dembrowski' (HP) | EBls
'Dentelle de Malines' (S) | EBls LRHS MAus MBri WAct
'Deschamps' (N) | EBls
'Desprez à Fleurs | CPou EBee EBls EWTr IArd LRHS
  Jaunes' (N) | MAus MRav SFam SPer SWCr WHCG
'Deuil de Paul | EBls
  Fontaine' (Mo)
Devon Maid' (Cl) | SWCr
'Devoniensis' (CIT) | see *R.* 'Climbing Devoniensis'
Devotion = 'Interfluco' | IDic
  (HT) **new**
Diadem | SWCr
= 'Tanmeda'PBR (F)
Diamond Border | ECnt
= 'Pouldiram'PBR (S)
'Diamond Jubilee' (HT) | EBls MBur SWCr
'Diana Armstrong' (HT) | NBat
Dick's Delight | ESty IDic SWCr
= 'Dicwhistle'PBR (GC)
'Dickson's Flame' (F) | SWCr
Die Welt = 'Diekor' (HT) | MBri NBat
'Diorama' (HT) | ENot MAus SWCr
'Directeur Alphand' (HP) | EBls WHCG
Disco Dancer | IDic
= 'Dicinfra'PBR (F)
Dixieland Linda | EBls
= 'Beadix' (ClHT)
Dizzy Heights | ESty GCoc MBri SWCr
= 'Fryblissful' (Cl)
'Docteur Andry' (HP) | EBls
'Docteur Grill' (T) | EBls MAus
Doctor Dick | MBri NBat NRog
= 'Cocbaden' (HT)
'Doctor Edward | EBls
  Deacon' (HT)
§ Doctor Goldberg | SWCr
= 'Gandol' (HT)
Doctor Jackson | MAus
= 'Ausdoctor' (S)
§ Doctor Jo | SWCr
= 'Fryatlanta' (F)

Doctor McAlpine   MBri
= 'Peafirst' (F/Patio)
'Doctor W. Van Fleet'   EBls MAus
(Ra/Cl)
'Doktor Eckener'   EBls
'Don Charlton' (HT)   NBat
'Don Juan' (Cl)   SWCr
§ 'Doncasteri'   EBls
'Doreen' (HT)   NRog
'Doris Tysterman' (HT)   CGro CTri EBls GGre GKir LStr
MAus MBri NRog SPer SWCr
'Dorothy Perkins' (Ra)   CGro CRHN CSBt CTri EBls GCoc
GGre LRHS MAus MRav NPer
NRog SPer SSea SWCr WHCG
'Dorothy Wheatcroft' (F)   SWCr
'Dorothy Wilson' (F)   EBls
'Dortmund'   EBls LGod LRHS MAus SPer SWCr
(ClHScB) ♀H4   WAct WHCG
Double Delight   CGro ESty GCoc GGre MBri MBur
= 'Andeli' (HT)   MRav NRog SPer SWCr
'Dream Girl' (Cl)   MAus MBri SFam
Dream Lover   MAsh MRav SWCr
= 'Peayetti'PBR (Patio)
'Dreaming Spires' (Cl)   CSBt ENot ESty MBri MMat MRav
SPer SSea SWCr
'Dresden Doll' (MinMo)   EBls MAus
Drummer Boy   SWCr
= 'Harvacity'PBR
(F/Patio)
Du Maître d'Ecole' (G)   EBls MAus MRav WHCG
Dublin Bay = 'Macdub'   CSBt CSam CTri EBee EBls EBre
(Cl) ♀H4   ECnt ELan ENot EPfP ESty GKir
IArd LGod LStr MAsh MBri MBur
MMat MRav NRog SPer SSea SWCr
WGer
'Duc de Fitzjames' (G)   EBls
'Duc de Guiche' (G) ♀H4   EBls MAus SFam SPer SSea SWCr
WAct WHCG
'Duchess of Portland'   see *R.* 'Portlandica'
'Duchesse d'Albe' (T)   EBls
'Duchesse   EBls MAus SFam SSea
d'Angoulême' (G)
'Duchesse   EBls
d'Auerstädt' (N)
'Duchesse de   EBls MAus MRav NBPC SWCr
Buccleugh' (G)   WLow
§ 'Duchesse de   EBee EBls LRHS MAus SFam SPer
Montebello' (G) ♀H4   WAct WHCG
'Duchesse de Rohan'   EBls
(CexHP)
'Duchesse de   EBls MAus SFam
Verneuil' (CeMo)
§ Duke Meillandina   SWCr
= 'Meipinjid'PBR (Min)
'Duke of Edinburgh' (HP)   EBls MAus
'Duke of Wellington' (HP)   EBee EBls
WHCG
'Duke of Windsor' (HT)   SPer SWCr
'Duke of York' (Ch)   EBls
'Dundee Rambler' (Ra)   EBls MAus
'Dupontii' (S)   EBee EBls EWTr LRHS MAus MRav
SFam SPer WAct WLow WOVN
XPep
'Dupuy Jamain' (HP)   EBls WHCG
'Dusky Maiden' (F)   CHad EBls MAus MBri WHCG
'Dutch Gold' (HT)   CGro CWSG MAus MBur MRav
NRog SPer SSea SWCr
'E.H. Morse'   see *R.* 'Ernest H.
Morse'
'Easlea's Golden   CSBt EBee EBls LRHS MAus MRav
Rambler' (Ra) ♀H4   SWCr WAct WHCG
'Easter Morning' (Min)   SWCr
Easy Cover   ECnt MAsh
= 'Pouleas'PBR (GC)

Easy Going   GCoc GGre IArd MAsh SCoo SWCr
= 'Harflow'PBR (F)
'Eblouissant' (Poly)   MRav
ecae   EBls LRHS MAus
- 'Helen Knight'   see *R.* 'Helen Knight'
'Eclair' (HP)   EBls WHCG
'Eddie's Jewel'   EBls MAus
(*moyesii* hybrid)
'Eden Rose' (HT)   EBls
Eden Rose '88   MBri SPer SWCr
= 'Meiviolin'PBR (ClHT)
'Edith Bellenden' (RH)   EBls
'Edward Hyams'   MAus
eglanteria   see *R. rubiginosa*
Eglantyne = 'Ausmak'PBR   CAbP CSBt EBre GCoc LRHS LStr
(S) ♀H4   MAsh MAus MBri MRav MWgw
SPer SWCr
Eleanor Annelise   GCoc
= 'Cocslightly' (HT)
Eleanor   ECnt
= 'Poulberin'PBR (S)
'Elegance' (ClHT)   EBls MAus
§ *elegantula* 'Persetosa' (S)   EBls ENot MAus SPer SWCr WAct
WHCG
§ Elina = 'Dicjana'PBR   CSBt EBee ECnt ENot ESty GGre
(HT) ♀H4   IDic LGod LStr MAus MBur MMat
MRav NBat NRog SPer SWCr
'Eliza Boëlle' (HP)   WHCG
'Elizabeth Harkness' (HT)   CWSG EBls MAus MBur SPer SWCr
Elizabeth of Glamis   CGro CTri CWSG EBls GCoc MBri
= 'Macel' (F)   NRog SPer SWCr
Elle = 'Meibderos'PBR   SWCr
(HT)
'Ellen Willmott' (HT)   MAus
'Ellen Willmott' (HT)   EBee EBls EMFP MAus SWCr
'Elmshorn' (S)   CBcs SWCr WHCG
'Else Poulsen' (Poly)   WHCG
Emanuel = 'Ausuel' (S)   MAus
'Emily Gray' (Ra)   CGro CSBt EBee EBls ECnt ENot
ESty EWTr GKir LRHS LStr MAsh
MAus MBur MMat MRav NPri
NRog SPer SSea SWCr WAct
WHCG
'Emma Wright' (HT)   MAus
'Emmerdale' (F)   WStI
'Empereur du Maroc' (HP)   EBls EMFP MAus MRav NBPC
SWCr WHCG WLow
'Empress Josephine'   see *R.* x *francofurtana* 'Empress
Josephine'
Empress Michiko   GCoc IDic
= 'Dicnifty'PBR (HT)
'Ena Harkness' (HT)   CGro CTri EBls GGre MBur NRog
SWCr WStI
§ 'Enfant de France' (HP)   EBls
x *engelmannii*   EBls
§ England's Rose   MAus SCoo SWCr
= 'Ausrace'PBR (S)
English Elegance   MAus
= 'Ausleaf' (S)
English Garden   CGro EBee EMFP ENot EPfP GGre
= 'Ausbuff'PBR (S)   LRHS LStr MAus MMat MRav SPer
SSea SWCr
'English Miss' (F) ♀H4   CSBt CTri EBls ECnt ESty GKir
LAst LStr MAsh MAus MBur MRav
SPer SPoG SSea SWCr WStI
'Eos' (*moyesii* hybrid)   EBls SSea
'Erfurt' (HM)   EBls EMFP MAus SPer SWCr
WHCG
§ 'Erinnerung an Brod' (S)   WHCG
§ 'Ernest H. Morse' (HT)   CSBt CTri CWSG EBls GCoc GKir
LAst MRav NRog SPer SSea SWCr
'Ernest May' (HT)   SSea
Escapade = 'Harpade'   EBls MAus SWCr
(F) ♀H4

Especially for You = 'Fryworthy'^{PBR} (HT) — CSBt CTri EBee ESty GCoc GGre LGod LStr MAsh SCoo SSea SWCr WWeb

Essex = 'Poulnoz'^{PBR} (GC) — ENot MMat MRav SPer SWCr WHCG

§ 'Estrellita de Oro' (Min) — SPer SWCr

'Etain' (Ra) — ECnt

§ 'Etendard' — MRav SPla SWCr WAct

Eternal Flame = 'Korassenet'^{PBR} (F) — ECnt MMat SWCr

'Ethel' (Ra) — EBee EMFP

'Etoile de Hollande' (HT) — CHad EBee ELan ENot GKir MAsh MMat NPri SFam SSea

'Etoile de Lyon' (T) — EBls

'Etude' (Cl) — WBVN

'Eugène Fürst' (HP) — EBls

'Eugénie Guinoisseau' (Mo) — EBls WHCG

Euphoria = 'Intereup'^{PBR} (GC/S) — GCoc IDic

Euphrates = 'Harunique' (*persica* hybrid) — MAus SWCr WAct

'Europeana' (F) — SWCr

'Eva' (HM) — EBls

'Evangeline' (Ra) — EBls MAus

Evelyn = 'Aussaucer'^{PBR} (S) ♡^{H4} — CGro CSBt EBee EMFP ENot EPfP ESty GCoc GGre LGod LRHS LStr MAus MMat MRav MWgw NPri SChu SPer SPla SSea SWCr

§ Evelyn Fison = 'Macev' (F) — CSBt ELan ENot EPfP GGre GKir MAus MMat MRav NRog SPer SWCr

Evening Light = 'Tarde Gris' (Min) (Cl) **new** — ESty

'Everest Double Fragrance' (F) — EBls

'Excelsa' (Ra) — CSBt CTri EBls EPfP GGre GKir IArd LGod MAsh MRav NRog NWea SSea SWCr WAct WStI

'Expectations' **new** — CSBt

§ Exploit = 'Meilider'^{PBR} (Cl) — GGre

§ Eye Paint = 'Maceye' (F) — MAus SMrm

'Eyecatcher' (F) — ECnt

Eyeopener = 'Interop'^{PBR} (S/GC) — EBls IDic SWCr

'F.E. Lester' — see *R*. 'Francis E. Lester'

§ 'F.J. Grootendorst' (Ru) — EBls LRHS MAus NRog SSea SWCr WAct

Fab = 'Bosconpea'^{PBR} (F) — GGre

'Fabvier' — see *R*. 'Colonel Fabvier'

Fairhope = 'Talfairhope' (Min) — NBat

§ Fairy Damsel = 'Harneatly' (Poly/GC) — EBls SWCr

§ Fairy Prince = 'Harnougette' (GC) — MAsh

Fairy Queen = 'Sperien' (Poly/GC) — IDic MAsh SSea SWCr

'Fairy Rose' — see *R*. 'The Fairy'

'Fairy Shell' (Patio) — MAsh

§ Fairy Snow = 'Holfairy' (S) — SWCr

§ Fairygold = 'Frygoldie'^{PBR} (Patio) — MBri

Fairyland = 'Harlayalong' (Poly) — EBls MAsh MBur SWCr

Falstaff = 'Ausverse' (S) — CSBt ECnt ESty MAus MBNS MBri SWCr

'Fantin-Latour' (*centifolia* hybrid) ♡^{H4} — CSam CTri EBee EBls ECnt ELan ENot EPfP EWTr GCoc LGod LRHS LStr MAsh MAus MBri MMat MRav MWgw NRog SFam SPer SSea SWCr WAct WHCG

fargesii hort. — see *R. moyesii* var. *fargesii*

farreri var. **persetosa** — see *R. elegantula* 'Persetosa'

Fascination = 'Jacoyel' (HT) — GKir LStr MBri SCoo

§ Fascination = 'Poulmax'^{PBR} (F) ♡^{H4} — CSBt ECnt ENot EPfP ESty GCoc LGod MAsh MAus MMat MRav SPer SPoG SSea SWCr

'Fashion Flame' (Min) — SWCr

Favourite Hit = 'Poululv' (Patio) **new** — ECnt

fedtschenkoana hort. — EBls LRHS MAus SPer WAct WHCG

fedtschenkoana Regel — SLPl

'Felicia' (HM) ♡^{H4} — CHad CSBt CSam EBee EBls ECnt ELan ENot EPfP EWTr GCoc GGre LGod LStr MAsh MAus MBri MMat MRav NRog SFam SPer SSea SWCr WAct WHCG WOVN WWeb

'Félicité Parmentier' (AxD) ♡^{H4} — CSam EBls EMFP LRHS MAsh MAus MRav SFam SPer SWCr WAct WHCG

§ 'Félicité Perpétue' (Ra) ♡^{H4} — CBcs EBee EBls ELan ENot EPfP GCoc GKir ISea LRHS LStr MAsh MAus MBri MMat MRav MWgw NBPC SFam SPer SSea SWCr WAct WHCG XPep

Felicity Kendal = 'Lanken' (HT) — SWCr

'Fellemberg' (ClCh) — EBls MAus SWCr WHCG XPep

Fellowship = 'Harwelcome'^{PBR} (F) ♡^{H4} — ECnt ENot ESty GCoc GGre LGod LStr MAsh MAus MBur MMat MRav SCoo SSea SWCr

'Ferdinand Pichard' (Bb) ♡^{H4} — CPou EBee EBls ECnt EMFP ENot EPfP LRHS MAsh MAus MBri MMat MRav MWgw NBPC SPer SSea SWCr WAct WFoF WGer WHCG WKif WOVN

§ Ferdy = 'Keitoli'^{PBR} (GC) — EBls ENot MRav SPer

Fergie = 'Ganfer'^{PBR} (F/Patio) — SWCr

Festival = 'Kordialo'^{PBR} (Patio) — ENot ESty LGod LStr MAus MMat MRav SPer SSea SWCr

Fiery Hit = 'Poulfiry'^{PBR} (Min) — ECnt MAsh SWCr

Fiery Sunblaze = 'Meineyta'^{PBR} (Min) — SWCr

Fiesta = 'Macfirinlin'^{PBR} (Patio) — MBri

Fifi = 'Hanfif' (F) — NBat

filipes — GIBF

- 'Brenda Colvin' — see *R*. 'Brenda Colvin'

§ - 'Kiftsgate' (Ra) ♡^{H4} — More than 30 suppliers

§ 'Fimbriata' (Ru) — CPou EBee EBls EWTr MAus MBri SPer SWCr WAct WHCG

Financial Times Centenary = 'Ausfin' (S) — MAus

Fiona = 'Meibeluxen'^{PBR} (S/GC) — EBls GGre SWCr

'Fire Princess' (Min) — SWCr

'Firecracker' (F) — EBls

Firefly = 'Macfrabro' (Min) — SWCr

Firestorm = 'Peazoe'^{PBR} (Patio) — SWCr

'First Love' (HT) — EBls

'Fisher and Holmes' (HP) — EBls MAus WAct WHCG

Fisherman's Friend = 'Auschild'^{PBR} (S) — MAus SPer

Flamenco = 'Poultika'^{PBR} (Cl) — ECnt MBri

Flash Dance = 'Poulyc004' (Cl) **new** — ECnt

'Fleur Cowles' (F) — MBur SWCr

'Flora' (Ra) — CRHN EBls MAus SFam

'Flora McIvor' (RH) — EBls MAus

'Florence Mary Morse' (S)   SDix

Florence Nightingale   MBur SPer
= 'Ganflor'^{PBR} (F)

Flower Carpet^{PBR}   see *R.* Pink Flower Carpet

Flower Carpet Coral   SCoo SPoG SWCr
= 'Noala'

Flower Carpet Red   ELan ENot GGre MAsh MMat
Velvet = 'Noare'^{PBR}   MRav SCoo WWeb

§ Flower Carpet Sunshine   ELan ENot EPfP GCoc GGre LStr
= 'Noason'^{PBR} (GC)   MAsh MMat MRav SCoo SWCr
    WWeb

§ Flower Carpet Twilight   CGro GGre LRHS
= 'Noatwi'^{PBR} (GC)

Flower Carpet Velvet   CGro EPfP GGre SWCr
(GC/S)

Flower Carpet White   CGro CTri ELan ENot EPfP GCoc
= 'Noaschnee'^{PBR}   GGre LRHS LStr MAsh MMat
(GC) ♥^{H4}   MRav SCoo SPer SPoG SSea SWCr
    WWeb

Flower Power   CSBt ECnt ESty GCoc GGre GKir
= 'Frycassia'^{PBR} (Patio)   LStr MAsh MAus MRav SSea SWCr
    WWeb

§ *foetida* (S)   EBls MAus

§ - 'Bicolor' (S)   EBls ENot LRHS MAus NRog SPer
    WAct

§ - 'Persiana' (S)   EBls MAus

foliolosa   EBls SLPl WHCG

Fond Memories   GCoc LStr SWCr WWeb
= 'Kirfelix'^{PBR} (Patio)

'Fondant Cascade'   ESty
(Patio/GC)

Forever Royal   MAsh SCoo SWCr
= 'Franmite' (F) **new**

Forever Young   IDic
= 'Jacimgol'^{PBR} (F)

forrestiana   EBls MAus WHCG

× *fortuneana* (Ra)   EBls WFar

Fortune's double yellow   see *R.* × *odorata* 'Pseudindica'

'Fountain' (HT/S)   EBls MAus SPer SWCr

Fragrant Cloud   CGro CTri CWSG EBls EBre ECnt
= 'Tanellis' (HT)   ENot EPfP ESty GCoc GGre GKir
    LStr MAsh MAus MBri MBur MMat
    MRav NBat NRog SPer SSea SWCr
    WWeb

'Fragrant Delight' (F) ♥^{H4}   CSBt ECnt GCoc GKir LAst LStr
    MRav SPer SWCr WWeb

Fragrant Dream   CGro ESty IDic LStr MBri SWCr
= 'Dicodour'^{PBR} (HT)

'Fragrant Hour' (HT)   MBur SWCr

Fragrant Memories   ENot ESty GCoc MAsh MMat SCoo
= 'Korpastato'^{PBR}   SWCr WOVN
(HT/S)

Frances Perry   GGre SWCr
= 'Bosrexcity'^{PBR} (F)

'Francesca' (HM)   CPou EBls LRHS MAus SFam SPer
    SWCr WAct WHCG

Francine Austin   LRHS MAus SPer SWCr WAct
= 'Ausram'^{PBR} (S/GC)

'Francis Dubreuil' (T)   EBls

§ 'Francis E. Lester'   CHad CRHN CSam EBee EBls
(HM/Ra) ♥^{H4}   EWTr LRHS MAus MBri SFam SPer
    SSea SWCr WAct WHCG

§ × *francofurtana*   CSam EBls MAsh MAus MRav SFam
'Empress Josephine'   SSea SWCr WAct WHCG
♥^{H4}

- 'Agatha'   EBls

'François Juranville'   CHad CPou CRHN CSBt EBee EBls
(Ra) ♥^{H4}   ENot EWTr GGre LRHS MAus
    MBri MRav NBPC NRog SPer
    SWCr WAct

'Frau Astrid Späth' (F)   NRog

§ 'Frau Karl Druschki' (HP)   EBls MAus WAct

'Fräulein Octavia   EBls
Hesse' (Ra)

'Fred Loads' (F/S) ♥^{H4}   EBls MAus MRav NBlu SWCr
    WLow

Freddie Mercury   MBur NBat
= 'Batmercury' (HT)

Free as Air   MBri
= 'Mehbronze'^{PBR}
(Patio)

Freedom = 'Dicjem'^{PBR}   ECnt ENot GCoc GGre IDic LGod
(HT) ♥^{H4}   LStr MAus MBur MMat MRav NBat
    NRog SPer SSea SWCr WWeb

'Freiherr von Marschall' (T)   EBls

'Frensham' (F)   CBcs EBls ENot LStr SSea SWCr

Friend for Life   GCoc GGre MAsh MRav SWCr
= 'Cocnanne'^{PBR} (F) ♥^{H4}

'Fritz Nobis' (S) ♥^{H4}   CAbP CHad EBls EMil ENot LRHS
    LStr MAus MMat MRav SPer SWCr
    WAct WHCG

Frothy = 'Macfrothy'^{PBR}   ECnt
(Patio)

'Fru Dagmar Hastrup'   CSBt CSam EBee EBls ECnt ELan
(Ru) ♥^{H4}   ENot EPfP GCoc GKir LBuc LStr
    MAus NRog SPer SWCr WAct
    WHCG WOVN

'Frühlingsanfang' (PiH)   EBls MAus SWCr WAct

'Frühlingsduft' (PiH)   EBls NRog SWCr

'Frühlingsgold' (PiH) ♥^{H4}   CBcs CGro EBls ELan ENot EPfP
    EWTr GCoc GKir LRHS LStr MAus
    MBri MMat MRav NRog NWea SPer
    SSea SWCr WAct WHCG WOVN

'Frühlingsmorgen' (PiH)   EBls ENot GCoc GKir LStr MAus
    MBri MMat MRav NPri NRog SMad
    SPer SSea SWCr WAct WHCG
    WOVN

'Frühlingsschnee' (PiH)   EBls

'Frühlingszauber'   EBls
(PiH) **new**

fuchianus   GIBF

'Fulgens'   see *R.* 'Malton'

Fulton Mackay   GCoc GGre SWCr
= 'Cocdana'^{PBR} (HT)

Fyvie Castle   GCoc SWCr
= 'Cocbamber' (HT)

'Gail Borden' (HT)   SWCr

§ *gallica* (G)   EBls ENot SSea

- 'Complicata'   see *R.* 'Complicata'

- 'Conditorum'   see *R.* 'Conditorum'

§ - var. *officinalis*   CAbP CHby CSam EBls EMFP ENot
(G) ♥^{H4}   GCoc GKir GPoy LRHS MAsh
    MAus MRav NRog SFam SPer SPoG
    SSea SWCr WAct WHCG
    WAct

- *rubus*   WAct

- 'Velutiniflora' (G)   EBls SSea

§ - 'Versicolor' (G) ♥^{H4}   More than 30 suppliers

Galway Bay   EBre GGre GKir LRHS MAsh MRav
= 'Macba' (ClHT)   SPer SWCr

§ Garden News   ECnt ESty
= 'Poulrim'^{PBR} (HT)

Garden Party   ENot MRav
= 'Kormollis'^{PBR} (F)

'Gardenia' (Ra)   EBee EWTr MAus SPer SWCr
    WHCG

'Gardiner's Pink' (Ra)   WHCG

'Garnette Carol'   see *R.* 'Carol Amling'

'Garnette Pink'   see *R.* 'Carol Amling'

'Gary Player' (HT)   NBat

'Général Galliéni' (T)   EBls

'Général Jacqueminot'   EBls MAus
(HP)

'Général Kléber' (CeMo)   EBls MAus MRav SFam SPer SSea
    SWCr WAct WHCG

§ 'Général Schablikine' (T)   EBls EMFP MAus

N *gentiliana* (Ra)   EBls LRHS MAus WHCG XPep

Gentle Touch = 'Diclulu'^{PBR}   CSBt CWSG EBls IDic MBri MMat
(Min/Patio)   MRav NRog SPer SPla SWCr

Geoff Hamilton
= 'Ausham'PBR (S)
CSBt EBls ENot ESty LRHS LStr MAsh MAus MBNS MMat SCoo SPer SWCr

'Georg Arends' (HP) — EBls MAus

'George Dickson' (HT) — EBls MAus

'George R. Hill' (HT) — NBat

'George Vancouver' (S) **new** — EBls

'Georges Vibert' (G) — EBls MAus WHCG

§ 'Geranium' (*moyesii* hybrid) ♥H4 — CBcs CGro CHad EBee ELan ENot EPfP EWTr GCoc GGre GKir IArd LGod LRHS LStr MAsh MAus MBri MMat MRav SPer SSea SWCr WAct WHCG WOVN

'Gerbe Rose' (Ra) — EBls MAus

Gertrude Jekyll = 'Ausbord'PBR (S) ♥H4 — More than 30 suppliers

'Ghislaine de Féligonde' (Ra/S) — CHad CPou EBee EBls EMFP EWTr LStr SMrm SPer SSea SWCr WHCG WPen

gigantea — EBls ISea

- 'Cooperi' — see *R.* 'Cooperi'

Ginger Syllabub = 'Harjolly' (Cl) — ESty GCoc GGre LStr MAsh SWCr

§ Gingernut = 'Coccrazy'PBR (Patio) — GCoc GGre MBri SWCr

Gipsy Boy — see *R.* 'Zigeunerknabe'

giraldii — EBls

Glad Tidings = 'Tantide'PBR (F) — CSBt CWSG LAst MBri MRav NRog SPer SWCr

Glamis Castle = 'Auslevel'PBR (S) — CBcs CSam CTri EBls EBre ESty GKir LRHS LStr MAus MBNS MBri MWgw SPer SWCr

§ *glauca* Pourr. (S) ♥H4 — More than 30 suppliers

'Glenfiddich' (F) — CGro CGre CTri CWSG GCoc GGre LStr MAus MBri MRav NPri NRog NWea SPer SSea SWCr WStI WWeb

'Glenn Dale' (Cl) — EBee

Glenshane = 'Dicvood'PBR (GC/S) — ESty IDic MRav SWCr

'Global Beauty' (HT) **new** — ESty

'Gloire de Bruxelles' (HP) — EBls

'Gloire de Dijon' (ClT) — More than 30 suppliers

'Gloire de Ducher' (HP) — MAus MRav SWCr WAct WHCG

'Gloire de France' (G) — EBls EWTr MAus MRav SWCr

'Gloire de Guilan' (D) — EBls MAus SWCr WAct WLow

'Gloire des Mousseuses' (CeMo) — EBls SFam SWCr WAct WHCG

'Gloire du Midi' (Poly) — MAus

'Gloire Lyonnaise' (HP) — EBee EBls EWTr WHCG

'Gloria Mundi' (Poly) — EBls SWCr

Gloriana = 'Chewpope'PBR (ClMin) — ESty MAus MBri SPer SSea SWCr

Glorious = 'Interictira'PBR (HT) — GCoc IDic MBri SWCr

Glorious = 'Leoglo' (HT) — NBat

Glowing Amber = 'Manglow'PBR (Min) — NBat SWCr

glutinosa — see *R. pulverulenta*

'Goethe' (CeMo) — EBls

Gold Bunny = 'Meifronuri' (F) — MBri

Gold Crown = see *R.* 'Goldkrone'

'Goldbusch' (RH) — EBls SSea WAct

'Golden Anniversary' (Patio) — ENot GCoc GGre LStr MAsh SPer SWCr

Golden Beauty = 'Korberbeni' **new** — ESty MMat

Golden Beryl = 'Manberyl' (Min) — NBat

Golden Celebration = 'Ausgold'PBR (S) ♥H4 — CSBt CWSG EBee EBre ECnt ENot ESty GCoc GGre GKir LGod LRHS LStr MAsh MAus MBri MMat MRav NPri SMad SPer SWCr WGer

'Golden Chersonese' (S) — EBls MAus NRog

§ Golden Days = 'Rugolda' (HT) — MBri

Golden Future = 'Horanymoll'PBR (Cl) — GGre SWCr

'Golden Glow' (Cl) — EBls

Golden Hands = 'Chessupremo'PBR (Min/Patio) — SWCr

Golden Hope = 'Mehpic'PBR (F) — MBri

§ Golden Jewel = 'Tanledolg'PBR (Patio) — ESty MAsh SWCr

Golden Jubilee = 'Cocagold' (HT) — CGro CTri ESty GCoc GGre MRav SWCr

Golden Kiss = 'Dicalways' (HT) — ECnt ESty GCoc IDic NBat SWCr

Golden Melody = 'Irene Churruca' (HT) — EBls

'Golden Memories' (F) **new** — ESty

Golden Mimi = 'Meispreyo' (Patio) — ESty

'Golden Moss' (Mo) — EBls

Golden Oldie = 'Fryescape' (HT) — GCoc

'Golden Ophelia' (HT) — EBls

'Golden Rambler' — see *R.* 'Alister Stella Gray'

'Golden Salmon Supérieur' (Poly) — EBls

'Golden Showers' (Cl) ♥H4 — More than 30 suppliers

'Golden Slippers' (F) — CBcs

'Golden Sunblaze' — see *R.* 'Rise 'n Shine'

§ Golden Symphonie = 'Meitoleil' (Min/Patio) — SWCr

Golden Trust = 'Hardish'PBR (Patio) — GGre LStr MAsh SWCr

Golden Wedding = 'Arokris'PBR (F/HT) — More than 30 suppliers

'Golden Wings' (S) ♥H4 — CHad CTri EBls ECnt ELan ENot EPfP GCoc LRHS LStr MAsh MAus MMat MRav SPer SSea SWCr WAct WHCG WOVN

Golden Years = 'Harween'PBR (F) — MAus SWCr

'Goldfinch' (Ra) — CHad EBee EBls EMFP LRHS LStr MAus MBri MBur MRav NBPC SFam SPer SSea SWCr WAct WHCG

'Goldilocks' (F) — NRog

§ 'Goldkrone' (HT) — SWCr

§ Goldstar = 'Candide' (HT) — ECnt SWCr

Good as Gold = 'Chewsunbeam'PBR (ClMin) — CSBt ECnt ESty LStr MBri NPri SPer SWCr WGer

Good Life = 'Cococircus'PBR (HT) — GCoc GGre MAsh SCoo SWCr

Good Luck = 'Burspec'PBR (F/Patio) — GCoc SPer SWCr

§ Gordon Snell = 'Dicwriter' (F) — IDic

Gordon's College = 'Cocjabby'PBR (F) ♥H4 — ESty GCoc

Grace = 'Auskeppy' (S) — CSBt ECnt LGod MAsh MAus MBri SWCr

'Grace Darling' (T) — EBls

Grace de Monaco = 'Meimit' (HT) — EBls

Gracious Queen = 'Bedqueen' (HT) — GCoc GGre LRHS SCoo WWeb

Graham Thomas = 'Ausmas'PBR (S) ♥H4 — More than 30 suppliers

Granada (HT)	EBls
Grand Hotel	ENot MBur SPer
= 'Mactel' (ClHT)	
Grand-mère Jenny	EBls
= 'Grem' (HT)	
'Grandpa Dickson' (HT)	CSBt CWSG EBls GGre GKir LGod MAsh MAus MBur MRav NPri SPer SWCr WWeb
Granny's Favourite (F)	GGre SWCr
Great Expectations	ENot
= 'Jacdal' (F)	
Great Expectations	CBcs
= 'Lanican' (HT)	
Great Expectations	CGro CSBt ECnt EPfP GCoc GGre IArd LGod LStr MAsh MBri MMat SCoo SPer SWCr WWeb
= 'Mackalves'[PBR] (F)	
§ 'Great Maiden's Blush' (A)	EBls GCoc GGre MRav NBPC SFam WAct
'Great News' (F)	MAus
'Great Ormond Street' (F)	EBls
'Great Western' (Bb)	EBls
Greenall's Glory	MAus SSea
= 'Kirmac'[PBR] (F/Patio)	
'Greenmantle' (RH)	EBls MAus
Greensleeves	EBls SPer SWCr
= 'Harlenten' (F)	
Greetings	GGre IDic MAsh MRav SWCr
= 'Jacdreco'[PBR] (F)	
Grenadine	ECnt SWCr
= 'Poulgrena'[PBR] (HT)	
'Grey Dawn' (F)	MBur SWCr
'Grimpant Cramoisi Supérieur' (ClCh)	EBls WHCG
'Grootendorst'	see *R.* 'F.J. Grootendorst'
'Grootendorst Supreme' (Ru)	MAus SPer SWCr
N 'Gros Choux de Hollande' hort. (Bb)	EBls WHCG
§ Grouse 2000	ENot
= 'Korteilhab'[PBR] (GC)	
Grouse = 'Korimro'[PBR] (S/GC) ♥[H4]	CTri EBls ENot GCoc MAus MMat MRav SPer WAct WOVN
'Gruss an Aachen' (Poly)	EBls EMFP EPfP LStr MAus SPer SWCr WAct WHCG
'Gruss an Teplitz' (China hybrid)	EBee EBls MAus SPer WHCG
'Guinée' (ClHT)	CHad CSBt EBee EBls EBre ECnt ELan ENot EPfP ESty EWTr GKir LRHS MAsh MAus MBur MMat MRav NPri SChu SPer SPla SSea SWCr WHCG WLow
'Gustav Grünerwald' (HT)	EBls MAus
Gwen Mayor	GCoc
= 'Cocover'[PBR] (HT)	
Gwent = 'Poulurt'[PBR] (GC)	CSBt ELan ENot GCoc LStr MAus MMat MRav NPri SPer SSea SWCr WAct WOVN WWeb
§ *gymnocarpa*	EBls ENot SPer SSea SWCr WAct WHCG
var. *willmottiae*	
Gypsy Boy	see *R.* 'Zigeunerknabe'
'Gypsy Jewel' (Min)	SWCr
'Hakuun' (F/Patio) ♥[H4]	ESty MAsh MAus SWCr
Hallé = 'Fryelectric' (HT)	ECnt
'Hamburger Phönix' (Ra)	CGro EBls SPer SWCr WAct
Hampshire	ENot MAus MRav SWCr
= 'Korhamp'[PBR] (GC)	
Hampton Palace	ECnt
= 'Poulgret'[PBR] (F)	
Hand in Hand	GGre MAsh SWCr WWeb
= 'Haraztec'[PBR] (Patio/Min)	
Handel = 'Macha' (Cl) ♥[H4]	CGro CSBt CTri CWSG EBls EBre ELan EPfP ESty GGre GKir LAst LRHS LStr MAsh MBri MBur MMat

	MRav NBlu NRog SPer SSea SWCr WWeb
Hannah Gordon	EBee ECnt ENot MBur MMat NBat
= 'Korweiso'[PBR] (F)	NRog SSea SWCr
'Hannah Hauxwell' (Patio/F)	NBat NRog SWCr
'Hanne' (HT)	NRog
'Hansa' (Ru)	EBee EBls ENot GCoc LBuc MAus SPer SWCr WHCG WOVN
Happy Anniversary	NBPC
= 'Bedfranc'[PBR]	
Happy Anniversary	CGro GGre GKir LStr MAsh MRav
= 'Delpre' (F)	SWCr WWeb
'Happy Birthday' (Min/Patio)	CWSG ESty GGre LStr SWCr
Happy Child	CWSG LRHS MAus SCoo SPer
= 'Auscomp'[PBR] (S)	SWCr
Happy Ever After	IDic SWCr
= 'Dicvanilla'[PBR] (F)	
'Happy Memories' (F)	EBls
Happy Retirement	ESty GCoc GGre LStr MAsh SCoo
= 'Tantoras'[PBR] (F)	SWCr
'Happy Thought' (Min)	CWSG
Happy Times	GGre MAsh SWCr
= 'Bedone'[PBR] (Patio/Min)	
Happy-go-lucky	SWCr
= 'Sunhap' (Patio)	
Harewood	MRav SWCr
= 'Taninaso'[PBR] (Patio/F)	
x *harisonii* (PiH)	MMat
§ – 'Harison's Yellow' (PiH)	EBls ENot MAus SPer SWCr
§ – 'Lutea Maxima' (PiH)	EBls
§ – 'Williams' Double Yellow' (PiH)	EBls GCoc MAus SWCr WAct
'Harry Edland' (F)	GGre SSea SWCr
'Harry Maasz' (GC/Cl)	EBls
'Harry Wheatcroft' (HT)	CBcs CGro EBls ESty GGre MAus MBur NRog SPer SWCr
Harvest Fayre	CGro CTri ENot IDic MMat MRav
= 'Dicnorth'[PBR] (F)	NRog SPer SWCr
'Headleyensis'	EBee EBls MAus WHCG
'Heart of England' (F)	MBur
Heart of Gold	GCoc
= 'Coctarlotte' (HT)	
new	
§ Heartbeat '97	GCoc LGod MAsh SWCr
= 'Cocorona'[PBR] (F)	
Heather Austin	LRHS MAus SWCr
= 'Auscook'[PBR] (S)	
§ 'Heather Muir' (*sericea* hybrid) (S)	EBls MAus
'Heaven Scent' (F)	NBat
Heavenly Rosalind	LRHS MAus
= 'Ausmash'[PBR] (S)	
§ 'Hebe's Lip' (DxSwB)	EBls MAus SWCr WAct
'Hector Deane' (HT)	EBls
'Heidi Jayne' (HT)	MBur SWCr
'Heinrich Schultheis' (HP)	EBls
§ 'Helen Knight' (*ecae* hybrid) (S)	EBls MAsh MAus MBri SSea SWCr WHCG
'Helen Traubel' (HT)	EBls
Helena = 'Poulna'[PBR] (S)	ECnt MAsh SWCr
helenae	CTri EBls GCal MAus SPer SWCr
– hybrid	WHCG
hemisphaerica (S)	EBls MAus SWCr
– 'Flora Plena'	WAct
hemsleyana	CHid
'Henri Fouquier' (G)	EBls
§ 'Henri Martin' (CeMo)	EBls MAus NRog SPer SWCr WAct WHCG
Henri Matisse	ESty
= 'Delstrobla' (HT)	
'Henry Nevard' (HP)	EBls MAus

'Her Majesty' (HP)	EBls MAsh
Her Majesty = 'Dicxotic'^{PBR} (F)	IDic SWCr
§ 'Herbstfeuer' (RH)	EBls MAus SPer SWCr
Heritage = 'Ausblush'^{PBR} (S)	CGro EBee EBls ECnt ELan EMFP ENot EPfP GCoc GGre GKir LGod LRHS LStr MAsh MAus MBri MMat MRav MWgw NPri SMad SPer SPla SSea SWCr WHCG WOVN WWeb
'Hermosa' (Ch)	EBls EMFP LRHS MAus MRav SPla SWCr WAct WHCG XPep
Hero = 'Aushero' (S)	MAus
Hertfordshire ⁴ = 'Kortenay'^{PBR} (GC) ♀^H	ENot MAus MMat MRav NPri SPer SWCr
Hi Society = 'Cocquation'^{PBR} (Patio)	GCoc
'Hiawatha' (Ra)	EBls SWCr
'Hidcote Gold' (S)	EBls MAus
'Hide and Seek' (F) **new**	GCoc
Hide and Seek = 'Diczodiac' (F) **new**	IDic
High Hopes = 'Haryup'^{PBR} (Cl) ♀^{H4}	CSBt EBee ECnt GGre LGod LRHS LStr MAsh MAus MBur MRav SPer SPla SPoG SWCr WHCG WWeb
§ 'Highdownensis' (*moyesii* hybrid) (S)	EBls ELan ENot MAus SFam SPer
Highfield = 'Harcomp'^{PBR} (Cl)	CSBt LGod MAus MBri MRav SPer SWCr
Hilda Murrell = 'Ausmurr' (S)	MAus
Hilde = 'Benhile' (Min) **new**	NBat
§ 'Hillieri' (S)	EBls MAus
'Hippolyte' (G)	EBls MAus
holodonta	see *R. moyesii* f. *rosea*
holy rose	see *R.* x *richardii*
Home of Time = 'Cocquamber'^{PBR} (HT)	ESty GCoc
'Home Sweet Home' (HT)	EBls
Home Sweet Home = 'Mailoeur' (Cl/G)	SSea SWCr
'Homère' (T)	EBls MAus
Honey Bunch = 'Cocglen'^{PBR} (F)	ESty GCoc LGod LStr MBri MRav SPer SWCr
Honeymoon	see *R.* 'Honigmond'
Honeywood = 'Fryfixit' (F)	ESty GCoc
§ 'Honigmond' (F)	CWSG SWCr
'Honorine de Brabant' (Bb)	CHad CPou EBee EBls LRHS MAus SFam SPer SPla SWCr WAct WHCG
'Horace Vernet' (HP)	EBls
horrida	see *R. biebersteinii*
'Horstmanns Rosenresli' (F)	EBls
Hot Gossip = 'Jacati' (Patio/Min)	GGre MBri SWCr
Hot Tamale = 'Jacpoy' (Min)	NBat
House Beautiful = 'Harbingo'^{PBR} (Patio)	GGre MAsh MRav SWCr
'Hugh Dickson' (HP)	EBls MAus SWCr
hugonis	see *R. xanthina* f. *hugonis*
- 'Plenissima'	see *R. xanthina* f. *hugonis*
'Hula Girl' (Min)	LGod
Humanity = 'Harcross'^{PBR} (F)	MRav SWCr
Hume's blush	see *R.* x *odorata* 'Odorata'
'Hunslet Moss' (Mo)	EBls
'Hunter' (Ru)	SWCr WAct
I Love You = 'Geelove'(HT)	ESty

Ice Cream = 'Korzuri'^{PBR} (HT) ♀^{H4}	CWSG ENot LStr MAus MMat MRav NPri SWCr
§ Iceberg = 'Korbin' (F) ♀^{H4}	CBcs CGro CSBt CWSG EBee EBls EBre ECnt ENot EPfP ESty GCoc GGre GKir LAst LGod LStr MAsh MAus MMat MRav NRog SPer SSea SWCr WWeb
'Iced Ginger' (F)	SPer SWCr
'Illusion' (Cl/F)	SWCr
'Ilse Krohn Superior' (Cl)	EBls
Imagination = 'Pouldrom' (F)	ECnt
'Impulse' (Patio)	GGre SWCr
In the Pink = 'Peaverity'^{PBR} (F)	GGre SWCr
Indian Summer = 'Peaperfume'^{PBR} (HT) ♀^{H4}	CSBt CWSG ESty GCoc GGre LAst LGod MBri MRav SWCr
* *indica* 'Major' **new**	XPep
'Indigo' (DPo)	CPou EBee EBls MAus WHCG
Ingrid Bergman = 'Poulman'^{PBR} (HT) ♀^{H4}	CSBt ECnt ENot ESty GCoc LGod LStr MAus MBur MMat MRav SWCr
§ Innocence = 'Cocoray'^{PBR} (Patio)	GCoc GGre SWCr
Intense Cover = 'Poultwool' (GC/S) **new**	MAsh
'Intermezzo' (HT)	MBur SWCr
§ Intrigue = 'Korlech'^{PBR} (F)	CSBt ENot LStr MBri MMat SSea
Invincible = 'Runatru'^{PBR} (F)	EBee ECnt MAus
'Ipsilanté' (G)	EBls MAus WAct WHCG
'Irene Av Danmark' (F)	EBls
'Irène Watts' (Ch)	EBee EBls ECre EMFP EPfP EWTr MAus SPla SWCr WAct WHCG
'Irene's Delight' (HT)	NRog
'Iris Foster'	NBat
'Irish Elegance' (HT)	EBls
Irish Eyes = 'Dicwitness'^{PBR} (F)	CWSG ECnt ENot EPfP ESty GCoc GGre IArd IDic LGod LStr MAsh MBri MRav NPri SCoo SPer SSea SWCr WWeb
'Irish Fireflame' (HT)	EBls
Irish Hope = 'Harexclaim'^{PBR} (F)	GGre MAsh SWCr
Irresistible = 'Tinresist' (Min/Patio)	NBat
Isabella = 'Poulisab'^{PBR} (S)	CPou CTri ECnt GGre MAsh SWCr
Isobel Derby = 'Horethel'^{PBR} (HT)	GGre SWCr
'Ispahan' (D) ♀^{H4}	CFee CHad EBls EGra EPfP EWTr LRHS MAsh MAus SFam SPer SSea SWCr WAct WHCG
'Ivory Fashion' (F)	EBls
§ x *jacksonii* 'Max Graf' (GC/Ru)	EBls ENot LRHS MAus MRav NRog WAct WFar
§ - White Max Graf = 'Korgram'^{PBR} (GC/Ru)	ENot MRav WAct
Jacobite rose	see *R.* x *alba* 'Alba Maxima'
'Jacpico'^{PBR}	see *R.* 'Pristine'
Jacqueline du Pré = 'Harwanna'^{PBR} (S) ♀^{H4}	CSBt EBee ECnt ENot GCoc LRHS MAus MRav SChu SPer SWCr WAct WHCG
Jacquenetta = 'Ausjac' (S)	MAus
N 'Jacques Cartier' hort.	see *R.* 'Marchesa Boccella'
'James Bourgault' (HP)	EBls
James Galway = 'Auscrystal' (S)	CSBt CWSG LGod MAus MBri SWCr
'James Mason' (G)	CSam EBls MAus MBri
'James Mitchell' (CeMo)	EBls MAus SWCr WHCG
'James Veitch' (DPoMo)	EBls MAus WHCG

'Jan Guest' (HT)　NRog
Jane Asher = 'Peapet'PBR　MBri SWCr
　(Min/Patio)
Jane Eyre　COtt MRav SWCr
　= 'Mehpark'PBR (Cl)
'Janet's Pride' (RH)　EBls MAus
§ 'Japonica' (CeMo)　MAus
§ Jardins de Bagatelle　MBur MRav SWCr
　= 'Meimafris'PBR (HT)
Jayne Austin　CSBt CWSG EBre ENot LRHS MAus
　= 'Ausbreak'PBR (S)　SMad SPer SWCr
JazzPBR (Cl)　see *R.* That's Jazz
Jean Kenneally　NBat
　= 'Tineally' (Min)
'Jean Mermoz' (Poly)　MAus NRog SMad SWCr
'Jean Rosenkrantz' (HP)　EBls
'Jean Sisley' (HT)　EBls
'Jeanie Deans' (RH)　MAus
'Jeanne de Montfort'　EBls MAus
　(CeMo)
§ Jemma Giblin　NBat
　= 'Horjemma' (Patio/F)
Jenny Charlton　NBat
　= 'Simway' (HT)
'Jenny Duval' misapplied　see *R.* 'Président de Sèze'
'Jenny Wren' (F)　EBls MAus
'Jenny's Dream' (HT)　LGod
Jenny's Rose = 'Cansit'　EBee ECnt
　(F)
'Jens Munk' (Ru)　WAct
'Jersey Beauty' (Ra)　EBls
'Jill Dando' (S)　EBls
Jill's Rose = 'Ganjil'PBR　SWCr
　(F)
Jilly Jewel = 'Benmfig'　NBat
　(Min)
'Jiminy Cricket' (F)　EBls NRog
'Joan Bell' (HT)　NRog
'Joanna Hill' (HT)　EBls
'Joanna Lumley' (HT)　MBur
'Joanne' (HT)　NRog
'Jocelyn' (F)　EBls
Joey's Palace　MAsh
　= 'Pouljoey'PBR
　(Patio) **new**
'John Cabot' (S)　SSea
John Clare　LRHS MAus MBri SWCr
　= 'Auscent'PBR (S)
'John Hopper' (HP)　EBls MAus SWCr
John Keats　SWCr
　= 'Meiroupis'PBR (S)
Johnnie Walker　ESty
　= 'Frygran'PBR (HT)
Jose Carreras　ECnt
　= 'Pouljose'PBR (HT)
'Josephine Bruce' (HT)　CBcs CSBt EBls LGod MBur MRav
　　NRog SWCr WStI
'Joseph's Coat' (S/Cl)　ENot IArd LGod LStr MBri MRav
　　NBlu SSea SWCr
Jubilee Celebration　MAus
　= 'Aushunter' (S) **new**
Jude the Obscure　CAbP ESty LRHS MAus
　= 'Ausjo'PBR (S)
§ Judi Dench　EPfP
　= 'Peahunder' (F)
'Judy Fischer' (Min)　LGod SWCr
'Julia Mannering' (RH)　MAus
'Julia's Rose'PBR (HT)　CGro LStr MAus MBur SPer
　　SWCr
'Juliet' (HP)　EBls
jundzillii　CFee
'Juno' (Ce)　EBls MAus WAct WHCG
'Just for You' (F)　GGre MAsh SWCr
'Just Jenny' (Min)　NBat

'Just Joey' (HT) ♀H4　CGro CSBt CWSG EBee EBls ECnt
　　ELan EPfP ESty GCoc GGre GKir
　　IArd LAst LGod LStr MAsh MAus
　　MBri MBur MMat MRav NPri NRog
　　SPer SSea SWCr WWeb
'Karl Foerster' (PiH)　EBls MAus
'Kassel' (S/Cl)　EBls
'Katharina Zeimet' (Poly)　EBls MAus NRog WAct
　　WHCG
Katherine Mansfield　CSBt MBur
　= 'Meilanein' (HT)
'Kathleen' (HM)　EBls
'Kathleen Ferrier' (F)　EBls SWCr
'Kathleen Harrop' (Bb)　EBls ENot LRHS LStr MAus MBur
　　SFam SPer SWCr WAct WHCG
§ Kathryn Morley　CAbP LRHS MAus MBri MWgw
　= 'Ausclub'PBR (F)　SWCr
'Katie' (ClF)　MBur SWCr
Katie Crocker　MBur
　= 'Sabbrindley' (F)
'Kazanlik' misapplied　see *R.* 'Professeur Emile Perrot'
Keep in Touch　SWCr
　= 'Hardrama'PBR (F)
Keepsake = 'Kormalda'　ENot MBur SWCr
　(HT)
'Ken 'n' Norma Bright'　NBat
　(HT)
Kent = 'Poulcov'PBR　CSBt ECnt ELan ENot EPfP ESty
　(S/GC) ♀H4　GCoc LStr MAsh MMat MRav NPri
　　SPer SPla SSea SWCr WAct WHCG
　　WWeb
'Kew Rambler' (Ra)　CRHN CSam EBee EBls MAus
　　MRav SFam SPer SWCr WHCG
'Kiftsgate'　see *R. filipes* 'Kiftsgate'
'Kilworth Gold' (HT)　SWCr
'Kim' (Patio)　NRog
Kind Regards　LAst SWCr
　= 'Peatiger' (F)
'King's Ransom' (HT)　CBcs CSBt EBls MMat MRav SPer
　　SWCr
'Kirsten Poulsen' (Poly)　EBls
Kiss 'n' Tell = 'Seakis'　MBur
　(Min)
'Kitty' (S) **new**　EBls
'Kitty Hawk' (Min)　NBat
Knock Out = 'Dadler' (F)　GCoc
x *kochiana*　EBls
§ 'Königin von Dänemark'　CHad CSam EBee EBls EMFP ENot
　(A) ♀H4　EPfP EWTr GCoc MAus MBri MMat
　　MRav MWgw SPer SSea SWCr
　　WAct WHCG
Korona = 'Kornita' (F)　NRog SPer SWCr
'Korresia' (F)　CSBt CTri EBls ECnt EPfP ESty
　　GCoc GGre GKir LGod LStr MAsh
　　MAus MBri MBur MMat MRav
　　NRog SPer SWCr
§ Kristin = 'Benmagic' (Min)　NBat
Kronenbourg = 'Macbo'　EBls
　(HT)
'Kronprinzessin Viktoria'　EBee EBls MAus WHCG
　(Bb)
L.D. Braithwaite　CSam CTri EBre ELan ENot EPfP
　= 'Auscrim'PBR (S) ♀H4　ESty GCoc GGre LGod LRHS LStr
　　MAus MRav NPri SPer SSea SWCr
　　WAct WHCG
La Bamba = 'Diczoom'　IDic
　(GC) **new**
'La Belle Distinguée' (RH)　EBls MAus WHCG
'La Belle Sultane'　see *R.* 'Violacea'
'La Follette' (Cl)　EBls
'La France' (HT)　EBls MAus MBur WLow
'La Mortola'　see *R. brunonii* 'La Mortola'
'La Noblesse' (Ce)　EBls
'La Perle' (Ra)　CRHN MAus

'La Reine' (HP) — EBls
'La Reine Victoria' — see *R.* 'Reine Victoria'
'La Rubanée' — see *R.* 'Centifolia Variegata'
La Sévillana — EBls ENot SPer SWCr WOVN
= 'Meigekanu'PBR
(F/GC)
'La Ville de Bruxelles' — EBls MAus MRav SFam SPer SWCr
(D) ♀H4 — WAct WHCG
'Lady Alice Stanley' (HT) — EBls
'Lady Barnby' (HT) — EBls
'Lady Belper' (HT) — EBls
'Lady Curzon' (Ru) — EBls MAus SWCr
'Lady Forteviot' (HT) — EBls
'Lady Gay' (Ra) — EBee WHCG
'Lady Godiva' (Ra) — MAus
'Lady Hillingdon' (T) — EWTr MAus
'Lady Hillingdon' (ClT) — see *R.* 'Climbing Lady Hillingdon'
'Lady Iliffe' (HT) — SWCr
Lady in Red = 'Sealady' — MBur
(Min)
Lady MacRobert — GCoc GGre
= 'Coclent' (F)
'Lady Mary Fitzwilliam' — EBls
(HT)
§ Lady Meillandina — CSBt SWCr
= 'Meilarco' (Min)
Lady Penelope — CSBt MAsh SSea SWCr
= 'Chewdor'PBR (ClHT)
§ 'Lady Penzance' (RH) ♀H4 — CBcs EBls MAus SPer SWCr WAct
§ Lady Rachel — EBee ECnt
= 'Candoodle' (F)
'Lady Romsey' (F) — EBls
Lady Rose = 'Korlady' — MAsh SWCr
(HT)
'Lady Sylvia' (HT) — CSBt CTri EBls MAus NRog SPer
SWCr WLow
Lady Taylor = 'Smitling' — MBur
(F/Patio)
'Lady Waterlow' (ClHT) — EBee EBls MAus SPer SWCr WHCG
laevigata (Ra) — EBls MAus SWCr XPep
- 'Anemonoides' — see *R.* 'Anemone'
- 'Cooperi' — see *R.* 'Cooperi'
'Lafter' (S) — EBls
'Lagoon' (F) — EBls
L'Aimant = 'Harzola'PBR — CSBt ENot ESty GCoc GGre LGod
(F) ♀H4 — LStr MAus MBur SWCr
'Lamarque' (N) — MAus
§ Lancashire — ECnt ENot ESty GCoc LStr MAus
= 'Korstesgli'PBR — MMat MRav SWCr
(GC) ♀H4
Lancashire Life — MBri
= 'Ruilanca' (F)
§ 'Lanei' (CeMo) — EBls
Laura Anne — GCoc
= 'Cocclarion' (HT)
§ Laura Ashley — MAus SWCr
= 'Chewharla'
(GC/ClMin)
Laura Ford — CSBt CTri EBre ENot ESty GGre
= 'Chewarvel'PBR — GKir LStr MAsh MAus MBri MMat
(ClMin) ♀H4 — MRav NBat NPri NRog SPer SSea
SWCr WWeb
'Laura Louisa' (Cl) — EBls
§ 'Laure Davoust' (Ra) — EBee
'Lavender Jewel' (Min) — MAus MBur
'Lavender Lassie' — CPou EMFP EWTr MAus SPer
(HM) ♀H4 — SWCr WHCG
'Lavender Pinocchio' (F) — MAus
§ Lawinia = 'Tanklewi'PBR — CSBt GKir LRHS LStr MAsh MRav
(ClHT) ♀H4 — NPri SPer SSea SWCr
'Lawrence Johnston' (Cl) — EBls LRHS MAus SFam SPer WAct
WLow
Lazy Days (F) — ECnt
'Le Havre' (HP) — EBls

'Le Rêve' (Cl) — EBls MAus SWCr
'Le Vésuve' (Ch) — EBls MAus
Leander = 'Auslea' (S) — MAus
Leaping Salmon — CGro CSBt EBee ECnt ELan GCoc
= 'Peamight'PBR (ClHT) — LAst LGod MAus MBri MRav SChu
SPer SSea SWCr WStI
'Leda' (D) — EBls MAus SFam SPer SSea SWCr
WAct
Leeds Castle — SWCr
= 'Tanrupeza'PBR (GC)
'Lemon Pillar' — see *R.* 'Paul's Lemon Pillar'
Léonardo de Vinci — CSBt
= 'Meideauri'PBR (F)
'Léonie Lamesch' (Poly) — EBls
'Léontine Gervais' (Ra) — CAbP CRHN LRHS MAus MBri
SWCr WAct
'Leo's Eye' **new** — SLon
Leslie's Dream — IDic
= 'Dicjoon'PBR (HT)
'Leverkusen' (Cl) ♀H4 — CHad EBee EBls LRHS MAus MRav
SPer SPla SSea SWCr WAct WHCG
'Leveson-Gower' (Bb) — EBls
'Ley's Perpetual' (ClT) — EBee EBls WHCG
x *lheritieriana* (Bs) — EBee
§ Lichtkönigin Lucia — SSea
= 'Korlillub' (S)
Life Begins at 40! (F) — SWCr
'Lilac Charm' (F) — EBls
Lilac Rose = 'Auslilac' (S) — MAus
Lilian Austin = 'Ausli' (S) — MAus MBri
Lilian Baylis — GGre SWCr
= 'Hardeluxe'PBR (F)
Liliana = 'Poulsyng'PBR (S) — ECnt MAsh SPla SWCr
§ Lilli Marlene = 'Korlima' — CSBt CWSG EBls ENot GCoc NRog
(F) — SPer SWCr
Lincoln Cathedral — GGre SPer SWCr
= 'Glanlin'PBR (HT)
Lincolnshire Poacher — NBat
= 'Glareabit' (HT)
Little Bo-peep — ENot MMat MRav
= 'Poullen'PBR
(Min/Patio) ♀H4
'Little Buckaroo' (Min) — LGod SPer SWCr
'Little Dorrit' (Poly) — NRog
'Little Flirt' (Min) — MAus SWCr
'Little Gem' (DPMo) — EBls MAus
Little Jackie = 'Savor' — NBat
(Min)
Little Muff = 'Horluisbond' — NBat
(Min)
Little Rambler — CBrm CSBt ECnt ELan ENot MAus
= 'Chewramb'PBR — MMat MRav SPer SWCr WGer
(MinRa) ♀H4 — WLow
§ Little Rascal — GGre WHPP
= 'Peaalamo'PBR
(Patio/Min)
'Little White Pet' — see *R.* 'White Pet'
Little Woman — IDic LStr SWCr
= 'Diclittle'PBR (Patio)
§ Liverpool Remembers — LGod
= 'Frystar'PBR (HT)
'Living Fire' (F) — NRog
Lochinvar — MAus
= 'Ausbilda' (S) **new**
'Long John Silver' (Cl) — EBls MAus
longicuspis hort. — see *R. mulliganii*
longicuspis Bertoloni — EBls SPla
(Ra)
- AC 2097 — GGar
§ - var. *sinowilsonii* (Ra) — EBls GCal MAus
aff. *longicuspis* — GGar
AC 1808 **new**
§ Lord Byron — MBri
= 'Meitosier'PBR (ClHT)

'Lord Louis' (HT)	MBur
'Lord Penzance' (RH)	CBgR EBls EMFP EWTr MRav SPer SWCr WAct
L'Oréal Trophy	MAus
= 'Harlexis' (HT)	
'Lorraine Lee' (T)	EBls
'Los Angeles' (HT)	EBls
'L'Ouche' misapplied	see *R*. 'Louise Odier'
'Louis Gimard' (CeMo)	EBls MAus SPer WAct WHCG
'Louis Philippe' (Ch)	EBls
'Louis XIV' (Ch)	CHad EBls WHCG
Louisa Stone	GGre SWCr
= 'Harbadge' (S)	
Louise Clements	EBls
= 'Clelou' (S)	
§ 'Louise Odier' (Bb)	EBee EBls ECnt EMFP ENot EPfP EWTr IArd LRHS LStr MAus MBri MRav MWgw SFam SPer SPla SSea SWCr WAct WHCG WLow WOVN
Love Knot	CSBt ECnt ESty SWCr WGor WWeb
= 'Chewglorious'^{PBR} (ClMin)	
'Love Token' (F)	MBur SWCr
Lovely Fairy = 'Spevu'^{PBR} (Poly/GC)	ECnt IDic MAsh SWCr WAct
Lovely Lady	CTri EBee ECnt ESty IDic LStr
= 'Dicjubell'^{PBR} (HT) ♥^{H4}	MAus MRav NBlu SWCr WWeb
'Lovely Meidiland' (Patio) **new**	MAsh
'Lovers' Meeting'^{PBR} (HT)	ESty GKir MBur MRav NRog SPer SSea SWCr WStI
Loving Memory	CGro CSBt CWSG EBee ECnt ENot
= 'Korgund'^{PBR} (HT)	GCoc GGre IArd LStr MBri MMat MRav NPri SPer SSea SWCr WWeb
Lucetta = 'Ausemi' (S)	MAus SPer
luciae	EBls
- var. *onoei*	CLyd EPot
'Lucilla' (Patio)	NBat
Lucky Duck	IDic
= 'Diczest'^{PBR} (Patio)	
'Lucy Ashton' (RH)	MAus
Ludlow Castle^{PBR}	see *R*. England's Rose
Luis Desamero	NBat
= 'Tinluis' (Min)	
'Lutea Maxima'	see *R*. x *harisonii* 'Lutea Maxima'
'Lykkefund' (Ra)	EBls MAus
'Lyon Rose' (HT)	EBls
'Ma Perkins' (F)	EBls SSea
'Ma Ponctuée' (DPMo)	EBls
'Mabel Morrison' (HP)	EBls MAus
Macartney rose	see *R*. *bracteata*
Macmillan Nurse	EBls
= 'Beamac' (S)	
'Macrantha' (Gallica hybrid)	EBls LRHS MAus SPer WAct
x *macrantha* 'Raubritter'	see *R*. 'Raubritter' ('Macrantha' hybrid)
macrophylla	MAus SWCr
- B&SWJ 2603	WCru
- 'Doncasteri'	see *R*. 'Doncasteri'
§ - 'Master Hugh' ♥^{H4} ex SS&W 7822	EBls MAus
Madam Speaker	MBur SWCr
= 'Meizuzes'^{PBR} (HT)	
'Madame Abel Chatenay' (HT)	EBls MAus
'Madame Alfred Carrière' (N) ♥^{H4}	More than 30 suppliers
'Madame Alice Garnier' (Ra)	CPou EBee EBls SPer
'Madame Antoine Mari' (T)	EBls
'Madame Berkeley' (T)	EBls
'Madame Bravy' (T)	EBls MAus

'Madame Butterfly' (HT)	EBls MAus MBur SFam SSea SWCr
§ 'Madame Caroline Testout' (HT)	EBee EWTr LRHS MRav SFam
'Madame Charles' (T)	EBls
'Madame d'Arblay' (Ra)	EBls
'Madame de Sancy de Parabère' (Bs)	EBls IArd MAus SFam WHCG
'Madame de Watteville' (T)	EBls
'Madame Delaroche-Lambert' (DPMo)	EBls MAus SWCr WAct WHCG
'Madame Driout' (CIT)	EBls WHCG
'Madame Eliza de Vilmorin' (HT)	EBls
'Madame Ernest Calvat' (Bb)	EBls MAus
'Madame Eugène Résal' misapplied	see *R*. 'Comtesse du Caÿla'
'Madame Gabriel Luizet' (HP)	EBls
'Madame Georges Bruant' (Ru)	EBls MAus
§ 'Madame Grégoire Staechelin' (ClHT) ♥^{H4}	CWSG EBee EBls EBre ECnt ELan EMFP ENot EPfP LRHS LStr MAus MBri MMat MRav NBlu NRog SChu SFam SPer SWCr WAct WHCG WWeb
'Madame Hardy' (ClD) ♥^{H4}	CPou CSBt CSam EBee EBls EMFP ENot EPfP GCoc LGod LRHS LStr MAus MBri MMat MRav SFam SPer SSea SWCr WAct WHCG WOVN
'Madame Isaac Pereire' (ClBb) ♥^{H4}	CHad CTri EBee EBls EBre ECnt ENot EPfP GCoc LGod LRHS LStr MAsh MAus MBri MMat MRav NBPC NRog SFam SMad SPer SSea SWCr WAct WHCG WLow
'Madame Jules Gravereaux' (ClT)	EBls MAus
'Madame Jules Thibaud' (Poly)	MAus
§ 'Madame Knorr' (DPo) ♥^{H4}	CPou EBee EBls EMFP ENot EPfP MAsh MRav MWgw SPer SSea SWCr WAct WLow WOVN
'Madame Laurette Messimy' (Ch)	EBls MAus WHCG
'Madame Lauriol de Barny' (Bb)WHCG	EBls MAus MRav SFam SWCr
'Madame Legras de Saint Germain' (AxN)	EBls LRHS MAus SFam SPer WAct WHCG
'Madame Lombard' (T)	EBls
'Madame Louis Laperrière' (HT)	EBls MAus SPer SWCr
'Madame Louis Lévêque' (DPMo)	EBls SWCr WHCG
'Madame Pierre Oger' (Bb)	EBee EBls ECnt ENot LRHS LStr MAsh MAus MRav SPer SSea SWCr WAct WLow
'Madame Plantier' (AxN)	EBee EBls LRHS MAus MRav SPer SSea SWCr WHCG WOVN
'Madame Scipion Cochet' (T)	EBls WHCG
'Madame Victor Verdier' (HP)	EBls
'Madame Wagram, Comtesse de Turenne' (T)	EBls
'Madame William Paul' (PoMo)	EBls
'Madame Zöetmans' (D)	EBls MAus
'Madeleine Selzer' (Ra)	EBls SWCr
'Madge' (HM)	SDix
Madrigal = 'Harextra'^{PBR} (S/F)	GGre SWCr
'Magenta' (S/HT)	EBls MAus SPer SWCr

Magenta Floorshow = 'Harfloorshow'^{PBR} (GC)   SWCr

Magic Carpet = 'Jaclover'^{PBR} (S/GC) ♀^{H4}   CWSG ECnt ENot EPfP GCoc IDic LGod LRHS MAus MRav SPer SSea

§ Magic Carrousel = 'Moorcar' (Min)   SWCr MAus

Magic Fire = 'Lapjaminal' (F)   GGre SWCr

Magic Hit = 'Poulhi004' **new**   MAsh SWCr

'Magna Charta' (HP)   EBls

'Magnifica' (RH)   EBls MAus

Maid of Kent^{PBR} (Cl)   CSBt SCoo SPer SWCr

'Maiden's Blush' Hort. (A) ♀^{H4}   CSam CTri EBls EBre ELan EMFP ENot LRHS MAus MRav SChu SFam SPer SSea SWCr WHCG

'Maiden's Blush' misapplied   see *R.* 'Great Maiden's Blush'

'Maiden's Blush, Great'   see *R.* 'Great Maiden's Blush'

'Maigold' (ClPiH) ♀^{H4}   CBcs CGro CSam CWSG EBee EBls ECnt ELan ENot EPfP GCoc GGre GKir LGod LRHS LStr MAsh MAus MBri MMat MRav MWgw NRog SMad SPer SSea SWCr WAct WHCG WWeb

§ *majalis*   EBls

Majestic = 'Poulpm001' (HT) **new**   ECnt

Make a Wish = 'Mehpat'^{PBR} (Min/Patio)   LStr MBri SWCr

'Malaga' (ClHT)   EBee ENot

Malcolm Sargent = 'Harwharry' (HT)   SWCr

Maltese rose   see *R.* 'Cécile Brünner'

§ 'Malton' (China hybrid)   EBls

Malvern Hills = 'Auscanary' (Ra)   CSBt MAus

Malverns = 'Kordehei' (GC)   ENot

Mandarin = 'Korcelin'^{PBR} (Min)   ESty LStr MMat SSea WWeb

'Manettii' (N)   EBls

'Manning's Blush' (RH)   CBgR EBls MAus MRav SSea WAct

'Mannington Cascade' (Ra)   EBls

'Mannington Mauve Rambler' (Ra)   EBls

'Manx Queen' (F)   MBur SWCr

Many Happy Returns = 'Harwanted'^{PBR} (S/F) ♀^{H4}   CGro CSBt CWSG EBee EBre ECnt ENot EPfP ESty GCoc GGre GKir LAst LGod LStr MAsh MBri MBur MMat MRav SPer SWCr WWeb

'Marbrée' (DPo)   EBls MAus

'Marcel Bourgouin' (G)   EBls

'Märchenland' (F/S)   EBls MAus

§ 'Marchesa Boccella' (DPo) ♀^{H4}   CPou CSam CTri EBee EBls EMFP ENot EPfP MAsh MAus MMat MRav SPer SPla SSea SWCr WAct

'Marcie Gandy' (HT)   SWCr

'Maréchal Davoust' (CeMo)   EBls MAus MRav SFam

'Maréchal Niel' (N)   CRHN EBls ERea MAus SPer SWCr WHCG WLow

'Margaret' (HT)   MBur SWCr

Margaret Chessum = 'Bossexpaint' (F) **new**   GGre

'Margaret Hall' (HT) **new**   NBat

Margaret Merril = 'Harkuly' (F/HT) ♀^{H4}   CSBt CWSG EBee EBls ECnt ELan EPfP ESty GCoc GGre GKir IArd LGod LStr MAsh MAus MBri MBur MMat MRav NRog SMad SPer SSea SWCr WHCG WWeb

'Margo Koster' (Poly)   EBls MAus NRog SWCr

Marguerite Anne = 'Cocredward'^{PBR} (F)   GCoc

'Marguérite Guillard' (HP)   EBls

'Marguerite Hilling' (S) ♀^{H4}   CAbP CTri EBls ENot GCoc GGre MAus MBri MMat MRav NRog SPer SSea SWCr WAct WHCG WOVN

Maria McGredy = 'Macturang'   MBri

x *mariae-graebnerae*   MAus SLPl WHCG

'Marie de Blois' (CeMo)   EBls

'Marie Louise' (D)   EBee EBls MAus SFam SWCr WAct WHCG

'Marie Pavic' (Poly)   CHad EBls MAus WHCG

'Marie van Houtte' (T)   EBls MAus

'Marie-Jeanne' (Poly)   EBls MAus

Marinette = 'Auscam'^{PBR} (S)   MAsh MAus SWCr

Marjorie Fair = 'Harhero' (Poly/S) ♀^{H4}   EBls ECnt GGre MAsh MAus MRav SPoG SWCr WAct

Marjorie Marshall = 'Hardenier'^{PBR} **new**   SWCr

'Marlena' (F/Patio)   GCoc MAus

Marry Me = 'Dicwonder'^{PBR} (Patio) ♀^{H4}   ESty IDic MBri SWCr

'Martha' (Bb)   EBls MAus

'Martha's Choice' (HT)   NBat

'Martin Frobisher' (Ru)   EBls MAus

'Mary' (Poly)   LStr

Mary Magdalene = 'Ausjolly'^{PBR} (S)   MAus SWCr

'Mary Manners' (Ru)   EBls SPer SWCr

Mary Pope = 'Korlasche' (HT)   ENot MRav

Mary Rose = 'Ausmary'^{PBR} (S) ♀^{H4}   CGro CHad CSBt CSam CTri CWSG EBee EBls ELan ENot EPfP ESty EWTr GCoc GGre GKir LGod LRHS LStr MAsh MAus MBri MMat MRav NPri SPer SSea SWCr

Mary Sumner = 'Macstra' (F)   MBur

'Mary Wallace' (Cl)   EBls MAus

Mary Webb = 'Auswebb' (S)   MAus MBri

'Masquerade' (F)   CBcs CGro CSBt CWSG EBls ENot LGod LStr MMat MRav NRog SPer SSea SWCr WStI

'Master Hugh'   see *R. macrophylla* 'Master Hugh'

Matangi = 'Macman' (F) ♀^{H4}   NRog SMad

Matawhero Magic^{PBR}   see *R.* Simply the Best

'Maude Elizabeth' (GC)   EBls

'Maurice Bernardin' (HP)   EBls

'Max Graf'   see *R.* x *jacksonii* 'Max Graf'

'Maxima'   see *R.* x *alba* 'Alba Maxima'

maximowicziana   GIBF

'May Queen' (Ra)   CPou CRHN EBee EBls EMFP LRHS MAsh MAus MBur MRav NLar SFam SPer SWCr WHCG

Mayor of Casterbridge = 'Ausbrid'^{PBR} (S)   LRHS MAus SWCr

'McGredy's Sunset' (HT)   NRog

'McGredy's Yellow' (HT)   EBls MBur

'Meg' (ClHT)   EBee EBls EWTr LRHS MAus SPer SSea SWCr WAct WHCG

'Meg Merrilies' (RH)   EBls MAus SSea SWCr WAct

Melody Maker = 'Dicqueen'^{PBR} (F)   CWSG IDic

Memento = 'Dicbar'^{PBR} (F) ♀^{H4}   ENot IDic SWCr

Memory Lane = 'Peavoodoo'^{PBR} (F)   SWCr

	'Mermaid' (Cl) ♥H3-4	CBcs CGro CRHN CSBt CWSG EBls ECnt ENot EPfP GCoc GKir LHop LRHS LStr MAus MMat MRav NRog SBra SPer SPla SSea SWCr WAct WBVN WHCG XPep
	'Merveille de Lyon' (HP)	EBls
§	Message = 'Meban' (HT)	SWCr
	'Meteor' (F/Patio)	SWCr
§	'Mevrouw Nathalie Nypels' (Poly) ♥H4	EBls LRHS LStr MAus MRav SPer SWCr WAct WKif WOVN
§	Michael Crawford = 'Poulvue'PBR (HT)	ECnt
	'Michèle Meilland' (HT)	EBls MAus
	x *micrugosa*	EBls MAus
	- 'Alba'	EBls MAus
	Middlesborough Football Club = 'Horflame' (HT)	NBat
	Mike Thompson = 'Sherired' (HT)	NBat
	'Millennium Rose 2000'PBR	see *R.* Rose 2000
	'Minnehaha' (Ra)	EBls EMFP LGod MAus SWCr
	mirifica stellata	see *R. stellata* var. *mirifica*
	Mischief = 'Macmi' (HT)	EBls GGre NRog SPer SWCr
	Miss Alice = 'Ausjake' (S)	MAus
§	Miss Dior = 'Harencens'PBR (S)	GGre
	'Miss Edith Cavell' (Poly)	EBls MAus
	Miss Flippins = 'Tuckflip' (Min)	NBat
	Miss Harp = 'Tanolg' (HT)	NRog
	'Miss Lowe' (Ch)	EBls
§	'Mister Lincoln' (HT)	EBls ESty LGod SPer SWCr
	Mistress Quickly = 'Ausky'PBR (S)	CTri LRHS MAus SWCr
	Misty Hit = 'Poulhi011' (Patio) **new**	ECnt
	'Mojave' (HT)	SWCr
	'Moje Hammarberg' (Ru)	ENot SWCr WAct
§	Molineux = 'Ausmol'PBR (S) ♥H4	CSBt CTri EBre ENot ESty GCoc GKir LRHS MAsh MAus MBri MMat SWCr
	'Monique' (HT)	EBls SWCr
	'Monsieur Tillier' (T)	EBls
	Moonbeam = 'Ausbeam' (S)	MAus MRav
	'Moonlight' (HM)	CHad CTri EBee EBls ECnt LRHS MAus MRav NRog SPer SWCr WAct WHCG
	'Morgengruss' (Cl)	SPer SWCr
	'Morlettii' (Bs)	EBee EBls EHol MRav WHCG
	'Morning Jewel' (ClF) ♥H4	GCoc NRog SPer SWCr
	Morning Mist = 'Ausfire' (S)	LRHS MAus
	Mortimer Sackler = 'Ausorts' (S) **new**	MAus
	moschata (Ra)	EBls MAus MRav SSea SWCr WAct
	- 'Autumnalis'	see *R.* 'Princesse de Nassau'
	- var. *nepalensis*	see *R. brunonii*
	Mother's Day = 'Moersdag' (Poly/F)	GGre GKir LAst LStr NPri SSea SWCr WWeb
	Mountain Snow = 'Aussnow' (Ra)	LRHS MAus
	Mountbatten = 'Harmantelle'PBR (F) ♥H4	CBcs CGro CWSG EBls ELan ENot EPfP GGre GKir LGod LStr MAsh MAus MBur SPer SSea SWCr
§	'Mousseline' (DPoMo)	EBls EMFP MAus MRav NBPC SPer SSea SWCr WAct WHCG
	'Mousseuse du Japon'	see *R.* 'Japonica'
	moyesii (S)	CDul CTri EBee EBls ELan ENot ISea MAus NRog NWea SPer SWCr WAct WOVN
	- 'Evesbatch' (S)	WAct
§	- var. *fargesii* (S)	EBls
	- 'Geranium'	see *R.* 'Geranium'
	- 'Highdownensis'	see *R.* 'Highdownensis'
	- 'Hillieri'	see *R.* 'Hillieri'
	- *holodonta*	see *R. moyesii* f. *rosea*
§	- f. *rosea* (S)	EBls ENot GCal
	- 'Sealing Wax'	see *R.* 'Sealing Wax'
	'Mozart' (HM)	NLar SWCr WHCG
	'Mr Bluebird' (MinCh)	MAus MBur SWCr WStI
	'Mr Chips' (HT)	MBur SWCr
	'Mrs Anthony Waterer' (Ru)	EBls MAus SPer SWCr WAct WHCG
	'Mrs Arthur Curtiss James' (ClHT)	EBee SWCr
	'Mrs B.R. Cant' (T)	EBls
	Mrs Doreen Pike = 'Ausdor'PBR (Ru)	LRHS MAus WAct
	'Mrs Foley Hobbs' (T)	EBls
	'Mrs Honey Dyson' (Ra)	CHad
	'Mrs John Laing' (HP)	EBee EBls EPfP LRHS MAus MRav NBPC SWCr WHCG
	'Mrs Oakley Fisher' (HT)	CHad EBls EMFP MAus MBri SPer SWCr WAct
	'Mrs Paul' (Bb)	EBls MAus
	'Mrs Pierre S. duPont' (HT)	EBls
	'Mrs Sam McGredy' (HT)	CSBt MAus
	'Mrs Walter Burns' (F/Patio)	SWCr
	'Mullard Jubilee' (HT)	SWCr
§	*mulliganii* (Ra) ♥H4	CDoC EBls EPfP MAus SWCr WHCG
	multibracteata (S)	EBls MAus WHCG
	multiflora (Ra)	EBls GIBF IFro LBuc MAus WPic
	- 'Carnea' (Ra)	EBls
	- var. *cathayensis* (Ra)	EBls
§	- 'Grevillei' (Ra)	EBee EBls MAus SPer SWCr
	- 'Platyphylla'	see *R. multiflora* 'Grevillei'
	- var. *watsoniana*	see *R. watsoniana*
	Mummy PBR	see *Rosa* Newly Wed
	'München' (HM)	EBls MAus
	mundi	see *R. gallica* 'Versicolor'
	- 'Versicolor'	see *R. gallica* 'Versicolor'
	'Mutabilis'	see *R.* x *odorata* 'Mutabilis'
	'My Choice' (HT)	SWCr
	'My Joy' (HT)	NBat
	'My Little Boy' (Min)	MBur
	My Love = 'Cogamo' (HT)	MBur
	My Mum = 'Webmorrow'	SWCr
	Myra = 'Battoo' (HT)	NBat
	Myriam = 'Cocgrand' (HT)	GCoc
	Mystique = 'Kirmyst' (F) **new**	SWCr
	'Nan of Painswick'	WAct
	'Nancy's Keepsake' (HT)	NBat
	'Narrow Water' (Ra)	EBee EBls SWCr WAct WHCG
§	'Nastarana' (N)	EBls
	'Nathalie Nypels'	see *R.* 'Mevrouw Nathalie Nypels'
	'National Trust' (HT)	EBls GGre IArd MAsh MMat NRog SPer
*	'Navie Viaud'	WAct
	'Nestor' (G)	EBls MAus
	'Nevada' (S) ♥H4	CGro CSBt ECnt ELan ENot EPfP GCoc GGre GKir IArd LGod LStr MAus MBri MMat MRav NRog SFam SPer SSea SWCr WAct WHCG WOVN
	New Age = 'Wekbipuhit' (F)	ESty GCoc SWCr
	'New Arrival' (Patio/Min)	GGre SWCr
§	'New Dawn' (Cl) ♥H4	More than 30 suppliers
	New Fashion = 'Poulholm'PBR (Patio)	ENot
	'New Look' (F)	SWCr

'New Penny' (Min)	MRav SWCr	
New Zealand	ESty NBat SWCr	
= 'Macgenev'^{PBR} (HT)		
§ Newly Wed	IDic	
= 'Dicwhynot'^{PBR}		
(Patio)		
News = 'Legnews' (F)	MAus SWCr	
Nice Day = 'Chewsea'^{PBR}	CGro CSBt CWSG ECnt ENot ESty	
(ClMin) ♀H4	GGre GKir LGod LStr MAsh MBri	
	MBur MMat MRav SPer SSea SWCr	
	WWeb	
'Nicola' (F)	SWCr	
Nigel Hawthorne	WAct	
= 'Harquibbler' (S)		
Night Light	ECnt MAsh MBri MBur SWCr	
= 'Poullight'^{PBR} (Cl)		
Nina = 'Mehnina'^{PBR} (S)	SWCr	
'Nina Weibull' (F)	ESty	
nitida	EBls ENot LRHS MAus NWea SPer	
	SSea SWCr WAct WHCG WHer	
	WOVN	
Noble Antony	ENot LRHS MAus MBri MMat	
= 'Ausway'^{PBR} (S)	MWgw SCoo SWCr WWeb	
§ 'Noisette Carnée' (N)	CHad CSam EBee EBls EMFP EPfP	
	MAus MBNS MBri MRav MWgw	
	NBPC SLPl SPer SSea SWCr WAct	
	WHCG WLow	
Norfolk = 'Poulfolk'^{PBR}	EBls ENot SPer SPla SSea SWCr	
(GC)		
Northamptonshire	EBls ENot MRav SWCr	
= 'Mattdor'^{PBR} (GC)		
'Northern Lights' (HT)	GCoc	
'Norwich Castle' (F)	EBls	
Norwich Cathedral	EBls	
= 'Beacath' (HT)		
'Norwich Pink' (Cl)	MAus	
'Norwich Salmon' (Cl)	MAus	
'Norwich Union' (F)	EBls MBri	
'Nostalgia' (Min)	ESty GGre	
Nostalgie	LStr MAsh SCoo SWCr	
= 'Taneiglat'^{PBR} (HT)		
'Nova Zembla' (Ru)	EBls MAus	
'Nozomi' (ClMin/GC) ♀H4	CGro CLyd EBls ECnt ENot ESty	
	GCoc GGre MAus MMat MRav	
	MWgw NWCA SMad SPer SSea	
	SWCr WAct WHCG WOVN WWeb	
'Nuits de Young'	EBee EBls ENot GCoc MAus SFam	
(CeMo) ♀H4	SSea SWCr WHCG	
'Nur Mahal' (HM)	EBls MAus SWCr WHCG	
nutkana (S)	EBls MAus	
§ - var. *hispida* (S)	EBls	
§ - 'Plena' (S) ♀H4	EBls ENot EPfP MAus MBri SFam	
	SWCr WAct WGer WHCG	
'Nymphenburg' (HM)	EBls ENot MAus SPer SWCr	
'Nypels' Perfection' (Poly)	MAus	
'Nyveldt's White' (Ru)	EBls MAus	
Octavia Hill	CSBt MRav NPri SPer SWCr	
= 'Harzeal'^{PBR} (F/S)		
Oddball = 'Horodd' (F)	SWCr	
x *odorata*	GIBF XPep	
* - 'Burmese Crimson' **new**	SLon	
- 'Fortune's Double	see *R.* x *odorata* 'Pseudindica'	
Yellow'		
§ - 'Mutabilis' (Ch) ♀H3-4	CHad CRHN EBls EBre ECre EHol	
	EMFP ENot EPfP GCoc MAus	
	MMat MRav NBPC SMad SMrm	
	SPer SSea SWCr WAct WBcn WCFE	
	WCot WHCG WOVN XPep	
§ - 'Ochroleuca' (Ch)	EBls	
§ - 'Odorata' (Ch)	EBls	
- old crimson China (Ch)	EBls WAct	
§ - 'Pallida' (Ch)	CBgR CHad EBls EMFP EPfP GCoc	
	LRHS MAus MMat MRav SPer SPla	
	SSea SWCr WAct WHCG	
§ - 'Pseudindica' (ClCh)	EBls MAus	
§ - Sanguinea Group (Ch)	EBls WHCG XPep	
§ - 'Viridiflora' (Ch)	EBls ENot LFol LRHS MAus MBur	
	MMat SMad SPer SSea SWCr WAct	
	WHCG	
'Oeillet Flamand'	see *R.* 'Oeillet Parfait'	
'Oeillet Panaché' (Mo)	WAct	
'Oeillet Parfait' (G)	EBls MAus	
officinalis	see *R. gallica* var. *officinalis*	
'Ohl' (G)	EBls	
'Oklahoma' (HT)	SWCr	
old blush China	see *R.* x *odorata* 'Pallida'	
old cabbage	see *R.* x *centifolia*	
Old John	IDic	
= 'Dicwillynilly'^{PBR} (F)		
old pink moss rose	see *R.* x *centifolia* 'Muscosa'	
Old Port = 'Mackati'^{PBR}	IArd	
(F)		
old red moss	see *R.* 'Henri Martin', *R.* 'Lanei'	
old velvet moss	see *R.* 'William Lobb'	
old yellow Scotch (PiH)	see *R.* x *harisonii* 'Williams'	
	Double Yellow'	
Olde Romeo	SWCr	
= 'Hadromeo' (HT)		
Oliver Twist	MBur	
= 'Sabbyron' (Patio)		
Olympic Palace	ECnt	
= 'Poulymp'^{PBR} (Min)		
'Omar Khayyám' (D)	EBls ENot MAus MRav SWCr	
§ 'Ombrée Parfaite' (G)	EBls	
Open Arms	ENot ESty MAus MMat MRav SPer	
= 'Chewpixcel'^{PBR}	SSea SWCr WGer	
(ClMin) ♀H4		
'Ophelia' (HT)	EBee EBls MAus	
Orange Floorshow	SWCr	
= 'Hargala'^{PBR} (GC)		
'Orange Honey' (Min)	MBur SWCr	
§ 'Orange Sensation' (F)	CTri CWSG EBls ENot MAus MMat	
	MRav NRog	
§ Orange Sunblaze	CSBt EBls ENot MMat MRav SPer	
= 'Meijikatar'^{PBR} (Min)	SSea SWCr	
'Orange Triumph' (Poly)	EBls	
Orangeade (F)	SWCr	
Oranges and Lemons	CGro ECnt ENot ESty GCoc GGre	
= 'Macoranlem'^{PBR}	LGod LStr MAus MBur MMat MRav	
(S/F)	SCoo SSea SWCr WWeb	
'Oriana' (HT)	MBur SWCr	
'Orient Express' (HT)	CWSG	
'Orpheline de Juillet'	see *R.* 'Ombrée Parfaite'	
Othello = 'Auslo'^{PBR} (S)	ESty MAus SPer WAct	
Our George = 'Kirrush'	WGor	
(Patio)		
§ Our Jubilee = 'Coccages'	ESty	
(HT)		
Our Love = 'Andour' (HT)	CWSG GGre SWCr	
Our Molly	IDic SWCr	
= 'Dicreason'^{PBR}		
(GC/S)		
Oxfordshire	ENot LStr MMat MRav NPri SSea	
= 'Korfullwind'^{PBR}	SWCr	
(GC) ♀H4		
Paddy McGredy	CGro NRog SWCr	
= 'Macpa' (F)		
Paddy Stephens	GGre	
= 'Macclack'^{PBR} (HT)		
Painted Moon	ESty IDic	
= 'Dicpaint'^{PBR} (HT)		
Panache = 'Poultop'^{PBR}	ECnt LStr MAsh SWCr	
(Patio)		
'Papa Gontier' (T)	EBls MAus	
'Papa Hémeray' (Ch)	EBls	
Papa Meilland = 'Meisar'	CGro CSBt EBls MAus MBur NRog	
(HT)	SPer SWCr	
Paper Anniversary **new**	SWCr	

'Papillon' (ClT) — EBls
'Pâquerette' (Poly) — EBls
'Parade' (Cl) ♀H4 — MAus MRav SWCr WHCG
Paradise = 'Weizeip' (HT) — SWCr
'Parkdirektor Riggers' (Cl) — CHad CRHN EBls LStr MAus MBri SPer SSea SWCr WHCG
Parks's yellow China — see *R.* x *odorata* 'Ochroleuca'
'Parkzierde' (Bb) — EBls
Parson's pink China — see *R.* x *odorata* 'Pallida'
Partridge — EBls MAus MMat SPer SWCr WAct
  = 'Korweirim'PBR (GC) — WOVN
'Party Girl' (Min) — NBat
Party Trick — IDic MBri
  = 'Dicparty'PBR (F)
parvifolia — see *R.* 'Burgundiaca'
Pas de Deux — ECnt MAsh SWCr
  = 'Poulhult'PBR (Cl)
Pascali = 'Lenip' (HT) — CTri EBls ENot EPfP GCoc GGre GKir MAus MBur MRav NRog SPer SSea SWCr
§ Pat Austin — CSBt ENot ESty LRHS MAus MBNS
  = 'Ausmum'PBR (S) ♀H4 — MBri MMat MRav SWCr
Patricia = 'Korpatri' (F) — SWCr
'Paul Crampel' (Poly) — EBls MAus NRog WAct
'Paul Lédé' (ClT) — see *R.* 'Climbing Paul Lédé'
'Paul Neyron' (HP) — EBls EMFP MAus SPer SWCr WHCG
'Paul Ricault' (CexHP) — EBls MAus
Paul Shirville — ELan ENot ESty GGre MAsh MAus MMat MRav NRog SPer SSea SWCr
  = 'Harqueterwife'PBR (HT) ♀H4
'Paul Transon' (Ra) ♀H4 — CPou CRHN EBee EBls EMFP LRHS MAus MBri MBur SPer SWCr
'Paul Verdier' (Bb) — EBls
'Paula Louise' (F) — NBat
§ 'Paulii' (Ru) — CArn EBls ENot MAus WAct WOVN
'Paulii Alba' — see *R.* 'Paulii'
'Paulii Rosea' (Ru/Cl) — EBls MAus WAct
'Paul's Early Blush' (HP) — EBls
'Paul's Himalayan Musk' (Ra) ♀H3-4 — CHad CRHN CSBt CSam EBee EBls EBre ECnt EMFP ENot EPfP EWTr IArd ISea LRHS LStr MAus MBri MRav MWgw SFam SPer SSea SWCr WAct WBVN WHCG WKif WLow WPic
'Paul's Lemon Pillar' (ClHT) — EBls EBre LRHS MAus MBNS NRog SPer SSea SWCr
'Paul's Perpetual White' (Ra) — EBee EBls EWTr WHCG
'Paul's Scarlet Climber' (Cl/Ra) — CGro CSBt EBls ECnt ELan ENot EPfP GGre GKir LGod LRHS LStr MAsh MAus MRav NBPC NPri SPer SSea SWCr WWeb
Paws = 'Beapaw' (S) — EBls
'Pax' (HM) — CPou EBee EBls EMFP MAus SWCr WHCG WKif
Peace = 'Madame A. Meilland' (HT) ♀H4 — CGro CSBt EBls ECnt ELan EPfP ESty GCoc GGre GKir LAst LGod LStr MAsh MAus MBri MBur MMat MRav NRog SPer SSea SWCr WWeb
Peace Sunblaze (Min) — see *R.* Lady Meillandina
Peacekeeper — CSBt GGre MAsh MRav SWCr
  = 'Harbella'PBR (F)
Peach Blossom — LRHS MAus SWCr
  = 'Ausblossom'PBR (S)
'Peach Dream' (Patio) — ESty
§ Peach Sunblaze — SWCr
  = 'Meixerul'PBR (Min)
Peach Surprise — ECnt
  = 'Poulrise'PBR (HT) **new**

§ Pearl Anniversary — GCoc GGre LStr MBri MRav SWCr
  = 'Whitston'PBR (Min/Patio)
Pearl Drift = 'Leggab' (S) — EBls MAus SPer SWCr WHCG
Pearly King — SWCr
  = 'Gendee'PBR (S) **new**
§ Peek-a-boo — ENot IDic SPer SWCr
  = 'Dicgrow'PBR (Min/Patio)
§ Peer Gynt = 'Korol' (HT) — ENot SWCr
Pegasus = 'Ausmoon'PBR (S) — LRHS LStr MAus MWgw SSea SWCr
'Pélisson' (CeMo) — EBls
§ *pendulina* — EBls GIBF MAus WHCG
  - 'Nana' — NHol
'Penelope' (HM) ♀H4 — More than 30 suppliers
'Penelope Plummer' (F) — EBls
Penny Lane — CGro CSBt ECnt ENot EPfP GCoc GGre LAst
  = 'Hardwell'PBR (Cl) ♀H4 — LGod LRHS LStr MAsh MAus MBri MBur MMat MRav MWgw NBat NBlu NPri SCoo SPer SSea SWCr WWeb
Pensioner's Voice — SWCr
  = 'Fryrelax'PBR (F)
x *penzanceana* — see *R.* 'Lady Penzance'
Perception — NBat
  = 'Harzippee'PBR (HT)
Perdita = 'Ausperd' (S) — LRHS MAus MRav SPer SWCr
§ Perestroika — ENot LStr MMat
  = 'Korhitom'PBR (F/Min)
Perfect Day = 'Poulrem' (F) — ECnt
§ Perfecta = 'Koralu' (HT) — EBls SWCr
'Perle des Jardins' (T) — EBls ENot MAus
'Perle des Panachées' (G) — EBls
§ 'Perle d'Or' (Poly) ♀H4 — CHad ECnt EMFP ENot EPfP GCoc LRHS MAus MMat NRog SChu SMad SPer SWCr WAct WHCG
'Perle von Hohenstein' (Poly) — EBls
'Pernille Poulsen' (F) — EBls
Perpetually Yours — CGro GCoc LGod LStr MAsh MRav SCoo SWCr
  = 'Harfable'PBR (Cl)
Persian yellow — see *R. foetida* 'Persiana'
Peter Beales — EBls
  = 'Cleexpert' (S)
Peter Pan — MAsh MAus SSea SWCr
  = 'Chewpan'PBR (Min)
Peter Pan — WWeb
  = 'Sunpete' (Patio)
'Petite de Hollande' (Ce) — EBls EMFP MAus SWCr WAct WHCG
Petite Folie = 'Meiherode' (Min) — SWCr
'Petite Lisette' (CexD) — EBls MAus WHCG
'Petite Orléannaise' (Ce) — EBls
Phab Gold — GCoc
  = 'Frybountiful'PBR (F)
§ Phantom = 'Maccatsan' (S/GC) — MBur
'Pharisäer' (HT) — EBls
§ Pheasant = 'Kordapt'PBR (GC) — ENot GCoc MAus MMat SPer SWCr WAct WHCG WOVN
Phillipa = 'Poulheart'PBR (S) — ECnt SWCr
Phoebe (Ru) — see *Rosa* 'Fimbriata'
phoenicia — EBls
'Phyllis Bide' (Ra) ♀H4 — CAbP CSam EBee EBls EMFP EPfP EWTr IArd LRHS LStr MAus SPer SSea SWCr WGer WHCG WLow
Picasso = 'Macpic' (F) — EBls

Piccadilly = 'Macar' (HT)	CGro CSBt CTri EBls ENot GGre GKir MMat MRav NBlu NRog SPer SSea SWCr
Piccolo = 'Tanolokip'^{PBR} (F/Patio)	ESty LStr MBri MRav SSea SWCr
Pickwick = 'Sabclive' (Patio)	MBur
'Picture' (HT)	EBls NRog SPer
'Pierre Notting' (HP)	EBls
Pigalle '84 = 'Meicloux' (F)	SWCr
'Pilgrim'^{PBR}	see *Rosa* The Pilgrim
§ *pimpinellifolia*	CDul EBls ECha ENot EWTr LBuc MAus MMat NWea SPer SSea SWCr WAct WBWf WHCG WOVN
- 'Altaica'	see *R. pimpinellifolia* 'Grandiflora'
§ - 'Andrewsii' ♀^{H4}	MAus MRav WAct
§ - double pink	EBls
§ - double white	CNat EBls GCoc IGor MAus SWCr WAct WBcn
- double yellow	see *R. x harisonii* 'Williams' Double Yellow'
§ - 'Dunwich Rose'	EBee EBls ENot EPfP LRHS MAus MBri MMat SPer SWCr WAct WHCG
- 'Falkland'	EBls ECha MAus
§ - 'Glory of Edzell'	EBls MAus
§ - 'Grandiflora'	EBls MAus SWCr
- - SF 18	ISea
- 'Harisonii'	see *R. x harisonii* 'Harison's Yellow'
- 'Irish Marbled'	EBls
- 'Lutea'	see *R. x harisonii* 'Lutea Maxima'
- 'Marbled Pink'	EBls MAus
- 'Mary, Queen of Scots'	EBls MAus SRms SWCr WAct
- 'Mrs Colville'	EBls MAus
- 'Ormiston Roy'	MAus
§ - 'Robbie'	WAct
- 'Single Cherry'	EBls MAus SSea
- 'Stanwell Perpetual'	see *R.* 'Stanwell Perpetual'
- 'Variegata' (v)	CArn
- 'William III'	EBls EWes MAus SLPl
Pink Abundance = 'Harfrothy'^{PBR} (F)	GGre MAsh SWCr
Pink Bells = 'Poulbells'^{PBR} (GC)	CGro EBls ENot GCoc MAus MMat SPer WHCG
'Pink Bouquet' (Ra)	CRHN
'Pink Drift = 'Poulcat'^{PBR} (Min/GC)	ENot
'Pink Favorite' (HT)	CSBt NRog SPer SWCr
Pink Fizz	SWCr
§ Pink Flower Carpet = 'Noatraum'^{PBR} (GC) ♀^{H4}	CSBt CTri EBre ELan ENot EPfP GCoc GGre GKir LRHS LStr MAsh MAus MMat MRav SCoo SPer SSea SWCr WWeb
'Pink Garnette'	see *R.* 'Carol Amling'
'Pink Grootendorst' (Ru) ♀^{H4}	EBls ENot EPfP LRHS LStr MAus NRog SPer SSea SWCr WAct WHCG
§ Pink Hit = 'Poutipe'^{PBR} (Min/Patio)	ECnt ENot MAsh MMat SWCr
Pink La Sevillana = 'Meigeroka'^{PBR} (F/GC)	SWCr
pink moss	see *R. x centifolia* 'Muscosa'
'Pink Parfait' (F)	EBls GGre MAus MBur NRog SMad SPer SSea SWCr
Pink Peace = 'Meibil' (HT)	ESty GGre MRav SWCr
Pink Pearl = 'Kormasyl' (HT)	ENot MRav
'Pink Perpétué' (Cl)	CGro CSBt CTri EBls EBre ECnt ELan ENot EPfP GCoc GGre GKir LAst LRHS MAsh MAus MBri MBur

	MMat MRav NBat NBlu NRog SPer SSea SWCr WWeb
'Pink Petticoat' (Min)	SWCr
Pink Pirouette = 'Harboul'^{PBR} (Patio)	ESty
'Pink Prosperity' (HM)	EBls MAus
'Pink Showers' (ClHT)	WAct
§ Pink Sunblaze = 'Meijidiro' (Min/Patio)	SWCr
Pink Surprise = 'Lenbrac' (Ru)	MAus
Pinocchio = 'Rosenmärchen' (F)	EBls
'Pinta' (HT)	EBls
pisocarpa	EBls
Playtime = 'Morplati' (F)	ENot MAus MRav
Pleine de Grâce = 'Lengra' (S)	EBls LRHS MAus WAct
'Plentiful' (F)	EBls MBri
Poetry in Motion = 'Harelan'^{PBR} (HT)	ESty GGre MBri NBat SWCr
Polar Star = 'Tanlarpost'^{PBR} (HT)	CSBt EBls ECnt ENot GGre LGod LStr MRav NRog SPer SWCr
x *polliniana*	SLPl
'Polly' (HT)	EBls NRog
polyantha grandiflora	see *R. gentiliana*
pomifera	see *R. villosa*
- 'Duplex'	see *R.* 'Wolley-Dod'
'Pompon Blanc Parfait' (A)	EBls MAus
'Pompon de Bourgogne'	see *R.* 'Burgundiaca'
'Pompon de Paris' (ClMinCh)	see *R.* 'Climbing Pompon de Paris'
§ 'Pompon de Paris' (MinCh)	EBls
'Pompon Panaché' (G)	EBls MAus
Portland rose	see *R.* 'Portlandica'
§ 'Portlandica'	EBls LRHS MAsh MAus SPer SSea SWCr WAct WHCG
Portmeirion = 'Ausguard'^{PBR} (S)	MAus SCoo SWCr
Pot o' Gold = 'Dicdivine'^{PBR} (HT)	IDic MAus MRav SPer SWCr
Pour Toi = 'Para Ti' (Min)	ENot MAus MMat MRav NPri SPer SWCr
Powder Puff (F)	SWCr
prairie rose	see *R. setigera*
Precious Moments = 'Lyopr'	GGre SWCr
'Precious Platinum' (HT)	LGod MRav SPer SWCr
Preservation = 'Bosiljurika'^{PBR} (S/F)	GGre SWCr
'Président de Sèze' (G) ♀^{H4}	EBls MAus SFam SPer SWCr WAct WHCG
President Heidar Aliyev = 'Cocosimber'^{PBR} (HT)	GCoc SWCr
'President Herbert Hoover' (HT)	EBls
'Prestige' (S)	NRog
Pretty in Pink = 'Dicumpteen'^{PBR} (GC)	ECnt IDic SWCr
Pretty Jessica = 'Ausjess' (S)	CTri GKir LRHS MAus MRav SPer
Pretty Lady = 'Scrivo'^{PBR} (F) ♀^{H4}	LStr MAus SWCr
Pretty Polly = 'Meitonje'^{PBR} (Min) ♀^{H4}	CGro CTri EPfP ESty GGre GKir LStr MAsh MBri MMat MRav SPoG SWCr WWeb
Pride of England = 'Harencore'^{PBR} (HT)	GCoc GGre MAsh MBur SWCr
'Prima Ballerina' (HT)	CGro CSBt CTri CWSG EBls ENot GCoc GGre GKir LAst LStr MAsh MMat MRav NBlu NRog SPer SSea SWCr

primula (S) ♀H3-4 — EBls EMFP ENot EWTr MAus SPer SSea SWCr WAct WHCG

'Prince Camille de Rohan' (HP) — EBls MAus WHCG

'Prince Charles' (Bb) — EBls MAus SWCr WHCG

Prince Palace = 'Poulzin'PBR (F) — ECnt MAsh

Prince Regent = 'Genpen' (S) — SSea

Princess Alexandra = 'Pouldra'PBR (S) — CTri ECnt MAsh SWCr

Princess Alice = 'Hartanna' (F) — LGod SWCr

Princess Nobuko = 'Coclistine' (HT) — GCoc

'Princess of Wales' (HP) — MMat

Princess of Wales = 'Hardinkum'PBR (F) ♀H4 — CGro CSBt EBee ECnt ENot GCoc GGre LStr MAsh MBri MBur MRav NPri SCoo SPer SWCr WWeb

Princess Royal = 'Dicroyal'PBR (HT) — GCoc IDic MBri

§ 'Princesse de Nassau' (Ra) — EBls MAus WAct WHCG

'Princesse Louise' (Ra) — CRHN MAus SFam

'Princesse Marie' misapplied — see *R.* 'Belvedere'

§ 'Pristine'PBR (HT) — IDic MAus SPer

N 'Professeur Emile Perrot' (D) — EBls SWCr WAct

'Prolifera de Redouté' misapplied — see *R.* 'Duchesse de Montebello'

'Prosperity' (HM) ♀H4 — CBcs CTri EBee EBls EMFP ENot EPfP GCoc LRHS MAus MMat MRav MWgw NRog SPer SWCr WAct WHCG WOVN

Prospero = 'Auspero' (S) — EBee MAus MBri WAct

x *pruhoniciana* 'Hillieri' — see *R.* 'Hillieri'

pulverulenta — EBls

Pure Bliss = 'Dictator'PBR (HT) — ECnt GCoc IDic

Pure Magic = 'Mattgrex' (Patio) — MAsh SWCr

'Purity' (Cl) — SWCr

'Purple Beauty' (HT) — MBur SWCr

Purple Tiger = 'Jacpurr'PBR (F) — ESty IDic SWCr

'Purpurtraum' (Ru) — WHCG

Pzazz = 'Poulzazz'PBR (Min/Patio) — ECnt

Quaker Star = 'Dicperhaps' (F) — IDic

quatre saisons — see *R.* x *damascena* var. *semperflorens*

'Quatre Saisons Blanche Mousseuse' (DMo) — EBls

Queen Elizabeth — see *R.* 'The Queen Elizabeth'

Queen Margarethe = 'Poulskov'PBR (F) — ECnt

Queen Mother = 'Korquemu'PBR (Patio) ♀H4 — CSBt EBls ELan ENot EPfP GCoc GGre LGod LRHS LStr MAsh MAus MBri MMat MRav NPri SPer SSea SWCr WWeb

'Queen of Bedders' (Bb) — EBls

Queen of Denmark — see *R.* 'Königin von Dänemark'

Queen of Hearts = 'Harford'PBR (S) **new** — MAsh

Queen of the Belgians — see *R.* 'Reine des Belges'

Queen's Palace = 'Poulelap'PBR (F) — ECnt

'Rachel' ambig. **new** — GCoc

Rachel = 'Tangust'PBR (HT) **new** — ESty SWCr

Racy Lady = 'Dicwaffle'PBR (HT) — IDic NBat

Radio Times = 'Aussal'PBR (S) — ESty MAus SWCr

Rainbow Magic = 'Dicxplosion'PBR (Patio) — ESty IDic SWCr

'Ralph Tizzard' (F) — SSea

'Rambling Rector' (Ra) ♀H4 — More than 30 suppliers

§ 'Ramona' (Ra) — EBls MAus

§ 'Raubritter' ('Macrantha' hybrid) — CAbP EBls MAus SPer SSea SWCr WAct WHCG

Ray of Hope = 'Cocnilly'PBR (F) — GCoc LGod MAsh SWCr

Ray of Sunshine = 'Cocclare'PBR (Patio) — GCoc MBri

'Raymond Carver' (S) — EBls

'Raymond Chenault' (Cl) — SWCr

Real Hit = 'Poulra007'PBR (Patio) **new** — ECnt

Rebecca (Patio) **new** — ESty

'Rebecca Claire' (HT) — SWCr

'Rebecca Kathleen' (F) — NBat

Reconciliation = 'Hartillery'PBR (HT) — ESty SWCr

§ Red Bells = 'Poulred'PBR (Min/GC) — CGro EBls ENot MAus MMat MRav SPer WHCG WOVN

Red Blanket = 'Intercell'PBR (S/GC) — CGro EBls ENot GCoc IDic MAus MRav SPer SWCr WAct WOVN

§ Red Coat = 'Auscoat' (F) — MAus

Red Dagmar = 'Speruge'PBR (S) — IDic

Red Devil = 'Dicam' (HT) — GGre MRav NBat NRog SWCr

'Red Grootendorst' — see *R.* 'F.J. Grootendorst'

Red Haze = 'Tanzahde'PBR (GC) **new** — SWCr

Red Meidiland = 'Meineble'PBR (GC) — CBrm SWCr

red moss — see *R.* 'Henri Martin'

Red New Dawn — see *R.* 'Etendard'

Red Rascal = 'Jacbed'PBR (S/Patio) — CSBt ECnt IDic SWCr

red rose of Lancaster — see *R. gallica* var. *officinalis*

Red Splendour = 'Davona' (F) — NRog

§ Red Sunblaze = 'Meirutral'PBR (Min) — SWCr WWeb

Red Trail = 'Interim'PBR (S/GC) — ESty

§ 'Red Wing' (S) — EBls MAus

§ Redgold = 'Dicor' (F) — GGre SWCr

Redouté = 'Auspale'PBR (S) — CAbP LRHS MAus SPer SWCr

Regensberg = 'Macyoumis'PBR (F/Patio) — ENot MAus MBri MRav NRog SPer SSea SWCr

§ 'Reine des Belges' (Cl) — EBls

'Reine des Centifeuilles' (Ce) — EBls SFam

'Reine des Violettes' (HP) — CHad CPou EBls EPfP EWTr IArd LGod LRHS LStr MAus MRav SChu SPer SWCr WAct WHCG

'Reine Marie Henriette' (ClHT) — EBls

'Reine Olga de Wurtenburg' (N) — EBls

§ 'Reine Victoria' (Bb) — EBee EBls EMFP EPfP LRHS LStr MAus MRav SPer SPla SWCr WAct

Remember Me = 'Cocdestin'PBR (HT) ♀H4 — CWSG EBls EBre ECnt ENot EPfP ESty GCoc GGre IArd LGod LStr MAsh MAus MBri MMat MRav NBat NRog SPer SSea SWCr WWeb

Remembrance	CTri ESty LGod LStr MAsh MRav	
= 'Harxampton'[PBR]	SPer SPoG SSea SWCr WWeb	
(F) ♀H4		
Renaissance	CSBt ESty GCoc GGre LStr MBur	
= 'Harzart'[PBR] (HT)	MRav SSea SWCr	
'René André' (Ra)	CRHN EBls EMFP MAus	
'René d'Anjou' (CeMo)	EBls MAus	
'Rescht'	see *R.* 'De Rescht'	
Rest in Peace	GGre SWCr	
= 'Bedswap' (Patio/F)		
'Rêve d'Or' (N)	CSam EBls MAus SPer SWCr	
	WHCG	
'Réveil Dijonnais' (ClHT)	EBls MAus	
'Reverend F. Page-Roberts'	EBls	
(HT)		
Rhapsody in Blue	CGro CSBt CTri ECnt ESty GGre	
= 'Frantasia' (S)	LGod LRHS MAsh MAus MBri	
	SCoo SWCr	
Richard Buckley	MBur	
= 'Smitshort' (F)		
§ x *richardii*	EBls MAus MRav SWCr WAct	
	WHCG	
Ring of Fire = 'Morefire'	MAsh SWCr	
(Patio)		
§ 'Rise 'n Shine' (Min)	LGod	
'Rival de Paestum' (T)	EBls MAus	
'River Gardens'	NPer	
'Rivers George IV' (S) **new**	EBls	
Road to Freedom	SWCr	
= 'Franlac' (F)		
Rob Roy = 'Cocrob' (F)	GCoc MBur SPer SWCr	
Robbie Burns	MAus SWCr	
= 'Ausburn' (PiH)		
'Robert le Diable' (Ce)	CPou EBee EBls MAus SPer SWCr	
	WAct WHCG	
'Robert Léopold' (Mo)	EBls	
'Robin Hood' (HM)	EBls SWCr	
Robin Redbreast	EBls IDic SWCr WGor	
= 'Interrob'[PBR]		
(Min/GC)		
§ Robusta = 'Korgosa' (Ru)	EBls ECnt MAus SSea SWCr	
'Roger Lambelin' (HP)	EBls ENot MAus	
Romance	MRav WWeb	
= 'Tanezamor'[PBR] (S)		
§ Romantic Hedgerose	ENot	
= 'Korworm' (F/S)		
Romantic Palace	ECnt MAsh	
= 'Poulmanti'[PBR] (F)		
§ Rosabell	ESty GCoc	
= 'Cocceleste'[PBR]		
(F/Patio)		
Rosalie Coral	ESty	
= 'Chewallop'[PBR]		
(ClMin)		
§ Rose 2000	GKir	
= 'Cocquetrum'[PBR] (F)		
'Rose à Parfum de l'Haÿ'	EBls	
(Ru)		
'Rose Ball' **new**	EBls	
§ 'Rose d'Amour' (S) ♀H4	CFee EBls ISea MAus WHCG	
'Rose de Meaux'	see *R.* 'De Meaux'	
'Rose de Meaux White'	see *R.* 'White de Meaux'	
'Rose de Rescht'	see *R.* 'De Rescht'	
'Rose des Maures'	see *R.* 'Sissinghurst Castle'	
misapplied		
'Rose d'Hivers' (D)	EBls	
'Rose d'Orsay' (S)	EBls	
'Rose du Maître d'Ecole'	see *R.* 'Du Maître d'Ecole'	
'Rose du Roi' (HP/DPo)	EBls MAus SWCr WAct WHCG	
'Rose du Roi à Fleurs	EBls MAus	
Pourpres' (HP)		
'Rose Edouard' (Bb)	EBls	
§ Rose Gaujard	EBls ENot GGre GKir LGod MAsh	
= 'Gaumo' (HT)	MBur MRav SWCr	

Rose Pearl	MMat	
= 'Korterschi'[PBR] **new**		
§ Roselina = 'Korsaku'[PBR]	ENot MMat	
(GC/Ru)		
§ 'Rose-Marie Viaud' (Ra)	CFee CPou CSam EBee MAus	
	SWCr WHCG	
'Rosemary Foster'	SSpi	
Rosemary Harkness	ESty LStr MRav SPer SWCr	
= 'Harrowbond'[PBR] (HT)		
'Rosemary Rose' (F)	EBls NRog SPer	
Rosenprofessor	see *R.* The Halcyon Days Rose	
'Roseraie de l'Haÿ' (Ru)	More than 30 suppliers	
♀H4		
'Rosette Delizy' (T)	EBls	
'Rosy Cheeks' (HT)	MBur SWCr	
Rosy Cushion	ENot IDic MAus MRav SPer SWCr	
= 'Interall'[PBR]	WAct WHCG WOVN	
(S/GC) ♀H4		
Rosy Future	CSBt ESty SWCr	
= 'Harwaderox'[PBR]		
(F/Patio)		
'Rosy Mantle' (Cl)	CBcs CSBt SPer SWCr	
§ Rote Max Graf	EBls ENot MMat MRav WAct	
= 'Kormax'[PBR] (GC/Ru)		
'Roundelay' (HT)	EBls MAus SWCr	
§ Roxburghe Rose	GCoc	
= 'Cocember' (HT)		
roxburghii (S)	CArn LEdu MBri SWCr WAct WHCG	
- f. *normalis* (S)	CFee EBls ISea	
- 'Plena'	see *R. roxburghii* f. *roxburghii*	
§ - f. *roxburghii* (d/S)	MAus	
'Royal Albert Hall' (HT)	EBls GCoc	
Royal Copenhagen	ECnt	
= 'Poulht001' (HT) **new**		
Royal Flush = 'Peapatio'	SWCr	
(F/Patio)		
'Royal Gold' (ClHT)	EBls ENot LAst MBri NRog SSea	
	SWCr WStI	
'Royal Highness' (HT)	EBls NRog SWCr	
'Royal Occasion' (F)	MRav SPer SWCr	
Royal Philharmonic	MBur	
= 'Hardeed'[PBR] (HT)		
Royal Salute = 'Macros'	ENot MMat MRav NRog	
(Min)		
'Royal Smile' (HT)	EBls	
Royal William	CSBt ECnt ELan ENot ESty GGre	
= 'Korzaun'[PBR]	GKir LGod LStr MAsh MAus MBri	
(HT) ♀H4	MBur MMat MRav NPri NRog SPer	
	SWCr WWeb	
Royal Worcester	SWCr	
= 'Trobroy'[PBR] (S)		
'Rubens' (HP)	EBls	
§ *rubiginosa*	CArn CCVT CDul CGro CRWN	
	EBls ENot EPfP GPoy IFro ILis	
	LBuc MAus MHer MMat MRav	
	SFam SPer SWCr WAct WMou	
rubra	see *R. gallica*	
rubrifolia	see *R. glauca*	
- 'Carmenetta'	see *R.* 'Carmenetta'	
'Rubrotincta'	see *R.* 'Hebe's Lip'	
rubus (Ra)	MAus MBNS	
- SF 96062	ISea	
- *velutescens*	WAct	
Ruby Anniversary	CGro CSBt CWSG ESty LStr MAsh	
= 'Harbonny'[PBR]	MRav SSea SWCr WWeb	
(Patio)		
Ruby Celebration	CWSG ESty SWCr	
= 'Peawinner'[PBR] (F)		
'Ruby Wedding' (HT)	More than 30 suppliers	
'Ruga' (Ra)	EBls	
rugosa (Ru)	CAgr CDul CLnd CTri EBee ENot	
	EPfP GKir LBuc MAus MBri MHer	
	MRav NBlu NWea SKee SPlb SWCr	
	WBVN WStI	

– 'Alba' (Ru) ♀H4	CBcs CCVT CDul EBee EBls ECGP ECnt ELan ENot EPfP EWTr GBin GGre LBuc LRHS LStr MAus MBri MMat MRav NWea SKee SPer SSea SWCr WAct WHen WOVN	
– 'Rubra' (Ru) ♀H4	CBcs CCVT CTri CWib ENot EPfP GGre LBuc MMat SPer WAct WHen	
– 'Scabrosa'	see *R.* 'Scabrosa'	
'Rugosa Atropurpurea' (Ru)	NRog	
'Rugspin' (Ru)	SWCr WAct	
'Ruhm von Steinfurth' (HP)	EBls	
'Rumba' (F)	SWCr	
Running Maid = 'Lenramp' (S/GC)	MAus	
Rush = 'Lenmobri' (S)	MAus	
Rushing Stream = 'Austream'PBR (GC)	MAus MBNS SWCr	
'Ruskin' (HPxRu)	EBls MAus SWCr	
'Russelliana' (Ra)	CRHN EBee EBls MAus SFam SSea WAct WHCG WRha	
Rutland = 'Poulshine'PBR (Min/GC)	ENot SWCr	
'Sadler's Wells' (S)	EBls	
'Safrano' (T)	EBls	
Saint Boniface = 'Kormatt'PBR (F/Patio)	CSBt ENot	
'Saint Catherine' (Ra)	CFee	
Saint Cecilia = 'Ausmit'PBR (S)	LRHS MAus MWgw SWCr	
'Saint Ethelberger' (S) **new**	EBls	
Saint John = 'Harbilbo'PBR (F)	CSBt MRav SWCr	
Saint John's rose	see *R.* x *richardii*	
Saint Mark's rose	see *R.* 'Rose d'Amour'	
'Saint Nicholas' (D)	CAbP EBls MAus	
'Saint Prist de Breuze' (Ch)	EBls	
Saint Swithun = 'Auswith'PBR (S)	GQui LRHS MAus SWCr	
'Salet' (DPMo)	EBls MAus WHCG	
'Sally Holmes'PBR (S) ♀H4	CHad EBls ENot GCoc MAus MBri MMat MRav MWgw SPer SWCr WAct WHCG	
Sally's Rose = 'Canrem' (HT)	EBee ECnt SWCr	
Salmo = 'Poulnoev'PBR (Patio)	ENot MBri MMat MRav	
Salsa = 'Poulslas' (Cl) **new**	ECnt	
§ Samaritan = 'Harverag'PBR (HT)	CSBt ESty GGre MAsh MRav SWCr	
sancta	see *R.* x *richardii*	
'Sander's White Rambler'[4] (Ra) ♀H	CRHN CSam CTri EBee EBls EMFP EPfP ESty LRHS MAus MRav NPri NRog SMad SPer SSea SWCr WAct WHCG WWeb	
'Sandringham Centenary'PBR (HT)	EBls	
'Sanguinea'	see *R.* x *odorata* Sanguinea Group	
'Sarah van Fleet' (Ru)	CGro CTri EBls ENot EPfP GCoc IArd LBuc LRHS LStr MAsh MAus MRav NRog SFam SPer SPla SWCr WAct WOVN	
Savoy Hotel = 'Harvintage'PBR (HT) ♀H4	CGro CSBt ECnt EPfP GGre LGod LStr MAus MRav SPer SPoG SWCr	
§ 'Scabrosa' (Ru) ♀H4	EBee EBls ECnt EMFP GCoc LRHS MAsh MAus SPer SSea SWCr WAct WHCG WOVN	
Scarlet Fire	see *R.* 'Scharlachglut'	
Scarlet Glow	see *R.* 'Scharlachglut'	

Scarlet Meidiland = 'Meikrotal'PBR (S/GC)	SWCr	
Scarlet Patio = 'Kortingle'PBR (Patio)	ENot MAsh MMat	
Scarlet Queen Elizabeth = 'Dicel' (F)	CBcs EBls GGre MBur MRav SWCr WStI	
'Scarlet Showers' (Cl)	SWCr	
'Scented Air' (F)	SPer	
Scentimental = 'Wekplapep'PBR (F)	MAsh MBri SCoo SWCr	
§ Scent-sation = 'Fryromeo'PBR (HT)	CWSG ESty GCoc MAsh MRav SCoo SWCr	
Scepter'd Isle = 'Ausland'PBR (S) ♀H4	CAbP CSBt ENot LRHS MAsh MAus MBri MMat NPri SCoo SPer SWCr	
§ 'Scharlachglut' (Cl/S) ♀H4	CPou EBls ENot LRHS MAus MBri MMat MRav SPer SWCr WAct WHCG WOVN	
* *schmidtiana*	CFee	
'Schneelicht' (Ru)	EBls MAus	
§ 'Schneezwerg' (Ru) ♀H4	EBls ENot GCoc MAus MBri MRav SPer SPla SSea SWCr WAct WHCG WOVN	
'Schoolgirl' (Cl)	CBcs CGro CSBt CTri EBls EBre ELan ENot EPfP ESty GGre GKir LAst LStr MAsh MBri MMat MRav NBlu NRog SPer SSea SWCr WWeb	
'Scintillation' (S/GC)	EBls MAus	
Scotch rose	see *R. pimpinellifolia*	
Scotch yellow (PiH)	see *R.* x *harisonii* 'Williams' Double Yellow'	
Scottish Special = 'Cocdapple' (Min/Patio)	MBri	
'Sea Pearl' (F)	ENot MRav SWCr	
'Seagull' (Ra) ♀H4	CGro CTri CWSG EBee EBls ECnt EMFP ESty EWTr GGre LGod LRHS LStr MAsh MRav NPri NRog NWea SMad SPer SPla SSea SWCr WHCG	
§ 'Sealing Wax' (*moyesii* hybrid)	EBls LRHS MBri WAct	
Selfridges = 'Korpriwa' (HT)	NBat NRog	
'Semiplena'	see *R.* x *alba* 'Alba Semiplena'	
sempervirens (Ra)	XPep	
'Sénateur Amic' (Cl)	EBls	
sericea (S)	CFee ITer MAus WHCG	
– CC 3306	WRos	
– CC 3926	WCot	
– SF 505	ISea	
– SF 95049	ISea	
– 'Heather Muir'	see *R.* 'Heather Muir' (*sericea* hybrid)	
* – var. *morrisonensis* B&SWJ 7139	WCru	
§ – subsp. *omeiensis* BWJ 7550 **new**	WCru	
– – f. *pteracantha* (S)	EBee EBls ELan ENot EPfP EWTr GGar MAus MMat MRav NRog NWea SMad SPer SSea SWCr WAct WOVN	
– – – 'Atrosanguinea' (S)	CArn	
– 'Red Wing'	see *R.* 'Red Wing'	
sertata	GIBF	
§ *setigera*	EBls GIBF MAus	
setipoda	EBls MAus SWCr WAct WFar WHCG	
seven sisters rose	see *R. multiflora* 'Grevillei'	
Sexy Rexy = 'Macrexy'PBR (F) ♀H4	CGro EBre EPfP ESty GCoc GGre GKir LStr MAsh MAus MBri MRav NBat NRog SPer SSea SWCr WWeb	
§ 'Shailer's White Moss' (CeMo)	EBee EBls LRHS MAus NRog SFam SWCr WHCG	
Sharifa Asma = 'Ausreef'PBR (S)	CSBt ELan ENot LRHS LStr MAus MBNS MMat MRav SPer SWCr WAct	

'Sheelagh Baird' (S/Poly)   SWCr

Sheila's Perfume   ECnt ESty GCoc GGre LStr MAsh
= 'Harsherry'PBR (HT/F)   MRav SPer SWCr

'Shepherd's Delight' (F)   SWCr

sherardii   WBWf

Shine On = 'Dictalent'PBR   CSBt ECnt ESty GGre IDic MAsh
(Patio) ♥H4   MBri MRav SPoG SWCr WWeb

Shining Flare = 'Hadflare'   SWCr
(HT)

Shining Light   GCoc MAsh SCoo SWCr
= 'Cocshimmer'PBR
(Patio)

Shining Ruby = 'Hadruby'   SWCr
(HT)

Shirley Spain   GCoc
= 'Cocharod' (F)

Shocking Blue   CSBt ECnt ENot MAus MMat MRav
= 'Korblue'PBR (F)   SPer SWCr

Shona = 'Dicdrum' (F)   IDic

Short 'n' Sweet   GGre
= 'Tinshort' (Min)

'Shot Silk' (HT)   CSBt EBee EBls MBur SWCr

Shrimp Hit   MAsh SWCr
= 'Poulshrimp'PBR
(Patio) **new**

'Shropshire Lass' (S)   LRHS MAus MBri SPer WLow

Sightsaver = 'Fryaffair'PBR   ESty
(HT)

§ Silver Anniversary   CGro CSBt CTri EBee ECnt ELan
= 'Poulari'PBR   ENot EPfP GCoc GGre GKir LAst
(HT) ♥H4   LGod LRHS LStr MAsh MAus MBri
    MMat MRav NPri SCoo SPer SSea
    SWCr WWeb

'Silver Jubilee' (HT) ♥H4   CBcs CGro CSBt EBee EBls EBre
    ECnt ENot EPfP ESty GCoc GGre
    IArd LGod LRHS LStr MAsh MAus
    MBur MBur MMat MRav NBat NBlu
    NRog SPer SSea SWCr WWeb

'Silver Lining' (HT)   EBls MBur SWCr

'Silver Moon' (Cl)   CRHN EBls

'Silver Wedding' (HT)   CGro CSBt CWSG EBls EBre ESty
    GCoc GGre IArd LAst LRHS MAus
    MBur MRav NRog SPer SWCr

Silver Wedding   CTri ESty GGre SWCr
Celebration (F)

§ Simba = 'Korbelma'PBR   ENot MMat
(HT)

Simon Robinson   SWCr
= 'Trobwich'PBR
(Min/GC)

Simply Heaven   EBee ESty GCoc IDic SWCr
= 'Diczombie'PBR (HT)

§ Simply Sunblaze   SWCr
= 'Meidipser' (Min)

§ Simply the Best   CGro CSBt ECnt ESty GCoc GGre
= 'Macamster'PBR (HT)   LGod LRHS LStr MAsh MBri MMat
    SCoo SPer SWCr WWeb

§ Singin' in the Rain   SWCr
= 'Macivy'PBR (F)

sinowilsonii   see *R. longicuspis* var. *sinowilsonii*

'Sir Cedric Morris' (Ra)   CRHN EBls SSea

Sir Clough = 'Ausclough'   MAus
(S)

Sir Edward Elgar   EBls LStr MAus MRav
= 'Ausprima'PBR (S)

'Sir Frederick Ashton'   EBls
(HT)

'Sir Joseph Paxton' (Bb)   CAbP MAus

Sir Neville Marriner   NBat
= 'Glanmusic' (F)

§ Sir Walter Raleigh   MAus MBri MRav SWCr
= 'Ausspry' (S)

Sir William Leech   NBat
= 'Hortropic' (HT)

§ 'Sissinghurst Castle' (G)   EBls

Smarty = 'Intersmart'PBR   CAbP IDic MAus MRav SPer SWCr
(S/GC)   WAct

Smooth Angel PBR (HT)   LGod

Smooth Lady = 'Hadlady'   LGod
(HT)

Smooth Prince   LGod
= 'Hadprince'PBR (HT)

§ 'Smooth Velvet'PBR (HT)   LGod SPer

Snow Carpet   EBls ENot ETow GCoc MAus
    WAct
= 'Maccarpe'PBR
(Min/GC)

'Snow Dwarf'   see *R.* 'Schneezwerg'

Snow Goose   CSBt MAus
= 'Auspom'PBR (Cl/S)

Snow Hit   ECnt SWCr
= 'Poulsnows'PBR
(Min/Patio)

'Snow Queen'   see *R.* 'Frau Karl Druschki'

§ Snow Sunblaze   CSBt MRav SPer SWCr
= 'Meigovin'PBR (Min)

Snowcap = 'Harfleet'PBR   ESty GGre
(Patio)

'Snowdon' (Ru)   EBls MAus

'Snowdrift' **new**   WHCG

'Snowflake' (Ra)   WHCG

'Soldier Boy' (Cl)   SWCr WHCG

§ Solitaire = 'Macyefre'PBR   MBri
(HT)

Solo Mio = 'Poulen002'PBR   CTri ECnt MAsh SWCr
(S)

§ 'Sombreuil' (ClT)   CHad EBee EBls EMFP EPfP IArd
    LRHS MAus MRav NBPC SChu
    SFam SPer SPla SWCr WAct WHCG
    WLow

Someday Soon   NBat
= 'Seasoon' (Min)

Something Special   ECnt GCoc SWCr
= 'Macwyo'PBR (HT)

'Sophie's Perpetual'   EBls EMFP ENot LRHS MAus MMat
(ClCh)   MRav SPer SWCr WAct WHCG
    XPep

Sophy's Rose   MAus MBri SWCr
= 'Auslot'PBR (S)

soulieana (Ra/S) ♥H3-4   EBls MAus SWCr WAct WKif

'Soupert et Notting'   LRHS MAus MRav SPer
(DPoMo)

'Southampton' (F) ♥H4   EBls GGre LStr MAus MMat MRav
    NRog SPer SSea SWCr WBVN

'Souvenir d'Alphonse   EBls ENot WHCG
Lavallée' (ClHP)

'Souvenir de Brod'   see *R.* 'Erinnerung an Brod'

'Souvenir de Claudius   EBee EBls MAus NRog SPer
Denoyel' (ClHP)

'Souvenir de François   EBls
Gaulain' (T)

'Souvenir de Jeanne   EBls WHCG
Balandreau' (HP)

'Souvenir de la Malmaison   see *R.* 'Climbing Souvenir de la
(ClBb)   Malmaison'

'Souvenir de la Malmaison'   EBls ENot GCoc LRHS
(Bb)   MAus MMat MRav NBPC SPer
    SWCr WAct

'Souvenir de Madame   CPou EBls EHol MAus MRav SWCr
Léonie Viennot' (ClT)

'Souvenir de Philémon   EBls MAus
Cochet' (Ru)

'Souvenir de Pierre Vibert'   EBls
(DPMo)

'Souvenir de Saint Anne's'   CHad EBee EBls EWTr MAus SWCr
(Bb)   WAct WHCG

'Souvenir d'Elise Vardon'   EBls
(T)

'Souvenir di Castagneto' (HP) — MRav

'Souvenir du Docteur Jamain' (ClHP) — CHad CPou EBee EBls EHol ENot LRHS LStr MAus SFam SMrm SPer SSea SWCr WAct WHCG WKif

'Souvenir du Président Carnot' (HT) — EBls

'Souvenir d'un Ami' (T) — EBls

spaldingii — see *R. nutkana* var. *hispida*

Spangles = 'Ganspa'[PBR] (F) — SWCr

'Spanish Beauty' — see *R*. 'Madame Grégoire Staechelin'

Sparkling Scarlet = 'Meihati' (ClF) — ELan GGre MAsh SWCr

Sparkling Yellow = 'Poulgode'[PBR] (GC/S) — ECnt MAsh SWCr

'Special Anniversary' — MAsh SWCr WWeb

Special Child = 'Tanaripsa' **new** — SWCr

Special Friend = 'Kirspec'[PBR] (Patio) — GCoc LStr

Special Occasion = 'Fryyoung'[PBR] (HT) — ENot ESty GCoc GGre MMat MRav SWCr

'Spectabilis' (Ra) — EBls WHCG

'Spek's Yellow' (HT) — EBls

'Spencer' misapplied — see *R*. 'Enfant de France'

spinosissima — see *R. pimpinellifolia*

Spirit of Freedom = 'Ausbite' (S) **new** — MAsh MAus

§ 'Splendens' (Ra) — EBls SLPl SSea SWCr WAct

'Spong' (G) — EBee EBls MAus SWCr WAct

St Piers = 'Harentrap'[PBR] (S) — GGre

§ St Tiggywinkle = 'Korbasren'[PBR] (GC) — ENot LGod MMat

§ 'Stanwell Perpetual' (PiH) — CTri EBls EMFP ENot EPfP EWTr GCoc LStr MBri MMat MRav NBPC SPer SSea SWCr WAct WHCG WOVN

'Star of Waltham' (HP) — WHCG

Star Performer = 'Chewpearl' (ClPatio) — CSBt ESty MAsh SWCr

Stardust = 'Peavandyke'[PBR] (Patio/F) — ESty GGre SWCr

Starina = 'Megabi' (Min) — SWCr

Starlight Express = 'Trobstar'[PBR] (Cl) — GKir MAsh SCoo SPer SWCr

'Stars 'n' Stripes' (Min) — LGod MAus SSea

Stella (HT) — EBls SWCr

stellata — MAus

§ - var. *mirifica* — EBls MAus SWCr

'Sterling Silver' (HT) — EBls LStr SWCr

Strawberries and Cream = 'Geestraw' (Min/Patio) — ESty

Strawberry Fayre = 'Arowillip'[PBR] (Min/Patio) — CTri GKir LAst MAsh MBri MRav SWCr WWeb

§ Sue Hipkin = 'Harzazz'[PBR] (HT) — MBur MRav SWCr

Sue Lawley = 'Macspash' (F) — SWCr

§ Suffolk = 'Kormixal'[PBR] (S/GC) — CGro CSBt ELan ENot GCoc LStr MAus MMat MRav NPri SPer SSea SWCr WAct WWeb

suffulta — see *R. arkansana* var. *suffulta*

Sugar and Spice = 'Peallure' (Patio) — SWCr

Sugar Baby = 'Tanabagus'[PBR] (Patio) — MAsh SWCr

Sugar 'n' Spice = 'Tinspice' (Min) — MAsh MRav SWCr

Suma = 'Harsuma'[PBR] (GC) — EPfP ESty GCoc SWCr WAct

Summer Breeze = 'Korelasting'[PBR] (Cl) — ENot MBri MMat MRav SWCr

Summer Dream = 'Frymaxicot'[PBR] (F) — CSBt LStr

§ Summer Dream = 'Jacshe' (HT) — LAst SWCr

§ Summer Fragrance = 'Tanfudermos' (HT) — CSBt GCoc MRav SWCr

Summer Gold = 'Poulreb'[PBR] (F) — ECnt ENot SWCr WWeb

'Summer Holiday' (HT) — MBur SPer

Summer Lady = 'Tanydal'[PBR] (HT) — MBur

'Summer Magic' (Patio) — GGre SWCr

Summer Palace = 'Poulcape'[PBR] (F/Patio) — ECnt MAsh SWCr

'Summer Sunrise' (GC) — EBls

'Summer Sunset' (GC) — EBls

Summer Wine = 'Korizont'[PBR] (Cl) ♀H4 — CSBt EBee ECnt ENot ESty MBri MMat SPer SSea SWCr

§ Sun Hit = 'Poulsun'[PBR] (Patio) — CGro CSBt ECnt ENot ESty GGre LGod MAsh MMat MRav SWCr WWeb

Sunblest = 'Landora' (HT) — CGro GGre MAsh MBur MRav NBlu NRog SWCr

Sunderland Supreme = 'Nossun' (HT) — NBat

Sunrise = 'Kormarter'[PBR] (Cl) — ESty MBur MMat MRav SWCr WGer

§ Sunseeker = 'Dicracer'[PBR] (F/Patio) — EPfP ESty GGre IDic LGod MAsh MRav SWCr WWeb

§ Sunset Boulevard = 'Harbabble'[PBR] (F) ♀H4 — CSBt ECnt ENot GGre GKir LGod LStr MAsh MAus MBri MMat MRav SCoo SPer SSea SWCr WWeb

Sunset Strip = 'Arocore' (Min) **new** — NBat

'Sunshine' (Poly) — SPer

'Sunsilk' (F) — SWCr

Sunsplash = 'Cocweaver' (HT) **new** — GCoc

Super Dorothy = 'Heldoro' (Ra) — MAus

Super Elfin = 'Helkleger'[PBR] (Ra) ♀H4 — CSam ECnt ENot LStr MMat MRav SPer SSea SWCr

Super Excelsa = 'Helexa' (Ra) — ENot ESty GGre LStr MAsh MAus MRav SSea SWCr

Super Fairy = 'Helsufair'[PBR] (Ra) — ECnt ENot ESty LStr MAus MMat MRav SPer SSea SWCr

§ Super Sparkle = 'Helfels'[PBR] (Ra) — CBrm EBee ECnt LStr SSea SWCr

§ Super Star = 'Tanorstar' (HT) — CTri EBls ENot GKir LStr MRav SWCr WWeb

'Surpasse Tout' (G) — EBls MAus WHCG

§ 'Surpassing Beauty of Woolverstone' (ClHP) — EBls WHCG

§ Surrey = 'Korlanum'[PBR] (GC) ♀H4 — CSBt CTri ECnt ELan ENot ESty LGod LStr MAus MMat MRav NPri SPer SPla SSea SWCr WAct

Susan Hampshire = 'Meinatac' (HT) — EBls MBur

Susan = 'Poulsue' (S) — EBee ECnt MAsh SWCr

Sussex = 'Poulave'[PBR] (GC) — CSBt ECnt ENot GCoc LStr MBur MMat MRav NPri SPer SSea SWCr

'Sutter's Gold' (HT) — EBls MAus MBur SWCr

Swan = 'Auswhite' (S) — GGre MAus SWCr

	Swan Lake = 'Macmed' (Cl)	EBee EBls ECnt ELan ENot EPfP ESty GGre GKir LGod LRHS MBur MMat MRav NPri SPer SSea SWCr WWeb
	Swany = 'Meiburenac' (Min/GC) ♀H4	CGro EBls ESty MAus SPer SWCr WHCG
	Sweet Bouquet = 'Sabchurchill' (HT)	MBur
	Sweet Caroline = 'Micaroline' (Min)	NBat
	Sweet Cover = 'Poulweeto'PBR **new**	MAsh
	Sweet Dream = 'Fryminicot'PBR (Patio) ♀H4	CGro CSBt EBre ECnt ELan ENot EPfP ESty GCoc GGre LAst LGod LStr MAsh MAus MBri MBur MMat MRav NBat NRog SPer SPla SSea SWCr WWeb
	'Sweet Fairy' (Min)	CSBt
	Sweet Juliet = 'Ausleap'PBR (S)	CAbP CHad CSBt CWSG EBee EBls EBre ESty GKir LGod LRHS MAsh MAus NBat NPri SPer SWCr
*	'Sweet Lemon Dream' (Patio) **new**	MAsh
	Sweet Magic = 'Dicmagic'PBR (Min/Patio) ♀H4	CGro CSBt CTri EBre ENot EPfP ESty GGre IDic LGod LStr MAsh MBri MMat MRav NBat SPla SWCr WWeb
	Sweet Memories = 'Whamemo' (Patio)	COtt CTri EBre ECnt EPfP ESty GCoc GKir LGod LStr MAsh MBur MRav SCoo SPer SPla SSea SWCr WGer WWeb
	'Sweet Repose' (F)	SWCr
	Sweet Revelation PBR	see *R.* Sue Hipkin
§	Sweet Symphonie = 'Meibarke'PBR (Patio)	ENot MBri MRav SWCr
	'Sweet Velvet' (F)	SWCr
	'Sweet Wonder' (Patio)	COtt EPfP ESty GKir MAsh SWCr
N	Sweetheart = 'Cocapeer'PBR (HT)	GCoc SWCr
	sweginzowii	GCal MAus
	- 'Macrocarpa'	EBls
	'Sydonie' (HP)	EBls WHCG
	'Sympathie' (ClHT)	ENot MMat SPer SSea SWCr
	'Talisman' (HT)	EBls
	Tall Story = 'Dickooky'PBR (F) ♀H4	EBls IDic SWCr WHCG WOVN
	'Tallyho' (HT)	EBls
	Tamora = 'Austamora' (S)	MAus
§	Tango = 'Macfirwal' (F)	NRog
	Tango = 'Poulyc005' (Cl) **new**	ECnt
	Tatton = 'Fryentice' (F)	MBri
	Tattoo = 'Poulyc0005' (Cl) **new**	ECnt
§	'Tausendschön' (Ra)	EBls
	'Tea Rambler' (Ra)	EBls
§	Tear Drop = 'Dicomo'PBR (Min/Patio)	IDic LStr SWCr
§	Teasing Georgia = 'Ausbaker'PBR (S)	ECnt LRHS MAus MBri SWCr
	'Temple Bells' (ClMin/GC)	NRog
	'Tenerife' (HT)	WStI
	Tequila Sunrise = 'Dicobey'PBR (HT) ♀H4	CTri ECnt ENot ESty GGre GKir IDic LStr MAsh MAus MBri MRav NRog SMrm SPer SSea SWCr WWeb
§	Terracotta = 'Meicobuis'PBR (HT)	MBur
	Tess of the D'Urbervilles = 'Ausmove'PBR (S)	MAus MBNS SWCr
	'Texas Centennial' (HT)	EBls
§	Thaïs = 'Memaj' (HT)	EBls
	Thank You = 'Chesdeep'PBR (Patio)	GCoc GGre MRav SWCr
	Thanks a Million (HT)	GGre SWCr
§	That's Jazz = 'Poulnorm'PBR (ClF)	EBee ECnt
§	The Alexandra Rose = 'Ausday'PBR	LRHS MAus MWgw SWCr
	'The Bishop' (CexG)	EBls MAus
	'The Bride' (T)	EBls
	The Compass Rose = 'Korwisco'PBR (S)	ENot MMat MRav SPer
	The Compassionate Friends = 'Harzodiac'PBR (F)	GGre SWCr
§	The Countryman = 'Ausman'PBR (S)	LRHS MAsh MAus MBri SWCr
§	The Daily Telegraph = 'Peahigh'PBR (S)	GGre MBri SWCr
	The Dark Lady = 'Ausbloom'PBR (S)	EBre LRHS MAsh MAus MBri SPer SWCr
	The Didgemere Rose = 'Fertry' (S)	GGre
	'The Doctor' (HT)	EBls SSea SWCr
§	The Dove = 'Tanamola'PBR (F)	ECnt SWCr
	'The Ednaston Rose' (Cl)	WHCG
§	'The Fairy' (Poly) ♀H4	CSBt CSam EBee EBls ECnt ELan ENot EPfP ESty GGre GKir LGod LStr MAsh MAus MBur MMat MRav NRog SMad SPer SPla SSea SWCr WAct WCFE WCot WHCG WOVN WWeb
	The Flower Arranger = 'Fryjam' (F)	LRHS
	'The Garland' (Ra) ♀H4	CRHN EBee EBls EMFP LRHS MAus SFam SPer SWCr WAct WHCG XPep
	The Generous Gardener = 'Ausdrawn' (S) **new**	MAus
§	The Halcyon Days Rose = 'Korparesni'PBR (F)	ENot MMat
	The Herbalist = 'Aussemi' (S)	LRHS MAus
	The Jubilee Rose	ECnt
	The Lady = 'Fryjingo'PBR (S) ♀H4	MAus SWCr
	The Maidstone Rose = 'Kordauerpa'PBR	ENot SWCr
	The Mayflower = 'Austilly' (S)	CSBt LGod MAus MBri SWCr
§	The McCartney Rose = 'Meizeli'PBR (HT)	GGre LStr SPer SWCr
	'The New Dawn'	see *R.* 'New Dawn'
	The Nun = 'Ausnun' (S)	MAus
	The Painter = 'Mactemaik'PBR (F)	LStr SSea
	The People's Princess = 'Geepeop'PBR (F)	MAsh SCoo SWCr
§	The Pilgrim = 'Auswalker'PBR (S)	CAbP CHad CSBt CSam EBee EBre EMFP ENot EPfP ESty GKir EWTr LRHS MAus MBri MMat MRav SChu SPer SPla SWCr WHCG
	The Prince = 'Ausvelvet'PBR (S)	LRHS LStr MAus MBNS MBri SPer SWCr
	The Prince's Trust = 'Harholding' (Cl)	GGre LStr MAsh SWCr
	'The Prioress' (S)	MAus
§	'The Queen Elizabeth' (F)	CBcs CGro CSBt CWSG EBls ECnt ENot GCoc GKir LGod LStr MAsh MBri MBur MMat MRav NRog SPer SSea SWCr WWeb
	The Reeve = 'Ausreeve' (S)	MAus
	The Scotsman = 'Poulscots'PBR (HT)	ECnt GCoc

The Seckford Rose — ENot MMat MRav
= 'Korpinrob' (S)

§ The Squire = 'Ausquire' — MAus
(S)

§ The Times Rose — ECnt ENot LGod LStr MAus MMat
= 'Korpeahn'PBR — MRav SPer SSea SWCr
(F) ♔H4

'Thelma' (Ra) — EBls MAus

'Thérèse Bugnet' (Ru) — EBls MAus

Thinking of You — ESty GCoc GGre LGod LStr MAsh
= 'Frydandy' (HT) — MBri SWCr WWeb

'Thisbe' (HM) — EBls MAus SWCr WAct WHCG XPep

§ Thomas Barton — LStr
= 'Meihirvin' (HT)

'Thoresbyana' — see *R.* 'Bennett's Seedling'

'Thoughts of You' (HT) — GGre

Thousand Beauties — see *R.* 'Tausendschön'

threepenny bit rose — see *R. elegantula* 'Persetosa'

'Tiara' (RH) — SWCr

Tiger Cub = 'Poulcub'PBR — ENot MMat
(Patio)

Tigris = 'Harprier' — WAct
(*persica* hybrid) (S)

'Till Uhlenspiegel' (RH) — EBls

Times Past = 'Harhilt' — ESty GCoc LStr SWCr
(Cl)

'Tina Turner' (HT) — MBur NBat SWCr

Tintinara — ECnt IDic
= 'Dicuptight'PBR (HT)

Tip Top = 'Tanope' — CBcs GKir NRog SPer
(F/Patio)

'Tipo Ideale' — see *R.* x *odorata* 'Mutabilis'

'Tipsy Imperial — EBls
Concubine' (T)

Titanic = 'Macdako'PBR — SWCr
(F)

Tivoli = 'Poulduce'PBR — ECnt ENot MAus
(HT)

'Toby Tristam' (Ra) — CRHN

'Tom Foster' (HT) — NBat

tomentosa — WBWf

Too Hot to Handle — SSea
= 'Macloupri'PBR (S/Cl)

Top Marks — CGro CSBt CTri ENot EPfP GCoc
= 'Fryministar'PBR — LAst LGod LStr MBri MRav NRog
(Min/Patio) — SCoo SPer SSea SWCr WStI
WWeb

'Top of the Bill' (Patio) — GGre SWCr

'Topeka' (F) — SWCr

Topkapi Palace — ECnt MAsh
= 'Poulthe'PBR (F)

§ Toprose = 'Cocgold'PBR — GCoc GGre GKir MAsh SWCr
(F)

'Topsi' (F/Patio) — NRog SPer

§ 'Tour de Malakoff' (Ce) — CSBt EBls EHol LRHS MAus MRav
NBPC SFam SPer SWCr WAct
WHCG

Tournament of Roses — MAus
= 'Jacient' (HT)

Tower Bridge = 'Haravis' — GGre SWCr
(HT)

§ Toynbee Hall — ENot
= 'Korwonder'PBR (F)

'Trade Winds' (HT) — SWCr

Tradescant = 'Ausdir'PBR — EBre LRHS MAus MBNS SWCr
(S)

§ Tradition '95 — MMat MRav SWCr
= 'Korkeltin'PBR
(Cl) ♔H4

Tranquility = 'Barout' (HT) — MBur SWCr

'Treasure Trove' (Ra) — CRHN EBls EMFP LRHS MAus
MBur SWCr WAct

Trevor Griffiths — LRHS MAus
= 'Ausold'PBR (S)

'Tricolore de Flandre' (G) — EBls MAus

'Trier' (Ra) — CPou EBee EBls MAus WHCG

'Trigintipetala' misapplied — see *R.* 'Professeur Emile Perrot'

'Triomphe de l'Exposition' — MAus
(HP)

'Triomphe du — EBls MAus
Luxembourg' (T)

triphylla — see *R.* x *beanii*

Troika = 'Poumidor' — CSBt ENot ESty GGre GKir LStr
(HT) ♔H4 — MAsh MAus MBur MMat MRav
SPer SPoG SWCr

Troilus = 'Ausoil' (S) — MAus

§ Tropico Sunblaze — SWCr
= 'Meiglassol'PBR (Min)

Trumpeter = 'Mactru' — CSBt EBee ECnt ENot ESty GGre
(F) ♔H4 — IArd LGod LStr MAsh MAus MBri
MBur MMat MRav NBat SPer SSea
SWCr WWeb

Tumbling Waters — ENot MMat MRav
= 'Poultumb'PBR (F/S)

'Tuscany' (G) — GCoc MAus WAct WHCG

'Tuscany Superb' (G) ♔H4 — CHad CPou CSam EBee EBls
EMFP ENot EPfP EWTr ISea LAst
LRHS MAus MMat MRav NBPC
SPer SSea SWCr WAct WHCG WKif
WLow

Twenty-fifth = 'Beatwe' (F) — EBls

§ Twenty-one Again! — MRav SWCr
= 'Meinimo'PBR (HT)

Twist = 'Poulstri'PBR (Cl) — ECnt ESty MAsh SWCr

Tynwald = 'Mattwyt'PBR — ENot LStr MMat SPer
(HT)

'Typhoon' (HT) — MBur

'Tzigane' (HT) — MBur SWCr

'Ulrich Brünner Fils' (HP) — EBls MAus

'Uncle Bill' (HT) — EBls

Uncle Walter = 'Macon' — EBls SWCr
(HT)

UNICEF = 'Cocjojo'PBR — GCoc
(F)

§ 'Unique Blanche' (Ce) — EBls MAus SSea

Valencia = 'Koreklia'PBR — CSBt ECnt ENot ESty LGod MAus
(HT) ♔H4 — MBur MMat NBat

§ Valentine Heart — CSBt ESty IArd IDic LGod MAsh
= 'Dicogle'PBR (F) ♔H4 — MAus MRav SPoG SWCr WWeb

Valerie Sykes — NBat
= 'Horflashrob' (F)

Valiant Heart = 'Poulberg' — ECnt
(F)

'Vanguard' (Ru) — EBls

'Vanity' (HM) — EBls MAus

'Variegata di Bologna' (Bb) — EBee EBls EMFP EPfP LRHS MAus
MRav SSea SWCr WAct

Variety Club = 'Haredge' — LGod MAsh SCoo SWCr
(Patio)

'Vatertag' (Min) — GGre

'Veilchenblau' (Ra) ♔H4 — CHad CRHN EBee EBls ECnt EGra
ELan ENot EPfP LGod LRHS LStr
MAsh MAus MBri MBur MRav
MWgw NPri SPer SSea SWCr WAct
WHCG

Velvet Fragrance — CSBt EBee ECnt ESty GCoc MAsh
= 'Fryperdee'PBR (HT) — MAus MBri MRav NBat SWCr

Velvet Hit = 'Poulria'PBR — ENot
(Patio)

'Venusta Pendula' (Ra) — EBls MAus

'Vermilion Patio' **new** — MAsh SWCr

Versailles Palace — SWCr
= 'Poulsail'PBR (F)

'Verschuren' (HT/v) — MBur

versicolor — see *R. gallica* 'Versicolor'

'Vick's Caprice' (HP) — EBls MAus

'Vicomtesse Pierre — EBls MAus
du Fou' (ClHT)

Vidal Sassoon   MBur SWCr
  = 'Macjuliat'^PBR (HT)
'Village Maid'   see *R.* 'Centifolia Variegata'
§ *villosa* L.   EBls MAus WAct
  - 'Duplex'   see *R.* 'Wolley-Dod'
'Violacea' (G)   EBee EBls MAus SSea SWCr WHCG
'Violette' (Ra)   CPou CRHN EBee EBls MAus WAct WHCG WHer

'Violinista Costa' (HT)   EBls
virginiana ♀H4   CFee EBls ENot GCal GIBF MAus MSte NWea SPer SWCr WAct WHCG WHen WOVN
  - 'Plena'   see *R.* 'Rose d'Amour'
'Virgo' (HT)   EBls
'Viridiflora'   see *R.* x *odorata* 'Viridiflora'
'Vivid' (Bourbon hybrid)   EBls
Voice of Thousands   NBat
  = 'Horsunsmile' (F)
'W.E. Lippiat' (HT)   EBls
Waltz = 'Poulkrid'^PBR (Cl)   ECnt MAsh SWCr
wardii var. *culta*   MAus
Warm Welcome   CBrm CGro EBre ECnt ENot EPfP
  = 'Chewizz'^PBR   ESty GGre GKir LGod LStr MAsh
  (ClMin) ♀H4   MAus MBri MMat MRav MWgw NBat NRog SMad SPer SSea SWCr WWeb
§ Warm Wishes   CSBt EBee ECnt ENot ESty GCoc
  = 'Fryxotic'^PBR   GGre GKir LAst LGod LStr MAsh
  (HT) ♀H4   MAus MBri MBur MMat SWCr WWeb
'Warrior' (F)   SPer
Warwick Castle   MAus SPer
  = 'Auslian'^PBR (S)
Warwickshire   ENot MMat MRav NPri SPer SWCr
  = 'Korkandel'^PBR (GC)   WOVN WWeb
§ *watsoniana* (Ra)   EBls
webbiana   EBls MAus SPer WHCG
'Wedding Day' (Ra)   CRHN CSBt CSam EBee EBls EBre ECnt ELan ENot EPfP ESty GGre LRHS LStr MAsh MAus MBNS MBri MBur MMat MRav MWgw SPer SSea SWCr WAct WHCG WLow WWeb
§ 'Wee Barbie'^PBR (Min)   SSea
Wee Cracker   ENot ESty GCoc GGre LGod MAsh
  = 'Cocmarris'^PBR   SWCr
  (Patio)
Wee Jock = 'Cocabest'^PBR (F/Patio)   GCoc GGre GKir MBri MRav SSea SWCr
'Weetwood' (Ra)   CRHN SPer
'Well Done' (Patio)   GGre SWCr
Welwyn Garden Glory   ESty SWCr
  = 'Harzumber'^PBR (HT)
'Wendy Cussons' (HT)   CBcs CGro CTri CWSG EBls GCoc GKir MAsh MBur MRav NRog SPer SWCr
Wenlock = 'Auswen' (S)   GGre MAus SPer SWCr
§ Westerland = 'Korwest'   MRav NBPC SWCr
  (F/S) ♀H4
'Westfield Star' (HT)   MAus
§ Westminster Pink   ECnt
  = 'Fryamour'^PBR (HT)
Where the Heart Is   GCoc
  = 'Cocoplan' (HT)
'Whisky Gill' (HT)   SWCr
Whisky Mac = 'Tanky'   CBcs CGro CSBt CTri CWSG EBls
  (HT)   ELan GCoc GGre MBri MBur MRav NPri NRog SPer SSea WWeb
'White Bath'   see *R.* 'Shailer's White Moss'
White Bells   EBls ENot MMat MRav SPer WHCG
  = 'Poulwhite'^PBR   WOVN
  (Min/GC)
§ 'White Cécile Brünner'   EBls MAus WHCG
  (Poly)

'White Christmas' (HT)   MBur SWCr
§ White Cloud   CSBt EBee ECnt ENot ESty LGod
  = 'Korstacha'^PBR   MMat MRav SWCr WHCG
  (S/ClHT) ♀H4
White Cloud = 'Savacloud'   MBri
  (Min)
'White Cockade' (Cl)   EBls GCoc MRav SPer SWCr
§ 'White de Meaux' (Ce)   EBls MAus
White Diamond   ESty IDic
  = 'Interamon'^PBR (S)
§ White Gold   GCoc GGre MAsh SCoo SWCr
  = 'Cocquiriam'^PBR (F)
'White Grootendorst' (Ru)   EBls MAus SSea WAct
White Knight (HT)   see *R.* Message = 'Meban' (HT)
White Knight = 'Poullaps'   EBee SWCr
  (ClHT/S)
White Meidiland   SWCr
  = 'Meicoublan'^PBR
  (S/GC)
white moss   see *R.* 'Comtesse de Murinais', *R.* 'Shailer's White Moss'
§ 'White Pet' (Poly) ♀H4   CHad CSBt CSam EBee ECnt EMFP ENot EPfP GCoc GGre LGod LRHS LStr MAus MBri MMat MRav NBPC SPer SPla SSea SWCr WAct WLow
* 'White Pet' sport (Cl)   GCal
white Provence   see *R.* 'Unique Blanche'
'White Queen Elizabeth'   EBls MBur
  (F)
white rose of York   see *R.* x *alba* 'Alba Semiplena'
'White Spray' (F)   EBls
'White Tausendschön'   MAus
  (Ra)
'White Wings' (HT)   CHad EBls MAus SPer SWCr WAct WHCG
N *wichurana* (Ra)   EBls MAus SWCr WHCG XPep
* - 'Nana'   MRav
  - 'Variegata' (Ra/v)   CSWP MCCP
* - 'Variegata Nana' (Ra/v)   MRav
'Wickwar' (Ra)   CSWP EBls EHol EPla GCal MSte SSpi SWCr WAct WHCG
§ Wife of Bath = 'Ausbath'   MAus MBri
  (S)
'Wilhelm' (HM)   EBls MAus MRav SPer SWCr WHCG
'Will Scarlet' (HM)   MAus SWCr
'Willhire Country' (F)   EBls
'William Allen Richardson'   EBls MAus SWCr WHCG
  (N)
'William and Mary' (S)   EBls
'William Cobbett' (F)   SSea
§ 'William Lobb' (CeMo)   CHad CRHN CSBt EBls EBre ENot
  ♀H4   EPfP EWTr LGod LRHS LStr MAsh MAus MBri MMat MWgw SChu SPer SSea SWCr WAct WHCG WKif WLow
William Morris   CSBt ECnt MAus MBri SWCr
  = 'Auswill'^PBR (S)
William Quarrier   GCoc
  = 'Coclager' (F)
'William R. Smith' (T)   EBls
William Shakespeare   CSBt LGod MAus
  2000 = 'Ausromeo' (S)
William Shakespeare   ENot GCoc GGre MBNS MBri SPer
  = 'Ausroyal'^PBR (S)   SSea WStI
'William Tyndale' (Ra)   EBee WHCG
'Williams' Double Yellow'   see *R.* x *harisonii* 'Williams' Double Yellow'
willmottiae   see *R. gymnocarpa* var. *willmottiae*
Wilton = 'Eurosa' **new**   SWCr
Wiltshire   CSBt ECnt ENot ESty LStr MMat
  = 'Kormuse'^PBR   MRav NPri SSea SWCr WOVN
  (S/GC) ♀H4

Winchester Cathedral = 'Auscat'PBR (S)	CSBt EBls EBre ECnt EMFP ENot EPfP ESty GGre LGod LRHS LStr MAsh MAus MBri MRav MWgw NPri SChu SMad SPer SWCr
Windflower = 'Auscross' (S)	LRHS MAus
Windrush = 'Ausrush' (S)	MAus SWCr WAct WHCG
Wine and Dine = 'Dicuncle'PBR (GC)	IDic
Winter Magic = 'Foumagic' (Min)	MBur
x *wintoniensis*	WAct WHCG
Wise Portia = 'Ausport' (S)	MAus
Wishing = 'Dickerfuffle'PBR (F/Patio)	IDic MAus SWCr
With Love = 'Andwit' (HT)	GGre SWCr
With Thanks = 'Fransmoov'PBR (HT)	LAst MBri SWCr
'Woburn Abbey' (F)	CWSG EBls SSea
§ 'Wolley-Dod' (S)	EBls LRHS MAus MRav SWCr
'Woman's Hour' (F/Patio)	EBls
§ *woodsii*	EBls IFro MAus WHCG
- var. *fendleri*	see *R. woodsii*
'Woolverstone'	see *R.* 'Surpassing Beauty of Woolverstone'
Wor Jackie = 'Kirworjackie' (HT)	NBat
Worcestershire = 'Korlalon'PBR (GC)	CSBt ENot ESty GCoc MAus MMat MRav SPer SWCr WWeb
World Peace 2000 = 'Peayellow'PBR (HT)	SWCr
§ *xanthina* 'Canary Bird' (S) ♀H4	More than 30 suppliers
§ - f. *hugonis* ♀H4	EBls MAus NRog SPer SWCr WAct WHCG
- f. *spontanea*	CArn EBls
'Xavier Olibo' (HP)	EBls
X-Rated = 'Tinx' (Min)	NBat
Yellow Button = 'Auslow' (S)	MBri WAct
'Yellow Cécile Brünner'	see *R.* 'Perle d'Or'
Yellow Charles Austin = 'Ausyel' (S)	MAus
§ Yellow Dagmar Hastrup = 'Moryelrug'PBR (Ru)	CBrm EBee ENot EPfP EWTr MAus MMat SPer SPla SWCr WAct WOVN
'Yellow Doll' (Min)	MAus SSea SWCr
'Yellow Dream' (Patio)	GGre SWCr
Yellow Flower CarpetPBR	see *Rosa* Flower Carpet Sunshine
'Yellow Patio' (Min/Patio)	LStr MAsh SSea SWCr
yellow Scotch	see *R.* x *harisonii* 'Williams' Double Yellow'
Yellow Sunblaze = 'Meitrisical' (Min)	CSBt SWCr
Yellow Sweet Magic = 'Dicyellmag' (Patio) **new**	IDic
'Yesterday' (Poly/F/S) ♀H4	EBls GKir MAsh MAus MRav SPoG SWCr
'Yolande d'Aragon' (HP)	EBls
York and Lancaster	see *R.* x *damascena* var. *versicolor*
Yorkshire = 'Korbarkeit'PBR (GC)	ENot GCoc LStr MMat MRav SSea SWCr
'Yorkshire Lady' (HT)	NBat
Young Quinn = 'Macbern' (HT)	MBur
'Yvonne Rabier' (Poly) ♀H4	EBls LStr MAus MRav SPer SSea SWCr WAct WHCG WLow
Zambra = 'Meicurbos' (F)	CBcs
'Zéphirine Drouhin' (Bb)	More than 30 suppliers
§ 'Zigeunerknabe' (S)	EBee EBls ECnt EMFP EWTr MAus MBri MRav SPer SSea SWCr WAct WHCG

Roscoea ✿ (Zingiberaceae)

alpina	CBct CBro CLAP CPLG EBee EBre EChP EHrv EHyt ERos GEdr GKir IBlr ITim MTho NLAp NMen NWCA SOkd SRms WCot WCru WLin WSan
- CC 1820	LEur WCot
- CC 3667	GEdr GKev
- pink-flowered	EUJe ITer WCom
auriculata	More than 30 suppliers
- early-flowering **new**	WCru
- 'Floriade'	CLAP IBlr LEur
- late-flowering **new**	WCru
- 'Special' **new**	CLAP
australis	CFir IBlr SOkd WCru
'Beesiana'	More than 30 suppliers
'Beesiana' pale-flowered	IBlr LEdu LEur WPnP
'Beesiana' white-flowered	CBct CDes CFwr CLAP EBee EHrv EPfP GEdr GSki IBlr LAst LPhx MBNS MMHG NBir WAbe WPnP
bhutanica **new**	IBlr
cautleyoides ♀H4	More than 30 suppliers
- CLD 687	GEdr
- Blackthorn strain	SBla
- var. *cautleyoides*	CDWL EBee
- 'Early Purple'	CLAP EBee
- hybrid	GSki MLLN
- 'Jeffrey Thomas'	CBct CFwr CLAP EBee EPot GEdr GSki IBlr LEur WCot
- 'Kew Beauty' ♀H4	CDes CFir CLAP EBre ETow GKir LEur MTed MTho SRms
- 'Kew Beauty' seedlings	EGle EMan GCal
- 'Purple Giant'	CLAP
- purple-flowered **new**	IBlr
- 'Reinier'	CLAP LEur WCot
cautleyoides x *humeana*	CLAP IBlr LEur
- 'Gestreept'	CLAP
- 'Himalaya' **new**	CLAP
humeana ♀H4	CBct CBro CFee CLAP EBee EBre EHyt ERos GBin GCrs GMac LAma LRHS SBla WCot WCru WPrP
- f. *lutea*	IBlr
- 'Purple Streaker'	CDes CLAP EBee WPGP
- 'Rosemoor Plum' **new**	CLAP
- f. *tyria*	IBlr
kunmingensis var. *elongatobractea*	IBlr LEur
- var. *kunmingensis* **new**	IBlr
- 'Monique'	CLAP IBlr LEur
procera	see *R. purpurea*
§ *purpurea*	More than 30 suppliers
- CC 3628	WCot
- L&S 20845	IBlr
- 'Brown Peacock'	CLAP LEur WCot
- var. *gigantea*	CFir CLAP LEur
- lilac-flowered	CDWL GSki
- 'Nico'	CLAP LEur WCot
- 'Niedrig' **new**	EBee
- pale-flowered	EBla
- 'Peacock'	CLAP LEur
- 'Peacock Eye'	CLAP LEur WCot
- 'Polaris'	LEur
- var. *procera*	see *R. purpurea*
- 'Red Gurkha' **new**	SBla
- short	CLAP
- tall	CLAP
§ *scillifolia*	CBro CDes CFir CFwr CPBP EPot ERos GBuc GCal GEdr GKir GSki IBlr LAma LEur LHop LRHS MAvo MTho NBir NMen NRog WCom WCot WCru WLin WPrP
- dark-flowered	CStu EBee EHrv

– pink-flowered	CBct EBee EChP EHrv GEdr IBlr LEur NMen WAbe
tibetica	CLAP EBee GCrs GEdr IBlr LEur NLAp WCru WOBN
– dark-flowered	WWst
tumjensis	CLAP EBee IBlr
'Vincent' **new**	WCot
'Yeti' **new**	CLAP

rosemary see *Rosmarinus officinalis*

Rosmarinus ✿ (*Lamiaceae*)

corsicus 'Prostratus'	see *R. officinalis* Prostratus Group
eriocalyx	XPep
lavandulaceus hort.	see *R. officinalis* Prostratus Group
lavandulaceus Noë	see *R. eriocalyx*
officinalis	More than 30 suppliers
– var. *albiflorus*	CArn CPrp CSev EBee ELau EPfP ESis GBar GPoy LRHS MBar MBow MHer MSwo NChi NHHG SChu SDow SHDw SLim SMac SPer SPlb STre WCHb WHHs WWpP WWye XPep
– – 'Lady in White'	CSBt EBee ELan EPfP LAst LRHS SDow SPer WHHs WJek
– 'Alderney'	CPrp MHer MWgw SDow
– var. *angustissimus* **new**	XPep
§ – – 'Benenden Blue' ♀H4	CMHG CSBt CSev CWib EBee EGoo ELau GBar GPoy LHop LRHS MAsh MHer MWgw NHHG SChu SDix SDow SMHy SMer SPer SPlb STre WEas WWye
– – 'Corsican Blue'	CArn EPfP GBar GPoy MHer NGHP SCro SDow SHDw SIde WBrE WPer XPep
– – 'Corsicus Prostratus'	CBcs ELau
– 'Arta'	SSpi
– 'Aureovariegatus'	see *R. officinalis* 'Aureus'
§ – 'Aureus' (v)	CPla GBar IBlr NHHG SDry WCHb WEas
– 'Baie d'Audierne' **new**	XPep
– 'Baie de Douarnenez' **new**	XPep
– 'Barbecue'PBR	MHer
– 'Barcelona' **new**	XPep
– 'Blue Boy'	MHer
– 'Blue Lagoon'	NGHP WCHb WJek
– 'Blue Rain' **new**	MHer NGHP
* – 'Boule'	CPrp WCHb XPep
– 'Cap Béar' **new**	XPep
– 'Capercaillie'	SDow
– 'Cisampo' **new**	XPep
– 'Collingwood Ingram'	see *R. officinalis* var. *angustissimus* 'Benenden Blue'
– dwarf, blue-flowered	ELau GBar
– dwarf, white-flowered **new**	WCHb
– 'Eve' **new**	XPep
– 'Farinole'	CPrp XPep
– 'Fastigiatus'	see *R. officinalis* 'Miss Jessopp's Upright'
– 'Fota Blue'	CArn CBod CPlt CPrp CSev CWib ELau EOHP GBar IArd MHer NHHG SAga SCro SDow SHDw SIde WCHb WHHs WJek WWye
– 'Golden Rain'	see *R. officinalis* 'Joyce DeBaggio'
– 'Gorizia'	SDow XPep
– 'Green Ginger'	CBod CPrp CSpe EChP EOHP GBin LHop MHer NCot NPer SDow WBcn WBry WCHb WHHs WMnd
– 'Guilded'	see *R. officinalis* 'Aureus'
– 'Gunnel's Upright'	GBar WRha
– 'Haifa'	CBgR CBod EBee WCHb

– 'Heavenly Blue'	GBar
– 'Henfield Blue'	SHDw
– 'Iden Blue'	SIde
– 'Iden Blue Boy'	SIde
– 'Iden Pillar'	SIde
§ – 'Joyce DeBaggio' (v)	MHer SDow
– 'Ken Taylor'	LPhx
– 'Lady in Blue'	WHHs
– *lavandulaceus*	see *R. officinalis* Prostratus Group
– 'Lérida' **new**	XPep
– 'Lilies Blue'	GPoy
– 'Lockwood Variety'	see *R. officinalis* (Prostratus Group) 'Lockwood de Forest'
– 'Loddon Pink'	WHHs
– 'Loupian' **new**	XPep
– 'Majorca Pink'	CBcs CChe CPrp CSBt CSam EBee EGoo ELau GAbr GBar MBow MHer MRav SDow SIde SLon SPer SRms SSto WCHb WHHs WSSM WWye XPep
– 'Maltese White'	CStr WCot
– 'Marenca' **new**	WCHb XPep
– 'Mason's Finest' **new**	SDow
– 'McConnell's Blue' ♀H4	CArn CDoC CPrp EBee EBre ELan ELau GAbr GBar LHop LRHS MAsh MBro MGos MRav MWat MWgw SDow SDry SHDw SPla WCHb WFar WHHs WHoo WPGP WTel WWye
– 'Minerve' **new**	XPep
§ – 'Miss Jessopp's Upright' ♀H4	More than 30 suppliers
– 'Montagnette' **new**	XPep
– 'Mrs Harding'	CBod CPrp EBee MHer
– 'Octopussy'	WBry
– 'Pat Vlasto'	CStr
§ – 'Primley Blue'	CArn CPrp CSam CSev CWSG EBee ECtt ELau GBar LRHS MAsh MHer MRav NGHP NHHG NJOw SChu SDow SIde SMer WCHb WHer WPer
§ – Prostratus Group	More than 30 suppliers
– – 'Capri'	EBee EOHP MRav NGHP
– – 'Gethsemane'	SIde
– – 'Jackman's Prostrate'	CBcs ECtt
§ – – 'Lockwood de Forest'	GBar
– – 'Punta di Canelle' **new**	XPep
– f. *pyramidalis*	see *R. officinalis* 'Miss Jessopp's Upright'
* – 'Rampant Boule'	SDow
– *repens*	see *R. officinalis* Prostratus Group
– 'Roman Beauty' **new**	LAst SVil
– 'Rosemarey' **new**	XPep
– 'Roseus'	CArn CMHG CPrp CSBt CWib EBee EChP ELan ELau EMil EPfP GPoy LHop LRHS MAnH MBct MHer NHHG SChu SDow SLim SMac WAbe WHHs WHer WMnd WPer WWeb WWye
– 'Russell's Blue'	WFar
– 'Saint Florent' **new**	XPep
– 'Santa Barbara Blue' **new**	XPep
– 'Sawyer's Select' **new**	MHer
– 'Sea Level'	CBod MBow WCHb
– 'Severn Sea' ♀H4	More than 30 suppliers
– 'Silver Sparkler' **new**	WPat
– 'Silver Spires' = 'Wolros'	LRav SIde
– 'Sissinghurst Blue' ♀H4	CArn CBcs CSev EBee ECha ELau ELan EMil EPfP GAbr GBar LAst LRHS MAsh MBow MRav NGHP SDow SIde SLim SPer SPlb SRms WCHb WCom WHHs WSel WWye XPep

- 'Sissinghurst White'	WHHs
- 'South Downs Blue'	SHDw
- 'Sudbury Blue'	EBee ELau EPfP GBar MHer NHHG SDow SHDw WEas WJek XPep
- 'Trusty'	GBar LHop LRHS WBcn XPep
- 'Tuscan Blue'	More than 30 suppliers
- 'Ulysse' **new**	XPep
- 'Variegatus'	see *R. officinalis* 'Aureus'
- 'Vicomte de Noailles'	ERea XPep
repens	see *R. officinalis* Prostratus Group

Rostrinucula (Lamiaceae)

dependens Guiz 18	CBot

Rosularia ✿ (Crassulaceae)

from Sandras Dag	LBee
alba	see *R. sedoides*
§ *chrysantha*	EBre EBur EMlt EPem ESis MHer NJOw NMen SIng SPlb WLow
- number 1	CWil LBee
crassipes	see *Rhodiola wallichiana*
§ *muratdaghensis*	EBur SChr SIng
pallida A. Berger	see *R. chrysantha*
platyphylla hort.	see *R. muratdaghensis*
rechingeri	CWil
§ *sedoides*	CWil LRHS MBar SChu SIng WPer WRHF WWin
§ - var. *alba*	EDAr EHol EPot GGar MBar NLAp SChu WTin WWin
sempervivum	CWil EWes NMen SChr WCot
§ - subsp. *glaucophylla*	CWil NSla WAbe
spatulata hort.	see *R. sempervivum* subsp. *glaucophylla*

Rothmannia (Rubiaceae)

capensis	EShb LRHS SOWG
§ *globosa*	ERea

Rubia (Rubiaceae)

manjith	GPoy
peregrina	CArn GPoy MSal
tinctorum	CArn ELau EOHP GBar GPoy GWCH MSal SWat WCHb WHer WWye

Rubus (Rosaceae)

RCB/Eq C-1	WCot
alceifolius Poiret	CFee CStr SDys SMac WGMN
arcticus	EPPr GGar GIBF MBro MCCP NLAp NLar SRms SRot WBea WCot WCru WPat
- subsp. *stellarcticus* 'Anna' (F)	ESim
- - 'Beata' (F)	ESim
- - 'Linda' (F)	ESim
- - 'Sofia' (F)	ESim
x *barkeri*	ECou WPGP
§ 'Benenden' ♀H4	More than 30 suppliers
'Betty Ashburner'	CAgr CDoC EBee ECrN ENot EPfP EWTr GQui LAst LBuc MGos MRav MWgw MWhi NArg NHol SPer WBVN WDin WTin
biflorus ♀H4	CBcs CFil CPle EBee EMon EPfP EWes LRHS MBlu SMac SSte
'Black Butte' **new**	SDea
'Boatsberry' **new**	SDea
'Boysenberry, Thornless' (F)	EMui GTwe LBuc LRHS SDea SPer
* *buergeri* 'Variegatus' (v)	NHol WMoo
calophyllus	CFil SSte WBor WPGP
calycinoides Hayata	see *R. pentalobus*
calycinoides Kuntze **new**	SSte

chamaemorus	GIBF GPoy
cissoides	WCot
cockburnianus (F)	CArn CBcs CPle CTri EBee EBre ELan ENot EPfP EWTr GKir LBuc LRHS MBlu MRav MSwo MWat NBea NHol NLRH NSti NWea SPer SPlb SRms SSte WDin WEas WFar
- 'Goldenvale' ♀H4	More than 30 suppliers
coreanus	CFil EPla
crataegifolius	CBrd SMac SSte WPat
'Emerald Spreader'	GKir LRHS MBri SBod WMoo
flagelliflorus	MBar
fockeanus hort.	see *R. pentalobus*
formosensis B&SWJ 1798	WCru
x *fraseri*	SSte WGMN
fruticosus 'Adrienne' (F)	EMui MAsh
- 'Ashton Cross' (F)	EMui GTwe LBuc
- 'Bedford Giant' (F)	CSBt ENot GTwe LRHS MGos MRav NRog SKee
- 'Black Satin' (F)	LRHS SDea
- 'Cook's Special' (F)	NRog
- 'Cottenham Green'	EMon
- 'Fantasia'PBR (F) ♀H4	EMui
- 'Godshill Goliath' (F)	SDea
- 'Helen'	CSut EMui MAsh SDea
- 'Himalayan Berry'	ENot
- 'Himalayan Giant' (F)	GTwe LBuc LRHS MRav NRog SDea SPer
- 'John Innes' (F)	CTri NRog
- 'Loch Ness'PBR (F) ♀H4	COtt CSBt EMui ENot GKir GTwe IArd LBuc LRHS MBri MGos SCoo SDea SPer
- 'Merton Thornless' (F)	CSBt CTri GTwe LRHS MGos NBee NRog WGwG
- 'No Thorn' (F)	SDea
- 'Oregon Thornless' (F)	CSBt EMui ENot GTwe MBri MRav SCoo SDea SKee SPer SRms
- 'Parsley Leaved' (F)	MRav NRog SDea
* - 'Sylvan' (F)	LRHS MCoo MGos
- 'Thornfree' (F)	SDea
- 'Variegatus' (v)	CBot IFro MBlu NHol NSti SSte WPat
- 'Veronique' (F)	EMui
- 'Waldo'	COtt CSBt CSam EMui LBuc LRHS MGos SDea
'Golden Showers' **new**	CWib
hakonensis B&SWJ 5555	WCru
henryi	CBot EPfP EPla LRHS MRav NLar NSti SLon SMac SSte WCot WFar
- var. *bambusarum*	CFil CMCN EBee EMan EPar EPfP EPla MCCP SBra WCru WPat WTin
hupehensis	SLPl SSte
ichangensis	CBot CPom CStr EPla LEdu SSte
idaeus 'Allgold'	see *R. idaeus* 'Fallgold'
- 'Augusta' (F)	EMui
- 'Aureus' (F)	ECha ELan EPla MRav NBid SDry SMac SSte WCot WFar
- 'Autumn Bliss'PBR (F) ♀H4	CSBt CSut CTri CWSG EMui ENot EPfP GKir GTwe LBuc LRHS MBri MGos MRav NBee NRog SCoo SDea SKee SPer
§ - 'Fallgold' (F)	EMui EPfP LRHS SKee SPer
- 'Galante' (F)	EMui
- 'Glen Ample'PBR (F) ♀H4	CAgr CSBt CSut CWSG EMui EPfP GTwe LBuc LRHS MBri SCoo SDea SKee SPer SPoG
- 'Glen Clova' (F)	CAgr CSBt CTri ENot GKir GTwe LRHS MRav NBee NBlu NRog SKee SPer
- 'Glen Lyon'PBR (F)	GTwe LBuc LRHS MBri SCoo
- 'Glen Magna'PBR (F)	CAgr CSBt CSut CWSG EMui GTwe LBuc LRHS MBri NRog SCoo SDea SKee

- 'Glen Moy'PBR (F) ♀H4	CSBt EMui EPfP GKir GTwe LRHS MBri MGos MRav NBee NRog SCoo SDea SKee
- 'Glen Prosen'PBR (F) ♀H4	CSBt EMui ENot GKir GTwe LRHS MBri MRav NRog SCoo SDea SKee SPer
- 'Glen Rosa'PBR (F)	GTwe LRHS SKee
- 'Glen Shee'PBR (F)	GTwe SKee
- 'Heritage' (F)	ENot LRHS MRav SCoo
- 'Julia' (F)	GTwe MCoo
- 'Leo'PBR (F) ♀H4	CSBt EMui GTwe MGos NRog SCoo SKee
- 'Malling Admiral' (F) ♀H4	COtt CTri EMui ENot GKir GTwe LRHS NRog SCoo SPer
- 'Malling Delight' (F) ♀H4	CSBt GKir GTwe LRHS MRav SCoo
- 'Malling Jewel' (F) ♀H4	COtt CSBt CTri EMui ENot GKir GTwe LBuc LRHS NBee NRog SDea SKee SPer
- 'Redsetter' (F)	EMui
- 'Ruby' (F)	EMui
- 'Summer Gold' (F)	GTwe
- 'Terri-Louise' (F)	EMui
- 'Tulameen' (F)	EMui MBri SCoo SKee
- 'Zeva Herbsternte' (F)	GTwe
illecebrosus (F)	ITer NLar SSte
irenaeus	CFil SSpi SSte WPGP
Japanese wineberry	see *R. phoenicolasius*
'Kenneth Ashburner'	CDoC GEil NLar SLPl WFar WTin
'King's Acre Berry' (F)	EMui
laciniatus	EHol EPla
lambertianus	CFil
leucodermis NNS 00-663	EPPr
lineatus	CBot CDoC CMCo CPLG CPle EBee EPfP GEil GKir LRHS NSti SDix SDry SMac SMad SSpi SSte WCru WDin WPGP WPat
x ***loganobaccus*** 'Brandywine' **new**	SDea
- 'LY 59' (F) ♀H4	EMui EPfP GTwe MRav NRog SDea SKee SRms
- 'LY 654' (F) ♀H4	CSam GKir GTwe LBuc LRHS MBri MGos SDea SPer
- thornless	CTri CWSG ECot GKir GTwe NRog SDea
'Margaret Gordon'	CPMA GKir MRav WHCG
microphyllus 'Variegatus' (v)	CRez EMan MGos WPat
§ ***nepalensis***	CAgr CDoC GEdr GKir LEdu NHol NLAp SSte
niveus	EPla
nutans	see *R. nepalensis*
odoratus	CPle CPom CTri ELan EPfP EWTr GEil MRav NPal SPer SSte WBor WCom WCot WHCG WTin
palmatus var. ***coptophyllus***	SLPl
parviflorus	CArn
- double (d)	EMon WCru
- 'Sunshine Spreader'	NPro WPat
parvus	ECou
pectinellus	WBcn
- var. ***trilobus***	CFee CPom GMac NLar SMac SSte
- - B&SWJ 16698	NPro
- - B&SWJ 1669B	GSki LPio WCru WMoo
peltatus	CFil NLar SSte WPGP
§ ***pentalobus***	CRez CTri ELan EMan EPla MBar MWhi NFor SMac WFar WWin
- B&SWJ 3878	WCru
- 'Emerald Carpet'	CAgr ECrN ESim NLar SBod
§ ***phoenicolasius***	CAgr EMui EPfP GEil GKir GTwe LEdu LRHS MBlu MBri MRav NRog NSti SDea SPer WAbb WCru WHCG
rolfei	EPPr SMac
- B&SWJ 3546	WCru
rosifolius	CBcs CSpe
- 'Coronarius' (d)	CFee CHar CPom CSpe ECrN ELan EMan EPPr LRHS MBow MRav NPro NSti SSte WFar WGwG WOVN
sachalinensis	GIBF
saxatilis	GIBF
setchuenensis	CMCN CSWP SSte
'Silvan' (F) ♀H4	EMui GTwe
spectabilis	CPle CPom CSev CWib ELan EPPr EPla MRav NHol SSte WCom WFar WRha
- 'Flore Pleno'	see *R. spectabilis* 'Olympic Double'
§ - 'Olympic Double' (d)	More than 30 suppliers
splendidissimus B&SWJ 2361	WCru
squarrosus	CPle ECou EHol EPla
'Sunberry' (F)	GTwe SDea
swinhoei B&SWJ 1735	WCru
taiwanicola	GEdr NLar NPSI SMac SSte WWhi
- B&SWJ 317	MHar NPro WCru
Tayberry Group (F) ♀H4	CSam CTri EMui ENot GKir GTwe LBuc MBri MGos NLar NRog SPer SRms
- 'Buckingham' (F)	CSut EMui GTwe LRHS MBri
- 'Medana Tayberry' (F)	LRHS SDea SKee
§ ***thibetanus*** ♀H4	More than 30 suppliers
- 'Silver Fern'	see *R. thibetanus*
treutleri	SSte
tricolor	CAgr CBcs CHEx CSBt CTri CWib EBee ECrN ENot EPfP GBri GIBF GKir LGro MRav MSwo MTis MWhi NFor NHol SDix SHBN SLon SMac SPer SSte WBod WDin WHCG WWin
- 'Dart's Evergreen'	SLPl
- 'Ness'	SLPl
tridel 'Benenden'	see *R.* 'Benenden'
trilobus B&SWJ 9096 **new**	WCru
'Tummelberry' (F)	GTwe
ulmifolius **new**	GEil
- 'Bellidiflorus' (d)	CBot ENot MBlu MRav MSwo NFor NSti SChu SDix SMac SPer WAbb WHal
ursinus	LEdu
'Veitchberry' (F)	EMui GTwe
volkensii	SSpi
Walberton Red = 'Odel'	SPer
xanthocarpus **new**	NLar
'Youngberry' (F)	SDea

Rudbeckia ✿ (*Asteraceae*)

Autumn Sun	see *R.* 'Herbstsonne'
californica	CSam MAnH MNrw WPer
deamii	see *R. fulgida* var. *deamii*
echinacea purpurea	see *Echinacea purpurea*
§ ***fulgida*** var. ***deamii*** ♀H4	More than 30 suppliers
- var. ***fulgida***	WHil
§ - var. ***speciosa*** ♀H4	CKno CM&M CSam CWCL ECha ECtt ELan EPfP ERou GAbr LRHS MHer NGdn SPer SPlb SRms SWal WEas WFar WMoo WPer WTel WTin WViv WWpP
- var. ***sullivantii*** 'Goldsturm' ♀H4	More than 30 suppliers
- 'Sun Baby'	CStr
- Viette's Little Suzy = 'Blovi'PBR	EBee EBre EMan LRHS WCra
glaucescens NNS 00-667	WCot
gloriosa	see *R. hirta*
'Golden Jubilee'	LRHS WWeb

'Goldquelle' (d) ♀H4	More than 30 suppliers
§ 'Herbstsonne' ♀H4	More than 30 suppliers
§ *hirta*	CHar EBre NBir
- 'Chim Chiminee' **new**	GFlt
- 'Goldilocks'	GWCH
- 'Irish Eyes'	LRHS LRav NChi
- var. *pulcherrima*	EBee EFou EPPr WWpP
- 'Sonora'	COtt
- 'Toto' ♀H3	CHrt LPVe SWvt WWpP
§ 'Juligold'	CPrp EBee EFou EMan LRHS NGdn
	SCro SMrm SPla SPoG SSpe WCAu
	WFar WWpP
July Gold	see *R.* 'Juligold'
laciniata	CBrm CStr EBee ECGN EChP ELan
	EMan EMon EPPr EPfP MCCP
	MDKP MFir NLar NOrc NSti SCro
	WCot WMoo
- var. *ampla*	MDKP
- 'Golden Glow'	see *R. laciniata* 'Hortensia'
§ - 'Hortensia' (d)	EMon EPla MFir
maxima	CBot CDes CFwr EBee EChP ECha
	EFou EMan EMon LPhx LRHS
	MAnH MAvo MBri MCCP NCGa
	NDov NLar NSti SChu SDix SMrm
	SPlb SUsu WAul WCot WFar WWpP
missouriensis	EBee SUsu
mollis	EBee
newmannii	see *R. fulgida* var. *speciosa*
nitida	IHMH
occidentalis	MLLN NVic WFar WPer
- 'Black Beauty'PBR	CSpe EChP EMan EPfP MBNS
	MMHG NBhm NSti WHHs WMnd
	WShp
- 'Green Wizard'	More than 30 suppliers
* *paniculata*	EFou WWpP
purpurea	see *Echinacea purpurea*
speciosa	see *R. fulgida* var. *speciosa*
subtomentosa	EBee EFou EMan EMon GCal LRHS
	MAvo MDKP NSti WCAu WOld
'Takao'	EBee MBnl MLLN NPro SUsu
	WGMN
triloba	CBri CFwr CMea CSam ECGN
	EFou EMan GBri LRHS NVic SCro
	WBea WCAu WFar WMoo WTin

rue see *Ruta graveolens*

Ruellia (Acanthaceae)

brittoniana 'Katie'	WCot
humilis	EBee EMan NLar SCro SIgm
	WCot
macrantha	MJnS
makoyana ♀H1	CHal CSev IBlr MBri SMur
malacosperma	WCot
'Mr Foster'	CHal
* *muralis*	MAvo

Rumex (Polygonaceae)

§ *acetosa*	CArn CHby CSev ELau GBar GPoy
	GWCH IHMH LRHS MBow MHer
	NBir NGHP NPri NSco SIde SWal
	WHer WLHH WSel WWye
- 'Abundance'	ELau
- subsp. *acetosa*	MAvo
'Saucy' (v)	
- 'De Belleville'	CPrp
- 'Profusion'	GPoy
- subsp. *vinealis*	EMan WCot
acetosella	CArn MSal WSel
alpinus	WCot
flexuosus	CRow EHoe EShb IBlr ITer NLar
	WWeb
hydrolapathum	CArn CHEx EMFW LPBA MSta
	SPlb WWpP

obtusifolius 'Golden	CNat
My Foot'	
patientia **new**	CAgr
sanguineus	CAgr CTri EMan EPAt EPza GBBs
	GGar IHMH LPBA MWgw NLar
	SWal WBrk WFar WMAq WMnd
	WWeb
- var. *sanguineus*	CArn CBgR CElw CRow CSev EBee
	EDAr EHoe ELan EPar EPla LRHS
	MHer MNrw MTho NBro NHol
	WHer WLHH WPer WSel WWye
* 'Schavel' **new**	CAgr
scutatus	CArn CHby CSev ELau GPoy MHer
	SIde SPlb WHHs WHbs WHer WJek
	WLHH WWye
- 'Silver Shield'	CRow EBee ELau EMar EPPr IBlr
	NBlu SIde WCHb WJek WLHH
venosus	MSal

Rumohra (Davalliaceae)

adiantiformis ♀H1	EFtx SEND WFib
- RCB/Arg D-2	WCot

Rupicapnos (Papaveraceae)

africana	SBla

Ruschia (Aizoaceae)

karrooica	SChr
uncinata	SChr

Ruscus ✿ (Ruscaceae)

aculeatus	CArn CRWN EBee ELan ENot EPfP
	GKir GPoy MRav NWea SAPC SArc
	SMad SRms SSta WDin WHer
	WPGP WRHF WStI WWye
- (f)	WMou
- (m)	WMou
- hermaphrodite	EPla EWes GCal SPer WGer
- var. *aculeatus*	GCal
'Lanceolatus' (f)	
- var. *angustifolius*	EPla MTed
Boiss.	
- - (f)	EPla
* - 'Wheeler's Variety' (f/m)	CPMA WPGP
hypoglossum	EPla MTed SEND SLon WRHF
racemosus	see *Danae racemosa*

Russelia (Scrophulariaceae)

§ *equisetiformis* ♀H1	CHll EShb SIgm SOWG XPep
juncea	see *R. equisetiformis*

Ruta (Rutaceae)

chalepensis	CArn XPep
§ - 'Dimension Two'	WHer
- prostrate	see *R. chalepensis* 'Dimension
	Two'
corsica	CArn
graveolens	CArn CDul EChP EFer EPfP GBar
	GPoy GWCH NBlu NPri SIde SPet
	WHHs WHer WJek WPer WWye
	XPep
- 'Jackman's Blue'	More than 30 suppliers
- 'Variegata' (v)	CBot ELan EMan EPAt GBar GEil
	NFor NPer SPer WBry WHer WJek
	WRHF
montana	EBee
prostrata	see *R. chalepensis* 'Dimension
	Two'

Ruttya (Acanthaceae)

fruticosa 'Scholesii'	ERea

x *Ruttyruspolia* (Acanthaceae)

'Phyllis van Heerden'	GFai

S

Sabal (Arecaceae)

§ *bermudana*	CRoM EAmu LPal WMul
causiarum	CRoM
domingensis	CRoM EAmu
etonia	LPal
mauritiiformis	WMul
§ *mexicana*	CRoM CTrC EAmu WMul
minor	CBrP CHEx CRoM CTrC EAmu
	LPal MPRe NPal WHPE WMul
palmetto	CArn CDoC CRoM CTrC EAmu
	LPal MPRe WMul WNor
princeps	see *S. bermudana*
'Riverside'	CRoM
rosei	LPal
texana	see *S. mexicana*
umbraculifera	MPRe
uresana	LPal

Saccharum (Poaceae)

arundinaceum **new**	EPPr
§ *baldwinii*	CBig
brevibarbe	CBig EBee EMan EPPr
var. *contortum*	
ravennae	CBig CCtw CPen EBee EHoe EMan
	EMon EPza EWes GBin LRav MSte
	NSti SMad SPlb WFar WWeb
strictum (Ell.) Ell. ex Nutt.	see *S. baldwinii*

sage see *Salvia officinalis*

sage, annual clary see *Salvia viridis*

sage, biennial clary see *Salvia sclarea*

sage, pineapple see *Salvia elegans* 'Scarlet Pineapple'

Sageretia (Rhamnaceae)

§ *thea*	STre
theezans	see *S. thea*

Sagina (Caryophyllaceae)

boydii	EWes
subulata	IHMH WShp
§ - var. *glabrata* 'Aurea'	CTri ECha ECtt EDAr EFer EMlt
	GKir LGro MBNS MOne MWhi
	NHol SIng SRms WEas WHal
	WMoo WPer WShp WWin WWpP

Sagittaria (Alismataceae)

'Bloomin Babe'	CRow
graminea	CRow
'Crushed Ice' (v)	
japonica	see *S. sagittifolia*
latifolia	COld EMFW LPBA NPer
* *leucopetala*	NArg NLar NPer
'Flore Pleno' (d)	
§ *sagittifolia*	CBen CDWL CRow CWat EHon
	EMFW EPfP LNCo LPBA MSta
	NArg SLon SWat WFar WMAq
	WWpP
- 'Flore Pleno' (d)	CDWL CRow CWat EMFW LPBA
	MSta SLon SWat WMAq WPnP
- var. *leucopetala*	WMAq

Saintpaulia (Gesneriaceae)

'Blue Dragon' **new**	WDib
'Bob Serbin' (d)	WDib
'Buffalo Hunt' **new**	WDib
'Centenary'	WDib
'Cherries 'n' Cream'	WDib
'Chiffon Fiesta' **new**	WDib
'Chiffon Mist' **new**	WDib
'Chiffon Moonmoth'	WDib
'Chiffon Stardust'	WDib
'Chiffon Vestor' **new**	WDib
'Coroloir' **new**	WDib
'Delft' **new**	WDib
'Golden Glow' **new**	WDib
'Halo's Aglitter'	WDib
'Irish Flirt' (d)	WDib
'Lemon Drop'	WDib
'Lemon Whip' **new**	WDib
'Love Spots'	WDib
'Lucky Lee Ann'	WDib
'Marching Band' **new**	WDib
'Mermaid'	WDib
'Midget Lillian'	WDib
'Midnight Flame' **new**	WDib
'Nubian Winter' **new**	WDib
'Otoe' **new**	WDib
'Powder Keg'	WDib
'Powwow' **new**	WDib
'Ramblin Magic'	WDib
'Rapid Transit' **new**	WDib
'Rob's Bamboozle' **new**	WDib
'Rob's Dust Storm' (d)	WDib
'Rob's Firebrand' **new**	WDib
'Rob's Gundaroo' (d)	WDib
'Rob's Heatwave' **new**	WDib
'Rob's Hopscotch' **new**	WDib
'Rob's Ice Ripples' (d)	WDib
'Rob's Mad Cat'	WDib
'Rob's Rinky Dink' (d)	WDib
'Rob's Sarsparilla' **new**	WDib
'Rob's Shadow Magic' (d)	WDib
'Rob's Sticky Wicket' **new**	WDib
'Rob's Toorooka' **new**	WDib
shumensis	WDib
'Sky Bandit'	WDib
'Tippy Toes' (d)	WDib
'Ultra Violet Halo' **new**	WDib

Salix ✿ (Salicaceae)

acutifolia	ELan GIBF NSti SPla WDin
- 'Blue Streak' (m) ♀H4	CDul CEnd CMHG CWiW EPfP
	EPla EWes MAsh MBlu MRav NBir
	SLon SMHy SWat WFar
- 'Pendulifolia' (m)	SBLw
aegyptiaca	CDoC CLnd ECrN MBlu NWea
	WMou
alba	CAgr CCVT CDul CLnd CWiW
	ECrN ENot GKir LBuc NWea SBLw
	WDin WMou WOrn
- f. *argentea*	see *S. alba* var. *sericea*
- 'Aurea'	CLnd CTho MRav WIvy WMou
- 'Belders' **new**	SBLw
- var. *caerulea*	CAgr CDul CLnd ENot MRav
	NWea WMou
- - 'Wantage Hall'	CWiW
- 'Cardinalis' (f)	CWiW
- 'Chermesina' hort.	see *S. alba* subsp. *vitellina* 'Britzensis'
- 'Dart's Snake'	CEnd CTho EBee ELan ENot EPfP
	LRHS MRav SCoo SPer WBcn
- 'Hutchinson's Yellow'	CDoC CTho MGos NWea WDin
- 'Liempde' (m)	ENot MRav SBLw
- 'Raesfeld'	CWiW
§ - var. *sericea* ♀H4	CBcs CDoC CLnd CMHG CTho
	ECrN ENot EPfP GKir MBlu MRav
	NFor NWea SBLw SHBN SPer
	WDin WGer WIvy WMou
- 'Splendens'	see *S. alba* var. *sericea*

- 'Tristis' ambig.	CDul CLnd CTri CWSG ECrN ELan GKir LRHS MBri MGos NBee NBlu NLar NWea SBLw SKee SLim SRms WDin WFar WHar
- 'Tristis' misapplied	see *S.* x *sepulcralis* var. *chrysocoma, S. humilis*
- subsp. ***vitellina*** ♀H4	CBrm CDul ENot EPfP GKir LBuc MBNS MBrN NWea SLon SWat WDin WIvy WMoo WPGP
§ - - 'Britzensis' (m) ♀H4	More than 30 suppliers
- 'Vitellina Pendula'	see *S. alba* 'Tristis'
- 'Vitellina Tristis'	see *S. alba* 'Tristis'
§ ***alpina***	CLyd GIBF NBir NHol
'Americana'	CWiW
amplexicaulis 'Pescara'	CWiW
amygdaloides	CWiW
'Aokautere'	CWiW
apoda (m)	EWes GIBF NBir WPer
§ ***arbuscula***	CBcs CNic GIBF NWCA WDin
arctica var. ***petraea***	MBro NHol NLAp WPat
arenaria	see *S. repens* var. *argentea*
aurita	LRav NLar NWea
babylonica	CEnd CTrG MSwo NBee SBLw SHBN WMou
- 'Annularis'	see *S. babylonica* 'Crispa'
§ - 'Crispa'	CDul CFai ELan EPla LHop NBlu NPro SMad SPla WBcn WFar
- 'Pan Chih-kang'	CWiW
§ - var. ***pekinensis***	CEnd
§ - - 'Tortuosa' ♀H4	More than 30 suppliers
* - 'Tortuosa Aurea'	MCCP SWvt WBrE
x ***basaltica*** (m)	GIBF
bicolor (f)	GIBF
- (m)	GIBF
'Blackskin'	CWiW
bockii	GKir LRHS LTwo MBar WCFE WFar
§ 'Bowles' Hybrid'	CAgr MRav WMou
'Boydii' (f) ♀H4	CFee EBee EPfP EPot GCrs GKir GTou ITim MBro MDun MGos NBir NFor NHol NMen NRya NSla SBla SIng SRms WAbe WFar WPat
§ 'Boyd's Pendulous' (m)	CFee CLyd CWib EHyt MBar
breviserrata	CLyd GIBF
caesia	GIBF NWCA
candida	GIBF
caprea	CAgr CBcs CCVT CDul CLnd CRWN CTri ECrN ENot EPfP GKir LBuc NWea SBLw SPer WDin WMou
- 'Black Stem'	CNat
- 'Curlilocks'	COtt MBar MSwo
§ - 'Kilmarnock' (m)	More than 30 suppliers
- var. ***pendula*** (m)	see *S. caprea* 'Kilmarnock' (m)
cascadensis	GIBF
cashmiriana	CFai CLyd MBro NHol NWCA WPat
* ***caspica rubra nana***	SWat
x ***cepusiensis*** (f)	GIBF
x ***cernua***	NWCA
'Chrysocoma'	see *S.* x *sepulcralis* var. *chrysocoma*
cinerea	CAgr CBcs CDoC ECrN ENot GKir LBuc NWea SBLw WDin
- 'Tricolor' (v)	CArn SLim
commutata	GIBF
§ ***cordata***	ECrN SLPl WDin
x ***cottetii***	EBee GIBF IArd MBar WDin
daphnoides	CBrm CCVT CDoC CDul CLnd CSam EBee ENot EPfP GKir LRHS MBrN MSwo NSti NWea SBLw SPer SPla SRms STre WDin WFar WMou
- 'Aglaia' (m)	CBcs CTri ECrN WIvy WMyn WPGP

- 'Meikle'	CAgr CWiW
- 'Netta Statham'	CWiW
- 'Ovaro Udine'	CWiW
- 'Oxford Violet'	ECrN WIvy
- 'Sinker'	WIvy
- 'Stewartstown'	CWiW
'E.A. Bowles'	see *S.* 'Bowles' Hybrid'
x ***ehrhartiana***	CNat
§ ***elaeagnos***	CAgr CCVT CDoC CLnd CTho CTri EBee ECrN ENot EPfP GKir LRHS MBlu MBrN MRav SLon SMHy SWat WDin WFar WIvy WMou
§ - subsp. ***angustifolia*** ♀H4	CDul ELan MRav MTis NLar NWea SRms STre WWin
'Elegantissima'	see *S.* x *pendulina* var. *elegantissima*
eriocephala	CWiW
'American Mackay'	
- 'Kerksii' (m)	CWiW
- 'Mawdesley'	CWiW
- 'Russelliana' (f)	CWiW
§ 'Erythroflexuosa'	More than 30 suppliers
exigua	More than 30 suppliers
fargesii	CBot CDoC CEnd CFee CFil EBee ELan EPfP GIBF GKir LEdu LHop LRHS MBlu MDun MGos MRav NSti SDix SSpi WCru WFar WPGP WPat
x ***finnmarchica***	GEdr GIBF NWCA
foetida (f)	GIBF
formosa	see *S. arbuscula*
fragilis	CCVT CDul CLnd ECrN GKir MRav NWea SBLw WDin WMou
- 'Legomey'	WIvy
x ***fruticosa*** 'McElroy'	CWiW
§ ***fruticulosa***	CBcs CTri GCrs GKev GKir GTou NWCA SBla SMrm WPat
'Fuiri-koriyanagi'	see *S. integra* 'Hakuro-nishiki'
furcata	see *S. fruticulosa*
glauca	CNat
- subsp. ***callicarpaea*** (f)	GIBF
glaucosericea	EBee
'Golden Curls'	see *S.* 'Erythroflexuosa'
gracilistyla	CTho ECrN NSti SLPl WMou WMyn
- 'Melanostachys' (m)	More than 30 suppliers
x ***grahamii*** (f)	GIBF
x ***greyi***	NPro
hastata (f)	GIBF
- 'Wehrhahnii' (m) ♀H4	More than 30 suppliers
helvetica ♀H4	CBcs ELan ENot EPfP GGar GKir LRHS MAsh MBar MBlu MBri MBro MDun MGos MRav NBee NBir NFor NWCA NWea SHBN SPer WDin WFar WHar WPat
herbacea	GIBF GTou NMen
hibernica	see *S. phylicifolia*
hookeriana	CLnd CMHG CTho EBee ELan EPla MBlu MBrN MRav SLPl SSpi WCFE WIvy WMou WTin
incana	see *S. elaeagnos*
integra 'Albomaculata'	see *S. integra* 'Hakuro-nishiki'
§ - 'Hakuro-nishiki' (v)	More than 30 suppliers
- 'Pendula' (f)	CEnd LRHS
irrorata	CLnd
'Jacquinii'	see *S. alpina*
kinuyanagi (m)	ELan EPla SMrm
§ ***koriyanagi***	CWiW WIvy
'Kumeti'	CWiW
'Kuro-me'	see *S. gracilistyla* 'Melanostachys'
x ***laestadiana***	GIBF
lanata ♀H4	More than 30 suppliers
- 'Drake's Hybrid'	NMen

- hybrid	WPat
- 'Mark Postill'	see *S.* 'Mark Postill'
- 'Stuartii'	see *S.* 'Stuartii'
lapponum	ESis GIBF GKir MBro NHol NWea SRms
- (m)	GIBF
- var. *daphneola* (f)	GIBF
- - (m)	GIBF
liliputa	see *S. turczaninowii*
§ *lindleyana*	NBir
lucida	EBee ECrN
'Maerd Brno' (f)	MBlu
magnifica ♀H4	CDul CEnd CFil CLnd CMCN EBee ELan EMil EPfP EPla GIBF GKir IDee LRHS MSte NSti NWea SDry SKee SMad SSpi SWat WCru WDin WFar WMou WPGP
§ 'Mark Postill' (f)	CDoC EBee EMil LHop LRHS MBNS SPla SPoG
matsudana 'Tortuosa'	see *S. babylonica* var. *pekinensis* 'Tortuosa'
- 'Tortuosa Aureopendula'	see *S.* 'Erythroflexuosa'
'Melanostachys'	see *S. gracilistyla* 'Melanostachys'
x *meyeriana*	WIvy
- 'Lumley' (f)	CWiW
x *mollissima*	CWiW
var. *hippophaifolia* 'Jeffries'	
- 'Notts Spaniard' (f)	CWiW
- - 'Stinchcombe'	WIvy
- 'Trustworthy' (f)	CWiW
- var. *undulata*	CWiW
'Kottenheider Weide'	
moupinensis	EPfP
§ *myrsinifolia*	EPla MBlu
§ *myrsinites*	GIBF
- var. *jacquiniana*	see *S. alpina*
myrtilloides	CLyd
- 'Pink Tassels' (m)	EHyt MBrN NWCA SIng WPat
myrtilloides x *repens*	see *S.* x *finnmarchica*
nakamurana	CFai CFee EPot EPla GIBF GKir LRHS MBro MRav NLap NLRH NPro WFar WIvy WPat
var. *yezoalpina*	
nepalensis	see *S. lindleyana*
nigricans	see *S. myrsinifolia*
nivalis	see *S. reticulata* subsp. *nivalis*
x *obtusifolia*	GIBF
onychiophylla (f)	GIBF
x *ovata*	CLyd NMen
§ x *pendulina*	CTho ECrN
var. *elegantissima*	
pentandra	CAgr CBot CDul CLnd ECrN LRav NWea WDin WFar WMou
- 'Patent Lumley'	CWiW
'Philip's Fancy'	NWCA
§ *phylicifolia*	ECrN WMou
- 'Malham'	CWiW
polaris	CLyd GIBF
x *punctata*	GIBF
§ *purpurea*	CBcs CDul GIBF MBrN NWea SRms WDin WMou
- 'Abbeys'	WIvy
- 'Brittany Green' (f)	CWiW
- 'Continental Reeks'	CWiW WIvy
- 'Dark Dicks' (f)	CWiW WIvy
- 'Dicky Meadows'	CAgr CWiW WIvy
- 'Goldstones'	CAgr CWiW WIvy
- f. *gracilis*	see *S. purpurea* 'Nana'
- 'Green Dicks'	CAgr CWiW WIvy
- 'Helix'	see *S. purpurea*
- 'Howki' (m)	WMou
- 'Irette' (m)	CWiW
- 'Jagiellonka' (f)	CWiW WIvy
- var. *japonica*	see *S. koriyanagi*

- subsp. *lambertiana*	CWiW WIvy
- 'Lancashire Dicks' (m)	CWiW
- 'Leicestershire Dicks' (m)	CWiW
- 'Light Dicks'	CWiW
- 'Lincolnshire Dutch'	CWiW
§ - 'Nana'	CLyd EPfP ESis MWhi NLar SLPl SLon SPer STre WAul WFar WMoo
- 'Nancy Saunders' (f)	CHad CTho CWiW EHoe EPPr EPla GBuc GGGa MBNS MBlu MBrN MBri MRav MSte NPro NSti SMHy SUsu WCot WIvy WPen
- 'Pendula' ♀H4	CEnd CWib EBee ECrN ENot LRHS MAsh MBar MBri MRav MSwo NBlu NHol NWea SPer SPoG WDin WStI
- 'Read'	CWiW
- 'Reeks'	CWiW
- 'Richartii' (f)	CWiW NSti
- 'Uralensis' (f)	CWiW
pyrenaica	CLyd EHyt GIBF NWCA
repens	ECrN GIBF GKir MBar SRms STre SWat WDin
§ - var. *argentea*	EBee ENot EPfP GIBF MBar MRav MWhi NWCA NWea SLim SPer WDin WFar WWin
- 'Armando' PBR **new**	MGos
- from Saint Kilda	GKir
- 'Iona' (m)	CLyd WStI
- *pendula*	see *S.* 'Boyd's Pendulous' (m)
- 'Voorthuizen' (f)	CWib EHol EHyt MBar MGos WDin WGer WStI
reticulata ♀H4	EPot GCrs GIBF GKir GTou NBir NLAp NMen NRya NSla NWoo WPat
§ - subsp. *nivalis*	GIBF
retusa	CTri GIBF GKir GTou MBro NBir NLAp WPat
retusa x *pyrenaica*	ECho
rosmarinifolia hort.	see *S. elaeagnos* subsp. *angustifolia*
x *rubens* 'Basfordiana' (m)	CDoC CDul CLnd CTho CWiW EPla EWes MBNS MRav NWea WMou WMyn
- 'Bouton Aigu'	CWiW
- 'Farndon'	CWiW
- 'Flanders Red'	CWiW
- 'Fransgeel Rood'	CWiW
- 'Glaucescens'	CWiW
- 'Golden Willow'	CWiW
- 'Jaune de Falaise'	CWiW
- 'Jaune Hâtive'	CWiW
- 'Laurina'	CWiW
- 'Natural Red'	CWiW
- 'Parsons'	CWiW
- 'Rouge Ardennais'	CWiW
- 'Rouge Folle'	CWiW
- 'Russet'	CWiW
x *rubra*	CWiW
- 'Abbey's Harrison'	CWiW
- 'Continental Osier'	CWiW
- 'Eugenei' (m)	CDul CTho ECrN EPla GQui MBlu SWat WBcn WIvy WMou WWin
- 'Fidkin'	CWiW
- 'Harrison's'	CWiW
- 'Harrison's Seedling A' (f)	CWiW
- 'Mawdesley'	CWiW
- 'Mawdesley Seedling A' (f)	CWiW
- 'Pyramidalis'	CWiW
'Scarlet Curls'	WPat
x *sepulcralis*	NWea
- 'Caradoc'	CWiW

§	- var. *chrysocoma*	CDoC CDul CSBt CWib EBee ECrN ENot EPfP EWTr GKir LBuc LPan LRHS MGos MWat NBea NBee SBLw SCoo SHBN SLim SPer WDin WOrn
	serpyllifolia	CLyd CTri EHyt GIBF MBro NHol NLAp NMen WPat
	serpyllifolia x *retusa*	NWCA
	serpyllum	see *S. fruticulosa*
	'Setsuka'	see *S. udensis* 'Sekka'
	x *simulatrix*	CLyd EBee EHyt GIBF MBar NWCA
	x *sobrina*	GIBF
	x *stipularis* (f)	CMHG NWea
§	'Stuartii'	GIBF MBar NMen NWCA SRms
	subopposita	CDul EBee ELan EWes MBNS MBar MBro NPro STre
	x *tetrapla*	GIBF
	thomasii	GIBF
	'Tora' PBR	LRav
	triandra	LRav WMou
	- 'Black German'	CWiW
	- 'Black Hollander'	CAgr CWiW WIvy
	- 'Black Maul'	CAgr CWiW
	- 'Grisette de Falaise'	CWiW
	- 'Grisette Droda'	CWiW
	- 'Long Bud'	CWiW
	- 'Noir de Challans'	CWiW
	- 'Noir de Touraine'	CWiW
	- 'Noir de Villaines'	CWiW WIvy
	- 'Rouge d'Orléans'	ECrN
	- 'Sarda d'Anjou'	CWiW
	- 'Semperflorens' (m)	CNat
	- 'Whissander'	CAgr CWiW WIvy
	x *tsugaluensis* 'Ginme' (f)	CMHG SLPl
§	*turczaninowii* (m)	GIBF
§	*udensis* 'Sekka' (m)	CMHG CTho EBee ECtt ELan EPar NBir NHol NWea STre SWat WFar WIvy WMou
	uva-ursi	CLyd GIBF
	viminalis	CCVT CDul CLnd EBee ECrN ENot LBuc NWea WDin WMou
	- 'Bowles' Hybrid'	see *S.* 'Bowles' Hybrid'
	- 'Brown Merrin'	CAgr WIvy
	- 'Green Gotz'	CWiW WIvy
	- 'Reader's Red' (m)	CAgr WIvy
	- 'Riefenweide'	WIvy
	- 'Yellow Osier'	CAgr WIvy
	vitellina 'Pendula'	see *S. alba* 'Tristis'
§	*waldsteiniana*	GIBF MBar NWCA
	x *wimmeriana*	SRms
	'Yelverton'	LRHS MRav SWat WWes

Salvia ❀ (*Lamiaceae*)

B&SWJ 9032 blue, from Guatamala	WCru
BWJ 9062 pale blue, from Guatamala	WCru
CC&McK 77	GTou
CD&R 1148	WHil
CD&R 1162	SPin
CD&R 3071	CStr SPin
acetabulosa	see *S. multicaulis*
aethiopis	CPle CSev CPle LPhx MLLN SDnm SPin WWye XPep
§ *africana*	CArn CPle CStr GGar LPio SPin WDyG WWye XPep
africana-caerulea	see *S. africana*
africana-lutea	see *S. aurea*
agnes	CStr LIck SPin
albimaculata	SBla SPin
algeriensis	LPhx SPin
'Allen Chickering' **new**	XPep
amarissima	CPle CStr SPin

'Amber'	EBee SUsu
ambigens	see *S. guaranitica* 'Blue Enigma'
§ *amplexicaulis*	CPle CTCP EPPr MAnH MGol MWrn NBPC NLar SBod SPin WCAu WPer WWin WWye XPep
angustifolia Cav.	see *S. reptans*
angustifolia Mich.	see *S. azurea*
'Anthony Parker' **new**	CPle MRod SDys SPin
apiana	CArn MGol MHer MSal SAga SGar SHFr SIgm SPin WCot XPep
argentea ♥H3	More than 30 suppliers
arizonica	CPle CPom CStr LIck MAsh MLLN MRod SDys SPin XPep
atrocyanea	CPle CSpe CStr EBlw LIck MAsh MLLN MRod SDys SGar SPin WDyG WOut WWye
aucheri	CPle GBar GBuc GCal
§ *aurea*	CBot CHal CHll CPle CSev CStr CTCP ELan EPAt GGar LHop LPio MHar MOak MSte SAga SGar SPin SSte WDyG WPer XPep
	- 'Kirstenbosch'	CPle CSev CStr EBee ECtt EMan EPPr GEil MAsh MLLN MRav NCGa SDys SPin WCot WOut WPer WWye
aurita **new**	SPin
austriaca	CPle EBee SHFr SPin WPer
§ *azurea*	CArn CPle CRWN EBee LPhx LPio MAsh MRod MSte SAga SBod SMrm SPin WOut WRha XPep
	- var. *grandiflora*	CStr MAsh SPin
bacheriana	see *S. buchananii*
§ *barrelieri*	CPle SHFr SPin WOut XPep
'Bee's Bliss' **new**	XPep
bertolonii	see *S. pratensis* Bertolonii Group
bicolor Des.	see *S. barrelieri*
blancoana	CArn CHrt CMea CPle CSLe CStr ECha ELau EMan EPAt GBar LEdu MAsh MHer MLLN MOak MSte MWgw NChi SAga SCro SDys SPin
blepharophylla	CPle CSpe CStr EBee ECtt EOrc EPAt LAst LHop LIck MAsh MHar MHer MSte MWat NCGa SAga SCro SDnm SPin WGwG WPen WWye
	- 'Diablo'	MAsh SDys
'Blue Chiquita' **new**	MRod
brachyantha	EBee
§ *buchananii* ♥H1+3	More than 30 suppliers
bulleyana misapplied	see *S. flava* var. *megalantha*
bulleyana	CBgR CBri EChP EMFP EMan EPAt EWes GBar LIck MDKP MHer NLar SDnm SHFr WCru WFar WLin
cacaliifolia ♥H1+3	CPle CPne CRHN CSpe CStr CWCL EBlw ECtt EOrc EPAt GBar MAsh MEHN MHer MLLN MNrw MSte MWat SGar SHFr SPin SSte SUsu WCom WOut WPPR WSHC WWye
cadmica	SPin
caerulea misapplied	see *S. guaranitica* 'Black and Blue'
caerulea L.	see *S. africana*
caespitosa	EHyt GEdr NWCA SBla
campanulata	CPle CPom LPhx SPin WCot
	- CC 4038	ITer
	- CC&McK 1071	CFir
canariensis	CDoC CFil CPle CStr EBee EPAt IGor MLLN MSte SHFr SPin WOut WSan WWye XPep
	- f. *candidissima*	XPep
candelabrum ♥H3-4	CArn CDes CMea CPle CSpe EBee EBlw ECtt EMan EOrc EPAt LPhx MAsh MHer MSte SAga SCro SDnm SHFr SPin WCHb WCot WKif WSHC WWye XPep

candidissima	SPin
canescens	XPep
cardinalis	see *S. fulgens*
carduacea	SPin
castanea	CPle CPom MHar SPin
- white-flowered **new**	SPin
§ *chamaedryoides*	CPle CPom CSev CStr CWCL EBee
	EBlw LPhx MAsh MRod NDov
	SAga SChu SDys SGar SPin SSpi
	WCom WPPR WSHC XPep
- var. *isochroma*	MAsh SDys
- 'Marine Blue' **new**	MRod
- silver	CBgR CStr LPhx MRod MSte SAga
	SPin WOut XPep
chamaedryoides	XPep
x *microphylla* **new**	
chamelaeagnea	CStr SDys SPin XPep
chapalensis	SAga SPin
chiapensis	CPle CStr EOrc MAsh MRod SPin
chinensis	see *S. japonica*
'Christine Yeo'	CDes CDoC CPle EBee EChP ECtt
	EPPr EPyc GGar LIck MAsh MDKP
	MRod MSte SDnm SDys SGar SPin
	SWal WDyG WGMN WMnd WOut
	WPGP WSHC WWye
cinnabarina	MAsh
cleistogama misapplied	see *S. glutinosa*
cleistogama	MHer
DeBary & Paul	
clevelandii	CPle MGol MHer MRod SDnm
	SPin WOut XPep
- 'Winnifred Gilman'	SDys SPin
clinopodioides **new**	SPin
coahuilensis	CMdw EBla LPhx MAsh MRod
	NDov SAga SGar SHFr SMrm SPin
	SUsu WSHC WWye
coccinea	EOrc MGol MHer MSte SHFr SPin
	WWye
- 'Brenthurst'	CStr SPin WGMN
- 'Coral Nymph'	CElw CHrt ECtt EOrc LDai LIck
	LRHS MGol SChu SDnm SDys SPin
	SWat
* - 'Indigo'	EPfP WSan
* - 'Lady in Red' ♀H3	CHrt CStr ECtt EOrc LIck MWgw
	SWat
- pink	SPin
* - 'Snow Nymph'	LIck
columbariae	SPin
concolor misapplied	see *S. guaranitica*
concolor Lamb.	CPle GCal MAsh SPin WDyG WOut
	WSHC WWye
confertiflora	More than 30 suppliers
corrugata	More than 30 suppliers
cristata **new**	WCot
cyanescens	CPle EPot SPin XPep
cyclostegia	EBee
darcyi	CHll CPle CPom CStr EChP EPyc
	LIck LPhx MAsh MRod SAga SDys
	SHFr SIgm SPin SSpi WHil WSHC
	XPep
davidsonii	SPin
'Dear Anja'	CPlt EFou EGle LHop LPhx NDov
	SCro
dentata	WCot WOut XPep
desoleana **new**	XPep
digitaloides BWJ 7777	WCru
discolor ♀H1	More than 30 suppliers
* - *nigra*	CMdw WDin
disermas	CPle SPin SPlb XPep
disjuncta **new**	CStr MRod SPin
divinorum	EOHP GPoy MGol MSal WGMN
dolichantha	EBee ECtt EMFP EShb GFlt MAnH
	MGol MWrn NBPC SBod SDnm
	SPin WGMN WHil WLin WWye

dolomitica	CStr SPin XPep
dombeyi	CStr SDys SPin
dominica	XPep
dorisiana	CPle CPne CSpe CStr ELan EOHP
	EPAt MAsh MLLN MSte SAga SDys
	SPin SSte WJek WOut WWye
dorrii	CStr SPin
eigii	SPin
§ *elegans*	CMHG CPle CSev CStr ELau EPAt
	EWes GEil LIck MAsh MSte NPPs
	NVic SCro WCom WFar WHil
	WOut WPPR WWye
- 'Frieda Dixon'	EBee EOHP
- 'Honey Melon'	EOHP MAsh
§ - 'Scarlet Pineapple'	More than 30 suppliers
- 'Sonoran Red' **new**	SDys
* - 'Tangerine Sage'	CArn CBri CDoC CPrp EBre ELau
	EOHP GBar GGar LFol MBow
	MGol MHer NGHP SDnm SPin
	SWal WBry WHHS
eremostachya	SPin
evansiana **new**	SPin
- BWJ 8013	WCru
fallax	CStr SPin
farinacea	SPin
- 'Alba'	LPVe
- 'Cirrus'	WHil
- 'Rhea'	LIck LRHS
- 'Strata'	EBre ECtt LRHS
- 'Victoria' ♀H3	EBre ELau LPVe MHer MRod SDys
flava **new**	SPin
§ - var. *megalantha*	CFai CHea CPle ELan EOrc GBin
	LRHS MFir MNrw NBPC NChi
	NGdn NSti WBor WFar WPer
	WWin WWye
forreri	CBAn CDes EBee MAsh SAga SDys
	SPin SSpi WPGP WSPU
- CD&R 1269	CPle CStr
§ *forsskaolii*	More than 30 suppliers
§ *fruticosa*	CArn CPle CPrp CStr ELau EOHP
	LRHS SIde XPep
§ *fulgens* ♀H3	CPle CPne CStr EPAt IFro ILis
	MAsh MHer SAga SGar SHFr SPer
	SPin WCHb WCom WFar WOut
	WRha WWye
gesneriiflora	CPle CPne CStr MAsh MHer
	MHom MSte SPin WGwG WWye
gilliesii	CStr MRod SPin XPep
§ *glutinosa*	CArn CHad CPle EBre EOrc EPAt
	EPPr GCal ITer LDai MNrw NBro
	SAga SPin SSpi WCAu WOut WPer
	WWye
grahamii	see *S. microphylla* var.
	microphylla
greggii	CBot CPle ECtt EWes LPio MAsh
	MHer MSte MTis SWat WGMN
	WKif WPer WWin XPep
- CD&R 1148	CPle LIck SDys WSPU
- 'Alba'	CBgR CHal CPle CSev EBee EOHP
	LIck MAsh MHer NBur NGHP
	SDys SPin WPPR WSHC WWol
	XPep
- 'Blush Pink'	see *S. microphylla* 'Pink Blush'
- 'Caramba' (v)	CFwr CSpe MAsh NGHP SAga
	SDnm SPin WCra WGMN WWol
- 'Dark Dancer' **new**	CPle
- 'Desert Blaze' (v)	CBAn CBgR CDes CDoC CPle CStr
	EBee EChP ECtt EMan LIck MAsh
	MDKP MHar NDov NGHP SCro
	SDys WCom WCot WHil WSPU
- 'Devon Cream'	see *S. greggii* 'Sungold'
- 'Forman's Red'	EBee XPep
- 'Keter's Red'	CPle MAsh MRod
- x *lycioides* misapplied	see *S. greggii* x *serpyllifolia*

– 'Magenta'	MDKP WHil	
– 'Navajo Cream' **new**	NPri	
– 'Navajo Dark Purple' **new**	NPri	
– 'Navajo Salmon Red' **new**	NPri	
– 'Navajo White' **new**	NPri	
– 'Peach' misapplied	see *S.* x *jamensis* 'Pat Vlasto'	
– 'Peach'	CDoC CPle CSpe EBee ELau EOrc EPfP LHop LPhx LPio LRHS MAsh MDKP MHer MLLN MSte NBrk NCGa NDov NGHP SAga SDnm SGar SPin SUsu SWal WMnd WPPR WWol	
– 'Plum Wine' **new**	CPle	
– 'Raspberry Royal'	see *S.* 'Raspberry Royale'	
– 'San Isidro Moon' **new**	CPle	
§ – x *serpyllifolia*	CPle EBee EMFP LPio MAsh MRod NGHP SBri SCro SDys SGar WGMN WHil WPPR WSHC WWol WWye	
– 'Sierra San Antonio'	see *S.* x *jamensis* 'Sierra San Antonio'	
– 'Sparkler' (v)	CPle	
– 'Stormy Pink'	CDes CSpe EBee MAsh WPGP	
– 'Sundown'	NGHP	
§ – 'Sungold'	CDes CPle CStr EBee EOrc EPfP GEil LHop LIck LPhx LRHS MAsh SAga SDys SPin SWal WHil WMnd WPPR WSan WWol	
– variegated **new**	CBot XPep	
– yellow	LPio LRHS XPep	
§ *guaranitica*	CBot CFil CHEx CHrt CPle CPne CTbh EBre ECtt LPio MHer SAga SDnm SPer SPin WCHb WPGP WSan WWye	
– 'Argentine Skies'	CPle CStr LIck LPhx LPio MAsh SAga SBla SChu SDys SMrm SPin WDyG WPGP WSHC WWye	
§ – 'Black and Blue'	CFil CKno CPLG CPle CPne CRHN CSWP CSev CStr EBee EBlw EPPr LIck LPhx MFOX MSte MWat SBri SDnm SGar SMrm SPin SVen WDyG WHil WPGP WPer WPrP WRha WWye	
§ – 'Blue Enigma' ♀H3-4	More than 30 suppliers	
haematodes	see *S. pratensis* Haematodes Group	
haenkei **new**	CStr MRod SPin	
heldreichiana	CSev CStr SPin	
henryi	MRod SPin	
heterochroa	EBee	
hians	CFir CPle EBee EOrc EPAt GBBs GBar LAst LPhx MBro MNrw SAga SBla SDnm SGar SMrm SPin SRms WCot WHoo WPer WWye	
hierosolymitana	CPle	
hispanica misapplied	see *S. lavandulifolia*	
hispanica L.	SPin	
horminum	see *S. viridis* var. *comata*	
huberi **new**	SPin	
hypargeia	CPle SPin	
indica	SPin XPep	
'Indigo Spires'	CHll CPle CSpe CStr EBee EBlw ECtt EOrc LPhx MAsh MHar MHom MLLN MRod NCGa SCro SMrm SPin SUsu WCom WDyG WOut WPPR WPen WSHC WWye	
interrupta	CPle CStr CWCL EHol EMan EOHP EPAt EWes LIck SAga SChu SHFr SMHy SPin WCom WOut WPen XPep	
involucrata ♀H3	CBri CDes CFir CPLG CPle CPom CSev CStr EOrc EPAt GCal GQui LPhx MAsh MHar MHer MRod	

		NBro NBur SCro SDys SMrm SPin SSte WOut WSHC
– 'Bethellii' ♀H3-4	More than 30 suppliers	
– 'Boutin' ♀H3	CPle GBri MAJR MAsh MLLN SAga SBri SDys	
§ – 'Hadspen'	CHad CHll CSam CStr LIck MSte SPin WCom WKif WWye	
– 'Mrs Pope'	see *S. involucrata* 'Hadspen'	
I – var. *puberula*	CPle SDys SPin	
iodantha	CPle MAsh SAga SPin WWye	
x *jamensis*	CStr MDKP SDys XPep	
– – CPN 5096	SAga	
– 'Cherry Queen'	CPle CStr MAsh SAga SDys WWye	
– 'Devantville'	CPle LPhx SAga	
– 'El Duranzo'	CPle LPio	
– 'Fuego'	LIck	
– 'James Compton'	EBee EBlw LIck LPio MSte SDys SGar SIgm WHoo	
– 'La Luna'	CPle CPom CSam CSev EBee ECtt EPfP LPhx LPio MAsh MHar MHer MSte NDov NPPs SAga SBri SDys SGar SPin SWal WCom WFar WMnd WPGP WPPR WSHC WWye	
– 'La Siesta'	CBAn CPle EBee LPio MAsh SDys	
– 'La Tarde'	CPle LPio MRod MSte SAga SCro SDys	
– 'Lemon Sorbet' **new**	SDys	
– 'Los Lirios' ♀H3-4	CBgR CPle CPom CStr EBee EOrc LIck MSte SAga SBri SDys SMrm SPin WCom WGMN WOut WPen WSPU	
* – 'Mauve'	SDys	
– 'Moonlight Over Ashwood' (v)	CPle MAsh SDys SPin	
– 'Moonlight Serenade'	CBAn CPle CSev CStr EBee EBlw EOrc MAsh MRod SAga SDys WHil WHoo WSPU	
§ – 'Pat Vlasto'	CPle CStr EBee LIck SDys SMrm SPin SWal WEas WPen WWye	
– 'Pleasant Pink'	CPle CSev EBee LIck MAsh SAga SPin	
§ – 'Sierra San Antonio'	CPle CSpe MAsh SDys	
§ *japonica*	CArn CPle CStr SPin WWye	
judaica	CPle CStr EBee EChP SPin XPep	
jurisicii	CArn CFir CPle CStr CWib EBee EOrc MWgw NLar SDnm SGar SIgm SPin SScr WOut WWye	
– 'Alba'	SPin	
– pink-flowered	CStr SPin	
* *karvinskii*	CStr SPin	
kuznetzovii	EBee	
lanceolata	XPep	
lanigera	SPin	
§ *lavandulifolia*	More than 30 suppliers	
lemmonii	see *S. microphylla* var. *wislizenii*	
leptophylla	see *S. reptans*	
leucantha ♀H1	More than 30 suppliers	
– 'Midnight'	LIck	
– 'Purple Velvet'	CPle MAsh MHar MRod SDys SPin	
– 'Santa Barbara'	MAsh SDys	
leucophylla	CBot CStr SIgm SPin WLin XPep	
– NNS 95-445	WCot	
longispicata	SPin	
lycioides misapplied	see *S. greggii* x *S. serpyllifolia*	
lycioides A. Gray	CHll CPle SDys SPin WDyG WGMN WHlf XPep	
lyrata	CBgR CPle EBee EMan EOHP EPAt MDKP MGol MSal MSph SAga SGar SHFr SPin SUsu WOut WWye	
	MSph SHar WHil	
– 'Burgundy Bliss'		
– 'Purple Knockout'	CFwr EBee EBlw EBre EChP EMFP EMan EMar EPyc GEil GSki LAst LPVe LPhx MDKP MSPs NGHP SAga SGar SPin WHrl WWeb	

macellaria misapplied	see *S. microphylla*	
macellaria Epling	CSam	
madrensis	CStr LIck MOak MRod SPin WCom WOut	
- 'Dunham' **new**	MAsh	
§ 'Maraschino'	CAbP CBri EBee EMan MAsh SDys SMrm WCot WMnd	
melissodora new	MRod	
mellifera	CArn CPle CStr SPin XPep	
merjamie	CPle CPom EBee SPin XPep	
- 'Mint-sauce'	CElw CPen CPla ELan EMan EMar MCCP MNrw SHFr WBea WPer	
mexicana	CPle LIck SPin SSpi WWye	
- T&K 550	CArn CBot	
- 'Limelight'	CStr WOut	
- var. **minor**	CPle MRod SAga	
- 'Tula' **new**	SDys	
meyeri new	MRod SPin	
§ **microphylla**	CArn CHrt CMHG CPle CPom ELau EOHP EOrc EPAt EWes GBar GGar LFol LHop MBow MHer NPPs NSti SBri SHFr SSpi SYvo WCom WCru WHCG WHHs WPPR WPer XPep	
- 'Cerro Potosi'	CBgR CBri CMdw CPle CPom CSev CSpe CStr EBee EBlw MAsh MRod MSte SAga SCro SDys SGar SHFr SMrm SPin WDyG WGMN WPen WWeb WWye	
- 'Dieciocho de Marzo' **new**	CPle	
* - 'Elmar'	EBee	
* - 'Huntingdon Red'	EOHP	
- 'Huntington' **new**	CPle	
- 'Kew Red' ♀H3-4	CBAn CDoC CPle CStr EBee MAsh MBro MNrw SAga SPin WHoo WPen	
- 'La Trinidad' **new**	CPle	
- 'Maraschino'	see *S.* 'Maraschino'	
§ - var. **microphylla**	More than 30 suppliers	
- - 'La Foux'	CHea CPle EBlw LPhx MAsh MDKP MRod SAga SCro SDys SMrm WSPU	
- - 'Newby Hall' ♀H3-4	CBrm CPle CStr EBee ECtt EOrc EWes GEil LIck LPhx MAsh MSte SChu WPGP	
- var. **neurepia**	see *S. microphylla* var. *microphylla*	
- 'Orange Door' **new**	CPle	
- 'Oregon Peach'	LRHS	
- 'Oxford'	CPle CStr SAga SDys SPin	
§ - 'Pink Blush' ♀H3-4	CAbP CKno CPle CPne EBee ECtt ELan EMan EOrc EPfP GBri LRHS MAsh MLLN MMil MRod MSte NGHP SAga SMrm SPin SSpi SWal WCom WHil WPGP WSHC	
- 'Pleasant View' ♀H3-4	CPle WOut	
- purple	EBee GCal WHHs	
- 'Red Velvet' **new**	CPle	
§ - 'Ruth Stungo' (v)	CPle SAga	
- 'San Carlos Festival'	CBAn EBee ECtt MAsh SDys SPin	
- 'Variegata' splashed	see *S. microphylla* 'Ruth Stungo'	
- 'Wild Watermelon'	CBAn CPle EBee MAsh SDys	
§ - var. **wislizeni**	CDoC CPle CStr SDys SPin WHil WPer	
- 'Zaragoza' **new**	CPle	
milliorhiza	CArn EBee MSal SPin	
miniata new	CPle CStr MAsh SDys SPin	
misella new	SPin	
moorcroftiana	MGol SDnm SPin	
'Mrs Beard' **new**	XPep	
muelleri misapplied	CDes CPom CSpe EBee EPyc MAsh SPin WCFE WCom WPGP XPep	

'Mulberry Wine'	CHll CPle EBee ECtt MAsh SAga SDys SPin WHil	
§ **multicaulis** ♀H4	CPle EBee EBlw ECha EMan EPyc ETow GBri MHer MSte SHFr WCot WEas WSHC	
munzii	XPep	
* **murrayi**	CAbP WCot	
namaensis	CStr SPin XPep	
napifolia	CPom CStr EBee GBBs GSki LPhx MGol MSPs NGar SAga SBod SDnm SPin WGMN WSPU	
nemorosa	EBee NLar SHFr SPin SRms WShp XPep	
- 'Amethyst' ♀H4	More than 30 suppliers	
- 'Caradonna'	EBee EChP EFou EMan IBal LDai MNrw MTis NMyG NPro SPoG SUsu WCot WHil	
- East Friesland	see *S. nemorosa* 'Ostfriesland'	
- 'Lubecca' ♀H4	CMHG EBee ECtt EFou EGle EHrv EMan EPfP EPla GEil LRHS MLLN NCGa SMrm SPer WCAu WMnd	
- 'Marcus' **new**	CPrp EBee EPfP LRHS MBNS NDov SUsu WCot	
- 'Midsummer'	MGol	
- 'Negrito'	EBee EGle SCro	
§ - 'Ostfriesland' ♀H4	More than 30 suppliers	
- 'Phoenix Pink'	LPhx	
- 'Pink Beauty' **new**	SCro	
- 'Plumosa'	see *S. nemorosa* 'Pusztaflamme'	
- 'Porzellan' ♀H4	ECtt	
§ - 'Pusztaflamme' ♀H4	CPrp CStr EBee EBre EChP ECha EMan ENot EPfP LBBr LRHS MCLN MMHG NPro NSti SAga SBla SCro SMrm SUsu WCAu WHoo WWeb	
- 'Rose Queen'	CBri CStr ECtt EMFP EPPr GKir GSki NBir SPer SPin SPla WFar WHHs WLow	
- 'Rosenwein'	CBri CSam EBee EMan GBuc LDai LPVe LPhx MDKP MWrn SMrm	
- 'Schwellenburg'	EBee	
§ - subsp. **tesquicola**	CPom EBee ECha EGle EGoo LPVe LPhx NLar SAga SMrm	
- 'Wesuwe'	CPle EBee EGle NDov NGby SCro	
neurepia	see *S. microphylla* var. *microphylla*	
nilotica	CArn CPle EBee EOrc EWll MGol SHFr SPin WHer XPep	
nipponica	CPle WPer	
- B&SWJ 5829	WCru	
- 'Fuji Snow' (v)	EBee EMan EWes MLLN	
nubicola	CBgR CPle CStr EMar GPoy LDai MWod SPin WLin WOut WWye XPep	
officinalis	More than 30 suppliers	
- 'Alba'	see *S. officinalis* 'Albiflora'	
§ - 'Albiflora'	ECtt EOHP GBar MAsh MLLN NGHP SPin WCHb WJek WPer XPep	
N - 'Aurea' ambig.	CWib EPar GPoy MBar NPri WShp	
- 'Berggarten'	CArn CBot CPrp EBee ECha ELau EMan EOHP EPfP GBar GCal GKir LHop LPhx LPio MAnH MHer MRav NSti SAga SChu SCro SDix SSvw WBry WCFE WHer WMnd XPep	
I - 'Blackcurrant'	CHal SPin WHHs	
§ - broad-leaved	CBot CSWP ELau MHer SWat WHHs WJek WWye	
- 'Crispa'	WCHb XPep	
- 'Extrakta'	EOHP	
- 'Herrenhausen'	MSte	
§ - 'Icterina' (v) ♀H4	More than 30 suppliers	
- 'Kew Gold'	ELau MRav WJek	
- **latifolia**	see *S. officinalis* broad-leaved	

– 'Minor'	EGoo WHer	
– narrow-leaved	see *S. lavandulifolia*	
* – 'Pink Splash' (v)	WCHb	
– *prostrata*	see *S. lavandulifolia*	
– 'Purpurascens' ♀H4	More than 30 suppliers	
– 'Purpurascens Variegata' (v)	CStr GBar MAsh NSti SPet WEas	
– 'Robin Hill'	GBar	
– 'Rosea'	WBcn WCHb WHer	
* – tangerine	EDAr LAst SPet	
– Tomentosa Group	CArn	
– 'Tricolor' (v)	More than 30 suppliers	
– 'Variegata'	see *S. officinalis* 'Icterina'	
– 'Wurzburg' **new**	CSam	
oppositiflora ♀H1+3	CBgR CPle CStr EMan LIck MAsh MHer MRod SDys SPin WPPR	
pachyphylla	SIgm SPin XPep	
pachystachya **new**	SPin	
palaestina **new**	XPep	
§ *patens* ♀H3	More than 30 suppliers	
– 'Alba' misapplied	see *S. patens* 'White Trophy'	
– 'Blue Trophy'	LIck	
– 'Cambridge Blue' ♀H3	More than 30 suppliers	
– 'Chilcombe'	CPle CPom CSam CStr EBee EBlw ECtt LIck MAsh MAvo MBow MHer MHer NPPs SAga SChu SDys SHFr SPin SSvw WCom WCra WHil WOut WPPR WSHC WWeb WWol WWye	
– 'Guanajuato'	More than 30 suppliers	
– 'Oxford Blue'	see *S. patens*	
– 'Royal Blue'	see *S. patens*	
– 'White Trophy'	CHal CPle CPom CStr EBee EChP ECtt EOrc ERou LDai LHop LIck LRHS MAsh MSte NGHP SDnm SGar SPin SWal WCom WFar WPPR WSHC WWeb WWol WWye	
penstemonoides	EBee XPep	
phlomoides	CTCP EBee MGol	
'Phyllis Fancy' **new**	CStr	
pinguifolia **new**	SPin	
polystachya	CPle MRod SPin WWye	
pratensis	CArn CFwr CPle CStr ELan EPAt LPio MSal MWgw SECG SGar SPin WOut WPer WWye XPep	
– 'Albiflora'	EBre LRHS	
§ – Bertolonii Group	SEND	
§ – Haematodes Group ♀H4	CBot CPle EBee EChP ECha ELan LDai MBro MNrw NDov NLar SBla SDnm SRms WPer WWye XPep	
– 'Indigo' ♀H4	CDes CPlt CStr EBee EBlw EBre EMan EPPr EPfP EWll LRHS MRav NDov NLar WAul WMnd	
– 'Lapis Lazuli'	CDes CPle CPlt EBee EMon LPhx	
– 'Pink Delight' **new**	EBee	
– 'Rhapsody in Blue' **new**	EBee WCot	
– 'Rosea'	CBgR CPle EBre ECha LPhx LRHS NDov SPin WWye	
prunelloides **new**	CStr SPin	
przewalskii	CBel CDes CHar CPle CPom CStr EFwa EOrc GIBF GSki IFro LPhx MGol MSal NBPC NBid NMRc SDnm SGar SHFr SMrm SPin WBVN WGMN WOut WPer WWye	
– ACE 1157	EBee WCot WCru	
– BWJ 7920	WCru	
– DJH 210524	EPPr	
'Purple Majesty'	CHea CHll CPle CPne CSev CSpe CStr EBee EMan LIck LPhx LPio MAsh MRod MSte NCGa SDys SMrm SPin SSpi SUsu WCom WSPU WSan WWye	
purpurea	CM&M CPle MGol SPin	
§ 'Raspberry Royale' ♀H3-4	More than 30 suppliers	

recognita	CBot CPle CPom CSpe LPhx WKif WSHC XPep	
§ *reflexa*	LIck	
regeliana misapplied	see *S. virgata*.	
regeliana Trautv.	CPle MLLN NBir SPin	
regla	CPle CStr MRod SDys SPin XPep	
– 'Jame' **new**	WCot	
repens	CPle CStr CTCP EBee IGor SDys SPin WDyG WWye	
– var. *repens*	SGar XPep	
§ *reptans*	CPle CSam CStr CWCL EPAt LHop LIck MAsh MHar SAga SPin WDyG WPer XPep	
ringens	CPom GFlt SPin XPep	
riparia misapplied	see *S. rypara*	
§ *riparia* Kunth	EPAt MAsh	
roborowskii	SPin	
roemeriana ♀H3	CPle CStr EBee EOrc LIck MAsh MDKP MHom NWCA SDnm SDys SPin WHil WPGP XPep	
'Royal Crimson Distinction' PBR	EBee	
rubescens	CStr MRod SPin	
rubiginosa **new**	MRod	
runcinata **new**	XPep	
rutilans	see *S. elegans* 'Scarlet Pineapple'	
rypara	CPle CPom SDys SPin	
sagittata	CSpe CStr MAsh MRod SPin	
* *sauntia* **new**	SPin	
scabiosifolia	CPom ECoo MGol SPin	
scabra	CFir CPle CStr EChP MGol MSte SDys SPin WCAu WOut WWye XPep	
sclarea	CArn CBot CHby CPle EBee ECtt EGoo ELau GPoy LRHS MHer MWat NChi NGHP NGdn SECG SIde SPin WCHb WHHs WHer WHoo WPer WWye XPep	
§ – var. *sclarea*	CKno EWTr MAnH NSti SPet WCra WWeb	
– var. *turkestanica* hort.	More than 30 suppliers	
§ – 'Vatican White'	CPle EBee EMar GKir LDai NLar SDnm WHil WWeb	
– white-bracted	CBri CWib ECoo EFWa EOHP GMac LHop MAnH NGHP NLar SBod SPin SWvt WCom WGwG WHHs WSHC XPep	
scutellarioides	CStr MLLN WOut	
semiatrata misapplied	see *S. chamaedryoides*	
semiatrata Zucc.	CPle CPom CSpe EBee EOrc EPAt LIck LPhx MAsh SAga SDys SPin WGMN WWye	
sessei	CStr MRod	
'Shirley's Creeper' **new**	XPep	
'Silke's Dream'	CPle MAsh MRod SDys SPin WSHC	
sinaloensis	CBgR CElw CFai CPle CSpe CStr EBee MAsh MDKP MHar MSte SAga SDys SPin WFar WGMN WOut WRha	
– 'Blue Eyes' **new**	SPer WWeb	
somalensis	CDoC CPle CStr MAsh SDys SHar SPin WOut XPep	
sonomensis	XPep	
spathacea ♀H3-4	CPle CPom CStr EMan GCal LHop LPhx SDys SIgm SPin WSHC WWye XPep	
splendens	CStr MRod SPin	
– 'Peach'	CStr SPin	
§ – 'Van-Houttei' ♀H3	CDoC CPle CStr LIck MAsh MLLN MRod SDys SPin WCom WGMN WWye	
sprucei	CStr SPin	
§ *staminea*	CPle CStr MGol SHFr SPin WSan WWye XPep	

stenophylla	CPle CTCP EBee EChP MGol SPin WGwG WOut WPer
stepposa	SPin XPep
x *superba* ♀H4	CBot CSBt ECtt ELan EOrc EPfP EWTr LAst LEdu LRHS MBri MHer MMil MWat SDix SMrm SPer SRms SSpe SSvw WHoo WMnd WWhi WWye
- 'Adrian'	SChu
- 'Forncett Dawn'	EFou EGle SChu
- 'Rubin' ♀H4	EBee SChu SCro SMrm
- 'Superba'	CSev ECha ECtt EFou EHrv LPhx MRav WCAu
§ x *sylvestris*	LAst WLin XPep
- 'Blauhügel' ♀H4	More than 30 suppliers
§ - 'Blaukönigin'	CBri EBee EPfP ERou EWTr GKir IBal IHMH LPVe LRHS MWat MWrn NArg NBPC NGHP NJOw NLar NMir NVic SIgm SPet SPlb SWvt WBea WBrk WFar WHil WLow WPer WWeb
- Blue Queen	see *S.* x *sylvestris* 'Blaukönigin'
- 'Lye End'	ECtt ERou MRav NCGa
§ - 'Mainacht' ♀H4	More than 30 suppliers
- May Night	see *S.* x *sylvestris* 'Mainacht'
- 'Rose Queen'	More than 30 suppliers
- 'Rügen'	CBgR EBee EChP EMan IBal LRHS MBri NDov WHil
- 'Schneehügel'	EBee EChP ECha EGle ELan EMan ENot EPPr EPfP GKir LAst LPVe MBNS MBri MMil NBPC NCGa NPri NPro SBla WCAu WHil WMnd WShp WWeb
- 'Tänzerin' ♀H4	EFou EGle LPhx NDov SChu SCro SDys SMHy SMrm WCot
- 'Viola Klose'	CMHG CStr EBee EBre EFou EGle EMan GCal GKir LPhx LRHS NCGa NLar NPPs SMrm SSvw WCAu WCot SMad SUsu
- 'Wissalink'	SMad SUsu
tachiei hort.	see *S. forsskaolii*
taraxacifolia	CPle CStr SCro SPin
tesquicola	see *S. nemorosa* subsp. *tesquicola*
tiliifolia	EBee MGol SDnm SHFr SPin SRms
tomentosa	CPle EBee ECoo MGol SPin
transcaucasica	see *S. staminea*
transsylvanica	CArn CBel CHea CPle EBee EChP EOrc EPAt EPPr EWTr LRHS MWgw MWrn SChu SCro SDnm SMrm SPin SWat WCAu WCom WPer XPep
- 'Blue Spire' **new**	MBri MWhi SSvw
'Trebah Lilac White'	CPle CPom EPyc MAsh MRod MSte NFla SCoo SDnm SDys SGar SPin WWye
'Trelawny Rose Pink'	EPyc LRHS MAsh MHar MSte SDnm SDys
'Trelissick Creamy Yellow'	ECtt EPyc LAst LRHS MAsh MRod MSte NFla SAsh SDnm SDys SPin
'Trenance Lilac Pink'	CPle EPyc LRHS MAsh MRod MSte SDnm SDys SGar SPin
'Trewithen Cerise'	CPle ECtt EPyc LAst LRHS MAsh MRod MSte NFla SAsh SCoo SDnm SPin SPoG
trijuga	SPin WOut
triloba	see *S. fruticosa*
tubifera **new**	SAga
uliginosa ♀H3-4	More than 30 suppliers
- 'African Skies'	NBrk SMrm WDyG
urica	CSpc MAsh SDys SPin
'Van-Houttei'	see *S. splendens* 'Van-Houttei'
'Vatican City'	see *S. sclarea* 'Vatican White'
verbenaca	CArn EPAt MBow MHer MSal NMir NSco SPin WOut WPer WWye XPep

- pink	WOut
verticillata	CArn CPle CPlt CStr EBee ECha EGoo EHrv GFlt LRHS MBro MGol MHer MWgw NSti SDys SPer SPin WCAu WOut WPer WWye XPep
- 'Alba'	CPle EBee ECGN EGle EOrc EPfP ERou EShb LRHS MRav MTis MWgw NGdn NSti SBla SPer SPin WCAu WHer WMnd WPer XPep
- subsp. *amasiaca*	SGar
- 'Hannay's Blue'	EFou
- 'Hannay's Purple'	EFou
- 'Purple Rain'	More than 30 suppliers
- 'Smouldering Torches'	LPhx SMHy
- 'White Rain'	CAbP EChP EFou EOMN LBBr
villicaulis	see *S. amplexicaulis*
§ *virgata* Jacq.	CBri CPle EBee SPin WCAu WOut WWye
viridis **new**	SPin
§ - var. *comata*	CArn EMar GSki NGHP SECG SIde WHHs WJek
- var. *viridis*	SBod WHrl
viscosa Sesse & Moc.	see *S. riparia*
viscosa Jacquin	CPle CStr CTCP SPin WOut WWye XPep
wagneriana	CStr SPin
'Waverly' **new**	CPle CStr
yunnanensis	EBee
- BWJ 7874	WCru

Salvinia (*Salviniaceae*)

auriculata	WDyG

Sambucus ✿ (*Caprifoliaceae*)

adnata	EBee
- B&SWJ 2252	WCru
caerulea	see *S. nigra* subsp. *cerulea*
callicarpa **new**	SSpi
canadensis	see *S. nigra* subsp. *canadensis*
chinensis	EBee
- B&SWJ 6542	WCru
coraensis	see *S. williamsii* subsp. *coreana*
ebulus	LEdu NSti SMad
- DJHC 0107	WCru
formosana	LEdu
- B&SWJ 1543	IFro WCru
* *himalayensis*	EWes
§ *javanica* B&SWJ 4047	WCru
kamtschatica	GIBF WHCr
nigra	CCVT CDul CElw CRWN ENot GKir GPoy GWCH IHMH LBuc MHer MSwo NWea SHFr SIde SMrm WDin WMou XPep
- 'Albomarginata'	see *S. nigra* 'Marginata'
- 'Albovariegata' (v)	CBri CDoC CDul EBee SSte
* - 'Ardwall'	GCal
N - 'Aurea' ♀H4	CBcs CDul CLnd CSBt EBee ECrN ELan ENot EPfP GKir MBar MRav NBee NWea SPer WDin WFar WSHC
- 'Aureomarginata' (v)	CBri EBee ECrN ELan EPfP GEil MRav NFor NLar NSti SHBN WCFE WFar
- Black Beauty = 'Gerda' ♀H4	More than 30 suppliers
- Black Lace = 'Eva'	CKno CSBt CSpe CWib ENor LAst LRHS MBri MDun NCGa NPro SCoo SPer WCot WGMN WGwG WHHs WWeb
- 'Cae Rhos Lligwy'	WHer
- subsp. *canadensis*	NWea
- - 'Aurea'	CWib MBar MBlu NWea WHar
- - 'Maxima'	EPfP SMad SMrm
- - 'York' (F)	CAgr

§	- subsp. *cerulea*	EPfP SMad
	- 'Frances' (v)	WBcn WCot
	- 'Godshill' (F)	CAgr SDea
	- 'Golden Locks'	MAsh MWgw
§	- 'Guincho Purple'	CBcs CBri CDoC CDul CWib EBee ECrN EHoe ELan EPfP GAbr GCal GEil IHMH ISea LRHS MBar MBlu MCCP MDun MHer MRav MSwo NFor SMrm WDin WFar WSHC
	- 'Heterophylla'	see *S. nigra* 'Linearis'
	- 'Ina' **new**	CAgr
	- f. *laciniata* ♥H4	CBcs CMHG EBee ELan EPfP EPla GAbr GKir MBlu MLLN MRav NBee NBee NFor NSti SChu SDix SLon SMHy SPer SSpi SSta WCFE WCot WDin WFar WPGP WSHC
§	- 'Linearis'	CFai CPMA ELan EPla GEil MRav NLar SPer
	- 'Long Tooth'	CNat
	- 'Luteovariegata' (v)	WBcn
	- 'Madonna' (v)	CBcs CMHG EBee EPla EWTr LRHS MBri MGos MLLN MRav NBee NLar SPer SPla WCot
§	- 'Marginata' (v)	CDul CMHG CPLG CWib EHoe GAbr GEil ISea LRHS MBar MGos MHer MLLN MRav SDix SLon SPer WCot WDin WFar WHar WWin
	- 'Marion Bull' (v)	CNat
	- 'Nana'	EMon
	- 'Plaque' (v)	CNat
	- 'Plena' (d)	EPla MInt SSte WCot
	- 'Pulverulenta' (v)	CBgR CDoC CHar EBee EPfP EPla GCal GKir LHop LRHS MLLN MRav SPer WBcn WCot WGMN WSHC WWeb
	- 'Purple Pete'	CNat
	- 'Purpurea'	see *S. nigra* 'Guincho Purple'
	- 'Pygmy'	EPla
	- 'Pyramidalis'	CPMA EPla MBlu NLar WCot
	- 'Samdal' (F)	CAgr
	- 'Samidan' (F)	CAgr
	- 'Samnor' (F)	CAgr
*	- 'Tenuifolia'	MRav NLar
	- 'Thundercloud'	CElw CMHG GKir LRHS MBri MTis NBee NChi NPro WBcn WCot WPat
	- 'Variegata'	see *S. nigra* 'Marginata'
	- f. *viridis*	CAgr CBgR CNat EMon
	racemosa	CAgr EPfP GIBF GWCH NWea WRha
	- 'Aurea'	CLnd EHoe GKir WGwG
	- 'Crûg Lace'	WCru
	- 'Goldenlocks'	CBgR EGra EWes GKir MGos MSwo NLar NPro SPer WBcn
	- 'Plumosa Aurea'	More than 30 suppliers
	- 'Sutherland Gold' ♥H4	More than 30 suppliers
	- 'Tenuifolia'	CMHG CPMA CSWP ELan EPfP LRHS NLar WPat
	wightiana	see *S. javanica*
§	*williamsii*	CMCN WFar
	subsp. *coreana*	

Samolus (Primulaceae)

	repens	CPBP ECou

Sanchezia (Acanthaceae)

	nobilis hort.	see *S. speciosa*
§	*speciosa*	CHal

Sandersonia (Colchicaceae)

	aurantiaca	CFwr CPne EPot LAma LRHS NRog WViv
I	- 'Phoenix' **new**	WViv

Sanguinaria (Papaveraceae)

	canadensis	More than 30 suppliers
	- f. *multiplex* (d)	CDes CLAP EMan EPPr GEdr GKir LRHS WPnP
	- - 'Paint Creek Double'	SSpi
	- - 'Plena' (d) ♥H4	More than 30 suppliers
	- 'Peter Harrison'	LPhx

Sanguisorba (Rosaceae)

§	*albiflora*	CDes CRow EBee EFou EGle ELan EMon EPPr ERou GBuc GMac MRav NLar NPro SChu SHop SMrm WBea WFar WPGP WTin WWin WWpP
	armena	MNrw SSvw WTin
	benthamiana	CHEx
	canadensis	CDes CKno CRow EBee EChP ECha EGle GCal GFlt GKir GPoy GSki LPhx MFir MSte MTis MWgw NVic SAga SDix SUsu WAul WBea WCAu WCot WFar WMoo WOld WTin WWye
*	*caucasica*	EBee EWes LPhx WWye
	dodecandra	CTCP
	hakusanensis	CDes CHar EBee ECha MNrw NBir NBro NPro WFar
	- B&SWJ 8709	WCru
	magnifica Schischk. & Kom.	CBot CDes CFir
	- *alba*	see *S. albiflora*
	menziesii	CDes CHar CKno EBee EFou EGle EPPr GBin GFlt LPhx NLar NPro SChu SOkh SUsu WCAu WCot WFar WPGP WPnP
§	*minor*	CAgr CArn CHby CKno CSam EBee ELau GAbr GBar GPoy MBar MBow MDun MGas MHer NArg NBro NGHP NMir NPri SIde SPlb WBri WBrk WCHb WHHs WHbs WHer WMoo WWye
	- subsp. *muricata*	GWCH
	obtusa	More than 30 suppliers
	- var. *albiflora*	see *S. albiflora*
	officinalis	CArn CBrm CHar CKno EBee ECGN EHrv EPfP GBar GBin IHMH MBow MHer NDov NMir NPPs NPro SECG SWat WCAu WMoo WRHF WWpP WWye
	- 'Arnhem'	CKno EBee EGle EPPr LPhx SMHy SOkh
	- 'Lemon Splash' (v) **new**	WCot
I	- 'Martin's Mulberry' **new**	EBee EWes
	- 'Pink Tanna'	CBgR EBee EFou EMon EPPr MBri SMHy SOkh WCAu WCot WHlf
	parviflora	see *S. tenuifolia* var. *parviflora*
	pimpinella	see *S. minor*
	'Pink Brushes'	LHop
	sitchensis	see *S. stipulata*
§	*stipulata*	CPlt EBee ECGN GCal IBlr MNrw WCom
	'Tanna'	More than 30 suppliers
	tenuifolia	CBrm CKno LPhx LRHS MSph NChi NLar NPro WAul WBea WCAu WMoo WWhi
	- 'Alba'	CDes CKno EBee GBuc GGar LPhx MBri MDun MSPs NPro SAga SMHy SOkh WCot WFar WPGP
§	- var. *parviflora*	CBot EBee MNrw NLar
	- - white	WTin
	- 'Pink Elephant'	CDes EBee GBin NSti
	- 'Purpurea'	CDes EBee NLar WFar
	- 'Stand Up Comedian' **new**	EBee NLar

Sanicula (*Apiaceae*)

europaea	EBee GBar GPoy MSal NSco WHer WTin WWye
* *fortunei* **new**	EBee
odorata **new**	EBee
orthacantha **new**	EBee

Sansevieria ✿ (*Dracaenaceae*)

trifasciata 'Golden Hahnii' (v) ♀H1	MBri
- 'Laurentii' (v) ♀H1	MBri

Santolina (*Asteraceae*)

benthamiana **new**	XPep
§ *chamaecyparissus* ♀H4	More than 30 suppliers
- var. *corsica*	see *S. chamaecyparissus* var. *nana*
- 'Double Lemon'	EBee EPfP SPla WCot
- 'Lambrook Silver'	CDoC CHar EBee ECtt EGoo ENot EPfP GKir LRHS MAsh SCoo SLim SPla WCra
- 'Lemon Queen'	CArn CBcs CBot CDoC CSLe EGoo ELau EPfP GBar GKir LAst LRHS MAsh MBow MGos MHer MSwo NBir NPri SIde SPla SWat WCHb WFar WHHs WPer XPep
§ - var. *nana* ♀H4	CBcs CBot EBee ECha ENot EPfP GKir LRHS MAsh MBar MDun MHer MRav MSwo NFor SPer SPoG SRms SWat WPer XPep
- 'Pretty Carol'	CAbP CBot EBee EBre ELan EMil EPfP EWTr GBar GKir LRHS MAsh NBrk NLRH SAga SIde SLim SPla WFar WGwG WHHs WWeb XPep
- 'Small-Ness'	CBot CDoC CLyd CStu EBee EGoo ELan EPfP ESis EWes GBar GEdr GKir LRHS MAsh MBro MHer MSte NMen SIng SLim SMrm SPer STre SWvt WCom WFar WPat WWeb
- subsp. *squarrosa*	XPep
incana	see *S. chamaecyparissus*
* *lindavica* **new**	XPep
'Oldfield Hybrid'	EChP MLan WCot XPep
pectinata	see *S. rosmarinifolia* subsp. *canescens*
§ *pinnata*	CArn CSLe CSev CTri MHer WPer
§ - subsp. *neapolitana* ♀H4	CArn CSBt CSev EBee ECha ECrN ELan ENot EPfP GBar LRHS MBri NFor NPri SDix SIde WCom WEas WHCG WSel WTin WWye XPep
- - cream	see *S. pinnata* subsp. *neapolitana* 'Edward Bowles'
§ - - 'Edward Bowles'	More than 30 suppliers
- - 'Sulphurea'	CHar CMea ECrN EGoo EPfP LPhx LRHS MAsh SPer WGwG WHHs WKif WPer WWhi WWpP XPep
rosmarinifolia	CArn CDoC ECrN ELau EWTr GWCH MRav MWhi SLon SPlb SRms WCHb WSel WShp WWye XPep
I - 'Caerulea' **new**	XPep
§ - subsp. *canescens*	EBee EPfP LRHS MRav WPer WWye
§ - subsp. *rosmarinifolia*	More than 30 suppliers
- - 'Primrose Gem' ♀H4	CBcs CBot CDoC CHar CSBt EBee EChP ECha ECrN ELau EMil ENor EPfP GBar GKir LHop LRHS MAsh MSwo NPPs NPri SBod SPer SPla SWvt WCot WPer WWye XPep
tomentosa	see *S. pinnata* subsp. *neapolitana*
virens	see *S. rosmarinifolia* subsp. *rosmarinifolia*

viridis	see *S. rosmarinifolia* subsp. *rosmarinifolia*

Sanvitalia (*Asteraceae*)

'Little Sun'	LRHS NPri SPet
'Sunbini'PBR	CSpe NPri

Sapindus (*Sapindaceae*)

saponaria	EGFP
var. *drummondii*	

Sapium (*Euphorbiaceae*)

japonicum	CFil CMCN EGFP WPGP
- B&SWJ 8744	WCru

Saponaria (*Caryophyllaceae*)

'Bressingham' ♀H4	CPBP EDAr EPfP LBee LRHS MTho NHol NMen SBla SBod SIng WAbe WPat WWin
caespitosa	EWes GTou NJOw NMen
x *lempergii* 'Max Frei'	CAbP CSam EBee EMan EPPr GBuc LPhx LRHS MSte SAga SBla SCro SDix SHar SScr WCot WOVN WSHC XPep
* 'Lilac Double'	MRav
lutea	CPBP
ocymoides ♀H4	More than 30 suppliers
- 'Alba'	ECha WFar
- 'Rubra Compacta' ♀H4	LRHS MTho NSla
- 'Snow Tip'	CBrm EDAr MWrn NDlv NLar WGor
- 'Splendens'	XPep
officinalis	CAgr CArn CBre CHby ELau GBar GPoy LEdu MHer MSal NGHP NSti SECG SIde SPlb WBrk WFar WHHs WHer WMoo WPer WWpP WWye
- 'Alba Plena' (d)	EBee EBre ECha ECoo GBar GKir NBrk NLar NSti WCHb WFar WHer WPer WRha WTin WWin
- 'Betty Arnold' (d)	WCot WTin
§ - 'Dazzler' (v)	ELau EMan EPPr GBar MRav NBir WCHb WHer
- 'Rosea Plena' (d)	CBre CFee CFwr CTCP EChP ECoo ELan ERou GKir LLWP LRHS MBri MHer NArg NBPC NBid NCot NGHP NGdn NOrc NVic SPer STes WBea WBrk WCAu WCHb WFar WMoo WPer
- 'Rubra Plena' (d)	CBre CHad EBee ELan MWhi NGHP NSti SHar WCHb WHer WRha WTin
- 'Variegata'	see *S. officinalis* 'Dazzler'
x *olivana* ♀H4	EDAr EMlt EPot MTho NMen SBla SIng WAbe WPat WRHF WWin
pamphylica	MNrw
pulvinaris	see *S. pumilio*
§ *pumilio*	GTou
'Rosenteppich'	SBla WPat
zawadskii	see *Silene zawadskii*

Saposhnikovia (*Apiaceae*)

divaricata	CArn MSal

Sarcococca ✿ (*Buxaceae*)

confusa ♀H4	More than 30 suppliers
hookeriana ♀H4	CFil CTrG ECot EPfP GSki LAst WBrE WFar WPGP
- B&SWJ 2585	WCru
- Sch 2396	EPla
- var. *digyna* ♀H4	More than 30 suppliers
- - 'Purple Stem'	CTri EHol EPfP EPla MGos MRav NLar WCru WDin WPGP WRHF
I - - 'Schillingii'	CDul
- var. *humilis*	More than 30 suppliers

orientalis	CAbP CFil CMCN CPMA ELan EPfP EPla LRHS MAsh MGos SLon SPla SSpi WFar WPGP WSpi
'Roy Lancaster'	see *S. ruscifolia* 'Dragon Gate'
ruscifolia	CBcs CMCN CPMA CSBt EBee EBre ECrN ELan ENot EPfP EPla GKir LRHS MAsh MGos MRav MSwo NCGa SLim SLon SMac SPer SRms SSpi WCru WFar WPGP
- var. *chinensis* ♀H4	CFil CPMA CSam EPfP EPla MRav WCru
- - L 713	EPla
§ - 'Dragon Gate'	CFil CPMA EPfP EPla LRHS LTwo MAsh SReu SSta WBcn WPGP
saligna	CBcs CFil CPMA EPfP NLar WBcn WCru
wallichii	CFil
- B&SWJ 2291	WCru
- B&SWJ 7285	WCru

Sarcopoterium (Rosaceae)

spinosum **new**	XPep

Sarmienta (Gesneriaceae)

repens ♀H2	NMen WAbe WCru

Sarothamnus see *Cytisus*

Sarracenia ✿ (Sarraceniaceae)

alata	CFwr CSWC MCCP SHmp WSSs
- 'Black Tube' **new**	WSSs
- heavily-veined	SHmp WSSs
- pubescent	CSWC WSSs
- 'Red Lid'	CSWC WSSs
- wavy lid	SHmp WSSs
- white-flowered **new**	WSSs
alata x *flava* var. *maxima*	CSWC
x *areolata*	CSWC WSSs
x *catesbyi* ♀H1	CFil CSWC WSSs
'Dixie Lace' **new**	CSWC
x *excellens* ♀H1	CSWC
x *exornata* (*alata* red x *purpurea* subsp. *venosa*)	CSWC
flava ♀H1	CFil CFwr CSWC EBla MCCP WSSs
- all green giant	see *S. flava* var. *maxima*
- var. *atropurpurea* **new**	WSSs
- 'Burgundy'	WSSs
- var. *cuprea*	WSSs
- var. *flava* **new**	WSSs
§ - var. *maxima*	CSWC WNor WSSs
- var. *ornata*	CSWC SHmp WSSs
- var. *rubricorpora* **new**	WSSs
- var. *rugelii*	SHmp WSSs
- veinless	CSWC
x *harperi*	CSWC
'Ladies in Waiting' **new**	CSWC
leucophylla ♀H1	CFwr CSWC EBla SHmp WSSs
- pubescent **new**	WSSs
- 'Schnell's Ghost' **new**	WSSs
'Lynda Butt'	SHmp WSSs
x *miniata*	SHmp
minor	CSWC SHmp WSSs
- 'Okee Giant'	CSWC EBla LHew WSSs
- 'Okefenokee Giant'	see *S. minor* 'Okee Giant'
minor x *oreophila*	CSWC
x *mitchelliana* ♀H1	CFwr
x *moorei*	WSSs
- 'Brook's Hybrid'	CSWC LHew WSSs
oreophila	CSWC SHmp WSSs
oreophila x *leucophylla*	CSWC
oreophila x *minor*	CSWC

x *popei*	CSWC
psittacina	CSWC SHmp WSSs
purpurea	CFil EBla NWCA
- subsp. *purpurea*	CFwr CSWC MCCP WSSs
- - f. *heterophylla*	CSWC WSSs
- subsp. *venosa*	CSWC SHmp WSSs
- - var. *burkii*	CSWC WSSs
- subsp. *venosa* x *oreophila*	CSWC
x *readii*	SHmp WSSs
- 'Farnhamii'	CSWC
x *rehderi*	SHmp
rubra	CSWC WSSs
- subsp. *alabamensis*	CSWC SHmp WSSs
- subsp. *gulfensis*	CSWC SHmp WSSs
* - - f. *heterophylla*	CSWC WSSs
- subsp. *jonesii*	CSWC WSSs
* - - f. *heterophylla*	CSWC
- subsp. *rubra*	CSWC WSSs
- subsp. *wherryi*	CSWC WSSs
- - giant form **new**	WSSs
- - yellow-flowered	CSWC WSSs

Saruma (Aristolochiaceae)

henryi	CPom EBee EMan LEur WCot

Sasa ✿ (Poaceae)

chrysantha hort.	see *Pleioblastus chino*
disticha 'Mirrezuzume'	see *Pleioblastus pygmaeus* 'Mirrezuzume'
glabra f. *albostriata*	see *Sasaella masamuneana* 'Albostriata'
kagamiana	EBee NLar
kurilensis	EBee EPAt EPla LPal MWht NMoo SDry WFar WJun
- 'Shima-shimofuri' (v)	EPfP EPla ERod SDry WJun
- short	EPla
megalophylla 'Nobilis'	see *S. senanensis* f. *nobilis*
nana	see *S. veitchii* f. *minor*
nipponica	CEnd SDry WJun
- 'Aureostriata'	SDry
oshidensis	EPla
§ *palmata*	CAbb CBcs CDul CHad COld CTrG CWib EBee EHoe ENot GFlt MCCP MWhi SEND WDin WFar WHer WPnP
- f. *nebulosa*	CBcs CBct CDoC CFir CHEx EBee EFul EHul ENot EPfP EPla EPza EWes MBrN MMoz MWht MWod NMoo SAPC SArc SDry SSto WDyG WFar WJun WMoo WMul
- 'Warley Place' (v)	SDry
quelpaertensis	EPla SDry
senanensis	SDry
§ - f. *nobilis*	SDry
tessellata	see *Indocalamus tessellatus*
tsuboiana	CBcs CDoC EBee EPla EPza LPal MAsh MMoz MWht NGdn NLar SDry WDyG WFar WMoo
§ *veitchii*	More than 30 suppliers
§ - f. *minor*	CBct EBee EPza MCCP MMoz

Sasaella (Poaceae)

bitchuensis hort.	SDry
glabra	see *S. masamuneana*
§ *masamuneana*	CDul CEnd EPla LAst
§ - 'Albostriata' (v)	CDoC CFil CMco COtt CWib EBee EPPr EPla ERod EWsh LEdu LPal MCCP MMoz MWht NGdn NMoo SDry SSto WDyG WFar WJun WMoo WMul WPGP WViv
- 'Aureostriata' (v)	COtt EPla GCal MMoz NPal SDry

§ **ramosa** CFwr CHEx EBee EPla LAst LEdu
MCCP MMoz MWht NMoo NRya
SDry WDin WMul

Sassafras (*Lauraceae*)
albidum CArn CFil CTho EPfP LRHS SSpi
WPGP
tzumu CFil WPGP

satsuma see *Citrus unshiu*

Satureja ✿ (*Lamiaceae*)
amani **new** XPep
§ **coerulea** ♀H4 EWes NBir NLAp
douglasii CArn EOHP SHDw WJek
I – 'Indian Mint' EDAr NGHP WLHH
georgiana **new** SSpi
hortensis CBod GPoy ILis MHer MLan WHHs
WHer WJek WLHH WSel
montana CArn ELau GPoy ILis LLWP MBri
MHer NMen SDix SIde SRms SRob
WCHb WHHs WHer WPer WWeb
WWye XPep
* – *citriodora* GPoy MHer XPep
– 'Coerulea' see *S. coerulea*
§ – subsp. *illyrica* LLWP WJek
– 'Purple Mountain' GPoy LLWP MHer
– *subspicata* see *S. montana* subsp. *illyrica*
parnassica LLWP WPer
repanda see *S. spicigera*
seleriana SScr
§ **spicigera** CArn CBod CLyd CNic CPBP EDAr
ELau EPot GBar GEdr LEdu LFol
LLWP MHer NBir NPri WCHb
WJek WLHH WSel WWin WWye
thymbra CArn EOHP LLWP SHDw WJek
XPep

Satyrium (*Orchidaceae*)
erectum **new** WCot
nepalense GGGa

Saurauia (*Actinidiaceae*)
subspinosa CHEx

Sauromatum (*Araceae*)
guttatum see *S. venosum*
§ **venosum** CHEx CKob CMea EAmu EBee
EMan EUJe ITer LAma LEur LRHS
MBri MOak MSph WCot WCru

Saururus (*Saururaceae*)
cernuus CHEx CRow CWat EHon ELan
EMFW EPAt EPfP LNCo LPBA MSta
SLon SRms SWat WMAq WWpP
chinensis CRow EBee WCru

Saussurea (*Asteraceae*)
albescens EMan WCot
auriculata HWJCM 490 WCru
stella **new** SScr

savory, summer see *Satureja hortensis*

savory, winter see *Satureja montana*

Saxegothaea (*Podocarpaceae*)
conspicua CBcs CDoC CMCN ECou EPla
IDee LCon SMad WCwm

Saxifraga ✿ (*Saxifragaceae*)
McB 1377 CLyd
SEP 22 CLyd EHyt
SEP 45 CLyd

McB 1397 from Nepal CLyd
'Ada' (x *petraschii*) (7) NMen
'Aemula' (x *borisii*) (7) NMen
§ 'Afrodite' (*sempervivum*) CLyd
(7)
aizoides (9) **new** WAbe
– var. *atrorubens* (9) NHol
aizoon see *S. paniculata*
'Aladdin' (x *borisii*) (7) NHol NMen
* 'Alan Hayhurst' (8) MDHE WAbe
'Alan Martin' CLyd
(x *boydilacina*) (7)
'Alba' (x *apiculata*) (7) ELan EMlt EPot GTou LRHS MBro
MHer NHol NLAp NMen NRya
NSla SBla SChu SPlb WCom WPat
WWin
'Alba' (x *arco-valleyi*) see *S.* 'Ophelia'
'Alba' (*oppositifolia*) (7) CLyd ELan EWes GKir GTou NDlv
NLAp NMen WAbe
'Albert Einstein' NMen
(x *apiculata*) (7)
'Albertii' (*callosa*) (8) see *S.* 'Albida'
§ 'Albida' (*callosa*) (8) GTou LRHS NLar SIng WAbe
WCom WWin
'Aldebaran' (x *borisii*) (7) NMen
'Alfons Mucha' (7) CLyd EHyt NMen
'Allendale Acclaim' EHyt NDlv NMen
(x *lismorensis*) (7)
'Allendale Accord' EHyt NDlv NMen
(*diapensioides*
x *lilacina*) (7)
'Allendale Allure' (7) NMen
'Allendale Andante' NMen
(x *arco-valleyi*) (7)
'Allendale Angel' EHyt NMen
(x *kepleri*) (7)
'Allendale Argonaut' (7) NDlv NMen
'Allendale Ballad' (7) NMen
'Allendale Ballet' (7) CLyd EHyt NMen
'Allendale Bamby' NMen
(x *lismorensis*) (7)
'Allendale Banshee' (7) NMen
'Allendale Beau' NMen
(x *lismorensis*) (7)
'Allendale Beauty' (7) NMen
'Allendale Betty' CLyd EHyt NMen
(x *lismorensis*) (7)
'Allendale Billows' (7) NMen
'Allendale Bonny' (7) NMen
'Allendale Boon' EHyt
(x *izari*) (7)
'Allendale Bounty' (7) NMen
'Allendale Bravo' EHyt NMen WAbe
(x *lismorensis*) (7)
'Allendale Cabal' (7) CLyd NMen
'Allendale Celt' EHyt NMen
(x *novacastelensis*) (7)
'Allendale Charm' (7) EHyt NMen
'Allendale Chick' (7) NMen
'Allendale Comet' (7) GCrs NMen
'Allendale Dance' (7) NMen
'Allendale Dream' (7) NMen
'Allendale Duo' (7) NMen
'Allendale Elegance' NMen
(7) **new**
'Allendale Elf' (7) **new** NMen
'Allendale Elite' (7) **new** NMen
'Allendale Enchantment' NMen
(7) **new**
'Allendale Envoy' (7) **new** NMen
'Allendale Epic' (7) **new** NMen
'Allendale Fairy' (7) **new** NMen
'Allendale Fame' (7) **new** NMen
'Allendale Frost' (7) **new** NMen

'Allendale Garnet' (7) — CLyd NDlv NMen
'Allendale Ghost' (7) **new** — NMen
'Allendale Goblin' (7) **new** — NMen
'Allendale Grace' (7) **new** — NMen
'Allendale Gremlin' (7) **new** — NMen
'Allendale Joy' (x *wendelacina*) (7) — NMen
'Allendale Pearl' (x *novacastelensis*) (7) — CLyd EHyt NMen
'Allendale Ruby' (7) — CLyd CPBP NDlv NMen
'Allendale Snow' (x *rayei*) (7) — NDlv NMen
'Alpenglow' (7) — NMen
alpigena (7) — CLyd NSla WAbe
'Amitie' (x *gloriana*) (7) — NMen
andersonii (7) — CLyd EHyt NDlv NMen NRya
- McB 1475 — NHol
'Andrea della Robbia' (7) — NMen
x *andrewsii* (8x11) — MDHE MTho WAbe
angustifolia Haw. — see S. *bypnoides*
'Anna' (x *fontanae*) (7) — NMen
'Anne Beddall' (x *goringiana*) (7) — CLyd NMen WAbe
'Aphrodite' (*sempervivum*) (7) — see S. 'Afrodite'
x *apiculata* sensu stricto hort. — see S. 'Gregor Mendel'
'Apple Blossom' (15) — ECtt GTou MDHE MOne NRya WGor
aquatica (15) — NLAp
§ 'Arco' (x *arco-valleyi*) (7) — NJOw
x *arco-valleyi* sensu stricto hort. — see S. 'Arco'
x *arendsii* (15) — MDHE WEas
- purple (15) — EBre
§ 'Aretiastrum' (x *boydii*) (7) — CLyd ITim NDlv NMen WOBN
'Ariel' (x *bornibrookii*) (7) — CLyd NMen
'Arthur' (x *anglica*) (7) — NMen
'Assimilis' (x *petraschii*) (7) — CLyd
'August Hayek' (x *leyboldii*) (7) — ITim NMen
'Aurea Maculata' (*cuneifolia*) — see S. 'Aureopunctata'
§ 'Aureopunctata' (x *urbium*) (11/v) — COkL EBee EBre ECha EMan GBuc GCal MHer MWgw NHol SLon SMrm SPer SPlb SRms WBro WCom WHen WMoo WWpP
'Baldensis' — see S. *paniculata* var. *baldensis*
'Ballawley Guardsman' (15) — ECho MBNS MDHE SIng
§ 'Beatrix Stanley' (x *anglica*) (7) — CLyd MHer NDlv NHol NLAp NMen NRya
'Becky Foster' (x *borisii*) (7) — NMen
'Beechcroft White' (15) — LRHS MDHE
'Bellisant' (x *bornibrookii*) (7) — CLyd NMen
'Berenika' (x *bertolonii*) (7) — NMen
'Beryl' (x *anglica*) (7) — NMen
'Bettina' (x *paulinae*) (7) — NMen
x *biasolettoi* sensu stricto hort. — see S. 'Phoenix'
x *bilekii* (7) — CLyd
'Birch Baby' (15) — SIng
'Black Beauty' (15) — CBcs CMea EBre ECho EMlt LRHS MDHE MHer NHol
'Black Forest Gateaux' (*fortunei*) (5) — CLAP
'Black Ruby' (*fortunei*) (5) — More than 30 suppliers
'Blackberry and Apple Pie' (*fortunei*) (5) — More than 30 suppliers
'Blaník' (x *borisii*) (7) — CLyd NMen

'Blanka' (x *borisii*) (7) — NMen
'Blütenteppich' (15) — WPer WShp
'Bob Hawkins' (15/v) — CLyd EBre ELan LRHS MDHE MHer NHol WWin
§ 'Bodensee' (x *bofmannii*) (7) — WPat
'Bohdalec' (x *megaseiflora*) (7) — NMen
'Bohemia' (7) — CLyd EHyt EPot NMen NSla SBla WAbe
'Bornmuelleri' (7) — NMen
'Boston Spa' (x *elisabethae*) (7) — CLyd ITim LRHS MBro MHer NDlv NHol NJOw NLAp NMen SChu SPlb WPat
'Brailes' (x *poluanglica*) (7) — CLyd ITim
'Bridget' (x *editbae*) (7) — CLyd CMea CNic GKir LRHS NDlv NHol NMen SIng WWin
'Brno' (x *elisabethae*) (7) — NHol NMen
bronchialis (10) — CLyd CNic
- var. *vespertina* — see S. *vespertina*
'Brookside' (*burseriana*) (7) — EPot ITim NMen
brunoniana — see S. *brunonis*
§ *brunonis* (1) — GAbr MDHE WCru
- CC&McK 108 — NWCA
bryoides (10) — CLyd GCrs GTou NRya NWCA
x *burnatii* Sünd (8) — CLyd EBre LRHS NDlv NLar NMen NPro WGor
burseriana (7) — GKir MBro NLAp NRya WAbe WGor
'Buster' (x *bardingii*) (7) — NMen
'Buttercup' (x *kayei*) (7) — CLyd EPot GEdr GTou MBro NHol NJOw NLAp NMen NWCA WHoo WPat
x *byam-groundsii* (7) — CLyd
caesia hort. (x *fritscbiana*) — see *Saxifraga* 'Krain'
caesia L. (8) — SRms
§ *callosa* (8) ♀H4 — ECGP EMlt GTou MBro MWat NHol NLAp SBla WEas WPat WTin
- var. *bellardii* — see S. *callosa*
- subsp. *callosa* (8) — SOkd
§ - - var. *australis* (8) — EMlt EPot MDHE NBro NHol NMen
- - var. *callosa* (8) — MDHE
- var. *lantoscana* — see S. *callosa* subsp. *callosa* var. *australis*
- *lingulata* — see S. *callosa*
callosa x *cochlearis* (8) — see S. Silver Farreri Group
'Cambridge Seedling' (7) — NMen
canaliculata (15) — MDHE NMen
x *canis-dalmatica* — see S. x *gaudinii*
§ 'Carmen' (x *elisabethae*) (7) — GKir LRHS MBro MOne NDlv NLAp NMen NRya WAbe WOBN
§ 'Carniolica' (*paniculata*) (8) — CLyd LRHS MBar MDHE NBro NMen NWCA SBla WCom
'Carniolica' (x *pectinata*) (8) — MDHE WAbe
'Carnival' (15) — COkL
carolinica — see S. 'Carniolica'
'Castor' (x *bilekii*) (7) — NMen
'Cathy Reed' (x *polulacina*) (7) — NMen
§ *caucasica* (7) **new** — EHyt
- var. *desoulavyi* — see S. *desoulavyi*
cebennensis (15) ♀H2 — CLyd CNic NMen NRya
- dwarf (15) — WAbe
'Cecil Davies' (8) — MDHE
cespitosa (15) — GKir MDHE WAbe
'Chambers' Pink Pride' — see S. 'Miss Chambers'
'Charlecote' (x *poluanglica*) (7) — ITim
'Charles Chaplin' **new** — CPBP

'Cheap Confections' CBct CBod CElw CHEx CLAP
  (*fortunei*) (4)   CM&M CMil CSpe CStr EBee EChP
    ECtt EMar EWll GAbr GFlt IPot
    LTwo MSte NHol NMen SMrm SPla
    WCot WFar WHil WLin WOld WPGP

§ *cherlerioides* (10)   ECtt MBNS NRya NVic WEas
'Cherry Pie' (*fortunei*) (5)   CBct CHea CLAP EMan EMar LHop
    LTwo MBNS MNrw NMyG WCot
    WShp
'Cherrytrees' (x *boydii*) (7)   NMen NSla
'Chetwynd' (*marginata*)   NMen WAbe
  (7)
'Chez Nous' (x *gloriana*)   CLyd NJOw NMen
  (7/v)
'Chodov' (7)   NMen
'Christine' (x *anglica*) (7)   CLyd NDlv NHol NLAp NMen
cinerea (7)   GCrs NMen
'Citronella' **new**   WAbe
'Claire Felstead'   GCrs
  (*cinerea* x *poluniniana*)
'Clare' (x *anglica*) (7)   NMen
'Clare Island' (15)   MDHE SIng
§ 'Clarence Elliott'   CLyd CMea CTri EHyt EWes GCal
  (*umbrosa*) (11) ♀H4   GKev GKir LRHS MHar MHer NFla
    NHol NRya NVic WAbe WCom
    WHoo WPat WWin
'Claudia' (x *borisii*) (7)   NMen
'Cleo' (x *boydii*) (7)   NMen
§ x *clibranii* (15)   MDHE SIng
§ 'Cloth of Gold' (*exarata*   CLyd EBre ECha ECtt ELan EMlt
  subsp. *moschata*) (15)   GTou LAst LRHS MBar MHer NHol
    NJOw NMen NRya SIng SPlb SRms
    WAbe WBVN WFar WWin
cochlearis (8)   EHyt ESis GEdr GKir LBee LRHS
    MOne MWat NBro NDlv NMen
    WAbe WCom WPer WWin
'Cockscomb'   EPot MDHE NJOw NLAp NMen
  (*paniculata*) (8)   SIng WAbe
columnaris (7)   NMen NSla
'Compacta' (*exarata*   MBro
  subsp. *moschata*) (15)
continentalis (15) **new**   NWCA
'Conwy Snow' (*fortunei*)   WAbe
  (5) **new**
'Conwy Star' (*fortunei*)   WAbe
  (5) **new**
'Coolock Gem' **new**   EHyt
'Coolock Kate'   EHyt NMen
'Cordata' (*burseriana*) (7)   NMen
'Corona' (x *boydii*) (7)   NHol NMen
'Corrennie Claret' (15)   EWes GTou
I 'Correvoniana' hort.   ECtt GKir LRHS MBro MHer MOne
  (*brevifolia*) (8)   NDlv NJOw NRya WCom WGor
    WWin
§ 'Corrie Fee' (*oppositifolia*)   GCrs GFlt GKir GTou SIng
  (7)
§ *cortusifolia* (5)   CHid CLAP EBee SSpi
  - B&SWJ 5879   WCru
  - var. *fortunei*   see *S. fortunei*
  - var. *stolonifera* (5)   WCru
  B&SWJ 6205
'Cotton Crochet'   EBee EChP EMan LAst MBNS
  (*fortunei*) (5/d)   MLLN NHol NMyG NPSI SMrm
    WBor WCot WFar WOld
cotyledon (8)   GCrs LBee LRHS MDHE NFor
    NHol WEas WPer
§ 'Cranbourne' (x *anglica*)   CLyd GCrs LRHS MBro NHol NLAp
  (7) ♀H4   NMen SBla SIng WCom WPat
'Cream Seedling'   EBre ESis NDlv NJOw NLAp NMen
  (x *elisabethae*) (7)
'Crenata' (*burseriana*) (7)   CLyd CMea EPot GCrs LRHS MBro
    NDlv NMen WAbe WHoo
'Crimson Rose'   see *S.* 'Rosea'
  (*paniculata*) (8)

§ *crustata* (8)   EHyt MDHE MDKP NMen SIng
  - var. *vochinensis*   see *S. crustata*
'Crystal Pink' (*fortunei*)   CBct CFai CMil EBee EChP EHrv
  (5/v)   EMil GAbr LAst LHop MBri MNrw
    MTis NBro NMen NMyG NPSI
    WCot WFar WGor WOld
'Crystalie' (x *biasolettoi*)   EPot LRHS MBro NMen NRya WPat
  (7)
'Cultrata' (*paniculata*) (8)   NBro
'Cumulus' (*iranica* hybrid)   CLyd CPBP EHyt GCrs NLAp
  (7) ♀H4   NMen SBla
cuneata (15)   GAbr NHol
§ *cuneifolia* (11)   CNic GGar IHMH LBee LRHS
    MHer MWat NDlv NFla NSti
    NWCA WRos
  - var. *capillipes*   see *S. cuneifolia* subsp. *cuneifolia*
§ - subsp. *cuneifolia* (11)   ECtt
* - var. *subintegra* (11)   ECho
cuscutiformis (5)   see *S.* 'Cuscutiformis'
§ 'Cuscutiformis'   CElw CHid CPLG EBee EBla
  (*stolonifera*) (5)   ETow GCal MRav SBla SRms
    WAbe WCru
cymbalaria (2)   EBur SIng
  - var. *huetiana* (2)   CNic
dahurica   see *S. cuneifolia*
'Dainty Dame'   CLyd LRHS NDlv NMen
  (x *arco-valleyi*) (7)
'Dana' (x *megaseiflora*)   CLyd NHol NMen
'Dartington Double'   EBre EMlt EWes GKir GTou LRHS
  (15/d)   MDHE NHol NLAp
'Dartington Double   MDHE NHol WCom
  White' (15/d)
'Dawn Frost' (7)   CLyd EHyt ITim NDlv NLAp NMen
    WAbe
'Delia' (x *hornibrookii*) (7)   CLyd ITim NMen
§ 'Denisa'   NMen
  (x *pseudokotschyi*) (7)
densa   see *S. cherlerioides*
'Dentata' (x *geum*)   see *S.* 'Dentata' (x *polita*)
§ 'Dentata' (x *polita*) (11)   CMea CStr ECha EPla GGar NVic
    SUsu WMoo
'Dentata' (x *urbium*)   see *S.* 'Dentata' (x *polita*)
§ *desoulavyi* (7)   GTou NMen
diapensioides (7)   CLyd WAbe
'Doctor Clay'   LBee MDHE NLAp NMen NRya
  (*paniculata*) (8)   WAbe
'Doctor Ramsey' (8)   EHyt EWes GEdr GTou LBee LRHS
    MBro NBro NDlv NJOw NLar
    NMen WAbe WGor
'Donald Mann' (15)   EWes
'Dorothy Milne' (7)   NMen
aff. *doyalana* (7)   CPBP NDlv
  - SEP 45   EHyt
'Drakula'   CLyd LRHS NDlv NMen SIng
  (*ferdinandi-coburgi*) (7)
'Dubarry' (15)   ECho EWes MDHE NRya
'Dulcimer' (x *petraschii*)   NMen
  (7)
'Duncan Lowe'   CLyd
  (*andersonii*) (7) ♀H4
'Dwight Ripley' (7) **new**   NMen WOBN
'Edgar Irmscher' (7)   CLyd NMen NWCA
'Edie Campbell' (15)   MDHE
'Edith' (x *edithae*) (7)   LRHS NJOw
'Edward Elgar'   NHol NMen
  (x *megaseiflora*) (7)
x *elegantissima* (15)   see *S.* x *clibranii*
'Elf' (7)   see *S.* 'Beatrix Stanley'
'Elf' (15)   ECtt LRHS NHol NMen SIng SRms
    WGor
x *elisabethae* sensu   see *Saxifraga* 'Carmen'
  stricto hort.
'Elizabeth Sinclair'   CLyd ITim NJOw NMen
  (x *elisabethae*) (7)

'Ellie Brinckerhoff' NMen
  (x *bornibrookii*) (7)
x *engleri* **new** CLyd
§ 'Ernst Heinrich' CLyd NMen NRya
  (x *heinrichii*) (7)
'Esther' (x *burnatii*) (8) CMea COkL EHyt EPot GCrs GKir
  LBee LRHS NHol NMen NWCA
  SBla SMer WAbe WHoo
§ 'Eulenspiegel' (x *geuderi*) CLyd EPot NMen
  (7)
'Eva Hanzlikova' (7) CPBP
exarata (15) LRHS NMen WAbe
§ - subsp. *moschata* (15) MDHE
fair maids of France see S. 'Flore Pleno'
'Fairy' (*exarata* ECtt ELan EPot WCom
  subsp. *moschata*) (15)
'Faldonside' (x *boydii*) CLyd CPBP MBro NDlv NHol
  (7) ♀H4 NLAp NMen NRya SBla WAbe
  WHoo WPat
'Falstaff' (*burseriana*) (7) CLyd
x *farreri* hort. (8) see S. Silver Farreri Group
§ 'Faust' (x *borisii*) (7) NMen WAbe
'Favorit' (x *bilekii*) (7) EHyt
§ *federici-augusti* CLyd GTou NSla WAbe
  subsp. *grisebachii*
  (7) ♀H2-3
'Ferdinand' (x *hofmannii*) NMen
  (7)
ferdinandi-coburgi CLyd ECtt LRHS NDlv NRya
  (7) ♀H4 NWCA WAbe WBrE
§ - var. *rhodopea* (7) CLyd EPot GCrs LRHS NDlv NMen
  SIng
'Findling' (15) EBre EMlt EPot IHMH LGro LRHS
  NJOw NMen WAbe WWin
'Five Color' (*fortunei*) CFai EBee MBnl NBPC NGdn SPer
  (5) **new** WGor
§ *flagellaris* (1) NMen WAbe
'Flavescens' misapplied see *Saxifraga* 'Lutea' (*paniculata*)
'Flavescens' Farrer NDlv
  (*paniculata*) **new**
'Flavescens' NBro
  (*paniculata*) (8)
x *fleischeri* (7) NMen
§ 'Flore Pleno' CFir EBee EWTr EWes MAvo NBir
  (*granulata*) (15/d) NLar NRya SIng WCom WFar
'Florissa' (*oppositifolia*) (7) CLyd WAbe
florulenta Schott, see S. *callosa*
  Nyman & Kotschy
'Flowers of Sulphur' see S. 'Schwefelblüte'
'Forsteriana' CBod
  (*petraea*) (15)
§ *fortunei* (5) ♀H4 CHEx EBee EBre EWTr ITim MRav
  NBir NHol SPer SRms SSpi WAbe
  WCru WMoo WWin
  - f. *alpina* CLAP
  - - from Hokkaido WCru
  - var. *incisolobata* (5) SSpi
  - var. *koraiensis* (5) WCru
    B&SWJ 8688 **new**
  - var. *obtusocuneata* (5) CLAP ECho EHyt LTwo NMen
  WAbe
  - f. *partita* CLAP WCru
  - var. *pilosissima* (5) WCru
    B&SWJ 8557 **new**
  - pink (5) CLAP NPSI WAbe WFar WTMC
  - var. *suwoensis* (5) **new** CLAP
'Foster's Gold' CLyd NMen
  (x *elisabethae*) (7)
'Four Winds' (15) EWes LRHS NHol NMen SIng
  WCom WMoo
'Francesco Redi' (7) NMen WAbe
'Francis Cade' (8) GAbr WAbe
'Frank Sinatra' NMen
  (x *paluanglica*) (7) **new**

'Franzii' (x *paulinae*) (7) NMen
'Friar Tuck' (x *boydii*) (7) NMen
'Friesei' (x *salmonica*) (7) CLyd EPot NLAp NMen
x *fritschiana* sensu see S. 'Krain'
  stricto hort. (8)
'Fumiko' (*fortunei*) (5) WCru
  B&SWJ 6124
'Funkii' (x *petraschii*) (7) NMen
funstonii **new** CGra
'Gaertneri' NMen
  (*mariae-theresiae*) (7)
'Gaiety' (15) ECho MDHE SIng
'Galaxie' CLyd NDlv NHol NMen WOBN
  (x *megaseiflora*) (7)
'Ganymede' NJOw NMen
  (*burseriana*) (7)
§ x *gaudinii* (8) CLyd ECtt ESis GGar GTou LRHS
  NDlv NMen NWCA SIng WGor
  WPer
'Gelber Findling' (7) EPot LRHS MDHE WAbe
'Gem' (x *irvingii*) (7) CLyd NDlv NLAp NMen
'General Joffre' (15) see S. 'Maréchal Joffre'
georgei (7) CLyd GCrs NDlv NLAp NMen
  - McB 1379 NHol
  - *hybrid* (7) GCrs
georgei x 'Winifred' **new** CLyd
'Gertie Pritchard' see S. 'Mrs Gertie Prichard'
  (x *megaseiflora*)
x *geuderi* sensu stricto see S. 'Eulenspiegel'
  hort.
§ x *geum* (11) CHid EBee EOrc MRav NWoo
  SMrm WFar WMoo
  - Dixter form (11) ECha SMHy SUsu WFar WWpP
'Glauca' (*paniculata* see S. 'Labradorica'
  var. *brevifolia*)
'Gleborg' (15) EWes MDHE
'Gloria' (*burseriana*) CLyd EHyt LRHS MBro NHol
  (7) ♀H4 NMen NSla SBla SIng WPat
x *gloriana* (7) see S. 'Godiva'
'Gloriosa' (x *gloriana*) (7) see S. 'Godiva'
§ 'Godiva' (x *gloriana*) (7) CLyd NMen
'Gold Dust' CLyd GCrs GTou NJOw NLAp
  (x *eudoxiana*) (7) NMen NRya WCom WWin
'Golden Falls' (15/v) EBre EMlt EWes GAbr GKir GTou
  LRHS MBNS MBro NHol NMen
  SPlb WCom WPat
Golden Prague see S. 'Zlatá Praha'
  (x *pragensis*)
'Goring White' (7) NMen
'Gothenburg' (7) CLyd EHyt NMen WAbe
'Grace' (x *arendsii*) (15/v) see S. 'Seaspray'
'Grace Farewell' EMlt GCrs LRHS MBar MBro NDlv
  (x *anglica*) (7) NHol NMen NRya NWCA SBla
  WCom WHoo
'Grandiflora' (*burseriana*) NHol
  (7)
granulata (15) CNic CRWN EDAr NLar NRya
  NSco
'Gratoides' (x *grata*) (7) NMen
§ 'Gregor Mendel' CLyd CMea EMlt GTou LRHS MBro
  (x *apiculata*) (7) ♀H4 NDlv NHol NJOw NLAp NMen
  SBla SRms WAbe WCom WHoo
  WTel
grisebachii see S. *federici-augusti* subsp.
  grisebachii
'Haagii' (x *eudoxiana*) (7) ELan GTou MBro NDlv NMen
  WTel
hallii see S. *marshallii*
'Harbinger' **new** WAbe
'Hareknoll Beauty' EPot MDHE NMen NRya SOkd
  WAbe
'Harlow Car' (7) CLyd NMen NSla
'Harlow Car' CPBP
  x *poluniniana* (7)

'Harold Bevington' | MDHE
(*paniculata*) (8)

'Harry Marshall' | CLyd NMen
(x *irvingii*) (7)

'Hartside Pink' | CLyd NWoo
(*umbrosa*) (11)

'Hartswood White' (15) | EBre MDHE MWat

'Harvest Moon' | CBct EBee MBnl NCGa NPri
(*stolonifera*) (5) **new**

'Hedwig' (x *malbyana*) | NHol NMen
(7)

x *heinreichii* sensu | see *S.* 'Ernst Heinrich'
stricto hort.

'Hi-Ace' (15/v) | CLyd EBre ECtt EMlt EPot GTou
MBro MHer NLAp SBla SPlb WFar

'Highdownensis' (8) | MDHE NDlv

'Hime' (*stolonifera*) (5) | WCru

'Hindhead Seedling' | CLyd ITim LRHS NDlv NJOw
(x *boydii*) (7) | NMen SIng WAbe

hirsuta (11) | EBla EBre EMar GGar IFro MDHE
NFla WCru

'Hirsuta' (x *geum*) | see *S.* x *geum*

'Hirtella' Ingwersen | MDHE
(*paniculata*) (8)

'His Majesty' (x *irvingii*) | NMen WAbe
(7)

'Hocker Edge' | CLyd ITim NDlv NMen WAbe
(x *arco-valleyi*) (7)

'Holden Seedling' (15) | ECtt EPot EWes MDHE

'Honnginton' | ITim

x *hornibrookii* (7) | NLAp WPat

hostii (8) | CLyd GTou LBee LRHS NHol
NJOw SIng WTin

§ - subsp. *hostii* (8) | GEdr MDHE

- - var. *altissima* (8) | STre

- subsp. *rhaetica* (8) | MDHE NBro NDlv NMen

'Hsitou Silver' (*stolonifera*) | CFee WCru
(5) B&SWJ 1980

'Hunscote' | ITim

hybrid JB 11 | NMen

§ *hypnoides* (15) | MOne

hypostoma (7) | CLyd

'Icelandica' (*cotyledon*) (8) | NHol

'Icicle' (x *elisabethae*) (7) | NMen WAbe

'Ignaz Dörfler' (7) | WAbe

imparilis | WCru

'Ingeborg' (15) | ECha LRHS MDHE SIng

iranica (7) | CLyd EHyt ITim NLAp NMen
WOBN

- pink (7) | EHyt

'Irene Bacci' (x *baccii*) (7) | CLyd NMen

'Iris Prichard' | CLyd ITim MBro WAbe WHoo
(x *hardingii*) (7)

'Irish' (15) | EPot MDHE

x *irvingii* (7) | NDlv

x *irvingii* sensu stricto | see *S.* 'Walter Irving'
hort.

jacquemontiana (1) | WAbe

'James Bremner' (15) | LRHS MDHE NBur NFla SIng

'Jan Palach' (x *krausii*) (7) | NMen

'Jason' (x *elisabethae*) (7) | NMen

'Jenkinsiae' (x *irvingii*) | CFee CLyd EBre EMlt ESis GKir
(7) ♀H4 | GTou LRHS MBro NDlv NHol
NLAp NMen NRya NWCA SBla
SChu SIng SMer WAbe WHoo WPat
WWin

§ 'Johann Kellerer' | ITim NDlv NSla SBla
(x *kellereri*) (7)

'John Tomlinson' | CLyd NMen NSla WOBN
(*burseriana*) (7)

'Josef Capek' | CLyd NMen
(x *megaseiflora*) (7)

'Josef Mánes' | NMen
(x *borisii*) (7)

'Joy' | see *S.* 'Kaspar Maria Sternberg'

'Joy Bishop' **new** | WAbe

'Judith Shackleton' | CLyd NMen WAbe
(x *abingdonensis*) (7)

'Juliet' | see *S.* 'Riverslea'

§ *juniperifolia* (7) | CLyd EBre GKir GTou LRHS MHer
NDlv NJOw NLAp NWCA SChu
SMer SRms

- subsp. *sancta* | see *S. sancta*

'Jupiter' (x *megaseiflora*) | CLyd LRHS NDlv NHol NLAp
(7) | NMen

'Kampa' (7) | CLyd

§ *karadzicensis* (7) | NMen

'Karasin' (7) | CLyd NMen

'Karel Capek' | CLyd CMea EPot ITim NDlv NHol
(x *megaseiflora*) (7) | NJOw NRya NSla SIng WAbe

'Karel Stivín' (x *edithae*) | CLyd NMen
(7)

'Kaspar Maria Sternberg' | CLyd MBro NHol NJOw NMen
(x *petraschii*) (7) | WPat

'Kath Dryden' | ITim NHol NLAp
(x *anglica*) (7)

'Kathleen Pinsent' (8) | CLyd MDHE NWCA SIng WAbe
♀H4 | WCom

'Kathleen' (x *polulacina*) (7) | CLyd NHol NLAp WOBN

x *kellereri* sensu stricto | see *S.* 'Johann Kellerer'
hort.

'Kew Gem' (x *petraschii*) | NMen
(7)

'Kewensis' (x *kellereri*) (7) | NMen WAbe

'Kineton' (7) | ITim NMen

'King Lear' (x *bursiculata*) | LRHS NMen SBla
(7)

'Kingscote White' (15) | ITim MDHE SIng

'Kinki Purple' (*stolonifera*) | WCru
(5) B&SWJ 4972

Kiss Me | see *S.* 'Miluj Me'

'Knapton Pink' (15) | EBre MDHE MOne NBlu NHol
NPri NRya SIng WAbe WCom

'Knapton White' (15) | MDHE SIng

§ x *kochii* (7) | EHyt

§ 'Kolbiana' (x *paulinae*) (7) | CLyd

'Koprvnik' (*paniculata*) | SIng
(8)

§ 'Krain' (x *fritschiana*) | NHol SIng SOkd
(7)

'Krákatit' (x *megaseiflora*) | NMen WAbe
(7)

'Krasava' (x *megaseiflora*) | CLyd CPBP NHol NMen
(7)

kusnezowiana (7) | SOkd

'Kyrillii' (x *borisii*) (7) | CLyd NMen

'Labe' (x *arco-valleyi*) (7) | CLyd CNic CPBP EPot LRHS NMen
SBla

§ 'Labradorica' (*paniculata*) | MDHE
(8)

'Lady Beatrix Stanley' | see *S.* 'Beatrix Stanley'

'Lagraveana' (*paniculata*) | NDlv NGar
(8)

x *landaueri* sensu stricto | see *S.* 'Leonore'
hort.

'Latonica' (*callosa*) (8) | EPot SOkd

'Lemon Hybrid' (x *boydii*) | NMen
(7)

'Lemon Spires' (7) | NMen

'Lenka' (x *byam-groundsii*) | NJOw NMen NSla WAbe
(7)

'Leo Gordon Godseff' | ITim LRHS NMen
(x *elisabethae*) (7)

§ 'Leonore' (x *landaueri*) (7) | LRHS

'Letchworth Gem') | GCal NWCA
(x *urbium*) (11

x *leyboldii* (7) | GTou

'Lidice' (7) | CLyd MBro NDlv NLAp NMen
WAbe WHoo

'Lilac Time' (x *youngiana*) NMen
(7)
lilacina (7)   CLyd EHyt NHol NMen WAbe
    WCom WPat
'Limelight' (*callosa*) (8)   MDHE
lingulata (8)   see *S. callosa*
'Lismore Carmine'   CLyd GCrs ITim NDlv NLAp NMen
(x *lismorensis*) (7)   NWCA
'Lismore Cherry' (7)   CLyd EHyt
'Lismore Gem'   NLAp NMen
(x *lismorensis*) (7)
'Lismore Mist'   CLyd EHyt
(x *lismorensis*) (7)
* 'Lismore Pink'   CLyd EPot ITim NDlv NLAp NMen
(x *lismorensis*) (7)   NWCA WCom
'Little Piggy' (*epipbylla*)   WCru
(5) **new**
longifolia (8)   NSla WGor
'Louis Armstrong' **new**   WAbe
Love Me   see *S.* 'Miluj Mne'
lowndesii (7)   EHyt
'Ludmila Subrová'   CLyd NMen
(x *bertolonii*) (7)
'Lusanna' (x *irvingii*) (7)   CLyd NHol
'Luschtinetz' (15)   MDHE
'Lutea' (*diapensioides*)   see *S.* 'Wilhelm Tell', 'Primulina'
'Lutea' (*marginata*)   see *S.* 'Faust'
§ 'Lutea' (*paniculata*) (8)   CNic GTou LBee LRHS MBro NBro
   ♥H4   NDlv NJOw NMen SChu WCom
'Luzníce'   NDlv NMen
(x *poluluteopurpurea*) (7)
macedonica   see *S. juniperifolia*
x **macnabiana** (8)   WOBN
'Magdalena'   NMen
(x *thomasiana*) (7)
'Major' (*cochlearis*) (8)   EPot LRHS NMen WGor
   ♥H4
§ 'Maréchal Joffre' (15)   MDHE WCom
'Margarete' (x *borisii*) (7)   CLyd NMen
marginata (7)   CLyd
- var. **balcanica**   see *S. marginata* var. *rocheliana*
- var. **boryi** (7)   CLyd EPot LRHS NMen
- var. **coriophylla** (7)   EPot NMen NWCA WAbe
- var. **karadzicensis**   see *S. karadzicensis*
§ - var. **rocheliana** (7)   CLyd EPot ITim LRHS NMen
- - 'Balkan' (7)   CLyd
'Maria Callas'   CLyd
(x *poluanglica*) (7)
'Maria Luisa'   GCrs NDlv NMen WAbe
(x *salmonica*) (7)
'Marianna' (x *borisii*) (7)   CLyd NDlv NMen NRya
'Maroon Beauty'   EBee ECtt EMan EMar MDKP MSPs
(*stolonifera*) (5)   WCot
'Mars' (x *elisabethae*) (7)   NMen
'Marshal Joffre' (15)   see *S.* 'Maréchal Joffre' (15)
§ **marshallii** (4)   WWin
§ 'Martha' (x *semmleri*) (7)   CLyd NMen
'Mary Golds' (7)   CLyd
matta-florida (7)   NMen
'May Queen' (7)   NHol NMen
x **megaseiflora** sensu   see *S.* 'Robin Hood'
stricto hort.
'Melrose' (x *salmonica*)   NMen
(7)
mertensiana (6)   CLyd EBee GTou NBir WCru
- var. **bulbifera** (6)   CNic
'Meteor' (7)   NJOw NRya
micranthidifolia (4)   CLAP EBee WPGP
(Milford Group)   NMen
   'Aldo Bacci' (7)
'Millstream Cream'   CLyd ITim NJOw NMen
(x *elisabethae*) (7)
§ 'Miluj Mne'   EPot ITim NDlv NLAp
(x *poluanglica*) (7)

'Minnehaha'   ITim WAbe
(x *elisabethae*) (7)
'Minor' (*cochlearis*) (8)   EHyt GTou LRHS MBro NHol
   ♥H4   NMen NWCA SChu SIng WHoo
    WPat
'Minor Glauca'   see *S.* 'Labradorica'
(*paniculata*)
'Minutifolia' (*paniculata*)   CPBP EPot LRHS MBro MDHE
(8)   NDlv NWCA WAbe WCom
§ 'Miss Chambers'   CMea EBee EMan MWgw SMHy
(x *urbium*) (11)   SUsu WCot WMoo WPen
'Mona Lisa' (x *borisii*) (7)   CLyd MBro NHol NLAp NMen
    WAbe WPat
§ 'Mondscheinsonate'   NHol
(x *boydii*) (7)
'Moonlight'   see *S.* 'Sulphurea'
'Moonlight Sonata'   see *S.* 'Mondscheinsonate'
(x *boydii*)
'Mortimer Pritchard' **new**   CLyd
moschata   see *S. exarata* subsp. *moschata*
'Mother of Pearl'   CLyd EPot NDlv NLAp NMen
(x *irvingii*) (7)
'Mother Queen'   CLyd MBro NHol NLAp WHoo
(x *irvingii*) (7)   WPat
'Mount Nachi' (*fortunei*)   More than 30 suppliers
(5)
'Mrs E. Piper' (15)   COkL MDHE
§ 'Mrs Gertie Prichard'   NHol NMen WAbe
(x *megaseiflora*) (7)
'Mrs Helen Terry'   CLyd EPot ITim LRHS NDlv NMen
(x *salmonica*) (7)
'Mrs Leng' (x *elisabethae*)   MDKP NMen
(7)
mutata (8)   CLyd SIng
'Myra' (x *anglica*) (7)   CLyd LRHS MBro NHol NMen
    NWCA WHoo WPat
'Myra Cambria'   NDlv NHol NMen
(x *anglica*) (7)
'Myriad' (7)   CLyd
'Nancye' (x *goringiana*)   CLyd EHyt ITim NDlv NLAp NMen
    WOBN
§ **nelsoniana** (4)   EBee NHol NJOw
nigroglandulifera   EBee
'Nimbus' (*iranica*) (7)   EHyt NMen WAbe
'Niobe' (x *pulvilacina*) (7)   CLyd EHyt NMen
nivalis (4)   NHol
'Norvegica' (*cotyledon*) (8)   GTou MDHE WWin
'Notata' (*paniculata*) (8)   NLAp NMen
'Nottingham Gold'   CLyd EPot NHol NJOw NMen
(x *boydii*) (7)
'Obristii' (x *salmonica*) (7)   NDlv NHol NMen NRya
§ **obtusa** (7)   NMen
'Ochroleuca'   NMen
(x *elisabethae*) (7)
'Odysseus' (*sancta*) (7)   NMen
'Olymp' (*scardica*) (7)   NMen
'Opalescent' (7)   CLyd NJOw NMen
§ 'Ophelia' (x *arco-valleyi*)   NHol NMen
(7)
oppositifolia (7)   GIBF GKir GTou MBNS MHer
    MOne NLAp NSla SPlb SRms WAbe
    WBVN WWin
- 'Corrie Fee'   see *S.* 'Corrie Fee'
- from Iceland   EHyt WAbe
* - subsp. **oppositifolia**   CLyd GAbr GCrs GTou NLAp
var. **latina** (7)
oppositifolia   see *S.* x *kochii*
x **biflora**
'Oriole' (x *boydii*) (7)   NMen
'Oxhill' (7)   ITim NMen
§ **paniculata** (8)   CNic EBre ESis GGar GKir GTou
    LRHS MBro MDKP MHer MWat
    NDlv NLAp NMen NSla SAga SPlb
    SRms WHoo

§ – var. **baldensis** (8) — CLyd EBre EHyt EMlt GKir GTou LRHS MBar MBro MWat NBro NDlv NHol NLap NMen NRya SBla SPlb WAbe WWin

– var. **brevifolia new** — COkL

§ – subsp. **cartilaginea** (8) — NHol SBla WAbe

– subsp. **kolenatiana** — see *S. paniculata* subsp. *cartilaginea*

– subsp. **neogaea** hort. (8) — see *S.* 'Labradorica'

paradoxa (15) — EPot LRHS SBla WGor

'Parcevalis' (x *finnisiae*) (7x9) — CLyd

'Parsee' (x *margoxiana*) (7) — NJOw NMen NRya

x **patens** (8x9) — NJOw

§ 'Paula' (x *paulinae*) (7) — NMen

'Peach Blossom' (7) — CLyd EPot GCrs LRHS NMen NRya SBla

'Peach Melba' **new** — WAbe

'Pearly Gates' (x *irvingii*) (7) — CLyd NMen NSla

'Pearly Gold' (15) — CMea LRHS NRya

'Pearly King' (15) — EBre ECho LRHS MHer NMen NPri WAbe WFar

'Pearly King' variegated (v) — COkL NHol

x **pectinata** Schott, Nyman & Kotschy (8) — see *S.* 'Krain'

pedemontana (15) — MDHE WAbe

– subsp. **cervicornis** (15) — MDHE

* – from Mount Kasbak (15) — CLyd MDHE

'Penelope' (x *boydilacina*) (7) — CLyd CMea EHyt EMlt EPot GCrs LRHS MBro NHol NMen SBla WAbe WCom WHoo WPat

pensylvanica (4) — GCal

'Perikles' (7) — NMen

'Peter Burrow' (x *poluanglica*) (7) ♀H4 — CLyd CPBP EHyt NLAp NMen NWCA WAbe

'Peter Pan' (15) — EMlt EPfP EPot GKir GTou LGro MBro MHer NHol NMen NPri NPro NRya WCom WPat

'Petra' (7) — CLyd EPot ITim NHol NJOw NMen

x **petraschii** (7) — CLyd ITim

§ 'Phoenix' (x *biasolettoi*) (7) — EHyt LRHS NMen WOBN

'Pilatus' (x *boydii*) (7) — NMen

'Pink Pagoda' (*rufescens*) (5) — WCru

'Pink Pearl' (7) — CMea NMen

'Pixie' (15) — CTri EBre ECtt EPot GAbr GKir LRHS NHol NLAp NMen NPri SIng SRms

'Pixie Alba' — see *S.* 'White Pixie'

'Plena' (*granulata*) — see *S.* 'Flore Pleno'

'Pollux' (x *boydii*) (7) — EPot NHol NMen

x **poluanglica** (7) — NLAp

poluniniana (7) — CLyd NHol NWCA

poluniniana x 'Winifred' — CLyd

'Pompadour' x (15) — LRHS MDHE NHol

'Popelka' (*marginata*) (7) — CLyd

porophylla (7) — NMen

– var. **thessalica** — see *S. sempervivum* f. *stenophylla*

aff. **porophylla** (7) — NWCA

'Portae' (x *fritschiana*) (8) — NJOw SIng

'Primrose Bee' (x *apiculata*) (7) — EPot

'Primrose Dame' (x *elisabethae*) (7) — MDKP NHol NMen WAbe WCom

'Primulaize' (9x11) — CLyd MBro NLar NMen

'Primulaize Salmon' (9x11) — NDlv NHol NWoo WCom WHoo WPer

§ 'Primulina' (x *malbyana*) (7) — NDlv NMen WOBN

§ 'Primuloides' (*umbrosa*) (11) ♀H4 — MBro NPri SRms SWvt WEas

'Prince Hal' (*burseriana*) (7) NMen — CLyd EPot LRHS NDlv NJOw NLAp

'Princess' (*burseriana*) (7) — CLyd EHyt LRHS NJOw NMen

'Probynii' (*cochlearis*) (8) — EPot MDHE MWat NDlv NMen WAbe

'Prometheus' (x *prosenii*) (7) — CLyd

'Prospero' (x *petraschii*) (7) — NMen

x **prosenii** sensu stricto hort. — see *S.* 'Regina'

'Pseudofranzii' (x *paulinae*) (7) — NWCA

x **pseudokotschyi** sensu stricto hort. — see *S.* 'Denisa'

'Pseudoscardica' (x *wehrhahnii*) (7) — NMen

'Pseudovaldensis' (*cochlearis*) (8) — CNic MDHE WAbe

pubescens new — WAbe

– subsp. **iratiana** (15) — NLAp

punctata Sternbo. (4) — see *S. nelsoniana*

* **punctissima** — NHol

'Pungens' (x *apiculata*) (7) — NDlv NHol NJOw NMen

'Purple Piggy' (*epiphylla*) (7) — CLAP WCru

'Purple Piggy' *stolonifera* (5) **new** — CFee

'Purpurea' (*fortunei*) — see *S.* 'Rubrifolia'

'Purpurteppich' (15) — MDHE WPer WShp

§ 'Pygmalion' (x *webrii*) (7) — CLyd NHol NMen WPat

'Pyramidalis' (*cotyledon*) (8) — EPfP EWTr SRms

'Pyrenaica' (*oppositifolia*) (7) — NMen

quadrifaria (7) — NHol

'Quarry Wood' (x *anglica*) (7) — CLyd ITim NHol NMen

'Rainsley Seedling' (8) — MDHE NBro NMen

ramulosa (7) — NMen

'Red Pixie' — COkL

'Red Poll' (x *poluanglica*) (7) — CLyd CPBP EHyt ITim NMen NRya WAbe

§ 'Regina' (x *prosenii*) (7) — CLyd ITim MHer NMen

retusa (7) — CLyd NLAp NMen NSla NWCA

'Rex' (*paniculata*) (8) — EHyt LBuc NHol NMen

'Riverslea' (x *bornibrookii*) (7) — CPBP LRHS MBro NHol NMen WOBN WPat

§ 'Robin Hood' (x *megaseiflora*) (7) — CLyd EPot LRHS MBro NHol NMen SBla WHoo WPat

'Rokujô' (*fortunei*) (5) — CLAP EBee GKir NLar NPro WFar WTMC

'Romeo' (x *bornibrookii*) (7) — CLyd

'Rosea' (*cortusifolia*) (5) — CLAP WOBN

'Rosea' (*paniculata*) (8) ♀H4 — EMlt GKir GTou LBee MBro NBro NDlv NHol NSla SBla SRms WTel WWin

'Rosea' (x *stuartii*) (7) — NDlv NMen

'Rosemarie' (x *anglica*) (7) — CLyd NHol NMen

'Rosenzwerg' (15) — LRHS

'Rosina Sündermann' (x *rosinae*) (7) — EPot NDlv

rotundifolia (12) — CLyd EBee GBin MDKP NHol SSpi

§ – subsp. **chrysospleniifolia** var. **rhodopea** (12) — WCru

'Roy Clutterbuck' (7) — NMen

'Rubella' (x *irvingii*) (7) — CLyd ITim

§ 'Rubrifolia' (*fortunei*) (5) — CLAP EBee EBre EChP ECha EHoe EMan GAbr GFlt IBal MAvo MBow NMen NMyG SMad SPet

		SSpi SWvt WAbe WCot WCru WFar WGer WLin WOld WSan WTMC WWeb
*	'Ruby Red'	NPro
*	'Ruby Wedding' (*cortusifolia*) (5) **new**	WCru
	rufescens (5) **new**	SOkd
	– BWJ 7510	WCru
	– BWJ 7684	WCru
	'Rusalka' (x *borisii*) (7)	CLyd NMen
	'Russell Vincent Prichard' (x *irvingii*) (7)	NHol NMen
	'Ruth Draper' (*oppositifolia*) (7)	NLAp NWCA WAbe
	'Ruth McConnell' (15)	CMea LRHS MDHE WCom
	'Sabrina' (x *fallsvillagensis*) (7)	CLyd
	'Saint John's' (x *fritschiana*) (8)	EBur MDHE NJOw WWin
	'Saint Kilda' (*oppositifolia*) (7)	GCrs GTou
	x *salmonica* sensu stricto hort.	see *S*. 'Salomonii'
§	'Salomonii' (x *salmonica*) (7)	CLyd ITim NDlv NMen SRms
	'Samo' (x *bertolonii*) (7)	CLyd NMen
	sancta (7)	CLyd EPot LRHS NMen SRms
	– subsp. *pseudosancta* (7)	see *S. juniperifolia*
	'Sandpiper' (7)	NHol
	sanguinea (1)	MDHE
	'Sanguinea Superba' (x *arendsii*) (15) ♀H4	MDHE SIng
	sarmentosa	see *S. stolonifera*
	'Sartorii'	see *S*. 'Pygmalion'
	'Saturn' (x *megaseiflora*) (7)	ITim NHol NMen
	'Sázava' (x *poluluteopurpurea*) (7)	CLyd ITim NMen WAbe
	scardica (7)	CPBP NBro NMen
	– var. *dalmatica*	see *S. obtusa*
	– f. *erythrantha* (7)	CLyd
	– subsp. *korabensis*	GCrs
	– var. *obtusa*	see *S. obtusa*
§	'Schelleri' (x *petraschii*) (7)	EHyt NJOw NMen
	'Schneeteppich' (15)	WCom WPer WShp
§	'Schwefelblüte' (15)	EBre GTou LRHS NFla NPri WCom WPat
	scleropoda (7)	NMen
§	'Seaspray' (x *arendsii*) (15/v)	EWes
	'Seissera' (*burseriana*) (7)	ITim NHol NMen
	x *semmleri* sensu stricto hort.	see *S*. 'Martha'
	sempervivum (7)	CLyd NMen NSla NWCA WTin
§	– f. *stenophylla* (7)	GTou MHer WAbe
	sendaica	WCru
	'Sendtneri' (8)	WAbe
	sibirica (14)	GTou
§	'Silver Cushion' (15/v)	CMea EBre ELan EPfP GAbr GTou LAst LRHS MBar MDHE NHol SIng SMer SPlb WAbe WCom WMoo
	'Silver Edge' (x *arco-valleyi*) (7)	NMen WAbe
	Silver Farreri Group (8)	NDlv NGar
	– 'Snowflake' (8)	MDHE NDlv
	'Silver Maid' (x *fritschiana*) (8)	NMen SOkd
	'Silver Mound'	see *S*. 'Silver Cushion'
	'Sir Douglas Haig' (15)	MDHE SIng
	'Snowcap' (*pubescens*) (15)	EHyt ITim NDlv NWCA

	'Snowdon' (*burseriana*) (7)	NMen
	'Somerset Seedling' (8)	MDHE
	'Sorrento' (*marginata*) (7)	NMen
§	'Southside Seedling' (8) ♀H4	More than 30 suppliers
	spathularis (11)	GKir MHar WCom WCot WEas WWin
	'Speciosa' (*burseriana*) (7)	NDlv
	'Splendens' (*oppositifolia*) (7) ♀H4	ELan EPfP GKev NDlv NHol NLAp NMen SBla SMer SRms WPat
	'Spotted Dog'	GEdr
	'Sprite' (15)	LRHS MDHE
	spruneri (7)	LRHS NMen SIng
	– var. *deorum* (7)	NMen
	'Stansfieldii' (*rosacea*) (15)	EBre GKir LRHS MDHE NBlu NHol NJOw NMen SPlb
*	'Stansfieldii Rosea' (15)	MDHE
§	'Stella' (x *stormonthii*) (7)	SBla
	stellaris (4)	GTou
	stenophylla	see *S. flagellaris*
	subsp. *stenophylla*	
	stolitzkae (7)	GCrs NLAp NMen NWCA WAbe
§	*stolonifera* (5) ♀H2	CArn CHEx CHal CPLG EBee ECho EWTr GBin LDai MHar NBro SBri SDix SIng SWvt WEas WFar WMoo
	'Stormonth's Variety'	see *S*. 'Stella'
	stribrnyi (7)	NMen
	– JCA 861-400	NWCA
	'Sturmiana' (*paniculata*) (8)	NMen SRms
	aff. *subsessiliflora* (7)	NWCA
	'Suendermannii' (x *kellereri*) (7)	NDlv
	'Suendermannii Major' (x *kellereri*) (7)	CLyd LRHS NRya NSla
	'Sugar Plum Fairy' (*fortunei*) (5)	CBcs CLAP EBee EChP EHrv EMan EMar GFlt LAst MBNS NBro NCot SPoG WCot WShp WTMC
§	'Sulphurea' (x *boydii*) (7)	CMea CNic CPBP LRHS NHol NMen NWCA SChu SIng WAbe WCom WHoo WPat
	'Sun Dance' (x *boydii*) (7)	NHol
	'Superba' (*callosa* var. *australis*) (8)	GCrs GTou MBro MDHE
	'Swan' (x *fallsvillagensis*) (7)	NMen
	'Sylva' (x *elisabethae*) (7)	NMen
	'Symons-Jeunei' (8)	MDHE WAbe
	'Tábor' (x *schottii*) (7)	NMen
	'Tamayura' (*fortunei*) (5)	EMan EMar MBNS NMyG WCot
	taygetea (12)	ETow
	'Theoden' (*oppositifolia*) (7) ♀H4	CLyd CMea EWes GCrs GTou NHol NJOw NLAp NWCA SBla
	'Theresia' (x *mariae-theresiae*) (7)	NMen
	'Thorpei' (7)	NMen
	'Timbalii' (x *gaudinii*) (8)	SIng
	'Timmy Foster' (x *irvingii*) (7)	CLyd NHol NMen NSla
	tombeanensis (7)	CLyd NMen
	'Tricolor' (*stolonifera*) (5) ♀H2	EBak LRHS SPer WFar
	trifurcata (15) **new**	GGar
	'Triumph' (x *arendsii*) (15)	EBre ECtt GTou LRHS NPri SBla WBVN
	'Tully' (x *elisabethae*) (7)	NHol WPat
	'Tumbling Waters' (8) ♀H4	EHyt EPot GAbr LHop LRHS MBro NHol NLAp NMen NSla NWCA SIng SOkd WAbe WCra WGor WPat WWin
§	'Tvuj Den' (x *poluanglica*) (7)	NDlv NMen WAbe WOBN

§ 'Tvuj Písen' | CLyd EHyt ITim NDlv NLAp
(x *poluanglica*) (7)

§ 'Tvuj Polibek' | EHyt EPot ITim MDKP NDlv NLAp
(x *poluanglica*) (7) | NMen SBla WAbe

§ 'Tvuj Pritel' | EMlt NDlv NLAp
(x *poluanglica*) (7)

§ 'Tvuj Usmev' | CLyd EHyt ITim NDlv NLAp NMen
(x *poluanglica*) (7)

§ 'Tvuj Uspech' | EHyt ITim NDlv NLAp NMen SBla
(x *poluanglica*) (7) | SOkd WAbe

'Tycho Brahe' | CLyd NMen WAbe
(x *doerfleri*) (7)

'Tysoe' (7) | ITim NMen

umbrosa (11) | CBrm EBee EBre ENot LRHS MRav
SPer SPlb SRms SWvt WCAu WHen
WMoo WWin

- 'Aurea' | see *S.* 'Aureopunctata'
- var. *primuloides* | see *S.* 'Primuloides'
'Unique' | see *S.* 'Bodensee'
x *urbium* (11) ♀H4 | CHEx EBee ELan ENot EPfP EPza
GKir LAst LEdu LGro MWgw NSti
SPet SRms WBVN WBor WBrk
WCFE WFar WPer

- *primuloides* | see *S.* 'Clarence Elliott'
'Elliott's Variety'
'Vaccariana' (*oppositifolia*) | ECho NHol
(7)
'Václav Hollar' | NMen
(x *gusmusii*) (7)
'Vahlii' (x *smithii*) (7) | NMen
'Valborg' | see *S.* 'Cranbourne'
'Valentine' | see *S.* 'Cranbourne'
'Valerie Finnis' | see *S.* 'Aretiastrum'
(Vanessa Group) | NMen
'Cio-Cio-San' (7)

I 'Variegata' | ECho ECtt EPfP GGar IHMH MBar
(*cuneifolia*) (11/v) | NBlu NVic SHFr SIng SPet SPlb
WCom WMoo WPer WTel
'Variegata' (*umbrosa*) | see *S.* 'Aureopunctata'
I 'Variegata' (x *urbium*) | EBee EPar EPfP GGar GKir LAst
(11/v) | LGro LRHS MRav NFor NLar NSti
NVic SRms SSto WBrk WEas WShp
WWin

vayredana (15) | GCrs NWCA WAbe
veitchiana (5) | NBro WCru
'Venetia' (*paniculata*) (8) | MDHE
'Vesna' (x *borisii*) (7) | CLyd NHol NJOw NLAp NMen
WWin

§ *vespertina* (10) | CGra
'Vincent van Gogh' | CLyd NHol NMen SRot WOBN
(x *borisii*) (7)
'Vladana' | CLyd EPot NHol NJOw NMen
(x *megaseiflora*) (7) | NRya
'Vlasta' (7) | CLyd NMen
'Vltava' (7) | CLyd NMen
'Volgeri' (x *bofmannii*) (7) | CLyd
'Wada' (*fortunei*) (5) | More than 30 suppliers
§ 'Wallacei' (15) | ECho MDHE NMen
'Walpole's Variety' (8) | CBrm WPer
§ 'Walter Ingwersen' | SIng SRms
(*umbrosa*) (11)
'Walter Ingwersen' | see *S.* 'Walter Ingwersen'
(*umbrosa* | (*umbrosa*)
var. *primuloides*)
§ 'Walter Irving' | CLyd ITim LRHS NHol NLAp
(x *irvingii*) (7) | NMen WAbe
'Weisser Zwerg' (15) | MDHE WAbe
'Wellesbourne' (7) | CLyd
'Welsh Dragon' (15) | MDHE WAbe
'Welsh Red' (15) | WAbe
'Welsh Rose' (15) | WAbe
wendelboi (7) | CLyd EHyt NMen WOBN
'Wendrush' | CLyd NMen
(x *wendelacina*) (7)

'Wendy' (x *wendelacina*) | NMen
(7)
'Wetterhorn' | CLyd
(*oppositifolia*) (7)
'Wheatley Lion' | NMen
(x *borisii*) (7)
'Wheatley Rose' (7) | CLyd ITim LRHS NHol
'White Cap' (x *boydii*) (7) | NHol NMen
§ 'White Pixie' (15) | CLyd ECtt EMlt EPfP GKir
LGro LRHS MHer NHol NJOw
NLAp NPri NPro NRya SBla SPlb
SRms
'White Star' (x *petraschii*) | see *S.* 'Schelleri'
'Whitehill' (8) | CLyd CMea EBre EGoo ELan EMlt
ESis GAbr GEdr GKir GTou LBee
LRHS MBro NBro NHol NLAp
NMen SIng SPet WCom WHoo
WPat WPer WTin WWin
'Whitlavei Compacta' | NWoo
(*hypnoides*) (15)
§ 'Wilhelm Tell' | NMen WOBN
(x *malbyana*) (7)
'William Boyd' | NSla WAbe
(x *boydii*) (7)
§ 'Winifred' (x *anglica*) (7) | CLyd GCrs NLAp NMen WAbe
'Winifred Bevington' | CLyd EBre EMlt EPot ESis GEdr
(8x11) | GTou ITim LBee LRHS MBro NBro
NDlv NHol NJOw NLAp NMen
NRya SIng WAbe WHoo WLin WPat
WPer
'Winston Churchill' (15) | EBre EPfP LRHS MBNS MDHE
NHol NPri SIng
'Winton' (x *paulinae*) (7) | NMen
'Wisley' (*federici-augusti* | MBro NHol NLAp NMen WCom
subsp. *grisebachii*) (7) | WHoo WPat
♀H2-3
'Wisley Primrose' | see *S.* 'Kolbiana'
'Yellow Rock' (7) | NRya
Your Day | see *S.* 'Tvuj Den'
Your Friend | see *S.* 'Tvuj Prítel'
Your Good Fortune | see *S.* 'Tvuj Uspech'
Your Kiss | see *S.* 'Tvuj Polibek'
Your Smile | see *S.* 'Tvuj Usmev'
Your Song | see *S.* 'Tvuj Písen'
Your Success | see *S.* 'Tvuj Uspech'
x *zimmeteri* (8x11) | CLyd EWes
§ 'Zlatá Praha' | CLyd CPBP NMen WAbe
(x *pragensis*) (7)
'Zlin' (7) | NMen

Scabiosa (Dipsacaceae)

africana | CElw
'Agnes Whitfield' **new** | EChP
alpina L. | see *Cephalaria alpina*
argentea **new** | EWes
atropurpurea | EBee EGoo SMrm
- 'Ace of Spades' | CDes CHad CSpe CWCL EBee
EBlw EChP LPio LRHS NPPs SMad
WCot WSan
§ - 'Chile Black' | More than 30 suppliers
§ - 'Chile Pepper' | CFai CHar EBee EMan EWll LHop
LIck MDKP MTis NCGa NCot NPri
SAga SPoG SUsu WWol
§ - 'Chilli Red' | EBee EBre ECoo GCal SAga
§ - 'Chilli Sauce' | CBcs CFai CHar EBee EMan EPfP
LHop LIck MTis NCGa NCot NPri
SUsu WCra WWol
- dark-flowered | CBri
§ - subsp. *maritima* | EBee
- 'Mixed Chile' **new** | SUsu
- 'Peter Ray' | CElw ECtt
banatica | see *S. columbaria*
'Betsy Trotwood' | LPio
'Burgundy Bonnets' | EBre LRHS NPPs

§ 'Butterfly Blue' — EBre ENot EPfP EWTr GKir IHMH LRHS MBNS MBnl MBri MCLN MWgw NDov NLar SCoo SMrm SPer SPla SWvt WAul WCAu WFar WShp WWhi

caucasica — CSam EPfP GFlt GKev LAst MBro NBlu NChi NPPs WBVN WFar WHoo WWin

- var. *alba* — EHrv EPfP MBow NBlu WFar WHoo

- 'Blausiegel' — CFir CMHG CSam EBee EChP LRHS MBNS NGdn SPet SPla WCAu

- 'Bressingham White' — SAsh
- 'Challenger' — SAsh
- 'Clive Greaves' ♀H4 — More than 30 suppliers
- 'Crimson Cushion' — CBcs CSpe EBee EBlw ECtt SMHy WCra

- 'Fama' — CFai CMdw CSpe EMan MBNS MHer MWgw NBir NLar SMrm SPlb SRms WBar WFar WHil WHoo

- 'Goldingensis' — EBee GKir GMac GWCH MBNS MHer NBPC NGdn NPri WPer

- House's hybrids — CSBt LPVe NGdn NVic SMac SRms WHil

- 'Isaac House' — NLar
- 'Kompliment' — ENot LRHS NChi NLar SCro
- 'Lavender Blue' — CHar NBPC WFar
- 'Miss Willmott' ♀H4 — CHad CM&M CSam CWCL EBee EChP ECha EFou ELan EPfP ERou EWTr GKir LAst LHop LRHS MBri MHer MWgw NPPs SPer SPet SPla SUsu SWvt WAul WCAu WCot WFar WMnd

- 'Moerheim Blue' — EBee ERou NGby
- 'Mount Cook' — SAsh
- Perfecta Series — CSpe EBee EChP LAst LPio LRHS NGdn NLar SMrm SWat

- - 'Perfecta Alba' — COIW CSpe EBee EChP EMan GKir LAst LPio MBro NChi NLar NOrc NPri SMrm STes SWat WHil WWhi

- - 'Perfecta Lilac Blue' — CWib STes
- 'Stäfa' — CKno CM&M EBee ERou EWTr LHop LRHS MBri MMHG MTis NLar SAsh SBla SMrm SPla SUsu WAul WFar WMnd

'Chile Black' — see *S. atropurpurea* 'Chile Black'
'Chile Pepper' — see *S. atropurpurea* 'Chile Pepper'
'Chile Red' — see *S. atropurpurea* 'Chilli Red'
'Chile Sauce' — see *S. atropurpurea* 'Chilli Sauce'
cinerea — CTCP ECoo
§ *columbaria* — CBgR EBee ECGP EWTr MLLN NLan NMir NPPs NSco NWCA SBri SECG SMrm SWal WHer WJek
* - *alba* — WShp
* - *alpina* **new** — CTCP
- 'Flower Power' **new** — EBee
- 'Nana' — CBrm CMdw EBee ECGP GEdr IBal LPVe NBir NGdn NLar NMen NPri WCFE WHil WSan
§ - subsp. *ochroleuca* — More than 30 suppliers
cretica — XPep
drakensbergensis — CHar EBee EMan GGar LPhx LPio MDKP MTPN
farinosa — CDes CMil CTCP EBee MHar MHer SAga SGar SMrm SUsu WPer
gigantea — see *Cephalaria gigantea*
graminifolia — EBre EDAr EMan GBuc LPio LRHS MDKP MWrn NBir NMen NPPs NWCA SRms WHil

- 'Pinkushion' — CStr
- *rosea* — EWes
'Helen Dillon' — CBgR CElw EBee EMan MBnl NCGa SMrm SOkh

'House's Novelty Mix' — SMac
hymnettia **new** — XPep
incisa **new** — CTCP EShb
'Irish Perpetual Flowering' — CMdw EMan NDov NPPs WCot
japonica — WHil WPer
- var. *acutiloba* — NChi WHil
- var. *alpina* — CHar CSpe CTCP EBee EChP ECoo EFou ESis GAbr GBuc GTou MBro MFir MLLN NBlu NGdn NPPs SRot WBea WCot WHoo WLin WRha WSan WTin
- - pink-flowered **new** — EFou
- 'Blue Diamonds' — IBal
lucida — CHea EBee EBre EChP EMan EPar EPfP GTou LRHS MBro MRav MWrn NHol NLAp NPPs NPri SAga SBla WCAu WCom WMnd WPGP WPat WPer
maritima — see *S. atropurpurea* subsp. *maritima*
'Midnight' — CMea CSpe
'Miss Havisham' — CElw EBee ECtt EMan LPio WCot WPGP
montana Mill. — see *Knautia arvensis*
montana (Bieb.) DC. — see *Knautia tatarica*
ochroleuca — see *S. columbaria* subsp. *ochroleuca*
parnassi — see *Pterocephalus perennis*
'Peggotty' — EBee EChP WCot
'Pink Buttons' — ECoo EOMN LAst MBNS MMHG SLon SPet SPla
'Pink Mist'PBR — EBee EBre EPfP EWTr GKir LRHS MBri MCLN NBir NLar SCoo SMrm SPer SRms WCAu WShp
prolifera — CTCP LPhx MWrn
pterocephala — see *Pterocephalus perennis*
'Rosie's Pink' — ECtt EMan SMrm
rumelica — see *Knautia macedonica*
'Satchmo' — see *S. atropurpurea* 'Chile Black'
silenifolia — MBri
songarica JJ&JH 90/216 — EBee
succisa — see *Succisa pratensis*
tatarica — see *Cephalaria gigantea*
tenuis — EMan LPhx MHer SHar WGMN
triandra — EBee LHop
ucranica — WOut XPep
'Ultra Violet' **new** — SHar

Scadoxus (Amaryllidaceae)
multiflorus — LAma LRHS MBri MOak NRog WCot
§ - subsp. *katherinae* ♀H1 — ERea
natalensis — see *S. puniceus*
§ *puniceus* — CDes ERea SYvo

Scaevola (Goodeniaceae)
aemula 'Blue Fan' — see *S. aemula* 'Blue Wonder'
§ - 'Blue Wonder'PBR — EMan LAst MOak NPer SHFr SMrm SWvt
- 'Petite' — CHal
Blauer Facher = 'Saphira'PBR — SMrm WWol
'Blue Ice' **new** — LAst
crassifolia — SPlb
'Zig Zag' **new** — LAst

Scandix (Apiaceae)
pecten-veneris — MSal

Schefflera (Araliaceae)
actinophylla ♀H1 — EBak SRms WMul
arboricola ♀H1 — SEND WMul XBlo
- B&SWJ 7040 — WCru

- 'Compacta' | MBri
- 'Gold Capella' ♀H1 | LRHS MBri SEND
- 'Trinetta' | MBri
delavayi **new** | CHEx WMul
digitata | CTrC
elegantissima ♀H1 | EShb
gracilis HWJ 622 **new** | WCru
hoi var. *fantsipanensis* | WCru
  B&SWJ 8228 **new**
impressa **new** | CHEx
microphylla B&SWJ 3872 | WCru
pueckleri **new** | WMul

Schima (*Theaceae*)

argentea | see *S. wallichii* subsp. *noronhae*
   | var. *superba*
wallichii | CFil
  subsp. *liukiuensis*
§ - subsp. *noronhae* | CHEx CPLG ISea SSpi WBod
  var. *superba*
- subsp. *wallichii* | ISea
  var. *khasiana*
* *yunnanensis* | GGGa

Schinus (*Anacardiaceae*)

molle | IDee XPep
polygamus | CBcs

Schisandra (*Schisandraceae*)

arisanensis B&SWJ 3050 | WCru
aff. *bicolor* BWJ 8151 | WCru
  new
chinensis | CAgr CArn EBee GPoy MSwo
   | WBVN WNor WSHC
- B&SWJ 4204 | WCru
grandiflora | CDoC EBee ECot ELan EPfP LRHS
   | MBlu MWgw SCoo
- B&SWJ 2245 | WCru
henryi | WCru
  subsp. *yunnanensis*
  B&SWJ 6546 **new**
nigra B&SWJ 5897 | WCru
propinqua var. *sinensis* | CBot CSPN MBlu NLar WCru
   | WSHC
- - BWJ 8148 | WCru
rubriflora | CHEx CRHN CSPN CTri
   | CWSG EBee EPfP LRHS MBlu
   | MDun MGos NRib NSti SHBN
   | SSpi
- (f) | CBcs ELan MGos SBra WSHC
- (m) | EMil NHol
rubriflora | WCru
  x *grandiflora*
sphenanthera | EBee ELan EMil EPfP GBin IMGH
   | LRHS MDun WSHC
verrucosa HWJ 664 | WCru

Schivereckia (*Brassicaceae*)

doerfleri | CNic

Schizachyrium (*Poaceae*)

§ *scoparium* | CBig CBri CBrm CFwr CKno
   | CWCL EBee EBre ECGN EHoe
   | EMan EPPr EPza EWes EWsh GSki
   | LPVe LRHS LRav MFan MWod
   | MWrn SUsu WDyG WWeb

Schizocentron see *Heterocentron*

Schizocodon see *Shortia*

Schizophragma (*Hydrangeaceae*)

* *corylieum* **new** | NLar
corylifolium | WCru

hydrangeoides | CBcs CDoC CFil EBee ELan EMil
   | EPfP GKir LRHS MAsh MBlu MBri
   | MDun MGos NPal SBra SLim SLon
   | SMur SPer SSpi SSta WDin WSHC
- B&SWJ 5954 | WCru
- B&SWJ 6119 | WCru
- B&SWJ 8505 from | WCru
  Ullüngdo
- 'Brookside Littleleaf' | see *Hydrangea anomala* subsp.
   | *petiolaris* var. *cordifolia*
   | 'Brookside Littleleaf'
- 'Moonlight' (v) | More than 30 suppliers
* f. *quelpartensis* | WCru
  B&SWJ 1160
- 'Roseum' ♀H4 | More than 30 suppliers
integrifolium ♀H4 | CBcs CFil CMac ELan EPfP LRHS
   | SDix SHBN SSpi
- var. *fauriei* | WSHC
- - B&SWJ 1701 | WCru
aff. *megalocarpum* | WCru
  BWJ 8150 **new**

Schizostachyum (*Poaceae*)

§ *funghomii* | EPla MMoz SDry WJun WPGP

Schizostylis ✿ (*Iridaceae*)

§ *coccinea* | More than 30 suppliers
- f. *alba* | More than 30 suppliers
- 'Anne' | WBro WHoo
- 'Ballyrogan Giant' | CFir CLAP EBee IBlr WPGP
- 'Cardinal' | MAvo WBro WFar
- 'Cindy Towe' **new** | EBee
- 'Elburton Glow' | MAvo WFar WHoo
- 'Fenland Daybreak' | CHar CLAP EBre EChP EFou EGle
   | GFlt GKir IBlr LIck LRHS MAvo
   | MLan NGdn NHol NLar SGar
   | SMrm SPet SSpe WBea WBro
   | WCAu WCra WFar WHoo
- 'Gigantea' | see *S. coccinea* 'Major'
- 'Grandiflora' | see *S. coccinea* 'Major'
- 'Hilary Gould' | CLAP GBuc IBlr MAvo NCGa SChr
   | WBea WBro WFar WHal
- 'Hint of Pink' | MAvo MDKP
- 'Jack Frost' **new** | MAvo
- 'Jennifer' ♀H4 | More than 30 suppliers
- late-flowering | NBPC
- 'Maiden's Blush' | CSpe EBee EBre ECGP EChP ECtt
   | EGle EHrv GEil GKir LIck LPio
   | LRHS MAvo MBnl MDKP MSte
   | NFla NLar WBVN WBro WCra WFar
   | WMoo WPnP
§ - 'Major' ♀H4 | More than 30 suppliers
* - 'Marietta' | CHid MAvo
- 'Molly Gould' | CStu EBee EHrv MAvo WBro WOut
   | WTin
- 'Mrs Hegarty' | More than 30 suppliers
- 'November Cheer' | EBee EBre ECot GKir IBlr LIck
   | LRHS MSte NBir NLar SMrm SSpe
   | WBro WCra WFar
- 'Pallida' | CMil CSam EBee ECha EGra EHrv
   | ELan EMan GBuc IBlr MAvo MRav
   | NBir WFar WMoo
- 'Peer Gynt' **new** | GFlt
- 'Pink Princess' **new** | CBro CPen MAvo
- 'Professor Barnard' | CFee CFwr CPrp CSpe EBee GCal
   | GMac IBlr LAst MSte NBir NBrk
   | SPla WBro WFar WMyn WOld
   | WPnn
- 'Red Dragon' | WFar
- 'Salmon Charm' | CLAP EBee EBre IBlr LRHS MAvo
   | WBro WFar
- 'Silver Pink' | IBlr
- 'Snow Maiden' | CAbP CFai CLAP ECtt GBuc IBal
   | LRHS MBNS WBro WLFP

§ - 'Sunrise' ♀H4 More than 30 suppliers
- 'Sunset' see *S. coccinea* 'Sunrise'
- 'Tambara' CFwr CLAP CMHG CMdw CPou
  EBee EHrv EMan GMac IBlr LHop
  NGdn WFar WMyn WPnP
- 'Viscountess Byng' CBro CFwr CHea CPrp CTri CWCL
  EBee EGle ERou GAbr GCal GEil
  IBlr LAst LRHS NPPs SPer WBea
  WFar WOld WPer
- 'Zeal Salmon' CBro CFee CFir CFwr CLAP CPou
  CPrp EBee ECha EGle GAbr IBlr
  LHop MRav NBir NBrk SCro SMHy
  SSpi WBro WFar WHil WMoo

Schoenoplectus (*Cyperaceae*)
§ **lacustris** EMFW EPAt EPza IHMH NArg
- subsp. EPza LNCo SLon
  tabernaemontani
- - 'Albescens' (v) CDWL CKno CWat EHon EMFW
  EPza LNCo LPBA MSta NArg SLon
  SWal SWat WCot WDyG WHal
  WPrP WWpP
- - 'Zebrinus' (v) More than 30 suppliers
  pungens MSta

Schoenus (*Cyperaceae*)
pauciflorus CFil CKno CWCL ECou EHoe
  EMan EWes GOrn MAvo NBro
  NChi SMrm WDyG WHal WMoo
  WPGP WPrP

Schotia (*Caesalpiniaceae*)
afra CKob
brachypetala CKob SOWG

Schrebera (*Oleaceae*)
alata CKob

Sciadopitys (*Sciadopityaceae*)
verticillata ♀H4 CBcs CDoC CKen CTho EHul GKir
  IDee ISea LBee LCon LLin LPan
  LRHS MAsh MBar MBri MDun
  MGos SLim SSpi SWvt WDin WEve
  WFar WNor WOrn
- 'Firework' CKen
- 'Globe' CKen
- 'Gold Star' CKen
- 'Golden Rush' CKen LLin MGos NLar
- 'Grüne Kugel' CKen
- 'Jeddeloh Compact' CKen
- 'Mecki' CKen LLin
- 'Picola' CKen
- 'Pygmy' CKen
- 'Shorty' CKen
- 'Sternschnuppe' CKen LLin NLar

Scilla (*Hyacinthaceae*)
adlamii see *Ledebouria cooperi*
amethystina see *S. litardierei*
amoena WCot WShi
autumnalis CAvo CNic CStu EPot LAma LRHS
  WShi
bifolia ♀H4 CAvo CBro CPom EPar EPot LAma
  LPhx LRHS NRog WShi
- 'Alba' LPhx LRHS
- 'Rosea' CPom EPar EPot LAma LRHS NRog
bithynica NGar SSpi WShi
campanulata see *Hyacinthoides hispanica*
chinensis see *S. scilloides*
cilicica LAma
greilhuberi WAbe WCot
hohenackeri ERos
- BSBE 811 WCot
hyacinthoides EHyt WBVN

ingridiae **new** WWst
italica see *Hyacinthoides italica*
japonica see *S. scilloides*
kraussii GIBF
libanotica see *Puschkinia scilloides* var.
  libanotica
liliohyacinthus CBro CRow EHyt IBlr MMHG SSpi
  WSHC
- 'Alba' ERos
lingulata CStu
- var. **ciliolata** CBro
§ **litardierei** CAvo CPom CStu EPot ERos GIBF
  LAma LPhx LRHS MBri NGar
  NMen WCot
messeniaca CPom GIBF SHel
- MS 38 WCot
- 'Grecian Sky' SIgm SUsu
§ **mischtschenkoana** CAvo CBro EHyt EPar EPfP
  EPot LAma LRHS NRog
  WDav
- 'Tubergeniana' ♀H4 CMea LPhx
monophylla ERos
  var. **tingitana** **new**
monophyllos CFil
morrisii ERos
natalensis **new** WCot WHil
non-scripta see *Hyacinthoides non-scripta*
nutans see *Hyacinthoides non-scripta*
persica ERos
- JCA 0.876.501 WCot
peruviana More than 30 suppliers
- SB&L 20/1 WCot
- 'Alba' CBcs CSWP CSpe EBee ECha
  LAma LPio MTho NRog SMrm
  WCot
* - var. **ciliata** S&L 311/2 WCot
* - var. **ifnense** WCot
- var. **venusta** S&L 311/2 WCot
pratensis see *S. litardierei*
puschkinioides LAma
reverchonii EHyt ERos
rosenii GCrs
- 'Bakuriani' **new** WWst
§ **scilloides** CBrm CBro EPot ERos GIBF SCnR
  SRot WCot
- MSF 782 SSpi
siberica ♀H4 CAvo EPfP LAma LRHS NMen
  NRog WPer WShi
- 'Alba' CBro EPar EPfP EPot LAma LRHS
  NRog WShi
- subsp. **armena** CHEx
- 'Spring Beauty' CBro CMea EPar EPot LAma LPhx
  LRHS MBri NRog SRms
- var. **taurica** ERos
'Tubergeniana' see *S. mischtschenkoana*
verna CDes ERos WHer WShi
vicentina see *Hyacinthoides vicentina*
violacea see *Ledebouria socialis*

Scindapsus (*Araceae*)
aureus see *Epipremnum aureum*
pictus (v) LRHS MBri

Scirpoides (*Cyperaceae*)
§ **holoschoenus** CBig CRWN

Scirpus (*Cyperaceae*)
angustifolius **new** LNCo
cernuus see *Isolepis cernua*
cyperinus CBrm CFwr
holoschoenus see *Scirpoides holoschoenus*
lacustris see *Schoenoplectus lacustris*
- 'Spiralis' see *Juncus effusus* f. *spiralis*
maritimus see *Bolboschoenus maritimus*

tabernaemontani	see *Schoenoplectus lacustris* subsp. *tabernaemontani*

Scleranthus (Illecebraceae)

biflorus	CTrC CWil EDAr EMlt EWes NDlv NWCA SPlb WPer
brockiei	CTrC
singuliflorus	WPat
uniflorus	CLyd CTrC EDAr EShb EWes GAbr NWCA SMad SPlb
– CC 466	NWCA
– compact **new**	SScr

Scoliopus (Trilliaceae)

bigelowii	CStu SBla SCnR SOkd WFar
hallii	SCnR SOkd WCru

Scolopendrium see *Asplenium*

Scolymus see *Cynara*

Scopolia (Solanaceae)

carniolica	CAvo CFir COld EBee ECGN EChP EGle ELan EMon EPar GCal GFlt GPoy IBlr LPhx MBlu MHar MSal MSte NChi NLar NSti SPlb WAul WCru WPGP
§ – var. **brevifolia**	CAvo EHrv EPPr LSpr SDys WBcn WTin
– – WM 9811	MPhe
– subsp. **hladnikiana**	see *S. carniolica* var. *brevifolia*
– 'Zwanenburg'	CAvo EBee EHrv EPPr EPar LEur WCot
lurida	see *Anisodus luridus*
physaloides	MSal
sinensis	see *Atropanthe sinensis*

Scorzonera (Asteraceae)

radiata	EBee
suberosa subsp. **cariensis**	EBee EHyt

Scrophularia (Scrophulariaceae)

aquatica	see *S. auriculata*
§ **auriculata**	EFWa ELau MHer MSal NPer WHer WWpP WWye
§ – 'Variegata' (v)	CArn EChP ECtt EHoe ELan ENot EPfP ERou GKir LPBA LRHS MBri MDun MHer MRav MSta MWat NSti SDnm SPer SPlb SRms WBea WCot WFar WHal WWin WWpP
buergeriana	MSal
– 'Lemon and Lime' misapplied	see *Teucrium viscidum* 'Lemon and Lime'
§ **canina** subsp. **hoppii**	EBee
grandiflora	CBgR EBee WFar WSan
juratensis	see *S. canina* subsp. *hoppii*
macrantha	WCot
marilandica	EBee
nodosa	CArn CRWN EBee ELau MSal NMir NSco WBri WCAu WHbs WHer WMoo WSel
– **tracheliodes**	CNat
– **variegata**	see *S. auriculata* 'Variegata'
scopolii	EBee
vernalis	EBee

Scutellaria ✿ (Lamiaceae)

albida	EBee EPPr
– subsp. **colchica**	MSPs
§ **alpina**	CLyd CPBP CPlt EMan GCrs GEdr LRHS NBlu NJOw SBla SPlb SRms SRot WBVN WGor WPer WShp
– 'Arcobaleno'	CBrm EBre EPPr LPVe NLar

– 'Greencourt'	EBee
altissima	CArn CTCP EBee ELan EMan EMar GBuc MBro MOne MSal NBro NCGa NPPs SHel SPlb SScr STes WBar WBea WCHb WHoo WMoo WPer WWin
'Amazing Grace'	EChP EWes
baicalensis	CArn EBee EMlt EPPr EWTr EWll GPoy IBlr MSal SBla SIgm SMac SPet SSvw WPer
barbata	MSal
californica NNS 98-511 **new**	WCot
canescens	see *S. incana*
columnae	IFro
diffusa	CPBP ECtt WPer
formosana 'China Blue'	CAbP EPfP
galericulata	EBee GPoy GWCH MHer MSal NVic SHar WCHb WHer WJek WWye
hastata	see *S. hastifolia*
§ **hastifolia**	CTri EBee ECot ECtt EDAr NFor NSti WPer
§ **incana**	CPlt CPom EBee ECGN ECGP EFou EHrv ELan EMan EWTr LHop LPhx LRHS NCGa NDov NSti SAga SMrm SSvw SUsu WCAu WMoo WSHC WWye
indica **new**	WCot
– var. **japonica**	see *S. indica* var. *parvifolia*
§ – var. **parvifolia**	CLyd CPBP CStu EBee EBur EHyt EMan EWes LBee LRHS NMen NWCA SBla SRot WPat
– – 'Alba'	CGra CLyd CPBP EHyt EMan ETow LBee LRHS LTwo SBla SSvw WPat
lateriflora	CArn CBod EBee ELau EOHP GBar GPoy MGol MSal SPoG WCHb WHbs WHer WJek WPer WSel WWye
novae-zelandiae	ECou EHyt LRHS MTho NWCA
orientalis	CPBP EBee ECtt LRHS NLAp SBla SMac SScr WLin WPat WWin
– subsp. **bicolor**	NWCA
– subsp. **carica**	WWye
– 'Eastern Star'	MWrn NArg SPet
– 'Eastern Sun' **new**	GFlt
– subsp. **pinnatifida**	EMlt NLar NWCA
pontica	NLar
prostrata	CMHG EMan LTwo NLAp WPat WWin
scordiifolia	CLyd CMea CMil CNic EBee ECha EMlt GKir IHMH MBro NRya NWCA SBla SRms SUsu WBVN WCom WFar WHal WHoo WTin WWeb WWin WWye
– 'Seoul Sapphire'	EBee EMan GCrs GEil SOkd WCot
serrata	EBee
suffrutescens **new**	XPep
supina	see *S. alpina*
tournefortii	EChP ECtt LLWP

seakale see *Crambe maritima*

Sebaea (Gentianaceae)

repens	SPlb
thomasii	GCrs SOkd WAbe

Securigera see *Coronilla*

Sedastrum see *Sedum*

Sedum ✿ (Crassulaceae)

B&SWJ 737	EGoo
§ 'Abbeydore'	CKno EBee EBre ECGP EChP EDAr

	EFou EGle EGoo EMan EMon	
	MAnH NSti WPGP WWeb	
acre	CTri EBre ECot GPoy MBar MHer	
	NBlu SECG SPlb WShp XPep	
- 'Aureum'	EDAr EMlt EPfP IHMH MBar MOne	
	NBlu NLar WFar WPat	
- 'Elegans'	ECtt EDAr GTou NJOw WShp	
§ - var. *majus*	CChe CNic	
- 'Minus'	EDAr WFar	
aggregatum	see *Orostachys aggregata*	
§ *aizoon*	EPfP SChu SIde SPlb	
- 'Aurantiacum'	see *S. aizoon* 'Euphorbioides'	
§ - 'Euphorbioides'	CMea EBee EBre ECha ECtt EGoo	
	ELan LDai LRHS MBNS MHer	
	MRav MWgw NLar NPro SGar SPer	
	SPlb WBea WFar WTin	
albescens	see *S. rupestre* f. *purpureum*	
alboroseum	see *S. erythrostictum*	
§ *album*	CHal EBre IHMH MBNS NBro	
	WPer	
§ - 'Chloroticum'	EDAr	
- 'Coral Carpet'	EDAr EPfP ESis EWTr GAbr IHMH	
	MBar MRav MWat NHol SChu SIng	
	WShp XPep	
- var. *micranthum*	see *S. album* 'Chloroticum'	
§ - subsp. *teretifolium*	CTri MBar SIng WShp	
'Murale'		
altissimum	see *S. sediforme*	
altum	EMon LPhx WFar WMoo	
amplexicaule	see *S. tenuifolium*	
§ *anacampseros*	CHEx CNic EGoo NHol WPer	
	WShp	
anglicum	MBow SChr	
athoum	see *S. album*	
atlanticum	see *S. dasyphyllum* subsp.	
	dasyphyllum var. *mesatlanticum*	
Autumn Joy	see *S.* 'Herbstfreude'	
§ 'Bertram Anderson' ♀H4	More than 30 suppliers	
bithynicum 'Aureum'	see *S. hispanicum* var. *minus*	
	'Aureum'	
'Black Emperor' **new**	EBee	
brevifolium	IHMH ITim MDHE	
'Carl'	CKno CPrp EBee EBre EChP ECha	
	EFou EGle EGoo EMan EMon	
	LHop LRHS MRav MSte MWgw	
	NBro NCGa NSti SUsu WCot WHil	
	WMnd	
caucasicum	WAbb WEas	
cauticola ♀H4	CLyd CNic COkL CSpe EDAr EMan	
	GCal GEdr MBrN MHer MRav	
	SMrm SRms SRot WAbe	
- from Lida	ECho	
§ - 'Lidakense'	CMea CStu CTri EBre ECtt EGle	
	EMan EMlt GKir LRHS MBar MBri	
	MTis NPPs NSla SBla SChu SIng	
	SRot WFar WRHF WShp	
- 'Purpurine' **new**	GCal	
- 'Robustum'	EBee EWll WShp	
cauticola x *tatarinowii*	EGoo EWes	
'Citrus Twist' **new**	EBee MBnl NPro	
confusum	EOas SChr SEND	
'Coral Sunset'	EGoo	
crassipes	see *Rhodiola wallichiana*	
crassularia	see *Crassula milfordiae*	
cryptomerioides	WCru	
B&SWJ 054		
cyaneum misapplied	see *S. takasui*	
cyaneum Rudolph	WAbe	
dasyphyllum	CNic GTou MBar MHer MOne	
	MWat NHol NRya NWCA SRms	
	XPep	
- subsp. *dasyphyllum*	CHEx CHal	
var. *glanduliferum*		
- - 'Lilac Mound'	MDHE	

§ - - var. *mesatlanticum*	CNic MDHE NBir	
- *mucronatis*	see *S. dasyphyllum* subsp.	
	dasyphyllum var. *mesatlanticum*	
divergens	XPep	
douglasii	see *S. stenopetalum* 'Douglasii'	
drymarioides	EBee	
'Dudley Field'	MHer	
'Eleanor Fisher'	see *S. telephium* subsp. *ruprechtii*	
ellacombeanum	see *S. kamtschaticum* var.	
	ellacombeanum	
§ *erythrostictum*	MTho	
- 'Frosty Morn' (v)	More than 30 suppliers	
§ - 'Mediovariegatum' (v)	COlW EBre EChP EGle EGoo ELan	
	EMon EPfP ERou IFro LRHS MBri	
	MHer MNrw MRav NBPC SAga	
	SGar SHBN SWvt WBrE WFar WHil	
	WMnd WMoo WPer WShp	
§ *ewersii*	CHEx CNic CSLe EBee EDAr EMon	
	GAbr GTou LRHS MHer NBro NLar	
	SPlb	
§ - var. *homophyllum* **new**	IHMH	
§ *fabaria*	EBee EChP EMan WAbb WCot	
	WEas	
fastigiatum	see *Rhodiola fastigiata*	
floriferum	see *S. kamtschaticum*	
forsterianum	LGro SPlb	
subsp. *elegans*		
frutescens	STre	
furfuraceum	NMen	
'Gold Mound' **new**	CStu LAst MGos	
* 'Green Expectations'	EBee EChP EGle MCLN MSph	
	MSte NSti	
gypsicola	EBee WPer	
'Harvest Moon'	EBur	
§ 'Herbstfreude' ♀H4	More than 30 suppliers	
heterodontum	see *Rhodiola heterodonta*	
hidakanum	CLyd ECtt EMFP GCrs GGar GTou	
	MBro NBro NHol NMen NPPs	
	SUsu WHoo WPat WTin	
§ *hispanicum*	ECho IHMH SPlb	
- 'Albescens'	CNic	
- *glaucum*	see *S. hispanicum* var. *minus*	
§ - var. *minus*	ECtt GTou MBar NPri NRya SChu	
	SIng SPlb WMoo	
§ - - 'Aureum'	ECha EDAr MBar NHol NJOw	
	WMoo WWpP	
humifusum	CPBP EBur EHyt ETow NHol	
	NWCA SIng	
hybridum	WEas	
- 'Immergrünchen'	COkL	
ishidae	see *Rhodiola ishidae*	
'Joyce Henderson'	CPrp CStr EBee EChP ECtt EGle	
	EMan EWTr LHop LPio MRav	
	NCGa NLar SBla SPer WBor WBrk	
	WCom WCot WEas WOld WRHF	
	WTin	
§ *kamtschaticum* ♀H4	MBar MHer WBea WFar WShp	
	WWpP	
§ - var. *ellacombeanum*	CNic EBre EDAr EGoo MHer	
♀H4	NMen WCot	
- - B&SWJ 8853	WCru	
§ - var. *floriferum*	CMea CNic COkL CTri EBre ECtt	
'Weihenstephaner	EDAr EGoo EMlt EPfP ESis GKir	
Gold'	IHMH LRHS MBar MHer MRav	
	MWat NBlu NFor NJOw NMen	
	NVic SChu SPlb SRms WFar WPat	
	XPep	
- var. *kamtschaticum*	CBrm CHEx CLyd CMea COkL	
'Variegatum' (v) ♀H4	EBee ECtt EDAr EMlt EPPr EPfP	
	LBee MHer MWat SBla SIng SRms	
	SRot SWvt WCot WEas WFar WShp	
- var. *middendorffianum*	see *S. middendorffianum*	
'Karlfunkenstein' **new**	GBin	
kirilovii	see *Rhodiola kirilovii*	

	laxum subsp. *heckneri*	SSpi
	lineare	CHEx LAst SSto
	- 'Variegatum' (v)	SChr
	litorale	EBee
§	*lydium*	GTou MBar MHer MOne SPlb WShp
	- 'Aureum'	see *S. hispanicum* var. *minus* 'Aureum'
	- 'Bronze Queen'	see *S. lydium*
	'Lynda Windsor'PBR	EBee EChP EMan EPfP MAsh MBNS MBri MCCP MCLN NPro NSti SPer SSpi WHil
	makinoi 'Ogon' **new**	CStu
	'Marchant's Dark Leaf' **new**	SMHy
	maweanum	see *S. acre* var. *majus*
	maximowiczii	see *S. aizoon*
§	*middendorffianum*	CLyd ECho EDAr EGoo EPPr GTou ITim MBrN MDHE MHer MWat NMen SRms SRot WHoo WWin
	monregalense	EDAr
	'Moonglow'	ECtt NMen
	moranense	CHal CNic ETow
	morganianum ♀H1	CHal EBak
	murale	see *S. album* subsp. *teretifolium* 'Murale'
N	*nevii* hort.	EGle SPlb
	nicaeense	see *S. sediforme*
	obcordatum	NMen
§	*obtusatum*	COkL ECtt EDAr GGar MBro NBro NJOw NSla
§	- subsp. *retusum*	WCot
§	*ochroleucum*	XPep
	oppositifolium	see *S. spurium* var. *album*
	oreganum	ECha EDAr ESis GAbr GTou IHMH MBar MWat NMen SPlb SRms SRot WBea WPer WShp WWin
	- 'Procumbens'	see *S. oreganum* subsp. *tenue*
§	- subsp. *tenue*	CNic MBro NHol NRya WPat
§	*oregonense*	CLyd EBur EOas GTou NJOw NMen
	oryzifolium 'Minor'	EBur
	oxypetalum	STre
	pachyclados	see *Rhodiola pachyclados*
	palmeri	CBel CHEx CNic CSpe EMan EOas ETow NBir SChr SDix XPep
	pilosum	NMen
	'Pink Chablis'PBR **new**	EBee EChP EMan MBnl WHil
§	*pluricaule*	EHyt SChu SPlb SRms SRot WAbe
	populifolium	CMHG ECha GCal MHer NChi SDry STre WCom WPer
	praealtum	EOas SChr
	pruinosum	see *S. spathulifolium* subsp. *pruinosum*
	pulchellum	MSPs
	purdyi	ITim NMen
§	'Purple Emperor'	More than 30 suppliers
	'Purple Leaf'	NSti
	'Red Rum'	LRHS
	reflexum L.	see *S. rupestre* L.
	reptans	NRya
	retusum	see *S. obtusatum* subsp. *retusum*
	rhodiola	see *Rhodiola rosea*
	'Ringmore Ruby'	WCot
	'Rose Carpet'	SWvt WCom WWeb
	rosea	see *Rhodiola rosea*
	rubroglaucum misapplied	see *S. oregonense*
	rubroglaucum Praeger	see *S. obtusatum*
	x *rubrotinctum*	CHEx CHal SChr XPep
	- 'Aurora'	SChr
§	'Ruby Glow' ♀H4	More than 30 suppliers
	'Ruby Port'	CSpe

§	*rupestre* L.	CAgr CNic EBre EPfP GGar MBNS MBar MHer MWhi NBlu SChu SPlb WHer WShp XPep
	- 'Angelina'	EMlt EPPr EWes NBir SUsu WCot
I	- 'Aureum' **new**	SIng
	- 'Minus'	CNic
	- 'Monstrosum Cristatum'	ITer NBir SMad
§	- f. *purpureum*	NRya
	ruprechtii	see *S. telephium* subsp. *ruprechtii*
	sarcocaule hort.	see *Crassula sarcocaulis*
§	*sediforme*	CArn EDAr XPep
	- *nicaeense*	see *S. sediforme*
	selskianum	COkL EBee GTou IHMH MOne WFar
	sexangulare	EDAr ESis GAbr IHMH MBar MHer MOne NRya SPlb SRms WBea WFar XPep
	sibiricum	see *S. hybridum*
§	*sieboldii*	CSam CStu WRHF
	- 'Mediovariegatum' (v) ♀H2-3	EBre EMan SPlb WPer
	'Silver Moon'	EBur MDHE
	spathulifolium	CAgr ECha EPot GTou MDKP MOne SChu WEas
	- 'Aureum'	EBur ECtt GKir GTou MBar NRya
	- 'Cape Blanco' ♀H4	More than 30 suppliers
§	- subsp. *pruinosum*	MDHE
	- 'Purpureum' ♀H4	EBre EDAr EPfP GAbr GKir GTou IHMH LBee LPVe LRHS MBar MBri MHer MWat NBlu NHol NJOw NMen NRya SBla SMer SPlb WAbe WBVN WCom WFar WPer WShp WWin
§	*spectabile* ♀H4	CArn CHrt CPrp EBee ELan EPfP LRHS MHer MRav NBlu SHFr SPer SPlb SRms WBea WBrk WCAu WFar WTel WTin WWin WWpP XPep
	- 'Abendrot'	EMon
	- 'Album' ♀H4	CHEx WOut
	- 'Brilliant' ♀H4	More than 30 suppliers
	- 'Brilliant Variegated' (v)	WShp
	- 'Carmen'	WMoo
	- 'Iceberg'	More than 30 suppliers
	- 'Indian Chief'	CM&M CPrp EBee EBre EChP EGle GKir LRHS SVil WFar WMnd WMoo WWpP
	- 'Lisa'	EMon MTPN NLar
	- 'Meteor'	CStr EBee MBNS MLLN MRav MSte NLar SMrm WBea WCAu WPer
*	- 'Mini'	ELan MRav
	- 'Pink Fairy'	WHil
	- 'Rosenteller'	EGle EMon SMrm
	- September Glow	see *S. spectabile* 'Septemberglut'
§	- 'Septemberglut'	EBre EFWa EGoo EMan EMon GKir NSti WCAu WCot
	- 'Stardust'	CFwr COIW CPrp EGle EGoo EMil EMon ENot EPfP ERou EWTr GBBs GLil LPVe LPio LRHS MBNS MHer MLLN NCGa SPer SPet WCAu WFar WGor WViv WWeb
	- 'Steve Ward' **new**	EWes
	- 'Variegatum'	see *S. erythrostictum* 'Mediovariegatum'
	spinosum	see *Orostachys spinosa*
	spurium	CHEx CWCL EGoo EWTr LGro MBNS NBlu SEND SRms WWpP
§	- var. *album*	EGoo NRya
*	- 'Atropurpureum'	ECha NFor
	- 'Coccineum'	EBre MBar MHer SSto WBVN
	- Dragon's Blood	see *S. spurium* 'Schorbuser Blut'
	- 'Erdblut'	EBre GKir LRHS NFla NMen
	- 'Fuldaglut'	CHal CNic COkL EBee EBre EDAr EHoe EMan EMlt ENot GBuc

	IHMH MBNS MWat NRya SChu SIng SMrm WBea WMoo WPer WShp WWin
- 'Green Mantle'	ECha ESis SMer SSto WWpP
- Purple Carpet	see *S. spurium* 'Purpurteppich'
- 'Purpureum'	EGoo SIng SRms
§ - 'Purpurteppich'	COkL EBre ESis GKir LGro LRHS MRav NBro NDov NHol NLar SRms
- 'Roseum'	EWll SRms
- 'Ruby Mantle'	NPro WBVN
§ - 'Schorbuser Blut' ♀H4	CMea EBee ECtt EDAr EPfP ESis GKir IHMH MBNS MBro MWat NChi NRya NVic SPlb SRms WEas WHoo WPat WRHF WShp WTin
I - 'Splendens Roseum'	LGro
- 'Summer Glory'	NLar WBea
- 'Tricolor'	see *S. spurium* 'Variegatum'
I - 'Variegatum' (v)	CNic ECha EDAr EGoo EHoe EMlt ESis LAst MBar MHer MRav NFla NRya SBod SIng SPlb WBea WEas WMoo WPat WWin
stefco	NRya
stenopetalum	IHMH SPlb
§ - 'Douglasii'	CNic MOne SRms
'Stewed Rhubarb Mountain'	CPrp EBee ECGP EChP ECtt EGle EMan EMon EWTr LDai LHop MBNS MRav MSte NDov SChu WCom WCot WHil WPGP
stoloniferum 'Variegata'	WWeb
'Strawberries and Cream'	CBrm CFwr CPrp EBee EChP EGle EMan EMon ERou GBin LAst LPhx LPio MBNS MBri MCCP MRav NBhm NBro NDov NMyG NPro NSti SChu WCAu WHil WWeb
stribrnyi	see *S. urvillei* Stribrnyi Group
'Sunset Cloud'	CMHG CSam EBee ECtt EGle EMon EWes GCal LRHS MRav
takasui	CLyd
takesimense B&SWJ 8518	WCru
§ ***tatarinowii***	CLyd EDAr
§ ***telephium***	CAgr CArn CHrt CMea MBNS MFOX NBir SRms WHil WWye
- 'Abbeydore'	see *S.* 'Abbeydore'
- 'Arthur Branch'	EPPr GBuc MNrw MSte MTho
- var. ***borderei***	CElw EBee EFWa EGle EMan EMon LHop LRHS
- 'El Cid'	EBee EWes
- subsp. ***fabaria***	see *S. fabaria*
* - 'Hester'	EBee EChP WWpP
- 'Jennifer'	EMan WCot
- 'Leonore Zuuntz'	WCot
- 'Matrona'	More than 30 suppliers
- subsp. ***maximum***	CBrm SChu
- - 'Atropurpureum' ♀H4	CBot CBrm CHad CMea EBee ECha ECoo EGle Elan EMan EMar EPfP LPVe MRav SChu SGar SWvt WCot WEas WMoo WWin
- - 'Gooseberry Fool'	ECtt EGle EGoo EMan EMon EOMN ERou LPhx LPio MAnH SHar WCot WWeb
- 'Mohrchen'	More than 30 suppliers
- 'Munstead Red'	More than 30 suppliers
§ - subsp. ***ruprechtii***	More than 30 suppliers
- - 'Hab Gray'	EBee EChP MSte NPPs WCot WWhi
- subsp. ***telephium*** 'Lynda et Rodney'	CKno EBee EGle EGoo EMan EMon MSph WCot
- - var. ***purpureum*** B&SWJ 8480 **new**	WCru
- 'Variegatum' (v)	COtt ECoo LRHS MDKP WHal WWin
- 'Veluwe se Wakel'	EBee

* - Washfield purple selection	EBee
§ ***tenuifolium***	EBur
- subsp. ***tenuifolium***	EBur
tetractinum	EFou
trollii	see *Rhodiola trollii*
§ ***urvillei*** Stribrnyi Group	CLyd
ussuriense	SUsu WOut
§ 'Vera Jameson' ♀H4	CPrp CSLe EBre EChP ECha EDAr EGle EHoe EMar ENot EPfP LRHS MBrN MFan MRav MWat NHol NPPs SBla SChu SHBN WCom WEas WFar WMoo WPer WWhi
'Washfield Purple'	see *Sedum* 'Purple Emperor'
'Weihenstephaner Gold'	see *S. kamtschaticum* var. *floriferum* 'Weihenstephaner Gold'
weinbergii	see *Graptopetalum paraguayense*
yezoense	see *S. pluricaule*

Seemannia see Gloxinia

Selaginella ✿ (Selaginellaceae)

apoda	MBri
braunii	NMar WCot
douglasii	NMar
emmeliana	see *S. pallescens*
helvetica	CStu
involvens	WRic
kraussiana ♀H1	CBgR CHal MBri NMar NRya WRic
- 'Aurea'	CHal GGar MBri NMar SMad
- 'Brownii' ♀H1	MBri NMar
- 'Variegata' (v) ♀H1	MBri
martensii 'Watsoniana'	NMar
moellendorfii	WRic
§ ***pallescens***	NMar
- 'Aurea'	NMar
sanguinolenta	SIng
uncinata ♀H1	WRic
vogelii	NMar

Selinum (Apiaceae)

carvifolium	EBee EMan MLLN MWgw NLar
tenuifolium	see *S. wallichianum*
§ ***wallichianum***	CHad CRow EChP EFou EGoo EMan EPla EWTr GBuc GGar LPhx MLLN NBid NCGa SIgm SMHy SMrm SSpi WHer WPGP WPrP WSHC WWhi
- EMAK 886	EBee GPoy MBri NSti SDix

Selliera (Goodeniaceae)

radicans	CStu ECou GGar

Semele (Ruscaceae)

androgyna	CHEx CRHN

Semiaquilegia (Ranunculaceae)

§ ***adoxoides***	EBee NPPs
- B&SWJ 1190	WCru
'Early Dwarf'	EDif
§ ***ecalcarata***	CPlt CPom CTCP EBee EBre EDAr EMan GBin GIBF LDai MNrw NLar NPPs SMrm SRms WCru WFar WPGP WPer WPrP WSan WWhi WWin
* - f. ***bicolor***	CPom WCru
- 'Flore Pleno' (d)	EBee EChP
simulatrix	see *S. ecalcarata*

Semiarundinaria (Poaceae)

from Korea	EPla
§ ***fastuosa*** ♀H4	CAbb CBig CDoC CHEx CTrC EAmu EBee EFul EPfP EPla ERod

	LPal MBri MMoz MWht NMoo NVic SAPC SArc SDix SDry SPlb WJun WMul
- var. *viridis*	EBee EPla ERod LPJP SDry WCru WJun
kagamiana	CDoC CPen EBee EPla MBri MMoz MWht NMoo SDry SEND WJun
§ *lubrica*	CFil WPGP
makinoi	EPla MWht WJun WPGP
nitida	see *Fargesia nitida*
§ *okuboi*	EPla ERod LPal MMoz MWht SEND WJun
villosa	see *S. okuboi*
yamadorii	EPla ERod MMoz MWht SDry WJun
- 'Brimscombe'	EPla SDry
yashadake	EPla ERod SDry WJun
- *kimmei*	CAbb CDoC CFil CPen EBee EPla ERod MAsh MMoz MPRe MWht NMoo SDry SEND WDyG WFar WJun WPGP

Sempervivella see *Rosularia*

Sempervivum ✿ (*Crassulaceae*)

from Sierra del Cadi	MOne NHol
from Sierra Nova	NDlv
'Abba'	MOne WHal WPer
acuminatum	see *S. tectorum* var. *glaucum*
'Adelmoed'	CWil
'Adeltruid'	NHol
'Adlerhorst'	GEdr NHol
'Aglow'	CWil MHom MOne NMen
'Aladdin'	CWil SRms
'Albernelli'	NHol
'Alchimist' **new**	MOne
'Alcithoë'	CWil MOne
'Aldo Moro'	CWil GAbr LBee MHom MOne NMen
'Alidae' **new**	MOne
allionii	see *Jovibarba allionii*
'Allison'	CWil
'Alluring'	GAbr
'Alpha'	CWil EBee EMlt ESis LBee LRHS MOne NHol NMen NPPs SIng SRms STre WHal WPer WTin
altum	CWil MHom NMen
'Amanda'	CWil NMen SRms WHoo WPer WTin
'Ambergreen'	NMen
'Andorra' ambig.	NHol
andreanum	CWil ESis MHom NBro NHol NMen SIng
'Apache'	CWil NMen
'Apollo'	NHol
'Apple Blossom'	CMea CWil GCrs NMen
arachnoideum ♀H4	More than 30 suppliers
- from Ararat	SDys
- from cascade piste 7 **new**	MOne
* - 'Abruzzii'	GCrs SIng
- 'Boria' **new**	MOne
- var. *bryoides*	CWil ESis NMen SIng WIvy WLin WPer
- 'Clairchen'	NHol NMen NSla
- cristate	CWil
* - *densum*	EBre EHyt EMlt NRya WAbe
- subsp. *doellianum*	see *S. arachnoideum* var. *glabrescens*
§ - var. *glabrescens*	EHyt NMen SDys
- - 'Album'	GCrs
- 'Kappa'	see *S.* 'Kappa'
- 'Laggeri'	see *S. arachnoideum* subsp. *tomentosum*
- 'Mole Harbord'	LRHS

* - 'Peña Prieta'	NHol
- red	NMen
- 'Rubrum'	COIW EPem LRHS MCCP MOne NFla WLow
- 'Sultan'	MOne
- subsp. *tomentosum* misapplied	see *S.* x *barbulatum* 'Hookeri'
§ - subsp. *tomentosum* ♀H4	CHal CWil EBee EBre EMlt EPot GKir LRHS MHer NHol NMen NPer NRya NWCA SChu SIng SRms WBrE WPer WWin
- - 'Minor'	NHol NJOw NMen SIng
§ - - 'Stansfieldii'	GAbr SDys SIng STre WHal
§ - 'White Christmas'	CWil
arachnoideum x *calcareum*	CWil NHol NMen WIvy WTin
- x *montanum*	SIng
- x *nevadense*	CWil SDys SIng
- x *pittonii*	CWil NHol NJOw NMen
arenarium	see *Jovibarba arenaria*
armenum	MOne NMen
'Aross'	CLyd CMea NMen
'Arrowheads Red'	MOne
'Artist'	CWil
arvernense	see *S. tectorum*
'Ashes of Roses'	EGoo EPot MHom MOne NMen WAbe WPer
'Asteroid'	CWil NMen
atlanticum	CWil GEdr MHom NDlv NJOw NMen NSla
- from Atlas Mts, Morocco	CWil
- from Oukaimaden	CWil MOne NHol NMen WTin
- 'Edward Balls'	CWil EPem MOne SDys
'Atlantis'	NHol
'Atropurpureum'	CHEx CWil GAbr MOne SRms WGor WIvy WPer
'Atropurpureum' Hemlich form **new**	MOne
§ 'Aymon Correvon'	MOne
balcanicum	EDAr NMen
ballsii	CWil NMen
- from Kambeecho	MHom
- from Smólikas	CWil MHom MOne NMen
- from Tschumba Petzi	CWil MHom SDys SIng
'Banderi'	CWil MOne
'Banjo' **new**	MOne
'Barbarosa' **new**	MOne
§ x *barbulatum*	NMen SDys SIng WPer
§ - 'Hookeri'	CWil MOne NLar NMen SIng WAbe WPer
'Bascour Zilver'	CWil GAbr SIng WHal
'Banyan'	MTPN
'Beaute'	CWil
'Bedazzled'	CWil
'Bedivere'	CLyd CPBP CWil LBee MOne NMen SRms
'Bedivere Crested'	CWil
'Bedley Hi'	MHom
'Bella Donna'	CWil MDHE MHom NHol NMen WPer
'Bella Meade'	CWil EPem NMen SRms WPer
'Bellotts Pourpre'	CWil NHol
'Bennerbroek'	MDHE
'Benny Hill'	CWil
'Bernstein'	MHer WHal
'Beta'	MHom NHol NMen WAbe WCom WPer WTin
'Bethany'	CWil NHol NMen WHal
'Bicolor'	EPfP
'Big Mal'	NHol
'Big Slipper'	EPem NHol
'Binstead'	NHol
'Birchmaier'	EDAr MOne
'Black Cap' **new**	MOne

'Black Claret'	NHol
'Black Knight'	CStu EMlt ESis LBee LRHS SBla SRms WHal
'Black Mini'	CWil EMlt MDKP NBir NMen SRms
'Black Mountain'	CWil LBee MOne
'Black Prince'	CLyd GCrs
'Black Velvet'	WCom WPer
'Bladon'	WPer
'Blari'	MOne
'Blood Tip'	CHEx CHal CLyd CWil EBee EHyt ESis GAbr GFlt ITim LBee LRHS MHer NHol NMen SChu SRms WCom WGor WHal WLow
'Blue Boy'	CWil EMlt ESis GAbr LBee MOne NHol SIng SRms WCom WHoo WPer
'Blue Moon'	CLyd MOne NMen
'Blue Time'	MOne SChu WTin
'Boissieri'	see *S. tectorum* subsp. *tectorum* 'Boissieri'
'Bold Chick'	MOne
'Booth's Red'	CLyd EPem MOne NMen SIng WGor
'Borealis' **new**	MOne
borisii	see *S. ciliosum* var. *borisii*
borissovae	CWil EDAr MHom NMen SDys
'Boromir'	CWil MOne SChu
'Bowles' Variety'	WPer
'Britta'	MOne SDys
'Brock'	MHer MHom NHol WPer
'Bronco'	CWil EBee LBee MHom MOne NMen SChu SRms SUsu WLow
'Bronze Pastel'	CLyd CWil MHom MOne NMen NSla SRms WTin
'Bronze Tower'	NHol
'Brown Owl'	CWil ESis MOne NHol SRms
'Brownii'	GAbr MOne NMen SBla WPer WTin
'Brunette'	GAbr
'Burgundy'	MOne
'Burgundy Velvet'	MOne SIng
'Burnatii'	CWil MOne NMen
'Butterbur'	CWil
'Butterfly' **new**	MOne
'Café'	CWil EGoo ESis NHol NMen SIng SRms WPer
'Cakor'	NHol
x *calcaratum*	EDAr SIng SRms
calcareum	CNic COlW CWil EHyt EPot MOne NBro NMen SPlb SRms WBVN WHoo WLow WPer
- from Alps, France	CWil MOne
- from Calde la Vanoise, France	CWil
- from Ceuze	CWil WIvy
- from Col Bayard, France	CWil MOne
- from Colle St Michael	CWil MOne NMen
- from Gleize	CWil MOne NHol NMen
- from Gorges du Cains	CWil MOne
- from Guillaumes, Mont Ventoux, France	CWil MOne NMen WHoo
- from Mont Ventoux, France	CWil MOne
- from Queyras	CWil MOne NMen
- from Route d'Annôt	CWil MOne
- from Triora	CWil MOne NHol NMen
- 'Atropurpureum'	SChu
- 'Benz'	SDys
- 'Extra'	CWil
- 'Greenii'	CWil ESis MOne NDlv NHol NMen SPlb
§ - 'Grigg's Surprise'	CWil EMlt MHer MOne NMen

- 'Limelight'	CMea CWil NMen SChu WHal WTin
- 'Monstrosum'	see *S. calcareum* 'Grigg's Surprise'
- 'Mrs Giuseppi'	CWil EBee EBre EMlt ESis GAbr LBee LRHS MOne NMen NOak SBla SChu SRms STre WAbe WPer
- 'Pink Pearl'	CWil EGoo MOne NMen SDys WTin
- 'Sir William Lawrence'	CMea CPBP CWil EPem ESis NMen SChu WHal WHoo WPer WTin
'Caldera'	NHol
* *callosum barnesii*	GAbr
'Cameo'	see *Jovibarba heuffelii* var. *glabra* 'Cameo'
'Canada Kate'	CWil NHol WPer
'Cancer'	MOne
'Candy Floss'	CWil MOne NMen SIng
cantabricum	CWil MDHE NMen
- subsp. *cantabricum* from Leitariegos	CWil ETow GAbr MHom MOne NMen
- from Lago de Enol	MOne
- from Navafria	CWil NHol SIng
- from Peña Prieta	NMen
- from Piedrafita, Spain	MOne
- from Riaño, Spain	CWil GAbr
- from San Glorio	CWil GAbr MOne NMen
- from Santander, Spain	NHol
- from Sierra del Cadi, Spain	CLyd
- from Ticeros	CWil MOne NMen
- from Valvernera	CWil
- subsp. *guadarramense*	see *S. vicentei* subsp. *paui*
- - from Lobo No. 1	CWil MOne
- - from Lobo No. 2	MOne
- - from Navafria No. 1	WTin
- - from Valvanera No. 1	NMen
- subsp. *urbionense*	CLyd CWil SIng
- - from Picos de Urbión, Spain	MOne NMen
cantabricum x *montanum* subsp. *stiriacum*	CWil WEas WTin
'Canth'	CWil NHol
'Caramel'	MOne
* 'Carinal'	NBir
* x *carlsii* **new**	MOne
'Carluke'	MOne
'Carmen'	CHal CWil GAbr MOne
'Carneus'	MOne NHol
'Carnival'	CHal NMen WPer
caucasicum	CWil EHol MHom MOne NMen SIng
'Cauticolum' **new**	MOne
'Cavo Doro'	CWil MDHE
'Centennial'	MOne
'Ceylon' **new**	MOne
'Chalen' **new**	MOne
charadzeae	CWil LBee NHol
'Cherry Frost'	CLyd ITim MOne
'Cherry Glow'	see *Jovibarba heuffelii* 'Cherry Glow'
'Chocolate'	CWil NHol
x *christii*	MOne NHol
'Christmas Time'	NHol
ciliosum ♀H4	CMea CPBP CWil NMen SChu SIng WLow
- from Ali Botusch	SDys
- from Ali Butús	GCrs
* - from Gallica	CLyd
- from Ochrid	NMen
§ - var. *borisii*	EMlt GCal GTou NDlv NMen SChr WHal
- var. *galicicum*	GCrs NMen
'Mali Hat'	

ciliosum × *ciliosum* var. *borisii*	CHal GEdr ITim NMen
ciliosum × *marmoreum*	CWil NMen
'Cindy'	CWil SRms
'Circlet'	CWil NMen
* *cistaceum*	WEas
'Clara Noyes'	WPer
'Clare'	CLyd EPem MHer MOne
'Clemanum' **new**	MOne
'Cleveland Morgan'	CWil EBre EPem LRHS MHom NBro NMen
'Climax'	EBee EPem ESis EWll MHom NMen SSto
'Cobweb Capers'	MHom MOne
'Cobweb Centre'	MOne NMen
'Collage'	CWil NHol
'Collecteur Anchisi'	CWil MOne NHol SDys
'Commander Hay' ♀H4	CHEx CLyd CMea CWil EPfP EWes GKev MHom NMen NPer SRms WEas WHal WLow WPer
'Comte de Congae'	MOne NMen
'Congo'	CWil MOne
'Conran'	NHol
'Corio' **new**	MOne
'Cornstone'	NHol
'Corona'	CWil ESis MOne NHol SRms WPer
'Corsair'	CWil ESis MBrN MOne NMen WGor WIvy WPer WTin
'Cranberry' **new**	MOne
'Cresta'	MOne
crested **new**	MOne
'Crimson Velvet'	CHEx CMea CWil EBee EDAr LBee MDHE MOne NHol WPer
§ 'Crispyn'	CBrm CLyd CWil EHyt EPot LBee MHom MOne NHol NMen WEas WPer
'Croky'	MOne
'Croton'	SIng WPer
'Cupream'	CWil MDHE NDlv SRms WPer
'Dakota'	CWil NHol NMen
'Dallas'	CLyd CWil MOne NHol NMen SRms
'Damask'	CWil LBee MDHE NMen WPer
'Dame Arsac'	MOne
'Dancer's Veil'	CWil
'Dark Beauty'	CLyd CMea CWil EHyt MOne NMen SIng WAbe WHal WHoo WLow WPer
'Dark Cloud'	CWil GAbr LBee WIvy WPer
'Dark Point'	CWil MHom MOne NMen
'Darkie'	CWil WPer
davisii	CWil
'De Kardijk'	CWil
'Deebra'	CWil
'Deep Fire'	CWil MOne NHol SRms WTin
× *degenianum*	GAbr WPer
'Delta'	NMen WHoo WTin
densum	see *S. tectorum*
'Diamant' **new**	MOne
'Diane'	CWil
* *dinaricum* **new**	EDAr
'Director Jacobs'	CWil EDAr GAbr MOne NHol NMen WEas WPer WTin WWin
'Doctor Roberts'	NHol
dolomiticum	NMen
dolomiticum × *montanum*	CWil MOne NBro NMen WTin
'Donarrose'	NHol
'Downland Queen'	CWil NHol
'Duke of Windsor'	MOne NMen
'Dusky'	CWil
'Dyke'	CTri CWil GAbr NHol NMen WHal
dzhavachischvilii	MOne NMen
'Edge of Night'	CWil NHol SRms

'Eefje'	CWil
'El Greco'	MOne
'El Toro'	MHom
'Elene' **new**	MOne
'Elgar'	CWil MOne WIvy WPer
'Elizabeth'	WPer
'Elvis'	CLyd CWil GAbr NMen
'Emerald Giant'	CWil MOne NHol SRms WPer WTin
'Emerson's Giant'	CWil MOne NMen
'Emma Jane'	MOne
'Emmchen'	CWil
'Engle's'	CLyd EBee EMlt LRHS MHer MOne NMen NPPs SChu SRms WHal WPer
'Engle's 13-2'	CWil MOne NBro NHol SChu
'Engle's Rubrum'	CPBP ESis GAbr GTou LBee NHol NMen
erythraeum	CLyd MHom NHol NMen SIng WAbe WHal
– from Pirin, Bulgaria	NMen
– from Rila, Bulgaria	NMen
– 'Red Velvet' **new**	MOne
'Excalibur'	CLyd CWil NMen WIvy
'Exhibita'	CWil SDys SRms
'Exorna'	CWil MHom MOne NMen WEas WPer
'Fair Lady'	CWil MHom MOne NMen
'Fame'	CWil MDHE MOne NHol
× *fauconnettii*	CWil NHol NMen SIng
– 'Thompsonii'	CWil MOne NHol NMen SIng
'Feldmaier'	MOne
'Festival'	NMen
'Feu de Printemps'	MOne
'Fiery Furness' **new**	MOne
'Fiesta'	WHal
fimbriatum	see *S.* × *barbulatum*
'Finerpointe'	MOne
'Fire Glint'	CWil MOne NHol SRms
'Firebird'	CWil NMen
'Firefly' **new**	MOne
'First Try'	MOne
'Flaming Heart'	CWil MBrN MOne NMen WPer
'Flamingo'	NMen
'Flamme' **new**	MOne
'Flander's Passion'	EMlt EPot LBee LRHS NMen SRms WPer
'Flasher'	CWil EMlt WEas WPer
'Fluweel'	MOne
'Fontanae'	MOne
'Forden'	CHEx MOne WGor
'Ford's Amability'	ESis SDys
'Ford's Shadows'	SDys
'Ford's Spring'	CLyd CWil MOne NHol NMen WIvy WPer WWin
'Freckles'	MOne
'Freeland'	WPer
'Frigidum'	NDlv
'Frolic'	SIng
'Frost and Flame'	NHol
'Frosty'	CWil MOne SRms
'Fuego'	CWil MHom MOne
× *funckii*	CWil EDAr IHMH MBrN NHol NMen SDys SIng WLin WPer WTin
'Furryness' **new**	MOne
'Fuzzy Wuzzy'	MOne
'Galahad'	CWil GAbr
'Gallivarda'	CWil
'Gambol'	NHol SIng
'Gamma'	CWil LBee LRHS NHol NMen SChu SDys SIng SRms WEas WTin
'Garnet'	WPer
'Gay Jester'	CTri CWil MOne WHoo WTin
'Gazelle'	WPer

	'Genevione'	CWil
	'Georgette'	CWil NMen SIng WPer
	'Ginger' **new**	MOne
	'Ginnie's Delight'	CWil NMen
	'Gipsy'	CWil
	giuseppii	CWil NHol NMen SIng WPer
	– from Peña Espigüete, Spain	CWil MOne NMen SDys
	– from Peña Prieta, Spain	CWil MOne NMen
	'Gizmo'	CWil
I	'Glaucum' **new**	MOne
	'Gleam'	MOne
	'Gloriosum'	GAbr WPer
	'Glowing Embers'	CWil ESis MHom MOne NMen WHal WPer
	'Goldie' **new**	MOne
	'Gollum'	EPem MOne
	'Granada'	GAbr GCrs NMen
	'Granat'	CLyd CWil EDAr IGor MHer MOne NMen SRms WCom WPer
	'Granby'	CWil LBee MOne NMen SDys
	grandiflorum	CWil NMen SIng WBrE WPer
	– 'Fasciatum'	CWil MOne NMen
	– from Valpine	MOne
	– 'Keston'	MOne
	grandiflorum x *ciliosum*	CWil MOne NMen
	grandiflorum x *montanum*	NMen
	'Grannie's Favourite' **new**	MOne
	'Grape Idol'	CWil
	'Grapetone'	MHom NMen SDys WHal
	'Graupurpur'	CWil
	'Gray Dawn'	CWil MHom
	'Green Apple'	CWil GAbr MHom NMen SDys
	'Green Disk'	CWil
	'Green Gables'	CWil WPer
	'Green Giant'	MTPN
	'Greenwich Time'	NMen
*	*greigii*	GEdr
	'Grenadier' **new**	MOne
	'Grey Ghost'	CWil NMen WIvy WPer
	'Grey Green'	CWil NHol
	'Grey Lady'	CMea CWil
	'Greyfriars'	CLyd CMea CWil EPot EWll LBee NMen WCom WGor WPer
	'Greyolla'	CLyd CWil WPer
	'Gruaud Larose'	NHol
	'Grünrand' **new**	MOne
	'Grünschnabel' **new**	MOne
	'Grünspan'	CWil
	'Grünspecht'	MOne
	'Gulle Dame'	CWil
	'Gypsy' **new**	MOne
	'Halemaumau'	CWil MOne
	'Hall's Hybrid'	CWil GAbr GEdr NBro SRms WCom
	'Happy'	CWil MOne NMen SRms WIvy WPer
	'Hart'	CWil EPem NHol NPPs SRms WTin
	'Hartside' **new**	MOne
	'Haullauer's Seedling' **new**	MOne
I	'Hausmanni' **new**	MOne
	'Havana'	CWil NMen
	'Hayling'	CWil LRHS MOne NHol NMen NPPs SRms WPer
	'Heavenly Joy'	NHol
	'Heigham Red'	CWil ESis GCrs LBee MCCP MOne NHol NMen WPer
I	'Heliotroop'	MOne SDys
	helveticum	see *S. montanum*
	'Hester'	CHEx CLyd CWil EPyc ESis GAbr MDHE NBro NMen SIng SRms WFar

	'Hey-Hey'	CLyd EMlt EPem EPot GCrs LBee LRHS MBrN NMen SIng SPlb SRms WAbe WLow WPer
	'Hidde'	CWil WPer
	'Hiddes Roosje'	MOne
	'Hirsutum'	see *Jovibarba allionii*
	hirtum	see *Jovibarba hirta*
	'Hispidulum' **new**	MOne
	'Hookeri'	see *S. x barbulatum* 'Hookeri'
	'Hopi'	CWil MOne NHol SRms
	'Hortulanus Smit'	NMen
	'Hot Shot'	CLyd
	'Hullabaloo'	EPem MOne
	'Hurricane'	MOne WPer
	'Icicle'	CMea CWil LRHS NBro NHol NLAp NMen SIng SRms WGor
	imbricatum	see *S. x barbulatum*
	'Imperial'	CLyd CWil MHom
	'Inge'	see *Jovibarba heuffelii* 'Inge'
	ingwersenii	MHom MOne SIng WLow
	'Interlace'	MOne
	'Iophon'	MOne
	'Irazu'	CWil GAbr MOne NMen SDys SRms WPer
	'Isaac Dyson'	SDys
*	*italicum* Ricci	NMen MHom
	'Itchen'	MOne NMen SIng
	'IWO'	CHEx NMen
	'Jack Frost'	CMea CWil EMlt MOne NBro NMen SChu
	'Jade' ambig. **new**	MOne
	'Jane'	MOne
	'Jelly Bean'	CWil ESis MOne NMen
	'Jet Stream'	CWil NMen SDys
	'Jewel Case'	CWil LRHS MOne NMen SIng SRms
	'John T.'	MOne WEas
	'Jolly Green Giant'	CWil MHom MOne
	'Jo's Spark'	CWil NSla
	'Jubilee'	CLyd CMea CWil EHyt ELan EMlt EPem EPot EPyc GAbr NHol NMen SRms WGor WLow WPer WWin
	'Jubilee Tricolor'	CSLe GFlt NHol NMen
	'Jungle Fires'	CWil EPot NHol SDys SRms
	'Jungle Shadows'	EDAr
	'Jupiter'	ESis
	'Jurato'	NHol
	'Justine's Choice'	CWil ESis SRms
	'Kalinda'	CLyd CWil MHom NMen
§	'Kappa'	CTri CWil MOne NBro NHol SDys SIng WPer
	'Katmai'	CWil NHol
	'Kelly Jo'	CLyd CWil EBee ESis EWll NBro NMen SIng WCot WTin
	'Kelut' **new**	MOne
	'Kermit'	MHom NMen
	'Kerneri'	NHol
	'Kibo'	MOne
	'Kimble'	WPer
	kindingeri	CLyd CWil EPem GTou MHer MHom NMen NWCA
	'King George'	CHal CLyd CTri CWil EPem ESis GAbr ITim LBee LRHS MOne NMen SChu SRms WBVN WGor WHal WHoo WPer WTin
	'Kip'	CMea NMen WIvy WPer
	'Kismet'	CWil NMen
	'Koko Flanel'	CWil
	'Kolagas Mayfair' **new**	MOne
	'Kolibri'	MDHE
	'Korspel Glory 4'	CWil
	'Korspelsegietje'	CWil
	kosaninii	CWil ESis LRHS MOne NHol NMen SIng WPer WTin

	– from Koprivnik	CLyd MOne NMen SDys WAbe
*	– from Visitor	CWil MOne
	– 'Hepworth'	NHol
	'Krakeling'	MOne
	'Kramers Purpur'	CWil NMen
	'Kramers Spinrad'	CHEx CLyd CMea CWil EMlt EPyc ESis GAbr LBee LEdu MOne NMen SChu SDys SIng WEas WHoo WTin
	'La Serenissima' **new**	MOne
	'Lady Kelly'	CLyd CMea MOne NMen WIvy
	'Launcelot'	WPer
	'Lavender and Old Lace'	CHEx CLyd CWil EMlt EPot GAbr GCrs LRHS MCCP NLAp NMen SChu WLow WPer
	'Laysan'	CWil NHol
	Le Clair's hybrid No. 4	NMen
	'Lennik's Glory'	see S. 'Crispyn'
	'Lentevur'	CWil
	'Lentezon'	CWil
	'Leocadia's Nephew'	CWil MOne NMen
	'Leon Smits'	CWil
	'Les Yielding' **new**	MOne
	'Lilac Time'	CLyd CWil EMlt GAbr GEdr LRHS MHer MOne NMen SChu SRms WHal WIvy WPer
I	'Linaria'	MTPN
	'Lipari'	CWil EWll SRms WLow
	'Lipstick'	CLyd NMen
	'Lively Bug'	CWil ESis ITim LBee SDys WPer
	'Lloyd Praeger'	see S. *montanum* subsp. *stiriacum* 'Lloyd Praeger'
	'Lonzo'	CWil SRms
	'Lustrous' **new**	MOne
	'Lynne's Choice'	CWil GAbr MOne SIng WHal WIvy
	macedonicum	CWil EDAr NDlv NMen WTin
	– from Ljuboten	MOne NMen
	'Madeleine'	CWil
	'Magic Spell'	CWil MOne NMen
	'Magical'	CWil
	'Magnificum'	CWil NMen
I	'Mahogany'	CHEx CLyd CTri CWil EWll LBee LRHS MOne NBlu NHol NMen SBla SChu SRms SWal WEas WGor WHal WLow
	'Maigret'	CWil WPer
	'Majestic'	CWil NMen
	'Malby's Hybrid'	see S. 'Reginald Malby'
	'Marella'	CWil WPer
	'Maria Laach'	CWil
	'Marijntje'	CWil NHol
	'Marjorie Newton'	CWil
§	*marmoreum*	CLyd CWil EMlt EPot LBee LRHS NMen SChu SRms STre WHal WPer
	– from Kanzas Gorge	EPot MOne NHol NMen
	– from Monte Tirone	CWil SDys
	– from Okol	CWil MOne NMen
	– 'Brunneifolium'	CLyd CWil EGoo EMlt GAbr LBee MOne NHol NMen SChu SIng WPer
	– subsp. *marmoreum* var. *dinaricum*	NMen
§	– 'Ornatum'	SRms
	'Matador'	MOne
	'Mate'	NMen
	'Maubi'	COkL CWil
	'Mauvine'	MOne NHol
	'Mayfair Imp' **new**	MOne
	'Medallion'	MOne
	'Meisse'	MOne
	'Melanie'	CWil MBrN NMen WIvy
	'Mercury'	CWil GAbr LRHS MDHE NBro NHol NMen SRms
	'Merkur'	MOne
	'Merlin'	CWil ESis
	'Midas'	CWil EMlt ESis
	'Mila' **new**	CLyd CWil
	'Minaret' **new**	MOne
	'Mini Frost'	CLyd CWil GAbr NMen SIng WPer
	'Minuet'	CWil
	'Missouri Rose'	NHol
	'Mixed Spice'	CMea CWil
	'Moerkerk's Merit'	CWil GAbr NHol NMen
	'Mondstein'	CWil MOne SRms
	'Montage'	CWil
§	*montanum*	CLyd CWil EBre GCrs LEdu LRHS NMen WPer
	– from Anchisis	MOne
	– from Arbizion	CWil MOne
	– from Windachtal	CWil NMen
	– subsp. *burnatii*	MHom SIng
	– subsp. *carpaticum*	CWil
	– – 'Cmiral's Yellow'	EMlt NMen WIvy
	– Fragell form	SChr
	– subsp. *montanum*	CWil
	– – var. *braunii*	NLAp WLow
	– 'Rubrum'	see S. 'Red Mountain'
§	– subsp. *stiriacum*	CWil MOne NMen SIng
§	– – 'Lloyd Praeger'	CWil LBee MOne NMen SDys
	'Monte Carlo'	CWil
	'More Honey'	CWil NMen SRms
	'Morning Glow'	WGor WHal
	'Mount Hood'	LRHS SRms WHal
	'Mrs Elliott'	MOne
	'Mulberry Wine'	CLyd CWil EBee LBee NHol
	'Myrrhine'	CWil
	'Mystic'	CLyd CWil EMlt MBrN NMen WPer
	nevadense	CWil EPot MOne NMen SRms
	– from Puerto de San Francisco	MOne
	– var. *hirtellum*	CWil NMen SIng
*	*nevadense* x *calopticum* **new**	WTin
	'Nico'	CWil SRms
	'Night Raven'	CLyd CMea WIvy
	'Nigrum'	see S. *tectorum* 'Nigrum'
	'Niobe'	MOne
	'Noir'	CWil EMFP EWll IHMH NBro NMen SChu
	'Norbert'	CWil SRms
	'Norne' **new**	MOne
	'Nortofts Beauty'	MOne
	'Nouveau Pastel'	CMea CWil MOne NMen NPPs WHal
	'Octet'	EPem MOne NMen SIng
	octopodes	CLyd MDHE NBir
	– var. *apetalum*	CWil EPem GAbr MOne NMen SIng SRms
	'Oddity'	CPBP CWil EDAr MHer NMen WBea WCot WPer
	'Ohio Burgundy'	CWil MDHE MOne NDlv NMen WAbe WPer WTin
	'Old Rose'	MOne
	'Olga'	CWil
	'Olivette'	MDHE NMen WPer WTin
	'Omega'	MOne WPer
	'Opitz'	CLyd WPer
	'Ornatum'	EPot MHer MOne NMen WAbe WEas WHal WIvy
	ossetiense	CWil GAbr MOne NMen SIng
	'Othello'	CHEx CHal CTri EBee EMFP GAbr NBir STre WCot WTin
	'Packardian'	CWil MOne NHol NMen
	'Painted Lady'	CWil
	'Palissander'	CWil GAbr MOne NMen
	'Pam Wain'	MHom NMen
	'Parade' **new**	MOne
	'Paricutin'	CWil SDys
	'Pastel'	CWil NMen SIng

patens	see *Jovibarba heuffelii*	
'Patrician'	CWil EMlt LBee LRHS SRms	
'Peach Blossom'	CWil	
'Pekinese'	CLyd CWil EMlt EPem EPot ESis	
	GEdr NBro NHol NMen SIng SRms	
	WCot WEas WPer WWin	
'Peterson's Ornatum'	MOne SDys	
'Petsy'	CWil SRms	
'Pilatus'	CWil SRms	
'Pink Astrid'	CWil ESis	
'Pink Cloud'	CWil SBla SRms	
'Pink Dawn'	CWil MOne	
'Pink Delight'	MOne	
'Pink Flamingoes'	MOne	
'Pink Lemonade'	MHom	
'Pink Mist'	WPer	
'Pink Puff'	CLyd CWil MHom MOne NMen	
	SRms	
'Pinkie'	CWil	
'Pippin'	CWil ESis SRms WPer	
'Piran'	CWil MOne	
pittonii	CHal CMea CWil EMlt GAbr GCrs	
	NMen WHal	
'Pixie'	CLyd CNic CWil GCrs MOne NDlv	
	NMen	
'Plum Mist'	NHol	
'Plumb Rose'	MOne NMen SChu	
'Pluto'	CWil NHol	
'Polaris'	CLyd CWil MHom	
'Poldark'	MOne	
'Pompeon'	MOne	
'Ponderosa'	CWil	
'Pottsii'	CWil GAbr MHer MOne	
'Powellii'	MOne	
'Prairie Sunset'	GCrs	
'Procton'	MOne	
'Proud Zelda'	GAbr MOne NMen	
'Pruhonice'	CWil MOne SRms	
'Pseudo-ornatum'	EMlt EPfP LBee LRHS SChu SRms	
'Pumaros'	NMen SDys	
pumilum	CWil MBar NMen	
– from Adyl Su No. 1	CWil	
– from Armchi	CWil SDys	
– from Armchi	MOne NMen	
x *ingwersenii*		
– from El'brus No. 1	CWil SIng	
– from Techensis	CWil NMen	
pumilum	GAbr	
x *arachnoideum*		
pumilum x *ingwersenii*	CWil WLow	
'Purdy'	MHom WAbe	
'Purdy's 50-6'	CWil	
'Purdy's 70-40' **new**	MOne	
'Purple Beauty'	CLyd CWil MOne	
'Purple King'	CMea CWil MHom SDys	
'Purpurriese'	CWil EDAr	
'Pygmalion'	GCrs SIng	
'Queen Amalia'	see *S. reginae-amaliae*	
'Quintessence'	CWil GCrs NHol SRms	
'Racy'	CWil	
'Radiant'	CWil	
'Ragtime'	MOne	
'Ramses'	MOne SDys	
'Raspberry Ice'	CLyd CMea CWil EMlt NBro NHol	
	NMen WPer	
'Rauer Kulm'	CWil	
'Rauheit' **new**	MOne	
'Red Ace'	CWil EWll GAbr NBro NMen SRms	
'Red Beam'	CWil MDHE MOne	
'Red Chips'	MHom	
'Red Cross' **new**	MOne	
'Red Delta'	CWil MOne NBir NMen	
'Red Devil'	CLyd CWil EHyt EMlt MOne NHol	
	NMen WTin	

'Red King'	MOne	
'Red Lion'	CWil	
'Red Lynn'	CWil	
§ 'Red Mountain'	CHEx CHal CWil EBee EMlt EWll	
	LBee LRHS MOne SRms	
'Red Pink' **new**	MOne	
'Red Robin'	EBee EMlt MOne	
'Red Rum'	WPer	
'Red Shadows'	CWil LBee WPer WTin	
'Red Spider'	MHom NBro NMen	
'Red Summer' **new**	MOne	
'Red Wings'	MOne NMen SRms	
'Regal'	MOne NMen	
'Reggy'	CWil	
'Regina'	NMen	
reginae	see *S. reginae-amaliae*	
§ *reginae-amaliae*	NHol	
– from Kambeecho No. 2	MDHE NMen SDys	
– from Mavri Petri	CLyd CWil MOne SDys SIng	
– from Sarpun	CWil NMen SDys WTin	
– from Vardusa	SDys	
§ 'Reginald Malby'	CTri EBre LRHS MDHE NMen	
	SRms	
'Reinhard'	CBrm CMea CWil EMlt EPot ESis	
	GAbr GEdr MBrN MCCP MDHE	
	MHer MOne NMen NPPs SIng	
	SRms WHal WPer	
'Remus'	CWil MOne NMen SDys SIng SRms	
	WGor	
'Rex'	NMen	
'Rhone'	CWil MOne	
* *richardii*	MBar	
'Risque'	CWil WPer	
'Rita Jane'	CLyd CWil MHom MOne NMen	
	WTin	
'Robin'	CLyd EBre EPot ITim LBee NBro	
	NHol NLar SRms WTin	
'Ronny'	CWil	
'Rose Splendour'	NHol	
x *roseum* **new**	MOne	
– 'Fimbriatum'	CWil GAbr LBee NDlv NHol WEas	
'Rosie'	CLyd CMea CPBP CWil EMlt EPot	
	ESis GAbr MCCP MOne NHol	
	NMen SIng SRms WHal WHoo	
	WPer WTin	
'Rotkopf'	CWil MOne NHol SChu SRms	
	WLow	
'Rotmantel'	SDys WTin	
'Rotsandsteinriese' **new**	MOne	
'Rotund'	CWil	
'Rouge'	CWil NMen	
'Royal Mail'	MOne	
'Royal Opera'	CWil MOne	
'Royal Ruby'	CWil EBre EMlt GAbr LBee LRHS	
	MBrN SChu SRms	
'Rubellum'	MOne	
'Rubikon Improved'	MOne	
'Rubin'	ECGP EGoo EPfP EPyc ESis GAbr	
	GEdr IHMH MCCP NBir NLAp	
	NMen SRms WAbe WEas WHoo	
	WPer WShp	
'Rubrum Ash'	CWil EHyt EPem GAbr MOne	
	NMen WAbe WTin	
'Rubrum Ornatum'	MHom	
'Rubrum Ray'	CWil ESis MOne SRms	
* 'Ruby Glow'	ESis	
'Russian River'	WHoo WTin	
'Rusty'	CWil WFar	
ruthenicum	LRHS MHom	
'Sabanum'	CLyd	
'Safara'	CWil	
'Saffron'	CWil MOne NMen	
'Saga'	EPem MHom MOne	
'Sanford's Hybrid'	MOne	

'Sarah'	MOne NMen	
'Sassy Frass'	CLyd NMen	
'Saturn'	CWil MOne NMen	
schlehanii	see *S. marmoreum*	
schnittspahnii **new**	MOne	
x *schottii* **new**	MOne	
'Seminole'	CWil MOne	
'Serena' **new**	MOne	
'Sharon's Pencil'	CWil	
'Sheila'	GAbr	
'Shirley Moore'	CWil MOne WTin	
'Shirley's Joy'	CHal GAbr NMen WTin	
'Sideshow'	CWil MOne	
'Sigma'	MOne	
'Silberkarneol' misapplied	see *S.* 'Silver Jubilee'	
'Silberspitz'	CWil ESis MHer MHom NBro	
	NMen WPer	
'Silver Cup'	CWil	
§ 'Silver Jubilee'	CMea CWil EDAr GAbr MDHE	
	NBro NDlv SPlb SRms WLow	
'Silver Queen'	CWil	
'Silver Thaw'	CWil EMlt NMen SIng WCot	
'Silverine'	CWil	
'Silvertone'	CWil	
Simonkaianum	see *Jovibarba hirta*	
'Sioux'	CLyd CPBP CWil ESis EWll GAbr	
	LBee MBrN NMen NPPs SIng WIvy	
	WPer WTin	
'Skrocki's Beauty'	see *S.* 'Shrocki's Bronze'	
§ 'Skrocki's Bronze'	CWil GAbr SChu WPer	
'Skrocki's Purple Rose'	CWil	
'Slabber's Seedling'	CWil	
'Smokey Jet'	CWil	
'Snowberger'	CLyd CMea CWil EBre EMlt EPem	
	EPot ESis LRHS MOne NMen SRms	
	WHal WPer	
'Soarte' **new**	MOne	
soboliferum	see *Jovibarba sobolifera*	
'Soothsayer'	CWil MOne NMen	
'Sopa'	CWil MOne NMen	
sosnowskyi	CWil MOne NMen	
'Soul'	CWil	
'Soul Sister'	CWil	
'Spanish Dancer'	CWil	
'Speciosum' **new**	MOne	
'Spherette'	CMea CWil NMen WPer	
'Spice'	MOne	
'Spider's Lair' **new**	SIng	
'Spinnelli'	MOne WTin	
'Spiver's Velvet'	MOne	
'Sponnier'	MOne	
'Spring Mist'	CMea CWil GFlt MOne NLar SRms	
	WGor WPer WTin	
'Sprite'	CWil ESis MOne NMen SDys WTin	
stansfieldii	see *S. arachnoideum* subsp.	
	tomentosum 'Stansfieldii'	
'Starburst'	CWil	
'Starion'	CWil MOne	
'Starshine'	MHer NHol NMen	
'State Fair'	CWil NHol SIng WPer	
* *stolonifera*	GAbr	
'Strawberry Fields'	CWil MOne	
'Strider'	WTin	
'Stuffed Olive'	CWil ESis MOne SDys	
I 'Subanum' **new**	MOne	
'Sun Waves'	CWil MOne NHol SDys	
'Sunrise'	MOne	
'Super Dome'	CWil	
'Superama'	CWil	
'Supernova'	MOne	
'Syston Flame'	CWil NMen	
'Tamberlane'	CWil	
'Tambimuttu'	CWil MOne	
'Tarita'	CWil	

'Tarn Hows'	MOne	
'Teck'	CWil	
§ *tectorum* ♀H4	CArn CHby CLyd COkL CPrp	
	CSam CWil EBee ELan EPfP GPoy	
	GTou LBee LRHS MBar MDHE	
	MHer NMen SIde SIng SPlb STre	
	WJek WWye	
– from Eporn	CWil MOne NMen	
– subsp. *alpinum*	CWil NMen SIng	
– 'Atropurpureum'	ELan NHol WCom WTin	
– 'Atrorubens'	NHol	
– 'Atroviolaceum'	CWil EDAr GCal NHol NLar WTin	
– var. *calcareum* **new**	MOne	
– subsp. *cantalicum*	SRms	
§ – var. *glaucum*	CWil NDlv WLow	
§ – 'Nigrum'	EHyt EMlt ESis LBee LRHS MHer	
	MOne NBro NHol NMen SDys	
	SRms WGor WTin	
– 'Red Flush'	CWil MBrN NMen SDys	
– 'Royanum'	ESis GAbr	
* – subsp. *sanguineum*	EDAr	
new		
– 'Sunset'	CWil GAbr NMen SDys WHal	
– subsp. *tectorum*	MOne	
§ – 'Atropurpureum'	CWil	
§ – – 'Boissieri'	CWil SRms WIvy	
– – 'Triste'	CWil EBee EMlt LBee LRHS MOne	
	SIng SRms WAbe	
– 'Violaceum'	CLyd MHom SIng SRms WAbe	
tectorum x *ciliosum*	WTin	
new		
– x *grandiflorum* **new**	MOne	
– x *zeleborii* **new**	WTin	
'Tederheid' **new**	MOne	
'Telfan'	MOne NMen	
'Tenburg' **new**	MOne	
'Terlamen'	CWil	
'Terracotta Baby'	CWil	
'Thayne'	NMen	
'The Rocket'	CWil	
thompsonianum	CWil ESis NDlv NHol NMen	
'Thunder'	CWil	
'Tiffany'	CBrm NHol WPer	
'Tiger Bay'	NHol	
'Tina'	WPer	
'Tip Top'	CWil	
'Titania'	CWil EPem NBro NMen WHal WTin	
'Tombago'	CWil MOne	
'Topaz'	CWil EBee EMlt LBee LRHS MOne	
	NMen SBla SChu SRms	
'Tordeur's Memory'	CWil LBee MOne NMen	
'Trail Walker'	CWil LBee MOne SRms	
transcaucasicum	CWil	
'Tree Beard'	CWil	
'Tristesse'	CLyd CWil MOne NMen WGor	
	WGwG	
'Truva'	MOne NMen	
'Twilight Blues'	CWil	
x *vaccarii*	NMen	
'Vanbaelen'	CWil GAbr NMen SDys	
'Vanessa'	CWil	
* *verschaffii*	EPem	
x *versicolor*	NHol	
'Veuchelen'	CWil MOne	
vicentei	CWil MHom NDlv NMen WTin	
– from Gaton	LBee MOne NMen	
§ – subsp. *paui*	NSla	
'Victorian'	MOne	
'Video'	CWil MHom NMen	
'Violet Queen'	CWil	
'Virgil'	CWil GAbr MBrN NMen SDys SIng	
	WCom WPer WTin	
'Virginus'	CLyd CWil	
'Vulcano'	CWil	

'Warners Pink'	MDKP
'Watermelon Rind'	MOne
webbianum	see *S. arachnoideum* subsp. *tomentosum*
'Webby Flame'	CWil
'Webby Ola'	NMen
'Weirdo'	CWil
'Wendy'	CLyd MOne NMen
'Westerlin'	CLyd CWil MOne NMen
'White Christmas'	see *S. arachnoideum* 'White Christmas'
'White Eyes'	SOkd SScr
'Whitening'	GAbr NMen
x **widderi**	SIng
'Wollcott's Variety'	CWil EBee EBre EPem ESis GAbr LRHS MDKP MOne NBir NMen WPer WTin
wulfenii	CWil NMen
* - **roseum new**	EDAr
'Zaza'	CWil
zeleborii	CHal SDys WHal
'Zenith'	CWil GAbr SRms
I 'Zenobia'	MHom
'Zenocrate'	CWil WHal
'Zepherin'	CWil
'Zilver Moon'	CWil
'Zircon'	NMen
'Zone'	CHEx NMen
'Zulu'	CWil

Senecio (*Asteraceae*)

§ **articulatus**	CHal EShb
aschenbornianus	GCal
aureus	see *Packera aurea*
bicolor subsp. **cineraria**	see *S. cineraria*
bidwillii	see *Brachyglottis bidwillii*
buchananii	see *Brachyglottis buchananii*
candicans	see *S. cineraria*
cannabifolius	GCal
canus NNS 99-459	SBla
chrysanthemoides	see *Euryops chrysanthemoides*
§ **cineraria**	XPep
- 'Ramparts'	WEas
- 'Silver Dust' ♀H3	CSLe EPfP LRHS
- 'White Diamond'	ECha LGro
compactus	see *Brachyglottis compacta*
confusus	ELan ERea ESlt SOWG
cyaneus new	SSpi
doria	LRHS WCot WFar
doronicum	WCot
glastifolius	ERea
'Goldplate' **new**	ITim
grandiflorus	CTbh
'Gregynog Gold'	see *Ligularia* 'Gregynog Gold'
greyi hort.	see *Brachyglottis* (Dunedin Group) 'Sunshine'
greyi Hook.	see *Brachyglottis greyi*
heritieri DC.	see *Pericallis lanata*
hoffmannii	EShb
integrifolius	NChi
subsp. **capitatus new**	
laxifolius hort.	see *Brachyglottis* (Dunedin Group) 'Sunshine'
'Leonard Cockayne'	see *Brachyglottis* 'Leonard Cockayne'
leucophyllus	SOkd
leucostachys	see *S. viravira*
macroglossus	CHll
- 'Variegatus' (v) ♀H1	CHal ERea EShb LAst SMur
macrospermus	WWhi
maritimus	see *S. cineraria*
mikanioides	see *Delairea odorata*
monroi	see *Brachyglottis monroi*
petasitis	CHEx

polyodon	CSpe CTCP EBla GBri MCCP MNrw SCro SSpi SUsu
- S&SH 29	CFir CPlt EBee
- subsp. **subglaber**	EMan EMon IFro
przewalskii	see *Ligularia przewalskii*
pulcher	CFil CSam ETow GBri LEdu MAvo MNrw MTho SMrm SUsu WCot WCru WPGP
reinholdii	see *Brachyglottis rotundifolia*
rowleyanus	EBak SMur
scandens	CMac ELan ERea MNrw MTho WCwm WHer WPGP
seminiveus	EBee
§ **serpens**	CHal CStu CTbh
§ **smithii**	CRow ELan EMan GFlt NBid NChi WBcn WCot WCru WFar
speciosus	NBir
spedenii	see *Brachyglottis spedenii*
squalidus	WHer
'Sunshine'	see *Brachyglottis* (Dunedin Group) 'Sunshine'
tamoides 'Variegatus' (v)	ERea
tanguticus	see *Sinacalia tangutica*
§ **viravira** ♀H3-4	CSLe EBee EGoo EHol ERea EShb LIck MRav MWgw SMad SMrm SPer WCom WCot WEas WSHC XPep

Senna (*Caesalpiniaceae*)

artemisioides ♀H1	CTrC SOWG XPep
§ **corymbosa**	CHEx CRHN ERea LRHS LRav SOWG SYvo XPep
didymobotrya	SOWG
x **floribunda**	XPep
hebecarpa	EMan
§ **marilandica**	EBee ELan ELau SIgm
§ **obtusifolia**	MSal
retusa	CHEx

Sequoia (*Cupressaceae*)

sempervirens ♀H4	CBcs CDoC CDul CLnd CMCN CTho CTrG ECrN EHul EPfP ERom GKir LCon LPan MAsh MLan SKee SLon WDin WEve WMou WNor
- 'Adpressa'	CDoC CDul CMac CSli CTho EBre EHul EOrn EPla GKir LCon LLin MAsh MBar MBri MGos NWea SLim WEve WFar
- 'Cantab' **new**	CDul
- 'Prostrata'	CDoC CDul CSli EBre EOrn LLin MBar MBri SLim

Sequoiadendron (*Cupressaceae*)

giganteum ♀H4	More than 30 suppliers
- 'Barabits Requiem'	MBlu MBri NLar SLim SMad
- 'Blue Iceberg'	CKen
- 'Cannibal'	MBlu
- 'Glaucum'	CDoC EMil LCon LPan MBlu MBri NLar SMad WEve
* - 'Glaucum Compactum'	MBri
- 'Greenpeace'	MBlu
- 'Hazel Smith'	MBlu
- 'Pendulum'	CDoC CKen EPfP ERod GTSp LCon LPan NLar SLim SMad SWvt WEve
- 'Peve Bonsai' **new**	NLar
- 'Pygmaeum'	MBlu NLar
- 'Variegatum' (v)	CDoC WBcn WEve

Serapias (*Orchidaceae*)

lingua	CDes CHdy EHyt LAma LEur SBla SCnR SSpi
- peach-flowered	WHil
parviflora	WHer

Serenoa (*Arecaceae*)

repens	CBrP CRoM LPal

Seriphidium (*Asteraceae*)

caerulescens	XPep
§ canum	EBee MHer
§ maritimum	CArn GGar ILis MHer NSti XPep
- subsp. **humifusum** **new**	WCot
§ nutans	CSLe EBee MWat MWgw
§ tridentatum	CArn EBee MGol
§ vallesiacum ♀H4	ECGP WEas XPep

Serissa (*Rubiaceae*)

foetida	see *S. japonica*
§ japonica	STre
- rosea	STre
- 'Sapporo' **new**	SSpi
- 'Variegata' (v)	CHal STre

Serratula (*Asteraceae*)

* minor	EBee
§ seoanei	CMea CTri EBee ECha EDAr EMan EMon LHop LPhx MHer MWat NJOw SAga SDix SIng SRms WCot WFar WPGP WPat WPrP WTin WWhi WWin
shawii	see *S. seoanei*
tinctoria	CArn CBgR ELau EMan GBar MSal NLar
- subsp. macrocephala	EBee EBre LRHS
wolffii	EBee

Sesamum (*Pedaliaceae*)

indicum	CArn

Sesbania (*Papilionaceae*)

punicea	SGar SOWG XPep

Seseli (*Apiaceae*)

elatum **new**	EBee
- subsp. **osseum**	CFil EBee LPio SIgm
globiferum	LPhx LPio SIgm
gummiferum	CArn CBot CFwr CSpe EBee EMan EMar LEdu LPhx LPio
hippomarathrum	SIgm WCot
libanotis	CSpe EBee LPhx LPio NDov NPPs SAga SIgm
pallasii	EBee SIgm
rigidum	EBee
varium	EBee LPio SIgm

Sesleria (*Poaceae*)

§ albicans	EPPr
§ argentea	GIBF
autumnalis	EMon EPPr LBBr LPhx
caerulea	CHrt CSam EBee EChP EHoe ELan EPza LAst LBuc LPVe LPhx MBar MBri MLLN MMoz MWgw MWhi SWal WWeb XPep
- subsp. calcarea	see *S. albicans*
- 'Malvern Mop'	CKno EBee WPGP
* candida	EPPr
cylindrica	see *S. argentea*
glauca	CRez EHoe NLar NOak NPro NSti SChu WPer
heufleriana	CElw CPlt EChP EHoe EMan EPPr EPla NLar SLPI SPlb WCot
insularis	CSWP EMon LRHS
'Morning Dew'	GCal
nitida	CBig CKno EBee EHoe EMan EMon EPPr LPhx LRHS MMoz WPGP

Setaria (*Poaceae*)

macrostachya ♀H3	CHrt CKno LPhx
palmifolia	CHEx CHll CKno CRoM EPPr WDyG WHal
viridis	CHrt NChi NSti WCot WTin

Setcreasea see *Tradescantia*

Severinia (*Rutaceae*)

buxifolia	SCit

shaddock see *Citrus maxima*

Shepherdia (*Elaeagnaceae*)

argentea	CAgr CBcs CPle GIBF NLar
rotundifolia	GIBF

Sherardia (*Rubiaceae*)

arvensis	MSal

Shibataea (*Poaceae*)

chinensis	EPla
kumasasa	CAbb CBcs CBig CDoC CHEx EHoe ENot EPfP EPla EPza ERod GCal GKir IBal LEdu LPal MBrN MCCP MGos MMoz MWhi MWht NMoo NVic SDry SLPI WJun WNor
- f. aureostriata	EPla SDry
lancifolia	EPla SDry WJun

Shortia (*Diapensiaceae*)

galacifolia	IBlr
- var. brevistyla	IBlr
x intertexta 'Ahlfeld' **new**	IBlr
- 'Leona'	IBlr
soldanelloides	IBlr SSpi
- f. alpina	IBlr
- var. ilicifolia	IBlr SSpi
- - 'Askival'	IBlr
- var. magna	IBlr
uniflora	IBlr WCru
* - var. kamtchatica	WCru
- var. kantoensis	IBlr
* - var. nana	WCru
- var. orbicularis	GCrs IBlr SSpi
'Grandiflora'	

Sibbaldia (*Rosaceae*)

procumbens	EBee GKir

Sibbaldiopsis (*Rosaceae*)

§ tridentata	CBgR EMar
- 'Lemon Mac'	SIng SMac
- 'Nuuk'	NBlu NHol SMac

Sibiraea (*Rosaceae*)

altaiensis	see *S. laevigata*
§ laevigata	CFil

Sibthorpia (*Scrophulariaceae*)

europaea	CHEx CPLG

Sida (*Malvaceae*)

acuta	MGol
hermaphrodita	EBee EMan WCot

Sidalcea (*Malvaceae*)

'Brilliant'	CDWL CM&M EBee EChP EMan EPfP LRHS MDKP NFla NPPs NSti SCro SPer WFar WLow WViv

candida	CSam EChP ECtt ELan EPPr EPfP EWTr GCal GGar IFro LAst LEdu LHop LRHS MBNS MRav MSte MWgw NCGa NGdn NSti SHel SPer SPla SUsu WCAu WCot WFar WLin WViv
- 'Bianca'	CBot EBee EHrv ERou LAst LPVe MFOX MSte NLar NPri WFar WHil WMoo WPer WWhi WWpP
- 'Shining Heart' **new**	CFwr
'Crimson King'	WFar
'Croftway Red'	CBcs CFir EBee ECGP ELan EMan EPfP GGar GKir LRHS MFir MRav SAga SChu SCro SHel SLon SPer SPet SWvt WCAu WMoo WSan
cusickii	EBee
'Elsie Heugh' ♀H4	More than 30 suppliers
hendersonii	EBee
hickmanii	EBee
subsp. **anomala**	
hirtipes	EBee
'Interlaken'	EBee NOrc
'Jimmy Whittet'	WBrE
'Little Princess' PBR	CFai CFir EBee EBre EMan GBri MBnl MBri NLar NPro WShp WWeb
'Loveliness'	CM&M EBee EChP ELan EMan LBBr MBnl MRav MWgw NBro NDov NGdn NLar SAga SVil WViv
malviflora	MFir NSti SChu SRms SYvo WWpP
- 'Alba'	WFar
'Mary Martin'	EMan
'Monarch'	MDKP WHil
'Moorland Rose Coronet'	WMoo
'Mr Lindbergh'	EBee EBre EMan EPfP ERou LRHS NHol SOkh WFar
'Mrs Borrodaile'	CM&M EBee ECtt EMan EMar GBuc LRHS MBNS MBnl MMil MRav MTis MWgw NBro NGdn NHol NPro SChu SHel WCAu WFar WMoo WWeb
'Mrs Galloway'	WFar
'Mrs T.Alderson'	EMan WFar WMoo
'My Love'	EBee EFou NDov
neomexicana	EBee EMan GCal MSPs NChi WBea WHil
'Oberon'	GBuc WEas WFar WMoo
oregana	NBid NGdn
-NNS 98-517 **new**	WCot
- 'Brilliant'	MBnl NPri WMoo WShp
- subsp. **spicata**	EPPr WMoo
- - NNS 98-518	WCot
'Party Girl'	More than 30 suppliers
'Präriebrand'	SAga
'Puck'	ECtt
'Purpetta'	EBee EChP MDKP MFOX NChi NLar STes WBea
reptans NNS 95-464	WCot
'Reverend Page Roberts'	MMHG MRav WCot WFar
'Rosaly'	CBrm EBee EChP LPVe MSPs MWrn NChi NLar NVic WGor
'Rosanna'	EChP LPVe LPhx MDKP NLar WBea WWeb WWpP
'Rose Queen'	EBee ECha ENot EPPr LHop LRHS MFOX MRav MTis SAga SChu SPer SRms WCAu WFar WMoo
'Rosy Gem'	CElw ECtt LRHS MBNS WFar WShp
Stark's hybrids	LRHS SRms WBea
'Sussex Beauty'	CMCo CSam EBee EMan EWTr MAvo MLLN MRav MSte NCiC NDov NGdn NPPs SChu WAul WCot WFar WMoo
'Sweet Joy'	SMrm
'The Duchess'	WFar
'William Smith' ♀H4	COtt CSam ECtt EGra EMar EPfP EWTr EWes LAst LRHS MBnl MCLN MLLN MRav MWrn NChi NCiC NGdn NOrc NPPs SOkh SPer SPla WCAu WFar
'Wine Red'	CPLG EBee ECGP ERou LHop MBnl MDKP SVil SWvt WHil

Sideritis (Lamiaceae)

cypria new	XPep
phlomoides new	EHyt
scordioides	XPep
syriaca	CArn EBee EMan EOHP EWll IFro SGar SHFr SIgm SSvw

Sieversia (Rosaceae)

pentapetala	see *Geum pentapetalum*

Silaum (Apiaceae)

silaus	WBWf

Silene (Caryophyllaceae)

acaulis	EDAr EMlt GTou LBee LRHS MTho NLar NMen SBla SRms WAbe
§ - subsp. **acaulis**	CGra SPlb SRms
- 'Alba'	CGra EPot EWes LRHS NLan SOkd WAbe
§ - subsp. **bryoides**	NWCA
- subsp. **elongata**	see *S. acaulis* subsp. *acaulis*
- subsp. **exscapa**	see *S. acaulis* subsp. *bryoides*
- 'Frances'	EPot GTou NMen NRya NSla NWCA WAbe
- 'Francis Copeland'	ECho NMen
- 'Helen's Double' (d)	EHyt
* - **minima**	CLyd EPot
- 'Mount Snowdon'	EDAr ELan EPfP EWes LBee LRHS NHol NLar NMen NRya NWCA SRms WPat
- 'Pedunculata'	see *S. acaulis* subsp. *acaulis*
alba	see *S. latifolia*
alpestris	CM&M EBee EPfP ESis MBar MHer MNrw MTho SRms SRot WBea WFar WMoo
- 'Flore Pleno' (d) ♀H4	CWCL EWes LBee LRHS NFor NSla WWin
* **andina** F&W 8174	NWCA
araratica new	WAbe
argaea new	CPBP EHyt
x **arkwrightii**	see *Lychnis* x *arkwrightii*
armeria	EBee
asclepiadea	GCrs
asterias	GBuc IFro IGor MBNS MHar MNrw NBid NBro NSti WDyG WPer WWin
- MESE 429	EBee
atropurpurea	CStu ECtt
- MESE 66	WAbe
bellidioides	EBee GGar WPGP
californica	NWCA
caroliniana	CBrm LPVe
subsp. **wherryi**	
chlorifolia new	NWCA
chungtienensis	EBee
§ **compacta**	NLar SMrm WCot
dinarica	WAbe
§ **dioica**	CArn CHrt CRWN EPfP MBow MHer NLan NLar NVic SWat WFar WHen WHer WMoo WRos WShi
- 'Clifford Moor' PBR (v)	EHoe LRHS NSti SCoo WCHb
- 'Compacta'	see *S. dioica* 'Minikin'
§ - 'Flore Pleno' (d)	CBgR EBee ECha GMac LLWP MNrw MRav MTho NBid NBro NGdn SMrm WEas WFar WHoo WPer WTin WWin

§ - 'Graham's Delight' (v) — ECoo EMon WCHb WHer WMoo
- 'Inane' — CBgR CNat EBlw MAvo MSph SHar WBea
- f. *lactea* — MHer
§ - 'Minikin' — CBgR CLyd EBre ECha EMon LRHS MAvo NBrk SPer WBea WCot WTin
- 'Pat Clissold' (v) — WCHb
- 'Pembrokeshire Pastel' (v) — MAvo
- 'Richmond' (d) — GBuc MInt
§ - 'Rosea Plena' (d) — CBre CM&M EBee EMan EMon MAnH MTho SChu SMrm WHer WPer
- 'Rubra Plena' — see *S. dioica* 'Flore Pleno'
- 'Thelma Kay' (d/v) — CBgR CFee CMil CSev EBee ECtt EMan EWes GBuc MDun NBid NLar WMoo WPGP
- 'Underdine' — EWes
- 'Variegata' — see *S. dioica* 'Graham's Delight'
elisabethae — SScr
§ *fimbriata* — CBot CBre CSpe CTCP EBee ECoo EHrv ELan EPyc EWTr GCal MMHG MRav MWat NGar NSti SBla SBri SChu SHel SMrm WAbb WCot WKif WRHF WSHC WTin WWye
- 'Marianne' — MNrw
firma RBS 0243 **new** — GKev
gallica — CTCP NLar
var. *quinquevulnera*
hookeri — MTho WBVN WCom
- Ingramii Group — CGra CPBP
inflata — see *S. vulgaris*
keiskei — CNic ECha WBVN
- var. *minor* — EWes LRHS MTho WAbe WWin
latifolia — CArn MBow MGas NMir NSco WHen WHer
- subsp. *alba* — CTCP GWCH
maritima — see *S. uniflora*
maroccana **new** — CRWN
morrisonmontana — WCru
B&SWJ 3149
multifida — see *S. fimbriata*
nutans — CArn MNrw SRms SSth WHer
* - var. *salmoniana* — WBWf
- var. *smithiana* — WBWf
orientalis — see *S. compacta*
parishii var. *latifolia* **new** — CPBP
petersonii — NWCA
pusilla — CHal NLar
regia — CDes EBee LRav MNrw SSpi WPGP
rubra — see *S. dioica*
saxifraga **new** — XPep
schafta ♀H4 — CHal EBre ECha ECtt EDAr EMlt EPfP GKir LRHS MBro MWat NBid NBlu NJOw NWCA SIng SPet SRms WFar WHoo WPer WWin
- 'Abbotswood' — see *Lychnis* x *walkeri* 'Abbotswood Rose'
- 'Robusta' — LRHS
§ - 'Shell Pink' — EWes LBee LRHS NBid NWCA WAbe WCom
sieboldii — see *Lychnis coronata* var. *sieboldii*
'Snowflake' — COkL
suksdorfii — CLyd CTCP EPot
tenuis — GBuc
- ACE 2429 — GBuc
thessalonica — MCCP WPat
undulata — GGar
§ *uniflora* — EBre ECtt EGoo EMar EMlt EPfP GGar IHMH MFir MWat NBid NBlu NBro NJOw NWoo SPlb SRms SWal WBar WFar WHen WHer WMoo

- 'Alba Plena' — see *S. uniflora* 'Robin Whitebreast'
I - 'Compacta' — CHid EMar ESis LPVe NDlv WBea WMoo
§ - 'Druett's Variegated' (v) — More than 50 suppliers
- 'Flore Pleno' — see *S. uniflora* 'Robin Whitebreast'
- pink-flowered **new** — LBee
§ - 'Robin Whitebreast' (d) — CHar CNic CSLe EBee ECha ECtt GCal GKir LPVe MBar MHer MTho MWat MWgw NBid NBro NOak SRms SRot WMoo WPer WShp WWin
- 'Rosea' — ECtt EMar GGar IHMH LRHS MRav NFor NJOw SMrm SPlb SRot SUsu WPer
- 'Silver Lining' (v) — GBuc
- 'Swan Lake' (d) — IHMH WCot
- 'Variegata' — see *S. uniflora* 'Druett's Variegated'
- Weisskehlchen — see *S. uniflora* 'Robin Whitebreast'
- 'White Bells' — CTri EBee ECtt EPfP SPet WBea WHoo WKif WSHC
vallesia — WPer
virginica — CDes EBee
§ *vulgaris* — CRWN MGas MHer NLan NMir NSco SECG
- subsp. *maritima* — see *S. uniflora*
waldsteinii — SScr
wallichiana — see *S. vulgaris*
'Wisley Pink' — CHal ECtt
yunnanensis — LPhx
§ *zawadskii* — GBuc MDKP MNrw SWal WPer WTin

Silphium (Asteraceae)

gracile — EBee
integrifolium — EBee SAga WCot
laciniatum — CArn EBee EMan LPhx SMad SMrm WCot
perfoliatum ♀H4 — CArn EBee GPoy LPhx NLar NSti SMad SMrm WCot WFar
terebinthinaceum — EBee LPhx SMad

Silybum (Asteraceae)

marianum — CArn CSpe CTCP EBee ECoo EFer ELan EMan EPAt EPar EPfP GPoy MSal MWgw NArg NGHP SECG SIde WFar WHer WWye
- 'Adriana' — ECoo EWll MSph NArg WBry

Simmondsia (Simmondsiaceae)

chinensis — MSal

Sinacalia (Asteraceae)

§ *tangutica* — CRow CSam EBee ECha EMan EPPr GGar MBNS MFOX NBid NBro NSti SDix SMrm WAbb WCru WDyG WFar

Sinarundinaria (Poaceae)

anceps — see *Yushania anceps*
jaunsarensis — see *Yushania anceps*
maling — see *Yushania maling*
murielae — see *Fargesia murielae*
nitida — see *Fargesia nitida*

Sinningia (Gesneriaceae)

'Blue Wonder' — MBri
* *caerulea* — WDib
§ *canescens* ♀H1 — CHal ERea
§ *cardinalis* — CHal EBak WDib
- 'Innocent' **new** — WDib
§ x *cardosa* — MBri
'Diego Rose' — MBri
'Duchess of York' — CSut
'Duke of York' — CSut

leucotricha	see *S. canescens*
§ *douglasii*	CSpe
nivalis	WDib
speciosa 'Etoile de Feu'	LAma MBri
- 'Hollywood'	LAma
- 'Kaiser Friedrich'	LAma MBri
- 'Kaiser Wilhelm'	LAma MBri
- 'Mont Blanc'	LAma MBri
- 'Violacea'	MBri
verticillata	see *S. douglasii*

Sinobambusa (*Poaceae*)

§ *intermedia*	EPla WJun
* *orthotropa*	CFil EPla WPGP
rubroligula	CFil EPla NMoo WPGP
tootsik	EPla SDry WJun
- var. *albovariegata* (v)	SDry
- 'Variegata'	see *S. tootsik* var. *albovariegata*

Sinocalycanthus (*Calycanthaceae*)

chinensis	CBcs CMCN CPMA CPle EPfP IDee
	IMGH NPal SMad SSpi WBVN
	WBod WFar WPGP

Sinofranchetia (*Lardizabalaceae*)

chinensis	CPLG GCal WCru

Sinojackia (*Styracaceae*)

xylocarpa	EPfP NLar SSpi WFar

Sinowilsonia (*Hamamelidaceae*)

henryi	CBcs

Siphocampylus (*Campanulaceae*)

foliosus CDPR 3240 **new**	WPGP

Sisymbrium (*Brassicaceae*)

§ *luteum*	SHar WHer

Sisyrinchium ✿ (*Iridaceae*)

from Andes Mts	EWes
from Tierra del Fuego	CRow
x *anceps*	see *S. angustifolium*
§ *angustifolium*	CMHG CNic EBur ECha GFlt GKir
	LPBA MBNS MBar MSal MWat NBir
	NChi NLAp SPlb SRms WPer
- *album*	GKir NChi NLar
§ *arenarium*	CPBP EBur EPot GEdr NMen
	NRya
atlanticum	ESis NBro SUsu WPer
bellum hort.	see *S. idahoense* var. *bellum*
bermudianum	see *S. angustifolium*
- 'Album'	see *S. graminoides* 'Album'
'Biscutella'	CHad CKno CLyd CPrp CTri EBur
	ECtt EDAr EWTr ITer ITim NMen
	NRya SChu SIng SPla SPlb SSth
	SWal SWvt WFar WGwG WHal
	WKif WMoo WTin
* 'Blue Ice'	CBrm CMea CPBP CWCL EBur
	EDAr MAvo MBro NHol SMrm
	WAbe WFar WHal WHoo WMoo
	WPat WPer
boreale	see *S. californicum*
brachypus	see *S. californicum* Brachypus Group
'Californian Skies'	More than 30 suppliers
§ *californicum*	CBen CBrm EBur EHon EMFW
	EPfP EShb ESis GAbr LPBA MBar
	MSta MWat NBid NBlu NBro SSth
	SWal WBVN WFar WMAq WPer
	WWin WWpP WWye WPGP
§ - Brachypus Group	CBro CHar ECtt EDAr EMlt EPot
	GGar GTou IHMH LPVe MBNS
	MNrw MOne MWgw NBir NJOw

	NLAp NLar NPri NVic SGar SPet
	SPlb SWat SWvt WBrE WLow
	WMoo WWpP
* *capsicum*	CPLG
§ *chilense*	ERos
coeleste	EBur
coeruleum	see *Gelasine coerulea*
commutatum	CHar EDAr ERos GBuc MNrw
	MWgw SGar SRot WBro
convolutum	EChP EMan LRHS MSph NDov
	NPPs WCot
cuspidatum	see *S. arenarium*
'Deep Seas'	NLar SUsu
demissum	CLyd CNic EBur
depauperatum	CLyd EBur MNrw WHer WMoo
	WPer
'Devon Blue'	WFar
'Devon Skies'	CHid CMCo CMHG CRez EBur
	MDKP SIng SWvt WAbe WFar
	WWin
douglasii	see *Olsynium douglasii*
'Dragon's Eye'	CElw EBur MBrN SIng SMHy SRot
	SSth SSvw SUsu WKif
'E.K. Balls'	More than 30 suppliers
elmeri	EBur
'Emmeline' **new**	EBur
filifolium	see *Olsynium filifolium*
fuscatum **new**	NRog
graminoides	EBur NBro SYvo WPer
§ - 'Album'	EBur GFlt GGar LRHS NBro
	WPer
grandiflorum	see *Olsynium douglasii*
'Hemswell Sky'	CLyd EBur EHoe LAst MDHE NRya
'Iceberg'	EBur SMHy SSth SUsu WKif
idahoense	ECha EDAr EMlt ESis GAbr GEdr
	GGar LRHS MHer NJOw NRya
	SPlb SRms
§ - 'Album' ♀H4	More than 30 suppliers
§ - var. *bellum*	CBro CMHG EBre EBur ELan EMlt
	EPfP GFlt GTou IHMH LRHS MBNS
	MNrw MWhi NMen NPri NWCA
	SIng SPet SRms SSto WCom WHen
	WMAq WPat WPer WSSM WWpP
	XPep
- - 'Pale Form'	SMHy
- - 'Rocky Point'	CElw CLyd CMCo CSpe EBee EBre
	EBur MBro NLAp SRot WCom
	WHoo WPat WWeb
- blue	EGra
iridifolium	see *S. micranthum*
junceum	see *Olsynium junceum*
littorale	CPLG EBur NLar WPer
macrocarpon ♀H2-3	CFee CGra CLyd CPBP EBur ERos
	ESis GTou LBee LRHS MAvo MDKP
	NJOw NMen SBla SBri SChr SIng
	SWal WLin WPer
'Marie'	EBur
'Marion'	CMea MAvo MSph NLar SBla SMHy
	SRot SSth SSvw SUsu WWye
'May Snow'	see *S. idahoense* 'Album'
'Miami' **new**	EBur
§ *micranthum*	CBro EBur
montanum	ERos IHMH
'Mrs Spivey'	EBur ECtt MBar MHer NBir NOak
	WBro WRHF
'North Star'	see *S.* 'Pole Star'
nudicaule x *montanum*	CFee CMHG EBur ITim MDHE
	MNrw NRya SRot WPer
palmifolium	CDes CFil GFlt MAnH MCCP
	MDKP SSpi
- JCA 2.880.010	WPGP
patagonicum	CPLG EBur EDAr ERos GBuc GFlt
	WPer
- F&W 9312	WCot

§	'Pole Star'	CFee CLyd CNic CSpe EBur EChP EMlt GTou IBlr LRHS WFar WHal WMoo WPer
	'Quaint and Queer'	CHea CM&M CMil CPLG CWCL EBur EChP ECha ECtt EGra EMar ERou MBrN MRav MTho MWgw NBir NBro NChi NJOw SHBN SWvt WBea WMnd WMoo WPer WWhi WWin WWpP WWye
I	'Raspberry'	CMea EBur WAbe
	scabrum	see *S. chilense*
	'Sisland Blue'	EBur EWes
	'Stars and Stripes'	LPBA
§	***striatum***	More than 30 suppliers
§	- 'Aunt May' (v)	More than 30 suppliers
	- 'Variegatum'	see *S. striatum* 'Aunt May'

Sium (Apiaceae)

	sisarum	ELau EOHP GBar GPoy MHer MSal

Skimmia ✿ (*Rutaceae*)

	anquetilia	MBar WBcn WBod
	arisanensis B&SWJ 7114	WCru
	x ***confusa***	EHol
	- 'Isabella'	SPer
	- 'Kew Green' (m) ♀H4	More than 30 suppliers
§	***japonica***	CMHG CTrw CWib EMil GKir GQui MGos SReu SSta WDin WFar WGwG WHCG WStI
	- (f)	CTrG CTri ELan ENot EPfP SPer SRms
	- B&SWJ 5053	WCru
	- 'Alba'	see *S. japonica* 'Wakehurst White'
	- 'Bowles' Dwarf Female' (f)	CMHG EBee EPla LRHS MBar MBri MGos NHol SLim SLon
	- 'Bowles' Dwarf Male' (m)	CMHG EBee EPla LRHS MBar MBri MHar SLim WBod
	- 'Bronze Knight' (m)	EBee ENot GBin LRHS MBar MRav NHol SLim
	- 'Chameleon'	LAst MRav
	- 'Claries Repens'	CDoC EPla LRHS SPer
	- 'Emerald King' (m)	LRHS MAsh MBar MBri MWgw WBcn WFar
N	- 'Foremanii'	see *S. japonica* 'Veitchii'
§	- 'Fragrans' (m) ♀H4	CDoC CSBt CSam CTri CTrw EBee ECrN ENot EPfP GKir LRHS MBar MBlu MGos MRav NCGa SHBN SLim SPer WBod WFar WGwG
	- 'Fragrant Cloud'	see *S. japonica* 'Fragrans'
	- 'Fragrantissima' (m)	LRHS MBri WBod
	- 'Fructu Albo'	see *S. japonica* 'Wakehurst White'
	- 'Highgrove Redbud' (f)	EBee LRHS MBar MGos SLim WBcn WBod
	- var. ***intermedia*** f. ***repens*** B&SWJ 5560	WCru
	- 'Keessen' (f)	WFar
	- 'Kew White' (f)	CAbP CBcs CDoC EBee EBre ECrN EPfP GKir IArd MBri MGos MLan MWat NHol SLon SSta WCFE WHCG
	- Luwian = 'Wanto'PBR	EBee LRHS NHol NPro WFar
	- 'Marlot'	EPfP MGos
	- 'Nymans' (f) ♀H4	CDoC CEnd CSam EBee EBre ELan EPfP GKir LRHS MAsh MBar MBri MRav MWht NDlv NHol SHBN SLim SMer SPer SPla SReu SSpi SSta WFar WStI
	- 'Oblata'	SMer
	- 'Obovata' (f)	EPla
	- 'Pigmy'	CPLG
	- 'Red Princess' (f)	LAst MAsh MBri WBcn
*	- 'Red Riding Hood'	NHol SLon
	- 'Redruth' (f)	CBcs CDoC CSBt CSam EBee GKir LAst LRHS MAsh MBar MGos

		MWat MWht NHol SLim SSta WBcn WWeb
§	- subsp. ***reevesiana***	More than 30 suppliers
	- - B&SWJ 3763	WCru
	- - ETOT 182	WPGP
	- - 'Chilan Choice'	EBee GKir LRHS MAsh SLim SPla SSta
	- - 'Fata Morgana' (m)	MGos
	- - var. ***reevesiana*** B&SWJ 3544	WCru
	- - 'Robert Fortune'	MBar
§	- Rogersii Group	CTri MBar MWat
	- - 'Dunwood'	MBar
	- - 'George Gardner'	MBar
	- - 'Helen Goodall' (f)	MBar
§	- - 'Nana Mascula' (m)	CTri
	- - 'Rockyfield Green'	MBar
	- - 'Snow Dwarf' (m)	LRHS MBar MBri
	- 'Rubella' (m) ♀H4	More than 30 suppliers
	- 'Rubinetta' (m)	CChe EBee EPfP GKir IArd MAsh MBar MGos NHol SLim WFar
	- 'Ruby Dome' (m)	LRHS MBar WBcn
	- 'Ruby King' (m)	CDoC CSBt ECrN GKir IArd LRHS MAsh MBar MWgw NHol
	- 'Scarlet Dwarf' (f)	EBee MBar
	- 'Scarlet Queen' (f)	CWib
	- 'Stoneham Red'	MBri
	- 'Tansley Gem' (f)	EPfP GKir LRHS MAsh MBar MBri MWht SSta WFar
	- 'Thelma King'	GKir LRHS
§	- 'Veitchii' (f)	CBcs CSBt CTri EBee ECrN ENot EPfP GKir IArd IMGH MAsh MBar MDun MGos MRav MSwo NHol SEND SHBN SLim SMer SPer SWvt WBod WDin WStI WTel
§	- 'Wakehurst White' (f)	CMHG CPle CSBt CTrw EPfP GKir MBar MRav SHBN SLim SLon SReu SSpi SSta WBod WCru WFar
	- 'White Gerpa'	MGos
	- 'Winifred Crook' (f)	EPla GKir MBar MBri
	- 'Winnie's Dwarf'	MGos
	- 'Wisley Female' (f)	CDoC CTri ECtt EPla NHol SAga
	laureola	CDoC CSam EBee ECot MRav NHol SRms WFar WSHC
	- 'Borde Hill' (f)	NPri
	- subsp. ***multinervia*** Sch 2154	WPGP
	'Olympic Flame'	EPfP GKir LRHS MGos NHol NPro SLim WFar
	reevesiana	see *S. japonica* subsp. *reevesiana*
	rogersii	see *S. japonica* Rogersii Group

Smallanthus (Asteraceae)

	uvedalius	MSal

Smilacina (Convallariaceae)

	atropurpurea	CBct EBee WCru
	dahurica	EBee
	formosana	CBct WHil
	- B&SWJ 349	WCru
	forrestii	EBee LEur WCru
	fusca	WCru
	henryi	EBee LEur WCru
	japonica	CBct EBee LEur WCru
	- B&SWJ 1179	WCru
	aff. ***japonica***	LEur
	oleracea	EBee GEdr WCru
	- B&SWJ 2148	WCru
	paniculata (Baker) F.T.Wang & T.Tang	EBee
	purpurea	EBee LEur
§	***racemosa*** ♀H4	More than 30 suppliers
	- var. ***amplexicaulis***	GCal MTed
	- - 'Emily Moody'	SSpi

salvinii B&SWJ 9000 **new**   WCru

stellata   CAvo CBct CHEx CRow EBee
EPPr EPar EPla EPot GBBs LEur
LHop MDun MLLN MRav NChi
NFla NGar SMac WAul WCru
WTin

stenolobum **new**   LEur

szechuanica   LEur WCru

tatsiensis   LEur

trifolia   EBee LEur

tubifera   EBee

Smilax (Smilacaceae)

B&SWJ 6628 from Thailand **new**   WCru

asparagoides 'Nanus'   see *Asparagus asparagoides*
'Myrtifolius'

aspera   CFil LEdu SMur WCru WPGP

- 'Silver Shield'   SSpi

china B&SWJ 4427   WCru

discotis   CBcs SEND

glaucophylla
B&SWJ 2971   WCru

nipponica B&SWJ 4331   WCru

rotundifolia   LEdu

sagittifolia   NArg

sieboldii   MRav

- B&SWJ 744   WCru

Smithiantha (Gesneriaceae)

'Little One'   WDib

Smyrnium (Apiaceae)

olusatrum   CArn CHrt CSev CSpe GBar IHMH
MGas MHer MSal SIde SWat WHbs
WHer WLHH WWye

perfoliatum   CPom CSpe EHrv ELan EMar EOrc
EPar EWes GBuc MFir NSti SDix
WCot WEas WSHC

- subsp. *rotundifolium*   EBee
MESE 337

Solandra (Solanaceae)

grandiflora misapplied   see *S. maxima*

grandiflora Swartz   ERea WMul

hartwegii   see *S. maxima*

longiflora   ERea

§ *maxima*   ERea SVen

Solanum (Solanaceae)

aviculare G.Forst.   XPep

bonariense **new**   XPep

crispum   EHol ISea MSwo WDin WStI

- 'Autumnale'   see *S. crispum* 'Glasnevin'

§ - 'Glasnevin' ♀H3   More than 30 suppliers

- 'Variegatum' (v)   WGwG

dulcamara   CArn GPoy MGol

- 'Hullavington' (v)   CNat

- 'Variegatum' (v)   CBcs CMac EBee ECrN EHoe EPfP
IBlr LRHS MAsh MBNS MBri NSti
SBra SPet WBVN WFar WSHC
WWeb

hispidum **new**   CHEx

horridum **new**   CHEx

jasminoides   see *S. laxum*

laciniatum   CArn CBrm CDoC CFwr CHEx
CPLG CSev CSpe CTCP EMan
EWes IBlr LHop MFir MLLN MTis
SAPC SArc SGar SHFr SNew

§ *laxum*   CBcs CDul EBee ECrN EPfP EShb
LRHS MSwo NSti SBra SCoo SPer
SPet SPoG SRms SWvt WDin WFar
WGwG WSHC XPep

- 'Album' ♀H3   More than 30 suppliers

- 'Album Variegatum' (v)   CWib ELan EPfP GQui LAst LRHS
MBNS NSti SBra WCot WRHF
WSHC

* - 'Aureovariegatum' (v)   CSBt CTrC EBee EPfP LRHS MGos
NBlu SCoo SLim SPer SPla SPlb
WBod WRHF WWeb

linearifolium   CHea SOkh WCot WPat WSPU

muricatum (F)   ESlt

- 'Lima' (F)   ECrN

- 'Quito' (F)   ECrN SSte

pseudocapsicum   MBri

- RCB/Arg R-4   WCot

- 'Ballon'   MBri

- variegated   EShb

quitoense (F)   MGol SSte WMul

§ *rantonnetii*   CHll ELan EMan ERea EShb IDee
MOak SOWG XPep

- 'Royal Robe'   CBcs CRHN GQui

* - 'Variegatum' (v)   ERea ESlt MOak WHil

salicifolium **new**   EShb

seaforthianum   SOWG

valdiviense   WDin

'Variegatum' (v)

wendlandii   ERea EShb

Soldanella (Primulaceae)

alpina   EBee GCrs GTou ITim MTho MWat
NMen SBla SIng SRms WAbe
WBVN WLin

I - 'Alba' **new**   WAbe

austriaca   WAbe

carpatica   EDAr EHyt ETow GTou LTwo NRya
SIng WAbe

- 'Alba'   EDAr GKev ITim MDKP NLAp
NSla SBla WAbe WOBN

carpatica x *pusilla*   CPBP NRya SBla

carpatica x *villosa*   MDKP

cyanaster   EBee EHyt NGar NRya NSla SBla
WAbe

dimoniei   CFee ITim NMen NSla NWCA SBla
WAbe

§ *hungarica*   CLyd MTho WAbe WLin

minima   CLyd EHyt GCrs GGar NBro NDlv
NGar NMen NRya NSla NWCA
SBla WAbe WLin WOBN

montana   CLAP CLyd CMea GCrs GFlt GTou
LTwo MTho NGar NJOw NLar
NMen SIng WAbe WRha

- subsp. *hungarica*   see *S. hungarica*

pindicola   EBee EHyt EMan EWes MBro
MOne NDlv NGar NJOw NMen
NWCA SIng WAbe WFar

pusilla   GFlt GGar ITim NSla WAbe

villosa   CDes CLAP EBee EBre GCrs GGar
LRHS MTho NGar NJOw NRya
NSla SAga SBla WAbe WFar WOBN
WSHC

Soleirolia (Urticaceae)

soleirolii   CHEx CHal CTri EPAt EPot LPBA
LRHS MBri MCCP MWhi SHFr SIng
STre WHer XPep

- 'Argentea'   see *S. soleirolii* 'Variegata'

§ - 'Aurea'   CHal CTri EPot SIng

- 'Golden Queen'   see *S. soleirolii* 'Aurea'

- 'Silver Queen'   see *S. soleirolii* 'Variegata'

§ - 'Variegata' (v)   CHal LPBA

Solenomelus (Iridaceae)

chilensis   see *S. pedunculatus*

§ *pedunculatus*   CFee CFil

- F&W 9606   CPBP WPGP

sisyrinchium   CPBP ERos

Solenopsis (*Campanulaceae*)

axillaris   see *Isotoma axillaris*

Solenostemon ✿ (*Lamiaceae*)

'Anne Boleyn'	CHal MOak
'Autumn'	CHal MOak
'Barnum'	MOak
'Beauty' (v)	CHal MOak
'Beauty of Lyons'	CHal MOak
'Beckwith's Gem'	CHal
'Bizarre Croton'	CHal MOak
'Black Dragon'	CHal
'Black Prince'	CHal MOak WDib
'Blackheart'	MOak
'Brilliant' (v)	MOak WDib
'Bronze Gloriosus'	MOak
'Buttercup'	CHal WDib
'Buttermilk' (v) ♀H1	CHal MOak
'Carnival' (v)	CHal MOak WDib
'Carousel'	CHal MOak
'Chamaeleon' (v)	CHal MOak WDib
'City of Liverpool'	CHal
'Combat'	CHal
'Copper Sprite'	CHal MOak
'Crimson Ruffles' (v) ♀H1	CHal MOak WDib
'Crimson Velvet'	CHal MOak
'Crinkly Bottom'	MOak
'Crown of Bohemia'	MOak
'Dairy Maid' (v)	CHal MOak
'Dazzler' (v)	CHal MOak
'Display'	CHal MOak
'Dolly' (v)	MOak
'Dracula'	CHal MOak
'Emerald Forest'	MOak
'Etna' (v)	CHal
'Fire Fingers'	LAst MOak
'Firebrand' (v) ♀H1	CHal MOak
'Firedance'	MOak
'Firefly'	CHal MOak
'Freckles' (v)	CHal MOak
'Funfair' (v)	CHal MOak
'Gloriosus'	CHal MOak
'Glory of Luxembourg' (v) ♀H1	CHal MOak
'Goldie'	CHal MOak
'Harvest Time'	MOak
'Holly' (v)	MOak
'Inky Fingers' (v)	CHal MOak
'Jean' (v)	CHal MOak
'Joseph's Coat' (v)	MOak
'Juliet Quartermain'	CHal MOak WDib
'Jupiter'	CHal MOak
'Kentish Fire'	CHal MOak
'Kiwi Fern' (v)	CHal MOak WDib
'Klondike'	CHal MOak
'Laing's Croton' (v)	CHal MOak
'Lemon Dash'	MOak
'Lemondrop'	CHal
'Leopard' (v)	MOak
'Lord Falmouth' ♀H1	CHal MOak WDib
'Melody'	CHal MOak
'Midas'	CHal MOak
'Midnight'	MOak
'Mission Gem' (v)	CHal LAst MOak WWol
'Molten Lava' (v)	MOak
'Mrs Pilkington' (v)	MOak
'Muriel Pedley' (v)	CHal MOak
'Nettie' (v)	MOak
'Ottoman'	CHal
'Paisley Shawl' (v) ♀H1	CHal WDib
'Palisandra'	CHrt CSpe
pentheri	CHal
'Percy Roots'	MOak

'Peter's Wonder'	CHal
'Phantom'	MOak
'Picturatus' (v) ♀H1	CHal WDib
'Pineapple Beauty' (v) ♀H1	CHal MOak SSte WDib
'Pineapplette' ♀H1	CHal MOak WDib WWol
'Pink Devil' (v)	MOak
'Pink Shawl'	MOak
'Poyton'	MOak
'Primrose Cloud'	MOak
'Primrose Spire'	MOak
'Purple Oak'	CHal LAst
'Raspberry Ripple'	CHal
'Red Croton'	CHal
'Red Mars'	MOak WDib
'Red Nettie' (v)	CHal MOak
'Red Paisley Shawl' (v)	MOak
'Red Rosie'	CHal
'Red Stinger'	CHal WWol
'Red Velvet'	CHal CHrt MOak WWol
'Rob Roy'	MOak
'Rose Blush' (v)	CHal LAst MOak WDib WWol
'Rosie'	MOak
'Roy Pedley'	CHal MOak
'Royal Scot' (v) ♀H1	CHal MOak WDib
'Salmon Plumes' (v)	CHal MOak
'Sam Cooke'	MOak
'Scarlet Ribbons'	CHal MOak
'Speckles'	CHal MOak
'Spire'	MOak
'Strawberry Jam'	CHal MOak
'Sunbeam' (v)	MOak
thyrsoideus	see *Plectranthus thyrsoideus*
'Tom Cooke'	MOak
'Treales' (v)	CHal MOak
'Vesuvius'	CHal MOak
'Walter Turner' (v) ♀H1	CHal MOak WDib WWol
'White Gem' (v)	MOak
'White Pheasant' (v)	MOak
'Winsome' (v)	CHal MOak WDib
'Winter Sun' (v)	CHal CHrt MOak
'Wisley Tapestry' (v) ♀H1	CHal MOak WDib
'Yellow Croton'	MOak

Solidago (*Asteraceae*)

Babygold	see *S.* 'Goldkind'
brachystachys	see *S. cutleri*
caesia	EBee ECha EMan EMon ERou EWes MFir MSte NBir WCot WMoo WOld WWpP
canadensis	CTri ELan NNor SPlb WFar WHer WSSM
§ - var. **scabra**	WOld WTin
'Cloth of Gold'	CBcs COtt EBee EBre GKir LRHS NPro NSti SMer SWvt WMnd WOld
§ 'Crown of Rays'	CLyd CPrp EBee EBre ECtt EFou ERou LRHS MRav MWgw NArg SHar SMer WFar WMnd WShp WWin
§ **cutleri**	CLyd EBee ELan ESis MBar MTho MWat NHol NJOw NLar SBla SPlb SRms WFar WPat WPer WWin
- **nana**	EWes
'Dzintra'	EBee
'Early Bird'	EFou
'Featherbush' **new**	EBre LRHS
§ **flexicaulis** 'Variegata' (v)	EBee EBre EChP ECoo ELan EMan EMar EMon EPfP GBin LRHS MHar NLar NSti WCAu WCot WFar WHer WHil WOld WPer
'Gardone' ♀H4	WFar
gigantea	EBee EMon WPer
glomerata	EMon NLar WPer
Golden Baby	see *S.* 'Goldkind'

'Golden Crown'	WViv
§ 'Golden Dwarf'	EFou LRHS WWeb
'Golden Falls'	EBre
'Golden Fleece'	see *S. sphacelata* 'Golden Fleece'
Golden Gate	WViv
= 'Dansolgold'PBR	
'Golden Rays'	see *S.* 'Goldstrahl'
'Golden Shower'	CSam MWat
'Golden Thumb'	see *S.* 'Queenie'
'Golden Wings'	CBre ERou MWat
'Goldenmosa' ♀H4	CRez CSBt CSam EBee EBre ECGN
	EMan ENot EPfP ERou EWTr LRHS
	MRav MWat SChu SPer WCot WFar
	WOld WShp
'Goldilocks'	LRHS NPri SMrm
§ 'Goldkind'	CHrt CM&M COIW CSBt EBee
	ECtt EPfP EPza ERou GKir IHMH
	MBow NArg NBPC NOrc SMer
	SPet SWal SWvt WBea WFar WMoo
	WRHF WSSM WShp WTin WWeb
	WWpP
§ 'Goldstrahl'	LRHS
Goldzwerg	see *S.* 'Golden Dwarf'
graminifolia	SAga
'Harvest Gold' **new**	ERou
hispida	EMon
hybrida	see x *Solidaster luteus*
'Laurin'	EBee EMil EPfP LRHS NLar WHoo
	WShp WTin
'Ledsham'	EBee EMFP WMnd
'Lemore'	see x *Solidaster luteus* 'Lemore'
'Leraft'	EBee
* *leuvalis*	CStr
'Linner Gold'	EFou
Monte d'Oro	WViv
= 'Dansolmonte'PBR	
Monte Solo	WViv
= 'Dansolsolo'PBR	
multiradiata	ESis
odora	MGol MSal
ohioensis	EBee
* 'Peter Pan'	ERou WFar
§ 'Queenie'	EBre ECha MHer NPro NVic SLon
	SPer SRms
rigida	LRHS MRav WCot WPer
– JLS 88002WI	EMon
– subsp. *humilis*	EBee
rugosa	ECha LPhx MTed MWgw WCot
– var. *aspera*	EMon
– 'Fireworks'	CBre CHVG CSam CStr EBee EChP
	EFou EMan EPPr LRHS MHar
	NBPC NDov NPPs SUsu WCot
	WHoo WOld WTin
sempervirens	EMon WCot
simplex var. *nana*	WPer
spathulata var. *nana*	NWCA
speciosa	WPer
§ *sphacelata* 'Golden	EBee LRHS WHoo WMnd
Fleece'	
Strahlenkrone	see *S.* 'Crown of Rays'
'Summer Sunshine' **new**	ERou
Sweety	MBri
= 'Barseven'PBR **new**	
'Tom Thumb'	MRav SRms WEas
uliginosa **new**	EShb
ulmifolia	EBee LRHS
virgaurea	CArn CBod EBee GPoy GWCH
	MHer NLar NSco WHer WJek WPer
	WSel WWye
– subsp. *alpestris*	CLyd NHol
var. *minutissima*	
– 'Paleface' **new**	EMon
– 'Praecox'	CM&M NHol
§ – 'Variegata' (v)	EHoe NPro

vulgaris 'Variegata'	see *S. virgaurea* 'Variegata'

x *Solidaster* (Asteraceae)

hybridus	see x *S. luteus*
§ *luteus*	CSBt CTri EBee EFou EWTr GBri
	GKir MBri MHar NGar SRms WEas
	WFar WWin
§ – 'Lemore' ♀H4	CElw CHea CPrp EBee EBre ECGN
	EFou ELan EMan ENot EPfP ERou
	EWsh GLil GMac LRHS MMil MRav
	MWat NPri NSti NVic SPer WCot
	WFar WLin
'Super'	CStr EBee EFou WCot WFar

Sollya (Pittosporaceae)

fusiformis	see *S. heterophylla*
§ *heterophylla* ♀H1	More than 30 suppliers
– 'Alba'	ELan LAst MAsh SMrm
– mauve	ECou WGwG
– pink	CBcs CFRD CSPN EOrc SAdn
	WGwG
– 'Pink Charmer'	EBee ELan EPfP ERea LRHS SBra
	SMrm SMur WSHC
parviflora	ITer

Sonchus (Asteraceae)

palustris	EMon

Sophora (Papilionaceae)

§ *davidii*	CWCL CWib ECou EPfP IDee
	MBlu MGos NPal SIgm SOWG
	WDin WPGP WSHC
flavescens	WCru
japonica ♀H4	CAbP CBcs CLnd CTho EBee EMil
	ENot EPfP EWTr LRHS MDun
	MGos MWhi SBLw SHBN SKee
	SMHT SPer SPlb WBVN WBod
	WDin WNor WOrn
– 'Pendula'	CDul LRHS SBLw SCoo
– 'Regent'	LPan
§ 'Little Baby'	CBcs CWib EPfP ERea LAst MCCP
	MGos SHFr SMur WPGP WPat
macrocarpa	CFil GQui SBra
microphylla	CHEx CPle CWCL EBee ECou EPfP
	LHop SAPC SArc SEND SIgm SVen
	WBVN WBod WCru WHer WPGP
– 'Dragon's Gold'	EBre ECou ELan EPfP ERea LRHS
	WDin
– 'Early Gold'	CBcs ERea GQui
– var. *fulvida*	ECou
– var. *longicarinata*	ECou
– Sun King	EMil LRHS MBlu MGos SCoo
= 'Hilsop'PBR ♀H4	
mollis	CPle
prostrata misapplied	see *S.* 'Little Baby'
prostrata Buch.	CBcs CBot ECou
– Pukaki form	ECou
secundiflora	MGol SIgm
tetraptera ♀H3	CAbP CBcs CDul CLnd CMac
	CPne EBee ECou EPfP GQui ISea
	MLan SEND SGar SPer SRms WPGP
viciifolia	see *S. davidii*

Sorbaria (Rosaceae)

SF 95205	ISea
aitchisonii	see *S. tomentosa* var. *angustifolia*
arborea	see *S. kirilowii*
aff. *assurgens*	WCru
BWJ 8185 **new**	
§ *kirilowii*	GEil GIBF IFro SLon
lindleyana	see *S. tomentosa*
rhoifolia	EPfP
sorbifolia	CAbP CBcs CMCo EBee ECrN EMil
	EWTr GEil GKir LRHS MBar MDun

	MTis MWhi NPro SEND SLPl SPer WCot WDin WFar
- var. **stellipila**	CFil GEil SLPl
- - B&SWJ 776	WCru
§ **tomentosa**	CAbP SHBN WHCG
§ - var. **angustifolia** ♀H4	CDul CTri EBee ELan ENot EPfP EWTr GKir IMGH LRHS MDun MGos MRav NPro SEND SLon SPer SSta WCru WEas WFar WHer
* - 'Anthony Waterer'	NPSI

Sorbus ✿ (Rosaceae)

CLD 310	GIBF
Harry Smith 12732	GKir LRHS MDun
§ **alnifolia**	CLnd CMCN CTho EPfP GFlt GIBF MBlu SLPl
americana	CLnd GIBF NWea
'Belmonte'	GKir LRHS SBLw
- **erecta**	see S. decora
aff. **amurensis**	WCru
B&SWJ 8665 **new**	WCru
anglica	CDul CNat
'Apricot'	CEnd GKir
'Apricot Lady'	GKir LRHS MAsh SSta
'Apricot Queen'	CLnd ECrN EMil GKir MAsh SBLw
aria	CCVT CDul CLnd CSBt ECrN EPfP GKir LBuc MBar NBee NWea SKee WDin WMou WOrn WStI
- 'Aurea'	CLnd MBlu WFar
- 'Chrysophylla'	CDul CSBt EBee ECrN GKir IMGH LRHS MBri MGos NWea SKee SLim SPer SPoG
- 'Decaisneana'	see S. aria 'Majestica'
- 'Gigantea'	CDul
- 'Lutescens' ♀H4	More than 30 suppliers
- 'Magnifica'	CDoC CDul CTho EBee ECrN ELan ENot EWTr LPan SBLw WDin
- 'Majestica' ♀H4	CDoC CDul CTho ECrN GIBF GKir LPan LRHS NWea SBLw SPer SPoG WDin WOrn
- 'Mitchellii'	see S. thibetica 'John Mitchell'
- 'Orange Parade' **new**	SBLw
- var. **salicifolia**	see S. rupicola
x **arnoldiana** 'Cerise Queen'	GKir
- 'Golden Wonder' **new**	SBLw
- 'Maidenblush' **new**	SBLw
- 'Schouten'	SBLw
aronioides misapplied	see S. caloneura
arranensis	CDul CNat GIBF
§ **aucuparia**	More than 30 suppliers
- 'Aspleniifolia'	CBcs CCVT CDul CLnd CMCN CSBt CTho EBee ECrN ENot GKir LPan LRHS MAsh MBri MDun MGos NWea SBLw SKee SLim SPer WDin WFar WOrn
I - 'Aurea' **new**	SBLw
§ - 'Beissneri'	CDul CLnd EBee EMil GKir MAsh MBri MGos NRog SKee
- Cardinal Royal = 'Michred'	CDoC EBee ECrN GQui LRHS
- 'Crème Lace'	EBee GKir
- 'Dirkenii'	CDul CLnd COtt CWSG EBee GKir IMGH LRHS MAsh MBri MDun SKee SLim WDin
- var. **edulis** (F)	CDul CLnd CTho LBuc MGos NPSI SBLw WDin
- - 'Rabina' (F)	ESim
- - 'Rosina' (F)	ESim
- - 'Rossica Major' (F)	CDoC CDul CTho ECrN GQui SBLw
§ - 'Fastigiata'	CDoC CDul CEnd CSBt CTri EBee ECrN EPfP GKir LRHS MAsh MGos

	MWat NBee NWea SBLw SHBN WDin WFar WStI
- 'Hilling's Spire'	CTho GKir LRHS MAsh MBri MLan SLPl
- 'Pendula'	EBee SBLw
- **pluripinnata**	see S. scalaris
- var. **rossica** Koehne	see S. aucuparia var. edulis
- 'Rossica Major'	see S. aucuparia var. edulis 'Rossica Major'
- 'Rowancroft Coral Pink'	see Sorbus 'Rowancroft Coral Pink'
- 'Sheerwater Seedling' ♀H4	CBcs CCVT CDoC CDul CLnd CMCN CTho EBee ECrN ELan ENot EPfP EWTr GKir LRHS MLan MRav MSwo NBee NBlu NPSI SCoo SLim SPer SSta WDin WFar WOrn WStI
- 'Weettra' **new**	SBLw
- 'Winterdown'	CNat
- var. **xanthocarpa** ♀H4	CLnd EBee ENot EPfP MGos NBee SBLw WDin
'Autumn Spires' **new**	LRHS
'Bellona'	WPat
'Burka'	WPat
§ **caloneura**	CBcs CFil EPla WHCr
'Carpet of Gold'	CLnd
cashmiriana Hedl. ♀H4	More than 30 suppliers
- 'Rosiness'	GKir LRHS MAsh MBri MDun SCoo SKee SLim
cashmiriana hort. pink-fruited	CLnd GKir LRHS SSpi
chamaemespilus	GIBF WPat
'Chamois Glow'	MAsh
'Chinese Lace'	CDul CEnd CLnd CMCN CTho EBee ECot ECrN EPfP GKir LRHS MAsh MBri MDun MGos MLan MSwo MWat NBea SHBN SKee SLim SMad SPer SSpi WDin WGor WOrn
§ **commixta**	CBcs CDul CEnd CLnd CMCN CTho EBee ECrN EPfP EPla GIBF GKir LRHS MBar MBri MGos MLan MRav MSwo NBea NBee SBLw SKee SLim SPer WDin WOrn WStI
- 'Embley' ♀H4	CBcs CCVT CLnd CMCN CSBt CSam CTho CTri EBee ECrN ELan ENot EPfP GKir LRHS MBar MGos MLan MRav SLim SSpi SSta WDin WOrn
- 'Jermyns'	GKir MAsh
- var. **rufoferruginea**	GKir GQui
- - B&SWJ 6078	WCru
conradinae misapplied	see S. pohuashanensis (Hance) Hedlund
conradinae Koehne	see S. esserteauana
'Copper Kettle'	GKir MBri
'Coral Beauty'	CLnd
'Covert Gold'	CEnd CLnd
croceocarpa	CDul CNat
cuspidata	see S. vestita
§ **decora** (Sarg.) C.K. Schneid.	CTho GIBF NBlu SBLw
* - 'Grootendorst'	CDul
- var. **nana**	see S. aucuparia 'Fastigiata'
devoniensis	CAgr CDul CNat CTho WMou
discolor misapplied	see S. commixta
discolor (Maxim.) Maxim.	CLnd CMCN EBee GKir MAsh MBlu MGos MSwo MWat NWea
domestica	CDul CLnd CMCN CTho ENot EPfP NWea SLPl SPer WDin
- 'Maliformis'	see S. domestica f. pomifera
§ - f. **pomifera**	EHol GIBF
dumosa	GIBF

'Eastern Promise'	CWSG ECrN EMil GKir LRHS MAsh MBlu MBri MGos MWat NLar SCoo SKee SLim SSta WDin
eminens	CDul CNat
§ *esserteauana*	CDoC CDul CLnd CTho EBee ENot
- 'Flava'	CTho GKir LRHS
'Fastigiata'	see *S. aucuparia* 'Fastigiata', *S. x thuringiaca* 'Fastigiata'
folgneri	CDoC CEnd
- 'Emiel'	MBlu
- 'Lemon Drop'	CDul CEnd CLnd GKir LRHS MAsh MBlu NLar SCoo SKee SMad SSpi
§ *foliolosa*	CDul EPfP GIBF MBlu NWea
- 'Lowndes'	CLnd
forrestii	EPfP GIBF GKir NBea NLar SLPl SSpi
* *fortunei*	CLnd
I *fruticosa* McAllister	CEnd CLnd EBee EPfP GIBF GKir MBri NWea SSpi SSta WPGP
- 'Koehneana'	see *S. koehneana*
'Ghose'	CEnd CLnd CTho GKir IMGH LRHS MBlu SCoo SKee SPer SSpi
'Golden Wonder'	see *S.* 'Lombarts Golden Wonder'
N *gonggashanica*	CLnd EGFP GKir
* *gorrodini*	CLnd
§ *graeca*	CDul CMCN GIBF SEND
harrowiana **new**	CDul
'Harvest Moon'	GKir GQui LRHS
hedlundii	GTSp IBlr WWes
helenae	GGGa GQui
hemsleyi	CLnd GIBF GKir MBri MDun
x *hostii*	CLnd EBee ENot LRHS MRav SPer
§ *hupehensis* C.K. Schneid. ♀H4	CBcs CDul CEnd CLnd CMCN CTho CTri EBee ECrN EPfP GIBF ISea LRHS MBar MRav NBee NWea SBLw SHBN SLPl SPer SSpi SSta WCru WCwm WDin WFar WNor WOrn
- SF 96268	ISea
- 'November Pink'	see *S. hupehensis* 'Pink Pagoda'
§ - var. *obtusa* ♀H4	CDoC CDul CLnd CMCN EPfP GIBF GKir MBlu MDun SFam SSpi SSta WDin
§ - 'Pink Pagoda'	CDoC CLnd CWSG CWib EBee EMui EPfP GKir IArd IMGH LRHS MAsh MGos MLan MSwo MWat NWea SCoo SKee SLim SLon SPer WDin
- 'Rosea'	see *S. hupehensis* var. *obtusa*
* - *roseoalba*	GKir
hybrida misapplied	see *S. x thuringiaca*
hybrida L.	ECrN NWea
- 'Gibbsii' ♀H4	CDoC CLnd ELan EPfP GKir LRHS MAsh MBri
insignis	CDoC GIBF
intermedia	CBcs CDul CLnd CSBt CTho CTri CWib EBee ECrN ENot GIBF GKir LRHS MGos NBee NBlu NPSI NWea SBLw WDin WMou WStI
- 'Brouwers'	ELan SBLw WMoo
'Joseph Rock'	More than 30 suppliers
§ x *kewensis*	CDul CLnd GKir NLar SPer SPlb WBrE
'Kirsten Pink'	CLnd CWib EBee ECrN GKir WFar
§ *koehneana* C.K. Schneid. ♀H4	CLnd CMCN ECrN EGra GBin GCrs GGGa GKir GQui LRHS MAsh MBri MDun NBlu NSla SHFr WPat WTin
aff. *koehneana*	GKir WCwm
- Harry Smith 12799	EPfP GKir MBri
'Kukula'	MDun
kurzii	GIBF
lanata hort.	see *S. vestita*
lancastriensis	CDul CNat CTho GIBF
latifolia	CLnd EBee ECrN ENot GIBF NWea SBLw WDin
'Leonard Messel'	CTho GKir LRHS MBri NBea
'Leonard Springer'	EBee ECrN ENot EPfP GQui SSta
leyana	WMou
§ 'Lombarts Golden Wonder'	CBcs CDoC CDul CLnd EBee GKir LPan MAsh NWea
matsumurana misapplied	see *S. commixta*
matsumurana (Makino) Koehne	GKir
megalocarpa	CBcs CDoC CFil CPMA GKir SSpi WCwm WNor WPGP
minima	CDul WMou
'Molly Sanderson'	IBlr SSta
monbeigii (Card.) Yü	CLnd GIBF
moravica 'Laciniata'	see *S. aucuparia* 'Beissneri'
mougeotii	GIBF GKir
multijuga	GIBF
§ *munda*	CMCN GBin GKir
'Peachi-Ness'	CLnd
'Pearly King'	CBcs CSam CTho EBee GKir LRHS MAsh NBea
§ 'Pink Pearl'	CDul GKir LRHS MDun
'Pink Veil' **new**	NBlu
'Pink-Ness'	GKir LRHS MBri SKee SLim
pogonopetala Koehne	GIBF
pohuashanensis hort.	see *S. x kewensis*
§ *pohuashanensis* (Hance) Hedlund	CTho GKir
porrigentiformis	CDul CNat CTho
poteriifolia	GCrs
prattii misapplied.	see *S. munda*
prattii Koehne **new**	CLnd
- var. *subarachnoidea*	see *S. munda*
pseudofennica	GIBF
N *pseudovilmorinii*	EMon GKir
- MF 93044	SSpi
randaiensis	GIBF
- B&SWJ 3202	SSpi WCru
'Ravensbill'	CTho GKir MBlu MBri
'Red Robin' **new**	NBlu
'Red Tip'	CDoC CDul CLnd MBar
reducta ♀H4	CBcs CEnd CMCN CSWP EPfP GBin GIBF GKir ISea ITim LRHS MBlu MBro NBlu NHol NWea SIng SPer SSpi SSta WDin WFar WNor
reflexipetala misapplied	see *S. commixta*
rehderiana misapplied	see *S. aucuparia*
rehderiana Koehne	CLnd GIBF GKir WNor
'Rose Queen' **new**	MBri
'Rowancroft Coral Pink'	CTho MBar MGos
§ *rupicola*	CDul CTho GIBF
'Salmon Queen'	CLnd
sambucifolia	GIBF
sargentiana ♀H4	More than 30 suppliers
§ *scalaris* Koehne	CBcs CDul CEnd CTho CTri EBee EPfP GKir IMGH LRHS MBri SKee SPer SPoG SSpi WDin WOrn
'Schouten'	ECrN ENot LRHS
scopulina hort.	see *S. aucuparia* 'Fastigiata'
setschwanensis	GGGa
sibirica	GIBF
'Signalman'	GKir LRHS
'Sunshine'	CDoC GKir LRHS MAsh MBri NBlu WDin
aff. *thibetica*	WCru
BWJ 7757a **new**	
§ - 'John Mitchell' ♀H4	CDul CLnd CMCN CTho ECrN ENot EPfP GKir GQui LPan LRHS MAsh MBlu MBri MGos MRav NBea NWea SBir SLim SPer WOrn WPat

§ x *thuringiaca* — CSBt NBea WMou
§ - 'Fastigiata' — CBcs CDoC CDul CLnd EBee ENot GKir MGos NBee SBLw SKee WDin
  torminalis — CCVT CLnd CTho CTri EBee ECrN EPfP GKir LBuc LRHS MBri MRav NWea SBLw SPer WDin WFar WMou WOrn
  umbellata — CMCN
  - var. *cretica* — see *S. graeca*
  ursina — see *S. foliolosa*
  x *vagensis* — CLnd GIBF WMou
  verrucosa var. *subulata* — WCru
    HWJ 579 **new**
§ *vestita* — CLnd CMCN CTho
  vexans — CDul CNat GIBF
  vilmorinii ♀H4 — More than 30 suppliers
  - 'Robusta' — see *S.* 'Pink Pearl'
  wardii — CBcs CLnd CTho GKir LRHS MBlu
  'White Swan' **new** — NBlu
  'White Wax' — CDul CWSG EMui EPfP MAsh MDun MGos MLan SBLw SPer WDin
  'Wilfrid Fox' — CLnd SHBN SLPl
  willmottiana — CDul
  wilsoniana — CLnd
  'Wisley Gold' **new** — LRHS

Sorghastrum (Poaceae)
  avenaceum — see *S. nutans*
§ *nutans* — CBig CKno CRWN ECGN ECha EMan SMad WMoo
  - 'Indian Steel' — CBig CBrm CFwr CPen EBee EChP EMan EPPr EPza LAst LIck LPVe MAnH MSte MWrn SMad

Sorghum (Poaceae)
  halepense — MSte

sorrel, common see *Rumex acetosa*

sorrel, French see *Rumex scutatus*

Souliea see *Actaea*

soursop see *Annona muricata*

Sparaxis (Iridaceae)
  bulbifera — EGrW
  elegans — EGrW EPot
  - 'Coccinea' — WCot
  grandiflora — EGrW WCot
    subsp. *grandiflora*
  hybrids — EGrW LAma
  parviflora **new** — WCot
  tricolor — EMui EPar MDun NRog

Sparganium (Sparganiaceae)
§ *erectum* — CRow ECoo EHon EMFW EMan EPAt LNCo LPBA MSta NArg NPer SWat WFar WHer WMAq WWpP
  ramosum — see *S. erectum*

Sparrmannia (Tiliaceae)
  africana ♀H1 — CAbb CBcs CHEx CHll CKob CPle EAmu ERea EShb GQui MBri SAPC SArc SDnm SMur SYvo
  - 'Variegata' (v) — ERea
  palmata — see *S. ricinocarpa*
§ *ricinocarpa* — CKob

Spartina (Poaceae)
  patens — EHoe EPPr

  pectinata — CBod CHEx EChP GBin GKir WFar
  - 'Aureomarginata' (v) — More than 30 suppliers

Spartium (Papilionaceae)
  junceum ♀H4 — CArn CBcs CDoC CDul CPLG CSBt CWCL CWib ECrN ELan EMil ENot EPfP LRHS MBri MGos MWat SArc SDix SHBN SLon SPer SRms WDin WStl WTel XPep
  - 'Brockhill Compact' — LRHS

Spartocytisus see *Cytisus*

Spathantheum (Araceae)
  orbignyanum — EBee WCot

Spathipappus see *Tanacetum*

Spathiphyllum (Araceae)
  'Viscount' — MBri
  wallisii — CHal EOHP LRHS MBri

spearmint see *Mentha spicata*

Speirantha (Convallariaceae)
§ *convallarioides* — CDes CFil CLAP CPom EBee ERos SOkd SSpi WCot WCru WPGP
  gardenii — see *S. convallarioides*

Spergularia (Caryophyllaceae)
  rupicola — CBrm CNic

Sphacele see *Lepechinia*

Sphaeralcea (Malvaceae)
  ambigua — EBee ELan XPep
  'Childerley' — EMan LHop SAga
  coccinea — EMan SPlb
  fendleri — CBcs CBot CHll CMHG CSam EOrc WWye
  - subsp. *venusta* — EBee XPep
  'Hopleys Lavender' — EBee EChP EMan LHop MAvo SAga SVil
  'Hyde Hall' — EBee EChP EPPr MAvo MCCP MMil SMrm WBor
  incana — EBee NPPs SMrm SPet
  malviflora — WPer
  miniata — CBot CHll ELan MLLN MOak SAga WCom
  munroana — CBot CBrm CMHG CSLe CSev CWCL EBee ELan EPPr LHop MOak WCFE WSHC XPep
  - 'Dixieland Pink' — WCom
  - 'Manor Nursery' (v) — ECGP EMan EWes LHop MAvo WCot
  - pale pink — CBot CSpe ECtt EMan LPhx SAga
* - 'Shell Pink' — ECGP
  'Newleaze Coral' — CWCL EMan EPPr LAst LHop LLWP MAvo SAga
  'Newleaze Pink' — LHop SAga
  parvifolia — EBee
  remota — EMan GFlt MGol SPlb
  rivularis — EBee EMan MGol
  umbellata — see *Phymosia umbellata*

Sphaeromeria (Asteraceae)
§ *capitata* — NWCA WLin

Spigelia (Loganiaceae)
  marilandica — EBee

Spilanthes (Asteraceae)
  acmella — see *Acmella oleracea*
  oleracea — see *Acmella oleracea*

Spiraea ✿ (*Rosaceae*)

'Abigail'	CDoC
albiflora	see *S. japonica* var. *albiflora*
arborea	see *Sorbaria kirilowii*
§ 'Arguta' ♀H4	More than 30 suppliers
x *arguta* 'Bridal Wreath'	see *S.* 'Arguta'
- 'Compacta'	see *S.* x *cinerea*
- 'Nana'	see *S.* x *cinerea*
bella	WHCG WTin
betulifolia	GEil MRav MWgw SMac WHCG
- var. *aemiliana*	CBot CWSG EBee EBre ECtt ESis
	GKir MAsh MGos NHol SLPl WFar
x *billardii* misapplied	see *Spiraea* x *pseudosalicifolia*
x *bumalda*	see *S. japonica* 'Bumalda'
- 'Wulfeni'	see *S. japonica* 'Walluf'
callosa 'Alba'	see *S. japonica* var. *albiflora*
§ *cantoniensis*	CPle MTed SLon
'Flore Pleno' (d)	
- 'Lanceata'	see *S. cantoniensis* 'Flore Pleno'
§ x *cinerea*	EPfP SSta
- 'Grefsheim' ♀H4	CBcs CDoC COtt CSBt EBee ECtt
	EMil ENot GKir LRHS MBri MGos
	SLim SPer SSta WCFE WDin WFar
	WRHF
crispifolia	see *S. japonica* 'Bullata'
decumbens	CPle
douglasii	EWTr MBar
formosana B&SWJ 1597	CPLG
§ x *foxii*	SLPl
fritschiana	SLPl SLon
hayatana **new**	SLon
hendersonii	see *Petrophytum hendersonii*
§ *japonica*	SBod SMer WFar
- 'Alba'	see *S. japonica* var. *albiflora*
§ - var. *albiflora*	More than 30 suppliers
- 'Allgold'	NBee
- 'Alpina'	see *S. japonica* 'Nana'
- 'Alpine Gold'	CFai MAsh NPro WWeb
- 'Anthony Waterer' (v)	CBcs CChe CSBt CWSG CWib
	EBre ECrN ELan ENot EPfP GKir
	LRHS MBar MBri MGos MRav
	MSwo NBee NWea SHBN SPer
	SRms WBVN WBod WDin WFar
	WGwG WHar WTel
- 'Blenheim'	SRms
§ - 'Bullata'	CFee CMHG EPfP GEdr MBar
	NWCA SRms WAbe WBod WHCG
§ - 'Bumalda'	GKir WFar
- 'Candlelight' ♀H4	CAbP CBcs CSBt CWSG EBee EBre
	EGra EPfP GKir LAst LRHS MAsh
	MBri MGos NHol SCoo SLim SPer
	SPla SPoG SWvt WGwG
§ - 'Crispa'	CRez EBee EPfP LRHS MBar NPro
	WFar WWeb
- 'Dart's Red' ♀H4	GKir LRHS SSta WWeb
- 'Firelight'	CAbP CBcs CChe CSBt EBee EBre
	ECrN ELan ENot EPfP GKir LHop
	LRHS MAsh MBri MGos MSwo
	NHol SCoo SLim SPer SPla SSta
	SWvt WBrE WGwG WStI
- var. *fortunei*	WHCG
'Atrosanguinea'	
- 'Froebelii'	GEil
- 'Glenroy Gold'	SLon WHen
- 'Gold Mound'	CMHG CWSG CWib EBee ECrN
	ELan ENot EPfP GKir LRHS MBar
	MHer MRav MSwo MWgw MWhi
	NBee NFor SHBN SHFr SPer SPlb
	SRms SWal WDin WFar WHar WStI
	WWeb
- 'Gold Rush'	CMHG MBNS WHCG
- Golden Princess	CTri CWSG EPfP GKir LAst LBuc
= 'Lisp'PBR ♀H4	LRHS MAsh MBar MGos NBee

	NHol SLon SMer SPer SReu SRms
	SSta WCFE WDin WFar WStI WWeb
- 'Goldflame'	More than 30 suppliers
- 'Little Princess'	CBcs CWSG CWib EBee ECrN
	EGra EMil ENot GKir LRHS MAsh
	MBar MBri MRav MSwo MWat
	MWhi NBee NHol SLim SPer SRms
	SSta SWvt WBVN WDin WFar
	WHar
- Magic Carpet	CBcs LRHS MAsh SCoo SPoG
= 'Walbuma'PBR ♀H4	
- 'Magnifica'	WHCG WPat
§ - 'Nana' ♀H4	CMHG CSBt EBee ENot ESis GEil
	MAsh MBar MRav MTho SRms
	WEas WHCG WPat WPer
- 'Nyewoods'	see *S. japonica* 'Nana'
- 'Shirobana'	see *S. japonica* var. *albiflora*
- 'Snow Cap'	CWib
§ - 'Walluf'	CFai CPle CTri CWib GEil NFor
	WBcn WHCG
- 'White Cloud'	ELan
- 'White Gold'PBR	CAbP ENor EPfP LAst LBuc LRHS
	MAsh NPro SPer
'Margaritae'	NPro SHBN SPer SWvt
micrantha **new**	CPLG
nipponica	CBcs MBar
- 'Halward's Silver'	CFai GEil LRHS MRav NHol NPro
	SLPl WBcn WBod
- 'June Bride'	NBlu
- 'Rotundifolia'	GEil
§ - 'Snowmound' ♀H4	More than 30 suppliers
- var. *tosaensis* hort.	see *S. nipponica* 'Snowmound'
- var. *tosaensis* (Yatabe)	LHop MWat SReu
Makino	
x *pachystachys*	GEil
palmata 'Elegans'	see *Filipendula purpurea*
	'Elegans'
§ *prunifolia* (d)	CDul CFai ECrN ELan GEil MBlu
	MRav SLon SPer WCom WHCG
	WTel WWin
- 'Plena'	see *S. prunifolia*
x *pseudosalicifolia*	GEil SHFr WWin
'Triumphans'	
salicifolia	GEil WFar
stevenii	SPer
'Summersnow'	SLPl
'Superba'	see *S.* x *foxii*
thunbergii ♀H4	CChe CWib CSBt CTri CWib EBee
	ENot EPfP MRav NWea SCoo SLim
	SMer SRms WDin WGwG WHCG
- 'Fujino Pink'	WDin
* - 'Mellow Yellow'	WFar WPen
- 'Mount Fuji'	CAbP CWib EBre EHoe GSki LRHS
	MGos NPro WBcn WFar
* - *rosea*	WBcn
- 'Tickled Pink'	CAbP LRHS
ulmaria	see *Filipendula ulmaria*
x *vanhouttei*	CBcs CSBt CTri EBee ENot EPfP
	MBar MHer MRav MSwo NLRH
	SGar SHBN SHFr SPer SPla SRms
	WDin WFar WTel
- 'Gold Fountain'	WBcn WFar
- Pink Ice = 'Catpan' (v)	CAbP CBcs CDoC CMHG COtt
	CSLe CWib EBee EHoe EMil EPfP
	LAst LHop LRHS MAsh MGos
	MLLN MTis NHol SGar SHBN SPer
	SPlb SWvt WDin WFar WHar WTel
	WWeb
veitchii	MRav WBcn
venusta 'Magnifica'	see *Filipendula rubra* 'Venusta'

Spiranthes (*Orchidaceae*)

aestivalis	SSpi
cernua	MS&S

- var. **odorata** <u>new</u> — CPom
- - 'Chadd's Ford' — More than 30 suppliers
  spiralis — SSpi

Spirodela (Lemnaceae)
§ **polyrhiza** — EMFW MSta

Spodiopogon (Poaceae)
  sibiricus — CBig CKno CWCL EBee ECGN
  EChP ECha EHoe EMan EMon
  EPPr EPza LBBr LEdu MSte NFor
  SMad

Sporobolus (Poaceae)
  airoides — EBee
  asper — EBee
  cryptandrus — EBee EPPr
  heterolepis — CBig CFwr EBee EHoe LHop LPhx
  MSPs SMad WPrP
  wrightii — EBee WSPU

Spraguea (Portulacaceae)
  'Powder Puff' — LRHS

Sprekelia (Amaryllidaceae)
  formosissima — CSpe CStu LAma LRHS NRog

Stachys (Lamiaceae)
  aethiopica 'Danielle' <u>new</u> — EBee ECtt LAst SPoG SVil
§ **affinis** — CArn CFir ELau GPoy LEdu
  albens — EOrc IFro
§ **albotomentosa** — CSpe EBee EMan GBri GEil LHop
  LPhx NBir SAga SHFr SSvw WCHb
  WCot WGMN
  alopecuros — WWin
  alpina — CNat EBee
  x **ambigua** — NSti
  atherocalyx — EBee
  balansae — NSti
  betonica — see *S. officinalis*
§ **byzantina** — More than 30 suppliers
§ - 'Big Ears' — CBAn EBee ECha EMan ENot
  EWTr LHop MAnH MBri MWat
  NDov SMrm WCAu WCot WFar
  WMnd WMoo
§ - 'Cotton Boll' — COIW EBee ECha EFou GCal
  GMac LRHS MBct MHar MWat
  SPer WCot
  - 'Countess Helen von — see *S. byzantina* 'Big Ears'
  Stein'
  - gold-leaved — see *S. byzantina* 'Primrose Heron'
  - large-leaved — see *S. byzantina* 'Big Ears'
  - 'Limelight' — EBee WCot
§ - 'Primrose Heron'^{PBR} — COtt EBre ECha ECot EMan EPfP
  LBBr LRHS NLar NOrc NSti SMer
  SPer SWvt WBry WCAu
  - 'Sheila McQueen' — see *S. byzantina* 'Cotton Boll'
  - 'Silver Carpet' — More than 30 suppliers
§ - 'Striped Phantom' (v) — EMan WCAu WCHb WCot WEas
  - 'Variegata' — see *S. byzantina* 'Striped Phantom'
  candida — EBee EHyt WPat
  chrysantha — EHyt LPhx SAga
  citrina — CMea GCal LRHS WCom WOut
  coccinea — CBot CPla EBee EChP ECtt EHrv
  EMan EOrc EWsh GBBs LRHS
  MCLN MHer MTis NBir SDnm
  SHFr SPet WCHb WHil WMoo
  WOut WPat WRos WSSM WSan
  WWin
  - 'El Salto' — WCom
  corsica — EBee WPGP
  cretica — EMan EOrc XPep
  - subsp. **salviifolia** <u>new</u> — XPep
  densiflora — see *S. monieri*

§ **discolor** — CMea EBee EChP EOrc EPPr MBro
  MLLN SBla SMac WCot WCru WLin
  WOut WPer WViv
  dregeana — SAga
  germanica — CNat CPen CPom EBee EMan
  NArg WBri WOut
  - subsp. **bithynica** — EBee
  glutinosa <u>new</u> — XPep
  grandiflora — see *S. macrantha*
  heraclea — EBee XPep
  'Hidalgo' — see *S. albotomentosa*
  iva — LPhx
  lanata — see *S. byzantina*
  lavandulifolia — EHyt
  longifolia <u>new</u> — WOut
§ **macrantha** — More than 30 suppliers
  - 'Alba' — EBee ECha WMoo
  - 'Hummelo' — see *S. monieri* 'Hummelo'
  - 'Nivea' — EBee EHrv ELan EMan GCal
  MMHG WPat
§ - 'Robusta' ♡^{H4} — CDes CStr EBee EBlw ELan GKir
  NBro NGdn SHel SVal WCAu WCot
  WRHF WWye
  - 'Rosea' — CBri CElw CMHG EBee EFou EGra
  ELan GFlt LLWP MCLN SCro SHel
  SPlb WEas WPer WRha WWye
  - 'Superba' — CBri EBee EChP EGra EPfP GKir
  IBal LAst LRHS MBow MBri MDun
  MMHG MRav SBla SMrm SPer
  SWvt WCAu WCHb WCom WCot
  WFar WMoo WWeb
  - 'Violacea' — CDes CStr EBee MAvo NChi WPGP
  marrubiifolia — EBee
  mexicana — EMan LPhx MDKP MMHG MSte
  WHil
§ **monieri** — CABP CM&M EBee EChP EGle
  EMan LRHS MAvo MCLN NLar
  SMrm WCot WOBN WOut WPer
  WViv
§ - 'Hummelo' — EBee EFou EGle EMan ENot EPPr
  EPfP GEil LHop LPhx MDKP NDov
  NLar SAga SMHy SMrm SUsu
  WCAu WWeb
* - **minor** <u>new</u> — GBin
* - 'Rosea' — EBee NDov SBla
  - 'Saharan Pink' — CBgR EBee WOut
  - 'Spitzweg' — EPPr SUsu
  nivea — see *S. discolor*
§ **officinalis** — CArn CRWN CSev CStr EBee GBar
  GPoy IHMH MGas MHer MSal
  NLan NMir WBea WHHs WHbs
  WHer WWye
  - 'Alba' — CArn CBot EBee MBri MCLN NBro
  NRya WCAu WCHb WCom WFar
  WHer WOut WRha WWye
  - mauve-flowered <u>new</u> — WTin
  - 'Rosea' — CMea SHop WCAu WCot WTin
  - 'Rosea Superba' — CBgR EBee ECha MCLN MDKP
  SIng WCAu WCot WFar WMoo
  - 'Wisley White' <u>new</u> — EBee
  olympica — see *S. byzantina*
  palustris — LPBA MGas MSta NLan NSco SHar
  WFar WOut
  plumosa — EBee XPep
  saxicola <u>new</u> — MDKP
  setifera — EBee
  spicata — see *S. macrantha*
  swainsonii <u>new</u> — XPep
  sylvatica — CArn EMan MGol NLan NSco WBri
  WHer
  - 'Hoskin's Variegated' (v) — WCHb WWpM
  - 'Huskers' (v) — EBee EPPr ITer MCCP
  thirkei — EBee WRHF XPep
  tuberifera — see *S. affinis*

Stachytarpheta (Verbenaceae)

mutabilis	SOWG

Stachyurus (Stachyuraceae)

chinensis	CBcs CMCN CPMA CPle IArd IDee LRHS MBri MGos NLar SPoG
- 'Celina'	MBlu MGos SMad
- 'Joy Forever' (v)	CEnd CMCN EPfP LTwo MBlu MGos SPoG SSpi
himalaicus	CFil IArd IDee NLar WPGP
- HWJCM 009	WCru
leucotrichus	CPMA
'Magpie' (v)	CFil CPMA EPfP LRHS NLar SLon SPer SSpi WCru WPGP
praecox ♀H4	More than 30 suppliers
§ - var. *matsuzakii*	CBcs CFil NBhm WPGP
- - B&SWJ 2817	WCru
- - 'Scherzo' (v)	WCru
* - 'Rubriflora'	CPMA ELan EPfP LRHS SSpi WFar
salicifolius	CFil CMCN SLon
sigeyosii B&SWJ 6915	WCru
szechuanensis	CBcs
aff. *szechuanensis*	WCru
BWJ 8153 **new**	
yunnanensis	CFil WPGP

Staehelina (Asteraceae)

dubia **new**	XPep

Staphylea (Staphyleaceae)

bumalda	CBcs CPMA EPfP NLar WPGP
colchica	CBcs ELan EPfP EWTr NPal WDin WSHC
- 'Rosea'	CBcs
holocarpa	CBcs CDul CPMA CPle EPfP MRav SSpi WBVN WFar
N - var. *rosea*	CPMA ENot EPfP SMad
N - 'Rosea'	CBcs CMCN MBlu MGos NLar SSpi
pinnata	CBcs CPMA EPfP LEdu NLar WHCr WNor WPat
trifolia	CAgr CBcs

Statice see *Limonium*

Stauntonia (Lardizabalaceae)

hexaphylla	CBcs CDoC CHEx CSam CTri EBee EHol EMan EPfP GQui LRHS MAsh MDun SAdn SBra SHGC SPer SReu SSpi SSta WBrE WPGP WSHC
- B&SWJ 4858	WCru
purpurea B&SWJ 3690	WCru

Stegnogramma (Thelypteridaceae)

pozoi	EFer

Stellaria (Caryophyllaceae)

graminea	NBid
holostea	CRWN MBow NMir NSco SECG WBri WHer WShi

Stemmacantha (Asteraceae)

carthamoides	MSal
centauriodes	EBlw ECGP ECha EGle GCal LPhx MAnH MAvo NBid SAga
rhapontica	EMan

Stenanthium (Melanthiaceae)

robustum	WPGP

Stenochlaena (Blechnaceae)

palustris	MBri

Stenomesson (Amaryllidaceae)

§ *miniatum*	CStu WCot

Stenotaphrum (Poaceae)

secundatum **new**	XPep
- 'Variegatum' (v) ♀H1	CHal EShb WDyG

Stephanandra (Rosaceae)

incisa	CBcs CPLG WHCG
§ - 'Crispa'	More than 30 suppliers
- 'Dart's Horizon'	SLPl
- 'Prostrata'	see *S. incisa* 'Crispa'
tanakae	CBcs CDoC CPLG CPle CTri ELan EPfP EWTr GKir IMGH LAst MBar MBlu MRav MWat NFor SHBN SLPl SLon SPer SPla WDin WFar WHCG WPat

Stephania (Menispermaceae)

japonica B&SWJ 2396	WCru
rotundifolia	EUJe

Stephanotis (Asclepiadaceae)

floribunda ♀H1	CBcs EBak GQui LRHS MBri SMur SOWG
- *variegata* (v)	SMur

Sterculia (Sterculiaceae)

rupestris **new**	EShb

Sternbergia (Amaryllidaceae)

candida	CBro LAma
- JCA 933000	SSpi WCot
§ *clusiana*	EHyt LAma
colchiciflora	EPot
fischeriana	CBro
greuteriana	SOkd
lutea	CAvo CBro CFwr EHyt EPot EWes LAma LPhx LRHS MRav MWat NMen NRog NWCA SDix SSpi WEas WLin WTin
- Angustifolia Group	CBro CDes EMon WCot
macrantha	see *S. clusiana*
sicula	CBro CFwr EHyt EPot WCot XPep
- var. *graeca*	EHyt
- 'John Marr' **new**	CDes

Stevia (Asteraceae)

rebaudiana	EBee EOHP GPoy MSal WJek

Stewartia ✿ (Theaceae)

gemmata	CFil MDun NLar WNor WPGP
'Korean Splendor'	see *S. pseudocamellia* Koreana Group
koreana	see *S. pseudocamellia* Koreana Group
malacodendron ♀H4	EPfP LRHS MBri SSpi
monadelpha	CMen EPfP SSpi WBod WNor
ovata	CBcs CMen SSpi
N - var. *grandiflora*	CMen GKir LRHS
pseudocamellia ♀H4	More than 30 suppliers
- var. *koreana*	see *S. pseudocamellia* Koreana Group
§ - Koreana Group ♀H4	CBcs CDul CEnd CFil CMCN CMen CTho ECrN EPfP LRHS MBri MDun NLar SPer SSpi WBod WDin WFar WNor WPGP
pteropetiolata	CBcs
- var. *koreana*	LRHS
rostrata	CBcs CFil CMCN GIBF MBlu WNor WPGP
serrata	CBcs CMen SSpi

sinensis ♀H4	CFil CMen CPMA EPfP MBlu MDun SMad SSpi SSta WNor WPGP

Sticherus (*Gleicheniaceae*)
urceolatus	WRic

Stigmaphyllon (*Malpighiaceae*)
ciliatum	ERea

Stilbocarpa (*Araliaceae*)
polaris **new**	SSpi

Stipa (*Poaceae*)
B&SWJ 2302 from Sikkim	EBee
§ *arundinacea*	More than 30 suppliers
- 'Autumn Tints'	EHoe EPza
- 'Golden Hue'	EHoe
barbata	CDes CFwr CKno CSpe EBee ECGN EGle EHoe EMan EWes LPhx LRHS MAvo NDov NOGN SCro SMad SMrm SPer SUsu WCom WCot WHal WHil WPGP WRos XPep
- 'Silver Feather'	CBig CHrt EPza EWsh LIck MAnH MWhi NBPC
boysterica	CFee
brachytricha	see *Calamagrostis brachytricha*
§ *calamagrostis*	More than 30 suppliers
- 'Lemperg'	EMan EPPr
capillata	CBel CBrm CFwr CKno COlW ECGN EChP EGle EHoe EPPr EWsh GBin GKir LPhx LRHS MCLN MWhi NBea NCGa NChi SMad SMrm SYvo WCot WHal WOVN WPGP WWpP WWye XPep
- 'Brautschleier'	CHrt CWib EPza GCal LIck SWal
* - 'Lace Veil'	CBig LRav
chrysophylla	CFil
- F&W 9321	WPGP
columbiana	MLLN
comata	EBee IFro NFor
elegantissima	CKno EHoe MGol
extremiorientalis	CBig CFwr CKno ECha EGle EPPr EPza GIBF GSki LAst NOGN SLPl WHal WWpP
gigantea ♀H4	More than 30 suppliers
- 'Gold Fontaene'	CDes CFir CKno EBee EMon EPPr EWes LPhx MMoz MNrw NDov SMad WPGP
grandis	CBig CBrm CKno EBlw ECha EPPr GBin WHal WMoo WPer WWpP
joannis	EBee GCal
lasiagrostis	see *S. calamagrostis*
lessingiana	CBre CFil CHrt CM&M CPLG CSam EBee EHul EPla GBin GIBF ITim SMac WPGP WPnP WWpP
offneri	CKno CStr EBee EPPr EWes LPhx NDov SBla SIgm
patens	EBee
pennata	CBcs CBig CKno COlW EBee EHoe EMan GBin GCal GKir LRav MFir NCGa NOak SMad SMer
pulcherrima	CKno EMan GCal MAvo SIgm XPep
- 'Windfeder'	CFir SLPl SMad SMrm
ramosissima **new**	CKno
robusta	EBee EPPr XPep
spartea	CBrm
splendens misapplied	see *S. calamagrostis*
§ *splendens* Trin.	CBig ECoo EFou EHoe EMan EPPr EWTr LEdu LPhx WFoF
stenophylla	see *S. tirsa*
stipoides **new**	GGar

tenacissima	CKno CSBt EBee ECha EFou EHoe EHul EPla EUJe GSki WBro WDin WMoo XPep
tenuifolia misapplied	see *S. tenuissima*
tenuifolia Steud.	CHar CMea CMil EHul EMar EPGN EPfP GGar GKir LRHS MBri MCLN MMil MRav MWgw MWrn NBea NBir NBro NChi NHol NSti NVic SIng SLon SPer WCAu WHal WMoo XPep
§ *tenuissima*	More than 30 suppliers
- 'Pony Tails'	CBig COlW EBee EDAr EPfP IBal LAst LRav MBNS MBar MLan MWgw NCGa NLar SCou SWvt WMnd
§ *tirsa*	GBin
turkestanica	EBee LPhx MAnH MMoz NDov SUsu SWat
ucrainica	LPhx
verticillata **new**	CKno

Stoebe (*Asteraceae*)
alopecuroides	SPlb

Stokesia (*Asteraceae*)
cyanea	see *S. laevis*
§ *laevis*	CFwr CHea EBee ECGP ECha EGle EPfP EWTr GKir LAst LRHS MBro NBro NFor NLar SMac SMrm SPet WBrE WCAu WFar WPer WSan
- 'Alba'	CHea CM&M CMea COlW EBee ECha EGle EHrv ELan EMan EPar EPfP ERou EWTr GKir GMac LAst LPhx LRHS MRav NBrk NHol NPPs SChu SPer SSpi STes
- 'Blue Star'	More than 30 suppliers
- 'Mary Gregory'	More than 30 suppliers
- mixed	CPou MLan
- 'Omega Skyrocket'	CBre CFai CFwr CMHG CPou EBee EChP EMan EMar ERou MLLN MWrn NBPC NHol NOak SMrm SOkh SSpi SUsu WBor WCAu WCot WFar WShp
- 'Purple Parasols'	More than 30 suppliers
- 'Silver Moon'	CBAn CFai CFwr CMHG EBee EChP EGle EMan EMar EMil GCal LAst LBBr MTPN MTis NBir NCot NPri SCro SHar SOkh SUsu SVil WCot WFar WTMC
- 'Träumerei'	EBee EChP EGle EMan EMar ERou LAst LRHS MTis NHol NPPs SLon SOkh SPet SWal WCAu WMnd WMoo
- 'Wyoming'	ERou

Stranvaesia see *Photinia*

x *Stranvinia* see *Photinia*

Stratiotes (*Hydrocharitaceae*)
aloides	CDWL CWat ECoo EHon EMFW EPAt LNCo LPBA MSta NArg SWat

strawberry see *Fragaria*

Strelitzia (*Strelitziaceae*)
alba	EAmu
nicolai	CAbb CHEx CRoM EAmu LPal WMul XBlo
reginae ♀H1	CAbb CBcs CBrP ELan ERea EShb ESlt GQui LEur LPal LPan LRHS MJnS NPal SAPC SArc SPlb SRms WMul XBlo
- 'Humilis'	XBlo

- 'Kirstenbosch Gold' — XBlo

Streptocarpella see *Streptocarpus*

Streptocarpus ✿ (*Gesneriaceae*)

	'Albatross' ♀H1	SBrm SDnm WDib
	'Amanda' Dibley ♀H1	WDib
	'Anne'	CSpe SBrm WDib
	'Athena'	WDib
	baudertii	WDib
	'Beryl'	WDib
	'Bethan' ♀H1	SBrm WDib
	'Beverley Ruth'	MOak
I	'Black Gardenia' **new**	WDib
	'Black Panther'	SBrm WDib
	'Blue Bird' **new**	MOak
	'Blue Gem'	WDib
	'Blue Heaven'	SBrm
	'Blue Ice' **new**	MOak
	'Blue Moon'	WDib
	'Blue Nymph'	WDib
	'Blue Pencil'	SBrm
§	'Blue Upstart'	MOak
	'Blushing Bride' (d)	SDnm WDib
	'Blushing Pink' **new**	MOak SBrm
	'Border Line' **new**	SBrm
*	'Boysenberry Delight'	WDib
	'Branwen'	SBrm SDnm WDib
	'Brimstone' **new**	MOak SBrm
	'Bristol's Black Bird' **new**	WDib
	'Bristol's Ice Castle' **new**	WDib
	'Bristol's Very Best' **new**	WDib
	'Buttons' **new**	SBrm
	caeruleus **new**	WDib
	candidus	WDib
	'Carol'	WDib
	'Carolyn Ann' **new**	MOak
	'Carys' ♀H1	WDib
	'Catrin' ♀H1	SBrm WDib
	caulescens	CHal WDib
*	- 'Compactus'	CHal
	- var. *pallescens*	WDib
	'Charlotte'	MOak WDib
	'Chorus Line' ♀H1	SDnm WDib
	'Clouds'	CSpe
	'Concord Blue'	WDib
	'Constant Nymph'	WDib
	'Copper Knob' **new**	MOak
	'Crystal Beauty' **new**	WDib
	'Crystal Blush' **new**	WDib
	'Crystal Ice' PBR ♀H1	WDib
	'Crystal Snow' **new**	WDib
	cyaneus	WDib
	- subsp. *polackii*	WDib
	'Cynthia' ♀H1	WDib
I	'Daphne' ♀H1	WDib
	'Dark Eyes Mary' **new**	SBrm
	'Dark Secret' **new**	SBrm
	'Demeter' **new**	SBrm
	'Diana'	SBrm WDib
	dunnii	SGar WDib
	'Elegance' **new**	MOak SBrm
	'Ella' **new**	MOak SBrm
	'Elsi'	SBrm SDnm WDib
	'Emily'	WDib
	'Emma'	SBrm WDib
	'Falling Stars' ♀H1	CSpe ERea SBrm WDib
	'Festival Wales'	SBrm WDib
	'Fiona'	SBrm WDib
	floribundus	WDib
	gardenii	WDib
	'Gillian' **new**	MOak
	glandulosissimus ♀H1	CHal SSte SVen WDib
	'Gloria' ♀H1	CSpe SBrm WDib

'Good Hope'	ERea
'Gower Daybreak' **new**	SBrm
'Gower Garnet' **new**	MOak
'Gower Midnight' **new**	MOak SBrm
'Grape Slush'	WDib
'Gwen' **new**	WDib
'Hannah Ellis' **new**	MOak SBrm
'Happy Snappy' ♀H1	SBrm SDnm WDib
'Heidi' ♀H1	SBrm SDnm WDib
'Helen' ♀H1	SBrm WDib
'Huge White'	CSpe
'Ida' **new**	MOak
'Inky Fingers' **new**	MOak SBrm
'Izzy' **new**	MOak SBrm
'Jane Elizabeth' **new**	MOak SBrm
'Jennifer' ♀H1	SBrm SDnm WDib
'Joanna'	SBrm WDib
johannis	WDib
'Judith' **new**	MOak
'Julie'	WDib
'Karen'	SBrm SDnm WDib
kentaniensis	WDib
'Kerry's Gold' **new**	MOak
'Kim' ♀H1	CSpe SBrm SDnm WDib
kirkii	WDib
'Kisie' **new**	MOak SBrm
'Largesse' **new**	SBrm
'Laura' ♀H1	SBrm WDib
'Lisa' ♀H1	SBrm
'Little Gem'	CSpe
'Louise'	SBrm WDib
'Lynne'	SBrm WDib
'Maassen's White' ♀H1	ERea SBrm WDib
'Magpie' **new**	MOak
'Mandy'	SDnm WDib
'Margaret'	SBrm WDib
'Marie'	WDib
'Mary' **new**	MOak SBrm
'Megan'	SBrm WDib
'Melanie' ♀H1	WDib
meyeri	WDib
'Midnight Flame'	ERea WDib
'Mini Nymph'	WDib
'Modbury Lady' **new**	MOak
modestus	WDib
'Moonlight' **new**	WDib
'Muse' **new**	MOak SBrm
'Neptune'	SBrm WDib
'Nia' **new**	WDib
'Nicola'	SBrm WDib
'Nita' **new**	MOak
'Olga'	WDib
'Olwen'	WDib
'Party Doll'	SBrm WDib
parviflorus	LEur
'Passion Pink'	MOak SBrm
'Patricia' **new**	MOak SBrm
'Paula' ♀H1	SBrm WDib
pentherianus	WDib
'Pink Fondant'	CSpe
'Pink Souffle'	SBrm SDnm WDib
'Plum Crazy'	SBrm
polyanthus subsp. *dracomontanus*	WDib
primulifolius	WDib
- subsp. *formosus*	WDib
prolixus	WDib
'Purple Haze' **new**	MOak
* 'Purple Passion'	SBrm
'Raspberry Dream' **new**	MOak
rexii	WDib
'Rhiannon'	SDnm WDib
'Rose Gower' **new**	MOak
'Rosebud'	SBrm WDib

'Rosemary' (d) — WDib
'Ruby' ♀H1 — SBrm WDib
'Ruby Anniversary' **new** — MOak
'Ruffled Lilac' — CSpe SBrm
'Sally' — SBrm WDib
'Samantha' **new** — MOak
'Sandra' — SDnm WDib
'Sarah' — WDib
saxorum ♀H1 — CHal EMan EOHP EShb Llck MBri MOak SRms SSte WDib WFar
- compact — EOHP WDib
'Sian' — SBrm SDnm WDib
silvaticus **new** — WDib
'Snow White' ♀H1 — CSpe SDnm WDib
'Something Special' — SBrm SDnm WDib
'Sophie' — WDib
'Southshore' **new** — WDib
'Spider' **new** — MOak
'Stacey' **new** — MOak SBrm
'Stella' ♀H1 — SBrm WDib
'Stephanie' **new** — WDib
stomandrus — WDib
'Strawberry Fondant' **new** — MOak SBrm
* 'Sugar Almond' — CSpe SBrm
'Susan' ♀H1 — WDib
'Swaybelle' **new** — SBrm
'Terracotta' — MOak SBrm
'Texas Hot Chilli' **new** — WDib
'Texas Sunrise' **new** — MOak
'Tina' ♀H1 — SBrm SDnm WDib
'Tracey' — WDib
'Turbulent Tide' **new** — SBrm
'Upstart' — see *S.* 'Blue Upstart'
variabilis **new** — WDib
'Velvet Underground' **new** — SBrm
'Vera' **new** — SBrm
'Violet Lace' — CSpe SBrm
wendlandii — WDib
'Wendy' — SBrm WDib
'White Wings' **new** — MOak SBrm
'Wiesmoor Red' — WDib
'Winifred' — SBrm WDib

Streptopus (Convallariaceae)

amplexifolius — CBro EBee GBuc WCru
- M&PS 98/022 — GCrs NLar
obtusatus — EBee
roseus — EBee GCrs GFlt LAma
simplex — EBee

Streptosolen (Solanaceae)

jamesonii ♀H1 — CHal CHll CPle CSev EBak ELan ERea EShb MOak WBod
- 'Fire Gold' — ERea

Strobilanthes (Acanthaceae)

anisophylla — WCot
atropurpurea misapplied — see *S. attenuata*
atropurpurea Nees — see *S. wallichii*
attenuata — More than 30 suppliers
- subsp. *nepalensis* — CLAP WOut WWye
- - TSS from Nepal — EBee EMar WRHF
- 'Out of the Ocean' — WOut
dyeriana (v) ♀H1 — CHal EBak EMan EShb WCot WRha
flexicaulis — EBee WCot
- B&SWJ 354 — WCru
nutans — CDes CLAP CPom CPou EBee WCot WPGP
rankanensis — CDes CLAP EBee EDAr
- B&SWJ 1771 — CPom WCru
violacea misapplied — CPrp ERea WPer
wallichii — CDes CLAP EBee EPPr NBPC NMRc SMHy WCAu WCot WCru WFar WPGP

Stromanthe (Marantaceae)

amabilis — see *Ctenanthe amabilis*
sanguinea — CHal MBri
'Stripestar' — MBri

Strongylodon (Papilionaceae)

macrobotrys — SOWG

Stuartia see *Stewartia*

Stylidium (Stylidiaceae)

affine — SPlb
soboliferum — ECou

Stylophorum (Papaveraceae)

diphyllum — CPou ECha EGle EMar EPar GKir LAma MRav MSal WAul WCru WFar WPnP
lasiocarpum — CPBP CPLG CPom EMan EMar EWTr GAbr MAnH NBPC NDlv SBri SGar WCot WCru WPrP WRos

Styphelia (Epacridaceae)

colensoi — see *Cyathodes colensoi*

Styrax (Styracaceae)

americanus — CBcs
confusus **new** — CMCN
formosanus — CFil WPGP
   var. *formosanus*
- - B&SWJ 3803 — WCru
hemsleyanus ♀H4 — CAbP CBcs CEnd CFil CPLG CTho EPfP LRHS MBlu SPer SSpi WBor WFar WNor WPGP
japonicus ♀H4 — More than 30 suppliers
- B&SWJ 4405 — WCru
§ - Benibana Group ♀H4 — SReu SSta
- - 'Pink Chimes' — CAbP CMCN CPLG CPMA ELan EPfP LRHS MBlu MBri MDun NBlu SKee SPer SSpi SSta
- 'Carillon' — LRHS
- 'Fargesii' — CDoC CFil CTho EPfP GKir LRHS MAsh MBri SSpi WFar
- 'Roseus' — see *S. japonicus* Benibana Group
- 'Sohuksan' **new** — CFil
obassia ♀H4 — CArn CBcs CMCN CPne CTho EPfP LPan LRHS MBlu MDun SSpi WBod WNor WPGP
- B&SWJ 6023 — WCru
odoratissimus — CFil
serrulatus — CFil

Suaeda (Chenopodiaceae)

vera **new** — XPep

Succisa (Dipsacaceae)

§ *pratensis* — CArn EBee ECoo MBow MHer NLan NLar NMen NSco NWCA SMHy SSpi WGwG WHer WJek WPrP
- *alba* — EBee MDKP
- 'Buttermilk' — CPlt SSpi
- 'Corinne Tremaine' (v) — WHer
- dwarf — NGby NRya
- 'Forest Pearls' **new** — SSpi
- 'Forest Pink' **new** — SSpi
- 'Peddar's Pink' — EBee EWes

sunberry see *Rubus* 'Sunberry'

Sutera (Scrophulariaceae)

'Blizzard'PBR — LAst SMrm WGor WWol
Candy Floss = 'Yasflos' — LAst

cordata　LHop
- 'Blue Showers' **new**　LAst
- 'Bridal Showers' **new**　NPri
- 'Lavender Showers' **new**　NPri
- pale pink　LAst
- 'Pink Domino'^{PBR}　ECtt LAst WGor
§ - 'Snowflake'　ECtt LAst LPVe MLan MOak NBlu
　　　　SCoo SPet
- 'Typhoon White P. **new**　LAst
jurassica　see *Jamesbrittenia jurassica*
neglecta　SPlb WPGP
Olympic Gold　ECtt LAst NPri SCoo
　= 'Prosutv' (v)
Sea Mist = 'Yagemil'^{PBR}　NPri

Sutherlandia (Papilionaceae)
frutescens　CArn GGar SPlb WCot WJek WSHC
　　　　XPep
* - var. *alba* **new**　WCot
- 'Prostrata'　EMan SIgm
montana　SIgm

Swainsona (Papilionaceae)
galegifolia　CHll
- 'Albiflora'　CSpe LPhx SBla SOWG

sweet cicely see *Myrrhis odorata*

Swertia (Gentianaceae)
bimaculata **new**　CTCP

Syagrus (Arecaceae)
§ **romanzoffiana**　CBrP CRoM EAmu LPJP LPal

x *Sycoparrotia* (Hamamelidaceae)
semidecidua　CBcs CFil CPMA GKir LRHS MBlu
　　　　NLar WPGP

Sycopsis (Hamamelidaceae)
sinensis　CMCN EPfP LRHS MBlu NLar
　　　　SDnm SMur SSpi WBcn WDin WFar
　　　　WSHC

Symphoricarpos (Caprifoliaceae)
albus　CDul EBee ECrN ENot MSwo
　　　　NWea WDin
- 'Constance Spry'　MTed SRms
§ - var. *laevigatus*　EBee ENot EPfP LBuc MBar
§ - 'Taff's White' (v)　WMoo
- 'Variegatus'　see *S. albus* 'Taff's White'
'Amethyst'　EBee
x *chenaultii* 'Hancock'　CSBt EBee ECrN ELan ENot EPfP
　　　　GEil MBar MRav MSwo MWat
　　　　NLRH NPro SHBN SPer WDin
　　　　WFar
x *doorenbosii*　EBee ENot GKir LRHS MBar MRav
'Magic Berry'　NWea
- 'Mother of Pearl'　EBee ELan ENot EPfP GKir LRHS
　　　　MBar MGos MRav NWea
- 'White Hedge'　CSBt ELan ENot LBuc LRHS MRav
　　　　NWea SPer WTel
orbiculatus　IMGH LRHS WGwG
- 'Albovariegatus'　see *S. orbiculatus* 'Taff's Silver
　　　　Edge'
- 'Argenteovariegatus'　see *S. orbiculatus* 'Taff's Silver
　　　　Edge'
- 'Bowles' Golden　see *S. orbiculatus* 'Foliis Variegatis'
　Variegated'
§ - 'Foliis Variegatis' (v)　CTri EBee ECrN EGra EHoe ELan
　　　　ENot EPfP GEil LRHS MGos MRav
　　　　NPro NSti SHBN SPer WDin WEas
　　　　WFar WGwG WHCG WSHC WWin
§ - 'Taff's Silver Edge' (v)　EBee EHoe LRHS MBar NSti
- 'Variegatus'　see *S. orbiculatus* 'Foliis Variegatis'

rivularis　see *S. albus* var. *laevigatus*

Symphyandra (Campanulaceae)
from Iran　EPPr WPGP
armena　CNic CTCP EBee EBur EDif ELan
　　　　EWTr GBuc NCGa NLar
asiatica　see *Hanabusaya asiatica*
cretica　EBee ECoo ETow MAvo MWrn
　　　　NPPs SMac SScr WOut WSPU
hofmannii　EBee EBur ELan EPyc MBro MTho
　　　　NBrk NLar NPri WFar WPer WRha
　　　　WWin
§ **ossetica**　CElw EBee ELan EMan MWrn
　　　　NCiC NWoo
§ **pendula**　CFir CTCP EBee EBre EChP EPfP
　　　　EWTr EWes GBuc LPVe MBNS
　　　　MLwd NJOw NLar WBar WFar
　　　　WPer WWeb
- *alba*　see *S. pendula*
wanneri　CTCP EBee EBur EChP EMan EPfP
　　　　LRHS NCGa NLar WWin
zangezura　CTCP EBee EBur EChP EMan
　　　　EWTr MLLN MLwd MWrn SGar
　　　　SHFr

Symphyotrichum see *Aster*

Symphytum (Boraginaceae)
asperum　CPom ECha ELan EMon GAbr
　　　　MRav MSal MTed NCot NLar
　　　　WBVN WCHb WMoo WTMC
* **azureum**　EBee MBri MSte NLar WCAu
　　　　WCHb WFar WMnd WTMC
'Belsay'　CSam GBuc
'Belsay Gold'　SDix
caucasicum　♀^{H4}　CElw CMHG CSam ECha ELau
　　　　EMFW EPar GBar GFlt GPoy IHMH
　　　　LEdu LRHS MAnH MBri MHar
　　　　MRav NSti SIde SSvw WCHb WHer
　　　　WMoo WRha WWpP WWye
- 'Eminence'　CMCo CMdw EBee EGoo WCHb
- 'Norwich Sky'　CKno EBee EChP MMil NMir
　　　　WCHb
cordatum　EMon
- MDM 94019　NGar
'Denford Variegated' (v)　CBgR CRow ITer MInt WBry
§ 'Goldsmith' (v)　More than 30 suppliers
grandiflorum　EBee EMFW ENot GPoy SPer
　　　　WHHs WShp
* - 'Sky-blue-pink' **new**　EBee NCot
'Hidcote Blue'　More than 30 suppliers
§ 'Hidcote Pink'　CPrp EBee EChP ECha ELau EPla
　　　　EPza EWsh LRHS MBow MRav
　　　　MSte MWgw NBir SLPl SUsu
　　　　WCAu WFar WMnd WMoo WPnP
　　　　WTMC
'Hidcote Variegated' (v)　WCHb
ibericum　More than 30 suppliers
- 'All Gold'　CSpe ECha ECtt ELau EWsh GSki
　　　　MBri MRav SLon WCAu WCru
　　　　WMoo WTMC
- 'Blaueglocken'　CBod CSev EBee EChP ECha
　　　　WMoo WPrP WSan
- dwarf　NPri WMoo
- 'Gold in Spring'　EBee EGoo GIBF NLar WCHb WFar
- 'Jubilee'　see *S.* 'Goldsmith'
- 'Lilacinum'　EBee WHer
- 'Pink Robins'　WCHb
- variegated (v)　WCot
- 'Variegatum'　see *S.* 'Goldsmith'
- 'Wisley Blue'　EBee EPfP EWTr IHMH NLar WBan
　　　　WFar WMnd WMoo WShp
'Lambrook Sunrise'　CLAP EBee LAst LHop LRHS MBri
　　　　MMil NBro NGHP NPri NSti SChu

SPla WCot WMoo WPnP WSan WTMC WWpP

'Langthorns Pink'   CPom ELan EMar GBar GBri GBuc GCal WCHb

'Mereworth'   see *Symphytum* x *uplandicum* 'Mereworth'

officinale   CAgr CArn COld CSev GBar GPoy MHer MNrw MSal NGHP NMir NPer SIde SRms WBrk WHer WWye

- 'Boraston White'   MHer WCHb
- var. **ochroleucum**   WHer WTMC

orientale   CAgr CPom EMon GCal STes WCHb

peregrinum   see *S.* x *uplandicum*

'Roseum'   see *S.* x *uplandicum*

'Rubrum'   CDes CPrp EBee EBlw ECot EHrv ELan ELau EPPr EPfP EWes GSki LAst LRHS MCLN MHer MSte NGHP NOrc SPer WCAu WCot WCru WHHs WPGP WSan WTMC

tuberosum   CArn CBre CElw COld CPom CSam ELau EOHP GPoy IHMH MBow MDun MFir MHer MSte NHol NSti SMac WBVN WCHb WFar WHer WRha WTMC WWye

§ x *uplandicum*   CSev CTri ELan ELau EMar GBar GPoy GWCH IHMH MHer MRav MSal SIde SPer WCHb WHHs WHbs WJek WWye

- 'Axminster Gold' (v)   CBct CDes CLAP CMea CPlt CRow EBee EMan IBlr ITer LHop LPhx NBid SAga SMrm SSpi WPGP
- 'Bocking 14'   CAgr CBod CHby CPrp GBar IHMH SIde
- 'Droitwich' (v) **new**   WCot

§ - 'Mereworth' (v)   CBct EBee ETow SMad WCHb

- 'Moorland Heather' **new**   WMoo
- 'Variegatum' (v) ♀H4   More than 30 suppliers

Symplocarpus (*Araceae*)

foetidus   EBee GIBF ITer SSpi WCot

Symplocos (*Symplocaceae*)

paniculata   CDul NLar WWes
pyrifolia   CFil

Syncarpha (*Asteraceae*)

eximia   SPlb

Syneilesis (*Asteraceae*)

aconitifolia   CLAP EBee
- B&SWJ 879   WCru
palmata   CLAP EBee WCot
- B&SWJ 1003   WCru
subglabrata   CLAP
- B&SWJ 298   WCot WCru

Syngonium (*Araceae*)

'Maya Red'   MBri
podophyllum ♀H1   XBlo
- 'Emerald Gem'   CHal
- 'Silver Knight'   MBri
- 'Variegatum' (v)   MBri
'White Butterfly'   CHal MBri

Synnotia see *Sparaxis*

Synthyris (*Scrophulariaceae*)

laciniata   ETow
missurica   CLAP ETow GBuc SSpi WLin
- var. **stellata**   CLAP EBee EHrv GCal GGar SBla SSpi WFar WPGP
pinnatifida   GBuc NWCA

---

reniformis   CLAP GBuc IBlr

Syringa ❀ (*Oleaceae*)

afghanica misapplied   see *S. protolaciniata*
amurensis   see *S. reticulata* subsp. *amurensis*
x *chinensis*   CTho WDin WFar
- 'Saugeana'   IDee SPer
x *diversifolia*   WBcn
  'William H. Judd'
emodi   WHCG
- 'Aurea'   IArd NLar
- 'Aureovariegata' (v)   CBcs CEnd CPMA LRHS MAsh MDun SSpi WDin
x *henryi* 'Alba'   WBcn
x *hyacinthiflora*   IArd
  'Clarke's Giant'
- 'Esther Staley' ♀H4   EBee ENot EPfP MRav SBLw
'Josee'   EBee SWvt WFar WPat WWeb
x *josiflexa* 'Bellicent' ♀H4   CDul CEnd CLnd CTho EBee ELan ENot EPfP GKir ISea MBar MRav NPri NSti SHBN SMur SPer SPlb SPoG SRms SSpi WDin WHCG WPat WPen WTel WWeb
- 'James MacFarlane'   NRib
- 'Lynette'   EPla NPro WBcn
§ - 'Royalty'   LBuc NBlu
josikaea   CLnd CSBt CTho LBuc MBar NLar SPer WHCG
komarovii   GIBF
- L 490   GGGa
§ - subsp. **reflexa**   CDul CTho EPfP MBar MGos MRav WDin WFar
§ x *laciniata* Mill.   CBot CDul CPMA EBee EHol EPfP GEil GKir LRHS MBri MRav NLar SMad SMur SPer SSpi WGor WHCG WKif WPGP WRHF
§ **meyeri**   More than 30 suppliers
  var. **spontanea**
  'Palibin' ♀H4
microphylla   see *S. pubescens* subsp. *microphylla*
- 'Superba'   see *S. pubescens* subsp. *microphylla* 'Superba'
'Minuet'   MGos NBlu
'Miss Canada'   EWTr MBri
palibiniana   see *S. meyeri* var. *spontanea* 'Palibin'
patula (Palibin) Nakai   see *S. pubescens* subsp. *patula*
patula misapplied   see *S. meyeri* var. *spontanea* 'Palibin'
pekinensis   see *S. reticulata* subsp. *pekinensis*
x *persica* ♀H4   CPLG CPMA CSam CTri EPfP EWTr GKir MGos MWat NLar SLon WTel XPep
- 'Alba' ♀H4   CBot CMil CPMA GQui WFar WHCG WPat
- var. *laciniata*   see *S.* x *laciniata*
pinnatifolia   IArd NLar WHCG WPGP
x *prestoniae*   EWTr LRHS MGos
  'Agnes Smith'
- 'Audrey'   MGos
- 'Coral'   WFar
- 'Desdemona'   SSpi
- 'Elinor' ♀H4   CMHG CPle EBee ENot MRav NSti SPer
- 'Hiawatha'   MGos WBcn
- 'Isabella'   MGos SLdr
- 'Kim'   CTho MRav NLar WRHF
- 'Nocturne'   LRHS MGos WFar
- 'Redwine'   LRHS MGos NBlu
- 'Royalty'   see *S.* x *josiflexa* 'Royalty'
§ **protolaciniata**   CMHG CPle EPla IDee SSta WAbe WFar
- 'Kabul'   EPfP NLar

§ **pubescens**   CBrm
    subsp. *microphylla*
§ - 'Superba' ♀H4   More than 30 suppliers
§ - subsp. *patula*   CMac CSBt EGra EPfP GEil GIBF
    LAst MAsh MRav MWat NWea
    SLon SPla SSta WFar WStI
§ - - 'Miss Kim' ♀H4   CDoC CSBt CWSG EBee EBre ENot
    EWTr GKir IArd LRHS MBri MBro
    MGos MRav MSwo NBPC NBlu
    NPro SHBN SLim SSta WDin WFar
    WHCG WPat
'Red Pixie' **new**   MBri
reflexa   see *S. komarovii* subsp. *reflexa*
§ *reticulata*   CPle GIBF
    subsp. *amurensis*
- 'Ivory Silk'   CTho CWSG EPfP IMGH MAsh
    MBri SKee
- var. *mandschurica*   see *S. reticulata* subsp. *amurensis*
§ - subsp. *pekinensis*   CMCN CPle CTho ECre
- - 'Pendula'   IArd IDee
x *swegiflexa*   CDul NLar
sweginzowii   CSam CTho EWTr LBuc SPer WFar
tomentella   CDul LBuc NWea SKee SRms
velutina   see *S. pubescens* subsp. *patula*
villosa   MWhi WBVN WDin
vulgaris   CLnd LBuc MBar NWea WBVN
    WBrE XPep
- var. *alba*   MBar
- 'Albert F. Holden'   WBcn
§ - 'Andenken an Ludwig   More than 30 suppliers
    Späth' ♀H4
- 'Aurea'   CNat EPla MRav NPro WBcn
- Beauty of Moscow   see *S. vulgaris* 'Krasavitsa Moskvy'
- 'Belle de Nancy' (d)   EBee ELan GKir MRav NBlu SBLw
    SHBN SLim WDin WGwG
- 'Charles Joly' (d) ♀H4   More than 30 suppliers
- 'Congo'   EBee ENot GKir MRav NMoo NPri
    SCoo SPer
- 'Edward J. Gardner' (d)   ECrN ENot LRHS MBri SPer
- 'Firmament' ♀H4   CTho ELan ENot EPfP GKir MRav
    NLar SCoo SHBN SPer
- 'G. J. Baardse' **new**   SBLw
- 'Général Pershing' **new**   SBLw
- 'Katherine Havemeyer'   More than 30 suppliers
    (d) ♀H4
§ - 'Krasavitsa Moskvy'   GKir LRHS MBri
- 'La Tour d'Auvergne'   SBLw
    new
- 'Madame Antoine   ECrN ENot GKir MRav
    Buchner' (d)
- 'Madame Lemoine'   More than 30 suppliers
    (d) ♀H4
- 'Masséna'   ENot MRav NPri SCoo
- 'Maud Notcutt'   ECrN ENot GBin NPri SCoo SPer
- 'Michel Buchner' (d)   CBcs EBee ENot GKir MAsh MBar
    MRav MWat NBee NBlu SBLw
    SKee SLim SPer
- 'Miss Ellen Willmott' (d)   MRav SBLw
- 'Mont Blanc' **new**   SBLw
- 'Mrs Edward Harding'   EBee ECrN ENot EPfP GKir LBuc
    (d) ♀H4   MGos NPri NWea
- 'Olivier de Serres'   SBLw
- 'Président Grévy' (d)   CDoC CLnd CMac SBLw SPer
- 'President Lincoln' **new**   SBLw
- 'Primrose'   CDoC CMac CSBt CTho EBee
    ECrN ELan ENot EPfP GBin GKir
    IArd LAst LRHS MAsh MBri MDun
    MGos MSwo SCoo SHBN SKee SPer SSta WBVN
    WDin WFar
- 'Sensation'   CDoC CPle CSBt CWSG EBee
    ECrN ENot EPfP GBin GKir IArd
    LAst LRHS MAsh MBri MDun MRav
    MSwo SCoo SHBN SKee SLdr SLim
    SPer SSta

- 'Souvenir d'Alice   GKir LRHS
    Harding' (d)
- 'Souvenir de Louis   see *S. vulgaris* 'Andenken an
    Spaeth'   Ludwig Späth'
- 'Sweetheart' **new**   MBri
- variegated (v)   SLim
- variegated double (d/v)   MTed WBcn
- 'Vestale' ♀H4   ENot MRav SCoo
wolfii   CArn CPLG GIBF MCCP WBVN
yunnanensis   CPLG CTho GIBF LTwo WDin
    WWin

Syringodea (Iridaceae)
luteonigra   CStu

Syzygium (Myrtaceae)
australe **new**   EShb
paniculatum   CTrC

T

Tabernaemontana (Apocynaceae)
coronaria   see *T. divaricata*
§ *divaricata*   ESlt SOWG

Tacca (Taccaceae)
chantrieri **new**   EAmu
- 'Ntum-ntum' **new**   EUJe
integrifolia   CKob EAmu

Tacitus see *Graptopetalum*

Tagetes (Asteraceae)
lemmonii   SHDw XPep
lucida   CArn EOHP MSal WJek
tenuifolia **new**   CArn

Talbotia (Velloziaceae)
elegans   CSpe WCot

Talinum (Portulacaceae)
calycinum   EWll WDyG
'Kingwood Gold'   CPla CWCL
okanoganense   CGra ETow
'Zoe'   CGra

tamarillo see *Cyphomandra betacea*

tamarind see *Tamarindus indica*

Tamarindus (Caesalpiniaceae)
indica (F)   ELau SPlb XBlo

Tamarix (Tamaricaceae)
africana   WWin
gallica   CSBt EBee ENot NWea SAPC SArc
    WSHC XPep
§ *parviflora*   EMil LRHS MGos
pentandra   see *T. ramosissima*
§ *ramosissima*   CDul CTrC CTri EBee EBre
    ECrN ELan EPfP GEil MBar SEND
    SMrm SRms SSta WDin WSHC
    WWeb
- 'Pink Cascade'   CSBt EBee ECrN EMil ENot EPfP
    GKir LRHS MBri MGos MRav NBlu
    SPer SWvt WDin WStI XPep
§ - 'Rubra' ♀H4   CChe CDoC EBee EMil ENot EPfP
    LRHS MBlu MGos SLon SPer WDin
- 'Summer Glow'   see *T. ramosissima* 'Rubra'
tetrandra ♀H4   More than 30 suppliers
- var. *purpurea*   see *T. parviflora*

Tamus (Dioscoreaceae)

communis	CArn MSal

Tanacetum ✿ (Asteraceae)

CC&McK 460	GTou
§ *argenteum*	EBee MRav MTho SIde SLon
- subsp. *canum*	EWes LRHS
§ *balsamita*	CArn CCge COld CPrp EBee ELan ELau EOHP GPoy MBri MHer MSal WHbs WJek WLHH WPer WSel WTin WWye XPep
§ - subsp. *balsamita*	CBod GPoy MSal SIde
§ - subsp. *balsamitoides*	CBod CPrp ELau GBar GWCH MHer NPri WJek WLHH WWye
- var. *tanacetoides*	see *T. balsamita* subsp. *balsamita*
- *tomentosum*	see *T. balsamita* subsp. *balsamitoides*
capitatum	see *Sphaeromeria capitata*
§ *cinerariifolium*	CArn CBod CPrp EChP EOHP GBar GPoy WPer XPep
§ *coccineum*	GPoy MSal NBPC SGar SRms WFar WSSM WWin
- 'Aphrodite' (d)	CPrp EBee ECtt WCAu WHil
- 'Beauty of Stapleford' **new**	WCAu WHil
- 'Bees' Jubilee'	ERou
- 'Bees' Pink Delight'	CPrp
- 'Brenda'	EBee EPfP LHop NLRH SPoG WHil
- 'Duro'	CFir EChP GBuc WHrl
- 'Eileen May Robinson' ♀H4	CBcs EBee ECot EHol EMar ENot EOMN EPfP MWgw WHil
- 'Evenglow'	CPrp EBee ECtt EPfP MRav WCAu WHil
- 'H.M. Pike'	CPrp
- 'James Kelway' ♀H4	CPrp EBee ECot ECtt EHol EMar EOMN EPfP EWll LRHS MBri MWrn NBir SRms WCAu WHer WHil
- 'King Size'	WFar
- 'Laurin'	EBee
- Robinson's giant flowered	SRms WMoo
- 'Robinson's Pink'	EBee EChP ELan ENot GKir LAst NOrc SRms WShp
- 'Robinson's Red'	CSBt CSam EBee EChP GKir IBal IHMH LAst LIck MBNS NOrc NPri NVic SRms SWvt WShp WWeb
I - 'Robinson's Rose' **new**	MBNS
* - *rubrum*	GWCH
- 'Sam Robinson'	WMoo
- 'Snow Cloud'	EBee ELan EOMN LRHS WCAu WHil
§ *corymbosum*	EBee SMHy WCot
§ - subsp. *clusii*	EBee
densum	ECho EPot WCFE
- subsp. *amani*	EBee ECha EMFP ESis GBar GTou LBee LGro LRHS MHer MWat SEND SPer SRms WCom WWin XPep
gossypinum **new**	WLin
§ *haradjanii*	CMea ECtt ELan EMlt MBro NFor NLAp SBla SChu WHer WSHC
herderi	see *Hippolytia herderi*
huronense	EBee
karelinii JJH 198	EBee
macrophyllum misapplied	see *Achillea grandifolia*
§ *macrophyllum* (Waldst. & Kit.) Sch.Bip.	EChP ECtt EMon EPPr GCal GKir LPhx WCot WPer
niveum	CArn EBee EOHP MSal WBea WBri WBry WCot
- 'Jackpot'	CWib EBee ENot EWes LRHS MWrn SHar SPoG SSvw WWeb
§ *parthenium*	CArn CBod ELau GBar GPoy IHMH MBow MHer NPer SECG SIde SRms WBri WHHs WHer WSSM WWye
- 'Aureum'	CHid CRow EBee ECha ELan ELau EMar EOHP EWes GBar GPoy IHMH LGro MBow MBri MHer NBlu NGHP SMad SPer SPlb SRms WCot WEas WHHs WHer WPer WSSM WWin WWpP
- double white (d)	CSWP GBar GPoy NPer SEND SRms
- 'Golden Ball'	ETow
- 'Golden Moss'	NVic
- 'Malmesbury'	CNat
- 'Minety'	CNat
- 'Plenum' (d)	EHrv
§ - 'Rowallane' (d)	CHea EBee EHol ELan GBuc GMac MAvo MBri MRav SUsu WCot
- 'Silver Ball'	LPVe
- 'Sissinghurst White'	see *T. parthenium* 'Rowallane'
- 'White Bonnet' (d)	EChP ERou NBrk WEas
poteriifolium	EBee EBre
ptarmiciflorum 'Silver Feather'	EChP ECha GFlt WJek
vulgare	CAgr CArn CBod CPrp CSev ECtt ELau GPoy IHMH MBow MHar MHer MSal NSco SIde WMoo WWpP WWye
- 'All Gold' **new**	WCAu
- var. *crispum*	CBod CPrp EBee ELau EOHP GBar GPoy MBri MHer SIde SMad WBea WCot WFar WHer WJek WRha WSel
- 'Isla Gold' (v)	CBos CElw EBee EGle EMon EPPr EWes GCal MHar NBid NSti SUsu WBea WBry WCHb WCot WFar WMoo WRha WWpP WWye
- 'Silver Lace' (v)	CElw EBee EMon GBri ITer NBrk NGHP NSti SEND WBVN WBea WCHb WFar WHer WMoo

Tanakaea (Saxifragaceae)

radicans	WCru

tangelo see *Citrus* x *tangelo*

tangerine see *Citrus reticulata*

tangor see *Citrus* x *nobilis* Tangor Group

Tapeinochilos (Costaceae)

ananassae	MOak

Taraxacum (Asteraceae)

albidum	CNat EBee WCot
- DJH 452	CHid
coreanum **new**	CNat
faeroense **new**	WCot
officinale agg. variegated (v) **new**	WCot
rubrifolium	CSpe

Tarchonanthus (Asteraceae)

camphoratus	CTrC

tarragon see *Artemisia dracunculus*

Tasmannia see *Drimys*

Taxodium (Cupressaceae)

§ *distichum* ♀H4	More than 30 suppliers
§ - var. *imbricatum*	CFil CMCN EPfP WPGP

- - 'Nutans' ♀H4	CBcs CEnd CTho EBre ECrN LCon LRHS MAsh MBlu MBri SKee SLim
- 'Minaret' **new**	MBlu
- 'Peve Minaret' **new**	NLar SLim
- 'Peve Yellow' **new**	SLim
- 'Secrest'	CBcs LRHS MBlu MBri SLim
mucronatum	CDoC CFil

Taxus ✿ (*Taxaceae*)

baccata ♀H4	More than 30 suppliers
- 'Adpressa Aurea' (v)	CKen EPla GKir MOne
- 'Adpressa Variegata' (m/v) ♀H4	CDoC EHul LCon MAsh SLim
- 'Aldenham Gold'	CKen
- 'Amersfoort'	CDoC EOrn EPla LCon MDun NLar WBcn
- 'Argentea Minor'	see *T. baccata* 'Dwarf White'
§ - Aurea Group	ENot SRms
I - 'Aurea Pendula'	EBre EOrn
I - 'Aureomarginata' (v)	CBcs CSBt EOrn GKir LEar MAsh SWvt WStI
- 'Autumn Shades'	CBcs
- 'Cavendishii' (f)	ECho
- 'Compacta'	EOrn EPla
- 'Corleys Coppertip'	CKen CSam EHul EOrn GKir LCon MAsh MBar MOne NLar SCoo SLim WEve WFar
- 'Cristata'	CKen
- 'David'	IArd NLar
- 'Dovastoniana' (f) ♀H4	CMac GKir LCon MBar NLar NWea WMou
- 'Dovastonii Aurea' (m/v) ♀H4	CMac EHul EOrn EPfP EPla GKir LBee LCon LPan LRHS MAsh MBar MBlu MBri NLar NWea SCoo SLim WCFE WDin
- 'Drinkstone Gold' (v)	EHul WBcn
§ - 'Dwarf White' (v)	EOrn EPla LCon MAsh SCoo WGor
- 'Elegantissima' (f/v)	ECrN EHul EPfP MTis SPoG WEve WFar
- 'Erecta' (f)	EHul SHBN
§ - 'Fastigiata' (f) ♀H4	More than 30 suppliers
- Fastigiata Aurea Group	CKen CLnd CWib ECrN EHul EPfP IArd LBuc LEar LLin LPan MAsh MGos NBee NBlu NGHP NHol NRar SKee SRms WBrE WFar WHar
- 'Fastigiata Aureomarginata' (m/v) ♀H4	CDoC CKen CMac EBre EHul EOrn EPfP GKir IMGH ISea LAst LBee LCon LEar LPan LRHS MBar MBri MGos MWat NWea SAga SLim SLon SPer SWvt WCFE WDin WEve WOrn
- 'Fastigiata Robusta' (f)	CDoC EBre EPfP EPla GKir LCon LRHS MBar MBri MOne SPoG WEve WFar WGer
- 'Goud Elsje'	CKen EOrn
- 'Green Column'	CKen MBlu
- 'Green Diamond'	CKen WBcn
- 'Hibernica'	see *T. baccata* 'Fastigiata'
- 'Icicle'	CBcs EPla LCon LLin MAsh MGos NLar
- 'Ivory Tower'	CBcs CKen LCon LLin MAsh MGos NLar WFar WGor
- 'Klitzeklein'	CKen
- 'Laurie'	SPoG
- 'Lutea' (f) **new**	ECrN
- 'Melfard'	CDoC EHul
- 'Nutans'	CDoC CKen CNic CSBt EHul EOrn IMGH LCon LLin MBar MOne NDlv SCoo
- 'Overeynderi'	EHul
- 'Pendula'	MRav
- 'Prostrata'	CMac WFar
- 'Pygmaea'	CKen

- 'Repandens' (f) ♀H4	CDoC EHul IArd LCon LPan MBar SHBN WCFE WDin WFar
I - - 'Repens Aurea' (v) ♀H4	CDoC CKen ECrN EHul EOrn EPfP LCon LLin LRHS MAsh MBar MBri MGos NHol WFar
- 'Semperaurea' (m) ♀H4	CBcs CDoC CMac EBre EHul EOrn GKir LBuc LCon LPan LRHS MAsh MBar MGos NBee NHol NWea SLim SPla WCFE WDin WFar
- 'Silver Spire' (v)	CKen MDKP WBcn
- 'Standishii' (f) ♀H4	More than 30 suppliers
- 'Summergold' (v)	CSli EBre EHul ELan ENot EPfP GKir LCon MAsh MBar MGos NBlu NHol SLim WDin WEve WFar WStI
- 'Washingtonii' (v)	IArd MBar SHBN
- 'White Icicle'	EOrn WGor
brevifolia	EPla
cuspidata 'Aurescens' (v)	CKen EPla SRms
- var. *nana*	CNic EHul EOrn LCon MBar MOne
- 'Robusta'	EHul LLin
- 'Straight Hedge'	CDoC EHul IMGH SLim WGor
x *media* 'Brownii'	EHul LBuc
- 'Hicksii' (f) ♀H4	CDul EBre EHul GKir IMGH LBuc LRHS MBar NWea SLim WFar
- 'Hillii'	MBar
- 'Lodi'	LBee
- 'Viridis'	MGos

Tayberry see *Rubus* Tayberry Group

Tecoma (*Bignoniaceae*)

x *alata*	SOWG
capensis ♀H1	CHEx CSev CTCP EBak EShb LRHS SHFr SOWG SYvo
- 'Aurea'	CSev SOWG
- 'Lutea'	LRHS
garrocha	EShb
'Orange Glow'	SOWG
ricasoliana	see *Podranea ricasoliana*
stans	SOWG

Tecomanthe (*Bignoniaceae*)

speciosa	ECou SOWG

Tecomaria see *Tecoma*

Tecophilaea (*Tecophilaeaceae*)

cyanocrocus ♀H2	CAvo CBro EHyt EPot GCrs LAma LRHS SBla SOkd WCom WCot
- 'Leichtlinii' ♀H2	CAvo CBro EHyt LAma LRHS SCnR SSpi
- 'Purpurea'	see *T. cyanocrocus* 'Violacea'
- Storm Cloud Group	GCrs
§ - 'Violacea'	CAvo CBro EHyt GCrs LRHS
violiflora	LAma

Tectaria (*Dryopteridaceae*)

gemmifera	GQui NMar

Telanthophora (*Asteraceae*)

grandifolia	CHEx SAPC SArc

Telekia (*Asteraceae*)

§ *speciosa*	More than 30 suppliers

Telesonix see *Boykinia*

Teline see *Genista*

Tellima (*Saxifragaceae*)

grandiflora	More than 30 suppliers
- 'Delphine' (v)	EMan EPPr SAga SUsu WCot
- 'Forest Frost'	EBee EMan NGdn NLar NSti WCot WGor WMoo WSkp

– Odorata Group	CBre EBee EChP ECha EGoo MRav NBrk NSti SBla WHen WMoo WWpP WWye
– 'Purpurea'	see *T. grandiflora* Rubra Group
– 'Purpurteppich'	EBee EBre ECha EGoo EHrv EMan GAbr GKir LHop LRHS MLwd MRav NGdn SChu WCot WMnd WMoo WTMC
§ – Rubra Group	More than 30 suppliers

Telopea (*Proteaceae*)
oreades	CTrC
speciosissima	CBcs CTrC SOWG SPlb SSpi
truncata	CDoC CFil SSpi WPGP

Templetonia (*Papilionaceae*)
retusa	ECou

Temu see *Blepharocalyx*

Tephroseris (*Asteraceae*)
integrifolia	EBee WHer

Tephrosia (*Papilionaceae*)
grandiflora	GFai
virginiana **new**	SUsu
vogelii **new**	CArn

Ternstroemia (*Theaceae*)
gymnanthera	see *T. japonica*
§ *japonica*	EPfP

Tetracentron (*Tetracentraceae*)
sinense	CFil CMCN EPfP GQui IArd LRHS NLar

Tetradenia (*Lamiaceae*)
riparia	EShb

Tetradium (*Rutaceae*)
§ *daniellii*	CFil CMCN EPfP GKir IArd NLar SSpi WBor WPGP
§ – Hupehense Group	CBcs CMCN CPle EBee GKir MBri SSpi WDin
glabrifolium	CFil EBee
– B&SWJ 3541	WCru
I *velutinum*	CMCN

Tetragonolobus see *Lotus*

Tetraneuris (*Asteraceae*)
brandegeei	WLin
§ *scaposa*	EBre EPot LRHS

Tetrapanax (*Araliaceae*)
B&SWJ 1925	CPLG
§ *papyrifer* ♀H2-3	CHEx NLar SAPC SArc WMul
– B&SWJ 7135	WCru
– 'Empress' **new**	WCru
– 'Rex' **new**	WCru WMul

Tetrapathaea see *Passiflora*

Tetrastigma (*Vitaceae*)
obtectum **new**	ECre
voinierianum ♀H1	ESlt MBri SAPC SArc WCot

Tetratheca (*Tremandraceae*)
ciliata var. *alba*	SOWG
thymifolia	ECou
– pink-flowered	SOWG

Teucridium (*Verbenaceae*)
parvifolium	GEil

Teucrium (*Lamiaceae*)
* *ackermannii*	CLyd EGoo LBee LRHS MBro NMen SBla SMac SUsu WAbe WHoo WPat WTin XPep
arduinoi	XPep
aroanium	CLyd CStu EPot LBee LRHS MWat NMen NWCA SBla SScr WAbe
asiaticum	EGoo XPep
betonicum **new**	WOut
bicolor	CPle IFro
botrys	EGoo MHer MSal
brevifolium **new**	XPep
canadense	MSal
chamaedrys misapplied	see *T.* x *lucidrys*
chamaedrys ambig.	CHal CPom CSam CWib ECrN GAbr GBar IHMH LRHS NJOw NWCA SLim SRms STre SVen WBrk WCAu WGMN WHbs WJek WSel WShp WTin WWeb XPep
chamaedrys L.	EGoo NGHP
– 'Nanum'	CLyd MBro NLAp WPat WWye
I – 'Rose'	WMoo
– 'Rose Carpet'	EChP ECrN EGoo EOrc WCom
– 'Variegatum' (v)	EGoo EMan GBar LLWP WCHb WCom WPer WRha
§ *cossonii*	XPep
§ *creticum*	WLin
divaricatum **new**	XPep
dunense **new**	XPep
flavum	EChP SGar SHFr WCHb WJek WOut WPGP XPep
– subsp. *grandiflorum*	XPep
fruticans	More than 30 suppliers
– 'Azureum' ♀H3	CBcs CBot CHar CM&M CPle CWCL CWSG EBee EChP LRHS MBro SBra SIgm SLim SPer WBod WEas XPep
– 'Collingwood Ingram'	EBee
– 'Compactum'	CDoC EBee EMan ENot EWTr LRHS MCCP SLon SPer SPla WAbe WBcn
– dark	SMrm
gnaphalodes **new**	XPep
hircanicum	More than 30 suppliers
– 'Purple Tails'	CWib WGwG WHHs
laciniatum **new**	XPep
lancifolium **new**	WOut
§ x *lucidrys*	More than 30 suppliers
– 'Pain de Sucre' **new**	EGoo
lucidum	XPep
marum	CArn EOHP MSal NMen SBla SIgm WJek XPep
– 'Feuilles Vertes' **new**	XPep
'Massif Central'	LRHS WWeb
massiliense misapplied	see *T.* x *lucidrys*
massiliense L.	EGoo EMan EOrc WHer XPep
microphyllum **new**	XPep
micropodioides	XPep
montanum	GBar LPVe NJOw SCro XPep
orientale **new**	XPep
polium	CArn CBAn CLyd CPLG MBro MWat NLAp SIgm WJek WPat XPep
– subsp. *aureum*	NWCA SBla XPep
– subsp. *capitatum* **new**	XPep
pyrenaicum	CHal CMea EBee EHyt EMan EPot GCrs GEdr MBro MHer NSla NWCA SBla SIng SScr WPat WWin WWye
rosmarinifolium	see *T. creticum*
rotundifolium	EBee
scordium	CNat
scorodonia	CArn COld CRWN CSev EGoo ELau EWTr GBar GPoy MFOX

	MHer MSal NMir WHHs WHer WJek WLHH WSSM WSel XPep
- 'Binsted Gold'	EBee EGoo EMan EMon EPPr LDai MHar
- 'Crispum'	CHby CRez ELau EMar EOrc GBar GEil MHar MHer MLLN MWat MWgw NBid NBro NJOw SOkh WBod WBrE WCHb WHoo WKif WMoo WPer WSel WTin
* - 'Crispum Aureomarginatum'	EBee EChP
§ - 'Crispum Marginatum' (v)	More than 30 suppliers
- 'Winterdown' (v)	CMea EBee EGoo EMan EPPr LHop MBro NPro SAga WCHb WHHs WHer WHil WHoo WLin
scorodonium 'Pant Gwyn' (v)	CNat
subspinosum	CLyd CMea CStu LBee LRHS MBro NLAp NMen NWCA WHoo WPat XPep
§ *viscidum* 'Lemon and Lime' (v)	EBee ECtt EMan EPPr LHop NSti SDnm WCot WPGP
webbianum	ECho
'Winterdown' **new**	GBri

Thalia (Marantaceae)

dealbata	CDWL CHEx EAmu GCal LPBA MJnS MSta NArg NLar SLon SSpi WDyG WMAq WMul WWpP
geniculata	CDWL WMul

Thalictrum (Ranunculaceae)

from Afghanistan	see *T. isopyroides*
ACE 1141	WCot
CC 3691	ITer
CC 4051	WCot
RCB/Arg P-14	WCot
actaeifolium	EBee
- var. *brevistylum* B&SWJ 8819 **new**	WCru
adiantifolium	see *T. minus* 'Adiantifolium'
alpinum	EBee NRya
angustifolium	see *T. lucidum*
aquilegiifolium	More than 30 suppliers
- var. *album*	More than 30 suppliers
- dwarf	CMea
* - 'Hybridum'	CHad EBlw WFar WMoo WPer
- Purple Cloud	see *T. aquilegiifolium* 'Thundercloud'
- 'Purpureum'	CPom CSev EBee ECGN LPio MBro MDun MTis NLar NPSI SPla WCAu WCru WHoo
- 'Roseum'	WCot
§ - 'Thundercloud' ♀H4	CFir CKno EBee EBre ECtt EPfP GCal GKir LRHS MBri MCLN NLar SWvt WBrE WCra WSpi WWeb
atriplex **new**	EBee
baicalense	EBee
§ *chelidonii*	CBos EBre GKir
- B&SWJ 2520	WCru
clavatum	CDes EBee
contortum	EBee SDys
coreanum	see *T. ichangense*
coriaceum	EBee
cultratum	EChP
- HWJCM 367	EBee NLar SSpi WCru
dasycarpum	EBee EMan MLLN NLar
* *decorum*	CBos CFwr GMac LPhx LPio NCGa NDov WCru WLFP WSHC WShp
§ *delavayi* ♀H4	More than 30 suppliers
- B&SWJ 7748	WCru
- var. *acuminatum* BWJ 7535 **new**	WCru

- - BWJ 7971	WCru
- 'Album'	CFwr CPLG CPlt CPom CSpe CWCL EBee EBre ECha EFou EGle GKir LPhx LPio LRHS MBro MCLN MTis NCGa NDov NLar NOak SPer WHoo WMoo WPrP
- 'Hewitt's Double' (d) ♀H4	More than 30 suppliers
diffusiflorum	CDes GBri GBuc GFlt GKir SBla WSHC
dioicum	EBee
dipterocarpum misapplied	see *T. delavayi*
dipterocarpum Franch. ACE 4.878.280	CMil
elegans **new**	EBee
'Elin'	CElw CFir CSpe EBee EBlw EMan ERou LHop MDKP NBir NCot WCot
fargesii	EBee
fendleri	GBin GBuc
- var. *polycarpum*	NHol
filamentosum	EMon
- B&SWJ 777	WCru
* - var. *tenuifolium* Heronswood	WCot
aff. *finetii* DJHC 473	CDes
flavum	EBee EBre EDAr GBBs GFlt GKir LPhx NBro SSpi SWat WBrE
§ - subsp. *glaucum* ♀H4	More than 30 suppliers
- 'Illuminator'	CBot CHad CHid CPar CSam EBee EGle EPPr GBri GFlt GKir LPio LRHS MOne MRav NHol NPri SMrm SPlb SUsu WCAu WCom WCot WCra WPnP WPrP WWhi
flexuosum	see *T. minus* subsp. *minus*
foetidum	EBee
aff. *foetidum* BWJ 7558 **new**	WCru
foliolosum B&SWJ 2705	WCru
- S&SH 382	GBri
grandiflorum **new**	EBee
§ *ichangense*	EBee GBri GKir SAga
§ *isopyroides*	CFir CPBP CPom CSev EBre EChP ELan EMar EPla EPot EPza GBin GBuc GKir GTou LAst LPio LRHS MRav MTis MWgw NChi NGdn SLon SRot SWal WCot WCru WDyG WTin
javanicum	EBee
- var. *puberulum* B&SWJ 6770 **new**	WCru
kiusianum	CBos CHea CLyd EChP ECha EDAr EGle ESis EWes GAbr GBuc GEdr GFlt GMac LRHS MTho NBir NMen NMyG SRot SWvt WAbe WCom WCot WFar WLin WOVN WWhi
- Kew form	SAga SRot
- white-flowered **new**	CFir
koreanum	see *T. ichangense*
§ *lucidum*	CPou EBee ELan EMan IHMH LPhx MAnH MRav NLar NSti SHar SMHy WCot WPrP
minus	CAgr CBos CMHG EBee EBre ECGP ELan EMan EMon GBuc MLLN NMrw NOak NSti WWye
§ - 'Adiantifolium'	EBee LPio MLLN MRav MWgw NFla NLar NOak SHar SRms WFar WOut WPer
§ - subsp. *minus*	EBee MLLN
§ - subsp. *olympicum*	WPer
- subsp. *saxatile*	see *T. minus* subsp. *olympicum*

- var. **sipellatum**	WCru
B&SWJ 5051	
morisonii	EBee
occidentale JLS 86255	MNrw
omeiense BWJ 8049 **new**	WCru
orientale	EBee EHyt SBla WPat
polygamum	see *T. pubescens*
§ **pubescens**	CBos EBee EBre ECha GBri LPhx
	MSal MTed NDov WPrP
punctatum	CBos MDun WAbe WPnP
- B&SWJ 1272	EMan GBin LPhx WCru
reniforme	CFir GMac LPio
- B&SWJ 2159	EMan
- B&SWJ 2610	EBee WCru
reticulatum new	WCru
rochebruneanum	More than 30 suppliers
rutaefolium	EBee
sachalinense new	GKev
RBS 0279 **new**	
simplex	LPio NHol
- var. **brevipes**	WCru
B&SWJ 4794	
speciosissimum	see *T. flavum* subsp. *glaucum*
sphaerostachyum	CBos CElw GKir IFro LRHS MBri
	SMrm WGer
squarrosum	EBee LPio LRHS MTed NPPs
tuberosum	CBos CDes CElw CMea EHyt GKir
	MLLN NLap SBla SMrm SSpi SUsu
	WCot WPat
- 'Rosie Hardy' **new**	WCot
uchiyamae	EBee EBre EGle GBri GFlt MDKP
	NDov WCot WGMN
venulosum	EBee
virgatum B&SWJ 2964	WCru

Thamnocalamus (Poaceae)

aristatus	EPfP EPla
crassinodus	EPla SDry
- dwarf	EPla
- 'Kew Beauty'	EFul EPfP EPla ERod MBrN MMoz
	MWht SDry WJun WPGP
- 'Lang Tang'	EFul EPla ERod WJun WPGP
- 'Merlyn'	EPla ERod MMoz SDry WJun
	WPGP
falcatus	see *Drepanostachyum*
	falcatum
falconeri	see *Himalayacalamus falconeri*
funghomii	see *Schizostachyum funghomii*
khasianus	see *Drepanostachyum*
	khasianum
maling	see *Yushania maling*
spathaceus hort.	see *Fargesia murielae*
§ **spathiflorus**	CFil EFul EPla SDry WJun
- subsp. **nepalensis**	EPla
§ **tessellatus**	CAbb EFul EPla MMoz SDry WDyG
	WJun

Thamnochortus (Restionaceae)

cinereus	CBig CTrC
insignis	CBig CCtw CTrC WMul WNor
	WPrP
lucens	CAbb
spicigerus	CBig

Thapsia (Apiaceae)

decipiens	see *Melanoselinum decipiens*
garganica	CArn EBee EMan SIgm
maxima	SIgm
villosa	SIgm

Thea see *Camellia*

Thelionema (Phormiaceae)

grande new	CWil

Thelypteris (Thelypteridaceae)

kunthii	WRic
limbosperma	see *Oreopteris limbosperma*
palustris	CPLG CRWN EBee EBlw EFer
	EMon EPza GEdr LEur LPBA MLan
	NHol NVic NWoo SRms WFib
	WRic
phegopteris	see *Phegopteris connectilis*

Themeda (Poaceae)

japonica	CBrm EHoe EPPr GIBF WDyG
triandra	EPza GIBF SMad

Thermopsis (Papilionaceae)

caroliniana	see *T. villosa*
fabacea	see *T. lupinoides*
lanceolata	CHad CPom CTri EBee ECGP
	EChP EMan GBin LSpr MBri MCLN
	MEHN MLLN MMil MTis NBPC
	NCGa NPri NSti SAga SMrm SOkh
	WAul WCAu WFar WHrl WPer
	WWye
§ **lupinoides**	CPne EBee ECGP ECha EHrv
	EWTr GLil LPio MGol NOrc WFar
	WPer
macrophylla 'Agnina'	EWes
new	
mollis	EBee NBid
montana	see *T. rhombifolia* var. *montana*
§ **rhombifolia**	EBee EFou ELan EPfP GGar LHop
var. **montana**	MNrw NOrc NPol NSti SGar SPer
	WAbb WBVN WPer
§ **villosa**	CMea EBee EMan GIBF MLLN
	MRav MSte NDov NLar SBla SDix
	SMHy WCom WCot WPGP

Thevetia (Apocynaceae)

peruviana	LRHS MSal SOWG

Thladiantha (Cucurbitaceae)

dubia	SDix

Thlaspi (Brassicaceae)

alpinum	EPot NJOw
bellidifolium	NBir
biebersteinii	see *Pachyphragma*
	macrophyllum
bulbosum	GEdr GTou
§ **cepaeifolium**	GTou NMen WBri
subsp. **rotundifolium**	
fendleri	MNrw
rotundifolium	see *T. cepaeifolium* subsp.
	rotundifolium

Thrinax (Arecaceae)

radiata	EAmu

Thryptomene (Myrtaceae)

saxicola new	ECou
- 'F.C. Payne'	CBcs

Thuja ✿ (Cupressaceae)

'Extra Gold'	see *T. plicata* 'Irish Gold'
'Gnome' **new**	IBal
§ **koraiensis**	IDee LCon MBar SLim WCwm
occidentalis	EBre LCon LLin MAsh MGos NHol
'Amber Glow'	SLim WEve
- Aurea Group	MBar
- 'Aureospicata'	EHul
- 'Bateman Broom' **new**	CKen
- 'Beaufort' (v)	CKen EHul MBar
- 'Caespitosa'	CFee CKen CNic LLin LRHS NHol
	NLar SPoG WEve WGor

-	'Cristata Aurea'	CKen
-	'Danica' ♀H4	CMac EBre EHul ENot EOrn GKir LCon LLin MAsh MBar NWea SBod SLim SMer SRms WCFE WEve WFar WLow WStI
-	'Dicksonii'	EHul
-	'Douglasii Aurea' (v)	CKen
-	'Ellwangeriana Aurea'	MGos
-	Emerald	see *T. occidentalis* 'Smaragd'
-	'Ericoides'	CDoC CTri EHul LRHS MBar SRms
-	'Europa Gold'	CDoC EHul GKir LBee MAsh MBar MGos NLar SLim
-	'Fastigiata'	MBar
-	'Filiformis'	CKen EBre EPla
-	'Globosa'	CMac MBar SBod WGor
I -	'Globosa Variegata' (v)	CKen MBar WEve
-	'Gold Drop'	CKen
-	'Golden Globe'	CDoC EBre EHul ENot EOrn LLin LPan MBar MGos SBod SCoo SLim SPla WDin
-	'Golden Minaret'	EHul
-	'Hetz Midget'	CKen EBre EHul EOrn IMGH LLin MBar NHol NLar SCoo SLim SMer SPlb SPoG WDin WFar
-	'Holmstrup' ♀H4	CDoC CMac CSBt CSli CWib EBre EHul ENot EOrn GKir LLin LRHS MAsh MBar NBee SLim SRms WCFE WDin WEve WFar WStI WTel
-	'Holmstrup's Yellow'	CKen EBre EGra EHul GKir LCon SCoo WBVN WCFE WEve
-	'Hoveyi'	CMac CTri EGra EHul WEve
-	'Linesville'	CKen
-	'Little Champion'	EHul
-	'Little Gem'	EHul GKir MGos NHol NPro SRms WDin WGor
-	'Lutea Nana' ♀H4	CMac EHul EOrn MBar NDlv WCFE
-	'Malonyana'	WCwm
-	'Marrisen's Sulphur'	CSli EBre EHul EOrn SLim SPla WBcn WEve
-	'Meineke's Zwerg' (v)	CKen NLar
-	'Miky'	CKen WBcn
-	'Ohlendorffii'	CDoC CKen EHul EOrn LLin MBar NHol
-	'Orientalis Semperaurescens'	see *Platycladus orientalis* 'Semperaurea'
I -	'Pumila Sudworth'	NHol
I -	'Pygmaea'	CKen MBar SLon
-	'Pyramidalis Aurea'	EBre ENot WEve
-	'Pyramidalis Compacta'	EBre EHul WGor
-	'Recurva Nana'	EHul MBar NHol
-	'Rheingold' ♀H4	More than 30 suppliers
§ -	'Smaragd' ♀H4	CDoC CDul CSBt CWib EBre ECrN EHul ENot EOrn EPfP GKir LBuc LCon LLin LPan LRHS MAsh MBar MGos NBee NBlu SBod SLim SPer SPla WCFE WEve WFar WOrn WStI
* -	'Smaragd Variegated' (v)	CKen
-	'Southport'	CKen MBri WEve
-	'Spaethii'	EHul EOrn
-	'Spiralis'	EHul IMGH MBar NLar WCFE
§ -	'Stolwijk' (v)	EHul EOrn LLin MBar MGos WBcn
-	'Sunkist'	CKen CMac CSBt CSli CWib EBre ECrN EHul ENot EOrn GKir LPan MAsh MBar MGos NHol SBod SLim SMer SPla WEve WFar
-	'Suzie'	LLin
-	'Teddy'	CFee EBre LCon LLin MAsh NLar SLim WEve WFar
-	'Tiny Tim'	CDoC CMac CNic CSBt CWib EHul ENot ESis IMGH LLin MAsh MBar MGos WEve WGor
-	'Trompenburg'	ECho EHul EOrn MAsh WBcn

-	'Wansdyke Silver' (v)	CMac EHul EOrn MBar SLim
-	'Wareana'	CMac
-	'Wareana Aurea'	see *T. occidentalis* 'Wareana Lutescens'
§ -	'Wareana Lutescens'	CWib EHul EOrn MBar WEve
-	'Woodwardii'	EHul MBar SMer
-	'Yellow Ribbon'	CSBt CSli EBre EHul GKir LCon LRHS MBar SLim SMer SPla WEve
orientalis		see *Platycladus orientalis*
plicata		CDul CTho EHul EPfP GIBF MBar MGos NBlu NWea SLim SPer WDin WMou
-	'Atrovirens' ♀H4	CTri EBre ECrN ENot GKir LBee LBuc LCon LPan LRHS MAsh MBar MBri MGos NBee NBlu SLim SMer SRms WDin WEve WHar
* -	'Atrovirens Aurea'	WBcn WEve
-	'Aurea' ♀H4	EHul LBee LRHS MAsh SLim SRms
-	'Brooks Gold'	CKen
-	'Can-can' (v)	EBre GKir
I -	'Cole's Variety'	CWib MBar SLim
-	'Collyer's Gold'	CBrm EHul MAsh NLar SRms
-	'Copper Kettle'	CBrm CKen CNic CSli EBre ECrN EGra EHul ENot GKir LCon MAsh MBar MBri NDlv NPro SCoo SLim WEve WGor
-	'Cuprea'	CKen EHul MBar
-	'Doone Valley'	CKen CSli EHul EOrn MBar NDlv NHol
-	'Emerald' PBR	WEve
-	'Fastigiata' ♀H4	CMac EBre LRHS WTel
-	'Gelderland'	EBre EHul SCoo SLim WEve WFar
-	'Gracilis Aurea'	ECho EHul WBcn
-	'Grüne Kugel'	CDoC
-	'Hillieri'	MBar
§ -	'Irish Gold' (v) ♀H4	CAbP CDul CMac EPla LCon LLin LRHS NPro SAga WBcn
-	'Rogersii'	CDoC CKen CMac CSli CTri EBre EHul EOrn EPfP GKir LCon LLin LRHS MAsh MBar MGos NBee NHol SRms WFar WTel
-	'Stolwijk's Gold'	see *T. occidentalis* 'Stolwijk'
-	'Stoneham Gold' ♀H4	CDoC CKen CMac EBre EGra EHul EOrn GKir LBee LCon LLin LRHS MAsh MBar MGos SBod SLim SMer SRms WCFE WEve WTel
-	'Sunshine'	CKen EBre
* -	'Windsor Gold'	EHul
-	'Winter Pink' (v)	CKen NLar
-	'Zebrina' (v)	CBcs CBrm CDoC CDul CMac CSBt CSli CWib EBre ECrN EHul ELan EOrn GKir LCon LLin MAsh MBar MGos MWat NBee NWea SLim SPer WCFE WDin WEve WFar WHar WTel
plicata × ***standishii***		WCwm
standishii		WCwm

Thujopsis (*Cupressaceae*)

dolabrata ♀H4		CBcs CTho CTrG ECrN EHul GKir LBee MBar MMHG NDlv NLar NWea SHBN SPer WBrE WDin WFar
-	'Aurea' (v)	CDoC CKen EBre EHul EOrn LCon LLin MBar MGos NLar SCoo SHBN SLim WBcn WEve
-	'Laetevirens'	see *T. dolabrata* 'Nana'
§ -	'Nana'	CDoC CKen CMac EBre EGra EHul EOrn IArd LCon LLin MBar SCoo SLim SRms STre WEve WFar
-	'Variegata' (v)	CDoC CDul CFee EBre EHul EOrn LCon LLin MBar NDlv SCoo SHFr SLim SPoG WDin WEve
koraiensis		see *Thuja koraiensis*

Thunbergia (Acanthaceae)
- *alata* — MBri SHFr SYvo
- - 'African Sunset' **new** — CSpe
- *coccinea* — LRHS MJnS
- *erecta* — CKob ELan ERea ESlt SOWG
- *fragrans* — ERea LRHS
- *grandiflora* ♀H1 — CHll ELan EPfP ERea ESlt MJnS SOWG WMul
- - 'Alba' — CHll WMul
- *gregorii* ♀H1+3 — CHll CSpe ERea LRHS SOWG
- - 'Sun Lady' — CSpe
- 'Lemon Star' **new** — CSpe
- *mysorensis* ♀H1 — ERea SOWG
- *natalensis* — CSpe
- 'Samantha' — CSpe

Thymbra (Lamiaceae)
- *spicata* **new** — XPep

thyme, caraway see *Thymus herba-barona*

thyme, garden see *Thymus vulgaris*

thyme, lemon see *Thymus x citriodorus*

thyme, wild see *Thymus serpyllum*

Thymus ✿ (Lamiaceae)
- from Turkey — EWes LLWP SHDw WWpP
- 'Anderson's Gold' — see *T. pulegioides* 'Bertram Anderson'
- *azoricus* — see *T. caespititius*
- 'Caborn Lilac Gem' — LLWP SHDw
- 'Caborn Purple Haze' **new** — LLWP
- § *caespititius* — CArn CLyd EBre ELau EPot GBar GPoy MHer NLRH NMen NRya SPlb SRot WCHb WPer
- *caespitosus* — GKir LLWP
- *camphoratus* — CArn CBod ELau EOHP EWes GBar LLWP LPhx MHer MWat NGHP SHDw WAbe WHHs WJek XPep
- - 'A Touch of Frost' — SHDw
- - 'Derry' — CSpe LLWP SHDw
- *capitatus* — CArn XPep
- *carnosus* misapplied — see *T. vulgaris* 'Erectus'
- *carnosus* Boiss. — GBar XPep
- 'Carol Ann' (v) — CBod ELau EWes GBar LLWP MBNS WWpP
- *cephalotos* — EHyt WAbe
- *ciliatus* — CArn LLWP WPer XPep
- *cilicicus* Boiss. & Bail. — EHyt ETow EWes GBar NMen SBla WAbe WCHb WJek WWye
- *cilicicus* Goteborg — ITim
- x *citriodorus* — CArn CHby CHrt EBre EDAr ELau GAbr GBar GPoy LGro LLWP MBow MBrN MHer NGHP SWal WBrE WFar WHHs WHen WJek WPer WSSM WShp WWpP WWye XPep
- - 'Archer's Gold' — see *T. pulegioides* 'Archer's Gold'
- - 'Argenteus' (v) — LLWP
- - 'Aureus' — see *T. pulegioides* 'Aureus'
- - 'Bertram Anderson' — see *T. pulegioides* 'Bertram Anderson'
- § - 'Golden King' (v) — CLyd EBre ECha EDAr ELan GBar LHop LLWP LRHS MBar MBri MBro MHer NGHP NSti WCHb WHoo WPer WSel WStI
- § - 'Golden Lemon' (v) — CArn GPoy LLWP WJek WWpP WWye
- - 'Golden Lemon' misapplied — see *T. pulegioides* 'Aureus'

- - 'Golden Queen' (v) — CMea COlW EDAr EOHP EPot ESis GBar LBBr MBow MHer NBlu NPri NSla SHDw SPer SPet SRms WFar WWin WWpP
- - 'Lemon Supreme' — LLWP
- - 'Lime' — LLWP
- - *repandus* — see *Thymus* 'Rosemary's Lemon Carpet'
- - 'Silver King' (v) — LLWP
- - 'Silver Posie' — see *T. vulgaris* 'Silver Posie'
- - 'Silver Queen' (v) ♀H4 — CBcs CLyd CSam EBre ECha EDAr ELan EMlt EOHP ESis GBar GGar GKir IBal LRHS MBar MHer NBlu NGHP NPPs SGar SPlb WCom WFar WShp WStI WWpP
- * - 'Variegatus' (v) — CMea GBar LHop MBri WFar WWin
- - 'Variegatus' misapplied — see *T. x citriodorus* 'Golden King'
- - 'Villa Nova' (v) — LLWP
- 'Coccineus' — see *Thymus* Coccineus Group
- § Coccineus Group ♀H4 — CArn ECha ECtt EDAr ELan ELau EMlt GAbr GKir GTou IHMH LGro LLWP LRHS MBar MBri MBro MHer NCGa NHol SBla SIng SRot WHen WHoo WPat WTel WWin
- § - 'Atropurpureus' misapplied — LLWP SHDw
- - 'Hardstoft Red' (v) — GBar LLWP
- - 'Purple Beauty' — LLWP
- - 'Purpurteppich' — LLWP
- - 'Red Elf' — GBar SHDw WJek
- 'Coccineus Major' — CMea EDAr GKir LRHS MHer SIde WAbe WCom WJek WSSM XPep
- *comosus* — EDAr GBar LLWP MHer SHDw WAbe WEas WPer
- 'Cow Green' **new** — LLWP
- 'Creeping Lemon' — ELau GBar LLWP MHer SHDw WHHs WJek
- 'Creeping Mauve' — LLWP
- 'Creeping Orange' — LLWP
- 'Dartmoor' — GBar GCal LLWP SHDw
- 'Desboro' — GBar LLWP MBNS MHer
- *doerfleri* — CLyd ECha LLWP WSel XPep
- - 'Bressingham' — CArn CMea EBre ECtt EDAr ELau EMlt GBar GKir LBee LGro LLWP LRHS MBro MHer NGHP SBla SIng SPlb SRms SWal WHHs WPat WPer WTel WWpP WWye
- 'Doone Valley' (v) — More than 30 suppliers
- *drucei* — see *T. polytrichus*
- 'E.B.Anderson' — see *T. pulegioides* 'Bertram Anderson'
- 'Eastgrove Pink' — LLWP SHDw
- 'Emma's Pink' — LLWP
- *erectus* — see *T. vulgaris* 'Erectus'
- * *ericoides* — EPot MHer WAbe
- 'Fragrantissimus' — CArn ELau EOHP GBar GPoy GWCH LLWP MHer MWat NGHP NPri SIde SPlb WHHs WHen WJek WPer WWye
- 'Gibson's Cave' **new** — LLWP
- 'Glenridding' **new** — LLWP
- 'Gowbarrow' **new** — LLWP
- * *gratian* **new** — SHDw
- 'Hans Stam' — LLWP
- 'Hardstoft Red' — see *T.* (Coccineus Group) 'Hardstoft Red'
- § 'Hartington Silver' (v) — More than 30 suppliers
- *herba-barona* — CArn CMea CTri ECha EDAr ELau EOHP GBar GPoy LEdu LLWP MBow MHer NFor NGHP NHol NRya SIde SRms STre WHHs WPer WWye XPep
- - 'Bob Flowerdew' — LLWP

	- *citrata*	see *T. herba-barona* 'Lemon-scented'
§	- 'Lemon-scented'	CArn ECha ELau GBar GPoy LLWP MHer MOne SHDw SIde SMHy WCHb
	'Highdown'	ECtt SHDw
	'Highdown Lemon' **new**	SHDw
	'Highdown Red' **new**	SHDw
	'Highland Cream'	see *T.* 'Hartington Silver'
	hirsutus	NBir XPep
	hyemalis	LLWP
	integer	SBla
	'Kurt'	LLWP SHDw
	'Lake District' **new**	LLWP
	lanuginosus hort.	see *T. pseudolanuginosus*
§	'Lavender Sea'	ELau EWes LLWP
	'Lemon Caraway'	see *T. herba-barona* 'Lemon-scented'
*	'Lemon Variegated' (v)	EDAr ELau GBar WHHs
	leucotrichus	MBro WCom WPat XPep
	'Lilac Time'	COkL EWes GBar LLWP MHer SHDw SPlb WCHb WHHs WJek
	longicaulis	CArn CLyd ECha EGoo ELau GBar LLWP MBNS WJek XPep
	'Low Force' **new**	LLWP
	marschallianus	see *T. pannonicus*
	mastichina	CArn GBar SBla SChu WHHs WWye XPep
	- 'Didi'	CArn LLWP MHer
	membranaceus	WAbe
	micans	see *T. caespititius*
	minus	see *Calamintha nepeta*
	montanus Waldst. & Kit.	see *T. pulegioides*
	neiceffii	CArn CLyd ECha ELau GBar LLWP NWCA WWpP XPep
	nummularius misapplied	see *T.* 'Pat Milne'
	odoratissimus	see *T. pallasianus* subsp. *pallasianus*
	'Orange Spice'	LLWP SHDw
	pallasianus	ELau LLWP SHDw
§	- subsp. *pallasianus*	CBod GBar MHer
§	*pannonicus*	LLWP MHer WPer
	parnassicus **new**	XPep
§	'Pat Milne'	ELau LGro
	'Peter Davis'	CArn EDAr GBar LHop LLWP MBNS MBow MHer NBir NCGa NGHP SBla SChu SIde WAbe WJek WLin
§	'Pink Ripple'	CBod CMea ELau EWes GBar LLWP MHer SHDw SMHy WCHb WHoo WJek
§	*polytrichus* misapplied	see *T. praecox*
§	*polytrichus* A. Kern. ex Borbás **new**	XPep
§	- subsp. *britannicus*	EPot GPoy LLWP NSti SHDw SPlb WJek WPer
	- 'Minor'	EPot LLWP WPer
§	- - 'Thomas's White' ♀H4	LLWP MHer
	- - variegated (v)	WLin
	'Porlock'	CMea CSev EDAr ELau ESis ETow GBar GPoy LLWP MHer NGHP NRya SIde SRms STre WHoo WJek WPer WWpP
	praecox	GBar LLWP MHer NLan NSco
	- 'Albiflorus'	WShp
	- subsp. *arcticus*	see *T. polytrichus* subsp. *britannicus*
	'Provence'	LLWP
§	*pseudolanuginosus*	More than 30 suppliers
	- 'Hall's Variety'	ELau GBar
	- 'Mountain Select'	LLWP SHDw
§	*pulegioides*	CArn CBod CHby ELau ESis GBar GPoy LLWP MBow MBri MHer

		NPri NRya SHDw SIde WHHs WJek WPer WWpP WWye
§	- 'Archer's Gold'	More than 30 suppliers
§	- 'Aureus' ♀H4	EBre EDAr EMlt ESis GBar GKir GTou LLWP LRHS MBar MBow MBri MBro NBlu NWCA SBla SPer WFar WHen WHoo
§	- 'Bertram Anderson' ♀H4	More than 30 suppliers
	- 'Foxley' (v)	CBod EHoe ELau LLWP MHer NGHP NPro NTHB SHDw SPlb WCHb WJek WWpP
	- 'Golden Dwarf'	LLWP
§	- 'Goldentime'	GBar GKir LGro LLWP LRHS NGHP WJek WSel
	- 'Sir John Lawes'	LLWP SHDw
	- 'Tabor'	NTHB SHDw WJek
	- variegated	GBar
	'Redstart'	CBod CLyd ECha ELau EOHP EPot GBar LBee LLWP LRHS SHDw WCHb
	richardii subsp. *nitidus*	STre WWye
	- 'Compactus Albus'	see *T. vulgaris* 'Snow White'
	'Rosalicht'	LLWP
	'Rosedrift'	LLWP SHDw
	'Rosemary's Lemon Carpet'	LLWP
	rotundifolius	ELau LLWP MHer SHDw XPep
§	'Ruby Glow'	EBre ELau EWes LLWP MHer MRav SHDw WJek
	serpyllum ambig.	CArn ELau GKir LLWP MBri NBlu SIde SIng SPet SPlb SRms WJek WPer WWpP
	serpyllum L.	WBVN XPep
	- var. *albus*	ECha ELau GKir GPoy GTou LLWP MBow MBro SBla SChu SIde SPer SRms WHHs WHoo WWye XPep
	- 'Albus Variegatus'	see *T.* 'Hartington Silver'
N	- 'Annie Hall'	CMea EDAr ELau EPot GAbr GBar LGro LLWP LRHS MBow MHer NFor NGHP SIde SIng WHHs WPer WWye
	- 'Atropurpureus'	see *T.* (Coccineus Group) 'Atropurpureus'
	- 'Barwinnock Snowdrift' (v)	GBar
	- *coccineus* 'Major'	see *T.* 'Coccineus Major'
N	- - 'Minor'	CHby EBre EDAr ELau GKir GTou SGar SRms WHHs
	- 'Conwy Rose'	WAbe
N	- 'East Lodge'	LLWP WWpP
	- 'Elfin'	CArn CLyd EDAr EPot EWes GTou LBee LRHS MBri MBro MHer NLAp SBla SHDw SPlb WAbe WBea XPep
	- 'Flossy'	LLWP
N	- 'Fulney Red'	EWes LLWP
	- 'Goldstream' (v)	CLyd CMea ELau ESis GBar IHMH LHop LLWP LRHS MBar MBri MHer NGHP NRya NSti SPlb SRms WCHb WHHs WPer
	- subsp. *lanuginosus*	see *T. pseudolanuginosus*
	- 'Lavender Sea'	see *T.* 'Lavender Sea'
	- 'Lemon Curd'	CBod CBrm ELau EOHP GBar LLWP MHer NGHP NSti SHDw SIde SPlb WCHb WJek WRHF WRha WSel WWye XPep
I	- 'Minimus'	More than 30 suppliers
	- 'Minor'	CArn ECtt GBar GWCH MBro NHol NMen NSla SBla SHDw WAbe WCom WLin WTin WWin XPep
N	- 'Minor Albus'	GBar
	- 'Minus'	see *T. serpyllum* 'Minor'
	- 'Petite'	EWes LLWP

N	- 'Pink Chintz' ♀H4	More than 30 suppliers
	- 'Pink Ripple'	see *T.* 'Pink Ripple'
	- subsp. *pulchellus*	LLWP
	- 'Purple Beauty'	see *Thymus* (Coccineus Group) 'Purple Beauty'
	- 'Purpurteppich'	see *Thymus* (Coccineus Group) 'Purpurteppich'
	- 'Pygmaeus' **new**	LLWP
	- 'Rainbow Falls' (v)	CBod GBar LLWP MBow MHer NFla NGHP NHol SHDw WBry WHHs
	- 'Red Elf'	see *Thymus* (Coccineus Group) 'Red Elf'
	- 'Roger's Snowdrift' **new**	LLWP
N	- 'Roseus'	EOHP GBar SIde
	- 'Ruby Glow'	see *T.* 'Ruby Glow'
N	- 'Russetings'	CBrm CLyd COkL ECtt EDAr ELau EPot GBar GGar LLWP MBar MHer NHol NMen SIde SIng SRms WWin WWpP WWye
N	- 'September'	LLWP MHer
N	- 'Snowdrift'	CArn CMea ECtt EDAr ELau EPot GBar LEdu MBar MBro MHer NHol NRya NSti SIde SPlb WJek WPat WPer WWpP
N	- 'Splendens'	LLWP WShp
	- 'Variegatus'	see *T.* 'Hartington Silver'
	- 'Vey'	EWes GBar LLWP MHer SHDw WCHb
	sibthorpii	CArn
N	'Silver Posie'	see *T. vulgaris* 'Silver Posie'
	'Snowdonia Imperial Beauty' **new**	LLWP
	'Snowdonia Lass' **new**	LLWP
	'Snowdonia Pink Gem' **new**	LLWP
	'Snowdonia Rosie' **new**	LLWP
	'Snowdonia Rowena' **new**	LLWP
	'Swaledale' **new**	LLWP
*	*taeniensis*	CArn
*	*valesiacus*	LLWP SHDw
	vulgaris	CArn CHby CSam CSev ECha EDAr ELau GPoy LLWP MBar MBow MBri MHer NBlu NGHP NVic SDix SPer SPlb SWal WHHs WJek WPer XPep
	- *albus*	GBar LLWP WHen
	- 'Aureus' hort.	see *T. pulegioides* 'Goldentime'
*	- 'Boule' **new**	XPep
*	- 'Compactus'	IBal LLWP
	- 'Diamantis'	LLWP
	- 'Dorcas White'	LLWP MHer WPer
	- 'English Winter'	GBar
§	- 'Erectus'	CArn CLyd CStu ETow GBar LLWP MHer WEas WPer WWye
	- French	ELau LLWP MHer SHDw SPlb
	- 'French Summer'	SIde
	- 'Golden Pins'	CArn GBar
	- 'Haute Vallée de l'Aude' **new**	XPep
	- 'Lemon Queen'	ELau
	- 'Lucy'	CPrp EOHP GBar LLWP
	- 'Pinewood'	GPoy LLWP MHer SMHy
	- pink	LLWP
	- 'Saint Chinian Blanc' **new**	XPep
	- 'Saint Chinian Rose' **new**	XPep
§	- 'Silver Posie'	More than 30 suppliers
§	- 'Snow White'	ELau EWes LLWP SHDw SWal WJek
	'Widecombe' (v)	LLWP SHDw
	zygis	CArn XPep

Tiarella (Saxifragaceae)

'Black Ruby'	CHid
'Black Snowflake'	CBAn EBee SHar
'Black Velvet' PBR	EBee MLLN NCGa SPer SRot WShp
collina	see *T. wherryi*
cordifolia ♀H4	More than 30 suppliers
- 'Eco Red Heart'	SSpi
- 'Glossy'	EBee GBuc GKir SSpi WPGP
- 'Oakleaf'	CLAP EBee EChP EMan EWTr GCal IBal MLan NBro NSti SOkh WCAu WPnP
- 'Rosalie'	see x *Heucherella alba* 'Rosalie'
- 'Running Tapestry'	CLAP WMoo WPnP
- 'Slick Rock'	EBee ECha EPPr
'Cygnet' PBR	CLAP EBee EMan LAst MLLN NCGa SHar SPer SRot WFar WMoo WShp
'Dark Star'	ECtt EFou
'Dunvegan'	EBee MLLN WMoo WShp
'Elizabeth Oliver'	CDes CLAP WPrP
'Freckles'	MRav
'Heronswood Mist' (v)	CBct CHar EBee EChP GBri MBNS NBPC NBro NCGa NPPs NSti STes SWvt WBea WCot WCra WShp
'Inkblot'	CBAn EBee EChP MLLN NBro SHar SMac SYvo WCAu WFar WMoo WPnP
'Iron Butterfly' PBR	CBAn CBct CBri CCol CDes CHar CHea CLAP EBee ECGP EFou EMan EMar EPPr EPfP GBin MLLN MRav MSte NBro NCGa NPPs SHar SPer SRot WFar WMoo WPGP WShp
'Jeepers Creepers'	MAvo MHar SHar
*	'Laciniate Runner'	CLAP
'Martha Oliver'	CLAP CRez EBee GBuc WHal WPGP WPrP WTin
'Martha Roderick'	CMea
'Mint Chocolate'	More than 30 suppliers
'Neon Lights'	CHar EBee MBnl NBro NCGa NGdn SHar SWvt WShp
§	'Ninja'	More than 30 suppliers
'Petite Pink Bouquet'	NGdn
'Pink Bouquet'	CLAP EBee EChP ECtt EHrv EMan LRHS MBNS MBnl MLLN MSph SOkh SPla WCot WFar WGMN WMoo
'Pink Skyrocket'	SHar
'Pinwheel'	EBee EBre ECha LRHS MRav WTMC
polyphylla	ELan EPar GAbr GBBs GBin LGro MLLN MRav MWrn SBri SMac SWal WBea WCru WFar WMoo WPnP
- 'Filigran'	MWrn NLar
- 'Moorgrün'	GCal WFar
- pink	CLAP EHrv EPar
'Skeleton Key'	CLAP LRHS WCot
'Skid's Variegated' (v)	CBct EBee EChP ECtt EMan EPPr LAst MBNS MSph NBPC NPro SWvt WCot WMoo WShp
'Spring Symphony' PBR	CHar CLAP CWCL EBee EBre GBin MBri NBir NCGa NLar NMyG NPPs SHar WFar WMoo WSpi
'Starfish'	EBee MLLN NPPs SHar WShp
'Tiger Stripe'	CLAP COtt EBee ECha EMan ENot EPfP LRHS MRav MWrn NBro SPer WFar WMoo WPnP WShp WSpi
trifoliata	ELan MRav SBla WFar
unifoliata	CMCo MSal
'Viking Ship' PBR	see x *Heucherella* 'Viking Ship'
§	*wherryi* ♀H4	More than 30 suppliers
- 'Bronze Beauty'	CLAP CMea COtt EChP EMar EPar GBuc LAst MAvo MRav NDov

	NHol NPPs NPro SAga SMHy SPla
	SSpi SWat WAbe WBrk WCot WFar
	WMoo WPGP WShp WSpi WWhi
- 'Green Velvet'	ECha
- 'Montrose'	CLAP EBee WPGP
- 'Skid's Variegated'	see *T.* 'Skid's Variegated'

Tibouchina (Melastomataceae)

graveolens	ERea
'Jules'	CBcs ESlt SOWG
organensis	CBcs CKno ERea GQui
paratropica	CPle CRHN SSpi
semidecandra hort.	see *T. urvilleana*
§ **urvilleana** ♀H1	CBcs CDoC CHEx CKno CRHN
	CSpe CTbh EBak EBee ECre ELan
	ERea ESlt ISea LPan LRHS MTis
	SAPC SArc SDnm SLon SOWG SPer
	SRms SYvo WCot WMul
- 'Edwardsii'	CSev EMan MLan NPSI SUsu
- 'Rich Blue Sun' **new**	CSpe
- variegated (v)	WCot

Tigridia ✿ (Iridaceae)

hybrids	SDeJ
lutea	SDeJ
multiflora	CFir
pavonia	CMdw CPLG CSpe EDif EMui ERea
	IGor LAma MBri NRog SPet
- 'Aurea'	CFwr EBee
- 'Lilacea'	EBee
- 'Speciosa'	CFwr EBee

Tilia ✿ (Tiliaceae)

americana	CDul CLnd CMCN EBee ENot NWea
- 'Dentata'	CDul
- 'Nova'	CDoC CTho SBLw
- 'Redmond'	CTho
amurensis	CMCN GIBF WMou
argentea	see *T. tomentosa*
begoniifolia	see *T. dasystyla*
'Blue Star'	ENot
'Chelsea Sentinel'	CDul
chenmoui	MBlu WMou
chinensis	CMCN
chingiana	CDul CMCN GKir LRHS MBlu SBir
	SKee
cordata ♀H4	CCVT CDul CLnd CSBt EBee ECrN
	ELan ENot EPfP GKir IMGH LBuc
	LPan MSwo NBee NWea SBLw
	SHBN SKee SPer WDin WMou WStI
§ - 'Böhlje'	CDul ECrN SBLw SLPl WMoo
- 'Dainty Leaf'	CDul
- 'Erecta'	see *T. cordata* 'Böhlje'
- 'Greenspire' ♀H4	CDoC CDul CLnd CTho CWib
	EBee ECrN ENot LPan LRHS NBee
	SBLw
- 'Lico'	WMou
- 'Morden'	WMou
- 'Plymtree Gold'	CEnd
- 'Swedish Upright'	CDul CLnd CTho
- 'Winter Orange'	CDul CEnd CRez LRHS MBlu SBir
	SKee WMou
§ **dasystyla**	CLnd CMCN
x **euchlora** ♀H4	CCVT CDul CLnd CMCN EBee
	ECrN ENot EPfP GKir LPan MBri
	MGos MWat NBee NWea SBLw
	SPer SSta WDin WFar WMou WOrn
x **europaea**	CDul CLnd CRWN ECrN ELan
	NWea SBLw WMou
- 'Pallida'	CDul CLnd CTho EBee SBLw SKee
	WMou
- 'Wratislaviensis' ♀H4	CDoC CDul CLnd CTho EPfP
	LRHS MAsh MBlu MBri NWea SKee
	SMad WMou

x **flavescens**	CDul SBLw
'Glenleven'	
'Hanwell'	ENot
henryana	CDoC CDul CEnd CMCN CTho
	CWib EBee EPfP ERod GKir IArd
	LRHS MBlu SBir SMad WDin
	WMou WPGP
- var. **subglabra**	WMou
§ **heterophylla**	CMCN CTho LRHS
- var. **michauxii**	CLnd
insularis	CMCN MBlu WMou
japonica	CDul CMCN WMou
kiusiana	CMCN GKir WMou
mandshurica	CMCN
maximowicziana	CDul SSta WPGP
mexicana	WMou
miqueliana	CMCN WMou
'Moltkei'	CLnd CMCN WPGP
mongolica	CDoC CLnd CMCN CTho EBee
	ENot EPfP GKir SMHT WMou
monticola	see *T. heterophylla*
oliveri	CDul CMCN GKir MBlu NWea SBir
	SKee WMou WPGP
'Palace Garden'	ENot
paucicostata	CMCN
'Petiolaris' ♀H4	CCVT CDoC CDul CEnd
	CLnd CMCN EBee ELan ENot EPfP
	GKir LRHS MBri MSwo NWea
	SBLw SHBN SKee SPer SSta WDin
	WMou
platyphyllos	CCVT CDoC CDul CLnd CMCN
	CSBt ECrN ENot EPfP GKir LBuc
	NBee NWea SBLw SCoo SKee SPer
	WDin WMou
- 'Aurea'	CDul CTho ECrN MBlu WMou
- 'Corallina'	see *T. platyphyllos* 'Rubra'
- 'Dakvorm' **new**	SBLw
- 'Delft'	SBLw
- 'Erecta'	see *T. platyphyllos* 'Fastigiata'
§ - 'Fastigiata'	CDul CTho EBee ECrN ENot SBLw
	SLPl
- 'Laciniata'	CDul CEnd CMCN CTho GKir
	WMou
- 'Orebro'	SLPl
* - 'Pendula'	CTho
§ - 'Rubra' ♀H4	CDoC CDul CLnd CTho EBee
	ECrN ENot EPfP GKir LBuc LRHS
	MBri MGos NWea SBLw SLPl WDin
	WFar WMou
- 'Tortuosa'	CDoC CTho WMou
§ **tomentosa**	CDul CLnd CMCN CTho ECrN
	ELan ENot GKir IMGH NWea
	SBLw SEND WDin WMou
- 'Brabant' ♀H4	CDoC CDul EBee ENot EPfP LPan
	SBLw
tuan	CMCN WMou
x **vulgaris**	see *T.* x *europaea*

Tillaea see *Crassula*

Tillandsia (Bromeliaceae)

aeranthos new	SChr
argentea ♀H1 **new**	MBri
cyanea ♀H1	LRHS MBri SMur
usneoides	CHal SHmp

Tipularia (Orchidaceae)

discolor	CDes

Tithonia (Asteraceae)

rotundifolia 'Torch'	SMrm

Tofieldia (Melanthiaceae)

pusilla	ERos

Tolmiea (Saxifragaceae)

menziesii	ECha LGro MBNS MBri MWgw NHol SPer WBrE WHrl WMoo WWpP
- 'Goldsplash'	see *T. menziesii* 'Taff's Gold'
- 'Maculata'	see *T. menziesii* 'Taff's Gold'
§ - 'Taff's Gold' (v) ♀H4	CRow EBee ECha EHoe EMar EOHP EPat EPar GAbr IHMH MBri MHer NBid NGdn NMRc NSti NVic SIng SPlb WBea WEas WGMN WHoo WMoo WTin WWpP WWye
- 'Variegata'	see *T. menziesii* 'Taff's Gold'

Tonestus (Asteraceae)

§ **lyallii**	NLAp WPer WWin
§ **pygmaeus**	NLAp WPat

Toona (Meliaceae)

§ **sinensis**	CMCN CPle CTho CWib EPfP EPla EWTr IDee WBVN WMul WPGP
- 'Flamingo' (v)	CBcs LRHS

Torenia (Scrophulariaceae)

concolor var.	MOak WCru
formosana B&SWJ 124	
Pink Moon = 'Dantopkmn'	LAst
'Purple Moon' **new**	LAst
Summer Wave Blue	WCot
= 'Sunrenilabu'	
* Summer Wave Series	SCoo

Torreya (Taxaceae)

californica new	CDul
grandis	EGFP

Townsendia (Asteraceae)

alpigena var. **alpigena**	CGra EHyt WLin
condensata	CPBP NSla
exscapa	EHyt
florifera	EMan EMlt
formosa	CBAn NBir
hookeri	CGra CPBP EHyt
incana	CGra CPBP CStu EHyt
jonesii	EHyt
leptotes	CGra
montana	see *T. alpigena* var. *alpigena*
nuttallii	CGra
§ **rothrockii**	CGra CPBP NMen
spathulata	CGra CPBP
wilcoxiana hort.	see *T. rothrockii*

Toxicodendron (Anacardiaceae)

vernicifluum	see *Rhus verniciflua*

Trachelium (Campanulaceae)

§ **asperuloides**	EHyt WAbe
caeruleum ♀H1	ERea SGar WBrE
- 'Purple Umbrella'	CPLG EMan
- 'White Umbrella'	EMan
jacquinii	MBro NWCA WPat
subsp. **rumelianum**	

Trachelospermum ✿ (Apocynaceae)

§ **asiaticum** ♀H2-3	More than 30 suppliers
- B&SWJ 4814	WCru
* - 'Aureum'	ERea LRHS
- 'Golden Memories'	EPfP SMur SSpi
- 'Goshiki' (v)	ERea GQui MGos SSpi
- var. **intermedium**	CFil WPGP
- B&SWJ 8733	WCru
- 'Nagaba' (v)	SSpi
- 'Theta'	SSpi
from Nanking, China	SLon

jasminoides ♀H2-3	More than 30 suppliers
- B&SWJ 5117	WCru
§ - 'Japonicum'	CRHN CSPN GCal IArd LRHS SBra SLPl SLon SPla SSpi
- 'Major'	CSPN CTrG SSpi WBcn
* - 'Oblanceolatum'	GCal
- 'Tricolor' (v)	CRHN GCal IArd SSpi SSta SWvt
- 'Variegatum' (v) ♀H2-3	More than 30 suppliers
- 'Waterwheel'	WBcn WSHC
- 'Wilsonii'	EPfP EShb GCal SWvt WBcn XPep
- - W 776	CMac CRHN CSPN CSam EBee EBre ELan EMil EPla GCal LRHS MCCP SAPC SArc SLim SPer SSpi SSta WCru WHar WPGP
majus misapplied	see *T. jasminoides* 'Japonicum'
majus Nakai	see *T. asiaticum*

Trachycarpus (Arecaceae)

§ **fortunei** ♀H3-4	More than 30 suppliers
- 'Nanus'	MGos
latisectus	CBrP EAmu LPJP LPal NPal WMul
martianus	CTrC EAmu LPJP LPal SChr WMul
nanus	LPal
takil	CBrP CKob CTrC EAmu ITer LPJP LPal NPal WMul
wagnerianus	CBrP CPHo EAmu EPla LPJP LPal MFan NPal SDry WMul WPGP

Trachystemon (Boraginaceae)

orientalis	CBre CBri CHEx CHid CPLG CSev EBee ECha EGol ELan EPar EPfP MFir MHar MRav NBid SDnm SLon WCAu WCot WCru WDyG WFar WHer WMoo WPnP WWin WWye

Tradescantia ✿ (Commelinaceae)

albiflora	see *T. fluminensis*
x **andersoniana**	see *T. Andersoniana Group*
W. Ludwig & Rohw. nom. inval.	
§ Andersoniana Group	IHMH MSal NFor NJOw SPet WEas WPer WWeb WWin WWpP
- 'Baby Doll'	EGle GKir
- 'Bilberry Ice'	More than 30 suppliers
- 'Blanca'	MWrn NChi
- 'Blue and Gold'	CBct EBre EHoe EPPr EPfP EPla GBuc LAst LHop LRHS MBNS MMHG NPri NPro NSti SPla STes SWvt WCAu WCra WMnd WWin
- 'Blue Stone'	CMea ECha ERou LPVe MBNS NPri SOkh SRms WFar WMoo WTin
- 'Bridal Veil'	CHll
- 'Caerulea Plena'	see *T. virginiana* 'Caerulea Plena'
- Carmine Glow	see *T.* (Andersoniana Group) 'Karminglut'
- 'Charlotte'	CStr EBee EChP ECha EGle LRHS MHar MOne NBro NGdn SChu WCAu WLow WMnd WShp WTMC
- 'Concord Grape'	More than 30 suppliers
- 'Croftway Blue'	SCro
- 'Danielle'	CRez EBee EChP EGle EPfP NGdn WTMC
- 'David's Blaby Blue'	MTed
- 'Domaine de Courson'	EBee LPio
- 'Gisela'	EFou
- 'In the Navy'	EBee EOMN ERou WCot
- 'Innocence'	More than 30 suppliers
- 'Iris Prichard'	CM&M CPrp EBee EChP ELan EPar EPfP EPla ERou LHop LRHS NCGa NLar SCro WFar
- 'Isis' ♀H4	CBcs CHar CMHG CPrp CSBt EChP ECtt EFou ELan EPar EPfP EPla GKir LRHS MRav MWgw NBir

	NCGa NGdn NOrc SBod SChu
	SPer SPla SWvt WMnd WTin WWin
§ – 'J.C. Weguelin' ♀H4	EBee EGle EMil EPfP GKir LRHS
	NBir NDlv SRms WMnd WShp
§ – 'Karminglut'	CHar EBee EBre EGle ELan EMan
	EPar EPfP ERou GKir IHMH MBri
	MNrw NBir NGdn NOrc NVic SVil
	WHoo WShp WWye
– 'Leonora'	COIW EBee ENot EPfP ERou LRHS
	NLar WShp
– 'Little Doll'	CElw EBee EBre ECtt EGle EMan
	ERou EWTr GBri GKir GMac LAst
	LRHS MBri MDKP MHar MLLN
	MSph MTed NBPC NBro NPri
	SOkh SVil WCot WFar WHil WTMC
	WWhi
– 'Little White Doll'	CM&M CPrp CSpe CStr EBee ERou
	GMac LAst MDKP MSph MSte
	NBPC SOkh SWvt WCot WLin
	WShp
– 'Mac's Double' (d) **new**	EBee
– 'Mariella'	EBee EGle SVil
– 'Mrs Loewer'	EMon
– 'Osprey' ♀H4	More than 30 suppliers
– 'Pauline'	CHar EBee EBre ECtt EFou EMan
	EPla ERou GKir LAst LRHS MCLN
	MNrw MRav NBir NCGa NHol
	NLar SChu SMer SWvt WFar WHoo
	WTel WTin WWin
– 'Purewell Giant'	CSBt EBee ECot EMil ERou LHop
	NBro NCGa NDlv NLar SChu SPer
	SWvt WGor WKif WMnd
– 'Purple Dome'	CHar EBee EBre ECtt EFou EPla
	GKir LAst LRHS MHar MRav
	MWgw NBir NBro NCGa NGdn
	SMac SPla STes WMnd WTin WWye
– 'Red Grape'	EBee EBre ECtt EFou EOMN ERou
	GKir LRHS MAvo MBNS MDKP
	NPro NSti SUsu WBor WCAu
– 'Rubra'	CPrp CSBt EBee EChP EPfP ERou
	LPVe MOne MWgw NDlv NOrc
	NPri SBod SChu SCro SRms WBar
	WMoo WShp
– 'Satin Doll' **new**	SPoG
– 'Sweet Kate'	EBre ERou MCCP MSph NBro SAga
	WBor
– 'Sylvana'	CM&M CRez EBee EGle SOkh SVil
	WCAu WHil
– 'Valour'	CWat EBee LRHS WFar
– 'Zwanenburg Blue'	CM&M CRez EBre EChP ECha
	EFou EMan EPyc ERou GKir LRHS
	MWgw NCGa SPlb WCom WLow
	WMnd WShp WTel
'Angel Eyes' **new**	MDKP
'Baerbel'	CSBt SBod
bracteata	ETow
brevicaulis	EBee ECha EFou EGra EMFP EPar
	EPla ERos GBuc LRHS MTho NBro
	NMen
'Bridesmaid'	MOak
canaliculata	see *T. ohiensis*
cerinthoides	CHal
fluminensis	SChr
– 'Albovittata' **new**	CHal
– 'Aurea' ♀H1	CHal MBri
– 'Laekenensis' (v)	CHal MBri
– 'Maiden's Blush' (v)	CHal CSpe MOak SGar SRms SVen
	WFoF
– 'Quicksilver' (v) ♀H1	CHal MBri
– 'Tricolor Minima' ♀H1	CHal
multiflora	see *Tripogandra multiflora*
navicularis	see *Callisia navicularis*
occidentalis	EBee
§ *ohiensis*	CFee EBee EMan LPBA

§ *pallida* ♀H2-3	CHal IBlr
§ – 'Purpurea' ♀H2-3	EShb MOak SVen
pendula	see *T. zebrina*
'Pink Chablis' **new**	ERou
'Purple Sabre'	LAst
purpurea	see *T. pallida* 'Purpurea'
sillamontana ♀H1	CHal EOas MBri
spathacea 'Vittata' ♀H1	CHal
'Tracey'	CM&M
tricolor	see *T. zebrina*
virginiana	CM&M EFWa MWhi
– 'Alba'	EWTr GCal WPer
§ – 'Caerulea Plena' (d)	CM&M CMHG EBee EChP EFou
	ELan EMan EPla ERou LRHS MRav
	NCGa NChi NLRH SChu SRms WFar
– 'Rubra'	CM&M LAst SPet SPlb
§ *zebrina* ♀H1	CHal SChr
– *discolor*	CHal
– *pendula*	see *T. zebrina*
– 'Purpusii' ♀H1	CHal SRms
– 'Quadricolor' (v) ♀H1	CHal

Tragopogon (Asteraceae)

crocifolius	CSpe EMan WCot WGMN
porrifolius	ILis SECG
pratensis	CArn NMir

Trapa (Trapaceae)

natans	NArg WFar

Trautvetteria (Ranunculaceae)

carolinensis	CTCP EBee WCru
var. *japonica*	
– var. *occidentalis*	GKir WCru

Trevesia (Araliaceae)

palmata	CKob WMul

Trichopetalum (Anthericaceae)

§ *plumosum*	CBro

Tricuspidaria see *Crinodendron*

Tricyrtis ✿ (Convallariaceae)

CC 3454	WCot
'Adbane'	CBct CLAP EBla ELan EMan EWes
	GBuc GKir LRHS MMHG NLar
	WCot WFar WRha WViv
affinis	CLAP GAbr GBuc GGar
– B&SWJ 2804	WCru
– B&SWJ 5847	WCru
– 'Variegata'	see *T.* 'Variegata' (*affinis* hybrid)
'Amanagowa'	CLAP WFar
bakeri	see *T. latifolia*
dilatata	see *T. macropoda*
'Eco Gold Spangles'	SSpi
'Empress' **new**	EBee EWes MAvo MCCP
flava	WCru
formosana ♀H4	More than 30 suppliers
– B&SWJ 306	CBct CLAP EBla WCot WCru WFar
	WRos
– B&SWJ 355	CBct LEur WCru WFar
– B&SWJ 3635	WFar
– B&SWJ 3712	WCru WFar
– B&SWJ 6705	CLAP WCru WPrP
– B&SWJ 6741	WCru
– dark	GAbr GBBs GKir LEur WFar
– 'Dark Beauty'	CDes CLAP EBee EHrv EMan GFlt
	GSki LEur LRHS MBnl MBri MCCP
	SUsu WFar WGMN WPrP
– 'Gilt Edge' (v) **new**	CFwr EBee EChP EPfP LAst MAvo
	MBNS MBnl MCCP NBro NMyG
– 'Lodge Farm'	EBla
– pale	GBBs LRHS WFar

- 'Purple Beauty' — CBct CFwr MDKP
- 'Samurai' (v) — CLAP CMil EBee EMan EPPr LEur WCot
- 'Seiryu' — LEur
- 'Shelley's' — CBct CLAP ETow GCal LEur NBro WPrP
- 'Small Wonder' **new** — WCru
§ - Stolonifera Group — CAvo CBcs CBro CM&M CMHG EBee EBlw EBre EHrv ELan EMan EMar EPfP LEdu LEur LHop LRHS MRav MTis MWgw NGdn NHol NSti SDix WCom WFar WMnd WPnP WWeb WWin
- 'Variegata' (v) — CBct CLAP EBee EBla GBBs LEur MLLN NBir WCru WFar
'Harlequin' — LEur NLar WFar
§ *hirta* — More than 30 suppliers
- B&SWJ 2827 — WCru
§ - 'Alba' — CSam EHrv GEdr WFar WWin
* - 'Albomarginata' (v) — CPrp CRez EBee EBlw EChP EMar EPPr EPfP LBuc LEur MCCP NCGa NHol SLon SSpi SWvt WCAu WMnd WPGP
- 'Golden Gleam' — CBct CHea EBla WCot WFar
- hybrids — CM&M WFar
- 'Kinkazan' — EBlw LEur WFar
- 'Makinoi Gold' — LEur WFar
- var. *masamunei* — WCru
- 'Matsukaze' — CLAP CPom WFar
- 'Miyazaki' — CBct CFir CHea CHid CLAP CPom EBee EFou EGle ELan EMan EPar GBuc LEur LRHS MHer MNrw NCGa NLar SMac SMad SMrm WBea WCot WFar
* - 'Nana' — WFar
- 'Silver Blue' — WFar
- 'Taiwan Atrianne' — CSam MBri
- 'Variegata' (v) — CLAP CPlt EBlw EFou EMan EWes GBuc LEur LHop SBla SMad SUsu WCot WCru WFar WPnP WPrP
- 'White Flame' (v) — WCot
N Hototogisu — More than 30 suppliers
ishiiana — CDes CLAP EBee EBla LEur WCru WFar WPGP
- var. *surugensis* — EBla LEur WCru WFar
'Ivory Queen' — WFar
japonica — see *T. hirta*
'Kohaku' — CBct CDes CLAP CPom EBla ELan LEur NPro WCot WCru WFar WPGP
lasiocarpa — CBct CLAP
- B&SWJ 3635 — CLAP EBla WCru WFar
- B&SWJ 7013 — WCru WPrP
§ *latifolia* — CBct EBlw EBre EChP ELan EMar EPPr EPot GAbr GBBs GEdr GFlt GGar LEur MNrw NGdn NLar WAul WCot WCru WFar WPnP WViv WWin
'Lemon Lime' (v) — CBct CBro CLAP EBla EMan LRHS MLLN MSph NPro SBla SUsu WFar
'Lightning Strike' (v) **new** — EBee WCot
'Lilac Towers' — CBct EBre EPar GBBs GKir WCru WFar WPnP
macrantha — GBBs GGar WWin
§ - subsp. *macranthopsis* — CBct CLAP EBla GEdr LEur SSpi WCot WCru WFar
macranthopsis — see *T. macrantha* subsp. *macranthopsis*
* *macrocarpa* — EChP GAbr WFar
N *macropoda* — CBct CFwr CHid CSam EBee EBla EDAr ELan EMan EPar EPfP GAbr GBuc ITim LAst MCCP NGdn NWCA SMac SMad WFar WMnd WViv

- B&SWJ 1271 — CBct EBla LEur WCru
- from Yungi Temple, China — CLAP EPPr WCot
- variegated (v) — WCru
maculata — WViv
- HWJCM 470 — WCru
nana — CBct CLAP WCru
- 'Raven's Back' — WCru
ohsumiensis — CBct CDes CLAP EBee EBla EBlw ECha EMan EPot GBuc GEdr LEur MTho SUsu WCru WFar WPGP
perfoliata — CLAP LEur WCru WFar
'Shimone' — CHid CLAP CStu EBlw ECha ELan GBuc LEur WFar WKif WPrP
'Shining Light' **new** — EBre
'Snow Fountain' — EBee
stolonifera — see *T. formosana* Stolonifera Group
'Tojen' — More than 30 suppliers
'Toki-no-mai' — EBee EBla WHil
'Tresahor White' — CBct
§ 'Variegata' (*affinis* hybrid) (v) — LEur WCru WFar WPnP
viridula — LEur
'Washfields' **new** — WPGP
'White Towers' — More than 30 suppliers
'White Towers' spotted — LEur

Trientalis (Primulaceae)
europaea — SOkd
- *rosea* — CNat

Trifolium (Papilionaceae)
alpinum — EBee WSan
badium — EBee
incarnatum — MHer WHer
ochroleucon — More than 30 suppliers
pannonicum — CFir CMea EBee EChP EHrv EMon GCal LPhx MLLN MSte NCot SEND SOkh SUsu WFar WPGP WSHC WTin
pratense — MHer NSco SECG
- 'Dolly North' — see *T. pratense* 'Susan Smith'
- 'Ice Cool' — see *T. repens* 'Green Ice'
- 'Nina' — CBgR CNat EBee EMan WCHb WWye
§ - 'Susan Smith' (v) — CElw CRow EBee EChP EHoe EMan EMlt EPPr EShb EWes IBlr LRHS MLLN MNrw MOak NGHP WCHb WFar WWpP
repens — COld EHrv NSco WCAu
- 'Cherhill' **new** — CNat
- 'Douglas Dawson' — CBgR EMan LDai
- 'Dragon's Blood' **new** — MBNS
- 'Gold Net' — see *T. pratense* 'Susan Smith'
- 'Good Luck' — CNat CRow MTho WWye
§ - 'Green Ice' — CBre CFwr CRow EBee EChP EMan MRav MTho NBir NSti WBea WCHb WCom WFar WHer WMoo WWye
- 'Harlequin' (v) — CBre EMlt MAvo MTho WBea WCot WDyG WFar WMoo WOut WPer WWpP WWye
- pale pink — CBgR
- 'Pentaphyllum' — see *T. repens* 'Quinquefolium'
- 'Purple Velvet' — EPPr MAvo
- 'Purpurascens' — CArn CBre EBee GCal GGar GMac ILis LRHS MAvo MBNS MHer MWgw NSti WBea WHen WKif WMoo WWhi
§ - 'Purpurascens Quadrifolium' — CNic CStu EChP ECha EDAr EWes NBid NGHP NMir NPer SIde SIng SPer SPlb WCHb WFar WRHF WWin WWpP WWye
- 'Quadrifolium' — EHoe EPar

§	– 'Quinquefolium'	EBee IHMH WShp
	– 'Tetraphyllum Purpurascens Purpureum'	see *T. repens* 'Purpurascens Quadrifolium'
*	– 'Velvet and Baize' (v)	CNat
	– 'Wheatfen'	CBre CPlt CRow EBee EMan GMac MRav MTho NDov NGHP NPer WBea WCHb WCom WCot WDyG WMoo
	– 'William'	CBre EMan MAvo MRav WCot WWye
	rubens	More than 30 suppliers
	– 'Peach Pink'	CCol CSpe EBee EChP EMan EMon LPhx MAvo MHar STes SUsu WCot WWpP
	– 'Red Feathers'	CFwr WRHF
	– white-flowered	LPhx

Triglochin (Juncaginaceae)

maritimum **new**	CRWN
palustre **new**	CRWN

Trigonella (Papilionaceae)

foenum-graecum	CArn MSal SIde WLHH

Trigonotis (Boraginaceae)

rotundifolia	EBee EMan

Trillidium see *Trillium*

Trillium ✿ (Trilliaceae)

	albidum	CLAP EHyt EPot GBuc GCrs GKir NMen SSpi WCru
	angustipetalum	CLAP EBee
	– hybrid	SSpi
	apetalon	EBee LAma WCru
	camschatcense	CLAP EBee GEdr GKir LAma LEur SSpi WAbe WCru
§	*catesbyi*	CBro CLAP EBee EHrv EPot GCrs GEdr LAma SSpi WCru
	cernuum	CLAP GKir LAma WCru
	chloropetalum	CBro EBee EPar ETow GKir SBla SSpi WCot WCru WKif
§	– var. *giganteum* ♀H4	CLAP GBuc GEdr NDov NWoo SSpi WAbe WCot WCru
	– 'Ice Creme'	SSpi
	– var. *rubrum*	see *T. chloropetalum* var. *giganteum*
	– 'Volcano'	SSpi
	– white	CLAP ECha SSpi
	cuneatum	CBcs CBro CFwr CLAP EBee EChP ECha ELan EPar EPfP EPot GAbr GBBs GBuc GEdr GFlt GGar LAma LEur LRHS MDun MTho NMen SBod SHBN SPer SSpi WCru WFar
	– red	GCrs
	cuneatum x *luteum*	EPot
	decipiens **new**	SSpi
	erectum ♀H4	More than 30 suppliers
§	– f. *albiflorum*	CBro CFir CLAP EBee EPot GBuc GEdr GKir LAma LEur SSpi WCru WPnP
	– 'Beige'	CLAP GBBs GCrs GEdr GSki
	– f. *luteum*	CLAP EPfP LAma SSpi WCru
	flexipes	CBro CLAP EBee EPot GCrs GEdr GKir LAma LEur WCru
	flexipes x *erectum*	CLAP GBuc GKir NMen WCru
	govanianum	EBee LAma WCru
	grandiflorum ♀H4	More than 30 suppliers
	– 'Flore Pleno' (d) ♀H4	EBre ECha EPar EPot ETow GBuc GKir MTho SOkd WCot
	– 'Jenny Rhodes'	IBlr
	– f. *roseum*	CLAP
	– 'Snowbunting' (d)	SOkd

	– white-flowered **new**	SSvw
	kurabayashii	CFil CLAP GFlt SSpi WPGP
	ludovicianum **new**	SSpi
§	*luteum* ♀H4	More than 30 suppliers
	nivale	EBee
	ovatum	CLAP GCrs GKir LAma
	– from Oregon	CLAP
	– var. *hibbersonii*	CBro CStu EHyt ETow GBuc GCrs GEdr LEur NMen
	– 'Roy Elliott'	NBir NMen
	parviflorum	CLAP EBee SSpi
	pusillum	CLAP EBee ELan EPot GBBs GEdr GGar GKev SSpi
	– var. *pusillum*	EHyt GCrs SBla
	– var. *virginianum*	CBro CLAP LAma WAbe WCru
	recurvatum	CBcs CPen EBee EHrv EPar EPot GAbr GEdr GKir GSki LAma LEur MDun NMen SHBN SPer WAbe WCru WFar WPnP
	rivale ♀H3	CBos CBro CElw CLAP CStu EHrv EPot GBuc GCrs ITim LAma NDov NGar NMen SBla SOkd SSpi WAbe WCot WFar
	– 'Purple Heart'	EPot GCrs GEdr
	rugelii	CBro CLAP EBee GBuc GCrs GEdr GKir LAma LEur NMen SSpi WCru
	– Askival hybrids	CLAP GBuc GCrs GKir NMen SSpi
	rugelii x *vaseyi*	GCrs GKir SSpi
	sessile	CHid CLAP EBee EPot EWTr GAbr GBBs GBuc GEdr GFlt GKir GSki LAma MAvo NBir NMyG SSpi WCAu WCot WCru WFar WGMN WHlf WKif WPnP WSHC WSan WShi
	– var. *luteum*	see *T. luteum*
	– purple	GKir
	– 'Rubrum'	see *T. chloropetalum* var. *giganteum*
	simile	CLAP GCrs GKir SSpi
	smallii	LAma WCru
	stamineum	CLAP EBee EPot GEdr SSpi
	stylosum	see *T. catesbyi*
	sulcatum	CBro CLAP EBee EPar EPot GBBs GBuc GCrs GEdr GKir NMen SSpi WCru WFar
	tschonoskii	EBee GEdr LAma SSpi WCru
	– var. *himalaicum*	LEur WCru
	underwoodii **new**	EBee SSpi
	undulatum	CLAP EBee EPot GEdr GGar LAma WCru
	vaseyi	CBro CLAP EHyt EPot GBBs GBuc GCrs GEdr GKir LAma LEur NMen SSpi WCru
	viride	CLAP NGby WCru WFar WPnP
	viridescens	CLAP EBee GEdr LAma SSpi

Trinia (Apiaceae)

glauca **new**	EBee

Triosteum (Caprifoliaceae)

pinnatifidum	CDes

Tripetaleia (Ericaceae)

§ *bracteata*	GKir

Tripleurospermum (Asteraceae)

§ *maritimum*	XPep

Tripogandra (Commelinaceae)

§ *multiflora*	CHal

Tripsacum (Poaceae)

dactyloides	EPPr

Tripterospermum (Gentianaceae)

*	aff. *chevalieri*	WCru
	B&SWJ 8359	
	cordifolium B&SWJ 081	WCru
	fasciculatum	WCru
	B&SWJ 7197	
	aff. *hirticalyx*	WCru
	B&SWJ 8264 **new**	
	japonicum	WAbe
	- B&SWJ 1168	WCru
	lanceolatum B&SWJ 085	WCru
	taiwanense B&SWJ 1205	WCru

Tripterygium (Celastraceae)

	regelii	CBcs CFil NLar WPGP
	- B&SWJ 5453	WCru

Trisetum (Poaceae)

	distichophyllum	EHoe

Tristagma (Alliaceae)

	F&W 9450 **new**	WCot
	uniflorum	see *Ipheion uniflorum*

Tristania (Myrtaceae)

	laurina	see *Tristaniopsis laurina*

Tristaniopsis (Myrtaceae)

§	*laurina*	CTrC

Triteleia (Alliaceae)

	californica	see *Brodiaea californica*
§	'Corrina'	CAvo EBee LPhx MNrw
	grandiflora	WCot
	hyacinthina	EBee ERos LAma LRHS
	ixioides	EBee ERos
	- var. *scabra*	ETow
	- 'Splendens'	EBee
	- 'Starlight'	CAvo EBee EPot GBBs GFlt WHil
§	*laxa*	CAvo CMea EBee EPot LAma NRog WCom
	- NNS 95-495	WCot
	- 'Allure'	EBee
§	- 'Koningin Fabiola'	CFwr CMea CTri EBee EMan GBBs GFlt LAma LPhx MBri NBir NRog WBrE WCot WPrP
	- Queen Fabiola	see *T. laxa* 'Koningin Fabiola'
§	*peduncularis*	EBee GKir LAma
	- NNS 95-499	WCot
	x *tubergenii*	EBee LAma
	uniflora	see *Ipheion uniflorum*

Trithrinax (Arecaceae)

	acanthocoma	CBrP CRoM LPal
	campestris	CBrP CTrC EAmu LPal WMul

Tritoma see *Kniphofia*

Tritonia (Iridaceae)

	crocata ♀H2-3	CPou EMui LPio NMen NRog WHer WHil
	- 'Baby Doll'	EBee
	- 'Pink Sensation'	CDes EBee
	- 'Prince of Orange'	CPou
	- 'Princess Beatrix'	CDes EBee
	- 'Serendipity' **new**	EBee
§	*disticha*	More than 30 suppliers
	subsp. *rubrolucens*	
	laxifolia	EBee
	lineata	CDes CPou EBee WPGP
	pallida	SPlb
	rosea	see *T. disticha* subsp. *rubrolucens*
	securigera	GGar

Tritoniopsis (Iridaceae)

	pulchra	CDes

Trochetiopsis (Sterculiaceae)

	melanoxylon **new**	EShb

Trochiscanthes (Apiaceae)

§	*nodiflora* **new**	EBee

Trochocarpa (Epacridaceae)

	thymifolia	SOkd WAbe
	- white-flowered **new**	SOkd

Trochodendron (Trochodendraceae)

	aralioides	CBcs CDoC CFil CHEx CTho EPfP GKir LRHS MGos SAPC SArc SHGC SLPl SLon SMad SPer SReu SSpi SSta WCot WDin
	- B&SWJ 6080 from Japan	WCru
	- B&SWJ 6727 from Taiwan	WCru

Trollius (Ranunculaceae)

	ACE 1187	GEdr
	acaulis	EBee EGle EWTr EWes GAbr LEur MTho NLAp NRya WFar WPat
	asiaticus	EBee GBuc GKir
	aff. *buddae* BWJ 7958 **new**	WCru
§	*chinensis*	EBee ECha GCal IHMH NChi SBla SRms SWat WBar
	- 'Golden Queen' ♀H4	More than 30 suppliers
	- 'Imperial Orange'	WWin
	'Cressida'	EBee
	x *cultorum* 'Alabaster'	CBos CDes CFir CLAP CMea CMil CRow EBee EMan EPfP ERou GBuc GKir MCLN MRav NBPC NLar SBla SMad SMrm WCFE WFar WPGP WTin
	- - seedlings	SSpi
	- 'Baudirektor Linne'	MRav NGdn WFar
	- Bressingham hybrids	EBre WFar
	- 'Byrne's Giant'	EBee WFar WPnP
	- 'Canary Bird'	ELan EMil EPfP GBri NGdn SMur SRms WCot
	- 'Cheddar'	COtt CPen EBee EGle ENot ERou MBri MCCP MRav MTis NBro NGdn NLar NPro NSti SMHy SOkh WCot WCra WFar WHil WPnP
	- 'Commander-in-chief'	CDes EBee EBre WFar WPGP WPnP
	- 'Earliest of All'	CDWL CSBt CSam EBee EGle EWTr GKir LRHS MBri NGby NGdn SPer SRms WCra WFar WHoo
	- 'Etna'	CDWL EBee EChP EGle ERou GKir GMac MBri WFar WLin WPnP WSan
§	- 'Feuertroll'	CDWL EBee ECha EMar MBNS NGby NPro SMur WCra WFar WHoo
	- Fireglobe	see *T.* x *cultorum* 'Feuertroll'
	- 'Glory of Leiden'	EBee
	- 'Golden Cup'	ECot NBir NGdn
	- 'Golden Monarch'	EPar WFar
	- 'Goldquelle' ♀H4	EHon SMur WWpP
	- 'Goliath'	WFar
	- 'Helios'	CSam EBee ECha SBla
	- 'Lemon Queen'	CDWL CWat EBee EChP EMan EPar EPfP ERou GCal GKir LPBA LRHS MBri MRav NBlu NFor SMrm SPer SWat WCAu WCra WFar WPnP WSpi WWin
	- 'Meteor'	WFar
	- 'Orange Crest'	EBee EGle GCal WFar

– 'Orange Globe'	NGby SMrm WFar WWeb
– 'Orange Princess' ♀H4	CDWL CSBt CWat EBee EBre
	EMFW ENot EPfP ERou GBin GKir
	LRHS MCCP NBro NLar NPri SPer
	SRms WAul WCra WLow WPnP
– 'Orange Queen'	MBri SWvt
– 'Prichard's Giant'	CDWL CM&M CRez EBee EChP
	EGle ELan EMan EMar NBro NGby
	WFar
– 'Salamander'	SMur
§ – 'Superbus' ♀H4	CDes CM&M CMHG EBee EBre
	EChP EFou EGle EHol ELan EPar
	EPfP GKir MBNS NGdn SPer SSpi
	WFar WLin WPnP
– 'T. Smith'	EBee EGle LBuc MTis NBro NGby
	WCot WCra WFar
* – 'Taleggio'	EMon NLar
– 'Yellow Beauty'	WFar
europaeus	More than 30 suppliers
– 'Superbus'	see *T.* x *cultorum* 'Superbus'
hondoensis	EBee EBre EPPr GBin GlBF GKir
	LEur NBur NLar NPro
ircuticus	EBee
laxus	EBee EWes
ledebourii hort.	see *T. chinensis*
papavereus	see *T. yunnanensis* var.
	yunnanensis
pumilus	CMea EBre ECha ELan EMlt GCrs
	ITim LBee LEur LRHS MBro MHer
	NChi NRya SPer SUsu WFar WPer
	WWeb
– ACE 1818	EPot GBuc WCot
– 'Wargrave'	NMen
ranunculinus	EBee
riederianus	EBee GKir
stenopetalus	EBee EChP ECha EWes GCal GKir
	MBri MRav WFar WPnP
yunnanensis	EBre GBuc GCrs GKir LRHS NBid
	NGby NWoo SHar WFar WPnP
	WWpP
– CD&R 2097	WCru
– f. *eupetalus* BWJ 7614	WCru
new	
§ – var. *yunnanensis*	EBee

Tropaeolum ✿ (*Tropaeolaceae*)

azureum	CPla
brachyceras	NLar WCot
ciliatum ♀H1	CBcs CBro CFil CFir CPla CPne
	CSam CStu EBee ELan EOrc EPot
	GCal LEur MPRe MTho NSti SMrm
	WBor WCot WCru WFar WHer
	WNor WPGP WViv
hookerianum subsp.	CFil ERos
austropurpureum	
– subsp. *hookerianum*	WCot
F&W 8630	
– – F&W 9467	WPGP
incisum	CFil SOkd
lepidum	CPla WCot
* *lucidum*	WCot
majus	WSel
– Alaska Series (v) ♀H3	CPrp SIde WJek WSel
* – 'Clive Innes'	ERea
– 'Crimson Beauty'	CSpe
§ – 'Darjeeling Double'	LRHS SMrm WCot WCru
(d) ♀H4	
– 'Darjeeling Gold' (d)	see *T. majus* 'Darjeeling Double'
– 'Empress of India'	CPrp LRHS WEas WJek
– 'Forest Flame'	LRHS
– 'Hermine Grashoff'	CSWP CSpe ERea LRHS MLLN
(d) ♀H2-3	NPer SMrm WCot
– 'Margaret Long' (d)	CSpe GCal LRHS MLLN SMrm
	WCot

* – 'Peaches and Cream'	WJek
– 'Red Wonder'	CHad CSWP CSpe LRHS NPri
	SMrm
– 'Ruffled Apricot'	CSpe
– Tom Thumb mixed	WJek
– 'Wina'	WJek
pentaphyllum	CFil CSpe EBee ECha ELan ETow
	GCal GCrs IBlr LTwo MTho WCot
polyphyllum	CDes CFil EBee ECha EHyt GBuc
	GCrs SBla SMHy WCot WPGP
	WTre
speciosum ♀H4	More than 30 suppliers
sylvestre	EBee WCru WPGP
tricolor ♀H1	CAvo CFil EHyt ELan EPot ETow
	MTho WBor WPat
tuberosum	CBcs CEnd EBee GPoy LRHS WBrE
	WPrP
– var. *lineamaculatum*	More than 30 suppliers
'Ken Aslet' ♀H3	
– var. *piliferum* 'Sidney'	CFil EBee IBlr WCru WPGP

Tsuga (*Pinaceae*)

canadensis	EHul GTSp LCon LPan MBar NBlu
	NWea SHBN WDin
– 'Abbott's Dwarf'	CKen MGos
§ – 'Abbott's Pygmy'	CKen
– 'Albospica' (v)	CDoC EOrn LRHS WGor
– 'Arnold Gold Weeper'	CKen
– 'Aurea' (v)	LCon MBar WBcn
– 'Baldwin Dwarf Pyramid'	MBar
– 'Beehive'	WGor
– 'Bennett'	EHul MBar
– 'Betty Rose' (v)	CKen
– 'Brandley'	CKen
§ – 'Branklyn'	CKen WBcn
– 'Cappy's Choice'	CKen
– 'Cinnamonea'	CKen
– 'Coffin'	CKen
– 'Cole's Prostrate'	CDoC CKen EOrn GKir LCon LLin
	MAsh MBar NHol NLar SHBN
– 'Coryhill' **new**	MAsh
– 'Creamey' (v)	CKen
– 'Curley'	CKen
– 'Curtis Ideal'	CKen
* – 'Everitt's Dense Leaf'	CKen
– 'Everitt's Golden'	CKen
– 'Fantana'	CDoC EBre EHul LBee LLin LRHS
	MAsh MBar NLar SCoo SLim
– 'Gentsch White' (v)	LLin MGos
– 'Golden Splendor'	LLin
– 'Horsford'	CKen NLar
– 'Hussii'	CKen LCon NLar
– 'Jacqueline Verkade'	CKen
– 'Jeddeloh' ♀H4	CDoC CMac CNic EBre EHul ENot
	EOrn EPot GKir IMGH LLin LRHS
	MBar MBri MGos NHol SLim WDin
	WEve WStI
– 'Jervis'	CDoC CKen LCon NLar
– 'Julianne'	CKen
– 'Kingsville Spreader'	CKen
– 'Little Joe'	CKen
I – 'Lutea'	CKen
– 'Many Cones'	CKen
– 'Minima'	CKen
– 'Minuta'	CDoC CKen EHul EOrn LBee LCon
	LLin LRHS MBar MGos SCoo SLon
	SPoG WGor
– 'Nana'	CMac EHul WDin
– 'Palomino'	CDoC CKen MBar
– 'Pendula' ♀H4	CBrm CDoC CKen EHul ENot
	EOrn LCon LRHS MAsh MBar MBri
	MOne NHol SLim WCwm WDin
	WEve WMou
– 'Pincushion'	CKen

- 'Prostrata'	see *T. canadensis* 'Branklyn'
- 'Pygmaea'	see *T. canadensis* 'Abbott's Pygmy'
- 'Rugg's Washington Dwarf'	CKen
- 'Snowflake'	CKen LCon MGos
- 'Stewart's Gem'	CKen
- 'Verkade Petite'	CKen
- 'Verkade Recurved'	CKen MBar WBcn
- 'Von Helms' Dwarf'	CKen
- 'Warnham'	CKen ECho EOrn LBee LRHS MBri SCoo
caroliniana	CKen
'La Bar Weeping'	
chinensis	GIBF
diversifolia	EPot
- 'Gotelli'	CKen
heterophylla ♀H4	CDoC CDul CLnd EBre ENot EPfP GKir LBuc LCon LRHS MBar NWea SHBN SMad SPer STre WDin WEve WFar
- 'Iron Springs'	CKen EOrn
- 'Laursen's Column'	CKen
menziesii	see *Pseudotsuga menziesii*
mertensiana	LCon WCwm
- 'Blue Star'	CKen MGos
- 'Elizabeth'	CKen
I - 'Glauca Nana'	CKen
- 'Quartz Mountain'	CKen
sieboldii 'Baldwin'	CKen
- 'Honeywell Estate'	CKen
- 'Nana'	CKen

Tsusiophyllum (*Ericaceae*)

tanakae	see *Rhododendron tsusiophyllum*

Tuberaria (*Cistaceae*)

guttata	WCru
lignosa	CMHG CMea CStu EMan GEdr SGar WAbe WCot

Tulbaghia ✿ (*Alliaceae*)

acutiloba	CAvo ERos
alliacea	CFee ERos WCot WPrP
alliacea x **violacea**	EBee
capensis	CFee LPio MHom
cepacea	CStu NBir
§ - var. **maritima**	CAvo CDes EBee ERos MHom WCot
coddii	CAvo CFee MHom WCot
coddii x **violacea**	CPne EBee
cominsii	CFil SCnR
cominsii x **violacea**	CAvo CDes CFil ERos MHom WPrP
dregeana	WCot
'Fairy Star'	CDes ERos WCot WOBN WPrP
fragrans	see *T. simmleri*
galpinii	CFil CPen EBee ERos SChr WCot
'John May's Special'	CDes CKno EBee EGra EMan MSph MSte WCot WPGP
leucantha	CAvo CStu EBee ERos SBla WCot
maritima	see *T. cepacea* var. *maritima*
Marwood seedling	MTPN
montana new	CDes EShb
natalensis	CAvo CPou EBee LPhx
- pink	ERos MHom SOkh WCot WPrP
§ **simmleri**	CPou EBee EBla ERos ESis EWes GAbr GSki LAma LPio MHom MSph WCot
- pink-flowered	CPen
- white-flowered	CPen CPou
verdoornia	WCot
violacea	More than 30 suppliers
* - 'Alba'	GSki LPio WFar
I - 'Fine Form'	SMHy
- 'John Rider'	WPer

* - **pallida**	CAvo CDes CMdw CPou EBee WCot WPrP
§ - 'Silver Lace' (v)	More than 30 suppliers
- 'Variegata'	see *T. violacea* 'Silver Lace'

Tulipa ✿ (*Liliaceae*)

'Abba' (2)	MBri NRog
'Abu Hassan' (3)	LAma MBri NRog
acuminata (15)	CBro CFwr LAma LPhx LRHS
'Ad Rem' (4)	LAma NRog
'Addis' (14) ♀H4	LAma
'African Queen' (3)	LAma
agenensis	WWst
aitchisonii	see *T. clusiana*
'Aladdin' (6)	LAma LRHS NRog
albertii (15)	LAma
'Albino' (3)	LAma
aleppensis (15)	LAma
'Alfred Cortot' (12) ♀H4	LAma
'Ali Baba' (14) ♀H4	MBri
'Allegretto' (11)	LAma MBri NRog
altaica (15) ♀H4	EPot LAma
amabilis	see *T. hoogiana*
'Ancilla' (12) ♀H4	CBro LAma NRog SGar
'Angélique' (11) ♀H4	CAvo CMea EPfP LAma LRHS MBri NBir NRog SPer WHal
'Anne Claire' (3)	LAma
'Apeldoorn' (4)	LAma LRHS MBri NRog
'Apeldoorn's Elite' (4) ♀H4	LAma LRHS NRog
'Apricot Beauty' (1) ♀H4	CHid EPfP LAma LRHS MBri NBir NRog SPer
'Apricot Jewel'	see *T. linifolia* (Batalinii Group) 'Apricot Jewel'
'Apricot Parrot' (10) ♀H4	LAma MBri NRog SPer
'Arabian Mystery' (3)	CAvo CMea LAma NBir NRog WHal
'Aristocrat' (5) ♀H4	LAma
'Artist' (8) ♀H4	EChP LAma NBir SPer
'Athleet' (3)	LAma LRHS
'Attila' (3)	LAma LRHS NRog
aucheriana (15) ♀H4	CBro EHyt EPot ERos LAma LRHS LTwo WWst
aximensis (15)	WWst
bakeri	see *T. saxatilis* Bakeri Group
'Ballade' (6) ♀H4	LAma MBri SPer
'Ballerina' (6) ♀H4	CAvo CBro CMea LAma LPhx MBri SPer WHal
batalinii	see *T. linifolia* Batalinii Group
'Beauty of Apeldoorn' (4)	LAma NRog
Beauty Queen (1)	NRog
'Bellflower' (7)	LAma
'Bellona' (3)	LAma
'Berlioz' (12)	LAma
'Bestseller' (1)	NRog
biebersteiniana (15)	LAma
§ **biflora** (15)	CBro EMar EPot LAma LRHS LTwo NRog
bifloriformis (15)	LRHS
'Big Chief' (4) ♀H4	LAma MBri
'Bing Crosby' (3)	LAma
'Black Hero' **new**	SPer
'Black Horse' **new**	LAma
'Black Parrot' (10) ♀H4	CAvo GFlt LAma LPhx LRHS MBri NRog
'Bleu Aimable' (5)	CAvo LAma LRHS
'Blue Heron' (7) ♀H4	LAma NRog
'Blue Parrot' (10)	LAma LRHS NRog
'Blushing Lady' (5)	LAma
'Bonanza' (11)	LAma LRHS
'Boule de Neige' (2)	LAma
'Boutade' **new**	NPer
'Bravissimo' (2)	MBri
'Brilliant Star' (1)	LAma MBri NRog

'Jan Reus' **new** — LAma
'Jeantine' (12) ♀H4 — EPfP
'Jewel of Spring' (4) ♀H4 — LAma
'Jimmy' (3) — NRog
'Jockey Cap' (14) — LAma
'Joffre' (1) — LAma MBri NRog
'Johann Strauss' (12) — CBro LAma MBri NRog
'Juan' (13) ♀H4 — LAma MBri
'Kansas' (3) — LAma
karabachensis **new** — WWst
'Karel Doorman' (10) — LAma
kaufmanniana (12) — CAvo EPot NRog
§ 'Kees Nelis' (3) — LAma MBri NRog
'Keizerskroon' (1) ♀H4 — LAma NRog
kolpakowskiana (15) ♀H4 — EChP EPfP LAma LRHS MBri / NJOw NRog
korolkowii — WWst
kurdica (15) — LAma LRHS
* 'Lady Diana' (14) — MBri
'Leen van der Mark' (3) — LAma
'Lefeber's Favourite' (4) — LAma
'Libretto Parrot' (10) — LAma
'Lilac Time' (6) — LAma
'Lilac Wonder' — see *T. saxatilis* (Bakeri Group) / 'Lilac Wonder'
'Lilliput' — see *T. humilis* 'Lilliput'
linifolia (15) ♀H4 — CAvo EChP EHyt EPar EPfP EPot / GIBF LAma LRHS NJOw NRog / NSla SSpi
§ - Batalinii Group (15) ♀H4 — CBro LAma MBri NRog
§ - - 'Apricot Jewel' (15) — CBro EPot
§ - - 'Bright Gem' (15) ♀H4 — CAvo CBro EPot GCrs LAma LRHS / MBri MBro NRog WCra WHoo
- - 'Bronze Charm' (15) — CAvo CBro CMea ECGP EPot / LAma LPhx MBri
- - 'Red Gem' (15) — LAma
- - 'Red Jewel' (15) — GFlt
- - 'Yellow Jewel' (15) — EPot GFlt LAma
§ - Maximowiczii Group (15) — CBro EPot LAma LPhx
'Little Beauty' (15) ♀H4 — CMea LAma
'Little Princess' **new** — LAma
'London' (4) — LAma
'Lucky Strike' (3) — LAma
§ 'Lustige Witwe' (3) — LAma
§ 'Lydia' (3) — LAma
§ 'Madame Lefeber' (13) — CBro MBri NRog
'Magier' (5) **new** — LAma
'Maja' (7) — LAma
'Mamasa' (5) — LAma
'March of Time' (14) — MBri
'Maréchal Niel' (2) — LAma
'Mariette' (6) — CBro LAma LRHS MBri SPer
'Marilyn' (6) — LAma LRHS NRog
'Marjolein' (6) ♀H4 — NRog
marjolletii (15) — CAvo CBro CMea LAma NRog
'Mary Ann' (14) — LAma
'Maureen' (5) ♀H4 — LAma
mauritiana (15) — LAma
maximowiczii — see *T. linifolia* Maximowiczii / Group
'Maytime' (6) — LAma MBri NRog SPer
'Maywonder' (11) ♀H4 — LAma MBri
'Menton' (5) — LAma
Merry Widow — see *T.* 'Lustige Witwe'
'Miss Holland' (3) — MBri
'Mona Lisa' (6) — LAma
'Monsella' (2) — NRog
§ *montana* (15) — CBro EPot GIBF LAma LPhx NBid
'Monte Carlo' (2/d) ♀H4 — LAma LRHS MBri
'Montreux' **new** — LAma
'Moonshine' (6) — NRog
'Mount Tacoma' (11) — CAvo LAma MBri NRog SPer
'Mr Van der Hoef' (2) — LAma MBri NRog

'Murillo' (2) — LAma
'My Lady' (4) ♀H4 — LAma
'Negrita' (3) — EMar LAma
neustruevae (15) — CBro EPot
'New Design' (3/v) — EMar LAma MBri SPer
'Orange Bouquet' (3) ♀H4 — LAma NRog
'Orange Elite' (14) — LAma MBri
'Orange Emperor' (13) ♀H4 — LAma LRHS MBri NRog SPer
'Orange Favourite' (10) — LAma LRHS
'Orange Sun' — see *T.* 'Oranjezon'
'Orange Triumph' (11) — MBri
'Oranje Nassau' (2) ♀H4 — LAma MBri NRog
§ 'Oranjezon' (4) ♀H4 — LAma
'Oratorio' (14) ♀H4 — LAma LRHS MBri
'Oriental Beauty' (14) ♀H4 — LAma LRHS NRog
'Oriental Splendour' (14) — EPfP LAma

orithyioides — WWst
orphanidea (15) — EPot LAma LRHS SCnR
- 'Flava' (15) — CBro EPot LAma LPhx
§ - Whittallii Group (15) ♀H4 — CAvo CMea LAma LPhx NRog

ostrowskiana (15) — LAma
'Oxford' (4) ♀H4 — LAma NRog
'Oxford's Elite' (4) — LAma
'Page Polka' (3) — LAma
'Palestrina' (3) — LAma
'Pandour' (14) — LAma MBri
'Parade' (4) ♀H4 — LAma MBri
passeriniana (15) — LAma
patens **new** — WWst
'Paul Richter' (3) — LAma
'Pax' (3) — LAma
'Peach Blossom' (2) — LAma LRHS MBri NRog SPer
'Perlina' (14) — LAma
persica — see *T. celsiana*
'Philippe de Comines' (5) — LAma
'Picture' (5) ♀H4 — LAma
'Pieter de Leur' **new** — EPfP LAma
'Pimpernel' (8/v) — LAma
'Pink Beauty' (1) — LAma
'Pink Impression' (4) ♀H4 — LAma
'Pinkeen' (13) — LAma
'Pinocchio' (14) — SGar
'Plaisir' (14) ♀H4 — LAma MBri
platystigma (15) — LAma
polychroma — see *T. biflora*
praestans (15) — CNic EPfP LAma
- 'Fusilier' (15) ♀H4 — CBro EMar EPot LAma LRHS MBri / NBir NJOw NRog SGar
- 'Unicum' (15/v) — LAma LRHS MBri NRog
- 'Van Tubergen's — LAma LRHS NJOw NRog / Variety' (15)
'Preludium' (3) — LAma
'President Kennedy' (4) ♀H4 — LAma
'Prince of Austria' (1) — LAma
'Princeps' (13) — CBro LAma MBri
'Prinses Irene' (3) ♀H4 — CMea LAma MBri NBir NRog SPer / WHal
'Professor Röntgen' (10) — LAma
pulchella humilis — see *T. humilis*
§ 'Purissima' (13) ♀H4 — CAvo CBro CMea LAma LRHS / NRog
'Purple Prince' (5) **new** — EPfP
'Queen Ingrid' (14) — LAma LRHS
'Queen of Bartigons' (5) ♀H4 — LAma NRog
'Queen of Marvel' (2) — NRog
'Queen of Night' (5) — CAvo CMea EMar EPfP GFlt LAma / LRHS MBri NRog SPer WHal
'Queen of Sheba' (6) ♀H4 — CAvo LAma NRog

'Rajka' (6)   LAma
'Red Emperor'   see *T.* 'Madame Lefeber'
'Red Georgette' (5) ♀H4   LRHS MBri NBir
'Red Parrot' (10)   LAma NRog
'Red Riding Hood' (14)   CAvo CBro CMea EPfP LAma LRHS
  ♀H4   MBri NBir LAma NRog SPer
'Red Shine' (6) ♀H4   CBro LAma MBri
'Red Wing' (7) ♀H4   LAma
Rembrandt mix   MBri
rhodopea   see *T. urumoffii*
'Ringo'   see *T.* 'Kees Nelis'
'Rococo' (10)   MBri
'Rosy Wings' (3)   LAma
'Sapporo' (6)   CAvo LAma
saxatilis (15)   CBro CNic EPfP LAma LRHS MBri
                                    NJOw NRog
§ – Bakeri Group (15)   CPou LAma
§ – – 'Lilac Wonder' (15)   CAvo CBro EChP EPot LAma MBri
  ♀H4   NRog
'Scarlet Baby' (12)   EPfP LRHS
'Schoonoord' (2)   LAma MBri NRog
schrenkii (15)   EPot LAma
'Scotch Lassie' (5)   LAma
'Shakespeare' (12)   CBro LAma NRog
'Shirley' (3)   CAvo EPfP LAma LRHS MBri
                                    NRog
'Showwinner' (12) ♀H4   CBro LAma MBri NRog
'Sigrid Undset' (5)   LAma
'Silentia' (3)   LAma
'Snow Parrot' (10)   CAvo
'Snowflake' (3)   LAma
'Snowpeak' (5)   LAma
sogdiana (15)   LAma
'Sorbet' (5) ♀H4   LAma
'Sparkling Fire' (14)   LAma
sprengeri (15) ♀H4   CAvo CBro CFil CLAP CNic ECGP
                                    ECha EPar LAma MRav SDix SOkd
                                    SSpi WIvy
  – Trotter's form (15)   WCot
'Spring Green' (8) ♀H4   CAvo CMea EMar EPfP LAma LRHS
                                    MBri NRog SPer WHal
'Spring Pearl' (13)   LAma
'Spring Song' (4)   LAma
stellata   see *T. clusiana* var. *stellata*
'Stockholm' (2) ♀H4   LAma
'Stresa' (12) ♀H4   CBro LAma LRHS
'Striped Apeldoorn' (4)   LAma NRog
  new
'Striped Bellona' (3)   NRog
subpraestans (15)   EPot LAma
'Sunray' (3)   LAma
'Susan Oliver' (8)   LAma
'Swan Wings' (7)   LAma
'Sweet Harmony' (5) ♀H4   LAma LRHS MBri
'Sweet Lady' (14)   LAma
'Sweetheart' (13)   CBro LAma MBri NRog SPer
sylvestris (15)   CAvo CBro EPar LAma LRHS
                                    MBow NRog SSpi WBWf WCot
                                    WHer WShi WTin
tarda (15) ♀H4   CAvo CBro EBla EPar EPfP EPot
                                    GFlt GIBF LAma LRHS MBri NJOw
                                    NRog
tetraphylla (15)   LAma
'Texas Flame' (10)   LAma LRHS MBri NRog
'Texas Gold' (10)   LAma NRog
'The First' (12)   CBro LAma
'Toronto' (14) ♀H4   EPfP LAma LRHS MBri
'Toulon' (13) ♀H4   MBri
'Towa' (14)   LAma
'Toyota' (5)   SPer
'Trinket' (14) ♀H4   LAma
'Triumphator' (2)   LAma
tschimganica (15)   LAma
tubergeniana (15)   LAma

  – 'Keukenhof' (15)   LAma
turkestanica (15) ♀H4   CBro CSWP EChP EMar EPar EPfP
                                    EPot GFlt LAma LPhx MBri NRog
                                    NSla WBrE WHoo
'Turkish Delight' **new**   NPer
'Uncle Tom' (11)   LAma MBri
§ *undulatifolia* (15)   LAma
'Union Jack' (5) ♀H4   LAma
'United States' (14) **new**   NPer
urumiensis (15) ♀H4   CAvo CBro EPot LAma MBri NJOw
                                    NRog WHoo
§ *urumoffii* (15)   LAma
'Valentine' (3) ♀H4   LAma
'Van der Neer' (1)   LAma
'Varinas' (3)   LAma
violacea   see *T. humilis* Violacea Group
'Vivaldi' (12)   LAma
'Vivex' (4) ♀H4   LAma
§ 'Vlammenspel' (1)   LAma
'Vuurbaak' (2)   LAma
vvedenskyi (15)   EPot LAma NRog
  – 'Tangerine Beauty' (15)   LRHS MBri
  ♀H4
'Weber's Parrot' (10)   MBri
'West Point' (6) ♀H4   CBro LAma MBNS MBri NRog
'White Dream' (3)   LAma LRHS
'White Elegance' (6)   CAvo SPer
'White Emperor'   see *T.* 'Purissima'
'White Parrot' (10)   CAvo LAma LRHS NRog
'White Swallow' (3)   NRog
'White Triumphator' (6)   CAvo CBro CMea GFlt LAma LPhx
  ♀H4   LRHS NBir NRog WHal
'White Virgin' (3)   LAma
whittallii   see *T. orphanidea* Whittallii Group
'Willem van Oranje' (2)   LAma
'Willemsoord' (2)   LAma LRHS MBri NRog
wilsoniana   see *T. montana*
'Yellow Dawn' (14)   LAma LRHS
'Yellow Emperor' (5)   MBri
'Yellow Empress' (13)   LAma
'Yellow Flight' (3)   LAma
'Yellow Present' (3)   LAma
'Yokohama' (3)   LAma NRog
'Zampa' (14) ♀H4   LAma
'Zombie' (13)   LAma
'Zomerschoon' (5)   LAma

tummelberry see *Rubus* 'Tummelberry'

Tunica see *Petrorhagia*

Tupistra (Convallariaceae)
aurantiaca B&SWJ 2267   WCru
chinensis **new**   EBee
  – 'Eco China Ruffles'   WCot
grandistigma **new**   EBee
nutans   CKob LEur

Turbina (Convolvulaceae)
corymbosa   MGol

Turnera (Turneraceae)
ulmifolia   MSal

Tussilago (Asteraceae)
farfara   CArn ELau GBar GPoy GWCH
                                    MHer MSal NSco WHer

Tutcheria (Theaceae)
§ *spectabilis*   EPfP

Tweedia (Asclepiadaceae)
§ *caerulea* ♀H2   CSpe EMan ERea LPhx LPio SHFr
                                    SPer SWal WEas WRos

- 'Heaven Born' **new**	EDif
- pink	LPio

Typha (Typhaceae)

angustifolia	CAgr CBen CRow CWat EHon EMFW EPAt EPza LNCo LPBA MSta NArg NBlu NPer SPlb SWat WFar WPnP WWpP WWye
latifolia	CAgr CBen CRow CWat EHon EMFW ENot EPza LPBA MSta NPer SWat WDyG WFar WHer WMAq WMyn WWpP WWye
- 'Variegata' (v)	CBen CDWL CRow CWat ELan EMFW EPza LPBA MSta NArg WCot WMAq WWpP
§ **laxmannii**	CBen CDWL CRow EHon EMFW EPza LPBA MSta NArg WPnP WWpP
minima	CBen CDWL CFwr CMHG CRow CStu CWat EHoe EHon EMFW EPfP EPza GBin LEdu LNCo LPBA MSta NArg NBlu NPer SCoo SMad SWal SWat WFar WMAq WPnP WRos WWpP
- var. **gracilis**	ENot
shuttleworthii	CRow WWpP
stenophylla	see *T. laxmannii*

Typhonium (Araceae)

horsfieldii new	EBee

U

ugli see *Citrus* x *tangelo* 'Ugli'

Ugni (Myrtaceae)

§ **molinae**	CDul CFir CPLG CPle CSBt CTrC IDee ISea LEdu MCCP MDun SHFr SLPl SOWG WCHb WDin WFar WGwG WJek WMoo WPic WSHC WWye XPep
- 'Flambeau' **new**	NLar

Ulex (Papilionaceae)

europaeus	CCVT CDoC CDul CRWN EBee ECrN EGoo ENot EPfP GPoy GWCH LBuc MCoo NWea SPer WDin WHar WMou
§ - 'Flore Pleno' (d) ♀H4	CBcs CBgR CDoC CSBt EBee EMon ENot EPfP EPla IArd MBlu MGos NLar NWea SHBN SPer WBcn WCot WFar WRHF
- 'Plenus'	see *U. europaeus* 'Flore Pleno'
- 'Prostratus'	MBar
gallii	WDin
- 'Mizen Head'	GCal GGGa GSki MBlu MWhi SLon WBcn
§ **minor**	EPla
nanus	see *U. minor*

Ulmus ✿ (Ulmaceae)

'Dodoens'	EWTr IArd LBuc MGos SBLw
§ **glabra**	CDul CRWN ECrN GKir NWea SBLw WDin
- 'Camperdownii'	CDoC CTho EBee ECrN ELan LRHS NBee SBLw SPer
- 'Exoniensis'	CDul CTho SBLw
- 'Gittisham'	CTho
- 'Horizontalis'	see *U. glabra* 'Pendula'
- 'Lutescens'	CDoC CEnd CTho CTri LRHS SBLw SKee SLim

- 'Nana'	WPat
§ - 'Pendula'	CDul LPan SBLw SLim
x *hollandica* 'Commelin'	SBLw
- 'Dampieri' **new**	SBLw
- 'Dampieri Aurea'	CBot CDul CEnd CLnd CTho EBee ELan EPfP GKir LBuc LRHS MAsh MBar MBlu MGos NBee NBlu SBLw SHBN SKee SLim SPer WDin WOrn WPat
- 'Groeneveld'	SBLw
- 'Jacqueline Hillier'	ELan EPfP EPla GEdr GEil IMGH LAst MBar MBro MGos NHol NLap NWea SBLw SLon SPer SSto STre WCFE WDin WFar WOld WPGP WPat
- 'Lobel'	CDul ENot MGos SBLw
- 'Wredei'	see *U.* x *hollandica* 'Dampieri Aurea'
laevis	CDul CTho ECrN
minor new	SBLw
- subsp. **sarniensis new**	SBLw
- 'Variegata' (v)	EPot SCoo
montana	see *U. glabra*
parvifolia	CMCN CTho ECrN NWea SMad STre WNor
- 'Frosty' (v)	ECho EPot
- 'Geisha' (v)	ELan EMil MAsh MGos NLap WBcn WPat
§ - 'Hokkaido'	LBee LTwo MBro NLAp NLar SBla WAbe WOBN WPat
- 'Pygmaea'	see *U. parvifolia* 'Hokkaido'
- 'Yatsubusa'	CLyd EPot ESis EWes LTwo NHol NLAp NLar SIng STre WBcn WPat
'Plantijn'	SBLw
procera	CDul CTho LBuc SBLw WDin
- 'Argenteovariegata' (v)	CDul CLnd CTho MAsh MGos SMad
pumila	CAgr CDul EPot WNor
rubra	MSal
'Sapporo Autumn Gold'PBR	WDin
x *vegeta* **new**	SBLw

Umbellularia (Lauraceae)

californica	CArn CPne IArd SAPC SArc WSHC

Umbilicus (Crassulaceae)

rupestris	CRWN EChP GEdr NWCA SChr WBri WCru WHer WShi WWye

Uncinia (Cyperaceae)

from Chile	GCal
egmontiana	CBri CElw EBla EChP EHoe EMan EPPr EPyc GFlt GSki LPhx MNrw NChi NHol SMac WCot WHrl WLeb WPnP WWpP
N **rubra**	More than 30 suppliers
uncinata	CFil CM&M ECha EMan GGar GSki LHop SDix SGar WCot
* - **rubra**	More than 30 suppliers

Uniola (Poaceae)

latifolia	see *Chasmanthium latifolium*

Urceolina (Amaryllidaceae)

miniata	see *Stenomesson miniatum*
peruviana	see *Stenomesson miniatum*

Urginea (Hyacinthaceae)

maritima	CArn EBee GCal LAma MNrw MSal

Urospermum (Asteraceae)

dalechampii	CDes COtt CSam EBee EBre ECha EMan GKir LLWP SAga WCot

Ursinia (*Asteraceae*)

alpina	CPBP
montana	NWCA

Urtica (*Urticaceae*)

dioica 'Chedglow' (v)	CNat
- subsp. *gracilis*	CNat
var. *procera*	
galeopsifolia	CNat

Utricularia (*Lentibulariaceae*)

alpina	CSWC
australis	EFEx
bisquamata	CSWC SHmp
blancheti	CSWC
calycifida	CSWC SHmp
dichotoma	CSWC EFEx
- var. *uniflora*	LHew
exoleta R. Brown	see *U. gibba*
§ *gibba*	EFEx
intermedia	EFEx
lateriflora	EFEx
livida	CSWC EFEx
longifolia	CSWC
macrorhiza **new**	CSWC
menziesii	EFEx
monanthos	CSWC EFEx
- from Queenstown, Tasmania	MCCP
nephrophylla	SHmp
novae-zelandiae	CSWC
ochroleuca	EFEx
praelonga	CSWC SHmp
pubescens	CSWC LHew SHmp
reniformis	CSWC EFEx SHmp
- *nana*	CSWC EFEx
sandersonii	CSWC SHmp
- blue	CSWC
subulata	EFEx
tricolor	CSWC SHmp
vulgaris	CDWL CSWC EFEx

Uvularia (*Convallariaceae*)

§ *caroliniana*	EBee IBlr
disporum	LAma
grandiflora ♀H4	More than 30 suppliers
- dwarf	IBlr LEur
- var. *pallida*	CAvo CBct CBos CPom EBee ECha EGle EHrv EMan EPar GBri GBuc IBlr LEur LPhx MRav SBla SMHy SOkh SUsu WAbe WCru WPGP WPnP
- 'Susie Lewis'	WCru
grandiflora × *perfoliata*	IBlr
perfoliata	CStu EBee ECha EDAr EGle EHyt EMan EPar EPfP EPla GBri GCrs GGar IBlr LAma LEur MRav SIng SSpi WBrE WCru WHil WIvy WPGP WPnP
pudica	see *U. caroliniana*
sessilifolia	CBct EBee EPPr EPar GBBs GCrs IBlr LAma NLar NMen SCnR SSvw WCru WIvy

V

Vaccaria (*Caryophyllaceae*)

§ *hispanica*	MSal
segetalis	see *V. hispanica*

Vaccinium ✿ (*Ericaceae*)

from Bolivia	EWes
arctostaphylos	SReu SSta
caespitosum	SOkd
'Cinderella'	SSta
consanguineum	SReu
corymbosum (F) ♀H4	CBcs ENot EPfP MBar MGos NBee SCoo SReu SSta WBVN WDin
- 'Berkeley' (F)	CTrh GTwe LBuc LRHS SDea
- 'Blue Ray' (F)	CWib SCoo
- 'Bluecrop' (F)	CTrh CWib EMui EPfP GKir GTwe LBuc LRHS MAsh MBri MGos NBee SCoo SDea SKee SPer SWvt WFar
- 'Bluegold' (F)	LRHS MAsh SCoo
- 'Bluejay' (F)	CTrh LRHS MAsh SCoo
- 'Bluetta' (F)	CWib GTwe LRHS SCoo WFar
- 'Concord' (F)	ENot SCoo
- 'Coville' (F)	EMui
- 'Darrow' (F) **new**	SPoG
- 'Duke' (F)	CTrh ELan EPfP GKir LRHS MAsh
- 'Earliblue' (F)	EMui LRHS MGos SDea
- 'Goldtraube' (F)	CTri CWSG CWib GKir MBlu MBri MGos SDea SKee WStI
- 'Herbert' (F)	CTrh EMui GTwe MGos SCoo
- 'Ivanhoe' (F)	CTrh SCoo
- 'Jersey' (F)	GKir LRHS MAsh MGos SCoo SDea
- 'Nelson' (F)	CTrh SCoo
- 'Northland' (F)	CWib GTwe SCoo SDea
- 'Patriot' (F)	CTrh CWib GTwe LRHS MGos SCoo
- 'Pioneer' (F)	MBar
- 'Spartan' (F)	GTwe LRHS SCoo
- 'Stanley' **new**	MAsh
- 'Sunrise' (F)	GTwe
- 'Top Hat' (F)	LRHS MAsh
- 'Toro' (F)	GTwe LRHS MAsh
- 'Weymouth' (F)	SDea
crassifolium	GKir LRHS MAsh
subsp. *sempervirens* 'Well's Delight' (F)	
cylindraceum ♀H4	CPLG EPfP MBro SSta WAbe WFar WPat
- 'Tinkerbelle'	ITim NLAp WAbe
delavayi	GGar GKir LRHS MAsh MBar MDun NRya SReu SSpi SSta WAbe WFar
donianum	see *V. sprengelii*
dunalianum	CBcs
- var. *caudatifolium* B&SWJ 1716	WCru
emarginatum	SSta
floribundum	CBcs CDoC CFil CMHG GGar GKir GTou IDee LRHS MAsh MDun NLar SPer SSpi SSta WPGP WPic
glaucoalbum ♀H3-4	CAbP CDoC CPLG EPfP GGGa GKir IDee LRHS MAsh MBar MRav SMad SPer SPoG SSpi WBod WDin SReu SSta
griffithianum	ELan GKir GTwe LRHS MAsh MBar
§ *macrocarpon* (F)	MBri NWCA SDea SRms
- 'CN' (F)	ESim MGos
- 'Early Black' (F)	CBcs MGos SLdr
- 'Franklin' (F)	EPot ESim
- 'Hamilton' (F)	CStu GCrs GEdr ITim LTwo NHol NLAp WPat
- 'McFarlin' (F)	EMui
- 'Olson's Honkers' (F)	ESim
- 'Pilgrim' (F)	ESim
mortinia	NMen
moupinense	CDoC GKir IMGH LRHS MAsh WAbe

- 'Variegatum' (v)	LTwo
myrtillus	GPoy MBar WDin
'Nimo Pink'	MBar
nummularia	CNic EHyt GEdr GKir ITim NLAp
	SReu SSpi WAbe WPic
ovatum	CBcs CMHG GBin IDee LRHS
	MBar MDun SPer SSta WPic
- 'Thundercloud'	CAbP LRHS MAsh
§ *oxycoccos* (F)	CArn GPoy WWes
padifolium	CFil WPGP
pallidum	IBlr
palustre	see *V. oxycoccos*
parvifolium	SReu
praestans	ESim GIBF NHol NLar
retusum	CTrw IDee WBod WDin WPic
sikkimense	GGGa
§ *sprengelii*	CBcs
uliginosum	GIBF
vitis-idaea	CNic EWTr GGar GPoy MBar
	MGos NLAp SRot WFar
- 'Autumn Beauty'	NLar
- 'Betsy Sinclair' **new**	CStu
- 'Compactum'	EWes NLAp
- Koralle Group ♀H4	EPfP MBar MBri MRav NHol WPat
- var. *minus*	EHyt GCrs GKir MAsh NLar NMen
	SOkd WAbe
- 'Red Pearl'	CSBt EPfP LRHS MAsh MGos
	MSwo SPer
* - 'Variegatum' (v)	EWes NLAp WPat

Valeriana (*Valerianaceae*)

'Alba'	see *Centranthus ruber* 'Albus'
alliariifolia	EMon GCal NBro NSti WCot
arizonica	CLyd CStu EDAr MSte
'Coccinea'	see *Centranthus ruber*
coreana	CFee
hardwickii	GPoy
jatamansii	CArn EBee GPoy
montana	GTou NBro NRya SRms SWat
moyanoi	CFil
officinalis	More than 30 suppliers
- subsp. *sambucifolia*	CFee CPom SHar WCAu WHil
* - 'Variegata' (v)	WCHb
phu 'Aurea'	More than 30 suppliers
* - 'Purpurea'	ECoo
pyrenaica	ECha EHrv SHar WCot
saxatilis	NRya
supina	NWCA
tatamana	WEas
wallrothii	WCot

Valerianella (*Valerianaceae*)

§ *locusta*	GPoy
olitoria	see *V. locusta*

Vallea (*Elaeocarpaceae*)

stipularis	CDoC CTCP
- var. *pyrifolia*	CPLG CPle

Vallota see *Cyrtanthus*

Vancouveria (*Berberidaceae*)

chrysantha	CDes CElw CFil CPom EBee ECha
	EMan ERos GBuc GEil IBlr LEur
	LHop MNrw MRav NLar NRya
	NWCA SSpi WCru WSHC
hexandra	CDes CElw CFil CPom EBee ECGN
	EHrv EMan EMon EPar EPla ERos
	GBuc GCal GEil GFlt GKir IBlr
	LEur NRya NSti SMad SSpi WAbe
	WBea WCru WTin WWin
planipetala	IBlr LEur SSpi WCru

veitchberry see *Rubus* 'Veitchberry'

Veltheimia (*Hyacinthaceae*)

§ *bracteata* ♀H1	CHal EBak IBlr SYvo WCot
§ *capensis* ♀H1	CSev MTPN
viridifolia Jacq.	see *V. bracteata*
viridifolia hort.	see *V. capensis*

x *Venidioarctotis* see *Arctotis*

Venidium see *Arctotis*

Veratrilla (*Gentianaceae*)

baillonii **new**	GKev

Veratrum ✿ (*Melanthiaceae*)

album	CFil ECha GBuc GIBF LRHS MRav
	SBla SChu SSpi WBrE WCot WCru
	WFar
- var. *flavum*	LPhx WCot WCru
- var. *oxysepalum*	WCru
californicum	CFil GCal IBlr WSHC
dolichopetalum	WCru
B&SWJ 4416	
formosanum	MMil MNrw
- B&SWJ 1575	WCru
maackii var. *maackii*	WCru
B&SWJ 5831	
nigrum ♀H4	CBos CBro CDes CFil CFir EMil
	GBuc GCal LPhx MMil MNrw
	NBPC NBhm NBir NChi NCot
	NGby NGdn NLar SChu SMad
	SMrm SPlb SPoG SSpi WCAu
	WCom WCot WFar WTin
stamineum	WCru
viride	EBee GFlt IBlr NLar SBla SSpi

Verbascum ✿ (*Scrophulariaceae*)

adzharicum	IFro MAnH MBro NBur WHoo
	WSan
- 'Charles Delight'	MSph
Allestree hybrids	CFee EHol EHrv EMar
'Annie May' **new**	ECoo LPhx
'Apricot Sunset'	ECoo LPhx MAnH
'Arctic Summer'	see *V. bombyciferum*
	'Polarsommer'
arcturus	WPer
'Aurora' **new**	LPhx
'Aztec Gold' **new**	LPhx
* *bakerianum*	EBla ECtt EMan MAnH MSPs
	MWrn NLRH WHil WMoo
'Banana and Custard'	CWCL EBee EOMN MAnH MBct
	SPet WSan
'Bill Bishop'	SIng
blattaria	EBee EHrv LIck LRHS MBow
	MNFA MWgw MWrn NBir SWat
	WEas WFar WHer WPer WWhi
- MESE 560	EBee
- f. *albiflorum*	CBot CBri CNic CSpe EBee ECGN
	EChP EMar ERou LHop LLWP
	LPhx LRHS MBro MHer MWrn
	NSti SGar SMHy WHer WPer WTin
- pink	CBri EBee EGoo NPPs STes WGMN
- yellow	CBri SWat WSan
* *boerhavii* bicolor	MAnH WRos
§ *bombyciferum*	CBre CSev EBlw EChP ECha NGdn
	NPSI NSti SRms WCot WSSM
	WWeb XPep
- BSSS 232	WCru
* - 'Arctic Snow' **new**	WWpP
§ - 'Polarsommer'	CBot CHrt CSam CSpe EBre EPfP
	ERou EWTr GGar GKir LRHS MBri
	MFan NBir NBlu NVic SPer SPet
	SRms SWat WLow WViv WWeb
- 'Silver Lining'	NBur NPer SDnm WBry

'Brookside'   ECoo LPhx MSte
'Broussa'   see *V. bombyciferum*
'Buttercup' **new**   CFai EBee EMan WHil
'Butterscotch'   MAnH MSph
'Caribbean Crush'   CFai CHar CSpe CWCL EBee ELan
                    EMan LAst LBuc MBNS MMil
                    NCGa NPri SDnm
(Caribbean Crush   EBee ENot EPfP
  Group) 'Mango'
'Catherine' **new**   WWeb
chaixii   CHea CSam EBee EBlw ECha ECtt
                    EHrv GAbr GBuc LRHS MMHG
                    MWgw NBir SBla WAul WFar
                    WMoo WPer
- 'Album' ♥H4   More than 30 suppliers
- 'Clent Sunrise'   NPri
- 'Helene Bowles' **new** CHar
chaixii x 'Wendy's   MAvo MDKP
  Choice'
'Charles Harper'   ECoo LPhx MSph MSte
'Claire' **new**   LPhx
'Clementine' **new**   LPhx
(Cotswold Group)   More than 30 suppliers
  'Cotswold Beauty'
  ♥H4
- 'Cotswold Queen' More than 30 suppliers
- 'Gainsborough' ♥H4 More than 30 suppliers
- 'Mont Blanc'   EBee EChP ECot EFou EHrv EMan
                    EMar LAst LPio LRHS MAnH MLLN
                    SChu SWat WSan
- 'Pink Domino' ♥H4 More than 30 suppliers
- 'Royal Highland' COlW EChP ECot ECtt EFou EHrv
                    ELan EMar EPfP ERou GKir LAst
                    LPio LRHS MAnH MAvo MCLN
                    MTis MWat NGdn NLar NSti SChu
                    SDnm SWat SWvt WCot WFar
                    WMnd WWeb
- 'White Domino'   EBee ERou LRHS MBNS NGby
                    NPri SPla WCAu WViv WWol
'Cotswold King'   CSpe EBee LHop LPio MBri MSph
                    NDov SDnm WCot WPGP WSan
creticum   EBee LPhx SUsu WPer
'Daisy Alice'   ECoo LPhx MAnH MSte
'Dark Lady' **new**   LPhx
§ *densiflorum*   CArn EBee ECoo ERou NFla WFar
                    WPer
'Dijon' **new**   ECtt EWes
dumulosum ♥H2-3 CSam EDAr EHyt EPot NWCA
                    WAbe
epixanthinum   CHar CPla ECoo EMan GMac ITer
                    MAnH MCCP MDKP MWrn NCGa
                    NLar
- MESE 552   EBee
'Golden Wings' ♥H2-3 CPla ECtt ITim NMen WAbe WPat
'Helen Johnson'   More than 30 suppliers
'Hiawatha' **new**   LPhx
'High Noon' **new**   LPhx
I x *hybridum*   EBee ECGP MAnH MHer MSPs
  'Copper Rose'   MWrn SPet WGMN WHil
- 'Snow Maiden'   CBri CPen EBee MAnH MBri MSPs
                    MWrn SDnm WBry WGMN WRHF
- 'Wega' **new**   CBot SSvw
'Innocence' **new**   MAvo
'Jackie'   More than 30 suppliers
'Jolly Eyes'   EBee EChP EMan MAvo MBnl MTis
                    NCGa NCot WSan
'June Johnson'   MAnH SHar WHil
'Kalypso' **new**   LPhx
'Klondike' **new**   LPhx
'Kynaston'   MAnH SHar
'Letitia' ♥H3   More than 30 suppliers
longifolium   LRHS WFar
- MESE 394   EBee
- var. *pannosum*   see *V. olympicum*

* *luridifolium* **new** WPGP
lychnitis   CArn LPhx WHer WOut
'Megan's Mauve'   CWCL EBee EBre ECot EMan EWll
                    NPSI NSti SLon SPer SWvt WSpi
                    WWeb
'Monster'   LPhx MAnH MSph MSte
'Moonshadow' **new**   LPhx
'Mystery Blonde' **new** LPhx
nigrum   CArn CHrt EBee ECtt EPfP GFlt
                    LRHS MAnH MBNS MBow MWrn
                    NChi NGHP NSti SBri SECG SEND
                    SMer SRob SWal WBVN WCAu
                    WCot WFar WHer WMoo WPer
                    WShp WWpP
- var. *album*   EBee LPio MAnH NGHP NLar
                    WCAu WMoo
'Nimrod' **new**   LPhx
'Norfolk Dawn'   ECoo LPhx MAnH MSte
§ *olympicum*   CHrt CPLG CSam EBee EBlw ECtt
                    EGoo ELan ENot EPfP GKir LPVe
                    LRHS MBNS MWgw NBPC NLRH
                    NOak SDix SEND SRob SWal WBry
                    WCAu WCot WFar WPer WShp
                    XPep
oreophilum   EBee
'Patricia'   ECoo LPhx MSph MSte
phlomoides   EMan WOut
phoeniceum   CArn EBee ECGN ELan EPfP LPVe
                    LRHS MWgw NBro NOak SBri
                    SECG SGar SMer SPet SPlb WAul
                    WBVN WEas WHen WPer WSSM
                    WShp WWeb WWin
* - 'Album'   CSpe EBee LIck WBrE
- 'Flush of Pink'   ECtt
- 'Flush of White' CBot EBre ECtt EGoo EMan ERou
                    LAst LPhx LRHS MSPs NChi NPri
                    SDnm SRob STes WGor WHen
                    WHil WMoo WWpP
- hybrids   CBot CSpe ECtt EGoo EMan MHer
                    NBid NBlu NChi NGdn NVic SRms
                    SWat WFar WGor WPer
- 'Violetta'   More than 30 suppliers
I 'Phoenix' **new**   LPhx
'Pink Ice'   MAvo
'Primrose Cottage' ECoo LPhx MAnH
pyramidatum   CBot EBee LPhx WHer
'Raspberry Ripple' CBAn EBee EBre ELan EMan EMar
                    ENot EPfP IHMH MAnH MAvo
                    NPSI SDnm SPer
'Raspberry Sorbet' CBAn EMan
rorippifolium   CFwr CHea EWll LPhx MSPs WCot
                    WHil
'Royal Candles' **new** NCot
'Southern Charm'   CWCL EChP ECtt EMan ERou EWll
                    LPVe LRHS MAnH MAvo MBct
                    MBri NChi NGHP NVic SDnm STes
                    WHil WSan WWpP
* 'Spica'   CBot EBee GMac MSPs NLar
spicatum   CBot WFar
spinosum   SBla
'Summer Sorbet'   EBee EBre ELan EMan ENot EPfP
                    SPer
* Sunset shades   MSph WWpP
thapsiforme   see *V. densiflorum*
thapsus   COld CSev EBee GFlt GPoy GWCH
                    MBow MHer NMir NSco SRob
                    WHHs WSel WWye
'Tilney Moonbeam'   ECtt EMar
undulatum   CArn
'Valerie Grace'   ECoo LPhx MAnH MSte
'Vernale'   CBot
'Virginia' **new**   LPhx
wiedemannianum   EBee LPhx SIgm WHer
'Yellow Johnson' **new** EMan NCot

Verbena (Verbenaceae)

'Adonis Light Blue' (G)	LRHS
'Aphrodite'	LAst
'Apple Blossom' (G)	LRHS
'Aveyron' (G)	GBri SChu
Aztec Series Aztec Lavender Improved = 'Balazlavi' **new**	LIck
- Aztec Magic Pink = 'Balazpima' PBR **new**	LIck
- Aztec Magic Plum **new**	NPri
- Aztec Magic Silver = 'Balazsilma' **new**	LIck NPri
- Aztec Red = 'Balazred' **new**	LIck NPri
- Aztec White = 'Balazwhit' **new**	LIck
'Betty Lee'	ECtt
'Blue Cascade' (G)	LAst
'Blue Prince' (G)	CSpe
§ *bonariensis* ♀H3-4	More than 30 suppliers
- variegated (v)	ITer
'Boon' (G)	ECtt
'Booty' (G)	ECtt
'Boughton House' (G)	MSte
bracteata	GEil
canadensis (G)	EBee SUsu
- 'Perfecta' (G)	MGol
'Candy Carousel' (G)	SPet
chamaedrifolia	see *V. peruviana*
'Claret' (G)	CBAn EBee GBri MAsh WPen WViv
corymbosa	CBrm CHea CHll CM&M CPen CRez EBee EChP ECha EGra EMan EPPr GBBs GSki LHop LLWP NBPC NLar SAga SBla SBod WCom WCot WPer WWpP
- 'Gravetye'	CHad CHrt GBuc GCal NCiC WFar
'Diamond Butterfly' (G)	WWol
'Diamond Carouselle' (G)	WWol
'Diamond Merci' (G)	LIck WWol
'Diamond Oranginia' (G) **new**	LIck WWol
'Diamond Rubiniana' (G) **new**	WWol
'Diamond Topaz' (G)	LIck WWol
'Edith Eddleman' (G)	CPlt EBee EChP ECtt LRHS MNrw
* 'Fiesta'	WCot
* 'Foxhunter' (G)	EMan
'Freefall'	GBri
gooddingii **new**	WCot
hastata	More than 30 suppliers
- 'Alba'	CBri CHar EBee EChP EMan EMon EPyc EWTr GBar GBuc GSki LDai MCCP MDKP MLLN NBPC STes WCAu WHrl WMoo WPer WTin WWin WWpP
- 'Rosea'	More than 30 suppliers
'Hidcote Purple' (G)	MSte
hispida (G)	EBee
'Homestead Purple' (G)	CHrt CSev EBee EBre ECGP EChP ECtt EMan ENor EPfP GSki LDai LIck MAsh MWgw SAga SCoo SGar SMrm SUsu WGwG
'Huntsman' (G)	GBuc
'Imagination' (G)	LRHS
incompta	EBee EMan
'Jenny's Wine' (G)	CElw ECtt EMan SMrm
N 'Kemerton' (G)	EMan
'La France' (G)	CHea CSam ECha ECtt EMan EPfP GBri LPhx MAnh SAga SChu SDix SMHy SMrm SOkh SUsu WHoo
Lanai Series 'Lanai Lavender Star' **new**	NPri
- 'Lanai Purple'	SCoo
'Lawrence Johnston' (G) ♀H3	MAJR WHen
litoralis	EBee
'Lois' Ruby'	CSam EPfP SAga SMHy SUsu
'Loveliness' (G)	EMan IBlr SMer
macdougalii	EBee EChP EGoo EMan GEil IFro MGol WWpP
officinalis	CArn CRWN EDAr GBar GPoy MGol MHer MSal SECG SIde WHer WJek WLHH WPer WSel WWye XPep
patagonica	see *V. bonariensis*
'Peach Blossom' (G)	WCot
'Peaches and Cream' (G) ♀H3	LRHS NPri
§ *peruviana* (G)	EBre EPfP MAsh SBla SChu SDix SIng SRms
'Pink Bouquet'	see *V. 'Silver Anne'*
'Pink Cascade'	NBlu
'Pink Parfait' (G)	CHal CHrt ECtt EMan EPfP LAst SMer SPet
'Pink Pearl' (G)	ECtt
platensis RCB/Arg P-2 **new**	WCot
'Purple Sissinghurst' (G)	CSam
'Raspberry Crush' (G)	LRHS
'Red Cascade'	SPet
§ *rigida* ♀H3	More than 30 suppliers
- 'Lilacina'	XPep
- 'Polaris'	CHad CHar CStr EBee IBal LHop LRHS SMrm SUsu WCAu WWpP
* 'Royal Purple'	EMan
§ 'Silver Anne' (G) ♀H3	CHrt CSam EBee ECtt EMan LDai SChu SDix SMer SUsu WEas WHen
§ 'Sissinghurst' (G) ♀H2-3	CSam CWCL ECtt EMan LAst NPri SIng SMrm SPoG SRms WEas WHen
* 'Snow Flurry'	CFir WCot
stricta	EBee EMan
Tapien Pink = 'Sunver' PBR (G)	LAst WWol
Tapien Salmon = 'Sunmaref' (G)	LAst WWol
Tapien Violet = 'Sunvop' PBR (G)	LAst WWol
Tapien White (G) **new**	LAst
Temari Blue = 'Sunmaribu' (G) **new**	LAst
Temari Coral Pink = 'Sunmariripi' PBR (G)	LAst SCoo
Temari Scarlet = 'Sunmarisu' PBR (G)	LAst SCoo
Temari Violet = 'Sunmariba' PBR (G)	SCoo
Temari White = 'Sunmaririho' PBR (G)	LAst WWol
'Tenerife'	see *V. 'Sissinghurst'*
tenuisecta (G)	WMoo WPer XPep
venosa	see *V. rigida*
Waterfall Blue = 'Dofall' PBR	CWCL NPri

Verbesina (Asteraceae)

alternifolia	CArn EMan MGol
- 'Goldstrahl'	EBee WCAu
helianthoides	CTCP EBee EWll

Vernonia (Asteraceae)

crinita	EBee ECha EFou MWat NLar SIgm SMad SSvw WCAu
- 'Mammuth'	EMan LHop LPhx WCot
fasciculata	EBee EChP EMan LRHS NLar SSvw WCAu WCot

gigantea new	EPAt
noveboracensis	EBee ECGN MGol SMrm WPer WWpP
- 'Albiflora'	NLar WPer

Veronica (Scrophulariaceae)

amethystina	see *V. spuria*
armena	CLyd EBre EWes MDKP MHer MSte MWat NLRH NMen NRya NWCA SBla SRot WFar
§ **austriaca**	MLLN WFar WMoo
- var. **dubia**	see *V. prostrata*
- 'Ionian Skies'	More than 30 suppliers
§ - subsp. **teucrium**	CArn EBee LPVe MFOX MWgw NDlv SMac SRms WFar WOut WPer
- - 'Blue Blazer'	SCro
- - 'Blue Fountain'	LLWP
- - 'Crater Lake Blue' ♀H4	ECha ECtt EFou ENot EOrc ERou GEil LHop LPhx LRHS MAvo MRav NBid NCGa NFor SAga SMrm SPla SPlb SRms WCom WCot WEas WFar WMnd WPer WWin
- - 'Kapitän'	ECha GBuc NCGa NPro SMrm WFar WPer
- - 'Knallblau'	EBee EFou EMil LRHS MBri NCGa SSvw
- - 'Königsblau'	EBee WBea
- - 'Royal Blue' ♀H4	EBee ECot EFou EMan EMlt EPfP GBuc GFlt LPio LRHS MWrn NOak NSti WBea WFar WMnd WMoo WWeb
- - 'Shirley Blue'	see *V.* 'Shirley Blue'
bachofenii new	WTin
beccabunga	CArn CBen CWat EHon ELan EMFW EPfP GPoy LNCo LPBA MGas MSta NArg NMir NPer NSco SWat WFar WHer WMAq WWpP
- var. **limosa new**	WWye
bellidioides	GTou
'Bergen's Blue'	EBee EChP MBri NLar NPro SCro
Blue Bouquet	see *V. longifolia* 'Blaubündel'
'Blue Indigo' **new**	CHar EBee EFou IBal
'Blue Spire'	SWat WPer
bombycina	ITim NWCA WLin
- subsp. **bolkardaghensis**	NMen
bonarota	see *Paederota bonarota*
caespitosa	CPBP EPot MDHE
- subsp. **caespitosa**	CLyd EHyt NMen WAbe
candida	see *V. spicata* subsp. *incana*
x **cantiana** 'Kentish Pink'	CStr EGoo GBuc MBro MHer SHel SIng SPla WBea WDyG WPer WSpi
caucasica	LPhx SAga WCru
chamaedrys	NMir XPep
§ - 'Miffy Brute' (v)	EBee MDKP MHar NBir NFla NHol NPro WCom WHer
- 'Pam' (v)	CBre EMan EPPr WCHb WWpP
- 'Variegata'	see *V. chamaedrys* 'Miffy Brute'
- 'Waterrow'	EMon
cinerea ♀H4	CLyd MBro SAga WEas WHoo WSHC
dabneyi	CDes
'Darwin's Blue' PBR	CMHG EBee EChP ECtt MBNS MBri WCot WGwG WHHs
'Ellen Mae'	EBee WCAu
'Eveline' **new**	EBee EMan EPfP MBNS WCot
exaltata	CWCL EBee ECGN EChP EMFP EMan GBuc LPhx MSte NBur NChi SAga WCot WPer
'Fantasy'	SMHy
filiformis	GWCH WShp
- 'Fairyland' (v)	CBgR EMan EMon EWes WCHb
formosa	see *Paederota formosa*
§ **fruticans**	GTou

fruticulosa	NWCA
gentianoides ♀H4	More than 30 suppliers
- 'Alba'	CMea EOrc GCal NBid NChi NSti SAga
- 'Barbara Sherwood'	EBee EBre GKir GMac MFir MLLN MNFA WCot
- 'Blue Streak' **new**	WHil
- 'Lilacina'	EBee LRHS
- 'Nana'	EOrc MMil WBrE
- 'Pallida'	EBee EMan ENot EPfP IHMH LRHS MBrN MRav MSph NPri SPlb WBor WFar WShp
- 'Robusta'	EBee GMac LRHS MSph NCGa SPet WMnd
- 'Tissington White'	More than 30 suppliers
- 'Variegata' (v)	More than 30 suppliers
'Goodness Grows'	EMan LAst LRHS SChu
grandis	EBee EChP EMan EWll GAbr MDKP MGol MHar MTis MWhi MWrn NBur NChi NLar NPPs SPoG WBVN WBrk WMoo WOut
x **guthrieana**	CNic EMlt GEdr NMen SRms SRot WCru WFar WPer
'Heraud'	EBee WCAu
incana	see *V. spicata* subsp. *incana*
* - 'Candidissima'	GCal
'Inspiration'	EFou LPhx SCro SMrm
* **keiskei** pink	ECtt
kellereri	see *V. spicata*
kiusiana	CPlt CStr EBee EBre EMan MDKP MTis MWrn NBPC NLar SMac SPoG
* - var. **maxima new**	CTCP
kotschyana	CPBP
liwanensis	EDAr NMen SScr XPep
- Mac&W 5936	EPot MDKP
longifolia	CSBt EBee ECGN ECha ELan EPfP EShb EWTr GWCH MFir MHar MWgw NPPs SMrm STes WBVN WBea WCom WEas WFar WMoo WWye
- 'Alba'	CHea EBee EChP ELan EMan EPfP WBea WCAu WMoo
§ - 'Blaubündel'	EBee ERou LPVe MDKP NGdn SMac WWeb
- 'Blauer Sommer'	EBee EChP EFou EMan LRHS NGdn WMnd
§ - 'Blauriesin'	CKno CM&M COlW CTri EBee ECGP EMil ERou GLil MBnl MBow MBri NFla NSti SMad SPer SSvw WFar WShp
- Blue Giantess	see *V. longifolia* 'Blauriesin'
- 'Blue John'	EBee EFou WCAu
- 'Fascination'	MOne NGdn NPro SMrm WSan
- 'Foerster's Blue'	see *V. longifolia* 'Blauriesin'
- 'Joseph's Coat' (v)	EBee EGle NBrk
- 'Lila Karina'	EBee WPer
- 'Lilac Fantasy'	EBee EFou WCAu
- 'Oxford Blue'	LRHS WRHF
- 'Rose Tone'	ECha ERou MDKP WGMN WMoo WSSM
- 'Rosea'	EBee EChP EOMN ERou MGol STes WBrE WPer
- 'Schneeriesin'	CKno CPrp EBee ECGP ECha EHrv LRHS MBnl MBri NBir SChu SPer WShp
lyallii	see *Parahebe lyallii*
macrostachya	EBee
'Martje'	SMrm
montana 'Corinne Tremaine' (v)	CBgR EBee EMan EMar EMon IFro IHMH LHop MBct MHar NBir NCGa SRms WCot WHer WRHF WWye
nipponica	SScr WPer
nummularia	NBur WPer

§ **wormskjoldii**	EBee EDAr EMlt IHMH LAst MAvo
	MBrN MBro NCGa NMen NWCA
	SBla SHel SRms WLin WPer WWin
- 'Alba'	EMlt MDHE MDKP WPer

Veronicastrum (Scrophulariaceae)

japonicum	ECGN
latifolium BWJ 8158 **new**	WCru
sibiricum BWJ 6352 **new**	WCru
villosulum	CPom WCot WCru
§ **virginicum**	CArn CHea CRow EBee EChP
	ECha ECtt EFou EHrv GKir NBir
	NSti SRms WHHs WMoo WPer
	WWhi WWin WWpP
- 'Alboroseum'	ECGN EMan WTin
- 'Album'	More than 30 suppliers
- 'Apollo'	CBre EBee EChP ECtt EFou EGle
	EMan EPfP ERou LAst LPhx LRHS
	MBri MWgw NBro NLar NSti
	SMHy WAul WCAu WHil WShp
	WTMC
- 'Diane'	CElw EBee EGle LPhx
- 'Fascination'	More than 30 suppliers
§ - var. **incarnatum**	CBri CKno EBee ECGN ELan EMan
	GKir LPhx LRHS MBow MRav
	MWgw NBro NDov NFla SMHy
	SPer STes SYvo WBor WFar
- - 'Pink Glow'	CHar EBee EBre ECtt EFou EHoe
	EHrv ELan EMan EMil EPfP EWTr
	GAbr GKir LHop LPhx MTis NBPC
	NGdn NSti SAga SMrm SOkh SPla
	WCAu WFar WMnd
- 'Lavendelturm'	CPlt EBee ECha EGle EMil LPhx
	LRHS NDov SOkh WCot WTMC
- 'Pointed Finger'	EFou SMrm SOkh
- **roseum**	see *V. virginicum* var. *incarnatum*
- var. **sibiricum**	CStr EBee ECha GCal NBid SBla
	SCro SVal WHoo WMoo
- 'Spring Dew'	CBre CElw EBee EChP EGle EMan
	ERou LPhx MWgw NBid NBro
	NDov NLar WCAu WMnd
- 'Temptation'	CHVG EBee EChP EFou EGle EMan
	ERou LPhx MAvo MTed NBro
	NDov NLar SMHy WCAu
'White Jolan'	CFir CHar

Verschaffeltia (Arecaceae)

splendida	XBlo

Verticordia (Myrtaceae)

chrysantha **new**	SOWG
longistylis **new**	SOWG
minutiflora **new**	SOWG
plumosa purple	SOWG

Vestia (Solanaceae)

§ **foetida** ♀H1	CBcs CPLG CPom CTCP CTrC
	CWib EChP EMan EPfP ERea
	MNrw SDnm SGar SHFr SOWG
	WHil WKif WPGP WPer WPic
	WSHC WWye
lycioides	see *V. foetida*

Vetiveria (Poaceae)

zizanioides	MSal

Viburnum ✿ (Caprifoliaceae)

acerifolium	CBcs CFil CPle GIBF WBod WFar
	WHCG WPat
alnifolium	see *V. lantanoides*
atrocyaneum	CFil CPle ISea WBcn WFar WHCG
	WPGP WPat
- B&SWJ 7272	WCru
awabuki	CFil CHEx EBee EPfP NLar WPGP

- B&SWJ 8404	WCru
- 'Emerald Lustre'	CDoC CHEx CSam
betulifolium	CAbP CBrd CFil CMCN CPLG
	CPMA CPle CTrw EPfP EPla GIBF
	MBlu NLar WHCG WPGP
- B&SWJ 1619	WCru
bitchiuense	CPMA CPle ELan WWes
x **bodnantense**	CBot CTri CTrw CWSG EBee
	MDun MRav MWat NDlv NFor
	WHar WStl WTel WWin
- 'Charles Lamont' ♀H4	More than 30 suppliers
- 'Dawn' ♀H4	More than 30 suppliers
- 'Deben' ♀H4	CDoC EBee ENot EPfP GKir LRHS
	MBlu MBri MRav MWya SKee SPer
	WBod WCru WDin WFar
bracteatum	CFil CPle EPfP
buddlejifolium	EPfP GEil GKir SSpi WBcn WCru
	WFar WHCG
burejaeticum	GIBF
x **burkwoodii**	More than 30 suppliers
- 'Anne Russell' ♀H4	More than 30 suppliers
- 'Chenaultii'	EPfP WCru WDin
- 'Compact Beauty'	EPfP WPat
- 'Conoy'	CPMA
- 'Fulbrook' ♀H4	CAbP CMHG EPfP LRHS MAsh
	MBri WDin WFar
- 'Mohawk'	CAbP CDoC CEnd CPMA ELan
	EPfP GKir LRHS MAsh MBri NLar
	SCoo SMur SPla SSpi SWvt WBcn
	WPGP WPat
- 'Park Farm Hybrid' ♀H4	CAbP CDoC CPMA CSam CTri
	CWSG EBee EBre ECrN ELan ENot
	EPfP GKir LAst LRHS MAsh MBro
	MRav MSwo NBea NSti SLPl SPer
	SRms WCru WPat
calvum **new**	GEil
x **carlcephalum** ♀H4	More than 30 suppliers
- 'Cayuga'	NLar WPat
* - 'Variegatum' (v)	CPMA
carlesii	CBcs CDul CWib EBee ENot EPfP
	GIBF GKir LRHS MBlu MRav NPri
	SCoo SLim SPer SReu WStl WTel
- 'Aurora' ♀H4	More than 30 suppliers
- 'Charis'	CMHG CPMA CSBt LRHS NLar
	WBcn WBod
- 'Compactum'	CPMA
- 'Diana'	CEnd CMHG CPMA EPfP GKir
	LRHS MAsh MBro MWya NLar SPer
	SSpi WPat WPen
- 'Marlou'	EPfP NLar
cassinoides	CPle EPfP GEil GKir NMen WFar
	WPat
'Chesapeake'	CBrm CDoC CMHG CPMA EBee
	EWes LRHS NLar NPro SEND
	WBcn WBod WWes
chingii	CFil CPMA CPle GGGa SLon WCru
	WPGP
'Chippewa' **new**	NLar
cinnamomifolium ♀H3	CAbP CBcs CBot CFil CHEx CPle
	ECre EPfP GEil GKir ISea LRHS
	MAsh NRib SAPC SArc SLon SMac
	SPer SSpi WBod WFar WHCG
	WPGP WSHC
cotinifolium	CPle
cylindricum	CBot CFil CMCN CPle EPfP SReu
	SSpi WBcn WCru WPGP
- B&SWJ 7239	WCru
- HWJCM 434	WCru
dasyanthum	CPle EPfP GIBF GKir IArd NLar
davidii ♀H4	More than 30 suppliers
- (f)	CBcs CDoC CDoC CSBt ELan EPfP
	GIBF GKir MAsh MDun MGos
	SHBN SPer SPla SReu SRms SSta
	WBod WPat

- (m)	CBcs CBot CDoC CSBt CWSG ELan EPfP GIBF GKir MAsh MDun MGos MRav SPer SPla SReu SRms SSta WBod WPat
dentatum	EPfP WPGP
- var. **deamii**	GIBF
§ - var. **pubescens**	CPle
dilatatum	CPne GIBF SSpi
- B&SWJ 4456	WCru
- 'Erie'	EPfP NLar
- 'Iroquois' **new**	EPfP
erosum B&SWJ 3585	WCru
erubescens	CPMA WFar WWes
- B&SWJ 8281	WCru
- var. **gracilipes**	CPle EPfP
'Eskimo'	CAbP CDul CPMA CWSG EBee ECrN EPfP GKir LAst LRHS MAsh MBNS MBlu MBro MGos MRav NBlu NMoo SLim SMur SReu SSpi SWvt WDin WFar WPat WWes
§ **farreri** ♀H4	More than 30 suppliers
- 'Album'	see *V. farreri* 'Candidissimum'
§ - 'Candidissimum'	CBot CFil EBee ELan EPfP GKir IArd IMGH LPio LRHS MMHG SKee SPer SSpi WBcn WPat
- 'December Dwarf'	NLar
- 'Farrer's Pink'	CAbP CPMA NHol NLar
- 'Fioretta'	ENot WFar
- 'Nanum'	CFil CPMA EPfP MBar MBrN MRav NHol NLar SChu WFar WHCG WPat
foetens	see *V. grandiflorum* f. *foetens*
foetidum	CPle
- var. **rectangulatum** B&SWJ 3637	WCru
fragrans Bunge	see *V. farreri*
'Fragrant Cloud'	ECrN MGos
furcatum ♀H4	EPfP GIBF IArd NLar SSpi WHCG
- B&SWJ 5939	WCru
x **globosum**	CAbP CBcs CDoC CEnd CFil
'Jermyns Globe'	CMHG EBee EPla GKir MBar MGos MRav MSte SLon SMur WBod WCru WDin WFar WHCG WPGP
grandiflorum	CPMA CSBt
§ - f. **foetens**	EPfP WBod
- 'Snow White'	ERea
harryanum	CFil CMHG CPle CPne EBee EPfP GEil GKir LRHS MBNS SMac SOWG WCru WFar WPGP WSHC
henryi	CAbP CFil CPle ECrN EPfP LRHS NLar WBcn WDin WHCG WPat
x **hillieri**	CAbP CFil CPle GBin MRav MWhi NRib WBcn WFar WHCG WKif
- 'Winton' ♀H4	CAbP CDoC EPfP EPla GEil GKir LRHS MBri MTis NPro SHBN SLim SLon SOWG SSpi WBod WCru WDin WFar WPGP
hupehense new	GEil
ichangense	NLar
japonicum	CFil CHEx CPle CSam EPfP GKir SHBN WPGP
x **juddii** ♀H4	More than 30 suppliers
koreanum	WBod
- B&SWJ 4231	WCru
lantana	CBgR CCVT CDul CLnd CRWN CTri ECrN ENot EWTr GKir GWCH LBuc MBow NWea SKee SPer WDin WFar WMou WStI
- 'Aureum'	CBot ECtt EHoe MBlu NLar WBcn
- 'Mohican'	NPro WWes
- 'Variefolium' (v)	CPMA
- 'Xanthocarpum'	GKir
§ **lantanoides**	EPfP GKir NLar SSpi
lentago	CAbP CBot CPle

lobophyllum	CPle EPfP GIBF NLar
luzonicum B&SWJ 3930	WCru
- var. **oblongum** B&SWJ 3549 **new**	WCru
macrocephalum	CPMA WDin
- f. **keteleeri**	CEnd CPMA CPle SSpi
mariesii	see *V. plicatum* f. *tomentosum* 'Mariesii'
nervosum B&SWJ 2251a	WCru
nudum	CPle EBee EPfP GIBF NLar WWes
- var. **angustifolium**	GIBF
- 'Pink Beauty'	CPMA CWSG LRHS MRav WFar WPGP
odoratissimum	CBcs CFil CPle EPfP IArd SHBN
misapplied	SSpi WSHC
odoratissimum	CHEx CPLG CSam SMur XPep
- B&SWJ 6913	WCru
- 'Emerald Lustre'	see *V. awabuki* 'Emerald Lustre'
- 'Oneida'	NLar WDin
opulus	More than 30 suppliers
- 'Aureum'	CBot CChe CDul CHar CMHG CSam CTri EBee EBre ECtt EHoe ELan EMil EPfP EWTr GKir LRHS MAsh MBar MGos MRav NHol SHBN SPer SSta WDin WFar WHCG WPat
- 'Compactum' ♀H4	More than 30 suppliers
N - 'Fructu Luteo'	ENot GKir
* - 'Harvest Gold'	EBee GKir SLim
- 'Nanum'	CAbP CPle EBee ELan EPla EPot ESis GKir MBar MRav NHol NMen NPro WDin WHCG WPat
- 'Notcutt's Variety' ♀H4	EBee ENot EPfP MGos SHBN SHFr SMur SRms WBcn WPat
- 'Park Harvest'	GKir LRHS MBri NLar NSti SLPl WPat
§ - 'Roseum' ♀H4	More than 30 suppliers
- 'Sterile'	see *V. opulus* 'Roseum'
* - 'Sterile Compactum'	IMGH
N - 'Xanthocarpum' ♀H4	CBcs CDoC CDul CMHG CSam EBee EBre EGra ELan EPfP GKir LAst LHop LRHS MBar MBlu MGos MRav MSwo MWat NHol SLPl SLon SPer SRms WBod WDin WFar WTel WWin
- 'Xanthocarpum Compactum'	EMon
parvifolium	NLar
N **plicatum**	CBot CDul CTri CWib ENot GKir IArd MBar WDin
- 'Nanum'	see *V. plicatum* f. *tomentosum* 'Nanum Semperflorens'
§ - f. **plicatum**	CBot
- - 'Grandiflorum'	CDoC CPle EPfP GKir LRHS MBar MBri SPer WBcn WHCG
- - 'Rotundifolium'	IArd NHol NLar SHBN WPat
- - 'Popcorn'	CAbP GKir LRHS MAsh SLon SReu SSpi SSta WPat
- - 'Rosace'	MBlu
- - 'Sterile'	see *V. plicatum* f. *plicatum*
- f. **tomentosum**	EWTr WDin WStI
- - 'Cascade'	EBee EWTr NLar SHBN SSpi
- - 'Dart's Red Robin'	ECtt LRHS NHol WBcn WPat
- - 'Lanarth'	More than 30 suppliers
§ - - 'Mariesii' ♀H4	More than 30 suppliers
§ - - 'Nanum Semperflorens'	CDoC CWSG EBee ECtt GEil IArd MBlu MBro MGos MRav NBlu NHol SHBN SPer WFar WHCG WPat WSHC
- - 'Pink Beauty' ♀H4	More than 30 suppliers
- - 'Rowallane'	EBee EPfP
- - 'Saint Keverne'	IArd SHBN SRob
- - 'Shasta'	CMCN COtt EPfP LRHS MBri NHol NLar SSpi WDin

- - 'Summer Snowflake'	CBrm CDoC CDul CEnd CMHG
	CWSG EBee ECrN ENot EPfP
	EWTr GKir LRHS MRav NHol
	SHBN SPer WDin WFar WHCG
- 'Watanabe'	see *V. plicatum* f. *tomentosum*
	'Nanum Semperflorens'
'Pragense' ♀H4	CAbP CBcs CDul CMCN EBee EPfP
	GEil GKir MBar MGos MRav NBlu
	NHol NRib SLon SPer WBod WDin
	WFar WHCG WPat
propinquum	CAbP
- B&SWJ 4009	WCru
pubescens	see *V. dentatum* var. *pubescens*
x *rhytidophylloides*	GKir WFar
- 'Alleghany'	NLar
- 'Dart's Duke'	ENot GKir LRHS MBri SLPl
- 'Holland'	EPla GKir
- 'Willowwood'	EBee LRHS MAsh NLar SMad SPer
	WPat
rhytidophyllum	CDul CHEx CSBt EBee ECrN ENot
	EPfP EWTr GKir ISea LPan MBar
	MGos MRav NBlu NWea SHBN
	SPer SReu SRms SSpi WAul WCFE
	WDin WFar WMoo WTel WWin
- 'Roseum'	CBot CPLG GEil MRav SLPl SWvt
- 'Variegatum' (v)	CPMA WBcn
§ *rigidum*	CFil WPGP
rufidulum **new**	NLar
sargentii	EPfP GBin GEil GIBF
- var. *calvescens* **new**	GEil
- f. *flavum* **new**	NLar
- 'Onondaga' ♀H4	More than 30 suppliers
- 'Susquehanna'	EPfP
semperflorens	see *V. plicatum* f. *tomentosum*
	'Nanum Semperflorens'
§ *setigerum*	CPle EPfP GIBF IArd NLar SLPl
	SSpi WPat
- 'Aurantiacum'	EPfP
sieboldii	CBcs CPle GIBF
- B&SWJ 2837	WCru
- 'Seneca'	EPfP NLar
subalpinum **new**	NLar
suspensum	CBcs
taiwanianum	WCru
B&SWJ 3009	
theiferum	see *V. setigerum*
tinus	More than 30 suppliers
- 'Bewley's Variegated' (v)	CBcs CDoC EBee ECrN EMil GKir
	MGos MRav SCoo SPer
I - 'Compactum'	EBee SPoG SWvt
- 'Eve Price' ♀H4	More than 30 suppliers
- 'French White' ♀H4	CBot CDoC CDul CWSG EBee
	ECrN EPfP EPla LRHS MAsh MBri
	MGos MRav MSwo SCoo STop
	SWvt WFar WPGP WWeb
- 'Gwenllian' ♀H4	More than 30 suppliers
- 'Israel'	EMil SPer SPla WFar
- 'Little Bognor'	LRHS NLar NPro
- 'Lucidum'	CBcs CSam SHBN SHGC WCFE
	WDin WFar
- 'Lucidum Variegatum' (v)	CFil CPMA EHol SDry SLim WPGP
- 'Macrophyllum'	LPan SWvt WBcn WWeb XPep
* - 'Pink Parfait'	MRav
- 'Pink Prelude'	ENot MWya
- 'Purpureum'	CBcs CSBt EBee ECrN EHoe EPfP
	EPla LRHS MAsh MRav MSwo
	SCoo SHBN SLPl SLim SPer SPoG
	WDin WFar WGwG WMoo WPat
	WWeb
- subsp. *rigidum*	see *V. rigidum*
- 'Spirit' **new**	SPoG
- 'Spring Bouquet'	MGos MWya NBee
- 'Variegatum' (v)	More than 30 suppliers
- 'Villa Noailles' **new**	XPep

tomentosum	see *V. plicatum*
trilobum	GIBF
- 'Bailey's Compact' **new**	WPat
urceolatum B&SWJ 6988	WCru
utile	CBot EPfP WFar WHCG WPGP
	WWes
wrightii	CPle EPfP MBro WHCG WPat
- var. *hessei*	EPfP GEil LRHS NLar

Vicia (Papilionaceae)
cracca	GWCH MBow NLan NSco
sepium	MGol NSco
sylvatica	CBgR WBWf

Victoria (Nymphaeaceae)
'Longwood Hybrid'	MSta

Vigna (Papilionaceae)
§ *caracalla*	MJnS

Viguiera (Asteraceae)
multiflora	WCot

Villarsia (Menyanthaceae)
bennettii	see *Nymphoides peltata*
	'Bennettii'

Vinca (Apocynaceae)
difformis ♀H3-4	CHad CHar COlW CStr CTri EBee
	ECha EMan LLWP LRHS NCGa SBri
	SDix SDry WHer WPic WWye
* - 'Alba'	CPom WCom
- subsp. *difformis*	CHid EMon
- Greystone form	CDoC CHid EPPr EPfP EPla
	LHop MBNS SCoo SEND WCAu
	WPnP
- 'Jenny Pym'	CBgR CFwr CHid CPom EBee EPPr
	GEil MAvo SMac SMad WCom
	WOut WWeb
- 'Oxford'	SLPl
- 'Snowmound'	CBgR MRav SMac
'Hidcote Purple'	see *V. major* var. *oxyloba*
major	More than 30 suppliers
- 'Alba'	GBuc WEas
- 'Caucasian Blue'	CFil EBee WPGP
- 'Elegantissima'	see *V. major* 'Variegata'
- var. *hirsuta* hort.	see *V. major* var. *oxyloba*
§ - subsp. *hirsuta* (Boiss.)	EMon MWgw WWye
Stearn	
- 'Honeydew' (v)	EMon
- 'Jason Hill'	EMon
§ - 'Maculata' (v)	CDoC CSBt EBee EMar EMon ENot
	EPAt LHop LRHS MBar MSwo
	NBPC NHol SDry SLim SPer WCru
	WDin WMoo WWeb
§ - var. *oxyloba*	CFis CNic COld CPLG CTri CWCL
	EBee ECtt ELan EMon EOrc EPla
	GSki LHop MRav SLPl SLim SMac
	SRms WHen WPic
- var. *pubescens*	see *V. major* subsp. *hirsuta*
- 'Reticulata' (v)	ELan EMon
- 'Surrey Marble'	see *V. major* 'Maculata'
§ - 'Variegata' (v) ♀H4	More than 30 suppliers
minor	CAgr CDoC CDul EBee ELan ENot
	EPar EPfP GAbr GKir GPoy MAsh
	MBar MBro MFir MHer MWat NBlu
	NPri NWea SHFr WBrE WDin WFar
	WStI WWye XPep
- f. *alba* ♀H4	CBcs CBel CBot CDoC EBee ECha
	EGoo EPfP LAst LRHS MAsh MBar
	MGos MHer MWgw NBlu NPri
	SHBN SMac SPer STre WCot WCru
	WStI WWpP WWye
- 'Alba Aureavariegata'	see *V. minor* 'Alba Variegata'

- f. *alba* 'Gertrude Jekyll' ♀H4 — More than 30 suppliers

§ - 'Alba Variegata' (v) — EBre EHoe EPPr EPla GKir LAst MAsh MBar MFir MGos MHer NChi NHol NPri NPro SPer SRms STre WBVN WBod WCot WEas WFar WHer WTel

§ - 'Argenteovariegata' (v) ♀H4 — More than 30 suppliers

§ - 'Atropurpurea' ♀H4 — More than 30 suppliers

- 'Aurea' — LBBr SPla

§ - 'Aureovariegata' (v) — CBcs CBot CChe GAbr GKir GPoy IHMH LAst LRHS MAsh MBar MFir MGos MRav NBlu NFor NHol NPri SPer SPlb WFar WHen WShp WTel WWye

- 'Azurea' — CHid

§ - 'Azurea Flore Pleno' (d) ♀H4 — More than 30 suppliers

* - 'Blue and Gold' — EGoo EMon

- 'Blue Cloud' — MLLN NHol

- 'Blue Drift' — EMon EWes MBNS MLLN MSwo NHol

- 'Blue Moon' — EBee ECtt NHol SPer SPla

- 'Bowles' Blue' — see *V. minor* 'La Grave'

- 'Bowles' Variety' — see *V. minor* 'La Grave'

- 'Burgundy' — EPar MWgw SRms WWye

- 'Caerulea Plena' — see *V. minor* 'Azurea Flore Pleno'

- 'Dartington Star' — see *V. major* var. *oxyloba*

- 'Double Burgundy' — see *V. minor* 'Multiplex'

- 'Garnet' — EWTr

- 'Green Carpet' — see *V. minor* 'Grüner Teppich'

§ - 'Grüner Teppich' — EMon WFar

- 'Illumination' (v) — More than 30 suppliers

§ - 'La Grave' ♀H4 — More than 30 suppliers

- 'Maculata' (v) — EGoo ELan SCoo WBcn

- 'Marie' **new** — LBuc MGos

- 'Marion Cran' — CEnd GSki

§ - 'Multiplex' (d) — CBgR EBee ECtt EMan EOrc EPPr EPar EPla LBuc MAsh MBar MInt NChi NHol NPri SRms WCFE WCru WHrl

- 'Persian Carpet' (v) — EMon

- 'Purpurea' — see *V. minor* 'Atropurpurea'

- 'Rubra' — see *V. minor* 'Atropurpurea'

- 'Sabinka' — CHid EGoo EMon EPla

- 'Silver Service' (d/v) — CHid EMan EMon EPPr GBuc MInt MRav NHol WCot WHoo

- 'Variegata' — see *V. minor* 'Argenteovariegata'

- 'Variegata Aurea' — see *V. minor* 'Aureovariegata'

- 'White Gold' — CChe EBee NHol NPri NPro

sardoa — EMon EPPr

Vincetoxicum (Asclepiadaceae)

§ *hirundinaria* — EBee GPoy LEdu WWye

nigrum — EMon NBur NChi WCot WTin

officinale — see *V. hirundinaria*

scandens **new** — CPLG

Viola ✿ (Violaceae)

'Abigail' (Vtta) — LPVe

'Achilles' (Va) — LPVe

'Ada Jackson' (ExVa) — WOFF

'Adelina' (Va) — LPVe

'Admiral' (Va) — GMac WWhi

'Admiration' (Va) — EBre GMac LPVe WBou WShp

adunca — NWCA

- var. *minor* — see *V. labradorica* Schrank.

aetolica — CTCP ESis WOut

'Agnes Cochrane' (ExVa) — WOFF

'Agneta' (Va) — LPVe

'Alanta' (Va) — LPVe SAga WWhi

§ *alba* — EWes NHol NMen WBrE WWin

I 'Alcea' (Va) — LPVe

'Alethia' (Va) — LPVe

'Alex Blackwood' (SP) — WOFF

'Alice' — CDev

'Alice Witter' (Vt) — CBre CDev CGro ECha NChi SHar

'Alice Wood' (ExVa) — WOFF

'Alice Woodall' (Va) — LPVe

* 'Alison' (Va) — GMac WBou WWhi

'Alma' (Va) — WOFF

'Amelia' (Va) — GMac LPVe WBou WWhi

'Amethyst' (C) — EBee

§ 'Amiral Avellan' (Vt) — CDev CGro WHer

'Andrena' (Va) — LPVe

'Angela' (Va) — LPVe

'Anita' (Va) — LPVe

'Ann' (SP) — WOFF

'Ann Kean' (Vtta) **new** — LPVe

'Ann Robb' (ExVa) — WOFF

'Anna' (Va) — LPVe

'Anna Leyns' (Va) — LPVe

'Annabelle' (Va) — LPVe

'Annaliese' (C) — LPVe

'Anne Mott' (Va) — LPVe

'Annette Ross' (Va) — LPVe

I 'Annie' (Vt) — CGro

'Annie Roberts' (FP) — WOFF

I 'Annona' (Va) — LPVe

'Anthea' (Va) — LPVe

'Antique Lace' (Va) — MHer

'Apollo' (Va) — LPVe

'Arabella' (Va) — EBee LPVe LRHS SChu SMrm WBou

arborescens — SSpi

'Ardross Gem' (Va) — CSam EBee EChP ECtt EDAr GAbr GKir GMac LPVe LRHS NChi WBou WCom WEas WFar WPer WWhi

arenaria — see *V. rupestris*

'Arkwright's Ruby' (Va) — LPVe LRHS SRms WWhi

'Artemis' (Va) — LPVe

'Ashvale Blue' (PVt) — CGro

'Aspasia' (Va) ♀H4 — GMac LPVe LRHS WBou WWhi

'Astrid' (Va) — LPVe

'Atalanta' (Vtta) — LPVe LRHS

'Athena' (Va) — LPVe

'Aurelia' (Va) — LPVe

'Aurora' (Va) — LPVe

'Avril' (Va) — LPVe

'Avril Lawson' (Va) — CElw GMac SHar WBou

'Azurella' — LRHS

'Baby Lucia' (Va) — CElw SRms

'Barbara' (Va) — LPVe WBou WOFF

'Barbara Cawthorne' (C) — LPVe

'Barnsdale Gem' — MBNS

'Baroness de Rothschild' (Vt) — CGro WHer

'Baronne Alice de Rothschild' (Vt) — CDev

'Beatrice' (Vtta) — WBou

'Becka' (Va) — LPVe

'Becky Groves' (Vt) — CGro

* *bella* — WEas

I 'Bella' (C) — EBee

§ 'Belmont Blue' (C) — EBre ECtt EWes GMac LBee LPVe LPhx LRHS MHer MRav NBir NCGa NChi NPPs SAga SBla SChu SMrm SPer SRms WBou WCom WFar WOut WSHC WWhi

'Bernard Cox' (FP) — WOFF

§ *bertolonii* — EBee WBou

'Beshlie' (Va) ♀H4 — EBee ECtt GMac LPVe MBNS SChu WBou WEas WTin

'Bessie Cawthorne' (C) — LPVe

'Bettina' (Va) — LPVe

'Betty' (Va) — WOFF

	'Betty Dale' (ExVa)	WOFF
	'Bianca' (Vtta)	LPVe
	biflora	CMHG CPla EBee EPar MTho NChi
	'Bishop's Belle' (FP)	WOFF
	'Blackfaulds Gem' (SP)	WOFF
	'Blue Bird' (Va)	GMac
	'Blue Butterfly' (C)	GMac WSHC
	'Blue Carpet' (Va)	GMac
	'Blue Cloud' (Va)	LPVe
	'Blue Diamond'	EBee
	'Blue Moon' (C)	SChu WBou WTin
	'Blue Moonlight' (C)	CBos CElw GBuc GMac LBee LRHS NChi
	'Blue Perfection' (Va)	LRHS WShp
	'Blue Tit' (Va)	SChu
	'Bonna Cawthorne' (Va)	LPVe
	'Boughton Blue'	see *V.* 'Belmont Blue'
	'Bournemouth Gem' (Vt)	CBre CDev CGro
§	'Bowles' Black' (T)	CArn CDev CSWP CSpe EBee EDAr EMlt ENor EPfP ESis LPVe LRHS MHer NBro SBla SMac SPla SRms WBea WBou WCAu WEas
	'Boy Blue' (Vtta)	ECtt LPVe
	'Bruneau' (dVt)	CGro EFou
*	'Bryony' (Vtta)	LPVe WBou
	bubanii	EBee GKev
	'Bullion' (Va)	LPVe WCot
	'Burncoose Yellow'	WBou
	'Buttercup' (Vtta)	EBee GMac LPVe SChu SIng SMrm WBou WWhi
	'Butterpat' (C)	GMac
	'Calantha' (Vtta)	LPVe
	'California' (Vt)	CDev
	'Callia' (Va)	LPVe
I	'Calliandra' (Vtta)	LPVe
	Can Can Series	WHer
	canadensis	CTCP EBee NWCA
	'Candida' (Vtta)	LPVe
	'Candy' **new**	CDev
	canina	NBro NPPs
*	- *alba*	CBre
	'Carina' (Vtta)	LPVe
	'Carola' (Va)	LPVe
I	'Cassandra' (Vtta)	LPVe
	'Catforth Blue Ribbon'	CElw
	'Catherine Williams' (ExVa)	WOFF
	'Cat's Whiskers'	CElw EBee GMac
	cazorlensis	CPBP SBla
	'Chandler's Glory' (Va)	LPVe
	'Chantal' (Vtta)	LPVe
	'Chantreyland' (Va)	NBir
	'Charles William Groves' (Vt)	CGro
	'Charlotte'	CSam WBou
	'Charlotte Mott' (Va)	LPVe
	'Cherub'	GMac
	'Christmas' (Vt)	CDev CGro
	'Christobel' (Va)	LPVe
	'Cinders' (Vtta)	GMac
	'Citrina' (Va)	LPVe
	'Claire' (Va)	LPVe
	'Clare Harrison' (Va)	LPVe
	'Cleeway Crimson' (FP)	WOFF
	'Clementina' (Va) ♀H4	CElw LPVe MRav
	'Cleo' (Va)	EBee GMac WBou
	'Clive Groves' (Vt)	CBre CDev CGro CHid
	'Clodagh' (Va)	LPVe
	'Clover' (Va)	LPVe
	'Coconut Sorbet'	LRHS
	'Coeur d'Alsace' (Vt)	CBre CDev CNic CPBP EBee EFou EPar LPhx NLar WCot WEas WWhi
	'Colette' (Va)	LPVe
	'Colleen' (Vtta)	LPVe
	'Colombine' (Vt) **new**	CGro

	'Columbine' (Va)	CBos CDev CElw CGro CSam EChP ESis GKir GMac LAst LPVe LPhx LRHS MHer NBir NWoo SAga SChu SIng SMrm SPer SSto WBou WCom WCot WEas WFar WKif WWhi
§	'Comte de Brazza' (dPVt)	CDev CGro GMac SHar WHer WRha WWeb
	'Comte de Chambord' (dVt)	NChi SHar WRha
	'Connie' (Va)	LPVe
	'Connigar'	CSam
	'Connor Glendinning' (ExVa)	WOFF
	'Coralie' (Vtta)	LPVe
	'Cordelia' (Va)	EBee LPVe SBla
	'Cornetto'	MBow MHer
*	'Cornish White'	CDev
	cornuta ♀H4	CElw CMea CPla EBee EOrc EPot GGar LPVe MBro MFir MWat NBir NBro NChi SMrm SPer SRms WBea WBou WFar WHen WHoo WRos WWpP
	- Alba Group ♀H4	More than 30 suppliers
§	- 'Alba Minor'	EBee EPfP EWes GMac IGor LPVe MBNS MBro MCLN NBro NChi NPPs SChu WAbe WCom WFar
	- blue	LPVe MHer WMoo WWhi
	- 'Brimstone'	CHea
	- 'Cleopatra' (C)	GMac
	- 'Clouded Yellow'	GMac MAnH
	- 'Compton Lane'	WCom
	- 'Eastgrove Blue Scented' (C)	see *V.* 'Eastgrove Blue Scented' (C)
	- 'Gypsy Moth' (C)	GMac NPPs
	- 'Icy But Spicy'	EHrv SSvw
	- Lilacina Group (C)	ECha LPVe MBro MRav MSte NChi SChu SMrm SWat WFar
	- 'Maiden's Blush'	EMan GMac NChi NPPs
	- 'Minor' ♀H4	CPla GMac LPVe LRHS MCLN NBro SBla WBou
	- 'Minor Alba'	see *V. cornuta* 'Alba Minor'
	- pale blue	LRHS
*	- 'Paris White'	EBee EPfP
	- 'Purple Gem'	GMac
	- Purpurea Group	CElw CMea ECha GBuc
	- 'Rosea'	ECha LPVe
	- 'Spider'	GMac WWhi
	- 'Variegata' (v)	LPVe
	- 'Victoria's Blush'	CSpe GMac MSte NBir NPPs SMrm WBou WWhi
	- 'Violacea'	GMac LRHS
	- 'Yellow King'	EBee EHrv
	corsica	EBee EMan LPVe NChi WOut XPep
*	'Cottage Garden' (Va)	LRHS
	'Countess of Shaftsbury' (dVt)	CDev
	'Cox's Moseley' (ExVa)	WOFF
	'Crepuscule' (Vt)	CGro
	'Cressida' (Va)	LPVe
§	*cucullata* ♀H4	SChu WFar WPrP
§	- 'Alba' (Vt)	CBro CGro ECGP EPar LLWP NBir NChi SRms SScr WEas
	- *rosea*	EWes
*	- 'Striata Alba'	LRHS MWgw NBro
*	'Cuty' (Va)	LRHS
I	'Czar'	see *Viola* 'The Czar'
§	'Czar Bleu' (Vt)	CDev
	'Daena' (Vtta)	CBos LPVe
	'Daisy Smith' (Va)	GMac SChu WBou
	'Dancing Geisha' (Vt)	CM&M EBee EMan IBal MBNS MSph MTPN NBPC SHar WAul WCot WWeb
	'Dartington Hybrid' (Va)	LPVe

'Daveron' (C)	LPVe	'Fabiola' (Vtta)	GMac LPVe NBir
'David Rhodes' (FP)	WOFF	'Famecheck Apricot' **new**	NChi
'David Wheldon' (Va)	LPVe WOFF	* 'Fantasy'	WBou
'Davina' (Va)	LPVe SChu	'Farewell' (ExVa)	WOFF
'Dawn' (Vtta)	EBee LPVe WBou WLin	'Felicity' (Va)	LPVe
'Deanna' (Va)	LPVe	'Finola Galway' (Va)	LPVe
'Decima' (Va)	LPVe	'Fiona' (Va)	EBee GMac LPVe MSte NChi SChu
declinata	EBee		WBou
'Delia' (Va)	GMac LPVe WBou	'Fiona Lawrenson' (Va)	LPVe
'Delicia' (Vtta)	LPVe NChi WBou	*flettii*	GFlt NChi
'Delmonden' (Va)	SBla	'Florence' (Va)	LPVe
delphinantha	CGra WLin	'Foxbrook Cream' (C)	EMan GBuc GMac LPVe WBou
'Delphine' (Va)	LPVe MLLN MSte NChi SChu		WCom WWhi
'Demeter' (Va)	LPVe	'Frances' (Va)	LPVe
'Desdemona' (Va)	EBee GMac WBou	'Frances Perry'	WWhi
'Desmonda' (Va)	LPVe SChu	'Francesca' (Va)	LPVe
'Devon Cream' (Va)	GMac WBou	'Freckles'	see *V. sororia* 'Freckles'
'Diana Groves'	CGro	'Frederica'	CDev
'Dimity' (Va)	LPVe	'Gary Caird' (FP)	WOFF
'Dione' (Vtta)	LPVe	I 'Gazania' (Va)	LPVe WBou
I 'Diosma' (Va)	LPVe	'George Carter' (FP)	WOFF
§ *dissecta*	GBin WCot WPer	'George Hughes' (FP)	WOFF
§ - var. *chaerophylloides*	CGro GKev MTho	'Georgina' (Va)	LPVe
f. *eizanensis*		'Geraldine' (Vtta)	LPVe
- var. *sieboldiana* **new**	CPMA	'Geraldine Cawthorne' (C)	LPVe
'Doctor Smart' (C)	LPVe	'Gina' (Vtta)	LPVe
'Dominique' (Va)	LPVe	'Gladys Findlay' (Va)	GMac LPVe WBou WOFF
'Dominy' (Vtta)	LPVe	'Gladys Hughes' (FP)	WOFF
'Donau' (Vt)	CBre CDev CGro	* 'Glenda'	WBou
'Double White' (dVt)	CGro NWCA	'Glenholme' **new**	GMac
dubyana	EBee GBuc	'Gloire de Verdon' (PVt)	CGro NWCA
'Duchesse de Parme'	CDev CGro GBar GMac IFro	'Gloriole' (Vt) **new**	CGro
(dPVt)	NWCA WHer	'Governor Herrick' (Vt)	CDev CGro WPer
'D'Udine' (dPVt)	CDev CGro GMac WHer	§ *gracilis*	CElw NBir WFar
'Dusk'	WBou	- 'Lutea'	CSam
'E.A. Bowles'	see *V.* 'Bowles' Black'	* - 'Magic'	SMrm
'Eastgrove Blue Scented'	EBee EMan GMac WBou WCot	- 'Major'	WBou
(C)	WEas WIvy WOut	'Green Goddess' [PBR] **new**	LAst MBNS NCGa
'Eastgrove Elizabeth	WEas WSHC	'Green Jade' (v)	CPla EMan MBNS NBir
Booth'		'Greenroyd Fancy' (ExVa)	WOFF
'Eastgrove Ice Blue' (C)	WBou WEas	'Grey Owl' (Va)	CMea EBee LBee LPVe LPhx LRHS
'Eastgrove Twinkle' (C)	WEas		SChu WBou WEas WKif WPGP
eizanensis	see *V. dissecta* var.	'Griselda' (Vtta)	LPVe
	chaerophylloides f. *eizanensis*	'Grovemount Blue' (C)	CMea
'Elaine Cawthorne' (C)	LPVe	§ *grypoceras* var. *exilis*	CNic CTCP EBee EHoe EMan EMlt
'Elaine Quin'	EBee NChi SChu WBou		EWll GBri NHol SChu SMad WCom
§ *elatior*	CElw CMea CNic CPla CPom	- 'Variegata' (v)	NBir
	CSWP EBee EMon EPPr EPar GAbr	'Gustav Wermig' (Vt)	GAbr LPVe WBou
	GBri GBuc LRHS MNrw NChi	'Gwen Cawthorne' (C)	LPVe
	SChu WCom WCot WPer WSHC	'H.H. Hodge' (ExVa)	WOFF
	WWye	'Hackpen'	CSam
§ *elegantula*	EBee	'Hadria Cawthorne' (C)	LPVe
'Elisha' (Va)	LPVe	'Hansa' (C)	CHid EBee NChi
'Elizabeth' (Va)	EBee ECtt LPVe NCGa SChu SMrm	'Haslemere'	see *V.* 'Nellie Britton'
	WBou	* 'Heaselands'	SMHy SMrm SUsu
'Elizabeth Cawthorne' (C)	LPVe	I 'Hebe' (Vtta)	LPVe
'Elizabeth Christie' (FP)	WOFF	§ *hederacea*	CDev CMHG ECou GQui MBNS
'Elizabeth McCallum' (FP)	WOFF		NBro SAga SRms WWye
'Elliot Adam' (Va)	EBee WBou WOut	- blue	CFee WPer
'Elsie Coombs' (Vt)	CDev WPer	- 'Putty'	ECou
'Emily Mott' (Va)	LPVe	'Helen' (Va)	EChP ECtt
'Emma' (Va)	CMea LPVe	'Helen W. Cochrane' (ExVa)	WOFF
'Emma Cawthorne' (C)	LPVe	'Helena' (Va)	LPVe SChu WBou
'Enterea' (Va)	LPVe	'Hera' (Va)	LPVe
erecta	see *V. elatior*	'Hespera' (Va)	LPVe
'Eris' (Va)	LPVe NChi	I 'Hesperis' (Va)	LPVe
'Eros' (Va)	LPVe	*heterophylla*	see *V. bertolonii*
'Etain' (Va)	CHar COlW EBee ECha ELan EWes	subsp. *epirota*	
	GBuc GMac LAst LPVe LPhx MSte	* 'Hetty Gatenby'	WBou WOFF
	NCGa NDov SUsu WBou WEas	'Hextable' (C)	LPVe
	WWhi	*hirsutula*	EBla EHrv
'Ethena' (Va)	LPVe	*hispida*	LPVe
'Etienne' (Va)	LPVe	'Hudsons Blue'	CElw WEas
'Evelyn Jackson' (Va)	WOFF	'Hugh Campbell' (ExVa)	WOFF

'Lynn' (Va)	LPVe	
'Lysander' (Va)	LPVe	
'Madame Armandine Pagès' (Vt)	CBre CDev EBee	
'Madelaine' (Va)	LPVe	
'Maggie' (Va)	LPVe	
'Maggie Mott' (Va) ♀H4	CElw EBee EBre ECha ECtt EDAr EOrc GAbr GBuc GKir GMac LHop LPVe LRHS MBri NChi NDov SBla SPer WBou WFar WWhi WWin	
'Magic'	EBee GMac SChu WBou	
'Magnifico'	LRHS	
'Malise' (Va)	LPVe	
'Malvena' (Vtta)	LPVe	
mandshurica	CDev CGro NWCA	
- f. *albiflora* **new**	GKev	
- 'Fuji Dawn' (v)	CGro CPla CRez EHoe EMan GKev ITer LRHS MFOX SIng WCot	
- var. *ikedaeana* black-centred **new**	GKev	
'Margaret' (Va)	WBou	
'Margaret Cawthorne' (C)	LPVe	
'Marian' (Va)	LPVe	
'Marie-Louise' (dPVt)	CDev CGro CTri EBee EPar	
'Marika' (Va)	LPVe	
* 'Mars'	MBnl NCGa SHar	
'Mars' (Va)	EBee LPVe MCCP	
'Marsland's Yellow' (Vtta)	LPVe	
'Martin' (Va) ♀H4	EBee ECha EFou EShb GMac LBee LPVe MMil MRav NDov SAga SChu SSto WBou WCom WFar WIvy WWin WWol	
'Mary Cawthorne' (C)	LPVe	
'Mauve Beauty' (Va)	LPVe	
'Mauve Haze' (Va)	GMac MSte WBou WEas	
'Mauve Radiance' (Va)	GMac LPVe NVic WBou	
'May Mott' (Va)	EBee GMac WBou	
'Mayfly' (Va)	GMac MSte WBou	
'Meena' (Vtta)	LPVe	
'Megumi' (Va)	LPVe	
'Melinda' (Vtta)	LPVe WBou	
* 'Melissa' (Va)	LPVe SChu	
'Mercury' (Va)	LPVe WBou	
'Merry Cheer' (C)	LPhx SUsu	
'Milkmaid' (Va)	EBee EFou EWll LBee NBir WWhi	
minor pale purple-flowered **new**	GKev	
'Miranda' (Vtta)	LPVe	
'Miss Brookes' (Va)	LPVe WBou WOFF	
'Misty Guy' (Vtta)	NChi WBou	
'Molly Sanderson' (Va) ♀H4	More than 30 suppliers	
I 'Mona' (Va)	LPVe	
'Monica' (Va)	LPVe SChu	
'Moonlight' (Va) ♀H4	EBee EBre ECha EDAr ELan GMac LBee LHop LPVe MHer SBla SChu WBou WCom WWhi	
'Moonraker'	NBir	
'Morvana' (Va)	LPVe	
'Morwenna' (Va)	LPVe WCom WWhi	
'Moseley Ideal' (ExVa)	WOFF	
'Mrs C.M. Snocken' (FP)	WOFF	
'Mrs Chichester' (Va)	GMac LPVe WBou WOFF	
'Mrs Cotterell'	EBee GBuc	
'Mrs David Lloyd George' (dVt)	CDev WHer	
'Mrs G. Robb' (ExVa)	WOFF	
'Mrs Lancaster' (Va)	CHid EBee EBre GMac LPVe MBNS NBir NChi SChu SRms WBou	
'Mrs M.B. Wallace' (ExVa)	WOFF	
'Mrs R. Barton' (Vt)	CDev CGro EBee	
'Mrs Staples'	EBee	

'Myfawnny' (Va)	CBos CElw CMea EBee ECtt EDAr ELan EWes GMac LBee LPVe LRHS NChi NPri SChu SMrm SRms WBou WFar WHil WWhi	
'Mylene' (Va)	LPVe	
'Myntha' (Vtta)	LPVe	
'Nadia' (Va)	LPVe	
'Naomi' (Va)	LPVe	
'Natasha' (Va)	LPVe	
'Neapolitan'	see *V.* 'Pallida Plena'	
§ 'Nellie Britton' (Va) ♀H4	EBee ECtt GMac LPVe SChu WWhi WWin	
'Nemesis' (Va)	LPVe	
'Neptune' (Va)	LPVe	
'Nerena' (Vtta)	LPVe	
'Nesta' (Vtta)	LPVe	
'Netta Statham'	see *V.* 'Belmont Blue'	
'Nicole' (Va)	LPVe	
'Nigra' (Va)	LPVe	
'Nina' (Va)	LPVe	
'Nona' (Va)	LPVe	
'Nora'	WBou	
'Norah Church' (Vt)	CDev CGro EBee SBla SHar	
'Norah Leigh' (Va)	ELau WBou	
obliqua	see *V. cucullata*	
'Octavia' (Va)	LPVe	
'Odile' (Va)	LPVe	
odorata	CAgr CArn CBcs CBod CDev CPrp CRWN CSWP EBee EGoo EPar EPfP EWTr GBar GMac GPoy LRHS MRav MWat NBlu NCGa SECG SIde SRms STes WBVN WCom WCot WWye	
- 'Alba'	CBre CDev CPom CSWP EBee EFou ELan EMan EPar EWTr GBar ILis LAst MHer NOak NPri SIde SRms WMoo WWhi WWye	
- 'Alba Plena' (d)	EPar NChi SBla WHer	
- apricot	see *V.* 'Sulphurea'	
- var. *dumetorum*	see *V. alba*	
- *flore-pleno* (d)	EPar	
- 'Forncett Mavis'	EFou	
- pink	see *V. odorata* Rosea Group	
- *rosea*	see *V. odorata* Rosea Group	
- Rosea Group (Vt)	CDes CGro EPar GBar GMac MRav WCot WWhi	
- 'Sisters'	CGro	
* - subsp. *subcarnea*	WBWf	
- 'Sulphurea'	see *V.* 'Sulphurea'	
'Olive Edmonds' (Va)	LPVe	
'Olwyn' (Va)	LPVe	
'Opéra' (Vt)	CGro	
'Orchid Pink' (Vt)	CGro SHar	
oreades	CPBP ETow	
'Oriana' (Va)	LPVe	
'Painted Lady' (Va)	GMac	
§ 'Pallida Plena' (dPVt)	CBre CDev CGro WHer	
palmata	NPro	
'Palmer's White' (Va)	LPVe WBou	
palustris	CRWN ELau WHer WShi	
'Pamela Zambra' (Vt)	CDev	
'Pandora' (Va)	LPVe	
papilionacea	see *V. sororia*	
'Parme de Toulouse' (dPVt)	CBre CDev CGro EBee NLar WWeb	
'Pat Creasy' (Va)	GMac WBou	
'Pat Kavanagh' (C)	GMac LPVe MWat NDov NPPs SMrm WBou	
'Patricia Brookes' (Va)	LPVe	
patrinii	EBee	
pedata	CBro CFai EBee EMan EPot LRHS SSpi WAbe WCot WHil WPer	
- 'Bicolor'	EBee WAbe	
pedatifida	CFai EMan MBNS MTho NJOw WCom WLin	

	– white-flowered	CFai WLin
	'Peggy Brookes' (FP)	WOFF
	pensylvanica	see *V. pubescens* var. *eriocarpa*
	'Peppered-palms'	CPla EBee EHrv LRHS WOut
	'Perle Rose' (Vt)	CDev CGro SBla
	'Pete'	SChu
	'Petra' (Vtta)	LPVe
	'Philippa Cawthorne' (C)	LPVe
	'Phoebe' (Va)	LPVe
	'Phyl Dove' (Vt)	CGro
	'Pickering Blue' (Va)	LPVe WBou
	'Pilar' (Va)	LPVe SChu
	'Pippa' (Vtta)	LPVe
	'Poppy' (Va)	LPVe
	'Priam' (Va)	LPVe
	'Primrose Cream' (Va)	LPVe
	'Primrose Dame' (Va)	EBee EBre LPVe MHer WBou
	'Primrose Pixie' (Va)	WBou
	'Prince Henry' (T)	LPVe
	'Prince John' (T)	LPVe LRHS NBlu
	'Princess Blue' (Princess Series)	NBlu
	'Princess Mab' (Vtta)	LPVe WBou
	'Princess of Prussia' (Vt)	CBre CDev EBee WHer
	'Princess of Wales'	see *V.* 'Princesse de Galles'
§	'Princesse de Galles' (Vt)	CDev CGro CM&M CTri EPar NSti SHar
§	*pubescens*	SRms
	var. *eriocarpa*	
	pumila	NChi
	'Purity' (Vtta)	GMac LPVe
	'Purple Wings' (Va)	WBou
	'Putty'	WCru
	'Queen Charlotte' (Vt)	CDev CGro CM&M EBee ENor EShb GEdr GMac ILis MHer MWgw NChi NJOw NWCA SSto WCot WMoo WWeb
	'Queen Victoria'	see *V.* 'Victoria Regina'
	'R.N. Denby' (ExVa)	WOFF
	'Ramona' (Va)	LPVe
	'Raven'	GMac LPhx SChu WBou
	'Ravenna' (Va)	LPVe
	'Rawson's White' (Vt)	CGro SHar
	'Rebecca' (Vtta)	More than 30 suppliers
	'Rebecca Cawthorne' (C)	LPVe
	'Red Charm' (Vt)	CM&M EBee MWgw
	'Red Giant' (Vt)	CGro SHar
	'Red Lion'	CDev
	'Red Queen' (Vt)	NSti
	reichei **new**	CRWN
	reichenbachiana	EPar
	'Reine des Blanches' (dVt)	EFou
	'Remora' (Vtta)	LPVe
	reniforme	see *V. hederacea*
	'Rhoda' (Va)	LPVe
	riviniana	CArn CRWN GWCH MBow MGas MHer NSco WHer WJek WShi
	– 'Ed's Variegated' (v)	EBee EMan EPPr WCot
§	– Purpurea Group	More than 30 suppliers
	– white	EWes NWoo
	'Rodney Davey' (Vt/v)	CPla EMan IFro NBir NBro
	'Rodney Fuller' (FP)	WOFF
	'Rodney Marsh'	NBir
	'Romilly' (Va)	LPVe
	'Rosalie' (Va)	LPVe
*	'Rosanna'	CDev
	'Roscastle Black'	CElw CMea CPlt EBee GMac LRHS MAnH MBNS SMrm WBou WCot WPGP WWhi
	'Rosemary Cawthorne' (C)	LPVe
	rotundifolia	EBee
	'Rowan Hood' (ExVa)	WOFF
	'Rowena' (Va)	LPVe

*	'Royal Elk'	CDev CGro
	'Royal Robe' (VT)	CDev CGro
*	'Rubra' (Vt)	WPer
§	*rupestris*	SHar
*	– *rosea*	CDev CNic CPla CPom EBee EDAr EWTr GAbr IFro LLWP MHer MWgw NSti NWCA STre WEas WHHs
	'Russian Superb' (Vt)	CDev
	'Ruth Blackall' (Va)	LPVe
*	'Ruth Elkins'	GMac LPVe WBou WOFF
	'Saint Helena' (Vt)	CBre CDev
	'Sally' (Vtta)	LPVe
	'Samantha' (Vtta)	LPVe
	'Sandra Louise' (C)	LPVe
	'Sarah Binnie' (ExVa)	WOFF
	'Saughton Blue' (Va)	LPVe
	schariensis	CPBP EWes
	selkirkii	CDev CNic CPla EHyt ITer NBro NWCA
	– 'Variegata' (v)	CGro GBri GBuc NBir
	septentrionalis	see *V. sororia*
	'Serena' (Va)	LPVe WBou
	'Sheila' (Va)	WBou
	'Sherbet Dip'	WBou
	'Shirobana'	NBir WCru
	'Sidborough Poppet'	EGoo EWes WPer
	'Sir Fred Warner' (Va)	LPVe
§	'Sissinghurst' (Va)	GMac LPVe MHer NBir
	'Sky Blue' (Va)	LPVe
	'Smugglers' Moon'	MSte SChu WBou
	'Snow Queen' (Va)	WWhi
	'Sophie' (Vtta)	LPVe SChu WBou
§	*sororia*	EBee ECha ELau EMan EPPr GSki LRHS MNrw MOne MRav MWgw NBro NRya WEas WPen
	– 'Albiflora' ♀H4	More than 30 suppliers
§	– 'Freckles'	More than 30 suppliers
	– 'Freckles' dark	EBee LHop SMac
	– 'Priceana'	CBre CCge CDes CDev CElw CM&M EBee EMan EOrc EWTr NBir NChi SMrm WPGP
	– 'Speckles' (v)	CGro EMon
	'Soula' (Vtta)	LPVe
*	'Spencer's Cottage'	WBou
*	'Stacey Proud' (v)	NPro
	'Steyning' (Va)	LPVe WBou
	stojanowii	CGro SBla WEas
§	'Sulphurea' (Vt)	CDev CGro CPBP CPMA CSWP EPar MHar MHer MMHG MRav NPPs NWCA SUsu WCom WCot WEas WPer WWhi
	'Sulphurea' lemon form (Vt) **new**	CGro
	'Susanah' (Vtta)	LPVe
	'Susie' (Va)	EWll WBou
	'Swanley White'	see *V.* 'Comte de Brazza'
	'Sylvia Hart'	MTho WPnP
	'Talitha' (Va)	GMac LPVe
	'Tamsin' (Va)	LPVe
	'Tanith' (Vt)	CBre CDev EBee
	'Thalia' (Vtta)	LPVe WBou
	'The Czar' (Vt)	CBre CGro ILis NChi
	'Thea' (Va)	LPVe
	'Thelma' (Va)	LPVe
	'Thetis' (Va)	LPVe
	'Thierry' (Va)	LPVe
	'Tiffany' (Va)	LPVe
	'Tiger Eyes'	CSpe EBla MBNS NCGa SWal
	'Tina' (Va)	LPVe WOFF
	'Tinpenny Purple' **new**	WTin
	'Titania' (Va)	CGro LPVe
	'Tom' (SP)	WOFF
	'Tom Tit' (Va)	LPVe WBou

'Tony Venison' (C/v) — CElw EBee EDAr EHoe EMan EPPr MBNS MTho WBou WCom WFar WHer

'Toulouse' — WHer

tricolor — CPrp GBar GPoy GWCH MHer NGHP NPri NSco SIde WHHs WHer WJek WSel

- 'Sawyer's Blue' — WPer

'Tullia' (Vtta) — LPVe

'Unity' (Vtta) — LPVe

'Velleda' (Vtta) — LPVe

velutina — see *V. gracilis*

'Venetia' (Va) — LPVe

'Venus' (Va) — LPVe

verecunda — GFlt NCGa

- B&SWJ 604a — WCru

§ - var. *yakusimana* — WOBN

'Victoria' — see *V. 'Czar Bleu'*

'Victoria Cawthorne' (C) — CElw EBee EMan GBuc GMac LPVe LPhx MAnH MHer MOne MSte NDov NPPs SBla SChu WBou WCom WEas WWhi

§ 'Victoria Regina' (Vt) — CBre CDev

'Victoria's Blush' (C) — CBos CSpe EBee ECtt GBuc MHer NChi WCom

'Violacea' (C) — LPVe

'Virginia' (Va) — GMac LPVe SChu WBou

'Virgo' (Va) — LPVe

'Vita' (Va) — GBuc GMac LPVe MBNS SBla SChu WBou WIvy WWhi

'Wanda' (Va) — LPVe

'Wasp' (Va) — GMac

'White Ladies' — see *V. cucullata* 'Alba'

'White Pearl' (Va) — GMac LPhx MLLN WBou

'White Perfection' — CWib LRHS MBNS

'White Superior' — CBcs EWll

'White Swan' (Va) — GMac LPVe NChi

'William' (Va) **new** — NDov

'William Fife' (ExVa) — WOFF

'William Snocken' (FP) — WOFF

'Winifred Jones' (Va) — WBou

'Winifred Warden' (Va) — MBNS

'Winona' (Vtta) — LPVe

'Winona Cawthorne' (C) — GMac LPVe NChi NDov NPPs SChu WWhi

'Wisley White' — EBee EWes WFar

'Woodlands Cream' (Va) — GMac MHer WBou WOFF

'Woodlands Lilac' (Va) — SChu WBou WOFF

'Woodlands White' (Va) — WBou WOFF

yakusimana — see *V. verecunda* var. *yakusimana*

'Zara' (Va) — WBou

'Zepherine' (Va) — LPVe

'Zoe' (Vtta) — EBee GMac LPVe NCGa NPri WBou WWol

'Zona' (Va) — LPVe

Viscaria (*Caryophyllaceae*)

vulgaris — see *Lychnis viscaria*

Vitaliana (*Primulaceae*)

§ *primuliflora* — CLyd ETow GCrs GKir GTou MBro NLAp NMen NRya NSla

- subsp. *praetutiana* — EHyt EPot MBro NHol NMen NWCA SBla WAbe WFar WLin WPat

- subsp. *tridentata* — NMen

Vitex (*Verbenaceae*)

agnus-castus — CAgr CArn CBcs CDul EBee EDAr ELau EShb GPoy LEdu LRHS MCCP MHer SIgm SLon SMad SPer WDin WFar WHer WSHC WWye XPep

- 'Alba' **new** — XPep

- 'Blue Spire' — CFwr

- 'Blushing Bride' **new** — WCot

- var. *latifolia* — EBee EPAt EPfP LRHS WDin XPep

I - 'Rosea' **new** — XPep

- 'Silver Spire' — ELan

incisa — see *V. negundo* var. *heterophylla*

lucens **new** — CHEx

negundo — CArn

§ - var. *heterophylla* — CPle

Vitis ✿ (*Vitaceae*)

'Abundante' (F) — WSuV

'Alden' (O/W) — WSuV

amurensis — EBee EPfP GIBF LAst LRHS

- B&SWJ 4138 — WCru

'Aurore' Seibel 5279 (W) — WSuV

'Baco Noir' (O/B) — GTwe SDea WSuV

Black Hamburgh — see *V. vinifera* 'Schiava Grossa'

'Black Strawberry' (B) — WSuV

§ 'Boskoop Glory' (F) — CMac EMil LBuc NBlu SCoo SDea SEND WSuV

'Brant' (O/B) ♀H4 — More than 30 suppliers

'Brilliant' (B) — WSuV

'Buffalo' (B) — WSuV

californica (F) — ERea

'Canadice' (O/R/S) — SDea WSuV

'Cascade' (O/B) — see *V. Seibel 13053*

Castel 19637 (B) — WSuV

'Chambourcin' (B) — WSuV

coignetiae ♀H4 — More than 30 suppliers

- B&SWJ 4744 — WCru

- from Korea — CBot

- - B&SWJ 4550 — WCru

- Claret Cloak = 'Frovit'PBR — EBee ELan ENot EPfP LRHS MAsh MRav SMur SPer SSpi WPGP WPat WWeb

- cut-leaved **new** — LAst

'Dalkauer' (W) — WSuV

I 'Diamond' (B) — WSuV

'Einset' (B/S) — WSuV

ficifolia — see *V. thunbergii*

flexuosa B&SWJ 5568 — WCru

- var. *choii* B&SWJ 4101 — WCru

§ 'Fragola' (O/R) — CAgr CMac EBee EBre EPfP EPla ERea EWTr GTwe MAsh MRav NVne SDea SEND SRms WCom WSuV

'Gagarin Blue' (O/B) — CAgr ERea GTwe NPer NVne SDea WSuV

'Glenora' (F/B/S) — ERea WSuV

henryana — see *Parthenocissus henryana*

'Himrod' (O/W/S) — ERea GTwe SDea WSuV

inconstans — see *Parthenocissus tricuspidata*

'Interlaken' (G/W) — ERea WSuV

'Kempsey Black' (B) — WSuV

'Kuibishevski' (O/R) — WSuV

labrusca 'Concord' (O/B) — ERea

Landot 244 (O/B) — WSuV

'Léon Millot' (O/G/B) — CSBt EMui ERea NVne SDea WSuV

'Maréchal Foch' (O/B) — WSuV

'Maréchal Joffre' (O/B) — GTwe NVne WSuV

'Muscat Bleu' (O/B) — ERea NVne WSuV

Oberlin 595 (O/B) — WSuV

'Orion' — EMui NVne WSuV

palmata — WCru

parsley-leaved — see *V. vinifera* 'Ciotat'

parvifolia — WPat

'Phönix' (O/W) — GTwe MBri MGos NVne SKee SLim WSuV

piasezkii — WCru

- B&SWJ 5236 — WCru

* 'Pink Strawberry' (O) — WSuV

'Pirovano 14' (O/B) — ERea GTwe SDea WSuV

§ 'Plantet' (O/B) — WSuV

* 'Poloske Muscat' (W) — WSuV

pseudoreticulata — CFil WPGP

* 'Queen of Esher' — GTwe MBri SKee SLim
quinquefolia — see *Parthenocissus quinquefolia*
Ravat 51 (O/W) — WSuV
'Regent'^{PBR} — CWSG GTwe MBri MCoo MGos NVne SKee SLim WSuV
'Reliance' (O/R/S) — ERea WSuV
'Rembrant' (R) — WSuV
riparia — WCru
'Rondo' (O/B) EM 6494-5 — EMui NVne WSuV
'Schuyler' (O/B) — ESim WSuV
Seibel (F) — EMui GTwe SDea
§ Seibel 13053 (O/B) — ERea LRHS MAsh SDea WSuV
Seibel 138315 (R) — WSuV
Seibel 5409 (W) — WSuV
Seibel 5455 — see V. 'Plantet'
Seibel 7053 — WSuV
Seibel 9549 — WSuV
'Seneca' (W) — WSuV
§ 'Seyval Blanc' (O/W) — CAgr ERea GTwe NVne SDea WSuV
Seyve Villard 12.375 — see V. 'Villard Blanc'
Seyve Villard 20.473 (F) — MAsh WSuV
Seyve Villard 5276 — see V. 'Seyval Blanc'
'Suffolk Seedless' (B/S) — WSuV
'Tereshkova' (O/B) — ERea SDea WSuV
'Thornton' (F/S) — WSuV
§ *thunbergii* B&SWJ 4702 — WCru
'Triomphe d'Alsace' (O/B) — CAgr CSBt LRHS NPer SDea WSuV
'Trollinger' — see V. *vinifera* 'Schiava Grossa'
'Vanessa' (O/R/S) — ERea SDea
§ 'Villard Blanc' (O/W) — WSuV
vinifera — NVne
- EM 323158B — WSuV
- 'Abouriou' (O/B) — WSuV
- 'Adelheidtraube' (F) — WSuV
- 'Albalonga' (W) — WSuV
§ - 'Alicante' (G/B) — ERea GTwe NVne SDea WSuV
- 'Apiifolia' — see V. *vinifera* 'Ciotat'
- 'Appley Towers' (G/B) — ERea
- 'Augusta Louise' (O/W) — WSuV
- 'Auxerrois' (O/W) — WSuV
- 'Bacchus' (O/W) — NVne SDea WSuV
- 'Baresana' (G/W) — WSuV
- 'Black Alicante' — see V. *vinifera* 'Alicante'
- 'Black Corinth' (G/B/S) — ERea
- 'Black Frontignan' (G/O/B) — ERea WSuV
- Black Hamburgh — see V. *vinifera* 'Schiava Grossa'
- 'Black Monukka' (G/B/S) — ERea WSuV
- 'Black Prince' (G/B) — WSuV
- 'Blauburger' (O/B) — WCru
- 'Blue Portuguese' — see V. *vinifera* 'Portugieser'
§ - 'Bouvier' (W) — WSuV
- 'Bouviertraube' — see V. *vinifera* 'Bouvier'
- 'Buckland Sweetwater' (G/W) — ERea GTwe MGos NVne SDea WSuV
- 'Cabernet Sauvignon' (O/B) — MAsh SDea WSuV
- 'Canners' (F/S) — ERea
- 'Canon Hall Muscat' (G/W) — ERea NVne
- 'Cardinal' (O/R) — ERea NVne WSuV
- 'Chaouch' (G/W) — ERea
- 'Chardonnay' (O/W) — MAsh NPer NVne SDea WSuV
§ - 'Chasselas' (G/O/W) — EMui ERea LRHS MAsh NVne SDea WSuV
- 'Chasselas de Fontainebleau' (F) — EMil
- 'Chasselas de Tramontaner' (F) — EMil
- 'Chasselas d'Or' — see V. *vinifera* 'Chasselas'
- 'Chasselas Rosé' (G/R) — ERea WSuV
- 'Chasselas Vibert' (G/W) — ERea WSuV
- 'Chenin Blanc' (O/W) — WSuV

§ - 'Ciotat' (F) — EPla ERea NVne SDea WBcn WCru WSuV
§ - 'Cot' (O/B) — WSuV
- 'Crimson Seedless' (R/S) — ERea
- 'Csabyongye' (W) — WSuV
- 'Dattier de Beyrouth' (W) — WSuV
- 'Dornfelder' (O/R) — EBee NVne SKee WSuV
- 'Dunkelfelder' (O/R) — NVne WSuV
- 'Early Van der Laan' (F) — EMil NBlu
- 'Ehrenfelser' (O/W) — WSuV
- 'Elbling' (O/W) — WSuV
- 'Excelsior' (W) — WSuV
- 'Faber' (O/W) — WSuV
- 'Ferdinand de Lesseps' — ERea
- 'Fiesta' (F/W/S) — WSuV
- 'Findling' (W) — NVne WSuV
- 'Flame' — ESim
- 'Flame Seedless' (R/S) — WSuV
- 'Forta' (W) — WSuV
- 'Foster's Seedling' (G/W) — ERea GTwe SDea WSuV
- 'Gamay Hâtif' (O/B) — ERea
- 'Gamay Hâtif des Vosges' (W) — WSuV
- 'Gamay Noir' (O/B) — WSuV
- 'Gamay Teinturier Group' (O/B) — WSuV
- 'Gewürztraminer' (O/R) — LRHS MAsh SDea WSuV
- 'Glory of Boskoop' — see V. 'Boskoop Glory'
- 'Golden Chasselas' — see V. *vinifera* 'Chasselas'
- 'Golden Queen' (G/W) — ERea
- 'Goldriesling' (O/W) — WSuV
- 'Gros Colmar' (G/B) — ERea
- 'Gros Maroc' (G/B) — ERea
- 'Grüner Veltliner' (O/W) — WSuV
- 'Gutenborner' (O/W) — WSuV
- 'Helfensteiner' (O/R) — WSuV
- 'Huxelrebe' (O/W) — NVne WSuV
- 'Incana' (O/B) — EBee EPfP EPla MRav WCFE WCom WCot WCru WSHC
- 'Juliaumsrebe' (O/W) — WSuV
- 'Kanzler' (O/W) — WSuV
- 'Kerner' (O/W) — NVne WSuV
- 'Kernling' (F) — NVne WSuV
- 'King's Ruby' (F/S) — ERea
- 'Lady Downe's Seedling' (G/B) — ERea
- 'Lady Hastings' (G/B) — ERea
- 'Lady Hutt' (G/W) — ERea
- 'Lakemont' (O/W/S) — ERea SKee
- 'Madeleine Angevine' (O/W) — CAgr CDul CSBt EMui ERea GTwe LRHS MAsh MGos NVne SDea WSuV
- 'Madeleine Celine' (B) — WSuV
- 'Madeleine Noire' — NVne
- 'Madeleine Royale' (G/W) — ERea WSuV
- 'Madeleine Silvaner' (O/W) — CSBt EMui ERea GTwe LRHS MAsh MGos NPer NVne SDea SPer WBVN WSuV
- 'Madresfield Court' (G/B) — ERea GTwe NVne WSuV
- 'Malbec' — see V. *vinifera* 'Cot'
- 'Merlot' (G/B) — NVne SDea WSuV
§ - 'Meunier' (B) — WSuV
- 'Mireille' (F) — GTwe SDea WSuV
- 'Morio Muscat' (O/W) — WSuV
- 'Mrs Pearson' (G/W) — ERea
- 'Mrs Pince's Black Muscat' (G/B) — ERea NVne
§ - 'Müller-Thurgau' (O/W) — EMui ERea GKir GTwe LRHS MAsh MGos SDea SPer WSuV
- 'Muscat Blanc à Petits Grains' (O/W) — SWvt WSuV
- 'Muscat Champion' (G/R) — ERea

- 'Muscat de Saumur' WSuV
  (O/W)
- 'Muscat Hamburg' (G/B) EMil EMui ERea MAsh MGos NVne
  SDea SWvt WSuV
- 'Muscat of Alexandria' CBcs CMac CRHN EHol EMui ERea
  (G/W) NVne SDea
- 'Muscat of Hungary' ERea
  (G/W)
- 'Muscat Ottonel' (O/W) WSuV
- 'Muscat Saint Laurent' WSuV
  (W)
- 'New York Muscat' (O/B) ERea WSuV
- 'No. 69' (W) WSuV
- 'Noir Hâtif de Marseilles' ERea WSuV
  (O/B)
- 'Oliver Irsay' (O/W) ERea WSuV
- 'Optima' (O/W) WSuV
- 'Ortega' (O/W) NVne WSuV
- 'Perle' (O/W) WSuV
- 'Perle de Czaba' EMil ERea WSuV
  (G/O/W)
- 'Perlette' (O/W/S) ERea WSuV
- 'Petit Rouge' (R) WSuV
- 'Pinot Blanc' (O/W) LRHS MAsh WSuV
- 'Pinot Gris' (O/B) SDea WSuV
- 'Pinot Noir' (O/B) NVne WSuV
- 'Plavac Mali' (B) WSuV
§ - 'Portugieser' (O/B) WSuV
- 'Précoce de Bousquet' WSuV
  (O/W)
- 'Précoce de Malingre' ERea SDea
  (O/W)
- 'Primavis Frontignan' WSuV
  (G/W)
- 'Prince of Wales' (G/B) ERea
- 'Purpurea' (O/B) ♀H4 More than 30 suppliers
- 'Regner' (O/W) MGos
- 'Reichensteiner' SDea WSuV
  (O/G/W)
- 'Reine Olga' (O/R) ERea
- 'Riesling' (O/W) LRHS MAsh WSuV
- 'Riesling-Silvaner see *V. vinifera* 'Müller-Thurgau'
- 'Rish Baba' ERea
- 'Royal Muscadine' NVne WSuV
  (G/O/W)
- 'Saint Laurent' (G/O/W) ERea WSuV
- 'Sauvignon Blanc' (O/W) NVne WSuV
- 'Scheurebe' (O/W) WSuV
§ - 'Schiava Grossa' (G/B/D) More than 30 suppliers
- 'Schönburger' (O/W) NVne SDea WSuV
- 'Schwarzriesling' see *V. vinifera* 'Meunier'
- 'Sémillon' MAsh
- 'Septimer' (O/W) WSuV
- 'Shiraz' (B) WSuV
- 'Siegerrebe' (O/W/D) EMui ERea GTwe LRHS MAsh
  NVne SDea WSuV
- 'Silvaner' (O/W) WSuV
- 'Spetchley Red' EBee WCru WPat WSPU
- strawberry grape see *V.* 'Fragola'
- 'Suffolk Red' (G/R/S) ERea
§ - 'Sultana' (W/S) EMui ERea GTwe NVne SDea
  WSuV
- 'Syrian' (G/W) ERea
- 'Teinturier Group (F) ERea
- 'Theresa' **new** MBri
- 'Thompson Seedless' see *V. vinifera* 'Sultana'
- 'Trebbiano' (G/W) ERea
* - 'Triomphe' (O/B) EMui NVne
- 'Triomphrebe' (W) WSuV
- 'Vitalis Gold' WWeb
- 'Vitalis Ruby' WWeb
- 'Wrotham Pinot' (O/B) NVne SDea WSuV
- 'Würzer' (O/W) WSuV
- 'Zweigeltrebe' (O/B) WSuV

* 'White Strawberry' (O/W) WSuV
- 'Zalagyöngye' (W) WSuV

Vriesea (Bromeliaceae)
carinata MBri
hieroglyphica new MBri
x **poelmanii** MBri
x **polonia** MBri
saundersii ♀H1 MBri
splendens ♀H1 MBri
'Vulkana' MBri

W

Wachendorfia (Haemodoraceae)
brachyandra EMan GCal
thyrsiflora CDes CFir CHEx CMCo CPLG
EBee GGar IGor SAga SHFr
WCFE WCot WDyG WFar
WPGP WPrP

Wahlenbergia (Campanulaceae)
albomarginata ECou EMan GTou LRHS NLAp
NLar NWCA
- 'Blue Mist' ECou
congesta CNic CPBP EHyt LRHS MDKP
WBVN
cuspidata new EPot
gloriosa GCrs GEdr GKev LBee LRHS MBro
NJOw NLAp NMen SScr WFar
WWin
pumilio see *Edraianthus pumilio*
pygmaea WHoo
§ **saxicola** CLyd CRow EHyt EMan GTou
NDlv NWCA
serpyllifolia see *Edraianthus serpyllifolius*
simpsonii GTou
tasmanica see *W. saxicola*
undulata CSpe CTCP

Waldsteinia (Rosaceae)
fragarioides WPer
geoides EBee EMan EPPr EPfP IHMM LRHS
NPro SPer WCom WShp
ternata More than 30 suppliers
§ - 'Mozaick' (v) GKir IBlr NBir NPro WCom
- 'Variegata' see *W. ternata* 'Mozaick'

Wallichia (Arecaceae)
densiflora CBrP CRoM LPal
disticha LPal

walnut, black see *Juglans nigra*

walnut, common see *Juglans regia*

Wasabia (Brassicaceae)
japonica CArn GPoy

Washingtonia (Arecaceae)
filifera ♀H1 CAbb CBrP CDoC CRoM EAmu
EShb EUJe LPal MBri SAPC SArc
SEND SPlb WMul
robusta CRoM CTrC EAmu LPal SChr SMad
SPlb WHPE WMul

Watsonia (Iridaceae)
aletroides CCtw CDes EBee LPio LRHS SAga
SIgm WCot
angusta CDes CPne IBlr ITer
- JCA 3.950.409 WCot

	ardernei	see *W. borbonica* subsp. *ardernei* 'Arderne's White'
	beatricis	see *W. pillansii*
I	'Best Red'	GCal LPio
§	*borbonica*	CCtw CPne CPou CWCL EShb IBlr LPio SAga SGar SWat WCot
	- subsp. *ardernei* hort.	see *W. borbonica* subsp. *ardernei* 'Arderne's White'
§	- - 'Arderne's White'	CBre CDes CPne EBee ERos GCal MSte SBla WPGP
	- subsp. *borbonica*	CDes EBee WPGP
	brevifolia	see *W. laccata*
	coccinea	CDes EBee WCot WPGP
	densiflora	CBcs CFil CPou EBee GFlt IBlr ITer MSte WCot
	'Flame' **new**	NCGa
	fourcadei	CPne EBee ITer WPGP
	- S&SH 89	CDes
	fulgens	CPne LEdu MSte
	galpinii	CFir IBlr
	gladioloides	CFil
§	*humilis*	CDes CFil CStu SSpi WPGP
	knysnana	CPou
§	*laccata*	CFir CPou EBee SChr SWat WCot
	lepida	CFil CPou
	marginata	CPou WCot
	- 'Star Spike'	WCot
	marlothii	CFil
	meriania	CFil CPou EBee GGar GSki IBlr WCot
	- var. *bulbillifera*	CFwr EBee GAbr GMac IBlr LPio LRHS
§	*pillansii*	CCtw CFil CHEx CPen CPne CPou CPrp CTrC EBee EBre EMan ERos GMac GSki IBlr LRHS SBla SIgm SMrm WCot
	- JCA 3.953.609	SSpi
	- pink-flowered **new**	CPen
	- salmon-flowered **new**	CPen
	pink	CDes EBee
	pyramidata	see *W. borbonica*
	roseoalba	see *W. humilis*
§	*spectabilis*	WFar
	'Stanford Scarlet'	CDes CPou EBee IBlr NCGa SBla WPGP WSHC
	stenosiphon	CPou EBee IBlr
	strubeniae	IBlr
	tabularis	GGar IBlr ITer WCot
	'Tresco Dwarf Pink'	CDes EBee EMan GCal LPio NGby WCot WPGP
	Tresco hybrids	CAbb CPne WCFE
	vanderspuyae	CCtw CPou EBee IBlr WCot
	watsonioides	WCot
	wilmaniae	CFil CPou IBlr ITer
	- JCA 3.955.200	SSpi

Wattakaka see *Dregea*

Wedelia (Asteraceae)

§	*texana*	EBee

Weigela ✿ (Caprifoliaceae)

CC 1231	CPLG
'Abel Carrière'	CMac CTri EBee ECtt EPfP GEil NWea SEND WCFE WFar WTel
'Avalanche' Lemoine	see *W. praecox* 'Avalanche'
'Avalanche' hort.	see *W.* 'Candida'
'Boskoop Glory'	GQui SPer
Briant Rubidor = 'Olympiade' (v)	More than 30 suppliers
'Brigela'PBR **new**	MBri
'Bristol Ruby'	More than 30 suppliers
§ 'Candida'	CTri ELan EWes GEil GSki LRHS MBar MRav NBlu NHol SPer WTel
Carnaval = 'Courtalor'PBR	COtt CWib GKir LPan LRHS WStI

'Conquête'	GEil GKir LAst SLon
coraeensis	CHll GEil IArd MBlu MMHG
- 'Alba'	GEil
'Davnik'	MTPN
decora	GEil GQui
'Emerald Edge'	WBcn
'Eva Rathke'	CBot CTri GKir NWea SCoo WFar WTel
'Evita'	MBar MGos WFar
floribunda	GEil
florida	CTrw EPfP MBar MWat SMer
- f. *alba*	CBcs WFar
* - 'Albovariegata' (v)	WBVN WBrE
- 'Bicolor'	CMac ELan
- 'Bristol Snowflake'	CBot EPfP GKir MBNS MBar MGos MHer MSwo NHol NLar SLon WBod
- 'Foliis Purpureis' ♀H4	More than 30 suppliers
- 'Java Red'	LRHS
- 'Pink Princess'	MSwo WWeb
- 'Samabor'	WFar
- 'Sunny Princess'	NHol
- 'Suzanne' (v)	CDul GEil LAst LRHS MGos NPro
- 'Tango'	CPMA ECtt LRHS MAsh MWya NPro WBcn WWeb
'Florida Variegata' (v) ♀H4	More than 30 suppliers
florida var. *venusta*	GEil
- 'Versicolor'	CBot CMHG CMac CPLG CWib GQui SLon SMrm WFar
- Wine and Roses = 'Alexandra'	CABP CBcs CDoC EBee EGra ELan ENot EPfP LAst MAsh NPri NSti SWvt WWeb
'Gold Rush'	NHol
'Golden Candy' **new**	NPro
'Gustave Malet'	GEil GQui
hortensis	GIBF
- 'Nivea'	CPle MBri NPro
- var. *rubra*	GEil
japonica	GEil
- 'Dart's Colourdream'	CFwr EBee ECtt EWes GKir MGos MRav NHol SCoo SLPl SLim SMer WBVN
'Jean's Gold'	ELan MGos MRav
'Kosteriana Variegata' (v)	CFwr CSLe EBee GEil LRHS MAsh SLon WFar
'Le Printemps'	GEil
'Looymansii Aurea'	CBot CMHG CTri ELan EPfP GEil GKir LAst LRHS MRav NHol SLon SPer WBod WDin WFar WHar WPen WWin
Lucifer = 'Courtared'PBR	CDoC EBee NHol NLar
'Marjorie'	IMGH
maximowiczii	CPLG CPle GQui GSki
§ *middendorffiana*	More than 30 suppliers
'Minuet'	EBee EPfP GSki MBar MGos MRav MSwo NPro WWeb
'Mme. le Couturier'	GEil
'Mont Blanc'	CBot GEil MMHG
Nain Rouge = 'Courtanin'PBR	EBee LRHS MBri NHol
'Nana Variegata' (v)	CPLG LRHS MBar MBri NBee NHol MBri
Naomi Campbell = 'Bokrashine'PBR **new**	MBri
'Newport Red'	EBee ENot GEil GKir LRHS MBNS MRav MWat NWea SMer WFar WGwG
'Pink Poppet'	CSBt EBre GTSp LAst LRHS MAsh NBPC SCoo SPoG SWvt
praecox	GIBF
§ - 'Avalanche'	ECtt MRav WStI
'Praecox Variegata' (v) ♀H4	CChe CTri EBee ELan EPfP GKir LAst LRHS MAsh MRav SMac SPer SPla SReu SRms WCFE WCru WFar WHCG WSHC

'Red Prince' ♀H4 — EBee ELan GEil GWCH LAst LRHS MGos MSwo SPoG WBod

'Ruby Queen'PBR — CDoC EPfP LRHS

'Rumba' — EMil EWTr GEil GSki MMHG MRav NPro

'Samba' — GEil LRHS

sessilifolia — see *Diervilla sessilifolia*

'Snowflake' — EBee ECtt NPri NPro SRms WDin WFar

'Styriaca' — GEil

subsessilis B&SWJ 1056 — WCru

'Victoria' — CDoC CHar CMHG CWib EBee ECtt ELan EPfP LAst LRHS MAsh MSwo SCoo SPer SPla WBrE WGor WHar WWeb

'Wessex Gold' (v) — CFai WHCG

Weinmannia (Cunoniaceae)

racemosa 'Kamahi' — CTrC

trichosperma — ISea SAPC SArc

Weldenia (Commelinaceae)

candida — EBla EHyt LTwo NMen SIng SOkd WAbe

Westringia (Lamiaceae)

angustifolia — ECou

brevifolia — ECou

– Raleighii Group — ECou

§ *fruticosa* ♀H1 — CArn CBcs CPLG CPle ECou WJek XPep

– 'Variegata' (v) — CPle GQui WJek

– 'Wynyabbie Gem' — EMan

longifolia — ECou

rigida 'Morning Light' (v) — EMan WCot

rosmariniformis — see *W. fruticosa*

'Smokie' **new** — SOWG

whitecurrant see *Ribes rubrum* (W)

Widdringtonia (Cupressaceae)

cedarbergensis — CPLG GGar

cupressoides — see *W. nodiflora*

§ *nodiflora* — GGar

schwarzii — CPLG GGar

Wigandia (Hydrophyllaceae)

caracasana — CKob

Wikstroemia (Thymelaeaceae)

gemmata — SCoo SSta

kudoi — WCru

wineberry see *Rubus phoenicolasius*

Wisteria ✿ (Papilionaceae)

§ *brachybotrys* — CMCN SLim

§ – murasaki-kapitan — CEnd

§ – 'Shiro-kapitan' — CEnd CHad CPMA CSPN CTri EBee ENot EPfP LRHS MAsh MBri MGos NHol SBra SHBN SLim SLon SPer WPGP

* – 'White Silk' — CEnd CPMA MGos

§ 'Burford' — CEnd CSPN EMui LRHS MAsh MBri MWat NBea NHol NRib SCoo SKee SLim WHar

'Caroline' — CBcs CDoC CEnd CMen CSBt CSPN EBee EPfP ERea GKir LRHS MBlu MGos NBea NBee SPer SSpi

floribunda — CBcs CRHN CRez CWib ELan LPan LRHS SBra SHBN WDin WNor

§ – 'Alba' ♀H4 — More than 30 suppliers

– 'Black Dragon' — see *W.* x *formosa* 'Yae-kokuryû' (d)

– 'Burford' — see *W.* 'Burford'

– 'Cannington' — SCoo SLim

* – 'Cascade' — MGos

§ – 'Domino' — CBcs CEnd EBee EPfP GKir LPan LRHS MAsh MBar MGos NBea NHol SBra SLim SPer SSta WFar WSHC WWeb

– 'Fragrantissima' — see *W. sinensis* 'Jako'

* – 'Harlequin' — CBcs CHad CSPN EBee LRHS MBro MGos

– 'Hon-beni' — see *W. floribunda* 'Rosea'

– 'Honey Bee Pink' — see *W. floribunda* 'Rosea'

– 'Honko' — see *W. floribunda* 'Rosea'

– 'Jakohn-fuji' — see *W. sinensis* 'Jako'

§ – 'Kuchi-beni' — CBcs CEnd CSBt CSPN EBee ECrN ELan EPfP GKir LRHS MGos SBra SLim SPer WWeb

– 'Lavender Lace' — see *W.* 'Lavender Lace'

– 'Lawrence' — CSPN LRHS MBri NBee WWeb

– 'Lipstick' — see *W. floribunda* 'Kuchi-beni'

– 'Longissima' — see *W. floribunda* 'Multijuga'

– 'Longissima Alba' — see *W. floribunda* 'Alba'

– 'Macrobotrys' — see *W. floribunda* 'Multijuga'

– 'Magenta' — ECrN LRHS

§ – 'Multijuga' ♀H4 — More than 30 suppliers

– Murasaki-naga — see *W. floribunda* 'Purple Patches'

– 'Nana Richin's Purple' — CEnd LRHS

– 'Peaches and Cream' — see *W. floribunda* 'Kuchi-beni'

– 'Pink Ice' — see *W. floribunda* 'Rosea'

§ – 'Purple Patches' — EBee GKir LRHS MGos NPri SLim

– Reindeer — see *W. sinensis* 'Jako'

§ – 'Rosea' ♀H4 — CBcs CEnd CMen CSPN CWib ECrN ELan ENot EPfP IMGH LBuc LPan LRHS MAsh MBar MBri MDun MGos MWgw NBea NHol SBra SLim SPer SWvt WDin WFar WStI WWeb

– 'Royal Purple' — ERea LRHS MBri WGor

– 'Russelliana' — EBee SLim

– 'Shiro-naga' — see *W. floribunda* 'Alba'

– 'Shiro-noda' — see *W. floribunda* 'Alba'

– 'Snow Showers' — see *W. floribunda* 'Alba'

– 'Violacea Plena' (d) — CDoC EBee LPan LRHS MGos MRav NPri SEND SHBN SPer SWvt WDin WFar WWeb

x *formosa* — SLim

– 'Black Dragon' (d) — see *W.* x *formosa* 'Yae-kokuryû'

– 'Domino' — see *W. floribunda* 'Domino'

– 'Issai' Wada pro parte — see *W. floribunda* 'Domino'

– 'Kokuryû' (d) — see *W.* x *formosa* 'Yae-kokuryû'

– 'Yae-kokuryû' (d) — CBcs CEnd CMen CSBt CSPN EBee ECrN ELan EPfP GKir LPan LRHS MAsh MBri MGos NBlu NHol SBra SHBN SLim SMad SPer SReu SSpi SSta SWvt WFar WGor

frutescens — WNor

– 'Alba' — see *W. frutescens* 'Nivea'

– 'Magnifica' — see *W. macrostachya* 'Magnifica'

§ – 'Nivea' — CMen

Kapitan-fuji — see *W. brachybotrys*

§ 'Lavender Lace' — CEnd EPfP LRHS

§ *macrostachya* — EBee MAsh

  'Magnifica'

multijuga 'Alba' — see *W. floribunda* 'Alba'

'Showa-beni' — CEnd LRHS SCoo SLim

sinensis ♀H4 — More than 30 suppliers

– 'Alba' ♀H4 — CBcs CDoC CHad CMen CWib EBee ECrN ELan ENot EPfP LBuc LPan LRHS MBar MWat NBlu SBra SEND SLim SPer SPla WDin WFar

– 'Amethyst' — CEnd CSBt CSPN EBee EPfP ERea LRHS MDun MGos MRav NSti SBra SPla SReu

– 'Blue Sapphire' — CMen CSPN EBee LRHS SBra WBod

- 'Consequa'	see *W. sinensis* 'Prolific'
§ - 'Jako'	CEnd NHol SBra
- 'Oosthoek's Variety'	see *W. sinensis* 'Prolific'
- 'Prematura'	see *W. floribunda* 'Domino'
- 'Prematura Alba'	see *W. brachybotrys* 'Shiro-kapitan'
§ - 'Prolific'	CSBt CSam CTri CWib EBee ELan
	EPfP LBuc LPan LRHS MBri MDun
	MGos NBlu NHol SBra SEND SKee
	SPer SPla SSpi SWvt WFar WPat
	WWeb
- 'Rosea'	CMen LPan SKee SWvt
venusta	see *W. brachybotrys* 'Shiro-kapitan'
- var. *violacea* hort.	see *W. brachybotrys* murasaki-kapitan
- var. *violacea* Rehder	see *W. brachybotrys* murasaki-kapitan
villosa	WNor

Withania (Solanaceae)
somnifera	CArn EOHP GPoy MSal SHDw

Wittsteinia (Alseuosmiaceae)
vacciniacea	EBee GEil WCru WWes

Wodyetia (Arecaceae)
bifurcata	EAmu LPal

Woodsia (Woodsiaceae)
intermedia	NBro
obtusa	CLAP EBee EBlw EFer EFtx EOMN
	GCal LAst LRHS WRic
polystichoides ♀H4	GQui

Woodwardia (Blechnaceae)
from Emei Shan, China	CLAP
areolata **new**	SSpi
blechnoides	NMar
fimbriata	CFwr CHid CLAP EOMN GCal
	MAsh NBlu NWCA SSpi WCot
	WFib WPGP
orientalis	WPic
- var. *formosana*	CLAP NMar
- - B&SWJ 6865	WCru
radicans ♀H3	CAbb CFil CHEx CLAP EBee GQui
	ISea NMar SAPC SArc WAbe WCot
	WFib WPic
unigemmata	CHEx CLAP EDAr SAPC SArc SSpi
	WAbe WFib WHal
virginica	CLAP

worcesterberry see *Ribes divaricatum*

Wulfenia (Scrophulariaceae)
amherstiana	CPas GCed SOkd
blechicii	GIBF
subsp. *rohlenae*	
carinthiaca	EBee GAbr GEdr GIBF MMHG
	MOne NBir NHol NLar
x *schwarzii*	EBee

Wyethia (Asteraceae)
helianthoides	EMan

X

Xanthium (Asteraceae)
sibiricum **new**	CArn

Xanthoceras (Sapindaceae)
sorbifolium ♀H3-4	CBcs CBot CFil CLnd CMCN CWib
	EBee ECrN ELan EPfP GKir IArd
	IDee MBlu MRav NHol NPSI SMad
	SSpi WDin WFar WNor WPGP WPat
	XPep

Xanthophthalmum (Asteraceae)
coronarium	CArn WJek
§ *segetum*	GWCH MBow WHer

Xanthorhiza (Ranunculaceae)
simplicissima	CBcs CFil CRow EBee EPfP GCal
	GEil LEdu NLar SDys SSpi WBor
	WPGP

Xanthorrhoea (Xanthorrhoeaceae)
australis	CPLG SPlb WGer
johnsonii	MGos SHmp WMul
preisii	LPan WMul

Xanthosoma (Araceae)
sagittifolium	CKob EAmu EUJe MJnS MOak
	WMul
violaceum	CDWL CKob EAmu EUJe LEur
	MJnS MOak WMul

Xerochrysum (Asteraceae)
bracteatum 'Coco'	CMHG EMan GMac WCot
- 'Dargan Hill Monarch'	CHll CMHG CSev CSpe SRms
- 'Skynet'	CSev GCal GMac
- 'Sundaze Magenta' **new**	LAst

Xeronema (Phormiaceae)
callistemon	CTrC

Xerophyllum (Melanthiaceae)
tenax	EPot GBuc GIBF WLin

Xylorhiza see *Machaeranthera*

Xyris (Xyridaceae)
juncea	ECou

Y

youngberry see *Rubus* 'Youngberry'

Ypsilandra (Melanthiaceae)
thibetica	EBee EBla LAma LEur NGar SSpi
	WCot

Yucca ✿ (Agavaceae)
aloifolia	CHEx EOas ISea LRHS MGos
	MPRe SAPC SArc SNew SPlb
	WMul
- 'Marginata' (v)	MPRe
- 'Purpurea'	SPlb
I - 'Spanish Bayonet' **new**	SEND
- 'Tricolor'	MPRe
- 'Variegata' (v)	LPal LPan SAPC SArc WHPE
angustifolia	see *Y. glauca*
angustissima	GCal
- NNS 99-509	WCot
arizonica	CBrP GCal
baccata	CTrC EOas GCal XPep
- NNS 99-510	WCot
brevifolia	CRoM WMul
carnerosana	CTrC WMul
§ *elata*	CTrC SChr
§ *elephantipes* ♀H1	LRHS MBri SEND SMur
- 'Jewel' (v)	EAmu SEND
- 'Puck' **new**	MPRe

faxoniana	EOas
filamentosa ♀H4	More than 30 suppliers
- 'Bright Edge' (v) ♀H3	More than 30 suppliers
- 'Color Guard' (v)	CTrC WCot
- 'Variegata' (v) ♀H3	CBcs CBot CDul EPfP LRHS MGos SAga SRms WDin WFar WGer
filifera	EOas
flaccida	CBcs NBee NBlu SDix SEND
- 'Golden Sword' (v) ♀H3	More than 30 suppliers
- 'Ivory' ♀H3-4	CDoC CEnd CHar CPMA EBee EBre ECrN ECtt ELan ENot EPfP GAbr GCal GKir LRHS MBlu MBri MGos MRav SLPl SMad SPer SRms SSta SSto STre WCot WLeb WPic WWeb
x *floribunda*	SAPC SArc
'Garland's Gold' (v)	CBcs CDoC GQui LRHS MAsh MBri MDun MGos WBod WFar WPat
§ *glauca*	CAbb CBcs CBrP CHEx CMHG CTrC EPfP GCal LRHS MBri SAPC SEND WBod WMul XPep
- var. *radiosa*	CTrC
gloriosa ♀H4	CBcs CDoC CDul CHEx CTri EGra ENot EPla EWTr LAst LPan LRHS LRav MPRe NPal SAPC SArc SEND SHBN SMad SSpi SWvt WBrE WHPE WMul WStI
- 'Aureovariegata'	see *Y. gloriosa* 'Variegata'
- 'Moon Frost' **new**	WCot
- 'Variegata' (v) ♀H4	More than 30 suppliers
guatemalensis	see *Y. elephantipes*
harrimaniae	GCal SIgm
kanabensis	GCal
navajoa	GCal
'Nobilis'	SDix
radiosa	see *Y. elata*
recurvifolia ♀H4	CHEx EOas EPfP MGos SAPC SArc
rigida	CBrP CTrC WMul
rostrata	CAbb CBrP CTrC EAmu EOas LPal SAPC SArc WHPE WMul XPep
schidigera	GCal WCot WMul
schottii	CAbb CBrP CTrC GCal
thompsoniana	CTrC GCal
torreyi	CTrC EOas GCal XPep
'Vittorio Emanuele II'	MTed
whipplei	CAbb CBot CBrP CCtw CDoC CFil CRoM EBee EOas GCal LEdu LRHS SAPC SEND SSpi WBrE WPGP XPep
- subsp. *intermedia* NNS 01-413 **new**	WCot
- subsp. *parishii*	SIgm
- - NNS 01-415	WCot
- subsp. *percursa* NNS 01-416 **new**	WCot
- subsp. *whipplei* NNS 01-417 **new**	WCot

Yushania (*Poaceae*)

§ *anceps*	CAbb CBcs CDoC CFil CHEx CHad EBee EFul EPfP EPla EPza GBin MGos MMoz MWht NVic SAPC SArc SDry WBrE WCru WDin WFar WMoo WPGP
§ - 'Pitt White'	CFil EBee EPla SDry WJun WPGP
- 'Pitt White Rejuvenated'	ERod
chungii	CFil EPla WPGP
maculata	EPla ERod MMoz MWht SDry WJun
§ *maling*	EPfP EPla ERod MMoz SDry WJun

Z

Zaluzianskya (*Scrophulariaceae*)

JCA 15665	WAbe
imported from USA	SSpi
capensis	CPLG
- 'Midnight Candy'	EMan
'Katherine'	EMan SIng SRot SScr
'Orange Eye' **new**	CStu
ovata	CPBP CPLG EHyt EPot GBri LPio LSpr MAvo MTho NBir NBur NJOw SAga SBla SIng SMrm WAbe WCom
* cf. *rostrata* DBG 219	ETow
'Semonkong'	CMdw EMan GCal LPio MSte WHil

Zamia (*Zamiaceae*)

fischeri	WMul
floridana	CRoM LPal
furfuracea	CBrP EAmu LPal WMul
muricata	LPal
neurophyllidia **new**	CBrP
pumila	CBrP WMul
roezlii	CBrP
skinneri	LPal
standleyi	CBrP
vazquezii	CBrP

Zamioculcas (*Araceae*)

zamiifolia	ESlt

Zantedeschia (*Araceae*)

§ *aethiopica* ♀H3	More than 30 suppliers
- B&SWJ 3959	WCru
- 'Apple Court Babe'	CElw CRow CStu GCal MNrw WDyG
- 'Crowborough' ♀H3	More than 30 suppliers
- 'Gigantea'	CHEx
- 'Glow'	MNrw WCot
- 'Green Goddess' ♀H3	More than 30 suppliers
- 'Little Gem'	LPio SMad
- 'Mr Martin'	CDes EBee EMan MNrw WCot WPGP
- 'Pershore Fantasia' (v)	EBee MNrw WCot WFar WPnP WSPU
- 'Tiny Tim' **new**	SChr
- 'Whipped Cream'	MNrw
- 'White Gnome'	CDes EBee WFar
- 'White Mischief' **new**	EBee
- 'White Pixie'	COtt EMan ENot WViv
- 'White Sail'	CLAP EBee EMan EMar EPza GCal LAst MNrw MRav WFib
albomaculata	CPLG EBee LAma MNrw NRog SGar
'Anneke'	EPfP SPer WBrE WViv
'Apricot Glow'	CHll WViv
'Aztec Gold'	CHEx
'Best Gold'	see Z. 'Florex Gold'
black	CSut
'Black Eyed Beauty'	CStu EMFW EMui IHMH LAma NRog WPnP WViv
'Black Magic'	EPfP LAma SPer WFar WViv
'Black Pearl'	LAma
'Bridal Blush'	LAma
'Cameo'	CSut EMui LAma MNrw WFar WViv
'Carmine Red'	MNrw WBrE
'Celeste'	WViv
'Chianti'	MNrw WViv
'Crystal Blush'	LAma
'Crystal Glow' **new**	WViv

'Dominique'	MNrw
elliottiana ♀H1	CBcs CFir CHal EUJe GQui ITer LAma MNrw NRog SWal WPnn WViv
'Flame'	EMui
§ 'Florex Gold'	CSut LAma WViv
'Galaxy'	WViv
'Golden Sun'	WViv
'Harvest Moon'	LAma
'Hot Shot'	WViv
'Kiwi Blush'	CABP CBot CDWL CFir CHEx CLAP CRow CSpe EBee ELan EMan ERou LPBA LRHS MAvo MCCP NPal SPla SSpi SVil WCot WFar WPnP WPnn WSan WViv
'Lavender Petite'	LAma
'Lilac Mist' **new**	WViv
'Lime Lady'	ECha
'Little Suzie'	WViv
'Majestic Red'	EMui WCot WViv
'Mango'	EMui IHMH LAma MNrw WCot WPnP WPnn WViv
'Maroon Dainty'	LAma
'Moonglow' **new**	WViv
'Mozart' **new**	WViv
'Pacific Pink'	WViv
'Pink Mist'	EBee EMar LAma MNrw WPnP
'Pink Persuasion'	EMui LAma MNrw SPer WFar WPnP WViv
'Pot of Gold' **new**	WViv
'Purple Haze'^{PBR}	WViv
red	IHMH
'Red Sox'^{PBR} **new**	WViv
rehmannii ♀H1	CStu GQui IHMH LAma MNrw NLar SRms WSPU WViv
– 'Little Dream'	WViv
salmon orange	IHMH
'Schwarzwalder'^{PBR}	WViv
'Sensation'	IHMH WViv
'Silver Lining'	LAma MNrw
'Solfatare'	LAma MNrw
'Treasure'	WCot WViv
'Yellow Queen'	WViv

Zanthorhiza see *Xanthorhiza*

Zanthoxylum (*Rutaceae*)

acanthopodium B&SWJ 7237 **new**	WCru
ailanthoides	CFil EPfP
– B&SWJ 8535	WCru
– from Japan	WPGP
americanum	CAgr CBcs CFil ELan
armatum	CAgr CFil WPGP
bungeanum	CAgr CFil WPGP
coreanum	CFil WPGP
molle **new**	CFil WPGP
oxyphyllum	CFil WPGP
piasezkii	CBcs
piperitum	CFil EBee SMad WBcn WPGP
– purple-leaved	CFil
planispinum	LEdu MRav
* *rhetsoides* **new**	CFil
schinifolium	CAgr CBcs LEdu SSpi
– B&SWJ 1245	WCru
simulans	CBcs CLnd MBlu
stenophyllum	CBcs

Zauschneria (*Onagraceae*)

arizonica	see *Z. californica* subsp. *latifolia*
§ *californica*	CBcs CBri CBrm CHll CMHG CSam EBee EPfP GQui NMen SLon WHrl WPnn

– 'Albiflora'	EOrc EPot WAbe
§ – subsp. *cana*	ECGP ECha MHar SChu SIgm XPep
– – 'Sir Cedric Morris'	EPfP LRHS MAsh SMur
– 'Catalina' **new**	XPep
– 'Clover Dale'	EWes
§ – 'Dublin' ♀H3	More than 30 suppliers
– 'Ed Carman'	EBee ECtt EMan EPPr MAvo
§ – subsp. *garrettii*	NWCA SDys SIgm XPep
– 'Glasnevin'	see *Z. californica* 'Dublin'
§ – subsp. *latifolia*	MBro SIgm WPnn XPep
– – NNS 95-512	NWCA
– – 'Sally Walker'	EWes
§ – subsp. *mexicana*	CWib EPot MHer SRms WAbe WCom
– 'Olbrich Silver'	CWCL EBee ECha EMan EWes LHop MAvo MBro NWCA SUsu WAbe WCom WCot WHil WHoo WPat WWin
– 'Schieffelin's Choice' **new**	XPep
– 'Sierra Salmon'	XPep
– 'Solidarity Pink'	CSpe EBee MTho WKif WPat WSHC XPep
– 'Western Hills' ♀H4	CBri CFir CLyd CSpe EBee ECtt LHop LPhx MRav NWCA SAga SBla SIgm SIng WAbe WCom WHoo WPGP XPep
cana villosa	see *Z. californica* subsp. *mexicana*
'Copton Ash Pink'	SIgm
I 'Pumilio'	NMen
§ *septentrionalis*	ETow SBla SIgm

Zebrina see *Tradescantia*

Zelkova ✿ (*Ulmaceae*)

carpinifolia	CDoC CDul CLnd CMCN CTho LRHS SBLw STre WDin WNor
serrata ♀H4	CBcs CDul CLnd CMCN CTho CWib EBee ECrN ELan EPfP EWTr GKir IArd LRHS MBar NBea NHol NPSI NPal NWea SBLw SPer STre WBod WCru WDin WFar WMou WNor WOrn
– B&SWJ 8491 from Korea	WCru
– 'Goblin'	CLnd MBro WPat
– 'Green Vase'	LPan LRHS MBlu SCoo SLim
– 'Variegata' (v)	CPMA MBlu MGos WBcn
– 'Yatsubusa'	STre
– 'Yrban Ruby'	MGos
sinica	CBcs CLnd CMCN STre WNor
x *verschaffeltii*	GKir

Zenobia (*Ericaceae*)

pulverulenta	More than 30 suppliers
– 'Blue Sky'	CMCN EPfP MBlu NLar SSpi WPGP
– pink-flowered **new**	MBlu

Zephyranthes ✿ (*Amaryllidaceae*)

atamasca	CStu ERos
brazosensis	CStu
candida	CAvo CBro CStu EBee EMan EMon EPot EPyc ERea ERos ITim LAma LEur LRHS NRog SDeJ SDix WCot
citrina	EBee EHyt EPot ERos LAma NRog WCot
drummondii	EBee WCot
flavissima	CBro EBee WCot WPGP WPrP
'Grandjax'	WCot
'La Buffa Rose'	WCot
lindleyana	WCot
macrosiphon	EBee
mexicana	ERos

minima   CStu EBee
'Prairie Sunset'   WCot
robusta   see *Habranthus robustus*
rosea   EBee EPot LAma SPet
sulphurea   LAma
verecunda   CStu

Zexmenia (*Asteraceae*)
hispida   see *Wedelia texana*

Zigadenus (*Melanthiaceae*)
elegans   CSam EBee EBre ECha EHyt EMan
                      EPar ERos LRHS SMad SSpi WBVN
                      WCom WWin
fremontii   CStu EBee EBla MDKP WCot
glaberrimus   SSpi
nuttallii   EBee EMan ERos MDKP WCot
                      WLin
venenosus   EBee

Zingiber (*Zingiberaceae*)
chrysanthum   CKob EUJe LEur
clarkei   CKob EUJe LEur MOak WMul
gracile **new**   CKob
'Midnight'   CKob MOak

mioga   CKob GPoy LEur MSal
officinale   CKob GPoy MOak MSal
purpureum   CKob
'Red Dwarf' **new**   CKob
rubens   CKob EUJe LEur
spectabile **new** CKob
'Yellow Delight' **new**   CKob
zerumbet   CKob EUJe GPoy LEur MOak
                      WMul
- 'Darceyi' (v)   CKob EUJe LEur MOak

Zizia (*Apiaceae*)
aptera   CDes EBee EMan EMar LPhx
aurea   EBee LPhx WTin

Ziziphus (*Rhamnaceae*)
§ *jujuba* (F)   CAgr LEdu LPan
- 'Lang' (F)   ERea
- 'Li' (F)   LPan
- var. *spinosa* **new**   CArn
sativa   see *Z. jujuba*

Zoysia (*Poaceae*)
matrella **new**   XPep
tenuifolia **new** XPep

BIBLIOGRAPHY

This is by no means exhaustive but lists some of the more useful works used in the preparation of the *RHS Plant Finder*. Included are websites, all of which were available on line in February/March 2002. The websites of raisers of new plants (not listed here) are also an invaluable source of information. The PBR grant holder will be found in the appropriate PBR source listed below.

GENERAL

Allan, H.H., et al. 2000. *Flora of New Zealand*. Wellington. (5 vols).

Altwegg, A., G. Fortgens & E. Siebler (eds.). 1996. *ISU Yearbook 1965-95*. Windisch, Germany: Internationale Stauden-Union.

Bailey, L.H. & E.Z. Bailey, et al. 1976. *Hortus Third*. New York: Macmillan.

Bean, W.J. 1988. *Trees and Shrubs Hardy in the British Isles*. (8th ed. edited by Sir George Taylor & D.L. Clarke & Supp. ed. D.L. Clarke). London: John Murray.

Beckett, K. (ed.). 1994. *Alpine Garden Society Encyclopaedia of Alpines*. Pershore, Worcs: AGS (2 vols).

Brickell, C. (ed.). 1996. *The Royal Horticultural Society A-Z Encyclopedia of Garden Plants*. London: Dorling Kindersley.

Brickell, C. (ed.). 1999. *The RHS New Encyclopedia of Plants and Flowers*. London: Dorling Kindersley.

Brummitt, R.K. & C.E. Powell (eds.). 1992. *Authors of Plant Names*. Kew: Royal Botanic Gardens.

Brummitt, R.K. (comp.). 1992. *Vascular Plant Families and Genera*. Kew: Royal Botanic Gardens.

Bond, P. & P. Goldblatt. 1984. *Plants of the Cape Flora: A Descriptive Catalogue*. Journal of South African Botany Supplementary Volume no. 13. Kirstenbosch, South Africa: National Botanic Gardens.

Bramwell, D. & Z.I. Bramwell. 1974. *Wild Flowers of the Canary Islands*. London: Stanley Thornes.

Castroviejo, S., M. Lainz, G. Lopez Gonzalez, P. Montserrat, F. Munoz Garmendia, J. Paiva & L. Villar (eds.). *Flora Iberica (vols 1-6, 7(2), 8) 1987-2000*. Plantas vasculares de la Peninsula Iberica e Islas Baleares. Madrid: Real Jardin Botanico, C.S.I.C.

Cave, Y. & V. Paddison. 1999. *The Gardener's Encyclopaedia of New Zealand Native Plants*. Auckland: Godwit.

Chittenden, F.J. & P.M. Synge (eds.). 1956. *The Royal Horticultural Society Dictionary of Gardening*. (2nd ed.). Oxford: Clarendon Press. (4 vols).

Clement, E.J. & M.C. Foster. 1994. *Alien Plants of the British Isles*. London: Botanical Society of the British Isles.

Cooke, I. 1998. *The Plantfinder's Guide to Tender Perennials*. Newton Abbot, Devon: David & Charles.

Cronquist, A., A.H. Holmgren, N.H. Holmgren, J.L. Reveal & P.H. Holmgren, et al. (eds.). *Intermountain Flora: Vascular Plants of the Intermountain West, USA (1986-97)*. (Vols 1, 3-6). New York: New York Botanical Garden.

Cullen, J. (ed.). 2001. *Handbook of North European Garden Plants*. Cambridge University Press.

Davis, P.H., R.R. Mill & K. Tan (eds.). 1965. *Flora of Turkey and the East Aegean Islands* (1965-1988) (Vols 1-10). Edinburgh University Press.

Forrest, M. (comp.) & E.C. Nelson (ed.). 1985. *Trees and Shrubs Cultivated in Ireland*. Dublin: Boethius Press for An Taisce.

Goldblatt, P. & J. Manning. 2000. *Cape Plants*. A Conspectus of the Cape Flora of South Africa. South Africa / USA: National Botanical Institute of South Africa / Missouri Botanical Garden.

Graf, A.B. 1963. *Exotica 3*. Pictorial Cyclopedia of Exotic Plants. (3rd ed.). New Jersey, USA: Roehrs

Graf, A.B. 1986. *Tropica*. Color Cyclopedia of Exotic Plants and Trees. (3rd ed.). New Jersey, USA: Roehrs

Greuter, W., et al. (eds.). 2000. *International Code of Botanical Nomenclature (Saint Louis Code)*. Königstein, Germany: Koeltz Scientific Books.

Greuter, W., R.K. Brummitt, E. Farr, N. Kilian, P.M. Kirk & P.C. Silva (comps.). 1993. *NCU-3*. *Names in Current Use for Extant Plant Genera*. Konigstein, Germany: Koeltz Scientific Books.

Grierson, A.J.C., D.G. Long & H.J. Noltie, et al. (eds.). 2001. *Flora of Bhutan*. Edinburgh: Royal Botanic Garden.

Griffiths, M. (ed.). 1994. *The New RHS Dictionary Index of Garden Plants*. London: Macmillan

Güner, A., N. Özhatay, T. Ekîm, K.H.C. Baser & I.C. Hedge. 2000. *Flora of Turkey and the East Aegean Islands*. Supplement 2. Vol. 11. Edinburgh: Edinburgh University Press.

Harkness, M.G. 1993. *The Bernard E. Harkness Seedlist Handbook*. (2nd ed.). London: Batsford.

Hickman, J.C. (ed.). 1993. *The Jepson Manual*. *Higher Plants of California*. Berkeley & Los Angeles: University of California Press.

Hillier, J. & A. Coombes (eds.). 2002. *The Hillier Manual of Trees & Shrubs*. (7th ed.). Newton Abbot, Devon: David & Charles.

Hirose, Y. & M. Yokoi. 1998. *Variegated Plants in Colour*. Iwakuni, Japan: Varie Nine

Hirose, Y. & M. Yokoi. 2001. *Variegated Plants in Colour*. Volume 2. Iwakuni, Japan: Varie Nine

Huxley, A., M. Griffiths & M. Levy (eds.). 1992. *The New RHS Dictionary of Gardening*. London: Macmillan.

Jacobsen, H. 1973. *Lexicon of Succulent Plants.* London: Blandford.

Jellitto, L. & W. Schacht. 1990. *Hardy Herbaceous Perennials.* Portland, Oregon: Timber Press. (2 vols).

Kelly, J. (ed.). 1995. *The Hiller Gardener's Guide to Trees and Shrubs.* Newton Abbot, Devon: David & Charles.

Krüssmann, G. & M.E. Epp (trans.). 1986. *Manual of Cultivated Broad-leaved Trees and Shrubs.* London: B.T. Batsford Ltd. (3 vols).

Leslie, A.C. (trans.). *New Cultivars of Herbaceous Perennial Plants 1985-1990.* Hardy Plant Society.

Mabberley, D.J. 1997. *The Plant-Book.* A Portable Dictionary of the Vascular Plants. (2nd ed.). Cambridge: Cambridge University Press.

McGregor, R.L., T.M. Barkley, R.E. Brooks & E.K. Schofield, et al. (eds.). 1987. *Flora of the Great Plains.* Lawrence, Kansas: University Press of Kansas.

Metcalf, L.J. 1987. *The Cultivation of New Zealand Trees and Shrubs.* Auckland: Reed Methuen.

Munz, P. 1973. *A Californian Flora and Supplement.* London: University of California Press.

Ohwi, J. 1965. *Flora of Japan.* Washington DC: Smithsonian Institution.

Phillips, R. & M. Rix. 1989. *Shrubs.* London: Pan

Phillips, R. & M. Rix. 1993. *Perennials.* London: Pan (2 vols).

Phillips, R. & M. Rix. 1997. *Conservatory and Indoor Plants.* London: Macmillan. (2 vols).

Platt, K. (comp.). 2000. *The Seed Search.* (4th ed.). Sheffield: Karen Platt

Polunin, O. & A. Stainton. 1984. *Flowers of the Himalaya.* Oxford: Oxford University Press.

Press, J.R. & M.J. Short (eds.). 1994. *Flora of Madeira.* London: Natural History Museum/HMSO.

Rehder, A. 1940. *Manual of Cultivated Trees and Shrubs Hardy in North America.* (2nd ed.). New York: Macmillan.

Stace, C. 1997. *New Flora of the British Isles.* (2nd ed.). Cambridge: Cambridge University Press.

Stainton, A. 1988. *Flowers of the Himalaya.* A Supplement. Oxford University Press.

Stearn, W.T. 1992. *Botanical Latin.* (4th ed.). Newton Abbot, Devon: David & Charles.

Stearn, W.T. 1996. *Stearn's Dictionary of Plant Names for Gardeners.* London: Cassell

Thomas, G.S. 1990. *Perennial Garden Plants.* A Modern Florilegium. (3rd ed.). London: Dent.

Thomas, G.S. 1992. *Ornamental Shrubs, Climbers & Bamboos.* London: John Murray

Trehane, P. (comp.). 1989. *Index Hortensis.* Volume 1: Perennials. Wimborne: Quarterjack

Trehane, P., et al. 1995. *International Code of Nomenclature for Cultivated Plants.* Wimborne, UK: Quarterjack

Tutin, T.G., et al. (ed.). 1993. *Flora Europaea.* Volume 1. Psilotaceae to Platanaceae. (2nd ed.). Cambridge University Press.

Tutin, T.G., et al. 1964. *Flora Europaea.* Cambridge University Press. Vols 1-5.

Hoffman, M.H.A., van de Laar, H.J., de Jong, P.C. & Geers, F. (eds). 2000. *Naamlijst van Houtige Gewassen.* (List of Names of Woody Plants). Boskoop, Netherlands: Boomteeltpraktijkonderzoek

Hoffman, M.H.A., van de Laar, H.J., de Jong, P.C. & Geers, F. (eds).2000. *Naamlijst van Vaste Plantem.* (List of Names of Perennials). Boskoop, Netherlands: Boomteeltpraktijkonderzoek

Walter, K.S. & H.J. Gillett (eds.). 1998. *1997 IUCN Red List of Threatened Plants.* Gland, Switzerland and Cambridge, UK: IUCN.

Walters, S.M. & J. Cullen, et al. (eds.). 2000. *The European Garden Flora.* Cambridge: Cambridge University Press. (6 vols).

Willis, J.C. & H.K. Airy-Shaw (ed.). 1973. *A Dictionary of the Flowering Plants and Ferns.* (8th ed.). Cambridge University Press.

GENERAL PERIODICALS

New, Rare and Unusual Plants.

The Hardy Plant Society. *The Hardy Plant.*

The Hardy Plant Society. *The Sport.*

Internationale Stauden-Union. *ISU Yearbook.*

Royal Horticultural Society. *The Garden.*

Royal Horticultural Society. *The Plantsman.*

Royal Horticultural Society. *The New Plantsman.*

GENERAL WEBSITES

International Plant Names Index. www.ipni.org

List of Plant Species. University of Waikato. http://cber.bio.waikato.ac.nz

Plant Breeders Rights - Database Search. http://www.affa.gov.au/content/pbr_database/search.cfm

2003. Canadian Plant Breeders' Rights Office. Canadian Food Inspection Agency. www.inspection.gc.ca/english/plaveg/pbrpov/pbrpove.shtml

2002. Australian Cultivar Registration Authority. www.anbg.gov.au/acra/

2002. Australian Plant Breeders' Rights List Online: The Commonwealth Department of Agriculture, Fisheries & Forestry. www.affa.gov.au/corporate_docs/publications/excel/pbr/accept.xls

2002. Australian Plant Names Index. Australian National Botanic Gardens, (comp.). www.anbg.gov.au/anbg/names.html

2002. Community Plant Variety Office List of Grants and Applications for Plant Variety Rights. www.cpvo.fr/en/default.html

2002. GRIN (Germplasm Resources Information Network) Taxonomy. www.ars-grin.gov/npgs/tax/index.html

2002. Flora of China Checklist. http://flora.huh.harvard.edu/china

2002. VAST TROPICOS. Missouri Botanical Garden.

http://mobot.mobot.org/W3T/Search/vast.html

2001. The Plants Database. Version 3.5. USDA, NRCS http://plants.usda.gov/

2001. US Patent Full-Text Database. US Patent and Trademark Office, (comp.). www.uspto.gov/patft/index.html

2000. Flora of North America Website. Morin, N.R., et al. http://hua.huh.harvard.edu/fna/index.html

2000. IOPI Provisional Global Plant Checklist. www.bgbm.fu-berlin.de/iopi/gpc/query.htm

2000. New Ornamentals Database. Hatch, L.C. (comp.) http://members.tripod.com.~Hatch_L/nosdex.html

1999. Flora Mesoamericana Internet Version (W3FM). Missouri Botanical Garden. www.mobot.org/fm/intro.html

1998. A Synonymized Checklist of the Vascular Flora of the United States, Puerto Rico and the Virgin Isles. BIOTA of North America Program. www.csdl.tamu.edu/FLORA/b98/check98.htm

GENERA

Acacia
Beckett, K.A. 1993. Some Australian Wattles in Cultivation. *The Plantsman* 15(3):131-47.

Simmons, M.H. 1987. *Acacias of Australia.* (2nd ed.). Melbourne: Nelson.

Acer
Harris, J.G.S. 2000. *The Gardener's Guide to Growing Maples.* Newton Abbot, Devon: David & Charles.

Van Gelderen, C.J. & D.M. Van Gelderen. 1999. *Maples for Gardens.* A Color Encyclopaedia. Portland, Oregon: Timber Press.

Vertrees, J.D. 2001. *Japanese Maples.* Momiji and Kaede. (3rd ed.). Portland, Oregon: Timber Press.

Actaea
Compton, J. 1992. *Cimicifuga* L. *Ranunculaceae. The Plantsman* 14(2):99-115.

Compton, J. 1992. *Cimicifuga.* A Bane of a Name for a Fine Plant. *The Garden* (RHS) 117(11):504-506.

Compton, J.A. & A. Culham. 2000. The Name is the Game. *The Garden* (RHS) 125(1):48-52.

Compton, J.A., A. Culham & S.L. Jury. 1998. Reclassification of *Actaea* to Include *Cimicifuga* and *Souliea* (*Ranunculaceae*): Phylogeny Inferred from Morphology, nrDNA ITS, and cpDNA trn_L-F Sequence Variation. *Taxon* 47:593-634.

Adiantum
Goudey, C.J. 1985. *Maidenhair Ferns in Cultivation.* Melbourne: Lothian.

Agapanthus
Snoeijer, W. 1998. *Agapanthus.* A Review. Gouda: Wim Snoeijer.

Agavaceae
Irish, M. & G. Irish. 2000. *Agaves, Yuccas and Related Plants.* A Gardener's Guide. Portland, Oregon: Timber Press.

Aizoaceae
Burgoyne, P., H. Hartmann, S. Hammer, P. Chesselet, E. van Jaarsveld, C. Klak, G. Smith, B. van Wyk & H. Kurzweil. 1998. *Mesembs of the World. Illustrated Guide to a Remarkable Succulent Group.* South Africa: Briza Publications.

Allium
Dadd, R. 1997. RHS Trials: Grand Alliums. *The Garden* (RHS) 122(9):658-661.

Davies, D. 1992. *Alliums. The Ornamental Onions.* London: B. T. Batsford Ltd.

Gregory, M., et al. 1998. *Nomenclator Alliorum.* London: RBG, Kew.

Mathew, B. 1996. *A Review of Allium Section Allium.* London: Royal Botanic Gardens, Kew.

Androsace
Smith, G. & D. Lowe. 1997. *The Genus Androsace.* Pershore, Worcs.: Alpine Garden Society Publications Limited.

Anemone, Japanese
McKendrick, M. 1990. Autumn Flowering Anemones. *The Plantsman* 12(3):140-151.

McKendrick, M. 1998. Japanese Anemones. *The Garden* (RHS) 123(9):628-633.

Anthemis
Leslie, A. 1997. Focus on Plants: *Anthemis tinctoria. The Garden* (RHS) 122(8):552-555.

Apiaceae
Ingram, T. 1993. *Umbellifers.* Pershore, Worcs.: Hardy Plant Society.

Pimenov, M.G. & M.V. Leonov. 1993. *The Genera of the Umbelliferae.* London: Royal Botanic Gardens, Kew.

Aquilegia
Munz, P.A. 1946. *Aquilegia:* the Cultivated and Wild Columbines. *Gentes Herb.* 7(1):1-150.

Arecaceae (Palmae, Palms)
Jones, D.L. 1995. *Palms Throughout the World.* Chatswood, NSW: Reed Books.

Uhl, N.W. & J. Dransfield. 1987. *Genera Palmarum.* A Classification of Palms Based on the Work of Harold E. Moore Jr. Lawrence, Kansas: Allen Press.

Argyranthemum
Cheek, R. 1993. La Belle Marguerite. *The Garden* (RHS) 118(8):350-355.

Humphries, C.J. 1976. A Revision of the Macaronesian Genus *Argyranthemum. Bull. Brit. Mus. (Nat. Hist.) Bot.* 5(4):145-240.

Arisaema
Pradhan, U.C. 1997. *Himalayan Cobra Lilies Arisaema.* Their Botany and Culture. (2nd ed.). Kalimpong, West Bengal, India: Primulaceae Books.

Arum
Bown, D. 2000. *Plants of the Arum Family.* (2nd ed.). Portland, Oregon: Timber Press.

Boyce, P. 1993. *The Genus Arum.* London: HMSO.

Aster
Picton, P. 1999. *The Gardener's Guide to Growing Asters.* Newton Abbot: David & Charles.

Ranson, E.R. 1946. *Michaelmas Daisies and Other Garden Asters.* London: John Gifford Ltd.

Astilbe

Noblett, H. 2001. *Astilbe.* A Guide to the Identification of Cultivars and Common Species. Cumbria: Henry Noblett.

Aubrieta

1975. *International Registration Authority Checklist.* Weihenstephan, Germany: (Unpublished).

Auricula

Baker, G. & P. Ward. 1995. *Auriculas.* London: Batsford.

Bamboos

Bell, M. 2000. *The Gardener's Guide to Growing Bamboos.* Newton Abbot: David & Charles.

Chao, C.S. 1989. *A Guide to Bamboos Grown in Britain.* RBG, Kew.

Ohrnberger, D. 1999. *The Bamboos of the World. Annotated Nomenclature and Literature of the Species and the Higher and Lower Taxa.* Amsterdam: Elsevier.

Begonia

Ingles, J. 1990. *American Begonia Society Listing of Begonia Cultivars.* Revised Edition Buxton Checklist. American Begonia Society.

Thompson, M.L. & E.J. Thompson. 1981. *Begonias.* The Complete Reference Guide. New York: Times Books.

Betula

Ashburner, K. & T. Schilling. 1985. *Betula utilis* and its Varieties. *The Plantsman* 7(2):116-125.

Ashburner, K.B. 1980. *Betula* - a Survey. *The Plantsman* 2(1):31-53.

Hunt, D. (ed.). 1993. *Betula: Proceedings of the IDS Betula Symposium 1992.* Richmond, Surrey: International Dendrology Society.

Bougainvillea

Bor, N.L. & M.B. Raizada. 1982. Some Beautiful Indian Climbers and Shrubs. *J. Bombay Nat. Hist. Soc.* (2nd Ed):291-304.

Choudhury, B. & B. Singh (comps.). 1981. *The International Bougainvillea Check List.* New Delhi: Indian Agricultural Research Institute.

Gillis, W.T. 1976. Bougainvilleas of Cultivation (*Nyctaginaceae*). *Baileya* 20(1):34-41.

Iredell, J. 1990. *The Bougainvillea Grower's Handbook.* Brookvale, Australia: Simon & Schuster.

Iredell, J. 1994. *Growing Bougainvilleas.* London: Cassell.

MacDaniels, L.H. 1981. A Study of Cultivars in *Bougainvillea* (*Nyctaginaceae*). *Baileya* 21(2):77-100.

Singh, B., R.S. Panwar, S.R. Voleti, V.K. Sharma & S. Thakur. 1999. *The New International Bougainvillea Check List.* (2nd ed.). New Delhi: Indian Agricultural Research Institute.

Bromeliaceae

Beadle, D.A. (comp.). 1998. *The Bromeliad Cultivar Registry.* The Bromeliad Society International.

Beadle, D.A. 1991. *A Preliminary Listing of all the Known Cultivar and Grex Names for the Bromeliaceae.* Corpus Christi, Texas: Bromeliad Society.

Luther, H.E. & E. Sieff. 2000. *An Alphabetical List of Bromeliad Binomials.* (7th ed.) Orlando, Florida: Bromeliad Society International.

Rauh, W. 1979. *Bromeliads for Home, Garden and Greenhouse.* Blandford, Dorset: Blandford Press.

Bulbs

Bryan, J.E. 1989. *Bulbs.* Vols. 1 & 2. Bromley, Kent: Christopher Helm.

Du Plessis, N. & G. Duncan. 1989. *Bulbous Plants of Southern Africa.* Cape Town: Tafelberg.

Grey-Wilson, C. & B. Mathew. 1981. *Bulbs.* London: Collins.

Leeds, R. 2000. *The Plantfinder's Guide to Early Bulbs.* Newton Abbot, Devon: David & Charles.

Phillips, R., M. Rix & B. Mathew (ed.). 1981. *The Bulb Book.* A Photographic Guide to Over 800 Hardy Bulbs. London: Ward Lock Ltd.

Royal General Bulbgrowers Association. 1991. *International Checklist for Hyacinths and Miscellaneous Bulbs.* Hillegom, The Netherlands: KAVB.

Buxus

Batdorf, L.R. 1995. *Boxwood Handbook.* A Practical Guide to Knowing and Growing Boxwood. Boyce, VA, USA: The American Boxwood Society.

Camellia

Gonos, A.A. (ed.). 1999. *Camellia Nomenclature.* (23rd Revd ed.). Southern California Camellia Society.

Savige, T.J. (comp.). 1993. *The International Camellia Register.* The International Camellia Society. (2 vols).

Savige, T.J. (comp.). 1997. *The International Camellia Register.* Supplement to volumes one and two. The International Camellia Society.

Campanula

Lewis, P. & M. Lynch. 1998. *Campanulas.* A Gardeners Guide. (2ND ED.). London: Batsford.

Canna

Cooke, I. 2001. *Gardener's Guide to Growing Cannas.* Newton Abbot, Devon: David & Charles.

Hayward, K. 2000. *Canna Handbook.* (Edition 1.01). Farnborough, Hants: Hart Canna.

Carnivorous Plants

D'Amato, P. 1998. *The Savage Garden.* Berkeley, USA: Ten Speed Press.

Pietropaulo, J. & P. Pietropaulo. 1986. *Carnivorous Plants of the World.* Oregon, USA: Timber Press.

Schlauer, J. (comp.). 2001. *Carnivorous Plant Database.* www2.labs.agilent.com/bot/cp_home

Slack, A. 1988. *Carnivorous Plants.* (Revd ed.). Sherborne, Dorset: Alphabooks.

Cercidiphyllum

Dosmann, M.S. 1999. Katsura: a Review of *Cercidiphyllum* in Cultivation and in the Wild. *The New Plantsman* 6(1):52-62.

Chaenomeles

Weber, C. 1963. Cultivars in the Genus *Chaenomeles. Arnoldia (Jamaica Plain)* 23(3):17-75.

Chrysanthemum (Dendranthema)

Brummitt, D. 1997. *Chrysanthemum* Once Again. *The Garden* (RHS) 122(9):662-663.

Gosling, S.G. (ed.). 1964. *British National Register of Chrysanthemums.* Whetstone, London: National Chrysanthemum Society.

National Chrysanthemum Society. 2000. *British National Register of Names of Chrysanthemums Amalgamated Edition 1964-1999.* Tamworth, Staffordshire: The National Chrysanthemum Society.

Cistus

Bygrave, P. & R.G. Page. 2002. *Cistus – a Guide to the Collection at Chelsea Physic Garden.* Wisley: NCCPG.

Citrus

Davies, F.S. & L.G. Albrigo. 1994. *Citrus.* Wallingford, Oxon: Cab International.

Saunt, J. 1990. *Citrus Varieties of the World.* An Illustrated Guide. Norwich: Sinclair

Clematis

Evison, R. 1998. *The Gardener's Guide to Growing Clematis.* Newton Abbot: David & Charles.

Fisk, J. 1989. *Clematis, the Queen of Climbers.* London: Cassell.

Fretwell, B. 1989. *Clematis.* London: Collins.

Grey-Wilson, C. 2000. *Clematis the Genus.* London: B.T. Batsford

Johnson, M. 2001. *The Genus Clematis.* Södertälje, Sweden: Magnus Johnsons Plantskola AB & Bengt Sundström.

Lloyd, C. & T.H. Bennett. 1989. *Clematis.* (Revd ed.). London: Viking.

Matthews, V. (comp.). 2002. *The International Clematis Register and Checklist 2002.* London: The Royal Horticultural Society.

Snoeijer, W. (comp.). 1991. *The Clematis Index.* Boskoop, Netherlands: Fopma.

Snoeijer, W. 1996. *Checklist of Clematis Grown in Holland.* Boskoop, Netherlands: Fopma.

Conifers

den Ouden, P. & B.K. Boom. 1965. *Manual of Cultivated Conifers.* The Hague: Martinus Nijhof.

Farjon, A. 1998. *World Checklist and Bibliography of Conifers.* London: Royal Botanic Gardens, Kew.

Krüssmann, G. & M.E. Epp (trans.). 1985. *Manual of Cultivated Conifers.* London: Batsford.

Lewis, J. & A.C. Leslie. 1987. *The International Conifer Register. Part 1. Abies to Austrotaxus.* London: Royal Horticultural Society.

Lewis, J. & A.C. Leslie. 1989. *The International Conifer Register. Part 2. Belis to Pherosphaera,* excluding the Cypresses. London: The Royal Horticultural Society.

Lewis, J. & A.C. Leslie. 1992. *The International Conifer Register. Part 3. The Cypresses.* London: The Royal Horticultural Society.

Lewis, J. & A.C. Leslie (ed.). 1998. *The International Conifer Register. Part 4 Juniperus.* London: The Royal Horticultural Society.

Welch, H.J. 1979. *Manual of Dwarf Conifers.* New York: Theophrastus.

Welch, H.J. 1991. *The Conifer Manual.* Volume 1. Dordrecht, The Netherlands: Kluwer Academic Publishers.

Welch, H.J. 1993. *The World Checklist of Conifers.* Bromyard, Herefordshire: Landsman's Bookshops Ltd.

Cornus

Howard, R.A. 1961. Registration Lists of Cultivar Names in *Cornus L.. Arnoldia (Jamaica Plain)* 21(2):9-18.

Corydalis

Lidén, M. & H. Zetterlund. 1997. *Corydalis. A Gardener's Guide and a Monograph of the Tuberous Species.* Pershore, Worcs.: AGS Publications Ltd.

Mathew, B. 2001. Earning their spurs (*Corydalis*). *The Garden* (RHS) 126(3):184-187.

Corylus

Crawford, M. 1995. *Hazelnuts: Production and Culture.* Dartington, Devon: Agroforestry Research Trust.

Game, M. 1995. Champion of the Cobnut. *The Garden* (RHS) 120(11):674-677.

Cotoneaster

Fryer, J. & B. Hylmö. 1998. Seven New Species of *Cotoneaster* in Cultivation. *The New Plantsman* 5(3):132-144.

Fryer, J. & B. Hylmö. 2001. Captivating Cotoneasters. *The New Plantsman* 8(4):227-238.

Fryer, J. 1996. Undervalued Versatility. *Cotoneaster. The Garden* (RHS) 121(11):709-715.

Crassulaceae

Eggli, U. & H. Hart. 1995. *Evolution and Systematics of the Crassulaceae.* Leiden, Netherlands: Backhuys Publishers.

Crocosmia

Dunlop, G. 1999. Bright Sparks. *The Garden* (RHS) 124(8):599-605.

Kostelijk, P.J. 1984. *Crocosmia* in Gardens. *The Plantsman* 5(4):246-253.

Crocus

Jacobsen, N., J. van Scheepen & M. Ørgaard. 1997. The *Crocus chrysanthus - biflorus* Cultivars. *The New Plantsman* 4(1):6-38.

Mathew, B. 1982. *The Crocus.* A Review of the Genus *Crocus (Iridaceae).* London: B.T. Batsford Ltd.

Cyclamen

Grey-Wilson, C. 1997. *Cyclamen. A Guide for Gardeners, Horticulturists & Botanists.* London: Batsford.

Cypripedium

Cribb, P. 1997. *The Genus Cypripedium.* Portland, Oregon: Timber Press.

Dahlia

American Dahlia Society website. www.dahlia.org

National Dahlia Society. 2001. *Classified Directory and Judging Rules.* (26th ed.) Marlow, Bucks: National Dahlia Society.

RHS & R. Hedge (comps.). 1969. *Tentative Classified List and International Register of Dahlia*

Names 1969. (& Supplements 1-12). London: The Royal Horticultural Society.

Daphne

Brickell, C. & R. White. 2000. A Quartet of New Daphnes. *The New Plantsman* 7(1):6-18.

Brickell, C. 2000. *Daphne.* Part 2: Henderson's Daphne. *The New Plantsman* 7(2):114-122.

Brickell, C.D. & B. Mathew. 1976. *Daphne. The Genus in the Wild and in Cultivation.* Woking, Surrey: Alpine Garden Society.

Grey-Wilson, C. (ed.). 2001. *The Smaller Daphnes.* The Proceedings of 'Daphne 2000', a Conference Held at the Royal Horticultural Society, Organised by the Joint Rock Garden Plant Committee. Pershore, Worcs: AGS Publications Ltd.

Delphinium

1949. *A Tentative Checklist of Delphinium Names.* London: Royal Horticultural Society.

1970. *A Tentative Check List of Delphinium Names.* Addendum to the 1949 tentative check-list of *Delphinium* names. London: The Royal Horticultural Society.

Leslie, A.C. 1995. The International Delphinium Register Supplement 1993-94. *The Delphinium Society Year Book 1995.*

Leslie, A.C. 1996. *The International Delphinium Register Cumulative Supplement 1970-1995.* London: The Royal Horticultural Society.

Leslie, A.C. 1996. The International Delphinium Register Supplement 1994-95. *The Delphinium Society Year Book 1996:*82-86.

Leslie, A.C. 1997. The International Delphinium Register Supplement 1995-96. *The Delphinium Society Year Book 1997:*106-108.

Leslie, A.C. 1998. The International Delphinium Register Supplement 1996-97. *The Delphinium Society Year Book 1998:*108-109.

Leslie, A.C. 1999. The International Delphinium Register Supplement 1997-98. *Delphinium Soc. Yearbook.*

Leslie, A.C. 2000. The International Delphinium Register Supplement 1998-99. *Delphinium Soc. Yearbook*

Dianthus

Bird, R. 1994. *Border Pinks.* London: B.T. Batsford Ltd.

Galbally, J. & E. Galbally. 1997. *Carnations and Pinks for Garden and Greenhouse.* Portland, Oregon: Timber Press.

Leslie, A.C. *The International Dianthus Register 1983-2000.* (2nd ed. & Supps 1-17). London: Royal Horticultural Society.

Diascia

Benham, S. 1987. *Diascia:* A Survey of the Species in Cultivation. *The Plantsman* 9(1):1-17.

Harrison, H. 1996. *Diascia (Scrophulariaceae). Hardy Plant* 18(1):41-47.

Lord, T. 1996. *Diascia* on Trial. *The Garden* (RHS) 121(4):192-194.

Dierama

Hilliard, O.M. & B.L. Burtt. 1991. *Dierama. The Harebells of Africa.* Johannesburg; London: Acorn Books.

Dionysia

Grey-Wilson, C. 1989. *The Genus Dionysia.* Woking, Surrey: Alpine Garden Society.

Douglasia

Mitchell, B. 1999. Celebrating the Bicentenary of David Douglas: a Review of *Douglasia* in Cultivation. *The New Plantsman* 6(2):101-108.

Dracaena

Bos, J.J., P. Graven, W.L.A. Hetterscheid & J.J. van de Wege. 1992. Wild and cultivated *Dracaena fragrans. Edinburgh J. Bot.* 49(3):311-331.

Echinacea

Vernon, J. 1999. Power Flowers. *The Garden* (RHS) 124(8):588-593.

Epimedium

Barker, D.G. 1996. *Epimediums and other herbaceous Berberidaceae.* Pershore, Worcs.: The Hardy Plant Society.

Stearn, W.T. 1937. Epimedium & Vancouveria, a Monograph. *J. Linn. Soc., Bot.* 51:409-535.

White, R. 1996. *Epimedium:* Dawning of a New Area. *The Garden* (RHS) 121(4):208-214.

Episcia

Dates, J.D. 1993. *The Gesneriad Register 1993.* Check List of Names with Descriptions of Cultivated Plants in the Genera *Episcia* & *Alsobia.* Galesburg, Illinois: American Gloxinia & Gesneriad Society, Inc.

Erica

Baker, H.A. & E.G.H. Oliver. 1967. *Heathers in Southern Africa.* Cape Town: Purnell.

Schumann, D., G. Kirsten & E.G.H. Oliver. 1992. *Ericas of South Africa.* Vlaeberg, South Africa: Fernwood Press.

Erodium

Clifton, R. 1994. *Geranium Family Species Checklist.* Part 1 *Erodium.* (4th ed.). The Geraniaceae Group.

Leslie, A.C. 1980. The Hybrid of *Erodium corsicum* With *Erodium reichardii. The Plantsman* 2:117-126.

Victor, D.X. (comp.). 2000. *Erodium Register of Cultivar Names.* The Geraniaceae Group.

Erythronium

Mathew, B. 1992. A Taxonomic and Horticultural Review of *Erythronium* L. (*Liliaceae*). *J. Linn. Soc., Bot.* 109:453-471.

Mathew, B. 1998. The Genus *Erythronium. Bull. Alpine Gard. Soc. Gr. Brit.* 66(3):308-321.

Euonymus

Brown, N. 1996. Notes on Cultivated Species of *Euonymus. The New Plantsman* 3(4):238-243.

Lancaster, C.R. 1982. *Euonymus* in Cultivation - Addendum. *The Plantsman* 4:61-64, 253-254.

Lancaster, R.C. 1981. An Account of *Euonymus* in Cultivation and its Availability in Commerce. *The Plantsman* 3(3):133-166.

Euphorbia
Turner, R. 1995. *Euphorbias. A Gardeners Guide.* London: Batsford.
Witton, D. 2000. *Euphorbias.* Pershore, Worcs: Hardy Plant Society.

Fagales
Govaerts, R. & D.G. Frodin. 1998. *World Checklist and Bibliography of Fagales.* Royal Botanic Gardens, Kew.

Fagus
Dönig, G. 1994. *Die Park-und Gartenformen der Rotbuche Fagus sylvatica L..* Erlangen, Germany: Verlag Gartenbild Heinz Hansmann.
Wyman, D. 1964. Registration List of Cultivar Names of *Fagus* L. *J. Arnold Arbor.* 24(1):1-8.

Fascicularia
Nelson, E.C. & G. Zizka. 1997. *Fascicularia (Bromeliaceae):* Which Species are Cultivated and Naturalized in Northwestern Europe. *The New Plantsman* 4(4):232-239.
Nelson, E.C., G. Zizka, R. Horres & K. Weising. 1999. Revision of the Genus *Fascicularia* Mez *(Bromeliaceae). Botanical Journal of the Linnean Society* 129(4):315-332.

Ferns
2001. *Checklist of World Ferns.* http://homepages.caverock.net.nz/~bj/fern/
Johns, R.J. 1996. *Index Filicum.* Supplementum Sextum pro annis 1976-1990. RBG, Kew.
Johns, R.J. 1997. *Index Filicum.* Supplementum Septimum pro annis 1991-1995. RBG, Kew.
Jones, D.L. 1987. *Encyclopaedia of Ferns.* Melbourne, Australia: Lothian.
Kaye, R. 1968. *Hardy Ferns.* London: Faber and Faber.
Rickard, M.H. 2000. *The Plantfinder's Guide to Garden Ferns.* Newton Abbot, Devon: David and Charles.
Rush, R. 1984. *A Guide to Hardy Ferns.* London: British Pteridological Society.

Fragaria
Day, D. (ed.). 1993. *Grower Digest 3: Strawberries.* (Revd ed.). London: Nexus Business Communications.

Fritillaria
Mathew, B., et al. 2000. *Fritillaria* Issue. *Bot. Mag.* 17(3):145-185.
Pratt, K. & M. Jefferson-Brown. 1997. *The Gardener's Guide to Growing Fritillaries.* Newton Abbot: David & Charles.
Turrill, W.B. & J.R. Sealy. 1980. *Studies in the Genus Fritillaria (Liliaceae).* Hooker's Icones Plantarum Vol 39 (1 & 2). Royal Botanic Garden Kew.

Fruit
1987. *Index of the Bush Fruit Collection at the National Fruit Trials 1987.* Faversham, Kent: MAFF.
Anon. 1997. *Catalogue of Cultivars in the United Kingdom National Fruit Collection.* Kent, UK: Brogdale Horticultural Trust.
Bowling, B.L. 2000. *The Berry Grower's Companion.* Portland, Oregon: Timber Press.

Hogg, R. 1884. *The Fruit Manual.* (5th ed.). London: Journal of Horticulture Office.

Fuchsia
Bartlett, G. 1996. *Fuchsias - A Colour Guide.* Marlborough, Wilts: Crowood Press.
Boullemier, Leo.B. (comp.). 1991. *The Checklist of Species, Hybrids and Cultivars of the Genus Fuchsia.* London, New York, Sydney: Blandford Press.
Boullemier, Leo.B. (comp.). 1995. *Addendum No. 1 to the 1991 Checklist of Species, Hybrids and Cultivars of the Genus Fuchsia.* Dyfed, Wales: The British Fuchsia Society.
Goulding, E. 1995. *Fuchsias: The Complete Guide.* London: Batsford.
Johns, E.A. 1997. *Fuchsias of the 19th and Early 20th Century.* An Historical Checklist of Fuchsia Species & Cultivars, pre-1939. Kidderminster, Worcs: The British Fuchsia Society
Nijhuis, M. 1994. *1000 Fuchsias.* London: Batsford.
Nijhuis, M. 1996. *500 More Fuchsias.* London: Batsford.
Van Veen, G. 2002. *Gelderse Fuchsia Info-site.* http://home-1.worldonline.nl/~veenvang/A_homepage.htm

Galanthus
Bishop, M., A. Davis & J. Grimshaw. 2001. Snowdrops. A monograph of cultivated *Galanthus.* Maidenhead: Griffin Press.
Davis, A.P., B. Mathew (ed.) & C. King (ill.). 1999. *The Genus Galanthus.* A Botanical Magazine Monograph. Oregon: Timber Press.

Gentiana
Bartlett, M. 1975. *Gentians.* Dorset: Blandford Press.
Halda, J.J. 1996. *The Genus Gentiana.* Dobré: Sen.
Wilkie, D. 1950. *Gentians.* (2nd ed Revised). London: Country Life.

Geranium
Bath, T. & J. Jones. 1994. *The Gardener's Guide to Growing Hardy Geraniums.* Newtton Abbot, Devon: David & Charles.
Clifton, R.T.F. 1995. *Geranium Family Species Check List Part 2.* Geranium. (4th Edition, issue 2). Dover: The Geraniaceae Group.
Jones, J., et al. 2001. *Hardy Geraniums for the Garden.* (3rd Edition, Revised and Enlarged). Pershore, Worcs: Hardy Plant Society.
Victor, D.X. 2000. *Geranium.* Register of Cultivar Names. The Geraniaceae Group. www.hardygeraniums.com/register_of_cultivar_names.htm
Yeo, P.F. 2002. *Hardy Geraniums.* (3rd ed.). Kent: Croom Helm.

Gesneriaceae
Dates, J.D. 1986. *The Gesneriad Register 1986.* Check List of Names with Descriptions of Intergeneric Hybrids in the Tribe *Gloxinieae.* Sugar Grove, Illinois: American Gloxinia & Gesneriad Society, Inc.
Dates, J.D. 1987. *The Gesneriad Register 1987.* Check List of Names with Descriptions of Cultivated Plants in the Genera *Bucinellina,*

Columnea, Dalbergaria, Pentadenia, Trichantha
Also Intergeneric Hybrids. Galesburg, Illinois:
American Gloxinia & Gesneriad Society, Inc.

Dates, J.D. 1990. *The Gesneriad Register 1990.*
Check List of Names with Descriptions of
Cultivated Plants in the Genus *Aeschynanthus.*
Galesburg, Illinois: American Gloxinia &
Gesneriad Society, Inc.

Gladiolus
1994. British Gladiolus Society List of Cultivars
Classified for Show Purposes 1994. Mayfield,
Derbyshire: British Gladiolus Society.

1997. British Gladiolus Society List of European
Cultivars Classified for Exhibition Purposes 1997.
Mayfield, Derbyshire: British Gladiolus Society.

1997. British Gladiolus Society List of New Zealand
Cultivars Classified for Exhibition Purposes 1997.
Mayfield, Derbyshire: British Gladiolus Society.

1997. British Gladiolus Society List of North
American Cultivars Classified for Exhibition
Purposes 1997. Mayfield, Derbyshire: British
Gladiolus Society.

1998. British Gladiolus Society List of European
Cultivars Classified for Exhibition Purposes 1998.
Mayfield, Derbyshire: British Gladiolus Society.

1998. British Gladiolus Society List of New Zealand
Cultivars Classified for Exhibition Purposes 1998.
Mayfield, Derbyshire: British Gladiolus Society.

1998. British Gladiolus Society List of North
American Cultivars Classified for Exhibition
Purposes 1998. Mayfield, Derbyshire: British
Gladiolus Society.

Goldblatt, P. & J. Manning. 1998. *Gladiolus in Southern
Africa.* Vlaeberg, South Africa: Fernwood Press.

Goldblatt, P. 1996. *Gladiolus in Tropical Africa.*
Systematics Biology and Evolution. Oregon:
Timber Press.

Lewis, G.J., A.A. Obermeyer & T.T. Barnard. 1972.
A Revision of the South African Species of
Gladiolus. J. S. African Bot. (Supp. Vol.)

Gleditsia
Santamour, F.S. & A.J. McArdle. 1983. Checklist of
Cultivars of Honeylocust (*Gleditsia triacanthos* L.).
J. Arboric. 9:271-276.

Grevillea
Olde, P. & N. Marriott. 1995. *The Grevillea Book.*
(3). Kenthurst, NSW: Kangaroo Press.

Haemanthus
Snijman, D. 1984. A Revision of the Genus
Haemanthus. J. S. African Bot. (Supp) 12:

Hamamelis
Coombes, A.J. 1996. Winter Magic. Introduction to
Witch Hazels. *The Garden* (RHS) 121(1):28-33.

Lane, C. 1998. *Hamamelis* in Small Spaces. *The
Garden* (RHS) 123(1):38-41.

Strand, C. 1998. Asian Witch Hazels and their
Hybrids: a History of *Hamamelis* in cultivation.
The New Plantsman 5(4):231-245.

Heathers
Nelson, E.C. Feb 2002. International Cultivar
Registration Authority for Heathers.
www.heathersociety.org.uk/registration.html

Nelson, E.C. & D.J. Small (eds.). 2000.
International Register of Heather Names. Volume 1
Hardy Cultivars & European Species. Part 1: A-C.
The Heather Society.

Nelson, E.C. & D.J. Small (eds.). 2000.
International Register of Heather Names. Volume 1
Hardy Cultivars & European Species. Part 2: D-I.
The Heather Society.

Nelson, E.C. & D.J. Small (eds.). 2000.
International Register of Heather Names. Volume 1
Hardy Cultivars & European Species. Part 3: J-P.
The Heather Society.

Nelson, E.C. & D.J. Small (eds.). 2000.
International Register of Heather Names. Volume 1
Hardy Cultivars & European Species. Part 4: Q-
Z. The Heather Society.

Small, D. & A. Small (comps.). 2001. *Handy Guide
to Heathers.* (3rd ed.) Creeting St Mary, Suffolk:
The Heather Society.

Underhill, T. 1990. *Heaths & Heathers.* The Grower's
Encyclopedia. Newton Abbot: David & Charles.

Hebe
Chalk, D. 1988. *Hebes & Parahebes.* Bromley, Kent:
Christopher Helm (Publishers) Ltd.

Hutchins, G. 1997. *Hebes: Here and There.* A
Monograph on the Genus *Hebe.* Caversham,
Berks: Hutchins & Davies.

Hedera
McAllister, H. 1988. Canary & Algerian Ivies. *The
Plantsman* 10(1):27-29.

McAllister, H.A. & A. Rutherford. 1990. *Hedera helix
& H. hibernica* in the British Isles. *Watsonia* 18:7-15.

Rose, P.Q. 1996. *The Gardener's Guide to Growing
Ivies.* David & Charles.

Rutherford, A., H. McAllister & R.R. Mill. 1993.
New Ivies from the Mediterranean Area and
Macaronesia. *The Plantsman* 15(2):115-128.

Hedychium
Schilling, T. 1982. A Survey of Cultivated
Himalayan and Sino-Himalayan *Hedychium*
Species. *The Plantsman* 4:129-149.

Spencer-Mills, L. 1996. Glorious *Hedychium. The
Garden* (RHS) 121(12):754-759.

Heliconia
Berry, F. & W.J. Kress. 1991. *Heliconia.* An Identification
Guide. Washington: Smithsonian Institution Press.

Helleborus
Mathew, B. 1989. *Hellebores.* Woking: Alpine
Garden Society.

Rice, G. & E. Strangman. 1993. *The Gardener's
Guide to Growing Hellebores.* Newton Abbot,
Devon: David and Charles.

Hemerocallis
Erhardt, W. 1988. *Hemerocallis Daylilies.* London: Batsford.

Grenfell, D. 1998. *The Gardener's Guide to Growing Daylilies*. Newton Abbott: David & Charles.

Kitchingman, R.M. 1985. Some Species and Cultivars of *Hemerocallis*. *The Plantsman* 7(2):68-89.

Monroe, W.E. (comp.). 1973. *Hemerocallis Check List July 1 1957 to July 1 1973*. American Hemerocallis Society Inc.

Monroe, W.E. (comp.). 1983. *Hemerocallis Check List July 1 1973 to July 1 1983*. American Hemerocallis Society.

Munson, R.W. 1993. *Hemerocallis - The Daylily*. Timber Press.

Petit, T.L. & J.P. Peat. 2000. *The Color Encyclopaedia of Daylilies*. Portland, Oregon: Timber Press.

Shield, J. 1997. *Daylily Database*. http://galagarden.com/release31.html

Webber, S. (ed.). 1988. *Daylily Encyclopaedia*. Damascus, Maryland: Webber Gardens.

Herbs

Page, M. & W. Stearn. *Culinary Herbs: A Wisley Handbook*.

Phillips, R. & N. Foy. 1990. *Herbs*. London: Pan Books Ltd.

Hibiscus

Beers, L. & J. Howie. 1990. *Growing Hibiscus*. (2nd ed.). Kenthurst, Australia: Kangaroo Press.

Chin, H.F. 1986. *The Hibiscus: Queen of Tropical Flowers*. Kuala Lumpur: Tropical Press Sdn. Bhd.

Walker, J. 1999. *Hibiscus*. London: Casell.

Hippeastrum

KAVB. 1980. *Alfabetische Lijst van de in Nederland in Cultuur Zijnde Amaryllis (Hippeastrum) Cultivars*. Hillegom, Netherlands: Koninklijke Algemeene Vereeniging Voor Bloembollencultur.

Read, V.M. 1998. Blooming Bold. *The Garden* (RHS) 123(10):734-737.

Hosta

Giboshi.com Hosta Database. www.giboshi.com

Grenfell, D. 1990. *Hosta*. London: Batsford.

Grenfell, D. 1993. *Hostas*. Pershore, Worcs: Hardy Plant Society.

Grenfell, D. 1996. *The Gardener's Guide to Growing Hostas*. Newton Abbot: David & Charles.

Schmid, W.G. 1991. *The Genus Hosta*. London: B.T. Batsford Ltd.

Hyacinthus

Clark, T. 2000. Focus on Plants: Treasures of the East (Hyacinths). *The Garden* (RHS) 125(9):672-675.

Stebbings, G. 1996. Heaven Scent. *The Garden* (RHS) 121(2):68-72.

Hydrangea

Church, G. 1999. *Hydrangeas*. London: Cassell.

Haworth-Booth, M. 1975. *The Hydrangeas*. London: Garden Book Club.

Lawson-Hall, T. & R. Brian. 1995. *Hydrangeas*. A Gardener's Guide. London: B T Batsford.

Mallet, C. 1992. *Hydrangeas. Species and Cultivars*. Volume 1. Varengeville Sur Mer: Centre d'Art Floral.

Mallet, C. 1994. *Hydrangeas. Species and Cultivars*. Volume 2. Varengeville Sur Mer: Editions Robert Mallet.

Hypericum

Lancaster, R. & N. Robson. 1997. Focus on Plants: Bowls of Beauty. *The Garden* (RHS) 122(8):566-571.

Ilex

Andrews, S. 1983. Notes on Some *Ilex* x *altaclerensis* Clones. *The Plantsman* 5(2):65-81.

Andrews, S. 1984. More Notes on Clones of *Ilex* x *altaclerensis*. *The Plantsman* 6(3):157-166. Erratum vol.6 p.256.

Andrews, S. 1985. Holly Berries of a Varied Hue. *The Garden* (RHS) 110(11):518-522.

Andrews, S. 1994. Hollies with a Difference. *The Garden* (RHS) 119(12):580-583,].

Dudley, T.R. & G.K. Eisenbeiss. 1992. *International Checklist of Cultivated Ilex*. Part 1 Ilex Opaca. Washington USA: United States Department of Agriculture.

Dudley, T.R. & G.K. Eisenbeiss. 1992. *International Checklist of Cultivated Ilex*. Part 2 Ilex crenata. United States National Arboretum: United States Department of Agriculture.

Galle, F.C. 1997. *Hollies: the Genus Ilex*. Portland, Oregon: Timber Press.

Iridaceae

Innes, C. 1985. *The World of Iridaceae. A Comprehensive Record*. Ashington, Sussex: Holly Gate International Ltd.

Iris

2000. *American Iris Society Database*. www.irisregister.com

Hoog, M.H. 1980. Bulbous Irises . *The Plantsman* 2(3):141-64.

Mathew, B. 1981. *The Iris*. London: Batsford.

Mathew, B. 1993. The Spuria Irises. *The Plantsman* 15(1):14-25.

Service, N. 1990. *Iris unguicularis*. *The Plantsman* 12(1):1-9.

Stebbings, G. 1997. *The Gardener's Guide to Growing Iris*. Newton Abbot: David & Charles.

The Species Group of the British Iris Society, (ed.). 1997. *A Guide to Species Irises*. Their Identification and Cultivation. Cambridge, UK: Cambridge University Press.

Kalmia

Jaynes, R.A. 1997. *Kalmia*. Mountain Laurel and Related Species. Oregon: Timber Press.

Pullen, A. 1997. *Kalmia latifolia*. *The Garden* (RHS) 122(6):400-403.

Kniphofia

Grant-Downton, R. 1997. Notes on *Kniphofia thomsonii* in Cultivation and in the Wild. *The New Plantsman* 4(3):148-156.

Taylor, J. 1985. *Kniphofia* - a Survey. *The Plantsman* 7(3):129-160.

Kohleria

Dates, J.D. (ed.) & F.N. Batcheller (comp.). 1985.

The Gesneriad Register 1985. Check List of Names with Descriptions of Cultivated Plants in the Genus *Kohleria.* Lincoln Acres, California: American Gloxinia and Gesneriad Society, Inc.

Lachenalia
Duncan, G,D. 1988. *The Lachenalia Hand Book.*

Lantana
Howard, R.A. 1969. A Check List of Names Used in the Genus *Lantana. J. Arnold Arbor.* 29(11):73-109.

Lathyrus
Norton, S. 1996. *Lathyrus. Cousins of Sweet Pea.* Surrey: NCCPG

Lavandula
McNaughton, V. 2000. *Lavender. The Grower's Guide.* Woodbridge, Suffolk: Garden Art Press
Tucker, A.O. & K.J.W. Hensen. 1985. The Cultivars of Lavender and Lavandin (*Labiatae*). *Baileya* 22(4):168-177.
Upson, T. 1999. Deep Purple. *The Garden* (RHS) 124(7):524-529.

Legumes
2000. *ILDIS.* International Legume Database and Information Service. www.ildis.org
Lewis, G.P. 1987. *Legumes of Bahia.* London: Royal Botanic Gardens, Kew.
Lock, J.M. & J. Heald. 1994. *Legumes of Indo-China.* London: Royal Botanic Gardens, Kew.
Lock, J.M. & K. Simpson. 1991. *Legumes of West Asia.* London: Royal Botanic Gardens, Kew.
Lock, J.M. 1989. *Legumes of Africa: A Checklist.* London: Royal Botanic Gardens, Kew.
Roskov, Yu.R., A.K. Sytin & G.P. Yakovlev. 1996. *Legumes of Northern Eurasia.* London: Royal Botanic Gardens, Kew.

Leptospermum
1963. Check List of *Leptospermum* Cultivars. *J. Roy. New Zealand Inst. Hort.* 5(5):224-30.
Dawson, M. 1997. A History of *Leptospermum scoparium* in Cultivation - Discoveries from the Wild. *The New Plantsman* 4(1):51-59.
Dawson, M. 1997. A History of *Leptospermum scoparium* in Cultivation - Garden Selections. *The New Plantsman* 4(2):67-78.

Lewisia
Davidson, B.L.R. 2000. *Lewisias.* Portland, Oregon: Timber Press.
Elliott, R. 1978. *Lewisias.* Woking: Alpine Garden Society.
Mathew, B. 1989. *The Genus Lewisia.* Bromley, Kent: Christopher Helm.

Liliaceae Sensu Lato
Mathew, B. 1989. Splitting the *Liliaceae. The Plantsman* 11(2):89-105.

Lilium
Leslie, A.C. *The International Lily Register 1982-2000.* (3rd Ed & Supps 1-18). London: Royal Horticultural Society.

Lonicera
Bradshaw, D. 1996. *Climbing Honeysuckles.* Surrey: NCCPG

Magnolia
Callaway, D. Sept 2002. www.magnoliasociety.org/index.html
Callaway, D.J. 1994. *Magnolias.* London: B.T. Batsford Ltd.
Frodin, D.G. & R. Govaerts. 1996. *World Checklist and Bibliography of Magnoliaceae.* London: Royal Botanic Garden, Kew.
Gardiner, J. 2000. *Magnolias.* A Gardeners' Guide. Portland, Oregon: Timber Press.
Hunt, D. (ed.). 1998. *Magnolias and their Allies.* Proceedings of an International Symposium, Royal Holloway, University of London, Egham, Surrey, UK, 12-13 April 1996. International Dendrology Society and The Magnolia Society.

Malus
Crawford, M. 1994. *Directory of Apple Cultivars.* Devon: Agroforestry Research Trust.
Fiala, J.L. 1994. *Flowering Crabapples.* The genus *Malus.* Portland, Oregon: Timber Press.
Morgan, J. & A. Richards. 1993. *The Book of Apples.* London: Ebury Press.
Parfitt, B. 1965. *Index of the Apple Collection at the National Fruit Trials.* Faversham, Kent: MAFF.
Rouèche, A. 2000. *Les Crets Fruits et Pomologie.* http://perso.club_internet.fr/lescret/index2.htm
Spiers, V. 1996. *Burcombes, Queenies and Colloggetts.* St Dominic, Cornwall: West Brendon.
Taylor, H.V. 1948. *The Apples of England.* London: Crosby Lockwood.

Meconopsis
Brickell, C. & E. Stevens. 2002. *Meconopsis* 'Lingholm'. *The New Plantsman* 1(2): 88-92
Cobb, J.L.S. 1989. *Meconopsis.* Bromley, Kent: Christopher Helm.
Grey-Wilson, C. 1992. A Survey of the Genus *Meconopsis* in Cultivation. The Plantsman 14(1):1-33
Stevens, E. & C. Brickell. 2001. Problems with the Big Perennial Poppies. *The New Plantsman* 8(1):48-61.
Stevens, E. 2001. Further Observations on the Big Perennial Blue Poppies. *The New Plantsman* 8(2):105-111.

Moraea
Goldblatt, P. 1986. *The Moraeas of Southern Africa. A Systematic Monograph of the Genera in South Africa, Lesotho, Swaziland, Transkei, Botswana, Namibia and Zimbabwe.* Kirstenbosch: National Botanic Gardens.

Narcissus
Blanchard, J.W. 1990. *Narcissus - a guide to wild daffodils.* Lye End Link, St John's, Woking, Surrey GU21 1SW: Alpine Garden Society.
Kington, S. (comp.). *The International Daffodil Register and Classified List.* www.rhs.org.uk/research/registerpages/DaffSearch.asp
Kington, S. (comp.). 1998. *The International*

Daffodil Register and Classified List 1998. First Supplement 1997-1998. London: RHS.

Kington, S. (comp.). 1999. *The International Daffodil Register and Classified List (1998)* Second Supplement. London: RHS.

Kington, S. (comp.). 2000. *The International Daffodil Register and Classified List (1998)* Third Supplement. London: RHS.

Throckmorton, T.D. (ed.). 1985. Daffodills to Show & Grow and Abridged Classified List of Daffodil Names. Hernando, Mississippi: RHS and American Daffodil Society.

Nematanthus

Arnold, P. 1978. *The Gesneriad Register 1978.* Check List of *Nematanthus.* American Gloxinia and Gesneriad Society, Inc.

Nerium

Pagen, F.J.J. 1987. Oleanders. *Nerium* L. and the oleander cultivars. Agricultural University Wageningen Papers.

Toogood, A. 1997. *Nerium oleander. The Garden* (RHS) 122(7):488-491.

Nymphaea

International Water Lily Society. 1993. *Identification of Hardy Nymphaea.* Stapely Water Gardens Ltd. Includes nomenclaturally adjusted contents page (1995) with Erratum & Addendum.

Knotts, K. & R. Sacher (comps.). 2000. *Provisional Check List of Names/Epithets of Nymphaea L..* International Waterlily & Water Gardening Society. Cocoa Beach, Florida.

Swindells, P. 1983. *Waterlilies.* London: Croom Helm.

Orchidaceae

Cribb, P. & C. Bailes. 1989. *Hardy Orchids.* Bromley, Kent: Christopher Helm.

Hunt, P.F. & D.B. Hunt. 1996. *Sander's List of Orchid Hybrids: Addendum 1991-1995.* London: Royal Horticultural Society.

Shaw, J.M.H. *The International Orchid Register.* www.rhs.org.uk/research/registration_orchids.asp

Orchidaceae: Add Pf03

Hunt, P.F. 2000. New Orchid Hybrids. *Orchid Rev.* 108(1233): Supplement.

Origanum

Paton, A. 1994. Three Membranous-bracted Species of *Origanum. Kew Mag.* 11(3):109-117.

White, S. 1998. *Origanum.* The Herb Marjoram and its Relatives. Surrey: NCCPG.

Paeonia

Harding, A. & R.G. Klehm. 1993. *The Peony.* London: Batsford.

Haworth-Booth, M. 1963. *The Moutan or Tree Peony.* London: Garden Book Club.

Kessenich, G.M. 1976. *Peonies.* (Variety Check List Pts 1-3). American Peony Society.

Osti, G.L. 1999. *The Book of Tree Paeonies.* Turin: Umberto Allemandi

Page, M. 1997. *The Gardener's Guide to Growing Paeonies.* Newton Abbott: David & Charles

Rogers, A. 1995. *Peonies.* Portland, Oregon: Timber Press

Wang, L., et al. 1998. *Chinese Tree Peony.* Beijing: China Forestry Publishing House.

Papaver

Grey-Wilson, C. 1998. Oriental Glories. *The Garden* (RHS) 123(5):320-325.

Grey-Wilson, C. 2000. *Poppies.* The Poppy Family in the Wild and in Cultivation. London: B.T. Batsford.

Passiflora

Vanderplank, J. 1996. *Passion Flowers.* (2nd ed.). London, England: Cassell.

Pelargonium

Clifton, R. 1999. *Geranium Family Species Checklist, Part 4 Pelargonium.* The Geraniaceae Group.

Complete Copy of the Spalding Pelargonium Checklist. (Unpublished). USA.

Abbott, P.G. 1994. *A Guide to Scented Geraniaceae.* Angmering, West Sussex: Hill Publicity Services.

Anon. 1978. *A Checklist and Register of Pelargonium Cultivar Names.* Part one A-B. Australian Pelargonium Society.

Bagust, H. 1988. *Miniature and Dwarf Geraniums.* London: Christopher Helm.

Clifford, D. 1958. *Pelargoniums.* London: Blandford Press.

Key, H. 2000. *1001 Pelargoniums.* London: Batsford.

Miller, D. 1996. *Pelargonium.* A Gardener's Guide to the Species and Cultivars and Hybrids. London: B. T. Batsford.

Van der Walt, J.J.A., et al. 1977. *Pelargoniums of South Africa.* (1-3). Kistenbosch, South Africa: National Botanic Gardens.

Penstemon

Lindgren, D.T. & B. Davenport. 1992. List and description of named cultivars in the genus *Penstemon* (1992). University of Nebraska.

Lord, T. 1994. Peerless Penstemons. *The Garden* (RHS) 119(7):304-309.

Nold, R. 1999. *Penstemons.* Portland, Oregon: Timber Press.

Way, D. & P. James. 1998. *The Gardener's Guide to Growing Penstemons.* Newton Abbott: David & Charles.

Phlomis

Mann Taylor, J. 1998. *Phlomis: The Neglected Genus.* Wisley: NCCPG.

Phlox

Harmer, J. & J. Elliott. 2001. *Phlox.* Pershore, Worcs: Hardy Plant Society

Stebbings, G. 1999. Simply Charming. *The Garden* (RHS) 124(7):518-521.

Wherry, E.T. 1955. The Genus *Phlox.* Morris Arboretum Monographs III.

Phormium

Heenan, P.B. 1991. *Checklist of Phormium Cultivars.* Royal New Zealand Institute of Horticulture.

McBride-Whitehead, V. 1998. Phormiums of the Future. *The Garden* (RHS) 123(1):42-45.

Pieris

Bond, J. 1982. *Pieris* - a Survey. *The Plantsman* 4(2):65-75.

Wagenknecht, B.L. 1961. Registration Lists of Cultivar Names in the Genus *Pieris* D. Don. *Arnoldia (Jamaica Plain)* 21(8):47-50.

Plectranthus

Miller, D. & N. Morgan. 2000. Focus on Plants: A New Leaf. *The Garden* (RHS) 125(11):842-845.

Shaw, J.M.H. 1999. Notes on the Identity of Swedish Ivy and Other Cultivated *Plectranthus. The New Plantsman* 6(2):71-74.

Pleione

Cribb, P. & I. Butterfield. 1999. *The Genus Pleione.* (2nd ed.). London: RBG Kew.

Poaceae

Clayton, W.D. & S.A. Renvoize. 1986. *Genera Graminum.* Grasses of the World. London: HMSO.

Darke, R. 1999. *The Colour Encyclopedia of Ornamental Grasses.* Sedges, Rushes, Restios, Cat-tails and Selected Bamboos. London: Weidenfeld & Nicolson.

Grounds, R. 1998. *The Plantfinder's Guide to Ornamental Grasses.* Newton Abott, Devon: David & Charles.

Ryves, T.B., E.J. Clement & M.C. Foster. 1996. *Alien Grasses of the British Isles.* London: Botanical Society of the British Isles.

Wood, T. 2002. *Garden Grasses, Rushes and Sedges.* (3rd ed.). Abingdon: John Wood.

Polemonium

Nichol-Brown, D. 1997. *Polemonium.* Teeside: Trimdon.

Potentilla

Davidson, C.G., R.J. Enns & S. Gobin. 1994. *A Checklist of Potentilla fruticosa: the Shrubby Potentillas.* Morden, Manitoba: Agriculture & Agri-Food Canada Research Centre. Data also on Plant Finder Reference Library professional version CD-ROM 1999/2000.

Miller, D.M. 2002. *RHS Plant and Trials Awards. Shrubby Potentilla.* London: RHS.

Primula

Fenderson, G.K. 1986. *A Synoptic Guide to the Genus Primula.* Lawrence, Kansas: Allen Press.

Green, R. 1976. *Asiatic Primulas.* Woking: The Alpine Garden Society.

Halda, J.J. 1992. *The Genus Primula in Cultivation and the Wild.* Denver, Colorado: Tethys Books.

Hecker, W.R. 1971. *Auriculas & Primroses.* London: Batsford.

Kohlein, F. 1984. *Primeln.* Stuttgart, Germany: Ulmer.

Richards, J. 1993. *Primula.* London: Batsford.

Smith, G.F., B. Burrow & D.B. Lowe. 1984. *Primulas of Europe and America.* Woking: Alpine Garden Society.

Wemyss-Cooke, T.J. 1986. *Primulas Old and New.* Newton Abbot: David & Charles.

Primula allionii

Archdale, B. & D. Richards. 1997. *Primula allionii Forms and Hybrids.* National Auricula & Primula Society, Midland & West Section.

Primula auricula hort.

Hawkes, A. 1995. Striped Auriculas. National Auricula & Primula Society, Midland & West Section.

Robinson, M.A. 2000. *Auriculas for Everyone.* How to Grow and Show Perfect Plants. Lewes: Guild of Master Craftsmen Publications.

Telford, D. 1993. *Alpine Auriculas.* National Auricula & Primula Society, Midland & West Section.

Ward, P. 1991. *Show Auriculas.* National Auricula & Primula Society, Midland & West Section.

Primula auricula hort.

Nicholle, G. 1996. *Border Auriculas.* National Auricula & Primula Society, Midland & West Section.

Primula auricula hort.

Baker, G. *Double Auriculas.* National Auricula & Primula Society, Midland & West Section.

Proteaceae

Rebelo, T. 1995. *Proteas.* A Field Guide to the Proteas of Southern Africa. Vlaeberg: Fernwood Press / National Botanical Institute.

Prunus

1986. *Index of the Cherry Collection at the National Fruit Trials 1986.* Faversham, Kent: MAFF.

Bultitude, J. *Index of the Plum Collection at the National Fruit Trials.* Faversham, Kent: MAFF.

Crawford, M. 1996. *Plums.* Dartington, Devon: Agroforestry Research Trust.

Crawford, M. 1997. *Cherries: Production and Culture.* Dartington, Devon: Agroforestry Research Trust.

Grubb, N.H. 1949. *Cherries.* London: Crosby Lockwood.

Jacobsen, A.L. 1992. *Purpleleaf Plums.* Portland, Oregon: Timber Press.

Jefferson, R.M. & K.K. Wain. 1984. *The Nomenclature of Cultivated Flowering Cherries (Prunus).* The Satu-Zakura Group. Washington: USDA.

Kuitert, W. 1999. *Japanese Flowering Cherries.* Oregon: Timber Press.

Smith, M.W.G. 1978. *Catalogue of the Plums at the National Fruit Trials.* Faversham, Kent: MAFF.

Taylor, H.V. 1949. *The Plums of England.* London: Crosby Lockwood.

Pulmonaria

Hewitt, J. 1994. *Pulmonarias.* Pershore, Worcs.: The Hardy Plant Society.

Hewitt, J. 1999. Well Spotted. *The Garden* (RHS) 124(2):98 - 103.

Pyracantha

Egolf, D.R. & A.O. Andrick. 1995. *A Checklist of Pyracantha Cultivars.* Agricultural Research Service.

Pyrus

Crawford, M. 1996. *Directory of Pear Cultivars.* Totnes, Devon: Agroforestry Research Institute.

Parfitt, B. 1981. *Index of the Pear Collection at the National Fruit Trials.* Faversham, Kent: MAFF.

Smith, M.W.G. 1976. *Catalogue of the British Pear.* Faversham, Kent: MAFF.

Quercus

Avalos, S.V. 1995. *Contribución al Concimiento del Género Quercus (Fagaceae) en el Estado de Guerrero, Mexico.* Mexico City: Facultad de Ciencias, UNAM.

Miller, H.A. & S.H. Lamb. 1985. *Oaks of North America.* Happy Camp, California: Naturegraph Publishers.

Mitchell, A. 1994. The Lucombe Oaks. *The Plantsman* 15(4):216-224.

Rhododendron

Argent, G., G. Fairweather & K. Walter. 1996. *Accepted Names in Rhododendron section Vireya.* Royal Botanic Garden, Edinburgh.

Argent, G., J. Bond, D. Chamberlain, P. Cox & A. Hardy. 1997. *The Rhododendron Handbook 1998.* Rhododendron Species in Cultivation. London: The Royal Horticultural Society.

Chamberlain, D.F. & S.J. Rae. 1990. A Revision of *Rhododendron* IV. Subgenus *Tsutsusi. Edinburgh J. Bot.* 47(2):

Chamberlain, D.F. 1982. A Revision of *Rhododendron* II. Subgenus *Hymenanthes. Notes Roy. Bot. Gard. Edinburgh* 39(2):

Cox, P. & K. Cox. 1988. *Encyclopedia of Rhododendron Hybrids.* London: Bt Batsford.

Cullen, J. 1980. A Revision of *Rhododendron* I. Subgenus *Rhododendron* sections *Rhododendron* and *Pogonanthum. Notes Roy. Bot. Gard. Edinburgh* 39(1):

Davidian, H.H. *The Rhododendron Species Volume IV.* Batsford.

Davidian, H.H. 1982. *The Rhododendron Species Volume I Lepidotes.* Batsford.

Davidian, H.H. 1989. *The Rhododendron Species Volume II.* Batsford.

Davidian, H.H. 1992. *Rhododendron Species Volume III Elepidotes.* Series *Neriiflorum - Thomsonii* Azaleastrum & Camtschaticum. Batsford.

Galle, F.C. 1985. *Azaleas.* Portland, Oregon: Timber Press.

Lee, F.P. 1958. *The Azalea Book.* New York: D. Van Nostrand Co. Ltd.

Leslie, A. (comp.). 1980. *The Rhododendron Handbook 1980.* London: The Royal Horticultural Society.

Leslie, A. *The International Rhododendron Register.* Checklist of Rhododendron Names Registered 1989-1994. (& Supps 28-39). London: RHS.

Salley, H.E. & H.E. Greer. 1986. *Rhododendron Hybrids.* A Guide to their Origins. London: Batsford.

Tamura, T. (ed.). 1989. *Azaleas in Kurume.* Kurume, Japan: International Azalea Festival '89.

Ribes

Crawford, M. 1997. *Currants and Gooseberries: Production and Culture.* Dartington, Devon: Agroforestry Research Trust.

Rosa

2002. *Help Me Find Roses.* www.helpmefind.com/sites/rrr/rosetest.html

Austin, D. 1988. *The Heritage of the Rose.* Woodbridge, Suffolk: Antique Collectors' Club.

Beales, P. 1992. *Roses.* London: Harvill.

Beales, P., T. Cairns, W. Duncan, G. Fagan, W. Grant, K. Grapes, P. Harkness, K. Hughes, J. Mattock & D. Ruston. 1998. *Botanica's Roses.* The Encyclopedia of Roses. UK: Grange Books PLC.

Cairns, T. (ed.). 2000. *Modern Roses XI.* The World Encyclopedia of Roses. London: Academic Press.

Dickerson, B.C. 1992. *The Old Rose Advisor.* Portland, Oregon: Timber Press.

Dobson, B.R. & P. Schneider (comps.). 1996. *Combined Rose List.*

Haw, S.G. 1996. Notes on Some Chinese and Himalayan Rose Species of Section *Pimpinellifoliae. The New Plantsman* 3(3):143-146.

McCann, S. 1985. *Miniature Roses.* Newton Abbot: David & Charles.

Phillips, R. & M. Rix. 1988. *Roses.* London: Macmillan.

Phillips, R. & M. Rix. 1993. *The Quest for the Rose.* London: BBC Books.

Thomas, G.S. 1995. *The Graham Stuart Thomas Rose Book.* London: John Murray.

Verrier, S. 1996. *Rosa Gallica.* Balmain, Australia: Florilegium.

Rosularia

Eggli, U. 1988. A Monographic Study of the Genus *Rosularia. Bradleya* (Suppl.) 6:1-118.

Saintpaulia

Moore, H.E. 1957. *African Violets, Gloxinias and Their Relatives.* A Guide to the Cultivated Gesneriads. New York: Macmillan

Salix

Newsholme, C. 1992. *Willows.* The Genus *Salix.* London: Batsford

Salvia

Clebsch, B. 1997. *A Book of Salvias.* Oregon: Timber Press.

Compton, J. 1994. Mexican Salvias in Cultivation. *The Plantsman* 15(4):193-215.

Saxifraga

Bland, B. 2000. *Silver Saxifrages.* Pershore, Worcs: AGS Publications.

Horný, R., K.M. Webr, J. Byam-Grounds & E. Zoulova (ill.). 1986. *Porophyllum Saxifrages.* Stamford, Lincolnshire: Byam-Grounds Publications.

Kohlein, F. 1984. *Saxifrages and Related Genera.* London: Batsford.

McGregor, M. (ed.). 2000. *Saxifrage 2000.* Driffield, E. Yorks: Saxifrage Society.

McGregor, M. 1995. *Saxifrages: The Complete Cultivars & Hybrids.* First Edition of the International Register of Saxifrages. (1st ed.).

Stocks, A. 1995. *Saxifragaceae*. Hardy Plant Society.

Webb, D.A. & R.J. Gornall. 1989. *Saxifrages of Europe*. Bromley, Kent: Christopher Helm.

Sedum

Evans, R.L. 1983. *Handbook of Cultivated Sedums*. Motcombe, Dorset: Ivory Head Press.

Stephenson, R. 1994. *Sedum*. The Cultivated Stonecrops. Portland, Oregon: Timber Press.

Sempervivum

Miklánek, M. *Sempervivum and Jovibarba List of Cultivars*. http://miklanek.tripod.com/MCS/cv.html

Mitchell, P.J. (comp.). 1985. *International Cultivar Register for Jovibarba, Rosularia, Sempervivum*. Volume One. Burgess Hill: The Sempervivum Society.

Sinningia

Dates, J.D. 1988. *The Gesneriad Register 1988*. Check List of Names with Descriptions of Cultivated Plants in the Genus *Sinningia*. Galesburg, Illinios: American Gloxinia and Gesneriad Society, Inc.

Solenostemon

Pedley, W.K. & R. Pedley. 1974. Coleus - A Guide to Cultivation and Identification. Edinburgh: Bartholemew.

Sorbus

McAllister, H. 1984. The Aucuparia Section of *Sorbus*. *The Plantsman* 6(4):248-255.

McAllister, H. 1996. *Sorbus*: Mountain Ash and its Relatives. *The Garden* (RHS) 121(9):561-567.

Snyers d'Attenhoven, C. 1999. *Sorbus* Lombart hybrids in Belgische Dendrologie. Belgium.

Wright, D. 1981. Sorbus - a Gardener's Evaluation. *The Plantsman* 3(2):65-98.

Streptocarpus

Arnold, P. 1979. *The Gesneriad Register 1979: Check List of Streptocarpus*. Binghamton, New York: American Gloxinia & Gesneriad.

Succulents

Eggli, U. & N. Taylor. 1994. *List of Names of Succulent Plants other than Cacti Published 1950-92*. London: Royal Botanic Gardens Kew.

Grantham, K. & P. Klaassen. 1999. *The Plantfinder's Guide to Cacti and Other Succulents*. Newton Abbot, Devon: David & Charles.

Syringa

Fiala, J.L. 1988. *Lilacs*. The Genus *Syringa*. London: Christopher Helm.

Rogers, O.M. 1976. *Tentative International Register of Cultivar Names in the Genus Syringa*. Research Report no. 49.

Vrugtman, F. 2000. *International Register of Cultivar Names in the Genus Syringa L. (Oleaceae)*. (Contribution No. 91). Hamilton, Canada: Royal Botanic Gardens.

Tillandsia

Kiff, L.F. 1991. *A Distributional Checklist of the Genus Tillandsia*. Encino, California: Botanical Diversions.

Trillium

Case, F.W.J. & R.B. Case. 1997. Trilliums. Portland, Oregon: Timber Press.

Jacobs, D.L. & R.L. Jacobs. 1997. *American Treasures*. Trilliums in Woodland Garden. Decatur, Georgia: Eco-Gardens.

Tulipa

van Scheepen, J. (ed.). 1996. Classified List and International Register of Tulip Names. Hillegom, The Netherlands: Koninklijke Algemeene Vereeniging Voor Bloembollencultuur.

Ulmus

Green, P.S. 1964. Registratration of Cultivar Names in *Ulmus*. *Arnoldia (Jamaica Plain)* 24:41-80.

Vegetables

1999. Official Journal of the European Communities. Common catalogue of varieties of vegetable species C167A. (21st ed.). Luxembourg: Office for Official Publications of the European Communities.

Phillips, R. & M. Rix. 1993. *Vegetables*. London: Pan Books Ltd.

Viola

Coombes, R.E. 1981. *Violets*. London: Croom Helm.

Farrar, R. 1989. *Pansies, Violas & Sweet Violets*. Reading: Hurst Village Publishing.

Fuller, R. 1990. *Pansies, Violas & Violettas*. The Complete Guide. Marlborough: The Crowood Press.

Perfect, E.J. 1996. *Armand Millet and his Violets*. High Wycombe: Park Farm Press.

Zambra, G.L. 1950. *Violets for Garden and Market*. (2nd Ed). London: Collingridge.

Vitis

Pearkes, G. 1989. *Vine Growing in Britain*. London: Dent.

Robinson, J. 1989. *Vines, Grapes and Wines*. London: Mitchell Beazley.

Watsonia

Goldblatt, P. 1989. *The Genus Watsonia*. A Systematic Monograph. South Africa: National Botanic Gardens.

Weigela

Howard, R.A. 1965. A Checklist of Cultivar Names in *Weigela*. *Arnoldia (Jamaica Plain)* 25:49-69.

Wisteria

Valder, P. 1995. *Wisterias*. A Comprehensive Guide. Australia: Florilegium.

Zauschneria

Raven, P.H. 1977. Generic and Sectional Delimitation in *Onagraceae*, Tribe *Epilobieae*. Ann. Missouri Bot. Gard. 63(2):326-340.

Robinson, A. 2000. Focus on Plants: Piping Hot (*Zauschneria* Cultivars). *The Garden* (RHS) 125(9):698-699.

INTERNATIONAL PLANT FINDERS

GERMANY

Erhardt, A. & W. (comp.). (4th ed. 2000). *PPP-Index, The European Plant Finder.* ISBN-3-8001-3183-8. 100,000 plants and seeds available from 2,000 European retail and wholesale nurseries. CD-ROM only. Orders: The Plant Press, 10 Market Street, Lewes, East Sussex, BN7 2NB, UK. T (01273) 476151. E-mail john@plantpress.com £39.99. Or Verlag Eugen Ulmer, PO Box 70 05 61, D-70574 Stuttgart. T +49 711-4507-121. E-mail: info@ulmer.de; website: www.ulmer.de

NETHERLANDS

Terra (2000/2001). *Plantenvinder voor de lage landen.* ISBN 90-6255-936-0. Approx. 50,000 plants and 150 nurseries. Orders: Uitgeverij Terra, POB 1080, 7230 AB Warnsveld, Netherlands. T +31 (575) 581310. F +31 (575) 525242. E-mail: info@terraboek.nl; website: www.terraboek.nl. €11.30.

NEW ZEALAND

Gaddum, M. (comp). (est. 1998). New Zealand Plant Finder www.plantfinder.co.nz. 45,000 plants and seeds, 1000 photos, 320 nurseries by paid subscription. Free search gives sample of nurseries. PO Box 2237, Gisborne, NZ.

UNITED KINGDOM

Pawsey, A (ed.). (21st birthday ed. 2003-2004). *Find that Rose!* Published May 2003. Lists over 3,100 varieties available in the UK with basic type, colour and fragrance codes. New varieties highlighted. Details of approx. 60 growers. How to find a rose with a particular Christian name or to celebrate a special event and where to see roses in bloom. For further information send SAE to: The Editor, 303 Mile End Road, Colchester, Essex CO4 5EA. To order, send a cheque for £3 made out to *Find That Rose!* to the above address.

USA

Hill, Susan & Narizny, Susan (comp.) (2000). *The Pacific North West Plant Locator 2000/2001.* ISBN 0-967 4907-1-5. Directory of sources for plants (no seeds) available at retail and mail order nurseries in Oregon, Washington and Idaho with complete nursery information. Includes a common name/botanical name index. Orders: Black-Eyed Susans Press, PMB 227, 6327-C, SW Capitol Highway, Portland, OR 97201-1937, USA. Email: susans@blackeyedsusanspress.com Price US$20 plus $4 p+p (USA) or $10 (outside USA). Website: www.blackeyedsusanspress.com

Burch, Derek (comp.) & Galletta, Kay (ed.). *PlantFinder.* A monthly magazine for the wholesale nursery and landscape industry giving current listings of plants and plant-related materials in the southern United States. Orders: Betrock Information Systems Inc., 7770 Davie Road Extension, Hollywood, Florida 33024-2516. Subscription cost US$69.95 (double for foreign mail subscriptions). Email: betrock@betrock.com Website: www.hortworld.com

Hutchinson, B. & A. (comp.). *The Plant & Supply Locator.* A monthly magazine for the wholesale nursery and landscape industry giving current listings of plants in the southeastern United States. Orders: Hutchinson Publishing Corp., 102 East Lee Road, Taylors, South Carolina 29687. T +1 (864) 292 9490.

Nurseries

The following nurseries stock between them
an unrivalled choice of plants but before making
a visit, please remember to check with the nursery
that the plant you seek is currently available.

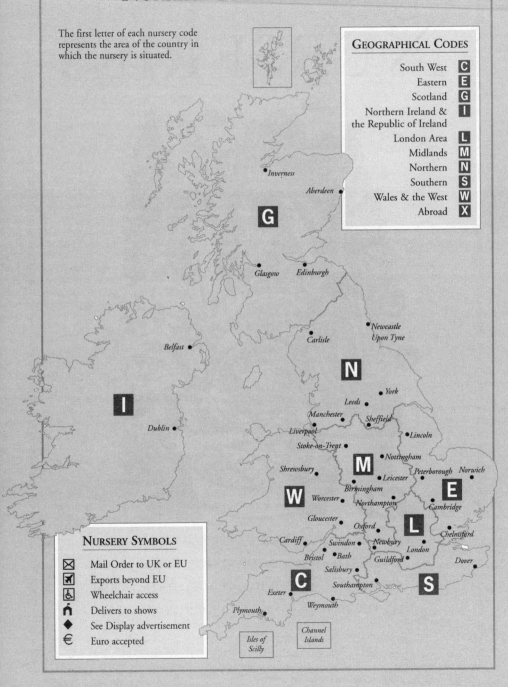

NURSERY CODES AND SYMBOLS

The first letter of each nursery code represents the area of the country in which the nursery is situated.

GEOGRAPHICAL CODES

South West	C
Eastern	E
Scotland	G
Northern Ireland & the Republic of Ireland	I
London Area	L
Midlands	M
Northern	N
Southern	S
Wales & the West	W
Abroad	X

NURSERY SYMBOLS

⊠ Mail Order to UK or EU
✈ Exports beyond EU
& Wheelchair access
ń Delivers to shows
◆ See Display advertisement
€ Euro accepted

USING THE THREE NURSERY LISTINGS

Your main reference from the Plant Directory is the Nursery Details by Code listing, which includes all relevant information for each nursery in order of nursery code. The Nursery Index by Name is an alphabetical list for those who know a nursery's name but not its code and wish to check its details in the main list. The Specialist Nurseries index is to aid those searching for a particular plant group.

1 NURSERY DETAILS BY CODE

Once you have found your plant in the Plant Directory, turn to this list to find out the name, address, opening times and other details of the nurseries whose codes accompany the plant.

KEY		
✉	Mail order to UK or EU	🏠 Delivers to shows
✈	Exports beyond EU	€ Euro accepted
♿	Wheelchair access	◆ See Display advertisement

A geographical code is followed by three letters reflecting the nursery's name

LLin

LINCLUDEN NURSERY ✉ ✈ 🏠 € ♿ ◆
Bisley Green, Bisley, Woking, Surrey, GU24 9EN
Ⓣ (01483) 797005
Ⓕ (01483) 474015
Ⓔ sales@lincludennursery.co.uk
Ⓦ www.lincludennursery.co.uk
Also supplies wholesale: Yes
Contact: Mr & Mrs J A Tilbury
Opening Times: 0930-1630 Tue-Sat all year excl. B/hols. Closed Chelsea week & Xmas.
Min Mail Order UK: Nmc
Min Mail Order EU: Nmc
Cat. Cost: 3 x 1st class
Credit Cards: Visa MasterCard Solo Switch
Specialities: Dwarf, slow-growing & unusual conifers.
Map Ref: L, C3
OS Grid Ref: SU947596

Refer to the box at the base of each right-hand page for a key to the symbols

A brief summary of the plants available plus any other special characteristics of the nursery

The map letter is followed by the map square in which the nursery is located

The Ordnance Survey national grid reference for use with OS maps

2 NURSERY INDEX BY NAME

If you seek a particular nursery, look it up in this alphabetical index. Note its code and turn to the Nursery Details by Code list for full information.

3 SPECIALIST NURSERIES

A list of 31 categories under which nurseries have classified themselves if they exclusively, or predominantly, supply this range of plants.

CONIFERS

How to Use the Nursery Listings

The details given for each nursery have been compiled from information supplied to us in answer to a questionnaire. In some cases, because of constraints of space, the entries have been slightly abbreviated.

Nurseries are not charged for their entries, and inclusion in no way implies a value judgement.

Nursery Details by Code (*page 782*)

Each nursery is allocated a code, for example SLan. The first letter of each code indicates the main area of the country in which the nursery is situated. In this example, S=Southern England. The remaining three letters reflect the nursery's name, in this case Langley Boxwood Nursery in Hampshire.

In this main listing the nurseries are given in alphabetical order of codes for quick reference from the Plant Directory. All of the nurseries' details, such as address, opening times, mail order service etc., will be found here.

Opening Times

Although opening times have been published as submitted and where applicable, it is always advisable, especially if travelling a long distance, to check with the nursery first. The initials NGS indicate that the nursery is open under the National Gardens Scheme.

Mail Order - ⊠ UK or EU

Many nurseries provide a mail order service which, in many cases, now extends to all members of the European Union. Where '**No minimum charge**' (**Nmc**) is shown please note that to send even one plant may involve the nursery in substantial postage and packing costs. Even so, some nurseries may not be prepared to send tender or bulky plants.

Export ⊠

Export refers to mail order beyond the European Union. Nurseries that are prepared to consider exporting are indicated. However, there is usually a substantial minimum charge and, in addition, all the costs of Phytosanitary Certificates and Customs have to be met by the purchaser.

Catalogue Cost

Some nurseries offer their catalogue free, or for a few stamps (the odd value quoted can usually be made up from a combination of first or second class stamps), but a large (at least A5) stamped addressed envelope is always appreciated as well. Overseas customers should use an equivalent number of International Reply Coupons (IRCs) in place of stamps.

Wheelchair Access ♿

Following readers' suggestions, this year we have asked nurseries to indicate if their premises are suitable for wheelchair users. The assessment of ease-of-access is entirely the responsibility of the individual nursery.

Specialities

Nurseries list here the plants or genera that they supply, together with other features about their service. Some hold National Collections of plants to which they may or may not charge an entry fee. Please enquire before visiting a Collection.

Delivery to Shows ♠

Many nurseries will deliver pre-ordered plants to flower shows for collection by customers. These are indicated by a marquee symbol. Contact the nursery for details of shows they attend.

Payment in Euros €

All Republic of Ireland nurseries will, of course, accept Euro payments.

A number of UK nurseries have indicated that they will accept payment in Euros. You should, however, check with the nursery concerned before making such a payment, as some will only accept cash and some only cheques, whilst others will expect the purchaser to pay bank charges.

Maps

If you wish to visit any of the nurseries you can find its approximate location on the relevant map (following p.917), unless the nursery has requested this is not shown (this usually applies to mail order only nurseries). Nurseries are also encouraged to provide their Ordnance Survey national grid reference for use with OS publications such as the Land Ranger series.

Nursery Index by Name (*page 907*)

For convenience, an alphabetical index of nurseries is included on p.907. This gives the names of all nurseries listed in the book in alphabetical order of nursery name together with their code.

Specialist Nurseries (*page 915*)

This list of nurseries has been introduced to help those with an interest in finding specialist categories of plant. Nurseries have been asked to classify themselves under one or more headings where this represents the type of plant they *predominantly* or *exclusively* have in stock. For example, if you wish to find a nursery specialising in ornamental grasses, look up 'Grasses' in the listing where you will find a list of nursery codes. Then turn to the Nursery Details by Code, for details of the nurseries.

Please note that not all nurseries shown here will have plants listed in the Plant Directory. This may be their choice or because the *RHS Plant Finder* does not list seeds or annuals and only terrestrial orchids and hardy cacti. For space

reasons, it is rare to find a nursery's full catalogue listed in the Plant Directory.

In all cases, please ensure you ring to confirm the range available before embarking on a journey to the nursery.

The specialist plant groups listed in this edition are:

Acid-loving	Grasses
Alpines/rock	Hedging
Aquatics/marginals	Herbs
Bamboos	Marginal/bog plants
British wild flowers	Orchids
Bulbous plants	Organic
Cacti & succulents	Ornamental trees
Carnivorous	Peat-free
Chalk-loving	Period plants
Climbers	Propagate to order
Coastal	Roses
Conifers	Seeds
Conservatory	Specimen-sized plants
Drought-tolerant	Topiary
Ferns	Tropical plants
Fruit	

Perennials and shrubs have been omitted as these are considered to be too general and serviced by a great proportion of the nurseries.

Deleted Nurseries

Every year a few nurseries ask to be deleted. This may be because they are about to move or close, or they are changing the way in which they trade. A small number do not reply and, as we have no current information concerning them, they are deleted.

Please, never use an old edition

Nursery Details
by Code

Please note that all these nurseries are listed in alphabetical order by their code. All nurseries are listed in alphabetical order by their name in the **Nursery Index by Name** on page xxx.

South West

CAbb   **Abbotsbury Sub-Tropical Gardens** ⊠ 🅐
Abbotsbury, Nr Weymouth, Dorset, DT3 4LA
Ⓣ (01305) 871344
Ⓕ (01305) 871344
Ⓔ info@abbotsburygardens.co.uk
Ⓦ www.abbotsburyplantsales.co.uk
Contact: David Sutton
Opening Times: 1000-1800 daily mid Mar-1st Nov. 1000-1500 Nov-mid Mar.
Min Mail Order UK: £10.00 + p&p
Cat. Cost: £2.00 + A4 Sae + 42p stamp
Credit Cards: Access Visa MasterCard Switch
Specialities: Less common & tender shrubs incl. palms, tree ferns, bamboos & plants from Australia, New Zealand & S. Africa.
Map Ref: C, C5

CAbP   **Abbey Plants** ⊠ 🅐
Chaffeymoor, Bourton, Gillingham, Dorset, SP8 5BY
Ⓣ (01747) 840841
Contact: K Potts
Opening Times: 1000-1300 & 1400-1700 Tue-Sat Mar-Nov. Dec-Feb by appt.
Cat. Cost: 2 x 2nd class
Credit Cards: None
Specialities: Flowering trees & shrubs. Shrub roses incl. many unusual varieties. Limited stock.
Map Ref: C, B5
OS Grid Ref: ST762304

CAbx   **Abraxas Gardens** ⊠ 🅐
7 Little Keyford Lane, Frome, Somerset, BA11 5BB
Ⓣ (01373) 472879
Ⓦ www.abraxasgardens.co.uk

Contact: Duncan Skene
Opening Times: Not open, mail order only.
Min Mail Order UK: £10.00
Cat. Cost: Free
Credit Cards: None
Specialities: *Crocosmia, Iris sibirica, Hemerocallis* (spiders, spider variants & unusual forms). Many recent introductions available only in small numbers.
Map Ref: C, B5
OS Grid Ref: ST775465

CAgr   **Agroforestry Research Trust** ⊠
46 Hunters Moon, Dartington, Totnes, Devon, TQ9 6JT
Ⓣ (01803) 840776
Ⓕ (01803) 840776
Ⓔ mail@agroforestry.co.uk
Ⓦ www.agroforestry.co.uk
Contact: Martin Crawford
Opening Times: Not open, mail order only.
Min Mail Order UK: No minimum charge
Min Mail Order EU: Nmc
Cat. Cost: 4 x 1st class
Credit Cards: MasterCard Visa
Specialities: Top & soft fruit. Mostly trees, shrubs & perennials. *Alnus, Berberis, Amelanchier, Carya, Elaeagnus, Juglans, Pinus, Quercus* & *Salix.* Also seeds. Some plants in small quantities only.

CArn   **Arne Herbs** ⊠ 🅜 € 🅐
Limeburn Nurseries, Limeburn Hill, Chew Magna, Bristol, BS40 8QW
Ⓣ (01275) 333399
Ⓕ (01275) 333399
Ⓔ lyman@lyman-dixon.freeserve.co.uk
Ⓦ www.arneherbs.co.uk
Also supplies wholesale: Yes
Contact: A Lyman-Dixon & Jenny Thomas
Opening Times: Most times, please check first.
Min Mail Order UK: Nmc
Min Mail Order EU: Nmc
Cat. Cost: £3.75 UK, 10 x IRC refundable on first order. Or Online.
Credit Cards: None

Specialities: Herbs, wild flowers & cottage flowers. A few plants ltd., please see catalogue for details. Will deliver to Farmers' Markets.
Map Ref: C, A5
OS Grid Ref: ST563638

CAvo   AVON BULBS ⊠
Burnt House Farm, Mid-Lambrook, South Petherton, Somerset, TA13 5HE
ⓣ (01460) 242177
ⓕ (01460) 242177
ⓔ info@avonbulbs.co.uk
ⓦ www.avonbulbs.co.uk
Contact: C Ireland-Jones
Opening Times: Thu, Fri, Sat mid Sep-end Oct & mid Feb-end Mar for collection of pre-booked orders.
Min Mail Order UK: £10.00 + p&p
Min Mail Order EU: £20.00 + p&p
Cat. Cost: 4 x 2nd class
Credit Cards: Visa Access Switch
Specialities: Mail order supply of a very wide range of smaller, often unusual bulbs.
Map Ref: C, B5

CBAn   BARBARA AUSTIN PERENNIALS LTD ⊠ ⋔ ⓖ
West Kington Nurseries, Pound Hill, West Kington, Nr Chippenham, Wiltshire, SN14 7JG
ⓣ (01249) 782822
ⓕ (01249) 782953
ⓔ sales@westkingtonnurseries.co.uk
Also supplies wholesale: Yes
Opening Times: 1000-1700 7 days, incl. B/hols Feb-Dec.
Cat. Cost: Free
Credit Cards: MasterCard Visa
Specialities: Herbaceous, alpines, *Buxus* & topiary. Herbaceous liners.
Map Ref: C, A5

CBcs   BURNCOOSE NURSERIES ⊠ ⊠ ⋔ ⓖ
Gwennap, Redruth, Cornwall, TR16 6BJ
ⓣ (01209) 860316
ⓕ (01209) 860011
ⓔ burncoose@eclipse.co.uk
ⓦ www.burncoose.co.uk
Also supplies wholesale: Yes
Contact: C H Williams
Opening Times: 0830-1700 Mon-Sat & 1100-1700 Sun.
Min Mail Order UK: Nmc
Min Mail Order EU: Nmc*
Cat. Cost: £1.50 incl. p&p
Credit Cards: Visa Access Switch
Specialities: Extensive range of over 3000 ornamental trees & shrubs and herbaceous. Rare & unusual *Magnolia, Rhododendron.*

Conservatory plants. 30 acre garden. *Note: individual quotations for EU sales.
Map Ref: C, D1
OS Grid Ref: SW742395

CBct   BARRACOTT PLANTS ⊠ ⋔ € ◆
Old Orchard, Calstock Road, Gunnislake, Cornwall, PL18 9AA
ⓣ (01822) 832234
ⓔ GEOFF@geoff63.freeserve.co.uk
Also supplies wholesale: Yes
Contact: Geoff Turner, Thelma Watson
Opening Times: 0900-1700 Thu-Sat, Mar-end Sep. Other times by appt.
Min Mail Order UK: £10.00
Cat. Cost: 2 x 1st class
Credit Cards: None
Specialities: Herbaceous plants: shade-loving, foliage & form. *Acanthus, Astrantia, Bergenia, Convallaria, Ligularia, Liriope, Roscoea, Smilacina, Symphytum* & *Tricyrtis.*
Map Ref: C, C3
OS Grid Ref: SX436702

CBdn   ANN & ROGER BOWDEN ⊠ ⊠ € ⓖ ◆
Cleave House, Sticklepath, Okehampton, Devon, EX20 2NL
ⓣ (01837) 840481
ⓕ (01837) 840482
ⓔ bowdenshosta@eclipse.co.uk
ⓦ www.hostas-uk.com
Contact: Ann & Roger Bowden
Opening Times: By appt. only.
Min Mail Order UK: Nmc
Min Mail Order EU: Nmc
Cat. Cost: 3 x 1st class
Credit Cards: Visa Access EuroCard Switch
Specialities: *Hosta* only. Nat. Coll. of modern hybrid *Hosta.*
Map Ref: C, C3
OS Grid Ref:

CBdw   BODWEN NURSERY ⊠
Pothole, St Austell, Cornwall, PL26 7DW
ⓣ No phone
Also supplies wholesale: Yes
Contact: John Geraghty
Opening Times: Not open.
Min Mail Order UK: Nmc
Cat. Cost: 2 x 2nd class
Credit Cards: None
Specialities: Japanese maples. Some rarer cultivars available in limited quantities only.

KEY			
⊠ Mail order to UK or EU	⋔ Delivers to shows		
⊠ Exports beyond EU	€ Euro accepted		
ⓖ Accessible by wheelchair	◆ See Display advertisement		

C

CBel BELMONT HOUSE NURSERY ✉ €
Little Horton, Devizes,
Wiltshire, SN10 3LJ
Ⓣ (01380) 860510
Ⓔ rcottis@supanet.com
Contact: Gordon Cottis
Opening Times: By appt. Please phone.
Min Mail Order UK: Nmc*
Min Mail Order EU: £2.50
Cat. Cost: 2 x 2nd class
Credit Cards: None
Specialities: *Helleborus* hybrids & true species,
Galanthus, Digitalis, Geranium, Pulmonaria.
*Note: mail order *Cyclamen* & *Galanthus* only,
Nov-Feb. *Galanthus* stock ltd & variable.
Other plants may be available in small
quantities.
Map Ref: C, A6
OS Grid Ref: SU042623

CBen BENNETT'S WATER LILY FARM ✉ ♿
Putton Lane, Chickerell, Weymouth,
Dorset, DT3 4AF
Ⓣ (01305) 785150
Ⓕ (01305) 781619
Ⓔ JB@waterlily.co.uk
Ⓦ www.waterlily.co.uk
Contact: J Bennett
Opening Times: Tue-Sun Apr-Aug, Tue-Sat
Sept & Mar.
Min Mail Order UK: £25.00 + p&p*
Min Mail Order EU: £25.00 + p&p
Cat. Cost: Sae for price list
Credit Cards: Visa Access MasterCard
Switch
Specialities: Aquatic plants. Nat. Coll. of
Water Lilies. *Note: mail order Apr-Sep only.
Map Ref: C, C5
OS Grid Ref: SY651797

CBgR BEGGAR'S ROOST PLANTS ♠ ♿
Lilstock, Bridgwater, Somerset, TA5 1SU
Ⓣ (01278) 741519
Ⓕ (01278) 741519
Contact: Rosemary FitzGerald, Kate Harris
Opening Times: By appt. only.
Credit Cards: None
Specialities: British native plants & their
garden-worthy varieties. Hardy ferns. Classic
perennials, incl. *Salvia* & winter interest
plants. Available in small quantities only.
Map Ref: C, B4
OS Grid Ref: ST168450

CBig THE BIG GRASS CO. ✉ ✉ ♠ €
Hookhill Plantation, Woolfardisworthy, East
Black Dog, Nr Crediton, Devon, EX17 4RX
Ⓣ (01363) 866146

Ⓕ (01363) 866146
Ⓔ alison@big-grass-co.co.uk
Ⓦ www.big-grass.com
Also supplies wholesale: Yes
Contact: Alison & Scott Evans
Opening Times: By appt. only.
Min Mail Order UK: Nmc
Min Mail Order EU: Nmc
Cat. Cost: 2 x 1st class
Credit Cards: None
Specialities: Grasses.
Map Ref: C, B3

CBla BLACKMORE & LANGDON LTD ✉ ✉
Pensford, Bristol, BS39 4JL
Ⓣ (01275) 332300
Ⓕ (01275) 332300/(01275) 331207
Ⓔ plants@blackmore-langdon.com
Ⓦ www.blackmore-langdon.com
Contact: J S Langdon
Opening Times: 0900-1700 Mon-Fri, 1000-
1600 Sat & Sun.
Min Mail Order UK: Nmc
Min Mail Order EU: Nmc
Cat. Cost: Sae 2 x 2nd class
Credit Cards: MasterCard Visa Switch
Specialities: *Phlox, Delphinium* & *Begonia.*
Also seeds.
Map Ref: C, A5

CBod BODMIN PLANT AND HERB
NURSERY ✉ ♿
Laveddon Mill, Laninval Hill, Bodmin,
Cornwall, PL30 5JU
Ⓣ (01208) 72837
Ⓕ (01208) 76491
Ⓔ bodminnursery@aol.com
Contact: Mark Lawlor
Opening Times: 0900-1800 (or dusk) 7 days.
Min Mail Order UK: Nmc
Cat. Cost: 2 x 1st class
Credit Cards: all major credit/debit cards
Specialities: Herbs, herbaceous & grasses,
aquatic, marginal & bog plants, plus interesting
range of shrubs. Wide range of fruit &
ornamental trees. New range of coastal, patio &
conservatory plants. Note: mail order herbs only.
Map Ref: C, C2
OS Grid Ref: SX053659

CBos BOSVIGO PLANTS
Bosvigo House, Bosvigo Lane, Truro,
Cornwall, TR1 3NH
Ⓣ (01872) 275774
Ⓕ (01872) 275774
Ⓔ bosvigo.plants@virgin.net
Ⓦ www.bosvigo.com
Contact: Wendy Perry

C

Opening Times: 1100-1800 Thu & Fri
Mar-end Sep.
Cat. Cost: 4 x 1st class
Credit Cards: None
Specialities: Rare & unusual herbaceous.
Map Ref: C, D2
OS Grid Ref: SW815452

CBot THE BOTANIC NURSERY ⊠ ♠ €
(Office) Bath Road, Atworth, Nr Melksham,
Wiltshire, SN12 8NU
Ⓜ 07850 328756
Ⓕ (01225) 700953
Ⓔ enquiries@thebotanicnursery.com
Ⓦ www.TheBotanicNursery.com
Contact: T & M Baker
Opening Times: 1000-1700 Fri & Sat +
themed openings - send for details. Closed
Nov-Feb.
Min Mail Order UK: 30p Sae for mail order
lists.
Cat. Cost: £1.00 coin
Credit Cards: Visa Access
Specialities: Rare hardy shrubs & perennials
for lime soils. *Eryngium, Papaver orientale*
cultivars, *Delphinium*. National Collection of
Digitalis. Note: nursery & plant sales at
Cottles Lane, nr Stonar School, Atworth, nr
Melksham.
Map Ref: C, A5

CBow BOWLEY PLANTS ◆
Church Farm, North End, Ashton Keynes,
Nr Swindon, Wiltshire,
SN6 6QR
Ⓣ (01285) 640352
Ⓜ 07855 524929
Contact: G P Bowley
Opening Times: 0900-1700 Tue, 1000-1600
Sat, 1300-1600 Sun, Mar-Oct incl.
Cat. Cost: 2 x 1st class
Credit Cards: None
Specialities: Variegated plants & coloured
foliage. Alpines, perennials. shrubs, ferns,
grasses, conifers & herbs.
Map Ref: C, A6
OS Grid Ref: SU043945

CBrd BROADLEAS GARDENS LTD
Broadleas, Devizes, Wiltshire, SN10 5JQ
Ⓣ (01380) 722035
Ⓕ (01380) 722035
Ⓔ carl.j.bishop@btinternet.com
Contact: Lady Anne Cowdray
Opening Times: 1400-1800 Wed, Thu & Sun
Apr-Oct.
Cat. Cost: 1 x 1st class
Credit Cards: None

Specialities: General range.
Map Ref: C, A6

CBre BREGOVER PLANTS ⊠ ♠
Hillbrooke, Middlewood, North Hill,
Nr Launceston, Cornwall, PL15 7NN
Ⓣ (01566) 782661
Contact: Jennifer Bousfield
Opening Times: 1100-1700 Wed-Fri Mar-
mid Oct and by appt.
Min Mail Order UK: Nmc*
Min Mail Order EU: Nmc
Cat. Cost: 2 x 1st class
Credit Cards: None
Specialities: Unusual hardy perennials grown
in small garden nursery. *Note: ltd. stocks,
mail order Oct-Mar only.
Map Ref: C, C2
OS Grid Ref: SX273752

CBri BRIDGEMAN & KENT
Plumtree Cottage, Bottlesford, Pewsey,
Wiltshire, SN9 6LW
Ⓣ (01672) 851845
Ⓕ (01672) 851845
Ⓔ anduff@bridgeman-kent.co.uk
Ⓦ www.nepeta.co.uk
Contact: Andrew Duff
Opening Times: By appt. only Mar-late Oct.
Cat. Cost: None issued
Credit Cards: None
Specialities: Herbaceous & bulbous perennials,
Nepeta. Limited numbers as wide range.
Map Ref: C, B6
OS Grid Ref: SU110590

CBrm BRAMLEY LODGE GARDEN
NURSERY € ⬓
Beech Tree Lane, Ipplepen, Newton Abbot,
Devon, TQ12 5TW
Ⓣ (01803) 813265
Ⓔ blnursery@btopenworld.com
Ⓦ www.bramleylodge-nursery.co.uk
Contact: Susan Young
Opening Times: 1000-1600 Thu-Sun Mar-
Oct, 1000-1600 Sun Nov-Feb.
Cat. Cost: 3 x 1st class
Credit Cards: None
Specialities: Grasses. Also trees, shrubs,
perennials & rock plants. Several small model
themed gardens.
Map Ref: C, C3
OS Grid Ref: SX828673

C

CBro BROADLEIGH GARDENS ✉ ♠ ♿
Bishops Hull, Taunton, Somerset, TA4 1AE
Ⓣ (01823) 286231
Ⓕ (01823) 323646
Ⓔ info@broadleighbulbs.co.uk
Ⓦ www.broadleighbulbs.co.uk
Contact: Lady Skelmersdale
Opening Times: 0900-1600 Mon-Fri for
viewing only. Orders collected if notice given.
Min Mail Order UK: Nmc
Min Mail Order EU: Nmc
Cat. Cost: 2 x 1st class
Credit Cards: Visa MasterCard
Specialities: Jan catalogue: bulbs in growth
(*Galanthus, Cyclamen* etc.) & herbaceous
woodland plants (trilliums, hellebores etc).
Extensive list of *Agapanthus*. June catalogue:
dwarf & unusual bulbs, *Iris* (DB & PC).
Nat. Coll. of Alec Grey hybrid daffodils.
Map Ref: C, B4

CBrP BROOKLANDS PLANTS ✉
25 Treves Road, Dorchester, Dorset, DT1 2HE
Ⓣ (01305) 265846
Ⓔ IanWatt@quicklink.freeserve.co.uk
Also supplies wholesale: Yes
Contact: Ian Watt
Opening Times: By appt. for collection only.
Min Mail Order UK: £25.00 + p&p
Min Mail Order EU: £25.00 + p&p
Cat. Cost: 2 x 2nd class
Credit Cards: None
Specialities: Palms & cycads. Over 100 species
from seedling to specimen size. *Agave, Yucca,
Dasylirion, Cordyline, Puya, Restio* & bamboo.
Note: some species available in small
quantities only.
Map Ref: C, C5

CBur BURNHAM NURSERIES ✉ ✉ ♠ ♿
Forches Cross, Newton Abbot,
Devon, TQ12 6PZ
Ⓣ (01626) 352233
Ⓕ (01626) 362167
Ⓔ mail@burnhamnurseries.co.uk
Ⓦ www.orchids.uk.com
Also supplies wholesale: Yes
Contact: Any member of staff
Opening Times: 1000-1600 Mon-Sun.
Min Mail Order UK: Nmc
Min Mail Order EU: £100.00 + p&p
Cat. Cost: A4 Sae + 44p stamp
Credit Cards: Visa Switch American Express
MasterCard
Specialities: All types of orchid except British
native types. Note: please ask for details on
export beyond EU.
Map Ref: C, C4

CCAT CIDER APPLE TREES ✉ €
Kerian, Corkscrew Lane, Woolston,
Nr North Cadbury,
Somerset, BA22 7BP
Ⓣ (01963) 441101
Also supplies wholesale: Yes
Contact: Mr J Dennis
Opening Times: By appt. only.
Min Mail Order UK: £7.20
Min Mail Order EU: £7.20
Cat. Cost: Free
Credit Cards: None
Specialities: *Malus* (speciality standard trees).
Map Ref: C, B5

**CCge COTTAGE GARDEN PLANTS AND
HERBS** ♠ ♿
North Lodge, Canonteign, Christow, Exeter,
Devon, EX6 7NS
Ⓣ (01647) 252950
Contact: Shirley Bennett
Opening Times: 1000-1700 w/ends &
B/hols Mar-Sep. Ring for private visit at
other times. Lectures given on 'Hardy
Geraniums' & 'Cottage Garden Plants'.
Credit Cards: None
Specialities: Cottage garden plants, herbs and
esp. hardy geraniums (over 200 kinds
available).
Map Ref: C, C3
OS Grid Ref: SX836829

CCha CHAPEL FARM HOUSE NURSERY € ♿
Halwill Junction, Beaworthy,
Devon, EX21 5UF
Ⓣ (01409) 221594
Ⓕ (01409) 221594
Contact: Robin or Toshie Hull
Opening Times: 0900-1700 Tue-Sat, 1000-
1600 Sun & B/hol Mons.
Cat. Cost: None issued.
Credit Cards: None
Specialities: Plants from Japan. Also
herbaceous. Japanese garden design service
offered.
Map Ref: C, C3

CChe CHERRY TREE NURSERY ♿
(Sheltered Work Opportunities)
off New Road Roundabout, Northbourne,
Bournemouth, Dorset, BH10 7DA
Ⓣ (01202) 593537 (01202) 590840
Ⓕ (01202) 590626
Also supplies wholesale: Yes
Contact: Stephen Jailler
Opening Times: 0830-1530 Mon-Fri, 0900-
1200 most Sats.
Cat. Cost: A4 Sae + 66p stamps

C

Credit Cards: None
Specialities: Hardy shrubs.
Map Ref: C, C6

CCol   COLD HARBOUR NURSERY ⊠ ♠
(Office) 28 Moor Road, Swanage,
Dorset, BH19 1RG
Ⓣ (01929) 423520 evenings
Ⓔ coldharbournursery@hotmail.com
Ⓦ www.dorset-perennials.co.uk
Contact: Steve Saunders
Opening Times: 1000-1700 Tue-Fri & most
w/ends 1st Mar-end Oct. Other times by appt.
Min Mail Order UK: £6.00 + p&p
Cat. Cost: 3 x 2nd class
Credit Cards: None
Specialities: Unusual herbaceous perennials
incl. hardy *Geranium,* daylilies & grasses.
Note: nursery is at Bere Road (opp. Silent
Woman Inn), Wareham.
Map Ref: C, C5

CCtw   CHURCHTOWN NURSERIES ⊠ ♠
Gulval, Penzance, Cornwall, TR18 3BE
Ⓣ (01736) 362626
Ⓕ (01736) 362626
Contact: C Osborne
Opening Times: 1000-1700 Apr-Sep, 1000-
1600 Oct-Mar or by appt.
Min Mail Order UK: £25.00 + p&p
Cat. Cost: 1 x 1st class Sae for list.
Credit Cards: None
Specialities: Good, ever-increasing, range of
shrubs, herbaceous & tender perennials &
ornamental grasses incl. some more unusual.
Map Ref: C, D1
OS Grid Ref: SW486317

CCVT   CHEW VALLEY TREES ⊠
Winford Road, Chew Magna, Bristol,
BS40 8QE
Ⓣ (01275) 333752
Ⓕ (01275) 333746
Ⓔ enquiries@chewvalleytreesandland
scapes.co.uk
Ⓦ www.chewvalleytreesandlandscapes.co.uk
Also supplies wholesale: Yes
Contact: J Scarth
Opening Times: 0800-1700 Mon-Fri all year.
0900-1600 7th Sep-25th May. Not open
B/hols.
Min Mail Order UK: Nmc*
Cat. Cost: Free
Credit Cards: Visa MasterCard Switch
Specialities: Native British & ornamental
trees, shrubs, apple trees & hedging. Partial
wheelchair access. *Note: max. plant height
for mail order 2.7m.

Map Ref: C, A5
OS Grid Ref: ST558635

CDes   DESIRABLE PLANTS ⊠
Pentamar, Crosspark, Totnes, Devon,
TQ9 5BQ*
Ⓣ (01803) 864489
Ⓔ sutton.totnes@lineone.net
Contact: Dr J J & Mrs S A Sutton
Opening Times: Not open, mail order only.
Min Mail Order UK: £15.00
Cat. Cost: 4 x 1st class
Credit Cards: None
Specialities: Choice & interesting herbaceous
plants by mail order. Cat. available May for
autumn dispatch. *Watsonia* & other S.
hemisphere *Iridaceae, Anemone, Crinum,
Arisaema, Thalictrum* & *Epimedium.* *Note:
nursery not at this address.

CDev   DEVON VIOLET NURSERY ⊠ ☒ € ⓑ
Rattery, South Brent, Devon, TQ10 9LG
Ⓣ (01364) 643033
Ⓕ (01364) 643033
Ⓔ virgin.violets@virgin.net
Ⓦ www.sweetviolets.co.uk
Also supplies wholesale: Yes
Contact: Robert Sidol, Sarah Bunting
Opening Times: All year round. Please ring
first.
Min Mail Order UK: £4.50
Min Mail Order EU: £5.50
Cat. Cost: 1 x 1st class
Credit Cards: None
Specialities: Violets & Parma violets. Nat.
Coll. of *Viola odorata.*
Map Ref: C, C3
OS Grid Ref: SX747620

CDob   SAMUEL DOBIE & SON ⊠
Long Road, Paignton, Devon, TQ4 7SX
Ⓣ (01803) 696411
Ⓕ (01803) 696450
Ⓦ www.dobies.co.uk
Contact: Customer Services
Opening Times: 0830-1700 Mon-Fri
(office). Also answerphone.
Min Mail Order UK: Nmc*
Cat. Cost: Free
Credit Cards: Visa MasterCard Switch
Delta
Specialities: Wide selection of popular flower
& vegetable seeds. Also includes young

KEY		
⊠ Mail order to UK or EU	♠ Delivers to shows	
☒ Exports beyond EU	€ Euro accepted	
ⓑ Accessible by wheelchair	◆ See Display advertisement	

C

plants, summer flowering bulbs & garden sundries. *Note: mail order to UK & Rep. of Ireland only.

CDoC   DUCHY OF CORNWALL ✉ ◆
Cott Road, Lostwithiel, Cornwall, PL22 0HW
Ⓣ (01208) 872668
Ⓕ (01208) 872835
Ⓔ sales@duchynursery.co.uk
Ⓦ www.duchyofcornwallnursery.co.uk
Contact: Tracy Wilson
Opening Times: 0900-1700 Mon-Sat, 1000-1700 Sun & B/hols.
Min Mail Order UK: Nmc
Cat. Cost: Cat £2.00 (stamps or cheque)
Credit Cards: Visa American Express Access Switch Delta
Specialities: Very wide range of garden plants incl. trees, shrubs, conifers, roses, perennials, fruit & half-hardy exotics.
Map Ref: C, C2
OS Grid Ref: SX112614

CDul   DULFORD NURSERIES ✉ ⬧
Cullompton, Devon, EX15 2DG
Ⓣ (01884) 266361
Ⓕ (01884) 266663
Ⓔ dulford.nurseries@virgin.net
Ⓦ www.dulford-nurseries.co.uk
Also supplies wholesale: Yes
Contact: Paul & Mary Ann Rawlings
Opening Times: 0730-1630 Mon-Fri.
Min Mail Order UK: Nmc
Min Mail Order EU: Nmc
Cat. Cost: Free
Credit Cards: None
Specialities: Native, ornamental & unusual trees & shrubs incl. oaks, maples, beech, birch, chestnut, ash, lime, *Sorbus* & pines.
Map Ref: C, C4
OS Grid Ref: SY062062

CDWL   DORSET WATER LILIES ✇ ń ⬧
Egerton Cottage, Corscombe, Dorchester, Dorset, DT2 0NU
Ⓣ (01935) 891668
Ⓕ (01935) 891946
Also supplies wholesale: Yes
Contact: Jane Hackett
Opening Times: 0900-1600 Mon & Fri only.
Cat. Cost: Free
Credit Cards: None
Specialities: Hardy & tropical water lilies, lotus, marginal & bogside plants. Note: nursery at Yeovil Road, Halstock, Nr Yeovil, Somerset BA22 9RR.
Map Ref: C, C5
OS Grid Ref: ST543083

CElw   ELWORTHY COTTAGE PLANTS ń ⬧
Elworthy Cottage, Elworthy, Nr Lydeard St Lawrence, Taunton, Somerset, TA4 3PX
Ⓣ (01984) 656427
Ⓔ mike@elworthy-cottage.co.uk
Ⓦ www.elworthy-cottage.co.uk
Contact: Mrs J M Spiller
Opening Times: 1000-1600 Wed, Thu & Fri mid Mar-end Aug & Thu only during Sep. Also by appt.
Cat. Cost: 3 x 2nd class
Credit Cards: None
Specialities: *Clematis* & unusual herbaceous plants esp. hardy *Geranium, Geum,* grasses, *Campanula, Crocosmia, Pulmonaria, Astrantia* & *Viola.* Note: nursery on B3188, 5 miles north of Wiveliscombe.
Map Ref: C, B4
OS Grid Ref: ST084349

CEnd   ENDSLEIGH GARDENS ✉ ⬧ ◆
Milton Abbot, Tavistock, Devon, PL19 0PG
Ⓣ (01822) 870235
Ⓕ (01822) 870513
Ⓔ Treemail@endsleigh-gardens.com
Ⓦ www.endsleigh-gardens.com
Contact: Michael Taylor
Opening Times: 0800-1700 Mon-Sat. 1000-1700 Sun (closed Sun Dec & Jan).
Min Mail Order UK: £12.00 + p&p
Cat. Cost: 2 x 1st class
Credit Cards: Visa Access Switch MasterCard
Specialities: Choice & unusual trees & shrubs incl. *Acer* & *Cornus* cvs. Old apples & cherries. Wisteria. Grafting service.
Map Ref: C, C3

CFai   FAIRHAVEN NURSERY ✉ ń
Clapworthy Cross, Chittlehampton, Umberleigh, Devon, EX37 9QT
Ⓣ (01769) 540528
Ⓔ fairhavennursery@hotmail.com
Contact: Derek & Pauline Burdett
Opening Times: 1000-1600 all year, but please check first.
Min Mail Order UK: £10.00 + p&p
Cat. Cost: 2 x 1st class
Credit Cards: None
Specialities: Propagate & grow wide selection of more unusual varieties of hardy trees, shrubs & perennials. Many grown in small batches that may not be ready for despatch on request. Orders taken for delivery when available.
Map Ref: C, B3

CFee   FEEBERS HARDY PLANTS ✉ ⬧ ◆
1 Feeber Cottage, Westwood, Broadclyst, Nr Exeter, Devon, EX5 3DQ

C

ⓣ (01404) 822118
Contact: Mrs E Squires
Opening Times: 1000-1700 Wed Mar-Jul &
Sep-Oct. Sat & Sun by prior appt.
Min Mail Order UK: Nmc*
Min Mail Order EU: Nmc
Cat. Cost: Sae + 36p stamp
Credit Cards: None
Specialities: Plants for wet clay soils, alpines
& hardy perennials incl. those raised by Amos
Perry. *Note: mail order ltd. Plants held in
small quantities unless grown from seed.
Accessible for wheelchairs in dry weather only.
Map Ref: C, C4

CFil FILLAN'S PLANTS ⊠
Tuckermarsh Gardens, Tamar Lane, Bere
Alston, Devon, PL20 7HN
ⓣ (01822) 840721
ⓕ (01822) 841551
ⓔ fillansplants@yahoo.co.uk
Also supplies wholesale: Yes
Contact: Mark Fillan
Opening Times: 1000-1700 Sat Mar-Sep &
by appt. any other time.
Min Mail Order UK: £20.00 + p&p
Cat. Cost: 3 x 1st class
Credit Cards: all major credit/debit cards
Specialities: Bamboos, *Hydrangea* & unusual
woody plants. Many plants available in small
quantities only.
Map Ref: C, C3
OS Grid Ref: SX444678

CFir FIR TREE FARM NURSERY ⊠ €
Tresahor, Constantine, Falmouth,
Cornwall, TR11 5PL
ⓣ (01326) 340593
ⓔ ftfnur@aol.com
ⓦ www.cornwallgardens.com
Contact: Jim Cave
Opening Times: 1000-1700 Thu-Sun 1st
Mar-30th Sep.
Min Mail Order UK: £25.00 + p&p
Min Mail Order EU: £40.00 + p&p
Cat. Cost: 6 x 1st class or cheque for £1.60
Credit Cards: Visa Access Delta Switch
Specialities: Over 4000 varieties of cottage
garden & rare perennials & 100 types of
Clematis.
Map Ref: C, D1

CFis MARGERY FISH GARDENS €
East Lambrook Manor, East Lambrook,
South Petherton, Somerset, TA13 5HL
ⓣ (01460) 240328
ⓕ (01460) 242344
ⓔ enquiries@eastlambrook.com

ⓦ www.eastlambrook.com
Contact: Mark Stainer
Opening Times: 1000-1700 1st Feb-31st Oct
7 days.
Credit Cards: Visa Switch MasterCard
Specialities: Hardy *Geranium, Euphorbia,
Helleborus* & herbaceous. National Collection
of hardy *Geranium* on site. All stock in small
quantities.
Map Ref: C, B5

CFRD FORD NURSERY ⋔
The Willows, Broom Lane, Oake, Taunton,
Somerset, TA4 1BE
ⓣ (01823) 461961
ⓕ (01823) 461961
Contact: Mr P F Dunn
Opening Times: 0900-1300 & 1400-1700
Mon-Fri. Sat & Sun by appt. only.
Cat. Cost: 3 x 2nd class
Specialities: Approx. 200 varieties of *Clematis*
and other climbers. Some available in small
quantities only.
Map Ref: C, B4
OS Grid Ref: ST160244

CFul RODNEY FULLER ⊠
Coachman's Cottage, Higher Bratton
Seymour, Wincanton, Somerset, BA9 8DA
ⓣ (01963) 34480
ⓔ coachmans@tinyworld.co.uk
Contact: Rodney Fuller
Opening Times: By appt. only.
Min Mail Order UK: £18.00 incl.
Cat. Cost: 2 x 1st class
Credit Cards: None
Specialities: *Helianthemum.*
Map Ref: C, B5

CFwr THE FLOWER BOWER ⊠
Woodlands, Shurton,
Stogursey, Nr Bridgwater,
Somerset, TA5 1QE
ⓣ (01278) 732134
ⓕ (01278) 732134
ⓔ flower.bower@virgin.net
Contact: Sheila Tucker
Opening Times: 1000-1700, open most days
mid-Mar-31st Oct, please phone first.
Min Mail Order UK: £10.00 + p&p*
Min Mail Order EU: £20.00 + p&p
Cat. Cost: 4 x 1st class
Credit Cards: None

KEY			
	⊠ Mail order to UK or EU	⋔ Delivers to shows	
	⊠ Exports beyond EU	€ Euro accepted	
	ⓑ Accessible by wheelchair	◆ See Display advertisement	

C

Specialities: Unusual perennials. Crocosmias, *Euphorbia*, hardy geraniums, *Phlox*, grasses, bamboos, ferns & bulbs*. Note: mail order Oct-end Apr only.
Map Ref: C, B4
OS Grid Ref: ST203442

CGra GRAHAM'S HARDY PLANTS ✉ ♘
Southcroft, North Road,
Timsbury, Bath, BA2 0JN
Ⓣ (01761) 472187
Ⓔ graplant@aol.com
Ⓦ www.members.aol.com/graplant
Contact: Graham Nicholls
Opening Times: Not open to the public. Mail order and show sales only.
Min Mail Order UK: £2.00 + p&p
Min Mail Order EU: £2.00 + p&p
Cat. Cost: 2 x 1st class or 2 x IRC
Credit Cards: None
Specialities: North American alpines esp. *Lewisia, Eriogonum, Penstemon, Campanula, Kelseya, Phlox.*
Map Ref: C, B5

CGro C W GROVES & SON ✉ ♿
West Bay Road, Bridport, Dorset, DT6 4BA
Ⓣ (01308) 422654
Ⓕ (01308) 420888
Ⓔ c.w.grovesandson@zetnet.co.uk
Ⓦ www.users.zetnet.co.uk/c.w.grovesandson/
Contact: C W Groves
Opening Times: 0830-1700 Mon-Sat, 1030-1630 Sun.
Min Mail Order UK: Nmc*
Min Mail Order EU: £15.00 + p&p
Cat. Cost: 1 x 1st class
Credit Cards: all major credit/debit cards
Specialities: Nursery & garden centre specialising in Parma & hardy *Viola*. *Note: mainly violets by mail order.
Map Ref: C, C5

CHad HADSPEN GARDEN & NURSERY € ♿
Hadspen House, Castle Cary,
Somerset, BA7 7NG
Ⓣ (01749) 813707
Ⓕ (01749) 813707
Ⓔ pope@hadspengarden.co.uk
Ⓦ www.hadspengarden.co.uk
Contact: N & S Pope
Opening Times: 1000-1700 Thu-Sun & B/hols. 1st Mar-1st Oct. Garden open at the same time.
Cat. Cost: 4 x 1st class
Credit Cards: all major credit/debit cards
Specialities: Large-leaved herbaceous. Old fashioned and shrub roses.
Map Ref: C, B5

CHal HALSWAY NURSERY ✉
Halsway, Nr Crowcombe, Taunton,
Somerset, TA4 4BB
Ⓣ (01984) 618243
Contact: T A & D J Bushen
Opening Times: Most days, please phone first.
Min Mail Order UK: £2.00 + p&p
Cat. Cost: 2 x 1st class*
Credit Cards: None
Specialities: *Coleus* & *Begonia* (excl. tuberous & winter flowering). Good range of greenhouse & garden plants. *Note: list for *Coleus* & *Begonia* only, no nursery list.
Map Ref: C, B4

CHar WEST HARPTREE NURSERY ♘ €
Bristol Road, West Harptree, Bath,
Somerset, BS40 6HG
Ⓣ (01761) 221370
Ⓕ (01761) 221989
Ⓔ bryn@herbaceousperennials.co.uk
Ⓦ www.herbaceousperennials.co.uk
Also supplies wholesale: Yes
Contact: Bryn & Helene Bowles
Opening Times: From 1000 Tue-Sun 1st Mar-30th Nov.
Cat. Cost: Large SAE for free names list.
Credit Cards: MasterCard Switch Visa
Specialities: Unusual herbaceous perennials & shrubs. Lilies, bulbs & grasses.
Map Ref: C, B5

CHby THE HERBARY ✉ ▥
161 Chapel Street, Horningsham, Warminster,
Wiltshire, BA12 7LU
Ⓣ (01985) 844442
Ⓜ 07773 661547
Ⓔ rosen@horningsham.fsnet.co.uk
Contact: Pippa Rosen
Opening Times: Apr-Oct by appt. only.
Min Mail Order UK: Nmc
Min Mail Order EU: Nmc
Cat. Cost: 2 x 1st class
Credit Cards: None
Specialities: Culinary, medicinal & aromatic herbs organically grown. Note: mail order all year for organic herb seed & large variety of organic bean seed.
Map Ref: C, B5
OS Grid Ref: ST812414

CHdy HARDY ORCHIDS ✉ ▥
New Gate Farm, Scotchey Lane, Stour
Provost, Gillingham, Dorset, SP8 5LT
Ⓣ (01747) 838368
Ⓕ (01747) 838308
Ⓔ hardyorchids@supanet.com

C

W www.hardyorchids.supanet.com
Contact: N J Heywood
Opening Times: By appt. only.
Min Mail Order UK: £10.00 + p&p
Min Mail Order EU: £10.00 + p&p
Cat. Cost: 2 x 1st class
Credit Cards: None
Specialities: Hardy orchids. *Cypripedium,
Dactylorhiza, Pleione, Anacamptis, Orchis,
Ophrys* & *Epipactis.*
Map Ref: C, B5
OS Grid Ref: ST778217

CHea   HEATHER BANK NURSERY ✉ ♠
Woodlands, 1 High Street, Littleton Panell,
Devizes, Wiltshire, SN10 4EL
T (01380) 812739
E mullanhbn.fsnet.co.uk
Contact: Mrs B Mullan
Opening Times: 0900-1800 Mon, Tue, Thu
& Fri & w/ends. Please check by phone first if
coming a long distance.
Min Mail Order UK: £10.00 + p&p
Cat. Cost: 3 x 1st class
Credit Cards: None
Specialities: *Campanula* & cottage garden
plants.
Map Ref: C, B6

CHEx   HARDY EXOTICS ✉ ♿
Gilly Lane, Whitecross, Penzance,
Cornwall, TR20 8BZ
T (01736) 740660
F (01736) 741101
W www.hardyexotics.co.uk
Contact: C Shilton/J Smith
Opening Times: 1000-1700 7 days Mar-
Oct, 1000-1700 Mon-Sat Nov-Feb. Please
phone first in winter months if travelling a
long way.
Min Mail Order UK: £50.00 + carriage
Min Mail Order EU: £100.00
Cat. Cost: £1.00 postal order or 4 x 1st class
(no cheques)
Credit Cards: Visa Access MasterCard
Connect Delta
Specialities: Largest collection in the UK
of trees, shrubs & herbaceous plants for
tropical & desert effects. Hardy & half-
hardy plants for gardens, patios &
conservatories.
Map Ref: C, D1
OS Grid Ref: SW524345

CHid   HIDDEN VALLEY NURSERY ✉ €
Umberleigh, Devon, EX37 9BU
T (01769) 560567
E lindleypla@tiscali.co.uk

W www.hiddenvalleynursery.co.uk
Contact: Linda & Peter Lindley
Opening Times: Daylight hours, but please
phone first.
Min Mail Order UK: Nmc*
Cat. Cost: 2 x 1st class
Credit Cards: None
Specialities: Hardy perennials esp. shade
lovers. *Note: mail order during Mar only.
Map Ref: C B3
OS Grid Ref: SS567205

CHll   HILL HOUSE NURSERY & GARDENS €
Landscove, Nr Ashburton, Devon, TQ13 7LY
T (01803) 762273
F (01803) 762273
E sacha@garden.demon.co.uk
W www.garden.demon.co.uk
Contact: Raymond, Sacha & Matthew
Hubbard
Opening Times: 1100-1700 7 days, all year.
Open all B/hols incl. Easter Sun. Tearoom
open 1st Mar-30th Sep.
Cat. Cost: None issued.
Credit Cards: Delta MasterCard Switch Visa
Specialities: 3000+ varieties of plants, most
propagated on premises, many rare or
unusual. The garden, open to the public, was
laid out by Edward Hyams. Pioneers of
glasshouse pests control by beneficial insects.
Map Ref: C, C3

CHrt   HORTUS NURSERY ✉ ♠ ♿
Shrubbery Bungalow, School Lane, Rousdon,
Lyme Regis, Dorset, DT7 3XW
T (01297) 444019
M 07747 043997
F (01297) 444019
E plants@hortusnursery.com
W www.hortusnursery.com
Contact: Marie-Elaine Houghton
Opening Times: 1000-1700 Wed-Sun, Mar-
Oct. Other times by appt.
Min Mail Order UK: Nmc
Cat. Cost: 2 x 1st class
Credit Cards: None
Specialities: Ornamental grasses &
perennials, particularly *Carex, Aster, Digitalis,
Euphorbia, Geranium* & *Penstemon.* Garden
open as nursery. Garden design & planting
service.
Map Ref: C, C4
OS Grid Ref: SY296914

KEY | ✉ Mail order to UK or EU   ♠ Delivers to shows
✉ Exports beyond EU   € Euro accepted
♿ Accessible by wheelchair   ◆ See Display advertisement

C

CHVG   HIDDEN VALLEY GARDENS ⬧
Treesmill, Nr Par, Cornwall, PL24 2TU
Ⓣ (01208) 873225
Ⓦ www.hiddenvalleygardens.co.uk
Contact: Mrs P Howard
Opening Times: 1000-1800 beginning Mar-end Oct 7 days. Please phone for directions.
Cat. Cost: none issued
Credit Cards: None
Specialities: Cottage garden plants, *Crocosmia, Iris sibirica* & many unusual perennials which can be seen growing in the garden. Note: some stock available in small quantities.
Map Ref: C, D2
OS Grid Ref: SX094567

CJas   JASMINE COTTAGE GARDENS ⬧
26 Channel Road, Walton St Mary, Clevedon, Somerset, BS21 7BY
Ⓣ (01275) 871850
Ⓔ margaret@bologrew.demon.co.uk
Ⓦ www.bologrew.pwp.blueyonder.co.uk
Contact: Mr & Mrs M Redgrave
Opening Times: May to Sep, daily by appt.
Min Mail Order UK: Nmc*
Cat. Cost: None issued
Credit Cards: None
Specialities: *Rhodochiton, Asarina, Maurandya, Dicentra macrocapnos, Salvia, Solenopsis, Isotoma*, half-hardy geraniums. *Note: mail order seed only.
Map Ref: C, A4
OS Grid Ref: ST405725

CKel   KELWAYS LTD ⬧ ⬧ ⬧ €
Langport, Somerset, TA10 9EZ
Ⓣ (01458) 250521
Ⓕ (01458) 253351
Ⓔ sales@kelways.co.uk
Ⓦ www.kelways.co.uk
Also supplies wholesale: Yes
Contact: Mr David Root
Opening Times: 0900-1700 Mon-Fri, 1000-1700 Sat, 1000-1600 Sun.
Min Mail Order UK: £4.00 + p&p
Min Mail Order EU: £8.00 + p&p
Cat. Cost: Free
Credit Cards: Visa Access
Specialities: *Paeonia, Iris, Hemerocallis* & herbaceous perennials. Nat. Coll. *Paeonia lactiflora*. *Note: mail order for *Paeonia, Iris* & *Hemerocallis* only.
Map Ref: C, B5

CKen   KENWITH NURSERY (GORDON HADDOW) ⬧ ⬧ € ⬧ ◆
Blinsham, Nr Torrington, Beaford, Winkleigh, Devon, EX19 8NT

Ⓣ (01805) 603274
Ⓕ (01805) 603663
Ⓔ conifers@kenwith63.freeserve.co.uk
Ⓦ www.kenwithnursery.co.uk
Contact: Gordon Haddow
Opening Times: 1000-1630 Wed-Sat Nov-Feb & by appt. 1000-1630 7 days Mar-Oct.
Min Mail Order UK: £10.00 + p&p*
Min Mail Order EU: £50.00 + p&p
Cat. Cost: 3 x 1st class
Credit Cards: Visa MasterCard EuroCard
Specialities: All conifer genera. Grafting a speciality. Many new introductions to UK. Nat. Coll. of Dwarf Conifers.
Map Ref: C, B3

CKno   KNOLL GARDENS ⬧ ⬧ ⬧
Hampreston, Stapehill, Nr Wimborne, Dorset, BH21 7ND
Ⓣ (01202) 873931
Ⓕ (01202) 870842
Ⓔ enquiries@knollgardens.co.uk
Ⓦ www.knollgardens.co.uk
Also supplies wholesale: Yes
Contact: N R Lucas
Opening Times: 1000-1700 (or dusk if earlier) Wed-Sun. Closed Xmas period.
Min Mail Order UK: Nmc
Cat. Cost: £1.40 cheque or order Online
Credit Cards: Visa MasterCard
Specialities: Grasses (main specialism). Select perennials. Nat. Collections of *Pennisetum, Phygelius* & deciduous *Ceanothus*.
Map Ref: C, C6

CKob   KOBAKOBA ⬧ ⬧ ⬧
2 High Street, Ashcott, Bridgwater, Somerset, TA7 9PL
Ⓣ (01458) 210700
Ⓜ 07870 624969
Ⓕ (01458) 210650
Ⓔ plants@kobakoba.co.uk
Ⓦ www.kobakoba.co.uk
Contact: Christine Smithee & David Constantine
Opening Times: Please phone for opening times.
Min Mail Order UK: Nmc
Min Mail Order EU: Nmc
Cat. Cost: 4 x 1st class/4 x IRC
Credit Cards: Visa MasterCard Delta
Specialities: Plants for tropical effect incl. *Ensete, Musa, Hedychium, Curcuma* & other *Zingiberaceae*. Conservatory & greenhouse plants.
Map Ref: C, B5
OS Grid Ref: ST4237

C

CLAP LONG ACRE PLANTS ✉ 🏃 ♿
South Marsh, Charlton Musgrove,
Nr Wincanton, Somerset, BA9 8EX
Ⓣ (01963) 32802
Ⓕ (01963) 32802
Ⓔ info@longacreplants.co.uk
Ⓦ www.longacreplants.co.uk
Contact: Nigel & Michelle Rowland
Opening Times: 1000-1700 Thu-Sat, Feb-
Apr, plus special open days 29-31 May,
19-21 Jun, 18-20 Jul, 25-27 Sep,
17-19 Oct 2003.
Min Mail Order UK: £15.00 + p&p
Min Mail Order EU: £30.00 + p&p
Cat. Cost: 3 x 1st class
Credit Cards: MasterCard Visa
Specialities: Ferns, lilies, woodland bulbs &
perennials. Nat. Coll. of *Asarum*.
Map Ref: C, B5

CLCN LITTLE CREEK NURSERY ✉ 🗷 ♿
39 Moor Road, Banwell, Weston-super-Mare,
Somerset, BS29 6EF
Ⓣ (01934) 823739
Ⓕ (01934) 823739
Contact: Rhys & Julie Adams
Opening Times: By appt only.
Min Mail Order UK: Nmc
Min Mail Order EU: Nmc
Cat. Cost: 3 x 1st class
Credit Cards: None
Specialities: Species *Cyclamen* (from seed),
Helleborus, Agapanthus & *Schizostylis*.
Map Ref: C, B4

CLnd LANDFORD TREES ✉ €
Landford Lodge, Landford, Salisbury,
Wiltshire, SP5 2EH
Ⓣ (01794) 390808
Ⓕ (01794) 390037
Ⓔ sales@landfordtrees.co.uk
Ⓦ www.landfordtrees.co.uk
Also supplies wholesale: Yes
Contact: C D Pilkington
Opening Times: 0800-1700 Mon-Fri.
Min Mail Order UK: Please enquire
Min Mail Order EU: Please enquire
Cat. Cost: Free
Credit Cards: None
Specialities: Deciduous ornamental trees.
Map Ref: C, B6
OS Grid Ref: SU247201

CLoc C S LOCKYER ✉ 🗷 🏃 € ◆
Lansbury, 70 Henfield Road, Coalpit Heath,
Bristol BS36 2UZ
Ⓣ (01454) 772219
Ⓕ (01454) 772219

Ⓔ sales@lockyerfuchsias.co.uk
Ⓦ www.lockyerfuchsias.co.uk
Also supplies wholesale: Yes
Contact: C S Lockyer
Opening Times: 1000-1300, 1430-1700
most days, please ring. Many open days &
coach parties. Limited wheelchair access.
Min Mail Order UK: 6 plants + p&p
Min Mail Order EU: £12.00 + p&p
Cat. Cost: 4 x 1st class
Credit Cards: None
Specialities: *Fuchsia*.
Map Ref: C, A5

CLyd LYDFORD ALPINE NURSERY ✉ 🏃
2 Southern Cottages, Lydford, Okehampton,
Devon, EX20 4BL
Ⓣ (01822) 820398
Contact: Julie & David Hatchett
Opening Times: 1000-1700 Tue & Thu Apr-
Oct & by appt. Nov-Mar by appt. only.
Closed 15th-29th Sep.
Min Mail Order UK: £10.00 + p&p*
Cat. Cost: Sae for saxifrage list.
Credit Cards: None
Specialities: *Saxifraga*. Very wide range of
choice & unusual alpines in small quantities.
*Note: mail order *Saxifraga* only.
Map Ref: C, C3
OS Grid Ref: SX504830

CM&M M & M PLANTS ♿
Lloret, Chittlehamholt, Umberleigh,
Devon, EX37 9PD
Ⓣ (01769) 540448
Ⓕ (01769) 540448
Contact: Mr M Thorne
Opening Times: 0930-1730 Tue-Sat, Apr-
Oct & 1000-1600 Tue-Sat, Nov-Mar &
B/hols. Sat by appt. Aug & Dec-Jan.
Cat. Cost: 3 x 1st class
Credit Cards: None
Specialities: Perennials. We also carry a good
range of alpines, shrubs, trees & roses.
Map Ref: C, B3

CMac MACPENNYS NURSERIES ✉
154 Burley Road, Bransgore, Christchurch,
Dorset, BH23 8DB
Ⓣ (01425) 672348
Ⓕ (01425) 673945
Contact: T & V Lowndes
Opening Times: 0800-1700 Mon-Fri,

C

0900-1700 Sat 1400-1700 Sun.
Closed Xmas & New Year.
Min Mail Order UK: Nmc
Cat. Cost: A4 Sae with 4 x 1st class
Credit Cards: Access Delta Access EuroCard
MasterCard Visa Switch Solo
Specialities: General. Nursery partial
accessible for wheelchairs.
Map Ref: C, C6

CMCN MALLET COURT NURSERY ⊠ ⊠ ♠ € ⬚
Curry Mallet, Taunton, Somerset, TA3 6SY
Ⓣ (01823) 481493
Ⓕ (01823) 481493
Ⓔ harris@malletcourt.freeserve.co.uk
Ⓦ www.malletcourt.co.uk
Also supplies wholesale: Yes
Contact: J G S & P M E Harris F.L.S.
Opening Times: 0900-1700 Mon-Fri.
Sat & Sun by appt.
Min Mail Order UK: Nmc*
Min Mail Order EU: Nmc
Cat. Cost: £1.50
Credit Cards: MasterCard Visa
Specialities: Maples, oaks, *Magnolia*, hollies &
other rare and unusual plants including those
from China & South Korea. *Note: mail order
Oct-Mar only.
Map Ref: C, B4

CMCo MEADOW COTTAGE PLANTS ♠ €
Pitt Hill, Ivybridge, Devon, PL21 0JJ
Ⓣ (01752) 894532
Also supplies wholesale: Yes
Contact: Mrs L P Hunt
Opening Times: By appt. only.
Cat. Cost: 2 x 2nd class
Credit Cards: None
Specialities: Hardy geranium, other hardy
perennials, ornamental grasses and bamboos.
Map Ref: C, D3

CMdw MEADOWS NURSERY ⊠ ♠
5 Rectory Cottages, Mells, Frome,
Somerset, BA11 3PA
Ⓣ (01373) 813025
Ⓕ (01373) 812268
Also supplies wholesale: Yes
Contact: Sue Lees & Eddie Wheatley
Opening Times: 1000-1800 Wed-Sun 1st
Feb-31st Oct & B/hols.
Min Mail Order UK: Nmc
Cat. Cost: 4 x 1st class
Credit Cards: None
Specialities: Hardy perennials, shrubs & some
conservatory plants. *Kniphofia*.
Map Ref: C, B5
OS Grid Ref: ST729492

CMea THE MEAD NURSERY ⬚
Brokerswood, Nr Westbury, Wiltshire,
BA13 4EG
Ⓣ (01373) 859990
Contact: Steve & Emma Lewis-Dale
Opening Times: 0900-1700 Wed-Sat &
B/hols, 1200-1700 Sun, 1st Feb-10th Oct.
Closed Easter Sun.
Cat. Cost: 5 x 1st class
Credit Cards: None
Specialities: Perennials, alpines, pot grown
bulbs and grasses.
Map Ref: C, B5
OS Grid Ref: ST833517

CMen MENDIP BONSAI STUDIO ♠
Byways, Back Lane, Downside, Shepton
Mallet, Somerset, BA4 4JR
Ⓣ (01749) 344274
Ⓕ (01749) 344274
Ⓔ jr.trott@ukonline.co.uk
Ⓦ www.mendipbonsai.co.uk
Contact: John Trott
Opening Times: By appt. only.
Cat. Cost: large sae for plant & workshop lists
Credit Cards: MasterCard Visa
Specialities: Bonsai & garden stock. Acers,
conifers, *Stewartia*. Operates education classes
in bonsai.
Map Ref: C, B5

CMHG MARWOOD HILL GARDENS ⬚
Barnstaple, Devon, EX31 4EB
Ⓣ (01271) 342528
Ⓔ malcolmpharoah@supanet.com
Ⓦ www.marwoodhillgardens.co.uk
Contact: Malcolm Pharoah
Opening Times: 1100-1700 7 days.
Cat. Cost: 3 x 1st class
Credit Cards: Visa Delta MasterCard Switch Solo
Specialities: Large range of unusual trees &
shrubs. *Eucalyptus*, alpines, *Camellia*, *Astilbe*,
bog plants & perennials. Nat. Colls. of *Astilbe*,
Tulbaghia & *Iris ensata*.
Map Ref: C, B3

CMil MILL COTTAGE PLANTS ⊠ ♠ ⬚
The Mill, Henley Lane, Wookey,
Somerset, BA5 1AP
Ⓣ (01749) 676966
Ⓔ mcp@tinyworld.co.uk
Contact: Sally Gregson
Opening Times: 1000-1800 Wed Mar-Sep or
by appt. Phone for directions.
Min Mail Order UK: £5.00 + p&p
Min Mail Order EU: £10.00 + p&p
Cat. Cost: 4 x 1st class
Credit Cards: None

Specialities: Unusual & period cottage plants esp. *Dierama, Papaver orientale,* hardy *Geranium,* ferns, & grasses. Also *Hydrangea aspera* & *H. serrata* cvs.
Map Ref: C, B5

CNat   NATURAL SELECTION ⊠ €
1 Station Cottages, Hullavington,
Chippenham, Wiltshire, SN14 6ET
Ⓣ (01666) 837369
Ⓔ martin@worldmutation.demon.co.uk
Ⓦ www.worldmutation.demon.co.uk
Contact: Martin Cragg-Barber
Opening Times: Please phone first.
Min Mail Order UK: £9.00 + p&p
Cat. Cost: £1.00 or 5 x 2nd class
Credit Cards: None
Specialities: Unusual British natives & others. Also seed.
Map Ref: C, A5
OS Grid Ref: ST898828

CNCN   NAKED CROSS NURSERIES ⊠ 🚻
Waterloo Road, Corfe Mullen, Wimborne,
Dorset, BH21 3SR
Ⓣ (01202) 693256
Ⓕ (01202) 693259
Also supplies wholesale: Yes
Contact: Peter French
Opening Times: 0900-1700 7 days.
Min Mail Order UK: 10 heathers
Cat. Cost: 2 x 1st class
Credit Cards: Visa American Express Switch MasterCard
Specialities: Heathers.
Map Ref: C, C6

CNic   NICKY'S ROCK GARDEN NURSERY 🚻 🚻
Broadhayes, Stockland, Honiton,
Devon, EX14 9EH
Ⓣ (01404) 881213
Ⓔ Dianabob.Dark@nickys.sagehost.co.uk
Contact: Diana & Bob Dark
Opening Times: 0900-dusk 7 days. Please phone first to check & for directions.
Cat. Cost: 3 x 1st class
Credit Cards: None
Specialities: Plants for rock gardens, scree, troughs, banks, walls & front of border & dwarf shrubs. Many unusual. Plants propagated in small numbers. Ring to check availability before travelling.
Map Ref: C, C4
OS Grid Ref: ST236027

CNMi   NEWPORT MILLS NURSERY ⊠
Wrantage, Taunton, Somerset, TA3 6DJ
Ⓣ (01823) 490231

Ⓜ 07950 035668
Contact: John Barrington, Rachel Pettitt
Opening Times: By appt. only.
Min Mail Order UK: Nmc
Min Mail Order EU: Nmc
Cat. Cost: Free
Credit Cards: None
Specialities: *Delphinium.* Mail order Apr-Sep for young delphiniums in 7cm pots. Dormant plants can be sent out in autumn/winter if requested. Some varieties only available in small quantities & propagated to order.
Map Ref: C, B4

COkL   OAK LEAF NURSERIES ⊠ 🚻
24 Crantock Drive, Almondsbury,
Bristol, BS32 4HG
Ⓣ (01454) 620180
Ⓜ 07718 667940
Also supplies wholesale: Yes
Contact: David Price
Opening Times: Not open, mail order only.
Min Mail Order UK: Nmc
Cat. Cost: 2 x 1st class
Credit Cards: None
Specialities: Wide range of rock & herbaceous plants, some unusual, incl. *Dianthus, Helianthemum, Lavandula, Hebe* & *Saxifraga.* Shrubs also a speciality.
Map Ref: C, A5

COld   THE OLD MILL HERBARY
Helland Bridge, Bodmin,
Cornwall, PL30 4QR
Ⓣ (01208) 841206
Ⓕ (01208) 841206
Ⓔ enquiries@oldmillherbary.co.uk
Ⓦ www.oldmillherbary.co.uk
Contact: Mrs B Whurr
Opening Times: 1000-1700 Thu-Tue Apr-30th Sep.
Cat. Cost: 6 x 1st class
Credit Cards: None
Specialities: Culinary, medicinal & aromatic herbs, shrubs, climbing & herbaceous plants.
Map Ref: C, C2
OS Grid Ref: SX065717

COIW   THE OLD WITHY GARDEN NURSERY ⊠
The Grange, Gweek, Helston,
Cornwall, TR12 6BE
Ⓣ (01326) 221171

K E Y		
⊠ Mail order to UK or EU	🚻 Delivers to shows	
🗷 Exports beyond EU	€ Euro accepted	
🚻 Accessible by wheelchair	◆ See Display advertisement	

C

Ⓕ (01326) 221171
Ⓔ WithyNursery@fsbdial.co.uk
Contact: Sheila Chandler or Nick Chandler
Opening Times: 1000-1700 Wed-Mon, mid Feb-end Oct. 1000-1730 7 days, Apr-Sep.
Min Mail Order UK: Nmc
Cat. Cost: 4 x 1st class
Credit Cards: MasterCard Visa Delta Switch
Specialities: Cottage garden plants, perennials, some biennials & grasses. Good selection of *Achillea, Eryngium, Euphorbia,* hardy geraniums, *Penstemon & Sedum.*
Map Ref: C, D1
OS Grid Ref: SW688255

COtt   OTTER NURSERIES LTD 🅱
Gosford Road, Ottery St. Mary,
Devon, EX11 1LZ
Ⓣ (01404) 815815
Ⓕ (01404) 815816
Ⓔ otter@otternurseries.co.uk
Contact: Mrs Pam Poole
Opening Times: 0800-1730 Mon-Sat, 1030-1630 Sun. Closed Xmas, Boxing Day & Easter Sun.
Cat. Cost: None issued
Credit Cards: Visa Access American Express Diners Switch
Specialities: Large garden centre & nursery with extensive range of trees, shrubs, conifers, climbers, roses, fruit & hardy perennials.
Map Ref: C, C4

CPar   PARKS PERENNIALS
242 Wallisdown Road, Wallisdown,
Bournemouth, Dorset, BH10 4HZ
Ⓣ (01202) 524464
Contact: S Parks
Opening Times: Apr-Oct most days, please phone first.
Cat. Cost: None issued.
Credit Cards: None
Specialities: Hardy herbaceous perennials.
Map Ref: C, C6

CPas   PASSIFLORA (NATIONAL COLLECTION) ⊠ ⊠ €
Lampley Road, Kingston Seymour, Clevedon,
Somerset, BS21 6XS
Ⓣ (01934) 833350
Ⓕ (01934) 877255
Ⓔ greenholm@lineone.net
Also supplies wholesale: Yes
Contact: John Vanderplank or Jane Lindsay
Opening Times: 0900-1300 & 1400-1700 Mon-Sat, May-Sep.
Min Mail Order UK: £20.00 + p&p
Min Mail Order EU: £30.00 + p&p

Cat. Cost: 3 x 1st class
Credit Cards: Visa Access EuroCard MasterCard
Specialities: *Passiflora.* Nat. Coll. of over 200 species & varieties. Note: retail nursery now at Kingston Seymour.
Map Ref: C, A4

CPBP   PARHAM BUNGALOW PLANTS ⊠ ñ €
Parham Lane, Market Lavington, Devizes,
Wiltshire, SN10 4QA
Ⓣ (01380) 812605
Ⓔ jjs@pbplants.freeserve.co.uk
Contact: Mrs D E Sample
Opening Times: Please ring first.
Min Mail Order UK: Nmc
Min Mail Order EU: Nmc
Cat. Cost: Sae
Credit Cards: None
Specialities: Alpines & dwarf shrubs.
Map Ref: C, B6

CPen   PENNARD PLANTS ⊠ ⊠ ñ €
3 The Gardens, East Pennard,
Shepton Mallet, Somerset, BA4 6TU
Ⓣ (01749) 860039
Ⓜ 07702 579627
Ⓕ (01749) 860232
Ⓔ sales@pennardplants.com
Ⓦ pennardplants.com
Contact: Chris Smith
Opening Times: By appt. only.
Min Mail Order UK: Nmc
Min Mail Order EU: Nmc
Cat. Cost: 2 x 1st class
Credit Cards: all major credit/debit cards
Specialities: Ornamental grasses, *Agapanthus, Crocosmia, Dierama, Kniphofia* & phormiums. Note: nursery at The Walled Garden at East Pennard.
Map Ref: C, B5

CPev   PEVERIL CLEMATIS NURSERY € 🅱
Christow, Exeter, Devon, EX6 7NG
Ⓣ (01647) 252937
Contact: Barry Fretwell
Opening Times: 1000-1300 & 1400-1730 Fri-Wed, 1000-1300 Sun. Dec-1st Mar closed.
Cat. Cost: 2 x 1st class
Credit Cards: None
Specialities: *Clematis.*
Map Ref: C, C3

CPhi   ALAN PHIPPS CACTI ⊠ €
62 Samuel White Road, Hanham,
Bristol, BS15 3LX
Ⓣ (0117) 9607591

C

W www.cactus-mail.com/alan-phipps/index.html
Contact: A Phipps
Opening Times: 10.00-1700 but prior phone call essential to ensure a greeting.
Min Mail Order UK: £5.00 + p&p
Min Mail Order EU: £20.00 + p&p
Cat. Cost: Sae or 2 x IRC (EC only)
Credit Cards: None
Specialities: *Mammillaria, Astrophytum* & *Ariocarpus.* Species & varieties will change with times. Ample quantities exist in spring. Ltd. range of *Agave.* Note: Euro accepted as cash only.
Map Ref: C, A5
OS Grid Ref: ST644717

CPHo   THE PALM HOUSE ⊠
8 North Street, Ottery St Mary, Devon, EX11 1DR
T (01404) 815450
E george@thepalmhouse.co.uk
W www.thepalmhouse.co.uk
Contact: George Gregory
Opening Times: By appt. only.
Min Mail Order UK: £15.00
Cat. Cost: 2 x 1st class
Credit Cards: None
Specialities: Palms.
Map Ref: C, C4
OS Grid Ref: SY098955

CPla   PLANT WORLD BOTANIC GARDENS ⊠ ⊠ € ⬡ ◆
St Marychurch Road, Newton Abbot, Devon, TQ12 4SE
T (01803) 872939
F (01803) 875018
E raybrown@plantworld-devon.co.uk
W www.plantworld-devon.co.uk
Also supplies wholesale: Yes
Contact: Ray Brown
Opening Times: 0930-1700 7 days a week, Apr (Easter if earlier)-Oct.
Min Mail Order UK: £8.00*
Min Mail Order EU: £20.00
Cat. Cost: 3 x 1st class or 2 x IRC.
Credit Cards: Visa Access EuroCard MasterCard
Specialities: Alpines & unusual herbaceous plants. 4 acre garden correctly planted out as the map of the world. Nat. Coll. of *Primula.* *Note: mail order for seed only.
Map Ref: C, C3

CPle   PLEASANT VIEW NURSERY ⊠ ⬡
Two Mile Oak, Nr Denbury, Newton Abbot, Devon, TQ12 6DG

T (01803) 813388 answerphone
Contact: Mrs B D Yeo
Opening Times: Nursery open 1000-1700 Wed-Fri mid Mar-end Sep (closed for lunch 1245-1330).
Min Mail Order UK: £20.00 + p&p
Min Mail Order EU: £20.00 + p&p (Salvias only)
Cat. Cost: 3 x 2nd class or 2 x IRC
Credit Cards: None
Specialities: *Salvia* & unusual shrubs for garden & conservatory. Nat. Colls. of *Salvia* & *Abelia.* Note: nursery off A381 at T.M. Oak Cross towards Denbury.
Map Ref: C, C3
OS Grid Ref: SX8368

CPLG   PINE LODGE GARDENS & NURSERY ⬡
Cuddra, Holmbush, St Austell, Cornwall, PL25 3RQ
T (01726) 73500
F (01726) 77370
E garden@pine-lodge.com
W www.pine-lodge.co.uk
Contact: Ray & Shirley Clemo
Opening Times: 1000-1700 7 days 12th Mar-31st Oct.
Cat. Cost: 5 x 2nd class
Credit Cards: None
Specialities: Rare & unusual shrubs & herbaceous, some from seed collected on plant expeditions each year. Nat. Coll. of *Grevillea.* Ltd. stocks of all plants.
Map Ref: C, D2
OS Grid Ref: SX045527

CPlt   PLANTAHOLICS ⬡
Hillside, Coombe Street, Penselwood, Wincanton, Somerset, BA9 8NF
T (01747) 840852
Also supplies wholesale: Yes
Contact: Jane Edmonds
Opening Times: For 2003 only 1000-1600 last Fri, Sat & Sun of each month, Mar-Sep, but please phone first. Opening under review for 2004.
Cat. Cost: None issued for 2003
Credit Cards: None
Specialities: Small nursery concentrating mainly on high performance perennials for various situations. Many unusual & most propagated on the nursery. Sales area

C

accessible for wheelchair customers.
Map Ref: C, B5

CPMA P M A PLANT SPECIALITIES ⊠ ⊠

Junker's Nursery Ltd., Lower Mead, West
Hatch, Taunton, Somerset, TA3 5RN
Ⓣ (01823) 480774
Ⓕ (01823) 481046
Ⓔ karan@junker.net
Ⓦ www.junker.net
Also supplies wholesale: Yes
Contact: Karan or Nick Junker
Opening Times: Strictly by appt. only.
Min Mail Order UK: Nmc
Min Mail Order EU: Nmc
Cat. Cost: 6 x 2nd class
Credit Cards: None
Specialities: Choice & unusual shrubs incl.
grafted *Acer palmatum, Cornus, Magnolia* & a
wide range of *Daphne.* Ltd. numbers of some
hard to propagate plants, esp. daphnes.
Reserve orders accepted.
Map Ref: C, B4

CPne PINE COTTAGE PLANTS ⊠ ⊠ ♠ €

Pine Cottage, Fourways, Eggesford,
Chulmleigh, Devon, EX18 7QZ
Ⓣ (01769) 580076
Ⓕ (01769) 581427
Ⓔ pcplants@supanet.com
Ⓦ www.pcplants.co.uk
Also supplies wholesale: Yes
Contact: Dick Fulcher
Opening Times: By appt. only. Special open
weeks for *Agapanthus*, 1000-1800 daily excl.
Sun mornings 21st Jul-24th Aug 2003.
Min Mail Order UK: £15.00 + p&p
Min Mail Order EU: £20.00 + p&p
Cat. Cost: 4 x 1st class
Credit Cards: None
Specialities: Nat. Coll. of *Agapanthus.* Note:
mail order *Agapanthus* from Oct-Jun. Some
cvs available in small quantities only.
Map Ref: C, B3

CPom POMEROY PLANTS

Tower House, Pomeroy Lane, Wingfield,
Trowbridge, Wiltshire, BA14 9LJ
Ⓣ (01225) 769551
Contact: Simon Young
Opening Times: Mar-Nov.
Please phone first.
Cat. Cost: None issued
Credit Cards: None
Specialities: Hardy, mainly species, herbaceous
perennials. Many unusual and often small
numbers. Specialities *Allium, Salvia* & shade-
lovers, esp. *Epimedium.*

Map Ref: C, B5
OS Grid Ref: ST817569

CPou POUNSLEY PLANTS ⊠ ♠ € ⬓

Pounsley Combe, Spriddlestone,
Brixton, Plymouth, Devon, PL9 0DW
Ⓣ (01752) 402873
Ⓕ (01752) 402873
Ⓔ pou599@aol.com
Ⓦ www.admin@pounsleyplants.com
Also supplies wholesale: Yes
Contact: Mrs Jane Hollow
Opening Times: Normally 1000-1700 Mon-
Sat but please phone first.
Min Mail Order UK: £10.00 + p&p*
Min Mail Order EU: £20.00 + p&p
Cat. Cost: 2 x 1st class
Credit Cards: None
Specialities: Unusual herbaceous perennials &
cottage plants. Selection of *Clematis* & old
roses. Large selection of South African
monocots. *Note: mail order Nov-Feb only.
Map Ref: C, D3
OS Grid Ref: SX521538

CPrp PROPERPLANTS.COM ⊠ ♠

Penknight, Edgcumbe Road, Lostwithiel,
Cornwall, PF22 0JD
Ⓣ (01208) 872291
Ⓕ (01208) 872291
Ⓔ info@Properplants.com
Ⓦ www.ProperPlants.com
Contact: Sarah Wilks
Opening Times: By appt. only.
Min Mail Order UK: Nmc
Min Mail Order EU: Nmc
Cat. Cost: 4 x 1st class
Credit Cards: all major credit/debit cards
Specialities: Wide range of unusual & easy
herbaceous perennials, ferns & grasses. Less
common herbs.

CQua QUALITY DAFFODILS ⊠ ⊠ €

14 Roscarrack Close, Falmouth,
Cornwall, TR11 4PJ
Ⓣ (01326) 317959
Ⓕ (01326) 317959
Ⓔ RAScamp@daffodils.uk.com
info.at.qualitydaffodils.co.uk
Ⓦ www.qualitydaffodils.co.uk
www.daffodils.uk.com
Also supplies wholesale: Yes
Contact: R A Scamp
Opening Times: Not open, mail order only.
Min Mail Order UK: Nmc
Min Mail Order EU: Nmc
Cat. Cost: 3 x 1st class
Credit Cards: all major credit/debit cards

C

Specialities: *Narcissus* hybrids & species.
Map Ref: C, D1

CRde   ROWDE MILL NURSERY € ⑤
Rowde, Devizes, Wiltshire, SN10 1SZ
ⓣ (01380) 723016
ⓕ (01380) 723016
ⓔ cholmeley@supanet.com
Contact: Mrs J Cholmeley
Opening Times: 1000-1700 Thu-Sun &
B/hol Mon Apr-Sep.
Cat. Cost: None issued
Credit Cards: None
Specialities: Wide range of hardy perennials,
all grown on the nursery. Plants offered in
pots or lifted from stockbeds.
Map Ref: C, A6

CRea   REALLY WILD FLOWERS ⊠ ⊠ €
H V Horticulture Ltd, Spring Mead,
Bedchester, Shaftesbury, Dorset, SP7 0JU
ⓣ (01747) 811778
ⓕ (01747) 811499
ⓔ rwflowers@aol.com
ⓦ www.reallywildflowers.co.uk
Also supplies wholesale: Yes
Contact: Grahame Dixie
Opening Times: Not open to public.
Min Mail Order UK: £40.00 + p&p
Min Mail Order EU: £100.00 + p&p
Cat. Cost: 3 x 1st class
Credit Cards: None
Specialities: Wild flowers for grasslands,
woodlands, wetlands & heaths. Seeds, orchids.
Advisory & soil analysis services.

CRez   REZARE NURSERIES
Rezare, Nr Treburley, Launceston,
Cornwall, PL15 9NX
ⓣ (01579) 370969
ⓔ rezarenurseries@aol.com
Contact: Kym & Rick Finney/Mel & Jim
Gearing
Opening Times: 1000-1730, 7 days mid Feb-
mid Nov. Other times by appt.
Cat. Cost: None issued
Credit Cards: MasterCard Visa
Specialities: Growers of a full & varied range
of choice & unusual plants of the highest
quality, incl. a good selection of herbaceous
perennials, shrubs & trees.
Map Ref: C, C2

CRHN   ROSELAND HOUSE NURSERY ⊠ ṅ
Chacewater, Truro, Cornwall, TR4 8QB
ⓣ (01872) 560451
ⓔ clematis@roselandhouse.co.uk
ⓦ www.roselandhouse.co.uk

Contact: C R Pridham
Opening Times: 1300-1800 Tue & Wed,
Apr-Sep.
Min Mail Order UK: Nmc
Cat. Cost: 2 x 1st class
Credit Cards: None
Specialities: Climbing & conservatory plants.
National Collection of *Clematis viticella* cvs.
Map Ref: C, D1

**CRoM   ROSEDOWN MILL PALMS AND
EXOTICS ⊠**
Hartland, Bideford, Devon, EX39 6AH
ⓣ (01237) 441527
ⓔ huwcol@aol.com
ⓦ www.rosedownmill.co.uk
Contact: Huw Collingbourne
Opening Times: By appt. only.
Min Mail Order UK: £25.00
Min Mail Order EU: £25.00
Cat. Cost: Sae for list
Credit Cards: None
Specialities: Palms, cycads, pachypodiums.
Map Ref: C, B2
OS Grid Ref: SS276248

CRow   ROWDEN GARDENS ⊠ ⊠ ⑤
Brentor, Nr Tavistock, Devon, PL19 0NG
ⓣ (01822) 810275
ⓕ (01822) 810275
ⓔ rowdengardens@btopenworld.com
Also supplies wholesale: Yes
Contact: John R L Carter
Opening Times: By appt only.
Min Mail Order UK: Nmc
Min Mail Order EU: Nmc
Cat. Cost: 6 x 1st class
Credit Cards: None
Specialities: Aquatics, damp loving &
associated plants incl. rare & unusual
varieties. Nat. Coll. of *Polygonum, Ranunculus
ficaria, Caltha* & Water *Iris*. Note: some stock
available in small quantities only.
Map Ref: C, C3

CRWN   THE REALLY WILD NURSERY ⊠ ⊠ ṅ €
19 Hoopers Way, Torrington,
Devon, EX38 7NS
ⓣ (01805) 624739
ⓔ thereallywildnursery@hotmail.com
ⓦ www.thereallywildnurserydevon.biz
Also supplies wholesale: Yes
Contact: Kathryn Moore

K E Y		
⊠ Mail order to UK or EU	ṅ Delivers to shows	
⊠ Exports beyond EU	€ Euro accepted	
⑤ Accessible by wheelchair	◆ See Display advertisement	

C

Opening Times: Not open.
Min Mail Order UK: £10.00 + p&p*
Min Mail Order EU: £20.00 + p&p
Cat. Cost: 3 x 1st class
Credit Cards: None
Specialities: Wildflowers, bulbs & seeds.
*Note: mail order all year round, grown to
order (plants in pots or plugs).

CSam   **Sampford Shrubs** ⊠ €
Sampford Peverell, Tiverton, Devon, EX16 7EN
Ⓣ (01884) 821164
Ⓔ martin@samshrub.co.uk
Ⓦ www.samshrub.co.uk
Contact: M Hughes-Jones & S Proud
Opening Times: 0900-1700 Thu-Sat, Feb.
0900-1700 7 days, Mar-Jun. 0900-1700 Thu-
Sat Jul-Nov. Mail order Oct-mid Mar.
Min Mail Order UK: £15.00 + p&p*
Cat. Cost: A5 Sae
Credit Cards: MasterCard Switch Solo Delta
Electron Maestro Visa
Specialities: Large displays of *Pulmonaria* &
Crocosmia. Nat. Coll. of *Helenium*. *Note:
mail order is for herbaceous & small shrubs
only from Oct-mid Mar.
Map Ref: C, B4
OS Grid Ref: ST043153

CSBt   **St Bridget Nurseries Ltd** ⊠ 🅖
Old Rydon Lane, Exeter, Devon, EX2 7JY
Ⓣ (01392) 873672
Ⓕ (01392) 876710
Ⓦ www.stbridgetnurseries.co.uk
Contact: Garden Centre Plant Advice
Opening Times: 0800-1700 Mon-Sat, 1030-
1630 Sun, 0900-1700 Bank Hols. Closed
Xmas Day, Boxing Day & Easter Sunday.
Min Mail Order UK: Nmc*
Cat. Cost: Free
Credit Cards: Visa MasterCard Switch Solo
Specialities: Large general nursery, with two
garden centres. *Note: mail order available
between Nov & Mar.
Map Ref: C, C4
OS Grid Ref: SX955905

CSdC   **Sherwood Cottage** €
Newton St Cyres, Exeter, Devon, EX5 5BT
Ⓣ (01392) 851589
Ⓔ vaughan.gallavan@connectfree.co.uk
Contact: Vaughan Gallavan
Opening Times: By appt. only.
Cat. Cost: 2 x 1st class
Credit Cards: None
Specialities: Magnolias, trees & shrubs. Nat.
Coll. of Knap Hill azaleas. Ghent & species
deciduous azaleas. Sherwood Garden new Nat.

Coll. of *Magnolia*. Stock in limited
quantities.
Map Ref: C, C3

CSev   **Lower Severalls Nursery** ⊠ 🅖
Crewkerne, Somerset, TA18 7NX
Ⓣ (01460) 73234
Ⓕ (01460) 76105
Ⓔ mary@lowerseveralls.co.uk
Ⓦ www.lowerseveralls.co.uk
Contact: Mary R Pring
Opening Times: 1000-1700 Fri-Wed 1st Mar-
20th Oct & Sun 1400-1700 May & Jun.
Min Mail Order UK: £20.00*
Cat. Cost: 4 x 1st class
Credit Cards: None
Specialities: Herbs, herbaceous &
conservatory plants. *Note: Mail order
perennials only.
Map Ref: C, B5
OS Grid Ref: ST457111

CSil   **Silver Dale Nurseries** € ◆
Shute Lane, Combe Martin, Devon, EX34 0HT
Ⓣ (01271) 882539
Ⓔ silverdale.nurseries@virgin.net
Contact: Roger Gilbert
Opening Times: 1000-1800 7 days.
Cat. Cost: 4 x 1st class
Credit Cards: Visa MasterCard EuroCard
Specialities: Nat. Coll. of *Fuchsia*. Hardy
fuchsias (cultivars and species).
Map Ref: C, B3

CSLe   **Silver Leaf Nurseries** ⊠ 🏠 🅖 ◆
Charmouth Road, Lyme Regis,
Dorset, DT7 3HF
Ⓣ (01297) 444655
Ⓕ (01297) 444655
Ⓔ woodberry@fsbdial.co.uk
Ⓦ www.silverleaf@woodberrydown.com
Also supplies wholesale: Yes
Contact: Chris Hughes
Opening Times: Most days. Please phone first.
Min Mail Order UK: £25.00
Cat. Cost: 4 x 1st class
Credit Cards: None
Specialities: Silver- & grey-leafed plants, incl.
many lavenders. Will propagate to order.
Map Ref: C, C4
OS Grid Ref: ST932343

CSli   **Slipps Garden Centre** 🅖
Butts Hill, Frome,
Somerset, BA11 1HR
Ⓣ (01373) 467013
Ⓕ (01373) 467013
Also supplies wholesale: Yes

Contact: James Hall
Opening Times: 0900-1730 Mon-Sat, 1000-1630 Sun.
Cat. Cost: None issued
Credit Cards: Visa Access MasterCard Delta Switch
Specialities: *Achillea.*
Map Ref: C, B5

CSpe   SPECIAL PLANTS ⊠ ♠ € ⓖ
Hill Farm Barn, Greenways Lane,
Cold Ashton, Chippenham,
Wiltshire, SN14 8LA
Ⓣ (01225) 891686
Ⓔ specialplants@bigfoot.com
Ⓦ www.specialplants.net
Contact: Derry Watkins
Opening Times: 1030-1630 7 days Mar-Sept.
Other times please ring first to check.
Min Mail Order UK: £10.00 + p&p*
Min Mail Order EU: £10.00 + p&p
Cat. Cost: 5 x 2nd class (sae only for seed list)
Credit Cards: MasterCard Visa Delta Switch
Electron Maestro
Specialities: Tender perennials, *Mimulus, Pelargonium, Salvia, Streptocarpus.* Hardy geraniums, *Anemone, Erysimum, Papaver, Viola* & grasses. Many varieties prop. in small numbers. New introductions of S. African plants. *Note: mail order Sep-Mar only.
Map Ref: C, A5
OS Grid Ref: ST749726

CSPN   SHERSTON PARVA NURSERY LTD
⊠ ⌧ ♠ € ⓖ
Malmesbury Road, Sherston,
Wiltshire, SN16 0NX
Ⓣ (01666) 841066
Ⓕ (01666) 841132
Ⓔ sales@sherstonparva.com
Ⓦ www.sherstonparva.com
Contact: Martin Rea
Opening Times: 1000-1700 7 days 1st Feb-31th Dec. Closed Jan.
Min Mail Order UK: Nmc
Min Mail Order EU: Nmc
Cat. Cost: Free
Credit Cards: MasterCard Delta Visa Switch
Specialities: *Clematis,* wall shrubs & climbers.
Map Ref: C, A5

CSto   STONE LANE GARDENS ⊠ ⓖ
Stone Farm, Chagford, Devon, TQ13 8JU
Ⓣ (01647) 231311
Ⓕ (01647) 231311
Ⓔ kenneth_ashburner@talk21.com
Ⓦ http://mythicgarden.users.btopenworld.com

Also supplies wholesale: Yes
Contact: Kenneth Ashburner
Opening Times: By appt. only.
Min Mail Order UK: £5.00
Cat. Cost: £3.00 for descriptive catalogue
Credit Cards: None
Specialities: Wide range of wild provenance *Betula* & *Alnus.* Interesting varieties of *Rubus, Sorbus* etc.
OS Grid Ref: SX709909

CStr   SUE STRICKLAND PLANTS ⊠ ♠
The Poplars, Isle Brewers, Taunton,
Somerset, TA3 6QN
Ⓣ (01460) 281454
Ⓕ (01460) 281454
Ⓔ sues@stricklandc.freeserve.co.uk
Contact: Sue Strickland
Opening Times: 0930-1430 Mon-Wed Mar-Jul & Sep-Oct, some Sun, please phone first. Other times by appt.
Min Mail Order UK: 4 plants
Cat. Cost: 2 x 1st class
Credit Cards: None
Specialities: *Salvia* & unusual herbaceous perennials incl. *Nepeta, Helianthus, Origanum* & grasses.
Map Ref: C, B4

CStu   STUCKEY'S ALPINES ♠
38 Phillipps Avenue, Exmouth,
Devon, EX8 3HZ
Ⓣ (01395) 273636
Ⓔ stuckeysalpines@aol.com
Contact: Roger & Brenda Stuckey
Opening Times: As NGS dates or by appt.
Cat. Cost: None issued
Credit Cards: None
Specialities: Alpines in general. Hardy & half-hardy bulbs. NZ *Clematis* hybrids. Extensive choice of plants, many in small quantities.
Map Ref: C, C4

CSut   SUTTONS SEEDS ⊠
Woodview Road, Paignton,
Devon, TQ4 7NG
Ⓣ (01803) 696321
Ⓕ (01803) 696345
Ⓦ www.suttons-seeds.co.uk
Contact: Customer Services
Opening Times: (Office) 0830-1700 Mon-Fri. Also answerphone.

C

Min Mail Order UK: Nmc
Cat. Cost: Free
Credit Cards: Visa MasterCard Switch Delta
Specialities: Over 1,000 varieties of flower &
vegetable seed, bulbs, plants & sundries.

CSWC   SOUTH WEST CARNIVOROUS
PLANTS ⊠ ♠
2 Rose Cottages, Culmstock, Cullompton,
Devon, EX15 3JJ
Ⓣ (01884) 841549
Ⓕ (01884) 841549
Ⓔ flytraps@littleshopofhorrors.co.uk
Ⓦ www.littleshopofhorrors.co.uk
Contact: Jenny Pearce & Alistair Pearce
Opening Times: By appt.
Min Mail Order UK: £10.00 + p&p
Min Mail Order EU: £20.00 + p&p
Cat. Cost: 2 x 2nd class
Credit Cards: all major credit/debit cards
Specialities: *Cephalotus, Nepenthes, Dionea,
Drosera, Darlingtonia, Sarracenia, Pinguicula
& Utricularia.* Specialists in hardy carnivorous
plants & *Dionea muscipula* cvs.
Map Ref: C, B4

CSWP   SONIA WRIGHT PLANTS ⊠ ☑ 🖼
Buckerfields Nursery, Ogbourne St George,
Marlborough, Wiltshire, SN8 1SG
Ⓣ (01672) 841065
Ⓕ (01672) 541047
Contact: Anyas Simon, Sonia Wright
Opening Times: 1000-1800 Wed-Sat, Mar-
Oct. 1000-1600 Fri-Sat, Nov-Feb.
Min Mail Order UK: £15.00 Primulas only*
Min Mail Order EU: £15.00 Primulas only
Cat. Cost: 4 x 1st class
Credit Cards: None
Specialities: Barnhaven polyanthus &
primroses. Grasses, grey-leaved plants, *Iris,
Euphorbia, Penstemon,* old roses. *Note: mail
order primroses only despatched autumn.
Nursery has moved to above address.
Map Ref: C, A6

CTbh   TREBAH ENTERPRISES LTD
Trebah, Mawnan Smith, Falmouth,
Cornwall, TR11 5JZ
Ⓣ (01326) 250448
Ⓕ (01326) 250781
Ⓔ mail@trebah-garden.co.uk
Ⓦ www.trebah-garden.co.uk
Contact: Plant Sales Staff
Opening Times: 1030-1700 all year.
Cat. Cost: None issued
Credit Cards: Visa Access EuroCard American
Express Switch Delta Electron MasterCard Solo
Specialities: Tree ferns, *Camellia, Gunnera* &

conservatory climbers.
Map Ref: C, D1
OS Grid Ref: SW770276

CTCP   TURNPIKE COTTAGE PLANTS ⊠ ☑ ♠
(office) Turnpike Cottage, Trow, Salcombe
Regis, Sidmouth, Devon, EX10 0PB
Ⓣ (01395) 515265
Ⓜ 07870 389889
Ⓕ (01395) 515265
Ⓔ plants@turnpike.fsbusiness.co.uk
Ⓦ www.echiums.com
Contact: Mike Burgess
Opening Times: 1000-1600 Tue-Sun,
Mar-Oct.
Min Mail Order UK: £5.00*
Min Mail Order EU: £5.00
Cat. Cost:
Credit Cards: all major credit/debit cards
Specialities: *Echium.* *Note: mail order seeds
only. Nursery at Popplefords, Newton
Poppleford, Sidmouth, Devon.
Map Ref: C, C4

CTho   THORNHAYES NURSERY ⊠
St Andrews Wood, Dulford, Cullompton,
Devon, EX15 2DF
Ⓣ (01884) 266746
Ⓕ (01884) 266739
Ⓔ trees@thornhayes.demon.co.uk
Ⓦ www.thornhayes-nursery.co.uk
Also supplies wholesale: Yes
Contact: K D Croucher
Opening Times: 0800-1600 Mon-Fri.
Min Mail Order UK: Nmc
Min Mail Order EU: Nmc
Cat. Cost: 5 x 1st class
Credit Cards: None
Specialities: A broad range of forms of
ornamental, amenity & fruit trees incl. West
Country apple varieties.
Map Ref: C, C4

CThr   THREE COUNTIES NURSERIES ⊠
Marshwood, Bridport, Dorset, DT6 5QJ
Ⓣ (01297) 678257
Ⓕ (01297) 678257
Contact: A & D Hitchcock
Opening Times: Not open.
Min Mail Order UK: Nmc
Cat. Cost: 2 x 2nd class
Credit Cards: Visa MasterCard
Specialities: Aquilegias.

CTrC   TREVENA CROSS NURSERIES ⊠ € 🖼
Breage, Helston,
Cornwall, TR13 9PS
Ⓣ (01736) 763880

(F) (01736) 762828
(E) sales@trevenacross.co.uk
(W) www.trevenacross.co.uk
Also supplies wholesale: Yes
Contact: Graham Jeffery, John Eddy
Opening Times: 0900-1700 Mon-Sat,
1030-1630 Sun.
Min Mail Order UK: Nmc
Min Mail Order EU: Nmc*
Cat. Cost: A5 Sae with 2 x 1st class
Credit Cards: Access Visa Switch
Specialities: South African, Australian & New
Zealand plants, incl. *Aloe, Protea,* tree ferns,
palms, *Restio,* hardy succulents & wide range
of other exotics. *Note: mail order to EU by
negotiation.
Map Ref: C, D1
OS Grid Ref: SW614284

CTrG   **TREGOTHNAN NURSERY** ⊠ ⊠ ♠ € ⅏
Estate Office, Tregothnan, Truro,
Cornwall, TR2 4AN
(T) (01872) 520325
(F) (01872) 520291
(E) bigplants@tregothnan.co.uk
(W) www.tregothnan.com
Also supplies wholesale: Yes
Contact: Jonathon Jones
Opening Times: By appt. for collection only.
Min Mail Order UK: £250.00
Min Mail Order EU: £500.00
Cat. Cost: On web.
Credit Cards: MasterCard Visa Delta
EuroCard
Specialities: Unusual & rare plants from own
stock. Extra large specimens available for
instant effect. Known wild origin plants.

CTrh   **TREHANE CAMELLIA NURSERY** ⊠ ♠ € ⅏
J Trehane & Sons Ltd, Stapehill Road,
Hampreston, Wimborne,
Dorset, BH21 7ND
(T) (01202) 873490
(F) (01202) 873490
Also supplies wholesale: Yes
Contact: Lorraine or Jeanette
Opening Times: 0900-1630 Mon-Fri all year
(excl. Xmas & New Year). 1000-1600 Sat-Sun
in spring & by special appt.
Min Mail Order UK: Nmc
Min Mail Order EU: Nmc
Cat. Cost: £1.70 cat./book
Credit Cards: Visa Access MasterCard
Specialities: Extensive range of *Camellia*
species, cultivars & hybrids. Many new
introductions. Evergreen azaleas, *Pieris,*
Magnolia & blueberries.
Map Ref: C, C6

CTri   **TRISCOMBE NURSERIES** ⊠ ⅏ ♦
West Bagborough, Nr Taunton,
Somerset, TA4 3HG
(T) (01984) 618267
(E) triscombe.nurseries2000@virgin.net
(W) www.triscombenurseries.co.uk
Contact: S Parkman
Opening Times: 0900-1300 & 1400-1730
Mon-Sat. 1400-1730 Sun & B/hols.
Min Mail Order UK: Nmc
Cat. Cost: 2 x 1st class
Credit Cards: None
Specialities: Trees, shrubs, roses, fruit,
Clematis, herbaceous & rock plants.
Map Ref: C, B4

CTrw   **TREWITHEN NURSERIES** ⊠ €
Grampound Road, Truro, Cornwall, TR2 4DD
(T) (01726) 882764
(F) (01726) 882301
(E) gardens@trewithen-estate.demon.co.uk
(W) www.trewithengardens.co.uk
Also supplies wholesale: Yes
Contact: M Taylor
Opening Times: 0800-1630 Mon-Fri.
Min Mail Order UK: Nmc
Cat. Cost: £1.25
Specialities: Shrubs, especially *Camellia* &
Rhododendron.
Map Ref: C, D2

CWat   **THE WATER GARDEN** ⊠ ⅏
Hinton Parva, Swindon, Wiltshire, SN4 0DH
(T) (01793) 790558
(F) (01793) 791298
(E) watergarden@supanet.com
Contact: Mike & Anne Newman
Opening Times: 1000-1700 Wed-Sun.
Min Mail Order UK: £10.00 + p&p
Cat. Cost: 4 x 1st class
Credit Cards: Visa Access Switch
Specialities: Water lilies, marginal & moisture
plants, oxygenators & alpines.
Map Ref: C, A6

CWCL   **WESTCOUNTRY NURSERIES (INC.**
WESTCOUNTRY LUPINS) ⊠ ♠ € ♦
Ford Hill Forge, Hartland, Bideford,
Devon, EX39 6EE
(T) (01237) 441208
(F) (01237) 441208
(E) SarahConibear@westcountry-
nurseries.co.uk

C

Ⓦ www.westcountry-nurseries.co.uk
Also supplies wholesale: Yes
Contact: Sarah Conibear
Opening Times: By appt. only.
Min Mail Order UK: £15.00
Min Mail Order EU: £50.00
Cat. Cost: 2 x 1st class + A5 Sae for full
colour cat.
Credit Cards: None
Specialities: *Lupinus, Lewisia, Hellebore*,
gentians, cyclamen, lavender, select perennials
& grasses.

CWDa   WESTDALE NURSERIES ⊠ ⊠ ♠ ⬚
Holt Road, Bradford-on-Avon,
Wiltshire, BA15 1TS
Ⓣ (01225) 863258
Ⓕ (01225) 863258
Ⓔ westdale.nurseries@talk21.com
Ⓦ www.westdalenurseries.co.uk
Also supplies wholesale: Yes
Contact: Louisa Bernal
Opening Times: 0900-1800 7 days.
Min Mail Order UK: £10.00 + p&p
Min Mail Order EU: £10.00 + p&p*
Cat. Cost: 4 x 1st class
Credit Cards: None
Specialities: *Bougainvillea, Geranium*,
conservatory plants. *Note: export beyond EU
by arrangement.
Map Ref: C, A5

CWdb   WOODBOROUGH GARDEN CENTRE ⬚
Nursery Farm, Woodborough, Nr Pewsey,
Wiltshire, SN9 5PF
Ⓣ (01672) 851249
Ⓕ (01672) 851249
Contact: Els M Brewin
Opening Times: 0900-1700 Mon-Sat, 1100-
1700 Sun.
Cat. Cost: None issued
Credit Cards: Access Diners EuroCard
MasterCard Switch Visa
Specialities: Wide range of shrubs, trees,
herbaceous, alpines & herbs. Large selection
of climbers esp. Clematis, & spring bulbs.
Map Ref: C, A6
OS Grid Ref: SU119597

CWGr   WINCHESTER GROWERS LTD. ⊠ ⊠ ⬚
Varfell Farm, Long Rock, Penzance,
Cornwall, TR20 8AQ
Ⓣ (01736) 851033
Ⓕ (01736) 851033
Ⓔ dahlias@wgltd.co.uk
Ⓦ www.wgltd.co.uk
Also supplies wholesale: Yes
Contact: Sarah Thomas

Opening Times: 1000-1600, 30th & 31st
Aug 2003. Other times by appt.
Min Mail Order UK: Nmc
Min Mail Order EU: Nmc
Cat. Cost: Free
Credit Cards: Visa Delta MasterCard Switch
Specialities: Nat. Coll. of *Dahlia*. Due to large
number of varieties, stock of some is limited.
Map Ref: C, D1

CWhi   WHITEHOUSE IVIES ⊠ ⊠ €
Blinsham Beaford, Winkleigh,
Devon, EX19 8NT
Also supplies wholesale: Yes
Contact: Gail Haddow
Opening Times: By appt. only.
Min Mail Order UK: £17.70 + p&p
Min Mail Order EU: £17.70 + p&p
Cat. Cost: £1.50 or 6 x 1st class
Credit Cards: Visa MasterCard EuroCard
Specialities: Ivy, over 350 varieties.
Map Ref: C, B3

CWib   WIBBLE FARM NURSERIES ⊠ ⊠ ♠ ⬚
Wibble Farm, West Quantoxhead,
Nr Taunton, Somerset, TA4 4DD
Ⓣ (01984) 632303
Ⓕ (01984) 633168
Ⓔ wibblefarmnurseries@hotmail.com
Also supplies wholesale: Yes
Contact: Mrs M L Francis
Opening Times: 0800-1700 Mon-Fri, 1000-
1600 Sat. All year excl. B/hols.
Min Mail Order UK: Nmc
Min Mail Order EU: Nmc
Cat. Cost: 2 x 1st class
Credit Cards: MasterCard Switch Visa
Specialities: Growers of a wide range of hardy
plants, many rare & unusual.
Map Ref: C, B4

CWil   FERNWOOD NURSERY ⊠ ⊠ € ⬚
Peters Marland, Torrington, Devon, EX38 8QG
Ⓣ (01805) 601446
Ⓔ hw@fernwood-nursery.co.uk
Ⓦ www.fernwood-nursery.co.uk
Contact: Howard Wills & Sally Wills
Opening Times: Any time by appt. Please
phone first.
Min Mail Order UK: Nmc
Min Mail Order EU: Nmc
Cat. Cost: Sae for list or £1.50 for houseleeks
booklet
Credit Cards: None
Specialities: Nat. Coll. of *Sempervivum,
Jovibarba, Rosularia* & *Phormium*.
Map Ref: C, C3
OS Grid Ref: SS479133

CWin   WINFRITH HOSTAS ⊠ € ⍟
5 Knoll Park, Gatemore Road, Winfrith
Newburgh, Dorchester, Dorset, DT2 8LD
Ⓣ (01305) 852935
Ⓦ www.winfrithhostas.co.uk
Also supplies wholesale: Yes
Contact: John Ledbury
Opening Times: By appt.
Min Mail Order UK: Nmc*
Cat. Cost: 2 x 1st class
Credit Cards: None
Specialities: *Hosta.* *Note: mail order available
from Oct-Mar only.
Map Ref: C, C5

CWiW   WINDRUSH WILLOW ⊠ ⌧ €
Higher Barn, Sidmouth Road, Aylesbeare,
Exeter, Devon, EX5 2JJ
Ⓣ (01395) 233669
Ⓕ (01395) 233669
Ⓔ windrushw@aol.com
Ⓦ www.windrushwillow.com
Also supplies wholesale: Yes
Contact: Richard Kerwood
Opening Times: By appt.
Min Mail Order UK: Nmc
Min Mail Order EU: Nmc
Cat. Cost: 2 x 1st class
Credit Cards: None
Specialities: *Salix.* Unrooted cuttings available
Dec-Mar.

CWoo   IAN AND ROSEMARY WOOD ⊠
Newlands, 28 Furland Road, Crewkerne,
Somerset, TA18 8DD
Ⓣ (01460) 74630
Ⓔ ianwood@ukgateway.net
Contact: Ian and Rosemary Wood
Opening Times: By appt. only. Primarily mail
order service.
Min Mail Order UK: Nmc
Cat. Cost: 2 x 1st or 2nd class
Credit Cards: None
Specialities: *Erythronium, Cyclamen* species &
dwarf *Narcissus* species. Note: some species
may only be available in small quantities, see
catalogue.
Map Ref: C, B5

CWrd   WARD ALPINES ⊠ ⌧ ⋔ €
Newton Farm Nursery, Hemyock,
Cullompton, Devon, EX15 3QS
Ⓣ (01823) 680410
Ⓕ (01823) 680410
Ⓦ www.wardalpines@btopenworld.com
Also supplies wholesale: Yes
Contact: J.F. & S.M. Ward
Opening Times: By appt only & when garden

open under NGS.
Min Mail Order UK: Nmc
Min Mail Order EU: Nmc
Cat. Cost: 3 x 1st class
Specialities: Wide range of *Gentiana sino-
ornata, Rhodohypoxis/Rhodoxis, Iris sibirica* &
I. ensata.
Map Ref: C, B4
OS Grid Ref: ST140123

CWri   NIGEL WRIGHT RHODODENDRONS ⍟
The Old Glebe, Eggesford, Chulmleigh,
Devon, EX18 7QU
Ⓣ (01769) 580632
Also supplies wholesale: Yes
Contact: Nigel Wright
Opening Times: By appt. only.
Cat. Cost: 2 x 1st class
Credit Cards: None
Specialities: *Rhododendron* only. 200 varieties
field grown, root-balled, some potted. For
collection only. Specialist grower.
Map Ref: C, B3
OS Grid Ref: SS6171

CWSG   WEST SOMERSET GARDEN CENTRE ⊠ ⍟
Mart Road, Minehead, Somerset, TA24 5BJ
Ⓣ (01643) 703812
Ⓕ (01643) 706470
Ⓔ wsgardencentre@compuserve.com
Ⓦ www.westsomersetgardencentre.co.uk
Contact: Mrs J K Shoulders
Opening Times: 0800-1700 Mon-Sat, 1000-
1600 Sun.
Min Mail Order UK: Nmc
Cat. Cost: Not available
Credit Cards: Access Visa Switch Solo
Specialities: Wide general range. *Ceanothus.*
Map Ref: C, B4

CWVF   WHITE VEIL FUCHSIAS ⊠ ⍟
Verwood Road, Three Legged Cross,
Wimborne, Dorset, BH21 6RP
Ⓣ (01202) 813998
Contact: A. C. Holloway
Opening Times: 0900-1300 & 1400-1700
Mon-Fri Jan-Dec, & Sat Jan-Aug. 0900-1300
Sun Jan-Jul, closed Sun Aug, closed Sat &
Sun Sep-Dec.
Min Mail Order UK: 8 plants
Cat. Cost: 3 x 1st class
Credit Cards: None
Specialities: Fuchsias.

E

EASTERN

EAmu   AMULREE EXOTICS ⊠ ♠ ⑤
(Office) Katonia Avenue, Maylandsea,
Essex, CM3 6AD
Ⓣ (01245) 425255
Ⓕ (01245) 425255
Ⓔ SDG@exotica.fsbusiness.co.uk
Ⓦ www.turn-it-tropical.co.uk
Also supplies wholesale: Yes
Contact: S Gridley
Opening Times: 0930-1730 7 days spring-
autumn, 1000-1630 7 days autumn-spring.
Min Mail Order UK: Nmc
Cat. Cost: 1 x 2nd class
Credit Cards: Visa MasterCard Electron Solo
Switch
Specialities: Hardy & half-hardy plants for
home, garden & conservatory. Palms,
bamboos, bananas, tree ferns, cannas, gingers
& much more. Note: nursery is at Tropical
Wings, Wickford Road, South Woodham
Ferrers.
Map Ref: E, D2

EAsh   ASHPOND PLANTS
Ashpond House, Oxborough Road, Stoke
Ferry, Norfolk, PE33 9TA
Ⓣ (01366) 500447
Contact: Claire Smith
Opening Times: 1200-1700 Fri & Sat
1st Apr-30th Sep (incl.)
Cat. Cost: None issued.
Credit Cards: None
Specialities: Cottage garden & unusual hardy
perennials. Some plants available in ltd.
quantities. Garden open.
Map Ref: E, B1
OS Grid Ref: TF708001

EBak   B & H M BAKER
Bourne Brook Nurseries, Greenstead Green,
Halstead, Essex, CO9 1RJ
Ⓣ (01787) 476369/472900
Also supplies wholesale: Yes
Contact: B, HM and C Baker
Opening Times: 0800-1630 Mon-Fri, 0900-
1200 & 1400-1630 Sat & Sun.
Cat. Cost: 2 x 1st class + 33p
Credit Cards: MasterCard Delta Visa Switch
Specialities: *Fuchsia* & conservatory plants.
Map Ref: E, C2

EBee   BEECHES NURSERY ⊠ ♠ ⑤
Village Centre, Ashdon, Saffron Walden,
Essex, CB10 2HB
Ⓣ (01799) 584362
Ⓕ (01799) 584421

Ⓔ sales@beechesnursery.co.uk
Ⓦ www.beechesnursery.co.uk
Contact: Alan Bidwell/Kevin Marsh
Opening Times: 0830-1700 Mon-Sat, 1000-
1700 Sun & B/hols.
Min Mail Order UK: £10.00*
Min Mail Order EU: £20.00
Cat. Cost: 6 x 2nd class herbaceous list
Credit Cards: Visa Access MasterCard
EuroCard Switch
Specialities: Herbaceous specialists &
extensive range of other garden plants. *Note:
mail order generally from Oct-Feb, Mar-Sep
where conditions permit. Trees NOT available
by mail order.
Map Ref: E, C2

**EBla   BLACKSMITHS COTTAGE
NURSERY ⊠ ♠ €**
Langmere, Green Road,
Langmere, Diss, Norfolk,
IP21 4QA
Ⓣ (01379) 740982, nursery (01379) 741917
Ⓕ (01379) 741917
Ⓔ Blackcottnursery@aol.com
Also supplies wholesale: Yes
Contact: Ben or Jill Potterton
Opening Times: 1000-1700 Fri-Sun Mar-Oct
& B/hols, or by appt.
Min Mail Order UK: Nmc
Min Mail Order EU: Nmc
Cat. Cost: 3 x 1st class
Credit Cards: None
Specialities: Hardy *Geranium, Digitalis,
Heuchera, Crocosmia, Polygonatum, Tricyrtis* &
Siberian *Iris*. Over 2000 species grown. Large
selection of shade plants.
Map Ref: E, C3

EBls   PETER BEALES ROSES ⊠ ▣
London Road,
Attleborough, Norfolk,
NR17 1AY
Ⓣ (01953) 454707
Ⓕ (01953) 456845
Ⓔ sales@classicroses.co.uk
Ⓦ www.classicroses.co.uk
Contact: Simon White
Opening Times: 0900-1700 Mon-Sat, 1000-
1600 Sun & B/hols.
Min Mail Order UK: Nmc
Min Mail Order EU: Nmc
Cat. Cost: Free
Credit Cards: Visa MasterCard Access Switch
Solo Delta JCB
Specialities: Old fashioned roses & classic
roses. Nat. Coll. of Species Roses.
Map Ref: E, C3

E

EBlw **BLACKWATER PLANTS** ☒ ♠ ⬚
Old Mill House Nursery, Guithavan Valley,
Witham, Essex, CM8 1HF
Ⓜ 07931 311108
Ⓔ blackwaterplants@ukonline.co.uk
Contact: Kirsty Bishop & Fiona Mildren
Opening Times: 1000-1700 7 days, within
larger nursery. Please ring for specific enquiries
before visiting, because of relocation to this
new site in Spring 2003.
Min Mail Order UK: £10.00
Cat. Cost: 2 x 1st class
Credit Cards: None
Specialities: Wide range of plants, many for
shade and moist soils, incl. grasses, bamboos,
ferns, palms & perennials. Peat free &
organic. Nat. Coll. of *Astrantia*.
Map Ref: E, D2

EBre **BLOOMS OF BRESSINGHAM** ☒ ⬚ ◆
Bressingham, Diss, Norfolk, IP22 2AB
Ⓣ (01379) 688585 orderline 0845 601 4019
Ⓕ (01379) 688678
Ⓔ sales@blooms-uk.com
Ⓦ www.blooms-online.co.uk
Contact: Anne Etheridge
Opening Times: 0900-1700 1st Nov-31st
Mar, 0900-1800 1st Apr-31st Oct, 7 days.
Closed Xmas, Boxing Day & Easter Sun.
Min Mail Order UK: £15.00
Cat. Cost: None issued, free mailing list sent
seasonally
Credit Cards: Visa Delta Switch MasterCard
Specialities: Wide general range. Many own
varieties. Focus on hardy ornamental plants &
grasses. Perennials. Rare perennials available in
small quantities under "Heritage Range".
Map Ref: E, C3

EBrk **BROOKSIDE NURSERY** ☒ ☒ ♠ € ⬚
Little Acre, Boston Road, New York,
Lincolnshire, LN4 4YP
Ⓣ (01526) 342156
Ⓕ (01526) 344654
Ⓔ alan.butler9@btopenworld.com
Ⓦ www.brookside-nursery.com
Also supplies wholesale: Yes
Contact: A J Butler
Opening Times: 1000-1700 Thu-Sun &
B/hol Mons. Please phone first.
Min Mail Order UK: Nmc
Min Mail Order EU: Nmc
Cat. Cost: 1 x 1st class
Credit Cards: Visa MasterCard Switch
Specialities: Cacti & succulent plants. Nat.
Coll. of *Sansevieria*.
Map Ref: E, B1

EBur **JENNY BURGESS** ☒ ☒ € ⬚
Alpine Nursery, Sisland,
Norwich, Norfolk, NR14 6EF
Ⓣ (01508) 520724
Contact: Jenny Burgess
Opening Times: Any time by appt.
Min Mail Order UK: £5.00 + p&p
Min Mail Order EU: £10.00 + p&p
Cat. Cost: 3 x 1st class
Credit Cards: None
Specialities: Alpines, *Sisyrinchium* &
Campanula. Nat. Coll. of *Sisyrinchium*.
Note: *Sisyrinchium* only by mail
order.
Map Ref: E, B3

ECGN **THE CONTENTED GARDENER
NURSERY** ☒ ♠
The Garden House,
42 Wragby Road, Bardney,
Lincolnshire, LN3 5XL
Ⓣ (01526) 397307
Ⓕ (01526) 397280
Ⓔ maryleeheykoop@aol.com
Ⓦ www.leeheykoop.co.uk
Contact: Lee Heykoop
Opening Times: Please phone to arrange a
visit.
Min Mail Order UK: £25.00 + £12.00 p&p
Cat. Cost: A4 Sae + 4 x 1st class
Credit Cards: None
Specialities: Perennials & grasses for
naturalistic planting in dry and damp and
woodland edge.
Map Ref: E, B1
OS Grid Ref: TF123698

ECGP **CAMBRIDGE GARDEN PLANTS** ♠ ⬚
The Lodge, Clayhithe Road, Horningsea,
Cambridgeshire, CB5 9JD
Ⓣ (01223) 861370
Contact: Mrs Nancy Buchdahl
Opening Times: 1100-1730 Thu-Sun
mid Mar-31st Oct.
Other times by appt.
Cat. Cost: 4 x 1st class
Credit Cards: None
Specialities: Hardy perennials incl. wide
range of *Geranium, Allium, Euphorbia,
Penstemon, Digitalis*. Some shrubs, roses &
Clematis.
Map Ref: E, C2
OS Grid Ref: TL497637

KEY		
☒ Mail order to UK or EU	♠ Delivers to shows	
☒ Exports beyond EU	€ Euro accepted	
⬚ Accessible by wheelchair	◆ See Display advertisement	

E

ECha   THE BETH CHATTO GARDENS LTD ✉ ♿
Elmstead Market, Colchester, Essex, CO7 7DB
Ⓣ (01206) 822007
Ⓕ (01206) 825933
Ⓔ info@bethchatto.fsnet.co.uk
Ⓦ www.bethchatto.co.uk
Contact: Beth Chatto
Opening Times: 0900-1700 Mon-Sat 1st
Mar-31st Oct. 0900-1600 Mon-Fri 1st Nov-
1st Mar. Closed Sun.
Min Mail Order UK: £20.00
Min Mail Order EU: Ask for details
Cat. Cost: £3.00 incl. p&p
Credit Cards: Visa Switch MasterCard
Specialities: Predominantly herbaceous. Many
unusual for special situations.
Map Ref: E, D3
OS Grid Ref: TM069238

ECho   CHOICE LANDSCAPES ✉ ♿ ♿ € ♿
Priory Farm, 101 Salts Road, West Walton,
Wisbech, Cambridgeshire, PE14 7EF
Ⓣ (01945) 585051
Ⓕ (01945) 580053
Ⓔ info@choicelandscapes.org
Ⓦ www.choicelandscapes.org
Contact: Michael Agg & Jillian Agg
Opening Times: 1000-1700 Tue-Sat 5th Mar-
31st Oct 2003 & 4th Feb-1st Nov 2004. Not
open on show dates, please phone. Other
times by appt.
Min Mail Order UK: Nmc
Min Mail Order EU: £10.00 + p&p
Cat. Cost: 6 x 1st class or 6 IRC
Credit Cards: Visa MasterCard Switch Solo
Specialities: Dwarf conifers, alpines, acers,
rhododendrons, hostas, bulbs, pines & lilies.
Map Ref: E, B1

EChP   CHOICE PLANTS ✉ ♿ € ♦
83 Halton Road, Spilsby,
Lincolnshire, PE23 5LD
Ⓣ (01790) 752361
Ⓕ (01790) 752524
Ⓔ jgunson@spilsby94.fsnet.co.uk
Ⓦ www.choiceplants.net
Contact: Joan Gunson
Opening Times: 1000-1700 Wed-Sun &
B/hol Mon Mar-Oct.
Min Mail Order UK: £20.00 + p&p*
Cat. Cost: 2 x 1st class
Credit Cards: None
Specialities: Hardy *Geranium, Crocosmia,
Hemerocallis, Iris* & a good selection of
unusual hardy perennials.
*Note: mail order Feb-May & Sep-Nov
only.
Map Ref: E, B1

ECml   CAMDOL NURSERIES ✉ ♿
c/o G W Topham & Son,
North East Farm, A428 Cambridge Road,
Eltisley, St Neots, Cambridgeshire, PE19 6TR
Ⓣ (01954) 719283
Ⓕ (01954) 718962
Ⓔ camilla@gwtopham.co.uk
Ⓦ www.camdolnurseries.co.uk
Also supplies wholesale: Yes
Contact: Camilla Prothero/William Topham
Opening Times: 0800-1600 Mon-Fri, office
opening hours.
Cat. Cost: 3 x 1st class
Credit Cards: all major credit/debit cards
Specialities: Trees, shrubs, aquatic plants.
Map Ref: E, C2
OS Grid Ref: TL285608

ECnt   CANTS OF COLCHESTER ✉ ♿
Nayland Road, Mile End, Colchester,
Essex, CO4 5EB
Ⓣ (01206) 844008
Ⓕ (01206) 855371
Ⓔ finder@cantsroses.co.uk
Ⓦ www.cantsroses.co.uk
Contact: Angela Pawsey
Opening Times: 0900-1300, 1400-1630
Mon-Fri. Sat varied, please phone first. Sun
closed.
Min Mail Order UK: Nmc*
Min Mail Order EU: Nmc
Cat. Cost: Free
Credit Cards: Visa MasterCard Delta Solo
Switch
Specialities: Roses. Unstaffed rose field can be
viewed dawn-dusk every day from end Jun-end
Sep. *Note: mail order end Oct-end Mar only.
Map Ref: E, C3

ECoo   PATRICIA COOPER ♿
Magpies Green Lane, Mundford,
Norfolk, IP26 5HS
Ⓣ (01842) 878496
Ⓔ magpiesnursery@handbag.com
Contact: Patricia Cooper
Opening Times: 0900-1700 Tue-Fri, 1000-
1700 Sat & Sun. Closed Mon.
Cat. Cost: Free
Credit Cards: None
Specialities: Unusual hardy perennials, grasses
& foliage plants.
Map Ref: E, C2

ECot   THE COTTAGE GARDEN ♿
Langham Road, Boxted, Colchester,
Essex, CO4 5HU
Ⓣ (01206) 272269
Ⓔ enquiries@thecottage-garden.co.uk

Ⓦ www.thecottage-garden.co.uk
Contact: Alison Smith
Opening Times: 0800-1700 7 days
spring & summer. 0800-1700 Thu-Mon
Sep-Feb.
Cat. Cost: Free leaflet
Credit Cards: Visa Access Connect Switch
Delta
Specialities: 400 varieties of shrubs, 500
varieties of herbaceous. Huge range of trees,
grasses, alpines, herbs, hedging, all home
grown. Garden antiques.
Map Ref: E, C3
OS Grid Ref: TM003299

ECou   COUNTY PARK NURSERY
Essex Gardens, Hornchurch, Essex,
RM11 3BU
Ⓣ (01708) 445205
Ⓦ www.countyparknursery.co.uk
Contact: G Hutchins
Opening Times: 0900-dusk Mon-Sat excl.
Wed, 1000-1700 Sun Mar-Oct. Nov-Feb by
appt. only.
Cat. Cost: 3 x 1st class
Credit Cards: None
Specialities: Alpines & rare and unusual
plants from New Zealand, Tasmania &
Falklands. Nat. Coll. of *Coprosma.* Many
plants in small quantities only.
Map Ref: E, D2

ECre   CREAKE PLANT CENTRE Ⓖ
Nursery View, Leicester Road, South Creake,
Fakenham, Norfolk, NR21 9PW
Ⓣ (01328) 823018
Contact: Mr T Harrison
Opening Times: 1000-1300 & 1400-1730 7
days excl. Xmas.
Cat. Cost: None issued
Credit Cards: None
Specialities: Unusual shrubs, herbaceous,
conservatory plants. Huge selection of hardy
Geranium.
Map Ref: E, B1

ECri   CRIN GARDENS ⊠
79 Partons Road, Kings Heath,
Birmingham, B14 6TD
Ⓣ 0121 443 3815
Ⓕ 0121 443 3815
Contact: M Milinkovic
Opening Times: Not open.
Min Mail Order UK: Nmc
Cat. Cost: 2 x 1st class
Credit Cards: None
Specialities: Lilies. Limited stock available on
first come, first served basis.

ECrN   CROWN NURSERY ⊠ Ⓖ
High Street, Ufford, Woodbridge,
Suffolk, IP13 6EL
Ⓣ (01394) 460755
Ⓕ (01394) 460142
Ⓔ enquiries@crown-nursery.co.uk
Ⓦ www.crown-nursery.co.uk
Also supplies wholesale: Yes
Contact: Jill Proctor
Opening Times: 0900-1700 (or dusk if
sooner) Mon-Sat.
Min Mail Order UK: Nmc
Cat. Cost: 2 x 1st class
Credit Cards: Visa Delta MasterCard
EuroCard JCB Switch
Specialities: Mature & semi-mature native,
ornamental & fruit trees.
Map Ref: E, C3
OS Grid Ref: TM292528

ECtt   COTTAGE NURSERIES ⊠ Ⓖ
Thoresthorpe, Alford, Lincolnshire,
LN13 0HX
Ⓣ (01507) 466968
Ⓕ (01507) 463409
Ⓔ bill@cottagenurseries.net
Ⓦ www.cottagenurseries.net
Also supplies wholesale: Yes
Contact: W H Denbigh
Opening Times: 0900-1700 7 days 1st Mar-
31st Oct, 1000-1600 Thu-Sun Nov-Feb.
Min Mail Order UK: Nmc
Cat. Cost: 3 x 1st class
Credit Cards: None
Specialities: Wide general range.
Map Ref: E, A2
OS Grid Ref: TF423716

EDAr   D'ARCY & EVEREST ⊠ ń € Ⓖ
(Office) PO Box 78, St Ives, Huntingdon,
Cambridgeshire, PE27 4UQ
Ⓣ (01480) 497672
Ⓜ 07715 374440/1
Ⓕ (01480) 466042
Ⓔ richard@darcyeverest.co.uk
Ⓦ www.darcyeverest.co,uk
Also supplies wholesale: Yes
Contact: Angela Whiting, Richard Oliver
Opening Times: By appt. only.
Min Mail Order UK: £10.00 + p&p
Min Mail Order EU: £50.00 + p&p
Cat. Cost: 6 x 1st class
Credit Cards: None

E

Specialities: Alpines, herbs & selected perennials. Note: nursery is at Pidley Sheep Lane (B1040), Somersham, Huntingdon.
Map Ref: E, C2
OS Grid Ref: 533276

EDif   DIFFERENT PLANTS ṅ
The Mellis Stud, Gate Farm, Cranley Green, Eye, Suffolk, IP23 7NX
Ⓣ (01379) 870291
Contact: Fleur Waters
Opening Times: Sat-Thu by appt. only, closed Fri. Plant stall Diss market Fri May-Sep.
Cat. Cost: 4 x 1st class
Credit Cards: None
Specialities: *Mimulus aurantiacus* & hybrids, *Arctotis* named & selected seed strains, half-hardy bulbous/cormous perennials incl. *Dietes, Aristea, Cypella, Tigridia* & *Anomatheca laxa*. Stocks of bulbs may be limited in numbers.
Map Ref: E, C3

EDsa   DARASINA NURSERY 🅐
Ingatestone Hall, Hall Lane, Ingatestone, Essex, CM4 9NR
Ⓣ (01277) 353235
Also supplies wholesale: Yes
Contact: Stephen Nelson
Opening Times: 1130-1730 Sat, Sun & B/hol, Easter Sat-end Sep. Other times by appt.
Cat. Cost: Free list
Credit Cards: None
Specialities: Courtyard style & container planting. Hardy & half-hardy shrubs incl. figs, *Pittosporum, Melianthus*. Many uncommon perennials, ferns, herbs & veg. plants.
Map Ref: E, D2
OS Grid Ref: TQ653987

EFam   FAMECHECK SPECIAL PLANTS ✉
Hilltrees, Wandlebury Hill (A1307), Cambridge, Cambridgeshire, CB2 4AD
Ⓣ (01223) 243734 long ring or after dark
Contact: Miss F Cook N.D.H.
Opening Times: 1000-1700 except Tue, Wed & Sat, all year unless frost. Other times by appt.
Min Mail Order UK: £5.00 + p&p
Cat. Cost: 2 x 1st class for list.
Credit Cards: None
Specialities: Daffodils, long-lasting & weatherproof cut-flower varieties. Bearded *Iris* & orange violets. Some only available in small quantities. About 1000 modern varieties, mostly imported. NCH status applied for daffodils & *Iris*.
Map Ref: E, C2

EFer   THE FERN NURSERY ✉ 🅐
Grimsby Road, Binbrook, Lincolnshire, LN8 6DH
Ⓣ (01472) 398092
Ⓔ richard@timm984fsnet.co.uk
Ⓦ www.fernnursery.co.uk
Also supplies wholesale: Yes
Contact: R N Timm
Opening Times: 0900-1700 Sat & Sun Apr-Oct or by appt.
Min Mail Order UK: Nmc*
Min Mail Order EU: Nmc
Cat. Cost: 2 x 1st class
Credit Cards: None
Specialities: Ferns & hardy perennials. *Note: only plants listed in the mail order part of the catalogue will be sent mail order.
Map Ref: E, A1
OS Grid Ref: TF212942

EFEx   FLORA EXOTICA ✉ 🗃 €
Pasadena, South-Green, Fingringhoe, Colchester, Essex, CO5 7DR
Ⓣ (01206) 729414
Contact: J Beddoes
Opening Times: Not open, mail order only.
Min Mail Order UK: Nmc
Min Mail Order EU: Nmc
Cat. Cost: 4 x 1st class
Credit Cards: None
Specialities: Exotic flora incl. orchids.

EFou   FOUR SEASONS ✉ €
Forncett St Mary, Norwich, Norfolk, NR16 1JT
Ⓣ (01508) 488344
Ⓕ (01508) 488478
Ⓔ mail@fsperennials.co.uk
Ⓦ www.fsperennials.co.uk
Contact: J P Metcalf & R W Ball
Opening Times: Not open, mail order only.
Min Mail Order UK: £15.00 + p&p
Cat. Cost: Free
Credit Cards: Visa MasterCard Switch
Specialities: Herbaceous perennials. *Anemone, Aster, Campanula, Chrysanthemum, Digitalis, Erigeron, Geranium, Helenium, Iris, Salvia* & grasses.

EFtx   FERNATIX ✉
Ivy Cottage, Ixworth Road, Honington, Suffolk, IP31 1QY
Ⓣ (01359) 269373
Ⓔ fernatix@supanet.com
Contact: Steven Fletcher & Kerry Robinson
Opening Times: By appt. only.
Min Mail Order UK: £15.00
Cat. Cost: 2 x 1st class

E

Credit Cards: None
Specialities: Ferns, hardy & greenhouse species & cultivars. Some available in ltd. numbers only.
Map Ref: E, C2

EFul FULBROOKE NURSERY ⊠
Home Farm, Westley Waterless, Newmarket, Suffolk, CB8 0RG
Ⓣ (01638) 507124
Ⓕ (01638) 507124
Ⓔ fulbrook@clara.net
Ⓦ www.fulbrooke.co.uk
Contact: Paul Lazard
Opening Times: By appt. most times incl. w/ends.
Min Mail Order UK: £5.50 + p&p
Min Mail Order EU: £6.00 + p&p
Cat. Cost: 3 x 1st class
Credit Cards: None
Specialities: Bamboos & grasses.
Map Ref: E, C2

EFWa FOUR WAYS GARDEN & NURSERY ⓖ
Duffins Farm, Cross Roads, Lotts Bridge, Three Holes, Wisbech, Cambridgeshire, PE14 9JG
Ⓣ (01354) 638315
Ⓔ vsteele@duffinsfarm.free-online.co.uk
Ⓦ www. duffins.free-online.co.uk
Contact: Verity Steele, Barry Weekes
Opening Times: 1000-1600 1st & 3rd Sat-Sun, Mon-Fri by appt & invitation.
Cat. Cost: 1 x 1st class
Credit Cards: None
Specialities: Hardy perennials, native plants, grasses, oenotheras.
Map Ref: E, B1
OS Grid Ref: TL512986

EGFP GRANGE FARM PLANTS ⊠ ⓖ
Grange Farm, 38 Fishergate Road, Sutton St James, Spalding, Lincolnshire, PE12 0EZ
Ⓣ (01945) 440240
Ⓜ 07751 532795
Ⓕ (01945) 440355
Ⓔ ellis.family@tinyonline.co.uk
Contact: M C Ellis
Opening Times: By appt. only.
Min Mail Order UK: Nmc
Cat. Cost: 1 x 1st class
Credit Cards: None
Specialities: Rare trees & shrubs, esp. *Juglans, Fraxinus*. Some species in limited supply.
Map Ref: E, B2
OS Grid Ref: TF3818

EGle GLEN CHANTRY €
Ishams Chase, Wickham Bishops, Essex, CM8 3LG
Ⓣ (01621) 891342
Ⓕ (01621) 891342
Contact: Sue Staines & Wol Staines
Opening Times: 1000-1600 Fri & Sat from 4th Apr-27th Sep. Sae for details.
Cat. Cost: 4 x 1st class
Credit Cards: None
Specialities: A wide & increasing range of perennials, many unusual. Partial wheelchair access.
Map Ref: E, D2

EGln GLENHIRST CACTUS NURSERY ⊠ ⊠
Station Road, Swineshead, Nr Boston, Lincolnshire, PE20 3NX
Ⓣ (01205) 820314
Ⓕ (01205) 820614
Ⓔ info@cacti4u.co.uk
Ⓦ www.cacti4u.co.uk
Contact: N C & S A Bell
Opening Times: Visitors welcome, but by telephone appt. only.
Min Mail Order UK: Nmc
Min Mail Order EU: Nmc
Cat. Cost: 2 x 1st class
Credit Cards: Visa MasterCard Switch Solo Electron
Specialities: Extensive range of cacti & succulent plants & seeds, incl. Christmas cacti & orchid cacti. Hardy & half-hardy desert plants. Display gardens. Palms, *Cordyline, Phormium* & other hardy architectural plants. Note: exports seeds only.
Map Ref: E, B1
OS Grid Ref: TF245408

EGlv GLENVILLE NURSERIES ⊠ ⓖ ◆
King John Bank, Walpole St Andrew, Wisbech, Cambridgeshire, PE14 7LD
Ⓣ (01945) 780020
Ⓕ (01945) 780078
Ⓔ brtowler@btopenworld.com
Ⓦ www.glenvillenurseries.co.uk
Also supplies wholesale: Yes
Contact: B R Towler
Opening Times: 1000-1600 Mon-Fri, Sat by arrangement, closed Sun.
Min Mail Order UK: £6.00 + p&p
Min Mail Order EU: £30.00 + p&p
Cat. Cost: 2 x 2nd class

E

Credit Cards: MasterCard Switch Delta Visa
Specialities: Young flowering, ornamental &
climbing shrubs. Also conifers.
Map Ref: E, B1
OS Grid Ref: TF487188

EGol   GOLDBROOK PLANTS ⊠ 🖾
Hoxne, Eye, Suffolk, IP21 5AN
ⓣ (01379) 668770
ⓕ (01379) 668770
Contact: Sandra Bond
Opening Times: 1000-1700 or dusk if earlier,
Thu-Sun Apr-Sep, Sat & Sun Oct-Mar or by
appt. Closed during Jan, Chelsea & Hampton
Court Shows.
Min Mail Order UK: £15.00 + p&p
Min Mail Order EU: £100.00 + p&p
Cat. Cost: 4 x 1st class
Credit Cards: None
Specialities: Very large range of *Hosta* (over
900), *Hemerocallis* & bog *Iris*.
Map Ref: E, C3

**EGoo   ELISABETH GOODWIN
NURSERIES** ⊠ 🏠 🖾
Elm Tree Farm, 1 Beeches Road, West Row,
Bury St Edmunds, Suffolk, IP28 8NP
ⓣ (01638) 713050
ⓔ elisabeth.goodwin@bushinternet.com
Also supplies wholesale: Yes
Contact: Elisabeth Goodwin
Opening Times: Any time by prior
arrangement.
Min Mail Order UK: Nmc
Cat. Cost: 4 x 1st class
Credit Cards: None
Specialities: Drought tolerant plants for both
sun & shade esp. *Dianthus, Helianthemum,
Sedum, Teucrium, Vinca*, grasses, *Aquilegia,
Digitalis, Achillea, Agastache* & *Onosma*. Some
plants grown in limited quantities.
Map Ref: E, C2

EGra   GRASMERE PLANTS ⊠ 🖾
Grasmere School Road, Terrington St John,
Wisbech, Cambridgeshire, PE14 7SE
ⓣ (01945) 880514
Contact: Roger Fleming
Opening Times: 1000-1700 Fri-Wed, closed
Thu, Mar-late Oct, other times by appt.
Please phone first. Garden open.
Min Mail Order UK: £15.00 + p&p*
Cat. Cost: 2 x 2nd class
Credit Cards: None
Specialities: Hardy perennials incl. *Geranium*
& grasses, shrubs & dwarf conifers. Some
stock available in small quantities only. *Note:
mail order perennials only.

Map Ref: E, B1
OS Grid Ref: 537143

**EGrW   THE GREAT WESTERN GLADIOLUS
NURSERY** ⊠ € ◆
PO Box 147, Shipdham, Thetford,
Norfolk, IP25 7BR
ⓣ (01362) 820870
ⓕ (01362) 820870
ⓔ gladioli@aol.com
ⓦ www.greatwesternglads.co.uk
Also supplies wholesale: Yes
Contact: Frank Hartnell
Opening Times: By appt. only.
Min Mail Order UK: Nmc
Min Mail Order EU: Nmc
Cat. Cost: 4 x 1st class (2 catalogues)
Credit Cards: None
Specialities: *Gladiolus* species & hybrids, corms
& seeds. Other South African bulbous plants.

EHan   HANGING GARDENS NURSERIES LTD
Ongar Road West, A414 Writtle,
Chelmsford, Essex, CM1 3NT
ⓣ (01245) 421020
ⓕ (01245) 422293
ⓔ @hangingardens.co.uk
ⓦ www.hangingardens.co.uk
Contact: Jim Drake & Bob Teasell
Opening Times: 0900-1800 Apr-Nov, 0900-
1700 Dec-Mar, 7 days.
Cat. Cost: None issued
Credit Cards: Access American Express Delta
EuroCard MasterCard Switch Visa
Specialities: *Clematis*, David Austin roses,
basket & patio plants, excellent range of hardy
nursery stock. Note: (office) 15 Further
Meadow, Writtle, Chelmsford CM1 3LE.
Map Ref: E, D2

EHea   THE HEATHER SOCIETY ⊠ €
Denbeigh, All Saints Road, Creeting St. Mary,
Ipswich, Suffolk, IP6 8PJ
ⓣ (01449) 711220
ⓕ (01449) 711220
ⓔ heathers@zetnet.co.uk
ⓦ www.heathersociety.org.uk
Contact: David & Anne Small
Opening Times: Not open.
Min Mail Order UK: Nmc for members.
£11.50 (incl. 1 yr membership)
Min Mail Order EU: Nmc for members,
£12.50 (incl. 1 yr membership).
Cat. Cost: 1 x 1st class
Credit Cards: Visa MasterCard
Specialities: Heathers. Mail order for Heather
Society members within the EU. Apr only.

E

EHoe   HOECROFT PLANTS ⊠ ♪ € ⓖ ◆
Severals, Grange Holt Road, Wood Norton,
Dereham, Norfolk, NR20 5BL
Ⓣ (01362) 684206
Ⓕ (01362) 684206
Ⓔ hoecroft@acedial.co.uk
Ⓦ www.hoecroft.co.uk
Contact: Jane Lister
Opening Times: 1000-1600 Thu-Sun 1st
Apr-1st Oct or by appt.
Min Mail Order UK: Nmc
Min Mail Order EU: Nmc
Cat. Cost: 5 x 2nd class/£1 coin
Credit Cards: None
Specialities: 240 varieties of variegated and
300 varieties of coloured-leaved plants in all
species. 270 grasses. Note: nursery 2 miles
north of Guist on B1110.
Map Ref: E, B3
OS Grid Ref: 8289

EHof   HOFFLANDS DAFFODILS ⊠ ⓧ
Little Totham Road, Goldhanger, Maldon,
Essex, CM9 8AP
Ⓣ (01621) 788678
Ⓕ (01621) 788445
Ⓔ Hofflands@care4free.net
Contact: John Pearson
Opening Times: By appt. only. Normally mail
order only.
Min Mail Order UK: Nmc
Min Mail Order EU: Nmc
Cat. Cost: Free
Credit Cards: MasterCard Visa
Specialities: *Narcissus*. Note: only available in
small quantities.

EHol   HOLKHAM GARDENS
Holkham Park, Wells-next-the-Sea,
Norfolk, NR23 1AB
Ⓣ (01328) 711636
Ⓔ info@holkhamgardens.com
Contact: Peter Gill, Trevor Gill
Opening Times: 1000-1700 7 days Mar-Oct.
1100-dusk 7 days Nov-Feb. Closed mid Dec-
early Jan.
Cat. Cost: 3 x 1st class
Credit Cards: Access Visa Switch MasterCard
Specialities: Wide range of shrubs, herbaceous
perennials, alpines, wall plants, climbers, roses,
conservatory plants and herbs, both common
& unusual. Some plants in limited supply.
Map Ref: E, B1

EHon   HONEYSOME AQUATIC NURSERY ⊠
The Row, Sutton, Nr Ely,
Cambridgeshire, CB6 2PF
Ⓣ (01353) 778889

Also supplies wholesale: Yes
Contact: Mrs L S Bond
Opening Times: At all times by appt. only.
Min Mail Order UK: Nmc
Cat. Cost: 2 x 1st class
Credit Cards: None
Specialities: Hardy aquatic, bog & marginal.
Map Ref: E, C2

EHrv   HARVEYS GARDEN PLANTS ⊠ ♪ € ⓖ
Mulberry Cottage, Bradfield St George,
Bury St Edmunds, Suffolk, IP30 0AY
Ⓣ (01284) 386777
Ⓕ (01284) 386777 & answerphone
Ⓔ roger@harveysgardenplants.co.uk
Ⓦ www.harveysgardenplants.co.uk
www.hellebore.co.uk
Contact: Roger Harvey
Opening Times: 0930-1700 Thu & Fri,
0930-1300 Sat, 15th Jan-30th Jun & 1st Sep-
31st Oct. Other times by arrangement.
Min Mail Order UK: £15.00 + p&p
Min Mail Order EU: Please enquire
Cat. Cost: 5 x 1st class
Credit Cards: all major credit/debit cards
Specialities: *Helleborus, Anemone, Epimedium,
Euphorbia, Eryngium, Astrantia, Pulmonaria*
& other herbaceous perennials. Woodland
plants, heleniums. Nat. Coll. of *Helenium*
being set up with NCCPG.
Map Ref: E, C2

EHul   HULL FARM ⊠
Spring Valley Lane, Ardleigh, Colchester,
Essex, CO7 7SA
Ⓣ (01206) 230045
Ⓕ (01206) 230820
Also supplies wholesale: Yes
Contact: J Fryer & Sons
Opening Times: 1000-1600 7 days excl.
Xmas.
Min Mail Order UK: £30.00 + p&p
Cat. Cost: 5 x 2nd class
Credit Cards: MasterCard Visa
Specialities: Conifers, grasses.
Map Ref: E, C3
OS Grid Ref: GR043274

EHyt   HYTHE ALPINES ⊠ ♪ € ⓖ
Methwold Hythe, Thetford,
Norfolk, IP26 4QH
Ⓣ (01366) 728543
Ⓕ (01366) 728543

⊠ Mail order to UK or EU	♪ Delivers to shows
ⓧ Exports beyond EU	€ Euro accepted
ⓖ Accessible by wheelchair	◆ See Display advertisement

KEY

E

Contact: Mike Smith
Opening Times: 1000-1700 Tue & Wed
Mar-Oct.
Min Mail Order UK: Nmc
Min Mail Order EU: Nmc
Cat. Cost: 6 x 1st class, 4 x IRCs
Credit Cards: None
Specialities: Rare & unusual alpines, rock
garden plants & bulbs for enthusiasts &
exhibitors.
Map Ref: E, C2

EJWh   JILL WHITE ⊠ ♠ €
St Davids', Recreation Way, Brightlingsea,
Essex, CO7 ONJ
ⓉT (01206) 303547
Also supplies wholesale: Yes
Contact: Jill White
Opening Times: By appt. only.
Min Mail Order UK: Nmc
Cat. Cost: Sae
Credit Cards: None
Specialities: *Cyclamen* species esp. *Cyclamen
parviflorum*. Also seed. Note: small quantities
only.
Map Ref: E, D3

EKMF   KATHLEEN MUNCASTER FUCHSIAS ♠ ⅏
18 Field Lane Morton, Gainsborough,
Lincolnshire, DN21 3BY
Ⓣ (01427) 612329
Ⓔ jim@smuncaster.freeserve.co.uk
Ⓦ www.kathleenmuncasterfuchsias.co.uk
Contact: Kathleen Muncaster
Opening Times: 1000-dusk Thu-Tue. After
mid-Jun please phone to check.
Cat. Cost: 2 x 1st class
Credit Cards: None
Specialities: *Fuchsia*. Nat. Coll. of Hardy
Fuchsia (full status).
Map Ref: E, A1

ELan   LANGTHORNS PLANTERY ⅏
High Cross Lane West,
Little Canfield, Dunmow,
Essex, CM6 1TD
Ⓣ (01371) 872611
Ⓕ (01371) 872611
Contact: E Cannon, P Seymour
Opening Times: 1000-1700 or dusk (if
earlier) 7 days excl. Xmas fortnight.
Cat. Cost: £1.50
Credit Cards: Visa Access Switch MasterCard
Delta
Specialities: Wide general range with many
unusual plants.
Map Ref: E, D2
OS Grid Ref: 592204

ELau   LAUREL FARM HERBS ⊠ ⅏
Main Road, Kelsale, Saxmundham,
Suffolk, IP13 2RG
Ⓣ (01728) 668223
Ⓔ seagontheherbman@aol.com
Ⓦ www.theherbfarm.co.uk
Contact: Chris Seagon
Opening Times: 1000-1700 Wed-Mon 1st
Mar-31st Oct. 1000-1500 Wed-Fri 1st Nov-
28th Feb.
Min Mail Order UK: 6 plants + p&p
Min Mail Order EU: 12 plants
Cat. Cost: Online only.
Credit Cards: Visa MasterCard Switch Delta
Specialities: Herbs esp. rosemary, thyme,
lavender, mint, comfrey & sage. Note: mail
orders accepted by email, phone or post.
Map Ref: E, C3

EMan   MANOR NURSERY ⊠ ⅏
Thaxted Road, Wimbish, Saffron Walden,
Essex, CB10 2UT
Ⓣ (01799) 513481
Ⓕ (01799) 513481
Ⓔ flora@gardenplants.co.uk
Ⓦ www.gardenplants.co.uk
Contact: William Lyall
Opening Times: 0900-1700 summer. 0900-
1600 winter. Closed Xmas.
Min Mail Order UK: Nmc
Cat. Cost: 4 x 2nd class
Credit Cards: Visa Access Switch EuroCard
MasterCard
Specialities: Uncommon perennials, grasses,
hardy *Geranium, Sedum* & cottage garden
plants. Variegated & coloured foliage plants.
Many newly introduced cultivars.
Map Ref: E, C2
OS Grid Ref:

EMar   LESLEY MARSHALL ⊠ ⅏
Uncommon Garden Plants, Islington Lodge
Cottage, Tilney All Saints, King's Lynn,
Norfolk, PE34 4SF
Ⓣ (01553) 765103
Ⓔ lesley.marshall@amserve.net
Contact: Lesley & Peter Marshall
Opening Times: 0930-1800 Mon, Wed, Fri-
Sun Mar-Oct.
Min Mail Order UK: 6 plants*
Cat. Cost: £1 refundable. £1 coin/4 x 1st class
Credit Cards: None
Specialities: Uncommon garden plants, hardy
perennials & plants for foliage effect.
Hemerocallis. Choice seed list. Some plants
available in ltd. quantities. *Note: mail order
Feb-Apr (spring list) & Sep-Nov (autumn list).
Map Ref: E, B1

E

EMcA   S M McArd (Seeds) ✉
39 West Road, Pointon, Sleaford,
Lincolnshire, NG34 0NA
Ⓣ (01529) 240765
Ⓕ (01529) 240765
Ⓔ seeds@smmcard.com
Ⓦ www.smmcard.com
Also supplies wholesale: Yes
Contact: Susan McArd
Opening Times: Not open, mail order only.
Min Mail Order UK: Nmc
Min Mail Order EU: Nmc
Cat. Cost: 2 x 2nd class
Credit Cards: None
Specialities: Unusual & giant vegetables esp.
tree (Egyptian) onion. Seeds & plants.

EMFP   Mills' Farm Plants & Gardens ✉
Norwich Road, Mendlesham,
Suffolk, IP14 5NQ
Ⓣ (01449) 766425
Ⓕ (01449) 766425
Ⓔ sue@millsfarmplants.co.uk
Ⓦ www.millsfarmplants.co.uk
Contact: Peter & Susan Russell
Opening Times: 0900-1730 Wed-Sun
Mar-Nov & B/hol Mon.
Min Mail Order UK: Nmc*
Min Mail Order EU: Nmc
Cat. Cost: 5 x 2nd class
Credit Cards: all major credit/debit cards
Specialities: Pinks, old roses, wide general
range. *Note: mail order for pinks & roses only.
Map Ref: E, C3
OS Grid Ref: TM119650

**EMFW   Mickfield Watergarden Centre
Ltd** ✉ ✉ € ♿
Debenham Road, Mickfield, Stowmarket,
Suffolk, IP14 5LP
Ⓣ (01449) 711336
Ⓕ (01449) 711018
Ⓔ mike@mickfield.co.uk
Ⓦ www.watergardenshop.co.uk
Also supplies wholesale: Yes
Contact: Mike & Yvonne Burch
Opening Times: 0930-1700 7 days.
Min Mail Order UK: Nmc
Min Mail Order EU: £25.00 + p&p
Cat. Cost: £1.00
Credit Cards: Visa Access MasterCard Switch
Specialities: Hardy aquatics, *Nymphaea* &
moisture lovers.
Map Ref: E, C3

EMic   Mickfield Hostas ✉ 🏃 € ♿
The Poplars, Mickfield, Stowmarket,
Suffolk, IP14 5LH

Ⓣ (01449) 711576
Ⓕ (01449) 711576
Ⓔ mickfieldhostas@btconnect.com
Ⓦ www.mickfieldhostas.co.uk
Contact: Mr & Mrs R L C Milton
Opening Times: For specified dates see
catalogue or website.
Min Mail Order UK: Nmc
Min Mail Order EU: Nmc
Cat. Cost: 4 x 1st class*
Credit Cards: Visa MasterCard
Specialities: *Hosta*, over 1000 varieties (some
subject to availability) mostly from USA. New
varieties become available during the season.
*Note: catalogue cost refunded on order.
Map Ref: E, C3

EMil   Mill Race Nursery € ♿
New Road, Aldham, Colchester,
Essex, CO6 3QT
Ⓣ (01206) 242521
Ⓕ (01206) 241616
Ⓔ admin@millracenursery.co.uk
Ⓦ www.millracenursery.co.uk
Also supplies wholesale: Yes
Contact: Bill Mathews
Opening Times: 0900-1730 7 days.
Cat. Cost: Sae + 2 x 1st class
Credit Cards: Access Visa Diners Switch
Specialities: Over 400 varieties of herbaceous
& many unusual trees, shrubs & climbers.
Map Ref: E, C2
OS Grid Ref: TL918268

EMlt   Malletts Nurseries ✉ ♿
Home Farm, Dell Corner Lane,
N. Burlingham, Norwich, Norfolk,
NR13 4SX
Ⓣ (01603) 713676
Ⓔ peter@mallettsnurseries.co.uk
Ⓦ www.mallettsnurseries.co.uk
Also supplies wholesale: Yes
Contact: Peter Mallett
Min Mail Order UK: Nmc
Cat. Cost: 4 x 1st class
Credit Cards: None
Specialities: Alpines.
Map Ref: E, B3
OS Grid Ref: TG362103

EMon   Monksilver Nursery ✉ €
Oakington Road, Cottenham,
Cambridgeshire, CB4 8TW

K E Y	✉ Mail order to UK or EU	🏃 Delivers to shows
	✉ Exports beyond EU	€ Euro accepted
	♿ Accessible by wheelchair	◆ See Display advertisement

E

Ⓣ (01954) 251555
Ⓕ (01223) 502887
Ⓔ plants@monksilver.com
Ⓦ www.monksilver.com
Contact: Joe Sharman & Alan Leslie
Opening Times: 1000-1600 Fri & Sat 1 Mar-30 Jun, 20 Sep + Fri & Sat Oct 2002.
Min Mail Order UK: £15.00 + p&p
Min Mail Order EU: £30.00 + p&p
Cat. Cost: 8 x 1st class
Credit Cards: None
Specialities: Herbaceous plants, grasses, *Anthemis, Arum, Helianthus, Lamium, Nepeta, Monarda, Salvia, Vinca*, sedges & variegated plants. Many NCCPG 'Pink Sheet' plants. Ferns.
Map Ref: E, C2

EMui   KEN MUIR LTD ⊠
Honeypot Farm, Rectory Road,
Weeley Heath, Essex, CO16 9BJ
Ⓣ 0870 7479111
Ⓕ (01255) 831534
Ⓔ info@kenmuir.co.uk
Ⓦ www.kenmuir.co.uk
Also supplies wholesale: Yes
Contact: Ming Yang, Claire Higgins
Opening Times: 1000-1600.
Min Mail Order UK: Nmc
Cat. Cost: Free
Credit Cards: Visa Access Switch
Specialities: Fruit.
Map Ref: E, D3

ENGS   NORTH GREEN SNOWDROPS ⊠
North Green Only, Stoven,
Beccles, Suffolk, NR34 8DG
Contact: John Morley
Opening Times: By appt. only.
Min Mail Order UK: Details in cat.
Min Mail Order EU: Details in cat.
Cat. Cost: 6 x 1st class
Credit Cards: Visa MasterCard Switch Delta
Specialities: *Galanthus*, a comprehensive range of cultivars.

ENor   NORFOLK LAVENDER ⊠ ▣ ▣
Caley Mill, Heacham, King's Lynn,
Norfolk, PE31 7JE
Ⓣ (01485) 570384
Ⓕ (01485) 571176
Ⓔ admin@norfolk-lavender.co.uk
Ⓦ www.norfolk-lavender.co.uk
Contact: Henry Head
Opening Times: 0930-1700 7 days.
Min Mail Order UK: £15.00 + p&p
Min Mail Order EU: £15.00 + p&p
Cat. Cost: 2 x 1st class

Credit Cards: Visa Access Switch
Specialities: Nat. Coll. of *Lavandula*.
Map Ref: E, B1

ENot   NOTCUTTS NURSERIES ⊠ ▣ €
Woodbridge, Suffolk, IP12 4AF
Ⓣ (01394) 383344
Ⓕ (01394) 445440
Ⓔ sales@notcutts.co.uk
Ⓦ www.notcutts.co.uk
Also supplies wholesale: Yes
Contact: Plant Adviser
Opening Times: Garden centres 0900-1800 Mon-Sat & 1030-1630 Sun.
Min Mail Order UK: £200.00 + p&p
Min Mail Order EU: £500.00 + p&p
Cat. Cost: £5.00 + £1.25
Credit Cards: Visa Access Switch Connect
Specialities: Wide general range. Specialist list of *Syringa*. Nat. Coll. of *Hibiscus*.
Map Ref: E, C3
OS Grid Ref: TM268487

EOas   OASIS ⊠
42 Greenwood Avenue, South Benfleet,
Essex, SS7 1LD
Ⓣ (01268) 757666
Ⓔ paul@oasisdesigns.co.uk
Ⓦ www.oasisdesigns.co.uk
Contact: Paul Spracklin
Opening Times: Strictly by appt. only.
Min Mail Order UK: Nmc*
Cat. Cost: None issued, see Website.
Credit Cards: None
Specialities: Small nursery offering a range of hardy & half-hardy exotic succulent plants incl. *Agave, Aloe, Beschorneria, Dasylirion, Nolina, Yucca* & *Cacti*. Most items held in limited quantities. *Note: mail order sent by overnight courier only.
Map Ref: E, D2

EOHP   OLD HALL PLANTS ⊠ €
1 The Old Hall, Barsham, Beccles,
Suffolk, NR34 8HB
Ⓣ (01502) 717475
Ⓔ info@oldhallplants.co.uk
Ⓦ www.oldhallplants.co.uk
Contact: Janet Elliott
Opening Times: By appt. most days, please phone first.
Min Mail Order UK: Nmc
Min Mail Order EU: Nmc
Cat. Cost: 4 x 1st class
Credit Cards: None
Specialities: Herbs, over 600 varieties grown. *Mentha, Plectranthus, Streptocarpus*. Partial wheelchair access.

E

Map Ref: E, C3
OS Grid Ref: TM395904

EOMN OLD MILL NURSERY
Pearson's Mill, Barrow Mere, Barton-on-
Humber, North Lincolnshire, DN18 6DD
Ⓣ (01469) 532389
Ⓜ 07831 253214
Ⓕ (01469) 531964
Contact: Andrew Robinson
Opening Times: 0900-1700 7 days, Mar-Oct.
Closed w/ends Nov-Feb.
Cat. Cost: 1 x 1st class for list
Credit Cards: None
Specialities: Over 600 varieties of herbaceous
plants and over 200 varieties of shrubs.
Map Ref: E, A1
OS Grid Ref: TA059217

EOrc ORCHARD NURSERIES ⊠ ⋔ ⍊
Tow Lane, Foston, Grantham,
Lincolnshire, NG32 2LE
Ⓣ (01400) 281354
Ⓕ (01400) 281354
Ⓔ orchnurs@lineone.net
Contact: Margaret Rose
Opening Times: Due to illness, by appt. only
in 2003.
Min Mail Order UK: No minimum charge
Cat. Cost: 5 x 2nd class
Credit Cards: None
Specialities: Small flowered *Clematis,* unusual
herbaceous esp. *Geranium, Helleborus, Hosta,*
Salvia. Many plants in small quantities only.
Sae for seed list, *Helleborus* in spring, others in
autumn.
Map Ref: E, B1
OS Grid Ref: SK857428

EOrn ORNAMENTAL CONIFERS ◆
22 Chapel Road, Terrington St Clement,
Kings Lynn, Norfolk, PE34 4ND
Ⓣ (01553) 828874
Ⓕ (01553) 828874
Contact: Peter Rotchell
Opening Times: 0930-1700 Thu-Tue, closed
Wed. Closed 20th Dec-2nd Feb.
Credit Cards: None
Specialities: Conifers.
Map Ref: E, B1

EPar PARADISE CENTRE ⊠ ⊠ ⋔ €
Twinstead Road, Lamarsh, Bures,
Suffolk, CO8 5EX
Ⓣ (01787) 269449
Ⓕ (01787) 269449
Ⓔ hedy@paradisecentre.com
Ⓦ www.paradisecentre.com

Contact: Hedy Stapel-Valk
Opening Times: 1000-1700 Sat-Sun &
B/hols or by appt. Easter-1st Nov.
Min Mail Order UK: £7.50 + p&p
Min Mail Order EU: £25.00 + p&p
Cat. Cost: 5 x 1st class
Credit Cards: Visa Access Diners
Specialities: Unusual bulbous & tuberous plants
including shade & bog varieties. Some seeds.
Map Ref: E, C2

EPAt P & A PLANT SUPPLIES LTD ⊠
The Nursery Sutton, Norwich,
Norfolk, NR12 9RA
Ⓣ (01692) 580424
Ⓕ (01692) 583327
Ⓔ info@suttongardencentre.com
Also supplies wholesale: Yes
Contact: Stewart Wright
Opening Times: 0900-1700 Mon-Sat, 1030-
1630 Sun.
Min Mail Order UK: Nmc
Cat. Cost: 4 x 1st class
Credit Cards: all major credit/debit cards
Specialities: Aquatic & bog plants, *Geranium,*
Salvia, Nymphaea.
Map Ref: E, B3
OS Grid Ref: TG385237

EPem PEMBROKE FARM NURSERY ⋔ € ⍊
Pembroke Farm, Barway, Ely,
Cambridgeshire, CB7 5UB
Ⓣ (01353) 722903
Ⓕ (01353) 722903
Ⓔ Pemcacti@aol.com/enquiries@
cactiandsucculents.co.uk
Ⓦ www.cactiandsucculents.co.uk
Also supplies wholesale: Yes
Contact: Richard & Sheena Drane
Opening Times: Any time by prior appt.
only.
Cat. Cost: None issued
Credit Cards: None
Specialities: *Cacti* & succulents incl. *Agave,*
Aloe & *Sempervivum.*
Map Ref: E, C2

EPfP THE PLACE FOR PLANTS € ⍊
East Bergholt Place, East Bergholt,
Suffolk, CO7 6UP
Ⓣ (01206) 299224
Ⓕ (01206) 299224
Contact: Rupert & Sara Eley

E

Opening Times: 1000-1700 (or dusk if earlier) 7 days. Closed Easter Sun. Garden open Mar-Oct.
Cat. Cost: 2 x 1st class
Credit Cards: Visa Access MasterCard EuroCard Delta Switch
Specialities: Wide range of specialist & popular plants. 15 acre mature garden.
Map Ref: E, C3

EPGN   PARK GREEN NURSERIES ⊠ ☒
Wetheringsett, Stowmarket, Suffolk, IP14 5QH
ⓣ (01728) 860139
ⓕ (01728) 861277
ⓔ nurseries@parkgreen.fsnet.co.uk
ⓦ www.parkgreen.co.uk
Contact: Richard & Mary Ford
Opening Times: 1000-1600 Mon-Fri & 1000-1300 Sat, 1 Mar-20 Sep.
Min Mail Order UK: Nmc
Min Mail Order EU: Nmc
Cat. Cost: 4 x 1st class
Credit Cards: Visa MasterCard Delta Switch
Specialities: *Hosta,* ornamental grasses & herbaceous.
Map Ref: E, C3
OS Grid Ref: TM136644

EPla   P W PLANTS ⊠ ♠ ▣ ◆
Sunnyside, Heath Road, Kenninghall, Norfolk, NR16 2DS
ⓣ (01953) 888212
ⓕ (01953) 888212
ⓔ pw.plants@paston.co.uk
ⓦ www.pwplants.co.uk
Contact: Paul Whittaker
Opening Times: Every Fri & last Sat in every month, plus all Sats Apr-Sep.
Min Mail Order UK: Nmc
Min Mail Order EU: Nmc
Cat. Cost: 5 x 1st class
Credit Cards: Visa MasterCard Switch JCB Solo
Specialities: Bamboos, grasses, choice shrubs & perennials. Note: does not deliver to Chelsea Show.
Map Ref: E, C3

EPot   POTTERTON & MARTIN ⊠ ☒ ♠ € ▣
Moortown Road, Nettleton, Caistor, Lincolnshire, LN7 6HX
ⓣ (01472) 851714
ⓕ (01472) 852580
ⓔ rob@pottertons.co.uk
ⓦ www.pottertons.co.uk
Also supplies wholesale: Yes
Contact: Robert Potterton
Opening Times: 0900-1630 7 days.

Min Mail Order UK: Nmc
Min Mail Order EU: Nmc
Cat. Cost: £1.00 in stamps
Credit Cards: MasterCard Switch Visa
Specialities: Alpines, dwarf bulbs, conifers & shrubs. Hardy orchids & *Pleione*. Seed list sent out in Nov.
Map Ref: E, A1
OS Grid Ref: TA091001

EPPr   THE PLANTSMAN'S PREFERENCE ⊠ ♠ ▣
(Office) Lynwood, Hopton Road, Garboldisham, Diss, Norfolk, IP22 2QN
ⓣ (01953) 681439 (office)
ⓜ (07799) 855559 (nursery)
ⓔ plantpref@aol.com
ⓦ www.plantpref.co.uk
Contact: Jenny & Tim Fuller
Opening Times: 0930-1700 Fri, Sat & Sun Mar-Oct. Other times by appt.
Min Mail Order UK: Nmc
Min Mail Order EU: Nmc
Cat. Cost: 4 x 1st class/IRCs. Also Online.
Credit Cards: None
Specialities: Hardy *Geranium* (450), grasses & sedges (600+). Unusual & interesting perennials. Note: nursery is at Hall Farm, Church Road, South Lopham, Diss.
Map Ref: E, C3
OS Grid Ref: TM041819

EPts   POTASH NURSERY ⊠ ♠ ▣
Cow Green, Bacton, Stowmarket, Suffolk, IP14 4HJ
ⓣ (01449) 781671
ⓔ enquiries@potashnursery.co.uk
ⓦ www.potashnursery.co.uk
Contact: M W Clare
Opening Times: 1000-1700 Fri-Sun & B/hol Mons mid Feb-end Jun.
Min Mail Order UK: £12.80
Cat. Cost: 4 x 1st class
Credit Cards: Visa Delta MasterCard
Specialities: *Fuchsia*.
Map Ref: E, C3
OS Grid Ref: TM0565NE

EPyc   PENNYCROSS PLANTS
Earith Road, Colne, Huntingdon, Cambridgeshire, PE28 3NL
ⓣ (01487) 841520
ⓔ plants@pennycross99.freeserve.co.uk
Also supplies wholesale: Yes
Contact: Janet M Buist
Opening Times: 0900-dusk Thu, 1400-dusk Fri, 1st Mar-31st Oct. Other times by appt.
Cat. Cost: 4 x 2nd class
Credit Cards: None

E

Specialities: Hardy perennials. Grasses. Some plants available in ltd. quantities only.
Map Ref: E, C2
OS Grid Ref: TL378759

EPza   PLANTAZIA ⊠ n̂ 🦽
Woodford Farm, Weston Green Road, Weston Longville, Norwich, Norfolk, NR9 5LG
Ⓣ (01603) 880757
Ⓕ (01603) 880757
Ⓔ plantazia.co@virgin.net
Ⓦ Plantazia-nursery.co.uk
Contact: Mike Read
Opening Times: 1000-1700, 7 days, 1st Mar-31st Oct. 1000-1600 Sat & Sun only Nov-Dec. Closed Jan & Feb. Mail order all year round.
Min Mail Order UK: Nmc
Cat. Cost: 4 x 1st class
Credit Cards: all major credit/debit cards
Specialities: Grasses, *Gunnera, Bamboo.*
Map Ref: E, B3
OS Grid Ref: TG090153

ER&R   RHODES & ROCKLIFFE ⊠ ☒ €
2 Nursery Road, Nazeing, Essex, EN9 2JE
Ⓣ (01992) 451598 (office hours)
Ⓕ (01992) 440673
Ⓔ RRBegonias@aol.com
Contact: David Rhodes or John Rockliffe
Opening Times: By appt.
Min Mail Order UK: £2.50 + p&p*
Min Mail Order EU: £5.00 + p&p
Cat. Cost: 2 x 1st class
Credit Cards: None
Specialities: *Begonia* species & hybrids. Nat. Coll. of *Begonia.* Plants propagated to order. *Note: mail order Apr-Sep only.
Map Ref: E, D2

ERea   READS NURSERY ⊠ ☒
Hales Hall, Loddon, Norfolk, NR14 6QW
Ⓣ (01508) 548395
Ⓕ (01508) 548040
Ⓔ plants@readsnursery.co.uk
Ⓦ www.readsnursery.co.uk
Contact: Stephen Read
Opening Times: 1000-1700 (dusk if earlier) Tue-Sat, 1100-1600 Sun & B/hols Easter-end Sep & by appt.
Min Mail Order UK: £10.00 + p&p
Min Mail Order EU: £10.00 + p&p
Cat. Cost: 4 x 1st class
Credit Cards: Visa Access Diners Switch
Specialities: Conservatory plants, vines, *Citrus,* figs & unusual fruits & nuts. Wall shrubs & climbers. Scented & aromatic hardy

plants. Box & yew hedging & topiary. UK grown. Nat. Colls. of *Citrus,* figs, vines.
Map Ref: E, B3

ERob   ROBIN SAVILL CLEMATIS SPECIALIST ⊠ ☒
(Office) 2 Bury Cottages, Bury Road, Pleshey, Chelmsford, Essex, CM3 1HB
Ⓣ (01245) 237380
Ⓕ (01245) 603882
Ⓔ clematis@madasafish.com
Also supplies wholesale: Yes
Contact: Robin Savill
Opening Times: Visitors by appt. only.
Min Mail Order UK: 1 plant + p&p
Min Mail Order EU: 1 plant + p&p
Cat. Cost: £2.50 or 10 x 1st class
Credit Cards: None
Specialities: Over 800 varieties of *Clematis* incl. many unusual species & cvs from around the world. Nat. Coll. of *Clematis viticella.*
Map Ref: E, D2

ERod   THE RODINGS PLANTERY ⊠ ☒ n̂ € 🦽
Anchor Lane, Abbess Roding, Essex, CM5 0JW
Ⓣ (01279) 876421
Ⓔ andy@bamboo100.fsnet.co.uk
Contact: Jane & Andy Mogridge
Opening Times: By appt. only. Occasional open days, please phone for details.
Min Mail Order UK: £15.00 + p&p
Min Mail Order EU: £500.00 + p&p
Cat. Cost: 3 x 1st class
Credit Cards: None
Specialities: *Bamboo.* Rare & unusual trees.
Map Ref: E, D2

ERom   THE ROMANTIC GARDEN ⊠ ☒ € 🦽 ◆
Swannington, Norwich, Norfolk, NR9 5NW
Ⓣ (01603) 261488
Ⓕ (01603) 864231
Ⓔ enquiries@romantic-garden-nursery.co.uk
Ⓦ www.romantic-garden-nursery.co.uk
Also supplies wholesale: Yes
Contact: John Powles/John Carrick
Opening Times: 1000-1700 Wed Fri & Sat all year.
Min Mail Order UK: £5.00 + p&p
Min Mail Order EU: £30.00 + p&p
Cat. Cost: 4 x 1st class

KEY: ⊠ Mail order to UK or EU   n̂ Delivers to shows   ☒ Exports beyond EU   € Euro accepted   🦽 Accessible by wheelchair   ◆ See Display advertisement

E

Credit Cards: Visa Access American Express
Specialities: Half-hardy & conservatory. *Buxus* topiary, ornamental standards, large specimens.
Map Ref: E, B3

ERos ROSEHOLME NURSERY ⊠ 🗷 ⬛
Roseholme Farm, Howsham, Market Rasen, Lincolnshire, LN7 6JZ
Ⓣ (01652) 678661
Ⓕ (01472) 852450
Ⓔ Pbcenterpr@aol.com
Also supplies wholesale: Yes
Contact: P B Clayton
Opening Times: By appt. for collection of orders.
Min Mail Order UK: Nmc
Min Mail Order EU: Nmc
Cat. Cost: 2 x 2nd class
Credit Cards: None
Specialities: Underground lines - bulbs, corms, rhizomes & tubers (esp. *Crocus, Iris*).
Map Ref: E, A1

ERou ROUGHAM HALL NURSERIES ⊠ 🗷 € ◆
Ipswich Road, Rougham, Bury St Edmunds, Suffolk, IP30 9LZ
Ⓣ 0800 970 7516
Ⓕ (01359) 271149
Ⓔ hardyperennials@aol.com
Ⓦ www.roughamhallnurseries.co.uk
Also supplies wholesale: Yes
Contact: A A & K G Harbutt
Opening Times: 1000-1600 7 days, 1st Mar-31st Oct.
Min Mail Order UK: Nmc*
Min Mail Order EU: Nmc
Cat. Cost: 5 x 1st class
Credit Cards: MasterCard Visa
Specialities: Hardy perennials esp. *Aster* (*n-a, n-b* & species), *Delphinium, Hemerocallis, Iris, Kniphofia, Papaver* & *Phlox*. Nat. Colls. of *Delphinium* & gooseberry. *Note: delphiniums for collection only, no mail order.
Map Ref: E, C2

ERsn SUE ROBINSON
21 Bederic Close, Bury St Edmunds, Suffolk, IP32 7DN
Ⓣ (01284) 764310
Ⓕ (01284) 764310
Contact: Sue Robinson
Opening Times: By appt. only.
Cat. Cost: None issued
Credit Cards: None
Specialities: Variegated & foliage plants. Garden open. Lectures at clubs & societies, group bookings welcome.

ESCh SHEILA CHAPMAN CLEMATIS ⊠ 🐾 ⬛
Crowther Nurseries, Ongar Road, Abridge, Romford, Essex, RM4 1AA
Ⓣ (01708) 688090
Ⓕ (01708) 688090
Ⓦ www.sheilachapman.co.uk
Contact: Sheila Chapman
Opening Times: 0930-1700 (or dusk in winter) all year excl. Xmas week.
Min Mail Order UK: Nmc
Cat. Cost: 4 x 1st class
Credit Cards: All major credit/debit cards
Specialities: Over 600 varieties of *Clematis*.
Map Ref: E, D2
OS Grid Ref: TL548197

ESgl SEAGATE IRISES ⊠ € ⬛
A17 Long Sutton By-Pass, Long Sutton, Lincolnshire, PE12 9RX
Ⓣ (01406) 365138
Ⓕ (01406) 365447
Ⓔ Sales@irises.co.uk
Ⓦ www.irises.co.uk
Also supplies wholesale: Yes
Contact: Julian Browse or Wendy Browse
Opening Times: 1000-1800 daily May-Sep. Please phone for appt. Oct-Apr.
Min Mail Order UK: 3 plants (£15.00)
Min Mail Order EU: Nmc carriage at cost.
Cat. Cost: £2.50, no stamps pls.
Credit Cards: Visa Access MasterCard Switch
Specialities: Bearded *Iris*, over 400 varieties, modern & historic tall bearded, medians & dwarfs. Many container grown available.
Map Ref: E, B1
OS Grid Ref: TF437218

EShb SHRUBLAND PARK NURSERIES ⊠ 🐾 € ⬛ ◆
Coddenham, Ipswich, IP6 9QJ
Ⓣ (01473) 833187
Ⓜ 07890 527744
Ⓕ (01473) 832838
Ⓔ gill@shrublandparknurseries.co.uk
Ⓦ www.shrublandparknurseries.co.uk
Also supplies wholesale: Yes
Contact: Gill Stitt
Opening Times: 1000-1700 (dusk if earlier) Wed-Sun. Other times by prior appt. Please ring to check during the 2 weeks either side of Xmas & for directions before visiting.
Min Mail Order UK: £10.00
Min Mail Order EU: £10.00
Cat. Cost: 3 x 1st class
Credit Cards: all major credit/debit cards
Specialities: An increasing range of conservatory & houseplants, incl. passion

flowers, succulents & architectural. Hardy
perennials & unusual annuals. Limited stock
of some items.
Map Ref: E, C3
OS Grid Ref: TM128524

ESim   CLIVE SIMMS ⊠
Woodhurst, Essendine, Stamford,
Lincolnshire, PE9 4LQ
Ⓣ (01780) 755615
Ⓔ clive_simms@lineone.net
Ⓦ www.clivesimms.com
Contact: Clive & Kathryn Simms
Opening Times: By appt. for collection only.
Min Mail Order UK: Nmc
Cat. Cost: 2 x 1st class
Specialities: Uncommon nut trees & unusual
fruiting plants. Only available in small
quantities.

ESis   SISKIN PLANTS ⊠
30 Jackson Road, Newbourne, Woodbridge,
Suffolk, IP12 4NR
Ⓣ (01394) 448068
Ⓕ (01394) 448502
Ⓔ info@siskinplants.co.uk
Ⓦ www.siskinplants.co.uk
Contact: Tricia Newell
Opening Times: Not open. Mail order only.
Min Mail Order UK: Nmc
Min Mail Order EU: Nmc
Cat. Cost: 3 x 2nd class
Credit Cards: None
Specialities: Alpines, sempervivums, small
perennials, grasses & dwarf shrubs esp. plants
for troughs and dwarf hebes.

ESlt   SCARLETTS QUALITY PLANTS ⊠ € ⓐ
Nayland Road, West Bergholt, Colchester,
Essex, CO6 3DH
Ⓣ (01206) 242533
Ⓕ (01206) 242530
Ⓔ info@scarletts.co.uk
Ⓦ www.scarletts.org
Also supplies wholesale: Yes
Contact: Kate Backhouse
Opening Times: By appt. only.
Min Mail Order UK: Nmc
Min Mail Order EU: Nmc
Cat. Cost: Free list
Credit Cards: MasterCard EuroCard Visa
Delta
Specialities: Conservatory plants. *Citrus.*
Map Ref: E, C2

ESou   SOUTHFIELD NURSERIES ⊠ ⋔ ⓐ ◆
Bourne Road, Morton, Nr Bourne,
Lincolnshire, PE10 0RH

Ⓣ (01778) 570168
Also supplies wholesale: Yes
Contact: Mr & Mrs B Goodey
Opening Times: 1000-1215 & 1315-1600 7
days. Nov-Jan by appt. only.
Min Mail Order UK: Nmc
Min Mail Order EU: Nmc
Cat. Cost: 3 x 1st class
Credit Cards: None
Specialities: A wide range of cacti &
succulents incl. some of the rarer varieties, all
grown on our own nursery.
Map Ref: E, B1
OS Grid Ref: TF094234

ESty   STYLE ROSES ⊠ ⋔ ⓐ
10 Meridian Walk, Holbeach, Spalding,
Lincolnshire, PE12 7NR
Ⓣ (01406) 424089
Ⓜ 07932 044093/07780 860415
Ⓕ (01406) 424089
Ⓔ styleroses@aol.com
Ⓦ www.styleroses.co.uk
Also supplies wholesale: Yes
Contact: Chris Styles, Margaret Styles
Opening Times: Vary, please phone.
Min Mail Order UK: Nmc
Min Mail Order EU: Nmc
Cat. Cost: Free
Credit Cards: None
Specialities: Roses: standard & bush roses.
Note: export subject to countries' plant health
requirements, carriage & export certificates
where required charged at cost.
Map Ref: E, B1

ESul   BRIAN & PEARL SULMAN ⊠ ⋔ ⓐ
54 Kingsway, Mildenhall, Bury St Edmunds,
Suffolk, IP28 7HR
Ⓣ (01638) 712297
Ⓕ (01638) 712297
Ⓔ pearl@sulmanspelargoniums.co.uk
Ⓦ www.sulmanspelargoniums.co.uk
Contact: Pearl Sulman
Opening Times: Not open, mail order only.
Open w/end 7th/8th Jun 2003, early Jun
2004 (phone for confirmation of dates).
Min Mail Order UK: £20.00
Min Mail Order EU: £20.00
Cat. Cost: 4 x 1st class
Credit Cards: Visa MasterCard
Specialities: *Pelargonium.* Some varieties only
available in small numbers.

E

Map Ref: E, C2
OS Grid Ref: TL715747

ETho **THORNCROFT CLEMATIS NURSERY** ⊠ ⊠ ♠ € ⑤
The Lings, Reymerston, Norwich,
Norfolk, NR9 4QG
ⓉTel (01953) 850407
ⒻFax (01953) 851788
ⒺEmail sales@thorncroft.co.uk
ⓌWeb www.thorncroft.co.uk
Contact: Ruth P Gooch
Opening Times: 1000-1630 Thu-Tue, Mar-
Oct, 1000-1500 Mon-Fri, Nov-Feb.
Min Mail Order UK: Nmc
Min Mail Order EU: £16.00
Cat. Cost: 6 x 2nd class
Credit Cards: MasterCard Solo Visa Delta
Switch
Specialities: *Clematis*. Note: does not export
to USA, Canada or Australia. Accepts euros
only as cash not cheques.
Map Ref: E, B3
OS Grid Ref: TG039062

ETow **TOWN FARM NURSERY** ⊠
Street House, The Street, Metfield, Harleston,
Norfolk, IP20 0LA
ⓉTel (01379) 586189
ⒺEmail david.baker@themail.co.uk
ⓌWeb www.madaboutplants.co.uk
Contact: F D Baker
Opening Times: Feb-Oct by appt. only.
Min Mail Order UK: £5.00 + p&p
Min Mail Order EU: £20.00 + p&p
Cat. Cost: Sae
Credit Cards: None
Specialities: Unusual alpines, border
perennials. Also seed. Limited stocks available.
Map Ref: E, C3

EUJe **URBAN JUNGLE** ⊠
The Nurseries, Ringland Lane, Old Costessey,
Norwich, Norfolk, NR8 5BG
ⓉTel (01603) 744997
ⒻFax (0709) 2366869
ⒺEmail liz@urbanjungle.uk.com
ⓌWeb www.urbanjungle.uk.com
Also supplies wholesale: Yes
Contact: Liz Browne
Opening Times: 1000-1700 Tue-Sun,
closed Mon, Mar-Oct, 1000-1600 Fri-Sun,
Nov-Feb. Open B/hols except Xmas Day
& Boxing Day.
Min Mail Order UK: Nmc
Min Mail Order EU: Nmc
Cat. Cost: 2 x 1st class
Credit Cards: all major credit/debit cards

Specialities: Exotic plants, gingers, bananas
and aroids.
Map Ref: E, B3

EWes **WEST ACRE GARDENS** ⊠ ♠ ⑤
West Acre, Kings Lynn, Norfolk, PE32 1UJ
ⓉTel (01760) 755562
Contact: J J Tuite
Opening Times: 1000-1700 7 days 1st Feb-
30th Nov. Other times by appt.
Min Mail Order UK: Nmc
Cat. Cost: 4 x 1st class
Credit Cards: Visa MasterCard Delta Switch
Specialities: Unusual shrubs, herbaceous &
alpines. Large selection of *Rhodohypoxis* &
grasses. Note: mail order Oct-Mar only.
Map Ref: E, B1
OS Grid Ref: TF792182

EWll **THE WALLED GARDEN** ⑤ ♦
Park Road, Benhall, Saxmundham,
Suffolk, IP17 1JB
ⓉTel (01728) 602510
ⒻFax (01728) 602510
ⒺEmail jim@thewalledgarden.co.uk
ⓌWeb www.thewalledgarden.co.uk
Contact: Jim Mountain
Opening Times: 0930-1700 Tue-Sun Mar-
Oct, Tue-Sat Nov-Feb.
Cat. Cost: 2 x 1st class
Credit Cards: Visa MasterCard Switch
Specialities: Tender & hardy perennials & wall
shrubs.
Map Ref: E, C3
OS Grid Ref: TM371613

EWoo **WOOTTEN'S PLANTS** ⊠ ⑤
Wenhaston, Blackheath, Halesworth,
Suffolk, IP19 9HD
ⓉTel (01502) 478258
ⒻFax (01502) 478888
ⒺEmail sales@woottensplants.co.uk
ⓌWeb www.woottensplants.co.uk
Contact: M Loftus
Opening Times: 0930-1700 7 days.
Min Mail Order UK: Nmc
Min Mail Order EU: Nmc
Cat. Cost: £2.50 illus. + £1.50 p&p
Credit Cards: Access Visa American Express
Switch
Specialities: *Pelargonium, Penstemon, Salvia,
Hemerocallis, Hosta, Auricula* & *Iris*. Grasses.
Map Ref: E, C3
OS Grid Ref: TM42714375

EWsh **WESTSHORES NURSERIES** ⊠
82 West Street, Winterton,
Lincolnshire, DN15 9QF

Ⓣ (01724) 733940
Ⓕ (01724) 733940
Ⓔ westshnur@aol.com
Contact: Gail & John Summerfield
Opening Times: 0930-1800 (or dusk) Wed-
Sun & B/hols 1st Mar-mid Nov.
Min Mail Order UK: £15.00*
Cat. Cost: 2 x 1st class
Credit Cards: None
Specialities: Ornamental grasses & herbaceous
perennials. *Note: mail order grasses only.
Map Ref: E, A1

EWTr WALNUT TREE GARDEN NURSERY ✉ €
Flymoor Lane, Rocklands, Attleborough,
Norfolk, NR17 1BP
Ⓣ (01953) 488163
Ⓕ (01953) 483187
Ⓔ jimnclare@aol.com
Ⓦ www.walnut-tree-garden-nursery.co.uk
Contact: Jim Paine & Clare Billington
Opening Times: 0900-1800 Tue-Sun Feb-
Nov & B/hols.
Min Mail Order UK: £30.00
Cat. Cost: 4 x 1st class
Credit Cards: Visa MasterCard Switch Solo
Map Ref: E, B1
OS Grid Ref: TL978930

SCOTLAND

GAbr ABRIACHAN NURSERIES ✉
Loch Ness Side, Inverness,
Scotland, IV3 8LA
Ⓣ (01463) 861232
Ⓕ (01463) 861232
Ⓔ info@lochnessgarden.com
Ⓦ www.lochnessgarden.com
Contact: Mr & Mrs D Davidson
Opening Times: 0900-1900 daily (dusk if
earlier) Feb-Nov.
Min Mail Order UK: Nmc
Min Mail Order EU: Nmc
Cat. Cost: 4 x 1st class
Credit Cards: None
Specialities: Herbaceous, *Primula,
Helianthemum,* hardy *Geranium, Sempervivum
& Primula auricula.*
Map Ref: G, B2
OS Grid Ref: NH571347

GBar BARWINNOCK HERBS ✉ €
Barrhill, by Girvan, Ayrshire,
Scotland, KA26 0RB
Ⓣ (01465) 821338
Ⓕ (01465) 821338
Ⓔ herbs.scotland@barwinnock.com
Ⓦ www.barwinnock.com

Contact: Dave & Mon Holtom
Opening Times: 1000-1700 7 days 1st Apr-
31st Oct.
Min Mail Order UK: Nmc
Min Mail Order EU: Nmc
Cat. Cost: Free
Credit Cards: all major credit/debit cards
Specialities: Culinary, medicinal, fragrant-
leaved plants & wild flowers organically
grown.
Map Ref: G, D2
OS Grid Ref: NX309772

GBBs BORDER BELLES ✉ ♶ ⓖ
Old Branxton Cottages, Innerwick, Nr
Dunbar, East Lothian, Scotland, EH42 1QT
Ⓣ (01368) 840325
Ⓕ (01368) 840325
Ⓔ borderbelles@whsmithnet.co.uk
Ⓦ www.borderbelles.com
Also supplies wholesale: Yes
Contact: Gillian Moynihan & Kirstie
Wenham
Opening Times: Please phone before visiting.
Min Mail Order UK: Nmc*
Min Mail Order EU: on request
Cat. Cost: 3 x 1st class
Credit Cards: None
Specialities: *Anemone, Allium, Campanula,
Diplarrhena,* hardy geraniums, *Hosta,
Trillium, Tricyrtis,* woodland plants incl.
Actaea, Mertensia & Mitchella. *Note: mail
order Oct-Mar only.
Map Ref: G, C3

GBin BINNY PLANTS ✉ ♶ €
West Lodge, Binny Estate, Ecclesmachen
Road, Nr Broxbourn, West Lothian,
Scotland, EH52 6NL
Ⓣ (01506) 858931
Ⓕ (01506) 858155
Ⓔ binnyplants@aol.com
Ⓦ www.binnyplants.co.uk
Also supplies wholesale: Yes
Contact: Billy Carruthers
Opening Times: 1000-1700 Thu-Mon 14
Mar-31 Oct.
Min Mail Order UK: Nmc*
Min Mail Order EU: £25.00
Cat. Cost: 3 x 1st class
Credit Cards: Visa MasterCard EuroCard
Specialities: Perennials incl. *Euphorbia,
Geranium, Hosta & Iris.* Plus large selection

G

G

of grasses & ferns. *Note: Mail order
Oct-Mar only.
Map Ref: G, C3

GBon BONHARD NURSERY
Murrayshall Road, Scone,
Perth, Scotland,
PH2 7PQ
ⓣ (01738) 552791
ⓕ (01738) 552939
Contact: Mr C Hickman
Opening Times: 0900-1700, or dusk if
earlier, 7 days.
Cat. Cost: Free (fruit trees & roses)
Credit Cards: Access EuroCard MasterCard
Switch Visa
Specialities: Herbaceous, conifers & alpines.
Fruit & ornamental trees. Shrub & species
roses.
Map Ref: G, C3

GBri BRIDGE END NURSERIES ♙ 🅐
Gretna Green, Dumfries & Galloway,
Scotland, DG16 5HN
ⓣ (01461) 800612
ⓕ (01461) 800612
ⓔ enquiries@bridgendnurseries.co.uk
ⓦ www.bridgendnurseries.co.uk
Contact: R Bird
Opening Times: 0930-1700 all year. Evenings
by appt.
Cat. Cost: None issued
Credit Cards: all major credit/debit cards
Specialities: Hardy cottage garden
perennials. Many unusual & interesting
varieties.
Map Ref: G, D3

GBuc BUCKLAND PLANTS ⊠ € 🅐
Whinnieliggate, Kirkcudbright,
Scotland, DG6 4XP
ⓣ (01557) 331323
ⓕ (01557) 331323
ⓦ www.bucklandplants.co.uk
Contact: Rob or Dina Asbridge
Opening Times: 1000-1700 Thu-Sun 1st
Mar-1st Nov.
Min Mail Order UK: £15.00 + p&p
Min Mail Order EU: £50.00 + p&p
Cat. Cost: 3 x 1st class
Credit Cards: all major credit/debit cards
Specialities: A very wide range of scarce
herbaceous & woodland plants incl. *Anemone,
Cardamine, Crocosmia, Erythronium,
Helleborus, Lilium, Meconopsis, Primula,
Tricyrtis* & *Trillium*.
Map Ref: G, D2
OS Grid Ref: NX719524

GCal CALLY GARDENS ⊠ 🅐
Gatehouse of Fleet, Castle Douglas,
Scotland, DG7 2DJ
ⓕ (01557) 815029. Also information line.
ⓦ www.callygardens.co.uk
Also supplies wholesale: Yes
Contact: Michael Wickenden
Opening Times: 1000-1730 Sat-Sun, 1400-
1730 Tue-Fri. Easter Sat-last Sun in Sept.
Min Mail Order UK: £15.00 + p&p
Cat. Cost: 3 x 1st class
Credit Cards: None
Specialities: Unusual perennials. *Agapanthus,
Crocosmia, Eryngium, Euphorbia,* hardy
Geranium & grasses. Some rare shrubs,
climbers & conservatory plants.
Map Ref: G, D2

GCed CEDAR COTTAGE PLANTS ⊠
Aberfoyle Road, Balfron Station, Glasgow,
Scotland, G63 0SQ
ⓣ (01360) 440701
ⓕ (01360) 440933
ⓔ rkpgreen@aol.com
Contact: Richard Green
Opening Times: By appt. only. Please phone.
Min Mail Order UK: Nmc
Cat. Cost: 3 x 1st class
Credit Cards: None
Specialities: Herbaceous perennials.
Map Ref: G, C2
OS Grid Ref: NS532918

GCoc JAMES COCKER & SONS ⊠ € 🅐
Whitemyres, Lang Stracht, Aberdeen,
Scotland, AB15 6XH
ⓣ (01224) 313261
ⓕ (01224) 312531
ⓔ sales@roses.uk.com
ⓦ www.roses.uk.com
Also supplies wholesale: Yes
Contact: Alec Cocker
Opening Times: 0900-1730 7 days.
Min Mail Order UK: Nmc
Min Mail Order EU: £4.55 + p&p
Cat. Cost: Free
Credit Cards: Visa MasterCard Delta Switch
Specialities: Roses.
Map Ref: G, B3

GCrs CHRISTIE'S NURSERY ⊠ 🅜 ♙ € 🅐 ◆
Downfield, Westmuir, Kirriemuir, Angus,
Scotland, DD8 5LP
ⓣ (01575) 572977
ⓕ (01575) 572977
ⓔ ianchristie@btconnect.com
ⓦ www.christiealpines.co.uk
Contact: Ian & Ann Christie

G

Opening Times: 1000-1700 Mon, Wed-Sat & Sun 1st Mar-31st Oct. Closed Tue & Sun.
Min Mail Order UK: 5 plants + p&p
Min Mail Order EU: On request
Cat. Cost: 4 x 1st class
Credit Cards: Access Delta EuroCard JCB MasterCard Switch Visa
Specialities: Alpines, esp. gentians, *Cassiope*, *Primula*, *Lewisia*, orchids, *Trillium* & ericaceous.
Map Ref: G, B3

GDea   **DEANSTON NURSERY** ✉ € ♿
Deanston Farm, Lochfoot, Dumfries & Galloway, Scotland, DG2 8QX
Ⓣ (01556) 690519
Ⓕ (01566) 690641
Ⓔ info@deanstonnursery.co.uk
Ⓦ www.deanstonnursery.co.uk
Contact: Susan McClelland
Opening Times: 1000-1800 (closed Mon & Tue) 1st Apr-30 Sep. 1000-1600 Sat & Sun only Mar-Oct.
Min Mail Order UK: Nmc
Min Mail Order EU: Nmc
Cat. Cost: 3 x 1st class
Credit Cards: all major credit/debit cards
Specialities: Wide and eclectic selection of unusual & interesting hardy perennials, organically grown, incl. herbs, grasses, native plants, bog plants, climbers. Also seeds.
Map Ref: G, D2
OS Grid Ref: NX860718

GEdr   **EDROM NURSERIES** ✉ 🛆 ♿
Coldingham, Eyemouth, Berwickshire, Scotland, TD14 5TZ
Ⓣ (01890) 771386
Ⓕ (01890) 71685
Ⓔ info@edromnurseries.co.uk
Ⓦ www.edromnurseries.co.uk
Contact: Mr Terry Hunt
Opening Times: 0900-1700 Mon-Sun, 1 Mar-30 Sep. Other times by appt.
Min Mail Order UK: Nmc
Min Mail Order EU: £20.00
Cat. Cost: 3 x 2nd class
Credit Cards: Visa MasterCard
Specialities: *Trillium, Arisaema, Primula, Gentiana, Meconopsis, Anemone* & other alpines.
OS Grid Ref: NT8866

GEil   **EILDON PLANTS** ✉ ♿
Lowood Nurseries, Melrose, Roxburghshire, Scotland, TD6 9BJ
Ⓣ (01896) 755530
Ⓕ (01896) 755530

Ⓔ sales@eildonplants.co.uk
Ⓦ www.eildonplants.co.uk
Also supplies wholesale: Yes
Contact: R Sinclair
Opening Times: 1000-1700 7 days Mar-Oct.
Min Mail Order UK: Nmc
Cat. Cost: 2 x 1st class
Credit Cards: None
Specialities: Outstanding collection of hardy shrubs & perennials. Old roses, tender perennials & conservatory plants.
Map Ref: G, C3

GEve   **EVELIX DAFFODILS** ✉ €
Aird Asaig, Evelix, Dornoch, Sutherland, Highland, Scotland, IV25 3NG
Ⓣ (01862) 810715
Ⓔ dugaldmacarthur@lineone.net
Contact: D C MacArthur
Opening Times: By appt. only.
Min Mail Order UK: Nmc
Min Mail Order EU: Nmc
Cat. Cost: 3 x 1st class, available end May
Credit Cards: None
Specialities: New *Narcissus* cultivars for garden display & exhibition. Many cultivars are in limited supply.
Map Ref: G, A2

GFai   **FAIRHOLM PLANTS** ✉
Fairholm, Larkhall, Lanarkshire, Scotland, ML9 2UQ
Ⓣ (01698) 881671
Ⓕ (01698) 888135
Ⓔ james_sh@btconnect.com
Contact: Mrs J M Hamilton
Opening Times: Apr-Oct by appt.
Min Mail Order UK: Nmc*
Cat. Cost: 1 x 2nd class for descriptive list.
Credit Cards: None
Specialities: *Abutilon* & unusual half hardy perennials esp. South African. Nat. Coll. of *Abutilon* cvs. *Note: mail order for young/small plants.
Map Ref: G, C2
OS Grid Ref: NS754515

GFle   **FLEURS PLANTS** ✉ €
2 Castlehill Lane, Abington Road, Symington, Biggar, Scotland, ML12 6SJ
Ⓣ (01899) 308528
Also supplies wholesale:
Contact: Jim Elliott

G

Opening Times: Please phone to arrange a visit.
Min Mail Order UK: £8.00 + p&p
Min Mail Order EU: £20.00 + p&p
Cat. Cost: Sae
Credit Cards: None
Specialities: *Primula, Meconopsis.*
Map Ref: G, C3

GFlt   Floreat Plants ⊠ ⋔ ⅖
9 Station Road, Bardowie, Glasgow,
Scotland, G62 6ET
Ⓣ (01360) 620241
Ⓜ 07960 792430, 07802 482253
Ⓕ (01360) 620241
Ⓔ floreatplants@ic24.net
Also supplies wholesale: Yes
Contact: Sue Bell, Carole Allen
Opening Times: 1000-1300 Wed, 1400-1600
Sun, Mar-Sep or by appt. at any other time.
Min Mail Order UK: Nmc
Cat. Cost: 3 x 1st class
Credit Cards: None
Specialities: Unusual range of alpines, bulbs &
herbaceous plants. Note: nursery at different
location, please phone for directions.
Map Ref: G, C2
OS Grid Ref: NS541809

GGar   Garden Cottage Nursery ⊠
Tournaig, Poolewe, Achnasheen, Highland,
Scotland, IV22 2LH
Ⓣ (01445) 781777
Ⓕ (01445) 781777
Ⓔ sales@gcnursery.co.uk
Ⓦ www.gcnursery.co.uk
Contact: Ben Rushbrooke
Opening Times: 1030-1800 Mon-Sat mid
Mar-mid Oct or by appt.
Min Mail Order UK: £10.00 + p&p
Cat. Cost: 4 x 2nd class
Credit Cards: None
Specialities: A wide range of plants esp. those
from the southern hemisphere, Asiatic
primulas & plants for coastal gardens.
Map Ref: G, A2
OS Grid Ref: NG878835

GGGa   Glendoick Gardens Ltd ⊠ ⊠
Glencarse, Perth, Scotland, PH2 7NS
Ⓣ (01738) 860205
Ⓕ (01738) 860630
Ⓔ sales@glendoick.com
Ⓦ www.glendoick.com
Also supplies wholesale: Yes
Contact: P A, E P & K N E Cox
Opening Times: 2003:1000-1600 Mon-Fri
only, 14 Apr-13 Jun. 2004: by appt. only.

1400-1700 1st & 3rd Sun in May. Garden
centre open 7 days.
Min Mail Order UK: £35.00 + p&p
Min Mail Order EU: £100.00 + p&p
Cat. Cost: £2.00 or £1.50 stamps
Credit Cards: Visa MasterCard Delta Switch
JCB
Specialities: Rhododendrons, azaleas and
ericaceous, *Primula* & *Meconopsis.* Plants from
wild seed. Many catalogue plants available at
garden centre.
Map Ref: G, C3

GGre   Greenhead Roses ⊠
Greenhead Nursery, Old Greenock Road,
Inchinnan, Renfrew, Scotland, PA4 9PH
Ⓣ (0141) 812 0121
Ⓕ (0141) 812 0121
Ⓔ greenheadnursery.aol.com
Also supplies wholesale: Yes
Contact: C N Urquhart
Opening Times: 1000-1700 7 days.
Min Mail Order UK: Nmc*
Min Mail Order EU: Nmc
Cat. Cost: Sae
Credit Cards: Visa Switch
Specialities: Roses. Wide general range, dwarf
conifers, trees, heathers, rhododendrons &
azaleas, shrubs, alpines, fruit, hardy herbaceous
& spring & summer bedding. *Note: mail
order for bush roses only, Oct-Mar.
Map Ref: G, C2

GIBF   Iain Brodie of Falsyde ⊠
(Office) Cuilalunn, Kinchurdy Road, Boat of
Garten, Invernesshire, Scotland, PH24 3BP
Ⓣ (01479) 831464
Ⓕ (01479) 831672
Ⓔ plants&seeds@falsyde.sol.co.uk
Contact: Iain Brodie of Falsyde
Opening Times: Please phone first.
Min Mail Order UK: £20.00
Min Mail Order EU: £30.00
Cat. Cost: 3 x 1st class (only available from
Oct)
Credit Cards: None
Specialities: *Betulaceae, Rosaceae* & *Ericaceae.*
Note: nursery is at Auchgourish Gardens, Boat
of Garten. Anchgourish Gardens are open
Apr-Sep.
Map Ref: G, B2

**GKev   Kevock Garden Plants &
Flowers** ⊠ ⊠ €
16 Kevock Road, Lasswade,
Midlothian, EH18 1HT
Ⓣ 0131 663 2089
Ⓜ 07811 321585

(F) 0131 663 2089
(E) kevockgarden@postmaster.co.uk
(W) www.kevockgarden.co.uk
Also supplies wholesale: Yes
Contact: Stella Rankin
Opening Times: Not open.
Min Mail Order UK: Nmc
Min Mail Order EU: Nmc
Cat. Cost: 4 x 1st class
Credit Cards: Visa MasterCard Switch
Specialities: Chinese & Himalayan plants. *Primula, Meconopsis, Iris.*

GKir   KIRKDALE NURSERY ⊠
Daviot, Nr Inverurie, Aberdeenshire,
Scotland, AB51 0JL
(T) (01467) 671264
(F) (01467) 671282
(E) kirkdalenursery@btconnect.com
(W) www.kirkdalenursery.co.uk
Contact: Geoff or Alistair
Opening Times: 1000-1700 7 days (summer),
1000-1600 7 days (winter).
Min Mail Order UK: £20.00 + p&p*
Cat. Cost: None issued
Credit Cards: Visa Access Switch
Specialities: Trees, herbaceous, grasses.
*Note: mail order strictly mid-Oct to mid-Mar, carriage at cost.
Map Ref: G, B3

GLbr   LADYBRAE FARM NURSERY ⊠ ◆
Ladybrae Farm, Ladysbridge, Banff,
Scotland, AB45 2JR
(T) (01261) 861259 (after 1800)
(E) francesbeasley@tiscali.co.uk
(W) www.ladybraefarmnursery.co.uk
Also supplies wholesale: Yes
Contact: Frances Beasley
Opening Times: 1000-1800 Mon-Sat,
1100-1600 Sun.
Min Mail Order UK: Nmc*
Cat. Cost: 2 x 1st class
Credit Cards: None
Specialities: Hardy ornamentals, esp. hardy geraniums, hebes. *Note: mail order Nov-Mar.
Map Ref: G, B3

GLil   LILLIESLEAF NURSERY ⊠ €
Garden Cottage Linthill, Melrose,
Roxburghshire, Scotland, TD6 9HU
(T) (01835) 870415
(F) (01835) 870415
(E) lleafnursery@aol.com
Also supplies wholesale: Yes
Contact: Teyl de Bordes
Opening Times: 0900-1700 Mon-Sat, 1000-1600 Sun. Dec-Feb, please phone first.

Min Mail Order UK: Nmc*
Min Mail Order EU: Nmc
Cat. Cost: 2 x 1st class
Credit Cards: Visa Access
Specialities: *Epimedium* & wide range of common & uncommon plants. Nat. Coll. of *Epimedium.* *Note: mail order of *Epimedium* only.
Map Ref: G, C3

GMac   ELIZABETH MACGREGOR ⊠ ⊠
Ellenbank, Tongland Road, Kirkcudbright,
Scotland, DG6 4UU
(T) (01557) 330620
(F) (01557) 330620
(E) elizabeth@violas.abel.co.uk
Contact: Elizabeth MacGregor
Opening Times: 1000-1700 Mon, Fri & Sat
May-Sep, or please phone.
Min Mail Order UK: 6 plants £13.20
Min Mail Order EU: £50.00 + p&p
Cat. Cost: 4 x 1st class or 5 x 2nd class
Credit Cards: Visa MasterCard
Specialities: Violets, violas & violettas, old and new varieties. *Campanula, Geranium, Penstemon, Aster, Primula, Iris* & other unusual herbaceous.
Map Ref: G, D2

GNor   SHEILA NORTHWAY AURICULAS ⊠ ⊠
Balmaclellan, Castle Douglas,
Kirkcudbrightshire, Scotland, DG7 3Qr
(T) (01644) 420661
Contact: Sheila Northway & M Northway
Opening Times: Mail order (Feb-Nov) & by appt. only.
Min Mail Order UK: £10.00 + p&p
Min Mail Order EU: £20.00+p&p, payment with order (normally 48 hr priority rate).
Cat. Cost: A4 Sae + 2 x 2nd class or 2 x IRCs.
Credit Cards: None
Specialities: *Primula allionii, P. auricula* plus a few other *Primula.*
Map Ref: G, D2

GOrn   ORNAMENTAL GRASSES ⊠
14 Meadowside of Craigmyle, Kemnay,
Inverurie, Aberdeenshire,
Scotland, AB51 5LZ
(T) (01467) 643544
Contact: John & Lois Frew
Opening Times: By appt.

G

Min Mail Order UK: Nmc
Min Mail Order EU: Nmc
Cat. Cost: 3 x 1st class
Credit Cards: None
Specialities: Ornamental grasses. Limited
stock of plants.
Map Ref: G, B3

GPoy   POYNTZFIELD HERB NURSERY ⊠ ⊠ € ⬙
Nr Balblair, Black Isle, Dingwall, Ross &
Cromarty, Highland, Scotland, IV7 8LX
Ⓣ (01381) 610352*
Ⓕ (01381) 610352
Ⓔ info@poyntzfieldherbs.co.uk
Ⓦ www.poyntzfieldherbs.co.uk
Contact: Duncan Ross
Opening Times: 1300-1700 Mon-Sat 1st
Mar-30th Sep, 1300-1700 Sun Apr-Aug.
Min Mail Order UK: £5.00 + p&p
Min Mail Order EU: £10.00 + p&p
Cat. Cost: 4 x 1st class
Credit Cards: All major credit/debit cards
Specialities: Over 400 popular, unusual &
rare herbs esp. medicinal. Also seeds. *Note:
phone between 1200-1300 & 1800-1900
only.
Map Ref: G, B2
OS Grid Ref: NH711642

GQui   QUINISH GARDEN NURSERY ⊠
Dervaig, Isle of Mull, Argyll,
Scotland, PA75 6QL
Ⓣ (01688) 400344
Ⓕ (01688) 400344
Ⓔ nick@Q-gardens.fsnet.co.uk
Ⓦ Q-gardens.org
Contact: Nicholas Reed
Opening Times: By appt. only.
Min Mail Order UK: Nmc
Min Mail Order EU: Nmc
Cat. Cost: 2 x 1st class
Credit Cards: None
Specialities: Choice garden shrubs &
conservatory plants.
Map Ref: G, C1

GSki   SKIPNESS PLANTS ⊠ ♬ ⬙
The Gardens Skipness, Nr Tarbert, Argyll,
Scotland, PA29 6XU
Ⓣ (01880) 760201
Ⓕ (01880) 760201
Ⓔ billmc@SKIPNESS.fsnet.co.uk
Also supplies wholesale: Yes
Contact: Bill & Joan McHugh
Opening Times: 0900-1800 Mon-Fri, 0900-
1600 Sat-Sun end Mar-Oct.
Min Mail Order UK: Nmc
Min Mail Order EU: Nmc

Cat. Cost: £1.00*
Credit Cards: Visa MasterCard Delta
Specialities: Unusual herbaceous perennials,
shrubs, climbers & grasses. *Note: Catalogue
cost refunded on first order.
Map Ref: G, C2

GTou   TOUGH ALPINE NURSERY ⊠ ⊠
Westhaybogs, Tough, Alford,
Aberdeenshire, Scotland, AB33 8DU
Ⓣ (01975) 562783
Ⓕ (01975) 563561
Ⓔ fred@alpines.co.uk
Ⓦ www.alpines.co.uk
Also supplies wholesale: Yes
Contact: Fred & Monika Carrie
Opening Times: 1st Mar-31st Oct. Please
check first.
Min Mail Order UK: Nmc
Min Mail Order EU: Nmc
Cat. Cost: 3 x 2nd class
Credit Cards: MasterCard Access Switch
Delta Visa
Specialities: Alpines.
Map Ref: G, B3
OS Grid Ref: 610114

GTSp   THE TREE SHOP ⊠ ⬙
Ardkinglas Estate Nurseries Ltd., Cairndow,
Argyll, Scotland, PA26 8BH
Ⓣ (01499) 600263
Ⓕ (01499) 600348
Ⓔ tree.shop@virgin.net
Ⓦ www.scottishtrees.co.uk
Contact: Glyn Toplis or Sally Hall
Opening Times: 0930-1800 Apr-Sep, 0930-
1700 Oct-Mar.
Min Mail Order UK: Nmc
Min Mail Order EU: Nmc
Cat. Cost: 2 x 1st class
Credit Cards: all major credit/debit cards
Specialities: Native species. Rare & unusual
conifers. Rhododendrons, plus an interesting
range of trees, shrubs & perennials. Many
plants available in small numbers only.
Map Ref: G, C2
OS Grid Ref: NN189127

GTwe   J TWEEDIE FRUIT TREES ⊠
Maryfield Road Nursery, Nr Terregles,
Dumfries, Scotland, DG2 9TH
Ⓣ (01387) 720880
Contact: John Tweedie
Opening Times: Please ring for times.
Collections by appt.
Min Mail Order UK: Nmc
Cat. Cost: Sae
Credit Cards: None

Specialities: Fruit trees & bushes. A wide range of old & new varieties.
Map Ref: G, D2

GUzu   UZUMARA ORCHIDS ☒ ☒ €
9 Port Henderson, Gairloch, Ross-shire, Scotland, IV21 2AS
Ⓣ (01445) 741228
Ⓕ (01445) 741228
Ⓔ i.la_croix@virgin.net
Ⓦ www.uzumaraorchids.com
Contact: Mrs I F La Croix
Opening Times: By appt only.
Min Mail Order UK: Nmc
Min Mail Order EU: Nmc
Cat. Cost: Sae
Credit Cards: None
Specialities: African & Madagascan orchids.

GWCH   WOODSIDE COTTAGE HERBS ☒
Woodside Cottage, Longriggend, Airdrie, Lanarkshire, Scotland, ML6 7RU
Ⓣ (01236) 843826
Ⓕ (01236) 842545
Ⓔ mail@herbscents.co.uk
Ⓦ herbscents.co.uk
Contact: Brenda Brown
Opening Times: By appt.only.
Min Mail Order UK: Nmc
Cat. Cost: 4 x 1st class
Credit Cards: Visa MasterCard Switch Solo
Specialities: Herbs, wild flowers & hardy plants incl. shrubs, grasses & cottage garden flowers.
Map Ref: G, C2
OS Grid Ref: NS824708

N. IRELAND & REPUBLIC

IArd   ARDCARNE GARDEN CENTRE €
Ardcarne, Boyle, Co. Roscommon, Ireland
Ⓣ 00 353 (0)79 67091
Ⓕ 00 353 (0)79 67341
Ⓔ ardcarne@indigo.ie
Ⓦ www.ardcarnegc.com
Contact: James Wickham, Mary Frances Dwyer, Kirsty Ainge
Opening Times: 0900-1800 Mon-Sat, 1400-1800 Sun & B/hols.
Credit Cards: Access Visa American Express
Specialities: Coastal plants, native & unusual trees, specimen plants & semi-mature trees. Wide general range.
Map Ref: I, B1

IBal   BALI-HAI MAIL ORDER NURSERY ☒ ☒ € ⓓ
42 Largy Road Carnlough, Ballymena, Co. Antrim, N. Ireland, BT44 0EZ
Ⓣ 028 2888 5289
Ⓕ 028 2888 5976
Ⓔ ianwscroggy@btopenworld.com
Ⓦ www.balihainursery.com
Also supplies wholesale: Yes
Contact: Mrs M E Scroggy
Opening Times: Mon-Sat by appt. only.
Min Mail Order UK: Nmc
Min Mail Order EU: Nmc
Cat. Cost: £1.50
Credit Cards: None
Specialities: *Hosta, Phormium*. Note: export beyond EU restricted to bare root perennials, no grasses.
Map Ref: I, A3

IBlr   BALLYROGAN NURSERIES ☒ ☒ ⓓ
The Grange, Ballyrogan, Newtownards, Co. Down, N. Ireland, BT23 4SD
Ⓣ (028) 9181 0451 (evenings)
Ⓔ gary.dunlop@btinternet.com
Also supplies wholesale: Yes
Contact: Gary Dunlop
Opening Times: Only open by appt.
Min Mail Order UK: £10.00 + p&p
Min Mail Order EU: £20.00 + p&p
Cat. Cost: 2 x 1st class
Credit Cards: None
Specialities: Choice herbaceous. *Agapanthus, Celmisia, Crocosmia, Euphorbia, Meconopsis, Rodgersia, Iris, Dierama* & *Phormium*. Note: limited exports beyond EU.
Map Ref: I, B3

ICar   CARNCAIRN DAFFODILS (BROUGHSHANE) ☒ ☒
Houston's Mill, 10 Buckna Road, Broughshane, Ballymena, Co. Antrim, N. Ireland, BT42 4NJ
Ⓣ (02825) 862805
Ⓕ (02825) 862700
Ⓔ broughshane@N.A.C.N..org
Also supplies wholesale: Yes
Contact: Sandy Wilson
Opening Times: Please phone in advance.
Min Mail Order UK: Nmc
Min Mail Order EU: Nmc
Cat. Cost: Free
Credit Cards: None

KEY		
☒ Mail order to UK or EU	⋔ Delivers to shows	
☒ Exports beyond EU	€ Euro accepted	
ⓓ Accessible by wheelchair	◆ See Display advertisement	

I

Specialities: Old & new *Narcissus* cultivars, mainly for show.
Map Ref: I, A3

ICro   CROCKNAFEOLA NURSERY €
Killybegs, Co. Donegal, Ireland
Ⓣ 00 353 (0)73 51018
Ⓕ 00 353 (0)73 51018
Ⓔ crocknafeola@hotmail.com
Contact: Fionn McKenna
Opening Times: Summer 0900-1800
Mon,Tues & Thurs-Sat, closed Wed,
1200-1800. Closes at dusk in winter.
Cat. Cost: None issued
Credit Cards: None
Specialities: Bedding plants, herbaceous perennials, rhododendrons, plants for containers, roses, plus shrubs & hedging for coastal areas.
Map Ref: I, D2

IDee   DEELISH GARDEN CENTRE ⊠ €
Skibbereen, Co. Cork, Ireland
Ⓣ 00 353 (0)28 21374
Ⓕ 00 353 (0)28 21374
Ⓔ deel@eircom.net
Contact: Bill & Rain Chase
Opening Times: 1000-1300 & 1400-1800
Mon-Sat, 1400-1800 Sun.
Min Mail Order UK: 100 Euros + p&p
Min Mail Order EU: 100 Euros + p&p
Cat. Cost: Sae
Credit Cards: Visa Access
Specialities: Unusual plants for the mild coastal climate of Ireland. Conservatory plants. Sole Irish agents for Chase Organic Seeds.

IDic   DICKSON NURSERIES LTD ⊠ ⊠
Milecross Road, Newtownards, Co. Down,
N. Ireland, BT23 4SS
Ⓣ (028) 9181 2206
Ⓕ (028) 9181 3366
Ⓔ mail@dickson-roses.co.uk
Ⓦ www.dickson-roses.co.uk
Also supplies wholesale: Yes
Contact: A P C Dickson OBE,
Linda Stewart
Opening Times: 0800-1230 & 1300-1700
Mon-Thu. 0800-1230 Fri. Closes at 1600
Mon-Thu Dec-Jan.
Min Mail Order UK: One plant
Min Mail Order EU: £25.00 + p&p
Cat. Cost: Free
Credit Cards: None
Specialities: Roses esp. modern Dickson varieties. Note: most varieties are available in limited quantities only.
Map Ref: I, B3

IFro   FROGSWELL NURSERY €
Cloonconlon, Straide, Foxford, Co. Mayo,
Ireland
Ⓣ 00 353 (0)94 31420
Ⓕ 00 353 (0)94 31420
Ⓔ jane@frogswell.com
Ⓦ www.frogswell.com
Contact: Jane Stanley
Opening Times: Please phone first. Garden open by appt., group bookings welcome.
Cat. Cost: 3 x 1st class
Credit Cards: None
Specialities: A small nursery growing unusual perennials & shrubs, many from seed sourced in Japan & South America, often in small quantities.
Map Ref: I, B1

IGor   GORTKELLY CASTLE NURSERY ⊠ €
Upperchurch, Thurles, Co. Tipperary, Ireland
Ⓣ 00 353 (0) 504 54441
Contact: Clare Beumer
Opening Times: Not open to the public.
Min Mail Order UK: Nmc
Min Mail Order EU: Nmc
Cat. Cost: 5 x 1st class (UK), 5 x 41c (Rep. of Ireland)
Credit Cards: None
Specialities: Choice perennials.
Map Ref: I, C2

IHMH   HUBERT MCHALE ⊠ €
Foghill, Carrowmore-Lacken, Ballina,
Co. Mayo, Ireland
Ⓣ 00 353 (0)96 34996
Ⓔ hubertmchale@eircom.net
Also supplies wholesale: Yes
Contact: Hubert McHale
Opening Times: By appt. only.
Min Mail Order UK: Nmc
Min Mail Order EU: Nmc
Cat. Cost: 2 x IRC
Credit Cards: None
Specialities: Perennial herbs, aquatics, foliage & rockery plants.
Map Ref: I, B1

ILis   LISDOONAN HERBS ⊠ € ⑤
98 Belfast Road, Saintfield, Co. Down,
N. Ireland, BT24 7HF
Ⓣ (028) 9081 3624
Ⓔ b.pilcher@pop.dial.pipex.com
Contact: Barbara Pilcher
Opening Times: Wed & Sat am. For other times, please phone to check.
Min Mail Order UK: Nmc
Min Mail Order EU: Nmc
Cat. Cost: 2 x 1st class

I

Credit Cards: None
Specialities: Aromatics, herbs, kitchen garden plants, period plants, some native species. Freshly cut herbs & salads. Some stock available in limited quanities only.
Map Ref: I, B3
OS Grid Ref: J390624

ILsc   LISCAHANE NURSERY €
Ardfert, Tralee, Co. Kerry,
Ireland
Ⓣ 00 353 (0)667 134222
Ⓕ 00 353 (0)667 134600
Contact: Dan Nolan/Bill Cooley
Opening Times: 1000-1800 Tue-Sat (summer), 1000-1700 Thu-Sat (winter). Sun please phone. Closed Mon.
Cat. Cost: None issued
Credit Cards: Visa Access Laser
Specialities: Coastal shelter plants.
Map Ref: I, D1

IMGH   M G H NURSERIES €
50 Tullyhenan Road, Banbridge, Co. Down, N. Ireland, BT32 4EY
Ⓣ (028) 4062 2795
Contact: Miss M G Heslip
Opening Times: 1000-1800 Thu, Fri & Sat & B/Hol Mons.
Cat. Cost: 3 x 1st class
Credit Cards: None
Specialities: Grafted conifers, holly, maples, box, ornamental trees & flowering shrubs.
Map Ref: I, B3

IOrc   ORCHARDSTOWN NURSERIES €
4 Miles Out, Cork Road, Waterford, Ireland
Ⓣ 00 353 (0)513 84273
Ⓕ 00 353 (0)513 84422
Ⓔ orchardstownplc@02.ie
Contact: Ron Dool
Opening Times: 0900-1800 Mon-Sat, 1400-1800 Sun.
Min Mail Order UK: Nmc*
Min Mail Order EU: Nmc
Cat. Cost: None issued
Credit Cards: Visa MasterCard
Specialities: Unusual hardy plants incl. shrubs, shrub roses, trees, climbers, *Rhododendron* species & water plants. *Note: only some plants mail order.
Map Ref: I, D2

IPot   THE POTTING SHED €
Bolinaspick, Camolin, Enniscorthy,
Co. Wexford, Ireland
Ⓣ 00 353 (0)548 3629
Ⓕ 00 353 (0)548 3540

Ⓔ sricher@iol.ie
Ⓦ www.camolinpottingshed.com
Contact: Susan Carrick
Opening Times: 1100-1800 Wed-Sat, 1300-1800 Sun, 2nd Apr-28th Sep 2003. Other times by appt.
Min Mail Order UK: Nmc
Min Mail Order EU: Nmc
Cat. Cost: 3 x 1st class
Credit Cards: MasterCard Visa
Specialities: Herbaceous & ornamental grasses.
Map Ref: I, C3

IRhd   RINGHADDY DAFFODILS €
Ringhaddy Road Killinchy, Newtownards, Co. Down, N. Ireland, BT23 6TU
Ⓣ (028) 9754 1007
Ⓕ (028) 9754 2276
Ⓔ ringdaff@nireland.com
Contact: Nial Watson
Opening Times: Not open.
Min Mail Order UK: £20.00 + p&p
Min Mail Order EU: £30.00 + p&p
Cat. Cost: £2.50 redeemable on order.
Credit Cards: None
Specialities: New daffodil varieties for exhibitors and hybridisers. Limited stock of some varieties.

IRya   RYANS NURSERIES €
Lissivigeen, Killarney, Co. Kerry, Ireland
Ⓣ 00 353 (0)64 33507
Ⓕ 00 353 (0)64 37520
Ⓔ tlryan@eircom.net
Ⓦ www.ryansnurseries.com
Contact: Mr T Ryan
Opening Times: 0900-1800 Mon-Sat 1400-1800 Sun.
Cat. Cost: None issued
Credit Cards: Visa Laser MasterCard
Specialities: *Camellia, Pieris, Acacia, Eucalyptus, Dicksonia*, azaleas & many tender and rare plants.
Map Ref: I, D1

ISea   SEAFORDE GARDENS €
Seaforde, Co. Down, N. Ireland, BT30 8PG
Ⓣ (028) 4481 1225
Ⓕ (028) 4481 1370
Ⓔ plants@seafordegardens.com
Ⓦ www.seafordegardens.com
Also supplies wholesale: Yes
Contact: P Forde

KEY: ⊠ Mail order to UK or EU ⋔ Delivers to shows
⊠ Exports beyond EU € Euro accepted
♿ Accessible by wheelchair ◆ See Display advertisement

I

Opening Times: 1000-1700 Mon-Fri all year.
1000-1700 Sat & 1300-1800 Sun mid Feb-
end Oct.
Min Mail Order UK: Nmc
Min Mail Order EU: Nmc
Cat. Cost: Free
Credit Cards: None
Specialities: Over 600 varieties of self-
propagated trees & shrubs. Nat. Coll. of
Eucryphia.
Map Ref: I, B3

ISsi   SEASIDE NURSERY ⊠ € ⌂
Claddaghduff, Co. Galway, Ireland
Ⓣ 00 353 (0)95 44687
Ⓕ 00 353 (0)95 44761
Ⓔ seaside@anu.ie
Ⓦ www.anu.ie/seaside/
Also supplies wholesale: Yes
Contact: Tom Dyck
Opening Times: 0900-1300 & 1400-1800
Mon-Sat, 1400-1800 Sun.
Min Mail Order UK: Nmc
Min Mail Order EU: Nmc
Cat. Cost: 3 Euros
Credit Cards: Visa MasterCard
Specialities: Plants & hedging suitable for
seaside locations. Rare plants originating from
Australia & New Zealand esp. *Phormium,
Astelia.*
Map Ref: I, B1

ITer   TERRA NOVA PLANTS ⊠ ⊠ €
Dromin, Kilmallock, Co. Limerick, Ireland
Ⓣ 00 353 (0)63 90744
Ⓔ terranovaplants@eircom.net
Ⓦ homepage.eircom.net/~terranovaplants
Contact: Deborah Begley
Opening Times: Garden & nursery open by
appt.
Min Mail Order UK: Nmc*
Min Mail Order EU: Nmc
Cat. Cost: 3 x IRC
Credit Cards: None
Specialities: Bulbous aroids, variegated plants,
unusual plants grown from seed. Large seedlist
in autumn. *Note: mail order dormant bulbs
& seeds only.
Map Ref: I, C2

ITim   TIMPANY NURSERIES &
GARDENS ⊠ ⊠ ⌂ ⌂
77 Magheratimpany Road, Ballynahinch, Co.
Down, N. Ireland, BT24 8PA
Ⓣ (028) 9756 2812
Ⓕ (028) 9756 2812
Ⓔ timpany@alpines.freeserve.co.uk
Ⓦ www.alpines.freeserve.co.uk

Also supplies wholesale: Yes
Contact: Susan Tindall
Opening Times: 1030-1730 Tue-Sat, Sun by
appt. Closed Mon excl. B/hols.
Min Mail Order UK: Nmc
Min Mail Order EU: £30.00 + p&p
Cat. Cost: £1.50
Credit Cards: Visa Access MasterCard
Specialities: *Celmisia, Androsace, Primula,
Saxifraga, Helichrysum, Dianthus, Meconopsis,
Primula auricula* & *Cassiope.*
Map Ref: I, B3

LONDON AREA

LAma   JACQUES AMAND ⊠ ⊠ ⌂ € ⌂
The Nurseries, 145 Clamp Hill, Stanmore,
Middlesex, HA7 3JS
Ⓣ (020) 8420 7110
Ⓕ (020) 8954 6784
Ⓔ bulbs@jacquesamand.co.uk
Also supplies wholesale: Yes
Contact: Stuart Chapman & John Amand
Opening Times: 0900-1700 Mon-Fri,
1000-1400 Sat-Sun. Limited Sun opening
in Dec & Jan.
Min Mail Order UK: Nmc
Min Mail Order EU: Nmc
Cat. Cost: 1 x 1st class
Credit Cards: Visa Access
Specialities: Rare and unusual species bulbs
esp. *Arisaema, Trillium, Fritillaria,* tulips.
Map Ref: L, B3

LAst   ASTERBY & CHALKCROFT NURSERIES
⌂ ◆
The Ridgeway, Blunham,
Bedfordshire, MK44 3PH
Ⓣ (01767) 640148
Ⓕ (01767) 640667
Ⓔ sales@asterbyplants.co.uk
Ⓦ www.asterbyplants.co.uk
Also supplies wholesale: Yes
Contact: Simon & Elizabeth Aldridge
Opening Times: 1000-1700 7 days. Closed
Xmas & Jan.
Cat. Cost: 2 x 1st class
Credit Cards: Visa MasterCard Switch
Specialities: Hardy shrubs & herbaceous.
Clematis & trees.
Map Ref: L, A3
OS Grid Ref: TL151497

LAyl   AYLETT NURSERIES LTD ⌂
North Orbital Road, London Colney,
St Albans, Hertfordshire, AL2 1DH
Ⓣ (01727) 822255
Ⓕ (01727) 823024

Ⓔ info@Aylettnurseries.co.uk
Ⓦ www.aylettnurseries.co.uk
Also supplies wholesale: Yes
Contact: Roger S Aylett
Opening Times: 0830-1730 Mon-Fri, 0830-1700 Sat, 1030-1630 Sun.
Cat. Cost: Free
Credit Cards: MasterCard Switch Visa Connect
Specialities: *Dahlia*. Note: trial grounds at Bowmans Farm nr Jct. 22 M25, at MacDonalds roundabout take B556 to Colney Heath on left hand side 500m.
Map Ref: L, B3
OS Grid Ref: TL169049

LBBr   BELL BAR NURSERY ♬ 🖫
Bulls Lane, Bell Bar, Nr Hatfield,
Hertfordshire, AL9 7BB
Ⓣ (01707) 650007
Ⓕ (01707) 650008
Ⓔ swener@globalnet.co.uk
Also supplies wholesale: Yes
Contact: S Wener
Opening Times: 0900-1630 Fri & Sat Mar-Nov. 1000-1600 Sun, Mar-Oct. Other times by appt.
Cat. Cost: 2 x 1st class
Credit Cards: None
Specialities: Hardy perennials, grasses, bulbs, ferns & bamboo. *Euphorbia, Geranium, Carex, Miscanthus, Molinia* & *Penstemon*.
Map Ref: L, B4
OS Grid Ref: TL243053

LBee   BEECHCROFT NURSERY 🖫
127 Reigate Road, Ewell, Surrey, KT17 3DE
Ⓣ (020) 8393 4265
Ⓕ (020) 8393 4265
Also supplies wholesale: Yes
Contact: C Kimber
Opening Times: 1000-1600 Mon-Sat, 1000-1400 Sun from Mar-Nov incl. Closed Sun Dec-Feb incl. & Xmas-New Year week.
Cat. Cost: None issued
Credit Cards: Visa Switch MasterCard
Specialities: Conifers & alpines.
Map Ref: L, C3

LBuc   BUCKINGHAM NURSERIES ⊠ 🗹 € 🖫 ◆
14 Tingewick Road, Buckingham, MK18 4AE
Ⓣ (01280) 822133
Ⓕ (01280) 815491
Ⓔ enquiries@buckingham-nurseries.co.uk
Ⓦ www.buckingham-nurseries.co.uk
Contact: R J & P L Brown
Opening Times: 0830-1730 (1800 in summer) Mon-Fri, 1000-1600 Sun. Late night

opening Thu 1930 (2000 in summer).
Min Mail Order UK: Nmc
Min Mail Order EU: Nmc
Cat. Cost: Free
Credit Cards: Visa MasterCard Switch
Specialities: Bare rooted and container grown hedging. Trees, shrubs, herbaceous perennials, alpines, grasses & ferns.
Map Ref: L, A2
OS Grid Ref: SP333675

LBut   BUTTERFIELDS NURSERY ⊠ 🗹
Harvest Hill, Bourne End,
Buckinghamshire, SL8 5JJ
Ⓣ (01628) 525455
Also supplies wholesale: Yes
Contact: I Butterfield
Opening Times: 0900-1300 & 1400-1700. Please phone beforehand in case we are attending shows.
Min Mail Order UK: Nmc*
Min Mail Order EU: £30.00 + p&p
Cat. Cost: 2 x 2nd class
Credit Cards: None
Specialities: Nat. Coll. of *Pleione*. *Dahlia* for collection. Scientific Award 1999. *Note: only *Pleione* by mail order.
Map Ref: L, B3

LCha   CHASE ORGANICS (GB) LTD ⊠ 🗹
Riverdene Business Park,
Molesey Road, Hersham,
Surrey, KT12 4RG
Ⓣ (01932) 253666
Ⓕ (01932) 252707
Ⓔ chaseorg@aol.com
Ⓦ www.organiccatalog.com
Contact: S Bossard
Opening Times: 0930-1630 Mon-Fri.
Min Mail Order UK: 80p p&p under £17.50*
Min Mail Order EU: No minimum charge (seed only).
Cat. Cost: Free
Credit Cards: Visa Access Switch MasterCard
Specialities: `The Organic Gardening Catalogue' offers vegetable, herb & flower seeds & garden sundries especially for organic gardeners. *Note: mail order plants only to UK, seeds to EU. Outside EU by arrangement.
Map Ref: L, C3

L

L

LChw CHADWELL SEEDS ☒ ☒
81 Parlaunt Road, Slough,
Buckinghamshire, SL3 8BE
Ⓣ (01753) 542823
Ⓕ (01753) 542823
Contact: Chris Chadwell
Min Mail Order UK: Nmc
Min Mail Order EU: Nmc
Cat. Cost: 3 x 2nd class
Credit Cards: None
Specialities: Seed collecting expedition
to the Himalayas. Separate general seed
list of Japanese, N. American & Himalayan
plants.

LCla CLAY LANE NURSERY ☒ ń
3 Clay Lane, South Nutfield, Nr Redhill,
Surrey, RH1 4EG
Ⓣ (01737) 823307
Ⓔ ken.claylane@talk21.com
Contact: K W Belton
Opening Times: 1000-1700 Tue-Sun 1st Feb-
31st Aug. Other times by appt. Please phone
before travelling.
Min Mail Order UK: £6.00*
Cat. Cost: 3 x 1st class
Credit Cards: None
Specialities: *Fuchsia*. *Note: mail order by
telephone pre-arangement only. Limited stock
of many varieties.
Map Ref: L, C4

LCon THE CONIFER GARDEN ☒ ń € ▣
Hare Lane Nursery, Little Kingshill,
Great Missenden,
Buckinghamshire, HP16 0EF
Ⓣ (01494) 862086 (0900-1800 hrs)
Ⓕ (01494) 862086
Ⓔ info@conifer garden.co.uk
Ⓦ www.conifergarden.co.uk
Contact: Mr & Mrs M P S Powell
Opening Times: Usually 1100-1600 Tue-
Wed, Fri & Sat. Please phone first.
Min Mail Order UK: Nmc*
Min Mail Order EU: Nmc
Cat. Cost: 2 x 1st class for list only
Credit Cards: None
Specialities: Conifers only, over 400 varieties
always in stock. *Note: mail order to UK only,
by overnight carrier.
Map Ref: L, B3
OS Grid Ref: SU895992

LCtg COTTAGE GARDEN NURSERY ◆
Barnet Road, Arkley, Barnet,
Hertfordshire, EN5 3JX
Ⓣ (020) 8441 8829
Ⓕ (020) 8531 3178

Ⓔ nurseryinfo@cottagegardennursery-
barnet.co.uk
Ⓦ www.cottagegardennursery-barnet.co.uk
Contact: David and Wendy Spicer
Opening Times: 0930-1700 Tue-Sat Mar-
Oct, 0930-1600 Tue-Sat Nov-Feb, 1000-1600
Sun & B/hol Mon all year.
Cat. Cost: None issued.
Credit Cards: Visa Access MasterCard Switch
Solo Delta
Specialities: General range of hardy shrubs,
trees & perennials. Architectural & exotics,
Fuchsia, seasonal bedding, patio plants.
Map Ref: L, B3
OS Grid Ref: TQ226958

LDai DAISY ROOTS ☒ ń
8 Gosselin Road, Bengeo, Hertford,
Hertfordshire, SG14 3LG
Ⓣ (01992) 582401
Ⓔ dayzroots@aol.com
Ⓦ www.plantpotty.net
Contact: Anne Godfrey
Opening Times: By appt. only & as NGS.
Min Mail Order UK: Nmc
Cat. Cost: 3 x 1st class
Credit Cards: None
Specialities: Ever-increasing range of choice &
unusual perennials, particularly *Agastache*,
Anthemis, Digitalis, Erysimum, Salvia & *Sedum*.
Map Ref: L, B4

LDea DEREK LLOYD DEAN ☒ ☒ ń
8 Lynwood Close,
South Harrow,
Middlesex, HA2 9PR
Ⓣ (020) 8864 0899
Ⓦ www.dereklloyddean.com
Contact: Derek Lloyd Dean
Opening Times: Not open, mail order only.
Min Mail Order UK: £2.50 + p&p
Min Mail Order EU: £2.50 + p&p
Cat. Cost: 2 x 1st class
Credit Cards: None
Specialities: Regal, angel, ivy & scented leaf
Pelargonium. Nat. Coll. of Angel *Pelargonium*.

LEar EARLSTONE NURSERY ☒
Earlstone Manor Farm, Burghclere,
Newbury, Berkshire, RG20 9NG
Ⓣ (01635) 278648
Ⓕ (01635) 278672
Ⓔ earlstonenursery@wistbray.com
Also supplies wholesale: Yes
Contact: B C Ginsberg or J Wallis
Opening Times: By appt.
Min Mail Order UK: £30.00 + p&p
Cat. Cost: Free

Credit Cards: None
Specialities: All varieties of *Buxus*. Topiary.
Taxus baccata & other varieties of *Taxus*.
Various varieties of *Ilex*.

LEdu   EDULIS ⊠ ⋔ €
1 Flowers Piece, Ashampstead,
Berkshire, RG8 8SG
Ⓣ (01635) 578113
Ⓕ (01635) 578113
Ⓔ edulis.2000@virgin.net
Ⓦ www.edulis.co.uk
Also supplies wholesale: Yes
Contact: Paul Barney
Opening Times: By appt. only.
Min Mail Order UK: £30.00 + p&p
Min Mail Order EU: £50.00 + p&p
Cat. Cost: 6 x 1st class
Credit Cards: None
Specialities: Unusual edibles, architectural
plants, permaculture plants.
Map Ref: L, B2

LEur   THE EUROPA NURSERY ⊠ ☒ ⋔
PO Box 17589, London, E1 4YN
Ⓣ (020) 7265 8131
Ⓕ (020) 7366 9892
Ⓔ europanurs@aol.com
Ⓦ www.europa-nursery.co.uk
Contact: Tim Branney & Adam Draper
Opening Times: Not open, mail order only.
Min Mail Order UK: Nmc
Min Mail Order EU: Nmc
Cat. Cost: 3 x 1st class
Credit Cards: None
Specialities: Extensive range of woodland &
shade-loving perennials, incl. rare & new
introductions. *Arisaema, Arum, Disporum,*
Epimedium, Hedychium, Lilium species, *Paris,*
Polygonatum, Smilacina, Tricyrtis, hardy ferns
& hardy orchids.

LFol   FOLIAGE SCENTED & HERB PLANTS
Walton Poor, Crocknorth Road, Ranmore
Common, Dorking, Surrey, RH5 6SX
Ⓣ (01483) 282273
Ⓕ (01483) 282273
Contact: Mrs Prudence Calvert
Opening Times: Open during Apr-Sep, please
phone for appt. if possible.
Cat. Cost: 3 x 2nd class
Credit Cards: None
Specialities: Herbs, aromatic & scented plants.

LGod   GODLY'S ROSES ⊠ ⓖ
Redbourn, St Albans, Hertfordshire, AL3 7PS
Ⓣ (01582) 792255
Ⓕ (01582) 794267

Also supplies wholesale: Yes
Contact: Colin Godly
Opening Times: 0900-1900 summer, 0900-
dusk winter, Mon-Fri. 0900-1800 Sat & Sun.
Min Mail Order UK: £4.50 + p&p
Cat. Cost: Free
Credit Cards: Visa Access American Express
Switch
Specialities: Roses.
Map Ref: L, B3
OS Grid Ref: TL096137

LGro   GROWING CARPETS ⊠ ⋔ € ⓖ
Christmas Tree House, High Street, Guilden
Morden, Nr Royston, Hertfordshire, SG8 0JP
Ⓣ (01763) 852705
Contact: Mrs E E Moore
Opening Times: Open by appt. only.
Min Mail Order UK: Nmc
Cat. Cost: 5 x 2nd class
Credit Cards: None
Specialities: Wide range of ground-covering
plants. Note: to avoid bad weather
conditions, mail order plants are only
dispatched in Apr, Sep-Oct on a first-come
first-served basis. Some plants available in
small numbers only.
Map Ref: L, A4
OS Grid Ref: TL278438

LHew   HEWITT-COOPER CARNIVOROUS
PLANTS ⊠ ⋔
76 Courtney Crescent, Carshalton on the
Hill, Surrey, SM5 4NB
Ⓣ (020) 8643 9307
Ⓕ (020) 8661 6583
Ⓔ nigel@nigelandpolly.fsnet.co.uk
Ⓦ www.hccarnivorousplants.co.uk
Contact: Nigel Hewitt-Cooper
Opening Times: By appt.
Min Mail Order UK: £10.00 + p&p*
Min Mail Order EU: £50.00
Cat. Cost: 1 x 1st class/1 x IRC
Credit Cards: Visa MasterCard
Specialities: Carnivorous plants. Some species
ltd. *Note: mail order May-Nov. Credit cards
not accepted for mail order.
Map Ref: L, C4

LHop   HOPLEYS PLANTS LTD ⊠ ⋔ ⓖ ◆
High Street, Much Hadham,
Hertfordshire, SG10 6BU
Ⓣ (01279) 842509

L

Ⓕ (01279) 843784
Ⓔ sales@hopleys.co.uk
Ⓦ www.hopleys.co.uk
Also supplies wholesale: Yes
Contact: Aubrey Barker
Opening Times: 0900-1700 Mon & Wed-Sat,
1400-1700 Sun. Closed Jan & Feb.
Min Mail Order UK: Nmc
Cat. Cost: 5 x 1st class
Credit Cards: Visa Access Switch
Specialities: Wide range of hardy & half-
hardy shrubs & perennials.
Map Ref: L, A4
OS Grid Ref: TL428196

LHyd HYDON NURSERIES ⊠ € ◆
Clock Barn Lane, Hydon Heath, Godalming,
Surrey, GU8 4AZ
Ⓣ (01483) 860252
Ⓕ (01483) 419937
Also supplies wholesale: Yes
Contact: A F George, Rodney Longhurst &
Mrs A M George
Opening Times: 0800-1245 & 1400-1700
Mon-Sat. Sun during May & by appt. Open
B/hols.
Min Mail Order UK: Nmc
Min Mail Order EU: £25.00 + p&p
Cat. Cost: £1.50 or 6 x 1st class or 8 x 2nd
class
Credit Cards: None
Specialities: Large and dwarf *Rhododendron,
yakushimanum* hybrids, azaleas (deciduous &
evergreen), *Camellia* & other trees & shrubs.
Specimen Rhododendrons. Conservatory:
scented tender rhododendrons & winter-
flowering camellias.
Map Ref: L, C3

LIck LOWER ICKNIELD FARM
NURSERIES ⊠ 🔊 ◆
Lower Icknield Way, Great Kimble,
Aylesbury, Buckinghamshire,
HP17 9TX
Ⓣ (01844) 343436
Ⓜ 0780 3979993
Ⓕ (01844) 343436
Ⓔ lowericknield@waitrose.com
Contact: S Baldwin, D Baldwin
Opening Times: 0900-1730 7 days excl.
Xmas-New Year.
Min Mail Order UK: £14.00*
Cat. Cost: 3 x 1st class. Argyranthemums only
Credit Cards: None
Specialities: Nat. Coll. of *Argyranthemum.*
Patio & basket plants. Tender & hardy
perennials. Salvias. Grasses.
*Note: mail order argyranthemums.

Map Ref: L, B3
OS Grid Ref: SP814058

LIri THE IRIS GARDEN ⊠ € ◆
47 Station Road, Barnet,
Hertfordshire, EN5 1PR
Ⓣ (020) 8441 1300
Ⓕ (020) 8441 1300
Ⓔ theirisgarden@aol.com
Ⓦ www.theirisgarden.co.uk
Contact: Clive Russell
Opening Times: Nursery not open. Visit our
iris exhibits at shows. Please phone for show
details.
Min Mail Order UK: £15.00 + p&p
Min Mail Order EU: £25.00 + p&p
Cat. Cost: 8 x 1st class.
Credit Cards: all major credit/debit cards
Specialities: Modern bearded & spuria *Iris*
from breeders in UK, USA, France, Italy &
Australia. Note: orders for bearded iris must
be received by end Jun & by end Aug for
spurias.

LKna KNAP HILL & SLOCOCK
NURSERIES ⊠ ⊠ 🔊
Barrs Lane, Knaphill, Woking,
Surrey, GU21 2JW
Ⓣ (01483) 481214/5
Ⓕ (01483) 797261
Ⓦ www.knaphillrhododendrons.co.uk
Also supplies wholesale: Yes
Contact: Mrs Joy West
Opening Times: 0900-1700 Mon-Fri by appt.
only.
Min Mail Order UK: Nmc
Min Mail Order EU: Nmc
Cat. Cost: 3 x 1st class
Credit Cards: Visa Access MasterCard
Specialities: Wide variety of rhododendrons &
azaleas.
Map Ref: L, C3

LLin LINCLUDEN NURSERY ⊠ ⊠ ṅ € 🔊 ◆
Bisley Green, Bisley, Woking, Surrey,
GU24 9EN
Ⓣ (01483) 797005
Ⓕ (01483) 474015
Ⓔ sales@lincludennursery.co.uk
Ⓦ www.lincludennursery.co.uk
Also supplies wholesale: Yes
Contact: Mr & Mrs J A Tilbury
Opening Times: 0930-1630 Tue-Sat all year
excl. B/hols. Closed Chelsea week & Xmas.
Min Mail Order UK: Nmc
Min Mail Order EU: Nmc
Cat. Cost: 3 x 1st class
Credit Cards: Visa MasterCard Solo Switch

Specialities: Dwarf, slow-growing & unusual conifers.
Map Ref: L, C3
OS Grid Ref: SU947596

LLWP **L W PLANTS** ⊠ ♠
23 Wroxham Way, Harpenden,
Hertfordshire, AL5 4PP
Ⓣ (01582) 768467
Ⓔ lwplants@waitrose.com
Ⓦ www.thymus.co.uk
Contact: Mrs M Easter
Opening Times: 1000-1700 most days, but please phone first.
Min Mail Order UK: £15.00 + p&p*
Cat. Cost: A5 Sae + 5 x 2nd class
Credit Cards: None
Specialities: Unusual hardy perennials & herbs esp. *Geranium, Penstemon* & *Thymus*. Nat. Colls. of *Thymus, Hyssopus* & *Satureja*. *Note: mail order late Sep-Apr, *Thymus* all year round & no minimum charge.
Map Ref: L, B3
OS Grid Ref: TL141153

LMil **MILLAIS NURSERIES** ⊠ ⊠ ♿ ◆
Crosswater Lane, Churt, Farnham,
Surrey, GU10 2JN
Ⓣ (01252) 792698
Ⓕ (01252) 792526
Ⓔ sales@rhododendrons.co.uk
Ⓦ www.rhododendrons.co.uk
Also supplies wholesale: Yes
Contact: David Millais
Opening Times: 1000-1300 & 1400-1700 Mon-Fri. Sat spring & autumn. Daily in May and early Jun.
Min Mail Order UK: £25.00 + p&p*
Min Mail Order EU: £60.00 + p&p
Cat. Cost: 4 x 1st class
Credit Cards: Visa Switch Delta MasterCard
Specialities: Rhododendrons, azaleas, magnolias & acers. *Note: mail order Oct-Apr only.
Map Ref: L, C3
OS Grid Ref: SU856397

LMor **MOREHAVENS** ⊠ ♿
Sandpit Hill, Buckland Common,
Tring, Hertfordshire, HP23 6NG
Ⓣ (01494) 758642
Ⓦ www.camomilelawns.co.uk
Also supplies wholesale: Yes
Contact: B Farmer
Opening Times: Only for collection.
Min Mail Order UK: £13.25 incl. p&p
Min Mail Order EU: £17.25
Cat. Cost: Free

Credit Cards: None
Specialities: Camomile 'Treneague'.
Map Ref: L, B3

LNCo **NATURE'S CORNER** ⊠
11 Bunyan Close, Pirton, Nr Hitchin,
Hertfordshire, SG5 3RE
Ⓣ (01462) 712519
Ⓔ DouglasCrawley@Naturescorners.co.uk
Ⓦ www.Naturescorners.co.uk
Contact: Douglas Crawley
Opening Times: Not open. Mail order only.
Min Mail Order UK: Nmc
Cat. Cost: 1 x 1st class
Specialities: *Nymphaea*.

LPal **THE PALM CENTRE** ⊠ ⊠ € ♿
Ham Central Nursery, opposite Riverside Drive, Ham Street, Ham, Richmond,
Surrey, TW10 7HA
Ⓣ (020) 8255 6191
Ⓕ (020) 8255 6192
Ⓔ mail@palmcentre.co.uk
Ⓦ www.palmcentre.co.uk
Also supplies wholesale: Yes
Contact: Martin Gibbons
Opening Times: 0900-1700 (dusk in winter) 7 days. Admin & Order Dept. 0900-1700 Mon-Fri.
Min Mail Order UK: £10.00 + p&p
Min Mail Order EU: £10.00 + p&p
Cat. Cost: Free
Credit Cards: Visa MasterCard Switch
Specialities: Palms & cycads, exotic & sub-tropical, hardy, half-hardy & tropical. Seedlings to mature trees. Also bamboos, tree ferns & other exotics.
Map Ref: L, B3

LPan **PANTILES PLANT & GARDEN CENTRE** ⊠ ⊠ ♠ ♿ ◆
Almners Road, Lyne, Chertsey, Surrey,
KT16 0BJ
Ⓣ (01932) 872195
Ⓕ (01932) 874030
Ⓔ sales@pantiles-nurseries.co.uk
Ⓦ www.pantiles-nurseries.co.uk
Also supplies wholesale: Yes
Contact: David Gillam
Opening Times: 0900-1800 Mon-Sat, 1100-1700 Sun summer. 0900-1700 Mon-Sat, 1000-1600 Sun winter.
Min Mail Order UK: £100.00 + p&p

KEY		
⊠ Mail order to UK or EU	♠ Delivers to shows	
⊠ Exports beyond EU	€ Euro accepted	
♿ Accessible by wheelchair	◆ See Display advertisement	

L

Min Mail Order EU: £100.00 + p&p
Cat. Cost: Free
Credit Cards: Visa Switch MasterCard
Specialities: Large trees, shrubs, conifers &
climbers in containers. Australasian & other
unusual plants. Selection of tree ferns from
New Zealand & Australia.
Map Ref: L, C3
OS Grid Ref: TQ0166

LPBA   PAUL BROMFIELD - AQUATICS ⊠ ⊠ € ♿
Maydencroft Lane, Gosmore, Hitchin,
Hertfordshire, SG4 7QD
Ⓣ (01462) 457399
Ⓜ 07801 656848
Ⓕ (01462) 422652
Ⓔ info@bromfieldaquatics.co.uk
Ⓦ www.bromfieldaquatics.co.uk
Also supplies wholesale: Yes
Contact: P Bromfield
Opening Times: 1000-1730 Mon-Sat Feb-
Oct. Please ring first. Order online at website.
Min Mail Order UK: £15.00 incl.
Min Mail Order EU: £100.00 incl.
Cat. Cost: 2 x 1st class
Credit Cards: Visa MasterCard Delta JCB
Switch
Specialities: Water lilies, marginals & bog.
Map Ref: L, A3

LPen   PENSTEMONS BY COLOUR ⊠
76 Grove Avenue, Hanwell, London, W7 3ES
Ⓣ (020) 8840 3199
Ⓕ (020) 8840 6415
Ⓔ debra.hughes1@virgin.net
Also supplies wholesale: Yes
Contact: Debra Hughes
Opening Times: Any time by appt.
Min Mail Order UK: £5.00 + p&p
Min Mail Order EU: £10.00 + p&p
Cat. Cost: Free
Credit Cards: None
Specialities: *Penstemon*.
Map Ref: L, B3

LPhx   PHOENIX PERENNIAL PLANTS ♠ ♿
Paice Lane, Medstead, Alton,
Hampshire, GU34 5PR
Ⓣ (01420) 560695
Ⓕ (01420) 563640
Ⓔ GreenFarmPlants.Marina.Christopher@
Care4free.net
Contact: Marina Christopher
Opening Times: 1000-1800 Thu-Sat, 20th
Mar-25th Oct 2003, except 10th-12th Jul
2003 when attending Hampton Court Flower
Show.
Cat. Cost: 4 x 1st class

Credit Cards: All major cards accepted.
Specialities: Small shrubs, sub-shrubs &
perennials, many uncommon. *Cistus,
Prostanthera, Achillea, Eryngium, Monarda,
Phlox, Verbascum*, bulbs & grasses. Note:
formerly Green Farm Plants, co-located with
Select Seeds LSss.
Map Ref: L, C2
OS Grid Ref: SU657362

LPio   PIONEER NURSERY ⊠ ♠ € ♿
Baldock Lane, Willian, Letchworth,
Hertfordshire, SG6 2AE
Ⓣ (01462) 675858
Ⓔ milly@pioneerplants.com
Ⓦ www.pioneerplants.com
Also supplies wholesale: Yes
Contact: Nick Downing
Opening Times: 0900-1700 Tue-Sat 1000-
1600 Sun, Mar-Oct, 1000-1600 Tue-Sat Nov,
Dec & Feb.
Min Mail Order UK: £15.00 + p&p
Min Mail Order EU: 30 Euros
Cat. Cost: Free
Credit Cards: MasterCard Visa
Specialities: *Salvia*, tender perennials. Wide
range of hard-to-find perennials & bulbs.
Map Ref: L, A3

LPJP   PJ'S PALMS AND EXOTICS ⊠ €
41 Salcombe Road, Ashford,
Middlesex, TW15 3BS
Ⓣ (01784) 250181
Contact: Peter Jenkins
Opening Times: Mail order only 1st Mar-
30th Nov. Visits by arrangement.
Min Mail Order UK: Nmc
Min Mail Order EU: Nmc
Cat. Cost: 2 x 1st class
Credit Cards: None
Specialities: Palms, bananas & other exotic
foliage plants, hardy & half-hardy.
Trachycarpus wagnerianus seeds available.
Note: plants available in small quantities.
Map Ref: L, B3

LPVe   PLANTA VERA ⊠ ♿
Lyne Hill Nursery, Farm Close, Lyne Crossing
Road, Chertsey, Surrey, KT16 0AT
Ⓣ (01932) 563011
Ⓕ (01932) 563011
Ⓔ PlantaVera@mmay45.fsnet.co.uk
Also supplies wholesale: Yes
Contact: Morris May
Opening Times: Not open.
Min Mail Order UK: £24.00 (12 plants)
Cat. Cost: Free availability list in Spring.
Credit Cards: None

Specialities: 415 named violas & violettas.
Note: mail order collection by arrangement.
Map Ref: L, C3

LRav   RAVEN VALLEY PLANT NURSERY
(Office) 3 Fairoaks Park, Aldershot Road,
Worplesdon, Guildford,
Surrey, GU3 3HG
ⓣ (01483) 234605
Ⓜ 07887 925945
Ⓔ ravenvalley@aol.com
Ⓦ www.plantzalive.com
Contact: Maria & Terry Milton
Opening Times: 1000-1600 (1700 in summer),
Sat, Sun & B/hols only. Or by arrangement,
please phone first. Closed Jan & Feb.
Cat. Cost: on floppy disc only. SAE
Credit Cards: None
Specialities: *Eucalyptus*, grasses. Note: nursery
is at Raven Valley, Mayfields, Woking.
Map Ref: L, C3

LRHS   WISLEY PLANT CENTRE (RHS) Ⓖ ◆
RHS Garden Wisley, Woking,
Surrey, GU23 6QB
ⓣ (01483) 211113
Ⓕ (01483) 212372
Ⓔ wisleyplantcentre@rhs.org.uk
Opening Times: 1000-1800 Mon-Sat 1100-
1700 Sun summer, 1000-1730 Mon-Sat 1000-
1600 Sun winter. Closed 25-26 Dec & Easter
Sun.
Cat. Cost: None issued
Credit Cards: MasterCard Access American
Express Switch Visa
Specialities: Very wide range, many rare &
unusual.
Map Ref: L, C3

LSee   SEEDS BY SIZE ⊠ ⊠ €
45 Crouchfield, Boxmoor, Hemel Hempstead,
Hertfordshire, HP1 1PA
ⓣ (01442) 251458
Ⓔ john-robert-size@seeds-by-size.co.uk
Ⓦ www.seeds-by-size.co.uk
Also supplies wholesale: Yes
Contact: Mr John Robert Size
Opening Times: Not open, mail order only.
Min Mail Order UK: Nmc
Min Mail Order EU: Nmc
Cat. Cost: 2 x 1st class
Credit Cards: None
Specialities: Flowers & vegetables. 1,400
varieties of vegetable, (175 cabbage, 99
cauliflower, 70 onion, 100 tomatoes) &
5,000 flowers such as 400 varieties of sweet
pea, 100 herbs. Note: cash only euro
payments.

**LSiH   SINO-HIMALAYAN PLANT
ASSOCIATION** ⊠ ⊠
81 Parlaunt Road, Slough,
Buckinghamshire, SL3 8BE
ⓣ (01753) 542823
Ⓕ (01753) 542823
Contact: Chris Chadwell
Min Mail Order UK: Nmc
Cat. Cost: None issued
Credit Cards: None
Specialities: Seed available for exchange to
members. Please apply for membership.

LSpr   SPRINGLEA NURSERY Ⓖ
Springlea, Seymour Plain, Marlow,
Bucks, SL7 3BZ
ⓣ (01628) 473366
Ⓜ 07761 213779
Contact: Mary Dean
Opening Times: Apr-Sep. Please check before
visiting. Garden open, see NGS for details.
Cat. Cost: None issued
Credit Cards: None
Specialities: Wide range of rare & unusual
shrubs & perennials incl. hardy *Geranium,
Pulmonaria, Primula*, bog plants, ground
cover & shade loving plants.
Map Ref: L, B3

LSss   SELECT SEEDS ⊠ ⋔ € Ⓖ
Paice Lane, Medstead,
Nr Alton, Hampshire, GU34 5PR
ⓣ (01420) 560695
Ⓕ (01420) 563640
Ⓔ GreenFarmPlants.Marina.Christopher@
Care4free.net
Contact: Marina Christopher
Opening Times: Not open. Mail order only.
Min Mail Order UK: £10.00
Cat. Cost: 3 x 1st class
Credit Cards: all major credit/debit cards
Specialities: Seeds. *Aconitum, Eryngium,
Thalictrum, Sanguisorba* & *Angelica*.
Note: co-located with Phoenix Perennial
Plants LPhx.
Map Ref: L, C2
OS Grid Ref: SU657362

LStr   HENRY STREET NURSERY ⊠
Swallowfield Road, Arborfield, Reading,
Berkshire, RG2 9JY
ⓣ (0118) 9761223
Ⓕ (0118) 9761417

L

L

Ⓔ info@henrystreet.co.uk
Ⓦ www.henrystreet.co.uk
Also supplies wholesale: Yes
Contact: Mr M C Goold
Opening Times: 0900-1730 Mon-Sat, 1030-1630 Sun.
Min Mail Order UK: Nmc
Min Mail Order EU: Nmc
Cat. Cost: Free
Credit Cards: Visa Access Switch
Specialities: Roses.
Map Ref: L, C3

LToo TOOBEES EXOTICS ⊠ ⊠ ♫ € ⛿
(Office) 20 Inglewood St Johns, Woking, Surrey, GU21 3HX
Ⓣ (01483) 797534 (nursery) (01483) 722600 (evenings)
Ⓕ (01483) 751995
Ⓔ bbpotter@compuserve.com
Ⓦ www.toobees-exotics.com
Contact: Bob Potter
Opening Times: 1000-1700 Thu-Sun & B/hol Mons, 17 Apr-28 Sep 2003. Other times by appointment.
Min Mail Order UK: Nmc
Min Mail Order EU: Nmc
Cat. Cost: Sae
Credit Cards: MasterCard Visa Delta Switch
Specialities: South African & Madagascan succulents, many rare & unusual species. Palms, tree ferns, air plants, carnivorous plants, *Euphorbia, Pachypodium*. Note: nursery is at Blackhorse Road, Woking.
Map Ref: L, C3

LTwo TWO JAYS ALPINES ◆
(Office) 35 Greenways, Luton, Bedfordshire, LU2 8BL
Ⓣ (01442) 864951
Ⓕ (01442) 864951
Ⓔ john.spokes@talk21.com
Contact: John Spokes
Opening Times: 0930-1730 or dusk if earlier, 7 days.
Cat. Cost: 3 x 2nd class
Specialities: Large range of alpines, herbaceous, shrubs, many in small quantities. Note: nursery is at Little Heath Farm, Little Heath Lane, Potten End, Berkhamstead.
Map Ref: L, A3

LVER THE VERNON GERANIUM NURSERY ⊠ ⛿
Cuddington Way, Cheam, Sutton, Surrey, SM2 7JB
Ⓣ (020) 8393 7616
Ⓕ (020) 8786 7437

Ⓔ mrgeranium@aol.com
Ⓦ www.geraniumsuk.com
Contact: Philip James & Liz Sims
Opening Times: 0930-1730 Mon-Sat, 1000-1600 Sun, 1st Mar-30th Jun.
Min Mail Order UK: Nmc
Min Mail Order EU: Nmc
Cat. Cost: £2.00 UK, £2.50 EU
Credit Cards: all major credit/debit cards
Specialities: *Pelargonium* & *Fuchsia*.
Map Ref: L, C4

MIDLANDS

MAAq AVON AQUATICS ⊠
Ilmington Road, Wimpstone, Stratford-upon-Avon, Warwickshire, CV37 8NR
Ⓣ (01789) 450638
Ⓕ (01789) 450967
Ⓔ avonaquatics@btinternet.com
Ⓦ www.avonaquatics.com
Also supplies wholesale: Yes
Contact: Rebecca Morgan & Richard Morgan
Opening Times: 0900-1700 Mon-Sat 1000-1600 Sun.
Min Mail Order UK: £20.00 + p&p
Credit Cards: Visa MasterCard Switch Solo
Specialities: Water lilies (70 varieties of *Nymphaea*), marginals (native), oxygenators & bog plants.
Map Ref: M, C2

MAJR A J ROBINSON ⊠
Sycamore Farm, Foston, Derbyshire, DE65 5PW
Ⓣ (01283) 815635
Ⓕ (01283) 815635
Contact: A J Robinson
Opening Times: By appt. for collection of plants only.
Min Mail Order UK: £12.50 argyranthemums only
Cat. Cost: 2 x 1st class
Credit Cards: None
Specialities: Extensive collection of tender perennials. Salvias. National Collection of *Argyranthemum*.
Map Ref: M, B2

MAln L A ALLEN ⊠
178 Hill Village Road, Four Oaks, Sutton Coldfield, W Midlands, B75 5JG
Ⓣ (0121) 308 0697
Ⓔ www.fidalgo.freeserve.co.uk
Also supplies wholesale: Yes
Contact: L A Allen
Opening Times: By prior appt.
Min Mail Order UK: Nmc

Min Mail Order EU: Nmc
Cat. Cost: 4 x 1st class
Credit Cards: None
Specialities: Nat. Coll. of *Primula auricula.*
Type: alpine *auricula,* show edged, show self,
doubles, stripes. Surplus plants from the
Collection so limited in numbers.

MAnH ARN HILL PLANTS ♪ €
62 West Lockinge, Wantage,
Oxfordshire, OX12 8QE
ⓉT (01235) 834312
Ⓜ 07879 862749
Ⓕ (01235) 862361
Ⓔ sally@arnhillplants.com
Ⓦ www.arnhillplants.com
Contact: Sally Hall
Opening Times: 1000-1730 Thu-Sat, 6th
Mar-31st Oct 2003.
Cat. Cost: 4 x 1st class
Credit Cards: None
Specialities: Wide range of unusual &
traditional hardy perennials and grasses.
Map Ref: M, D2
OS Grid Ref: SU423878

MAsh ASHWOOD NURSERIES LTD ⊠ ♿
Greensforge, Kingswinford,
W Midlands, DY6 0AE
Ⓣ (01384) 401996
Ⓕ (01384) 401108
Ⓔ ashwoodnurs@hotmail.com
Ⓦ www.ashwood-nurseries.co.uk
Contact: John Massey & Philip Baulk
Opening Times: 0900-1800 Mon-Sat &
0930-1800 Sun excl. Xmas & Boxing Day.
Min Mail Order UK: Nmc
Min Mail Order EU: Nmc
Cat. Cost: 6 x 1st class
Credit Cards: Visa Access MasterCard
Specialities: Large range of hardy plants &
dwarf conifers. Nat. Colls. of *Lewisia* &
Cyclamen species. *Hellebores, Hepatica, Salvia.*
Note: mail order seeds, special packs only.
Map Ref: M, C2

MAus DAVID AUSTIN ROSES LTD ⊠ ✈ € ♿
Bowling Green Lane, Albrighton,
Wolverhampton, WV7 3HB
Ⓣ (01902) 376377
Ⓕ (01902) 372142
Ⓔ retail@davidaustinroses.co.uk
Ⓦ www.davidaustinroses.com
Also supplies wholesale: Yes
Contact: Retail Dept
Opening Times: 0900-1700 Mon-Fri, 1000-
1800 Sat, Sun & B/hols. Until dusk Nov-Mar.
Min Mail Order UK: Nmc

Min Mail Order EU: Nmc
Cat. Cost: Free
Credit Cards: Switch Visa MasterCard
Specialities: Roses. Nat. Coll. of English Roses.
Map Ref: M, B1

MAvo AVONDALE NURSERY ♪ ♿
(Office) 3 Avondale Road, Earlsdon,
Coventry, Warwickshire, CV5 6DZ
Ⓣ (024) 766 73662
Ⓜ 07979 093096
Ⓕ (024) 766 73662
Ⓔ enquiries@avondalenursery.co.uk
Ⓦ www.avondalenursery.co.uk
Contact: Brian Ellis
Opening Times: 1000-1230, 1400-1700 7
days 1st Mar-15th Oct. Closed Sun pm Jul-
Aug. Other times by appt.
Cat. Cost: 4 x 1st class
Credit Cards: None
Specialities: Rare & unusual perennials esp.
*Campanula, Eryngium, Leucanthemum, Geum,
Crocosmia, Pulmonaria* & grasses. Note:
nursery is at Smith's Nursery, 3 Stoneleigh
Road, Baginton, Nr Coventry.
Map Ref: M, C2

MBar BARNCROFT NURSERIES ⊠ ♿
Dunwood Lane, Longsdon, Nr Leek,
Stoke-on-Trent, Staffordshire, ST9 9QW
Ⓣ (01538) 384310
Ⓕ (01538) 384310
Ⓦ www.barncroftnurseries.co.uk
Also supplies wholesale: Yes
Contact: S Warner
Opening Times: 0930-1730 or dusk if earlier
Fri-Sun all year, plus Mon-Thu 0930-1730
Mar-Dec.
Min Mail Order UK: £10.00 + p&p
Cat. Cost: £2.50 incl. p&p
Credit Cards: None
Specialities: Extensive range of over 2000
heathers, conifers, shrubs, trees, climbers,
dwarf grasses & rhododendrons. Display
garden containing 400 heather cvs.
Map Ref: M, B1

**MBct BARCOTE GARDEN HERBACEOUS
PLANTS**
Barcote Garden, Faringdon,
Oxfordshire, SN7 8PP
Ⓣ (01367) 870600
Contact: Christine Smith

M

M

Opening Times: By arrangement Mar-Sep. Closed Oct-Feb.
Cat. Cost: Sae for plant list.
Credit Cards: None
Specialities: Herbaceous perennials. Small quantities of all plants listed. Ferns.
Map Ref: M, D2
OS Grid Ref: SU322977

MBlu **BLUEBELL NURSERY & ARBORETUM**
⊠ ♠ € ⌂
Annwell Lane, Smisby, Nr Ashby de la Zouch, Derbyshire, LE65 2TA
Ⓣ (01530) 413700
Ⓕ (01530) 417600
Ⓔ sales@bluebellnursery.com
Ⓦ www.bluebellnursery.com
Contact: Robert & Suzette Vernon
Opening Times: 0900-1700 Mon-Sat & 1030-1630 Sun Mar-Oct, 0900-1600 Mon-Sat (not Sun) Nov-Feb. Closed 24th Dec-4th Jan. Closed Easter Sun.
Min Mail Order UK: Nmc
Min Mail Order EU: Nmc
Cat. Cost: £1.30 + 2 x 1st class
Credit Cards: Visa Access Switch
Specialities: Uncommon trees & shrubs. Display garden & arboretum.
Map Ref: M, B1

MBnl **BENSLEY NURSERIES** ♠ ⌂
(office) 7 Bensley Close, Chellaston, Derby, Derbyshire, DE73 1TL
Ⓣ (01332) 690546
Ⓜ 07968 951019
Ⓕ (01332) 690546
Ⓔ verygreenfingers@hotmail.com
Contact: Mairi Longdon
Opening Times: 1030-1630 Mon-Thu, 1st Mar-31st Oct. Other times by appt.
Cat. Cost: 4 x 1st class
Credit Cards: None
Specialities: Choice & unusual perennials esp. *Achillea, Geranium, Geum, Helenium, Heuchera, Pulmonaria* & grasses. Note: nursery is at White Gables, Dale Road, Stanley, Derbyshire.
Map Ref: M, B2
OS Grid Ref: SK417398

MBNS **BARNSDALE GARDENS** ♠ ⌂
Exton Avenue, Exton, Oakham, Rutland, LE15 8AH
Ⓣ (01572) 813200
Ⓕ (01572) 813346
Ⓔ office@barnsdalegardens.co.uk
Ⓦ www.barnsdalegardens.co.uk
Contact: Nick or Sue Hamilton

Opening Times: 0900-1700 Mar-May & Sep-Oct, 0900-1900 Jun-Aug, 1000-1600 Nov-Feb, 7 days. Closed 23th & 25th Dec.
Cat. Cost: A5 + 5 x 2nd class
Credit Cards: Visa Access MasterCard Switch Delta American Express
Specialities: Choice & unusual garden plants. Over 70 varieties of *Penstemon*, over 170 varieties of *Hemerocallis*.
Map Ref: M, B3

MBow **BOWDEN HALL NURSERY** ⊠
(Office) Malcoff Farmhouse, Malcoff, Chapel-en-le-Frith, High Peak, Derbyshire, SK23 0QR
Ⓣ (01663) 751969
Ⓜ 07867 502775
Ⓕ (01663) 751469
Ⓔ info@bowdenhallnursery.co.uk
Ⓦ www.bowdenhallnursery.co.uk
Contact: Julie Norfolk
Opening Times: 1030-1700 Wed-Sun & B/hols from 1st Mar. Other times by appt.
Min Mail Order UK: £12.00 + p&p*
Cat. Cost: 5 x 1st class or £1.75 (cat. also growing guide and handbook)
Credit Cards: None
Specialities: Herbs, wild flowers & hardy cottage garden plants & some old roses. Plants grown in peat-free compost using organic fertilisers. *Note: mail order excl. roses. Nursery at Bowden Hall, Bowden, Chapel-en-le-Frith, High Peak.
Map Ref: M, A2
OS Grid Ref: SK065817

MBPg **BARNFIELD PELARGONIUMS** ⊠
Barnfield, Off Wilnecote Lane, Belgrave, Tamworth, Staffordshire, B77 2LF
Ⓣ (01827) 250123
Ⓕ (01827) 250123
Ⓔ brianandjenniewhite@hotmail.com
Contact: Jennie & Brian White
Opening Times: Not open to the public.
Min Mail Order UK: £3.50
Min Mail Order EU: £6.00
Cat. Cost: 2 x 1st class
Credit Cards: None
Specialities: Over 160 varieties of scented leaf pelargoniums. Note: stock available in limited quantities only.

MBri **BRIDGEMERE NURSERIES** € ⌂
Bridgemere, Nr Nantwich, Cheshire, CW5 7QB
Ⓣ (01270) 521100
Ⓕ (01270) 520215
Ⓔ info@bridgemere.co.uk

Ⓦ www.bridgemere.co.uk
Contact: Keith Atkey, Nigel Snow
Opening Times: 0900-1800 7 days, except Xmas Day & Boxing Day.
Cat. Cost: None issued
Credit Cards: Visa Access MasterCard Switch
Specialities: Perennials, shrubs, trees, roses, climbers, rhododendrons & azaleas, alpines, heathers, bamboos, ferns, grasses, aquatics, houseplants.
Map Ref: M, B1
OS Grid Ref: SJ727435

MBrN   BRIDGE NURSERY € 🔊
Tomlow Road, Napton-on-the-Hill, Nr Rugby, Warwickshire, CV47 8HX
Ⓣ (01926) 812737
Ⓦ www.Bridge-Nursery.co.uk
Also supplies wholesale: Yes
Contact: Christine Dakin & Philip Martino
Opening Times: 1000-1600 Fri-Sun 1st Feb-22nd Dec. Other times by appt.
Cat. Cost: 4 x 1st class
Credit Cards: None
Specialities: Ornamental grasses, sedges & bamboos. Also range of shrubs & perennials.
Map Ref: M, C2
OS Grid Ref: SP463625

MBro   BROADSTONE NURSERIES
13 The Nursery, High Street, Sutton Courtenay, Abingdon, Oxfordshire, OX14 4UA
Ⓣ (01235) 847557 (evenings preferred)
Contact: J Shackleton
Opening Times: 1400-1700 Tue, 1400-1800 Sat (except show days). By appt. on other days/times.
Cat. Cost: 3 x 1st class
Credit Cards: None
Specialities: Plants for rock garden, scree, troughs & borders. Lime tolerant hardy alpines, perennials & unusual plants. Small selection choice shrubs.
Map Ref: M, D3

MBSH   BRITISH SEED HOUSES LTD ✉ 🗷 €
Camp Road, Witham St Hughs, Lincoln, LN6 9QJ
Ⓣ (01522) 868714
Ⓕ (01522) 868095
Ⓔ seeds@bshlincoln.co.uk
Ⓦ www.britishseedhouses.com
Also supplies wholesale: Yes
Contact: Simon Taylor
Opening Times: 0800-1730 Mon-Fri excl. B/hols.
Min Mail Order UK: £50.00 + p&p

Min Mail Order EU: £50.00 + p&p
Cat. Cost: 2 x 1st class
Credit Cards: all major credit/debit cards
Specialities: Seed.

MBur   BURROWS ROSES ✉
Meadow Croft, Spondon Road, Dale Abbey, Derby, DE7 4PQ
Ⓣ (01332) 668289
Ⓕ (01332) 668289
Contact: Stuart & Diane Burrows
Opening Times: Not open, mail order only.
Min Mail Order UK: No minimum order, up to 3 plants £2.50 p&p
Min Mail Order EU: £4.50 + p&p
Cat. Cost: 2 x 1st class
Credit Cards: None
Specialities: Roses only.

MCad   CADDICK'S CLEMATIS NURSERY ✉ 🔊
Lymm Road, Thelwall, Warrington, Cheshire, WA13 0UF
Ⓣ (01925) 757196
Ⓕ (01925) 268357
Ⓦ www.caddicks-clematis.co.uk
Contact: Mrs D Caddick
Opening Times: 1000-1700 Tue-Sat 8th Feb-31st Oct, 1100-1600 Sun. Nov by arrangement. 1100-1600 B/hols. Closed Dec & Jan.
Min Mail Order UK: £13.90 + p&p
Min Mail Order EU: £13.90 + p&p
Cat. Cost: 4 x 1st class UK, £2.00 or credit card EU & Eire.
Credit Cards: Visa Access MasterCard Switch
Specialities: *Clematis.*
Map Ref: M, A1

MCCP   COLLECTORS CORNER PLANTS ✉
33 Rugby Road, Clifton-upon-Dunsmore, Rugby, Warwickshire, CV23 0DE
Ⓣ (01788) 571881
Contact: Pat Neesam
Opening Times: By appt. only.
Min Mail Order UK: £10.00
Cat. Cost: 6 x 1st class
Credit Cards: None
Specialities: General range of choice herbaceous perennials, grasses, shrubs, palms, ferns & bamboos.
Map Ref: M, C3

M

M

MCLN   COUNTRY LADY NURSERY 🔲
Lilac Cottage, Chapel Lane,
Gentleshaw, Nr Rugeley,
Staffordshire, WS15 4ND
(T) (01543) 675520
(F) (01543) 675520
(W) www.countryladynursery.co.uk
Contact: Mrs Sylvia Nunn
Opening Times: 1000-1700 Thu-Sun &
B/hol Mons Mar-end Sep. Other times by
appt. Nursery will cease trading end Sep 2003
due to retirement.
Cat. Cost: 4 x 1st class
Credit Cards: None
Specialities: Wide range of unusual perennials
incl. hardy *Geranium, Heuchera, Penstemon,
Hosta, Hemerocallis, Achillea, Phlox* & *Papaver*.
1 acre show garden.
Map Ref: M, B1
OS Grid Ref: SK052119

MCls   COLES PLANT CENTRE 🔲
624 Uppingham Road, Thurnby,
Leicestershire, LE7 9QB
(T) (0116) 241 8394
(F) (0116) 243 2311
(E) info@colesplantcentre.co.uk
(W) www.colesplantcentre.co.uk
Also supplies wholesale: Yes
Contact: Mark Goddard
Opening Times: 0800-1700 Mon-Fri, 0900-
1700 Sat & Sun.
Credit Cards: MasterCard Switch
Specialities: Fruit, Ornamental Trees &
Shrubs.
Map Ref: M, B3

MCoo   COOL TEMPERATE ✉
10 Ivy Grove, New Basford,
Nottingham, NG7 7LZ
(T) (0115) 847 8302
(F) (0115) 847 8302
(E) philcorbett53@hotmail.com
(W) www.cooltemperate.co.uk
Also supplies wholesale: Yes
Contact: Phil Corbett
Opening Times: Not open, mail order only.
Min Mail Order UK: Nmc
Min Mail Order EU: Nmc
Cat. Cost: 2 x 1st class
Credit Cards: None
Specialities: Tree fruit, soft fruit, nitrogen-
fixers, hedging, own-root fruit trees.

MCre   CRESCENT PLANTS ✉ 🌱
34 The Crescent, Cradley Heath,
W Midlands, B64 7JS
(T) (0121) 550 2628

(F) (0121) 550 2732
(E) ian@auriculas.co.uk
(W) www.auriculas.co.uk
Also supplies wholesale: Yes
Contact: Ian Goddard
Min Mail Order UK: Nmc
Min Mail Order EU: Nmc
Cat. Cost: 2 x 1st class
Credit Cards: None
Specialities: Named varieties of *Primula
auricula* incl. show, alpine, double, striped &
border types. Also seed.

MDHE   DHE PLANTS ✉
(Office) Rose Lea, Darley House Estate,
Darley Dale, Matlock,
Derbyshire, DE4 2QH
(T) (01629) 732512
Contact: Peter M Smith
Opening Times: 1000-1700 Tue-Sat, 1030-
1630 Sun. Please phone first.
Min Mail Order UK: Nmc*
Cat. Cost: 2 x 1st class
Credit Cards: None
Specialities: Alpines esp. *Erodium* (70+),
Helianthemum & *Saxifraga*. *Note: mail order
Oct-Mar only. Nursery stock is at Robert
Young Floral Centre, Bakewell Rd, Matlock.
Map Ref: M, B1

MDKP   D K PLANTS 🌱
(Office) 19 Harbourne Road, Cheadle, Stoke
on Trent, Staffordshire, ST10 1JU
(T) (01538) 754460
(M) 07779 545015
Contact: Dave Knox
Opening Times: 0900-2000 (or dusk if earlier)
Mon-Tue & Thu-Fri. Other times by appt.
Cat. Cost: 4 x 1st + A4 Sae
Credit Cards: None
Specialities: Unusual hardy alpines &
perennials. All grown on the nursery. Note:
nursery is at new roundabout across from
Queen's Arms pub, Freehay Crossroads,
Cheadle.
Map Ref: M, B1

MDun   DUNGE VALLEY GARDENS € 🔲
Windgather Rocks, Kettleshulme, High Peak,
Derbyshire, SK23 7RF
(T) (01663) 733787
(F) (01663) 733787
(E) sales@dungevalley.f9.co.uk
(W) www.dungevalley.f9.co.uk
Also supplies wholesale: Yes
Contact: David Ketley
Opening Times: 1030-1700 Tue-Sat 1st Apr-
15th Jun, Thu-Sun 19th Jun-31st Aug. Open

M

B/Hols & w/ends Mar. Otherwise by appt.
Cat. Cost: A5 Sae
Credit Cards: MasterCard Visa
Specialities: *Rhododendron* species & hybrids.
Magnolias, trees, shrubs & perennials, some
rare & wild collected. *Meconopsis, Trillium,*
acers & bamboos.
Map Ref: M, A2
OS Grid Ref: SJ989777

MEHN ELIZABETH HOUSE NURSERY ⋔ € ♿
Weedon Lois, Towcester,
Northamptonshire, NN12 8PN
Ⓣ (01327) 860056
Ⓕ (01327) 860779
Also supplies wholesale: Yes
Contact: Lindsey Cartwright
Opening Times: 1000-1700 Thu-Sat, Mar-
Oct. Closed Aug.
Cat. Cost: 2 x 1st class
Credit Cards: None
Specialities: Wide range of hardy perennials.
Map Ref: M, C3
OS Grid Ref: SP604472

MFan FANCYPLANTS ✉ ⋔
9 Meadow Close, Stretton on Dunsmore,
Rugby, Warwickshire, CV23 9NL
Ⓣ (024) 7654 3010
Ⓕ (024) 7654 0665
Ⓔ style@fancyplants.co.uk
Contact: Mandy Alexander
Opening Times: Not open. Mail order only.
Min Mail Order UK: £10.00
Cat. Cost: 2 x 1st class
Credit Cards: None
Specialities: Designer plants for year-round
structure & style. Emphasis on exotic &
contemporary foliage plants incl. ornamental
grasses, bamboos, hardy palms, tree ferns,
cordylines & *Phormium, Hosta, Heuchera.*
Map Ref: M, C2
OS Grid Ref: SP412729

MFie FIELD HOUSE NURSERIES ✉
Leake Road, Gotham,
Nottinghamshire, NG11 0JN
Ⓣ (0115) 9830278
Ⓕ (0115) 9831486
Ⓔ dlvwjw@field-house-alpines.fsbusiness.co.uk
Contact: Doug Lochhead & Valerie A
Woolley
Opening Times: 0900-1700 Fri-Wed or by appt.
Min Mail Order UK: Min. order 4 plants*
Min Mail Order EU: £30.00
Cat. Cost: 4 x 1st or 4 x IRCs
Credit Cards: Visa Access
Specialities: *Primula*, auriculas, alpines & rock

plants. 3 Nat. Colls. of *Primula* and *P.
auricula.* *Note: mail order for *Primula,*
auriculas & seeds only.
Map Ref: M, B3

MFir THE FIRS NURSERY ✉ ♿
Chelford Road, Henbury, Macclesfield,
Cheshire, SK10 3LH
Ⓣ (01625) 426422
Ⓕ (01625) 426422
Contact: Fay J Bowling
Opening Times: 1000-1700 Tue & Thu-Sat,
Mar-Sep.
Min Mail Order UK: £10.00 + p&p
Cat. Cost: 2 x 1st class
Credit Cards: None
Specialities: Wide range of herbaceous
perennials, many available in small quantities.
Map Ref: M, A2
OS Grid Ref: SJ885735

MFOX FOX COTTAGE PLANTS ⋔ ♿
Yew Tree Farm, Thatchers Lane, Tansley,
Matlock, Derbyshire, DE4 5FD
Ⓣ (01629) 57493
Ⓜ 07787 963966
Ⓕ (01629) 57493
Contact: Mrs Avril Buckley
Opening Times: 1200-1700 daily Feb-Oct.
Nov-Jan by appt. Please ring to confirm.
Cat. Cost: 2 x 1st class
Credit Cards: None
Specialities: Unusual hardy & tender perennials.
Stock available in small quantities only.
Map Ref: M, C2
OS Grid Ref: SK324594

MGas LINDA GASCOIGNE WILD FLOWERS
17 Imperial Road, Kibworth Beauchamp,
Leicestershire, LE8 0HR
Ⓣ (0116) 2793959
Contact: Linda Gascoigne
Opening Times: By appt. only.
Cat. Cost: 3 x 1st class
Credit Cards: None
Specialities: Wide range of wild flowers &
plants to attract wildlife. No peat used.
Map Ref: M, C3

MGol GOLDEN COTTAGE PLANTS ✉ ▣
Golden Cottage, Scarcliffe Lanes,
Upper Langwith, Mansfield,
Nottinghamshire, NG20 9RQ

KEY		
✉ Mail order to UK or EU	⋔ Delivers to shows	
▣ Exports beyond EU	€ Euro accepted	
♿ Accessible by wheelchair	◆ See Display advertisement	

Ⓣ (07971) 743567
Ⓔ sacredplants@onetel.net.uk
Contact: C Coleman
Opening Times: By appt. only.
Min Mail Order UK: Nmc
Min Mail Order EU: Nmc
Cat. Cost: 2 x 1st class
Credit Cards: None
Specialities: Ethnobotanical plants and seeds.
Hardy, tropical & sub-tropical. All plants
& seeds only available in limited quantity
ie 2 plants/person/species.

M **MGos** **Goscote Nurseries Ltd** ⊠ € ⬚ ◆
Syston Road, Cossington,
Leicestershire, LE7 4UZ
Ⓣ (01509) 812121
Ⓕ (01509) 814231
Ⓔ sales@goscote.co.uk
Ⓦ www.goscote.co.uk
Contact: Derek Cox, James Toone
Opening Times: 7 days, closed between Xmas
& New Year.
Min Mail Order UK: £50.00 + p&p
Min Mail Order EU: £150.00 + p&p
Cat. Cost: 5 x 1st class
Credit Cards: Visa Access MasterCard Delta
Switch
Specialities: Japanese maples, rhododendrons
& azaleas, *Magnolia, Camellia, Pieris* & other
Ericaceae. Ornamental trees & shrubs,
conifers, fruit, heathers, alpines, *Clematis* &
unusual climbers. Show Garden to visit.
Map Ref: M, B3

MHar **Harts Green Nursery**
89 Harts Green Road, Harborne,
Birmingham, B17 9TZ
Ⓣ (0121) 427 5200
Contact: B Richardson
Opening Times: 1400-1730 Wed Apr-Jul &
Sep. Other times, excl. Aug, by appt.
Cat. Cost: None issued.
Credit Cards: None
Specialities: Hardy perennials. Some in small
quantities only.
Map Ref: M, C2
OS Grid Ref: SP030845

MHer **The Herb Nursery** ⬚ ◆
Thistleton, Oakham, Rutland, LE15 7RE
Ⓣ (01572) 767658
Ⓕ (01572) 768021
Contact: Peter Bench
Opening Times: 0900-1800 (or dusk) 7 days
excl. Xmas-New Year.
Cat. Cost: A5 Sae.
Credit Cards: None

Specialities: Herbs, wild flowers, cottage
garden plants, scented-leaf pelargoniums.
Map Ref: M, B3

MHom **Homestead Plants** ⊠
The Homestead, Normanton, Bottesford,
Nottingham, NG13 0EP
Ⓣ (01949) 842745
Ⓕ (01949) 842745
Contact: Mrs S Palmer
Opening Times: By appt.
Min Mail Order UK: Nmc
Cat. Cost: 4 x 2nd class
Credit Cards: None
Specialities: Unusual hardy & half-hardy
perennials, especially *Helleborus* & *Paeonia*
species. *Hosta, Jovibarba, Sempervivum* &
Heliotrope. Most available only in small
quantities.
Map Ref: M, B3
OS Grid Ref: SK812407

MHrb **The Herb Garden** ⬚
Kingston House Estate, Race Farm Lane,
Kingston Bagpuize, Oxfordshire,
OX13 5AU
Ⓣ (01865) 823101
Ⓕ (01865) 820159
Ⓔ vcjw37@yahoo.com
Ⓦ www.KingstonHerbGarden.co.uk
Contact: Val Williams
Opening Times: As for Kingston House Open
Days, or phone nursery for appt. Sae for
details.
Cat. Cost: 2 x 1st class
Credit Cards: None
Specialities: Small nursery specialising in the
more unusual lavenders. Herbs, dye plants &
lavenders in a walled garden setting. Check
web site for availability.
Map Ref: M, D2

MIDC **Ian and Deborah Coppack** ⊠ ⬚ ◆
Woodside, Langley Road, Langley,
Macclesfield, Cheshire,
SK11 0DG
Ⓣ (01260) 253308
Ⓕ (01260) 253308
Ⓔ coppack@worldonline.co.uk
Also supplies wholesale: Yes
Contact: Ian & Deborah Coppack
Opening Times: 0900-1700 Mar-Sep.
Min Mail Order UK: Nmc
Cat. Cost: 2 x 1st class
Credit Cards: None
Specialities: *Hosta.*
Map Ref: M, A2
OS Grid Ref: 938715

M INTAKES FARM
Sandy Lane, Longsdon, Stoke-on-Trent,
Staffordshire, ST9 9QQ
ⓣ (01538) 398452
Contact: Mrs Kathleen Inman
Opening Times: By appt. only.
Cat. Cost: None issued
Credit Cards: None
Specialities: Double, variegated & unusual
forms of British natives & cottage garden
plants.
Map Ref: M, B1

MJac JACKSON'S NURSERIES
Clifton, Campville, Nr Tamworth,
Staffordshire, B79 0AP
ⓣ (01827) 373307
ⓕ (01827) 373307
Also supplies wholesale: Yes
Contact: N Jackson
Opening Times: 0900-1800 Mon Wed-Sat,
1000-1700 Sun.
Cat. Cost: 2 x 1st class
Credit Cards: None
Specialities: Fuchsia.
Map Ref: M, B1

MJnS JUNGLE SEEDS AND GARDENS ✉
PO Box 45, Watlington SPDO,
Oxfordshire, OX49 5YR
ⓣ (01491) 614765
ⓕ (01491) 614765
ⓔ enquiry@junglegardens.co.uk
ⓦ www.junglegardens.co.uk
Contact: Penny White
Opening Times: By appt. only to collect plants.
Min Mail Order UK: Nmc
Cat. Cost: 2 x 1st class
Credit Cards: Visa MasterCard Switch
Specialities: Hardy, semi-hardy &
conservatory exotics. Some items limited
availability.

MKay KAYES GARDEN NURSERY
1700 Melton Road, Rearsby,
Leicestershire, LE7 4YR
ⓣ (01664) 424578
ⓔ hazelkaye.kgn@nascrnet
Contact: Hazel Kaye
Opening Times: 1000-1700 Tue-Sat & B/hols
1000-1200 Sun Mar-Oct. By appt. Nov, Dec
& Feb. Closed Jan.
Cat. Cost: 2 x 1st class
Credit Cards: None
Specialities: Herbaceous, climbers & aquatic
plants. Grasses.
Map Ref: M, B3
OS Grid Ref: SK648140

MLan LANE END NURSERY
Old Cherry Lane, Lymm,
Cheshire, WA13 0TA
ⓣ (01925) 752618
ⓔ sawyer@laneend.u-net.com
ⓦ www.laneend.u-net.com
Contact: I Sawyer
Opening Times: 0930-1730 Thu-Tue Feb-
Dec.
Cat. Cost: None issued
Credit Cards: None
Specialities: Award of Garden Merit plants
with a wide range of choice & unusual
shrubs, trees, perennials & ferns.
Map Ref: M, A1
OS Grid Ref: SJ664850

MLea LEA RHODODENDRON GARDENS
LTD ✉ ✉ ♿
Lea, Matlock, Derbyshire, DE4 5GH
ⓣ (01629) 534380/534260
ⓕ (01629) 534260
Contact: Peter Tye
Opening Times: 1000-1730 7 days 20 Mar-
30 Jun. Out of season by appt.
Min Mail Order UK: £15.00 + p&p
Min Mail Order EU: £15.00 + p&p
Cat. Cost: 30p + Sae
Credit Cards: all major credit/debit cards
Specialities: Rhododendrons & azaleas.
Map Ref: M, B1
OS Grid Ref: SK324571

MLLN LODGE LANE NURSERY & GARDENS ♉
Lodge Lane, Dutton, Nr Warrington,
Cheshire, WA4 4HP
ⓣ (01928) 713718
ⓕ (01928) 713718
ⓔ rod@lodgelanenursery.co.uk
ⓦ www.lodgelanenursery.co.uk
Contact: Rod or Diane Casey
Opening Times: 1000-1700 Wed-Sun &
B/hols, mid Mar-mid Sep. By appt. outside
these dates.
Cat. Cost: 3 x 1st class
Credit Cards: None
Specialities: Unusual perennials & shrubs
incl. *Allium, Campanula, Digitalis, Penstemon,
Euphorbia, Geranium, Heuchera, Inula,
Kniphofia* & ornamental grasses. National
Collection of *Inula* from Tatton Park.
Map Ref: M, A1
OS Grid Ref: SJ586779

M

KEY		
✉ Mail order to UK or EU	♉ Delivers to shows	
✉ Exports beyond EU	€ Euro accepted	
♿ Accessible by wheelchair	◆ See Display advertisement	

M

MLwd   **Linward Hardy Plants** ✉ ň
17 Roland Avenue, Nuthall,
Nottingham, NG16 1BB
Ⓣ (0115) 854 5283
Ⓔ Edds@ntlworld.com
Ⓦ www.linwardhardyplants.co.uk
Contact: Edward Seeley & Linda Scott
Opening Times: By prior arrangement only.
Min Mail Order UK: Nmc
Cat. Cost: 50p coin
Credit Cards: None
Specialities: Hardy *Geranium, Digitalis* &
unusual hardy perennials. Some stock in
limited quantities. Enquiries always welcome.
Map Ref: M, B3
OS Grid Ref: SK522438

MMat   **Mattock's Roses** ✉
Freepost, The Rose Nurseries, Nuneham
Courtenay, Oxfordshire, OX44 9PY
Ⓣ 08457 585652
Ⓕ (01865) 343166
Ⓔ roses@mattocks.co.uk
Ⓦ www.mattocks.co.uk
Contact: Sales Office
Opening Times: 0900-1800 Mon-Sat, 1030-
1630 Sun.
Min Mail Order UK: Nmc
Cat. Cost: Free
Credit Cards: Visa MasterCard Switch
Specialities: Roses.
Map Ref: M, D3

MMHG   **Morton Hall Gardens** ✉ ň
Morton Hall, Ranby,
Retford, Nottinghamshire, DN22 8HW
Ⓣ (01777) 702530
Ⓔ mortonhall@business77.freeserve.co.uk
Contact: Gill McMaster
Opening Times: By appt.only
Min Mail Order UK: £5.00 + p&p
Cat. Cost: 3 x 1st class
Credit Cards: None
Specialities: Shrubs & perennials.
Map Ref: M, A3

MMil   **Mill Hill Plants** ◆
Mill Hill House, Elston Lane,
East Stoke, Newark,
Nottinghamshire, NG23 5QJ
Ⓣ (01636) 525460
Ⓜ 07713 176507
Ⓔ millhill@talk21.com
Ⓦ http://come.to/mill.hill.plants&garden
Contact: G M Gregory
Opening Times: 1000-1730 Fri-Sun & B/hols
Mar-Oct & by appt.
Cat. Cost: none issued

Credit Cards: None
Specialities: Hardy perennials, many unusual.
Nat. Coll. of *Berberis*.
Map Ref: M, B3

MMoz   **Mozart House Nursery Garden** ň
84 Central Avenue, Wigston,
Leicestershire, LE18 2AA
Ⓣ (0116) 288 9548
Contact: Des Martin
Opening Times: By appt. only.
Cat. Cost: 5 x 1st class
Credit Cards: None
Specialities: *Bamboo*, ornamental grasses,
rushes & sedges, ferns.
Map Ref: M, C3

MNew   **Newington Nurseries** € ▣ ◆
Newington, Wallingford,
Oxfordshire, OX10 7AW
Ⓣ (01865) 400533
Ⓕ (01865) 891766
Ⓔ newington@connectfree.co.uk
Ⓦ www.newington-nurseries.co.uk
Contact: Mrs A T Hendry
Opening Times: 1000-1700 Tues-Sun Mar-
Oct, 1000-1600 Tues-Sun Nov-Feb.
Cat. Cost: 4 x 1st class & A4 sae
Credit Cards: Access MasterCard Visa Switch
Specialities: Unusual cottage garden plants,
alpines, hardy exotics, conservatory plants &
herbs. Nat. Coll. of *Alocasia* (*Araceae*).
Map Ref: M, D3

MNFA   **The Nursery Further Afield** ▣
Evenley Road, Mixbury, Nr Brackley,
Northamptonshire, NN13 5YR
Ⓣ (01280) 848808
Contact: Gerald Sinclair
Opening Times: 1000-1700 Wed-Sat Mar-early
Oct. Also Sun & Mon on NGS open days.
Cat. Cost: 2 x 1st class
Credit Cards: None
Specialities: Hardy perennials, many unusual,
incl. *Anemone, Aster, Campanula, Geranium,
Hemerocallis* & *Iris sibirica*. Nat. Coll. of
Hemerocallis.
Map Ref: M, C3
OS Grid Ref: SP608344

MNHC   **The National Herb Centre** ▣
Banbury Road, Warmington,
Nr Banbury, Oxfordshire, OX17 1DF
Ⓣ (01295) 690999
Ⓕ (01295) 690034
Ⓦ www.herbcentre.co.uk
Contact: Nick Turner
Opening Times: 0900-1730 Mon-Sat,

1030-1700 Sun.
Credit Cards: all major credit/debit cards
Specialities: Herbs

MNrw NORWELL NURSERIES ⊠ ń 🖳 ◆
Woodhouse Road, Norwell, Newark,
Nottinghamshire, NG23 6JX
Ⓣ (01636) 636337
Ⓔ wardha@aol.com
Also supplies wholesale: Yes
Contact: Dr Andrew Ward
Opening Times: 1000-1700 Mon, Wed-Fri &
Sun (Wed-Mon May & Jun). By appt. Aug &
20th Oct-1st Mar.
Min Mail Order UK: £12.00 + p&p
Cat. Cost: 3 x 1st class
Credit Cards: None
Specialities: A large collection of unusual &
choice herbaceous perennials & alpines esp.
Penstemon, hardy *Geranium, Geum,* summer
bulbs, grasses & woodland plants. Gardens
open.
Map Ref: M, B3

MOak OAKLAND NURSERIES ⊠ 🖾 ń
147 Melton Road, Burton-on-the-Wolds,
Loughborough, Leicestershire, LE12 5TQ
Ⓣ (01509) 880646
Ⓕ (01509) 889294
Ⓔ tim@joakland.freeserve.co.uk
Ⓦ www.oaklandnurseries.co.uk
Also supplies wholesale: Yes
Contact: Tim & John Oakland
Opening Times: Strictly by appt. Apr-Sep.
Min Mail Order UK: £15.00 + p&p
Min Mail Order EU: £15.00 + p&p
Cat. Cost: 4 x 1st class
Credit Cards: MasterCard Visa
Specialities: Tender perennials, *Canna, Coleus,*
Caladium, Abutilon, Streptocarpus,
conservatory & exotic plants. Some *Canna*
available in limited quantities, *Coleus*
propagate to order. Note: export *Canna /*
Caladium only as dormant plants.
Map Ref: M, B3
OS Grid Ref: SK615214

MOne ONE HOUSE NURSERY ⊠ ń 🖳 ◆
Buxton New Road, Macclesfield,
Cheshire, SK11 0AD
Ⓣ (01625) 427087
Contact: Miss J L Baylis
Opening Times: 1000-1700 Tue-Sun & B/hol
Mons Mar-Oct, Nov-Feb ring for opening
times.
Min Mail Order UK: Nmc*
Cat. Cost: 3 x 1st class
Credit Cards: None

Specialities: Alpines & perennials. Good
range of *Primula auricula, Sempervivum,*
dwarf *Rhododendron,* dwarf conifers & bulbs.
*Note: mail order for *Sempervivum* & double
primroses only.
Map Ref: M, A2
OS Grid Ref: SJ943741

MPet PETER GRAYSON (SWEET PEA
SEEDSMAN) ⊠ 🖾
34 Glenthorne Close, Brampton,
Chesterfield, Derbyshire, S40 3AR
Ⓣ (01246) 278503
Ⓕ (01246) 278503
Also supplies wholesale: Yes
Contact: Peter Grayson
Opening Times: Not open, mail order only.
Min Mail Order UK: Nmc
Min Mail Order EU: Nmc
Cat. Cost: C5 Sae, 1 x 2nd class
Credit Cards: None
Specialities: *Lathyrus* species & cvs. Large
collection of old-fashioned sweet peas & over
100 Spencer sweet peas incl. own cultivars
and collection of old-fashioned cottage
garden annuals & perennials.

MPhe PHEDAR NURSERY ⊠ 🖾 €
Bunkers Hill, Romiley, Stockport,
Cheshire, SK6 3DS
Ⓣ (0161) 430 3772
Ⓕ (0161) 430 3772
Also supplies wholesale: Yes
Contact: Will McLewin
Opening Times: Frequent esp. in spring but
very irregular. Please phone to arrange appt.
Min Mail Order UK: Nmc
Min Mail Order EU: Nmc
Cat. Cost: 2 x A5 AE or address labels +
4 x 1st class
Credit Cards: None
Specialities: *Helleborus, Paeonia.* Note: non-
EU exports subject to destination & on an
ad hoc basic only. Please contact nursery for
details. Ltd. stock of some rare items.
Map Ref: M, A2
OS Grid Ref: SJ936897

MPkF PACKHORSE FARM NURSERY ń 🖳
Sandyford House, Lant Lane, Tansley,
Matlock, Derbyshire, DE4 5FW
Ⓣ (01629) 57206
Ⓜ 07974 095752

M

Ⓕ (01629) 57206
Contact: Hilton W. Haynes
Opening Times: 1000-1700 Tues & Wed.
Any other time by appt. only.
Cat. Cost: £1.50
Credit Cards: None
Specialities: Acer, rare stock is limited in
supply. Other more unusual hardy shrubs,
trees & conifers.
Map Ref: M, B2
OS Grid Ref: SK322617

M

MPRe   PLANTS FOR ALL REASONS ⊠
Woodshoot Nurseries, King's Bromley,
Burton-upon-Trent, Staffordshire, DE13 7HN
Ⓣ (01543) 472233
Ⓕ (01543) 472115
Ⓔ sales@plants-for-all-reasons.com
Ⓦ www.plants-for-all-reasons.com
Also supplies wholesale: Yes
Contact: Richard Flint
Opening Times: Retail by appt. Wholesale on
site, please phone for details.
Min Mail Order UK: £20.00 + p&p
Cat. Cost: 2 x 1st class
Credit Cards: None
Specialities: *Phormium, Pittosporum,
Tropaeolum,* daphnes, palms, agaves & acacias.
Partial wheelchair access.
Map Ref: M, B2
OS Grid Ref: SK127164

MRav   RAVENSTHORPE NURSERY ⊠ ♿
6 East Haddon Road, Ravensthorpe,
Northamptonshire, NN6 8ES
Ⓣ (01604) 770548
Ⓕ (01604) 770548
Ⓔ ravensthorpenursery@hotmail.com
Contact: Jean & Richard Wiseman
Opening Times: 1000-1800 (dusk if earlier)
Tue-Sun. Also B/hol Mons.
Min Mail Order UK: Nmc
Min Mail Order EU: Nmc
Cat. Cost: None issued.
Credit Cards: Visa MasterCard
Specialities: Over 2,600 different trees, shrubs
& perennials with many unusual varieties.
Search & delivery service for large orders,
winter months only.
Map Ref: M, C3
OS Grid Ref: SP665699

MRod   RODBASTON COLLEGE ⊠
Rodbaston, Penkridge, Staffordshire, ST19 5PH
Ⓣ (01785) 712209
Also supplies wholesale: Yes
Contact: Yoke van der Meer
Opening Times: By appt.

Min Mail Order UK: £10.00*
Min Mail Order EU: £15.00
Cat. Cost: 2 x 1st class
Credit Cards: None
Specialities: Salvias. Nat. Coll. of 'New World'
Salvia. *Note: mail order small size plugs only.
Stock available in limited quantities only.
Map Ref: M, B1

MS&S   S & S PERENNIALS ⊠
24 Main Street, Normanton Le Heath,
Leicestershire, LE67 2TB
Ⓣ (01530) 262250
Contact: Shirley Pierce
Opening Times: Afternoons only, otherwise
please phone.
Min Mail Order UK: Nmc
Cat. Cost: 2 x 1st class
Credit Cards: None
Specialities: *Erythronium, Fritillaria,* hardy
Cyclamen, dwarf *Narcissus, Hepatica &
Anemone.* Note: stock available in small
quantities only.
Map Ref: M, B1

MSal   SALLEY GARDENS ⊠ ▣ € ♿
32 Lansdowne Drive, West Bridgford,
Nottinghamshire, NG2 7FJ
Ⓣ (0115) 9233878 evenings
Contact: Richard Lewin
Opening Times: 0900-1700 Sun-Wed,
1st Apr-30th Sep and by appt.
Min Mail Order UK: Nmc
Min Mail Order EU: Nmc
Cat. Cost: Sae
Credit Cards: None
Specialities: Medicinal plants esp. from North
America & China. Dye plants, herbs, spices,
seeds. Some species available in limited
quantities only. Note: nursery is at Simkins
Farm, Adbolton Lane, West Bridgford, Notts.
Map Ref: M, B3

MSGs   SHOWGLADS ⊠
105 Derby Road, Bramcote,
Nottingham, NG9 3GZ
Ⓣ (0115) 925 5498
Ⓔ rogerbb@lineone.net
Contact: Roger Braithwaite
Opening Times: Not open.
Min Mail Order UK: £3.25
Cat. Cost: 2 x 1st class
Credit Cards: None
Specialities: *Gladiolus.*

MSph   SPRINGHILL PLANTS ⋔
(Office) 18 Westfields, Abingdon,
Oxfordshire, OX14 1BA

Ⓣ (01235) 530889 after 1800
Ⓜ 07790 863378.
Contact: Caroline Cox
Opening Times: Apr-Sep by appt. only. Please phone first.
Cat. Cost: 75p or 3 x 1st class
Credit Cards: None
Specialities: Small nursery offering a wide range of unusual & garden-worthy perennials & shrubs. Many AGM & rare plants available. Some stock available in small quantities. Note: nursery is at Buildings Farm, Gozzard's Ford, Nr Marcham, Abingdon.
Map Ref: M, D2

MSPs   STRACHAN'S PLANTS ⊠ ⋔ ⓰
(Office) 4 Staple Hall Road, Northfield, Birmingham, B31 3TH
Ⓣ (0121) 478 1038 (1800-2100 hrs)
Ⓜ 07960 340396, 07903 553020 (day)
Ⓔ andy.strachan@care4free.net
Also supplies wholesale: Yes
Contact: Julie Dyhouse or Andy Strachan
Opening Times: 0900-1700 Mon-Fri, Mar-Oct, but please phone first to confirm as attend a lot of shows.
Min Mail Order UK: Nmc
Cat. Cost: 2 x 1st class + A5 sae to office address for list.
Credit Cards: None
Specialities: Small nursery specialising in rare & unusual perennials & old favourites. Note: nursery is at CLM, Newtown, Offenham, Evesham, Worcs. WR11 5RZ.
Map Ref: W, C5

MSta   STAPELEY WATER GARDENS LTD ⊠ ⊠
London Road, Stapeley, Nantwich, Cheshire, CW5 7LH
Ⓣ (01270) 623868
Ⓕ (01270) 624919
Ⓔ stapeleywg@btinternet.com
Ⓦ www.stapelywatergardens.co.uk
Also supplies wholesale: Yes
Contact: Mr Dean Barratt
Opening Times: From 0900 Mon-Fri, 1000 Sat, Sun & B/hols all year excl. Xmas Day. Please check closing times.
Min Mail Order UK: Nmc
Min Mail Order EU: Nmc
Cat. Cost: £2.00 handbook, price list free
Credit Cards: Visa Access MasterCard Switch
Specialities: World's largest water garden centre. Full range of hardy water lilies, aquatic, bog & poolside plants. Nat. Coll. of *Nymphaea* (UK & France).
Map Ref: M, B1

MSte   STEVENTON ROAD NURSERIES €
Steventon Road, East Hanney, Wantage, Oxfordshire, OX12 0HS
Ⓣ (01235) 868828
Ⓕ (01235) 763670
Ⓔ johngraham.steventonroadnursery@virgin.net
Ⓦ www.steventonroadnurseries.co.uk
Also supplies wholesale: Yes
Contact: John Graham
Opening Times: 0900-1700 Mon-Fri, 1000-1700 Sat & Sun Mar-Nov. Winter by appt.
Cat. Cost: 4 x 1st class
Credit Cards: None
Specialities: Tender & hardy perennials.
Map Ref: M, D2

MSwo   SWALLOWS NURSERY ⊠
Mixbury, Brackley, Northamptonshire, NN13 5RR
Ⓣ (01280) 847721
Ⓕ (01280) 848611
Ⓔ enq@swallowsnursery.co.uk
Ⓦ www.swallowsnursery.co.uk
Also supplies wholesale: Yes
Contact: Chris Swallow
Opening Times: 0900-1300 & 1400-1700 (earlier in winter) Mon-Fri, 0900-1300 Sat.
Min Mail Order UK: Nmc
Cat. Cost: 2 x 1st class
Credit Cards: Visa MasterCard Switch
Specialities: Growing a wide range, particularly shrubs, trees, roses and heathers.
Map Ref: M, C3
OS Grid Ref: SP607336

MTed   TED BROWN UNUSUAL PLANTS €
1 Croftway, Markfield, Leicester, LE67 9UG
Ⓣ (01530) 244517
Also supplies wholesale: Yes
Contact: Ted Brown
Opening Times: From 1000 Sat, Sun & B/hols Mar-Nov. Other times by appt.
Cat. Cost: None issued
Credit Cards: None
Specialities: Mainly herbaceous, many unusual. Bamboos.
Map Ref: M, B3

MTho   A & A THORP
Bungalow No 5, Main Street, Theddingworth, Leicestershire, LE17 6QZ
Ⓣ (01858) 880496

M

M

MTis   TISSINGTON NURSERY 🏠 ♿

Contact: Anita & Andrew Thorp
Opening Times: 1000-1700.
Cat. Cost: 4 x 1st class
Credit Cards: None
Specialities: Unusual plants or those in short supply.
Map Ref: M, C3

MTis   TISSINGTON NURSERY 🏠 ♿
Tissington, Nr Ashbourne,
Derbyshire,
DE6 1RA
Ⓣ (01335) 390650
Ⓕ (01335) 390693
Ⓔ info@tissingtonnursery.co.uk
Ⓦ www.tissingtonnursery.co.uk
Contact: Mrs Sue Watkins
Opening Times: 1000-1800 daily 1st Mar-30th Sep incl. Easter Sun & B/hols.
Cat. Cost: 3 x 1st class
Credit Cards: Visa MasterCard
Specialities: Perennials, shrubs & climbers incl. unusual varieties. Some available only in very ltd. numbers.
Map Ref: M, B1
OS Grid Ref: SK176521

MTiv   PHILIP TIVEY & SON ✉
28 Wanlip Road, Syston,
Leicestershire, LE7 8PA
Ⓣ 0116 269 2968
Ⓕ 0116 269 2968
Ⓔ chris.tivey@ntlworld.com
Also supplies wholesale: Yes
Contact: Chris Tivey
Opening Times: 1000-1500 daily.
Min Mail Order UK: £8.00 + p&p
Cat. Cost: Sae
Credit Cards: None
Specialities: *Dahlia*. Note: small quantities only.

MTPN   SMART PLANTS ✉ 🏠 ♿
Sandy Hill Lane, Off Overstone Road,
Moulton, Northampton, NN3 7JB
Ⓣ (01604) 454106
Contact: Stuart Smart
Opening Times: 1030-1700 Thu, Fri & Sat, other times by appt.
Min Mail Order UK: Nmc*
Cat. Cost: 3 x 1st class
Credit Cards: None
Specialities: Wide range of herbaceous, alpines, shrubs, grasses, hardy *Geranium*, *Sempervivum* & succulents.
*Note: mail order of *Sempervivum*, succulents only.
Map Ref: M, C3

MWar   WARD FUCHSIAS ✉
5 Pollen Close, Sale, Cheshire, M33 3LS
Ⓣ (0161) 282 7434
Contact: K Ward
Opening Times: 0930-1700 Tue-Sun Feb-Jun incl. B/hols.
Min Mail Order UK: Nmc
Cat. Cost: Free
Credit Cards: None
Specialities: *Fuchsia*.
Map Ref: M, A2

MWat   WATERPERRY GARDENS LTD ✉ ♿
Waterperry, Nr Wheatley,
Oxfordshire, OX33 1JZ
Ⓣ (01844) 339226/254
Ⓕ (01844) 339883
Ⓔ office@waterperrygardens.fsnet.co.uk
Ⓦ www.waterperrygardens.co.uk
Contact: Mr R Jacobs
Opening Times: 0900-1730 Mon-Fri, 0900-1800 Sat & Sun summer. 0900-1700 winter.
Min Mail Order UK: Nmc*
Cat. Cost: 75p
Credit Cards: Visa MasterCard Switch American Express
Specialities: General, plus Nat. Coll. of *Saxifraga* (*Porophyllum*). Reasonable wheelchair access. *Note: limited mail order, please phone for information.
Map Ref: M, D3
OS Grid Ref: SP630064

MWgw   WINGWELL NURSERY ✉
Top Street, Wing,
Oakham, Rutland, LE15 8SE
Ⓣ (01572) 737727
Ⓕ (01572) 737788
Ⓔ dejardin.design@btinternet.com
Ⓦ www.wingwellnursery.com
Contact: Rose Dejardin
Opening Times: 1000-1700 daily Mar-Dec.
Min Mail Order UK: Nmc*
Cat. Cost: £1.00 for descriptive cat.
Credit Cards: all major credit/debit cards
Specialities: Herbaceous perennials. *Note: mail order Oct-Mar for herbaceous plants, grasses & ferns only.
Map Ref: M, B3
OS Grid Ref: SP892029

MWhe   A D & N WHEELER 🏠
Pye Court, Willoughby,
Rugby, Warwickshire,
CV23 8BZ
Ⓣ (01788) 890341
Ⓕ (01788) 890341
Contact: Mrs N Wheeler

Opening Times: 1000-1630 7 days mid Feb-late Jun. Other times please phone for appt.
Cat. Cost: 3 x 1st class
Credit Cards: None
Specialities: *Fuchsia, Pelargonium* & hardy *Geranium.*
Map Ref: M, C3

MWhi **WHITEHILL FARM NURSERY** ⊠ € ♿
Whitehill Farm, Burford, Oxfordshire, OX18 4DT
ⓣ (01993) 823218
ⓕ (01993) 822894
Contact: P J M Youngson
Opening Times: 0900-1800 (or dusk if earlier) 7 days.
Min Mail Order UK: £5.00 + p&p
Min Mail Order EU: £5.00 + p&p
Cat. Cost: 4 x 1st class*
Credit Cards: None
Specialities: Grasses & bamboos, less common shrubs, perennials & trees.
*Note: £1.00 of catalogue cost refunded on 1st order.
Map Ref: M, D2
OS Grid Ref: SP268113

MWht **WHITELEA NURSERY** ⊠ ♿
Whitelea Lane, Tansley, Matlock, Derbyshire, DE4 5FL
ⓣ (01629) 55010
ⓔ whitelea@nursery-stock.freeserve.co.uk
ⓦ www.nursery-stock.freeserve.co.uk
Contact: David Wilson
Opening Times: By appt.
Min Mail Order UK: No minimum charge*
Cat. Cost: 2 x 1st class
Credit Cards: None
Specialities: *Bamboo*, ivies. Substantial quantities of 30 cvs & species of bamboo, remainder stocked in small numbers only.
*Note: palletised deliveries only at present.
Map Ref: M, B1
OS Grid Ref: SK325603

MWod **WOODLANDS GRANGE** ♘
Plantation Lane, Hopwas, Nr Tamworth, Staffordshire, B78 3AS
ⓣ (01827) 311567
ⓕ (01827) 54144
ⓔ enquiries@woodlandsgrange.co.uk
ⓦ www.woodlandsgrange.co.uk
Contact: Sean Bradnack, Jim Bliss
Opening Times: 0830-1700 Mon-Sat, 1030-1630 Sun. Late night opening during season, please phone for details.
Cat. Cost: 2 x 1st class

Credit Cards: all major credit/debit cards
Specialities: Ornamental grasses & *Bamboo.*
Map Ref: M, B1

MWrn **WARREN HILLS NURSERY** ⊠ ♘ ♿
Warren Hills Cottage, Warren Hills Road, Coalville, Leicestershire, LE67 4UY
ⓣ (01530) 812350
ⓔ warrenhills@tinyworld.co.uk
Contact: Penny Waters or Bob Taylor
Opening Times: By appt. only, please phone.
Min Mail Order UK: £10.00 + p&p
Cat. Cost: 4 x 1st class
Credit Cards: None
Specialities: *Astrantia, Campanula, Dierama, Penstemon, Heuchera, Nepeta.* Nat. Coll. of *Astrantia.*
Map Ref: M, B1

MWya **WYATTS** ♘ € ♿
Hill Barn Farm, Great Rollright, Chipping Norton, Oxfordshire, OX7 5SH
ⓣ (01608) 684835 (01608) 684990
ⓕ (01608) 684990
ⓔ wyatts@callnetuk.com
ⓦ www.cotswoldgardenplants.co.uk
Contact: John Wyatt or Christine Chittenden
Opening Times: 0900-1700 7 days 21st Oct-1st Mar, 0930-1800 2nd Mar-20th Oct.
Cat. Cost: 2 x 1st class
Credit Cards: MasterCard Switch Delta Visa
Specialities: Many unusual, rare & exotic plants, shrubs & trees incl. *Daphne, Euonymus, Viburnum, Clematis, Cornus* & *Acer.* Alpines, fruit trees & cane fruit. Please check availability list.
Map Ref: M, C2
OS Grid Ref: SP317313

NORTHERN

NABC **ASKHAM BRYAN COLLEGE NURSERY** ♿
Askham Bryan, York, YO23 3FR
ⓣ (01904) 772277
ⓕ (01904) 772288
ⓦ www.askham-bryan.ac.uk
Contact: Don Buckle
Opening Times: 1000-1500 Thu & Fri.
Min Mail Order UK: No minimum charge
Cat. Cost: Free
Credit Cards: None
Specialities: Hardy shrubs, perennials, esp. *Daphne, Hosta.* Nat. Coll. of *Spiraea.*

⊠ Mail order to UK or EU	♘ Delivers to shows
✈ Exports beyond EU	€ Euro accepted
♿ Accessible by wheelchair	◆ See Display advertisement

KEY

M

Map Ref: N, C2
OS Grid Ref: SE553476

NArg ARGHAM VILLAGE NURSERY ⊠ &
Argham Grange, Grindale, Bridlington,
East Yorkshire, YO16 4XZ
Ⓣ (01723) 892141
Ⓕ (01723) 892141
Ⓔ geoffpickering@arghamvillage.co.uk
Ⓦ www.arghamvillage.co.uk
Contact: Geoff Pickering
Opening Times: 1000-1700 Mar-Oct,
1130-1500 Nov-Feb, 7 days.
Min Mail Order UK: £50.00 + p&p
Cat. Cost: 4 x 1st class
Credit Cards: Visa MasterCard Delta
Specialities: Herbaceous perennials. Aquatic
plants, marginals, bog, alpines, rock plants.
Map Ref: N, C3

NAsh ASHTONS NURSERY GARDENS ⊠ &
Mythop Road, Lytham, Lytham St Annes,
Lancashire, FY8 4JP
Ⓣ (01253) 736627/794808
Ⓕ (01253) 735311
Ⓔ info@ashtons-lytham.co.uk
Ⓦ www.ashtons-lytham.co.uk
Also supplies wholesale: Yes
Contact: T M Ashton
Opening Times: 0900-1700 daily.
Min Mail Order UK: Nmc
Cat. Cost: None issued
Credit Cards: MasterCard Visa Switch Delta
American Express
Specialities: Herbaceous plants. Hardy shrubs.
Map Ref: N, D1

NBat BATTERSBY ROSES ⊠ €
Peartree Cottage, Old Battersby, Great Ayton,
Cleveland, TS9 6LU
Ⓣ (01642) 723402
Ⓔ battersbyroses@lineone.net
Ⓦ www.battersbyroses.8m.com
Contact: Eric & Avril Stainthorpe
Opening Times: 1000-dusk most days.
Min Mail Order UK: Nmc
Min Mail Order EU: Nmc
Cat. Cost: Sae
Credit Cards: None
Specialities: Exhibition roses incl. some
American & Canadian miniatures.
Map Ref: N, C2

NBea BEAMISH CLEMATIS NURSERY €
Burntwood Cottage, Stoney Lane, Beamish,
Co. Durham, DH9 0SJ
Ⓣ (0191) 370 0202
Ⓕ (0191) 370 0202

Ⓦ www.beamishclematisnursery.co.uk
Contact: Colin Brown or Jan Wilson
Opening Times: 0900-1700 Wed-Mon,
closed Tue. Closed Easter Sun & Xmas week.
Cat. Cost: 3 x 1st class
Credit Cards: None
Specialities: *Clematis*, climbers, shrubs &
ornamental trees.
Map Ref: N, B2

NBee BEECHCROFT NURSERIES ⊠ &
Bongate, Appleby-in-Westmorland,
Cumbria, CA16 6UE
Ⓣ (01768) 351201
Ⓕ (01768) 351201
Contact: Roger Brown
Opening Times: 0900-1700 Tue-Sun, closed
Mon.
Min Mail Order UK: Nmc*
Cat. Cost: Sae for tree list.
Credit Cards: None
Specialities: Hardy field-grown trees &
shrubs. *Note: mail order trees Nov-Mar
only.
Map Ref: N, C1

NBhm BEETHAM NURSERIES &
Pool Darkin Lane Beetham,
Nr Milnthorpe, Cumbria, LA7 7AP
Ⓣ (01539) 563630
Ⓕ (01539) 564487
Contact: S & L Abbit
Opening Times: 0900-1730 Summer, 0900-
dusk Winter.
Cat. Cost: None issued
Credit Cards: Visa American Express Switch
Specialities: Comprehensive range of Trees,
Shrubs & Herbaceous Plants. Many unusual
varieties.
Map Ref: N, C1

NBid BIDE-A-WEE COTTAGE GARDENS ⊠ &
Stanton, Netherwitton,
Morpeth, Northumberland,
NE65 8PR
Ⓣ (01670) 772262
Ⓔ bideaweecg@aol.com
Contact: Mark Robson
Opening Times: 1330-1700 Sat & Wed 26th
Apr-30th Aug 2003.
Min Mail Order UK: Nmc
Cat. Cost: 3 x 1st class
Credit Cards: None
Specialities: Unusual herbaceous perennials,
Primula, grasses. Nat. Coll. of *Centaurea*
(provisional status).
Map Ref: N, B2
OS Grid Ref: NZ132900

NBir   **BIRKHEADS COTTAGE GARDEN NURSERY** ⊠
Nr Causey Arch, Sunniside,
Newcastle upon Tyne, NE16 5EL
ⓣ (01207) 232262
Ⓜ 07778 447920
Ⓕ (01207) 232262
Ⓔ birkheads.nursery@virgin.net
Ⓦ www.birkheadscottagenursery.co.uk
Contact: Mrs Christine Liddle
Opening Times: 1000-1700 every day Mar-end Oct. Winter opening Nov-Feb (please phone first). Groups by appt.
Min Mail Order UK: £30.00*
Cat. Cost: None issued
Credit Cards: None
Specialities: Hardy herbaceous perennials, grasses, bulbs & herbs. *Allium, Campanula, Digitalis, Euphorbia, Geranium, Primula.* Max. 30 of any plant propagated each year. *Note: mail order Nov-Feb only. Orders taken all year for winter deliveries.
Map Ref: N, B2
OS Grid Ref: NZ220569

NBlu   **BLUNDELL'S NURSERIES** ♿
68 Southport New Road Tarleton, Preston, Lancashire, PR4 6HY
ⓣ (01772) 815442
Ⓔ jerplusjeff@aol.com
Also supplies wholesale: Yes
Contact: Any member of staff
Opening Times: 0900-1700 daily excl. Weds. Closed Dec-Feb.
Cat. Cost: None issued
Credit Cards: None
Specialities: Trees, shrubs, incl. topiary & large specimens, conifers. *Clematis* & other climbers, perennials, alpines, ferns, heathers, herbs, hanging basket, bedding, conservatory plants, aquatics, hedging, roses. Garden design service available.
Map Ref: N, D1

NBPC   **THE BARN PLANT CENTRE & GIFT SHOP** ♿
The Square, Scorton,
Preston, Lancashire,
PR3 1AU
ⓣ (01524) 793533
Ⓕ (01524) 793533
Ⓔ neil.anderton@virgin.net
Ⓦ www.plantsandgifts.co.uk
Contact: Neil Anderton, Karen Macleod
Opening Times: 0900-1700 Mon-Sat, 1000-1800 Sun.
Cat. Cost: 2 1st class
Credit Cards: all major credit/debit cards

Specialities: 600 varieties of perennials. Old roses.
Map Ref: N, C1
OS Grid Ref: GR501487

NBrk   **T H BARKER & SONS** ⊠ ♿
Baines Paddock Nursery,
Haverthwaite, Ulverston,
Cumbria, LA12 8PF
ⓣ (015395) 58236
Ⓔ rachel@thbarker.demon.co.uk
Ⓦ www.ukclematis.co.uk
Contact: W E Thornley
Opening Times: 0930-1730 Wed-Mon 1st Feb-30th Nov. Closed Tue.
Min Mail Order UK: 2 plants
Cat. Cost: £1.00 (Clematis & Climbers)
Credit Cards: None
Specialities: *Clematis, Lonicera* & other climbers. Cottage garden plants esp. hardy *Geranium, Aster, Ranunculus, Iris* & *Viola.* Many rare. Most stock grown on the nursery.
Map Ref: N, C1

NBro   **BROWNTHWAITE HARDY PLANTS** ♿
Fell Yeat, Casterton,
Kirkby Lonsdale, Lancashire, LA6 2JW
ⓣ (015242) 71340 (after 1800).
Contact: Chris Benson
Opening Times: Tue-Sun 1st Apr-30th Sep.
Cat. Cost: 3 x 1st class*
Credit Cards: None
Specialities: Herbaceous perennials & grasses incl. *Geranium, Hosta, Iris*, especially *I. ensata* & *I. sibirica, Heucherella, Tiarella, Primula auricula* & *P. sieboldii.* *(Sae for *P. auricula* mail order list.)
Map Ref: N, C1

NBur   **BURTON AGNES HALL NURSERY** ⊠ ♿
Burton Agnes Hall Preservation Trust Ltd,
Estate Office, Burton Agnes, Driffield,
East Yorkshire, YO25 0ND
ⓣ (01262) 490324
Ⓕ (01262) 490513
Ⓔ burton.agnes@farmline.com
Ⓦ www.burton-agnes.com
Contact: Mrs S Cunliffe-Lister
Opening Times: 1100-1700 Apr-Oct.
Min Mail Order UK: £15.00 + p&p*
Min Mail Order EU: £15.00 + p&p
Cat. Cost: 4 x 1st class
Credit Cards: None

Specialities: Large range perennials & alpines. Many unusual varieties esp. *Penstemon, Osteospermum, Digitalis, Anemone, Geranium.* Nat. Coll. of *Campanula.* *Note: mail order Nov-Mar only.
Map Ref: N, C3

NCGa CATH'S GARDEN PLANTS ⊠ ⋒ ⬚
Eriskay, 2 Sea View, Nether Kellet, Carnforth, Lancashire, LA6 1EG
ⓣ (01524) 735567 office, (015395) 61126 nursery
ⓕ (01524) 735567
ⓔ cath@cathsgardenplants.fsbusiness.co.uk
ⓦ www.cathsgardenplants.gbr.cc
Also supplies wholesale: Yes
Contact: Cath Sanderson
Opening Times: 1030-1700 Fri-Mon, Apr-Oct.
Min Mail Order UK: Nmc
Min Mail Order EU: £25.00
Cat. Cost: 4 x 1st class
Credit Cards: None
Specialities: Wide variety of perennials, incl. uncommon varieties & selections of grasses, ferns, shrubs & climbing plants. Note: nursery is at Heaves Hotel, Levens, Nr Kendal, Cumbria.
Map Ref: N, C1
OS Grid Ref: SD497867

NChi CHIPCHASE CASTLE NURSERY ⋒ ⬚
Chipchase Castle, Wark, Hexham, Northumberland, NE48 3NT
ⓣ (01434) 230083
ⓦ www.northernperennials.co.uk
Contact: Suzanne Newell & Janet Beakes
Opening Times: 1000-1700 Thu-Sun & B/hol Mons Easter (or 1st Apr)-mid Oct.
Cat. Cost: A5 sae for list
Credit Cards: None
Specialities: Unusual herbaceous esp. *Erodium, Eryngium, Geranium* & *Viola.* Some plants only available in small numbers. Suitable for accompanied wheelchair users.
Map Ref: N, B2

NChl CHILTERN SEEDS ⊠ ⊠ € ◆
Bortree Stile, Ulverston, Cumbria, LA12 7PB
ⓣ (01229) 581137 (24 hrs)
ⓕ (01229) 584549
ⓔ info@chilternseeds.co.uk
ⓦ www.chilternseeds.co.uk
Opening Times: Normal office hours, Mon-Fri.
Min Mail Order UK: Nmc
Min Mail Order EU: Nmc
Cat. Cost: 3 x 2nd class
Credit Cards: Visa Access American Express Switch MasterCard EuroCard

Specialities: Over 4,600 items of all kinds - wild flowers, trees, shrubs, cacti, annuals, houseplants, vegetables & herbs.

NCiC CICELY'S COTTAGE GARDEN PLANTS
43 Elmers Green, Skelmersdale, Lancashire, WN8 6SG
ⓣ (01695) 720790
ⓔ maureen.duncan@ic24.net
Contact: Maureen Duncan
Opening Times: Please phone to avoid disappointment as opening times vary.
Cat. Cost: Free plant list
Credit Cards: None
Specialities: Shrubs, hardy, half-hardy & tender perennials incl. *Penstemon.* Traditional & unusual cottage garden plants & pelargoniums. Stock available in small quantities.
Map Ref: N, D1

NCot COTTAGE GARDEN PLANTS ⊠
1 Sycamore Close, Whitehaven, Cumbria, CA28 6LE
ⓣ (01946) 695831
ⓔ jnprkss@aol.com
ⓦ www.cottagegardenplants.com
Contact: Mrs J Purkiss
Opening Times: By appt. only. For garden, consult local press & radio for charity openings.
Min Mail Order UK: Nmc
Cat. Cost: 3 x 1st class sae
Credit Cards: None
Specialities: Hardy perennials incl. *Geranium, Polemonium, Primula* & bog plants.
Map Ref: N, C1

NCro CROSTON CACTUS ⊠ ⋒ ⬚
43 Southport Road, Eccleston, Chorley, Lancashire, PR7 6ET
ⓣ (01257) 452555
ⓔ desert.plants@lineone.net
ⓦ www.croston-cactus.co.uk
Contact: John Henshaw
Opening Times: 0930-1700 Wed-Sat & by appt.
Min Mail Order UK: £5.00 + p&p
Min Mail Order EU: £10.00 + p&p
Cat. Cost: 2 x 1st or 2 x IRCs
Credit Cards: None
Specialities: Mexican cacti, *Echeveria* hybrids & some bromeliads & *Tillandsia.*
Map Ref: N, D1

NDlv DALESVIEW NURSERY ⊠ ⊠ ⬚
24 Braithwaite Edge Road, Keighley, West Yorkshire, BD22 6RA

Ⓣ (01535) 606531
Also supplies wholesale: Yes
Contact: David Ellis & Eileen Morgan
Opening Times: 1000-1700 Wed-Sun &
B/hols.
Min Mail Order UK: Nmc
Min Mail Order EU: Nmc
Cat. Cost: 4 x 1st class
Credit Cards: None
Specialities: Dwarf *Hebe, Saxifraga, Primula, Rhododendron, Fuchsia* & conifers.
Map Ref: N, C2

NDov   DOVE COTTAGE NURSERY ⓦ
23 Shibden Hall Road,
Halifax,
West Yorkshire, HX3 9XA
ⓉT (01422) 203553
Ⓔ dovecottage.nursery@virgin.net
Ⓦ www.dovecottagenursery.co.uk
Contact: Stephen & Kim Rogers
Opening Times: 1000-1800 Wed-Sun &
B/hols Feb-Sep.
Cat. Cost: 4 x 1st class
Credit Cards: Switch Solo Delta Electron Visa
MasterCard
Specialities: *Helleborus* & selected perennials
& grasses for naturalistic planting.
Map Ref: N, D2
OS Grid Ref: SE115256

NEqu   EQUATORIAL PLANT CO. ⊠ ⊠ ⋔ €
7 Gray Lane, Barnard Castle,
Co. Durham, DL12 8PD
Ⓣ (01833) 690519
Ⓕ (01833) 690519
Ⓔ equatorialplants@teesdaleonline.co.uk
Also supplies wholesale: Yes
Contact: Dr Richard Warren
Opening Times: By appt. only.
Min Mail Order UK: Nmc
Min Mail Order EU: Nmc
Cat. Cost: Free
Credit Cards: Visa Access
Specialities: Laboratory raised orchids only.

**NFir   FIR TREES PELARGONIUM
NURSERY** ⊠ ⋔ ⓦ
Stokesley, Middlesbrough,
Cleveland, TS9 5LD
Ⓣ (01642) 713066
Ⓕ (01642) 713066
Ⓦ www.firtreespelargoniums.co.uk
Contact: Helen Bainbridge
Opening Times: 1000-1600 7 days 15th Mar-
30th Sep, 1000-1600 Mon-Fri 1st Oct-15th
Mar.
Min Mail Order UK: £2.50 + p&p

Cat. Cost: 4 x 1st class
Credit Cards: MasterCard Visa Switch
Specialities: All types of *Pelargonium* - fancy
leaf, regal, decorative regal, oriental regal, angel,
miniature, zonal, ivy leaf, stellar, scented, dwarf,
unique, golden stellar & species.
Map Ref: N, C2

NFla   FLAXTON HOUSE NURSERY
Flaxton, York, North Yorkshire, Y060 7RJ
Ⓣ (01904) 468753
Contact: Mrs H Williams
Opening Times: 1000-1700 Tue-Sun 1st
Mar-31st Oct.
Cat. Cost: 2 x 1st class
Credit Cards: None
Specialities: Wide general range of
herbaceous & alpines with many unusual
plants. Selection of climbers & shrubs. Ltd.
quantities so phone before travelling.
Map Ref: N, C2
OS Grid Ref: 467462

NFor   FORD NURSERY ⊠
Castle Gardens, Ford,
Berwick-upon-Tweed, TD15 2PZ
Ⓣ (01890) 820379
Ⓕ (01890) 820594
Ⓔ Ford.nursery@which.net
Ⓦ www.FordNursery.co.uk
Contact: Sarah Glass & Roy Harmeston
Opening Times: 1000-1730 7 days Mar-Oct,
1000-1630 Mon-Fri Nov-Feb.
Min Mail Order UK: Nmc
Cat. Cost: Free
Credit Cards: Visa Access Switch
Specialities: Over 1200 different species of
container grown hardy ornamental shrubs,
perennials, trees & herbs, climbers & grasses.
Map Ref: N, A2

NGar   GARDENSCAPE ⊠ ⋔ €
Fairview, Smelthouses, Summerbridge,
Harrogate, North Yorkshire, HG3 4DH
Ⓣ (01423) 780291
Ⓜ 07801 232024
Ⓕ (01423) 780291
Ⓔ mdmyers@gardenscape.co.uk
Ⓦ www.gardenscape.co.uk
Contact: Michael D Myers
Opening Times: By appt.
Min Mail Order UK: £10.00 + p&p
Min Mail Order EU: £30.00

KEY		
⊠ Mail order to UK or EU	⋔ Delivers to shows	
⊠ Exports beyond EU	€ Euro accepted	
ⓦ Accessible by wheelchair	◆ See Display advertisement	

Cat. Cost: 3 x 1st class
Credit Cards: None
Specialities: Woodland plants & alpines, snowdrops. Nat. Colls. of *Anemone nemorosa*, *Hepatica* & *Primula marginata*.
Map Ref: N, C2
OS Grid Ref: SE195644

NGby   GILBEY'S PLANTS ✉ ♦ € ⬚
(office) 42 Park Street, Masham, Ripon, North Yorkshire, HG4 4HN
Ⓣ (01765) 689927 (01845) 525285
Ⓕ (01765) 689927
Ⓔ gilbeyplants@aol.com
Also supplies wholesale: Yes
Contact: Giles N Gilbey
Opening Times: 1000-1700 Mon-Sat, 1400-1700 Sun, 1st Mar-1st Oct. Winter by appt. only.
Min Mail Order UK: Nmc*
Min Mail Order EU: Nmc
Cat. Cost: 4 x 1st class
Credit Cards: None
Specialities: Unusual hardy perennials & ferns. *Note: mail order Oct-Mar only. Nursery at The Walled Garden, Cemetery Road, Thirsk YO7 4DL.
Map Ref: N, C2

NGdn   GARDEN HOUSE NURSERIES ⬚
The Square, Dalston, Carlisle, Cumbria, CA5 7LL
Ⓣ (01228) 710297
Ⓔ david@gardenhousenursery.co.uk
Ⓦ www.gardenhousenursery.co.uk
Contact: David Hickson
Opening Times: 0900-1700 7 days Mar-Oct.
Cat. Cost: None issued, plant list on web
Credit Cards: None
Specialities: *Geranium, Hosta, Hemerocallis, Iris*, grasses, bamboos & *Penstemon*.
Map Ref: N, B1
OS Grid Ref: NY369503

NGHP   GREEN GARDEN HERBS & PLANTS ♦ ⬚
13 West Bank, Carlton, North Yorkshire, DN14 9PZ
Ⓣ (01405) 860708
Ⓜ 079499 06290
Ⓕ (01405) 860708
Ⓔ green@gardenherbs.fsnet.co.uk
Also supplies wholesale: Yes
Contact: Sarah Clark, Stefan Vida
Opening Times: 1000-1700 Wed-Mon, closed Tue, Mar-Sep. Other times by appt.
Cat. Cost: 4 x 2nd class
Credit Cards: Visa
Specialities: Herbs. Note: nursery has moved

(May 02) to 13 West Bank, Carlton, North Yorks.
Map Ref: N, D3
OS Grid Ref: SE626242

NGSd   GRANGE SIDE NURSERIES ⬚
Grange Cottage, Thorpe Lane, Cawood, Selby, Yorkshire, YO8 3SG
Ⓣ (01757) 268274
Ⓕ (01757) 268274
Ⓔ sale@grangesidenurseries.co.uk
Ⓦ www.grangesidenurseries.co.uk
Also supplies wholesale: Yes
Contact: Michael & Lynne Johnstone
Opening Times: 1000-1700, early spring-autumn. 1000-1600 rest of year.
Credit Cards: all major credit/debit cards
Specialities: Perennials. Alpines.

NHal   HALLS OF HEDDON ✉ ✉ ⬚
(Office) West Heddon Nurseries, Heddon-on-the-wall, Northumberland, NE15 0JS
Ⓣ (01661) 852445
Ⓕ (01661) 852398
Ⓔ hallsofheddon@breathemail.net
Ⓦ www.hallsofheddon.co.uk
Also supplies wholesale: Yes
Contact: Judith Lockey
Opening Times: 0900-1700 Mon-Sat 1000-1700 Sun.
Min Mail Order UK: Nmc
Min Mail Order EU: £25.00 + p&p*
Cat. Cost: 3 x 2nd class
Credit Cards: None
Specialities: *Chrysanthemum* & *Dahlia*. Wide range of herbaceous. *Note: mail order *Dahlia* & *Chrysanthemum* only. EU & export *Dahlia* tubers only.
Map Ref: N, B2

NHer   HERTERTON HOUSE GARDEN NURSERY
Hartington, Cambo, Morpeth, Northumberland, NE61 4BN
Ⓣ (01670) 774278
Contact: Mrs M Lawley & Mr Frank Lawley
Opening Times: 1330-1730 Mon Wed Fri-Sun 1st Apr-end Sep. (Earlier or later in the year weather permitting.)
Cat. Cost: None issued
Credit Cards: None
Specialities: Country garden flowers.
Map Ref: N, B2

NHHG   HARDSTOFT HERB GARDEN
Hall View Cottage, Hardstoft, Pilsley, Nr Chesterfield, Derbyshire, S45 8AH
Ⓣ (01246) 854268
Contact: Lynne & Steve Raynor

Opening Times: 1000-1700 daily 15th
Mar-15th Sep. Closed Tue excl. Easter &
B/hol weeks.
Cat. Cost: Free
Credit Cards: MasterCard Switch Delta Visa
Specialities: Wide range of herbs. Over 40
lavenders & 12 rosemary. Scented
pelargoniums. Nat. Coll. of *Echinacea.*
Map Ref: N, D2

NHol   HOLDEN CLOUGH NURSERY
☒ ☒ ń ⅃ ◆
Holden, Bolton-by-Bowland, Clitheroe,
Lancashire, BB7 4PF
Ⓣ (01200) 447615
Ⓕ (01200) 447615
Ⓔ enquiries@holdencloughnursery.co.uk
Ⓦ www.holdencloughnursery.co.uk
Also supplies wholesale: Yes
Contact: P J Foley
Opening Times: 0900-1630 Mon-Sat all year
& B/hol Mons, 1300-1630 Easter Sun + Sun
May B/hol w/ends. Closed 25th Dec-2nd Jan
2004 & Good Fri. Please phone first to check
opening times.
Min Mail Order UK: Nmc
Min Mail Order EU: Nmc
Cat. Cost: £1.40
Credit Cards: MasterCard Visa Delta
Specialities: Large general list incl. *Primula,
Saxifraga, Sempervivum, Jovibarba, Astilbe,*
grasses, *Hosta,* heathers & *Rhododendron.*
Seasonal mail order on some items.
Map Ref: N, C2
OS Grid Ref: SD773496

NHor   HORN'S GARDEN CENTRE
Dixon Estate, Shotton Colliery,
Co. Durham, DH6 2PX
Ⓣ (0191) 526 2987
Ⓕ (0191) 526 2889
Contact: G Horn & Theresa Horn
Opening Times: 0900-1730 Mon-Sat 1000-
1600 Sun, all year excl. Easter Mon.
Credit Cards: Visa EuroCard MasterCard
Access Switch American Express Delta
Specialities: *Fuchsia,* pelargoniums. Wide
range of trees, shrubs & perennials.
Map Ref: N, B2

NIng   INGLEFIELD SPECIALITY PLANTS ⅃ ◆
Windermere Road, Staveley, Cumbria, LA8 9LY
Ⓣ (01539) 821142
Ⓕ (01539) 822774
Ⓦ www.inglefieldplants.co.uk
Contact: Michael & Elizabeth Tullis
Opening Times: 1000-1700 7 days, times
may vary Dec-Feb, please contact for details.

Credit Cards: all major credit/debit cards
Specialities: Specimen plants, Mediterranean
& conservatory plants. Available to order and
in small quantities.
OS Grid Ref: SD469984

NJOw   JOHN OWEN NURSERIES
20 West Bank, Carlton, Nr Goole,
East Yorkshire, DN14 9PZ
Ⓣ (01405) 861415
Ⓜ 07762 650131
Ⓕ (01405) 861415
Ⓔ johnowen-nurseries@njow.fsnet.co.uk
Also supplies wholesale: Yes
Contact: John D W Owen
Opening Times: 1000-1700 Thu-Sat, 1st
Mar-31st Oct & B/hols.
Cat. Cost: 3 x 2nd class
Credit Cards: None
Specialities: Alpines & perennials, especially
*Allium, Campanula, Dianthus, Oxalis,
Primula* & *Saxifraga.* A few varieties available
in small quantities only.
Map Ref: N, D3
OS Grid Ref: SE629243

NLan   LANDLIFE WILDFLOWERS LTD ☒
National Wildflower Centre,
Court Hey Park, Liverpool, L16 3NA
Ⓣ (0151) 737 1819
Ⓕ (0151) 737 1820
Ⓔ gill@landlife.org.uk
Ⓦ www.wildflower.org.uk
Also supplies wholesale: Yes
Contact: Gillian Watson
Opening Times: 1000-1700, 7 days, 1 Apr-
30 Sep only.
Min Mail Order UK: £30.00 (plants), no
min. for seeds.
Cat. Cost: Sae + 2 x 2nd class
Credit Cards: Visa Delta Access Switch Solo
Specialities: Wild herbaceous plants & seeds.
Cafe & shop. Visitor centre, admission
charge.
Map Ref: N, D1

NLAp   LANESIDE ALPINES ☒ ń
74 Croston Road, Garstang, Preston,
Lancashire, PR3 1HR
Ⓣ (01995) 605537
Ⓜ 0794 6659661
Ⓔ jcrhutch@aol.com
Contact: Jeff Hutchings

N

N

Opening Times: By appt. only.
Min Mail Order UK: Nmc*
Cat. Cost: Sae
Specialities: Alpines, incl. gentians, *Penstemon*
species, primulas, show auriculas, *Saxifraga,*
dwarf evergreen shrubs, celmisias, New
Zealand plants, planted bowls & planted tufa.
*Note: mail order from autumn 2003. Many
species available in small numbers only.
Map Ref: N, D1

NLar   LARCH COTTAGE NURSERIES ✉ € ♿ ◆
Melkinthorpe, Penrith, Cumbria, CA10 2DR
Ⓣ (01931) 712404
Ⓕ (01931) 712727
Ⓔ plants@larchcottage.freeserve.co.uk
Ⓦ www.larchcottagenurseries.co.uk
www.larchcottagenurseries.com
Contact: Joanne McCulloch/Peter Stott
Opening Times: Daily from 1000-1730.
Min Mail Order UK: Nmc
Min Mail Order EU: Nmc
Cat. Cost: £2.50
Credit Cards: Visa Access Switch Delta Solo
Specialities: Unusual & old fashioned
perennials. Rare & dwarf conifers. Unusual
shrubs & trees.
Map Ref: N, C1
OS Grid Ref: NY315602

NLLv   LEEDS LAVENDER ✉
Greenscapes Nursery, Brandon Crescen,
Shadwell, Leeds, LS17 9JH
Ⓣ (0113) 2892922
Ⓦ www.leedslavender.co.uk
Also supplies wholesale: Yes
Contact: Ruth Dorrington
Opening Times: 1330-1630 Tue-Thu, 1000-
1700 Fri, Sat, Sun, Mar-Sep or by appt.
Min Mail Order UK: Nmc
Cat. Cost: 2 x 1st class
Credit Cards: None
Specialities: *Lavandula*. Limited varieties peat
free.
Map Ref: N, D2

NLRH   LITTLE RED HEN NURSERIES ✉
91 Denholme Road, Oxenhope, Keighley,
West Yorkshire, BD22 9SJ
Ⓣ (01535) 643786
Ⓔ louise@redhens.co.uk
Ⓦ www.redhens.co.uk
Also supplies wholesale: Yes
Contact: Louise Harris
Opening Times: Please phone first.
Min Mail Order UK: Nmc
Cat. Cost: Free
Credit Cards: None

Specialities: Small nursery with ltd. stock.
Details in catalogue or on website.
Map Ref: N, D2
OS Grid Ref: SE045343

NMar   J & D MARSTON ✉
Culag Green Lane, Nafferton, Driffield,
East Yorkshire, YO25 0LF
Ⓣ (01377) 254487
Ⓕ (01377) 254487
Contact: D & Mrs JK Marston
Opening Times: 1350-1700 Sat & Sun
Easter-mid Sep. Other times by appt.
Min Mail Order UK: £20.00 + p&p
Min Mail Order EU: £60.00 + carriage
Cat. Cost: 4 x 1st class
Credit Cards: None
Specialities: Hardy & greenhouse ferns only.
Map Ref: N, C3

NMen   MENDLE NURSERY ✉ ⌂ ♿
Holme, Scunthorpe, Lincolnshire, DN16 3RF
Ⓣ (01724) 850864
Ⓔ annearnshaw@lineone.net
Ⓦ www.mendlenursery.com
Contact: Mrs A Earnshaw
Opening Times: 1000-1600 Tue-Sun.
Min Mail Order UK: Nmc
Min Mail Order EU: Nmc*
Cat. Cost: 3 x 1st class
Credit Cards: None
Specialities: Many unusual alpines esp.
Saxifraga & *Sempervivum.*
Map Ref: N, D3
OS Grid Ref: SE925070

NMir   MIRES BECK NURSERY ✉ ♿
Low Mill Lane, North Cave, Brough,
East Riding Yorkshire, HU15 2NR
Ⓣ (01430) 421543
Also supplies wholesale: Yes
Contact: Irene Tinklin & Martin Rowland
Opening Times: 1000-1600 Wed-Sat 1st
Mar-30th Sep. 1000-1500 Wed-Fri 1st Oct-
30th Nov & by appt.
Min Mail Order UK: Nmc*
Min Mail Order EU: Nmc*
Cat. Cost: 3 x 1st class
Credit Cards: None
Specialities: Wild flower plants of Yorkshire
provenance. *Note: mail order for wild flower
plants, plugs & seeds only.
Map Ref: N, D3
OS Grid Ref: SE889316

NMoo   MOOR MONKTON NURSERIES ✉
Moor Monkton, York Road, Nr York,
Yorkshire, YO26 8JJ

Ⓣ (01904) 738770
Ⓕ (01904) 738770
Ⓔ sales@bamboo-uk.co.uk
Ⓦ www.bamboo-uk.co.uk
Contact: Peter Owen
Opening Times: 0900-1700.
Min Mail Order UK: Nmc*
Cat. Cost: 5 x 2nd class or email for details.
Credit Cards: None
Specialities: Bamboos, palms, unusual trees, shrubs & perennials. *Note: Mail order for bamboo only.
Map Ref: N, C2

NMRc   MILLRACE NURSERY ⓖ
84 Selby Road, Garforth, Leeds, LS25 1LP
Ⓣ (0113) 286 9233
Ⓕ (0113) 286 9908
Contact: C Carthy
Opening Times: 1000-1700 7 days, Apr & May. 1000-1700 Mon, Tue, Thu-Sat & B/hols, Mar & Jun-Oct, closed Wed.
Cat. Cost: 2 x 1st class
Credit Cards: None
Specialities: Unusual perennials, especially drought-resistant, incl. hardy geraniums, alliums, campanulas, penstemons, potentillas & veronicas. Some plants in small numbers only.
Map Ref: N, D2

NMyG   MARY GREEN ⊠ ή
The Walled Garden, Hornby, Lancaster, Lancashire, LA2 8LD
Ⓣ (01257) 270821
Ⓜ 07778 910348
Ⓕ (01257) 270821
Ⓔ Marygreenplants@aol.com
Contact: Mary Green
Opening Times: By appt. only.
Min Mail Order UK: £10.00
Cat. Cost: 4 x 1st class
Credit Cards: None
Specialities: Choice herbaceous perennials, incl. hostas, astilbes & geraniums.
Map Ref: N, C1
OS Grid Ref: SD588688

NNew   NEWTON HILL ALPINES € ⓖ
335 Leeds Road, Newton Hill, Wakefield, West Yorkshire, WF1 2JH
Ⓣ (01924) 377056
Ⓔ s.vigors@nmsi.ac.uk
Also supplies wholesale: Yes
Contact: Sheena Vigors
Opening Times: 0900-1700 Fri-Wed all year. Closed Thu. Please phone first.

Cat. Cost: 2 x 1st class
Credit Cards: None
Specialities: Alpines esp. *Saxifraga*, also *Erica*, conifers & dwarf shrubs.
Map Ref: N, D2
OS Grid Ref: SE328229

NNor   NORCROFT NURSERIES ⊠ ⓖ
Roadends, Intack, Southwaite, Carlisle, Cumbria, CA4 0LH
Ⓣ (016974) 73933
Ⓜ 07789 050633
Ⓕ (016974) 73969
Ⓔ stellaandkeithbell@sbell44.fsnet.co.uk
Also supplies wholesale: Yes
Contact: Keith Bell
Opening Times: Every afternoon excl. Mon but open B/hols.
Min Mail Order UK: Nmc
Cat. Cost: 2 x 2nd class
Credit Cards: None
Specialities: Hardy herbaceous, ornamental grasses, hostas, *Lilium*, aquatics.
Map Ref: N, B1
OS Grid Ref: NY474433

NOaD   OAK DENE NURSERIES ⊠
10 Back Lane, West Royston, Barnsley, South Yorkshire, S71 4SB
Ⓣ (01226) 722253
Ⓕ (01226) 722253
Also supplies wholesale: Yes
Contact: J Foster or G Foster
Opening Times: 0900-1800 1st Apr-30th Sep, 1000-1600 1st Oct-31st Mar. (Closed 1230-1330.)
Min Mail Order UK: Please phone for further information.
Cat. Cost: None issued.
Credit Cards: None
Specialities: Cacti, succulents & South African *Lachenalia* bulbs.
Map Ref: N, D2

NOak   OAK TREE NURSERY ⊠ ή
Mill Lan, Barlow, Selby, North Yorkshire, YO8 8EY
Ⓣ (01757) 618409
Contact: Gill Plowes
Opening Times: By appt. only.
Min Mail Order UK: £10.00 + p&p
Cat. Cost: 2 x 1st class
Credit Cards: None

N

Specialities: Cottage garden plants, grasses
& ferns.
Map Ref: N, D3

NOGN   THE ORNAMENTAL GRASS
NURSERY ⊠ ⋔ ⧉
Church Farm, Westgate, Rillington,
Malton, North Yorkshire, YO17 8LN
Ⓣ (01944) 758247
Ⓜ 07813 327886
Ⓕ (01944) 758247
Ⓔ sales@ornamentalgrass.co.uk
Ⓦ www.ornamentalgrass.co.uk
Also supplies wholesale: Yes
Contact: Angela Kilby
Opening Times: 0930-1600 Tue-Thu & Sat
1st Apr-mid Oct.
Min Mail Order UK: Nmc
Cat. Cost: 4 x 1st class
Credit Cards: None
Specialities: Ornamental grasses, bamboos,
ferns, hostas & herbaceous perennials.
Map Ref: N, C3

NOrc   ORCHARD HOUSE NURSERY
Orchard House, Wormald Green,
Nr Harrogate, North Yorkshire, HG3 3NQ
Ⓣ (01765) 677541
Ⓕ (01765) 677541
Also supplies wholesale: Yes
Contact: Mr B M Corner
Opening Times: 0800-1630 Mon-Fri.
Cat. Cost: 4 x 1st class
Credit Cards: None
Specialities: Herbaceous perennials, ferns,
grasses, water plants & unusual cottage garden
plants.
Map Ref: N, C2

NPal   THE PALM FARM ⊠ Ⓜ € ⧉
Thornton Hall Gardens, Station Road,
Thornton Curtis, Nr Ulceby,
Humberside, DN39 6XF
Ⓣ (01469) 531232
Ⓕ (01469) 531232
Ⓔ bill@thepalmfarm.com
Ⓦ www.thepalmfarm.com
Also supplies wholesale: Yes
Contact: W W Spink
Opening Times: 1400-1700 7 days in
summer. Please phone for winter times.
Min Mail Order UK: £11.00 + p&p
Min Mail Order EU: £25.00 + p&p
Cat. Cost: 1 x 2nd class
Credit Cards: None
Specialities: Hardy & half-hardy palms,
unusual trees, shrubs & conservatory plants.
Note: some plants available only in small

quantities. Payment in euros accepted only if
purchaser pays bank commission.
Map Ref: N, D3

NPar   GERRY PARKER PLANTS ⊠ ⋔ € ⧉
9 Cotherstone Road, Newton Hall,
Durham, DH1 5YN
Ⓣ (0191) 386 8749
Ⓔ Gerryparker@btinternet.com
Contact: G Parker
Opening Times: Open by appt.
Min Mail Order UK: Nmc
Min Mail Order EU: Nmc
Cat. Cost: 3 x 1st class
Credit Cards: None
Specialities: Woodland plants, bulbs, border
plants, all suited to clay soils. Many in small
quantities.
Map Ref: N, B2

NPen   PENTON MILL
RHODODENDRONS ⊠ Ⓜ € ⧉
Penton, Carlisle, Cumbria,
CA6 5QU
Ⓣ (01228) 577336
Ⓕ (01228) 577336
Ⓔ acrhodos@onetel.net.uk
Contact: Alan J Clark
Opening Times: By appt. only.
Min Mail Order UK: £20.00 + p&p
Min Mail Order EU: £50.00 + p&p
Cat. Cost: 6 x 1st class
Credit Cards: Access Visa Not for telephone
orders
Specialities: Rhododendrons & azaleas &
moisture loving primulas. Note: nursery
formerly Muncaster Castle.
Map Ref: N, B1
OS Grid Ref: NY434764

NPer   PERRY'S PLANTS ⧉
The River Garden, Sleights,
Whitby, North Yorkshire,
YO21 1RR
Ⓣ (01947) 810329
Ⓕ (01947) 810940
Ⓔ perry@rivergardens.fsnet.co.uk
Contact: Pat & Richard Perry
Opening Times: 1000-1700 mid-March to
Oct.
Cat. Cost: Large (A4) Sae
Credit Cards: None
Specialities: *Lavatera, Malva, Erysimum,
Euphorbia, Anthemis, Osteospermum* & *Hebe.*
Uncommon hardy & container plants &
aquatic plants.
Map Ref: N, C3
OS Grid Ref: NZ869082

NPoe **POETS COTTAGE SHRUB NURSERY** 🚾
Lealholm, Whitby,
North Yorkshire, YO21 2AQ
Ⓣ (01947) 897424
Contact: Hilda Rees
Opening Times: 0900-1700 Mar-Christmas,
1300-1530 Jan & Feb, 7 days.
Cat. Cost: None issued.
Credit Cards: None
Specialities: Dwarf conifers, *Acer* &
herbaceous.
Map Ref: N, C3

NPol **POLEMONIUM PLANTERY** ✉ 🏃 🚾
28 Sunnyside Terrace, Trimdon Grange,
Trimdon Station, Co. Durham, TS29 6HF
Ⓣ (01429) 881529
Ⓔ polemoniumnpc@aol.com
Ⓦ www.polemonium.co.uk
Also supplies wholesale: Yes
Contact: David or Dianne Nichol-Brown
Opening Times: Open for Red Cross, 25 May
2003 & for NGS, 26 May 2003. Other times
by appt. only.
Min Mail Order UK: £10.00
Cat. Cost: Sae for list
Credit Cards: None
Specialities: Nat. Coll. of *Polemonium* &
related genera, plus some rare North American
plants. The collection holds scientific status.
Map Ref: N, B2
OS Grid Ref: NZ369353

NPPs **PENNINE PERENNIALS**
15 Mount View, Uppermill, Saddleworth,
Manchester, OL3 6DB
Ⓣ (01457) 872494/873110
Ⓔ pennineperennials@btinternet.com
Contact: Sarah Crawcour, Helen Grainger
Opening Times: Mar-Oct by appt. only.
Cat. Cost: A5 sae for plant list
Credit Cards: None
Specialities: Unusual hardy perennials,
particularly those suitable for Pennine areas.
Note: nursery at different address in same
village.
Map Ref: N, D2

NPri **PRIMROSE COTTAGE NURSERY** 🚾 ◆
Ringway Road, Moss Nook, Wythenshawe,
Manchester, M22 5WF
Ⓣ (0161) 437 1557
Ⓕ (0161) 499 9932
Ⓔ info@primrosecottagenursery.co.uk
Ⓦ www.primrosecottagenursery.co.uk
Contact: Caroline Dumville
Opening Times: 0830-1730 Mon-Sat, 0930-
1730 Sun (summer). 0815-1700 Mon-Sat,

0930-1700 Sun (winter).
Cat. Cost: 2 x 1st class
Credit Cards: all major credit/debit cards
Specialities: Hardy herbaceous perennials,
alpines, herbs, roses, patio & hanging basket
plants. Shrubs.
Map Ref: N, D2

NPro **PROUDPLANTS** 🏃
East of Eden Nurseries, Ainstable, Carlisle,
Cumbria, CA4 9QN
Ⓣ (01768) 896604
Ⓕ (01768) 896604
Contact: Roger Proud
Opening Times: 0900-1800 7 days Mar-Nov.
Other times by appt.
Cat. Cost: None issued
Credit Cards: None
Specialities: Interesting & unusual shrubs &
perennials esp. dwarf & ground cover plants.
Map Ref: N, B1
OS Grid Ref: HA1336186

NPSI **PLANTS OF SPECIAL INTEREST** 🚾 ◆
4 High Street, Braithwell, Nr Rotherham,
South Yorkshire, S66 7AL
Ⓣ (01709) 790642
Ⓕ (01709) 790342
Ⓔ info@psinursery.co.uk
Ⓦ www.psinursery.co.uk
Contact: Rita Ann Dunstan
Opening Times: 1000-1700 Tue-Sun Jan-
Dec, & B/hol Mons. Closed Xmas.
Cat. Cost: None issued.
Credit Cards: Access Switch Visa MasterCard
Specialities: Selection of herbaceous plants
esp. *Zantedeschia* & grasses. Specimen shrubs,
semi-mature trees & architectural plants.
Note: nursery in centre of Braithwell opp.
Red Lion public house.
Map Ref: N, D2

NRar **RARER PLANTS** 🚾
Ashfield House, Austfield Lane, Monk
Fryston, Leeds, LS25 5EH
Ⓣ (01977) 682263
Contact: Anne Watson
Opening Times: 1000-1600 Sat & Sun 20th
Feb-1st Apr.
Cat. Cost: Sae
Credit Cards: None
Specialities: *Helleborus* & *Galanthus*.
Map Ref: N, D2

	KEY		
	✉ Mail order to UK or EU	🏃 Delivers to shows	
	✈ Exports beyond EU	€ Euro accepted	
	🚾 Accessible by wheelchair	◆ See Display advertisement	

N

N

NRib   **RIBBLESDALE NURSERIES** € ⬚
Newsham Hall Lane, Woodplumpton,
Preston, Lancashire, PR4 0AS
ⓣ (01772) 863081
ⓔ ribblesdale99@hotmail.com
Also supplies wholesale: Yes
Contact: James Hart
Opening Times: 0900-1730 daily.
0900-1900 Thu Apr-Jul. Closed Mon
Aug-Easter.
Credit Cards: Visa MasterCard Delta
Switch
Specialities: Trees, shrubs & perennials.
Conifers, hedging, alpines, fruit, climbers,
herbs, aquatics, ferns & conservatory plants.
Map Ref: N, D1
OS Grid Ref: SD515351

NRob   **W ROBINSON & SONS LTD** ⊠ ⬚ € ⬚
Sunny Bank, Forton, Nr Preston,
Lancashire, PR3 0BN
ⓣ (01524) 791210
ⓕ (01524) 791933
ⓔ info@mammothonion.co.uk
ⓦ www.mammothonion.co.uk
Also supplies wholesale: Yes
Contact: Miss Robinson
Opening Times: 0900-1700 7 days Mar-Jun,
0800-1700 Mon-Fri Jul-Feb.
Min Mail Order UK: Nmc
Min Mail Order EU: Nmc
Cat. Cost: Free
Credit Cards: Visa Access American Express
Switch
Specialities: Mammoth vegetable seed.
Onions, leeks, tomatoes & beans. Range of
vegetable plants in the spring.

NRog   **R V ROGER LTD** ⊠ ⬚
The Nurseries, Malton Road (A.169),
Pickering, North Yorkshire,
YO18 8EA
ⓣ (01751) 472226
ⓕ (01751) 476749
ⓔ sales@rvrogers.co.uk
ⓦ www.rvroger.co.uk
Also supplies wholesale: Yes
Contact: I M Roger, S Murfitt, N Perkins
Opening Times: 0900-1700 Mon-Sat, 1300-
1700 Sun. Closed 25th Dec-2nd Jan.
Min Mail Order UK: Nmc
Min Mail Order EU: Nmc
Cat. Cost: £1.50
Credit Cards: Visa Access Switch MasterCard
Specialities: General list, hardy in north of
England.
Map Ref: N, C3
OS Grid Ref: SE801827

NRya   **RYAL NURSERY** ⊠ ⌂ ⬚
East Farm Cottage, Ryal,
Northumberland,
NE20 0SA
ⓣ (01661) 886562
ⓕ (01661) 886918
ⓔ alpines@ryal.freeserve.co.uk
Also supplies wholesale: Yes
Contact: R F Hadden
Opening Times: Mar-Jul 1300-1600 Mon-
Tue but please phone first, 1000-1600 Sun &
other times by appt.
Min Mail Order UK: £5.00 + p&p
Min Mail Order EU: £5.00 + p&p
Cat. Cost: Sae
Credit Cards: None
Specialities: Alpine & woodland plants.
Mainly available in small quantities only.
Map Ref: N, B2
OS Grid Ref: NZ015744

NSco   **SCOTT'S WILDFLOWERS** ⊠ ⬚
Swallow Hill Barn, 31 Common Side,
Distington, Workington, Cumbria,
CA14 4PU
ⓣ (01946) 830486
ⓔ wildflowers@btinternet.com
ⓦ www.scottswildflowers.co.uk
Also supplies wholesale: Yes
Contact: Ted Scott
Opening Times: 1000-1600 Mar-Oct, 1130-
1500 Nov-Feb, 7 days.
Min Mail Order UK: £6.00 + p&p
Cat. Cost: 3 x 1st class
Credit Cards:
Specialities: Native British wildflowers.
Map Ref: N, C1

NScw   **SCAWSBY HALL NURSERIES** ⊠ ⬚
Barnsley Road, Scawsby, Doncaster,
South Yorkshire,
DN5 7UB
ⓣ (01302) 782585
ⓕ (01302) 782585
ⓔ mail@scawsbyhallnurseries.co.uk
ⓦ www.scawsbyhallnurseries.co.uk
Contact: David Lawson
Opening Times: 0930-1730 Mon-Sat, 1100-
1700 Sun, Mar-Sep, 0930-1630 Mon-Sat
1100-1630 Sun, Oct-Feb.
Min Mail Order UK: Nmc
Min Mail Order EU: Nmc
Cat. Cost: None issued
Credit Cards: Visa MasterCard Switch Solo
Specialities: A wide range of herbaceous
perennials, hardy shrubs & indoor plants.
Map Ref: N, D3
OS Grid Ref: SE542049

NShi **SHIRLEY'S PLANTS** ⊠ ň
6 Sandheys Drive, Church Town, Southport,
Merseyside, PR9 9PQ
Ⓣ (01704) 213048
Ⓜ 07951 834066
Ⓦ www.stbegonias.com
Contact: Shirley & Terry Tasker
Opening Times: By appt. only.
Min Mail Order UK: Nmc
Cat. Cost: 2 x 1st class
Credit Cards: None
Specialities: Nat. Coll. of *Begonia* species &
hybrids.
Map Ref: N, D1
OS Grid Ref: SD355183

NSla **SLACK TOP ALPINES** ⊠ ň €
Hebden Bridge, West Yorkshire, HX7 7HA
Ⓣ (01422) 845348
Also supplies wholesale: Yes
Contact: M R or R Mitchell
Opening Times: 1000-1700 Wed-Sun 1st Mar-
30th Sep & B/hol Mons 1st Mar-31st Oct.
Min Mail Order UK: £10.00
Cat. Cost: Sae
Credit Cards: None
Specialities: Alpine & rockery plants.
*Gentiana, Saxifraga, Primula, Hepatica,
Paeonia* & *Pulsatilla.*
Map Ref: N, D2
OS Grid Ref: SD977286

NSpr **SPRINGWOOD PLEIONES** ⊠ ň € ♿
35 Heathfield, Leeds, LS16 7AB
Ⓣ (0113) 261 1781
Ⓔ ken@pleiones.com
Ⓦ www.pleiones.com
Contact: Ken Redshaw
Opening Times: By appt. only.
Min Mail Order UK: £3.00 + p&p
Min Mail Order EU: £3.00 + p&p
Cat. Cost: 1 x 1st class
Credit Cards: None
Specialities: *Pleione.*
Map Ref: N, D2
OS Grid Ref: SE265400

NSti **STILLINGFLEET LODGE
NURSERIES** ⊠ ♿
Stillingfleet,
North Yorkshire, YO19 6HP
Ⓣ (01904) 728506
Ⓕ (01904) 728506
Ⓔ vanessa.cook@still-lodge.freeserve.co.uk
Ⓦ www.stillingfleetlodgenurseries.co.uk
Contact: Vanessa Cook
Opening Times: 1000-1600 Tue Wed Fri &
Sat 1st Apr-18th Oct.

Min Mail Order UK: Nmc*
Cat. Cost: 8 x 2nd class
Credit Cards: None
Specialities: Foliage & unusual perennials.
Hardy *Geranium, Pulmonaria,* variegated
plants & grasses. Nat. Coll. of *Pulmonaria.*
*Note: mail order Nov-mid Mar only.
Map Ref: N, C2

NTay **TAYLORS NURSERIES** ⊠ ň ♿ ◆
Sutton Road, Sutton, Doncaster,
South Yorkshire, DN6 9JZ
Ⓣ (01302) 700716
Ⓕ (01302) 708415
Also supplies wholesale: Yes
Contact: John Taylor
Opening Times: 1000-1600, 15th Feb-15th
Nov. Phone for opening times 16th Nov-14th
Feb.
Min Mail Order UK: 1 plant + p&p
Cat. Cost: free
Credit Cards: all major credit/debit cards
Specialities: *Clematis* (over 300 varieties).
Map Ref: N, D2
OS Grid Ref: SE552121

NTHB **TAVISTOCK HERB NURSERY** ⊠ ň
Tavistock, Preston Old Road, Clifton,
Lancashire, Pr4 0ZA
Ⓣ (01772) 683505
Ⓕ (01772) 683505
Ⓔ tavistockherbs@themail.co.uk
Also supplies wholesale: Yes
Contact: Mrs C Jones
Opening Times: By appt. only.
Min Mail Order UK: Nmc
Cat. Cost: 2 x 1st class stamps
Credit Cards: None
Specialities: Herbs. *Mentha* & *Thymus*
species. Note: main nursery at Garstang
Road, Barton, near Preston, Lancs.
Map Ref: N, D1

NVic **THE VICARAGE GARDEN** ⊠ ♿
Carrington, Urmston, Manchester, M31 4AG
Ⓣ (0161) 775 2750
Ⓕ (0161) 775 3679
Ⓔ info@vicaragebotanicalgardens.co.uk
Ⓦ www.vicaragebotanicalgardens.co.uk
Contact: Paul Haine
Opening Times: 0900-1700 Mon-Sat, closed
Thu. 1000-1630 Sun all year.
Min Mail Order UK: £10.00 + p&p

KEY		
⊠ Mail order to UK or EU	ň Delivers to shows	
▣ Exports beyond EU	€ Euro accepted	
♿ Accessible by wheelchair	◆ See Display advertisement	

N

Min Mail Order EU: £25.00 + p&p
Cat. Cost: 2 x 2nd class for list
Credit Cards: all major credit/debit cards
Specialities: Herbaceous, alpines, grasses, ferns. Free admission to 7 acre gardens.
Map Ref: N, D2
OS Grid Ref: SJ729926

NVne THE VINE HOUSE ⊠
3 Elm Street, Skelmanthorpe, Huddersfield, Yorkshire, HD8 9BH
Ⓣ (01484) 865964
Ⓔ sales@thevinehouse.fsnet.co.uk
Ⓦ www.thevinehouse.fsnet.co.uk
Also supplies wholesale: Yes
Contact: Stuart Smith
Opening Times: Visitors by arrangement.
Min Mail Order UK: 20
Cat. Cost: Sae
Credit Cards: None
Specialities: *Vitis*, mostly *Vitis vinifera*.
Map Ref: N, D2

NWCA WHITE COTTAGE ALPINES ⊠ ⋔ ▣
Sunnyside Nurseries, Hornsea Road, Sigglesthorne, East Yorkshire, HU11 5QL
Ⓣ (01964) 542692
Ⓕ (01964) 542692
Ⓔ plants@whitecottagealpines.co.uk
Ⓦ www.whitecottagealpines.co.uk
Contact: Sally E Cummins
Opening Times: 1000-1700 (or dusk) Thu-Sun & B/hol Mon 1 Mar-30 Sep. If travelling far, please phone first.
Min Mail Order UK: £7.50 + p&p
Min Mail Order EU: £15.00 + p&p by card or sterling cheque only.
Cat. Cost: 4 x 1st class
Credit Cards: Visa MasterCard Switch
Specialities: Alpines & rock plants. 500+ species incl. American, dwarf *Salix* & *Helichrysum*. Note: euro payments by card only.
Map Ref: N, C3

NWea WEASDALE NURSERIES LTD. ⊠ €
Newbiggin-on-Lune, Kirkby Stephen, Cumbria, CA17 4LX
Ⓣ (01539) 623246
Ⓕ (01539) 623277
Ⓔ sales@weasdale.com
Ⓦ www.weasdale.com
Contact: Andrew Forsyth
Opening Times: 0830-1730 Mon-Fri. Closed w/ends, B/hols, Xmas-New Year.
Min Mail Order UK: Nmc*
Min Mail Order EU: Nmc
Cat. Cost: £1.50 or 6 x 1st class, £2 by credit/debit card

Credit Cards: Visa MasterCard Switch Delta Access Solo
Specialities: Hardy forest trees, hedging, broadleaved & conifers. Specimen trees & shrubs grown at 850 feet. Mail order a speciality. *Note: mail order Nov-Apr only.
Map Ref: N, C1

NWit D S WITTON ⊠
26 Casson Drive, Harthill, Sheffield, Yorkshire, S26 7WA
Ⓣ (01909) 771366
Ⓕ (01909) 771366
Ⓔ donshardyeuphorbias@btopenworld.com
Ⓦ www.donshardyeuphorbias.btinternet.co.uk
Contact: Don Witton
Opening Times: By appt. only.
Min Mail Order UK: Nmc*
Cat. Cost: 1 x 1st class + sae
Specialities: Nat. Coll. of Hardy *Euphorbia*. Over 130 varieties. *Note: mail order *Euphorbia* seed only.
Map Ref: N, D2
OS Grid Ref: SK494812

NWoo WOODLANDS COTTAGE NURSERY ▣
Summerbridge, Harrogate, North Yorkshire, HG3 4BT
Ⓣ (01423) 780765
Ⓔ annstark@btinternet.com
Ⓦ www.woodlandscottagegarden.co.uk
Contact: Mrs Ann Stark
Opening Times: By appt. only, mid Mar-mid Sep.
Cat. Cost: 2 x 1st class
Credit Cards: None
Specialities: Herbs, plants for shade & hardy perennials. Plants available in small quantities only.
Map Ref: N, C2
OS Grid Ref: SE195631

NZep ZEPHYRWUDE IRISES ⊠
48 Blacker Lane Crigglestone, Wakefield, West Yorkshire, WF4 3EW
Ⓣ (01924) 252101
Ⓜ 07813 978165
Ⓔ zephyrwude@aol.com
Ⓦ http://hometown.aol.co.uk/zephyrwude
Contact: Richard L Brook
Opening Times: Mail order only. Viewing by appt. 0900-dusk most days May-early June, peak late May. Phone 0900-2300.
Min Mail Order UK: £15.00 + p&p
Min Mail Order EU: £15.00 + p&p
Cat. Cost: 1 x 1st class
Credit Cards: None

Specialities: Bearded *Iris*, 1970s-80s hybrids only. Mainly 12" dwarf & intermediate, a few tall. Catalogue available Apr-Sep. Delivery Aug-Oct only.
Map Ref: N, D2
OS Grid Ref: SE302161

SOUTHERN

SAdn ASHDOWN FOREST GARDEN CENTRE & NURSERY 🔲
Duddleswell, Ashdown Forest,
Nr Uckfield, East Sussex,
TN22 3JP
Ⓣ (01825) 712300
Ⓕ (01825) 712732
Contact: Victoria Tolton
Opening Times: 0900-1730 winter, 0900-1900 summer.
Credit Cards: all major credit/debit cards
Specialities: *Lavandula*.
Map Ref: S, C4

SAga AGAR'S NURSERY ✉ 🔯 € 🔲
Agars Lane, Hordle, Lymington,
Hampshire, SO41 0FL
Ⓣ (01590) 683703
Contact: Diana Tombs, Debbie Ursell
Opening Times: 1000-1700 Fri-Wed Mar-Oct, 1000-1600 Fri-Wed Nov, Dec & Feb.
Min Mail Order UK: £14.00*
Cat. Cost: 2 x 1st class (plugs only)
Credit Cards: None
Specialities: *Penstemon* & *Salvia*. Also wide range of hardy plants incl. shrubs, climbers & herbaceous. *Note: plugs only by mail order.
Map Ref: S, D2

SAPC ARCHITECTURAL PLANTS (CHICHESTER) LTD ✉ 🔯 € 🔲 ◆
Lidsey Road Nursery,
Westergate, Nr Chichester,
West Sussex, PO20 6SU
Ⓣ (01243) 545008
Ⓕ (01243) 545009
Ⓔ chichester@architecturalplants.com
Ⓦ www.architecturalplants.com
Also supplies wholesale: Yes
Contact: Christine Shaw
Opening Times: 1000-1600 Sun-Fri all year. Closed Sat & B/hol Mons. Open Good Fri.
Min Mail Order UK: Nmc
Min Mail Order EU: £150.00 + p&p
Cat. Cost: Free
Credit Cards: all major credit/debit cards
Specialities: Architectural plants & hardy exotics esp. evergreen broadleaved trees & seaside exotics, trees & spiky plants,

yuccas/agaves. Note: second nursery near Horsham, Code SArc.
Map Ref: S, D3

SArc ARCHITECTURAL PLANTS ✉ 🔯 € 🔲 ◆
Cooks Farm, Nuthurst,
Horsham, West Sussex,
RH13 6LH
Ⓣ (01403) 891772
Ⓕ (01403) 891056
Ⓔ enquiries@architecturalplants.com
Ⓦ www.architecturalplants.com
Also supplies wholesale: Yes
Contact: Sarah Chandler & Rachel Hannibal
Opening Times: 0900-1700 Mon-Sat, closed Sun.
Min Mail Order UK: Nmc
Min Mail Order EU: £150.00 + p&p
Cat. Cost: Free
Credit Cards: all major credit/debit cards
Specialities: Architectural plants & hardy exotics. Note: second nursery near Chichester, code SAPC.
Map Ref: S, C3

SAsh ASHENDEN NURSERY 🔯
Cranbrook Road, Benenden,
Cranbrook, Kent,
TN17 4ET
Ⓣ (01580) 241792
Ⓕ (01580) 241792
Contact: Kevin McGarry, Julia Shrimplin
Opening Times: By appt. Please phone.
Cat. Cost: 1 x 1st class Sae
Credit Cards: None
Specialities: Rock garden plants, perennials & ornamental grasses.

SBai STEVEN BAILEY LTD ✉ 🔯 🔲
Silver Street, Sway, Lymington,
Hampshire, SO41 6ZA
Ⓣ (01590) 682227
Ⓕ (01590) 683765
Ⓦ www.steven-bailey.co.uk
Also supplies wholesale: Yes
Contact: Stef Bailey
Opening Times: 1000-1300 & 1400-1630 Mon-Fri all year. 1000-1300 & 1400-1600 Sat Mar-Jun excl. B/hols.
Min Mail Order UK: Quote
Min Mail Order EU: Quote
Cat. Cost: 2 x 2nd class
Credit Cards: Visa MasterCard Switch

S

Specialities: Carnations, pinks, *Alstroemeria* & penstemons.
Map Ref: S, D2

SBir BIRCHFLEET NURSERY
Nyewood, Petersfield, Hampshire, GU31 5JQ
Ⓣ (01730) 821636
Ⓕ (01730) 821636
Ⓔ gammoak@aol.com
Also supplies wholesale: Yes
Contact: John & Daphne Gammon
Opening Times: By appt. only. Please phone.
Cat. Cost: 2 x 1st class
Credit Cards: None
Specialities: Oaks. Beech. Nat. Coll. of *Liquidambar*. Note: nursery accessible for wheelchairs in dry weather.
Map Ref: S, C3

S **SBla BLACKTHORN NURSERY €** Ⓖ
Kilmeston, Alresford, Hampshire, SO24 0NL
Ⓣ (01962) 771796
Ⓕ (01962) 771071
Contact: A R & S B White, M Ellis
Opening Times: 0900-1700 Fri & Sat only 7th Mar-28th Jun and 5th-27th Sep 2003. 0900-1700 Fri & Sat only 5th Mar-26th Jun and 3rd-25th Sep 2004.
Cat. Cost: Plant list for 3 x 1st class
Credit Cards: None
Specialities: Choice perennials & alpines, esp. *Daphne, Epimedium, Helleborus* & *Hepatica*.
Map Ref: S, C2

SBLw BRIAN LEWINGTON ⊠ Ⓖ
(office) 9 Meadow Rise, Horam, Heathfield, East Sussex, TN21 0LZ
Ⓣ (01435) 810124
Ⓕ (01435) 810124
Ⓔ BHLewington@aol.com
Ⓦ www.treesandhedges.co.uk
Also supplies wholesale: Yes
Contact: Brian Lewington
Opening Times: By appt. only.
Min Mail Order UK: Nmc
Specialities: Larger size trees and hedging. Note: nursery is at Leverett Farm, Dallington, nr Heathfield, Sussex.
Map Ref: S, D4
OS Grid Ref: TQ578172

SBod BODIAM NURSERY Ⓖ
Cowfield Cottage Bodiam, Robertsbridge, East Sussex, TN32 5RA
Ⓣ (01580) 830811
Ⓕ (01580) 831989
Contact: Danielle Seymour
Opening Times: 1000-1700 7 days.

Closed Mon & Fri, Nov-Feb.
Cat. Cost: 4 x 1st class
Credit Cards: Visa MasterCard Solo JCB
Specialities: Herbaceous perennials, grasses, conifers, *Camellia* & climbers. Also offers an organic range of herbaceous perennials.
Map Ref: S, C5

SBra J BRADSHAW & SON ⊠ ⋔ ♦
Busheyfield Nursery, Herne, Herne Bay, Kent, CT6 7LJ
Ⓣ (01227) 375415
Ⓕ (01227) 375415
Also supplies wholesale: Yes
Contact: D J Bradshaw & Martin Bradshaw
Opening Times: 1000-1700 Tue-Sat 1st Mar-31st Oct & B/hol Mons. Other times by appt. only.
Min Mail Order UK: 2 plants + p&p
Cat. Cost: Sae + 2 x 1st class
Credit Cards: Visa MasterCard Switch
Specialities: *Clematis, Lonicera*, other climbers & wall shrubs.
Map Ref: S, C5
OS Grid Ref: TR174646

SBri BRICKWALL COTTAGE NURSERY Ⓖ
1 Brickwall Cottages, Frittenden, Cranbrook, Kent, TN17 2DH
Ⓣ (01580) 852425
Ⓔ suemartin@brickcot.fsnet.co.uk
Contact: Sue Martin
Opening Times: 1000-1700 Sats 29th Mar, 24th May, 27th Sep 2003 or by appt.
Cat. Cost: 2 x 1st class
Credit Cards: None
Specialities: Hardy perennials. Stock ltd. in quantity. *Geum, Potentilla*, herbaceous.
Map Ref: S, C5
OS Grid Ref: TQ815410

SBrm BRAMBLY HEDGE ⊠
Mill Lane, Sway, Hampshire, SO41 8LN
Ⓣ (01590) 683570
Ⓔ swaystreps@lineone.net
Contact: Kim Williams
Opening Times: 1000-1400 certain Sats, Jun-Oct, phone or write for dates.
Min Mail Order UK: Nmc*
Cat. Cost: 9"x 7" sae
Credit Cards: None
Specialities: National Collection of *Streptocarpus*. *Note: mail order Mar-Oct, small quantities only available.
Map Ref: S, D2
OS Grid Ref: SZ294973

SCam **CAMELLIA GROVE NURSERY** ⊠ ☒ ň €
Market Garden, Lower Beeding,
West Sussex, RH13 6PP
Ⓣ (01403) 891143
Ⓕ (01403) 891336
Ⓔ rhs20@camellia-grove.com
Ⓦ www.camellia-grove.com
Also supplies wholesale: Yes
Contact: Chris Loder
Opening Times: 7 days, by appt. only. This is
so we can give you our undivided attention.
Min Mail Order UK: Nmc
Min Mail Order EU: £100.00 +p&p
Cat. Cost: 2 x 1st class
Specialities: Camellias & azaleas.
Map Ref: S, C3

SChr **JOHN CHURCHER** ⊠ ☒
47 Grove Avenue, Portchester, Fareham,
Hampshire, PO16 9EZ
Ⓣ (023) 9232 6740
Ⓔ John@plants-palms.freeserve.co.uk
Contact: John Churcher
Opening Times: By appt. only. Please phone.
Min Mail Order UK: Nmc
Min Mail Order EU: Nmc
Cat. Cost: 4 x 1st class
Credit Cards: None
Specialities: Hardy *Opuntia, Agave, Aloe,*
succulents, palms, treeferns, plus small general
range of attractive species, hardy & half-hardy.
Map Ref: S, D2
OS Grid Ref: SU614047

SChu **CHURCH HILL COTTAGE**
GARDENS ⊠ € ♿
Charing Heath, Ashford, Kent, TN27 0BU
Ⓣ (01233) 712522
Ⓕ (01233) 712522
Contact: Mr M & J & Mrs M Metianu
Opening Times: 1000-1700 1st Feb-30th
Nov Tue-Sun & B/hol Mons. Other times by
appt.
Min Mail Order UK: £10.00 + p&p
Cat. Cost: 4 x 1st class
Credit Cards: None
Specialities: Unusual hardy plants, *Dianthus,*
Hosta, ferns, *Viola* & alpines.
Map Ref: S, C5

SCit **THE CITRUS CENTRE** ⊠
West Mare Lane, Marehill, Pulborough,
West Sussex, RH20 2EA
Ⓣ (01798) 872786
Ⓕ (01798) 874880
Ⓔ enquiries@citruscentre.co.uk
Ⓦ www.citruscentre.co.uk
Also supplies wholesale: Yes

Contact: Amanda & Chris Dennis
Opening Times: 0930-1730 Wed-Sun. Phone
for Xmas & B/hol opening times.
Min Mail Order UK: Nmc
Min Mail Order EU: Nmc
Cat. Cost: Sae
Credit Cards: Visa Access
Specialities: *Citrus* & *Citrus* relatives.
Map Ref: S, D3

SCnR **COLIN ROBERTS** ⊠
Tragumna, Morgay Wood Lane, Three Oaks,
Guestling, East Sussex, TN35 4NF
Ⓜ 07718 029909
Ⓕ (01424) 814308
Contact: Colin Roberts
Opening Times: Not open.
Min Mail Order UK: £20.00
Cat. Cost: 2 x 1st class
Credit Cards: None
Specialities: Dwarf bulbs & woodland plants
incl. many rare & unusual, in small numbers.

SCog **COGHURST NURSERY** ⊠ ň € ♿
Ivy House Lane, Near Three Oaks, Hastings,
East Sussex, TN35 4NP
Ⓣ (01424) 756228
Ⓕ (01424) 428944
Ⓔ rotherview@btinternet.com
Also supplies wholesale: Yes
Contact: R Bates & W Bates
Opening Times: 0930-1600 7 days.
Min Mail Order UK: Nmc
Min Mail Order EU: Nmc
Cat. Cost: 4 x 1st class
Credit Cards: all major credit/debit cards
Specialities: *Camellia.* Note: nursery is on the
same site as Rotherview Nursery.
Map Ref: S, D5

SCoo **COOLING'S NURSERIES LTD** ♿
Rushmore Hill, Knockholt, Sevenoaks,
Kent, TN14 7NN
Ⓣ (01959) 532269
Ⓕ (01959) 534092
Ⓔ Plantfinder@coolings.co.uk
Ⓦ www.coolings.co.uk
Contact: Mark Reeve & Gary Carvosso
Opening Times: 0900-1700 Mon-Sat &
1000-1630 Sun.
Cat. Cost: None issued
Credit Cards: Visa Access Switch Electron
Delta MasterCard

S

Specialities: Large range of perennials, conifers & bedding plants. Some unusual shrubs.
Map Ref: S, C4

SCou   COOMBLAND GARDENS ✉ ⌷
Coombland, Coneyhurst, Billingshurst,
West Sussex, RH14 9DG
Ⓣ (01403) 741727
Ⓕ (01403) 741727
Ⓔ coombland@lineone.net
Ⓦ www.coombland.co.uk
Contact: David Browne
Opening Times: 1400-1600 Mon-Fri Mar-end Oct. B/hols & other times by appt. only.
Min Mail Order UK: £20.00 + p&p
Min Mail Order EU: 8 plants + p&p*
Cat. Cost: 5 x 1st class
Credit Cards: Visa MasterCard Delta
Specialities: Nat. Coll. of Hardy *Geranium*. Choice herbaceous. Seeds. *Note: hardy geraniums only to EU. Restricted wheelchair access.
Map Ref: S, C3

SCrf   CROFTERS NURSERIES € ⌷
Church Hill, Charing Heath, Near Ashford,
Kent, TN27 0BU
Ⓣ (01233) 712798
Ⓕ (01233) 712798
Ⓔ croftersch@hotmail.com
Contact: John & Sue Webb
Opening Times: 1000-1700. Closed Sun-Tue. Please check first.
Cat. Cost: 3 x 1st class
Credit Cards: None
Specialities: Fruit, ornamental trees & conifers. Old apple varieties. Small number of *Prunus serrula* with grafted ornamental heads.
Map Ref: S, C5
OS Grid Ref: TQ923493

SCro   CROFTWAY NURSERY ✉ ♙ € ⌷
Yapton Road, Barnham,
Bognor Regis, West Sussex, PO22 0BH
Ⓣ (01243) 552121
Ⓕ (01243) 552125
Ⓔ sales@croftway.co.uk
Ⓦ www.croftway.co.uk
Also supplies wholesale: Yes
Contact: Graham Spencer
Opening Times: 0900-1700 Mon-Sat, 1000-1600 Sun. Closed 1st Dec-28th Feb except by appt.
Min Mail Order UK: Nmc
Min Mail Order EU: Nmc
Cat. Cost: Free
Credit Cards: Visa Access Switch American Express MasterCard

Specialities: Wide general range, emphasis on perennials. Specialists in *Iris*, hardy *Geranium*, *Salvia, Hemerocallis* & *Penstemon*.
Map Ref: S, D3
OS Grid Ref: SU969039

SDay   A LA CARTE DAYLILIES ✉ € ◆
Little Hermitage, St Catherine's Down,
Nr Ventnor, Isle of Wight, PO38 2PD
Ⓣ (01983) 730512
Ⓔ andy@ukdaylilies.com
Ⓦ www.ukdaylilies.com
Contact: Jan & Andy Wyers
Opening Times: By appt. only.
Min Mail Order UK: Nmc
Min Mail Order EU: Nmc
Cat. Cost: 3 x 1st class
Credit Cards: None
Specialities: *Hemerocallis*. Nat. Colls. of Miniature & Small Flowered *Hemerocallis* & Large Flowered *Hemerocallis* (post-1960 award-winning cultivars).

SDea   DEACON'S NURSERY ✉ ⌷ € ◆
Moor View, Godshill, Isle of Wight,
PO38 3HW
Ⓣ (01983) 840750 (24 hrs) (01983) 522243
Ⓕ (01983) 523575
Ⓔ deacons.nursery@btopenworld.com
Ⓦ www.deaconsnurseryfruits.co.uk
Also supplies wholesale: Yes
Contact: G D & B H W Deacon
Opening Times: 0800-1600 Mon-Fri May-Sep, 0800-1700 Mon-Fri 0800-1200 Sat Oct-Apr.
Min Mail Order UK: Nmc
Min Mail Order EU: Nmc
Cat. Cost: Free
Credit Cards: Visa Access Switch
Specialities: Over 300 varieties of apple, old & new, pears, plums, gages, damsons, cherries. Modern soft fruit, grapes, hops, nuts & family trees.
Map Ref: S, D2

SDeJ   DE JAGER & SONS ✉ ⌷ ⌷
The Nurseries,
Marden, Kent, TN12 9BP
Ⓣ (01622) 831235
Ⓕ (01622) 832416
Ⓔ PdeJag@aol.com
Ⓦ www.dejagerflowerbulbs.co.uk
Also supplies wholesale: Yes
Contact: Mrs B Pavey
Opening Times: 0900-1700 Mon-Fri
Min Mail Order UK: £15.00 + p&p
Min Mail Order EU: £15.00 + p&p
Cat. Cost: Free

Credit Cards: Visa Access
Specialities: Wide general range esp. bulbs.
Lilium, Tulipa, Narcissus species &
miscellaneous. Large range of perennials.
Map Ref: S, C4

SDix GREAT DIXTER NURSERIES ⊠ 🖔
Northiam, Rye, East Sussex, TN31 6PH
ⓣ (01797) 253107
ⓕ (01797) 252879
ⓔ nursery@greatdixter.co.uk
ⓦ www.greatdixter.co.uk
Contact: K Leighton
Opening Times: 0900-1230 & 1330-1700
Mon-Fri, 0900-1200 Sat all year. Also 1400-
1700 Sat, Sun & B/hols Apr-Oct.
Min Mail Order UK: £15.00 + p&p
Min Mail Order EU: £15.00 + p&p
Cat. Cost: 4 x 1st class
Credit Cards: Access Switch Visa MasterCard
Solo Delta
Specialities: *Clematis,* shrubs and plants.
Gardens open. Note: plants dispatched Sep-
Mar only.
Map Ref: S, C5

SDnm DENMANS GARDEN,
(JOHN BROOKES LTD) 🖔
Clock House, Denmans, Fontwell,
Nr Arundel, West Sussex, BN18 0SU
ⓣ (01243) 542808
ⓕ (01243) 544064
ⓔ denmans@denmans-garden.co.uk
ⓦ www.denmans-garden.co.uk
Contact: Michael Neve & Clare Scherer
Opening Times: 0900-1700 7 days 1st Mar-
31st Oct.
Cat. Cost: £2.50
Credit Cards: Visa MasterCard
Specialities: Rare and unusual plants.
Map Ref: S, D3

SDow DOWNDERRY NURSERY ⊠ ☒ ♙ € 🖔
Pillar Box Lane, Hadlow,
Nr Tonbridge,
Kent, TN11 9SW
ⓣ (01732) 810081
ⓕ (01732) 811398
ⓔ info@downderry-nursery.co.uk
ⓦ www.downderry-nursery.co.uk
Also supplies wholesale: Yes
Contact: Dr S J Charlesworth
Opening Times: 1000-1700 1st May-31 Oct
& by appt.
Min Mail Order UK: Nmc
Min Mail Order EU: Nmc
Cat. Cost: 3 x 1st class
Credit Cards: Delta MasterCard Switch Visa

Specialities: Nat. Colls. of *Lavandula*
and *Rosmarinus.*
Map Ref: S, C4

SDry DRYSDALE GARDEN EXOTICS ⊠
Bowerwood Road, Fordingbridge,
Hampshire, SP6 1BN
ⓣ (01425) 653010
Contact: David Crampton
Opening Times: 0930-1730 Wed-Fri, 1000-
1730 Sun. Closed 24th Dec-2nd Jan incl.
Min Mail Order UK: £10.00 + p&p
Min Mail Order EU: £15.00 + p&p
Cat. Cost: 3 x 1st class
Credit Cards: None
Specialities: Plants for exotic & foliage effect.
Plants for Mediterranean gardens. Nat. Coll.
of Bamboos.
Map Ref: S, D1

SDys DYSONS NURSERIES ⊠ ♙ 🖔
Great Comp Garden, Platt, Sevenoaks,
Kent, TN15 8QS
ⓣ (01732) 886154
ⓔ william.dyson@ukgateway.net
ⓦ www.greatcomp.co.uk
Also supplies wholesale: Yes
Contact: William T Dyson
Opening Times: 1100-1800 7 days 1st Apr-
31st Oct. Other times by appt.
Min Mail Order UK: £9.00 + p&p
Cat. Cost: 4 x 1st class
Credit Cards: None
Specialities: Salvias, especially New World
species and cultivars.
Map Ref: S, C4

SECG THE ENGLISH COTTAGE GARDEN
NURSERY ⊠
2 Hurst Poultry Farm, Giggers Green Road,
Aldington, Kent, TN25 7BU
ⓣ (01233) 720907
ⓕ (01233) 720907
ⓔ enquiries@englishplants.co.uk
ⓦ www.englishplants.co.uk
Also supplies wholesale: Yes
Contact: Teresa Sinclair
Opening Times: 7 days, please phone first.
Min Mail Order UK: Nmc
Cat. Cost: Free
Credit Cards: MasterCard Visa Switch
Specialities: Small nursery offering variety of
traditional cottage garden plants, wildflowers

S

KEY		
⊠ Mail order to UK or EU	♙ Delivers to shows	
☒ Exports beyond EU	€ Euro accepted	
🖔 Accessible by wheelchair	◆ See Display advertisement	

& herbs. Notes: ltd. stock of some wildflowers. Credit cards accepted for online orders only.

SEND   EAST NORTHDOWN FARM ✉ € ♿ ◆
Margate, Kent, CT9 3TS
Ⓣ (01843) 862060
Ⓕ (01843) 860206
Ⓔ friend.northdown@ukonline.co.uk
Ⓦ www.botanyplants.co.uk
Also supplies wholesale: Yes
Contact: Louise & William Friend
Opening Times: 0900-1700 Mon-Sat, 1000-1700 Sun all year. Closed Xmas week & Easter Sun.
Min Mail Order UK: £15.00
Cat. Cost: Available online only.
Credit Cards: Visa Switch MasterCard
Specialities: Chalk & coast-loving plants.
Map Ref: S, B6

SFai   FAIRWEATHER'S GARDEN
CENTRE ✉ ☒ € ♿
High Street, Beaulieu, Hampshire, SO42 7YB
Ⓣ (01590) 612113
Ⓕ (01590) 612615
Ⓔ chrisfairweather@waitrose.com
Ⓦ www.fairweathers.co.uk
Also supplies wholesale: Yes
Contact: Christopher Fairweather
Opening Times: 0930-1700 7 days.
Min Mail Order UK: Nmc
Min Mail Order EU: Nmc
Cat. Cost: 2 x 1st class
Credit Cards: Visa MasterCard
Specialities: Nat. Coll. of *Vireya* Rhododendrons. Our main collection, at local nursery, can be viewed by appt.
Map Ref: S, D2

SFam   FAMILY TREES ✉ ♿ ◆
Sandy Lane, Shedfield, Hampshire, SO32 2HQ
Ⓣ (01329) 834812
Contact: Philip House
Opening Times: 0930-1230 Wed & Sat mid Oct-end May.
Min Mail Order UK: Nmc
Min Mail Order EU: Nmc
Cat. Cost: Free
Credit Cards: None
Specialities: Fruit & ornamental trees. Trained fruit tree specialists: standards, espaliers, cordons. Other trees, old-fashioned & climbing roses, evergreens. Trees, except evergreens, sold bare rooted. Large specimens in pots.
Map Ref: S, D2

SGar   GARDEN PLANTS ✉ ♨
Windy Ridge, Victory Road, St Margarets-at-Cliffe, Dover, Kent, CT15 6HF
Ⓣ (01304) 853225
Ⓔ GardenPlants@GardenPlants-nursery.co.uk
Ⓦ www.GardenPlants-nursery.co.uk
Also supplies wholesale: Yes
Contact: Teresa Ryder & David Ryder
Opening Times: 1000-1700 (closed Wed).
Min Mail Order UK: Nmc
Cat. Cost: 2 x 1st class + A5 sae
Credit Cards: None
Specialities: Unusual perennials, *Penstemon* & *Salvia*. Plantsman's garden open to view. Map essential for first visit.
Map Ref: S, C6
OS Grid Ref: TR358464

SGrm   GRIMSDYKE HOUSE ✉ ☒
12 Southcourt Avenue, Bexhill-on-Sea, East Sussex, TN39 3AR
Ⓣ (01424) 221452
Ⓕ (01424) 221452
Ⓔ bougainvilleaplants@grimsdykehouse.freeserve.co.uk
Ⓦ www.bougainvilleaplants.com
www.bougainvilleaplants.co.uk
Also supplies wholesale: Yes
Contact: AP Hamilton
Opening Times: 0900-1700 Mon-Fri, 0900-1200 Sat & Sun.
Min Mail Order UK: £6.00
Min Mail Order EU: £6.00
Cat. Cost: 3 x 1st class
Credit Cards: None
Specialities: *Bougainvillea*. Note: export only express airmail & phytocertificate, all costed individually. Nursery open for pre-arranged collection only.
Map Ref: S, D5

SHar   HARDY'S COTTAGE GARDEN
PLANTS ✉ ♨ ♿
Freefolk Priors, Freefolk, Whitchurch, Hampshire, RG28 7NJ
Ⓣ (01256) 896533
Ⓕ (01256) 896572
Ⓔ hardy@cottagegardenplants.fsnet.co.uk
Ⓦ www.hardys-plants.co.uk
Also supplies wholesale: Yes
Contact: Rosy Hardy
Opening Times: 1000-1700 7 days 1st Mar-31st Oct.
Min Mail Order UK: Nmc
Min Mail Order EU: Nmc
Cat. Cost: 8 x 1st class.
Credit Cards: Visa Access Electron Switch Solo

Specialities: Hardy *Geranium* & other herbaceous both old & new. Collection of *Viola odorata* & Parma violets now available. Note: a charge of £2.00 is made for delivery of pre-ordered plants to shows.
Map Ref: S, C2

SHay   HAYWARD'S CARNATIONS ⊠
The Chace Gardens, Stakes Road, Purbrook, Waterlooville, Hampshire, PO7 5PL
Ⓣ (023) 9226 3047
Ⓕ (023) 9226 3047
Also supplies wholesale: Yes
Contact: A N Hayward
Opening Times: 0930-1700 Mon-Fri.
Min Mail Order UK: £10.00 + p&p
Min Mail Order EU: £50.00 + p&p
Cat. Cost: 1 x 1st class
Credit Cards: None
Specialities: Hardy pinks & border carnations (*Dianthus*). Greenhouse perpetual carnations.
Map Ref: S, D2

SHBN   HIGH BANKS NURSERIES 🅖
Slip Mill Road, Hawkhurst, Kent, TN18 5AD
Ⓣ (01580) 754492
Ⓕ (01580) 754450
Also supplies wholesale: Yes
Contact: Jeremy Homewood
Opening Times: 0800-1700 (1630 in winter) daily.
Cat. Cost: £1.50 (stamps) + A4 Sae
Credit Cards: all major credit/debit cards
Specialities: Wide general range with many unusual plants. Minimum of 250,000 plants on site at any one time. Many unusual plants. Open ground stock ltd. between Nov and Feb.
Map Ref: S, C5

SHDw   HIGHDOWN NURSERY ⊠ ⊠ ⋔ € 🅖
New Hall Lane, Small Dole, Nr Henfield, West Sussex, BN5 9YH
Ⓣ (01273) 492976
Ⓕ (01273) 492976
Ⓔ highdown.herbs@btinternet.com
Also supplies wholesale: Yes
Contact: A G & J H Shearing
Opening Times: 0900-1700 7 days.
Min Mail Order UK: £10.00 + p&p
Min Mail Order EU: £10.00 + p&p
Cat. Cost: 3 x 1st class
Credit Cards: Visa MasterCard Delta JCB EuroCard
Specialities: Herbs. Note: partial wheelchair access.
Map Ref: S, D3

SHel   HELLYER'S GARDEN PLANTS ⊠ ◆
Orchards, off Wallage Lane*, Rowfant, Nr Crawley, West Sussex, RH10 4NJ
Ⓣ (01342) 718280
Ⓕ (01342) 718280
Ⓔ penelope.hellyer@hellyers.co.uk
Ⓦ www.hellyers.co.uk
Contact: Penelope Hellyer
Opening Times: 1300-1700 Wed-Sat Mar-Oct & by prior appt.
Min Mail Order UK: Nmc
Cat. Cost: 4 x 1st + A5 Sae (1st class).
Credit Cards: None
Specialities: Hardy plants for sun/shade. Small selection of climbers, shrubs. 100+ varieties of hardy *Geranium*. Some stock in ltd. quantities; small numbers available through propagation service. Note: mail order mainland Britain only. *Wallage Lane is off the B2028 equidistant Crawley Down & Turners Hill.
Map Ref: S, C4
OS Grid Ref: TQ334373

SHFr   SUE HARTFREE ⊠
25 Crouch Hill Court, Lower Halstow, Nr Sittingbourne, Kent, ME9 7EJ
Ⓣ (01795) 842426
Contact: Sue Hartfree
Opening Times: Any time by appt. Please phone first. .
Min Mail Order UK: £20.00 + p&p
Min Mail Order EU: £30.00 + p&p
Cat. Cost: A5 Sae + 4 x 1st class
Credit Cards: None
Specialities: Rare & unusual plants for the garden & conservatory incl. many varieties of *Salvia*. Some plants available in small quantities, but can be propagated to order. Garden open.
Map Ref: S, C5
OS Grid Ref: TQ860672

SHGC   HAMBROOKS GROWING CONCERN ⊠ ⊠ ⋔ 🅖
Wangfield Lane, Curdridge, Southampton, Hampshire, SO32 2DA
Ⓣ (01489) 780505/779993
Ⓕ (01489) 785396
Ⓔ steveharding@hambrooks.co.uk
Ⓦ www.hambrooks.co.uk
Also supplies wholesale: Yes
Contact: Stephen Harding

S

Opening Times: 0730-1800 Mon-Fri.
Min Mail Order UK: Nmc
Min Mail Order EU: Nmc
Cat. Cost: 2 x 1st class
Credit Cards: all major credit/debit cards
Specialities: Specimen stock, herbaceous,
conifers, shrubs, grasses, climbers & hedging.
Map Ref: S, D2
OS Grid Ref: SU523141

SHHo HIGHFIELD HOLLIES ⊠ ⊠ ◆
Highfield Farm, Hatch Lane, Liss,
Hampshire, GU33 7NH
Ⓣ (01730) 892372
Ⓕ (01730) 894853
Ⓔ louise@highfieldhollies.com
Ⓦ www.highfieldhollies.com
Contact: Mrs Louise Bendall
Opening Times: By appt.
Min Mail Order UK: Nmc
Min Mail Order EU: £500 + p&p
Cat. Cost: £2.00 for illustrated cat.
Credit Cards: None
Specialities: 100+ species & cultivars *Ilex* incl.
specimen trees, hedging & topiary. Some in
short supply.
Map Ref: S, C3
OS Grid Ref: SU787276

SHmp HAMPSHIRE CARNIVOROUS
PLANTS ⊠ ⊠ ⋔ €
Ya-Mayla, Allington Lane, West End,
Southampton, Hampshire, SO30 3HQ
Ⓣ (023) 8047 3314
Ⓜ 07703 258296
Ⓕ (023) 8047 3314
Ⓔ matthew@msoper.freesave.co.uk
Ⓦ www.hampshire-carnivorous.co.uk
Also supplies wholesale: Yes
Contact: Matthew Soper
Opening Times: By appt. only.
Min Mail Order UK: Nmc
Min Mail Order EU: £50.00 + p&p
Cat. Cost: 2 x 2nd class
Credit Cards: Visa MasterCard
Specialities: Carnivorous plants esp.
Nepenthes, Heliamphora, Sarracenia, Pinguicula
& *Utricularia.*

SHol HOLLY GATE CACTUS NURSERY ⊠ €
Billingshurst Road, Ashington,
West Sussex, RH20 3BB
Ⓣ (01903) 892 930
Ⓔ info@hollygatecactus.co.uk
Ⓦ www.hollygatecactus.co.uk
Also supplies wholesale: Yes
Contact: Mr T M Hewitt
Opening Times: 0900-1700 7 days Feb-Oct,

0900-1600 Nov-Jan.
Min Mail Order UK: £5.00 + p&p
Min Mail Order EU: £10.00 + p&p
Cat. Cost: 2 x 1st class
Credit Cards: None
Specialities: *Cacti* & succulents, plants &
seeds. World famous cactus garden.
Map Ref: S, D3
OS Grid Ref: TQ133175

SHom HOME PLANTS
52 Dorman Ave, North Aylesham,
Canterbury, Kent, CT3 3BW
Ⓣ (01304) 841746
Contact: Stuart & Sue Roycroft
Opening Times: By appt. only, please phone
first.
Cat. Cost: SAE for list
Credit Cards: None
Specialities: *Phygelius.* Nat. Coll. Holder
status applied for. Limited stock, please
phone first.

SHop HOPALONG NURSERY ⊞
Crabtree Close, Fairseat, Sevenoaks,
Kent, TN15 7JR
Ⓣ (01732) 822422
Ⓕ (01732) 822422
Ⓔ jon@hopalongnursery.co.uk
Ⓦ www.hopalongnursery.co.uk
Contact: Jon Clark
Opening Times: 1000-1700 Wed-Sat, 1100-
1600 Sun, 1st Mar-31st Oct. Open B/hols.
Cat. Cost: £2.00 or free Online
Credit Cards: None
Specialities: Unusual hardy herbaceous
perennials, grasses, ferns, *Cistus.* Some plants
in small quantities.
Map Ref: S, C4
OS Grid Ref: TQ632613

SHvs HARVEST NURSERIES ⊠ €
Harvest Cottag, Boonshill Farm, Iden,
Nr Rye, East Sussex, TN31 7QA
Ⓣ (01797) 230583
Ⓔ harvest.nurseries@virgin.net
Contact: D A Smith
Opening Times: Not open, mail order only.
Min Mail Order UK: Nmc
Min Mail Order EU: £20.00 + p&p
Cat. Cost: 2 x 1st class
Credit Cards: None
Specialities: *Epiphyllum* & wide range of
succulents. Descriptive catalogue.

SIde IDEN CROFT HERBS ⊠ ⊞ ◆
Frittenden Road, Staplehurst, Kent,
TN12 0DH

S

Ⓣ (01580) 891432
Ⓕ (01580) 892416
Ⓔ idencroft.herbs@dial.pipex.com
Ⓦ www.herbs-uk.com
Contact: Tracey Pearman
Opening Times: 0900-1700 Mon-Sat &
1100-1700 Sun & B/hols during summer.
Open all winter with reduced hours - please
phone to confirm prior to visit.
Min Mail Order UK: Nmc
Min Mail Order EU: Nmc
Cat. Cost: 2 x 1st class for descriptive list.
Credit Cards: all major credit/debit cards
Specialities: Herbs, aromatic & wild flower
plants & plants for bees & butterflies. Nat.
Colls. of *Mentha, Nepeta* & *Origanum*.
Wheelchairs available at nursery. Note: exports
seed only.
Map Ref: S, C5

SIgm TIM INGRAM ♠ €
Copton Ash, 105 Ashford Road, Faversham,
Kent, ME13 8XW
Ⓣ (01795) 535919
Contact: Dr T J Ingram
Opening Times: 1400-1800 Tue-Fri & Sat-
Sun Mar-Oct. Nov-Feb by appt.
Cat. Cost: 4 x 1st class
Credit Cards: None
Specialities: Unusual perennials, alpines &
plants from Mediterranean-type climates incl.
Lupinus, Penstemon, Salvia & umbellifers. Ltd.
stock of some rarer plants.
Map Ref: S, C5
OS Grid Ref: TR015598

SIng W E TH. INGWERSEN LTD ♠
Birch Farm Nursery, Gravetye, East Grinstead,
West Sussex, RH19 4LE
Ⓣ (01342) 810236
Ⓔ info@ingwersen.co.uk
Ⓦ www.ingwersen.co.uk
Contact: M P & M R Ingwersen
Opening Times: 0900-1600 daily excl. Sun &
B/hols, Mar-Sep. 0900-1600 Mon-Fri Oct-
Feb.
Cat. Cost: 2 x 1st class
Credit Cards: None
Specialities: Very wide range of hardy plants
mostly alpines. Also seed.
Map Ref: S, C4

SIri IRIS OF SISSINGHURST ⊠ € ◆
Plummers Farmhouse, Biddenden Road,
Sissinghurst, Kent, TN17 2JP
Ⓣ (01580) 715137
Ⓔ irisofs@aol.com
Contact: Margaret Roberts

Opening Times: 1000-1700 following
w/ends: 19th-20th Apr, 17th-18th May, 31st
May-1st Jun, 7th-8th Jun, 6th-7th Sep 2003.
Other times by appt.
Min Mail Order UK: Nmc
Min Mail Order EU: Nmc
Cat. Cost: 2 x 1st class
Credit Cards: None
Specialities: *Iris,* short, intermediate & tall
bearded, sibirica & many species.
Map Ref: S, C5

SKee KEEPERS NURSERY ⊠
Gallants Court, Gallants Lane, East Farleigh,
Maidstone, Kent, ME15 0LE
Ⓣ (01622) 726465
Ⓕ (01622) 726465
Ⓔ info@keepers-nursery.co.uk
Ⓦ www.keepers-nursery.co.uk
Contact: Hamid Habibi
Opening Times: All reasonable hours by appt.
Min Mail Order UK: Nmc
Cat. Cost: 2 x 1st class. Free by email.
Credit Cards: Visa MasterCard American
Express Switch Solo
Specialities: Old & unusual top fruit
varieties. Top fruit propagated to order.
Map Ref: S, C4

SKen KENT STREET NURSERIES ⊠ €
Sedlescombe, Battle, East Sussex, TN33 0SF
Ⓣ (01424) 751134
Ⓔ peter@1066-countryplants.co.uk
Ⓦ www.1066-countryplants.co.uk
Also supplies wholesale: Yes
Contact: P Stapley
Opening Times: 0900-1800 7 days.
Min Mail Order UK: £6.50
Min Mail Order EU: Nmc
Cat. Cost: 2 x 1st class, email, or on web
Credit Cards: MasterCard Visa
Specialities: *Pelargonium,* bedding &
perennials.
Map Ref: S, D5
OS Grid Ref: 790155

SLan LANGLEY BOXWOOD
NURSERY ⊠ ✖ € ♿ ◆
Rake, Nr Liss, Hampshire, GU33 7JL
Ⓣ (01730) 894467
Ⓕ (01730) 894703
Ⓔ sales@boxwood.co.uk
Ⓦ www.boxwood.co.uk

Also supplies wholesale: Yes
Contact: Russell Coates
Opening Times: 0900-1630 Mon-Fri, 1000-1600 Sat. Please phone for directions.
Min Mail Order UK: £20.00 + p&p
Min Mail Order EU: £100.00 + p&p
Cat. Cost: 4 x 1st class
Credit Cards: MasterCard Visa
Specialities: Buxus species, cultivars & hedging. Good range of topiary, *Taxus,* and 'character-pruned' specimens. Nat. Coll. of *Buxus.* Evergreen topiary & hedging.
Map Ref: S, C3
OS Grid Ref: SU812290

SLau THE LAURELS NURSERY ⋔ €
Benenden, Cranbrook, Kent, TN17 4JU
Ⓣ (01580) 240463
Ⓕ (01580) 240463
Ⓦ www.thelaurelsnursery.co.uk
Also supplies wholesale: Yes
Contact: Peter or Sylvia Kellett
Opening Times: 0800-1700 Mon-Thu, 0800-1600 Fri, 0900-1200 Sat, Sun by appt. only.
Cat. Cost: Free
Credit Cards: None
Specialities: Open ground & container ornamental trees, shrubs & climbers incl. flowering cherries, birch, beech & *Wisteria.*
Map Ref: S, C5
OS Grid Ref: TQ815313

SLay LAYHAM GARDEN CENTRE & NURSERY ✉ ♿
Lower Road, Staple, Nr Canterbury, Kent, CT3 1LH
Ⓣ (01304) 813267
Ⓕ (01304) 814007
Ⓔ layham@gcstaple.fsnet.co.uk
Also supplies wholesale: Yes
Contact: Ellen Wessel
Opening Times: 0900-1700 7 days.
Min Mail Order UK: Nmc
Min Mail Order EU: £25.00 + p&p
Cat. Cost: Free
Credit Cards: Visa Switch MasterCard
Specialities: Roses, herbaceous, shrubs, trees & hedging plants.
Map Ref: S, C6
OS Grid Ref: TR276567

SLBF LITTLE BROOK FUCHSIAS ♿
Ash Green Lane, West Ash Green, Nr Aldershot, Hampshire, GU12 6HL
Ⓣ (01252) 329731
Ⓔ carol.gubler@business.ntl.com
Ⓦ www.littlebrookfuchsias.co.uk
Also supplies wholesale: Yes

Contact: Carol Gubler
Opening Times: 0900-1700 Wed-Sun 1st Jan-6th Jul.
Cat. Cost: 50p + Sae
Credit Cards: None
Specialities: Fuchsias, old & new.
Map Ref: S, C3

SLdr LODER PLANTS ✉ ✉ ⋔ €
Market Garden, Lower Beeding, West Sussex, RH13 6PP
Ⓣ (01403) 891412
Ⓕ (01403) 891336
Ⓔ rhspf@rhododendrons.com
Ⓦ www.rhododendrons.com
Also supplies wholesale: Yes
Contact: Chris Loder
Opening Times: 7 days, by appt. only so we can give you our undivided attention.
Min Mail Order UK: Nmc
Min Mail Order EU: £100.00 + p&p
Cat. Cost: 2 x 1st class
Credit Cards: Visa Access
Specialities: Rhododendrons & azaleas in all sizes. *Camellia, Acer, Hydrangea* & ferns.
Map Ref: S, C3

SLim LIME CROSS NURSERY ♿
Herstmonceux, Hailsham, East Sussex, BN27 4RS
Ⓣ (01323) 833229
Ⓕ (01323) 833944
Ⓔ LimeCross@aol.com
Ⓦ www.Limecross.co.uk
Also supplies wholesale: Yes
Contact: J A Tate, Mrs A Green
Opening Times: 0830-1700 Mon-Sat & 1000-1600 Sun.
Cat. Cost: 2 x 1st class
Credit Cards: Visa MasterCard Delta Switch
Specialities: Conifers, trees & shrubs, climbers.
Map Ref: S, D4

SLon LONGSTOCK PARK NURSERY ✉ ♿
Longstock, Stockbridge, Hampshire, SO20 6EH
Ⓣ (01264) 810894
Ⓕ (01264) 810924
Ⓔ longstocknursery@leckfordestate.co.uk
Ⓦ www.longstocknursery.co.uk
Contact: David Roberts
Opening Times: 0830-1630 Mon-Sat all year excl. Xmas & New Year, & 1100-1700 Sun Mar-Oct.
Min Mail Order UK: Min. postal charge

£8.50 for parcels up to 10kg mainland UK.
Cat. Cost: £2.00 cheque incl. p&p
Credit Cards: Visa Access Switch MasterCard
Specialities: A wide range, over 2000 varieties,
of trees, shrubs, perennials, climbers, aquatics
& ferns. Nat. Colls. of *Buddleja* & *Clematis
viticella*. Note: no trees over 2m high sent by
mail order.
Map Ref: S, C2

SLPl   LANDSCAPE PLANTS ⊠ ⊠ ⬙
Cattamount, Grafty Green, Maidstone,
Kent, ME17 2AP
Ⓣ (01622) 850245
Ⓕ (01622) 858063
Ⓔ tomladell@aol.com
Also supplies wholesale: Yes
Contact: Tom La Dell
Opening Times: By appt. only.
Min Mail Order UK: £100.00 + p&p
Min Mail Order EU: £200.00 + p&p
Cat. Cost: 2 x 1st class
Credit Cards: None
Specialities: Garden & landscape shrubs &
perennials.
Map Ref: S, C5
OS Grid Ref: TQ772468

**SMac   MACGREGORS PLANTS FOR
           SHADE ⊠ ⋔ ⬙**
Carters Clay Road, Lockerley, Romsey,
Hampshire, SO51 0GL
Ⓣ (01794) 340256
Ⓕ (01794) 341828
Ⓔ bowrons@macgregorsplants.demon.co.uk
Ⓦ www.macgregors-shadeplants.co.uk
Also supplies wholesale: Yes
Contact: Irene & Stuart Bowron
Opening Times: 1000-1600 most days, or by
appt. Please phone before travelling.
Min Mail Order UK: Nmc*
Cat. Cost: 3 x 1st class
Credit Cards: MasterCard Visa
Specialities: Shade-loving & shade tolerant
plants & other less usual shrubs & perennials.
Limited stock of rarer plants. Nat. Collection
of *Phygelius*. *Note: mail order restricted to
small nos. sent by 24hr carrier.
Map Ref: S, C2
OS Grid Ref: SU308239

SMad   MADRONA NURSERY ⊠ ⋔ € ⬙
Pluckley Road, Bethersden,
Kent, TN26 3DD
Ⓣ (01233) 820100
Ⓕ (01233) 820091
Contact: Liam MacKenzie
Opening Times: 1000-1700 Sat-Tue 15th

Mar-28th Oct. Closed 6th-20th Aug.
Min Mail Order UK: Nmc
Cat. Cost: Free
Credit Cards: Visa MasterCard American
Express JCB Switch
Specialities: Unusual shrubs, conifers &
perennials. *Eryngiums, Pseudopanax.*
Map Ref: S, C5
OS Grid Ref: TQ918419

**SMer   MERRYFIELD NURSERIES
           (CANTERBURY) LTD ⊠ ⬙**
Stodmarsh Road, Canterbury, Kent, CT3 4AP
Ⓣ (01227) 462602
Ⓔ merry-field@tinyonline.co.uk
Contact: Mrs A Downs
Opening Times: 1000-1600 Mon, 0900-
1730 Tue-Sat, 1000-1700 Sun B/hol Mons.
Min Mail Order UK: £10.00 + p&p
Cat. Cost: None issued
Credit Cards: Access Visa Switch
Specialities: Wide range of shrubs, conifers,
herbaceous, many unusual.
Map Ref: S, C5

SMHT   MOUNT HARRY TREES ◆
Offham, Lewes, East Sussex, BN7 3QW
Ⓣ (01273) 474456
Ⓕ (01273) 474266
Contact: A Renton
Opening Times: By appt.
Cat. Cost: 2 x 1st class
Credit Cards: None
Specialities: Deciduous trees, specialising in
heavy-standard to semi-mature sizes, incl.
Sorbus varieties.
Map Ref: S, D4
OS Grid Ref: TQ313913

SMHy   MARCHANTS HARDY PLANTS ⋔ ⬙
2 Marchants Cottages, Ripe Road, Laughton,
East Sussex, BN8 6AJ
Ⓣ (01323) 811737
Ⓕ (01323) 811737
Contact: Graham Gough
Opening Times: 0930-1730 Wed-Sat,
12th Mar-25th Oct 2003.
Cat. Cost: 4 x 1st class
Specialities: Uncommon herbaceous
perennials. *Agapanthus, Kniphofia, Sedum,*
choice grasses, *Miscanthus, Molinia.*
Map Ref: S, D4
OS Grid Ref: TQ506119

S

SMrm   MERRIMENTS GARDENS €
Hawkhurst Road, Hurst Green,
East Sussex, TN19 7RA
(T) (01580) 860666
(F) (01580) 860324
(E) markbuchele@beeb.net
(W) www.merriments.co.uk
Contact: Mark Buchele
Opening Times: 0930-1730 Mon-Sat, 1030-1730 Sun (or dusk in winter).
Cat. Cost: Online only
Credit Cards: Visa Access American Express
Specialities: Unusual shrubs. Tender & hardy perennials.
Map Ref: S, C4

SMur   MURRELLS PLANT & GARDEN CENTRE 🖳
Broomers Hill Lane, Pulborough,
West Sussex, RH20 2DU
(T) (01798) 875508
(F) (01798) 872695
Contact: Clive Mellor
Opening Times: 0900-1730 summer, 0900-1700 winter, 1000-1600 Sun.
Cat. Cost: 3 x 1st class
Credit Cards: Switch MasterCard Visa Solo
Specialities: Shrubs, trees & herbaceous plants incl. many rare & unusual varieties.
Map Ref: S, D3

SNew   NEW FOREST PALMS & EXOTICS
Hollybush Cottage, Pauls Lane,
Sway, Lymington,
Hampshire, SO41 6BR
(T) (01590) 683864
(M) 07870 483972
(E) Paulsnursery@farmersweekly.net
(W) www.newforestpalms.co.uk
Also supplies wholesale: Yes
Contact: F R Toyne
Opening Times: 1000-1700 Tue-Sun Mar-Oct. 1000-1500 Tue-Sun Nov-Feb. Closed Mon. Closed Jan.
Cat. Cost: 2 x 1st class
Credit Cards: Visa MasterCard
Specialities: Ornamental grasses & plants for the Mediterranean look. Note: nursery 300 yards down lane from the cottage.
Map Ref: S, D2
OS Grid Ref: SZ292978

SNut   NUTLIN NURSERY 🔊 🖳
Crowborough Road, Nutley,
Nr Uckfield,
East Sussex, TN22 3HU
(T) (01825) 712670
(F) (01825) 712670

Contact: Mrs Morven Cox
Opening Times: Phone in evening (before 2100) before visiting.
Cat. Cost: 1 x 1st class
Credit Cards: None
Specialities: *Hydrangea, Wisteria,* hardy ferns. Largely grown peat free.
Map Ref: S, C4
OS Grid Ref: TQ4428

SOkd   OAKDENE NURSERY ✉ 🖂 🔊
Street End Lane, Broad Oak, Heathfield,
East Sussex, TN21 8TU
(T) (01435) 864382
Contact: David Sampson
Opening Times: 0900-1700 Wed-Sat excl. B/hols. Sun by appt.
Min Mail Order UK: £10.00
Min Mail Order EU: £25.00
Cat. Cost: 2 x 1st class
Credit Cards: None
Specialities: Rare & unusual alpines. Woodland plants.
Map Ref: S, C4

SOkh   OAKHURST NURSERY 🔊
Mardens Hill,
Crowborough,
East Sussex, TN6 1XL
(T) (01892) 653273
(F) (01892) 653273
(E) sandy.colton@tesco.net
Contact: Stephanie Colton
Opening Times: 1100-1700 most days mid Apr-mid Sep. Other times &, if travelling, please phone first esp. at w/ends.
Cat. Cost: 2 x 1st class
Credit Cards: None
Specialities: Common & uncommon herbaceous perennials in small quantities to enable as wide a range as possible.
Map Ref: S, C4
OS Grid Ref: TQ324501

SOWG   THE OLD WALLED GARDEN ✉ €
Oxonhoath, Hadlow, Kent, TN11 9SS
(T) (01732) 810012
(F) (01732) 810856
(E) amyrtle@aol.com
(W) www.theoldwalledgarden.co.uk
Also supplies wholesale: Yes
Contact: John & Heather Angrave
Opening Times: 0900-1700 Mon-Fri. W/ends by appt.
Min Mail Order UK: Nmc
Cat. Cost: 4 x 1st class
Credit Cards: None
Specialities: Many rare & unusual shrubs.

Wide range of conservatory plants esp. Australian. Nat. Coll. of *Callistemon*.
Map Ref: S, C4

SPer PERRYHILL NURSERIES LTD ⊠ ♠ &
Hartfield, East Sussex,
TN7 4JP
Ⓣ (01892) 770377
Ⓕ (01892) 770929
Ⓔ sales@perryhillnurseries.co.uk
Ⓦ www.perryhillnurseries.co.uk
Contact: P J Chapman
Opening Times: 0900-1700 7 days 1st Mar-31st Oct. 0900-1630 1st Nov-28th Feb.
Min Mail Order UK: Nmc*
Cat. Cost: £2.00 or on web
Credit Cards: Visa Access MasterCard EuroCard Switch
Specialities: Wide range of trees, shrubs, conifers, *Rhododendron* etc. Over 1300 herbaceous varieties, over 500 rose varieties. *Note: mail order despatch depends on size & weight of plants.
Map Ref: S, C4
OS Grid Ref: TQ480375

SPet PETTET'S NURSERY ♠ € &
Poison Cross, Eastry, Sandwich,
Kent, CT13 0EA
Ⓣ (01304) 613869
Ⓕ (01304) 613869
Ⓔ terry@pettetsnursery.fsnet.co.uk
Ⓦ www.pettetsnursery.co.uk
Also supplies wholesale: Yes
Contact: T & EHP Pettet
Opening Times: 0900-1700 daily Mar-Jun. 1000-1600 daily Jul-Nov.
Credit Cards: None
Specialities: Climbers, shrubs, herbaceous perennials, alpines, pelargoniums, fuchsias.
Map Ref: S, C6

SPin JOHN AND LYNSEY'S PLANTS
2 Hillside Cottages, Trampers Lane,
North Boarhunt, Fareham,
Hampshire,
PO17 6DA
Ⓣ (01329) 832786
Contact: Mrs Lynsey Pink
Opening Times: By appt. only.
Cat. Cost: None issued
Credit Cards: None
Specialities: Mainly *Salvia* with a wide range of other unusual perennials. Limited stock, be will be happy to propagate to order. Garden design & consultation service also available.
Map Ref: S, D2
OS Grid Ref: SU603109

SPla PLAXTOL NURSERIES ⊠ &
The Spoute, Plaxtol, Sevenoaks, Kent,
TN15 0QR
Ⓣ (01732) 810550
Ⓕ (01732) 810149
Ⓔ info@plaxtol-nurseries.co.uk
Ⓦ www.plaxtol-nurseries.co.uk
Contact: Tessa, Donald & Jenny Forbes
Opening Times: 1000-1700 7 days. Closed 2 weeks from Xmas Eve.
Min Mail Order UK: £10.00 + p&p*
Min Mail Order EU: £30.00 + p&p
Cat. Cost: 2 x 1st class
Credit Cards: Visa American Express MasterCard
Specialities: Hardy shrubs & herbaceous esp. for flower arrangers. Old-fashioned roses, ferns & climbers. *Note: mail order Nov-Mar only.
Map Ref: S, C4
OS Grid Ref: TQ611535

SPlb PLANTBASE € &
Lamberhurst Vineyard,
Lamberhurst Down, Lamberhurst,
Kent, TN3 8ER
Ⓣ (01892) 891453
Ⓕ (01892) 891453
Ⓔ graham@plantbase.freeserve.co.uk
Contact: Graham Blunt
Opening Times: 1000-1700 7 days Mar-Oct.
Cat. Cost: 2 x 1st class
Credit Cards: Visa Switch Access MasterCard Delta
Specialities: Wide range of alpines, perennials, shrubs, climbers, waterside plants, herbs, Australasian shrubs & South African plants.
Map Ref: S, C5

SPoG THE POTTED GARDEN NURSERY
Ashford Road, Bearsted, Maidstone,
Kent, ME14 4NH
Ⓣ (01622) 737801
Ⓕ (01622) 632459
Ⓔ sales@pottedgarden.fsnet.co.uk
Contact: Robert Brookman
Opening Times: 0900-1730 (dusk in winter) 7 days. Closed Xmas, Boxing Day & New Year's Day.
Credit Cards: Visa MasterCard Switch Electron Delta Solo
Map Ref: S, C5

S

S

SPol **POLLIE'S PERENNIALS AND DAILY LILY NURSERY** ⊠
Lodore, Mount Pleasant Lane,
Sway, Lymington,
Hampshire, SO41 8LS
Ⓣ (01590) 682577
Ⓕ (01590) 682577
Ⓔ terry@maasz.fsnet.co.uk
Contact: Pollie Maasz
Opening Times: 0930-1730 Apr-Sep, any other time by appt., especially during daylily season mid-May-mid-Aug.
Min Mail Order UK: £4.50*
Cat. Cost: Free
Credit Cards: None
Specialities: *Hemerocallis,* also less commonly available hardy perennials. Stock available in small quantities only. Nat. Collection of spider & unusual form *Hemerocallis* applied for. *Note: mail order, daylilies only.
Map Ref: S, D2

SPop **POPS PLANTS** ⊠ ⊠ n̂ €
Pops Cottage, Barford Lane, Downton,
Salisbury, Wiltshire, SP5 3PZ
Ⓣ (01725) 511421
Ⓕ (01425) 653472
Ⓔ mail@popsplants
Ⓦ www.popsplants.com
Contact: G Dawson or L Roberts
Opening Times: By appt. only.
Min Mail Order UK: Nmc
Min Mail Order EU: Nmc
Cat. Cost: £2.00 for colour brochure.
Credit Cards: None
Specialities: *Primula auricula.* Some varieties in limited numbers.

SRat **UNUSUAL PLANTS AT RATSBURY** €
Smallhythe Road, Tenterden, Kent, TN30 7LU
Ⓣ (01580) 762066
Ⓔ Ratsbury@aol.com
Contact: Jane Kirk
Opening Times: Please phone before visiting.
Credit Cards: None
Specialities: Unusual and traditional cottage garden plants.
Map Ref: S, C5
OS Grid Ref: TQ887322

SReu **G REUTHE LTD** ⊠
Crown Point Nursery, Sevenoaks Road,
Ightham, Nr Sevenoaks, Kent, TN15 0HB
Ⓣ (01732) 810694
Ⓕ (01732) 862166
Contact: C & P Tomlin
Opening Times: 0900-1630 Mon-Sat (closed Wed). 1000-1630 Sun & B/hols Apr & May

only, occasionally in Jun, please check.
Closed Jan, Jul & Aug.
Min Mail Order UK: £30.00 + p&p
Min Mail Order EU: £500.00*
Cat. Cost: £2.00
Credit Cards: Visa Access
Specialities: Rhododendrons & azaleas, trees, shrubs & climbers. *Note: mail order certain plants only to EU.
Map Ref: S, C4

SRiv **RIVER GARDEN NURSERIES** ⊠ n̂ € ⊡
Troutbeck, Otford,
Sevenoaks, Kent, TN14 5PH
Ⓣ (01959) 525588
Ⓕ (01959) 525810
Ⓔ box@river-garden.co.uk
Ⓦ www.river-garden.co.uk
Also supplies wholesale: Yes
Contact: Jenny Alban Davies
Opening Times: By appt. only.
Min Mail Order UK: £10.00 + p&p
Min Mail Order EU: £50.00 + p&p
Cat. Cost: 2 x 1st class
Credit Cards: all major credit/debit cards
Specialities: *Buxus* species, cultivars & hedging. *Buxus* topiary.
Map Ref: S, C4
OS Grid Ref: TQ523593

SRms **RUMSEY GARDENS** ⊠ ⊡ ◆
117 Drift Road, Clanfield, Waterlooville,
Hampshire, PO8 0PD
Ⓣ (023) 9259 3367
Ⓔ info@rumsey-gardens.co.uk
Ⓦ www.rumsey-gardens.co.uk
Contact: Mr N R Giles
Opening Times: 0900-1700 Mon-Sat & 1000-1700 Sun & B/hols. Closed Sun Nov-Feb.
Min Mail Order UK: Nmc
Min Mail Order EU: Nmc
Cat. Cost: On web
Credit Cards: Visa MasterCard Switch
Specialities: Wide general range. Nat. Coll. of *Cotoneaster.*
Map Ref: S, D2

SRob **ROBINS NURSERY** ⊡
Coldharbour Road,
Upper Dicker, Hailsham,
East Sussex, BN27 3PY
Ⓜ 07798 527634
Ⓔ stuart@robnurse.free-online.co.uk
Ⓦ www.robnurse.free-online.co.uk
Contact: Stuart Dye
Opening Times: 1100-1700 Sat & Sun, Mar-Oct.

Cat. Cost: Free
Credit Cards: None
Specialities: Small retail nursery specialising in herbaceous plants, incl. *Euphorbia* & *Echium*. All plants grown at nursery in peat-free compost.
Map Ref: S, D4
OS Grid Ref: TQ561109

SRos   ROSEWOOD DAYLILIES ⊠
70 Deansway Avenue, Sturry, Nr Canterbury, Kent, CT2 0NN
Ⓣs (01227) 711071
Ⓕ (01227) 711071
Ⓔ Rosewoodgdns@aol.com
Contact: Chris Searle
Opening Times: By appt. only. Please phone.
Min Mail Order UK: Nmc
Cat. Cost: 2 x 1st class
Credit Cards: None
Specialities: *Hemerocallis,* mainly newer American varieties. *Agapanthus.*
Map Ref: S, C5

SRot   ROTHERVIEW NURSERY ⊠ ⋔ € ♿
Ivy House Lane, Three Oaks, Hastings, East Sussex, TN35 4NP
Ⓣ (01424) 756228
Ⓕ (01424) 428944
Ⓔ rotherview@btinternet.com
Also supplies wholesale: Yes
Contact: Ray Bates
Opening Times: 1000-1700 Mar-Oct, 1000-1530 Nov-Feb, 7 days.
Min Mail Order UK: £10.00 + p&p
Min Mail Order EU: £20.00 + p&p
Cat. Cost: 4 x 1st class
Credit Cards: all major credit/debit cards
Specialities: Alpines. Note: nursery is on same site as Coghurst Camellias.
Map Ref: S, D5

SScr   SCREE GARDENS € ♿
56 Valley Drive, Loose, Maidstone, Kent, ME15 9TL
Ⓣ (01622) 746941
Contact: Michael Brett
Opening Times: 1000-1700 Sat & Sun Apr-Aug. Garden open under NGS. Please phone first.
Cat. Cost: 1 x 2nd class for list
Credit Cards: None
Specialities: Rock garden, scree, trough & herbaceous plants.
Map Ref: S, C5

SSea   SEALE NURSERIES ⊠ ♿ ◆
Seale Lane, Seale, Farnham, Surrey, GU10 1LD
Ⓣ (01252) 782410

Ⓔ plants@sealesuperroses.com
Ⓦ www.sealesuperroses.com
Contact: David & Catherine May
Opening Times: Tue-Sun & B/hol Mons. Closed 25th Dec-8th Jan 2004.
Min Mail Order UK: £10.00 + p&p
Cat. Cost: 5 x 1st class
Credit Cards: Visa Switch Access Delta
Specialities: Roses & *Pelargonium.* Some varieties in short supply, please phone first.
Map Ref: S, C3
OS Grid Ref: SU887477

SSpe   SPELDHURST NURSERIES ♿
Langton Road, Speldhurst, Tunbridge Wells, Kent, TN3 0NR
Ⓣ (01892) 862682
Ⓕ (01892) 862682
Ⓔ VistasLtd@aol.com
Contact: Christine & Stephen Lee
Opening Times: 1000-1700 Wed-Sat excl. Jan. 1000-1700 Sun Mar-Jul & Sep-Oct.
Cat. Cost: 4 x 1st class for list.
Credit Cards: MasterCard Visa Switch Delta
Specialities: Herbaceous.
Map Ref: S, C4

SSpi   SPINNERS GARDEN €
School Lane, Boldre, Lymington, Hampshire, SO41 5QE
Ⓣ (01590) 673347
Ⓕ (01590) 679506
Ⓔ kevin@hughes83.fsnet.co.uk
Ⓦ www.spinnersgarden.com
Contact: Peter Chappell & Kevin Hughes
Opening Times: 1000-1700 Tue-Sat. Sun & Mon by appt. only.
Cat. Cost: 3 x 1st class
Credit Cards: None
Specialities: Less common trees & shrubs esp. *Acer, Magnolia,* species & lace-cap *Hydrangea.* Woodland & bog plants. Nat. Coll. of *Trillium.*
Map Ref: S, D2
OS Grid Ref: SZ323981

SSpr   SPRINGBANK NURSERIES ⊠ ⊠
Winford Road, Newchurch, Sandown, Isle of Wight, PO36 0JX
Ⓣ (01983) 865444
Ⓕ (01983) 868670
Also supplies wholesale: Yes
Contact: K Hall

K E Y		
⊠ Mail order to UK or EU	⋔ Delivers to shows	
⊠ Exports beyond EU	€ Euro accepted	
♿ Accessible by wheelchair	◆ See Display advertisement	

Opening Times: 7 days Sep-Oct. Collections by appt. Specific open days to be advertised.
Min Mail Order UK: £10.00 + p&p
Min Mail Order EU: £25.00 + p&p
Cat. Cost: 6 x 1st class
Credit Cards: None
Specialities: *Nerine sarniensis* hybrids (over 600 varieties) & some species. Nat. Coll. of *Nerine*.
Map Ref: S, D2

SSta   STARBOROUGH NURSERY ✉ ⓖ
Starborough Road, Marsh Green, Edenbridge, Kent, TN8 5RB
Ⓣ (01732) 865614
Ⓕ (01732) 862166
Contact: C & P Tomlin
Opening Times: 0900-1600 Thu-Sat, or by appt. Closed Jan, Jul & Aug.
Min Mail Order UK: £30.00 + p&p
Min Mail Order EU: £500.00*
Cat. Cost: £2.00
Credit Cards: Visa Access
Specialities: Rare and unusual shrubs especially *Daphne, Acer*, rhododendrons & azaleas, *Magnolia* & *Hamamelis*. *Note: certain plants only to EU.
Map Ref: S, C4

SSte   STENBURY NURSERY ✉ ⋔ €
Smarts Cross, Southford, Nr Whitwell, Isle of Wight, PO38 2AG
Ⓜ 07909 525343
Ⓔ stenburyiow@aol.com
Contact: Mr B Clarke
Opening Times: 1000-1600 Sat & Sun 21st Mar-1st Oct.
Min Mail Order UK: £20.00*
Min Mail Order EU: £20.00
Cat. Cost: 2 x 1st class
Credit Cards: None
Specialities: *Passiflora, Melaleuca, Callistemon* & other Australian plants. Rubus sp. Note: mail order Apr-Sep, for *Passiflora* only.
Map Ref: S, D2

SSth   SOUTHEASE PLANTS € ⓖ
Corner Cottage, Southease, Nr Lewes, East Sussex, BN7 3HX
Ⓣ (01273) 513681
Ⓕ (01273) 513681
Contact: Adrian Orchard
Opening Times: 1100-1700 Wed-Sat, 1400-1700 Sun & by appt.
Cat. Cost: 2 x 1st class
Credit Cards: None
Specialities: A small nursery concentrating on hellebores, with a small range of herbaceous perennials, biennials &

annuals in ltd. quantities.
Map Ref: S, D4
OS Grid Ref: TQ422052

SSto   STONE CROSS GARDEN CENTRE ⓖ ◆
Rattle Road, Pevensey, Sussex, BN24 5EB
Ⓣ (01323) 763250
Ⓕ (01323) 763195
Ⓔ gardencentre@stone-cross-nurseries.co.uk
Ⓦ www.stone-cross-nurseries.co.uk
Also supplies wholesale: Yes
Contact: Mrs J Birch
Opening Times: 0830-1730 Mon-Sat & 1000-1600 Sun & B/hols.
Cat. Cost: None issued
Credit Cards: Visa Access Switch
Specialities: *Hebe* & *Clematis*, evergreen shrubs. Lime tolerant & coastal shrubs & plants.
Map Ref: S, D4
OS Grid Ref: 6104

SSvw   SOUTHVIEW NURSERIES ✉ ⋔ € ◆
Chequers Lane, Eversley Cross, Hook, Hampshire, RG27 0NT
Ⓣ (0118) 9732206
Ⓕ (0118) 9736160
Ⓔ Mark@Trenear.freeserve.co.uk
Also supplies wholesale: Yes
Contact: Mark & Elaine Trenear
Opening Times: Mail order only. Orders for collection by prior arrangement.
Min Mail Order UK: Nmc
Cat. Cost: Free
Credit Cards: None
Specialities: Unusual hardy plants, specialising in old fashioned pinks & period plants. Nat. Coll. of Old Pinks. Orders by prior arrangement only.
Map Ref: S, C3

STes   TEST VALLEY NURSERY ⋔ €
Stockbridge Road, Timsbury, Romsey, Hampshire, SO51 0NG
Ⓣ (01794) 368881
Ⓕ (01794) 368493
Ⓔ jbenn@onetel.net.uk
Contact: Julia Benn
Opening Times: 1000-1600 Tue-Sun Apr-mid Aug, or by appt.
Cat. Cost: 3 x 2nd class
Credit Cards: None
Specialities: Small nursery with range of herbaceous perennials, specialising in unusual & new varieties. Ltd. quantities of some varieties. Phone first to avoid disappointment.
Map Ref: S, C2

STil   **TILE BARN NURSERY** ☒ ☒ €
Standen Street, Iden Green, Benenden,
Kent, TN17 4LB
Ⓣ (01580) 240221
Ⓕ (01580) 240221
Ⓔ tilebarn.nursery@virgin.net
Ⓦ www.tilebarn-cyclamen.co.uk
Also supplies wholesale: Yes
Contact: Peter Moore
Opening Times: 0900-1700 Wed-Sat.
Min Mail Order UK: £10.00 + p&p
Min Mail Order EU: £25.00 + p&p
Cat. Cost: Sae
Credit Cards: None
Specialities: *Cyclamen* species.
Map Ref: S, C5
OS Grid Ref: TQ805301

STop   **SUSSEX TOPIARY** ☒ ◆
Naldretts Lane, Bucks Green,
Horsham,
West Sussex, RH12 3JF
Ⓣ (01403) 823131
Ⓜ 07870 268662
Ⓔ sussextopiary@zoom.co.uk
Also supplies wholesale: Yes
Contact: Denis De Ambrosi
Opening Times: 1000-1700 Wed-Mon,
closed Tue.
Min Mail Order UK: £5.00
Min Mail Order EU: Nmc
Cat. Cost: 2 x 1st class
Credit Cards: None
Specialities: Specimen plants, trainers,
hedging, box species.
Map Ref: S, C4
OS Grid Ref: TQ082329

STre   **PETER TRENEAR** ☒ ⓖ
Chantreyland, Chequers Lane, Eversley Cross,
Hampshire, RG27 0NX
Ⓣ (0118) 9732300
Ⓔ peter@babytrees.co.uk
Ⓦ www.babytrees.co.uk
Contact: Peter Trenear
Opening Times: 0900-1630 Mon-Sat.
Min Mail Order UK: £5.00 + p&p
Cat. Cost: 1 x 1st class
Credit Cards: None
Specialities: Trees, shrubs, conifers & *Pinus*.
Map Ref: S, C3
OS Grid Ref: SU795612

SUsu   **USUAL & UNUSUAL PLANTS** ♠ €
Onslow House, Magham Down, Hailsham,
East Sussex, BN27 1PL
Ⓣ (01323) 840967
Ⓕ (01323) 844725

Ⓔ jennie@onslow.clara.net
Contact: Jennie Maillard
Opening Times: 0930-1730 Wed-Sat &
B/Hol Mons 12 Mar-31 Oct.
Cat. Cost: Sae + 75p
Credit Cards: None
Specialities: Small quantities of a wide
variety of unusual perennials esp. *Erysimum,
Euphorbia,* hardy *Geranium, Salvia* & grasses.
Map Ref: S, D4
OS Grid Ref: TQ607113

SVal   **VALE NURSERY** ☒
Heath Cottage, Hayes Lane, Stockbury
Valley, Sittingbourne, Kent, ME9 7QH
Ⓣ (01795) 844004
Ⓕ (01795) 842991
Ⓔ info@valenursery.co.uk
Ⓦ www.valenursery.co.uk
Opening Times: Not open, mail order only.
Min Mail Order UK: £10.00
Cat. Cost: Free
Specialities: Herbaceous perennials. Limited
quantities of some stock.

SVen   **VENTNOR BOTANIC GARDEN**
Undercliff Drive, Ventnor,
Isle of Wight,
PO38 1UL
Ⓣ (01983) 855397
Ⓕ (01983) 856756
Ⓔ simon@vbg1.demon.co.uk
Ⓦ http://botanic.co.uk
Contact: Simon Goodenough & Jan Wyers
Opening Times: 1000-1700 7 days Mar-Oct.
Cat. Cost: None issued
Credit Cards: MasterCard Visa
Map Ref: S, D2

SVil   **THE VILLAGE NURSERIES** ♠ € ⓖ ◆
Sinnocks, West Chiltington,
Pulborough, West Sussex, RH20 2JX
Ⓣ (01798) 813040
Ⓕ (01798) 817240
Ⓔ petermanfield@aol.com
Ⓦ www.village-nurseries.co.uk
Contact: Peter Manfield
Opening Times: 0900-1800 or dusk, 7 days.
Cat. Cost: None issued
Credit Cards: Visa Delta MasterCard Switch
Solo
Specialities: Wide range of hardy perennials
& grasses, incl. many new varieties. Selected

K E Y	☒ Mail order to UK or EU	♠ Delivers to shows
	☒ Exports beyond EU	€ Euro accepted
	ⓖ Accessible by wheelchair	◆ See Display advertisement

shrubs, conifers, climbers & trees.
Map Ref: S, D3
OS Grid Ref: TQ095182

SWal WALLACE PLANTS ♠
Lewes Road Nursery, Lewes Road, Laughton,
East Sussex, BN8 6BN
Ⓣ (01323) 811729
Ⓔ sjk@wallaceplants.fsnet.co.uk
Contact: Simon Wallace
Opening Times: 0930-1800 or dusk 7 days
incl B/hols.
Cat. Cost: 3 x 1st class
Credit Cards: None
Specialities: Ornamental grasses, hebes, hardy
fuchsias, salvias, penstemons, unusual plants.
Map Ref: S, D4
OS Grid Ref: TQ513126

S

SWat WATER MEADOW NURSERY ✉ ☒ ♠ €
Cheriton, Nr Alresford, Hampshire, SO24 0QB
Ⓣ (01962) 771895
Ⓕ (01962) 771895
Ⓔ plantaholic@onetel.net.uk
Ⓦ www.plantaholic.co.uk
Also supplies wholesale: Yes
Contact: Mrs Sandy Worth
Opening Times: 1000-1700 Wed-Sat Mar-Jul
or by appt.
Min Mail Order UK: £10.00 + p&p
Min Mail Order EU: £50.00 + p&p
Cat. Cost: 6 x 1st class or £1.50 cheque
Credit Cards: Visa MasterCard
Specialities: Water lilies, extensive water
garden plants, unusual herbaceous perennials,
aromatic herbs & wildflowers. Nat. Coll. of
Papaver orientale group.
Map Ref: S, C2

SWCr WYCH CROSS NURSERIES ⬚
Wych Cross, Forest Row,
East Sussex, RH18 5JW
Ⓣ (01342) 822705
Ⓕ (01342) 825329
Ⓔ roses@wychcross.co.uk
Ⓦ www.wychcross.co.uk
Contact: J Paisley
Opening Times: 0900-1730 Mon-Sat.
Cat. Cost: Free
Credit Cards: Visa MasterCard Delta Switch
Specialities: Roses.
Map Ref: S, C4

SWvt WOLVERTON PLANTS LTD € ⬚ ◆
Wolverton Common, Tadley, Hampshire,
RG26 5RU
Ⓣ (01635) 298453
Ⓕ (01635) 299075

Ⓔ Julian@wolvertonplants.co.uk
Ⓦ www.wolvertonplants.co.uk
Also supplies wholesale: Yes
Contact: Julian Jones
Opening Times: 0900-1800 (or dusk Nov-
Feb), 7 days. Closed Xmas/New Year.
Cat. Cost: Online
Credit Cards: all major credit/debit cards
Map Ref: S, C2
OS Grid Ref: SU555589

SYvo YVONNE'S PLANTS
66 The Ridgway, Woodingdean, Brighton,
Sussex, BN2 6PD
Ⓣ (01273) 300883
Ⓔ yvonnesplants@clanlaw.org.uk
Ⓦ www.clanlaw.org.uk/yvonnesplants
Contact: Mrs Yvonne Law
Opening Times: Mar-Oct by appt. only and
Open Day 1000-1600 Sat 26 Apr 2003.
Cat. Cost: None issued, plant list Online
Credit Cards: None
Specialities: Conservatory, tender &
herbaceous perennials, incl. *Cestrum,
Agapanthus, Canna, Fuchsia, Hedychium* &
grasses.
Map Ref: S, D4
OS Grid Ref: TQ360056

WALES AND THE WEST

WAba ABACUS NURSERIES ✉
Drummau Road, Skewen, Neath,
West Glamorgan, Wales, SA10 6NW
Ⓣ (01792) 817994 (evenings)
Ⓔ plants@abacus-nurseries.co.uk
Ⓦ www.abacus-nurseries.co.uk
Also supplies wholesale: Yes
Contact: David Hill
Opening Times: Not open to the public.
Collection by arrangement.
Min Mail Order UK: Nmc
Min Mail Order EU: Nmc
Cat. Cost: 1 x 2nd class
Credit Cards: None
Specialities: *Dahlia*, outdoor spray
chrysanthemums.
Map Ref: W, D3
OS Grid Ref:

WAbb ABBEY DORE COURT GARDEN ⬚
Abbey Dore Court, Abbey Dore,
Herefordshire, HR2 0AD
Ⓣ (01981) 240419
Ⓕ (01981) 240419
Contact: Mrs C Ward
Opening Times: 1100-1730 31st Mar-30th
Sep. Closed Mon, Wed & Fri.

Open B/hol Mons.
Cat. Cost: None issued
Credit Cards: None
Specialities: Shrubs & hardy perennials, many unusual, which may be seen growing in the garden. *Astrantia, Crocosmia, Potentilla, Pulmonaria* & *Sedum.*
Map Ref: W, C4

WAbe **ABERCONWY NURSERY** ♠ &
Graig, Glan Conwy, Colwyn Bay, Conwy, Wales, LL28 5TL
Ⓣ (01492) 580875
Contact: Dr & Mrs K G Lever
Opening Times: 1000-1700 Tue-Sun Feb-Oct.
Cat. Cost: 2 x 2nd class
Credit Cards: Visa MasterCard
Specialities: Alpines, including specialist varieties, esp. autumn gentians, *Saxifraga* & dwarf ericaceous. Shrubs, incl. large range of *Cistus*, & woodland plants incl. *Helleborus* & *Epimedium.*
Map Ref: W, A3
OS Grid Ref: SH799744

WAct **ACTON BEAUCHAMP ROSES** ⊠ ☒
Acton Beauchamp, Worcestershire, WR6 5AE
Ⓣ (01531) 640433
Ⓕ (01531) 640802
Contact: Lindsay Bousfield
Opening Times: 1400-1700 Wed-Sun Mar-Oct, 1000-1700 B/hol Mon. Also by appt.
Note: Nov-Feb mail order only.
Min Mail Order UK: Nmc
Min Mail Order EU: Nmc
Cat. Cost: 3 x 1st class
Credit Cards: Visa MasterCard
Specialities: Species roses, old roses, modern shrub, English, climbers, ramblers & ground-cover roses.
Map Ref: W, C4
OS Grid Ref: SO683492

WAul **AULDEN FARM** ♠ &
Aulden, Leominster, Herefordshire, HR6 0JT
Ⓣ (01568) 720129
Ⓔ pf@auldenfarm.co.uk
Ⓦ www.auldenfarm.co.uk
Contact: Alun & Jill Whitehead
Opening Times: 1000-1700 Tue & Thu Apr-Aug.
Cat. Cost: 2 x 1st class
Credit Cards: None
Specialities: Hardy herbaceous perennials, with a special interest in *Hemerocallis* & *Iris ensata.*
Map Ref: W, C4

WBad **BADSEY LAVENDER FIELDS** &
Badsey Fields Lane, Evesham, Worcestershire, WR11 5EX
Ⓣ (01386) 832124
Ⓕ (01386) 832124
Also supplies wholesale: Yes
Contact: Phil Hodgetts
Opening Times: 0900-1800 7 days excl. Xmas week.
Cat. Cost: 2 x 1st class
Credit Cards: None
Specialities: Lavenders.
Map Ref: W, C5

WBan **THE GARDEN AT THE BANNUT** &
Bringsty, Herefordshire, WR6 5TA
Ⓣ (01885) 482206
Ⓕ (01885) 482206
Ⓔ everettbannut@zetnet.co.uk
Ⓦ www.bannut.co.uk
Contact: Daphne Everett
Opening Times: 1400-1700 Wed, Sat, Sun & B/hols Easter-end Sep & by appt.
Specialities: *Penstemon, Calluna, Erica* & *Daboecia.*
Map Ref: W, C4
OS Grid Ref: SO691546

WBar **BARNCROFT NURSERIES** &
Olden Lane, Ruyton-xi-Towns, Shrewsbury, Shropshire, SY4 1JD
Ⓣ (01939) 261619
Also supplies wholesale: Yes
Contact: Mrs R E Eccleston
Opening Times: 1000-1730 Tue-Sat 1000-1600 Sun. Closed throughout Jan. Open B/hols.
Cat. Cost: none available
Credit Cards: None
Specialities: Wide range of unusual herbaceous plants, shrubs, water plants, water lily ponds & ferns, as well as cottage garden favourites.
Map Ref: W, B4

WBcn **BEACON'S NURSERIES** &
Tewkesbury Road, Eckington, Nr Pershore, Worcestershire, WR10 3DE
Ⓣ (01386) 750359
Ⓔ Jonathan@Beaconsnurseries.fsnet.co.uk
Also supplies wholesale: Yes
Contact: Jonathan Beacon
Opening Times: 0900-1300 & 1400-1700

W

KEY
⊠ Mail order to UK or EU   ♠ Delivers to shows
☒ Exports beyond EU   € Euro accepted
& Accessible by wheelchair   ◆ See Display advertisement

Mon-Sat & 1400-1700 Sun.
(Closed 25th Dec-1st Jan.)
Cat. Cost: 2 x 1st class
Credit Cards: None
Specialities: Shrubs, camellias, herbaceous, aquatics, conifers, climbing plants & hollies.
Map Ref: W, C5

WBea   BEACONS' BOTANICALS ⊠ ń
Banc-y-Felin, Carregsawdde, Llangadog,
Carmarthenshire, Wales, SA19 9DA
Ⓣ (01550) 777992
Ⓔ chrisandsuewill@bushinternet.com
Contact: Mrs S H Williams
Opening Times: Most weekdays, please phone first.
Min Mail Order UK: £10.00 + p&p
Cat. Cost: 2 x 1st class
Credit Cards: None
Specialities: Hardy *Geranium, Allium, Campanula, Persicaria*, unusual mints & hardy bulbs, *Veronica*. Extensive range of rare & unusual herbaceous plants.
Map Ref: W, C3

WBod   BODNANT GARDEN NURSERY LTD ⊠ ☑
Tal-y-Cafn, Colwyn Bay, Clwyd,
Wales, LL28 5RE
Ⓣ (01492) 650731
Ⓕ (01492) 650863
Ⓔ sales@bodnant.co.uk
Ⓦ www.bodnant.co.uk
Contact: Sian Grindley
Opening Times: All year.
Min Mail Order UK: Nmc
Min Mail Order EU: Nmc
Cat. Cost: £2.00*
Credit Cards: Visa MasterCard Switch Connect American Express
Specialities: *Rhododendron, Camellia, Magnolia.* Wide range of unusual trees and shrubs. *Note: catalogue cost refundable with 1st order.
Map Ref: W, A3

WBor   BORDERVALE PLANTS ń ⌂
Nantyderi, Sandy Lane, Ystradowen,
Cowbridge, Vale of Glamorgan,
Wales, CF71 7SX
Ⓣ (01446) 774036
Ⓔ nyd@btopenworld.com
Ⓦ www.bordervale.co.uk
Contact: Claire E Jenkins
Opening Times: 1000-1700 Fri-Sun & B/hols mid Mar-mid Oct. Other times by appt.
Cat. Cost: 2 x 1st class large sae or on website.
Credit Cards: None

Specialities: Unusual herbaceous perennials trees & shrubs, as well as cottage garden plants, many displayed in the 2 acre garden.
Map Ref: W, D3
OS Grid Ref: ST022776

WBou   BOUTS COTTAGE NURSERIES ⊠ ń
Bouts Lane, Inkberrow,
Worcestershire, WR7 4HP
Ⓣ (01386) 792923
Ⓦ www.boutsviolas.co.uk
Contact: M & S Roberts
Opening Times: Not open to the public.
Min Mail Order UK: Nmc
Min Mail Order EU: Nmc
Cat. Cost: Sae
Credit Cards: None
Specialities: Viola.

WBrE   BRON EIFION NURSERY ⊠ ⌂
Bron Eifion, Criccieth, Gwynedd,
Wales, LL52 0SA
Ⓣ (01766) 522890
Ⓔ Stress2k@btinternet.com
Contact: Suzanne Evans
Opening Times: 1000-dusk 7 days 1st Mar-31st Oct. 1st Nov-29th Feb by appt. only.
Min Mail Order UK: £30.00 + p&p
Min Mail Order EU: £50.00 + p&p
Cat. Cost: 4 x 2nd class
Credit Cards: None
Specialities: *Kalmia, Daphne, Embothrium*, plants for coastal regions & wide range of hardy plants.
Map Ref: W, B2

WBri   BRINGSTY NURSERY ⊠ ⌂
Bringsty Common, Nr Bromyard,
Herefordshire, WR6 5UW
Ⓣ (01886) 821482
Ⓔ jennifer@bringstyherbs.fsnet.co.uk
Contact: Ms JM Powles
Opening Times: 1000-1700 Wed-Sun 1 Apr-30 Sep.
Min Mail Order UK: £10.00
Cat. Cost: 3 x 1st class
Credit Cards: None
Specialities: Over 350 varieties of container grown medicinal, decorative & culinary herbs. Rockery & cottage garden plants. Wild flowers. Some stock is limited where hard to raise.
Map Ref: W, C4

WBrk   BROCKAMIN PLANTS ń ⌂
Brockamin, Old Hills, Callow End,
Worcestershire, WR2 4TQ
Ⓣ (01905) 830370

ⓔ dickstonebrockamin@tinyworld.co.uk
Contact: Margaret Stone
Opening Times: By appt. only.
Cat. Cost: 3 x 2nd class
Credit Cards: None
Specialities: Hardy perennials, especially
hardy geraniums and some asters. Sells at
Gardeners' Markets. Stock available in small
quantities only.
Map Ref: W, C5
OS Grid Ref: SO830488

WBro   BROOK FARM PLANTS ⊠ ⓖ
Boulsdon Lane, Newent, Gloucestershire,
GL18 1JH
ⓣ (01531) 822534
ⓔ sally@brookfarmplants.co.uk
ⓦ www.brookfarmplants.co.uk
Contact: Mrs S E Keene
Opening Times: Visitors welcome most times
by appt.
Min Mail Order UK: Nmc
Cat. Cost: 3 x 2nd class
Credit Cards: None
Specialities: *Digitalis, Papaver, Schizostylis* &
other unusual perennials. Some stock may be
limited availability, but can be grown to order.
Map Ref: W, C4

WBry   JULIA'S GARDEN ⋔ €
Bryn Ffynnon Fields Nursery, Bontuchel,
Ruthin, Clwyd, Wales, LL15 2BL
ⓜ 07967 229139
ⓔ julia@juliasgarden.fsbusiness.co.uk
Contact: Julia White
Opening Times: By appt. only.
Cat. Cost: 2 x 1st class
Credit Cards: Visa MasterCard
Specialities: Traditional cottage plants & herbs
incl. *Alcea, Mentha, Origanum, Digitalis* &
Angelica.
Map Ref: W, A3

WBuc   BUCKNELL NURSERIES ⊠
Bucknell, Shropshire, SY7 0EL
ⓣ (01547) 530606
ⓕ (01547) 530699
Also supplies wholesale: Yes
Contact: A N Coull
Opening Times: 0800-1700 Mon-Fri &
1000-1300 Sat.
Min Mail Order UK: Nmc
Cat. Cost: Free
Credit Cards: None
Specialities: Bare rooted hedging conifers &
forest trees.
Map Ref: W, C4
OS Grid Ref: 737355

WBVN   BANWY VALLEY NURSERY ⓖ
Foel, Llangadfan, Nr Welshpool, Powys,
Wales, SY21 0PT
ⓣ (01938) 820281
ⓕ (01938) 820281
ⓔ banwy.valley@virgin.net
Contact: Syd Luck
Opening Times: 1000-1700 Tue-Sun.
Open B/hols.
Cat. Cost: 2 x 1st class
Credit Cards: None
Specialities: Perennials, shrubs, incl. climbers,
ornamental & fruit trees. Ever expanding
range of magnolias & rhododendrons. All
grown on the nursery.
Map Ref: W, B3
OS Grid Ref: SH993107

WBWf   BRITISH WILDFLOWERS ⊠ ⓖ
Marked Ash Cottage, Rushbury,
Church Stretton, Shropshire,
SY6 7EL
ⓣ (01584) 841539
Also supplies wholesale: Yes
Contact: Spencer Stoves
Opening Times: By appt. only.
Min Mail Order UK: Nmc
Cat. Cost: 1 x 1st class stamp
Credit Cards: None
Specialities: British wildflowers of known
British origin only.
Map Ref: W, B4
OS Grid Ref: SO516908

WCAu   CLAIRE AUSTIN HARDY PLANTS
⊠ € ⓖ ◆
The Stone House, Cramp Pool,
Shifnal, Shropshire,
TF11 8PE
ⓣ (01952) 463700
ⓕ (01952) 463111
ⓔ enquiries@claireaustin-hardyplants.co.uk
ⓦ www.claireaustin-hardyplants.co.uk
Contact: Claire Austin
Opening Times: 0900-1600 Mon-Fri, Nov-
Feb. 1000-1600 7 days, Mar-Oct.
Min Mail Order UK: Nmc
Min Mail Order EU: £50.00 + p&p
Cat. Cost: Free
Credit Cards: MasterCard Visa Switch
Specialities: *Paeonia, Iris, Hemerocallis* &
hardy plants.
Map Ref: W, B4

W

KEY		
⊠ Mail order to UK or EU	⋔ Delivers to shows	
☒ Exports beyond EU	€ Euro accepted	
ⓖ Accessible by wheelchair	◆ See Display advertisement	

WCel   CELYN VALE EUCALYPTUS
NURSERIES ⊠ ☒ € ◆
Carrog, Corwen, Clwyd,
Wales, LL21 9LD
Ⓣ (01490) 430671
Ⓕ (01490) 430671
Ⓔ info@eucalyptus.co.uk
Ⓦ www.eucalyptus.co.uk
Also supplies wholesale: Yes
Contact: Andrew McConnell & Paul Yoxall
Opening Times: 0900-1600 Mon-Fri Jan-Nov. Please phone first outside these days.
Min Mail Order UK: 3 plants + p&p
Min Mail Order EU: 3 plants + p&p
Cat. Cost: 2 x 1st class
Credit Cards: Switch Delta Solo Electron
MasterCard Visa
Specialities: Hardy *Eucalyptus* & *Acacia*.
Map Ref: W, A3
OS Grid Ref: SJ116452

W **WCFE   CHARLES F ELLIS €**
(Office) Barn House, Wormington,
Nr Broadway, Worcestershire, WR12 7NL
Ⓣ (01386) 584077 (nursery)
Ⓕ (01386) 584491
Contact: Charles Ellis
Opening Times: 1000-1600 7 days 1st Apr-30th Sep.
Cat. Cost: None issued.
Credit Cards: None
Specialities: Wide range of more unusual shrubs, conifers & climbers. Note: Nursery is at Oak Piece Farm Nursery, Stanton, Broadway.
Map Ref: W, C5

WCHb   THE COTTAGE HERBERY ♫
Mill House, Boraston, Nr Tenbury Wells,
Worcestershire, WR15 8LZ
Ⓣ (01584) 781575
Ⓕ (01584) 781483
Ⓦ www.thecottageherbery.co.uk
Contact: K & R Hurst
Opening Times: By appt. only. Order collection service available.
Cat. Cost: 5 x 1st class
Credit Cards: None
Specialities: Over 600 varieties of herbs.
Aromatic & scented foliage plants, esp.
Symphytum, Lamium, Monarda, Ajuga, Lobelia
& seeds.
Map Ref: W, C4

WChG   CHENNELS GATE GARDENS &
NURSERY ⌂
Eardisley, Herefordshire, HR3 6LT
Ⓣ (01544) 327288

Contact: Mark Dawson
Opening Times: 1000-1700 7 days Mar-Oct.
Cat. Cost: 2 x 2nd class
Credit Cards: None
Specialities: Interesting & unusual cottage garden plants, grasses, hedging & shrubs.
Map Ref: W, C4

WCom   COMPTON LANE NURSERIES ⊠
Little Compton, Moreton-in-Marsh,
Gloucestershire, GL56 0SJ
Ⓣ (01608) 674578
Ⓕ (01608) 674877
Also supplies wholesale: Yes
Contact: Chris Brown
Opening Times: 1000-1700 Tue-Sat Feb-Oct.
Min Mail Order UK: £15.00 + p&p*
Cat. Cost: 5 x 1st class, sae for separate mail order list.
Credit Cards: None
Specialities: Mainly alpines/herbaceous & a few unusual shrubs. *Saxifraga, Primula, Cyclamen, Viola, Philadelphus, Hebe.* *Note: mail order Oct-Mar.
Map Ref: W, C5

WCot   COTSWOLD GARDEN
FLOWERS ⊠ ☒ ♫ €
Brown's Nursery, Gibbs Lane, Offenham,
Evesham, Worcestershire, WR11 8RR
Ⓣ (01386) 422829 mail order (01386) 422829
Ⓕ (01386) 49844
Ⓔ info@cgf.net
Ⓦ www.cgf.net
Also supplies wholesale: Yes
Contact: Bob Brown/Vicky Parkhouse/Andy Houghton
Opening Times: 0900-1730 Mon-Fri all year.
1000-1730 Sat & Sun Mar-Sep, Sat & Sun Oct-Feb by appt.
Min Mail Order UK: Nmc
Min Mail Order EU: Nmc
Cat. Cost: Free
Credit Cards: MasterCard Access Diners Visa
Switch
Specialities: A very wide range of easy & unusual perennials. Nat. Coll. of *Lysimachia*.
Map Ref: W, C5
OS Grid Ref: SP077426

WCra   CRANESBILL NURSERY ⊠ € ⌂
White Cottage, Stock Green,
Nr Redditch, Worcestershire, B96 6SZ
Ⓣ (01386) 792414
Ⓕ (01386) 792280
Ⓔ smandjbates@aol.com
Contact: Mrs S M Bates

Opening Times: 1000-1700 19th Mar-30th Sep. Closed Wed & Thu. Aug by appt. only. Please contact for w/end opening.
Min Mail Order UK: Nmc
Min Mail Order EU: Nmc
Cat. Cost: 4 x 1st class
Credit Cards: all major credit/debit cards
Specialities: Hardy geraniums & other herbaceous plants.
Map Ref: W, C5

WCru   CRÛG FARM PLANTS 🔘
Griffith's Crossing,
Nr Caernarfon,
Gwynedd, Wales, LL55 1TU
Ⓣ (01248) 670232
Ⓔ bleddyn&sue@crug-farm.co.uk
Ⓦ www.crug-farm.co.uk
Also supplies wholesale: Yes
Contact: B and S Wynn-Jones
Opening Times: 1000-1800 Thu-Sun last Sat Feb-last Sun Sep, plus B/hols.
Cat. Cost: 3 x 2nd class
Credit Cards: Visa Access Delta MasterCard
Specialities: Shade plants, climbers, hardy *Geranium, Pulmonaria*, rare shrubs, *Tropaeolum*, herbaceous & bulbous incl. self-collected new introductions from the Far East. Nat. Colls. of *Coriaria, Paris* & *Polygonatum*.
Map Ref: W, A2
OS Grid Ref: SH509652

WCwm   CWMRHAIADR NURSERY ✉
Glaspwll, Machynlleth,
Powys, Wales, SY20 8UB
Ⓣ (01654) 702223
Ⓕ (01654) 702223
Ⓔ glynne.jones@btinternet.com
Contact: Glynne Jones
Opening Times: By appt. only. Please phone. Garden open under NGS.
Min Mail Order UK: £10.00*
Cat. Cost: 2 x 1st class
Credit Cards: None
Specialities: *Acer* species. Camellias, rhododendrons & magnolias. Rarer conifer species & clones. *Note: mail order Nov & Mar only.
Map Ref: W, B3

WDav   MARTIN DAVIS PLANTS ✉ 👤 €
Osric, 115 Calton Road,
Gloucester, GL1 5ES
Ⓣ (01452) 539749
Ⓔ martin@osrics.freeserve.co.uk
Contact: Martin Davis
Opening Times: By appt. only.
Min Mail Order UK: Nmc*

Min Mail Order EU: Nmc
Cat. Cost: 4 x 1st class
Credit Cards: None
Specialities: *Allium, Lilium, Canna*, dwarf bearded *Iris* & other bulbous/rhizomatous subjects. *Note: mail order for bulbs Oct-Jan, for plants Mar-May, limited stock.
Map Ref: W, D5

WDib   DIBLEY'S NURSERIES ✉ 👤 € 🔘 ◆
Llanelidan, Ruthin,
Denbighshire, LL15 2LG
Ⓣ (01978) 790677
Ⓕ (01978) 790668
Ⓔ sales@dibleys.com
Ⓦ www.dibleys.com
Also supplies wholesale: Yes
Contact: R Dibley
Opening Times: 1000-1700 7 days Mar-Oct.
Min Mail Order UK: Nmc
Min Mail Order EU: Nmc
Cat. Cost: Free
Credit Cards: Visa Access Switch Electron Solo
Specialities: *Streptocarpus, Columnea, Solenostemon* & other gesneriads & *Begonia*. Nat. Coll. of *Streptocarpus*.
Map Ref: W, A3

WDin   DINGLE NURSERIES €
Welshpool, Powys, Wales, SY21 9JD
Ⓣ (01938) 555145
Ⓕ (01938) 555778
Ⓔ kerry@dinglenurseries.co.uk
Ⓦ www.dinglenurseries.co.uk
Also supplies wholesale: Yes
Contact: Kerry Hamer
Opening Times: 0900-1700 Wed-Mon.
Cat. Cost: Free plant list
Credit Cards: MasterCard Switch EuroCard Delta Visa
Specialities: Largest range of trees & shrubs in Wales. Wide seasonal selection of garden plants incl. roses, herbaceous perennials, conifers & barerooted forestry, hedging & fruit. All sizes incl. many mature specimens.
Map Ref: W, B4

WDyf   DYFFRYN NURSERIES ✉ 👤 € 🔘
Home Farm, Dyffryn, Cardiff,
Wales, CF5 6JU
Ⓣ (02920) 592085
Ⓕ (02920) 593462

W

KEY		
✉ Mail order to UK or EU		👤 Delivers to shows
🗹 Exports beyond EU		€ Euro accepted
🔘 Accessible by wheelchair		◆ See Display advertisement

Ⓔ sales@dyffryn-nurseries.co.uk
Ⓦ www.dyffryn-nurseries.co.uk
Also supplies wholesale: Yes
Contact: Victoria Hardaker
Opening Times: 0800-1600 Mon-Fri, 1100-1600 Sat & Sun.
Min Mail Order UK: £25.00
Min Mail Order EU: £25.00
Cat. Cost: Information on request
Credit Cards: MasterCard Access Switch Delta Visa
Specialities: Native & exotic mature, hardy specimen & architectural plants.
Map Ref: W, D3

WDyG **DYFFRYN GWYDDNO NURSERY** ⊠ ṅ ◆
Dyffryn Farm, Lampeter Velfrey, Narberth, Pembrokeshire, Wales, SA67 8UN
Ⓣ (01834) 861684
Ⓔ sally.polson@virgin.net
Ⓦ www.pembrokeshireplants.co.uk
Contact: Mrs S L Polson
Opening Times: 1000-1700 Mon-Thu Apr-Oct & many Sun. Phone for details or an appt. for other times.
Min Mail Order UK: Nmc*
Cat. Cost: 2 x 2nd class
Specialities: Eclectic, yet wide-ranging, from tender salvias & grasses to bog. Peat free & principled. *Note: mail order via web site.
Map Ref: W, D2
OS Grid Ref: SR138148

WEas **EASTGROVE COTTAGE GARDEN NURSERY** ⬤
Sankyns Green Nr Shrawley, Little Witley, Worcestershire, WR6 6LQ
Ⓣ (01299) 896389
Ⓦ www.eastgrove.co.uk
Contact: Malcolm & Carol Skinner
Opening Times: 1400-1700 Thu-Sun 17th Apr-31st Jul & B/hol Mons. Closed Aug. 1400-1700 Thu-Sat 4th Sep-11th Oct plus Sun 5th Oct.
Cat. Cost: On web
Credit Cards: None
Specialities: Unique cottage garden & arboretum. Many varieties of *Viola, Iris, Dianthus* & *Aquilegia*, plus a wide range of old favourites & many unusual plants. RHS Partnership garden.
Map Ref: W, C5
OS Grid Ref: SO795644

WEll **ELLWOOD PENSTEMONS** ⊠
Ellwood House, Fern Road, Ellwood, Coleford, Gloucestershire, GL16 7LY
Ⓣ (01594) 833839

Contact: Yvonne Shorthouse
Opening Times: Visitors welcome at most times Mon-Sat Apr-Oct, please phone first.
Min Mail Order UK: Nmc
Cat. Cost: 3 x 1st class
Credit Cards: None
Specialities: Penstemons. Will propagate to order. Stock ltd. as propagated on site.
Map Ref: W, D4
OS Grid Ref: SO591082

WEve **EVERGREEN CONIFER CENTRE** ⊠ ⬤ ◆
Tenbury Road, Rock, Nr Kidderminster, Worcestershire, DY14 9RB
Ⓣ (01299) 266581
Ⓕ (01299) 266755
Ⓔ brian@evergreen-conifers.co.uk
Ⓦ www.evergreen-conifers.co.uk
Also supplies wholesale: Yes
Contact: Mr B Warrington
Opening Times: 0900-1700 (dusk in winter) Mon-Sat.
Min Mail Order UK: Nmc*
Cat. Cost: 4 x 1st class for list
Credit Cards: Electron Visa MasterCard Switch Solo
Specialities: Conifers mainly but also acers, heathers, trees, evergreen shrubs. *Note: mail order conifers only.
Map Ref: W, C4

WFar **FARMYARD NURSERIES** ⊠ ⊠ ⬤ ◆
Llandysul, Dyfed, Wales, SA44 4RL
Ⓣ (01559) 363389 (01267) 220259
Ⓕ (01559) 362200
Ⓔ richard@farmyardnurseries.co.uk
Ⓦ www.farmyardnurseries.co.uk
Also supplies wholesale: Yes
Contact: Richard Bramley
Opening Times: 1000-1700 7 days excl. Xmas, Boxing & New Year's Day.
Min Mail Order UK: Nmc
Min Mail Order EU: £50.00 + p&p
Cat. Cost: 4 x 1st class
Credit Cards: Visa Switch MasterCard
Specialities: Excellent general range esp. *Helleborus, Hosta, Tricyrtis* & *Schizostylis*, plus shrubs, trees, climbers, alpines & esp. herbaceous. Nat. Coll. of *Tricyrtis*.
Map Ref: W, C2

WFFs **FABULOUS FUCHSIAS**
The Martins, Stanley Hill, Bosbury, Nr Ledbury, Herefordshire, HR8 1HE
Ⓣ (01531) 640298
Ⓔ afuchsia@excite.com
Contact: Angela Thompson

Opening Times: By appt. only. Sells at local plant fairs.
Cat. Cost: 3 x 1st class
Credit Cards: None
Specialities: *Fuchsia*: hardy, bush, trailing, species, triphyllas, unusual varieties, many available in small quantities only.

WFib FIBREX NURSERIES LTD ⊠ 🗷 🏠
Honeybourne Road, Pebworth, Stratford-on-Avon, Warwickshire, CV37 8XP
Ⓣ (01789) 720788
Ⓕ (01789) 721162
Ⓔ sales@fibrex.co.uk
Ⓦ www.fibrex.co.uk
Also supplies wholesale: Yes
Contact: U Key-Davis & R L Godard-Key
Opening Times: 1030-1700 Mon-Fri, 1200-1700 Sat & Sun Mar-Jul. 1030-1600 Mon-Fri Aug-Feb. Office hours 0930-1700 Mon-Fri all year excl. last 2 wks Dec/1st wk Jan.
Min Mail Order UK: £10.00 + p&p
Min Mail Order EU: £20.00 + p&p
Cat. Cost: 2 x 2nd class
Credit Cards: MasterCard Visa
Specialities: *Hedera*, ferns, *Pelargonium* & *Helleborus*. National Collections of *Pelargonium* & *Hedera*. Note: plant collections subject to time of year, please check by phone.
Map Ref: W, C5
OS Grid Ref: SP1246

WFoF FLOWERS OF THE FIELD
Field Farm, Weobley, Herefordshire, HR4 8QJ
Ⓣ (01544) 318262
Ⓕ (01544) 318262
Ⓔ flowerofthefield@tesco.net
Also supplies wholesale: Yes
Contact: Kathy Davies
Opening Times: 0900-1900 7 days.
Cat. Cost: 2 x 1st class
Credit Cards: None
Specialities: Cut flowers eg lilies, chrysanthemums, carnations, freesias & gladioli. Traditional, unusual perennials & grasses, shrubs, trees, herbs. Summer & winter hanging baskets, bedding. Nursery partially accessible for wheelchairs.
Map Ref: W, C4

WGei W G GEISSLER
Winsford, Kingston Road, Slimbridge, Gloucestershire, GL2 7BW
Ⓣ (01453) 890340
Ⓕ (01453) 890340
Ⓔ geissler.w@virgin.net
Ⓦ www.t.mann.taylor.clara.net/ptero.html

http://freespace.virgin.net/geissler.w/
Contact: W G Geissler
Opening Times: 0900-1700 Mar-Nov.
Cat. Cost: None issued.
Credit Cards: None
Specialities: Hardy cacti & succulents & related books. Nat. Colls. of *Opuntia* (sect. *Tephrocactus*) & *Pterocactus*.
Map Ref: W, D4

WGer FRON GOCH GARDEN CENTRE 🖢
Pant Road, Llanfaglan, Caernarfon, Gwynedd, Wales, LL54 5RL
Ⓣ (01286) 672212
Ⓕ (01286) 678912
Ⓔ info@frongoch-gardencentre.co.uk
Ⓦ www.frongoch-gardencentre.co.uk
Contact: RA & Mrs V Williams
Opening Times: 0900-1800 Mon-Sat, 1030-1630 Sun all year.
Cat. Cost: None issued
Credit Cards: MasterCard Switch Visa
Specialities: Wide range of trees, shrubs, conifers & herbaceous perennials, ferns & grasses; emphasis on plants for coastal & damp sites.
Map Ref: W, A2

WGHP GREEN HILL PLANTS
46 Edde Cross Street, Ross-on-Wye, Herefordshire, HR9 7BZ
Ⓣ (01989) 567850
Ⓜ 07977 555089 (during opening hours)
Ⓔ elizabeth@greenhillplants.co.uk
Contact: Darren or Elizabeth Garman
Opening Times: 1000-1700 Thu, Fri & Sat, Easter-end Sep (closed one week in Aug, phone for details). Other times by appt. only, please phone.
Cat. Cost: 3 x 1st class
Credit Cards: None
Specialities: Herbs, grasses, herbaceous perennials & ornamental willows. Note: nursery located at Goodrich Court Walled Garden, Goodrich Court Stables, Goodrich HR9 6HT.
Map Ref: W, C4
OS Grid Ref: SO569200

WGMN GREEN MAN NURSERY ⊠ 🏠 🖢
Grove House, Haimwood, Llandrinio, Powys, SY22 6SQ
Ⓣ (01691) 830065

W

Ⓕ (01691) 830065
Ⓔ plants@GreenManNursery.co.uk
Ⓦ www.GreenManNursery.co.uk
Contact: Pamela Rundle
Opening Times: 1000-1700 daily, but please phone first.
Min Mail Order UK: Nmc
Cat. Cost: 2 x 1st class
Credit Cards: None
Map Ref: W, B4
OS Grid Ref: SJ310166

WGor   GORDON'S NURSERY ⊠ ▣
1 Cefnpennar Cottages, Cefnpennar,
Mountain Ash, Mid-Glamorgan,
Wales, CF45 4EE
Ⓣ (01443) 474593
Ⓕ (01443) 475835
Ⓔ gordonsnursery@compuserve.com
Ⓦ http:\\ourworld.compuserve.com/
homepages/gordonsnursery
Contact: D A Gordon
Opening Times: 1000-1800 7 days 1st Mar-31st Oct. 1100-1600 Sat & Sun 1st Nov-28th Feb.
Min Mail Order UK: Nmc*
Cat. Cost: 3 x 1st class
Credit Cards: Visa MasterCard Switch Solo Electron
Specialities: Shrubs, perennials, alpines & dwarf conifers. *Note: mail order only available in some cases, please check for conditions in catalogue.
Map Ref: W, D3
OS Grid Ref: SO037012

WGwG   GWYNFOR GROWERS ⊠ ♋ € ▣
Gwynfor, Pontgarreg, Llangranog, Llandysul,
Ceredigion, Wales, SA44 6AU
Ⓣ (01239) 654151
Ⓕ (01239) 654152
Ⓔ anne@gwynfor-growers.fsnet.co.uk
Also supplies wholesale: Yes
Contact: Anne & Bob Seaman
Opening Times: 1000-1700 Wed-Sun & B/hol Mons. Closed 25th Dec-1st Feb.
Min Mail Order UK: £30.00
Min Mail Order EU: £30.00
Cat. Cost: 4 x 1st class
Credit Cards: None
Specialities: Good general range specialising in herbaceous plants & *Fuchsia*.
Map Ref: W, C2
OS Grid Ref: SN331536

WGWT   GRAFTED WALNUT TREES ⊠ € ▣
The Manse, Capel Isaac, Llandeilo,
Camarthenshire, Wales, SA19 7TN

Ⓣ (01558) 669043
Ⓔ gary@graftedwalnuts.co.uk
Ⓦ www.graftedwalnuts.co.uk
Also supplies wholesale: Yes
Contact: Gary Wignall
Opening Times: 0900-1800 Mon-Fri. Nursery visits by appt. only.
Min Mail Order UK: Nmc
Cat. Cost: 3 x 1st class
Credit Cards: None
Specialities: Grafted walnut trees incl. nut bearing varieties of English walnut, ornamental forms of English & black walnut, minor species & hybrids. Ltd. supply of ornamental varieties.
Map Ref: W, C3
OS Grid Ref: SN580266

WHal   HALL FARM NURSERY ♋ €
Vicarage Lane, Kinnerley,
Nr Oswestry, Shropshire,
SY10 8DH
Ⓣ (01691) 682135
Ⓕ (01691) 682135
Ⓔ hallfarmnursery@ukonline.co.uk
Ⓦ www.hallfarmnursery.co.uk
Contact: Christine & Nick Ffoulkes-Jones
Opening Times: 1000-1700 Tue-Sat 1st Mar-11th Oct 2003.
Cat. Cost: 4 x 1st class
Credit Cards: None
Specialities: Unusual herbaceous plants incl. hardy *Geranium, Pulmonaria,* grasses, bog plants & pool marginals, late-flowering perennials, foliage plants. Nursery partially accessible for wheelchairs.
Map Ref: W, B4
OS Grid Ref: SJ333209

WHar   HARLEY NURSERY ▣
Harley, Shropshire,
SY5 6LP
Ⓣ (01952) 510241
Ⓕ (01952) 510222
Ⓔ Harleynurseries@farmersweekly.net
Contact: Duncan Murphy, Moira Murphy, Michael Birt
Opening Times: 0900-1730 Mon-Sat, 1000-1750 Sun & B/hols. Winter hours 1000-1600 Sun & B/hols.
Cat. Cost: 2 x 1st class
Credit Cards: Visa Access
Specialities: Wide range of ornamental & fruit trees. Own grown shrubs, climbers, wide range of hedging plants year round. Conservation & wildlife plants & native trees a speciality.
Map Ref: W, B4

W

WHbs **HERBS AT MYDDFAI** 🔲
Beiliglas, Myddfai, Nr Llandovery,
Carmarthenshire, Wales, SA20 0QB
Ⓣ (01550) 720494
Ⓕ (01550) 720628
Ⓔ gill@myddfai.com
Ⓦ www.myddfai.com
Contact: Gill Swan
Opening Times: 1400-1800 Tue-Sat Apr-Oct,
or by appt.
Cat. Cost: 2 x 1st class
Credit Cards: None
Specialities: Herbs & wild flowers. Organic.
Map Ref: W, C3
OS Grid Ref: SN781310

WHCG **HUNTS COURT GARDEN & NURSERY** 🔲
North Nibley, Dursley,
Gloucestershire, GL11 6DZ
Ⓣ (01453) 547440
Ⓕ (01453) 549944
Ⓔ keith@huntscourt.fsnet.co.uk
Contact: T K & M M Marshall
Opening Times: Nursery & garden 0900-
1700 Tue-Sat excl. Aug. Also by appt. See
NGS for Sun openings.
Cat. Cost: 5 x 2nd class
Credit Cards: None
Specialities: Old roses species & climbers.
Hardy *Geranium, Penstemon* & unusual
shrubs.
Map Ref: W, D4

WHCr **HERGEST CROFT GARDENS**
Kington, Herefordshire, HR5 3EG
Ⓣ (01544) 230160
Ⓕ (01544) 232031
Ⓔ gardens@hergest.kc3.co.uk
Ⓦ www.hergest.co.uk
Contact: Stephen Lloyd
Opening Times: 1230-1730 7 days Apr-Oct,
1200-1800 7 days May-Jun.
Cat. Cost: None issued
Credit Cards: None
Specialities: *Acer, Betula* & unusual woody
plants.
Map Ref: W, C4

WHen **HENLLYS LODGE PLANTS** 🔲
Henllys Lodge, Beaumaris,
Anglesey, Gwynedd,
Wales, LL58 8HU
Ⓣ (01248) 810106
Ⓔ cranesbill@hugheslane.freeserve.co.uk
Contact: Mrs E Lane
Opening Times: 1100-1700 Mon Wed Fri Sat
Sun & by appt. Apr-Oct.

Cat. Cost: 2 x 1st class
Credit Cards: None
Specialities: Hardy *Geranium,* ground cover
& cottage style perennials.
Map Ref: W, A3
OS Grid Ref: SH601773

WHer **THE HERB GARDEN & HISTORICAL PLANT NURSERY** ✉
Pentre Berw, Gaerwen, Anglesey, Gwynedd,
Wales, LL60 6LF
Ⓣ (01248) 422208
Ⓜ 07751 583958
Ⓔ The_Herb-Garden@hotmail.com
Ⓦ www.HistoricalPlants.co.uk
Contact: Corinne & David Tremaine-
Stevenson
Opening Times: By appt. only.
Min Mail Order UK: £15.00 + p&p
Min Mail Order EU: £50.00 + p&p sterling
only.
Cat. Cost: List £2.00 in stamps
Credit Cards: None
Specialities: Wide range of herbs, rare natives
& wild flowers; rare & unusual & historical
perennials & old roses.
Map Ref: W, A2

WHHs **HERITAGE HERBS** ✉ 🏃 € 🔲
Gwynfor, Pontgarreg, Ceredigion, SA44 6AU
Ⓣ (01239) 654151
Ⓕ (01239) 654152
Ⓔ info@heritageherbs.co.uk
Ⓦ www.heritageherbs.co.uk
Also supplies wholesale: Yes
Contact: Anne & Bob Seaman
Opening Times: 1000-1700 Wed-Sun &
B/hol Mons. Closed 25th Dec-1st Feb.
Min Mail Order UK: £30.00
Min Mail Order EU: £30.00
Cat. Cost: 4 x 1st class
Credit Cards: None
Specialities: Herbs
Map Ref: W, C2
OS Grid Ref: SN331536

WHil **HILLVIEW HARDY PLANTS**
✉ 🗷 🏃 € 🔲 ◆
(off B4176) Worfield, Nr Bridgnorth,
Shropshire, WV15 5NT
Ⓣ (01746) 716454
Ⓕ (01746) 716454
Ⓔ hillview@themutual.net

W

Ⓦ www.hillviewhardyplants.com
Also supplies wholesale: Yes
Contact: Ingrid Millington, John Millington
Opening Times: 0900-1700 Mon-Sat Mar-mid Oct. At other times, please phone first.
Min Mail Order UK: £10.00 + p&p
Min Mail Order EU: £10.00 + p&p
Cat. Cost: 4 x 2nd class
Credit Cards: all major credit/debit cards
Specialities: Choice herbaceous perennials incl. *Aquilegia, Astrantia, Auricula, Primula, Crocosmia, Eucomis, Phlox, Schizostylis, Verbascum, Acanthus.*
Map Ref: W, B4
OS Grid Ref: SO772969

WHlf   HAYLOFT PLANTS ⊠
Little Court, Rous Lench, Evesham, Worcestershire, WR11 4UL
Ⓣ (01386) 793361
Ⓕ (01386) 793761
Ⓔ hayloftplants@talk21.com
Contact: Yvonne Walker
Opening Times: Not open, mail order only.
Min Mail Order UK: Nmc
Min Mail Order EU: Nmc
Cat. Cost: Free
Credit Cards: all major credit/debit cards

WHoo   HOO HOUSE NURSERY € ◆
Hoo House, Gloucester Road, Tewkesbury, Gloucestershire, GL20 7DA
Ⓣ (01684) 293389
Ⓕ (01684) 293389
Ⓔ nursery@hoohouse.co.uk
Also supplies wholesale: Yes
Contact: Robin & Julie Ritchie
Opening Times: 1000-1700 Mon-Sat.
Cat. Cost: 3 x 1st class
Credit Cards: None
Specialities: Wide range of herbaceous & alpines - many unusual, incl. *Campanula, Geranium* & *Penstemon.* Nat. Colls. of *Platycodon* & *Gentiana asclepiadea* cvs.
Map Ref: W, C5
OS Grid Ref: SO893293

WHPE   HYDE COTTAGE PALMS & EXOTICS ⊠ Ⓖ
Church Road, Crowle, Worcestershire, WR7 4AT
Ⓣ (01905) 381632
Ⓕ 0871 242 2240
Ⓔ palmsandexotics@tiscali.co.uk
Ⓦ www.palmsandexotics.co.uk
Contact: Rochford Dyer
Opening Times: 0900-1800 Mon-Sat, 1000-1600 Sun. Close at dusk in winter.
Min Mail Order UK: £8.50

Cat. Cost: 2 x 1st class
Credit Cards: None
Specialities: *Bamboo* (6 species), palms (10 sp.), tree ferns (3 sp.), *Yucca* (4 sp.), *Hedychium* (8 sp.) & unusual shrubs.
Map Ref: W, C5
OS Grid Ref: SO922562

WHPP   HP PLANTS ⊠
Yew Tree House, High Street, Hillesley, Wooton-under-Edge, Gloucestershire, GL12 7RD
Ⓜ 07767 897331
Ⓦ www.hpplants.com
Contact: Pauline Mapp
Opening Times: Mail order or by appt. only.
Min Mail Order UK: Nmc
Cat. Cost: Free
Credit Cards: None
Specialities: Pelargoniums

WHrl   HARRELLS HARDY PLANTS
(Office) 15 Coxlea Close, Evesham, Worcestershire, WR11 4JS
Ⓣ (01386) 443077
Ⓕ (01386) 443852
Ⓔ enicklin@evesham11.fsnet.co.uk
Ⓦ www.harrellshardyplants.co.uk
Contact: Liz Nicklin & Kate Phillips
Opening Times: By appt. only. Please phone before visiting.
Min Mail Order UK:
Cat. Cost: 3 x 1st class
Credit Cards: None
Specialities: A developing nursery offering wide range of hardy plants, new & old, many unusual. Note: nursery located off Rudge Rd, Evesham. Please phone for directions or see catalogue.
Map Ref: W, C5
OS Grid Ref: SP033443

WIvo   IVOR MACE NURSERIES ⊠
2 Mace Lane, Ynyswen, Treorci, Rhondda, Mid-Glamorgan, Wales, CF42 6DS
Ⓣ (01656) 302680 day (01443) 775531 evening
Ⓔ ivormace@hotmail.com
Contact: I Mace
Opening Times: Not open. Plants can be seen growing. By appt.
Min Mail Order UK: £5.00 + p&p*
Cat. Cost: Sae
Specialities: Large exhibition chrysanthemums.
*Note: delivery by mail order or collection during Feb & Mar only.
Map Ref: W, C3

W

WIvy   IVYCROFT PLANTS ⊠ ⧉
Upper Ivington, Leominster,
Herefordshire, HR6 0JN
Ⓣ (01568) 720344
Ⓔ rogerandsue@ivycroft.freeserve.co.uk
Ⓦ www.ivycroft.freeserve.co.uk
Contact: Roger Norman
Opening Times: 0900-1600 Wed & Thu
Mar-Sep. Other times by appt., please
phone.
Min Mail Order UK: Nmc*
Cat. Cost: 2 x 1st class
Credit Cards: None
Specialities: *Cyclamen, Galanthus, Salix,*
alpines & herbaceous. *Note: mail order
Feb/Mar *Galanthus* & *Salix* only.
Map Ref: W, C4
OS Grid Ref: SO464562

WJek   JEKKA'S HERB FARM ⊠ ⊠ ⋔ €
Rose Cottage, Shellards Lane,
Alveston, Bristol,
BS35 3SY
Ⓣ (01454) 418878
Ⓕ (01454) 411988
Ⓔ farm@jekkasherbfarm.com
Ⓦ www.jekkasherbfarm.com
Also supplies wholesale: Yes
Contact: Jekka McVicar
Opening Times: By appt. only.
Min Mail Order UK: Nmc
Min Mail Order EU: Nmc*
Cat. Cost: 4 x 1st class
Credit Cards: Visa MasterCard Delta Switch
Specialities: Culinary, medicinal, aromatic,
decorative herbs. *Note: individual quotations
for EU Sales. Soil Association licensed herb
farm.
Map Ref: W, D4

WJun   JUNGLE GIANTS ⊠ ⊠ € ⧉
Burford House Gardens,
Tenbury Wells, Worcestershire,
WR15 8HQ
Ⓣ (01584) 819885
Ⓕ (01584) 819779
Ⓔ bamboo@junglegiants.co.uk
Ⓦ www.junglegiants.co.uk
Also supplies wholesale: Yes
Contact: Michael Brisbane
Opening Times: 7 days. By appt. only please.
Min Mail Order UK: £25.00 + p&p
Min Mail Order EU: £100.00 + p&p
Cat. Cost: 2 x 1st class
Credit Cards: Access MasterCard Visa
Specialities: *Bamboo.*
Map Ref: W, C4
OS Grid Ref: SO580682

WKif   KIFTSGATE COURT GARDENS ⧉
Kiftsgate Court, Chipping Camden,
Gloucestershire, GL55 6LW
Ⓣ (01386) 438777
Ⓕ (01386) 438777
Ⓔ kiftsgte@aol.com
Ⓦ www.kiftsgate.co.uk
Contact: Mrs J Chambers
Opening Times: 1400-1800 Wed, Thu &
Sun 1st Apr-30th Sep & B/hol Mons. Also
Mon & Sat in Jun & Jul.
Cat. Cost: None issued
Credit Cards: None
Specialities: Small range of unusual plants.
Map Ref: W, C5

WKin   KINGSTONE COTTAGE PLANTS ⊠
Weston-under-Penyard,
Ross-on-Wye, Herefordshire, HR9 7PH
Ⓣ (01989) 565267
Contact: Mr M Hughes
Opening Times: By appt. and as under NGS.
Min Mail Order UK: Nmc
Min Mail Order EU: Nmc
Cat. Cost: 2 x 1st class
Credit Cards: None
Specialities: Nat. Coll. of *Dianthus.*
Map Ref: W, C4

WLav   THE LAVENDER GARDEN ⊠ ⋔ €
Ashcroft Nurseries, Nr Ozleworth,
Kingscote, Tetbury,
Gloucestershire, GL8 8YF
Ⓣ (01453) 860356 (01453) 549286
Also supplies wholesale: Yes
Contact: Andrew Bullock
Opening Times: 1100-1700 Sat & Sun.
Weekdays variable, please phone.
Min Mail Order UK: £10.00 + p&p
Min Mail Order EU: £20.00 + p&p
Cat. Cost: 2 x 1st class
Credit Cards: None
Specialities: *Lavandula, Buddleja,* plants to
attract butterflies. Herbs, wild flowers.
Map Ref: W, D5
OS Grid Ref: ST798948

WLeb   LEBA ORCHARD - GREEN'S LEAVES ⊠ ⋔
Lea Bailey, Nr Ross-on-Wye,
Herefordshire, HR9 5TY
Ⓣ (01989) 750303
Also supplies wholesale: Yes
Contact: Paul Green

W

KEY		
⊠ Mail order to UK or EU	⋔ Delivers to shows	
⊠ Exports beyond EU	€ Euro accepted	
⧉ Accessible by wheelchair	◆ See Display advertisement	

Opening Times: By appt. only, w/ends preferred.
Min Mail Order UK: £10.00 + p&p
Min Mail Order EU:
Cat. Cost: 3 x 2nd class
Credit Cards: None
Specialities: Ornamental grasses, sedges & phormiums. Increasing range of rare & choice shrubs, also some perennials.
Map Ref: W, C4

WLFP   LINNETT FARM PLANTS ⊠ ⊠
Ullingswick, Hereford,
Herefordshire, HR1 3JQ
Ⓣ (01432) 820337
Contact: Basil Smith
Opening Times: Not open.
Min Mail Order UK: £15.00 + p&p
Min Mail Order EU: £15.00 + p&p
Cat. Cost: Free
Credit Cards: None
Specialities: Hardy *Cyclamen* for the garden, named *Helleborus, Dierama* & *Schizostylis.* Also seeds. Note: nursery formerly CTDA.

WLHH   LAWTON HALL HERBS
Lawton Hall, Eardisland,
Herefordshire, HR6 9AX
Ⓣ (01568) 709215
Ⓔ herbs@lawtonhall.co.uk
Ⓦ www.LawtonHall.co.uk
Contact: Alexandra Fox
Opening Times: 1030-1830 Wed-Mon, closed Tue.
Cat. Cost: 1 x 1st class
Credit Cards: None
Specialities: Herbs, culinary, aromatic & medicinal.
Map Ref: W, C4

WLin   LINGEN NURSERY AND GARDEN ⊠
Lingen, Nr Bucknell,
Shropshire, SY7 0DY
Ⓣ (01544) 267720
Ⓕ (01544) 267720
Ⓔ kim&maggie@lingen.freeserve.co.uk
Ⓦ www.lingennursery.co.uk
Also supplies wholesale: Yes
Contact: Kim W Davis
Opening Times: 1000-1700 Thu-Mon Feb-Oct. Closed Tue-Wed all year.
Min Mail Order UK: Nmc
Min Mail Order EU: £20.00 + p&p
Cat. Cost: 3 x 1st class
Credit Cards: Visa MasterCard
Specialities: Alpines, rock plants, herbaceous esp. *Androsace, Aquilegia, Campanula, Iris, Primula,* auriculas & *Penstemon.*

Nat. Coll. of Herbaceous *Campanula* & housing *Iris sibirica.*
Map Ref: W, C4
OS Grid Ref: SO366669

WLow   LOWER SPRING NURSERY ⬚
Kenley, Shrewsbury, Shropshire, SY5 6PA
Ⓣ (01952) 510589
Ⓕ (01952) 510589
Ⓔ plants@lowerspring.fsworld.co.uk
Also supplies wholesale: Yes
Contact: Jo and Andy Jackson
Opening Times: 0900-1700 Wed-Sun & B/hols, Mar-Oct. Winter by arrangement.
Credit Cards: None
Specialities: Fragrant perennials & shrubs with some more unusual varieties. Also a good range of cacti, succulents & alpines. Available in limited quantities.
Map Ref: W, B4
OS Grid Ref: SJ580006

WLun   LUNNON NURSERY ⊠ €
Little Lunnon, Broughton Green, Hanbury,
Nr Droitwich, Worcestershire, WR9 7EF
Ⓣ (01905) 391316
Ⓕ (01905) 391316
Also supplies wholesale: Yes
Contact: John Farmer
Opening Times: By appt. only. Please phone first.
Min Mail Order UK: Nmc
Cat. Cost: 2 x 1st class
Credit Cards: None
Specialities: *Euphorbia.* Grafted trees. Wide range of hardy perennials, shrubs & trees.
Map Ref: W, C5

WMal   MARSHALL'S MALMAISON ⊠ ⬚ ♫ € ⬚
4 The Damsells, Tetbury,
Gloucestershire, GL8 8JA
Ⓣ (01666) 502589
Also supplies wholesale: Yes
Contact: J M Marshall
Opening Times: By appt. only.
Min Mail Order UK: £17.00 incl. p&p
Min Mail Order EU: £30.00 incl p&p
Cat. Cost: 1st class Sae
Credit Cards: None
Specialities: Nat. Coll. of Malmaison Carnations.
Map Ref: W, D5

WMAq   MEREBROOK WATER PLANTS ⊠ ⬚
Merebrook Farm, Hanley Swan,
Worcestershire, WR8 0DX
Ⓣ (01684) 310950
Ⓔ enquiries@pondplants.co.uk

Ⓦ www.pondplants.co.uk
Contact: Roger Kings & Biddi Kings
Opening Times: 1000-1600 Thu-Tue
Easter-Sep.
Min Mail Order UK: Nmc
Min Mail Order EU: £20.00
Cat. Cost: Free
Credit Cards: Access Visa Switch Delta
Specialities: *Nymphaea* & other aquatic plants.
Extensive display gardens open to the public
(no charge). International Waterlily & Water
Gardening Soc. accredited collection.
Map Ref: W, C5
OS Grid Ref: SO802425

WMnd   MYND HARDY PLANTS ⊠
Delbury Hall Estate, Diddlebury, Craven
Arms, Shropshire, SY7 9DH
Ⓣ (01547) 530459
Ⓕ (01547) 530459
Ⓔ sales@myndplants.co.uk
Ⓦ www.myndplants.co.uk
Also supplies wholesale: Yes
Contact: Steve Adams
Opening Times: 1000-1700 Mon, Wed-Sat,
closed Tues, 1100-1700 Sun, Easter-end Sep.
Other times phone for appt.
Min Mail Order UK: Nmc
Min Mail Order EU: Nmc
Cat. Cost: 4 x 2nd class
Credit Cards: Visa MasterCard
Specialities: Herbaceous plants.
Map Ref: W, B4
OS Grid Ref: SO510852

WMoo   MOORLAND COTTAGE PLANTS ⊠ ♿
Rhyd-y-Groes, Brynberian, Crymych,
Pembrokeshire, Wales, SA41 3TT
Ⓣ (01239) 891363
Ⓔ jenny@moorlandcottageplants.co.uk
Ⓦ www.moorlandcottageplants.co.uk
Contact: Jennifer Matthews
Opening Times: 1000-1800 daily excl. Wed
end Feb-end Sep.
Min Mail Order UK: See cat. for details.
Cat. Cost: 4 x 1st class
Credit Cards: None
Specialities: Traditional & unusual hardy
perennials. Many rarities. Cottage garden
plants; plants for woodland & shade; moisture
lovers; ornamental grasses & colourful ground
cover. Display garden open for NGS.
Map Ref: W, C2
OS Grid Ref: SN091343

WMou   MOUNT PLEASANT TREES €
Rockhampton, Berkeley,
Gloucestershire, GL13 9DU

Ⓣ (01454) 260348
Also supplies wholesale: Yes
Contact: P & G Locke
Opening Times: By appt. only.
Cat. Cost: 3 x 2nd class
Credit Cards: None
Specialities: Wide range of trees for forestry,
hedging, woodlands & gardens esp. *Tilia,
Populus* & *Platanus.*
Map Ref: W, D4

WMul   MULU NURSERIES ⊠ ☒ ♠ € ♿
Longdon Hill, Wickhamford, Evesham,
Worcestershire, WR11 7RP
Ⓣ (01386) 833171
Ⓕ (01386) 833136
Ⓔ plants@mulu.co.uk
Ⓦ www.mulu.co.uk
Also supplies wholesale: Yes
Contact: Andy Bateman
Opening Times: 1000-1800 or dusk 7 days.
Min Mail Order UK: Nmc
Min Mail Order EU: £25.00 + p&p
Cat. Cost: free
Credit Cards: Visa MasterCard Delta Switch
Specialities: Exotic plants, hardy & tender
incl. bananas, gingers, palms, tree ferns,
aroids.
Map Ref: W, C5
OS Grid Ref: SP060417

WMyn   MYNYDD PENCARREG WATER PLANTS
Gwarffynnon Farm, Pencarreg,
Carmarthenshire, Wales, SA48 8ED
Ⓣ (01570) 480452
Ⓔ david.bull@ukonline.co.uk
Contact: Katie Bull
Opening Times: Fri-Sun, Mar-Oct or by appt.
Cat. Cost: 2 x 2nd class
Credit Cards: None
Specialities: Water lilies, marginals, moisture-
loving plants, bog primulas & willows.
Map Ref: W, C3
OS Grid Ref: SN56974347

WNor   NORFIELDS ⊠ ☒ ♠ €
Llangwm Arboretum, Usk,
Monmouthshire, NP15 1NQ
Ⓣ (01291) 650306
Ⓕ (01291) 650577
Ⓔ andrew@norfields.co.uk
Ⓦ www.Norfields.co.uk
Also supplies wholesale: Yes

W

KEY		
⊠ Mail order to UK or EU	♠ Delivers to shows	
☒ Exports beyond EU	€ Euro accepted	
♿ Accessible by wheelchair	◆ See Display advertisement	

Contact: Andrew Norfield
Opening Times: Not open.
Min Mail Order UK: £3.00 + p&p
Min Mail Order EU: £3.00 + p&p
Cat. Cost: 2 x 1st class
Credit Cards: None
Specialities: Wide range of tree seedlings for growing on. *Acer, Betula, Stewartia* & pre-treated seed.

WOBN   OLD BARN NURSERY ⊠ ⋔ €
Llwynglas, Llwynteg, Ffynnon-ddrain,
Carmarthen, Carmarthenshire,
Wales, SA33 6EE
Ⓣ (01267) 237275
Ⓔ oldbarnnursery@aol.com
Also supplies wholesale: Yes
Contact: G B J Smith & M Scott
Opening Times: Not open. Mail order only.
Min Mail Order UK: £10.00
Min Mail Order EU: £10.00
Cat. Cost: 2 x 1st class
Credit Cards: None
Specialities: Alpines, many unusual, in small numbers. *Rhodohypoxis* in profusion. *Agapanthus* & wide range of *Iris*, some in small numbers.

WOFF   OLD FASHIONED FLOWERS ⊠
Cleeway, Eardington, Bridgnorth,
Shropshire, WV16 5JT
Ⓣ (01746) 766909
Ⓔ jand.cm@virgin.net
Contact: John Snocken
Opening Times: By appt. only.
Min Mail Order UK: Nmc
Min Mail Order EU: Nmc
Cat. Cost: 2 x 2nd class
Credit Cards: None
Specialities: Show pansies, fancy pansies & exhibition violas. Nat. Coll. of Florists' Violas & Pansies. Some bedding violas.
Map Ref: W, B4
OS Grid Ref: 723907

WOld   OLD COURT NURSERIES ⊠ ☑ € ⅆ
Colwall, Nr Malvern,
Worcestershire, WR13 6QE
Ⓣ (01684) 540416
Ⓕ (01684) 565314
Ⓔ picton@dircon.co.uk
Ⓦ www.autumnasters.co.uk
Also supplies wholesale:
Contact: Paul & Meriel Picton
Opening Times: 1100-1700 Wed-Sun May-Oct, 7 days 2nd week Sep-2nd week Oct.
Min Mail Order UK: Nmc*
Min Mail Order EU: Nmc

Cat. Cost: 1 x 1st class
Credit Cards: None
Specialities: Nat. Coll. of Michaelmas Daisies. Herbaceous perennials. *Note: mail order for *Aster* only.
Map Ref: W, C4
OS Grid Ref: SO759430

WOrn   ORNAMENTAL TREE NURSERIES ⊠ ⅆ
Broomy Hill Gardens, Cobnash, Kingsland,
Herefordshire, HR6 9QZ
Ⓣ (01568) 708016
Ⓕ (01568) 709022
Ⓔ enquiries@ornamental-trees.co.uk
Ⓦ www.ornamental-trees.co.uk
Also supplies wholesale: Yes
Contact: Russell Mills
Opening Times: 0900-1700 Mon-Sat. 1000-1600 Sun.
Min Mail Order UK: £9.95
Cat. Cost: 2 x 2nd class
Credit Cards: Visa Switch MasterCard Access Delta American Express
Specialities: Ornamental trees.
Map Ref: W, C4

WOut   OUT OF THE COMMON WAY ⊠ ⋔
(Office) Penhyddgan, Boduan, Pwllheli,
Gwynedd, Wales, LL53 8YH
Ⓣ (01758) 721577 (Office) (01407) 720431 (Nursery)
Ⓔ jo.davidson@virgin.net
Contact: Joanna Davidson (nursery) Margaret Mason (office & mail order)
Opening Times: By arrangement.
Min Mail Order UK: Nmc
Min Mail Order EU: Nmc
Cat. Cost: Sae 33p (2nd class)
Credit Cards: None
Specialities: *Lobelia, Nepeta, Geranium, Salvia, Digitalis, Lavandula, Stachys* & *Veronica*. Note: some plants propagated in small quantities only. Nursery is at Pandy Treban, Bryngwran, Anglesey.
Map Ref: W, A2
OS Grid Ref: SH370778

WOVN   THE OLD VICARAGE NURSERY ⊠ ⋔
Lucton, Leominster, Herefordshire,
HR6 9PN
Ⓣ (01568) 780538
Ⓕ (01568) 780818
Contact: Mrs R M Flake
Opening Times: By appt.
Min Mail Order UK: Nmc
Cat. Cost: 2 x 1st class
Credit Cards: None
Specialities: Roses: old roses; climbers

& ramblers; species & ground cover.
Euphorbia & half-hardy *Salvia.*
Map Ref: W, C4

WP&B **P & B Fuchsias** ⊠ ⋔ € ⓐ
Maes y Gwaelod, Penclawdd Road, Penclawdd,
Swansea, West Glamorgan, Wales, SA4 3RB
ⓣ (01792) 851669
ⓕ (01792) 851779
ⓔ pbfuchsias@fuchsias.u-net.com
ⓦ www.fuchsias.u-net.com
Contact: Paul Fisher
Opening Times: 0900-1800 7 days 1 Mar-30
Sep.
Min Mail Order UK: £9.00 (6 plants @
£1.50 incl. P&P)
Cat. Cost: 3 x 1st class
Credit Cards: None
Specialities: Fuchsias. Hybrid & species. Note:
cuttings only available Mar-May. Very ltd.
quantities of each.
Map Ref: W, D3

WPat **Chris Pattison** ⊠ ⋔ €
Brookend, Pendock,
Gloucestershire,
GL19 3PL
ⓣ (01531) 650480
ⓕ (01531) 650480
ⓔ cpplants@redmarley.freeserve.co.uk
ⓦ www.chrispattison.fsnet.co.uk
Also supplies wholesale: Yes
Contact: Chris Pattison
Opening Times: 0900-1700 Mon-Fri.
W/ends by appt. only.
Min Mail Order UK: £10.00 +p&p*
Cat. Cost: 3 x 1st class
Credit Cards: None
Specialities: Choice, rare shrubs & alpines.
Grafted stock esp. Japanese maples &
Liquidambar. Wide range of *Viburnum,*
Phormium, dwarf willows & dwarf ericaceous
shrubs. *Note: mail order Nov-Feb only.
Map Ref: W, C5
OS Grid Ref: SO781327

WPen **Penpergwm Plants** ⓐ
Penpergwm Lodge, Abergavenny,
Gwent,
Wales, NP7 9AS
ⓣ (01873) 840422/840208
ⓕ (01873) 840470/840208
ⓔ boyle@penpergwm.co.uk
ⓦ www.penplants.com
Contact: Mrs J Kerr/Mrs S Boyle
Opening Times: 28th Mar-29 Sep 2002, 27th
Mar-28th Sep 2003, Thu-Sun 1400-1800.
Cat. Cost: 2 x 1st class

Credit Cards: None
Specialities: Hardy perennials.
Map Ref: W, D4

WPer **Perhill Nurseries** ⊠ €
Worcester Road, Great Witley,
Worcestershire, WR6 6JT
ⓣ (01299) 896329
ⓕ (01299) 896990
ⓔ PerhillP@aol.com
ⓦ www.hartlana.co.uk/perhill/
Also supplies wholesale: Yes
Contact: Duncan Straw
Opening Times: 0900-1700 Mon-Sat, 1000-
1600 Sun, 1st Feb-15th Oct & by appt.
Min Mail Order UK: Nmc
Min Mail Order EU: £10.00
Cat. Cost: 6 x 2nd class
Credit Cards: MasterCard Delta Switch
EuroCard Visa Maestro
Specialities: 2500+ varieties of rare, unusual
alpines & herbaceous perennials incl. *Penstemon,*
Campanula, Salvia, Thymus, herbs, *Veronica.*
Map Ref: W, C4
OS Grid Ref: 763656

WPGP **Pan-Global Plants** ⊠ ⓐ
The Walled Garden, Frampton Court,
Frampton-on-Severn,
Gloucestershire, GL2 7EU
ⓣ (01452) 741641
ⓜ 07801 275138
ⓕ (01453) 768858
ⓦ www.panglobalplants.com
Contact: Nick Macer
Opening Times: 1100-1700 Wed-Sun
1st Feb-31st Oct. Also B/hols. Closed 2nd
Sun in Sep. Winter months by appt., please
phone first.
Min Mail Order UK: £50.00
Cat. Cost: 4 x 1st class
Credit Cards: MasterCard Visa Solo Delta
American Express
Specialities: A plantsman's nursery offering a
wide selection of rare & desirable trees,
shrubs, herbaceous, bamboos, exotics,
climbers, ferns etc. Specialities incl. *Magnolia,*
Hydrangea & *Bamboo.*
Map Ref: W, D5

WPhl **Just Phlomis** ⊠ ⓐ
Sunningdale, Grange Court, Westbury-on-
Severn, Gloucestershire, GL14 1PL

W

Ⓣ (01452) 760268
Ⓕ (01452) 760268
Ⓔ phlomis@manntaylor.com
Ⓦ www.manntaylor.com/phlomis.html
Contact: J Mann Taylor
Opening Times: By appt. only.
Min Mail Order UK: £7.50 + p&p
Cat. Cost: 2 x 2nd class
Credit Cards: None
Specialities: Nat. Coll. of *Phlomis*.
Map Ref: W, D4
OS Grid Ref: SO727164

WPic   THE PICTON CASTLE TRUST NURSERY 🅰
Picton Castle, Haverfordwest, Pembrokeshire,
Wales, SA62 4AS
Ⓣ (01437) 751326
Ⓕ (01437) 751326
Ⓔ pct@pictoncastle.freeserve.co.uk
Ⓦ www.pictoncastle.co.uk
Contact: D L Pryse Lloyd
Opening Times: 1030-1700 7 days except
Mon Apr-Oct. Other times by arrangement.
Cat. Cost: 1 x 1st class
Credit Cards: None
Specialities: Woodland & unusual shrubs.
Herbs.
Map Ref: W, D2

WPnn   THE PERENNIAL NURSERY
Rhosygilwen, Llanrhian Road, St Davids,
Pembrokeshire, Wales, SA62 6DB
Ⓣ (01437) 721954
Ⓕ (01437) 721954
Ⓔ pdsymons@tiscali.co.uk
Contact: Mrs Philipa Symons
Opening Times: 1030-1730 Mar-Oct. Nov-
Feb by appt.
Credit Cards: None
Specialities: Herbaceous perennials & alpines.
Tender perennials esp. *Argyranthemum*.
Coastal plants.
Map Ref: W, C1
OS Grid Ref: SM775292

WPnP   PENLAN PERENNIALS ✉ ☑ ⋒ € 🅰
Penlan Farm, Penrhiwpal, Llandysul,
Ceredigion, Wales, SA44 5QH
Ⓣ (01239) 851244
Ⓕ (01239) 851244
Ⓔ rcain@penlanfarm.co.uk
Ⓦ www.penlanperennials.co.uk
Contact: Richard & Jane Cain
Opening Times: 0930-1730 Wed-Sun Mar-
Sep & B/hols. Other times by appt.
Min Mail Order UK: Nmc*
Min Mail Order EU: Nmc

Cat. Cost: 4 x 2nd class
Credit Cards: None
Specialities: Aquatic, marginal & bog plants.
Shade-loving & woodland perennials, ferns &
grasses. *Note: mail order all year, next day
delivery.
Map Ref: W, C2
OS Grid Ref: SN344457

WPPR   PERSHORE PLANT RAISERS ✉ €
Pensham, Pershore, Worcestershire, WR10 3HB
Ⓣ (01386) 554672
Ⓕ (01386) 556555
Also supplies wholesale: Yes
Contact: Edward Wilson
Opening Times: 1000-1600 Mar-Oct, Mon-Sat.
Min Mail Order UK: £11.00
Min Mail Order EU: £12.00
Cat. Cost: 2 x 1st class
Credit Cards: None
Specialities: *Penstemon, Salvia, Diascia*. Note:
mail order Mar-May & Sep-Nov.
Map Ref: W, C5

WPrP   PRIME PERENNIALS ✉ ⋒
Llety Moel, Rhos-y-Garth, Llanilar,
Nr Aberystwyth, Ceredigion, Wales,
SY23 4SG
Ⓣ (01974) 241505
Ⓜ 07890 708142
Contact: Elizabeth Powney
Opening Times: Open by appt. only.
Min Mail Order UK: Nmc*
Min Mail Order EU: Nmc
Cat. Cost: 4 x 1st class
Credit Cards: None
Specialities: Unusual & interesting perennials,
bulbs & grasses. *Dierama, Tulbaghia,
Kniphofia, Tricyrtis* & many others grown in
peat free compost. Nursery 650ft above sea
level. *Note: mail order Apr-Dec.
Map Ref: W, C3

WRha   RHANDIRMWYN PLANTS
2 Tremcecynog, Rhandirmwyn,
Nr Llandovery, Carmarthenshire, Wales,
SA20 0NU
Ⓣ (01550) 760220
Ⓕ (01550) 760399
Contact: Sara Fox/Thomas Sheppard
Opening Times: Open most days, but please
ring first to avoid disappointment.
Cat. Cost: none issued.
Credit Cards: None
Specialities: 1000+ varieties & species incl.
aquilegias, campanulas, chrysanthemums,
digitalis, geraniums, geums, *Lychnis, Mentha,
Monarda, Origanum*, primulas, *Rosmarinus*,

salvias & violas. Stock limited in quantity but not variety!
Map Ref: W, C3
OS Grid Ref: SN796428

WRHF   **RED HOUSE FARM** ⑤
Flying Horse Lane, Bradley Green,
Nr Redditch, Worcestershire, B96 6QT
Ⓣ (01527) 821269
Ⓕ (01527) 821674
Ⓔ contact@redhousefarmgardenandnursery.co.uk
Ⓦ www.redhousefarmgardenandnursery.co.uk
Contact: Mrs Maureen Weaver
Opening Times: 0900-1700 Mon-Sat all year.
1000-1700 Sun & B/hols.
Cat. Cost: 2 x 1st class
Credit Cards: None
Specialities: Cottage garden perennials.
Map Ref: W, C5
OS Grid Ref: SO986623

WRic   **RICKARD'S HARDY FERNS LTD** ⊠
Carreg y Fedwen, Fling, Tregarth, Nr Bangor,
Gwynedd,
Ⓣ (01248) 602944
Ⓕ (01248) 602944
Also supplies wholesale: Yes
Contact: Richard Hayward
Opening Times: 0900-1700 Mon & Wed-Fri,
1100-1700 Sat & Sun Mar-Oct. 1100-1600
Nov-Mar by appt. only.
Min Mail Order UK: £30.00 + p&p*
Min Mail Order EU: £50.00 + p&p*
Cat. Cost: 5 x 1st class or 6 x 2nd class
Credit Cards: None
Specialities: Ferns, hardy & half-hardy, tree
ferns. *Note: UK customers order with ltd.
cheque. EU customers confirm availability
before ordering. Rare items in ltd. numbers,
year round availability not guaranteed.
Map Ref: W, C4
OS Grid Ref: GR592667

WRos   **ROSEMARY'S FARMHOUSE NURSERY** ⑤
Llwyn-y-moel-gau, Llanfihangel, Llanfyllin,
Powys, Wales, SY22 5JE
Ⓣ (01691) 648196
Ⓕ (01691) 648196
Ⓔ rosemary@farmhouse-nursery.fsnet.co.uk
Contact: Rosemary Pryce
Opening Times: 1000-1700 most days all
year, but advisable to phone to confirm.
Cat. Cost: None issued.
Credit Cards: None
Specialities: Unusual perennials & ornamental
grasses. Hardy geraniums.
Map Ref: W, B3
OS Grid Ref: SJ083149

WSan   **SANDSTONES COTTAGE GARDEN**
PLANTS ⊠ ⋔ € ⑤
58 Bolas Heath, Great Bolas,
Shropshire, TF6 6PS
Ⓣ (01952) 541657
Ⓜ 07801 338133
Ⓕ (01952) 541657
Ⓔ pbrelsforth@supernet.com
Ⓦ www.sandstonesplants.cwc.net
www.sandstoneplants.mcmail.com
Contact: Joanne Brelsforth/Paul Brelsforth
Opening Times: By appt. only.
Min Mail Order UK: £10.00 + p&p
Min Mail Order EU: £25.00 + p&p
Cat. Cost: 4 x 1st class
Credit Cards: all major credit/debit cards
Specialities: Unusual & interesting hardy
perennials. Specialising in plants for shade &
moist areas.
Map Ref: W, B4

WSel   **THE SELSLEY HERB NURSERY** ⋔ ⑤
Hayhedge Lane, Bisley, Stroud,
Gloucestershire, GL6 7AN
Ⓣ (01452) 770073
Ⓕ (01452) 770879
Contact: Rob Wimperis
Opening Times: 1000-1700 Tue-Sat, 1400-
1700 Sun & B/hols Mar-Oct. Nov-Feb
variable, please phone to check. only.
Cat. Cost: 4 x 1st class
Credit Cards: MasterCard Visa
Specialities: Culinary, aromatic & medicinal
herbs & selected garden plants.
Map Ref: W, D5
OS Grid Ref: SO058906

WSHC   **STONE HOUSE COTTAGE NURSERIES** ⑤
Stone, Nr Kidderminster,
Worcestershire,
DY10 4BG
Ⓣ (01562) 69902
Ⓕ (01562) 69960
Ⓔ louisa@shcn.co.uk
Ⓦ www.shcn.co.uk
Contact: J F & L N Arbuthnott
Opening Times: 1000-1730 Wed-Sat. &
B/hol Mon. By appt. only Oct-Mar.
Cat. Cost: Sae
Credit Cards: None
Specialities: Small general range esp. wall
shrubs, climbers & unusual plants.
Map Ref: W, C5

W

W

WShi   JOHN SHIPTON (BULBS) ⊠ ⊠ €
Y Felin, Henllan Amgoed, Whitland,
Dyfed, Wales,
SA34 0SL
Ⓣ (01994) 240125
Ⓕ (01994) 241180
Ⓔ bluebell@zoo.co.uk
Ⓦ www.bluebellbulbs.co.uk
Also supplies wholesale: Yes
Contact: John Shipton & Alison Foot
Opening Times: By appt. only.
Min Mail Order UK: Nmc
Min Mail Order EU: Nmc
Cat. Cost: Sae
Credit Cards: None
Specialities: Native British bulbs, & bulbs &
plants for naturalising.
Map Ref: W, D2
OS Grid Ref: SN188207

WShp   SHIPLEY GARDENS ⬚
Holme Lacy, Herefordshire,
HR2 6LS
Ⓣ (01432) 870356
Ⓔ rmacadie@aol.com
Contact: Bob Macadie
Opening Times: 1000-1800 (or dusk) 7 days,
Mar-end Nov.
Credit Cards: all major credit/debit
cards
Specialities: Wide range of hardy perennials.
Garden open to the public every day from 1st
Apr-31 Nov.
Map Ref: W, C4
OS Grid Ref: 563357

WSpi   SPINNEYWELL NURSERY ⊠ ◆
Waterlane, Oakridge, Bisley,
Glos, GL6 7PH
Ⓣ (01452) 770092
Ⓕ (01452) 770151
Ⓔ wendy.spinneywell@virgin.net
Ⓦ www.goto.nu/spinneywell
Also supplies wholesale: Yes
Contact: Wendy Asher
Opening Times: 1000-1700 Wed-Sat, 1st
Mar-end Nov. 1000-1600 Wed-Sat, 1st Dec-
end Feb. Please check opening hours during
May 2003.
Min Mail Order UK: £10.00 + p&p
Min Mail Order EU: £30.00 + p&p
Cat. Cost: 6 x 1st class
Credit Cards: None
Specialities: *Buxus, Taxus* & unusual
herbaceous & shrubs. Hellebores, euphorbias,
Ceanothus, hardy geraniums.
Map Ref: W, C5
OS Grid Ref: SO9204

**WSPU   PERSHORE COLLEGE OF
HORTICULTURE** ⬚
Specialist Plant Unit & Plant Centre,
Avonbank, Pershore,
Worcestershire, WR10 3JP
Ⓣ (01386) 561385
Ⓕ (01386) 555601
Also supplies wholesale: Yes
Contact: Jo Yates (Plant Centre)
Opening Times: (Plant centre) 0900-1700
Mon-Sat, 1030-1630 Sun.
Cat. Cost: £1.00
Credit Cards: Visa Access
Specialities: Nat. Coll. of *Penstemon*. Open for
viewing 0800-1630 Mon-Fri.
Map Ref: W, C5

WSSM   SOUTH SHROPSHIRE MEADOW ⊠
Brays Tenement, Marton Hill, Welshpool,
Powys, Wales, SY21 8JY
Ⓣ (01938) 580030
Ⓕ (01938) 580030
Ⓔ SouthShropshireM@aol.com
Ⓦ www.southshropshiremeadow.co.uk
Contact: Kate Nicholls
Opening Times: Not open to the public.
Min Mail Order UK: Nmc
Cat. Cost: 2 x 1st stamps
Credit Cards: all major credit/debit cards
Specialities: Quality hardy perennials and
cottage garden plants. Stock available in
limited quanitites, please contact for details.
Note: credit cards only accepted for online
orders.

WSSs   SHROPSHIRE SARRACENIAS ⊠ ⊠ ṅ ⬚
5 Field Close, Malinslee, Telford,
Shropshire, TF4 2EH
Ⓣ (01952) 501598
Ⓔ mking1@compuserve.com
Ⓦ www.carnivorousplants.uk.com
Contact: Mike King
Opening Times: By appt. only.
Min Mail Order UK: Nmc
Min Mail Order EU: Nmc
Cat. Cost: 2 x 1st class
Credit Cards: None
Specialities: *Sarracenia*. Some stock limited.
Nat. Collection Holder status applied for.
Map Ref: W, B4
OS Grid Ref: SJ689085

WStI   ST ISHMAEL'S NURSERIES ⬚
Haverfordwest, Pembrokeshire,
Wales, SA62 3SX
Ⓣ (01646) 636343
Ⓕ (01646) 636343
Ⓔ info@stishmaelsgc.co.uk

ⓦ www.st-ishmaelsgardencentre.co.uk
Contact: Mr D & Mrs H Phippen
Opening Times: 0900-1730 Mon-Sat,
summer. 0900-1700 Mon-Sat, winter. Sun
open at 10.00.
Cat. Cost: None issued
Credit Cards: Visa Diners Access Switch Delta
MasterCard EuroCard
Specialities: Wide general range.
Map Ref: W, D1

WSuV SUNNYBANK VINE NURSERY ☒ ☒
The Old Trout Inn, Dulas,
Herefordshire, HR2 0HL
ⓣ (01981) 240256
ⓔ http://vinenursery@hotmail.com
ⓦ vinenursery.netfirms.com
Also supplies wholesale: Yes
Contact: B R Edwards
Opening Times: Not open, mail order only.
Min Mail Order UK: £8.00 incl. p&p
Min Mail Order EU: £10.00 incl. p&p*
Cat. Cost: Sae
Credit Cards: None
Specialities: Vines. *Note: EU sales by
arrangement.
Map Ref: W, C4

WTan TAN-Y-LLYN NURSERIES
Meifod, Powys, Wales, SY22 6YB
ⓣ (01938) 500370
ⓕ (01938) 500303
ⓔ callumjohnston@tanyllyn.the-nursery.co.uk
ⓦ www.tanyllyn.the-nursery.co.uk
Contact: Callum Johnston
Opening Times: 1000-1700 Tue-Fri Mar-Jun
and at other times by appt.
Cat. Cost: 2 x 1st class
Credit Cards: None
Specialities: Herbs, alpines, perennials.
Map Ref: W, B3
OS Grid Ref: SJ167125

WTel TELLING AND COATES ☒
64A Church Street, Charlton Kings,
Cheltenham, Gloucestershire,
GL53 8AS
ⓣ (01242) 514472
ⓔ tellingandcoates@freenet.co.uk
ⓦ www.tellingandcoates.freeola.net
Also supplies wholesale: Yes
Contact: John Coates
Opening Times: Nursery open 0830-1300 &
1400-1730 Mar-Nov, closed Sun, Wed &
B/hols. Dec-Feb by appt. only
Min Mail Order UK: Nmc
Cat. Cost: 3 x 1st class or 4 x 2nd class
Credit Cards: None

Specialities: A traditional hardy plant nursery
offering a wide range of shrubs, climbers,
heathers, alpines & herbaceous plants at
reasonable prices.
Map Ref: W, C5
OS Grid Ref: SO966205

WTin TINPENNY PLANTS ☒
Tinpenny Farm, Fiddington, Tewkesbury,
Gloucestershire, GL20 7BJ
ⓣ (01684) 292668
ⓔ Tinpenny@btinternet.com
Contact: Elaine Horton
Opening Times: 1200-1700 Tue-Thu or by
appt.
Cat. Cost: 2 x 1st class
Credit Cards: None
Specialities: Wide range of hardy garden-
worthy plants esp. *Helleborus, Iris* &
Sempervivum. Small nursery will propagate to
order rare plants from own stock.
Map Ref: W, C5
OS Grid Ref: SO919318

WTMC TIR MAB CYNAN NURSERY
Brithdir, Dolgellau, Gwynedd,
Wales, LL40 2RW
ⓣ (01341) 450339
ⓕ (01341) 450339
ⓦ www.tirmabcynan.nursery@
btopenworld.com
Also supplies wholesale: Yes
Contact: Jim Haunch
Opening Times: 1000-dusk, Easter-1 Oct.
Cat. Cost: None issued
Specialities: Hardy *Geranium, Hemerocallis,*
hostas, ferns, *Iris,* a wide range of hardy
perennials & sought after plants.
Map Ref: W, B3

WTre TREASURES OF TENBURY LTD ☒ € ☒
Burford House Gardens, Tenbury Wells,
Worcestershire, WR15 8HQ
ⓣ (01584) 810777
ⓕ (01584) 810673
ⓔ treasures@burford.co.uk
ⓦ www.burford.co.uk
Contact: Mike Humphries
Opening Times: 1000-1800 (dusk in winter)
7 days.
Min Mail Order UK: Nmc
Min Mail Order EU: Nmc
Cat. Cost: 4 x 1st class stamps

K	☒ Mail order to UK or EU	🛉 Delivers to shows
E	☒ Exports beyond EU	€ Euro accepted
Y	☒ Accessible by wheelchair	◆ See Display advertisement

W

Credit Cards: Visa Access Switch
Specialities: *Clematis* and herbaceous,
bamboos, trees & shrubs. Nat. Coll. of
Clematis.
Map Ref: W, C4

WViv VIV MARSH POSTAL PLANTS
⊠ ⊠ € 🖳 ◆
Walford Heath, Shrewsbury,
Shropshire, SY4 2HT
Ⓣ (01939) 291475
Ⓕ (01939) 290743
Ⓔ mail@PostalPlants.co.uk
Ⓦ www.PostalPlants.co.uk
Also supplies wholesale: Yes
Contact: Mr Viv Marsh
Opening Times: 1000-1600 7 days, Mar-Oct.
Min Mail Order UK: Nmc
Min Mail Order EU: Nmc
Cat. Cost: 5 x 1st class or 2 x IRCs (£1 refund
on first order)
Credit Cards: Visa MasterCard Switch
Specialities: Rare & routine herbaceous
perennials. Worldwide plant introductions,
incl. new *Alstroemeria, Zantedeschia,
Gypsophila, Aster* & *Solidago.*Note: mail order
beyond Europe Oct-Feb only when plants are
dormant.
Map Ref: W, B4
OS Grid Ref: SJ446198

WVKB VAL-KERR BRUGMANSIAS ⊠ 🔥 € 🖳
61 Green Lane Bayston Hill, Shrewsbury,
Shropshire, SY3 0Nr
Ⓣ (01743) 236246
Ⓕ (01743) 246716
Ⓔ brugmansias:hotmail.com
Contact: Luigi Valducci
Opening Times: 0900-1700 by appt. only.
Min Mail Order UK: Nmc
Credit Cards: all major credit/debit cards
Specialities: Brugmansias. Note: nursery main
site at Meole Brace Garden Club, Vicarage
Road, Shrewsbury.

WWeb WEBBS OF WYCHBOLD € ◆
Wychbold, Droitwich,
Worcestershire, WR9 0DG
Ⓣ (01527) 861777
Ⓕ (01527) 861284
Ⓔ olly@webbsofwychbold.co.uk
Ⓦ www.webbsofwychbold.co.uk
Also supplies wholesale: Yes
Contact: Olly Spencer
Opening Times: 0900-1800 Mon-Fri winter.
0900-2000 Mon-Fri summer. 0900-1800 Sat
& 1030-1630 Sun all year. Closed Xmas Day,
Boxing Day & Easter Sun.

Cat. Cost: None issued
Credit Cards: Visa Access American Express
Specialities: Hardy trees & shrubs, climbers,
conifers, alpines, heathers, herbaceous, herbs,
roses, fruit & aquatics. Nat. Coll. of Shrubby
Potentilla.
Map Ref: W, C5

WWes WESTONBIRT ARBORETUM ⊠
(Forest Enterprise) The National Arboretum,
Tetbury, Gloucestershire, GL8 8QS
Ⓣ (01666) 880544
Ⓕ (01666) 880386
Ⓔ plant.centre@forestry.gsi.gov.uk
Ⓦ www.westonbirtarboretum.com
Contact: Julia Wickens, Sarah Landers
Opening Times: 1000-1730 7 days summer,
1000-1700 winter.
Min Mail Order UK: Nmc*
Cat. Cost: None issued.
Credit Cards: Visa Access Switch Solo Delta
Specialities: Japanese maples & general range of
trees & shrubs, many choice & rare. Specimen
trees. Most plants available in small numbers
only. *Note: mail order Dec-Mar only.
Map Ref: W, D5

WWhi WHIMBLE NURSERY 🖳
Kinnerton, Presteigne, Powys, Wales, LD8 2PD
Ⓣ (01547) 560413
Ⓔ whimble@btopenworld.com
Contact: Liz Taylor
Opening Times: 1030-1730 Wed-Sun (closed
Mon & Tue except B/hol Mons) Apr-mid Oct.
Cat. Cost: 5 x 1st class*
Credit Cards: None
Specialities: Mainly herbaceous, some
unusual. Small collections of *Achillea,
Crocosmia, Geranium, Viola.* *Note: send sae
for plant list (no descriptions).
Map Ref: W, C4

WWHy WELSH HOLLY ⊠ 🖳
Llyn-y-Gors Tenby Road, St Clears,
Carmarthenshire, Wales,
SA33 4JP
Ⓣ (01994) 231789
Ⓕ (01994) 231789
Ⓔ info@welsh-holly.co.uk
Ⓦ www.welsh-holly.co.uk
Also supplies wholesale: Yes
Contact: Philip Lanc
Opening Times: By appt. only.
Min Mail Order UK: Nmc
Cat. Cost: 2 x 1st class
Credit Cards: None
Specialities: Hollies. Limited stock of less
common plants.

WWin WINTERGREEN NURSERIES [&]
Bringsty Common, Bringsty,
Worcestershire, WR6 5UJ
(T) (01886) 821858 (eves.)
Contact: S Dodd
Opening Times: 1000-1730 Wed-Sun 1st
Mar-31st Oct & by appt.
Cat. Cost: 2 x 2nd class
Credit Cards: None
Specialities: General, esp. alpines & herbaceous.
Map Ref: W, C4
OS Grid Ref: SO708555

WWol WOOLMANS PLANTS LTD [⊠] €
The Plant Centre, Knowle Hill, Evesham,
Worcestershire, WR11 7EN
(T) (01386) 833022
(F) (01386) 832915
(E) sales@woolman.co.uk
(W) www.woolman.co.uk
Also supplies wholesale: Yes
Contact: John Woolman
Opening Times: 0900-1700 Mon-Fri.
Min Mail Order UK: Nmc
Min Mail Order EU: Nmc
Cat. Cost: Free
Credit Cards: MasterCard Visa Switch
Specialities: *Chrysanthemum,* hanging basket
& patio plants, *Dahlia,* perennials.
Map Ref: W, C5

WWpP WATERPUMP PLANTS [⊠]
Waterpump Farm, Ryeford, Ross-on-Wye,
Herefordshire, HR9 7PU
(T) (01989) 750177
Contact: Mrs E Sugden
Opening Times: 1100-1700 Wed-Sun Apr-
Sep or by appt.
Min Mail Order UK: £15.00
Cat. Cost: 4 x 1st class
Credit Cards: None
Specialities: Hardy geraniums, aquatics,
moisture loving and many unusual herbaceous
plants. Organically grown. Some stock in
limited quantities, but can be grown to order.
Map Ref: W, C4
OS Grid Ref: SO642226

WWst WESTONBIRT PLANTS [⊠] [⊠] €
9 Westonbirt Close, Worcester, WR5 3RX
(T) (01905) 350429 (answerphone)
(F) (01905) 350429
Contact: Garry Dickerson
Opening Times: Not open, strictly mail order
only.
Min Mail Order UK: Nmc
Min Mail Order EU: Nmc
Cat. Cost: 3 x 1st class

Credit Cards: None
Specialities: *Iris, Fritillaria, Erythronium,*
particular interest in *Iris* species, + *Crocus,
Corydalis, Lilium, Arisaema, Trillium, Arum*
& tulip species. Many rare plants in ltd.
numbers.

WWye THE NURTONS GARDEN & NURSERY
[&] ◆
Tintern, Chepstow, Gwent,
Wales, NP16 7NX
(T) (01291) 689253
(F) (01291) 689253
(E) elsa.adrian@thenurtons.fsnet.co.uk
(W) www.thenurtons.co.uk
Contact: Adrian & Elsa Wood
Opening Times: 1030-1700 Wed-Mon,
mid Feb-mid Oct. Other times by appt.
(closed Tue).
Cat. Cost: 3 x 1st class
Credit Cards: None
Specialities: Wide range of unusual
perennials, aromatic and medicinal herbs,
Salvia, grasses & sedges. Soil Association
symbol. Cert UK 5.
Map Ref: W, D4
OS Grid Ref: SO536011

ABROAD

XB&T B & T WORLD SEEDS [⊠] [⊠] €
Paguignan, 34210 Olonzac, France
(T) 00 33 (0) 4689 12963
(F) 00 33 (0) 4689 13039
(E) lesley@b-and-t-world-seeds.com
(W) www.b-and-t-world-seeds.com
Also supplies wholesale: Yes
Contact: Lesley Sleigh
Min Mail Order UK: £10.00
Min Mail Order EU: £10.00
Cat. Cost: £10 Europe, £14 elsewhere.
Credit Cards: Visa MasterCard
Specialities: Master list contains over 40,000
items. 700 sub-lists available. Exports seed
only. Catalogue/botanical reference system
available on CD Rom. SeedyRom (TM)
catalogue £20 worldwide.

XBlo TABLE BAY VIEW NURSERY [⊠] [⊠]
(Office) 60 Molteno Road, Oranjezicht,
Cape Town, 8001 South Africa
(T) 00 27 21 683 5108/424 4854
(F) 00 27 21 683 5108

X

Ⓔ info@tablebayviewnursery.co.za
Contact: Terence Bloch
Opening Times: No personal callers.
Min Mail Order UK: £15.00 + p&p
Min Mail Order EU: £15.00
Cat. Cost: £3.40 (cheque/postal order)
Credit Cards: None
Specialities: Tropical & sub-tropical ornamental & fruiting plants.

XDoo   IGNACE VAN DOORSLAER ⊠ ⋔ €
Kapellendries 52, B 9090,
Melle Gontrode, Belgium
Ⓣ 0032 (09) 252 11 23
Ⓕ 0032 (09) 252 44 55
Also supplies wholesale: Yes
Contact: Ignace van Doorslaer
Opening Times: 6 days per week, by appt.
Min Mail Order UK: Depends on weight*
Min Mail Order EU: Depends on weight*
Cat. Cost: Free
Credit Cards: None
Specialities: *Agapanthus.* *Note: invoice sent when transport charges known. £ stirling accepted. Located 12km south of Gent. Will deliver to shows in Belgium, France & Holland.

XFro   FROSCH EXCLUSIVE PERENNIALS ⊠ ☒ €
Am Brunnen 14,
D-85551 Kirchheim,
Germany
Ⓣ 00 49 172 842 2050

Ⓕ 00 49 9077 5565
Ⓔ info@cypripedium.de
Ⓦ www.cypripedium.de
Also supplies wholesale: Yes
Contact: Michael Weinert
Opening Times: Not open, mail order only. 0700-2200.
Min Mail Order UK: £120.00 + p&p
Min Mail Order EU: £120.00 + p&p
Cat. Cost: None issued.
Credit Cards: None
Specialities: *Cypripedium* hybrids. Hardy orchids.

XPep   PÉPINIÈRE FILIPPI ⊠ €
RN 113, 34140 Meze,
France
Ⓣ 04 67 43 88 69
Ⓕ 04 67 43 84 59
Ⓔ olivier.filippi@wanadoo.fr
Ⓦ www.jardin-sec.com
Also supplies wholesale: Yes
Contact: Olivier Filippi
Opening Times: 0900-1200 & 1330-1730 Mon-Fri, 0900-1200 Sat, Sep-Jun. Closed Sun & B/hols. 0830-1200 Mon-Sat, Jul-Aug.
Min Mail Order UK: 30 Euros
Min Mail Order EU: 30 Euros
Cat. Cost: 10 Euros or Online
Credit Cards: Visa MasterCard
Specialities: *Cistus* and botanical range of Mediterranean plants. CCVS French National Collection of *Cistus.*

NURSERY INDEX
BY NAME

Nurseries that are included in the *RHS Plant Finder* for the first time this year (or have been reintroduced) are marked in **bold type**. Full details of the nurseries will be found in **Nursery Details by Code** on page xxx. For a key to the geographical codes, see the start of **Nurseries**.

A La Carte Daylilies	SDay	Bali-hai Mail Order Nursery	IBal
Abacus Nurseries	WAba	Ballyrogan Nurseries	IBlr
Abbey Dore Court Garden	WAbb	Banwy Valley Nursery	WBVN
Abbey Plants	CAbP	Barcote Garden Herbaceous Plants	MBct
Abbotsbury Sub-Tropical Gardens	CAbb	T H Barker & Sons	NBrk
Aberconwy Nursery	WAbe	**Barn Plant Centre & Gift Shop, The**	**NBPC**
Abraxas Gardens	CAbx	Barncroft Nurseries	WBar
Abriachan Nurseries	GAbr	Barncroft Nurseries	MBar
Acton Beauchamp Roses	WAct	**Barnfield Pelargoniums**	**MBPg**
Agar's Nursery	SAga	Barnsdale Gardens	MBNS
Agroforestry Research Trust	CAgr	Barracott Plants	CBct
L A Allen	MAln	Barwinnock Herbs	GBar
Jacques Amand	LAma	Battersby Roses	NBat
Amulree Exotics	EAmu	Beacon's Nurseries	WBcn
Architectural Plants	SArc	Beacons' Botanicals	WBea
Architectural Plants (Chichester) Ltd	SAPC	Peter Beales Roses	EBls
Ardcarne Garden Centre	IArd	Beamish Clematis Nursery	NBea
Argham Village Nursery	NArg	Beechcroft Nurseries	NBee
Arn Hill Plants	MAnH	Beechcroft Nursery	LBee
Arne Herbs	CArn	Beeches Nursery	EBee
Ashdown Forest Garden	SAdn	Beetham Nurseries	NBhm
Centre & Nursery		Beggar's Roost Plants	CBgR
Ashenden Nursery	SAsh	Bell Bar Nursery	LBBr
Ashpond Plants	EAsh	Belmont House Nursery	CBel
Ashtons Nursery Gardens	NAsh	Bennett's Water Lily Farm	CBen
Ashwood Nurseries Ltd	MAsh	**Bensley Nurseries**	**MBnl**
Askham Bryan College Nursery	NABC	Bide-A-Wee Cottage Gardens	NBid
Asterby & Chalkcroft Nurseries	LAst	Big Grass Co., The	CBig
Aulden Farm	WAul	Binny Plants	GBin
Barbara Austin Perennials Ltd	CBAn	Birchfleet Nursery	SBir
Claire Austin Hardy Plants	WCAu	Birkheads Cottage Garden Nursery	NBir
David Austin Roses Ltd	MAus	Blackmore & Langdon Ltd	CBla
Avon Aquatics	MAAq	Blacksmiths Cottage Nursery	EBla
Avon Bulbs	CAvo	Blackthorn Nursery	SBla
Avondale Nursery	MAvo	Blackwater Plants	EBlw
Aylett Nurseries Ltd	LAyl	Blooms of Bressingham	EBre
B & T World Seeds	XB&T	Bluebell Nursery & Arboretum	MBlu
Badsey Lavender Fields	WBad	Blundell's Nurseries	NBlu
Steven Bailey Ltd	SBai	Bodiam Nursery	SBod
B & H M Baker	EBak	Bodmin Plant and Herb Nursery	CBod

Deanston Nursery	GDea	Flora Exotica	EFEx
Deelish Garden Centre	IDee	**Floreat Plants**	**GFlt**
Denmans Garden, (John Brookes Ltd)	**SDnm**	Flower Bower, The	CFwr
Desirable Plants	CDes	Flowers of the Field	WFoF
Devon Violet Nursery	CDev	Foliage Scented & Herb Plants	LFol
DHE Plants	MDHE	Ford Nursery	CFRD
Dibley's Nurseries	WDib	Ford Nursery	NFor
Dickson Nurseries Ltd	IDic	Four Seasons	EFou
Different Plants	EDif	Four Ways Garden & Nursery	EFWa
Dingle Nurseries	WDin	Fox Cottage Plants	MFOX
Samuel Dobie & Son	CDob	Frogswell Nursery	IFro
Ignace van Doorslaer	XDoo	Fron Goch Garden Centre	WGer
Dorset Water Lilies	**CDWL**	Frosch Exclusive Perennials	XFro
Dove Cottage Nursery	NDov	Fulbrooke Nursery	EFul
Downderry Nursery	SDow	Rodney Fuller	CFul
Drysdale Garden Exotics	SDry	Garden at the Bannut, The	WBan
Duchy of Cornwall	CDoC	Garden Cottage Nursery	GGar
Dulford Nurseries	CDul	Garden House Nurseries	NGdn
Dunge Valley Gardens	MDun	Garden Plants	SGar
Dyffryn Gwyddno Nursery	WDyG	Gardenscape	NGar
Dyffryn Nurseries	WDyf	Linda Gascoigne Wild Flowers	MGas
Dysons Nurseries	SDys	W G Geissler	WGei
Earlstone Nursery	LEar	Gilbey's Plants	NGby
East Northdown Farm	SEND	Glen Chantry	EGle
Eastgrove Cottage Garden Nursery	WEas	Glendoick Gardens Ltd	GGGa
Edrom Nurseries	GEdr	Glenhirst Cactus Nursery	EGln
Edulis	LEdu	Glenville Nurseries	EGlv
Eildon Plants	GEil	Godly's Roses	LGod
Elizabeth House Nursery	MEHN	Goldbrook Plants	EGol
Charles F Ellis	WCFE	Golden Cottage Plants	MGol
Ellwood Penstemons	WEll	Elisabeth Goodwin Nurseries	EGoo
Elworthy Cottage Plants	CElw	Gordon's Nursery	WGor
Endsleigh Gardens	CEnd	Gortkelly Castle Nursery	IGor
English Cottage Garden Nursery, The	**SECG**	Goscote Nurseries Ltd	MGos
Equatorial Plant Co.	NEqu	Grafted Walnut Trees	WGWT
Europa Nursery, The	LEur	Graham's Hardy Plants	CGra
Evelix Daffodils	GEve	Grange Farm Plants	EGFP
Evergreen Conifer Centre	WEve	**Grange Side Nurseries**	**NGSd**
Fabulous Fuchsias	**WFFs**	Grasmere Plants	EGra
Fairhaven Nursery	CFai	Peter Grayson (Sweet Pea Seedsman)	MPet
Fairholm Plants	GFai	Great Dixter Nurseries	SDix
Fairweather's Garden Centre	SFai	Great Western Gladiolus Nursery, The	EGrW
Famecheck Special Plants	EFam	Green Garden Herbs & Plants	NGHP
Family Trees	SFam	**Green Hill Plants**	**WGHP**
Fancyplants	**MFan**	**Green Man Nursery**	**WGMN**
Farmyard Nurseries	WFar	Mary Green	NMyG
Feebers Hardy Plants	CFee	Greenhead Roses	GGre
Fern Nursery, The	EFer	Grimsdyke House	SGrm
Fernatix	**EFtx**	C W Groves & Son	CGro
Fernwood Nursery	CWil	Growing Carpets	LGro
Fibrex Nurseries Ltd	WFib	Gwynfor Growers	WGwG
Field House Nurseries	MFie	Hadspen Garden & Nursery	CHad
Fillan's Plants	CFil	Hall Farm Nursery	WHal
Fir Tree Farm Nursery	CFir	Halls of Heddon	NHal
Fir Trees Pelargonium Nursery	NFir	Halsway Nursery	CHal
Firs Nursery, The	MFir	Hambrooks Growing Concern	SHGC
Flaxton House Nursery	NFla	Hampshire Carnivorous Plants	SHmp
Fleurs Plants	GFle	Hanging Gardens Nurseries Ltd	EHan

Lower Icknield Farm Nurseries	LIck	New Forest Palms & Exotics	SNew
Lower Severalls Nursery	CSev	Newington Nurseries	MNew
Lower Spring Nursery	WLow	Newport Mills Nursery	CNMi
Lunnon Nursery	WLun	Newton Hill Alpines	NNew
Lydford Alpine Nursery	CLyd	Nicky's Rock Garden Nursery	CNic
M & M Plants	CM&M	Norcroft Nurseries	NNor
M G H Nurseries	IMGH	Norfields	WNor
Ivor Mace Nurseries	WIvo	Norfolk Lavender	ENor
Elizabeth MacGregor	GMac	North Green Snowdrops	ENGS
MacGregors Plants for Shade	SMac	Sheila Northway Auriculas	GNor
Macpennys Nurseries	CMac	Norwell Nurseries	MNrw
Madrona Nursery	SMad	Notcutts Nurseries	ENot
Mallet Court Nursery	CMCN	Nursery Further Afield, The	MNFA
Malletts Nurseries	EMlt	Nurtons Garden & Nursery, The	WWye
Manor Nursery	EMan	(formerly Wye Valley Plants)	
Marchants Hardy Plants	SMHy	Nutlin Nursery	SNut
Margery Fish Gardens	CFis	Oak Dene Nurseries	NOaD
Lesley Marshall	EMar	Oak Leaf Nurseries	COkL
Marshall's Malmaison	Wmal	Oak Tree Nursery	NOak
J & D Marston	NMar	Oakdene Nursery	SOkd
Marwood Hill Gardens	CMHG	Oakhurst Nursery	SOkh
Mattock's Roses	MMat	Oakland Nurseries	MOak
S M McArd (Seeds)	EMcA	Oasis	EOas
Hubert McHale	IHMH	Old Barn Nursery	WOBN
Mead Nursery, The	CMea	Old Court Nurseries	WOld
Meadow Cottage Plants	CMCo	Old Fashioned Flowers	WOFF
Meadows Nursery	CMdw	Old Hall Plants	EOHP
Mendip Bonsai Studio	**CMen**	Old Mill Herbary, The	COld
Mendle Nursery	NMen	**Old Mill Nursery**	**EOMN**
Merebrook Water Plants	WMAq	Old Vicarage Nursery, The	WOVN
Merriments Gardens	SMrm	Old Walled Garden, The	SOWG
Merryfield Nurseries (Canterbury) Ltd	SMer	Old Withy Garden Nursery, The	COIW
Mickfield Hostas	EMic	One House Nursery	MOne
Mickfield Watergarden Centre Ltd	EMFW	Orchard House Nursery	NOrc
Mill Cottage Plants	CMil	Orchard Nurseries	EOrc
Mill Hill Plants	MMil	Orchardstown Nurseries	IOrc
Mill Race Nursery	EMil	Ornamental Conifers	EOrn
Millais Nurseries	LMil	Ornamental Grass Nursery, The	NOGN
Millrace Nursery	NMRc	Ornamental Grasses	GOrn
Mills' Farm Plants & Gardens	EMFP	Ornamental Tree Nurseries	WOrn
Mires Beck Nursery	NMir	Otter Nurseries Ltd	COtt
Monksilver Nursery	EMon	Out of the Common Way	WOut
Moor Monkton Nurseries	NMoo	John Owen Nurseries	NJOw
Moorland Cottage Plants	WMoo	**P & A Plant Supplies Ltd**	**EPAt**
Morehavens	LMor	P & B Fuchsias	WP&B
Morton Hall Gardens	MMHG	P M A Plant Specialities	CPMA
Mount Harry Trees	SMHT	P W Plants	EPla
Mount Pleasant Trees	WMou	**Packhorse Farm Nursery**	**MPkF**
Mozart House Nursery Garden	MMoz	Palm Centre, The	LPal
Mulu Nurseries	WMul	Palm Farm, The	NPal
Kathleen Muncaster Fuchsias	EKMF	**Palm House, The**	**CPHo**
Murrells Plant & Garden Centre	SMur	Pan-Global Plants	WPGP
Mynd Hardy Plants	WMnd	Pantiles Plant & Garden Centre	LPan
Mynydd Pencarreg Water Plants	**WMyn**	Paradise Centre	EPar
Naked Cross Nurseries	CNCN	Parham Bungalow Plants	CPBP
National Herb Centre, The	**MNHC**	Park Green Nurseries	EPGN
Natural Selection	CNat	Gerry Parker Plants	NPar
Nature's Corner	**LNCo**	Parks Perennials	CPar

Shrubland Park Nurseries	EShb	Toobees Exotics	LToo
Silver Dale Nurseries	CSil	Tough Alpine Nursery	GTou
Silver Leaf Nurseries	CSLe	Town Farm Nursery	ETow
Clive Simms	ESim	Treasures of Tenbury Ltd	WTre
Sino-Himalayan Plant Association	LSiH	Trebah Enterprises Ltd	CTbh
Siskin Plants	ESis	**Tree Shop, The**	**GTSp**
Skipness Plants	GSki	Tregothnan Nursery	CTrG
Slack Top Alpines	NSla	Trehane Camellia Nursery	CTrh
Slipps Garden Centre	CSli	Peter Trenear	STre
Smart Plants	MTPN	Trevena Cross Nurseries	CTrC
South Shropshire Meadow	**WSSM**	Trewithen Nurseries	CTrw
South West Carnivorous Plants	CSWC	Triscombe Nurseries	CTri
Southease Plants	SSth	Turnpike Cottage Plants	CTCP
Southfield Nurseries	ESou	J Tweedie Fruit Trees	GTwe
Southview Nurseries	SSvw	Two Jays Alpines	LTwo
Special Plants	CSpe	Unusual Plants at Ratsbury	SRat
Speldhurst Nurseries	SSpe	**Urban Jungle**	**EUJe**
Spinners Garden	SSpi	Usual & Unusual Plants	SUsu
Spinneywell Nursery	**WSpi**	Uzumara Orchids	GUzu
Springbank Nurseries	SSpr	**Val-Kerr Brugmansias**	**WVKB**
Springhill Plants	MSph	Vale Nursery	SVal
Springlea Nursery	**LSpr**	Ventnor Botanic Garden	SVen
Springwood Pleiones	NSpr	Vernon Geranium Nursery, The	LVER
Stapeley Water Gardens Ltd	MSta	Vicarage Garden, The	NVic
Starborough Nursery	SSta	Village Nurseries, The	SVil
Stenbury Nursery	SSte	Vine House, The	NVne
Steventon Road Nurseries	MSte	Viv Marsh Postal Plants	WViv
Stillingfleet Lodge Nurseries	NSti	Wallace Plants	SWal
Stone Cross Garden Centre	**SSto**	Walled Garden, The	EWll
Stone House Cottage Nurseries	WSHC	Walnut Tree Garden Nursery	EWTr
Stone Lane Gardens	CSto	**Ward Alpines**	**CWrd**
Strachan's Plants	MSPs	Ward Fuchsias	MWar
Henry Street Nursery	LStr	Warren Hills Nursery	MWrn
Sue Strickland Plants	CStr	Water Garden, The	CWat
Stuckey's Alpines	CStu	Water Meadow Nursery	SWat
Style Roses	ESty	Waterperry Gardens Ltd	MWat
Brian & Pearl Sulman	ESul	Waterpump Plants	WWpP
Sunnybank Vine Nursery	WSuV	Weasdale Nurseries Ltd.	NWea
Sussex Topiary	STop	Webbs of Wychbold	WWeb
Suttons Seeds	CSut	**Welsh Holly**	**WWHy**
Swallows Nursery	**MSwo**	West Acre Gardens	EWes
Table Bay View Nursery	XBlo	West Harptree Nursery	CHar
Tan-y-Llyn Nurseries	WTan	West Somerset Garden Centre	CWSG
Tavistock Herb Nursery	NTHB	Westcountry Nurseries	CWCL
Taylors Nurseries	NTay	(inc. Westcountry Lupins)	
Telling and Coates	WTel	Westdale Nurseries	CWDa
Terra Nova Plants	ITer	Westonbirt Arboretum	WWes
Test Valley Nursery	STes	Westonbirt Plants	WWst
Thorncroft Clematis Nursery	ETho	Westshores Nurseries	EWsh
Thornhayes Nursery	CTho	A D & N Wheeler	MWhe
A & A Thorp	MTho	Whimble Nursery	WWhi
Three Counties Nurseries	**CThr**	White Cottage Alpines	NWCA
Tile Barn Nursery	STil	Jill White	EJWh
Timpany Nurseries & Gardens	ITim	**White Veil Fuchsias**	**CWVF**
Tinpenny Plants	WTin	Whitehill Farm Nursery	MWhi
Tir Mab Cynan Nursery	WTMC	Whitehouse Ivies	CWhi
Tissington Nursery	MTis	Whitelea Nursery	MWht
Philip Tivey & Son	**MTiv**	Wibble Farm Nurseries	CWib

SPECIALIST NURSERIES

Nurseries have classified themselves under the following headings where they *exclusively* or *predominantly* supply this range of plants. Plant groups are set out in alphabetical order. Refer to **Nursery Details by Code** on page xxx for details of the nurseries whose codes are listed under the plant group which interests you. See page xxx for a fuller explanation.

ACID-LOVING PLANTS

CMen CTrh CWrd CWri
EHea GGar GGGa GWCH
LHyd LMil MGos MLea
NDlv NLAp NPen SCam
SFai SHmp SRot WAbe
WCru WMyn WPic

ALPINE/ROCK PLANTS

CAvo CBAn CBrm CCha
CFul CGra CLyd CM&M
CMea COkL CPBP CPla
CWil CWrd ECho EHyt
EMlt EPot ESis GCrs GTou
ITim LGro LPVe MAAq
MCre MDHE MNew
MOne MS&S NArg NBro
NDlv NHol NJOw NLAp
NPol NRya NSla NWCA
NWoo SIgm SIng SPop
SRot SScr WAbe WBrE
WBri WGor WHoo WOBN
WPat WPer XFro

AQUATIC PLANTS

CBen CBod CDWL CRow
CWat EHon EMFW IHMH
LNCo LPBA MAAq MSta
NArg SWat WMAq WMyn
WPnP WRic WWpP

BAMBOOS

CBct CDul CPen EAmu
EFul ERod EPla GBin
LEdu MBrN MFan
MMoz MWhi MWht
MWod NGdn NMoo
NOGN SAPC SArc SDry
WAbb WHPE WJun WMul
WPGP

BRITISH WILD FLOWERS

CArn COld CRea CRWN
GBar GWCH MGas MSal
NHHG NLan NMir NPol
NSco NTHB SECG SWat
WBri WLav WBWf WHbs
WHer WHHs WJek WShi

BULBOUS PLANTS

CAvo CBro CMea CPou
CQua CWoo ECho ECri
EDif EFam EGrW EHyt
EMui EPot ERos GCrs
GEve IBal LPhx MNrw
MS&S NOaD NSla
WDav WOBN WShi WWst
XBlo

CACTI & SUCCULENTS

CPhi CTrC EBrk EGln
EOas ESou LToo NCro
NOaD SChr SHol SHvs

CARNIVOROUS PLANTS

CSWC SHmp WSSs

CHALK-LOVING PLANTS

CBot CKel CSev EFam
LPhx SEND SLon SMHT
SYvo XPep

CLIMBERS

CRHN CSPN CTri CWhi
ECot EHan ELan EOrc
ESCh ETho MCad MNew
NBea NBrk NSti SBra
SLau SLay WAct WCru
WFib WSHC

COASTAL PLANTS

CTbh GGar IBal SChr
SEND WBrE WPnn XPep

CONIFERS

CKen CLnd CMen CTho
ECho EOrn LCon LLin
MGos MPkF SLim WEve
WGor

CONSERVATORY PLANTS

CRHN CRoM CTbh
CWDa EBak ECot EOHP
EShb ESlt GFai GGGa
LDea LHyd LToo MJnS
MOak MNew NPal SGrm
SYvo WDib WRic XBlo

DROUGHT TOLERANT

CKno CSLe ECha EOas
EFam EGoo LSss MHrb
SChr SEND SIgm SUsu
WBad WBry XPep

FERNS

CLAP CFwr CRow CRWN
ECha EFer EFtx EMon
GBin LEur LPBA Mmoz
NHol NMar NMyG NPal
NWoo SArc SHmp SNut
SRot WAbe WFib WHal
WRic

FRUIT

CAgr CCAT CTho CTri
GTwe ECrN EMui ESim
LEdu MCoo SFam SKee
WGWT WOrn WSuV XBlo

GRASSES

CBig CBod CBrm CFwr
CKno CM&M CMea CPen
CPla CRWN CStr ECGN
ECha ECot EFul EGle
EHoe ELan EPla EPPr EPyc
GBin GCal GDea GIBF
GOrn LEdu LPhx LRav
LSss MAAq MBrN MFan
MMoz MNrw MWhi
MWod NBea NBro NGdn
NHol NMoo NOGN NSti
SHel SUsu SWal SYvo
WAbb WHal WLeb WMoo
WPer WPGP WWye

HEDGING

CCVT CDul CLnd CTrG
CTri ECot ECrN ERom
IHMH IMGH LBuc LEar
LRav MHrb MCoo NBee
SBLw SCam SLan SRiv
WAct WBad WBrE WCel
WDin WEve WLav WMou
WOrn WWeb

HERBS

CAgr CArn CCha CHby
CSev COld ELau EOHP
GBar GDea GWCH LFol
LGro LLWP IHMH ILis
MGol MHer MHrb MSal
MWhi NHHG NLLv NPol
NTHB NWoo SECG
SHDw SWat WBad WBri
WBry WCHb WHbs
WHHs WJek WLav WLHH
WPer WSel WWye

MARGINAL/BOG PLANTS

CDWL CLAP COld CRow
CWat CWrd GGar LPBA
NPen WHal WMoo WMyn
WPnP WShi WWpP

ORCHIDS

CBur CHdy EFEx EPot
GCrs LEur NEqu NSpr
XFro

ORGANIC

CHby COld EBlw GBar

GDea LEdu LLWP MSal
Npol WCHb WGWT
WHbs WJek WShi WMyn
WWpP

ORNAMENTAL TREES

CBdw CCAT CCVT
CDul CEnd CLnd CM&M
CMen CPMA CTho CTri
ECot ECrN EGFP ELan
EMui ERod ERom GIBF
IMGH LPan LRav MGos
MPkF NBea NBee SBir
SBLw SLau SLay SMHT
WBrE WCel WGWT
WMou WNor WOrn
WPGP

PALMS

CPHo CRoM CTrC EAmu
EGln NPal SAPC SArc
WHPE WMul

PEAT FREE

CAbx CBri CHby CElw
CHea CKno CKob
CMdw CMea CPen CPom
CRHN CRWN CSam
CSev EBla EBlw ECGN
ECml EGoo ILis LEdu
MEHN MGas MMoz MPhe
MRod MSal NGby NLRH
NOGN NPol NSco SECG
SCou SRob SVen SYvo
WCHb WHbs WGWT
WHoo WJek WMal WPnP
WPrP WRha WSel WShi
WWpP

PERIOD PLANTS

CArn CKel EMFP IBal ILis
SKee SSvw WAct WHer
WSpi

PROPAGATE TO ORDER

CAbx CBre CDul CElw
CHdy CKel CMen CMdw
CRHN CRWN CSLe CTho
CWDa EBla ECho ECtt
EGFP EPyc EShb GBin
GFai IHMH ILis LGro
LHyd LLWP LMil MDHE
MMoz MOak MRod

NCro NLLv NPen NPol
NTHB NRya NShi NWoo
SCou SECG SHDw SHel
SLan SLau SLon SRiv SSea
SWat WBad WFFs WFib
WHer WHil WJek WJun
WLav WMal WOBN
WP&B WPrP WSSs WTin
WVKB WWHy WWpP
XBlo

ROSES

CPou ECnt EMFP GCoc
IDic MAus MBur MMat
SFam SSea SWCr

SEEDS

CAgr CDob CHby CPas
CPla CSut EGrW EMcA
GDea GIBF MGol LCha
LSee LSss MSal MJnS
NChl NLan NOGN NRob
SCou WHen WJek WLFP
WNor

SPECIMEN SIZED PLANTS

CCVT CDul CKel CMen
CPhi CPMA CTho
CTrG CTrh CWDa EAmu
EBla ECho ECot ECrN
EGol ELan ELau ESlt
ESou GGGa GIBF LPan
LPVe LRav MBrN MOak
NArg NCro NHol NPal
NPen NPSI SBLw
SCam SEND SFai SFam
SHGC SHmp SLan
WBad WBrE WCel WDin
WEve WJek WJun WHPE
WOrn WPat WRic WSpi
WWeb

TOPIARY

CBAn ECot ERom LEar
LPan SLan SRiv WEve
WWeb

TROPICAL PLANTS

CDWL CRoM CTrC
CWDa EAmu EOas EShb
EUJe LToo MFan MJnS
MOak SAPC WCru WHPE
WMul

INDEX MAP

The maps on the following pages show the approximate location of the nurseries whose details are listed in this directory.

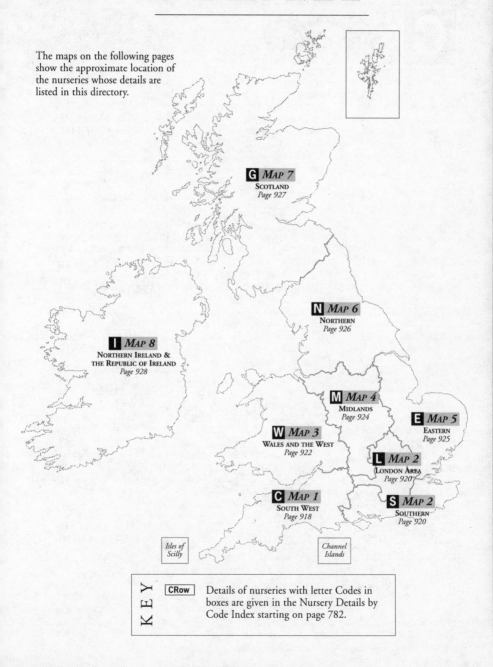

G *MAP 7*
SCOTLAND
Page 927

I *MAP 8*
NORTHERN IRELAND &
THE REPUBLIC OF IRELAND
Page 928

N *MAP 6*
NORTHERN
Page 926

M *MAP 4*
MIDLANDS
Page 924

E *MAP 5*
EASTERN
Page 925

W *MAP 3*
WALES AND THE WEST
Page 922

L *MAP 2*
LONDON AREA
Page 920

C *MAP 1*
SOUTH WEST
Page 918

S *MAP 2*
SOUTHERN
Page 920

Isles of Scilly

Channel Islands

K E Y   `CRow`   Details of nurseries with letter Codes in boxes are given in the Nursery Details by Code Index starting on page 782.

MAP ONE

C SOUTH WEST

Llanelli
Swansea
Neath
Port Talbot
Bridgend

Ilfracombe
Combe Martin
CSil
CMHG
Barnstaple

Bideford
CRoM
CHid
CFai
CM&M
CWhi
CPne
CBig
CKen
CWri

CWil
CCha
CBdn
CSdC

Okehampton
CLyd
CPev

Launceston
CRow
CCge
CBre
CEnd
CPla
COld
CRez
Tavistock
Newton Abbot
Wadebridge
CBct
CPle

Bodmin
CHll
CBod
Liskeard
CDev
CBrm
CDoC
CFil
Plymouth

Newquay
CMCo
CTrw
St Austell
CHVG
CPou
CRHN
CPLG
Truro
CBos
CTrG
St Ives
CWGr
Redruth
Camborne
CHex
CBcS
CCtw
CTrC
CFir
Falmouth
Penzance
CTbh
COIW
CQua

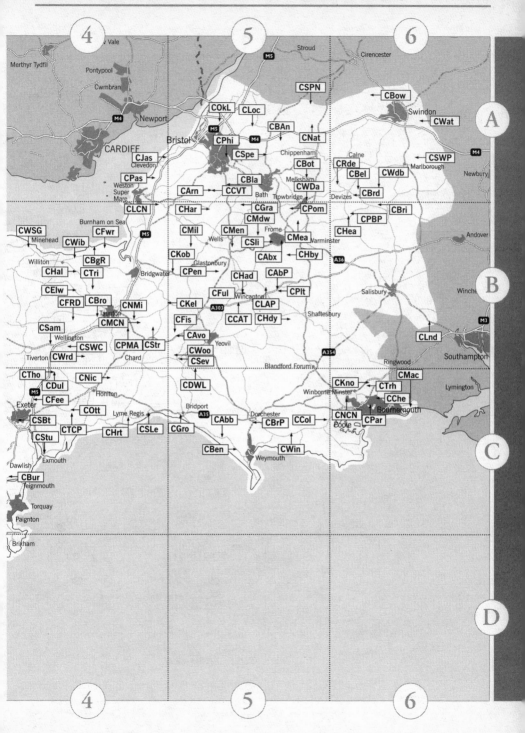

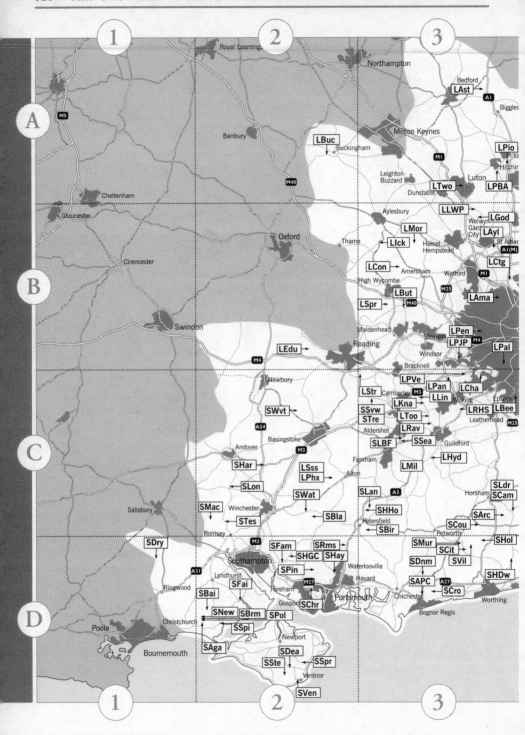

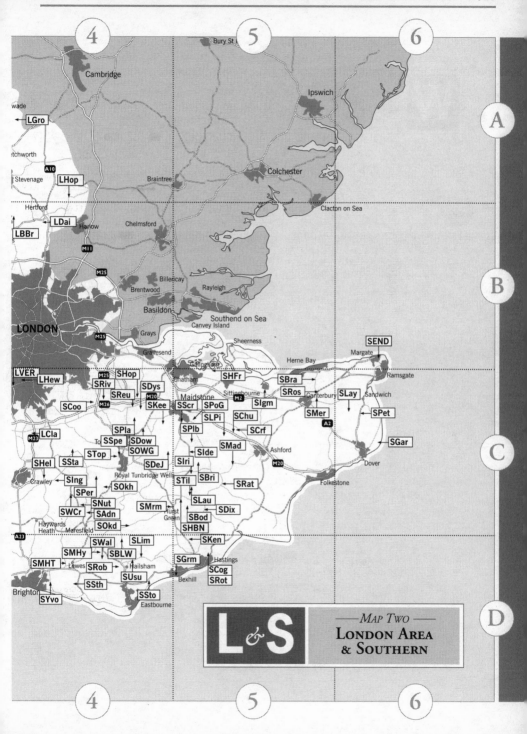

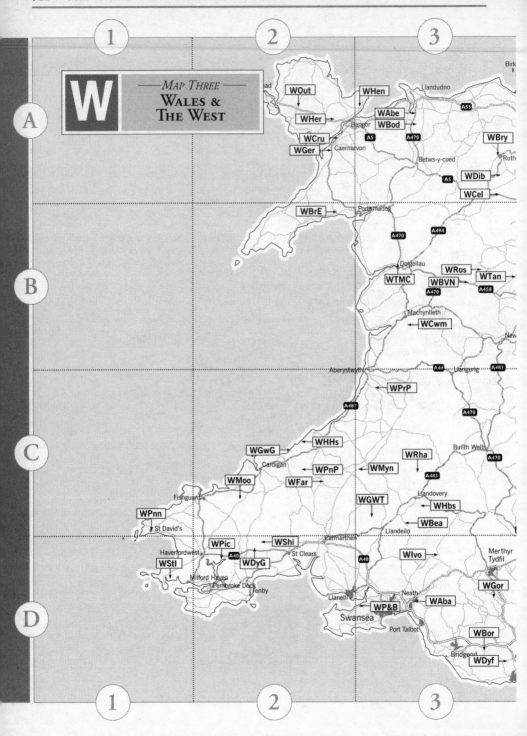

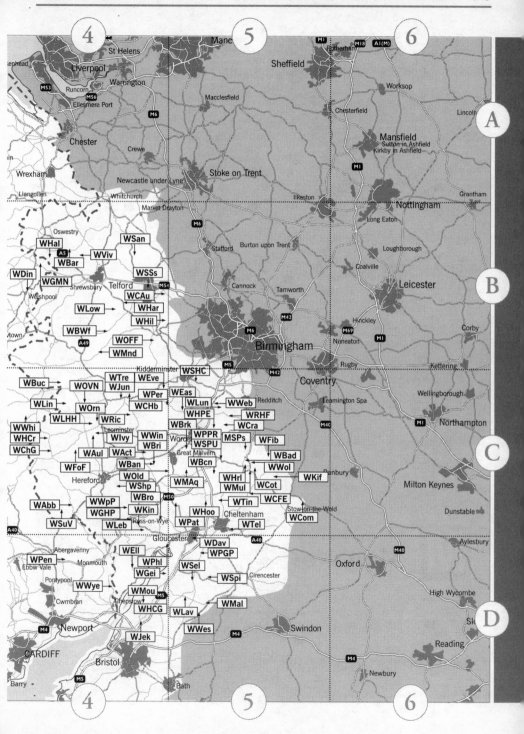

Grid references (top): 1 | 2 | 3

Grid references (left): A | B | C | D

Grid references (bottom): 1 | 2 | 3

Map labels / town names

Blackpool, Lytham St. Anne's, Southport, Preston, Keighley, Nelson, Burnley, Accrington, Bradford, Halifax, Brighouse, Leeds, Pudsey, Batley, Dewsbury, Wakefield, Castleford, Kingston upon Hull, Scunthorpe

Crosby, Litherland, Bootle, Wallasey, Birkenhead, Bebington, Skelmersdale, Wigan, Leigh, St. Helens, MANCHESTER, Huddersfield, Barnsley, Rotherham, SHEFFIELD, Doncaster, Lincoln

Liverpool, Runcorn, Widnes, Knutsford, Chester, Macclesfield, Chesterfield, Worksop, Newark-on-Trent, Mansfield, Sutton in Ashfield, Ashfield, Grantham

Wrexham, Crewe, Nantwich, Newcastle under Lyme, Stoke on Trent, Ashbourne, Ilkeston, Derby, Nottingham, Long Eaton, Melton Mowbray

Shrewsbury, Stafford, Burton upon Trent, Loughborough, Coalville, Leicester, Uppingham, Peterborough, Corby

Telford, Cannock, Tamworth, Hinckley, Nuneaton, Kettering, Wellingborough, Northampton

Kidderminster, Birmingham, Coventry, Rugby, Bedford, Milton Keynes, Letchworth

Worcester, Redditch, Royal Leamington Spa, Banbury, Luton

Great Malvern, Hereford, Woodstock, Chipping Norton, Leighton Buzzard, Dunstable, Aylesbury, Hemel Hempstead, St. Albans, Watford, High Wycombe

Pontypool, Cwmbran, Burford, Oxford, Slough, Windsor, Bracknell

Newport, CARDIFF, Bristol, Bath, Swindon, Faringdon, Wallingford, Maidenhead, Reading, Newbury, Leatherhead, Woking, Epsom, Trowbridge, Staines

Motorways
M6, M66, M62, M53, M56, M54, M42, M40, M5, M4, M1, M18, M69, A1(M), A1, A6, A50, A5, A34, A40, M25

Boxed location codes
MWar, MCad, MLan, MPhe, MBow, MFir, MOne, MDun, MIDC, MLLN, MBar, MInt, MDHE, MFOX, MPKF, MLEa, MWht, MNrw, MLwd, MMil, MHom, MDKP, MTis, MBnl, MSta, MBri, MAJR, MBlu, MSal, MFie, MOak, MHer, MBNS, MRod, MCLN, MPRe, MTed, MKay, MGos, MCls, MWgw, MAus, MWod, MJac, MS&S, MWrn, MMoz, MGas, MTho, MAsh, MHar, MAvo, MFan, MCCP, MWhe, MBrN, MMHG, MRav, MTPN, MAAq, MEHN, MSwo, MNFA, MWya, MWhi, MWat, MSph, MMat, MHrb, MBct, MSte, MNew, MBro, MAnH

Map legend
M — MAP FOUR — MIDLANDS

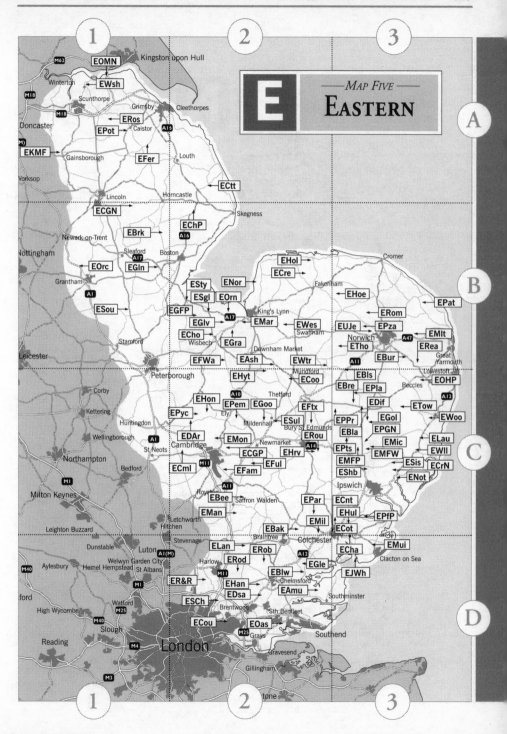

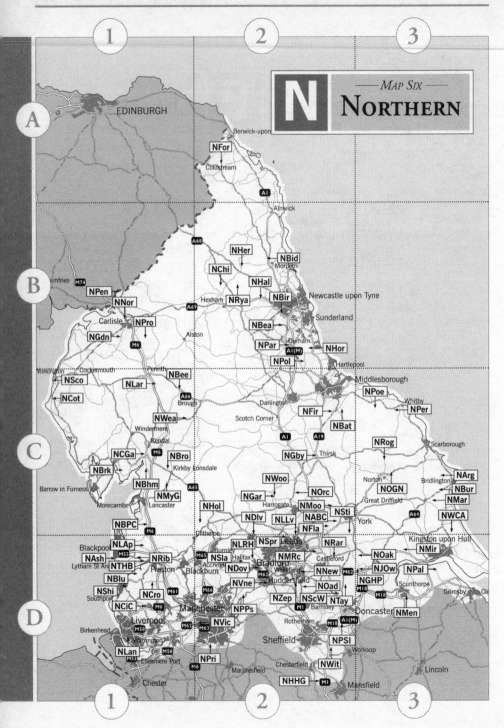

1 **2** **3**

N — MAP SIX — **NORTHERN**

EDINBURGH

A

Berwick-upon-

NFor

Coldstream

A1

Alnwick

B

Dumfries M74

NHer

NBid

Morpeth

NChi

NPen

NHal

NNor

NRya

NBir

Newcastle upon Tyne

Hexham

A69

Carlisle

NPro

NBea

Sunderland

A68

NGdn

NPar

Durham

NHor

M6

A1(M)

NPol

Hartlepool

Workington Cockermouth Penrith

NBee

Middlesborough

NSco

NLar

NPoe

Whitby

NCot

A66

Brough

Darlington

NFir

NPer

NWea

Scotch Corner

NBat

Windermere

Kendal

A1

A19

C

NCGa

M6

NBro

NGby

Thirsk

NRog

Scarborough

NBrk

Kirkby Lonsdale

Norton

NArg

Barrow in Furness

NBhm

A65

NWoo

NOGN

Bridlington

NBur

Morecambe Lancaster

NMyG

NGar

NOrc

Great Driffield

NMar

NHol

Harrogate

NMoo

NSti

York

NWCA

NDlv

NLLv

NABC

A64

Clitheroe

NFla

Kingston upon Hull

NBPC

M6

NLRH

NSpr

Leeds

NRar

NMir

Blackpool

Burnley

Halifax

Castleford

NOak

NLAp

M55

NRib

M65

NSla

NMRc

NNew

NJOw

NPal

NAsh

Accrington

Bradford

Wakefield

M62

NTHB

Preston

Blackburn

NDov

Huddersfield

NOad

NGHP

Scunthorpe

Lytham St An

NBlu

NVne

M62

M18

NShi

Southport

NCro

M61

NZep

NScW

NTay

Grimsby Cle

Barnsley

M1

NCiC

M6

Manchester

NPPs

Rotherham

Doncaster

NMen

D

Liverpool

M58

M62

M63

NVic

M18

A1(M)

Birkenhead

Warrington

Sheffield

NPSl

Worksop

Lincoln

NLan

M56

Chesterfield

NWit

M53

NPri

M6

Ellesmere Port

Macclesfield

NHHG

M1

Mansfield

Chester

1 **2** **3**

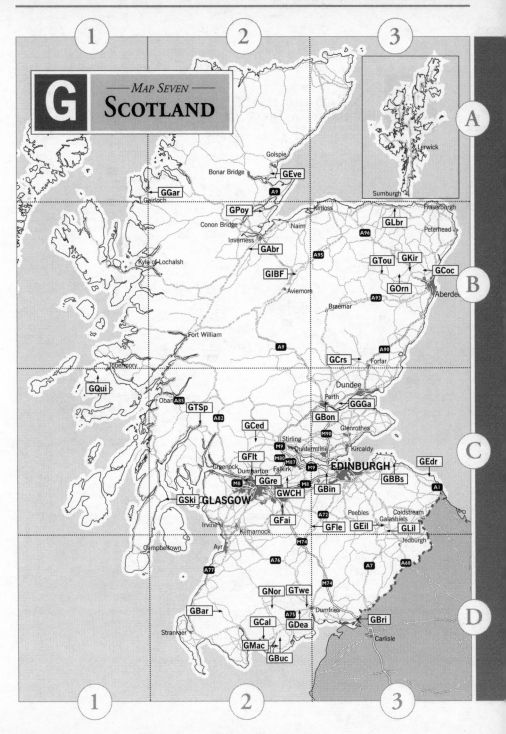

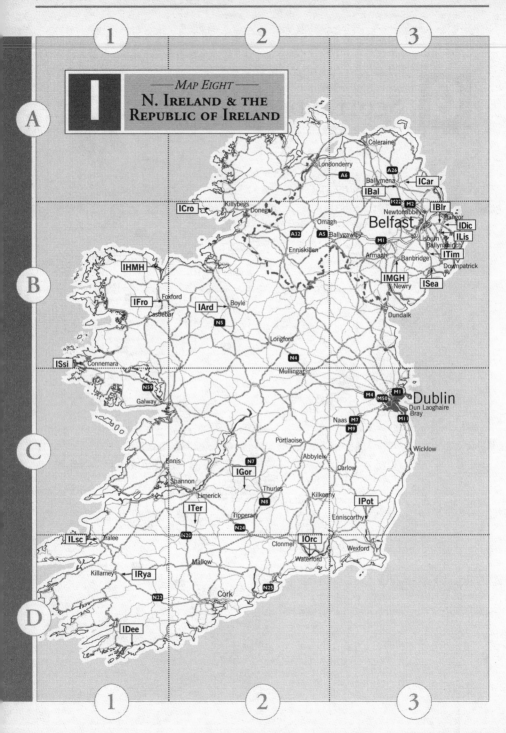

MAP EIGHT
N. IRELAND & THE REPUBLIC OF IRELAND

A

B

C

D

1   2   3

Coleraine
Londonderry
A26
Ballymena **ICar**
IBal
A6
A422 M2 **IBlr**
Killybegs Newtonabbey Bangor
ICro Donegal Belfast **IDic**
A32 A5 Ballygawley M1 **ILis**
Omagh Lisburn
Enniskillen Armagh Ballynahinch **ITim**
Banbridge Downpatrick
IHMH Newry **IMGH**
ISea
Foxford **IFro** Boyle
Castlebar **IArd**
N5 Dundalk
Longford
N4
Mullingar
ISsi Connemara
N59 Dublin
Galway M4 M1 Dun Laoghaire
M50 Bray
Naas M7 M1
M9
Portlaoise Wicklow
Ennis Abbyleix
N7 Carlow
Shannon **IGor**
Limerick Thurles
N8 Kilkenny
ITer Tipperary **IPot**
N24 Enniscorthy
ILsc Tralee N20
Clonmel **IOrc** Wexford
Mallow Waterford
Killarney **IRya**
N22 Cork N25
IDee

1   2   3

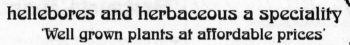

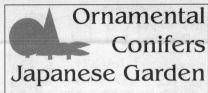

948

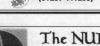

INDEX OF ADVERTISERS

The HARDY PLANT SOCIETY

Explores, encourages and conserves all that is best in gardens

The Hardy Plant Society encourages interest in growing hardy perennial plants and provides members with information about familiar and less well known perennial plants that flourish in our gardens, how to grow them and where they may obtained. This friendly society offers a range of activities locally and nationally, giving members plenty of opportunity to meet other keen gardeners to share ideas and information in a convivial atmosphere. The activities and work of the Society inform and encourage the novice gardener, stimulate and enlighten the more knowledgeable, and entertain and enthuse all gardeners bonded by a love for, and an interest in, hardy perennial plants.

LOCAL GROUPS

There are over 40 local groups across the UK and national members are invited to join the group nearest to them. Each group offers a wide range of gardening activities including informative lectures, garden visits and plant plus educational and social events throughout the year. Most groups produce their own newsletters. Full details of how to join a local group are sent out to new members.

SPECIALIST GROUPS AND GARDENING BY POST

Specialist Groups produce their own newsletters and organise meetings and events for fellow enthusiasts. The Correspondents Group ensures that members who are unable to attend meetings can exchange gardening ideas and information.

SEED DISTRIBUTION

Every member can join in the annual Seed Distribution Scheme by obtaining or donating hardy perennial seed. The Seed List offers over 2,500 tempting varieties of rare, unusual and familiar seeds and is sent to every member in December.

Please see overleaf for an application form

SHOWS AND EVENTS

Exhibits at major shows throughout the country let visitors see hardy plants in bloom and leaf in their natural season and more information about the work of the Society is available. Events hosted by local group members are also organised, from plant study days to residential weekends to garden visits. The Society also organises overseas garden tours.

CONSERVATION

The Hardy Plant Society is concerned about the conservation of garden plants and is working towards ensuring that older, rarer and lesser-known perennial plants are conserved and made available to gardeners generally.

PUBLICATIONS AND THE SLIDE LIBRARY

The Society's journal, *The Hardy Plant*, is published twice a year and regular newsletters provide information on all the Society's events, activities, interests and group contacts. The Society also publishes a series of booklets on special plant families which include Hardy Geraniums, Penstemons, Pulmonarias, Hostas, Grasses, Euphorbias, Phlox, Campanulas for the garden and Umbellifers. Other publications for members include a B&B list and a gardens to visit list. The Slide Library has a wide range of hardy plant slides available on loan.

INFORMATION ABOUT THE SOCIETY IS AVAILABLE FROM:

The Administrator
Mrs Pam Adams
The Hardy Plant Society
Little Orchard
Great Comberton
Pershore
Worcestershire WR10 3DP

Tel: 01386 710317
Fax: 01386 710117
E-mail: admin@hardy-plant.org.uk
Website: www.hardy-plant.org.uk

The HARDY PLANT SOCIETY

MEMBERSHIP APPLICATION FOR 2003

The Annual Subscriptions are:
Single £10.00 per year (one member)
Joint £12.00 per year (two members at the same address)

• Subscriptions are renewable annually on **1 January**.
• Subscriptions of members joining after 1 October are valid until the end of the following year.
• Overseas members are requested to pay in pounds sterling by International Money Order
or by credit card. An optional charge of £6.00 is made for airmail postage outside Western Europe of
all literature, if preferred.

Please fill in the details in BLOCK CAPITALS, tear off this form and send it with your payment to the
Administrator or telephone the Administrator with details of your credit card.

Please tick the type of membership required

☐   Single £10.00 per year (one member)

☐   Joint £12.00 per year (two members at one address)

☐   Airmail postage £6.00 per year (optional for members outside Western Europe)

NAME/S ....

ADDRESS ....

....

.... POST CODE ....

TELEPHONE NUMBER ....

I enclose a cheque/postal order* payable to **THE HARDY PLANT SOCIETY** (in pounds sterling ONLY) for £...........

OR
Please debit my Visa/Master Card* by the sum of £ ....
(* delete as required)

CARD NUMBER ☐☐☐☐ ☐☐☐☐ ☐☐☐☐ ☐☐☐☐

EXPIRY DATE ☐☐☐☐

Name as embossed on card ....

Signature ....

Please print your name and address clearly, tear out the page and send it to
The Administrator at the address overleaf

The Hardy Plant Society is a Registered Charity, number 208080

THE NATIONAL PLANT COLLECTIONS®

National Council for the Conservation of Plants & Gardens

Patron: HRH The Prince of Wales

THE LOST GARDEN OF BRITAIN

We have a long history of gardening, plant collecting and breeding in the British Isles so our gardens contain an amazing diversity of plants. Due to the imperatives of marketing and fashion, the desire for 'new' varieties and the practicalities of bulk cultivation, many plants unique to British gardens have been lost. This diversity is important as a genetic resource for the future and as a cultural link to the past.

WHAT IS THE NATIONAL COUNCIL FOR THE CONSERVATION OF PLANTS & GARDENS?

The NCCPG's mission is to conserve, document and make available this resource for the benefit of horticulture, education and science. The main conservation vehicle is the National Plant Collection® scheme where individuals or organisations undertake to preserve a group of related plants in trust for the future. Our 41 local groups across Britain support the administration of the scheme, the collection holders and propagate rare plants; working to promote the conservation of cultivated plants.

WHO ARE THE NATIONAL PLANT COLLECTION® HOLDERS?

Collection holders come from every sector of horticulture, amateur and professional. Almost half of the existing 630 National Collections are in private ownership and include allotments, back gardens and large estates. 21% of collections are found in nurseries, which range from large commercial concerns to the small specialist grower. 20 local authorities are involved in the scheme, including Sir Harold Hillier Gardens & Arboretum (Hampshire County Council) and Leeds City Council each caring for 11 collections. Universities, agricultural colleges, schools, arboreta and botanic gardens all add to the diversity, and there are also a number of collections on properties belonging to English Heritage, The National Trust and The National Trust for Scotland.

> *Please see overleaf for Membership Application Form*

WHAT DO COLLECTION HOLDERS DO?

Collection holders subscribe to the scheme's ideals and stringent regulations. As well as protecting the living plants in their chosen group, they also work on areas including education, scientific research and nomenclature, with the common aim of conserving cultivated plants.

HOW CAN YOU HELP?

You can play your part in supporting plant conservation by becoming a national member of NCCPG. Regular journals and newsletters will keep you informed of how your support is helping to save our plant biodiversity. Join your local group for the opportunity to play a more active role in plant conservation through co-operation with collection holders, a varied programme of talks, plant sales, involvement in local horticultural shows and nursery visits.

HOW TO JOIN:

Please contact
Genevieve Melbourne Webb
The General Administrator
NCCPG National Office
RHS Garden, Wisley
Woking, Surrey GU23 6QP

Tel: 01483 211465
Fax: 01483 212404
E-mail: info@nccpg.org.uk
Website: www.nccpg.com

'The NCCPG seeks to conserve, document, promote and make available Britain and Ireland's great biodiversity of garden plants for the benefit of horticulture, education and science'

MEMBERSHIP APPLICATION

Title _____ Name _____
(e.g. Mr, Mrs)

Address _____

_____

_____

Postcode _____ Tel _____

College (*if applying for Student Membership*)

_____

I/We wish to apply for national membership of The National Council for the Conservation of Plants & Gardens (The Company) and wish to receive copies of The Plant Heritage Journal.

I/We enclose subscription of £ _____ made payable to: **'The National Council for the Conservation of Plants & Gardens'** *or*

I/We wish to pay by direct debit and enclose £ _____
completed mandate form for

I/We wish to be sent information about _____ (place tick ✓ in box)
our local group.

I/We would like to receive details of the following to support the work of NCCPG:

● Donation _____   ● Legacies _____   (place tick ✓ in box(es))

Instruction to your Bank or Building Society to pay by Direct Debit

DIRECT Debit

Originators Identification Number   NCCPG use only

| 9 | 7 | 4 | 2 | 1 | 2 | |

Name and full postal address of your Bank or Building Society
The Manager, (BLOCK CAPITALS, PLEASE)

_____ Bank/Building Society

Address _____

_____ Postcode _____

Name(s) of Account Holders _____

_____

Bank sort code (top right hand corner of your cheque) _____

Bank/Building Society account no. _____

Signature _____ Date _____

Instruction to your Bank or Building Society
Please pay The National Council for the Conservation of Plants & Gardens Direct Debits from the account detailed in the instruction subject to the safeguards assured by the Direct Debit Guarantee. I understand that this instruction may remain with the NCCPG and if so, details will be passed electronically to my Bank/ Building Society.

Banks & Building Societies may not accept Direct Debit instructions for some types of account.

This Guarantee is offered by all Banks and Building Societies that take part in the Direct Debit Scheme. The efficiency and security of the scheme is monitored and protected by your own Bank or Building Society.

If the amounts to be paid or the payments dates change, you will be told of this at least six weeks in advance.

If an error is made by The National Council for the Conservation of Plants and Gardens or your Bank or Building Society, you are guaranteed a full and immediate refund from your branch of the amount paid.

You can cancel a Direct Debit at any time, by writing to your Bank or Building Society. Please also send a copy to NCCPG National Office.

National Membership Fees: (Group rates vary)
Individual   £10.00   Corporate   50.00
Student (in full time education)   £4.00

Credit Card Payments - if you prefer your Credit/Debit card please fill in the following:

Card No _____

Expires end _____ Amount £ _____

Name on Card _____

Signature _____ Date _____

GIFT AID

In April 2000 measures were introduced to help charities reclaim the tax that supporters have already paid on their contributions.

Please complete the Gift Aid Declaration below to increase the value of your support for the NCCPG at no additional cost to yourself.

I would like the NCCPG (Reg. Charity No 1004009) to reclaim the tax on all contributions I make on or after the date of this declaration.

I understand that I must pay an amount of income tax or capital gains tax at least equal to the tax the charity reclaims on my donation in the tax year.

Signature _____

Date _____

(Please note that Gift Aid is only applicable if you are a UK tax payer)

Please complete this membership form and send with remittance to:
NCCPG National Office,
RHS Garden, Wisley, Woking, Surrey GU23 6QP